The
OFFICIAL
ENCYCLOPEDIA
of
BASEBALL
NINTH REVISED EDITION

The
OFFICIAL
ENCYCLOPEDIA
of
BASEBALL

NINTH REVISED EDITION

by

Hy TURKIN and S. C. THOMPSON

Revisions by Pete Palmer

DOLPHIN BOOKS
DOUBLEDAY & COMPANY, INC.
GARDEN CITY, NEW YORK
1977

THE OFFICIAL ENCYCLOPEDIA OF BASEBALL was originally published by A. S. Barnes and Company, Inc., in 1951. The Dolphin Edition is published by arrangement with A. S. Barnes and Company, Inc.

Dolphin Edition, 1977

CONTENTS

PREFACE

It took an earthquake to start this book.

One evening in September, 1944, Hy Turkin felt his chair shake and saw his living-room pictures sway. To an abstemious sportswriter the deduction was simple: an earthly tremor. So he phoned his paper, the *New York Daily News*. His report was included in a Page Two story of the major earthquake that had rocked the Atlantic seaboard.

Next morning, S. C. Thompson read the account, complete with name and address. Discovering therefrom that Turkin lived only about a fungo-hit from his home, Thompson decided to go around the corner and introduce himself to his sports-minded neighbor. "I'd like you to visit my house sometime, Hy, and look over my baseball collection. I know you'll find it interesting."

Interesting? It proved to be overwhelming. His profession as a musician in Broadway shows provided "Tommy" with spare time and money. These he parlayed with an unquenchable thirst for big league data to amass one of the most exhaustive files in baseball history.

Almost 20 years had gone into the collection of this statistical "diamond" treasure. But it took less than 20 minutes to fully appreciate the immensity of his compilation. Thus began a paired project dedicated to presenting sports fans the most complete baseball compendium ever attempted. Thompson, in several years at his sideline job as statistician in the Al Munro Elias Baseball Bureau, had perfected his technique of collecting and collating data. Turkin burrowed through musty ledgers in Health Departments of distant cities, and interviewed the ever-thinning legion of 19th century heroes of the game, seeking vital data of the more obscure players of bygone years.

The entire project was slanted toward publication in baseball's Jubilee Year, 1951.

This all-time register offered the fascinating challenge of a private-detective job. Every clue had to be tracked down. For instance, a yellowed newspaper in the public library dated 1892, carried an agate line about a certain rookie being signed by a National League team after pitching three shutouts for the University of Maryland. Needed—full name, birthplace and birthdate of this player. Next step—a wire sent to the registrar of the college.

Came the reply: "No school record for such a name. However, it might interest you to know that before 1895 it was not necessary for a boy to be enrolled at this college in order to play for its baseball team!"

A better source proved to be the obituary columns. It's boring and slightly ghoulish to snoop through death notices in the newspapers 365 days a year, but any item involving an old ballplayer was quickly followed up by a letter

to the Board of Health in the city where the player died, enclosing a dollar for a photostatic copy of the death certificate. The return document bore the authentic full name, age and birthplace. It also invariably revealed the man to be one to four years older than his "baseball age." The latter is a stock-in-trade fib every player uses to attract pro scouts in the beginning and to shield time's true toll from managers toward the end of an active career.

So some leads died. But others, which literally led to the graveyard, brought rewards of vital information. Thompson trekked to four cemeteries in Philadelphia to copy data directly off the tombstones of former major leaguers. Turkin visited the Indian reservation burial grounds of Chief Sockalexis and learned the famous outfielder's true birthdate from a plaque placed there by the Penobscot tribe.

The project continued to grow, with years of interviewing baseball officials and players . . . of searching through private collections . . . of comparing notes with assorted amateur statisticians . . . of chasing all over the country for original box scores that would help reconstruct season averages of the very first professional league, the National Association 1871-75, all of whose official records were destroyed in a fire . . . of bringing compass and steel tape to ballparks to plot the playing area and measure the height of every fence . . . of pumping league publicity directors . . . of writing and rewriting and editing.

To pour such oceans of effort into a job, long before any sign of financial backing or official endorsement, proves it was a labor of love. Writing baseball history is never as much fun as playing it, watching it or even reading it. The authors will therefore be ever grateful for encouragement early and late, from such experts as Ernest J. Lanigan, Frank G. Marcellus, Thomas P. Shea, Lee Allen, Phil Redelheim and Harry Simmons who made possible The Jubilee Edition.

Fifty thousand copies of the Jubilee Edition were sold and it was obvious that a new edition would have to be placed in print before too long. Work started on the Revised Edition directly after the Jubilee Edition was issued, and five years later, in 1956, the First Revised Edition, greatly expanded, was published.

It was expected that another five years would be permitted to pass before issuing still another revised work. But the face of baseball was altered with the shifts of two franchises to the West Coast; the major league audience was now spread from border to border, and the ever-increasing televising of games created additional interest and new fans. As a result work on a Second Revised Edition was speeded and many more facts had to be added, rechecked and verified for the ever-growing All-Time Register of Players and Managers. Many had to be called to help, and among them were George S. Hipp of Indianapolis, Indiana, Robert McConnell of Wilmington, Delaware, Joseph M. Overfield of Buffalo, New York, Ralph E. Lin Weber of Toledo ,Ohio, Robert A. Styer of Seattle, Washington, and Clarence Blasco

of Kirkwood, Missouri. Their contributions were enormous in helping the Fourth Revised Edition arrive on schedule.

Following the deaths of Mr. Turkin and Mr. Thompson, after publication of the Third Edition, Roger Treat, author-editor of *The Official Encyclopedia of Baseball,* was chosen to prepare the Fourth Edition. Mr. Treat died in 1969 and the Fifth and Sixth Editions were edited by his daughter-in-law, and assistant, Mrs. Peter Rowe Treat. Pete Palmer, currently the editor of *The All-Time Rosters of Major League Baseball Clubs,* was selected to edit the Seventh Edition.

Special gratitude must be recorded for the help received from the National and American League offices, John Phillips of the Howe News Bureau, Don Harrison of Naugatuck, Connecticut, and Bill Haber of New York City.

1 EVOLUTION OF BASEBALL

Historical Origin

Just when, where, and by whom baseball was introduced in its most primitive form has made historians dig as far back as the early days of civilization to supply some evidence of the origin of a game which is now perhaps one of the most highly-specialized of all team skills.

No matter the amount of scientific probing into its earlier beginnings the game has been placed in various birthplaces . . . France . . . England . . . the United States, and some have even drawn strong hints that the first bat-and-ball activity can be traced to the era of the caveman. Then there is that school of diamond thought which insists all evolution should be traced from 1884, many years after the first recorded activity, since that is the year overhand pitching was first introduced. Others are just as certain that a form of the game which bears some facsimile to the present-day sport was in vogue many centuries ago.

However, most of the unbiased probers have come to accept the version unearthed by Robert William Henderson in his book, *Ball, Bat and Bishop* (Rockport Press, 1947). Henderson, as the librarian of the Racquet and Tennis Club of New York, had an abiding interest in bat-and-ball games. Also, his role as supervisory chief of the main reading room in the New York Public Library and his 35 years of research on game origins come through this volume as clear-cut, complete and convincing.

Quoting eminent anthropologists, Henderson repeatedly proves that all modern ball games are derived from religious rites of ancient times, with fertility (of crops or people) as the main theme. He places the first recorded "batting contest" in Egypt some 5,000 years ago.

Stick-wielding worshippers of the Egyptian god of agriculture, Osiris, would place his image on a cart and try to rush it into the Temple of Papremis. An army of priests, also wielding wooden clubs, would line up just outside the Temple and try to fight them back. Though many heads were split in this annual affair, it was only mock combat and more of a traditional drama around crop-planting-time.

As for games with a ball, these sprang up not as natural amusement but also as an offshoot of rituals. Egyptian king-gods and high priests used a ball as the central symbol of Springtime ceremonies. Authorities disagree as to whether the ball represented the sun (which is the source of life) or the mummified head of Osiris (symbol of growth and fertility). But in either case it is an object of potency, and so ball-tossing "games" or "rituals" became common among women. Archaeologists have found pictures of semi-nude women playing ball, carved into the tomb of Beni Hasan, which was built before 2,000 B.C.

Ancient Greeks and Romans played ball. The Romans built "ball rooms" in their bath houses. But in these cultures ball-playing was strictly for conditioning, much as the medicine ball is used in our modern gymnasium. The ball games that climaxed religious rites spread from the Egyptians to the Arabs and finally into southern Europe by way of the invading Moors.

11

Noticing how tremendously popular were the pagan fertility rites, the Christian church decided to adopt it in their Easter ceremony. Islamic customs had reached southwestern France, and records show that early in the 12th century, in the high church of Vienna, the Archbishop would pass a ball back and forth with clerics lined up for the processional. After the services, the Archbishop threw the ball among the assembled people, who followed the Moorish custom of splitting into "teams."

The popular custom spread throughout France and Spain. Even the Cathedral of Rheims wound up Easter services with a ball game. Contending teams developed two different styles of propelling the ball: either they kicked it (leading eventually to modern soccer and football) or they swatted it with a stick (leading to games like lacrosse, golf and . . . eventually . . . baseball!). The French called these early mass games "la soule."

When the ball-playing phase of the medieval Easter festival crossed the English Channel, the British soon developed a variation nearer the modern game of baseball, called stoolball. It first was played in a churchyard, with a pitcher trying to throw the ball against an upturned stool and an opponent trying to punch or bat the ball away before it reached the "home" stool.

The game soon spread over the countryside. Milkmaids added a second stool, then a third, fourth and more "bases" to be circled after striking the ball. When players added the rule that a runner could be put out by being hit with a thrown ball, this led into the more familiar British youngsters' game of rounders . . . the French game of "poison ball" . . . and our own "Massachusetts game" of baseball in the 1800's. In rounders, the stools were replaced by wooden posts driven into the ground. These posts or "bases" were sometimes called "goals," so that researcher Henderson found 18th-century references to "goal ball" and "base ball" in Britain.

American Development

English immigrants brought the game of rounders to these shores. When there weren't enough boys to make up two full teams, they would play variations so commonly known to sandlot youngsters of today: One Old Cat, Two Old Cat, etc. In One Old Cat, only one base is used, and the game requires only three players: pitcher, catcher and batter. More men, more bases, higher "Old Cats."

Sometimes called rounders, other times baseball, a game closely resembling our present national pastime was played in the United States long before its supposed invention by Doubleday in 1839. Dr. Oliver Wendell Holmes told of playing baseball while at Harvard in 1829. Henderson's scholarly volume mentions other similar evidence.

Helping prove his contention that the American game of baseball is derived directly from the British game of rounders, Henderson reveals that the first U. S. book to deal with baseball was Robin Carver's *Book of Sports,* printed in 1834 in Boston. In the preface, Carver admits being "indebted" to a London book published six years earlier, *The Boy's Own Book.* The latter explains in detail the game of rounders, including a lettered diagram for placing the posts (bases) in the shape of a diamond.

Carver's book copies the rules for rounders almost verbatim—yet the Bostonian calls this game "base, or goal ball." Carver's book is notable in another respect: it printed the first American picture of the game.

Baseball was still a waddling infant with uncertain step when a bewhiskered surveyor named Alexander J. Cartwright put it on a solid footing in 1845. For several years, he had been playing the game with fellow New Yorkers of high

social standing. Tired of haphazard games, he proposed a regular organization and proceeded to sign enough men to make a formal ball club, the first in history.

Cartwright headed a committee to frame a standard set of rules. Drawing heavily upon the popular Carver's *Book of Sports* and exercising excellent judgment in using the best phases of play in the community, Cartwright proposed a list of rules which was adopted September 23, 1845. Much of that original code still is in force today. Here are some of the more interesting provisions (with the authors' comments appended in parentheses) :

(1) Bases shall be from home to second, and first to third, 42 paces equidistant. (Remember, a pace is three feet, making that home-to-second distance 126 feet as compared with the present 127 feet, 3⅜ inches. Also, the infield was made square, not an elongated diamond.)

(2) The game is to consist of 21 counts or aces, but at the conclusion an equal number of hands must be played. (An ace meant a run, hand was an out.)

(3) The ball must be pitched, not thrown for the bat. (This meant underhand pitching only.)

(4) A ball knocked outside the range of first or third base is foul.

(5) Three balls being struck at and missed, and the last one caught is a hand out; if not caught is considered fair and the striker bound to run.

(6) A ball being struck or tipped, and caught either flying or on the first bound, is a hand out.

(7) A player running the bases shall be out if the ball is in the hands of an adversary on the base and the runner is touched by it before he makes his base; it being understood, however, that in no instance is a ball to be thrown at him. (This put it out of the rounders class.)

(8) A player running, who shall prevent an adversary from catching or getting the ball before making his base, is a hand out.

(9) Three hands out, all out.

(10) No ace or base can be made on a foul strike.

(11) But one base allowed when the ball bounds out of the field when struck.

Since the Knickerbockers were about to lose their playing field, in midtown Manhattan, a committee went looking for a new site. They took the ferry across the Hudson River and ended their hunt at the Elysian Fields, Hoboken, New Jersey. That was the home field for the elegant Knickerbockers the next year when they accepted a challenge from a group called the New York Nine.

Though all teams in those days were amateur, this first recorded match in history was for the side bet of a dinner per player. On this ill-starred afternoon of June 19, 1846, the Knickerbockers suffered just about the worst defeat in their 37-year career—23 to 1 in four innings. One of the New York players named Davis was fined six cents for swearing at the umpire, who was Cartwright himself.

Though the Knickerbockers didn't play a match game again for five years, their rules were universally adopted by many other clubs which sprang up in this period. The Elysian Fields drew clubs like the Gothams, Eagles, Empires and Mutuals. The Baltics played in Harlem, the Unions in the Bronx and the Atlantic, Excelsior, Putnam and Eckford clubs in Brooklyn.

In Philadelphia, an organization named the Olympic Club antedated the Knickerbockers, but played town ball from 1833 on and didn't switch to baseball until 1860. In New England, teams still "soaked" the runner with the ball, but the game grew rapidly there after the Olympic Club of Boston became the first to organize in that area.

By May of 1857 there were so many clubs in the field that the Knickerbockers begrudgingly called a convention in New York. They accomplished little beyond

Here is where it all began, the Elysian Fields in Hoboken, N. J., on June 19, 1846 where the first game under the Cartwright rules was played. No admission was charged to see the New York team rout the Knickerbockers, 23-1.

fixing the rules for the coming season: the complete Knickerbocker set, with the one important exception that nine innings, not 21 runs, constituted a game.

Three delegates from each of 25 different clubs flocked to the next convention, March 10, 1858. This time they formed the game's first league, the National Association of Base Ball Players. Their rules gained nationwide prestige, and the game was on its way to becoming the national pastime, though still amateur.

In its first season of operation, the new league capitalized on the natural Brooklyn-New York rivalry by staging a series of All-Star Games between teams from those cities. Because of the cost of fixing up the Fashion Race Course on Long Island for the opening game on July 20, 1858, an admission fee of 50 cents was charged. This is the first time fans were ever asked to pay at the gate. For the record, a crowd of 1,500 saw New York beat Brooklyn, 22 to 18.

The year 1860 saw the first tour by an organized baseball club. The Excelsiors of Brooklyn visited central and western New York and thumped all opposition. Later they traveled to Philadelphia and Baltimore to beat picked teams. The triumphal tour was heralded throughout the sports world, and more and more baseball teams began springing up all over the country.

Baseball suffered a sharp readjustment from 1861–65. In those years of Civil War, the number of clubs in and around New York City dwindled from 62 to 28. The championship went to the Atlantic Club of Brooklyn in 1861, 1864–65, but the Eckfords of New York finished first in 1862 and repeated with an unbeaten slate in 1863.

While the grade of league ball deteriorated during the war, the game's gospel was spread so effectively through intermingling of the troops from far-separated states that valuable groundwork was laid for post-war expansion. In Army camps and prison stockades, soldiers from both sides were teaching and learning this popular game.

Post-Civil War Highlights

Veterans coming home from the Civil War found baseball changed in one important aspect—an 1864 rule abolished the "out" for a fair hit caught on one bounce. There were even bigger surprises in store, for the game was headed for a record post-war boom, just as it was to flourish immediately after later wars.

The league's annual convention in 1866 drew representatives from more than 100 clubs. The next year the number rose to 237, including over 100 from states as far west as Ohio, Wisconsin, Illinois and Indiana.

Increasing interest in the midwest built up a natural rivalry between sections of the country. However, since all clubs were supposedly 100 per cent amateur at this time, no one could afford an extended trip till a group of government clerks and college students representing the Nationals of Washington, D. C., started out in July, 1867 for a 3,000-mile tour of the west. The club bore all its own expenses. Since the Nationals did not share in any of the gate receipts, the trip cost $5,000.

Washington won every game of that memorable trip but one—losing to the Forest City Club of Rockford, Illinois. Pitching for the winners that day was a 17-year old boy named A. G. Spalding, who had learned the game from an invalided Civil War veteran in his home town.

Spalding, who later became a great player, famous clubowner and successful sporting goods dealer, also figured in the first eastern trip taken by an amateur western team. Early in 1870, a group of businessmen in Rockford pooled $7,000

Pitching deliveries—improper and legal—under the game's earliest rules. A pitch (left) was illegal if delivered from above the hip line. A legal delivery was made with an underhand toss to the plate.

to underwrite their hometown heroes' junket. The trip was highly successful, including Spalding victories over the Atlantics and Nationals.

Though baseball was booming, its lone league was steadily waning. Heavy betting surrounded each game, and soon some players were blatantly "throwing" games in return for bribes. The league was powerless . . . or at least it didn't choose to use any disciplinary powers it had.

By the late 1860's, amateurism was a sham. Star players either were being paid sub rosa or with semipro inducements like sinecure jobs with local merchants. Al Reach, who like Spalding later became a wealthy sporting goods manufacturer and publisher of the annual baseball guide, was the first admittedly pro player, drawing a regular salary from the Philadelphia club in 1864.

The straw that really broke the amateur association's back was Cincinnati's determination to organize an out-and-out pro club in 1869. Harry Wright, captain and center fielder, drew $1,200, and lured his brother George, a brilliant shortstop, from the Unions club by paying him $1,400. Pitcher Asa Brainard drew $1,100 and third baseman Fred Waterman an even thousand. The rest got $800 each: Doug Allison, C; Charles Gould, 1B; Charles Sweazy, 2B; Andy Leonard, LF; Cal McVey, RF, and Dick Hurley, substitute. That made a total payroll of $9,500.

Playing every prominent club between California and Massachusetts, the legendary Red Stockings never lost a game all season. They won 65 and drew one—when the Haymakers of Troy, New York, pulled their team off the field in the sixth inning because of an argument over a foul tip with the score 17 to 17. The club traveled 11,877 miles and played before 200,000 people, and upon their triumphal return "home" (Gould was the only actual Cincinnatian) were greeted by club president Aaron Champion who exulted at the victory banquet, "I'd rather be president of the Cincinnati Reds than of the United States!"

The winning streak carried over into the next season, including a triumphant tour of the deep south. However, the historic string was snapped at 92 when the Atlantics of Brooklyn pulled the tremendous upset on the Capitoline Grounds. The date: June 14, 1870. The Atlantics were ready to quit when the score stood 5 to 5 at the end of nine innings, but Harry Wright insisted that the rules called for extra innings. The argument was brought to the attention of official scorer Henry Chadwick, pioneer baseball writer who later framed many of baseball's official rules and edited the game's guides for half a century.

Chadwick decreed that the game should go on. Cincinnati scored twice in the 11th, but lost when the home team came back with three. Some accounts of that final rally report that a fan climbed on outfielder Cal McVey while he was chasing Joe Start's fly, which went for a triple.

Despite this heartbreaking defeat . . . and another to the Atlantics later in the season . . . the Red Stockings succeeded in transforming the entire baseball picture of America. Purely amateur clubs couldn't hope to keep up with finished professionals like Cincinnati. At first, rival clubs tried proselyting, scouting and semipro-type bonuses. By the end of 1870 halfway measures were proven too weak, and the time was ripe for formation of the first professional league in history.

II MAJOR LEAGUE HISTORY

National Association

The diamond success of the Cincinnati Red Stockings spurred other cities in the midwest to seek the same national publicity which a baseball team had brought to the Rhineland.

"Why can't we attain similar status?" was the cry of civic leaders through the west and the east. Cincinnati had showed them how a successful baseball team can bring fame to a metropolis, and civic pride more than profit provided the impetus toward the formation of baseball's first professional league.

If smart business operators had taken time to examine the financial ledgers of the Cincinnati Baseball Club of the day they would have shied away from such a speculative venture. The Red Stockings, although the most artistic success of their time, were a profound financial failure even if their statements were marked in black ink

Baseball's No. 1 attraction, which had awakened a spirit of sport among promoters in other cities, showed a net profit of ONE DOLLAR AND THIRTY-NINE CENTS the preceding year, scarcely a sum to excite industrial giants to get on the baseball bandwagon.

The figures were not deceiving. The Red Stocking gate receipts amounted to $29,726.26; salaries and expenses in maintaining the club totalled $29,724.87. Net profit: $1.39. Yet Harry Wright's red-hued heroes had reaped so much glory for the Rhineland City that almost all the other leading clubs were turning professional, too.

With the amateur National Association withering away from sheer impotence, Father Chadwick campaigned in his *New York Clipper* columns for formation of a professional group. Al Wright echoed this in his *Philadelphia Mercury*. Another powerful advocate was Nick Young, secretary of the Washington club, who was later to become secretary of the National Association and president of the National League.

Ten club delegates held a preliminary parley on March, 4, 1871. Two weeks later, on St. Patrick's Day, they met again in Collier's Cafe, on New York's Broadway and 13th Street. There, in a smoky gaslit hallroom adjoining the Cafe (saloon), pro baseball suffered its real birth pangs, for that meeting established the National Association of Professional Base-Ball Players.

After electing James N. Kerns of Troy, New York, as president, they drew up a set of championship rules, but no fixed schedule. Every club was to play each of the others a best three-out-of five series, and the team with the best record at the end of the season was entitld to fly the championship streamer (also called the "whip pennant") at its ballpark for a year. The entry fee was fixed at $10 per club.

Brooklyn's Eckfords thought the organization too loosely knit to survive. They wouldn't risk the $10 fee for a chance to be recognized as champions of the United States. So the NAPBBP (generally shortened to NA) started the season with the remaining nine clubs represented at that meeting: Athletics, of Philadelphia; Bostons, of Boston; White Stockings, of Chicago; Haymakers, of Troy;

Olympics, of Washington; Forest City, of Rockford, Illinois; Kekiongas, of Fort Wayne, Indiana; Mutuals, of New York, and Forest City, of Cleveland.

When the Kekionga franchise wilted in August, the Eckfords belatedly decided that professional league baseball was here to stay, so they paid their $10 and replaced Kekionga. But a special post-season convention nullified their games because of the late entry, and they were stricken from the league standings.

It is ironic that the Kekionga club, the only one not to weather the season, won the opening game by 2 to 0. Not only was this noteworthy as the first pro league game of record, but it was also the lowest-scoring game in the first four years of the league. Here are the highlights of that historic inaugural:

The Kekiongas won the toss and sent Forest City to bat. Bobby Mathews threw the first pitch, a ball. James (Deacon) White was the first batter and he led off with the first major league hit, a double. Gene Kimball followed with a fly to second, but when White took too long a lead, Tom Carey pulled an unassisted double play.

There were several other "famous firsts" in that game. In the second inning, Art Allison struck out. However, Jim Lennon missed the third strike, and Allison reached base safely. Lennon atoned for his error in the home half of the inning by scoring the first run, which also proved to be the winning run. He doubled and came in on Joe McDermott's single. Kekionga had the game clinched by the ninth, but was ready to take its last batting turn anyway when a sudden rainfall caused umpire Boake to call a halt.

FOREST CITY (Cleveland) at KEKIONGA (Fort Wayne)

May 4, 1871

CLEVELAND	AB	R	H	O	A	FORT WAYNE	AB	R	H	O	A
J. White, c	4	0	3	9	0	Williams, rf	4	0	0	4	0
Kimball, 2b	4	0	0	3	4	Mathews, p	4	0	0	1	0
Pabor, cf	4	0	0	0	0	Foran, 3b	3	0	1	2	0
Allison, rf	4	0	1	2	0	Goldsmith, 2b	3	0	0	3	1
E. White, lf	3	0	0	1	0	Lennon, c	3	1	1	9	1
Pratt, p	3	0	0	1	0	Carey, ss	3	0	0	3	1
Sutton, 3b	3	0	1	0	0	Mincher, lf	3	0	0	2	0
Carleton, 1b	3	0	0	6	0	McDermott, cf	3	0	1	0	1
Bass, ss	3	0	0	2	3	Kelly, 1b	3	1	1	3	0
Totals	31	0	5	24	7	Totals	29	2	4	27	4

Cleveland	000	000	000	--- 0
Fort Wayne	010	010	00x	--- 2

(Called, in 9th: rain)

First base by errors—Cleveland 4, Fort Wayne 0. Two base hits—J. White, Lennon. Double play—Carey (unassisted). Walks, by—Mathews, 1, Pratt 1. Strikeouts, by—Mathews 6. Passed balls—J. White 2, Lennon 1. Umpire—J. L. Boake. Time—2 hours.

Chicago quickly displaced Kekionga as league leader by winning its first seven straight games. Unbeaten, the White Stockings invaded New York on June 5 to meet the Mutuals, owned by the notorious political potentate, Boss Tweed. Despite the 50-cent admission fee, a record 6,000 crowd jammed the

stands, and 3,000 others watched from beyond the fences, perched on neighboring roofs or wagons. Pushcart owners charged 10 cents for standing room on their vehicles.

The Mutuals brought great joy to Gotham fans by beating Chicago, 8 to 5. The New Yorkers continued on a winning streak of their own that soon put them in first place. Incidentally, though at first they refused to share their gate receipts, the Mutuals finally agreed to grant the visiting club one-third of the gross.

New York fortunes sagged in July. George Zettlein proceeded to pitch Chicago back into the league lead. However, the most destructive cow of all time, Mrs. O'Leary's bovine villain, ruined more than a good part of the city of Chicago by kicking over that fateful kerosene lamp in a barn on October 8. Rockford players entering the city that day saw the colossal blaze that seared the lakefront grounds as well as millions of dollars of other property. No ballpark . . . no game . . . and, as it turned out, no pennant.

The demoralized White Stockings had to play their remaining games on the road, where they lost the last three straight and the flag. In the game that decided the championship, October 30, Chicago was "home team" at the Union Grounds, Brooklyn, where the Athletics took a 4–1 decision behind the fine efforts of the league's ace pitcher, ex-cricketeer Dick McBride, and the batting champion, Long Levi Meyerle (.403) .

Still, it took a post-season decision by the NA's championship committee to determine the whip-pennant winner. Two games which the Athletics had lost to Rockford were declared forfeited to the Philadelphia team because Rockford had used an ineligible player, W. Scott Hastings.

Boston's failure to finish on top, due to an untimely series of player injuries, upset the experts of the day. The Beaneaters had taken over more than the Red Stocking nickname of the old invincible Cincinnati club. They had the four key players: the Wright brothers, McVey and Gould. They also bore the same "professional" stamp of competence as their famed predecessors. There was less gambling and swearing and fighting in Boston games than anywhere else in the circuit, so Harry Wright's team was respected.

Even more brilliant an organizer and leader than a player, bewhiskered Harry Wright bolstered his Red Stocking nucleus in Boston by proselyting A. G. Spalding, destined to become the NA's greatest pitcher, Ross Barnes and Fred Cone from the 1870 Rockfords.

In 1872, it was decided to name a player as NA president. The honor went to Bob Ferguson, famed captain-third baseman of Brooklyn's Atlantics. Chicago, not sufficiently recovered from the big fire, dropped out of pro ball for two years. Rockford quit, and its best player, Adrian Constantine (Cap) Anson, switched to the Athletics to continue a big league career that lasted 27 years, an all-time record.

Four new clubs swelled the NA to 11 teams in '72. A vital new rule allowed pitchers to use snap and jerk deliveries, though still restricted to underhand serves, thereby opening the door to curve ball pitching. Spalding never threw a curve in his life. The rugged Westerner relied on contol and change of pace, and these proved enough to carry Boston to four straight pennants, by steadily wider margins, from 1872–75. Boston added two more diamond immortals to its rolls in '73, Deacon White and James (Orator) O'Rourke.

The monotony of Boston triumphs (one local paper gloated that Boston Conquers All with this headline in Latin: "BOSTON OMNIA VINCIT") was only a minor factor in the demise of the NA. Gamblers infested the ranks so badly that the public was fast losing confidence in pro games.

Boston, scourge of the first league, took NA titles from 1872 through '75. Standing (l. to r.): McVey, Spalding, White, Barnes. Seated: O'Rourke, Leonard, George Wright, Harry Wright, Hall, Schaefer, Beals.

Open pool-selling on the day's results used to take place right in the park. As much as $20,000 would be bet on a game, with the expected consequence of widespread bribery and open intimidation of umpires and players. Toughs who had come to the park mainly to bet would pour profanity at a player whose error or strikeout hurt the club they were backing. Compounded with this were growing evils such as liquor-selling on the premises, contract-jumping and player desertions.

Small wonder the NA proved a pushover for the logical reform wave leading to the formation of the National League in 1876.

National League

When William A. Hulbert of Chicago died in 1882, the National League passed a resolution "that to him alone is due the credit of having founded the National League, and to his able leadership, sound judgment and impartial management is the success of the league chiefly due."

True enough. Yet if Hulbert had been able to hear his eulogy, the walrus-mustached pioneer would have insisted that A. G. Spalding be credited with an "assist" in the founding of baseball's first indestructible league.

The Hulbert-Spalding saga goes back to 1875. Early that year, owners of the weak Chicago franchise offered the club presidency to Hulbert, a successful businessman who was a die-hard rooter for the die-easy White Stockings team of his home city. He asked for a few weeks to consider the offer.

The next time the champion Bostons came to Chicago, Hulbert visited their star pitcher, Spalding himself, and told how thousands of Chicago fans were wild for a winning team but couldn't get one because of constant player piracy on the part of Eastern clubs, which dominated professional baseball. He emphasized the other growing evils in the sport, including gambling, and

Spalding nodded sympathetically. Finally Hulbert spoke of his own proffered job and urged in earnest tones:

"Spalding, you've no business playing in Boston. You're a Western boy and you belong right here. If you come to Chicago to play and manage next season, I'll accept the presidency of this club, and we'll give those fellows a fight for their lives."

Promise of a handsome contract dispelled any remaining doubt in Spalding's mind. Shaking hands to seal the deal, he promised to bring Chicago a real contender for 1876. In June of 1875, Hulbert visited Boston, where Spalding helped him sign teammates Ross Barnes, Cal McVey and Deacon Jim White. Then they went to Philadelphia, where they secretly signed Cap Anson and Ezra Sutton, who had been recruited earlier by Spalding. Sutton later backed out because of pressure from the Athletics' fans and officials.

Every effort was made to keep the signings a secret till the end of the season, since a man contracting in midseason to play with a different club the next year was subject to automatic expulsion by the NA . . . though this threat was rarely invoked. Chicagoans were bursting with too much pride and joy to keep the coup quiet for more than a few weeks. When the entire story came to light in a Chicago newspaper, tremors were felt throughout the league.

Bostonians felt bitter over the defection of their Big Four. Boys followed them on the street, hooting, "Oh, you seceders! Your White Stockings will get dirty." With the country still feeling the scourge of post-Civil War reconstruction, the term "seceder" was still as vile an epithet as a New Englander could summon.

Stung by criticism, the Big Four leaned over backward to prove their integrity. Spalding led the league's pitchers, Barnes paced the batters. Boston never lost a game all year on home grounds. Their season's won-lost of 71–8 meant a winning percentage of .899, which never has been matched in major league history.

Worried over rumors of his expulsion at the next NA convention, Spalding visited Hulbert's home at the end of the season. Chicago's enterprising president reassured him, "Why, they can't expel you. They wouldn't dare. In the eyes of the public, you six players are stronger than the whole Association."

Hulbert put Spalding further at ease by vowing that regardless of any action by the Association, the newly signed players would be paid for the entire 1876 season. Then the wavy-haired, silver-tongued executive became engrossed in deep thought. Suddenly he jumped up and said, "Spalding, I have a new scheme. Let us anticipate the Eastern cusses and organize a new association before their March meeting. Then we'll see who'll do the expelling!"

They held daily conferences thereafter. In one of these, Hulbert suggested, "Let us get away from the old, wornout title, 'National Association of Base Ball Players,' and call it 'The National League of Professional Base Ball Clubs.'" His idea here was to organize reform on a responsible business basis of clubs rather than depend on a flabby federation of players.

When they had determined most of the principles of their projected league, Hulbert and Spalding had Judge Orrick C. Bishop of St. Louis draw up a formal constitution. The jurist also framed a standard form of player's contract designed to end the evil of "revolving" (jumping).

In January of 1876, Hulbert summoned officials of the Cincinnati, St. Louis and Louisville clubs to a secret meeting in Louisville. The downtrodden Westerners gave Hulbert an enthusiastic vote of confidence. Most important, they assigned power of attorney to him and Charles A. Fowles of St. Louis in dealing with Eastern clubs.

Hulbert and Fowles sent a circular letter to the remaining NA teams, asking for a conference "on matters of interest to the game at large, with special reference

Charley Comiskey, St. Louis leader of AA days; first owner of the Chicago (AL) White Sox.

John Montgomery Ward, brilliant all-around performer; he won 84 games in 1879 and '80.

Hoss Radbourn, Providence pitching great of the 80s.

Pop Anson, NA pioneer; he played the longest, 27 years.

to reformation of existing abuses." Time: 12 noon, Wednesday, February 2, 1876. Place: Hulbert's suite in the Grand Central Hotel, Broadway at Third Street, New York City.

Impelled by curiosity, caution and common sense, the Eastern club presidents all came—G. W. Thompson of Philadelphia, N. T. Appolonio of Boston, M. G. Bulkeley of Hartford and W. H. Cammeyer of the New York Mutuals. According to Spalding's historical volume, *America's National Game,* Hulbert locked the door of his room, put the key in his pocket, turned to the puzzled magnates and said, "Gentlemen, you have no occasion for uneasiness. I locked the door simply to prevent any intrusions from without . . . and incidentally to make it impossible for any of you to leave until I have finished what I have to say. I promise not to take more than an hour."

In that historic hour, Hulbert expertly outlined all the evils that were demoralizing the players and fans. He proved that the NA was either unable or unwilling to correct the abuses. He climaxed his remarks by producing a copy of the model constitution for a new National League. Chicago's spellbinder won their support on the spot, and the NL was born right then and there.

One of the first steps taken by the new league was to raise the franchise fee from $10 to $100. To insure sizeable gate receipts, so that payrolls could be met, membership was limited to cities of at least 75,000 population. Bookmaking and liquor selling were banned on league ball-grounds. Players found guilty of betting or taking bribes were to be expelled from professional baseball.

When it came to election of officers, Hulbert diplomatically appeased the uneasy Easterners by plumping for "one of their own" for the presidency of

the league, Hartford's esteemed Morgan G. Bulkeley. Backed unanimously, Bulkeley accepted. Never more than a league figurehead, he quit a year later to pursue a political career that saw him elected Mayor of Hartford, Governor of Connecticut and U. S. Senator. Hulbert succeeded Bulkeley and ruled the league with an iron hand until his death in 1882.

For that inaugural season of 1876, the NL decided on five home games and five road games round-robin style between the charter member clubs—New York, Boston, Hartford, Philadelphia, Chicago, St. Louis, Cincinnati and Louisville. They played three times a week, making 70 games for each team. Admission was pegged at 50 cents, though tickets were sold for a dime after the third inning had been played.

With rain delaying the other openers, the first game in NL history was played at Philadelphia on Saturday, April 22, 1876. Boston won by a score of 6 to 5. Jim (Orator) O'Rourke of the winners made the first hit, and teammate Tom McGinley the first run, while Ezra Sutton, who had changed his mind about jumping to Chicago with Spalding, committed the first error. The full box score follows:

BOSTON (6)	AB	R	H	PO	A	E		PHILADELPHIA (5)	AB	R	H	PO	A	E
G. Wright, ss	4	2	1	2	2	0		Force, ss	5	0	1	0	4	1
Leonard, 2b	4	0	2	0	4	1		Eggler, cf	5	0	0	4	1	1
O'Rourke, cf	5	1	2	0	0	0		Fisler, 1b	5	1	3	13	0	1
Murnane, 1b	6	1	2	8	0	0		Meyerle, 2b	5	1	1	3	2	0
Schafer, 3b	5	1	1	1	0	1		Sutton, 3b	5	0	0	1	0	2
McGinley, c	5	1	0	8	0	3		Coons, c	4	2	2	1	2	3
Manning, rf	4	0	0	4	0	0		Hall, lf	4	0	2	1	0	0
Parks, lf	4	0	0	3	0	1		Fouser, rf	4	0	0	3	1	1
Borden, p	3	0	0	1	1	1		Knight, p	4	1	1	1	3	2
Totals	40	6	8	27	7	7		Totals	41	5	10	27	13	11

Boston	012	010	002 --- 6
Philadelphia	010	003	001 --- 5

Earned runs—Boston 1, Philadelphia 2. Total bases on hits—Boston 9, Philadelphia 12. First base on errors—Boston 6, Philadelphia 3. Left on bases—Boston 7, Philadelphia 9. Double plays—Eggler-Coons, Force-Fouser-Fisler. Umpire—Mr. William McLean. Time—2:05. Attendance—3,000.

As the season rolled on, gambling and drinking were markedly reduced, though not wiped out completely. Hulbert's dream of conquest came true in that very first year as his beloved Chicagos, bolstered by Boston's Big Four and Cap Anson, romped off with the pennant. However, Hulbert's brainchild league was threatened in midseason when the Philadelphia and New York clubs, fearing they would lose money on long road trips, refused to play their return games in the West.

Boasting the bulk of the NL's population, the Philadelphia and New York franchises announced, "The league needs us more than we need them." They were counting on the old practice of the NA, which condoned such offenses. But when Hulbert ascended to the league presidency at the December, 1876, meetings, he saw to it that both clubs were expelled.

There was further trial-by-fire the next year, but Hulbert had the courage and conviction to guide the league according to its avowed principles. Cincinnati, disheartened by a last-place finish in 1876, failed to pay its dues the next year. Though the league was already reduced to six members, Hulbert insisted

They started it all, William A. Hulbert and Ban Johnson. Through their efforts, the National and American Leagues were organized. Hulbert was the NL's second president; Johnson was the first in the AL.

Cincinnati be dropped, too. This season of 1877 also saw a prearranged league schedule, another Hulbert innovation, instead of the old plan whereby it was left to club secretaries to arrange series with other league teams.

With Spalding retiring from the mound in 1877, Tommy Bond of Boston became the hotshot pitcher of the season, leading his club to the pennant. But the Beaneaters' return to glory was vitiated by the game's worst scandal of the 19th century. Embarking on a road trip late in the season with the pennant practically clinched, Louisville proceeded to lose games with such regularity that the club's vice-president, Charles E. Chase, initiated an investigation.

Struck by the great number of telegrams received daily by Louisville's substitute player, Al Nichols, Chase asked him for a written authorization to open all his wires, since he was one of the players suspected of dealing with gamblers. Nichols refused.

"Your refusal is an admission of guilt," Chase insisted. "That means you're barred for life."

"All right, then," muttered Nichols. "Open them."

Damning, damaging evidence was brought to light. Several of the Grays players had been taking bribes from Eastern gamblers, telegraphing the code word "sash" for games that they agreed to throw. Faced with the wires, George Hall and Jim Devlin confessed, implicating Nichols and Bill Craver. Devlin had been the team's star pitcher. Outfielder Hall was the team captain and the league's first home run king, with five for the 1876 season.

Chase suspended the four players for life. Though Devlin was a personal friend of his, league president Hulbert sustained the decision, and none of the four ever played professional baseball again. Devlin visited every annual league meeting thereafter, humbly repenting and begging for reinstatement. It never

was granted. Ironically, he ended his days enforcing law and order as a member of the Philadelphia city police force.

Though expulsion of the crooked players insured the league of a stronger footing in the country's estimation, it caused several immediate headaches. Bereft of its star players, Louisville dropped out of the league. So did St. Louis, which had secretly negotiated for the ill-fated four to join them the following season . . . until the gambling scandal broke. Hartford couldn't draw at home, and had to give up the ghost.

Cincinnati was reinstated for 1878. Indianapolis, Milwaukee and Providence were rounded up by Hulbert, to make the NL a six-club circuit again. Indianapolis and Milwaukee had to quit after one season, but the Providence team prospered for eight years, never finishing worse than third. These were the halcyon days in Rhode Island, which toasted the Wright brothers, George and Harry, and the immortal pitcher, Charles Radbourn.

The 1879 season was distinguished for several reasons. It saw the institution of the reserve rule by the Boston club's thrifty president, Arthur H. Soden, allowing each club exclusive bargaining rights with a designated five of its players for the following season. The number of reserve players rapidly increased, finally reaching the 100 per cent figure under which all professional sports operate in America today.

In 1879, too, Hulbert expanded the NL to eight teams. This is the number of clubs it has fielded until 1962; except for the turbulent 90's when the collapse of two rival leagues caused the league to expand to an even dozen clubs.

From 1880–82, Cap Anson's Chicago White Stockings ran roughshod over the league. Featuring such colorful stars as King Kelly, Silver Flint, Ed Williamson and Larry Corcoran, the flamboyant Westerners rang up three straight pennants. Club president Hulbert and secretary Spalding decked the team out in expensive uniforms, put them up at the best hotels and had the White Stockings ride to the ballpark in open barouches drawn by white horses.

The NL faced a series of crises in 1882. Hulbert died of heart failure that April. Soden presided over the league strictly as a fill-in. It was not until December that a capable successor was found in Abraham G. Mills, former Civil War soldier and brilliant lawyer who had played and served as club president for the old Washington Olympics. Also, that year, Dick Higham became the first (and last) umpire convicted of collusion with gamblers, and was instantly fired.

But the sharpest threat of all came from a newly-founded major league, the American Association, which charged only half the NL's admission fee and played Sunday ball (which was expressly forbidden in the NL constitution). The popular AA ran franchises in large cities which had dropped out of the NL for one reason or another. And it weathered player piracy by the senior circuit. The NL monopoly of professional baseball was at an end.

Mills set to work realistically. Rather than embark on a suicidal war with the AA, the new NL president formulated a live-and-let-live National Agreement. Under this historic document, all organized major and minor leagues agreed to honor existing player contracts. The AA and NL clubs were each allowed to bind 14 players via reserve clause. Blacklists of dishonest players were to be mutually recognized.

With interleague peace came prosperity in 1883. Attendances boomed. Gearing his league for full-blown competition with the AA, Mills made two small fading franchises, Troy and Worcester, transfer their players to the great cities of New York and Philadelphia. He also adopted the AA's plan of hiring a staff of league

umpires, free from all club control, and paying them on a yearly basis. To bolster the league further, he reinstated 15 players who had been suspended for minor offenses.

A scant year later, war thundered across baseball's plains again. St. Louis realtor Henry V. Lucas organized the Union Association in 1884 specifically to fight the "outrageous" reserve rule. His UA stole players wholesale from the AA and NL, though the latter circuits pitched into a secret cash pool to pay bonuses to would-be jumpers from their leagues.

Soon after Charlie Sweeney of Providence NL had struck out 19 batters in one game for a new record, the star-struck UA plucked him with a heavily-moneyed hand. That left poor Providence with only one able-bodied pitcher, Radbourn . . . who happened to be under temporary suspension for insubordination. Manager Frank Bancroft raised the ban. The 30-year-old right-hander proceeded to earn his nickname of Old Hoss by pitching the last 38 consecutive games. Radbourn won 60 games that season, the last 18 in a row, against only 12 defeats. He not only clinched the pennant but added a World Series fillip with three straight victories to sweep the interleague playoffs.

With three major leagues and 34 clubs operating in 1884, there simply were not enough cash customers to go around. The UA sank in a sea of red ink. NL president Mills, who had temporized with the AA, felt no mercy toward the insurgent UA.

Over Mills' bitter objection, UA founder Lucas was admitted into the NL as head of a new St. Louis franchise in 1885. When the league over-rode his decision to blacklist the contract-jumping players, welcoming them back instead upon payment of a fine, Mills resigned in protest. Nick Young, a conciliatory Washingtonian who had served as league secretary continuously since 1876, was elevated to the presidency, and he held the post for 18 years.

Baseball pioneers were Henry Chadwick (left), who designed the rules changes in the 19th century, and Branch Rickey, who created the game's 'farm' system which supplied an endless stream of minor league players to the majors.

Now owner and president of the Chicago NL club, Spalding exulted in two more league pennants, 1885–86. But when his team blew the winner-take-all World Series to the underdog St. Louis Browns in '86, he angrily sold his league batting champion, King Kelly, to Boston for the record price of $10,000. The next year he shipped Kelly's batterymate, pitcher John Clarkson, to the same team for the same fabulous fee. Having won five times in seven years, Chicago now entered an era of NL pennant drought that lasted 20 years . . . so the lucrative sales turned out to be poor deals indeed.

Another major player deal of that period involved the end of Buffalo's franchise in the NL. Detroit bought Buffalo's "Big Four" of Dan Brouthers, Deacon White (who had been a member of the original "Big Four" in Boston a decade earlier), Hardy Richardson and Jack Rowe for $8,500, and entered the league in 1886. These four sluggers made Detroit a strong contender the first year, world champions the next.

Stovepipe-hatted Jim Mutrie lorded it when his Giants brought New York the flag in 1888 and '89, abetted by the fearless backstopping of Buck Ewing, the blazing pitching of Tim Keefe and the classic shortstopping of John Montgomery Ward. However, around this time the lesser-clarioned classification rule came to life . . . a veritable bombshell that exploded into another three-league war in 1890.

John T. Brush, president of the Indianapolis club, fathered the classification rule, designed to clamp a ceiling on ever-growing player salaries. Players were to be graded according to ability from class A to E, corresponding salaries to range from $2,500 down to $1,500.

This unjust and unworkable harness was slipped over the players at a time when John Montgomery Ward, leader of their benevolent organization (called the Brotherhood), was out of the country on a world tour with Spalding's squads. As brilliant a lawyer as he was a shortstop, Ward approached the magnates upon his return to protest, but was brushed off with the statement, "There is nothing to discuss." It was too late to organize any resistance for the 1889 season, but the next year Ward obtained financial backing for a Players' League, which drew most of the best players from the AA and NL.

The 1890 season was disastrous for all. Aggregate deficit for the three leagues ran close to a million dollars. Brooklyn was represented in all three leagues, but was proudest of its NL team which won the 1890 pennant.

Though they outdrew their rivals, the PL had to surrender at the close of 1890. But this peaceful settlement quickly touched off a disastrous battle destined to doom the AA, as the surviving leagues squabbled over the player spoils.

Somehow, the Athletics AA team forgot to include their PL jumpers, Louis Bierbauer and Harry Stovey, on their reserve list. Bierbauer (father of musical comedy star Elsie Janis) was claimed by Pittsburgh NL, and irate Philadelphians shouted "Pirates!", a nickname that stuck to Pittsburgh. Boston NL claimed Stovey, former home-run and base-stealing king. When the board of arbitration deprived the A's of both their straying stars, the entire junior circuit angrily rebelled by withdrawing from the National Agreement.

The cold war between the former friendly enemies lasted just one year. The AA began to raid the NL's players in the fall of 1891 . . . but the senior league meanwhile maneuvered a series of deals that brought over four of the best franchises from the AA. That spelled finis for the AA.

From 1892–1900, the NL reigned alone. It listed a dozen clubs, shrinking to eight in the depression following the Spanish-American War. During the Gay Nineties, Frank Selee managed five pennant winners and Ned Hanlon the other five. Selee's star in Boston was Charles (Kid) Nichols, who notched at least

20 victories in each of his first 10 seasons. Hanlon led the boisterous, brainy Baltimore Orioles to 1894-95-96 flags, thanks to the brillance of Wee Willie Keeler, John McGraw, Hughie Jennings, et al. Hanlon switched to Brooklyn in '99 and brought along most of his Oriole prodigies, a combination that rang up two quick pennants.

But the new century brought new woes to the NL. The public now was ready for a second major league. Not so the NL. It fought the inevitable trend with its worst weapon: smugness. Far worse, the league was wracked internally by a secret plot to reorganize baseball's entire structure on a syndicate basis. Behind all this was Andrew Freedman, subway contractor who owned the New York franchise.

First of the vital challenges which the NL bungled developed when a zealous ex-sportswriter named Ban Johnson came to the league meeting, hat in hand, to discuss Eastern franchises for his soundly-organized American League in 1901. Instead of hearing his proposition, the NL sneaked an adjournment and left Johnson standing foolishly in the foyer.

Smallest but mightiest New York Giant was John McGraw, a fiery third baseman, a crafty manager. He created an early Polo Grounds dynasty.

This spelled "war," and Ban waged it brilliantly. First, he pulled out of the National Agreement with the NL. Then he raided the haughty enemy's ranks with devastating sweeps. Star players of the NL were practically "sitting ducks" for Johnson the hunter, since the old league was still operating under a player salary limit of $2,400. Of 182 AL players that first season, 111 came directly from the NL, including Cy Young, Nap Lajoie, Jimmy Collins and Clark Griffith.

In the summer of 1901, the NL made its next mistake. To patch up its riddled ranks it abrogated the National Agreement and thereby made all minor leaguers

fair game. New suggestions of truce with the AL were immediately squashed by the Freedman faction.

Prior to the league's winter meetings of 1901, Freedman gathered his fellow conspirators from the Cincinnati, Boston and St. Louis clubs. At a parley on his estate at Red Bank, New Jersey, they worked out a master plan to syndicate the league, issuing preferred stock to the league "trust" and common stock among the clubs, with Freedman's henchmen to get the lion's share.

With the four remaining clubs solidly opposed to syndicate baseball, the matter came to a showdown at the annual meeting in December. Freedman's group wanted Nick Young as league president again. The opposition put up Spalding, by now a million-dollar sporting goods dealer, who still bore tremendous prestige as a constant crusader for the sport. Twenty-five times they balloted. Twenty-five times the vote was 4 to 4.

When the Freedman clique finally left the room, Spalding was elected "Unanimously." Spalding seized league papers and records, but had to resign the following March when a New York court granted a permanent injunction against him. Instead of a league president, the circuit was ruled by a three-man "compromise board" the rest of the season.

In April of that tumultuous 1902 campaign, the Pennsylvania Supreme Court granted an injunction against Lajoie, who had jumped from Philadelphia NL to the A's, and ordered his return to the NL club. Johnson's antidote was to switch Lajoie to Cleveland and keep him out of the state of Pennsylvania. It was a hollow victory for the NL.

Three months later, the new league suffered a real jolt when John McGraw deserted Baltimore to manage the Giants under Freedman's banner. It was to

Tinker (left) to Evers (right) to Chance, the fabulous trio which carried the Chicago Cubs to early 20th century glory in the National League. All three were simultaneously placed in the Hall of Fame.

be Freedman's last triumph. He sold out his baseball holdings at the year's end to John T. Brush, opening the avenue to NL settlement on a sensible candidate for president, young Harry C. Pulliam.

When Pulliam initiated truce talks with the AL early in 1903, Brush sought to employ the injunction weapon his predecessor had used successfully against Spalding. Brush bristled at the AL for moving the Baltimore franchise, which wilted after McGraw's flight, to New York, not far from his Polo Grounds. However, Brush was persuaded to drop the court action, and by August full-scale peace reigned with the signing of a new National Agreement. The AL-NL olive branch became a tangible reality that fall when their teams tangled in the first modern World Series.

On the field of battle, a bowlegged "Flying Dutchman" called Honus Wagner performed daily miracles at shortstop and wielded a murderous bat to bring Pittsburgh pennants in 1901–02–03. Christy Mathewson's pitching genius featured Giant victories the next two years. But the Cubs dominated the NL for the rest of that dead-ball decade. The Tinker-Evers-Chance combination came out on top in 1906–07–08 and '10, with a 104-games-won second-place team to show for that one-year gap.

Chicago's 1906 array set an all-time mark by winning 116 games. But the '08 team roused its fandom most. That was the year Chicago, New York and Pittsburgh all came down the stretch neck-and-neck. In the last Cub visit to New York, the last game of the series was tied with two out in the ninth, with Moose McCormick on third and Fred Merkle on first, when Al Bridwell lashed a clean hit to center. McCormick scampered in with the "winning" run, and the joyous crowd swarmed on the field. But . . .

The big "but" centered around the actions of Merkle, then a 19-year-old substitute first baseman. Noticing Bridwell's drive landing safely, and McCormick scampering home with ease, Merkle veered away on his run toward second and headed for the clubhouse in centerfield instead.

The throw from the outfield landed near third base, and amid the confusion of people streaming on the field, Giant coach Joe McGinnity grabbed the ball and threw it into the stands. Floyd Kroh, Cub pitcher not in the game, retrieved it, and second baseman Johnny Evers was credited with putting out Merkle for the inning-ending force out at second base. As umpire Hank O'Day was led off the field by police, he kept shouting, "The man is out. The game has got to go on." By now there were too many people on the field to resume play, so O'Day called the game on account of darkness.

At first the game went into the books as a Giant victory. If this result had remained, the New Yorkers would have won the flag by a full game from Chicago and Pittsburgh. However, after considerable official delay, the league board of directors ordered the game replayed. On October 8, one day after the scheduled close of the season, the teams tangled at the Polo Grounds. Heroic Matty, who had won 37 games that season for the Giants, lost this crucial one to his lifelong rival, Mordecai (Three-Fingered) Brown, 4 to 2.

The modern era of offensive baseball unfolded when the leagues sanctioned the use of a cork-center ball in 1911. The AL placed 35 hitters in the .300 circle that season. Over in the NL, Frank (Wildfire) Schulte of the Cubs broke all home-run records with a total of 21. Apparently a master of offense as well as defense, McGraw led the Giants to successive pennants in 1911–12–13; but the Little Napoleon met his Waterloo in the World Series each of those years.

Assassination of an archduke in far off Serbia touched off a world war in 1914. Baseball faced virtual assassination around the same time, as the newly-formed Federal League sued to have the entire structure of organized ball invalidated

by the courts. Time proved a valuable ally for the old leagues. The lawsuit languished. On the field, the inexperienced Feds failed to find the gold mine they had envisioned. With the world situation steadily worsening in 1916, FL ring-leaders surrendered to generous settlement terms by the NL and AL . . . ending the last major league "war" after over-all losses totalling perhaps $10,000,000.

In the two troubled years of FL activity, the NL sprang two of the most surprising winners of all. Boston's "Miracle Team" rose from last place on July 19, 1914, to a breathtaking pennant finish and a sweep of the World Series. The next year, Philadelphia took its first NL championship as Grover Alexander notched 31 victories.

Congress declared war just before the baseball season opened in 1917. Catcher Hank Gowdy of the Braves was the first to enlist, but the bulk of hundreds of major leaguers who joined the armed forces did not leave until the following season. McGraw won another pennant with his Giants in '17.

Baseball had tougher going in 1918. Army drafting claimed many star players. "Work or fight" was the national slogan, with orders from Washington curtailing the season to Labor Day.

The post-war boom took most magnates by surprise. Attendance records were set in many parks in 1919. The World Series drew almost a quarter of a million dollars more than the previous all-time high, the half million dollar Series of 1912. Amidst such prosperity, baseball suffered a near-fatal blow upon the revelation that the infamous Chicago "Black Sox" had thrown the 1919 Series to Cincinnati.

Between its sturdy new Commissioner, Judge Landis, and its astounding new home-run hero, Babe Ruth, baseball recaptured public confidence and enthusiasm. The game headed for unprecedented prosperity. Sunday baseball was legalized in New York in 1920, and the Gotham crowds were rewarded with topnotch teams in both leagues. Quite a bit more portly, but not a mite mellower than in his firebreathing Oriole days, McGraw rose to the apex of his managerial career by conquering all NL rivals with his Giants of 1921-22-23-24, the longest unbroken reign in league history.

McGraw now had 10 flags in 21 years. He never won another. But a bright new dynasty was about to dawn: nine flags in the next 21 years for the St. Louis Cardinals. Guiding genius behind this plethora of pennants was Branch Rickey, who had a versatile background as country schoolmaster, college football coach, lawyer, big league catcher, major league scout, manager in both major leagues, etc. Rickey finally found his perfect niche in baseball as a general manager.

Joining the impoverished Cards in 1919, Rickey hit upon a brilliant scheme. It was the only way his team could become a contender in a league where rich clubs like McGraw's Giants regularly paid outlandish prices for star players of rival teams. "Let's grow our own talent," Rickey told St. Louis clubowner Sam Breadon. "We can round up promising young prospects and develop them on our own minor league clubs."

It was simple enough to find minor clubs as a framework for a "farm system." The critical test was to discover enough diamond nuggets in-the-rough. Rickey himself had a matchless gift for evaluating the baseball potential of even the most callow teen-ager . . . "putting a dollar sign on a muscle," his admirers termed it. But he couldn't transmit such talent to his scouts, so he told them this rule-of-thumb to use on a prospect: "Can he run? Can he throw? Can he hit?"

It's World Series time, and here's part of stylishly-attired crowd which attended 1905 classic between Athletics and Giants. Derby hats and milady's best bonnet add to the festive atmosphere.

In 1926, the first of a long string of home-grown Cardinal champions hit the headlines. Player-manager Rogers Hornsby spurred them on to trample seven league rivals, and they went on to whip the vaunted Yankees in the Series. It was the beginning of a familiar pattern of St. Louis pennants—Bill McKechnie's Cards of '28; Gabby Street's crew of 1930 and '31; Frankie Frisch's Gashouse Gang of 1934; Billy Southworth's lean-and-hungry kids from '42 through '44, and Eddie Dyer, the slow-speaking and quick-thinking Texan, led the Redbirds to a tight victory over the slam-bang Red Sox in 1946.

Rickey was gone from St. Louis when the Cards registered pennants in 1943 and 1946, but those title teams were still mainly his farm products. When he switched to Brooklyn in 1943, the Dodgers already were blessed with a widespread farm system established by one of the many Rickey proteges in major league front offices, Larry MacPhail. Flatbush farmhands fashioned two more flags under Rickey, 1947 and 1949.

In between Card pennant winners, the NL turned up other worthy titlists. Big Poison and Little Poison, those deadly-hitting Waner brothers, brought Pittsburg home in front in 1927. Two years later, a former minor league infielder named Joe McCarthy managed the Cubs for the first of his nine big league pennants.

Replacing Rogers Hornsby as Cub manager on August 2, 1932, first baseman Charlie Grimm drove his team to the top in the two remaining months. That depression year also saw probably the greatest manager of all time, John McGraw, retire in ill health. The sulphuric-tongued, trigger-brained taskmaster's last official move was typically brilliant. Passing over more popular candidates, he handpicked as successor his coldly efficient first baseman, Bill Terry, who proceeded to win the world championship in his first full season at the helm, 1933. Terry and the Giants repeated as pennant winners in 1936–37.

Terry's pacemakers of 1934 were overtaken on the last day of the race by the

fantastic Gashouse Gang of St. Louis. This was the most colorful club since the old Orioles. They had Pepper Martin, who used his chest to slide on or to stop hard-hit grounders; Dizzy Dean, 30-game winner who outdid his lurid boasts; fun-loving Rip Collins on first base; Lippy Durocher, literally a howling success at shortstop, and similar characters. But manager Frankie Frisch, still the old "Fordham Flash" at second base, could match any of his charges for verve, nerve and deeds of derring-do. These were worthy world champions.

A month after the 1934 World Series, John A. Heydler retired as league president after 18 years of distinguished service in that post. He was followed by Ford C. Frick, former Hoosier schoolmaster, front-line baseball writer and radio sportscaster, who had joined the league as service bureau director the preceding year. Frick's blend of tact, intelligence and devotion to the game earned him continuous re-election, and eventually the post as commissioner.

The same 1934 meetings that elected Frick also voted to allow Leland Stanford (Larry) MacPhail to institute night baseball in his Cincinnati ball-park, and the first game was played on May 24, 1935 when the Reds beat the Phillies, 4 to 1. It proved an instant success. Chicago took the pennant in 1935, and also won in 1938, but increasing night ball revenue enabled general manager MacPhail to plow funds into a farm system that developed pennant winners at Cincinnati in 1939–40.

Redhaired MacPhail was gone from the Reds by the time his farm talent matured into title winners. The boldly imaginative "Barnum" went to work reviving the arid Dodger franchise, and by 1941 he had fashioned a flag for Flatbush. However, Larry suffered his bitterest disappointment just before entering war service in the Fall of 1942, for his star-studded Dodgers frittered

Judge Kenesaw Mountain Landis signs contract which makes him baseball's first commissioner. Club owners gathered at the historic scene are (l. to r.) Phil Ball, Browns; Barney Dreyfuss, Pirates; Connie Mack, Athletics; Clark Griffith, Senators; Jacob Ruppert, Yankees; Frank Navin, Tigers; Sam Breadon, Cardinals; Charles Ebbets, Dodgers; James C. Dunn, Indians; Charles Stoneham, Giants; Garry Herrmann, Reds; Harry Frazee, Red Sox; William Veeck, Cubs; Bob Quinn, Braves. Partially hidden from view are William F. Baker, Phillies, standing behind Ebbets, and Charles A. Comiskey, White Sox, standing behind Dunn.

away a 10½-game lead in August to the Cardinal youngsters. St. Louis repeated as rulers the next two years, which saw hundreds of big leaguers doff playing flannels to don military uniforms.

Baseball weathered World War II, despite severe travel restrictions, thanks to a heartening "green light" letter from President Franklin D. Roosevelt, who lauded the game's contribution to the nation's morale.

Bolstered by the effective pitching of Hank Borowy, a $100,000 waiver "cast-off" from the Yankees, the Cubs captured the 1945 pennant. That year was also notable for the signing of Jackie Robinson, first Negro in modern pro baseball, by the Dodgers' farm club of Montreal.

Baseball's new Commissioner, former U. S. Senator Albert B. (Happy) Chandler, was hardly in office a year when the Mexican League raided the major rosters heavily in the spring of 1946. Chandler warned all contract jumpers that they would be banned from organized baseball for five years, but dozens of them ignored the warning to scoop up the free-flowing pesos south of the border.

Despite the loss of its star pitcher, Max Lanier, and two others who went along on the "Mexican hayride," St. Louis spurted in the last week and finished the season in a tie with Brooklyn, the first deadlock in league history. The Cards swept the two-game playoff and went on to greater glory by outhustling the heavily-favored Red Sox in the Series.

Between the Mexican League threat and a near-successful attempt at player unionization by a Boston lawyer named Bob Murphy, the perturbed clubowners made many important concessions in 1946. The players organized a permanent committee, which had no trouble gaining beneficent terms like a $5,000 salary minimum; pension fund to be bolstered by club payments; limitation of salary cuts to 25 per cent in one season and a shortened spring training season.

Brooklyn's "Peck's Bad Boy," Leo Durocher, climaxed a series of run-ins with baseball's top brass by popping off during the spring training exhibition season of 1947 against his former boss, Yankee general manager MacPhail. Commissioner Chandler clamped down with a year's suspension for the Dodger manager. Called out of semi-retirement to lead the Flock, Burt Shotton succeeded in winning the flag, thanks to the spark of a flock of Rickey farm products, notably Jackie Robinson, who won the base-stealing title in his rookie season.

Billy Southworth skillfully piloted a collection of oldsters in Boston uniform to first place in 1948. The next year, with Shotton replacing Durocher in mid-season, Brooklyn won another flag, bolstered by batting-king Robinson. The game was jolted early in 1949 when stranded Mexican Leaguers brought lawsuits for being blacklisted by pro baseball. Commissioner Chandler wisely declared a general amnesty in June of that year, and later made an out-of-court settlement with the last challenger of the legality of the reserve clause, Danny Gardella.

Bonuses boomed in post-war years. Half a dozen prospects collected more than $50,000 each to sign with pro teams. One of the heaviest investors in this costly market was a young Delaware millionaire, Bob Carpenter, who owned the lowly Phillies. The policy paid off. Fashioned mainly by general manager Herb Pennock, who unfortunately died of a heart attack before his handiwork blossomed into Philadelphia's first pennant in 35 years, the Phillie Whiz Kids won all the NL marbles in 1950. It took a 10th-inning homer on the last day of the season by Dick Sisler, son of the first base immortal, to bring the Phils the decision over Brooklyn's fast finishers. Serving as chief Dodger scout at the time, George Sisler sat in the stands on that final day and watched his son's homer kayo the pennant hopes of the club he was working for.

The league lost a president when Frick was named Commissioner of Baseball, replacing Chandler who resigned July 15, 1951 when he learned his con-

tract wouldn't be renewed. Frick was handed a three-year pact at $65,000 a year and brought in his manager of the service bureau, Charley Segar, to serve as secretary-treasurer.

Warren C. Giles, head of the Cincinnati Reds, was elected to Frick's vacant post and Dave Grote, who handled the publicity of the Rhinelanders, was appointed manager of the service bureau.

Perhaps the most historic dash toward a pennant since the run of Boston's Miracle Braves in 1914, occurred in 1951 when the New York Giants, after being 13½ games behind Brooklyn in mid-August, finally caught the Dodgers, but only after the two clubs finished the season in a dead tie upon conclusion of the regular playing schedule. The stage was now set for the second league playoff in five years.

The Giants, after winning the first of the best-of-three-game playoff series, 3 to 1, lost the second clash 10 to 0. What followed provided perhaps the most dramatic climax recorded in the league's history.

Leading 4 to 1 entering the ninth inning of the final clash, the Dodgers needed but three outs to win the pennant. But they were to get only one. With one run in and runners on second and third base for the Giants, Dodger manager Chuck Dressen replaced starting pitcher Don Newcombe with Ralph Branca. Bobby Thomson was at the plate, and he represented the winning run. After Branca threw one strike, Thomson swung on the next pitch and lofted it into the left field stands for a home run, a 5–4 Giant victory and the league flag.

The Dodgers were winners in 1952 and '53, the latter year a notable one since it marked the first franchise shift in 53 years.

The shift was made March 18, 1953 when the Perini brothers, Lou and Charles, announced the transfer of their Boston Braves to Milwaukee. Sagging attendance figures and apathy on the part of the fans to adequately support the Braves were the reasons given by the Perinis for the switch.

Milwaukee proved a gold lode. In the first 13 home dates at the beer capital the Braves drew a total of 302,667, more than had flocked through the portals of Braves' Field for all of their 1952 home dates. A season attendance mark of 1,826,397 was a new league standard.

Milwaukee continued to prosper in 1954 when 2,131,388 paid to watch the third place Braves. The financial success of the Braves started baseball owners thinking of new diamond horizons, where television could be controlled in an intelligent manner and people would pay to see their heroes in the flesh instead of watching them from their own living room.

The Giants were 1954 champions, sweeping Cleveland in the Series, and the Dodgers bounced back to win in 1955 and '56. In both these seasons the Milwaukee attendance continued above the two million mark and these high figures evidently began to start a couple of clubowners wondering just how they could also increase their own gate receipts. Brooklyn president Walter O'Malley made a significant move in '56 when he took his Brooklyn team to Jersey City, New Jersey where the Dodgers played seven "home" games, one with each league rival. This started the speculation that the Dodgers would soon depart from Brooklyn permanently.

The Dodgers again played seven games in Jersey City in 1957, the year Milwaukee drew a record attendance of 2,215,404—the fourth straight season the Braves topped the two-million mark. On the field, the Braves rewarded their faithful with their first pennant, climaxed by a World Series victory over the Yankees.

The most historic events of the year—in fact in the history of baseball—

were the announcements, first by the New York Giants, then by the Brooklyn Dodgers, that their teams were leaving the vast metropolitan New York area for the West Coast. On August 19, Horace Stoneham, president of the Giants, announced that his club would leave New York at the end of the season and move to San Francisco. Brooklyn's O'Malley made it official on October 8 when he stated the Dodgers would be transferred to Los Angeles. Both owners cited old parks and limited parking facilities as main reasons for the shifts, but the unlimited possibilities of pay-television and the opportunity to acquire vast real estate properties were other vital factors in the move to the West.

Milwaukee repeated as pennant winners in 1958, the year the league took on a coast-to-coast "new look." The Dodgers, who were unable to get immediate approval for construction of a new stadium in the Chavez Ravine area of Los Angeles, played their games in the vast Los Angeles Memorial Coliseum, a field constructed specifically for football, and drew 1,845,556 fans. The Giants moved into much-smaller Seals' Stadium, where they attracted 1,272,625 fans.

These attendance figures represented an increase over the previous season when both teams were located in the East. However the Dodgers became involved in legal battles and delays over the construction of their new playing area; the Giants had little trouble in obtaining permission to start construction on a new park which was scheduled to be ready for the 1960 season.

Los Angeles set a new single-day league attendance mark on April 18 when 78,672 fans saw the Dodgers play the Giants in the first major league game ever to be played on the Pacific Coast.

A proposed third major league, headed by Branch Rickey and Congressional hearings into the laws governing organized baseball, overshadowed the events on the playing field to a considerable extent in 1959. When Congress failed to pass the Kefauver bill and the game's status remained unchanged Rickey's embryo Continental League was dealt a body blow from which it never recovered. The successful move to the West Coast by the Dodgers and Giants created a demand for expansion which was discussed in great detail by both leagues without reaching an agreement.

On the playing field the Dodgers, participating in their third play-off, defeated the Braves and went on to win the World Championship from the White Sox in a Series that shattered the former attendance mark of 86,288 set at Cleveland in 1948. Playing in the huge Los Angeles Coliseum the Dodgers bettered that record in all three home games. The first game drew 92,394 fans, the second was witnessed by 92,650 while the third game saw the largest crowd in World Series history—92,796—a record topped only by the Campanella benefit exhibition against the Yankees which drew 93,103, largest turnout in Major League history.

Definite expansion plans for both major leagues after the demise of Branch Rickey's proposed Continental League marked 1960 as a year of dramatic development. First, the National, then the American edged into the lead in the expansion race with President Cronin's American League finally emerging as the winner by voting to expand to ten clubs in 1961, while the more conservative National decided to withhold their plans until 1962.

On the field the swash-buckling Pirates landed Pittsburgh its first pennant since 1927. Their specialty was coming from behind to win games apparently hopelessly lost. They won 23 games during the season in their final turn at bat— 12 of these after two were out. Warren Spahn of the Braves won 21 games. It was the eleventh time in his major league career in which he had won 20 or more games per season. Established as preseason favorites, the Giants folded completely after the sudden discharge of Skipper Bill Rigney on June 18th. The

Cubs tried a novel but unsuccessful move when Manager Charlie Grimm and radio announcer Lou Boudreau switched jobs. Boudreau, however, had no more success than "Jolly Chollie" and the club finished a bad seventh, just one game ahead of the perpetual cellar-dwelling Phillies.

The underdog Reds surprised all of the experts by winning the 1961 flag despite the presence of some slightly "shopworn" players. In the race all of the way, they finished four games ahead of the favored Los Angeles Dodgers. It was the first Cincinnati pennant since 1940. On August 16th their double header with the Dodgers at the Coliseum in Los Angeles set a National League record for double headers when 72,140 fans witnessed the twin bill. The Pirates, winners in 1960, collapsed completely and finished a poor 6th. Phil Wrigley's innovation of installing a staff of coaches rather than a single manager failed miserably to improve the Cubs who finished a poor 7th just ahead of the perennial cellar-dwellers, the Phils, who rounded out their 4th consecutive year trailing the pack. Starting on July 23rd, they lost 28 out of 29 games setting a 20th century record of 23 losses in a row.

The 1962 National League season was marked by the Senior Circuit's expansion into a ten-club league, the first time the league has had more than the conventional 8 clubs since 1899. The clubs were poorly balanced and the result, while tense with the Giants, Dodgers and Reds fighting for the pennant, was just another season for the rest of the league. The Giants and Dodgers had to go into a play-off as they finished in a dead heat at the end of the regular season, the Giants winning two of the three play-off games. The Dodgers opened the season in their magnificent new Chavez Ravine Stadium. Maury Wills of the Dodgers was the toast of the league when he stole 104 bases, surpassing the immortal Ty Cobb's 1915 record of 96. Stan (The Man) Musial added a few more records to his already bulging collection when he passed Honus Wagner for the most total hits in National League history and moved past Tris Speaker in the all-time hit total where he is surpassed only by the great Ty Cobb. On the debit side of the ledger was the extremely poor showing of the New York Mets under Casey Stengel who set a new record for losses in a single season by dropping 120 decisions while the floundering Cubs lost 100 games for the first time in their National League history.

The Dodgers bounced back in 1963, taking the flag behind a superlative pitching staff headed by Sandy Koufax. Wild and inconsistent as a youngster, the Dodger southpaw's fast ball now was complemented by gilt-edge control. Sandy won 25 of 30 decisions, struck out a modern league record of 306 and tossed 11 shutouts in firmly establishing himself as baseball's premier pitcher. The Cardinals made a great bid in late season, winning 19 of 20 games to move within one game of the Dodgers, but Los Angeles terminated the streak and ended the Red Birds' flag hopes by sweeping a three-game series in St. Louis. Musial, who had announced his retirement at the club's annual summer picnic, was honored by the home fans on the season's final day and The Man wrote an appropriate ending to his fabulous success story by hitting singles in his final two at bats. Stan closed out his illustrious career with 3,630 hits and a host of records.

With Musial in his first year as a Cardinal vice-president, the Red Birds overhauled the Phillies on the final day to win the 1964 pennant. Philadelphia, which seemed to have an insurmountable lead with two weeks left, proceeded to drop 10 straight games and a one-team race became a four-team affair as the Cards, Reds and Giants surged into late contention. With only three days to go, all four had a chance, and the Giants didn't fall by the wayside until the next-to-last-day. St. Louis wrapped it up on the final day by whipping the lowly

Mets, 11–5, after losing to them the two previous days. Had the Cards lost the finale, the race would have ended in a three-way tie. Perhaps more startling than the Cards' triumph was the resignation of their pilot, Johnny Keane, one day after their World Series victory over the Yankees. And more surprising still was that Keane succeeded Yogi Berra at the Yankee helm. Berra was fired the same day that Keane quit the Cards. The year also marked the opening of the Mets' magnificent new home, Shea Stadium, named after William Shea, the New York attorney who was instrumental in returning National League ball to New York. The Phils' ace, Jim Bunning, gave the new park a proper christening by pitching a perfect game there June 21. Koufax also tossed a 1964 no-hitter, the third of his career, tying him with Bob Feller, Cy Young and Larry Corcoran. Houston's Ken Johnson also had a hitless gem, but his came in a losing cause. Cincinnati scored a ninth-inning run on two errors—one by Johnson—to win, 1–0.

Koufax, Don Drysdale, newcomer Claude Osteen and a marvelous bullpen brought the pennant flag to Los Angeles in 1965 and '66. Sandy smashed all modern strikeout marks with 382 in '65 and also won 26 games, including a record fourth no-hitter, which happened to be a perfect game. The peerless Dodger southpaw reached a high of 27 victories and fanned 317 batters in '66. Both years presented ding-dong pennant races, too, with the Giants challenging strongly both times and the Pirates, boasting a wrecking crew second to none, figuring prominently in '66. Houston had its new stadium, the $20,500,000 Astrodome, ready for the 1965 season and both St. Louis and Atlanta had new playing areas in 1966. Atlanta also had a new ball team, the Milwaukee Braves shifting operations to the Georgia capital that year after an abortive attempt the year before.

The 1965 season was marred by an incident at San Francisco August 22 when the Giants' mound star, Juan Marichal, struck Dodger catcher John Roseboro over the head with a bat. Marichal drew a $1,750 fine and a nine-day suspension for his "unprovoked and obnoxious" assault.

Although only 30 years old, Koufax announced his retirement in November, 1966, saying his aching left arm could endure no more pain. With Koufax gone, the Dodgers fell into the second division and the Cardinals, now managed by Red Schoendienst, a long time Red Bird star, climbed to the top led by the slugging of Orlando Cepeda, the running of Lou Brock and a well-balanced mound staff. Pittsburgh's Roberto Clemente continued to win more laurels, capturing his fourth batting crown with a career high of .357. Only Musial, Hornsby and Wagner won more often. At the winter meetings in Mexico City the league voted to expand to 12 clubs and began accepting franchise applications.

The Cardinals again breezed to the pennant in 1968. Bob Gibson led the Cards by setting a new league E.R.A. mark of 1.12. The league expanded to 12 teams in 1969, adding the Montreal Expos, the first major league team outside the United States, and the San Diego Padres. Two divisions were established, the East with Chicago, Montreal, New York, Philadelphia, Pittsburgh and St. Louis, and the West with Atlanta, Cincinnati, Houston, Los Angeles, San Diego and San Francisco.

The amazing New York Mets ran away with the championship, winning 27 more games than the previous season. Gil Hodges made good use of his entire roster. He relied mainly on a solid pitching staff, led by Tom Seaver, Jerry Koosman and Tug McGraw, and hitting topped by Cleon Jones. The Atlanta Braves won the West in a close race, but were swept aside by the Mets in the playoff. In December of 1969, Charles (Chub) Feeney was elected president of the National League, succeeding the retiring Warren Giles.

The next three years resulted in a battle between the Pittsburgh Pirates and

the Cincinnati Reds, with only one close division race. That was in 1971, when the Reds had an off year, and the Giants edged the Dodgers by a game on the final day. The Reds easily whipped the Pirates in the playoff of 1970, and the Pirates returned the favor to the Giants the following year. 1972 marked the first close championship series, as the Reds nipped the Bucs in five games. The Mets bounced back in 1973 to win the East title in the closest race in major league history. With only two days remaining, a five-way tie was still possible. New York went on to edge the Reds in five games in the playoff. The Mets made the miracle Braves' feat in 1914 look like a cinch. The New Yorkers were in last place on August 31st, then went on to pass five clubs in a month. The Braves had been in last place on July 19th, but moved up to fourth on July 21st and were second on August 31st.

Tom Seaver was the top performer for the Mets over the period, winning the Cy Young award in 1969, 1973 and 1975. Steve Carlton had the best individual season mark, winning 27 games for the lowly Phillies in 1972. Ferguson Jenkins of the Cubs strung six 20-win seasons in a row through 1972. Willie McCovey was the number one hitter for the three years through 1970, but was then hobbled by injuries. Pete Rose won three batting titles and led the Reds to their playoff victory in 1972. Johnny Bench, winner of two MVP awards, along with Joe Morgan, Tony Perez and Dave Concepcion were large contributors to the Reds' success, while Gary Nolan, when healthy, and Don Gullett were their most effective pitchers.

The leader of the Pirates was Roberto Clemente, whose tragic death in an airplane crash in 1972 shocked the baseball world. Clemente was aided by slugger Willie Stargell and hurler Steve Blass. Willie Mays ended his glorious career in 1973 after 22 years, while Hank Aaron just kept rolling along, setting a new league record for fewest at-bats per home run in 1973 and finally breaking Babe Ruth's lifetime homer record in 1974. Hank moved to the AL in 1975, and when he retired after 1976, he had set new lifetime marks for games, at-bats, total bases and runs batted in as well. Lou Brock set an all-time stolen base mark with 118 in 1974.

The Reds and Pirates moved into new stadiums in 1970, as did the Phils a year later. This left only the Cubs with a park built before 1960. Artificial turf was installed in six of the fields.

The Dodgers won in 1974, beating out Cincinnati in a close race and whipping Pittsburgh in the playoffs. But the Reds came back in 1975 to win 108 games, the best record in over twenty years. Again the Pirates bit the dust in the championship series.

In 1976, the Reds took the West for the fifth time in seven years and won their second straight World Series. This was the first time since 1922 that an NL team had performed the feat. The Phils won the East, but were swept aside by Cincinnati, who became the first team to win seven post-season games in a row. Bill Madlock won his second straight batting title, while Randy Jones won at least twenty games two years in a row for lowly San Diego. Mike Schmidt led in homers for the third successive year and hammered out four in one game as well.

American League

The groundwork for the formation of the American League actually was started nine years before its official beginning in 1901. Byron (Ban) Johnson, a minister's son, and Charles Albert Comiskey, player-manager of the Cincinnati team in the unwieldy National League, began their dreams of secession and a new diamond empire in the beer parlors of the Rhineland, as early as 1892.

The 27-year-old Johnson, who conducted a no-holds barred baseball column for the *Cincinnati Gazette,* held no particular affection for John T. Brush, club-owner of the local nine. But, for Comiskey, Johnson had nothing but admiration. Brush, a clothing magnate, was the target of some of Ban's choicest and most sulphuric adjectives, and was severely criticized for what Johnson claimed were "stingy tactics" which he said were harming the local franchise.

Comiskey, recognizing in Johnson an alert and imaginative mind who envisioned greater horizons for baseball, soon convinced clubowners anxious to reform the old Western Association that Ban was their man to head the league. Johnson, who went to the league's convention as a reporter, returned as its new president, mainly because Commy was so lavish in his praise of the sports writer.

Comiskey himself left Cincinnati at the close of the 1894 season to take a managerial post with Sioux City, where he started on a club-owning career which was to make him one of the game's most powerful and influential figures.

Johnson tackled his new assignment in typical fashion, hard-hitting and hard-working, and his eyes were cocked continuously at major-league status. He was especially alert for defections in the NL ranks and kept his ears close to the ground for rumblings of discontent.

Ban made his initial move in 1896, after Connie Mack had been fired as Pittsburgh pilot for making caustic comments against the second-guessing of a critical front office. Ban snapped up Mack for his league, offering the lean catcher-manager a bonus which consisted of part-interest in the Milwaukee club. Three years later, a series of bold and shrewd moves by Ban convinced him that his dreams of an American League were not too far removed from reality.

When the NL dropped four of its dozen clubs after the 1899 season, Johnson persuaded Charles Somers, Great Lakes shipping tycoon, to take over the vacated Cleveland franchise. Somers "steered" the league in its roughest period, over the next two years. Ban also set up a club in Buffalo. It took Commy's engineering, though, before Jim Hart, owner of the Chicago NL team, allowed Comiskey to switch his St. Paul team to Chicago's South Side. Hart never thought fans would tolerate the stockyard smells to see a ball game in that rundown district of town.

At this point, prestige-wise Johnson announced that his circuit was changing its name from the Western to the American League. Commy's team won the 1900 pennant after a prosperous season for the league in general. Johnson was now ready for the master stroke. Using as a pretext the rumored re-organization of the old American Association as a direct threat against his league, Ban sought NL permission to expand into Baltimore, Washington and Philadelphia. Unable to obtain even the courtesy of an audience with the haughty Nationals, Johnson launched open warfare.

First, Ban scrapped the National Agreement, so that all players became fair game in the eyes of rival leagues. He forestalled an AA-inspired plan to move into Boston by sending Connie Mack to the Hub to lease a plot for a ballpark (using Somers' bankroll). Somers, who had loaned Comiskey money to build a park in Chicago, also had a financial finger in the Philadelphia club, as well as his own titular Cleveland franchise.

The AL's expansion to the East proved popular, and the dissension-ridden rival league lost customers. Johnson's full-fledged major league began official operations on Wednesday, April 24, 1901. Other teams were rained out that day, but there was a gala inaugural in Chicago, which was destined to win the flag with Clark Griffith as manager and Comiskey now in the front office. The first American League box score:

CLEVELAND (2)	AB	R	H	PO	A	E		CHICAGO (8)	AB	R	H	PO	A	E
Pickering, rf	4	0	1	0	0	0		Hoy, cf	5	0	1	3	0	0
McCarthy, lf	4	0	2	4	0	0		Jones, rf	2	2	1	4	0	0
Genins, cf	4	0	0	1	0	0		Mertes, lf	3	2	1	4	0	0
LaChance, 1b	4	1	1	13	0	1		Shugart, ss	2	2	0	4	4	0
Bradley, 3b	4	0	0	2	5	0		Isbell, 1b	3	1	1	8	0	0
Beck, 2b	2	0	2	0	4	0		Hartman, 3b	4	0	1	0	5	1
Hallman, ss	3	1	0	1	3	1		Brain, 2b	4	0	0	1	3	0
Wood, c	4	0	1	2	2	0		Sullivan, c	4	1	2	2	0	0
Hoffer, p	4	0	0	1	0	0		Patterson, p	4	0	0	1	1	0
Totals	33	2	7	24	14	2		Totals	31	8	7	27	13	1

Cleveland	000	100	100	---	2
Chicago	250	000	10x	---	8

Left on base—Chicago 5, Cleveland 3. Two base hit—Beck. Double plays—Shugart-Isbell, Hoffer-Hallman-LaChance. Struck out—by Hoffer 1. Bases on balls—off Patterson 2, Hoffer 6. Umpire—Connolly. Time—1:30. Attendance—14,500.

Johnson's platform of "clean baseball and more 25-cent seats" drew increasing patronage. Star players kept streaming toward the better-paying AL. Ban backed his umpires religiously, even though it brought him head-on against such personal friends as Clark Griffith. Griff took the censure in good grace. Not so John McGraw, who couldn't shed his "Old Orioles" stripe. In midseason of 1902, irascible McGraw sold out his Baltimore holdings and jumped back to the NL. Johnson's answer was to move the Baltimore franchise to New York for 1903— despite politicians' threats to run city streets through his ballpark—and the AL finally had an eight-club alignment.

Connie Mack's A's were hard hit by an injunction that cost them the services of Nap Lajoie and other NL "jumpers." But an erratic southpaw named Rube Waddell came in from the Coast to strong-arm Mack's team to the 1902 pennant.

By now, the NL knew it had had enough. At a peace meeting in January of 1903, the old circuit tried the old stratagem that worked against the AA— offering to absorb the stronger teams of the rival circuit. Johnson and his fellow delegates snapped out of their seats, reached for their hats and stomped out of the conference. Four days later, there was a different tone at the interleague meeting. The NL asked only that Johnson promise not to invade Pittsburgh. Ban nodded. They shook hands, signed a preliminary agreement that established the dual-major league principle and finally set up a joint committee to settle ownership of disputed players.

Cy Young, still a 28-game winner at the age of 36, led Boston to the 1903 pennant. Teammate Bill Dinneen, who won 21, beat the Pirates three times in the ensuing World Series.

Hairbreadth finishes featured AL races the next few years. Of these, none brought greater satisfaction to Johnson than the 1906 campaign. Ban exulted along with his crony, Commy, whose Chicago "Hitless Wonders" put together 19 straight victories at one stage to finish on top of the heap. Then they deflated the mighty Cubs in baseball's first intracity World Series.

From 1907–09, it was all Detroit. Hughie Jennings managed this triumphant

Tiger pack. As one of the "Old Orioles," Hughie was used to blood-and-thunder aggressiveness on the field. But he had to admit none of his former teammates could approach the fierce, flaming will-to-win of his young outfielder, a tight-lipped Georgian named Ty Cobb. A basepath terror and batting wonder, Cobb captured the hitting crown all three of these pennant-winning seasons . . . and nine times afterward. His lifetime average over 24 years was a stratospheric .367, just one of the dozens of records still held by the "Georgia Peach."

Connie Mack's A's ruled the roost for four of the first five years after the cork ball came into use. Boasting the "Hundred thousand dollar infield" of McInnis-Collins-Barry-Baker, and the iron-armed pitching trio of Bender-Plank-Coombs, the White Elephants trumpeted triumphantly in 1910–11, 1913–14.

Boston's Red Sox, with a famed outfield trio of Speaker-Hooper-Lewis, also bagged four flags around that time: 1912, 1915–16, 1918. Comiskey's club in Chicago won the other pair of pennants in the second decade of this century. League overlord Johnson chortled as his clubs of this period posted four Series successes over the Giants of McGraw, his despised enemy ever since the 1902 desertion of Baltimore.

The Damon-Pythias bond between Johnson and Comiskey was strained when the AL chief suspended a White Sox outfielder for three days. Returning from a fishing trip that week, Ban sent Commy his best catch. Back came a bitter wire: "Do you think I can play that fish in left field?" The rift widened into an angry feud when Commy's infamous "Black Sox" were exposed for throwing the 1919 World Series.

Tris Speaker and his world champion Clevelands of 1920 were overshadowed by the eruption of the Sox scandal. Along came Babe Ruth, to fire the imagination with his wondrous homers, and Judge K. M. Landis, to restore faith in the game, and baseball was back on the glory road of sportsdom's Golden Era.

Ruth already had gained fame as a Red Sox pitching star and a part-time outfielder who could practically knock the cover off the ball. But his light shone brightest after his sale to the Yankees, who had never won a pennant. Babe helped dispel the title famine by whacking the unbelievable total of 59 homers in 1921. His howitzer at the plate enabled New York to stay on top in 1922 and 1923. In the latter year, his team moved from the National League's Polo Grounds into its own million dollar ballpark, Yankee Stadium, which was suitably tagged "The House that Ruth Built."

After 17 seasons with a trailing team, old faithful Walter Johnson, greatest pitcher in AL history, broke into two World Series when his Senators won in 1924–25. Manager Bucky Harris was the "Boy Wonder" at the helm each time.

The next phase of league history featured the "Murderers' Row" Yankee champions of 1926–27–28. Beer baron Col. Jacob Ruppert made a fetish of success, and the Yankee owner had the right men to insure it—richly experienced Edward G. Barrow as general manager, clever little Miller Huggins as field pilot and Babe Ruth backboning a lineup of "window breakers" like Lou Gehrig, Bob Meusel, Tony Lazzeri, et al. Babe hit 60 homers in 1927, the all-time record.

Even as these awe-inspiring Yanks enjoyed the spotlight, other real titans were bowing out in the wings. Ty Cobb and Tris Speaker closed their active careers after spending the 1928 season side by side in the A's outfield. Walter Johnson and Ban Johnson quit in 1927, the former after winning more than 400 games and the latter after broken-heartedly losing his long vendetta against the all-powerful Commissioner.

Ban Johnson's successor as AL president was Cleveland's chief executive, Ernest S. Barnard. Johnson and Barnard both died suddenly in 1931, as did

Comiskey. Gentlemanly Will Harridge rose to the presidency after 20 years in the league office as secretary.

Coincident with the cataclysmic Wall Street crash of 1929 was Connie Mack's return to baseball prosperity. Buoyant as ever in his late 60's, the league's managerial dean paraded to three straight pennants from 1929–31. Four of his aces came from Jack Dunn's Baltimore club, which had spawned Babe Ruth earlier. Dunn received upwards of $150,000 for Lefty Grove, George Earnshaw, Max Bishop and Joe Boley. Mack's fame finally transcended baseball's halls, and he received the Bok Award in 1929 for distinguished service to the city of Philadelphia.

An NL managerial castoff, Joe McCarthy, came to the Yankees to restore the regal sway of the Bronx Bombers. Holdovers from the Huggins regime helped him nail the flag in 1932. A frustrated runnerup each of the next three years, McCarthy finally hit his stride in 1936 for seven pennants in the next eight seasons and four straight world championships.

The renewed dynasty started in the rookie season of Joe DiMaggio, a fisherman's son grown into a graceful outfielder second only to Ruth in New York annals. It continued unabated as the farm chain, master-minded by Barrow and George Weiss, developed a string of summa cum laude graduates—Joe Gordon, Charlie Keller, Spud Chandler, Phil Rizzuto, Hank Borowy, et al. These youngsters were balanced with ageless veterans of topnotch caliber, like Lefty Gomez, Bill Dickey, Red Ruffing and Frank Crosetti. Tommy Henrich was a free-agent bargain at $20,000 in 1937.

Detroit's slow but slugging club of 1940 interrupted the Yank pennant monopoly. Cries of "Break up the Yankees" were often raised, but it took the tail end of World War II to do it. After the Yankees won in 1941, '42 and '43 the lowly Browns, under Luke Sewell, won their only AL title in 1944. Detroit, with slim Hal Newhouser and bespectacled Dizzy Trout as the 1–2 mound punch, won in 1945. The next year was the payoff for long-suffering Tom Yawkey, who had poured millions into the Red Sox for more than a decade before finally realizing a pennant. It was powered by batting king Ted Williams, baseball's most feared slugger since Babe Ruth.

With diamond dynamo Larry MacPhail operating as one-third owner of the Yanks in 1947, world championship days were back in the Bronx. Larry brought Bucky Harris back from the managerial boneyard to guide this club.

Cleveland interrupted a new Yankee era of domination in 1948, beating Boston in the league's first post-season playoff after the Indians and the Red Sox had concluded the regular season with identical records. Lou Boudreau, manager-shortstop, paced the Tribe down the stretch with his great hitting and fielding, and it was his momentum which enabled Cleveland to down Boston in an unprecedented one-game, sudden-death playoff battle at the Hub's Fenway Park.

The Yankees resumed their old position at the top of the heap for the next five years (1949–53), Casey Stengel leading a new group of Bombers to five straight world championships, a new record in the annals of the game. This was the same Stengel who had been found deficient as a manager of the Boston and Brooklyn entries of the NL.

It was Cleveland again which temporarily halted the fantastic Yankee pennant pushes. Al Lopez, who once played for Stengel in the NL, whipped his teacher in 1954. The Indians rolled up an impressive total of 111 victories—an all-time AL season high—but were humiliated in the Series when they dropped four straight to the New York Giants. It was the first AL post-season defeat in eight years.

During the Indians' drive they established another record, this for attendance for a single day when 84,587 stormed Municipal Stadium on September 12 to see the Tribe belt the Yankees in a doubleheader.

The Korean conflict, during the '50s, claimed several players who previously had served in the forces during World War II. Ted Williams, who held a reserve commission in the Marine Air Corps, was recalled to active duty soon after the start of the '52 year, not to return until the '53 campaign was well under way.

Perhaps the most startling developments of the early '50s were the franchise shifts which left St. Louis and Philadelphia bereft of AL representation for the first time since Ban Johnson organized the loop.

The St. Louis Browns were transferred to Baltimore on September 29, 1953 for a total reported to be $2,475,000. The Philadelphia Athletics were to go one year later, being bought by Arnold Johnson and associates for the sum of approximately three and one half million dollars. Both clubs drew well in their initial season, the Orioles pulling 1,060,910 through the gates in '54 and the Athletics, despite a sixth-place finish, attracting 1,393,054 in '55.

It was the same old AL story as the 1950s drew to a close—too much Yankee dominance. The greatest baseball dynasty ever created won pennants from 1955 through '58, but only got an even break in Series competition, losing the '55 and '57 sets to Brooklyn and Milwaukee. For manager Stengel it made nine pennants in 10 years.

Ted Williams remained the game's most provocative personality, and in 1956 created some sort of history by getting stung with a record-equaling fine of $5,000. The Boston thumper was penalized this amount by his club when he spat in the direction of the stands after the fans in his home park booed for desultory play.

Although the Yankees had the vast Metropolitan area to themselves in 1958 their attendance dropped some 68,000 over their 1957 total. Many theories were advanced for this fall-off, but there was no doubt that the day and night televising of games was beginning to take its toll of the attendance.

Will Harridge, president of the AL since 1931, startled the mid-winter league 1958 meeting when he announced his retirement. He gave no reasons for his decision but many believed that Harridge was bowing out due to the many problems baseball would be forced to face in the next few years. Talk of a third league, a demand by the players for 20 per cent of all gate, concession and television monies and constant discussion on the problems of television and how it should be regulated were some of the factors which, many believed, decided to make the 72-year-old Harridge announce his retirement. Joe Cronin, former star shortstop and manager of Boston and Washington, Hall-of-Famer, and general manager of the Red Sox, was named as his successor.

Picked to win their fifth straight pennant in 1959 the Yankees suddenly found themselves in the unfamiliar surroundings of the cellar where they landed on May 20th. From there they waged an up-hill battle but they were never able to regain their former prestige winding up in third place, 15 games behind the pennant-winning White Sox. Early Wynn of the White Sox was the biggest winner in the majors with 22 victories. Meanwhile the magnates were experiencing "growing pains." Expansion fever was at a high pitch due to the threat of Branch Rickey's Continental League. Suddenly the American League voted to study the request of Minneapolis-St. Paul for a spot in the junior circuit. Cronin's loop proposed expansion to nine clubs for each league by taking a franchise in Minneapolis-St. Paul and granting the National a club in New York. The National rejected this plan claiming they were "not interested" in expansion at the time.

With the Continental League on the ropes due to the pigeon-holing of the Kefauver bill in 1960, the American League once more discussed expansion and decided to go into action as soon as the National advised them of similar word. Meeting in Chicago on July 18th the National League cast a solid vote in favor of the move. When the senior circuit voted to add Houston and New York to the loop in 1962 the American League broke all speed records by boosting their league to 10 clubs. They authorized Calvin Griffith of the Washington club to make his move to Minneapolis-St. Paul, approved a new franchise for Washington to a syndicate headed by General Elwood Quesada, head of the FAA, and awarded a Los Angeles franchise to a group led by cowboy singer Gene Autry and TV tycoon Bob Reynolds. Starting from scratch it was a herculean task to field two brand new major league clubs in less than four months and the result was the wildest talent scramble in major league history.

The year also witnessed the dissolution of the game's most successful managerial team when both General Manager George Weiss and Manager Casey Stengel, of the New York Yankees, were relieved of their posts. This pair had guided the Yanks to ten pennants and seven World Championships in the last twelve years. Another unusual managerial shift occurred in 1960 when Jimmie Dykes of the Tigers and Joe Gordon of the Indians switched jobs. The American League launched the 1961 season with the first 10-club league in its history and also embarked on a marathon 162-games schedule. The new clubs, Minneapolis and Los Angeles, had rough going finishing 7th and 8th respectively. The Yankees, as usual, topheavy favorites did not disappoint their followers and repeated for their 12th pennant in 15 years. Under a new manager, Ralph Houk who assumed the helm after the departure of Casey Stengel, they did not lose their stride and not only copped the flag but continued on to take the Reds four games to one in the World Series. The big guns were Roger Maris who topped the famous Bambino's Home Run record by clouting 61, Mickey Mantle who was right behind him with 54 and pitcher Ed Ford who copped 25 decisions while losing only 4. In winning the pennant on his first try, manager Houk joined three of freshman managers, namely Bucky Harris, Joe Cronin, and Eddie Dyer. The Tigers under Bob Scheffing proved to be the surprise club of the year setting the pace for the first half of the season. Unfortunately the Tigers lacked the pitching depth necessary to stay in front but they were topped only by the Yanks in batting. Norm Cash won the batting crown with an average of .361 while Al Kaline and Rocky Colavito helped the cause with Kaline hitting .324 and Rocky clubbing 45 homers. The newly-born Angels surprised their followers by winning a respectable 70 victories.

It was the old, old story again in 1962 when the Yanks won their 10th flag in the past 12 years. However, they faced unexpected opposition from the two new clubs, the Minnesota Twins and the Los Angeles Angels who finished second and third respectively and gave the Yanks a run for their money, in fact, the Yanks could not find the magic wand until the final two weeks of the season when the Twins and Angels ran out of gas. General manager Fred Haney, the man of the hour in the Angels' set-up made some astounding deals which kept the club in the running until the very end. It was the most surprising club in the history of the game. Early Wynn was one of the tragic figures of the campaign. Trying hard for his 300th victory, he missed on several occasions and had to wait until the middle of the 1963 season to achieve the magic 300. Freshman Bo Belinsky, Earl Wilson and Bill Monbouquette of the Bosox and Jack Kralick of the Minnesota Twins all pitched no-hit games while 20-game winners included Dick Donovan, Ralph Terry, Ray Herbert and Camilo Pascual.

The Yankees continued their dynasty into 1963 and '64, winning two more

pennants to extend their streak to five. The only other club to win five consecutive flags was the Yankees of 1949–53. They won in '63 with their two big sluggers, Micky Mantle and Roger Maris, incapacitated much of the way; they won in '64 under a freshman manager, Yogi Berra, who succeeded Ralph Houk when the latter moved up to general manager. The Bombers won in a breeze in '63, finishing 10½ games in front of Chicago. But the 1964 race was a three-team affair between New York, Chicago and Baltimore, and the Bombers didn't clinch their 29th American League pennant until the next-to-last day.

Berra was fired the day after the World Series ended, despite his success during the season and extending the Cardinals to seven games in the Series. He was replaced by Johnny Keane, his opposite number on the Cards, who had resigned the same day Berra got the ax. The major change in the Yankee structure, however, took place in August when Dan Topping and Del Webb sold 80 per cent of their stock to the Columbia Broadcasting System. Webb sold his remaining 10 per cent to CBS six months later.

Minnesota rookie outfielder Tony Oliva burst onto the scene in 1964 and won the batting title with a .323 average and ranked first in several other batting departments. He repeated in 1965 with a .321 figure, helping the Twins to their first flag. Minnesota was a power club led by all-round shortstop Zoilo Versalles, who did everything well enough to earn the Most Valuable Player award. The Yankees surprised everybody by dropping to sixth place, their lowest finish since 1925 when they wound up seventh.

The Baltimore Orioles, bolstered by the acquisition of Frank Robinson in an inter-league trade with Cincinnati, captured the 1966 flag handily, finishing nine games ahead of the defending champion Twins. Robby won the Triple Crown with a .316 average, 49 home runs and 122 runs batted in and also was instrumental in the Birds' four-game sweep of the Dodgers in the World Series. Nothing much to talk about during the regular season, the Baltimore pitching staff held Los Angeles to a record low of two runs. The Angels' new park in Anaheim was unveiled, a triple-decked structure built in less than two years at a cost of $24,000,000. The Yankees continued their plunge downward and wound up in the league basement, only the third time in their proud 64-year history that they finished so poorly. There were other developments in Gotham, too. Keane was let out as manager on May 7 and replaced by Houk, who relinquished his front office duties. And then, in mid-September, Dan Topping sold his remaining stock in the club to CBS and Michael Burke, 50, a network vice-president and a former football player at the University of Pennsylvania, was named president. A month later, Lee MacPhail, son of the old baseball magnate, was added to the front office team as general manager.

The Boston Red Sox, ninth in 1966 and a study in futility for most of the post-Korean War era, produced one of the biggest surprises in history by winning the 1967 pennant, and on the final day, too. Their kingpin was Carl Yastrzemski, the sometimes moody leftfielder, who won the Triple Crown in even more heroic fashion than had Frank Robinson. Yaz seemed to hit game-winning homers or throw out runners at the plate nearly every day as he tied the Twins' Harmon Killebrew in homers with 44 and led in RBI's (121) and batting (.326). Boston had to withstand a furious four-team race to win, though, a race in which Minnesota, Detroit, Chicago and the Red Sox took turns holding the lead. Chicago, which had a woeful batting attack, was the first to drop out, two days before the end, but the others hung on until the final day.

Boston defeated Minnesota twice, on the final Saturday and Sunday, to assure itself of at least a tie, and then had to await the outcome of the Tigers' double-

header with the Angels. Detroit won the opener, but California spoiled the Tigers' pennant plans by taking the nightcap.

Charlie O. Finley, the controversial owner of the Kansas City Athletics, obtained permission to move the club to Oakland when the league met in October. The AL owners considered Finley's shift and expansion in one package. What came out of it was the Oakland Athletics and new franchises in Kansas City and Seattle, the latter two to begin operation in 1969.

Denny McLain led the Detroit Tigers to a comfortable twelve-game margin in the 1968 pennant race. McLain (31–6) was the first 30-game winner since Dizzy Dean in 1934. He also led in winning percentage, complete games and innings pitched. Jim (Catfish) Hunter of Oakland pitched the first regular season perfect game in 46 years.

With the expansion to 12 teams in 1969, the league was split into two divisions, East and West. Baltimore, Boston, Cleveland, Detroit, New York and Washington made up the East, while California, Chicago, Minnesota, Oakland and the two new teams, Kansas City and Seattle, made up the West. The Championship Series, a three-of-five clash between division winners to determine the league World Series representative, was also adopted.

The Baltimore Orioles, sparked by Frank Robinson, ran roughshod over the other clubs for the first three years, and also won nine straight playoff games. Manager Earl Weaver had essentially the same lineup for these years, including Brooks Robinson, "Boog" Powell, Paul Blair, Mark Belanger and pitchers Dave McNally, Jim Palmer and Mike Cuellar. The Birds topped the Twins in 1969 and 1970 as well as Oakland in 1971.

Detroit came back to win the East Crown in 1972. This was one of the closest races in league history, with four clubs still alive in the final week. The Tigers won the crucial first game of the final series of two with Boston to beat the Red Sox by half a game. The player strike had shortened the season by a week, leaving Detroit with one more game than Boston.

Meanwhile, in the West, the Oakland Athletics were beginning to move. Their manager was Dick Williams, who had guided the Red Sox to the 1967 pennant. In his third year at Oakland (1971) the A's became the first team in three years to come within ten games of the Orioles, but lost the playoff in three straight. In 1972 Oakland fought off the White Sox in the West and then nipped Detroit in the championship series in five games. Oakland continued its winning ways in 1973, gaining revenge over the Orioles in the playoff three games to two. Each team had won its division easily.

Reggie Jackson, Sal Bando, Joe Rudi, Bert Campaneris, Gene Tenace and pitchers Jim Hunter, Ken Holtzman, Vida Blue and Rollie Fingers formed the nucleus of the team which took over from Baltimore as the league's best. Oakland won again in 1974, beating the Orioles in the playoffs. They then went on to take their third straight World Series, the first time this feat had been accomplished in over twenty years. The Athletics led the Western Division once more in 1975, but were denied a chance at their fourth world championship by the rejuvenated Boston Red Sox. The Sox benefited from the play of super rookie Fred Lynn, who became the first player in history to win both MVP and rookie awards the same year.

Carl Yastrzemski won his third batting title in 1968 and lost out by less than a point in 1970. Rod Carew won five batting titles, leading in 1969 and 1972 through 1975. Harmon Killebrew topped the league in homers for the sixth time in 1969. Nolan Ryan of California set a new major league strikeout record in 1973 and also threw four no-hitters. Wilbur Wood of the White Sox,

once the league's best relief pitcher, won 20 games as a starter in 1974, giving 90 wins in four years.

After only one season, the Seattle club was switched to Milwaukee for 1970. Milwaukee made another move in 1972—to the East Division, as Bob Short moved his Washington club to Texas and the West.

The AL had their best season for attendance in history in 1973, aided by the new designated hitter rule which allowed a permanent pinch-hitter for the pitcher. It was announced in October that Joe Cronin would move from league president to chairman of the board, and that Lee MacPhail would take over as president for 1974.

A great deal of news continued to be made off the field. Hank Aaron came over from the NL in 1975 to finish his career with Milwaukee. Cleveland made news when they hired Frank Robinson, who became the first black manager in the majors, also in 1975. The biggest story concerned Jim "Catfish" Hunter. Relieved of his obligation to Oakland due to a breach of contract by Athletics owner Charles O. Finley, the Catfish went on the open market and was able to sell his services to the Yankees for a reported three-plus million dollars.

The Yankees were back on top in 1976 for the first time in twelve years, with the help of the Catfish and Thurman Munson. Kansas City won a close race from Oakland in the West and extended the Yanks to five games in the championship series. The Royals became the first expansion AL team to manage a first place finish. The usual fireworks occurred in Oakland. Faced with the likely defection through free agent status of several more of his stars, Finley tried to sell Vida Blue to New York and Joe Rudi and Rollie Fingers to Boston. Commissioner Kuhn voided the sales, stating that it was not in the best interests of baseball. Detroit's newcomer, Mark "The Bird" Fidrych regularly attracted crowds of 50,000 with his fine pitching and unique style of enthusiasm.

American Association

In the earlier years of the National League many of the mid-western cities were envious of the financial inroads the league had made, especially in hinterland towns which were not of major league status. Touring Easterners from the NL drew heavy gates in exhibitions played in Western areas, and the West soon started to sound out several cities as prospective entries in a new major circuit.

H. D. (Denny) Knight of Pittsburgh and Justus Thorner of Cincinnati rounded up a half dozen clubs and went into the field in 1882, avowed rivals of the NL. The newly-founded American Association was now in business.

With prideful, suspicious Soden acting as NL president, Eastern reception was openly hostile, extending to bold player raids and the coining of a favorite epithet. "Beer and Whiskey League," they termed the AA, deriding the fact that financial backers of the new circuit mainly derived their income from alcohol.

On the other side of the fence, name-calling consisted of tagging the NL the "rich man's league." To court the "plain workingmen" clientele, the AA slashed the admission price to half its rival's 50-cent standard, featured Sunday baseball (then expressly forbidden in the NL under threat of expulsion) and dispensed beer in the stands.

Cincinnati won the first AA flag behind the pitching of bespectacled Will White. The novelty of good baseball in fertile cities, bringing a host of new Western heroes into the diamond limelight, resulted in a prosperous inaugural season. The AA added two more franchises for 1883. Thanks to newly-elected president A. G. Mills, the NL wisely made peace with its lusty young rival, and under the National Agreement they operated as dual major leagues.

The most fabulous figure in AA history was not any of its new playing heroes, but a bulbous-nosed German immigrant named Chris Von der Ahe. Owner of a pleasure resort in the St. Louis suburbs, the hearty and generous "sport" became interested in baseball as a means of attracting customers to his place. But he was smart enough to know how ignorant he was of the game's intricacies, so Chris relied on the judgment of Alfred H. Spink, a zealous baseball writer and guiding spirit of the game in early St. Louis days.

Another colorful character who helped develop the Browns was Ted Sullivan, railroad concessionaire who sponsored a powerful team in Dubuque, Iowa. Ted brought the newly-formed Browns his best men, including first baseman Charlie Comiskey. St. Louis finished a close second to the pennant-winning Athletics in 1883, slumped in '84, and the next year, with Commy at the helm, started a streak of four straight pennants.

Though Al Spink, who founded *The Sporting News* soon afterward, and Comiskey, who revolutionized first base play, were the guiding geniuses behind the Browns' dynasty, expansive Von der Ahe swaggered under such sustained success and unabashedly proclaimed himself "the smartest feller in baseball." On the contrary, Chris' petulant orders to dispose of several important players after his crushing World Series loss to Detroit in 1887 proved costly. Commy repeated the flag in '88, but was nipped in quest of a fifth straight pennant by a Brooklyn team that had bought the standout players who incurred the displeasure of the St. Louis baron.

War with the Players' League in 1890 crippled the AA. Unable to meet budgets on a 25-cent-admission plank, several key clubs deserted to the NL. A year later, the AA withdrew from the National Agreement . . . only to lose the "cold war" when more clubowners secretly capitulated to the NL.

Despite its inglorious finish, the AA played a valuable role in baseball history. It pioneered reforms which the NL eventually adopted, like league control of umpires, Sunday baseball and the percentage system of determining pennant winners. Healthy competition also forced the NL to draft a National Agreement that served as a basis for present-day pacts guiding major and minor league operations.

Union Association

Insisting that the reserve rule "reserves all that is good for the owners, leaving the remainder for the players," St. Louis millionaire Henry V. Lucas embarked on a one-man crusade to end the players' "bondage." He organized the Union Association as a third major league in 1884. George Wright, given the concession of manufacturing the official ball for the circuit, agreed to run the Boston franchise. Thorner came in with his Cincinnati club after the AA founder thought he had received short shrift in his circuit.

Widely-traveled Ted Sullivan was dispatched to round up players willing to ignore the reserve clause binding them to the AA or NL. Before the season started, the Unions had about 50 of these. But most of the recruits suddenly repented and stayed with their old clubs. As owner of the St. Louis Maroons franchise, Lucas was able to ante up extra bonus money to keep his reserve-clause jumpers in line, so the UA's "angel" wound up with an overpowering pennant-winner that won its first 20 games and quickly killed interest in the "race." Only five clubs finished the season, though a dozen participated.

Unwilling to draw any distinction between breaking a current contract or the holdover clause, both the AA and NL raided UA ranks in the early months, and kidnapped many players who had drawn heavy advances in salary. On July 1, the UA declared open warfare and started to induce the stars of rival leagues to jump in mid-season, too.

The three-way war was too costly all around. Weaker clubs in the UA folded in profusion. Only in St. Louis, where Lucas unstintingly gave his fans the best in players and accommodations—including dozens of caged canaries strewn about the stands—was there any sustained prosperity.

When the UA expired at the end of the season, Lucas opportunistically snapped up the Cleveland NL franchise (which he had helped ruin by mid-season player raids) for $2,500. As part of his price for peace, Lucas insisted on moving into the NL. He transferred his Cleveland holding to St. Louis, paid Von der Ahe $5,000 for territorial privileges and ungraciously absented himself from the UA's dissolution meeting in order to concentrate on his new NL interest.

Players' League

The one-year stand of the Players' League (1890) was actually a movement motivated by players who were members of the National Brotherhood of Professional Players. This was a benevolent organization which used dues of five dollars a month from its members to aid its sick and needy.

After the 1885 season, the NL and AA magnates set a ceiling on players salaries and forbade any cash advances during the off-season. John Montgomery Ward, later a successful attorney, served as the Brotherhood's spokesman in protesting the salary scale of $2,000. Although the salary limit never was enforced, though kept on the books, additional grievances were fought successfully by the Brotherhood which demanded, and received, official recognition in 1887.

While Ward was away on a world tour, the magnates instituted the unfair

Classification System of scaling players' salaries. Upon his return, the brilliant Giant shortstop couldn't even get an audience with the NL. Declaring lack of good faith on the part of the league, the Brotherhood published a Declaration of Independence on November 4, 1889, and lined up financial support for a Players' League in 1890.

Players in the new circuit signed three-year contracts at their 1889 figure, which could be raised at the discretion of the club, but not slashed. Even more interesting, the PL abandoned the reserve rule by allowing players to switch clubs at will at the close of the season. However, the latter plan never got a trial, since the league lived only one year.

The secession movement was populer. Four out of five NL regulars jumped to the PL. Though forced to operate with makeshift lineups, the NL magnates boldly took on the insurgents by scheduling and re-scheduling games in order to conflict with PL contests in the same city. In New York, only a wall separated games played simultaneously by the rival leagues.

Spalding, appointed head of a "war committee" of the NL, offered King Kelly a $10,000 bribe plus a three-year League contract "at any figure you want to write in" to skip back. But the colorful "King Kel" couldn't go back on his Brotherhood mates and turned down the offer. Kelly went on to pilot the PL pennant-winners in Boston.

Rainy weather in the late stages of the race hurt PL attendances, and inexperienced magnates quickly lost heart at the reverses. A few sold out to eager NL rivals, and the Brotherhood collapsed. All contract-jumpers were restored to their original clubs without penalty.

Federal League

Unlike the Union Association and Players' League, which became third major leagues principally on "reform" platforms, the Federal League moved into the baseball picture strictly in the spirit of a capital investment. When coal magnate James A. Gilmore became president of the FL in September, 1913, it was still a sectional minor league operating in the Midwest.

Gilmore had the gift of gab, and soon sold a group of businessmen on the wisdom of backing a third major league. Glib Jim painted a rosy financial picture, dipping heavily into the figure of the "Half million dollar World Series" of 1912, which netted each of the competing clubs almost $150,000. As a clincher, he accented the advertising value of owning a ball club which daily made nation-wide headlines.

The spellbinder convinced the Ward baking brothers, who took the Brooklyn franchise; Charles Weeghman, who owned a chain of Chicago restaurants; Harry Sinclair, oil tycoon who took the Newark Club; Phil Ball, St. Louis ice king; Otto Stifel, wealthy brewer, and others.

Gilmore then went to work on the players. His first conquest was Joe Tinker of Cub fame, who was hired to manage the Chicago Whales. Other established stars followed. Even though they didn't fall for the greenback bait, such standouts as Ty Cobb and Tris Speaker had their salaries doubled to keep them from joining the "outlaw league."

Eight new ballparks were built within three months, including the Chicago plant that is now known as Wrigley Field. Indianapolis nosed out Chicago in a close race in 1914, while Chicago shaded St. Louis by one percentage point the next year. Only the imminence of American entry into the World War persuaded the FL magnates to listen to peace feelers from the AL and NL.

The price of peace came high. First, the Feds insisted that their rivals assume

the $385,000 worth of FL player contracts. Weeghman was permitted to buy the Cubs and Ball the Browns. Payments spread over five to 20 years were to reimburse the Ward interests, Sinclair and Pittsburgh backers. Of the many Fed players sold back to the majors, the highest price went for Benny Kauff, the "Ty Cobb of the Feds," whom the Giants snapped up for $35,000.

The settlement made no provision for the Baltimore club, which thereupon instituted an anti-trust suit against organized baseball that went all the way to the U. S. Supreme Court before Justice Holmes finally ruled in 1922 the sport was not "interstate commerce."

CLUB STANDINGS YEAR-BY-YEAR

CLUB STANDINGS YEAR-BY-YEAR
F indicates where club finished at end of season. x indicates did not finish season. t indicates
finished in a tie for this position. p indicates playoff used to break tie at end of scheduled season.

1871—NATIONAL ASSOCIATION

CLUB	F	W	L	PCT	MGR
ATH	1	22	7	.759	Hayhurst
CHI	2	20	9	.690	Foley
BOS	3	22	10	.688	Wright
OLY	4	16	15	.516	Young
HAY	5	15	15	500	Pike
					Craver
MUT	6	16	18	.471	Ferguson
CLE	7	10	19	.345	Pabor
KEK	8x	7	21	.250	Deane
					Lennon
ROK	9	6	20	.231	Waldo

1872—NATIONAL ASSOCIATION

CLUB	F	W	L	PCT	MGR
BOS	1	38	8	.826	Wright
ATH	2	31	15	.674	Hayhurst
L BAL	3	35	19	.648	Henderson
MUT	4	35	21	.625	Pearce
HAY	5x	15	10	.600	Wood
CLE	6x	6	15	.286	Hastings
ATL	7	9	28	.243	Ferguson
OLY	8x	2	7	.222	Young
MAN	9x	5	19	.208	Putnam
ECK	10	3	26	.103	Clinton
					Wood
NAT	11x	0	11	.000	Miller

1873—NATIONAL ASSOCIATION

CLUB	F	W	L	PCT	MGR
BOS	1	43	16	.729	Wright
PHI	2	36	16	.692	Young, G.
L BAL	3	34	22	.607	Henderson
ATH	4	28	23	.549	Hayhurst
MUT	5	29	25	.537	Cammeyer
ATL	6	17	37	.315	Ferguson
NAT	7	8	31	.205	Young, N.
RES	8x	2	21	.087	Benjamin
MAR	9x	0	6	.000	Smith

1874—NATIONAL ASSOCIATION

CLUB	F	W	L	PCT	MGR
BOS	1	52	18	.743	Wright
MUT	2	42	23	.646	Higham
ATH	3	33	22	.600	Hayhurst
PHI	4	29	29	.500	Craver
CHI	5	28	31	.475	Young, N.
ATL	6	23	32	.418	Ferguson
HAR	7	15	38	.283	Pike
L BAL	8	9	38	.191	Henderson

1875—NATIONAL ASSOCIATION

CLUB	F	W	L	PCT	MGR
BOS	1	71	8	.899	Wright
ATH	2	53	20	.726	Hayhurst
HAR	3	54	28	.659	Ferguson
ST.L	4	37	28	.569	Graffen
PHI	5	37	31	.544	Young, G
MUT	6	31	38	.449	Hicks
CHI	7	30	37	.448	Wood
RS	8x	4	15	.211	Sweazy
NAT	9x	5	23	.179	Childs
N H	10	7	40	.149	Gould
CEN	11x	2	12	.143	Craver
WES	12x	1	12	.077	Trimble
ATL	13	2	42	.045	Pabor

1876—NATIONAL LEAGUE

CLUB	F	W	L	PCT	MGR
CHI	1	52	14	.788	Spalding
St. L	2	45	19	.703	Graffen
HAR	3	47	21	.691	Ferguson
BOS	4	39	31	.557	Wright, W.
LOU	5	30	36	.455	Fulmer
MUT	6	21	35	.375	Cammeyer
ATH	7	14	45	.237	Wright, A.
CIN	8	9	56	.135	Gould

1877—NATIONAL LEAGUE

CLUB	F	W	L	PCT	MGR
BOS	1	42	18	.700	Wright
LOU	2	35	25	.583	Chapman
HAR	3	31	27	.534	Ferguson
ST.L	4	28	32	.467	Lucas
					McManus
CHI	5	26	33	.441	Spalding
CIN	6	15	42	.263	Pike
					Addy

1878—NATIONAL LEAGUE

CLUB	F	W	L	PCT	MGR
BOS	1	41	19	.683	Wright
CIN	2	37	23	.617	McVey
PRO	3	33	27	.550	Ware
CHI	4	30	30	.500	Ferguson
IND	5	24	36	.400	Clapp
MIL	6	15	45	.250	Chapman

1879—NATIONAL LEAGUE

CLUB	F	W	L	PCT	MGR
PRO	1	55	23	.705	Wright, G.
BOS	2	49	29	.628	Wright, W.
BUF	3t	44	32	.579	McGunnigle
CHI	3t	44	32	.579	Anson
CIN	5	38	36	.514	White, J. L.
					McVey
SYR	6x	15	27	.357	Smith
CLE	7	24	53	.312	McCormick
TRO	8	19	56	.253	Ferguson

1880—NATIONAL LEAGUE

CLUB	F	W	L	PCT	MGR
CHI	1	67	17	.798	Anson
PRO	2	52	32	.619	Bullock
CLE	3	47	37	.559	McCormick
TRO	4	41	42	.494	Ferguson
WOR	5	40	43	.482	Bancroft
					Brown
BOS	6	40	44	.476	Wright, W
BUF	7	24	58	.293	McGunnigle
					Crane
CIN	8	21	59	.263	Clapp

1881—NATIONAL LEAGUE

CLUB	F	W	L	PCT	MGR
CHI	1	56	28	.667	Anson
PRO	2	47	37	.559	Bullock
					Morrow
BUF	3	45	38	.542	O'Rourke
DET	4	41	43	.488	Bancroft
TRO	5	39	45	.464	Ferguson
BOS	6	38	45	.458	Wright, W
CLE	7	36	48	.429	McCormick
WOR	8	32	50	.390	Brown

1882—NATIONAL LEAGUE

CLUB	F	W	L	PCT	MGR
CHI	1	55	29	.655	Anson
PRO	2	52	32	.619	Wright, W
BOS	3t	45	39	.536	Morrill
BUF	3t	45	39	.536	O'Rourke
CLE	5	42	40	.512	Evans
DET	6	42	41	.506	Bancroft
TRO	7	35	48	.422	Ferguson
WOR	8	18	66	.214	Brown
					Bond
					Chapman

1882—AMERICAN ASSOCIATION

CLUB	F	W	L	PCT	MGR
CIN	1	54	26	.675	Fulmer
ECL	2	44	35	.557	Dyler
					Reccius
					Maskrey
ATH	3	40	35	.533	Sharsig
					Mason
ALL	4	39	39	.500	Pratt
ST.L	5	36	43	.456	Cuthbert
					Sullivan
BAL	6	19	54	.260	Myers

1883—NATIONAL LEAGUE

CLUB	F	W	L	PCT	MGR
BOS	1	63	35	.643	Burdock
					Morrill
CHI	2	59	39	.602	Anson
PRO	3	58	40	.592	Wright, W
CLE	4	55	42	.567	Bancroft
BUF	5	52	45	.536	O'Rourke
N Y	6	46	50	.479	Clapp
DET	7	40	58	.408	Chapman
PHI	8	17	81	.173	Ferguson

1883—AMERICAN ASSOCIATION

CLUB	F	W	L	PCT	MGR
ATH	1	66	32	.673	Knight
					Mason
					Sharsig
St. L	2	65	33	.663	Sullivan
					Comiskey
CIN	3	62	36	.633	Snyder
MET	4	54	42	.563	Mutrie
ECL	5	52	45	.536	Reccius
					Maskrey
					Gerhardt
COL	6	32	65	.330	Phillips
ALL	7	30	68	.306	Pratt
					Butler
					Battin
BAL	8	28	68	.292	Barnie

1884—NATIONAL LEAGUE

CLUB	F	W	L	PCT	MGR
PRO	1	84	28	.750	Bancroft
BOS	2	73	38	.658	Morrill
BUF	3	64	47	.577	O'Rourke
CHI	4t	62	50	.554	Anson
N Y	4t	62	50	.554	Price
PHI	6	39	73	.348	Wright, W
CLE	7	35	77	.313	Hackett
DET	8	28	84	.250	Chapman

1884—AMERICAN ASSOCIATION

CLUB	F	W	L	PCT	MGR
MET	1	75	32	.701	Mutrie
COL	2	69	39	.639	Schmelz
ECL	3	68	40	.630	Gerhardt
					Walsh
St. L	4	67	40	.626	Williams
					Von der Ahe
CIN	5	68	41	.624	Snyder
					White
BAL	6	63	43	.594	Barnie
ATH	7	61	46	.570	Mason
					Sharsig
TOL	8	46	58	.442	Morton
BRO	9	40	64	.385	Taylor
VIR	10	12	30	.286	Moses
ALL	11	30	78	.278	Battin
					Creamer
					Ferguson
					McKnight
					Phillips
IND	12	29	78	.271	Gifford
					Watkins
NAT	13x	12	51	.190	Hollingshead

1884—UNION ASSOCIATION

CLUB	F	W	L	PCT	MGR
St. L	1	91	16	.850	Sullivan / Dunlap
MIL	2x	8	3	.727	McKee
CIN	3	68	35	.660	O'Leary / Crane
BAL	4	56	48	.538	Levis / Henderson
BOS	5	58	51	.532	Murnane / Furniss / Morse
CHI	6x	33	35	.485	Hengle
NAT	7	47	66	.416	Scanlon
PIT	8x	7	10	.412	Battin / Ellick
KEY	9x	21	46	.313	Malone / Pratt
St. P	10	2	6	.250	Thompson
ALT	11x	6	19	.240	Curtis
K C	12	14	63	.182	Sullivan
WIL	13x	2	15	.118	Simmons

1885—NATIONAL LEAGUE

CLUB	F	W	L	PCT	MGR
CHI	1	87	25	.776	Anson
N Y	2	85	27	.758	Mutrie
PHI	3	56	54	.509	Wright, W
PRO	4	53	57	.481	Bancroft
BOS	5	46	66	.410	Morrill
DET	6	41	67	.379	Morton / Watkins
BUF	7	38	74	.339	Chapman / Hughson / Galvin
St. L	8	36	72	.333	Dunlap / Fine / Lucas

1885—AMERICAN ASSOCIATION

CLUB	F	W	L	PCT	MGR
St. L	1	79	33	.705	Comiskey
CIN	2	63	49	.563	Caylor
ALL	3	56	55	.505	Phillips
ATH	4	55	57	.491	Knight / Mason / Sharsig
BRO	5t	53	59	.473	Doyle / Hackett / Byrne
ECL	5t	53	59	.473	Hart
MET	7	44	64	.407	Gifford
BAL	8	41	68	.376	Barnie

1886—NATIONAL LEAGUE

CLUB	F	W	L	PCT	MGR
CHI	1	90	34	.725	Anson
DET	2	87	36	.707	Watkins
N Y	3	75	44	.630	Mutrie
PHI	4	71	43	.622	Wright, W
BOS	5	56	61	.478	Morrill
St. L	6	43	79	.352	Schmelz
K C	7	30	91	.247	Rowe
WAS	8	28	92	.233	Scanlon / Gaffney

1886—AMERICAN ASSOCIATION

CLUB	F	W	L	PCT	MGR
St. L	1	93	46	.669	Comiskey
ALL	2	80	57	.584	Phillips
BRO	3	76	61	.555	Byrne
ECL	4	66	70	.485	Hart
CIN	5	65	72	.471	Caylor
ATH	6	63	73	.467	Simmons / Mason / Sharsig
MET	7	53	82	.393	Gifford / Ferguson
BAL	8	48	83	.366	Barnie

1887—NATIONAL LEAGUE

CLUB	F	W	L	PCT	MGR
DET	1	79	45	.637	Watkins
PHI	2	75	48	.610	Wright, W
CHI	3	71	50	.587	Anson
N Y	4	68	55	.553	Mutrie
BOS	5	61	60	.504	Morrill
PIT	6	55	69	.444	Phillips
WAS	7	46	76	.377	Gaffney / Dennis
IND	8	37	89	.294	Fogel / Burnham / Thomas

1887—AMERICAN ASSOCIATION

CLUB	F	W	L	PCT	MGR
St. L	1	95	40	.704	Comiskey
CIN	2	81	54	.600	Schmelz
BAL	3	77	58	.570	Barnie
ECL	4	76	60	.559	Kelly
ATH	5	64	69	.481	Bancroft / Mason / Sharsig
BRO	6	60	74	.448	Byrne
MET	7	44	89	.331	Ferguson / Caylor / Orr
CLE	8	39	92	.298	Williams

1888—NATIONAL LEAGUE

CLUB	F	W	L	PCT	MGR
N Y	1	84	47	.641	Mutrie
CHI	2	77	58	.578	Anson
PHI	3	69	61	.531	Wright, W
BOS	4	70	64	.522	Morrill
DET	5	68	63	.519	Watkins / Leadley
PIT	6	66	68	.493	Phillips
IND	7	50	85	.370	Spence
WAS	8	48	86	.358	Hewitt / Sullivan / Whitney

1888—AMERICAN ASSOCIATION

CLUB	F	W	L	PCT	MGR
St. L	1	92	43	.681	Comiskey
BRO	2	88	52	.629	McGunnigle
ATH	3	81	52	.609	Sharsig
CIN	4	80	54	.597	Schmelz
BAL	5	57	80	.416	Barnie
CLE	6	50	82	.378	Williams / Loftus
ECL	7	48	87	.360	Kerins / Davidson
K C	8	43	89	.326	Rowe / Barkley / Watkins

1889—NATIONAL LEAGUE

CLUB	F	W	L	PCT	MGR
N Y	1	83	43	.659	Mutrie
BOS	2	83	45	.648	Hart
CHI	3	67	65	.508	Anson
PHI	4	63	64	.496	Wright, W
PIT	5	61	71	.462	Phillips / Dunlap / Hanlon
CLE	6	61	72	.459	Loftus
IND	7	59	75	.440	Bancroft / Glasscock
WAS	8	41	83	.331	Morrill / Irwin

1889—AMERICAN ASSOCIATION

CLUB	F	W	L	PCT	MGR
BRO	1	93	44	.679	McGunnigle
St. L	2	90	45	.667	Comiskey
ATH	3	75	58	.564	Sharsig
CIN	4	76	63	.547	Schmelz
BAL	5	70	65	.519	Barnie
COL	6	60	78	.435	Buckenberger

(Continued)

1889-American Association (Cont.)

CLUB	F	W	L	PCT	MGR
K C	7	55	82	.401	Watkins / Manning
ECL	8	27	111	.195	Davidson / Brown / Means / McKinney / Shannon / Wolf / Chapman

1890—NATIONAL LEAGUE

CLUB	F	W	L	PCT	MGR
BRO	1	86	43	.667	McGunnigle
CHI	2	83	53	.610	Anson
PHI	3	78	53	.595	Wright, W
CIN	4	78	55	.586	Loftus
BOS	5	76	57	.571	Selee
N Y	6	63	68	.481	Mutrie
CLE	7	44	88	.333	Schmelz / Leadley
PIT	8	23	114	.168	Hecker

1890—AMERICAN ASSOCIATION

CLUB	F	W	L	PCT	MGR
ECL	1	88	44	.667	Chapman
COL	2	79	55	.590	Buckenberger / Sullivan / Schmelz
St. L	3	78	58	.574	McCarthy / Roseman / Campau
TOL	4	68	64	.515	Morton
ROC	5	63	63	.500	Powers
BAL	6	15	19	.441	Barnie
SYR	7	55	72	.433	Fessenden / Frazer
ATH	8	54	78	.409	Sharsig
BRO	9x	26	73	.263	Kennedy

1890—PLAYERS' LEAGUE

CLUB	F	W	L	PCT	MGR
BOS	1	81	48	.628	Kelly
BRO	2	76	56	.576	Ward
N Y	3	74	57	.565	Ewing
CHI	4	75	62	.547	Comiskey
PHI	5	68	63	.519	Hilt / Fogarty / Buffinton
PIT	6	60	68	.469	Hanlon
CLE	7	55	75	.423	Faatz / Larkin / Tebeau
BUF	8	36	96	.273	Rowe

1891—NATIONAL LEAGUE

CLUB	F	W	L	PCT	MGR
BOS	1	87	51	.630	Selee
CHI	2	82	53	.607	Anson
N Y	3	71	61	.538	Mutrie
PHI	4	68	69	.496	Wright, W
CLE	5	65	74	.468	Leadley / Tebeau
BRO	6	61	76	.445	Ward
CIN	7	56	81	.409	Loftus
PIT	8	55	80	.407	Hanlon / McGunnigle

1891—AMERICAN ASSOCIATION

CLUB	F	W	L	PCT	MGR
BOS	1	93	42	.689	Irwin
St. L	2	86	52	.623	Comiskey
MIL	3	21	15	.583	Cushman
BAL	4	71	64	.526	Barnie / Van Haltren
ATH	5	73	66	.525	Sharsig / Wood / Barnie
COL	6	61	76	.445	Schmelz
CIN	7x	43	57	.430	Kelly
ECL	8	55	84	.396	Chapman
WAS	9	44	91	.326	Trott / Snyder / Shannon / Griffin

1892—NATIONAL LEAGUE

CLUB	F	W	L	PCT	MGR
BOS	1	102	48	.680	Selee
CLE	2	93	56	.624	Tebeau
BRO	3	95	59	.617	Ward
PHI	4	87	66	.569	Wright, W
CIN	5	82	68	.547	Comiskey
PIT	6	80	73	.523	{Burns / Buckenberger}
CHI	7	70	76	.479	Anson
N Y	8	71	80	.470	Powers
LOU	9	63	89	.414	{Pfeffer / Chapman}
WAS	10	58	93	.384	{Barnie / Irwin / Richardson / Wagner}
ST.L	11	56	94	.373	Von der Ahe
BAL	12	46	101	.313	{Van Haltren / Waltz / Hanlon}

1893—NATIONAL LEAGUE

CLUB	F	W	L	PCT	MGR
BOS	1	86	44	.662	Selee
PIT	2	81	48	.628	Buckenberger
CLE	3	73	55	.570	Tebeau
PHI	4	72	57	.558	Wright, W
N Y	5	68	64	.515	Ward
BRO	6t	65	63	.508	Foutz
CIN	6t	65	63	.508	Comiskey
BAL	8	60	70	.462	Hanlon
CHI	9	57	71	.445	Anson
ST.L	10	57	75	.432	Watkins
LOU	11	50	75	.400	Barnie
WAS	12	40	89	.310	{Wagner / O'Rourke}

1894—NATIONAL LEAGUE

CLUB	F	W	L	PCT	MGR
BAL	1	89	39	.695	Hanlon
N Y	2	88	44	.667	Ward
BOS	3	83	49	.629	Selee
PHI	4	71	56	.559	Irwin
BRO	5	70	61	.534	Foutz
CLE	6	68	61	.527	Tebeau
PIT	7	65	65	.500	{Buckenberger / Mac'k}
CHI	8	57	75	.432	Anson
ST.L	9	56	76	.424	Miller
CIN	10	54	75	.419	Comiskey
WAS	11	45	87	.341	Schmelz
LOU	12	36	94	.277	Barnie

1895—NATIONAL LEAGUE

CLUB	F	W	L	PCT	MGR
BAL	1	87	43	.669	Hanlon
CLE	2	84	46	.646	Tebeau
PHI	3	78	53	.595	Irwin
CHI	4	72	58	.554	Anson
BOS	5t	71	60	.542	Selee
BRO	5t	71	60	.542	Foutz
PIT	7	71	61	.538	Mack
CIN	8	66	64	.508	Ewing
N Y	9	66	65	.504	{Davis / Doyle / Watkins}
WAS	10	43	85	.336	Schmelz
ST.L	11	39	92	.298	{Buckenberger / Quinn / Phelan / Von der Ahe}
LOU	12	35	96	.267	McCloskey

1896—NATIONAL LEAGUE

CLUB	F	W	L	PCT	MGR
BAL	1	90	39	.698	Hanlon
CLE	2	80	48	.625	Tebeau
CIN	3	77	50	.606	Ewing
BOS	4	74	57	.565	Selee
CHI	5	71	57	.555	Anson
PIT	6	66	63	.512	Mack
N Y	7	64	67	.489	{Irwin / Joyce}

(Continued)

1896-National League (Cont.)

CLUB	F	W	L	PCT	MGR
PHI	8	62	68	.477	Nash
BRO	9t	58	73	.443	Foutz
WAS	9t	58	73	.443	Schmelz
ST.L	11	40	90	.306	{Diddlebock / Latham / Conner / Dowd}
LOU	12	38	93	.290	{McCloskey / McGunnigle}

1897—NATIONAL LEAGUE

CLUB	F	W	L	PCT	MGR
BOS	1	93	39	.705	Selee
BAL	2	90	40	.693	Hanlon
N Y	3	83	48	.634	Joyce
CIN	4	76	56	.576	Ewing
CLE	5	69	62	.527	Tebeau
BRO	6t	61	71	.462	Barnie
WAS	6t	61	71	.462	{Schmelz / Brown}
PIT	8	60	71	.458	Donovan
CHI	9	59	73	.447	Anson
PHI	10	55	77	.417	Stallings
LOU	11	52	78	.400	{Rogers / Clarke}
ST.L	12	29	102	.221	{Dowd / Nicol / Hallman / Von der Ahe}

1898—NATIONAL LEAGUE

CLUB	F	W	L	PCT	MGR
BOS	1	102	47	.685	Selee
BAL	2	96	53	.644	Hanlon
CIN	3	92	60	.605	Ewing
CHI	4	85	65	.567	Burns
CLE	5	81	68	.544	Tebeau
PHI	6	78	71	.523	{Stallings / Shettsline}
N Y	7	77	73	.513	{Joyce / Anson}
PIT	8	72	76	.486	Watkins
LOU	9	70	81	.464	Clarke
BRO	10	54	91	.372	{Barnie / Griffin / Ebbets}
WAS	11	51	101	.336	{Brown / Doyle / McGuire / Irwin}
ST.L	12	39	111	.260	Hurst

1899—NATIONAL LEAGUE

CLUB	F	W	L	PCT	MGR
BRO	1	88	42	.677	Hanlon
BOS	2	95	57	.625	Selee
PHI	3	94	58	.618	Shettsline
BAL	4	84	58	.592	McGraw
ST.L	5	83	66	.557	Tebeau
CIN	6	83	67	.553	Ewing
PIT	7	76	73	.510	{Watkins / Donovan}
CHI	8	75	73	.507	Burns
LOU	9	75	77	.493	Clarke
N Y	10	60	86	.411	{Day / Hoey}
WAS	11	53	95	.358	Irwin
CLE	12	20	134	.129	{Cross / Quinn}

1900—NATIONAL LEAGUE

CLUB	F	W	L	PCT	MGR
BRO	1	82	54	.603	Hanlon
PIT	2	79	60	.568	Clarke
PHI	3	75	63	.543	Shettsline
BOS	4	66	72	.478	Selee
CHI	5t	65	75	.464	Loftus
ST.L	5t	65	75	.464	{Tebeau / Heilbroner}
CIN	7	62	77	.446	Allen
N Y	8	60	78	.435	{Ewing / Davis}

1901—NATIONAL LEAGUE

CLUB	F	W	L	PCT	MGR
PIT	1	90	49	.647	Clarke
PHI	2	83	57	.593	Shettsline
BRO	3	79	57	.581	Hanlon
ST.L	4	76	64	.543	Donovan
BOS	5	69	69	.500	Selee
CHI	6	53	86	.381	Loftus
N Y	7	52	85	.380	Davis
CIN	8	52	87	.374	McPhee

1901—AMERICAN LEAGUE

CLUB	F	W	L	PCT	MGR
CHI	1	83	53	.610	Griffith
BOS	2	79	57	.581	Collins
DET	3	74	61	.548	Stallings
PHI	4	74	62	.544	Mack
BAL	5	68	65	.511	McGraw
WAS	6	61	72	.459	Manning
CLE	7	54	82	.397	McAleer
MIL	8	48	89	.350	Duffy

1902—NATIONAL LEAGUE

CLUB	F	W	L	PCT	MGR
PIT	1	103	36	.741	Clarke
BRO	2	75	63	.543	Hanlon
BOS	3	73	64	.533	Buckenberger
CIN	4	70	70	.500	{McPhee / Bancroft / Kelley}
CHI	5	68	69	.496	Selee
ST.L	6	56	78	.410	Donovan
PHI	7	56	81	.409	Shettsline
N Y	8	48	88	.353	{Fogel / Smith / McGraw}

1902—AMERICAN LEAGUE

CLUB	F	W	L	PCT	MGR
PHI	1	83	53	.610	Mack
ST.L	2	78	58	.574	McAleer
BOS	3	77	60	.562	Collins
CHI	4	74	60	.552	Griffith
CLE	5	69	67	.507	Armour
WAS	6	61	75	.449	Loftus
DET	7	52	83	.385	Dwyer
BAL	8	50	88	.362	{McGraw / Robinson}

1903—NATIONAL LEAGUE

CLUB	F	W	L	PCT	MGR
PIT	1	91	49	.650	Clarke
N Y	2	84	55	.604	McGraw
CHI	3	82	56	.594	Selee
CIN	4	74	65	.532	Kelley
BRO	5	70	66	.515	Hanlon
BOS	6	58	80	.420	Buckenberger
PHI	7	49	86	.363	Zimmer
ST.L	8	43	94	.314	Donovan

1903—AMERICAN LEAGUE

CLUB	F	W	L	PCT	MGR
BOS	1	91	47	.659	Collins
PHI	2	75	60	.556	Mack
CLE	3	77	63	.550	Armour
N Y	4	72	62	.537	Griffith
DET	5	65	71	.478	Barrow
ST.L	6	65	74	.468	McAleer
CHI	7	60	77	.438	Callahan
WAS	8	43	94	.314	Loftus

1904—NATIONAL LEAGUE

CLUB	F	W	L	PCT	MGR
N Y	1	106	47	.693	McGraw
CHI	2	93	60	.608	Selee
CIN	3	88	65	.575	Kelley
PIT	4	87	66	.569	Clarke
ST.L	5	75	79	.487	Nichols
BRO	6	56	98	.366	Hanlon
BOS	7	55	98	.360	Buckenberger
PHI	8	52	100	.342	Duffy

1904—AMERICAN LEAGUE

CLUB	F	W	L	PCT	MGR
BOS	1	95	59	.617	Collins
N Y	2	92	59	.609	Griffith
CHI	3	89	65	.578	Callahan / Jones
CLE	4	86	65	.570	Armour
PHI	5	81	70	.536	Mack
ST.L	6	65	87	.428	McAleer
DET	7	62	90	.408	Barrow / Lowe
WAS	8	38	113	.251	Kittredge / Donovan

1905—NATIONAL LEAGUE

CLUB	F	W	L	PCT	MGR
N Y	1	105	48	.686	McGraw
PIT	2	96	57	.627	Clarke
CHI	3	92	61	.601	Selee / Chance
PHI	4	83	69	.546	Duffy
CIN	5	79	74	.516	Kelley
ST.L	6	58	96	.377	Nichols / Burke / Robison
BOS	7	51	103	.331	Tenney
BRO	8	48	104	.316	Hanlon

1905—AMERICAN LEAGUE

CLUB	F	W	L	PCT	MGR
PHI	1	92	56	.621	Mack
CHI	2	92	60	.605	Jones
DET	3	79	74	.516	Armour
BOS	4	78	74	.513	Collins
CLE	5	76	78	.494	Lajoie
N Y	6	71	78	.477	Griffith
WAS	7	64	87	.421	Stahl
ST.L	8	54	99	.354	McAleer

1906—NATIONAL LEAGUE

CLUB	F	W	L	PCT	MGR
CHI	1	116	36	.763	Chance
N Y	2	96	56	.632	McGraw
PIT	3	93	60	.608	Clarke
PHI	4	71	82	.464	Duffy
BRO	5	66	86	.434	Donovan
CIN	6	64	87	.424	Hanlon
ST.L	7	52	98	.347	McCloskey
BOS	8	49	102	.324	Tenney

1906—AMERICAN LEAGUE

CLUB	F	W	L	PCT	MGR
CHI	1	93	58	.616	Jones
N Y	2	90	61	.596	Griffith
CLE	3	89	64	.582	Lajoie
PHI	4	78	67	.538	Mack
ST.L	5	76	73	.510	McAleer
DET	6	71	78	.477	Armour
WAS	7	55	95	.367	Stahl, G.
BOS	8	49	105	.318	Collins / Stahl, C.

1907—NATIONAL LEAGUE

CLUB	F	W	L	PCT	MGR
CHI	1	107	45	.704	Chance
PIT	2	91	63	.591	Clarke
PHI	3	83	64	.566	Murray
N Y	4	82	71	.536	McGraw
BRO	5	65	83	.439	Donovan
CIN	6	66	87	.431	Hanlon
BOS	7	58	90	.392	Tenney
ST.L	8	52	101	.340	McCloskey

1907—AMERICAN LEAGUE

CLUB	F	W	L	PCT	MGR
DET	1	92	58	.613	Jennings
PHI	2	88	57	.607	Mack
CHI	3	87	64	.576	Jones
CLE	4	85	67	.559	Lajoie
N Y	5	70	78	.473	Griffith

(Continued)

1907-American League (Cont.)

CLUB	F	W	L	PCT	MGR
ST.L	6	69	83	.454	McAleer
BOS	7	59	90	.396	Young / Huff / Unglaub / McGuire
WAS	8	49	102	.325	Cantillon

1908—NATIONAL LEAGUE

CLUB	F	W	L	PCT	MGR
CHI	1	99	55	.643	Chance
N Y	2t	98	56	.636	McGraw
PIT	2t	98	56	.636	Clarke
PHI	4	83	71	.539	Murray
CIN	5	73	81	.474	Ganzel
BOS	6	63	91	.409	Kelley
BRO	7	53	101	.344	Donovan
ST.L	8	49	105	.318	McCloskey

1908—AMERICAN LEAGUE

CLUB	F	W	L	PCT	MGR
DET	1	90	63	.588	Jennings
CLE	2	90	64	.584	Lajoie
CHI	3	88	64	.579	Jones
ST.L	4	83	69	.546	McAleer
BOS	5	75	79	.487	McGuire / Lake
PHI	6	68	85	.444	Mack
WAS	7	67	85	.441	Cantillon
N Y	8	51	103	.331	Griffith / Elberfeld

1909—NATIONAL LEAGUE

CLUB	F	W	L	PCT	MGR
PIT	1	110	42	.724	Clarke
CHI	2	104	49	.680	Chance
N Y	3	92	61	.601	McGraw
CIN	4	77	76	.504	Griffith
PHI	5	74	79	.484	Murray
BRO	6	55	98	.359	Lumley
ST.L	7	54	98	.355	Bresnahan
BOS	8	45	108	.294	Bowerman / Smith

1909—AMERICAN LEAGUE

CLUB	F	W	L	PCT	MGR
DET	1	98	54	.645	Jennings
PHI	2	95	58	.621	Mack
BOS	3	88	63	.583	Lake
CHI	4	78	74	.513	Sullivan
N Y	5	74	77	.490	Stallings
CLE	6	71	82	.464	Lajoie / McGuire
ST.L	7	61	89	.407	McAleer / O'Connor
WAS	8	42	110	.276	Cantillon

1910—NATIONAL LEAGUE

CLUB	F	W	L	PCT	MGR
CHI	1	104	50	.676	Chance
N Y	2	91	63	.591	McGraw
PIT	3	86	67	.562	Clarke
PHI	4	78	75	.510	Dooin
CIN	5	75	79	.487	Griffith
BRO	6	64	90	.416	Dahlen
ST.L	7	63	90	.412	Bresnahan
BOS	8	53	100	.346	Lake

1910—AMERICAN LEAGUE

CLUB	F	W	L	PCT	MGR
PHI	1	102	48	.680	Mack
N Y	2	88	63	.583	Stallings / Chase
DET	3	86	68	.558	Jennings
BOS	4	81	72	.529	Donovan
CLE	5	71	81	.467	McGuire
CHI	6	68	85	.444	Duffy
WAS	7	66	85	.437	McAleer
ST.L	8	47	107	.305	O'Connor

1911—NATIONAL LEAGUE

CLUB	F	W	L	PCT	MGR
N Y	1	99	54	.647	McGraw
CHI	2	92	62	.597	Chance
PIT	3	85	69	.552	Clarke
PHI	4	79	73	.520	Dooin
ST.L	5	75	74	.503	Bresnahan
CIN	6	70	83	.458	Griffith
BRO	7	64	86	.427	Dahlen
BOS	8	44	107	.291	Tenney

1911—AMERICAN LEAGUE

CLUB	F	W	L	PCT	MGR
PHI	1	101	50	.669	Mack
DET	2	89	65	.578	Jennings
CLE	3	80	73	.523	McGuire / Stovall
CHI	4	77	74	.5099	Duffy
BOS	5	78	75	.5098	Donovan
N Y	6	76	76	.500	Chase
WAS	7	64	90	.416	McAleer
ST.L	8	45	107	.296	Wallace

1912—NATIONAL LEAGUE

CLUB	F	W	L	PCT	MGR
N Y	1	103	48	.682	McGraw
PIT	2	93	58	.616	Clarke
CHI	3	91	59	.607	Chance
CIN	4	75	78	.490	O'Day
PHI	5	73	79	.480	Dooin
ST.L	6	63	90	.412	Bresnahan
BRO	7	58	95	.379	Dahlen
BOS	8	52	101	.340	Kling

1912—AMERICAN LEAGUE

CLUB	F	W	L	PCT	MGR
BOS	1	105	47	.691	Stahl
WAS	2	91	61	.599	Griffith
PHI	3	90	62	.592	Mack
CHI	4	78	76	.506	Callahan
CLE	5	75	78	.490	Davis / Birmingham
DET	6	69	84	.451	Jennings
ST.L	7	53	101	.344	Wallace / Stovall
N Y	8	50	102	.329	Wolverton

1913—NATIONAL LEAGUE

CLUB	F	W	L	PCT	MGR
N Y	1	101	51	.664	McGraw
PHI	2	88	63	.583	Dooin
CHI	3	88	65	.575	Evers
PIT	4	78	71	.523	Clarke
BOS	5	69	82	.457	Stallings
BRO	6	65	84	.436	Dahlen
CIN	7	64	89	.418	Tinker
ST.L	8	51	99	.340	Huggins

1913—AMERICAN LEAGUE

CLUB	F	W	L	PCT	MGR
PHI	1	96	57	.627	Mack
WAS	2	90	64	.584	Griffith
CLE	3	86	66	.566	Birmingham
BOS	4	79	71	.527	Stahl / Carrigan
CHI	5	78	74	.513	Callahan
DET	6	66	87	.431	Jennings
N Y	7	57	94	.377	Chance
ST.L	8	57	96	.373	Stovall / Austin / Rickey

1914—NATIONAL LEAGUE

CLUB	F	W	L	PCT	MGR
BOS	1	94	59	.614	Stallings
N Y	2	84	70	.545	McGraw
ST.L	3	81	72	.529	Huggins
CHI	4	78	76	.506	O'Day
BRO	5	79	77	.487	Robinson
PHI	6	74	80	.481	Dooin
PIT	7	69	85	.448	Clarke
CIN	8	60	94	.390	Herzog

1914—AMERICAN LEAGUE

CLUB	F	W	L	PCT	MGR
PHI	1	99	53	.651	Mack
BOS	2	91	62	.595	Carrigan
WAS	3	81	73	.526	Griffith
DET	4	80	73	.523	Jennings
ST.L	5	71	82	.464	Rickey
CHI	6t	70	84	.455	Callahan
N Y	6t	70	84	.455	Chance / Peckinpaugh
CLE	8	51	102	.333	Birmingham

1914—FEDERAL LEAGUE

CLUB	F	W	L	PCT	MGR
IND	1	88	65	.575	Phillips
CHI	2	87	67	.565	Tinker
BAL	3	84	69	.549	Knabe
BUF	4	80	71	.530	Schlafly
BRO	5	77	77	.500	Bradley
K C	6	69	84	.451	Stovall
PIT	7	64	88	.421	Gessler / Oakes
ST.L	8	61	89	.407	Brown / Jones

1915—NATIONAL LEAGUE

CLUB	F	W	L	PCT	MGR
PHI	1	90	62	.592	Moran
BOS	2	83	69	.546	Stallings
BRO	3	80	72	.527	Robinson
CHI	4	73	80	.477	Bresnahan
PIT	5	73	81	.474	Clarke
ST.L	6	72	81	.471	Huggins
CIN	7	71	83	.461	Herzog
N Y	8	69	83	.454	McGraw

1915—AMERICAN LEAGUE

CLUB	F	W	L	PCT	MGR
BOS	1	101	50	.669	Carrigan
DET	2	100	54	.649	Jennings
CHI	3	93	61	.604	Rowland
WAS	4	85	68	.556	Griffith
N Y	5	69	83	.454	Donovan
ST.L	6	63	91	.409	Rickey
CLE	7	57	95	.375	Birmingham / Fohl
PHI	8	43	109	.283	Mack

1915—FEDERAL LEAGUE

CLUB	F	W	L	PCT	MGR
CHI	1	86	66	.566	Tinker
ST.L	2	87	67	.565	Jones
PIT	3	86	67	.562	Oakes
K C	4	81	72	.533	Stovall
NEW	5	80	72	.526	Phillips / McKechnie
BUF	6	74	78	.487	Schlafly / Blair / Lord
BRO	7	70	82	.461	Magee / Ganzel
BAL	8	47	107	.305	Knabe

1916—NATIONAL LEAGUE

CLUB	F	W	L	PCT	MGR
BRO	1	94	60	.610	Robinson
PHI	2	91	62	.595	Moran
BOS	3	89	63	.586	Stallings
N Y	4	86	66	.566	McGraw
CHI	5	67	86	.438	Tinker
PIT	6	65	89	.422	Callahan
CIN	7	60	93	.392	Herzog / Wingo / Mathewson
ST.L	7t	60	93	.392	Huggins

1916—AMERICAN LEAGUE

CLUB	F	W	L	PCT	MGR
BOS	1	91	63	.591	Carrigan
CHI	2	89	65	.578	Rowland
DET	3	87	67	.565	Jennings
N Y	4	80	74	.519	Donovan
ST.L	5	79	75	.513	Jones
CLE	6	77	77	.500	Fohl
WAS	7	76	77	.497	Griffith
PHI	8	36	117	.235	Mack

1917—NATIONAL LEAGUE

CLUB	F	W	L	PCT	MGR
N Y	1	98	56	.636	McGraw
PHI	2	87	65	.572	Moran
ST.L	3	82	70	.539	Huggins
CIN	4	78	76	.506	Mathewson
CHI	5	74	80	.481	Mitchell
BOS	6	72	81	.471	Stallings
BRO	7	70	81	.464	Robinson
PIT	8	51	103	.331	Callahan / Wagner / Bezdek

1917—AMERICAN LEAGUE

CLUB	F	W	L	PCT	MGR
CHI	1	100	54	.649	Rowland
BOS	2	90	62	.592	Barry
CLE	3	88	66	.571	Fohl
DET	4	78	75	.510	Jennings
WAS	5	74	79	.484	Griffith
N Y	6	71	82	.464	Donovan
ST.L	7	57	97	.370	Jones
PHI	8	55	98	.359	Mack

1918—NATIONAL LEAGUE

CLUB	F	W	L	PCT	MGR
CHI	1	84	45	.651	Mitchell
N Y	2	71	53	.573	McGraw
CIN	3	68	60	.531	Mathewson / Groh
PIT	4	65	60	.520	Bezdek
BRO	5	57	69	.452	Robinson
PHI	6	55	68	.447	Moran
BOS	7	53	71	.427	Stallings
ST.L	8	51	78	.395	Hendricks

1918—AMERICAN LEAGUE

CLUB	F	W	L	PCT	MGR
BOS	1	75	51	.595	Barrow
CLE	2	73	54	.575	Fohl
WAS	3	72	56	.563	Griffith
N Y	4	60	63	.488	Huggins
ST.L	5	58	64	.475	Jones / Austin / Burke
CHI	6	57	67	.460	Rowland
DET	7	55	71	.437	Jennings
PHI	8	52	76	.402	Mack

1919—NATIONAL LEAGUE

CLUB	F	W	L	PCT	MGR
CIN	1	96	44	.686	Moran
N Y	2	87	53	.621	McGraw
CHI	3	75	65	.536	Mitchell
PIT	4	71	68	.511	Bezdek
BRO	5	69	71	.493	Robinson
BOS	6	57	82	.410	Stallings
ST.L	7	54	83	.394	Rickey
PHI	8	47	90	.343	Coombs / Cravath

1919—AMERICAN LEAGUE

CLUB	F	W	L	PCT	MGR
CHI	1	88	52	.629	Gleason
CLE	2	84	55	.604	Fohl / Speaker
N Y	3	80	59	.576	Huggins
DET	4	80	60	.571	Jennings
ST.L	5	67	72	.4820	Burke
BOS	6	66	71	.4817	Barrow
WAS	7	56	84	.400	Griffith
PHI	8	36	104	.257	Mack

1920—NATIONAL LEAGUE

CLUB	F	W	L	PCT	MGR
BRO	1	93	61	.604	Robinson
N Y	2	86	68	.558	McGraw
CIN	3	82	71	.536	Moran
PIT	4	79	75	.513	Gibson
CHI	5t	75	79	.487	Mitchell
ST.L	5t	75	79	.487	Rickey
BOS	7	62	90	.408	Stallings
PHI	8	62	91	.405	Cravath

1920—AMERICAN LEAGUE

CLUB	F	W	L	PCT	MGR
CLE	1	98	56	.636	Speaker
CHI	2	96	58	.623	Gleason
N Y	3	95	59	.617	Huggins
ST.L	4	76	77	.497	Burke
BOS	5	72	81	.471	Barrow
WAS	6	68	84	.447	Griffith
DET	7	61	93	.396	Jennings
PHI	8	48	106	.312	Mack

1921—NATIONAL LEAGUE

CLUB	F	W	L	PCT	MGR
N Y	1	94	59	.614	McGraw
PIT	2	90	63	.588	Gibson
ST.L	3	87	66	.569	Rickey
BOS	4	79	74	.516	Mitchell
BRO	5	77	75	.507	Robinson
CIN	6	70	83	.458	Moran
CHI	7	64	89	.418	Evers / Killefer
PHI	8	51	103	.331	Donovan / Wilhelm

1921—AMERICAN LEAGUE

CLUB	F	W	L	PCT	MGR
N Y	1	98	55	.641	Huggins
CLE	2	94	60	.610	Speaker
ST.L	3	81	73	.526	Fohl
WAS	4	80	73	.523	McBride
BOS	5	75	79	.487	Duffy
DET	6	71	82	.464	Cobb
CHI	7	62	92	.403	Gleason
PHI	8	53	100	.346	Mack

1922—NATIONAL LEAGUE

CLUB	F	W	L	PCT	MGR
N Y	1	93	61	.604	McGraw
CIN	2	86	68	.558	Moran
PIT	3t	85	69	.552	Gibson / McKechnie
ST.L	3t	85	69	.552	Rickey
CHI	5	80	74	.520	Killefer
BRO	6	76	78	.494	Robinson
PHI	7	57	96	.373	Wilhelm
BOS	8	53	100	.346	Mitchell

1922—AMERICAN LEAGUE

CLUB	F	W	L	PCT	MGR
N Y	1	94	60	.610	Huggins
ST.L	2	93	61	.604	Fohl
DET	3	79	75	.513	Cobb
CLE	4	78	76	.507	Speaker
CHI	5	77	77	.500	Gleason
WAS	6	69	85	.448	Milan
PHI	7	65	89	.422	Mack
BOS	8	61	93	.396	Duffy

1923—NATIONAL LEAGUE

CLUB	F	W	L	PCT	MGR
N Y	1	95	58	.621	McGraw
CIN	2	91	63	.591	Moran
PIT	3	87	67	.565	McKechnie
CHI	4	83	71	.539	Killefer
ST.L	5	79	74	.516	Rickey
BRO	6	76	78	.494	Robinson
BOS	7	54	100	.351	Mitchell
PHI	8	50	104	.325	Fletcher

1923—AMERICAN LEAGUE

CLUB	F	W	L	PCT	MGR
N Y	1	98	54	.645	Huggins
DET	2	83	71	.539	Cobb
CLE	3	82	71	.536	Speaker
WAS	4	75	78	.490	Bush
ST.L	5	74	78	.487	Fohl / Austin
PHI	6	69	83	.454	Mack
CHI	7	69	85	.448	Gleason
BOS	8	61	91	.401	Chance

1924—NATIONAL LEAGUE

CLUB	F	W	L	PCT	MGR
N Y	1	93	60	.608	McGraw
BRO	2	92	62	.597	Robinson
PIT	3	90	63	.588	McKechnie
CIN	4	83	70	.542	Hendricks
CHI	5	81	72	.530	Killefer
ST.L	6	65	89	.422	Rickey
PHI	7	55	96	.364	Fletcher
BOS	8	53	100	.346	Bancroft

1924—AMERICAN LEAGUE

CLUB	F	W	L	PCT	MGR
WAS	1	92	62	.597	Harris
N Y	2	89	63	.586	Huggins
DET	3	86	68	.558	Cobb
ST.L	4	74	78	.487	Sisler
PHI	5	71	81	.467	Mack
CLE	6	67	86	.438	Speaker
BOS	7	67	87	.435	Fohl
CHI	8	66	87	.431	Evers

1925—NATIONAL LEAGUE

CLUB	F	W	L	PCT	MGR
PIT	1	95	58	.621	McKechnie
N Y	2	86	66	.566	McGraw
CIN	3	80	73	.523	Hendricks
ST.L	4	77	76	.503	Rickey / Hornsby
BOS	5	70	83	.458	Bancroft
BRO	6t	68	85	.444	Robinson
PHI	6t	68	85	.444	Fletcher
CHI	8	68	86	.442	Killefer / Maranville / Gibson

1925—AMERICAN LEAGUE

CLUB	F	W	L	PCT	MGR
WAS	1	96	55	.636	Harris
PHI	2	88	64	.579	Mack
ST.L	3	82	71	.536	Sisler
DET	4	81	73	.526	Cobb
CHI	5	79	75	.513	Collins
CLE	6	70	84	.455	Speaker
N Y	7	69	85	.448	Huggins
BOS	8	47	105	.309	Fohl

1926—NATIONAL LEAGUE

CLUB	F	W	L	PCT	MGR
ST.L	1	89	65	.578	Hornsby
CIN	2	87	67	.565	Hendricks
PIT	3	84	69	.549	McKechnie
CHI	4	82	72	.532	McCarthy
N Y	5	74	77	.490	McGraw
BRO	6	71	82	.464	Robinson
BOS	7	66	86	.434	Bancroft
PHI	8	58	93	.384	Fletcher

1926—AMERICAN LEAGUE

CLUB	F	W	L	PCT	MGR
N Y	1	91	63	.591	Huggins
CLE	2	88	66	.571	Speaker
PHI	3	83	67	.553	Mack
WAS	4	81	69	.540	Harris
CHI	5	81	72	.529	Collins
DET	6	79	75	.513	Cobb
ST.L	7	62	92	.403	Sisler
BOS	8	46	107	.301	Fohl

1927—NATIONAL LEAGUE

CLUB	F	W	L	PCT	MGR
PIT	1	94	60	.610	Bush
ST.L	2	92	61	.601	O'Farrell
N Y	3	92	62	.597	McGraw
CHI	4	85	68	.556	McCarthy
CIN	5	75	78	.490	Hendricks
BRO	6	65	88	.425	Robinson
BOS	7	60	94	.390	Bancroft
PHI	8	51	103	.331	McInnis

1927—AMERICAN LEAGUE

CLUB	F	W	L	PCT	MGR
N Y	1	110	44	.714	Huggins
PHI	2	91	63	.591	Mack
WAS	3	85	69	.552	Harris
DET	4	82	71	.536	Moriarty
CHI	5	70	83	.458	Schalk
CLE	6	66	87	.431	McCallister
ST.L	7	59	94	.386	Howley
BOS	8	51	103	.331	Carrigan

1928—NATIONAL LEAGUE

CLUB	F	W	L	PCT	MGR
ST.L	1	95	59	.617	McKechnie
N Y	2	93	61	.604	McGraw
CHI	3	91	63	.591	McCarthy
PIT	4	85	67	.559	Bush
CIN	5	78	74	.513	Hendricks
BRO	6	77	76	.503	Robinson
BOS	7	50	103	.327	Slattery / Hornsby
PHI	8	43	109	.283	Shotton

1928—AMERICAN LEAGUE

CLUB	F	W	L	PCT	MGR
N Y	1	101	53	.656	Huggins
PHI	2	98	55	.641	Mack
ST.L	3	82	72	.532	Howley
WAS	4	75	79	.487	Harris
CHI	5	72	82	.468	Schalk / Blackburne
DET	6	68	86	.442	Moriarty
CLE	7	62	92	.403	Peckinpaugh
BOS	8	57	96	.373	Carrigan

1929—NATIONAL LEAGUE

CLUB	F	W	L	PCT	MGR
CHI	1	98	54	.645	McCarthy
PIT	2	88	65	.575	Bush / Ens
N Y	3	84	67	.556	McGraw
ST.L	4	78	74	.513	McKechnie / Southworth
PHI	5	71	82	.464	Shotton
BRO	6	70	83	.458	Robinson
CIN	7	66	88	.429	Hendricks
BOS	8	56	98	.364	Fuchs / Evers

1929—AMERICAN LEAGUE

CLUB	F	W	L	PCT	MGR
PHI	1	104	46	.693	Mack
N Y	2	88	66	.571	Huggins / Fletcher
CLE	3	81	71	.533	Peckinpaugh
ST.L	4	79	73	.520	Howley
WAS	5	71	81	.467	Johnson
DET	6	70	84	.455	Harris
CHI	7	59	93	.388	Blackburne
BOS	8	58	96	.377	Carrigan

1930—NATIONAL LEAGUE

CLUB	F	W	L	PCT	MGR
ST.L	1	92	62	.597	Street
CHI	2	90	64	.584	McCarthy / Hornsby
N Y	3	87	67	.565	McGraw
BRO	4	86	68	.558	Robinson
PIT	5	80	74	.519	Ens
BOS	6	70	84	.455	McKechnie
CIN	7	59	95	.383	Howley
PHI	8	52	102	.338	Shotton

1930—AMERICAN LEAGUE

CLUB	F	W	L	PCT	MGR
PHI	1	102	52	.662	Mack
WAS	2	94	60	.610	Johnson
N Y	3	86	68	.558	Shawkey
CLE	4	81	73	.526	Peckinpaugh
DET	5	75	79	.487	Harris
ST.L	6	64	90	.416	Killefer
CHI	7	62	92	.403	Bush
BOS	8	52	102	.338	Wagner

1931—NATIONAL LEAGUE

CLUB	F	W	L	PCT	MGR
ST.L	1	101	53	.656	Street
N Y	2	87	65	.572	McGraw
CHI	3	84	70	.545	Hornsby
BRO	4	79	73	.520	Robinson
PIT	5	75	79	.487	Ens
PHI	6	66	88	.429	Shotton
BOS	7	64	90	.416	McKechnie
CIN	8	58	96	.377	Howley

1931—AMERICAN LEAGUE

CLUB	F	W	L	PCT	MGR
PHI	1	107	45	.704	Mack
N Y	2	94	59	.614	McCarthy
WAS	3	92	62	.597	Johnson
CLE	4	78	76	.506	Peckinpaugh
ST.L	5	63	91	.409	Killefer
BOS	6	62	90	.408	Collins
DET	7	61	93	.396	Harris
CHI	8	56	97	.366	Bush

1932—NATIONAL LEAGUE

CLUB	F	W	L	PCT	MGR
CHI	1	90	64	.584	Hornsby / Grimm
PIT	2	86	68	.558	Gibson
BRO	3	81	73	.526	Carey
PHI	4	78	76	.506	Shotton
BOS	5	77	77	.500	McKechnie
N Y	6t	72	82	.468	McGraw / Terry
ST.L	6t	72	82	.468	Street
CIN	8	60	94	.390	Howley

1932—AMERICAN LEAGUE

CLUB	F	W	L	PCT	MGR
N Y	1	107	47	.695	McCarthy
PHI	2	94	60	.610	Mack
WAS	3	93	61	.604	Johnson
CLE	4	87	65	.572	Peckinpaugh
DET	5	76	75	.503	Harris
ST.L	6	63	91	.409	Killefer
CHI	7	49	102	.325	Fonseca
BOS	8	43	111	.279	Collins / McManus

1933—NATIONAL LEAGUE

CLUB	F	W	L	PCT	MGR
N Y	1	91	61	.599	Terry
PIT	2	87	67	.565	Gibson
CHI	3	86	68	.558	Grimm
BOS	4	83	71	.539	McKechnie
ST.L	5	82	71	.536	Street / Frisch
BRO	6	65	88	.425	Carey
PHI	7	60	92	.395	Shotton
CIN	8	58	94	.382	Bush

1933—AMERICAN LEAGUE

CLUB	F	W	L	PCT	MGR
WAS	1	99	53	.651	Cronin
N Y	2	91	59	.607	McCarthy
PHI	3	79	72	.523	Mack
CLE	4	75	76	.497	Peckinpaugh / Johnson
DET	5	75	79	.487	Harris / Baker

(Continued)

1933—American League (Cont.)

CLUB	F	W	L	PCT	MGR
CHI	6	67	83	.447	Fonseca
BOS	7	63	86	.423	McManus
ST.L	8	55	96	.364	Killefer / Sothoron / Hornsby

1934—NATIONAL LEAGUE

CLUB	F	W	L	PCT	MGR
ST.L	1	95	58	.621	Frisch
N Y	2	93	60	.608	Terry
CHI	3	86	65	.570	Grimm
BOS	4	78	73	.517	McKechnie
PIT	5	74	76	.493	Gibson / Traynor
BRO	6	71	81	.467	Stengel
PHI	7	56	93	.376	Wilson
CIN	8	52	99	.344	O'Farrell / Shotton / Dressen

1934—AMERICAN LEAGUE

CLUB	F	W	L	PCT	MGR
DET	1	101	53	.656	Cochrane
N Y	2	94	60	.610	McCarthy
CLE	3	85	69	.552	Johnson
BOS	4	76	76	.500	Harris
PHI	5	68	82	.453	Mack
ST.L	6	67	85	.441	Hornsby
WAS	7	66	86	.434	Cronin
CHI	8	53	99	.349	Fonseca / Dykes

1935—NATIONAL LEAGUE

CLUB	F	W	L	PCT	MGR
CHI	1	100	54	.649	Grimm
ST.L	2	96	58	.623	Frisch
N Y	3	91	62	.595	Terry
PIT	4	86	67	.562	Traynor
BRO	5	70	83	.458	Stengel
CIN	6	68	85	.444	Dressen
PHI	7	64	89	.418	Wilson
BOS	8	38	115	.248	McKechnie

1935—AMERICAN LEAGUE

CLUB	F	W	L	PCT	MGR
DET	1	93	58	.616	Cochrane
N Y	2	89	60	.597	McCarthy
CLE	3	82	71	.536	Johnson / O'Neill
BOS	4	78	75	.510	Cronin
CHI	5	74	78	.487	Dykes
WAS	6	67	86	.438	Harris
ST.L	7	65	87	.428	Hornsby
PHI	8	58	91	.389	Mack

1936—NATIONAL LEAGUE

CLUB	F	W	L	PCT	MGR
N Y	1	92	62	.597	Terry
CHI	2t	87	67	.565	Grimm
ST.L	2t	87	67	.565	Frisch
PIT	4	84	70	.545	Traynor
CIN	5	74	80	.481	Dressen
BOS	6	71	83	.461	McKechnie
BRO	7	67	87	.435	Stengel
PHI	8	54	100	.351	Wilson

1936—AMERICAN LEAGUE

CLUB	F	W	L	PCT	MGR
N Y	1	102	51	.667	McCarthy
DET	2	83	71	.539	Cochrane
CHI	3	81	70	.5364	Dykes
WAS	4	82	71	.5359	Harris
CLE	5	80	74	.519	O'Neill
BOS	6	74	80	.481	Cronin
ST.L	7	57	95	.375	Hornsby
PHI	8	53	100	.346	Mack

1937—NATIONAL LEAGUE

CLUB	F	W	L	PCT	MGR
N Y	1	95	57	.625	Terry
CHI	2	93	61	.604	Grimm
PIT	3	86	68	.558	Traynor
ST.L	4	81	73	.526	Frisch
BOS	5	79	73	.520	McKechnie
BRO	6	62	91	.405	Grimes
PHI	7	61	92	.399	Wilson
CIN	8	56	98	.364	Dressen / Wallace

1937—AMERICAN LEAGUE

CLUB	F	W	L	PCT	MGR
N Y	1	102	52	.662	McCarthy
DET	2	89	65	.578	Cochrane
CHI	3	86	68	.558	Dykes
CLE	4	83	71	.539	O'Neill
BOS	5	80	72	.526	Cronin
WAS	6	73	80	.477	Harris
PHI	7	54	97	.358	Mack
ST.L	8	46	108	.299	Hornsby / Bottomley

1938—NATIONAL LEAGUE

CLUB	F	W	L	PCT	MGR
CHI	1	89	63	.586	Grimm / Hartnett
PIT	2	86	64	.573	Traynor
N Y	3	83	67	.553	Terry
CIN	4	82	68	.547	McKechnie
BOS	5	77	75	.507	Stengel
ST.L	6	71	80	.470	Frisch / Gonzales
BRO	7	69	80	.463	Grimes
PHI	8	45	105	.300	Wilson / Lobert

1938—AMERICAN LEAGUE

CLUB	F	W	L	PCT	MGR
N Y	1	99	53	.651	McCarthy
BOS	2	88	61	.591	Cronin
CLE	3	86	66	.566	Vitt
DET	4	84	70	.545	Cochrane / Baker
WAS	5	75	76	.497	Harris
CHI	6	65	83	.439	Dykes
ST.L	7	55	97	.362	Street / Melillo
PHI	8	53	99	.349	Mack

1939—NATIONAL LEAGUE

CLUB	F	W	L	PCT	MGR
CIN	1	97	57	.630	McKechnie
ST.L	2	92	61	.601	Blades
BRO	3	84	69	.549	Durocher
CHI	4	84	70	.545	Hartnett
N Y	5	77	74	.510	Terry
PIT	6	68	85	.444	Traynor
BOS	7	63	88	.417	Stengel
PHI	8	45	106	.298	Prothro

1939—AMERICAN LEAGUE

CLUB	F	W	L	PCT	MGR
N Y	1	106	45	.702	McCarthy
BOS	2	89	62	.589	Cronin
CLE	3	87	67	.565	Vitt
CHI	4	85	69	.552	Dykes
DET	5	81	73	.526	Baker
WAS	6	65	87	.428	Harris
PHI	7	55	97	.362	Mack
ST.L	8	43	111	.279	Haney

1940—NATIONAL LEAGUE

CLUB	F	W	L	PCT	MGR
CIN	1	100	53	.654	McKechnie
BRO	2	88	65	.575	Durocher
ST.L	3	84	69	.549	Blades / Gonzales / Southworth

(Continued)

1940-National League (Cont.)

CLUB	F	W	L	PCT	MGR
PIT	4	78	76	.506	Frisch
CHI	5	75	79	.487	Hartnett
N Y	6	72	80	.474	Terry
BOS	7	65	87	.428	Stengel
PHI	8	50	103	.327	Prothro

1940—AMERICAN LEAGUE

CLUB	F	W	L	PCT	MGR
DET	1	90	64	.584	Baker
CLE	2	89	65	.578	Vitt
N Y	3	88	66	.571	McCarthy
BOS	4t	82	72	.532	Cronin
CHI	4t	82	72	.532	Dykes
ST.L	6	67	87	.435	Haney
WAS	7	64	90	.416	Harris
PHI	8	54	100	.351	Mack

1941—NATIONAL LEAGUE

CLUB	F	W	L	PCT	MGR
BRO	1	100	54	.649	Durocher
ST.L	2	97	56	.634	Southworth
CIN	3	88	66	.571	McKechnie
PIT	4	81	73	.526	Frisch
N Y	5	74	79	.484	Terry
CHI	6	70	84	.455	Wilson
BOS	7	62	92	.403	Stengel
PHI	8	43	111	.279	Prothro

1941—AMERICAN LEAGUE

CLUB	F	W	L	PCT	MGR
N Y	1	101	53	.656	McCarthy
BOS	2	84	70	.545	Cronin
CHI	3	77	77	.500	Dykes
CLE	4t	75	79	.487	Peckinpaugh
DET	4t	75	79	.487	Baker
ST.L	6t	70	84	.455	Haney / Sewell
WAS	6t	70	84	.455	Harris
PHI	8	64	90	.416	Mack

1942—NATIONAL LEAGUE

CLUB	F	W	L	PCT	MGR
ST.L	1	106	48	.688	Southworth
BRO	2	104	50	.675	Durocher
N Y	3	85	67	.559	Ott
CIN	4	76	76	.500	McKechnie
PIT	5	66	81	.449	Frisch
CHI	6	68	86	.442	Wilson
BOS	7	59	89	.399	Stengel
PHI	8	42	109	.278	Lobert

1942—AMERICAN LEAGUE

CLUB	F	W	L	PCT	MGR
N Y	1	103	51	.669	McCarthy
BOS	2	93	59	.612	Cronin
ST.L	3	82	69	.543	Sewell
CLE	4	75	79	.487	Boudreau
DET	5	73	81	.474	Baker
CHI	6	66	82	.446	Dykes
WAS	7	62	89	.411	Harris
PHI	8	55	99	.357	Mack

1943—NATIONAL LEAGUE

CLUB	F	W	L	PCT	MGR
ST.L	1	105	49	.682	Southworth
CIN	2	87	67	.565	McKechnie
BRO	3	81	72	.529	Durocher
PIT	4	80	74	.519	Frisch
CHI	5	74	79	.484	Wilson
BOS	6	68	85	.444	Stengel
PHI	7	64	90	.416	Harris / Fitzsimmons
N Y	8	55	98	.359	Ott

1943—AMERICAN LEAGUE

CLUB	F	W	L	PCT	MGR
N Y	1	98	56	.636	McCarthy
WAS	2	84	69	.549	Bluege
CLE	3	82	71	.536	Boudreau
CHI	4	82	72	.532	Dykes
DET	5	78	76	.506	O'Neill
ST.L	6	72	80	.474	Sewell
BOS	7	68	84	.447	Cronin
PHI	8	49	105	.318	Mack

1944—NATIONAL LEAGUE

CLUB	F	W	L	PCT	MGR
ST.L	1	105	49	.682	Southworth
PIT	2	90	63	.588	Frisch
CIN	3	89	65	.578	McKechnie
CHI	4	75	79	.487	Wilson Johnson Grimm
N Y	5	67	87	.435	Ott
BOS	6	65	89	.422	Coleman
BRO	7	63	91	.409	Durocher
PHI	8	61	92	.399	Fitzsimmons

1944—AMERICAN LEAGUE

CLUB	F	W	L	PCT	MGR
ST.L	1	89	65	.578	Sewell
DET	2	88	66	.571	O'Neill
N Y	3	83	71	.539	McCarthy
BOS	4	77	77	.500	Cronin
CLE	5t	72	82	.468	Boudreau
PHI	5t	72	82	.468	Mack
CHI	7	71	83	.461	Dykes
WAS	8	64	90	.416	Bluege

1945—NATIONAL LEAGUE

CLUB	F	W	L	PCT	MGR
CHI	1	98	56	.636	Grimm
ST.L	2	95	59	.617	Southworth
BRO	3	87	67	.565	Durocher
PIT	4	82	72	.532	Frisch
N Y	5	78	74	.513	Ott
BOS	6	67	85	.441	Coleman Bissonette
CIN	7	61	93	.396	McKechnie
PHI	8	46	108	.299	Fitzsimmons Chapman

1945—AMERICAN LEAGUE

CLUB	F	W	L	PCT	MGR
DET	1	88	65	.575	O'Neill
WAS	2	87	67	.565	Bluege
ST.L	3	81	70	.536	Sewell
N Y	4	81	71	.533	McCarthy
CLE	5	73	72	.503	Boudreau
CHI	6	71	78	.477	Dykes
BOS	7	71	83	.461	Cronin
PHI	8	52	98	.347	Mack

1946—NATIONAL LEAGUE

CLUB	F	W	L	PCT	MGR
ST.L	1p	98	58	.628	Dyer
BRO	2p	96	60	.615	Durocher
CHI	3	82	71	.536	Grimm
BOS	4	81	72	.529	Southworth
PHI	5	69	85	.448	Chapman
CIN	6	67	87	.435	McKechnie Gowdy
PIT	7	63	91	.409	Frisch Davis
N Y	8	61	93	.396	Ott

1946—AMERICAN LEAGUE

CLUB	F	W	L	PCT	MGR
BOS	1	104	50	.675	Cronin
DET	2	92	62	.597	O'Neill
N Y	3	87	67	.565	McCarthy Dickey Neun
WAS	4	76	78	.494	Bluege

(Continued)

1946-American League (Cont.)

CLUB	F	W	L	PCT	MGR
CHI	5	74	80	.481	Dykes Lyons
CLE	6	68	86	.442	Boudreau
ST.L	7	66	88	.429	Sewell Taylor
PHI	8	49	105	.318	Mack

1947—NATIONAL LEAGUE

CLUB	F	W	L	PCT	MGR
BRO	1	94	60	.610	Sukeforth Shotton
ST.L	2	89	65	.578	Dyer
BOS	3	86	68	.558	Southworth
N Y	4	81	73	.526	Ott
CIN	5	73	81	.474	Neun
CHI	6	69	85	.448	Grimm
PHI	7t	62	92	.403	Chapman
PIT	7t	62	92	.403	Herman Burwell

1947—AMERICAN LEAGUE

CLUB	F	W	L	PCT	MGR
N Y	1	97	57	.630	Harris
DET	2	85	69	.552	O'Neill
BOS	3	83	71	.539	Cronin
CLE	4	80	74	.519	Boudreau
PHI	5	78	76	.506	Mack
CHI	6	70	84	.455	Lyons
WAS	7	64	90	.416	Bluege
ST.L	8	59	95	.383	Ruel

1948—NATIONAL LEAGUE

CLUB	F	W	L	PCT	MGR
BOS	1	91	62	.595	Southworth
ST.L	2	85	69	.552	Dyer
BRO	3	84	70	.545	Durocher Shotton
PIT	4	83	71	.539	Meyer
N Y	5	78	76	.506	Ott Durocher
PHI	6	66	88	.429	Chapman Cooke Sawyer
CIN	7	64	89	.418	Neun Walters
CHI	8	64	90	.416	Grimm

1948—AMERICAN LEAGUE

CLUB	F	W	L	PCT	MGR
CLE	1p	97	58	.626	Boudreau
BOS	2p	96	59	.619	McCarthy
N Y	3	94	60	.610	Harris
PHI	4	84	70	.545	Mack
DET	5	78	76	.506	O'Neill
ST.L	6	59	94	.386	Taylor
WAS	7	56	97	.366	Kuhel
CHI	8	51	101	.336	Lyons

1949—NATIONAL LEAGUE

CLUB	F	W	L	PCT	MGR
BRO	1	97	57	.630	Shotton
ST.L	2	96	58	.623	Dyer
PHI	3	81	73	.526	Sawyer
BOS	4	75	79	.487	Southworth Cooney
N Y	5	73	81	.474	Durocher
PIT	6	71	83	.461	Meyer
CIN	7	62	92	.403	Walters Sewell
CHI	8	61	93	.396	Grimm Frisch

1949—AMERICAN LEAGUE

CLUB	F	W	L	PCT	MGR
N Y	1	97	57	.630	Stengel
BOS	2	96	58	.623	McCarthy
CLE	3	89	65	.578	Boudreau
DET	4	87	67	.565	Rolfe
PHI	5	81	73	.526	Mack
CHI	6	63	91	.409	Onslow
ST.L	7	53	101	.344	Taylor
WAS	8	50	104	.324	Kuhel

1950—NATIONAL LEAGUE

CLUB	F	W	L	PCT	MGR
PHI	1	91	63	.591	Sawyer
BRO	2	89	65	.578	Shotton
N Y	3	86	68	.558	Durocher
BOS	4	83	71	.539	Southworth
ST.L	5	78	75	.510	Dyer
CIN	6	66	87	.431	Sewell
CHI	7	64	89	.418	Frisch
PIT	8	57	96	.373	Meyer

1950—AMERICAN LEAGUE

CLUB	F	W	L	PCT	MGR
N Y	1	98	56	.636	Stengel
DET	2	95	59	.617	Rolfe
BOS	3	94	60	.610	McCarthy O'Neill
CLE	4	92	62	.597	Boudreau
WAS	5	67	87	.435	Harris
CHI	6	60	94	.390	Onslow Corriden
ST.L	7	58	96	.377	Taylor
PHI	8	52	102	.338	Mack

1951—NATIONAL LEAGUE

CLUB	F	W	L	PCT	MGR
N Y	1p	98	59	.624	Durocher
BRO	2p	97	60	.618	Dressen
ST.L	3	81	73	.526	Marion
BOS	4	76	78	.494	Southworth Holmes
PHI	5	73	81	.474	Sawyer
CIN	6	68	86	.442	Sewell
PIT	7	64	90	.416	Meyer
CHI	8	62	92	.403	Frisch Cavarretta

1951—AMERICAN LEAGUE

CLUB	F	W	L	PCT	MGR
N Y	1	98	56	.636	Stengel
CLE	2	93	61	.604	Lopez
BOS	3	87	67	.565	O'Neill
CHI	4	81	73	.526	Richards
DET	5	73	81	.474	Rolfe
PHI	6	70	84	.455	Dykes
WAS	7	62	92	.403	Harris
ST.L	8	52	102	.338	Taylor

1952—NATIONAL LEAGUE

CLUB	F	W	L	PCT	MGR
BRO	1	96	57	.627	Dressen
N Y	2	92	62	.597	Durocher
ST.L	3	88	66	.571	Stanky
PHI	4	87	67	.565	Sawyer O'Neill
CHI	5	77	77	.500	Cavarretta
CIN	6	69	85	.448	Sewell Hornsby
BOS	7	64	89	.418	Holmes Grimm
PIT	8	42	112	.273	Meyer

1952—AMERICAN LEAGUE

CLUB	F	W	L	PCT	MGR
N Y	1	95	59	.617	Stengel
CLE	2	93	61	.604	Lopez
CHI	3	81	73	.526	Richards
PHI	4	79	75	.513	Dykes
WAS	5	78	76	.506	Harris
BOS	6	76	78	.494	Boudreau
ST.L	7	64	90	.416	Hornsby Marion
DET	8	50	104	.325	Rolfe Hutchinson

1953—NATIONAL LEAGUE

CLUB	F	W	L	PCT.	MGR
BRO	1	105	49	.682	Dressen
MIL	2	92	62	.597	Grimm
PHI	3t	83	71	.539	O'Neill
St.L	3t	88	71	.539	Stanky
N Y	5	70	84	.455	Durocher
CIN	6	68	86	.442	Hornsby, Mills
CHI	7	65	89	.422	Cavarretta
PIT	8	50	104	.325	Haney

1953—AMERICAN LEAGUE

CLUB	F	W	L	PCT.	MGR
N Y	1	99	52	.656	Stengel
CLE	2	92	62	.597	Lopez
CHI	3	89	65	.578	Richards
BOS	4	84	69	.549	Boudreau
WAS	5	76	76	.500	Harris
DET	6	60	94	.390	Hutchinson
PHI	7	59	95	.383	Dykes
St.L	8	54	100	.351	Marion

1954—NATIONAL LEAGUE

CLUB	F	W	L	PCT.	MGR
N Y	1	97	57	.630	Durocher
BRO	2	92	62	.597	Alston
MIL	3	89	65	.578	Grimm
PHI	4	75	79	.487	O'Neill, Moore
CIN	5	74	80	.481	Tebbetts
St.L	6	72	82	.468	Stanky
CHI	7	64	90	.416	Hack
PIT	8	53	101	.344	Haney

1954—AMERICAN LEAGUE

CLUB	F	W	L	PCT.	MGR
CLE	1	111	43	.721	Lopez
N Y	2	103	51	.669	Stengel
CHI	3	94	60	.610	Richards, Marion
BOS	4	69	85	.448	Boudreau
DET	5	68	86	.442	Hutchinson
WAS	6	66	88	.429	Harris
BAL	7	54	100	.351	Dykes
PHI	8	51	103	.331	Joost

1955—NATIONAL LEAGUE

CLUB	F	W	L	PCT.	MGR
BRO	1	98	55	.641	Alston
MIL	2	85	69	.552	Grimm
N Y	3	80	74	.519	Durocher
PHI	4	77	77	.500	Smith
CIN	5	75	79	.487	Tebbetts
CHI	6	72	81	.471	Hack
St.L	7	68	86	.442	Stanky, Walker
PIT	8	60	94	.390	Haney

1955—AMERICAN LEAGUE

CLUB	F	W	L	PCT.	MGR
N Y	1	96	58	.623	Stengel
CLE	2	93	61	.604	Lopez
CHI	3	91	63	.591	Marion
BOS	4	84	70	.545	Higgins
DET	5	79	75	.513	Harris
K C	6	63	91	.409	Boudreau
BAL	7	57	97	.370	Richards
WAS	8	53	101	.344	Dressen

1956—NATIONAL LEAGUE

CLUB	F	W	L	PCT.	MGR
BRO	1	93	61	.604	Alston
MIL	2	92	62	.597	Grimm, Haney
CIN	3	91	63	.591	Tebbetts
St.L	4	76	78	.494	Hutchinson
PHI	5	71	83	.461	Smith
N Y	6	67	87	.435	Rigney
PIT	7	66	88	.429	Bragan
CHI	8	60	94	.390	Hack

1956—AMERICAN LEAGUE

CLUB	F	W	L	PCT.	MGR
N Y	1	97	57	.630	Stengel
CLE	2	88	66	.571	Lopez
CHI	3	85	69	.552	Marion
BOS	4	84	70	.545	Higgins
DET	5	82	72	.532	Harris
BAL	6	69	85	.448	Richards
WAS	7	59	95	.383	Dressen
K C	8	52	102	.338	Boudreau

1957—NATIONAL LEAGUE

CLUB	F	W	L	PCT.	MGR
MIL	1	95	59	.617	Haney
St.L	2	87	67	.565	Hutchinson
BRO	3	84	70	.545	Alston
CIN	4	80	74	.519	Tebbetts
PHI	5	77	77	.500	Smith
N Y	6	69	85	.448	Rigney
CHI t	7t	62	92	.403	Scheffing
PIT t	7t	62	92	.403	Bragan, Murtaugh

1957—AMERICAN LEAGUE

CLUB	F	W	L	PCT.	MGR
N Y	1	98	56	.636	Stengel
CHI	2	90	64	.584	Lopez
BOS	3	82	72	.532	Higgins
DET	4	78	76	.506	Tighe
BAL	5	76	76	.500	Richards
CLE	6	76	77	.497	Farrell
K C	7	59	94	.386	Boudreau, Craft
WAS	8	55	99	.357	Dressen, Lavagetto

1958—NATIONAL LEAGUE

CLUB	F	W	L	PCT.	MGR
MIL	1	92	62	.597	Haney
PIT	2	84	70	.545	Murtaugh
S F	3	80	74	.519	Rigney
CIN	4	76	78	.494	Tebbetts, Dykes
St.L	5t	72	82	.468	Hutchinson, Hack
CHI	5t	72	82	.468	Scheffing
L A	7	71	83	.461	Alston
PHI	8	69	85	.448	Smith, Sawyer

1958—AMERICAN LEAGUE

CLUB	F	W	L	PCT.	MGR
N Y	1	92	62	.597	Stengel
CHI	2	82	72	.532	Lopez
BOS	3	79	75	.513	Higgins
CLE	4	77	76	.503	Bragan, Gordon
DET	5	77	77	.500	Tighe, Norman
BAL	6	74	79	.484	Richards
K C	7	73	81	.474	Craft
WAS	8	61	93	.396	Lavagetto

1959—NATIONAL LEAGUE

CLUB	F	W	L	PCT.	MGR
L A	1p	88	68	.564	Alston
MIL	2p	86	70	.551	Haney
S F	3	83	71	.539	Rigney
PIT	4	78	76	.506	Murtaugh
CHI	5t	74	80	.481	Scheffing
CIN	5t	74	80	.481	Smith, Hutchinson
St.L	7	71	83	.461	Hemus
PHI	8	64	90	.416	Sawyer

1959—AMERICAN LEAGUE

CLUB	F	W	L	PCT.	MGR.
CHI	1	94	60	.610	Lopez
CLE	2	89	65	.578	Gordon
N Y	3	79	75	.513	Stengel
DET	4	76	78	.494	Norman, Dykes, Higgins
BOS	5	75	79	.487	York, Jurges
BAL	6	74	80	.481	Richards
K C	7	66	88	.429	Craft
WAS	8	63	91	.409	Lavagetto

1960—NATIONAL LEAGUE

CLUB	F	W	L	PCT.	MGR
PIT	1	95	59	.617	Murtaugh
MIL	2	88	66	.571	Dressen
St.L	3	86	68	.558	Hemus
L A	4	82	72	.532	Alston
S F	5	79	75	.513	Rigney, Sheehan
CIN	6	67	87	.435	Hutchinson
CHI	7	60	94	.390	Grimm, Boudreau
PHI	8	59	95	.383	Sawyer, Mauch

1960—AMERICAN LEAGUE

CLUB	F	W	L	PCT.	MGR
N Y	1	97	57	.630	Stengel
BAL	2	89	65	.578	Richards
CHI	3	87	67	.565	Lopez
CLE	4	76	78	.494	Gordon, White, Dykes
WAS	5	73	81	.474	Lavagetto
DET	6	71	83	.461	Dykes, Hitchcock, Gordon
BOS	7	65	89	.422	Jurges, Higgins
K C	8	58	96	.377	Elliott

1961—NATIONAL LEAGUE

CLUB	F	W	L	PCT.	MGR
CIN	1	93	61	.604	Hutchinson
L A	2	89	65	.578	Alston
S F	3	85	69	.552	Dark
MIL	4	83	71	.539	Dressen, Tebbetts
St.L	5	80	74	.519	Hemus, Keane
PIT	6	75	79	.487	Murtaugh
CHI	7	64	90	.416	Himsl, Craft, Tappe, Klein
PHI	8	47	107	.305	Mauch

1961—AMERICAN LEAGUE

CLUB	F	W	L	PCT.	MGR
N Y	1	109	53	.673	Houk
DET	2	101	61	.623	Scheffing
BAL	3	95	67	.586	Richards, Harris, Hitchcock
CHI	4	86	76	.531	Lopez
CLE	5	78	83	.484	Dykes, Harder
BOS	6	76	86	.469	Higgins
MIN	7	70	90	.438	Lavagetto, Mele
L A	8	70	91	.435	Rigney, Gordon, Bauer
K C	9t	61	100	.379	Gordon, Bauer
WAS	9t	61	100	.379	Vernon

1962—NATIONAL LEAGUE

CLUB	F	W	L	PCT.	MGR
S F	1p	103	62	.624	Dark
L A	2p	102	63	.618	Alston
CIN	3	98	64	.605	Hutchinson
PIT	4	93	68	.578	Murtaugh
MIL	5	86	76	.531	Tebbetts
St.L	6	84	78	.519	Keane
PHI	7	81	80	.503	Mauch
HOU	8	64	96	.400	Craft
CHI	9	59	103	.364	Tappe, Klein, Metro
N Y	10	40	120	.250	Stengel

1962—AMERICAN LEAGUE

CLUB	F	W	L	PCT.	MGR
N Y	1	96	66	.593	Houk
MIN	2	91	71	.562	Mele
L A	3	86	76	.531	Rigney
DET	4	85	76	.528	Scheffing
CHI	5	85	77	.525	Lopez
CLE	6	80	82	.494	McGaha
BAL	7	77	85	.475	Hitchcock
BOS	8	76	84	.475	Higgins
K C	9	72	90	.444	Bauer
WAS	10	60	101	.373	Vernon

1963—NATIONAL LEAGUE

CLUB	F	W	L	PCT.	MGR
L A	1	99	63	.611	Alston
St.L	2	93	69	.574	Keane
S F	3	88	74	.543	Dark
PHI	4	87	75	.537	Mauch
CIN	5	86	76	.531	Hutchinson
MIL	6	84	78	.516	Bragan
CHI	7	82	80	.506	Kennedy
PIT	8	74	88	.457	Murtaugh
HOU	9	66	96	.407	Craft
N Y	10	51	111	.315	Stengel

1963—AMERICAN LEAGUE

CLUB	F	W	L	PCT.	MGR
N Y	1	104	57	.646	Houk
CHI	2	94	68	.580	Lopez
MIN	3	91	70	.565	Mele
BAL	4	86	76	.531	Hitchcock
CLE	5t	79	83	.488	Tebbetts
DET	5t	79	83	.488	{Scheffing, Dressen}
BOS	7	76	85	.472	Pesky
K C	8	73	89	.451	Lopat
L A	9	70	91	.435	Rigney
WAS	10	56	106	.346	{Vernon, Hodges}

1964—NATIONAL LEAGUE

CLUB	F	W	L	PCT.	MGR
St.L	1	93	69	.574	Keane
CIN	2t	92	70	.568	Hutchinson
PHI	2t	92	70	.568	Mauch
S F	4	90	72	.556	Dark
MIL	5	88	74	.543	Bragan
L A	6t	80	82	.494	Alston
PIT	6t	80	82	.494	Murtaugh
CHI	8	76	86	.469	Kennedy
HOU	9	66	96	.407	{Craft, Harris}
N Y	10	53	109	.327	Stengel

1964—AMERICAN LEAGUE

CLUB	F	W	L	PCT.	MGR
N Y	1	99	63	.611	Berra
CHI	2	98	64	.605	Lopez
BAL	3	97	65	.599	Bauer
DET	4	85	77	.525	Dressen
L A	5	82	80	.506	Rigney
CLE	6t	79	83	.488	Tebbetts
MIN	6t	79	83	.488	Mele
BOS	8	72	90	.444	{Pesky, Herman}
WAS	9	62	100	.383	Hodges
K C	10	57	105	.352	{Lopat, McGaha}

1965—NATIONAL LEAGUE

CLUB	F	W	L	PCT.	MGR
L A	1	97	65	.599	Alston
S F	2	95	67	.586	Franks
PIT	3	90	72	.556	Walker
CIN	4	89	73	.549	Sisler
MIL	5	86	76	.531	Bragan
PHI	6	85	76	.528	Mauch
St.L	7	80	81	.497	Schoendienst
CHI	8	72	90	.444	{Kennedy, Klein}
HOU	9	65	97	.401	Harris
N Y	10	50	112	.309	{Stengel, Westrum}

1965—AMERICAN LEAGUE

CLUB	F	W	L	PCT.	MGR
MIN	1	102	60	.630	Mele
CHI	2	95	67	.586	Lopez
BAL	3	94	68	.580	Bauer
DET	4	89	73	.549	Dressen
CLE	5	87	75	.537	Tebbetts
N Y	6	77	85	.475	Keane
CAL	7	75	87	.463	Rigney
WAS	8	70	92	.432	Hodges
BOS	9	62	100	.383	Herman
K C	10	59	103	.364	{McGaha, Sullivan}

1966—NATIONAL LEAGUE

CLUB	F	W	L	PCT.	MGR
L A	1	95	67	.586	Alston
S F	2	93	68	.578	Franks
PIT	3	92	70	.568	Walker
PHI	4	87	75	.537	Mauch
ATL	5	85	77	.525	{Bragan, Hitchcock}
St.L	6	83	79	.512	Schoendienst
CIN	7	76	84	.495	{Heffner, Bristol}
HOU	8	72	90	.444	Hatton
N Y	9	66	95	.410	Westrum
CHI	10	59	103	.364	Durocher

1966—AMERICAN LEAGUE

CLUB	F	W	L	PCT.	MGR
BAL	1	97	63	.606	Bauer
MIN	2	89	73	.549	Mele
DET	3	88	74	.543	{Dressen, Swift, Skaff}
CHI	4	83	79	.512	Stanky
CLE	5	81	81	.500	{Tebbetts, Strickland}
CAL	6	80	82	.494	Rigney
K C	7	74	86	.463	Dark
WAS	8	71	88	.447	Hodges
BOS	9	72	90	.444	{Herman, Runnels}
N Y	10	70	89	.440	{Keane, Houk}

1967—NATIONAL LEAGUE

CLUB	F	W	L	PCT.	MGR
St.L	1	101	60	.627	Schoendienst
S F	2	91	71	.562	F·anks
CHI	3	87	74	.540	Durocher
CIN	4	87	75	.537	Bristol
PHI	5	82	80	.506	Mauch
PIT	6	81	81	.500	{Walker, Murtaugh}
ATL	7	77	85	.475	{Hitchcock, Silvestri}
L A	8	73	89	.451	Alston
HOU	9	69	93	.426	Hatton
N Y	10	61	101	.377	{Westrum, Parker}

1967—AMERICAN LEAGUE

CLUB	F	W	L	PCT.	MGR
BOS	1	92	70	.568	Williams
DET	2t	91	71	.562	Smith
MIN	2t	91	71	.562	{Mele, Ermer}
CHI	4	89	73	.549	Stanky
CAL	5	84	77	.522	Rigney
BAL	6t	76	85	.472	Bauer
WAS	6t	76	85	.472	Hodges
CLE	8	75	87	.463	Adcock
N Y	9	72	90	.444	Houk
K C	10	62	99	.385	{Dark, Appling}

1968—NATIONAL LEAGUE

CLUB	F	W	L	PCT.	MGR
St.L	1	97	65	.599	Schoendienst
S F	2	88	74	.543	Franks
CHI	3	84	78	.519	Durocher
CIN	4	83	79	.512	Bristol
ATL	5	81	81	.500	Harris
PIT	6	80	82	.494	Shepard
L A	7t	76	86	.469	Alston
PHI	7t	76	86	.469	{Mauch, Myatt, Skinner}
N Y	9	73	89	.451	Hodges
HOU	10	72	90	.444	{Hatton, Walker}

1968—AMERICAN LEAGUE

CLUB	F	W	L	PCT.	MGR
DET	1	103	59	.636	Smith
BAL	2	91	71	.562	{Bauer, Weaver}
CLE	3	86	75	.534	Dark
BOS	4	86	76	.531	Williams
N Y	5	83	79	.512	Houk
OAK	6	82	80	.506	Bob Kennedy
MIN	7	79	83	.488	Ermer
CAL	8t	67	95	.414	Rigney
CHI	8t	67	95	.414	{Stanky, Moss, Lopez}
WAS	10	65	96	.404	Lemon

1969—NATIONAL LEAGUE EASTERN DIVISION

CLUB	F	W	L	PCT.	MGR
N Y	1	100	62	.617	Hodges
CHI	2	92	70	.568	Durocher
PIT	3	88	74	.543	{Shepard, Grammas}
St.L	4	87	75	.537	Schoendienst
PHI	5	63	99	.389	{Skinner, Myatt}
MON	6	52	110	.321	Mauch

1969—NATIONAL LEAGUE WESTERN DIVISION

CLUB	F	W	L	PCT.	MGR
ATL	1	93	69	.574	Harris
S F	2	90	72	.556	King
CIN	3	89	73	.549	Bristol
L A	4	85	77	.525	Alston
HOU	5	81	81	.500	Walker
S D	6	52	110	.321	Gomez

1969—AMERICAN LEAGUE EASTERN DIVISION

CLUB	F	W	L	PCT.	MGR
BAL	1	109	53	.673	Weaver
DET	2	90	72	.556	Smith
BOS	3	87	75	.537	{R. Williams, Popowski}
WAS	4	86	76	.531	T. Williams
N Y	5	80	81	.497	Houk
CLE	6	62	99	.385	Dark

1969—AMERICAN LEAGUE WESTERN DIVISION

CLUB	F	W	L	PCT.	MGR
MIN	1	97	65	.599	Martin
OAK	2	88	74	.543	{Bauer, McNamara}
CAL	3	71	91	.438	{Rigney, Phillips}
K C	4	69	93	.426	Gordon
CHI	5	68	94	.420	{Lopez, Gutteridge}
SEA	6	64	98	.395	Schultz

1970—NATIONAL LEAGUE EASTERN DIVISION

CLUB	F	W	L	PCT.	MGR
CHI	1	89	73	.549	Murtaugh
CHI	2	84	78	.519	Durocher
N Y	3	83	79	.512	Hodges
St.L	4	76	86	.469	Schoendienst
PHI	5	73	88	.453	Lucchesi
MON	6	73	89	.451	Mauch

1970—NATIONAL LEAGUE WESTERN DIVISION

CLUB	F	W	L	PCT.	MGR
CIN	1	102	60	.630	Anderson
LA	2	87	74	.540	Alston
SF	3	86	76	.531	{King, Fox}
HOU	4	79	83	.488	Walker
ATL	5	76	86	.469	Harris
SD	6	63	99	.389	Gomez

1970—AMERICAN LEAGUE EASTERN DIVISION

UB	F	W	L	PCT.	MGR
L	1	108	54	.667	Weaver
S	2	93	69	.574	Houk
S	3	87	75	.537	Kasko
TE	4	79	83	.488	Smith
E	5	76	86	.469	Dark
AS	6	70	92	.432	T. Williams

1970—AMERICAN LEAGUE WESTERN DIVISION

UB	F	W	L	PCT.	MGR
N	1	98	64	.605	Rigney
K	2	89	73	.549	McNamara
L	3	86	76	.531	Phillips
	4t	65	97	.401	Metro, Lemon
	4t	65	97	.401	Bristol
I	6	56	106	.346	Gutteridge, Adair, Tanner

1971—NATIONAL LEAGUE EASTERN DIVISION

UB	F	W	L	PCT.	MGR
T	1	97	65	.599	Murtaugh
L	2	90	72	.556	Schoendienst
I	3t	83	79	.512	Durocher
	3t	83	79	.510	Hodges
N	5	71	90	.441	Mauch
I	6	67	95	.414	Lucchesi

1971—NATIONAL LEAGUE WESTERN DIVISION

UB	F	W	L	PCT.	MGR
	1	90	72	.556	Fox
	2	89	73	.549	Alston
L	3	82	80	.506	Harris
U	4t	79	83	.488	Walker
N	4t	79	83	.488	Anderson
	6	61	100	.379	Gomez

1971—AMERICAN LEAGUE EASTERN DIVISION

UB	F	W	L	PCT.	MGR
L	1	101	57	.639	Weaver
T	2	91	71	.562	Martin
	3	85	77	.525	Kasko
	4	82	80	.506	Houk
AS	5	63	96	.396	T. Williams
E	6	60	102	.370	Dark, Lipon

1971—AMERICAN LEAGUE WESTERN DIVISION

UB	F	W	L	PCT.	MGR
K	1	101	60	.627	R. Williams
	2	85	76	.528	Lemon
I	3	79	83	.488	Tanner
L	4	76	86	.469	Phillips
N	5	74	86	.463	Rigney
L	6	69	92	.429	Bristol

1972—NATIONAL LEAGUE EASTERN DIVISION

UB	F	W	L	PCT.	MGR
C	1	96	59	.619	Virdon
I	2	85	70	.548	Durocher, Lockman
	3	83	73	.532	Berra
	4	75	81	.481	Schoendienst
N	5	70	86	.449	Mauch
I	6	59	97	.378	Lucchesi, Owens

1972—NATIONAL LEAGUE WESTERN DIVISION

CLUB	F	W	L	PCT.	MGR
CIN	1	95	59	.617	Anderson
HOU	2	84	69	.549	Walker, Parker, Durocher
LA	3	85	70	.548	Alston
ATL	4	70	84	.455	Harris, Mathews
SF	5	69	86	.445	Fox
SD	6	58	95	.379	Gomez, Zimmer

1972—AMERICAN LEAGUE EASTERN DIVISION

CLUB	F	W	L	PCT.	MGR
DET	1	86	70	.551	Martin
BOS	2	85	70	.548	Kasko
BAL	3	80	74	.519	Weaver
NY	4	79	76	.510	Houk
CLE	5	72	84	.462	Aspromonte
MIL	6	65	91	.417	Bristol, McMillan, Crandall

1972—AMERICAN LEAGUE WESTERN DIVISION

CLUB	F	W	L	PCT.	MGR
OAK	1	93	62	.600	R. Williams
CHI	2	87	67	.565	Tanner
MIN	3	77	77	.500	Rigney, Quilici
KC	4	76	78	.494	Lemon
CAL	5	75	80	.484	Rice
TEX	6	54	100	.351	T. Williams

1973—NATIONAL LEAGUE EASTERN DIVISION

CLUB	F	W	L	PCT.	MGR
NY	1	82	79	.509	Berra
St.L	2	81	81	.500	Schoendienst
PIT	3	80	82	.494	Virdon, Murtaugh
MON	4	79	83	.488	Mauch
CHI	5	77	84	.478	Lockman
PHI	6	71	91	.438	Ozark

1973—NATIONAL LEAGUE WESTERN DIVISION

CLUB	F	W	L	PCT.	MGR
CIN	1	99	63	.611	Anderson
LA	2	95	66	.590	Alston
SF	3	88	74	.543	Fox
HOU	4	82	80	.506	Durocher
ATL	5	76	85	.472	Mathews
SD	6	60	102	.370	Zimmer

1973—AMERICAN LEAGUE EASTERN DIVISION

CLUB	F	W	L	PCT.	MGR
BAL	1	97	65	.599	Weaver
BOS	2	89	73	.549	Kasko, Popowski
DET	3	85	77	.525	Martin, Schultz
NY	4	80	82	.494	Houk
MIL	5	74	88	.457	Crandall
CLE	6	71	91	.438	Aspromonte

1973—AMERICAN LEAGUE WESTERN DIVISION

CLUB	F	W	L	PCT.	MGR
OAK	1	94	68	.580	Williams
KC	2	88	74	.543	McKeon
MIN	3	81	81	.500	Quilici
CAL	4	79	83	.488	Winkles
CHI	5	77	85	.475	Tanner
TEX	6	57	105	.352	Herzog, Wilber, Martin

1974—NATIONAL LEAGUE EASTERN DIVISION

CLUB	F	W	L	PCT.	MGR
PIT	1	88	74	.543	Murtaugh
St. L	2	86	75	.534	Schoendienst
PHI	3	80	82	.494	Ozark
MON	4	79	82	.491	Mauch
NY	5	71	91	.438	Berra
CHI	6	66	96	.407	Lockman, Marshall

1974—NATIONAL LEAGUE WESTERN DIVISION

CLUB	F	W	L	PCT.	MGR
LA	1	102	60	.630	Alston
CIN	2	98	64	.605	Anderson
ATL	3	88	74	.543	Mathews, King
HOU	4	81	81	.500	Gomez
SF	5	72	90	.444	Fox, Westrum
SD	6	60	102	.370	McNamara

1974—AMERICAN LEAGUE EASTERN DIVISION

CLUB	F	W	L	PCT.	MGR
BAL	1	91	71	.562	Weaver
NY	2	89	73	.549	Virdon
BOS	3	84	78	.519	Johnson
CLE	4	77	85	.475	Aspromonte
MIL	5	76	86	.469	Crandall
DET	6	72	90	.444	Houk

1974—AMERICAN LEAGUE WESTERN DIVISION

CLUB	F	W	L	PCT.	MGR
OAK	1	90	72	.556	Dark
TEX	2	84	76	.525	Martin
MIN	3	82	80	.506	Quilici
CHI	4	80	80	.500	Tanner
KC	5	77	85	.475	McKeon
CAL	6	68	94	.420	Winkles, Herzog, Williams

1975—NATIONAL LEAGUE EASTERN DIVISION

CLUB	F	W	L	PCT.	MGR
PIT	1	92	69	.571	Murtaugh
PHI	2	86	76	.531	Ozark
NY	3t	82	80	.506	Berra, McMillan
St. L	3t	82	80	.506	Schoendienst
CHI	5t	75	87	.463	Marshall
MON	5t	75	87	.463	Mauch

1975—NATIONAL LEAGUE WESTERN DIVISION

CLUB	F	W	L	PCT.	MGR
CIN	1	108	54	.667	Anderson
LA	2	88	74	.543	Alston
SF	3	80	81	.497	Westrum
SD	4	71	91	.438	McNamara
ATL	5	67	94	.416	King
HOU	6	64	97	.398	Gomez, Virdon

1975—AMERICAN LEAGUE EASTERN DIVISION

CLUB	F	W	L	PCT.	MGR
BOS	1	95	65	.594	Johnson
BAL	2	90	69	.566	Weaver
NY	3	83	77	.519	Virdon, Martin
CLE	4	79	80	.497	Robinson
MIL	5	68	94	.420	Crandall, Kuenn
DET	6	57	102	.358	Houk

1975—AMERICAN LEAGUE WESTERN DIVISION

CLUB	F	W	L	PCT.	MGR
OAK	1	98	64	.605	Dark
KC	2	91	71	.562	McKeon, Herzog
TEX	3	79	83	.488	Martin, Lucchesi
MIN	4	76	83	.478	Quilici
CHI	5	75	86	.466	Tanner
CAL	6	72	89	.447	Williams

1976—NATIONAL LEAGUE EASTERN DIVISION

CLUB	F	W	L	PCT.	MGR
PHI	1	101	61	.623	Ozark
PIT	2	92	70	.568	Murtaugh
N Y	3	86	76	.531	Frazier
CHI	4	75	87	.463	Marshall
St.L	5	72	90	.444	Schoendienst
MON	6	55	107	.340	Kuehl, Fox

1976—NATIONAL LEAGUE WESTERN DIVISION

CLUB	F	W	L	PCT.	MGR
CIN	1	102	60	.630	Anderson
L A	2	92	70	.568	Alston, Lasorda
HOU	3	80	82	.494	Virdon
S F	4	74	88	.457	Rigney
S D	5	73	89	.451	McNamara
ATL	6	70	92	.432	Bristol

1976—AMERICAN LEAGUE EASTERN DIVISION

CLUB	F	W	L	PCT.	MGR
N Y	1	97	62	.610	Martin
BAL	2	88	74	.543	Weaver
BOS	3	83	79	.512	Johnson, Zimmer
CLE	4	81	78	.509	Robinson
DET	5	74	87	.460	Houk
MIL	6	66	95	.410	Grammas

1976—AMERICAN LEAGUE WESTERN DIVISION

CLUB	F	W	L	PCT.	MGR
K C	1	90	72	.556	Herzog
OAK	2	87	74	.540	Tanner
MIN	3	85	77	.525	Mauch
CAL	4t	76	86	.469	Williams, Sherry
TEX	4t	76	86	.469	Lucchesi
CHI	6	64	97	.398	Richards

CHAMPIONSHIP SERIES

Beginning in 1969, the American and National Leagues were split into two six-club divisions, East and West. As a result, a post season best-of-five series was initiated to determine each league's representative in the World Series.

1969 —— NATIONAL LEAGUE

New York (East) 3 games vs. Atlanta (West) 0 games

Oct. 4	at Atlanta	New York 9, Atlanta 5
Oct. 5	at Atlanta	New York 11, Atlanta 6
Oct. 6	at New York	New York 7, Atlanta 4

1969 —— AMERICAN LEAGUE

Baltimore (East) 3 games vs. Minnesota (West) 0 games

Oct. 4	at Baltimore	Baltimore 4, Minnesota 3
Oct. 5	at Baltimore	Baltimore 1, Minnesota 0
Oct. 6	at Minnesota	Baltimore 11, Minnesota 2

1970 — NATIONAL LEAGUE

Cincinnati (West) 3 games vs. Pittsburgh (East) 0 games

Oct. 3	at Pittsburgh	Cincinnati 3, Pittsburgh 0
Oct. 4	at Pittsburgh	Cincinnati 3, Pittsburgh 1
Oct. 5	at Cincinnati	Cincinnati 3, Pittsburgh 2

1970 — AMERICAN LEAGUE

Baltimore (East) 3 games vs. Minnesota (West) 0 games

Oct. 3	at Minnesota	Baltimore 10, Minnesota 6
Oct. 4	at Minnesota	Baltimore 11, Minnesota 3
Oct. 5	at Baltimore	Baltimore 6, Minnesota 1

1971 — NATIONAL LEAGUE

Pittsburgh (East) 3 games vs. San Francisco (West) 1 game
Oct. 2   at San Francisco   San Francisco 5, Pittsburgh 4
Oct. 3   at San Francisco   Pittsburgh 9, San Francisco 4
Oct. 5   at Pittsburgh   Pittsburgh 2, San Francisco 1
Oct. 6   at Pittsburgh   Pittsburgh 9, San Francisco 5

1971 — AMERICAN LEAGUE

Baltimore (East) 3 games vs. Oakland (West) 0 games
Oct. 3   at Baltimore   Baltimore 5, Oakland 3
Oct. 4   at Baltimore   Baltimore 5, Oakland 1
Oct. 5   at Oakland   Baltimore 5, Oakland 3

1972 — NATIONAL LEAGUE

Cincinnati (West) 3 games vs. Pittsburgh (East) 2 games
Oct. 7   at Pittsburgh   Pittsburgh 5, Cincinnati 1
Oct. 8   at Pittsburgh   Cincinnati 5, Pittsburgh 3
Oct. 9   at Cincinnati   Pittsburgh 3, Cincinnati 2
Oct. 10   at Cincinnati   Cincinnati 7, Pittsburgh 1
Oct. 11   at Cincinnati   Cincinnati 4, Pittsburgh 3

1972 — AMERICAN LEAGUE

Oakland (West) 3 games vs. Detroit (East) 2 games
Oct. 7   at Oakland   Oakland 3, Detroit 2
Oct. 8   at Oakland   Oakland 5, Detroit 0
Oct. 10   at Detroit   Detroit 3, Oakland 0
Oct. 11   at Detroit   Detroit 4, Oakland 3
Oct. 12   at Detroit   Oakland 2, Detroit 1

1973 — NATIONAL LEAGUE

New York (East) 3 games vs. Cincinnati (West) 2 games
Oct. 6   at Cincinnati   Cincinnati 2, New York 1
Oct. 7   at Cincinnati   New York 5, Cincinnati 0
Oct. 8   at New York   New York 9, Cincinnati 2
Oct. 9   at New York   Cincinnati 2, New York 1
Oct. 10   at New York   New York 7, Cincinnati 2

1973 — AMERICAN LEAGUE

Oakland (West) 3 games vs. Baltimore (East) 2 games
Oct. 6   at Baltimore   Baltimore 6, Oakland 0
Oct. 7   at Baltimore   Oakland 6, Baltimore 3
Oct. 9   at Oakland   Oakland 2, Baltimore 1
Oct. 10   at Oakland   Baltimore 5, Oakland 4
Oct. 11   at Oakland   Oakland 3, Baltimore 0

1974 — NATIONAL LEAGUE

Los Angeles (West) 3 games vs. Pittsburgh (East) 1 game
Oct. 5   at Pittsburgh   Los Angeles 3, Pittsburgh 0
Oct. 6   at Pittsburgh   Los Angeles 5, Pittsburgh 2
Oct. 8   at Los Angeles   Pittsburgh 7, Los Angeles 0
Oct. 9   at Los Angeles   Los Angeles 12, Pittsburgh 1

1974 —— AMERICAN LEAGUE

Oakland (West) 3 games vs. Baltimore (East) 1 game
Oct. 5   at Oakland   Baltimore 6, Oakland 3
Oct. 6   at Oakland   Oakland 5, Baltimore 0
Oct. 8   at Baltimore   Oakland 1, Baltimore 0
Oct. 9   at Baltimore   Oakland 2, Baltimore 1

1975 — NATIONAL LEAGUE

Cincinnati (West) 3 games vs. Pittsburgh (East) 0 games
Oct. 4   at Cincinnati   Cincinnati 8, Pittsburgh 3
Oct. 5   at Cincinnati   Cincinnati 6, Pittsburgh 1
Oct. 7   at Pittsburgh   Cincinnati 5, Pittsburgh 3

1975 — AMERICAN LEAGUE

Boston (East) 3 games vs. Oakland (West) 0 games
Oct. 4   at Boston   Boston 7, Oakland 1
Oct. 5   at Boston   Boston 6, Oakland 3
Oct. 7   at Oakland   Boston 5, Oakland 3

1976 — NATIONAL LEAGUE

Cincinnati (West) 3 games vs. Philadelphia (East) 0 games

Oct. 9   at Philadelphia   Cincinnati 6, Philadelphia 3
Oct. 10   at Philadelphia   Cincinnati 6, Philadelphia 2
Oct. 12   at Cincinnati   Cincinnati 7, Philadelphia 6

1976 — AMERICAN LEAGUE

New York (East) 3 games vs. Kansas City (West) 2 games

Oct. 9   at Kansas City   New York 4, Kansas City 1
Oct. 10   at Kansas City   Kansas City 7, New York 3
Oct. 12   at New York   New York 5, Kansas City 3
Oct. 13   at New York   Kansas City 7, New York 4
Oct. 14   at New York   New York 7, Kansas City 6

EVOLUTION OF MAJOR LEAGUE CITIES
(alphabetically)

The letters in parenthesis indicate the league. (n) National Association; (N) National League; (a) American Association; (U) Union Association; (p) Players League; (A) American League; (F) Federal League.

ALTOONA: (U) 1884.
ATLANTA: (N) 1966 to date.
BALTIMORE: (n) 1872–74, listed as Lord Baltimore in club standings; also had second club in league in 1873, listed as Marylands in club standings; (a) 1882–91; (U) 1884; (N) 1892–99; (A) 1901–02; 1954 to date; (F) 1914–15.
BOSTON: (n) 1871–75; (N) 1876–1952; (U) 1884; (p) 1890; (a) 1891; (A) 1901 to date.
BROOKLYN: (n) 1872–75, listed as Atlantics in club standings; also had second club in league in 1872, listed as Eckfords in club standings; (a) 1884–90; (p) 1890; (N) 1890 1957; (F) 1914–15.
BUFFALO: (N) 1879–85; (p) 1890; (F) 1914–15.
CALIFORNIA: (A) 1965 to date.
CHICAGO: (n) 1871, 1874–75; (N) 1876 to date; (U) 1884; (p) 1890; (A) 1901 to date; (F) 1914–15.
CINCINNATI: (N) 1876–80, 1890 to date; (a) 1882–89, 1891; (U) 1884.
CLEVELAND: (n) 1871–72; (N) 1879–84, 1889–99; (a) 1887–88; (p) 1890; (A) 1901 to date.
COLUMBUS: (a) 1883–84, 1889–91.
DETROIT: (N) 1881–88; (A) 1901 to date.
ELIZABETH: (n) 1873, listed as Resolutes in club standings.
FT. WAYNE: (n) 1871, listed as Kekiongas in club standings.
HARTFORD: (n) 1874–75; (N) 1876–77.
HOUSTON: (N) 1962 to date.
INDIANAPOLIS: (N) 1878, 1887–89; (a) 1884; (F) 1914.
KANSAS CITY: (U) 1884; (N) 1886; (a) 1888–89; (F) 1914–15; (A) 1955–67, 1969 to date.
KEOKUK: (n) 1875, listed as Westerns in club standings.
LOS ANGELES: (N) 1958 to date; (A) 1961–64.
LOUISVILLE: (N) 1876–77; 1892–99; (a) 1882–91, listed as Eclipse in club standings.
MIDDLETOWN: (n) 1872, listed as Mansfields in club standings.
MILWAUKEE: (N) 1878, 1953–65; (U) 1884; (a) 1891; (A) 1901, 1970 to date.
MINNESOTA: (A) 1961 to date (Minneapolis-St. Paul).
MONTREAL: (N) 1969 to date.
NEWARK: (F) 1915.
NEW HAVEN: (n) 1875.
NEW YORK: (n) 1871–75, listed as Mutuals in club standings; (N) 1876, listed as Mutuals in club standings; 1883–1957, 1962–date; (a) 1883–87, listed as Metropolitans in club standings; (p) 1890; (A) 1903 to date.
OAKLAND: (A) 1968 to date.
PHILADELPHIA: (n) 1871–75, listed as Athletics in club standings; also had second club in league, 1873–75; also had third club in league in 1875, listed as Centennials in club standings; (N) 1876, listed as Athletics in club standings;

1883 to date; (a) 1882–91, listed as Athletics in club standings; (U) 1884, listed as Keystone in club standings; (p) 1890; (A) 1901–54.

PITTSBURGH: (a) 1882–86, listed as Allegheny in club standings; (U) 1884; (N) 1887 to date; (p) 1890; (F) 1914–15.

PROVIDENCE: (N) 1878–85.

RICHMOND: (a) 1884, listed as Virginia in club standings.

ROCKFORD: (n) 1871.

ROCHESTER: (a) 1890.

ST. LOUIS: (n) 1875, listed as Red Stockings in club standings; also had second club in league; (N) 1876–77, 1885–86, 1892 to date; (a) 1882–91; (U) 1884; (A) 1902–53; (F) 1914–15.

ST. PAUL: (U) 1884.

SAN DIEGO: (N) 1969 to date.

SAN FRANCISCO: (N) 1958 to date.

SEATTLE: (A) 1969.

SYRACUSE: (N) 1879; (a) 1890.

TEXAS: (A) 1972–date.

TOLEDO: (a) 1884, 1890.

TROY: (n) 1871–72, listed as Haymakers in club standings; (N) 1879–82.

WASHINGTON: (n) 1871, listed as Olympics in club standings; in 1872 had two clubs in league, listed as Olympics and Nationals in club standings; 1873, 1875, listed as Nationals in club standings; (a) 1884, listed as Nationals in club standings; 1891; (U) 1884, listed as Nationals in club standings; (N) 1886–89; 1892–99; (A) 1901–71.

WILMINGTON: (U) 1884.

WORCESTER: (N) 1880–82.

NATIONAL LEAGUE

ANNUAL ATTENDANCE

1901 —	1,920,031	1939 —	4,707,177
1902 —	1,683,012	1940 —	4,389,693
1903 —	2,390,362	1941 —	4,777,647
1904 —	2,664,271	1942 —	4,353,353
1905 —	2,734,310	1943 —	3,769,342
1906 —	2,781,213	1944 —	3,974,588
1907 —	2,640,220	1945 —	5,260,703
1908 —	3,512,108	1946 —	8,902,107
1909 —	3,496,420	1947 —	10,388,470
1910 —	3,494,544	1948 —	9,770,743
1911 —	3,231,768	1949 —	9,484,718
1912 —	2,735,759	1950 —	8,320,616
1913 —	2,831,531	1951 —	7,244,002
1914 —	1,707,397	1952 —	6,339,148
1915 —	2,430,142	1953 —	7,419,721
1916 —	3,051,634	1954 —	8,013,519
1917 —	2,361,136	1955 —	7,674,412
1918 —	1,372,127	1956 —	8,649,567
1919 —	2,878,203	1957 —	8,819,601
1920 —	4,036,575	1958 —	10,164,596
1921 —	3,986,984	1959 —	9,994,525
1922 —	3,941,820	1960 —	10,684,963
1923 —	4,069,817	1961 —	8,731,502
1924 —	4,340,644	1962 —	11,360,159
1925 —	4,353,704	1963 —	11,382,227
1926 —	4,920,399	1964 —	12,045,190
1927 —	5,309,917	1965 —	13,581,136
1928 —	4,881,097	1966 —	15,015,471
1929 —	4,925,713	1967 —	12,971,430
1930 —	5,446,532	1968 —	11,785,358
1931 —	4,583,815	1969 —	15,094,946
1932 —	3,841,334	1970 —	16,662,198
1933 —	3,162,821	1971 —	17,324,857
1934 —	3,200,105	1972 —	15,529,730
1935 —	3,657,309	1973 —	16,675,322
1936 —	3,903,691	1974 —	16,978,314
1937 —	4,204,228	1975 —	16,600,490
1938 —	4,560,837	1976 —	16,660,529

AMERICAN LEAGUE

ANNUAL ATTENDANCE

1901 —	1,683,584	1939 —	4,270,602
1902 —	2,206,454	1940 —	5,433,791
1903 —	2,344,888	1941 —	4,911,956
1904 —	3,024,028	1942 —	4,200,216
1905 —	3,120,752	1943 —	3,696,569
1906 —	2,938,076	1944 —	4,798,158
1907 —	3,398,764	1945 —	5,580,420
1908 —	3,611,366	1946 —	9,621,182
1909 —	3,739,570	1947 —	9,486,069
1910 —	3,270,689	1948 —	11,150,099
1911 —	3,339,514	1949 —	10,730,647
1912 —	3,263,631	1950 —	9,142,361
1913 —	3,526,805	1951 —	8,882,674
1914 —	2,747,591	1952 —	8,293,896
1915 —	2,484,684	1953 —	6,964,076
1916 —	3,451,885	1954 —	7,922,364
1917 —	2,858,858	1955 —	8,942,971
1918 —	1,707,999	1956 —	7,893,683
1919 —	3,654,236	1957 —	8,196,218
1920 —	5,084,300	1958 —	7,296,034
1921 —	4,620,328	1959 —	9,149,454
1922 —	4,874,355	1960 —	9,226,526
1923 —	4,602,589	1961 —	10,163,016
1924 —	5,255,439	1962 —	10,015,056
1925 —	5,186,851	1963 —	9,094,847
1926 —	4,912,583	1964 —	9,235,151
1927 —	4,612,951	1965 —	8,860,764
1928 —	4,221,188	1966 —	10,166,738
1929 —	4,662,470	1967 —	11,336,923
1930 —	4,685,730	1968 —	11,317,387
1931 —	3,883,292	1969 —	12,134,745
1932 —	3,133,232	1970 —	12,085,135
1933 —	2,926,210	1971 —	11,868,560
1934 —	3,763,606	1972 —	11,438,538
1935 —	3,688,007	1973 —	13,433,604
1936 —	4,178,922	1974 —	13,047,294
1937 —	4,735,835	1975 —	13,189,423
1938 —	4,445,684	1976 —	14,657,802

NATIONAL LEAGUE SINGLE GAME ATTENDANCE

Atlanta	53,775	(vs. L.A., Apr. 8, 1974) *
Chicago	46,572	(vs. Bro., May 18, 1947)
Cincinnati	52,526	(vs. L.A., Apr. 7, 1975)
Houston	50,908	(vs. L.A., June 22, 1966) *
Los Angeles	78,672	(vs. S.F., Apr. 18, 1958)
Montreal	34,331	(vs. Phi., Sept. 15, 1973)
New York	56,738	(vs. L.A., June 23, 1968)
Philadelphia	60,492	(vs. L.A., July 5, 1976) *
Pittsburgh	51,695	(vs. St.L., Apr. 6, 1973)
St. Louis	50,548	(vs. N.Y., Sept. 14, 1975)
San Diego	49,618	(vs. Cin., July 5, 1975) *
San Francisco	44,256	(vs. Atl., Sept. 1, 1973)

*Night Game

AMERICAN LEAGUE SINGLE GAME ATTENDANCE

Baltimore	48,042	(vs. Cal., May 17, 1975) *
Boston	36,350	(vs. N.Y., Aug. 7, 1956)
California	53,591	(vs. N.Y., July 13, 1962) *
Chicago	53,940	(vs. N.Y., June 8, 1951) *
Cleveland	78,382	(vs. Chi., Aug. 20, 1948) *
Detroit	57,888	(vs. Cle., Sept. 26, 1948)
Kansas City	39,474	(vs. Oak., June 29, 1974) *
Milwaukee	48,160	(vs. Cle., Apr. 11, 1975)
Minnesota	45,890	(vs. K.C., July 4, 1973)
New York	74,747	(vs. Bos., May 26, 1947) *
Oakland	48,758	(vs. Det., June 6, 1970)
Texas	39,269	(vs. Bal., June 1, 1974) *

*Night Game

III ALL-TIME REGISTER
OF
PLAYERS AND MANAGERS

This All-Time Register intends to cover every man who ever appeared in a regularly scheduled major league game since the birth of professional league play in 1871. There are gaps, but they have been plugged considerably since publication of the initial edition of the *Encyclopedia*, many by readers who were willing to supply the pegs which fitted holes; others by former players or members of their families.

This historic compilation consists of an alphabetical listing of all players and managers in the majors from 1871 through 1976 Information is arranged as follows:

Last name, followed by first and middle names, then nickname in parentheses, ONLY if the information is available. Birthplace, birthdate, death date. Year-by-year playing record, including club, league, positions played, total number of games played and playing performance. The last line carries the bats and throws of the player and his lifetime batting average or his won-lost lifetime total if a pitcher, or both.

KEY TO ABBREVIATIONS

Teams:

ALL (Allegheny) ; ALT (Altoona) ; ATH (Athletics) ; ATL (Braves) ; BAL (Baltimore) ; BOS (Boston) ; BRO (Brooklyn) ; BUF (Buffalo) ; CAL (California) ; CEN (Centennials) ; CHI (Chicago) ; CIN (Cincinnati) ; CLE (Cleveland) ; COL (Columbus) ; DET (Detroit) ; ECK (Eckford) ; ECL (Eclipse) ; HAR (Hartford) ; HOU (Houston) ; IND (Indianapolis) ; KC (Kansas City) ; KEK (Kekiongas) ; KEO (Keokuk) ; KEY (Keystone) ; LA (Los Angeles) ; LB (Lord Baltimore) ; LOU (Louisville) ; MAN (Mansfield) ; MAR (Maryland) ; MET (Metropolitans) ; MIL (Milwaukee) ; MINN (Minnesota) ; MON (Montreal) ; MUT (Mutuals) ; NAT (Nationals) ; NEW (Newark) ; NH (New Haven) ; NY (New York) ; OAK (Oakland) ; OLY (Olympics) ; PHI (Philadelphia) ; PIT (Pittsburgh) ; PRO (Providence) ; RES (Resolutes) ; RIC (Richmond) ; ROC (Rochester) ; ROK (Rockford) ; RS (Red Stockings) ; St.L (St. Louis; SD (San Diego) ; SEA (Seattle) ; SF (San Francisco) ; SYR (Syracuse) ; TEX (Texas) ; TOL (Toledo) ; TRO (Troy) ; VIR (Virginia) ; WAS (Washington) ; WIL (Wilmington) ; WOR (Worcester) .

LEAGUES

NA—National Association
N—National League
AA—American Association
U—Union Association
P—Players League
A—American League
F—Federal League

A dash indicates no record available
(Used for batting average before 1876)

BL—bats left
BR—bats right
BB—bats both

POSITIONS

1—First base
2—Second base
S—Shortstop
3—Third base
O—Outfield
C—Catcher
P—Pitcher
H—Pinch hitter
M—Manager
D—Designated hitter
ALL—Played all positions

TL—throws left
TR—throws right

ALL-TIME REGISTER

NOTE:

Certain Latin-American players who include their mother's maiden name in parentheses after their own last name are so indicated. Nicknames are shown in quotation marks for all players who are usually called by any name other than their own given first name. Games pitched are shown in the GP column for any player who appeared as a pitcher in fewer games than his total for any season. Total games pitched are also shown in the GP column for lifetime if less than the total number of games played lifetime. Players who appeared in ten or more games as the designated hitter for American League teams beginning in 1973 show the symbol 'D' in the position column.

AARON, HENRY LOUIS "HANK"
B.FEB.5,1934 MOBILE,ALA.

YR	CL	LEA	POS	GP	G	REC
1954	MIL	N	O		122	.280
1955	MIL	N	2-O		153	.314
1956	MIL	N	O		153	.328
1957	MIL	N	O		151	.322
1958	MIL	N	O		153	.326
1959	MIL	N	3-O		154	.355
1960	MIL	N	2-O		153	.292
1961	MIL	N	3-O		155	.327
1962	MIL	N	1-O		156	.323
1963	MIL	N	O		161	.319
1964	MIL	N	2-O		145	.328
1965	MIL	N	O		150	.318
1966	ATL	N	2-O		158	.279
1967	ATL	N	2-O		155	.307
1968	ATL	N	1-O		160	.287
1969	ATL	N	1-O		147	.300
1970	ATL	N	1-O		150	.298
1971	ATL	N	1-O		139	.327
1972	ATL	N	1-O		129	.265
1973	ATL	N	O		120	.301
1974	ATL	N	O		112	.268
1975	MIL	A	O-D		137	.234
1976	MIL	A	O-D		85	.229
		BRTR			3298	.305

AARON, TOMMIE LEE
B.AUG.5,1939 MOBILE,ALA.

YR	CL	LEA	POS	GP	G	REC
1962	MIL	N	1-2-3-O		141	.231
1963	MIL	N	1-2-3-O		72	.200
1965	MIL	N	1		8	.188
1968	ATL	N	1-3-O		98	.244
1969	ATL	N	1-O		49	.250
1970	ATL	N	1-O		44	.206
1971	ATL	N	1-3		25	.226
		BRTR			437	.229

ABADIE, JOHN
B.NOV.4,1858 PHILADELPHIA,PA.
D.MAY 17,1905

YR	CL	LEA	POS	GP	G	REC
1875	CEN	NA	1		11	-
	ATL	NA	1		1	-
					12	-

ABBATICCHIO, EDWARD JAMES "BATTY"
B.APR.15,1877 LATROBE,PA.
D.JAN.6,1957

YR	CL	LEA	POS	GP	G	REC
1897	PHI	N	2		3	.300
1898	PHI	N	3		20	.262
1903	BOS	N	2-S		133	.227
1904	BOS	N	S		154	.256
1905	BOS	N	S		153	.279
1907	PIT	N	2		147	.262
1908	PIT	N	2		144	.250
1909	PIT	N	S		23	.230
1910	PIT	N	S		1	.000
	BOS	N	S		47	.247
		BRTR			825	.255

ABBEY, BERT WOOD
B.NOV.29,1869 ESSEX,VT.
D.JUNE 11,1962

YR	CL	LEA	POS	GP	G	REC
1892	WAS	N	P		21	6-15
1893	CHI	N	P		8	3-5
1894	CHI	N	P		11	2-7
1895	CHI	N	P		2	0-1
	BRO	N	P		8	4-3
1896	BRO	N	P		19	8-8
		BRTR			69	23-39

ABBEY, CHARLES S.
B.1867 OMAHA,NEB.

YR	CL	LEA	POS	GP	G	REC
1893	WAS	N	O		31	.277
1894	WAS	N	O		129	.318
1895	WAS	N	O		133	.275
1896	WAS	N	O		75	.255
1897	WAS	N	O		78	.264
					446	.283

ABBOTT, FREDERICK H.
(REAL NAME FREDERICK H. VANDEMANN)
B.OCT.21,1873 VERSAILLES,OHIO
D.JUNE 11,1935

YR	CL	LEA	POS	GP	G	REC
1903	CLE	A	C		76	.271
1904	CLE	A	C		42	.168
1905	PHI	N	C		39	.195
		BRTR			157	.226

ABBOTT, LEANDER FRANKLIN "BIG DAN"
B.MAR.16,1862 WESTON,OHIO
D.FEB.13,1930

YR	CL	LEA	POS	GP	G	REC
1890	TOL	AA	P		3	1-2
		TR				

ABBOTT, ODY CLEON "ODD"
B.SEPT.5,1888 PITTSBURGH,PA.
D.APR.13,1933

YR	CL	LEA	POS	GP	G	REC
1910	STL	N	O		21	.186
		BRTR				

ABBOTT, WILLIAM GLENN "GLENN"
B.FEB.16,1951 LITTLE ROCK,ARK.

YR	CL	LEA	POS	GP	G	REC
1973	OAK	A	P		5	1-0
1974	OAK	A	P		19	5-7
1975	OAK	A	P		30	5-5
1976	OAK	A	P		19	2-4
		BRTR			73	13-16

ABER, ALBERT JULIUS "LEFTY"
B.JULY 31,1927 CLEVELAND,OHIO

YR	CL	LEA	POS	GP	G	REC
1950	CLE	A	P		1	1-0
1953	CLE	A	P		6	1-1
	DET	A	P		17	4-3
1954	DET	A	P		32	5-11
1955	DET	A	P		39	6-3
1956	DET	A	P		42	4-4
1957	DET	A	P		28	3-3
	KC	A	P		3	0-0
		BLTL			168	24-25

ABERCROMBIE, DAVID
B.1840 FALKIRK,SCOTLAND
D.SEPT.2,1916

YR	CL	LEA	POS	GP	G	REC
1871	TRO	NA	S		1	.000

ABERNATHIE, WILLIAM EDWARD
B.JAN.30,1930 TORRANCE,CAL.

YR	CL	LEA	POS	GP	G	REC
1952	CLE	A	P		1	0-0
		BRTR				

ABERNATHY, TALMADGE LAFAYETTE "TED"
B.OCT.30,1921 BYNUM,N.C.

YR	CL	LEA	POS	GP	G	REC
1942	PHI	A	P		1	0-0
1943	PHI	A	P		5	0-3
1944	PHI	A	P		1	0-0
		BRTL			7	0-3

ABERNATHY, THEODORE WADE "TED"
B.MAR.6,1933 STANLEY,N.C.

YR	CL	LEA	POS	GP	G	REC
1955	WAS	A	P		40	5-9
1956	WAS	A	P		5	1-3
1957	WAS	A	P		26	2-10
1960	WAS	A	P		2	0-0
1963	CLE	A	P		43	7-2
1964	CLE	A	P		53	2-6
1965	CHI	N	P		84	4-6
1966	CHI	N	P		10	1-3
	ATL	N	P		38	4-4
1967	CIN	N	P		70	6-3
1968	CIN	N	P		78	10-7
1969	CHI	N	P		56	4-3
1970	CHI	N	P		11	0-0
	STL	N	P		11	1-0
	KC	A	P		36	9-3
1971	KC	A	P		63	4-6
1972	KC	A	P		45	3-4
		BRTR			681	63-69

ABERNATHY, VIRGIL WOODROW "WOODY"
B.FEB.1,1915 FOREST CITY,N.C.

YR	CL	LEA	POS	GP	G	REC
1946	NY	N	P		15	1-1
1947	NY	N	P		1	0-0
		BLTL			16	1-1

ABERSON, CLIFFORD ALEXANDER "KIF"
B.AUG.28,1921 CHICAGO,ILL.
D.JUNE 23,1973 VALLEJO,CAL.

YR	CL	LEA	POS	GP	G	REC
1947	CHI	N	O		47	.279
1948	CHI	N	O		12	.188
1949	CHI	N	O		4	.000
		BRTR			63	.251

ABLES, HARRY TERRELL "HANS"
B.OCT.4,1884 TERRELL,TEX.
D.FEB.8,1951

YR	CL	LEA	POS	GP	G	REC
1905	STL	A	P		6	0-3
1909	CLE	A	P		6	1-1
1911	NY	A	P		3	0-1
		BRTL			15	1-5

ABRAMS, CALVIN ROSS
B.MAR.2,1924 PHILADELPHIA,PA.

YR	CL	LEA	POS	GP	G	REC
1949	BRO	N	O		8	.083
1950	BRO	N	O		38	.205
1951	BRO	N	O		67	.280
1952	BRO	N	O		10	.200
	CIN	N	O		71	.278
1953	PIT	N	O		119	.286
1954	PIT	N	O		17	.143
	BAL	A	O		115	.293
1955	BAL	A	1-O		118	.243
1956	CHI	A	O		4	.333
		BLTL			567	.269

ABRAMS, GEORGE ALLEN
B.NOV.9,1899 SEATTLE,WASH.

YR	CL	LEA	POS	GP	G	REC
1923	CIN	N	P		3	0-0
		BRTR				

ABREU, JOSEPH LAWRENCE
B.MAY 24,1916 OAKLAND,CAL.

YR	CL	LEA	POS	GP	G	REC
1942	CIN	N	2-3		9	.214
		BRTR				

YR	CL	LEA	POS	GP	G	REC

ABSTEIN, WILLIAM HENRY
"BIG BILL"
B.FEB.2,1883 ST.LOUIS,MO.
D.APR.8,1940

YR	CL	LEA	POS	GP	G	REC
1906	PIT	N	O		8	.200
1909	PIT	N	1		135	.260
1910	STL	A	1		25	.149
	BRTR				168	.242

ACEVEDO, ARNULFO (ESPINOSA)
(SEE ARNULFO ACEVEDO ESPINOSA)

ACHENBACH, CHARLES SHUH
(PLAYED UNDER NAME OF
RAYMOND CHARLES)

ACKER, THOMAS JAMES "TOM"
B.MAR.7,1930 PATERSON,N.J.

1956	CIN	N	P	29	4- 3
1957	CIN	N	P	49	10- 5
1958	CIN	N	P	38	4- 3
1959	CIN	N	P	37	1- 2
	BRTR			153	19-13

ACKLEY, FLORIAN FREDERICK
"FRITZ"
B.APR.10,1937 HAYWARD,WIS.

1963	CHI	A	P	2	1- 0
1964	CHI	A	P	3	0- 0
	BLTR			5	1- 0

ACOSTA, BALMADERO MERITO
B.MAY 19,1896 HAVANA,CUBA
D.NOV.17,1963 MIAMI,FLA.

1913	WAS	A	O	12	.250
1914	WAS	A	O	38	.257
1915	WAS	A	O	72	.209
1916	WAS	A	O	5	.125
1918	WAS	A	O	3	.000
	PHI	A	O	49	.302
	BLTL			179	.252

ACOSTA, CECILIO (MIRANDA)
"CY"
B.NOV.22,1946 SABINO,MEXICO

1972	CHI	A	P	26	3- 0
1973	CHI	A	P	48	10- 6
1974	CHI	A	P	27	0- 3
1975	PHI	N	P	6	0- 0
	BRTR			107	13- 9

ACOSTA, EDUARDO ELIXBET "ED"
B.MAR.9,1944 BOQUETE,PANAMA

1970	PIT	N	P	3	0- 0
1971	SD	N	P	8	3- 3
1972	SD	N	P	46	3- 6
	BBTR			57	6- 9
	BR 1970				

ACOSTA, JOSE "ACOSTICA"
B.MAR.4,1891 SAN ANTONIO DEL
RIO BLANCO,CUBA

1920	WAS	A	P	17	5- 4
1921	WAS	A	P	33	5- 4
1922	CHI	A	P	5	0- 2
	BRTR			55	10-10
	BB 1920				

ADAIR, JAMES AUDREY "CHOPPY"
B.JAN.25,1908 WAXAHACHAIE,TEX.

1931	CHI	N	S	18	.276
	BRTR				

ADAIR, KENNETH JERRY
"JERRY"
B.DEC.17,1936 TULSA,OKLA.

1958	BAL	A	2-S	11	.105
1959	BAL	A	2-S	12	.314
1960	BAL	A	2	3	.200
1961	BAL	A	2-S-3	133	.264
1962	BAL	A	2-S-3	139	.284
1963	BAL	A	2	109	.228
1964	BAL	A	2	155	.248
1965	BAL	A	2	157	.259
1966	BAL	A	2	17	.088
	CHI	A	2-S	105	.243
1967	CHI	A	2	28	.204
	BOS	A	2-S-3	89	.291
1968	BOS	A	1-2-S-3	74	.216
1969	KC	A	2-S-3	126	.250
1970	KC	A	2	7	.148
	BRTR			1165	.254

ADAIR, MARION DANNE "BILL"
B.FEB.10,1913 MOBILE,ALA.
NON-PLAYING MANAGER
CHI(A) 1970 (INTERIM)

ADAMS, ACE TOWNSEND
B.MAR.2,1914 WILLOWS,CAL.

1941	NY	N	P	38	4- 1
1942	NY	N	P	61	7- 4
1943	NY	N	P	70	11- 7
1944	NY	N	P	65	8-11
1945	NY	N	P	65	11- 9
1946	NY	N	P	3	0- 1
	BRTR			302	41-33

ADAMS, CHARLES BENJAMIN "BABE"
B.MAY 18,1883 TIPTON,IND.
D.JULY 28,1968 SILVER SPRING,MD

1906	STL	N	P	1	0- 1
1907	PIT	N	P	4	2- 2
1909	PIT	N	P	25	12- 3
1910	PIT	N	P	34	18- 9
1911	PIT	N	P	40	22-12
1912	PIT	N	P	28	11- 8
1913	PIT	N	P	43	21-10
1914	PIT	N	P	40	13-16
1915	PIT	N	P	40	14-14
1916	PIT	N	P	16	2- 9
1918	PIT	N	P	3	1- 1
1919	PIT	N	P	34	17-10
1920	PIT	N	P	35	17-13
1921	PIT	N	P	25	14- 5
1922	PIT	N	P	27	8-11
1923	PIT	N	P	26	13- 7
1924	PIT	N	P	9	3- 1
1925	PIT	N	P	33	6- 5
1926	PIT	N	P	19	2- 3
	BLTR			482	196-140

ADAMS, CHARLES DWIGHT "RED"
B.OCT.7,1921 PARLIER,CAL.

1946	CHI	N	P	8	0- 1
	BRTR				

ADAMS, DANIEL LESLIE
B.JUNE 19,1889 ST.LOUIS,MO.
D.OCT.6,1964 ST.LOUIS,MO.

1914	KC	F	P	36	4- 9
1915	KC	F	P	11	0- 2
	BRTR			47	4-11

ADAMS, EARL JOHN "SPARKY"
B.AUG.26,1897 NEWTOWN,PA.

1922	CHI	N	2	11	.250
1923	CHI	N	S-O	95	.289
1924	CHI	N	2-S	117	.280
1925	CHI	N	2-S	149	.287
1926	CHI	N	2-3	154	.309
1927	CHI	N	2-S-3	146	.292
1928	PIT	N	2-S	135	.276
1929	PIT	N	2-S-3	74	.260
1930	STL	N	2-3	137	.314
1931	STL	N	3	143	.293
1932	STL	N	3	31	.276
1933	STL	N	S-3	8	.167
	CIN	N	S-3	137	.262
1934	CIN	N	2-3	87	.252
	BRTR			1424	.286

ADAMS, ELVIN CLARK "BUSTER"
B.JUNE 24,1916 TRINIDAD,COL.

1939	STL	N	H	2	.000
1943	STL	N	O	8	.091
	PHI	N	O	111	.256
1944	PHI	N	O	151	.283
1945	PHI	N	O	14	.232
	STL	N	O	140	.292
1946	STL	N	O	81	.185
1947	PHI	N	O	69	.247
	BRTR			576	.266

ADAMS, GEORGE
B.GRAFTON,MASS.

1879	SYR	N	1-O	4	.214

ADAMS, GLENN CHARLES
B.OCT.4,1947 NORTHBRIDGE,MASS.

1975	SF	N	O	61	.300
1976	SF	N	O	69	.243
	BLTR			130	.274

ADAMS, HAROLD DOUGLAS "DOUG"
B.JAN.27,1943 BLUE RIVER,WIS.

1969	CHI	A	C	8	.214
	BLTR				

ADAMS, HERBERT LOREN "HERB"
B.APR.14,1918 OAK PARK,ILL.

1948	CHI	A	O	5	.273
1949	CHI	A	O	56	.293
1950	CHI	A	O	34	.203
	BLTL			95	.261

ADAMS, JAMES IRWIN "WILLIE"
B.SEPT.27,1890 CLEARFIELD,PA.
D.JUNE 18,1937

1912	STL	A	P	13	2- 3
1913	STL	A	P	4	0- 1
1914	PIT	F	P	15	1- 1
1918	PHI	A	P	32	5-12
	PHI	A	P	1	0- 0
				65	8-17

ADAMS, JAMES J.
B.ST.LOUIS,MO.

1890	STL	AA	C	1	.250

ADAMS, JOHN BERTRAM
B.JUNE 21,1891 WHARTON,TEX.
D.JUNE 24,1940

1910	CLE	A	C	5	.230
1911	CLE	A	C	2	.250
1912	CLE	A	C	20	.204
1915	PHI	N	C	24	.111
1916	PHI	N	C	11	.231
1917	PHI	N	C	43	.206
1918	PHI	N	C	84	.176
1919	PHI	N	C-1	78	.233
	BBTR			267	.202

ADAMS, JOSEPH EDWARD
B.OCT.28,1877 COWDEN,ILL.
D.OCT.8,1952

1902	STL	N	P	1	0- 0
	TL				

ADAMS, KARL TUTWEILER "REBEL"
B.AUG.11,1891 COLUMBUS,GA.

1914	CIN	N	P	4	0- 0
1915	CIN	N	P	26	1- 9
				30	1- 9

ADAMS, REUBEN ALEXANDER
B.DEC.23,1879 PARIS,TEX.
D.MAR.10,1955

1905	WAS	A	P	8	2- 6
	BLTL				

ADAMS, RICHARD LEROY
B.APR.8,1920 TJOLOMNE,CAL.

1947	PHI	A	1-O	37	.202
	BRTL				

ADAMS, ROBERT ANDREW
B.JAN.20,1910 BIRMINGHAM,ALA.

1931	PHI	N	P	1	0- 1
1932	PHI	N	P	4	0- 0
	BRTR			5	0- 1

ADAMS, ROBERT BURDETTE
B.JAN.21,1899 BEDFORD,IND.
D.SEPT.6,1944

1925	BOS	A	P	2	0- 0
	BRTR				

ADAMS, ROBERT HENRY "BOBBY"
B.DEC.21,1921 TUOLUMNE,CAL.

1946	CIN	N	2-3-O	94	.244
1947	CIN	N	2	81	.272
1948	CIN	N	2-3	87	.298
1949	CIN	N	2-3	107	.253
1950	CIN	N	2-3	115	.282
1951	CIN	N	2-3-O	125	.266
1952	CIN	N	3	154	.283
1953	CIN	N	3	150	.275
1954	CIN	N	2-3	110	.269
1955	CIN	N	2-3	64	.273
	CHI	A	2-3	28	.095
1956	BAL	A	2-3	41	.225
1957	CHI	N	2-3	60	.251
1958	CHI	N	1-2-3	62	.281
1959	CHI	N	1	3	.000
	BRTR			1281	.269

ADAMS, ROBERT MICHAEL "MIKE"
B.JULY 24,1948 CINCINNATI,OHIO

1972	MIN	A	O	3	.333
1973	MIN	A	O	55	.212
1976	CHI	N	2-3-O	25	.138
	BRTR			83	.198

ADAMS, SPENCER DEWEY
B.JUNE 21,1898 LAYTON,UTAH
D.NOV.25,1970 SALT LAKE CITY,
UTAH

1923	PIT	N	2-S	25	.250
1925	WAS	A	2-S-3	39	.272
1926	NY	A	2	28	.120
1927	STL	A	2-3	88	.266
	BLTR			180	.256

YR	CL	LEA	POS	GP	G	REC

ADAMSON, JOHN MICHAEL "MIKE"
B.SEP.13,1947 SAN DIEGO,CAL.
1967	BAL	A	P		3	0- 1
1968	BAL	A	P		2	0- 2
1969	BAL	A	P		6	0- 1
	BRTR				11	0- 4

ADCOCK, JOSEPH WILBUR "JOE"
B.OCT.30,1927 COUSHATTA,LA.
1950	CIN	N	1-O		102	.293
1951	CIN	N	O		113	.243
1952	CIN	N	1-O		117	.278
1953	MIL	N	1		157	.285
1954	MIL	N	1		133	.308
1955	MIL	N	1		84	.264
1956	MIL	N	1		137	.291
1957	MIL	N	1		65	.287
1958	MIL	N	1-O		105	.275
1959	MIL	N	1-O		115	.292
1960	MIL	N	1		138	.298
1961	MIL	N	1		152	.285
1962	MIL	N	1		121	.248
1963	CLE	A	1		97	.251
1964	LA	N	1		118	.268
1965	CAL	A	1		122	.240
1966	CAL	A	1		83	.273
	BRTR				1959	.277
NON-PLAYING MANAGER CLE(A) 1967

ADDIS, ROBERT GORDON "BOB"
B.NOV.6,1925 MINERAL,OHIO
1950	BOS	N	O		16	.250
1951	BOS	N	O		85	.276
1952	CHI	N	O		93	.295
1953	CHI	N	O		10	.167
	PIT	N	H		4	.000
	BLTR				208	.281

ADDY, ROBERT EDWARD "MAGNET"
B.1838 ROCHESTER,N.Y.
D.APR.10,1910
1871	ROK	NA	2-S		24	-
1873	PHI	NA	2		10	-
	BOS	NA	O		31	-
1874	HAR	NA	2-S-3		50	-
1875	PHI	NA	2-O		69	.263
1876	CHI	N	O		33	.272
1877	CIN	N	M-O		57	.278
	BLTR				274	-

ADERHOLT, MORRIS WOODROW
B.SEPT.13,1916 MT.OLIVE,N.C.
D.MAR.18,1955
1939	WAS	A	2		7	.200
1940	WAS	A	2		1	.000
1941	WAS	A	2-3		11	.143
1944	BRO	N	O		17	.271
1945	BRO	N	O		39	.217
	BOS	N	2-O		31	.333
	BLTR				106	.267

ADKINS, GRADY EMMETT
"BUTCHER BOY"
B.JUNE 29,1897 LITTLE ROCK,ARK.
D.MAR.31,1966 LITTLE ROCK,ARK.
1928	CHI	A	P	36	39	10-16
1929	CHI	A	P	31	37	2-11
	BRTR			67	76	12-27

ADKINS, JOHN DEWEY
B.MAY 11,1918 NORCATUR,KAN.
1942	WAS	A	P		1	0- 0
1943	WAS	A	P		7	0- 0
1949	CHI	N	P		30	2- 4
	BRTR				38	2- 4

ADKINS, MERLE THERON "DOC"
B.AUG.5,1872 TROY,WIS.
D.FEB.21,1934
1902	BOS	A	P		4	1- 1
1903	NY	A	P		2	0- 1
	TR				6	1- 2

ADKINS, RICHARD EARL
B.MAR.3,1920 ELECTRA,TEX.
D.SEPT.12,1955 ELECTRA,TEX.
| 1942 | PHI | A | S | | 3 | .143 |
| | BRTR | | | | | |

ADKINSON, HENRY MAGEE
B.SEPT.1,1874 CHICAGO,ILL.
D.MAY 1,1923
| 1895 | STL | N | O | | 1 | .400 |

ADLESH, DAVID GEORGE "DAVE"
B.JULY 15,1943 LONG BEACH,CAL.
1963	HOU	N	C		6	.000
1964	HOU	N	C		3	.200
1965	HOU	N	C		15	.147
1966	HOU	N	C		3	.000
1967	HOU	N	C		39	.181
1968	HOU	N	C		40	.183
	BRTR				106	.168

AGEE, TOMMIE LEE
B.AUG.9,1942 MAGNOLIA,ALA.
1962	CLE	A	O		5	.214
1963	CLE	A	O		13	.148
1964	CLE	A	O		13	.167
1965	CHI	A	O		10	.158
1966	CHI	A	O		160	.273
1967	CHI	A	O		158	.234
1968	NY	N	O		132	.217
1969	NY	N	O		149	.271
1970	NY	N	O		153	.286
1971	NY	N	O		113	.285
1972	NY	N	O		114	.227
1973	HOU	N	O		83	.235
	STL	N	O		26	.177
	BRTR				1129	.255

AGGANIS, HARRY "GREEK"
B.APR.30,1930 LYNN,MASS.
D.JUNE 27,1955
1954	BOS	A	1		132	.251
1955	BOS	A	1		25	.313
	BLTL				157	.261

AGLER, JOSEPH ABRAM
B.JUNE 12,1887 BEACH CITY,OHIO
D.APR.26,1971 MASSILLON,OHIO
1912	WAS	A	1		2	.000
1914	BUF	F	1-O		135	.272
1915	BUF	F	1		25	.178
	BAL	F	1-2		70	.214
	BLTL				232	.246

AGNEW, SAMUEL LESTER "SLAM"
B.APR.12,1887 FARMINGTON,MO.
D.JULY 19,1951
1913	STL	A	C		104	.208
1914	STL	A	C		113	.212
1915	STL	A	C		104	.203
1916	BOS	A	C		40	.209
1917	BOS	A	C		85	.200
1918	BOS	A	C		72	.166
1919	WAS	A	C		42	.235
	BRTR				560	.204

AGUIRRE, HENRY JOHN "HANK"
B.JAN.31,1932 AZUSA,CAL.
1955	CLE	A	P		4	2- 0
1956	CLE	A	P		16	3- 5
1957	CLE	A	P		10	1- 1
1958	DET	A	P		44	3- 4
1959	DET	A	P		3	0- 0
1960	DET	A	P		37	5- 3
1961	DET	A	P		45	4- 4
1962	DET	A	P		42	16- 8
1963	DET	A	P		38	14-15
1964	DET	A	P		32	5-10
1965	DET	A	P		32	14-10
1966	DET	A	P		30	3- 9
1967	DET	A	P		31	0- 1
1968	LA	N	P		25	1- 2
1969	CHI	N	P		41	1- 0
1970	CHI	N	P		17	3- 0
	BBTL				447	75-72
	BR 1955-64					

AHEARN, CHARLES
B.TROY,N.Y.
| 1880 | TRO | N | C | | 1 | .250 |

AINSMITH, EDWARD WILBUR "DORF"
B.FEB.4,1892 CAMBRIDGE,MASS.
1910	WAS	A	C		33	.192
1911	WAS	A	C		61	.222
1912	WAS	A	C		60	.226
1913	WAS	A	C		77	.210
1914	WAS	A	C		58	.225
1915	WAS	A	C		47	.200
1916	WAS	A	C		51	.170
1917	WAS	A	C		125	.191
1918	WAS	A	C		96	.212
1919	DET	A	C		114	.272
1920	DET	A	C		69	.231
1921	DET	A	C		35	.276
	STL	N	C		27	.290
1922	STL	N	C		119	.293
1923	STL	N	C		82	.213
	BRO	N	C		2	.200
1924	NY	N	C		10	.600
	BRTR				1066	.232

AITCHISON, RALEIGH LEONIDAS
B.DEC.5,1887 TYNDALL,S.D.
D.SEPT.26,1958
1911	BRO	N	P		1	0- 1
1914	BRO	N	P		26	12- 7
1915	BRO	N	P		7	0- 4
	BRTL				34	12-12

AITON, GEORGE WILSON
B.DEC.29,1890 KINGMAN,KAN.
D.AUG.16,1976 VAN NUYS,CAL.
| 1912 | STL | A | O | | 10 | .235 |
| | BBTR | | | | | |

AKE, JOHN LECKIE
B.AUG.29,1861 ALTOONA,PA.
D.MAY 11,1887
| 1884 | BAL | AA | S-3-O | | 13 | .208 |

AKER, JACK DELANE
B.JULY 13,1940 TULARE,CAL.
1964	KC	A	P	9	10	0- 1
1965	KC	A	P		34	4- 3
1966	KC	A	P		66	8- 4
1967	KC	A	P		57	3- 8
1968	OAK	A	P		54	4- 4
1969	SEA	A	P		15	0- 2
	NY	A	P		38	8- 4
1970	NY	A	P		41	4- 2
1971	NY	A	P		41	4- 4
1972	NY	A	P		4	0- 0
	CHI	N	P		48	6- 6
1973	CHI	N	P		47	4- 5
1974	ATL	N	P		17	0- 1
	NY	N	P		24	2- 1
	BRTR			495	496	47-45

AKERS, ALBERT EARL
B.NOV.1,1887 SHELBYVILLE,IND.
| 1912 | WAS | A | P | | 5 | 0- 0 |
| | BRTR | | | | | |

AKERS, THOMAS ERNEST "BUMP"
B.DEC.25,1904 CHATTANOOGA,TENN.
D.APR.13,1962
1929	DET	A	S		24	.265
1930	DET	A	S-3		85	.278
1931	DET	A	S		29	.197
1932	BOS	N	3		36	.258
	BRTR				174	.261

ALBANESE, JOSEPH PETER "JOE"
B.JUNE 26,1933 NEW YORK,N.Y.
| 1958 | WAS | A | P | | 6 | 0- 0 |
| | BRTR | | | | | |

ALBERTS, AUGUSTUS PETER
B.1861 READING,PA.
D.MAY 7,1912
1884	PIT	AA	S		2	.200
	WAS	U	S		4	.250
1888	CLE	AA	S-3		101	.192
1891	MIL	AA	3		12	.100
	BRTR				119	.186

ALBERTS, FREDERICK JOSEPH "CY"
B.JAN.14,1882 GRAND RAPIDS,MICH.
D.AUG.27,1917
| 1910 | STL | N | P | | 4 | 1- 2 |

ALBERTS, JAMES
(PLAYED UNDER NAME OF
ALVIN JAMES DOLAN)

ALBOSTA, EDWARD JOHN "RUBE"
B.OCT.27,1918 SAGINAW,MICH.

YR	CL	LEA	POS	GP	G	REC
1941	BRO	N	P		2	0- 2
1946	PIT	N	P		17	0- 6
	BRTR				19	0- 8

ALBRECHT, EDWARD ARTHUR
B.FEB.28,1929 ST. LOUIS CO.,MO.

YR	CL	LEA	POS	GP	G	REC
1949	STL	A	P		1	1- 0
1950	STL	A	P		2	0- 1
	BRTR				3	1- 1

ALBRIGHT, JOHN HAROLD
B.JUNE 30,1921 ST.PETERSBURG,FL

YR	CL	LEA	POS	GP	G	REC
1947	PHI	N	S		41	.232
	BRTR					

ALBURY, VICTOR "VIC"
B.MAY 12,1947 KEY WEST,FLA.

YR	CL	LEA	POS	GP	G	REC
1973	MIN	A	P		14	1- 0
1974	MIN	A	P		32	8- 9
1975	MIN	A	P	32	33	6- 7
1976	MIN	A	P		23	3- 1
	BLTL			101	102	18-17

ALCALA, SANTO
(REAL NAME
SANTO ANIBAL (ALCALA))
B.JAN.23,1952 DOMINICAN REPULIC

YR	CL	LEA	POS	GP	G	REC
1976	CIN	N	P		30	11- 4
	BRTR					

ALCARAZ, ANGEL LUIS (ACOSTA)
"LUIS"
B.JULY 20,1941 HUMACAO,P.R.

YR	CL	LEA	POS	GP	G	REC
1967	LA	N	2		17	.233
1968	LA	N	2-S-3		41	.151
1969	KC	A	2-S-3		22	.253
1970	KC	A	2		35	.167
	BRTR				115	.192

ALCOCK, JOHN FORBES "SCOTTY"
B.NOV.29,1885 WOOSTER,OHIO
D.JAN.30,1973 WOOSTER,OHIO

YR	CL	LEA	POS	GP	G	REC
1914	CHI	A	3		54	.173
	BRTR					

ALDERSON, DALE LEONARD
B.MAR.8,1918 BELDEN,NEB.

YR	CL	LEA	POS	GP	G	REC
1943	CHI	N	P		4	0- 1
1944	CHI	N	P		12	0- 0
	BRTR				16	0- 1

ALDRIDGE, VICTOR EDDINGTON
B.OCT.25,1893 INDIAN SPRGS.,IND
D.APR.17,1973 TERRE HAUTE,IND.

YR	CL	LEA	POS	GP	G	REC
1917	CHI	N	P		30	6- 6
1918	CHI	N	P		3	0- 1
1922	CHI	N	P		36	16-15
1923	CHI	N	P		30	16- 9
1924	CHI	N	P		32	15-12
1925	PIT	N	P		30	15- 7
1926	PIT	N	P		30	10-13
1927	PIT	N	P		35	15-10
1928	NY	N	P		22	4- 7
	BRTR				248	97-80

ALENO, CHARLES "CHUCK"
B.FEB.19,1918 ST.LOUIS,MO.

YR	CL	LEA	POS	GP	G	REC
1941	CIN	N	1-3		54	.243
1942	CIN	N	2-3		7	.143
1943	CIN	N	O		7	.300
1944	CIN	N	1-S-3		50	.165
	BRTR				118	.209

ALEXANDER, DAVID DALE "MOOSE"
B.APR.26,1903 GREENVILLE,TENN.

YR	CL	LEA	POS	GP	G	REC
1929	DET	A	1		155	.343
1930	DET	A	1		154	.326
1931	DET	A	1		135	.325
1932	DET	A	1		23	.250
	BOS	A	1		101	.372
1933	BOS	A	1		94	.281
	BRTR				662	.331

ALEXANDER, DOYLE LAFAYETTE
B.SEP.4,1950 CORDOVA,ALA.

YR	CL	LEA	POS	GP	G	REC
1971	LA	N	P		17	6- 6
1972	BAL	A	P		35	6- 8
1973	BAL	A	P		29	12- 8
1974	BAL	A	P		30	6- 9
1975	BAL	A	P		32	8- 8
1976	BAL	A	P		11	3- 4
	NY	A	P		19	10- 5
	BRTR				173	51-48

ALEXANDER, GARY WAYNE
B.MAR.27,1953 LOS ANGELES,CAL.

YR	CL	LEA	POS	GP	G	REC
1975	SF	N	C		3	.000
1976	SF	N	C		23	.178
	BRTR				26	.171

ALEXANDER, GROVER CLEVELAND
"PETE"
B.FEB.26,1887 ST.PAUL,NEB.
D.NOV.4,1950 ST.PAUL,NEB.

YR	CL	LEA	POS	GP	G	REC
1911	PHI	N	P		48	28-13
1912	PHI	N	P		46	19-17
1913	PHI	N	P		47	22- 8
1914	PHI	N	P	46	48	27-15
1915	PHI	N	P		49	31-10
1916	PHI	N	P	48	49	33-12
1917	PHI	N	P	45	47	30-13
1918	CHI	N	P		3	2- 1
1919	CHI	N	P		30	16-11
1920	CHI	N	P		46	27-14
1921	CHI	N	P		31	15-13
1922	CHI	N	P		33	16-13
1923	CHI	N	P		39	22-12
1924	CHI	N	P		21	12- 5
1925	CHI	N	P		32	15-11
1926	CHI	N	P		7	3- 3
	STL	N	P		23	9- 7
1927	STL	N	P		37	21-10
1928	STL	N	P		34	16- 9
1929	STL	N	P		22	9- 8
1930	PHI	N	P		9	0- 3
	BRTR			696	701	373-208

ALEXANDER, HUGH
B.JULY 10,1917 BUFFALO,MO.

YR	CL	LEA	POS	GP	G	REC
1937	CLE	A	P		7	.091
	BRTR					

ALEXANDER, MATTHEW "MATT"
B.JAN.30,1947 SHREVEPORT,LA.

YR	CL	LEA	POS	GP	G	REC
1973	CHI	N	O		12	.200
1974	CHI	N	2-3-0		45	.204
1975	OAK	A	2-0-R-D		63	.100
1976	OAK	A	O-R		61	.033
	BBTR				181	.141

ALEXANDER, ROBERT SOMERVILLE
B.AUG.7,1922 VANCOUVER,B.C.,CAN

YR	CL	LEA	POS	GP	G	REC
1955	BAL	A	P		4	1- 0
1957	CLE	A	P		5	0- 1
	BRTR				9	1- 1

ALEXANDER, WALTER E.
B.MAR.5,1891 ATLANTA,GA.

YR	CL	LEA	POS	GP	G	REC
1912	STL	A	C		37	.175
1913	STL	A	C		42	.141
1915	STL	A	C		1	.000
	NY	A	C		25	.250
1916	NY	A	C		36	.256
1917	NY	A	C		20	.137
	BRTR				161	.189

ALEXANDER, WILLIAM HENRY "NIN"
B.NOV.24,1858 PANA,ILL.
D.DEC.22,1933

YR	CL	LEA	POS	GP	G	REC
1884	KC	U	C-S-O		19	.127
	STL	AA	C-O		1	.000
					20	.119

ALLEN, ARTEMUS WARD "NICK"
B.SEPT.14,1889 NORTON,KAN.
D.OCT.16,1939 HINES,ILL.

YR	CL	LEA	POS	GP	G	REC
1914	BUF	F	C		31	.235
1915	BUF	F	C		83	.205
1916	CHI	N	C		5	.063
1918	CIN	N	C		37	.260
1919	CIN	N	C		15	.320
1920	CIN	N	C		43	.271
	BRTR				214	.231

ALLEN, BERNARD KEITH "BERNIE"
B.APR.16,1939 E. LIVERPOOL,O.

YR	CL	LEA	POS	GP	G	REC
1962	MIN	A	2		159	.269
1963	MIN	A	2		139	.240
1964	MIN	A	2		74	.214
1965	MIN	A	2-3		19	.231
1966	MIN	A	2-3		101	.238
1967	WAS	A	2		87	.193
1968	WAS	A	2-3		120	.241
1969	WAS	A	2-3		122	.247
1970	WAS	A	2-3		104	.234
1971	WAS	A	2-3		97	.266
1972	NY	A	2-3		84	.227
1973	NY	A	2		17	.228
	MON	N	2-3		16	.180
	BLTR				1139	.239

ALLEN, CYRUS ALBAN "DICK"
B.1855 GIRARD,PA.
D.APR.21,1915

YR	CL	LEA	POS	GP	G	REC
1879	SYR	N	3-O		11	.184
	CLE	N	3-O		16	.117
					27	.165

ALLEN, ETHAN NATHAN
B.JAN.1,1904 CINCINNATI,OHIO

YR	CL	LEA	POS	GP	G	REC
1926	CIN	N	O		18	.308
1927	CIN	N	O		111	.295
1928	CIN	N	O		129	.305
1929	CIN	N	O		143	.292
1930	CIN	N	O		21	.271
	NY	N	O		76	.307
1931	NY	N	O		94	.329
1932	NY	N	O		54	.175
1933	STL	N	O		91	.241
1934	PHI	N	O		145	.330
1935	PHI	N	O		156	.307
1936	PHI	N	O		30	.296
	CHI	N	O		91	.295
1937	STL	A	O		103	.316
1938	STL	A	O		19	.303
	BRTR				1281	.300

ALLEN, FLETCHER MANSON "SLED"
B.AUG.23,1886 WEST PLAINS,MO.
D.OCT.16,1959

YR	CL	LEA	POS	GP	G	REC
1910	STL	A	C		14	.095
	TR					

ALLEN, FRANK LEON
B.AUG.26,1889 NEWBERN,ALA.
D.JULY 30,1933

YR	CL	LEA	POS	GP	G	REC
1912	BRO	N	P		20	3- 9
1913	BRO	N	P		34	4-18
1914	BRO	N	P	36	37	8-14
	PIT	F	P		1	1- 0
1915	PIT	F	P		41	23-13
1916	BOS	N	P		19	8- 2
1917	BOS	N	P		29	3-11
	BRTL			180	181	50-67

ALLEN, HAROLD ANDREW "HANK"
B.JULY 23,1940 WAMPUM,PA.

YR	CL	LEA	POS	GP	G	REC
1966	WAS	A	O		9	.387
1967	WAS	A	O		116	.233
1968	WAS	A	2-3-O		68	.219
1969	WAS	A	2-3-O		109	.277
1970	WAS	A	O		22	.211
	MIL	A	1-2-O		28	.230
1972	CHI	A	3		9	.143
1973	CHI	A	C-1-2-3-O		28	.103
	BPTR				389	.241

ALLEN, HEZEKIAH "HAM"
B.NORWALK,CONN.

YR	CL	LEA	POS	GP	G	REC
1872	MAN	NA	S-O		16	.169
1884	PHI	N	C		1	.667
					17	.189

ALLEN, HORACE TANNER "PUG"
B.JUNE 11,1899 DELAND,FLA.

YR	CL	LEA	POS	GP	G	REC
1919	BRO	N	O		4	.000
	BLTR					

ALLEN, JESSE HALL
B.MAY 1,1868 COLUMBIANA,OHIO
D.APR.16,1946

YR	CL	LEA	POS	GP	G	REC
1893	CLE	N	C		1	.000
	BRTR					

ALLEN, JOHN MARSHALL
B.OCT.27,1890 BERKELEY SPRINGS,
W.VA.
D.SEPT.24,1967

YR	CL	LEA	POS	GP	G	REC
1914	BAL	F	P		1	0- 0
	BRTR					

YR CL LEA POS GP   G   REC

ALLEN, JOHN THOMAS
B.SEPT.30,1905 LENOIR,N.C.
D.MAR.29,1959
```
1932 NY  A  P        33  17- 4
1933 NY  A  P        25  15- 7
1934 NY  A  P        13   5- 2
1935 NY  A  P        23  13- 6
1936 CLE A  P    36  37  20-10
1937 CLE A  P        24  15- 1
1938 CLE A  P        30  14- 8
1939 CLE A  P    28  34   9- 7
1940 CLE A  P        32   9- 8
1941 STL A  P        20   2- 5
     BRO N  P        11   3- 0
1942 BRO N  P        27  10- 6
1943 BRO N  P        17   5- 1
     NY  N  P        15   1- 3
1944 NY  N  P    18  24   4- 7
     BRTR       352 365 142-75
```

ALLEN, LLOYD CECIL
B.MAY 8,1950 MERCED,CAL.
```
1969 CAL A  P         4   0- 1
1970 CAL A  P         8   1- 1
1971 CAL A  P        54   4- 6
1972 CAL A  P        42   3- 7
1973 CAL A  P         5   0- 0
     TEX A  P        23   0- 6
1974 TEX A  P        14   0- 1
     CHI A  P         6   0- 1
1975 CHI A  P         3   0- 2
     BRTR            159   8-25
```

ALLEN, MYRON S.
B.MAR.22,1854 RONDOUT,N.Y.
D.MAR.8,1924
```
1883 NY  N  P         1   0- 1
1886 BOS N  1         2    .000
1887 CLE AA O       117    .330
1888 KC  AA O        37    .215
                  1 157   0- 1
                          .304
```

ALLEN, RICHARD ANTHONY "DICK"
B.MAR.8,1942 WAMPUM,PA.
```
1963 PHI N  3-O      10    .292
1964 PHI N  3       162    .318
1965 PHI N  S-3     161    .302
1966 PHI N  3-O     141    .317
1967 PHI N  2-S-3   122    .307
1968 PHI N  3-O     152    .263
1969 PHI N  1       118    .288
1970 STL N  1-3-O   122    .279
1971 LA  N  1-3-O   155    .295
1972 CHI A  1-3     148    .308
1973 CHI A  1-2      72    .316
1974 CHI A  1-2     128    .301
1975 PHI N  1       119    .233
1976 PHI N  1        85    .268
     BRTR          1695    .293
```

ALLEN, ROBERT
B.1896
```
1919 PHI A  O        11    .094
     BRTR
```

ALLEN, ROBERT EARL
"THIN MAN"
B.JULY 2,1914 SMITHVILLE,TENN.
```
1937 PHI N  P         3   0- 1
     BRTR
```

ALLEN, ROBERT GILMAN
B.JULY 10,1867 MARION,OHIO
D.MAY 14,1943
```
1890 PHI N  S       133    .225
1891 PHI N  S       117    .227
1892 PHI N  S       148    .229
1893 PHI N  S       123    .283
1894 PHI N  S        40    .253
1897 BOS N  S        33    .309
1900 CIN N  M-S       5    .175
     BRTR           599    .246
```

ALLEN, ROBERT GRAY "BOB"
B.OCT.23,1937 TATUM,TEX.
```
1961 CLE A  P        48   3- 2
1962 CLE A  P        30   1- 1
1963 CLE A  P        43   1- 2
1966 CLE A  P        36   2- 2
1967 CLE A  P        47   0- 5
     BLTL           204   7-12
```

ALLEN, RONALD FREDRICK "RON"
B.DEC.23,1943 WAMPUM,PA.
```
1972 STL N  1         7    .091
     BBTR
```

ALLEY, LEONARD EUGENE "GENE"
B.JULY 10,1940 RICHMOND,VA.
```
1963 PIT N  2-S-3    17    .216
1964 PIT N  2-S-3    81    .211
1965 PIT N  2-S-3   153    .252
1966 PIT N  S       147    .299
1967 PIT N  S       152    .287
1968 PIT N  2-S     133    .245
1969 PIT N  2-S-3    82    .246
1970 PIT N  2-S-3   121    .244
1971 PIT N  S-3     114    .227
1972 PIT N  S-3     119    .248
1973 PIT N  S-3      76    .203
     BRTR          1195    .254
```

ALLIE, GAIR ROOSEVELT
B.OCT.28,1931 STATESVILLE,N.C.
```
1954 PIT N  S-3     121    .199
     BRTR
```

ALLIETTA, ROBERT GEORGE "BOB"
B.MAY 1,1952 NEW BEDFORD,MASS.
```
1975 CAL A  C        21    .178
     BRTR
```

ALLISON, ANDREW K.
B.1848 NEW YORK,N.Y.
```
1872 ECK NA 1-O      25    .140
```

ALLISON, ARTHUR ALGERNON
B.JAN.29,1849 PHILADELPHIA,PA.
D.FEB.25,1916
```
1871 CLE NA O        29    -
1872 CLE NA O        18    .261
1873 RES NA C-1-O    22    -
1875 NAT NA C-1-O    25    -
     HAR NA 2-O      35    -
1876 LOU N  1-O      31    .205
                    160    -
```

ALLISON, DOUGLASS L. "DONA"
B.1846 PHILADELPHIA,PA.
D.DEC.19,1916
```
1871 OLY NA C        27    -
1872 TRO NA C-S      23    .319
     ECK NA C        18    .299
1873 RES NA C-O      17    -
     MUT NA C        11    -
1874 MUT NA C-O      65    -
1875 HAR NA C-1      60    -
1876 HAR N  C        43    .256
1877 HAR N  C        29    .148
1878 PRO N  C        18    .267
1879 PRO N  C         1    .000
1883 BAL AA C         1    .500
     BRTR           313    -
```

ALLISON, MARK PENDLETON
B.JAN.23,1887 OWENSBORO,KY.
D.MAR.13,1964 ST.JOSEPH,MO.
```
1911 STL A  P         3   2- 1
1912 STL A  P        31   6-17
1913 STL A  P        11   1- 2
     BRTR            45   9-20
```

ALLISON, MILO HENRY
B.OCT.16,1890 ELK RAPIDS,MICH.
D.JUNE 18,1957
```
1913 CHI N  O         2    .333
1914 CHI N  O         1   1.000
1916 CLE A  O        14    .263
1917 CLE A  O        32    .143
     BLTR            49    .213
```

ALLISON, WILLIAM ANDREW
B.SEPT.18,1848 PHILADELPHIA,PA.
D.JUNE 12,1923
```
1872 ECK NA 1-O       3    .182
```

ALLISON, WILLIAM ROBERT "BOB"
B.JULY 11,1934 RAYTOWN,MO.
```
1958 WAS A  O        11    .200
1959 WAS A  O       150    .261
1960 WAS A  1-O     144    .251
1961 MIN A  1-O     159    .245
1962 MIN A  O       149    .266
1963 MIN A  O       148    .271
1964 MIN A  1-O     149    .287
1965 MIN A  1-O     135    .233
1966 MIN A  O        70    .220
1967 MIN A  O       153    .258
1968 MIN A  1-O     145    .247
1969 MIN A  1-O      81    .228
1970 MIN A  1-O      47    .208
     BRTR          1541    .255
```

ALMADA, MELO BALDOMERO "MEL"
B.FEB.7,1914 HWATABAMPO,SONORA,
MEXICO
```
1933 BOS A  O        14    .341
1934 BOS A  O        23    .233
1935 BOS A  1-O     151    .290
1936 BOS A  O        96    .253
1937 BOS A  O        32    .236
     WAS A  O       100    .309
1938 WAS A  O        47    .244
     STL A  O       102    .342
1939 STL A  O        42    .239
     BRO N  O        39    .214
     BLTL           646    .284
```

ALMEIDA, RAFAEL D. "MIKE"
B.JULY 30,1887 HAVANA,CUBA
```
1911 CIN N  3        29    .313
1912 CIN N  3        16    .220
1913 CIN N  3        50    .262
     BRTR            95    .270
```

ALMON, WILLIAM FRANCIS "BILL"
B.NOV.21,1952 PROVIDENCE,R.I.
```
1974 SD  N  S        16    .316
1975 SD  N  S         6    .400
1976 SD  N  S        14    .246
     BRTR            36    .286
```

ALOMA, LUIS (BARBA) "WITTO"
B.JULY 23,1923 HAVANA,CUBA
```
1950 CHI A  P        42   7- 2
1951 CHI A  P        25   6- 0
1952 CHI A  P        25   3- 1
1953 CHI A  P        24   2- 0
     BRTR           116  18- 3
```

ALOMAR, SANTOS (CONDE)
"SANDY"
B.OCT.19,1943 SALINAS,P.R.
```
1964 MIL N  S           19  .249
1965 MIL N  2-S         67  .241
1966 ATL N  2-S         31  .091
1967 NY  N  2-S-3       15  .000
     CHI A  2-S         12  .200
1968 CHI A  2-S-3-O    133  .253
1969 CAL A  2           22  .224
     CAL A  2          134  .250
1970 CAL A  2-S-3      162  .251
1971 CAL A  2-S        162  .260
1972 CAL A  2-S        155  .239
1973 CAL A  2-S        121  .238
1974 CAL A  2-S-3-O     46  .222
     NY  A  2           76  .269
1975 NY  A  2-S        151  .239
1976 NY  A  1-2-S-3-    67  .239
            O
     BBTR            1373  .245
     BR 1964 (PART), 65-66
```

ALOU, FELIPE ROJAS
(REAL NAME
FELIPE ROJAS (ALOU))
B.MAY 12,1935 HAINA,D.R.
```
1958 SF  N  O         75  .253
1959 SF  N  O         95  .275
1960 SF  N  O        106  .264
1961 SF  N  O        132  .289
1962 SF  N  O        154  .316
1963 SF  N  O        157  .281
1964 MIL N  1-O      121  .253
1965 MIL N  1-S-3-O  143  .297
1966 ATL N  1-S-3-O  154  .327
1967 ATL N  1-O      140  .274
1968 ATL N  O        160  .317
1969 ATL N  O        123  .282
1970 OAK A  1-O      154  .271
1971 OAK A  2          2  .250
     NY  A  1-O      131  .289
1972 NY  A  1-O      120  .278
1973 NY  A  1-O       93  .236
     MON N  1-O       19  .208
1974 MIL A  O          3  .000
     BRTR          2082  .286
```

YR	CL	LEA	POS	GP	G	REC

ALOU, JESUS MARIA ROJAS
(REAL NAME
JESUS MARIA ROJAS (ALOU))
B.MAR.24,1942 HAINA,D.R.

YR	CL	LEA	POS	GP	G	REC
1963	SF	N	O		16	.250
1964	SF	N	O		115	.274
1965	SF	N	O		143	.298
1966	SF	N	O		110	.259
1967	SF	N	O		129	.292
1968	SF	N	O		120	.263
1969	HOU	N	O		115	.248
1970	HOU	N	O		117	.306
1971	HOU	N	O		122	.279
1972	HOU	N	O		52	.312
1973	HOU	N	O		28	.236
	OAK	A	O		36	.306
1974	OAK	A	O-O		96	.268
1975	NY	N	O		62	.265
	BRTR				1261	.279

ALOU, MATEO ROJAS "MATTY"
(REAL NAME
MATEO ROJAS (ALOU))
B.DEC.20,1938 HAINA,D.R.

YR	CL	LEA	POS	GP	G	REC
1960	SF	N	O		4	.333
1961	SF	N	O		81	.310
1962	SF	N	O		78	.292
1963	SF	N	O		63	.145
1964	SF	N	O		110	.264
1965	SF	N	P-O	1	117	0- 0
						.231
1966	PIT	N	O		141	.342
1967	PIT	N	1-O		139	.338
1968	PIT	N	O		146	.332
1969	PIT	N	O		162	.331
1970	PIT	N	O		155	.297
1971	STL	N	1-O		149	.315
1972	STL	N	1-O		108	.314
	OAK	A	1-O		32	.281
1973	NY	A	1-O		123	.296
	STL	N	1-O		11	.273
1974	SD	N	1-O		48	.198
	BLTL	1	1667		0- 0	
						.307

**ALPERMAN, CHARLES AUGUSTUS
"WHITEY"**
B.NOV.10,1879 ETNA,PA.
D.DEC.25,1942

YR	CL	LEA	POS	GP	G	REC
1906	BRO	N	2-S		127	.252
1907	BRO	N	2		138	.233
1908	BRO	N	2		57	.197
1909	BRO	N	2		108	.248
	BRTR				430	.237

ALSTON, THOMAS EDISON "TOM"
B.JAN.31,1931 GREENSBORO,N.C.

YR	CL	LEA	POS	GP	G	REC
1954	STL	N	1		66	.246
1955	STL	N	1		13	.125
1956	STL	N	1		3	.000
1957	STL	N	1		9	.294
	BLTR				91	.244

ALSTON, WALTER EMMONS "SMOKEY"
B.DEC.1,1911 VENICE,OHIO

YR	CL	LEA	POS	GP	G	REC
1936	STL	N	1		1	.000
	BRTR					

NON-PLAYING MANAGER
BRO(N) 1954-57, LA(N) 1958-76

ALTEN, ERNEST MATTHIAS "LEFTY"
B.DEC.1,1894 AVON,OHIO

YR	CL	LEA	POS	GP	G	REC
1920	DET	A	P		14	0- 1
	BRTL					

ALTENBURG, JESSE HOWARD
B.JAN.2,1893 ASHLEY,MICH.
D.MAR.12,1973 LANSING,MICH.

YR	CL	LEA	POS	GP	G	REC
1916	PIT	N	O		8	.429
1917	PIT	N	O		11	.176
	BLTR				19	.290

**ALTIZER, DAVID TILDEN
"FILIPINO"**
B.NOV.6,1876 PEORIA,ILL.
D.MAY 14,1964 PLEASANT HILL,ILL

YR	CL	LEA	POS	GP	G	REC
1906	WAS	A	S		115	.256
1907	WAS	A	1-S-O		147	.269
1908	WAS	A	O		66	.218
	CLE	A	S-O		30	.227
	CHI	A	1-O		116	.233
1910	CIN	N	S		3	.600
1911	CIN	N	S		26	.227
	BLTR				503	.250

ALTMAN, GEORGE LEE
B.MAR.20,1933 GOLDSBORO,N.C.

YR	CL	LEA	POS	GP	G	REC
1959	CHI	N	O		135	.245
1960	CHI	N	1-O		119	.266
1961	CHI	N	1-O		138	.303
1962	CHI	N	1-O		147	.318
1963	STL	N	O		135	.274
1964	NY	N	O		124	.230
1965	CHI	N	1-O		90	.235
1966	CHI	N	1-O		88	.222
1967	CHI	N	1-O		15	.111
	BLTR				991	.269

ALTOBELLI, JOSEPH "JOE"
B.MAY 26,1932 DETROIT,MICH.

YR	CL	LEA	POS	GP	G	REC
1955	CLE	A	1		42	.200
1957	CLE	A	1-O		83	.207
1961	MIN	A	1-O		41	.221
	BLTL				166	.210

ALTROCK, NICHOLAS "NICK"
B.SEPT.15,1876 CINCINNATI,OHIO
D.JAN.20,1965 WASHINGTON,D.C.

YR	CL	LEA	POS	GP	G	REC
1898	LOU	N	P		11	3- 4
1902	BOS	A	P		3	1- 2
1903	BOS	A	P		3	0- 3
	CHI	A	P		11	4- 2
1904	CHI	A	P		38	21-13
1905	CHI	A	P	40	41	21-10
1906	CHI	A	P		38	20-13
1907	CHI	A	P		30	8-12
1908	CHI	A	P		23	3- 7
1909	CHI	A	P		5	1- 4
	WAS	A	P-O	9	12	1- 3
						.350
1912	WAS	A	P		1	0- 0
1913	WAS	A	P		4	0- 0
1914	WAS	A	P		1	0- 0
1915	WAS	A	P		1	0- 0
1918	WAS	A	P		6	1- 2
1919	WAS	A	P		1	0- 0
1924	WAS	A	P		1	0- 0
1929	WAS	A	O		1	1.000
1931	WAS	A	H		1	.000
1933	WAS	A	H		1	.000
	BBTL			226	233	84-75
						.178

ALUSIK, GEORGE JOSEPH
B.FEB.11,1935 ASHLEY,PA.

YR	CL	LEA	POS	GP	G	REC
1958	DET	A	O		2	.000
1961	DET	A	O		15	.143
1962	DET	A	H		2	.000
	KC	A	1-O		90	.273
1963	KC	A	O		87	.267
1964	KC	A	1-O		102	.240
	BRTR				298	.256

ALVARADO, LUIS CESAR
B.JAN.15,1949 LA JAS,P.R.

YR	CL	LEA	POS	GP	G	REC
1968	BOS	A	S		11	.130
1969	BOS	A	S		6	.000
1970	BOS	A	S-3		59	.224
1971	CHI	A	2-S		99	.216
1972	CHI	A	2-S-3		103	.213
1973	CHI	A	2-S-3		79	.232
1974	CHI	A	2-S-3		8	.100
	STL	N	S		17	.139
	CLE	A	2-S		61	.219
1976	STL	N	2		16	.286
	BRTR				459	.214

**ALVAREZ, JESUS MANUEL ORLANDO
(MONGE) "ORLANDO"**
B.FEB.28,1952 RIO GRANDE,P.R.

YR	CL	LEA	POS	GP	G	REC
1973	LA	N	H		4	.250
1974	LA	N	O		2	.000
1975	LA	N	H		4	.000
1976	CAL	A	O		15	.167
	BRTR				25	.157

ALVAREZ, OSWALDO GONZALES
B.OCT.19,1933 BOLONDRON,CUBA

YR	CL	LEA	POS	GP	G	REC
1958	WAS	A	2-S-3		87	.209
1959	DET	A	H		8	.500
	BRTR				95	.212

ALVAREZ, ROGELIO (HERNANDEZ)
B.APR.18,1938 PINAR DEL RIO,
CUBA

YR	CL	LEA	POS	GP	G	REC
1960	CIN	N	1		3	.111
1962	CIN	N	1		14	.214
	BRTR				17	.189

ALVIS, ROY MAXWELL "MAX"
B.FEB.2,1938 JASPER,TEX.

YR	CL	LEA	POS	GP	G	REC
1962	CLE	A	3		12	.216
1963	CLE	A	3		158	.274
1964	CLE	A	3		107	.252
1965	CLE	A	3		159	.247
1966	CLE	A	3		157	.245
1967	CLE	A	3		161	.256
1968	CLE	A	3		131	.223
1969	CLE	A	S-3		66	.225
1970	MIL	A	3		62	.183
	BRTR				1013	.247

ALVORD, WILLIAM C. "UNCLE BILL"
B.ST.LOUIS,MO.

YR	CL	LEA	POS	GP	G	REC
1885	STL	N	3		2	.000
1889	KC	AA	3		50	.221
1890	TOL	AA	3		120	.283
1891	CLE	N	3		13	.282
	WAS	AA	3		81	.235
1893	CLE	N	3		3	.250
					269	.256

**ALYEA, GARRABRANT RYERSON
"BRANT"**
B.DEC.8,1940 PASSAIC,N.J.

YR	CL	LEA	POS	GP	G	REC
1965	WAS	A	1-O		8	.231
1968	WAS	A	O		53	.267
1969	WAS	A	1-O		104	.249
1970	MIN	A	O		94	.291
1971	MIN	A	O		79	.177
1972	OAK	A	O		20	.194
	STL	N	O		13	.158
	BRTR				371	.247

AMALFITANO, JOHN JOSEPH "JOEY"
B.JAN.23,1934 SAN PEDRO,CAL.

YR	CL	LEA	POS	GP	G	REC
1954	NY	N	2-3		9	.000
1955	NY	N	S-3		36	.227
1960	SF	N	2-S-3-O		106	.277
1961	SF	N	2-3		109	.255
1962	HOU	N	2-3		117	.237
1963	SF	N	2-3		54	.175
1964	CHI	N	1-2-S		100	.241
1965	CHI	N	2-S		67	.271
1966	CHI	N	2-S-3		41	.158
1967	CHI	N	H		4	.000
	BRTR				643	.244

AMARO, RUBEN (MORA)
B.JAN.6,1936 VERA CRUZ,MEXICO

YR	CL	LEA	POS	GP	G	REC
1958	STL	N	2-S		40	.224
1960	PHI	N	S		92	.231
1961	PHI	N	1-2-S		135	.257
1962	PHI	N	1-S		79	.243
1963	PHI	N	1-S-3		115	.217
1964	PHI	N	1-2-S-3-O		129	.264
1965	PHI	N	1-2-S		118	.212
1966	NY	A	S		14	.217
1967	NY	A	1-S-3		130	.223
1968	NY	A	1-S		47	.122
1969	CAL	A	1-2-S-3		41	.222
	BRTR				940	.234

AMBLER, WAYNE HARPER
B.NOV.8,1915 ABINGTON,PA.

YR	CL	LEA	POS	GP	G	REC
1937	PHI	A	2		56	.216
1938	PHI	A	S		120	.234
1939	PHI	A	2-S		95	.211
	BRTR				271	.224

AMES, LEON KESSLING "RED"
B.AUG.2,1882 WARREN,OHIO
D.OCT.8,1936 WARREN,OHIO

YR	CL	LEA	POS	GP	G	REC
1903	NY	N	P		2	2- 0
1904	NY	N	P		16	4- 6
1905	NY	N	P		34	19- 7
1906	NY	N	P		31	12-10
1907	NY	N	P		39	10-12
1908	NY	N	P		18	7- 4
1909	NY	N	P		34	15-10
1910	NY	N	P		33	12-11
1911	NY	N	P		34	11-10
1912	NY	N	P		33	11- 5
1913	NY	N	P		8	2- 1
	CIN	N	P		31	11-13
1914	CIN	N	P		47	15-23
1915	CIN	N	P		17	2- 4
	STL	N	P		15	9- 3
1916	STL	N	P		45	11-16
1917	STL	N	P		43	15-10
1918	STL	N	P		27	9-14
1919	STL	N	P		23	3- 5
	PHI	N	P		3	0- 2
	BBTR			533	180-166

YR CL LEA POS GP   G   REC

AMOLE, MORRIS GEORGE "DOC"
B.JULY 5,1878 COATESVILLE,PA.
D.MAR.7,1912
1897 BAL N P   10   4- 4
1898 WAS N P   7   0- 6
                      17   4-10

AMOR, VICENTE ALVAREZ
B.AUG.9,1932 HAVANA,CUBA
1955 CHI N P   4   0- 1
1957 CHI N P   9   1- 2
        BRTR   13   1- 3

AMOROS, EDMUNDO ISASI "SANDY"
B.JAN.30,1932 MATANZAS,CUBA
1952 BRO N O   20 .250
1954 BRO N O   79 .274
1955 BRO N O   119 .247
1956 BRO N O   114 .260
1957 BRO N O   106 .277
1959 LA N H   5 .200
1960 LA N O   9 .143
     DET A O   65 .149
        BLTL   517 .255

ANCKER, WALTER
B.APR.10,1894 NEW YORK,N.Y.
D.FEB.13,1954
1915 PHI A P   4   0- 1
        BRTR

ANDERSEN, LARRY EUGENE
B.MAY 6,1953 PORTLAND,ORE.
1975 CLE A P   3   0- 0
        BRTR

ANDERSON, ALFRED WALTON
B.JAN.28,1915 GAINESVILLE,GA.
1941 PIT N S   70 .215
1942 PIT N S   54 .271
1946 PIT N H   2 .000
        BRTR   126 .238

ANDERSON, ANDY HOLM
B.NOV.13,1922 BREMERTON,WASH.
1948 STL A 1-2-S   51 .276
1949 STL A 2-S-3   71 .125
        BRTR   122 .184

ANDERSON, ARNOLD REVOLA "RED"
B.JUNE 19,1912 LAWTON,IOWA
D.AUG.7,1972 SIOUX CITY,IOWA
1937 WAS A P   2   0- 1
1940 WAS A P   2   1- 1
1941 WAS A P   32   4- 6
        BRTR   36   5- 8

ANDERSON, DAVID S. "VARNEY"
B.OCT.10,1868 CHESTER,PA.
D.MAR.22,1897
1889 PHI N P   3   0- 2
1890 PHI N P   6   1- 2
     PIT N P   13   2-11
                      22   3-15

ANDERSON, DWAIN CLEAVEN
B.NOV.23,1947 OAKLAND,CAL.
1971 OAK A 2-S-3   16 .270
1972 OAK A S-3   3 .000
     STL N 2-S-3   57 .267
1973 STL N S-O   18 .118
     SD N S-3   53 .121
1974 CLE A 2   2 .333
        BRTR   149 .203

ANDERSON, EDWARD JOHN "GOAT"
B.JAN.13,1880 CLEVELAND,OHIO
D.MAR.15,1923
1907 PIT N O   121 .206
        TR

ANDERSON, FERRELL JACK
B.JAN.9,1918 MAPLE CITY,KAN.
1946 BRO N C   79 .245
1953 STL N C   18 .286
        BRTR   97 .251

ANDERSON, GEORGE JENDRUS "ANDY"
(BORN GEORGE ANDREW JENDRUS)
B.SEPT.26,1889 CLEVELAND,OHIO
D.MAY 28,1962 CLEVELAND,OHIO
1914 BRO N F O   97 .310
1915 BRO N F O   134 .259
1918 STL N O   35 .295
        BLTR   266 .282

ANDERSON, GEORGE LEE "SPARKY"
B.FEB.22,1934 BRIDGEWATER,S.DAK
1959 PHI N 2   152 .218
        BRTR
NON-PLAYING MANAGER
CIN(N) 1970-76

ANDERSON, HAROLD
B.FEB.10,1904 ST.LOUIS,MO.
D.MAY 1,1974 ST.LOUIS,MO.
1932 CHI A O   9 .250
        BRTR

ANDERSON, HARRY WALTER
B.SEPT.10,1931 NORTH EAST,MD.
1957 PHI N O   118 .268
1958 PHI N 1-O   140 .301
1959 PHI N O   142 .240
1960 PHI N 1-O   38 .247
     CIN N 1-O   42 .167
1961 CIN N H   4 .250
        BLTR   484 .264

ANDERSON, JOHN CHARLES
B.NOV.23,1932 ST.PAUL,MINN.
1958 PHI N P   5   0- 0
1960 BAL A P   4   0- 0
1962 STL N P   5   0- 0
     HOU N P   10   0- 0
        BRTR   24   0-0

ANDERSON, JOHN FREDERICK "FRED"
B.DEC.11,1885 CALAHAN,N.C.
D.NOV.8,1957
1909 BOS A P   1   0- 0
1913 BOS A P   10   0- 6
1914 BUF F P   38 13-15
1915 BUF F P   36 19-13
1916 NY N P   38   9-13
1917 NY N P   38   8- 8
1918 NY N P   18   4- 2
        BRTR   179 53-57

ANDERSON, JOHN JOSEPH "HONEST JOHN"
B.DEC.14,1873 SASBOURG,NORWAY
D.JULY 23,1949
1894 BRO N O   16 .301
1895 BRO N O   103 .296
1896 BRO N 1-O   104 .314
1897 BRO N O   116 .332
1898 BRO N O   6 .158
     WAS N O   108 .305
     BRO N 1-O   19 .275
1899 BRO N 1-O   112 .274
1901 MIL N 1   138 .339
1902 STL A 1-O   126 .284
1903 STL A 1   139 .285
1904 NY A 1-O   143 .281
1905 NY A O   25 .212
     WAS A O   100 .295
1906 WAS A O   151 .271
1907 WAS A 1-O   87 .288
1908 CHI A O   123 .262
        BBTR   1616 .293

ANDERSON, LAWRENCE DENNIS "LARRY"
B.DEC.3,1952 MAYWOOD,CAL.
1974 MIL A P   2   0- 0
1975 MIL A P   8   1- 0
        BRTR   10   1- 0

ANDERSON, MICHAEL ALLEN "MIKE"
B.JUNE 22,1951 FLORENCE,S.C.
1971 PHI N O   26 .247
1972 PHI N O   36 .194
1973 PHI N O   87 .254
1974 PHI N 1-O   145 .251
1975 PHI N 1-O   115 .259
1976 STL N 1-O   86 .291
        BRTR   495 .254

ANDERSON, NORMAN CRAIG "CRAIG"
B.JULY 1,1938 WASHINGTON,D.C.
1961 STL N P   25   4- 3
1962 NY N P   50   3-17
1963 NY N P   3   0- 2
1964 NY N P   4   0- 1
        BRTR   82   7-23

ANDERSON, ROBERT CARL "BOB"
B.SEP.29,1935 E. CHICAGO,IND.
1957 CHI N P   8   0- 1
1958 CHI N P   17   3- 3
1959 CHI N P   37 12-13
1960 CHI N P   38 39   9-11
1961 CHI N P   57   7-10
1962 CHI N P   57   2- 7
1963 DET A P   32   3- 1
        BRTR   246 247 36-46

ANDERSON, VARNEY SAMUEL "VARN"
B.JUNE 18,1866 GENEVA,ILL.
D.NOV.5,1941 ROCKFORD,ILL.
1889 IND N P   1   0- 1
1894 WAS N P   2   0- 2
1895 WAS N P   26   9-16
1896 WAS N P   2   0- 1
        BRTR   31   9-20

ANDERSON, WALTER JOHN "LEFTY"
B.SEP.25,1897 GRAND RAPIDS,MICH
1917 PHI A P   14   0- 0
1919 PHI A P   3   1- 1
        BLTL   17   1- 1

ANDERSON, WILLIAM
1889 LOU AA P   1   0- 1

ANDERSON, WILLIAM EDWARD "LEFTY"
B.DEC.3,1896 BOSTON,MASS.
1925 BOS N P   2   0- 0
        BRTL

ANDERSON, WINGO CHARLIE
B.AUG.13,1886 ALVARADO,TEX.
D.DEC.19,1950
1910 CIN N P   7   0- 0
        BLTL

ANDRE, JOHN EDWARD
B.JAN.3,1925 BROCKTON,MASS.
1955 CHI N P   22   0- 1
        BLTR

ANDRES, ERNEST HENRY "JUNIE"
B.JAN.11,1918 JEFFERSONVILLE, IND.
1946 BOS A 3   15 .098
        BRTR

ANDREW, KIM DARRELL
B.NOV.14,1953 GLENDALE,CAL.
1975 BOS A 2   2 .500
        BRTR

ANDREWS, ELBERT DEVORE
B.DEC.11,1902 GREENWOOD,S.C.
1925 PHI A P   6   0- 0
        BLTR

ANDREWS, FRED
B.MAY 4,1952 LAFAYETTE,LA.
1976 PHI N 2   4 .667
        BRTR

ANDREWS, GEORGE EDWARD "ED"
B.APR.5,1859 PAINSVILLE,OHIO
D.AUG.12,1934
1884 PHI N 2   108 .221
1885 PHI N 2-O   103 .266
1886 PHI N O   106 .249
1887 PHI N O   103 .354
1888 PHI N O   123 .238
1889 PHI N 2-O   10 .282
     IND N O   40 .306
1890 BRO P O   95 .258
1891 CIN AA O   83 .210
        BPTR   771 .263

ANDREWS, HERBERT CARL "HUB"
B.AUG.31,1922 BURBANK,OKLA.
1947 NY N P   7   0- 0
1948 NY N P   1   0- 0
        BRTR   8   0-0

YR	CL LEA POS	GP	G	REC

ANDREWS, IVY PAUL "POISON"
B.MAY 6,1907 DORA,ALA.
D.NOV.24,1970 BIRMINGHAM,ALA.

YR	CL LEA POS	GP	G	REC
1931	NY A P		7	2- 0
1932	NY A P		4	2- 1
	BOS A P	25	27	8- 6
1933	BOS A P	34	36	7-13
1934	STL A P		43	4-11
1935	STL A P		50	13- 7
1936	STL A P		36	7-12
1937	CLE A P		20	3- 4
1937	NY A P		11	3- 2
1938	NY A P		19	1- 3
	BRTR	249	253	50-59

ANDREWS, JAMES P.
B.JUNE 6,1859 SHELBURNE FALLS, MASS.

1890	CHI N O		53	.188

ANDREWS, JOHN RICHARD
B.FEB.9,1949 MONTEREY PARK,CAL.

1973	STL N P		16	1- 1
	BLTL			

ANDREWS, MICHAEL JAY "MIKE"
B.JULY 9,1943 LOS ANGELES,CAL.

1966	BOS A 2		5	.167
1967	BOS A 2-S	142		.263
1968	BOS A 2-S-3	147		.271
1969	BOS A 2	121		.293
1970	BOS A 2	151		.253
1971	CHI A 1-2	109		.282
1972	CHI A 1-2	148		.220
1973	CHI A 1-2-3-D	53		.201
	OAK A 2	18		.190
	BRTR	894		.258

ANDREWS, NATHAN HARDY "NATE"
B.SEPT.30,1913 PEMBROKE,N.C.

1937	STL N P		4	0- 0
1939	STL N P		11	1- 2
1940	CLE A P		6	0- 1
1941	CLE A P		2	0- 0
1943	BOS N P		36	14-20
1944	BOS N P		37	16-15
1945	BOS N P	21	22	7-12
1946	CIN N P		7	2- 4
	NY N P		3	1- 0
	BRTR	127	128	41-54

ANDREWS, ROBERT PATRICK "ROB"
B.DEC.11,1952 SANTA MONICA,CAL.

1975	HOU N 2-S	103		.238
1976	HOU N 2-S	109		.256
	BRTR	212		.249

ANDREWS, STANLEY JOSEPH "POLO"
(REAL NAME STANLEY JOSEPH ANDRUSKEWICZ)
B.APR.17,1917 LYNN,MASS.

1939	BOS N C		13	.231
1940	BOS N C		19	.182
1944	BRO N C		4	.125
1945	BRO N C		21	.163
	PHI N C		13	.333
	BRTR		70	.215

ANDREWS, WILLIAM WALTER
B.SEPT.18,1859 PHILADELPHIA,PA.
D.JAN.20,1940

1884	LOU AA 1		15	.185
1885	PRO N 3		1	.000
1888	LOU AA 1		27	.202
			43	.191

ANDRUS, FREDERICK HOTHAM
B.AUG.23,1850 WASHINGTON,MICH.
D.NOV.30,1937 DETROIT,MICH.

1876	CHI N O		8	.306
1884	CHI N P		1	0- 0
	BRTR	1	9	0- 0
				.286

ANDRUS, WILLIAM MORGAN "ANDY"
B.JULY 25,1907 BEAUMONT,TEX.

1931	WAS A 3		3	.000
1937	PHI N 3-		3	.000
	BRTR		6	.000

ANDRUSKEWICZ, STANLEY JOSEPH
(PLAYED UNDER NAME OF STANLEY JOSEPH ANDREWS)

ANDUJAR, JOAQUIN
B.DEC.12,1952 SAN PEDRO DE MACORIS,D.R.

1976	HOU N P		28	9-10
	BBTR			

ANGELINI, NORMAN STANLEY "NORM"
B.SEP.24,1947 SAN FRANCISCO,CAL.

1972	KC A P		21	2- 1
1973	KC A P		7	0- 0
	BLTL		28	2- 1

ANGLEY, THOMAS SAMUEL
B.OCT.2,1904 BALTIMORE,MD.
D.OCT.26,1952

1929	CHI N C		5	.250
	BLTR			

ANIBAL, SANTO (ALCALA)
(SEE SANTO ALCALA)

ANKENMAN, FREDERICK NORMAN "PAT"
B.DEC.23,1912 HOUSTON,TEX.

1936	STL N S		1	.000
1943	BRO N S		1	.500
1944	BRO N 2-S		13	.250
	BRTR		15	.241

ANNIS, WILLIAM PERLEY
B.MAY 24,1857 STONEHAM,MASS.

1884	BOS N O		26	.184

ANSON, ADRIAN CONSTANTINE "CAP"
B.APR.11,1851 MARSHALLTOWN,IOWA
D.APR.14,1922 CHICAGO,ILL.

1871	ROK NA C-2-3		24	-
1872	ATH NA 3		45	.381
1873	ATH NA C-1-2-3-O		50	-
1874	ATH NA 1-S-3-O		54	-
1875	ATH NA C-1-3-O		69	.318
1876	CHI N 3		66	.343
1877	CHI N C-3		59	.337
1878	CHI N 2-O		59	.336
1879	CHI N M-1		49	.407
1880	CHI N M-1-2-S-3		84	.338
1881	CHI N M-C-1-S		84	.399
1882	CHI N M-C-1		82	.362
1883	CHI N M-P- C-1	2	98	0- 0 .307
1884	CHI N M-P- C-1-S	1	111	0- 0 .337
1885	CHI N M-C-1		112	.310
1886	CHI N M-1		125	.371
1887	CHI N M-1		122	.421
1888	CHI N M-1		134	.343
1889	CHI N M-1		134	.341
1890	CHI N M-1		139	.311
1891	CHI N M-1		136	.294
1892	CHI N M-1		147	.274
1893	CHI N M-1		101	.322
1894	CHI N M-1		83	.394
1895	CHI N M-1		122	.338
1896	CHI N M-1		106	.335
1897	CHI N M-1		112	.302
	BRTR	3	2507	0- 0

NON-PLAYING MANAGER NY(N) 1898

ANTOLICK, JOSEPH
B.SEPT.13,1916 HOKENSAUQUA,PA.

1944	PHI N C		4	.333
	BRTR			

ANTONELLI, JOHN AUGUST "JOHNNY"
B.APR.12,1930 ROCHESTER,N.Y.

1948	BOS N P		4	0- 0
1949	BOS N P		22	3- 7
1950	BOS N P		20	2- 3
1953	MIL N P		31	12-12
1954	NY N P		39	21- 7
1955	NY N P		38	14-16
1956	NY N P	41	49	20-13
1957	NY N P	40	47	12-18
1958	SF N P	41	47	16-13
1959	SF N P	40	43	19-10
1960	SF N P	41	42	6- 7
1961	CLE A P	11	12	0- 4
	MIL N P		9	1- 0
	BLTL	377	403	126-110

ANTONELLI, JOHN LAWRENCE
B.JULY 15 1915 MEMPHIS,TENN.

1944	STL N 1-2-3		8	.190
1945	STL N 3		2	.000
	PHI N 1-2-S-3	125		.256
	BRTR		135	.252

ANTONELLO, WILLIAM JAMES "BILL"
B.MAY 19,1927 BROOKLYN,N.Y.

1953	BRO N O		40	.163
	BRTR			

APARICIO, LUIS ERNESTO
B.APR.29,1934 MARACAIBO,VENEZ.

1956	CHI A S	152		.266
1957	CHI A S	143		.257
1958	CHI A S	145		.266
1959	CHI A S	152		.257
1960	CHI A S	153		.277
1961	CHI A S	156		.272
1962	CHI A S	153		.241
1963	BAL A S	146		.250
1964	BAL A S	146		.266
1965	BAL A S	144		.225
1966	BAL A S	151		.276
1967	BAL A S	134		.233
1968	CHI A S	155		.264
1969	CHI A S	156		.280
1970	CHI A S	146		.313
1971	BOS A S	125		.232
1972	BOS A S	110		.257
1973	BOS A S	132		.271
	BRTR	2599		.262

APODACA, ROBERT JOHN "BOB"
B.JAN.31,1950 LOS ANGELES,CAL.

1973	NY N P		1	0- 0
1974	NY N P		35	6- 6
1975	NY N P		46	3- 4
1976	NY N P		43	3- 7
	BRTR		125	12-17

APPLEGATE, FREDERICK ROMAINE
B.MAY 9,1879 WILLIAMSPORT,PA.

1904	PHI A P		3	1- 2
	BRTR			

APPLETON, EDWARD SAM "WHITEY"
B.FEB.29,1892 ARLINGTON,TEX.
D.JAN.27,1932

1915	BRO N P		34	4-10
1916	BRO N P		14	1- 2
	BRTR		48	5-12

APPLETON, PETER WILLIAM "JAKE"
(PLAYED UNDER NAME OF
PETER WILLIAM JABLONOWSKI IN
1927-33; REST OF CAREER UNDER
NAME OF PETER WILLIAM APPLETON,
AFTER CHANGING NAME LEGALLY)
B.MAY 20,1904 TERRYVILLE,CONN.
D.JAN.18,1974 TRENTON,N.J.

1927	CIN N P		6	2- 1
1928	CIN N P-O	31	32	3- 4
				.323
1930	CLE A P		39	8- 7
1931	CLE A P	29	30	4- 4
1932	CLE A P		4	0- 0
	BOS A P		11	0- 3
1933	NY A P		1	0- 0
1936	WAS A P		38	14- 9
1937	WAS A P		35	8-15
1938	WAS A P		43	7- 9
1939	WAS A P		40	5-10
1940	CHI A P		25	4- 0
1941	CHI A P		13	0- 3
1942	CHI A P		4	0- 0
	STL A P		14	1- 1
1945	STL A P		2	0- 0
	WAS A P		6	1- 0
	BRTR	341	343	57-66
				.233

YR CL LEA POS GP G REC

APPLING, LUCIUS BENJAMIN "LUKE"
B.APR.2,1908 HIGH POINT,N.C.

YR	CL	LEA	POS	GP	G	REC
1930	CHI	A	S		6	.308
1931	CHI	A	S		96	.232
1932	CHI	A	2-S-3		139	.274
1933	CHI	A	S		151	.322
1934	CHI	A	S		118	.303
1935	CHI	A	S		153	.307
1936	CHI	A	S		138	.388
1937	CHI	A	S		154	.317
1938	CHI	A	S		81	.303
1939	CHI	A	S		148	.314
1940	CHI	A	S		150	.348
1941	CHI	A	S		154	.314
1942	CHI	A	S		142	.262
1943	CHI	A	S		155	.328
1945	CHI	A	S		18	.362
1946	CHI	A	S		149	.309
1947	CHI	A	S-3		139	.306
1948	CHI	A	S-3		139	.314
1949	CHI	A	S		142	.301
1950	CHI	A	1-2-S		50	.234
		BRTR			2422	.310

NON-PLAYING MANAGER KC(A) 1967

ARAGON, ANGEL VALDES JR. "JACK"
B.NOV.20,1915 HAVANA,CUBA

YR	CL	LEA	POS	GP	G	REC
1941	NY	N	H		1	.000
		BRTR				

ARAGON, ANGEL VALDES SR. "PETE"
B.AUG.2,1893 HAVANA,CUBA
D.JAN.24,1952

YR	CL	LEA	POS	GP	G	REC
1914	NY	A	O		6	.142
1916	NY	A	3-O		12	.208
1917	NY	A	S-3-O		14	.067
		BRTR			32	.123

ARCHDEACON, MAURICE JOHN "FLASH"
B.DEC.14,1898 ST.LOUIS,MO.
D.SEPT.5,1954

YR	CL	LEA	POS	GP	G	REC
1923	CHI	A	O		22	.402
1924	CHI	A	O		95	.319
1925	CHI	A	O		10	.111
		BLTL			127	.333

ARCHER, FREDERICK MARVIN "LEFTY"
B.MAR.7,1910 JOHNSON CITY,TENN.

YR	CL	LEA	POS	GP	G	REC
1936	PHI	A	P		6	2- 3
1937	PHI	A	P		1	0- 0
		BLTL			7	2- 3

ARCHER, JAMES PATRICK
B.MAY 13,1883 DUBLIN,IRELAND
D.MAR.29,1958

YR	CL	LEA	POS	GP	G	REC
1904	PIT	N	C		7	.157
1907	DET	A	C		18	.119
1909	CHI	N	C		80	.230
1910	CHI	N	C-1		89	.259
1911	CHI	N	C		112	.252
1912	CHI	N	C		120	.283
1913	CHI	N	C		111	.266
1914	CHI	N	C		79	.258
1915	CHI	N	C		97	.243
1916	CHI	N	C		77	.220
1917	CHI	N	C		2	.000
1918	PIT	N	C-1		24	.155
	BRO	N	C		9	.273
	CIN	N	C-1-O		9	.269
		BRTR			834	.250

ARCHER, JAMES WILLIAM "JIM"
B.MAY 25,1933 WYTHEVILLE,VA.

YR	CL	LEA	POS	GP	G	REC
1961	KC	A	P		39	9-15
1962	KC	A	P		18	0- 1
		BRTL			57	9-16

ARCHIE, GEORGE ALBERT
B.APR.27,1914 NASHVILLE,TENN.

YR	CL	LEA	POS	GP	G	REC
1938	DET	A	H		3	.000
1941	WAS	A	1-3		105	.269
	STL	A	1		9	.379
1946	STL	A	1		4	.182
		BRTR			121	.273

ARCIA, JOSE RAIMUNDO (ORTA)
B.AUG.22,1943 HAVANA,CUBA

YR	CL	LEA	POS	GP	G	REC
1968	CHI	N	2-S-3-O		59	.190
1969	SD	N	1-2-S-3-O		120	.215
1970	SD	N	2-S-3-O		114	.223
		BRTR			293	.215

ARDELL, DANIEL MIERS
B.MAY 27,1941 SEATTLE,WASH.

YR	CL	LEA	POS	GP	G	REC
1961	LA	A	1		7	.250
		BLTL				

ARDIZOLA, RINALDO JOSEPH "RUGGER"
B.NOV.20,1919 NOVARA,ITALY

YR	CL	LEA	POS	GP	G	REC
1947	NY	A	P		1	0- 0
		BRTR				

ARDNER, JOSEPH A. "OLD HOSS"
B.FEB.29,1858 MT.VERNON,OHIO
D.SEPT.15,1935

YR	CL	LEA	POS	GP	G	REC
1884	CLE	N	2-3		26	.174
1890	CLE	N	2		84	.223
		BRTR			110	.212

ARELLANES, FRANK JULIAN
B.JAN.28,1882 SANTA CRUZ,CAL.
D.DEC.13,1918

YR	CL	LEA	POS	GP	G	REC
1908	BOS	A	P		12	4- 3
1909	BOS	A	P	45	46	16-12
1910	BOS	A	P		18	4- 7
		BRTR		75	76	24-22

ARFT, HENRY IRVEN "BOW WOW"
B.JAN.28,1922 MANCHESTER,MO.

YR	CL	LEA	POS	GP	G	REC
1948	STL	A	1		69	.238
1949	STL	A	H		6	.200
1950	STL	A	1		98	.268
1951	STL	A	1		112	.261
1952	STL	A	1		15	.143
		BLTL			300	.253

ARIAS, RODOLFO (MARTINEZ) "RUDY"
B.JUNE 6,1932 CAMAGUEY,CUBA

YR	CL	LEA	POS	GP	G	REC
1959	CHI	A	P		34	2- 0
		BLTL				

ARLETT, RUSSELL LORIS "BUZZ"
B.JAN.3,1899 OAKLAND,CAL.
D.MAY 16,1964 MINNEAPOLIS,MINN.

YR	CL	LEA	POS	GP	G	REC
1931	PHI	N	1-O		121	.313
		BBTR				

ARLICH, DONALD LOUIS "DON"
B.FEB.15,1943 WAYNE,MICH.

YR	CL	LEA	POS	GP	G	REC
1965	HOU	N	P		1	0- 0
1966	HOU	N	P		7	0- 1
		BLTL			8	0- 1

ARLIN, STEPHEN RALPH "STEVE"
B.SEP.25,1945 SEATTLE,WASH.

YR	CL	LEA	POS	GP	G	REC
1969	SD	N	P		4	0- 1
1970	SD	N	P		2	1- 0
1971	SD	N	P		36	9-19
1972	SD	N	P		38	10-21
1973	SD	N	P		34	11-14
1974	SD	N	P		16	1- 7
	CLE	A	P		11	2- 5
		BRTR			141	34-67

ARMAS, ANTONIO RAFAEL (MACHADO) "TONY"
B.JULY 12,1953 ANZOATEGUI,VENEZ.

YR	CL	LEA	POS	GP	G	REC
1976	PIT	N	O		4	.333
		BRTR				

ARMBRISTER, EDISON ROSANDA "ED"
B.JULY 4,1948 NASSAU,BAHAMAS

YR	CL	LEA	POS	GP	G	REC
1973	CIN	N	O		18	.216
1974	CIN	N	O		9	.286
1975	CIN	N	O		59	.185
1976	CIN	N	O		73	.295
		BRTR			159	.241

ARMBRUST, ORVILLE MARTIN
B.MAR.2,1910 GURDON,ARK.
D.OCT.2,1967 MOBILE,ALA.

YR	CL	LEA	POS	GP	G	REC
1934	WAS	A	P		3	1- 0
		BRTR				

ARMBRUSTER, CHARLES A.
B.1882 CINCINNATI,OHIO

YR	CL	LEA	POS	GP	G	REC
1905	BOS	A	C		35	.198
1906	BOS	A	C		72	.144
1907	BOS	A	C		23	.100
	CHI	A	C		1	.000
		TR			131	.149

ARMBRUSTER, HARRY "ARMY"
B.MAR.20,1882 CINCINNATI,OHIO
D.DEC.10,1953 CINCINNATI,OHIO

YR	CL	LEA	POS	GP	G	REC
1906	PHI	A	O		91	.238
		BLTL				

ARMOUR, WILLIAM R.
B.SEPT.3,1869 HOMESTEAD,PA.
D.DEC.2,1922 MINNEAPOLIS,MINN.
NON-PLAYING MANAGER
CLE(A) 1902-04, DET(A) 1905-06

ARMSTRONG, GEORGE NOBLE "DODO"
B.JUNE 3,1925 ORANGE,N.J.

YR	CL	LEA	POS	GP	G	REC
1946	PHI	A	C		8	.167
		BRTR				

ARMSTRONG, HOWARD ELMER
B.DEC.2,1889 GEAUGA CO.,OHIO
D.MAR.8,1926

YR	CL	LEA	POS	GP	G	REC
1911	PHI	A	P		1	0- 1
		TR				

ARMSTRONG, SAMUEL
B.FT.WAYNE,IND.

YR	CL	LEA	POS	GP	G	REC
1871	KEK	NA	O		13	-

ARNDT, HARRY J.
B.FEB.12,1879 SOUTH BEND,IND.
D.MAR.24,1921

YR	CL	LEA	POS	GP	G	REC
1902	DET	A	1-O		10	.135
	BAL	A	2-S-3-O		67	.257
1905	STL	N	2		111	.243
1906	STL	N	3		67	.270
1907	STL	N	1		9	.130
					264	.248

ARNOLD, CHRISTOPHER PAUL "CHRIS"
B.NOV.6,1947 LONG BEACH,CAL.

YR	CL	LEA	POS	GP	G	REC
1971	SF	N	2		6	.231
1972	SF	N	2-S-3		51	.226
1973	SF	N	C-2-3		49	.296
1974	SF	N	2-S-3		78	.241
1975	SF	N	2-O		29	.195
1976	SF	N	1-2-S-3		60	.217
		BRTR			273	.237

ARNOLD, WILLIS S. "BILLY"
B.MAR.2,1851 MIDDLETOWN,CONN.
D.JAN.17,1899

YR	CL	LEA	POS	GP	G	REC
1872	WAS	NA	M-O		2	.125

ARNOVICH, MORRIS "SNOOKER"
B.NOV.16,1910 SUPERIOR,WIS.
D.JULY 20,1959

YR	CL	LEA	POS	GP	G	REC
1936	PHI	N	O		13	.313
1937	PHI	N	O		117	.290
1938	PHI	N	O		139	.275
1939	PHI	N	O		134	.324
1940	PHI	N	O		39	.199
	CIN	N	O		62	.284
1941	NY	N	O		85	.280
1946	NY	N	O		1	.000
		BRTR			590	.287

ARNTZEN, ORIE EDGAR "OLD FOLKS"
B.OCT.18,1909 BEVERLY,ILL.
D.JAN.28,1970 CEDAR RAPIDS,IOWA

YR	CL	LEA	POS	GP	G	REC
1943	PHI	A	P		32	4-13
		BRTR				

ARRIGO, GERALD WILLIAM "JERRY"
B.JUNE 12,1941 CHICAGO,ILL.

YR	CL	LEA	POS	GP	G	REC
1961	MIN	A	P		7	0- 1
1962	MIN	A	P		1	0- 0
1963	MIN	A	P		5	1- 2
1964	MIN	A	P		41	7- 4
1965	CIN	N	P	27	28	2- 4
1966	CIN	N	P		3	0- 0
	NY	N	P		17	3- 3
1967	CIN	N	P		32	6- 6
1968	CIN	N	P		36	12-10
1969	CIN	N	P		20	4- 7
1970	CHI	A	P		5	0- 3
		BLTL		194	195	35-40

ARROYO, FERNANDO "FRED"
B.MAR.21,1952 SACRAMENTO,CAL.

YR	CL	LEA	POS	GP	G	REC
1975	DET	A	P		14	2- 1
		BRTR				

ARROYO, LUIS ENRIQUE
B.FEB.18,1927 PENUELAS,P.R.

YR	CL	LEA	POS	GP	G	REC
1955	STL	N	P		35	11- 8
1956	PIT	N	P		18	3- 3
1957	PIT	N	P	54	56	3-11
1959	CIN	N	P		10	1- 0
1960	NY	A	P		29	5- 1
1961	NY	A	P		65	15- 5
1962	NY	A	P		27	1- 3
1963	NY	A	P		6	1- 1
		BLTL		244	246	40-32

YR	CL	LEA	POS	GP	G	REC

ARROYO, RUDOLPH "RUDY"
B.JUNE 19,1950 NEW YORK,N.Y.
1971 STL N P 9 0-1
BLTL

ARUNDEL, HARVEY
B.1857 PHILADELPHIA,PA.
D.MAR.25,1904
1875 ATL NA O 1 .000
1882 PIT AA P-S 14 4-10
.192
1884 PRO N P 1 1-0
16 5-10
.183

ARUNDEL, JOHN THOMAS "TUG"
B.JUNE 22,1862 AUBURN,N.Y.
D.SEPT.5,1912
1882 ATH AA C 1 .000
1884 TOL AA C 14 .087
1887 IND N C 43 .236
1888 WAS N C 16 .196
74 .199

ASBELL, JAMES MARION
"BIG TRAIN"
B.JUNE 22,1914 DALLAS TEX.
D.JULY 6,1967 SAN MATEO,CAL.
1938 CHI N O 17 .182
BRTR

ASBJORNSON, ROBERT ANTHONY
"CASPER"
(NAME CHANGED TO ASBY)
B.JUNE 19,1909 CONCORD,MASS.
D.JAN.21,1970 WILLIAMSPORT,PA.
1928 BOS A C 6 .187
1929 BOS A C 17 .103
1931 CIN N C 45 .305
1932 CIN N C 29 .172
BRTR 97 .235

ASH, KENNETH LOWTHER
B.SEPT.16,1901 ANMOORE,W.VA.
1925 CHI A P 2 0-0
1928 CIN N P 9 3-3
1929 CIN N P-O 29 30 1-5
.143
1930 CIN N P 16 17 2-0
BRTR 56 58 6-8
.133

ASHBURN, RICHIE "WHITEY"
B.MAR.19,1927 TILDEN,NEB.
1948 PHI N O 117 .333
1949 PHI N O 154 .284
1950 PHI N O 151 .303
1951 PHI N O 154 .344
1952 PHI N O 154 .282
1953 PHI N O 156 .330
1954 PHI N O 153 .313
1955 PHI N O 140 .338
1956 PHI N O 154 .303
1957 PHI N O 156 .297
1958 PHI N O 152 .350
1959 PHI N O 153 .266
1960 CHI N O 151 .291
1961 CHI N O 109 .257
1962 NY N 2-O 135 .306
BLTR 2189 .308

ASHBY, ALAN DEAN
B.JULY 8,1951 LONG BEACH,CAL.
1973 CLE A C 11 .172
1974 CLE A C 10 .143
1975 CLE A C-1-3 90 .224
1976 CLE A C-1-3 89 .239
BLTR 200 .227
BB 1973-75

ASHFORD, THOMAS STEVE "TUCKER"
B.DEC.4,1954 MEMPHIS,TENN.
1976 SD N 3 4 .600
BRTR

ASMUSSEN, THOMAS WILLIAM
B.SEPT.26,1878 CHICAGO,ILL.
D.AUG.21,1963 ARLINGTON HEIGHTS
ILL.
1907 BOS N C 2 .000
TR

ASPROMONTE, KENNETH JOSEPH "KEN"
B.SEP.22,1931 BROOKLYN,N.Y.
1957 BOS A 2 24 .269
1958 BOS A 2 6 .125
WAS A 2-S-3 92 .225
1959 WAS A 1-2-S-O 70 .244
1960 WAS A H 4 .000
CLE A 2-3 117 .290
1961 LA A 2 66 .223
CLE A 2 22 .229
1962 CLE A 2-3 20 .143
MIL N 2-3 34 .291
1963 CHI N 1-2 20 .147
BRTR 475 .249
NON-PLAYING MANAGER
CLE(A) 1972-74

ASPROMONTE, ROBERT THOMAS "BOB"
B.JUNE 19,1938 BROOKLYN,N.Y.
1956 BRO N H 1 .000
1960 LA N S-3 21 .182
1961 LA N 2-S-3 47 .241
1962 HOU N 2-S-3 149 .266
1963 HOU N 1-3 136 .214
1964 HOU N 3 157 .280
1965 HOU N 1-S-3 152 .263
1966 HOU N 1-S-3 152 .252
1967 HOU N 3 137 .294
1968 HOU N 1-S-3-O 124 .225
1969 ATL N 2-S-3-O 82 .253
1970 ATL N 1-S-3-O 62 .213
1971 NY N 3 104 .225
BRTR 1324 .252

ASSELSTINE, BRIAN HANLY
B.SEPT.23,1953 SANTA BARBARA,CAL
1976 ATL N O 11 .212
BLTR

ASTROTH, JOSEPH HENRY "JOE"
B.SEPT.1,1922 EAST ALTON,ILL.
1945 PHI A C 10 .059
1946 PHI A C 4 .143
1949 PHI A C 55 .243
1950 PHI A C 39 .327
1951 PHI A C 64 .246
1952 PHI A C 104 .249
1953 PHI A C 82 .296
1954 PHI A C 77 .221
1955 KC A C 101 .252
1956 KC A C 8 .077
BRTR 544 .254

ATHERTON, CHARLES MORGAN
HERBERT "PREXY"
B.OCT.19,1873 NEW BRUNSWICK,N.J
D.DEC.19,1935
1899 WAS N 3 63 .240

ATKINS, FRANK MONTGOMERY
"TOMMY"
B.DEC.9,1887 PANCAU,NEB.
D.MAY 7,1956
1909 PHI A P 1 0-0
1910 PHI A P 15 3-2
BLTL 16 3-2

ATKINS, JAMES CURTIS
B.MAR.10,1921 BIRMINGHAM,ALA.
1950 BOS A P 1 0-0
1952 BOS A P 3 0-1
BLTR 4 0-1

ATKINSON, ALBERT W.
B.MAR.9,1861 CLINTON,ILL.
D.JUNE 17,1952 ELKHORN TOWNSHIP
MO.
1884 ATH AA P 22 11-11
CHI U P-O 12 5-7
.278
PIT U P-O 8 9 2-6
.121
BAL U P 8 3-5
1886 ATH AA P 43 25-17
1887 ATH AA P 16 5-9
109 110 51-55
.183

ATKINSON, EDWARD
B.BALTIMORE,MD.
1873 NAT NA O 2 .000

ATKINSON, HUBERT BERLEY
B.JUNE 2,1906 CHICAGO,ILL.
D.FEB.12,1961
1927 WAS A H 1 .000

ATKINSON, WILLIAM CECIL GLENN
"BILL"
B.OCT.4,1954 CHATHAM,ONT.,CAN.
1976 MON N P 4 0-0
BLTR

ATTREAU, RICHARD GILBERT
B.APR.8,1899 CHICAGO,ILL.
D.JULY 5,1964 CHICAGO,ILL.
1926 PHI N 1 17 .230
1927 PHI N 1 44 .205
BLTL 61 .215

ATWELL, MAURICE DAILEY "TOBY"
B.MAR.8,1924 LEESBURG,VA.
1952 CHI N C 107 .290
1953 CHI N C 24 .230
PIT N C 53 .245
1954 PIT N C 96 .289
1955 PIT N C 71 .213
1956 PIT N C 12 .111
MIL N C 15 .167
BLTR 378 .260

ATWOOD, WILLIAM FRANKLIN
B.SEPT.11,1912 ROME,GA.
1936 PHI N C 71 .302
1937 PHI N C 87 .244
1938 PHI N C 102 .196
1939 PHI N C 4 .000
1940 PHI N C 78 .192
BRTR 342 .229

ATZ, JACOB HENRY
B.JULY 1,1879 WASHINGTON,D.C.
D.MAY 22,1945
1902 WAS A 2 3 .100
1907 CHI A 3 4 .125
1908 CHI A 2 83 .194
1909 CHI A 2 119 .236
BRTR 209 .218

AUBREY, HARVEY HERBERT
B.JULY 5,1880 ST.JOSEPH,MO.
D.SEPT.18,1953 BALTIMORE,MD.
1903 BOS N S 94 .212
TR

AUERBACH, FREDERICK STEVEN
"RICK"
B.FEB.15,1950 WOODLAND HILLS,CAL
1971 MIL A S 79 .203
1972 MIL A S 153 .218
1973 MIL A S 6 .100
1974 LA N 2-S-3 45 .342
1975 LA N 2-S-3 85 .224
1976 LA N 2-S-3 36 .128
BRTR 404 .229

AUGUSTINE, DAVID RALPH "DAVE"
B.NOV.28,1949 FOLLANSBEE,W.VA.
1973 PIT N O 11 .286
1974 PIT N O 18 .182
BRTR 29 .207

AUGUSTINE, GERALD LEE "JERRY"
B.JULY 24,1952 KEWAUNEE,WIS.
1975 MIL A P 5 2-0
1976 MIL A P 39 9-12
BLTL 44 11-12

AUKER, ELDON LEROY "SUBMARINE"
B.SEPT.21,1910 NORCATUR,KAN.
1933 DET A P 15 3-3
1934 DET A P 43 15-7
1935 DET A P 36 18-7
1936 DET A P 35 13-16
1937 DET A P 39 43 17-9
1938 DET A P 27 11-10
1939 BOS A P 31 9-10
1940 STL A P 38 16-11
1941 STL A P 34 37 14-15
1942 STL A P 35 51 14-13
BRTR 333 356 130-101

AULDS, LEYCESTER DOYLE
B.DEC.21,1920 FARMERVILLE,LA.
1947 BOS A C 3 .250
BRTR

AULT, DOUGLAS REAGAN "DOUG"
B.MAR.9,1950 BEAUMONT,TEX.
1976 TEX A 1 9 .300
BRTL

AUST, DENNIS KAY
B.NOV.25,1940 TECUMSEH,NEB.

YR	CL	LEA	POS	G	REC
1965	STL	N	P	6	0- 0
1966	STL	N	P	9	0- 1
		BRTR		15	0- 1

AUSTIN, HENRY C.
B.BROOKLYN,N.Y.
D.SEPT.3,1895

YR	CL	LEA	POS	G	REC
1873	RES	NA	O	22	-

AUSTIN, JAMES PHILIP "PEPPER"
B.DEC.8,1879 SWANSEA,WALES
D.MAR.6,1965 LAGUNA BEACH,CAL.

YR	CL	LEA	POS	G	REC
1909	NY	A	S-3	136	.231
1910	NY	A	3	133	.218
1911	STL	A	3	148	.261
1912	STL	A	3	149	.252
1913	STL	A	M-3	142	.273
1914	STL	A	3	130	.238
1915	STL	A	3	141	.266
1916	STL	A	3	129	.207
1917	STL	A	3	127	.239
1918	STL	A	M-S-3	110	.264
1919	STL	A	3	106	.237
1920	STL	A	3	83	.271
1921	STL	A	S	27	.273
1922	STL	A	3	15	.290
1923	STL	A	M-H	1	.000
1925	STL	A	3	1	.000
1926	STL	A	3	1	.500
1929	STL	A	3	1	.000
		BBTR		1580	.247

AUSTIN, RICK GERALD
B.OCT.27,1946 SEATTLE,WAS.

YR	CL	LEA	POS	G	REC
1970	CLE	A	P	31	2- 5
1971	CLE	A	P	23	0- 0
1975	MIL	A	P	32	2- 3
1976	MIL	A	P	3	0- 0
		BRTL		89	4- 8

AUTRY, ALBERT "AL"
B.FEB.29,1952 MODESTO,CAL.

YR	CL	LEA	POS	G	REC
1976	ATL	N	P	1	1- 0
		BRTR			

AUTRY, MARTIN GORDON "CHICK"
B.MAR.5,1903 MARTINDALE,TEX.
D.JAN.26,1950

YR	CL	LEA	POS	G	REC
1924	NY	A	C	2	.000
1926	CLE	A	C	3	.143
1927	CLE	A	C	16	.255
1928	CLE	A	C	22	.300
1929	CHI	A	C	43	.208
1930	CHI	A	C	34	.253
		BRTR		120	.245

AUTRY, WILLIAM ASKEW
B.JAN.2,1885 HUMBOLDT,TENN.
D.JAN.16,1976 SANTA ROSA,CAL.

YR	CL	LEA	POS	G	REC
1907	CIN	N	O	7	.200
1909	CIN	N	1	9	.182
	BOS	N	1	61	.196
		BLTL		77	.199

AVERILL, EARL DOUGLAS
B.SEP.9,1931 CLEVELAND,O.

YR	CL	LEA	POS	G	REC
1956	CLE	A	C	42	.237
1958	CLE	A	3	17	.182
1959	CLE	N	C-2-3-0	74	.237
1960	CHI	N	C-3-0	52	.235
	CHI	A	C	10	.214
1961	LA	A	C-2-0	115	.266
1962	LA	A	C-0	92	.219
1963	PHI	N	C-1-3-0	47	.268
		BRTR		449	.242

AVERILL, HOWARD EARL "ROCK"
B.MAY 21,1902 SNOHOMISH,WASH.

YR	CL	LEA	POS	G	REC
1929	CLE	A	O	152	.330
1930	CLE	A	O	139	.339
1931	CLE	A	O	155	.333
1932	CLE	A	O	153	.314
1933	CLE	A	O	151	.301
1934	CLE	A	O	154	.313
1935	CLE	A	O	140	.288
1936	CLE	A	O	152	.378
1937	CLE	A	O	156	.299
1938	CLE	A	O	134	.330
1939	CLE	A	O	24	.273
	DET	A	O	87	.262
1940	DET	A	O	64	.280
1941	BOS	N	O	8	.118
		BLTR		1669	.316

AVILA, ROBERTO FRANCISCO (GONZALEZ) "BOBBY"
B.JUNE 7,1926 VERA CRUZ,MEXICO

YR	CL	LEA	POS	G	REC
1949	CLE	A	2	31	.214
1950	CLE	A	2-S	80	.299
1951	CLE	A	2	141	.305
1952	CLE	A	2	150	.300
1953	CLE	A	2	141	.286
1954	CLE	A	2-S	143	.341
1955	CLE	A	2	141	.272
1956	CLE	A	2	138	.224
1957	CLE	A	2-3	129	.268
1958	CLE	A	2-3	113	.253
1959	BAL	A	2-3-0	20	.170
	BOS	A	2	22	.244
	MIL	N	2	51	.238
		BRTR		1300	.281

AVREA, JAMES EPHERIUM "JAY"
B.JULY 6,1923 ALVARADO,TEX.

YR	CL	LEA	POS	G	REC
1950	CIN	N	P	2	0- 0
		BRTR			

AYALA, BENIGNO (FELIX) "BENNY"
B.FEB.7,1951 YAUCO,P.R.

YR	CL	LEA	POS	G	REC
1974	NY	N	O	23	.235
1976	NY	N	O	22	.115
		BRTR		45	.202

AYDELOTTE, JACOB S.
B.MARION,IND.

YR	CL	LEA	POS	G	REC
1884	IND	AA	P-O	12	5- 7
					.114
1886	ATH	AA	P	2	0- 2
				14	5- 9
					.098

AYERS, WILLIAM OSCAR
B.AUG.27,1918 NEWNAN,GA.

YR	CL	LEA	POS	G	REC
1947	NY	N	P	13	0- 3
		BRTR			

AYERS, YANCEY WYATT "DOC"
B.APR.21,1891 HILLSVILLE,VA.
D.MAY 26,1968 DRAPER,VA.

YR	CL	LEA	POS	G	REC
1913	WAS	A	P	4	2- 1
1914	WAS	A	P	49	12-16
1915	WAS	A	P	40	15- 9
1916	WAS	A	P	43	5- 9
1917	WAS	A	P	40	11-10
1918	WAS	A	P	40	10-12
1919	WAS	A	P	12	2- 6
	DET	A	P	23	4- 3
1920	DET	A	P	46	7-14
1921	DET	A	P	2	0- 0
		BRTR		299	68-80

AYLWARD, RICHARD JOHN "DANDY"
B.JUNE 4,1925 BALTIMORE,MD.

YR	CL	LEA	POS	G	REC
1953	CLE	A	C	4	.000
		BRTR			

AZCUE, JOSE JOAQUIN (LOPEZ) "JOE"
B.AUG.18,1939 CIENFUEGOS,CUBA

YR	CL	LEA	POS	G	REC
1960	CIN	N	C	14	.097
1962	KC	A	C	72	.229
1963	KC	A	C	2	.000
	CLE	A	C	94	.284
1964	CLE	A	C	83	.273
1965	CLE	A	C	111	.230
1966	CLE	A	C	98	.275
1967	CLE	A	C	86	.251
1968	CLE	A	C	115	.280
1969	CLE	A	C	7	.292
	BOS	A	C	19	.216
	CAL	A	C	80	.218
1970	CAL	A	C	114	.242
1972	CAL	A	C	3	.000
	MIL	A	C	11	.143
		BRTR		909	.252

BABB, CHARLES AMOS
B.FEB.20,1873 PORTLAND,ORE.
D.MAR.20,1954

YR	CL	LEA	POS	G	REC
1903	NY	N	S	121	.248
1904	BRO	N	S	151	.265
1905	BRO	N	1-S	74	.187
		BBTR		346	.243

BABE, LOREN ROLLAND
B.JAN.11,1928 PISGAH,IOWA

YR	CL	LEA	POS	G	REC
1952	NY	A	3	12	.095
1953	NY	A	3	5	.333
	PHI	A	S-3	103	.224
		BLTR		120	.223

BABICH, JOHN CHARLES
B.MAY 14,1913 ALBION,CAL.

YR	CL	LEA	POS	G	REC
1934	BRO	N	P	25	7-11
1935	BRO	N	P	37	7-14
1936	BOS	N	P	3	0- 0
1940	PHI	A	P	31	14-13
1941	PHI	A	P	16	2- 7
		BRTR		112	30-45

BABINGTON, CHARLEY PERCY
B.MAY 4,1895 CRANSTON,R.I.
D.MAR.22,1957

YR	CL	LEA	POS	G	REC
1915	NY	N	O	28	.242
		BRTR			

BACKMAN, LESTER JOHN
B.MAR.20,1888 CLEVES,OHIO
D.NOV.8,1975 CINCINNATI,OHIO

YR	CL	LEA	POS	G	REC
1909	STL	N	P	21	3-11
1910	STL	N	P	26	6- 7
		TR		47	9-18

BACON, EDGAR SUTER
B.APR.8,1895 FRANKLIN CO.,KY.
D.OCT.2,1963 FRANKFURT,KY.

YR	CL	LEA	POS	G	REC
1917	PHI	A	P	4	0- 0

BACSIK, MICHAEL JAMES "MIKE"
B.APR.1,1952 DALLAS,TEX.

YR	CL	LEA	POS	G	REC
1975	TEX	A	P	7	1- 2
1976	TEX	A	P	23	3- 2
		BRTR		30	4- 4

BACZEWSKI, FREDERICK JOHN
B.MAY 15,1926 ST.PAUL,MINN.

YR	CL	LEA	POS	G	REC
1953	CHI	N	P	9	0- 0
	CIN	N	P	24	11- 4
1954	CIN	N	P	29	6- 6
1955	CIN	N	P	1	0- 0
		BLTL		63	17-10

BADEN, ARTHUR HERMAN
B.SEPT.21,1886 ST.LOUIS,MO.
D.APR.5,1957 ST.LOUIS,MO.

YR	CL	LEA	POS	G	REC
1904	STL	A	O	2	.000
		BRTR			

BADER, LORE VERNE "KING"
B.APR.27,1888 BADER,ILL.
D.JUNE 2,1973 LE ROY,KAN.

YR	CL	LEA	POS	G	REC
1912	NY	N	P	2	2- 0
1917	BOS	A	P	15	2- 0
1918	BOS	A	P	5	1- 3
		BLTR		22	5- 3

BADGRO, MORRIS HIRAM "RED"
B.DEC.1,1902 ORILLA,WASH.

YR	CL	LEA	POS	G	REC
1929	STL	A	O	54	.284
1930	STL	A	O	89	.239
		BLTR		143	.257

BAECHT, EDWARD JOSEPH
B.MAY 15,1907 BADEN,OKLA.
D.AUG.15,1957 QUARRY TOWNSHIP, ILL.

YR	CL	LEA	POS	G	REC
1926	PHI	N	P	28	2- 0
1927	PHI	N	P	1	0- 1
1928	PHI	N	P	9	1- 1
1931	CHI	N	P	22	2- 4
1932	CHI	N	P	1	0- 0
1937	STL	A	P	3	0- 0
		BRTR		64	5- 6

BAERWALD, RUDOLPH FRED
(PLAYED UNDER NAME OF JOHN BELL)

BAGBY, JAMES CHARLES JR.
B.SEPT.8,1916 CLEVELAND,OHIO

YR	CL	LEA	POS	GP	G	REC
1938	BOS	A	P	43	45	15-11
1939	BOS	A	P		21	5- 5
1940	BOS	A	P-O	36	44	10-16
						.203
1941	CLE	A	P	33	35	9-15
1942	CLE	A	P	38	39	17- 9
1943	CLE	A	P-S	36	41	17-14
						.268
1944	CLE	A	P	13	14	4- 5
1945	CLE	A	P		25	8-11
1946	BOS	A	P		21	7- 6
1947	PIT	N	P		37	5- 4
		BRTR		303	322	97-96
						.226

YR	CL	LEA	POS	GP	G	REC

BAGBY, JAMES CHARLES JACOB SR. "SARGE"
B.OCT.5,1889 BARNETT,GA.
D.JULY 28,1954

YR	CL	LEA	POS	GP	G	REC
1912	CIN	N	P		5	2- 0
1916	CLE	A	P	48	51	16-15
1917	CLE	A	P		49	23-13
1918	CLE	A	P	45	47	17-16
1919	CLE	A	P	35	37	17-11
1920	CLE	A	P	48	49	31-12
1921	CLE	A	P	40	41	14-12
1922	CLE	A	P		25	4- 5
1923	PIT	N	P		21	3- 2
	BBTR			316	325	127-86

BAGWELL, WILLIAM MALLORY "BIG BILL"
B.FEB.24,1897 CHOUDRANT,LA.
D.OCT.5,1976 CHOUDRANT,LA.

YR	CL	LEA	POS	GP	G	REC
1923	BOS	N	O		56	.290
1925	PHI	A	O		36	.300
	BLTL				92	.294

BAHNSEN, STANLEY RAYMOND "STAN"
B.DEC.15,1944 COUNCIL BLUFFS,IA.

YR	CL	LEA	POS	GP	G	REC
1966	NY	A	P		4	1- 1
1968	NY	A	P	37	17-12	
1969	NY	A	P	40	9-16	
1970	NY	A	P	36	14-11	
1971	NY	A	P	36	14-12	
1972	CHI	A	P	43	44	21-16
1973	CHI	A	P	42	18-21	
1974	CHI	A	P	38	12-15	
1975	CHI	A	P	12	4- 6	
	OAK	A	P	21	6- 7	
1976	OAK	A	P	35	8- 7	
	BRTR			344	345	124-124

BAHR, EDSON GARFIELD
B.JUNE 26,1920 ROUCEAU,SASK., CANADA

YR	CL	LEA	POS	GP	G	REC
1946	PIT	N	P	27	29	8- 6
1947	PIT	N	P	19	21	3- 5
	BRTR			46	50	11-11

BAHRET, FRANK J.

YR	CL	LEA	POS	GP	G	REC
1884	BAL	U	O		1	.000
	IND	AA	C-O		5	.071
					6	.056

BAICHLY, GROVER
B.JAN 7,1890 TOLEDO,ILL.
D.JUNE 30,1956

YR	CL	LEA	POS	GP	G	REC
1914	STL	A	P		4	0- 0
	BRTR					

BAILEY, ABRAHAM LINCOLN "SWEETBREADS"
B.FEB.12,1895 JOLIET,ILL.
D.SEPT.27,1939

YR	CL	LEA	POS	GP	G	REC
1919	CHI	N	P		21	3- 5
1920	CHI	N	P		21	1- 2
1921	CHI	N	P		3	0- 0
	BRO	N	P		7	0- 0
	BRTR				52	4- 7

BAILEY, ARTHUR EUGENE "GENE"
B.NOV.25,1893 PEARSALL,TEX.
D.NOV.14,1973 HOUSTON,TEX.

YR	CL	LEA	POS	GP	G	REC
1917	PHI	A	O		5	.083
1919	BOS	N	O		4	.333
1920	BOS	N	O		13	.083
	BOS	A	O		46	.230
1923	BRO	N	1-O		127	.265
1924	BRO	N	O		18	.239
	BRTR				213	.247

BAILEY, FRED MIDDLETON "PENNY"
B.AUG.16,1895 MT.HOPE,W.VA.
D.AUG.16,1972 HUNTINGTON,W.VA.

YR	CL	LEA	POS	GP	G	REC
1916	BOS	N	O		6	.100
1917	BOS	N	O		50	.191
1918	BOS	N	O		9	.250
	BLTL				65	.185

BAILEY, HARRY LOUIS
B.NOV.19,1884 SHAWNEE,OHIO
D.OCT.27,1967 SEATTLE,WASH.

YR	CL	LEA	POS	GP	G	REC
1911	NY	A	O		5	.111
	BLTR					

BAILEY, HARVEY FRANCIS
B.NOV.24,1876 ADRIAN,MICH.
D.JULY 11,1922

YR	CL	LEA	POS	GP	G	REC
1899	BOS	N	P		12	6- 4
1900	BOS	N	P		4	0- 1
	TL				16	6- 5

BAILEY, JAMES HOPKINS
B.DEC.16,1934 STRAWBERRY PLAINS,TENN.

YR	CL	LEA	POS	GP	G	REC
1959	CIN	N	P		3	0- 1
	BBTL					

BAILEY, LEMUEL "KING"
B.CINCINNATI,OHIO
D.JUNE 2,1952

YR	CL	LEA	POS	GP	G	REC
1895	CIN	N	P		1	1- 0
	BLTL					

BAILEY, LONAS EDGAR "ED"
B.APR.15,1931 STRAWBERRY PLAINS,TENN.

YR	CL	LEA	POS	GP	G	REC
1953	CIN	N	C		2	.375
1954	CIN	N	C		73	.197
1955	CIN	N	C		21	.205
1956	CIN	N	C		118	.300
1957	CIN	N	C		122	.261
1958	CIN	N	C		112	.250
1959	CIN	N	C		121	.264
1960	CIN	N	C		133	.261
1961	CIN	N	C		12	.302
	SF	N	C-O		107	.238
1962	SF	N	C		96	.232
1963	SF	N	C		105	.263
1964	MIL	N	C		95	.262
1965	SF	N	C-1		24	.107
	CHI	N	C-1		66	.253
1966	CAL	A	H		5	.000
	BLTR				1212	.256

BAILEY, ROBERT SHERWOOD "BOB"
B.OCT.13,1942 LONG BEACH,CAL.

YR	CL	LEA	POS	GP	G	REC
1962	PIT	N	3		14	.167
1963	PIT	N	S-3		154	.228
1964	PIT	N	S-3-O		143	.281
1965	PIT	N	3-O		159	.256
1966	PIT	N	3-O		126	.279
1967	LA	N	1-S-3-O		116	.227
1968	LA	N	S-3-O		105	.227
1969	MON	N	1-3-O		111	.265
1970	MON	N	1-3-O		131	.287
1971	MON	N	1-3-O		157	.251
1972	MON	N	1-3-O		143	.233
1973	MON	N	3-O		151	.273
1974	MON	N	3-O		152	.280
1975	MON	N	3-O		106	.273
1976	CIN	N	3-O		69	.298
	BRTR				1837	.258

BAILEY, STEVEN JOHN "STEVE"
B.FEB.12,1942 BRONX,N.Y.

YR	CL	LEA	POS	GP	G	REC
1967	CLE	A	P		32	2- 5
1968	CLE	A	P		2	0- 1
	BRTR				34	2- 6

BAILEY, WILLIAM F.
B.APR.12,1889 FT.SMITH,ARK.
D.NOV.2,1926

YR	CL	LEA	POS	GP	G	REC
1907	STL	A	P		6	4- 1
1908	STL	A	P		22	3- 5
1909	STL	A	P	31	38	9-11
1910	STL	A	P		34	3-18
1911	STL	A	P		5	0- 4
1912	STL	A	P		3	0- 0
1914	BAL	F	P		19	7- 9
1915	BAL	F	P		30	4-15
	CHI	F	P		11	6- 5
1918	DET	A	P		8	1- 2
1921	STL	N	P		19	2- 5
1922	STL	N	P		12	0- 2
	BLTL			200	207	39-77

BAILOR, ROBERT MICHAEL "BOB"
B.MAR.10,1951 CONNELLSVILLE,PA.

YR	CL	LEA	POS	GP	G	REC
1975	BAL	A	2-S		5	.143
1976	BAL	A	S		9	.333
	BRTR				14	.231

BAIN, HERBERT LOREN
B.JULY 4,1922 STAPLES,MINN.

YR	CL	LEA	POS	GP	G	REC
1945	NY	N	P		3	0- 0
	BRTR					

BAIR, CHARLES DOUGLAS "DOUG"
B.AUG.22,1949 DEFIANCE,OHIO

YR	CL	LEA	POS	GP	G	REC
1976	PIT	N	P		4	0- 0
	BRTR					

BAIRD, ALBERT WELLS
B.JUNE 2,1895 CLEBURNE,TEX.

YR	CL	LEA	POS	GP	G	REC
1917	NY	N	2		10	.292
1919	NY	N	2-S-3		38	.241
	BRTR				48	.251

BAIRD, HOWARD DOUGLASS "DOUG"
B.SEPT.27,1891 ST.CHARLES,MO.
D.JUNE 13,1967 THOMASVILLE,GA.

YR	CL	LEA	POS	GP	G	REC
1915	PIT	N	3-O		145	.219
1916	PIT	N	2-3-O		128	.216
1917	PIT	N	3		43	.259
	STL	N	3		104	.253
1918	STL	N	3		82	.247
1919	PHI	N	3		66	.260
	STL	N	2-3-O		16	.260
	BRO	N	3		20	.167
1920	BRO	N	H		6	.333
	NY	N	3		7	.125
	BRTR				617	.234

BAIRD, ROBERT ALLEN "BOB"
B.JAN.16,1940 KNOXVILLE,TENN.
D.APR.11,1974 CHATTANOOGA,TENN.

YR	CL	LEA	POS	GP	G	REC
1962	WAS	A	P		3	0- 1
1963	WAS	A	P		5	0- 3
	BLTL				8	0- 4

BAKELY, EDWARD ENOCH
B.APR.17,1864 BLACKWOOD,N.J.
D.FEB.17,1915

YR	CL	LEA	POS	GP	G	REC
1883	ATH	AA	P-O		9	5- 4
						.139
1884	KEY	U	P-1-	39	43	14-24
			O			.134
	WIL	U	P		2	0- 2
	KC	U	P-O	5	6	2- 2
						.167
1888	CLE	AA	P		60	25-33
1889	CLE	N	P		34	12-22
1890	CLE	P	P		44	13-26
1891	WAS	AA	P		12	2-10
	BAL	AA	P		13	4- 2
	BRTR			218	223	77-125
						.154

BAKENHASTER, DAVID LEE "DAVE"
B.MAR.5,1945 COLUMBUS,O.

YR	CL	LEA	POS	GP	G	REC
1964	STL	N	P		2	0- 0
	BRTR					

BAKER, ALBERT JONES
B.FEB.28,1906 BATESVILLE,MISS.

YR	CL	LEA	POS	GP	G	REC
1938	BOS	A	P		3	0- 0
	BRTR					

BAKER, CHARLES
B.HUDSON,MASS.

YR	CL	LEA	POS	GP	G	REC
1884	CHI	U	2-S-O		11	.167
	PIT	U	O		3	.083
					14	.148

BAKER, CHARLES "SMILING BOCK"
B.JULY 17,1878 TROY,N.Y.

YR	CL	LEA	POS	GP	G	REC
1901	CLE	A	P		1	0- 1
	PHI	A	P		1	0- 1
					2	0- 2

BAKER, DELMER DAVID
B.MAY 3,1892 SHERWOOD,ORE.
D.SEP.11,1973 SAN ANTONIO,TEX.

YR	CL	LEA	POS	GP	G	REC
1914	DET	A	C		43	.214
1915	DET	A	C		68	.246
1916	DET	A	C		61	.153
	BRTR				172	.209

NON-PLAYING MANAGER
DET(A) 1933,38-42

BAKER, ERNEST G.
B.AUG.8,1875 THREE RIVERS,MICH.
D.OCT.25,1945

YR	CL	LEA	POS	GP	G	REC
1905	CIN	N	P		1	0- 0

BAKER, EUGENE WALTER "GENE"
B.JUNE 15,1925 DAVENPORT,IOWA

YR	CL	LEA	POS	GP	G	REC
1953	CHI	N	2		7	.227
1954	CHI	N	2		135	.275
1955	CHI	N	2		154	.268
1956	CHI	N	2		140	.258
1957	CHI	N	2		12	.250
	PIT	N	2-S-3		111	.266
1958	PIT	N	2-S-3		29	.250
1960	PIT	N	2-3		33	.243
1961	PIT	N	3		9	.100
	BRTR				630	.265

```
YR   CL LEA POS  GP    G    REC        YR   CL LEA POS  GP    G    REC        YR   CL LEA POS  GP    G    REC

BAKER, FLOYD WILSON                    BAKER, JOHNNIE B. "DUSTY"              BALCENA, ROBERT RUDOLPH 'BOBBY'
B.OCT.10,1918 LURAY,VA.                B.JUNE 15,1949 RIVERSIDE,CAL.          B.AUG.1,1928 SAN PEDRO,CAL.
1943 STL A  S-3      22   .174         1968 ATL N  O        6   .400          1956 CIN N  O        7   .000
1944 STL A  2-S      44   .175         1969 ATL N  O        3   .000                    BRTL
1945 CHI A  2-3      82   .250         1970 ATL N  O       13   .292
1946 CHI A  3         9   .250         1971 ATL N  O       29   .226          BALDSCHUN, JACK EDWARD
1947 CHI A  2-3     105   .264         1972 ATL N  O      127   .321          B.OCT.16,1936 GREENVILLE,O.
1948 CHI A  2-S-3   104   .215         1973 ATL N  O      159   .288          1961 PHI N  P       65   5- 3
1949 CHI A  2-S-3   125   .260         1974 ATL N  O      149   .256          1962 PHI N  P       67  12- 7
1950 CHI A  2-3-O    83   .317         1975 ATL N  O      142   .261          1963 PHI N  P       65  11- 7
1951 CHI A  3        82   .263         1976 LA   N  O      112   .242          1964 PHI N  P       71   6- 9
1952 WAS A  2-S-3    79   .262                BRTR       740   .273           1965 PHI N  P       65   5- 8
1953 WAS A  3         9   .000                                                1966 CIN N  P       42   1- 5
     BOS A  2-3      81   .273         BAKER, KIRTLY                          1967 CIN N  P        9   0- 0
1954 BOS A  2-3      21   .200         B.JUNE 24,1869 AURORA,IND.             1969 SD  N  P       61   7- 2
     PHI N  2-3      23   .227         D.APR.15,1927                          1970 SD  N  P       12   1- 0
1955 PHI N  3         5   .000         1890 PIT N  P       23   2-19                  BRTR       457  48-41
     BLTR           874   .251         1893 BAL N  P       19   3-10
                                       1894 BAL N  P        2   0- 0          BALDWIN, CHARLES BUSTED 'LADY'
                                       1898 WAS N  P        6   1- 3          B.APR.8,1859 ORMEL,N.Y.
BAKER, FRANK                           1899 WAS N  P       12   1- 8          D.MAR.7,1937 HASTINGS,MICH.
B.JAN.11,1944 BARTOW,FLA.                                  62   7-40          1884 MIL U  P-O      2    7   1- 1
1969 CLE A  O        52   .256                                                                              .214
1971 CLE A  O        73   .210         BAKER, NEAL VERNON                     1885 DET N  P-O     20   31  11- 9
     BLTR           125   .232         B.APR.30,1904 LAPORTE,TEX.                                           .241
                                       1927 PHI A  P        5   0- 0          1886 DET N  P       56   57  42-13
                                              BRTR                            1887 DET N  P            24  13-10
BAKER, FRANK WATTS                                                            1890 BRO N  P             2   1- 0
B.OCT.29,1946 MERIDIAN,MISS.           BAKER, NORMAN LESLIE                        BUF N  P             7   2- 5
1970 NY  A  S        35   .231         B.OCT.14,1862 PHILADELPHIA,PA.              BLTL       117  134  73-41
1971 NY  A  S        43   .139         1883 PIT AA P-O      3    4   0- 2                                   .226
1973 BAL A  1-2-S-3  44   .190                                     .000
1974 BAL A  2-S-3    24   .172         1885 LOU AA P       25  13-12          BALDWIN, CLARENCE GEOGHAN 'KID'
     BLTR           146   .191         1890 BAL AA P        2   1- 1          B.NOV.1,1864 NEWPORT,KY.
                                                      30   31  14-15          D.JULY 12,1897
                                                                  .143        1884 KC  U  C-2-3-O   49   .202
BAKER, GEORGE F.                                                                   CHI U  C          1  1.000
B.1859 ST.LOUIS,MO.                    BAKER, PHILIP                          1885 CIN AA P-C-     3   26   0- 0
1883 BAL AA C-S      6   .227          B.SEPT.19,1856 PHILADELPHIA,PA.                2-3-O              .147
1884 STL U  C       64   .171          D.JUNE 4,1940                          1886 CIN AA C-O     86   .238
1885 STL N  C-2-3-O  39   .122         1883 BAL AA C-S-O    27   .280          1887 CIN AA C-O     96   .262
1886 KC  N  C        1   .250          1884 WAS U  C-1      83   .282          1888 CIN AA C-1-O   66   .220
                   110   .159          1886 WAS N  1-O      81   .221          1889 CIN AA C-1-3-O 60   .248
                                                          191   .257          1890 CIN N  C        21   .153
                                                                                   ATH AA C        24   .239
BAKER, HOWARD FRANCIS                  BAKER, THOMAS CALVIN                          BRTR       2  429   0- 0
B.MAR.1,1888 BRIDGEPORT,CONN.          "RATTLESNAKE"                                                       .227
D.JAN.16,1964 BRIDGEPORT,CONN.         B.JUNE 11,1913 NURSERY,TEX.
1912 CLE A  3        11   .167         1935 BRO N  P       11   1- 0          BALDWIN, DAVID GEORGE "DAVE"
1914 CHI A  3        15   .277         1936 BRO N  P       37   1- 8          B.MAR.30,1938 TUCSON,ARIZ.
1915 CHI A  H         2   .000         1937 BRO N  P        7   0- 1          1966 WAS A  P        4   0- 0
     NY  N  3         1   .000              NY  N  P       13   1- 0          1967 WAS A  P       58   2- 4
     BRTR            29   .220         1938 NY  N  P        2   0- 0          1968 WAS A  P       40   0- 2
                                              BRTR        70   3- 9          1969 WAS A  P       43   2- 4
                                                                             1970 MIL A  P       28   2- 1
BAKER, JACK EDWARD                     BAKER, THOMAS HENRY "TOM"              1973 CHI A  P        3   0- 0
B.MAY 4,1950 BIRMINGHAM,ALA.           B.MAY 6,1934 PORT TOWNSEND,WASH.             BRTR       176   6-11
1976 BOS A  1       12   .130          1963 CHI N  P       10   0- 1
     BRTR                                     BLTL                            BALDWIN, FRANK DEWITT
                                                                             B.DEC.25,1928 CALIFON,N.J.
                                       BAKER, TRACY LEE                       1953 CIN N  C        16   .100
BAKER, JESSE                           B.1891 PENDLETON,ORE                         BRTR
(REAL NAME MICHAEL SILVERMAN)          D.MAR.14,1975 PLACERVILLE,CAL.
B.1896                                 1911 BOS A  1        1   .000          BALDWIN, HENRY CLAY
1919 WAS A  S        1   .000                 BRTR                            B.JUNE 13,1894 PHILADELPHIA,PA.
                                                                             D.FEB.24,1964 PHILADELPHIA,PA.
                                       BAKER, WILLIAM PRESLEY                 1927 PHI N  S-3      6   .313
BAKER, JESSE ORMOND                    B.FEB.22,1911 PAW CREEK,N.C.                  BRTR
B.JUNE 3,1888 ANDERSON ISLAND,         1940 CIN N  C       27   .217
WASH.                                  1941 CIN N  C        2   .000          BALDWIN, HOWARD EDWARD 'HARRY'
D.SEPT.26,1972 TACOMA,WASH.                 PIT N  C       35   .224          B.JUNE 3,1900 BALTIMORE,MD.
1911 CHI A  P       22   2- 7          1942 PIT N  C       18   .118          D.JAN.23,1958 BALTIMORE,MD.
     BLTL                              1943 PIT N  C       63   .273          1924 NY  N  P       10   3- 1
                                       1946 PIT N  C-1     53   .239          1925 NY  N  P        1   0- 0
                                       1948 STL N  C       45   .294                BRTR        11   12   3- 1
BAKER, JOHN FRANKLIN                   1949 STL N  C       20   .133
"FRANK" OR "HOME RUN"                         BRTR       263   .253
B.MAR.13,1886 TRAPPE,MD.                                                      BALDWIN, MARCUS ELMORE 'FIDO'
D.JUNE 28,1963 TRAPPE,MD.              BALAS, MITCHELL FRANCIS 'MIKE'         B.OCT.29,1863 PITTSBURGH,PA.
1908 PHI A  3        9   .290          (REAL NAME                             D.NOV.10,1929
1909 PHI A  3      148   .305          MITCHELL FRANCIS BALASKI)              1887 CHI N  P       38   40  19-17
1910 PHI A  3      146   .283          B.MAY 17,1910 LOWELL,MASS.             1888 CHI N  P       28   30  13-15
1911 PHI A  3      148   .334          1938 BOS N  P        1   0- 0          1889 COL AA P       63   64  26-34
1912 PHI A  3      149   .347                 BRTR                            1890 CHI P  P            58  32-21
1913 PHI A  3      149   .336                                                 1891 PIT N  P            54  20-28
1914 PHI A  3      150   .319          BALASKI, MITCHELL FRANCIS              1892 PIT N  P            57  25-27
1916 NY  A  3      100   .269          (PLAYED UNDER NAME OF                  1893 PIT N  P             5   1- 1
1917 NY  A  3      146   .282          MITCHELL FRANCIS BALAS)                     NY  N  P            35  12-19
1918 NY  A  3      126   .306                                                      BRTR       338  343 148-162
1919 NY  A  3      141   .293          BALAZ, JOHN LAWRENCE
1921 NY  A  3       94   .294          B.NOV.24,1950 TORONTO,ONT.,CAN.
1922 NY  A  3       69   .277          1974 CAL A  O       14   .238          BALDWIN, O. F.
     BLTR         1575   .307          1975 CAL A  O-D     45   .242          B.YOUNGSTOWN,OHIO
                                              BRTR        59   .241          1908 STL N  P        4   1- 3
```

YR	CL	LEA	POS	GP	G	REC

BALDWIN, RICKEY ALAN "RICK"
B.JUNE 1,1953 FRESNO,CAL.

YR	CL	LEA	POS	GP	G	REC
1975	NY	N	P		54	3- 5
1976	NY	N	P		11	0- 0
	BLTR				65	3- 5

BALDWIN, ROBERT HARVEY "BILL"
B.JUNE 9,1951 TAZEWELL,VA.

1975	DET	A	O		30	.221
1976	NY	N	O		9	.273
	BLTL				39	.231

BALENTI, MICHAEL RICHARD "CALUMET"
B.JULY 3,1886 ALTUS,OKLA.
D.AUG.4,1955

1911	CIN	N	S		7	.250
1913	STL	A	S		70	.181
	BRTR				77	.183

BALES, WESLEY OWEN "LEE"
B.DEC.4,1944 LOS ANGELES,CAL.

1966	ATL	N	2-3		12	.063
1967	HOU	N	2-S		19	.111
	BBTR				31	.093

BALL, ARTHUR
B.1874 CHICAGO,ILL.
D.DEC.26,1915

1894	STL	N	2		1	.333
1898	BAL	N	3		25	.175
	TR				26	.181

BALL, CORNELIUS 'NEAL'
B.APR.22,1881 GRANDHAVEN,MICH.
D.OCT.15,1957

1907	NY	A	S		15	.205
1908	NY	A	S		132	.247
1909	NY	A	S		8	.214
	CLE	A	S		96	.255
1910	CLE	A	S		53	.210
1911	CLE	A	2-3		116	.296
1912	CLE	A	2		38	.233
	BOS	A	2		17	.182
1913	BOS	A	2		21	.172
	BRTR				496	.251

BALL, JAMES CHANDLER
B.1885 HARFORD,COUNTY,MD.

1907	BOS	N	C		11	.150
1908	BOS	N	C		6	.133
	TR				17	.145

BALLENGER, PELHAM ASHBY
B.FEB.6,1894 GILREATH MILL,S.C.
D.DEC.8,1948 W.GANTT TOWNSHIP, S.C.

| 1928 | WAS | A | 2-3 | | 3 | .111 |
| | BRTR | | | | | |

BALLINGER, MARK ALAN
B.JAN.31,1949 GLENDALE,CAL.

| 1971 | CLE | A | P | | 18 | 1- 2 |
| | BRTR | | | | | |

BALLOU, NOBLE WINFRED "WIN"
B.NOV.30,1897 WILLIAMSBURG,KY.
D.JAN.30,1963 SAN FRANCISCO,CAL

1925	WAS	A	P		10	1- 1
1926	STL	A	P		43	10-10
1927	STL	A	P		21	5- 6
1929	BRO	N	P		25	2- 3
	BRTL				99	18-20

BALSAMO, ANTHONY FRED
B.NOV.21,1937 BROOKLYN,N.Y.

| 1962 | CHI | N | P | | 18 | 0- 1 |
| | BRTR | | | | | |

BAMBERGER, GEORGE IRVIN
B.AUG.1,1925 STATEN ISLAND,N.Y.

1951	NY	N	P		2	0- 0
1952	NY	N	P	5	6	0- 0
1959	BAL	A	P		3	0- 0
	BRTR			10	11	0- 0

BAMBERGER, HAROLD EARL "DUTCH"
B.OCT.29,1924 LEBANON,PA.

| 1948 | NY | N | P | | 7 | .083 |
| | BLTR | | | | | |

BANCROFT, DAVID JAMES "BEAUTY"
B.APR.20,1892 SIOUX CITY,IOWA
D.OCT.9,1972 SUPERIOR,WIS.

1915	PHI	N	S		153	.254
1916	PHI	N	S		142	.212
1917	PHI	N	S		127	.243
1918	PHI	N	S		125	.265
1919	PHI	N	S		92	.272
1920	PHI	N	S		42	.276
	NY	N	S		108	.308
1921	NY	N	S		153	.319
1922	NY	N	S		156	.321
1923	NY	N	2-S		107	.304
1924	BOS	N	M-S		79	.279
1925	BOS	N	M-S		128	.319
1926	BOS	N	M-S		127	.311
1927	BOS	N	M-S		111	.243
1928	BRO	N	S		149	.247
1929	BRO	N	S		104	.277
1930	NY	N	S		10	.059
	BBTR				1913	.279

BANCROFT, FRANK CARTER
B.MAY 9,1846 LANCASTER,MASS.
D.MAR.31,1921
NON-PLAYING MANAGER
WOR(N) 1880, DET(N) 1881-82,
CLE(N) 1883, PRO(N) 1884-85,
ATH(AA) 1887, IND(N) 1889
AND CIN(N) 1902.

BANDO, SALVATORE LEONARD "SAL"
B.FEB.13,1944.CLEVELAND,O.

1966	KC	A	3		11	.292
1967	KC	A	3		47	.192
1968	OAK	A	3-0		162	.251
1969	OAK	A	3		162	.281
1970	OAK	A	3		155	.263
1971	OAK	A	3		153	.271
1972	OAK	A	2-3		152	.236
1973	OAK	A	3		162	.286
1974	OAK	A	3		146	.243
1975	OAK	A	3		160	.230
1976	OAK	A	S-3		158	.240
	BRTR				1468	.255

BANE, EDWARD NORMAN "EDDIE"
B.MAR.22,1952 CHICAGO,ILL.

1973	MIN	A	P		23	0- 5
1975	MIN	A	P		4	3- 1
1976	MIN	A	P	17	18	4- 7
	BRTL			44	45	7-13

BANEY, RICHARD LEE "DICK"
B.NOV.1,1946 FULLERTON,CAL.

1969	SEA	A	P		9	1- 0
1973	CIN	N	P		11	2- 1
1974	CIN	N	P		22	1- 0
	BRTR				42	4- 1

BANKHEAD, DANIEL ROBERT "DAN"
B.MAY 3,1921 EMPIRE,ALA.
D.MAY 2,1976 HOUSTON,TEX.

1947	BRO	N	P		4	0- 0
1950	BRO	N	P		41	9- 4
1951	BRO	N	P	7	15	0- 1
	BRTR			52	62	9- 5

BANKS, ERNEST "ERNIE"
B.JAN.31,1931 DALLAS,TEX.

1953	CHI	N	S		10	.314
1954	CHI	N	S		154	.275
1955	CHI	N	S		154	.295
1956	CHI	N	S		139	.297
1957	CHI	N	S-3		156	.285
1958	CHI	N	S		154	.313
1959	CHI	N	S		155	.304
1960	CHI	N	S		156	.271
1961	CHI	N	1-S-0		138	.278
1962	CHI	N	1-3		154	.269
1963	CHI	N	1		130	.227
1964	CHI	N	1		157	.264
1965	CHI	N	1		163	.265
1966	CHI	N	1-3		141	.272
1967	CHI	N	1		151	.276
1968	CHI	N	1		150	.246
1969	CHI	N	1		155	.253
1970	CHI	N	1		72	.252
1971	CHI	N	1		39	.193
	BRTR				2528	.274

BANKS, GEORGE EDWARD
B.SEP.24,1938 PACOLET MILLS,S.C.

1962	MIN	A	3-0		63	.252
1963	MIN	A	3		25	.155
1964	MIN	A	H		1	.000
	CLE	A	2-3-0		9	.294
1965	CLE	A	3		4	.200
1966	CLE	A	H		4	.250
	BRTR				106	.219

BANKS, WILLIAM J.
(REAL NAME WILLIAM J. YERRICK)
B.FEB.26,1873 DANVILLE,PA.
D.SEPT.8,1936 DANVILLE,PA.

1895	BOS	N	P		1	1- 0
1896	BOS	N	P		4	0- 3
					5	1- 3

BANKSTON, WILBORN EVERETT
B.MAY 25,1893 BARNESVILLE,GA.

| 1915 | PHI | A | O | | 11 | .142 |
| | BLTR | | | | | |

BANNING, JAMES M.
B.ST.PAUL,MINN.

1888	WAS	N	C		1	.000
1889	WAS	N	C		2	.000
	BLTR				3	.000

BANNISTER, ALAN
B.SEPT.3,1951 MONTEBELLO,CAL.

1974	PHI	N	S-O		26	.120
1975	PHI	N	2-S-O		24	.262
1976	CHI	A	2-S-3-O		73	.248
	BRTR				123	.238

BANNOCK

1871	CHI	NA	3		3	-
1875	CHI	NA	3		2	.000
					5	-

BANNON, JAMES HENRY "FOXY"
B.MAY 5,1871 AMESBURY,MASS.
D.MAR.24,1948

1893	STL	N	P-O	2	23	0- 1
						.363
1894	BOS	N	O		127	.336
1895	BOS	N	O		121	.339
1896	BOS	N	O		87	.256
	BR			2	358	0- 1
						.320

BANNON, THOMAS EDWARD "WARD SIX"
B.MAY 8,1869 AMESBURY,MASS.
D.JAN.26,1950

1895	NY	N	1-0		37	.266
1896	NY	N	O		2	.143
					39	.267

BANTA, JOHN KAY "JACK"
B.JUNE 24,1925 HUDSON,KAN.

1947	BRO	N	P		3	0- 1
1948	BRO	N	P		2	0- 1
1949	BRO	N	P		48	10- 6
1950	BRO	N	P		16	4- 4
	BLTR				69	14-12

BAPTIST, ALFREDO CLAUDINO (GRIFFIN)
(SEE ALFREDO CLAUDINO GRIFFIN)

BARBARE, WALTER LAWRENCE "DINTY"
B.AUG.11,1891 GREENVILLE,S.C.
D.OCT.28,1965 GREENVILLE,S.C.

1914	CLE	A	S		15	.308
1915	CLE	A	3		77	.191
1916	CLE	A	3		13	.229
1918	BOS	A	3		13	.172
1919	PIT	N	2-3		85	.273
1920	PIT	N	S		57	.274
1921	BOS	N	S		134	.302
1922	BOS	N	1-2-3		106	.231
	BRTR				500	.260

BARBARY, DONALD ODELL "RED"
B.JUNE 20,1920 SIMPSONVILLE,S.C

| 1943 | WAS | A | H | | 1 | .000 |
| | BRTR | | | | | |

```
YR   CL LEA POS  GP    G    REC        YR    CL LEA POS. GP    G    REC        YR    CL LEA POS  GP     G    REC

BARBEAU, WILLIAM JOSEPH "JAP"          BARE, RAYMOND DOUGLAS "RAY"            BARNABE, CHARLES EDWARD
B.JUNE 10,1882 NEW YORK,N.Y.           B.APR.15,1949 MIAMI,FLA.              B.JUNE 12,1900 RUSSELL GULCH,
D.SEPT.10,1969 MILWAUKEE,WIS.          1972 STL N P         14   0- 1        COLO.
1905 CLE A 3         12  .237          1974 STL N P         10   1- 2        1927 CHI A P   17   18   0- 5
1906 CLE A 3         42  .194          1975 DET A P         29   8-13        1928 CHI A P    7   11   0- 2
1909 PIT N 3         85  .220          1976 DET A P         30   7- 8              BLTL      24   29   0- 7
      STL N 3        44  .251               BRTR          83  16-24
1910 STL N 2-3-0  7      .227                                                BARNES, EMILE DEERING "RED"
      BRTR         190   .224          BARFOOT, CLYDE RAYMOND "FOOTS"        B.DEC.25,1904 SUGGSVILLE,ALA.
                                       B.JULY 8,1891 RICHMOND,VA.           D.JULY 3,1959
BARBEE, DAVID MONROE                   D.MAR.11,1971 HIGHLAND PARK,CAL      1927 WAS A O         3   .364
B.MAY 7,1905 GREENSBORO,N.C.           1922 STL N P         42   4- 5        1928 WAS A O       114   .305
D.JULY 1,1968 ALBERMARLE,N.C.          1923 STL N P   33    37   3- 3        1929 WAS A O        72   .200
1926 PHI A O         19  .173          1926 DET A P         11   1- 2        1930 WAS A O        12   .167
1932 PIT N O         97  .257               BRTR      86    90   8-10              CHI A O        85   .248
      BRTR         116  .246                                                      BLTR         286   .269
                                       BARGER, EROS BOLLIVAR "CY"
BARBER, CHARLES D.                     B.MAY 18,1885 JAMESTOWN,KY.          BARNES, EVERETT DUANE "EPPIE"
B.1854 MARTINSBURG,PA.                 D.SEPT.23,1964 COLUMBIA,KY.          B.DEC.1,1900 OSSINING,N.Y.
D.NOV.23,1910                          1906 NY  A P          2   0- 0        1923 PIT N 1         2   .500
1884 CIN U 2         48  .190          1907 NY  A P          1   0- 0        1924 PIT N 1         2   .000
                                       1910 BRO N P         35  15-15              BLTL           4   .143
                                       1911 BRO N P   30    42  11-15
BARBER, STEPHEN DAVID "STEVE"          1912 BRO N P   16    17   1- 9        BARNES, FRANK
B.FEB.22,1939 TAKOMA PARK,MD.          1914 PIT F P         33  10-16        B.AUG.26,1928 GREENVILLE,MISS.
1960 BAL A P   36   10- 7              1915 PIT F P         34   9- 8        1957 STL N P    3    4   0- 1
1961 BAL A P   37   18-12                    BLTR     151   164  46-63       1958 STL N P    8   13   1- 1
1962 BAL A P   28    9- 6                                                    1960 STL N P         4   0- 1
1963 BAL A P   39   20-13              BARKER, ALFRED                              BRTR      15   21   1- 3
1964 BAL A P   36    9-13              B.JAN.18,1839 ROCKFO-D,ILL.
1965 BAL A P   37   15-10              D.SEPT.15,1912                        BARNES, FRANK SAMUEL "LEFTY"
1966 BAL A P   25   10- 5              1871 ROK NA O         1    -          B.JAN.9,1901 DALLAS,TEX.
1967 BAL A P   15    4- 9                                                    D.SEPT.27,1967
      NY  A P   17    6- 9             BARKER, LEONARD HAROLD "LEN"          1929 DET A P         4   0- 1
1968 NY  A P   20    6- 5              B.JULY 7,1955 FORT KNOX,KY.          1930 NY  A P         3   0- 1
1969 SEA A P   25    4- 7              1976 TEX A P          2   1- 0              BLTL           7   0- 2
1970 CHI N P    5    0- 1                    BRTR
      ATL N P    5    0- 1                                                   BARNES, JESSE LAWRENCE
1971 ATL N P   39    3- 1              BARKER, RAYMOND HERRELL "RAY"         "JESS" OR "NUBBY"
1972 ATL N P    5    0- 0              B.MAR.12,1936 MARTINSBURG,W.VA.      B.AUG.26,1892 GUTHRIE,OKLA.
      CAL A P   34    4- 4             1960 BAL A O          5   .000        D.SEPT.9,1961
1973 CAL A P   50    3- 2              1965 CLE A 1         11   .000        1915 BOS N P         9   3- 0
1974 SF  N P   13    0- 1                    NY  A 1-3      98   .254        1916 BOS N P        33   6-14
      BLTL      466 121-106            1966 NY  A 1         61   .187        1917 BOS N P   50   53  13-21
                                       1967 NY  A 1         17   .077        1918 NY  N P         9   6- 1
BARBER, STEVEN LEE "STEVE"                   BLTR          192   .214        1919 NY  N P   38   46  25- 9
B.MAR.13,1948 GRAND RAPIDS,MICH.                                            1920 NY  N P   43   45  20-15
1970 MIN A P   18   19   0- 0          BARKLEY, JOHN DUNCAN "RED"           1921 NY  N P        42  15- 9
1971 MIN A P    4    6   1- 0          B.SEPT.19,1914 CHILDRESS,TEX.        1922 NY  N P        37  13- 8
      BRTR      22   25   1- 0         1937 STL A 2         31   .267        1923 NY  N P        12   3- 1
                                       1939 BOS N S-3       12   .000              BOS N P        31  10-14
BARBER, TYRUS TURNER "TURNER"          1943 BRO N S         20   .314        1924 BOS N P        37  15-20
B.JULY 9,1894 ST.LOUIS,MO.                   BRTR           63   .264        1925 BOS N P        32  11-16
D.OCT.20,1968 MILAN,TENN.                                                   1926 BRO N P        31  10-11
1915 WAS A O         20  .302          BARKLEY, SAMUEL WILSON               1927 BRO N P        18   2-10
1916 WA3 A U         15  .212          B.MAY 19,1859 WHEEELING,W.VA.              BLTR     422  435 152-149
1917 CHI N O          7  .214          D.APR.20,1912
1918 CHI N 1-O       55  .236          1884 TOL AA 2       104   .300        BARNES, JOHN FRANCIS "HONEY"
1919 CHI N O         76  .313          1885 STL AA 1-2      96   .179        B.JAN.31,1900 FULTON,N.Y.
1920 CHI N 1-O       94  .265          1886 PIT AA 2       122   .269        1926 NY  A C         1   .000
1921 CHI N O        127  .314          1887 PIT N 1-2       90   .286              BLTR
1922 CHI N 1-O       84  .309          1888 KC  AA M-2     116   .220
1923 BRO N O         13  .217          1889 KC  AA 2        45   .277        BARNES, JUNIE SHOAF "LEFTY"
      BLTR         491  .289                 TR           573   .279        B.DEC.1,1911 LINWOOD,N.C.
                                                                            D.DEC.31,1963 JACKSONVILLE,N.C.
BARBERICH, FRANK                       BARLOW, MICHAEL ROSWELL "MIKE"       1934 CIN N P         2   0- 0
B.FEB.3,1882 ASTORIA,N.Y.              B.APR.30,1948 STAMFORD,N.Y.                BLTL
D.MAY 1,1965 OCALA,FLA.                1975 STL N P          9   0- 0
1907 BOS N P    2    1- 0              1976 HOU N P         16   2- 2        BARNES, LUTHER OWENS "LUTE"
1910 BOS A P    2    0- 0                    BLTR           25   2- 2        B.APR.28,1947 FOREST CITY,IOWA
      BBTR       4    1- 0                                                   1972 NY  N 2-S      24   .236
                                       BARLOW, THOMAS H.                     1973 NY  N H         3   .500
BARBIERI, JAMES PATRICK "JIM"          1872 ATL NA C-S      35   .276              BRTR          27   .243
B.SEP.15,1941 SCHENECTADY,N.Y.         1873 ATL NA C        23    -
1966 LA  N O         39  .280                MUT NA C        1    -          BARNES, ROBERT AVERY "LEFTY"
      BLTR                                   ATL NA C       31    -          B.JAN.6,1902 WASHBURN,ILL.
                                       1874 HAR NA S        32    -          1924 CHI A P         2   0- 0
BARCLAY, CURTIS CORDELL "CURT"         1875 NH  NA S         1    -                BLTL
B.AUG.22,1931 CHICAGO,ILL.                   ATL NA 2        1   .000
1957 NY  N P   37    9- 9                                   124    -         BARNES, ROSCOE CONKLING "ROSS"
1958 SF  N P    6    1- 0                                                    B.MAY 8,1850 MT.MORRIS,N.Y.
1959 SF  N P    1    0- 0              BARMES, BRUCE RAYMOND "SQUEAKY"      D.FEB.8,1915
      BRTR       44  10- 9             B.OCT.23,1929 VINCENNES,IND.         1871 BOS NA 2-S     33   .374
                                       1953 WAS A O          5   .200        1872 BOS NA 2       45   .404
                                             BLTR                           1873 BOS NA 2-3     60   .406
BARCLAY, GEORGE OLIVER                                                      1874 BOS NA 2       52   .353
"DEERFOOT"                             BARNA, HERBERT PAUL "BABE"           1875 BOS NA 2-O     78   .372
B.MAY 16,1876 MILLVILLE,PA.            B.MAR.2,1915 CLARKSBURG,W.VA.        1876 CHI N 2        66   .404
D.APR.3,1909                           D.MAY 18,1972 CHARLESTON,W.VA.       1877 CHI N 2        22   .272
1902 STL N O        137  .301          1937 PHI A H         14   .389        1879 CIN N 2-S      76   .256
1903 STL N U        107  .248          1938 PHI A O          9   .133        1881 BOS N 2-S      69   .271
1904 STL N O        103  .200          1941 NY  N O         10   .214              BRTR         501   .350
      BOS N O        24  .226          1942 NY  N O        104   .257
1905 BOS N O         28  .176          1943 NY  N O         40   .204        BARNES, SAMUEL THOMAS
                    399  .249                BOS A O         30   .170        B.DEC.18,1899 JACKSON,ALA.
                                             BLTR          207   .232        1921 DET A 2         7   .182
                                                                                  BLTL
```

YR	CL	LEA	POS	GP	G	REC

BARNES, VIRGIL JENNINGS "ZEKE"
B.MAR.5,1897 CIRCLEVILLE,KAN.
D.JULY 24,1958

YR	CL	LEA	POS	GP	G	REC
1919	NY	N	P		1	0-0
1920	NY	N	P		1	0-1
1922	NY	N	P		22	1-0
1923	NY	N	P		22	2-3
1924	NY	N	P		35	16-10
1925	NY	N	P		32	15-11
1926	NY	N	P		31	8-13
1927	NY	N	P		35	14-11
1928	NY	N	P		10	3-3
	BOS	N	P		16	2-7
	BRTR				205	61-59

BARNES, WILLIAM H.
B.INDIANAPOLIS,IND.
1884 STP U O 8 .161

BARNEY, EDMOND
B.JAN.23,1890 AMERY,WIS.
D.OCT.4,1967 RICE LAKE,WIS.

YR	CL	LEA	POS	GP	G	REC
1915	NY	A	O		11	.191
	PIT	N	O		32	.273
1916	PIT	N	O		45	.197
	BLTR				88	.224

BARNEY, REX EDWARD
B.DEC.19,1924 OMAHA,NEB.

YR	CL	LEA	POS	GP	G	REC
1943	BRO	N	P		9	2-2
1946	BRO	N	P		16	2-5
1947	BRO	N	P		28	5-2
1948	BRO	N	P		44	15-13
1949	BRO	N	P		38	9-8
1950	BRO	N	P		20	2-1
	BRTR				155	35-31

BARNHART, CLYDE LEE "POOCH"
B.DEC.29,1895 BUCK VALLEY,PA.

YR	CL	LEA	POS	GP	G	REC
1920	PIT	N	3		12	.326
1921	PIT	N	3		124	.258
1922	PIT	N	3-O		75	.330
1923	PIT	N	O		114	.324
1924	PIT	N	O		102	.276
1925	PIT	N	O		142	.325
1926	PIT	N	O		76	.192
1927	PIT	N	O		108	.319
1928	PIT	N	O		61	.296
	BRTR				814	.295

BARNHART, EDGAR VERNON "BARNEY"
B.SEPT.16,1904 COLUMBIA,MO.
1924 STL A P 1 0-0
BLTR

BARNHART, LESLIE EARL "BARNEY"
B.FEB.23,1905 HOXIE,KAN.
D.OCT.7,1971 SCOTTSDALE,ARIZ.

YR	CL	LEA	POS	GP	G	REC
1928	CLE	A	P		2	0-1
1930	CLE	A	P		1	1-0
	BRTR				3	1-1

BARNHART, VICTOR DEE
B.SEPT.1,1922 HAGERSTOWN,MD.

YR	CL	LEA	POS	GP	G	REC
1944	PIT	N	S		1	.500
1945	PIT	N	S-3		71	.269
1946	PIT	N	H		2	.000
	BRTR				74	.270

BARNICLE, GEORGE BERNARD "BARNEY"
B.AUG.26,1917 FITCHBURG,MASS.

YR	CL	LEA	POS	GP	G	REC
1939	BOS	N	P		6	2-2
1940	BOS	N	P		13	1-0
1941	BOS	N	P		1	0-1
	BRTR				20	3-3

BARNIE, WILLIAM S.
B.JAN.26,1853 NEW YORK,N.Y.
D.JULY 15,1900

YR	CL	LEA	POS	GP	G	REC
1874	HAR	NA	C-S-O		44	-
1875	WES	NA	C-O		10	-
	MUT	NA	C-O		10	-
1883	BAL	AA	M-C-S-O		17	.200
					81	-

NON-PLAYING MANAGER
BAL(AA) 1884-91, ATH(AA) 1891,
WAS(N) 1892, LOU(N) 1893-94
AND BRO(N) 1897-98.

BARNOWSKI, EDWARD ANTHONY "ED"
B.AUG.23,1943 SCRANTON,PA.

YR	CL	LEA	POS	GP	G	REC
1965	BAL	I	P	4	0	0
1966	BAL	A	P	2	0-1	
	BRTR			6	0-0	

BARONE, RICHARD ANTHONY "DICK"
B.OCT.13,1962 SAN JOSE,CAL.
1960 PIT N S 3 .000
BRTR

BARR, HYDER EDWARD "SCOTTY"
B.OCT.6,1886 BRISTOL,TENN.
D.DEC.2,1934 FT.WORTH,TEX.

YR	CL	LEA	POS	GP	G	REC
1908	PHI	A	2		19	.143
1909	PHI	A	O		22	.079
	BRTR				41	.112

BARR, JAMES LELAND "JIM"
B.FEB.10,1948 LYNWOOD,CAL.

YR	CL	LEA	POS	GP	G	REC
1971	SF	N	P		17	1-1
1972	SF	N	P		44	8-10
1973	SF	N	P		41	11-17
1974	SF	N	P	44	56	13-9
1975	SF	N	P	35	38	13-14
1976	SF	N	P	37	41	15-12
	BRTR			218	237	61-63

BARR, ROBERT ALEXANDER
B.MAR.12,1909 NEWTON,MASS.
1935 BRO N P 2 0-0
BRTR

BARR, ROBERT MC CLELLAND
B.1856 WASHINGTON,D.C.
D.MAR.11,1930

YR	CL	LEA	POS	GP	G	REC
1883	PIT	AA	P-1-O	28		6-18
						.230
1884	WAS	AA	P-1-O	39		9-24
						.152
	IND	AA	P-O	18		3-11
						.188
1886	WAS	N	P	22		4-18
1890	ROC	AA	P	57		28-25
1891	NY	N	P	5		0-3
					169	50-99
						.204

BARR, STEVEN CHARLES "STEVE"
B.SEPT.8,1951 ST.LOUIS,MO.

YR	CL	LEA	POS	GP	G	REC
1974	BOS	A	P	1		1-0
1975	BOS	A	P	3		0-1
1976	TEX	A	P	20		2-6
	BLTL			24		3-7

BARRAGAN, FACUNDO ANTHONY "CUNO"
B.JUNE 20,1932 SACRAMENTO,CAL.

YR	CL	LEA	POS	GP	G	REC
1961	CHI	N	C		10	.214
1962	CHI	N	C		58	.201
1963	CHI	N	C		1	.000
	BRTR				69	.202

BARRETT, CHARLES HENRY "RED"
B.FEB.14,1915 SANTA BARBARA,CAL.

YR	CL	LEA	POS	GP	G	REC
1937	CIN	N	P		1	0-0
1938	CIN	N	P		6	2-0
1939	CIN	N	P		2	0-0
1940	CIN	N	P		3	1-0
1943	BOS	N	P		38	12-18
1944	BOS	N	P		42	9-16
1945	BOS	N	P		9	2-3
	STL	N	P		36	21-9
1946	STL	N	P		23	3-2
1947	BOS	N	P		36	11-12
1948	BOS	N	P		34	7-8
1949	BOS	N	P		23	1-1
	BRTR				253	69-69

BARRETT, FRANCIS JOSEPH
B.JULY 1,1913 FT.LAUDERDALE,FLA

YR	CL	LEA	POS	GP	G	REC
1939	STL	N	P		1	0-1
1944	BOS	A	P		38	8-7
1945	BOS	A	P		37	4-3
1946	BOS	N	P		23	2-4
1950	PIT	N	P		5	1-2
	BRTR				104	15-17

BARRETT, JAMES ERIGENA
B.MAR.28,1875 ATHOL,MASS.
D.OCT.24,1921

YR	CL	LEA	POS	GP	G	REC
1899	CIN	N	O		26	.374
1900	CIN	N	O		138	.316
1901	DET	A	O		136	.294
1902	DET	A	O		136	.304
1903	DET	A	O		136	.315
1904	DET	A	O		162	.264
1905	DET	A	O		18	.254
1906	CIN	N	O		5	.000
1907	BOS	A	O		106	.243
1908	BOS	A	O		3	.125
	BLTR				866	.291

BARRETT, JOHN JOSEPH "JACK"
B.DEC.18,1915 LOWELL,MASS.
D.AUG.17,1974 SEABROOK BEACH, N.H.

YR	CL	LEA	POS	GP	G	REC
1942	PIT	N	O		111	.247
1943	PIT	N	O		130	.231
1944	PIT	N	O		149	.269
1945	PIT	N	O		142	.256
1946	PIT	N	O		32	.169
	BOS	N	O		24	.233
	BLTL				588	.251

BARRETT, MARTIN
B.CENTRAL FALLS,R.I.
1884 BOS N C 3 .000

BARRETT, RICHARD OLIVER
(SEE TRACY SOUTER BARRETT)

BARRETT, ROBERT SCHLEY "JUMBO"
B.JAN.27,1901 ATLANTA,GA.

YR	CL	LEA	POS	GP	G	REC
1923	CHI	N	H		3	.333
1924	CHI	N	1-2-3		54	.241
1925	CHI	N	2-3		14	.313
	BRO	N	H		1	.000
1927	BRO	N	3		99	.259
1929	BOS	N	3		68	.270
	BRTR				239	.260

BARRETT, TRACY SOUTER "KEWPIE"
(ALSO PLAYED UNDER NAMES OF
RICHARD OLIVER, 1933 AND
RICHARD OLIVER BARRETT 1934-43.
B.SEPT.28,1906 MONTOURSVILLE,PA
D.NOV.7,1966 SEATTLE,WASH.

YR	CL	LEA	POS	GP	G	REC
1933	PHI	A	P		15	4-4
1934	BOS	N	P		15	1-3
1943	CHI	N	P		15	0-4
	PHI	N	P		23	10-9
1944	PHI	N	P		37	12-18
1945	PHI	N	P		36	8-20
	BRTR				141	35-58

BARRETT, WILLIAM
B.WASHINGTON,D.C.

YR	CL	LEA	POS	GP	G	REC
1871	KEK	NA	C		1	-
1872	OLY	NA	C		1	.000
	ATL	NA	O		7	.267
1873	BAL	NA	O		1	-
					10	-

BARRETT, WILLIAM JOSEPH "WHISPERING BILL"
B.MAY 28,1900 CAMBRIDGE,MASS.
D.JAN.26,1951

YR	CL	LEA	POS	GP	G	REC
1921	PHI	A	P	4	14	1-0
1923	CHI	A	O		44	.271
1924	CHI	A	S-O		119	.271
1925	CHI	A	2-S-3-O		81	.363
1926	CHI	A	O		111	.307
1927	CHI	A	O		147	.286
1928	CHI	A	2-O		76	.277
1929	CHI	A	O		3	.000
	BOS	A	O		111	.270
1930	BOS	A	O		6	.176
	WAS	A	H		6	.000
	BRTR			4	718	1-0
						.288

BARRIOS, FRANCISCO JAVIER (JIMENEZ)
B.JUNE 10,1953 HERMOSILLO,MEX.

YR	CL	LEA	POS	GP	G	REC
1974	CHI	A	P		2	0-0
1976	CHI	A	P		35	5-9
	BRTR				37	5-9

BARRON, DAVID IRENUS "RED"
B.JUNE 21,1900 CLARKSVILLE,GA.
1929 BOS N O 10 .190
BRTR

BARRON, FRANK JOHN
B.AUG.6,1890 ST.MARY'S,W.VA.
D.SEPT.18,1964 ST.MARY'S,W.VA.
1914 WAS A P 1 0-0
BLTL

BARROW, EDWARD GRANT "COUSIN ED"
B.MAY 10,1868 SPRINGFIELD,ILL.
D.DEC.15,1953 PORT CHESTER,N.Y.
NON-PLAYING MANAGER
DET(A) 1903-34, BOS(A) 1918-20.

YR	CL LEA POS	GP	G	REC

BARROWS, FRANK LEWIS
B.BOSTON,MASS.
D.SEPT.24,1901

YR	CL LEA POS	GP	G	REC
1871	BOS NA 2-0		20	-
1874	BAL NA O		16	-
			36	-

BARROWS, ROLAND "CUKE"
B.OCT.20,1883 RAYMOND,ME.
D.FEB.10,1955

YR	CL LEA POS	GP	G	REC
1909	CHI A O		4	.150
1910	CHI A O		6	.200
1911	CHI A O		13	.195
1912	CHI A O		8	.231
	BLTR		31	.190

BARRY, EDWARD "JUMBO"
B.FREEPORT,IND.

YR	CL LEA POS	GP	G	REC
1905	BOS A P	7		1- 2
1906	BOS A P	3		0- 3
1907	BOS A P	2		0- 1
	TL	12		1- 6

BARRY, HARDIN
B.MAR.26,1891 SUSANVILLE,CAL.

YR	CL LEA POS	GP	G	REC
1912	PHI A P	3		0- 0
	BRTR			

BARRY, JOHN C. "SHAD"
B.SEPT.28,1876 NEWBURGH,N.Y.
D.NOV.27,1936

YR	CL LEA POS	GP	G	REC
1899	WAS N O		75	.303
1900	BOS N 2-S-O		66	.261
1901	BOS N O		11	.179
	PHI N 3-O		63	.245
1902	PHI N 1-O		138	.302
1903	PHI N 1-O		138	.276
1904	PHI N O		33	.205
	CHI N 1-O		72	.262
1905	CHI N 1		26	.212
	CIN N 1		126	.324
1906	CIN N 1-O		73	.287
	STL N 1-O		62	.249
1907	STL N O		81	.248
1908	STL N O		71	.228
	NY N O		31	.149
	BRTR		1066	.270

BARRY, JOHN JOSEPH "JACK"
B.APR.26,1887 MERIDEN,CONN.
D.APR.23,1961

YR	CL LEA POS	GP	G	REC
1908	PHI A 2		40	.222
1909	PHI A S		124	.215
1910	PHI A S		145	.259
1911	PHI A S		127	.265
1912	PHI A S		139	.261
1913	PHI A S		135	.275
1914	PHI A S		140	.242
1915	PHI A S		54	.218
	BOS A 2		78	.265
1916	BOS A 2		94	.203
1917	BOS A 4-2		116	.214
1919	BOS A 2		31	.241
	BRTR		1223	.243

BARRY, RICHARD DONOVAN "RICH"
B.SEP.12,1940 BERKELEY,CAL.

YR	CL LEA POS	GP	G	REC
1969	PHI N O		20	.188
	BRTR			

BARRY, THOMAS ARTHUR
B.APR.10,1879 ST.LOUIS,MO.
D.JUNE 4,1946

YR	CL LEA POS	GP	G	REC
1904	PHI N P	1		0- 1

BARTELL, RICHARD WILLIAM
"ROWDY DICK"
B.NOV.22,1907 CHICAGO,ILL.

YR	CL LEA POS	GP	G	REC
1927	PIT N S		1	.000
1928	PIT N 2-S		72	.305
1929	PIT N 2-S		143	.302
1930	PIT N S		129	.320
1931	PHI N S		135	.289
1932	PHI N S		154	.308
1933	PHI N S		152	.271
1934	PHI N S		146	.310
1935	NY N S		137	.262
1936	NY N S		145	.298
1937	NY N S		128	.306
1938	NY N S		127	.262
1939	NY N S		105	.238
1940	DET A S		139	.233
1941	DET A S		5	.167
	NY N S-3		104	.303
1942	NY N S-3		90	.244
1943	NY N S-3		99	.270
1946	NY N 2-3		5	.000
	BRTR		2016	.284

BARTHELSON, ROBERT EDWARD
B.JULY 15,1924 NEW HAVEN,CONN.

YR	CL LEA POS	GP	G	REC
1944	NY N P	7		1- 1
	BRTR			

BARTHOLD, JOHN FRANCIS
B.APR.14,1882 PHILADELPHIA,PA.
D.NOV.4,1946

YR	CL LEA POS	GP	G	REC
1904	PHI A P	4		0- 1
	BBTR			

BARTHOLOMEW, LESTER JUSTIN
B.APR.4,1905 MADISON,WIS.
D.SEPT.19,1972 BARRINGTON,ILL.

YR	CL LEA POS	GP	G	REC
1928	PIT N P	6		0- 0
1932	CHI N P	3		0- 0
	BRTL	9		0-0

BARTIROME, ANTHONY JOSEPH
B.MAY 9,1932 PITTSBURGH,PA.

YR	CL LEA POS	GP	G	REC
1952	PIT N 1		124	.220
	BLTL			

BARILEY, BOYD OWEN
B.FEB.11,1921 CHICAGO,ILL.

YR	CL LEA POS	GP	G	REC
1943	BRO N S		9	.048
	BRTR			

BARTLEY, WILLIAM JACKSON
B.JAN.8,1885 CINCINNATI,OHIO
D.MAY 17,1965 CINCINNATI,OHIO

YR	CL LEA POS	GP	G	REC
1903	NY N P	1		0- 0
1906	PHI A P	3		0- 0
1907	PHI A P	15		0- 0
	BRTR	19		0- 0

BARTLING, IRVING HENRY
B.JUNE 27,1916 BAY CITY,MICH.
D.JUNE 12,1973 WESTLAND,MICH.

YR	CL LEA POS	GP	G	REC
1938	PHI A S		14	.174
	BRTR			

BARTON, CARROLL R. "BUCK"
B.1893 WASHINGTON,D.C.

YR	CL LEA POS	GP	G	REC
1914	WAS A P	1		0- 0

BARTON, HARRY LAMB
B.JAN.20,1875 CHESTER,PA.
D.JAN.25,1955

YR	CL LEA POS	GP	G	REC
1905	PHI A C		18	.167
	BBTR			

BARTON, ROBERT WILBUR "BOB"
B.JULY 30,1941 NORWOOD,O.

YR	CL LEA POS	GP	G	REC
1965	SF N C		4	.571
1966	SF N C		43	.176
1967	SF N C		7	.211
1968	SF N C		46	.261
1969	SF N C		49	.170
1970	SD N C		61	.218
1971	SD N C		121	.250
1972	SD N C		29	.193
1973	CIN N C		3	.000
1974	SD N C		30	.235
	BRTR		393	.226

BARTON, VINCENT DAVID
B.FEB.1,1908 EDMONTON,ALBERTA,
CANADA
D.SEPT.13,1973 TORONTO,ONT.,CAN

YR	CL LEA POS	GP	G	REC
1931	CHI N O		66	.238
1932	CHI N O		36	.224
	BLTR		102	.233

BARTOSCH, DAVID ROBERT
B.MAR.24,1917 ST.LOUIS,MO.

YR	CL LEA POS	GP	G	REC
1945	STL N O		24	.255
	BRTR			

BARTSON, CHARLES FRANKLIN
B.MAR.13,1865 PEORIA,ILL.
D.JUNE 9,1936 PEORIA,ILL.

YR	CL LEA POS	GP	G	REC
1890	CHI P P		26	9-14

BASGALL, ROMANUS "MONTY"
B.FEB.8,1922 PFEIFER,KAN.

YR	CL LEA POS	GP	G	REC
1948	PIT N 2		38	.216
1949	PIT N 2-3		107	.218
1951	PIT N 2		55	.209
	BRTR		200	.215

BASHANG, ALBERT
B.AUG.22,1888 CINCINNATI,OHIO
D.JUNE 23,1967 CINCINNATI,OHIO

YR	CL LEA POS	GP	G	REC
1912	DET A O		6	.167
1918	BRO N O		2	.200
	BBTR		8	.174

BASHORE, WALTER FRANKLIN
B.OCT.6,1909 HARRISBURG,PA.

YR	CL LEA POS	GP	G	REC
1936	PHI N O		10	.200
	BRTR			

BASINSKI, EDWIN FRANK "BAZOOKA"
B.NOV.4,1922 BUFFALO,N.Y.

YR	CL LEA POS	GP	G	REC
1944	BRO N 2-S		39	.257
1945	BRO N 2-S		108	.262
1947	PIT N 2		56	.199
	BRTR		203	.244

BASKETTE, JAMES BLAIN "BIG JIM"
"BIG JIM"
B.DEC.10,1887 ATHENS,TENN.
D.JULY 30,1942

YR	CL LEA POS	GP	G	REC
1911	CLE A P	4		1- 2
1912	CLE A P	29		8- 4
1913	CLE A P	2		0- 0
	BRTR	35		9- 6

BASS, JOHN E.
B.1850 BALTIMORE,MD.

YR	CL LEA POS	GP	G	REC
1871	CLE NA 3		23	-
1872	ATL NA O		1	.250
1877	HAR N O		1	.250
			25	-

BASS, NORMAN DELANEY "NORM"
B.JAN.21,1939 LAUREL,MISS.

YR	CL LEA POS	GP	G	REC
1961	KC A P	40	41	11-11
1962	KC A P		22	2- 6
1963	KC A P		3	0- 0
	BRTR	65	66	13-17

BASS, RICHARD WILLIAM
B.JULY 7,1906 ROGERSVILLE,TENN.

YR	CL LEA POS	GP	G	REC
1939	WAS A P	1		0- 1
	BRTR			

BASS, WILLIAM C. "DOC"
B.CINCINNATI,OHIO

YR	CL LEA POS	GP	G	REC
1918	BOS N O		1	1.000

BASSETT, CHARLES EDWIN
B.FEB.9,1863 LINCOLN,R.I.
D.MAY 28,1942

YR	CL LEA POS	GP	G	REC
1884	PRO N 2-S-3-O		21	.144
1885	PRO N 2-S-3		81	.143
1886	KC N S		90	.260
1887	IND N 2		119	.270
1888	IND N 2		128	.241
1889	IND N 2		126	.253
1890	NY N 2		100	.239
1891	NY N 3		130	.266
1892	NY N 2-3		34	.185
	LOU N 2-3		78	.213
	TR		907	.237

BASSLER, JOHN LANDIS
B.JUNE 3,1895 LANCASTER,PA.

YR	CL LEA POS	GP	G	REC
1913	CLE A C		1	.000
1914	CLE A C		43	.182
1921	DET A C		119	.307
1922	DET A C		121	.323
1923	DET A C		135	.298
1924	DET A C		124	.346
1925	DET A C		121	.279
1926	DET A C		66	.305
1927	DET A C		81	.285
	BLTR		811	.304

YR	CL	LEA	POS	GP	G	REC

BASTIAN, CHARLES J.
B.JULY 4,1860 PHILADELPHIA,PA.
D.JAN.18,1932

YR	CL	LEA	POS	GP	G	REC
1884	WIL	U	P-2-S	1	17	0- 0
						.200
	KC	U	2		11	.255
1885	PHI	N	S		104	.167
1886	PHI	N	2		104	.217
1887	PHI	N	2-S		60	.275
1888	PHI	N	2		80	.192
1889	CHI	N	S		46	.135
1890	CHI	P	2-S		80	.186
1891	CIN	AA	2		1	.000
	PHI	N	S		1	.000
	BRTR			1	504	0- 0
						.198

BATCH, EMIL "HEINE"
B.JAN.21,1880 BROOKLYN,N.Y.
D.AUG.23,1926 BROOKLYN,N.Y.

YR	CL	LEA	POS	GP	G	REC
1904	BRO	N	3		28	.255
1905	BRO	N	3		145	.252
1906	BRO	N	O		52	.256
1907	BRO	N	O		106	.247
	BRTR				331	.251

BATCHELDER, JOSEPH EDMUND
B.JULY 11,1898 WENHAM,MASS.

YR	CL	LEA	POS	GP	G	REC
1923	BOS	N	P		4	1- 0
1924	BOS	N	P		3	0- 0
1925	BOS	N	P		4	0- 0
	BRTL				11	1- 0

BATEMAN, JOHN ALVIN
B.JULY 21,1942 KILLEEN,TEX.

YR	CL	LEA	POS	GP	G	REC
1963	HOU	N	C		128	.210
1964	HOU	N	C		74	.190
1965	HOU	N	C		45	.197
1966	HOU	N	C		131	.279
1967	HOU	N	C		76	.190
1968	HOU	N	C		111	.249
1969	MON	N	C		74	.209
1970	MON	N	C		139	.237
1971	MON	N	C		139	.242
1972	MON	N	C		18	.241
	PHI	N	C		82	.222
	BRTR				1017	.230

BATES, BUSH

YR	CL	LEA	POS	GP	G	REC
1889	KC	AA	P		1	0- 1

BATES, CHARLES RICHARD "DICK"
B.OCT.7,1945 MCARTHUR,O.

YR	CL	LEA	POS	GP	G	REC
1969	SEA	A	P		1	0- 0
	BLTR					

BATES, CHARLES WILLIAM
B.SEPT.17,1905 PHILADELPHIA,PA.

YR	CL	LEA	POS	GP	G	REC
1927	PHI	A	O		9	.237
	BRTR					

BATES, DELBERT OAKLEY "DEL"
B.JUNE 12,1940 SEATTLE,WASH.

YR	CL	LEA	POS	GP	G	REC
1970	PHI	N	C		22	.133
	BLTR					

BATES, FRANK CHARLES
B.CHATTANOOGA,TENN.

YR	CL	LEA	POS	GP	G	REC
1898	CLE	N	P		4	2- 1
1899	STL	N	P		4	0- 0
	CLE	N	P		20	1-19
					28	3-20

BATES, HUBERT EDGAR "BUD"
B.MAR.16,1913 LOS ANGELES,CAL.

YR	CL	LEA	POS	GP	G	REC
1939	PHI	N	O		15	.259
	BRTR					

BATES, JOHN WILLIAM
B.AUG.21,1882 STEUBENVILLE,OHIO
D.FEB.10,1949

YR	CL	LEA	POS	GP	G	REC
1906	BOS	N	O		140	.252
1907	BOS	N	O		119	.260
1908	BOS	N	O		117	.258
1909	BOS	N	O		60	.288
	PHI	N	O		73	.293
1910	PHI	N	O		131	.305
1911	CIN	N	O		147	.292
1912	CIN	N	O		81	.289
1913	CIN	N	O		131	.278
1914	CIN	N	O		58	.252
	CHI	N	O		9	.125
	BAL	F	O		59	.307
	BLTL				1125	.278

BATES, RAYMOND
B.FEB.8,1890 PATERSON,N.J.
D.AUG.15,1970 TUCSON,ARIZ.

YR	CL	LEA	POS	GP	G	REC
1913	CLE	A	3		20	.167
1917	PHI	A	3		127	.237
	BRTR				147	.233

BATISTA, RAFAEL
(REAL NAME
RAFAEL ROBLE (BATISTA))
B.NOV.21,1945 INGENIO CONSUELO,
P.R.

YR	CL	LEA	POS	GP	G	REC
1973	HOU	N	1		12	.267
1975	HOU	N	H		10	.300
	BLTL				22	.280

BATSCH, WILLIAM MC KINLEY
B.MAY 18,1892 MINGO JUNCTION,O.
D.DEC.31,1963 CANTON,OHIO

YR	CL	LEA	POS	GP	G	REC
1916	PIT	N	H		1	.000
	BRTR					

BATTAM, LAWRENCE
B.MAY 1,1878 BROOKLYN,N.Y.
D.JAN.27,1938

YR	CL	LEA	POS	GP	G	REC
1895	NY	N	3		2	.250

BATTEN, GEORGE BERNARD
B.OCT.7,1891 HADDONFIELD,N.J.
D.AUG.4,1972 NEW PORT RICHEY,
FLA.

YR	CL	LEA	POS	GP	G	REC
1912	NY	A	2		1	.000
	BRTR					

BATTEY, EARL JESSE
B.JAN.5,1935 LOS ANGELES,CAL.

YR	CL	LEA	POS	GP	G	REC
1955	CHI	A	C		5	.286
1956	CHI	A	C		4	.250
1957	CHI	A	C		48	.174
1958	CHI	A	C		68	.226
1959	CHI	A	C		26	.219
1960	WAS	A	C		137	.270
1961	MIN	A	C		133	.302
1962	MIN	A	C		148	.280
1963	MIN	A	C		147	.285
1964	MIN	A	C		131	.272
1965	MIN	A	C		131	.297
1966	MIN	A	C		115	.255
1967	MIN	A	C		48	.165
	BRTR				1141	.270

BATTIN, JOSEPH V.
B.NOV.11,1851 PHILADELPHIA,PA.
D.DEC.11,1937

YR	CL	LEA	POS	GP	G	REC
1871	CLE	NA	O		1	-
1873	ATH	NA	O		1	-
1874	ATH	NA	2-S-O		51	-
1875	STL	NA	2-3		63	.263
1876	STL	N	3		64	.294
1877	STL	N	P-2-3-O	1	57	0- 0
						.199
1882	PIT	AA	3		28	.207
1883	PIT	AA	M-P-3	1	96	0- 0
						.202
1884	PIT	AA	M-3		43	.178
	PIT	U	M-3		18	.197
	BAL	U	2-3		17	.086
1890	SYR	AA	3		29	.194
	BRTR			2	468	0- 0
						-

BATTLE, JAMES MILTON
B.MAR.26,1904 CELESTE,TEX.
D.SEPT.30,1965 CHICO,CAL.

YR	CL	LEA	POS	GP	G	REC
1927	CHI	A	S-3		6	.375
	BRTR					

BATTON, CHRISTOPHER SEAN "CHRIS"
B.AUG.24,1954 LOS ANGELES,CAL.

YR	CL	LEA	POS	GP	G	REC
1976	OAK	A	P		2	0- 0
	BRTR					

BATTS, MATTHEW DANIEL "MATT"
B.OCT.16,1921 SAN ANTONIO,TEX.

YR	CL	LEA	POS	GP	G	REC
1947	BOS	A	C		7	.500
1948	BOS	A	C		46	.314
1949	BOS	A	C		60	.242
1950	BOS	A	C		75	.273
1951	BOS	A	C		11	.138
	STL	A	C		79	.302
1952	DET	A	C		56	.237
1953	DET	A	C		116	.278
1954	DET	A	C		12	.286
	CHI	A	C		55	.228
1955	CIN	N	C		26	.254
1956	CIN	N	H		3	.000
	BRTR				546	.269

BAUCKER, JOHN "STUD"
B.PHILADELPHIA,PA.

YR	CL	LEA	POS	GP	G	REC
1875	NH	NA	C-2-S-3		19	-

BAUER, HENRY ALBERT "HANK"
B.JULY 31,1922 E.ST.LOUIS,ILL.

YR	CL	LEA	POS	GP	G	REC
1948	NY	A	O		19	.180
1949	NY	A	O		103	.272
1950	NY	A	O		113	.320
1951	NY	A	O		118	.296
1952	NY	A	O		141	.293
1953	NY	A	O		133	.304
1954	NY	A	O		114	.294
1955	NY	A	C-O		139	.278
1956	NY	A	O		147	.241
1957	NY	A	O		137	.259
1958	NY	A	O		128	.268
1959	NY	A	O		114	.238
1960	KC	A	O		95	.275
1961	KC	A	M-O		43	.264
	BRTR				1544	.277

NON-PLAYING MANAGER
KC(A) 1962, BAL(A) 1964-68,
OAK(A) 1969

BAUER, LOUIS WALTER
B.NOV.30,1898 EGG HARBOR,N.J.

YR	CL	LEA	POS	GP	G	REC
1918	PHI	A	P		1	0- 0

BAUERS, ALBERT J.
B.1850 COLUMBUS,OHIO
D.SEPT.6,1913

YR	CL	LEA	POS	GP	G	REC
1884	COL	AA	P		3	1- 2
1886	STL	N	P		4	0- 4
	TL				7	1- 6

BAUERS, RUSSELL LEE
B.MAY 10,1915 TOWNSEND,WIS.

YR	CL	LEA	POS	GP	G	REC
1936	PIT	N	P		1	0- 0
1937	PIT	N	P		34	13- 6
1938	PIT	N	P		40	13-14
1939	PIT	N	P		15	2- 4
1940	PIT	N	P		15	0- 2
1941	PIT	N	P		8	1- 3
1946	CHI	N	P		15	2- 1
1950	STL	A	P		1	0- 0
	BLTR				129	31-30

BAUMANN, CHARLES JOHN "PADDY"
B.DEC.20,1885 INDIANAPOLIS,IND.
D.NOV.20,1969 INDIANAPOLIS,IND.

YR	CL	LEA	POS	GP	G	REC
1911	DET	A	2		26	.256
1912	DET	A	3-O		13	.262
1913	DET	A	2		49	.298
1914	DET	A	2		3	.000
1915	NY	A	2-3		76	.292
1916	NY	A	3-O		79	.287
1917	NY	A	2		49	.218
	BRTR				295	.268

BAUMANN, FRANK MATT
B.JULY 1,1933 ST.LOUIS,MO.

YR	CL	LEA	POS	GP	G	REC
1955	BOS	A	P		7	2- 1
1956	BOS	A	P		7	2- 1
1957	BOS	A	P		4	1- 0
1958	BOS	A	P		10	2- 2
1959	BOS	A	P		26	6- 4
1960	CHI	A	P		47	13- 6
1961	CHI	A	P	53	55	10-13
1962	CHI	A	P		40	7- 6
1963	CHI	A	P		24	2- 1
1964	CHI	A	P		22	0- 3
1965	CHI	N	P		4	0- 1
	BLTL			244	246	45-38

BAUMER, JAMES SLOAN "JIM"
B.JAN.29,1931 TULSA,OKLA.

YR	CL	LEA	POS	GP	G	REC
1949	CHI	A	S		8	.400
1961	CIN	N	2		10	.125
	BRTR				18	.206

BAUMGARDNER, GEORGE WASHINGTON
B.JULY 22,1891 BARBOURSVILLE,
W.VA.
D.DEC.13,1970 BARBOURSVILLE,
W.VA.

YR	CL	LEA	POS	GP	G	REC
1912	STL	A	P		30	11-14
1913	STL	A	P		38	10-19
1914	STL	A	P		45	14-13
1915	STL	A	P		7	0- 2
1916	STL	A	P		4	1- 0
	BLTR				124	36-48

YR	CL	LEA	POS	GP	G	REC

BAUMGARTNER, HARRY E.
B.OCT.8,1892 S.PITTSBURG,TENN.
D.DEC.3,1930

YR	CL	LEA	POS	GP	G	REC
1920	DET	A	P		9	0- 1
		BL				

BAUMGARTNER, JOHN EDWARD
B.MAY 29,1931 BIRMINGHAM,ALA.

1953	DET	A	3		7	.185
		BRTR				

BAUMGARTNER, STANWOOD FULTON
B.DEC.14,1894 HOUSTON,TEX.
D.OCT.4,1955

1914	PHI	N	P		15	2- 2
1915	PHI	N	P		16	0- 2
1916	PHI	N	P		1	0- 0
1921	PHI	N	P	22	31	3- 6
1922	PHI	N	P		6	1- 1
1924	PHI	A	P		36	13- 6
1925	PHI	A	P		37	6- 3
1926	PHI	A	P		10	1- 1
		BLTL		143	152	26-21

BAUMHOLTZ, FRANK CONRAD
B.OCT.7,1919 MIDVALE,OHIO

1947	CIN	N	O		151	.283
1948	CIN	N	O		128	.296
1949	CIN	N	O		27	.235
	CHI	N	O		58	.226
1951	CHI	N	O		146	.284
1952	CHI	N	O		103	.325
1953	CHI	N	O		133	.306
1954	CHI	N	O		90	.297
1955	CHI	N	O		105	.289
1956	PHI	N	O		76	.270
1957	PHI	N	H		2	.000
		BLTL			1019	.293

BAUSEWINE, GEORGE
B.MAR.22,1869 PHILADELPHIA,PA.
D.JULY 29,1947

1889	ATH	AA	P		7	1- 4

BAUTA, EDUARDO (GALVEZ) "ED"
B.JAN.6,1935 FLORIDA CAMAGUEY, CUBA

1960	STL	N	P		9	0- 0
1961	STL	N	P		13	2- 0
1962	STL	N	P		20	1- 0
1963	STL	N	P		38	3- 4
	NY	N	P		9	0- 0
1964	NY	N	P		8	0- 2
		BRTR			97	6- 6

BAXES, DIMITRIOS S.
B.JULY 5,1928 SAN FRANCISCO,CAL

1959	LA	N	3		11	.303
	CLE	A	2-3		77	.239
		BRTR			88	.246

BAXES, MICHAEL "MIKE"
B.DEC.18,1930 SAN FRANCISCO,CAL

1956	KC	A	2-S		73	.226
1958	KC	A	2-S		73	.212
		BRTR			146	.217

BAXTER, JOHN
B.SPOKANE,WASH.

1907	STL	N	1		6	.190

BAY, HARRY ELBERT "DEERFOOT"
B.JAN.17,1878 PONTIAC,ILL.
D.MAR.20,1952

1901	CIN	N	O		34	.205
1902	CIN	N	O		6	.375
	CLE	A	O		108	.287
1903	CLE	A	O		141	.310
1904	CLE	A	O		132	.260
1905	CLE	A	O		143	.298
1906	CLE	A	O		68	.275
1907	CLE	A	O		34	.179
1908	CLE	A	H		2	.000
		BLTL			668	.280

BAYER, CHRISTOPHER A. "BURLEY" "BURLEY"
B.DEC.19,1875 LOUISVILLE,KY.
D.MAY.30,1933

1899	LOU	N	S		1	.000

BAYLESS, HARRY OWEN "DICK"
B.SEPT.6,1883 JOPLIN,MO.
D.DEC.16,1920

1908	CIN	N	O		19	.225

BAYLOR, DON EDWARD
B.JUNE 28,1949 AUSTIN,TEX.

1970	BAL	A	O		8	.235
1971	BAL	A	O		1	.000
1972	BAL	A	1-O		102	.253
1973	BAL	A	1-O		118	.286
1974	BAL	A	1-O		137	.272
1975	BAL	A	1-O		145	.282
1976	OAK	A	1-O-O		157	.247
		BRTR			668	.267

BAYNE, WILLIAM LEAR "BEVERLY"
B.APR.18,1899 PITTSBURGH,PA.

1919	STL	A	P		2	1- 1
1920	STL	A	P		18	5- 6
1921	STL	A	P		47	11- 5
1922	STL	A	P		26	4- 5
1923	STL	A	P		19	2- 2
1924	STL	A	P		22	1- 3
1928	CLE	A	P		37	2- 5
1929	BOS	A	P		27	5- 5
1930	BOS	A	P		1	0- 0
		BLTL			199	31-32

BEACH, JACKSON
B.ALEXANDRIA,VA.

1884	WAS	AA	O		8	.094

BEALL, JOHN WOOLF
B.MAR.12,1882 BELTSVILLE,MD.
D.JUNE 14,1926

1913	CLE	A	H		6	.167
	CHI	A	O		17	.267
1915	CIN	N	O		10	.232
1916	CIN	N	O		6	.333
1918	STL	N	O		19	.224
		BLTR			58	.257

BEALL, ROBERT BROOKS "BOB"
B.APR.24,1948 PORTLAND,ORE.

1975	ATL	N	1		20	.226
		BBTL				

BEALL, WALTER ESAU
B.JULY 29,1899 WASHINGTON,D.C.
D.JAN.28,1959

1924	NY	A	P		4	2- 0
1925	NY	A	P		8	0- 1
1926	NY	A	P		20	2- 4
1927	NY	A	P		1	0- 0
1929	WAS	A	P		3	1- 0
		BRTR			36	5- 5

BEALS, THOMAS L.
(PLAYED UNDER NAME OF
W. THOMAS IN 1871 AND 1873)
D.NOV.9,1911

1871	OLY	NA	2-0		10	.194
1872	OLY	NA	2-S-0		9	.282
1873	NAT	NA	C-2-0		37	-
1874	BOS	NA	1-2-0		19	.204
1875	BOS	NA	2-0		35	.293
1880	CHI	N	2-0		13	.149
					123	-

BEAM, ALEXANDER RODGER
B.NOV.21,1870 JOHNSTOWN,PA.
D.APR.17,1938

1889	PIT	N	P		2	1- 1

BEAM, ERNEST
B.1867 MANSFIELD,OHIO
D.SEPT.13,1918

1895	PHI	N	P		9	0- 2

BEAMON, CHARLES ALONZO
B.DEC.25,1934 OAKLAND,CAL.

1956	BAL	A	P		2	2- 0
1957	BAL	A	P		4	0- 0
1958	BAL	A	P	21	22	1- 3
		BRTR		27	28	3- 3

BEAN, BELVEDERE BENTON "BILL"
B.APR.23,1906 MULLIN,TEX.

1930	CLE	A	P		23	3- 3
1931	CLE	A	P		4	0- 1
1933	CLE	A	P		27	1- 2
1934	CLE	A	P		21	5- 1
1935	CLE	A	P		1	0- 0
	WAS	A	P		10	2- 0
		BRTR			86	11- 7

BEAN, JOSEPH WILLIAM
B.MAR.18,1874 BOSTON,MASS.
D.FEB.15,1961

1902	NY	N	S		50	.235
		TR				

BEARD, CRAMER THEODORE "TED"
B.JAN.7,1921 WOODSBORO,MD.

1948	PIT	N	O		25	.198
1949	PIT	N	O		14	.083
1950	PIT	N	O		61	.232
1951	PIT	N	O		22	.188
1952	PIT	N	O		15	.182
1957	CHI	A	O		38	.205
1958	CHI	A	O		19	.091
		BLTL			194	.198

BEARD, MICHAEL RICHARD "MIKE"
B.JUNE 21,1950 LITTLE ROCK,ARK.

1974	ATL	N	P		6	0- 0
1975	ATL	N	P		*34	4- 0
1976	ATL	N	P		30	0- 2
		BLTL			70	4- 2

BEARD, OLIVER PERRY
B.MAY 2,1862 LEXINGTON,KY.
D.MAY 28,1929

1889	CIN	AA	S		141	.293
1890	CIN	N	S		122	.268
1891	LOU	AA	2		68	.247
		BRTR			331	.273

BEARD, RALPH WILLIAM
B.FEB.11,1929 CINCINNATI,OHIO

1954	STL	N	P		13	0- 4
		BRTR				

BEARDEN, HENRY EUGENE "GENE"
B.SEPT.5,1920 LEXA,ARK.

1947	CLE	A	P		1	0- 0
1948	CLE	A	P		37	20- 7
1949	CLE	A	P		32	8- 8
1950	CLE	A	P		14	1- 3
	WAS	A	P-1	12	14	3- 5
						.227
1951	WAS	A	P		1	0- 0
	DET	A	P		37	3- 4
1952	STL	A	P	34	45	7- 8
1953	CHI	A	P	25	31	3- 3
		BLTL		193	212	45-38
						.236

BEARE, GARY RAY
B.AUG.22,1952 SAN DIEGO,CAL.

1976	MIL	A	P		6	2- 3
		BRTR				

BEARNARTH, LAWRENCE DONALD "LARRY"
B.SEP.11,1941 NEW YORK,N.Y.

1963	NY	N	P		58	3- 8
1964	NY	N	P		44	5- 5
1965	NY	N	P		40	3- 5
1966	NY	N	P		29	2- 3
1971	MIL	A	P		2	0- 0
		BRTR			173	13-21

BEATIN, EBENEZER AMBROSE
B.AUG.10,1866 BALTIMORE,MD.
D.MAY 9,1925

1887	DET	N	P		2	1- 1
1888	DET	N	P		16	5- 7
1889	CLE	N	P		37	20-14
1890	CLE	N	P		53	22-31
1891	CLE	N	P		5	1- 4
		BRTR			113	49-57

BEATLE, DAVID
B.1861 NEW YORK,N.Y.

1884	DET	N	C-0		1	.000

BEATTY, DESMOND "DESPERATE"
B.1893 NEW YORK,N.Y.
D.OCT.6,1969 NORWAY,MAINE

1914	NY	N	3		1	.000
		BRTR				

BEAUCHAMP, JAMES EDWARD "JIM"
B.AUG.21,1939 VINITA,OKLA.

1963	STL	N	H		4	.000
1964	HOU	N	1-0		23	.164
1965	HOU	N	1-0		24	.189
	MIL	N	1		4	.000
1967	ATL	N	H		4	.000
1968	CIN	N	1-0		31	.263
1969	CIN	N	1-0		43	.250
1970	HOU	N	O		31	.192
	STL	N	1-0		44	.259
1971	STL	N	1-0		77	.235
1972	NY	N	1-0		58	.242
1973	NY	N	1		50	.279
		BRTR			393	.231

BEAUMONT, CLARENCE HOWETH "GINGER"
B.JULY 23,1876 ROCHESTER,WIS.
D.APR.10,1956 BURLINGTON,WIS.

YR	CL	LEA	POS	GP	G	REC
1899	PIT	N	O		104	.350
1900	PIT	N	O		138	.282
1901	PIT	N	O		132	.328
1902	PIT	N	O		131	.357
1903	PIT	N	O		141	.341
1904	PIT	N	O		153	.301
1905	PIT	N	O		97	.328
1906	PIT	N	O		78	.265
1907	BOS	N	O		149	.322
1908	BOS	N	O		121	.267
1909	BOS	N	O		111	.263
1910	CHI	N	O		56	.267
	BLTR				1411	.311

BEAZLEY, JOHN ANDREW "NIG"
B.MAY 25,1919 NASHVILLE,TENN.

YR	CL	LEA	POS	GP	G	REC
1941	STL	N	P		1	1- 0
1942	STL	N	P		43	21- 6
1946	STL	N	P		19	7- 5
1947	BOS	N	P		9	2- 0
1948	BOS	N	P		3	0- 1
1949	BOS	N	P		1	0- 0
	BRTR				76	31-12

BECANNON, JAMES MELVILLE "BUCK"
B.AUG.22,1859 NEW YORK,N.Y.
D.NOV.5,1923

YR	CL	LEA	POS	GP	G	REC
1884	MET	AA	P		1	1- 0
1885	MET	AA	P		10	2- 8
1887	NY	N	3		1	.000
				11	12	3- 8
						.238

BECHTEL, GEORGE A.
B.1848 PHILADELPHIA,PA.

YR	CL	LEA	POS	GP	G	REC
1871	ATH	NA	P-3-	3	21	1- 2
			O			.360
1872	MUT	NA	1-O		52	.302
1873	PHI	NA	P-O	3	52	1- 2
						-
1874	PHI	NA	P-O	4	31	1- 3
						-
1875	CEN	NA	P		14	2-12
	ATH	NA	P-O	4	34	3- 1
						-
1876	LOU	N	O		14	.182
	MUT	N	O		2	.273
				28	220	8-20

BECK, CLYDE EUGENE "JERSEY"
B.JAN.6,1902 BASSETT,CAL.

YR	CL	LEA	POS	GP	G	REC
1926	CHI	N	2		30	.198
1927	CHI	N	2-3		117	.258
1928	CHI	N	S-3		131	.257
1929	CHI	N	S-3		54	.211
1930	CHI	N	2-S		83	.213
1931	CIN	N	S-3		53	.154
	BRTR				468	.232

BECK, ERWIN THOMAS "DUTCH"
B.JULY 19,1878 TOLEDO,OHIO
D.DEC.22,1916

YR	CL	LEA	POS	GP	G	REC
1899	BRO	N	S		7	.158
1901	CLE	A	2		135	.283
1902	CIN	N	1-2-O		43	.305
	DET	A	1-O		41	.304
	BRTR				226	.298

BECK, FRANK J.
B.1862 POUGHKEEPSIE,N.Y.

YR	CL	LEA	POS	GP	G	REC
1884	PIT	AA	P		3	0- 3
	BAL	U	P-O	2	6	0- 2
						.208
	TR			5	9	0- 5
						.257

BECK, FREDERICK THOMAS
B.NOV.17,1887 HAVANA,ILL.
D.MAR.12,1962

YR	CL	LEA	POS	GP	G	REC
1909	BOS	N	1-O		88	.198
1910	BOS	N	O		153	.275
1911	CIN	N	O		41	.184
	PHI	N	O		64	.281
1914	CHI	F	1		158	.279
1915	CHI	F	1		121	.219
	BLTL				625	.251

BECK, GEORGE F.
B.1889 MOLINE,ILL.

YR	CL	LEA	POS	GP	G	REC
1914	CLE	A	P		1	0- 0
	BRTR					

BECK, RICHARD HENRY "RICH"
B.JAN.21,1941 PASCO,WASH.

YR	CL	LEA	POS	GP	G	REC
1965	NY	A			3	2- 1
	BBTR					

BECK, WALTER WILLIAM "BOOM-BOOM"
B.OCT.16,1904 DECATUR,ILL.

YR	CL	LEA	POS	GP	G	REC
1924	STL	A	P		1	0- 0
1927	STL	A	P		3	1- 0
1928	STL	A	P		16	2- 3
1933	BRO	N	P		43	12-20
1934	BRO	N	P		22	2- 6
1939	PHI	N	P		34	7-14
1940	PHI	N	P		29	4- 9
1941	PHI	N	P		34	1- 9
1942	PHI	N	P	26	27	0- 1
1943	PHI	N	P		4	0- 0
1944	DET	A	P		28	1- 2
1945	CIN	N	P		11	2- 4
	PIT	N	P		14	6- 1
	BRTR			265	266	38-69

BECK, ZINN BERTRAM
B.SEPT.30,1889 STEUBENVILLE,O.

YR	CL	LEA	POS	GP	G	REC
1913	STL	N	3		10	.218
1914	STL	N	S-3		137	.232
1915	STL	N	3		70	.233
1916	STL	N	3		62	.223
1918	NY	A	1		11	.000
	BRTR				290	.227

BECKENDORF, HENRY WARD "HEINE"
B.JUNE 15,1884 NEW YORK,N.Y.
D.SEPT.15,1949

YR	CL	LEA	POS	GP	G	REC
1909	DET	A	C		15	.259
1910	DET	A	C		3	.429
	WAS	A	C		37	.146
	BRTR				55	.182

BECKER, BEALS
B.JULY 5,1886 EL DORADO,KAN.
D.AUG.16,1943

YR	CL	LEA	POS	GP	G	REC
1908	PIT	N	O		17	.154
	BOS	N	O		43	.275
1909	BOS	N	O		152	.245
1910	NY	N	O		46	.286
1911	NY	N	O		55	.262
1912	NY	N	O		125	.264
1913	CIN	N	O		30	.296
	PHI	N	O		88	.324
1914	PHI	N	O		138	.325
1915	PHI	N	O		112	.246
	BLTL				806	.276

BECKER, CHARLES S. "BUCK"
B.OCT.14,1888 WASHINGTON,D.C.
D.JULY 30,1928

YR	CL	LEA	POS	GP	G	REC
1911	WAS	A	P		11	3- 5
1912	WAS	A	P		4	0- 0
	BLTL				15	3- 5

BECKER, HEINZ REINHARD "DUTCH"
B.AUG.26,1915 BERLIN,GERMANY

YR	CL	LEA	POS	GP	G	REC
1943	CHI	N	1		24	.145
1945	CHI	N	1		67	.286
1946	CHI	N	H		9	.286
	CLE	A	1		50	.299
1947	CLE	A	H		2	.000
	BBTR				152	.263
	BL 1946					

BECKER, JOSEPH EDWARD
B.JUNE 25,1908 ST.LOUIS,MO.

YR	CL	LEA	POS	GP	G	REC
1936	CLE	A	C		22	.180
1937	CLE	A	C		18	.333
	BRTR				40	.241

BECKER, MARTIN HENRY
B.DEC.25,1889 TIFFIN,OHIO
D.SEPT.25,1957

YR	CL	LEA	POS	GP	G	REC
1915	NY	N	O		17	.250
	BBTL					

BECKER, ROBERT CHARLES
B.AUG.15,1875 SYRACUSE,N.Y.
D.OCT.11,1951

YR	CL	LEA	POS	GP	G	REC
1897	PHI	N	P		5	0- 2
1898	PHI	N	P		1	0- 0
					6	0- 2

BECKERT, GLENN ALFRED
B.OCT.12,1940 PITTSBURGH,PA.

YR	CL	LEA	POS	GP	G	REC
1965	CHI	N	2		154	.239
1966	CHI	N	2-S		153	.287
1967	CHI	N	2		146	.280
1968	CHI	N	2		155	.294
1969	CHI	N	2		131	.291
1970	CHI	N	2-O		143	.288
1971	CHI	N	2		131	.342
1972	CHI	N	2		120	.270
1973	CHI	N	2		114	.255
1974	SD	N	2-3		64	.256
1975	SD	N	3		9	.375
	BRTR				1320	.283

BECKLEY, JACOB PETER "JAKE" OR "EAGLE EYE"
B.AUG.4,1867 HANNIBAL,MO.
D.JUNE 25,1918 KANSAS CITY,MO.

YR	CL	LEA	POS	GP	G	REC
1888	PIT	N	1		71	.342
1889	PIT	N	1		123	.300
1890	PIT	P	1		121	.325
1891	PIT	N	1		129	.291
1892	PIT	N	1		152	.250
1893	PIT	N	1		131	.324
1894	PIT	N	1		132	.344
1895	PIT	N	1		131	.324
1896	PIT	N	1		54	.244
	NY	N	1		45	.297
1897	NY	N	1		18	.268
	CIN	N	1		96	.336
1898	CIN	N	1		116	.299
1899	CIN	N	1		135	.333
1900	CIN	N	1		138	.343
1901	CIN	N	1		140	.300
1902	CIN	N	P-1	1	129	0- 1
						.331
1903	CIN	N	1		119	.327
1904	STL	N	1		142	.325
1905	STL	N	1		134	.286
1906	STL	N	1		85	.247
1907	STL	N	1		32	.209
	BLTL			1	2373	0- 1
						.309

BECKMAN, JAMES JOSEPH
B.MAR.1,1907 CINCINNATI,OHIO

YR	CL	LEA	POS	GP	G	REC
1927	CIN	N	P		4	0- 1
1928	CIN	N	P		6	0- 1
	BRTR				10	0- 2

BECKMANN, WILLIAM ALOYSIUS
B.DEC.8,1907 CLAYTON,MO.

YR	CL	LEA	POS	GP	G	REC
1939	PHI	A	P		27	7-11
1940	PHI	A	P		34	8- 4
1941	PHI	A	P		22	5- 9
1942	PHI	A	P		5	0- 1
	STL	N	P		2	1- 0
	BRTR				90	21-25

BECQUER, JULIO (VELLEGAS)
B.DEC.20,1931 HAVANA,CUBA

YR	CL	LEA	POS	GP	G	REC
1955	WAS	A	1		10	.214
1957	WAS	A	1		105	.226
1958	WAS	A	1-O		86	.238
1959	WAS	A	1		108	.268
1960	WAS	A	P-1	1	110	0- 0
						.252
1961	LA	A	1		11	.000
	MIN	A	P-1-O	1	57	0- 0
						.238
1963	MIN	A	H		1	.000
	BLTL			2	488	0- 0
						.244

BEDELL, HOWARD WILLIAM "HOWIE"
B.SEP.29,1935 CLEARFIELD,PA.

YR	CL	LEA	POS	GP	G	REC
1962	MIL	N	O		58	.196
1968	PHI	N	H		9	.143
	BLTR				67	.193

BEDFORD, JAMES ELDRED
B.MAR.26,1902 HUDSON,N.Y.
D.JUNE 27,1962

YR	CL	LEA	POS	GP	G	REC
1925	CLE	A	2		2	.000
	TR					

BEDGOOD, PHILLIP BURLETTE
B.MAR.8,1898 HARRISON,GA.
D.NOV.8,1927

YR	CL	LEA	POS	GP	G	REC
1922	CLE	A	P		1	1- 0
1923	CLE	A	P		9	0- 2
	BRTR				10	1- 2

YR	CL	LEA	POS	GP	G	REC

BEDIENT, HUGH CARPENTER
B.OCT.23,1889 GERRY,N.Y.
D.JULY 21,1965 JAMESTOWN,N.Y.

YR	CL	LEA	POS	GP	G	REC
1912	BOS	A	P		41	20-10
1913	BOS	A	P		43	15-14
1914	BOS	A	P		42	8-12
1915	BUF	F	P		53	16-18
		BRTR			179	59-54

BEDNAR, ANDREW JACKSON
B.AUG.16,1908 STREATOR,ILL.
D.NOV.26,1937 GRAHAM,TEX.

YR	CL	LEA	POS	GP	G	REC
1930	PIT	N	P		2	0- 0
1931	PIT	N	P		3	0- 0
		BRTR			5	0- 0

BEEBE, FREDERICK LEONARD
B.DEC.31,1880 LINCOLN,MO.
D.OCT.30,1957 ELGIN,ILL.

YR	CL	LEA	POS	GP	G	REC
1906	CHI	N	P		14	6- 1
	STL	N	P		20	.9- 9
1907	STL	N	P		31	7-19
1908	STL	N	P		29	5-13
1909	STL	N	P		44	15-21
1910	CIN	N	P		35	12-14
1911	PHI	N	P		9	3- 3
1916	CLE	A	P		21	5- 3
		BRTR			203	62-83

BEECHER, EDWARD
B.AUG.27,1873 ST.LOUIS,MO.

YR	CL	LEA	POS	GP	G	REC
1897	STL	N	0		3	.333
1898	CLE	N	0		8	.200
					11	.257

BEECHER, EDWARD C.
B.JULY 2,1859 GUILFORD,CONN.
D.SEPT.12,1935

YR	CL	LEA	POS	GP	G	REC
1887	PIT	N	0		40	.272
1889	WAS	N	0		41	.296
1890	BUF	P	P-0	1	126	0- 1
						.357
1891	WAS	AA	0		56	.233
	ATH	AA	0		16	.205
	BL			1	279	0- 1
						.299

BEECHER, LEROY
B.MAY 10,1884 SWANTON,OHIO
D.OCT.11,1952

YR	CL	LEA	POS	GP	G	REC
1907	NY	N	P		2	0- 2
1908	NY	N	P		2	0- 0
		BLTR			4	0- 2

BEELER, JOSEPH SAM "JODIE"
D.OCT.26,1921 DALLAS,TEX.

YR	CL	LEA	POS	GP	G	REC
1944	CIN	N	2-3		3	.000
		BRTR				

BEENE, FRED RAY
B.NOV.24,1942 ANGLETON,TEX.

YR	CL	LEA	POS	GP	G	REC
1968	BAL	A	P		1	0- 0
1969	BAL	A	P		2	0- 0
1970	BAL	A	P		4	0- 0
1972	NY	A	P	29	30	1- 3
1973	NY	A	P		19	6- 0
1974	NY	A	P		6	0- 0
	CLE	A	P	32	33	4- 4
1975	CLE	A	P	19	20	1- 0
		BBTR		112	115	12- 7
		BR 1968				

BEERS, CLARENCE SCOTT
B.DEC.9,1918 EL DORADO,KAN.

YR	CL	LEA	POS	GP	G	REC
1948	STL	N	P		1	0- 0

BEGGS, JOSEPH STANLEY "FIREMAN"
B.NOV.4,1913 RANKIN,PA.

YR	CL	LEA	POS	GP	G	REC
1938	NY	A	P		14	3- 2
1940	CIN	N	P		37	12- 3
1941	CIN	N	P		37	4- 3
1942	CIN	N	P		38	6- 5
1943	CIN	N	P		39	7- 6
1944	CIN	N	P		1	1- 0
1946	CIN	N	P		28	12-10
1947	CIN	N	P		11	0- 3
	NY	N	P		32	.3- 3
1948	NY	N	P		1	0- 0
		BRTR			238	48-35

BEGLEY, EDWARD N.
B.1863 NEW YORK,N.Y.
D.JULY 28,1919

YR	CL	LEA	POS	GP	G	REC
1884	NY	N	P-0	31	32	12-18
						.181
1885	MET	AA	P-0		15	4- 9
						.173
				46	47	16-27
						.179

BEGLEY, EUGENE I.
B.1863 BROOKLYN,N.Y.

YR	CL	LEA	POS	GP	G	REC
1886	NY	N	C		3	.111

BEGLEY, JAMES LAWRENCE "IMP"
B.SEPT.19,1903 SAN FRANCISCO,
CAL.

YR	CL	LEA	POS	GP	G	REC
1924	CIN	N	2		2	.200
		BRTR				

BEHAN, CHARLES FREDERICK "PETE"
B.DEC.11,1887 DALLAS CITY,PA.
D.JAN.21,1957

YR	CL	LEA	POS	GP	G	REC
1921	PHI	N	P		2	0- 1
1922	PHI	N	P		7	4- 2
1923	PHI	N	P	30	34	3-12
		BRTR		39	43	7-15

BEHEL, STEPHEN ARNOLD DOUGLAS
B.ROCKFORD,ILL.

YR	CL	LEA	POS	GP	G	REC
1884	MIL	U	0		9	.222
1886	MET	AA	0		59	.208
					68	.211

BEHNEY, MELVIN BRIAN "MEL"
B.SEP.2,1947 NEWARK,N.J.

YR	CL	LEA	POS	GP	G	REC
1970	CIN	N	P		5	0- 2
		BLTL				

BEHRMAN, HENRY BERNARD "HANK"
B.JUNE 27,1921 BROOKLYN,N.Y.

YR	CL	LEA	POS	GP	G	REC
1946	BRO	N	P		47	11- 5
1947	BRO	N	P		40	5- 3
	PIT	N	P		10	0- 2
1948	BRO	N	P		34	5- 4
1949	NY	N	P		43	3- 3
		BRTR			174	24-17

BEJMA, ALOYSIUS FRANK "OLLIE"
B.SEPT.12,1907 SOUTH BEND,IND.

YR	CL	LEA	POS	GP	G	REC
1934	STL	A	2-S-3-0		95	.271
1935	STL	A	2-S-3		64	.192
1936	STL	A	2		67	.259
1939	CHI	A	2		90	.251
		BRTR			316	.245

BELANGER, MARK HENRY
B.JUNE 8,1944 PITTSFIELD,MASS.

YR	CL	LEA	POS	GP	G	REC
1965	BAL	A	S		11	.333
1966	BAL	A	S		8	.158
1967	BAL	A	2-S-3		69	.174
1968	BAL	A	S		145	.208
1969	BAL	A	S		150	.287
1970	BAL	A	S		145	.218
1971	BAL	A	S		150	.266
1972	BAL	A	S		113	.186
1973	BAL	A	S		154	.226
1974	BAL	A	S		155	.225
1975	BAL	A	S		152	.226
1976	BAL	A	S		153	.270
		BRTR			1405	.235

BELANGIO, PROSPER ALBERT
(PLAYED UNDER NAME OF
PROSBY ALBERT BLANCHE)

BELARDI, CARROLL WAYNE
B.SEPT.5,1930 ST.HELENA,CAL.

YR	CL	LEA	POS	GP	G	REC
1950	BRO	N	1		10	.000
1951	BRO	N	H		3	.333
1953	BRO	N	1		69	.239
1954	BRO	N	H		11	.222
	DET	A	1		88	.232
1955	DET	A	H		3	.000
1956	DET	A	1-0		79	.279
		BLTL			263	.242

BELDEN, IRA A.
B.APR.16,1874 CLEVELAND,OHIO
D.JULY 15,1916

YR	CL	LEA	POS	GP	G	REC
1897	CLE	N	0		8	.250

BELINSKY, ROBERT "BO"
B.DEC.7,1936 NEW YORK,N.Y.

YR	CL	LEA	POS	GP	G	REC
1962	LA	A	P	33	34	10-11
1963	LA	A	P		13	2- 9
1964	LA	A	P		23	9- 8
1965	PHI	N	P	30	31	4- 9
1966	PHI	N	P		9	0- 2
1967	HOU	N	P		27	3- 9
1969	PIT	N	P		8	0- 3
1970	CIN	N	P		3	0- 0
		BLTL		146	148	28-51

BELL, CHARLES C.
B.AUG.2,1868 CINCINNATI,OHIO
D.FEB.7,1937

YR	CL	LEA	POS	GP	G	REC
1889	KC	AA	P		1	1- 0
1891	LOU	AA	P		11	3- 8
	CIN	AA	P		4	1- 0
					16	5- 8

BELL, DAVID GUS "BUDDY"
B.AUG.27,1951 PITTSBURGH,PA.

YR	CL	LEA	POS	GP	G	REC
1972	CLE	A	3-0		132	.255
1973	CLE	A	3-0		156	.268
1974	CLE	A	3		116	.262
1975	CLE	A	3		153	.271
1976	CLE	A	1-3		159	.281
		BRTR			716	.269

BELL, DAVID RUSSELL "GUS"
B.NOV.15,1928 LOUISVILLE,KY.

YR	CL	LEA	POS	GP	G	REC
1950	PIT	N	0		111	.282
1951	PIT	N	0		149	.278
1952	PIT	N	0		131	.250
1953	CIN	N	0		151	.300
1954	CIN	N	0		153	.299
1955	CIN	N	0		154	.308
1956	CIN	N	0		150	.292
1957	CIN	N	0		121	.292
1958	CIN	N	0		112	.252
1959	CIN	N	0		168	.293
1960	CIN	N	0		143	.262
1961	CIN	N	0		103	.255
1962	NY	N	0		30	.149
	MIL	N	0		79	.285
1963	MIL	N	H		3	.333
1964	MIL	N	H		3	.000
		BLTR			1741	.281

BELL, FERN LEE "DANNY"
B.JAN.21,1913 ADA,OKLA.

YR	CL	LEA	POS	GP	G	REC
1939	PIT	N	0		83	.286
1940	PIT	N	H		6	.000
		BRTR			89	.283

BELL, FRANK GUSTAV
B.1863 CINCINNATI,OHIO
D.APR.14,1891

YR	CL	LEA	POS	GP	G	REC
1885	BRO	AA	C-3-0		10	.167

BELL, GARY
B.NOV.17,1936 SAN ANTONIO,TEX.

YR	CL	LEA	POS	GP	G	REC
1958	CLE	A	P		33	12-10
1959	CLE	A	P		44	16-11
1960	CLE	A	P	28	30	9-10
1961	CLE	A	P		34	12-16
1962	CLE	A	P		57	10- 9
1963	CLE	A	P		58	8- 5
1964	CLE	A	P		56	8- 6
1965	CLE	A	P		60	6- 5
1966	CLE	A	P		40	14-15
1967	CLE	A	P		9	1- 5
	BOS	A	P		29	12- 8
1968	BOS	A	P		35	11-11
1969	SEA	A	P		13	2- 6
	CHI	A	P		23	0- 0
		BRTR		519	521	121-117

BELL, GEORGE GLENN "FARMER"
B.NOV.2,1874 GREENWOOD,N.Y.
D.DEC.25,1941

YR	CL	LEA	POS	GP	G	REC
1907	BRO	N	P		35	8-16
1908	BRO	N	P		29	4-15
1909	BRO	N	P		33	16-15
1910	BRO	N	P		44	10-27
1911	BRO	N	P		19	5- 6
		BRTR			160	43-79

YR	CL	LEA	POS	GP	G	REC

BELL, HERMAN S. "HI"
B.JULY 16,1895 LOUISVILLE,KY.
D.JUNE 7,1949

1924	STL	N	P		28	3- 8
1926	STL	N	P		27	6- 6
1927	STL	N	P		25	1- 3
1929	STL	N	P		7	0- 2
1930	STL	N	P		39	4- 3
1932	NY	N	P		35	8- 4
1933	NY	N	P		38	6- 5
1934	NY	N	P		22	4- 3
		BRTR			221	32-34

BELL, JERRY HOUSTON
B.OCT.6,1947 MADISON,TENN.

1971	MIL	A	P		8	2- 1
1972	MIL	A	P		25	5- 1
1973	MIL	A	P		31	9- 9
1974	MIL	A	P		5	1- 0
		BBTR			69	17-11

BELL, JOHN
(REAL NAME
RUDOLPH FRED BAERWALD)
B.JAN.1,1881 WASSAU,WIS.
D.JULY 28,1955

| 1907 | NY | A | O | | 17 | .212 |
| | | BRTR | | | | |

BELL, KEVIN ROBERT
B.JULY 13,1955 LOS ANGELES,CAL.

| 1976 | CHI | A | 3 | | 68 | .248 |
| | | BRTR | | | | |

BELL, LESTER ROWLAND
B.DEC.14,1901 HARRISBURG,PA.

1923	STL	N	S		15	.373
1924	STL	N	3		17	.246
1925	STL	N	S-3		153	.285
1926	STL	N	3		155	.325
1927	STL	N	S-3		115	.259
1928	BOS	N	3		153	.277
1929	BOS	N	3		139	.298
1930	CHI	N	3		74	.278
1931	CHI	N	3		75	.282
		BRTR			896	.290

BELL, RALPH A. "LEFTY"
B.1889

| 1912 | CHI | A | P | | 2 | 0- 0 |
| | | BLTL | | | | |

BELL, ROY CHESTER "BEAU"
B.AUG.20,1907 BELLVILLE,TEX.

1935	STL	A	1-3-O		76	.250
1936	STL	A	1-O		155	.344
1937	STL	A	1-O		156	.340
1938	STL	A	O		147	.262
1939	STL	A	O		11	.219
	DET	A	O		54	.239
1940	CLE	A	1-O		120	.279
1941	CLE	A	1-O		48	.192
		BRTR			767	.297

BELL, WILLIAM SAMUEL
B.OCT.24,1933 GOLDSBORO,N.C.
D.OCT.11,1962

1952	PIT	N	P		4	0- 1
1955	PIT	N	P		1	0- 0
		BRTR			5	0- 1

BELLA, JOHN
B.AUG.23,1932 GREENWICH,CONN.

1957	NY	A	O		5	.100
1959	KC	A	1-O		47	.207
		BRTL			52	.196

BELLAN, ESTEBAN ENRIQUE
B.1850 CUBA
D.AUG.8,1932

1871	TRO	NA	S-3		29	.213
1872	TRO	NA	S-3-O		23	.278
1873	MUT	NA	3		7	-
					59	-

BELLMAN, JOHN CHARLES
B.LOUISVILLE,KY.

| 1889 | STL | AA | C | | 1 | .500 |

BELLOIR, ROBERT EDWARD "ROB"
B.JULY 13,1948 HEIDELBERG,GER.

1975	ATL	N	2-S		43	.219
1976	ATL	N	2-S-3		30	.200
		BRTR			73	.212

BEMIS, HARRY PARKER
B.FEB.1,1874 FARMINGTON,N.H.
D.MAY.23,1947

1902	CLE	A	C-2-O		93	.311
1903	CLE	A	C		93	.258
1904	CLE	A	C		95	.225
1905	CLE	A	C		69	.292
1906	CLE	A	C		93	.274
1907	CLE	A	C		65	.250
1908	CLE	A	C		91	.224
1909	CLE	A	C		42	.187
1910	CLE	A	C		61	.215
		BRTR			702	.254

BENCH, JOHNNY LEE
B.DEC.7,1947 OKLAHOMA CITY,OKLA.

1967	CIN	N	C		26	.163
1968	CIN	N	C		154	.275
1969	CIN	N	C		148	.293
1970	CIN	N	C-1-3-O		158	.293
1971	CIN	N	C-1-3-O		149	.238
1972	CIN	N	C-1-3-O		147	.270
1973	CIN	N	C-1-3-O		152	.253
1974	CIN	N	C-1-3		160	.280
1975	CIN	N	C-1-O		142	.283
1976	CIN	N	C-1-O		135	.234
		BRTR			1371	.268

BENDER, CHARLES ALBERT "CHIEF"
B.MAY 5,1883 BRAINERD,MINN.
D.MAY 22,1954 PHILADELPHIA,PA.

1903	PHI	A	P		36	43	17-15
1904	PHI	A	P		28	29	7-14
1905	PHI	A	P			35	15-10
1906	PHI	A	P		37	44	15-10
1907	PHI	A	P		33	45	16- 8
1908	PHI	A	P			20	8- 9
1909	PHI	A	P		34	40	18- 8
1910	PHI	A	P		30	36	23- 5
1911	PHI	A	P		31	32	17- 5
1912	PHI	A	P			27	13- 8
1913	PHI	A	P			48	19- 9
1914	PHI	A	P			28	17- 3
1915	BAL	F	P			26	4-16
1916	PHI	N	P		27	28	7- 7
1917	PHI	N	P			20	8- 2
1925	CHI	A	P			1	0- 0
		BRTR		461	502	204-129

BENEDICT, ARTHUR M.
B.MAR.31,1862 CORNWALL,ILL.

| 1883 | PHI | N | 2 | | 3 | .267 |
| | | BRTR | | | | |

BENES, JOSEPH ANTHONY "BANANAS"
B.JAN.8,1901 LONG ISLAND CITY,
N.Y.

| 1931 | STL | N | 2-S-3 | | 10 | .167 |
| | | BRTR | | | | |

BENGE, RAYMOND ADELPHIA "RAY"
B.APR.22,1902 JACKSONVILLE,TEX.

1925	CLE	A	P		2	1- 0
1926	CLE	A	P		8	1- 0
1928	PHI	N	P	40	42	8-18
1929	PHI	N	P	38	43	11-15
1930	PHI	N	P		38	11-15
1931	PHI	N	P		38	14-18
1932	PHI	N	P		41	13-12
1933	BRO	N	P		37	10-17
1934	BRO	N	P		36	14-12
1935	BRO	N	P		23	9- 9
1936	BOS	N	P		21	7- 9
	PHI	N	P		15	1- 4
1938	CIN	N	P		9	1- 1
		BRTR		346	353	101-130

BENGOUGH, BERNARD OLIVER "BENNY"
B.JULY 27,1898 NIAGARA FALLS,
N.Y.
D.DEC.22,1968 PHILADELPHIA,PA.

1923	NY	A	C		19	.132
1924	NY	A	C		11	.312
1925	NY	A	C		95	.258
1926	NY	A	C		36	.381
1927	NY	A	C		31	.247
1928	NY	A	C		58	.267
1929	NY	A	C		23	.194
1930	NY	A	C		44	.235
1931	STL	A	C		40	.250
1932	STL	A	C		54	.252
		BRTR			411	.255

BENIQUEZ, JUAN JOSE (TORRES)
B.MAY 13,1950 SAN SEBASTIAN,P.R.

1971	BOS	A	S		16	.298
1972	BOS	A	S		33	.242
1974	BOS	A	O		106	.267
1975	BOS	A	3-0-O		78	.291
1976	TEX	A	2-O		145	.255
		BRTR			378	.267

BENJAMIN, ALFRED STANLEY "STAN"
B.MAY 20,1914 FRAMINGHAM,MASS.

1939	PHI	N	3-O		12	.140
1940	PHI	N	O		8	.222
1941	PHI	N	1-2-3-O		129	.235
1942	PHI	N	1-O		78	.224
1945	CLE	A	O		14	.333
		BRTR			241	.229

BENJAMIN, JOHN W.
B.1837 ELIZABETH,N.J.
D.NOV.14,1895
NON-PLAYING MANAGER RES(NA)1873

BENN, HENRY OMER
B.JAN.25,1890 VIOLA,WIS.
D.JUNE 4,1967 MADISON,WIS.

| 1914 | CLE | A | P | | 1 | 0- 0 |
| | | BRTR | | | | |

BENNERS, ISSAC B.
B.PHILADELPHIA,PA.

1884	BRO	AA	O		49	.209
	WIL	U	O		6	.045
					55	.191

BENNETT, CHARLES WESLEY
B.NOV.21,1854 NEW CASTLE,PA.
D.FEB.24,1927

1878	MIL	N	C-O		48	.246
1880	WOR	N	C-O		50	.223
1881	DET	N	C-O		76	.301
1882	DET	N	C-1-2-3		80	.304
1883	DET	N	C-2-O		89	.301
1884	DET	N	C-1-2-S-O		88	.264
1885	DET	N	C-3-O		91	.269
1886	DET	N	C		69	.242
1887	DET	N	C		46	.363
1888	DET	N	C		72	.263
1889	BOS	N	C		80	.230
1890	BOS	N	C		85	.213
1891	BOS	N	C		74	.215
1892	BOS	N	C		32	.201
1893	BOS	N	C		58	.218
		BRTR			1038	.262

BENNETT, DAVID HANS "DAVE"
B.NOV.7,1945 BERKELEY,CAL.

| 1964 | PHI | N | P | | 1 | 0- 0 |
| | | BRTR | | | | |

BENNETT, DENNIS JOHN
B.OCT.5,1939 OAKLAND,CAL.

1962	PHI	N	P		31	9- 9
1963	PHI	N	P		23	9- 5
1964	PHI	N	P		41	12-14
1965	BOS	A	P		34	5- 7
1966	BOS	A	P		16	3- 3
1967	BOS	A	P		13	4- 3
	NY	N	P		8	1- 1
1968	CAL	A	P		16	0- 5
		BLTL			182	43-47

BENNETT, FRANCIS ALLEN "CHIP"
B.OCT.27,1905 MARDELA SPRINGS,
MD.
D.MAR.18,1966 WILMINGTON,DEL.

1927	BOS	A	P		4	0- 1
1928	BOS	A	P		1	0- 0
		BRTR			5	0- 1

BENNETT, HERSCHEL EMMETT
B.SEPT.21,1896 SPRINGFIELD,MO.
D.SEPT.9,1964 SPRINGFIELD,MO.

1923	STL	A	O		5	.000
1924	STL	A	O		41	.330
1925	STL	A	O		93	.279
1926	STL	A	O		80	.266
1927	STL	A	O		93	.266
		BLTR			312	.276

BENNETT, JAMES FRED "RED"
B.MAR.15,1902 ATKINS,ARK.
D.MAY 12,1957

1928	STL	A	O		7	.250
1931	PIT	N	O		32	.281
		BRTR			39	.278

YR	CL	LEA	POS	GP	G	REC

BENNETT, JOSEPH HARLEY "BUGS"
(SEE JOSEPH MORRIS)

BENNETT, JOSEPH ROSENBLUM
B.JULY 2,1900 NEW YORK,N.Y.
| 1923 | PHI | N | 3 | | 1 | .000 |
| | BRTR | | | | | |

BENNETT, JUSTIN TITUS "PUG"
B.FEB.20,1874 PONCA,NEB.
D.SEPT.12,1935
1906	STL	N	2		153	.262
1907	STL	N	2		86	.222
	TR				239	.248

BENSON, ALLEN WILBERT
B.JULY 12,1908 HURLEY,S.DAK.
| 1934 | WAS | A | P | | 2 | 0- 1 |
| | BRTR | | | | | |

BENSON, VERNON ADAIR
B.SEPT.19,1924 GRANITE QUARRY,
N.C.
1943	PHI	A	H		2	.000
1946	PHI	A	O		7	.000
1951	STL	N	3-O		13	.261
1952	STL	N	3		20	.191
1953	STL	N	H		13	.000
	BLTR				55	.202

BENTLEY, CYRUS G.
B.WATERBURY,CONN.
| 1872 | MAN | NA | P-O | | 23 | 1-13 |
| | | | | | | .239 |

BENTLEY, JOHN NEEDLES "JACK"
B.MAR.8,1895 SANDY SPRINGS,MD.
D.OCT.24,1969 OLNEY,MD.
1913	WAS	A	P		3	0- 0
1914	WAS	A	P		30	5- 7
1915	WAS	A	P		4	0- 2
1916	WAS	A	P		2	0- 0
1923	NY	N	P	31	52	13- 8
1924	NY	N	P	28	46	16- 5
1925	NY	N	P-1	29	64	11- 9
			O			.303
1926	PHI	N	P-1	7	75	0- 2
						.258
	NY	N	P	1	3	0- 0
1927	NY	N	P		8	0- 0
	BLTL			143	287	45-33
						.291

BENTON, JOHN ALTON "AL"
B.MAR.18,1911 NOBLE,OKLA.
1934	PHI	A	P		32	7- 9
1935	PHI	A	P		27	3- 4
1938	DET	A	P		19	5- 3
1939	DET	A	P		57	6- 8
1940	DET	A	P		42	6-10
1941	DET	A	P		38	15- 6
1942	DET	A	P		35	7-13
1945	DET	A	P		31	13- 8
1946	DET	A	P		28	11- 7
1947	DET	A	P		36	6- 7
1948	DET	A	P		30	2- 2
1949	CLE	A	P		40	9- 6
1950	CLE	A	P		36	4- 2
1952	BOS	A	P		24	4- 3
	BRTR				455	98-88

BENTON, JOHN CLEVELAND "RUBE"
B.JUNE 27,1890 CLINTON,N.C.
D.DEC.12,1937
1910	CIN	N	P		12	0- 1
1911	CIN	N	P		6	3- 3
1912	CIN	N	P		50	18-20
1913	CIN	N	P		23	11- 7
1914	CIN	N	P		41	16-18
1915	CIN	N	P		34	6-13
	PIT	N	P		1	0- 0
	NY	N	P		10	3- 5
1916	NY	N	P		38	16- 8
1917	NY	N	P		35	15- 9
1918	NY	N	P		3	1- 2
1919	NY	N	P		35	17-11
1920	NY	N	P		33	9-16
1921	NY	N	P		18	5- 2
1923	CIN	N	P		33	14-10
1924	CIN	N	P		32	7- 9
1925	CIN	N	P		33	9-10
	BLTL			437	150-144

BENTON, LAWRENCE JAMES
B.NOV.20,1897 CINCINNATI,OHIO
D.APR.3,1953 CINCINNATI,OHIO
1923	BOS	N	P		35	5- 9
1924	BOS	N	P		30	5- 7
1925	BOS	N	P	31	32	14- 7
1926	BOS	N	P	43	45	14-14
1927	BOS	N	P		11	4- 2
	NY	N	P		31	13- 5
1928	NY	N	P		42	25- 9
1929	NY	N	P	39	41	11-17
1930	NY	N	P		8	1- 3
	CIN	N	P		35	7-12
1931	CIN	N	P		38	10-15
1932	CIN	N	P		35	6-13
1933	CIN	N	P		34	10-11
1934	CIN	N	P		16	0- 1
1935	BOS	N	P		29	2- 3
	BRTR			455	462	127-128

BENTON, SIDNEY WRIGHT
B.AUG.4,1895 BUCKNER,ARK.
| 1922 | STL | N | P | | 1 | 0- 0 |
| | BRTR | | | | | |

BENTON, STANLEY W. "RABBIT"
B.SEPT.29,1901 LEXINGTON,KY.
| 1922 | PHI | N | 2 | | 6 | .211 |
| | BRTR | | | | | |

BENZ, JOSEPH LOUIS
"JOE" OR "BUTCHER BOY"
B.JAN.21,1886 NEW ALSACE,IND.
D.APR.22,1957 CHICAGO,ILL.
1911	CHI	A	P		12	3- 3
1912	CHI	A	P		41	13-17
1913	CHI	A	P		33	7-10
1914	CHI	A	P		48	14-19
1915	CHI	A	P		39	15-11
1916	CHI	A	P		28	5
1917	CHI	A	P		19	7- 3
1918	CHI	A	P		29	7- 8
1919	CHI	A	P		1	0- 0
	BRTR			250	75-75

BERARDINO, JOHN "BERNIE"
B.MAY 1,1917 LOS ANGELES,CAL.
1939	STL	A	2		126	.256
1940	STL	A	2-S-3		142	.258
1941	STL	A	S-3		128	.271
1942	STL	A	1-2-S-3		29	.284
1946	STL	A	2		144	.265
1947	STL	A	2		90	.261
1948	CLE	A	1-2-S-3		66	.190
1949	CLE	A	2-S-3		50	.191
1950	CLE	A	2-3		4	.400
	PIT	N	2-3		40	.206
1951	STL	A	1-2-3-O		39	.227
1952	CLE	A	1-2-S-3		35	.094
	PIT	N	2		19	.143
	BRTR			912	.249

BERBERET, LOUIS JOSEPH
B.NOV.20,1929 LONG BEACH,CAL.
1954	NY	A	C		5	.400
1955	NY	A	C		2	.400
1956	WAS	A	C		95	.261
1957	WAS	A	C		99	.261
1958	WAS	A	C		5	.167
	BOS	A	C		57	.210
1959	DET	A	C		100	.216
1960	DET	A	C		85	.194
	BLTR			448	.230

BERG, MORRIS "MOE"
B.MAR.2,1902 NEW YORK,N.Y.
D.MAY 29,1972 BELLEVILLE,N.J.
1923	BRO	N	2-S		49	.186
1926	CHI	A	S		41	.221
1927	CHI	A	C-2		35	.247
1928	CHI	A	C		76	.246
1929	CHI	A	C		107	.287
1930	CHI	A	C		20	.115
1931	CLE	A	C		10	.077
1932	WAS	A	C		75	.236
1933	WAS	A	C		40	.185
1934	WAS	A	C		33	.244
	CLE	A	C		29	.258
1935	BOS	A	C		38	.286
1936	BOS	A	C		39	.240
1937	BOS	A	C		47	.255
1938	BOS	A	C		10	.333
1939	BOS	A	C		14	.273
	BRTR			663	.243

BERGAMO, AUGUST SAMUEL
B.FEB.14,1918 DETROIT,MICH.
1944	STL	N	1-O		80	.286
1945	STL	N	1-O		94	.316
	BLTL			174	.305

BERGEN, MARTIN
B.OCT.25,1871 N.BROOKFIELD,MASS
D.JAN.19,1900
1896	BOS	N	C		62	.267
1897	BOS	N	C		83	.247
1898	BOS	N	C		120	.289
1899	BOS	N	C		71	.257
	TR			336	.268

BERGEN, WILLIAM ALOYSIUS
B.JUNE 13,1873 N.BROOKFIELD,
MASS.
D.DEC.19,1943
1901	CIN	N	C		82	.172
1902	CIN	N	C		89	.181
1903	CIN	N	C		58	.227
1904	BRO	N	C		94	.182
1905	BRO	N	C		76	.190
1906	BRO	N	C		103	.161
1907	BRO	N	C		51	.159
1908	BRO	N	C		99	.175
1909	BRO	N	C		112	.139
1910	BRO	N	C		89	.161
1911	BRO	N	C		84	.132
	BRTR			937	.170

BERGER, CHARLES "HEINE"
B.JAN.7,1882 LASALLE,ILL.
D.FEB.10,1954
1907	CLE	A	P		14	3- 3
1908	CLE	A	P		29	13- 8
1909	CLE	A	P		34	13-14
1910	CLE	A	P		13	3- 4
	TR			90	32-29

BERGER, CLARENCE EDWARD
B.NOV.1,1894 E.CLEVELAND,OHIO
D.JUNE 30,1959 WASHINGTON,D.C.
| 1914 | PIT | N | O | | 5 | .083 |
| | BLTR | | | | | |

BERGER, JOHN HENNE
B.AUG.28,1902 PHILADELPHIA,PA.
1922	PHI	A	C		2	1.000
1927	WAS	A	C		9	.267
	BRTR			11	.353

BERGER, JOHN HENRY "TUN"
B.DEC.6,1867 PITTSBURGH,PA.
D.JUNE 10,1907
1890	PIT	N	C-S-O		104	.266
1891	PIT	N	C-2		37	.240
1892	WAS	N	S		25	.142
					166	.241

BERGER, JOSEPH AUGUST "FATS"
B.DEC.20,1886 ST.LOUIS,MO.
D.MAR.5,1956
1913	CHI	A	2		77	.215
1914	CHI	A	S		47	.155
	BRTR			124	.191

BERGER, LOUIS WILLIAM "BOZE"
B.MAY 12,1910 BALTIMORE,MD.
1932	CLE	A	S		1	.000
1935	CLE	A	1-2-S-3		124	.258
1936	CLE	A	1-2-S-3		28	.173
1937	CHI	A	3		52	.238
1938	CHI	A	2-S		118	.217
1939	BOS	A	S		20	.300
	BRTR			343	.236

BERGER, WALTER ANTONE
B.OCT.10,1905 CHICAGO,ILL.
1930	BOS	N	O		151	.310
1931	BOS	N	O		156	.323
1932	BOS	N	1-O		145	.307
1933	BOS	N	O		137	.313
1934	BOS	N	O		150	.298
1935	BOS	N	O		150	.295
1936	BOS	N	O		138	.288
1937	BOS	N	O		30	.274
	NY	N	O		59	.291
1938	NY	N	O		16	.188
	CIN	N	O		99	.307
1939	CIN	N	O		97	.258
1940	CIN	N	H		2	.000
	PHI	N	1-O		20	.317
	BRTR			1350	.300

YR	CL	LEA	POS	GP	G	REC

BERGH, JOHN BAPTIST
B.OCT.8,1857 BOSTON,MASS.
D.APR.16,1883

1876	ATH	N	C		1	.000
1880	BOS	N	C		11	.167
					12	.152

BERGHAMMER, MARTIN ANDREW "PEPPER"
B.JUNE 18,1888 ELLIOTT,PA.
D.DEC.21,1957

1911	CHI	A	2		2	.000
1913	CIN	N	S		74	.218
1914	CIN	N	S		77	.223
1915	PIT	F	S		132	.238
			BLTR		285	.230

BERGMAN, ALFRED HENRY "DUTCH"
B.SEPT.27,1890 PERU,IND.
D.JUNE 21,1961

| 1916 | CLE | A | 2 | | 7 | .214 |
| | | | BRTR | | | |

BERGMAN, DAVID BRUCE "DAVE"
B.JUNE 6,1953 EVANSTON,ILL.

| 1975 | NY | A | O | | 7 | .000 |
| | | | BLTL | | | |

BERKELBACH, FRANK P.
B.PHILADELPHIA,PA.

| 1884 | CIN | AA | O | | 6 | .231 |

BERKENSTOCK, NATHAN
B.1883 PENNSYLVANIA
D.FEB.23,1900

| 1871 | ATH | NA | O | | 1 | .000 |

BERLY, JOHN CHAMBERS
B.MAY 24,1903 NATCHITOCHES,LA.

1924	STL	N	P		4	0- 0
1931	NY	N	P		27	7- 8
1932	PHI	N	P		21	1- 2
1933	PHI	N	P		13	2- 3
			BRTR		65	10-13

BERMAN, ROBERT LEON
B.JAN.24,1899 NEW YORK,N.Y.

| 1918 | WAS | A | C | | 2 | .000 |
| | | | BRTR | | | |

BERNARD, CURTIS HENRY
B.FEB.1,1879 PARKERSBURG,W.VA.
D.APR.10,1955

1900	NY	N	O		19	.243
1901	NY	N	O		19	.192
			TR		38	.217

BERNARD, JOSEPH

| 1909 | STL | N | P | | 1 | 0- 0 |

BERNARD, WILLIAM HENRY "STRAWBERRY BILL"
B.MAR.16,1871 CLARENCE,N.Y.
D.MAR.30,1949 SAN DIEGO,CAL.

1899	PHI	N	P		17	6- 5
1900	PHI	N	P		28	14-11
1901	PHI	A	P	30	31	17-11
1902	PHI	A	P		1	1- 0
	CLE	A	P		27	17- 6
1903	CLE	A	P		20	14- 5
1904	CLE	A	P		38	21-13
1905	CLE	A	P		22	6-14
1906	CLE	A	P		31	16-15
1907	CLE	A	P		8	0- 1
			BBTR	222	223	112-81

BERNHARDT, JUAN RAMON
B.AUG.31,1953 SAN PEDRO DE
MACORIS,D.R.

| 1976 | NY | A | 3-O | | 10 | .190 |
| | | | BRTR | | | |

BERNHARDT, WALTER JACOB
B.MAY 20,1893 ROULETTE,PA.
D.JULY 26,1958

| 1918 | NY | A | P | | 1 | 0- 0 |
| | | | BRTR | | | |

BERNIER, CARLOS RODRIGUEZ
B.JAN.28,1929 JUANA DIAZ,P.R.

| 1953 | PIT | N | O | | 105 | .213 |
| | | | BRTR | | | |

BERO, JOHN GEROGE
B.DEC.22,1923 GARY,W.VA.

1948	DET	A	2		4	.000
1951	STL	A	2-S		61	.213
			BLTR		65	.201

BERRA, LAWRENCE PETER "YOGI"
B.MAY,12;1925 ST.LOUIS,MO.

1946	NY	A	C		7	.364
1947	NY	A	C-O		83	.280
1948	NY	A	C-O		125	.305
1949	NY	A	C		116	.277
1950	NY	A	C		151	.322
1951	NY	A	C		141	.294
1952	NY	A	C		142	.273
1953	NY	A	C		137	.296
1954	NY	A	C-3		151	.307
1955	NY	A	C		147	.272
1956	NY	A	C-O		140	.298
1957	NY	A	C-O		134	.251
1958	NY	A	C-1-O		122	.266
1959	NY	A	C-O		131	.284
1960	NY	A	C-O		120	.276
1961	NY	A	C-O		119	.271
1962	NY	A	C		86	.224
1963	NY	A	C		64	.293
1965	NY	N	C		4	.222
			BLTR		2120	.285

NON-PLAYING MANAGER
NY(A) 1964, NY(N) 1972-75

BERRENS, JOSEPH

| 1912 | CHI | A | O | | 2 | .250 |

BERRES, RAYMOND FREDERICK "RAY"
B.AUG.31,1907 KENOSHA,WIS.

1934	BRO	N	C		39	.215
1936	BRO	N	C		105	.240
1937	PIT	N	C		2	.167
1938	PIT	N	C		40	.230
1939	PIT	N	C		81	.229
1940	PIT	N	C		21	.188
	BOS	N	C		85	.192
1941	BOS	N	C		120	.201
1942	NY	N	C		12	.188
1943	NY	N	C		20	.143
1944	NY	N	C		16	.471
1945	NY	N	C		20	.167
			BRTR		561	.216

BERRY, ALLEN KENT "KEN"
B.MAY 10,1941 KANSAS CITY,MO.

1962	CHI	A	O		3	.333
1963	CHI	A	2-O		4	.200
1964	CHI	A	O		12	.375
1965	CHI	A	O		157	.218
1966	CHI	A	O		147	.271
1967	CHI	A	O		147	.241
1968	CHI	A	O		153	.252
1969	CHI	A	O		130	.232
1970	CHI	A	O		141	.276
1971	CAL	A	O		111	.221
1972	CAL	A	O		119	.289
1973	CAL	A	O		136	.284
1974	MIL	A	O-D		98	.240
1975	CLE	A	O		25	.200
			BRTR		1383	.255

BERRY, CHARLES FRANCIS
B.OCT.18,1902 PHILIPSBURG,N.J.
D.SEPT.6,1972 EVANSTON,ILL.

1925	PHI	A	C		10	.214
1928	BOS	A	C		80	.260
1929	BOS	A	C		77	.242
1930	BOS	A	C		88	.289
1931	BOS	A	C		111	.283
1932	BOS	A	C		10	.188
	CHI	A	C		72	.305
1933	CHI	A	C		86	.255
1934	PHI	A	C		99	.268
1935	PHI	A	C		62	.253
1936	PHI	A	C		13	.059
1938	PHI	A	C		1	.000
			BRTR		709	.267

BERRY, CHARLES JOSEPH
B.SEPT.6,1860 ELIZABETH,N.J.
D.FEB.16,1940

1884	ALT	U	2		7	.269
	KC	U	2-3-O		29	.267
	CHI	U	2		5	.118
	PIT	U	2		2	.100
			BRTR		43	.243

BERRY, CLAUDE ELZY "ADMIRAL"
B.FEB.14,1880 LOSANTVILLE,IND.
D.FEB.1,1974 RICHMOND,IND.

1904	CHI	A	C		3	.000
1906	PHI	A	C		10	.226
1907	PHI	A	C		8	.291
1914	PIT	F	C		124	.243
1915	PIT	F	C		99	.192
			BRTR		244	.224

BERRY, CORNELIUS JOHN "NEIL"
B.JAN.11,1922 KALAMAZOO,MICH.

1948	DET	A	2-S		87	.266
1949	DET	A	2-S		109	.237
1950	DET	A	2-S-3		38	.256
1951	DET	A	2-S-3		67	.229
1952	DET	A	S-3		73	.228
1953	STL	A	2-S-3		57	.283
	CHI	A	2		5	.125
1954	BAL	A	S		5	.111
			BRTR		441	.244

BERRY, JONAS ARTHUR "JITTERY JOE"
B.DEC.16,1904 HUNTSVILLE,ARK.
D.SEPT.27,1958

1942	CHI	N	P		2	0- 0
1944	PHI	A	P		53	10- 8
1945	PHI	A	P		52	8- 7
1946	PHI	A	P		5	0- 1
	CLE	A	P		21	3- 6
			BLTR		133	21-22

BERRY, JOSEPH HOWARD JR. "NIG"
B.DEC.31,1896 PHILADELPHIA,PA.
D.APR.29,1976 PHILADELPHIA,PA.

1921	NY	N	2		9	.333
1922	NY	N	H		6	.000
			BBTR		15	.333

BERRY, JOSEPH HOWARD SR "HODGE"
B.SEPT.10,1872 WHEELING,W.VA.
D.MAR.3,1961

| 1902 | PHI | N | C | | 1 | .250 |
| | | | BBTR | | | |

BERRY, THOMAS HANEY
B.DEC.31,1842 CHESTER,PA.
D.JUNE 15,1915

| 1871 | ATH | NA | O | | 1 | .250 |

BERTAINA, FRANK LOUIS
B.APR.14,1944 SAN FRANCISCO,CAL.

1964	BAL	A	P		6	1- 0
1965	BAL	A	P		2	0- 0
1966	BAL	A	P		16	2- 5
1967	BAL	A	P		5	1- 1
	WAS	A	P	18	19	6- 5
1968	WAS	A	P		27	7-13
1969	WAS	A	P		14	1- 3
	BAL	A	P		3	0- 0
1970	STL	N	P		8	1- 2
			BLTL	99	100	19-29

BERTE, HARRY
B.MAY 10,1872 COVINGTON,KY.

| 1903 | STL | N | 2-S | | 4 | .357 |
| | | | TR | | | |

BERTELL, RICHARD GEORGE "DICK"
B.NOV.21,1935 OAK PARK,ILL.

1960	CHI	N	C		5	.133
1961	CHI	N	C		92	.273
1962	CHI	N	C		77	.302
1963	CHI	N	C		100	.233
1964	CHI	N	C		112	.238
1965	CHI	N	C		34	.214
	SF	N	C		22	.188
1967	CHI	N	C		2	.167
			BRTR		444	.250

BERTHRONG, HENRY W. "HARRY"
B.JAN.1,1844 MUMFORD,N.Y.
D.APR.28,1928 CHELSEA,MASS.

| 1871 | OLY | NA | 2-3-O | | 17 | .244 |
| | | | TR | | | |

BERTOIA, RENO PETER
B.JAN.8,1935 ST.VITO,UDINE, ITALY

YR	CL	LEA	POS	GP	G	REC
1950	DET	A	2		1	.000
1954	DET	A	2-S-3		54	.162
1955	DET	A	S-3		38	.206
1956	DET	A	2-3		22	.182
1957	DET	A	2-S-3		97	.275
1958	DET	A	S-3-O		86	.233
1959	WAS	A	2-S-3		90	.237
1960	WAS	A	2-3		121	.265
1961	MIN	A	3		35	.212
	KC	A	2-3		39	.242
	DET	A	2-S-3		24	.217
1962	DET	A	2-S-3		5	.000
	BRTR				612	.244

BERTRAND, ROMAN MATHIAS "LEFTY"
B.FEB.28,1909 COBDEN,MINN.

YR	CL	LEA	POS	GP	G	REC
1936	PHI	N	P		1	0- 0
	BRTL					

BESANA, FREDERICK CYRIL "FRED"
B.APR.5,1931 LINCOLN,CAL.

YR	CL	LEA	POS	GP	G	REC
1956	BAL	A	P		7	1- 0
	BRTL					

BESCHER, ROBERT HENRY
B.FEB.25,1884 LONDON,OHIO
D.NOV.29,1942

YR	CL	LEA	POS	GP	G	REC
1908	CIN	N	O		32	.272
1909	CIN	N	O		117	.240
1910	CIN	N	O		150	.250
1911	CIN	N	O		153	.275
1912	CIN	N	O		145	.281
1913	CIN	N	O		141	.258
1914	NY	N	O		135	.270
1915	STL	N	O		130	.263
1916	STL	N	O		151	.235
1917	STL	N	O		42	.155
1918	CLE	A	O		25	.333
	BBTL				1221	.258

BESSE, HERMAN
B.AUG.16,1911 ST.LOUIS,MO.
D.AUG.13,1972 LOS ANGELES,CAL.

YR	CL	LEA	POS	GP	G	REC
1940	PHI	A	P		17	0- 3
1941	PHI	A	P		6	2- 0
1942	PHI	A	P	30	34	2- 9
1943	PHI	A	P	5	7	1- 1
1946	PHI	A	P		7	0- 2
	BLTL			65	71	5-15

BESSENT, FRED DONALD "DON"
B.MAR,31,1931 JACKSONVILLE,FLA.

YR	CL	LEA	POS	GP	G	REC
1955	BRO	N	P		24	8- 1
1956	BRO	N	P		38	4- 3
1957	BRO	N	P		27	1- 3
1958	LA	N	P		19	1- 0
	BRTR				108	14- 7

BESTICK

YR	CL	LEA	POS	GP	G	REC
1872	ECK	NA	C		4	.214

BETCHER, FRANKLIN LYLE
(REAL NAME FRANKLIN LYLE BETTGER)
B.FEB.15,1888 PHILADELPHIA,PA.

YR	CL	LEA	POS	GP	G	REC
1910	STL	N	S		27	.202
	BBTR					

BETHEA, WILLIAM LAMAR "BILL"
B.JAN.1,1942 HOUSTON,TEX.

YR	CL	LEA	POS	GP	G	REC
1964	MIN	A	2-S		10	.167
	BRTR					

BETHKE, JAMES CHARLES "JIM"
B.NOV.5,1946 FALLS CITY,NEB.

YR	CL	LEA	POS	GP	G	REC
1965	NY	N	P		25	2- 0
	BRTR					

BETTENCOURT, LAWRENCE JOSEPH
B.SEPT.22,1907 NEWARK,CAL.

YR	CL	LEA	POS	GP	G	REC
1928	STL	A	3		67	.283
1931	STL	A	O		74	.257
1932	STL	A	3-O		27	.133
	BRTR				168	.258

BETTGER, FRANKLIN LYLE
(PLAYED UNDER NAME OF FRANKLIN LYLE BETCHER)

BETTS, FRED

YR	CL	LEA	POS	GP	G	REC
1913	CIN	N	P		1	0- 0

BETTS, HAROLD M.
B.1880 ST.LOUIS,MO.

YR	CL	LEA	POS	GP	G	REC
1903	STL	N	P		1	0- 1
	BRTR					

BETTS, WALTER MARTIN "HUCK"
B.FEB.18,1897 MILLSBORO,DEL.

YR	CL	LEA	POS	GP	G	REC
1920	PHI	N	P		27	1- 1
1921	PHI	N	P		32	3- 7
1922	PHI	N	P		7	1- 0
1923	PHI	N	P	19	20	2- 4
1924	PHI	N	P	37	38	7-10
1925	PHI	N	P	35	37	4- 5
1932	BOS	N	P		31	13-11
1933	BOS	N	P		35	11-11
1934	BOS	N	P		40	17-10
1935	BOS	N	P		44	2- 9
	BRTR			307	311	61-68

BETZEL, CHRISTIAN FREDERICK ALBERT JOHN HENRY DAVID "BRUNO"
B.DEC.6,1894 CELINA,OHIO
D.FEB.7,1965 W.HOLLYWOOD,FLA.

YR	CL	LEA	POS	GP	G	REC
1914	STL	N	2-3		7	.000
1915	STL	N	3		117	.251
1916	STL	N	2-3		142	.233
1917	STL	N	2-O		106	.217
1918	STL	N	2-3-O		76	.222
	BRTR				448	.231

BEVACQUA, KURT ANTHONY
B.JAN.23,1947 MIAMI BEACH,FLA.

YR	CL	LEA	POS	GP	G	REC
1971	CLE	A	2-S-3-O		55	.204
1972	CLE	A	3-O		19	.114
1973	KC	A	1-2-3-O-D		99	.257
1974	PIT	N	3-O		18	.114
	KC	A	1-2-S-3		39	.211
1975	MIL	A	1-2-S-3		104	.229
1976	MIL	A	2		12	.143
	BRTR				346	.222

BEVAN, JOSEPH HAROLD "HAL"
B.NOV.15,1930 NEW ORLEANS,LA.
D.OCT.5,1968 NEW ORLEANS,LA.

YR	CL	LEA	POS	GP	G	REC
1952	BOS	A	3		1	.000
	PHI	A	3		8	.353
1955	KC	A	3		3	.000
1961	CIN	N	H		3	.333
	BRTR				15	.292

BEVANS, E. P.
B.1848 NEW YORK

YR	CL	LEA	POS	GP	G	REC
1871	TRO	NA	2		3	.333
1872	ATL	NA	2-S-O		10	.205
	TR				13	.237

BEVENS, FLOYD CLIFFORD "BILL"
B.OCT.20,1916 HUBBARD,ORE.

YR	CL	LEA	POS	GP	G	REC
1944	NY	A	P		8	4- 1
1945	NY	A	P		29	13- 9
1946	NY	A	P		31	16-13
1947	NY	A	P		28	7-13
	BRTR				96	40-36

BEVIL, LOUIS EUGENE
(REAL NAME LOUIS EUGENE BEVILACQUA)
B.NOV.27,1922 DIXON,ILL.
D.FEB.1,1973 DIXON,ILL.

YR	CL	LEA	POS	GP	G	REC
1942	WAS	A	P		4	0- 1
	BBTR					

BEVILACQUA, LOUIS EUGENE
(PLAYED UNDER NAME OF LOUIS EUGENE BEVIL)

BEVILLE, CHARLES E. "CANDY"

YR	CL	LEA	POS	GP	G	REC
1901	BOS	A	P		3	0- 2

BEVILLE, HENRY MONTE
B.FEB.24,1875 DUBLIN,IND.
D.JAN.24,1955

YR	CL	LEA	POS	GP	G	REC
1903	NY	A	C		82	.194
1904	NY	A	C-1		9	.273
	DET	A	C		53	.225
	BLTR				144	.210

BEZDEK, HUGO FRANK
B.APR.1,1884 PRAGUE,CZECH*KIA
D.SEPT.19,1952
NON-PLAYING MANAGER
PIT (N) 1917-19

BIANCO, THOMAS ANTHONY "TOMMY"
B.DEC.16,1952 ROCKVILLE CNTR,N.Y

YR	CL	LEA	POS	GP	G	REC
1975	MIL	A	1-3		18	.176
	BBTR					

BIASATTI, HENRY ARCADO "HANK"
B.JAN.14,1925 BEANO,ITALY

YR	CL	LEA	POS	GP	G	REC
1949	PHI	A	1		21	.083
	BLTL					

BIBBY, JAMES BLAIR "JIM"
B.OCT.29,1944 FRANKLINTON,N.C.

YR	CL	LEA	POS	GP	G	REC
1972	STL	N	P		6	1- 3
1973	STL	N	P		6	0- 2
	TEX	A	P	26	27	9-10
1974	TEX	A	P		41	19-19
1975	TEX	A	P		12	2- 6
	CLE	A	P		24	5- 9
1976	CLE	A	P		34	13- 7
	BRTR			149	150	49-56

BICKFORD, VERNON EDGELL "VERN"
B.AUG.17,1920 HELLIER,KY.
D.MAY 6,1960

YR	CL	LEA	POS	GP	G	REC
1948	BOS	N	P		33	11- 5
1949	BOS	N	P		37	16-11
1950	BOS	N	P		40	19-14
1951	BOS	N	P		25	11- 9
1952	BOS	N	P		26	7-12
1953	MIL	N	P		20	2- 3
1954	BAL	A	P		1	0- 1
	BRTR				182	66-57

BICKHAM, DANIEL DENISON
B.OCT.31,1864 DAYTON,OHIO
D.MAR.3,1951

YR	CL	LEA	POS	GP	G	REC
1886	CIN	AA	P		1	1- 0

BICKNELL, CHARLES STEPHEN "BUD"
B.OCT.31,1928 PLAINFIELD,N.J.

YR	CL	LEA	POS	GP	G	REC
1948	PHI	N	P		17	0- 1
1949	PHI	N	P		13	0- 0
	BRTR				30	0- 1

BIELASKI, OSCAR
B.MAR.21,1847 WASHINGTON,D.C.
D.NOV.9,1911

YR	CL	LEA	POS	GP	G	REC
1872	NAT	NA	U		10	.170
1873	NAT	NA	O		38	-
1874	BAL	NA	1-2-O		25	-
1875	CHI	NA	O		52	-
1876	CHI	N	O		31	.206
	BRTR				156	-

BIEMILLER, HARRY LEE
B.OCT.9,1898 BALTIMORE,MD.
D.MAY 25,1965 ORLANDO,FLA.

YR	CL	LEA	POS	GP	G	REC
1920	WAS	A	P		5	1- 0
1925	CIN	N	P		23	0- 1
	BRTR				28	1- 1

BIERBAUER, LOUIS W.
B.SEPT.23,1865 ERIE,PA.
D.FEB.1,1926

YR	CL	LEA	POS	GP	G	REC
1886	ATH	AA	2		137	.244
1887	ATH	AA	2		126	.302
1889	ATH	AA	2		130	.313
1888	ATH	AA	2		134	.279
1890	BRO	P	2		132	.319
1891	PIT	N	2		117	.202
1892	PIT	N	2		153	.240
1893	PIT	N	2		128	.298
1894	PIT	N	2		131	.301
1895	PIT	N	2		119	.255
1896	PIT	N	2		57	.277
1897	STL	N	2		12	.217
1898	STL	N	2		4	.000
	BRTR				1380	.275

BIERMAN, CHARLES S.
B.1845 HOBOKEN,N.J.
D.AUG.4,1879 HOBOKEN,N.J.

YR	CL	LEA	POS	GP	G	REC
1871	KEK	NA	1		1	.000

YR	CL	LEA	POS	GP	G	REC

BIGBEE, CARSON LEE "SKEETER"
B.MAR.31,1895 WATERLOO,ORE.
D.OCT.17,1964 PORTLAND,ORE.

YR	CL	LEA	POS	GP	G	REC
1916	PIT	N	2-O		43	.250
1917	PIT	N	2-O		133	.239
1918	PIT	N	O		92	.255
1919	PIT	N	O		125	.276
1920	PIT	N	O		137	.280
1921	PIT	N	O		147	.323
1922	PIT	N	O		150	.350
1923	PIT	N	O		123	.299
1924	PIT	N	O		89	.262
1925	PIT	N	O		66	.238
1926	PIT	N	O		42	.221
	BLTR				1147	.287

BIGBEE, LYLE RANDOLPH "AL"
B.AUG.22,1893 SWEET HOME,ORE.
D.AUG.5,1942

YR	CL	LEA	POS	GP	G	REC
1920	PHI	A	P	12	37	0- 3
1921	PIT	N	P	5	5	0- 0
	BLTR			17	42	0- 3

BIGELOW, ELLIOT ALLARDICE "BABE"
B.OCT.13,1897 TARPON SPRINGS, FLA.
D.AUG.10,1933

YR	CL	LEA	POS	GP	G	REC
1929	BOS	A	O		100	.285
	BLTL					

BIGGS, CHARLES ORVAL
B.SEPT.15,1906 FRENCH LICK,IND.
D.MAY 24,1954

YR	CL	LEA	POS	GP	G	REC
1932	CHI	A	P		6	1- 1
	BRTR					

BIGLER, IVAN EDWARD
B.DEC.13,1894 BRADFORD,OHIO

YR	CL	LEA	POS	GP	G	REC
1917	STL	A	1		1	.000
	BRTR					

BIGNELL, GEORGE WILLIAM
B.JULY 18,1858 TAUNTON,MASS.
D.JAN.16,1925

YR	CL	LEA	POS	GP	G	REC
1884	MIL	U	C		4	.222

BIITTNER, LAWRENCE DAVID "LARRY"
B.JULY 27,1945 POCAHONTAS,IA.

YR	CL	LEA	POS	GP	G	REC
1970	WAS	A	H		2	.000
1971	WAS	A	1-O		66	.257
1972	TEX	A	1-O		137	.259
1973	TEX	A	1-O		83	.252
1974	MON	N	O		18	.269
1975	MON	N	O		121	.315
1976	MON	N	O		11	.188
	CHI	N	1-O		78	.245
	BLTL				516	.249

BILBREY, JAMES MELVIN
B.APR.20,1924 MONTEREY,TENN.

YR	CL	LEA	POS	GP	G	REC
1949	STL	A	P		1	0- 0
	BRTR					

BILDILLI, EMIL "HILL BILLY"
B.SEPT.16,1914 DIAMOND,IND.
D.SEPT.16,1946

YR	CL	LEA	POS	GP	G	REC
1937	STL	A	P		4	0- 1
1938	STL	A	P		5	1- 2
1939	STL	A	P		2	1- 1
1940	STL	A	P	28	29	2- 4
1941	STL	A	P		2	0- 0
	BRTL			41	42	4- 8

BILKO, STEPHEN THOMAS "STEVE"
B.NOV.13,1928 NANTICOKE,PA.

YR	CL	LEA	POS	GP	G	REC
1949	STL	N	1		6	.294
1950	STL	N	1		10	.182
1951	STL	N	1		21	.222
1952	STL	N	1		20	.264
1953	STL	N	1		154	.251
1954	STL	N	1		8	.143
	CHI	N	1		47	.239
1958	CIN	N	1		31	.264
	LA	N	1		47	.208
1960	DET	A	1		78	.207
1961	LA	A	1-O		114	.279
1962	LA	A	1		64	.287
	BRTR				600	.249

BILLIARD, HARRY P.
B.NOV.21,1885 WOOSTER,OHIO
D.JUNE 3,1923

YR	CL	LEA	POS	GP	G	REC
1908	NY	A	P		6	0- 0
1914	IND	F	P		32	8- 7
1915	NEW	F	P		14	0- 1
	BRTR				52	8- 8

BILLINGHAM, JOHN EUGENE "JACK"
B.FEB.21,1943 ORLANDO,FLA.

YR	CL	LEA	POS	GP	G	REC
1968	LA	N	P		50	3- 0
1969	HOU	N	P		52	6- 7
1970	HOU	N	P		46	13- 9
1971	HOU	N	P		33	10-16
1972	CIN	N	P		36	12-12
1973	CIN	N	P		40	19-10
1974	CIN	N	P		36	19-11
1975	CIN	N	P		33	15-10
1976	CIN	N	P		34	12-10
	BRTR				360	109-85

BILLINGS, HASKELL CLARK "JOSH"
B.SEPT.27,1907 NEW YORK,N.Y.

YR	CL	LEA	POS	GP	G	REC
1927	DET	A	P		10	5- 4
1928	DET	A	P		21	5-10
1929	DET	A	P		8	0- 1
	BRTR				39	10-15

BILLINGS, JOHN AUGUSTUS "JOSH"
B.NOV.30,1891 GRANTVILLE,KAN.

YR	CL	LEA	POS	GP	G	REC
1913	CLE	A	C		1	.000
1914	CLE	A	C		10	.250
1915	CLE	A	C		7	.246
1916	CLE	A	C		22	.160
1917	CLE	A	C		66	.178
1918	CLE	A	C		2	.333
1919	STL	A	C		38	.198
1920	STL	A	C		66	.278
1921	STL	A	C		20	.217
1922	STL	A	C		5	.429
1923	STL	A	C		4	.000
	BRTR				241	.217

BILLINGS, RICHARD ARLIN "DICK"
B.DEC.4,1942 DETROIT,MICH.

YR	CL	LEA	POS	GP	G	REC
1968	WAS	A	3-O		12	.182
1969	WAS	A	3-O		27	.135
1970	WAS	A	C		11	.250
1971	WAS	A	C-3-O		116	.246
1972	TEX	A	C-1-3-O		133	.254
1973	TEX	A	C-1-O		81	.179
1974	TEX	A	C-O		16	.226
	STL	N			1	.200
1975	STL	N	H		3	.000
	BRTR				400	.227

BINKOWSKI, GEORGE EUGENE
(PLAYED UNDER NAME OF
GEORGE EUGENE BINKS)

BINKS, GEORGE EUGENE "BINGO"
(REAL NAME
GEORGE EUGENE BINKOWSKI)
B.JULY 11,1916 CHICAGO,ILL.

YR	CL	LEA	POS	GP	G	REC
1944	WAS	A	O		5	.250
1945	WAS	A	1 -O		145	.278
1946	WAS	A	O		65	.194
1947	PHI	A	1-O		104	.258
1948	PHI	A	O		17	.098
	STL	A	1-O		15	.217
	BLTL				351	.254

BIRAS, STEPHEN ALEXANDER
B.FEB.26,1922 E.ST.LOUIS,ILL.
D.APR.21,1965 ST.LOUIS,MO.

YR	CL	LEA	POS	GP	G	REC
1944	CLE	A	2		2	1.000
	BRTR					

BIRCHALL, A. JUDSON "JUD"
B.1858 PHILADELPHIA,PA.
D.DEC.22,1887

YR	CL	LEA	POS	GP	G	REC
1882	ATH	AA	2-O		75	.263
1883	ATH	AA	O		95	.230
1884	ATH	AA	O		53	.262
					223	.256

BIRD, FRANK ZEPHERIN "DODO"
B.MAR.19,1869 SPENCER,MASS.
D.MAY 20,1958

YR	CL	LEA	POS	GP	G	REC
1892	STL	N	C		17	.196
	BRTR					

BIRD, GEORGE R.
B.JUNE 23,1850 STILMAN VALLEY, ILL.
D.NOV.9,1940

YR	CL	LEA	POS	GP	G	REC
1871	ROK	NA	O		25	-

BIRD, JAMES DOUGLAS "DOUG"
B.MAR.5,1950 CORONA,CAL.

YR	CL	LEA	POS	GP	G	REC
1973	KC	A	P		54	4- 4
1974	KC	A	P		55	7- 6
1975	KC	A	P		51	9- 6
1976	KC	A	P		39	12-10
	BRTR				199	32-26

BIRD, JAMES EDWARD "RED"
B.APR.25,1895 STEPHENVILLE,TEX.
D.MAR.23,1972 MURFREESBORO,ARK.

YR	CL	LEA	POS	GP	G	REC
1921	WAS	A	P		1	0- 0
	BLTL					

BIRDSALL, DAVID SOLOMON
B.JULY 16,1839 NEW YORK,N.Y.
D.JAN.30,1896

YR	CL	LEA	POS	GP	G	REC
1871	BOS	NA	C-O		31	-
1872	BOS	NA	C-O		14	.179
1873	BOS	NA	O		3	-
	BRTR				48	-

BIRKOFER, RALPH JOSEPH "LEFTY"
B.NOV.5,1909 CINCINNATI,OHIO
D.MAR.16,1971 CINCINNATI,OHIO

YR	CL	LEA	POS	GP	G	REC
1933	PIT	N	P		9	4- 2
1934	PIT	N	P		41	11-12
1935	PIT	N	P	37	38	9- 7
1936	PIT	N	P		34	7- 5
1937	BRO	N	P	11	12	0- 2
	BLTL			132	134	31-28

BIRMINGHAM, JOSEPH LEO "DODE"
B.AUG.6,1884 ELMIRA,N.Y.
D.APR.24,1946

YR	CL	LEA	POS	GP	G	REC
1906	CLE	A	O		10	.275
1907	CLE	A	O		136	.235
1908	CLE	A	O		122	.213
1909	CLE	A	O		100	.289
1910	CLE	A	O		104	.229
1911	CLE	A	3-O		125	.304
1912	CLE	A	M-O		107	.255
1913	CLE	A	M-O		47	.282
1914	CLE	A	M-O		19	.128
	BRTR				770	.253
NON-PLAYING MANAGER CLE(A) 1915						

BIRRER, WERNER JOSEPH "BABE"
B.JULY 4,1928 BUFFALO,N.Y.

YR	CL	LEA	POS	GP	G	REC
1955	DET	A	P		36	4- 3
1956	BAL	A	P		4	0- 0
1958	LA	N	P		16	0- 0
	BRTR				56	4- 3

BISCAN, FRANK STEPHEN "PORKY"
B.MAR.13,1920 MT.OLIVE,ILL.
D.MAY 22,1959

YR	CL	LEA	POS	GP	G	REC
1942	STL	A	P		11	0- 1
1946	STL	A	P		16	1- 1
1948	STL	A	P		47	6- 7
	BLTL				74	7- 9

BISCHOFF, JOHN GEORGE "SMILEY"
B.OCT.28,1897 GRANITE CITY,ILL.

YR	CL	LEA	POS	GP	G	REC
1925	CHI	A	C		7	.091
	BOS	A	C		41	.278
1926	BOS	A	C		59	.260
	BRTR				107	.262

BISHOP, CHARLES TULLER
B.JAN.1,1924 ATLANTA,GA.

YR	CL	LEA	POS	GP	G	REC
1952	PHI	A	P		6	2- 2
1953	PHI	A	P	39	40	3-14
1954	PHI	A	P	20	22	4- 6
1955	KC	A	P		4	1- 0
	BRTR			69	72	10-22

BISHOP, FRANK
B.CHICAGO,ILL.

YR	CL	LEA	POS	GP	G	REC
1884	CHI	U	S-3		4	.200

BISHOP, JAMES MORTON
B.JAN.22,1898 MONTGOMERY CITY, MO.
D.SEPT.17,1973 MONTGOMERY CITY, MO.

YR	CL	LEA	POS	GP	G	REC
1923	PHI	N	P		15	0- 3
1924	PHI	N	P		7	0- 1
	BRTR				22	0- 4

BISHOP, LLOYD CLIFTON
B.APR.25,1890 CONWAY SPRINGS, KAN.
D.JUNE 17,1968 WICHITA,KAN.

YR	CL	LEA	POS	GP	G	REC
1914	CLE	A	P		3	0- 1
	BRTR					

YR	CL	LEA	POS	GP	G	REC

BISHOP, MAX FREDERICK "TILLY"
B.SEPT.5,1899 WAYNESBORO,PA.
D.FEB.24,1962

YR	CL	LEA	POS	GP	G	REC
1924	PHI	A	2		91	.255
1925	PHI	A	2		105	.280
1926	PHI	A	2		122	.265
1927	PHI	A	2		117	.277
1928	PHI	A	2		126	.316
1929	PHI	A	2		129	.232
1930	PHI	A	2		130	.252
1931	PHI	A	2		130	.294
1932	PHI	A	2		114	.254
1933	PHI	A	2		117	.294
1934	BOS	A	1-2		97	.261
1935	BOS	A	1-2-S		60	.230
		BLTR			1338	.271

BISHOP, WILLIAM H. "LEFTY"
B.OCT.22,1900 HOUTZDALE,PA.
D.FEB.14,1956 ST.JOSEPH,MO.

YR	CL	LEA	POS	GP	G	REC
1921	PHI	A	P	2		0- 0
		BLTL				

BISHOP, WILLIAM R.
B.DEC.27,1869 ADAMSBURG,PA.
D.DEC.15,1932

YR	CL	LEA	POS	GP	G	REC
1886	PIT	AA	P	2		0- 1
1887	PIT	N	P	4		0- 4
1889	CHI	N	P	2		0- 0
				8		0- 5

BISLAND, RIVINGTON MARTIN
B.FEB.17,1890 NEW YORK,N.Y.
D.JAN.11,1973 SALTZBURG,AUSTRIA

YR	CL	LEA	POS	GP	G	REC
1912	PIT	N	H	1		.000
1913	STL	A	S	12		.136
1914	CLE	A	S	18		.105
		BRTR		31		.117

BISSONETTE, DELPHIA LOUIS "DEL"
B.SEPT.6,1899 WINTHROP,ME.
D.JUNE 9,1972 AUGUSTA,MAINE

YR	CL	LEA	POS	GP	G	REC
1928	BRO	N	1		155	.320
1929	BRO	N	1		116	.281
1930	BRO	N	1		146	.336
1931	BRO	N	1		152	.290
1933	BRO	N	1		35	.246
		BLTL			604	.305

NON-PLAYING MANAGER BOS(N) 1945

BITHORN, HIRAM GABRIEL "HI"
B.MAR.18,1916 SANTURCE,P.R.
D.DEC.29,1951

YR	CL	LEA	POS	GP	G	REC
1942	CHI	N	P	38		9-14
1943	CHI	N	P	39		18-12
1946	CHI	N	P	26		6- 5
1947	CHI	A	P	2		1- 0
		BRTR		105		34-31

BITTMAN, HENRY "RED"
B.CINCINNATI,OHIO

YR	CL	LEA	POS	GP	G	REC
1889	KC	AA	2		4	.286

BIVIN, JAMES NATHANIEL
B.DEC.11,1909 JACKSON,MISS.

YR	CL	LEA	POS	GP	G	REC
1935	PIT	N	P	47		2- 9
		BRTR				

BLACK, DAVID
B.APR.19,1892 CHICAGO,ILL.
D.OCT.27,1936

YR	CL	LEA	POS	GP	G	REC
1914	CHI	F	P	9		1- 0
1915	CHI	F	P	21		3- 2
	BAL	F	P	12		4- 8
1923	BOS	A	P	2		0- 0
				44		8-10

BLACK, DONALD PAUL "DON"
B.JULY 20,1916 SALIX,IOWA
D.APR.21,1959

YR	CL	LEA	POS	GP	G	REC
1943	PHI	A	P	33		6-16
1944	PHI	A	P	29		10-12
1945	PHI	A	P	26		5-11
1946	CLE	A	P	18		1- 2
1947	CLE	A	P	30		10-12
1948	CLE	A	P	18		2- 2
		BRTR		154		34-55

BLACK, JOHN B.
(REAL NAME JOHN FALCNOR HADDOW)
B.FEB.23,1890 COVINGTON,KY.

YR	CL	LEA	POS	GP	G	REC
1911	STL	A	1		54	.150
		BRTR				

BLACK, JOHN WILLIAM "JIGGY"
B.AUG.12,1899 PHILADELPHIA,PA.
D.JAN.14,1968 PHILADELPHIA,PA.

YR	CL	LEA	POS	GP	G	REC
1924	CHI	A	2		6	.200
		BLTR				

BLACK, JOSEPH "JOE"
B.FEB.8,1924 PLAINFIELD,N.J.

YR	CL	LEA	POS	GP	G	REC
1952	BRO	N	P	56	57	15- 4
1953	BRO	N	P		34	6- 3
1954	BRO	N	P		5	0- 0
1955	BRO	N	P		6	1- 0
	CIN	N	P		32	5- 2
1956	CIN	N	P	32	34	3- 2
1957	WAS	A	P		7	0- 1
		BRTR		172	175	30-12

BLACK, ROBERT BENJAMIN "BOB"
B.DEC.10,1862 CINCINNATI,OHIO
D.MAR.21,1933

YR	CL	LEA	POS	GP	G	REC
1884	KC	U	P-2- 16	38		3- 9
		S-0				.245

BLACK, WILLIAM CARROLL "BUD"
B.JULY 9,1932 UNIVERSITY CITY,
MO.

YR	CL	LEA	POS	GP	G	REC
1952	DET	A	P	2		0- 1
1955	DET	A	P	3		1- 1
1956	DET	A	P	5		1- 1
		BRTR		10		2- 3

BLACKABY, ETHAN ALLEN
B.JULY 24,1940 CINCINNATI,O.

YR	CL	LEA	POS	GP	G	REC
1962	MIL	N	O		6	.154
1964	MIL	N	O		9	.083
		BLTL			15	.120

BLACKBURN, EARL STUART
B.NOV.1,1892 LEESVILLE,OHIO
D.AUG.4,1966 MANSFIELD,OHIO

YR	CL	LEA	POS	GP	G	REC
1912	PIT	N	C	1		.000
	CIN	N	C	1		.000
1913	CIN	N	C	17		.259
1915	BOS	N	C	3		.167
1916	BOS	N	C	47		.273
1917	CHI	N	C	2		.000
		BRTR		71		.262

BLACKBURN, FOSTER EDWIN
B.JAN.6,1895 CHICAGO,ILL.

YR	CL	LEA	POS	GP	G	REC
1915	KC	F	P	7		0- 1
1921	CHI	A	P	1		0- 0
				8		0- 1

BLACKBURN, GEORGE W.
"SMILING GEORGE"
B.SEPT.21,1871 OZARK,MO.

YR	CL	LEA	POS	GP	G	REC
1897	BAL	N	P	5		2- 2

BLACKBURN, JAMES RAY "JIM"
B.JUNE 19,1924 WARSAW,KY.
D.OCT.26,1969 CINCINNATI,OHIO

YR	CL	LEA	POS	GP	G	REC
1948	CIN	N	P	16		0- 2
1951	CIN	N	P	2		0- 0
		BRTR		18		0- 2

BLACKBURN, RONALD HAMILTON
B.APR.23,1935 MT.AIRY,N.C.

YR	CL	LEA	POS	GP	G	REC
1958	PIT	N	P	38		2- 1
1959	PIT	N	P	26		1- 1
		BRTR		64		3- 2

BLACKBURNE, RUSSELL AUBREY
"LENA"
B.OCT.23,1886 CLIFTON HEIGHTS,
PA.
D.FEB.29,1968 RIVERSIDE,N.J.

YR	CL	LEA	POS	GP	G	REC
1910	CHI	A	S		75	.174
1912	CHI	A	S		5	.000
1914	CHI	A	2		144	.222
1915	CHI	A	3		96	.216
1918	CIN	N	S		125	.228
1919	BOS	N	1-2-S-3		31	.272
	PHI	N	1-3		72	.197
1927	CHI	A	H		1	1.000
1929	CHI	A	M-P		1	0- 0
		BRTR		1	550	0- 0

NON-PLAYING MANAGER CHI(A) 1928

BLACKERBY, GEORGE FRANCIS
B.NOV.10,1906 OKLAHOMA CITY,
OKLA.

YR	CL	LEA	POS	GP	G	REC
1928	CHI	A	O		30	.253
		BRTR				

BLACKSTONE, ROBERT J.
(PLAYED UNDER NAME OF
ROBERT J. BLAKISTON)

BLACKWELL, EWELL "WHIP"
B.OCT.23,1922 FRESNO,CAL.

YR	CL	LEA	POS	GP	G	REC
1942	CIN	N	P		2	0- 0
1946	CIN	N	P		33	9-13
1947	CIN	N	P		33	22- 8
1948	CIN	N	P		22	7- 9
1949	CIN	N	P		30	5- 5
1950	CIN	N	P		40	17-15
1951	CIN	N	P	38	39	16-15
1952	CIN	N	P		23	3-12
	NY	A	P		5	1- 0
1953	NY	A	P		8	2- 0
1955	NY	A	P		2	0- 1
		BRTR		236	237	82-78

**BLACKWELL, FREDRICK WILLIAM
"BLACKY"**
B.SEPT.7,1893 BOWLING GREEN,KY.
D.DEC.8,1975 MORGANTOWN,KY.

YR	CL	LEA	POS	GP	G	REC
1917	PIT	N	C		3	.200
1918	PIT	N	C		8	.153
1919	PIT	N	C		24	.215
		BLTR			35	.205

BLACKWELL, TIMOTHY P "TIM"
B.AUG.19,1952 SAN DIEGO,CAL.

YR	CL	LEA	POS	GP	G	REC
1974	BOS	A	C		44	.246
1975	BOS	A	C		59	.197
1976	PHI	N	C		4	.250
		BBTR			107	.221

BLADES, FRANCIS RAYMOND "RAY"
B.AUG.6,1896 MT.VERNON,ILL.

YR	CL	LEA	POS	GP	G	REC
1922	STL	N	S-3-O		37	.300
1923	STL	N	3-O		98	.246
1924	STL	N	2-3-O		131	.311
1925	STL	N	3-O		122	.342
1926	STL	N	O		107	.305
1927	STL	N	O		61	.317
1928	STL	N	O		51	.235
1930	STL	N	O		45	.396
1931	STL	N	O		35	.284
1932	STL	N	O		80	.229
		BRTR			767	.301

NON-PLAYING MANAGER
ST.LOUIS(N) 1939-40

BLAEDT, RICHARD ALAN "RICK"
B.DEC.9,1946 SANTA CRUZ,CAL.

YR	CL	LEA	POS	GP	G	REC
1969	CHI	N	O		10	.154
1975	NY	A	O		52	.222
		BRTR			62	.215

BLAEHOLDER, GEORGE FRANKLIN
B.JAN.26,1904 ORANGE,CAL.
D.DEC.29,1947

YR	CL	LEA	POS	GP	G	REC
1925	STL	A	P		2	0- 0
1927	STL	A	P		1	0- 1
1928	STL	A	P		38	10-15
1929	STL	A	P		42	14-15
1930	STL	A	P		37	11-13
1931	STL	A	P		35	11-15
1932	STL	A	P		42	14-14
1933	STL	A	P		38	15-19
1934	STL	A	P		39	14-18
1935	STL	A	P		6	1- 1
	PHI	A	P		23	6-10
1936	CLE	A	P		35	8- 4
		BRTR			338	104-125

BLAEMIRE, RAE BERTRAM
B.FEB.18,1914 GARY,IND.

YR	CL	LEA	POS	GP	G	REC
1941	NY	N	C		2	.400
		BRTR				

BLAIR, CLARENCE VICK "FOOTSIE"
B.JULY 13,1903 TEXARKANA,TEX.

YR	CL	LEA	POS	GP	G	REC
1929	CHI	N	1-2-3		26	.319
1930	CHI	N	2-3		134	.273
1931	CHI	N	1-2		86	.258
		BLTR			246	.273

BLAIR, DENNIS HERMAN
B.JUNE 5,1954 MIDDLETOWN,OHIO

YR	CL	LEA	POS	GP	G	REC
1974	MON	N	P		22	11- 7
1975	MON	N	P		30	8-15
1976	MON	N	P		5	0- 2
		BRTR			57	19-24

BLAIR, LOUIS NATHAN "BUDDY"
B.SEPT.15,1914 COLUMBIA,MISS.

YR	CL	LEA	POS	GP	G	REC
1942	PHI	A	3		137	.279
		BLTR				

YR	CL	LEA	POS	GP	G	REC

BLAIR, PAUL L   D
B.FEB.1,1944 CUSHING,OKLA.

YR	CL	LEA	POS	GP	G	REC
1964	BAL	A	O		8	.000
1965	BAL	A	O		119	.234
1966	BAL	A	O		133	.277
1967	BAL	A	O		151	.293
1968	BAL	A	3-O		141	.211
1969	BAL	A	O		150	.285
1970	BAL	A	3-O		133	.267
1971	BAL	A	O		141	.262
1972	BAL	A	O		142	.233
1973	BAL	A	O		146	.281
1974	BAL	A	O		151	.261
1975	BAL	A	1-O		140	.218
1976	BAL	A	O		145	.197
	BRTR				1700	.254
	BB 1971 (PART)					

BLAIR, WALTER ALLEN "HEAVY"
B.OCT.13,1883 LANDRUS,PA.
D.AUG.20,1948

1907	NY	A	C		7	.173
1908	NY	A	C		76	.190
1909	NY	A	C		42	.209
1910	NY	A	C		6	.227
1911	NY	A	C		85	.194
1914	BUF	F	C		127	.239
1915	BUF	F	M-C		98	.224
	BRTR				441	.215

BLAIR, WILLIAM ELLSWORTH
B.SEPT.17,1863 PITTSBURGH,PA.
D.FEB.22,1890

1888	ATH	AA	P	5	1- 4	
	TL					

BLAISDELL, HOWARD CARLETON "DICK"
B.JUNE 18,1862 BRADFORD,MASS.
D.AUG.20,1886

1884	KC	U	P-O	4	0- 3	
						.295

BLAKE, EDWARD JAMES
B.DEC.23,1925 GRANITE CITY,ILL.

1951	CIN	N	P	3	0- 0	
1952	CIN	N	P	2	0- 0	
1953	CIN	N	P	1	0- 0	
1957	KC	A	P	2	0- 0	
	BRTR			8	0- 0	

BLAKE, HENRY C.
B.JUNE 16,1874 PORTSMOUTH,OHIO
D.OCT.14,1919

1894	CLE	N	O		73	.286
1895	CLE	N	O		83	.280
1896	CLE	N	O		102	.242
1897	CLE	N	O		31	.256
1898	CLE	N	O		137	.245
1899	STL	N	O		94	.238
					520	.257

BLAKE, JOHN FREDERICK "SHERIFF"
B.SEPT.17,1899 ANSTED,W.VA.

1920	PIT	N	P		6	0- 0
1924	CHI	N	P		29	6- 6
1925	CHI	N	P		36	10-18
1926	CHI	N	P		39	11-12
1927	CHI	N	P		32	13-14
1928	CHI	N	P	34	35	17-11
1929	CHI	N	P	35	38	14-13
1930	CHI	N	P	34	36	10-14
1931	CHI	N	P		16	0- 4
	PHI	N	P		14	4- 5
1937	STL	A	P		15	2- 2
	STL	N	P		14	0- 3
	BBTR			304	310	87-102

BLAKELY, LINCOLN HOWARD "BINK" "BINK"
B.FEB.12,1913 OAKLAND,CAL.

1934	CIN	N	O		34	.225
	BRTR					

BLAKISTON, ROBERT J.
(REAL NAME
ROBERT J. BLACKSTONE)
B.OCT.2,1855 SAN FRANCISCO,CAL.
D.DEC.25,1918

1882	ATH	AA	2-3-O		72	.242
1883	ATH	AA	1-3-O		40	.249
1884	ATH	AA	1-2-S-3-		33	.266
			O			
1884	IND	AA	1-O		6	.200
					151	.248

BLANCHARD, JOHN EDWIN "JOHNNY"
B.FEB.26,1933 MINNEAPOLIS,MINN.

1955	NY	A	C		1	.000
1959	NY	A	C-1-O		49	.169
1960	NY	A	O		53	.242
1961	NY	A	C-O		93	.305
1962	NY	A	C-1-O		93	.232
1963	NY	A	O		76	.225
1964	NY	A	C-1-O		77	.255
1965	NY	A	C		12	.147
	KC	A	C-O		52	.200
	MIL	N	O		10	.100
	BLTR				516	.239

BLANCHE, PROSBY ALBERT
(REAL NAME PROSPER BELANGIO)
B.SEPT.21,1909 SOMERVILLE,MASS.

1935	BOS	N	P		6	0- 0
1936	BOS	N	P		11	0- 1
	BRTR				17	0- 1

BLANCO, DAMASO (CARIPE)
B.DEC.11,1941 CURIEPE,VENEZ.

1972	SF	N	2-S-3		39	.350
1973	SF	N	2-S-3		28	.000
1974	SF	N	H		5	.000
	BRTR				72	.212

BLANCO, GILBERT HENRY "GIL"
B.DEC.15,1945 PHOENIX,ARIZ.

1965	NY	A	P	17	1- 1	
1966	KC	A	P	11	2- 4	
	BLTL			28	3- 5	

BLANCO, OSWALDO C. (DIAZ) "OSSIE"
(BORN CARLOS OSVALDO BLANCO)
B.SEP.8,1945 CARACAS,VENEZ.

1970	CHI	A	1-O		34	.197
1974	CLE	A	1		18	.194
	BRTR				52	.196

BLANDING, FRED JAMES "FRITZ"
B.FEB.8,1888 REDLANDS,CAL.
D.JULY 16,1950

1910	CLE	A	P		6	2- 2
1911	CLE	A	P	29	30	7-11
1912	CLE	A	P		39	18-14
1913	CLE	A	P		41	15-10
1914	CLE	A	P	29	30	3- 9
	BRTR			144	146	45-46

BLANK

1909	STL	N	C		1	.000

BLANK, FREDERICK AUGUST
B.JUNE 18,1874 DESOTO,MO.
D.FEB.5,1936

1894	CIN	N	P	1	0- 1	
	BLTL					

BLANKENSHIP, CLIFFORD DOUGLAS
B.APR.10,1880 COLUMBUS,GA.
D.APR.26,1956

1905	CIN	N	1		15	.196
1907	WAS	A	C		37	.225
1909	WAS	A	C		39	.250
	BRTR				91	.225

BLANKENSHIP, HOMER "SI"
B.AUG.4,1902 BONHAM,TEX.
D.JUNE 22,1974 LONGVIEW,TEX.

1922	CHI	A	P	4	0- 0	
1923	CHI	A	P	4	1- 1	
1928	PIT	N	P	5	0- 2	
	BRTR			13	1- 3	

BLANKENSHIP, THEODORE
B.MAY 10,1901 BONHAM,TEX.
D.JAN.14,1945 ATOKA,OKLA.

1922	CHI	A	P		24	8-10
1923	CHI	A	P		44	9-14
1924	CHI	A	P		25	7- 6
1925	CHI	A	P		40	17- 8
1926	CHI	A	P		29	13-10
1927	CHI	A	P		38	12-17
1928	CHI	A	P		27	9-11
1929	CHI	A	P		8	0- 2
1930	CHI	A	P		7	2- 1
	BRTR				242	77-79

BLANKS, LARVELL
B.JAN.28,1950 DEL RIO,TEX.

1972	ATL	N	2-S-3		33	.329
1973	ATL	N	2-S-3		17	.222
1974	ATL	N	S		3	.250
1975	ATL	N	2-S		141	.234
1976	CLE	A	2-S-3		104	.280
	BRTR				298	.259

BLANTON, DARRELL ELIJAH "CY"
B.MAR.3,1909 WAURIKA,OKLA.
D.SEPT.13,1945

1934	PIT	N	P		1	0- 1
1935	PIT	N	P		35	18-13
1936	PIT	N	P		44	13-15
1937	PIT	N	P		36	14-12
1938	PIT	N	P		29	11- 7
1939	PIT	N	P		10	2- 3
1940	PHI	N	P		13	4- 3
1941	PHI	N	P		28	6-13
1942	PHI	N	P		6	0- 4
	BLTR				202	68-71

BLASINGAME, DON LEE
B.MAR.16,1932 CORINTH,MISS.

1955	STL	N	2-S		5	.375
1956	STL	N	2-S-3		150	.261
1957	STL	N	2		154	.271
1958	STL	N	2		143	.274
1959	STL	N	2		150	.289
1960	SF	N	2		136	.235
1961	SF	N	H		3	.000
	CIN	N	2		123	.222
1962	CIN	N	2		141	.281
1963	CIN	N	2-3		18	.161
	WAS	A	2		69	.256
1964	WAS	A	2		143	.267
1965	WAS	A	2		129	.223
1966	WAS	A	2-S		68	.215
	KC	A	2		12	.158
	BLTR				1444	.258

BLASINGAME, WADE ALLEN
B.NOV.22,1943 DEMING,N.MEX.

1963	MIL	N	P		2	0- 0
1964	MIL	N	P	28	29	9- 5
1965	MIL	N	P		38	16-10
1966	ATL	N	P	16	18	3- 7
1967	ATL	N	P		10	1- 0
	HOU	N	P	15	16	4- 7
1968	HOU	N	P		22	1- 2
1969	HOU	N	P	26	27	0- 5
1970	HOU	N	P		13	3- 3
1971	HOU	N	P		30	9-11
1972	HOU	N	P		10	0- 0
	NY	A	P		12	0- 1
	BLTL			222	227	46-51

BLASS, STEPHEN ROBERT "STEVE"
B.APR.18,1942 CANAAN,CONN.

1964	PIT	N	P		24	5- 8
1966	PIT	N	P		34	11- 7
1967	PIT	N	P		32	6- 8
1968	PIT	N	P-O	33	35	18- 6
						.138
1969	PIT	N	P		38	16-10
1970	PIT	N	P		31	32	10-12
1971	PIT	N	P		33	34	15- 8
1972	PIT	N	P		33	35	19- 8
1973	PIT	N	P		23	24	3- 9
1974	PIT	N	P		1	0- 0
	BRTR			282	295	103-76
						.172

BLATERIC, STEPHEN LAWRENCE "STEVE"
B.MAR.20,1944 DENVER,COLO.

1971	CIN	N	P		2	0- 0
1972	NY	A	P		1	0- 0
1975	CAL	A	P		2	0- 0
	BRTR				5	0- 0

BLATNICK, JOHN LOUIS "JOHNNY"
B.MAR.10,1921 BRIDGEPORT,PHIO

1948	PHI	N	O		121	.260
1949	PHI	N	O		6	.125
1950	PHI	N	O		4	.250
	STL	N	O		7	.150
	BRTR				138	.253

YR	CL LEA POS	GP	G	REC

BLATTNER, ROBERT GARNETT "BUDDY"
B.FEB.8,1920 ST.LOUIS,MO.

1942	STL N	2-S	19		.043
1946	NY N	1-2	126		.255
1947	NY N	2-3	55		.261
1948	NY N	2	8		.200
1949	PHI N	2-S-3	64		.247
	BRTR		272		.247

BLAUVELT, HENRY R.
B.ROCHESTER,N.Y.

| 1890 | ROC AA | P | | 2 | 0- 1 |

BLAYLOCK, GARY NELSON
B.OCT.11,1931 CLARKTON,MO.

1959	STL N	P	26	31	4- 5
	NY A	P		15	0- 1
	BRTR		41	46	4- 6

BLAYLOCK, MARVIN EDWARD "MARV"
B.SEPT.30,1929 FT.SMITH,ARK.

1950	NY N	H	1		.000
1955	PHI N	1-0	113		.208
1956	PHI N	1-0	136		.254
1957	PHI N	1-0	37		.154
	BLIL		287		.235

BLAYLOCK, ROBERT EDWARD "BOB"
B.JUNE 28,1935 CHATTANOOGA,OKLA

1956	STL N	P	14	1- 6
1959	STL N	P	3	0- 1
	BRTR		17	1- 7

BLEFARY, CURTIS LEROY "CURT"
B.JULY 5,1943 BROOKLYN,N.Y.

1965	BAL A	O	144		.260
1966	BAL A	1-0	131		.255
1967	BAL A	1-0	155		.242
1968	BAL A	C-1-0	137		.200
1969	HOU N	1-0	155		.253
1970	NY A	1-0	99		.212
1971	NY A	1-0	21		.194
	OAK A	C-2-3-0	50		.218
1972	OAK A	1-2-0	8		.455
	SD N	C-1-3-0	74		.196
	BLTR		974		.237

BLEMKER, RAYMOND
B.AUG.9,1937 HUNTINGBURG,IND.

| 1960 | KC A | P | | 1 | 0- 0 |
| | BRTL | | | | |

BLESSITT, ISAIAH "IKE"
B.SEP.30,1949 DETROIT,MICH.

| 1972 | DET A | O | | 4 | .000 |
| | BRTR | | | | |

BLETHEN, CLARENCE WALDO "CLIMAX"
B.JULY 11,1893 DOVER-FOXCROFT, MAINE
D.APR.11,1973 FREDERICK,MD.

1923	BOS A	P	5	0- 0
1929	BRO N	P	2	0- 0
	BLTR		7	0- 0

BLEWETT, ROBERT LAWRENCE
B.JUNE 28,1877 FOND DU LAC,WIS.
D.MAR.17,1958

| 1902 | NY N | P | 5 | 0- 2 |
| | BLTL | | | |

BLIGH, EDWIN FORREST "NED"
B.JUNE 30,1864 BROOKLYN,N.Y.
D.APR.18,1892

1886	BAL AA	C	3		.000
1888	CIN AA	C-0	3		.000
1889	COL AA	C	27		.126
1890	COL AA	C	8		.214
	LOU AA	C	24		.154
	BRTR		65		.151

BLISS, ELMER WARD
B.MAR.9,1875 PENFIELD,PA.
D.MAR.18,1962

1903	NY A	P	1	1- 0
1904	NY A	P	1	0- 0
	BLTR		2	1- 0

BLISS, F. E.
B.MILWAUKEE,WIS.

| 1878 | MIL N | 3-0 | | 2 | .125 |

BLISS, JOHN JOSEPH ALFRED
B.JAN.9,1883 VANCOUVER,WASH.
D.OCT.23,1968 TEMPLE CITY,CAL.

1908	STL N	C	43		.213
1909	STL N	C	32		.221
1910	STL N	C	16		.063
1911	STL N	C	85		.229
1912	STL N	C	49		.246
	BRTR		225		.219

BLOCHOWICZ, JAMES JOHN
(PLAYED UNDER NAME OF JAMES JOHN BLOCK)

BLOCK, JAMES JOHN "BRUNO"
(REAL NAME JAMES JOHN BLOCHOWICZ)
B.MAR.14,1885 WISCONSIN RAPIDS, WIS.
D.AUG.6,1937

1907	WAS A	C	24		.140
1910	CHI A	C	55		.210
1911	CHI A	C	39		.304
1912	CHI A	C	46		.257
1914	CHI F	C	45		.212
	BRTR		209		.234

BLOCK, SEYMOUR "CY"
B.MAY 4,1922 BROOKLYN,N.Y.

1942	CHI N	2-3	9		.364
1945	CHI N	2-3	2		.143
1946	CHI N	3	6		.231
	BRTR		17		.302

BLOGG, WESLEY C.
B.NORFOLK,VA.

| 1883 | PIT AA | C-1-0 | 9 | | .147 |

BLOMBERG, RONALD MARK "RON"
B.AUG.23,1948 ATLANTA,GA.

1969	NY A	O	4		.500
1971	NY A	O	64		.322
1972	NY A	1	107		.268
1973	NY A	1-0	100		.329
1974	NY A	0-0	90		.311
1975	NY A	0-0	34		.255
1976	NY A	H	1		.000
	BLTR		400		.302

BLONG, JOSEPH MYLES
B.SEPT.17,1853 ST.LOUIS,MO.
D.SEPT.27,1892 ST.LOUIS,MO.

1875	RS	NA	P-0	13	16	3-10
						—
1876	STL N	O		62		.233
1877	STL N	P-2-	25	58	10- 9
		O				.216
	BRTR		38	136	13-19
						—

BLOODWORTH, JAMES HENRY "JIMMY"
B.JULY 26,1917 TALLAHASSEE,FLA.

1937	WAS A	2	15		.220
1939	WAS A	2	83		.289
1940	WAS A	1-2-3	119		.245
1941	WAS A	2-S-3	142		.245
1942	DET A	2-S	137		.242
1943	DET A	2	129		.241
1946	DET A	2	76		.245
1947	PIT N	2	88		.250
1949	CIN N	1-2-3	134		.261
1950	CIN N	2	4		.214
	PHI N	1-2-3	54		.229
1951	PHI N	1-2	21		.143
	BRTR		1002		.248

BLOOMFIELD, CLYDE STALCUP "BUD"
B.JAN.5,1936 OKLAHOMA CITY,OKLA.

1963	STL N	3	1		.000
1964	MIN A	2-S	7		.143
	BRTR		8		.143

BLOTT, JOHN LEONARD
B.AUG.24,1902 GIRARD,OHIO
D.JUNE 11,1964 ANN ARBOR,MICH.

| 1924 | CIN N | C | 2 | | .000 |
| | BRTR | | | | |

BLUE, BIRD WAYNE
B.DEC.14,1876 BETTSVILLE,OHIO
D.DEC.14,1928

1908	STL A	C	11		.375
	PHI A	C	6		.167
	TR		17		.286

BLUE, LUZERNE ATWELL "LU"
B.MAR.5,1897 WASHINGTON,D.C.
D.JULY 28,1958

1921	DET A	1	153		.308
1922	DET A	1	145		.300
1923	DET A	1	129		.284
1924	DET A	1	108		.311
1925	DET A	1	150		.307
1926	DET A	1	128		.287
1927	DET A	1	112		.260
1928	STL A	1	154		.281
1929	STL A	1	151		.293
1930	STL A	1	117		.235
1931	CHI A	1	155		.304
1932	CHI A	1	112		.249
1933	BRO N	1	1		.000
	BBTL		1615		.287

BLUE, VIDA ROCHELLE
B.JULY 28,1949 MANSFIELD,LA.

1969	OAK A	P	12	1- 1
1970	OAK A	P	6	2- 0
1971	OAK A	P	39	24- 8
1972	OAK A	P	25	27	6-10
1973	OAK A	P	37	20- 9
1974	OAK A	P	40	17-15
1975	OAK A	P	39	22-11
1976	OAK A	P	37	18-13
	BBTL	235	238	110-67
	BL 1969			

BLUEGE, OSWALD LOUIS "OSSIE"
B.OCT.24,1900 CHICAGO,ILL.

1922	WAS A	3	19		.197
1923	WAS A	3	109		.245
1924	WAS A	3	117		.281
1925	WAS A	S-3	143		.287
1926	WAS A	3	139		.271
1927	WAS A	3	146		.274
1928	WAS A	3	146		.283
1929	WAS A	2-S-3	64		.295
1930	WAS A	3	134		.290
1931	WAS A	3	152		.272
1932	WAS A	3	149		.258
1933	WAS A	3	140		.261
1934	WAS A	S-3-0	99		.246
1935	WAS A	2-S-3	100		.263
1936	WAS A	2-S-3	90		.288
1937	WAS A	S	42		.283
1938	WAS A	2-S	58		.261
1939	WAS A	1	18		.153
	BRTR		1867		.272
NON-PLAYING MANAGER				
WAS(A) 1943-47				

BLUEGE, OTTO ADAM "SQUEAKY"
B.JULY 20,1910 CHICAGO,ILL.

1932	CIN N	H	1		.000
1933	CIN N	2-S-3	108		.213
	BRTR		109		.213

BLUEJACKET, JAMES
B.JULY 8,1887 ADAIR,OKLA.
D.MAR.26,1947

1914	BRO F	P	17	4- 4
1915	BRO F	P	24	10-11
1916	CIN N	P	3	0- 1
	BRTR		44	14-16

BLUHM, HARVEY FRED "RED"
D.JUNE 27,1894 CLEVELAND,OHIO
D.MAY 7,1952

| 1918 | BOS A | H | 1 | | .000 |
| | BRTR | | | | |

BLUME, CLINTON WILLIS
B.OCT.17,1900 BROOKLYN,N.Y.
D.JUNE 12,1973 ISLIP,L.I.,N.Y.

1922	NY N	P	1	1- 0
1923	NY N	P	12	2- 0
	BRTR		13	3- 0

BLYLEVEN, RIK AALBERT "BERT"
B.APR.6,1951 ZEIST,HOLLAND

1970	MIN A	P	27	10- 9
1971	MIN A	P	38	16-15
1972	MIN A	P	39	17-17
1973	MIN A	P	40	20-17
1974	MIN A	P	37	17-17
1975	MIN A	P	35	15-10
1976	MIN A	P	12	4- 5
	TEX A	P	24	9-11
	BRTR		252	108-100

BLYZKA, MICHAEL JOHN "MIKE"
B.DEC.25,1928 HAMTRAMCK,MICH.

YR	CL	LEA	POS	GP	G	REC
1953	STL	A	P		33	2- 6
1955	BAL	A	P		37	1- 5
	BRTR				70	3-11

BOAK, CHESTER ROBERT "CHET"
B.JUNE 19,1935 NEW CASTLE,PA.

YR	CL	LEA	POS	GP	G	REC
1960	KC	A	2		5	.154
1961	WAS	A	2		5	.000
	BRTR				10	.100

BOARDMAN, CHARLES LOUIS
B.APR.27,1893 SENECA FALLS,N.Y.
D.AUG.10,1968 SACRAMENTO,CAL.

YR	CL	LEA	POS	GP	G	REC
1913	PHI	A	P		2	0- 2
1914	PHI	A	P		2	0- 0
1915	STL	N	P		3	1- 0
	BLTL				7	1- 2

BOARDMAN, FREDERICK
B.CHICAGO,ILL.

YR	CL	LEA	POS	GP	G	REC
1874	BAL	NA	O		1	-

BOBB, MARK RANDALL "RANDY"
B.JAN.1,1948 LOS ANGELES,CAL.

YR	CL	LEA	POS	GP	G	REC
1968	CHI	N	C		7	.125
1969	CHI	N	C		3	.000
	BRTR				10	.100

BOCCABELLA, JOHN DOMINIC
B.JUNE 29,1941 SAN FRANCISCO,CAL

YR	CL	LEA	POS	GP	G	REC
1963	CHI	N	1		24	.189
1964	CHI	N	1-O		9	.391
1965	CHI	N	1-O		6	.333
1966	CHI	N	C-1-O		75	.228
1967	CHI	N	C-1-O		25	.171
1968	CHI	N	C-O		7	.071
1969	MON	N	C		40	.105
1970	MON	N	C-1-3		61	.269
1971	MON	N	C-1-3		74	.220
1972	MON	N	C-1-3		83	.227
1973	MON	N	C-1		118	.233
1974	SF	N.	C		29	.138
	BRTR				551	.219

BOCEK, MILTON FRANCIS
B.JULY 16,1912 CHICAGO,ILL.

YR	CL	LEA	POS	GP	G	REC
1933	CHI	A	O		11	.364
1934	CHI	A	O		19	.211
	BRTR				30	.267

BOCHTE, BRUCE ANTON
B.NOV.12,1950 PASADENA,CAL.

YR	CL	LEA	POS	GP	G	REC
1974	CAL	A	1-O		57	.270
1975	CAL	A	1		107	.285
1976	CAL	A	1-O		146	.258
	BLTL				310	.270

BOCKMAN, JOSEPH EDWARD "EDDIE"
B.JULY 26,1920 SANTA ANA,CAL.

YR	CL	LEA	POS	GP	G	REC
1946	NY	A	3		4	.083
1947	CLE	A	2-S-3		46	.258
1948	PIT	N	2-3		70	.239
1949	PIT	N	2-3		79	.223
	BRTR				199	.230

BODIE, FRANK L. "PING"
(REAL NAME
FRANCESCO STEPHANO PEZZOLO)
B.OCT.8,1887 SAN FRANCISCO,CAL.
D.DEC.17,1961

YR	CL	LEA	POS	GP	G	REC
1911	CHI	A	2-O		145	.288
1912	CHI	A	O		137	.294
1913	CHI	A	O		127	.265
1914	CHI	A	O		107	.229
1917	PHI	A	O		148	.291
1918	NY	A	O		91	.256
1919	NY	A	O		134	.278
1920	NY	A	O		129	.295
1921	NY	A	O		31	.172
	BRTR				1049	.276

BOECKEL, NORMAN D. "TONY"
B.AUG.25,1894 LOS ANGELES,CAL.
D.FEB.16,1924

YR	CL	LEA	POS	GP	G	REC
1917	PIT	N	3		64	.265
1919	PIT	N	3		45	.250
	BOS	N	3		95	.249
1920	BOS	N	3		153	.268
1921	BOS	N	3		153	.313
1922	BOS	N	3		119	.289
1923	BOS	N	S-3		148	.298
	BRTR				777	.282

BOEHLER, GEORGE HENRY
B.JAN.2,1892 LAWRENCEBURG,IND.
D.JUNE 23,1958

YR	CL	LEA	POS	GP	G	REC
1912	DET	A	P		4	1- 2
1913	DET	A	P		1	0- 1
1915	DET	A	P		9	1- 1
1916	DET	A	P		5	1- 1
1920	STL	A	P		3	0- 1
1921	STL	A	P		1	0- 0
1923	PIT	N	P		10	1- 3
1926	BRO	N	P	26	11	1- 0
1914	DET	A	P		18	2- 3
	BRTR			61	62	7-12

BOEHLING, JOHN JOSEPH "JOE"
B.MAR.20,1892 RICHMOND,VA.
D.SEPT.8,1941

YR	CL	LEA	POS	GP	G	REC
1912	WAS	A	P		3	0- 0
1913	WAS	A	P		38	17- 7
1914	WAS	A	P		27	12- 8
1915	WAS	A	P		41	13-13
1916	WAS	A	P		28	9-10
	CLE	A	P		11	2- 4
1917	CLE	A	P		14	1- 6
1920	CLE	A	P		3	0- 1
	BLTL				165	54-49

BOEHMER, LEONARD JOSEPH "LEN"
B.JUNE 28,1941 FLINT HILL,MO.

YR	CL	LEA	POS	GP	G	REC
1967	CIN	N	2		2	.000
1969	NY	A	1-2-S-3		45	.176
1971	NY	A	3		3	.000
	BRTR				50	.164

BOERNER, LAURENCE HYER
B.JAN.21,1905 STAUNTON,VA.

YR	CL	LEA	POS	GP	G	REC
1932	BOS	A	P		21	0- 4
	BRTR					

BOGART, JOHN RENZIE "BIG JOHN"
B.SEPT.21,1901 BLOOMSBURG,PA.

YR	CL	LEA	POS	GP	G	REC
1920	DET	A	P		4	2- 1
	BRTR					

BOGGS, RAYMOND JOSEPH "LEFTY"
B.DEC.12,1904 REAMSVILLE,KAN.

YR	CL	LEA	POS	GP	G	REC
1928	BOS	N	P		4	0- 0
	BLTL					

BOGGS, THOMAS WINTON "TOMMY"
B.OCT.25,1955 POUGHKEEPSIE,N.Y.

YR	CL	LEA	POS	GP	G	REC
1976	TEX	A	P		13	1- 7
	BRTR					

BOGLE, WARREN FREDERICK
B.OCT.19,1946 LYNDHURST,N.J.

YR	CL	LEA	POS	GP	G	REC
1968	OAK	A	P		16	0- 0
	BLTL					

BOHEN, LEO J. "PAT"
B.OCT.20,1891 NAPA,CAL.
D.APR.9,1942

YR	CL	LEA	POS	GP	G	REC
1913	PHI	A	P		1	0- 1
1914	PIT	N	P		1	0- 0
	BRTR				2	0- 1

BOHN, CHARLES
B.1857 CLEVELAND,OHIO
D.AUG.1,1903

YR	CL	LEA	POS	GP	G	REC
1882	LOU	AA	P-O	2	4	1- 1
						.154

BOHNE, SAMUEL ARTHUR
(REAL NAME SAMUEL ARTHUR COHEN)
B.OCT.22,1896 SAN FRANCISCO,CAL

YR	CL	LEA	POS	GP	G	REC
1916	STL	N	S		14	.237
1921	CIN	N	2-3		153	.285
1922	CIN	N	2-S		112	.274
1923	CIN	N	1-2-S-3		139	.252
1924	CIN	N	2-S-3		100	.255
1925	CIN	N	1-2-S-3-O		73	.257
1926	CIN	N	2		25	.204
	BRO	N	S-3		47	.200
	BRTR				663	.261

BOISCLAIR, BRUCE ARMAND
B.DEC.9,1952 PUTNAM,CONN.

YR	CL	LEA	POS	GP	G	REC
1974	NY	N	O		7	.250
1976	NY	N	O		110	.287
	BLTL				117	.285

BOKELMANN, RICHARD WERNER
B.OCT.26,1926 ARLINGTON
HEIGHTS,ILL.

YR	CL	LEA	POS	GP	G	REC
1951	STL	N	P		20	3- 3
1952	STL	N	P		11	0- 1
1953	STL	N	P		3	0- 0
	BRTR				34	3- 4

BOKEN, ROBERT ANTHONY
B.FEB.23,1908 MARYVILLE,ILL.

YR	CL	LEA	POS	GP	G	REC
1933	WAS	A	2-S-3		55	.278
1934	WAS	A	2		11	.222
	CHI	A	2-S		81	.236
	BRTR				147	.247

BOKINA, JOSEPH
B.APR.7,1910 NORTHAMPTON,MASS.

YR	CL	LEA	POS	GP	G	REC
1936	WAS	A	P		5	0- 2
	BRTR					

BOLAND

YR	CL	LEA	POS	GP	G	REC
1875	ATL	NA	O		1	-

BOLAND, BERNARD ANTHONY
B.JAN.21,1892 ROCHESTER,N.Y.
D.SEPT.12,1973 DETROIT,MICH.

YR	CL	LEA	POS	GP	G	REC
1915	DET	A	P		47	13- 6
1916	DET	A	P	47	49	10- 3
1917	DET	A	P	43	45	16-11
1918	DET	A	P		29	14-10
1919	DET	A	P		35	14-16
1920	DET	A	P		4	0- 2
1921	STL	A	P		8	1- 4
	BRTR			213	217	68-52

BOLAND, EDWARD JOHN
B.APR.18,1912 LONG ISLAND CITY,
N.Y.

YR	CL	LEA	POS	GP	G	REC
1934	PHI	N	O		8	.300
1935	PHI	N	O		30	.213
1944	WAS	A	O		19	.271
	BLTL				57	.257

BOLD, CHARLES DICKENS "DUTCH"
B.OCT.27,1894 KARLSKRONA,SWEDEN

YR	CL	LEA	POS	GP	G	REC
1914	STL	A	1		2	.000
	BRTR					

BOLDEN, WILLIAM HORACE
"BIG BILL"
B.MAY 9,1894 DANDRIDGE,TENN.

YR	CL	LEA	POS	GP	G	REC
1919	STL	N	P		3	0- 1
	BRTR					

BOLEN, STEWART O'NEAL
B.OCT.12,1902 JACKSON,ALA.

YR	CL	LEA	POS	GP	G	REC
1926	STL	A	P		5	0- 0
1927	STL	A	P		3	0- 1
1931	PHI	N	P		28	3-12
1932	PHI	N	P		5	0- 0
	BLTL				41	3-13

BOLES, CARL THEODORE
B.OCT.31,1934 CENTER POINT,ARK.

YR	CL	LEA	POS	GP	G	REC
1962	SF	N	O		19	.375

BOLEY, JOHN PETER "JOE"
(REAL NAME JOHN PETER BOLINSKY)
B.JULY 26,1898 MAHANOY CITY,PA.
D.DEC.30,1962

YR	CL	LEA	POS	GP	G	REC
1927	PHI	A	S		118	.311
1928	PHI	A	S		132	.264
1929	PHI	A	S		91	.251
1930	PHI	A	S		121	.276
1931	PHI	A	S		67	.228
1932	PHI	A	S		10	.206
	CLE	A	S		1	.250
	BRTR				540	.269

BOLGER, JAMES CYRIL "DUTCH"
B.FEB.23,1932 CINCINNATI,OHIO

YR	CL	LEA	POS	GP	G	REC
1950	CIN	N	O		2	.000
1951	CIN	N	H		2	.000
1954	CIN	N	O		5	.333
1955	CHI	N	O		64	.206
1957	CHI	N	3-O		112	.275
1958	CHI	N	O		84	.225
1959	CLE	A	H		8	.000
	PHI	N	O		35	.083
	BRTR				312	.229

YR	CL	LEA	POS	GP	G	REC

BOLIN, BOBBY DONALD
B.JAN.29,1939 SMYRNA,S.C.

1961	SF	N	P		37	2- 2
1962	SF	N	P		41	7- 3
1963	SF	N	P		47	10- 6
1964	SF	N	P	38	39	6- 9
1965	SF	N	P		45	14- 6
1966	SF	N	P		36	11-10
1967	SF	N	P		37	6- 8
1968	SF	N	P		34	10- 5
1969	SF	N	P		30	7- 7
1970	MIL	A	P		32	5-11
	BOS	A	P		6	2- 0
1971	BOS	A	P		52	5- 3
1972	BOS	A	P		21	0- 1
1973	BOS	A	P		39	3- 4
		BRTR		495	496	88-75

BOLINSKY, JOHN PETER
(PLAYED UNDER NAME OF
JOHN PETER BOLEY)

BOLLING, FRANK ELMORE
B.NOV.16,1931 MOBILE,ALA.

1954	DET	A	2		117	.236
1956	DET	A	2		102	.281
1957	DET	A	2		146	.259
1958	DET	A	2		154	.269
1959	DET	A	2		127	.266
1960	DET	A	2		139	.254
1961	MIL	N	2		148	.262
1962	MIL	N	2		122	.271
1963	MIL	N	2		142	.244
1964	MIL	N	2		120	.199
1965	MIL	N	2		148	.264
1966	ATL	N	2		75	.211
		BRTR			1540	.254

BOLLING, JOHN EDWARD
B.FEB.20,1918 MOBILE,ALA.

1939	PHI	N	1		69	.289
1944	BRO	N	1		56	.351
		BLTL			125	.313

BOLLING, MILTON JOSEPH "MILT"
B.AUG.9,1930 MISSISSIPPI CITY,
MISS.

1952	BOS	A	S		11	.222
1953	BOS	A	S		109	.263
1954	BOS	A	S-3		112	.249
1955	BOS	A	S		6	.200
1956	BOS	A	2-S-3		45	.212
1957	BOS	A	H		1	.000
	WAS	A	2-S-3		91	.227
1958	DET	A	2-S-3		24	.194
		BRTR			400	.241

BOLLO, GREGORY GENE "GREG"
B.NOV.16,1943 DETROIT,MICH.

1965	CHI	A	P		15	0- 0
1966	CHI	A	P		3	0- 1
		BRTR			18	0- 1

BOLLWEG, DONALD RAYMOND "DON"
B.FEB.12,1921 WHEATON,ILL.

1950	STL	N	1		4	.182
1951	STL	N	1		6	.111
1953	NY	A	1-O		70	.297
1954	PHI	A	1		103	.224
1955	KC	A	1		12	.111
		BLTR			195	.243

BOLTON, CECIL GLENN
B.FEB.13,1904 BOONEVILLE,MISS.

1928	CLE	A	1		4	.154
		BLTR				

BOLTON, WILLIAM CLIFTON "CLIFF"
B.APR.10,1907 GREENSBORO,N.C.

1931	WAS	A	C		23	.255
1933	WAS	A	C-O		33	.410
1934	WAS	A	C		42	.270
1935	WAS	A	C		110	.304
1936	WAS	A	C		86	.291
1937	DET	A	C		27	.263
1941	WAS	A	C		14	.000
		BLTR			335	.291

BOND, THOMAS HENRY
B.APR.2,1856 NEW YORK,N.Y.
D.JAN.24,1941 BOSTON,MASS.

1874	ATL	NA	P		55	23-31
1875	HAR	NA	P-1-	39	71	19-16
			2-O			-
1876	HAR	N	P		45	32-13
1877	BOS	N	P-O	58	61	40-17
						.228
1878	BOS	N	P		59	40-19
1879	BOS	N	P	62	65	42-19
1880	BOS	N	P-1-	56	74	26-29
			O			.216
1881	BOS	N	P		3	0- 3
1882	WOR	N	M-P-	2	8	0- 0
			O			.125
1884	BOS	U	P-3-	23	36	12- 9
			O			.291
	IND	AA	P-O	5	7	0- 5
						.136
		BRTR		407	484	234-161
						-

BOND, WALTER FRANKLIN "WALT"
B.OCT.10,1937 DENMARK,TENN.
D.SEP.14,1967 HOUSTON,TEX.

1960	CLE	A	O		40	.221
1961	CLE	A	O		38	.173
1962	CLE	A	O		12	.380
1964	HOU	N	1-O		148	.254
1965	HOU	N	1-O		117	.263
1967	MIN	A	O		10	.313
		BLTR			365	.256

BONDS, BOBBY LEE
B.MAR.15,1946 RIVERSIDE,CAL.

1968	SF	N	O		81	.254
1969	SF	N	O		158	.259
1970	SF	N	O		157	.302
1971	SF	N	O		155	.288
1972	SF	N	O		153	.259
1973	SF	N	O		160	.283
1974	SF	N	O		150	.256
1975	NY	A	O-D		145	.270
1976	CAL	A	O		99	.265
		BRTR			1258	.272

BONE, GEORGE DRUMMOND
B.AUG.27,1874 NEW HAVEN,CONN.
D.MAY 28,1918

1901	MIL	A	S		12	.292
		TR				

BONETTI, JULIO JAMES PAUL
B.JULY 4,1912 SAN FRANCISCO,CAL
D.JUNE 17,1952

1937	STL	A	P		28	4-11
1938	STL	A	P		17	2- 3
1940	CHI	N	P		1	0- 0
		BRTR			46	6-14

BONEY, HENRY TATE "HANEY"
B.OCT.28,1905 WALLACE,N.C.

1927	NY	N	P		3	0- 0
		BRTR				

**BONGIOVANNI, ANTHONY THOMAS
"NINO"**
B.DEC.21,1913 NEW ORLEANS,LA.

1938	CIN	N	O		2	.286
1939	CIN	N	O		66	.258
		BLTL			68	.259

BONHAM, ERNEST EDWARD "TINY"
B.AUG.16,1913 IONE,CAL.
D.SEPT.15,1949

1940	NY	A	P		12	9- 3
1941	NY	A	P		23	9- 6
1942	NY	A	P		28	21- 5
1943	NY	A	P		28	15- 8
1944	NY	A	P		26	12- 9
1945	NY	A	P		18	8-11
1946	NY	A	P		18	5- 8
1947	PIT	N	P		33	11- 8
1948	PIT	N	P		22	6-10
1949	PIT	N	P		18	7- 4
		BRTR		231	103-72

BONHAM, WILLIAM GORDON "BILL"
B.OCT.1,1948 GLENDALE,CAL.

1971	CHI	N	P		33	2- 1
1972	CHI	N	P		19	1- 1
1973	CHI	N	P		44	7- 5
1974	CHI	N	P	44	48	11-22
1975	CHI	N	P	38	40	13-15
1976	CHI	N	P		32	9-13
		BRTR		210	216	43-57

BONIKOWSKI, JOSEPH PETER
B.JAN.16,1941 PHILADELPHIA,PA.

1962	MIN	A	P		30	5- 7
		BRTR				

BONIN, ERNEST LUTHER "BONNIE"
B.JAN.13,1888 GREEN HILL,IND.
D.JAN.3,1966 SYCAMORE,OHIO

1913	STL	A	H		1	.000
1914	BUF	F	O		21	.173
		BLTR			22	.171

BONNER, FRANK J.
B.AUG.20,1869 LOWELL,MASS.
D.DEC.31,1905

1894	BAL	N	2		27	.301
1895	BAL	N	3		11	.295
	STL	N	S		14	.132
1896	BRO	N	2		7	.185
1899	WAS	N	2		85	.276
1902	CLE	A	2		34	.278
	PHI	A	2		11	.182
1903	BOS	N	2-S		46	.220
		TR			235	.254

BONNESS, WILLIAM JOHN
B.DEC.15,1923 CLEVELAND,OHIO

1944	CLE	A	P		2	0- 1
		BRTL				

BONO, ADLAI WENDELL "GUS"
B.AUG.29,1895 DOE RUN,MO.
D.DEC.3,1948

1920	WAS	A	P		4	0- 2
		BRTR				

BONURA, HENRY JOHN "ZEKE"
B.SEPT.20,1908 NEW ORLEANS,LA.

1934	CHI	A	1		127	.302
1935	CHI	A	1		138	.295
1936	CHI	A	1		148	.330
1937	CHI	A	1		116	.345
1938	WAS	N	1		137	.289
1939	NY	N	1		123	.321
1940	NY	N	1		79	.273
	CHI	N	1		49	.264
		BRTR			917	.307

BOOE, EVERETT LITTLE
B.SEPT.28,1891 MEEKVILLE,N.C.
D.MAY 21,1969 KENEDY,TEX.

1913	PIT	N	O		29	.200
1914	IND	F	O		19	.233
	BUF	F	O		73	.220
		BLTR			121	.217

BOOKER, RICHARD LEE "BUDDY"
B.MAY 28,1942 LYNCHBURG,VA.

1966	CLE	A	C		18	.214
1968	CHI	A	C		5	.000
		BLTR			23	.182

BOOL, ALBERT J.
B.AUG.24,1897 LINCOLN,NEB.

1928	WAS	A	C		2	.143
1930	PIT	N			78	.259
1931	BOS	N			49	.188
		BRTR			129	.237

BOOLES, SEABRON JAMES
B.JULY 14,1880 BERNICE,LA.
D.MAR.16,1955

1909	CLE	A	P		4	0- 1
		BLTL				

BOONE, GEORGE M.
B.LOUISVILLE,KY.

1891	LOU	AA	P		4	1- 0

BOONE, ISSAC MORGAN "IKE"
B.FEB.17,1897 SAMANTHA,ALA.
D.AUG.1,1958

1922	NY	N	O		2	.500
1923	BOS	A	O		5	.267
1924	BOS	A	O		128	.333
1925	BOS	A	O		133	.330
1927	CHI	A	O		29	.226
1930	BRO	N	O		40	.297
1931	BRO	N	H		6	.200
1932	BRO	N	H		13	.143
		BLTR			356	.319

BOONE, JAMES ALBERT "DAN"
B.JAN.19,1898 SAMANTHA,ALA.
D.MAY 11,1968 TUSCALOOSA,ALA.

YR	CL	LEA	POS	GP	G	REC
1919	PHI	A	P		3	0- 1
1921	DET	A	P		1	0- 0
1922	CLE	A	P		11	4- 6
1923	CLE	A	P		27	4- 6
	BRTR				42	8-13

BOONE, LUTE JOSEPH "LUKE"
B.MAY 6,1890 PITTSBURGH,PA.

YR	CL	LEA	POS	G	REC
1913	NY	A	S	6	.250
1914	NY	A	2	106	.222
1915	NY	A	2	130	.204
1916	NY	A	3	46	.185
1918	PIT	N	2-S	27	.198
	BRTR			315	.208

BOONE, RAYMOND OTIS "IKE"
B.JULY 27,1923 SAN DIEGO,CAL.

YR	CL	LEA	POS	G	REC
1948	CLE	A	S	6	.400
1949	CLE	A	S	86	.252
1950	CLE	A	S	109	.301
1951	CLE	A	S	151	.233
1952	CLE	A	2-S-3	103	.263
1953	CLE	A	S	34	.241
	DET	A	S-3	101	.312
1954	DET	A	S-3	148	.295
1955	DET	A	3	135	.284
1956	DET	A	3	131	.308
1957	DET	A	1-3	129	.273
1958	DET	A	1	39	.237
	CHI	A	1	77	.244
1959	CHI	A	1	9	.238
	KC	A	1-3	61	.273
	MIL	N	1	13	.200
1960	MIL	N	1	7	.250
	BOS	A	1	34	.205
	BRTR			1373	.275

BOONE, ROBERT RAYMOND "BOB"
B.NOV.19,1947 SAN DIEGO,CAL.

YR	CL	LEA	POS	G	REC
1972	PHI	N	C	16	.275
1973	PHI	N	C	145	.261
1974	PHI	N	C	146	.242
1975	PHI	N	C-3	97	.246
1976	PHI	N	C-1	121	.271
	BRTR			525	.256

BOOTH, AMOS SMITH "DARLING"
B.SEPT.4,1852 CINCINNATI,OHIO
D.JULY 11,1921

YR	CL	LEA	POS	GP	G	REC
1876	CIN	N	P-C-	1	63	0- 1
			S-3			.253
1877	CIN	N	P-C-	12	43	1- 7
			2-S-3-O			.170
1880	CIN	N	O		1	.000
1882	BAL	AA	3		1	.000
	LOU	AA	2		1	.000
	BRTR			13	109	1- 8
						.219

BOOTH, EDGAR H.
B.BROOKLYN,N.Y.

YR	CL	LEA	POS	G	REC
1872	MAN	NA	2-O	24	.336
	ATL	NA	2-O	14	.250
1873	RES	NA	2-O	18	-
	ATL	NA	O	13	-
1874	ATL	NA	O	44	-
1875	MUT	NA	2-O	68	-
1876	MUT	N	O	57	.213
				238	-

BOOZER, JOHN MORGAN
B.JULY 6,1938 COLUMBIA,S.C.

YR	CL	LEA	POS	GP	G	REC
1962	PHI	N	P		9	0- 0
1963	PHI	N	P		26	3- 4
1964	PHI	N	P	22	23	3- 4
1966	PHI	N	P		2	0- 0
1967	PHI	N	P		28	5- 4
1968	PHI	N	P		38	2- 2
1969	PHI	N	P		46	1- 2
	BRTR			171	172	14-16

BORBON, PEDRO (RODRIGUEZ)
B.DEC.2,1946 VALVERDE,MAO,D.R.

YR	CL	LEA	POS	G	REC
1969	CAL	A	P	22	2- 3
1970	CIN	N	P	12	0- 2
1971	CIN	N	P	3	0- 0
1972	CIN	N	P	62	8- 3
1973	CIN	N	P	80	11- 4
1974	CIN	N	P	73	10- 7
1975	CIN	N	P	67	9- 5
1976	CIN	N	P	69	4- 3
	BRTR			388	44-27

BORCHERS, GEORGE BENARD "CHIEF"
B.APR.18,1869 SACRAMENTO,CAL.
D.OCT.24,1938 SACRAMENTO,CAL.

YR	CL	LEA	POS	G	REC
1888	CHI	N	P	10	4- 5
1895	LOU	N	P	1	0- 1
	BBTB			11	4- 6

BORDAGARAY, STANLEY GEORGE "FRENCHY"
B.JAN.3,1912 COALINGS,CAL.

YR	CL	LEA	POS	G	REC
1934	CHI	A	O	29	.322
1935	BRO	N	O	120	.282
1936	BRO	N	2-O	125	.315
1937	STL	N	3-O	96	.293
1938	STL	N	O	81	.282
1939	CIN	N	2-O	63	.197
1941	NY	A	O	36	.260
1942	BRO	N	O	48	.241
1943	BRO	N	3-O	89	.302
1944	BRO	N	3-O	130	.281
1945	BRO	N	3-O	113	.256
	BRTR			930	.283

BORDEN, JOSEPH EMLEY
(PLAYED UNDER NAME OF
JOSEPH EMLEY JOSEPHS IN 1875)
B.MAY 9,1854 JACOBSTOWN,N.J.
D.OCT.14,1929

YR	CL	LEA	POS	GP	G	REC
1875	PHI	NA	P		7	2- 4
1876	BOS	N	P-O	24	32	12-12
						.202
	BRTR			31	39	14-16
						-

BORDETZKI, ANTONIO
(PLAYED UNDER NAME OF
ANTHONY VINCENT BRIEF)

BORGMANN, GLENN DENNIS
B.MAY 25,1950 PATERSON,N.J.

YR	CL	LEA	POS	G	REC
1972	MIN	A	C	56	.234
1973	MIN	A	C	12	.265
1974	MIN	A	C	128	.252
1975	MIN	A	C	125	.207
1976	MIN	A	C	24	.246
	BRTR			345	.233

BORK, FRANK BERNARD
B.JULY 13,1940 BUFFALO,N.Y.

YR	CL	LEA	POS	G	REC
1964	PIT	N	P	33	2- 2
	BRTL				

BORKOWSKI, ROBERT VILARIAN
B.JAN.27,1927 DAYTON,OHIO

YR	CL	LEA	POS	G	REC
1950	CHI	N	1-O	85	.273
1951	CHI	N	O	58	.157
1952	CIN	N	1-O	126	.252
1953	CIN	N	1-O	94	.269
1954	CIN	N	1-O	73	.265
1955	CIN	N	1-O	25	.167
	BRO	N	O	9	.105
	BRTR			470	.251

BORLAND, THOMAS BRUCE "TOM"
B.FEB.14,1933 EL DORADO,KAN.

YR	CL	LEA	POS	G	REC
1960	BOS	A	P	26	0- 4
1961	BOS	A	P	1	0- 0
	BLTL			27	0- 4

BOROM, EDWARD JONES "RED"
B.OCT.30,1915 SPARTANBURG,S.C.

YR	CL	LEA	POS	G	REC
1944	DET	A	2	7	.071
1945	DET	A	2-S-3	55	.269
	BLTR			62	.250

BOROS, STEPHEN "STEVE"
B.SEP.3,1936 FLINT,MICH.

YR	CL	LEA	POS	G	REC
1957	DET	A	S-3	24	.146
1958	DET	A	2	6	.000
1961	DET	A	3	116	.270
1962	DET	A	2-3	116	.228
1963	CHI	N	1-O	41	.211
1964	CIN	N	3	117	.257
1965	CIN	N	3	2	.000
	BRTR			422	.245

BOROWY, HENRY LUDWIG "HANK"
B.MAY 12,1916 BLOOMFIELD,N.J.

YR	CL	LEA	POS	GP	G	REC
1942	NY	A	P		25	15- 4
1943	NY	A	P		29	14- 9
1944	NY	A	P		35	17-12
1945	NY	A	P		18	10- 5
	CHI	N	P		15	11- 2
1946	CHI	N	P	32	33	12-10
1947	CHI	N	P	40	41	8-12
1948	CHI	N	P		39	5-10
1949	PHI	N	P		28	12-12
1950	PHI	N	P		3	0- 0
1950	PIT	N	P		11	1- 3
	DET	A	P		13	1- 1
1951	DET	A	P		26	2- 2
	BRTR			314	316	108-82

BORTON, WILLIAM BAKER "BABE"
B.AUG.14,1888 MARION,ILL.

YR	CL	LEA	POS	G	REC
1912	CHI	A	1	31	.371
1913	CHI	A	1	28	.275
	NY	A	1	33	.121
1915	STL	F	1	159	.289
1916	STL	A	1	66	.225
	BLTL			317	.271

BOSCH, DONALD JOHN "DON"
B.JULY 15,1942 SAN FRANCISCO,CAL

YR	CL	LEA	POS	G	REC
1966	PIT	N	O	3	.000
1967	NY	N	O	44	.140
1968	NY	N	O	50	.171
1969	MON	N	O	49	.179
	BBTR			146	.164

BOSETTI, RICHARD ALAN "RICK"
B.AUG.5,1953 REDDING,CAL.

YR	CL	LEA	POS	G	REC
1976	PHI	N	O	13	.278
	BRTR				

BOSMAN, RICHARD ALLEN "DICK"
B.FEB.17,1944 KENOSHA,WIS.

YR	CL	LEA	POS	GP	G	REC
1966	WAS	A	P		13	2- 6
1967	WAS	A	P	7	8	3- 1
1968	WAS	A	P		46	2- 9
1969	WAS	A	P	31	32	14- 5
1970	WAS	A	P		36	16-12
1971	WAS	A	P		35	12-16
1972	TEX	A	P		29	8-10
1973	TEX	A	P		7	2- 5
	CLE	A	P		22	1- 8
1974	CLE	A	P		25	7- 5
1975	CLE	A	P		6	0- 2
	OAK	A	P		22	11- 4
1976	OAK	A	P		27	4- 2
	BRTR			306	308	82-85

BOSS, ELMER HARLEY "LEFFY"
B.NOV.19,1908 HODGE,LA.
D.MAY 15,1964 NASHVILLE,TENN.

YR	CL	LEA	POS	G	REC
1928	WAS	A	1	12	.250
1929	WAS	A	1	28	.273
1930	WAS	A	1	3	.000
1933	CLE	A	1	112	.269
	BLTL			155	.268

BOSSER, MELVIN EDWARD
B.FEB.8,1920 JOHNSTOWN,PA.

YR	CL	LEA	POS	G	REC
1945	CIN	N	P	7	2- 0
	BRTR				

BOSTICK, HENRY LANDERS
(REAL NAME
HENRY LANDERS LIFSIT)
B.JAN.12,1895 BOSTON,MASS.

YR	CL	LEA	POS	G	REC
1915	PHI	A	3	2	.000
	BRTR				

BOSTOCK, LYMAN WESLEY
B.NOV.22,1950 BIRMINGHAM,ALA.

YR	CL	LEA	POS	G	REC
1975	MIN	A	O	98	.282
1976	MIN	A	O	128	.323
	BLTR			226	.305

BOSWELL, ANDREW COTTRELL
B.SEPT.5,1874 NEW GRETNA,N.J.
D.FEB.3,1936

YR	CL	LEA	POS	GP	G	REC
1895	NY	N	P		5	2- 2
	WAS	N	P-1	6	7	1- 3
						.231
				11	12	3- 5
						.200

YR	CL	LEA	POS	GP	G	REC

BOSWELL, DAVID WILSON "DAVE"
B.JAN.20,1945 BALTIMORE,MD.

YR	CL	LEA	POS	GP	G	REC
1964	MIN	A	P		4	2- 0
1965	MIN	A	P	27	36	6- 5
1966	MIN	A	P	28	32	12- 5
1967	MIN	A	P	37	44	14-12
1968	MIN	A	P	34	37	10-13
1969	MIN	A	P	39	40	20-12
1970	MIN	A	P	18	20	3- 7
1971	DET	A	P		3	0- 0
	BAL	A	P		15	1- 2
		BRTR		205	231	68-56

BOSWELL, KENNETH GEORGE "KEN"
B.FEB.23,1946 AUSTIN,TEX.

YR	CL	LEA	POS	GP	G	REC
1967	NY	N	2-3		11	.225
1968	NY	N	2		75	.261
1969	NY	N	2		102	.279
1970	NY	N	2		105	.254
1971	NY	N	2		116	.273
1972	NY	N	2		100	.211
1973	NY	N	2-3		76	.227
1974	NY	N	2-3-0		96	.216
1975	HOU	N	2-3		86	.242
1976	HOU	N	2-3-0		91	.262
		BLTR			858	.250

BOTTARINI, JOHN CHARLES
B.SEPT.14,1911 CROCKETT,CAL.

YR	CL	LEA	POS	GP	G	REC
1937	CHI	N	C		26	.275
		BRTR				

BOTTOMLEY, JAMES LEROY
"SUNNY JIM"
B.APR.23,1900 OGLESBY,ILL.
D.DEC.11,1959 ST.LOUIS,MO.

YR	CL	LEA	POS	GP	G	REC
1922	STL	N	1		37	.325
1923	STL	N	1		134	.371
1924	STL	N	1-2		137	.316
1925	STL	N	1		153	.367
1926	STL	N	1		154	.299
1927	STL	N	1		152	.303
1928	STL	N	1		149	.325
1929	STL	N	1		146	.314
1930	STL	N	1		131	.304
1931	STL	N	1		108	.348
1932	STL	N	1		91	.296
1933	CIN	N	1		145	.250
1934	CIN	N	1		142	.284
1935	CIN	N	1		107	.258
1936	STL	A	1		140	.298
1937	STL	A	M-1		65	.239
		BLTL			1991	.309

BOTZ, ROBERT ALLEN
B.APR.28,1935 MILWAUKEE,WIS.

YR	CL	LEA	POS	GP	G	REC
1962	LA	A	P		35	2- 1
		BRTR				

BOUCHEE, EDWARD FRANCIS "ED"
B.MAR.7,1933 LIVINGSTON,MONT.

YR	CL	LEA	POS	GP	G	REC
1956	PHI	N	1		9	.273
1957	PHI	N	1		154	.293
1958	PHI	N	1		89	.257
1959	PHI	N	1		136	.285
1960	PHI	N	1		22	.262
	CHI	N	1		98	.237
1961	CHI	N	1		112	.248
1962	NY	N	1		50	.161
		BLTL			670	.265

BOUCHER, ALEXANDER FRANCIS "BO"
B.DEC.10,1881 FRANKLIN,MASS.
D.JUNE 23,1974 TORRANCE,CAL.

YR	CL	LEA	POS	GP	G	REC
1914	STL	F	3		147	.232
		BRTR				

BOUCHER, MEDRIC T.
B.1889

YR	CL	LEA	POS	GP	G	REC
1914	BAL	F	C		14	.235
	PIT	F	C		1	.000
		BRTR			15	.235

BOUDREAU, LOUIS "LOU"
B.JULY 17,1917 HARVEY,ILL.

YR	CL	LEA	POS	GP	G	REC
1938	CLE	A	3		1	.000
1939	CLE	A	S		53	.258
1940	CLE	A	S		155	.295
1941	CLE	A	S		148	.257
1942	CLE	A	M-S		147	.283
1943	CLE	A	M-C-S		152	.286
1944	CLE	A	M-C-S		150	.327
1945	CLE	A	M-S		97	.306
1946	CLE	A	M-S		140	.293
1947	CLE	A	M-S		150	.307
1948	CLE	A	M-C-S		152	.355
1949	CLE	A	M-1-2-S-3		134	.284
1950	CLE	A	M-1-2-S-3		81	.269
1951	BOS	A	1-S-3		82	.267
1952	BOS	A	M-S-3		4	.000
		BRTR			1646	.295

NON-PLAYING MANAGER
BOS(A) 1953-54, KC(A) 1955-57,
CHI(N) 1960

BOULDIN, CARL EDWARD
B.SEP.17,1939 GERMANTOWN,KY.

YR	CL	LEA	POS	GP	G	REC
1961	WAS	A	P		2	0- 1
1962	WAS	A	P	6	7	1- 2
1963	WAS	A	P		10	2- 2
1964	WAS	A	P	9	10	0- 3
		BBTR	27	29	3- 8
	BL 1961					

BOULTES, JAKE JOHN
B.AUG.6,1884 ST.LOUIS,MO.
D.DEC.24,1955

YR	CL	LEA	POS	GP	G	REC
1907	BOS	N	P	24	29	5- 9
1908	BOS	N	P		17	3- 5
1909	BOS	N	P		1	0- 0
		TR	42	47	8-14

BOURQUE, PATRICK DANIEL "PAT"
B.MAR.23,1947 WORCESTER,MASS.

YR	CL	LEA	POS	GP	G	REC
1971	CHI	N	1		14	.189
1972	CHI	N	1		11	.259
1973	CHI	N	1		57	.209
	OAK	A	1-0		23	.190
1974	OAK	A	1		73	.229
	MIN	A	1		23	.219
		BLTL		201	.215

BOUTHILLIER, ARTHUR E.
(PLAYED UNDER NAME OF
ARTHUR E. BUTLER)

BOUTON, JAMES ALAN "JIM"
B.MAR.8,1939 NEWARK,N.J.

YR	CL	LEA	POS	GP	G	REC
1962	NY	A	P	36	38	7- 7
1963	NY	A	P		40	21- 7
1964	NY	A	P		38	18-13
1965	NY	A	P	30	31	4-15
1966	NY	A	P		24	3- 8
1967	NY	A	P		17	1- 0
1968	NY	A	P		12	1- 1
1969	SEA	A	P		57	2- 1
	HOU	N	P		16	0- 2
1970	HOU	N	P		29	4- 6
		BRTR	299	302	61-60

BOWA, LAWRENCE ROBERT "LARRY"
B.DEC.6,1945 SACRAMENTO,CAL.

YR	CL	LEA	POS	GP	G	REC
1970	PHI	N	2-S		145	.250
1971	PHI	N	S		159	.249
1972	PHI	N	S		152	.250
1973	PHI	N	S		122	.211
1974	PHI	N	S		162	.275
1975	PHI	N	S		136	.305
1976	PHI	N	S		156	.248
		BBTR		1032	.257

BOWCOCK, BENJAMIN JAMES "BENNY"
B.OCT.28,1879 FALL RIVER,MASS.
D.JUNE 16,1961 NEW BEDFORD,MASS

YR	CL	LEA	POS	GP	G	REC
1903	STL	A	2		14	.300
		BRTR				

BOWDEN, DAVID TIMON "TIM"
B.AUG.15,1891 MCDONOUGH,GA.
D.OCT.25,1949

YR	CL	LEA	POS	GP	G	REC
1914	STL	A	0		6	.285

BOWEN, EMMONS JOSEPH "CHICK"
B.JULY 26,1897 NEW HAVEN,CONN.
D.AUG.9,1948

YR	CL	LEA	POS	GP	G	REC
1919	NY	N	0		3	.200
		BRTR				

BOWEN, SUTHERLAND MC COY
B.FEB.17,1871 KINGSTON,IND.
D.JAN.25,1925

YR	CL	LEA	POS	GP	G	REC
1896	NY	N	P		2	0- 1
		BRTR				

BOWENS, SAMUEL EDWARDS "SAM"
B.MAR.23,1939 WILMINGTON,N.C.

YR	CL	LEA	POS	GP	G	REC
1963	BAL	A	0		15	.333
1964	BAL	A	0		139	.263
1965	BAL	A	0		84	.163
1966	BAL	A	0		89	.210
1967	BAL	A	0		62	.183
1968	WAS	A	0		57	.191
1969	WAS	A	0		33	.193
		BRTR		479	.223

BOWERMAN, FRANK EUGENE "MIKE"
B.DEC.5,1868 ROMEO,MICH.
D.NOV.30,1948

YR	CL	LEA	POS	GP	G	REC
1895	BAL	N	C		1	.000
1896	BAL	N	C		4	.125
1897	BAL	N	C		33	.323
1898	BAL	N	C		5	.438
	PIT	N	C		62	.278
1899	PIT	N	C-1		107	.269
1900	NY	N	C		73	.256
1901	NY	N	C		52	.217
1902	NY	N	C-1		99	.253
1903	NY	N	C		59	.276
1904	NY	N	C		90	.232
1905	NY	N	C-1		90	.269
1906	NY	N	C-1		87	.228
1907	NY	N	G 1		90	.260
1908	BOS	N	C		74	.228
1909	BOS	N	M-C		27	.212
		BRTR		953	.255

BOWERS, GROVER BILL
B.MAR.25,1923 PARKIN,ARK.

YR	CL	LEA	POS	GP	G	REC
1949	CHI	A	0		26	.192
		BLTR				

BOWERS, STEWART COLE
B.FEB.26,1915 NEW FREEDOM,PA.

YR	CL	LEA	POS	GP	G	REC
1935	BOS	A	P	10	11	2- 1
1936	BOS	A	P		6	0- 0
1937	BOS	A	P		1	0- 0
		BBTR	17	18	2- 1

BOWES, FRANK C.
B.1865 BATH,N.Y.
D.JAN.21,1895

YR	CL	LEA	POS	GP	G	REC
1890	BRO	AA	C		62	.207
		TR				

BOWLER, GRANT TIERNEY
B.OCT.24,1907 DENVER,COL.
D.JUNE 25,1968 DENVER,COLO.

YR	CL	LEA	POS	GP	G	REC
1931	CHI	A	P		13	0- 1
1932	CHI	A	P		4	0- 0
		BRTR	17	0- 1

BOWLES, CHARLES JAMES
B.MAR.15,1918 NORWOOD,MASS.

YR	CL	LEA	POS	GP	G	REC
1943	PHI	A	P	2	3	1- 1
1945	PHI	A	P	8	13	0- 3
		BRTR	10	16	1- 4

BOWLES, EMMETT JEROME
B.AUG.2,1898 WANETTE,OKLA.
D.SEPT.3,1959

YR	CL	LEA	POS	GP	G	REC
1922	CHI	A	P		1	0- 0
		BRTR				

BOWLIN, LOIS WELDON
"WELDON" OR "HOSS"
B.DEC.10,1940 PARAGOULD,ARK.

YR	CL	LEA	POS	GP	G	REC
1967	KC	A	3		2	.200
		BRTR				

BOWLING, STEPHEN SHADDON "STEVE"
B.JUNE 26,1952 TULSA,OKLA.

YR	CL	LEA	POS	GP	G	REC
1976	MIL	A	0		14	.167

BOWMAN, ALVAH EDSON "ABE"
B.JAN.25,1893 GREENUP,ILL.

YR	CL	LEA	POS	GP	G	REC
1914	CLE	A	P	22	2- 7
1915	CLE	A	P	2	0- 1
		BRTR	24	2- 8

BOWMAN, ELMARI WILHELM
B.MAR.19,1900 PROCTOR,VT.

YR	CL	LEA	POS	GP	G	REC
1920	WAS	A	H		2	.000
		BRTR				

YR	CL	LEA	POS	GP	G	REC

BOWMAN, ERNEST FERRELL "ERNIE"
B.JULY 28,1935 JOHNSON CITY, TENN.

YR	CL	LEA	POS	GP	G	REC
1961	SF	N	2-S-3		38	.211
1962	SF	N	2-S-3		46	.190
1963	SF	N	2-S-3		81	.184
	BRTR				165	.190

BOWMAN, JOSEPH EMIL
B.JUNE 17,1910 ARGENTINE,KAN.

YR	CL	LEA	POS	GP	G	REC
1932	PHI	A	P		7	0- 1
1934	NY	N	P	30	31	5- 4
1935	PHI	N	P-O	33	49	7-10
						.194
1936	PHI	N	P	40	44	9-20
1937	PIT	N	P	30	35	8- 8
1938	PIT	N	P	17	18	3- 4
1939	PIT	N	P	37	70	10-14
1940	PIT	N	P	32	57	9-10
1941	PIT	N	P	18	22	3- 2
1944	BOS	A	P	26	59	12- 8
1945	BOS	A	P	3	9	0- 2
	CIN	N	P	25	29	11-13
	BLTR			298	430	77-96
						.221

BOWMAN, ROBERT JAMES
B.OCT.3,1911 KEYSTONE,W.VA.
D.SEPT.4,1972 BLUEFIELD,W.VA.

YR	CL	LEA	POS	GP	G	REC
1939	STL	N	P		51	13- 5
1940	STL	N	P		28	7- 5
1941	NY	N	P		29	6- 7
1942	CHI	N	P		1	0- 0
	BRTR				109	26-17

BOWMAN, ROBERT LEROY "BOB"
B.MAY 10,1931 WILLITS,CAL.

YR	CL	LEA	POS	GP	G	REC
1955	PHI	N	O		3	.000
1956	PHI	N	O		6	.188
1957	PHI	N	O		99	.266
1958	PHI	N	O		91	.288
1959	PHI	N	P-O	5	57	0- 1
						.127
	BRTR			5	256	0- 1
						.249

BOWMAN, ROGER CLINTON
B.AUG.18,1927 AMSTERDAM,N.Y.

YR	CL	LEA	POS	GP	G	REC
1949	NY	N	P		2	0- 0
1951	NY	N	P		9	2- 4
1952	NY	N	P		2	0- 0
1953	PIT	N	P		30	0- 4
1955	PIT	N	P		7	0- 3
	BRT				50	2-11

BOWMAN, SUMNER SALLADE
B.FEB.9,1867 MILLERSBURG,PA.
D.JAN.11,1954

YR	CL	LEA	POS	GP	G	REC
1890	PHI	N	P		4	1- 0
	PIT	N	P		10	2- 7
1891	ATH	AA	P-O	8	14	2- 5
						.215
	TL			22	28	5-12
						.258

BOWMAN, WILLIAM G.
B.CHICAGO,ILL.

YR	CL	LEA	POS	GP	G	REC
1891	CHI	N	C		15	.088

BOWSER, JAMES H. "RED"
B.GREENSBURG,PA.

YR	CL	LEA	POS	GP	G	REC
1910	CHI	A	O		1	.000

BOWSFIELD, EDWARD OLIVER "TED"
B.JAN.10,1935 VERNON,B.C.,CANADA

YR	CL	LEA	POS	GP	G	REC
1958	BOS	A	P	16	17	4- 2
1959	BOS	A	P		5	0- 1
1960	BOS	A	P		17	1- 2
	CLE	A	P		11	3- 4
1961	LA	A	P	41	46	11- 8
1962	LA	A	P	34	44	9- 8
1963	KC	A	P		43	5- 7
1964	KC	A	P	50	52	4- 7
	BRTL			215	235	37-39

BOYD, FRANK C. "JAKE"
B.NORFOLK,VA.

YR	CL	LEA	POS	GP	G	REC
1894	WAS	N	P		6	0- 3
1895	WAS	N	P-O	14	46	1- 7
						.284
1896	WAS	N	P		4	1- 2
	TL			32	56	2-12
						.257

BOYD, FRANK JAY
B.APR.2,1868 WEST MIDDLETOWN,PA
D.DEC.16,1937

YR	CL	LEA	POS	GP	G	REC
1893	CLE	N	C		1	.200
	BRTR					

BOYD, GARY LEE
B.AUG.22,1946 PASADENA,CAL.

YR	CL	LEA	POS	GP	G	REC
1969	CLE	A	P		8	0- 2
	BRTR					

BOYD, RAYMOND C.
B.FEB.11,1887 HORTONVILLE,IND.
D.FEB.11,1920

YR	CL	LEA	POS	GP	G	REC
1910	STL	A	P		3	0- 2
1911	CIN	N	P		7	3- 3
	BRTR				10	3- 5

BOYD, ROBERT RICHARD "BOB"
B.OCT.1,1926 POTTS CAMP,MISS.

YR	CL	LEA	POS	GP	G	REC
1951	CHI	A	1		12	.167
1953	CHI	A	1-O		55	.297
1954	CHI	A	1-O		29	.179
1956	BAL	A	1-O		70	.311
1957	BAL	A	1-O		141	.318
1958	BAL	A	1		125	.309
1959	BAL	A	1		128	.265
1960	BAL	A	1		71	.317
1961	KC	A	1		26	.229
	MIL	N	1		36	.244
	BLTL				693	.293

BOYD, WILLIAM J.

YR	CL	LEA	POS	GP	G	REC
1872	MUT	NA	S-3-O		35	.254
1873	ATL	NA	3-O		48	-
1874	HAR	NA	3-O		26	-
1875	ATL	NA	1-2-3-O		36	-
					145	-

BOYER, CLETIS LEROY "CLETE"
B.FEB.9,1937 CASSVILLE,MO.

YR	CL	LEA	POS	GP	G	REC
1955	KC	A	2-S-3		47	.241
1956	KC	A	2-3		67	.217
1957	KC	A	2-3		10	.000
1959	NY	A	S-3		47	.175
1960	NY	A	S-3		124	.242
1961	NY	A	S-3-O		148	.224
1962	NY	A	3		158	.272
1963	NY	A	2-S-3		152	.251
1964	NY	A	S-3		147	.218
1965	NY	A	S-3		148	.251
1966	NY	A	S-3		154	.240
1967	ATL	N	S-3		154	.245
1968	ATL	N	3		71	.227
1969	ATL	N	3		144	.250
1970	ATL	N	S-3		134	.246
1971	ATL	N	S-3		30	.245
	BRTR				1725	.242

BOYER, CLOYD VICTOR "JUNIOR"
B.SEPT.1,1927 LIBERTY,MO.

YR	CL	LEA	POS	GP	G	REC
1949	STL	N	P		4	0- 0
1950	STL	N	P		36	7- 7
1951	STL	N	P		19	2- 5
1952	STL	N	P	23	24	6- 6
1955	KC	A	P		30	5- 5
	BRTR			112	113	20-23

BOYER, KENTON LLOYD "KEN"
B.MAY 20,1931 LIBERTY,MO.

YR	CL	LEA	POS	GP	G	REC
1955	STL	N	S-3		147	.264
1956	STL	N	3		150	.306
1957	STL	N	3-O		142	.265
1958	STL	N	S-3-O		150	.307
1959	STL	N	S-3		149	.309
1960	STL	N	3		151	.304
1961	STL	N	3		153	.329
1962	STL	N	3		160	.291
1963	STL	N	3		159	.285
1964	STL	N	3		162	.295
1965	STL	N	3		144	.260
1966	NY	N	1-3		136	.266
1967	NY	N	1-3		56	.235
	CHI	A	1-3		57	.261
1968	CHI	A	1-3		10	.125
	LA	N	1-3		83	.271
1969	LA	N	1		25	.206
	BRTR				2034	.287

BOYLE, EDWARD J.
B.MAY 8,1874 CINCINNATI,OHIO
D.FEB.20,1941

YR	CL	LEA	POS	GP	G	REC
1896	LOU	N	C		3	.111
	PIT	N	C		2	.000
					5	.071

BOYLE, HENRY J. "HANDSOME"
B.SEPT.20,1860 PHILADELPHIA,PA.

YR	CL	LEA	POS	GP	G	REC
1884	STL	U	P-O	18	49	16- 2
						.260
1885	STL	N	P-2-O	42	72	15-25
						.201
1886	STL	N	P		30	9-15
1887	IND	N	P		41	13-24
1888	IND	N	P		37	15-22
1889	IND	N	P		44	20-23
	TR			203	273	88-111
						.224

BOYLE, JAMES JOHN
B.JAN.19,1904 CINCINNATI,OHIO
D.DEC.24,1958

YR	CL	LEA	POS	GP	G	REC
1926	NY	N	C		1	.000
	BRTR					

BOYLE, JOHN ANTHONY "HONEST JOHN"
B.MAR.22,1866 CINCINNATI,OHIO
D.JAN.7,1913

YR	CL	LEA	POS	GP	G	REC
1886	CIN	AA	C		1	.250
1887	STL	AA	C		88	.240
1888	STL	AA	C		71	.245
1889	STL	AA	C		99	.250
1890	CHI	P	C-S-3		100	.257
1891	STL	AA	C-S		120	.280
1892	NY	N	C-1		116	.201
1893	PHI	N	1		117	.305
1894	PHI	N	1		116	.291
1895	PHI	N	1		133	.254
1896	PHI	N	C		39	.288
1897	PHI	N	C-1		73	.259
1898	PHI	N	C-1		6	.091
	BRTR				1079	.259

BOYLE, JOHN BELLEW
B.JULY 9,1889 MORRIS,ILL.
D.APR.3,1971 FT.LAUDERDALE,FLA.

YR	CL	LEA	POS	GP	G	REC
1912	PHI	N	S-3		15	.280
	BLTR					

BOYLE, RALPH FRANCIS "BUZZ"
B.FEB.9,1910 CINCINNATI,OHIO

YR	CL	LEA	POS	GP	G	REC
1929	BOS	N	O		17	.263
1930	BOS	N	O		1	.000
1933	BRO	N	O		93	.299
1934	BRO	N	O		128	.305
1935	BRO	N	O		127	.272
	BLTL				366	.293

BOYLES, HARRY "STRETCH"
B.NOV.29,1912 GRANITE CITY,ILL.

YR	CL	LEA	POS	GP	G	REC
1938	CHI	A	P		9	0- 4
1939	CHI	A	P		2	0- 0
	BRTR				11	0- 4

BRABENDER, EUGENE MATTHEW "GENE"
B.AUG.16,1941 MADISON,WIS.

YR	CL	LEA	POS	GP	G	REC
1966	BAL	A	P		31	4- 3
1967	BAL	A	P		14	6- 4
1968	BAL	A	P		37	6- 7
1969	SEA	A	P	40	41	13-14
1970	MIL	A	P		29	6-15
	BRTR			151	152	35-43

BRACK, GILBERT HERMAN "GIBBY"
B.MAR.29,1908 CHICAGO,ILL.
D.JAN.20,1960

YR	CL	LEA	POS	GP	G	REC
1937	BRO	N	O		112	.274
1938	BRO	N	O		40	.214
	PHI	N	O		72	.287
1939	PHI	N	1-O		91	.289
	BRTR				315	.279

BRACKEN, JOHN JAMES
B.APR.14,1881 CLEVELAND,OHIO
D.JULY 16,1954

YR	CL	LEA	POS	GP	G	REC
1901	CLE	A	P		12	4- 8
	BRTR					

BRACKINRIDGE, JOHN CALHOUN
B.DEC.24,1880 HARRISBURG,PA.
D.MAR.20,1953

YR	CL	LEA	POS	GP	G	REC
1904	PHI	N	P		7	0- 2

BRADEY, DONALD EUGENE "DON"
B.OCT.4,1934 CHARLOTTE,N.C.

YR	CL	LEA	POS	GP	G	REC
1964	HOU	N	P		3	0- 2
	BRTR					

`YR  CL LEA POS   GP   G    REC`

BRADFORD, CHARLES WILLIAM "BUDDY"
B.JULY 25,1944 MOBILE,ALA.
```
1966 CHI A  O          14   .143
1967 CHI A  O          24   .100
1968 CHI A  O         103   .217
1969 CHI A  O          93   .256
1970 CHI A  O          32   .187
     CLE A  3-O        75   .196
1971 CLE N  O          20   .158
     CIN N  O          79   .200
1972 CHI A  O          35   .271
1973 CHI A  O          53   .238
1974 CHI A  O          39   .333
1975 CHI A  O          25   .155
     STL N  O          50   .272
1976 CHI A  O          55   .219
     BRTR             697   .226
```

BRADFORD, HENRY VICTOR "VIC"
B.MAR.5,1916 BROWNSVILLE,TENN.
```
1943 NY  N  P           6   .200
     BRTR
```

BRADFORD, WILLIAM D.
B.AUG.28,1924 CHOCTAW,ARK.
```
1956 KC  A  P           1   0- 0
     BRTR
```

BRADLEY, FREDERICK LANGDON
B.JULY 31,1920 PARSONS,KAN.
```
1948 CHI A  P           8   0- 0
1949 CHI A  P           1   0- 0
     BRTR               9   0- 0
```

BRADLEY, GEORGE H. "FOGHORN"
B.1853 MILFORD,MASS.
D.APR.3,1900
```
1876 BOS N  P          22   11- 9
     BRTR
```

BRADLEY, GEORGE WASHINGTON "GRIN"
B.JULY 13,1852 READING,PA.
D.OCT.2,1931
```
1875 STL NA P-3        58   31-25
                            .228
1876 STL N  P          64   45-19
1877 CHI N  P-1- 50    55   19-23
          3-0               .243
1879 TRO N  P          61   13-40
1880 PRO N  P-1- 22    78   12- 9
          3-0               .226
1881 DET N  S           1   .000
     CLE N  P-S-  7    61    3- 4
                            .252
1882 CLE N  P-1- 17    29    7-10
                            .183
1883 CLE N  S           4   .313
     ATH AA P-1- 27    77   17- 7
          3-0               .238
1884 CLE N  U  P-S 34  52   21-13
                            .202
1886 ATH AA S          13   .149
1888 BAL AA S           1   .000
     BRTR  332  554   168-150
                            .229
```

BRADLEY, GEORGE WASHINGTON
B.APR.4,1918 GREENWOOD,ARK.
```
1946 STL A  O           4   .167
     BRTR
```

BRADLEY, HERBERT THEODORE
B.JAN.3,1904 AGENDA,KAN.
D.OCT.16,1959
```
1927 BOS A  P           6   1- 1
1928 BOS A  P          15   0- 3
1929 BOS A  P           3   0- 0
     BRTR              24   1- 4
```

BRADLEY, HUGH FREDERICK "CARUS"
B.MAY 23,1885 GRAFTON,MASS.
D.JAN.26,1949
```
1910 BOS A  1          32   .169
1911 BOS A  1          12   .300
1912 BOS A  1          40   .190
1914 PIT F  1         118   .302
1915 PIT F  1          26   .288
     BRO F  1          37   .246
     NEW F  1          12   .094
     BRTR             277   .257
```

BRADLEY, J. NICHOLAS "NICK"
B.ALTOONA,PA.
D.JAN.16,1889
```
1884 WAS U  O           1   .000
```

BRADLEY, JOHN THOMAS
B.SEPT.20,1893 DENVER,COLO.
```
1916 CLE A  C           2   .667
     BRTR
```

BRADLEY, THOMAS WILLIAM "TOM"
B.MAR.16,1947 ASHEVILLE,N.C.
```
1969 CAL A  P           3   0- 1
1970 CAL A  P          17   2- 5
1971 CHI A  P    45    48   15-15
1972 CHI A  P    40    43   15-14
1973 SF  N  P          35   13-12
1974 SF  N  P          30   8-11
1975 SF  N  P          13   2- 3
     BRTR  183  189    55-61
```

BRADLEY, WILLIAM JOSEPH "BILL"
B.FEB.13,1878 CLEVELAND,OHIO
D.MAR.11,1954
```
1899 CHI N  3          35   .307
1900 CHI N  1-3       120   .288
1901 CLE A  3         133   .296
1902 CLE A  3         136   .341
1903 CLE A  3         137   .315
1904 CLE A  3         154   .300
1905 CLE A  3         145   .268
1906 CLE A  3          82   .275
1907 CLE A  3         139   .223
1908 CLE A  S-3       148   .243
1909 CLE A  3          95   .186
1910 CLE A  3          61   .196
1914 BRO F  M-H        7    .500
1915 KC  F  3          66   .192
     BRTR            1458   .272
```

BRADSHAW, DALLAS CARL "WINDY"
B.NOV.23,1895 WOLF CREEK,ILL.
D.DEC.11,1939 HERRIN,ILL.
```
1917 PHI A  2           2   .000
     BLTR
```

BRADSHAW, GEORGE THOMAS
B.SEPT.12,1924 SALISBURY,N.C.
```
1952 WAS A  C          10   .217
     BRTR
```

BRADSHAW, JOE SIAH
B.AUG.17,1897 ROELLEN,TENN.
```
1929 BRO N  P           2   0- 0
     BRTR
```

BRADY, CLIFFORD FRANCIS
B.MAR.6,1897 ST.LOUIS,MO.
D.SEPT.25,1974 BELLEVILLE,ILL.
```
1920 BOS A  2          53   .228
     BRTR
```

BRADY, CORNELIUS JOSEPH "NEAL"
B.MAR.4,1897 COVINGTON,KY.
D.JUNE 19,1947
```
1915 NY  A  P           2   0- 0
1917 NY  A  P           2   1- 0
1925 CIN N  P          20   1- 3
     BRTR              24   2- 3
```

BRADY, FREDERICK
(SEE WILLIAM LORENZ KOPF)

BRADY, JAMES JOSEPH "JIM"
B.MAR.2,1936 JERSEY CITY,N.J.
```
1956 DET A  P           6   0- 0
     BLTL
```

BRADY, JAMES WARD "KING"
B.MAY 28,1881 ELMER,N.J.
D.AUG.21,1947 ALBANY,N.Y.
```
1905 PHI N  P           2   1- 1
1906 PIT N  P           3   1- 1
1907 PIT N  P           1   0- 0
1908 BOS A  P           1   1- 0
1912 BOS N  P           1   0- 0
     BRTR               8   3- 2
```

BRADY, ROBERT JAY
B.NOV.8,1922 LEWISTOWN,PA.
```
1946 BOS N  C           3   .200
1947 BOS N  H           1   .000
     BLTR               4   .167
```

BRADY, STEPHEN A.
B.JULY 14,1851 WORCESTER,MASS.
D.NOV.2,1917
```
1874 HAR NA 3-O        25   -
1875 NAT NA 1-2-O      18   -
     CHI NA O           1   -
1883 MET AA 1-O        97   .280
1884 MET AA           112   .269
1885 MET AA           108   .296
1886 MET AA O         123   .234
                      484   -
```

BRADY, THOMAS
B.HARTFORD,CONN.
```
1875 HAR NA O           1   .000
```

BRADY, WILLIAM A. "KING"
B.1888
D.APR.12,1917
```
1912 BOS N  P           1   0- 0
```

BRAGAN, ROBERT RANDALL "NIG"
B.OCT.30,1918 BIRMINGHAM,ALA.
```
1940 PHI N  S-3       132   .222
1941 PHI N  2-S-3     154   .251
1942 PHI N  C-2-S-3   109   .218
1943 BRO N  C-3        74   .264
1944 BRO N  C-2-S-3    94   .267
1947 BRO N  C          25   .194
1948 BRO N  C           9   .167
     BRTR             597   .240
```
NON-PLAYING MANAGER
PIT(N) 1956-57, CLE(A) 1958,
MIL(N) 1963-65, ATL(N) 1966

BRAGGINS, RICHARD NCALF
B.DEC.25,1879 MERCER,PA.
```
1901 CLE A  P           4   1- 2
     BRTR
```

BRAIN, DAVID LEONARD
B.JAN.24,1879 HEREFORD,ENGLAND
D.MAY 25,1959
```
1901 CHI A  2           5   .350
1903 STL N  S-3       118   .231
1904 STL N  S-3-O     125   .266
1905 STL N  S-3        41   .228
     PIT N  S-3        82   .257
1906 BOS N  3         139   .250
1907 BOS N  3         133   .279
1908 CIN N  O          16   .109
     NY  N  O           9   .076
     BRTR             668   .254
```

BRAINARD, ASA "COUNT"
B.1841 ALBANY,N.Y.
D.DEC.10,1888
```
1871 OLY NA P          30   13-15
1872 OLY NA P           9   2- 7
     MAN NA P-2         7   0- 2
                            .161
1873 BAL NA P-O        15   5- 7
1874 BAL NA P-2-O      46   5-23
     TR               107   25-54
```

BRAINERD, FREDERICK F.
B.FEB.17,1892 CHAMPAIGN,ILL.
D.APR.17,1959
```
1914 NY  N  2           2   .500
1915 NY  N  1-3        91   .201
1916 NY  N  3           2   .000
     BRTR              95   .202
```

BRAITHWOOD, ALFRED
B.FEB.15,1892 FAYETTE CITY,PA.
D.NOV.24,1960
```
1915 PIT F  P           1   0- 0
```

BRAME, ERVIN BECKHAM
B.OCT.12,1901 LAFAYETTE,KY.
D.NOV.22,1949
```
1928 PIT N  P    24    35   7- 4
1929 PIT N  P    37    59   16-11
1930 PIT N  P    32    50   17- 8
1931 PIT N  P    26    48   9-13
1932 PIT N  P    23    26   3- 1
     BLTR  142  218    52-37
```

BRAMHALL, ARTHUR WASHINGTON
B.FEB.22,1910 CHICAGO,ILL.
```
1935 PHI N  S-3         2   .000
     BRTR
```

YR	CL LEA POS	GP	G	REC

BRANCA, RALPH THEODORE JOSEPH "HAWK"
B.JAN.6,1926 MT.VERNON,N.Y.

1944	BRO N P		21	0- 2
1945	BRO N P		16	5- 6
1946	BRO N P		24	3- 1
1947	BRO N P		43	21-12
1948	BRO N P		36	14- 9
1949	BRO N P		34	13- 5
1950	BRO N P		43	7- 9
1951	BRO N P		42	13-12
1952	BRO N P		16	4- 2
1953	BRO N P		7	0- 0
	DET A P		17	4- 7
1954	DET A P		17	3- 3
	NY A P		5	1- 0
1956	BRO N P		1	0- 0
	BRTR		322	88-68

BRANCATO, ALBERT "BRONK"
B.MAY 29,1919 PHILADELPHIA,PA.

1939	PHI A P		21	.206
1940	PHI A S-3		107	.191
1941	PHI A S-3		144	.234
1945	PHI A S		10	.118
	BRTR		282	.214

BRANCH, HARVEY ALFRED
B.FEB.8,1939 MEMPHIS,TENN.

| 1962 | STL N P | | 1 | 0- 1 |
| | BRTL | | | |

BRANCH, NORMAN DOWNS "RED"
B.MAR.22,1916 SPOKANE,WASH.

1941	NY A P		27	5- 1
1942	NY A P		10	0- 1
	BRTR		37	5- 2

BRAND, RONALD GEORGE "RON"
B.JAN.13,1940 THOUSAND OAKS,CAL.

1963	PIT N C-2-3		46	.288
1965	HOU N C-3-0		117	.235
1966	HOU N C-2-3-0		56	.244
1967	HOU N C-2-0		84	.242
1968	HOU N C-3-0		43	.160
1969	MON N C-0		103	.258
1970	MON N C-2-S-3-0		72	.238
1971	MON N C-2-S-3-0		47	.214
	BRTR		568	.239

BRANDOM, CHESTER MILTON "CHICK"
B.MAR.31,1887 OKLAHOMA CITY, OKLA.
D.OCT.7,1958

1908	PIT N P		3	1- 0
1909	PIT N P		13	1- 0
1915	NEW F P		16	1- 1
	TR		32	3- 1

BRANDON, DARRELL G.
B.JULY 8,1940 NACOGDOCHES,TEX.

1966	BOS A P	40	41	8- 8
1967	BOS A P		39	5-11
1968	BOS A P		8	0- 0
1969	SEA A P		8	0- 1
	MIN A P		3	0- 0
1971	PHI N P		52	6- 6
1972	PHI N P		42	7- 7
1973	PHI N P		36	2- 4
	BRTR	228	229	28-37

BRANDT, EDWARD ARTHUR "BIG ED"
B.FEB.17,1905 SPOKANE,WASH.
D.NOV.1,1944

1928	BOS N P	38	39	9-21
1929	BOS N P	26	29	8-13
1930	BOS N P		41	4-11
1931	BOS N P	33	34	18-11
1932	BOS N P		35	16-16
1933	BOS N P	41	47	18-14
1934	BOS N P	40	48	16-14
1935	BOS N P	29	31	5-19
1936	BRO N P	38	43	11-13
1937	PIT N P		33	11-10
1938	PIT N P		24	5- 4
	BLTL	378	404	121-146

BRANDT, JOHN GEORGE "JACKIE"
B.APR.28,1934 OMAHA,NEB.

1956	STL N O		27	.286
	NY N O		98	.299
1958	SF N O		18	.250
1959	SF N 1-2-3-0		137	.270
1960	BAL A 1-3-0		145	.254
1961	BAL A 3-0		139	.297
1962	BAL 3-0		143	.255
1963	BAL A 3-0		142	.248
1964	BAL A O		137	.243
1965	BAL A O		96	.243
1966	PHI N O		82	.250
1967	PHI N O		16	.105
	HOU N 1-3-0		41	.236
	BRTR		1221	.262

BRANDT, WILLIAM GEORGE
B.MAR.21,1918 AURORA,IND.

1941	PIT N P		2	0- 1
1942	PIT N P		3	1- 1
1943	PIT N P		29	4- 1
	BRTR		34	5- 3

BRANNAN, OTIS OWEN
B.MAR.13,1902 GREENBRIER,ARK.
D.JUNE 6,1967 LITTLE ROCK,ARK.

1928	STL A 2		135	.244
1929	STL A 2		23	.294
	BPTR		158	.249

BRANOM, EDGAR DUDLEY "DUD"
B.NOV.30,1897 SULPHUR SPRINGS, TEX.

| 1927 | PHI A 1 | | 30 | .234 |
| | BLTL | | | |

BRANSFIELD, WILLIAM EDWARD "KITTY"
B.JAN.7,1875 WORCESTER,MASS.
D.MAY.1,1947

1898	BOS N C		5	.222
1901	PIT N 1		139	.274
1902	PIT N 1		100	.308
1903	PIT N 1		127	.265
1904	PIT N 1		139	.223
1905	PIT N 1		151	.259
1906	PHI N 1		139	.275
1907	PHI N 1		92	.233
1908	PHI N 1		143	.304
1909	PHI N 1		138	.292
1910	PHI N 1		110	.239
	CHI N 1		23	.256
1911	CHI N 1		3	.400
	BRTR		1309	.270

BRASHEAR, NORMAN C. "KITTY"
B.AUG.27,1877 MANSFIELD,OHIO
D.DEC.22,1934

| 1902 | STL N 1-2-S-0 | | 106 | .284 |

BRASHEAR, ROY PARKS
B.JAN.3,1874 ASHTABULA,OHIO
D.APR.20,1951

1899	LOU N P		3	1- 0
1903	PHI N 2		20	.227
	TR		23	1- 0
				.231

BRATCHER, JOSEPH WARLICK
B.JULY 22,1900 GRAND SALINE,TEX

| 1924 | STL N O | | 4 | .000 |
| | BLTR | | | |

BRATCHI, FREDERICK OSCAR
B.JAN.16,1892 ALLIANCE,OHIO

1921	CHI A O		16	.286
1926	BOS A O		72	.275
1927	BOS A H		1	.000
	BRTR		89	.276

BRAUN, JOHN PAUL
B.DEC.26,1939 MADISON,WIS.

| 1964 | MIL N P | | 1 | 0- 0 |
| | BRTR | | | |

BRAUN, STEPHEN RUSSELL "STEVE"
B.MAY 8,1948 TRENTON,N.J.

1971	MIN A 2-S-3-0		128	.254
1972	MIN A 2-S-3-0		121	.289
1973	MIN A 3-0		115	.283
1974	MIN A 3-0		129	.280
1975	MIN A 1-2-0		136	.302
1976	MIN A 3-0-0		122	.288
	BLTR		751	.284

BRAVO, ANGEL ALFONSO (URDANETA)
B.AUG.4,1942 MARACAIBO,VENEZ.

1969	CHI A O		27	.289
1970	CIN N O		65	.277
1971	CIN N H		5	.200
	SD N O		52	.155
	BLTL		149	.248

BRAXTON, EDGAR GARLAND
B.JUNE 10,1900 SNOW CAMP,N.C.
D.FEB.25,1966 NORFOLK,VA.

1921	BOS N P		17	.1- 3
1922	BOS N P		25	1- 2
1925	NY A P		3	1- 1
1926	NY A P		37	5- 1
1927	WAS A P		58	10- 9
1928	WAS A P		38	13-11
1929	WAS A P		37	12-10
1930	WAS A P		15	3- 2
	CHI A P		19	4-10
1931	CHI A P		17	0- 3
	STL A P		11	0- 0
1933	STL A P		5	0- 1
	BBTL		282	50-53

BRAY, CLARENCE WILBUR "BUSTER"
B.APR.1,1913 BIRMINGHAM,ALA.

| 1941 | BOS N O | | 4 | .091 |
| | BLTL | | | |

BRAZILL, FRANK LEO
B.AUG.11,1899 SPANGLER,PA.
D.NOV.3,1976 OAKLAND,CAL.

1921	PHI A 1		66	.271
1922	PHI A 3		6	.077
	BLTR		72	.258

BRAZLE, ALPHA EUGENE "COTTON"
B.OCT.19,1913 LOYAL,OKLA.
D.OCT.24,1973 GRAND JUNCTION, COLO.

1943	STL N P		13	8- 2
1946	STL N P		37	11-10
1947	STL N P		44	14- 8
1948	STL N P	42	45	10- 6
1949	STL N P		39	14- 8
1950	STL N P	46	47	11- 9
1951	STL N P		56	6- 5
1952	STL N P		46	12- 5
1953	STL N P		60	6- 7
1954	STL N P		58	5- 4
	BLTL	441	445	97-64

BREAZEALE, JAMES LEO "JIM"
B.OCT.3,1949 HOUSTON,TEX.

1969	ATL N 1		2	.000
1971	ATL N 1		10	.190
1972	ATL N 1-3		52	.247
	BLTR		64	.234

BRECHEEN, HARRY DAVID "THE CAT"
B.OCT.14,1914 BROKEN BOW,OKLA.

1940	STL N P		3	0- 0
1943	STL N P		29	9- 6
1944	STL N P	30	31	16- 5
1945	STL N P		24	15- 4
1946	STL N P	36	37	15-15
1947	STL N P		29	16-11
1948	STL N P		33	20- 7
1949	STL N P		32	14-11
1950	STL N P		27	8-11
1951	STL N P		24	8- 4
1952	STL N P		25	7- 5
1953	STL A P	26	27	5-13
	BLTL	318	321	133-92

BRECKINRIDGE, WILLIAM ROBERTSON
B.OCT.27,1906 TULSA,OKLA.
D.AUG.23,1958

| 1929 | PHI A P | | 3 | 0- 0 |
| | BRTR | | | |

BREEDEN, DANNY RICHARD
B.JUNE 27,1942 ALBANY,GA.

1969	CIN N C		3	.125
1971	CHI N C		25	.154
	BRTR		28	.151

BREEDEN, HAROLD NOEL "HAL"
B.JUNE 28,1944 ALBANY,GA.

1971	CHI N 1		23	.139
1972	MON N 1-0		42	.230
1973	MON N 1		105	.275
1974	MON N 1		79	.247
1975	MON N 1		24	.135
	BRTL		273	.243

```
YR   CL LEA POS  GP    G    REC

BREEDING, MARVIN EUGENE "MARV"
B.MAR.8,1934 DECATUR,ALA.
1960 BAL A  2          152  .267
1961 BAL A  2           90  .209
1962 BAL A  2-S-3       95  .246
1963 WAS A  2-S-3       58  .274
     LA  N  2-S-3       20  .167
        BRTR          415  .250

BREITENSTEIN, ALONZO
B.NOV.8,1857 UTICA,N.Y.
D.JUNE 19,1932
1883 PHI N  P            1   0- 1

BREITENSTEIN, THEODORE P.
B.JUNE 1,1869 ST.LOUIS,MO.
D.MAY 3,1935
1891 STL AA P            5   0- 1
1892 STL N  P      34   38 14-20
1893 STL N  P           41 19-20
1894 STL N  P           53 27-25
1895 STL N  P      51   66 18-30
1896 STL N  P      43   48 17-26
1897 CIN N  P      35   39 23-12
1898 CIN N  P      36   39 21-14
1899 CIN N  P      24   33 14-10
1900 CIN N  P      22   33 10-10
1901 STL N  P            3   0- 3
        BLTL     347  398 163-171

BREMER, HERBERT T. FREDERICK
B.OCT.25,1913 CHICAGO,ILL.
1937 STL N  C           11  .212
1938 STL N  C           50  .219
1939 STL N  C            9  .111
        BRTR           70  .212

BRENEGAN, SELMAR G.
B.SEPT.2,1891 GALESVILLE,WIS.
D.APR.20,1956
1914 PIT N  C            1  .000
        BLTR

BRENNAN, ADDISON FOSTER "AD"
B.JULY 18,1887 LAHARPE,KAN.
D.JAN.7,1962
1910 PHI N  P      19   21   2- 0
1911 PHI N  P            5   3- 1
1912 PHI N  P           27  11- 9
1913 PHI N  P           40  14-12
1914 CHI F  P           16   5- 5
1915 CHI F  P           19   3- 9
1918 WAS A  P            2   0- 0
     CLE A  P            1   0- 0
        BLTL     129  131  38-36

BRENNAN, JAMES A.
B.1862 ST.LOUIS,MO.
D.OCT.18,1904
1884 STL U  C-0         45  .210
1885 STL N  3-0          3  .100
1888 KC  AA C           34  .174
1889 ATH AA C           31  .214
1890 CLE P  C-3         59  .251
                       172  .217

BRENNAN, JAMES DONALD "DON"
B.DEC.2,1903 AUGSTA,ME.
D.APR.26,1953
1933 NY  A  P           18   5- 1
1934 CIN N  P           28   4- 3
1935 CIN N  P           38   5- 5
1936 CIN N  P           41   5- 2
1937 CIN N  P           10   1- 1
     NY  N  P            6   1- 0
        BRTR          141  21-12

BRENNEMAN, JAMES LEROY "JIM"
B.FEB.13,1941 SAN DIEGO,CAL.
1965 NY  A  P            3   0- 0
        BRTR

BRENNER, DELBERT HENRY "BERT"
B.JULY 18,1887 MINNEAPOLIS,MINN
D.APR.11,1971 ST.LOUIS PARK,
MINN.
1912 CLE A  P            2   1- 0
        BRTR

BRENTON, LYNN DAVIS "BUCK"
B.OCT.7,1893 PEORIA,ILL.
1913 CLE A  P            1   0- 0
1915 CLE A  P           11   2- 3
1920 CIN N  P            5   2- 1
1921 CIN N  P           17   1- 8
                        34   5-12


BRENZEL, WILLIAM RICHARD
B.MAR.3,1910 OAKLAND,CAL.
1932 PIT N  C            9  .042
1934 CLE A  C           15  .216
1935 CLE A  C           52  .218
        BRTR           76  .198

BRESNAHAN, ROGER PHILIP "DUKE"
B.JUNE 14,1880 TOLEDO,OHIO
D.DEC.4,1944 TOLEDO,OHIO
1897 WAS N  P            7   4- 1
1900 CHI N  C            1   .000
1901 BAL A  P-C    1    86   0- 0
                             .262
1902 BAL A  C-3-0      66   .273
     NY  N  C-1-S-3-   50   .292
                   0
1903 NY  N  0         111   .350
1904 NY  N  0         107   .284
1905 NY  N  C          95   .302
1906 NY  N  C-0       124   .281
1907 NY  N  C         104   .253
1908 NY  N  C         139   .283
1909 STL N  M-C        69   .244
1910 STL N  M-C        78   .278
1911 STL N  M-C        78   .278
1912 STL N  M-C        48   .333
1913 CHI N  C          69   .228
1914 CHI N  C         101   .278
1915 CHI N  M-C        77   .204
        BRTR      8 1410   4- 1
                             .279


BRESSLER, RAYMOND BLOOM "RUBE"
B.OCT.23,1894 BROOKVILLE,PA.
D.NOV.7,1966 MT.WASHINGTON,OHIO
1914 PHI A  P           29  10- 4
1915 PHI A  P      32   33   4-17
1916 PHI A  P            4   0- 3
1917 CIN N  P            3   0- 0
1918 CIN N  P-0    17   23   8- 5
                             .274
1919 CIN N  P-0    13   61   2- 4
                             .206
1920 CIN N  P-1    10   21   2- 0
                             .267
1921 CIN N  0         109   .307
1922 CIN N  1-0        52   .264
1923 CIN N  1-0        54   .277
1924 CIN N  1-0       115   .347
1925 CIN N  1-0        97   .348
1926 CIN N  1-0        86   .357
1927 CIN N  0         124   .291
1928 BRO N  0         145   .295
1929 BRO N  0         136   .318
1930 BRO N  0         109   .299
1931 BRO N  0          67   .281
1932 PHI N  0          27   .229
     STL N  0          10   .158
        BRTL    108 1305  26-33
                             .302

BRESSOUD, EDWARD FRANCIS "EDDIE"
B.MAY 2,1932 LOS ANGELES,CAL.
1956 NY  N  S          49   .227
1957 NY  N  S          49   .268
1958 SF  N  2-S-3      66   .263
1959 SF  N  1-2-S-3   104   .251
1960 SF  N  S         116   .225
1961 SF  N  2-S-3      59   .211
1962 BOS A  S         153   .277
1963 BOS A  S         140   .260
1964 BOS A  S         158   .293
1965 BOS A  S-3-0     107   .226
1966 NY  N  1-2-S-3   133   .225
1967 STL N  S-3        52   .134
        BRTR         1186   .252

BRETON, JOHN FREDERICK "JIM"
B.JULY 15,1891 CHICAGO,ILL.
D.MAY 30,1973 BELOIT,WIS.
1913 CHI A  2-3        12   .173
1914 CHI A  3          81   .212
1915 CHI A  3          16   .139
        BRTR          109   .202

BRETT, GEORGE HOWARD
B.MAY 15,1953 WHEELING,W.VA.
1973 KC  A  3          13   .125
1974 KC  A  S-3       133   .282
1975 KC  A  S-3       159   .308
1976 KC  A  S-3       159   .333
        BLTR          464   .306


BRETT, HERBERT JAMES "DUKE"
B.MAY 23,1900 LAWRENCEVILLE,VA.
D.NOV.25,1974 ST.PETERSBURG,FLA
1924 CHI N  P            1   0- 0
1925 CHI N  P           10   1- 1
        BRTR           11   1- 1

BRETT, KENNETH ALVEN "KEN"
B.SEP.18,1948 BROOKLYN,N.Y.
1967 BOS A  P            1   0- 0
1969 BOS A  P            8   2- 3
1970 BOS A  P           41   8- 9
1971 BOS A  P           49   0- 3
1972 MIL A  P      26   31   7-12
1973 PHI N  P      31   37  13- 9
1974 PIT N  P      27   63  13- 9
1975 PIT N  P      23   26   9- 5
1976 NY  A  P            2   0- 0
     CHI A  P      27   33  10-12
        BLTL     215  251  62-62

BREUER, MARVIN HOWARD
"BABY FACE"
B.APR.29,1914 ROLLA,MO.
1939 NY  A  P            1   0- 0
1940 NY  A  P           27   8- 9
1941 NY  A  P           26   9- 7
1942 NY  A  P           27   8- 9
1943 NY  A  P            5   0- 1
        BRTR           86  25-26

BREWER, JAMES THOMAS "JIM"
B.NOV.17,1937 MERCED,CAL.
1960 CHI N  P       5    6   0- 3
1961 CHI N  P           36   1- 7
1962 CHI N  P            6   0- 1
1963 CHI N  P           29   3- 2
1964 LA  N  P           34   4- 3
1965 LA  N  P      19   20   3- 2
1966 LA  N  P           13   0- 2
1967 LA  N  P           30   5- 4
1968 LA  N  P           54   8- 3
1969 LA  N  P           59   7- 6
1970 LA  N  P           58   7- 6
1971 LA  N  P           55   6- 5
1972 LA  N  P           51   8- 7
1973 LA  N  P           56   6- 8
1974 LA  N  P           24   4- 4
1975 LA  N  P           21   3- 1
     CAL A  P           21   1- 0
1976 CAL A  P           13   3- 1
        BLTL     584  586  69-65

BREWER, JOHN HERNDON "BUDDY"
B.JULY 21,1919 LONG BEACH,CAL.
1944 NY  N  P           14   1- 4
1945 NY  N  P           28   8- 6
1946 NY  N  P            1   0- 0
        BRTR           43   9-10

BREWER, THOMAS AUSTIN "TOM"
B.SEPT.3,1931 CHERAW,S.C.
1954 BOS A  P      33   37  10- 9
1955 BOS A  P      31   33  11-10
1956 BOS A  P      32   38  19- 9
1957 BOS A  P      32   45  16-13
1958 BOS A  P      33   42  12-12
1959 BOS A  P      36   47  10-12
1960 BOS A  P      34   45  10-15
1961 BOS A  P      10   18   3- 2
        BRTR     241  305  91-82

BREWSTER, CHARLES LAWRENCE
B.DEC.17,1916 MARTHAVILLE,LA.
1943 CIN N  2-S         7   .125
     PHI N  S          49   .220
1944 CHI N  S          10   .250
1946 CLE A  S           3   .000
        BRTR           69   .221

BRICE, ALAN HEALY
B.OCT.1,1937 NEW YORK,N.Y.
1961 CHI A  P            3   0- 1

BRICKELL, FRITZ DARRELL
B.MAR.19,1935 WICHITA,KAN.
D.OCT.15,1965 WICHITA,KAN.
1958 NY  A  2            2   .000
1959 NY  A  2-S         18   .256
1961 LA  A  S           21   .122
        BRTR           41   .187
```

YR	CL	LEA	POS	GP	G	REC

BRICKELL, GEORGE FREDERICK
B.NOV.8,1906 SAFFORDVILLE,KAN.
D.APR.8,1961

1926	PIT	N	O		24	.345
1927	PIT	N	O		32	.286
1928	PIT	N	O		81	.322
1929	PIT	N	O		60	.314
1930	PIT	N	O		68	.297
	PHI	N	O		53	.246
1931	PHI	N	O		130	.253
1932	PHI	N	O		45	.333
1933	PHI	N	O		8	.308
	BLTR				501	.281

BRICKLEY, GEORGE VINCENT
B.JULY 19,1894 EVERETT,MASS.
D.FEB.23,1947 EVERETT,MASS.

| 1913 | PHI | A | O | | 5 | .166 |
| | BRTR | | | | | |

BRICKNER, RALPH HAROLD
B.MAY 2,1926 CINCINNATI,OHIO

| 1952 | BOS | A | P | | 14 | 3- 1 |
| | BRTR | | | | | |

BRIDEWESER, JAMES EHRENFELD
B.FEB.13,1927 LANCASTER,OHIO

1951	NY	A	S		2	.375
1952	NY	A	2-S-3		42	.263
1953	NY	A	S		7	1.000
1954	BAL	A	2-S		73	.265
1955	CHI	A	2-S-3		34	.207
1956	CHI	A	S		10	.182
	DET	A	2-S-3		70	.218
1957	BAL	A	2-S-3		91	.268
	BRTR				329	.252

BRIDGES, EVERETT LAMAR "ROCKY"
B.AUG.7,1927 REFUGIO,TEX.

1951	BRO	N	2-S-3		63	.254
1952	BRO	N	2-S-3		51	.196
1953	CIN	N	2-S-3		122	.227
1954	CIN	N	2-S-3		53	.231
1955	CIN	N	2-S-3		95	.286
1956	CIN	N	2-S-3-O		71	.211
1957	CIN	N	S		5	.000
	WAS	A	2-S-3		120	.228
1958	WAS	A	2-S-3		116	.263
1959	DET	A	2-S		116	.268
1960	DET	A	S-3		10	.200
	CLE	A	S-3		10	.333
	STL	N	2		3	.000
1961	LA	A	2-S-3		84	.240
	BRTR				919	.247

BRIDGES, MARSHALL
B.JUNE 2,1931 JACKSON,MISS.

1959	STL	N	P		27	6- 3
1960	STL	N	P		20	2- 2
	CIN	N	P		14	4- 0
1961	CIN	N	P		13	0- 1
1962	NY	A	P		52	8- 4
1963	NY	A	P		23	2- 0
1964	WAS	A	P		17	0- 3
1965	WAS	A	P		40	1- 2
	BBTL				206	23-15
	BR 1962-65					

BRIDGES, THOMAS JEFFERSON DAVIS
B.DEC.28,1906 GORDONSVILLE,TENN
D.APR.19,1968 NASHVILLE,TENN.

1930	DET	A	P		8	3- 2
1931	DET	A	P		35	8-16
1932	DET	A	P		34	14-12
1933	DET	A	P		33	14-12
1934	DET	A	P		36	22-11
1935	DET	A	P		36	21-10
1936	DET	A	P		39	23-11
1937	DET	A	P		34	15-12
1938	DET	A	P		25	13- 9
1939	DET	A	P		29	17- 7
1940	DET	A	P		29	12- 9
1941	DET	A	P		25	9-12
1942	DET	A	P		23	9- 7
1943	DET	A	P		25	12- 7
1945	DET	A	P		4	1- 0
1946	DET	A	P		9	1- 1
	BRTR				424	194-138

BRIDWELL, ALBERT HENRY
B.JAN.4,1884 FRIENDSHIP,OHIO
D.JAN.24,1969 PORTSMOUTH,OHIO

1905	CIN	N	3-O		74	.252
1906	BOS	N	S		120	.227
1907	BOS	N	S		140	.218
1908	NY	N	S		147	.285
1909	NY	N	S		145	.294
1910	NY	N	S		141	.276
1911	NY	N	S		76	.270
	BOS	N	S		51	.291
1912	BOS	N	S		31	.236
1913	CHI	N	S		136	.240
1914	STL	F	S		117	.234
1915	STL	F	2-3		63	.226
	BLTR				1241	.255

BRIEF, ANTHONY VINCENT "BUNNY"
(REAL NAME ANTONIO BORDETSKI)
B.JULY 3,1892 BIG RAPIDS,MICH.
D.FEB.10,1963 MILWAUKEE,WIS.

1912	STL	A	1-O		15	.310
1913	STL	A	1		84	.217
1915	CHI	A	1		48	.214
1917	PIT	N	1		36	.217
	BRTR				183	.223

BRIGGS, CHARLES R.

| 1884 | CHI | U | 2-O | | 50 | .171 |

BRIGGS, DANIEL LEE "DAN"
B.NOV.18,1952 SCOTIA,CAL.

1975	CAL	A	1-O		13	.226
1976	CAL	A	1-O		77	.214
	BLTL				90	.215

BRIGGS, GRANT
B.PHILADELPHIA,PA.

1890	SYR	AA	C		86	.179
1891	LOU	AA	C		1	.250
1892	STL	N	C-O		23	.070
1895	LOU	N	C		1	.000
					111	.163

BRIGGS, HERBERT T. "BUTTONS"
B.FEB.18,1876 GLENVILLE,OHIO
D.FEB.18,1911

1896	CHI	N	P		22	12- 8
1897	CHI	N	P		22	5-17
1898	CHI	N	P		5	1- 4
1904	CHI	N	P		34	19-11
1905	CHI	N	P		20	9-10
	BRTR				103	46-50

BRIGGS, JOHN EDWARD
B.MAR.10,1944 PATERSON,N.J.

1964	PHI	N	1-O		61	.258
1965	PHI	N	O		93	.236
1966	PHI	N	O		81	.282
1967	PHI	N	O		106	.232
1968	PHI	N	1-O		110	.254
1969	PHI	N	1-O		124	.238
1970	PHI	N	O		110	.270
1971	PHI	N	O		10	.182
	MIL	A	1-O		125	.264
1972	MIL	A	1-O		135	.266
1973	MIL	A	O		142	.246
1974	MIL	A	O		154	.253
1975	MIL	A	O		28	.297
	MIN	A	1-O		87	.231
	BLTL				1366	.253

BRIGGS, JOHN TIFT
B.JAN.24,1934 NATOMA,CAL.

1956	CHI	N	P		3	0- 0
1957	CHI	N	P		3	0- 1
1958	CHI	N	P		20	5- 5
1959	CLE	A	P		4	0- 1
1960	CLE	A	P		21	4- 2
	KC	A	P		8	0- 2
	BRTR				59	9-11

BRIGHT, HARRY JAMES
B.SEP.22,1929 KANSAS CITY,MO.

1958	PIT	N	3		15	.250
1959	PIT	N	2-3-O		40	.250
1960	PIT	N	H		4	.000
1961	WAS	A	C-2-3		72	.240
1962	WAS	A	C-1-3		113	.273
1963	CIN	N	1		1	.000
	NY	A	1-3		60	.236
1964	NY	A	1		4	.200
1965	CHI	N	H		27	.280
	BRTR				336	.255

BRILES, NELSON KELLEY
B.AUG.5,1943 DORRIS,CAL.

1965	STL	N	P		37	3- 3
1966	STL	N	P		49	4-15
1967	STL	N	P		49	14- 5
1968	STL	N	P		33	19-11
1969	STL	N	P		36	15-13
1970	STL	N	P		30	6- 7
1971	PIT	N	P		37	8- 4
1972	PIT	N	P		28	14-11
1973	PIT	N	P		33	14-13
1974	KC	A	P		18	5- 7
1975	KC	A	P		24	6- 6
1976	TEX	A	P		32	11- 9
	BRTR				406	119-103

BRILL, JOHN
B.ASTORIA,N.Y.

| 1884 | DET | N | P-O | | 13 | 2-10 |
| | | | | | | .130 |

BRILLHEART, JAMES BENSON
B.SEPT.28,1903 DUBLIN,VA.
D.SEPT.2,1972 RADFORD,VA.

1922	WAS	A	P		31	4- 6
1923	WAS	A	P		12	0- 1
1927	CHI	N	P		32	4- 2
1931	BOS	A	P		11	0- 0
	BRTL				86	8- 9

BRINKER, WILLIAM HUTCHINSON "DODE"
B.AUG.30,1883 WARRENSBURG,MO.
D.FEB.5,1965 ARCADIA,CAL.

| 1912 | PHI | N | 3-O | | 9 | .222 |
| | BBTR | | | | | |

BRINKMAN, CHARLES ERNEST "CHUCK"
B.SEP.16,1944 CINCINNATI,O.

1969	CHI	A	C		14	.067
1970	CHI	A	C		9	.250
1971	CHI	A	C		15	.200
1972	CHI	A	C		35	.135
1973	CHI	A	C		62	.187
1974	CHI	A	C		8	.143
	PIT	N	C		4	.143
	BRTR				147	.172

BRINKMAN, EDWIN ALBERT "ED"
B.DEC.8,1941 CINCINNATI,O.

1961	WAS	A	3		4	.091
1962	WAS	A	S-3		54	.165
1963	WAS	A	S		145	.228
1964	WAS	A	S		132	.224
1965	WAS	A	S		154	.185
1966	WAS	A	S		158	.229
1967	WAS	A	S		109	.188
1968	WAS	A	2-S-O		77	.187
1969	WAS	A	S		151	.266
1970	WAS	A	S		158	.262
1971	DET	A	S		159	.228
1972	DET	A	S		156	.203
1973	DET	A	S		162	.237
1974	DET	A	S-3		153	.221
1975	STL	N	S		28	.240
	TEX	A	3		1	.000
	NY	A	2-S-3		44	.175
	BRTR				1845	.224

BRINKOPF, LEON CLARENCE
B.OCT.20,1926 CAPE GIRARDEAU,MO

| 1952 | CHI | N | S | | 9 | .182 |
| | BRTR | | | | | |

BRIODY, CHARLES F. "ALDERMAN"
B.AUG.13,1858 LANSINGBURG,N.Y.

1880	TRO	N	C		1	.000
1882	CLE	N	C		52	.263
1883	CLE	N	C-1-2-3		39	.232
1884	CLE	N	C-O		43	.169
	CIN	U	C		23	.326
1885	STL	N	C-2-3		61	.195
1886	KC	N	C		55	.237
1887	DET	N	C		32	.277
1888	KC	AA	C		13	.208
					319	.234

BRISSIE, LELAND VICTOR "LOU"
B.JUNE 5,1924 ANDERSON,S.C.

YR	CL	LEA	POS	GP	G	REC
1947	PHI	A	P		1	0- 1
1948	PHI	A	P		39	14-10
1949	PHI	A	P		34	16-11
1950	PHI	A	P		46	7-19
1951	PHI	A	P		2	0- 2
	CLE	A	P		54	4- 3
1952	CLE	A	P		42	3- 2
1953	CLE	A	P		16	0- 0
	BLTL				234	44-48

BRISTOL, JAMES DAVID "DAVE"
B.JUNE 23,1933 MACON,GA.
NON-PLAYING MANAGER
CIN(N) 1966-69, MIL(A) 1970-72,
ATL(N) 1976

BRISTOW, GEORGE
B.1871 PAPPAW,ILL.

YR	CL	LEA	POS	GP	G	REC
1899	CLE	N	O		3	.125

BRITT, JAMES E.

YR	CL	LEA	POS	GP	G	REC
1872	ATL	NA	P		35	8-27
1873	ATL	NA	P		23	9-14
	MUT	NA	P		1	0- 1
	ATL	NA	P		30	7-22
					89	24-64

BRITTAIN, AUGUST SCHUSTER
B.NOV.29,1912 WILMINGTON,N.C.
D.FEB.16,1974 WILMINGTON,N.C.

YR	CL	LEA	POS	GP	G	REC
1937	CIN	N	C		3	.167
	BRTR					

BRITTIN, JOHN ALBERT "JACK"
1950 PHI N P ... 3 0-0
B.MAR.4,1926 ATHENS,ILL.

YR	CL	LEA	POS	GP	G	REC
1950	PHI	N	P		3	0- 0
1951	PHI	N	P		3	0- 0
	BRTR				6	0- 0

BRITTON, JAMES ALAN "JIM"
B.MAR.25,1944 N.TONAWANDA,N.Y.

YR	CL	LEA	POS	GP	G	REC
1967	ATL	N	P		2	0- 2
1968	ATL	N	P		34	4- 6
1969	ATL	N	P		24	7- 5
1971	MON	N	P		16	2- 3
	BRTR				76	13-16

BRITTON, STEPHEN GILBERT "GIL"
B.SEPT.21,1891 PARSONS,KAN.

YR	CL	LEA	POS	GP	G	REC
1913	PIT	N	S		3	.000
	BRTR					

BROACA, JOHN JOSEPH
B.OCT.3,1909 LAWRENCE,MASS.

YR	CL	LEA	POS	GP	G	REC
1934	NY	A	P		26	12- 9
1935	NY	A	P		29	15- 7
1936	NY	A	P		37	12- 7
1937	NY	A	P		7	1- 4
1939	CLE	A	P		22	4- 2
	BRTR				121	44-29

BROBERG, PETER SVEN "PETE"
B.MAR.2,1940 WEST PALM BEACH,FLA

YR	CL	LEA	POS	GP	G	REC
1971	WAS	A	P		18	5- 9
1972	TEX	A	P		39	5-12
1973	TEX	A	P	22	23	5- 9
1974	TEX	A	P		12	0- 4
1975	MIL	A	P		38	14-16
1976	MIL	A	P		20	1- 7
	BRTR			149	150	30-57

BROCK, JOHN ROY
B.OCT.16,1897 HAMILTON,ILL.
D.OCT.27,1951 CLAYTON,MO.

YR	CL	LEA	POS	GP	G	REC
1917	STL	N	O		7	.400
1918	STL	N	C-O		27	.212
	BRTR				34	.263

BROCK, LOUIS CLARK "LOU"
B.JUNE 18,1939 EL DORADO,ARK.

YR	CL	LEA	POS	GP	G	REC
1961	CHI	N	O		4	.091
1962	CHI	N	O		123	.263
1963	CHI	N	O		148	.258
1964	CHI	N	O		52	.251
	STL	N	O		103	.348
1965	STL	N	O		155	.288
1966	STL	N	O		156	.285
1967	STL	N	O		159	.299
1968	STL	N	O		159	.279
1969	STL	N	O		157	.298
1970	STL	N	O		155	.304
1971	STL	N	O		157	.313
1972	STL	N	O		153	.311
1973	STL	N	O		160	.297
1974	STL	N	O		153	.306
1975	STL	N	O		136	.309
1976	STL	N	O		133	.301
	BLTL				2263	.296

BROCKETT, LOUIS ALBERT "KING"
B.JULY 23,1880 CARMI,ILL.
D.SEPT.19,1960

YR	CL	LEA	POS	GP	G	REC
1907	NY	A	P		10	1- 3
1909	NY	A	P		26	10- 8
1911	NY	A	P	17	19	2- 4
	TR			53	55	13-15

BRODERICK, MATTHEW T.
B.DEC.2,1876 LATTIMER MINES,PA.
D.FEB.22,1941

YR	CL	LEA	POS	GP	G	REC
1903	BRO	N	2		2	.000
	TR					

BRODIE, WALTER SCOTT "STEVE"
B.SEPT.11,1868 ROANOKE,VA.
D.OCT.29,1933 BALTIMORE,MD.

YR	CL	LEA	POS	GP	G	REC
1890	BOS	N	O		132	.295
1891	BOS	N	O		134	.266
1892	STL	N	2-O		154	.256
1893	STL	N	O		107	.336
	BAL	N	O		25	.372
1894	BAL	N	O		129	.369
1895	BAL	N	O		130	.365
1896	BAL	N	O		132	.294
1897	PIT	N	O		100	.298
1898	PIT	N	O		42	.274
	BAL	N	O		23	.286
1899	DAL	N	O		138	.309
1901	BAL	A	O		84	.310
1902	NY	N	O		109	.281
	BL				1439	.308

BRODOWSKI, RICHARD STANLEY
B.JULY 26,1932 BAYONNE,N.J.

YR	CL	LEA	POS	GP	G	REC
1952	BOS	A	P		20	5- 5
1955	BOS	A	P		16	1- 0
1956	WAS	A	P		7	0- 3
1957	WAS	A	P		6	0- 1
1958	CLE	A	P		5	1- 0
1959	CLE	A	P		18	2- 2
	BRTR				72	9-11

BROGLIO, ERNEST GILBERT "ERNIE"
B.AUG.27,1935 BERKELEY,CAL.

YR	CL	LEA	POS	GP	G	REC
1959	STL	N	P		35	7-12
1960	STL	N	P		52	21- 9
1961	STL	N	P		29	9-12
1962	STL	N	P		34	12- 9
1963	STL	N	P		39	18- 8
1964	STL	N	P		11	3- 5
	CHI	N	P		18	4- 7
1965	CHI	N	P		26	1- 6
1966	CHI	N	P		15	2- 6
	BRTR				259	77-74

BROHAMER, JOHN ANTHONY "JACK"
B.FEB.26,1950 MAYWOOD,CAL.

YR	CL	LEA	POS	GP	G	REC
1972	CLE	A	2-3		136	.233
1973	CLE	A	2		102	.220
1974	CLE	A	2		101	.270
1975	CLE	A	2		69	.244
1976	CHI	A	2-3		119	.251
	BLTR				527	.243
	BB 1972 (PART)					

BRONDELL, KENNETH LEROY
B.OCT.17,1921 BRADSHAW,NEB.

YR	CL	LEA	POS	GP	G	REC
1944	NY	N	P	7	8	0- 1
	BRTR					

BRONKIE, HERMAN CHARLES "DUTCH"
B.MAR.31,1885 S.MANCHESTER,CONN
D.MAY 27,1968 SOMERS,CONN.

YR	CL	LEA	POS	GP	G	REC
1910	CLE	A	S-3		5	.181
1911	CLE	A	3		2	.167
1912	CLE	A	3		6	.000
1914	CHI	N	3		1	1.000
1918	STL	N	3		18	.221
1919	STL	A	2-3		67	.255
1922	STL	A	3		23	.281
	BRTR				122	.240

BRONSTAD, JAMES WARREN "JIM"
B.JUNE 22,1936 FT.WORTH,TEX.

YR	CL	LEA	POS	GP	G	REC
1959	NY	A	P		16	0- 3
1963	WAS	A	P	25	27	1- 3
1964	WAS	A	P		4	0- 1
	BRTR			45	47	1- 7

BROOKENS, EDWARD DWAIN "IKE"
B.JAN.3,1949 CHAMBERSBURG,PA.

YR	CL	LEA	POS	GP	G	REC
1975	DET	A	P		3	0- 0
	BRTR					

BROOKS, F. HARRY
B.PHILADELPHIA,PA.

YR	CL	LEA	POS	GP	G	REC
1886	MET	AA	P		1	0- 1

**BROOKS, JONATHAN JOSEPH
"MANDY"**
(REAL NAME
JONATHAN JOSEPH BROZEK)
B.AUG.18,1898 MILWAUKEE,WIS.
D.JUNE 17,1962

YR	CL	LEA	POS	GP	G	REC
1925	CHI	N	O		90	.281
1926	CHI	N	O		26	.188
	BRTR				116	.270

BROOKS, ROBERT "BOB"
B.NOV.1,1945 LOS ANGELES,CAL.

YR	CL	LEA	POS	GP	G	REC
1969	OAK	A	O		29	.241
1970	OAK	A	O		7	.333
1972	OAK	A	O		15	.179
1973	CAL	A	O		4	.143
	BRTR				55	.231

BROSKIE, SIGMUND THEODORE "SIG"
B.MAR.23,1911 ISELIN,PA.
D.MAY 17,1975 CANTON,OHIO

YR	CL	LEA	POS	GP	G	REC
1940	BOS	N	C		11	.273
	BRTR					

BROSNAN, JAMES PATRICK "JIM"
B.OCT.24,1929 CINCINNATI,O.

YR	CL	LEA	POS	GP	G	REC
1954	CHI	N	P		18	1- 0
1956	CHI	N	P		30	5- 9
1957	CHI	N	P		41	5- 5
1958	CHI	N	P		8	3- 4
	STL	N	P		33	8- 4
1959	STL	N	P		20	1- 3
	CIN	N	P		26	8- 3
1960	CIN	N	P		57	7- 2
1961	CIN	N	P		53	10- 4
1962	CIN	N	P		48	4- 4
1963	CIN	N	P		6	0- 1
	CHI	A	P		45	3- 8
	BRTR				385	55-47

BROSSEAU, FRANKLIN LEE "FRANK"
B.JULY 31,1944 DRAYTON,N.D.

YR	CL	LEA	POS	GP	G	REC
1969	PIT	N	P		2	0- 0
1971	PIT	N	P		1	0- 0
	BRTR				3	0- 0

BROTTEM, ANTON CHRISTIAN "TONY"
B.APR.30,1892 HALSTAD,MINN.
D.AUG.5,1929

YR	CL	LEA	POS	GP	G	REC
1916	STL	N	C		26	.182
1918	STL	N	1		2	.000
1921	WAS	A	C		4	.147
	PIT	N	C		30	.242
	BRTR				62	.218

BROUGHTON, CECIL CALVERT "CAL"
B.DEC.28,1860 MAGNOLIA,WIS.
D.MAR.15,1939

YR	CL	LEA	POS	GP	G	REC
1883	CLE	N	C		4	.167
	BAL	AA	C-O		9	.188
1884	MIL	U	C-O		11	.308
1885	STL	AA	C		3	.083
	MET	AA	C		12	.356
1888	DET	N	C		1	.000
	BRTR				40	.257

```
YR  CL LEA POS  GP    G    REC
```

BROUTHERS, ARTHUR H.
B.NOV.25,1882 MONTGOMERY,ALA.
D.SEPT.28,1959 CHARLESTON,S.C.
1906 PHI A   3   36   .208
        TR

BROUTHERS, DENNIS "BIG DAN"
B.MAY 8,1858 SYLVAN LAKE,N.Y.
D.AUG.3,1932 E.ORANGE,N.J.
1879 TRO N P-1   2   39   0- 2
                            .273
1880 TRO N 1   3   .154
1881 BUF N 1   65   .318
1882 BUF N 1   84   .367
1883 BUF N P-1-3 2   97   0- 0
                            .371
1884 BUF N 1-3   90   .325
1885 BUF N 1   98   .358
1886 DET N 1   121   .370
1887 DET N 1   122   .419
1888 DET N 1   129   .306
1889 BOS N 1   126   .373
1890 BOS P 1   123   .345
1891 BOS AA 1   130   .352
1892 BRO N 1   152   .335
1893 BRO N 1   75   .348
1894 BAL N 1   123   .344
1895 BAL N 1   5   .261
     LOU N 1   24   .296
1896 PHI N 1   57   .330
1904 NY N 1   2   .000
     BLTL   4   1665   0- 2
                            .348

BROVIA, JOSEPH JOHN "JOE"
B.FEB.18,1922 DAVENPORT,CAL.
1955 CIN N H   21   .111
     BLTR

BROWER, FRANK WILLARD
"TURKEYFOOT"
B.MAR.26,1893 GAINESVILLE,VA.
D.NOV.20,1960 BALTIMORE,MD.
1920 WAS A O   36   .311
1921 WAS A O   83   .261
1922 WAS A O   139   .293
1923 CLE A 1   126   .285
1924 CLE A P-1-O 1   66   0- 0
                            .280
     BLTR   1   450   0- 0
                            .286

BROWER, LOUIS LESTER
B.JULY 1,1900 CLEVELAND,OHIO
1931 DET A S   21   .161
     BRTR

BROWN, ALTON LEO
B.APR.16,1928 NORFOLK,VA.
1951 WAS A P   7   0- 0
     BRTR

BROWN, CARROLL WILLIAM
"BOARDWALK"
B.FEB.20,1887 WOODBURY,N.J.
1911 PHI A P   2   0- 1
1912 PHI A P   35 13-11
1913 PHI A P   44 18-11
1914 PHI A P   15   1- 6
     NY A P   20   5- 5
1915 NY A P   19   21   3- 5
     BRTR   135   137 40-39

BROWN, CHARLES E.
B.1878 BALTIMORE,MD.
1897 CLE N P   4   1- 3
     TL

BROWN, CHARLES EDWARD "BUSTER"
B.AUG.31,1881 BOONE,IOWA
D.FEB.9,1914
1905 STL N P   23   8-11
1906 STL N P   32   8-16
1907 STL N P   9   2- 7
     PHI N P   21   8- 5
1908 PHI N P   4   0- 0
1909 PHI N P   7   0- 0
     BOS N P   18   4- 8
1910 BOS N P   46   9-23
1911 BOS N P   42   8-18
1912 BOS N P   31   4-15
1913 BOS N P   2   0- 0
     BRTR   235 51-103

BROWN, CHARLES ROY "CURLY"
B.DEC.9,1888 SPRING HILL,KAN.
D.JUNE 10,1968 SPRING HILL,KAN.
1911 STL A P   3   0- 2
1912 STL A P   16   1- 3
1913 STL A P   2   1- 1
1915 CIN N P   9   0- 2
     BLTL   30   2- 8

BROWN, CLINTON HAROLD "CLINT"
B.JULY 8,1903 GUY'S MILLS,PA.
D.DEC.31,1955
1928 CLE A P   2   0- 1
1929 CLE A P   3   0- 2
1930 CLE A P   35 11-13
1931 CLE A P   39 11-15
1932 CLE A P   37   39 15-12
1933 CLE A P   33   34 11-12
1934 CLE A P   17   4- 3
1935 CLE A P   23   4- 3
1936 CHI A P   38   6- 2
1937 CHI A P   53   7- 7
1938 CHI A P   8   1- 3
1939 CHI A P   61 11-10
1940 CHI A P   37   4- 6
1941 CLE A P   41   3- 3
1942 CLE A P   7   1- 1
     BLTR   434   437 89-93

BROWN, CURTIS "CURT"
B.SEP.14,1945 SACRAMENTO,CAL.
1973 MON N O   1   .000
     BRTR

BROWN, DELOS HIGHT
B.SEPT.9,1892 CENTRALIA,ILL.
1914 CHI A H   1   .000
     BRTR

BROWN, DRUMMOND NICHOLS
B.JAN.31,1885 TAFT,CAL.
D.JAN.24,1927 PARKVILLE,MO.
1913 BOS N C   15   .324
1914 KC F C   30   .207
1915 KC F C   77   .239
     BRTR   122   .242

BROWN, EDWARD P.
B.CHICAGO,ILL.
1882 STL AA P-2-O 1   17   0- 0
                            .177
1884 TOL AA 3   42   .174
     TR   1   59   0- 0
                            .175

BROWN, EDWARD WILLIAM "EDDIE"
B.JULY 17,1892 MILLIGAN,NEB.
D.SEPT.10,1956
1920 NY N O   3   .125
1921 NY N O   70   .281
1924 BRO N O   114   .308
1925 BRO N O   153   .306
1926 BOS N O   153   .328
1927 BOS N O   155   .306
1928 BOS N O   142   .268
     BRTR   790   .303

BROWN, EDWIN RANDOLPH "RANDY"
B.AUG.29,1944 LEESBURG,FLA.
1969 CAL A C-O   13   .160
1970 CAL A C   5   .000
     BLTR   18   .138

BROWN, ELMER YOUNG "SHOOK"
B.MAR.25,1883 SOUTHPORT,IND.
D.JAN.23,1955
1911 STL A P   5   2- 1
1912 STL A P   23   4- 8
1913 BRO N P   3   0- 0
1914 BRO N P   11   1- 2
1915 BRO N P   1   0- 0
     BLTR   43   7-11

BROWN, FRED HERBERT
B.APR.12,1879 OSSIPEE,N.H.
D.FEB.3,1955
1901 BOS N O   7   .125
1902 BOS N O   1   .000
     BRTR   8   .111

BROWN, FREEMAN
B.JAN.31,1845 HUBBARDSTOWN,MASS
D.DEC.27,1916
NON-PLAYING MANAGER
WOR(N) 1880-82

BROWN, HECTOR HAROLD
"HAL" OR "SKINNY"
B.DEC.11,1924 GREENSBORO,N.C.
1951 CHI A P   3   4   0- 0
1952 CHI A P   24   51   2- 3
1953 BOS A P   30 11- 6
1954 BOS A P   40   1- 8
1955 BOS A P   2   1- 0
     BAL A P   15   25   0- 4
1956 BAL A P   35   42   0- 7
1957 BAL A P   25   30   7- 8
1958 BAL A P-3   19   21   7- 5
                            .148
1959 BAL A P   31 11- 9
1960 BAL A P   30 12- 5
1961 BAL A P   27 10- 6
1962 BAL A P   22   6- 4
     NY A P   2   0- 1
1963 HOU N P   26   5-11
1964 HOU N P   27   3-15
     BRTR   358   410 85-92
                            .169

BROWN, ISSAC "IKE"
B.APR.13,1942 MEMPHIS,TENN.
1969 DET A 2-S-3-O   70   .229
1970 DET A 2-3-O   56   .287
1971 DET A 1-2-S-3-   59   .255
           O
1972 DET A 1-2-S-3-   51   .250
           O
1973 DET A 1-3-O   42   .289
1974 DET A 3   2   .000
     BRTR   280   .256

BROWN, JACKIE GENE
B.MAY 31,1943 HOLDENVILLE,OKLA.
1970 WAS A P   24   2- 2
1971 WAS A P   14   3- 4
1973 TEX A P   25   5- 5
1974 TEX A P   35 13-12
1975 TEX A P   17   5- 5
     CLE A P   25   1- 2
1976 CLE A P   32   9-11
     BRTR   172   38-41

BROWN, JAMES DONALDSON "MOOSE"
B.MAR.31,1897 LAUREL,IND.
1915 STL N O   1   .500
1916 PHI A O   14   .233
     BRTR   15   .244

BROWN, JAMES ROBERSON
B.APR.25,1912 JAMESVILLE,N.C.
1937 STL N 2-S   138   .276
1938 STL N 2-S-3   108   .301
1939 STL N 2-S   147   .298
1940 STL N 2-S-3   107   .280
1941 STL N 2-O   132   .306
1942 STL N 2-S-3   145   .256
1943 STL N 2-S-3   34   .182
1946 PIT N 2-S-3   79   .241
     BBTR   890   .279

BROWN, JAMES W. H.
B.LOCKHAVEN,PA.
1884 ALT U P-O   11   21   2- 9
                            .239
     NY N P   1   0- 1
     STP U P-1-O   6   1- 3
                            .313
1886 ATH AA P   1   0- 1
                 19   29   3-14
                            .237

BROWN, JERALD RAY "JAKE"
B.MAR.3,1948 SUMRALL,MISS.
1975 SF N O   41   .209
     BRTR

BROWN, JOHN J. "AD"
B.TRENTON,N.J.
1897 BRO N P   2   0- 2

BROWN, JOHN LINDSAY "RED"
B.JULY 22,1913 MASON,TEX.
D.JAN.1,1967 SAN ANTONIO,TEX.
1937 BRO N S   48   .270
     BRTR

BROWN, JOPHERY CLIFFORD
B.JAN.22,1945 GRAMBLING,LA.
1968 CHI N P   1   0- 0
     BLTR

YR	CL	LEA	POS	GP	G	REC

BROWN, JOSEPH E.
B.APR.4,1859 WARREN,PA.
D.JUNE 28,1888

YR	CL	LEA	POS	GP	G	REC
1884	CHI	N	P-C-	7	15	3- 2
			1-0			.220
1885	BAL	AA	P-2	4	5	0- 4
						.158
				11	20	3- 6
						.205

BROWN, JOSEPH HENRY
B.JULY 31,1900 LITTLE ROCK,ARK.
D.MAR.7,1950 LOS ANGELES,CAL.

| 1927 | CHI | A | P | | 1 | 0- 0 |
| | | | BRTR | | | |

BROWN, LARRY LESLIE
B.MAR.1,1940 SHINNSTON,W.VA.

1963	CLE	A	2-S		74	.255
1964	CLE	A	2-S		115	.230
1965	CLE	A	2-S		124	.253
1966	CLE	A	2-S		105	.229
1967	CLE	A	S		152	.227
1968	CLE	A	S		154	.234
1969	CLE	A	2-S-3		132	.239
1970	CLE	A	2-S-3		72	.258
1971	CLE	A	2-S-3		13	.220
	OAK	A	2-3		70	.196
1972	OAK	A	2-3		47	.183
1973	BAL	A	2-3		17	.250
1974	TEX	A	2-S-3		54	.197
			BRTR		1129	.233

BROWN, LEON
B.NOV.16,1949 SACRAMENTO,CAL.

| 1976 | NY | N | O | | 64 | .214 |
| | | | BBTR | | | |

BROWN, LEWIS J. "BLOWER"
B.FEB.1,1858 LEOMINSTER,MASS.
D.JAN.16,1889

1876	BOS	N	C		45	.207
1877	BOS	N	C-1		58	.253
1878	PRO	N	P-C-	1	57	0- 0
			1-0			.315
1879	PRO	N	C-O		51	.262
	CHI	N	1		6	.273
1881	DET	N	1		27	.243
	PRO	N	1-O		18	.228
1883	BOS	N	1		14	.236
	LOU	AA	C-1		14	.197
1884	BOS	U	P-C-	1	84	1- 0
			1-0			.236
			BRTR	2	374	1- 0
						.252

BROWN, LLOYD ANDREW
B.DEC.25,1904 BEEVILLE,TEX.
D.JAN.14,1974 OPALOCKA,FLA.

1925	BRO	N	P		17	0- 3
1928	WAS	A	P		27	4- 4
1929	WAS	A	P		40	8- 7
1930	WAS	A	P		38	16-12
1931	WAS	A	P		42	15-14
1932	WAS	A	P		46	15-12
1933	STL	A	P		8	1- 6
	BOS	A	P		33	8-11
1934	CLE	A	P		38	5-10
1935	CLE	A	P		42	8- 7
1936	CLE	A	P		24	8-10
1937	CLE	A	P		31	2- 6
1940	PHI	N	P		18	1- 3
			BLTL		404	91-105

BROWN, MACE STANLEY
B.MAY 21,1909 NORTH ENGLISH,IA.

1935	PIT	N	P		18	4- 1
1936	PIT	N	P		47	10-11
1937	PIT	N	P		50	7- 2
1938	PIT	N	P		51	15- 9
1939	PIT	N	P		47	9-13
1940	PIT	N	P		48	10- 9
1941	PIT	N	P		1	0- 0
	BRO	N	P		24	3- 2
1942	BOS	A	P		34	9- 3
1943	BOS	A	P		49	6- 6
1946	BOS	A	P		18	3- 1
			BRTR		387	76-57

BROWN, MORDECAI PETER CENTENNIAL "THREE FINGER"
B.OCT.19,1876 NYESVILLE,IND.
D.FEB.14,1948 TERRE HAUTE,IND.

1903	STL	N	P		26	9-13
1904	CHI	N	P		27	15- 9
1905	CHI	N	P		30	17- 9
1906	CHI	N	P		36	26- 6
1907	CHI	N	P	34	35	20- 6
1908	CHI	N	P		44	29- 9
1909	CHI	N	P		50	27- 9
1910	CHI	N	P		46	25-14
1911	CHI	N	P		53	21-11
1912	CHI	N	P	15	16	5- 6
1913	CIN	N	P		39	11-12
1914	STL	F	M-P		26	11- 5
	BRO	F	P		9	3- 6
1915	CHI	F	P		35	17- 8
1916	CHI	N	P		12	2- 3
			BBTR	482	484	238-126

BROWN, MYRL LINCOLN
B.OCT.10,1897 WAYNESBORO,PA.

| 1922 | PIT | N | P | | 7 | 3- 1 |
| | | | BRTR | | | |

BROWN, NORMAN
B.FEB.1,1919 EVERGREEN,N.C.

1943	PHI	A	P		1	0- 0
1946	PHI	A	P		4	0- 1
			BBTR		5	0- 1

BROWN, OLIVER S.
B.1849 BROOKLYN,N.Y.
D.SEPT.23,1932 BROOKLYN,N.Y.

1872	ATL	NA	O		4	.059
1874	BAL	NA	S		1	.000
1875	ATL	NA	1-O		3	.000
					8	.036

BROWN, OLLIE LEE
B.FEB.11,1944 TUSCALOOSA,ALA.

1965	SF	N	O		6	.200
1966	SF	N	O		115	.233
1967	SF	N	O		120	.267
1968	SF	N	O		40	.232
1969	SD	N	O		151	.264
1970	SD	N	O		139	.292
1971	SD	N	O		145	.273
1972	SD	N	O		23	.171
	OAK	A	O		20	.241
	MIL	A	3-O		66	.279
1973	MIL	A	O-O		97	.280
1974	HOU	N	O		27	.217
	PHI	N	O		43	.242
1975	PHI	N	O		84	.303
1976	PHI	N	O		92	.254
			BRTR		1168	.265

BROWN, OSCAR LEE
B.FEB.8,1946 LONG BEACH,CAL.

1969	ATL	N	O		7	.250
1970	ATL	N	O		28	.383
1971	ATL	N	O		27	.209
1972	ATL	N	O		76	.226
1973	ATL	N	O		22	.207
			BRTR		160	.244

BROWN, PAUL DWAYNE
B.JUNE 18,1941 FT.SMITH,ARK.

1961	PHI	N	P		5	0- 1
1962	PHI	N	P		23	0- 6
1963	PHI	N	P		6	0- 1
1968	PHI	N	P		2	0- 0
			BRTR		36	0- 8

BROWN, PAUL PERCIVAL "RAY"
B.JAN.31,1889 CHICAGO,ILL.
D.MAY 29,1953 LOS ANGELES,CAL.

| 1909 | CHI | N | P | | 1 | 1- 0 |

BROWN, RICHARD ERNEST "DICK"
B.JAN.17,1935 SHINNSTON,W.VA.
D.APR.12,1970 BALTIMORE,MD.

1957	CLE	A	C		34	.263
1958	CLE	A	C		68	.237
1959	CLE	A	C		48	.220
1960	CHI	A	C		16	.163
1961	DET	A	C		93	.266
1962	DET	A	C		134	.241
1963	BAL	A	C		59	.246
1964	BAL	A	C		88	.257
1965	BAL	A	C		96	.231
			BRTR		636	.244

BROWN, RICHARD P. "STUB"
B.AUG.3,1870 BALTIMORE,MD.
D.MAR.11,1948

1893	BAL	N	P		11	0- 0
1894	BAL	N	P		9	4- 2
1897	CIN	N	P		2	0- 2
			TL		22	4- 4

BROWN, ROBERT M.
NON-PLAYING MANAGER LOU(AA)1889

BROWN, ROBERT M.
B.1891

| 1914 | BUF | F | P | | 15 | 0- 0 |
| | | | BRTR | | | |

BROWN, ROBERT MURRAY
B.APR.1,1911 DORCHESTER,MASS.

1930	BOS	N	P		3	0- 0
1931	BOS	N	P		3	0- 1
1932	BOS	N	P		35	14- 7
1933	BOS	N	P		6	0- 0
1934	BOS	N	P		16	1- 3
1935	BOS	N	P	15	16	1- 8
1936	BOS	N	P		2	0- 2
			BRTR	80	81	16-21

BROWN, ROBERT WILLIAM "DOC"
B.OCT.25,1924 SEATTLE,WASH.

1946	NY	A	S-3		7	.333
1947	NY	A	S-3-O		69	.300
1948	NY	A	2-S-3-O		113	.300
1949	NY	A	3-O		104	.283
1950	NY	A	3		95	.267
1951	NY	A	3		103	.268
1952	NY	A	3		29	.247
1954	NY	A	3		28	.217
			BLTR		548	.279

BROWN, SAMUEL WAKEFIELD
B.MAY 21,1878 WEBSTER,PA.
D.NOV.8,1931

1906	BOS	N	C		65	.208
1907	BOS	N	C		66	.190
			BRTR		131	.199

BROWN, THOMAS MICHAEL "BUCKSHOT"
B.DEC.6,1927 BROOKLYN,N.Y.

1944	BRO	N	S		46	.164
1945	BRO	N	S-O		57	.245
1947	BRO	N	S-3-O		15	.235
1948	BRO	N	1-3		54	.241
1949	BRO	N	O		41	.303
1950	BRO	N	O		48	.291
1951	BRO	N	O		11	.160
	PHI	N	1-2-3-O		78	.219
1952	PHI	N	1-O		18	.160
	CHI	N	1-2-S		61	.320
1953	CHI	N	S-O		65	.196
			BRTR		494	.241

BROWN, THOMAS T.
B.SEP.21,1860 LIVERPOOL,ENGLAND
D.OCT.27,1927

1882	BAL	AA	P-O	2	46	0- 0
						.293
1883	COL	AA	P-S-O	2	97	0- 2
						.276
1884	COL	AA	P-O	2	107	1- 1
						.275
1885	PIT	AA	O		108	.304
1886	PIT	AA	O		114	.280
1887	PIT	N	O		46	.284
	IND	N	O		36	.223
1888	BOS	N	O		107	.247
1889	BOS	N	O		88	.232
1890	BOS	P	O		127	.277
1891	BOS	AA	O		137	.323
1892	LOU	N	O		153	.232
1893	LOU	N	O		121	.253
1894	LOU	N	O		130	.251
1895	STL	N	O		87	.226
	WAS	N	O		31	.227
1896	WAS	N	O		113	.299
1897	WAS	N	M-O		116	.287
1898	WAS	N	M-O		15	.164
			BLTR	6	1779	1- 3
						.269

BROWN, THOMAS WILLIAM "TOM"
B.DEC.12,1940 READING,PA.

| 1963 | WAS | A | 1-O | | 61 | .147 |
| | | | BBTL | | | |

YR	CL	LEA	POS	GP	G	REC

BROWN, WALTER GEORGE "JUMBO"
B.APR.30,1907 GREENE,R.I.
D.OCT.2,1966 FREEPORT,N.Y.

YR	CL	LEA	POS	GP	G	REC
1925	CHI	N	P		2	0- 0
1927	CLE	A	P		8	0- 2
1928	CLE	A	P		5	0- 1
1932	NY	A	P		19	5- 2
1933	NY	A	P		21	7- 5
1935	NY	A	P		20	6- 5
1936	NY	A	P		20	1- 4
1937	CIN	N	P		4	1- 0
	NY	N	P		4	1- 0
1938	NY	N	P		43	5- 3
1939	NY	N	P		31	4- 0
1940	NY	N	P		41	2- 4
1941	NY	N	P		31	1- 5
	BRTR				249	33-31

BROWN, WALTER IRVING
B.APR.23,1915 JAMESTOWN,N.Y.

1947	STL	A	P		19	1- 0
	BRTR					

BROWN, WILLARD
B.1866 SAN FRANCISCO,CAL.
D.DEC.20,1897

1887	NY	N	C		47	.261
1888	NY	N	C		17	.271
1889	NY	N	C		33	.259
1890	NY	P	C-1		59	.274
1891	PHI	N	1		112	.242
1893	BAL	N	1		7	.129
	LOU	N	1		111	.320
1894	LOU	N	1		13	.192
	STL	N	1		17	.257
	BRTR				416	.268

BROWN, WILLARD JESSE
B.JUNE 26,1915 SHREVEPORT,LA.

1947	STL	A	O		21	.179
	BRTR					

BROWN, WILLIAM JAMES "GATES"
B.MAY 2,1939 CRESTLINE,O.

1963	DET	A	O		55	.268
1964	DET	A	O		123	.272
1965	DET	A	O		96	.256
1966	DET	A	O		88	.266
1967	DET	A	O		51	.187
1968	DET	A	1-O		67	.370
1969	DET	A	O		60	.204
1970	DET	A	O		81	.226
1971	DET	A	O		82	.338
1972	DET	A	O		103	.230
1973	DET	A	O-O		125	.236
1974	DET	A	O		73	.242
1975	DET	A	H		47	.171
	BLTR				1051	.257

BROWN, WILLIAM VERNA
B.JULY 8,1893 COLEMAN,TEX.
D.MAY 13,1965 LUBBOCK,TEX.

1912	STL	A	O		9	.200
	BLTL					

BROWNE, BYRON ELLIS
B.DEC.27,1942 ST.JOSEPH,MO.

1965	CHI	N	O		4	.000
1966	CHI	N	O		120	.243
1967	CHI	N	O		10	.158
1968	HOU	N	O		10	.231
1969	STL	N	O		22	.226
1970	PHI	N	O		104	.248
1971	PHI	N	O		58	.206
1972	PHI	N	O		21	.190
	BRTR				349	.236

BROWNE, GEORGE E.
B.NOV.4,1876 WASHINGTON,D.C.
D.DEC.9,1920

1901	PHI	N	O		8	.192
1902	PHI	N	O		68	.237
	NY	N	O		55	.348
1903	NY	N	O		141	.313
1904	NY	N	O		149	.283
1905	NY	N	O		127	.293
1906	NY	N	O		121	.264
1907	NY	N	O		121	.260
1908	BOS	N	O		138	.228
1909	CHI	N	O		12	.200
	WAS	A	O		103	.272
1910	WAS	A	O		7	.182
	CHI	A	O		30	.241
1911	BRO	N	O		7	.333
1912	PHI	N	H		6	.200
	BLTR				1093	.274

BROWNE, JAMES WILLIAM EARL "SNITZ"
B.MAR.5,1911 LOUISVILLE,KY.

1935	PIT	N	1		9	.250
1936	PIT	N	1-O		8	.304
1937	PHI	N	1-O		105	.292
1938	PHI	N	1		21	.257
	BLTL				143	.283

BROWNE, PRENTICE ALMONT
B.MAR.21,1929 PEERSKILL,N.Y.

1962	HOU	N	1		65	.210
	BLTL					

BROWNING, CALVIN DUANE
B.MAR.16,1938 BURNS FLAT,OKLA.

1960	STL	N	P		1	0- 0
	BLTL					

BROWNING, FRANK "DUTCH"
B.OCT.29,1882 FALMOUTH,KY.
D.MAY 20,1948

1910	DET	A	P		11	2- 2
	BRTR					

BROWNING, LOUIS ROGER "PETE"
B.JULY 17,1861 LOUISVILLE,KY.
D.SEPT.10,1905 LOUISVILLE,KY.

1882	LOU	AA	2-S-3		69	.382
1883	LOU	AA	1-2-S-3-O		83	.349
1884	LOU	AA	P-1-3-O	1	105	0- 1 .341
1885	LOU	AA	O		113	.367
1886	LOU	AA	O		112	.339
1887	LOU	AA	O		134	.471
1888	LOU	AA	O		99	.313
1889	LOU	AA	O		83	.253
1890	CLE	P	O		118	.391
1891	PIT	N	O		50	.287
	CIN	N	O		51	.362
1892	LOU	N	O		21	.260
	CIN	N	O		81	.300
1893	LOU	N	O		57	.371
1894	STL	N	O		2	.143
	BRO	N	O		1	1.000
	BRTR			1	1179	0- 1 .355

BROZEK, JONATHAN JOSEPH
(PLAYED UNDER NAME OF
JONATHAN JOSEPH BROOKS)

BRUBAKER, BRUCE ELLSWORTH
B.DEC.29,1941 HARRISBURG,PA.

1967	LA	N	P		1	0- 0
1970	MIL	A	P		1	0- 0
	BRTR				2	0- 0

BRUBAKER, WILBUR LEE "BILL"
B.NOV.7,1910 CLEVELAND,OHIO

1932	PIT	N	3		7	.417
1933	PIT	N	3		2	.000
1934	PIT	N	3		3	.333
1935	PIT	N	3		6	.000
1936	PIT	N	3		145	.289
1937	PIT	N	3		120	.254
1938	PIT	N	3		45	.295
1939	PIT	N	2-3		100	.232
1940	PIT	N	1-S-3		38	.192
1943	BOS	N	1-3		13	.421
	BRTR				479	.264

BRUCE, LOUIS
B.JAN.16,1877 FRANKLIN CO.,N.Y.
D.FEB.9,1968

1904	PHI	A	P-O	1	30	0- 1 .277
	BLTR					

BRUCE, ROBERT JAMES "BOB"
B.MAY 16,1933 DETROIT,MICH.

1959	DET	A	P		2	0- 1
1960	DET	A	P		34	4- 7
1961	DET	A	P		14	1- 2
1962	HOU	N	P		32	10- 9
1963	HOU	N	P	30	32	5- 9
1964	HOU	N	P	35	37	15- 9
1965	HOU	N	P		35	9-18
1966	HOU	N	P		25	3-13
1967	ATL	N	P		12	2- 3
	BRTR			219	223	49-71

BRUCKBAUER, FREDERICK JOHN
B.MAY 27,1938 NEW ULM,MINN.

1961	MIN	A	P		1	0- 0
	BRTR					

BRUCKER, EARLE FRANCIS JR.
B.JAN.21,1927 LOS ANGELES,CAL.

1948	PHI	A	C		2	.167
	BLTR					

BRUCKER, EARLE FRANCIS SR.
B.MAY 6,1901 ALBANY,N.Y.

1937	PHI	A	C		102	.259
1938	PHI	A	C		53	.374
1939	PHI	A	C		62	.291
1940	PHI	A	C		23	.196
1943	PHI	A	H		1	.000
	BRTR				241	.290

BRUCKMILLER, ANDREW
B.JAN.1,1882 PITTSBURGH,PA.
D.JAN.12,1970 MC KEESPORT,PA.

1905	DET	A	P		1	0- 0
	BRTR					

BRUGGY, FRANK LEO
B.MAY 4,1891 ELIZABETH,N.J.
D.APR.5,1959

1921	PHI	N	C		96	.310
1922	PHI	N	C		53	.279
1923	PHI	A	C		54	.210
1924	PHI	A	C		50	.265
1925	CIN	N	C		6	.214
	BRTR				259	.277

BRUMLEY, TONY MIKE "MIKE"
B.JULY 10,1938 GRANITE,OKLA.

1964	WAS	A	C		136	.244
1965	WAS	A	C		79	.208
1966	WAS	A	C		9	.111
	BLTR				224	.229

BRUNER, JACK RAYMOND
B.JULY 1,1924 WATERLOO,IOWA

1949	CHI	A	P		4	1- 2
1950	CHI	A	P		9	0- 0
	STL	A	P		13	1- 2
	BLTL				26	2- 4

BRUNER, WALTER ROY
B.FEB.10,1918 LOUISVILLE,KY.

1939	PHI	N	P		4	0- 4
1940	PHI	N	P		2	0- 0
1941	PHI	N	P		13	0- 3
	BRTR				19	0- 7

BRUNET, GEORGE STUART
B.JUNE 8,1935 HOUGHTON,MICH.

1956	KC	A	P		6	0- 0
1957	KC	A	P		5	0- 1
1959	KC	A	P		2	0- 0
1960	KC	A	P		3	0- 2
	MIL	N	P		17	2- 0
1961	MIL	N	P		5	0- 0
1962	HOU	N	P		17	2- 4
1963	HOU	N	P		5	0- 3
	BAL	A	P		16	0- 1
1964	LA	A	P		10	2- 2
1965	CAL	A	P		41	9-11
1966	CAL	A	P		41	13-13
1967	CAL	A	P		40	11-19
1968	CAL	A	P		39	13-17
1969	CAL	A	P		23	6- 7
	SEA	A	P		12	2- 5
1970	WAS	A	P		24	8- 6
	PIT	N	P		12	1- 1
1971	STL	N	P		7	0- 1
	BRTL				324	69-93

BRUNO, THOMAS MICHAEL "TOM"
B.JAN.26,1953 CHICAGO,ILL.

1976	KC	A	P		12	1- 0
	BRTR					

BRUNSBERG, ARLO ADOLPH
B.AUG.15,1940 FERTILE,MINN.

1966	DET	A	C		2	.333
	BLTR					

BRUSH, ROBERT
B.MAR.8,1875 OSAGE,IOWA
D.APR.2,1944 SAN BERNADINO,CAL.

1907	BOS	N	1		2	.000

```
YR   CL LEA POS   GP    G    REC
```

BRUTON, WILLIAM HARON "BILL"
B.DEC.22,1929 PANOLA,ALA.
```
1953 MIL N  O          151      .250
1954 MIL N  O          142      .284
1955 MIL N  O          149      .275
1956 MIL N  O          147      .272
1957 MIL N  O           79      .278
1958 MIL N  O          100      .280
1959 MIL N  O          133      .289
1960 MIL N  O          151      .286
1961 DET A  O          160      .257
1962 DET A  O          147      .278
1963 DET A  O          145      .256
1964 DET A  O          106      .277
          BLTR        1610      .273
```

BRUYETTE, EDWARD
B.AURORA,ILL.
```
1901 MIL A  O           28      .180
          TR
```

BRYAN, WILLIAM RONALD "BILLY"
B.DEC.4,1938 MORGAN,GA.
```
1961 KC  A  C            9      .158
1962 KC  A  C           25      .149
1963 KC  A  C           24      .169
1964 KC  A  C           93      .241
1965 KC  A  C          108      .252
1966 KC  A  C-1         32      .132
     NY  A  C-1         27      .217
1967 NY  A  C           16      .167
1968 WAS A  C           40      .204
          BLTR         374      .216
```

BRYANT, CLAIBORNE HENRY "CLAY"
B.NOV.16,1911 LYNCHBURG,VA.
```
1935 CHI N  P      9   12    1- 2
1936 CHI N  P     26   32    1- 2
1937 CHI N  P     38   47    9- 3
1938 CHI N  P     44   50   19-11
1939 CHI N  P      4   28    2- 1
1940 CHI N  P      8   16    0- 1
          BRTR   129  185   32-20
```

BRYANT, DONALD RAY "DON"
B.JULY 13,1941 JASPER,FLA.
```
1966 CHI N  C           13      .308
1969 HOU N  C           31      .186
1970 HOU N  C           15      .208
          BRTR          59      .220
```

BRYANT, G.
```
1885 DET N  2            1      .000
```

BRYANT, RONALD RAYMOND "RON"
B.NOV.12,1947 REDLANDS,CAL.
```
1967 SF  N  P      1         0- 0
1969 SF  N  P     16         4- 3
1970 SF  N  P     34         5- 8
1971 SF  N  P     27         7-10
1972 SF  N  P     35        14- 7
1973 SF  N  P     41   42   24-12
1974 SF  N  P     41         3-15
1975 STL N  P     10         0- 1
          BBTL   205  206   57-56
```

BRYE, STEPHEN ROBERT "STEVE"
B.FEB.4,1949 ALAMEDA,CAL.
```
1970 MIN A  O            9      .182
1971 MIN A  O           28      .224
1972 MIN A  O          100      .241
1973 MIN A  O           92      .263
1974 MIN A  O          135      .283
1975 MIN A  O           86      .252
1976 MIN A  O           87      .264
          BRTR         537      .261
```

BRYNAN, CHARLES R.
B.PHILADELPHIA,PA.
```
1888 CHI N  P      3         2- 1
1891 BOS N  P      1         0- 0
          BRTR     4         2- 1
```

BUBSER, HAROLD FRED
B.SEPT.28,1895 CHICAGO,ILL.
```
1922 CHI A  H            3      .000
          BRTR
```

BUCHA, JOHN GEORGE
B.JAN.22,1925 ALLENTOWN,PA.
```
1948 STL N  C            2      .000
1950 STL N  C           22      .139
1953 DET A  C           60      .222
          BRTR          84      .205
```

BUCHANAN, JAMES FORREST
B.JULY 1,1876 CHATHAM HILL,VA.
D.JUNE 15,1949 RANDOLPH,NEB.
```
1905 STL A  P     22         7- 9
          BLTR
```

BUCHEK, GERALD PETER "JERRY"
B.MAY 9,1942 ST.LOUIS,MO.
```
1961 STL N  S           31      .133
1963 STL N  S            3      .250
1964 STL N  2-S-3       35      .200
1965 STL N  2-S-3       55      .247
1966 STL N  2-S-3      100      .236
1967 NY  N  2-S-3      124      .236
1968 NY  N  2-3-O       73      .182
          BRTR         421      .220
```

BUCHER, JAMES QUINTER
B.MAR.24,1912 MANASSAS,VA.
```
1934 BRO N  2           47      .226
1935 BRO N  2-3-O      123      .302
1936 BRO N  2-3-O      110      .251
1937 BRO N  2-3        125      .253
1938 STL N  2           17      .228
1944 BOS A  2-3         80      .274
1945 BOS A  2-3         52      .225
          BLTR         554      .265
```

BUCKENBERGER, ALBERT C.
B.JAN.31,1861 DETROIT,MICH.
D.JULY 1,1917
NON-PLAYING MANAGER
COL(AA) 188.-90, PIT(N) 1892-94
STL(N) 1895 AND BOS(N) 1902-04

BUCKEYE, GARLAND MAIERS "GOB"
B.OCT.16,1897 HERON LAKE,MINN.
D.NOV.14,1975 STONE LAKE,WIS.
```
1918 WAS A  P      1         0- 0
1925 CLE A  P     30        13- 8
1926 CLE A  P     32         6- 9
1927 CLE A  P     35        10-17
1928 CLE A  P      9         1- 5
     NY  N  P      1         0- 0
          BBTL   108        30-39
```

BUCKINGHAM, EDWARD TAYLOR
B.MAY 12,1874 METUCHEN,N.J.
D.JULY 30,1942 BRIDGEPORT,CONN.
```
1895 WAS N  P      1         0- 1
```

BUCKLES, JESS ROBERT "JIM"
B.MAY 20,1890 LORDSBURG,CAL.
D.AUG.2,1975 WESTMINSTER,CAL.
```
1916 NY  A  P      2         0- 0
          BLTL
```

BUCKLEY, JOHN EDWARD
B.MAR.20,1870 MARLBORO,MASS.
D.MAY 4,1942
```
1890 BUF P  P      4         1- 3
```

BUCKLEY, RICHARD D.
B.SEPT.21,1858 TROY,N.Y.
D.DEC.12,1929
```
1888 IND N  C-3         71      .273
1889 IND N  C           65      .258
1890 NY  N  C           70      .255
1891 NY  N  C           67      .211
1892 STL N  C          106      .220
1893 STL N  C            7      .057
1894 STL N  C           28      .169
     PHI N  C           39      .302
1895 PHI N  C           29      .255
          TR           482      .243
```

BUCKNER, WILLIAM JOSEPH "BILL"
B.DEC.14,1949 VALLEJO,CAL.
```
1969 LA  N  H            1      .000
1970 LA  N  1-O         28      .191
1971 LA  N  1-O        108      .277
1972 LA  N  1-O        105      .319
1973 LA  N  1-O        140      .275
1974 LA  N  1-O        145      .314
1975 LA  N  O           92      .243
1976 LA  N  1-O        154      .301
          BLTL         773      .289
```

BUDD
```
1890 CLE P  O            1      .000
```

BUDDIN, DONALD THOMAS
B.MAY 5,1934 TURBEVILLE,S.C.
```
1956 BOS A  S          114      .239
1958 BOS A  S          136      .237
1959 BOS A  S          151      .241
1960 BOS A  S          124      .245
1961 BOS A  S          115      .263
1962 HOU N  S-3         40      .163
     DET A  2-S-3       31      .229
          BRTR         711      .241
```

BUDNICK, MICHAEL JOE
B.SEPT.15,1919 ASTORIA,ORE.
```
1946 NY  N  P           35      2- 3
1947 NY  N  P            7      0- 0
          BRTR          42      2- 3
```

BUELOW, CHARLES JOHN
B.JAN.12,1877 DUBUQUE,IOWA
D.MAY 4,1951
```
1901 NY  N  3           19      .112
          BRTR
```

BUELOW, FREDERICK WILLIAM "FRITZ"
B.FEB.13,1876 BERLIN,GERMANY
D.DEC.27,1933
```
1899 STL N  C            7      .285
1900 STL N  C            7      .235
1901 DET A  C           69      .229
1902 DET A  C-1         64      .223
1903 DET A  C           90      .222
1904 DET A  C           42      .115
     CLE A  C           42      .180
1905 CLE A  C           74      .174
1906 CLE A  C           34      .163
1907 STL A  C           26      .147
          BRTR         455      .182
```

BUES, ARTHUR FREDERICK
B.MAR.3,1888 MILWAUKEE,WIS.
D.NOV.7,1954
```
1913 BOS N  3            2      .000
1914 CHI N  2-3         14      .227
          BRTR          16      .222
```

BUFFINGTON, CHARLES G.
B.JUNE 14,1861 FALL RIVER,MASS.
D.SEPT.23,1907 FALL RIVER,MASS.
```
1882 BOS N  P-1-O   15        2- 3
                                     .250
1883 BOS N  P-1- 37 86       24-13
           O                         .237
1884 BOS N  P-1- 65 84       40-14
           O                         .263
1885 BOS N  P-1- 50 82       23-27
           O                         .239
1886 BOS N  P-1  17 44        7-10
                                     .289
1887 PHI N  P-O  38 66       21-17
                                     .296
1888 PHI N  P       44       28-15
1889 PHI N  P       43       26-17
1890 PHI P  M-P     41       19-13
1891 BOS AA P       56       27- 9
1892 BAL N  P       13        5- 8
          BRTR  409 574  222-146
                                     .253
```

BUFORD, DONALD ALVIN "DON"
B.FEB.2,1937 LINDEN,TEX.
```
1963 CHI A  2-3         12      .286
1964 CHI A  2-3        135      .262
1965 CHI A  2-3        155      .283
1966 CHI A  2-3-O      163      .244
1967 CHI A  2-3-O      156      .241
1968 BAL A  2-3-O      130      .282
1969 BAL A  2-3-O      144      .291
1970 BAL A  2-3-O      144      .272
1971 BAL A  O          122      .290
1972 BAL A  O          125      .206
          BBTR        1286      .264
```

BUKER, CYRIL OWEN
B.FEB.5,1919 GREENWOOD,WIS.
```
1945 BRO N  P           42      7- 2
          BLTR
```

BUKER, HARRY L. "HAPPY"
```
1884 DET N  S-O         30      .136
```

YR	CL	LEA	POS	GP	G	REC

BUHL, ROBERT RAY "BOB"
B.AUG.12,1928 SAGINAW,MICH.

YR	CL	LEA	POS	GP	G	REC
1953	MIL	N	P		30	13- 8
1954	MIL	N	P		31	2- 7
1955	MIL	N	P		38	13-11
1956	MIL	N	P		38	18- 8
1957	MIL	N	P		34	18- 7
1958	MIL	N	P		11	5- 2
1959	MIL	N	P		31	15- 9
1960	MIL	N	P		36	16- 9
1961	MIL	N	P		32	9-10
1962	MIL	N	P		1	0- 1
	CHI	N	P		34	12-13
1963	CHI	N	P		37	11-14
1964	CHI	N	P		36	15-14
1965	CHI	N	P		32	13-11
1966	CHI	N	P		1	0- 0
	PHI	N	P		32	6- 8
1967	PHI	N	P		3	0- 0
	BRTR				457	166-132
	BB 1958-60, 66					

BULLARD, GEORGE DONALD "CURLEY"
B.OCT.24,1928 LYNN,MASS.

YR	CL	LEA	POS	GP	G	REC
1954	DET	A	S		4	.000
	BRTR					

BULLIS, SIMON D. 'SIM'
B.1862 ENGLAND
D.JAN.14,1908

YR	CL	LEA	POS	GP	G	REC
1884	TOL	AA	C-O		13	.067

BULLOCK, JAMES LEONARD
B.JAN.13,1845 BRISTOL,R.I.
D.AUG.12,1912
NON-PLAYING MANAGER
PRO(N) 1880-81

BULLOCK, MALTON JOSEPH
B.OCT.12,1914 BILOXI,MISS.

YR	CL	LEA	POS	GP	G	REC
1936	PHI	A	P		12	0- 2
	BLTL					

BUMBRY, ALONZA BENJAMIN "AL"
B.APR.21,1947 FREDERICKSBURG,VA.

YR	CL	LEA	POS	GP	G	REC
1972	BAL	A	O		9	.364
1973	BAL	A	O		110	.337
1974	BAL	A	O		94	.233
1975	BAL	A	3-O-D		114	.269
1976	BAL	A	O-O		133	.251
	BLTR				460	.274

BUNCE, JOSHUA
B.BROOKLYN,N.Y.

YR	CL	LEA	POS	GP	G	REC
1877	HAR	N	O		1	.000

BUNKER, WALLACE EDWARD "WALLY"
B.JAN.25,1945 SEATTLE,WASH.

YR	CL	LEA	POS	GP	G	REC
1963	BAL	A	P		1	0- 1
1964	BAL	A	P		29	19- 5
1965	BAL	A	P		34	10- 8
1966	BAL	A	P	29	30	10- 6
1967	BAL	A	P		29	3- 7
1968	BAL	A	P		18	2- 0
1969	KC	A	P		35	12-11
1970	KC	A	P		24	2-11
1971	KC	A	P		7	2- 3
	BRTR			206	207	60-52

BUNNING, JAMES PAUL DAVID "JIM"
B.OCT.23,1931 COVINGTON,KY.

YR	CL	LEA	POS	GP	G	REC
1955	DET	A	P		15	3- 5
1956	DET	A	P		15	5- 1
1957	DET	A	P		45	20- 8
1958	DET	A	P	35	36	14-12
1959	DET	A	P		40	17-13
1960	DET	A	P	36	38	11-14
1961	DET	A	P		38	17-11
1962	DET	A	P	41	41	19-10
1963	DET	A	P	39	41	12-13
1964	PHI	N	P		41	19- 8
1965	PHI	N	P		39	19- 9
1966	PHI	N	P		43	19-14
1967	PHI	N	P		40	17-15
1968	PIT	N	P		27	4-14
1969	PIT	N	P		25	10- 9
	LA	N	P		9	3- 1
1970	PHI	N	P	34	35	10-15
1971	PHI	N	P	29	31	5-12
	BRTR			591	601	224-184

BURBACH, WILLIAM DAVID "BILL"
B.AUG.22,1947 DICKEYVILLE,WIS.

YR	CL	LEA	POS	GP	G	REC
1969	NY	A	P		31	6- 8
1970	NY	A	P		4	0- 2
1971	NY	A	P		2	0- 1
	BRTR				37	6-11

BURBRINK, NELSON EDWARD
B.DEC.28,1921 CINCINNATI,OHIO

YR	CL	LEA	POS	GP	G	REC
1955	STL	N	C		58	.276
	BRTR					

BURCH, ALBERT WILLIAM
B.OCT.7,1883 ALBANY,N.Y.
D.OCT.5,1926

YR	CL	LEA	POS	GP	G	REC
1906	STL	N	O		91	.266
1907	STL	N	O		48	.227
	BRO	N	O		36	.292
1908	BRO	N	O		116	.243
1909	BRO	N	O		152	.271
1910	BRO	N	O		83	.236
1911	BRO	N	O		46	.228
	BLTR				572	.254

BURCH, EARNEST W.
B.1858 DEKALB CO.,ILL.

YR	CL	LEA	POS	GP	G	REC
1884	CLE	N	O		31	.201
1886	BRO	AA	O		114	.253
1887	BRO	AA	O		48	.400
	BL				193	.285

BURCHART, LARRY WAYNE
B.FEB.8,1946 TULSA,OKLA.

YR	CL	LEA	POS	GP	G	REC
1969	CLE	A	P		29	0- 2
	BRTR					

BURCHELL, FREDERICK DUFF
B.JULY 15,1879 PERTH AMBOY,N.J.
D.NOV.20,1951 JORDAN,N.Y.

YR	CL	LEA	POS	GP	G	REC
1903	PHI	N	P		6	0- 3
1907	BOS	A	P		2	0- 1
1908	BOS	A	P	31	32	10- 8
1909	BOS	A	P		10	3- 3
	BRTL				50	13-15

BURDA, EDWARD ROBERT "BOB"
B.JULY 16,1938 ST.LOUIS,MO.

YR	CL	LEA	POS	GP	G	REC
1962	STL	N	O		7	.071
1965	SF	N	1-O		31	.111
1966	SF	N	1-O		37	.163
1969	SF	N	1-O		97	.230
1970	SF	N	1-O		28	.261
	MIL	A	1-O		78	.248
1971	STL	N	1-O		65	.296
1972	BOS	A	1-O		45	.164
	BLTL				388	.224

BURDETTE, FREDDIE THOMASON
B.SEP.15,1936 MOULTRIE,GA.

YR	CL	LEA	POS	GP	G	REC
1962	CHI	N	P		8	0- 0
1963	CHI	N	P		4	0- 0
1964	CHI	N	P		18	1- 0
	BRTR				30	1- 0

BURDETTE, SELVA LEWIS "LEW"
B.NOV.22,1926 NITRO,W.VA.

YR	CL	LEA	POS	GP	G	REC
1950	NY	A	P		2	0- 0
1951	BOS	N	P		3	0- 0
1952	BOS	N	P		45	6-11
1953	MIL	N	P		46	15- 5
1954	MIL	N	P	38	39	15-14
1955	MIL	N	P	42	45	13- 8
1956	MIL	N	P	39	45	19-10
1957	MIL	N	P	37	41	17- 9
1958	MIL	N	P	40	47	20-10
1959	MIL	N	P	41	52	21-15
1960	MIL	N	P	45	46	19-13
1961	MIL	N	P	40	42	18-11
1962	MIL	N	P	37	39	10- 9
1963	MIL	N	P	15	17	6- 5
	STL	N	P		21	3- 8
1964	STL	N	P		8	1- 0
	CHI	N	P		28	9- 9
1965	CHI	N	P	7	8	0- 2
	PHI	N	P		19	3- 3
1966	CAL	A	P		54	7- 2
1967	CAL	A	P		19	1- 0
	BRTR			626	666	203-144

BURDICK, WILLIAM B.
B.1862 JANESVILLE,WIS.

YR	CL	LEA	POS	GP	G	REC
1888	IND	N	P		31	10-10
1889	IND	N	P		9	0- 3
	BRTR				40	10-13

BURDOCK, JOHN JOSEPH "BLACK JACK"
B.1851 BROOKLYN,N.Y.
D.NOV.28,1931

YR	CL	LEA	POS	GP	G	REC
1872	ATL	NA	C-2-S		35	.250
1873	ATL	NA	C-2		55	-
1874	MUT	NA	3		61	-
1875	HAR	NA	2-3		74	-
1876	HAR	N	2		69	.248
1877	HAR	N	2-3		58	.260
1878	BOS	N	2		60	.260
1879	BOS	N	2		84	.240
1880	BOS	N	2		84	.256
1881	BOS	N	2-S		73	.237
1882	BOS	N	2		82	.239
1883	BOS	N	M-2		96	.330
1884	BOS	N	2		84	.267
1885	BOS	N	2		45	.142
1886	BOS	N	2		59	.217
1887	BOS	N	2		64	.305
1888	BOS	N	2		21	.202
	BRO	AA	2		69	.125
1891	BRO	N	2		3	.083
	BRTR				1176	-

BURG, JOSEPH PETER "PETE"
B.JUNE 4,1882 CHICAGO,ILL.

YR	CL	LEA	POS	GP	G	REC
1910	BOS	N	S-3		13	.348
	TR					

BURGESS, FORREST HARRILL "SMOKY"
B.FEB.6,1927 CAROLEEN,N.C.

YR	CL	LEA	POS	GP	G	REC
1949	CHI	N	C		46	.268
1951	CHI	N	C		94	.251
1952	PHI	N	C		110	.296
1953	PHI	N	C		102	.292
1954	PHI	N	C		108	.368
1955	PHI	N	C		7	.190
	CIN	N	C		116	.306
1956	CIN	N	C		90	.275
1957	CIN	N	C		90	.283
1958	CIN	N	C		99	.283
1959	PIT	N	C		114	.297
1960	PIT	N	C		120	.294
1961	PIT	N	C		100	.303
1962	PIT	N	C		103	.328
1963	PIT	N	C		91	.280
1964	PIT	N	C		68	.246
	CHI	A	H		7	.200
1965	CHI	A	C		80	.286
1966	CHI	A	C		79	.313
1967	CHI	A	H		77	.133
	BLTR				1691	.295

BURGESS, THOMAS ROLAND
B.SEPT.1,1927 LONDON,ONT.,CAN.

YR	CL	LEA	POS	GP	G	REC
1954	STL	N	O		17	.048
1962	LA	A	1-O		87	.196
	BLTL				104	.177

BURGMEIER, THOMAS HENRY "TOM"
B.AUG.2,1943 ST.PAUL,MINN.

YR	CL	LEA	POS	GP	G	REC
1968	CAL	A	P-O	56	71	1- 4
						.000
1969	KC	A	P-O	31	47	3- 1
						.167
1970	KC	A	P		41	42	6- 6
1971	KC	A	P		67	68	9- 7
1972	KC	A	P			51	6- 2
1973	KC	A	P			6	0- 0
1974	MIN	A	P	50	51	5- 3
1975	MIN	A	P	46	47	5- 8
1976	MIN	A	P		57	8- 1
	BLTL			405	440	43-32
						.212

BURGO, WILLIAM ROSS
B.NOV.5,1922 JOHNSTOWN,PA.

YR	CL	LEA	POS	GP	G	REC
1943	PHI	A	O		17	.371
1944	PHI	A	O		27	.239
	BRTR				44	.297

BURICH, WILLIAM MAX
B.MAY 29,1918 CALUMET,MICH.

YR	CL	LEA	POS	GP	G	REC
1942	PHI	N	S-3		25	.288
1946	PHI	N	3		2	.000
	BRTR				27	.284

YR	CL	LEA	POS	GP	G	REC

BURK, CHARLES SANDFORD "SANDY"
B.APR.22,1887 COLUMBUS,OHIO
D.OCT.11,1934

YR	CL	LEA	POS	GP	G	REC
1910	BRO	N	P		4	0- 3
1911	BRO	N	P		13	1- 3
1912	BRO	N	P		2	0- 0
	STL	N	P		12	1- 3
1913	STL	N	P		19	0- 2
1915	PIT	F	P		2	0- 0
	BRTR				52	2-11

BURK, MACK EDWIN
B.APR.21,1935 NACOGDOCHES,TEX.

YR	CL	LEA	POS	GP	G	REC
1956	PHI	N	C		15	1.000
1958	PHI	N	H		1	.000
	BRTR				16	.500

BUPKAM, CHAUNCEY DE PEW "CHRIS"
B.OCT.13,1892 BENTON HARBOR, MICH.
D.MAY 9,1964 KALAMAZOO,MICH.

YR	CL	LEA	POS	GP	G	REC
1915	STL	A	H		1	.000
	BLTR					

BURKART, ELMER ROBERT "SWEDE"
B.FEB.1,1917 PHILADELPHIA,PA.

YR	CL	LEA	POS	GP	G	REC
1936	PHI	N	P		2	0- 0
1937	PHI	N	P		7	0- 0
1938	PHI	N	P		2	0- 1
1939	PHI	N	P		5	1- 0
	BRTR				16	1- 1

BURKE, DANIEL F.
B.OCT.25,1868 S.ABINGTON,MASS.
D.MAR.20,1933

YR	CL	LEA	POS	GP	G	REC
1890	ROC	AA	O		30	.286
	SYR	AA	C		9	.000
1892	BOS	N	C		1	.000
					40	.206

BURKE, EDWARD O.
B.OCT.6,1866 NORTHUMBERLAND,PA.
D.NOV.26,1907

YR	CL	LEA	POS	GP	G	REC
1890	PHI	N	O		100	.280
	PIT	N	O		32	.225
1891	MIL	AA	O		34	.224
1892	CIN	N	2-O		14	.139
	NY	N	2-O		83	.266
1893	NY	N	O		135	.289
1894	NY	N	O		138	.299
1895	NY	N	O		39	.256
	CIN	N	O		56	.279
1896	CIN	N	O		122	.342
1897	CIN	N	O		94	.289
	BRTR				847	.284

BURKE, FRANK ALOYSIUS
B.FEB.16,1880 CARBON,CO.,PA.
D.SEPT.17,1946

YR	CL	LEA	POS	GP	G	REC
1906	NY	N	O		8	.222
1907	BOS	N	O		36	.178
	TR				44	.181

BURKE, GLENN LAWRENCE
B.NOV.16,1952 OAKLAND,CAL.

YR	CL	LEA	POS	GP	G	REC
1976	LA	N	O		25	.239
	BRTR					

BURKE, JAMES TIMOTHY "SUNSET"
B.OCT.12,1874 ST.LOUIS,MO.
D.MAR.26,1942

YR	CL	LEA	POS	GP	G	REC
1898	CLE	N	3		13	.111
1899	STL	N	2		2	.333
1901	MIL	A	S-3		64	.207
	CHI	A	3		41	.248
	PIT	N	3		34	.211
1902	PIT	N	2-S-3-O		55	.296
1903	STL	N	2-3		113	.285
1904	STL	N	3		118	.227
1905	STL	N	M-3		122	.225
	BRTR				562	.243

NON-PLAYING MANAGER
STL(A) 1918-20

BURKE, JOHN PATRICK
B.JAN.27,1877 HAZELTON,PA.
D.AUG.4,1950

YR	CL	LEA	POS	GP	G	REC
1902	NY	N	P-O	2	4	0- 1
						.153
	BRTR					

BURKE, JOSEPH M.
B.CINCINNATI,OHIO
D.DEC.29,1896

YR	CL	LEA	POS	GP	G	REC
1890	STL	AA	3		2	.571
1891	CIN	AA	2		1	.250
					3	.455

BURKE, LEO PATRICK
B.MAY 6,1934 HAGERSTOWN,MD.

YR	CL	LEA	POS	GP	G	REC
1958	BAL	A	3-O		7	.455
1959	BAL	A	2-3		5	.200
1961	LA	A	H		6	.000
1962	LA	A	S-3-O		19	.266
1963	STL	N	3-O		30	.204
	CHI	N	1-2		27	.184
1964	CHI	N	C-1-2-3-O		59	.262
1965	CHI	N	C-O		12	.200
	BRTR				165	.239

BURKE, LESLIE KINGSTON "BUCK"
B.DEC.18,1902 LYNN,MASS.
D.MAY 6,1975 DANVERS,MASS.

YR	CL	LEA	POS	GP	G	REC
1923	DET	A	2-3		9	.090
1924	DET	A	2		72	.253
1925	DET	A	2		77	.289
1926	DET	A	2		38	.227
	BLTR				196	.258

BURKE, MICHAEL E.
B.CINCINNATI,OHIO
D.JUNE 6,1889

YR	CL	LEA	POS	GP	G	REC
1879	CIN	N	S-3-O		29	.222
	BRTR					

BURKE, PATRICK EDWARD
B.MAY 13,1902 ST.LOUIS,MO.
D.JULY 7,1965 ST.LOUIS,MO.

YR	CL	LEA	POS	GP	G	REC
1924	STL	A	3		1	.000
	BRTR					

BURKE, ROBERT JAMES
B.JAN.23,1907 JOLIET,ILL.
D.FEB.8,1971 STUART,FLA.

YR	CL	LEA	POS	GP	G	REC
1927	WAS	A	P		36	3- 2
1928	WAS	A	P		26	2- 4
1929	WAS	A	P		37	6- 0
1930	WAS	A	P		24	3- 4
1931	WAS	A	P		30	8- 3
1932	WAS	A	P	22	23	3- 6
1933	WAS	A	P		25	4- 3
1934	WAS	A	P	37	41	8- 8
1935	WAS	A	P	15	16	1- 8
1937	PHI	N	P		2	0- 0
	BLTL			254	260	38-46

BURKE, WALTER R.
B.CALIFORNIA
D.MAR.3,1911

YR	CL	LEA	POS	GP	G	REC
1882	BUF	N	P-O		1	0- 1
						.000
1883	BUF	N	P-O		1	0- 0
						.200
1884	BOS	U	P-O	39	45	19-15
						.212
1887	DET	N	P		2	0- 1
				43	49	19-17
						.209

BURKE, WILLIAM IGNATIUS
B.JULY 11,1889 CLINTON,MASS.
D.FEB.9,1967 WORCESTER,MASS.

YR	CL	LEA	POS	GP	G	REC
1910	BOS	N	P	19	20	1- 0
1911	BOS	N	P		2	0- 1
	BLTL			21	22	1- 1

BURKETT, JESSE CAIL "CRAB"
B.DEC.4,1868 WHEELING,W.VA.
D.MAY 27,1953 WORCESTER,MASS.

YR	CL	LEA	POS	GP	G	REC
1890	NY	N	P-O	14	101	3-11
						.306
1891	CLE	N	O		40	.271
1892	CLE	N	O		145	.277
1893	CLE	N	O		124	.372
1894	CLE	N	O		124	.357
1895	CLE	N	O		132	.423
1896	CLE	N	O		133	.410
1897	CLE	N	O		128	.383
1898	CLE	N	O		148	.345
1899	STL	N	O		138	.402
1900	STL	N	O		142	.360
1901	STL	N	O		142	.382
1902	STL	A	P-S-3-O	1	137	0- 1
						.306
1903	STL	A	O		133	.296
1904	STL	A	O		147	.273
1905	BOS	A	O		149	.257
	BLTL			15	2063	3-12
						.342

BURKHART, WILLIAM KENNETH "KEN"
B.NOV.18,1916 KNOXVILLE,TENN.

YR	CL	LEA	POS	GP	G	REC
1945	STL	N	P		42	18- 8
1946	STL	N	P		25	6- 3
1947	STL	N	P		34	3- 6
1948	STL	N	P	20	21	0- 0
	CIN	N	P		16	0- 3
1949	CIN	N	P		11	0- 0
	BRTR			148	149	27-20

BURLESON, RICHARD PAUL "RICK"
B.APR.29,1951 LYNWOOD,CAL.

YR	CL	LEA	POS	GP	G	REC
1974	BOS	A	2-S-3		114	.284
1975	BOS	A	S		158	.252
1976	BOS	A	S		152	.291
	BRTR				424	.274

BURNETT, HERCULES H.
B.AUG.13,1869 LOUISVILLE,KY.

YR	CL	LEA	POS	GP	G	REC
1888	LOU	AA	O		1	.000
1895	LOU	N	O		5	.411
					6	.333

BURNETT, JOHN HENDERSON
B.NOV.1,1906 BARTOW,FLA.
D.AUG.12,1959

YR	CL	LEA	POS	GP	G	REC
1927	CLE	A	2		17	.000
1928	CLE	A	S		3	.500
1929	CLE	A	S-3		19	.152
1930	CLE	A	S-3		54	.312
1931	CLE	A	2-S-3		111	.300
1932	CLE	A	2-S		129	.297
1933	CLE	A	2-S-3		83	.272
1934	CLE	A	S-3-O		72	.293
1935	STL	A	2-S-3		70	.223
	BLTR				558	.283

BURNETT, JOHN P.

YR	CL	LEA	POS	GP	G	REC
1907	STL	N	O		59	.238

BUPNETTE, WALLACE HARPER
B.JUNE 20,1929 BLAIRS,VA.

YR	CL	LEA	POS	GP	G	REC
1956	KC	A	P		18	6- 8
1957	KC	A	P		38	7-11
1958	KC	A	P		12	1- 1
	BRTR				68	14-20

BURNHAM, GEORGE WALTER "WATCH"
B.MAY 20,1860 ALBION,MICH.
D.NOV.18,1904
NON-PLAYING MANAGER IND(N) 1887

BURNS, DENNIS
B.MAY 24,1899 TIFF CITY,MO.
D.MAY 21,1969 TULSA,OKLA.

YR	CL	LEA	POS	GP	G	REC
1923	PHI	A	P		3	2- 1
1924	PHI	A	P		37	6- 8
	BRTR				40	8- 9

BURNS, EDWARD JAMES
B.OCT.31,1888 SAN FRANCISCO,CAL
D.JUNE 1,1942

YR	CL	LEA	POS	GP	G	REC
1912	STL	N	C		1	.000
1913	PHI	N	C		17	.200
1914	PHI	N	C		70	.259
1915	PHI	N	C		67	.241
1916	PHI	N	C		78	.333
1917	PHI	N	C		20	.204
1918	PHI	N	C		68	.207
	BRTR				321	.229

BURNS, GEORGE HENRY "TIOGA"
B.JAN.31,1893 NILES,OHIO

YR	CL	LEA	POS	GP	G	REC
1914	DET	A	1		137	.291
1915	DET	A	1		105	.253
1916	DET	A	1		135	.286
1917	DET	A	1		119	.226
1918	PHI	A	1		130	.352
1919	PHI	A	1-O		126	.296
1920	PHI	A	1		21	.259
	CLE	A	1		45	.242
1921	BOS	A	1-O		84	.361
1922	BOS	A	1		147	.306
1923	BOS	A	1		146	.328
1924	CLE	A	1		129	.310
1925	CLE	A	1		127	.336
1926	CLE	A	1		151	.358
1927	CLE	A	1		140	.319
1928	CLE	A	1		82	.249
	NY	A	1		4	.500
1929	NY	A	1		9	.000
	PHI	A	1		29	.265
	BRTR				1866	.307

YR	CL	LEA	POS	GP	G	REC

BURNS, GEORGE JOSEPH
B.NOV.24,1889 UTICA,N.Y.
D.AUG.15,1966 GLOVERSVILLE,N.Y.

YR	CL	LEA	POS	GP	G	REC
1911	NY	N	O		6	.059
1912	NY	N	O		29	.294
1913	NY	N	O		150	.286
1914	NY	N	O		154	.303
1915	NY	N	O		155	.272
1916	NY	N	O		155	.279
1917	NY	N	O		152	.302
1918	NY	N	O		119	.290
1919	NY	N	O		139	.303
1920	NY	N	O		154	.287
1921	NY	N	O		149	.299
1922	CIN	N	O		156	.285
1923	CIN	N	O		154	.274
1924	CIN	N	O		93	.256
1925	PHI	N	O		88	.292
		BRTR			1853	.287

BURNS, JAMES "FARMER"
B.ASHTABULA,OHIO

1901	STL	N	P		1	0- 0
		TR				

BURNS, JAMES M.
B.QUINCY,ILL.

1888	KC	AA	O		15	.273
1889	KC	AA	O		133	.303
1891	WAS	AA	O		20	.313
					168	.303

BURNS, JOHN IRVING "SLUG"
B.AUG.31,1907 CAMBRIDGE,MASS.
D.APR.18,1975 BOSTON,MASS.

1930	STL	A	1		8	.300
1931	STL	A	1		144	.260
1932	STL	A	1		150	.305
1933	STL	A	1		144	.288
1934	STL	A	1		154	.257
1935	STL	A	1		143	.286
1936	STL	A	1		9	.214
	DET	A	1		138	.283
		BLTL			890	.280

BURNS, JOHN JOSEPH
B.MAY 13,1877 AVOCA,PA.
D.JUNE 24,1957

1903	DET	A	2		10	.256
1904	DET	A	2		4	.125
		BRTR			14	.211

BURNS, JOSEPH FRANCIS
B.MAR.26,1889 IPSWICH,MASS.

1910	CIN	N	H		1	1.000
1913	DET	A	O		4	.309
		BLTL			5	.357

BURNS, JOSEPH FRANCIS
B.FEB.25,1900 TRENTON,N.J.

1924	CHI	A	C		8	.105
		BRTR				

BURNS, JOSEPH JAMES
B.JUNE 17,1916 BRYN MAWR,PA.
D.JUNE 24,1974 BRYN MAWR,PA.

1943	BOS	N	3-O		52	.208
1944	PHI	A	2-3		28	.240
1945	PHI	A	1-3-O		31	.256
		BRTR			111	.230

BURNS, PATRICK

1884	BAL	AA	1		6	.154
	BAL	U	1		1	.500
					7	.200

BURNS, RICHARD SIMON
B.DEC.26,1863 HOLYOKE,MASS.
D.NOV.11,1890

1883	DET	N	P-O	15	36	2-12
						.192
1884	CIN	U	P-O	41	68	25-16
						.315
1885	STL	N	P-O	1	14	0- 0
						.218
		BL		57	118	27-28
						.271

BURNS, THOMAS EVERETT
B.MAR.30,1857 HONESDALE,PA.
D.MAR.19,1902

1880	CHI	N	P-C-	1	82	0- 0
			S-3			.309
1881	CHI	N	2-S-3		84	.277
1882	CHI	N	2-S		84	.247
1883	CHI	N	2-S-O		97	.293
1884	CHI	N	S-3		82	.245
1885	CHI	N	2-S		111	.271
1886	CHI	N	3		111	.276
1887	CHI	N	3		115	.317
1888	CHI	N	3		134	.238
1889	CHI	N	3		136	.257
1890	CHI	N	3		139	.277
1891	CHI	N	3		57	.231
1892	PIT	N	M-3-O		12	.210
		BRTR		1	1244	0- 0
						.271

NON-PLAYING MANAGER
CHI(N) 1898-99

BURNS, THOMAS P. "OYSTER"
B.SEPT.6,1862 PHILADELPHIA,PA.
D.NOV.16,1928 BROOKLYN,N.Y.

1884	WIL	U	S		2	.143
	BAL	AA	P-2-	2	36	0- 0
			3-O			.304
1885	BAL	AA	P-2-	11	76	7- 4
			S-O			.229
1887	BAL	AA	S-3		140	.401
1888	BAL	AA	S-O		77	.308
	BRO	AA	2-S-O		52	.286
1889	BRO	AA	O		132	.316
1890	BRO	N	O		119	.284
1891	BRO	N	O		122	.281
1892	BRO	N	O		139	.310
1893	BRO	N	O		107	.279
1894	BRO	N	O		126	.358
1895	BRO	N	O		17	.192
	NY	N	O		33	.298
		BRTR		13	1178	7- 4
						.310

BURNS, WILLIAM
B.HAGERSTOWN,MD.

1902	BAL	A	H		1	1.000

BURNS, WILLIAM THOMAS
"SLEEPY BILL"
B.JAN.29,1880 SAN SABA,TEX.
D.JUNE 6,1953

1908	WAS	A	P		23	6-11
1909	WAS	A	P		6	2- 0
	CHI	A	P		20	7-13
1910	CHI	A	P		1	0- 0
	CIN	N	P		31	8-13
1911	CIN	N	P		6	0- 0
	PHI	N	P		21	3- 7
1912	DET	A	P		6	1- 4
		BBTL			114	27-48

BURNSIDE, PETER WILLITS "PETE"
B.JULY 2,1930 EVANSTON,ILL.

1955	NY	N	P		2	1- 0
1957	NY	N	P		10	1- 4
1958	SF	N	P		6	0- 0
1959	DET	A	P		30	1- 3
1960	DET	A	P		31	7- 7
1961	WAS	A	P		33	4- 9
1962	WAS	A	P		40	5-11
1963	BAL	A	P		6	0- 1
	WAS	A	P		38	0- 1
		BRTL			196	19-36

BURPO, GEORGE HARVIE
B.OCT.7,1922 JENKINS,KY.

1946	CIN	N	P		2	0- 0
		BRTL				

BURR, ALEXANDER THOMSON
B.NOV.1,1893 CHICAGO,ILL.
D.NOV.1,1918

1914	NY	A	O		1	.000
		BRTR				

BURRELL, FRANK ANDREW "BUSTER"
B.DEC.22,1867 E.WEYMOUTH,MASS.
D.MAY 8,1962

1891	NY	N	C		15	.075
1895	BRO	N	C		10	.160
1896	BRO	N	C		58	.307
1897	BRO	N	C		31	.238
		BRTR			114	.243

BURRELL, HARRY J.
B.1866 E.WEYMOUTH,MASS.
D.DEC.11,1914

1891	STL	AA	P		9	3- 2

BURRIGHT, LARRY ALLEN
B.JULY 10,1937 ROSEVILLE,ILL.

1962	LA	N	2-S		115	.205
1963	NY	N	2-S-3		41	.220
1964	NY	N	2		3	.000
		BRTR			159	.205

BURRIS, ALVA BURTON
B.JAN.28,1874 WARWICK,MD.
D.MAR.24,1938

1894	PHI	N	P		1	0- 0

BURRIS, BERTRAM RAY "RAY"
B.AUG.22,1950 IDABEL,OKLA.

1973	CHI	N	P		31	1- 1
1974	CHI	N	P	40	41	3- 5
1975	CHI	N	P	36	38	15-10
1976	CHI	N	P	37	39	15-13
		BRTR		144	149	34-29

BURRIS, PAUL ROBERT
B.JULY 21,1923 HICKORY,N.C.

1948	BOS	N	C		2	.500
1950	BOS	N	C		10	.174
1952	BOS	N	C		55	.220
1953	MIL	N	C		2	.000
		BRTR			69	.219

BURROUGHS, HENRY F.
B.1845 DETROIT,MICH.

1871	OLY	NA	3-O		12	9222
1872	OLY	NA	O		2	.125
					14	.211

BURROUGHS, JEFFREY ALAN "JEFF"
B.MAR.7,1951 LONG BEACH,CAL.

1970	WAS	A	O		6	.167
1971	WAS	A	O		59	.232
1972	TEX	A	1-O		22	.185
1973	TEX	A	1-O		151	.279
1974	TEX	A	1-O		152	.301
1975	TEX	A	O		152	.226
1976	TEX	A	O		158	.237
		BRTR			700	.255

BURROWS, JOHN
B.OCT.30,1913 WINNFIELD,LA.

1943	PHI	A	P		4	0- 1
	CHI	N	P		23	0- 2
1944	CHI	N	P		3	0- 0
		BRTL			30	0- 3

BURRUS, MAURICE LENNON "DICK"
B.JAN.29,1898 HATTERAS,N.C.
D.FEB.2,1972 ELIZABETH CITY,N.J

1919	PHI	A	1		70	.258
1920	PHI	A	1		71	.185
1925	BOS	N	1		152	.340
1926	BOS	N	1		131	.270
1927	BOS	N	1		72	.318
1928	BOS	N	1		64	.270
		BLTL			560	.291

BURT, FRANK J.
B.CAMDEN,N.J.

1882	BAL	AA	O		10	.108

BURTON, ELLIS NARRINGTON
B.AUG.12,1936 LOS ANGELES,CAL.

1958	STL	N	O		8	.233
1960	STL	N	O		29	.214
1963	CLE	A	O		26	.194
	CHI	N	O		93	.230
1964	CHI	N	O		42	.190
1965	CHI	N	O		17	.175
		BBTR			215	.216

BURTON, JIM SCOTT
B.OCT.27,1949 ROYAL OAK,MICH.

1975	BOS	A	P		29	1- 2
		BRTL				

BURTSCHY, EDWARD FRANK "MOE"
B.APR.18,1922 CINCINNATI,OHIO

1950	PHI	A	P		9	0- 1
1951	PHI	A	P		7	0- 0
1954	PHI	A	P		46	5- 4
1955	KC	A	P		7	2- 0
1956	KC	A	P		21	3- 1
		BRTR			90	10- 6

YR	CL	LEA	POS	GP	G	REC

BURWELL, RICHARD MATTHEW
B.JAN.23,1940 ALTON,ILL.

YR	CL	LEA	POS	GP	G	REC
1960	CHI	N	P		3	0- 0
1961	CHI	N	P		2	0- 0
		BRTR			5	0- 0

BURWELL, WILLIAM EDWIN
B.MAY 27,1895 JARBALO,KAN.
D.JUNE 11,1973 ORMOND BEACH,FLA

YR	CL	LEA	POS	GP	G	REC
1920	STL	A		33	35	6- 4
1921	STL	A	P		33	2- 4
1928	PIT	N	P		4	1- 0
		BLTR		70	72	9- 8

NON-PLAYING MANAGER PIT(N) 1947

BUSBY, JAMES FRANKLIN "JIM"
B.JAN.8,1927 KENEDY,TEX.

YR	CL	LEA	POS	GP	G	REC
1950	CHI	A	O		18	.208
1951	CHI	A	O		143	.283
1952	CHI	A	O		16	.128
	WAS	A	O		129	.244
1953	WAS	A	O		150	.312
1954	WAS	A	O		155	.298
1955	WAS	A	O		47	.230
	CHI	A	O		99	.243
1956	CLE	A	O		135	.235
1957	CLE	A	O		30	.189
	BAL	A	O		86	.250
1958	BAL	A	3-O		113	.237
1959	BOS	A	O		61	.225
1960	BOS	A	O		1	.000
	BAL	A	O		79	.258
1961	BAL	A	O		75	.258
1962	HOU	N	C O		15	.182
		BRTR			1352	.263

BUSBY, PAUL MILLER "RED"
B.AUG.25,1918 WAYNESBORO,MISS.

YR	CL	LEA	POS	GP	G	REC
1941	PHI	N	O		10	.313
1943	PHI	N	O		26	.250
		BLTR			36	.268

BUSBY, STEVEN LEE "STEVE"
B.SEP.29,1949 BURBANK,CAL.

YR	CL	LEA	POS	GP	G	REC
1972	KC	A	P		5	3- 1
1973	KC	A	P		37	16-15
1974	KC	A	P		38	22-14
1975	KC	A	P		34	18-12
1976	KC	A	P		13	3- 3
		BRTR			127	62-45

BUSCH, EDGAR JOHN
B.NOV.6,1917 LEBANON,ILL.

YR	CL	LEA	POS	GP	G	REC
1943	PHI	A	S		4	.294
1944	PHI	A	2-S-3		140	.271
1945	PHI	A	1-2-S-3		126	.250
		BRTR			270	.262

BUSCHHORN, DONALD LEE "DON"
B.APR.29,1946 INDEPENDENCE,MO.

YR	CL	LEA	POS	GP	G	REC
1965	KC	A	P	12	13	0- 1
		BRTR				

BUSH, GUY TERRELL
B.AUG.23,1905 ABERDEEN,MISS.

YR	CL	LEA	POS	GP	G	REC
1923	CHI	N	P		1	0- 0
1924	CHI	N	P		16	2- 5
1925	CHI	N	P		42	6-13
1926	CHI	N	P		35	13- 9
1927	CHI	N	P		36	10-10
1928	CHI	N	P		42	15- 6
1929	CHI	N	P		50	18- 7
1930	CHI	N	P		46	15-10
1931	CHI	N	P		39	16- 8
1932	CHI	N	P		40	19-11
1933	CHI	N	P		41	20-12
1934	CHI	N	P	40	41	18-10
1935	PIT	N	P		41	11-11
1936	PIT	N	P		16	1- 3
	BOS	N	P		15	4- 5
1937	BOS	N	P	32	33	8-15
1938	STL	N	P		6	0- 1
1945	CIN	N	P		4	0- 0
		BRTR		542	544	176-136

BUSH, LESLIE AMBROSE
"BULLET JOE"
B.NOV.27,1892 BRAINERD,MINN.
D.NOV.1,1974 FT.LAUDERDALE,FLA.

YR	CL	LEA	POS	GP	G	REC
1912	PHI	A	P		1	0- 0
1913	PHI	A	P		39	13- 7
1914	PHI	A	P		38	16-12
1915	PHI	A	P		25	5-15
1916	PHI	A	P	40	41	15-22
1917	PHI	A	P		37	11-17
1918	BOS	A	P		36	15-15
1919	BOS	A	P		5	0- 0
1920	BOS	A	P	35	45	15-15
1921	BOS	A	P	36	51	16- 9
1922	NY	A	P		39	26- 7
1923	NY	A	P	37	38	19-15
1924	NY	A	P	39	60	17-16
1925	STL	A	P-O	33	57	14-14
						.254
1926	WAS	A	P	12	17	1- 8
	PIT	N	P	19	28	6- 6
1927	PIT	N	P	5	10	1- 2
	NY	N	P		3	1- 1
1928	PHI	A	P	11	15	2- 1
		BRTR		490	585	193-182
						.242

BUSH, OWEN JOSEPH "DONIE"
B.OCT.8,1887 INDIANAPOLIS,IND.
D.MAR.28,1972 INDIANAPOLIS,IND.

YR	CL	LEA	POS	GP	G	REC
1908	DET	A	S		20	.294
1909	DET	A	S		157	.273
1910	DET	A	S		142	.262
1911	DET	A	S		150	.232
1912	DET	A	S		144	.231
1913	DET	A	S		152	.251
1914	DET	A	S		157	.252
1915	DET	A	S		155	.228
1916	DET	A	S		145	.225
1917	DET	A	S		147	.281
1918	DET	A	S		128	.234
1919	DET	A	S		129	.244
1920	DET	A	S		141	.263
1921	DET	A	2-S		104	.279
	WAS	A	S		23	.238
1922	WAS	A	3		41	.238
1923	WAS	A	M-2-3		10	.409
		BBTR			1945	.250

NON-PLAYING MANAGER
PIT(N) 1927-29, CHI(A) 1930-31,
AND CIN(N) 1933

BUSHELMAN, JOHN FRANCIS
B.AUG.29,1885 CINCINNATI,OHIO
D.OCT.26,1955

YR	CL	LEA	POS	GP	G	REC
1909	CIN	N	P		1	0- 1
1911	BOS	A	P		3	0- 1
1912	BOS	A	P		3	1- 0
		BRTR			7	1- 2

BUSHEY, FRANCIS CLYDE
B.AUG.1,1906 WHEATON,KAN.
D.MAR.18,1972 TOPEKA,KAN.

YR	CL	LEA	POS	GP	G	REC
1927	BOS	A	P		1	0- 0
1930	BOS	A	P		11	0- 1
		BRTR			12	0- 1

BUSHONG, ALBERT JOHN "DOC"
B.SEPT.15,1856 PHILADELPHIA,PA.
D.AUG.19,1908

YR	CL	LEA	POS	GP	G	REC
1875	ATL	NA	C		1	.600
1876	ATH	N	C		5	.048
1880	WOR	N	C-O		37	.163
1881	WOR	N	C		75	.229
1882	WOR	N	C		69	.152
1883	CLE	N	C		61	.172
1884	CLE	N	C		60	.231
1885	STL	AA	C		85	.265
1886	STL	AA	C		107	.229
1887	STL	AA	C		53	.295
1888	BRO	AA	C		69	.220
1889	BRO	AA	C		25	.163
1890	BRO	N	C		16	.234
		BRTR			663	.219

BUSKEY, JOSEPH HENRY
B.DEC.18,1902 CUMBERLAND,MD.
D.APR.11,1949

YR	CL	LEA	POS	GP	G	REC
1926	PHI	N	S		5	.000
		BRTR				

BUSKEY, THOMAS WILLIAM "TOM"
B.FEB.20,1947 HARRISBURG,PA.

YR	CL	LEA	POS	GP	G	REC
1973	NY	A	P		8	0- 1
1974	NY	A	P		4	0- 1
	CLE	A	P		51	2- 6
1975	CLE	A	P		50	5- 3
1976	CLE	A	P		39	5- 4
		BRTR			152	12-15

BUSSE, RAYMOND EDWARD "RAY"
B.SEP.25,1948 DAYTONA BEACH,FLA.

YR	CL	LEA	POS	GP	G	REC
1971	HOU	N	S-3		10	.147
1973	STL	N	S		24	.143
	HOU	N	S-3		15	.059
1974	HOU	N	3		19	.206
		BRTR			68	.148

BUTCHER, ALBERT MAXWELL "MAX"
B.SEPT.21,1910 HOLDEN,W.VA.
D.SEPT.15,1957

YR	CL	LEA	POS	GP	G	REC
1936	BRO	N	P	38	42	6- 6
1937	BRO	N	P	39	40	11-15
1938	BRO	N	P	24	25	5- 4
	PHI	N	P		12	4- 8
1939	PHI	N	P		19	2-13
	PIT	N	P		14	4- 4
1940	PIT	N	P	35	36	8- 9
1941	PIT	N	P		33	17-12
1942	PIT	N	P		24	5- 8
1943	PIT	N	P		33	10- 8
1944	PIT	N	P		36	13-11
1945	PIT	N	P		28	10- 8
		BRTR		334	342	95-106

BUTCHER, HENRY JOSEPH
B.JULY 12,1887 CHICAGO,ILL.

YR	CL	LEA	POS	GP	G	REC
1911	CLE	A	O		38	.240
1912	CLE	A	O		24	.195
		BRTR			62	.223

BUTKA, EDWARD LUKE
B.JAN.7,1919 CANONSBURG,PA.

YR	CL	LEA	POS	GP	G	REC
1943	WAS	A	1		3	.333
1944	WAS	A	1		15	.195
		BRTR			18	.220

BUTLAND, WILBURN RUE "BILL"
B.MAR.22,1918 TERRE HAUTE,IND.

YR	CL	LEA	POS	GP	G	REC
1940	BOS	A	P		1	1- 2
1942	BOS	A	P		23	7- 1
1946	BOS	A	P		5	1- 0
1947	BOS	A	P		1	0- 0
		BRTL			32	9- 3

BUTLER, ARTHUR EDWARD
(REAL NAME
ARTHUR EDWARD BOUTHILLIER)
B.DEC.19,1887 FALL RIVER,MASS.

YR	CL	LEA	POS	GP	G	REC
1911	BOS	N	3		19	.176
1912	PIT	N	2		43	.273
1913	PIT	N	2-S		82	.280
1914	STL	N	S		86	.201
1915	STL	N	S		130	.254
1916	STL	N	O		86	.209
		BRTR			446	.241

BUTLER, CECIL DEAN
B.OCT.23,1937 DALLAS,GA.

YR	CL	LEA	POS	GP	G	REC
1962	MIL	N	P		9	2- 0
1964	MIL	N	P		2	0- 0
		BRTR			11	2- 0

BUTLER, CHARLES THOMAS
B.MAY 12,1906 GREEN COVE
SPRINGS,FLA.
D.MAY 10,1964 ST.SIMON'S
ISLAND,GA.

YR	CL	LEA	POS	GP	G	REC
1933	PHI	N	P		1	0- 0
		BRTL				

BUTLER, FRANK DEAN "GOLDBRICK"
B.JULY 18,1860 SAVANNAH,GA.
D.JULY 10,1945

YR	CL	LEA	POS	GP	G	REC
1895	NY	N	O		5	.272
		BLTL				

BUTLER, FRANK E. "KID"
B.1862 BOSTON,MASS.
D.APR.9,1921 BOSTON,MASS.

YR	CL	LEA	POS	GP	G	REC
1884	BOS	U	O		70	.160

BUTLER, ISSAC B.
B.AUG.22,1873 MONTCALM CO.,MICH
D.MAR.17,1948 OAKLAND,CAL.

YR	CL	LEA	POS	GP	G	REC
1902	BAL	A	P-O	15	18	2-11
						.115
		TR				

BUTLER, JOHN ALBERT
(PLAYED UNDER NAME OF
FREDERICK KING IN 1901)
B.JULY 26,1879 S.BOSTON,MASS.
D.FEB.2,1950 BOSTON,MASS.

YR	CL	LEA	POS	GP	G	REC
1901	MIL	A	C		1	.500
1904	STL	N	C		12	.167
1906	BRO	N	C		1	.000
1907	BRO	N	C		29	.127
	BRTR				43	.145

BUTLER, JOHN STEPHEN
"TROLLEY LINE"
B.MAR.20,1894 EUREKA,KAN.
D.APR.29,1967 LONG BEACH,CAL.

YR	CL	LEA	POS	GP	G	REC
1926	BRO	N	S-3		147	.269
1927	BRO	N	S-3		149	.238
1928	CHI	N	'3		62	.270
1929	STL	N	S-3		17	.164
	BRTR				375	.252

BUTLER, ORMOND HOOK
B.NOV.1854 WEST VIRGINIA
D.SEPT.12,1915 MT.HOPE,MD.
NON-PLAYING MANAGER PIT(AA)1883

BUTLER, RICHARD H.
B.BROOKLYN,N.Y.

YR	CL	LEA	POS	GP	G	REC
1897	LOU	N	C		10	.184
1899	WAS	N	C		12	.263
					22	.224

BUTLER, W. J.
B.1861 NEW ORLEANS,LA.

YR	CL	LEA	POS	GP	G	REC
1884	IND	AA	O		9	.206

BUTLER, WILLIAM FRANKLIN "BILL"
B.MAR.12,1947 HYATTSVILLE,MD.

YR	CL	LEA	POS	GP	G	REC
1969	KC	A	P		34	9-10
1970	KC	A	P		25	4-12
1971	KC	A	P		14	1- 2
1972	CLE	A	P		6	0- 0
1974	MIN	A	P		26	4- 6
1975	MIN	A	P		23	5- 4
	BLTL				128	23-34

BUTLER, WILLIS EVERETT "KID"
B.AUG.9,1887 FRANKLIN,PA.
D.FEB.22,1964

YR	CL	LEA	POS	GP	G	REC
1907	STL	A	3		20	.220
	BRTR					

BUTTERS, THOMAS ARDEN "TOM"
B.APR.8,1938 DELAWARE,O.

YR	CL	LEA	POS	GP	G	REC
1962	PIT	N	P		4	0- 0
1963	PIT	N	P		6	0- 0
1964	PIT	N	P		28	2- 2
1965	PIT	N	P		5	0- 1
	BRTR				43	2- 3

BUTTERY, FRANK
B.JUNE 16,1851 NORWALK,CONN.
D.DEC.16,1902 SILVER MINE,CONN.

YR	CL	LEA	POS	GP	G	REC
1872	MAN	NA	P-3-O		17	1- 2
						.295

BUXTON, RALPH STANLEY
B.JUNE 7,1914 WEYBURN,SASK.,CAN

YR	CL	LEA	POS	GP	G	REC
1938	PHI	A	P		5	0- 1
1949	NY	A	P		14	0- 1
	BRTR				19	0- 2

BUZAS, JOSEPH JOHN
B.OCT.2,1919 ALPHA,N.J.

YR	CL	LEA	POS	GP	G	REC
1945	NY	A	S		30	.262
	BRTR					

BUZHARDT, JOHN WILLIAM
B.AUG.17,1936 PROSPERITY,S.C.

YR	CL	LEA	POS	GP	G	REC
1958	CHI	N	P		6	3- 0
1959	CHI	N	P		31	4- 5
1960	PHI	N	P	30	32	5-16
1961	PHI	N	P		41	6-18
1962	CHI	A	P		28	8-12
1963	CHI	A	P	19	20	9- 4
1964	CHI	A	P		31	10- 8
1965	CHI	A	P	32	34	13- 8
1966	CHI	A	P	33	34	6-11
1967	CHI	A	P		28	3- 9
	BAL	A	P		7	0- 1
	HOU	N	P		1	0- 0
1968	HOU	N	P		39	4- 4
	BRTR			326	332	71-96

BYERLY, ELDRED WILLIAM "BUD"
B.OCT.26,1920 WEBSTER GROVES,MO

YR	CL	LEA	POS	GP	G	REC
1943	STL	N	P		2	1- 0
1944	STL	N	P		9	2- 2
1945	STL	N	P		33	4- 5
1950	CIN	N	P		4	0- 1
1951	CIN	N	P	40	41	2- 1
1952	CIN	N	P		12	0- 1
1956	WAS	A	P		25	2- 4
1957	WAS	A	P		47	6- 6
1958	WAS	A	P		17	2- 0
	BOS	A	P		18	1- 2
1959	SF	N	P		11	1- 0
1960	SF	N	P		19	1- 0
	BRTR			237	238	22-22

BYERS, JOHN WILLIAM "BIG BILL"
"BIG BILL"
B.BALTIMORE,MD.

YR	CL	LEA	POS	GP	G	REC
1904	STL	N	C		17	.217
	TR					

BYRD, HARRY GLADWIN
B.FEB.3,1925 DARLINGTON,S.C.

YR	CL	LEA	POS	GP	G	REC
1950	PHI	A	P		6	0- 0
1952	PHI	A	P		37	15-15
1953	PHI	A	P		40	11-20
1954	NY	A	P		25	9- 7
1955	BAL	A	P		14	3- 2
	CHI	A	P		25	4- 6
1956	CHI	A	P		3	0- 1
1957	DET	A	P		37	4- 3
	BRTR				187	46-54
	BB 1955					

BYRD, SAMUEL DEWEY
B.OCT.15,1907 BREMEN,GA.

YR	CL	LEA	POS	GP	G	REC
1929	NY	A	O		62	.312
1930	NY	A	O		92	.284
1931	NY	A	O		115	.270
1932	NY	A	O		105	.297
1933	NY	A	O		85	.280
1934	NY	A	O		106	.246
1935	CIN	N	O		121	.262
1936	CIN	N	O		59	.248
	BRTR				745	.274

BYRNE, CHARLES H.
B.SEPT.1843 NEW YORK,N.Y.
D.JAN.4,1898
NON-PLAYING MANAGER
BRO(AA) 1885-87

BYRNE, GERALD WILFRED
B.FEB.2,1907 PARNELL,MICH.
D.AUG.11,1955

YR	CL	LEA	POS	GP	G	REC
1929	CHI	A	P		3	0- 1
	BRTR					

BYRNE, JOHN K.
(PLAYED UNDER NAME OF
JOHN K. O'BRIEN)

BYRNE, ROBERT MATHEW
B.DEC.31,1885 ST.LOUIS,MO.
D.DEC.31,1964 WAYNE,PA.

YR	CL	LEA	POS	GP	G	REC
1907	STL	N	3		149	.256
1908	STL	N	3		126	.191
1909	STL	N	3		105	.214
	PIT	N	3		46	.256
1910	PIT	N	3		148	.296
1911	PIT	N	3		152	.259
1912	PIT	N	3		130	.288
1913	PIT	N	3		113	.270
	PHI	N	3		19	.224
1914	PHI	N	2-3		126	.272
1915	PHI	N	2-3		105	.209
1916	PHI	N	2-3		48	.234
1917	PHI	N	2-3		13	.357
	CHI	A	2		1	.000
	BRTR				1281	.253

BYRNE, THOMAS JOSEPH "TOMMY"
B.DEC.31,1919 BALTIMORE,MD.

YR	CL	LEA	POS	GP	G	REC
1943	NY	A	P	11	13	2- 1
1946	NY	A	P	4	14	0- 1
1947	NY	A	P		4	0- 0
1948	NY	A	P		31	8- 5
1949	NY	A	P	32	35	15- 7
1950	NY	A	P	31	34	15- 9
1951	NY	A	P		9	2- 1
	STL	A	P	19	34	4-10
1952	STL	A	P	29	40	7-14
1953	CHI	A	P	6	18	2- 0
	WAS	A	P	6	14	0- 5
1954	NY	A	P	5	7	3- 2
1955	NY	A	P	27	45	16- 5
1956	NY	A	P	37	44	7- 3
1957	NY	A	P	30	35	4- 6
	BLTL			281	377	85-69

BYRNES, JAMES JOSEPH
B.JAN.5,1880 SAN FRANCISCO,CAL.
D.JULY 31,1941

YR	CL	LEA	POS	GP	G	REC
1906	PHI	A	C		10	.167

BYRNES, MILTON JOHN "SKIPPY"
B.NOV.15,1916 ST.LOUIS,MO.

YR	CL	LEA	POS	GP	G	REC
1943	STL	A	O		129	.280
1944	STL	A	O		128	.295
1945	STL	A	1-O		133	.249
	BRTL				390	.274

CABALLERO, RALPH JOSEPH "PUTSY"
B.NOV.5,1927 NEW ORLEANS,LA.

YR	CL	LEA	POS	GP	G	REC
1944	PHI	N	3		4	.000
1945	PHI	N	3		9	.000
1947	PHI	N	2-3		2	.143
1948	PHI	N	2-3		113	.245
1949	PHI	N	2-S		29	.279
1950	PHI	N	2-S-3		46	.167
1951	PHI	N	2-S-3		84	.186
1952	PHI	N	2-S-3		35	.238
	BRTR				322	.228

CABELL, ENOS MILTON
B.OCT.8,1949 FORT RILEY,KAN.

YR	CL	LEA	POS	GP	G	REC
1972	BAL	A	1		3	.000
1973	BAL	A	1-3		32	.208
1974	BAL	A	1-2-3-O		80	.241
1975	HOU	N	1-3-O		117	.264
1976	HOU	N	1-3		144	.273
	BRTR				376	.262

CABRERA, ALFREDO A.
B.1883 CANARY ISLANDS

YR	CL	LEA	POS	GP	G	REC
1913	STL	N	S		1	.000
	TR					

CADORE, LEON JOSEPH "CADDY"
B.NOV.20,1891 CHICAGO,ILL.
D.MAR.16,1958

YR	CL	LEA	POS	GP	G	REC
1915	BRO	N	P		7	0- 2
1916	BRO	N	P		1	0- 0
1917	BRO	N	P		37	13-13
1918	BRO	N	P		2	1- 0
1919	BRO	N	P	35	37	14-12
1920	BRO	N	P		35	15-14
1921	BRO	N	P		35	13-14
1922	BRO	N	P		29	8-15
1923	BRO	N	P	8	9	4- 1
	CHI	A	P		1	0- 1
1924	NY	N	P		2	0- 0
	BRTR			192	195	68-72

CADY, CHARLES B.
B.CHICAGO,ILL.

YR	CL	LEA	POS	GP	G	REC
1883	CLE	N	P-O	1	3	0- 1
						.000
1884	CHI	U	P-O	4	6	2- 0
						.095
	KC	U	2		1	.000
				5	10	2- 1
						.056

CADY, FORREST LEROY "HICK"
B.JAN.26,1886 BISHOP HILL,ILL.
D.MAR.3,1946

YR	CL	LEA	POS	GP	G	REC
1912	BOS	A	C		47	.259
1913	BOS	A	C		39	.242
1914	BOS	A	C		61	.258
1915	BOS	A	C		78	.278
1916	BOS	A	C		78	.191
1917	BOS	A	C		17	.152
1918	CLE	A	H		1	.000
1919	PHI	N	C		34	.214
	BRTR				355	.239

```
YR  CL LEA POS  GP    G    REC
```

CAFEGO, THOMAS
B.AUG.21,1911 WHIPPLE,W.VA.
D.OCT.29,1961
```
1937 STL A  O           4    .000
     BLTR
```

CAFFIE, JOSEPH CLIFFORD "JOE"
B.FEB.14,1931 RAMER,ALA.
```
1956 CLE A  O          12    .342
1957 CLE A  O          32    .270
     BLTR              44    .291
```

CAFFYN, BENJAMIN THOMAS
B.FEB.10,1880 PEORIA,ILL.
D.NOV.22,1942
```
1906 CLE A  O          30    .194
```

CAHILL, JOHN FRANCIS
B.PHILADELPHIA,PA.
D.NOV.1,1901
```
1884 COL AA P-O  1    59    1- 0
                            .210
1886 STL N  O        125    .198
1887 IND N  O         68    .231
     BR          1   252    1- 0
                            .211
```

CAHILL, THOMAS H.
B.OCT.1868 FALL RIVER,MASS.
D.DEC.25,1894
```
1891 LOU AA P-C-S    119    0- 0
                            .263
```

CAIN, LESLIE "LES"
B.JAN.13,1948 SAN LUIS OBISPO, CAL.
```
1968 DET A  P          8    1- 0
1970 DET A  P         29   12- 7
1971 DET A  P    26   27   10- 9
1972 DET A  P          5    0- 2
     BLIL        68   69   23-19
```

CAIN, MERRITT PATRICK "SUGAR"
B.APR.5,1908 MACON,GA.
D.APR.3,1975 ATLANTA,GA.
```
1932 PHI A  P         10    3- 4
1933 PHI A  P    38   39   13-12
1934 PHI A  P         36    9-17
1935 PHI A  P          6    0- 5
     STL A  P    30   31    9- 8
1936 STL A  P          4    1- 1
     CHI A  P         31   14-10
1937 CHI A  P         18    4- 2
1938 CHI A  P          5    0- 1
     BRTR       178  180   53-60
     BB 1932-33
```

CAIN, ROBERT MAX "BOB"
B.OCT.16,1924 LONGFORD,KAN.
```
1949 CHI A  P          6    0- 0
1950 CHI A  P    34   35    9-12
1951 CHI A  P          4    1- 2
     DET A  P         35   11-10
1952 STL A  P    29   35   12-10
1953 STL A  P    32   34    4-10
1954 CHI A  H          1    .000
     BLTL       140  150   37-44
                            .196
```

CAITHAMER, GEORGE THEODORE "SIDEL"
B.JULY 22,1910 CHICAGO,ILL.
D.JUNE 1,1954
```
1934 CHI A  C          5    .316
     BRTR
```

CALDERONE, SAMUEL FRANCIS "SAM"
B.FEB.6,1926 BEVERLY,N.J.
```
1950 NY  N  C         34    .299
1953 NY  N  C         35    .222
1954 MIL N  C         22    .379
     BRTR             91    .291
```

CALDWELL, BRUCE
B.FEB.8,1906 ASHTON,R.I.
D.FEB.15,1959 WEST HAVEN,CONN.
```
1928 CLE A  O         18    .222
1932 BRO N  1          7    .091
     BRTR             25    .184
```

CALDWELL, CHARLES WILLIAM
B.AUG.2,1901 BRISTOL,VA.
D.NOV.1,1957
```
1925 NY  A  P          3    0- 0
     BRTR
```

CALDWELL, EARL WELTON "TEACH"
B.APR.9,1905 SPARKS,TEX.
```
1928 PHI N  P          5    1- 4
1935 STL A  P          6    3- 2
1936 STL A  P         41    7-16
1937 STL A  P          9    0- 0
1945 CHI A  P         27    6- 7
1946 CHI A  P         39   13- 4
1947 CHI A  P         40    1- 4
1948 CHI A  P         25    1- 5
     BOS A  P          8    1- 1
     BRTR            200   33-43
```

CALDWELL, RALPH GRANT
B.JAN.18,1884 PHILADELPHIA,PA.
```
1904 PHI N  P          6    3- 3
1905 PHI N  P          7    1- 1
     BLTL              4    4- 4
```

CALDWELL, RALPH MICHAEL "MIKE"
B.JAN.22,1949 TARBORO,N.C.
```
1971 SD  N  P          6    1- 0
1972 SD  N  P         42    7-11
1973 SD  N  P    55   56    5-14
1974 SF  N  P         31   14- 5
1975 SF  N  P         38    7-13
1976 SF  N  P         50    1- 7
     BRTL       222  223   35-50
```

CALDWELL, RAYMOND BENJAMIN "RUBE"
B.APR.26,1888 CORYDON,PA.
D.AUG.17,1967 SALAMANCA,N.Y.
```
1910 NY  A  P          6    1- 0
1911 NY  A  P    41   59   14-14
1912 NY  A  P    30   39    8-16
1913 NY  A  P    27   51    9- 8
1914 NY  A  P    31   58   17- 9
1915 NY  A  P    37   72   19-16
1916 NY  A  P    20   45    5-12
1917 NY  A  P    36   63   13-16
1918 NY  A  P-O  24   65    9- 8
                            .291
1919 BOS A  P    17   31    5- 4
     CLE A  P          8    1- 0
1920 CLE A  P    34   41   20-10
1921 CLE A  P         37    6- 6
     BLTR       347  575  133-120
                            .240
```

CALHOUN, JOHN CHARLES
B.DEC.14,1879 ALLEGHENY,PA.
D.FEB.27,1947
```
1902 STL N  1-3-O     17    .156
     BRTR
```

CALHOUN, WILLIAM DAVITTE "MARY"
B.JUNE 23,1890 CARTERSVILLE,GA.
D.FEB.11,1955
```
1913 BOS N  1          6    .076
     BLTL
```

CALIGIURI, FREDERICK JOHN
B.OCT.22,1918 W.HICKORY,PA.
```
1941 PHI A  P          5    2- 2
1942 PHI A  P         13    0- 3
     BRTR             18    2- 5
```

CALIHAN, WILLIAM T.
B.1869 OSWEGO,N.Y.
D.DEC.20,1917
```
1890 ROC AA P         48   18-13
1891 ATH AA P         16    5- 7
                      64   23-20
```

CALLAGHAN, MARTIN FRANCIS
B.JUNE 9,1900 NORWOOD,MASS.
D.JUNE 24,1975 NORFOLK,MASS.
```
1922 CHI N  O         74    .257
1923 CHI N  O         61    .225
1928 CIN N  O         81    .290
1930 CIN N  O         79    .276
     BLTL            295    .270
```

CALLAHAN, DAVID JOSEPH
B.JULY 20,1888 OTTAWA,ILL.
```
1910 CLE A  O         13    .181
1911 CLE A  O          6    .250
     BLTR             19    .194
```

CALLAHAN, EDWARD J.
B.BOSTON,MASS.
```
1884 STL U  O          1    .000
     KC  U  S          1    .250
     BOS U  O          4    .357
                       6    .286
```

CALLAHAN, JAMES J.
B.MARLBORO,MASS.
```
1902 NY  N  O          1    .000
```

CALLAHAN, JAMES JOSEPH
B.MAR.18,1874 FITCHBURG,MASS.
D.OCT.4,1934
```
1894 PHI N  P          9    2- 3
1897 CHI N  P-2- 23   90   13-10
         S-O                .308
1898 CHI N  P    31   42   20-11
1899 CHI N  P    35   45   21-12
1900 CHI N  P         33   12-16
1901 CHI A  P    27   45   15- 7
1902 CHI A  P-S- 34   68   16-14
         O                 .239
1903 CHI A  M-P-3 3  118    1- 2
                            .290
1904 CHI A  M-2-O    132    .263
1905 CHI A  O         96    .272
1911 CHI A  O        120    .281
1912 CHI A  M-O      111    .272
1913 CHI A  M-O        6    .222
     BRTR       195  915  100-75
                            .275
```
NON-PLAYING MANAGER
CHI(A) 1914 AND PIT(N) 1916-17

CALLAHAN, JAMES W.
B.MOBERLY,MO.
```
1898 STL N  P          2    0- 2
```

CALLAHAN, JOSEPH THOMAS
B.OCT.8,1916 E.BOSTON,MASS.
D.MAY 24,1949 S.BOSTON,MASS.
```
1939 BOS N  P          4    1- 0
1940 BOS N  P          6    0- 2
     BRTR             10    1- 2
```

CALLAHAN, LEO DAVID
B.AUG.9,1890 BOSTON,MASS.
```
1913 BRO N  O         33    .171
     PHI N  O         81    .230
     BLTL            114    .221
```

CALLAHAN, PATRICK J.
B.NEW YORK,N.Y.
```
1884 IND AA 3         61    .263
```

CALLAHAN, RAYMOND JAMES "PAT"
B.AUG.29,1891 ASHLAND,WIS.
D.JAN.23,1973 OLYMPIA,WASH.
```
1915 CIN N  P          3    0- 0
     BLTL
```

CALLAHAN, WESLEY LEROY
B.JULY 3,1888 LYONS,IND.
D.SEPT.13,1953
```
1913 STL N  S          7    .285
     TR
```

CALLAWAY, FRANK BURNETT
B.FEB.26,1898 KNOXVILLE,TENN.
```
1921 PHI A  S         14    .240
1922 PHI A  2         29    .270
     BRTR             43    .255
```

CALLISON, JOHN WESLEY "JOHNNY"
B.MAR.12,1939 QUALLS,OKLA.
```
1958 CHI A  O         18    .297
1959 CHI A  O         49    .173
1960 PHI N  O         99    .260
1961 PHI N  O        138    .266
1962 PHI N  O        157    .300
1963 PHI N  O        157    .284
1964 PHI N  O        162    .274
1965 PHI N  O        160    .262
1966 PHI N  O        155    .276
1967 PHI N  O        149    .261
1968 PHI N  O        121    .244
1969 PHI N  O        134    .265
1970 CHI N  O        147    .264
1971 CHI N  O        103    .210
1972 NY  A  O         92    .258
1973 NY  A  O-D       45    .176
     DLTR           1886    .264
```

CALMUS, RICHARD LEE "DICK"
B.JAN.7,1944 LOS ANGELES,CAL.
```
1963 LA  N  P         21    3- 1
1967 CHI N  P          1    0- 0
     BRTR             22    3- 1
```

YR	CL	LEA	POS	GP	G	REC

CALVERT LEO PAUL EMILE "PAUL"
B.OCT.6,1917 MONTREAL,QUE.,CAN.

YR	CL	LEA	POS	GP	G	REC
1942	CLE	A	P		1	0- 0
1943	CLE	A	P		5	0- 0
1944	CLE	A	P		35	1- 3
1945	CLE	A	P		1	0- 0
1949	WAS	A	P	34	35	6-17
1950	DET	A	P		32	2- 2
1951	DET	A	P		1	0- 0
	BRTR			109	110	9-22

CALVO, JACINTO (GONZALEZ) "JACK"
(BORN JACINTO DEL CALVO)
B.JUNE 11,1894 HAVANA,CUBA
D.JUNE 15,1965 MIAMI,FLA.

YR	CL	LEA	POS	GP	G	REC
1913	WAS	A	O		16	.242
1920	WAS	A	O		17	.043
	BLTL				33	.161

CAMBRIA, FREDERICK DENNIS "FRED"
B.JAN.22,1948 CAMBRIA HEIGHTS, N.Y.

YR	CL	LEA	POS	GP	G	REC
1970	PIT	N	P		6	1- 2
	BRTR					

CAMELLI, HENRY RICHARD "HANK"
B.DEC.12,1915 GLOUCESTER,MASS.

YR	CL	LEA	POS	GP	G	REC
1943	PIT	N	C		1	.000
1944	PIT	N	C		63	.296
1945	PIT	N	C		1	.000
1946	PIT	N	C		42	.208
1947	BOS	N	C		52	.193
	BRTR				159	.229

CAMERON, JOHN WILLIAM
B.1885 BOSTON,MASS.

YR	CL	LEA	POS	GP	G	REC
1906	BOS	N	P-O	2	18	0- 0
						.180

CAMILLI, ADOLPH LOUIS "DOLPH"
B.APR.23,1907 SAN FRANCISCO,CAL

YR	CL	LEA	POS	GP	G	REC
1933	CHI	N	1		16	.224
1934	CHI	N	1		32	.275
	PHI	N	1		102	.212
1935	PHI	N	1		156	.261
1936	PHI	N	1		151	.315
1937	PHI	N	1		131	.339
1938	BRO	N	1		146	.251
1939	BRO	N	1		157	.290
1940	BRO	N	1		142	.287
1941	BRO	N	1		149	.285
1942	BRO	N	1		150	.252
1943	BRO	N	1		95	.247
1945	BOS	A	1		63	.212
	BLTL				1490	.277

CAMILLI, DOUGLAS JOSEPH "DOUG"
B.SEP.22,1936 PHILADELPHIA,PA.

YR	CL	LEA	POS	GP	G	REC
1960	LA	N	C		6	.333
1961	LA	N	C		13	.133
1962	LA	N	C		45	.284
1963	LA	N	C		49	.162
1964	LA	N	C		50	.179
1965	WAS	A	C		75	.192
1966	WAS	A	C		44	.206
1967	WAS	A	C		30	.183
1969	WAS	A	C		1	.333
	BRTR				313	.199

CAMILLI, LOUIS STEVEN "LOU"
B.SEP.24,1946 EL PASO,TEX.

YR	CL	LEA	POS	GP	G	REC
1969	CLE	A	3		13	.000
1970	CLE	A	2-S-3		16	.000
1971	CLE	A	2-S		39	.198
1972	CLE	A	2-S		39	.146
	BBTR				107	.146

CAMMEYER, G. WILLIAM HENRY
B.MAR.20,1821 NEW YORK,N.Y.
D.SEPT.4,1898
NON-PLAYING MANAGER
MUT(NA) 1873 AND MUT(N) 1876

CAMNITZ, R. HARRY
B.OCT.26,1884 HUSTONVILLE,KY.
D.JAN.6,1951

YR	CL	LEA	POS	GP	G	REC
1909	PIT	N	P		1	0- 0
1911	STL	N	P		2	1- 0
	BRTR				3	1- 0

CAMNITZ, SAMUEL HOWARD "HOWIE"
B.AUG.22,1881 COVINGTON,KY.
D.MAR.2,1960

YR	CL	LEA	POS	GP	G	REC
1904	PIT	N	P		10	1- 2
1906	PIT	N	P		2	1- 0
1907	PIT	N	P		31	13- 8
1908	PIT	N	P		38	16- 9
1909	PIT	N	P		41	25- 6
1910	PIT	N	P		38	12-13
1911	PIT	N	P		40	20-15
1912	PIT	N	P		41	22-12
1913	PIT	N	P		36	6-17
	PHI	N	P		9	3- 3
1914	PIT	F	P		36	14-19
1915	PIT	F	P		4	0- 0
	BRTR				326	133-104

CAMP, HOWARD LEE "RED"
B.JULY 1,1894 MUMFORD,ALA.
D.MAY 8,1960 EASTABOGA,ALA.

YR	CL	LEA	POS	GP	G	REC
1917	NY	A	O		5	.286
	BLTR					

CAMP, LLEWELLYN ROBERT
B.FEB.22,1868 COLUMBUS,OHIO
D.OCT.1,1948

YR	CL	LEA	POS	GP	G	REC
1892	STL	N	3		43	.204
1893	CHI	N	3		38	.268
1894	CHI	N	2		8	.156
	TR				89	.229

CAMP, RICK LAMAR
B.JUNE 10,1953 TRION,GA.

YR	CL	LEA	POS	GP	G	REC
1976	ATL	N	P		5	0- 1
	BRTR					

CAMP, WINFIELD SCOTT "KID"
B.1870 COLUMBUS,OHIO
D.MAR.2,1895

YR	CL	LEA	POS	GP	G	REC
1892	PIT	N	P		4	0- 2
1894	CHI	N	P		3	0- 1
					7	0- 3

CAMPANELLA, ROY
B.NOV.19,1921 PHILADELPHIA,PA.

YR	CL	LEA	POS	GP	G	REC
1948	BRO	N	C		83	.258
1949	BRO	N	C		130	.287
1950	BRO	N	C		126	.281
1951	BRO	N	C		143	.325
1952	BRO	N	C		128	.269
1953	BRO	N	C		144	.312
1954	BRO	N	C		111	.207
1955	BRO	N	C		123	.318
1956	BRO	N	C		124	.219
1957	BRO	N	C		103	.242
	BRTR				1215	.276

CAMPANERIS, DAGBERTO BLANCO "BERT" OR "CAMPY"
(BORN DAGBERTO CAMPANERIA)
B.MAR.9,1942 PUEBLO NUEVO,CUBA

YR	CL	LEA	POS	GP	G	REC
1964	KC	A	S-3-O		67	.257
1965	KC	A	ALL	1	144	0- 0
						.270
1966	KC	A	S		142	.267
1967	KC	A	S		147	.248
1968	OAK	A	S-O		159	.276
1969	OAK	A	S		135	.260
1970	OAK	A	S		147	.279
1971	OAK	A	S		134	.251
1972	OAK	A	S		149	.240
1973	OAK	A	S		151	.250
1974	OAK	A	S		134	.290
1975	OAK	A	S		137	.265
1976	OAK	A	S		149	.256
	BRTR			1	1795	0- 0
						.262

CAMPANIS, ALEXANDER SEBASTIAN
B.NOV.2,1916 COS,DODECANESE IS.

YR	CL	LEA	POS	GP	G	REC
1943	BRO	N	2		7	.100
	BBTR					

CAMPANIS, JAMES ALEXANDER "JIM"
B.FEB.9,1944 NEW YORK,N.Y.

YR	CL	LEA	POS	GP	G	REC
1966	LA	N	C		1	.000
1967	LA	N	C		41	.161
1968	LA	N	C		4	.091
1969	KC	A	C		30	.157
1970	KC	A	C-O		31	.130
1973	PIT	N	H		6	.167
	BRTR				113	.147

CAMPAU, CHARLES C. "COUNT"
B.OCT.17,1863 DETROIT,MICH.
D.APR.3,1938

YR	CL	LEA	POS	GP	G	REC
1888	DET	N	O		70	.203
1890	STL	AA	M-O		74	.274
1894	WAS	N	O		2	.142
					146	.245

CAMPBELL, ARCHIBALD STEWART "ARCHIE" OR "IRON MAN"
B.OCT.20,1903 MAPLEWOOD,N.J.

YR	CL	LEA	POS	GP	G	REC
1928	NY	A	P		13	0- 1
1929	WAS	A	P		4	0- 1
1930	CIN	N	P		23	2- 4
	BRTR				40	2- 6

CAMPBELL, ARTHUR VINCENT "VIN"
B.JAN.30,1888 ST.LOUIS,MO.
D.NOV.16,1969 WHITE HALL,MD.

YR	CL	LEA	POS	GP	G	REC
1908	CHI	N	O		1	.000
1910	PIT	N	O		74	.326
1911	PIT	N	O		21	.312
1912	BOS	N	O		145	.296
1914	IND	F	O		133	.315
1915	NEW	F	O		127	.314
	BLTR				501	.310

CAMPBELL, BRUCE DOUGLAS
B.OCT.20,1909 CHICAGO,ILL.

YR	CL	LEA	POS	GP	G	REC
1930	CHI	A	O		5	.500
1931	CHI	A	O		4	.412
1932	CHI	A	O		7	.222
	STL	A	O		139	.285
1933	STL	A	O		148	.277
1934	STL	A	O		138	.279
1935	CLE	A	O		80	.325
1936	CLE	A	O		76	.372
1937	CLE	A	O		134	.301
1938	CLE	A	O		133	.290
1939	CLE	A	O		130	.287
1940	DET	A	O		103	.283
1941	DET	A	O		141	.275
1942	WAS	A	O		122	.278
	BLTR				1360	.290

CAMPBELL, CLARENCE "SOUP"
B.MAR.7,1917 SPARTA,VA.

YR	CL	LEA	POS	GP	G	REC
1940	CLE	A	O		35	.226
1941	CLE	A	O		104	.250
	BLTR				139	.246

CAMPBELL, DAVID WILSON "DAVE"
B.JAN.14,1942 MANISTEE,MICH.

YR	CL	LEA	POS	GP	G	REC
1967	DET	A	1		2	.000
1968	DET	A	2		9	.125
1969	DET	A	1-2-3		32	.103
1970	SD	N	2		154	.219
1971	SD	N	1-2-S-3-	108		.227
			O			
1972	SD	N	2-3		33	.240
1973	SD	N	1-2-3		33	.224
	STL	N	2		13	.000
	HOU	N	1-3-O		9	.267
1974	HOU	N	1-2-3-O		35	.087
	BRTR				428	.213

CAMPBELL, HUGH
D.1881

YR	CL	LEA	POS	GP	G	REC
1873	RES	NA	P-2-O		19	2-15
						-

CAMPBELL, JAMES ROBERT "JIM"
B.JUNE 24,1937 PALO ALTO,CAL.

YR	CL	LEA	POS	GP	G	REC
1962	HOU	N	C		27	.221
1963	HOU	N	C		55	.222
	BRTR				82	.221

CAMPBELL, JAMES ROBERT "JIM"
B.JAN.10,1943 HARTSVILLE,S.C.

YR	CL	LEA	POS	GP	G	REC
1970	STL	N	H		13	.231
	BLTR					

CAMPBELL, JOHN MILLARD
B.SEPT.13,1907 WASHINGTON,D.C.

YR	CL	LEA	POS	GP	G	REC
1933	WAS	A	P		1	0- 0
	BRTR					

CAMPBELL, JOSEPH EARL "JOE"
B.MAR.10,1944 LOUISVILLE,KY.

YR	CL	LEA	POS	GP	G	REC
1967	CHI	N	O		1	.000
	BRTR					

CAMPBELL, MARC THADDEUS
B.NOV.29,1884 PUNXSUTAWNEY,PA.
D.FEB.13,1946 NEW BETHLEHEM,PA.

YR	CL	LEA	POS	GP	G	REC
1907	PIT	N	S		2	.250
	BLTR					

YR	CL	LEA	POS	GP	G	REC

CAMPBELL, MICHAEL
B.NEW JERSEY
| 1873 | RES | NA | 1-S-O | 20 | | - |

CAMPBELL, PAUL MC LAUGHLIN
B.SEPT.1,1917 PAW CREEK,N.C.
1941	BOS	A	H	1		.000
1942	BOS	A	O	26		.067
1946	BOS	A	1	28		.115
1948	DET	A	1	59		.265
1949	DET	A	1	87		.278
1950	DET	A	H	3		.000
		BLTL		204		.255

CAMPBELL, RONALD THOMAS "RON"
B.APR.5,1940 CHATTANOGA,TENN.
1964	CHI	N	2	26		.272
1965	CHI	N	H	2		.000
1966	CHI	N	S-3	24		.217
		BRTR		52		.247

CAMPBELL, SAMUEL
B.PHILADELPHIA,PA.
| 1890 | ATH | AA | 2 | 2 | | .000 |

CAMPBELL, WILLIAM GILTHORPE "GILLY"
B.FEB.13,1908 KANSAS CITY,KAN.
D.FEB.21,1973 LOS ANGELES,CAL.
1933	CHI	N	C	46		.281
1935	CIN	N	C-1-O	88		.257
1936	CIN	N	C-1	89		.268
1937	CIN	N	C	18		.275
1938	BRO	N	C	54		.246
		BLTR		295		.263

CAMPBELL, WILLIAM JAMES "BILL"
B.NOV.5,1873 PITTSBURGH,PA.
D.OCT.6,1957 CINCINNATI,OHIO
1905	STL	N	P	2	1- 1
1907	CIN	N	P	3	2- 0
1908	CIN	N	P	55	12-13
1909	CIN	N	P	30	7-11
		BLTL		70	22-25

CAMPBELL, WILLIAM RICHARD "BILL"
B.AUG.9,1948 HIGHLAND PARK,MICH.
1973	MIN	A	P	28	3- 3
1974	MIN	A	P	63	8- 7
1975	MIN	A	P	47	4- 6
1976	MIN	A	P	78	17- 5
		BLTR		216	32-15

CAMPFIELD, WILLIAM HOLTON "SAL"
B.FEB.19,1868 MEADVILLE,PA.
D.MAY 16,1952
| 1896 | NY | N | P | 6 | 0- 1 |
| | | BRTR | | | |

CAMPISI, SALVATORE JOHN "SAL"
B.AUG.11,1942 BROOKLYN,N.Y.
1969	STL	N	P	7	1- 0
1970	STL	N	P	37	2- 2
1971	MIN	A	P	6	0- 0
		BRTR		50	3- 2

CAMPOS, FRANCISCO JOSE (LOPEZ) "FRANK"
B.MAY 11,1924 HAVANA,CUBA
1951	WAS	A	O	8		.423
1952	WAS	A	O	53		.259
1953	WAS	A	H	10		.111
		BLTL		71		.279

CANAVAN, HUGH EDWARD
B.MAY 13,1897 WORCESTER,MASS.
| 1918 | BOS | N | P | 16 | 0- 4 |
| | | BLTL | | | |

CANAVAN, JAMES E.
B.NOV.26,1866 NEW BEDFORD,MASS.
D.MAY 27,1949
1891	CIN	AA	S	91		.253
	MIL	AA	2-S	34		.268
1892	CHI	N	2	118		.166
1893	CIN	N	O	118		.238
1894	CIN	N	O	100		.293
1897	BRO	N	2	63		.222
		BRTR		524		.231

CANDELARIA, JOHN ROBERT
B.NOV.6,1953 NEW YORK,N.Y.
1975	PIT	N	P	18	8- 6
1976	PIT	N	P	32	16- 7
		BLTL		50	24-13

CANDINI, MARIO CAIN "MILO"
B.AUG.3,1917 MANTECA,CAL.
1943	WAS	A	P	28	11- 7
1944	WAS	A	P	28	6- 7
1946	WAS	A	P	9	2- 0
1947	WAS	A	P	38	3- 4
1948	WAS	A	P	35	2- 3
1949	WAS	A	P	3	0- 0
1950	PHI	N	P	18	1- 0
1951	PHI	N	P	15	1- 0
		BRTR		174	26-21

CANNELL, WIRT VIRGIN "RIP"
B.JAN.23,1880 NAPLES,ME.
D.AUG.26,1948
1904	BOS	N	O	93		.234
1905	BOS	N	O	154		.247
		BLTL		247		.242

CANNIZZARO, CHRISTOPHER JOHN "CHRIS"
B.MAY 3,1938 OAKLAND,CAL.
1960	STL	N	C	7		.222
1961	STL	N	C	6		.500
1962	NY	N	C-O	59		.241
1963	NY	N	C	16		.242
1964	NY	N	C	60		.311
1965	NY	N	C	114		.183
1968	PIT	N	C	25		.241
1969	SD	N	C	134		.220
1970	SD	N	C	111		.279
1971	SD	N	C	21		.190
	CHI	N	C	71		.213
1972	LA	N	C	73		.240
1973	LA	N	C	17		.190
1974	SD	N	C	26		.183
		BRTR		740		.235

CANTILLON, JOSEPH D. "PONGO"
B.AUG.19,1861 JANESVILLE,WIS.
D.JAN.31,1930 HICKMAN,KY.
NON-PLAYING MANAGER
WAS(A) 1907-09

CANTRELL, GUY DEWEY "GUNNER"
B.APR.9,1904 CLARITA,OKLA.
D.JAN.31,1961
1925	BRO	N	P	14	1- 0
1927	BRO	N	P	6	0- 0
	PHI	N	P	2	0- 2
1930	DET	A	P	16	1- 5
		BRTR		38	2- 7

CANTWELL, BENJAMIN CALDWELL
B.APR.13,1902 MILAN,TENN.
D.DEC.4,1962
1927	NY	N	P	5	1- 1
1928	NY	N	P	7	1- 0
	BOS	N	P	22	3- 3
1929	BOS	N	P	27	4-13
1930	BOS	N	P	31	34	9-15
1931	BOS	N	P	33	40	7- 9
1932	BOS	N	P		37	13-11
1933	BOS	N	P	40	49	20-10
1934	BOS	N	P	27	29	5-11
1935	BOS	N	P	39	41	4-25
1936	BOS	N	P	34	35	9- 9
1937	NY	N	P		1	0- 1
	BRO	N	P		13	0- 0
		BRTR		316	340	76-108

CANTWELL, MICHAEL JOSEPH
B.JAN.15,1896 WASHINGTON,D.C.
D.JAN.9,1953
1916	NY	A	P	1	0- 0
1919	PHI	N	P	5	1- 3
1920	PHI	N	P	5	0- 3
		BLTL		11	1- 6

CANTWELL, THOMAS ALOYSIUS
B.DEC.23,1888 WASHINGTON,D.C.
D.APR.1,1968 WASHINGTON,D.C.
1909	CIN	N	P	6	1- 0
1910	CIN	N	P	2	0- 0
		BLTR		8	1- 0

CANTZ, BARTHOLOMEW L.
B.JAN.29,1860 PHILADELPHIA,PA.
D.FEB.12,1943
1888	BAL	AA	C	37		.165
1889	BAL	AA	C	21		.158
1890	ATH	AA	C	5		.096
				63		.157

CAPILLA, DOUGLAS EDMUND "DOUG"
B.JAN.7,1952 HONOLULU,HAWAII
| 1976 | STL | N | P | 7 | 1- 0 |
| | | BLTL | | | |

CAPRA, LEE WILLIAM "BUZZ"
B.OCT.1,1947 CHICAGO,ILL.
1971	NY	N	P	3	0- 1
1972	NY	N	P	14	3- 2
1973	NY	N	P	24	2- 7
1974	ATL	N	P	39	16- 8
1975	ATL	N	P	12	4- 7
1976	ATL	N	P	5	0- 1
		BRTR		97	25-26

CAPRI, PATRICK NICHOLAS
B.NOV.7,1918 NEW YORK,N.Y.
| 1944 | BOS | N | 2 | 7 | | .000 |
| | | BRTR | | | |

CAPRON, RALPH EARL
B.MAR.11,1893 MINNEAPOLIS,MINN.
1912	PIT	N	O	1		.000
1913	PHI	N	O	5		.000
		BLTR		6		.000

CARAWAY, CECIL BRADFORD PATRICK "PAT"
B.SEPT.26,1905 ERATH CO.,TEX.
D.JUNE 9,1974 EL PASO,TEX.
1930	CHI	A	P		38	10-10
1931	CHI	A	P	51	52	10-24
1932	CHI	A	P		19	2- 6
		BLTL		108	109	22-40

CARBINE, JOHN C.
B.1852 SYRACUSE,N.Y.
1875	WES	NA	1	10		-
1876	LOU	N	1	6		.150
				16		-

CARBO, BERNARDO "BERNIE"
B.AUG.5,1947 DETROIT,MICH.
1969	CIN	N	H	4		.000
1970	CIN	N	O	125		.310
1971	CIN	N	O	106		.219
1972	CIN	N	O	19		.143
	STL	N	3-O	99		.258
1973	STL	N	O	111		.286
1974	BOS	A	O-O	117		.249
1975	BOS	A	O-O	107		.257
1976	BOS	A	O-O	17		.236
	MIL	A	O-O	69		.235
		BLTR		774		.260

CARDEN, JOHN BRUTON
B.MAY 19,1921 KILLEEN,TEX.
D.FEB.8,1949 MEXIA,TEX.
| 1946 | NY | N | P | 1 | 0- 0 |
| | | BRTR | | | |

CARDENAL, JOSE ROSARIO DOMEC
(REAL NAME
JOSE ROSARIO DOMEC (CARDENAL))
B.OCT.7,1943 MATANZAS,CUBA
1963	SF	N	O	9		.200
1964	SF	N	O	20		.000
1965	CAL	A	2-S-O	134		.250
1966	CAL	A	O	154		.276
1967	CAL	A	O	108		.236
1968	CLE	A	O	157		.257
1969	CLE	A	3-O	146		.257
1970	STL	N	O	148		.293
1971	STL	N	O	89		.243
	MIL	A	O	53		.258
1972	CHI	N	O	143		.291
1973	CHI	N	O	145		.303
1974	CHI	N	O	143		.293
1975	CHI	N	O	154		.317
1976	CHI	N	O	136		.299
		BRTR		1739		.277

YR	CL	LEA	POS	GP	G	REC

CARDENAS, LEONARDO ALFONSO (LAZARO) "LEO" OR "CHICO"
B.DEC.17,1938 MATANZAS,CUBA

YR	CL	LEA	POS	GP	G	REC
1960	CIN	N	S		48	.232
1961	CIN	N	S		74	.308
1962	CIN	N	S		153	.294
1963	CIN	N	S		158	.235
1964	CIN	N	S		163	.251
1965	CIN	N	S		156	.287
1966	CIN	N	S		160	.255
1967	CIN	N	S		108	.256
1968	CIN	N	S		137	.235
1969	MIN	A	S		160	.280
1970	MIN	A	S		160	.247
1971	MIN	A	S		153	.264
1972	CAL	A	S		150	.223
1973	CLE	A	S-3		72	.215
1974	TEX	A	S-3		34	.272
1975	TEX	A	2-S-3		55	.235
		BRTR			1941	.257

CARDINAL, CONRAD SETH
B.MAR.30,1942 BROOKLYN,N.Y.

YR	CL	LEA	POS	GP	G	REC
1963	HOU	N	P		6	0- 1
		BRTR				

CARDONI, ARMAND JOSEPH "BIG BEN"
B.AUG.21,1921 JESSUP,PA.
D.APR.2,1969 JESSUP,PA.

YR	CL	LEA	POS	GP	G	REC
1943	BOS	N	P		11	0- 0
1944	BOS	N	P	22	29	0- 6
1945	BOS	N	P		3	0- 0
		BRTR		36	43	0- 6

CARDWELL, DONALD EUGENE "DON"
B.DEC.7,1935 WINSTON-SALEM,N.C.

YR	CL	LEA	POS	GP	G	REC
1957	PHI	N	P		30	4- 8
1958	PHI	N	P		16	3- 6
1959	PHI	N	P	25	26	9-10
1960	PHI	N	P		5	1- 2
	CHI	N	P	31	33	8-14
1961	CHI	N	P	39	40	15-14
1962	CHI	N	P		41	7-16
1963	PIT	N	P		33	13-15
1964	PIT	N	P		4	1- 2
1965	PIT	N	P		37	13-10
1966	PIT	N	P		32	6- 6
1967	NY	N	P	26	27	5- 9
1968	NY	N	P	29	30	7-13
1969	NY	N	P		30	8-10
1970	NY	N	P		16	0- 2
	ATL	N	P		16	2- 1
		BRTR		410	416	102-138

CAREW, RODNEY CLINE "ROD"
B.OCT.1,1945 GATUN,PANAMA

YR	CL	LEA	POS	GP	G	REC
1967	MIN	A	2		137	.292
1968	MIN	A	2-S		127	.273
1969	MIN	A	2		123	.332
1970	MIN	A	1-2		51	.366
1971	MIN	A	2-3		147	.307
1972	MIN	A	2		142	.318
1973	MIN	A	2		149	.350
1974	MIN	A	2		153	.364
1975	MIN	A	1-2		143	.359
1976	MIN	A	1-2		156	.331
		BLTR			1328	.328

CAREY, ANDREW ARTHUR "ANDY" (REAL NAME ANDREW ARTHUR NORDSTROM)
B.OCT.18,1931 OAKLAND,CAL.

YR	CL	LEA	POS	GP	G	REC
1952	NY	A	S-3	16		.150
1953	NY	A	2-S-3	51		.321
1954	NY	A	3	122		.302
1955	NY	A	3	135		.257
1956	NY	A	3	132		.237
1957	NY	A	3	85		.255
1958	NY	A	3	102		.286
1959	NY	A	3	41		.257
1960	NY	A	3-0	4		.333
	KC	A	3	102		.233
1961	KC	A	3	39		.244
	CHI	A	3	56		.266
1962	LA	N	3	53		.234
		BRTR		938		.260

CAREY, GEORGE C. "SCOOPS"
B.DEC.4,1870 E.LIVERPOOL,OHIO
D.DEC.17,1916

YR	CL	LEA	POS	GP	G	REC
1895	BAL	N	1		123	.271
1898	LOU	N	1		8	.187
1902	WAS	A	1		120	.316
1903	WAS	A	1		48	.198
		BRTR			299	.275

CAREY, MAX GEORGE (REAL NAME MAXIMILIAN CARNARIUS)
B.JAN.11,1890 TERRE HAUTE,IND.
D.MAY 30,1976 MIAMI,FLA.

YR	CL	LEA	POS	GP	G	REC
1910	PIT	N	0		2	.500
1911	PIT	N	0		122	.258
1912	PIT	N	0		150	.302
1913	PIT	N	0		154	.277
1914	PIT	N	0		156	.243
1915	PIT	N	0		140	.254
1916	PIT	N	0		154	.264
1917	PIT	N	0		155	.296
1918	PIT	N	0		126	.274
1919	PIT	N	0		66	.307
1920	PIT	N	0		130	.289
1921	PIT	N	0		140	.309
1922	PIT	N	0		155	.329
1923	PIT	N	0		153	.308
1924	PIT	N	0		149	.297
1925	PIT	N	0		133	.343
1926	PIT	N	0		86	.222
	BRO	N	0		27	.260
1927	BRO	N	0		144	.266
1928	BRO	N	0		108	.247
1929	BRO	N	0		19	.304
		BBTR			2469	.285

NON-PLAYING MANAGER
BRO(N) 1932-33

CAREY, THOMAS FRANCIS ALOYSIUS "SCOOPS"
B.OCT.11,1906 HOBOKEN,N.J.
D.FEB.21,1970 ROCHESTER,N.Y.

YR	CL	LEA	POS	GP	G	REC
1935	STL	A	2		76	.291
1936	STL	A	2		134	.273
1937	STL	A	2-S		130	.275
1939	BOS	A	2-S		54	.242
1940	BOS	A	2-S-3		43	.323
1941	BOS	A	2-S		24	.200
1942	BOS	A	2		1	1?000
1946	BOS	A	2		3	.200
		BRTR			465	.275

CAREY, THOMAS JOHN (REAL NAME J. J. NORTON)
B.1849 BROOKLYN,N.J.
D.FEB.13,1899

YR	CL	LEA	POS	GP	G	REC
1871	KEK	NA	2		19	–
1872	BAL	NA	1-2-S-3		41	.296
			0			
1873	BAL	NA	2-S-3		55	–
1874	MUT	NA	2-S		64	–
1875	HAR	NA	S		85	–
1876	HAR	N	S		68	.301
1877	HAR	N	S		60	.255
1878	PRO	N	S		59	.251
1879	CLE	N	S		80	.238
		TR			531	–

CARGO, ROBERT J. "CHIC"
B.1871 PITTSBURGH,PA.
D.APR.27,1904

YR	CL	LEA	POS	GP	G	REC
1892	PIT	N	S		2	.200
		BRTR				

CARISCH, FREDERICK BEHLMER
B.NOV.14,1881 FOUNTAIN CITY,WIS

YR	CL	LEA	POS	GP	G	REC
1903	PIT	N	C		5	.352
1904	PIT	N	C-1		36	.248
1905	PIT	N	C		30	.206
1906	PIT	N	C		4	.083
1912	CLE	A	C		24	.275
1913	CLE	A	C		81	.216
1914	CLE	A	C		40	.216
1923	DET	A	C		2	.000
		BRTR			222	.228

CARL, FREDERICK E.
B.1858 BALTIMORE,MD.
D.JULY 30,1897

YR	CL	LEA	POS	GP	G	REC
1889	LOU	AA	2-0		25	.202

CARL, LEWIS
B.BALTIMORE,MD.

YR	CL	LEA	POS	GP	G	REC
1874	BAL	NA	C		1	.000

CARLETON, JAMES
B.1849 NEW YORK

YR	CL	LEA	POS	GP	G	REC
1871	CLE	NA	1		29	–
1872	CLE	NA	1		7	.316
					36	–

CARLETON, JAMES OTTO "TEX"
B.AUG.19,1906 COMANCHE,TEX.

YR	CL	LEA	POS	GP	G	REC
1932	STL	N	P		44	10-13
1933	STL	N	P	44	46	17-11
1934	STL	N	P	40	41	16-11
1935	CHI	N	P		31	11- 8
1936	CHI	N	P		35	14-10
1937	CHI	N	P	32	34	16- 8
1938	CHI	N	P		33	10- 9
1940	BRO	N	P		34	6- 6
		BBTR		293	298	100-76

CARLIN, JAMES ARTHUR
B.FEB.23,1918 WYLAM,ALA.

YR	CL	LEA	POS	GP	G	REC
1941	PHI	N	3-0		16	.143
		BRTR				

CARLISLE, WALTER G. "ROSY"
B.JULY 6,1883 YEADON,ENGLAND
D.MAY 27,1945

YR	CL	LEA	POS	GP	G	REC
1908	BOS	A	0		3	.100

CARLOCK, JOHN H.

YR	CL	LEA	POS	GP	G	REC
1912	CLE	A	H		1	.000

CARLOS, FRANCISCO MANUEL "CISCO"
B.SEP.17,1940 MONROVIA,CAL.

YR	CL	LEA	POS	GP	G	REC
1967	CHI	A	P		2	2- 0
1968	CHI	A	P		29	4-14
1969	CHI	A	P		25	4- 3
	WAS	A	P		6	1- 1
1970	WAS	A	P		5	0- 0
		BRTR			73	11-18

CARLSEN, DONALD HERBERT "DON"
B.OCT.15,1926 CHICAGO,ILL.

YR	CL	LEA	POS	GP	G	REC
1948	CHI	N	P		1	0- 0
1951	PIT	N	P		7	2- 3
1952	PIT	N	P		5	0- 1
		BRTR			13	2- 4

CARLSON, HAROLD GUST
B.MAY 17,1892 ROCKFORD,ILL.
D.MAY 28,1930

YR	CL	LEA	POS	GP	G	REC
1917	PIT	N	P		34	7-11
1918	PIT	N	P		3	0- 1
1919	PIT	N	P		22	8-10
1920	PIT	N	P		39	14-13
1921	PIT	N	P		31	4- 8
1922	PIT	N	P		39	9-12
1923	PIT	N	P		4	0- 0
1924	PHI	N	P	38	39	8-17
1925	PHI	N	P	35	38	13-14
1926	PHI	N	P	35	38	17-12
1927	PHI	N	P	11	12	4- 5
	CHI	N	P		27	12- 8
1928	CHI	N	P		20	3- 2
1929	CHI	N	P		31	11- 5
1930	CHI	N	P		8	4- 2
		BRTR		377	385	114-120

CARLSON, JOSEPH MARTIN NAPOLEON (PLAYED UNDER NAME OF JOSEPH MARTIN NAPOLEON MUNSON)

CARLSON, LEON ALTON
B.FEB.17,1897 JAMESTOWN,N.Y.
D.SEPT.15,1961

YR	CL	LEA	POS	GP	G	REC
1920	WAS	A	P		3	0- 0
		BRTR				

CARLSTROM, ALBIN OSCAR "SWEDE"
B.OCT.26,1886 ELIZABETH,N.J.
D.APR.28,1935

YR	CL	LEA	POS	GP	G	REC
1911	BOS	A	S		2	.167
		BRTR				

CARLTON, STEVEN NORMAN "STEVE"
B.DEC.22,1944 MIAMI,FLA.

YR	CL	LEA	POS	GP	G	REC
1965	STL	N	P		15	0- 0
1966	STL	N	P		9	3- 3
1967	STL	N	P		30	14- 9
1968	STL	N	P	34	35	13-11
1969	STL	N	P	31	32	17-11
1970	STL	N	P		34	10-19
1971	STL	N	P		37	20- 9
1972	PHI	N	P		41	27-10
1973	PHI	N	P		40	13-20
1974	PHI	N	P		39	16-13
1975	PHI	N	P		37	15-14
1976	PHI	N	P		35	20- 7
		BLTL		382	384	168-126

YR	CL LEA POS	GP	G	REC

CARLYLE, HIRAM CLEO
B.SEPT.7,1903 FAIRBURN,GA.
D.NOV.12,1967 LOS ANGELES,CAL.
1927 BOS A O 95 .234
BLTR

CARLYLE, ROY EDWARD "DIZZY"
B.DEC.10,1900 BUFORD,GA.
D.NOV.22,1956
1925 WAS A O 1 .000
BOS A O 93 .326
1926 BOS A O 45 .285
NY A O 35 .385
BLTR 174 .318

CARMEL, LEON JAMES "DUKE"
B.APR.23,1937 NEW YORK,N.Y.
1959 STL N O 10 .130
1960 STL N 1-O 4 .000
1963 STL N 1-O 57 .227
NY N 1-O 47 .235
1965 NY A 1 6 .000
BLTL 124 .211

CARMEN, GEORGE W.
B.DOYLESTOWN,PA
1890 ATH AA S 25 .151

CARMICHAEL, CHESTER RALPH
B.SEPT.9,1888 EATON,IND.
D.AUG.23,1960
1909 CIN N P 2 0- 0
BRTR

CARNARIUS, MAXIMILIAN
(PLAYED UNDER NAME OF
MAX GEORGE CAREY)

CARNETT, EDWIN ELLIOTT "LEFTY"
B.OCT.21,1916 SPRINGFIELD,MO.
1941 BOS N P 2 0- 0
1944 CHI A P-1-O 2 126 0- 0
.276
1945 CLE A P-O 2 30 0- 0
.219
BLTR 6 158 0- 0
.268

CARNEY, JOHN JOSEPH "JACK"
B.NOV.10,1866 SALEM,MASS.
D.OCT.19,1925 LITCHFIELD,N.H.
1889 WAS N 1-O 69 .230
1890 BUF P 1 28 .262
CLE P O 25 .344
1891 CIN AA 1 91 .276
MIL AA 1 30 .291
BRTR 243 .270

CARNEY, PATRICK JOSEPH "DOC"
B.AUG.7,1876 HOLYOKE,MASS.
D.JAN.9,1953
1901 BOS N O 13 .302
1902 BOS N P-O 2 137 0- 1
.266
1903 BOS N P-O 10 102 4- 4
.240
1904 BOS N P-O 5 76 0- 2
.204
BLTL 17 328 4- 7
.245

CARNEY, WILLIAM J.
B.1878 ST.PAUL,MINN.
1904 CHI N P 2 .000

CARPENTER, LEWIS EMMETT
B.AUG.16,1915 WOODSTOCK,GA.
1943 WAS A P 4 0- 0
BRTR

CARPENTER, PAUL CALVIN
B.AUG.12,1894 GRANVILLE,OHIO
D.MAR.14,1968 NEWARK,OHIO
1916 PIT N P 5 0- 0
BRTR

CARPENTER, ROBERT LOUIS
B.DEC.12,1917 CHICAGO,ILL.
1940 NY N P 5 2- 0
1941 NY N P 29 11- 6
1942 NY N P 28 11-10
1946 NY N P 12 1- 3
1947 NY N P 2 0- 0
CHI N P 4 0- 1
BRTR 80 25-20

CARPENTER, WARREN WILLIAM
"HICK"
B.AUG.16,1855 GRAFTON,MASS.
D.APR.18,1937
1879 SYR N 1-3-O 63 .201
1880 CIN N 1-3 76 .243
1881 WOR N 3 82 .209
1882 CIN AA 3 80 .354
1883 CIN AA 3 94 .308
1884 CIN AA 3-O 109 .265
1885 CIN AA 3 112 .291
1886 CIN AA 3 111 .221
1887 CIN AA 3 127 .269
1888 CIN AA 3 135 .269
1889 CIN AA 1-3 123 .257
1892 STL N 3 1 .333
BRTL 1113 .264

CARPIN, FRANK DOMINIC
B.SEP.14,1938 BROOKLYN,N.Y.
1965 PIT N P 39 3- 1
1966 HOU N P 10 1- 0
BLTL 49 4- 1

CARR, CHARLES CARBITT
B.DEC.27,1876 COATESVILLE,PA.
D.NOV.25,1932
1898 WAS N 1 20 .197
1901 PHI A 1 2 .125
1903 DET A 1 135 .282
1904 DET A 1 91 .270
CLE A 1 32 .223
1905 CLE A 1 89 .235
1906 CIN N 1 22 .191
1914 IND F 1 115 .292
BRTR 506 .251

CARR, LEWIS SMITH
B.AUG.15,1872 UNION SPRINGS,N.Y
D.JUNE 15,1954
1901 PIT N S 9 .233
TR

CARRASQUEL, ALEJANDRO ALEXANDER
APARICIO "ALEX"
(REAL NAME
ALEJANDRO CARRASQUEL ELROY)
B.JULY 24,1912 CARACAS,VENEZ.
D.AUG.19,1969 CARACAS,VENEZ.
1939 WAS A P 40 5- 9
1940 WAS A P 28 6- 2
1941 WAS A P 35 6- 2
1942 WAS A P 35 7- 7
1943 WAS A P 39 11- 7
1944 WAS A P 43 8- 7
1945 WAS A P 35 7- 5
1949 CHI A P 3 0- 0
BRTR 258 50-39

CARRASQUEL, ALFONSO (COLON)
"CHICO"
B.JAN.23,1928 CARACAS,VENEZ.
1950 CHI A S 141 .282
1951 CHI A S 147 .264
1952 CHI A S 100 .248
1953 CHI A S 149 .279
1954 CHI A S 155 .255
1955 CHI A S 145 .256
1956 CLE A S-3 141 .243
1957 CLE A S 125 .276
1958 CLE A S-3 49 .256
KC A S-3 59 .213
1959 BAL A 1-2-S-3 114 .223
BRTR 1325 .258

CARREON, CAMILO (GARCIA) "CAM"
B.AUG.6,1937 COLTON,CAL.
1959 CHI A C 1 .000
1960 CHI A C 8 .235
1961 CHI A C 78 .271
1962 CHI A C 106 .256
1963 CHI A C 101 .274
1964 CHI A C 37 .274
1965 CLE A C 19 .231
1966 BAL A C 4 .222
BRTR 354 .264

CARRICK, WILLIAM MARTIN
"DOUGHNUT BILL"
B.SEPT.5,1873 ERIE,PA.
D.MAR.7,1932
1898 NY N P 5 3- 1
1899 NY N P 44 16-25
1900 NY N P 42 19-21
1901 WAS A P 42 15-22
1902 WAS A P-O 31 33 12-17
.187
TR 164 166 65-86
.161

CARRIGAN, WILLIAM FRANCIS
"ROUGH"
B.OCT.22,1883 LEWISTON,ME.
D.JULY 8,1969 LEWISTON,ME.
1906 BOS A C 37 .211
1908 BOS A C 57 .235
1909 BOS A C 94 .296
1910 BOS A C 114 .249
1911 BOS A C 72 .289
1912 BOS A C 87 .263
1913 BOS A M-C 85 .242
1914 BOS A M-C 81 .253
1915 BOS A M-C 46 .200
1916 BOS A M-C 33 .270
BRTR 706 .257
NON-PLAYING MANAGER
BOS(A) 1927-29

CARRITHERS, DONALD GEORGE "DON"
B.SEP.15,1949 LYNWOOD,CAL.
1970 SF N P 11 2- 1
1971 SF N P 22 5- 3
1972 SF N P 25 26 4- 8
1973 SF N P 25 28 1- 2
1974 MON N P 22 5- 2
1975 MON N P 19 5- 3
1976 MON N P 34 35 6-12
BRTR 158 163 28-31

CARROLL, CLAY PALMER
B.MAY 2,1941 CLANTON,ALA.
1964 MIL N P 11 2- 0
1965 MIL N P 19 0- 1
1966 ATL N P 73 8- 7
1967 ATL N P 42 6-12
1968 ATL N P 10 0- 1
CIN N P 58 7- 7
1969 CIN N P 71 12- 6
1970 CIN N P 65 9- 4
1971 CIN N P 61 10- 4
1972 CIN N P 65 6- 4
1973 CIN N P 53 8- 8
1974 CIN N P 57 12- 5
1975 CIN N P 56 7- 5
1976 CHI A P 29 4- 4
BRTR 670 91-68

CARROLL, DORSEY LEE "DIXIE"
B.MAY 9,1892 PADUCAH,KY.
1919 BOS N O 15 .265
BLTR

CARROLL, E. "CHICK"
B.CHICAGO,ILL.
1884 WAS U O 4 .200

CARROLL, EDGAR FLEISCHER
B.JULY 27,1907 BALTIMORE,MD.
1929 BOS A P 24 1- 0
BRTR

CARROLL, FREDERICK HERBERT
B.JULY 2,1864 SACRAMENTO,CAL.
D.NOV.7,1904
1884 COL AA C-O 69 .283
1885 PIT AA C 69 .263
1886 PIT AA C-1 122 .292
1887 PIT N C-1-O 101 .380
1888 PIT N O 96 .243
1889 PIT N C-O 90 .330
1890 PIT P C-O 111 .302
1891 PIT N O 87 .228
BRTR 745 .295

CARROLL, JOHN E. "SCRAPPY"
B.AUG.15,1860 BUFFALO,N.Y.
D.NOV.14,1942
1884 STP U 3-O 9 .083
1885 BUF N 2-O 12 .056
1887 CLE AA O 57 .252
1892 CHI N 3 1 .000
79 .206

YR	CL	LEA	POS	GP	G	REC

CARROLL, OWEN THOMAS "OWNIE"
B.NOV.11,1902 KEARNY,N.J.
D.JUNE 8,1975 ORANGE,N.J.

YR	CL	LEA	POS	GP	G	REC
1925	DET	A	P-O	10	11	2- 2
						.375
1927	DET	A	P	31	37	10- 6
1928	DET	A	P	34	43	16-12
1929	DET	A	P	34	37	9-17
1930	DET	A	P		6	0- 5
	NY	A	P	10	11	0- 1
	CIN	N	P		3	0- 1
1931	CIN	N	P	29	30	3- 9
1932	CIN	N	P	32	35	10-19
1933	BRO	N	P	33	34	13-15
1934	BRO	N	P	26	28	1- 3
		BRTR		248	275	64-90
						.200

CARROLL, PATRICK
B.PHILADELPHIA,PA.
D.FEB.14,1916

YR	CL	LEA	POS	GP	G	REC
1884	ALT	U	C-O		11	.255
	KEY	U	C		5	.158
					16	.229

CARROLL, RALPH ARTHUR "DOC"
B.DEC.28,1891 WORCESTER,MASS.

YR	CL	LEA	POS	GP	G	REC
1916	PHI	A	C		10	.091
		BRTR				

CARROLL, RICHARD T.
B.JULY 21,1884 CLEVELAND,OHIO
D.NOV.22,1945

YR	CL	LEA	POS	GP	G	REC
1909	NY	A	P		2	0- 0

CARROLL, SAMUEL "CLIFF"
B.OCT.18,1859 LAY GROVE,IOWA
D.JUNE 29,1923

YR	CL	LEA	POS	GP	G	REC
1882	PRO	N	O		10	.121
1883	PRO	N	O		58	.264
1884	PRO	N	O		112	.261
1885	PRO	N	O		104	.232
1886	WAS	N	O		111	.228
1887	WAS	N	O		101	.276
1888	PIT	N	O		7	.107
1890	CHI	N	O		136	.285
1891	CHI	N	O		130	.255
1892	STL	N	O		100	.273
1893	BOS	N	O		120	.234
		BB			989	.256

CARROLL, THOMAS EDWARD "TOM"
B.SEPT.17,1936 JAMAICA,N.Y.

YR	CL	LEA	POS	GP	G	REC
1955	NY	A	S		14	.333
1956	NY	A	S-3		36	.353
1959	KC	A	S-3		14	.143
		BRTR			64	.300

CARROLL, THOMAS MICHAEL "TOM"
B.NOV.5,1952 ORISKANY,N.Y.

YR	CL	LEA	POS	GP	G	REC
1974	CIN	N	P		16	4- 3
1975	CIN	N	P		12	4- 1
		BLTR			28	8- 4

CARSEY, WILFRED "KID"
B.OCT.22,1870 NEW YORK,N.Y.

YR	CL	LEA	POS	GP	G	REC
1891	WAS	AA	P	53	59	14-33
1892	PHI	N	P		35	19-16
1893	PHI	N	P	35	36	22-12
1894	PHI	N	P	31	32	16-14
1895	PHI	N	P		41	24-17
1896	PHI	N	P		24	11-13
1897	PHI	N	P		6	4- 2
	STL	N	P		13	1- 7
1898	STL	N	P		33	1-12
1899	CLE	N	P		9	1- 8
	WAS	N	P		7	1- 2
	NY	N	S-3		5	-333
1901	BRO	N	P		2	1- 0
		BRTR	289	302	115-136	
						.212

CARSON, ALEXANDER JAMES "SOLDIER"
B.NEW YORK,N.Y.

YR	CL	LEA	POS	GP	G	REC
1910	CHI	N	P		2	0- 0
	TR					

CARSON, WALTER LLOYD "KIT"
B.NOV.15,1912 COLTON,CAL.

YR	CL	LEA	POS	GP	G	REC
1934	CLE	A	O		5	.278
1935	CLE	A	O		16	.227
		BLTL			21	.250

CARSWELL, FRANK WILLIS "TEX"
B.NOV.6,1919 PALESTINE,TEX.

YR	CL	LEA	POS	GP	G	REC
1953	DET	A	O		16	.267
		BRTR				

CARTER, ARNOLD LEE "HOOK"
B.MAR.14,1918 RAINELLE,W.VA.

YR	CL	LEA	POS	GP	G	REC
1944	CIN	N	P	33	37	11- 7
1945	CIN	N	P	13	19	2- 4
		BLTL	46	56	13-11	

CARTER, CONRAD POWELL "NICK"
B.MAY 19,1879 OATLANDS,VA.
D.NOV.23,1961

YR	CL	LEA	POS	GP	G	REC
1908	PHI	A	P		17	2- 5
		TR				

CARTER, GARY EDMUND
B.APR.8,1954 CULVER CITY,CAL.

YR	CL	LEA	POS	GP	G	REC
1974	MON	N	C-O		9	.407
1975	MON	N	C-3-O	144		.270
1976	MON	N	C-O		91	.219
		BRTR			244	.256

CARTER, JOHN HOWARD "HOWIE"
B.OCT.13,1904 NEW YORK,N.Y.

YR	CL	LEA	POS	GP	G	REC
1926	CIN	N	2-S		5	.000
		BRTR				

CARTER, OTIS LEONARD "BLACKIE"
B.SEPT.30,1902 LANGLEY,S.C.

YR	CL	LEA	POS	GP	G	REC
1925	NY	N	O		1	.000
1926	NY	N	O		5	.235
		BRTR			6	.190

CARTER, PAUL WARREN "NICK"
B.MAY.1,1894 LAKE PARK,GA.

YR	CL	LEA	POS	GP	G	REC
1914	CLE	A	P		5	1- 3
1915	CLE	A	P	11	12	1- 2
1916	CHI	N	P		8	2- 2
1917	CHI	N	P		23	5- 8
1918	CHI	N	P		21	3- 2
1919	CHI	N	P	28	29	5- 4
1920	CHI	N	P		31	3- 6
		BLTR	127	129	20-27	

CARTER, SOLOMON MOBLEY
B.DEC.23,1908 PICAYUNE,MISS.

YR	CL	LEA	POS	GP	G	REC
1931	PHI	A	P		2	0- 0
		BRTR				

CARTWRIGHT, EDWARD CHARLES "JUMBO"
B.OCT.6,1859 JOHNSTOWN,PA.
D.1924 FLORIDA

YR	CL	LEA	POS	GP	G	REC
1890	STL	AA	1		75	.281
1894	WAS	N	1		132	.292
1895	WAS	N	1		121	.327
1896	WAS	N	1		131	.274
1897	WAS	N	1		33	.250
		BRTR			492	.292

CARTY, RICARDO ADOLFO JACOBO "RICO"
B.SEP.1,1939 SAN PEDRO DE
MACORIS,D.R.

YR	CL	LEA	POS	GP	G	REC
1963	MIL	N	H		2	.000
1964	MIL	N	O		133	.330
1965	MIL	N	O		83	.310
1966	ATL	N	C-1-3-O	151		.326
1967	ATL	N	1-O		134	.255
1969	ATL	N	O		104	.342
1970	ATL	N	O		136	.366
1972	ATL	N	O		86	.277
1973	TEX	A	O-O		86	.232
	CHI	N	O		22	.214
	OAK	A	H		7	.250
1974	CLE	A	1-O		33	.363
1975	CLE	A	1-O-O	118		.308
1976	CLE	A	1-O-O	152		.310
		BRTR		1247	.308	

CARUTHERS, ROBERT LEE "PARISIAN BOB"
B.JAN.5,1864 MEMPHIS,TENN.
D.AUG.5,1911 PEORIA,ILL.

YR	CL	LEA	POS	GP	G	REC
1884	STL	AA	P-O	13	23	7- 2
						.253
1885	STL	AA	P		60	40-13
1886	STL	AA	P-O	45	86	30-14
						.342
1887	STL	AA	P-O	38	98	29- 9
						.459
1888	BRO	AA	P-O	45	94	29-15
						.230
1889	BRO	AA	P	55	57	40-12
1890	BRO	N	P-O	34	71	22-11
						.265
1891	BRO	N	P	34	47	17-17
1892	STL	N	P-O	10	142	2- 8
						.277
1893	CHI	N	P		1	0- 0
	CIN	N	O		13	.286
		BLTR	335	692	216-101	
						.301

CARY, SCOTT RUSSELL "RED"
B.APR.11,1923 KENDALLVILLE,IND.

YR	CL	LEA	POS	GP	G	REC
1947	WAS	A	P		23	3- 1
		BLTL				

CASALE, JERRY JOSEPH
B.SEPT.27,1933 BROOKLYN,N.Y.

YR	CL	LEA	POS	GP	G	REC
1958	BOS	A	P		2	0- 0
1959	BOS	A	P		31	13- 8
1960	BOS	A	P		29	2- 9
1961	LA	A	P		13	1- 5
	DET	A	P		3	0- 0
1962	DET	A	P		18	1- 2
		BRTR		96	17-24	

CASANOVA, PAULINO (ORTIZ) "PAUL"
B.DEC.31,1941 COLON,CUBA

YR	CL	LEA	POS	GP	G	REC
1965	WAS	A	C		5	.308
1966	WAS	A	C		122	.254
1967	WAS	A	C		141	.248
1968	WAS	A	C		96	.196
1969	WAS	A	C		124	.216
1970	WAS	A	C		104	.229
1971	WAS	A	C		94	.203
1972	ATL	N	C		49	.206
1973	ATL	N	C		82	.216
1974	ATL	N	C		42	.202
		BRTR		859	.225	

CASCARELLA, JOSEPH THOMAS
B.JUNE 28,1907 PHILADELPHIA,PA.

YR	CL	LEA	POS	GP	G	REC
1934	PHI	A	P		42	12-15
1935	PHI	A	P		9	1- 6
	BOS	A	P		6	0- 3
1936	BOS	A	P		10	0- 2
	WAS	A	P		22	9- 8
1937	WAS	A	P		10	0- 5
	CIN	N	P		11	1- 2
1938	CIN	N	P		33	4- 7
		BRTR		143	27-48	

CASE, CHARLES EMMETT
B.SEPT.7,1879 SMITH LANDING,O.
D.JAN.30,1918

YR	CL	LEA	POS	GP	G	REC
1901	CIN	N	P		3	1- 2
1904	PIT	N	P		18	10- 5
1905	PIT	N	P		31	12-10
1906	PIT	N	P		2	1- 1
		BRTR		54	24-18	

CASE, GEORGE WASHINGTON
B.NOV.11,1915 TRENTON,N.J.

YR	CL	LEA	POS	GP	G	REC
1937	WAS	A	O		22	.289
1938	WAS	A	O		107	.305
1939	WAS	A	O		128	.302
1940	WAS	A	O		154	.293
1941	WAS	A	O		153	.271
1942	WAS	A	O		125	.320
1943	WAS	A	O		141	.294
1944	WAS	A	O		119	.249
1945	WAS	A	O		123	.294
1946	CLE	A	O		118	.225
1947	WAS	A	O		36	.150
		BRTR		1226	.282	

YR	CL LEA POS	GP	G	REC

CASEY, DANIEL MAURICE
B.NOV.20,1862 BINGHAMTON,N.Y.
D.FEB.8,1943

YR	CL	LEA	POS	GP	G	REC
1884	WIL	U	P		2	1- 1
1885	DET	N	P		12	4- 8
1886	PHI	N	P		44	25-19
1887	PHI	N	P		44	28-13
1888	PHI	N	P,		33	14-19
1889	PHI	N	P		18	8-10
1890	SYR	AA	P		48	20-22
	BRTL				201	100-92

CASEY, DENNIS PATRICK
B.MAR.30,1858 BINGHAMTON,N.Y.
D.JAN.19,1909

YR	CL	LEA	POS	GP	G	REC
1882	DET	N	2-3		9	.231
1884	WIL	U	O		2	.167
	BAL	AA	O		38	.274
1885	BAL	AA	O		64	.282
1887	NY	N	2		1	.000
	BLTR				114	.272

CASEY, HUGH THOMAS
B.OCT.14,1913 ATLANTA,GA.
D.JULY 3,1951

YR	CL	LEA	POS	GP	G	REC
1935	CHI	N	P		13	0- 0
1939	BRO	N	P		40	15-10
1940	BRO	N	P	44	45	11- 8
1941	BRO	N	P		45	14-11
1942	BRO	N	P		50	6 3
1946	BRO	N	P		46	11- 5
1947	BRO	N	P		46	10- 4
1948	BRO	N	P		22	3- 0
1949	PIT	N	P		33	4- 1
	NY	A	P		4	1- 0
	BRTR			343	344	75-42

CASEY, JAMES PATRICK "DOC"
B.MAR.15,1870 LAWRENCE,MASS.
D.DEC.31,1936 DETROIT,MICH.

YR	CL	LEA	POS	GP	G	REC
1898	WAS	N	3		28	.270
1899	WAS	N	3		9	.118
	BRO	N	3		136	.267
1900	BRO	N	3		1	.333
1901	DET	A	3		131	.200
1902	DET	A	3		132	.275
1903	CHI	N	3		112	.290
1904	CHI	N	3		136	.268
1905	CHI	N	3		142	.232
1906	BRO	N	3		149	.233
1907	BRO	N	3		138	.231
	BLTR				1114	.253

CASEY, JOSEPH FELIX
B.AUG.15,1887 BOSTON,MASS.
D.JUNE 2,1966 MELROSE,MASS.

YR	CL	LEA	POS	GP	G	REC
1909	DET	A	C		3	.200
1910	DET	A	C		23	.164
1911	DET	A	C		15	.152
1918	WAS	A	C		8	.235
	BRTR				49	.188

CASEY, WILLIAM B.
B.ST.LOUIS,MO.

YR	CL	LEA	POS	GP	G	REC
1887	ATH	AA	P		1	0- 0

CASH, DAVID "DAVE"
B.JUNE 11,1948 UTICA,N.Y.

YR	CL	LEA	POS	GP	G	REC
1969	PIT	N	2		18	.279
1970	PIT	N	2		64	.314
1971	PIT	N	2-S-3		123	.289
1972	PIT	N	2		99	.282
1973	PIT	N	2-3		116	.271
1974	PHI	N	2		162	.300
1975	PHI	N	2		162	.305
1976	PHI	N	2		160	.284
	BRTR				904	.291

CASH, NORMAN DALTON "NORM"
B.NOV.10,1934 JUSTICEBURG,TEX.

YR	CL	LEA	POS	GP	G	REC
1958	CHI	A	O		13	.250
1959	CHI	A	1		58	.240
1960	DET	A	1-O		121	.286
1961	DET	A	1		159	.361
1962	DET	A	1-O		148	.243
1963	DET	A	1		147	.270
1964	DET	A	1		144	.257
1965	DET	A	1		142	.266
1966	DET	A	1		160	.279
1967	DET	A	1		152	.242
1968	DET	A	1		127	.263
1969	DET	A	1		142	.280
1970	DET	A	1		130	.259
1971	DET	A	1		135	.283
1972	DET	A	1		137	.259
1973	DET	A	1		121	.262
1974	DET	A	1		53	.228
	BLTL				2089	.271

CASH, RONALD FORREST "RON"
B.NOV.20,1949 ATLANTA,GA.

YR	CL	LEA	POS	GP	G	REC
1973	DET	A	3-O		14	.410
1974	DET	A	1-3		20	.226
	BRTR				34	.297

CASHION, JAY CARL
B.JUNE 6,1891 MECKLENBURG,N.C.
D.NOV.17,1935

YR	CL	LEA	POS	GP	G	REC
1911	WAS	A	P	11	21	2- 3
1912	WAS	A	P	26	42	11- 6
1913	WAS	A	P-O	3	9	1- 2
						.294
1914	WAS	A	P		?	0- 1
	BLTR			42	74	14-12
						.247

CASKEY, CRAIG DOUGLAS
B.DEC.11,1949 VISALIA,CAL.

YR	CL	LEA	POS	GP	G	REC
1973	MON	N	P		9	0- 0
	BRTL					

CASKIN, EDWARD JAMES
B.DEC.30,1851 DANVERS,MASS.

YR	CL	LEA	POS	GP	G	REC
1879	TRO	N	C-S		67	.259
1880	TRO	N	C-S		82	.231
1881	TRO	N	S		62	.226
1883	NY	N	2-S		93	.238
1884	NY	N	C-S		97	.232
1885	STL	N	C-S-3		70	.179
1886	NY	N	S		1	.500
					472	.230

CASSADY, HARRY D.
B.JULY 20,1880 BELLEFLOWER,ILL.

YR	CL	LEA	POS	GP	G	REC
1904	PIT	N	O		11	.214
1905	WAS	A	O		10	.128
					21	.181

CASSIAN, EDWIN
B.CONNECTICUT

YR	CL	LEA	POS	GP	G	REC
1891	PHI	N	P		6	1- 3
	WAS	AA	P		7	0- 0
					13	1- 3

CASSIDY, JOHN P.
B.1855 BROOKLYN,N.Y.
D.JULY 3,1891

YR	CL	LEA	POS	GP	G	REC
1875	ATL	NA	P-1-	25	40	1-24
			2-O			-
	NH	NA	1		6	-
1876	HAR	N	O		12	.271
1877	HAR	N	P-O	2	60	1- 1
						.378
1878	CHI	N	O		60	.261
1879	TRO	N	1-O		8	.176
1880	TRO	N	2-O		83	.253
1881	TRO	N	O		84	.219
1882	TRO	N	3-O		28	.176
1883	PRO	N	1-2-O		89	.237
1884	BRO	AA	O		106	.263
1885	BRO	AA	O		54	.211
	TL			27	630	2-25
						-

CASSIDY, JOSEPH PHILLIP
B.FEB.8,1883 CHESTER,PA.
D.MAR.25,1906

YR	CL	LEA	POS	GP	G	REC
1904	WAS	A	S-3-O		152	.234
1905	WAS	A	S		151	.215
	BRTR				303	.225

CASSIDY, PETER FRANCIS
B.APR.8,1873 WILMINGTON,DEL.
D.JULY 9,1929

YR	CL	LEA	POS	GP	G	REC
1896	LOU	N	1		48	.221
1899	BRO	N	S-3		6	.150
1899	WAS	N	1		45	.315
	BRTR				99	.261

CASSINI, JACK DEMPSEY "GABBY"
B.OCT.26,1920 DEARBORN,MICH.

YR	CL	LEA	POS	GP	G	REC
1949	PIT	N	H		8	.000
	BRTR					

CASTER, GEORGE JASPER "JG"
B.AUG.4,1907 COLTON,CAL.
D.DEC.19,1955

YR	CL	LEA	POS	GP	G	REC
1934	PHI	A	P		5	3- 2
1935	PHI	A	P	25	26	1- 4
1937	PHI	A	P	34	37	12-19
1938	PHI	A	P		42	16-20
1939	PHI	A	P		28	9- 9
1940	PHI	A	P		36	4-19
1941	STL	A	P		32	3- 7
1942	STL	A	P		39	8- 2
1943	STL	A	P		35	6- 8
1944	STL	A	P		42	6- 6
1945	STL	A	P		10	1- 2
1946	DET	A	P		22	5- 1
	DET	A	P		26	2- 1
	BRTR			376	380	76-100

CASTIGLIA, JAMES VINCENT
B.SEPT.30,1918 PASSAIC,N.J.

YR	CL	LEA	POS	GP	G	REC
1942	PHI	A	C		16	.389
	BLTR					

CASTIGLIONE, PETER PAUL "PETE"
B.FEB.13,1921 GREENWICH,CONN.

YR	CL	LEA	POS	GP	G	REC
1947	PIT	N	S		13	.280
1948	PIT	N	S		4	.000
1949	PIT	N	S-3-O		118	.268
1950	PIT	N	1-2-S-3		94	.255
1951	PIT	N	S-3		132	.261
1952	PIT	N	1-3-O		67	.266
1953	PIT	N	3		45	.208
	STL	N	2-S-3		67	.173
1954	STL	N	3		5	.000
	BRTR				545	.255

CASTINO, VINCENT CHARLES
B.OCT.11,1918 WILLISVILLE,ILL.
D.MAR.6,1967 SACRAMENTO,CAL.

YR	CL	LEA	POS	GP	G	REC
1943	CHI	A	C		33	.228
1944	CHI	A	C		29	.231
1945	CHI	A	C		26	.216
	BRTR				88	.227

CASTLE, DONALD HARDY "DON"
B.FEB.1,1950 KOKOMO,IND.

YR	CL	LEA	POS	GP	G	REC
1973	TEX	A	H		4	.308
	BLTL					

CASTLE, JOHN FRANCIS
B.JUNE 1,1883 HONEY BROOK,PA.
D.APR.15,1929

YR	CL	LEA	POS	GP	G	REC
1910	PHI	N	O		2	.250

CASTLEMAN, CLYDELL "SLICK"
B.SEPT.8,1914 DONELSON,TENN.

YR	CL	LEA	POS	GP	G	REC
1934	NY	N	P		7	1- 0
1935	NY	N	P		29	15- 6
1936	NY	N	P	29	30	4- 7
1937	NY	N	P		23	11- 6
1938	NY	N	P	21	22	4- 5
1939	NY	N	P		12	1- 2
	BRTR			121	123	36-26

CASTLEMAN, FOSTER EPHRAIM
B.JAN.1,1931 NASHVILLE,TENN.

YR	CL	LEA	POS	GP	G	REC
1954	NY	N	O		13	.250
1955	NY	N	2-3		15	.214
1956	NY	N	2-S-3		124	.226
1957	NY	N	2-S-3		18	.162
1958	BAL	A	2-S-3-O		98	.170
	BRTR				268	.205

CASTLETON, ROY J. C.
B.1886 SALT LAKE CITY,UTAH

YR	CL	LEA	POS	GP	G	REC
1907	NY	A	P		3	1- 1
1909	CIN	N	P		4	1- 1
1910	CIN	N	P		4	1- 2
	BRTL				11	3- 4

CASTNER, PAUL HENRY "LEFTY"
B.FEB.16,1897 ST.PAUL,MINN.

YR	CL	LEA	POS	GP	G	REC
1923	CHI	A	P		6	0- 0
	BLTL					

YR	CL	LEA	POS	GP	G	REC

CASTRO, LOUIS M. "JUD"
B.1877 COLUMBIA,SOUTH AMERICA

| 1902 | PHI | A | 2-S-3-O | 41 | | .248 |
| | | TR | | | | |

CASTRO, WILLIAM RADHAMES (CHECO) "BILL"
B.DEC.13,1953 SANTIAGO,D.R.

1974	MIL	A	P		8	0- 0
1975	MIL	A	P		18	3- 2
1976	MIL	A	P		39	4- 6
		BRTR			65	7- 8

CATER, DANNY ANDERSON
B.FEB.25,1940 AUSTIN,TEX.

1964	PHI	N	1-3-O	60		.296
1965	CHI	A	1-3-O	142		.270
1966	CHI	A	O	21		.183
	KC		1-3-O	116		.292
1967	KC	A	1-3-O	142		.270
1968	OAK	A	1-2-O	147		.290
1969	OAK	A	1-2-O	152		.262
1970	NY	A	1-3-O	155		.301
1971	NY	A	1-3	121		.276
1972	BOS	A	1	92		.237
1973	BOS	A	1-3	63		.313
1974	BOS	A	1-O	56		.246
1975	STL	N	1	22		.229
		BRTR		1289		.276

CATES, ELI ELDO
B.JAN.28,1877 GREENSFORK,IND.
D.MAY 29,1964 RICHMOND,IND.

| 1908 | WAS | A | P | | 40 | 4- 8 |
| | | BRTR | | | | |

CATHER, THEODORE P.
B.MAY 20,1889 CHESTER,PA.
D.APR.9,1945 ELKTON,MD.

1912	STL	N	O		5	.421
1913	STL	N	P-1-	1	67	0- 0
			O			.213
1914	STL	N	O		39	.273
	BOS	N	O		50	.296
1915	BOS	N	O		40	.206
		BRTR		1	201	0- 0
						.252

CATHEY, HARDIN "ABNER"
B.JULY 6,1919 BURNS,TENN.

| 1942 | WAS | A | P | | 12 | 1- 1 |
| | | BRTR | | | | |

CATON, JAMES HOWARD ."HOWDY"
B.JULY 16,1896 ZANESVILLE,OHIO
D.JAN.8,1948

1917	PIT	N	S		14	.211
1918	PIT	N	S		80	.234
1919	PIT	N	S-3-O		39	.176
1920	PIT	N	S		98	.236
		BRTR			231	.226

CATTANACH, JOHN LECKIE
B.MAY 10,1863 PROVIDENCE,R.I.
D.NOV.10,1926

1884	PRO	N	P-O		1	0- 1
						.000
	STL	U	P		2	1- 1
					3	1- 2
						.000

CATTERSON, THOMAS HENRY
B.AUG.25,1884 ARTIC,R.I.
D.FEB.5,1920

1908	BRO	N	O		18	.191
1909	BRO	N	O		9	.222
		BL			27	.200

CAULFIELD, JOHN JOSEPH "JAKE"
B.NOV.23,1919 SAN FRANCISCO,CAL

| 1946 | PHI | A | S-3 | | 44 | .277 |
| | | BRTR | | | | |

CAUSEY, CECIL ALGERNON "RED"
B.AUG.11,1893 GEORGETOWN,FLA.
D.NOV.11,1960 AVON PARK,FLA.

1918	NY	N	P		29	11- 6
1919	NY	N	P	19	21	9- 3
	BOS	N	P		10	4- 5
1920	PHI	N	P	35	44	7-14
1921	PHI	N	P	7	8	3- 3
	NY	N	P	7	9	1- 1
1922	NY	N	P	24	25	4- 3
		BRTR		131	146	39-35

CAUSEY, JAMES WAYNE "WAYNE"
B.DEC.26,1936 RUSTON,LA.

1955	BAL	A	2-S-3	68		.194
1956	BAL	A	2-3	53		.170
1957	BAL	A	2-3	14		.200
1961	KC	A	2-S-3	104		.276
1962	KC	A	2-S-3	117		.252
1963	KC	A	S-3	139		.280
1964	KC	A	2-S-3	157		.281
1965	KC	A	2-S-3	144		.261
1966	KC	A	S-3	28		.228
	CHI	A	2-S-3	78		.244
1967	CHI	A	2-S	124		.226
1968	CHI	A	2	59		.180
	CAL	A	2	4		.000
	ATL	N	2-S-3	16		.108
		BLTR		1105		.252

CAVANAUGH, PATRICK JOHN
B.1900 READING,PA.

| 1919 | PHI | N | 3 | | 1 | .000 |

CAVARETTA, PHILIP JOSEPH "PHIL"
B.JULY 19,1916 CHICAGO,ILL.

1934	CHI	N	1		7	.381
1935	CHI	N	1	146		.275
1936	CHI	N	1	124		.273
1937	CHI	N	1-O	106		.286
1938	CHI	N	1-O	92		.239
1939	CHI	N	1	22		.273
1940	CHI	N	1	65		.280
1941	CHI	N	1-O	107		.286
1942	CHI	N	1-O	136		.270
1943	CHI	N	1-O	143		.291
1944	CHI	N	1-O	152		.321
1945	CHI	N	1-O	132		.355
1946	CHI	N	1-O	139		.294
1947	CHI	N	1-O	127		.314
1948	CHI	N	1-O	111		.279
1949	CHI	N	1-O	105		.294
1950	CHI	N	1-O	82		.273
1951	CHI	N	M-1	89		.311
1952	CHI	N	M-1	41		.238
1953	CHI	N	M-H	27		.286
1954	CHI	A	1-O	71		.316
1955	CHI	A	1	6		.000
		BLTL		2030		.293

CAVENEY, JAMES CHRISTOPHER "IKE"
B.DEC.10,1896 SAN FRANCISCO,CAL
D.JULY 6,1949

1922	CIN	N	S	118		.238
1923	CIN	N	S	138		.277
1924	CIN	N	2-S	95		.273
1925	CIN	N	S	115		.249
		BRTR		466		.260

CAVET, TILLAR H. "PUG"
B.DEC.26,1889 MCGREGOR,TEX.
D.AUG.4,1966 SAN LUIS OBISPO, CAL.

1911	DET	A	P		1	0- 0
1914	DET	A	P		31	7- 7
1915	DET	A	P		17	4- 3
		TL			49	11-10

CAYLOR, OLIVER PERRY
B.DEC.14,1849 DAYTON,OHIO
D.OCT.19,1897
NON-PLAYING MANAGER
CIN(AA)1885-86 AND MET(AA)1887

CECCARELLI, ARTHUR EDWARD "ART"
B.APR.2,1930 NEW HAVEN,CONN.

1955	KC	A	P	31		4- 7
1956	KC	A	P	3		0- 1
1957	BAL	A	P	20		0- 5
1959	CHI	N	P	18		5- 5
1960	CHI	N	P	7		0- 0
		BRTL		79		9-18
		BB 1957				

CECIL, REX ROLSTON
B.OCT.8,1916 LINDSAY,OKLA.
D.OCT.30,1966 LONG BEACH,CAL.

1944	BOS	A	P		11	4- 5
1945	BOS	A	P		7	2- 5
		BLTR			18	6-10

CEDENO, CESAR
B.FEB.25,1951 SANTO DOMINGO,D.R.

1970	HOU	N	O		90	.310
1971	HOU	N	1-O	161		.264
1972	HOU	N	O	139		.320
1973	HOU	N	O	139		.320
1974	HOU	N	O	160		.269
1975	HOU	N	O	131		.288
1976	HOU	N	O	150		.297
		BRTR		970		.294

CENTER, MARVIN EARL "PETE"
B.APP.22,1914 HAZEL GREEN,KY.

1942	CLE	A	P		1	0- 0
1943	CLE	A	P		24	1- 2
1945	CLE	A	P		31	6- 3
1946	CLE	A	P		21	0- 2
		BRTR			77	7- 7

CEPEDA, ORLANDO MANUEL
B.SEP.17,1937 PONCE,P.R.

1958	SF	N	1	148		.312
1959	SF	N	1-3-O	151		.317
1960	SF	N	1-O	151		.297
1961	SF	N	1-O	152		.311
1962	SF	N	1-O	162		.306
1963	SF	N	1-O	156		.316
1964	SF	N	1-O	142		.304
1965	SF	N	1-O	33		.176
1966	SF	N	1-O	19		.286
	STL	N	1	123		.303
1967	STL	N	1	151		.325
1968	STL	N	1	157		.248
1969	ATL	N	1	154		.257
1970	ATL	N	1	148		.305
1971	ATL	N	1	71		.276
1972	ATL	N	1	28		.298
	OAK	A	H		3	.000
1973	BOS	A	D	142		.289
1974	KC	A	D	33		.215
		BRTR		2124		.297

CERMAK, EDWARD
B.JULY 23,1881 CLEVELAND,OHIO
D.NOV.22,1911

| 1901 | CLE | A | O | | 1 | .000 |

CERONE, RICHARD ALDO "RICK"
B.MAY 19,1954 NEWARK,N.J.

1975	CLE	A	C		7	.250
1976	CLE	A	C		7	.125
		BRTR			14	.179

CERV, ROBERT HENRY "BOB"
B.MAY 5,1926 WESTON,NEB.

1951	NY	A	O		12	.214
1952	NY	A	O		36	.241
1953	NY	A	H		8	.000
1954	NY	A	O		56	.260
1955	NY	A	O		55	.341
1956	NY	A	O		54	.304
1957	KC	A	O	124		.272
1958	KC	A	O	141		.305
1959	KC	A	O	125		.285
1960	KC	A	O	23		.256
	NY	A	1-O	87		.250
1961	LA	A	O	18		.158
	NY	A	1-O	57		.271
1962	NY	A	O	14		.118
	HOU	N	O		19	.226
		BRTR		829		.276

CEY, RONALD CHARLES "RON"
B.FEB.15,1948 TACOMA,WASH.

1971	LA	N	H		2	.000
1972	LA	N	3		11	.270
1973	LA	N	3	152		.245
1974	LA	N	3	159		.262
1975	LA	N	3	158		.283
1976	LA	N	3	145		.277
		BRTR		627		.267

CHACON, ELIO (RODIRGUEZ)
B.OCT.26,1936 CARACAS,VENEZ.

1960	CIN	N	2-O		49	.181
1961	CIN	N	2-O		61	.265
1962	NY	N	2-S	118		.236
		BRTR		228		.232

YR	CL	LEA	POS	GP	G	REC

CHADBOURNE, CHESTER JAMES
B.OCT.26,1884 PARKMAN,ME.
D.JUNE 23,1943

YR	CL	LEA	POS	GP	G	REC
1906	BOS	A	2		11	.302
1907	BOS	A	O		10	.289
1914	KC	F	O		147	.275
1915	KC	F	O		152	.224
1918	BOS	N	O		27	.260
	BLTR				347	.255

CHADRAUN, WILLIAM
(PLAYED UNDER NAME OF
WILLIAM CHOUNEAU)

CHAGNON, LEON WILBUR "SHAG"
B.SEPT.28,1903 PITTSFIELD,N.H.
D.JULY 30,1953

1929	PIT	N	P		1	0- 0
1930	PIT	N	P		18	0- 3
1932	PIT	N	P		30	9- 6
1933	PIT	N	P		39	6- 4
1934	PIT	N	P		33	4- 1
1935	NY	N	P		14	0- 2
	BRTR				135	19-16

CHAKALES, ROBERT EDWARD "CHICK"
B.AUG.10,1927 ASHEVILLE,N.C.

1951	CLE	A	P		17	3- 4
1952	CLE	A	P		5	1- 2
1953	CLE	A	P		7	0- 2
1954	CLE	A	P		3	2- 0
	BAL	A	P		38	3- 7
1955	CHI	A	P		7	0- 0
	WAS	A	P		29	2- 3
1956	WAS	A	P		43	4- 4
1957	WAS	A	P		4	0- 1
	BOS	A	P		18	0- 2
	BRTR				171	15-25

CHALK, DAVID LEE "DAVE"
B.AUG.30,1950 DEL RIO,TEX.

1973	CAL	A	S		24	.232
1974	CAL	A	S-3		133	.252
1975	CAL	A	3		149	.273
1976	CAL	A	S-3		142	.217
	BRTR				448	.248

CHALMERS, GEORGE W. "DUT"
B.JUNE 7,1888 ABERDEEN,SCOTLAND
D.AUG.5,1960

1910	PHI	N	P		4	1- 1
1911	PHI	N	P		38	13-10
1912	PHI	N	P		12	3- 4
1913	PHI	N	P		26	3-10
1914	PHI	N	P		3	0- 3
1915	PHI	N	P		26	8- 9
1916	PHI	N	P		12	1- 4
	BRTR				121	29-41

CHAMBERLAIN, WILLIAM VINCENT
B.APR.21,1909 STOUGHTON,MASS.

| 1932 | CHI | A | P | | 12 | 0- 5 |
| | BRTL | | | | | |

CHAMBERLIN, JOSEPH JEREMIAH
B.MAY 10,1910 SAN FRANCISCO,CAL

| 1934 | CHI | A | S-3 | | 43 | .241 |
| | BRTR | | | | | |

CHAMBERLIN, ELTON P. "ICEBERG"
B.NOV.5,1867 BUFFALO,N.Y.
D.SEPT.22,1929

1886	LOU	AA	P-O	4	6	0- 3
						.150
1887	LOU	AA	P		37	18-16
1888	LOU	AA	P		26	9- 8
	STL	AA	P-O		20	11- 2
						.080
1889	STL	AA	P		53	35-15
1890	STL	AA	P		5	2- 3
	COL	AA	P		28	13- 7
1891	ATH	AA	P	51	54	21-22
1892	CIN	N	P		44	19-23
1893	CIN	N	P		27	14- 9
1894	CIN	N	P		20	9-11
1896	CLE	N	P		2	0- 1
	BRTR			317	322	151-120
						.195

CHAMBERS, CLIFFORD DAY "LEFTY"
B.JAN.10,1922 PORTLAND,ORE.

1948	CHI	N	P		29	2- 9
1949	PIT	N	P		34	13- 7
1950	PIT	N	P		37	12-15
1951	PIT	N	P		10	3- 6
	STL	N	P		21	11- 6
1952	STL	N	P		26	4- 4
1953	STL	N	P		32	3- 6
	BLTL				189	48-53

CHAMBERS, JOHN MONROE
B.SEPT.10,1911 COPPER HILL,TENN

| 1937 | STL | N | P | | 2 | 0- 0 |
| | BLTR | | | | | |

CHAMBERS, ROME J.
B.KERNERSVILLE,N.C.

| 1900 | BOS | N | P | | 1 | 0- 0 |
| | BLTL | | | | | |

CHAMBERS, WILLIAM CHRISTOPHER
B.SEPT.13,1889 CAMERON,W.VA.
D.MAR.27,1962

| 1910 | STL | N | P | | 1 | 0- 0 |

CHAMBLISS, CARROLL CHRISTOPHER
"CHRIS"
B.DEC.26,1948 DAYTON,O.

1971	CLE	A	1		111	.275
1972	CLE	A	1		121	.292
1973	CLE	A	1		155	.273
1974	CLE	A	1		17	.328
	NY	A	1		110	.243
1975	NY	A	1		150	.304
1976	NY	A	1		156	.293
	BLTR				820	.283

CHAMPION, BUFORD BILLY "BILL"
B.SEP.18,1947 SHELBY,N.C.

1969	PHI	N	P		23	5-10
1970	PHI	N	P		7	0- 2
1971	PHI	N	P		37	3- 5
1972	PHI	N	P	30	32	4-14
1973	MIL	A	P		37	5- 8
1974	MIL	A	P		31	11- 4
1975	MIL	A	P		27	6- 6
1976	MIL	A	P		10	0- 1
	BRTR			202	204	34-50

CHAMPION, ROBERT MICHAEL "MIKE"
B.FEB.10,1955 MONTGOMERY,ALA.

| 1976 | SD | N | 2 | | 11 | .237 |
| | BRTR | | | | | |

CHANCE, FRANK LEROY "HUSK"
B.SEPT.9,1877 FRESNO,CAL.
D.SEPT.15,1924 LOS ANGELES,CAL.

1898	CHI	N	C-O		42	.288
1899	CHI	N	C		57	.289
1900	CHI	N	C		48	.304
1901	CHI	N	O		63	.289
1902	CHI	N	C-1-O		67	.284
1903	CHI	N	1		123	.327
1904	CHI	N	1		124	.310
1905	CHI	N	M-1		115	.316
1906	CHI	N	M-1		136	.319
1907	CHI	N	M-1		109	.293
1908	CHI	N	M-1		126	.272
1909	CHI	N	M-1		92	.271
1910	CHI	N	M-1		87	.298
1911	CHI	N	M-1		29	.239
1912	CHI	N	M-1		2	.200
1913	NY	A	M-1		11	.208
1914	NY	A	M-1		1	.000
	BRTR				1232	.297
NON-PLAYING MANAGER BOS(A) 1923

CHANCE, ROBERT "BOB"
B.JUNE 10,1940 STATESBORO,GA.

1963	CLE	A	O		16	.288
1964	CLE	A	1-O		120	.279
1965	WAS	A	1-O		72	.256
1966	WAS	A	1		37	.175
1967	WAS	A	1		27	.214
1969	CAL	A	1		5	.143
	BLTR				277	.261

CHANCE, WILMER DEAN
"DEAN"
B.JUNE 1,1941 WAYNE,O.

1961	LA	A	P		5	0- 2
1962	LA	A	P		50	14-10
1963	LA	A	P		45	13-18
1964	LA	A	P		46	20- 9
1965	CAL	A	P		36	15-10
1966	CAL	A	P		41	12-17
1967	MIN	A	P		41	20-14
1968	MIN	A	P		43	16-16
1969	MIN	A	P		20	5- 4
1970	CLE	A	P		45	9- 8
	NY	N	P		3	0- 1
1971	DET	A	P		31	4- 6
	BRTR				406	128-115

CHANDLER, EDWARD OLIVER
B.FEB.6,1922 PINSON,ALA.

| 1947 | BRO | N | P | | 15 | 0- 1 |

CHANDLER, SPURGEON FERDINAND
"SPUD"
B.SEPT.12,1909 COMMERCE,GA.

1937	NY	A	P		12	7- 4
1938	NY	A	P		23	14- 5
1939	NY	A	P		11	3- 0
1940	NY	A	P		27	8- 7
1941	NY	A	P		28	10- 4
1942	NY	A	P		24	16- 5
1943	NY	A	P		30	20- 4
1944	NY	A	P		1	0- 0
1945	NY	A	P		4	2- 1
1946	NY	A	P		34	20- 8
1947	NY	A	P		17	9- 5
	BRTR				211	109-43

CHANEY, DARREL LEE
B.MAR.9,1948 HAMMOND,IND.

1969	CIN	N	S		93	.191
1970	CIN	N	2-S-3		57	.232
1971	CIN	N	2-S-3		10	.125
1972	CIN	N	2-S-3		83	.250
1973	CIN	N	2-S-3		105	.181
1974	CIN	N	2-S-3		117	.200
1975	CIN	N	2-S-3		71	.219
1976	ATL	N	2-S-3		153	.252
	BBTR				689	.222
BL 1973 (PART), 74-75

CHANEY, ESTY CLEON
B.JAN.29,1891 HADLEY,PA.
D.FEB.9,1952

1913	BOS	A	P		1	0- 0
1914	BRO	F	P		1	0- 0
	BRTR				2	0- 0

CHANNELL, LESTER CLARK
"GOAT" OR "GINT"
B.MAR.3,1886 CRESTLINE,OHIO
D.MAY 8,1954 DENVER,COLO.

1910	NY	A	O		6	.263
1914	NY	A	O		1	1.000
	BLTL				7	.300

CHANT, CHARLES JOSEPH "CHARLIE"
B.AUG.7,1951 BELL,CAL.

1975	OAK	A	O		5	.000
1976	STL	N	O		15	.143
	BRTR				20	.105

CHAPLIN, BERT E.
B.1896 PELZER,S.C.

1920	BOS	A	C		4	.250
1921	BOS	A	C		3	.000
1922	BOS	A	C		28	.189
	BLTR				35	.182

CHAPLIN, JAMES BAILEY "TINY"
B.JULY 13,1905 LOS ANGELES,CAL.
D.MAR.25,1939

1928	NY	N	P		12	0- 2
1930	NY	N	P		19	2- 6
1931	NY	N	P		16	3- 0
1936	BOS	N	P		40	10-15
	BRTR				87	15-23

CHAPMAN, CALVIN LOUIS
B.DEC.20,1912 COURTLAND,MISS.

1935	CIN	N	2-S		15	.340
1936	CIN	N	2-O		96	.247
	BLTR				111	.265

YR	CL	LEA	POS	GP	G	REC

CHAPMAN, EDWIN VOLNEY
B.NOV.28,1905 COURTLAND,MISS.
| 1933 | WAS | A | P | | 6 | 0- 0 |
| | | | BBTR | | | |

CHAPMAN, FREDERICK JOSEPH
B.NOV.24,1872 LITTLE COOLEY,PA.
D.DEC.14,1957
| 1887 | ATH | AA | P | | 1 | 1- 0 |
| | | | BRTR | | | |

CHAPMAN, FREDERICK WILLIAM
B.JULY 17,1916 LIBERTY,S.C.
1939	PHI	A	SS		15	.286
1940	PHI	A	SS		26	.159
1941	PHI	A	2-S-3		35	.159
			BRTR		76	.193

CHAPMAN, GLENN JUSTICE "PETE"
B.JAN.21,1908 CAMBRIDGE CITY,
IND.
| 1934 | BRO | N | 2-O | | 67 | .280 |
| | | | BRTR | | | |

CHAPMAN, HARRY E.
B.OCT.26,1887 SEVERANCE,KAN.
D.OCT.21,1918
1912	CHI	N	C		1	.250
1913	CHI	N	C		2	.500
1914	STL	F	C		59	.209
1915	STL	F	C		62	.198
1916	STL	A	C		18	.097
			BRTR		142	.195

CHAPMAN, JOHN CURTIS
B.MAY 8,1843 BROOKLYN,N.Y.
D.JUNE 10,1916
1874	ATL	NA	1-O		53	–
1875	STL	NA	O		41	.246
1876	LOU	N	O		17	.235
			TR		111	–
NON-PLAYING MANAGER
LOU(N) 1877, MIL(N) 1878,
WOR(N) 1882, DFT(N) 1883-84,
BUF(N) 1885, LOU(AA) 1889-91
AND LOU(N) 1892

CHAPMAN, JOHN JOSEPH
B.OCT.15,1899 CENTRALIA,PA.
D.NOV.3,1953
| 1924 | PHI | A | S | | 19 | .282 |
| | | | BRTR | | | |

CHAPMAN, RAYMOND JOHNSON "RAY"
B.JAN.15,1891 MCHENRY,KY.
D.AUG.17,1920
1912	CLE	A	S		31	.312
1913	CLE	A	S		140	.254
1914	CLE	A	2-S		106	.275
1915	CLE	A	S		154	.270
1916	CLE	A	2-S-3		109	.231
1917	CLE	A	S		156	.302
1918	CLE	A	S		128	.267
1919	CLE	A	S		115	.300
1920	CLE	A	S		111	.303
			BRTR		1050	.278

CHAPMAN, SAMUEL BLAKE "SAM"
B.APR.11,1916 TIBURON,CAL.
1938	PHI	A	O		114	.259
1939	PHI	A	1-O		140	.269
1940	PHI	A	O		134	.276
1941	PHI	A	O		143	.322
1945	PHI	A	O		9	.200
1946	PHI	A	O		146	.261
1947	PHI	A	O		149	.252
1948	PHI	A	O		123	.258
1949	PHI	A	O		154	.278
1950	PHI	A	O		144	.251
1951	PHI	A	O		18	.169
	CLE	A	1-O		94	.228
			BRTR		1368	.266

CHAPMAN, WILLIAM BENJAMIN "BEN"
B.DEC.25,1908 NASHVILLE,TENN.
1930	NY	A	2-3		138	.316
1931	NY	A	2-O		149	.315
1932	NY	A	O		151	.299
1933	NY	A	O		147	.312
1934	NY	A	O		149	.308
1935	NY	A	O		140	.289
1936	NY	A	O		36	.266
	WAS	A	O		97	.332
1937	WAS	A	O		35	.262
	BOS	A	O		113	.307
1938	BOS	A	O		127	.340
1939	CLE	A	O		149	.290
1940	CLE	A	O		143	.286
1941	WAS	A	O		28	.255
	CHI	A	O		57	.226
1944	BRO	N	P	11	20	5- 3
1945	BRO	N	P	10	13	3- 3
	PHI	N	M-P-	3	24	0- 0
				3-O		.314
1946	PHI	N	M-P	1		0- 0
			BRTR	25	1717	8- 6
						.302
NON-PLAYING MANAGER
PHI(N) 1947-48

CHAPPELL, LA VERNE ASHFORD "LARRY"
B.FEB.19,1890 MC CLUSKEY,ILL.
D.NOV.8,1918 SAN FRANCISCO,CAL.
1913	CHI	A	O		60	.229
1914	CHI	A	O		21	.231
1915	CHI	A	H		1	.000
1916	CLE	A	O		3	.000
	BOS	N	O		20	.226
1917	BOS	N	O		3	.000
			BLTR		108	.225

CHAPPELLE, WILLIAM HOGAN "BIG BILL"
B.MAR.22,1884 WATERLOO,N.Y.
D.DEC.31,1944
1908	BOS	N	P		13	2- 4
1909	BOS	N	P		5	1- 1
	CIN	N	P		1	0- 0
1914	BRO	F	P		16	4- 2
			BRTR		35	7- 7

CHARLES, EDWIN DOUGLAS "ED"
B.APR.29,1933 DAYTONA BEACH,FLA.
1962	KC	A	2-3		147	.288
1963	KC	A	3		158	.267
1964	KC	A	3		150	.241
1965	KC	A	2-S-3		134	.269
1966	KC	A	1-3-O		118	.286
1967	KC	A	3		19	.246
	NY	N	3		101	.238
1968	NY	N	1-3		117	.276
1969	NY	N	3		61	.207
			BRTR		1005	.263

CHARLES, RAYMOND "CHAPPY"
(REAL NAME
CHARLES SHUM ACHENBACH)
B.MAR.25,1881 PHILLIPSBURG,N.J.
D.AUG.4,1959 BETHLEHEM,PA.
1908	STL	N	2-S-3		119	.205
1909	STL	N	2-S		99	.236
	CIN	N	2-S		13	.256
1910	CIN	N	S		4	.133
			BRTR		235	.219

CHARTAK, MICHAEL GEORGE
B.APR.28,1917 BROOKLYN,N.Y.
D.JULY 25,1967 CEDAR RAPIDS,IA.
1940	NY	A	O		11	.133
1942	NY	A	O		5	.000
	WAS	A	O		24	.217
	STL	A	O		73	.249
1943	STL	A	1-O		108	.256
1944	STL	A	1-O		35	.236
			BLTL		256	.243

CHARTON, FRANK LANE "PETE"
B.DEC.21,1942 JACKSON,TENN.
| 1964 | BOS | A | P | | 25 | 0- 2 |
| | | | BLTR | | | |

CHASE, HAROLD HOMER "PRINCE HAL"
B.FEB.13,1883 LOS GATOS,CAL.
D.MAY 18,1947
1905	NY	A	1		126	.249
1906	NY	A	1		151	.323
1907	NY	A	1		125	.287
1908	NY	A	1		106	.257
1909	NY	A	1		118	.283
1910	NY	A	M-1		130	.290
1911	NY	A	M-1		133	.315
1912	NY	A	1		131	.274
1913	NY	A	1-2-O		39	.228
	CHI	A	1		102	.281
1914	CHI	A	1		58	.267
	BUF	F	1		75	.354
1915	BUF	F	1		145	.284
1916	CIN	N	1-2-O		142	.339
1917	CIN	N	1		152	.277
1918	CIN	N	1-O		74	.301
1919	NY	N	1		110	.284
			BRTL		1917	.291

CHASE, KENDALL FAY "LEFTY"
B.OCT.6,1913 ONEONTA,N.Y.
1936	WAS	A	P		1	0- 0
1937	WAS	A	P		14	4- 3
1938	WAS	A	P		32	9-10
1939	WAS	A	P		32	10-19
1940	WAS	A	P		35	15-17
1941	WAS	A	P		33	6-18
1942	BOS	A	P		13	5- 1
1943	BOS	A	P		7	0- 4
	NY	N	P	21	23	4-12
			BLTL	188	190	53-84

CHATHAM, CHARLES L. "BUSTER"
B.DEC.25,1901 WEST,TEX.
D.DEC.15,1975 WACO,TEX.
| 1930 | BOS | N | S-3 | | 112 | .267 |
| 1931 | BOS | N | S-3 | | 17 | .227 |

CHATTERTON, JAMES M.
B.OCT.14,1864 BROOKLYN,N.Y.
D.DEC.15,1944 TEWKSBURY,MASS.
| 1884 | KC | U | P-1- | 1 | 4 | 0- 1 |
| | | | O | | | .125 |

CHAVARRIA, OSVALDO "OSSIE"
B.AUG.5,1940 COLON,PANAMA
1966	KC	A	1-2-S-3-	86	.241
			O			
1967	KC	A	2-S-3-O	38	.102
			BRTR		124	.208

CHAVEZ, NESTOR ISAIAS (SILVA)
B.JULY 6,1947 CHACAO,VENEZ.
D.MAR.16,1969 MARACAIBO,VENEZ.
| 1967 | SF | N | P | | 2 | 1- 0 |
| | | | BRTR | | | |

CHEADLE, DAVID BAIRD "DAVE"
B.FEB.19,1952 GREENSBORO,N.C.
| 1973 | ATL | N | P | | 2 | 0- 1 |
| | | | BLTL | | | |

CHECH, CHARLES WILLIAM
B.APR.27,1878 MADISON,WIS.
D.JAN.31,1938
1905	CIN	N	P		39	13-13
1906	CIN	N	P		11	1- 4
1908	CLE	A	P		27	11- 7
1909	BOS	A	P		17	7- 6
			BRTR		94	32-30

CHEEK, HARRY G.
B.KANSAS CITY,MO.
| 1910 | PHI | N | C | | 2 | .500 |
| | | | TR | | | |

CHEEVES, VIRGIL EARL "CHIEF"
B.FEB.12,1901 OKLAHOMA CITY,
OKLA.
1920	CHI	N	P		5	0- 0
1921	CHI	N	P		37	11-12
1922	CHI	N	P		39	12-11
1923	CHI	N	P		19	3- 4
1924	CLE	A	P		8	0- 0
1927	NY	N	P		3	0- 0
			BRTR		111	26-27

YR   CL LEA POS GP   G   REC

CHELINI, ITALO VINCENT "CHILLY"
B.OCT.10,1914 SAN FRANCISCO,CAL.
D.AUG.25,1972 SAN FRANCISCO,CAL.
1935 CHI A	P		2	0- 0
1936 CHI A	P		18	4- 3
1937 CHI A	P		4	0- 1
BLTL			24	4- 4

CHENEY, LAWRENCE RUSSELL
B.MAY 2,1886 BELLEVILLE,KAN.
D.JAN.6,1969 DAYTONA BEACH,FLA.
1911 CHI N	P		3	1- 0
1912 CHI N	P		42	26-10
1913 CHI N	P	54	56	21-14
1914 CHI N	P		50	20-18
1915 CHI N	P		25	8- 9
BRO N	P		5	0- 2
1916 BRO N	P		41	18-12
1917 BRO N	P		35	8-12
1918 BRO N	P	32	33	11-13
1919 BRO N	P		9	1- 3
BOS N	P		8	0- 2
PHI N	P		9	2- 5
BRTR		313	316	116-100

CHENEY, THOMAS EDGAR "TOM"
B.OCT.14,1934 MORGAN,GA.
1957 STL N	P		4	0- 1
1959 STL N	P		11	0- 1
1960 PIT N	P		11	2- 2
1961 PIT N	P		1	0- 0
WAS A	P	10	13	1- 3
1962 WAS A	P		37	7- 9
1963 WAS A	P	23	26	8- 9
1964 WAS A	P		15	1- 3
1966 WAS A	P		3	0- 1
BRTR		115	121	19 29

CHERVINKO, PAUL
B.JULY 28,1910 TRAUGER,PA.
D.JUNE 3,1976 DANVILLE,ILL.
1937 BRO N	C		30	.146
1938 BRO N	C		12	.148
BRTR			42	.147

CHESBRO, JOHN DWIGHT
"HAPPY JACK"
B.JUNE 5,1874 N.ADAMS,MASS.
D.NOV.6,1931 CONWAY,MASS.
1899 PIT N	P		19	6- 9
1900 PIT N	P		29	15-13
1901 PIT N	P		33	21- 9
1902 PIT N	P		34	27- 6
1903 NY A	P		40	21-15
1904 NY A	P		55	41-13
1905 NY A	P		41	20-13
1906 NY A	P		48	24-16
1907 NY A	P		29	9-10
1908 NY A	P		44	14-20
1909 NY A	P		8	0- 3
BOS A	P		2	0- 2
BRTR		382	198-129

CHESNES, ROBERT VINCENT "BOB"
B.MAY 6,1921 OAKLAND,CAL.
1948 PIT N	P		25	39	14- 6
1949 PIT N	P		27	42	7-13
1950 PIT N	P		9	3- 3
BBTR		61	90	24-22

CHETKOVICH, MITCHELL
B.JULY 21,1917 FAIRPOINT,OHIO
D.AUG.24,1971 GRASS VALLEY,CAL.
| 1945 PHI N | P | | 4 | 0- 0 |
| BRTR | | | | |

CHILD, HARRY STEPHEN PATRICK
B.MAY 23,1905 BALTIMORE,MD.
D.NOV.8,1972 ALEXANDRIA,VA.
| 1930 WAS A | P | | 5 | 0- 0 |
| BLTR | | | | |

CHILDERS
B.ST.LOUIS,MO.
| 1895 LOU N | P | | 1 | 0- 0 |

CHILDS, A. F.
NON-PLAYING MANAGER NAT(NA)1875

CHILDS, CLARENCE ALGERNON
"CUPID"
B.AUG.8,1867 CALVERT CO.,MD.
D.NOV.8,1912 BALTIMORE,MD.
1888 PHI N	2		2	.000
1890 SYR AA	2		136	.344
1891 CLE N	2		141	.295
1892 CLE N	2		144	.335
1893 CLE N	2		122	.332
1894 CLE N	2		117	.365
1895 CLE N	2		120	.312
1896 CLE N	2		132	.348
1897 CLE N	2		114	.336
1898 CLE N	2		109	.289
1899 STL N	2		125	.266
1900 CHI N	2		138	.243
1901 CHI N	2		63	.257
BLTR			1463	.313

CHILDS, PETER PIENE
B.NOV.15,1871 PHILADELPHIA,PA.
D.FEB.15,1922
1901 STL N	2		8	.609
CHI N	2		60	.221
1902 PHI N	2		120	.192
TR			188	.217

CHILES, PEARCE NUGET
"WHAT'S THE USE"
B.MAY 28,1867 DEEPWATER,MO.
1899 PHI N	1-0		81	.329
1900 PHI N	1-0		28	.220
			109	.301

CHILES, RICHARD FRANCIS "RICH"
B.NOV-22,1949 SACRAMENTO,CAL.
1971 HOU N	O		67	.227
1972 HOU N	O		9	.273
1973 NY N	O		8	.120
1976 HOU N	O		5	.500
BLTL			89	.220

CHIOZZA, DINO JOSEPH "DYNAMO"
B.JUNE 30,1912 NEW ORLEANS,LA.
D.APR.23,1972 MEMPHIS,TENN.
| 1935 PHI N | S | | 2 | .000 |
| BLTR | | | | |

CHIOZZA, LOUIS PEO
B.MAY 17,1910 TALLULAH,LA.
D.FEB.28,1971 MEMPHIS,TENN.
1934 PHI N	2-3-O		134	.304
1935 PHI N	2-3		124	.284
1936 PHI N	2-3-O		144	.297
1937 NY N	3-O		117	.232
1938 NY N	2-O		57	.235
1939 NY N	3		40	.268
BLTR			616	.277

CHIPMAN, ROBERT HOWARD "BOB"
B.OCT.11,1918 BROOKLYN,N.Y.
D.NOV.8,1973 HUNTINGTON,N.Y.
1941 BRO N	P		1	1- 0
1942 BRO N	P		2	0- 0
1943 BRO N	P		1	0- 0
1944 BRO N	P		11	3- 1
CHI N	P		26	9- 9
1945 CHI N	P		25	4- 5
1946 CHI N	P		34	6- 5
1947 CHI N	P	32	33	7- 6
1948 CHI N	P		34	2- 1
1949 CHI N	P		38	7- 8
1950 BOS N	P		27	7- 7
1951 BOS N	P		33	4- 3
1952 BOS N	P		29	1- 1
BLTL		293	294	51-46

CHIPPLE, WALTER JOHN
(REAL NAME
WALTER JOHN CHLIPALA)
B.SEPT.26,1919 UTICA,N.Y.
| 1945 WAS A | O | | 18 | .136 |
| BRTR | | | | |

CHITI, HARRY
B.NOV.16,1932 KINCAID,ILL.
1950 CHI N	C		3	.333
1951 CHI N	C		9	.355
1952 CHI N	C		32	.274
1955 CHI N	C		113	.231
1956 CHI N	C		72	.212
1958 KC A	C		103	.268
1959 KC A	C		55	.272
1960 KC A	C		58	.221
DET A	C		37	.163
1961 DET A	C		5	.083
1962 NY N	C		15	.195
BRTR			502	.238

CHITTUM, NELSON BOYD
B.MAR.25,1933 HARRISONBURG,VA.
1958 STL N	P		13	0- 1
1959 BOS A	P		21	3- 0
1960 BOS A	P		6	0- 0
BRTR			40	3- 1

CHLIPALA, WALTER JOHN
(PLAYED UNDER NAME OF
WALTER JOHN CHIPPLE)

CHLUPSA, ROBERT JOSEPH "BOB"
B.SEP.16,1945 NEW YORK,N.Y.
1970 STL N	P		14	0- 2
1971 STL N	P		1	0- 0
BRTR			15	0- 2

CHOATE, DONALD LEON
B.JULY 2,1938 POTOSI,MO.
| 1960 SF N | P | | 4 | 0- 0 |
| BRTR | | | | |

CHOUINARD, FELIX GEORGE
B.OCT.5,1887 HINES,ILL.
D.APR.28,1955 HINES,ILL.
DECEASED
1910 CHI A	O		24	.195
1911 CHI A	2-O		14	.157
1914 PIT F	2-O		5	.440
BRO F	2-O		15	.366
BAL F	2-O		26	.217
1915 BRO F	2-O		4	.500
BLTR			88	.244

CHOUNEAU, WILLIAM "CHIEF"
(REAL NAME WILLIAM CHADRAUN)
B.SEPT.2,1889 CLOQUET,MINN.
D.SEPT.17,1948
| 1910 CHI A | P | | 1 | 0- 0 |
| TR | | | | |

CHOZEN, HARRY KENNETH
B.SEPT.27,1915 WINNEBAGO,MINN.
| 1937 CIN N | C | | 1 | .250 |
| BRTR | | | | |

CHRISLEY, BARBRA O'NEIL "NEIL"
B.DEC.16,1932 CALHOUN FALLS,S.C.
1957 WAS A	O		26	.157
1958 WAS A	3-O		105	.215
1959 DET A	O		65	.132
1960 DET A	1-O		96	.255
1961 MIL N	H		10	.222
BLTR			302	.210

CHRISTENBURY, LLOYD REID
B.OCT.19,1893 MECKLENBURG CO.,
N.C.
D.DEC.13,1944
1919 BOS N	O		7	.290
1920 BOS N	2-S-O		65	.208
1921 BOS N	2		62	.352
1922 BOS N	2-3-O		71	.250
BLTR			205	.271

CHRISTENSEN, BRUCE RAY
B.FEB.22,1948 MADISON,WIS.
| 1971 CAL A | S | | 29 | .270 |

CHRISTENSEN, WALTER NIELS
"SEACAP"
B.OCT.24,1899 SAN FRANCISCO,CAL.
1926 CIN N	O		114	.350
1927 CIN N	O		57	.254
BLTL			171	.315

YR	CL	LEA	POS	GP	G	REC

CHRISTENSON, LARRY RICHARD
B.NOV.10,1953 EVERETT,WASH.

YR	CL	LEA	POS	GP	G	REC
1973	PHI	N	P		10	1- 4
1974	PHI	N	P		10	1- 1
1975	PHI	N	P		29	11- 6
1976	PHI	N	P		32	13- 8
		BRTR			81	26-19

CHRISTIAN, ROBERT CHARLES "BOB"
B.OCT.17,1945 CHICAGO,ILL.
D.FEB.20,1974 SAN DIEGO,CAL.

1968	DET	A	1-0		3	.333
1969	CHI	A	0		39	.217
1970	CHI	A	0		12	.267
		BRTR			54	.224

CHRISTMAN, H. B.
B.DAYTON,OHIO

| 1888 | KC | AA | C | | 1 | .250 |

CHRISTMAN, MARQUETTE JOSEPH "MARK"
B.OCT.21,1913 MAPLEWOOD,MO.
D.OCT.9,1976 ST.LOUIS,MO.

1938	DET	A	S-3		95	.248
1939	DET	A	S		6	.250
	STL	A			79	.216
1943	STL	A	1-2-S-3		98	.271
1944	STL	A	1-3		148	.271
1945	STL	A	3		78	.277
1946	STL	A	S-3		128	.258
1947	WAS	A	2-S		110	.223
1948	WAS	A	2-S-3		120	.259
1949	WAS	A	1-2-S-3		49	.214
		BRTR			911	.253

CHRISTOPHER, JOSEPH O'NEAL "JOE"
B.DEC.13,1935 FREDERIKSTED,V.I.

1959	PIT	N	0		15	.000
1960	PIT	N	0		50	.232
1961	PIT	N	0		76	.263
1962	NY	N	0		119	.244
1963	NY	N	0		64	.221
1964	NY	N	0		154	.300
1965	NY	N	0		148	.249
1966	BOS	A	0		12	.077
		BRTR			638	.260

CHRISTOPHER, LOYD EUGENE
B.DEC.31,1919 POINT RICHMOND, CAL.

1945	BOS	A	0		8	.286
	CHI	N			1	.000
1947	CHI	A	0		7	.217
		BRTR			16	.243

CHRISTOPHER, RUSSELL ORMAND
B.SEPT.12,1907 POINT RICHMOND, CAL.
D.DEC.5,1954

1942	PHI	A	P		30	4-13
1943	PHI	A	P		24	5- 8
1944	PHI	A	P		35	14-14
1945	PHI	A	P	33	34	13-13
1946	PHI	A	P		30	5- 7
1947	PHI	A	P		44	10- 7
1948	CLE	A	P		45	3- 2
		BRTR		241	242	54-64

CHURCH, EMORY NICHOLAS "BUBBA"
B.SEPT.12,1925 BIRMINGHAM,ALA.

1950	PHI	N	P		31	39	8- 6
1951	PHI	N	P		38	39	15-11
1952	PHI	N	P			2	0- 0
	CIN	N		29	32	5- 9
1953	CIN	N	P	11	12	3- 3
	CHI	N			27	4- 5
1954	CHI	N	P			8	1- 3
1955	CHI	N	P			3	0- 0
		BRTR		147	162	36-37

CHURCH, HIRAM LINCOLN
B.CENTRAL SQUARE,N.Y.

| 1890 | BRO | AA0 | | | 3 | .125 |

CHURCH, LEONARD "LEN"
B.MAR.21,1942 CHICAGO,ILL.

| 1966 | CHI | N | P | | 4 | 0- 1 |
| | | BBTR | | | | |

CHURN, CLARENCE NOTTINGHAM
B.FEB.1,1930 BRIDGETOWN,VA.

1957	PIT	N	P		5	0- 0
1958	CLE	A	P		6	0- 0
1959	LA	N	P		14	3- 2
		BRTR			25	3- 2

CHURRY, JOHN
B.NOV.26,1901 JOHNSTOWN,PA.

1924	CHI	N	C		6	.143
1925	CHI	N	C		3	.500
1926	CHI	N	C		2	.000
1927	CHI	N	C		1	1.000
		BRTR			12	.278

CIAFFONE, LAWRENCE THOMAS
B.AUG.17,1924 BROOKLYN,N.Y.

| 1951 | STL | N | 0 | | 5 | .000 |
| | | BRTR | | | | |

CICERO, JOSEPH FRANCIS "DODE"
B.NOV.18,1910 ATLANTIC CITY,N.J

1929	BOS	A	0		10	.313
1930	BOS	A	3-0		18	.167
1945	PHI	A	3-0		12	.158
		BRTR			40	.222

CICOTTE, ALVA WARREN "AL"
B.DEC.23,1929 MELVINDALE,MICH.

1957	NY	A	P		20	2- 2
1958	WAS	A	P	8	9	0- 3
	DET	A	P	14	15	3- 1
1959	CLE	A	P		26	3- 1
1961	STL	N	P		29	2- 6
1962	HOU	N	P		5	0- 0
		BRTR		102	104	10-13

CICOTTE, EDWARD VICTOR "KNUCKLES"
B.JUNE 19,1884 DETROIT,MICH.
D.MAY 5,1969 DETROIT,MICH.

1905	DET	A	P		4	4- 0
1908	BOS	A	P	38	39	11-12
1909	BOS	A	P		26	13- 5
1910	BOS	A	P		36	15-11
1911	BOS	A	P		35	11-14
1912	BOS	A	P		9	1- 2
	CHI	A	P		20	9- 8
1913	CHI	A	P		41	18-12
1914	CHI	A	P		45	11-16
1915	CHI	A	P	39	40	13-11
1916	CHI	A	P		44	15- 7
1917	CHI	A	P		49	28-12
1918	CHI	A	P		38	12-19
1919	CHI	A	P		40	29- 7
1920	CHI	A	P		37	21-10
		BBTR		501	503	211-146

CIESLAK, THADDEUS WALTER "TED"
B.NOV.22,1916 MILWAUKEE,WIS.

| 1944 | PHI | N | 3-0 | | 85 | .245 |
| | | BRTR | | | | |

CIHOCKI, ALBERT JOSEPH
B.MAY 7,1924 NANTICOKE,PA.

| 1945 | CLE | A | 2-S-3 | | 92 | .212 |
| | | BRTR | | | | |

CIHOCKI, EDWARD JOSEPH "CY"
B.MAY 9,1909 WILMINGTON,DEL.

1932	PHI	A	0		1	.000
1933	PHI	A	S		33	.144
		BRTR			34	.143

CIMINO, PETER WILLIAM "PETE"
B.OCT.17,1942 PHILADELPHIA,PA.

1965	MIN	A	P		1	0- 0
1966	MIN	A	P		35	2- 5
1967	CAL	A	P		46	3- 3
1968	CAL	A	P		4	0- 0
		BRTR			86	5- 8

CIMOLI, GINO NICHOLAS
B.DEC.18,1929 SAN FRANCISCO,CAL.

1956	BRO	N	0		73	.111
1957	BRO	N	0		142	.293
1958	LA	N	0		109	.246
1959	STL	N	0		143	.279
1960	PIT	N	0		101	.267
1961	PIT	N	0		21	.299
	MIL	N	0		37	.197
1962	KC	A	0		152	.275
1963	KC	A	0		145	.263
1964	KC	A	0		4	.000
	BAL	A	0		38	.138
1 65	CAL	A	0		4	.000
		BRTR			969	.265

CIOLA, LOUIS ALEXANDER
B.SEPT.6,1922 NORFOLK,VA.

| 1943 | PHI | A | P | | 12 | 1- 3 |
| | | BRTR | | | | |

CIPRIANI, FRANK DOMINICK
B.APR.14,1941 BUFFALO,N.Y.

| 1961 | KC | A | 0 | | 13 | .250 |
| | | BRTR | | | | |

CISAR, GEORGE
B.AUG.25,1915 CHICAGO,ILL.

| 1937 | BRO | N | P | | 20 | .207 |
| | | BRTR | | | | |

CISCO, GALEN BERNARD
B.MAR.7,1937 ST.MARY'S,O.

1961	BOS	A	P	17	18	2- 4
1962	BOS	A	P		23	4- 7
	NY	N	P		4	1- 1
1963	NY	N	P		51	7-15
1964	NY	N	P		36	6-19
1965	NY	N	P		35	4- 8
1967	BOS	A	P		11	0- 1
1969	KC	A	P		15	1- 1
		BRTR		192	193	25-56

CISSELL, CHALMER WILLIAM "BILL"
B.JAN.3,1904 PERRYVILLE,MO.
D.MAR.15,1949

1928	CHI	A	S		125	.260
1929	CHI	A	S		152	.280
1930	CHI	A	2-S-3		141	.271
1931	CHI	A	2-S		109	.220
1932	CHI	A	S		12	.256
	CLE	A	2-S		131	.320
1933	CLE	A	2-S-3		112	.230
1934	BOS	A	2		102	.267
1937	PHI	A	2		34	.265
1938	NY	N	2		38	.268
		BRTR			956	.267

CLABAUGH, JOHN WILLIAM "MOOSE"
B.NOV.13,1901 ALBANY,MO.

| 1926 | BRO | N | 0 | | 11 | .071 |
| | | BLTR | | | | |

CLACK, ROBERT S. "GENTLEMAN BOB"
B.1851 BROOKLYN,N.Y.
D.OCT.22,1933

1874	ATL	NA	0		30	-
1875	ATL	NA	0		17	-
1876	CIN	N	P-1-	1	31	0- 0
			2-3-0			.154
		BRTR		1	78	0- 0

CLAIRE, DAVID MATTHEW
B.NOV.17,1897 LUDINGTON,MICH.
D.JAN.7,1956 LAS VEGAS,NEV.

| 1920 | DET | A | S | | 3 | .000 |
| | | BRTR | | | | |

CLANCEY, WILLIAM EDWARD
B.APR.12,1878 REDFIELD,N.Y.
D.FEB.10,1948

| 1905 | PIT | N | 1 | | 56 | .229 |
| | | TR | | | | |

CLANCY, ALBERT HARRISON
B.AUG.14,1888 SANTA FE,N.MEX.
D.OCT.17,1951

| 1911 | STL | A | 3 | | 3 | .000 |
| | | BRTR | | | | |

CLANCY, JOHN WILLIAM "BUD"
B.SEPT.15,1900 ODELL,ILL.
D.SEPT.26,1968 OTTUMWA,IOWA

1924	CHI	A	1		13	.257
1925	CHI	A	1		4	.000
1926	CHI	A	1		12	.342
1927	CHI	A	1		130	.300
1928	CHI	A	1		130	.271
1929	CHI	A	1		92	.283
1930	CHI	A	1		68	.244
1932	BRO	N	1		53	.306
1934	PHI	N	1		20	.245
		BLTL			522	.281

CLANTON, EUCAL CURT
B.FEB.19,1898 POWELL,MO.

| 1922 | CLE | A | 1 | | 1 | .000 |
| | | BLTL | | | | |

CLAPP, AARON BRONSON
B.JULY 1856 ITHACA,N.Y.
D.JAN.13,1914

| 1879 | TRO | N | 1-0 | | 34 | .272 |
| | | TR | | | | |

CLAPP, JOHN EDGAR
B.JULY 17,1851 ITHACA,N.Y.
D.DEC.18,1904

YR	CL	LEA	POS	GP	G	REC
1872	MAN	NA	C		19	.306
1873	ATH	NA	C-2-S		43	-
1874	ATH	NA	C-S-O		39	-
1875	ATH	NA	C		59	.248
1876	STL	N	C		64	.298
1877	STL	N	C-1-O		60	.316
1878	IND	N	M-1-O		60	.296
1879	BUF	N	C		67	.265
1880	CIN	N	M-C-O		79	.280
1881	CLE	N	C-O		65	.253
1883	NY	N	M-C-O		19	.178
		BRTR			574	-

CLARE, DANIEL J. "DENNY"
B.BROOKLYN,N.Y.

YR	CL	LEA	POS	GP	G	REC
1872	ATL	NA	2		2	.143

CLAREY, DOUGLAS WILLIAM "DOUG"
B.APR.20,1954 LOS ANGELES,CAL.

YR	CL	LEA	POS	GP	G	REC
1976	STL	N	2		9	.250
		BRTR				

CLARK, ALFRED ALOYSIUS "ALLIE"
B.JUNE 16,1923 S.AMBOY,N.J.

YR	CL	LEA	POS	GP	G	REC
1947	NY	A	O		24	.373
1948	CLE	A	1-3-O		81	.310
1949	CLE	A	1-O		35	.176
1950	CLE	A	O		59	.215
1951	CLE	A	O		3	.300
	PHI	A	3-O		56	.248
1952	PHI	A	1-O		71	.274
1953	PHI	A	O		20	.203
	CHI	A	1-O		9	.067
		BRTR			358	.262

CLARK, ALFRED ROBERT "DAD"
B.JUL.16,1873 SAN FRANCISCO,CAL
D.JULY 26,1956 OGDEN,UTAH

YR	CL	LEA	POS	GP	G	REC
1902	CHI	N	1		12	.186
		BLTL				

CLARK, BAILEY EARL "EARL"
B.NOV.6,1907 WASHINGTON,D.C.
D.JAN.16,1938

YR	CL	LEA	POS	GP	G	REC
1927	BOS	N	O		13	.273
1928	BOS	N	O		20	.304
1929	BOS	N	O		84	.315
1930	BOS	N	O		82	.296
1931	BOS	N	O		16	.220
1932	BOS	N	O		50	.250
1933	BOS	N	O		7	.348
1934	STL	A	O		13	.171
		BRTR			293	.291

CLARK, DANIEL CURRAN
B.JAN.18,1894 MERIDIAN,MISS.
D.MAY 23,1937 MERIDIAN,MISS.

YR	CL	LEA	POS	GP	G	REC
1922	DET	A	2		83	.292
1924	BOS	A	3		104	.277
1927	STL	N	O		58	.236
		BLTR			245	.277

CLARK, EDWARD C.
B.CINCINNATI,OHIO

YR	CL	LEA	POS	GP	G	REC
1886	ATH	AA	P		1	0- 1
1891	COL	AA	P		5	1- 2
					6	1- 3

CLARK, GLEN ESTER
B.MAR.7,1941 AUSTIN,TEX.

YR	CL	LEA	POS	GP	G	REC
1967	ATL	N	H		4	.000
		BBTR				

CLARK, GEORGE MYRON
B.MAY 19,1891 SMITHLAND,IOWA
D.NOV.14,1940

YR	CL	LEA	POS	GP	G	REC
1913	NY	A	P		11	0- 1
		BRTL				

CLARK, HARRY "PEP"
B.MAR.20,1883 PAULDING,OHIO
D.JUNE 8,1965 MILWAUKEE,WIS.

YR	CL	LEA	POS	GP	G	REC
1903	CHI	A	3		15	.308
		BRTR				

CLARK, HARVEY DANIEL "GINGER"
B.MAR.7,1879 WOOSTER,OHIO
D.MAY 10,1943

YR	CL	LEA	POS	GP	G	REC
1902	CLE	A	P		1	1- 0
		BRTR				

CLARK, JACK ANTHONY
B.NOV.10,1955 NEW BRIGHTON,PA.

YR	CL	LEA	POS	GP	G	REC
1975	SF	N	3-O		8	.235
1976	SF	N	O		26	.225
		BRTR			34	.227

CLARK, JAMES
(REAL NAME JAMES PETROSKY)
B.SEPT.21,1927 BAGLEY,PA.

YR	CL	LEA	POS	GP	G	REC
1948	WAS	A	S-3		9	.250
		BRTR				

CLARK, JAMES EDWARD "JIM"
B.APR.30,1947 KANSAS CITY,KAN.

YR	CL	LEA	POS	GP	G	REC
1971	CLE	A	1-O		13	.167
		BRTR				

CLARK, JAMES F.
B.DEC.26,1887 BROOKLYN,N.Y.

YR	CL	LEA	POS	GP	G	REC
1911	STL	N	O		14	.176
1912	STL	N	O		2	.000
		BRTR			16	.125

CLARK, JOHN CARROLL "CAP"
B.SEPT.19,1909 SNOW CAMP,N.C.
D.FEB.16,1957

YR	CL	LEA	POS	GP	G	REC
1938	PHI	N	C		52	.257
		BLTR				

CLARK, MELVIN EARL "MEL"
B.JULY 7,1926 LETART,W.VA.

YR	CL	LEA	POS	GP	G	REC
1951	PHI	N	O		10	.323
1952	PHI	N	3-O		47	.225
1953	PHI	N	O		60	.298
1954	PHI	N	O		83	.240
1955	PHI	N	O		10	.156
1957	DET	A	O		5	.000
		BRTR			215	.277

CLARK, MICHAEL JOHN "MIKE"
B.FEB.12,1922 CAMDEN,N.J.

YR	CL	LEA	POS	GP	G	REC
1952	STL	N	P		12	2- 0
1953	STL	N	P		23	1- 0
		BRTR			35	3- 0

CLARK, OWEN F. "SPIDER"
B.SEPT.16,1857 BROOKLYN,N.Y.
D.FEB.8,1892

YR	CL	LEA	POS	GP	G	REC
1889	WAS	N	C		37	.255
1890	BUF	P	C-2-O		69	.268
		TR			106	.257

CLARK, PHILIP JAMES "PHIL"
B.OCT.3,1932 ALBANY,GA.

YR	CL	LEA	POS	GP	G	REC
1958	STL	N	P	7	8	0- 1
1959	STL	N	P	7	7	0- 1
		BRTR		14	15	0- 2

CLARK, RICKEY CHARLES
B.MAR.21,1946 MT.CLEMENS,MICH.

YR	CL	LEA	POS	GP	G	REC
1967	CAL	A	P		32	12-11
1968	CAL	A	P		21	1-11
1969	CAL	A	P		6	0- 0
1971	CAL	A	P		11	2- 1
1972	CAL	A	P	26	27	4- 9
		BRTR		96	97	19-32

CLARK, ROBERT H.
B.MAR.18,1863 COVINGTON,KY.
D.AUG.21,1919

YR	CL	LEA	POS	GP	G	REC
1886	BRO	AA	C		72	.228
1887	BRO	AA	C		47	.289
1888	BRO	AA	C		45	.245
1889	BRO	AA	C		53	.245
1890	BRO	N	C		43	.218
1891	CIN	N	C		15	.132
1893	LOU	N	C		11	.103
		BRTR			286	.239

CLARK, ROBERT WILLIAM
B.AUG.22,1897 NEWPORT,PA.
D.MAY 18,1944

YR	CL	LEA	POS	GP	G	REC
1920	CLE	A	P		11	1- 2
1921	CLE	A	P		5	0- 0
		BRTR			16	1- 2

CLARK, RONALD BRUCE "RON"
B.JAN.14,1943 FT.WORTH,TEX.

YR	CL	LEA	POS	GP	G	REC
1966	MIN	A	3		5	1.000
1967	MIN	A	3		20	.167
1968	MIN	A	2-S-3		104	.185
1969	MIN	A	3		5	.125
	SEA	A	1-2-S-3		57	.196
1971	OAK	A	H		2	.000
1972	OAK	A	2-3		14	.267
	MIL	A	2-3		22	.185
1975	PHI	N	H		1	.000
		BRTR			230	.189

CLARK, ROYAL ELLIOTT "PEPPER"
B.MAY 11,1874 NEW HAVEN,CONN.
D.NOV.1,1925

YR	CL	LEA	POS	GP	G	REC
1902	NY	N	O		20	.139

CLARK, WILLIAM H. "DAD"
B.JAN.7,1865 OSWEGO,N.Y.
D.JUNE 3,1911

YR	CL	LEA	POS	GP	G	REC
1888	CHI	N	P		3	2- 0
1891	COL	AA	P		5	0- 0
1894	NY	N	P		16	2- 4
1895	NY	N	P		32	18-14
1896	NY	N	P		43	16-27
1897	NY	N	P		6	0- 3
	LOU	N	P		7	3- 3
1898	LOU	N	P		1	0- 1
		BBTR			113	41-52

CLARK, WILLIAM OTIS
"WEE WILLIE"
B.AUG.16,1872 PITTSBURGH,PA.
D.NOV.13,1932 PITTSBURGH,PA.

YR	CL	LEA	POS	GP	G	REC
1895	NY	N	1		22	.261
1896	NY	N	1		65	.303
1897	NY	N	1		118	.282
1898	PIT	N	1		57	.310
1899	PIT	N	1		79	.282
					341	.289

CLARK, WILLIAM OTIS "OTIE"
B.MAY 22,1918 BOSCOBEL,WIS.

YR	CL	LEA	POS	GP	G	REC
1945	BOS	A	P		12	4- 4
		BRTR				

CLARK, WILLIAM WATSON "WATTY"
B.MAY 16,1902 ST.JOSEPH,LA.
D.MAR.4,1972 CLEARWATER,FLA.

YR	CL	LEA	POS	GP	G	REC
1924	CLE	A	P		12	1- 3
1927	BRO	N	P		27	7- 2
1928	BRO	N	P		40	12- 9
1929	BRO	N	P	41	42	16-19
1930	BRO	N	P		44	13-13
1931	BRO	N	P		34	14-10
1932	BRO	N	P		40	20-12
1933	BRO	N	P		11	2- 4
	NY	N	P		16	3- 4
1934	NY	N	P		5	1- 2
	BRO	N	P		17	2- 0
1935	BRO	N	P	33	34	13- 8
1936	BRO	N	P		33	7-11
1937	BRO	N	P		2	0- 0
		BLTL		355	357	111-97

CLARK, WILLIAM WINFIELD
B.APR.11,1875 CIRCLEVILLE,OHIO
D.APR.15,1959

YR	CL	LEA	POS	GP	G	REC
1897	LOU	N	2		4	.176
		BRTR				

CLARKE, ALAN TOMAS "LEFTY"
B.MAR.8,1896 CLARKSVILLE,MD.
D.MAR.11,1975 CHEVERLY,MD.

YR	CL	LEA	POS	GP	G	REC
1921	CIN	N	P		1	0- 1
		BBTL				

CLARKE, ARTHUR FRANKLIN
"ARCHIE"
B.MAY 6,1865 BROOKLINE,MASS.
D.NOV.14,1949 BROOKLINE,MASS.

YR	CL	LEA	POS	GP	G	REC
1890	NY	N	C-2-3-O		101	.225
1891	NY	N	C		46	.188
					147	.214

YR	CL	LEA	POS	GP	G	REC

CLARKE, FRED CLIFFORD
B.OCT.3,1872 WINTERSET,IOWA
D.AUG.14,1960 WINFIELD,KAN.

YR	CL	LEA	POS	G	REC
1894	LOU	N	O	76	.275
1895	LOU	N	O	132	.354
1896	LOU	N	O	131	.327
1897	LOU	N	M-O	129	.406
1898	LOU	N	M-O	147	.318
1899	LOU	N	M-O	147	.348
1900	PIT	N	M-O	103	.281
1901	PIT	N	M-O	128	.316
1902	PIT	N	M-O	114	.321
1903	PIT	N	M-O	102	.351
1904	PIT	N	M-O	70	.306
1905	PIT	N	M-O	137	.299
1906	PIT	N	M-O	110	.309
1907	PIT	N	M-O	144	.289
1908	PIT	N	M-O	151	.265
1909	PIT	N	M-O	152	.287
1910	PIT	N	M-O	118	.263
1911	PIT	N	M-O	101	.324
1913	PIT	N	M-O	9	.077
1914	PIT	N	M-H	2	.000
1915	PIT	N	M-O	1	.500
		BLTR		2204	.315

NON-PLAYING MANAGER PIT(N) 1912

CLARKE, HARRY CORSON
B.1861
D.MAR.3,1923

1889	WAS	N	C	1	.000

CLARKE, HENRY TEFFT
B.AUG.28,1875 BELLEVUE,NEB.
D.MAR.28,1950

1897	CLE	N	P	8	3- 5
1898	CHI	N	P	2	1- 0
		BRTR		10	4- 5

CLARKE, HORACE MEREDITH
B.JUNE 2,1940 FREDERIKSTED,V.I.

1965	NY	A	2-S-3	51	.259
1966	NY	A	2-S-3	96	.266
1967	NY	A	2	143	.272
1968	NY	A	2	148	.230
1969	NY	A	2	156	.285
1970	NY	A	2	158	.251
1971	NY	A	2	159	.250
1972	NY	A	2	147	.241
1973	NY	A	2	148	.263
1974	NY	A	2	24	.234
	SD	N	2	42	.189
		BBTR		1272	.256

CLARKE, JAY JUSTIN "NIG"
B.DEC.15,1882 AMHERSTBURG,ONT., CANADA
D.JUNE 15,1949 RIVER ROUGE,MICH

1905	CLE	A	C	6	.182
	DET	A	C	2	.400
	CLE	A	C	37	.202
1906	CLE	A	C	57	.358
1907	CLE	A	C	120	.269
1908	CLE	A	C	97	.241
1909	CLE	A	C	55	.274
1910	CLE	A	C	21	.155
1911	STL	A	C	82	.215
1919	PHI	N	C	26	.242
1920	PIT	N	C	3	.000
		BLTR		506	.254

CLARKE, JOSHUA BALDWIN "PEPPER"
B.MAR.8,1879 WINFIELD,KAN.
D.JULY 2,1962

1898	LOU	N	O	6	.167
1905	STL	N	2-O	46	.257
1908	CLE	A	O	131	.242
1909	CLE	A	O	4	.000
1911	BOS	N	O	30	.233
		BLTR		217	.239

CLARKE, RICHARD GREY
B.SEPT.26,1912 FULTON,ALA.

1944	CHI	A	3	63	.260
		BRTR			

CLARKE, RUFUS RIVERS
B.APR.13,1900 ESTILL,S.C.

1923	DET	A	P	5	1- 1
1924	DET	A	P	2	0- 0
		BRTR		7	1- 1

CLARKE, SUMPTER ELLIS
B.OCT.18,1897 SAVANNAH,GA.

1920	CHI	N	3	1	.333
1923	CLE	A	O	1	.000
1924	CLE	A	O	45	.227
		BRTR		47	.224

CLARKE, THOMAS ALOYSIUS
B.MAY 9,1888 NEW YORK,N.Y.
D.AUG.14,1945

1909	CIN	N	C	17	.250
1910	CIN	N	C	56	.278
1911	CIN	N	C	82	.241
1912	CIN	N	C	72	.281
1913	CIN	N	C	114	.264
1914	CIN	N	C	113	.262
1915	CIN	N	C	96	.288
1916	CIN	N	C	78	.237
1917	CIN	N	C	58	.291
1918	CHI	N	C	1	.000
		BRTR		687	.265

CLARKE, VIBERT ERNESTO
B.JUNE 8,1929 COLON,PANAMA
D.JUNE 14,1970 CRISTOBAL,C.Z.

1955	WAS	A	P	7	0- 0
		BLTL			

CLARKE, WILLIAM JONES "BOILERYARD"
B.OCT.18,1868 NEW YORK,N.Y.
D.JULY 29,1959

1893	BAL	N	C	47	.194
1894	BAL	N	C	27	.270
1895	BAL	N	C	60	.297
1896	BAL	N	C	77	.290
1897	BAL	N	C	63	.274
1898	BAL	N	C	77	.245
1899	BOS	N	C	60	.229
1900	BOS	N	C	71	.320
1901	WAS	A	C	109	.284
1902	WAS	A	C	87	.262
1903	WAS	A	C-1	126	.239
1904	WAS	A	C-1	85	.213
1905	NY	N	1	27	.180
		BRTR		916	.260

CLARKE, WILLIAM STUART
B.JAN.24,1907 OAKLAND,CAL.

1929	PIT	N	S-3	57	.264
1930	PIT	N	2	4	.444

CLARKSON, ARTHUR HAMILTON "DAD"
B.AUG.31,1866 CAMBRIDGE,MASS.
D.JAN.6,1911

1891	NY	N	P	5	0- 2
1892	BOS	N	P	1	0- 0
1893	STL	N	P	21	12- 9
1894	STL	N	P	27	9-18
1895	STL	N	P	11	1- 6
	BAL	N	P	17	13- 4
1896	BAL	N	P	7	3- 2
				89	38-41

CLARKSON, JAMES BUSTER "BUS"
B.MAR.13,1918 COLUMBIA,S.C.

1952	BOS	N	S-3	14	.200
		BRTR			

CLARKSON, JOHN GIBSON
B.JULY 1,1861 CAMBRIDGE,MASS.
D.FEB.4,1909 CAMBRIDGE,MASS.

YR	CL	LEA	POS	GP	G	REC
1882	WOR	N	P-1		3	1- 1
						.364
1884	CHI	N	P-1-3-O		20	10- 3
						.261
1885	CHI	N	P-3-	70	72	52-16
			O			.215
1886	CHI	N	P	53	55	35-17
1887	CHI	N	P	59	61	38-21
1888	BOS	N	P		54	33-20
1889	BOS	N	P		72	48-19
1890	BOS	N	P		44	26-18
1891	BOS	N	P		55	34-19
1892	BOS	N	P		16	9- 7
	CLE	N	P		27	17-10
1893	CLE	N	P		34	16-16
1894	CLE	N	P		16	8- 8
		BRTR		523	529	327-175
						.225

CLARKSON, WALTER HAMILTON
B.NOV.3,1878 CAMBRIDGE,MASS.
D.OCT.10,1946

1904	NY	A	P	13	2- 2
1905	NY	A	P	8	2- 2
1906	NY	A	P	32	9- 4
1907	NY	A	P	6	0- 0
1907	CLE	A	P	16	5- 7
1908	CLE	A	P	2	0- 0
		TR		77	18-15

CLARKSON, WILLIAM HENRY "BLACKIE"
B.SEPT.27,1899 PORTSMOUTH,VA.
D.AUG.27,1971 RALEIGH,N.C.

YR	CL	LEA	POS	GP	G	REC
1927	NY	N	P	26	28	3- 9
1928	NY	N	P		4	0- 0
	BOS	N	P		19	0- 2
1929	BOS	N	P		2	0- 1
		BRTR		51	53	3-12

CLARY, ELLIS "CAT"
B.SEPT.11,1916 VALDOSTA,GA.

1942	WAS	A	2	76	.275
1943	WAS	A	3	73	.256
	STL	A	2-S-3	23	.275
1944	STL	A	2-3	25	.265
1945	STL	A	2-3	26	.211
		BRTR		223	.263

CLASET, GOWELL SYLVESTER "LEFTY"
B.NOV.26,1907 BATTLE CREEK,MICH

1933	PHI	A	P	8	2- 0
		BBTL			

CLAUSEN, FRED WILLIAM "FRITZ"
B.APR.26,1869 NEW YORK,N.Y.
D.FEB.11,1960

1892	LOU	N	P	24	9-13
1893	LOU	N	P	9	1- 3
	CHI	N	P	10	5- 3
1894	CHI	N	P	2	0- 1
1896	LOU	N	P	2	0- 1
		BRTL		47	15-21

CLAUSS, ALBERT STANLEY "LEFTY"
B.JUNE 24,1891 NEW HAVEN,CONN.
D.SEPT.13,1952

1913	DET	A	P	4	0- 2
		BRTL			

CLAY, DAIN ELMER "SNIFFY"
B.JULY 10,1919 HICKSVILLE,OHIO

1943	CIN	N	O	49	.269
1944	CIN	N	O	110	.250
1945	CIN	N	O	153	.280
1946	CIN	N	O	121	.228
		BRTR		433	.258

CLAY, FREDERICK C. "BILL"
B.NOV.23,1874 BALTIMORE,MD.
D.OCT.12,1917

1902	PHI	N	O	3	.250
		TR			

CLEARY, JOSEPH CHRISTOPHER
B.DEC.3,1920 CORK,IRELAND

1945	WAS	A	P	1	0- 0
		BRTR			

CLEMENS, CHESTER SPURGEON
B.MAY 10,1918 SAN FERNANDO,CAL.

1939	BOS	N	O	9	.217
1944	BOS	N	O	19	.176
		BRTR		28	.200

CLEMENS, CLEMENT LAMBERT "COUNT"
(REAL NAME CLEMENT LAMBERT ULATOWSKI)
B.NOV.2,1886 CHICAGO,ILL.
D.NOV.2,1967 ST.PETERSBURG,FLA.

1914	CHI	F	C	12	.154
1915	CHI	F	C	11	.136
1916	CHI	N	C	10	.000
		BRTR		33	.111

YR	CL	LEA	POS	GP	G	REC

CLEMENS, DOUGLAS HORACE "DOUG"
B.JUNE 9,1939 LEESPORT,PA.

YR	CL	LEA	POS	GP	G	REC
1960	STL	N	O		1	.000
1961	STL	N	O		6	.167
1962	STL	N	O		48	.237
1963	STL	N	O		5	.167
1964	STL	N	O		33	.205
	CHI	N	O		54	.279
1965	CHI	N	O		128	.221
1966	PHI	N	1-O		79	.256
1967	PHI	N	O		69	.178
1968	PHI	N	O		29	.211
	BLTR				452	.229

CLEMENS, ROBERT BAXTER
B.AUG.9,1886 MT.HEBRON,MO.
D.APR.5,1964 MARSHALL,MO.

1914	STL	A	O		8	.214
	BRTR					

CLEMENSEN, JOHN WILLIAM MELVILLE "BILL"
B.JUNE 20,1919 NEW BRUNSWICK, N.J.

1939	PIT	N	P		12	0- 1
1941	PIT	N	P		2	1- 0
1946	PIT	N	P		1	0- 0
	BRTR				15	1- 1

CLEMENT, WALLACE OAKES
B.JULY 21,1881 AUBURN,ME.
D.NOV.1,1953 CORAL GABLES,FLA.

1908	PHI	N	O		12	.242
1909	PHI	N	O		3	.000
	BRO	N	O		88	.256
	BLTR				103	.251

CLEMENTE, ROBERTO WALKER
D.AUG.18,1934 CAROLINA,P.R.
D.DEC.31,1972 SAN JUAN,P.R.

1955	PIT	N	O		124	.255
1956	PIT	N	2-3-O		147	.311
1957	PIT	N	O		111	.253
1958	PIT	N	O		140	.289
1959	PIT	N	O		105	.296
1960	PIT	N	O		144	.314
1961	PIT	N	O		146	.351
1962	PIT	N	O		144	.312
1963	PIT	N	O		152	.320
1964	PIT	N	O		155	.339
1965	PIT	N	O		152	.329
1966	PIT	N	O		154	.317
1967	PIT	N	O		147	.357
1968	PIT	N	O		132	.291
1969	PIT	N	O		138	.345
1970	PIT	N	O		108	.352
1971	PIT	N	O		132	.341
1972	PIT	N	O		102	.312
	BRTR				2433	.317

CLEMENTS, EDWARD
B.PHILADELPHIA,PA.

1890	PIT	N	S		1	.000

CLEMENTS, JOHN J. "JACK"
B.JULY 24,1864 PHILADELPHIA,PA.
D.MAY 23,1941 NORRISTOWN,PA.

1884	KEY	U	C-S-O		41	.289
	PHI	N	C		8	.240
1885	PHI	N	C-O		52	.191
1886	PHI	N	C		54	.205
1887	PHI	N	C		63	.306
1888	PHI	N	C		85	.247
1889	PHI	N	C		78	.284
1890	PHI	N	C		97	.315
1891	PHI	N	C		105	.305
1892	PHI	N	C		102	.270
1893	PHI	N	C		90	.290
1894	PHI	N	C		47	.343
1895	PHI	N	C		84	.389
1896	PHI	N	C		50	.362
1897	PHI	N	C		49	.239
1898	STL	N	C		85	.268
1899	CLE	N	C		4	.167
1900	BOS	N	C		16	.307
	BLTL				1110	.288

CLEMONS, LANCE LEVIS
B.JULY 7,1947 PHILADELPHIA,PA.

1971	KC	A	P		10	1- 0
1972	STL	N	P		3	0- 1
1974	BOS	A	P		6	1- 0
	BLTL				19	2- 1

CLEMONS, VERNE JAMES "STINGER" OR "TUBBY"
B.SEPT.8,1891 CLEMONS,IOWA
D.MAY 5,1959 BAY PINES,FLA.

1916	STL	A	C		3	.000
1919	STL	N	C		88	.264
1920	STL	N	C		112	.281
1921	STL	N	C		117	.320
1922	STL	N	C		71	.256
1923	STL	N	C		57	.285
1924	STL	N	C		25	.321
	BRTR				473	.287

CLENDENON, DONN ALVIN
B.JULY 15,1935 NEOSHO,MO.

1961	PIT	N	O		9	.314
1962	PIT	N	1-O		80	.302
1963	PIT	N	1		154	.275
1964	PIT	N	1		133	.282
1965	PIT	N	1-3		162	.301
1966	PIT	N	1		155	.299
1967	PIT	N	1		131	.249
1968	PIT	N	1		158	.257
1969	MON	N	1-O		38	.240
	NY	N	1-O		72	.252
1970	NY	N	1		121	.288
1971	NY	N	1		88	.247
1972	STL	N	1		61	.191
	BRTR				1362	.274

CLEVELAND, ELMER E.
B.1862 WASHINGTON,D.C.
D.OCT.8,1913

1884	CIN	U	2		26	.281
1888	NY	N	3		10	.270
	PIT	N	3		30	.204
1891	COL	AA	3		12	.142
	BRTR				78	.228

CLEVELAND, REGINALD LESLIE "REGGIE"
B.MAY 23,1948 SWIFT CURRENT, SASK.,CANADA

1969	STL	N	P		1	0- 0
1970	STL	N	P		16	0- 4
1971	STL	N	P		34	12-12
1972	STL	N	P		33	14-15
1973	STL	N	P		32	14-10
1974	BOS	A	P		41	12-14
1975	BOS	A	P		31	13- 9
1976	BOS	A	P		41	10- 9
	BRTR				229	75-73

CLEVENGER, TRUMAN EUGENE "TEX"
B.JULY 9,1932 VISALIA,CAL.

1954	BOS	A	P	23	25	2- 4
1956	WAS	A	P		20	0- 0
1957	WAS	A	P		52	7- 6
1958	WAS	A	P		55	9- 9
1959	WAS	A	P		50	8- 5
1960	WAS	A	P		53	5-11
1961	LA	A	P		12	2- 1
	NY	A	P		21	1- 1
1962	NY	A	P	21	22	2- 0
	BRTR			307	310	36-37

CLIFT, HARLOND BENTON ""DARKIE"
B.AUG.12,1912 EL RENO,OKLA.

1934	STL	A	3		147	.260
1935	STL	A	2-3		137	.295
1936	STL	A	3		152	.302
1937	STL	A	3		155	.306
1938	STL	A	3		149	.290
1939	STL	A	3		151	.270
1940	STL	A	3		150	.273
1941	STL	A	3		154	.255
1942	STL	A	S-3		143	.274
1943	STL	A	3		105	.232
	WAS	A	3		8	.300
1944	WAS	A	3		12	.159
1945	WAS	A	3		119	.211
	BRTR				1582	.272

CLIFTON, HERMAN EARL "FLEA"
B.DEC.12,1909 CINCINNATI,OHIO

1934	DET	A	2-3		16	.063
1935	DET	A	2-S-3		43	.255
1936	DET	A	2-S-3		13	.192
1937	DET	A	2-S-3		15	.116
	BRTR				87	.200

CLINE, JOHN "MONK"
B.LOUISVILLE,KY.

1882	BAL	AA	2-S-3-O		45	.222
1884	LOU	AA	S-O		94	.287
1885	LOU	AA	3-O		2	.222
1888	KC	AA	O		73	.243
1891	LOU	AA	O		19	.304
					233	.277

CLINE, TYRONE ALEXANDER "TY"
B.JUNE 15,1939 HAMPTON,S.C.

1960	CLE	A	O		7	.308
1961	CLE	A	O		12	.209
1962	CLE	A	O		118	.248
1963	MIL	N	O		72	.236
1964	MIL	N	1-O		101	.302
1965	MIL	N	1-O		123	.191
1966	CHI	N	O		7	.353
	ATL	N	1-O		42	.254
1967	ATL	N	O		10	.000
	SF	N	O		64	.270
1968	SF	N	1-O		116	.223
1969	MON	N	1-O		101	.239
1970	MON	N	H		2	.500
	CIN	N	1-O		48	.270
1971	CIN	N	1-O		69	.196
	BLTL				892	.238

CLINES, EUGENE "GENE"
B.OCT.6,1946 SAN PABLO,CAL.

1970	PIT	N	O		31	.405
1971	PIT	N	O		97	.308
1972	PIT	N	O		107	.334
1973	PIT	N	O		110	.263
1974	PIT	N	O		107	.225
1975	NY	N	O		82	.227
1976	TEX	A	O-D		116	.274
	BRTR				650	.278

CLINGMAN, WILLIAM FREDERICK
B.NOV.21,1869 CINCINNATI,OHIO
D.MAY 14,1958

1890	CIN	N	S		7	.258
1891	CIN	AA	2		1	.200
1895	PIT	N	3		108	.261
1896	LOU	N	3		120	.230
1897	LOU	N	3		115	.232
1898	LOU	N	S-3		154	.262
1899	LOU	N	S		108	.267
1900	CHI	N	S		46	.201
1901	WAS	A	S		137	.245
1903	CLE	A	2-S-3		21	.286
	BBTR				817	.248

CLINTON, JAMES LAWRENCE "BIG JIM"
B.AUG.10,1850 NEW YORK,N.Y.
D.SEPT.3,1921

1872	ECK	NA	M-2-S-3-O	24		.188
1873	RES	NA	3-O		8	–
1874	ATL	NA	1-2-O		4	–
1875	ATL	NA	P-1- 13		22	1-12
			2-O			–
1876	LOU	N	P-O	2	16	0- 1
						.338
1882	WOR	N	O		26	.163
1883	BAL	AA	2-O		94	.305
1884	BAL	AA	O		105	.281
1885	CIN	AA	O		98	.239
1886	BAL	AA	O		23	.183
	BRTR			15	420	1-13
						–

CLINTON, LUCIEAN LOUIS "LOU"
B.OCT.13,1937 PONCA CITY,OKLA.

1960	BOS	A	O		96	.228
1961	BOS	A	O		17	.255
1962	BOS	A	O		114	.294
1963	BOS	A	O		148	.232
1964	BOS	A	O		37	.258
	LA	A	O		91	.248
1965	CAL	A	O		89	.243
	KC	A	O		1	.000
	CLE	A	O		12	.176
1966	NY	A	O		80	.220
1967	NY	A	O		6	.500
	BRTR				691	.247

CLOLO, CARLOS
(PLAYED UNDER NAME OF CHARLES LOUIS HALL)

YR	CL	LEA	POS	GP	G	REC

CLONINGER, TONY LEE
B.AUG.13,1940 LINCOLN CO.,N.C.

YR	CL	LEA	POS	GP	G	REC
1961	MIL	N	P		19	7- 2
1962	MIL	N	P		24	8- 3
1963	MIL	N	P		41	9-11
1964	MIL	N	P		38	19-14
1965	MIL	N	P	40	41	24-11
1966	ATL	N	P	39	47	14-11
1967	ATL	N	P		16	4- 7
1968	ATL	N	P		8	1- 3
	CIN	N	P	17	21	4- 3
1969	CIN	N	P	35	36	11-17
1970	CIN	N	P		30	9- 7
1971	CIN	N	P		28	3- 6
1972	STL	N	P		17	0- 2
	BRTR			352	366	113-97

CLOSTER, ALAN EDWARD "AL"
B.JUNE 15,1943 CREIGHTON,NEB.

1966	WAS	A	P		1	0- 0
1971	NY	A	P		14	2- 2
1972	NY	A	P		2	0- 0
1973	ATL	N	P		4	0- 0
	BLTL				21	2- 2

CLOUGH, EDGAR GEORGE "BIG ED"
B.OCT.28,1906 WICONISCO,PA.
D.JAN.30,1944 HARRISBURG,PA.

1924	STL	N	O		7	.071
1925	STL	N	P		3	0- 1
1926	STL	N	P		1	0- 0
	BLTL			4	11	0- 1
						.111

CLOWERS, WILLIAM P.
B.AUG.14,1897 SAN ANTONIO,TEX.

1926	BOS	A	P		2	0- 0
	BLTL					

CLYDE, DAVID EUGENE
B.APR.22,1955 KANSAS CITY,KAN.

1973	TEX	A	P		18	4- 8
1974	TEX	A	P		28	3- 9
1975	TEX	A	P		1	0- 1
	BLTL				47	7-18

CLYDE, THOMAS KNOX
B.AUG.17,1923 WACHAPREAGUE,VA.

1943	PHI	A	P		4	0- 0
	BRTR					

CLYMER, OTIS EDGAR
B.JAN.27,1880 PINE GROVE,PA.
D.FEB.27,1926

1905	PIT	N	O		90	.296
1906	PIT	N	O		11	.244
1907	PIT	N	O		16	.227
	WAS	A	O		57	.316
1908	WAS	A	O		110	.253
1909	WAS	A	O		45	.196
1913	CHI	N	O		30	.229
	BOS	N	O		14	.324
	BLTR				373	.267

CLYMER, WILLIAM JOHNSTON "DERBY DAY BILL"
B.DEC.18,1873 PHILADELPHIA,PA.
D.DEC.26,1936

1891	ATH	AA	S		3	.000

COAKLEY, ANDREW JAMES
(PLAYED UNDER NAME OF
JACK MC ALLISTER IN 1902)
B.NOV.20,1882 PROVIDENCE, R.I.
D.SEPT.27,1963 NEW YORK,N.Y.

1902	PHI	A	P		3	2- 1
1903	PHI	A	P		6	0- 3
1904	PHI	A	P		11	7- 4
1905	PHI	A	P		34	20- 8
1906	PHI	A	P		22	7- 8
1907	CIN	N	P		37	17-16
1908	CIN	N	P		32	8-18
	CHI	N	P		4	2- 0
1909	CHI	N	P		1	0- 1
1911	NY	A	P		2	0- 1
	BLTR				152	63-60

COAN, GILBERT FITZGERALD "GIL"
B.MAY 18,1924 MONROE,N.C.

1946	WAS	A	P		59	.209
1947	WAS	A	O		11	.500
1948	WAS	A	O		111	.218
1949	WAS	A	O		104	.303
1950	WAS	A	O		135	.303
1951	WAS	A	O		107	.205
1952	WAS	A	O		68	.196
1953	WAS	A	O		94	.279
1954	BAL	A	O		61	.238
1955	BAL	A	O		17	.176
	CHI	A	O		9	.154
	NY	N	O		4	.000
1956	NY	N	H		918	.254
	BLTR					

COATES, JAMES ALTON "JIM"
B.AUG.4,1932 FARNHAM,VA.

1956	NY	A	P		2	0- 0
1959	NY	A	P		37	6- 1
1960	NY	A	P		35	13- 3
1961	NY	A	P		43	11- 5
1962	NY	A	P		50	7- 6
1963	WAS	A	P		20	2- 4
	CIN	N	P		9	0- 0
1965	CAL	A	P		17	2- 0
1966	CAL	A	P		9	1- 1
1967	CAL	A	P		25	1- 2
	BRTR				247	43-22

COBB, GEORGE WASHINGTON
B.SAN FRANCISCO,CAL.

1892	BAL	N	P	47	49	9-38

COBB, HERBERT EDWARD
B.AUG.6,1904 PINETOPS,N.C.

1929	STL	A	P		1	0- 0
	BRTR					

COBB, JOSEPH STANLEY
(REAL NAME
JOSEPH STANLEY SERAFIN)
B.JAN.24,1895 HUDSON,PA.
D.DEC.24,1947

1918	DET	A	C		1	.000
	BRTR					

**COBB, TYRUS RAYMOND "TY"
OR "THE GEORGIA PEACH"**
B.DEC.18,1886 NARROWS BANKS CO. GA.
D.JULY 17,1961 ATLANTA,GA.

1905	DET	A	O		41	.240
1906	DET	A	O		97	.320
1907	DET	A	O		150	.350
1908	DET	A	O		150	.324
1909	DET	A	O		156	.377
1910	DET	A	O		140	.385
1911	DET	A	O		146	.420
1912	DET	A	O		140	.410
1913	DET	A	2-O		122	.390
1914	DET	A	C		97	.368
1915	DET	A	O		156	.369
1916	DET	A	O		145	.371
1917	DET	A	O		152	.383
1918	DET	A	1-O		111	.382
1919	DET	A	O		124	.384
1920	DET	A	O		112	.334
1921	DET	A	M-O		128	.389
1922	DET	A	M-O		137	.401
1923	DET	A	M-O		145	.340
1924	DET	A	M-O		155	.338
1925	DET	A	M-P-	1	121	0- 0
			O			.378
1926	DET	A	M-O		79	.339
1927	PHI	A	O		134	.357
1928	PHI	A	O		95	.323
	BLTR			1	3033	0- 0
						.367

COBLE, DAVID LAMAR
B.DEC.24,1915 MONROE,N.C.
D.OCT.15,1971 ORLANDO,FLA.

1939	PHI	N	C		15	.280
	BRTR					

COCHRAN, ALVAH JACKSON "GOAT"
B.JAN.31,1891 CONCORD,GA.
D.MAY 23,1947

1915	CIN	N	P		1	0- 0
	BRTR					

COCHRAN, GEORGE LESLIE
B.FEB.12,1889 RUSK,TEX.

1918	BOS	A	3		25	.127
	TR					

COCHRANE, GORDON STANLEY "MICKEY"
B.APR.6,1903 BRIDGEWATER,MASS.
D.JUNE 28,1962 LAKE FOREST,ILL.

1925	PHI	A	C		134	.331
1926	PHI	A	C		120	.273
1927	PHI	A	C		126	.338
1928	PHI	A	C		131	.293
1929	PHI	A	C		135	.331
1930	PHI	A	C		130	.357
1931	PHI	A	C		122	.349
1932	PHI	A	C		139	.293
1933	PHI	A	C		130	.322
1934	DET	A	M-C		129	.320
1935	DET	A	M-C		115	.319
1936	DET	A	M-C		44	.270
1937	DET	A	M-C		27	.306
	BLTR				1482	.320

NON-PLAYING MANAGER DET (A)1938

COCKMAN, JAMES
B.APR.26,1873 GUELPH,ONT.,CAN.
D.SEPT.28,1947 GUELPH,ONT.,CAN.

1905	NY	A	3		13	.076
	BRTR					

COCREHAM, EUGENE
B.NOV.14,1890 LULING,TEX.
D.DEC.27,1945

1913	BOS	N	P		1	0- 1
1914	BOS	N	P		15	3- 4
1915	BOS	N	P		1	0- 0
	BRTR				17	3- 5

COFFEY, JOHN FRANCIS
B.JAN.28,1888 NEW YORK,N.Y.
D.FEB.14,1966 NEW YORK,N.Y.

1909	BOS	N	S		73	.186
1918	DET	A	2		22	.209
	BOS	A	2-3		15	.159
	BRTR				110	.188

COFFEY, JOHN JOSEPH
B.AUG.8,1893 OSWAYA,PA.

1912	DET	A	3		1	.000
	TR					

COFFMAN, GEORGE DAVID "SLICK"
B.DEC.11,1910 VETO,ALA.

1937	DET	A	P		28	7- 5
1938	DET	A	P		39	4- 4
1939	DET	A	P		23	2- 1
1940	STL	A	P	31	32	2- 2
	BRTR			121	122	15-12

COFFMAN, SAMUEL RICHARD "DICK"
B.DEC.18,1906 VETO,ALA.
D.MAR.24,1972 ATHENS,ALA.

1927	WAS	A	P		5	0- 1
1928	STL	A	P		29	4- 5
1929	STL	A	P		27	1- 1
1930	STL	A	P		38	8-18
1931	STL	A	P		32	9-13
1932	STL	A	P		9	5- 3
	WAS	A	P		22	1- 6
1933	STL	A	P		21	3- 7
1934	STL	A	P		40	9-10
1935	STL	A	P		41	5-11
1936	NY	N	P		42	7- 5
1937	NY	N	P		42	8- 3
1938	NY	N	P		51	4- 4
1939	NY	N	P		28	1- 2
1940	BOS	N	P		31	1- 5
1945	PHI	N	P		14	2- 1
	BRTR				472	72-95

COGAN, RICHARD HENRY
B.DEC.5,1871 PATERSON,N.J.
D.MAY 2,1948

1897	BAL	N	P		1	0- 0
1899	CHI	N	P		8	2- 3
1900	NY	N	P		3	0- 0
					12	2- 3

COGGINS, FRANKLIN "FRANK"
B.MAY.22,1944 GRIFFIN,GA.

1967	WAS	A	2		19	.307
1968	WAS	A	2		62	.175
1972	CHI	N	H		6	.000
	BBTR				87	.215

YR	CL	LEA	POS	GP	G	REC

COGGINS, RICHARD ALLEN "RICH"
B.DEC.7,1950 INDIANAPOLIS,IND.
1972	BAL	A	O	16		.333
1973	BAL	A	O	110		.319
1974	BAL	A	O	113		.243
1975	MON	N	O	13		.270
	NY	A	O	51		.224
1976	NY	A	O	7		.250
	CHI	A	O	32		.156
	BLTL			342		.265

COGSWELL, EDWARD
B.FEB.25,1854 ENGLAND
D.JULY 27,1888
1879	BOS	N	1	49		.322
1880	TRO	N	1	47		.301
1882	WOR	N	1	13		.122
	BR			109		.291

COHEN, ALTA ALBERT "SCHOOLBOY"
B.DEC.25,1910 NEW YORK,N.Y.
1931	BRO	N	O	1		.667
1932	BRO	N	O	9		.156
1933	PHI	N	O	19		.188
	BLTL			29		.194

COHEN, ANDREW HOWARD
B.OCT.25,1904 BALTIMORE,MD.
1926	NY	N	2-S	32		.257
1928	NY	N	2	129		.274
1929	NY	N	2	101		.294
	BRTR			262		.281

COHEN, HARRY
(PLAYED UNDER NAME OF
HARRY KANE)

COHEN, HYMAN
B.JAN.29,1931 BROOKLYN,N.Y.
| 1955 | CHI | N | P | 7 | | 0- 0 |
| | BRTR | | | | | |

COHEN, REUBEN
(PLAYED UNDER NAME OF
REUBEN EWING)

COHEN, SAMUEL ARTHUR
(PLAYED UNDER NAME OF
SAMUEL ARTHUR BOHNE)

COHEN, SYDNEY HARRY
B.MAY 7,1908 BALTIMORE,MD.
1934	WAS	A	P-O	3	4	1- 1
						.273
1936	WAS	A	P		19	0- 2
1937	WAS	A	P		33	2- 4
	BBTL			55	56	3- 7
						.152

COHN, PHILIP
(PLAYED UNDER NAME OF
PHILIP COONEY)

COKER, JIMMIE GOODWIN
B.MAR.28,1936 HOLLY HILL,S.C.
1958	PHI	N	C	2		.167
1960	PHI	N	C	81		.214
1961	PHI	N	C	11		.400
1962	PHI	N	H	5		.000
1963	SF	N	C	4		.200
1964	CIN	N	C	11		.313
1965	CIN	N	C	24		.246
1966	CIN	N	C-O	50		.252
1967	CIN	N	C	45		.186
	BRTR			233		.231

COLAVITO, ROCCO DOMENICO "ROCKY"
B.AUG.10,1933 BRONX,N.Y.
1955	CLE	A	O		5	.444
1956	CLE	A	O		101	.276
1957	CLE	A	O		134	.252
1958	CLE	A	P-1-O	1	143	0- 0
						.303
1959	CLE	A	O		154	.257
1960	DET	A	O		145	.249
1961	DET	A	O		163	.290
1962	DET	A	O		161	.273
1963	DET	A	O		160	.271
1964	KC	A	O		160	.274
1965	CLE	A	O		162	.287
1966	CLE	A	O		151	.238
1967	CLE	A	O		63	.241
	CHI	A	O		60	.221
1968	LA	N	O		40	.204
	NY	A	P-O	1	39	1- 0
						.220
	BRTR			2	1841	1- 0
						.266

COLBERT, NATHAN "NATE"
B.APR.9,1946 ST.LOUIS,MO.
1966	HOU	N	H		19	.000
1968	HOU	N	1-O		20	.151
1969	SD	N	1		139	.255
1970	SD	N	1-3		156	.259
1971	SD	N	1		156	.264
1972	SD	N	1		151	.250
1973	SD	N	1		145	.270
1974	SD	N	1-O		119	.207
1975	DET	A	1		45	.147
	MON	N	1		38	.173
1976	MON	N	1-O		14	.200
	OAK	A	H		2	.000
	BRTR				1004	.243

COLBERT, VINCENT NORMAN "VINCE"
B.DEC.20,1945 WASHINGTON,D.C.
1970	CLE	A	P		23	1- 1
1971	CLE	A	P	50	52	7- 6
1972	CLE	A	P	22	23	1- 7
	BRTR			95	98	9-14

COLBORN, JAMES WILLIAM "JIM"
B.MAY 22,1946 SANTA PAULA,CAL.
1969	CHI	N	P		6	1- 0
1970	CHI	N	P		34	3- 1
1971	CHI	N	P		14	0- 1
1972	MIL	A	P		39	7- 7
1973	MIL	A	P		43	20-12
1974	MIL	A	P		33	10-13
1975	MIL	A	P		36	11-13
1976	MIL	A	P		32	9-15
	BRTR				237	61-62

COLCLOUGH, THOMAS BERNARD
B.OCT.8,1870 CHARLESTON,S.C.
D.DEC.10,1919
1893	PIT	N	P		8	2- 0
1894	PIT	N	P		19	7- 7
1895	PIT	N	P		8	1- 1
1899	NY	N	P		14	4- 5
	BRTR				49	14-13

COLE, ALBERT GEORGE "BERT"
B.JULY 1,1898 SAN FRANCISCO,CAL
D.MAY 30,1975 SAN MATEO,CAL.
1921	DET	A	P	20	30	7- 4
1922	DET	A	P	24	27	1- 6
1923	DET	A	P	52	58	13- 5
1924	DET	A	P	28	33	3- 9
1925	DET	A	P		14	2- 3
	CLE	A	P		13	1- 1
1927	CHI	A	P		27	1- 4
	BLTL			177	202	28-32

COLE, DAVID BRUCE "DAVE"
B.AUG.29,1930 WILLIAMSPORT,MD.
1950	BOS	N	P		4	0- 1
1951	BOS	N	P		23	2- 4
1952	BOS	N	P		22	1- 1
1953	MIL	N	P		10	0- 1
1954	CHI	N	P	18	19	3- 8
1955	PHI	N	P		7	0- 3
	BRTR			84	85	6-18

COLE, EDWARD WILLIAM
(REAL NAME
EDWARD WILLIAM KISLEAISKAS)
B.MAR.25,1911 WILKES-BARRE,PA.
1938	STL	A	P		36	1- 5
1939	STL	A	P		6	0- 2
	BRTR				42	1- 7

COLE, LEONARD LESLIE "KING"
B.APR.15,1886 TOLEDO,IOWA
D.JAN.6,1916
1909	CHI	N	P		1	1- 0
1910	CHI	N	P		33	20- 4
1911	CHI	N	P		32	18- 7
1912	CHI	N	P		8	1- 2
	PIT	N	P		12	2- 2
1914	NY	A	P		33	11- 9
1915	NY	A	P		10	2- 3
	BRTR				129	55-27

COLE, RICHARD ROY "DICK"
B.MAY 6,1926 LONG BEACH,CAL.
1951	STL	N	2		15	.194
	PIT	N	2-S		42	.236
1953	PIT	N	1-2-S		97	.272
1954	PIT	N	2-S-3		138	.270
1955	PIT	N	2-S-3		77	.226
1956	PIT	N	2-S-3		72	.212
1957	MIL	N	1-2-3		15	.071
	BRTR				456	.249

COLE, WILLIS RUSSEL
B.JAN.6,1882 MILTON JUNCTION,
WIS.
D.OCT.11,1965
1909	CHI	A	O		46	.236
1910	CHI	A	O		22	.175
	BRTR				68	.216

COLEMAN, CLARENCE "CHOO CHOO"
B.AUG.25,1937 ORLANDO,FLA.
1961	PHI	N	C		34	.128
1962	NY	N	C		55	.250
1963	NY	N	C-O		106	.178
1966	NY	N	C		6	.188
	BLTR				201	.197

COLEMAN, CURTIS HANCOCK
B.FEB.18,1888 SALEM,ORE.
| 1912 | NY | A | 3 | | 12 | .263 |
| | BLTR | | | | | |

COLEMAN, GERALD FRANCIS "JERRY"
B.SEPT.14,1924 SAN JOSE,CAL.
1949	NY	A	2-S		128	.275
1950	NY	A	2-S		153	.287
1951	NY	A	2-S		121	.249
1952	NY	A	2		11	.405
1953	NY	A	2-S		8	.200
1954	NY	A	2-S-3		107	.217
1955	NY	A	2-S-3		43	.229
1956	NY	A	2-S-3		80	.257
1957	NY	A	2-S-3		72	.268
	BRTR				723	.263

COLEMAN, GORDON CALVIN "GORDY"
B.JULY 5,1934 ROCKVILLE,MD.
1959	CLE	A	1		6	.533
1960	CIN	N	1		66	.271
1961	CIN	N	1		150	.287
1962	CIN	N	1		136	.277
1963	CIN	N	1		123	.247
1964	CIN	N	1		89	.242
1965	CIN	N	1		108	.302
1966	CIN	N	1		91	.251
1967	CIN	N	1		4	.000
	BLTR				773	.273

COLEMAN, JOHN
B.BRISTOL,PA.
| 1890 | PHI | N | P | | 1 | 0- 0 |

COLEMAN, JOHN
B.JEFFERSON CITY,MO.
| 1895 | STL | N | P | | 2 | 0- 1 |

YR	CL	LEA	POS	GP	G	REC

COLEMAN, JOHN FRANCIS
B.MAR.6,1863 SARATOGA SPGS.,N.Y
B.MAY 31,1922

YR	CL	LEA	POS	GP	G	REC
1883	PHI	N	P-O	63	89	13-48
						.232
1884	PHI	N	P-1-O	19	43	5-14
						.245
	ATH	AA	P-O	2	30	0- 2
						.196
1885	ATH	AA	P-O	4	97	1- 3
						.309
1886	ATH	AA	P-O	2	122	1- 1
						.252
	PIT	AA	O		10	.333
1887	PIT	N	O		115	.334
1888	PIT	N	1-O		115	.230
1889	ATH	AA	P		6	3- 2
1890	PIT	N	P		3	0- 2
	BLTR			99	630	23-72
						.267

BB 1887

COLEMAN, JOSEPH HOWARD "JOE"
B.FEB.3,1947 BOSTON,MASS.

YR	CL	LEA	POS	GP	G	REC
1965	WAS	A	P		2	2- 0
1966	WAS	A	P		1	1- 0
1967	WAS	A	P		28	8- 9
1968	WAS	A	P	33	34	12-16
1969	WAS	A	P		40	12-13
1970	WAS	A	P		39	8-12
1971	DET	A	P		39	20- 9
1972	DET	A	P		40	19-14
1973	DET	A	P		40	23-15
1974	DET	A	P		41	14-12
1975	DET	A	P		31	10-18
1976	DET	A	P		12	2- 5
	CHI	N	P		39	2- 8
	BRTR			385	386	133-131

COLEMAN, JOSEPH PATRICK
B.JULY 30,1922 MEDFORD,MASS.

YR	CL	LEA	POS	GP	G	REC
1942	PHI	A	P		1	0- 1
1946	PHI	A	P		4	0- 2
1947	PHI	A	P	32	6-12	
1948	PHI	A	P	33	14-13	
1949	PHI	A	P	33	13-14	
1950	PHI	A	P		15	0- 5
1951	PHI	A	P		28	1- 6
1953	PHI	A	P		21	3- 4
1954	BAL	A	P	33	13-17	
1955	BAL	A	P		6	0- 1
	DET	A	P		17	2- 1
	BRTR			223	52-76	

COLEMAN, PARKE EDWARD "ED"
B.DEC.1,1902 CANBY,ORE.
D.AUG.5,1964 OREGON CITY,ORE.

YR	CL	LEA	POS	GP	G	REC
1932	PHI	A	O		26	.342
1933	PHI	A	O		102	.281
1934	PHI	A	O		101	.280
1935	PHI	A	O		10	.077
	STL	A	O		108	.287
1936	STL	A	O		92	.292
	BLTR			439	.285	

COLEMAN, PIERCE D. "PERCY"
B.CINCINNATI,OHIO

YR	CL	LEA	POS	GP	G	REC
1897	STL	N	P		12	1- 5
1898	CIN	N	P		1	0- 1
					13	1- 6

COLEMAN, RAYMOND LEROY "RAY"
B.JUNE 4,1922 DUNSMUIR,CAL.

YR	CL	LEA	POS	GP	G	REC
1947	STL	A	O		110	.259
1948	STL	A	O		17	.172
	PHI	A	O		68	.243
1950	STL	A	O		117	.271
1951	STL	A	O		91	.282
	CHI	A	O		51	.276
1952	CHI	A	O		85	.215
	STL	A	O		20	.196
	BLTR			559	.258	

COLEMAN, ROBERT HUNTER
B.SEPT.26,1890 HUNTINGBURG,IND.
D.JULY 16,1959

YR	CL	LEA	POS	GP	G	REC
1913	PIT	N	C		24	.180
1914	PIT	N	C		73	.266
1916	CLE	A	C		19	.214
	BRTR			116	.241	

NON-PLAYING MANAGER
BOS (N) 1944-45

COLEMAN, WALTER GARY "RIP"
B.JULY 31,1931 TROY,N.Y.

YR	CL	LEA	POS	GP	G	REC
1955	NY	A	P		10	2- 1
1956	NY	A	P		29	3- 5
1957	KC	A	P		19	0- 7
1959	KC	A	P		29	2-10
	BAL	A	P		3	0- 0
1960	BAL	A	P		5	0- 2
	BLTL			95	7-25	

COLES, CADWALLADER R. "CAD"
B.JAN.17,1885 AUGUSTA,GA.
D.JUNE 30,1942

YR	CL	LEA	POS	GP	G	REC
1915	KC	F	O		77	.253
	BLTR					

COLES, CHARLES EDWARD
B.JUNE 27,1931 FREDERICKTOWN,PA

YR	CL	LEA	POS	GP	G	REC
1958	CIN	N	O		5	.182
	BLTL					

COLETTA, CHRISTOPHER MICHAEL "CHRIS"
B.AUG.2,1944 BROOKLYN,N.Y.

YR	CL	LEA	POS	GP	G	REC
1972	CAL	A	O		14	.300
	BLTL					

COLGAN, WILLIAM H.
B.E.ST.LOUIS,ILL.

YR	CL	LEA	POS	GP	G	REC
1884	PIT	AA	C		48	.166

COLIVER, WILLIAM J.
B.1867 DETROIT,MICH.
D.MAR.24,1888

YR	CL	LEA	POS	GP	G	REC
1885	BOS	N	O		1	.000

COLLAMORE, ALLAN EDWARD
B.JUNE 5,1887 WORCESTER,MASS.

YR	CL	LEA	POS	GP	G	REC
1911	PHI	A	P		2	0- 0
1914	CLE	A	P		27	3- 7
1915	CLE	A	P	11	13	2- 5
	BRTR		40	42	5-12	

COLLARD, EARL CLINTON "HAP"
B.AUG.29,1900 WILLIAMS,ARIZ.
D.JULY 9,1968 JAMESTOWN,CAL.

YR	CL	LEA	POS	GP	G	REC
1927	CLE	A	P		4	0- 0
1928	CLE	A	P		1	0- 0
1930	PHI	N	P	30	31	6-12
	BRTR		35	36	6-12	

COLLIER, ORLIN EDWARD
B.FEB.17,1907 E.PRAIRIE,MO.
D.SEPT.9,1944

YR	CL	LEA	POS	GP	G	REC
1931	DET	A	P		2	0- 1
	BRTR					

COLLIFLOWER, JAMES HARRY "COLLIE"
B.MAR.11,1869 PETERSVILLE,MD.
D.AUG.14,1961

YR	CL	LEA	POS	GP	G	REC
1899	CLE	N	P		21	1-11
	BLTL					

COLLINS, CHARLES "CHUB"
B.1857 DUNDAS,ONT.,CANADA
D.MAY 20,1914

YR	CL	LEA	POS	GP	G	REC
1884	BUF	N	2-S		45	.177
	IND	AA	2		38	.229
1885	DET	N	S		14	.179
					97	.197

COLLINS, CYRIL WILSON
B.MAY 7,1889 PULASKI,TENN.
D.FEB.28,1941

YR	CL	LEA	POS	GP	G	REC
1913	BOS	N	O		16	.333
1914	BOS	N	O		27	.257
	BRTR			43	.263	

COLLINS, DANIEL THOMAS
B.JULY 12,1854
D.SEPT.21,1883

YR	CL	LEA	POS	GP	G	REC
1874	CHI	NA	P-S		3	1- 1
						-
1876	LOU	N	O		7	-.143
					10	1- 1
						-

COLLINS, DAVID S "DAVE"
B.OCT.20,1952 RAPID CITY,S.D.

YR	CL	LEA	POS	GP	G	REC
1975	CAL	A	O-D		93	.266
1976	CAL	A	O-D		99	.263
	BBTL			192	.265	

COLLINS, EDWARD TROWBRIDGE JR.
B.NOV.23,1916 LANSDOWNE,PA.

YR	CL	LEA	POS	GP	G	REC
1939	PHI	A	O		32	.238
1941	PHI	A	O		80	.242
1942	PHI	A	O		20	.235
	BLTR			132	.241	

COLLINS, EDWARD TROWBRIDGE SR.
(PLAYED UNDER NAME OF
EDWARD T. SULLIVAN IN 1906)
B.MAY 2,1887 MILLERTOWN,N.Y.
D.MAR.25,1951 BOSTON,MASS.

YR	CL	LEA	POS	GP	G	REC
1906	PHI	A	3		6	.200
1907	PHI	A	S		14	.320
1908	PHI	A	2-S		102	.273
1909	PHI	A	2		153	.346
1910	PHI	A	2		153	.322
1911	PHI	A	2		132	.365
1912	PHI	A	2		153	.348
1913	PHI	A	2		148	.345
1914	PHI	A	2		152	.344
1915	CHI	A	2		155	.332
1916	CHI	A	2		155	.308
1917	CHI	A	2		156	.289
1918	CHI	A	2		97	.276
1919	CHI	A	2		140	.319
1920	CHI	A	2		153	.369
1921	CHI	A	2		139	.337
1922	CHI	A	2		154	.324
1923	CHI	A	2		145	.360
1924	CHI	A	2		152	.349
1925	CHI	A	M-2		118	.346
1926	CHI	A	M-2		106	.344
1927	PHI	A	2		95	.338
1928	PHI	A	S		36	.303
1929	PHI	A	H		9	.000
1930	PHI	A	H		3	.500
	BLTR			2826	.333	

COLLINS, HARRY WARREN "RIP"
B.FEB.26,1896 WEATHERFORD,TEX.
D.MAY 27,1968 BRYAN,TEX.

YR	CL	LEA	POS	GP	G	REC
1920	NY	A	P		36	14- 8
1921	NY	A	P		28	11- 5
1922	BOS	A	P		32	14-11
1923	DET	A	P		17	3- 7
1924	DET	A	P	34	37	14- 7
1925	DET	A	P		26	6-11
1926	DET	A	P	30	31	8- 8
1927	DET	A	P		30	13- 7
1929	STL	A	P		26	11- 6
1930	STL	A	P		35	9- 7
1931	STL	A	P		17	5- 5
	BBTR	311	315	108-82		

BR 1924-31

COLLINS, HUBERT B.
B.APR.5,1864 LOUISVILLE,KY.
D.MAY 21,1892

YR	CL	LEA	POS	GP	G	REC
1886	LOU	AA	O		27	.287
1887	LOU	AA	O		129	.349
1888	LOU	AA	2-O		114	.321
	BRO	AA	2		12	.295
1889	BRO	AA	2		138	.268
1890	BRO	N	2		129	.278
1891	BRO	N	2-O		107	.284
1892	BRO	N	O		20	.302
	BRTR			676	.300	

COLLINS, JAMES ANTHONY "RIP"
B.MAR.30,1905 ALTOONA,PA.
D.APR.16,1970 NEW HAVEN,N.Y.

YR	CL	LEA	POS	GP	G	REC
1931	STL	N	1		89	.301
1932	STL	N	1-O		149	.279
1933	STL	N	1		132	.310
1934	STL	N	1		154	.333
1935	STL	N	1		150	.313
1936	STL	N	1		103	.292
1937	CHI	N	1		115	.274
1938	CHI	N	1		143	.267
1941	PIT	N	1-O		49	.210
	BBTL			1084	.296	

YR	CL	LEA	POS	GP	G	REC

COLLINS, JAMES JOSEPH "JIMMY"
B.JAN.16,1873 BUFFALO,N.Y.
D.MAR.6,1943 BUFFALO,N.Y.

YR	CL	LEA	POS	GP	G	REC
1895	BOS	N	3		11	.205
	LOU	N	3		93	.286
1896	BOS	N	3		83	.300
1897	BOS	N	3		133	.346
1898	BOS	N	3		152	.337
1899	BOS	N	3		151	.275
1900	BOS	N	3		142	.299
1901	BOS	A	M-3		138	.329
1902	BOS	A	M-3		105	.325
1903	BOS	A	M-3		130	.296
1904	BOS	A	M-3		156	.265
1905	BOS	A	M-3		131	.276
1906	BOS	A	M-3		37	.275
1907	BOS	A	3		41	.294
	PHI	A	3		100	.273
1908	PHI	A	3		115	.217
	BRTR				1718	.294

COLLINS, JOHN EDGAR "ZIP"
B.MAY 2,1892 BROOKLYN,N.Y.

YR	CL	LEA	POS	GP	G	REC
1914	PIT	N	O		49	.242
1915	PIT	N	O		101	.293
	BOS	N	O		5	.308
1916	BOS	N	O		93	.209
1917	BOS	N	O		8	.148
1921	PHI	A	O		24	.282
	BLTL				280	.253

COLLINS, JOHN FRANCIS "SHANO"
B.DEC.4,1885 CHARLESTOWN,MASS.
D.SEPT.10,1973

YR	CL	LEA	POS	GP	G	REC
1910	CHI	A	1-O		97	.197
1911	CHI	A	1		106	.262
1912	CHI	A	1-O		153	.290
1913	CHI	A	O		148	.239
1914	CHI	A	O		154	.274
1915	CHI	A	1-O		153	.257
1916	CHI	A	O		143	.243
1917	CHI	A	O		82	.234
1918	CHI	A	O		103	.274
1919	CHI	A	O		63	.279
1920	CHI	A	1		133	.303
1921	BOS	A	O		141	.286
1922	BOS	A	O		135	.271
1923	BOS	A	O		97	.231
1924	BOS	A	1-O		89	.292
1925	BOS	A	O		2	.333
	BRTR				1799	.264

NON-PLAYING MANAGER
BOSTON (A) 1931-32

COLLINS, JOSEPH EDWARD "JOE"
(REAL NAME
JOSEPH EDWARD KOLLONIGE)
B.DEC.3,1922 SCRANTON,PA.

YR	CL	LEA	POS	GP	G	REC
1948	NY	A	H		5	.200
1949	NY	A	1		7	.100
1950	NY	A	1-O		108	.234
1951	NY	A	1-O		125	.286
1952	NY	A	1		122	.280
1953	NY	A	1-O		127	.269
1954	NY	A	1		130	.271
1955	NY	A	1-O		105	.234
1956	NY	A	1-O		100	.225
1957	NY	A	1-O		79	.201
	BLTL				908	.256

COLLINS, KEVIN MICHAEL
B.AUG.4,1946 SPRINGFIELD,MASS.

YR	CL	LEA	POS	GP	G	REC
1965	NY	N	S-3		11	.174
1967	NY	N	2		4	.100
1968	NY	N	2-S-3		58	.201
1969	NY	N	3		16	.150
	MON	N	2-3		52	.240
1970	DET	A	1		25	.208
1971	DET	A	2-3-O		35	.268
	BLTR				201	.209

COLLINS, ORTH STEIN "BUCK"
B.APR.27,1880 LAFAYETTE,IND.
D.DEC.13,1949

YR	CL	LEA	POS	GP	G	REC
1904	NY	A	O		5	.352
1909	WAS	A	P-O	1	8	0- 0
						.000
	BLTR			1	13	0- 0
						.250

COLLINS, PHILIP EUGENE "FIDGETY PHIL"
B.AUG.27,1901 CHICAGO,ILL.
D.AUG.14,1948

YR	CL	LEA	POS	GP	G	REC
1923	CHI	N	P		1	1- 0
1929	PHI	N	P	43	59	9- 7
1930	PHI	N	P	47	55	16-11
1931	PHI	N	P	42	44	12-16
1932	PHI	N	P		43	14-12
1933	PHI	N	P	42	43	8-13
1934	PHI	N	P	45	48	13-18
1935	PHI	N	P		3	0- 2
	STL	N	P		26	7- 6
	BRTR			292	322	80-85

COLLINS, RAYMOND WILLISTON
B.FEB.11,1887 COLCHESTER,VT.
D.JAN.9,1970 BURLINGTON,VT.

YR	CL	LEA	POS	GP	G	REC
1909	BOS	A	P		12	4- 3
1910	BOS	A	P		35	13-11
1911	BOS	A	P		31	11-12
1912	BOS	A	P		27	14- 8
1913	BOS	A	P		30	19- 8
1914	BOS	A	P		39	20-13
1915	BOS	A	P		25	5- 7
	BLTL				199	86-62

COLLINS, ROBERT JOSEPH "RIP"
B.SEPT.19,1909 PITTSBURGH,PA.
D.APR.9,1969 PITTSBURGH,PA.

YR	CL	LEA	POS	GP	G	REC
1940	CHI	N	C		47	.208
1944	NY	N	C		3	.333
	BRTR				50	.211

COLLINS, THARON PATRICK "PAT"
B.SEPT.13,1896 SWEET SPRGS.,MO.
D.MAY 19,1960

YR	CL	LEA	POS	GP	G	REC
1919	STL	A	C		11	.143
1920	STL	A	C		23	.214
1921	STL	A	C		58	.243
1922	STL	A	C		63	.307
1923	STL	A	C		85	.177
1924	STL	A	C		32	.315
1926	NY	A	C		102	.286
1927	NY	A	C		92	.275
1928	NY	A	C		70	.220
1929	BOS	N	C		7	.000
	BRTR				543	.254

COLLINS, WILLIAM J.
B.1863 DUBLIN,IRELAND
D.JUNE 8,1893 NEW YORK,N.Y.

YR	CL	LEA	POS	GP	G	REC
1887	MET	AA	C		1	.250
1889	ATH	AA	C		1	.200
1890	ATH	AA	C		1	.000
1891	CLE	N	C		2	.000
1892	STL	N	O		1	.000
	BR				6	.143

COLLINS, WILLIAM SHIRLEY
B.MAR.27,1882 CHESTERTON,IND.
D.JUNE 26,1961 SAN BERNADINO, CAL.

YR	CL	LEA	POS	GP	G	REC
1910	BOS	N	O		151	.241
1911	BOS	N	O		17	.149
	CHI	N	O		7	.333
1913	BRO	N	O		32	.189
1914	BUF	F	O		20	.146
	BBTR				227	.224

COLLUM, JACK DEAN "JACKIE"
B.JUNE 21,1927 VICTOR,IA.

YR	CL	LEA	POS	GP	G	REC
1951	STL	N	P		3	2- 1
1952	STL	N	P		2	0- 0
1953	STL	N	P		7	0- 0
	CIN	N	P		30	7-11
1954	CIN	N	P		36	7- 3
1955	CIN	N	P		32	9- 8
1956	STL	N	P		38	6- 2
1957	CHI	N	P		9	1- 1
	BRO	N	P		3	0- 0
1958	LA	N	P		2	0- 0
	MIN	A	P		8	0- 2
1962	CLE	A	P		1	0- 0
	BLTL				171	32-28

COLMAN, FRANK LOYD
B.MAR.2,1918 LONDON,ONT.,CANADA

YR	CL	LEA	POS	GP	G	REC
1942	PIT	N	O		10	.135
1943	PIT	N	O		32	.271
1944	PIT	N	1-O		99	.270
1945	PIT	N	1-O		77	.209
1946	PIT	N	1-O		26	.170
	NY	A	O		5	.267
1947	NY	A	O		22	.107
	BLTL				271	.228

COLPAERT, RICHARD CHARLES "DICK"
B.JAN 3,1944 FRASER,MICH.

YR	CL	LEA	POS	GP	G	REC
1970	PIT	N	P		8	1- 0
	BRTR					

COLSON, LOYD ALBERT
B.NOV.4,1947 WELLINGTON,TEX.

YR	CL	LEA	POS	GP	G	REC
1970	NY	A	P		1	0- 0
	BRTR					

COLTON, LAWRENCE ROBERT "LARRY"
B.JUNE 8,1942 LOS ANGELES,CAL.

YR	CL	LEA	POS	GP	G	REC
1968	PHI	N	P		1	0- 0
	BLTR					

COLUCCIO, ROBERT PASQUALI "BOB"
B.OCT.2,1951 CENTRALIA,WASH.

YR	CL	LEA	POS	GP	G	REC
1973	MIL	A	O-D		124	.224
1974	MIL	A	O		138	.223
1975	MIL	A	O		22	.194
	CHI	A	O		61	.205
	BRTR				345	.219

COMBS, EARLE BRYAN "COLONEL"
B.MAY 14,1899 PEBWORTH,KY.
D.JULY 21,1976 RICHMOND,KY.

YR	CL	LEA	POS	GP	G	REC
1924	NY	A	O		24	.400
1925	NY	A	O		150	.343
1926	NY	A	O		145	.299
1927	NY	A	O		152	.356
1928	NY	A	O		149	.310
1929	NY	A	O		142	.345
1930	NY	A	O		137	.344
1931	NY	A	O		130	.318
1932	NY	A	O		144	.321
1933	NY	A	O		122	.298
1934	NY	A	O		63	.319
1935	NY	A	O		89	.282
	BLTR				1455	.325

COMBS, MERRILL RUSSELL "MERL"
B.DEC.11,1919 LOS ANGELES,CAL.

YR	CL	LEA	POS	GP	G	REC
1947	BOS	A	3		17	.221
1949	BOS	A	S-3		14	.208
1950	BOS	A	H		1	.000
	WAS	A	S		37	.245
1951	CLE	A	S		19	.179
1952	CLE	A	2-S		52	.165
	BLTR				140	.202

COMELLAS, JORGE
B.DEC.7,1916 HAVANA,CUBA

YR	CL	LEA	POS	GP	G	REC
1945	CHI	N	P		7	0- 2
	BRTR					

COMER, HARRY WAYNE "WAYNE"
B.FEB.3,1944 SHENANDOAH,VA.

YR	CL	LEA	POS	GP	G	REC
1967	DET	A	O		4	.333
1968	DET	A	C-O		48	.125
1969	SEA	A	C-3-O		147	.245
1970	MIL	A	O		13	.059
	WAS	A	3-O		77	.233
1972	DET	A	O		27	.111
	BRTR				316	.229

COMISKEY, CHARLES ALBERT "COMMY"
B.AUG.19,1859 CHICAGO,ILL.
D.OCT.26,1931 EAGLE RIVER,WIS.

YR	CL	LEA	POS	GP	G	REC
1882	STL	AA	P-1	1	78	0- 1
						.244
1883	STL	AA	1		95	.290
1884	STL	AA	1		108	.241
1885	STL	AA	M-1		83	.260
1886	STL	AA	M-1		131	.260
1887	STL	AA	M-1		125	.368
1888	STL	AA	M-1		137	.271
1889	STL	AA	M-1		137	.288
1890	CHI	P	M-1		88	.248
1891	STL	AA	M-1		139	.257
1892	CIN	N	M-1		140	.223
1893	CIN	N	M-1		62	.225
1894	CIN	N	M-1		59	.265
	BRTR			1	1382	0- 1
						.269

COMMAND, JAMES DALTON "JIM"
B.OCT.15,1929 GRAND RAPIDS,MICH

YR	CL	LEA	POS	GP	G	REC
1954	PHI	N	3		9	.222
1955	PHI	N	H		5	.000
	BLTR				14	.174

YR	CL LEA POS	GP	G	REC

COMOROSKY, ADAM
B.DEC.9,1905 SWOYERSVILLE,PA.
D.MAR.2,1951

YR	CL LEA POS	GP	G	REC
1926	PIT N O		8	.267
1927	PIT N O		18	.230
1928	PIT N O		51	.295
1929	PIT N O		127	.321
1930	PIT N O		152	.313
1931	PIT N O		99	.243
1932	PIT N O		108	.286
1933	PIT N O		64	.264
1934	CIN N O		127	.258
1935	CIN N O		59	.248
	BRTR		813	.285

COMPTON, ANNA SEBASTIAN "PETE"
B.SEPT.28,1889 SAN MARCOS,TEX.

1911	STL A O		28	.272
1912	STL A O		100	.280
1913	STL A O		61	.180
1915	STL F O		2	.250
	BOS N O		35	.241
1916	BOS N O		34	.302
	PIT N O		5	.100
1918	NY N O		21	.217
	BLTL		286	.239

COMPTON, HARRY LEROY "JACK"
B.MAR.9,1882 LANCASTER,OHIO

1911	CIN N P		8	1- 1
	BRTR			

COMPTON, MICHAEL LYNN "MIKE"
B.AUG.15,1944 STAMFORD,CONN.

1970	PHI N C		47	.164
	BRTR			

COMPTON, ROBERT CLINTON "BOB"
B.NOV.1,1950 MONTGOMERY,ALA.

1972	CHI N P		1	0- 0
	BLTL			

COMSTOCK, RALPH REMICK
B.NOV.24,1887 TOLEDO,OHIO
D.SEPT.13,1966 TOLEDO,OHIO

1913	DET A P		10	2- 5
1915	BOS A P		3	1- 0
	PIT F P		12	3- 3
1918	PIT N P		15	5- 6
	BRTR		40	11-14

CONATSER, CLINTON ASTOR "CLINT"
B.JULY 24,1921 LOS ANGELES,CAL.

1948	BOS N O		90	.277
1949	BOS N O		53	.263
	BRTR		143	.271

**CONCEPCION, DAVID ISMAEL
(BENITEZ) "DAVE"**
B.JUNE 17,1948 ARAGUA,VENEZ.

1970	CIN N 2-S		101	.260
1971	CIN N 2-S-3-O		130	.205
1972	CIN N 2-S-3		119	.209
1973	CIN N S-O		89	.287
1974	CIN N S-O		160	.281
1975	CIN N S-3		140	.274
1976	CIN N S		152	.281
	BRTR		891	.261

CONDE, RAMON LUIS
B.DEC.29,1934 JUANA DIAZ,P.R.

1962	CHI A 3		14	.000
	BRTR			

CONE, H. B.
B.TEXAS

1915	PHI A P		1	0- 0

CONE, JOSEPH FREDERICK
B.MAY 1848 ROCKFORD,ILL.
D.APR.13,1909

1871	BOS NA O		18	-

**CONGALTON, WILLIAM MILLAR
"BUNK"**
B.JAN.24,1875 GUELPH,ONT.,CAN.
D.AUG.16,1937

1902	CHI N O		47	.245
1905	CLE A O		12	.369
1906	CLE A O		117	.320
1907	CLE A O		9	.182
	BOS A O		124	.286
			309	.293

CONGER, RICHARD
B.APR.3,1921 LOS ANGELES,CAL.
D.FEB.16,1970 LOS ANGELES,CAL.

1940	DET A P		2	1- 0
1941	PIT N P		2	0- 0
1942	PIT N P	2	3	0- 0
1943	PHI N P		13	2- 7
	BPTR	19	20	3- 7

**CONIGLIARO, ANTHONY RICHARD
"TONY"**
B.JAN.7,1945 REVERE,MASS.

1964	BOS A O		111	.290
1965	BOS A O		138	.269
1966	BOS A O		150	.265
1967	BOS A O		95	.287
1969	BOS A O		141	.255
1970	BOS A O		146	.266
1971	CAL A O		74	.222
1975	BOS A O		21	.123
	BRTR		876	.264

**CONIGLIARO, WILLIAM MICHAEL
"BILLY"**
B.AUG.15,1947 REVERE,MASS.

1969	BOS A O		32	.288
1970	BOS A O		114	.271
1971	BOS A O		101	.262
1972	MIL A O		52	.230
1973	OAK A 2-O		48	.200
	BRTR		347	.256

CONKWRIGHT, ALLEN HOWARD "RED"
B.DEC.4,1897 SEDALIA,MO.

1920	DET A P		5	2- 1
	BRTR			

CONLAN, JOHN BERTRAND "JOCKO"
B.DEC.6,1902 CHICAGO,ILL.

1934	CHI A O		63	.249
1935	CHI A O		65	.286
	BLTL		128	.263

CONLEY, DONALD EUGENE "GENE"
B.NOV.10,1930 MUSKOGEE,OKLA.

1952	BOS N P		4	0- 3
1954	MIL N P		28	14- 9
1955	MIL N P		22	11- 7
1956	MIL N P		31	8- 9
1957	MIL N P		35	9- 9
1958	MIL N P		26	0- 6
1959	PHI N P		25	12- 7
1960	PHI N P		29	8-14
1961	BOS A P		33	11-14
1962	BOS A P		34	15-14
1963	BOS A P		9	3- 4
	BRTR		276	91-96

CONLEY, EDWARD J.
B.JULY 10,1864 SANDWICH,MASS.
D.OCT.16,1894 CUMBERLAND,R.I.

1884	PRO N P		8	4- 4

CONLEY, JAMES PATRICK "SNIPE"
B.APR.25,1894 SCHUYLKILL HAVEN,
PA.

1914	BAL F P		35	4- 6
1915	BAL F P		25	1- 4
1918	CIN N P		5	2- 0
	BRTR		65	7-10

CONLEY, ROBERT BURNS
B.FEB.1,1934 NEWPORT NEWS,VA.

1958	PHI N P		2	0- 0
	BRTR			

CONLON, ARTHUR JOSEPH
B.DEC.10,1898 WOBURN,MASS.

1923	BOS N 2-S-3		59	.218
	BRTR			

CONN, ALBERT THOMAS "BERT"
B.SEPT.22,1879 PHILADELPHIA,PA.
D.NOV.2,1944

1898	PHI N P		1	0- 0
1900	PHI N P		6	0- 1
1901	PHI N 2		5	.222
	TR	7	12	0- 1
				.267

CONNALLY, GEORGE WALTER "SARGE"
B.AUG.31,1898 MCGREGOR,TEX.

1921	CHI A P		5	0- 1
1923	CHI A P		3	0- 0
1924	CHI A P		44	7-13
1925	CHI A P		40	6- 7
1926	CHI A P		31	6- 5
1927	CHI A P		43	10-15
1928	CHI A P		28	2- 5
1929	CHI A P		11	0- 0
1931	CLE A P		17	5- 5
1932	CLE A P		35	8- 6
1933	CLE A P		41	5- 3
1934	CLE A P		5	0- 0
	BRTR		303	49-60

**CONNASTER, BROADUS MILBURN
"BRUCE"**
B.SEPT.19,1902 SEVIERVILLE,TENN
D.JAN.28,1971 TERRE HAUTE,IND.

1931	CLE A 1		12	.286
1932	CLE A 1		23	.233
	BRTR		35	.257

CONNAUGHTON, FRANK H.
B.JAN.1,1869 CLINTON,MASS.
D.DEC.1,1942 BOSTON,MASS.

1894	BOS N S		38	.337
1896	NY N S-O		83	.257
1906	BOS N 2-S		12	.205
	BRTR		133	.278

CONNELL, EUGENE JOSEPH
B.MAY 10,1906 HAZELTON,PA.
D.AUG.31,1937

1931	PHI N C		6	.250
	BRTR			

CONNELL, JOSEPH BERNARD
B.JAN.16,1902 BETHLEHEM,PA.

1926	NY N H		2	.000
	BLTL			

CONNELL, PETER J.
B.BROOKLYN,N.Y.

1886	MET AA 3		1	.000

CONNELL, TERENCE G.
B.JUNE 17,1855 PHILADELPHIA,PA.
D.MAR.25,1924

1874	CHI NA P-C		1	0- 0
				.000

CONNELLY, JOHN M. "RED"
B.1857
D.MAR.1,1896

1886	STL N O		2	.000

CONNELLY, THOMAS MARTIN
B.OCT.20,1898 CHICAGO,ILL.

1920	NY A O		1	.000
1921	NY A O		4	.200
	BLTR		5	.167

**CONNELLY, WILLIAM WIRT
"WILD BILL"**
B.JUNE 29,1925 ALBERTA,VA.

1945	PHI A P		2	1- 1
1950	CHI A P		2	0- 0
	DET A P		2	0- 0
1952	NY N P		11	5- 0
1953	NY N P		8	0- 1
	BLTR		25	6- 2

**CONNOLLY, EDWARD JOSEPH JR.
"ED"**
B.DEC.3,1939 BROOKLYN,N.Y.

1964	BOS A P		27	4-11
1967	CLE A P		15	2- 1
	BLTL		42	6-12

CONNOLLY, EDWARD JOSEPH SR
B.JULY 17,1908 BROOKLYN,N.Y.
D.NOV.12,1963 PITTSFIELD,MASS.

1929	BOS A C		5	.000
1930	BOS A C		27	.188
1931	BOS A C		42	.075
1932	BOS A C		75	.225
	BRTR		149	.178

YR CL LEA POS GP G REC

CONNOLLY, JOSEPH ALOYSIUS
B.FEB.12,1888 N.SMITHFIELD,R.I.
D.SEPT.1,1943
```
1913 BOS N  O        126  .281
1914 BOS N  O        120  .306
1915 BOS N  O        104  .298
1916 BOS N  O         62  .227
     BLTR            412  .288
```

CONNOLLY, JOSEPH GEORGE "COASTER"
B.JUNE 4,1896 SAN FRANCISCO,CAL
D.MAR.30,1960
```
1921 NY  N  O          2  .000
1922 CLE A  O         12  .244
1923 CLE A  O         52  .303
1924 BOS A  O         14  .100
     BRTR             80  .268
```

CONNOLLY, MERVIN THOMAS "BUD"
B.MAY 25,1901 SAN FRANCISCO,CAL
D.JUNE 12,1964 BERKELEY,CAL.
```
1925 BOS A  S-3       43  .261
     BRTR
```

CONNOLLY, THOMAS FRANCIS "BLACKIE"
B.DEC.30,1892 BOSTON,MASS.
D.MAY 14,1966 BOSTON,MASS.
```
1915 WAS A  3-0       50  .184
     BLTR
```

CONNOR, JAMES MATTHEW
(REAL NAME
JAMES MATTHEW O'CONNOR)
B.MAY 11,1867 PORT JERVIS,N.Y.
D.SEPT.3,1950
```
1892 CHI N  2         10  .057
1897 CHI N  2         77  .296
1898 CHI N  2        136  .225
1899 CHI N  2-3       66  .206
     BRTR            289  .235
```

CONNOR, JOHN
B.LASALLE,ILL.
D.OCT.13,1932
```
1884 BOS N  P          7  1- 4
1885 BUF N  P          1  0- 1
     LOU AA P          4  1- 3
                      12  2- 8
```

CONNOR, JOSEPH
```
1895 STL N  3          2  .000
```

CONNOR, JOSEPH FRANCIS
B.DEC.8,1874 WATERBURY,CONN.
D.NOV.8,1957
```
1900 BOS N  C          7  .200
1901 MIL A  C-2-O     38  .272
     CLE A  C-2-O     38  .138
1905 NY  A  C-1        8  .271
     BRTR             91  .209
```

CONNOR, ROGER
B.JULY 1,1857 WATERBURY,CONN.
D.JAN.4,1931 WATERBURY,CONN.
```
1880 TRO N  3         83  .332
1881 TRO N  1         84  .288
1882 TRO N  1-3-0     79  .327
1883 NY  N  1         96  .361
1884 NY  N  2-3-0    112  .316
1885 NY  N  1        110  .371
1886 NY  N  1        118  .354
1887 NY  N  1        127  .382
1888 NY  N  1        134  .291
1889 NY  N  1        131  .316
1890 NY  P  1        123  .372
1891 NY  N  1        123  .293
1892 PHI N  1        153  .285
1893 NY  N  1        135  .322
1894 NY  N  1-0       22  .293
     STL N  1         99  .318
1895 STL N  1        104  .326
1896 STL N  M-1      126  .282
1897 STL N  1         22  .229
     BLTL           1981  .327
```

CONNORS, JEREMIAH
B.PHILADELPHIA,PA.
```
1892 PHI N  O          1  .000
```

CONNORS, JOSEPH P.
B.1850 NEW YORK
```
1871 TRO NA 1-2-0      7  .182
```

YR CL LEA POS GP G REC

CONNORS, JOSEPH P.
B.PHILADELPHIA,PA.
```
1884 ALT U  P-3-  1    3  0- 1
            O             .100
     KC  U  P-O    2    3  0- 1
                          .091
                  3    6  0- 2
                          .095
```

CONNORS, KEVIN JOSEPH "CHUCK"
B.APR.10,1921 BROOKLYN,N.Y.
```
1949 BRO N  H          1  .000
1951 CHI N  1         66  .239
     BLTL             67  .238
```

CONNORS, MERVYN JAMES "MIKE"
B.JAN.23,1915 BERKELEY,CAL.
```
1937 CHI A  3         28  .233
1938 CHI A  1         24  .355
     BRTR             52  .279
```

CONNORS, WILLIAM JOSEPH "BILL"
B.NOV.2,1941 SCHENECTADY,N.Y.
```
1966 CHI N  P         11  0- 1
1967 NY  N  P          6  0- 1
1968 NY  N  P          9  0- 1
     BRTR             26  0- 2
```

CONOVER, THEODORE "HUCK"
B.MAR.10,1868 LEXINGTON,KY.
D.JULY 27,1910
```
1889 CIN AA P          1  0- 0
```

CONROY, BENJAMIN EDWARD
B.1871 PHILADELPHIA,PA.
```
1890 ATH AA 2-S      116  .175
```

CONROY, WILLIAM EDWARD "WID"
B.APR.5,1877 PHILADELPHIA,PA.
D.DEC.6,1959
```
1901 MIL A  S        131  .269
1902 PIT N  S-O       95  .241
1903 NY  A  3        125  .277
1904 NY  A  S-3      140  .249
1905 NY  A  S-3-0    101  .273
1906 NY  A  S-O      148  .245
1907 NY  A  S-O      140  .234
1908 NY  A  3        141  .237
1909 WAS A  3        139  .244
1910 WAS A  3-0      103  .254
1911 WAS A  3-0      106  .232
     BRTR           1369  .250
```

CONROY, WILLIAM FREDERICK "PEP"
B.JAN.9,1899 CHICAGO,ILL.
D.JAN.23,1970 CHICAGO,ILL.
```
1923 WAS A  3         18  .133
     BRTR
```

CONROY, WILLIAM GORDON
B.FEB.26,1915 BLOOMINGTON,ILL.
```
1935 PHI A  C          1  .250
1936 PHI A  C          1  .500
1937 PHI A  C         26  .200
1942 BOS A  C         83  .200
1943 BOS A  C         39  .180
1944 BOS A  C         19  .213
     BRTR            169  .199
```

CONSOLO, WILLIAM ANGELO "BILLY"
B.AUG.18,1934 CLEVELAND,OHIO
```
1953 BOS A  2-3       47  .215
1954 BOS A  2-S-3     91  .227
1955 BOS A  2          8  .222
1956 BOS A  2         48  .182
1957 BOS A  2-S-3     68  .270
1958 BOS A  2-S-3     46  .125
1959 BOS A  S         10  .214
     WAS A  2-S       79  .213
1960 WAS A  2-S-3    100  .207
1961 MIN A  2-S-3     11  .000
1962 PHI N  H         13  .400
     LA  A  2-S-3     28  .100
     KC  A  S         54  .240
     BRTR            603  .221
```

CONSTABLE, JIMMY LEE
B.JUNE 14,1933 JONESBORO,TENN.
```
1956 NY  N  P          3  0- 0
1957 NY  N  P         16  1- 1
1958 SF  N  P          9  1- 0
     CLE A  P          6  0- 1
     WAS A  P         15  0- 1
1962 MIL N  P          3  1- 1
1963 SF  N  P          4  0- 0
     BBTL             56  3- 4
```

YR CL LEA POS GP G REC

CONSUEGRA, SANDALIO SIMEON CASTELLON "SANDY"
B.SEPT.3,1920 SANTA CLARA,CUBA
```
1950 WAS A  P    21   24  7- 8
1951 WAS A  P         40  7- 8
1952 WAS A  P         30  6- 0
1953 WAS A  P          4  0- 0
     CHI A  P         29  7- 5
1954 CHI A  P-3       39  16- 3
                          .229
1955 CHI A  P         44  6- 5
1956 CHI A  P         28  1- 2
     BAL A  P          4  1- 1
1957 BAL A  P          5  0- 0
     NY  N  P          4  0- 0
     BRTR       248  251  51-32
                          .170
```

CONWAY, CHARLES CONNELL
B.APR.28,1896 YOUNGSTOWN,OHIO
D.SEPT.12,1968 YOUNGSTOWN,OHIO
```
1911 WAS A  O          2  .333
     BRTR
```

CONWAY, JACK CLEMENTS
B.JULY 30,1919 BRYAN,TEX.
```
1941 CLE A  S          2  .500
1946 CLE A  2-S-3     68  .225
1947 CLE A  2-S-3     34  .180
1948 NY  N  2-S-3     24  .245
     BRTR            128  .223
```

CONWAY, JAMES P.
B.CLIFTON,PA.
```
1884 BRO AA P-S- 13   14  3- 9
            O             .133
1885 ATH AA P-O        2  1- 1
                          .167
1889 KC  AA P         41  18-19
     TR          56   57  22-29
                          .191
```

CONWAY, JEROME PATRICK
B.JUNE 7,1901 HOLYOKE,MASS.
```
1920 WAS A  P          1  0- 0
     BLTL
```

CONWAY, OWEN SYLVESTER
B.OCT.23,1890 NEW YORK,N.Y.
D.MAR.13,1942
```
1915 PHI A  3          4  .067
```

CONWAY, PETER J.
B.OCT.30,1866 BURMONT,PA.
D.JAN.14,1903
```
1885 BUF N  P-1- 27   29  10-17
            S             .111
1886 KC  N  P-O  31   52  5-16
                          .235
     DET N  P         11  6- 5
1887 DET N  P    18   24  8-10
1888 DET N  P         45  31-14
1889 PIT N  P          3  2- 1
     BR         135  164  62-63
                          .227
```

CONWAY, RICHARD BUTLER
B.APR.25,1866 LOWELL,MASS.
D.SEPT.9,1926
```
1886 BAL AA P          9  2- 7
1887 BOS N  P    25   39  9-15
1888 BOS N  P          6  4- 1
     BLTR        40   54  15-23
```

CONWAY, RICHARD DANIEL "RIP"
B.APR.18,1896 WHITE BEAR,MINN.
D.DEC.3,1971 ST.PAUL,MINN.
```
1918 BOS N  2         14  .167
```

CONWAY, WILLIAM F.
B.NOV.28,1861 LOWELL,MASS.
D.DEC.18,1943
```
1884 PHI N  C          1  .000
1886 BAL AA C          7  .142
                       8  .111
```

CONWELL, EDWARD JAMES "IRISH"
B.JAN.29,1890 CHICAGO,ILL.
```
1911 STL N  3          1  .000
     BRTR
```

CONYERS, HERBERT LEROY "HERB"
B.JAN.8,1921 COWGILL,MO.
D.SEPT.16,1964 CLEVELAND,OHIO
```
1950 CLE A  1          7  .333
     BLTR
```

YR	CL	LEA	POS	GP	G	REC

CONZELMAN, JOSEPH HARRISON
B.JULY 14,1889 BRISTOL,CONN.

YR	CL	LEA	POS	GP	G	REC
1913	PIT	N	P		2	0- 1
1914	PIT	N	o		33	5- 6
1915	PIT	N	P		18	1- 1
		BRTR			53	6- 8

COOGAN, DALE ROGER
B.AUG.14,1930 LOS ANGELES,CAL.

1950	PIT	N	1		53	.240
		BLTL				

COOGAN, DANIEL GEORGE
B.FEB.16,1875 PHILADELPHIA,PA.
D.OCT.28,1942

1895	WAS	N	S		21	.203

COOK, EARL DAVID
B.DEC.10,1911 LEMONVILLE,ONT.,
CANADA

1941	DET	A	P		1	0- 0
		BRTR				

COOK, FREDERICK RUSSELL
(PLAYED UNDER NAME OF
FREDERICK RUSSELL WINCHELL)

COOK, JAMES FITCHIE
B.NOV.10,1879 DUNDEE,ILL.
D.JUNE 17,1949

1903	CHI	N	O		8	.120
		BRTR				

COOK, LUTHER A. "DOC"
B.JUNE 24,1889 FORT WORTH,TEX.
D.JUNE 30,1973 LAWRENCEBURG,
TENN.

1913	NY	A	O		20	.264
1914	NY	A	O		131	.283
1915	NY	A	O		132	.271
1916	NY	A	O		4	.100
		BLTR			287	.274

COOK, PAUL
B.MAY 5,1863 CALEDONIA,N.Y.
D.MAY 26,1905

1884	PHI	N	C		3	.083
1886	LOU	AA	C-1		68	.205
1887	LOU	AA	C-1		63	.267
1888	LOU	AA	C		53	.200
1889	LOU	AA	C		81	.236
1890	BRO	P	C-1		59	.242
1891	LOU	AA	C		39	.232
	STL	AA	C		7	.179
		BRTR			373	.227

COOK, RAYMOND CLIFFORD "CLIFF"
B.AUG.20,1936 DALLAS,TEX.

1959	CIN	N	3		9	.381
1960	CIN	N	3-O		54	.208
1961	CIN	N	3		4	.000
1962	CIN	N	3		6	.000
	NY	N	3-O		40	.232
1963	NY	N	1-3-O		50	.142
		BRTR			163	.201

COOK, ROLLIN EDWARD
B.OCT.5,1890 TOLEDO,OHIO
D.AUG.11,1975 TOLEDO,OHIO

1915	STL	A	P		5	0- 0
		BRTR				

COOK, RONALD WAYNE "RON"
B.JULY 11,1947 JEFFERSON,TEX.

1970	HOU	N	P	41	43	4- 4
1971	HOU	N	P	5	6	0- 4
		BLTL		46	49	4- 8

COOKE, ALLEN LINDSEY "DUSTY"
B.JUNE 23,1907 SWEPSONVILLE,N.C

1930	NY	A	O		92	.255
1931	NY	A	O		27	.333
1932	NY	A	O		3	.000
1933	BOS	A	O		119	.291
1934	BOS	A	O		74	.244
1935	BOS	A	O		100	.306
1936	BOS	A	O		111	.273
1938	CIN	N	O		82	.275
		BLTR			608	.291
NON-PLAYING MANAGER PHI(N) 1948

COOKE, FREDERICK B.
B.PAULDING,OHIO

1897	CLE	N	O		5	.295

COOLEY, DUFF C. "SIR RICHARD"
B.MAR.29,1873 LEAVENWORTH,KAN.
D.AUG.9,1937

1893	STL	N	O		26	.359
1894	STL	N	O		52	.299
1895	STL	N	O		132	.340
1896	STL	N	O		40	.302
	PHI	N	O		64	.301
1897	PHI	N	O		131	.327
1898	PHI	N	O		148	.317
1899	PHI	N	1		94	.280
1900	PHI	N	1		65	.200
1901	BOS	N	O		60	.270
1902	BOS	N	1-O		134	.297
1903	BOS	N	O		138	.289
1904	BOS	N	O		122	.272
1905	DET	A	O		97	.247
		BLTR			1303	.295

COOMBS, CECIL LYSANDER
B.MAR.18,1888 MOWEAGUA,ILL.

1914	CHI	A	O		7	.173
		BRTR				

COOMBS, DANIEL BERNARD "DANNY"
B.MAR.23,1942 LINCOLN,ME.

1963	HOU	N	P		1	0- 0
1964	HOU	N	P		7	1- 1
1965	HOU	N	P		26	0- 2
1966	HOU	N	P		2	0- 0
1967	HOU	N	P		6	3- 0
1968	HOU	N	P		40	4- 3
1969	HOU	N	P		8	0- 1
1970	SD	N	P		35	10-14
1971	SD	N	P		19	1- 6
		BRTL			144	19-27

COOMBS, JOHN WESLEY
"COLBY JACK"
B.NOV.18,1882 LEGRANDE,IOWA
D.APR.15,1957

1906	PHI	A	P	23	24	10-11
1907	PHI	A	P	23	24	6- 9
1908	PHI	A	P-O	26	78	7- 5
						.255
1909	PHI	A	P	30	37	12-11
1910	PHI	A	P	45	46	31- 9
1911	PHI	A	P	47	52	28-12
1912	PHI	A	P	40	54	21-10
1913	PHI	A	P		1	0- 0
1914	PHI	A	P		2	0- 0
1915	BRO	N	P		29	15-10
1916	BRO	N	P		27	13- 8
1917	BRO	N	P-O	31	32	7-11
1918	BRO	N	P-O	27	46	8-14
						.168
1920	DET	A	P		2	0- 0
		BBTR		356	457	158-111
						.235
NON-PLAYING MANAGER PHI(N) 1919

COOMBS, RAYMOND FRANK "BOBBY"
B.FEB.2,1908 GOODWINS MILLS,ME.

1933	PHI	A	P		21	0- 1
1943	NY	N	P		9	0- 1
		BRTR			30	0- 2

COONEY, JAMES EDWARD "SCOOPS"
B.AUG.24,1894 CRANSTON,R.I.

1917	BOS	A	2		11	.222
1919	NY	N	S		5	.214
1924	STL	N	2-S-3		110	.295
1925	STL	N	2-S-O		54	.273
1926	CHI	N	S		141	.251
1927	CHI	N	S		33	.242
	PHI	N	S		76	.270
1928	BOS	N	S		18	.137
		BRTR			448	.262

COONEY, JAMES JOHN
B.JULY 9,1865 CRANSTON,R.I.
D.JULY 2,1903

1890	CHI	N	S		135	.271
1891	CHI	N	S		118	.250
1892	CHI	N	S		84	.171
	WAS	N	S		6	.154
		BRTR			343	.243

COONEY, JOHN WALTER
B.MAR.18,1901 CRANSTON,R.I.

1921	BOS	N	P		8	0- 1
1922	BOS	N	P		4	1- 2
1923	BOS	N	P-1-O	23	42	3- 5
						.379
1924	BOS	N	P-1-O	34	55	8- 9
						.254
1925	BOS	N	P-1-O	31	54	14-14
						.320
1926	BOS	N	P-1	19	64	3- 3
						.302
1927	BOS	N	H		10	.000
1928	BOS	N	P	24	33	3- 7
1929	BOS	N	P-O	14	41	2- 3
						.319
1930	BOS	N	P	2	4	0- 0
1935	BRO	N	O		10	.310
1936	BRO	N	O		130	.282
1937	BRO	N	O		120	.293
1938	BOS	N	1-O		120	.271
1939	BOS	N	O		118	.274
1940	BOS	N	1-O		108	.318
1941	BOS	N	1-O		123	.319
1942	BOS	N	1-O		74	.207
1943	BRO	N	1		37	.206
1944	BRO	N	O		7	.750
	NY	A	O		10	.125
		BRTL		159	1172	34-44
						.286
NON-PLAYING MANAGER BOS(N) 1949

COONEY, PHILIP
(REAL NAME PHILIP COHN)
B.SEPT.14,1886 PATERSON,N.J.

1905	NY	A	3		1	.000
		BRTR				

COONEY, ROBERT DANIEL
B.JULY 12,1907 GLENS FALLS,N.Y.
D.MAY 4,1976 GLENS FALLS,N.Y.

1931	STL	A	P		5	0- 3
1932	STL	A	P	23	24	1- 2
		BRTR		28	29	1- 5

COONEY, WILLIAM A. "CUSH"
B.APR.4,1887 BOSTON,MASS.
D.NOV.6,1928

1909	BOS	N	P		5	0- 0
1910	BOS	N	P		8	0- 0
		TR			13	0- 0

COONS, WILBUR K.
B.PHILADELPHIA,PA.
D.AUG.30,1915

1875	ATH	NA	C		3	-
1876	ATH	N	C-O		54	.225
					57	-

COOPER, ARLEY WILBUR
B.FEB.24,1892 BEARSVILLE,W.VA.
D.AUG.7,1973 ENCINO,CAL.

1912	PIT	N	P		6	3- 0
1913	PIT	N	P		30	5- 3
1914	PIT	N	P		40	16-15
1915	PIT	N	P		38	5-16
1916	PIT	N	P		44	12-11
1917	PIT	N	P		41	17-11
1918	PIT	N	P		38	19-14
1919	PIT	N	P		36	19-13
1920	PIT	N	P		44	24-15
1921	PIT	N	P		38	22-14
1922	PIT	N	P		41	23-14
1923	PIT	N	P		39	17-19
1924	PIT	N	P		38	20-14
1925	PIT	N	P		32	12-14
1926	CHI	N	P		8	2- 1
	DET	A	P		8	0- 4
		BRTL			521	216-178

COOPER, CALVIN ASA
B.AUG.11,1924 GREAT FALLS,S.C.

1948	WAS	A	P		1	0- 0
		BRTR				

COOPER, CECIL CELESTER
B.DEC.20,1949 BRENHAM,TEX.

1971	BOS	A	1		14	.310
1972	BOS	A	1		12	.235
1973	BOS	A	1		30	.238
1974	BOS	A	1-O		121	.275
1975	BOS	A	1-O		106	.311
1976	BOS	A	1-O		123	.282
		BLTL			406	.283

YR	CL	LEA	POS	GP	G	REC

COOPER, CLAUDE WILLIAM
B.APR.1,1892 TROUPE,TEX.
D.JAN.21,1974 PLAINVIEW,TEX.

YR	CL	LEA	POS	GP	G	REC
1913	NY	N	O		27	.300
1914	BRO	F	O		110	.239
1915	BRO	F	1-O		152	.291
1916	PHI	N	O		56	.192
1917	PHI	N	O		24	.103
	BLTL				369	.258

COOPER, GUY EVANS
B.JAN.28,1893 ROME,GA.
D.AUG.2,1951

YR	CL	LEA	POS	GP	G	REC
1914	NY	A	P		1	0- 0
	BOS	A	P		10	1- 1
1915	BOS	A	P		1	0- 0
	BBTR				12	1- 1

COOPER, MORTON CECIL "MORT"
B.MAR.2,1913 ATHERTON,MO.
D.NOV.17,1958

YR	CL	LEA	POS	GP	G	REC
1938	STL	N	P		4	2- 1
1939	STL	N	P	45	47	12- 6
1940	STL	N	P		38	11-12
1941	STL	N	P		29	13- 9
1942	STL	N	P		37	22- 7
1943	STL	N	P		37	21- 8
1944	STL	N	P		34	22- 7
1945	STL	N	P		4	2- 0
	BOS	N	P		20	7- 4
1946	BOS	N	P		28	13-11
1947	BOS	N	P		10	2- 5
	NY	N	P		8	1- 5
1949	CHI	N	P		1	0- 0
	BRTR			295	297	128-75

COOPER, ORGE PATTERSON
B.NOV.26,1917 ALBEMARLE,N.C.

YR	CL	LEA	POS	GP	G	REC
1946	PHI	A	P		1	0- 0
1947	PHI	A	1		13	.250
	BRTR			1	14	0- 0
						.250

COOPER, WILLIAM WALKER "WALK"
B.JAN.8,1915 ATHERTON,MO.

YR	CL	LEA	POS	GP	G	REC
1940	STL	N	C		6	.316
1941	STL	N	C		68	.245
1942	STL	N	C		125	.281
1943	STL	N	C		122	.319
1944	STL	N	C		112	.317
1945	STL	N	C		4	.389
1946	NY	N	C		87	.268
1947	NY	N	C		140	.305
1948	NY	N	C		91	.266
1949	NY	N	C		42	.211
	CIN	N	C		82	.280
1950	CIN	N	C		15	.191
	BOS	N	C		102	.329
1951	BOS	N	C		109	.313
1952	BOS	N	C		102	.235
1953	MIL	N	C		53	.219
1954	PIT	N	C		14	.200
	CHI	N	C		57	.310
1955	CHI	N	C		54	.279
1956	CHI	N	C		40	.265
1957	STL	N	C		48	.269
	BRTR				1473	.285

COOPER, WILLIE G.
(PLAYED UNDE- NAME OF
WILLIAM G. NANCE)

COPELAND, MAYS
B.AUG.31,1913 MOUNTAIN VIEW,ARK

YR	CL	LEA	POS	GP	G	REC
1935	STL	N	P		1	0- 0
	BRTR					

COPPOLA, HENRY PETER
B.AUG.6,1913 E.DOUGLAS,MASS.

YR	CL	LEA	POS	GP	G	REC
1935	WAS	A	P		19	3- 4
1936	WAS	A	P		6	0- 0
	BRTR				25	3- 4

CORBETT, EUGENE LOUIS
B.OCT.25,1913 WINONA,MINN.

YR	CL	LEA	POS	GP	G	REC
1936	PHI	N	1		6	.143
1937	PHI	N	2-3		7	.333
1938	PHI	N	1		24	.080
	BLTR				37	.120

CORBETT, JOSEPH
B.DEC.4,1875 SAN FRANCISCO,CAL.
D.MAY 3,1945

YR	CL	LEA	POS	GP	G	REC
1895	WAS	N	P		8	0- 3
1896	BAL	N	P		8	3- 1
1897	BAL	N	P	35	36	24- 8
1904	STL	N	P		14	5- 9
	BRTR			65	66	32-21

CORBIN, ALTON RAY
"RAY"
B.FEB.12,1949 LIVE OAK,FLA.

YR	CL	LEA	POS	GP	G	REC
1971	MIN	A	P		52	8-11
1972	MIN	A	P	31	34	8- 9
1973	MIN	A	P		51	8- 5
1974	MIN	A	P		29	7- 6
1975	MIN	A	P		18	5- 7
	BRTR			181	184	36-38

CORBITT, CLAUDE ELLIOTT
B.JULY 21,1915 SUNBURY,N.C.

YR	CL	LEA	POS	GP	G	REC
1945	BRO	N	3		2	.500
1946	CIN	N	S		82	.248
1948	CIN	N	2-S-3		87	.256
1949	CIN	N	2-S-3		44	.181
	BRTR				215	.243

CORCORAN, ARTHUR ANDREW "BUNNY"
B.NOV.23,1894 ROXBURY,MASS.
D.JULY 27,1958 CHELSEA,MASS.

YR	CL	LEA	POS	GP	G	REC
1915	PHI	A	3		1	.000
	TR					

CORCORAN, JOHN A.
B.1873 CINCINNATI,OHIO
D.NOV.1,1901

YR	CL	LEA	POS	GP	G	REC
1895	PIT	N	S-3		6	.150

CORCORAN, JOHN H.
B.LOWELL,MASS.

YR	CL	LEA	POS	GP	G	REC
1884	BRO	AA	C		52	.215

CORCORAN, LAWRENCE J.
B.AUG.10,1861 BROOKLYN,N.Y.
D.OCT.14,1891

YR	CL	LEA	POS	GP	G	REC
1880	CHI	N	P-S-	57	70	43-14
			O			.221
1881	CHI	N	P-S-	45	47	31-14
			O			.222
1882	CHI	N	P-3		41	27-13
						.207
1883	CHI	N	P-2-2	52	66	31-21
			S-O			.207
1884	CHI	N	P-S-	59	63	35-23
			O			.230
1885	CHI	N	P-S		7	5- 2
						.227
	NY	N	P-O		2	1- 1
						.375
1886	NY	N	O		1	.000
	WAS	N	P-O	1	21	0- 1
						.185
1887	IND	N	P		3	0- 2
	TR			265	321	173-91
						.218

CORCORAN, M.

YR	CL	LEA	POS	GP	G	REC
1884	CHI	N	P		1	0- 1

CORCORAN, MICHAEL JOSEPH
B.AUG.26,1882 BUFFALO,N.Y.
D.DEC.9,1950

YR	CL	LEA	POS	GP	G	REC
1910	CIN	N	3		14	.217
	BRTR					

CORCORAN, THOMAS WILLIAM
"TOMMY" OR "CORKY"
B.JAN.4,1869 NEW HAVEN,CONN.
D.JUNE 25,1960 PLAINFIELD,CONN.

YR	CL	LEA	POS	GP	G	REC
1890	PIT	P	S		123	.219
1891	ATH	AA	S		132	.252
1892	BRO	N	S		151	.237
1893	BRO	N	S		115	.281
1894	BRO	N	S		129	.302
1895	BRO	N	S		128	.277
1896	BRO	N	S		132	.299
1897	CIN	N	2-S		108	.288
1898	CIN	N	S		153	.244
1899	CIN	N	S		135	.279
1900	CIN	N	S		128	.242
1901	CIN	N	S		30	.184
1902	CIN	N	2-S		137	.251
1903	CIN	N	S		115	.246
1904	CIN	N	S		150	.230
1905	CIN	N	S		151	.248
1906	CIN	N	S		117	.207
1907	NY	N	2		62	.265
	BRTR				2196	.257

COREY, EDWARD N.
B.APR.10,1900 CHICAGO,ILL.

YR	CL	LEA	POS	GP	G	REC
1918	CHI	A	P		1	0- 0
	BRTR					

COREY, FREDERICK HARRISON
B.1857 S.KINGSTON,R.I.
D.NOV.27,1912

YR	CL	LEA	POS	GP	G	REC
1878	PRO	N	P-1-	4	6	1- 3
			?			.125
1880	WOR	N	P-1-	24	41	9- 8
			S-O			.162
1881	WOR	N	P-S-	23	51	6-14
			U			.221
1882	WOR	N	P-1-	16	63	1-15
			S-3-O			.247
1883	ATH	AA	P-2-	20	71	9- 5
			S-3-O			.254
1884	ATH	AA	3		106	.273
1885	ATH	AA	P-3	1	95	1- 0
						.252
	BRTR			88	433	27-45
						.245

CORGAN, CHARLES HOWARD
B.DEC.4,1902 WAGONER,OKLA.
D.JUNE 13,1928 WAGONER,OKLA.

YR	CL	LEA	POS	GP	G	REC
1925	BRO	N	S		14	.170
1927	BRO	N	2		19	.263
	BBTR				33	.221

CORHAN, ROY "IRISH"
B.OCT.21,1887 INDIANAPOLIS,IND.
D.NOV.24,1958

YR	CL	LEA	POS	GP	G	REC
1911	CHI	A	S		43	.213
1916	STL	N	S		92	.210
	BRTR				135	.211

CORKHILL, JOHN STEWART "POP"
B.APR.11,1858 PARKESBURG,PA.
D.APR.4,1921

YR	CL	LEA	POS	GP	G	REC
1883	CIN	AA	2-S-O		86	.222
1884	CIN	AA	P-1-	1	111	1- 0
			S-3-O			.276
1885	CIN	AA	P-1-	5	112	1- 4
			O			.291
1886	CIN	AA	P-1-	1	129	0- 0
			S-O			.283
1887	CIN	AA	P-O	5	127	0- 0
						.330
1888	CIN	AA	P-1-	1	118	0- 0
			2-O			.271
	BRO	AA	O		19	.386
1889	BRO	AA	O		138	.258
1890	BRO	N	O		51	.225
1891	ATH	AA	O		83	.211
	CIN	N	O		1	.000
	PIT	N	O		41	.231
1892	PIT	N	O		67	.191
	BLTR			13	1083	2- 4
						.265

CORKINS, MICHAEL PATRICK "MIKE"
B.MAY 25,1946 RIVERSIDE,CAL.

YR	CL	LEA	POS	GP	G	REC
1969	SD	N	P		6	1- 3
1970	SD	N	P	24	25	5- 6
1971	SD	N	P		8	0- 0
1972	SD	N	P		47	6- 9
1973	SD	N	P	47	48	5- 8
1974	SD	N	P	25	30	2- 2
	BRTR			157	164	19-28

YR	CL	LEA	POS	GP	G	REC

CORRALES, PATRICK "PAT"
B.MAR.20,1941 LOS ANGELES,CAL.

YR	CL	LEA	POS	GP	G	REC
1964	PHI	N	H		2	.000
1965	PHI	N	C		63	.224
1966	STL	N	C		28	.181
1968	CIN	N	C		20	.268
1969	CIN	N	C		29	.264
1970	CIN	N	C		43	.236
1971	CIN	N	C		40	.181
1972	CIN	N	C		2	.000
	SD	N	C		44	.193
1973	SD	N	C		29	.208
	BRTR				300	.216

CORRELL, VICTOR CROSBY "VIC"
B.FEB.5,1946 WASHINGTON,D.C.

1972	BOS	A	C		1	.500
1974	ATL	N	C		73	.238
1975	ATL	N	C		103	.215
1976	ATL	N	C		69	.225
	BRTR				246	.226

CORRIDEN, JOHN MICHAEL JR.
B.JAN.6,1920 LOGANSPORT,IND.

| 1946 | BRO | N | H | | 1 | .000 |
| | BBTR | | | | | |

CORRIDEN, JOHN MICHAEL SR. "RED"
B.SEPT.4,1887 LOGANSPORT,IND.
D.SEPT.28,1959

1910	STL	A	S		26	.155
1912	DET	A	3		38	.203
1913	CHI	N	S		46	.175
1914	CHI	N	S		107	.230
1915	CHI	N	S		6	.000
	BRTR				223	.205

NON-PLAYING MANAGER CHI(A) 1950

CORRIDON, FRANK J. "FIDDLER"
B.NOV.25,1880 NEWPORT,R.I.
D.FEB.21,1941

1904	CHI	N	P	12	19	5- 5
	PHI	N	P		12	6- 5
1905	PHI	N	P		35	11-13
1907	PHI	N	P	37	38	17-14
1908	PHI	N	P		27	14-10
1909	PHI	N	P		27	11- 7
1910	STL	N	P		30	6-14
	BRTR	180	188			70-68

CORRIGAN

| 1884 | CHI | U | 2-0 | | 2 | .143 |

CORTAZZO, JOHN FRANK "JESS"
B.SEPT.26,1904 WILMERDING,PA.
D.MAR.4,1963 PITTSBURGH,PA.

| 1923 | CHI | A | H | | 1 | .000 |
| | BRTR | | | | | |

CORWIN, ELMER NATHAN "AL"
B.DEC.3,1926 NEWBURGH,N.Y.

1951	NY	N	P		15	5- 1
1952	NY	N	P	21	23	6- 1
1953	NY	N	P	48	54	6- 4
1954	NY	N	P	20	23	1- 3
1955	NY	N	P		13	0- 1
	BRTR	117	128			18-10

COSCARART, JOSEPH MARVIN
B.NOV.18,1911 ESCONDIDO,CAL.

1935	BOS	N	2-S-3		86	.236
1936	BOS	N	3		104	.245
	BRTR				190	.241

COSCARART, PETER JOSEPH
B.JUNE 16,1916 ESCONDIDO,CAL.

1938	BRO	N	2		32	.152
1939	BRO	N	2		115	.277
1940	BRO	N	2		143	.237
1941	BRO	N	2-S		43	.127
1942	PIT	N	2-S		133	.228
1943	PIT	N	2-S-3		133	.242
1944	PIT	N	2-S-0		139	.264
1945	PIT	N	2-S		123	.242
1946	PIT	N	S		3	.500
	BRTR	864				.243

COSGROVE, MICHAEL JAMES "MIKE"
B.FEB.17,1951 PHOENIX,ARIZ.

1972	HOU	N	P		7	0- 1
1973	HOU	N	P		13	1- 1
1974	HOU	N	P		45	7- 3
1975	HOU	N	P		32	1- 2
1976	HOU	N	P		22	3- 4
	BLTL				119	12-11

COSMAN, JAMES HENRY "JIM"
B.FEB.19,1943 BROCKPORT,N.Y.

1966	STL	N	P		1	1- 0
1967	STL	N	P		10	1- 0
1970	CHI	N	P		1	0- 0
	BRTR				12	2- 0

COSTELLO, DANIEL FRANCIS "DASHING DAN"
B.SEPT.9,1891 JESSUP,PA.
D.MAR.26,1936

1913	NY	A	H		2	.500
1914	PIT	N	O		21	.297
1915	PIT	N	O		71	.216
1916	PIT	N	O		60	.239
	BLTR				154	.243

COSTELLO, J. A. (REAL NAME KENNETH LELAND NASH)

COTE, HENRY JOSEPH
B.FEB.19,1864 TROY,N.Y.
D.APR.28,1940

1894	LOU	N	C		10	.313
1895	LOU	N	C		10	.265
					20	.288

COTE, WARREN PETER "PETE"
B.AUG.30,1902 CAMBRIDGE,MASS.

| 1926 | NY | N | H | | 2 | .000 |
| | BRTR | | | | | |

COTTER, DANIEL JOSEPH
B.APR.14,1867 BOSTON,MASS.
D.SEPT.14,1935

| 1890 | BUF | P | P | | 1 | 0- 1 |

COTTER, EDWARD CHRSITOPHER
B.JULY 4,1904 HARTFORD,CONN.
D.JUNE 14,1959

| 1926 | PHI | N | S-3 | | 17 | .308 |
| | BRTR | | | | | |

COTTER, HARVEY LOUIS "HOOKS"
B.MAY.22,1900 HOLDEN,MO.
D.AUG.6,1955

1922	CHI	N	1		1	19000
1924	CHI	N	1		98	.261
	BLTL				99	.264

COTTER, RICHARD RAPHAEL
B.OCT.23,1890 MANCHESTER,N.H.

1911	PHI	N	C		17	.283
1912	CHI	N	C		26	.278
	TR				43	.280

COTTER, THOMAS B.
B.SEPT.30,1866 WALTHAM,MASS.
D.NOV.22,1906

| 1891 | BOS | AA | C | | 5 | .273 |

COTTIER, CHARLES KEITH "CHUCK"
B.JAN.8,1936 DELTA,COLO.

1959	MIL	N	2		10	.125
1960	MIL	N	2		95	.227
1961	DET	A	2-S		10	.286
	WAS	A	2		101	.234
1962	WAS	A	2		136	.242
1963	WAS	A	2-S-3		113	.205
1964	WAS	A	2-S-3		73	.168
1965	WAS	A	H		7	.000
1968	CAL	A	2-3		33	.194
1969	CAL	A	2		2	.000
	BRTR	580				.220

COTTRELL, ENSIGN STOVER
B.AUG.29,1888 HOOSICK FALLS,N.Y
D.FEB.27,1947

1911	PIT	N	P		1	0- 0
1912	CHI	N	P		1	0- 0
1913	PHI	A	P		1	0- 0
1914	BOS	N	P		1	0- 1
1915	NY	A	P		7	0- 1
	BLTL				11	0- 2

COUCH, JOHN DANIEL
B.MAR.31,1891 VAUGHN,MONT.
D.DEC.8,1975 PALO ALTO,CAL.

1917	DET	A	P		3	0- 0
1922	CIN	N	P		43	16- 9
1923	CIN	N	P		19	2- 7
	PHI	N	P	11	12	2- 4
1924	PHI	N	P		37	4- 8
1925	PHI	N	P		34	5- 6
	BLTR	147	148			29-34

COUGHLAN, EDWARD E.
B.HARTFORD, CONN.

| 1884 | BUF | N | P-O | | 2 | 0- 0 |
| | | | | | | .250 |

COUGHLIN, DENNIS F.

| 1872 | NAT | NA | 2-S-3-0 | | 8 | .324 |

COUGHLIN, WILLIAM E. "ROSCOE"
B.MAR.15,1868 WALPOLE,MASS.
D.MAR.20,1951

1890	CHI	N	P		11	4- 7
1891	NY	N	P		8	3- 4
	TR				19	7-11

COUGHLIN, WILLIAM PAUL "BILL"
B.JULY 12,1878 SCRANTON,PA.
D.MAY 7,1943 SCRANTON,PA.

1899	WAS	N	3		5	.100
1901	WAS	A	3		137	.277
1902	WAS	A	2-S-3		121	.298
1903	WAS	A	3		125	.251
1904	WAS	A	3		64	.261
	DET	A	3		56	.355
1905	DET	A	3		138	.252
1906	DET	A	3		147	.235
1907	DET	A	3		134	.243
1908	DET	A	3		119	.215
	BRTR	1046				.252

COUGHTRY, JAMES MARLAN "MARLAN"
B.SEPT.11,1934 HOLLYWOOD,CAL.

1960	BOS	A	2-3		15	.158
1962	LA	A	2-3		11	.182
	KC	A	3		6	.182
	CLE	A	H		3	.500
	BLTR				35	.185

COULSON, ROBERT JACKSON
B.JUNE 17,1887 DONORA,PA.
D.SEPT.11,1953

1908	CIN	N	O		8	.333
1910	BRO	N	O		25	.247
1911	BRO	N	O		145	.234
1914	PIT	F	O		18	.203
	BRTR	196				.233

COULTER, THOMAS LEE "TOM"
B.JUNE 5,1945 STEUBENVILLE,O.

| 1969 | STL | N | 2 | | 6 | .316 |
| | BBTR | | | | | |

COUMBE, FREDERICK NICHOLAS "FRITZ"
B.DEC.13,1891 ANTRIM,PA.

1914	BOS	A	P		17	1- 2
	CLE	A	P		15	1- 5
1915	CLE	A	P	31	35	4- 7
1916	CLE	A	P	29	31	7- 5
1917	CLE	A	P	34	35	8- 6
1918	CLE	A	P	30	32	13- 7
1919	CLE	A	P		8	1- 1
1920	CIN	N	P-O		5	0- 1
						.231
1921	CIN	N	P	28	31	3- 4
	BLTL	197	209			38-38
						.199

COURTNEY, CLINTON DAWSON "SCRAP IRON"
B.MAR.16,1927 HALL SUMMIT,LA.
D.JUNE 16,1975 ROCHESTER,N.Y.

1951	NY	A	C		1	.000
1952	STL	A	C		119	.286
1953	STL	A	C		106	.251
1954	BAL	A	C		122	.270
1955	CHI	A	C		19	.378
	WAS	A	C		75	.298
1956	WAS	A	C		101	.300
1957	WAS	A	C		91	.267
1958	WAS	A	C		134	.251
1959	WAS	A	C		72	.233
1960	BAL	A	C		83	.227
1961	KC	A	C		1	.000
	BAL	A	C		22	.267
	BLTR	946				.268

```
YR  CL LEA POS  GP    G    REC
```

COURTNEY, ERNEST E.
B.1879 DES MOINES,IOWA
```
1902 BOS N S-O        40   .212
     BAL A 3           1   .500
1903 NY  A S          25   .241
     DET A 3          23   .253
1905 PHI N 3         155   .275
1906 PHI N 3         112   .236
1907 PHI N 1-3       130   .243
1908 PHI N 3          42   .181
     BLTR            528   .245
```

COURTNEY, HENRY SEYMOUR
B.NOV.19,1898 ASHEVILLE,N.C.
```
1919 WAS A P          4    3- 0
1920 WAS A P         37    8-11
1921 WAS A P    30   32    6- 9
1922 WAS A P          5    0- 1
     CHI A P         18    5- 6
     BLTL   94   96   22-27
```

COUSINEAU, EDWARD THOMAS
B.DEC.16,1899 WATERTOWN,MASS.
D.JULY 14,1951
```
1923 BOS N C          1  1.000
1924 BOS N C          3   .000
1925 BOS N C          1   .000
     BRTR             5   .500
```

COVELESKI, HARRY FRANK
"GIANT KILLER"
(REAL NAME
HARRY FRANK KOWALEWSKI)
B.APR.23,1886 SHAMOKIN,PA.
D.AUG.4,1950
```
1907 PHI N P          4    1- 0
1908 PHI N P          6    4- 1
1909 PHI N P         24    6-10
1910 CIN N P          7    1- 1
1914 DET A P         44   22-12
1915 DET A P         50   23-13
1916 DET A P         44   21-10
1917 DET A P         16    4- 6
1918 DET A P          3    0- 1
     BBTL           198   82-54
```

COVELESKI, STANLEY ANTHONY
(REAL NAME
STANISLAUS KOWALEWSKI)
B.JULY 13,1890 SHAMOKIN,PA.
```
1912 PHI A P          3    2- 1
1916 CLE A P         44   15-12
1917 CLE A P    45   46   19-14
1918 CLE A P         38   22-13
1919 CLE A P         43   24-12
1920 CLE A P         41   24-14
1921 CLE A P         43   23-13
1922 CLE A P         35   17-14
1923 CLE A P         33   13-14
1924 CLE A P         37   15-16
1925 WAS A P         32   20- 5
1926 WAS A P         36   14-11
1927 WAS A P          5    2- 1
1928 NY  A P         12    5- 1
     BRTR  447 448  215-141
```

COVENEY, JOHN PATRICK
B.1883 S.NATICK,MASS.
D.MAY 29,1961 COCHITUATE,MASS.
```
1903 STL N C          3   .200
     TR
```

COVINGTON, CHESTER ROGERS
"CHET"
B.NOV.6,1910 CAIRO,ILL.
D.JUNE 11,1976 PEMBROKE PARK,
FLA.
```
1944 PHI N P         19    1 -1
     BBTL
```

COVINGTON, CLARENCE CALVERT
"TEX"
B.NOV.18,1894 DENISON,TEX.
D.JAN.4,1963 DENISON,TEX.
```
1913 STL A 1         20   .150
1917 BOS N 1         17   .197
1918 BOS N O          3   .333
     BLTR            40   .178
```

COVINGTON, JOHN WESLEY "WES"
B.MAR.27,1932 LAURINBURG,N.C.
```
1956 MIL N O         75   .283
1957 MIL N O         96   .284
1958 MIL N O         90   .330
1959 MIL N O        103   .279
1960 MIL N O         95   .249
1961 MIL N O          9   .190
     CHI A O         22   .288
     KC  A O         17   .159
     PHI N O         57   .303
1962 PHI N O        116   .283
1963 PHI N O        119   .303
1964 PHI N O        129   .280
1965 PHI N O        101   .247
1966 CHI N O          9   .091
     LA  N O         37   .121
     BLTR          1075   .279
```

COVINGTON, WILLIAM WILKES
B.MAR.17,1887 HENRYVILLE,TENN.
D.DEC.10,1931
```
1911 DET A P         17    7- 1
1912 DET A P         14    3- 4
     BLTR            31   10- 5
```

COWAN, BILLY ROLLAND
B.AUG.28,1938 CALHOUN CITY,MISS.
```
1963 CHI N O         14   .250
1964 CHI N O        139   .241
1965 NY  N 2-S-O     82   .179
     MIL N O         19   .185
1967 PHI N 2-3-O     34   .153
1969 NY  A 1-O       32   .167
     CAL A O         28   .304
1970 CAL A 1-3-O     68   .276
1971 CAL A 1-O       74   .276
1972 CAL A H          3   .000
     BRTR           493   .236
```

COWENS, ALFRED EDWARD "AL"
B.OCT.25,1951 LOS ANGELES,CAL.
```
1974 KC  A 3-O      110   .242
1975 KC  A O        120   .277
1976 KC  A O        152   .265
     DRTR           382   .263
```

COX, ELMER JOSEPH "DICK"
B.SEPT.30,1897 PASADENA,CAL.
D.JUNE 1,1966 MORRO BAY,CAL.
```
1925 BRO N O        122   .329
1926 BRO N O        124   .296
     BRTR           246   .314
```

COX, ERNEST THOMPSON
B.FEB.19,1894 BIRMINGHAM,ALA.
D.APR.29,1974 BIRMINGHAM,ALA.
```
1922 CHI A P          1    0- 0
     BLTR
```

COX, FRANK BERNHARDT "RUNT"
B.MAR.17,1858 WALTHAM,MASS.
D.1928
```
1884 DET N S         27   .127
```

COX, GEORGE MELVIN
B.NOV.15,1904 SHERMAN,TEX.
```
1928 CHI A P         26    1- 2
     BRTR
```

COX, GLENN MELVIN
B.FEB.3,1931 MONTEBELLO,CAL.
```
1955 KC  A P          2    0- 2
1956 KC  A P          3    0- 2
1957 KC  A P         10    1- 0
1958 KC  A P          2    0- 0
     BRTR            17    1- 4
```

COX, JAMES CHARLES "JIM"
B.MAY 28,1950 BLOOMINGTON,ILL.
```
1973 MON N 2          9   .133
1974 MON N 2         77   .220
1975 MON N 2         11   .259
1976 MON N 2         13   .172
     BRTR           110   .215
```

COX, JOSEPH CASEY
"CASEY"
B.JULY 3,1941 LONG BEACH,CAL.
```
1966 WAS A P         66    4- 5
1967 WAS A P         54    7- 4
1968 WAS A P          4    0- 1
1969 WAS A P         52   12- 7
1970 WAS A P         37    8-12
1971 WAS A P         54    5- 7
1972 TEX A P         35    3- 5
     NY  A P          5    0- 1
1973 NY  A P          1    0- 0
     BRTR           308   39-42
```

COX, LARRY EUGENE
B.SEP.11,1947 BLUFFTON,OHIO
```
1973 PHI N C          1   .000
1974 PHI N C         30   .170
1975 PHI N C         11   .200
     BRTR            42   .172
```

COX, LESLIE WARREN
B.AUG.14,1905 JUNCTION,TEX.
D.OCT.14,1934 SAN ANGELO,TEX.
```
1926 CHI A P          2    0- 1
     BRTR
```

COX, PLATEAU REX
B.FEB.16,1896 HENCHER,N.C.
```
1920 DET A P          3    0- 0
     BLTR
```

COX, ROBERT JOE "BOB"
B.MAY 21,1941 TULSA,OKLA.
```
1968 NY  A 3        135   .229
1969 NY  A 2-3       85   .215
     BRTR           220   .225
```

COX, TERRY LEE
B.MAR.30,1949 ODESSA,TEX.
```
1970 CAL A P          3    0- 0
     BRTR
```

COX, WILLIAM DONALD
B.JUNE 23,1913 ASHMORE,ILL.
```
1936 STL N P          2    0- 0
1937 CHI A P          3    1- 0
1938 CHI A P          7    0- 2
     STL A P    22    24    1- 4
1939 STL A P          4    0- 2
1940 STL A P    12    13    0- 1
     BRTR            50    53    2- 9
```

COX, WILLIAM RICHARD "BILLY"
B.AUG.29,1919 NEWPORT,PA.
```
1941 PIT N S         10   .270
1946 PIT N S        121   .290
1947 PIT N S        132   .274
1948 BRO N 2-S-3     88   .249
1949 BRO N 3        100   .234
1950 BRO N 2-S-3    119   .257
1951 BRO N S-3      142   .279
1952 BRO N 2-S-3    116   .259
1953 BRO N 2-S-3    100   .291
1954 BRO N 2-S-3     77   .235
1955 BAL A 2-S-3     53   .211
     BRTR          1058   .262
```

COYLE, WILLIAM CLAUDE
B.PITTSBURGH,PA.
```
1893 BOS N P          1    0- 1
     TR
```

COYNE
```
1914 PHI A 3          1   .000
     TR
```

COZART, CHARLES RHUBIN
B.OCT.17,1919 LENOIR,N.C.
```
1945 BOS N P          5    1- 0
     BRTL
```

CRABB, JAMES ROY
B.AUG.23,1890 MONTICELLO,IOWA
D.MAR.30,1940
```
1912 CHI A P          2    0- 0
     PHI N P          7    2- 5
     BRTR             9    2- 5
```

CRABLE, GEORGE E.
B.1866 BROOKLYN,N.Y.
```
1910 BRO N P          2    0- 0
     BLTL
```

YR	CL	LEA	POS	GP	G	REC

CRABTREE, C. C.
(PLAYED UNDER NAME OF
CHARLES E. MC DONALD)

CRABTREE, ESTEL CRAYTON
B.AUG.19,1903 CRABTREE,OHIO
D.JAN.4,1967 LOGAN,OHIO

1929	CIN	N	H		1	.000
1931	CIN	N	1-3-O	117		.269
1932	CIN	N	O	108		.274
1933	STL	N	O	23		.265
1941	STL	N	3-O	77		.341
1942	STL	N	H	10		.333
1943	CIN	N	O	95		.276
1944	CIN	N	1-O	58		.286
	BRTL			489		.281

CRADDOCK, WALTER ANDERSON
B.MAR.25,1932 OAX,W.VA.

1955	KC	A	P		4	0- 2
1956	KC	A	P		2	0- 2
1958	KC	A	P		23	0- 3
					29	0- 7

CRAFT, HARRY FRANCIS "WILDFIRE"
B.APR.19,1915 ELLISVILLE,MISS.

1937	CIN	N	O		10	.310
1938	CIN	N	O	151		.270
1939	CIN	N	O	134		.257
1940	CIN	N	1-O	115		.244
1941	CIN	N	O	119		.249
1942	CIN	N	O		37	.177
	BRTR			566		.253
NON-PLAYING MANAGER
KC(A) 1957-59, CHI(N) 1961
HOU(N) 1962-64

CRAFT, MAURICE M. "MOLLIE"
B.NOV.28,1896 NORFOLK,VA.

1916	WAS	A	P		3	0- 1
1917	WAS	A	P		8	0- 0
1918	WAS	A	P		3	0- 0
1919	WAS	A	P		16	0- 3
	BRTR				30	0- 4

CRAGHEAD, HOWARD OLIVER
B.MAY 25,1908 FRESNO,CAL.
D.JULY 15,1962

1931	CLE	A	P		4	0- 0
1933	CLE	A	P		11	0- 0
	BRTR				15	0- 0

CRAIG, GEORGE MCCARTHY "LEFTY"
B.NOV.15,1887 PHILADELPHIA,PA.
D.APR.23,1911

1907	PHI	A	P		2	0- 0
	TL					

CRAIG, PETER JOEL "PETE"
B.JULY 10,1940 LASALLE,ONT.,CAN.

1964	WAS	A	P		2	0- 0
1965	WAS	A	P		3	0- 3
1966	WAS	A	P		1	0- 0
	BLTR				6	0- 3

CRAIG, ROGER LEE
B.FEB.17,1931 DURHAM,N.C.

1955	BRO	N	P		21	5- 3
1956	BRO	N	P		35	12-11
1957	BRO	N	P		32	6- 9
1958	LA	N	P		9	2- 1
1959	LA	N	P		29	11- 5
1960	LA	N	P		21	8- 3
1961	LA	N	P		40	5- 6
1962	NY	N	P		42	10-24
1963	NY	N	P		46	5-22
1964	STL	N	P		39	7- 9
1965	CIN	N	P		40	1- 4
1966	PHI	N	P		14	2- 1
	BRTR			368		74-98

CRAM, GERALD ALLEN
B.DEC.9,1947 LOS ANGELES,CAL.

1969	KC	A	P		5	0- 1
1974	NY	N	P		10	0- 1
1975	NY	N	P		4	0- 1
1976	KC	A	P		4	0- 0
	BRTR				23	0- 3

CRAMER, ROGER MAXWELL "DOC"
B.JULY 22,1906 BEACH HAVEN,N.J.

1929	PHI	A	O		2	.000
1930	PHI	A	O		30	.232
1931	PHI	A	O		65	.260
1932	PHI	A	O		92	.336
1933	PHI	A	O	152		.295
1934	PHI	A	O	153		.311
1935	PHI	A	O	149		.332
1936	BOS	A	O	154		.292
1937	BOS	A	O	133		.305
1938	BOS	A	P-O	1	148	0- 0
						.301
1939	BOS	A	O		137	.311
1940	BOS	A	O		150	.303
1941	WAS	A	O		154	.273
1942	DET	A	O		151	.263
1943	DET	A	O		140	.300
1944	DET	A	O		143	.292
1945	DET	A	O		141	.275
1946	DET	A	O		68	.294
1947	DET	A	O		73	.268
1948	DET	A	O		4	.000
	BLTR			1	2239	0- 0
						.296

CRAMER, WILLIAM B.
B.BROOKLYN,N.Y.
D.AUG.12,1885

1883	NY	N	O		2	.125

CRAMER, WILLIAM WENDELL
B.MAY 22,1891 BEDFORD,IND.
D.SEPT.11,1966 FORT WAYNE,IND.

1912	CIN	N	P		1	0- 0
	BRTR					

CRANDALL, DELMAR WESLEY "DEL"
B.MAR.5,1930 ONTARIO,CAL.

1949	BOS	N	C		67	.263
1950	BOS	N	C-1		79	.220
1953	MIL	N	C	116		.272
1954	MIL	N	C	138		.242
1955	MIL	N	C	133		.236
1956	MIL	N	C	112		.238
1957	MIL	N	C-1-O	118		.253
1958	MIL	N	C	131		.272
1959	MIL	N	C	150		.257
1960	MIL	N	C	142		.294
1961	MIL	N	C		15	.200
1962	MIL	N	C-1	107		.297
1963	MIL	N	C-1		86	.201
1964	SF	N	C		69	.231
1965	PIT	N	C		60	.214
1966	CLE	A	C		50	.231
	BRTR			1573		.254
NON-PLAYING MANAGER
MIL(A) 1972-75

CRANDALL, JAMES OTIS "DOC"
B.OCT.8,1887 WADENA,IND.
D.AUG.17,1951

1908	NY	N	P		32	12-12
1909	NY	N	P		30	6- 4
1910	NY	N	P	42	43	17- 4
1911	NY	N	P	41	50	15- 5
1912	NY	N	P	37	50	13- 7
1913	NY	N	P		24	4- 4
	STL	N	H		2	.000
	NY	N	P	11	15	0- 0
1914	STL	F	P-2	27	115	12- 9
						.312
1915	STL	F	P	51	81	21-15
1916	STL	A	P	2	16	0- 0
1918	BOS	N	P	5	14	1- 2
	BRTR			302	479	101-62
						.286

CRANE, EDWARD NICHOLAS
"CANNON-BALL"
B.MAY 1864 S.BOSTON,MASS.
D.SEPT.19,1896

1884	BOS	U	P-C-	2	99	0- 2
			O			.304
1885	PRO	N	P-O		1	0- 0
						.000
	BUF	N	O		13	.269
1886	WAS	N	P-O	10	80	2- 6
						.171
1888	NY	N	P		12	5- 6
1889	NY	N	P		28	14-10
1890	NY	P	P		44	16-23
1891	CIN	AA	P-O	32	34	14-17
						.145
	CIN	N	P		14	2-10
1892	NY	N	P		40	14-26
1893	NY	N	P		10	2- 4
	BRO	N	P		3	0- 2
	BRTR			196	378	69-106
						.236

CRANE, SAMUEL BYREN "LUCKY"
B.SEPT.13,1894 HARRISBURG,PA.
D.NOV.12,1955

1914	PHI	A	S		2	.000
1915	PHI	A	S		8	.087
1916	PHI	A	S		2	.250
1917	WAS	A	S		32	.179
1920	CIN	N	2-S-3-O		54	.215
1921	CIN	N	S		73	.233
1922	BRO	N	S		3	.250
	BRTR			174		.208

CRANE, SAMUEL NEWHALL
B.JAN.2,1854 SPRINGFIELD,MASS.
D.JUNE 26,1925

1873	RES	NA	2		1	-
1875	ATL	NA	1-O		21	-
1880	BUF	N	M-2-O		10	.125
1883	MET	AA	2-O		97	.234
1884	CIN	U	M-2		68	.231
1885	DET	N	2		68	.191
1886	STL	N	2		37	.175
1887	WAS	N	2		7	.312
1890	NY	N	1-O		2	.000
	PIT	N	2-S		22	.200
	NY	N	2		2	.000
	BRTR			384		-

CRAUSE, CLARENCE
(PLAYED UNDER NAME OF
CLARENCE CROSS)

CRAVATH, CLIFFORD CARLTON
"GAVVY"
B.MAR.23,1881 SAN DIEGO,CAL.
D.MAY 23,1963 LAGUNA BEACH,CAL.

1908	BOS	A	O		94	.256
1909	CHI	A	O		18	.061
	WAS	A	O		4	1.000
1912	PHI	N	O		130	.284
1913	PHI	N	O		147	.341
1914	PHI	N	O		149	.298
1915	PHI	N	O		150	.285
1916	PHI	N	O		137	.283
1917	PHI	N	O		140	.280
1918	PHI	N	O		121	.232
1919	PHI	N	M-O		83	.341
1920	PHI	N	M-O		46	.289
	BRTR			1219		.287

CRAVER, WILLIAM H.
B.1844 TROY,N.Y.
D.JUNE 17,1901

1871	TRO	NA	M-C-1-2-S		27	.303
1872	BAL	NA	C-1-2-3-O		33	.278
1873	BAL	NA	C-1-2-S-O		38	-
1874	PHI	NA	M-C-2		55	-
1875	CEN	NA	M-1-2-S-3		14	-
1875	ATH	NA	C-2		55	.314
1876	MUT	N	C-2		56	.222
1877	LOU	N	S		57	.263
	BRTR			335		-

CRAWFORD, CHARLES LOWRIE
"LARRY"
B.APR.27,1914 SWISSVALE,PA.

1937	PHI	N	P		6	0- 0
	BLTL					

YR	CL	LEA	POS	GP	G	REC

CRAWFORD, CLIFFORD RANKIN "PAT"
B.JAN.28,1902 SOCIETY HILL,S.C.

YR	CL	LEA	POS	GP	G	REC
1929	NY	N	1		65	.298
1930	NY	N	1-2		25	.276
	CIN	N	1-2		76	.290
1933	STL	N	1-2-3		91	.268
1934	STL	N	2-3		61	.271
	BLTR				318	.280

CRAWFORD, FORREST A.
B.MAY 10,1881 ROCKDALE,TEX.
D.MAR.27,1908

YR	CL	LEA	POS	GP	G	REC
1906	STL	N	S		45	.207
1907	STL	N	S		7	.227
	TR				52	.210

CRAWFORD, GEORGE

YR	CL	LEA	POS	GP	G	REC
1890	ATH	AA	O		5	.111

CRAWFORD, GLENN MARTIN
B.DEC.2,1918 NORTH BRANCH,MICH.
D.JAN.2,1972 SAGINAW,MICH.

YR	CL	LEA	POS	GP	G	REC
1945	STL	N	O		4	.000
	PHI	N	2-S-O		82	.295
1946	PHI	N	1		1	.000
	BLTR				87	.291

CRAWFORD, JAMES FREDERICK "JIM"
B.SEP.29,1950 CHICAGO,ILL.

YR	CL	LEA	POS	GP	G	REC
1973	HOU	N	P		48	2- 4
1975	HOU	N	P		44	3- 5
1976	DET	A	P		32	1- 8
	BLTL				124	6-17

CRAWFORD, KENNETH
B.PITTSBURGH,PA.

YR	CL	LEA	POS	GP	G	REC
1915	BAL	F	1-O		23	.244
	BL					

CRAWFORD, RUFUS "JAKE"
B.MAR.30,1928 CAMPBELL,MO.

YR	CL	LEA	POS	GP	G	REC
1952	STL	A	O		7	.182
	BRTR					

CRAWFORD, SAMUEL EARL "WAHOO SAM"
B.APR.18,1880 WAHOO,NEB.
D.JUNE 15,1968 HOLLYWOOD,CAL.

YR	CL	LEA	POS	GP	G	REC
1899	CIN	N	O		31	.308
1900	CIN	N	O		96	.270
1901	CIN	N	O		124	.334
1902	CIN	N	O		140	.333
1903	DET	A	O		137	.332
1904	DET	A	O		150	.247
1905	DET	A	1-O		154	.297
1906	DET	A	1-O		145	.295
1907	DET	A	O		144	.323
1908	DET	A	1-O		152	.311
1909	DET	A	1-O		156	.314
1910	DET	A	O		154	.289
1911	DET	A	O		146	.378
1912	DET	A	O		149	.325
1913	DET	A	1-O		153	.316
1914	DET	A	O		157	.314
1915	DET	A	O		156	.299
1916	DET	A	O		100	.286
1917	DET	A	1-O		61	.173
	BLTL				2505	.309

CRAWFORD, WILLIE MURPHY
B.SEP.7,1946 LOS ANGELES,CAL.

YR	CL	LEA	POS	GP	G	REC
1964	LA	N	O		10	.313
1965	LA	N	O		52	.148
1966	LA	N	R		6	.000
1967	LA	N	O		4	.250
1968	LA	N	O		61	.251
1969	LA	N	O		129	.247
1970	LA	N	O		109	.234
1971	LA	N	O		114	.281
1972	LA	N	O		96	.251
1973	LA	N	O		145	.295
1974	LA	N	O		139	.295
1975	LA	N	O		124	.263
1976	STL	N	O		120	.304
	BLTR				1109	.272

CREAMER, GEORGE W.
(REAL NAME GEORGE W. TRIEBEL)
B.1855 PHILADELPHIA,PA.
D.JUNE 27,1886

YR	CL	LEA	POS	GP	G	REC
1878	MIL	N	2-O		50	.212
1879	SYR	N	2-S-O		15	.213
1880	WOR	N	2		83	.202
1881	WOR	N	2		79	.209
1882	WOR	N	2		81	.228
1883	PIT	AA	2		89	.243
1884	PIT	AA	M-2		100	.185
	BRTR				497	.216

CREE, WILLIAM FRANKLIN "BIRDIE"
B.OCT.23,1882 KHEDIVE,PA.
D.NOV.8,1942

YR	CL	LEA	POS	GP	G	REC
1908	NY	A	O		21	.269
1909	NY	A	O		104	.262
1910	NY	A	O		134	.287
1911	NY	A	O		137	.348
1912	NY	A	O		50	.332
1913	NY	A	O		147	.271
1914	NY	A	O		77	.309
1915	NY	A	O		74	.214
	BRTR				744	.292

CREEDEN, CORNELIUS STEPHEN
B.JULY 21,1915 DANVERS,MASS.
D.NOV.30,1969 SANTA ANA,CAL.

YR	CL	LEA	POS	GP	G	REC
1943	BOS	N	H		5	.250
	BLTL					

CREEDEN, PATRICK FRANCIS
B.MAY 23,1907 NEWBURYPORT,MASS.

YR	CL	LEA	POS	GP	G	REC
1931	BOS	A	2		5	.000
	BLTR					

CREEGAN, MARTIN
B.SAN FRANCISCO,CAL.

YR	CL	LEA	POS	GP	G	REC
1884	WAS	U	C-1-3-O		9	.152

CREEL, JACK DALTON "TEX"
B.APR.23,1917 KYLE,TEX.

YR	CL	LEA	POS	GP	G	REC
1945	STL	N	P	26	35	5- 4
	BRTR					

CREELY, AUGUST
B.ST.LOUIS,MO.

YR	CL	LEA	POS	GP	G	REC
1890	STL	AA	S		4	.000

CREGAN, PETER "PEEKSKILL PETE"
B.APR.13,1875 KINGSTON,N.Y.
D.MAY 18,1945

YR	CL	LEA	POS	GP	G	REC
1899	NY	N	O		1	.000
1903	CIN	N	O		6	.111
	BRTR				7	.095

CREGER, BERNARD ODELL
B.MAR.21,1927 WYTHEVILLE,VA.

YR	CL	LEA	POS	GP	G	REC
1947	STL	N	S		15	.188
	BRTR					

CREMINS, ROBERT ANTHONY
B.FEB.15,1906 PELHAM MANOR,N.Y.

YR	CL	LEA	POS	GP	G	REC
1927	BOS	A	P		4	0- 0
	BLTL					

CRESPI, FRANK ANGELO JOSEPH "CREEPY"
B.FEB.16,1918 ST.LOUIS,MO.

YR	CL	LEA	POS	GP	G	REC
1938	STL	N	S		7	.263
	STL	N	H		15	.172
1940	STL	N	S-3		3	.273
1941	STL	N	2		146	.279
1942	STL	N	2-S		93	.243
	BRTR				264	.263

CRESS, WALKER JAMES
B.MAR.6,1918 BEN HUR,VA.

YR	CL	LEA	POS	GP	G	REC
1948	CIN	N	P	30	31	0- 1
1949	CIN	N	P		3	0- 0
	BRTR			33	34	0- 1

CRIDER, JERRY STEPHEN
B.SEP.2,1941 SIOUX FALLS,S.D.

YR	CL	LEA	POS	GP	G	REC
1969	MIN	A	P		21	1- 0
1970	CHI	A	P		32	4- 7
	BRTR				53	5- 7

CRIGER, LOUIS
B.FEB.6,1872 ELKHART,IND.
D.MAY 14,1934

YR	CL	LEA	POS	GP	G	REC
1896	CLE	N	C		2	.000
1897	CLE	N	C		38	.230
1898	CLE	N	C		81	.273
1899	STL	N	C		75	.256
1900	STL	N	C		76	.266
1901	BOS	A	C		69	.240
1902	BOS	A	C-O		86	.259
1903	BOS	A	C		96	.197
1904	BOS	A	C		98	.217
1905	BOS	A	C		109	.198
1906	BOS	A	C		6	.214
1907	BOS	A	C		75	.181
1908	BOS	A	C		84	.190
1909	STL	A	C		74	.170
1910	NY	A	C		27	.189
1912	STL	A	C		1	.000
	BRTR				997	.223

CRIMIAN JOHN MELVIN "JACK"
B.FEB.17,1926 PHILADELPHIA,PA.

YR	CL	LEA	POS	GP	G	REC
1951	STL	N	P		11	1- 0
1952	STL	N	P		5	0- 0
1956	KC	A	P	54	55	4- 8
1957	DET	A	P		4	0- 1
	BRTR			74	75	5- 9

CRISCOLA, ANTHONY PAUL
B.JULY 9,1915 WALLA WALLA,WASH.

YR	CL	LEA	POS	GP	G	REC
1942	STL	A	O		91	.297
1943	STL	A	O		29	.154
1944	CIN	N	O		64	.229
	BLTR				184	.248

CRISHAM, PATRICK LEWIS
B.JUNE 4,1877 AMESBURY,MASS.
D.JUNE 12,1915

YR	CL	LEA	POS	GP	G	REC
1899	BAL	N	1		44	.303

CRISP, JOSEPH SHELBY
B.JULY 8,1889 HIGGINSVILLE,MO.
D.FEB.5,1939

YR	CL	LEA	POS	GP	G	REC
1910	STL	A	C		1	.000
1911	STL	A	C		1	1.000
	BRTR				2	.500

CRISS, DODE
B.MAR.12,1885 SHERMAN,MISS.
D.SEPT.8,1955

YR	CL	LEA	POS	GP	G	REC
1908	STL	A	P-O	1	64	0- 1
						.341
1909	STL	A	P	10	35	1- 4
1910	STL	A	P-O	3	70	2- 1
						.231
1911	STL	A	P-O	4	58	0- 2
						.253
	BLTR			18	227	3- 8
						.276

CRISS, HARRY
(PLAYED UNDER NAME OF HUGH I. DALY)

CRIST, CHESTER A.
B.MADISONVILLE,OHIO

YR	CL	LEA	POS	GP	G	REC
1906	PHI	N	C		5	.000
	TR					

CRISTALL, WILLIAM A.
B.SEPT.12,1878 BUFFALO,N.Y.
D.JAN.29,1939

YR	CL	LEA	POS	GP	G	REC
1901	CLE	A	P		6	1- 4
	TR					

CRISTANTE, LEO DANTE
B.DEC.10,1926 DETROIT,MICH.

YR	CL	LEA	POS	GP	G	REC
1951	PHI	N	P		10	1- 1
1955	DET	A	P		20	0- 1
	BRTR				30	1- 2

CRITCHLEY, MORRIS A.
B.PITTSBURGH,PA.
D.MAR.7,1910

YR	CL	LEA	POS	GP	G	REC
1882	PIT	AA	P		1	1- 0
	STL	AA	P		4	0- 3
					5	1- 3

YR	CL	LEA	POS	GP	G	REC

CRITZ, HUGH MELVILLE
B.SEPT.17,1900 STARKVILLE,MISS.
1924	CIN	N	2-S	102		.322
1925	CIN	N	2	144		.277
1926	CIN	N	2	155		.270
1927	CIN	N	2	113		.278
1928	CIN	N	2	153		.296
1929	CIN	N	2-S	107		.247
1930	CIN	N	2	28		.231
1930	NY	N	2	124		.265
1931	NY	N	2	66		.290
1932	NY	N	2	151		.276
1933	NY	N	2	133		.246
1934	NY	N	2	137		.242
1935	NY	N	2	65		.187
		BRTR		1478		.268

CROCKER, CLAUDE ARTHUR
B.JULY 20,1925 CAROLEEN,N.C.
1944	BRO	N	P	2		0- 0
1945	BRO	N	P	1		0- 0
		BRTR		3		0- 0

CROCKETT, DANIEL SOLOMON
B.OCT.5,1875 LAMMOOR,VA.
D.FEB.23,1961
| 1901 | DET | A | 1 | 28 | | .291 |

CROFT, ARTHUR F.
B.JAN.23,1855 ST.LOUIS,MO.
D.MAR.16,1884
1875	RS	NA	O	19		-
1877	STL	N	1-2-O	54		.233
1878	IND	N	1-O	57		.162
				130		-

CROFT, HENRY T.
B.CHICAGO,ILL.
1899	LOU	N	O	1		.000
	PHI	N	2	2		.143
1901	CHI	N	O	3		.333
				6		.250

CROLIUS, FRED JOSEPH
B.DEC.16,1876 JERSEY CITY,N.J.
D.AUG.25,1960
1901	BOS	N	O	50		.238
1902	PIT	N	O	9		.263
				59		.239

CROMARTIE, WARREN LIVINGSTON
B.SEPT.29,1953 MIAMI BEACH,FLA.
1974	MON	N	O	8		.176
1976	MON	N	O	33		.210
		BLTL		41		.204

CROMPTON, EDWARD
B.FEB.12,1889 LIVERPOOL,ENGLAND
D.SEPT.28,1930
1909	STL	A	O	17		.157
1910	CIN	N	O	1		.000
		BLTL		18		.154

CROMPTON, HERBERT BRYAN
B.NOV.7,1912 MILAN,ILL.
D.AUG.5,1963 MOLINE,ILL.
1937	WAS	A	C	2		.333
1945	NY	A	C	36		.192
		BRTR		38		.196

CRONE, RAYMOND HAYES "RAY"
B.AUG.7,1931 MEMPHIS,TENN.
1954	MIL	N	P	19		1- 0
1955	MIL	N	P	33		10- 9
1956	MIL	N	P	35		11-10
1957	MIL	N	P	11		3- 1
	NY	N	P	25		4- 8
1958	SF	N	P	14		1- 2
		BRTR		137		30-30

CRONIN, DANIEL
B.1857 S.BOSTON,MASS.
D.NOV.30,1885
1884	CHI	U	2	1		.250
	KC	U	O	1		.000
				2		.111

CRONIN, JAMES JOHN
B.AUG.7,1906 RICHMOND,CAL.
| 1929 | PHI | A | 2 | 25 | | .232 |
| | | BBTR | | | | |

CRONIN, JOHN J.
B.MAY 26,1874 W.NEW BRIGHTON,
S.I.,N.Y.
D.JULY 12,1929
1895	BRO	N	P	2		0- 0
1898	PIT	N	P	4		2- 2
1899	CIN	N	P	5		2- 2
1901	DET	A	P	31		12-16
1902	DET	A	P	4		1- 0
	BAL	A	P	9		2- 5
	NY	N	P-O	13	19	5- 6
						.167
1903	NY	N	P	20		6- 4
1904	BRO	N	P	40		11-22
		BRTR		128	134	41-57
						.181

CRONIN, JOSEPH EDWARD "JOE"
B.OCT.12,1906 SAN FRANCISCO,CAL
1926	PIT	N	2-S	38		.265
1927	PIT	N	S	12		.227
1928	WAS	A	S	63		.243
1929	WAS	A	S	145		.282
1930	WAS	A	S	154		.346
1931	WAS	A	S	156		.306
1932	WAS	A	S	143		.318
1933	WAS	A	M-S	152		.309
1934	WAS	A	M-S	127		.284
1935	BOS	A	M-1-S	144		.295
1936	BOS	A	M-S-3	81		.281
1937	BOS	A	M-S	148		.307
1938	BOS	A	M-S	143		.325
1939	BOS	A	M-S	143		.308
1940	BOS	A	M-S-3	149		.285
1941	BOS	A	M-S-3-O	143		.311
1942	BOS	A	M-1-S-3	45		.304
1943	BOS	A	M-3	59		.312
1944	BOS	A	M-1	76		.241
1945	BOS	A	M-3	3		.375
		BRTR		2124		.302
NON-PLAYING MANAGER
WAS(A) 1933-34, BOS(A) 1935-47

CRONIN, WILLIAM PATRICK
B.DEC.26,1902 W.NEWTON,MASS.
1928	BOS	N	C	3		.000
1929	BOS	N	C	6		.111
1930	BOS	N	C	66		.253
1931	BOS	N	C	51		.206
		BRTR		126		.232

CROOKE, THOMAS A.
B.WASHINGTON,D.C.
D.APR.5,1929 QUANTICO,VA.
1909	WAS	A	1	3		.286
1910	WAS	A	1	8		.182
		TR		11		.207

CROOKS, JOHN CHARLES
B.NOV.9,1866 ST.PAUL,MINN.
D.JAN.29,1918
1889	COL	AA	2	12		.323
1890	COL	AA	2	135		.221
1891	COL	AA	2	138		.240
1892	STL	N	2-3	127		.213
1893	STL	N	3	128		.251
1895	WAS	N	2	118		.291
1896	WAS	N	2-3	24		.280
	LOU	N	2	37		.232
1898	STL	N	2	71		.238
				790		.244

CROSBY, EDWARD CARLTON "ED"
B.MAY 26,1949 LONG BEACH,CAL.
1970	STL	N	2-S-3	38		.253
1972	STL	N	2-S-3	101		.217
1973	STL	N	2-S-3	22		.128
	CIN	N	2-S	36		.216
1974	CLE	A	2-S-3	37		.209
1975	CLE	A	2-S-3	61		.234
1976	CLE	A	3	2		.500
		BLTR		297		.220

CROSBY, GEORGE W.
B.CHICAGO,ILL.
| 1884 | CHI | N | P | 3 | | 1- 2 |

CROSBY, KENNETH STEWART "KEN"
B.DEC.15,1947 NEW DENVER,B.C.,
CANADA
1975	CHI	N	P	9		1- 0
1976	CHI	N	P	7		0- 0
		BRTR		16		1- 0

**CROSETTI, FRANK PETER JOSEPH
"CROW"**
B.OCT.4,1910 SAN FRANCISCO,CAL.
1932	NY	A	S-3	116		.241
1933	NY	A	S	136		.253
1934	NY	A	S-3	138		.265
1935	NY	A	S	87		.256
1936	NY	A	S	151		.288
1937	NY	A	S	149		.234
1938	NY	A	S	157		.263
1939	NY	A	S	152		.233
1940	NY	A	S	145		.194
1941	NY	A	S-3	50		.223
1942	NY	A	2-S-3	74		.242
1943	NY	A	S	95		.233
1944	NY	A	S	55		.239
1945	NY	A	S	130		.238
1946	NY	A	S	28		.288
1947	NY	A	2-S	3		.000
1948	NY	A	2-S	17		.286
		BRTR		1683		.245

CROSS, AMOS C.
B.1861 CZECHOSLOVAKIA
D.JULY 16,1888
1885	LOU	AA	C	35		.295
1886	LOU	AA	C-1	74		.276
1887	LOU	AA	C	9		.257
				118		.280

CROSS, CLARENCE
(REAL NAME CLARENCE CRAUSE)
B.MAR.4,1856 ST.LOUIS,MO.
D.JUNE 23,1931
1884	ALT	U	3	2		.572
	KEY	U	S	2		.143
	KC	U	S	25		.212
1887	MET	AA	S	16		.245
				45		.222

CROSS, FRANK A.
B.CLEVELAND,OHIO
| 1901 | CLE | A | O | 1 | | .600 |
| | | TR | | | | |

CROSS, GEORGE LEWIS "LEW"
B.JAN.9,1872 MANCHESTER,N.H.
D.APR.5,1929
1893	CIN	N	P	2		0- 2
1894	CIN	N	P	9		2- 4
				11		2- 6

CROSS, JOFFRE JAMES "JEFF"
B.AUG.28,1918 TULSA,OKLA.
1942	STL	N	S	1		.250
1946	STL	N	2-S-3	49		.217
1947	STL	N	2-S-3	51		.102
1948	STL	N	H	2		.000
	CHI	N	2-S	16		.100
		BRTR		119		.162

CROSS, LAVE NAPOLEON
B.MAY 12,1866 MILWAUKEE,WIS.
D.SEPT.6,1927 PHILADELPHIA,PA.
1887	LOU	AA	C	54		.327
1888	LOU	AA	C	47		.213
1889	ATH	AA	C	55		.226
1890	PHI	P	C	60		.299
1891	ATH	AA	C-3-O	109		.302
1892	PHI	N	C-3-O	134		.262
1893	PHI	N	C-3	94		.302
1894	PHI	N	3	120		.388
1895	PHI	N	3	124		.277
1896	PHI	N	S-3	106		.261
1897	PHI	N	2-3	88		.261
1898	STL	N	3	151		.319
1899	CLE	N	M-3	38		.263
	STL	N	3	103		.304
1900	STL	N	3	16		.300
	BRO	N	3	117		.292
1901	PHI	A	3	100		.331
1902	PHI	A	3	137		.339
1903	PHI	A	3	137		.292
1904	PHI	A	3	155		.290
1905	PHI	A	3	146		.266
1906	WAS	A	3	130		.263
1907	WAS	A	3	41		.199
		BRTR		2262		.293

YR	CL	LEA	POS	GP	G	REC

CROSS, MONTFORD MONTGOMERY "MONTE"
B.AUG.31,1869 PHILADELPHIA,PA.
D.JUNE 21,1934

YR	CL	LEA	POS	GP	G	REC
1892	BAL	N	S		15	.160
1894	PIT	N	S		13	.404
1895	PIT	N	S		108	.255
1896	STL	N	S		124	.264
1897	STL	N	S		130	.288
1898	PHI	N	S		149	.259
1899	PHI	N	S		153	.259
1900	PHI	N	S		130	.200
1901	PHI	N	S		139	.197
1902	PHI	A	S		137	.207
1903	PHI	A	S		138	.245
1904	PHI	A	S		153	.182
1905	PHI	A	S		78	.270
1906	PHI	A	S		134	.200
1907	PHI	A	S		77	.206
	BRTR				1678	.233

CROSSIN, FRANK PATRICK
B.JUNE 15,1891 LUZERNE,PA.
D.DEC.6,1965 KINGSTON,PA.

YR	CL	LEA	POS	GP	G	REC
1912	STL	A	C		7	.277
1913	STL	A	C		3	.333
1914	STL	A	C		43	.122
	BRTR				53	.147

CROTHERS, DOUGLAS
B.ST.LOUIS,MO.

YR	CL	LEA	POS	GP	G	REC
1884	KC	U	P	3	4	1- 2
1885	MET	AA	P		18	7-11
				21	22	8-13

CROTTY, JOSEPH
B.CINCINNATI,OHIO

YR	CL	LEA	POS	GP	G	REC
1882	LOU	AA	C		5	.100
	STL	A	C-O		8	.133
1884	CIN	U	C		20	.287
1885	LOU	AA	C		39	.172
1886	MET	AA	C		12	.205
	BR				84	.199

CROUCH, JACK ALBERT "ROXY"
B.OCT.12,1903 SALISBURY,N.C.
D.AUG.25,1972 LEESBURG,FLA.

YR	CL	LEA	POS	GP	G	REC
1930	STL	A	C		6	.143
1931	STL	A	C		8	.000
1933	STL	A	C		19	.167
	CIN	N	C		10	.125
	BRTR				43	.125

CROUCH, WILLIAM ELMER
B.AUG.20,1910 WILMINGTON,DEL.

YR	CL	LEA	POS	GP	G	REC
1939	BRO	N	P		6	4- 0
1941	PHI	N	P		20	2- 3
	STL	N	P		18	1- 2
1945	STL	N	P		6	1- 0
	BBTR				50	8- 5

CROUCH, WILLIAM HENRY "SKIP"
B.DEC.3,1886 MARSHALLTON,DEL.
D.DEC.22,1945

YR	CL	LEA	POS	GP	G	REC
1910	STL	A	P		1	0- 0

CROUCHER, FRANK DONALD "DINGLE"
B.JULY 23,1914 SAN ANTONIO,TEX.

YR	CL	LEA	POS	GP	G	REC
1939	DET	A	S		97	.269
1940	DET	A	2-S-3		37	.105
1941	DET	A	S		136	.254
1942	WAS	A	2		26	.277
	BRTR				296	.251

CROUSE, CLYDE ELLSWORTH "BUCK"
B.JAN.6,1897 MUNCIE,IND.

YR	CL	LEA	POS	GP	G	REC
1923	CHI	A	C		23	.257
1924	CHI	A	C		94	.259
1925	CHI	A	C		54	.352
1926	CHI	A	C		49	.237
1927	CHI	A	C		85	.239
1928	CHI	A	C		78	.252
1929	CHI	A	C		45	.272
1930	CHI	A	C		42	.254
	BLTR				470	.262

CROWDER, ALVIN FLOYD "GENERAL"
B.JAN.11,1899 WINSTON-SALEM,N.C
D.APR.3,1972 WINSTON-SALEM,N.C.

YR	CL	LEA	POS	GP	G	REC
1926	WAS	A	P		19	7- 4
1927	WAS	A	P		15	4- 7
	STL	A	P		21	3- 5
1928	STL	A	P		41	21- 5
1929	STL	A	P		40	17-15
1930	STL	A	P		13	3- 7
	WAS	A	P		27	15- 9
1931	WAS	A	P		44	18-11
1932	WAS	A	P	50	51	26-13
1933	WAS	A	P		52	24-15
1934	WAS	A	P		29	4-10
	DET	A	P		9	5- 1
1935	DET	A	P		33	16-10
1936	DET	A	P		9	4- 3
	BLTR			402	403	167-115

CROWE, GEORGE DANIEL "BIG GEORGE"
B.MAR.22,1923 WHITELAND,IND.

YR	CL	LEA	POS	GP	G	REC
1952	BOS	N	1		73	.258
1953	MIL	N	1		47	.286
1955	MIL	N	1		104	.281
1956	CIN	N	1		77	.250
1957	CIN	N	1		133	.271
1958	CIN	N	1-2		111	.275
1959	STL	N	1		77	.301
1960	STL	N	1		73	.236
1961	STL	N	H		7	.143
	BLTL				702	.270

CROWELL, MINOT JOY
B.SEPT.5,1892 ROXBURY,MASS.
D.SEPT.30,1962

YR	CL	LEA	POS	GP	G	REC
1915	PHI	A	P		10	2- 6
1916	PHI	A	P		9	0- 5
	BRTR				19	2-11

CROWELL, WILLIAM THEODORE
B.NOV.6,1865 CUMMINSVILLE,OHIO
D.JULY 24,1935

YR	CL	LEA	POS	GP	G	REC
1887	CLE	AA	P		45	13-32
1888	CLE	AA	P		18	0-12
	LOU	AA	P		7	5- 2
	BRTR				70	18-46

CROWLEY, EDGAR JEWEL
B.AUG.20,1906 WATKINSVILLE,GA.
D.APR.14,1970 BIRMINGHAM,ALA.

YR	CL	LEA	POS	GP	G	REC
1928	WAS	A	3		2	.000
	BRTR					

CROWLEY, JOHN A.
B.JAN.12,1862 LAWRENCE,MASS.
D.SEPT.23,1896

YR	CL	LEA	POS	GP	G	REC
1884	PHI	N	C		44	.244

CROWLEY, TERRENCE MICHAEL "TERRY"
B.FEB.16,1947 STATEN ISLAND,N.Y.

YR	CL	LEA	POS	GP	G	REC
1969	BAL	A	1-O		7	.333
1970	BAL	A	1-O		83	.257
1971	BAL	A	1-O		18	.174
1972	BAL	A	1-O		97	.231
1973	BAL	A	1-O-O		54	.208
1974	CIN	N	1-O		84	.240
1975	CIN	N	1-O		66	.268
1976	ATL	N	H		7	.000
	BAL	A	1-O		33	.246
	BLTL				449	.236

CROWLEY, WILLIAM MICHAEL
B.APR.8,1857 PHILADELPHIA,PA.
D.JULY 14,1891

YR	CL	LEA	POS	GP	G	REC
1875	PHI	NA	1-2-3-O		9	-
1877	LOU	N	C-2-S-3-O		61	.281
1879	BUF	N	C-O		59	.282
1880	BUF	N	C-O		82	.261
1881	BOS	N	O		71	.254
1883	ATH	AA	1-O		24	.265
	CLE	N	O		11	.317
1884	BOS	N	O		103	.265
1885	BUF	N	O		92	.241
	BRTR				512	-

CROWSON, THOMAS WOODROW WILSON "WOODY"
B.SEPT.9,1918 HARTNETT CO.,N.C.
D.AUG.14,1947

YR	CL	LEA	POS	GP	G	REC
1945	PHI	A	P		1	0- 0
	BRTR					

CRUISE, WALTON EDWIN
B.MAY 6,1890 CHILDERSBURG,ALA.
D.JAN.9,1975 SYLACAUGA,ALA.

YR	CL	LEA	POS	GP	G	REC
1914	STL	N	O		95	.227
1916	STL	N	O		3	.667
1917	STL	N	O		153	.295
1918	STL	N	O		70	.271
1919	STL	N	1-O		9	.095
	BOS	N	O		73	.216
1920	BOS	N	O		91	.278
1921	BOS	N	O		108	.346
1922	BOS	N	1-O		104	.278
1923	BOS	N	O		21	.211
1924	BOS	N	O		9	.444
	BLTR				736	.277

CRUM, CALVIN CARL
B.1892 MATTOON,ILL.
D.DEC.7,1945

YR	CL	LEA	POS	GP	G	REC
1917	BOS	N	P		1	0- 0
1918	BOS	N	P		1	0- 1
	BRTR				2	0- 1

CRUMLING, EUGENE LEON
B.APR.5,1922 WRIGHTSVILLE,PA.

YR	CL	LEA	POS	GP	G	REC
1945	STL	N	C		6	.083

CRUMP, ARTHUR ELLIOTT
B.NOV.29,1901 NORFOLK,VA.

YR	CL	LEA	POS	GP	G	REC
1924	NY	N	O		1	.000
	BLTL					

CRUMPLER, RAY MAXTON
B.JULY 8,1895 CLINTON,N.C.

YR	CL	LEA	POS	GP	G	REC
1920	DET	A	P		4	1- 0
1925	PHI	N	P		3	0- 0
	BLTL				7	1- 0

CRUTCHER, RICHARD LOUIS
B.JULY 15,1891 FRANKFORT,KY.
D.JUNE 19,1952

YR	CL	LEA	POS	GP	G	REC
1914	BOS	N	P		33	5- 6
1915	BOS	N	P		14	2- 2
	BRTR				47	7- 8

CRUTHERS, CHARLES PRESTON "PRES"
B.SEPT.8,1890 PHILADELPHIA,PA.

YR	CL	LEA	POS	GP	G	REC
1913	PHI	A	2		5	.235
1914	PHI	A	2		4	.200
	BRTR				9	.219

CRUZ, CIRILO (DILAN) "TOMMY"
B.FEB.15,1951 ARROYO,P.R.

YR	CL	LEA	POS	GP	G	REC
1973	STL	N	O		3	.000
	BLTL					

CRUZ, HECTOR LOUIS (DILAN)
B.APR.2,1953 ARROYO,P.R.

YR	CL	LEA	POS	GP	G	REC
1973	STL	N	O		11	.000
1975	STL	N	3-O		23	.146
1976	STL	N	3		151	.228
	BRTR				185	.217

CRUZ, HENRY (ACOSTA)
B.FEB.27,1952 CHRISTIANSTED,V.I.

YR	CL	LEA	POS	GP	G	REC
1975	LA	N	O		53	.266
1976	LA	N	O		49	.182
	BLTL				102	.225

CRUZ, JOSE (DILAN)
B.AUG.8,1947 ARROYO,P.R.

YR	CL	LEA	POS	GP	G	REC
1970	STL	N	O		6	.353
1971	STL	N	O		83	.274
1972	STL	N	O		117	.235
1973	STL	N	O		132	.227
1974	STL	N	1-O		107	.261
1975	HOU	N	O		120	.257
1976	HOU	N	O		133	.303
	BLTL				698	.261

CUBBAGE, MICHAEL LEE "MIKE"
B.JUL.21,1950 CHARLOTTESVILLE,VA

YR	CL	LEA	POS	GP	G	REC
1974	TEX	A	2-3		9	.000
1975	TEX	A	2-3		58	.224
1976	TEX	A	2-3		14	.219
	MIN	A	2-3		104	.260
	BLTR				185	.241

CUCCINELLO, ALFRED EDWARD
B.AUG.26,1915 LONG ISLAND CITY, N.Y.

YR	CL	LEA	POS	GP	G	REC
1935	NY	N	2-3		54	.248
	BRTR					

CUCCINELLO, ANTHONY FRANCIS "COOCH"
B.NOV.8,1907 LONG ISLAND CITY, N.Y.

YR	CL	LEA	POS	GP	G	REC
1930	CIN	N	2-S-3		125	.312
1931	CIN	N	2		154	.315
1932	BRO	N	2		154	.281
1933	BRO	N	2-3		134	.252
1934	BRO	N	2-3		140	.261
1935	BRO	N	2-3		102	.292
1936	BOS	N	2		150	.308
1937	BOS	N	2		152	.271
1938	BOS	N	2		147	.265
1939	BOS	N	2		81	.306
1940	BOS	N	3		34	.270
	NY	N	2-3		88	.208
1942	BOS	N	2-3		40	.202
1943	BOS	N	2-S-3		13	.000
	CHI	A	3		34	.272
1944	CHI	A	2-3		38	.262
1945	CHI	A	3		118	.308
	BRTR				1704	.280

CUCCURULLO, ARTHUR JOSEPH "COOKIE"
B.FEB.8,1919 ASBURY PARK,N.J.

1943	PIT	N	P		1	0- 1
1944	PIT	N	P	32	36	2- 1
1945	PIT	N	P		29	1- 3
	BLTL			62	66	3- 5

CUDWORTH, JAMES ALARIC
B.AUG.22,1858 FAIRHAVEN,MASS.
D.DEC.21,1943

1884	KC	U	P-1-0		29	0- 0
						.134
	BRTR					

CUELLAR, CHARLES JESUS PATRICK "CHARLIE"
B.SEPT.24,1917 TAMPA,FLA.

| 1950 | CHI | A | P | | 2 | 0- 0 |
| | BRTR | | | | | |

CUELLAR, MIGUEL ANGEL "MIKE"
B.MAY 8,1937 SANTA CLARA,CUBA

1959	CIN	N	P		2	0- 0
1964	STL	N	P		32	5- 5
1965	HOU	N	P		25	1- 4
1966	HOU	N	P		38	12-10
1967	HOU	N	P	36	38	16-11
1968	HOU	N	P		28	8-11
1969	BAL	A	P		39	23-11
1970	BAL	A	P	40	41	24- 8
1971	BAL	A	P		38	20- 9
1972	BAL	A	P		35	18-12
1973	BAL	A	P		38	18-13
1974	BAL	A	P		38	22-10
1975	BAL	A	P		36	14-12
1976	BAL	A	P		26	4-13
	BLTL			451	454	185-129

CUETO, DAGOBERTO (CONCEPCION)
B.AUG.14,1937 SAN LIUS,CUBA

| 1961 | MIN | A | P | | 7 | 1- 3 |
| | BRTR | | | | | |

CUETO, MANUEL
B.FEB.8,1892 GUANAJAY,CUBA
D.JUNE 29,1942 HAVANA,CUBA

1914	STL	F	S-3		15	.100
1917	CIN	N	C-2-0		56	.200
1918	CIN	N	C-2-S-0		47	.296
1919	CIN	N	3-0		29	.250
	BRTR				147	.229

CUGG, JOHN J.
B.JERSEY CITY,N.J.

| 1884 | BAL | U | C | | 3 | .083 |

CULBERSON, DELBERT LEON "LEE"
B.AUG.6,1919 ADAIRSVILLE,GA.

1943	BOS	A	O		80	.272
1944	BOS	A	O		75	.238
1945	BOS	A	O		97	.275
1946	BOS	A	3-O		59	.313
1947	BOS	A	3-O		47	.238
1948	WAS	A	O		12	.172
	BRTR				370	.266

CULLEN, JOHN J.
B.MARYSVILLE,CAL.

| 1884 | WIL | U | S-O | | 9 | .194 |

CULLEN, JOHN PATRICK "JACK"
B.OCT.6,1939 NEWARK,N.J.

1962	NY	A	P		2	0- 0
1965	NY	A	P		12	3- 4
1966	NY	A	P		5	1- 0
	BRTR				19	4- 4

CULLEN, TIMOTHY LEO "TIM"
B.FEB.16,1942 SAN FRANCISCO,CAL.

1966	WAS	A	2-3		18	.235
1967	WAS	A	2-S-3-O		124	.236
1968	CHI	A	2		72	.200
	WAS	A	2-S-3		47	.272
1969	WAS	A	2-S-3		119	.209
1970	WAS	A	2-S		123	.214
1971	WAS	A	2-S		125	.191
1972	OAK	A	2-S-3		72	.261
	BRTR				700	.220

CULLENBINE, ROY JOSEPH
B.OCT.18,1914 NASHVILLE,TENN.

1938	DET	A	O		25	.284
1939	DET	A	O		75	.240
1940	BRO	N	O		22	.180
	STL	A	1-O		86	.230
1941	STL	A	1-O		149	.317
1942	STL	A	O		38	.193
	WAS	A	O		64	.286
	NY	A	1-O		21	.364
1943	CLE	A	1-O		138	.289
1944	CLE	A	O		154	.284
1945	CLE	A	3-O		8	.077
	DET	A	O		146	.277
1946	DET	A	1-O		113	.335
1947	DET	A	1		142	.224
	BBTR				1181	.276

CULLER, RICHARD BROADUS "DICK"
B.JAN.15,1915 HIGH POINT,N.C.
D.JUNE 16,1964 CHAPEL HILL,N.C.

1936	PHI	A	2-S		9	.237
1943	CHI	A	2-S-3		53	.216
1944	BOS	N	S		8	.071
1945	BOS	N	S-3		136	.262
1946	BOS	N	S		134	.255
1947	BOS	N	S		77	.248
1948	CHI	N	2-S		48	.169
1949	NY	N	S		7	.000
	BRTR				472	.244

CULLOP, HENRY NICHOLAS "NICK"
B.OCT.16,1900 ST.LOUIS,MO.

1926	NY	A	O		2	.500
1927	WAS	A	O		15	.217
	CLE	A	P-O	1	32	0- 0
						.235
1929	BRO	N	O		13	.195
1930	CIN	N	O		7	.182
1931	CIN	N	O		104	.263
	BRTR			1	173	0- 0
						.249

CULLOP, NORMAN ANDREW
B.SEPT.17,1887 CHILHOWIE,VA.
D.APR.15,1961

1913	CLE	A	P		23	3- 7
1914	CLE	A	P		1	0- 1
	KC	F	P		44	14-19
1915	KC	F	P		44	22-11
1916	NY	A	P		27	13- 6
1917	NY	A	P		30	5- 9
1921	STL	A	P		4	0- 2
	BLTL				173	57-55

CULLOTON, BERNARD ALOYSIUS "BUD"
B.MAY 19,1898 KINGSTON,N.Y.

1925	PIT	N	P		9	0- 1
1926	PIT	N	P		4	0- 0
	BRTR				13	0- 1

CULP, BENJAMIN BALDY
B.JAN.19,1914 PHILADELPHIA,PA.

1942	PHI	N	C		1	.000
1943	PHI	N	C		10	.208
1944	PHI	N	C		4	.000
	BRTR				15	.192

CULP, RAYMOND LEONARD "RAY"
B.AUG.6,1941 ELGIN,TEX.

1963	PHI	N	P		34	14-11
1964	PHI	N	P		30	8- 7
1965	PHI	N	P		33	14-10
1966	PHI	N	P		34	7- 4
1967	CHI	N	P		30	8-11
1968	BOS	A	P		35	16- 6
1969	BOS	A	P		32	17- 8
1970	BOS	A	P		33	17-14
1971	BOS	A	P		35	14-16
1972	BOS	A	P		16	5- 8
1973	BOS	A	P		10	2- 6
	BRTR				322	122-101

CULP, WILLIAM EDWARD
B.JUNE 11,1887 BELLAIRE,OHIO
D.SEPT.3,1969 ARNOLD,PA.

| 1910 | PHI | N | P | | 4 | 0- 0 |
| | BBTR | | | | | |

CULVER, GEORGE RAYMOND
B.JULY 8,1943 SALINAS,CAL.

1966	CLE	A	P		5	0- 2
1967	CLE	A	P		53	7- 3
1968	CIN	N	P	42	49	11-16
1969	CIN	N	P		32	5- 7
1970	STL	N	P		11	3- 3
	HOU	N	P		32	3- 3
1971	HOU	N	P		59	5- 8
1972	HOU	N	P		45	6- 2
1973	LA	N	P		28	4- 4
	PHI	N	P		14	3- 1
1974	PHI	N	P		14	1- 0
	BRTR			335	342	48-49

CUMBERLAND, JOHN SHELDON
B.MAY 10,1947 WESTBROOK,ME.

1968	NY	A	P		1	0- 0
1969	NY	A	P		2	0- 0
1970	NY	A	P		15	3- 4
	SF	N	P		7	2- 0
1971	SF	N	P		45	9- 6
1972	SF	N	P		9	0- 4
	STL	N	P		14	1- 1
1974	CAL	A	P		17	0- 1
	BRTL				110	15-16

CUMMINGS, JOHN WILLIAM "JACK"
B.APR.1,1904 PITTSBURGH,PA.
D.OCT.5,1962 W.MIFFLIN,PA.

1926	NY	N	C		7	.313
1927	NY	N	C		43	.363
1928	NY	N	C		33	.333
1929	NY	N	H		3	.333
	BOS	N	H		3	.167
	BRTR				89	.338

CUMMINGS, WILLIAM ARTHUR "CANDY"
B.OCT.17,1848 WARE,MASS.
D.MAY 17,1924 TOLEDO,OHIO

1872	MUT	NA	P		55	31-21
1873	BAL	NA	P-3		42	27-14
						-
1874	PHI	NA	P		54	28-26
1875	HAR	NA	P-O		52	35-12
						-
1876	HAR	N	P		24	15- 8
1877	CIN	N	P-O		19	5-14
						.200
	BRTR				246	141-95
						-

CUNNINGHAM, BRUCE LEE
B.SEP.29,1906 SAN FRANCISCO,CAL

1929	BOS	N	P	17	19	4- 6
1930	BOS	N	P	36	37	5- 6
1931	BOS	N	P	33	34	3-12
1932	BOS	N	P		18	1- 0
	BRTR			104	108	13-24

YR CL LEA POS GP   G   REC

CUNNINGHAM, ELLSWORTH BERT "BERT"
B.NOV.25,1866 WILMINGTON,DEL.
D.MAY 14,1952
1887 BRO AA P		3	0- 2
1888 BAL AA P		51	22-29
1889 BAL AA P	37	40	15-19
1890 PHI P P		15	3-10
BUF P P		29	10-15
1891 BAL AA P		31	11-14
1895 LOU N P	28	31	11-16
1896 LOU N P	23	24	7-14
1897 LOU N P		30	15-14
1898 LOU N P		43	28-15
1899 LOU N P	37	43	18-16
1900 CHI N P		8	5- 3
1901 CHI N P		1	0- 1
BRTR	336	349	145-168

CUNNINGHAM, GEORGE HAROLD
B.JULY 13,1894 STURGEON LAKE, MINN.
D.MAR.10,1972 CHATTANOOGA,TENN.
1916 DET A P		35	7-10
1917 DET A P		44	2- 7
1918 DET A P-O	27	56	6- 7
			.223
1919 DET A P	17	26	1- 1
1921 DET A O		1	.000
BRTR	123	162	16-25
			.224

CUNNINGHAM, JOSEPH ROBERT "JOE"
B.AUG.27,1931 SADDLE RIVER,N.J.
1954 STL N 1		85	.284
1956 STL N 1		4	.000
1957 STL N 1-O		122	.318
1958 STL N 1-O		131	.312
1959 STL N 1-O		144	.345
1960 STL N 1-O		139	.280
1961 STL N 1-O		113	.286
1962 CHI A 1-O		149	.295
1963 CHI A 1		67	.286
1964 CHI A 1		48	.250
WAS A 1		49	.214
1965 WAS A 1		95	.229
1966 WAS A 1		3	.125
BLTL		1141	.291

CUNNINGHAM, RAYMOND LEE
B.JAN.17,1908 MESQUITE,TEX.
1931 STL N 3		3	.000
1932 STL N 2-3		11	.182
BRTR		14	.154

CUNNINGHAM, RUDOLPH "MIKE"
B.STROUDSBURG,PA.
| 1906 PHI A P | | 6 | 0- 0 |
| TR | | | |

CUNNINGHAM WILLIAM ALOYSIUS
B.JUL.30,1895 SAN FRANCISCO,CAL
D.SEPT.26,1953
1921 NY N O		40	.276
1922 NY N 3-O		85	.327
1923 NY N 2-O		79	.271
1924 BOS N O		114	.272
BRTR		318	.286

CUNNINGHAM, WILLIAM JAMES
B.JUNE 9,1888 SCHENECTADY,N.Y.
D.FEB.21,1946 SCHENECTADY,N.Y.
1910 WAS A 2		22	.297
1911 WAS A 2		94	.190
1912 WAS A 2		8	.185
BRTR		124	.208

CUPPY, GEORGE JOSEPH "NIG"
(REAL NAME
GEORGE JOSEPH KOPPE)
B.JULY 3,1869 EATON,OHIO
D.JULY 27,1922
1892 CLE N P		43	27-16
1893 CLE N P		28	17-11
1894 CLE N P	40	41	21-16
1895 CLE N P		42	26-16
1896 CLE N P	40	41	25-15
1897 CLE N P		17	10- 6
1898 CLE N P		16	9- 7
1899 STL N P		21	10- 8
1900 BOS N P		17	8- 4
1901 BOS A P		17	4- 6
TR	281	283	157-105

CURLEY, WALTER JAMES "DOC"
B.MAR.12,1874 UPTON,MASS.
D.SEPT.23,1920 WORCESTER,MASS.
| 1899 CHI N 2 | | 10 | .105 |
| BRTR | | | |

CURRAN, SIMON FRANCIS "SAM"
B.OCT.30,1874 DORCHESTER,MASS.
D.MAY 19,1936
| 1902 BOS N P | | 1 | 0- 0 |

CURREN, PETER
B.BALTIMORE,MD.
| 1876 ATH N C-O | | 3 | .333 |

CURRENCE, DELANCY LAFAYETTE "LAFAYETTE"
B.DEC.3,1951 ROCK HILL,S.C.
| 1975 MIL A P | | 8 | 0- 2 |
| BBTL | | | |

CURRIE, CLARENCE F.
B.DEC.30,1878 GLENCOE,ONT.,CAN.
D.JULY 15,1941 LITTLE CHUTE,WIS
1902 CIN N P		10	3- 4
STL N P		13	7- 5
1903 CIN N P		22	4-12
CHI N P		6	1- 2
BRTR		51	15-23

CURRIE, MURPHY ARCHIBALD
B.AUG.31,1893 FAYETTEVILLE,N.C.
D.JUNE 23,1939 ASHEBORO,N.C.
| 1916 STL N P | | 6 | 0- 0 |
| BRTR | | | |

CURRIE, WILLIAM CLEVELAND
B.NOV.29,1928 LEARY,GA.
| 1955 WAS A P | | 3 | 0- 0 |
| BRTR | | | |

CURRIN, PERRY GILMORE
B.SEPT.27,1920 WASHINGTON,D.C.
| 1947 STL A S | | 3 | .000 |
| BLTR | | | |

CURRY, GEORGE ANTHONY "TONY"
B.DEC.12,1938 NASSAU,BAHAMAS
1960 PHI N O		95	.261
1961 PHI N O		15	.194
1966 CLE A H		19	.125
BLTL		129	.246

CURRY, GEORGE JAMES "SOLDIER BOY"
B.DEC.23,1888 BRIDGEPORT,CONN.
D.OCT.5,1963 STRATFORD,CONN.
| 1911 STL A P | | 3 | 0- 3 |
| BRTR | | | |

CURRY, JAMES L.
B.MAR.10,1893 CAMDEN,N.J.
D.AUG.2,1938 LAKELAND,N.J.
1909 PHI A 2		1	.250
1911 NY A 2		4	.182
1918 DET A 2		5	.250
BPTR		10	.229

CURRY, WESLEY
B.APR.1,1860 WILMINGTON,DEL.
D.MAY 19,1933 PHILADELPHIA,PA.
| 1884 RIC AA P | | 2 | 0- 2 |

CURTIS, CLIFTON GARFIELD
B.JULY 3,1883 DELWARE,OHIO
D.APR.23,1943
1909 BOS N P		10	4- 5
1910 BOS N P		43	6-24
1911 BOS N P		12	1- 8
CHI N P		4	0- 2
PHI N P		8	3- 1
1912 PHI N P		10	2- 5
BRO N P		19	4- 7
1913 BRO N P		30	8- 9
BRTR		136	28-61

CURTIS, EDWIN R.
NON-PLAYING MANAGER ALT(U) 1884

CURTIS, EUGENE "EUDE"
B.MAY 7,1877 BETHANY,W.VA.
D.JAN.2,1918
| 1903 PIT N O | | 5 | .421 |

CURTIS, FREDERICK
| 1905 NY A 1 | | 2 | .222 |

CURTIS, HARRY ALBERT
B.FEB.19,1888 PORTLAND,ME.
D.AUG.1,1951
| 1907 NY N C | | 6 | .222 |
| TR | | | |

CURTIS, JACK PATRICK
B.JAN.11,1937 RHODHISS,N.C.
1961 CHI N P		31	10-13
1962 CHI N P		4	0- 2
MIL N P		30	4- 4
1963 CLE A P		4	0- 0
BLTL		69	14-19

CURTIS, JOHN DUFFIELD "JACK"
B.MAR.9,1948 NEWTON,MASS.
1970 BOS A P		1	0- 0
1971 BOS A P		5	2- 2
1972 BOS A P	26	27	11- 8
1973 BOS A P		35	13-13
1974 STL N P	33	34	10-14
1975 STL N P		39	8- 9
1976 STL N P	37	38	6-11
BLTL	176	179	50-57

CURTIS, VERNON EUGENE "TURKEY"
B.MAY 24,1920 CAIRO,ILL.
1943 WAS A P		2	0- 0
1944 WAS A P		3	0- 1
1946 WAS A P		11	0- 0
BRTR		16	0- 1

CURTISS, ERVIN DUANE "TACKS"
B.DEC.27,1861 COLDWATER,MICH.
D.FEB.14,1945
1891 CIN N O		27	.266
WAS AA O		29	.252
BL		56	.257

CURTWRIGHT, GUY PAXTON
B.OCT.18,1912 HENDERSON,TEX.
1943 CHI A O		138	.291
1944 CHI A O		72	.253
1945 CHI A O		98	.281
1946 CHI A O		23	.200
BRTR		331	.276

CUSHMAN, CHARLES H.
B.MAY 25,1850 NEW YORK,N.Y.
D.JUNE 29,1909
NON-PLAYING MANAGER MIL(AA)1891

CUSHMAN, EDGAR LEANDER
B.MAR.27,1852 EAGLEVILLE,OHIO
D.SEPT.26,1915
1883 BUF N P-O		7	4- 3
			.200
1884 MIL U P		4	4- 0
1885 ATH AA P		10	3- 7
MET AA P		22	8-14
1886 MET AA P		38	17-21
1887 MET AA P		26	11-14
1890 TOL AA P		39	17-20
BRTL		146	64-79
			.177

CUSHMAN, HARVEY BARNES
B.JULY 10,1877 ROCKLAND,ME.
D.DEC.27,1920 EMSWORTH,PA.
| 1902 PIT N P | | 4 | 0- 4 |

CUSICK, ANTHONY DANIEL
B.1860 FALL RIVER,MASS.
1884 WIL U C-2-S-3-O		11	.147
1884 PHI N C		9	.143
1885 PHI N C-O		39	.177
1886 PHI N C		27	.221
1887 PHI N C		7	.358
		93	.196

CUSICK, JOHN PETER "JACK"
B.JUNE 12,1928 WEEHAWKEN,N.J.
1951 CHI N S		65	.177
1952 BOS N S-3		49	.167
BRTR		114	.174

YR	CL	LEA	POS	GP	G	REC

CUTHBERT, EDGAR EDWARD "NED"
B.JUNE 20,1845 PHILADELPHIA,PA.
D.FEB.6,1905

1871	ATH	NA	C-O		28	.278
1872	ATH	NA	O		46	.328
1873	PHI	NA	O		50	-
1874	CHI	NA	C-O		58	-
1875	STL	NA	C-O		65	.266
1876	STL	N	O		62	.242
1877	CIN	N	O		12	.175
1882	STL	AA	M-O		60	.219
1883	STL	AA	1-O		21	.158
1884	BAL	U	O		42	.193
		BRTR			444	-

CUTSHAW, GEORGE WILLIAM
B.JULY 29,1886 WILMINGTON,ILL.
D.AUG.22,1973 SAN DIEGO,CAL.

1912	BRO	N	2		102	.280
1913	BRO	N	2		147	.267
1914	BRO	N	2		153	.257
1915	BRO	N	2		154	.246
1916	BRO	N	2		154	.260
1917	BRO	N	2		135	.259
1918	PIT	N	2		126	.285
1919	PIT	N	2		139	.242
1920	PIT	N	2		131	.252
1921	PIT	N	2		98	.340
1922	DET	A	2		132	.267
1923	DET	A	2		45	.223
		BRTR			1516	.265

CUYLER, HAZEN SHIRLEY "KIKI"
B.AUG.30,1899 HARRISVILLE,MICH.
D.FEB.11,1950 ANN ARBOR,MICH.

1921	PIT	N	O		1	.000
1922	PIT	N	H		1	.000
1923	PIT	N	O		11	.250
1924	PIT	N	O		117	.354
1925	PIT	N	O		153	.357
1926	PIT	N	O		157	.321
1927	PIT	N	O		85	.309
1928	CHI	N	O		133	.285
1929	CHI	N	O		139	.360
1930	CHI	N	O		156	.355
1931	CHI	N	O		154	.330
1932	CHI	N	O		110	.291
1933	CHI	N	O		70	.317
1934	CHI	N	O		142	.338
1935	CHI	N	O		45	.274
	CIN	N	O		62	.251
1936	CIN	N	O		144	.326
1937	CIN	N	O		117	.271
1938	BRO	N	O		82	.273
		BRTR			1879	.321

CVENGROS, MICHAEL JOHN
D.DEC.1,1901 PANA,ILL.
D.AUG.2,1970 HOT SPRINGS,ARK.

1922	NY	N	P	1		0- 1
1923	CHI	A	P	41		12-13
1924	CHI	A	P	26		3-12
1925	CHI	A	P	22		3- 9
1927	PIT	N	P	23		2- 1
1929	CHI	N	P	32	33	5- 4
		BLTL		145	146	25-40

CYPERT, ALFRED BOYD "CY"
B.AUG.8,1889 LITTLE ROCK,ARK.
D.JAN.9,1973 WASHINGTON,D.C.

| 1914 | CLE | A | 3 | | 1 | .000 |
| | | BRTR | | | | |

D'ACQUISTO, JOHN FRANCIS
B.DEC.24,1951 SAN DIEGO,CAL.

1973	SF	N	P	7		1- 1
1974	SF	N	P	38	39	12-14
1975	SF	N	P	10		2- 4
1976	SF	N	P	28		3- 8
		BRTR		83	84	18-27

DADE, LONNIE PAUL "PAUL"
B.DEC.7,1951 SEATTLE,WASH.

1975	CAL	A	3-O	11		.200
1976	CAL	A	2-3-O	13		.111
		BRTR		24		.179

DAGENHARD, JOHN DOUGLAS
B.APR.25,1917 MAGNOLIA,OHIO

| 1943 | BOS | N | P | 2 | | 1- 0 |
| | | BRTR | | | | |

DAGLIA, PETER GEORGE
B.FEB.28,1906 NAPA,CAL.
B.MAR.11,1952

| 1932 | CHI | A | P | 12 | | 2- 4 |
| | | BRTR | | | | |

DAGRES, ANGELO GEORGE
B.AUG.22,1934 NEWBUPYPORT,MASS.

| 1955 | BAL | A | O | 8 | | .267 |
| | | BLTL | | | | |

DAHL, JAY STEVEN
B.DEC.6,1945 SAN BERNARDINO,CAL.
D.JUNE 20,1965 SALISBURY,4.C.

| 1963 | HOU | N | P | 1 | | 0- 1 |
| | | BBTL | | | | |

DAHLEN, WILLIAM FREDERICK "BAD BILL"
B.JAN.5,1871 GLENS FALLS,N.Y.
D.DEC.5,1950 BROOKLYN,N.Y.

1891	CHI	N	S-3-O	135		.263
1892	CHI	N	S-3	143		.294
1893	CHI	N	S-O	115		.311
1894	CHI	N	S-3	121		.362
1895	CHI	N	S	131		.273
1896	CHI	N	S	125		.361
1897	CHI	N	S	75		.296
1898	CHI	N	S	141		.290
1899	BRO	N	S	122		.281
1900	BRO	N	S	134		.259
1901	BRO	N	S	130		.261
1902	BRO	N	S	136		.267
1903	BRO	N	S	138		.262
1904	NY	N	S	145		.268
1905	NY	N	S	148		.242
1906	NY	N	S	143		.240
1907	NY	N	S	143		.207
1908	BOS	N	S	144		.239
1909	BOS	N	S	57		.233
1910	BRO	N	M-H	3		.000
1911	BRO	N	M-S	1		.000
		BRTR		2430		.277

NON-PLAYING MANAGER
BRO(N) 1912-13

DAHLGREN, ELLSWORTH TENNEY "BABE"
B.JUN.15,1912 SAN FRANCISCO,CAL

1935	BOS	A	1		149	.263
1936	BOS	A	1		16	.281
1937	NY	A	H		1	.000
1938	NY	A	1-3		27	.186
1939	NY	A	1		144	.235
1940	NY	A	1		155	.264
1941	BOS	N	1-3		44	.235
	CHI	N	1		99	.281
1942	CHI	N	1		17	.214
	STL	A	H		2	.000
	BRO	N	1		17	.173
1943	PHI	N	C-1-S-3	136		.288
1944	PIT	N	1	158		.289
1945	PIT	N	1	144		.250
1946	STL	A	1	28		.175
		BRTR		1137		.261

DAHLKE, JEROME ALEXANDER
B.JUNE 8,1930 WAUSAU,WIS.

| 1956 | CHI | A | P | 5 | | 0- 0 |
| | | BRTR | | | | |

DAILEY, CORNELIUS F. "CON"
B.SEPT.11,1864 BLACKSTONE,MASS.
D.JUNE 14,1928 BROOKLYN,N.Y.

1884	KEY	U	C		2	.000
1885	PRO	N	C-1-O		59	.260
1886	BOS	N	C		50	.239
1887	BOS	N	C		33	.217
1888	IND	N	C		57	.218
1889	IND	N	C		60	.251
1890	BRO	P	C-1		46	.253
1891	BRO	N	C		53	.296
1892	BRO	N	C		78	.243
1893	BRO	N	C		58	.286
1894	BRO	N	C		65	.269
1895	BRO	N	C		40	.233
1896	BRO	N/	C		1	.000
	CHI	N	C		9	.075
					611	.258

DAILEY, JOHN J.
B.BROOKLYN,N.Y.
D.JAN.8,1898

1875	NAT	NA	2-S-3	25		-
	ATH	NA	1-O	2		.125
				27		-

DAILEY, SAMUEL L.
B.MAR.31,1905 KANSAS CITY,KAN.

| 1929 | PHI | N | P | 20 | | 2- 2 |
| | | BLTR | | | | |

DAILEY, VINCENT PERRY
B.DEC.25,1864 OSCEOLA,PA.
D.NOV.14,1919

| 1890 | CLE | N | O | | 64 | .288 |

DAILEY, WILLIAM GARLAND "BILL"
B.MAY 13,1935 ARLINGTON,VA.

1961	CLE	A	P	12		1- 0
1962	CLE	A	P	27		2- 2
1963	MIN	A	P	66		6- 3
1964	MIN	A	P	14		1- 2
		BRTR		119		10- 7

DAILY, EDWARD M.
B.SEPT.7,1862 PROVIDENCE,R.I.
D.OCT.21,1891

1885	PHI	N	P-O		49	26-22
						.206
1886	PHI	N	P-O	26	78	13- 9
						.226
1887	PHI	N	P-O	6	25	0- 4
						.306
	WAS	N	P-O	1	80	0- 1
						.296
1888	WAS	N	P-O	8	110	2- 4
						.225
1889	COL	AA	O		137	.254
1890	BRO	AA	P-O	30	93	9-15
						.250
	NY	N	P		4	2- 1
	LOU	AA	P-O	12	23	6- 2
						.244
1891	LOU	AA	P-O	15	22	4- 8
						.277
	WAS	AA	P-O	4	17	0- 0
						.206
		BRTR		155	638	62-66
						.250

DAISEY, GEORGE K.

| 1884 | ALT | U | O | | 1 | .000 |

DAL CANTON, JOHN BRUCE "BRUCE"
B.JUNE 15,1942 CALIFORNIA,PA.

1967	PIT	N	P	8		2- 1
1968	PIT	N	P	7		1- 1
1969	PIT	N	P	57		8- 2
1970	PIT	N	P	41		9- 4
1971	KC	A	P	25		8- 6
1972	KC	A	P	35		6- 6
1973	KC	A	P	32		4- 3
1974	KC	A	P	31		8-10
1975	KC	A	P	4		0- 2
	ATL	N	P	26		2- 7
1976	ATL	N	P	42		3- 5
		BRTR		308		51-47

DALE, EMMETT EUGENE "GENE"
B.JUNE 16,1889 ST.LOUIS,MO.
D.MAR.20,1958

1911	STL	N	P	5		0- 2
1912	STL	N	P	19	20	0- 5
1915	CIN	N	P	49		18-17
1916	CIN	N	P	17		3- 4
		BRTR		90	91	21-28

DALEY, JOHN FRANCIS
B.MAY 25,1887 PITTSBURGH,PA.

| 1912 | STL | A | S | 17 | | .173 |
| | | BRTR | | | | |

DALEY, JUD LAWRENCE
B.MAR.14,1887 S.COVENTRY,CONN.
D.JAN.26,1967 GASDEN,ALA.

1911	BRO	N	O	16		.231
1912	BRO	N	O	61		.256
		BLTR		77		.250

YR   CL LEA POS GP   G   REC   YR   CL LEA POS   GP   G   REC   YR   CL LEA POS   GP   G   REC

DALEY, LEAVITT LEO "BUD"
B.OCT.7,1932 ORANGE,CAL.
1955	CLE	A	P		2	0- 1
1956	CLE	A	P		14	1- 0
1957	CLE	A	P		34	2- 8
1958	KC	A	P		26	3- 2
1959	KC	A	P		39	16-13
1960	KC	A	P		37	16-16
1961	KC	A	P		16	4- 8
	NY	A	P		23	8- 9
1962	NY	A	P		43	7- 5
1963	NY	A	P		1	0- 0
1964	NY	A	P		13	3- 2
	BLTL				248	60-64

DALEY, PETER HARVEY "PETE"
D.JAN.14,1930 GRASS VALLEY,CAL.
1955	BOS	A	C	17	.220
1956	BOS	A	C	59	.267
1957	BOS	A	C	78	.225
1958	BOS	A	C	27	.321
1959	BOS	A	C	65	.225
1960	KC	A	C-0	73	.263
1961	WAS	A	C	72	.192
	BRTR			391	.239

DALEY, THOMAS FRANCIS "PETE"
B.NOV.13,1884 DUBOIS,PA.
D.DEC.2,1934
1908	CIN	N	0	13	.108
1913	PHI	A	0	59	.260
1914	PHI	A	0	28	.241
	NY	A	0	67	.258
1915	NY	A	0	10	.250
	BLTR			177	.243

DALEY, WILLIAM
B.JUNE 27,1868 POUGHKEEPSIE,N.Y
D.MAY 4,1922
1889	BOS	N	P		9	3- 3
1890	BOS	P	P		47	20-12
1891	BOS	AA	P	19	20	9- 5
	TL			75	76	32-20

DALLESSANDRO, NICHOLAS DOMINIC "DIM DOM"
B.OCT.3,1913 READING,PA.
1937	BOS	A	0	68	.231
1940	CHI	N	0	107	.268
1941	CHI	N	0	140	.272
1942	CHI	N	0	96	.261
1943	CHI	N	0	87	.222
1944	CHI	N	0	117	.305
1946	CHI	N	0	65	.225
1947	CHI	N	0	66	.287
	BLTL			746	.267

DALRYMPLE, ABNER FRANK
B.SEPT.9,1857 WARREN,ILL.
D.JAN.25,1939
1878	MIL	N	0	60	.356
1879	CHI	N	0	67	.300
1880	CHI	N	0	84	.332
1881	CHI	N	0	81	.323
1882	CHI	N	0	84	.294
1883	CHI	N	0	80	.297
1884	CHI	N	0	110	.310
1885	CHI	N	0	113	.274
1886	CHI	N	0	82	.232
1887	PIT	N	0	92	.300
1888	PIT	N	0	56	.224
1891	MIL	AA	0	31	.315
	BLTR			940	.298

DALRYMPLE, CLAYTON ERROL "CLAY"
B.DEC.3,1936 CHICO,CAL.
1960	PHI	N	C	82	.272
1961	PHI	N	C	129	.220
1962	PHI	N	C	123	.276
1963	PHI	N	C	142	.252
1964	PHI	N	C	127	.238
1965	PHI	N	C	103	.213
1966	PHI	N	C	114	.245
1967	PHI	N	C	101	.172
1968	PHI	N	C	85	.207
1969	BAL	A	C	37	.238
1970	BAL	A	C	13	.219
1971	BAL	A	C	23	.204
	BLTR			1079	.233

DALRYMPLE, MICHAEL
B.ST.LOUIS,MO.
| 1915 | STL | A | 3 | | 3 | .000 |
| | TR | | | | | |

DALTON, TALBOT PERCY "JACK"
B.JULY 3,1885 HENDERSON,TENN.
1910	BRO	N	0	72	.227
1914	BRO	N	0	128	.319
1915	BUF	F	0	132	.294
1916	DET	A	0	8	.182
	BRTR			340	.287

DALY, BERT
B.APR.8,1882 BAYONNE,N.J.
D.SEPT.4,1952
| 1903 | PHI | A | 2-S-3 | 10 | .190 |
| | TR | | | | |

DALY, GEORGE JOSEPH
B.JULY 28,1887 BUFFALO,N.Y.
D.DEC.12,1957
| 1909 | NY | N | P | | 3 | 0- 3 |
| | BRTR | | | | | |

DALY, HUGH I. "ONE ARM"
(REAL NAME HARRY CRISS)
B.1857 BALTIMORE,MD.
1882	BUF	N	P		29	15-14
1883	CLE	N	P-0		42	24-18
						.109
1884	CHI	U	P-2-S-0		47	22-25
						.235
	PIT	U	P		10	5- 4
	WAS	U	P		2	1- 1
1885	STL	N	P		11	3- 8
1886	WAS	N	P		6	0- 6
1887	CLE	AA	P		17	4-12
	BRTR				164	74-88
						.155

DALY, JAMES J. "SUN"
B.JAN.6,1865 RUTLAND,VT.
D.APR.30,1938
1891	MIL	AA	0		1	.000
1892	BAL	N	0		13	.229
					14	.216

DALY, JOSEPH JOHN
B.SEPT.21,1868 CONSHOHOCKEN,PA.
D.MAR.21,1943
1890	ATH	AA	P		20	0- 1
1891	CLE	N	0		1	.000
1892	BOS	N	C		1	.000
					22	0- 1
						.175

DALY, THOMAS DANIEL
B.DEC.12,1891 ST.JOHN,N.B.,CAN.
D.NOV.7,1946 MEDFORD,MASS.
1913	CHI	A	C	1	.000
1914	CHI	A	0	61	.233
1915	CHI	A	0	29	.191
1916	CLE	A	C	31	.219
1918	CHI	A	C	1	.000
1919	CHI	N	C	25	.220
1920	CHI	N	C	44	.311
1921	CHI	N	C	51	.238
	BRTR			243	.239

DALY, THOMAS PETER "TIDO"
B.FEB.7,1866 PHILADELPHIA,PA.
D.OCT.29,1939
1887	CHI	N	C	74	.269
1888	CHI	N	C	65	.191
1889	WAS	N	C	69	.300
1890	BRO	N	C	82	.243
1891	BRO	N	C	61	.293
1892	BRO	N	C-3-0	120	.255
1893	BRO	N	2-3	126	.306
1894	BRO	N	2	123	.338
1895	BRO	N	2	122	.289
1896	BRO	N	2	64	.280
1898	BRO	N	2	23	.329
1899	BRO	N	2	143	.312
1900	BRO	N	2	98	.313
1901	BRO	N	2	132	.310
1902	CHI	A	2	137	.231
1903	CHI	A	2	45	.201
	CIN	N	2	79	.293
	BBTR			1563	.284

DAM, ELBRIDGE RUST "BILL"
B.APR.4,1885 CAMBRIDGE,MASS.
D.JUNE 22,1930
| 1909 | BOS | N | 0 | | 1 | .500 |

DAMASKA, JACK LLOYD
B.AUG.21,1937 BEAVER FALLS,PA.
| 1963 | STL | N | 2-0 | | 5 | .200 |
| | BRTR | | | | | |

DAMMAN, WILLIAM HENRY A.
B.AUG.9,1872 CHICAGO,ILL.
D.DEC.6,1948
1897	CIN	N	P		16	7- 5
1898	CIN	N	P		28	16- 8
1899	CIN	N	P		9	2- 1
	BLTL				53	25-14

DAMRAU, HARRY ROBERT
B.1892 NEW YORK,N.Y.
| 1915 | PHI | A | 3 | 16 | .196 |
| | BRTR | | | | |

DANEY, ARTHUR LEE
B.JULY 9,1904 TALIHINA,OKLA.
| 1928 | PHI | A | P | | 1 | 0- 0 |
| | BRTR | | | | | |

DANFORTH, DAVID CHARLES
B.MAR.7,1890 GRANGER,TEX.
D.SEPT.19,1970 BALTIMORE,MD.
1911	PHI	A	P		14	5- 2
1912	PHI	A	P		3	0- 0
1916	CHI	A	P		28	6- 5
1917	CHI	A	P		50	11- 6
1918	CHI	A	P		39	6-15
1919	CHI	A	P		15	1- 2
1922	STL	A	P		20	5- 2
1923	STL	A	P		38	16-14
1924	STL	A	P		41	15-12
1925	STL	A	P		38	7- 9
	BLTL				286	72-67

DANIEL, CHARLES EDWARD
D.SEPT.17,1933 BLUFFTON,ARK.
| 1957 | DET | A | P | | 1 | 0- 0 |
| | BRTR | | | | | |

DANIEL, HANDLEY JACOB "JAKE"
B.APR.22,1912 ROANOKE,ALA.
| 1937 | BRO | N | 1 | 12 | .185 |
| | BLTL | | | | |

DANIELS, BENNIE
B.JUNE 17,1932 TUSCALOOSA,ALA.
1957	PIT	N	P		1	0- 1
1958	PIT	N	P		8	0- 3
1959	PIT	N	P	34	36	7- 9
1960	PIT	N	P		10	1- 3
1961	WAS	A	P		32	12-11
1962	WAS	A	P		44	7-16
1963	WAS	A	P-0	35	36	5-10
						.152
1964	WAS	A	P		33	8-10
1965	WAS	A	P		33	9-13
	BLTR			230	233	45-76
						.170

DANIELS, BERTRAM ELMER
B.OCT.13,1882 DANVILLE,ILL.
D.JUNE 6,1958
1910	NY	A	1-3-0	95	.253
1911	NY	A	0	131	.286
1912	NY	A	0	133	.274
1913	NY	A	0	93	.216
1914	CIN	N	0	71	.219
	BRTR			523	.255

DANIELS, CHARLES L.
B.JULY 1,1861 ROXBURY,MASS.
| 1884 | BOS | U | P-0 | 2 | 3 | 0- 2 |
| | | | | | | .273 |

DANIELS, FREDERICK CLINTON
B.DEC.28,1924 GASTONIA,N.C.
| 1945 | PHI | N | 2-3 | | 76 | .200 |
| | BRTR | | | | | |

DANIELS, HAROLD JACK
B.DEC.21,1927 CHESTER,PA.
| 1952 | BOS | N | 0 | 106 | .187 |
| | BLTL | | | | |

DANIELS, LAWRENCE LONG "LAW"
B.1862 NEWTON,MASS.
D.JAN.7,1929
1887	BAL	AA	C	47	.287
1888	KC	AA	C	61	.205
				108	.240

YR	CL	LEA	POS	GP	G	REC

DANIELS, PETER J.
"SMILING PETE"
B.APR.8,1864 COUNTY CAVAN,
IRELAND
D.FEB.13,1928

YR	CL	LEA	POS	GP	G	REC
1890	PIT	N	P		4	1- 2
1898	STL	N	P		10	1- 6
					14	2- 8

DANNER, HENRY FREDERICK "BUCK"
B.JUNE 8,1891 DEDHAM,MASS.
D.SEPT.19,1949 BOSTON,MASS.

YR	CL	LEA	POS	GP	G	REC
1915	PHI	A	S		3	.250
		BRTR				

DANNING, HARRY "THE HORSE"
B.SEPT.6,1911 LOS ANGELES,CAL.

YR	CL	LEA	POS	GP	G	REC
1933	NY	N	C		3	.000
1934	NY	N	C		53	.330
1935	NY	N	C		65	.243
1936	NY	N	C		32	.159
1937	NY	N	C		93	.288
1938	NY	N	C		120	.306
1939	NY	N	C		135	.313
1940	NY	N	C		140	.300
1941	NY	N	C-1		130	.244
1942	NY	N	C		119	.279
		BRTR			890	.285

DANNING, IKE
B.JAN.20,1905 LOS ANGELES,CAL.

YR	CL	LEA	POS	GP	G	REC
1928	STL	A	C		2	.500
		BRTR				

DANTONIO, JOHN JAMES "FATS"
B.DEC.31,1919 NEW ORLEANS,LA.

YR	CL	LEA	POS	GP	G	REC
1944	BRO	N	C		3	.143
1945	BRO	N	C		47	.250
		BRTR			50	.244

DANZIG, HAROLD P. "BABE"
B.APR.30,1887 BINGHAMTON,N.Y.
D.JUL.14,1931 SAN FRANCISCO,CAL

YR	CL	LEA	POS	GP	G	REC
1909	BOS	A	1		6	.143
		BRTR				

DAPPER, CLIFFORD ROLAND
B.JAN.2,1920 LOS ANGELES,CAL.

YR	CL	LEA	POS	GP	G	REC
1942	BRO	N	C		8	.471
		BRTR				

DARBY, GEORGE W. "DEACON"
B.ALEXANDRIA,VA.

YR	CL	LEA	POS	GP	G	REC
1893	CIN	N	P		4	2- 1
	PHI	N	P		4	0- 0
		BLTR			8	2- 1

DARCY, PATRICK LEONARD "PAT"
B.MAY 12,1950 TROY,OHIO

YR	CL	LEA	POS	GP	G	REC
1974	CIN	N	P		6	1- 0
1975	CIN	N	P		27	11- 5
1976	CIN	N	P		11	2- 3
		BLTR			44	14- 8

DARINGER, CLIFFORD CLARENCE
"SHANTY"
B.APR.10,1885 HAYDEN,IND.
D.DEC.26,1971 SACRAMENTO,CAL.

YR	CL	LEA	POS	GP	G	REC
1914	KC	F	S-3		60	.247
		BLTR				

DARINGER, ROLLA HARRISON
B.NOV.15,1888 N.VERNON,IND.
D.MAY 23,1974 SEYMOUR,IND.

YR	CL	LEA	POS	GP	G	REC
1914	STL	N	S		2	.500
1915	STL	N	S		10	.087
		BLTR			12	.148

DARK, ALVIN RALPH "BLACKIE"
B.JAN.7,1922 COMANCHE,OKLA.

YR	CL	LEA	POS	GP	G	REC
1946	BOS	N	S-0		15	.231
1948	BOS	N	S		137	.322
1949	BOS	N	S-3		130	.276
1950	NY	N	S		154	.279
1951	NY	N	S		156	.303
1952	NY	N	S		151	.301
1953	NY	N	P-2-	1	155	0- 0
			S-3-0			.300
1954	NY	N	S		154	.293
1955	NY	N	S		115	.282
1956	NY	N	S		48	.252
	STL	N	S		100	.286
1957	STL	N	S-3		140	.290
1958	STL	N	S-3		18	.297
	CHI	N	3		114	.295
1959	CHI	N	1-S-3		136	.264
1960	PHI	N	1-3		55	.242
	MIL	N	1-2-3-0		50	.298
		BRTR		1	1828	0- 0
						.289

NON-PLAYING MANAGER
SF(N) 1961-64, KC(A) 1966-67,
CLE(A) 1968-71, OAK(A) 1974-75

DARLING, DELL CONRAD
"WIENERWURST"
B.DEC.21,1863 ERIE,PA.
D.NOV.21,1904

YR	CL	LEA	POS	GP	G	REC
1883	BUF	N	C		5	.158
1887	CHI	N	C-0		38	.411
1888	CHI	N	C		20	.213
1889	CHI	N	C		35	.191
1890	CHI	P	C-1		58	.259
1891	STL	AA	C		17	.137
		BR			173	.266

DARNELL, ROBERT JACK
B.NOV.6,1930 WEWOKA,OKLA.

YR	CL	LEA	POS	GP	G	REC
1954	BRO	N	P		6	0- 0
1956	BRO	N	P		1	0- 0
		BRTR			7	0- 0

DARRAGH, JAMES S.
B.JULY 17,1866 EBENSBURG,PA.
D.AUG.12,1939 ROCHESTER,PA.

YR	CL	LEA	POS	GP	G	REC
1891	LOU	AA	P		1	1- 0

DARROW, GEORGE F.
B.JULY 12,1905 BELOIT,KAN.

YR	CL	LEA	POS	GP	G	REC
1934	PHI	N	P		17	2- 6
		BLTL				

DARWIN, ARTHUR BOBBY LEE "BOBBY"
B.FEB.16,1943 LOS ANGELES,CAL.

YR	CL	LEA	POS	GP	G	REC
1962	LA	A	P		1	0- 1
1969	LA	N	P	3	6	0- 0
1971	LA	N	0		11	.250
1972	MIN	A	0		145	.267
1973	MIN	A	0		145	.252
1974	MIN	A	0		152	.264
1975	MIN	A	0-0		48	.219
	MIL	A	0-0		55	.247
1976	MIL	A	0		25	.247
	BOS	A	0-0		43	.179
		BRTR			634	0- 1
						.252

DASHIELL, JOHN WALLACE "WALLY"
B.MAY 9,1901 JEWETT,TEX.
D.MAY 20,1972 PENSACOLA,FLA.

YR	CL	LEA	POS	GP	G	REC
1924	CHI	A	S		1	.000

DASHNER, LEE CLARE "LEFTY"
B.APR.25,1887 RENAULT,ILL.
D.DEC.16,1960

YR	CL	LEA	POS	GP	G	REC
1913	CLE	A	P		1	0- 0
		BBTL				

DASSO, FRANCIS JOSEPH NICHOLAS
B.AUG.31,1917 CHICAGO,ILL.

YR	CL	LEA	POS	GP	G	REC
1945	CIN	N	P		16	4- 5
1946	CIN	N	P		2	0- 0
		BRTR			18	4- 5

DAUB, DANIEL WILLIAM
B.JAN.12,1869 MIDDLETOWN,OHIO
D.MAR.25,1951

YR	CL	LEA	POS	GP	G	REC
1892	CIN	N	P		5	1- 1
1893	BRO	N	P		12	6- 6
1894	BRO	N	P		28	10-15
1895	BRO	N	P		20	10-10
1896	BRO	N	P		27	14-11
1897	BRO	N	P		18	5-11
					110	46-54

DAUBERT, HARRY J.
B.JUNE 19,1892 COLUMBUS,OHIO
D.JAN.8,1944 DETROIT,MICH.

YR	CL	LEA	POS	GP	G	REC
1915	PIT	N	S		1	.000
		BRTR				

DAUBERT, JACOB ELLSWORTH "JAKE"
B.MAY 15,1885 LLEWELLYN,PA.
D.OCT.9,1924 CINCINNATI,OHIO

YR	CL	LEA	POS	GP	G	REC
1910	BRO	N	1		144	.264
1911	BRO	N	1		149	.307
1912	BRO	N	1		145	.308
1913	BRO	N	1		139	.350
1914	BRO	N	1		126	.329
1915	BRO	N	1		150	.301
1916	BRO	N	1		127	.316
1917	BRO	N	1		125	.261
1918	BRO	N	1		108	.308
1919	CIN	N	1		140	.276
1920	CIN	N	1		142	.304
1921	CIN	N	1		136	.306
1922	CIN	N	1		156	.336
1923	CIN	N	1		125	.292
1924	CIN	N	1		102	.281
		BLTL			2014	.303

DAUER, RICHARD FREMONT "RICH"
B.JULY 27,1952 SAN BERNARDINO,
CAL.

YR	CL	LEA	POS	GP	G	REC
1976	BAL	A	2		11	.103
		BRTR				

DAUGHERTY, HAROLD RAY "DOC"
B.OCT.12,1927 PARIS,PA.

YR	CL	LEA	POS	GP	G	REC
1951	DET	A	H		1	.000
		BRTR				

DAUGHTERS, ROBERT FRANCIS "RED"
B.AUG.5,1914 CINCINNATI,OHIO

YR	CL	LEA	POS	GP	G	REC
1937	BOS	A	H		1	.000
		BRTR				

DAUSS, GEORGE AUGUST "HOOKS"
B.SEPT.22,1889 INDIANAPOLIS,IND
D.JULY 27,1963 ST.LOUIS,MO.

YR	CL	LEA	POS	GP	G	REC
1912	DET	A	P		2	0- 1
1913	DET	A	P		33	13-12
1914	DET	A	P		45	18-15
1915	DET	A	P		46	23-13
1916	DET	A	P		39	18-12
1917	DET	A	P	37	38	17-14
1918	DET	A	P		33	13-16
1919	DET	A	P		34	21- 9
1920	DET	A	P		38	13-21
1921	DET	A	P		32	10-15
1922	DET	A	P		39	13-13
1923	DET	A	P		50	21-13
1924	DET	A	P		40	12-11
1925	DET	A	P		35	16-11
1926	DET	A	P		35	12- 7
		BRTR		538	539	220-183

DAVALILLO, POMPEYO ROMERO
"YO-YO"
B.JULY 5,1931 CABIMAS,VENEZUELA

YR	CL	LEA	POS	GP	G	REC
1953	WAS	A	S		19	.293
		BRTR				

DAVALILLO, VICTOR JOSE "VIC"
B.JULY 31,1936 CABIMAS,VENEZ.

YR	CL	LEA	POS	GP	G	REC
1963	CLE	A	0		90	.292
1964	CLE	A	0		150	.270
1965	CLE	A	0		142	.301
1966	CLE	A	0		121	.250
1967	CLE	A	0		139	.287
1968	CLE	A	0		51	.239
	CAL	A	0		93	.298
1969	CAL	A	1-0		33	.155
	STL	N	P-0	2	63	0- 0
						.265
1970	STL	N			111	.311
1971	PIT	N	1-0		99	.285
1972	PIT	N	1-0		117	.318
1973	PIT	N	1-0		59	.181
	OAK	A	1-0		37	.188
1974	OAK	A	0		17	.174
		BLTL		2	1322	0- 0
						.279

YR	CL	LEA	POS	GP	G	REC

DA VANON, FRANK GERALD "GERRY"
B.AUG.21,1945 OCEANSIDE,CAL.

YR	CL	LEA	POS	GP	G	REC
1969	SD	N	2-S	24		.136
	STL	N	S	16		.300
1970	STL	N	2-3	11		.111
1971	BAL	A	1-2-S-3	38		.235
1973	CAL	A	2-S-3	41		.245
1974	STL	N	2-S-3-0	30		.150
1975	HOU	N	2-S-3	32		.278
1976	HOU	N	2-S-3	61		.290
		BRTR		253		.238

DAVENPORT, CLAUDE EDWIN
B.MAY 28,1898 RUNGE,TEX.

YR	CL	LEA	POS	GP	G	REC
1920	NY	N	P	1		0- 0
		BRTR				

DAVENPORT, DAVID W. "DAVIE"
B.FEB.20,1890 DE RIDDER,LA.
D.OCT.16,1954

YR	CL	LEA	POS	GP	G	REC
1914	CIN	N	P	10		2- 2
	STL	F	P	33		10-15
1915	STL	F	P	55		22-18
1916	STL	A	P	59		12-11
1917	STL	A	P	47		17-17
1918	STL	A	P	31		10-11
1919	STL	A	P	24		2-11
		BRTR		259		75-85

DAVENPORT, JAMES HOUSTON "JIM"
B.AUG.17,1933 SILURIA,ALA.

YR	CL	LEA	POS	GP	G	REC
1958	SF	N	S-3	134		.256
1959	SF	N	S-3	123		.258
1960	SF	N	S-3	112		.251
1961	SF	N	3	137		.278
1962	SF	N	3	144		.297
1963	SF	N	2-S-3	147		.252
1964	SF	N	2-S-3	116		.236
1965	SF	N	2-S-3	106		.251
1966	SF	N	1-2-S-3	111		.249
1967	SF	N	2-S-3	124		.275
1968	SF	N	2-S-3	113		.224
1969	SF	N	1-S-3-0	112		.241
1970	SF	N	3	22		.243
		BRTR		1501		.258

DAVENPORT, JOUBERT LUM
B.JUNE 27,1900 TUCSON,ARIZ.
D.APR.21,1961

YR	CL	LEA	POS	GP	G	REC
1921	CHI	A	P	13	15	0- 3
1922	CHI	A	P	9	12	1- 1
1923	CHI	A	P		2	0- 0
1924	CHI	A	P		1	0- 0
		BLTL		25	30	1- 4

DAVIAULT, RAYMOND JOSEPH ROBERT
B.MAY 27,1934 MONTREAL,QUE.,CAN

YR	CL	LEA	POS	GP	G	REC
1962	NY	N	P	36		1- 5
		BRTR				

DAVIDSON, CLAUDE BOUCHER "DAVEY"
B.OCT.13,1896 ROXBURY,MASS.
D.APR.18,1956 WEYMOUTH,MASS.

YR	CL	LEA	POS	GP	G	REC
1918	PHI	A	2	31		.185
1919	WAS	A	3	2		.375
		BLTR		33		.202

DAVIDSON, HOMER HURD
B.OCT.14,1884 CLEVELAND,OHIO
D.JULY 26,1948

YR	CL	LEA	POS	GP	G	REC
1908	CLE	A	C-0	9		.000
		TR				

DAVIDSON, MORDECAI H.
B.NOV.30,1846 PORT WASHINGTON,O
D.SEPT.6,1940
NON-PLAYING MANAGER
LOU(AA) 1888-89

DAVIDSON, THOMAS EUGENE "TED"
B.OCT.4,1939 LAS VEGAS,NEV.

YR	CL	LEA	POS	GP	G	REC
1965	CIN	N	P	24		4- 3
1966	CIN	N	P	54		5- 4
1967	CIN	N	P	9		1- 0
1968	CIN	N	P	23		1- 0
	ATL	N	P	4		0- 0
		BRTL		114		11- 7

DAVIDSON, WILLIAM J. "DAVEY"
B.MAY 10,1887 LAFAYETTE,IND.
D.MAR.13,1915 DETROIT,MICH.

YR	CL	LEA	POS	GP	G	REC
1909	CHI	N	0	2		.142
1910	BRO	N	0	131		.238
1911	BRO	N	0	74		.233
		BRTR		207		.235

DAVIE, GERALD LEE
B.FEB.10,1933 DETROIT,MICH.

YR	CL	LEA	POS	GP	G	REC
1959	DET	A	P	11		2- 2
		BRTR				

DAVIES, GEORGE WASHINGTON
B.FEB.22,1868 COLUMBUS,WIS.
D.SEPT.22,1906

YR	CL	LEA	POS	GP	G	REC
1891	MIL	AA	P	12		7 -5
1892	CLE	N	P	25		10-15
1893	CLE	N	P	3		0- 1
	NY	N	P	4		1- 2
				44		18-23

DAVIES, LLOYD GARRISON "CHICK"
B.MAR.6,1892 PEABODY,MASS.
D.SEPT.5,1973 MIDDLETOWN,CONN.

YR	CL	LEA	POS	GP	G	REC
1914	PHI	A	P	1	19	1- 0
1915	PHI	A	P-0	4	56	0- 2
						.182
1925	NY	N	P-0	2	4	0- 0
						.000
1926	NY	N	P		38	2- 4
	BLTL			45	117	3- 6
						.196

DAVIS, ALFONZO DEFORD "LEFTY"
B.FEB.4,1875 NASHVILLE,TENN.
D.FEB.4,1919

YR	CL	LEA	POS	GP	G	REC
1901	BRO	N	0	25		.209
	PIT	N	0	88		.308
1902	PIT	N	0	59		.291
1903	NY	A	0	108		.245
1907	CIN	N	0	70		.229
		BLTL		350		.264

DAVIS, ARTHUR WILLARD "BILL"
B.JUNE 6,1942 GRACEVILLE,MINN.

YR	CL	LEA	POS	GP	G	REC
1965	CLE	A	H	10		.300
1966	CLE	A	1	23		.158
1969	SD	N	1	31		.175
		BLTL		64		.181

DAVIS, BRYSHEAR BARNETT "BROCK"
B.OCT.19,1943 OAKLAND,CAL.

YR	CL	LEA	POS	GP	G	REC
1963	HOU	N	0	34		.200
1964	HOU	N	0	1		.000
1966	HOU	N	0	10		.148
1970	CHI	N	0	6		.000
1971	CHI	N	0	106		.256
1972	MIL	A	0	85		.318
		BLTL		242		.260

DAVIS, CURTIS BENTON "COONSKIN"
B.SEPT.7,1904 GREENFIELD,MO.
D.OCT.12,1965 COVINA,CAL.

YR	CL	LEA	POS	GP	G	REC
1934	PHI	N	P		51	19-17
1935	PHI	N	P	44	46	16-14
1936	PHI	N	P	10	11	2- 4
	CHI	N	P		24	11- 9
1937	CHI	N	P		28	10- 5
1938	STL	N	P		40	12- 8
1939	STL	N	P	49	63	22-16
1940	STL	N	P		14	0- 4
	BRO	N	P		22	8- 7
1941	BRO	N	P	28	31	13- 7
1942	BRO	N	P		32	15- 6
1943	BRO	N	P		31	10-13
1944	BRO	N	P		31	10-11
1945	BRO	N	P		24	10-10
1946	BRO	N	P		1	0- 0
		BRTR		429	449	158-131

DAVIS, FRANK TALMADGE "DIXIE"
B.OCT.12,1890 WILSON MILLS,N.C.
D.FEB.4,1944

YR	CL	LEA	POS	GP	G	REC
1912	CIN	N	P		7	0- 1
1915	CHI	A	P		2	0- 0
1918	PHI	N	P	17	18	0- 2
1920	STL	A	P		38	18-12
1921	STL	A	P		39	16-16
1922	STL	A	P		25	11- 6
1923	STL	A	P		19	4- 6
1924	STL	A	P		29	11-13
1925	STL	A	P		35	12- 7
1926	STL	A	P		27	4- 8
		BRTR		238	239	76-71

DAVIS, GEORGE ALLEN
B.MAR.29,1890 LANCASTER,N.Y.
D.JUNE 4,1961

YR	CL	LEA	POS	GP	G	REC
1912	NY	A	P	10		1- 5
	BOS	N	P	2		0- 0
1914	BOS	N	P	9		3- 3
1915	BOS	N	P	15		3- 3
		BBTR		36		7-11

DAVIS, GEORGE STACEY
B.AUG.23,1870 COHOES,N.Y.
D.OCT.17,1940 PHILADELPHIA,PA.

YR	CL	LEA	POS	GP	G	REC
1890	CLE	N	0	134		.264
1891	CLE	N	P-3-	1	136	0- 0
			0			.292
1892	CLE	N	S-3-0	143		.253
1893	NY	N	3	133		.373
1894	NY	N	3	124		.345
1895	NY	N	M-3	110		.330
1896	NY	N	S-3	124		.315
1897	NY	N	S	131		.358
1898	NY	N	S	121		.306
1899	NY	N	S	111		.348
1900	NY	N	M-S	113		.325
1901	NY	N	M-S-3	130		.309
1902	CHI	A	1-S	132		.298
1903	NY	N	S	4		.250
1904	CHI	A	S	152		.256
1905	CHI	A	S	151		.278
1906	CHI	A	S	133		.277
1907	CHI	A	S	132		.238
1908	CHI	A	2-S	128		.217
1909	CHI	A	1	28		.132
		BBTR		2370		0- 0
						.297

DAVIS, GEORGE WILLIS "KIDDO"
B.FEB.12,1902 BRIDGEPORT,CONN.

YR	CL	LEA	POS	GP	G	REC
1926	NY	A	0	1		.000
1932	PHI	N	0	137		.309
1933	NY	N	0	126		.258
1934	STL	N	0	16		.303
	PHI	N	0	100		.293
1935	NY	N	0	47		.264
1936	NY	N	0	47		.239
1937	NY	N	0	56		.263
	CIN	N	0	40		.257
1938	CIN	N	0	5		.278
		BRTR		575		.282

DAVIS, HARRY ALBERT "STINKY"
B.MAY 7,1908 SHREVEPORT,LA.

YR	CL	LEA	POS	GP	G	REC
1932	DET	A	1	141		.269
1933	DET	A	1	66		.214
1937	STL	A	1	120		.276
		BLTL		327		.264

DAVIS, HARRY H. "JASPER"
B.JULY 19,1873 PHILADELPHIA,PA.
D.AUG.11,1947

YR	CL	LEA	POS	GP	G	REC
1895	NY	N	1	7		.333
1896	NY	N	1	64		.254
	PIT	N	1-0	43		.206
1897	PIT	N	1-3	107		.309
1898	PIT	N	1	58		.290
	LOU	N	1-2-0	36		.227
	WAS	N	1	1		.000
1899	WAS	N	1	18		.188
1901	PHI	A	1	117		.307
1902	PHI	A	1-0	132		.308
1903	PHI	A	1	101		.298
1904	PHI	A	1	102		.308
1905	PHI	A	1	149		.284
1906	PHI	A	1	145		.292
1907	PHI	A	1	149		.266
1908	PHI	A	1	147		.248
1909	PHI	A	1	149		.268
1910	PHI	A	1	139		.248
1911	PHI	A	1	57		.197
1912	CLE	A	M-1	2		.000
1913	PHI	A	C-1	8		.444
1914	PHI	A	1	7		.333
1915	PHI	A	1	5		.167
1916	PHI	A	0	4		.167
1917	PHI	A	H	1		.000
		BRTR		1748		.277

DAVIS, HERMAN THOMAS "TOMMY"
B.MAR.21,1939 BROOKLYN,N.Y.

YR	CL	LEA	POS	GP	G	REC
1959	LA	N	H	1		.000
1960	LA	N	3-O	110		.276
1961	LA	N	3-O	132		.278
1962	LA	N	3-O	163		.346
1963	LA	N	3-O	146		.326
1964	LA	N	O	152		.275
1965	LA	N	O	17		.250
1966	LA	N	3-O	100		.313
1967	NY	N	1-O	154		.302
1968	CHI	A	1-O	132		.268
1969	SEA	A	1-O	123		.271
	HOU	N	O	24		.241
1970	HOU	N	O	57		.282
	CHI	N	O	11		.262
	OAK	A	1-O	66		.290
1971	OAK	A	1-2-3-O	79		.324
1972	CHI	N	1-O	15		.269
	BAL	A	1-O	26		.256
1973	BAL	A	1-O	137		.306
1974	BAL	A	D	158		.289
1975	BAL	A	D	116		.283
1976	CAL	A	1-O	72		.265
	KC	A	H	8		.263
	BRTR			1999		.294

DAVIS, ISSAC MARION
B.JUNE 14,1895 PUEBLO,COL.

YR	CL	LEA	POS	GP	G	REC
1919	WAS	A	S	7		.000
1924	CHI	A	S	10		.242
1925	CHI	A	S	146		.240
	BRTR			163		.235

DAVIS, J. IRA "SLATS"
B.JULY 8,1870 BROOKLYN,N.Y.
D.DEC.21,1942

YR	CL	LEA	POS	GP	G	REC
1899	NY	N	1-S	6		.250

DAVIS, JACKE SYLVESTA
B.MAR.5,1936 CARTHAGE,TEX.

YR	CL	LEA	POS	GP	G	REC
1962	PHI	N	O	48		.213
	BRTR					

DAVIS, JAMES BENNETT
B.SEPT.15,1925 RED BLUFF,CAL.

YR	CL	LEA	POS	GP	G	REC
1954	CHI	N	P	46	11- 7	
1955	CHI	N	P	42	7-11	
1956	CHI	N	P	46	5- 7	
1957	STL	N	P	10	0- 1	
	NY	N	P	10	1- 0	
	BBTL			154	24-26	

DAVIS, JAMES J. "JUMBO"
B.NEW YORK,N.Y.
D.FEB.1921

YR	CL	LEA	POS	GP	G	REC
1884	KC	U	3	7		.222
1886	BAL	AA	3	59		.185
1887	BAL	AA	S-3	130		.345
1888	KC	AA	3	122		.266
1889	KC	AA	3	62		.258
	STL	AA	S-O	2		.000
1890	STL	AA	3	21		.250
	BRO	AA	3	37		.284
1891	WAS	AA	3	18		.250
	LTR			458		.278

DAVIS, JOHN A. "DAISY"
B.1858 BOSTON,MASS.

YR	CL	LEA	POS	GP	G	REC
1884	STL	AA	P	28	11-12	
	BOS	N	P-O	5	1- 3	
						.050
1885	BOS	N	P	11	5- 6	
				44	17-21	
						.159

DAVIS, JOHN HUMPHREY
B.JULY 15,1916 LAUREL RUN,PA.

YR	CL	LEA	POS	GP	G	REC
1941	NY	N	3	21		.214
	BRTR					

DAVIS, JOHN WILBUR "BUD"
B.DEC.7,1889 MERRY POINT,VA.
D.MAY 26,1967

YR	CL	LEA	POS	GP	G	REC
1915	PHI	A	P	20	1- 2	
	BLTR					

DAVIS, LAWRENCE COLUMBUS
"CRASH"
B.JULY 14,1919 CANON,GA.

YR	CL	LEA	POS	GP	G	REC
1940	PHI	A	2-S	23		.269
1941	PHI	A	1-2	39		.219
1942	PHI	A	1-2-S	86		.224
	BRTR			148		.230

DAVIS, OTIS ALLEN "SCAT"
B.SEPT.24,1920 CHARLESTON,ARK.

YR	CL	LEA	POS	GP	G	REC
1946	BRO	N	H	1		.000
	BLTL					

DAVIS, RAYMOND THOMAS "PEACHES"
B.MAY 25,1910 GLASS,TEX.

YR	CL	LEA	POS	GP	G	REC
1936	CIN	N	P	26	8- 8	
1937	CIN	N	P	42	11-13	
1938	CIN	N	P	29	7-12	
1939	CIN	N	P	20	1- 0	
	BLTR			117	27-33	

DAVIS, ROBERT BRANDON
B.SEPT.10,1928 WILMINGTON,DEL.

YR	CL	LEA	POS	GP	G	REC
1952	PIT	N	O	55		.179
1953	PIT	N	O	12		.205
	BRTR			67		.187

DAVIS, ROBERT EDWARD
B.SEPT.11,1933 NEW YORK,N.Y.

YR	CL	LEA	POS	GP	G	REC
1958	KC	A	P	8	0- 4	
1960	KC	A	P	21	0- 0	
	BRTR			29	0- 4	

DAVIS, ROBERT JOHN EUGENE "BOB"
B.MAR.1,1952 PRYOR,OKLA.

YR	CL	LEA	POS	GP	G	REC
1973	SD	N	C	5		.091
1975	SD	N	C	43		.234
1976	SD	N	C	51		.205
	BRTR			51		.205

DAVIS, RONALD EVERETTE "RON"
B.OCT.21,1941 ROANOKE RAPIDS,N.C

YR	CL	LEA	POS	GP	G	REC
1962	HOU	N	O	6		.214
1966	HOU	N	O	48		.247
1967	HOU	N	O	94		.256
1968	HOU	N	O	52		.212
	STL	N	O	33		.177
1969	PIT	N	O	62		.234
	BRTR			295		.233

DAVIS, THOMAS J.

YR	CL	LEA	POS	GP	G	REC
1890	CLE	N	O	6		.214

DAVIS, THOMAS OSCAR "TOD"
B.JULY 24,1925 LOS ANGELES,CAL.

YR	CL	LEA	POS	GP	G	REC
1949	PHI	A	2-S-3	31		.267
1951	PHI	A	2-3	11		.067
	BRTR			42		.233

DAVIS, VIRGIL LAWRENCE "SPUD"
B.DEC.20,1904 BIRMINGHAM,ALA.

YR	CL	LEA	POS	GP	G	REC
1928	STL	N	C	2		.200
	PHI	N	C	67		.282
1929	PHI	N	C	98		.342
1930	PHI	N	C	106		.313
1931	PHI	N	C	120		.326
1932	PHI	N	C	125		.336
1933	PHI	N	C	141		.349
1934	STL	N	C	107		.300
1935	STL	N	C-1	102		.317
1936	STL	N	C	112		.273
1937	CIN	N	C	76		.268
1938	CIN	N	C	12		.167
	PHI	N	C	70		.247
1939	PHI	N	C	87		.307
1940	PIT	N	C	99		.326
1941	PIT	N	C	57		.252
1944	PIT	N	C	54		.301
1945	PIT	N	C	23		.242
	BRTR			1458		.308

NON-PLAYING MANAGER PIT(N) 1946

DAVIS, WILEY ANDERSON
B.AUG.1,1875 BLOUNT CO.,TENN.
D.SEPT.22,1942

YR	CL	LEA	POS	GP	G	REC
1896	CIN	N	P	2	0- 0	
	BRTR					

DAVIS, WILLIAM HENRY "WILLIE"
B.APR.15,1940 MINERAL SPRINGS,
ARK.

YR	CL	LEA	POS	GP	G	REC
1960	LA	N	O	22		.318
1961	LA	N	O	128		.254
1962	LA	N	O	157		.285
1963	LA	N	O	156		.245
1964	LA	N	O	157		.294
1965	LA	N	O	142		.238
1966	LA	N	O	153		.284
1967	LA	N	O	143		.257
1968	LA	N	O	160		.250
1969	LA	N	O	129		.311
1970	LA	N	O	146		.305
1971	LA	N	O	158		.309
1972	LA	N	O	149		.289
1973	LA	N	O	152		.285
1974	MON	N	O	153		.295
1975	TEX	A	O	42		.249
	STL	N	O	98		.291
1976	SD	N	O	141		.268
	BLTL			2386		.279

DAVIS, WOODROW WILSON
B.APR.25,1913 NICHOLLS,GA.

YR	CL	LEA	POS	GP	G	REC
1938	DET	A	P	2	0- 0	
	BLTR					

DAVISON, MICHAEL LYNN "MIKE"
B.AUG.4,1945 GALESBURG,ILL.

YR	CL	LEA	POS	GP	G	REC
1969	SF	N	P	1	0- 0	
1970	SF	N	P	31	3- 5	
	BLTL			32	3- 5	

DAWSON, ANDRE FERNANDO
B.JULY 10,1954 MIAMI,FLA.

YR	CL	LEA	POS	GP	G	REC
1976	MON	N	O	24		.235
	BRTR					

DAWSON, RALPH FENTON "JOE"
B.MAR.9,1898 BOW,WASH.

YR	CL	LEA	POS	GP	G	REC
1924	CLE	A	P	4	1- 2	
1927	PIT	N	P	20	3- 7	
1928	PIT	N	P	31	7- 7	
1929	PIT	N	P	4	0- 1	
	BRTR			59	11-17	

DAWSON, REXFORD PAUL
B.FEB.10,1889 SKAGIT CO.,WASH.
D.OCT.20,1958

YR	CL	LEA	POS	GP	G	REC
1913	WAS	A	P	1	0- 0	
	BLTR					

DAY, CHARLES FREDERICK "BOOTS"
B.AUG.31,1947 ILION,N.Y.

YR	CL	LEA	POS	GP	G	REC
1969	STL	N	O	11		.000
1970	CHI	N	O	11		.250
	MON	N	O	41		.269
1971	MON	N	O	127		.283
1972	MON	N	O	128		.233
1973	MON	N	O	101		.275
1974	MON	N	O	52		.185
	BLTL			471		.256

DAY, CLYDE HENRY "PEA RIDGE"
B.AUG.26,1899 PINEVILLE,MO.
D.MAR.21,1934 KANSAS CITY,MO.

YR	CL	LEA	POS	GP	G	REC
1924	STL	N	P	3	1- 1	
1925	STL	N	P	17	2- 4	
1926	CIN	N	P	4	0- 0	
1931	BRO	N	P	22	2- 2	
	BRTR			46	5- 7	

DAY, JOHN B.
B.MAR.2,1847 PORTLAND,CONN.
D.JAN.25,1925
NON-PLAYING MANAGER MY(N) 1899

DAY, WILLIAM
B.JULY 28,1867 WILMINGTON,DEL.
D.AUG.6,1923

YR	CL	LEA	POS	GP	G	REC
1889	PHI	N	P	3	0- 3	
1890	PHI	N	P	4	1- 1	
	PIT	N	P	7	0- 7	
	TR			14	1-11	

DEAGLE, LORENZO BURROUGHS "REN"
B.JUNE 26,1858 NEW YORK,N.Y.
D.DEC.24,1937

YR	CL	LEA	POS	GP	G	REC
1883	CIN	AA	P-S	19	10- 8	
						.130
1884	CIN	AA	P	3	2- 1	
	LOU	AA	P-O	12	4- 6	
						.114
	BRTR			34	16-15	
						.109

YR	CL	LEA	POS	GP	G	REC

DEAL, CHARLES ALBERT
B.OCT.30,1891 WILKINSBURG,PA.

YR	CL	LEA	POS	GP	G	REC
1912	DET	A	3		41	.225
1913	DET	A	3		16	.220
	BOS	N	3		10	.309
1914	BOS	N	3		79	.210
1915	STL	F	3		65	.314
1916	STL	A	3		23	.135
	CHI	N	3		2	.250
1917	CHI	N	3		135	.254
1918	CHI	N	3		119	.239
1919	CHI	N	3		116	.289
1920	CHI	N	3		129	.240
1921	CHI	N	3		115	.289
			BRTR		850	.256

DEAL, ELLIS FERGASON "COT"
B.JAN.23,1923 ARAPAHO,OKLA.

YR	CL	LEA	POS	GP	G	REC
1947	BOS	A	P	5	6	0- 1
1948	BOS	A	P		4	1- 0
1950	STL	N	P		3	0- 0
1954	STL	N	P		33	2- 3
			BBTR	45	46	3- 4
			BL 1947-48			

DEAL, FREDERICK LINDSAY
B.SEPT.3,1916 LENOIR,N.C.

YR	CL	LEA	POS	GP	G	REC
1939	BRO	N	O			.000
			BLTR			

DEAL, JOHN WESLEY "SNAKE"
B.JAN.21,1079 CUNSHOHOCKEN,PA.
D.MAY 9,1944

YR	CL	LEA	POS	GP	G	REC
1906	CIN	N	1		65	.208
			BRTR			

DEALEY, PATRICK E.
B.MOOSUP,CONN.
D.JAN.1925

YR	CL	LEA	POS	GP	G	REC
1884	STP	U	C-O		5	.143
1885	BOS	N	C-1-S-3		34	.230
1886	BOS	N	C		14	.333
1887	WAS	N	C-S		56	.286
1890	SYR	AA	P-C		18	0- 1
						.174
			BRTR		127	0- 1
						.256

DEAN, ALFRED LOVILL "CHUBBY"
B.AUG.24,1916 MT.AIRY,N.C.
D.DEC.21,1970 RIVERSIDE,CAL.

YR	CL	LEA	POS	GP	G	REC
1936	PHI	A	1		111	.287
1937	PHI	A	P-1	2	104	1- 0
						.262
1938	PHI	A	P	6	16	2- 1
1939	PHI	A	P	54	80	5- 8
1940	PHI	A	P-1	30	67	6-13
						.289
1941	PHI	A	P-1	18	27	2- 4
						.237
	CLE	A	P-1	8	17	1- 4
						.167
1942	CLE	A	P	27	70	8-11
1943	CLE	A	P	17	41	5- 5
			BLTL	162	533	30-46
						.274

DEAN, CHARLES WILSON "DORRY"
B.NOV.6,1852 CINCINNATI,OHIO
D.MAY 4,1935

YR	CL	LEA	POS	GP	G	REC
1874	BAL	NA	2-O		47	-
1876	CIN	N	P-S-	30	34	4-26
			O			.257
			BRTR	30	81	4-26

DEAN, JAMES HARRY
B.MAY 12,1915 ROCKMART,GA.
D.JUNE 1,1960

YR	CL	LEA	POS	GP	G	REC
1941	WAS	A	P	2		0- 0
			BRTR			

DEAN, JAY HANNA "DIZZY"
B.JAN.16,1911 LUCAS,ARK.
D.JULY 17,1974 RENO,NEVADA

YR	CL	LEA	POS	GP	G	REC
1930	STL	N	P		1	1- 0
1932	STL	N	P	46	47	18-15
1933	STL	N	P	48	51	20-18
1934	STL	N	P	50	51	30- 7
1935	STL	N	P	50	53	28-12
1936	STL	N	P		51	24-13
1937	STL	N	P		27	13-10
1938	CHI	N	P		13	7- 1
1939	CHI	N	P		19	6- 4
1940	CHI	N	P		10	3- 3
1941	CHI	N	P		1	0- 0
1947	STL	A	P		1	0- 0
			BRTR	317	325	150-83

DEAN, PAUL DEE "DAFFY"
B.AUG.14,1913 LUCAS,ARK.

YR	CL	LEA	POS	GP	G	REC
1934	STL	N	P		39	19-11
1935	STL	N	P		46	19-12
1936	STL	N	P		17	5- 5
1937	STL	N	P		1	0- 0
1938	STL	N	P		5	3- 1
1939	STL	N	P		16	0- 1
1940	NY	N	P		27	4- 4
1941	NY	N	P		5	0- 0
1943	STL	A	P		3	0- 0
			BRTR	159		50-34

DEAN, TOMMY DOUGLAS
B.AUG.30,1945 IUKA,MISS.

YR	CL	LEA	POS	GP	G	REC
1967	LA	N	S		12	.143
1969	SD	N	2-S		101	.176
1970	SD	N	S		61	.222
1971	SD	N	2-S-3		41	.114
			BKTR	215		.180

DEAN, WAYLAND OGDEN
B.JUNE 20,1903 RICHWOOD,W.VA.
D.APR.10,1930

YR	CL	LEA	POS	GP	G	REC
1924	NY	N	P		26	6-12
1925	NY	N	P		33	10- 7
1926	PHI	N	P	33	63	8-16
1927	PHI	N	P	2	3	0- 1
	CHI	N	P		2	0- 0
			BBTR	96	127	24-36

DEANE, JOHN HENRY
B.MAY 6,1846 TRENTON,N.J.
D.MAY 31,1925

YR	CL	LEA	POS	GP	G	REC
1871	KEK	NA	M-O		5	-

DEAR, PAUL STANFORD "BUDDY"
B.DEC.1,1905 NORFOLK,VA.

YR	CL	LEA	POS	GP	G	REC
1927	WAS	A	2	2		.000
			BRTR			

DE ARMOND, CHARLES HOMMER
B.FEB.13,1877 OKEANA,OHIO
D.DEC.17,1933

YR	CL	LEA	POS	GP	G	REC
1903	CIN	N	3		11	.297
			BRTR			

DEASLEY, JAMES "SACK"
B.PHILADELPHIA,PA.

YR	CL	LEA	POS	GP	G	REC
1884	WAS	U	S		31	.216
	KC	U	S		13	.175
					44	.207

DEASLEY, THOMAS H. "PAT"
B.NOV.17,1857 PHILADELPHIA,PA.
D.APR.1,1943

YR	CL	LEA	POS	GP	G	REC
1881	BOS	N	C-1-S-O		43	.229
1882	BOS	N	C-S-C-O		66	.267
1883	STL	AA	C-O		53	.250
1884	STL	AA	C		73	.202
1885	NY	N	C-S		52	.256
1886	NY	N	C		38	.265
1887	NY	N	C		29	.362
1888	WAS	N	C		34	.157
			BRTR	388		.246

DE BERRY, JOHN HERMAN "HANK"
B.DEC.29,1893 SAVANNAH,TENN.
D.SEPT.10,1951

YR	CL	LEA	POS	GP	G	REC
1916	CLE	A	C		15	.273
1917	CLE	A	C		25	.273
1922	BRO	N	C		85	.301
1923	BRO	N	C		78	.285
1924	BRO	N	C		77	.243
1925	BRO	N	C		67	.259
1926	BRO	N	C		48	.287
1927	BRO	N	C		68	.234
1928	BRO	N	C		82	.252
1929	BRO	N	C		68	.262
1930	BRO	N	C		35	.295
			BRTR		648	.267

DE BERRY, JOSEPH H.
B.NOV.29,1899 SOUTHERN PINES, N.C.
D.OCT.9,1944

YR	CL	LEA	POS	GP	G	REC
1920	STL	A	P		10	2- 4
1921	STL	A	P		10	0- 1
			BLTR		20	2- 5

DEBUS, ADAM JOSEPH
B.JULY 10,1893 CHICAGO,ILL.

YR	CL	LEA	POS	GP	G	REC
1917	PIT	N	S-3		38	.229
			BRTR			

DE BUSSCHERE, DAVID ALBERT "DAVE"
B.OCT.16,1940 DETROIT,MICH.

YR	CL	LEA	POS	GP	G	REC
1962	CHI	A	P		12	0- 0
1963	CHI	A	P		24	3- 4
			BRTR		36	3- 4

DECATUR, ARTHUR RUE
B.JAN.14,1893 CLEVELAND,OHIO
D.APR.25,1966 TALLADEGA,ALA.

YR	CL	LEA	POS	GP	G	REC
1922	BRO	N	P		29	3- 4
1923	BRO	N	P		36	3- 3
1924	BRO	N	P		31	10- 9
1925	BRO	N	P		1	0- 0
	PHI	N	P		25	4-13
1926	PHI	N	P		2	0- 0
1927	PHI	N	P		29	3- 5
			BRTR		153	23-34

DE CINCES, DOUGLAS VERNON "DOUG"
B.AUG.29,1950 BURBANK,CAL.

YR	CL	LEA	POS	GP	G	REC
1973	BAL	A	2-S-3		10	.111
1974	BAL	A	3		1	.000
1975	BAL	A	1-2-S-3		61	.251
1976	BAL	A	1-2-S-3		129	.234
			BRTR		201	.235

DECKER, EDWARD HARRY
B.SEPT.3,1854 LOCKPORT,ILL.

YR	CL	LEA	POS	GP	G	REC
1879	SYR	N	C-1-O		3	.100
1882	STL	AA	2		2	.250
1884	DET	N	C-O		4	.286
	KC	U	C-O		23	.136
1886	CIN	N	C-O		15	.203
	WAS	N	C-3		6	.143
1889	PHI	N	C-2		11	.103
1890	PHI	N	C-1-O		5	.368
	PIT	N	C		90	.273
			BRTR		159	.236

DECKER, GEORGE A "GENTLEMAN GEORGE"
B.JUNE 1,1869 YORK,PA.
D.JUNE 9,1909

YR	CL	LEA	POS	GP	G	REC
1892	CHI	N	2-O		79	.231
1893	CHI	N	1-2-O		81	.276
1894	CHI	N	1-O		89	.310
1895	CHI	N	O		70	.291
1896	CHI	N	1-O		106	.281
1897	CHI	N	1-O		109	.307
1898	STL	N	1		64	.263
	LOU	N	1-O		42	.315
1899	LOU	N	1		38	.234
	WAS	N	1-O		4	.000
					682	.281

DECKER, GEORGE HENRY "JOE"
B.JUNE 16,1947 STORM LAKE,IA.

YR	CL	LEA	POS	GP	G	REC
1969	CHI	N	P		4	1- 0
1970	CHI	N	P		24	2- 7
1971	CHI	N	P	21	22	3- 2
1972	CHI	N	P		5	1- 0
1973	MIN	A	P		29	10-10
1974	MIN	A	P		37	16-14
1975	MIN	A	P		10	1- 3
1976	MIN	A	P		13	2- 7
			BRTR	143	144	36-43

YR	CL	LEA	POS	GP	G	REC

DEDE, ARTHUR RICHARD
B.JULY 12,1895 BROOKLYN,N.Y.
D.SEPT.6,1971 KEENE,N.H.

YR	CL	LEA	POS	GP	G	REC
1916	BRO	N	C		1	.000
		BRTR				

DEDEAUX, RAOUL
B.FEB.17,1915 NEW ORLEANS,LA.

| 1935 | BRK | N | S | | 2 | .250 |
| | | BRTR | | | | |

DEE, JAMES D.
B.BUFFALO,N.Y.

| 1884 | PIT | AA | S | | 13 | .136 |

DEE, MAURICE LEO "SHORTY"
B.OCT.4,1889 HALIFAX,N.S.,CAN.
D.AUG.12,1971 JAMACIA PLAIN,
MASS.

| 1915 | STL | A | S | | 1 | .000 |
| | | BRTR | | | | |

DEEGAN, W. JOHN "DUMMY"
B.NEW YORK,N.Y.

| 1901 | NY | N | P | | 2 | 0- 2 |

DEERING, JOHN THOMAS
B.JUNE 25,1878 LYNN,MASS.
D.FEB.15,1943

1903	DET	A	P		11	3- 8
	NY	A	P		9	3- 1
		TR			20	6- 9

DEES, CHARLES HENRY "CHARLIE"
B.JUNE 24,1935 BIRMINGHAM,ALA.

1963	LA	A	1		60	.307
1964	LA	A	1		26	.077
1965	CAL	A	1		12	.156
		BLTL			98	.265

DE FATE, CLYDE HERBERT "TONY"
B.FEB.22,1895 KANSAS CITY,MO.
D.SEPT.3,1963 NEW ORLEANS,LA.

1917	STL	N	S		14	.143
	DET	A	2		3	.000
		BRTR			17	.133

DE GERICK, MICHAEL ARTHUR
B.APR.1,1943 NEW YORK,N.Y.

1961	CHI	A	P		1	0- 0
1962	CHI	A	P		1	0- 0
		BRTR			2	0- 0

DE GROFF, EDWARD ARTHUR "RUBE"
B.SEPT.2,1879 HYDE PARK,N.Y.
D.DEC.17,1955

1905	STL	N	O		15	.250
1906	STL	N	O		1	.000
					16	.233

DEHLMAN, HERMAN J.
B.1850 CATASAUQUA,PA.
D.MAR.13,1885

1872	ATL	NA	1		35	.201
1873	ATL	NA	1		54	-
1874	ATL	NA	1		53	-
1875	STL	NA	1		64	.215
1876	STL	N	1		64	.178
1877	STL	N	1-O		32	.185
					302	-

DEIDEL, JAMES LAWRENCE "JIM"
B.JUNE 6,1949 DENVER,COL.

| 1974 | NY | A | C | | 2 | .000 |
| | | BRTR | | | | |

DEININGER, OTTO CHARLES "PEP"
B.OCT.10,1877 WASSERALFINGEN,
GERMANY
D.SEPT.25,1950

1902	BOS	A	P		2	0- 1
1908	PHI	N	O		1	.000
1909	PHI	N	O		46	.260
		BLTL		2	49	0- 1
						.263

DEISEL, EDWARD "PAT"
B.APR.29,1876 RIPLEY,OHIO
D.APR.17,1948

1902	BRO	N	C		1	.667
1903	CIN	N	C		2	.000
		BRTR			3	.667

DEITRICK, WILLIAM ALEXANDER
B.APR.20,1902 HANOVER CO.,VA.
D.MAY 6,1946

1927	PHI	N	S		5	.167
1928	PHI	N	O		52	.200
		BRTR			57	.198

DEJAN, MICHAEL DAN "MIKE"
B.JAN.13,1915 CLEVELAND,OHIO
D.FEB.2,1953 W.LOS ANGELES,CAL.

| 1940 | CIN | N | O | | 12 | .188 |
| | | BLTL | | | | |

DE JESUS, IVAN (ALVAREZ)
B.JAN.9,1953 SANTURCE,P.R.

1974	LA	N	S		3	.333
1975	LA	N	S		63	.184
1976	LA	N	S-3		22	.171
		BRTR			88	.183

DEKONING, WILLIAM CALLAHAN
B.DEC.19,1919 BROOKLYN,N.Y.

| 1945 | NY | N | C | | 3 | .000 |
| | | BRTR | | | | |

DE LA CRUZ, TOMAS
B.SEPT.18,1914 MARIANAO,CUBA
D.SEPT.6,1958

| 1944 | CIN | N | P | 34 | 36 | 9- 9 |
| | | BRTR | | | | |

DE LA HOZ, MIGUEL ANGEL "MIKE"
B.OCT.2,1939 HAVANA,CUBA

1960	CLE	A	S-3		49	.256
1961	CLE	A	2-S-3		61	.260
1962	CLE	A	2		12	.083
1963	CLE	A	2-S-3-O		67	.267
1964	MIL	N	2-S-3		78	.291
1965	MIL	N	1-2-S-3		81	.256
1966	ATL	N	2-S-3		71	.218
1967	ATL	N	2-S-3		74	.203
1969	CIN	N	H		1	.000
		BRTR			494	.251

**DELAHANTY, EDWARD JAMES
"BIG ED"**
B.OCT.30,1867 CLEVELAND,OHIO
D.JULY 2,1903 FORT ERIE,ONT.,
CAN.

1888	PHI	N	2		74	.227
1889	PHI	N	2-O		54	.292
1890	CLE	P	2-S-O		115	.296
1891	PHI	N	1-O		128	.249
1892	PHI	N	O		120	.312
1893	PHI	N	O		132	.370
1894	PHI	N	O		114	.400
1895	PHI	N	O		116	.399
1896	PHI	N	1-O		122	.394
1897	PHI	N	O		129	.377
1898	PHI	N	O		142	.334
1899	PHI	N	O		145	.408
1900	PHI	N	1		130	.319
1901	PHI	N	1-O		138	.357
1902	WAS	A	1-O		123	.376
1903	WAS	A	O		43	.338
		BRTR			1825	.346

**DELAHANTY, FRANK GEORGE
"PUDGIE"**
B.DEC.29,1885 CLEVELAND,OHIO
D.JULY 22,1966 CUYAHOGA,OHIO

1905	NY	A	1-O		9	.240
1906	NY	A	O		92	.238
1907	CLE	A	O		15	.173
1908	NY	A	O		37	.256
1914	BUF	F	O		79	.212
	PIT	F	O		42	.213
1915	PIT	F	O		14	.238
		BRTR			288	.219

DELAHANTY, JAMES CHRISTOPHER
B.JUNE 20,1882 CLEVELAND,OHIO
D.OCT.17,1953

1901	CHI	N	3		16	.174
1902	NY	N	O		7	.231
1904	BOS	N	2-3		138	.285
1905	BOS	N	O		124	.258
1906	CIN	N	3		112	.280
1907	STL	A	2-3		33	.219
	WAS	A	2-3		108	.293
1908	WAS	A	2		82	.317
1909	WAS	A	2		88	.221
	DET	A	2		48	.253
1910	DET	A	2		106	.293
1911	DET	A	1-2		144	.339
1912	DET	A	2-3-0		78	.286
1914	BRO	F	2		74	.284
1915	BRO	F	1		16	.250
		BRTR			1174	.283

DELAHANTY, JOSEPH NICHOLAS
B.OCT.18,1875 CLEVELAND,OHIO
D.JAN.9,1936

1907	STL	N	O		6	.303
1908	STL	N	O		138	.255
1909	STL	N	2-O		111	.214
		BRTR			255	.238

DELAHANTY, THOMAS JAMES
B.MAR.9,1872 CLEVELAND,OHIO
D.JAN.10,1951

1894	PHI	N	2		1	.250
1896	CLE	N	3		15	.216
	PIT	N	S		1	.333
1897	LOU	N	2		1	.333
		TR			18	.224

DE LANCEY, WILLIAM L.
B.CUMMINSVILLE,OHIO

| 1890 | CLE | N | 2 | | 36 | .189 |

DE LANCEY, WILLIAM PINKNEY
B.NOV.28,1911 GREENSBORO,N.C.
D.NOV.28,1946

1932	STL	N	C		8	.192
1934	STL	N	C		93	.316
1935	STL	N	C		103	.279
1940	STL	N	C		15	.222
		BLTR			219	.289

DELANEY, ARTHUR D. "SWEDE"
(REAL NAME ARTHUR D. HELENIUS)
B.JAN.5,1897 CHICAGO,ILL.
D.MAY 2,1970 HAYWARD,CAL.

1924	STL	N	P		8	1- 0
1928	BOS	N	P		39	9-17
1929	BOS	N	P		20	3- 5
		BRTR			67	13-22

DE LA ROSA, JESUS
B.JULY 28,1953 SANTO DOMINGO,D.R

| 1975 | HOU | N | H | | 3 | .333 |
| | | BRTR | | | | |

DEL CALVO, JACINTO
(PLAYED UNDER NAME OF
JACINTO CALVO)

DEL GRECO, ROBERT GEORGE "BOBBY"
B.APR.7,1933 PITTSBURGH,PA.

1952	PIT	N	O		99	.217
1956	PIT	N	3-O		14	.200
	STL	N	O		102	.215
1957	CHI	N	O		20	.200
	NY	A	O		8	.429
1958	NY	A	O		12	.200
1960	PHI	N	O		100	.237
1961	PHI	N	2-3-O		41	.259
	KC	A	O		74	.230
1962	KC	A	O		132	.254
1963	KC	A	3-O		121	.212
1965	PHI	N	O		8	.000
		BRTR			731	.229

DELHI, LEE WILLIAM "FLAME"
B.NOV.5,1890 LOS ANGELES,CAL.
D.MAY 9,1966

| 1912 | CHI | A | P | | 1 | 0- 0 |
| | | BRTR | | | | |

DELIS, JUAN FRANCISCO
B.FEB.27,1928 SANTIAGO,CUBA

| 1955 | WAS | A | 2-3-O | | 54 | .189 |
| | | BRTR | | | | |

YR	CL	LEA	POS	GP	G	REC

DELKER, EDWARD ALBERT
B.APR.17,1907 DE ALTO,PA.
```
1929 STL N  2-S-3    22   .150
1931 STL N  3          1   .500
1932 STL N  2         20   .119
     PHI N  2         30   .161
1933 PHI N  2-3       25   .171
     BRTR            98   .155
```

DELL, WILLIAM GEORGE "WHEEZER"
B.JUNE 11,1887 TUSCARORA,NEV.
D.AUG.24,1966 INDEPENDENCE,CAL.
```
1912 STL N  P          3   0- 0
1915 BRO N  P         40  11-10
1916 BRO N  P         32   8- 9
1917 BRO N  P         17   0- 4
     BRTR            92  19-23
```

DELMAS, BERT CHARLES
B.MAY 5,1912 SAN FRANCISCO,CAL.
```
1933 BRO N  2         12   .250
     BLTR
```

DELOCK, IVAN MARTIN "IKE"
B.NOV.11,1929 HIGHLAND PARK,MICH
```
1952 BOS A  P         39   4- 9
1953 BOS A  P         23   3- 1
1955 BOS A  P         29   9- 7
1956 BOS A  P         48  13- 7
1957 BOS A  P         49   9- 8
1958 BOS A  P         31  14- 8
1959 BOS A  P         28  11- 6
1960 BOS A  P         24   9-10
1961 BOS A  P         28   6- 9
1962 BOS A  P         17   4- 5
1963 BOS A  P          6   1- 2
     BAL A  P          7   1- 3
     BRTR           329  84-75
```

DE LOS SANTOS, RAMON (GENERO)
B.JAN.19,1949 SANTO DOMINGO,D.R.
```
1974 HOU N  P         12   1- 1
     BLTL
```

DEL SAVIO, GARTON ORVILLE
B.NOV.26,1914 NEW YORK,N.Y.
```
1943 PHI N  S              .091
     BRTR
```

DELSING, JAMES HENRY "JIM"
B.NOV.13,1925 RUDOLPH,WIS.
```
1948 CHI A  O         20   .190
1949 NY  A  O          9   .350
1950 NY  A  H         12   .400
     STL A  O         69   .263
1951 STL A  O        131   .249
1952 STL A  O         93   .255
     DET A  O         33   .274
1953 DET A  O        138   .288
1954 DET A  O        122   .248
1955 DET A  O        114   .239
1956 DET A  O         10   .000
     CHI A  O         55   .122
1960 KC  A  O         16   .250
     BLTR           822   .255
```

DE MAESTRI, JOSEPH PAUL "OATS"
B.DEC.9,1928 SAN FRANCISCO,CAL.
```
1952 CHI A  2-S-3     56   .203
     STL A  2-S-3     81   .226
1953 PHI A  S        111   .255
1954 PHI A  2-S-3    146   .230
1955 KC  A  S        123   .249
1956 KC  A  2-S      133   .233
1957 KC  A  S        135   .245
1958 KC  A  S        139   .219
1959 KC  A  S        118   .244
1960 NY  A  2-S       49   .229
1961 NY  A  2-S-3     30   .146
     BRTR          1121   .236
```

DEMAREE, ALBERT WENTWORTH
B.SEPT.8,1884 QUINCY,ILL.
D.MAY 2,1962 LOS ANGELES,CAL.
```
1912 NY  N  P          2   1- 0
1913 NY  N  P         31  13- 4
1914 NY  N  P         38  10-17
1915 PHI N  P         32  14-11
1916 PHI N  P         39  19-14
1917 CHI N  P         24   5- 9
     NY  N  P         15   4- 5
1918 NY  N  P         26   8- 6
1919 BOS N  P         25   6- 6
     BLTR           232  80-72
```

DEMAREE, JOSEPH FRANKLIN "FRANK"
(REAL NAME
JOSEPH FRANKLIN DIMARIA)
B.JUNE 10,1910 WOODLAND,CAL.
D.AUG.30,1958
```
1932 CHI N  O         23   .250
1933 CHI N  O        134   .272
1935 CHI N  O        107   .325
1936 CHI N  O        154   .350
1937 CHI N  O        154   .324
1938 CHI N  O        129   .273
1939 NY  N  O        150   .304
1940 NY  N  O        121   .302
1941 NY  N  O         16   .171
     BOS N  O         48   .230
1942 BOS N  O         64   .225
1943 STL N  O         39   .291
1944 STL N  O         16   .255
     BRTR          1155   .299
```

DEMARRISS, FRED
B.1865 NASHUA,N.H.
```
1890 CHI N  P          1   0- 0
     TR
```

DE MARS, WILLIAM LESTER "KID"
B.AUG.26,1925 BROOKLYN,N.Y.
```
1948 PHI A  2-S-3     18   .172
1950 STL A  S-3       61   .247
1951 STL A  S          1   .250
     BRTR            80   .237
```

DE MERIT, JOHN STEPHEN
B.JAN.0,1936 WEST BEND,WIS.
```
1957 MIL N  O         33   .147
1958 MIL N  O          3   .667
1959 MIL N  O         11   .200
1961 MIL N  O         32   .162
1962 NY  N  O         14   .188
     BRTR            93   .174
```

DEMERY, LAWRENCE CALVIN "LARRY"
B.JUNE 4,1953 BAKERSFIELD,CAL.
```
1974 PIT N  P    19    21   6- 6
1975 PIT N  P    45    49   7- 5
1976 PIT N  P    36    40  10- 7
     BRTR       100   110  23-18
```

DEMETER, DONALD LEE "DON"
B.JUNE 25,1935 OKLAHOMA CITY,
OKLA
```
1956 BRO N  O          3   .333
1958 LA  N  O         43   .189
1959 LA  N  O        139   .256
1960 LA  N  O         64   .274
1961 LA  N  O         15   .172
     PHI N  1-O      106   .257
1962 PHI N  1-3-O    153   .307
1963 PHI N  1-3-O    154   .258
1964 DET A  1-O      134   .256
1965 DET A  1-O      122   .278
1966 DET A  1-O       32   .212
     BOS A  1-O       73   .292
1967 BOS A  3-O       20   .279
     CLE A  3-O       51   .207
     BRTR          1109   .265
```

DEMETER, STEVEN "STEVE"
B.JAN.27,1935 HOMER CITY,PA.
```
1959 DET A  3         11   .111
1960 CLE A  3          4   .000
     BRTR            15   .087
```

DE MILLER, HARRY
B.NOV.12,1867 WOOSTER,OHIO
D.OCT.19,1928
```
1892 STL N  S          1   .000
     BR
```

DEMMITT, CHARLES RAYMOND "RAY"
B.FEB.2,1884 ILLIOPOLIS,ILL.
D.FEB.19,1956
```
1909 NY  A  O        119   .241
1910 STL A  O         10   .173
1914 DET A  O          1   .000
     CHI A  O        145   .258
1915 CHI A  O          9   .000
1917 STL A  O         14   .283
1918 STL A  O        116   .281
1919 STL A  O         79   .238
     BLTR           493   .257
```

DE MOLA, DONALD JOHN "DON"
B.JULY 5,1952 GLEN COVE,N.Y.
```
1974 MON N  P         25   1- 0
1975 MON N  P         60   4- 7
     BRTR            85   5- 7
```

DE MONTREVILLE, EUGENE NAPOLEON
B.MAR.26,1874 ST.PAUL,MINN.
D.FEB.18,1935 MEMPHIS,TENN.
```
1894 PIT N  S          2   .250
1895 WAS N  S         12   .227
1896 WAS N  S        130   .349
1897 WAS N  2-S      132   .349
1898 BAL N  2-S      151   .325
1899 CHI N  2         83   .286
     BAL N  2         60   .276
1900 BRO N  2         63   .250
1901 BOS N  2-3      140   .305
1902 BOS N  2-3      123   .269
1903 WAS A  2         11   .292
1904 STL A  2          4   .111
     BRTR           911   .308
```

DE MONTREVILLE, LEON "LEE"
B.SEPT.23,1879 ST.PAUL,MINN.
D.MAR.23,1962
```
1903 STL N  S         20   .243
     TR
```

DE MOTT, BENJAMIN HARRISON
B.APR.2,1889 GREEN VILLAGE,N.J.
D.JULY 5,1963 SOMERVILLE,N.J.
```
1910 CLE A  P          9   0- 3
1911 CLE A  P          2   0- 1
     BRTR            11   0- 4
```

DEMPSEY, CORNELIUS FRANCIS "CON"
B.SEP.16,1923 SAN FRANCISCO,CAL
```
1951 PIT N  P          3   0- 2
     BRTR
```

DEMPSEY, JOHN RIKARD "RICK"
B.SEP.13,1949 FAYETTEVILLE,TENN.
```
1969 MIN A  C          5   .500
1970 MIN A  C          5   .000
1971 MIN A  C          6   .308
1972 MIN A  C         25   .200
1973 NY  A  C          6   .182
1974 NY  A  C-O       43   .239
1975 NY  A  C-O-D     71   .262
1976 NY  A  C-O       21   .119
     BAL A  C-O       59   .213
     BRTR           241   .225
```

DENEHY, WILLIAM FRANCIS "BILL"
B.MAR.31,1946 MIDDLETOWN,CONN.
```
1967 NY  N  P         15   1- 7
1968 WAS A  P          3   0- 0
1971 DET A  P         31   0- 3
     BBTR            49   1-10
     BL 1971
```

DENIENS
```
1914 CHI F  C          1   .000
```

DENNEHY, THOMAS FRANCIS "TOD"
B.MAY 12,1899 PHILADELPHIA,PA.
```
1923 PHI N  O          9   .250
     BLTL
```

DENNING, OTTO GEORGE
B.DEC.28,1913 HAYS,KAN.
```
1942 CLE A  C-O       92   .210
1943 CLE A  1         37   .240
     BRTR           129   .215
```

DENNIS, DONALD RAY "DON"
B.MAR.3,1942 UNIONTOWN,KAN.
```
1965 STL N  P         41   2- 3
1966 STL N  P         38   4- 2
     BRTR            79   6- 5
```

DENNIS, WALTER L.
B.1853 WASHINGTON,D.C.
D.SEPT.10,1889
NON-PLAYING MANAGER WAS(N) 1887

```
YR   CL LEA POS GP    G    REC      YR   CL LEA POS GP    G    REC      YR   CL LEA POS GP    G    REC
```

DENNY, JEREMIAH "JERRY"
B.MAR.16,1859 NEW YORK,N.Y.
D.AUG.15,1927
```
1881 PRO N  3              84   .240
1882 PRO N  3              84   .246
1883 PRO N  3              98   .274
1884 PRO N  C-1-2-3  108        .251
1885 PRO N  3              83   .223
1886 STL N  3             119   .257
1887 IND N  3             122   .340
1888 IND N  S-3           126   .261
1889 IND N  3             133   .282
1890 NY  N  3             114   .212
1891 NY  N  3               4   .250
     CLE N  3              36   .229
     PHI N  1-3            19   .301
1893 LOU N  S             44   .251
1894 LOU N  3             60   .274
          BRTR            1234  .263
```

DENNY, JOHN ALLEN
B.NOV.8,1952 PRESCOTT,ARIZ.
```
1974 STL N  P          2   0- 0
1975 STL N  P      25 26  10- 7
1976 STL N  P         30  11- 9
          BRTR     57 58  21-16
```

DENT, ELLIOTT ESTILL "EDDIE"
B.DEC.8,1887 BALTIMORE,MD.
D.JULY 15,1974 CLAYTON,GA.
```
1909 BRO N  P          6   2- 4
1911 BRO N  P          5   2- 1
1912 BRO N  P          1   0- 0
          BRTR        12   4- 5
```

DENT, RUSSELL EARL "BUCKY"
B.NOV.25,1951 SAVANNAH,GA.
```
1973 CHI A  S         40   .248
1974 CHI A  S        154   .274
1975 CHI A  S        157   .264
1976 CHI A  S        158   .246
          BRTR       509   .260
```

DENTE, SAMUEL JOSEPH "BLACKIE"
B.APR.26,1922 HARRISON,N.J.
```
1947 BOS A  3         46   .232
1948 STL A  S-3       98   .270
1949 WAS A  S        153   .273
1950 WAS A  2-S-3    155   .239
1951 WAS A  2-S-3     88   .238
1952 CHI A  1-2-S-3-  62   .221
            O
1953 CHI A  S          2   .000
1954 CLE A  2-S       68   .266
1955 CLE A  2-S-3     73   .257
          BRTR       745   .252
```

DENZER, ROGER
B.OCT.5,1871 LESUEUR CO.,MINN.
D.SEPT.18,1949
```
1897 CHI N  P         12   3- 6
1901 NY  N  P         11   2- 5
          TR          23   5-11
```

DE PAUGHER, MICHAEL H.
B.SAN FRANCISCO,CAL.
```
1884 IND N  C          2   .250
```

DE PHILLIPS, ANTHONY ANDREW
B.SEPT.20,1913 NEW YORK,N.Y.
```
1943 CIN N  C         35   .100
          BRTR
```

DERBY, EUGENE A.
B.TROY,N.Y.
```
1885 BAL AA P-C-O     10   0- 1
                           .129
```

DERBY, GEORGE H. "JONAH"
B.JULY 6,1857 WEBSTER,MASS.
D.JULY 4,1925
```
1881 DET N  P-O  55  59  29-26
                           .186
1882 DET N  P-O  36  38  16-20
                           .202
1883 BUF N  P-O      15   3-11
                           .237
          BLTR  106 112  48-57
                           .199
```

DERRICK, CLAUDE LESTER "DEEK"
B.JUNE 11,1886 CLAYTON,GA.
D.JULY 15,1974 CLAYTON,GA.
```
1910 PHI A  S          2   .000
1911 PHI A  2         36   .230
1912 PHI A  S         21   .241
1913 NY  A  S         22   .292
1914 CIN N  S          3   .333
1914 CHI N  S         28   .219
          BRTR       112   .242
```

DERRICK, JAMES MICHAEL "MIKE"
B.SEPT.19,1943 COLUMBIA,S.C.
```
1970 BOS A  1-O       24   .212
          BLTR
```

DERRINGER, SAMUEL PAUL "DUKE"
B.OCT.7,1906 SPRINGFIELD,KY.
```
1931 STL N  P         35  18- 8
1932 STL N  P         39  11-14
1933 STL N  P          3   0- 2
     CIN N  P         33   7-25
1934 CIN N  P         47  15-21
1935 CIN N  P         45  22-13
1936 CIN N  P         51  19-19
1937 CIN N  P         43  10-14
1938 CIN N  P         41  21-14
1939 CIN N  P         38  25- 7
1940 CIN N  P         37  20-12
1941 CIN N  P         29  12-14
1942 CIN N  P         29  10-11
1943 CHI N  P         32  10-14
1944 CHI N  P         42   7-13
1945 CHI N  P         35  16-11
          BRTR       579 223-212
```

DERRINGTON, CHARLES JAMES "JIM"
B.NOV.29,1939 SOUTH GATE,CAL.
```
1956 CHI A  P          1   0- 1
1957 CHI A  P         20   0- 1
          BLTL        21   0- 2
```

DERRY, ALVA RUSSELL "RUSS"
B.OCT.7,1917 PRINCETON,MO.
```
1944 NY  A  O         38   .254
1945 NY  A  O         78   .225
1946 PHI A  O         69   .207
1949 STL N  H          2   .000
          BLTR       187   .224
```

DESAUTELS, EUGENE ABRAHAM "RED"
B.JUNE 13,1907 WORCESTER,MASS.
```
1930 DET A  C         42   .190
1931 DET A  C          3   .091
1932 DET A  C         28   .236
1933 DET A  C         30   .143
1937 BOS A  C         96   .243
1938 BOS A  C        108   .291
1939 BOS A  C         76   .243
1940 BOS A  C         71   .225
1941 CLE A  C         66   .201
1942 CLE A  C         62   .247
1943 CLE A  C         68   .205
1945 CLE A  C         10   .111
1946 PHI A  C         52   .215
          BRTR       712   .233
```

DE SHONG, JAMES BROOKLYN
B.NOV.30,1909 HARRISBURG,PA.
```
1932 PHI A  P          6   0- 0
1934 NY  A  P         31   6- 7
1935 NY  A  P         29   4- 1
1936 WAS A  P     34 35  18-10
1937 WAS A  P         37  14-15
1938 WAS A  P         31   5- 8
1939 WAS A  P          7   0- 3
          BRTR    175 176  47-44
```

DES JARDIEN, PAUL RAYMOND "SHORTY"
B.AUG.24,1893 COFFEYVILLE,KAN.
D.MAR.7,1956
```
1916 CLE A  P          1   0- 0
          BRTR
```

DESSAU, FRANK ROLLAND "RUBE"
B.MAR.29,1883 NEW GALILEE,PA.
D.MAY 6,1952
```
1907 BOS N  P          2   0- 1
1910 BRO N  P         19   2- 3
          BBTR        21   2- 4
```

DETORE, GEORGE FRANCIS
B.NOV.11,1906 UTICA,N.Y.
```
1930 CLE A  3          3   .167
1931 CLE A  S-3       30   .267
          BRTR        33   .250
```

DETTORE, THOMAS ANTHONY "TOM"
B.NOV.17,1947 CANONSBURG,PA.
```
1973 PIT N  P         12   0- 1
1974 CHI N  P         16   3- 5
1975 CHI N  P         36   5- 4
1976 CHI N  P          4   0- 1
          BRTR        68   8-11
```

DETWEILER, ROBERT STERLING "DUCKY"
B.FEB.15,1919 TRUMBAUERSVILLE, PA.
```
1942 BOS N  3         12   .318
1946 BOS N  H          1   .000
          BRTR        13   .311
```

DEUTSCH, MELVIN ELLIOTT
B.JULY 26,1915 CALDWELL,TEX.
```
1946 BOS A  P          3   0- 0
          BRTR
```

DEVENS, CHARLES
B.JAN.1,1910 MILTON,MASS.
```
1932 NY  A  P          1   1- 0
1933 NY  A  P         14   3- 3
1934 NY  A  P          1   1- 0
          BRTR        16   5- 3
```

DEVINE, PAUL ADRIAN "ADRIAN"
B.DEC.2,1951 GALVESTON,TEX.
```
1973 ATL N  P         24   2- 3
1975 ATL N  P          5   1- 0
1976 ATL N  P         48   5- 6
          BRTR        77   8- 9
```

DEVINE, WALTER JAMES "JIM"
B.OCT.5,1858 BROOKLYN,N.Y.
D.JAN.11,1905
```
1883 BAL AA P-O        2   1- 1
                           .222
1886 NY  N  O          1   .000
          TL           2   3   1- 1
                           .167
```

DEVINE, WILLIAM PATRICK "MICKEY"
B.MAY 9,1892 ALBANY,N.Y.
D.OCT.1,1937
```
1918 PHI N  C          4   .125
1920 BOS A  C          8   .201
1925 NY  N  C-3       21   .273
          BRTR        33   .226
```

DEVINEY, HAROLD J. "HAL"
B.APR.11,1893 NEWTON,MASS.
D.JAN.5,1933
```
1920 BOS A  P          1   0- 0
          BRTR
```

DE VIVEIROS, BERNARD JOHN
B.APR.19,1901 OAKLAND,CAL.
```
1924 CHI A  S          1   .000
1927 DET A  S         24   .227
          BRTR        25   .217
```

DEVLIN, ARTHUR MC ARTHUR
B.OCT.16,1879 WASHINGTON,D.C.
D.SEPT.18,1948
```
1904 NY  N  3        130   .281
1905 NY  N  3        153   .246
1906 NY  N  3        148   .299
1907 NY  N  3        143   .277
1908 NY  N  3        157   .253
1909 NY  N  3        143   .265
1910 NY  N  3        147   .260
1911 NY  N  3         95   .278
1912 BOS N  1-S-3    124   .289
1913 BOS N  3         73   .229
          BRTR      1313   .269
```

DEVLIN, JAMES ALEXANDER
B.1849 PHILADELPHIA,PA.
D.OCT.10,1883
```
1873 PHI NA 1-S-3-O  21    -
1874 CHI NA 1-3-O    44    -
1875 CHI NA P-1-O    70   6-14
                           -
1876 LOU N  P        68  30-35
1877 LOU N  P        61  35-25
          BRTR      264  71-74
                           -
```

YR CL LEA POS GP G REC

DEVLIN, JAMES H.
B.APR.16,1866 TROY,N.Y.
D.DEC.14,1900 TROY,N.Y.

YR	CL	LEA	POS	GP	G	REC
1886	NY	N	P		1	0- 0
1887	PHI	N	P		2	0- 2
1888	STL	AA	P		12	6- 5
1889	STL	AA	P		9	4- 2
	TL				24	10- 9

DEVLIN, JAMES RAYMOND
B.AUG.25,1922 PLAINS,PA.

YR	CL	LEA	POS	GP	G	REC
1944	CLE	A	C		1	.000
	BLTR					

DE VOGT, REX EUGENE
B.JAN.4,1888 CLARE,MICH.
D.NOV.9,1935 ALMA,MICH.

YR	CL	LEA	POS	GP	G	REC
1913	BOS	N	C		3	.000

DEVORE, JOSHUA D.
B.NOV.13,1887 MURRAY CITY,OHIO
D.OCT.5,1954

YR	CL	LEA	POS	GP	G	REC
1908	NY	N	O		5	.167
1909	NY	N	O		23	.160
1910	NY	N	O		130	.304
1911	NY	N	O		149	.280
1912	NY	N	O		106	.275
1913	NY	N	O		16	.190
	CIN	N	O		66	.267
	PHI	N	O		23	.282
1914	NY	N	O		30	.302
	BOS	N	O		51	.227
	BLTR				599	.278

DE VORMER, ALBERT E.
B.AUG.19,1891 GRAND RAPIDS,MICH
D.AUG.29,1966 GRAND RAPIDS,MICH

YR	CL	LEA	POS	GP	G	REC
1918	CHI	A	C		8	.315
1921	NY	A	C		22	.347
1922	NY	A	C		24	.203
1923	BOS	A	C		74	.258
1927	NY	N	C		68	.248
	BRTR				196	.261

DEVOY, WALTER JOSEPH
B.MAR.4,1885 ST.LOUIS,MO.
D.DEC.17,1953

YR	CL	LEA	POS	GP	G	REC
1909	STL	A	O		19	.247

DEWALD, CHARLES H.
D.1867 ASHLAND,OHIO

YR	CL	LEA	POS	GP	G	REC
1890	CLE	P	P		2	2- 0
	TL					

DEXTER, CHARLES DANA
B.JUNE 15,1876 EVANSVILLE,IND.
D.JUNE 9,1934

YR	CL	LEA	POS	GP	G	REC
1896	LOU	N	C-O		98	.284
1897	LOU	N	C-O		63	.292
1898	LOU	N	O		112	.311
1899	LOU	N	O		76	.262
1900	CHI	N	C		35	.201
1901	CHI	N	1-3-O		112	.278
1902	CHI	N	1-3-O		70	.227
	BOS	N	2-S-3-O		49	.257
1903	BOS	N	O		120	.223
	TR				735	.265

DIBUT, PEDRO
B.NOV.18,1892 CIENFUEGOS,CUBA

YR	CL	LEA	POS	GP	G	REC
1924	CIN	N	P		7	3- 0
1925	CIN	N	P		1	0- 0
	BRTR				8	3- 0

DICKEN, PAUL FRANKLIN
B.OCT.2,1943 DELAND,FLA.

YR	CL	LEA	POS	GP	G	REC
1964	CLE	A	H		11	.000
1966	CLE	A	H		2	.000
	BRTR				13	.000

DICKERMAN, LEO LOUIS
B.OCT.31,1897 DESOTO,MO.

YR	CL	LEA	POS	GP	G	REC
1923	BRO	N	P		35	8-12
1924	BRO	N	P		7	0- 0
	STL	N	P		18	7- 4
1925	STL	N	P		29	4-11
	BRTR				89	19-27

DICKERSON, GEORGE CLARK
B.DEC.1,1892 RENNER,TEX.
D.JULY 9,1938

YR	CL	LEA	POS	GP	G	REC
1917	CLE	A	P		1	0- 0
	BRTR					

DICKERSON, LEWIS PESSANO
"BUTTERCUP"
B.OCT.11,1858 TYASKIN,MD.
D.JULY 23,1920

YR	CL	LEA	POS	GP	G	REC
1878	CIN	N	O		30	.309
1879	CIN	N	O		80	.294
1880	TRO	N	S-O		30	.189
	WOR	N	O		31	.316
1881	WOR	N	O		80	.316
1883	PIT	AA	2-S-O		80	.283
1884	BAL	U	3-O		46	.357
	BAL	AA	O		13	.232
	LOU	AA	O		8	.138
1885	BUF	N	S-O		5	.048
	BLTR				403	.286

DICKEY, GEORGE WILLARD "SKEETS"
B.JULY 10,1915 KENSETT,ARK.
D.JUNE 16,1976 DEWITT,ARK.

YR	CL	LEA	POS	GP	G	REC
1935	BOS	A	C		5	.000
1936	BOS	A	C		10	.043
1941	CHI	A	C		32	.200
1942	CHI	A	C		59	.233
1946	CHI	A	C		37	.192
1947	CHI	A	C		83	.223
	BBTR				226	.204

DICKEY, WILLIAM MALCOLM
B.JUNE 6,1907 BASTROP,LA.

YR	CL	LEA	POS	GP	G	REC
1928	NY	A	C		10	.200
1929	NY	A	C		130	.324
1930	NY	A	C		109	.339
1931	NY	A	C		130	.327
1932	NY	A	C		108	.310
1933	NY	A	C		130	.318
1934	NY	A	C		104	.322
1935	NY	A	C		120	.279
1936	NY	A	C		112	.362
1937	NY	A	C		140	.332
1938	NY	A	C		132	.313
1939	NY	A	C		128	.302
1940	NY	A	C		106	.247
1941	NY	A	C		109	.284
1942	NY	A	C		82	.295
1943	NY	A	C		85	.351
1946	NY	A	M-C		54	.261
	BLTR				1789	.313

DICKMAN, GEORGE EMERSON
B.NOV.12,1916 BUFFALO,N.Y.

YR	CL	LEA	POS	GP	G	REC
1936	BOS	A	P		1	0- 0
1938	BOS	A	P		32	5- 5
1939	BOS	A	P		48	8- 3
1940	BOS	A	P		35	8- 6
1941	BOS	A	P		9	1- 1
	BRTR				125	22-15

DICKSHOT, JOHN OSCAR "UGLY"
(REAL NAME
JOHN OSCAR DICKSUS)
B.JAN.24,1912 WAUKEGAN,ILL.

YR	CL	LEA	POS	GP	G	REC
1936	PIT	N	O		9	.222
1937	PIT	N	O		82	.254
1938	PIT	N	O		29	.229
1939	NY	N	O		10	.235
1944	CHI	A	O		62	.253
1945	CHI	A	O		130	.302
	BRTR				322	.276

DICKSON, JAMES EDWARD "JIM"
B.APR.20,1938 PORTLAND,ORE.

YR	CL	LEA	POS	GP	G	REC
1963	HOU	N	P		13	0- 1
1964	CIN	N	P		4	1- 0
1965	KC	A	P		68	3- 2
1966	KC	A	P		24	1- 0
	BLTR				109	5- 3

DICKSON, MURRY MONROE
B.AUG.21,1916 TRACY,MO.

YR	CL	LEA	POS	GP	G	REC
1939	STL	N	P		1	0- 0
1940	STL	N	P		1	0- 0
1942	STL	N	P	36	37	6- 3
1943	STL	N	P		31	8- 2
1946	STL	N	P		47	15- 6
1947	STL	N	P		47	13-16
1948	STL	N	P	42	43	12-16
1949	PIT	N	P		44	12-14
1950	PIT	N	P	51	52	10-15
1951	PIT	N	P	45	46	20-16
1952	PIT	N	P	43	47	14-21
1953	PIT	N	P		45	10-19
1954	PHI	N	P		40	10-20
1955	PHI	N	P		36	12-11
1956	PHI	N	P		3	0- 3
	STL	N	P	28	32	13- 8
1957	STL	N	P		14	5- 3
1958	KC	A	P	27	28	9- 5
	NY	A	P		6	1- 2
1959	KC	A	P		38	2- 1
	BRTR			625	638	172-181

DICKSON, WALTER R.
B.1882 GREENVILLE,TEX.
D.DEC.10,1918

YR	CL	LEA	POS	GP	G	REC
1910	NY	N	P		12	1- 0
1912	BOS	N	P		36	3-19
1913	BOS	N	P		19	6- 7
1914	PIT	F	P		40	9-19
1915	PIT	F	P		27	7- 5
	BRTR				134	26-50

DICKSUS, JOHN OSCAR
(PLAYED UNDER NAME OF
JOHN OSCAR DICKSHOT)

DIDDLEBOCK, HENRY H.
B.JUNE 27,1854 PHILADELPHIA,PA.
D.FEB.5,1900 PHILADELPHIA,PA.
NON-PLAYING MANAGER STL(N) 1896

DIDIER, ROBERT DANIEL "BOB"
B.FEB.16,1949 HATTIESBURG,MISS.

YR	CL	LEA	POS	GP	G	REC
1969	ATL	N	C		114	.256
1970	ATL	N	C		57	.149
1971	ATL	N	C		51	.219
1972	ATL	N	C		13	.300
1973	DET	A	C		7	.455
1974	BOS	A	C		5	.071
	BBTR				247	.229

DIEHL, ERNEST GUY
B.OCT.27,1877 CINCINNATI,OHIO
D.NOV.6,1958

YR	CL	LEA	POS	GP	G	REC
1903	PIT	N	O		1	.333
1904	PIT	N	S-O		12	.162
1906	BOS	N	S		3	.545
1909	BOS	N	O		1	.500
	BRTR				17	.255

DIEHL, GEORGE KRAUSE
B.FEB.25,1918 ALLENTOWN,PA.

YR	CL	LEA	POS	GP	G	REC
1942	BOS	N	P		1	0- 0
1943	BOS	N	P		1	0- 0
	BRTR				2	0- 0

DIERING, CHARLES EDWARD ALLEN
"CHUCK"
B.FEB.5,1923 ST.LOUIS,MO.

YR	CL	LEA	POS	GP	G	REC
1947	STL	N	O		105	.216
1948	STL	N	O		7	.000
1949	STL	N	O		131	.263
1950	STL	N	O		89	.250
1951	STL	N	O		64	.259
1952	NY	N	O		41	.174
1954	BAL	A	O		128	.258
1955	BAL	A	S-3-O		137	.256
1956	BAL	A	3-O		50	.186
	BRTR				752	.249

YR	CL	LEA	POS	GP	G	REC

DIERKER, LAWRENCE EDWARD "LARRY"
B.SEP.22,1946 HOLLYWOOD,CAL.

YR	CL	LEA	POS	GP	G	REC
1964	HOU	N	P		3	0- 1
1965	HOU	N	P		26	7- 8
1966	HOU	N	P		29	10- 8
1967	HOU	N	P		15	6- 5
1968	HOU	N	P	32	33	12-15
1969	HOU	N	P		39	20-13
1970	HOU	N	P		37	16-12
1971	HOU	N	P		24	12- 6
1972	HOU	N	P		31	15- 8
1973	HOU	N	P		14	1- 1
1974	HOU	N	P		33	11-10
1975	HOU	N	P		34	14-16
1976	HOU	N	P		28	13-14
	BRTR			345	346	137-117

DIETRICH, WILLIAM JOHN "BULLFROG"
B.MAR.29,1910 PHILADELPHIA,PA.

YR	CL	LEA	POS	GP	G	REC
1933	PHI	A	P		8	0- 1
1934	PHI	A	P	39	40	11-12
1935	PHI	A	P	43	44	7-13
1936	PHI	A	P		21	4- 6
	WAS	A	P		5	0- 1
	CHI	A	P		14	4- 4
1937	CHI	A	P		29	8-10
1938	CHI	A	P		8	2- 4
1939	CHI	A	P		25	7- 8
1940	CHI	A	P		23	10- 6
1941	CHI	A	P		19	5- 8
1942	CHI	A	P		26	6-11
1943	CHI	A	P		26	12-10
1944	CHI	A	P		36	16-17
1945	CHI	A	P		18	7-10
1946	CHI	A	P		11	3- 3
1947	PHI	A	P		11	5- 2
1948	PHI	A	P		4	1- 2
	BRTR			366	368	108-128

DIETZ, LLOYD ARTHUR "DUTCH"
B.FEB.9,1912 CINCINNATI,OHIO
D.OCT.29,1972 BEAUMONT,TEX.

YR	CL	LEA	POS	GP	G	REC
1940	PIT	N	P	4	6	0- 1
1941	PIT	N	P		33	7- 2
1942	PIT	N	P		40	6- 9
1943	PIT	N	P	8	10	0- 3
	PHI	N	P		21	1- 1
	BRTR			106	110	14-16

DIETZ, RICHARD ALLEN "DICK"
B.SEP.18,1941 CRAWFORDSVILLE, IND.

YR	CL	LEA	POS	GP	G	REC
1966	SF	N	C		13	.043
1967	SF	N	C		56	.225
1968	SF	N	C		98	.272
1969	SF	N	C		79	.230
1970	SF	N	C		148	.300
1971	SF	N	C		142	.252
1972	LA	N	C		27	.161
1973	ATL	N	C-1		83	.295
	BRTR			646		.261

DIETZEL, LEROY LOUIS "ROY"
B.JAN.9,1931 BALTIMORE,MD.

YR	CL	LEA	POS	GP	G	REC
1954	WAS	A	2-3	9		.238
	BRTR					

DIFANI, CLARENCE JOSEPH "JAY"
B.DEC.21,1923 CRYSTAL CITY,MO.

YR	CL	LEA	POS	GP	G	REC
1948	WAS	A	H		2	.000
1949	WAS	A	2		2	1.000
	BRTR				4	.333

DIGGS, REESE WILSON
B.SEPT.22,1915 MATHEWS,VA.

YR	CL	LEA	POS	GP	G	REC
1934	WAS	A	P		4	1- 2
	BBTR					

DIGNAN, STEPHEN E.
B.MAY.16,1859 BOSTON,MASS.
D.JULY 11,1881

YR	CL	LEA	POS	GP	G	REC
1880	BOS	N	O		8	.324
	WOR	N	O		3	.300
					11	.318

DI LAURO, JACK EDWARD
B.MAR.3,1943 AKRON,OHIO

YR	CL	LEA	POS	GP	G	REC
1969	NY	N	P		23	1- 4
1970	HOU	N	P	42	43	1- 3
	BBTL			65	66	2- 7

DILLARD, DAVID DONALD "DON"
B.JAN.8,1937 GREENVILLE,S.C.

YR	CL	LEA	POS	GP	G	REC
1959	CLE	A	H		10	.400
1960	CLE	A	O		6	.143
1961	CLE	A	O		74	.272
1962	CLE	A	O		95	.230
1963	MIL	N	O		67	.235
1965	MIL	N	O		20	.158
	BLTR				272	.244

DILLARD, ROBERT LEE "PAT"
B.JUNE 12,1874 CHATTANOOGA,TENN
D.JULY 22,1907

YR	CL	LEA	POS	GP	G	REC
1900	STL	N	3-O		44	.237

DILLARD, STEPHEN BRADLEY "STEVE"
B.FEB.8,1951 MEMPHIS,TENN.

YR	CL	LEA	POS	GP	G	REC
1975	BOS	A	2		1	.400
1976	BOS	A	2-S-3		57	.275
	BRTR				58	.279

DILLHOEFER, WILLIAM MARTIN "PICKLES"
B.OCT.13,1894 CLEVELAND,OHIO
D.FEB.22,1922

YR	CL	LEA	POS	GP	G	REC
1917	CHI	N	C		42	.126
1918	PHI	N	C		8	.090
1919	STL	N	C		45	.213
1920	STL	N	C		76	.263
1921	STL	N	C		76	.241
	BRTR				247	.223

DILLINGER, HARLEY HUGH
B.OCT.30,1894 POMEROY,OHIO
D.JAN.8,1959

YR	CL	LEA	POS	GP	G	REC
1914	CLE	A	P		10	0- 1
	BRTL					

DILLINGER, ROBERT BERNARD "DUKE"
B.SEPT.17,1918 GLENDALE,CAL.

YR	CL	LEA	POS	GP	G	REC
1946	STL	A	S-3		83	.280
1947	STL	A	3		137	.294
1948	STL	A	3		153	.321
1949	STL	A	3		137	.324
1950	PHI	A	3		84	.309
	PIT	N	3		58	.288
1951	PIT	N	3		12	.233
	CHI	A	3		89	.301
	BRTR				753	.306

DILLMAN, WILLIAM HOWARD "BILL"
B.MAY 25,1945 TRENTON,N.J.

YR	CL	LEA	POS	GP	G	REC
1967	BAL	A	P	32	33	5- 9
1970	MON	N	P		18	2- 3
	BRTR			50	51	7-12

DILLON, FRANK EDWARD "POP"
B.OCT.17,1873 NORMAL,ILL.
D.SEPT.12,1931

YR	CL	LEA	POS	GP	G	REC
1899	PIT	N	1		30	.258
1900	PIT	N	1		5	.111
1901	DET	A	1		75	.298
1902	DET	A	1		66	.205
	BAL	A	1		2	.286
1904	BRO	N	1		134	.258
	BL				312	.255

DILLON, PACKARD ANDREW
B.ST.LOUIS,MO.
D.JAN.9,1890

YR	CL	LEA	POS	GP	G	REC
1875	RS	NA	C		3	-

DILLON, STEPHEN EDWARD "STEVE"
B.MAR.20,1943 YONKERS,N.Y.

YR	CL	LEA	POS	GP	G	REC
1963	NY	N	P		1	0- 0
1964	NY	N	P		2	0- 0
	BLTL				3	0- 0

DILONE, MIGUEL ANGEL (REYES)
B.NOV.1,1954 SANTIAGO,D.R.

YR	CL	LEA	POS	GP	G	REC
1974	PIT	N	O		12	.000
1975	PIT	N	O		18	.000
1976	PIT	N	O		16	.235
	BBTR				46	.160

DI MAGGIO, DOMINIC PAUL "DOM"
OR "THE LITTLE PROFESSOR"
B.FEB.12,1918 SAN FRANCISCO,CAL.

YR	CL	LEA	POS	GP	G	REC
1940	BOS	A	O		108	.301
1941	BOS	A	O		144	.283
1942	BOS	A	O		151	.286
1946	BOS	A	O		142	.316
1947	BOS	A	O		136	.283
1948	BOS	A	O		155	.285
1949	BOS	A	O		145	.307
1950	BOS	A	O		141	.328
1951	BOS	A	O		146	.296
1952	BOS	A	O		128	.294
1953	BOS	A	H		3	.333
	BRTR				1399	.298

DI MAGGIO, JOSEPH PAUL "JOLTIN' JOE"
OR "THE YANKEE CLIPPER"
B.NOV.25,1914 MARTINEZ,CAL.

YR	CL	LEA	POS	GP	G	REC
1936	NY	A	O		138	.323
1937	NY	A	O		151	.346
1938	NY	A	O		145	.324
1939	NY	A	O		120	.381
1940	NY	A	O		132	.352
1941	NY	A	O		139	.357
1942	NY	A	O		154	.305
1946	NY	A	O		132	.290
1947	NY	A	O		141	.315
1948	NY	A	O		153	.320
1949	NY	A	O		76	.346
1950	NY	A	1-O		139	.301
1951	NY	A	O		116	.263
	BRTR				1736	.325

DI MAGGIO, VINCENT PAUL "VINCE"
B.SEPT.6,1912 MARTINEZ,CAL.

YR	CL	LEA	POS	GP	G	REC
1937	BOS	N	O		132	.256
1938	BOS	N	O		150	.228
1939	CIN	N	O		8	.071
1940	CIN	N	O		2	.250
	PIT	N	O		110	.289
1941	PIT	N	O		151	.267
1942	PIT	N	O		143	.238
1943	PIT	N	S-O		157	.248
1944	PIT	N	3-O		109	.240
1945	PHI	N	O		127	.257
1946	PHI	N	O		6	.211
	NY	N	O		15	.000
	BRTR				1110	.249

DIMARIA, JOSEPH FRANKLIN
(PLAYED UNDER NAME OF
JOSEPH FRANKLIN DEMAREE)

DIMITRIHOFF, DIMITRI IVANOVICH
(PLAYED UNDER NAME OF
ALEXANDER JOHN SCHAUER)

DINEEN, KERRY MICHAEL
B.JULY 1,1952 ENGLEWOOD,N.J.

YR	CL	LEA	POS	GP	G	REC
1975	NY	A	O		7	.364
1976	NY	A	O		4	.286
	BLTL				11	.345

DINGES, VANCE GEORGE
B.MAY 29,1917 ELIZABETH,N.J.

YR	CL	LEA	POS	GP	G	REC
1945	PHI	N	1-O		109	.287
1946	PHI	N	1-O		50	.308
	BLTL				159	.291

DINNEEN, WILLIAM HENRY "BIG BILL"
B.APR.5,1876 SYRACUSE,N.Y.
D.JAN.13,1955

YR	CL	LEA	POS	GP	G	REC
1898	WAS	N	P	26	27	9-16
1899	WAS	N	P	36		14-18
1900	BOS	N	P		37	21-16
1901	BOS	N	P		40	16-19
1902	BOS	A	P-O	42	44	21-20 .134
1903	BOS	A	P		34	21-11
1904	BOS	A	P		39	24-15
1905	BOS	A	P		31	14-14
1906	BOS	A	P		28	8-19
1907	BOS	A	P		7	0- 4
	STL	A	P		22	7-11
1908	STL	A	P		27	14- 7
1909	STL	A	P		17	6- 7
	BRTR			386	389	175-177 .193

DIORIO, RONALD MICHAEL "MIKE"
B.JULY 15,1946 WATERBURY,CONN.

YR	CL	LEA	POS	GP	G	REC
1973	PHI	N	P		23	0- 0
1974	PHI	N	P		2	0- 0
	BRTR				25	0- 0

DI PIETRO, ROBERT LOUIS PAUL
B.SEPT.1,1927 SAN FRANCISCO,CAL

YR	CL	LEA	POS	GP	G	REC
1951	BOS	A	O		4	.091
BRTR						

DISCH, GEORGE CHARLES
B.MAR.15,1879 BENTON CO.,MO.

YR	CL	LEA	POS	GP	G	REC
1905	DET	A	P		8	0- 2

DISTASO, ALEC JOHN
B.DEC.23,1948 LOS ANGELES,CAL.

YR	CL	LEA	POS	GP	G	REC
1969	CHI	N	P		2	0- 0
BRTR						

DISTEL, GEORGE ADAM
B.APR.15,1896 MADISON,IND.
D.FEB.12,1967 MADISON,IND.

YR	CL	LEA	POS	GP	G	REC
1918	STL	N	2-S		8	.176

DITMAR, ARTHUR JOHN "ART"
B.APR.3,1929 REVERE,MASS.

YR	CL	LEA	POS	GP	G	REC
1954	PHI	A	P		14	1- 4
1955	KC	A	P		35	12-12
1956	KC	A	P		44	12-22
1957	NY	A	P		46	8- 3
1958	NY	A	P		38	9- 8
1959	NY	A	P		38	13- 9
1960	NY	A	P	34	36	15- 9
1961	NY	A	P		12	2- 3
	KC	A	P		20	0- 5
1962	KC	A	P		6	0- 2
BRTR				287	289	72-77

DITTMER, JOHN DOUGLAS "JACK"
B.JAN.10,1928 ELKADER,IOWA

YR	CL	LEA	POS	GP	G	REC
1952	BOS	N	2		93	.193
1953	MIL	N	2		138	.266
1954	MIL	N	2		66	.245
1955	MIL	N	2		38	.125
1956	MIL	N	2		44	.245
1957	DET	A	2-3		16	.227
BLTR					395	.232

DIXON, JOHN CRAIG "SONNY"
B.NOV.5,1924 CHARLOTTE,N.C.

YR	CL	LEA	POS	GP	G	REC
1953	WAS	A	P		43	5- 8
1954	WAS	A	P		16	1- 2
	PHI	A	P		38	5- 7
1955	KC	A	P		2	0- 0
1956	NY	A	P		3	0- 1
BBTR					102	11-18

DIXON, LEO MICHAEL
B.SEPT.6,1897 CHICAGO,ILL.

YR	CL	LEA	POS	GP	G	REC
1925	STL	A	C		76	.224
1926	STL	A	C		33	.191
1927	STL	A	C		36	.194
1929	CIN	N	C		14	.167
BRTR					159	.206

DOAK, WILLIAM LEOPOLD "SPITTIN' BILL"
B.JAN.28,1891 PITTSBURGH,PA.
D.NOV.26,1954

YR	CL	LEA	POS	GP	G	REC
1912	CIN	N	P		1	0- 0
1913	STL	N	P		15	2- 8
1914	STL	N	P		36	19- 6
1915	STL	N	P		38	16-18
1916	STL	N	P		29	12- 8
1917	STL	N	P		44	16-20
1918	STL	N	P		31	9-15
1919	STL	N	P		31	13-14
1920	STL	N	P		39	20-12
1921	STL	N	P		32	15- 6
1922	STL	N	P		37	11-13
1923	STL	N	P		30	8-13
1924	STL	N	P		11	2- 1
	BRO	N	P		21	11- 5
1927	BRO	N	P		27	11- 8
1928	BRO	N	P		28	3- 8
1929	STL	N	P		3	1- 2
BRTR					453	169-157

DOAN, WALTER RUDOLPH
B.MAR.12,1887 BELLEVUE,IDAHO
D.OCT.19,1935 W.BRANDYWINE,PA.

YR	CL	LEA	POS	GP	G	REC
1909	CLE	A	P-O	1	4	0- 1
						.167
1910	CLE	A	P		6	0- 0
BLTR				7	10	0- 1
						.188

DOBB, JOHN KENNETH "LEFTY"
B.NOV.15,1901 MUSKEGON,MICH.

YR	CL	LEA	POS	GP	G	REC
1924	CHI	A	P		2	0- 0
TL						

DOBBEK, DANIEL JOHN "DAN"
B.DEC.6,1934 ONTONAGON,MICH.

YR	CL	LEA	POS	GP	G	REC
1959	WAS	A	O		16	.250
1960	WAS	A	O		110	.218
1961	MIN	A	O		72	.168
BLTR					198	.208

DOBBS, JOHN GORDON
B.JUNE 3,1876 CHATTANOOGA,TENN.
D.SEPT.9,1934

YR	CL	LEA	POS	GP	G	REC
1901	CIN	N	O		108	.276
1902	CIN	N	O		63	.287
	CHI	N	O		59	.310
1903	CHI	N	O		16	.230
	BRO	N	O		110	.237
1904	BRO	N	O		95	.248
1905	BRO	N	O		123	.254
BLTR					574	.263

DOBENS, RAYMOND JOSEPH
B.JULY 28,1906 NASHUA,N.H.

YR	CL	LEA	POS	GP	G	REC
1929	BOS	A	P		11	0- 0
BLTL						

DOBERNIC, ANDREW JOSEPH "JESS"
B.NOV.20,1918 MT.OLIVE,ILL.

YR	CL	LEA	POS	GP	G	REC
1939	CHI	A	P		4	0- 1
1948	CHI	N	P		54	7- 2
1949	CHI	N	P		4	0- 0
	CIN	N	P		14	0- 0
BRTR					76	7- 3

DOBSON, CHARLES THOMAS "CHUCK"
B.JAN.10,1944 KANSAS CITY,MO.

YR	CL	LEA	POS	GP	G	REC
1966	KC	A	P		14	4- 6
1967	KC	A	P	32	33	10-10
1968	OAK	A	P		35	12-14
1969	OAK	A	P		35	15-13
1970	OAK	A	P		41	16-15
1971	OAK	A	P		30	15- 5
1973	OAK	A	P		1	0- 1
1974	CAL	A	P		5	2- 3
1975	CAL	A	P		9	0- 2
BRTR				202	203	74-69

DOBSON, JOSEPH GORDON "JOE" OR "BURRHEAD"
B.JAN.20,1917 DURANT,OKLA.

YR	CL	LEA	POS	GP	G	REC
1939	CLE	A	P		35	2- 3
1940	CLE	A	P		40	3- 7
1941	BOS	A	P		27	12- 5
1942	BOS	A	P		30	11- 9
1943	BOS	A	P		25	7-11
1946	BOS	A	P		32	13- 7
1947	BOS	A	P		33	18- 8
1948	BOS	A	P		38	16-10
1949	BOS	A	P		33	14-12
1950	BOS	A	P		39	15-10
1951	CHI	A	P		28	7- 6
1952	CHI	A	P		29	14-10
1953	CHI	A	P		23	5- 5
1954	BOS	A	P		2	0- 0
BRTR					414	137-103

DOBSON, PATRICK EDWARD "PAT"
B.FEB.12,1942 DEPEW,N.Y.

YR	CL	LEA	POS	GP	G	REC
1967	DET	A	P		28	1- 2
1968	DET	A	P		47	5- 8
1969	DET	A	P		49	5-10
1970	SD	N	P		38	14-15
1971	BAL	A	P		38	20- 8
1972	BAL	A	P		38	16-18
1973	ATL	N	P		12	3- 7
	NY	A	P		22	9- 8
1974	NY	A	P		39	19-15
1975	NY	A	P		33	11-14
1976	CLE	A	P		35	16-12
BRTR					381	119-117

DOBY, LAWRENCE EUGENE "LARRY"
B.DEC.13,1924 CAMDEN,S.C.

YR	CL	LEA	POS	GP	G	REC
1947	CLE	A	1-2-S		29	.156
1948	CLE	A	O		121	.301
1949	CLE	A	O		147	.280
1950	CLE	A	O		142	.326
1951	CLE	A	O		134	.295
1952	CLE	A	O		140	.276
1953	CLE	A	O		149	.263
1954	CLE	A	O		153	.272
1955	CLE	A	O		131	.291
1956	CHI	A	O		140	.268
1957	CHI	A	O		119	.288
1958	CLE	A	O		89	.283
1959	DET	A	O		18	.218
	CHI	A	1-O		21	.241
BLTR					1533	.283

DOCKINS, GEORGE WOODROW "LEFTY"
B.MAY 5,1917 CLYDE,KAN.

YR	CL	LEA	POS	GP	G	REC
1945	STL	N	P		31	8- 6
1947	BRO	N	P		4	0- 0
BLTL					35	8- 6

DODD, ONA MELVIN
B.OCT.14,1886 SPRINGTOWN,TEX.
D.MAR.31,1929

YR	CL	LEA	POS	GP	G	REC
1912	PIT	N	2		5	.000
BRTR						

DODGE, JOHN LEWIS
B.APR.27,1893 BOLIVAR,TENN.
D.JUNE 19,1916

YR	CL	LEA	POS	GP	G	REC
1912	PHI	N	2-S-3		30	.120
1913	PHI	N	3		3	.333
	CIN	N	3		94	.243
BRTR					127	.215

DODGE, SAMUEL EDWARD
B.DEC.19,1899 PHILADELPHIA,PA.

YR	CL	LEA	POS	GP	G	REC
1921	BOS	A	P		1	0- 0
1922	BOS	A	P		3	0- 1
BRTR					4	0- 1

DOE, ALFRED GEORGE "COUNT"
B.APR.8,1864 GLOUCESTER,MASS.
D.OCT.4,1938

YR	CL	LEA	POS	GP	G	REC
1890	BUF	P	P		1	0- 1
	PIT	P	P		1	0- 1
					2	0- 2

DOERR, ROBERT PERSHING "BOBBY"
B.APR.7,1918 LOS ANGELES,CAL.

YR	CL	LEA	POS	GP	G	REC
1937	BOS	A	2		55	.224
1938	BOS	A	2		145	.289
1939	BOS	A	2		127	.318
1940	BOS	A	2		151	.291
1941	BOS	A	2		132	.282
1942	BOS	A	2		144	.290
1943	BOS	A	2		155	.270
1944	BOS	A	2		125	.325
1946	BOS	A	2		151	.271
1947	BOS	A	2		146	.258
1948	BOS	A	2		140	.285
1949	BOS	A	2		139	.309
1950	BOS	A	2		149	.294
1951	BOS	A	2		106	.289
BRTR					1865	.288

DOHENY, EDWARD R.
B.NOV.24,1874 NORTHFIELD,VT.
D.DEC.29,1916

YR	CL	LEA	POS	GP	G	REC
1895	NY	N	P		3	0- 3
1896	NY	N	P		17	7- 7
1897	NY	N	P		10	6- 4
1898	NY	N	P		28	8-19
1899	NY	N	P		35	14-16
1900	NY	N	P		18	4-14
1901	NY	N	P		9	2- 4
	PIT	N	P		11	6- 3
1902	PIT	N	P		21	17- 4
1903	PIT	N	P		27	16- 8
BLTL					179	80-82

DOHERTY, JOHN MICHAEL
B.AUG.22,1951 WOBURN,MASS.

YR	CL	LEA	POS	GP	G	REC
1974	CAL	A	1		74	.256
1975	CAL	A	1		30	.202
BLTL					104	.240

DOLAN, ALVIN JAMES "COZY"
(REAL NAME JAMES ALBERTS)
B.DEC.6,1882 OSKOSH,WIS.
D.DEC.10,1958

YR	CL	LEA	POS	GP	G	REC
1909	CIN	N	3		3	.167
1911	NY	A	3		19	.304
1912	NY	A	3		17	.200
	PHI	N	3		11	.280
1913	PHI	N	3		55	.262
	PIT	N	3		35	.203
1914	STL	N	3-O		126	.240
1915	STL	N	O		111	.280
1922	NY	N	H		1	.000
BRTR					378	.252

DOLAN, E. L. "BIDDY"

YR	CL	LEA	POS	GP	G	REC
1914	IND	F	1		31	.223
BR						

DOLAN, JOHN
B.SEPT.12,1867 NEWPORT,KY.
D.MAY 8,1948

YR	CL	LEA	POS	GP	G	REC
1890	CIN	N	P		2	1 -1
1891	COL	AA	P	27	28	13-10
1893	STL	N	P		3	0- 2
1895	CHI	N	P		2	0- 1
		TR		34	35	14-14

DOLAN, JOSEPH
B.FEB.24,1873 BALTIMORE,MD.
D.MAR.24,1938

YR	CL	LEA	POS	G	REC
1896	LOU	N	S	44	.219
1897	LOU	N	2-S	35	.210
1899	PHI	N	2	60	.256
1900	PHI	N	2-3	70	.194
1901	PHI	N	2	5	.071
	PHI	A	S-3	97	.219
		TR		311	.215

DOLAN, PATRICK HENRY "COZY"
B.DEC.3,1872 CAMBRIDGE,MASS.
D.MAR.29,1907

YR	CL	LEA	POS	GP	G	REC
1892	WAS	N	P		5	2- 2
1895	BOS	N	P		23	11- 9
1896	BOS	N	P		6	1- 4
1900	CHI	N	O		13	.205
1901	CHI	N	O		43	.262
	BRO	N	O		62	.280
1902	BRO	N	O		140	.283
1903	CHI	A	1		28	.250
	CIN	N	O		93	.288
1904	CIN	N	1-O		126	.284
1905	CIN	N	1		22	.234
	BOS	N	O		112	.275
1906	BOS	N	O		152	.248
		BLTL		34	825	14-15
						.271

DOLAN, THOMAS J.
B.JAN.10,1859 NEW YORK,N.Y.
D.JAN.16,1913

YR	CL	LEA	POS	GP	G	REC
1879	STL	N	C		1	.000
1882	BUF	N	C-3-O		22	.157
1883	STL	AA	P-C-O	1	78	0- 0
						.222
1884	STL	AA	C		35	.263
	STL	U	C-3-O		20	.194
1885	STL	N	C		3	.222
1886	STL	N	C		15	.250
	BAL	AA	C		37	.153
1888	STL	AA	C		11	.194
1891	STL	AA	C		1	.000
		TR		1	223	0- 0
						.203

DOLE, W. C.

YR	CL	LEA	POS	G	REC
1875	NH	NA	O	1	-

DOLJACK, FRANK JOSEPH "DOLIE"
B.OCT.10,1908 CLEVELAND,OHIO
D.JAN.23,1948

YR	CL	LEA	POS	G	REC
1930	DET	A	O	20	.257
1931	DET	A	O	63	.278
1932	DET	A	O	8	.385
1933	DET	A	O	42	.286
1934	DET	A	O	56	.233
1943	CLE	A	O	3	.000
		BRTR		192	.269

DOLL, ARTHUR JAMES "MOOSE"
B.MAY 7,1913 CHICAGO,ILL.

YR	CL	LEA	POS	GP	G	REC
1935	BOS	N	C		3	.100
1936	BOS	N	P		1	0- 1
1938	BOS	N	P		3	0- 0
		BRTR		4	7	0- 1
						.154

DOMEC, JOSE ROSARIO (CARDENAL)
(SEE JOSE ROSARIO
DOMEC CARDENAL)

DONAHUE, CHARLES MICHAEL "SHE"
B.JUNE 29,1877 OSWEGO,N.Y.
D.AUG.28,1947

YR	CL	LEA	POS	G	REC
1904	STL	N	S	4	.267
	PHI	N	S-3	56	.215
		BRTR		60	.219

DONAHUE, FRANCIS ROSTELL "RED"
B.JAN.23,1873 WATERBURY,CONN.
D.AUG.25,1913

YR	CL	LEA	POS	G	REC
1893	NY	N	P	2	0- 1
1895	STL	N	P	1	0- 1
1896	STL	N	P	33	7-23
1897	STL	N	P	44	11-33
1898	PHI	N	P	34	17-16
1899	PHI	N	P	34	22- 7
1900	PHI	N	P	26	16-10
1901	PHI	N	P	35	20-13
1902	STL	A	P	35	22-11
1903	STL	A	P	14	6- 4
	CLE	A	P	19	6-13
1904	CLE	A	P	35	18-14
1905	CLE	A	P	20	6-11
1906	DET	A	P	29	13-14
		BRTR		361	164-171

DONAHUE, JAMES AUGUSTUS
B.JAN.8,1862 LOCKPORT,ILL.
D.APR.19,1935

YR	CL	LEA	POS	G	REC
1886	MET	AA	C-O	50	.201
1887	MET	AA	C	60	.345
1888	KC	AA	C	87	.241
1889	KC	AA	C	67	.238
1891	COL	AA	C	77	.217
		TR		341	.245

DONAHUE, JOHN AUGUSTUS "JIGGS"
B.JULY 13,1879 SPRINGFIELD,OHIO
D.JULY 19,1913

YR	CL	LEA	POS	G	REC
1900	PIT	N	C	3	.200
1901	PIT	N	C	2	.000
	MIL	A	C	37	.305
1902	STL	A	C-1	29	.250
1904	CHI	A	1	102	.251
1905	CHI	A	1	149	.287
1906	CHI	A	1	154	.257
1907	CHI	A	1	157	.259
1908	CHI	A	1	93	.204
1909	CHI	A	1	2	.000
	WAS	A	1	84	.237
		BLTL		812	.256

DONAHUE, JOHN FRANCIS "JIGGS"
B.APR.19,1894 ROXBURY,MASS.
D.OCT.3,1949

YR	CL	LEA	POS	G	REC
1923	BOS	A	O	10	.343
		BBTR			

DONAHUE, JOHN STEPHEN MICHAEL "DEACON"
B.JUNE 23,1920 CHICAGO,ILL.

YR	CL	LEA	POS	G	REC
1943	PHI	N	P	2	0- 0
1944	PHI	N	P	6	0- 2
		BRTR		8	0- 2

DONAHUE, PATRICK WILLIAM
B.NOV.8,1884 SPRINGFIELD,OHIO
D.JAN.31,1966 SPRINGFIELD,OHIO

YR	CL	LEA	POS	G	REC
1908	BOS	A	C	35	.198
1909	BOS	A	C	64	.239
1910	BOS	A	C	2	.000
	PHI	A	C	16	.143
	CLE	A	C	2	.167
		BRTR		119	.212

DONAHUE, TIMOTHY CORNELIUS "BRIDGET"
B.JUNE 8,1870 RAYNHAM,MASS.
D.JUNE 12,1902

YR	CL	LEA	POS	G	REC
1891	BOS	AA	C	3	.000
1895	CHI	N	C	62	.271
1896	CHI	N	C	54	.226
1897	CHI	N	C	53	.234
1898	CHI	N	C	117	.236
1899	CHI	N	C	90	.250
1900	CHI	N	C	65	.239
1902	WAS	A	C	3	.250
		BLTR		447	.241

DONALD, RICHARD ATLEY "SWAMPY"
B.AUG.19,1912 MORTON,MISS.

YR	CL	LEA	POS	G	REC
1938	NY	A	P	2	0- 1
1939	NY	A	P	24	13- 3
1940	NY	A	P	24	8- 3
1941	NY	A	P	22	9- 5
1942	NY	A	P	20	11- 3
1943	NY	A	P	22	6- 4
1944	NY	A	P	30	13-10
1945	NY	A	P	9	5- 4
		BLTR		153	65-33

DONALDS, EDWARD ALEXANDER "SKIPPER"
B.JUNE 22,1885 GALLIPOLIS,OHIO
D.JULY 3,1950

YR	CL	LEA	POS	G	REC
1912	CIN	N	P	1	1- 0
		BRTR			

DONALDSON, JOHN DAVID
B.MAY 5,1943 CHARLOTTE,N.C.

YR	CL	LEA	POS	G	REC
1966	KC	A	2	15	.133
1967	KC	A	2-S	105	.276
1968	OAK	A	2-S-3	127	.220
1969	OAK	A	2	12	.077
	SEA	A	2-S-3	95	.234
1970	OAK	A	2-S-3	41	.247
1974	OAK	A	2-3	10	.133
		BLTR		405	.238

DONDERO, LEONARD PETER
B.SEPT.19,1903 NEWARK,CAL.

YR	CL	LEA	POS	G	REC
1929	STL	A	3	19	.194
		BRTR			

DONLIN, MICHAEL JOSEPH "TURKEY MIKE"
B.MAY 30,1878 ERIE,PA.
D.SEPT.24,1933 HOLLYWOOD,CAL.

YR	CL	LEA	POS	GP	G	REC
1899	STL	N	P-O	1	67	0- 0
						.329
1900	STL	N	1		77	.327
1901	BAL	A	1-O		122	.340
1902	CIN	N	P-S-O	1	33	0- 0
						.294
1903	CIN	N	O		124	.351
1904	CIN	N	O		59	.356
	NY	N	O		37	.280
1905	NY	N	O		150	.356
1906	NY	N	O		30	.314
1908	NY	N	O		155	.334
1911	NY	N	O		12	.333
	BOS	N	O		56	.318
1912	PIT	N	O		77	.316
1914	NY	N	O		35	.161
		BLTL		2	1034	0- 0
						.334

DONNELLEY, FRANCIS N.
B.OCT.7,1869 TAMAROA,ILL.
D.FEB.3,1953

YR	CL	LEA	POS	G	REC
1893	CHI	N	P	6	3- 1
1894	CHI	N	P	1	0- 0
				7	3- 1

DONNELLY, EDWARD "BUCK"
B.JULY 29,1880 HAMPTON,N.Y.
D.NOV.28,1957 RUTLAND,VT.
(REAL NAME EDWARD O'DONNELL)

YR	CL	LEA	POS	GP	G	REC
1911	BOS	N	P		5	3- 2
1912	BOS	N	P	37	38	5-10
		BRTR		42	43	8-12

DONNELLY, EDWARD VINCENT
B.DEC.10,1934 ALLEN,MICH.

YR	CL	LEA	POS	G	REC
1959	CHI	N	P	9	1- 1
		BRTR			

DONNELLY, JAMES B.
B.JULY 19,1865 NEW HAVEN,CONN.
D.MAR.5,1915

YR	CL	LEA	POS	G	REC
1884	KC	U	C-3	6	.130
	IND	AA	S-3	40	.249
1885	DET	N	1-3	55	.232
1886	KC	N	P-3	113	0- 1
					.201
1887	WAS	N	3	117	.229
1888	WAS	N	3	122	.201
1889	WAS	N	3	4	.154
1890	STL	AA	3	11	.344
1891	COL	AA	3	17	.241
1896	BAL	N	3	104	.330
1897	PIT	N	3	43	.177
	NY	N	3	23	.205
1898	STL	N	3	1	1.000
		BR		656	0- 1
					.234

DONNELLY, SYLVESTER URBAN "BLIX"
B.JAN.21,1915 OLIVIA,MINN.
D.JUNE 20,1976 OLIVIA,MINN.

YR	CL	LEA	POS	GP	G	REC
1944	STL	N	P		27	2- 1
1945	STL	N	P		31	8-10
1946	STL	N	P		13	1- 2
	PHI	N	P		12	3- 4
1947	PHI	N	P		38	4- 6
1948	PHI	N	P		26	5- 7
1949	PHI	N	P		23	2- 1
1950	PHI	N	P		14	2- 4
1951	BOS	N	P		6	0- 1
		BRTR			190	27-36

DONNELLY, T. J.

YR	CL	LEA	POS	GP	G	REC
1871	KEK	NA	3-O		9	.233
1873	NAT	NA	2-S-O		30	-
1874	PHI	NA	2-S-O		5	-
					44	-

DONOHUE, JAMES THOMAS "JIM"
B.OCT.31,1938 ST.LOUIS,MO.

YR	CL	LEA	POS	GP	G	REC
1961	DET	A	P		14	1- 1
	LA	A	P		38	4- 6
1962	LA	A	P		12	1- 0
	MIN	A	P		6	0- 1
		BRTR			70	6- 8

DONOHUE, JOSEPH F.
B.1869 SYRACUSE,N.Y.
D.NOV.12,1894

YR	CL	LEA	POS	GP	G	REC
1891	PHI	N	O		6	.317

DONOHUE, PETER JOSEPH
B.NOV.5,1900 ATHENS,TEX.

YR	CL	LEA	POS	GP	G	REC
1921	CIN	N	P		21	7- 6
1922	CIN	N	P		33	18- 9
1923	CIN	N	P		42	21-15
1924	CIN	N	P	35	36	16- 9
1925	CIN	N	P	42	43	21-14
1926	CIN	N	P		47	20-14
1927	CIN	N	P		33	6-16
1928	CIN	N	P		23	7-11
1929	CIN	N	P		32	10-13
1930	CIN	N	P		8	1- 3
	NY	N	P		18	7- 6
1931	NY	N	P		4	0- 1
	CLE	A	P		2	0- 0
1932	BOS	N	P		4	0- 1
		BRTR		344	346	134-118

DONOSO, LINO GALATA
B.SEPT.23,1922 HAVANA,CUBA

YR	CL	LEA	POS	GP	G	REC
1955	PIT	N	P		25	4- 6
1956	PIT	N	P		3	0- 0
		BLTL			28	4- 6

DONOVAN, FREDERICK M.
B.CLEVELAND,OHIO

YR	CL	LEA	POS	GP	G	REC
1895	CLE	N	C		3	.083

DONOVAN, JEREMIAH FRANCIS
B.SEPT.3,1876 LOCK HAVEN,PA.
D.JUNE 27,1938 ST.PETERSBURG, FLA.

YR	CL	LEA	POS	GP	G	REC
1906	PHI	N	C		53	.199
		BRTR				

DONOVAN, MICHAEL BERCHMAN
B.OCT.18,1881 BROOKLYN,N.Y.
D.FEB.3,1938 NEW YORK,N.Y.

YR	CL	LEA	POS	GP	G	REC
1904	CLE	A	S		2	..000
1908	NY	A	3		5	.157
		BRTR			7	.143

DONOVAN, PATRICK JOSEPH "PATSY"
B.MAR.16,1865 COUNTY CORK, IRELAND
D.DEC.25,1953 LAWRENCE,MASS.

YR	CL	LEA	POS	GP	G	REC
1890	BOS	N	O		32	.245
	BRO	N	O		26	.380
1891	LOU	AA	O		98	.319
	WAS	AA	O		17	.200
1892	WAS	N	O		40	.252
	PIT	N	O		88	.311
1893	PIT	N	O		110	.331
1894	PIT	N	O		133	.306
1895	PIT	N	O		126	.316
1896	PIT	N	O		129	.316
1897	PIT	N	M-O		120	.326
1898	PIT	N	O		147	.302
1899	PIT	N	M-O		123	.296
1900	STL	N	O		127	.324
1901	STL	N	O		129	.294
1902	STL	N	M-O		126	.309
1903	STL	N	M-O		105	.327
1904	WAS	A	M-O		125	.239
1906	BRO	N	M-O		7	.238
1907	BRO	N	M-O		1	.000
		BLTL			1809	.304

NON-PLAYING MANAGER BRO(N) 1908
BOS(A) 1910-11

DONOVAN, RICHARD EDWARD "DICK"
B.DEC.7,1927 BOSTON,MASS.

YR	CL	LEA	POS	GP	G	REC
1950	BOS	N	P		10	0- 2
1951	BOS	N	P		8	0- 0
1952	BOS	N	P		7	0- 2
1954	DET	A	P		2	0- 0
1955	CHI	A	P	29	40	15- 9
1956	CHI	A	P	34	44	12-10
1957	CHI	A	P	28	30	16- 6
1958	CHI	A	P		34	15-14
1959	CHI	A	P		31	9-10
1960	CHI	A	P		33	6- 1
1961	WAS	A	P	23	24	10-10
1962	CLE	A	P		34	20-10
1963	CLE	A	P	30	31	11-13
1964	CLE	A	P	30	31	7- 9
1965	CLE	A	P		12	1- 3
		BLTR		345	371	122-99

DONOVAN, THOMAS JOSEPH
B.JULY 7,1879 LOCK HAVEN,PA.
D.FEB.20,1955 WILLIAMSPORT,PA.

YR	CL	LEA	POS	GP	G	REC
1901	BRO	N	O		18	.253
		BRTR				

DONOVAN, WILLARD EARL
B.JULY 6,1916 MAYWOOD,ILL.

YR	CL	LEA	POS	GP	G	REC
1942	BOS	N	P		31	3- 6
1943	BOS	N	P		7	1- 0
		BRTL			38	4- 6

DONOVAN, WILLIAM EDWARD "WILD BILL"
B.OCT.13,1876 LAWRENCE,MASS.
D.DEC.9,1923 FORSYTH,N.Y.

YR	CL	LEA	POS	GP	G	REC
1898	WAS	N	P-O	11	30	1- 6
						.178
1899	BRO	N	P		4	1- 2
1900	BRO	N	P		5	1- 2
1901	BRO	N	P		41	25-15
1902	BRO	N	P-1	34	46	17-15
			2-O			.169
1903	DET	A	P	36	39	17-15
1904	DET	A	P	34	44	17-16
1905	DET	A	P	34	46	18-14
1906	DET	A	P	25	28	9-15
1907	DET	A	P	32	37	25- 4
1908	DET	A	P	29	30	18- 7
1909	DET	A	P	21	22	8- 7
1910	DET	A	P		26	18- 7
1911	DET	A	P	20	24	10- 9
1912	DET	A	P		6	1- 0
1915	NY	A	M-P		10	0- 3
1916	NY	A	M-P		1	0- 0
1918	DET	A	P		2	0- 0
		BRTR		369	441	186-137
						.196

NON-PLAYING MANAGER NY(A) 1917
PHI(N) 1921

DOOIN, CHARLES SEBASTIAN "RED"
B.JUNE 12,1879 CINCINNATI,OHIO
D.MAY 14,1952

YR	CL	LEA	POS	GP	G	REC
1902	PHI	N	C-O		87	.228
1903	PHI	N	C		53	.218
1904	PHI	N	C		104	.242
1905	PHI	N	C		108	.250
1906	PHI	N	C		107	.245
1907	PHI	N	C		96	.211
1908	PHI	N	C		132	.248
1909	PHI	N	C		140	.224
1910	PHI	N	M-C		94	.242
1911	PHI	N	M-C		74	.328
1912	PHI	N	M-C		69	.234
1913	PHI	N	M-C		55	.256
1914	PHI	N	M-C		53	.178
1915	CIN	N	C		10	.323
	NY	N	C		46	.218
1916	NY	N	C		15	.118
		BRTR			1243	.240

DOOLAN, MICHAEL JOSEPH "DOC"
(REAL NAME
MICHAEL JOSEPH DOOLITTLE)
B.MAY 7,1880 ASHLAND,PA.
D.NOV.1,1951

YR	CL	LEA	POS	GP	G	REC
1905	PHI	N	S		135	.254
1906	PHI	N	S		154	.230
1907	PHI	N	S		145	.204
1908	PHI	N	S		129	.234
1909	PHI	N	S		147	.219
1910	PHI	N	S		148	.263
1911	PHI	N	S		145	.238
1912	PHI	N	S		146	.258
1913	PHI	N	S		151	.218
1914	BAL	F	S		144	.243
1915	BAL	F	S		119	.195
	CHI	F	S		24	.256
1916	CHI	N	S		28	.211
	NY	N	S		18	.240
1918	BRO	N	2		92	.179
		BRTR			1725	.231

DOOLITTLE, MICHAEL JOSEPH
(PLAYED UNDER NAME OF
MICHAEL JOSEPH DOOLAN)

DOOMS, HARRY E. "JACK"
B.ST.LOUIS,MO.
D.DEC.1899

YR	CL	LEA	POS	GP	G	REC
1892	LOU	N	O		1	.000

DORAN, JOHN F.
B.1873 NEW JERSEY

YR	CL	LEA	POS	GP	G	REC
1891	LOU	AA	P		17	5- 9
		TL				

DORAN, THOMAS J. "LONG TOM"
B.DEC.2,1880 WESTCHESTER CO., N.Y.
D.JUNE 22,1910

YR	CL	LEA	POS	GP	G	REC
1904	BOS	A	C		5	.000
1905	BOS	A	C		3	.000
	DET	A	C		29	.165
1906	BOS	A	C		2	.000
		TR			39	.146

DORAN, WILLIAM JAMES
B.JUN.14,1900 SAN FRANCISCO,CAL

YR	CL	LEA	POS	GP	G	REC
1922	CLE	A	3		3	.500
		BLTR				

DO REGO, ANTONE
(PLAYED UNDER NAME OF
ANTONE REGO)

DORGAN, JEREMIAH F.
B.1856 MERIDEN,CONN.
D.JUNE 10,1891

YR	CL	LEA	POS	GP	G	REC
1880	WOR	N	C-O		9	.229
1882	ATH	AA	C-O		45	.287
1884	IND	AA	O		34	.294
	BRO	AA	C		4	.308
1885	DET	N	O		39	.285
		TR			131	.286

DORGAN, MICHAEL CORNELIUS
B.OCT.2,1853 MIDDLETOWN,CONN.
D.APR.26,1909 SYRACUSE,N.Y.

YR	CL	LEA	POS	GP	G	REC
1877	STL	N	C-S-3-O	60		.308
1879	SYR	N	1-3-O	59		.266
1880	PRO	N	P-3-	1	76	0- 0
			O			.246
1881	WOR	N	1-S-O	51		.254
	DET	N	1-3-O	8		.229
1883	NY	N	P-C-	4	62	0- 1
			O			.235
1884	NY	N	P-C- 14	79		8- 6
			2-O			.276
1885	NY	N	O		88	.325
1886	NY	N	O		118	.292
1887	NY	N	O		71	.295
1890	SYR	AA	O		31	.219
		BRTR		19	703	8- 7
						.273

DORISH, HARRY "FRITZ"
B.JULY 13,1923 SWOYERSVILLE,PA.

YR	CL	LEA	POS	GP	G	REC
1947	BOS	A	P		41	7- 8
1948	BOS	A	P		9	0- 1
1949	BOS	A	P		8	0- 0
1950	STL	A	P	29	30	4- 9
1951	STL	A	P-3	32		5- 6
						.258
1952	CHI	A	P		39	8- 4
1953	CHI	A	P		55	10- 6
1954	CHI	A	P		37	6- 4
1955	CHI	A	P		13	2- 0
	BAL	A	P		35	3- 3
1956	BAL	A	P		13	0- 0
	BOS	A	P		15	0- 2
		BRTR		323	324	45-43
						.157

DORMAN, CHARLES DWIGHT "CURLEY"
B.OCT.3,1905 JACKSONVILLE,ILL.

YR	CL	LEA	POS	GP	G	REC
1928	CLE	A	O		25	.364
		BRTR				

DORMAN, CHARLES WILLIAM
B.APR.23,1898 SAN FRANCISCO,CAL
D.NOV.15,1928 SAN FRANCISCO,CAL

YR	CL	LEA	POS	GP	G	REC
1923	CHI	A	C		1	.500
		BRTR				

DORNER, AUGUSTUS
B.AUG.18,1876 CHAMBERSBURG,PA.
D.MAY 4,1956

YR	CL	LEA	POS	GP	G	REC
1902	CLE	A	P		4	3- 1
1903	CLE	A	P		12	3- 5
1906	CIN	N	P		2	0- 0
	BOS	N	P		34	8-26
1907	BOS	N	P		36	12-16
1908	BOS	N	P		38	8-19
1909	BOS	N	P		5	1- 2
		BRTR		131		35-69

DORR, CHARLES ALBERT "BERT"
B.OMAHA,NEB.
D.JUNE 19,1914

YR	CL	LEA	POS	GP	G	REC
1882	STL	AA	P		8	3- 5

DORSETT, CALVIN LEAVELLE "PREACHER"
B.JUNE 10,1913 LONE OAK,TEX.
D.OCT.22,1970 ELK CITY,OKLA.

YR	CL	LEA	POS	GP	G	REC
1940	CLE	A	P		1	0- 0
1941	CLE	A	P		5	0- 1
1947	CLE	A	P		2	0- 0
		BRTR			8	0- 1

DORSEY, JEREMIAH
B.1885 OAKLAND,CAL.

YR	CL	LEA	POS	GP	G	REC
1911	PIT	N	O		2	.000

DORSEY, MICHAEL JEREMIAH "JERRY"
B.1854 CANADA
D.NOV.3,1938 AUBURN,N.Y.

YR	CL	LEA	POS	GP	G	REC
1884	BAL	U	P-O		2	0- 1
						.000

DOSCHER, JOHN HENRY JR. "JACK"
B.JULY 27,1880 TROY,N.Y.
D.MAY 27,1971 PARK RIDGE,ILL.

YR	CL	LEA	POS	GP	G	REC
1903	CHI	N	P		1	0- 1
	BRO	N	P		3	0- 0
1904	BRO	N	P		2	0- 1
1905	BRO	N	P		11	1- 5
1906	BRO	N	P		2	0- 1
1908	CIN	N	P		6	1- 3
		BLTL		25		2-11

DOSCHER, JOHN HENRY SR. "HERM"
B.DEC.20,1852 NEW YORK,N.Y.
D.MAR.20,1934 BUFFALO,N.Y.

YR	CL	LEA	POS	GP	G	REC
1872	ATL	NA	O		6	.346
1873	ATL	NA	O		1	-
1875	NAT	NA	S-3	21		-
1879	TRO	N	3		46	.223
1881	CLE	N	3		5	.211
1882	CLE	N	3-O		25	.240
					104	-

DOTTER, GARY RICHARD
B.AUG.7,1942 ST.LOUIS,MO.

YR	CL	LEA	POS	GP	G	REC
1961	MIN	A	P		2	0- 0
1963	MIN	A	P		2	0- 0
1964	MIN	A	P		3	0- 0
		BLTL			7	0- 0

DOTTERER, HENRY JOHN "DUTCH"
B.NOV.11,1931 SYRACUSE,N.Y.

YR	CL	LEA	POS	GP	G	REC
1957	CIN	N	C		4	.083
1958	CIN	N	C		11	.250
1959	CIN	N	C		52	.267
1960	CIN	N	C		33	.228
1961	WAS	A	C		7	.263
		BRTR		107		.248

DOTY, ELMER L. "BABE"
B.DEC.17,1867 LYONS,N.Y.
D.NOV.20,1929

YR	CL	LEA	POS	GP	G	REC
1890	TOL	AA	P	1		1- 0
		BRTR				

DOUGHERTY, CHARLES
B.FEB.7,1862 DARLINGTON,WIS.
D.FEB.18,1925

YR	CL	LEA	POS	GP	G	REC
1884	ALT	U	2-S-3-O	23		.259

DOUGHERTY, PATRICK HENRY
B.OCT.27,1876 BOLIVAR,N.Y.
D.APR.30,1940

YR	CL	LEA	POS	GP	G	REC
1902	BOS	A	3-O		106	.335
1903	BOS	A	O		139	.332
1904	BOS	A	O		59	.268
	NY	A	O		96	.289
1905	NY	A	O		116	.263
1906	NY	A	O		12	.170
	CHI	A	O		75	.238
1907	CHI	A	O		148	.270
1908	CHI	A	O		138	.278
1909	CHI	A	O		139	.285
1910	CHI	A	O		127	.248
1911	CHI	A	O		76	.289
		BLTR		1231		.284

DOUGHERTY, THOMAS JAMES "SUGAR BOY"
B.MAY 30,1881 CHICAGO,ILL.
D.NOV.6,1953

YR	CL	LEA	POS	GP	G	REC
1904	CHI	A	P	1		0- 0
		BLTR				

DOUGLAS, CHARLES WILLIAM "WHAMMY"
B.FEB.17,1935 CARRBORO,N.C.

YR	CL	LEA	POS	GP	G	REC
1957	PIT	N	P		11	3- 3
		BRTR				

DOUGLAS, JOHN FRANKLIN
B.SEPT.14,1918 BECKLEY,W.VA.

YR	CL	LEA	POS	GP	G	REC
1945	BRO	N	1		5	.000
		BLTL				

DOUGLAS, PHILIP BROOKS "SHUFFLIN' PHIL"
B.JUNE 17,1890 CEDARTOWN,GA.
D.AUG.1,1952 SEQUATCHIE VALLEY, TENN.

YR	CL	LEA	POS	GP	G	REC
1912	CHI	A	P		3	0- 1
1914	CIN	N	P		45	11-18
1915	CIN	N	P		8	1- 5
	BRO	N	P		20	5- 5
	CHI	N	P		4	1- 1
1917	CHI	N	P		51	14-20
1918	CHI	N	P		25	10- 9
1919	CHI	N	P		25	10- 6
	NY	N	P		8	2- 4
1920	NY	N	P		46	14-10
1921	NY	N	P		40	15-10
1922	NY	N	P		24	11- 4
		BRTR		299		94-93

DOUGLAS, WILLIAM B. "KLONDIKE"
B.MAY 10,1872 BOSTON,PA.
D.DEC.13,1953

YR	CL	LEA	POS	GP	G	REC
1896	PHI	N	O		79	.268
1897	STL	N	C-1-O	127		.327
1898	PHI	N	1		146	.266
1899	PHI	N	C		72	.264
1900	PHI	N	C		45	.306
1901	PHI	N	C		47	.333
1902	PHI	N	C-1-O	107		.235
1903	PHI	N	1		97	.255
1904	PHI	N	1		3	.333
		BLTR		723		.278

DOUGLASS, ASTYANAX SAUNDERS
B.SEPT.19,1899 COVINGTON,TEX.
D.JAN.26,1975 EL PASO,TEX.

YR	CL	LEA	POS	GP	G	REC
1921	CIN	N	C		4	.143
1925	CIN	N	C		7	.176
		BLTR			11	.174

DOUGLASS, LAWRENCE HOWARD
B.JUNE 5,1892 JELLICO,TENN.

YR	CL	LEA	POS	GP	G	REC
1915	BAL	F	P		2	1- 0

DOUTHIT, TAYLOR LEE
B.APR.22,1901 LITTLE ROCK,ARK.

YR	CL	LEA	POS	GP	G	REC
1923	STL	N	O		9	.185
1924	STL	N	O		53	.277
1925	STL	N	O		30	.274
1926	STL	N	O		139	.308
1927	STL	N	O		130	.262
1928	STL	N	O		154	.295
1929	STL	N	O		150	.336
1930	STL	N	O		154	.303
1931	STL	N	O		36	.331
	CIN	N	O		95	.262
1932	CIN	N	O		96	.243
1933	CIN	N	O		1	.000
	CHI	N	O		27	.225
		BRTR		1074		.291

DOW, CLARENCE G.
B.OCT.11,1854 CHARLESTOWN,MASS.
D.MAR.11,1893

YR	CL	LEA	POS	GP	G	REC
1884	BOS	U	O		1	.333

DOWD, JAMES JOSEPH
B.FEB.16,1889 HOLYOKE,MASS.
D.DEC.20,1960

YR	CL	LEA	POS	GP	G	REC
1910	PIT	N	P		1	0- 0

DOWD, JOHN LEO
B.JAN.3,1891 S.WEYMOUTH,MASS.

YR	CL	LEA	POS	GP	G	REC
1912	NY	A	S		10	.194
		BRTR				

DOWD, RAYMOND BERNARD "SNOOKS"
B.DEC.2,1897 SPRINGFIELD,MASS.
D.APR.4,1962

YR	CL	LEA	POS	GP	G	REC
1919	DET	A	H		1	.000
	PHI	A	2-S-3		13	.158
1926	BRO	N	2		2	.000
		BRTR			16	.077

DOWD, THOMAS JEFFERSON "BUTTERMILK TOMMY"
B.APR.20,1869 HOLYOKE,MASS.
D.JULY 2,1933

YR	CL	LEA	POS	GP	G	REC
1891	BOS	AA	O		4	.167
	WAS	AA	2		105	.252
1892	WAS	N	2-3-O		141	.246
1893	STL	N	O		131	.294
1894	STL	N	O		123	.267
1895	STL	N	O		127	.325
1896	STL	N	M-2-O		125	.266
1897	STL	N	M-2-O		35	.269
	PHI	N	O		90	.290
1898	STL	N	O		139	.243
1899	CLE	N	O		146	.275
1901	BOS	A	O		138	.270
		BRTR		1304		.272

DOWIE, JOSEPH E.
B.NEW ORLEANS,LA.
D.SEPT.3,1893

YR	CL	LEA	POS	GP	G	REC
1889	BAL	AA	O		20	.240

DOWLING, DAVID BARCLAY "DAVE"
B.AUG.23,1942 BATON ROUGE,LA.

YR	CL	LEA	POS	GP	G	REC
1964	STL	N	P		1	0- 0
1966	CHI	N	P		1	1- 0
		BRTL			2	1- 0

```
YR  CL LEA POS  GP   G   REC
```

DOWLING, HENRY PETER "PETE"
B.KENTUCKY
D.JUNE 30,1905
```
1897 LOU N P         4   1- 3
1898 LOU N P        35  13-17
1899 LOU N P        35  13-18
1901 MIL A P        10   3- 5
     CLE A P        34   8-15
     TL            118  38-58
```

DOWLING, RODNEY J.
(PLAYED UNDER NAME OF
ROBERT J. GLENALVIN)

DOWNEY, ALEXANDER CUMMINGS "RED"
B.FEB.6,1889 AURORA,IND.
D.JULY 10,1949
```
1909 BRO N O        19  .256
     BLTL
```

DOWNEY, THOMAS EDWARD
B.JAN.1,1884 LAWRENCE,MASS.
D.AUG.3,1961 PASSAIC,N.J.
```
1909 CIN N S       119  .231
1910 CIN N S-3     109  .270
1911 CIN N S       106  .261
1912 PHI N 3        54  .292
     CHI N 3        13  .182
1914 BUF F 2-S     151  .223
1915 BUF F 2-3      90  .199
     BRTR          642  .241
```

DOWNING, ALPHONSO ERWIN "AL"
B.JUNE 28,1941 TRENTON,N.J.
```
1961 NY  A P         5   0- 1
1962 NY  A P         1   0- 0
1963 NY  A P        24  13- 5
1964 NY  A P    37  40  13- 8
1965 NY  A P    35  36  12-14
1966 NY  A P        30  10-11
1967 NY  A P        31  14-10
1968 NY  A P        15   3- 3
1969 NY  A P        30   7- 5
1970 OAK A P        10   3- 3
     MIL A P        17   2-10
1971 LA  N P        37  20- 9
1972 LA  N P        31   9- 9
1973 LA  N P        30   9- 9
1974 LA  N P        21   5- 6
1975 LA  N P        22   2- 1
1976 LA  N P        17   1- 2
     BRTL   393 397 123-106
```

DOWNING, BRIAN JAY
B.OCT.9,1950 LOS ANGELES,CAL.
```
1973 CHI A C-3-O    34  .178
1974 CHI A C-O     108  .225
1975 CHI A C       138  .240
1976 CHI A C-O     104  .256
     BRTR          384  .237
```

DOWNS, DAVID RALPH "DAVE"
B.JUNE 21,1952 LOGAN,UTAH
```
1972 PHI N P         4   1- 1
     BRTR
```

DOWNS, JEROME WILLIS "RED"
B.AUG.23,1883 NEOLA,IOWA
D.OCT.12,1939
```
1907 DET A 2-O     105  .219
1908 DET A 2        84  .221
1912 BRO N 2         9  .250
     CHI N 2        43  .263
     BRTR          241  .227
```

DOWSE, THOMAS JOSEPH
B.AUG.12,1866 IRELAND
D.DEC.14,1946 RIVERSIDE,CAL.
```
1890 CLE N O        40  .207
1891 COL AA C       55  .217
1892 CIN N P-C   1  40   0- 1
                        .173
     CIN N C         1  .000
     PHI N C        16  .170
     WAS N C-O       6  .261
     BRTR      1 158   0- 1
                        .196
```

DOYLE, CORNELIUS J.
B.1858 HOLYOKE,MASS.
D.JAN.18,1927
```
1883 PHI N O        16  .203
1890 TOL AA 3        1  .000
                    17  .197
```

DOYLE, EDWARD H.
B.ILLINOIS
D.FEB.6,1929
```
1882 STL AA P        3   0- 3
```

DOYLE, HOWARD JAMES "DANNY"
B.JAN.24,1917 MCLOUD,OKLA.
```
1943 BOS A C        13  .209
     BBTR
```

DOYLE, JAMES FRANCIS
B.DEC.25,1881 SYRACUSE,N.Y.
D.FEB.1,1912
```
1910 CIN N 3         7  .191
1911 CHI N 3       127  .282
     BRTR          134  .277
```

DOYLE, JESS HERBERT
B.APR.14,1898 KNOXVILLE,TENN.
D.APR.5,1961
```
1925 DET A P        45   4- 7
1926 DET A P         2   0- 0
1927 DET A P         7   0- 0
1931 STL A P         1   0- 0
     BRTR           55   4- 7
```

DOYLE, JOHN A.
B.NOVA SCOTIA,CANADA
```
1884 PIT AA O       23  .203
```

DOYLE, JOHN JOSEPH "JACK"
B.OCT.25,1870 KILLORGLIN,IRE.
D.DEC.31,1958 HOLYOKE,MASS.
```
1889 COL AA C-2-O   11  .355
1890 COL AA P-C  1  76   1- 0
                        .272
1891 CLE N C-3-O    64  .263
1892 CLE N C-1-O    22  .300
     NY  N C-2-O    86  .295
1893 NY  N C-O      80  .322
1894 NY  N 1       105  .369
1895 NY  N M-1      78  .316
1896 BAL N 1       118  .345
1897 BAL N 1       114  .356
1898 WAS N M-1-2    42  .285
     NY  N 1        79  .297
1899 NY  N 1       117  .308
1900 NY  N 1       130  .273
1901 CHI N 1        73  .241
1902 NY  N 1        50  .300
     WAS A C-1-2-O  78  .238
1903 BRO N 1       139  .313
1904 BRO N 1         8  .227
     PHI N 1        64  .220
1905 NY  A 1         1  .000
     BRTR     1 1535   1- 0
                        .302
```

DOYLE, JOSEPH J.
B.APR.9,1838 NEW YORK,N.Y.
D.JAN.7,1906 WHITE PLAINS,N.Y.
NON-PLAYING MANAGER BRO(AA)1885

DOYLE, JOSEPH K.
B.CINCINNATI,OHIO
```
1872 NAT NA 2-S      8  .222
```

DOYLE, JUDD BRUCE "SLOW JOE"
B.SEPT.15,1881 CLAY CENTER,KAN.
D.NOV.21,1947
```
1906 NY  A P         9   2- 2
1907 NY  A P        29  11-11
1908 NY  A P        12   1- 1
1909 NY  A P        17   8- 6
1910 NY  A P         3   0- 2
     CIN N P         5   0- 0
     BRTR           75  22-22
```

DOYLE, LAWRENCE JOSEPH "LAUGHING LARRY"
B.JULY 31,1886 CASEYVILLE,ILL.
D.MAR.1,1974 SARANAC LAKE,N.Y.
```
1907 NY  N 2        69  .260
1908 NY  N 2       102  .308
1909 NY  N 2       144  .302
1910 NY  N 2       151  .285
1911 NY  N 2       141  .310
1912 NY  N 2       143  .330
1913 NY  N 2       132  .280
1914 NY  N 2       145  .260
1915 NY  N 2       150  .320
1916 NY  N 2       113  .264
     CHI N 2         9  .436
1917 CHI N 2       135  .254
1918 NY  N 2        75  .261
     NY  N 2       113  .289
1920 NY  N 2       137  .285
     BLTR         1759  .290
```

DOYLE, PAUL SINNOTT
B.OCT.2,1939 PHILADELPHIA,PA.
```
1969 ATL N P        36   2- 0
1970 CAL A P        40   3- 1
     SD  N P         9   0- 2
1972 CAL A P         2   0- 0
     BLTL           87   5- 3
```

DOYLE, ROBERT DENNIS "DENNY"
B.JAN.17,1944 GLASGOW,KY.
```
1970 PHI N 2       112  .208
1971 PHI N 2        95  .231
1972 PHI N 2       123  .249
1973 PHI N 2       116  .273
1974 CAL A 2-S     147  .260
1975 CAL A 2-3       8  .067
     BOS A 2 S-S    89  .310
1976 BOS A 2       117  .250
     BLTR          807  .252
```

DOYLE, WILLIAM CARL
B.JULY 30,1912 KNOXVILLE,TENN.
D.SEPT.4,1951
```
1935 PHI A P        14   2- 7
1936 PHI A P         8   0- 3
1939 BRO N P         5   1- 2
1940 BRO N P         3   0- 0
     STL N P        21   3- 3
     BRTR           51   6-15
```

DOZIER, WILLIAM JOSEPH "BUZZ"
B.AUG.31,1927 WACO,TEX.
```
1947 WAS A P         2   0- 0
1949 WAS A P         2   0- 0
     BRTR            4   0- 0
```

DRABOWSKY, MYRON WALTER "MOE"
B.JULY 21,1935 OZANNA,POLAND
```
1956 CHI N P         9   2- 4
1957 CHI N P        36  13-15
1958 CHI N P        22   9-11
1959 CHI N P        31   5-10
1960 CHI N P    32  33   3- 1
1961 MIL N P        16   0- 2
1962 CIN N P        23   2- 6
     KC  A P        10   1- 1
1963 KC  A P        26   7-13
1964 KC  A P    53  54   5-13
1965 KC  A P        14   1- 5
1966 BAL A P        44   6- 0
1967 BAL A P        43   7- 5
1968 BAL A P        45   4- 4
1969 KC  A P        52  11- 9
1970 KC  A P        24   1- 2
     BAL A P        21   4- 2
1971 STL N P        51   6- 1
1972 STL N P        30   1- 1
     CHI A P         7   0- 0
     BRTR   589 591  88-105
```

DRAGO, RICHARD ANTHONY "DICK"
B.JUNE 25,1945 TOLEDO,OHIO
```
1969 KC  A P        41  11-13
1970 KC  A P        35   9-15
1971 KC  A P        35  17-11
1972 KC  A P    34  35  12-17
1973 KC  A P    37  38  12-14
1974 BOS A P        33   7-10
1975 BOS A P        40   2- 2
1976 CAL A P        43   7- 8
     BRTR   298 300  77-90
```

DRAKE
```
1884 WAS AA O        2  .286
```

```
YR  CL LEA POS  GP    G    REC
```

DRAKE, DELOS DANIEL
B.DEC.3,1886 GIRARD,OHIO
D.OCT.3,1965 FINDLAY,OHIO
1911 DET A O   95   .279
1914 STL F 1-O   138   .252
1915 STL F O   99   .265
　　　BRTR   332   .264

DRAKE, LARRY FRANCIS
B.MAY 4,1921 DALLAS,TEX.
1945 PHI A O   1   .000
1948 WAS A O   4   .286
　　　BLTR   5   .222

DRAKE, LOGAN GAFFNEY "L.G."
B.DEC.26,1900 SPARTANBURG,S.C.
D.JUNE 1,1940 COLUMBIA,S.C.
1922 CLE A P   1   0- 0
1923 CLE A P   4   0- 0
1924 CLE A P   5   0- 1
　　　BRTR   10   0- 1

DRAKE, SAMUEL HARRISON "SAMMY"
B.OCT.7,1934 LITTLE ROCK,ARK.
1960 CHI N 2-3   15   .067
1961 CHI N O   13   .000
1962 NY N 2   25   .192
　　　BBTR   53   .153

DRAKE, SOLOMON LOUIS "SOLLY"
B.OCT.23,1930 N.LITTLE ROCK,ARK
1956 CHI N O   65   .256
1959 LA N O   9   .250
　　　PHI N O   67   .145
　　　BBTR   141   .232

DRAKE, THOMAS KENDALL
B.AUG.7,1914 BIRMINGHAM,ALA.
1939 CLE A P   8   8   0- 1
1941 BRO N P-O   10   11   1- 1
　　　　　　　　　　　　　　　 .400
　　　BRTR   18   19   1- 2
　　　　　　　　　　　　　　　 .286

DRAUBY, JACOB C.
B.1865 HARRISBURG,PA.
1892 WAS N 3   10   .205

DREESEN, WILLIAM RICHARD
B.JULY 26,1904 NEW YORK,N.Y.
D.NOV.9,1971 MT.VERNON,N.Y.
1931 BOS N 3   48   .222
　　　BLTR

DREISEWERD, CLEMENT JOHN "STEAMBOAT"
B.JAN.24,1916 OLD MONROE,MO.
1944 BOS A P   7   2- 4
1945 BOS A P   2   0- 1
1946 BOS A P   20   4- 1
1948 STL A P   13   0- 2
　　　NY N P   4   0- 0
　　　BLTL   46   6- 8

DRENNAN, K. JOHN
1904 DET A 1   1   .000

DRESCHER, WILLIAM CLAYTON
B.MAY 23,1921 CONGERS,N.Y.
D.MAY 15,1968 CONGERS,N.Y.
1944 NY A C   4   .143
1945 NY A C   48   .270
1946 NY A C   5   .333
　　　BRTR   57   .266

DRESSEN, CHARLES WALTER "CHUCK"
B.SEPT.20,1898 DECATUR,ILL.
D.AUG.10,1966 DETROIT,MICH.
1925 CIN N 2-3-O   76   .274
1926 CIN N S-3-O   127   .266
1927 CIN N S-3   144   .292
1928 CIN N 3   135   .291
1929 CIN N 2-3   110   .244
1930 CIN N 2-3   33   .211
1931 CIN N 3   5   .067
1933 NY N 3   16   .222
　　　BRTR   646   .272
NON-PLAYING MANAGER
CIN(N) 1934-37, BRO(N)1951-53,
WAS(A) 1955-57, MIL(N) 1960-61
DET(A) 1963-66

DRESSEN, LEO AUGUST "LEE"
B.JULY 23,1889 ELLINWOOD,KAN.
D.JUNE 30,1931 DILLER,NEB.
1914 STL N 1   46   .233
1918 DET A 1   31   .178
　　　BLTL   77   .205

DRESSER, EDWARD
1898 BRO N S   1   .250

DRESSER, ROBERT U.
B.OCT.4,1878 NEWTON,MASS.
D.JULY 27,1924 DUXBURY,MASS.
1902 BOS N P   1   0- 1
　　　TL

DRESSLER, ROBERT ANTHONY "ROB"
B.FEB.2,1954 PORTLAND,ORE.
1975 SF N P   3   1- 0
1976 SF N P   25   3-10
　　　BRTR   28   4-10

DREW, DAVID
1884 KEY U P-2   1   2   0- 0
　　　　　　　　　　　　　　　 .444
　　　WAS U 1-S-O   13   .327
　　　　　　　　　 1   15   0- 0
　　　　　　　　　　　　　　　 .344

DREWS, FRANK JOHN
B.MAY 25,1916 BUFFALO,N.Y.
D.APR.22,1972 BUFFALO,N.Y.
1944 BOS N 2   46   .206
1945 BOS N 2   49   .204
　　　BRTR   95   .205

DREWS, KARL AUGUST
B.FEB.22,1920 ELTINGEVILLE,S.I.
N.Y.
D.AUG.15,1963 DANIA,FLA.
1946 NY A P   3   0- 1
1947 NY A P   30   6- 6
1948 NY A P   19   2- 3
　　　STL A P   20   3- 2
1949 STL A P   31   4-12
1951 PHI N P   5   1- 0
1952 PHI N P   33 14-15
1953 PHI N P   47   9-10
1954 PHI N P   8   1- 0
　　　CIN N P   22   4- 4
　　　BRTR   218 44-53

DRIESSEN, DANIEL "DAN"
B.JULY 29,1951 HILTON HEAD,S.C.
1973 CIN N 1-3-O   102   .301
1974 CIN N 1-3-O   150   .281
1975 CIN N 1-O   88   .281
1976 CIN N 1-O   98   .247
　　　BRTR   438   .281

DRILL, LEWIS L.
B.MAY 9,1877 BROWERVILLE,MINN.
D.JULY 4,1969 ST.PAUL,MINN.
1902 WAS A C-2-S-O   37   .272
　　　BAL A C-1   2   .250
　　　WAS A C-2-S-O   32   .250
1903 WAS A C   51   .252
1904 WAS A C   43   .394
　　　DET A C-1   51   .225
1905 DET A C   72   .261
　　　BRTR   288   .255

DRISCOLL, JAMES BERNARD "JIM"
B.MAY 14,1944 MEDFORD,MASS.
1970 OAK A 2-S   21   .192
1972 TEX A 2-3   15   .000
　　　BLTR   36   .143

DRISCOLL, JOHN F. "DENNY"
B.NOV.19,1855 LOWELL,MASS.
D.JULY 11,1886
1880 BUF N P-O   6   18   1- 3
　　　　　　　　　　　　　　　 .136
1882 PIT AA P   22 13- 9
1883 PIT AA P-C-3-O   41 18-21
　　　　　　　　　　　　　　　 .185
1884 LOU AA P-O   13   7- 6
　　　　　　　　　　　　　　　 .167
1885 BUF N 2   7   .158
　　　　　　　 82   101 39-39
　　　　　　　　　　　　　　　 .160

DRISCOLL, JOHN LEO "PADDY"
B.JAN.11,1896 EVANSTON,ILL.
D.JUNE 28,1968 CHICAGO,ILL.
1917 CHI N 2   13   .107
　　　BRTR

DRISCOLL, MICHAEL COLUMBUS
B.OCT.19,1892 N.ABINGTON,MASS.
D.MAR.21,1953
1916 PHI A P   1   0- 1
　　　BRTR

DRISSEL, MICHAEL F. "MIKE"
B.DEC.19,1864 ST.LOUIS,MO.
D.FEB.26,1913 ST.LOUIS,MO.
1885 STL AA C   6   .056
　　　BRTR

DROHAN, DAVID
(PLAYED UNDER NAME OF
DAVID ROWAN)

DROHAN, THOMAS F.
B.AUG.26,1888 FALL RIVER,MASS.
D.SEPT.17,1926
1913 WAS A P   2   0- 0
　　　BRTR

DROPO, WALTER "MOOSE"
B.JAN.30,1924 MOOSUP,CONN.
1949 BOS A 1   11   .146
1950 BOS A 1   136   .322
1951 BOS A 1   99   .239
1952 BOS A 1   37   .265
　　　DET A 1   115   .279
1953 DET A 1   152   .248
1954 DET A 1   107   .281
1955 CHI A 1   141   .280
1956 CHI A 1   125   .266
1957 CHI A 1   93   .256
1958 CHI A 1   28   .192
1959 CIN N 1   63   .290
　　　CIN N 1   26   .103
　　　BAL A 1-3   62   .278
1960 BAL A 1-3   79   .268
1961 BAL A 1   14   .259
　　　BRTR   1288   .270

DROTT, RICHARD FRED "DICK"
B.JULY 1,1936 CINCINNATI,OHIO
1957 CHI N P   38 15-11
1958 CHI N P   39   7-11
1959 CHI N P   8   1- 2
1960 CHI N P   23   0- 6
1961 CHI N P   35   1- 4
1962 HOU N P   6   1- 0
1963 HOU N P   27   2-12
　　　BRTR   176 27-46

DRUCKE, LOUIS FRANK
B.DEC.3,1888 WACO,TEX.
D.SEPT.22,1955
1909 NY N P   3   2- 1
1910 NY N P   34 12-10
1911 NY N P   15   4- 4
1912 NY N P   1   0- 0
　　　TR   53 18-15

DRUHOT, CARL A. "COLLIE"
B.SEPT.1,1882 OHIO
D.FEB.5,1918
1906 CIN N P   14   6- 8
　　　STL N P   5   2- 1
1907 STL N P   2   0- 2
　　　BLTL   21   8-11

DRYSDALE, DONALD SCOTT "DON"
B.JULY 23,1936 VAN NUYS,CAL.
1956 BRO N P   25   26   5- 5
1957 BRO N P   34   37 17- 9
1958 LA N P   44   47 12-13
1959 LA N P   44   46 17-13
1960 LA N P   41 15-14
1961 LA N P   40 13-10
1962 LA N P   43 25- 9
1963 LA N P   42 19-17
1964 LA N P   40 18-16
1965 LA N P   44   58 23-12
1966 LA N P   40   46 13-16
1967 LA N P   38 13-16
1968 LA N P   31 14-12
1969 LA N P   12   5- 4
　　　BRTR   518 547 209-166

YR	CL	LEA	POS	GP	G	REC

DUBIEL, WALTER JOHN "MONK"
B.FEB.12,1919 HARTFORD,CONN.
D.OCT.25,1969 HARTFORD,CONN.

YR	CL	LEA	POS	GP	G	REC
1944	NY	A	P	30	31	13-13
1945	NY	A	P		26	10- 9
1948	PHI	N	P	37	38	8-10
1949	CHI	N	P	32	33	6- 9
1950	CHI	N	P		39	6-10
1951	CHI	N	P		22	2- 2
1952	CHI	N	P		1	0- 0
	BRTR			187	190	45-53

DUBUC, JEAN JOSEPH OCTAVE "CHAUNCEY"
B.SEPT.15,1888 ST.JOHNSBURY,VT.
D.AUG.28,1958

1908	CIN	N	P		16	5- 6
1909	CIN	N	P		19	2- 5
1912	DET	A	P		37	17-10
1913	DET	A	P	36	66	16-14
1914	DET	A	P	36	69	13-14
1915	DET	A	P	40	60	17-12
1916	DET	A	P	36	52	10- 8
1918	BOS	A	P		5	0- 1
1919	NY	N	P	36	37	6- 4
	BRTR			261	360	86-74

DUCKWORTH, JAMES RAYMOND "JIM"
B.MAY 24,1939 NATIONAL CITY,CAL.

1963	WAS	A	P		37	4-12
1964	WAS	A	P		30	1- 6
1965	WAS	A	P		17	2- 2
1966	WAS	A	P		5	0- 3
	KC	A	P		8	0- 2
	BRTR			97	7-25

DUDLEY, ELZIE CLISE
B.AUG.8,1904 GRAHAM,N.C.

1929	BRO	N	P	35	36	6-14
1930	BRO	N	P		21	2- 4
1931	PHI	N	P	30	44	8-14
1932	PHI	N	P	13	23	1- 1
1933	PIT	N	P		1	0- 0
	BLTR			100	125	17-33

DUDLEY, ERNEST
(PLAYED UNDER NAME OF ERNEST DUDLEY LEE)

DUDRA, JOHN JOSEPH
B.MAY 27,1918 ASSUMPTION,ILL.
D.OCT.24,1965

1941	BOS	N	1-2-S-3	14	.360
	BRTR				

DUFF, CECIL ELBA "LARRY"
B.NOV.30,1896 RADERSBURG,MONT.

1922	CHI	A	P		3	1- 1
	BLTR					

DUFF, PATRICK HENRY
B.MAY 6,1875 PROVIDENCE,R.I.
D.SEPT.11,1925

1906	WAS	A	C		1	.000
	TR				*	

DUFFALO, JAMES FRANCIS "JIM"
B.NOV.25,1935 HELVETIA,PA.

1961	SF	N	P	24	25	5- 1
1962	SF	N	P		24	1- 2
1963	SF	N	P		34	4- 2
1964	SF	N	P		35	5- 1
1965	SF	N	P		2	0- 1
	CIN	N	P		22	0- 1
	BRTR			141	142	15- 8

DUFFEE, CHARLES EDWARD "HOME RUN"
B.JAN.27,1866 MOBILE,ALA.
D.DEC.24,1894

1889	STL	AA	O		137	.245
1890	STL	AA	O		98	.274
1891	COL	AA	O		137	.302
1892	WAS	N	O		129	.252
1893	CIN	N	O		4	.200
	BR				505	.266

DUFFIE, JOHN BROWN
B.OCT.4,1945 GREENWOOD,S.C.

1967	LA	N	P		2	0- 2
	BRTR					

DUFFY, BERNARD A.
B.AUG.18,1893 VINSON,OKLA.
D.FEB.9,1962

1913	PIT	N	P		3	0- 0
	BRTR					

DUFFY, EDWARD C.
B.1844 IRELAND

1871	CHI	NA	S-3		25	-

DUFFY, FRANK THOMAS
B.OCT.14,1946 OAKLAND,CAL.

1970	CIN	N	S		6	.182
1971	CIN	N	S		13	.188
	SF	N	2-S-3		21	.179
1972	CLE	A	S		130	.239
1973	CLE	A	S		116	.263
1974	CLE	A	S		158	.233
1975	CLE	A	S		146	.243
1976	CLE	A	S		133	.212
	BRTR				723	.236

DUFFY, HUGH
B.NOV.26,1866 CRANSTON,R.I.
D.OCT.19,1954 BOSTON,MASS.

1888	CHI	N	O		71	.282
1889	CHI	N	O		136	.311
1890	CHI	P	O		137	.328
1891	BOS	AA	O		127	.340
1892	BOS	N	O		146	.302
1893	BOS	N	O		131	.378
1894	BOS	N	O		124	.438
1895	BOS	N	O		131	.352
1896	BOS	N	O		131	.302
1897	BOS	N	O		134	.341
1898	BOS	N	O		151	.319
1899	BOS	N	O		147	.279
1900	BOS	N	O		50	.298
1901	MIL	A	M-O		78	.308
1904	PHI	N	M-O		16	.261
1905	PHI	N	M-O		15	.307
1906	PHI	N	M-H		1	.000
	BRTR				1726	.329
NON-PLAYING MANAGER
CHI(A) 1910-11, BOS(A) 1921-22

DUGAN, DANIEL PHILLIP
B.FEB.22,1907 PLAINFIELD,N.J.
D.JUNE 25,1968 GREEN BROOK TOWNSHIP,N.J.

1928	CHI	A	P	1	0- 0
1929	CHI	A	P	19	1- 4
	BLTL			20	1- 4

DUGAN, E.

1884	KC	U	O	3	.000

DUGAN, EDWARD J.
B.1864 BROOKLYN,N.Y.

						.114
1884	RIC	AA	P-2	20	21	5-15

DUGAN, JOSEPH ANTHONY "JUMPING JOE"
B.MAY.12,1897 MAHANOY CITY,PA.

1917	PHI	A	S		43	.194
1918	PHI	A	2-S		120	.195
1919	PHI	A	2-S		104	.271
1920	PHI	A	2-S-3		123	.322
1921	PHI	A	3		119	.295
1922	BOS	A	S-3		84	.281
	NY	A	3		60	.294
1923	NY	A	3		146	.283
1924	NY	A	3		148	.302
1925	NY	A	3		102	.292
1926	NY	A	3		123	.288
1927	NY	A	3		112	.269
1928	NY	A	3		94	.276
1929	BOS	N	3		60	.304
1931	DET	A	3		8	.235
	BRTR				1446	.280

DUGAN, WILLIAM E.
B.1864 KINGSTON,N.Y.

1884	RIC	AA	C		8	.040

DUGAS, AUGUSTIN JOSEPH "GUS"
B.MAR.24,1907 ST.JEAN DEMATHA, QUE.,CANADA

1930	PIT	N	O		9	.290
1932	PIT	N	O		55	.237
1933	PIT	N	1-O		37	.169
1934	WAS	A	O		24	.053
	BLTL				125	.209

DUGDALE, DANIEL EDWARD
B.OCT.28,1864 PEORIA,ILL.
D.MAY 9,1934 SEATTLE,WASH.

1886	KC	N	C		12	.175
1894	WAS	N	C		33	.217
					45	.207

DUGEY, OSCAR JOSEPH "JAKE"
B.OCT.25,1893 PALESTINE,TEX.
D.JAN.1,1966 DALLAS,TEX.

1913	BOS	N	S-3		5	.250
1914	BOS	N	2-O		58	.193
1915	PHI	N	2		42	.154
1916	PHI	N	2		41	.220
1917	PHI	N	2		44	.194
1920	BOS	N	H		5	.000
	BRTR				195	.194

DUGGAN, JAMES ELMER "MER"
B.JUNE 3,1884 WHITELAND,IND.
D.DEC.5,1951

1911	STL	A	1		1	.000
	BLTL					

DUGGLEBY, WILLIAM JAMES "FROSTY BILL"
B.MAR.16,1874 UTICA,N.Y.
D.AUG.30,1944

1898	PHI	N	P		9	3- 3
1901	PHI	N	P	33	19-12
1902	PHI	A	P		2	1- 1
	PHI	N	P		31	11-17
1903	PHI	N	P		36	13-18
1904	PHI	N	P		32	12-14
1905	PHI	N	P		38	18-16
1906	PHI	N	P		42	13-19
1907	PHI	N	P		5	1- 2
	PIT	N	P		9	0- 2
	TR				237	91-104

DUKE, MARTIN F. "DUCK"
B.COLUMBUS,OHIO
D.DEC.31,1898

1891	WAS	AA	P		4	0- 4
	TL					

DUKES, NOBLE JAN "JAN"
B.AUG.16,1945 CHEYENNE,WYO.

1969	WAS	A	P		8	0- 2
1970	WAS	A	P		5	0- 0
1972	TEX	A	P		3	0- 0
	BLTL				16	0- 2

DUKES, THOMAS EARL "TOM"
B.AUG.31,1942 KNOXVILLE,TENN.

1967	HOU	N	P		17	0- 2
1968	HOU	N	P		43	2- 2
1969	SD	N	P		13	1- 0
1970	SD	N	P		53	1- 6
1971	BAL	A	P		28	1- 5
1972	CAL	A	P		7	0- 1
	BRTR				161	5-16

DULIBA, ROBERT JOHN "BOB"
B.JAN.9,1935 GLEN LYON,PA.

1959	STL	N	P		11	0- 1
1960	STL	N	P		27	4- 4
1962	STL	N	P		28	2- 0
1963	LA	A	P		6	1- 1
1964	LA	A	P		58	6- 4
1965	BOS	A	P		39	4- 2
1967	KC	A	P		7	0- 0
	BRTR				176	17-12

DUMONT, GEORGE HENRY "PEA SOUP"
B.NOV.13,1895 MINNEAPOLIS,MINN.
D.OCT.13,1956

1915	WAS	A	P		6	2- 1
1916	WAS	A	P		17	2- 2
1917	WAS	A	P		37	5-14
1918	WAS	A	P		4	1- 1
1919	BOS	A	P		13	0- 4
	BRTR				77	10-22

DUMOVICH, NICHOLAS
B.JAN.2,1902 LOS ANGELES,CAL.

1923	CHI	N	P		28	3- 5
	BLTL					

YR	CL	LEA	POS	GP	G	REC

DUNCAN, DAVID EDWIN "DAVE"
B.SEP.26,1945 DALLAS,TEX.

YR	CL	LEA	POS	GP	G	REC
1964	KC	A	C		25	.170
1967	KC	A	C		34	.188
1968	OAK	A	C		82	.191
1969	OAK	A	C		58	.126
1970	OAK	A	C		86	.259
1971	OAK	A	C		103	.253
1972	OAK	A	C		121	.218
1973	CLE	A	C		95	.233
1974	CLE	A	C-1		136	.200
1975	BAL	A	C		96	.205
1976	BAL	A	C		93	.204
			BRTR		929	.214

DUNCAN, JAMES WILLIAM "JIM"
B.JULY 1,1871 SALTZBURG,PA.
D.OCT.16,1901 FOXBURG,PA.

1899	WAS	N	C		15	.234
	CLE	N	C		30	.231
			BRTR		45	.232

DUNCAN, LOUIS BAIRD "PAT"
B.OCT.6,1893 COALTON,OHIO
D.JULY 17,1960

1915	PIT	N	O		3	.200
1919	CIN	N	O		31	.244
1920	CIN	N	O		154	.295
1921	CIN	N	O		145	.308
1922	CIN	N	O		151	.327
1923	CIN	N	O		147	.327
1924	CIN	N	O		96	.270
			BRTR		727	.307

DUNCAN, VERNON VAN DUKE
B.JAN.6,1890 CLAYTON,N.C.
D.JUNE 1,1954

1913	PHI	N	O		8	.416
1914	BAL	F	O		157	.287
1915	BAL	F	3-O		146	.269
			BLTR		311	.280

DUNDON, AUGUSTUS JOSEPH
B.JULY 10,1874 COLUMBUS,OHIO
D.SEPT.1,1940 PITTSBURGH,PA.

1904	CHI	A	2		108	.234
1905	CHI	A	2		106	.192
1906	CHI	A	2		33	.135
			BRTR		247	.204

DUNDON, EDWARD JOSEPH "DUMMY"
B.JULY 10,1859 COLUMBUS,OHIO
D.AUG.18,1893

1883	COL	AA	P-2	19	26	3-16
			O			.161
1884	COL	AA	P-O	10	26	5- 4
						.140
		TR		29	52	8-20
						.151

DUNEGAN, JAMES WILLIAM "JOE"
B.AUG.6,1947 BURLINGTON,IOWA

1970	CHI	N	P	7	10	0- 2
			BRTR			

DUNGAN, SAMUEL MORRISON
B.JAN.29,1866 FRENDALE,CAL.
D.MAR.16,1939

1892	CHI	N	O		113	.291
1893	CHI	N	O		107	.310
1894	CHI	N	O		10	.237
	LOU	N	O		8	.333
1900	CHI	N	O		6	.266
1901	WAS	A	1-O		137	.324
	BR				381	.309

DUNHAM, LELAND HUFFIELD "LEE"
B.JUNE 9,1902 ATLANTA,ILL.
D.MAY 1,1961

1926	PHI	N	1		5	.250
			BLTL			

DUNHAM, WILEY H.
B.PIKETON,OHIO

1902	STL	N	P		7	2- 3

DUNKLE, EDWARD PERKS "DAVEY"
B.AUG.30,1872 HOMESTEAD,PA.
D.NOV.19,1941

1897	PHI	N	P		7	5- 2
1898	PHI	N	P		9	1- 5
1899	WAS	N	P		4	0- 2
1903	CHI	A	P		11	5- 5
	WAS	A	P		14	5- 8
1904	WAS	A	P	12	13	2- 9
			BBTR	57	58	18-31

DUNLAP, FREDERICK C.
"SURE SHOT"
B.MAY 21,1859 PHILADELPHIA,PA.
D.DEC.1,1902

1880	CLE	N	2		84	.273
1881	CLE	N	2-3		78	.324
1882	CLE	N	2		82	.278
1883	CLE	N	2		90	.328
1884	STL	U	M-P-	1	81	0- 0
			2-O			.420
1885	STL	N	M-2		106	.269
1886	STL	N	M-2		73	.281
	DET	N	M-2		49	.284
1887	DET	N	M-2		64	.326
1888	PIT	N	M-2		81	.261
1889	PIT	N	M-2		121	.235
1890	PIT	N	2		17	.172
	NY	P	2		1	.000
1891	WAS	AA	2		7	.200
			BRTR	1	934	0- 0
						.295

DUNLAP, GRANT LESTER
B.DEC.20,1923 STOCKTON,CAL.

1953	STL	N	O		16	.353
			BRTR			

DUNLAP, WILLIAM JAMES
B.MAY 1,1909 THREE RIVERS,MASS.

1929	BOS	N	O		10	.414
1930	BOS	N	O		16	.069
			BRTR		26	.241

DUNLEAVY, JOHN FRANCIS
B.SEPT.14,1879 HARRISON,N.J.
D.APR.12,1944 S.NORWALK,CONN.

1903	STL	N	P-O	14	52	6- 8
						.249
1904	STL	N	P-O	7	51	1- 4
						.236
1905	STL	N	O		119	.241
				21	222	7-12
						.241

DUNLOP, GEORGE HENRY
B.JULY 19,1888 MERIDEN,CONN.
D.DEC.12,1972 MERIDEN,CONN.

1913	CLE	A	S-3	7	.222	
1914	CLE	A	S	1	.000	
			BRTR	8	.190	

DUNN, JAMES WILLIAM
B.FEB.25,1931 VALDOSTA,GA.

1952	PIT	N	P		3	0- 0
			BRTR			

DUNN, JOHN JOSEPH "JACK"
B.OCT.6,1872 MEADVILLE,PA.
D.OCT.22,1928 TOWSON,MD.

1897	BRO	N	P	25	34	16- 9
1898	BRO	N	P	37	45	15-21
1899	BRO	N	P	38	39	21-12
1900	BRO	N	P		8	3- 5
	PHI	N	P		10	4- 5
1901	PHI	N	P		2	0- 1
	BAL	A	P-S-	6	96	3- 3
			3			.247
1902	NY	N	P-2-	3	96	0- 3
			S-3-O			.211
1903	NY	N	2-S-3		72	.241
1904	NY	N	P-3	1	55	0- 0
						.309
			BRTR	130	457	62-59
						.247

DUNN, JOSEPH EDWARD
B.MAR.11,1885 SPRINGFIELD,OHIO
D.MAR.19,1944

1908	BRO	N	C		20	.172
1909	BRO	N	C		7	.160
			BRTR		27	.169

DUNN, RONALD RAY "RON"
B.JAN.24,1950 OKLAHOMA CITY,OKLA

1974	CHI	N	2-3		23	.294
1975	CHI	N	2-3-O		32	.159
			BRTR		55	.241

DUNN, STEPHEN
B.DEC.21,1858 LONDON,ONT.,CAN.
D.MAY 5,1933 LONDON,ONT.,CAN.

1884	STP	U	1-2		9	.242

DUNNING, ANDREW J.
B.NEW YORK,N.Y.

1889	PIT	N	P		2	0- 2
1891	NY	N	P		1	0- 0
					3	0- 2

DUNNING, STEVEN JOHN "STEVE"
B.MAY 15,1949 DENVER,COLO.

1970	CLE	A	P		19	4- 9
1971	CLE	A	P	31	32	8-14
1972	CLE	A	P	16	20	6- 4
1973	CLE	A	P		4	0- 2
	TEX	A	P	23	27	2- 6
1974	TEX	A	P		1	0- 0
1976	CAL	A	P		4	0- 0
	MON	N	P		32	2- 6
			BRTR	130	139	22-41

DUPEE, FRANK OLIVER
B.APR.29,1877 MONCTON,VT.
D.AUG.14,1956 PORTLAND,ME.

1901	CHI	A	P		1	0- 0
			TR			

DUPREE, MICHAEL DENNIS "MIKE"
B.MAY 29,1953 KANSAS CITY,KAN.

1976	SD	N	P		12	0- 0
			BRTR			

DURBIN, BLAINE ALONZO "KID"
B.1887 LAMAR,MO.
D.SEPT.11,1943 KIRKWOOD,MO.

1907	CHI	N	P	5	10	0- 1
1908	CHI	N	O		14	.363
1909	CIN	N	H		6	.200
	PIT	N	H		1	.000
			BLTL	5	31	0- 1
						.271

DUREN, RINOLD GEORGE "RYNE"
B.FEB.22,1929 CAZENOVIA,WIS.

1954	BAL	A	P		1	0- 0
1957	KC	A	P		14	0- 3
1958	NY	A	P		44	6- 4
1959	NY	A	P		41	3- 6
1960	NY	A	P		42	3- 4
1961	NY	A	P		4	0- 1
	LA	A	P		40	6-12
1962	LA	A	P		42	2- 9
1963	PHI	N	P	33	34	6- 2
1964	PHI	N	P		2	0- 0
	CIN	N	P		26	0- 2
1965	PHI	N	P		6	0- 0
	WAS	A	P		16	1- 1
			BRTR	311	312	27-44

DURHAM, DONALD GARY "DON"
B.MAR.21,1949 YOSEMITE,KY.

1972	STL	N	P	10	14	2- 7
1973	TEX	A	P	15	16	0- 4
			BRTR	25	30	2-11

DURHAM, EDWARD FANT
B.AUG.17,1908 CHESTER,S.C.
D.APR.27,1976 CHESTER,S.C.

1929	BOS	A	P		14	1- 0
1930	BOS	A	P		33	4-15
1931	BOS	A	P	38	39	8-10
1932	BOS	A	P	34	35	6-13
1933	CHI	A	P		24	10- 6
			BLTR	143	145	29-44

DURHAM, JAMES GARFIELD
B.OCT.7,1881 DOUGLASS,KAN.

1902	CHI	A	P-O	3	5	1- 1
						.066

DURHAM, JOSEPH VANN "JOE"
B.JULY 31,1932 NEWPORT NEWS,VA.

1954	BAL	A	O		10	.225
1957	BAL	A	O		77	.185
1959	STL	N	O		6	.000
			BRTR		93	.188

DURHAM, LOUIS G. "BULL"
B.1881 BOLIVAR,N.Y.

1904	BRO	N	P		2	1- 0
1907	WAS	A	P		2	0- 0
1908	NY	N	P		1	0- 0
1909	NY	N	P		4	0- 0
			TR		9	1- 0

DURNBAUGH, ROBERT EUGENE "BOBBY"
B.JAN.15,1933 DAYTON,OHIO

1957	CIN	N	S		2	.000
			BRTR			

YR CL LEA POS GP G   REC

DURNING, GEORGE WARREN
B.MAY 9,1902 PHILADELPHIA,PA.

YR	CL	LEA	POS	GP	G	REC
1925	PHI	N	O		5	.357
	BRTR					

DURNING, RICHARD KNOTT "RICH"
B.OCT.10,1892 LOUISVILLE,KY.
D.SEP.23,1948

YR	CL	LEA	POS	GP	G	REC
1917	BRO	N	P		1	0- 0
1918	BRO	N	P		1	0- 0
	BLTL				2	0- 0

DUROCHER, LEO ERNEST "LIPPY"
B.JULY 27,1905 W.SPRINGFIELD,
MASS.

YR	CL	LEA	POS	GP	G	REC
1925	NY	A	S		2	.000
1928	NY	A	2-S		102	.270
1929	NY	A	S		106	.246
1930	CIN	N	2-S		119	.243
1931	CIN	N	S		121	.227
1932	CIN	N	S		143	.217
1933	CIN	N	S		16	.216
	STL	N	S		123	.258
1934	STL	N	S		146	.260
1935	STL	N	S		143	.265
1936	STL	N	S		136	.286
1937	STL	N	S		135	.203
1938	BRO	N	S		141	.219
1939	BRO	N	M-S		116	.277
1940	BRO	N	M-2-S		62	.231
1941	BRO	N	M-S		18	.286
1943	BRO	N	M-S		6	.222
1945	BRO	N	M-2		2	.200
	BRTR				1637	.247

   BB 1928-29
NON-PLAYING MANAGER
BRO(N) 1942, 1944, 1946, 1948,
NY(N) 1948-55, CHI(N) 1966-72,
HOU(N) 1972-73

DURRETT, ELMER CHARLES "RED"
B.FEB.3,1921 SHERMAN,TEX.

YR	CL	LEA	POS	GP	G	REC
1944	BRO	N	O		11	.156
1945	BRO	N	O		8	.125
	BLTL				19	.146

DURST, CEDRIC MONTGOMERY
B.AUG.23,1896 AUSTIN,TEX.
D.FEB.16,1971 SAN DIEGO,CAL.

YR	CL	LEA	POS	GP	G	REC
1922	STL	A	O		15	.333
1923	STL	A	1-O		45	.212
1926	STL	A	O		80	.237
1927	NY	A	O		65	.248
1928	NY	A	O		74	.252
1929	NY	A	O		92	.257
1930	NY	A	O		8	.188
	BOS	A	O		102	.243
	BLTL				481	.244

DURYEA, JAMES WHITNEY
"CYCLONE JIM"
B.SEPT.7,1862 OSAGE,IOWA
D.AUG.7,1942

YR	CL	LEA	POS	GP	G	REC
1889	CIN	AA	P-O	54	55	32-21
						.268
1890	CIN	N	P		32	17-13
1891	CIN	N	P		11	2- 8
	STL	AA	P		4	1- 1
1892	CIN	N	P-O		11	3- 5
						.111
	WAS	N	P		16	2-12
1893	WAS	N	P		17	5- 8
	BRTR			145	146	62-68
						.192

DUSAK, ERVIN FRANK "FOUR SACK"
B.JULY 29,1920 CHICAGO,ILL.

YR	CL	LEA	POS	GP	G	REC
1941	STL	N	O		6	.143
1942	STL	N	3-O		12	.185
1946	STL	N	2-3-O		100	.240
1947	STL	N	3-O		111	.284
1948	STL	N	P-2-	1	114	0- 0
			S-3-O			.209
1949	STL	N	H		1	.000
1950	STL	N	P-O	14	23	0- 2
						.083
1951	STL	N	P		5	0- 0
	PIT	N	P-2-3-O		21	0- 1
	PIT	N	P-2-	3	21	0- 1
			3-O			.308
1952	PIT	N	O		20	.222
	BRTR			23	413	0- 3
						.243

DUSER, CARL ROBERT
B.JULY 22,1932 HAZELTON,PA.

YR	CL	LEA	POS	GP	G	REC
1956	KC	A	P		2	1- 1
1958	KC	A	P		1	0- 0
	BLTL				3	1- 1

DUSTAL, ROBERT ANDREW "BOB"
B.SEP.28,1935 SAYREVILLE,N.J.

YR	CL	LEA	POS	GP	G	REC
1963	DET	A	P		7	0- 1

DUZEN, WILLIAM GEORGE
B.FEB.21,1870 BUFFALO,N.Y.
D.MAR.11,1944

YR	CL	LEA	POS	GP	G	REC
1890	BUF	P	P		2	0- 2
	BRTR					

DWIGHT
B.CHICAGO,ILL.

YR	CL	LEA	POS	GP	G	REC
1884	KC	U	C-O		12	.268

DWYER, JAMES EDWARD "JIM"
B.JAN.3,1950 EVERGREEN PARK,ILL.

YR	CL	LEA	POS	GP	G	REC
1973	STL	N	O		28	.193
1974	STL	N	1-O		74	.279
1975	STL	N	O		21	.194
	MON	N	O		60	.286
1976	MON	N	O		50	.185
	NY	N	O		11	.154
	BLTL				244	.242

DWYER, JOHN E.
B.CHICAGO,ILL.

YR	CL	LEA	POS	GP	G	REC
1882	CLE	N	C-O		1	.000

DWYER, JOHN FRANCIS "FRANK"
B.MAR.25,1868 LEE,MASS.
D.FEB.4,1943

YR	CL	LEA	POS	GP	G	REC
1888	DET	N	P		5	4- 1
1889	CHI	N	P	29	33	16-12
1890	CHI	P	P		16	1- 7
1891	CIN	AA	P-2-	29	34	13-18
			O			.250
	MIL	AA	P		10	4- 4
	CIN	N	P		14	2- 6
1892	STL	N	P		46	20-10
	CIN	N	P		32	18-14
1893	CIN	N	P	39	49	18-19
1894	CIN	N	P		34	18-13
1895	CIN	N	P		35	25-10
1896	CIN	N	P	27	35	17-12
1897	CIN	N	P		29	16-10
1898	CIN	N	P		5	0- 5
	BRTR			354	377	173-141
						.233

NON-PLAYING MANAGER DET(A) 1902

DWYER, JOSEPH MICHAEL "DOUBLE"
B.MAR.27,1904 ORANGE,N.J.

YR	CL	LEA	POS	GP	G	REC
1937	CIN	N	H		12	.273
	BLTL					

DYCK, JAMES ROBERT "JIM"
B.FEB.3,1922 OMAHA,NEB.

YR	CL	LEA	POS	GP	G	REC
1951	STL	A	3		4	.067
1952	STL	A	3-O		122	.269
1953	STL	A	3-O		112	.213
1954	CLE	A	H		2	1.000
1955	BAL	A	3-O		61	.279
1956	BAL	A	O		11	.217
	CIN	N	1-3		18	.091
	BRTR				330	.245

DYER, BENJAMIN FRANKLIN
B.FEB.13,1893 CHICAGO,ILL.
D.AUG.7,1959

YR	CL	LEA	POS	GP	G	REC
1914	NY	N	2-S		7	.250
1916	NY	N	S-3		7	.211
1917	DET	A	S		4	.308
1917	DET	A	S		30	.209
1918	DET	A	P		13	0- 0
1919	DET	A	3		44	.247
	BRTR				105	0- 0
						.238

DYER, DON ROBERT "DUFFY"
B.AUG.15,1945 DAYTON,OHIO

YR	CL	LEA	POS	GP	G	REC
1968	NY	N	C		1	.333
1969	NY	N	C		29	.257
1970	NY	N	C		59	.209
1971	NY	N	C		59	.231
1972	NY	N	C-O		94	.231
1973	NY	N	C		70	.185
1974	NY	N	C		63	.211
1975	PIT	N	C		48	.227
1976	PIT	N	C		69	.223
	BRTR				492	.220

DYER, EDWIN HAWLEY "EDDIE"
B.OCT.11,1900 MORGAN CITY,LA.
D.APR.20,1964 HOUSTON,TEX.

YR	CL	LEA	POS	GP	G	REC
1922	STL	N	P	2	6	0- 0
1923	STL	N	P-O	4	35	2- 1
						.267
1924	STL	N	P-O	29	50	8-11
						.237
1925	STL	N	P		31	4- 3
1926	STL	N	P		6	1- 0
1927	STL	N	P		1	0- 0
	BLTL			73	129	15-15
						.223

NON-PLAYING MANAGER
STL(N) 1946-50

DYGERT, JAMES HENRY "SUNNY JIM"
B.JULY 5,1884 UTICA,N.Y.
D.FEB.8,1936

YR	CL	LEA	POS	GP	G	REC
1905	PHI	A	P		6	1- 3
1906	PHI	A	P		35	11-13
1907	PHI	A	P		42	20- 9
1908	PHI	A	P		41	11-15
1909	PHI	A	P		32	8- 5
1910	PHI	A	P		19	4- 4
	TR				175	55-49

DYKES, JAMES JOSEPH "JIMMY"
B.NOV.10,1896 PHILADELPHIA,PA.
D.JUNE 15,1976 PHILADELPHIA,PA.

YR	CL	LEA	POS	GP	G	REC
1918	PHI	A	2		59	.188
1919	PHI	A	2		17	.184
1920	PHI	A	2-3		142	.256
1921	PHI	A	2		155	.274
1922	PHI	A	3		145	.275
1923	PHI	A	2-S		124	.252
1924	PHI	A	2-3		110	.312
1925	PHI	A	2-S-3		122	.325
1926	PHI	A	2-3		124	.287
1927	PHI	A	P-1-	2	121	0- 0
			3			.324
1928	PHI	A	2-S-3		85	.277
1929	PHI	A	2-S-3		119	.327
1930	PHI	A	3		125	.301
1931	PHI	A	S-3		101	.273
1932	PHI	A	S-3		153	.265
1933	CHI	A	3		151	.260
1934	CHI	A	M-1-2-3		127	.268
1935	CHI	A	M-1-2-3		117	.288
1936	CHI	A	M-3		127	.267
1937	CHI	A	M-1-3		30	.306
1938	CHI	A	M-2		26	.303
1939	CHI	A	M-3		2	.000
	BRTR			2	2282	0- 0
						.280

NON-PLAYING MANAGER
CHI(A) 1940-46, PHI(A) 1951-53,
BAL(A) 1954, CIN(N) 1958,
DET(A) 1959-60, CLE(A) 1960-61

DYLER, JOHN F.
B.LOUISVILLE,KY.

YR	CL	LEA	POS	GP	G	REC
1882	LOU	AA	M-O		1	.000

EADDY, DONALD JOHNSON "DON"
B.FEB.16,1934 GRAND RAPIDS,MICH

YR	CL	LEA	POS	GP	G	REC
1959	CHI	N	3		15	.000
	BRTR					

EAGAN, CHARLES EUGENE "TRUCK"
B.AUG.10,1877 OAKLAND,CAL.
D.MAR.19,1949

YR	CL	LEA	POS	GP	G	REC
1901	PIT	N	S		4	.083
	CLE	A	2-3		5	.176
					9	.138

EAGAN, WILLIAM "BAD BILL"
B.JUNE 1,1869 CAMDEN,N.J.
D.FEB.14,1905

YR	CL	LEA	POS	GP	G	REC
1891	STL	AA	2		81	.222
1893	CHI	N	2		6	.300
1898	PIT	N	2		16	.328
					103	.240

EAGLE, WILLIAM
B.ROCKVILLE,MD.

YR	CL	LEA	POS	GP	G	REC
1898	WAS	N	O		4	.333

EAKLE, CHARLES EMORY
B.SEPT.27,1887 MARYLAND
D.JUNE 15,1959 BALTIMORE,MD.

YR	CL	LEA	POS	GP	G	REC
1915	BAL	F	2		2	.286

```
YR   CL LEA POS  GP    G    REC          YR    CL LEA POS  GP    G    REC          YR   CL LEA POS  GP    G   REC

EARL, HOWARD J.                          EAST, CARLTON W.                          EAVES, VALLIE ENNIS "CHIEF"
B.FEB.21,1867 PALMYRA,N.Y.               B.AUG.27,1893 MARLETTA,VA.               B.SEPT.6,1911 ALLEN,OKLA.
D.DEC.23,1916                            D.JAN.15,1953                             1935 PHI A  P         3    1- 2
1890 CHI N 2-0        92    .247         1915 STL A  P          1    0- 0          1939 CHI A  P         2    0- 1
1891 MIL AA O         30    .254         1924 WAS A  O          2    .333          1940 CHI A  P         5    0- 2
                     122    .248              BLTL       1    3    0- 0            1941 CHI N  P        12    3- 3
                                                                   .286           1942 CHI N  P         2    0- 0
EAPLE, WILLIAM MOFFAT                                                                   BRTR           24    4- 8
"GLOBETROTTER"                           EAST, GORDON HUGH
B.NOV.10,1867 PHILADELPHIA,PA.           B.JULY 7,1919 BIRMINGHAM,ALA.            EAYRS, EDWIN
D.MAY 30,1946                            1941 NY  N  P          2    1- 1          B.NOV.10,1890 BLACKSTONE,MASS.
1889 CIN AA C-1-0     53    .269         1942 NY  N  P          4    0- 2          D.NOV.30,1969 WARWICK,R.I.
1890 STL AA C         23    .212         1943 NY  N  P    13   17    1- 3          1913 PIT N  P          4    0- 0
1892 PIT N  C          5    .500              BRTR      19   23    2- 6            1920 BOS N  P-O   7   87    1- 2
1893 PIT N  C         26    .317                                                                            .328
1894 LOU N  C         19    .377         EAST, HARRY H.                            1921 BOS N  P     2   15    0- 0
     BRO N  C-2       14    .321         B.ST.LOUIS,MO.                                 BRO N  O            8    .167
     BRTR            140    .297         1882 BAL AA 3          1    .000               BLTL     13  114    1- 2
                                                                                                            .306
EARLEY, ARNOLD CARL                      EASTER, LUSCIOUS LUKE
B.JUNE 4,1933 LINCOLN PARK,MICH.         "LUKE"                                    EBBETS, CHARLES HERCULES
1960 BOS A  P         2    0- 1          B.AUG.4,1921 ST.LOUIS,MO.                 B.OCT.29,1859 NEW YORK,N.Y.
1961 BOS A  P        33    2- 4          1949 CLE A  O         21    .222          D.APR.18,1925
1962 BOS A  P        38    4- 5          1950 CLE A  1-0      141    .280          NON-PLAYING MANAGER BRO(N) 1898
1963 BOS A  P        53    3- 7          1951 CLE A  1        128    .270
1964 BOS A  P        25    1- 1          1952 CLE A  1        127    .263          EBRIGHT, HIRAM C. "BUCK"
1965 BOS A  P        57    0- 1          1953 CLE A  1         68    .303          B.JUNE 12,1859 LANCASTER CO.,PA
1966 CHI N  P        13    2- 1          1954 CLE A  H          6    .167          D.OCT.24,1916
1967 HOU N  P         2    0- 0               BLTR            491    .273          1889 WAS N  3         15    .254
     BLTL           223   12-20                                                         BRTR
                                         EASTERLING, PAUL
EARLEY, THOMAS FRANCIS ALOYSIUS          B.SEPT.28,1905 REIDSVILLE,GA.            ECCLES, HARRY JOSIAH "BUGS"
B.FEB.19,1918 ROXBURY,MASS.              1928 DET A  O         43    .325          B.JULY 9,1893 KENNEDY,N.Y.
1938 BOS N  P         2    1- 0          1930 DET A  O         29    .202          D.JUNE 2,1955
1939 BOS N  P        14    1- 4          1938 PHI A  O          4    .286          1915 PHI A  P          5    0- 1
1940 BOS N  P         4    2- 0               BRTR            76    .275                BLTL
1941 BOS N  P   33   34    6- 8
1942 BOS N  P        27    6-11          EASTERLY, JAMES MORRIS "JAMIE"           ECHOLS, JOHN GRESHAM
1945 BOS N  P   11   13    2- 1          B.FEB.17,1953 HOUSTON,TEX.               B.JAN.9,1917 ATLANTA,GA.
     BRTR       91   94   18-24          1974 ATL N  P          3    0- 0          D.NOV.13,1972 ATLANTA,GA.
                                         1975 ATL N  P         21    2- 9          1939 STL N  2          2    .000
EARLY, JACOB WILLARD "JAKE"              1976 ATL N  P          4    1- 1               BRTR
B.MAY 19,1915 KING'S MOUNTAIN,                BBTL            28    1--8
N.C.                                                                              ECKERSLEY, DENNIS LEE
1939 WAS A  C        32    .262          EASTERLY, THEODORE HARRISON              B.OCT.3,1954 OAKLAND,CAL.
1940 WAS A  C        80    .257          B.APR.20,1885 LINCOLN,NEB.               1975 CLE A  P         34   13- 7
1941 WAS A  C       104    .287          D.JULY 6,1951 CLEAR LAKE                 1976 CLE A  P         36   13-12
1942 WAS A  C       104    .204          HIGHLANDS,CAL.                                BRTR            70   26-19
1943 WAS A  C       126    .258          1909 CLE A  C         98    .261
1946 WAS A  C        64    .201          1910 CLE A  C-O      110    .306          ECKERT, ALBERT GEORGE
1947 STL A  C        87    .224          1911 CLE A  C-O       99    .324          B.MAY 17,1908 MILWAUKEE,WIS.
1948 WAS A  C        97    .220          1912 CLE A  C         65    .296          D.APR.20,1974 MILWAUKEE,WIS.
1949 WAS A  C        53    .246               CHI A            28    .364          1930 CIN N  P          2    0- 1
     BLTR           747    .241          1913 CHI A  C         60    .235          1931 CIN N  P         14    0- 1
                                         1914 KC  F  C        134    .331          1935 STL N  P          2    0- 0
EARNSHAW, GEORGE LIVINGSTON              1915 KC  F  C        110    .267               BLTL            18    0- 2
"MOOSE"                                       BLTR           704    .299
B.FEB.15,1900 NEW YORK,N.Y.                                                       ECKERT, CHARLES WILLIAM "BUZZ"
D.DEC.1,1976 LITTLE ROCK,ARK.            EASTERWOOD, ROY CHARLES                  B.AUG.8,1897 PHILADELPHIA,PA.
1928 PHI A  P        26    7- 7          B.JAN.12,1915 WAXAHACHIE,TEX.            1919 PHI A  P          2    0- 1
1929 PHI A  P        44   24- 8          1944 CHI N  C         17    .212          1920 PHI A  P          2    0- 0
1930 PHI A  P        49   22-13               BRTR                                1922 PHI A  P         21    0- 2
1931 PHI A  P        43   21- 7                                                        BRTR            25    0- 3
1932 PHI A  P        36   19-13          EASTON, JOHN DAVID
1933 PHI A  P        21    5-10          B.MAR.4,1933 TRENTON,N.J.                ECKHARDT, OSCAR GEORGE "OX"
1934 CHI A  P        33   14-11          1955 PHI N  H          1    .000          B.DEC.23,1901 YORKTOWN,TEX.
1935 CHI A  P         3    1- 2          1959 PHI N  H          3    .000          D.APR.22,1951 YORKTOWN,TEX.
     BRO N  P        25    8-12               BRTR             4    .000          1932 BOS N  H          8    .250
1936 BRO N  P        19    4- 9                                                   1936 BRO N  O         16    .182
     STL N  P        20    2- 1          EASTON, JOHN E.                               BLTR            24    .192
     BRTR           319  127-93          B.1867 BRIDGEPORT,OHIO
                                         1889 COL AA P          4    1- 0          EDDY, DONALD EUGENE "DON"
EASLER, MICHAEL ANTHONY "MIKE"          1890 COL AA P         37   14-13          B.OCT.25,1946 MASON CITY,IOWA
B.NOV.29,1950 CLEVELAND,OHIO             1891 COL AA P         15    5-10          1970 CHI A  P          7    0- 0
1973 HOU N  O         6    .000               STL AA P          9    4- 3          1971 CHI A  P         22    0- 2
1974 HOU N  H        15    .067               COL AA P-O   3    6    0- 3               BRTL            29    0- 2
1975 HOU N  H         5    .000                                    .105
1976 CAL A  O        21    .241          1892 STL N  P          5    2- 3          EDELEN, EDWARD JOSEPH
     BLTR            47    .173          1894 PIT N  P          3    0- 1          B.MAR.16,1912 BRYANTOWN,MD.
                                                            76   79   26-33        1932 WAS A  P          2    0- 0
EASON, MALCOLM WAYNE                                                .194               BRTR
B.MAR.13,1879 BROOKVILLE,PA.
D.APR.16,1970 DOUGLAS,ARIZ.              EASTWICK, RAWLINS JACKSON                EDELMAN, JOHN ROGERS
1900 CHI N  P         1    1- 0          "RAWLY"                                   B.JULY 27,1935 PHILADELPHIA,PA.
1901 CHI N  P        25    8-17          B.OCT.24,1950 CAMDEN,N.J.                1955 MIL N  P          5    0- 0
1902 CHI N  P         6    1- 1          1974 CIN N  P          8    0- 0               BRTR
     BOS N  P        25    9-14          1975 CIN N  P         58    5- 3
1903 DET A  P         7    2- 4          1976 CIN N  P         71   11- 5
1905 BRO N  P   27   29    5-20               BRTR           137   16- 8
1906 BRO N  P   34   36   10-17
     TR        125  129   36-73          EATON, ZEBULON VANCE "RED"
                                         B.FEB.2,1920 COOLEEMEE,N.C.
                                         1944 DET A  P          8    0- 0
                                         1945 DET A  P         26    4- 2
                                              BRTR            35    4- 2
```

YR CL LEA POS GP   G   REC

EDEN, CHARLES M.
B.JAN.18,1855 LEXINGTON,KY.
D.SEPT.17,1920
1877 CHI N O   15 .218
1879 CLE N O   81 .272
1884 PIT AA P-O   1   32 C- 1
                              .3C5
1885 PIT AA P-O   3   98 1- 2
                              .264
       BRTR   4   226 1- 3
                              .269

EDEN, EDWARD MICHAEL "MIKE"
B.MAY 22,1949 FORT CLAYTON,
CANAL ZONE
1976 ATL N 2   5 .000
       BBTR

EDINGTON, JACOB FRANK "STUMP"
B.JULY 4,1891 LYONS,IND.
D.NOV.11,1969 BASTROP,LA.
1912 PIT N O   15 .302
       BLTL

EDGERTON, WILLIAM ALBERT "BILL"
B.AUG.16,1941 SOUTH BEND,IND.
1966 KC A P   6 C- 1
1967 KC A P   7 1- 0
1969 SEA A P   4 C- 1
       BLTL   17 1- 2

EDMONDSON, GEORGE HENDERSON
B.MAY 28,1896 WAXAHACHIE,TEX.
D.JULY 11,1973 WACO,TEX.
1922 CLE A P   2 0- 0
1923 CLE A P   1 0- 0
1924 CLE A P   5 0- 0
       BRTR   8 0- 0

EDMONDSON, PAUL MICHAEL
B.FEB.12,1943 KANSAS CITY,KAN.
D.FEB.13,1970 SANTA BARBARA,CAL.
1969 CHI A P   14 1- 6
       BRTR

EDMONDSON, ROBERT E.
B.APR.30,1879 PARIS,KY.
D.AUG.14,1931 LAWRENCE,KAN.
1908 WAS A O   26 .188
       BRTR

EDMONDSTON, SAMUEL SHERWOOD
"BIG SAM"
B.AUG.30,1883 WASHINGTON,D.C.
1906 WAS A P   3 0- 1
1907 WAS A P   1 0- 0
       BLTL   4 0- 1

EDMONSON, EDWARD EARL "EDDIE"
B.NOV.20,1889 HOPEWELL,PA.
D.MAY 10,1971 LEESBURG,FLA.
1913 CLE A 1-0   2 .C00
       BLTR

EDWARDS
1875 ATL NA O   1 -

EDWARDS, ALBERT
B.1896 FREEPORT,L.I.,N.Y.
1915 PHI A 2   2 .000
       TR

EDWARDS, CHARLES BRUCE
"BRUCE" OR "BULL"
B.JULY 15,1923 QUINCY,ILL.
D.APR.25,1975 SACRAMENTO,CAL.
1946 BRO N C   92 .267
1947 BRO N C   130 .296
1948 BRO N C-1-3-0   96 .276
1949 BRO N C-3-0   64 .209
1950 BRO N C-1   50 .183
1951 BRO N C   17 .250
       CHI N C-1   51 .234
1952 CHI N C-2   50 .245
1954 CHI N H   4 .000
1955 WAS A C-3   30 .175
1956 CIN N C-2-3   7 .200
       BRTR   591 .256

EDWARDS, FOSTER HAMILTON
"EDDIE"
B.SEPT.1,1903 HOLSTEIN,IOWA
1925 BOS N P   1 0- C
1926 BOS N P   3 2- 0
1927 BOS N P   29   33 2- 8
1928 BOS N P   21 2- 1
1930 NY A P   2 0- 0
       BRTR   56   6C 6- 9

EDWARDS, HENRY ALBERT "HANK"
B.JAN.29,1919 ELMWOOD PLACE,O.
1941 CLE A O   16 .221
1942 CLE A O   13 .250
1943 CLE A O   92 .276
1946 CLE A O   124 .301
1947 CLE A O   108 .26C
1948 CLE A O   55 .269
1949 CLE A O   5 .267
       CHI N O   58 .290
1950 CHI N O   41 .364
1951 BRO N H   35 .226
       CIN N O   41 .315
1952 CIN N O   74 .283
       CHI A O   8 .333
1953 STL A O   65 .198
       BLTL   735 .280

EDWARDS, HOWARD RODNEY "DOC"
B.DEC.10,1937 VARNEY,W.VA.
1962 CLE A C   53 .273
1963 CLE A C   10 .258
       KC A C   71 .250
1964 KC A C-1   97 .224
1965 KC A C   6 .150
       NY A C   45 .190
1970 PHI N C   35 .269
       BRTR   317 .238

EDWARDS, JAMES CORBETTE
"LITTLE JOE"
B.DEC.14,1894 BANNER,MISS.
D.JAN.19,1965 PONTOTOC,MISS.
1922 CLE A P   25 3- 8
1923 CLE A P   38 10-10
1924 CLE A P   10 4- 3
1925 CLE A P   13 C- 3
       CHI A P   9 1- 2
1926 CHI A P   32 6- 9
1928 CIN N P   18 2- 2
       BRTL   145 26-37

EDWARDS, JOHN ALBAN "JOHNNY"
B.JUNE 10,1938 COLUMBUS,OHIO
1961 CIN N C   52 .186
1962 CIN N C   133 .254
1963 CIN N C   148 .259
1964 CIN N C   126 .281
1965 CIN N C   114 .267
1966 CIN N C   98 .191
1967 CIN N C   80 .206
1968 STL N C   85 .239
1969 HOU N C   151 .232
1970 HOU N C   140 .221
1971 HOU N C   106 .233
1972 HOU N C   108 .268
1973 HOU N C   79 .244
1974 HOU N C   50 .222
       BLTR   1470 .242

EDWARDS, SHERMAN STANLEY
B.JULY 25,1909 MT.IDA,ARK.
1934 CIN N P   1 0- 0
       BRTR

EELLS, HARRY A.
B.FEB.14,1881 IDA GROVE,IOWA
D.OCT.15,1940 LOS ANGELES,CAL.
1906 CLE A P   14 4- 5
       BRTR

EGAN, ALOYSIUS JEROME "WISH"
B.JUNE 16,1881 EVERETT,MICH.
D.APR.13,1951
1902 DET A P   3 1- 2
1905 STL N P   23 5-16
1906 STL N P   16 2- 9
                          42 8-27

EGAN, ARTHUR AUGUSTUS "BEN"
B.NOV.20,1883 AUGUSTA,N.Y.
D.FEB.18,1968 SHERRILL,N.Y.
1908 PHI A C   2 .143
1912 PHI A C   48 .174
1914 CLE A C   29 .227
1915 CLE A C   42 .108
       BRTR   121 .164

EGAN, JAMES
B.1838 ANSONIA,CONN.
D.SEPT.26,1884
1882 TRO N P-C- 14   29 4- 6
              O   .181

EGAN, JOHN JOSEPH "RIP"
B.JULY 9,1871 PHILADELPHIA,PA.
D.DEC.22,1950
1894 WAS N P   1 0- 0

EGAN, RICHARD JOSEPH
B.JUNE 23,1884 PORTLAND,ORE.
D.JUNE 30,1947
1908 CIN N 2   18 .206
1909 CIN N 2   126 .275
1910 CIN N 2   134 .245
1911 CIN N 2   152 .249
1912 CIN N 2   149 .247
1913 CIN N 2-S   60 .282
1914 BRO N S   106 .226
1915 BRO N 2   3 .000
       BOS N 2-0   83 .264
1916 BOS N 2   83 .223
       BRTR   914 .250

EGAN, RICHARD WALLIS "DICK"
B.MAR.24,1937 BERKELEY,CAL.
1963 DET A P   20 0- 1
1964 DET A P   23 0- 0
1966 CAL A P   11 0- 0
1967 LA N P   20 1- 1
       BLTL   74 1- 2

EGAN, THOMAS PATRICK "TOM"
B.JUNE 9,1946 LOS ANGELES,CAL.
1965 CAL A C   18 .263
1966 CAL A C   7 .000
1967 CAL A C   1 .000
1968 CAL A C   16 .116
1969 CAL A C   46 .192
1970 CAL A C   79 .230
1971 CHI A C-1   85 .239
1972 CHI A C   50 .191
1974 CAL A C   43 .117
1975 CAL A C   28 .229
       BRTR   373 .200
       BB 1974 (PART), 75

EGGERT, ELMER ALBERT
B.JAN.29,1902 ROCHESTER,N.Y.
D.APR.9,1971 ROCHESTER,N.Y.
1927 BOS A P   5 0- C
       BRTR

EGGLER, DAVID DANIEL
B.APR.30,1851 BROOKLYN,N.Y.
D.APR.5,1902
1871 MUT NA O   33 -
1872 MUT NA O   56 .346
1873 MUT NA O   54 -
1874 PHI NA 2-0   58 -
1875 ATH NA O   66 .288
1876 ATH N O   39 .295
1877 CHI N O   33 .265
1879 BUF N O   77 .208
1883 BAL AA O   53 .194
       BUF N O   38 .245
1884 BUF N O   58 .198
1885 BUF N O   6 .083
       BRTR   571 -

EHMKE, HOWARD JOHN
B.APR.24,1894 SILVER CREEK,N.Y.
D.MAR.17,1959
1915 BUF F P   18 C- 2
1916 DET A P   5 3- 1
1917 DET A P   35 10-15
1919 DET A P   33 17-10
1920 DET A P   38 15-18
1921 DET A P   30 13-14
1922 DET A P   45 17-17
1923 BOS A P   43 20-17
1924 BOS A P   45   46 19-17
1925 BOS A P   34 9-20
1926 BOS A P   14 3-10
       PHI A P   20   21 12- 8
1927 PHI A P   30 12-10
1928 PHI A P   23 9- 8
1929 PHI A P   11 7- 2
1930 PHI A P   3 0- 1
       BRTR   427   429 166-166

EHRET, PHILIP SYDNEY "RED"
B.AUG.31,1868 LOUISVILLE,KY.
D.JULY 28,1940

YR	CL	LEA	POS	GP	G	REC
1888	KC	AA	P-O	7	16	4- 3
						.186
1889	LOU	AA	P	47	66	9-29
1890	LOU	AA	P		42	24-13
1891	LOU	AA	P		26	13-12
1892	PIT	N	P		40	18-19
1893	PIT	N	P		36	17-17
1894	PIT	N	P		41	18-22
1895	STL	N	P		31	6-20
1896	CIN	N	P		33	18-15
1897	CIN	N	P		27	10-10
1898	LOU	N	P		12	3- 7
		BRTR		342	370	140-167
						.220

EHRHARDT, WELTON CLAUDE "RUBE"
B.NOV.20,1894 BEECHER,ILL.

YR	CL	LEA	POS	GP	G	REC
1924	BRO	N	P		15	5- 3
1925	BRO	N	P		36	10-14
1926	BRO	N	P		44	2- 5
1927	BRO	N	P		46	3- 7
1928	BRO	N	P		28	1- 3
1929	CIN	N	P		24	1- 2
		BRTR			193	22-34

EIBEL, HENRY HACK "HACK"
B.DEC.6,1893 BROOKLYN,N.Y.
D.OCT.16,1945

YR	CL	LEA	POS	GP	G	REC
1912	CLE	A	O		1	.000
1920	BOS	A	P	3	29	0- 0
		BLTL		3	30	0- 0
						.174

EICHRODT, FREDERICK GEORGE
B.JAN.6,1903 CHICAGO,ILL.
D.JULY 14,1965 INDIANAPOLIS,IND

YR	CL	LEA	POS	GP	G	REC
1925	CLE	A	O		15	.230
1926	CLE	A	O		37	.313
1927	CLE	A	O		85	.221
1931	CHI	A	O		34	.214
		BRTR			171	.234

EILERS, DAVID LOUIS "DAVE"
B.DEC.3,1936 OLDENBURG,TEX.

YR	CL	LEA	POS	GP	G	REC
1964	MIL	N	P		6	0- 0
1965	MIL	N	P		6	0- 0
	NY	N	P		11	1- 1
1966	NY	N	P		23	1- 1
1967	HOU	N	P		35	6- 4
		BRTR			81	8- 6

EISENHART, JACOB HENRY
B.OCT.3,1922 PERKASIE,PA.

YR	CL	LEA	POS	GP	G	REC
1944	CIN	N	P		1	0- 0
		BLTL				

EISENSTAT, HARRY
B.OCT.10,1915 BROOKLYN,N.Y.

YR	CL	LEA	POS	GP	G	REC
1935	BRO	N	P		2	0- 1
1936	BRO	N	P		5	1- 2
1937	BRO	N	P		13	3- 3
1938	DET	A	P		32	9- 6
1939	DET	A	P		10	2- 2
	CLE	A	P		26	6- 7
1940	CLE	A	P		27	1- 4
1941	CLE	A	P		21	1- 1
1942	CLE	A	P		29	2- 1
		BLTL			165	25-27

EITELJORG, EDWARD HENRY
B.OCT.14,1871 BERLIN,GERMANY
D.DEC.7,1942

YR	CL	LEA	POS	GP	G	REC
1890	CHI	N	P		1	0- 0
1891	WAS	AA	P		8	2- 6
					9	2- 6

ELAND

YR	CL	LEA	POS	GP	G	REC
1873	MAR	NA	O		1	.000

ELBERFELD, NORMAN ARTHUR "KID"
B.APR.13,1875 POMEROY,OHIO
D.JAN.13,1944

YR	CL	LEA	POS	GP	G	REC
1898	PHI	N	3		13	.228
1899	CIN	N	S		41	.259
1901	DET	A	S		122	.309
1902	DET	A	S		139	.265
1903	DET	A	S		35	.323
	NY	A	S		90	.290
1904	NY	A	S		122	.256
1905	NY	A	S		108	.262
1906	NY	A	S		99	.306
1907	NY	A	S		120	.271
1908	NY	A	M-S		19	.196
1909	NY	A	S-3		106	.237
1910	WAS	A	3		127	.250
1911	WAS	A	2-3		127	.272
1914	BRO	N	S		30	.226
		BRTR			1298	.270

ELDER, GEORGE REZIN
B.MAR.10,1923 LOUISVILLE,KY.

YR	CL	LEA	POS	GP	G	REC
1949	STL	A	O		41	.250
		BLTR				

ELDER, HENRY KNOX "HEINE"
B.AUG.23,1890 SEATTLE,WASH.

YR	CL	LEA	POS	GP	G	REC
1913	DET	A	P		1	0- 0
		BLTL				

ELIA, LEE CONSTANTINE
B.JULY 16,1937 PHILADELPHIA,PA.

YR	CL	LEA	POS	GP	G	REC
1966	CHI	A	S		80	.205
1968	CHI	N	2-S-3		15	.176
		BRTR			95	.203

ELKO, PETER
B.JUNE 17,1918 WILKES-BARRE,PA.

YR	CL	LEA	POS	GP	G	REC
1943	CHI	N	3		9	.133
1944	CHI	N	3		7	.227
		BRTR			16	.173

ELLAM, ROY
B.JULY 11,1887 CONSHOHOCKEN,PA.
D.OCT.28,1948

YR	CL	LEA	POS	GP	G	REC
1909	CIN	N	S		10	.190
1918	PIT	N	S		26	.130
		BRTR			36	.143

ELLER, HORACE OWEN "HOD"
B.JULY 5,1894 MUNCIE,IND.
D.JULY 18,1961

YR	CL	LEA	POS	GP	G	REC
1917	CIN	N	P		37	10- 5
1918	CIN	N	P		37	16-12
1919	CIN	N	P		38	19- 9
1920	CIN	N	P-1-	35	38	13-12
			2			.253
1921	CIN	N	P		13	2- 2
		BRTR		160	163	60-40
						.221

ELLERBE, FRANCIS ROGERS
"FRANK" OR "GOVERNOR"
B.DEC.25,1895 MARION,S.C.

YR	CL	LEA	POS	GP	G	REC
1919	WAS	A	S		28	.276
1920	WAS	A	S-3		101	.292
1921	WAS	A	S		10	.200
	STL	A	S		105	.288
1922	STL	A	S		91	.246
1923	STL	A	S		18	.184
1924	STL	A	S		21	.194
	CLE	A	S		46	.261
		BRTR			420	.268

ELLICK, JOSEPH J.
B.1856 CINCINNATI,OHIO

YR	CL	LEA	POS	GP	G	REC
1875	RS	NA	S-3-O		7	-
1878	MIL	N	P-C-3		3	0- 0
						.154
1880	WOR	N	3		5	.053
1884	CHI	U	C-2-S-O		72	.253
	PIT	U	M-S		18	.167
	KC	U	2-O		2	.000
	BAL	U	S-O		7	.148
					114	0- 0
						-

ELLINGSEN, H. BRUCE
B.APR.26,1949 POCATELLO,IDAHO

YR	CL	LEA	POS	GP	G	REC
1974	CLE	A	P		16	1- 1
		BLTL				

ELLIOT, LAWRENCE LEE "LARRY"
B.MAR.5,1938 SAN DIEGO,CAL.

YR	CL	LEA	POS	GP	G	REC
1962	PIT	N	O		8	.300
1963	PIT	N	H		4	.000
1964	NY	N	O		80	.228
1966	NY	N	O		65	.246
		BLTL			157	.236

ELLIOTT, ALLEN CLIFFORD
B.DEC.25,1897 ST.LOUIS,MO.

YR	CL	LEA	POS	GP	G	REC
1923	CHI	N	1		53	.250
1924	CHI	N	1		10	.143
		BLTR			63	.242

ELLIOTT, CARTER WARD
B.NOV.28,1897

YR	CL	LEA	POS	GP	G	REC
1921	CHI	N	S		12	.250
		BLTR				

ELLIOTT, CLAUDE J.
B.NOV.17,1879 PARDEEVILLE,WIS.
D.JUNE 21,1923

YR	CL	LEA	POS	GP	G	REC
1904	CIN	N	P		10	4- 6
	NY	N	P		3	0- 1
1905	NY	N	P		10	2- 1
		BRTR			23	6- 8

ELLIOTT, EUGENE BIRMINGHOUSE
B.FEB.8,1889 FAYETTE CITY,PA.
D.JAN.5,1976 HUNTINGDON,PA.

YR	CL	LEA	POS	GP	G	REC
1911	NY	A	3		5	.077
		BLTR				

ELLIOTT, HAROLD H. "ROWDY"
B.JULY 8,1890 BLOOMINGTON,ILL.
D.FEB.12,1934

YR	CL	LEA	POS	GP	G	REC
1910	BOS	N	C		1	.000
1916	CHI	N	C		23	.255
1917	CHI	N	C		85	.251
1918	CHI	N	C		5	.000
1920	BRO	N	C		41	.241
		BRTR			155	.241

ELLIOTT, HARRY LEWIS
B.DEC.30,1925 SAN FRANCISCO,CAL

YR	CL	LEA	POS	GP	G	REC
1953	STL	N	O		24	.254
1955	STL	N	O		68	.256
		BRTR			92	.256

ELLIOTT, HERBERT GLENN
"GLENN" OR "LEFTY"
B.NOV.11,1919 SAPULPA,OKLA
D.JULY 27,1969 PORTLAND,ORE.

YR	CL	LEA	POS	GP	G	REC
1947	BOS	N	P		11	0- 1
1948	BOS	N	P		1	1- 0
1949	BOS	N	P		22	3- 4
		BLTL			34	4- 5

ELLIOTT, HOWARD WILLIAM "ACE"
B.MAY 29,1903 MT.CLEMENS,MICH.
D.APR.25,1963 HONOLULU,HAWAII

YR	CL	LEA	POS	GP	G	REC
1929	PHI	N	P		40	3- 7
1930	PHI	N	P		48	6-11
1931	PHI	N	P		16	0- 2
1932	PHI	N	P		16	2- 4
		BRTR			120	11-24

ELLIOTT, JAMES THOMAS "JUMBO"
B.OCT.22,1900 ST.LOUIS,MO.
D.JAN.7,1970 TERRE HAUTE,IND.

YR	CL	LEA	POS	GP	G	REC
1923	STL	A	P		1	0- 0
1925	BRO	N	P		3	0- 2
1927	BRO	N	P		30	6-13
1928	BRO	N	P		41	9-14
1929	BRO	N	P		6	1- 2
1930	BRO	N	P		35	10- 7
1931	PHI	N	P		52	19-14
1932	PHI	N	P		39	11-10
1933	PHI	N	P	35	36	6-10
1934	PHI	N	P		3	0- 1
	BOS	N	P		7	1- 1
		BRTL		252	253	63-74

ELLIOTT, RANDY LEE
B.JUNE 5,1951 OXNARD,CAL.

YR	CL	LEA	POS	GP	G	REC
1972	SD	N	O		14	.204
1974	SD	N	1-O		13	.212
		BRTR			27	.207

YR CL LEA POS GP G REC

ELLIOTT, ROBERT IRVING
"BOB" OR "MR. TEAM"
B.NOV.26,1916 SAN FRANCISCO,CAL
D.MAY 4,1966 SAN DIEGO,CAL.

YR	CL	LEA	POS	GP	G	REC
1939	PIT	N	O		32	.333
1940	PIT	N	O		148	.292
1941	PIT	N	O		141	.273
1942	PIT	N	3-O		143	.297
1943	PIT	N	2-S-3		156	.315
1944	PIT	N	S-3		143	.298
1945	PIT	N	3-O		144	.290
1946	PIT	N	3-O		140	.263
1947	BOS	N	3		150	.317
1948	BOS	N	3		151	.283
1949	BOS	N	3		139	.280
1950	BOS	N	3		142	.305
1951	BOS	N	3		136	.285
1952	NY	N	3-O		98	.228
1953	STL	A	3		48	.250
	CHI	A	3-O		67	.260
	BRTR				1978	.289

NON-PLAYING MANAGER KC(A) 1960

ELLIS, BENJAMIN F.
B.POTTSVILLE,PA.

YR	CL	LEA	POS	GP	G	REC
1896	PHI	N	S		4	.063

ELLIS, DOCK PHILLIP
B.MAR.11,1945 LOS ANGELES,CAL.

YR	CL	LEA	POS	GP	G	REC
1968	PIT	N	P	26	27	6- 5
1969	PIT	N	P	35	37	11-17
1970	PIT	N	P	30	38	13-10
1971	PIT	N	P	31	44	19- 9
1972	PIT	N	P	25	36	15- 7
1973	PIT	N	P	28	29	12-14
1974	PIT	N	P	26	30	12- 9
1975	PIT	N	P	27	30	8- 9
1976	NY	A	P		32	17- 8
	BBTR			260	303	113-88

ELLIS, GEORGE WILLIAM "RUBE"
B.NOV.17,1885 DOWNEY,CAL.
D.MAR.13,1938

YR	CL	LEA	POS	GP	G	REC
1909	STL	N	O		145	.268
1910	STL	N	O		141	.258
1911	STL	N	O		148	.250
1912	STL	N	O		109	.269
	BLTL				543	.260

ELLIS, JAMES RUSSELL "JIM"
B.MAR.25,1945 TULARE,CAL.

YR	CL	LEA	POS	GP	G	REC
1967	STL	N	P		8	1- 1
1969	STL	N	P		2	0- 0
	BRTL				10	1- 1

ELLIS, JOHN CHARLES
B.AUG.21,1948 NEW LONDON,CONN.

YR	CL	LEA	POS	GP	G	REC
1969	NY	A	C		22	.290
1970	NY	A	C-1-3		78	.248
1971	NY	A	C-1		83	.244
1972	NY	A	C-1		52	.294
1973	CLE	A	C-1-D		127	.270
1974	CLE	A	C-1-D		128	.285
1975	CLE	A	C-1		92	.230
1976	TEX	A	C		11	.419
	BRTR				593	.266

ELLIS, ROBERT WALTER "BOB"
B.JULY 3,1950 GRAND RAPIDS,MICH.

YR	CL	LEA	POS	GP	G	REC
1971	MIL	A	3-O		36	.198
1974	MIL	A	3-O		22	.292
1975	MIL	A	O		6	.286
	BRTR				64	.229

ELLIS, SAMUEL JOSEPH "SAMMY"
B.FEB.11,1941 YOUNGSTOWN,OHIO

YR	CL	LEA	POS	GP	G	REC
1962	CIN	N	P		8	2- 2
1964	CIN	N	P		52	10- 3
1965	CIN	N	P		44	22-10
1966	CIN	N	P	41	43	12-19
1967	CIN	N	P		32	8-11
1968	CAL	A	P		42	9-10
1969	CHI	A	P		10	0- 3
	BLTR			229	231	63-58

ELLISON, GEORGE RUSSELL
B.1897

YR	CL	LEA	POS	GP	G	REC
1920	CLE	A	P		1	0- 0
	BRTR					

ELLISON, HERBERT SPENCER "BERT"
B.NOV.15,1895 RUTLAND,ARK.
D.AUG.11,1955 SAN FRANCISCO,CAL

YR	CL	LEA	POS	GP	G	REC
1916	DET	A	3		2	.125
1917	DET	A	1		9	.172
1918	DET	A	2		7	.260
1919	DET	A	2		56	.216
1920	DET	A	1		61	.219
	BRTR				135	.215

ELLSWORTH, RICHARD CLARK "DICK"
B.MAR.22,1940 LUSK,WYO.

YR	CL	LEA	POS	GP	G	REC
1958	CHI	N	P		1	0- 1
1960	CHI	N	P		31	7-13
1961	CHI	N	P		37	10-11
1962	CHI	N	P		37	9-20
1963	CHI	N	P		37	22-10
1964	CHI	N	P		37	14-18
1965	CHI	N	P		36	14-15
1966	CHI	N	P		38	8-22
1967	PHI	N	P		32	6- 7
1968	BOS	A	P		31	16- 7
1969	BOS	A	P		2	0- 0
	CLE	A	P		34	6- 9
1970	CLE	A	P		29	3- 3
1971	MIL	A	P		14	0- 0
	MIL	A	P		11	0- 1
	BLTL				407	115-137

ELMORE, VERDO WILSON
B.DEC.10,1899 GORDO,ALA.
D.AUG.5,1969 BIRMINGHAM,ALA.

YR	CL	LEA	POS	GP	G	REC
1924	STL	A	O		7	.176
	BLTR					

ELROY, ALEJANDRO CARRASQUEL
(PLAYED UNDER NAME OF
ALEJANDRO CARRASQUEL)

ELSH, EUGENE ROY
B.MAR.1,1896 PENNSGROVE,N.J.

YR	CL	LEA	POS	GP	G	REC
1923	CHI	A	O		81	.249
1924	CHI	A	O		60	.306
1925	CHI	A	1-O		32	.188
	BRTR				173	.262

ELSTON, DONALD RAY "DON"
B.APR.6,1929 CAMPBELLSTOWN,OHIO

YR	CL	LEA	POS	GP	G	REC
1953	CHI	N	P		2	0- 1
1957	BRO	N	P		1	0- 0
	CHI	N	P		39	6- 7
1958	CHI	N	P		69	9- 8
1959	CHI	N	P		65	10- 8
1960	CHI	N	P		60	8- 9
1961	CHI	N	P		58	6- 7
1962	CHI	N	P		57	4- 8
1963	CHI	N	P		51	4- 1
1964	CHI	N	P		48	2- 5
	BRTR				450	49-54

ELY, FREDERICK WILLIAM "BONES"
B.JUNE 7,1863 GIRARD,PA.
D.JAN.10,1952

YR	CL	LEA	POS	GP	G	REC
1884	BUF	N	P-O	1		0- 1
						.000
1886	LOU	AA	P-O	5	10	0- 4
						.147
1890	SYR	AA	S-O		118	.263
1891	BRO	N	S		31	.171
1892	BAL	N	S		1	0- 1
1893	STL	N	S		44	.263
1894	STL	N	S		127	.305
1895	STL	N	S		118	.260
1896	PIT	N	S		126	.287
1897	PIT	N	S		133	.282
1898	PIT	N	S		148	.210
1899	PIT	N	S		138	.288
1900	PIT	N	S		130	.242
1901	PIT	N	S		62	.219
	PHI	A	S		45	.223
1902	WAS	A	S		105	.263
	BRTR			7	1337	0- 6
						.259

EMBREE, CHARLES WILLARD "RED"
B.AUG.30,1919 EL MONTE,CAL.

YR	CL	LEA	POS	GP	G	REC
1941	CLE	A	P		1	0- 1
1942	CLE	A	P		19	3- 4
1944	CLE	A	P		3	0- 1
1945	CLE	A	P		8	4- 4
1946	CLE	A	P		28	8-12
1947	CLE	A	P	27	28	8-10
1948	NY	A	P		20	5- 3
1949	STL	A	P	35	40	3-13
	BRTR			141	147	31-48

EMBREY, CHARLES AKIN "SLIM"
B.AUG.7,1901 COLUMBIA,TENN.
D.OCT.10,1947

YR	CL	LEA	POS	GP	G	REC
1923	CHI	A	P		1	0- 0
	BRTR					

EMERSON, CHESTER ARTHUR "CHUCK"
B.OCT.27,1889 STOW,ME.
D.JULY 2,1971 AUGUSTA,ME.

YR	CL	LEA	POS	GP	G	REC
1911	PHI	A	O		7	.222
1912	PHI	A	H		1	.000
	BLTR				8	.211

EMERY, CALVIN WAYNE "CAL"
B.JUNE 28,1937 CENTRE HALL,PA.

YR	CL	LEA	POS	GP	G	REC
1963	PHI	N	1		16	.158
	BLTL					

EMERY, HERRICK SMITH "SPOKE"
B.DEC.10,1898 BAY CITY,MICH.
D.JUNE 2,1975 CAPE CANAVERAL,
FLA.

YR	CL	LEA	POS	GP	G	REC
1924	PHI	N	O		5	.667
	BRTR					

EMIG, CHARLES H.
B.BELLEVUE,KY.

YR	CL	LEA	POS	GP	G	REC
1896	LOU	N	P		1	0- 1

EMMER, FRANK WILLIAM
B.FEB.17,1896 CRESTLINE,OHIO
D.OCT.18,1963

YR	CL	LEA	POS	GP	G	REC
1916	CIN	N	2-S-3-O		42	.146
1926	CIN	N	S		80	.196
	BRTR				122	.182

EMMERICH, ROBERT G.
B.AUG.1,1897 NEW YORK,N.Y.
D.NOV.23,1948

YR	CL	LEA	POS	GP	G	REC
1923	BOS	N	O		13	.083
	BRTR					

EMMERICH, WILLIAM PETER "SLIM"
B.SEPT.29,1919 ALLENTOWN,PA.

YR	CL	LEA	POS	GP	G	REC
1945	NY	N	P		31	4- 4
1946	NY	N	P		2	0- 0
	BRTR				33	4- 4

EMSLIE, ROBERT DANIEL
B.JAN.27,1859 GUELPH,ONT.,CAN.
D.APR.26,1943

YR	CL	LEA	POS	GP	G	REC
1883	BAL	AA	P-O		28	9-16
						.153
1884	BAL	AA	P	50	51	32-18
1885	BAL	AA	P		13	2-10
	ATH	AA	P-O		4	0- 3
						.083
	TR			95	96	43-47
						.187

ENDICOTT, WILLIAM FRANKLIN
B.SEPT.4,1918 ACORN,MO.

YR	CL	LEA	POS	GP	G	REC
1946	STL	N	O		20	.200
	BLTL					

ENGEL, JOSEPH WILLIAM
B.MAR.12,1893 WASHINGTON,D.C.
D.JUNE 12,1969 CHATTANOOGA,TENN

YR	CL	LEA	POS	GP	G	REC
1912	WAS	A	P		17	1- 5
1913	WAS	A	P		36	8- 9
1914	WAS	A	P		35	7- 5
1915	WAS	A	P		11	1- 3
1917	CIN	N	P		1	0- 1
1919	CLE	A	P		1	0- 0
1920	WAS	A	P		1	0- 0
	BRTL				102	17-23

ENGLE, ARTHUR CLYDE
"CLYDE" OR "HACK"
B.MAR.19,1884 DAYTON,OHIO
D.DEC.26,1939

YR	CL	LEA	POS	GP	G	REC
1909	NY	A	O		135	.278
1910	NY	A	3		6	.200
	BOS	A	3		105	.266
1911	BOS	A	1-3		146	.270
1912	BOS	A	1-2		57	.234
1913	BOS	A	1		143	.290
1914	BOS	A	1		55	.194
	BUF	F	3		32	.259
1915	BUF	F	2-3-O		141	.263
1916	CLE	A	3		11	.133
	BRTR				831	.266

YR	CL	LEA	POS	GP	G	REC

ENGLE, CHARLES
B.AUG.27,1903 BROOKLYN,N.Y.
1925	PHI	A	S		1	.000
1926	PHI	A	S		19	.105
1930	PIT	N	2-S-3		67	.264
		BRTR			87	.251

ENGLISH, CHARLES DEWIE
B.APR.8,1910 DARLINGTON,S.C.
1932	CHI	A	3		24	.317
1933	CHI	A	2		3	.444
1936	NY	N	2		6	.000
1937	CIN	N	2-3		17	.238
		BRTR			50	.287

ENGLISH, ELWOOD GEORGE "WOODY"
B.MAR.2,1907 GRANVILLE,OHIO
1927	CHI	N	S		87	.290
1928	CHI	N	S		116	.299
1929	CHI	N	S		144	.276
1930	CHI	N	S-3		156	.335
1931	CHI	N	S-3		156	.319
1932	CHI	N	S-3		127	.272
1933	CHI	N	S-3		105	.261
1934	CHI	N	S-3		109	.278
1935	CHI	N	S-3		34	.202
1936	CHI	N	S-3		64	.247
1937	BRO	N	2-S		129	.238
1938	BRO	N	3		34	.250
		BRTR			1261	.286

ENGLISH, GILBERT RAYMOND
B.JULY 2,1909 TRINITY,N.C.
1931	NY	N	3		3	.000
1932	NY	N	S-3		59	.225
1936	DET	A	3		1	.000
1937	DET	A	2		18	.262
	BOS	N	3		79	.290
1938	BOS	N	3		53	.248
1944	BRO	N	2-S-3		27	.152
		BRTR			240	.245

ENNIS, DELMER "DEL"
B.JUNE 8,1925 PHILADELPHIA,PA.
1946	PHI	N	O		141	.313
1947	PHI	N	O		139	.275
1948	PHI	N	O		152	.290
1949	PHI	N	O		154	.302
1950	PHI	N	O		153	.311
1951	PHI	N	O		144	.267
1952	PHI	N	O		151	.289
1953	PHI	N	O		152	.285
1954	PHI	N	1-O		145	.261
1955	PHI	N	O		146	.296
1956	PHI	N	O		153	.260
1957	STL	N	O		136	.286
1958	STL	N	O		106	.261
1959	CIN	N	O		5	.333
	CHI	A	O		26	.219
		BRTR			1903	.284

ENNIS, RUSSELL ELWOOD "HACK"
B.MAR.10,1897 SUPERIOR,WIS.
D.JAN.21,1949
| 1926 | WAS | A | C | | 1 | .000 |
| | | BRTR | | | | |

ENRIGHT, GEORGE ALBERT
B.MAY 9,1954 NEW BRITAIN,CONN.
| 1976 | CHI | A | C | | 2 | .000 |
| | | BRTR | | | | |

ENRIGHT, JOHN PERCY
B.1896 FORT WORTH,TEX.
| 1917 | NY | A | P | | 1 | 0- 1 |
| | | BRTR | | | | |

ENS, ANTON "MUTZ"
B.NOV.8,1884 ST.LOUIS,MO.
D.JUNE 28,1950
| 1912 | CHI | A | 1 | | 3 | .000 |
| | | BLTL | | | | |

ENS, JEWEL WINKLEMEYER
B.AUG.24,1889 ST.LOUIS,MO.
D.JAN.17,1950
1922	PIT	N	1-2-S-3		47	.295
1923	PIT	N	1-3		12	.267
1924	PIT	N	1		5	.300
1925	PIT	N	1		3	.200
		BRTR			67	.290
NON-PLAYING MANAGER
PIT(N) 1929-31

ENWRIGHT, CHARLES MICHAEL
B.OCT.6,1887 SACRAMENTO,CAL.
D.JAN.19,1917
| 1909 | STL | N | S | | 3 | .142 |
| | | BLTR | | | | |

ENYART, TERRY GENE
B.OCT.10,1950 IRONTON,OHIO
| 1974 | MON | N | P | | 2 | 0- 0 |
| | | BRTL | | | | |

ENZENROTH, CLARENCE HERMAN "JACK"
B.NOV.4,1889 MINERAL POINT,WIS.
D.FEB.21,1944
1914	STL	A	C		3	.167
	KC	F	C		24	.166
1915	KC	F	C		14	.158
		BRTR			41	.165

ENZMANN, JOHN
B.MAR.4,1890 BROOKLYN,N.Y.
1914	BRO	N	P		7	1- 0
1918	CLE	A	P		30	5- 7
1919	CLE	A	P		14	1- 2
1920	PHI	N	P	16	17	2- 3
		BRTR		67	68	9-12

EPPERLY, ALBERT PAUL "TUB"
B.MAY 7,1918 GLIDDEN,IOWA
1938	CHI	N	P		9	2- 0
1950	BRO	N	P		5	0- 0
		BLTR			14	2- 0

EPPS, AUBREY LEE "YO-YO"
B.MAR.3,1914 MEMPHIS,TENN.
| 1935 | PIT | N | C | | 1 | 8750 |
| | | BRTR | | | | |

EPPS, HAROLD FRANKLIN
B.MAR.26,1914 ATHENS,GA.
1938	STL	N	O		17	.300
1940	STL	N	O		11	.200
1943	STL	A	O		8	.286
1944	STL	A	O		22	.177
	PHI	A	O		67	.262
		BLTL			125	.253

EPSTEIN, MICHAEL PETER "MIKE"
B.APR.4,1943 BRONX,N.Y.
1966	BAL	A	1		6	.182
1967	BAL	A	1		9	.154
	WAS	A	1		96	.229
1968	WAS	A	1		123	.234
1969	WAS	A	1		131	.278
1970	WAS	A	1		140	.256
1971	WAS	A	1		24	.247
	OAK	A	1		104	.234
1972	OAK	A	1		138	.270
1973	TEX	A	1		27	.188
	CAL	A	1		91	.215
1974	CAL	A	1		18	.161
		BLTL			907	.244

ERAUTT, EDWARD LORENZ SEBASTIAN "EDDIE"
B.SEPT.26,1924 PORTLAND,ORE.
1947	CIN	N	P		36	4- 9
1948	CIN	N	P		2	0- 0
1949	CIN	N	P		39	4-11
1950	CIN	N	P		33	4- 2
1951	CIN	N	P		30	0- 0
1953	CIN	N	P		4	0- 0
	STL	N	P		20	3- 1
		BRTR			164	15-23

ERAUTT, JOSEPH MICHAEL "JOE"
B.SEPT.1,1921 VIBANK,SASK.,CAN.
D.OCT.6,1976 PORTLAND,ORE.
1950	CHI	A	C		16	.222
1951	CHI	A	C		16	.160
		BRTR			32	.186

ERICKSON, DONALD LEE
B.DEC.13,1931 SPRINGFIELD,ILL.
| 1958 | PHI | N | P | | 9 | 0- 1 |
| | | BRTR | | | | |

ERICKSON, ERIC GEORGE "SWAT"
B.MAR.13,1895 GOTHENBURG,SWEDEN
D.MAY 19,1965 JAMESTOWN,N.Y.
1914	NY	N	P		1	0- 1
1916	DET	A	P		7	0- 2
1918	DET	A	P		12	4- 5
1919	DET	A	P		3	0- 2
	WAS	A	P		20	5-10
1920	WAS	A	P		39	12-16
1921	WAS	A	P		32	8-10
1922	WAS	A	P		30	4-12
		BRTR			144	33-58

ERICKSON, HAROLD JAMES "HAL"
B.JULY 17,1919 PORTLAND,ORE.
| 1953 | DET | A | P | | 18 | 0- 1 |
| | | BRTR | | | | |

ERICKSON, HENRY NELS
B.NOV.11,1908 CHICAGO,ILL.
D.DEC.13,1964 LOUISVILLE,KY.
| 1935 | CIN | N | C | | 37 | .261 |
| | | BRTR | | | | |

ERICKSON, PAUL WALFORD "AB"
B.DEC.14,1915 ZION,ILL.
1941	CHI	N	P		32	5- 7
1942	CHI	N	P		18	1- 6
1943	CHI	N	P		15	1- 3
1944	CHI	N	P		33	5- 9
1945	CHI	N	P		28	7- 4
1946	CHI	N	P		32	9- 7
1947	CHI	N	P		40	7-12
1948	CHI	N	P		3	0- 0
	PHI	N	P		4	2- 0
	NY	N	P		2	0- 0
		BRTR			207	37-48

ERICKSON, RALPH LIEF
B.JUNE 25,1906 DUBOIS,IDAHO
1929	PIT	N	P		1	0- 0
1930	PIT	N	P		7	1- 0
		BLTL			8	1- 0

ERMER, CALVIN COOLIDGE "CAL"
B.NOV.10,1924 BALTIMORE,MD.
| 1947 | WAS | A | 2 | | 1 | .000 |
| | | BRTR | | | | |
NON-PLAYING MANAGER
MIN(A) 1967-68

ERNAGA, FRANK JOHN
B.AUG.22,1930 SUSANVILLE,CAL.
1957	CHI	N	O		20	.314
1958	CHI	N	H		9	.125
		BRTR			29	.279

ERRICKSON, RICHARD MERRIWELL
B.MAR.5,1914 VINELAND,N.J.
1938	BOS	N	P		34	9- 7
1939	BOS	N	P		28	6- 9
1940	BOS	N	P		34	12-13
1941	BOS	N	P		38	6-12
1942	BOS	N	P		21	2- 5
	CHI	N	P		13	1- 1
		BLTR			168	36-47

ERSKINE, CARL DANIEL
B.DEC.13,1926 ANDERSON,IND.
1948	BRO	N	P		17	6- 3
1949	BRO	N	P		22	8- 1
1950	BRO	N	P		22	7- 6
1951	BRO	N	P		46	16-12
1952	BRO	N	P	33	34	14- 6
1953	BRO	N	P	39	43	20- 6
1954	BRO	N	P	38	39	18-15
1955	BRO	N	P	31	42	11- 8
1956	BRO	N	P	31	32	13-11
1957	BRO	N	P	15	21	5- 3
1958	LA	N	P	31	32	4- 4
1959	LA	N	P		10	0- 3
		BRTR		335	360	122-78

ERSKINE, JAMES
(PLAYED UNDER NAME OF
ERSKINE JOHN MAYER)

ERSKINE, SAMUEL FRANKEL
(PLAYED UNDER NAME OF
SAMUEL FRANKEL MAYER)

```
YR  CL LEA POS   GP    G    REC
```

ERWIN, ROSS EMIL "TEX"
B.DEC.22,1885 FORNEY,TEX.
D.APR.5,1953
```
1907 DET A C          4   .200
1910 BRO N C         68   .188
1911 BRO N C         74   .271
1912 BRO N C         59   .211
1913 BRO N C         20   .258
1914 BRO N C          7   .500
     CIN N C         14   .306
     BLTR          246   .237
```

ESCALERA, SATURNINO CUADRADO "NINO"
B.NOV.29,1929 SANTURCE,P.R.
```
1954 CIN N 1-S-O     73   .159
     BLTR
```

ESCHEN, JAMES GOODRICH
B.AUG.21,1893 BROOKLYN,N.Y.
D.SEPT.27,1960
```
1915 CLE A  O        15   .239
     BRTR
```

ESCHEN, LAWRENCE EDWARD
B.SEPT.22,1920 SUFFERN,N.Y.
```
1942 PHI A 2-S       12   .000
```

ESMOND, JAMES J.
B.OCT.8,1889 ALBANY,N.Y.
D.JUNE 26,1948
```
1911 CIN N S         59   .273
1912 CIN N S         82   .195
1914 IND F S        150   .295
1915 NEW F S        155   .258
     BRTR          446   .264
```

ESPER, CHARLES H. "DUKE"
B.JULY 28,1868 SALEM,N.J.
D.AUG.31,1910
```
1890 ATH AA P        19   7- 8
     PIT N  P         2   0- 2
     PHI N  P         6   4- 0
1891 PHI N  P        34  20-13
1892 PHI N  P        19  13- 6
     PIT N  P        11   1- 0
1893 WAS N  P        40  12-26
1894 WAS N  P        15   6- 9
     BAL N  P        16   9- 2
1895 BAL N  P        27  12-12
1896 BAL N  P        19  14- 5
1897 STL N  P         8   1- 6
1898 STL N  P        10   3- 5
     TL            226 102-94
```

ESPINOSA, ARNULFO ACEVEDO "NINO"
(REAL NAME
ARNULFO ACEVEDO (ESPINOSA))
B.AUG.15,1953 VILLIA ALTAGRACIA,
D.R.
```
1974 NY N N P         2   0- 0
1975 NY N N P         2   0- 1
1976 NY N N P        12   4- 4
     BRTR           16   4- 5
```

ESPOSITO, SAMUEL "SAMMY"
B.DEC.15,1931 CHICAGO,ILL.
```
1952 CHI A S          1   .250
1955 CHI A S          3   .000
1956 CHI A 2-S-3     81   .228
1957 CHI A 2-S-3-O   94   .205
1958 CHI A 2-S-3-O   98   .247
1959 CHI A 2-S-3     69   .167
1960 CHI A 2-S-3     57   .182
1961 CHI A 2-S-3     63   .170
1962 CHI A 2-S-3     75   .235
1963 CHI A R          1   .000
     KC  A 2-S-3     18   .200
     BRTR          560   .207
```

ESSEGIAN, CHARLES ABRAHAM "CHUCK"
B.AUG.9,1931 BOSTON,MASS.
```
1958 PHI N O         39   .246
1959 STL N O         17   .179
     LA  N O         24   .304
1960 LA  N O         52   .215
1961 BAL A H          1   .000
     KC  A O          4   .333
     CLE A O         60   .289
1962 CLE A O        106   .274
1963 KC  A O        101   .225
     BRTR          404   .255
```

ESSIAN, JAMES SARKIS "JIM"
B.JAN.2,1951 DETROIT,MICH.
```
1973 PHI N C          2   .000
1974 PHI N C-1-3     17   .100
1975 PHI N C          2  1.000
1976 CHI A C-1-3     78   .246
     BRTR           99   .233
```

ESSICK, WILLIAM EARL "VINEGAR BILL"
B.DEC.18,1881 GRAND RIDGE,ILL.
D.OCT.11,1951
```
1906 CIN N P          6   1- 1
1907 CIN N P          3   0- 2
     TR              9   1- 3
```

ESTALELLA, ROBERTO MENDEZ
B.APR.25,1911 CARDENAS,CUBA
```
1935 WAS A 3         15   .314
1936 WAS A H         13   .222
1939 WAS A O         82   .275
1941 STL A O         46   .241
1942 WAS A 3-O      133   .277
1943 PHI A O        117   .259
1944 PHI A 1-O      140   .298
1945 PHI A O        126   .299
1949 PHI A O          8   .250
     BRTR          680   .282
```

ESTELLE, RICHARD HENRY "DICK"
B.JAN.18,1942 LAKEWOOD,N.J.
```
1964 SF N P           6   1- 2
1965 SF N P           6   0- 0
     BBTL            12   1- 2
```

ESTERBROOK, THOMAS JOHN "DUDE"
B.JUNE 29,1857 NEW BRIGHTON,
S.I.,N.Y.
D.APR.30,1901
```
1880 BUF N C-1-2-S-  63   .241
           O
1882 CLE N 1-O       45   .246
1883 MET AA 3        41   .250
1884 MET AA 3       112   .408
1885 NY N 3-O        88   .256
1886 NY N 3         123   .361
1887 MET AA S        26   .224
1888 IND N 1         64   .219
     LOU AA 1        23   .226
1889 LOU AA 1        11   .309
1890 NY N 1          45   .289
1891 BRO N 2          3   .375
     BRTR          644   .278
```

ESTERDAY, HENRY
B.SEPT.16,1864 PHILADELPHIA,PA.
```
1884 KEY U S         28   .250
1888 KC AA S        114   .195
1889 COL AA S       105   .175
1890 COL AA S        52   .145
     ATH AA S        19   .154
     LOU AA S         7   .087
     BRTR          325   .177
```

ESTOCK, GEORGE JOHN
B.NOV.2,1924 STIRLING,N.J.
```
1951 BOS N P         37   0- 1
     BRTR
```

ESTRADA, CHARLES LEONARD "CHUCK"
B.FEB.15,1938 SAN LUIS OBISPO,
CAL.
```
1960 BAL A P            36  18-11
1961 BAL A P            33  15- 9
1962 BAL A P     34  38   9-17
1963 BAL A P             8   3- 2
1964 BAL A P     17  18   3- 2
1966 CHI N P             9   1- 1
1967 NY N P             9   1- 2
     BRTR      146 151  50-44
```

ESTRADA, FRANCISCO (SOTO) "FRANK"
B.FEB.12,1948 NAVOJOA,SONORA,MEX
```
1971 NY N C           1   .500
     BRTR
```

ESTRADA, OSCAR
B.FEB.15,1904 HAVANA,CUBA
```
1929 STL A P          1   0- 0
     BLTL
```

ETCHEBARREN, ANDREW AUGUSTE "ANDY"
B.JUNE 20,1943 WHITTIER,CAL.
```
1962 BAL A C          2   .333
1965 BAL A C          5   .167
1966 BAL A C        121   .221
1967 BAL A C        112   .215
1968 BAL A C         74   .233
1969 BAL A C         73   .249
1970 BAL A C         78   .243
1971 BAL A C         70   .270
1972 BAL A C         71   .202
1973 BAL A C         54   .257
1974 BAL A C         62   .222
1975 BAL A C          8   .200
     CAL A C         31   .280
1976 CAL A C        103   .227
     BRTR          864   .234
```

ETCHISON, CLARENCE HAMPTON "BUCK"
B.JAN.27,1918 BALTIMORE,MD.
```
1943 BOS N 1         10   .316
1944 BOS N 1        109   .214
     BLTL          119   .220
```

ETHERIDGE, BOBBY LAMAR
B.NOV.25,1942 GREENVILLE,MISS.
```
1967 SF N 3          40   .226
1969 SF N S-3        56   .260
     BRTR           96   .244
```

ETTEN, NICHOLAS RAYMOND THOMAS "NICK"
B.SEPT.19,1913 CHICAGO,ILL.
```
1938 PHI A 1         22   .259
1939 PHI A 1         43   .252
1941 PHI N 1        151   .311
1942 PHI N 1        139   .264
1943 NY A 1         154   .271
1944 NY A 1         154   .293
1945 NY A 1         152   .285
1946 NY A 1         108   .232
1947 PHI N 1         14   .244
     BLTL          937   .277
```

EUBANK, JOHN FRAMKLIN
B.SEPT.9,1872 SERVIA,IND.
D.NOV.3,1958
```
1905 DET A P          7   2- 0
1906 DET A P     23  26   4-10
1907 DET A P         15   2- 3
     BRTR       45  48   8-13
```

EUBANKS, UEL MELVIN "POSS"
B.FEB.14,1903 QUINLAN,TEX.
D.NOV.21,1954
```
1922 CHI N P          2   0- 0
     BRTR
```

EUNICK, FERNANDAS BOWEN
B.APR.22,1892 BALTIMORE,MD.
D.DEC.9,1959 BALTIMORE,MD.
```
1917 CLE A 3          1   .000
     BRTR
```

EUSTACE, FRANK JOHN
B.NOV.7,1873 NEW YORK,N.Y.
D.OCT.20,1932
```
1896 LOU N S         25   .163
```

EVANS, ALFRED HUBERT "AL"
B.SEPT.28,1916 KENLY,N.C.
```
1939 WAS A C          7   .333
1940 WAS A C         14   .320
1941 WAS A C         53   .277
1942 WAS A C         74   .229
1944 WAS A C         14   .091
1945 WAS A C         51   .260
1946 WAS A C         88   .254
1947 WAS A C         99   .241
1948 WAS A C         93   .259
1949 WAS A C        109   .271
1950 WAS A C         90   .235
1951 BOS A C         12   .125
     BRTR          704   .250
```

EVANS, CHICKERING F.
B.SEPT.10,1888 ARLINGTON,VT.
D.SEPT.2,1916
```
1909 BOS N P          4   0- 0
1910 BOS N P         13   1- 1
     BRTR           17   1- 4
```

EVANS, DARRELL WAYNE
B.MAY 26,1947 PASADENA,CAL.

YR	CL	LEA	POS	GP	G	REC
1969	ATL	N	3		12	.231
1970	ATL	N	3		12	.318
1971	ATL	N	3-0		89	.242
1972	ATL	N	3		125	.254
1973	ATL	N	1-3		161	.281
1974	ATL	N	3		160	.240
1975	ATL	N	1-3		156	.243
1976	ATL	N	1-3		44	.173
	SF	N	1-3		92	.222
	BLTR				851	.247

EVANS, DWIGHT MICHAEL "DEWEY"
B.NOV.3,1951 SANTA MONICA,CAL.

YR	CL	LEA	POS	GP	G	REC
1972	BOS	A	O		18	.263
1973	BOS	A	O		119	.223
1974	BOS	A	O		133	.281
1975	BOS	A	O		128	.274
1976	BOS	A	O		146	.242
	BRTR				544	.258

EVANS, J. FORD
B.DEC.15,1844 AKRON,OHIO
NON-PLAYING MANAGER CLE(N) 1882

EVANS, JACOB "BLOODY JAKE"
B.BALTIMORE,MD.
D.FEB.3,1907

YR	CL	LEA	POS	GP	G	REC
1875	NH	NA	O		1	-
1879	TRO	N	O		70	.230
1880	TRO	N	P-S-	1		
			O			.255
1881	TRO	N			81	.242
1882	WOR	N	P-2-	1		
			S-O			.212
1883	CLE	N	P-2-	1	89	0- 0
			3-O			.235
1884	CLE	N	2-S-O		80	.258
1885	BAL	AA	O		20	.205
	TR			3	468	0- 1
						-

EVANS, JOSEPH PATTON
B.MAY 15,1895 MERIDIAN,MISS.
D.AUG.9,1953

YR	CL	LEA	POS	GP	G	REC
1915	CLE	A	3		42	.257
1916	CLE	A	3		33	.146
1917	CLE	A	3		132	.290
1918	CLE	A	3		79	.263
1919	CLE	A	S		21	.071
1920	CLE	A	O		56	.349
1921	CLE	A	O		57	.333
1922	CLE	A	O		75	.269
1923	WAS	A	3-0		106	.263
1924	STL	A	O		77	.254
1925	STL	A	O		55	.314
	BRTR				733	.259

EVANS, LE ROY
B.MAR.19,1874 KNOXVILLE,TENN.

YR	CL	LEA	POS	GP	G	REC
1897	STL	N	P		2	0- 1
	LOU	N	P		9	5- 4
1898	WAS	N	P		7	3- 3
1899	WAS	N	P		7	3- 2
1902	NY	N	P		19	8-11
	BRO	N	P		13	5- 6
1903	BRO	N	P		15	5- 9
	STL	A	P		7	1- 5
	BRTR				79	30-41

EVANS, LOUIS RICHARD "STEVE"
B.FEB.17,1885 CLEVELAND,OHIO
D.DEC.28,1943

YR	CL	LEA	POS	GP	G	REC
1908	NY	N	O		2	.333
1909	STL	N	O		143	.259
1910	STL	N	O		151	.241
1911	STL	N	O		150	.294
1912	STL	N	O		135	.283
1913	STL	N	O		97	.249
1914	BRO	F	1-O		145	.355
1915	BRO	F	O		63	.289
	BAL	F	O		87	.319
	BLTL				973	.288

EVANS, RUSSELL EARL "RED"
B.NOV.12,1906 CHICAGO,ILL.

YR	CL	LEA	POS	GP	G	REC
1936	CHI	A	P	17	18	0- 3
1939	BRO	N	P		24	1- 8
	BRTR			41	42	1-11

EVANS, WILLIAM ARTHUR
B.AUG.3,1911 ELVINE,MO.

YR	CL	LEA	POS	GP	G	REC
1932	CHI	A	P		7	0- 0
	BBTL					

EVANS, WILLIAM JAMES
B.FEB.10,1894 ROCKINGHAM CO.,
N.C.

YR	CL	LEA	POS	GP	G	REC
1916	PIT	N	P		13	2- 5
1917	PIT	N	P		8	0- 4
1919	PIT	N	P		7	0- 4
	BRTR				28	2-13

EVANS, WILLIAM LAWRENCE "BILLY"
B.MAR.25,1919 QUANAH,TEX.

YR	CL	LEA	POS	GP	G	REC
1949	CHI	A	P		4	0- 1
1951	BOS	A	P		9	0- 0
	BRTR				13	0- 1

EVERETT, WILLIAM L. "WILD BILL"
B.DEC.13,1868 FT.WAYNE,IND.
D.JAN.19,1938

YR	CL	LEA	POS	GP	G	REC
1895	CHI	N	3		133	.356
1896	CHI	N	3-0		131	.333
1897	CHI	N	3		90	.314
1898	CHI	N	1		149	.325
1899	CHI	N	1		136	.309
1900	CHI	N	1		23	.236
1901	WAS	A	1		33	.189
	TR				695	.320

EVERITT, EDWARD LEON "LEON"
B.JAN.12,1947 MARSHALL,TEX.

YR	CL	LEA	POS	GP	G	REC
1969	SD	N	P	5	6	0- 1
	BLTR					

EVERS, JOHN JOSEPH "CRAB"
B.JULY 22,1883 TROY,N.Y.
D.MAR.28,1947 ALBANY,N.Y.

YR	CL	LEA	POS	GP	G	REC
1902	CHI	N	2-S		25	.225
1903	CHI	N	2		123	.293
1904	CHI	N	2		152	.265
1905	CHI	N	2		99	.276
1906	CHI	N	2		154	.255
1907	CHI	N	2		151	.250
1908	CHI	N	2		123	.300
1909	CHI	N	2		126	.263
1910	CHI	N	2		125	.263
1911	CHI	N	2		44	.226
1912	CHI	N	2		143	.341
1913	CHI	N	M-2		136	.285
1914	BOS	N	2		139	.279
1915	BOS	N	2		83	.263
1916	BOS	N	2		71	.216
1917	BOS	N	2		24	.176
	PHI	N	2		56	.231
1922	CHI	A	2		1	.000
1929	BOS	N	M-2		1	.000
	BLTR				1776	.270

NON-PLAYING MANAGER
CHI(N) 1921, CHI(A) 1924

EVERS, JOSEPH FRANCIS
B.SEPT.10,1891 TROY,N.Y.
D.JAN.4,1949

YR	CL	LEA	POS	GP	G	REC
1913	NY	N	3		1	.000
	BRTR					

EVERS, THOMAS FRANCIS
B.MAR.31,1852 TROY,N.Y.
D.MAR.23,1925

YR	CL	LEA	POS	GP	G	REC
1882	BAL	AA	2		1	.000
1884	WAS	U	2		106	.234
					107	.232

EVERS, WALTER ARTHUR "HOOT"
B.FEB.8,1921 ST.LOUIS,MO.

YR	CL	LEA	POS	GP	G	REC
1941	DET	A	O		1	.000
1946	DET	A	O		81	.266
1947	DET	A	O		126	.296
1948	DET	A	O		139	.314
1949	DET	A	O		132	.303
1950	DET	A	O		143	.323
1951	DET	A	O		116	.224
1952	DET	A	H		1	1.000
	BOS	A	O		106	.262
1953	BOS	A	O		99	.240
1954	BOS	A	O		6	.000
	NY	N	O		12	.091
	DET	A	O		30	.183
1955	BAL	A	O		60	.238
	CLE	A	O		39	.288
1956	CLE	A	H		3	.000
	BAL	A	O		48	.241
	BRTR				1142	.278

EWELL
B.WASHINGTON,D.C.

YR	CL	LEA	POS	GP	G	REC
1871	CLE	NA	O		1	.000

EWING, GEORGE LEMUEL "LONG BOB"
B.APR.24,1873 NEW HAMPSHIRE,O.
D.JUNE 20,1947

YR	CL	LEA	POS	GP	G	REC
1902	CIN	N	P-O	15	19	5- 6
						.171
1903	CIN	N	P	29	31	14-13
1904	CIN	N	P	26	30	11-12
1905	CIN	N	P	40	42	21-12
1906	CIN	N	P		33	13-14
1907	CIN	N	P	41	44	17-19
1908	CIN	N	P		37	17-15
1909	CIN	N	P		31	11-12
1910	PHI	N	P		34	16-14
1911	PHI	N	P		4	0- 2
1912	STL	N	P		1	0- 0
	BRTR			291	306	125-119
						.195

EWING, JOHN "LONG JOHN"
B.JUNE 1,1863 CINCINNATI,OHIO
D.APR.23,1893

YR	CL	LEA	POS	GP	G	REC
1883	STL	AA	O		1	.000
1884	CIN	U	O		1	.000
	WAS	U	O		1	.200
1888	LOU	AA	P		21	8-13
1889	LOU	AA	P	40	47	7-30
1890	NY	P	P		35	19-10
1891	NY	N	P		31	21-10
	TR			127	131	55-63
						.186

EWING, REUBEN
(REAL NAME REUBEN COHEN)
B.NOV.30,1899 ODESSA,RUSSIA
D.OCT.5,1970 W.HARTFORD,CONN.

YR	CL	LEA	POS	GP	G	REC
1921	STL	N	O		3	.000

EWING, SAMUEL JAMES "SAM"
B.APR.9,1949 LEWISBURG,TENN.

YR	CL	LEA	POS	GP	G	REC
1973	CHI	A	1		11	.150
1976	CHI	A	1-0		19	.220
	BLTL				30	.197

EWING, WILLIAM "BUCK"
B.OCT.17,1859 HOAGLANDS,OHIO
D.OCT.20,1906 CINCINNATI,OHIO

YR	CL	LEA	POS	GP	G	REC
1880	TRO	N	C-O		13	.152
1881	TRO	N	C-S-3-O		65	.243
1882	TRO	N	P-C-	1	72	0- 0
			3			.273
1883	NY	N	C-2-S-O		85	.306
1884	NY	N	P-C-	1	88	0- 1
			S-O			.278
1885	NY	N	P-C-	1	81	0- 1
			1-S-3-O			.304
1886	NY	N	C-O		70	.309
1887	NY	N	2-3		76	.365
1888	NY	N	C-3		103	.306
1889	NY	N	P-C	2	96	0- 0
						.326
1890	NY	P	M-P-	1	83	0- 1
			C			.349
1891	NY	N	C-2		14	.340
1892	NY	N	C-1		97	.319
1893	CLE	N	O		114	.371
1894	CLE	N	O		53	.255
1895	CIN	N	M-1		103	.316
1896	CIN	N	M-1		67	.282
1897	CIN	N	M-1		1	.000
	BRTR			6	1281	0- 3
						.311

NON-PLAYING MANAGER
CIN(N) 1898-99, NY(N) 1900

EWOLDT, ARTHUR LEE "SHERIFF"
B.JAN.8,1894 PAULINA,IOWA

YR	CL	LEA	POS	GP	G	REC
1919	PHI	A	O		9	.233
	BRTR					

EYRICH, GEORGE LINCOLN
B.MAR.3,1925 READING,PA.

YR	CL	LEA	POS	GP	G	REC
1943	PHI	N	P		9	0- 0
	BRTR					

EZZELL, HOMER ESTELL
B.FEB.28,1896 VICTORIA,TEX.

YR	CL	LEA	POS	GP	G	REC
1923	STL	A	3		88	.247
1924	BOS	A	S-3		90	.271
1925	BOS	A	2-3		58	.285
	BRTR				236	.265

YR CL LEA POS GP G REC

FAATZ, JAYSON S. "JAY"
B.OCT.24,1860 WEEDSPORT,N.Y.
D.APR.10,1923
1884 PIT AA	1		29	.230
1888 CLE AA	1		120	.264
1889 CLE N	1		115	.230
1890 BUF P	1		32	.200
BRTR			296	.242
NON-PLAYING MANAGER CLE(N) 1890

FABER, URBAN CHARLES "RED"
B.SEPT.6,1888 CASCADE,IOWA
D.SEPT.25,1976 CHICAGO,ILL.
1914 CHI A	P		40	10- 9
1915 CHI A	P		50	24-13
1916 CHI A	P		35	17- 9
1917 CHI A	P		41	16-13
1918 CHI A	P		11	5- 1
1919 CHI A	P		25	11- 9
1920 CHI A	P		40	23-13
1921 CHI A	P		43	25-15
1922 CHI A	P		43	21-17
1923 CHI A	P	32	33	14-11
1924 CHI A	P		21	9-11
1925 CHI A	P		34	12-11
1926 CHI A	P		27	15- 8
1927 CHI A	P		18	4- 7
1928 CHI A	P		27	13- 9
1929 CHI A	P		31	13-13
1930 CHI A	P		29	8-13
1931 CHI A	P		44	10-14
1932 CHI A	P		42	2-11
1933 CHI A	P		36	3- 4
BBTR		669	670	255-211

FABRIQUE, ALBERT LA VERNE "BUNNY"
B.DEC.23,1887 CLINTON,MICH.
D.JAN.10,1960
1916 BRO N	S		2	.000
1917 BRO N	S		25	.205
BBTR			27	.200

FACE, ELROY LEON "ROY"
B.FEB.20,1928 STEPHENTOWN,N.Y.
1953 PIT N	P	41	43	6- 8
1955 PIT N	P	42	43	5- 7
1956 PIT N	P	68	69	12-13
1957 PIT N	P		59	4- 6
1958 PIT N	P		57	5- 2
1959 PIT N	P	57	58	18- 1
1960 PIT N	P		68	10- 8
1961 PIT N	P		62	6-12
1962 PIT N	P		63	8- 7
1963 PIT N	P		56	3- 9
1964 PIT N	P		55	3- 3
1965 PIT N	P		16	5- 2
1966 PIT N	P		54	6- 6
1967 PIT N	P		61	7- 5
1968 PIT N	P		43	2- 4
DET A	P		2	0- 0
1969 MON N	P		44	4- 2
BBTR		848	853	104-95
BR 1953-59				

FAETH, ANTHONY JOSEPH
B.JULY 8,1894 ABERDEEN,S.C.
1919 CLE A	P		6	0- 0
1920 CLE A	P		13	0- 0
BRTR			19	0- 0

FAGAN, EVERETT JOSEPH
B.JAN.13,1919 POTTERSVILLE,N.J.
1943 PHI A	P		18	2- 6
1946 PHI A	P		20	0- 1
BRTR			38	2- 7

FAGAN, WILLIAM A. "CLINKERS"
B.LANSINGBURG,N.Y.
1887 MET AA	P		6	1- 4
1888 KC AA	P	17	18	6-11
		23	24	7-15

FAGIN, FREDERICK H.
B.CINCINNATI,OHIO
| 1895 STL N | C | | 1 | .333 |

FAHEY, FRANCIS R.
B.JAN.22,1896 MILFORD,MASS.
D.MAR.19,1954
| 1918 PHI A | P | | 10 | 0- 0 |
| BBTR | | | | |

FAHEY, HOWARD SIMPSON
B.JUNE 24,1892 MEDFORD,MASS.
D.OCT.24,1971 CLEARWATER,FLA.
| 1912 PHI A | S | | 5 | .000 |
| BRTR | | | | |

FAHEY, WILLIAM ROGER "BILL"
B.JUNE 14,1950 DETROIT,MICH.
1971 WAS A	C	2	.000
1972 TEX A	C	39	.168
1974 TEX A	C	6	.250
1975 TEX A	C	21	.297
1976 TEX A	C	38	.250
BLTR		106	.212

FAHR, GERALD WARREN "JERRY"
B.DEC.9,1926 MARMADUKE,ARK.
| 1951 CLE A | P | | 5 | 0- 0 |
| BRTR | | | | |

FAHRER, CLARENCE WILLIE "PETE"
B.MAR.10,1890 HOLGATE,OHIO
D.JUNE 10,1967
| 1914 CIN N | P | | 5 | 0- 0 |
| TR | | | | |

FAIN, FERRIS ROY "BURRHEAD"
B.MAY.29,1922 SAN ANTONIO,TEX.
1947 PHI A	1	136	.291
1948 PHI A	1	145	.281
1949 PHI A	1	150	.263
1950 PHI A	1	151	.282
1951 PHI A	1-O	117	.344
1952 PHI A	1	145	.327
1953 CHI A	1	128	.256
1954 CHI A	1	65	.302
1955 DET A	1	58	.264
CLE A	1	56	.254
BLTL		1151	.290

FAIRBANK, JAMES LEE
B.MAR.17,1881 DEANSBORO,N.Y.
D.DEC.27,1955
1903 PHI A	P		1	0- 0
1904 PHI A	P		3	0- 1
			4	0- 1

FAIRCLOTH, JAMES LAMAR "RAGS"
B.AUG.19,1892 KENTON,TENN.
| 1919 PHI N | P | | 2 | 0- 0 |
| BRTR | | | | |

FAIREY, JAMES BURKE "JIM"
B.SEP.22,1944 ORANGEBURG,S.C.
1968 LA N	O	99	.199
1969 MON N	O	20	.286
1970 MON N	O	92	.242
1971 MON N	O	92	.245
1972 MON N	O	86	.234
1973 LA N	H	10	.222
BLTL		399	.235

FAIRLY, RONALD RAY "RON"
B.JULY 12,1938 MACON,GA.
1958 LA N	O	15	.283
1959 LA N	O	118	.238
1960 LA N	O	14	.108
1961 LA N	1-O	111	.322
1962 LA N	1-O	147	.278
1963 LA N	1-O	152	.271
1964 LA N	1	150	.256
1965 LA N	1-O	158	.274
1966 LA N	1-O	117	.288
1967 LA N	1-O	153	.220
1968 LA N	1-O	141	.234
1969 LA N	1-O	30	.219
MON N	1-O	70	.289
1970 MON N	1-O	119	.288
1971 MON N	1-O	146	.257
1972 MON N	1-O	140	.278
1973 MON N	1-O	142	.298
1974 MON N	1-O	101	.245
1975 STL N	1-O	107	.301
1976 STL N	1	73	.264
OAK A	1	15	.239
BLTL		2219	.267

FALCH, ANTON
| 1884 MIL U | C-O | | 5 | .471 |

FALCONE, PETER "PETE"
B.OCT.1,1953 BROOKLYN,N.Y.
1975 SF N	P	34	12-11
1976 STL N	P	32	12-16
BLTL		66	24-27

FALK, BIBB AUGUST "JOCKEY"
B.JAN.27,1899 AUSTIN,TEX.
1920 CHI A	O	7	.294
1921 CHI A	O	152	.285
1922 CHI A	O	131	.298
1923 CHI A	O	87	.307
1924 CHI A	O	138	.352
1925 CHI A	O	154	.301
1926 CHI A	O	155	.345
1927 CHI A	O	145	.327
1928 CHI A	O	98	.290
1929 CLE A	O	126	.310
1930 CLE A	O	82	.325
1931 CLE A	O	79	.304
BLTL		1354	.314

FALK, CHESTER EMANUEL
B.MAY.15,1905 AUSTIN,TEX.
1925 STL A	P	13	17	0- 0
1926 STL A	P	18	19	4- 4
1927 STL A	P		9	1- 0
BLTL		40	45	5- 4

FALKENBERG, FREDERICK PETER "CY"
B.DEC.17,1880 CHICAGO,ILL.
D.APR.14,1961
1903 PIT N	P		10	1- 5
1905 WAS A	P		12	4- 4
1906 WAS A	P		40	14-20
1907 WAS A	P	32	33	5-18
1908 WAS A	P		17	6- 1
CLE A	P		8	2- 5
1909 CLE A	P		24	10- 9
1910 CLE A	P		37	14-13
1911 CLE A	P	15	16	8- 5
1913 CLE A	P		39	23-10
1914 IND F	P		49	25-16
1915 NEW F	P		16	4- 6
BRO F	P		16	7- 8
1917 PHI A	P		15	2- 6
BRTR		330	332	125-126

FALLENSTEIN, EDWARD JOSEPH "JACK"
B.DEC.23,1908 NEWARK,N.J.
D.NOV.24,1971 ORANGE,N.J.
1931 PHI N	P		24	0- 0
1933 BOS N	P	9	11	2- 1
BRTR		33	35	2- 1

FALLON, GEORGE DECATUR "FLASH"
B.JULY 8,1916 JERSEY CITY,N.J.
1937 BRO N	2		4	.250
1943 STL N	2		36	.231
1944 STL N	2-S-3		69	.199
1945 STL N	2-S		24	.236
BRTR			133	.216

FALSEY, PETER JAMES
B.APR.24,1891 NEW HAVEN,CONN.
| 1914 PIT N | P | | 3 | 0- 0 |
| BLTL | | | | |

FANNON, CLIFFORD BRYSON "CLIFF" OR "MULE"
B.MAY 13,1924 LOUISA,KY.
D.DEC.11,1966 SANDUSKY,OHIO
1945 STL A	P		5	0- 0
1946 STL A	P	27	5- 2
1947 STL A	P	26	6- 8
1948 STL A	P	34	48	10-14
1949 STL A	P	30	37	8-14
1950 STL A	P	25	33	5- 9
1951 STL A	P	7	8	0- 2
1952 STL A	P	10	11	0- 2
BLTR		164	195	34-51

FANNING, JOHN JACOB
B.1863 S.ORANGE,N.J.
D.JUNE 10,1917
1889 IND N	P		1	0- 1
1894 PHI N	P		6	1- 3
			7	1- 4

FANNING, WILLIAM JAMES "JIM"
B.SEPT.14,1927 CHICAGO,ILL.
1954 CHI N	C	11	.184
1955 CHI N	C	5	.000
1956 CHI N	C	1	.250
1957 CHI N	C	47	.180
BRTR		64	.170

YR	CL	LEA	POS	GP	G	REC

FANOK, HARRY MICHAEL
B.MAY 11,1940 WHIPPANY,N.J.
1963	STL	N	P		12	2- 1
1964	STL	N	P		4	0- 0
	BBTR				16	2- 1

FANOVICH, FRANK JOSEPH
B.JAN.11,1922 NEW YORK,N.Y.
1949	CIN	N	P		29	0- 2
1953	PHI	A	P		26	0- 3
	BLTL				55	0- 5

FANWELL, HARRY CLAYTON
B.OCT.16,1886 PATAPSCO,MD.
D.JULY 15,1965 BALTIMORE,MD.
| 1910 | CLE | A | P | | 17 | 2- 9 |
| | BBTR | | | | | |

FANZONE, CARMEN RONALD
B.AUG.30,1943 DETROIT,MICH.
1970	BOS	A	3		10	.200
1971	CHI	N	1-3-0		12	.186
1972	CHI	N	1-2-S-3-	86		.225
			0			
1973	CHI	N	1-3-0		64	.273
1974	CHI	N	1-2-3-0		65	.190
	BRTR				237	.224

FARLEY, ROBERT JACOB "BOB"
B.NOV.15,1937 WATSONTOWN,PA.
1961	SF	N	1-0		13	.100
1962	CHI	A	1		35	.189
	DET	A	1-0		36	.160
	BLTL				84	.163

FARLEY, THOMAS T.
B.CHICAGO,ILL.
| 1884 | WAS | AA | O | | 13 | .213 |

FARMER, ALEXANDER JOHNSON
B.MAY 9,1880 NEW YORK,N.Y.
D.MAR.5,1920
| 1908 | BRO | N | C | | 12 | .167 |
| | BRTR | | | | | |

FARMER, EDWARD JOSEPH "ED"
B.OCT.18,1949 EVERGREEN PARK,ILL
1971	CLE	A	P		43	5- 4
1972	CLE	A	P		46	2- 5
1973	CLE	A	P		16	0- 2
	DET	A	P		24	3- 0
1974	PHI	N	P		14	2- 1
	BRTR				143	12-12

FARMER, FLOYD HASKELL "JACK"
B.JULY 14,1892 GRANVILLE,TENN.
D.MAY 21,1970 COLUMBIA,LA.
1916	PIT	N	2-0		55	.271
1918	CLE	A	O		7	.222
	BRTR				62	.269

FARMER, WILLIAM
B.PHILADELPHIA,PA.
1888	PIT	N	C		2	.000
	ATH	AA	C		3	.167
	BRTR				5	.125

FARRAR, SIDNEY DOUGLAS
B.AUG.10,1859 PARIS HILL,ME.
D.MAY 7,1935
1883	PHI	N	1		98	.230
1884	PHI	N	1		110	.246
1885	PHI	N	1		111	.245
1886	PHI	N	1		118	.248
1887	PHI	N	1		115	.344
1888	PHI	N	1		130	.246
1889	PHI	N	1		130	.268
1890	PHI	P	1		127	.251
	TR				939	.262

FARRELL, CHARLES ANDREW "DUKE"
B.AUG.31,1866 OAKDALE,MASS.
D.FEB.15,1925
1888	CHI	N	C-O		63	.232
1889	CHI	N	C-O		100	.263
1890	CHI	P	C-1		117	.296
1891	BOS	AA	C-3-O		122	.304
1892	PIT	N	3-O		152	.230
1893	WAS	N	C-3		122	.296
1894	NY	N	C		112	.282
1895	NY	N	C-3		89	.283
1896	NY	N	C		45	.279
	WAS	N	C-3		37	.326
1897	WAS	N	C		65	.327
1898	WAS	N	C-1		88	.316
1899	WAS	N	C		5	.333
	BRO	N	C		78	.294
1900	BRO	N	C		73	.277
1901	BRO	N	C-1		76	.293
1902	BRO	N	C-1		72	.237
1903	BOS	A	C		17	.404
1904	BOS	A	C		67	.219
1905	BOS	A	C		7	.238
	BBTR			1507		.280

FARRELL, EDWARD STEPHEN "DOC"
B.DEC.26,1902 JOHNSON CITY,N.Y.
D.DEC.20,1966 LIVINGSTON,N.J.
1925	NY	N	2-S-3		27	.214
1926	NY	N	S		67	.287
1927	NY	N	S-3		42	.387
	BOS	N	2-S-3		110	.292
1928	BOS	N	S		134	.215
1929	BOS	N	2		5	.125
	NY	N	2-3		63	.213
1930	STL	N	S		23	.213
	CHI	N	S		46	.292
1932	NY	A	2		26	.175
1933	NY	A	2-S		44	.269
1935	BOS	A	2		4	.286
	BRTP			591		.260

FARRELL, JOHN "HARTFORD JACK"
D.FEB.10,1914
| 1874 | HAR | NA | O | | 3 | - |

FARRELL, JOHN A. "MOOSE"
B.JULY 5,1857 NEWARK,N.J.
D.NOV.15,1916
1879	SYR	N	2		54	.304
	PRO	N	2		12	.260
1880	PRO	N	2		77	.270
1881	PRO	N	2-0		83	.237
1882	PRO	N	2		84	.254
1883	PRO	N	2		93	.304
1884	PRO	N	2-3		109	.220
1885	PRO	N	2		67	.206
1886	PHI	N	2		23	.171
	WAS	N	2		42	.252
1887	WAS	N	2-S		86	.264
1888	BAL	AA	2-S		103	.197
1889	BAL	AA	S		42	.204
	BRTR			875		.241

FARRELL, JOHN J.
B.JUNE 16,1892 CHICAGO,ILL.
D.MAR.24,1918
1914	CHI	F	2		157	.240
1915	CHI	F	2		69	.213
	BBTR			226		.232

FARRELL, JOHN STEPHEN
B.DEC.4,1876 COVINGTON,KY.
D.MAY 14,1921
1901	WAS	A	2-O		135	.277
1902	STL	N	2-S		139	.255
1903	STL	N	2		130	.272
1904	STL	N	2		130	.255
1905	STL	N	2		6	.182
	TR			540		.264

FARRELL, JOSEPH F.
B.1858 BROOKLYN,N.Y.
D.APR.18,1893
1882	DET	N	2-S-3		66	.246
1883	DET	N	3		98	.246
1884	DET	N	3		108	.225
1886	BAL	AA	2-3		72	.212
				344		.233

FARRELL, MAJOR KERBY "KERBY"
B.SEPT.3,1913 LEAPWOOD,TENN.
D.DEC.17,1975 NASHVILLE,TENN.
1943	BOS	N	P-1	5	85	0- 1
						.268
1945	CHI	A	1		103	.258
	BLTL			5	188	0- 1
						.262
NON-PLAYING MANAGER CLE(A) 1957

FARRELL, RICHARD JOSEPH "TURK"
B.APR.8,1934 BOSTON,MASS.
1956	PHI	N	P		1	0- 1
1957	PHI	N	P		52	10- 2
1958	PHI	N	P		54	8- 9
1959	PHI	N	P		38	1- 6
1960	PHI	N	P		59	10- 6
1961	PHI	N	P		5	2- 1
	LA	N	P		50	6- 6
1962	HOU	N	P		43	10-20
1963	HOU	N	P		34	14-13
1964	HOU	N	P		32	11-10
1965	HOU	N	P		33	11-11
1966	HOU	N	P		32	6-10
1967	HOU	N	P		7	1- 0
	PHI	N	P		50	9- 6
1968	PHI	N	P		54	4- 6
1969	PHI	N	P		46	3- 4
	BRTR				590	106-111

FARRELL, W.
| 1883 | BAL | AA | S | | 2 | .000 |

FARROW, JOHN JACOB
B.1852 VERPLANCK'S POINT,N.Y.
D.DEC.31,1914
1873	RES	NA	C-1-3-0		10	-
1874	ATL	NA	C-2		27	-
1884	BRO	AA	C		16	.190
	TR				53	-

FAST
B.MILWAUKEE,WIS.
| 1887 | IND | N | P | | 4 | 0- 1 |

FAST, DARCY RAE
B.MAR.10,1947 DALLAS,ORE.
| 1968 | CHI | N | P | | 8 | 0- 1 |
| | BLTL | | | | | |

FASZHOLZ, JOHN EDWARD "JACK"
B.APR.11,1927 ST.LOUIS,MO.
| 1953 | STL | N | P | | 4 | 0- 0 |
| | BRTR | | | | | |

FAUL, WILLIAM ALVAN "BILL"
B.APR.21,1940 CINCINNATI,OHIO
1962	DET	A	P		1	0- 0
1963	DET	A	P		28	5- 6
1964	DET	A	P		1	0- 0
1965	CHI	N	P		17	6- 6
1966	CHI	N	P		17	1- 4
1970	SF	N	P		7	0- 0
	BRTR				71	12-16

FAULKNER, JAMES LEROY
B.JULY 27,1900 BEATRICE,NEB.
D.JUNE 2,1962
1927	NY	N	P		3	1- 0
1928	NY	N	P		38	9- 8
1930	BRO	N	P		2	0- 0
	BBTL				43	10- 8
	BL 1927					

FAUSETT, ROBERT SHAW "BUCK"
B.APR.8,1908 SHERIDAN,ARK.
1944	CIN	N	P-3	2	13	0- 0
						.097
	BLTR					

FAUST, CHARLES VICTOR "VIC"
B.OCT.9,1883 MARION,KAN.
D.JUNE 18,1915
| 1911 | NY | N | P | | 2 | 0- 0 |

FAUTSCH, JOSEPH R.
B.1889
D.MAR.16,1971 NEW HOPE,MINN.
| 1916 | CHI | A | P | | 1 | 0- 0 |
| | BRTR | | | | | |

FAUVER, CLAYTON KING
B.AUG.1,1872 N.EATON,OHIO
D.MAR.3,1942
| 1899 | LOU | N | P | | 1 | 1- 0 |
| | BB | | | | | |

YR	CL	LEA	POS	GP	G	REC

FAZIO, ERNEST JOSEPH "ERNIE"
B.JAN.25,1942 OAKLAND,CAL.

YR	CL	LEA	POS	GP	G	REC
1962	HOU	N	S		12	.083
1963	HOU	N	2-S-3		102	.184
1966	KC	A	2-S		27	.206
	BRTR				141	.182

FEAR, LUVERN CARL "VERN"
B.AUG.21,1924 EVERLY,IOWA

1952	CHI	N	P		4	0- 0
	BBTR					

FEDEROFF, ALFRED "AL"
B.JULY 11,1925 BAIRDFORD,PA.

1951	DET	A	2		2	.000
1952	DET	A	2-S		74	.242
	BRTR				76	.238

FEE, JOHN
B.1870 CARBONDALE,PA.
D.MAR.4,1913

1889	IND	N	P		7	2- 2

FEHRING, WILLIAM PAUL
B.MAY 31,1912 COLUMBUS,IND.

1934	CHI	A	C		1	.000
	BBTR					

FEINBERG, EDWARD
B.SEPT.20,1918 PHILADELPHIA,PA.

1938	PHI	N	S-O		10	.150
1939	PHI	N	2-S		6	.222
	BBTR				16	.184

FELDERMAN, MARVIN WILFRED
B.DEC.17,1917 BELLEVUE,IOWA

1942	CHI	N	C		3	.167
	BRTR					

FELDMAN, HARRY
B.NOV.10,1919 NEW YORK,N.Y.
D.MAR.16,1962

1941	NY	N	P		3	1- 1
1942	NY	N	P		31	7- 1
1943	NY	N	P	31	44	4- 5
1944	NY	N	P	40	54	11-13
1945	NY	N	P	35	38	12-13
1946	NY	N	P		3	0- 2
	BRTR			143	173	35-35

FELIX, AUGUST GUENTHER
B.MAY 24,1895 CINCINNATI,OHIO
D.MAY 12,1960

1923	BOS	N	2-3-O		139	.273
1924	BOS	N	O		59	.211
1925	BOS	N	O		121	.307
1926	BRO	N	O		134	.280
1927	BRO	N	O		130	.265
	BRTR				583	.274

FELIX, HARRY
B.1877 BROOKLYN,N.Y.
D.OCT.18,1961

1901	NY	N	P		1	0- 0
1902	PHI	N	P-3	9	16	1- 3
						.111
	TR			10	17	1- 3
						.105

FELLER, JACK LELAND
B.DEC.10,1936 ADRIAN,MICH.

1958	DET	A	C		1	.000
	BRTR					

**FELLER, ROBERT WILLIAM ANDREW
"BOB" OR "RAPID ROBERT"**
B.NOV.3,1918 VAN METER,IOWA

1936	CLE	A	P		14	5- 3
1937	CLE	A	P		26	9- 7
1938	CLE	A	P		39	17-11
1939	CLE	A	P		39	24- 9
1940	CLE	A	P		43	27-11
1941	CLE	A	P		44	25-13
1945	CLE	A	P		9	5- 3
1946	CLE	A	P		48	26-15
1947	CLE	A	P		42	20-11
1948	CLE	A	P		44	19-15
1949	CLE	A	P		36	15-14
1950	CLE	A	P		35	16-11
1951	CLE	A	P		33	22- 8
1952	CLE	A	P		30	9-13
1953	CLE	A	P		25	10- 7
1954	CLE	A	P		19	13- 3
1955	CLE	A	P		25	,4- 4
1956	CLE	A	P		19	0- 4
	BRTR				570	266-162

FELSCH, OSCAR EMIL "HAPPY"
B.AUG.22,1891 MILWAUKEE,WIS.
D.AUG.17,1964 MILWAUKEE,WIS.

1915	CHI	A	O		121	.248
1916	CHI	A	O		146	.301
1917	CHI	A	O		152	.308
1918	CHI	A	O		53	.252
1919	CHI	A	O		135	.275
1920	CHI	A	O		142	.338
	BRTR				749	.290

FELSKE, JOHN FREDERICK
B.MAY 30,1942 CHICAGO,ILL.

1968	CHI	N	C		4	.000
1972	MIL	A	C-1		37	.138
1973	MIL	A	C-1		13	.136
	BRTR				54	.135

FENNELLY, FRANCIS JOHN
B.FEB.18,1860 FALL RIVER,MASS.
D.AUG.4,1920

1884	WAS	AA	2-S-O		62	.288
	CIN	AA	S		28	.369
1885	CIN	AA	S		112	.259
1886	CIN	AA	S		132	.258
1887	CIN	AA	S		134	.368
1888	CIN	AA	2-S-O		112	.191
	ATH	AA	S		15	.239
1889	ATH	AA	S		137	.259
1890	BRO	AA	S		47	.251
	BRTR				779	.278

FENNER, HORACE ALFRED "HOD"
B.JULY 17,1897 MARTIN,MICH.

1921	CHI	A	P		2	0- 0
	BRTR					

FENWICK, ROBERT RICHARD "BOBBY"
B.DEC.10,1946 OKINAWA

1972	HOU	N	2-S-3		36	.180
1973	STL	N	2		5	.167
	BRTR				41	.179

FERENS, STANLEY
B.MAR.5,1919 WENDELL,PA.

1942	STL	A	P		19	3- 4
1946	STL	A	P		34	2- 9
	BBTL				53	5-13

FERGUSON, CHARLES AUGUSTUS
B.MAY 10,1875 OKEMOS,MICH.
D.MAY 17,1931

1901	CHI	N	P		1	0- 0

FERGUSON, CHARLES J.
B.APR.17,1863 CHARLOTTESVILLE,
VA.
D.APR.29,1888

1884	PHI	N	P-O	46	51	20-22
						.251
1885	PHI	N	P-O	46	59	26-19
						.306
1886	PHI	N	P-O	43	71	32- 9
						.252
1887	PHI	N	P-2	33	69	21-10
						.412
	BBTR			168	250	99-60
						.313

FERGUSON, GEORGE CECIL
B.AUG.19,1886 ELLSWORTH,IND.
D.SEPT.5,1943

1906	NY	N	P		22	2- 1
1907	NY	N	P		15	3- 2
1908	BOS	N	P		37	11-11
1909	BOS	N	P		36	5-23
1910	BOS	N	P		26	7- 7
1911	BOS	N	P		6	1- 3
	TR				142	29-47

**FERGUSON, JAMES ALEXANDER
"ALEX"**
B.FEB.16,1897 MONTCLAIR,N.J.
D.APR.28,1976 CAMARILLO,CAL.

1918	NY	A	P		1	0- 0
1921	NY	A	P		17	3- 1
1922	BOS	A	P		39	9-16
1923	BOS	A	P		34	9-13
1924	BOS	A	P		41	14-17
1925	BOS	A	P		5	0- 2
	NY	A	P		21	4- 2
	WAS	A	P		7	5- 1
1926	WAS	A	P		19	3- 4
1927	PHI	N	P		31	8-16
1928	PHI	N	P		34	5-10
1929	PHI	N	P		5	1- 2
	BRO	N	P		3	0- 1
	BRTR				257	61-85

FERGUSON, JOSEPH VANCE "JOE"
B.SEP.19,1946 SAN FRANCISCO,CAL.

1970	LA	N	C		5	.250
1971	LA	N	C		36	.216
1972	LA	N	C-O		8	.292
1973	LA	N	C-O		136	.263
1974	LA	N	C-O		111	.252
1975	LA	N	C-O		66	.208
1976	LA	N	C-O		54	.222
	STL	N	C-O		71	.201
	BRTR				487	.238

FERGUSON, ROBERT LESTER
B.APR.18,1919 BIRMINGHAM,ALA.

1944	CIN	N	P		9	0- 3
	BRTR					

FERGUSON, ROBERT V.
B.1845 BROOKLYN,N.Y.
D.MAY 3,1894

1871	MUT	NA	M-C-2-3		34	-
1872	ATL	NA	M-3		35	.262
1873	ATL	NA	M-P-	1	53	0- 1
					3	-
1874	ATL	NA	M-P-	1	56	0- 1
			C-3			-
1875	HAR	NA	M-3		84	-
1876	HAR	N	M-3		69	.264
1877	HAR	N	M-P-	3	58	1- 1
					2	.256
1878	CHI	N	M-S		60	.334
1879	TRO	N	M-3		29	.252
1880	TRO	N	M-2		82	.262
1881	TRO	N	M-2		84	.287
1882	TRO	N	M-2-S		79	.254
1883	PHI	N	M-P-	1	85	0- 0
					2	-
						.256
1884	PIT	AA	M-1-3-O		10	.154
	BBTR			6	818	1- 3
						-

NON-PLAYING MANAGER
MET(AA) 1886-87

FERNANDES, EDWARD PAUL
B.MAR.11,1918 OAKLAND,CAL.

1940	PIT	N	C		28	.121
1946	CHI	A	C		14	.250
	BBTR				42	.185

FERNANDEZ, FRANK
B.APR.16,1943 STATEN ISLAND,N.Y.

1967	NY	A	C-O		9	.214
1968	NY	A	C-O		51	.170
1969	NY	A	C-O		89	.223
1970	OAK	A	C-O		94	.214
1971	OAK	A	C		4	.111
	WAS	A	C-O		18	.100
	CHI	N	C		17	.171
1972	CHI	N	C		3	.000
	BRTR				285	.199

FERNANDEZ, FROILAN "NANNY"
B.OCT.25,1918 WILMINGTON,CSL.

1942	BOS	N	3-O		145	.255
1946	BOS	N	S-3-O		115	.255
1947	BOS	N	S-3-O		83	.206
1950	PIT	N	3		65	.258
	BRTR				408	.248

FERNANDEZ, HUMBERTO (PEREZ) "CHICO"
B.MAR.2,1932 HAVANA,CUBA

YR	CL	LEA	POS	GP	G	REC
1956	BRO	N	S		34	.227
1957	PHI	N	S		149	.262
1958	PHI	N	S		148	.230
1959	PHI	N	2-S		45	.211
1960	DET	A	S		133	.241
1961	DET	A	S-3		133	.248
1962	DET	A	1-S-3		141	.249
1963	DET	A	S		15	.143
	NY	N	2-S-3		58	.200
	BRTR				856	.240

FERNANDEZ, LORENZO MARTO (MOSQUERA) "CHICO"
B.APR.23,1939 HAVANA,CUBA

1968	BAL	A	2-S		24	.111
	BRTR					

FERRARA, ALFRED JOHN "AL"
B.DEC.22,1939 BROOKLYN,N.Y.

1963	LA	N	O		21	.159
1965	LA	N	O		41	.210
1966	LA	N	O		63	.270
1967	LA	N	O		122	.277
1968	LA	N	O		2	.143
1969	SD	N	O		138	.260
1970	SD	N	O		138	.277
1971	SD	N	O		17	.118
	CIN	N	O		32	.182
	BRTR				574	.259

FERRARESE, DONALD HUGH "DON"
B.JUNE 19,1929 OAKLAND,CAL.

1955	BAL	A	P		6	0- 0
1956	BAL	A	P		36	4-10
1957	BAL	A	P		8	1- 1
1958	CLE	A	P		28	3- 4
1959	CLE	A	P		15	5- 3
1960	CHI	A	P		5	0- 1
1961	BAL	A	P-O	42	43	5-12
						.171
1962	PHI	N	P		5	0- 1
	STL	N	P		38	1- 4
	BRTL			183	184	19-36
						.156

FERRARO, MICHAEL DENNIS "MIKE"
B.AUG.18,1944 KINGSTON,N.Y.

1966	NY	A	3		10	.179
1968	NY	A	3		23	.161
1969	SEA	A	H		5	.000
1972	MIL	A	2-S-3		124	.255
	BRTR				162	.232

FERRAZZI, WILLIAM JOSEPH
B.APR.19,1912 QUINCY,MASS.

1935	PHI	A	P		3	1- 2
	BRTR					

FERRELL, RICHARD BENJAMIN "RICK"
B.OCT.12,1905 DURHAM,N.C.

1929	STL	A	C		64	.229
1930	STL	A	C		101	.268
1931	STL	A	C		117	.306
1932	STL	A	C		126	.315
1933	STL	A	C		22	.250
	BOS	A	C		118	.297
1934	BOS	A	C		132	.297
1935	BOS	A	C		133	.301
1936	BOS	A	C		121	.312
1937	BOS	A	C		18	.308
	WAS	A	C		86	.229
1938	WAS	A	C		135	.292
1939	WAS	A	C		87	.281
1940	WAS	A	C		103	.273
1941	WAS	A	C		21	.273
	STL	A	C		100	.252
1942	STL	A	C		99	.223
1943	STL	A	C		74	.239
1944	WAS	A	C		99	.277
1945	WAS	A	C		91	.266
1947	WAS	A	C		37	.303
	BRTR				1884	.281

FERRELL, WESLEY CHEEK "WES"
B.FEB.2,1908 GREENSBORO,N.C.
D.DEC.9,1976 SARASOTA,FLA.

1927	CLE	A	P		1	0- 0
1928	CLE	A	P		2	0- 2
1929	CLE	A	P	43	43	21-10
1930	CLE	A	P	43	53	25-13
1931	CLE	A	P	40	48	22-12
1932	CLE	A	P	38	55	23-13
1933	CLE	A	P-O	28	61	11-12
						.271
1934	BOS	A	P	26	34	14- 5
1935	BOS	A	P	41	75	25-14
1936	BOS	A	P	39	61	20-15
1937	BOS	A	P	12	18	3- 6
	WAS	A	P	25	53	11-13
1938	WAS	A	P	23	26	13- 8
	NY	A	P		5	2- 2
1939	NY	A	P		3	1- 2
1940	BRO	N	P	1	2	0- 0
1941	BOS	N	P		4	2- 1
	BRTR			374	548	193-128
						.280

FERRER, SERGIO (MARPERO)
B.JAN.29,1951 SANTURCE,P.R.

1974	MIN	A	2-S		24	.281
1975	MIN	A	2-S		32	.247
	BBTR				56	.261

FERRICK, THOMAS JEROME "TOM"
B.JAN.6,1915 NEW YORK,N.Y.

1941	PHI	A	P		36	8-10
1942	CLE	A	P		31	3- 2
1946	CLE	A	P		9	0- 0
	STL	A	P		25	4- 1
1947	WAS	A	P		31	1- 7
1948	WAS	A	P		37	2- 5
1949	STL	A	P	50	51	6- 4
1950	STL	A	P		16	1- 3
	NY	A	P		30	8- 4
1951	NY	A	P		9	1- 1
	WAS	A	P		22	2- 0
1952	WAS	A	P		27	4- 3
	BRTR			323	324	40-40

FERRIS, ALBERT SAYLES "HOBE"
B.DEC.7,1877 PROVIDENCE,R.I.
D.MAR.18,1938

1901	BOS	A	2		138	.251
1902	BOS	A	2		133	.251
1903	BOS	A	2		141	.250
1904	BOS	A	2		156	.221
1905	BOS	A	2		141	.220
1906	BOS	A	2		130	.244
1907	BOS	A	2		143	.241
1908	STL	A	3		148	.270
1909	STL	A	2-3		148	.216
	BRTR				1278	.240

FERRISS, DAVID MEADOW "DAVE" OR "BOO"
B.DEC.5,1921 SHAW,MISS.

1945	BOS	A	P	35	61	21-10
1946	BOS	A	P	40	45	25- 6
1947	BOS	A	P	33	52	12-11
1948	BOS	A	P		31	7- 3
1949	BOS	A	P		4	0- 0
1950	BOS	A	P		1	0- 0
	BLTR			144	194	65-30

FERRY, ALFRED JOSEPH "CY"
B.SEPT.27,1878 HUDSON,N.Y.
D.SEPT.27,1938

1904	DET	A	P		3	0- 1
1905	CLE	A	P		1	0- 0
	BRTR				4	0- 1

FERRY, JOHN FRANCIS
B.APR.7,1887 PITTSFIELD,MASS.
D.AUG.29,1954

1910	PIT	N	P		6	1- 2
1911	PIT	N	P		26	6- 4
1912	PIT	N	P		11	2- 0
1913	PIT	N	P		4	1- 0
	BRTR				47	10- 6

FERSON, ALEXANDER "COLONEL"
B.JULY 14,1866 PHILADELPHIA,PA.

1889	WAS	N	P		35	17-17
1890	BUF	P	P		10	1- 5
1892	BAL	N	P		2	0- 1
	TR				47	18-23

FESSENDEN, WALLACE CLIFTON
B.WATERTOWN,MASS.
NON-PLAYING MANAGER SYR(AA)1890

FETTE, LOUIS HENRY WILLIAM "LOU"
B.MAR.15,1907 ALMA,MO.

1937	BOS	N	P	35	36	20-10
1938	BOS	N	P		33	11-13
1939	BOS	N	P		27	10-10
1940	BOS	N	P		7	0- 5
	BRO	N	P		2	0- 0
1945	BOS	N	P		5	0- 2
	BRTR			109	110	41-40

FETZER, WILLY MCKINNON
B.JUNE 24,1884 CONCORD,N.C.

1906	PHI	A	O		1	.000

FEWSTER, WILSON LLOYD "CHICK"
B.NOV.10,1895 BALTIMORE,MD.
D.APR.16,1945

1917	NY	A	2		11	.222
1918	NY	A	2		5	.500
1919	NY	A	S-O		81	.283
1920	NY	A	S		21	.286
1921	NY	A	2-O		66	.280
1922	NY	A	2-O		44	.228
	BOS	A	O		23	.316
1923	BOS	A	2-S		90	.236
1924	CLE	A	2		101	.267
1925	CLE	A	2-3		93	.248
1926	BRO	N	2		105	.243
1927	BRO	N	H		4	.000
	BRTR				644	.258

FICK, JOHN RALPH
B.MAY 18,1921 BALTIMORE,MD.
D.JUNE 9,1958 SOMERS POINT,N.J.

1944	PHI	N	P		4	0- 0
	BLTL					

FIDRYCH, MARK STEVEN "BIRD"
B.AUG.14,1954 WORCESTER,MASS.

1976	DET	A	P		31	19- 9
	BRTR					

FIEBER, CLARENCE THOMAS
B.SEPT.4,1913 SAN FRANCISCO,CAL

1932	CHI	A	P		3	1- 0
	BLTL					

FIELD, JAMES C.
B.APR.24,1863 PHILADELPHIA,PA.
D.MAY 13,1953

1883	COL	AA	1		75	.239
1884	COL	AA	1		105	.229
1885	PIT	AA	1		56	.245
	BAL	AA	1		38	.213
1890	ROC	AA	1		51	.190
1898	WAS	N	1		5	.095
					330	.228

FIELD, SAMUEL JAY
B.OCT.12,1848 PHILADELPHIA,PA.
D.OCT.28,1904

1875	CEN	NA	C-O		3	-
	NAT	NA	C		5	-
1876	CIN	N	C-2		4	.000
	BRTR				12	-

FIELDS, GEORGE W.

1872	MAN	NA	S-3-O		17	.282

FIELDS, JOHN JAMES "JOCKO"
B.OCT.20,1864 CORK,IRELAND
D.OCT.14,1950

1887	PIT	N	O		39	.298
1888	PIT	N	O		44	.195
1889	PIT	N	C-O		74	.311
1890	PIT	P	C-2-O		127	.277
1891	PIT	N	C		19	.239
	PHI	N	C		8	.233
1892	NY	N	C		17	.268
	BRTR				328	.274

FIENE, LOUIS HENRY "BIG FINN"
B.DEC.29,1884 FT.DODGE,IOWA
D.DEC.22,1964

1906	CHI	A	P		6	1- 1
1907	CHI	A	P		4	0- 1
1908	CHI	A	P		1	0- 1
1909	CHI	A	P	13	15	2- 2
	BRTR			24	26	3- 5

YR	CL	LEA	POS	GP	G	REC

FIFE, DANNY WAYNE
B.OCT.5,1949 HARRISBURG,ILL.

YR	CL	LEA	POS	GP	G	REC
1973	MIN	A	P		10	3-2
1974	MIN	A	P		4	0-0
		BRTR			14	3-2

FIFIELD, JOHN PROCTOR
B.OCT.5,1871 ENFIELD,N.H.
D.NOV.27,1939

YR	CL	LEA	POS	GP	G	REC
1897	PHI	N	P		24	4-20
1898	PHI	N	P		20	11-9
1899	PHI	N	P		13	3-8
	WAS	N	P-3	6	7	2-4
						.200
				63	64	20-41
						.200

FIGGEMEIER, FRANK Y.
B.APR.25,1873 ST.LOUIS,MO.

YR	CL	LEA	POS	GP	G	REC
1894	PHI	N	P		1	0-1

FIGUEROA, EDUARDO (PADILLA) "ED"
B.OCT.14,1948 CIALES,P.R.

YR	CL	LEA	POS	GP	G	REC
1974	CAL	A	P		25	2-8
1975	CAL	A	P		33	16-13
1976	NY	A	P		34	19-10
		BRTR			92	37-31

FILE, LAWRENCE SAMUEL
B.MAY 18,1922 CHESTER,PA.

YR	CL	LEA	POS	GP	G	REC
1940	PHI	N	S-3		7	.077
		BRTR				

FILES, CHARLES EDWARD "EDDIE"
B.MAY 19,1883 PORTLAND,ME.
D.MAY.10,1954

YR	CL	LEA	POS	GP	G	REC
1908	PHI	A	P		2	0-0
		BRTR				

FILIPOWICZ, STEPHEN CHARLES "FLIP"
B.JUNE 28,1921 DONORA,PA.
D.FEB.21,1975 WILKES-BARRE,PA.

YR	CL	LEA	POS	GP	G	REC
1944	NY	N	C-O		15	.195
1945	NY	N	O		35	.205
1948	CIN	N	O		7	.346
		BRTR			57	.223

FILLEY, MARCUS LUCIUS
B.FEB.28,1912 TROY,N.Y.

YR	CL	LEA	POS	GP	G	REC
1934	WAS	A	P		1	0-0
		BRTR				

FILLINGIM, DANA
B.NOV.6,1893 SEALE,ALA.
D.FEB.3,1961

YR	CL	LEA	POS	GP	G	REC
1915	PHI	A	P		8	0-4
1918	BOS	N	P		14	7-6
1919	BOS	N	P		32	6-13
1920	BOS	N	P	37	38	12-21
1921	BOS	N	P	44	45	15-10
1922	BOS	N	P		25	5-9
1923	BOS	N	P	35	36	1-9
1925	PHI	N	P		5	1-0
		BLTR		200	203	47-72

FINCHER, WILLIAM ALLEN
B.MAY 26,1894 ATLANTA,GA.
D.MAY 8,1946

YR	CL	LEA	POS	GP	G	REC
1916	STL	A	P		12	0-1
		BRTR				

FINE, BENJAMIN J.
NON-PLAYING MANAGER STL(N) 1885

FINE, THOMAS MORGAN "TOMMY"
B.OCT.10,1914 CLEBURNE,TEX.

YR	CL	LEA	POS	GP	G	REC
1947	BOS	A	P		9	1-2
1950	STL	A	P	14	16	0-1
		BBTR		23	2-3	1-3

FINGERS, ROLAND GLEN "ROLLIE"
B.AUG.25,1946 STEUBENVILLE,OHIO

YR	CL	LEA	POS	GP	G	REC
1968	OAK	A	P		1	0-0
1969	OAK	A	P		60	6-7
1970	OAK	A	P		45	7-9
1971	OAK	A	P		48	4-6
1972	OAK	A	P		65	11-9
1973	OAK	A	P		62	7-8
1974	OAK	A	P		76	9-5
1975	OAK	A	P	75	76	10-6
1976	OAK	A	P		70	13-11
		BRTR		502	503	67-61

FINIGAN, JAMES LEROY "JIM"
B.AUG.19,1928 QUINCY,ILL.

YR	CL	LEA	POS	GP	G	REC
1954	PHI	A	3		136	.302
1955	KC	A	2-3		150	.255
1956	KC	A	2-3		91	.216
1957	DET	A	2-3		64	.270
1958	SF	N	2-3		23	.200
1959	BAL	A	2-S-3		48	.252
		BRTR			512	.264

FINK, HERMAN ADAM
B.AUG.22,1911 LANDIS,N.C.

YR	CL	LEA	POS	GP	G	REC
1935	PHI	A	P		5	0-3
1936	PHI	A	P		34	8-16
1937	PHI	A	P		28	2-1
		BRTR			67	10-20

FINLAYSON, PEMBROKE
B.JULY 31,1888 CHERAW,S.C.
D.MAR.6,1912

YR	CL	LEA	POS	GP	G	REC
1908	BRO	N	P		1	0-0
1909	BRO	N	P		1	0-0
		BRTR			2	0-0

FINLEY, ROBERT EDWARD
B.NOV.25,1915 ENNIS,TEX.

YR	CL	LEA	POS	GP	G	REC
1943	PHI	N	C		28	.259
1944	PHI	N	C		94	.249
		BRTR			122	.252

FINLEY, WILLIAM JAMES
B.OCT.4,1863 NEW YORK,N.Y.
D.OCT.6,1912

YR	CL	LEA	POS	GP	G	REC
1886	NY	N	C-O		13	.188

FINN, CORNELIUS FRANCIS "NEAL"
B.JAN.24,1904 BROOKLYN,N.Y.
D.JULY 7,1933

YR	CL	LEA	POS	GP	G	REC
1930	BRO	N	2		87	.278
1931	BRO	N	2		118	.274
1932	BRO	N	3		65	.238
1933	PHI	N	2		51	.237
		BRTR			321	.262

FINNERAN, JOSEPH IGNATIUS "HAPPY"
B.OCT.29,1892 E.ORANGE,N.J.
D.FEB.3,1942

YR	CL	LEA	POS	GP	G	REC
1912	PHI	N	P		14	0-2
1913	PHI	N	P		3	0-0
1914	BRO	F	P		27	12-11
1915	BRO	F	P		37	10-12
1918	DET	A	P		6	1-2
	NY	A	P		23	3-6
		BRTR			110	26-33

FINNEY, HAROLD WILSON
B.JULY 30,1907 LAFAYETTE,ALA.

YR	CL	LEA	POS	GP	G	REC
1931	PIT	N	C		10	.308
1932	PIT	N	C		31	.212
1933	PIT	N	C		56	.233
1934	PIT	N	C		5	.000
1936	PIT	N	C		21	.000
		BRTR			123	.203

FINNEY, LOUIS KLOPSCHE "LOU"
B.AUG.13,1910 BUFFALO,ALA.
D.APR.22,1966 LAFAYETTE,ALA.

YR	CL	LEA	POS	GP	G	REC
1931	PHI	A	O		9	.376
1933	PHI	A	O		74	.267
1934	PHI	A	1-O		92	.279
1935	PHI	A	1-O		109	.273
1936	PHI	A	1-O		151	.302
1937	PHI	A	1-O		92	.251
1938	PHI	A	1-O		122	.275
1939	PHI	A	O		9	.136
	BOS	A	1-O		95	.325
1940	BOS	A	1-O		130	.320
1941	BOS	A	1-O		127	.288
1942	BOS	A	1-O		113	.285
1944	BOS	A	1-O		68	.287
1945	BOS	A	H		2	.000
	STL	A	1-3-O		57	.277
1946	STL	A	O		16	.300
1947	PHI	N	H		4	.000
		BLTR			1270	.287

FIORE, MICHAEL GARRY JOSEPH "MIKE"
B.OCT.11,1944 BROOKLYN,N.Y.

YR	CL	LEA	POS	GP	G	REC
1968	BAL	A	1-O		6	.059
1969	KC	A	1-O		107	.274
1970	KC	A	1-O		25	.181
	BOS	A	1-O		41	.140
1971	BOS	A	1		51	.177
1972	STL	N	1-O		17	.100
	SD	N	H		7	.000
		BLTL			254	.227

FIRTH, THEODORE JOHN
B.PHILADELPHIA,PA.
D.APR.18,1885

YR	CL	LEA	POS	GP	G	REC
1884	RIC	AA	P		1	0-1

FISCHER, CHARLES WILLIAM "CARL"
B.NOV.5,1905 MEDINA,N.Y.
D.DEC.10,1963 MEDINA,N.Y.

YR	CL	LEA	POS	GP	G	REC
1930	WAS	A	P		8	1-1
1931	WAS	A	P		46	13-9
1932	WAS	A	P		12	3-2
	STL	A	P		24	3-7
1933	DET	A	P		35	11-15
1934	DET	A	P		20	6-4
1935	DET	A	P		3	0-1
	CHI	A	P		24	5-5
1937	CLE	A	P		2	0-1
	WAS	A	P		17	4-5
		BRTL			191	46-50

FISCHER, HENRY WILLIAM "HANK"
B.JAN.11,1940 YONKERS,N.Y.

YR	CL	LEA	POS	GP	G	REC
1962	MIL	N	P		29	2-3
1963	MIL	N	P		31	4-3
1964	MIL	N	P	37	38	11-10
1965	MIL	N	P	31	32	8-9
1966	ATL	N	P		14	2-3
	CIN	N	P		11	0-6
	BOS	A	P		6	2-3
1967	BOS	A	P		9	1-2
		BRTR		168	170	30-39

FISCHER, REUBEN WALTER
B.SEPT.19,1918 CARLOCK,S.D.

YR	CL	LEA	POS	GP	G	REC
1941	NY	N	P		2	1-0
1943	NY	N	P		22	5-10
1944	NY	N	P		38	6-14
1945	NY	N	P		31	3-8
1946	NY	N	P		15	1-2
		BRTR			108	16-34

FISCHER, WILLIAM CHARLES
B.MAR.2,1891 NEW YORK,N.Y.
D.SEPT.4,1945

YR	CL	LEA	POS	GP	G	REC
1913	BRO	N	C		62	.267
1914	BRO	N	C		43	.257
1915	CHI	F	C		105	.326
1916	CHI	N	C		65	.197
	PIT	N	C		42	.254
1917	PIT	N	C		95	.286
		BLTR			412	.273

FISCHER, WILLIAM CHARLES "BILL"
B.OCT.11,1930 WAUSAU,WIS.

YR	CL	LEA	POS	GP	G	REC
1956	CHI	A	P		3	0-0
1957	CHI	A	P		33	7-8
1958	CHI	A	P		17	2-3
	DET	A	P		22	2-4
	WAS	A	P		3	0-3
1959	WAS	A	P		34	9-11
1960	WAS	A	P		20	3-5
	DET	A	P		20	5-3
1961	DET	A	P		26	3-2
	KC	A	P		15	1-0
1962	KC	A	P		34	4-12
1963	KC	A	P		45	9-6
1964	MIN	A	P		9	0-1
		BRTR			281	45-58

FISHBURNE, SAMUEL
B.JUNE 2,1895 HAVERHILL,MASS.

YR	CL	LEA	POS	GP	G	REC
1919	STL	N	1-2		9	.333
		BRTR				

FISHEL, LEO
B.DEC.13,1877 BABYLON,L.I.,N.Y.

YR	CL	LEA	POS	GP	G	REC
1899	NY	N	P		1	0-1

YR	CL	LEA	POS	GP	G	REC

FISHER
B.JOHNSTOWN,PA.

YR	CL	LEA	POS	GP	G	REC
1884	KEY	U	P-1	8	10	1- 7
						.222
	WIL	U	S-O	8		.069
1885	BUF	N	P	1		0- 1
				9	19	1- 8
						.143

FISHER, AUGUST HARRIS "GUS"
B.OCT.21,1885 POTTSBOROUGH,TEX.
D.APR.8,1972 PORTLAND,ORE.

YR	CL	LEA	POS	G	REC
1911	CLE	A	C	70	.261
1912	NY	A	C	4	.200
	BLTR			74	.258

FISHER, CHAUNCY BURR
"WHOA BILL"
B.JAN.8,1872 ANDERSON,IND.
D.APR.27,1939

YR	CL	LEA	POS	G	REC
1893	CLE	N	P	3	0- 2
1894	CLE	N	P	3	0- 2
	CIN	N	P	12	2-10
1896	CIN	N	P	20	9- 7
1897	BRO	N	P	18	8- 7
1901	NY	N	P	1	0- 1
	STL	N	P	1	0- 0
	BRTR			58	19-29

FISHER, CLARENCE HENRY
B.AUG.27,1898 LETART,W.VA.
D.NOV.2,1965 POINT PLEASANT,
W.VA.

YR	CL	LEA	POS	G	REC
1919	WAS	A	P	2	0- 0
1920	WAS	A	P	2	0- 1
	BRTR			4	0- 1

FISHER, DONALD RAYMOND
B.FEB.6,1916 CLEVELAND,OHIO
D.JULY 29,1973 MAYFIELD HEIGHTS
OHIO

YR	CL	LEA	POS	G	REC
1945	NY	N	P	2	1- 0
	BRTR				

FISHER, EDDIE GENE
B.JULY 16,1936 SHREVEPORT,LA.

YR	CL	LEA	POS	G	REC
1959	SF	N	P	17	2- 6
1960	SF	N	P	3	1- 0
1961	SF	N	P	15	0- 2
1962	CHI	A	P	57	9- 5
1963	CHI	A	P	33	9- 8
1964	CHI	A	P	59	6- 3
1965	CHI	A	P	82	15- 7
1966	CHI	A	P	23	1- 3
	BAL	A	P	44	5- 3
1967	BAL	A	P	46	4- 3
1968	CLE	A	P	54	4- 2
1969	CAL	A	P	52	3- 2
1970	CAL	A	P	67	4- 4
1971	CAL	A	P	57	10- 8
1972	CAL	A	P	43	4- 5
	CHI	A	P	6	0- 1
1973	CHI	A	P	26	6- 7
	STL	N	P	6	2- 1
	BRTR			690	85-70

FISHER, FREDERICK BROWN "FRITZ"
B.NOV.28,1941 ADRIAN,MICH.

YR	CL	LEA	POS	G	REC
1964	DET	A	P	1	0- 0
	BLTL				

FISHER, GEORGE ALOYS "SHOWBOAT"
B.JAN.16,1899 JENNINGS,IOWA

YR	CL	LEA	POS	G	REC
1923	WAS	A	O	13	.240
1924	WAS	A	O	15	.219
1930	STL	N	O	92	.374
1932	STL	A	O	18	.182
	BLTR			138	.335

FISHER, HARRY C.
B.PHILADELPHIA,PA.

YR	CL	LEA	POS	G	REC
1884	KC	U	S-3	10	.195
	CHI	U	3	1	.667
	CLE	N	C-2	6	.130
1889	LOU	AA	O	1	.000
				18	.147

FISHER, HARRY DEVEREUX
B.JAN.3,1926 NEWBURY,ONT.,CAN.

YR	CL	LEA	POS	GP	G	REC
1951	PIT	N	H		3	.000
1952	PIT	N	P	8	15	1- 2
	BLTR			8	18	1- 2
						.278

FISHER, JOHN GUS "RED"
B.JUNE 22,1887 PITTSBURGH,PA.
D.JAN.31,1940

YR	CL	LEA	POS	G	REC
1910	STL	A	O	23	.125
	TR				

FISHER, JOHN HOWARD "JACK"
B.MAR.4,1939 FROSTBURG,MD.

YR	CL	LEA	POS	GP	G	REC
1959	BAL	A	P		27	1- 6
1960	BAL	A	P		40	12-11
1961	BAL	A	P		36	10-13
1962	BAL	A	P	32	33	7- 9
1963	SF	N	P		36	6-10
1964	NY	N	P		40	10-17
1965	NY	N	P		43	8-24
1966	NY	N	P		38	11-14
1967	NY	N	P		39	9-18
1968	CHI	A	P		35	8-13
1969	CIN	N	P		34	4- 4
	BRTR			400	401	86-139

FISHER, MAURICE WAYNE
B.FEB.16,1931 WELLS CO.,IND.

YR	CL	LEA	POS	G	REC
1955	CIN	N	P	1	0- 0
	BRTR				

FISHER, NEWTON
B.JUNE 18,1871 NASHVILLE,TENN.
D.FEB.28,1947 CHICAGO,ILL.

YR	CL	LEA	POS	G	REC
1898	PHI	N	C	9	.154
	BRTR				

FISHER, RAYMOND LYLE "CHIC"
B.OCT.4,1887 MIDDLEBURY,VT.

YR	CL	LEA	POS	G	REC
1910	NY	A	P	15	5- 3
1911	NY	A	P	29	10-11
1912	NY	A	P	17	2- 8
1913	NY	A	P	43	11-17
1914	NY	A	P	29	10-11
1915	NY	A	P	30	18-11
1916	NY	A	P	31	11- 8
1917	NY	A	P	23	8- 9
1919	CIN	N	P	26	14- 5
1920	CIN	N	P	33	10-11
	BRTR			276	99-95

FISHER, ROBERT TAYLOR
B.NOV.3,1886 NASHVILLE,TENN.
D.AUG.4,1963 JACKSONVILLE,FLA.

YR	CL	LEA	POS	G	REC
1912	BRO	N	S	82	.233
1913	BRO	N	S	132	.262
1914	CHI	N	S	15	.300
1915	CHI	N	S	147	.287
1916	CIN	N	2-S-O	61	.272
1918	STL	N	2	63	.317
1919	STL	N	2	3	.273
	BRTR			503	.276

FISHER, THOMAS CHALMERS "RED"
B.NOV.1,1880 ANDERSON,IND.
D.SEPT.3,1972 ANDERSON,IND.

YR	CL	LEA	POS	GP	G	REC
1902	DET	A	P		1	0- 0
1904	BOS	N	P	31	36	6-16
	BRTR			32	37	6-16

FISHER, THOMAS GENE "TOM"
B.APR.4,1942 CLEVELAND,OHIO

YR	CL	LEA	POS	G	REC
1967	BAL	A	P	2	0- 0
	BRTR				

FISHER, WILBUR MC CULLOUGH
B.JULY 18,1894 GREENBOTTAM,W.VA
D.OCT.24,1960 WELCH,W.VA.

YR	CL	LEA	POS	G	REC
1916	PIT	N	H	1	.000
	BRTR				

FISHER, WILLIAM CHARLES
"CHEROKEE"
B.1844 PHILADELPHIA,PA.
D.SEPT.26,1912

YR	CL	LEA	POS	GP	G	REC
1871	ROK	NA	P-1- 22	25		5-17
			O			-
1872	BAL	NA	P-3- 11	44		8- 3
			O			.205
1873	ATH	NA	P-1- 4	49		2- 2
			O			-
1874	HAR	NA	P-S- 35	52		13-22
			3-O			-
1875	PHI	NA	P-O 39	40		22-17
						.231
1876	CIN	N	P-1- 25	35		4-20
			S-O			.248
1877	CHI	N	3	1		.000
1878	PRO	N	P	1		0- 1
	BRTR			137	248	54-82
						-

FISK, CARLTON ERNEST "PUDGE"
B.DEC.26,1947 BELLOWS FALLS,VT.

YR	CL	LEA	POS	G	REC
1969	BOS	A	C	2	.000
1971	BOS	A	C	14	.313
1972	BOS	A	C	131	.293
1973	BOS	A	C	135	.246
1974	BOS	A	C	52	.299
1975	BOS	A	C	79	.331
1976	BOS	A	C	134	.255
	BRTR			547	.277

FISK, MAXIMILIAN PATRICK
B.1888 ROSELAND,IND.

YR	CL	LEA	POS	G	REC
1914	CHI	F	P	39	12-12
	BRTR				

FISLER, WESTON DICKSON
B.JULY 5,1841 CAMDEN,N.J.
D.DEC.26,1922

YR	CL	LEA	POS	G	REC
1871	ATH	NA	1-2	28	.333
1872	ATH	NA	2	46	.327
1873	ATH	NA	1-2	43	-
1874	ATH	NA	1-2	37	.343
1875	ATH	NA	1-2-O	57	.276
1876	ATH	N	1-2-O	59	.286
				270	-

FITTERY, PAUL CLARENCE
B.OCT.10,1891 LEBANON,PA.
D.JAN.28,1974 CARTERSVILLE,GA.

YR	CL	LEA	POS	GP	G	REC
1914	CIN	N	P		11	0- 2
1917	PHI	N	P	17	19	1- 1
	BBTL			28	30	1- 3

FITZBERGER, CHARLES CASPAR
B.FEB.13,1905 BALTIMORE,MD.
D.JAN.25,1965 BALTIMORE,MD.

YR	CL	LEA	POS	G	REC
1928	BOS	N	H	7	.286
	BLTL				

FITZGERALD, DENNIS S.
B.BOSTON,MASS.

YR	CL	LEA	POS	G	REC
1890	ATH	AA	S	2	.429

FITZGERALD, EDWARD RAYMOND
B.MAY 21,1924 SANTA YNEZ,CAL.

YR	CL	LEA	POS	G	REC
1948	PIT	N	C	102	.267
1949	PIT	N	C	75	.263
1950	PIT	N	C	6	.067
1951	PIT	N	C	55	.227
1952	PIT	N	C-3	51	.233
1953	PIT	N	C	6	.118
	WAS	A	C	88	.250
1954	WAS	A	C	115	.289
1955	WAS	A	C	74	.237
1956	WAS	A	C	64	.304
1957	WAS	A	C	45	.272
1958	WAS	A	C-1	58	.263
1959	WAS	A	C	19	.194
	CLE	A	C	49	.271
	BRTR			807	.260

FITZGERALD, HOWARD CHUMNEY
"LEFTY"
B.MAY 16,1902 EAGLE LAKE,TEX.
D.FEB.27,1959

YR	CL	LEA	POS	G	REC
1922	CHI	N	O	10	.330
1924	CHI	N	O	7	.158
1926	BOS	A	O	31	.258
	BLTL			48	.259

FITZGERALD, JOHN FRANCIS
B.SEPT.15,1934 BROOKLYN,N.Y.

YR	CL	LEA	POS	G	REC
1958	SF	N	P	1	0- 0
	BLTL				

FITZGERALD, JOHN H.
B.MAY 30,1870 NATICK,MASS.

YR	CL	LEA	POS	G	REC
1891	BOS	AA	P	6	2- 1

FITZGERALD, JOHN T.
B.LEADVILLE,COL.

YR	CL	LEA	POS	GP	G	REC
1890	ROC	AA	P		12	3- 8
1891	LOU	AA	P	31	32	12-17
1892	LOU	N	P		4	1- 3
				47	48	16-28

FITZGERALD, JUSTIN HOWARD
"MIKE"
B.JUNE 22,1890 SAN MATEO,CAL.
D.JAN.17,1945

YR	CL	LEA	POS	G	REC
1911	NY	A	O	16	.270
1918	PHI	N	O	66	.293
	BLTR			82	.288

YR	CL	LEA	POS	GP	G	REC

FITZGERALD, MATTHEW WILLIAM
B.AUG.31,1880 ALBANY,N.Y.
D.SEPT.22,1949
```
1906 NY  N  C            4   .500
1907 NY  N  C            6   .133
     TR                 10   .200
```

FITZGERALD, RAYMOND FRANCIS
B.DEC.5,1904 WESTFIELD,MASS.
```
1931 CIN N  H            1   .000
     BRTR
```

FITZKE, PAUL FREDERICK HERMAN
B.JULY 30,1900 LACROSSE,WIS.
D.JUNE 30,1950
```
1924 CLE A  P            1   0- 0
     BRTR
```

FITZMAURICE, SHAUN EARLE
B.AUG.25,1942 WORCESTER,MASS.
```
1966 NY  N  O            9   .154
     BRTR
```

FITZMORRIS, ALAN JAMES "AL"
B.MAR.21,1946 BUFFALO,N.Y.
```
1969 KC  A  P            7   1- 1
1970 KC  A  P      43   45   8- 5
1971 KC  A  P           36   7- 5
1972 KC  A  P      38   39   2- 5
1973 KC  A  P           15   8- 3
1974 KC  A  P           34  13- 6
1975 KC  A  P           35  16-12
1976 KC  A  P      35   37  15-11
     BBTR         243  248  70-48
```

FITZPATRICK, EDWARD HENRY
B.DEC.9,1889 PHILLIPSBURG,PA.
D.OCT.23,1965 BETHLEHEM,PA.
```
1915 BOS N  2-O        105   .221
1916 BOS N  2-O         83   .213
1917 BOS N  2-3-O       63   .253
     BRTR              251   .227
```

FITZSIMMONS, FREDERICK LANDIS
"FAT FREDDIE"
B.JULY 28,1901 MISHAWAKA,IND.
```
1925 NY  N  P           10   6- 3
1926 NY  N  P           37  14-10
1927 NY  N  P           42  17-10
1928 NY  N  P           40  20- 9
1929 NY  N  P           37  15-11
1930 NY  N  P           41  19- 7
1931 NY  N  P           35  18-11
1932 NY  N  P           35  11-11
1933 NY  N  P           36  16-11
1934 NY  N  P           38  18-14
1935 NY  N  P           18   4- 8
1936 NY  N  P           28  10- 7
1937 NY  N  P            6   2- 2
     BRO N  P           13   4- 8
1938 BRO N  P           27  11- 8
1939 BRO N  P           27   7- 9
1940 BRO N  P           20  16- 2
1941 BRO N  P           13   6- 1
1942 BRO N  P            1   0- 0
1943 BRO N  P            9   3- 4
     BRTR              513 217-146
```
NON-PLAYING MANAGER
PHI(N) 1943-45

FITZSIMMONS, THOMAS WILLIAM
B.APR.6,1890 OAKLAND,CAL.
D.DEC.20,1971 OAKLAND,CAL.
```
1919 BRO N  3            4   .000
     BRTR
```

FLACK, MAX JOHN
B.FEB.5,1890 BELLEVILLE,ILL.
D.JULY 31,1975 BELLEVILLE,ILL.
```
1914 CHI F  O          135   .253
1915 CHI F  O          141   .315
1916 CHI N  O          141   .258
1917 CHI N  O          131   .248
1918 CHI N  O          123   .257
1919 CHI N  O          116   .294
1920 CHI N  O          135   .302
1921 CHI N  O          133   .301
1922 CHI N  O           17   .222
     STL N  O           66   .292
1923 STL N  O          128   .291
1924 STL N  O           67   .263
1925 STL N  O           79   .249
     BLTL             1412   .279
```

FLAGER, WALTER LEONARD
B.NOV.3,1921 CHICAGO HEIGHTS,
ILL.
```
1945 CIN N  S           21   .212
     PHI N  2-S         49   .250
     BLTR               70   .241
```

FLAGSTEAD, IRA "PETE"
B.SEPT.22,1893 MONTAGUE,MICH.
D.MAR.13,1940
```
1917 DET A  O            4   .000
1919 DET A  O           97   .331
1920 DET A  O          110   .235
1921 DET A  S-O         85   .305
1922 DET A  O           44   .308
1923 DET A  O            1   .000
     BOS A  O          109   .312
1924 BOS A  O          149   .304
1925 BOS A  O          148   .280
1926 BOS A  O           98   .299
1927 BOS A  O          131   .285
1928 BOS A  O          140   .290
1929 BOS A  O           16   .325
     WAS A  O           16   .143
     PIT N  O           26   .280
1930 PIT N  O           44   .250
     BRTR             1218   .290
```

FLAHERTY, P. J.
B.WORCESTER,MASS.
```
1881 WOR N  O            1   .000
     BLTL
```

FLAHERTY, PATRICK HENRY
B.JUNE 24,1862 ST.LOUIS,MO.
D.JAN.30,1946
```
1894 LOU N  3           38   .295
```

FLAHERTY, PATRICK JOSEPH
B.JUNE 29,1876 CARNEGIE,PA.
D.JAN.23,1968 ALEXANDRIA,LA.
```
1899 LOU N  P            7   2- 3
1900 PIT N  P            4   0- 1
1903 CHI A  P           39  11-25
1904 CHI A  P            5   3- 2
     PIT N  P      29   31  19- 9
1905 PIT N  P      27   29  10-10
1907 BOS N  P      27   35  12-15
1908 BOS N  P           31  12-18
1910 PHI N  P-O   1    2   0- 0
                            .500
1911 BOS N  P-O   2   23   0- 2
                            .287
     BLTL         172  206  69-85
                            .196
```

FLAIR, ALBERT DELL "BROADWAY"
B.JULY 24,1918 NEW ORLEANS,LA.
```
1941 BOS A  1           10   .200
     BLTL
```

FLANAGAN, CHARLES JAMES
B.DEC.31,1891 OAKLAND,CAL.
D.JAN.8,1930
```
1913 STL A  3            4   .000
     BRTR
```

FLANAGAN, EDWARD F. "SLEEPY"
B.SEPT.15,1861 LOWELL,MASS.
D.NOV.10,1926
```
1887 ATH AA 1           19   .277
1889 LOU AA 1           23   .247
                        42   .255
```

FLANAGAN, JAMES PAUL "STEAMER"
B.APR.20,1881 WILKES-BARRE,PA.
D.APR.21,1947
```
1905 PIT N  O            7   .280
```

FLANAGAN, MICHAEL KENDALL "MIKE"
B.DEC.16,1951 MANCHESTER,N.H.
```
1975 BAL A  P            2   0- 1
1976 BAL A  P           20   3- 5
     BLTL               22   3- 6
```

FLANIGAN, RAYMOND ARTHUR
B.JAN.8,1923 MORGANTOWN,W.VA.
```
1946 CLE A  P            3   0- 1
     BRTR
```

FLANIGAN, THOMAS ANTHONY "TOM"
B.SEPT.6,1934 CINCINNATI,OHIO
```
1954 CHI A  P            2   0- 0
1958 STL N  P            1   0- 0
     BRTL                3   0- 0
```

FLASKAMPER, RAYMOND HAROLD
B.OCT.13,1901 ST.LOUIS,MO.
```
1927 CHI A  S           26   .221
     BBTR
```

FLATER, JOHN WILLIAM "JACK"
B.SEPT.22,1883 WESTMINSTER,MD.
D.MAR.20,1970 WESTMINSTER,MD.
```
1908 PHI A  P            5   1- 3
     TR
```

FLAVIN, JOHN THOMAS
B.MAY 7,1942 ALBANY,CAL.
```
1964 CHI N  P            5   0- 1
     BLTL
```

FLEET, FRANK H.
B.1848 NEW YORK,N.Y.
D.JUNE 13,1900
```
1871 MUT NA P            1   0- 1
1872 ECK NA 2-3-O       13   .190
1873 RES NA P-1-   3    21   0- 3
            2-S-3             -
1874 ATH NA C-2-O       19     -
1875 STL NA P            3   2- 1
     ATL NA P-C-   2    25   0- 1
            2-S              -
                   8    82   2- 1
                              -
```

FLEITAS, ANGEL FELIX HUSTA
B.NOV.10,1918 LOS ABRENS,CUBA
```
1948 WAS A  S           15   .077
     BRTR
```

FLEMING, LESLIE FLETCHER
"BILL"
B.JULY 31,1913 LOS ANGELES,CAL.
```
1940 BOS A  P           10   1- 2
1941 BOS A  P           16   1- 1
1942 CHI N  P           33   5- 6
1943 CHI N  P           11   0- 1
1944 CHI N  P      39   40   9-10
1946 CHI N  P           14   0- 1
     BRTR         123  124  16-21
```

FLEMING, LESLIE HARVEY "MOE"
B.AUG.7,1915 SINGLETON,TEX.
```
1939 DET A  O            8   .000
1941 CLE A  1            2   .250
1942 CLE A  1          156   .292
1945 CLE A  1-O         42   .329
1946 CLE A  1-O         99   .278
1947 CLE A  1          103   .242
1949 PIT N  1           24   .258
     BLTL              434   .277
```

FLEMING, THOMAS VINCENT
"SLEUTH"
B.1879 BUSTLETON,PA.
D.DEC.26,1957
```
1899 NY  N  O           20   .257
1902 PHI N  O            5   .375
1904 PHI N  O            2   .000
                        27   .261
```

FLETCHER
```
1872 ECK NA O            2   .250
```

FLETCHER, ARTHUR
B.JAN.5,1885 COLLINSVILLE,ILL.
D.FEB.6,1950
```
1909 NY  N  S           29   .214
1910 NY  N  S           44   .224
1911 NY  N  S-3        108   .319
1912 NY  N  S          129   .282
1913 NY  N  S          136   .297
1914 NY  N  S          135   .286
1915 NY  N  S          149   .254
1916 NY  N  S          133   .286
1917 NY  N  S          151   .260
1918 NY  N  S          124   .263
1919 NY  N  S          127   .277
1920 NY  N  S           41   .254
     PHI N  S          102   .297
1922 PHI N  S          110   .280
     BRTR             1518   .277
```
NON-PLAYING MANAGER
PHI(N) 1923-26, NY(A) 1929

FLETCHER, ELBURT PRESTON
B.MAR.18,1916 DORCHESTER,MASS.

YR	CL	LEA	POS	GP	G	REC
1934	BOS	N	1		8	.500
1935	BOS	N	1		39	.236
1937	BOS	N	1		148	.247
1938	BOS	N	1		147	.272
1939	BOS	N	1		35	.245
	PIT	N	1		102	.303
1940	PIT	N	1		147	.273
1941	PIT	N	1		151	.288
1942	PIT	N	1		145	.289
1943	PIT	N	1		154	.283
1946	PIT	N	1		148	.256
1947	PIT	N	1		69	.242
1949	BOS	N	1		122	.261
	BLTL				1415	.271

FLETCHER, O. FRANK
B.MAR.6,1891 HILDRETH,ILL.
D.OCT.7,1974 ST.PETERSBURG,FLA.

YR	CL	LEA	POS	GP	G	REC
1914	PHI	N	H		1	.000
	BRTR					

FLETCHER, SAMUEL S.

YR	CL	LEA	POS	GP	G	REC
1909	BRO	N	P		1	0- 1
1912	CIN	N	P		2	0- 0
	TR				3	0- 1

FLETCHER, THOMAS WAYNE
B.JUNE 28,1942 ELMIRA,N.Y.

YR	CL	LEA	POS	GP	G	REC
1962	DET	A	P		1	0- 0
	BBTL					

FLETCHER, VANOIDE "VAN"
B.AUG.6,1928 EAST BEND,N.C.

YR	CL	LEA	POS	GP	G	REC
1955	DET	A	P		9	0- 0

FLICK, ELMER HARRISON
B.JAN.11,1876 BEDFORD,OHIO
D.JAN.9,1971 BEDFORD,OHIO

YR	CL	LEA	POS	GP	G	REC
1898	PHI	N	O		133	.319
1899	PHI	N	O		125	.343
1900	PHI	N	O		138	.378
1901	PHI	N	O		138	.336
1902	PHI	A	O		11	.324
	CLE	A	O		110	.293
1903	CLE	A	O		142	.299
1904	CLE	A	O		149	.303
1905	CLE	A	O		131	.306
1906	CLE	A	O		157	.311
1907	CLE	A	O		147	.302
1908	CLE	A	O		9	.212
1909	CLE	A	O		66	.255
1910	CLE	A	O		24	.265
	BLTR				1480	.315

FLICK, LEWIS MILLER "NOISY"
B.FEB.18,1915 BRISTOL,TENN.

YR	CL	LEA	POS	GP	G	REC
1943	PHI	A	O		1	.600
1944	PHI	A	O		19	.114
	BLTL				20	.175

FLINN, DON RAPHIEL
B.NOV.17,1892 HUCKABY,TEX.
D.MAR.9,1959

YR	CL	LEA	POS	GP	G	REC
1917	PIT	N	O		14	.298
	BRTR					

FLINT, FRANK SYLVESTER "SILVER"
B.AUG.3,1855 PHILADELPHIA,PA.
D.JAN.14,1892

YR	CL	LEA	POS	GP	G	REC
1875	RS	NA	C-3		17	-
1878	IND	N	C		60	.228
1879	CHI	N	C		75	.290
1880	CHI	N	C-0		71	.167
1881	CHI	N	C-1-0		80	.310
1882	CHI	N	C-0		81	.250
1883	CHI	N	C-0		84	.265
1884	CHI	N	C		71	.207
1885	CHI	N	C-0		67	.208
1886	CHI	N	C		49	.202
1887	CHI	N	C		48	.282
1888	CHI	N	C		22	.181
1889	CHI	N	C		15	.232
	BRTR				740	-

FLITCRAFT, HILDRETH MILTON "HILLY"
B.AUG.21,1923 WOODSTOWN,N.J.

YR	CL	LEA	POS	GP	G	REC
1942	PHI	N	P		3	0- 0
	BLTL					

FLOHR, MORITZ HERMAN "DUTCH"
B.AUG.15,1911 CANISTEO,N.Y.

YR	CL	LEA	POS	GP	G	REC
1934	PHI	A	P		15	0- 2
	BLTL					

FLOOD, CURTIS CHARLES "CURT"
B.JAN.18,1938 HOUSTON,TEX.

YR	CL	LEA	POS	GP	G	REC
1956	CIN	N	H		5	.000
1957	CIN	N	2-3		3	.333
1958	STL	N	3-0		121	.261
1959	STL	N	2-0		121	.255
1960	STL	N	3-0		140	.237
1961	STL	N	O		132	.322
1962	STL	N	O		151	.296
1963	STL	N	O		158	.302
1964	STL	N	O		162	.311
1965	STL	N	O		156	.310
1966	STL	N	O		160	.267
1967	STL	N	O		134	.335
1968	STL	N	O		150	.301
1969	STL	N	O		153	.285
1971	WAS	A	O		13	.200
	BRTR				1759	.293

FLOOD, TIMOTHY A.
B.MAR.13,1877 MONTGOMERY CITY, MO.
D.JUNE 15,1929

YR	CL	LEA	POS	GP	G	REC
1899	STL	N	2		9	.333
1902	BRO	N	2-0		131	.228
1903	BRO	N	2		87	.249
	BRTR				227	.239

FLORENCE, PAUL ROBERT "PEP"
B.APR.23,1901 CHICAGO,ILL.

YR	CL	LEA	POS	GP	G	REC
1926	NY	N	C		76	.229
	BBTR					

FLORES, JESSE SANDOVAL
B.NOV.2,1916 GUADALAJARA,MEXICO

YR	CL	LEA	POS	GP	G	REC
1942	CHI	N	P		4	0- 1
1943	PHI	A	P		31	12-14
1944	PHI	A	P		27	9-11
1945	PHI	A	P		29	7-10
1946	PHI	A	P		29	9- 7
1947	PHI	A	P		28	4-13
1950	CLE	A	P		28	3- 3
	BRTR				176	44-59

FLOWERS, BENNETT "BEN"
B.JUNE 15,1927 GOLDSBORO,N.C.

YR	CL	LEA	POS	GP	G	REC
1951	BOS	A	P		1	0- 0
1953	BOS	A	P		32	1- 4
1955	DET	A	P		4	0- 0
	STL	N	P		4	1- 0
1956	STL	N	P		3	1- 1
	PHI	N	P		32	0- 2
	BRTR				76	3- 7

FLOWERS, CHARLES RICHARD
B.1850 PHILADELPHIA,PA.
D.OCT.5,1892

YR	CL	LEA	POS	GP	G	REC
1871	TRO	NA	2-S		21	.303
1872	ATH	NA	S		3	.235
					24	.294

FLOWERS, CHARLES WESLEY "WES"
B.AUG.13,1913 WYNNE,ARK.

YR	CL	LEA	POS	GP	G	REC
1940	BRO	N	P		5	1- 1
1944	BRO	N	P		9	1- 1
	BLTL				14	2- 2

FLOWERS, D'ARCY RAYMOND "JAKE"
B.MAR.16,1902 CAMBRIDGE,MD.
D.DEC.27,1962

YR	CL	LEA	POS	GP	G	REC
1923	STL	N	2-S-3		13	.094
1926	STL	N	2		40	.270
1927	BRO	N	S		67	.234
1928	BRO	N	2		103	.274
1929	BRO	N	2		46	.200
1930	BRO	N	2		89	.320
1931	BRO	N	2-S		22	.226
	STL	N	2-S		45	.248
1932	STL	N	3		67	.255
1933	BRO	N	2-S-3-0		78	.233
1934	CIN	N	H		13	.333
	BRTR				583	.255

FLOYD, LESLIE ROE "BUBBA"
B.JUNE 23,1917 DALLAS,TEX.

YR	CL	LEA	POS	GP	G	REC
1944	DET	A	S		3	.444
	BRTR					

FLOYD, ROBERT NATHAN "BOB"
B.OCT.20,1943 HAWTHORNE,CAL.

YR	CL	LEA	POS	GP	G	REC
1968	BAL	A	S		5	.111
1969	BAL	A	2-3		39	.202
1970	BAL	A	2-S		3	.000
	KC	A	S-3		14	.326
1971	KC	A	2-S-3		31	.152
1972	KC	A	2-3		61	.179
1973	KC	A	2-S		51	.333
1974	KC	A	2-S-3		10	.111
	BRTR				214	.219

FLUHRER, JOHN L.
(ALSO PLAYED UNDER NAME OF
WM. G. MORRIS 1 GAME IN 1915)
B.JAN.3,1894 ADRIAN,MICH.
D.JULY 17,1946

YR	CL	LEA	POS	GP	G	REC
1915	CHI	N	O		7	.400
	BRTR					

FLINN, CORNELIUS FRANCIS XAVIER "CARNEY"
B.JAN.23,1875 CINCINNATI,OHIO
D.FEB.10,1947

YR	CL	LEA	POS	GP	G	REC
1894	CIN	N	P		2	0- 1
1896	NY	N	P		3	0- 0
	WAS	N	P		4	0- 1
	BLTL				9	0- 2

FLYNN, EDWARD J.
B.CHICAGO,ILL.

YR	CL	LEA	POS	GP	G	REC
1887	CLE	AA	3		7	.215

FLYNN, GEORGE A. "DIBBY"
B.MAY 24,1870 CHICAGO,ILL.
D.DEC.28,1901

YR	CL	LEA	POS	GP	G	REC
1896	CHI	N	O		29	.267

FLYNN, JOHN A. "JOCKO"
B.JUNE 30,1864 LAWRENCE,MASS.
D.DEC.30,1907

YR	CL	LEA	POS	GP	G	REC
1886	CHI	N	P-O	32	56	24- 6
						.200
1887	CHI	N	O		1	.000
				32	57	24- 6
						.200

FLYNN, JOHN ANTHONY
B.SEPT.7,1883 PROVIDENCE,R.I.
D.MAR.23,1935

YR	CL	LEA	POS	GP	G	REC
1910	PIT	N	1		93	.274
1911	PIT	N	1-3		32	.214
1912	WAS	A	1		20	.169
	BRTR				145	.251

FLYNN, JOSEPH
B.PHILADELPHIA,PA.

YR	CL	LEA	POS	GP	G	REC
1884	KEY	U	C-1-S-0		50	.244
	BOS	U	C-1-0		9	.233
					59	.242

FLYNN, MICHAEL E.
B.LOWELL,MASS.

YR	CL	LEA	POS	GP	G	REC
1891	BOS	AA	C		1	.000

FLYNN, ROBERT DOUGLAS "DOUG"
B.APR.18,1951 LEXINGTON,KY.

YR	CL	LEA	POS	GP	G	REC
1975	CIN	N	2-S-3		89	.268
1976	CIN	N	2-S		93	.283
	BRTR				182	.277

FLYNN, WILLIAM "CLIPPER"
B.1850 NEW YORK
D.NOV.11,1881

YR	CL	LEA	POS	GP	G	REC
1871	TRO	NA	1-3-0		29	.311
1872	OLY	NA	1		9	.220
					38	.291

FLYTHE, STUART MCGUIRE
B.DEC.5,1911 CONWAY,N.C.
D.OCT.18,1963

YR	CL	LEA	POS	GP	G	REC
1936	PHI	A	P		17	0- 0
	BRTR					

FODGE, EUGENE ARLEN "GENE"
B.JULY 8,1931 SOUTH BEND,IND.

YR	CL	LEA	POS	GP	G	REC
1958	CHI	N	P		16	1- 1
	BRTR					

YR	CL LEA POS	GP	G	REC

FOGARTY, JAMES G.
B.FEB.12,1864 SAN FRANCISCO,CAL
D.MAY 20,1891
1884 PHI N	P-2-	1	95	0- 0
	S-3-O			.211
1885 PHI N	2-S-3-O	111	.231	
1886 PHI N	O		76	.292
1887 PHI N	O		126	.365
1888 PHI N	O		120	.235
1889 PHI N	O		128	.258
1890 PHI P	M-O		91	.251
	BR	1	747	0- 0
				.268

FOGARTY, JOSEPH J.
B.SAN FRANCISCO,CAL.
1885 STL N	O		2	.125

FOGEL, HORACE S.
B.MAR.2,1861 MACUNGIE,PA.
D.NOV.15,1928
NON-PLAYING MANAGER
IND(N) 1887, NY(N) 1902

FOHL, LEO ALEXANDER "LEE"
B.NOV.28,1879 PITTSBURGH,PA.
D.OCT.30,1965 CLEVELAND,OHIO
1902 PIT N	C		1	.000
1903 CIN N	C		4	.357
	BLTR		5	.294
NON-PLAYING MANAGER
CLE(A) 1915-19, STL(A) 1921-23,
BOS(A) 1924-26

FOILES, HENRY LEE "HANK"
B.JUNE 10,1929 RICHMOND,VA.
1953 CIN N	C		5	.154
	CLE A	C	7	.143
1955 CLE A	C		62	.261
1956 CLE A	C		1	.000
	PIT N	C	79	.212
1957 PIT N	C		109	.270
1958 PIT N	C		104	.205
1959 PIT N	C		53	.225
1960 KC A	C		6	.571
	CLE A	C	24	.279
	DET A	C	26	.250
1961 BAL A	C		43	.274
1962 CIN N	C		43	.275
1963 CIN N	C		1	.000
	LA A	C	41	.214
1964 LA	A H		4	.250
	BRTR		608	.243

FOLEY, CHARLES JOSEPH "CURRY"
B.JAN.20,1858 MILLTOWN,IRELAND
D.OCT.20,1898
1879 BOS N	P-O	18	35	5- 8
				.313
1880 BOS N	P-1-	28	78	14-14
	O			.285
1881 BUF N	P-1-	6	83	2- 4
	O			.256
1882 BUF N	P-O	1	84	0- 0
				.305
1883 BUF N	P-O	1	23	1- 0
				.270
	TL	54	303	22-26
				.283

FOLEY, JOHN J
B.HANNIBAL,MO.
1885 PRO N	P		1	0- 1

FOLEY, RAYMOND KIRWIN
B.JUNE 23,1907 MISSOURI CITY,MO
1928 NY N	P		2	.000
	BLTR			

FOLEY, THOMAS J.
B.AUG.16,1842 CASHEL,IRELAND
D.NOV.3,1926
1871 CHI NA	M-C-3-O	18	-	

FOLEY, WILLIAM BROWN
B.NOV.15,1855 CHICAGO,ILL.
D.NOV.12,1916
1875 CHI NA	3		3	-
1876 CIN N	C-3		58	.226
1877 CIN N	3		56	.188
1878 MIL N	C-3		55	.271
1879 CIN N	2-3-O		55	.213
1881 DET N	2-3		5	.118
1884 CHI U	3		18	.294
	BRTR		250	-

FOLI, TIMOTHY JOHN "TIM"
B.DEC.8,1950 CULVER CITY,CAL.
1970 NY	N S-3		5	.364
1971 NY	N 2-S-3-O		97	.226
1972 MON	N 2-S		149	.241
1973 MON	N 2-S-O		126	.240
1974 MON	N S-3		121	.254
1975 MON	N 2-S		152	.238
1976 MON	N S		149	.264
	BRTR		799	.245

FOLKERS, RICHARD NEVIN "RICH"
B.OCT.17,1946 WATERLOO,IOWA
1970 NY	N P		16	0- 2
1972 STL	N P		9	1- 0
1973 STL	N P		34	4- 4
1974 STL	N P		55	6- 2
1975 SD	N P		45	6-11
1976 SD	N P		33	2- 3
	BLTL		192	19-22

FONDY, DEE VIRGIL
B.OCT.31,1924 SLATON,TEX.
1951 CHI N	1		49	.271
1952 CHI N	1		145	.300
1953 CHI N	1		150	.309
1954 CHI N	1		141	.285
1955 CHI N	1		150	.265
1956 CHI N	1		137	.269
1957 CHI N	1		11	.314
	PIT N	1	95	.313
1958 CIN N	1-O		89	.218
	BLTL		967	.283

FONSECA, LEWIS ALBERT "LEW"
B.JAN.21,1899 OAKLAND,CAL.
1921 CIN N	1-2-O		82	.276
1922 CIN N	2		81	.361
1923 CIN N	1-2		65	.270
1924 CIN N	1-2		20	.228
1925 PHI N	1-2		126	.319
1927 CLE A	1-2		112	.311
1928 CLE A	1-3		75	.327
1929 CLE A	1		148	.369
1930 CLE A	1		40	.279
1931 CLE A	1		26	.370
	CHI A	1-2-O	121	.299
1932 CHI A	M-P-	1	18	0- 0
	O			.135
1933 CHI A	M-1		23	.203
	BRTR	1	937	0- 0
				.316
NON-PLAYING MANAGER CHI(A) 1934

FOOR, JAMES EMERSON "JIM"
B.JAN.13,1949 ST.LOUIS,MO.
1971 DET A	P		3	0- 0
1972 DET A	P		7	1- 0
1973 PIT N	P		3	0- 0
	BLTL		13	1- 0

FOOTE, BARRY CLIFTON
B.FEB.16,1952 SMITHFIELD,N.C.
1973 MON N	C		6	.667
1974 MON N	C		125	.262
1975 MON N	C		118	.194
1976 MON N	C-1		105	.234
	BRTR		354	.233

FORAN, JAMES H.
B.1848 NEW YORK
1871 KEK NA	1-O		19	-

FORCE, DAVID W. "WEE DAVEY"
B.JULY 27,1849 NEW YORK,N.Y.
D.JUNE 21,1918
1871 OLY NA	S-3		32	-
1872 TRO NA	S-3		25	.414
	BAL NA	3	18	.409
1873 BAL NA	P-S-3		48	1- 1
				-
1874 CHI NA	S-3-O		59	-
1875 ATH NA	S		77	.312
1876 ATH N	S		60	.228
1877 STL N	S-3		58	.258
1879 BUF N	S		78	.209
1880 BUF N	2-O		78	.162
1881 BUF N	2-S-3-O		75	.179
1882 BUF N	2-S-3		73	.241
1883 BUF N	2-S-3		95	.213
1884 BUF N	2-S		102	.208
1885 BUF N	2-S-3		71	.225
1886 WAS N	S		68	.181
	BRTR		1017	1- 1
				-

FORD, DARNELL GLENN "DAN"
B.MAY 19,1952 LOS ANGELES,CAL.
1975 MIN A	O		130	.280
1976 MIN A	O		145	.267
	BRTR		275	.273

FORD, E. L.
B.RICHMOND,VA.
1884 RIC AA	1-S		2	.000

FORD, EDWARD CHARLES "WHITEY"
B.OCT.21,1928 NEW YORK,N.Y.
1950 NY	A P		20	9- 1
1953 NY	A P	32	33	18- 6
1954 NY	A P		34	16- 8
1955 NY	A P		39	18- 7
1956 NY	A P		31	19- 6
1957 NY	A P		24	11- 5
1958 NY	A P		30	14- 7
1959 NY	A P		35	16-10
1960 NY	A P		33	12- 9
1961 NY	A P		39	25- 4
1962 NY	A P		38	17- 8
1963 NY	A P		38	24- 7
1964 NY	A P		39	17- 6
1965 NY	A P	37	38	16-13
1966 NY	A P		22	2- 5
1967 NY	A P		7	2- 4
	BLTL	498	500	236-106

FORD, EUGENE MATTHEW
B.JUNE 23,1913 FT.DODGE,IOWA
1936 BOS N	P		2	0- 0
1938 CHI A	P		4	0- 0
	BRTR		6	0- 0

FORD, EUGENE WYMAN
B.APR.16,1881 MILTON,N.S.,CAN.
D.AUG.23,1973 DUNEDIN,FLA.
1905 DET A	P		7	0- 2
	BRTR			

FORD, HORACE HILLS "HOD"
B.JULY 23,1897 NEW HAVEN,CONN.
1919 BOS N	2		10	.214
1920 BOS N	2-S		88	.241
1921 BOS N	2-S		152	.279
1922 BOS N	2-S		143	.271
1923 BOS N	2-S		111	.271
1924 PHI N	2		145	.272
1925 BRO N	S		66	.273
1926 CIN N	3		57	.279
1927 CIN N	2-S		115	.274
1928 CIN N	S		149	.241
1929 CIN N	2-S		140	.276
1930 CIN N	2-S		132	.231
1931 CIN N	2-S-3		84	.229
1932 STL N	S		1	.000
	BOS N	2-S	40	.274
1933 BOS N	S		5	.067
	BRTR		1446	.263

FORD, PERCIVAL EDMUND WENTWORTH "WENTY"
B.NOV.25,1946 NASSAU,BAHAMAS
1973 ATL N	P		4	1- 2
	BRTR			

FORD, RUSSELL WILLIAM
B.APR.25,1883 BRANDON,MAN.,CAN.
D.JAN.24,1960
1909 NY	A P		1	0- 0
1910 NY	A P		36	26- 6
1911 NY	A P		37	22-11
1912 NY	A P	36	39	13-21
1913 NY	A P		33	11-18
1914 BUF F	P		35	21- 6
1915 BUF F	P		21	5- 9
	BRTR	199	202	98-71

FORD, THEODORE HENRY "TED"
B.FEB.7,1947 VINELAND,N.J.
1970 CLE A	O		26	.174
1971 CLE A	O		74	.194
1972 TEX A	O		129	.235
1973 CLE A	O		11	.225
	BRTR		240	.219

FORD, THOMAS W.
B.CHATTANOOGA,TENN.
1890 COL AA	P		1	0- 1
	BRO AA	P-S	10	0- 6
				.034
			11	0- 7
				.032

YR	CL	LEA	POS	GP	G	REC

FOREMAN, AUGUST "HAPPY"
B.JULY 20,1897 MEMPHIS,TENN.
D.FEB.13,1953

YR	CL	LEA	POS	GP	G	REC
1924	CHI	A	P		5	0- 0
1926	BOS	A	P		3	0- 0
			BLTL		8	0- 0

FOREMAN, FRANCIS ISAIAH "MONKEY"
B.MAY 1,1863 BALTIMORE,MD.
D.NOV.19,1957

YR	CL	LEA	POS	GP	G	REC
1884	CHI	U	P-O		3	1- 0
						.091
	KC	U	P		1	0- 1
1885	BAL	AA	P-O		3	2- 1
						.286
1889	BAL	AA	P	51	54	25-21
1890	CIN	N	P		24	13-11
1891	CIN	N	P		1	0- 0
	WAS	A	P	44	49	22-22
1892	WAS	N	P	11	2- 5
	BAL	N	P		5	0- 2
1893	NY	N	P		2	0- 1
1895	CIN	N	P		25	11-14
1896	CIN	N	P		22	12- 6
1901	BOS	A	P		1	0- 1
	BAL	A	P		23	13- 7
1902	BAL	A	P		2	0- 2
			BLTL	218	226	101-94
						.227

FOREMAN, JOHN DAVIS "BROWNIE"
B.AUG.6,1875 BALTIMORE,MD.
D.OCT.10,1926

YR	CL	LEA	POS	GP	G	REC
1895	PIT	N	P		19	8- 7
1896	PIT	N	P		9	3- 4
	CIN	N	P		5	2- 3
			BLTL		33	13-14

FORMAN, WILLIAM ORANGE "BILL"
B.OCT.10,1886 VENANGO,PA.
D.OCT.3,1958 UNIONTOWN,PA.

YR	CL	LEA	POS	GP	G	REC
1909	WAS	A	P		2	0- 2
1910	WAS	A	P		1	0- 0
			BBTR		3	0- 2

FORNIELES, JOSE MIGUEL (TORRES) "MIKE"
B.JAN.18,1932 HAVANA,CUBA

YR	CL	LEA	POS	GP	G	REC
1952	WAS	A	P		4	2- 2
1953	CHI	A	P		39	8- 7
1954	CHI	A	P	15	16	1- 2
1955	CHI	A	P	26	28	6- 3
1956	CHI	A	P		6	0- 1
	BAL	A	P	30	33	4- 7
	BOS	A	P	25	26	8- 7
1957	BAL	A	P	15	16	2- 6
1958	BOS	A	P		37	4- 6
1959	BOS	A	P		46	5- 3
1960	BOS	A	P		70	10- 5
1961	BOS	A	P		57	9- 8
1962	BOS	A	P		42	3- 6
1963	BOS	A	P		9	0- 0
	MIN	A	P		11	1- 1
			BRTR	432	440	63-64

FORSCH, KENNETH ROTH "KEN"
B.SEP.8,1946 SACRAMENTO,CAL.

YR	CL	LEA	POS	GP	G	REC
1970	HOU	N	P		4	1- 2
1971	HOU	N	P		33	8- 8
1972	HOU	N	P		30	6- 8
1973	HOU	N	P		46	9-12
1974	HOU	N	P		70	8- 7
1975	HOU	N	P		34	4- 8
1976	HOU	N	P		52	4- 3
			BRTR	269	40-48

FORSCH, ROBERT HERBERT "BOB"
B.JAN.13,1950 SACRAMENTO,CAL.

YR	CL	LEA	POS	GP	G	REC
1974	STL	N	P	19	20	7- 4
1975	STL	N	P	34	35	15-10
1976	STL	N	P	32	35	8-10
			BRTR	85	90	30-24

FORSTER, TERRY JAY
B.JAN.14,1952 SIOUX FALLS,S.D.

YR	CL	LEA	POS	GP	G	REC
1971	CHI	A	P		45	2- 3
1972	CHI	A	P	62	63	6- 5
1973	CHI	A	P	51	53	6-11
1974	CHI	A	P		59	7- 8
1975	CHI	A	P		17	3- 3
1976	CHI	A	P		29	2-12
			BLTL	263	266	26-42

FORSTER, THOMAS W.
B.MAY 1,1858 NEW YORK,N.Y.
D.JULY 17,1946

YR	CL	LEA	POS	GP	G	REC
1882	DET	N	2-3		20	.098
1884	PIT	AA	S-3		35	.212
1885	MET	AA	2		57	.220
1886	MET	AA	2		84	.205
					196	.200

FORSYTHE, CLARENCE
B.ST.LOUIS,MO.

YR	CL	LEA	POS	GP	G	REC
1915	BAL	F	3		1	.000
			TR			

FORTUNE, GARRETT REESE "GARY"
B.OCT.11,1894 HIGH POINT,N.C.
D.SEPT.23,1955

YR	CL	LEA	POS	GP	G	REC
1916	PHI	N	P		1	0- 1
1918	PHI	N	P		8	0- 2
1920	BOS	A	P		14	0- 2
			BBTR		23	0- 5

FOSNOW, GERALD EUGENE "JERRY"
B.SEP.21,1940 DESHLER,OHIO

YR	CL	LEA	POS	GP	G	REC
1964	MIN	A	P		7	0- 1
1965	MIN	A	P		29	3- 3
			BRTL		36	3- 4

FOSS, GEORGE DUEWARD "DEEBY"
B.JUNE 16,1898 REGISTER,VA.
D.NOV.10,1969 MIAMI,FLA.

YR	CL	LEA	POS	GP	G	REC
1921	WAS	A	3		4	.000
			BRTR			

FOSS, LAWRENCE CURTIS
B.APR.18,1936 CASTLETON,KAN.

YR	CL	LEA	POS	GP	G	REC
1961	PIT	N	P		3	1- 1
1962	NY	N	P		5	0- 1
			BRTR		8	1- 2

FOSSE, RAYMOND EARL "RAY"
B.APR.4,1947 MARION,ILL.

YR	CL	LEA	POS	GP	G	REC
1967	CLE	A	C		7	.063
1968	CLE	A	C		1	.000
1969	CLE	A	C		37	.172
1970	CLE	A	C		120	.307
1971	CLE	A	C-1	133	.276
1972	CLE	A	C-1	134	.241
1973	OAK	A	C		143	.254
1974	OAK	A	C		69	.196
1975	OAK	A	C-1-2	82	.140
1976	CLE	A	C-1	90	.301
			BRTR		816	.254

FOSTER, ALAN BENTON
B.DEC.8,1946 PASADENA,CAL.

YR	CL	LEA	POS	GP	G	REC
1967	LA	N	P		4	0- 1
1968	LA	N	P		3	1- 1
1969	LA	N	P		24	3- 9
1970	LA	N	P		33	10-13
1971	CLE	A	P	36	37	8-12
1972	CAL	A	P		8	0- 1
1973	STL	N	P		35	13- 9
1974	STL	N	P	31	33	7-10
1975	SD	N	P	17	19	3- 1
1976	SD	N	P	26	29	3- 6
			BRTR	217	225	48-63

FOSTER, CLARENCE FRANCIS "POP"
B.APR.8,1878 NEW HAVEN,CONN.
D.APR.16,1944

YR	CL	LEA	POS	GP	G	REC
1898	NY	N	O		31	.281
1899	NY	N	O		88	.305
1900	NY	N	O		20	.286
1901	WAS	A	O		104	.271
	CHI	A	O		11	.281
			TR		254	.285

FOSTER, EDWARD CUNNINGHAM "KID"
B.FEB.13,1887 CHICAGO,ILL.
D.JAN.15,1937 WASHINGTON,D.C.

YR	CL	LEA	POS	GP	G	REC
1910	NY	A	3		30	.132
1912	WAS	A	3		154	.285
1913	WAS	A	3		106	.247
1914	WAS	A	3		156	.282
1915	WAS	A	2-3		154	.275
1916	WAS	A	2-3		158	.253
1917	WAS	A	2-3		143	.235
1918	WAS	A	3		129	.283
1919	WAS	A	3		120	.263
1920	BOS	A	2-3		117	.259
1921	BOS	A	2-3		120	.284
1922	BOS	A	3		48	.211
	STL	A	3		37	.306
1923	STL	A	2		27	.180
			BRTR		1499	.264

FOSTER, EDWARD LEE
D.MAR.2,1929

YR	CL	LEA	POS	GP	G	REC
1908	CLE	A	P		6	1- 0

FOSTER, ELMER ELLSWORTH
D.JULY 22,1946 DEEPHAVEN,MINN.

YR	CL	LEA	POS	GP	G	REC
1884	ATH	AA	C-O		3	.167
	KEY	U	C		1	.333
1886	MET	AA	O		18	.206
1888	NY	N	O		37	.147
1889	NY	N	O		2	.000
1890	CHI	N	O		27	.247
1891	CHI	N	O		4	.187
			TR		92	.191

FOSTER, GEORGE "RUBE"
B.JAN.5,1888 LEHIGH,OKLA
D.MAR.1,1976 BOKOSHE,OKLA.

YR	CL	LEA	POS	GP	G	REC
1913	BOS	A	P	19	20	3- 4
1914	BOS	A	P		32	14- 8
1915	BOS	A	P	38	40	20- 9
1916	BOS	A	P	34	38	14- 7
1917	BOS	A	P		17	8- 7
			BRTR	140	147	59-35

FOSTER, GEORGE ARTHUR
B.DEC.1,1948 TUSCALOOSA,ALA.

YR	CL	LEA	POS	GP	G	REC
1969	SF	N	O		9	.400
1970	SF	N	O		9	.316
1971	SF	N	O		36	.267
	CIN	N	O		104	.234
1972	CIN	N	O		59	.200
1973	CIN	N	O		17	.282
1974	CIN	N	O		106	.264
1975	CIN	N	1-O		134	.300
1976	CIN	N	1-O		144	.306
			BRTR		618	.275

FOSTER, LARRY LYNN
B.DEC.24,1937 LANSING,MICH.

YR	CL	LEA	POS	GP	G	REC
1963	DET	A	P		1	0- 0
			BLTR			

FOSTER, LEONARD NORRIS "LEO"
B.FEB.2,1951 COVINGTON,KY.

YR	CL	LEA	POS	GP	G	REC
1971	ATL	N	S		9	.000
1973	ATL	N	S		3	.167
1974	ATL	N	2-S-3-O	72	.196
1976	NY	N	2-S		24	.203
			BRTR		108	.187

FOSTER, OSCAR E. "REDDY"
B.1867 RICHMOND,VA.
D.DEC.19,1908

YR	CL	LEA	POS	GP	G	REC
1896	NY	N	O		1	.000

FOSTER, ROY
B.JULY 29,1945 BIXBY,MISS.

YR	CL	LEA	POS	GP	G	REC
1970	CLE	A	O		139	.268
1971	CLE	A	O		125	.245
1972	CLE	A	O		73	.224
			BRTR		337	.253

FOTHERGILL, ROBERT ROY "BOB" OR "FATTY"
B.AUG.16,1897 MASSILLON,OHIO
D.MAR.20,1938 DETROIT,MICH.

YR	CL	LEA	POS	GP	G	REC
1922	DET	A	O		42	.322
1923	DET	A	O		101	.315
1924	DET	A	O		54	.301
1925	DET	A	O		71	.353
1926	DET	A	O		110	.367
1927	DET	A	O		143	.359
1928	DET	A	O		111	.317
1929	DET	A	O		115	.350
1930	DET	A	O		54	.254
	CHI	A	O		52	.311
1931	CHI	A	O		108	.282
1932	CHI	A	O		116	.295
1933	BOS	A	O		28	.344
			BRTR		1105	.326

FOUCAULT, STEVEN RAYMOND "STEVE"
B.OCT.3,1949 DULUTH,MINN.

YR	CL	LEA	POS	GP	G	REC
1973	TEX	A	P		32	2- 4
1974	TEX	A	P		69	8- 9
1975	TEX	A	P		59	8- 4
1976	TEX	A	P		46	8- 8
			BLTR		206	26-25

FOURNIER, F. HENRY "FRENCHY"
B.SYRACUSE,N.Y.

YR	CL	LEA	POS	GP	G	REC
1894	CIN	N	P		6	1- 3
			TL			

YR	CL	LEA	POS	GP	G	REC

FOURNIER, JACQUES FRANK "JACK"
B.SEPT.29,1891 AU SABLE,MICH.
D.SEPT.5,1973 TACOMA,WASH.

YR	CL	LEA	POS	GP	G	REC
1912	CHI	A	1		35	.192
1913	CHI	A	1-0		68	.234
1914	CHI	A	1-0		109	.311
1915	CHI	A	1-0		126	.322
1916	CHI	A	1		105	.240
1917	CHI	A	H		1	.000
1918	NY	A	1		27	.350
1920	STL	N	1		141	.306
1921	STL	N	1		149	.343
1922	STL	N	P-1	1	128	0- 0
						.294
1923	BRO	N	1		133	.351
1924	BRO	N	1		154	.334
1925	BRO	N	1		145	.350
1926	BRO	N	1		87	.284
1927	BOS	N	1		122	.283
		BLTR		1	1530	0- 0
						.313

FOUSER, WILLIAM C.
B.1855 PHILADELPHIA,PA.
D.MAR.1,1919

YR	CL	LEA	POS	GP	G	REC
1876	ATH	N	2-0		21	.135

FOUTZ, DAVID LUTHER "SCISSORS"
B.SEPT.7,1856 CARROLL CO.,MD.
D.MAR.5,1897

YR	CL	LEA	POS	GP	G	REC
1884	STL	AA	P-0	23	32	15- 6
						.233
1885	STL	AA	P-1	47	65	33-14
						.250
1886	STL	AA	P-0	57	89	41-16
						.282
1887	STL	AA	P-0	36	103	24-12
						.393
1888	BRO	AA	P-1-	19	140	12- 7
			0			.283
1889	BRO	AA	P-1	4	138	4- 0
						.286
1890	BRO	N	P-1	4	129	3- 1
						.302
1891	BRO	N	P-1	6	130	3- 3
						.262
1892	BRO	N	P-0	22	53	12- 9
						.199
1893	BRO	N	M-1-0		130	.272
1894	BRO	N	M-1		73	.310
1895	BRO	N	M-0		28	.304
1896	BRO	N	M-1-0		2	.250
		BRTR		218	1112	147-68
						.286

FOUTZ, FRANK HAYES
B.APR.8,1877 BALTIMORE,MD.
D.DEC.25,1961

YR	CL	LEA	POS	GP	G	REC
1901	BAL	A	1		20	.236
		BRTR				

FOWLER, JESSE PETER
B.OCT.30,1897 SPARTANBURG,S.C.
D.SEPT.23,1973 COLUMBIA,S.C.

YR	CL	LEA	POS	GP	G	REC
1924	STL	N	P	13		1- 1
		BRTL				

FOWLER, JOHN ARTHUR "ART"
B.JULY 3,1922 CONVERSE,S.C.

YR	CL	LEA	POS	GP	G	REC
1954	CIN	N	P	40		12-10
1955	CIN	N	P	46		11-10
1956	CIN	N	P	45		11-11
1957	CIN	N	P	33		3- 0
1959	LA	N	P	36		3- 4
1961	LA	A	P	53		5- 8
1962	LA	A	P	48		4- 3
1963	LA	A	P	57		5- 3
1964	LA	A	P	4		0- 2
		BRTR		362		54-51

FOWLER, JOSEPH CHESTER "GINK"
B.NOV.11,1900 WACO,TEX.

YR	CL	LEA	POS	GP	G	REC
1923	CIN	N	S		11	.333
1924	CIN	N	2-S-3		59	.333
1925	CIN	N	S		6	.400
1926	BOS	N	3		2	.125
		BLTR			78	.326

FOWLER, RICHARD JOHN "DICK"
B.MAR.30,1921 TORONTO,ONT.,CAN.
D.MAY 22,1972 ONEONTA,N.Y.

YR	CL	LEA	POS	GP	G	REC
1941	PHI	A	P	4		1- 2
1942	PHI	A	P	31	32	6-11
1945	PHI	A	P	7	11	1- 2
1946	PHI	A	P		32	9-16
1947	PHI	A	P		36	12-11
1948	PHI	A	P		29	15- 8
1949	PHI	A	P		31	15-11
1950	PHI	A	P		11	1- 5
1951	PHI	A	P		22	5-11
1952	PHI	A	P		18	1- 2
		BRTR		221	226	66-79

FOX, CHARLES FRANCIS "IRISH"
B.OCT.7,1922 NEW YORK,N.Y.

YR	CL	LEA	POS	GP	G	REC
1942	NY	N	C		3	.429
		BRTR				

NON-PLAYING MANAGER
SF(N) 1970-74, MON(N) 1976

FOX, ERVIN "PETE"
B.MAR.8,1909 EVANSVILLE,IND.
D.JULY 5,1966 DETROIT,MICH.

YR	CL	LEA	POS	GP	G	REC
1933	DET	A	0		128	.288
1934	DET	A	0		128	.285
1935	DET	A	0		131	.321
1936	DET	A	0		73	.305
1937	DET	A	0		148	.331
1938	DET	A	0		155	.293
1939	DET	A	0		161	.296
1940	DET	A	0		93	.289
1941	BOS	A	0		73	.302
1942	BOS	A	0		77	.262
1943	BOS	A	0		127	.288
1944	BOS	A	0		121	.315
1945	BOS	A	0		66	.245
		BRTR			1461	.298

FOX, GEORGE B. "PADDY"
B.JAN.2,1869
D.MAY 8,1914 PHILADELPHIA,PA.

YR	CL	LEA	POS	GP	G	REC
1891	LOU	AA	3		6	.105
1899	PIT	N	C		13	.243
					19	.200

FOX, HENRY H.

YR	CL	LEA	POS	GP	G	REC
1902	PHI	N	P	1		0- 0

FOX, HOWARD FRANCIS "HOWIE"
B.MAR.1,1921 COBURG,ORE.
D.OCT.9,1955

YR	CL	LEA	POS	GP	G	REC
1944	CIN	N	P	2		0- 0
1945	CIN	N	P	45		8-13
1946	CIN	N	P	4		0- 0
1948	CIN	N	P	34	35	6- 9
1949	CIN	N	P	38	41	6-19
1950	CIN	N	P	34	35	11- 8
1951	CIN	N	P		40	9-14
1952	PHI	N	P		13	2- 7
1954	BAL	A	P		38	1- 2
		BRTR		248	253	43-72

FOX, JACOB NELSON "NELLIE"
B.DEC.25,1927 ST.THOMAS,PA.
D.DEC.1,1975 BALTIMORE,MD.

YR	CL	LEA	POS	GP	G	REC
1947	PHI	A	2		7	.000
1948	PHI	A	2		3	.154
1949	PHI	A	2		88	.255
1950	CHI	A	2		130	.247
1951	CHI	A	2		147	.313
1952	CHI	A	2		152	.296
1953	CHI	A	2		154	.285
1954	CHI	A	2		155	.319
1955	CHI	A	2		154	.311
1956	CHI	A	2		154	.296
1957	CHI	A	2		155	.317
1958	CHI	A	2		155	.300
1959	CHI	A	2		156	.306
1960	CHI	A	2		150	.289
1961	CHI	A	2		159	.251
1962	CHI	A	2		157	.267
1963	CHI	A	2		137	.260
1964	HOU	N	2		133	.265
1965	HOU	N	1-2-3		21	.268
		BLTR			2367	.288

FOX, JOHN JOSEPH
B.FEB.7,1859 ROXBURY,MASS.
D.APR.18,1893

YR	CL	LEA	POS	GP	G	REC
1881	BOS	N	P-1-	17	30	6- 8
			0			.178
1883	BAL	AA	P-1-0		23	6-14
						.168
1884	PIT	AA	P-S	7	8	1- 6
						.240
1886	WAS	N	P		1	0- 1
				48	62	13-29
						.179

FOX, JOHN PAUL
B.MAY 21,1885 READING,PA.
D.JUNE 28,1963 READING,PA.

YR	CL	LEA	POS	GP	G	REC
1908	PHI	A	0		8	.209
		BRTR				

FOX, TERRENCE EDWARD "TERRY"
B.JULY 31,1935 CHICAGO,ILL.

YR	CL	LEA	POS	GP	G	REC
1960	MIL	N	P		5	0- 0
1961	DET	A	P		39	5- 2
1962	DET	A	P	44	47	3- 1
1963	DET	A	P		46	8- 6
1964	DET	A	P		32	4- 3
1965	DET	A	P		42	6- 4
1966	DET	A	P		6	0- 1
	PHI	N	P	36	38	3- 2
		BRTR		248	253	29-19

FOX, WILLIAM H.
B.JAN.15,1872 STURBRIDGE,MASS.
D.MAY 6,1946

YR	CL	LEA	POS	GP	G	REC
1897	WAS	N	?-S		6	.250
1901	CIN	N	2		44	.183
		BBTP			48	.191

FOXEN, WILLIAM H.
B.MAY 31,1884 TENAFLY,N.J.
D.APR.17,1937

YR	CL	LEA	POS	GP	G	REC
1908	PHI	N	P		22	7- 7
1909	PHI	N	P		18	3- 7
1910	PHI	N	P		16	5- 5
	CHI	N	P		2	0- 0
1911	CHI	N	P		3	1- 1
		BLTL			61	16-20

FOXX, JAMES EMORY "JIMMIE" OR "BEAST"
B.OCT.22,1907 SUDLERSVILLE,MD.
D.JULY 21,1967 MIAMI,FLA.

YR	CL	LEA	POS	GP	G	REC
1925	PHI	A	C		10	.667
1926	PHI	A	C		26	.313
1927	PHI	A	1		61	.323
1928	PHI	A	C-1-3		118	.328
1929	PHI	A	1		149	.354
1930	PHI	A	1		153	.335
1931	PHI	A	1-3		139	.291
1932	PHI	A	1-3		154	.364
1933	PHI	A	1		149	.356
1934	PHI	A	1		150	.334
1935	PHI	A	C-1-3		147	.346
1936	BOS	A	1-0		155	.338
1937	BOS	A	1		150	.285
1938	BOS	A	1		149	.349
1939	BOS	A	P-1	1	124	0- 0
						.360
1940	BOS	A	1-3		144	.297
1941	BOS	A	1-3-0		135	.300
1942	BOS	A	1		30	.270
	CHI	N	C-1		70	.205
1944	CHI	N	C-3		15	.050
1945	PHI	N	P-1-	9	89	1- 0
			3			.268
		BRTR		10	2317	1- 0
						.325

FOY, JOSEPH ANTHONY "JOE"
B.FEB.21,1943 NEW YORK,N.Y.

YR	CL	LEA	POS	GP	G	REC
1966	BOS	A	S-3		151	.262
1967	BOS	A	3-0		130	.251
1968	BOS	A	3-0		150	.225
1969	KC	A	1-2-S-3-	145		.262
			0			
1970	NY	N	3		99	.236
1971	WAS	A	2-S-3		41	.234
		BRTR			716	.248

YR	CL LEA POS	GP	G	REC

FOYTACK, PAUL EUGENE
B.NOV.16,1930 SCRANTON,PA.
1953 DET A	P		6	0- 0
1955 DET A	P		22	0- 1
1956 DET A	P		43	15-13
1957 DET A	P		38	14-11
1958 DET A	P		39	15-13
1959 DET A	P		39	14-14
1960 DET A	P	28	29	2-11
1961 DET A	P		32	11-10
1962 DET A	P		29	10- 7
1963 DET A	P		9	0- 1
LA A	P	25	26	5- 5
1964 LA	P		2	0- 1
BRTR	312	314	86-87

FRAILING, KENNETH DOUGLAS "KEN"
B.JAN.19,1948 MARION,WIS.
1972 CHI A	P		4	1- 0
1973 CHI A	P		10	0- 0
1974 CHI N	P	55	58	6- 9
1975 CHI N	P		41	2- 5
1976 CHI N	P		6	1- 2
BLTL	116	119	10-16

FRANCIS, EARL COLEMAN
B.JULY 14,1935 SLAB FORK,W.VA.
1960 PIT N	P		7	1- 0
1961 PIT N	P		23	2- 8
1962 PIT N	P		36	9- 8
1963 PIT N	P	33	34	4- 6
1964 PIT N	P		2	0- 1
1965 STL N	P		2	0- 0
BRTR	103	104	16-23

FRANCIS, OSMAN B.
B.OCT.4,1859 GREENTOWN,OHIO
D.MAY 2,1947
| 1890 CHI N | P | | 1 | 0- 0 |

FRANCIS, RAY JAMES
B.MAR.8,1893 SHERMAN,TEX.
D.JULY 14,1932
1922 WAS A	P		39	7-18
1923 DET A	P	33	37	4- 8
1925 NY A	P		4	0- 0
BOS A	P		6	0- 2
BLTL	82	86	11-28

FRANCONA, JOHN PATSY "TITO"
B.NOV.4,1933 ALIQUIPPA,PA.
1956 BAL A	1-O	139	.258
1957 BAL A	1-O	97	.233
1958 CHI A	O	41	.258
DET A	1-O	45	.246
1959 CLE A	1-O	122	.363
1960 CLE A	1-O	147	.292
1961 CLE A	1-O	155	.301
1962 CLE A	1	158	.272
1963 CLE A	1-O	142	.228
1964 CLE A	1-O	111	.248
1965 STL N	1-O	81	.259
1966 STL N	1-O	83	.212
1967 PHI N	1-O	27	.205
ATL N	1-O	82	.248
1968 ATL N	1-O	122	.286
1969 ATL N	1-O	51	.295
OAK A	1-O	32	.341
1970 OAK A	1-O	32	.242
MIL A	1	52	.231
BLTL	1719	.272

FRANK, CHARLES
B.MAY 30,1870 MOBILE,ALA.
D.MAY 24,1922
1893 STL N	O	40	.331
1894 STL N	O	80	.246
		120	.272

FRANK, FREDERICK
B.MAR.11,1874 LOUISA,KY.
D.MAR.27,1950
| 1898 CLE N | O | 17 | .208 |

FRANKHOUSE, FREDERICK MELOY
B.APR.9,1904 PORT ROYAL,PA.
1927 STL N	P		8	5- 1
1928 STL N	P	21	22	3- 2
1929 STL N	P	30	34	7- 2
1930 STL N	P	8	9	2- 3
BOS N	P		27	7- 6
1931 BOS N	P		26	8- 8
1932 BOS N	P	37	40	4- 6
1933 BOS N	P		43	16-15
1934 BOS N	P		37	17- 9
1935 BOS N	P		40	11-15
1936 BRO N	P	41	42	13-10
1937 BRO N	P	33	39	10-13
1938 BRO N	P	30	31	3- 5
1939 BOS N	P		23	0- 2
BRTR	402	421	106-97

FRANKLIN
| 1884 WAS U | O | | 1 | .000 |

FRANKLIN, JAMES WILFORD "JACK"
B.OCT.20,1919 PARIS,ILL.
| 1944 BRO N | P | | 1 | 0- 0 |
| BRTR |

FRANKLIN, JOHN WILLIAM "JAY"
B.MAR.16,1953 ARLINGTON,VA.
| 1971 SD N | P | | 3 | 0- 1 |
| BRTR |

FRANKLIN, MURRAY ASHER "MOE"
B.APR.1,1914 CHICAGO,ILL.
1941 DET A	S-3	13	.300
1942 DET A	2-S	48	.260
BRTR	61	.262

FRANKS, HERMAN LOUIS
B.JAN.4,1914 PRICE,UTAH
1939 STL N	C	17	.059
1940 BRO N	C	65	.183
1941 BRO N	C-O	57	.201
1947 PHI A	C	8	.200
1948 PHI A	C	40	.224
1949 NY N	C	1	.667
BLTR	188	.195
NON-PLAYING MANAGER
SF(N) 1965-68

FRASER, CHARLES CARROLTON "CHICK"
B.MAR.17,1874 SCOTLAND
D.MAY 8,1940 WENDELL,IOWA
1896 LOU N	P	41	43	13-25
1897 LOU N	P		36	15-17
1898 LOU N	P		26	7-19
CLE N	P		6	2- 3
1899 PHI N	P	35	37	21-13
1900 PHI N	P		26	16-10
1901 PHI A	P	40	43	20-15
1902 PHI N	P		27	12-13
1903 PHI N	P	31	32	12-17
1904 PHI N	P	42	44	13-24
1905 BOS N	P	39	45	15-21
1906 CIN N	P		31	10-20
1907 CIN N	P		22	8- 5
1908 CHI N	P		26	11- 9
1909 CHI N	P		1	0- 0
BRTR	429	445	175-211

FRASIER, VICTOR PATRICK
B.AUG.5,1906 RUSTON,LA.
1931 CHI A	P	46	13-15
1932 CHI A	P	29	3-13
1933 CHI A	P	10	1- 1
DET A	P	20	5- 5
1934 DET A	P	8	1- 3
1937 BOS N	P	3	0- 0
1939 CHI A	P	10	0- 1
BRTR	126	23-38

FRAZER, GEORGE KASSON
B.JAN.7,1861 SYRACUSE,N.Y.
D.FEB.5,1913
NON-PLAYING MANAGER SYR(AA)1890

FRAZIER, JOSEPH FILMORE "JOE"
B.OCT.6,1922 LIBERTY,N.C.
1947 CLE A	O	9	.071
1954 STL N	1-O	81	.295
1955 STL N	O	58	.200
1956 STL N	O	14	.211
CIN N	O	10	.235
BAL A	O	45	.257
BLTR	217	.241
NON-PLAYING MANAGER NY(N) 1976

FREDERICK, JOHN HENRY
B.JAN.26,1901 DENVER,COL.
1929 BRO N	O	148	.328
1930 BRO N	O	142	.334
1931 BRO N	O	146	.270
1932 BRO N	O	118	.299
1933 BRO N	O	147	.308
1934 BRO N	O	104	.296
BLTL	805	.307

FREED, EDWARD CHARLES
B.AUG.22,1919 CENTRE VALLEY,PA.
| 1942 PHI N | O | 13 | .303 |
| BRTR |

FREED, ROGER VERNON
B.JUNE 2,1946 LOS ANGELES,CAL.
1970 BAL A	1-O	4	.154
1971 PHI N	C-O	118	.221
1972 PHI N	O	73	.225
1974 CIN N	1	6	.333
1976 MON N	1-O	8	.200
BRTR	209	.221

FREEHAN, WILLIAM ASHLEY "BILL"
B.NOV.29,1941 DETROIT,MICH.
1961 DET A	C	4	.400
1963 DET A	C-1	100	.243
1964 DET A	C-1	144	.300
1965 DET A	C	130	.234
1966 DET A	C-1	136	.234
1967 DET A	C-1	155	.282
1968 DET A	C-1-O	155	.263
1969 DET A	C-1	143	.262
1970 DET A	C	117	.241
1971 DET A	C-O	148	.277
1972 DET A	C-1	111	.262
1973 DET A	C-1	110	.234
1974 DET A	C-1	130	.297
1975 DET A	C-1	120	.246
1976 DET A	C-1	71	.270
BRTR	1774	.262

FREEMAN, ALEXANDER VERNON "BUCK"
B.JULY 5,1896 MART,TEX.
1921 CHI N	P		38	9-10
1922 CHI N	P		11	0- 1
BBTR	49	9-11

FREEMAN, HARVEY B. "POKE"
B.OCT.22,1897 OTSEGO,MICH.
D.JAN.10,1970 KALAMAZOO,MICH.
| 1921 PHI A | P | | 18 | 1- 4 |
| BRTR |

FREEMAN, HERSHELL BASKIN "HERSH" OR "BUSTER"
B.JULY 1,1928 GADSDEN,ALA.
1952 BOS A	P		4	1- 0
1953 BOS A	P		18	1- 4
1955 BOS A	P		2	0- 0
CIN N	P-3	52	53	7- 4
				.167
1956 CIN N	P		64	14- 5
1957 CIN N	P		52	7- 2
1958 CIN N	P		3	0- 0
CHI N	P		9	0- 1
BRTR	204	205	30-16
				.143

FREEMAN, JAMES JEREMIAH "JERRY"
B.1882
DECEASED
1908 WAS A	1	154	.252
1909 WAS A	1	19	.167
		173	.245

FREEMAN, JIMMY LEE
B.JUNE 29,1951 CARLSBAD,N.MEX.
1972 ATL N	P	6	8	2- 2
1973 ATL N	P	13	14	0- 2
BLTL	19	22	2- 4

FREEMAN, JOHN EDWARD
B.JAN.24,1901 BOSTON,MASS.
D.APR.14,1958
| 1927 BOS A | O | 4 | .000 |
| BRTR |

YR	CL LEA POS	GP	G	REC

FREEMAN, JOHN F. "BUCK"
B.OCT.30,1871 CATASAQUA,PA.
D.JUNE 25,1949

1891	WAS AA P	6		0- 0
1898	WAS N O	29		.368
1899	WAS N O	155		.318
1900	BOS N 1-O	109		.300
1901	BOS A 1	129		.346
1902	BOS N O	138		.311
1903	BOS A O	141		.285
1904	BOS A O	157		.278
1905	BOS A 1-O	130		.240
1906	BOS A 1-O	121		.250
1907	BOS A O	4		.167
	BLTL	6 1119		0- 0
				.294

FREEMAN, JULIUS B.
B.1869 OMAHA,NEB.

| 1888 | STL AA P | 1 | | 0- 1 |

FREEMAN, MARK PRICE
B.DEC.7,1930 MEMPHIS,TENN.

1959	KC A P	3		0- 0
	NY A P	1		0- 0
1960	CHI N P	30		3- 3
	BRTR	34		3- 3

FREESE, EUGENE LEWIS "GENE"
B.JAN.8,1934 WHEELING,W.VA.

1955	PIT N 2-3	134		.253
1956	PIT N 2-3	65		.208
1957	PIT N 2-3-O	114		.283
1958	PIT N 3	17		.167
	STL N 2-S-3	62		.257
1959	PHI N 2-3	132		.268
1960	CHI A 3	127		.273
1961	CIN N 2-3	152		.277
1962	CIN N 3	18		.143
1963	CIN N 3-O	66		.244
1964	PIT N 3	99		.225
1965	PIT N 3	43		.263
	CHI A 3	17		.281
1966	CHI A 3	48		.208
	HOU N 2-3-O	21		.091
	BRTR	1115		.254

FREESE, GEORGE WALTER "BUD"
B.SEPT.12,1926 WHEELING,W.VA.

1953	DET N H	1		.000
1955	PIT N 3	51		.257
1961	CHI N H	9		.286
	BRTR	61		.257

FREEZE, CARL ALEXANDER "JAKE"
B.APR.25,1900 FT.SMITH,ARK.

| 1925 | CHI A P | 2 | | 0- 0 |
| | BRTR | | | |

FREGOSI, JAMES LOUIS "JIM"
B.APR.4,1942 SAN FRANCISCO,CAL.

1961	LA A S	11		.222
1962	LA A S	58		.291
1963	LA A S	154		.287
1964	LA A S	147		.277
1965	CAL A S	161		.277
1966	CAL A 1-S	162		.252
1967	CAL A S	151		.290
1968	CAL A S	159		.244
1969	CAL A S	161		.260
1970	CAL A 1-S	158		.278
1971	CAL A 1-S-O	107		.233
1972	NY N 1-S-3	101		.232
1973	NY N 1-S-3-O	45		.234
	TEX A 1-S-3	45		.268
1974	TEX A 1-3	78		.261
1975	TEX A 1-3-O	77		.262
1976	TEX A 1-3-O	58		.233
	BRTR	1833		.265

FREIBERGER, VERN DONALD
B.DEC.19,1923 DETROIT,MICH.

| 1941 | CLE A 1 | 2 | | .125 |
| | BRTL | | | |

FREIGAU, HOWARD EARL "TY"
B.AUG.1,1902 DAYTON,OHIO
D.JULY 18,1932

1922	STL N S-3	3		.000
1923	STL N 1-2-S-3-	113		.263
	O			
1924	STL N 3	98		.269
1925	STL N S	9		.154
	CHI N 1-S-3	117		.307
1926	CHI N 3	140		.270
1927	CHI N 3	30		.233
1928	BRO N S-3	17		.206
	BOS N 2-S	52		.257
	BRTR	579		.272

FREISLEBEN, DAVID JAMES "DAVE"
B.OCT.31,1951 CORAOPOLIS,PA.

1974	SD N P	33		9-14
1975	SD N P	36		5-14
1976	SD N P	34		10-13
	BRTR	103		24-41

FREITAS, TONY
B.MAY 5,1908 MILL VALLEY,CAL.

1932	PHI A P	23		12- 5
1933	PHI A P	19		2- 4
1934	CIN N P	30	31	6-12
1935	CIN N P		31	5-10
1936	CIN N P		4	0- 2
	BRTL	107	108	25-33

FRENCH, CHARLES CALVIN
B.OCT.12,1883 INDIANAPOLIS,IND.
D.MAR.30,1962

1909	BOS A 2-S	51		.251
1910	BOS A 2	9		.200
	CHI A 2	45		.165
	BLTR	105		.207

FRENCH, FRANK ALEXANDER "PAT"
B.SEPT.22,1893 DOVER,N.H.
D.JULY 13,1969 BATH,MAINE

| 1917 | PHI A O | 4 | | .000 |
| | BRTR | | | |

FRENCH, LAWRENCE HERBERT
B.NOV.1,1908 VISALIA,CAL.

1929	PIT N P	30		7- 5
1930	PIT N P	42		17-18
1931	PIT N P	39		15-13
1932	PIT N P	47		18-16
1933	PIT N P	47		18-13
1934	PIT N P	49		12-18
1935	CHI N P	42		17-10
1936	CHI N P	43		18- 9
1937	CHI N P	42		16-10
1938	CHI N P	43		10-19
1939	CHI N P	36		15- 8
1940	CHI N P	40		14-14
1941	CHI N P	26		5-14
	BRO N P	6		0- 0
1942	BRO N P	38		15- 4
	BBTL	570		197-171
	BR 1929-33, 35-39			

FRENCH, RAYMOND EDWARD
B.JAN.9,1897 ALMEDA,CAL.

1920	NY A S	2		.000
1922	BRO N S	43		.219
1924	CHI A S	37		.179
	BRTR	82		.193

FRENCH, RICHARD JAMES "JIM"
B.AUG.13,1941 WARREN,OHIO

1965	WAS A C	13		.297
1966	WAS A C	10		.208
1967	WAS A C	6		.063
1968	WAS A C	59		.194
1969	WAS A C	63		.184
1970	WAS A C-O	69		.211
1971	WAS A C	14		.146
	BLTR	234		.196

FRENCH, WALTER EDWARD "PIGGY"
B.JULY 12,1899 MOORESTOWN,N.J.

1923	PHI A O	16		.231
1925	PHI A O	67		.370
1926	PHI A O	112		.305
1927	PHI A O	109		.304
1928	PHI A O	49		.257
1929	PHI A O	45		.267
	BLTR	398		.303

FRENCH, WILLIAM
B.BALTIMORE,MD.

| 1873 | MAR NA P-1-O | 5 | | 0- 1 |
| | | | | - |

FREY, BENJAMIN RUDOLPH
B.APR.6,1906 DEXTER,MICH.
D.NOV.1,1937

1929	CIN N P	3		1- 2
1930	CIN N P	44		11-18
1931	CIN N P	34		8-12
1932	STL N P	2		0- 2
	CIN N P	28		4-10
1933	CIN N P	37	38	6- 4
1934	CIN N P	39	41	11-16
1935	CIN N P		38	6-10
1936	CIN N P	31	32	10- 8
	BRTR	256	260	57-82

FREY, LINUS REINHARD "LONNY"
B.AUG.23,1912 ST.LOUIS,MO.

1933	BRO N S	34		.319
1934	BRO N S-3	125		.284
1935	BRO N 2-S	131		.262
1936	BRO N 2-S	148		.279
1937	CHI N 2-S	78		.278
1938	CIN N 2-S	124		.265
1939	CIN N 2	125		.291
1940	CIN N 2	150		.266
1941	CIN N 2	146		.254
1942	CIN N 2	141		.266
1943	CIN N 2	144		.263
1946	CIN N 2-O	111		.246
1947	CIN N 2	24		.209
	NY A 2	24		.179
1948	NY A H	1		.000
	NY N 2	29		.255
	BLTR	1535		.269
	BL 1939-43, 46-48			

FRIAS, JESUS MARIA (ANDUJAR) "PEPE"
B.JULY 14,1948 SAN DE PEDRO DE MACORIS,D.R.

1973	MON N 2-S-3-O	100		.231
1974	MON N 2-S-3-O	75		.214
1975	MON N 2-S-3	51		.125
1976	MON N 2-S-O	76		.248
	BRTR	302		.218

FRIBERG, BERNARD ALBERT "BARNEY"
B.AUG.18,1899 MANCHESTER,N.H.
D.DEC.8,1958

1919	CHI N O	8		.200
1920	CHI N 2-O	50		.211
1922	CHI N 1-2-3-O	97		.311
1923	CHI N 3	146		.318
1924	CHI N 3	142		.279
1925	CHI N 1-3	44		.257
	PHI N P-2-	1	91	0- 0
	S-3-O			.270
1926	PHI N 2	144		.268
1927	PHI N 3	111		.233
1928	PHI N S	52		.202
1929	PHI N S-O	128		.301
1930	PHI N 2-S-O	105		.341
1931	PHI N 2-3	103		.261
1932	PHI N 2	61		.240
1933	BOS A 2-S-3	17		.317
	BRTR	1 1299		0- 0
				.280

FRICANO, MARION JOHN
B.JULY 15,1923 BRANT,N.Y.
D.MAY 18,1976 TIJUANA,MEX.

1952	PHI A P	2		1- 0
1953	PHI A P	39	46	9-12
1954	PHI A P	37	42	5-11
1955	KC A P	10		0- 0
	BRTR	88	100	15-23

FRIDAY, GRIER WILLIAM "SKIPPER"
B.OCT.24,1896 LINCOLNTON,N.C.

| 1923 | WAS A P | 7 | | 0- 1 |
| | BRTR | | | |

FRIDLEY, JAMES RILEY "JIM"
B.SEPT.6,1924 PHILIPPI,W.VA.

1952	CLE A O	62		.251
1954	BAL A O	85		.246
1958	CIN N O	5		.222
	BRTR	152		.248

FRIED, ARTHUR EDWIN "CY"
B.JULY 23,1897 SAN ANTONIO,TEX.
D.OCT.10,1970 SAN ANTONIO,TEX.

| 1920 | DET A P | 2 | | 0- 0 |
| | BLTL | | | |

YR	CL	LEA	POS	GP	G	REC

FRIEDRICH, ROBERT GEORGE
B.AUG.30,1909 CINCINNATI,OHIO
| 1932 | WAS | A | P | | 2 | 0- 0 |
| | | BRTR | | | | |

FRIEL, PATRICK HENRY
B.JUNE 11,1860 LEWISBURG,W.VA.
D.JAN.15,1924
1890	SYR	AA	O		62	.238
1891	ATH	AA	O		2	.286
					64	.243

FRIEL, WILLIAM EDWARD
B.APR.1,1876 RENOVO,PA.
D.DEC.24,1959
1901	MIL	A	3-O		106	.271
1902	STL	A	ALL	1	79	0- 0
						.239
1903	STL	A	2-3		98	.223
		BLTR		1	283	0- 0
						.245

FRIEND, DANIEL SEBASTIAN
B.MAY 19,1873 CHILLICOTHE,OHIO
D.JUNE 1,1942
1895	CHI	N	P		5	2- 2
1896	CHI	N	P		33	19-14
1897	CHI	N	P	23	24	12-11
1898	CHI	N	P		2	0- 2
		TL		63	64	33-29

FRIEND, FRANK B.
B.WASHINGTON,D.C.
D.SEPT.8,1897
| 1896 | LOU | N | C | | 2 | .200 |

FRIEND, OWEN LACEY "RED"
B.MAR.21,1927 GRANITE CITY,ILL.
1949	STL	A	2		2	.375
1950	STL	A	2-S-3	119		.237
1953	DET	A	2	31		.177
	CLE	A	2-S-3	34		.235
1955	BOS	A	2-S	14		.262
	CHI	N	S-3	6		.100
1956	CHI	N	H	2		.000
		BRTR		208		.227

FRIEND, ROBERT BARTMESS "BOB"
B.NOV.24,1930 LAFAYETTE,IND.
1951	PIT	N	P		34	6-10
1952	PIT	N	P		35	7-17
1953	PIT	N	P		32	8-11
1954	PIT	N	P		35	7-12
1955	PIT	N	P		44	14- 9
1956	PIT	N	P		49	17-17
1957	PIT	N	P		40	14-18
1958	PIT	N	P		38	22-14
1959	PIT	N	P		35	8-19
1960	PIT	N	P		38	18-12
1961	PIT	N	P		41	14-19
1962	PIT	N	P		39	18-14
1963	PIT	N	P		39	17-16
1964	PIT	N	P		35	13-18
1965	PIT	N	P		34	8-12
1966	NY	A	P		12	1- 4
	NY	N	P		22	5- 8
		BRTR			602	197-230

FRIERSON, ROBERT LAWRENCE "BUCK"
B.JULY 29,1917 CHICOTA,TEX.
| 1941 | CLE | A | O | | 5 | .273 |
| | | BRTR | | | | |

FRIES, PETER J.
B.CHICAGO,ILL.
1883	COL	AA	P		3	0- 3
1884	IND	AA	O		1	.250
		TL		3	4	0- 3
						.267

FRILL, JOHN EDMOND
B.APR.3,1879 READING,PA.
D.SEPT.29,1918
1910	NY	A	P		10	2- 2
1912	STL	A	P		3	1- 0
	CIN	N	P		3	1- 0
		BRTL			16	4- 2

FRINK, FRED FERDINAND
B.AUG.25,1911 MACON,GA.
| 1934 | PHI | N | O | | 2 | .000 |
| | | BRTR | | | | |

FRISBEE, CHARLES AUGUSTUS
B.FEB.2,1874 DOWS,IOWA
D.NOV.7,1954
1899	BOS	N	O		39	.331
1900	NY	N	O		4	.153
		BBTR			43	.316

FRISCH, FRANK FRANCIS "FRANKIE"
OR "THE FORDHAM FLASH"
B.SEPT.9,1898 BRONX,N.Y.
D.MAR.12,1973 ELKTON,MD.
1919	NY	N	2-S-3		54	.226
1920	NY	N	3		110	.280
1921	NY	N	2-3		153	.341
1922	NY	N	2-S-3		132	.326
1923	NY	N	2-3		151	.348
1924	NY	N	2-S-3		145	.328
1925	NY	N	2-S-3		120	.331
1926	NY	N	2		135	.314
1927	STL	N	2		153	.337
1928	STL	N	2		141	.300
1929	STL	N	2-3		138	.334
1930	STL	N	2-3		133	.346
1931	STL	N	2		131	.311
1932	STL	N	2-3		115	.292
1933	STL	N	M-2-S		147	.303
1934	STL	N	M-2-3		140	.305
1935	STL	N	M-2-3		103	.294
1936	STL	N	M-2-3		93	.274
1937	STL	N	M-2		17	.219
		BBTR			2311	.316
NON-PLAYING MANAGER STL(N)1938,
PIT(N) 1940-46, CHI(N) 1949-51

FRISELLA, DANIEL VINCENT "DANNY"
B.MAR.4,1946 SAN FRANCISCO,CAL.
1967	NY	N	P		14	1- 6
1968	NY	N	P		19	2- 4
1969	NY	N	P		3	0- 0
1970	NY	N	P		30	8- 3
1971	NY	N	P		53	8- 5
1972	NY	N	P		39	5- 8
1973	ATL	N	P		42	1- 2
1974	ATL	N	P		36	3- 4
1975	SD	N	P		65	1- 6
1976	STL	N	P		18	0- 0
	MIL	A	P		32	5- 2
		BLTR			351	34-40

FRISK, JOHN EMIL
B.OCT.15,1874 KALKASKA,MICH.
D.JAN.27,1922
1899	CIN	N	P		9	3- 6
1901	DET	A	P	12	19	5- 3
1905	STL	A	O		127	.261
1907	STL	A	H		5	.250
		BLTR		21	160	8- 9
						.266

FRITZ, CHARLES CORNELIUS
B.JUNE 18,1882 MOBILE,ALA.
D.JULY 31,1944
| 1907 | PHI | A | P | | 1 | 1- 0 |
| | | TL | | | | |

FRITZ, HARRY KOCH "DUTCHMAN"
B.SEPT.30,1890 PHILADELPHIA,PA.
D.NOV.4,1974 COLUMBUS,OHIO
1913	PHI	A	3		5	.000
1914	CHI	F	3		63	.229
1915	CHI	F	3		72	.240
		BRTR			140	.228

FRITZ, LAWRENCE JOSEPH "LARRY"
B.FEB.14,1949 E.CHICAGO,IND.
| 1975 | PHI | N | H | | 1 | .000 |
| | | BLTL | | | | |

FROATS, WILLIAM JOHN "BILL"
B.OCT.20,1930 NEW YORK,N.Y.
| 1955 | DET | A | P | | 1 | 0- 0 |
| | | BLTL | | | | |

FROCK, SAMUEL W.
B.DEC.23,1882 BALTIMORE,MD.
D.NOV.3,1925
1907	BOS	N	P		5	1- 3
1909	PIT	N	P		8	2- 1
1910	PIT	N	P		1	0- 0
	BOS	N	P		45	12-19
1911	BOS	N	P		4	0- 1
		BRTR			63	15-24

FROELICH, WILLIAM PALMER "BEN"
B.NOV.12,1887 PITTSBURGH,PA.
D.SEPT.1,1916
| 1909 | PHI | N | C | | 1 | .000 |
| | | TR | | | | |

FROMME, ARTHUR HENRY
B.SEPT.3,1883 QUINCY,ILL.
D.AUG.24,1956
1906	STL	N	P		5	1- 4
1907	STL	N	P		23	5-13
1908	STL	N	P		20	5-13
1909	CIN	N	P		37	19-13
1910	CIN	N	P		11	3- 4
1911	CIN	N	P		38	10-11
1912	CIN	N	P		43	16-19
1913	CIN	N	P		9	1- 4
	NY	N	P		26	11- 6
1914	NY	N	P		38	9- 5
1915	NY	N	P		4	0- 1
		BRTR			254	80-93

FRY, JOHNSON
B.NOV.21,1901 HUNTINGTON,W.VA.
D.APR.7,1959
| 1923 | CLE | A | P | | 1 | 0- 0 |
| | | BRTR | | | | |

FRYE, CHARLES ANDREW
B.JULY 17,1914 HICKORY,N.C.
D.MAY 25,1945
| 1940 | PHI | N | P | 15 | 18 | 0- 6 |
| | | BRTR | | | | |

FRYMAN, WOODROW THOMPSON "WOODY"
B.APR.15,1940 EWING,KY.
1966	PIT	N	P		36	12- 9
1967	PIT	N	P		28	3- 8
1968	PHI	N	P		34	12-14
1969	PHI	N	P		36	12-15
1970	PHI	N	P		27	8- 6
1971	PHI	N	P		37	10- 7
1972	PHI	N	P		23	4-10
	DET	A	P		16	10- 3
1973	DET	A	P		34	6-13
1974	DET	A	P		27	6- 9
1975	MON	N	P		38	9-12
1976	MON	N	P		34	13-13
		BRTL			370	105-119

FUCHS, CHARLES THOMAS
B.NOV.18,1912 UNION CITY,N.J.
1942	DET	A	P		9	3- 3
1943	PHI	N	P		17	2- 7
	STL	A	P		13	0- 0
1944	BRO	N	P		8	1- 0
		BBTR			47	6-10

FUCHS, EMIL EDMUND "JUDGE"
B.APR.17,1878 HAMBURG,GERMANY
D.DEC.5,1961
NON-PLAYING MANAGER BOS(N) 1929

FUENTES, MIGUEL (PINET)
B.MAY 10,1946 LOIZA,P.R.
D.JAN.29,1970 LOIZA,P.R.
| 1969 | SEA | A | P | | 8 | 1- 3 |
| | | BRTR | | | | |

FUENTES, RIGOBERTO (PEAT) "TITO"
B.JAN.4,1944 HAVANA,CUBA
1965	SF	N	2-S-3		26	.208
1966	SF	N	2-S		133	.261
1967	SF	N	2-S		133	.209
1969	SF	N	S-3		67	.295
1970	SF	N	2-S-3		123	.267
1971	SF	N	2		152	.273
1972	SF	N	2		152	.264
1973	SF	N	2-3		160	.277
1974	SF	N	2		108	.249
1975	SD	N	2		146	.280
1976	SD	N	2		135	.263
		BBTR			1335	.264
		BR 1965-67, 70 (PART)				

FUHR, OSCAR LAWRENCE
B.AUG.22,1893 DEFIANCE,OHIO
D.MAR.27,1975 DALLAS,TEX.
1921	CHI	N	P		1	0- 0
1924	BOS	A	P		23	3- 6
1925	BOS	A	P		38	0- 6
		BLTL			62	3-12

YR	CL	LEA	POS	GP	G	REC

FUHRMAN, ALFRED GEORGE "OLLIE"
B.JULY 20,1896 JORDAN,MINN.
D.JAN.11,1969 PEORIA,ILL.
1922 PHI A C 7 .333
BBTR

FULGHUM, JAMES LAVOISIER "DOT"
B.JULY 4,1900 VALDOSTA,GA.
D.NOV.11,1947 MIAMI,FLA.
1921 PHI A S 2 .000
BRTR

FULLER, CHARLES F. "NIG"
1902 BRO N C 3 .000
BRTR

FULLER, EDWARD A.
B.MAR.22,1869 WASHINGTON,D.C.
1886 WAS N P 1 0- 1

FULLER, FRANK EDWARD "RABBIT"
B.JAN.1,1895 DETROIT,MICH.
D.OCT.29,1965 WARREN,MICH.
1915 DET A 2 14 .156
1916 DET A 2 20 .100
1923 BOS A 2 6 .238
BRTR 40 .177

FULLER, HENRY W. "HARRY"
B.DEC.5,1862 CINCINNATI,OHIO
D.DEC.12,1895
1891 STL AA 3 1 .000

FULLER, JAMES HARDY "JIM"
B.NOV.28,1950 BETHESDA,MD.
1973 BAL A 1-0 9 .115
1974 BAL A 1-0 64 .222
BRTR 73 .209

FULLER, JOHN EDWARD
B.JAN.29,1950 LYNWOOD,CAL.
1974 ATL N O 3 .333
BLTL

FULLER, VERN GORDON "VERN"
B.MAR.1,1944 MENOMONIE,WIS.
1964 CLE A H 2 .000
1966 CLE A 2 16 .234
1967 CLE A 2-S 73 .223
1968 CLE A 2-S-3 97 .242
1969 CLE A 2-3 108 .236
1970 CLE A 1-2-3 29 .182
BRTR 325 .232

FULLER, WILLIAM BENJAMIN "SHORTY"
B.OCT.10,1867 CINCINNATI,OHIO
D.APR.11,1904
1888 WAS N S 49 .182
1889 STL AA S 140 .228
1890 STL AA S 130 .271
1891 STL AA 2-S 135 .219
1892 NY N S 138 .236
1893 NY N S 130 .247
1894 NY N S 95 .282
1895 NY N S 126 .227
1896 NY N S 17 .180
BRTR 960 .239

FULLERTON, CURTIS HOOPER
B.SEPT.13,1898 ELLSWORTH,ME.
D.JAN.2,1975 WINTHROP,MASS.
1921 BOS A P 4 0- 1
1922 BOS A P 31 1- 4
1923 BOS A P 37 2-15
1924 BOS A P 33 7-12
1925 BOS A P 4 0- 3
1933 BOS A P 6 0- 2
BLTR 115 10-37

FULLIS, CHARLES PHILIP "CHICK"
B.FEB.27,1904 GIRARDVILLE,PA.
D.MAR.28,1946
1928 NY N O 11 .000
1929 NY N O 86 .288
1930 NY N O 13 .000
1931 NY N O 89 .328
1932 NY N O 96 .298
1933 PHI N 3-O 151 .309
1934 PHI N O 28 .225
STL N O 69 .261
1936 STL N O 47 .281
BRTR 590 .295

FULMER, CHARLES J.
B.FEB.13,1851 PHILADELPHIA,PA.
D.FEB.15,1940
1871 ROK NA 1-S 16 -
1872 MUT NA S-3 36 .302
1873 PHI NA C-S 49 -
1874 PHI NA S-3 57 -
1875 PHI NA S-3 68 .222
1876 LOU N M-S 66 .272
1879 BUF N 2 75 .266
1880 BUF N 2 11 .152
1882 CIN AA M-S 79 .277
1883 CIN AA S 82 .247
1884 CIN AA S-3-0 30 .177
STL AA 2 1 .000
TR 570 -

FULMER, CHRISTOPHER
B.JULY 4,1858 TAMAQUA,PA.
D.NOV.9,1931 TAMAQUA,PA.
1875 ATL NA O 1 .500
1884 WAS U C-1-0 47 .282
1886 BAL AA C 79 .251
1887 BAL AA C 56 .368
1888 BAL AA C 51 .179
1889 BAL AA C 16 .278
250 .275

FULTZ, DAVID LEWIS
B.MAY 29,1875 STAUNTON,VA.
D.OCT.30,1959
1898 PHI N O 16 .196
1899 PHI N S-3 2 .400
BAL N 3-O 54 .304
1901 PHI A 2-O 132 .295
1902 PHI A 2 O 129 .300
1903 NY A O 78 .240
1904 NY A O 96 .278
1905 NY A O 122 .332
BRTR 629 .275

FUNK, ELIAS CALVIN "LIZ"
B.OCT.28,1904 LA CYGNE,KAN.
D.JAN.16,1968 NORMAN,OKLA.
1929 NY A H 1 .000
1930 DET A O 140 .275
1932 CHI A O 122 .259
1933 CHI A O 10 .222
BLTL 273 .267

FUNK, FRANKLIN RAY "FRANK"
B.AUG.30,1935 WASHINGTON,D.C.
1960 CLE A P 9 4- 2
1961 CLE A P 56 11-11
1962 CLE A P 47 2- 1
1963 MIL N P 25 26 3- 3
BRTR 137 138 20-17

FUNKHOUSER, LEONIDAS P.
(PLAYED UNDER NAME OF
LEONIDAS P. LEE)

FURILLO, CARL ANTHONY "CARL" OR "ROCKY"
B.MAR.8,1922 STONY CREEK MILLS, PA.
1946 BRO N O 117 .284
1947 BRO N O 124 .295
1948 BRO N O 108 .297
1949 BRO N O 142 .324
1950 BRO N O 153 .305
1951 BRO N O 158 .295
1952 BRO N O 134 .247
1953 BRO N O 132 .344
1954 BRO N O 150 .294
1955 BRO N O 140 .314
1956 BRO N O 149 .289
1957 BRO N O 119 .306
1958 LA N O 122 .290
1959 LA N O 50 .290
1960 LA N O 8 .200
BRTR 1806 .299

FURNISS, THOMAS
B.CONNECTICUT
NON-PLAYING MANAGER BOS(U) 1884

FUSSELBACH, EDWARD L.
B.JULY 4,1858 PHILADELPHIA,PA.
1882 STL AA P-C- 2 35 0- 2
O .219
1884 BAL U C 65 .286
1885 ATH AA C 5 .316
1888 LOU AA O 1 .250
2 106 0- 2
.267

FUSSELL, FREDERICK MORRIS
B.OCT.7,1897 SHERIDAN,MO.
D.OCT.23,1966 SYRACUSE,N.Y.
1922 CHI N P 3 1- 1
1923 CHI N P 28 3- 5
1928 PIT N P 28 8- 9
1929 PIT N P 21 2- 2
BLTL 80 14-17

FUSSELMAN, LESTER LEROY
B.MAR.7,1921 PRYOR,OKLA.
D.MAY 21,1970 CLEVELAND,OHIO
1952 STL N C 32 .159
1953 STL N C 11 .250
BRTR 43 .169

GABLER, FRANK HAROLD "GABBO"
B.NOV.6,1911 E.HIGHLANDS,CAL.
D.NOV.1,1967 LONG BEACH,CA6.
1935 NY N P 26 2- 1
1936 NY N P 43 9- 8
1937 NY N P 6 0- 0
BOS N P 19 4- 7
1938 BOS N P 1 0- 0
CHI A P 18 1- 7
BRTR 113 16-23

GABLER, JOHN RICHARD
B.OCT.2,1930 KANSAS CITY,MO.
1959 NY A P 3 1- 1
1960 NY A P 21 3- 3
1961 WAS A P 29 34 3- 8
BBTR 53 58 7-12

GABLER, WILLIAM LOUIS
B.AUG.4,1931 ST.LOUIS,MO.
1958 CHI N H 3 .000
BLTR

GABLES, KENNETH HARLIN
B.JAN.31,1919 WALNUT GROVE,MO.
D.JAN.2,1960
1945 PIT N P 29 11- 7
1946 PIT N P 32 2- 4
1947 PIT N P 1 0- 0
BRTR 62 13-11

GABRIELSON, LEONARD GARY "LEN"
B.FEB.14,1940 OAKLAND,CAL.
1960 MIL N O 4 .000
1963 MIL N 1-3-0 46 .217
1964 MIL N 1-O 24 .184
CHI N 1-O 89 .246
1965 CHI N 1-O 28 .250
SF N 1-O 80 .301
1966 SF N 1-O 94 .217
1967 CAL A O 11 .083
LA N O 90 .261
1968 LA N O 108 .270
1969 LA N 1-O 83 .270
1970 LA N 1-O 43 .190
BLTR 708 .253

GABRIELSON, LEONARD HILBOURNE
B.SEPT.8,1916 OAKLAND,CAL.
1939 PHI N 1 5 .222
BLTL

GADDY, JOHN WILSON
B.FEB.5,1916 WADESBORO,N.C.
1938 BRO N P 2 2- 0
BRTR

GAEDEL, EDWARD CARL "EDDIE"
B.JUNE 8,1925 CHICAGO,ILL.
D.JUNE 19,1961
1951 STL A H 1 .000
BR

GAFFKE, FABIAN SEBASTIAN
B.AUG.5,1913 MILWAUKEE,WIS.
1936 BOS A O 15 .127
1937 BOS A O 54 .288
1938 BOS A C-O 15 .100
1939 BOS A O 1 .000
1941 CLE A O 4 .250
1942 CLE A O 40 .164
BRTR 129 .227

GAFFNEY, JOHN H.
B.JUNE 29,1855 ROXBURY,MASS.
D.AUG.8,1913 NEW YORK,N.Y.
NON-PLAYING MANAGER
WAS(N) 1886-87

YR	CL	LEA	POS	GP	G	REC

GAGLIANO, PHILIP JOSEPH "PHIL"
B.DEC.27,1941 MEMPHIS,TENN.

YR	CL	LEA	POS	G	REC
1963	STL	N	2-3	10	.400
1964	STL	N	1-2-3-0	40	.259
1965	STL	N	2-3-0	122	.240
1966	STL	N	1-2-3-0	90	.254
1967	STL	N	1-2-S-3	73	.221
1968	STL	N	2-3-0	53	.229
1969	STL	N	1-2-3-0	62	.227
1970	STL	N	1-2-3	18	.188
	CHI	N	1-2-3	26	.150
1971	BOS	A	2-3-0	47	.324
1972	BOS	A	1-2-3-0	52	.256
1973	CIN	N	1-2-3-0	63	.290
1974	CIN	N	1-2-3	46	.065
		BRTR		702	.238

GAGLIANO, RALPH MICHAEL
B.OCT.8,1946 MEMPHIS,TENN.

YR	CL	LEA	POS	G	REC
1965	CLE	A	R	1	.000
		BLTR			

GAGNIER, EDWARD J.
B.APR.16,1883 PARIS,FRANCE
D.SEPT.13,1946

YR	CL	LEA	POS	G	REC
1914	BRO	F	S	94	.182
1915	BRO	F	2	19	.260
	BUF	F	2	2	.000
		BRTR		115	.191

GAGNON, HAROLD DENNIS "CHICK"
B.SEPT.27,1897 MILLBURY,MASS.
D.APR.30,1970 WILMINGTON,DEL.

YR	CL	LEA	POS	G	REC
1922	DET	A	S	9	.250
1924	WAS	A	S	4	.200
		BRTR		13	.222

GAGUS, CHARLES
B.SAN FRANCISO,CAL.

YR	CL	LEA	POS	G	REC
1884	WAS	U	P-S-O	42	11- 9
					.240

GAINER, DELLOS CLINTON
"DEL" OR "SHERIFF"
B.NOV.10,1886 MONTROSE,W.VA.
D.JAN.29,1947

YR	CL	LEA	POS	G	REC
1909	DET	A	1	2	.200
1911	DET	A	1	70	.302
1912	DET	A	1	51	.240
1913	DET	A	1	104	.270
1914	DET	A	1	1	.000
	BOS	A	1	38	.238
1915	BOS	A	1	82	.295
1916	BOS	A	1	56	.253
1917	BOS	A	1	52	.308
1919	BOS	A	1-0	47	.237
1922	STL	N	1-0	43	.268
		BRTR		546	.273

GAINES, ARNESTA JOE
"JOE"
B.NOV.22,1936 BRYAN,TEX.

YR	CL	LEA	POS	G	REC
1960	CIN	N	0	11	.200
1961	CIN	N	0	5	.000
1962	CIN	N	0	64	.231
1963	BAL	A	0	66	.286
1964	BAL	A	0	16	.154
	HOU	N	0	89	.254
1965	HOU	N	0	100	.227
1966	HOU	N	0	11	.077
		BRTR		362	.241

GAINES, WILLARD ROLAND "NEMO"
B.DEC.23,1897 FAIRFAX CO.,VA.

YR	CL	LEA	POS	G	REC
1921	WAS	A	P	4	0- 0
		BLTL			

GAISER, FREDERICK JACOB
B.AUG.31,1885 STUTTGART,GERMANY
D.OCT.9,1918 TRENTON,N.J.

YR	CL	LEA	POS	G	REC
1938	STL	N	P	1	0- 0

GALAN, AUGUST JOHN "AUGIE"
B.MAY 25,1912 BERKELEY,CAL.

YR	CL	LEA	POS	G	REC
1934	CHI	N	2	66	.260
1935	CHI	N	0	154	.314
1936	CHI	N	0	145	.264
1937	CHI	N	0	147	.252
1938	CHI	N	0	110	.286
1939	CHI	N	0	148	.304
1940	CHI	N	2-0	68	.230
1941	CHI	N	0	65	.208
	BRO	N	0	17	.259
1942	BRO	N	1-2-0	69	.263
1943	BRO	N	1-0	139	.287
1944	BRO	N	2-0	151	.318
1945	BRO	N	1-3-0	152	.307
1946	BRO	N	1-3-0	99	.310
1947	CIN	N	0	124	.314
1948	CIN	N	0	54	.286
1949	NY	N	1-0	22	.059
	PHI	A	0	12	.308
		BBTR		1742	.287
		BL 1944-49			

GALATZER, MILTON "MILT"
B.MAY 4,1907 CHICAGO,IL..
D.JAN.29,1976 SAN FRANCISCO,CAL

YR	CL	LEA	POS	GP	G	REC
1933	CLE	A	1-0		57	.238
1934	CLE	A	0		49	.270
1935	CLE	A	0		93	.301
1936	CLE	A	P-0	1	49	0- 0
						.237
1939	CIN	N	1		3	.000
		BLTL		1	251	0- 0
						.268

GALAZEWSKI, STANLEY JOSEPH
(PLAYED UNDER NAME OF
STANLEY JOSEPH GALLE)

GALEHOUSE, DENNIS WARD "DENNY"
B.DEC.7,1911 MARSHALLVILLE,OHIO

YR	CL	LEA	POS	G	REC
1934	CLE	A	P	1	0- 0
1935	CLE	A	P	5	1- 0
1936	CLE	A	P	36	8- 7
1937	CLE	A	P	36	9-14
1938	CLE	A	P	36	7- 8
1939	BOS	A	P	30	9-10
1940	BOS	A	P	25	6- 6
1941	STL	A	P	30	9-10
1942	STL	A	P	32	12-12
1943	STL	A	P	31	11-11
1944	STL	A	P	24	9-10
1946	STL	A	P	30	8-12
1947	STL	A	P	9	1- 3
	BOS	A	P	21	11- 7
1948	BOS	A	P	27	8- 8
1949	BOS	A	P	2	0- 0
		BRTR		375	109-118

GALLAGHER, ALAN MITCHELL EDWARD
GEORGE PATRICK HENRY "AL"
B.OCT.19,1945 SAN FRANCISCO,CAL.

YR	CL	LEA	POS	G	REC
1970	SF	N	3	109	.266
1971	SF	N	3	136	.277
1972	SF	N	3	82	.223
1973	SF	N	0	5	.222
	CAL	A	2-S-3	110	.273
		BRTR		442	.263

GALLAGHER, D. F.

YR	CL	LEA	POS	G	REC
1901	CLE	A	0	2	.000

GALLAGHER, DOUGLAS EUGENE
B.FEB.21,1940 FREMONT,OHIO

YR	CL	LEA	POS	G	REC
1962	DET	A	P	9	0- 4
		BRTL			

GALLAGHER, EDWARD JOHN "JACKIE"
B.JULY 23,1903 PROVIDENCE,R.I.

YR	CL	LEA	POS	G	REC
1923	CLE	A	0	1	1.000
		BLTR			

GALLAGHER, EDWARD MICHAEL
"LEFTY"
B.NOV.28,1910 DORCHESTER,MASS.

YR	CL	LEA	POS	G	REC
1932	BOS	A	P	9	0- 3
		BBTL			

GALLAGHER, JAMES E.
B.FINDLAY,OHIO
D.MAR.29,1894

YR	CL	LEA	POS	G	REC
1886	WAS	N	S	1	.200

GALLAGHER, JOHN C.
B.1894 PITTSBURGH,PA.

YR	CL	LEA	POS	G	REC
1915	BAL	F	2	40	.200
		BRTR			

GALLAGHER, JOSEPH EMMETT
"MUSCLES"
B.MAR.7,1914 BUFFALO,N.Y.

YR	CL	LEA	POS	G	REC
1939	NY	A	0	14	.244
	STL	A	0	71	.282
1940	STL	A	0	23	.271
	BRO	N	0	57	.264
		BRTR		165	.273

GALLAGHER, LAWRENCE KIRBY "GIL"
B.SEPT.5,1896 WASHINGTON,D.C.
D.JAN.6,1957

YR	CL	LEA	POS	G	REC
1922	BOS	N	S	7	.045
		BBTR			

GALLAGHER, ROBERT COLLINS "BOB"
B.JULY 7,1948 NEWTON,MASS.

YR	CL	LEA	POS	G	REC
1972	BOS	A	H	7	.000
1973	HOU	N	1-0	71	.264
1974	HOU	N	1-0	102	.172
1975	NY	N	0	33	.133
		BLTL		213	.220

GALLAGHER, WILLIAM H.
B.1875 LOWELL,MASS.

YR	CL	LEA	POS	G	REC
1896	PHI	N	S	14	.327

GALLAGHER, WILLIAM JOHN
B.PHILADELPHIA,PA.

YR	CL	LEA	POS	GP	G	REC
1883	BAL	AA	P-S-3	6	16	0- 3
			O			.159
	PHI	N	0		2	.000
1884	KEY	U	P		3	1- 2
	TL			9	21	1- 5
						.133

GALLE, STANLEY JOSEPH
(REAL NAME
STANLEY JOSEPH GALAZEWSKI)
B.FEB.7,1919 MILWAUKEE,WIS.

YR	CL	LEA	POS	G	REC
1942	WAS	A	3	13	.111
		BRTR			

GALLIA, MELVIN ALLYS "BERT"
B.OCT.14,1891 BEEVILLE,TEX.

YR	CL	LEA	POS	GP	G	REC
1912	WAS	A	P		2	0- 0
1913	WAS	A	P		30	1- 5
1914	WAS	A	P		2	0- 0
1915	WAS	A	P		43	16-10
1916	WAS	A	P		49	17-13
1917	WAS	A	P	42	44	9-13
1918	STL	A	P		19	7- 6
1919	STL	A	P		34	12-14
1920	STL	A	P		2	0- 1
	PHI	N	P	18	19	2- 6
		BRTR		241	244	64-68

GALLIGAN, JOHN T.
B.1868 EASTON,PA.
D.JULY 17,1906

YR	CL	LEA	POS	G	REC
1889	LOU	AA	0	31	.167

GALLIVAN, PHILIP JOSEPH
B.MAY 29,1907 SEATTLE,WASH.
D.NOV.24,1969 ST.PAUL,MINN.

YR	CL	LEA	POS	G	REC
1931	BRO	N	P	6	0- 1
1932	CHI	N	P	13	1- 3
1934	CHI	N	P	35	4- 7
		BRTR		54	5-11

GALLOWAY, CLARENCE EDWARD
"CHICK"
B.AUG.4,1896 CLINTON,S.C.
D.NOV.7,1969 CLINTON,S.C.

YR	CL	LEA	POS	G	REC
1919	PHI	A	S	17	.143
1920	PHI	A	S	98	.202
1921	PHI	A	S-3	131	.265
1922	PHI	A	S	155	.324
1923	PHI	A	S	134	.278
1924	PHI	A	S	129	.276
1925	PHI	A	S	149	.241
1926	PHI	A	S	133	.240
1927	PHI	A	S	77	.265
1928	DET	A	S-3	53	.264
		BRTR		1076	.264

GALLOWAY, JAMES CATO "BAD NEWS"
B.SEPT.16,1887 IREDELL,TEX.
D.MAY 3,1950

YR	CL	LEA	POS	G	REC
1912	STL	N	2	21	.185
		BBTR			

YR	CL	LEA	POS	GP	G	REC

GALVIN, JAMES F. "PUD"
B.DEC.25,1856 ST.LOUIS,MO.
D.MAR.7,1902 PITTSBURGH,PA.

1875	STL	NA	P-O	6	11	4- 2
						.146
1879	BUF	N	P	65	66	37-27
1880	BUF	N	P-O	55	64	20-34
						.211
1881	BUF	N	P-O	53	62	29-24
						.211
1882	BUF	N	P-O		54	28-22
						.213
1883	BUF	N	P-O	73	79	44-29
						.220
1884	BUF	N	P		68	46-21
1885	BUF	N	M-P		32	12-19
	PIT	AA	P-O		11	3- 8
						.108
1886	PIT	AA	P		50	29-21
1887	PIT	N	P		49	28-20
1888	PIT	N	P		50	23-25
1889	PIT	N	P		40	23-17
1890	PIT	P	P		26	11-14
1891	PIT	N	P		28	15-13
1892	PIT	N	P		11	5- 6
	STL	N	P		15	5- 6
	BRTR			686	716	362-308
						.203

GALVIN, JAMES JOSEPH
B.AUG.11,1907 SOMERVILLE,MASS.

| 1930 | BOS | N | H | | 2 | .000 |
| | BRTR | | | | | |

GALVIN, JOHN
B.BRROKLYN,N.Y.
D.MAY 1904

1872	ATL	NA	2		1	.000
1874	ATL	NA	2		1	.000
					2	.000

GALVIN, LOUIS
B.HAVERILL,MASS.
D.JUNE 17,1895

| 1884 | STP | U | P | | 3 | 0- 2 |

GAMBLE, JOHN ROBERT
B.FEB.10,1948 RENO,NEV.

1972	DET	A	S		6	.000
1973	DET	A	R		7	.000
	BRTR				13	.000

GAMBLE, LEE JESSE
B.JUNE 28,1910 RENOVO,PA.

1935	CIN	N	O		2	.500
1938	CIN	N	O		53	.320
1939	CIN	N	O		72	.267
1940	CIN	N	O		38	.143
	BLTR				165	.266

GAMBLE, OSCAR CHARLES
B.DEC.20,1949 RAMER,ALA.

1969	CHI	N	O		24	.225
1970	PHI	N	O		88	.262
1971	PHI	N	O		92	.221
1972	PHI	N	1-O		74	.237
1973	CLE	A	O-D		113	.267
1974	CLE	A	O-D		135	.291
1975	CLE	A	O-D		121	.261
1976	NY	A	O		110	.232
	BLTR				757	.256

GAMBLE, ROBERT
B.1867 HAZELTON,PA.

| 1888 | ATH | AA | P | | 1 | 0- 1 |

GAMMON, JOHN FRANCIS
(PLAYED UNDER NAME OF
JOHN FRANCIS SMITH)

GAMMONS, JOHN ASHLEY "DAFF"
B.MAR.17,1876 NEW BEDFORD,MASS.
D.SEPT.24,1963 E.GREENWICH,R.I.

| 1901 | BOS | N | O | | 26 | .211 |

GANDIL, CHARLES ARNOLD "CHICK"
B.JAN.19,1887 ST.PAUL,MINN.
D.DEC.13,1970 CALISTOGA,CAL.

1910	CHI	A	1		77	.193
1912	WAS	A	1		117	.305
1913	WAS	A	1		147	.318
1914	WAS	A	1		145	.259
1915	WAS	A	1		136	.291
1916	CLE	A	1		146	.259
1917	CHI	A	1		149	.273
1918	CHI	A	1		114	.271
1919	CHI	A	1		115	.290
	BRTR				1146	.276

GANDY, ROBERT BRINKLEY
B.AUG.25,1893 JACKSONVILLE,FLA.
D.JUNE 19,1945

| 1916 | PHI | N | O | | 1 | .000 |
| | BLTR | | | | | |

GANLEY, ROBERT STEPHEN
B.APR.23,1875 LOWELL,MASS.
D.OCT.10,1945

1905	PIT	N	O		32	.315
1906	PIT	N	O		134	.258
1907	WAS	A	O		154	.276
1908	WAS	A	O		150	.239
1909	WAS	A	O		16	.209
	PHI	A	O		83	.207
	BLTL				569	.254

GANNON, JAMES EDWARD "GUSSIE"
B.NOV.26,1873 ERIE,PA.
D.APR.12,1966 ERIE,PA.

| 1895 | PIT | N | P | | 1 | 0- 0 |

GANNON, WILLIAM G.
B.NEW HAVEN,CONN.
D.APR.26,1927 FT.WORTH,TEX.

1898	STL	N	P		1	0- 1
1901	CHI	N	O		15	.159
				1	16	0- 1
						.167

GANTENBEIN, JOSEPH STEPHEN "SEP"
B.AUG.25,1916 SAN FRANCISCO,CAL

1939	PHI	A	2-3		111	.290
1940	PHI	A	1-S-3-O		75	.239
	BLTR				186	.272

GANTNER, JAMES ELMER "JIM"
B.JAN.5,1954 FOND DU LAC,WIS.

| 1976 | MIL | A | 3 | | 26 | .246 |
| | BLTR | | | | | |

GANZEL, CHARLES WILLIAM
B.JUNE 18,1862 WATERFORD,WIS.
D.APR.7,1914

1884	STP	U	C-O		7	.208
1885	PHI	N	C-O		33	.168
1886	PHI	N	C		1	.000
	DET	N	L		53	.276
1887	DET	N	C		55	.285
1888	DET	N	C-2		93	.248
1889	BOS	N	C-O		71	.265
1890	BOS	N	C		38	.269
1891	BOS	N	C		68	.259
1892	BOS	N	C		51	.270
1893	BOS	N	C-O		69	.282
1894	BOS	N	C		65	.278
1895	BOS	N	C		74	.265
1896	BOS	N	C		44	.262
1897	BOS	N	C		27	.274
	BRTR				749	.264

GANZEL, FOSTER PERE "BABE"
B.MAY 23,1901 MALDEN,MASS.

1927	WAS	A	O		13	.437
1928	WAS	A	O		10	.077
	BRTR				23	.311

GANZEL, JOHN HENRY
B.APR.7,1874 KALAMAZOO,MICH.
D.JAN.14,1959

1898	PIT	N	1		14	.111
1900	CHI	N	1		78	.272
1901	NY	N	1		139	.220
1903	NY	N	1		129	.285
1904	NY	A	1		129	.261
1907	CIN	N	1		143	.254
1908	CIN	N	M-1		108	.250
	BRTR				740	.253

NON-PLAYING MANAGER BRO(F) 1915

GARAGIOLA, JOSEPH HENRY "JOE"
B.FEB.12,1926 ST.LOUIS,MO.

1946	STL	N	C		74	.237
1947	STL	N	C		77	.257
1948	STL	N	C		24	.107
1949	STL	N	C		81	.261
1950	STL	N	C		34	.318
1951	STL	N	C		27	.194
	PIT	N	C		72	.255
1952	PIT	N	C		118	.273
1953	PIT	N	C		27	.233
	CHI	N	C		74	.272
1954	CHI	N	C		63	.281
	NY	N	C		5	.273
	BLTR				676	.257

GARBACH, NATHANIEL MICHAEL
(PLAYED UNDER NAME OF
NATHANIEL MICHAEL GARBARK)

GARBACH, ROBERT MICHAEL
(PLAYED UNDER NAME OF
ROBERT MICHAEL GARBARK)

GARBARK, NATHANIEL MICHAEL
(REAL NAME
NATHANIEL MICHAEL GARBACH)
B.FEB.3,1916 HOUSTON,TEX.

1944	NY	A	C		89	.261
1945	NY	A	C		60	.216
	BRTR				149	.244

GARBARK, ROBERT MICHAEL
(REAL NAME
ROBERT MICHAEL GARBACH)
D.NOV.13,1909 HOUSTON,TEX.

1934	CLE	A	C		5	.000
1935	CLE	A	C		6	.333
1937	CHI	N	C		1	.000
1938	CHI	N	C		23	.259
1939	CHI	N	C		24	.143
1944	PHI	A	C		18	.261
1945	BOS	A	C		68	.261
	BRTR				145	.248

GARBER, HENRY EUGENE "GENE"
B.NOV.13,1947 LANCASTER,PA.

1969	PIT	N	P		2	0- 0
1970	PIT	N	P		14	0- 3
1972	PIT	N	P		4	0- 0
1973	KC	A	P	48	49	9- 9
1974	KC	A	P		17	1- 2
	PHI	N	P		34	4- 0
1975	PHI	N	P		71	10-12
1976	PHI	N	P		59	9- 3
	BRTR			249	250	33-29

GARDER, ROBERT MITCHELL
B.SEPT.10,1928 HUNKERS,PA.

| 1956 | PIT | N | P | | 2 | 0- 0 |
| | BRTR | | | | | |

GARBOWSKI, ALEXANDER
B.JUNE 25,1925 YONKERS,N.Y

| 1952 | DET | A | H | | 2 | .000 |
| | BRTR | | | | | |

GARCIA, ALFONSO RAFAEL "KIKO"
B.OCT.14,1953 MARTINEZ,CAL.

| 1976 | BAL | A | S | | 11 | .219 |
| | BRTR | | | | | |

GARCIA, EDWARD MIGUEL "MIKE"
B.NOV.17,1923 SAN GABRIEL,CAL.

1948	CLE	A	P		1	0- 0
1949	CLE	A	P		41	14- 5
1950	CLE	A	P		33	11-11
1951	CLE	A	P		47	20-13
1952	CLE	A	P		46	22-11
1953	CLE	A	P		38	18- 9
1954	CLE	A	P		45	19- 8
1955	CLE	A	P		38	11-13
1956	CLE	A	P		35	11-12
1957	CLE	A	P		38	12- 8
1958	CLE	A	P		6	1- 0
1959	CLE	A	P		29	3- 6
1960	CHI	A	P		15	0- 0
1961	WAS	A	P		16	0- 1
	BRTR			428	142-97

YR	CL	LEA	POS	GP	G	REC

GARCIA, PEDRO MODESTO (DELFI)
B.APR.17,1950 GUAYAMA,P.R.
1973	MIL	A	2		160	.245
1974	MIL	A	2		141	.199
1975	MIL	A	2		98	.225
1976	MIL	A	2		41	.217
	DET	A	2		77	.198
	BRTR				517	.221

GARCIA, RALPH
B.DEC.14,1948 LOS ANGELES,CAL.
1972	SD	N	P		3	0- 0
1974	SD	N	P		8	0- 0
	BRTR				11	0- 0

GARCIA, RAMON GARCIA
B.MAR.5,1924 LA ESPERANZA,CUBA
| 1948 | WAS | A | P | | 4 | 0- 0 |
| | BRTR | | | | | |

GARCIA, VINICIO UZGANGA "CHICO"
B.DEC.13,1928 VERA CRUZ,MEXICO
| 1954 | BAL | A | 2 | | 39 | .113 |
| | BRTR | | | | | |

GARDELLA, ALFRED STEVE "AL"
B.JAN.11,1918 NEW YORK,N.Y.
| 1945 | NY | N | 1-0 | | 17 | .077 |
| | BLTL | | | | | |

GARDELLA, DANIEL LEWIS "DANNY"
B.FEB.26,1920 NEW YORK,N.Y.
1944	NY	N	O		47	.250
1945	NY	N	1-0		121	.272
1950	STL	N	H		1	.000
	BLTL				169	.268

GARDINER, ARTHUR CECIL
B.DEC.26,1899 BROOKLYN,N.Y.
| 1923 | PHI | N | P | | 1 | 0- 0 |
| | BRTR | | | | | |

GARDNER, ALEXANDER
B.APR.28,1861 TORONTO,ONT.,CAN.
D.JUNE 18,1926
| 1884 | WAS | AA | C | | 1 | .000 |

GARDNER, ARTHUR JUNIOR "ART"
B.SEPT.21,1952 MADDEN,MISS.
| 1975 | HOU | N | P | | 13 | .194 |
| | BLTL | | | | | |

GARDNER, EARL M.
B.JAN.24,1885 SPARTA,ILL.
D.MAR.2,1943
1908	NY	A	2		20	.213
1909	NY	A	2		22	.329
1910	NY	A	2		86	.244
1911	NY	A	2		102	.263
1912	NY	A	2		43	.281
	BRTR				273	.263

GARDNER, FRANKLIN W. "GID"
B.AUG.1,1859 E.CAMBRIDGE,MASS.
D.AUG.1,1914
1879	TRO	N	P		2	0- 2
1880	CLE	N	P-0	9	10	2- 7
						.200
1883	BAL	AA	P-2-	1	42	1- 0
			3-0			.290
1884	BAL	AA	O		41	.203
	CHI	U	P-3-	1	20	0- 0
			O			.173
	PIT	U	2-0		16	.254
	BAL	U	S		1	.250
1885	BAL	AA	P-2	1	44	0- 1
						.219
1887	IND	N	2-0		18	.306
1888	WAS	N	2		2	.200
				14	196	3-10
						.238

GARDNER, FREDERICK
B.PALMER,MASS.
| 1887 | BAL | AA | P | | 4 | 0- 1 |

GARDNER, GLENN MILESO
B.JAN.25,1916 BURNSVILLE,N.C.
D.JULY 7,1964 ROCHESTER,N.Y.
| 1945 | STL | N | P | | 17 | 3- 1 |
| | BRTR | | | | | |

GARDNER, HARRY
B.SEPT.20,1888 PORTLAND,ORE.
D.AUG.2,1961
1911	PIT	N	P		13	1- 1
1912	PIT	N	P		1	0- 0
			TR		14	1- 1

GARDNER, JAMES ANDERSON
B.OCT.4,1874 PITTSBURGH,PA.
D.APR.24,1905
1895	PIT	N	P		10	8- 2
1897	PIT	N	P		28	5- 5
1898	PIT	N	P		32	10-13
1899	PIT	N	P		7	1- 1
1902	CHI	N	P		3	1- 2
			TR		80	25-23

GARDNER, RAYMOND VINCENT
B.OCT.25,1901 FREDERICK,MD.
D.MAY 3,1968 FREDERICK,MD.
1929	CLE	A	S		82	.262
1930	CLE	A	S		33	.077
	BRTR				115	.253

GARDNER, RICHARD FRANK "ROB"
B.DEC.19,1944 BINGHAMTON,N.Y.
1965	NY	N	P		5	0- 2
1966	NY	N	P	41	43	4- 8
1967	CHI	N	P		18	0- 2
1968	CLE	A	P		5	0- 0
1970	NY	A	P		1	1- 0
1971	OAK	A	P		4	0- 0
	NY	A	P		2	0- 0
1972	OAK	A	P		20	8- 5
1973	OAK	A	P		3	0- 0
	MIL	A	P		10	1- 1
	BRTL			109	111	14-18

GARDNER, WILLIAM FREDERICK "BILLY"
B.JULY 19,1927 NEW LONDON,CONN.
1954	NY	N	2-S-3		62	.213
1955	NY	N	2-S-3		59	.203
1956	BAL	A	2-S-3		144	.231
1957	BAL	A	2-S		154	.262
1958	BAL	A	2-S		151	.225
1959	BAL	A	2-S-3		140	.217
1960	WAS	A	2-S		145	.257
1961	MIN	A	2-3		45	.234
	NY	A	2-3		41	.212
1962	NY	A	2-3		4	.000
	BOS	A	2-S-3		53	.271
1963	BOS	A	2-3		36	.190
	BRTR				1034	.237

GARDNER, WILLIAM LAWRENCE "LARRY"
B.MAY 13,1886 ENOSBURG FALLS,VT
D.MAR.12,1976 ST.GEORGE,VT.
1908	BOS	A	3		3	.300
1909	BOS	A	3		19	.297
1910	BOS	A	2		113	.283
1911	BOS	A	2-3		138	.284
1912	BOS	A	3		143	.315
1913	BOS	A	3		131	.282
1914	BOS	A	3		155	.259
1915	BOS	A	3		127	.258
1916	BOS	A	3		148	.308
1917	BOS	A	3		146	.265
1918	PHI	A	3		127	.285
1919	CLE	A	3		139	.300
1920	CLE	A	3		154	.310
1921	CLE	A	3		153	.319
1922	CLE	A	3		137	.285
1923	CLE	A	3		52	.253
1924	CLE	A	3		38	.200
	BLTR				1923	.289

GARFIELD, WILLIAM MILTON
B.OCT.26,1867 ELYRIA,OHIO
D.DEC.16,1941
1889	PIT	N	P		4	0- 2
1890	CLE	N	P		8	1- 7
			TR		12	1- 9

GARIBALDI, ARHUR E.
B.AUG.21,1909 SAN FRANCISCO,CAL
D.OCT.20,1967 SACRAMENTO,CAL.
| 1936 | STL | N | 2-3 | | 71 | .276 |
| | BRTR | | | | | |

GARIBALDI, ROBERT ROY "BOB"
B.MAR.3,1942 STOCKTON,CAL.
1962	SF	N	P		9	0- 0
1963	SF	N	P		4	0- 1
1966	SF	N	P		1	0- 0
1969	SF	N	P		1	0- 1
	BLTR				15	0- 2

GARLAND, LOUIS LYMAN
B.JULY 16,1905 ARCHIE,MO.
| 1931 | CHI | A | P | | 7 | 0- 2 |
| | BRTR | | | | | |

GARLAND, MARCUS WAYNE "WAYNE"
B.OCT.26,1950 NASHVILLE,TENN.
1973	BAL	A	P		4	0- 1
1974	BAL	A	P		20	5- 5
1975	BAL	A	P		29	2- 5
1976	BAL	A	P		38	20- 7
	BRTR				91	27-18

GARMAN, MICHAEL DOUGLAS "MIKE"
B.SEP.16,1949 CALDWELL,IDAHO
1969	BOS	A	P		2	1- 0
1971	BOS	A	P		3	1- 1
1972	BOS	A	P		3	0- 1
1973	BOS	A	P		12	0- 0
1974	STL	N	P		64	7- 2
1975	STL	N	P		66	3- 8
1976	CHI	N	P		47	2- 4
	BRTR				197	14-16

GARMS, DEBS C. "TEX"
B.JUNE 26,1908 BANGS,TEX.
1932	STL	A	O		34	.284
1933	STL	A	O		78	.317
1934	STL	A	O		91	.293
1935	STL	A	O		10	.267
1937	BOS	N	3-0		125	.259
1938	BOS	N	3-0		117	.315
1939	BOS	N	3-0		132	.298
1940	PIT	N	3-0		103	.355
1941	PIT	N	3-0		83	.264
1943	STL	N	S-3-0		90	.257
1944	STL	N	3-0		73	.301
1945	STL	N	3-0		74	.336
	BLTR				1010	.293

GARNER, PHILIP MASON "PHIL"
B.APR.30,1949 JEFFERSON CITY, TENN.
1973	OAK	A	3		9	.000
1974	OAK	A	2-S-3		30	.179
1975	OAK	A	2-S		160	.246
1976	OAK	A	2		159	.261
	BRTR				358	.251

GARONI, WILLIAM
B.JULY 28,1877 FT.LEE,N.J.
D.SEPT.9,1914
| 1899 | NY | N | P | | 3 | 0- 1 |

GARR, RALPH ALLEN
B.DEC.12,1945 RUSTON,LA.
1968	ATL	N	H		11	.286
1969	ATL	N	O		22	.222
1970	ATL	N	O		37	.281
1971	ATL	N	O		154	.343
1972	ATL	N	O		134	.325
1973	ATL	N	O		148	.299
1974	ATL	N	O		143	.353
1975	ATL	N	O		151	.278
1976	CHI	A	O		136	.300
	BLTR				936	.315

GARRETT, CLARENCE RAYMOND
B.MAR.6,1891 READER,W.VA.
| 1915 | CLE | A | P | | 4 | 2- 2 |
| | BRTR | | | | | |

GARRETT, GREGORY "GREG"
B.MAR.12,1948 ATASCADERO,CAL.
1970	CAL	A	P		32	5- 6
1971	CIN	N	P		2	0- 1
	BBTL				34	5- 7

YR	CL	LEA	POS	GP	G	REC

GARRETT, HENRY ADRIAN "ADE"
B.JAN.3,1943 BROOKSVILLE,FLA.

YR	CL	LEA	POS	GP	G	REC
1966	ATL	N	O		4	.000
1970	CHI	N	H		3	.000
1971	OAK	A	O		14	.143
1972	OAK	A	O		14	.000
1973	CHI	N	C-O		36	.222
1974	CHI	N	C-1-O		10	.000
1975	CHI	N	1		16	.095
	CAL	A	C-1-O-O		37	.262
1976	CAL	A	C-1		29	.125
	BLTR				163	.185

GARRETT, RONALD WAYNE "WAYNE"
B.DEC.3,1947 BROOKSVILLE,FLA.

YR	CL	LEA	POS	GP	G	REC
1969	NY	N	2-S-3		124	.218
1970	NY	N	2-S-3		114	.254
1971	NY	N	2-3		56	.213
1972	NY	N	2-3		111	.232
1973	NY	N	2-3		140	.256
1974	NY	N	S-3		151	.224
1975	NY	N	S-3		107	.266
1976	NY	N	2-3		80	.223
	MON	N	2-3		59	.243
	BLTR				942	.237

GARRIDO, GIL GONZALO
B.JUNE 26,1941 PANAMA CITY,PAN.

YR	CL	LEA	POS	GP	G	REC
1964	SF	N	S		14	.080
1968	ATL	N	S		18	.208
1969	ATL	N	S		82	.220
1970	ATL	N	2-S-3		101	.264
1971	ATL	N	2-S-3		79	.216
1972	ATL	N	2-S-3		40	.267
	BRTR				334	.237

GARRIOTT, CECIL VIRGIL
B.AUG.15,1916 HARRISTOWN,ILL.

YR	CL	LEA	POS	GP	G	REC
1946	CHI	N	H		6	.000
	BLTR					

GARRISON, CLIFFORD GARRY
B.AUG.13,1906 MEEKER,OKLA.

YR	CL	LEA	POS	GP	G	REC
1928	BOS	A	P		6	0- 0
	BRTR					

GARRISON, ROBERT FORD "ROCKY"
B.AUG.29,1915 GREENVILLE,S.C.

YR	CL	LEA	POS	GP	G	REC
1943	BOS	A	O		36	.279
1944	BOS	A	O		13	.245
	PHI	A	O		121	.269
1945	PHI	A	O		6	.304
1946	PHI	A	O		9	.108
	BRTR				185	.262

GARRITY, FRANCIS JOSEPH "HANK"
B.FEB.4,1908 BOSTON,MASS.
D.SEPT.3,1962

YR	CL	LEA	POS	GP	G	REC
1931	CHI	A	C		8	.214
	BRTR					

GARRY, JAMES THOMAS
B.SEP.21,1869 GREAT BARRINGTON, MASS
D.JAN.15,1917

YR	CL	LEA	POS	GP	G	REC
1893	BOS	N	P		1	0- 1

GARVER, NED FRANKLIN
B.DEC.25,1925 NEY,OHIO

YR	CL	LEA	POS	GP	G	REC
1948	STL	A	P	38	46	7-11
1949	STL	A	P	41	55	12-17
1950	STL	A	P-O	37	51	13-18
						.286
1951	STL	A	P	33	49	20-12
1952	STL	A	P	21	24	7-10
	DET	A	P		1	1- 0
1953	DET	A	P		30	11-11
1954	DET	A	P	35	36	14-11
1955	DET	A	P		33	12-16
1956	DET	A	P		6	0- 2
1957	KC	A	P		24	6-13
1958	KC	A	P		31	12-11
1959	KC	A	P		32	10-13
1960	KC	A	P		28	4- 9
1961	LA	A	P		12	0- 3
	BRTR			402	458	129-157
						.218

GARVEY, STEVEN PATRICK "STEVE"
B.DEC.22,1948 TAMPA,FLA.

YR	CL	LEA	POS	GP	G	REC
1969	LA	N	H		3	.333
1970	LA	N	2-3		34	.269
1971	LA	N	3		81	.227
1972	LA	N	1-3		96	.269
1973	LA	N	1-O		114	.304
1974	LA	N	1		156	.312
1975	LA	N	1		160	.319
1976	LA	N	1		162	.317
	BRTR				806	.301

GARVIN, VIRGIL LEE
B.JAN.1,1874 NAVASOTA,TEX.
D.JUNE 16,1908

YR	CL	LEA	POS	GP	G	REC
1896	PHI	N	P		2	0- 1
1899	CHI	N	P		22	9-13
1900	CHI	N	P		28	11-17
1901	MIL	A	P		37	8-21
1902	CHI	A	P		23	9-10
	BRO	N	P		2	1- 1
1903	BRO	N	P		38	15-18
1904	BRO	N	P		23	6-15
	NY	A	P		2	0- 1
	TR				177	59-97

GASPAR, HARRY LAMBERT
B.APR.28,1883 KINGSLEY,IOWA
D.MAY.14,1940 ORANGE,CAL.

YR	CL	LEA	POS	GP	G	REC
1909	CIN	N	P		44	19-11
1910	CIN	N	P		48	15-17
1911	CIN	N	P		44	10-17
1912	CIN	N	P		7	1- 3
	BRTR				143	45-48

GASPAR, RODNEY EARL "ROD"
B.APR.3,1946 LONG BEACH,CAL.

YR	CL	LEA	POS	GP	G	REC
1969	NY	N	O		118	.228
1970	NY	N	O		11	.000
1971	SD	N	O		16	.118
1974	SD	N	1-O		33	.214
	BBTR				178	.208

GASSAWAY, CHARLES CASON "SHERIFF"
B.AUG.12,1918 GASSAWAY,TENN.

YR	CL	LEA	POS	GP	G	REC
1944	CHI	N	P		2	0- 1
1945	PHI	A	P		24	4- 7
1946	CLE	A	P		13	1- 1
	BLTL				39	5- 9

GASTALL, THOMAS EVERETT "TOM"
B.JUNE 13,1933 FALL RIVER,MASS.
D.SEPT.20,1956

YR	CL	LEA	POS	GP	G	REC
1955	BAL	A	C		20	.148
1956	BAL	A	C		32	.196
	BRTR				52	.181

GASTFIELD, EDWARD "ED"
B.AUG.1,1865 CHICAGO,ILL.
D.DEC.1,1899

YR	CL	LEA	POS	GP	G	REC
1884	DET	N	C-1-O		22	.063
1885	DET	N	P		1	0- 0
	CHI	N	C		1	.000
					24	0- 0
						.059

GASTON, ALEXANDER NATHANIEL
B.MAR.12,1893 NEW YORK,N.Y.

YR	CL	LEA	POS	GP	G	REC
1920	NY	N	C		4	.100
1921	NY	N	C		20	.227
1922	NY	N	C		16	.192
1923	NY	N	C		22	.205
1926	BOS	A	C		98	.223
1929	BOS	A	C		55	.224
	BRTR				215	.218

GASTON, CLARENCE EDWIN
B.MAR.17,1944 SAN ANTONIO,TEX.

YR	CL	LEA	POS	GP	G	REC
1967	ATL	N	O		9	.120
1969	SD	N	O		129	.230
1970	SD	N	O		146	.318
1971	SD	N	O		141	.228
1972	SD	N	O		111	.269
1973	SD	N	O		133	.250
1974	SD	N	O		106	.213
1975	ATL	N	1-O		64	.241
1976	ATL	N	1-O		69	.291
	BRTR				908	.257

GASTON, NATHANIEL MILTON "MILT"
B.JAN.27,1896 RIDGEFIELD PARK, N.J.

YR	CL	LEA	POS	GP	G	REC
1924	NY	A	P		28	5- 3
1925	STL	A	P		42	15-14
1926	STL	A	P		32	10-18
1927	STL	A	P		37	13-17
1928	WAS	A	P		28	6-12
1929	BOS	A	P		39	12-19
1930	BOS	A	P		38	13-20
1931	BOS	A	P		23	2-13
1932	CHI	A	P		28	7-17
1933	CHI	A	P		30	8-12
1934	CHI	A	P		29	6-19
	BRTR				354	97-164
	BB 1933					

GASTON, WELCOME THORNBURG
B.DEC.19,1872 GUERNSEY CO.,OHIO
D.DEC.13,1944

YR	CL	LEA	POS	GP	G	REC
1898	BRO	N	P		2	1- 1
1899	BRO	N	P		1	0- 1
	TL				3	1- 2

GASTREICH, HENRY CARL
(PLAYED UNDER NAME OF HENRY CARL GASTRIGHT)

GASTRIGHT, HENRY CARL
(REAL NAME HENRY CARL GASTREICH)
B.MAR.29,1865 COVINGTON,KY.
D.OCT.9,1937

YR	CL	LEA	POS	GP	G	REC
1889	COL	AA	P		31	11-13
1890	COL	AA	P		50	26-14
1891	COL	AA	P		35	12-19
1892	WAS	N	P		12	2- 6
1893	PIT	N	P		9	3- 2
	BOS	N	P		20	12- 4
1894	BRO	N	P		16	3- 4
1896	CIN	N	P		2	0- 1
	BRTR				175	69-63

GATEWOOD, AUBREY LEE
B.NOV.17,1938 N.LITTLE ROCK,ARK.

YR	CL	LEA	POS	GP	G	REC
1963	LA	A	P		4	1- 1
1964	LA	A	P	15	23	3- 3
1965	CAL	A	P		46	4- 5
1970	ATL	N	P		3	0- 0
	BRTR			68	76	8- 9

GATINS, FRANK ANTHONY
B.MAR.6,1873 JOHNSTOWN,PA.
D.NOV.8,1911

YR	CL	LEA	POS	GP	G	REC
1898	WAS	N	S		16	.250
1901	BRO	N	3		49	.229
					65	.234

GAULE, MICHAEL JOHN
B.AUG.4,1869 BALTIMORE,MD.
D.JAN.24,1918

YR	CL	LEA	POS	GP	G	REC
1889	LOU	AA	O		1	.000
	BLTL					

GAUTREAU, WALTER PAUL "DOC"
B.JULY 26,1901 CAMBRIDGE,MASS.
D.AUG.23,1970 SALT LAKE CITY,UT

YR	CL	LEA	POS	GP	G	REC
1925	PHI	A	2		4	.000
	BOS	N	2		68	.262
1926	BOS	N	2		79	.267
1927	BOS	N	2		87	.246
1928	BOS	N	2		23	.278
	BRTR				261	.257

GAUTREAUX, SIDNEY ALLEN "PUDGE"
B.MAY 4,1913 NEW ORLEANS,LA.

YR	CL	LEA	POS	GP	G	REC
1936	BRO	N	C		75	.268
1937	BRO	N	C		11	.100
	BBTR				86	.247

GAW, GEORGE JOSEPH "CHIPPY"
B.MAR.13,1892 NEWTON,MASS.

YR	CL	LEA	POS	GP	G	REC
1920	CHI	N	P		6	1- 1
	TR					

GAZELLA, MICHAEL
B.OCT.13,1896 OLYPHANT,PA.

YR	CL	LEA	POS	GP	G	REC
1923	NY	A	2-S-3		8	.077
1926	NY	A	S-3		66	.232
1927	NY	A	3		54	.278
1928	NY	A	3		32	.232
	BRTR				160	.241

YR	CL	LEA	POS	GP	G	REC

GEAR, DALE DUDLEY
B.FEB.2,1876 LONE ELM,KAN.
D.SEPT.23,1951

YR	CL	LEA	POS	GP	G	REC
1896	CLE	N	P		2	0- 2
1897	CLE	N	O		7	.167
1901	WAS	A	P-O	23	58	3-11
						.236
				25	67	3-13
						.239

GEARHART, LLOYD WILLIAM "GARY"
B.AUG.10,1923 NEW LEBANON,OHIO

| 1947 | NY | N | O | | 73 | .246 |
| | | BRTL | | | | |

GEARIN, DENNIS JOHN "DINTY"
B.OCT.14,1897 PROVIDENCE,R.I.
D.MAR.11,1959

1923	NY	N	P		6	1- 1
1924	NY	N	P	6	10	1- 2
	BOS	N	P		1	0- 1
		BLTL		13	17	2- 4

GEARY, EUGENE FRANCIS JOSEPH "HUCK"
B.JAN.22,1917 BUFFALO,N.Y.

1942	PIT	N	S		9	.227
1943	PIT	N	S		46	.151
		BLTR			55	.160

GEARY, ROBERT NORTON "SPEED"
B.MAY 10,1893 CINCINNATI,OHIO

1918	PHI	A	P		16	3- 5
1919	PHI	A	P		9	0- 3
1921	CIN	N	P		10	1- 1
		BRTR			35	4- 9

GEBHARD, ROBERT HENRY "BOB"
B.JAN.3,1943 LAMBERTON,MINN.

1971	MIN	A	P		17	1- 2
1972	MIN	A	P		13	0- 1
1974	MON	N	P		1	0- 0
		BRTR			31	1- 3

GEBRIAN, PETER "GABE"
B.AUG.10,1923 BAYONNE,N.J.

| 1947 | CHI | A | P | | 27 | 2- 3 |
| | | BRTR | | | | |

GEDDES, JAMES LEE "JIM"
B.MAR.23,1949 COLUMBUS,OHIO

1972	CHI	A	P	5	6	0- 0
1973	CHI	A	P	6	6	0- 0
		BRTR		11	12	0- 0

GEDEON, ELMER JOHN
B.APR.15,1917 CLEVELAND,OHIO
D.APR.15,1944

| 1939 | WAS | A | O | | 5 | .200 |
| | | BRTR | | | | |

GEDEON, ELMER JOSEPH "JOE"
B.DEC.5,1893 SACRAMENTO,CAL.
D.MAY 19,1941

1913	WAS	A	P-O	1	26	0- 0
						.188
1914	WAS	A	O		4	.000
1916	NY	A	2		122	.211
1917	NY	A	2		33	.239
1918	STL	A	2		123	.213
1919	STL	A	2		120	.254
1920	STL	A	2		153	.292
		BRTR		1	581	0- 0
						.244

GEDNEY, ALFRED W., "COUNT"
B.MAY 10,1849 BROOKLYN,N.Y.
D.MAR.26,1922

1872	TRO	NA	O		9	.413
	ECK	NA	O		18	.158
1873	MUT	NA	O		54	-
1874	ATH	NA	1-O		54	-
1875	MUT	NA	P-O		68	1- 0
						-
					203	1- 0
						-

GEE, JOHN ALEXANDER "WHIZ"
B.DEC.7,1915 SYRACUSE,N.Y.

1939	PIT	N	P		3	1- 2
1941	PIT	N	P		3	0- 2
1943	PIT	N	P		15	4- 4
1944	PIT	N	P		4	0- 0
	NY	N	P		4	0- 0
1945	NY	N	P		2	0- 0
1946	NY	N	P		13	2- 4
		BLTL			44	7-12

GEER, WILLIAM HENRY HARRISON
B.AUG.13,1849 SYRACUSE,N.Y.
D.JAN.5,1922

1874	MUT	NA	O		2	-
1875	NH	NA	2-S-3-O		37	-
1878	CIN	N	2-S		62	.215
1880	WOR	N	S-O		2	.000
1884	KEY	U	S		8	.226
	BRO	AA	S		107	.226
1885	LOU	AA	S		14	.113
		TR			232	-

GEHRIG, HENRY LOUIS "LOU"
OR "THE IRON HORSE"
B.JUNE 19,1903 NEW YORK,N.Y.
D.JUNE 2,1941 NEW YORK,N.Y.

1923	NY	A	1		13	.423
1924	NY	A	1		10	.500
1925	NY	A	1-O		126	.295
1926	NY	A	1		155	.313
1927	NY	A	1		155	.373
1928	NY	A	1		154	.374
1929	NY	A	1		154	.300
1930	NY	A	1		154	.379
1931	NY	A	1		155	.341
1932	NY	A	1		156	.349
1933	NY	A	1		152	.334
1934	NY	A	1-S		154	.363
1935	NY	A	1		149	.329
1936	NY	A	1		155	.324
1937	NY	A	1		157	.351
1938	NY	A	1		157	.295
1939	NY	A	1		8	.143
		BLTL			2164	.340

GEHRING, HENRY
B.JAN.24,1881 ST.PAUL,MINN.
D.APR.18,1912

1907	WAS	A	P	14	20	3- 7
1908	WAS	A	P		5	0- 1
				19	25	3- 8

GEHRINGER, CHARLES LEONARD "CHARLEY" OR "THE MECHANICAL MAN"
B.MAY 11,1903 FOWLERVILLE,MICH.

1924	DET	A	2		5	.545
1925	DET	A	2		8	.167
1926	DET	A	2		123	.277
1927	DET	A	2		133	.317
1928	DET	A	2		154	.320
1929	DET	A	2		155	.339
1930	DET	A	2		154	.330
1931	DET	A	2		101	.311
1932	DET	A	2		152	.298
1933	DET	A	2		155	.325
1934	DET	A	2		154	.356
1935	DET	A	2		150	.330
1936	DET	A	2		154	.354
1937	DET	A	2		144	.371
1938	DET	A	2		152	.306
1939	DET	A	2		118	.325
1940	DET	A	2		139	.313
1941	DET	A	2		127	.220
1942	DET	A	2		45	.267
		BLTR			2323	.320

GEHRMAN, PAUL ARTHUR "DUTCH"
B.MAY 3,1914 MT.ANGEL,ORE.

| 1937 | CIN | N | P | | 2 | 0- 1 |
| | | BRTR | | | | |

GEIER, PHILIP LOUIS "LITTLE PHIL"
B.NOV.5,1875 WASHINGTON,D.C.
D.SEPT.25,1967

1896	PHI	N	O		17	.232
1897	PHI	N	2-O		88	.285
1900	CIN	N	O		29	.273
1901	PHI	A	O		50	.236
	MIL	A	O		10	.184
1904	BOS	N	O		148	.243
		BLTR			342	.252

GEIGER, GARY MERLE
B.APR.4,1937 SAND RIDGE,ILL.

1958	CLE	A	P-3-O	1	91	0- 0
						.231
1959	BOS	A	O		120	.245
1960	BOS	A	O		77	.302
1961	BOS	A	O		140	.232
1962	BOS	A	O		131	.249
1963	BOS	A	1-O		121	.263
1964	BOS	A	O		5	.385
1965	BOS	A	O		24	.200
1966	ATL	N	O		78	.262
1967	ATL	N	O		69	.162
1969	HOU	N	O		93	.224
1970	HOU	N	O		5	.250
		BLTR		1	954	0- 0
						.246

GEISHERT, VERNON WILLIAM "VERN"
B.JAN.10,1946 MADISON,WIS.

| 1969 | CAL | A | P | | 11 | 1- 1 |
| | | BRTR | | | | |

GEISS, EMIL M.
B.CHICAGO,ILL.

1882	BAL	AA	P-O		13	4- 9
						.159
1887	CHI	N	P		3	0- 1
		BR			16	4-10
						.140

GEISS, WILLIAM
B.1860 CHICAGO,ILL.

1884	DET	N	P-1-	1	75	0- 0
			2-O			.177
1891	STL	AA	2		76	.323
				1	151	0- 0
						.253

GELBERT, CHARLES MAGNUS
B.JAN.26,1906 SCRANTON,PA.
D.JAN.13,1967 EASTON,PA.

1929	STL	N	S		146	.262
1930	STL	N	S		139	.304
1931	STL	N	S		131	.289
1932	STL	N	S		122	.268
1935	STL	N	2-S-3		62	.292
1936	STL	N	S-3		93	.229
1937	CIN	N	2-S-3		43	.193
	DET	A	S		20	.085
1939	WAS	A	S-3		68	.255
1940	WAS	A	P-2-	2	22	0- 0
			S-3			.370
	BOS	A	3		30	.198
		BRTR		2	876	0- 0
						.267

GELNAR, JOHN RICHARD
B.JUNE 25,1943 GRANITE,OKLA

1964	PIT	N	P		7	0- 0
1967	PIT	N	P		10	0- 1
1969	SEA	A	P	39	40	3-10
1970	MIL	A	P		53	4- 3
1971	MIL	A	P		2	0- 0
		BRTR		111	112	7-14

GENEWICH, JOSEPH EDWARD
B.JAN.15,1897 ELMIRA,N.Y.

1922	BOS	N	P		6	0- 2
1923	BOS	N	P		43	13-14
1924	BOS	N	P		34	10-19
1925	BOS	N	P		34	12-10
1926	BOS	N	P		37	8-16
1927	BOS	N	P		40	11- 8
1928	BOS	N	P		13	3- 7
	NY	N	P		26	11- 4
1929	NY	N	P	21	25	3- 7
1930	NY	N	P	18	21	2- 5
		BRTR		272	279	73-92

GENINS, C. FRANK "FRENCHY"
B.NOV.2,1866 ST.LOUIS,MO.
D.SEPT.30,1922

1892	CIN	N	S		31	.195
	STL	N	S		14	.167
1895	PIT	N	3-O		64	.253
1901	CLE	A	O		26	.232
		TR			135	.228

GENOVESE, GEORGE MICHAEL
B.FEB.22,1923 STATEN ISLAND,N.Y

| 1950 | WAS | A | H | | 3 | .000 |
| | | BLTR | | | | |

YR	CL	LEA	POS	GP	G	REC

GENTILE, JAMES EDWARD "JIM"
B.JUNE 3,1934 SAN FRANCISCO,CAL.

YR	CL	LEA	POS	GP	G	REC
1957	BRO	N	1		4	.167
1958	LA	N	1		12	.133
1960	BAL	A	1		138	.292
1961	BAL	A	1		148	.302
1962	BAL	A	1		152	.251
1963	BAL	A	1		145	.248
1964	KC	A	1		136	.251
1965	KC	A	1		38	.246
	HOU	N	1		81	.242
1966	HOU	N	1		49	.243
	CLE	A	1		33	.128
	BLTL				936	.260

GENTILE, SAMUEL CHRISTOPHER
B.OCT.12,1916 CHARLESTOWN,MASS.

YR	CL	LEA	POS	GP	G	REC
1943	BOS	N	H		8	.250
	BLTR					

GENTRY, GARY EDWARD
B.OCT.6,1946 PHOENIX,ARIZ.

YR	CL	LEA	POS	GP	G	REC
1969	NY	N	P		35	13-12
1970	NY	N	P		32	9- 9
1971	NY	N	P		32	12-11
1972	NY	N	P		32	7-10
1973	ATL	N	P	16	17	4- 6
1974	ATL	N	P		3	0- 0
1975	ATL	N	P		7	1- 1
	BRTR			157	158	46-49

GENTRY, HARVEY WILLIAM
B.MAY 27,1926 WINSTON-SALEM,N.C

YR	CL	LEA	POS	GP	G	REC
1954	NY	N	H		5	.250
	BLTR					

GENTRY, JAMES RUFFUS "RUFE"
B.MAY 18,1918 WINSTON-SALEM,N.C

YR	CL	LEA	POS	GP	G	REC
1943	DET	A	P		4	1- 3
1944	DET	A	P		37	18-14
1946	DET	A	P		2	0- 0
1947	DET	A	P		1	0- 0
1948	DET	A	P		4	0- 0
	BRTR			48	13-17

GEORGE, ALEXANDER THOMAS "ALEX"
B.SEPT.27,1938 KANSAS CITY,MO.

YR	CL	LEA	POS	GP	G	REC
1955	KC	A	S		5	.100
	BLTR					

GEORGE, CHARLES PETER "GREEK"
B.DEC.25,1912 WAYCROSS,GA.

YR	CL	LEA	POS	GP	G	REC
1935	CLE	A	C		2	.000
1936	CLE	A	C		23	.195
1938	BRO	N	C		7	.200
1941	CHI	N	C		35	.156
1945	PHI	A	C		51	.174
	BRTR			118	.177

GEORGE, THOMAS EDWARD "LEFTY"
B.AUG.13,1886 PITTSBURGH,PA.
D.MAY 13,1955

YR	CL	LEA	POS	GP	G	REC
1911	STL	A	P		27	3-10
1912	CLE	A	P		11	0- 5
1915	CIN	N	P		7	2- 2
1918	BOS	N	P		10	1- 5
	BLTL			55	6-22

GEORGE, WILLIAM M.
B.JAN.27,1865 BELLAIRE,OHIO
D.AUG.23,1916

YR	CL	LEA	POS	GP	G	REC
1887	NY	N	P		13	3- 9
1888	NY	N	P-O	4	9	2- 1
						.230
1889	NY	N	O		3	.267
	COL	AA	P-O	3	5	0- 0
						.308
	BRTL			20	30	5-10
						.220

GEORGY, OSCAR JOHN
B.NOV.25,1918 NEW ORLEANS,LA.

YR	CL	LEA	POS	GP	G	REC
1938	NY	N	1		1	0- 0
	BRTR					

GERAGHTY, BENJAMIN RAYMOND
B.JULY 19,1912 JERSEY CITY,N.J.
D.JUNE 18,1963 JACKSONVILLE,FLA

YR	CL	LEA	POS	GP	G	REC
1936	BRO	N	S		51	.194
1943	BOS	N	2-S-3		8	.000
1944	BOS	N	2-3		11	.250
	BRTR			70	.199

GERARD, DAVID FREDERICK
B.AUG.6,1936 NEW YORK,N.Y.

YR	CL	LEA	POS	GP	G	REC
1962	CHI	N	P		39	2- 3
	BRTR					

GERBER, WALTER "SPOOKS"
B.AUG.18,1891 COLUMBUS,OHIO
D.JUNE 19,1951

YR	CL	LEA	POS	GP	G	REC
1914	PIT	N	S		17	.241
1915	PIT	N	S-3		56	.194
1917	STL	A	S		14	.308
1918	STL	A	S		56	.240
1919	STL	A	S		140	.227
1920	STL	A	S		154	.279
1921	STL	A	S		114	.278
1922	STL	A	S		153	.267
1923	STL	A	S		154	.281
1924	STL	A	S		148	.272
1925	STL	A	S		72	.272
1926	STL	A	S		131	.270
1927	STL	A	S		142	.224
1928	STL	A	S		6	.222
	BOS	A	S		104	.217
1929	BOS	A	2-S		61	.165
	BRTR			1522	.257

GERBERMAN, GEORGE ALOIS
B.MAR.8,1942 EL CAMPO,TEX.

YR	CL	LEA	POS	GP	G	REC
1962	CHI	N	P		1	0- 0
	BRTR					

GERHARDT, ALLEN RUSSELL "RUSTY"
B.AUG.13,1950 BALTIMORE,MD.

YR	CL	LEA	POS	GP	G	REC
1974	SD	N	P		23	2- 1
	BBTL			23	2- 1

GERHARDT, JOSEPH JOHN "MOVEUP"
B.FEB.14,1855 WASHINGTON,D.C.
D.MAR.11,1922

YR	CL	LEA	POS	GP	G	REC
1872	NAT	NA	2		1	-
1873	NAT	NA	S		13	-
1874	BAL	NA	S		14	-
1875	MUT	NA	2-S-3-O		59	-
1876	LOU	N	1-2		65	.258
1877	LOU	N	1-2-S-O		59	.304
1878	CIN	N	2		61	.303
1879	CIN	N	1-2-3		78	.199
1881	DET	N	2-3		80	.242
1883	LOU	AA	M-2		77	.270
1884	LOU	AA	M-2		108	.220
1885	NY	N	2		112	.155
1886	NY	N	2		123	.190
1887	NY	N	3		1	.000
	MET	AA	2		85	.277
1890	BRO	AA	2		97	.211
	STL	AA	2-3		37	.260
1891	LOU	AA	2		2	.000
	BRTR			1072	-

GERHEAUSER, ALBERT "AL"
B.JUNE 24,1917 ST.LOUIS,MO.
D.MAY 28,1972 SPRINGFIELD,MO.

YR	CL	LEA	POS	GP	G	REC
1943	PHI	N	P		38	10-19
1944	PHI	N	P	30	32	8-16
1945	PIT	N	P		32	5-10
1946	PIT	N	P-O	35	36	2- 2
						.333
1948	STL	A	P		14	0- 3
	BLTL			149	152	25-50
						.209

GERKEN, GEORGE HERBERT
B.JULY 28,1903 CHICAGO,ILL.

YR	CL	LEA	POS	GP	G	REC
1927	CLE	A	O		6	.214
1928	CLE	A	O		38	.226
	BRTR			44	.225

GERKIN, STEPHEN PAUL "SPLINTER"
B.NOV.19,1915 GRAFTON,W.VA.

YR	CL	LEA	POS	GP	G	REC
1945	PHI	A	P		21	0-12
	BRTR					

GERLACH, JOHN GLENN
B.MAY 11,1917 SHULLSBURG,WIS.

YR	CL	LEA	POS	GP	G	REC
1938	CHI	A	S		9	.280
1939	CHI	A	3		3	1.000
	BRTR			12	.333

GERMAN, LESTER STANLEY
B.JUNE 1,1869 BALTIMORE,MD.
D.JUNE 10,1934 GERMANTOWN,MD.

YR	CL	LEA	POS	GP	G	REC
1890	BAL	AA	P		16	4-10
1893	NY	N	P	18	20	10- 8
1894	NY	N	P	17	19	7- 8
1895	NY	N	P	20	31	7-13
1896	NY	N	P		3	1- 1
	WAS	N	P		23	2-18
1897	WAS	N	P-2	7	19	4- 3
						.311
				104	131	35-61
						.252

GERNER, EDWIN FREDERICK
B.JULY 22,1897 PHILADELPHIA,PA.
D.MAY 15,1970 PHILADELPHIA,PA.

YR	CL	LEA	POS	GP	G	REC
1919	CIN	N	P		5	1- 0
	BLTL					

GERNERT, RICHARD EDWARD "DICK"
B.SEPT.12,1929 READING,PA.

YR	CL	LEA	POS	GP	G	REC
1952	BOS	A	1		102	.243
1953	BOS	A	1		139	.253
1954	BOS	A	1		14	.261
1955	BOS	A	1		7	.200
1956	BOS	A	1-O		106	.291
1957	BOS	A	1-O		99	.237
1958	BOS	A	1		122	.237
1959	BOS	A	1-O		117	.262
1960	CHI	A	1-O		52	.250
	DET	A	1-O		21	.300
1961	DET	A	1		6	.200
	CIN	N	1		40	.302
1962	HOU	N	1		10	.208
	BRTR			835	.254

GERONIMO, CESAR FRANCISCO
B.MAR.11,1948 EL SEIBO,D.R.

YR	CL	LEA	POS	GP	G	REC
1969	HOU	N	O		28	.250
1970	HOU	N	O		47	.243
1971	HOU	N	O		94	.220
1972	CIN	N	O		120	.275
1973	CIN	N	O		139	.210
1974	CIN	N	O		150	.281
1975	CIN	N	O		148	.257
1976	CIN	N	O		149	.307
	BLTL			875	.267

GERTENRICH, LOUIS WILHELM
B.MAY 4,1875 CHICAGO,ILL.
D.OCT.23,1933

YR	CL	LEA	POS	GP	G	REC
1901	MIL	A	O		2	.333
1903	PIT	N	O		1	.000
					3	.143

GERVAIS, LUCIEN EDWARD "LEFTY"
B.JULY 6,1890 GROVER,WIS.
D.OCT.19,1950 LOS ANGELES,CAL.

YR	CL	LEA	POS	GP	G	REC
1913	BOS	N	P		6	0- 1
	BLTL					

GESSLER, HARRY HOMER "DOC"
B.DEC.23,1880 INDIANA,PA.
D.DEC.26,1924

YR	CL	LEA	POS	GP	G	REC
1903	DET	A	O		29	.238
	BRO	N	O		43	.247
1904	BRO	N	O		89	.290
1905	BRO	N	1		119	.290
1906	BRO	N	1		9	.242
	CHI	N	O		22	.253
1908	BOS	A	O		128	.308
1909	BOS	A	O		111	.299
	WAS	A	O		17	.182
1910	WAS	A	O		145	.259
1911	WAS	A	O		128	.282
	BLTR			840	.280
NON-PLAYING MANAGER PIT(F) 1914						

GESSNER, CHARLES J.
B.PHILADELPHIA,PA.

YR	CL	LEA	POS	GP	G	REC
1886	ATH	AA	P		1	0- 1

GETTEL, ALLEN JONES "AL"
B.SEPT.17,1917 NORFOLK,VA.

YR	CL	LEA	POS	GP	G	REC
1945	NY	A	P		27	9- 8
1946	NY	A	P		26	6- 7
1947	CLE	A	P	31	34	11-10
1948	CLE	A	P		5	0- 1
	CHI	A	P-2	22	24	8-10
						.241
1949	CHI	A	P		19	2- 5
	WAS	A	P		16	0- 2
1951	NY	N	P		30	1- 2
1955	NY	N	P		8	1- 0
	BRTR			184	189	38-45
						.228

GETTIG, CHARLES H.
(REAL NAME
CHARLES H. GETTINGER)
B.1875 CUMBERLAND,MD.

YR	CL	LEA	POS	GP	G	REC
1896	NY	N	P		6	1- 0
1897	NY	N	P-S	2	20	1- 1
						.203
1898	NY	N	P-O	37	55	5- 4
						.248
1899	NY	N	P	15	31	7- 8
					60	112	14-13
						.239

YR	CL	LEA	POS	GP	G	REC

GETTINGER, CHARLES H.
(PLAYED UNDER NAME OF
CHARLES H. GETTIG)

GETTINGER, THOMAS L.
B.1870 MOBILE,ALA.

YR	CL	LEA	POS	GP	G	REC
1889	STL	AA	O		3	.455
1890	STL	AA	O		59	.260
1895	LOU	N	P-O	1	60	0- 1
						.281
	BLTL			1	122	0- 1
						.277

GETTMAN, JACOB JOHN "QUICK"
B.OCT.25,1875 FRANK,RUSSIA
D.OCT.4,1956

YR	CL	LEA	POS	GP	G	REC
1897	WAS	N	O		37	.315
1898	WAS	N	O		140	.279
1899	WAS	N	O		16	.226
	BBTL				193	.280

GETZ, GUSTAVE
B.AUG.3,1889 PITTSBURGH,PA.
D.MAY 28,1969 KEANSBURG,N.J.

YR	CL	LEA	POS	GP	G	REC
1909	BOS	N	3		40	.223
1910	BOS	N	3		47	.194
1914	BRO	N	3		55	.248
1915	BRO	N	3		130	.258
1916	BRO	N	3		40	.219
1917	CIN	N	2-3		7	.286
1918	CLE	A	3		6	.066
	PIT	N	3		7	.200
	BRTR				332	.219

GETZEIN, CHARLES H. "PRETZELS"
B.FEB.14,1864 CHICAGO,IL.
D.JUNE 19,1932

YR	CL	LEA	POS	GP	G	REC
1884	DET	N	P		17	5-12
1885	DET	N	P-O	38	39	12-26
						.211
1886	DET	N	P		43	31-11
1887	DET	N	P		43	29-13
1888	DET	N	P		45	18-26
1889	IND	N	P		41	19-22
1890	BOS	N	P		42	23-17
1891	BOS	N	P-O	11	13	4- 6
						.189
	CLE	N	P		1	0- 1
1892	STL	N	P		14	5- 9
	BRTR			295	298	146-143
						.207

GEYER, JACOB BOWMAN "RUBE"
B.MAR.22,1885 ALLEGHENY,PA.
D.OCT.12,1962 WAHKON,MINN.

YR	CL	LEA	POS	GP	G	REC
1910	STL	N	P		4	0- 1
1911	STL	N	P		29	9- 6
1912	STL	N	P		41	7-14
1913	STL	N	P		30	1- 5
	BRTR			104	17-26

GEYGAN, JAMES EDWARD "CHAPPIE"
B.JUNE 3,1903 COLUMBUS,OHIO
D.MAR.15,1966 COLUMBUS,OHIO

YR	CL	LEA	POS	GP	G	REC
1924	BOS	A	S		33	.256
1925	BOS	A	S		3	.182
1926	BOS	A	3		4	.300
	BRTR				40	.252

**GHARRITY, EDWARD PATRICK
"PATSY"**
B.MAR.13,1892 PARNELL,IOWA
D.OCT.10,1966 BELOIT,WIS.

YR	CL	LEA	POS	GP	G	REC
1916	WAS	A	C-1		39	.228
1917	WAS	A	1		76	.284
1918	WAS	A	C		4	.250
1919	WAS	A	C-O		111	.271
1920	WAS	A	C-1		131	.245
1921	WAS	A	C		121	.310
1922	WAS	A	C		96	.256
1923	WAS	A	C-1		93	.207
1929	WAS	A	H		3	.000
1930	WAS	A	1		2	.000
	BRTR				676	.249

GIALLOMBARDO, ROBERT PAUL "BOB"
B.MAY 20,1938 BROOKLYN,N.Y.

YR	CL	LEA	POS	GP	G	REC
1958	LA	N	P	6	8	1- 1
	BLTL					

GIANNINI, JOSEPH FRANCIS
B.SEPT.8,1888 SAN FRANCISCO,CAL
D.SEPT.26,1942

YR	CL	LEA	POS	GP	G	REC
1911	BOS	A	S		1	.500
	BLTR					

GIARD, JOSEPH OSCAR "PECO"
B.OCT.7,1898 WARE,MASS.
D.JULY 10,1956

YR	CL	LEA	POS	GP	G	REC
1925	STL	A	P		30	10- 5
1926	STL	A	P		22	3-10
1927	NY	A	P		16	0- 0
	BLTL				68	13-15

GIBBON, JOSEPH CHARLES "JOE"
B.APR.10,1935 HICKORY,MISS.

YR	CL	LEA	POS	GP	G	REC
1960	PIT	N	P		27	4- 2
1961	PIT	N	P	30	31	13-10
1962	PIT	N	P		19	3- 4
1963	PIT	N	P	37	40	5-12
1964	PIT	N	P	28	29	10- 7
1965	PIT	N	P		31	4- 9
1966	SF	N	P		37	4- 6
1967	SF	N	P		28	6- 2
1968	SF	N	P		29	1- 2
1969	SF	N	P		16	1- 3
	PIT	N	P		35	5- 1
1970	PIT	N	P		41	0- 1
1971	CIN	N	P		50	5- 6
1972	CIN	N	P		2	0- 0
	HOU	N	P		9	0- 0
	BRTL			419	424	61-65
	BB 1967-68					

GIBBS, JERRY DEAN "JAKE"
B.NOV.7,1938 GRENADA,MISS.

YR	CL	LEA	POS	GP	G	REC
1962	NY	A	3		2	.000
1963	NY	A	C		4	.250
1964	NY	A	C		3	.167
1965	NY	A	C		37	.221
1966	NY	A	C		62	.258
1967	NY	A	C		116	.233
1968	NY	A	C		124	.213
1969	NY	A	C		71	.224
1970	NY	A	C		49	.301
1971	NY	A	C		70	.218
	BLTR				538	.233

GIBSON, CHARLES E.
B.1877 PHILADELPHIA,PA.

YR	CL	LEA	POS	GP	G	REC
1905	STL	A	C		1	.000
	TR					

GIBSON, CHARLES GRIFFIN
B.NOV.21,1899 LAGRANGE,GA.

YR	CL	LEA	POS	GP	G	REC
1924	PHI	A	C		12	.133
	BRTR					

GIBSON, FRANK GILBERT
B.SEPT.27,1890 OMAHA,NEB.
D.APR.27,1961

YR	CL	LEA	POS	GP	G	REC
1913	DET	A	C		20	.140
1921	BOS	N	C		63	.264
1922	BOS	N	C-1		66	.299
1923	BOS	N	C		41	.300
1924	BOS	N	C-1-3		90	.310
1925	BOS	N	C-1		104	.278
1926	BOS	N	C		24	.340
1927	BOS	N	C		60	.222
	BBTR				468	.274
	BL 1913					

GIBSON, GEORGE "MOON"
B.JULY 22,1880 LONDON,ONT.,CAN.
D.JAN.25,1967 LONDON,ONT.,CAN.

YR	CL	LEA	POS	GP	G	REC
1905	PIT	N	C		44	.178
1906	PIT	N	C		81	.178
1907	PIT	N	C		110	.220
1908	PIT	N	C		140	.228
1909	PIT	N	C		150	.265
1910	PIT	N	C		143	.259
1911	PIT	N	C		98	.209
1912	PIT	N	C		95	.240
1913	PIT	N	C		48	.280
1914	PIT	N	C		102	.285
1915	PIT	N	C		120	.251
1916	PIT	N	C		33	.202
1917	NY	N	C		35	.171
1918	NY	N	C		4	.500
	BRTR				1203	.236

NON-PLAYING MANAGER
PIT(N) 1920-22, CHI(N) 1925,
PIT(N) 1932-34

GIBSON, JOHN RUSSELL "RUSS"
B.MAY 6,1939 FALL RIVER,MASS.

YR	CL	LEA	POS	GP	G	REC
1967	BOS	A	C		49	.203
1968	BOS	A	C-1		76	.225
1969	BOS	A	C		85	.251
1970	SF	N	C		24	.232
1971	SF	N	C		25	.193
1972	SF	N	C		5	.167
	BRTR				264	.228

GIBSON, LEIGHTON B.
B.1866 LANCASTER,PA.

YR	CL	LEA	POS	GP	G	REC
1888	ATH	AA	C		1	.000
	TR					

GIBSON, NORWOOD R.
B.MAR.11,1877 PEORIA,ILL.
D.JULY 7,1959

YR	CL	LEA	POS	GP	G	REC
1903	BOS	A	P		25	11- 9
1904	BOS	A	P		33	17-14
1905	BOS	A	P		24	5-10
1906	BOS	A	P		5	0- 2
	TR				87	33-35

GIBSON, ROBERT "BOB"
B.NOV.9,1935 OMAHA,NEB.

YR	CL	LEA	POS	GP	G	REC
1959	STL	N	P	13	21	3- 5
1960	STL	N	P	27	40	3- 6
1961	STL	N	P	35	40	13-12
1962	STL	N	P	32	42	15-13
1963	STL	N	P	36	41	18- 9
1964	STL	N	P		40	19-12
1965	STL	N	P	38	42	20-12
1966	STL	N	P	35	46	21-12
1967	STL	N	P	24	27	13- 7
1968	STL	N	P	34	35	22- 9
1969	STL	N	P	35	37	20-13
1970	STL	N	P	34	40	23- 7
1971	STL	N	P		31	16-13
1972	STL	N	P		34	19-11
1973	STL	N	P		25	12-10
1974	STL	N	P		33	11-13
1975	STL	N	P		22	3-10
	BRTR			528	596	251-174

GIBSON, ROBERT CHARLES
B.AUG.20,1869 DUNCANSVILLE,PA.

YR	CL	LEA	POS	GP	G	REC
1890	CHI	N	P		1	1- 0
	PIT	N	P-O		3	0- 2
						.231
					4	1- 2
						.176

GIBSON, SAMUEL BRAXTON
B.AUG.5,1900 HIGH POINT,N.C.

YR	CL	LEA	POS	GP	G	REC
1926	DET	A	P	35	36	12- 9
1927	DET	A	P		33	11-12
1928	DET	A	P		20	5- 8
1930	NY	A	P		2	0- 1
1932	NY	N	P		41	4- 8
	BLTR			131	132	32-38

GICK, GEORGE EDWARD
B.OCT.18,1915 DUNNINGTON,IND.

YR	CL	LEA	POS	GP	G	REC
1937	CHI	A	P		1	0- 0
1938	CHI	A	P		1	0- 0
	BBTR				2	0- 0

GIDEON, JAMES LESLIE "JIM"
B.SEPT.26,1953 TAYLOR,TEX.

YR	CL	LEA	POS	GP	G	REC
1975	TEX	A	P	1	0- 0
	BRTR					

GIEBEL, JOSEPH HENRY
B.NOV.30,1891 WASHINGTON,D.C.

YR	CL	LEA	POS	GP	G	REC
1913	PHI	A	C		1	.333
	BRTR					

GIEBELL, FLOYD KARL
B.DEC.10,1914 PENNSBORO,W.VA.

YR	CL	LEA	POS	GP	G	REC
1939	DET	A	P		9	1- 1
1940	DET	A	P		2	2- 0
1941	DET	A	P		17	0- 0
	BLTR				28	3- 1

GIEL, PAUL ROBERT
B.FEB.29,1932 WINONA,MINN.

YR	CL	LEA	POS	GP	G	REC
1954	NY	N	P		6	0- 0
1955	NY	N	P		34	4- 4
1958	SF	N	P		29	4- 5
1959	PIT	N	P		4	0- 0
1960	PIT	N	P		16	2- 0
1961	MIN	A	P	12	15	1- 0
	KC	A	P		1	0- 0
	BRTR			102	105	11- 9

GIFFORD, JAMES H.
B.OCT.18,1845 WARREN,N.Y.
D.DEC.19,1901
NON-PLAYING MANAGER
IND(AA) 1884, MET(AA) 1885-86

YR	CL LEA POS	GP	G	REC

GIGGIE, ROBERT THOMAS "BOB"
B.AUG.13,1933 DORCHESTER,MASS.
1959	MIL N	P	13		1- 0
1960	MIL N	P	3		0- 0
	KC A	P	10		1- 0
1962	KC A	P	4		1- 1
	BRTR		30		3- 1

GIGON, NORMAN PHILIP "NORM"
B.MAY 12,1938 TEANECK,N.J.
| 1967 | CHI N | 2-3-O | 34 | | .171 |
| | BRTR | | | | |

GIL, TOMAS GUSTAVO (GUILLEN) "GUS"
B.APR.19,1940 CARACAS,VENEZ.
1967	CHI A	1-2	51		.115
1969	SEA A	2-S-3	92		.222
1970	MIL A	2-3	64		.185
1971	MIL A	2-3	14		.156
	BRTR		221		.186

GILBERT, ANDREW
B.JULY 18,1916 LATROBE,PA.
1942	BOS A	O	6		.091
1946	BOS A	O	2		.000
	BRTR		8		.083

GILBERT, BENNETT HAROLD ROCHEFORT
(PLAYED UNDER NAME OF
BENNETT HAROLD ROCHEFORT)

GILBERT, CHARLES MADER
B.JULY 8,1919 NEW ORLEANS,LA.
1940	BRO N	O	57		.266
1941	CHI N	O	39		.279
1942	CHI N	O	74		.184
1943	CHI N	O	8		.150
1946	CHI N	O	15		.077
	PHI N	O	88		.242
1947	PHI N	O	83		.237
	BLTL		364		.229

GILBERT, DREW EDWARD
B.JULY 26,1935 KNOXVILLE,TENN.
| 1959 | CIN N | O | 7 | | .150 |
| | BLTR | | | | |

GILBERT, HAROLD JOSEPH "TOOKIE"
B.APR.4,1929 NEW ORLEANS,LA.
D.JUNE 23,1967 NEW ORLEANS,LA.
1950	NY N	1	113		.220
1953	NY N	1	70		.169
	BLTR		183		.203

GILBERT, HARRY
| 1890 | PIT N | 2 | 2 | | .250 |

GILBERT, JOE DENNIS
B.APR.20,1952 JASPER,TEX.
1972	MON N	P	22		0- 1
1973	MON N	P	21		1- 2
	BRTL		43		1- 3

GILBERT, JOHN G.
B.JAN.8,1864 POTTSTOWN,PA.
D.NOV.12,1903
| 1890 | PIT N | S | 2 | | .000 |

GILBERT, JOHN ROBERT "JACKRABBIT"
B.SEPT.14,1875 RHINEBECK,N.Y.
D.JULY 7,1941
1898	WAS N	O	2		.167
	NY N	O	1		.250
1904	PIT N	O	25		.241
			28		.237

GILBERT, LAWRENCE WILLIAM
B.DEC.3,1891 NEW ORLEANS,LA.
D.FEB.17,1965 NEW ORLEANS,LA.
1914	BOS N	O	72		.268
1915	BOS N	O	45		.151
	BLTL		117		.230

GILBERT, PETER
B.SEPT.6,1867 BALTIC,CONN.
D.JAN.1,1912
1890	BAL AA	3	29		.262
1891	BAL AA	3	137		.229
1892	BAL N	3	4		.200
1894	BRO N	3	6		.000
	LOU N	3	28		.287
	TR		204		.234

GILBERT, WALTER JOHN
B.DEC.19,1901 OSCODA,MICH.
D.SEPT.8,1958
1928	BRO N	3	39		.203
1929	BRO N	3	143		.304
1930	BRO N	3	150		.294
1931	BRO N	3	145		.266
1932	CIN N	3	114		.214
	BRTR		591		.269

GILBERT, WILLIAM
B.HAVRE DE GRACE,MD.
| 1892 | BAL N | P | 2 | | 0- 1 |

GILBERT, WILLIAM OLIVER
B.JUNE 21,1876 TRENTON,N.J.
D.AUG.8,1927
1901	MIL A	2	127		.269
1902	BAL A	S	130		.243
1903	NY N	2	128		.252
1904	NY N	2	146		.253
1905	NY N	2	115		.247
1906	NY N	2	98		.231
1908	STL N	2	89		.214
1909	STL N	2	12		.172
	BRTR		845		.246

GILBREATH, RODNEY JOE "ROD"
B.SEP.24,1952 LAUREL,MISS.
1972	ATL N	2-3	18		.237
1973	ATL N	3	29		.284
1974	ATL N	2	3		.333
1975	ATL N	2-S-3	90		.243
1976	ATL N	2-S-3	116		.251
	BRTR		256		.252
	DB 1975 (PAK?)				

GILBRETH, WILLIAM FREEMAN "BILL"
B.SEP.3,1947 ABILENE,TEX.
1971	DET A	P	9		2- 1
1972	DET A	P	2		0- 0
1974	CAL A	P	3		0- 0
	BLTL		14		2- 1

GILE, DONALD LOREN "DON"
B.APR.19,1935 MODESTO,CAL.
1959	BOS A	C	3		.200
1960	BOS A	C-1	29		.176
1961	BOS A	C-1	8		.278
1962	BOS A	1	18		.049
	BRTR		58		.150

GILHAM, GEORGE LEWIS
B.SEPT.8,1899 SHAMOKIN,PA.
D.APR.25,1937
1920	STL N	C	1		.000
1921	STL N	C	1		.000
	BRTR		2		.000

GILHOOLEY, FRANK PATRICK "FLASH"
B.JUNE 10,1892 TOLEDO,OHIO
D.JULY 11,1959
1911	STL N	O	1		.000
1912	STL N	O	13		.224
1913	NY A	O	24		.341
1914	NY A	O	1		.667
1915	NY A	O	1		.000
1916	NY A	O	58		.278
1917	NY A	O	54		.242
1918	NY A	O	112		.276
1919	BOS A	O	48		.241
	BLTR		312		.271

GILKS, ROBERT JAMES
B.JULY 2,1867 CINCINNATI,OHIO
D.AUG.20,1944
1887	CLE AA	P-O	11	22	6- 5
					.333
1888	CLE AA	3-O	118		.232
1889	CLE N	O	52		.238
1890	CLE N	P-O	4	130	2- 2
					.213
1893	BAL N	O	15		.274
	BRTR		15	337	8- 7
					.234

GILL, EDWARD JAMES
B.AUG.7,1896 SOMERVILLE,MASS.
| 1919 | WAS A | P | 16 | | 1- 1 |
| | BLTR | | | | |

GILL, GEORGE LLOYD
B.FEB.13,1909 CATCHINGS,MISS.
1937	DET A	P	31		11- 4
1938	DET A	P	24		12- 9
1939	DET A	P	3		0- 1
	STL A	P	27		1-12
	BRTR		85		24-26

GILL, HAROLD EDMUND "HADDIE"
B.JAN.23,1899 BROCKTON,MASS.
D.AUG.1,1932
| 1923 | CIN N | P | 1 | | 0- 0 |
| | BLTL | | | | |

GILL, JAMES C.
B.ST.LOUIS,MO.
| 1889 | STL AA | 2-O | 2 | | .250 |

GILL, JOHN WESLEY "PATCHEYE"
B.MAR.27,1906 NASHVILLE,TENN.
1927	CLE A	O	21		.216
1928	CLE A	H	2		.000
1931	WAS A	O	8		.267
1934	WAS A	O	13		.245
1935	CHI N	H	3		.333
1936	CHI N	O	71		.253
	BLTR		118		.245

GILL, WARREN DARST
B.DEC.21,1878 LADOGA,IND.
D.NOV.26,1952
| 1908 | PIT N | 1 | 25 | | .224 |
| | TR | | | | |

GILLELAND, SAMUEL
(PLAYED UNDER NAME OF
SAMUEL GILLEN)

GILLEN, SAMUEL
(REAL NAME SAMUEL GILLELAND)
B.1870 ALLEGHENY,PA.
D.MAY 13,1905
1893	PIT N	S	3		.000
1897	PHI N	S	74		.258
			77		.253

GILLEN, THOMAS J.
B.MAY 18,1862 PHILADELPHIA,PA.
D.JAN.26,1889
1884	KEY U	C-O	28		.149
	PHI N	C	1		.333
1886	DET N	C	2		.400
			31		.154

GILLENWATER, CARDEN EDISON
B.MAY 13,1918 RICEVILLE,TENN.
1940	STL N	O	7		.160
1943	BRO N	O	8		.176
1945	BOS N	O	144		.288
1946	BOS N	O	99		.228
1948	WAS A	O	77		.244
	BRTR		335		.260

GILLENWATER, CLARAL LEWIS
B.MAY 20,1900 SIMS,IND.
| 1923 | CHI A | P | 5 | | 1- 3 |
| | BRTR | | | | |

GILLESPIE, JAMES
B.BUFFALO,N.Y.
| 1890 | BUF P | O | 1 | | .000 |

GILLESPIE, JOHN PATRICK
B.FEB.25,1900 OAKLAND,CAL.
D.FEB.15,1954
| 1922 | CIN N | P | 31 | | 3- 3 |
| | BRTR | | | | |

GILLESPIE, PATRICK PETER "PETE"
B.NOV.30,1851 CARBONDALE,PA.
D.MAY 5,1910
1880	TRO N	O	82		.242
1881	TRO N	O	83		.277
1882	TRO N	O	72		.265
1883	NY N	O	95		.314
1884	NY N	O	97		.264
1885	NY N	O	102		.292
1886	NY N	O	98		.272
1887	NY N	O	74		.293
	BL		703		.279

GILLESPIE, PAUL ALLEN
B.SEPT.18,1920 CARTERSVILLE,GA.
1942	CHI N	C	5		.250
1944	CHI N	C	9		.269
1945	CHI N	C-O	75		.288
	BLTR		89		.283

YR	CL	LEA	POS	GP	G	REC

GILLESPIE, ROBERT WILLIAM "BUNCH"
B.OCT.8,1918 COLUMBUS,OHIO

YR	CL	LEA	POS	GP	G	REC
1944	DET	A	P	7		0- 1
1947	CHI	A	P	25		5- 8
1948	CHI	A	P	25		0- 4
1950	BOS	A	P	1		0- 0
		BRTR		58		5-13

GILLIAM, JAMES WILLIAM "JIM" OR "JUNIOR"
B.OCT.17,1928 NASHVILLE,TENN.

YR	CL	LEA	POS	GP	G	REC
1953	BRO	N	2	151		.278
1954	BRO	N	2-O	146		.282
1955	BRO	N	2-O	147		.249
1956	BRO	N	2-O	153		.300
1957	BRO	N	2-O	149		.250
1958	LA	N	2-3-O	147		.261
1959	LA	N	2-3	145		.282
1960	LA	N	2-3	151		.248
1961	LA	N	2-3-O	144		.244
1962	LA	N	2-3-O	160		.270
1963	LA	N	2-3	148		.282
1964	LA	N	2-3-O	116		.228
1965	LA	N	2-3-O	111		.280
1966	LA	N	1-2-3	88		.217
		BBTR		1956		.265

GILLIFORD, PAUL GANT
B.JAN.12,1945 BRYN MAWR,PA.

YR	CL	LEA	POS	GP	G	REC
1967	BAL	A	P	2		0- 0
		BRTL				

GILLIGAN, ANDREW BERNARD "BARNEY"
B.JAN.3,1856 CAMBRIDGE,MASS.
D.APR.1,1934

YR	CL	LEA	POS	GP	G	REC
1875	ATL	NA	C-O	2		-
1879	CLE	N	C-O	52		.170
1880	CLE	N	C-S-O	28		.179
1881	PRO	N	C-2-S-O	45		.218
1882	PRO	N	C-S	55		.223
1883	PRO	N	C	72		.198
1884	PRO	N	C-1-3	80		.244
1885	PRO	N	C-S-O	69		.214
1886	WAS	N	C	82		.190
1887	WAS	N	C	27		.242
1888	DET	N	C	1		.200
		BRTR		513		-

GILLIGAN, JOHN PATRICK
B.OCT.18,1885 CHICAGO,ILL.

YR	CL	LEA	POS	GP	G	REC
1909	STL	A	P	3		1- 2
1910	STL	A	P	9		0- 3
		BBTR		12		1- 5

GILLIS, GRANT
B.JAN.24,1901 GROVE HILL,ALA.

YR	CL	LEA	POS	GP	G	REC
1927	WAS	A	S	10		.222
1928	WAS	A	S	24		.253
1929	BOS	A	2	28		.247
		BRTR		62		.245

GILMAN, PITKIN CLARK
B.MAR.14,1864 EATON TOWNSHIP,O.
D.AUG.17,1950

YR	CL	LEA	POS	GP	G	REC
1884	CLE	N	O	2		.100
1893	CLE	N	3	2		.285
		BLTL		4		.176

GILMORE, ERNEST GROVER
B.NOV.1,1888 CHICAGO,ILL.
D.NOV.25,1919

YR	CL	LEA	POS	GP	G	REC
1914	KC	F	O	138		.282
1915	KC	F	O	119		.282
		BLTL		257		.282

GILMORE, FRANK T.
B.APR.27,1864 WEBSTER,MASS.
D.JULY 22,1929

YR	CL	LEA	POS	GP	G	REC
1886	WAS	N	P	9		4- 4
1887	WAS	N	P	27		7-20
1888	WAS	N	P	13		1-10
		BR		49		12-34

GILMORE, JAMES
B.BALTIMORE,MD.

YR	CL	LEA	POS	GP	G	REC
1875	NAT	NA	C-2-3	5		-

GILMORE, LEONARD PRESTON "MEOW"
B.NOV.3,1918 CLINTON,IND.

YR	CL	LEA	POS	GP	G	REC
1944	PIT	N	P	1		0- 1
		BRTR				

GILPATRICK, GEORGE F.
B.FEB.28,1875 HOLDEN,MO.
D.DEC.15,1941

YR	CL	LEA	POS	GP	G	REC
1898	STL	N	P	7		0- 1

GILROY

YR	CL	LEA	POS	GP	G	REC
1874	CHI	NA	C	8		-
1875	ATH	NA	O	1		.000
				9		-

GILROY, JOHN N.
B.OCT.26,1875 WASHINGTON,D.C.
D.AUG.4,1897

YR	CL	LEA	POS	GP	G	REC
1895	WAS	N	P	11		1- 4
1896	WAS	N	P	1		0- 0
				12		1- 4

GILSON, HAROLD "HAL"
B.FEB.9,1942 LOS ANGELES,CAL.

YR	CL	LEA	POS	GP	G	REC
1968	STL	N	P	13		0- 2
	HOU	N	P	2	3	0- 0
		BRTL		15	16	0- 2

GING, WILLIAM JOSEPH
B.NOV.7,1872 ELMIRA,N.Y.
D.SEPT.14,1950

YR	CL	LEA	POS	GP	G	REC
1899	BOS	N	P	1		1- 0

GINGRAS, JOSEPH JOHN E.
B.JAN.10,1893 NEW YORK,N.Y.
D.SEPT.6,1947

YR	CL	LEA	POS	GP	G	REC
1915	KC	F	P	2		0- 0
		BRTR				

GINN, TINSLEY RUCKER
B.SEPT.26,1891 ROYSTON,GA.
D.AUG.30,1931 ATLANTA,GA.

YR	CL	LEA	POS	GP	G	REC
1914	CLE	A	O	2		.000
		BLTR				

GINSBERG, MYRON NATHAN "JOE"
B.OCT.11,1926 NEW YORK,N.Y.

YR	CL	LEA	POS	GP	G	REC
1948	DET	A	C	11		.361
1950	DET	A	C	36		.232
1951	DET	A	C	102		.260
1952	DET	A	C	113		.221
1953	DET	A	C	18		.302
	CLE	A	C	46		.284
1954	CLE	A	C	3		.500
1956	KC	A	C	71		.246
	BAL	A	C	15		.071
1957	BAL	A	C	85		.274
1958	BAL	A	C	61		.211
1959	BAL	A	C	65		.181
1960	BAL	A	C	14		.267
	CHI	A	C	28		.253
1961	CHI	A	C	6		.000
	BOS	A	C	19		.250
1962	NY	N	C	2		.000
		BLTR		695		.241

GIONFRIDDO, ALBERT FRANCIS "AL"
B.MAR.8,1922 DYSART,PA.

YR	CL	LEA	POS	GP	G	REC
1944	PIT	N	O	4		.167
1945	PIT	N	O	122		.284
1946	PIT	N	O	64		.255
1947	PIT	N	H	1		.000
	BRO	N	H	37		.177
		BLTL		228		.266

GIORDANO, THOMAS ARTHUR
B.OCT.9,1925 NEWARK,N.J.

YR	CL	LEA	POS	GP	G	REC
1953	PHI	A	2	11		.175
		BRTR				

GIRARD, CHARLES A.
B.1886 BROOKLYN,N.Y.

YR	CL	LEA	POS	GP	G	REC
1910	PHI	N	P	7		1- 2

GIULIANI, ANGELO JOHN "TONY"
B.NOV.24,1912 ST.PAUL,MINN.

YR	CL	LEA	POS	GP	G	REC
1936	STL	A	C	71		.217
1937	STL	A	C	19		.302
1938	WAS	A	C	46		.217
1939	WAS	A	C	54		.250
1940	BRO	N	C	1		.000
1941	BRO	N	C	3		.000
1943	WAS	A	C	49		.226
		BRTR		243		.233

GIUSTI, DAVID JOHN "DAVE"
B.NOV.27,1939 SENECA FALLS,N.Y.

YR	CL	LEA	POS	GP	G	REC
1962	HOU	N	P	22	26	2- 3
1964	HOU	N	P		8	0- 0
1965	HOU	N	P		38	8- 7
1966	HOU	N	P	34	41	15-14
1967	HOU	N	P	37	43	11-15
1968	HOU	N	P	37	38	11-14
1969	STL	N	P		22	3- 7
1970	PIT	N	P		66	9- 3
1971	PIT	N	P		58	5- 6
1972	PIT	N	P		54	7- 4
1973	PIT	N	P		67	9- 2
1974	PIT	N	P		64	7- 5
1975	PIT	N	P		61	5- 4
1976	PIT	N	P		40	5- 4
		BRTR		608	626	97-88

GLADD, JAMES WALTER
B.OCT.2,1922 FT.GIBSON,OKLA.

YR	CL	LEA	POS	GP	G	REC
1956	NY	N	C		4	.091
		BRTR				

GLADDING, FRED EARL
B.JUNE 28,1936 FLAT ROCK,MICH.

YR	CL	LEA	POS	GP	G	REC
1961	DET	A	P		8	1- 0
1962	DET	A	P		6	0- 0
1963	DET	A	P		22	1- 1
1964	DET	A	P		42	7- 4
1965	DET	A	P		46	6- 2
1966	DET	A	P		51	5- 0
1967	DET	A	P		42	6- 4
1968	HOU	N	P		7	0- 0
1969	HOU	N	P		57	4- 8
1970	HOU	N	P		63	7- 4
1971	HOU	N	P		48	4- 5
1972	HOU	N	P		42	5- 6
1973	HOU	N	P		16	2- 0
		BLTR		450		48-34

GLADE, FREDERICK MONROE "LUCKY"
B.JAN.25,1876 DUBUQUE,IOWA
D.NOV.21,1934

YR	CL	LEA	POS	GP	G	REC
1902	CHI	N	P		1	0- 1
1904	STL	A	P		36	19-15
1905	STL	A	P		32	6-24
1906	STL	A	P		35	15-15
1907	STL	A	P		32	13- 9
1908	NY	A	P		5	0- 4
		BRTR		141		53-68

GLADMAN, JOHN H. "BUCK"
B.1864 WASHINGTON,D.C.

YR	CL	LEA	POS	GP	G	REC
1883	PHI	N	3		1	.000
1884	WAS	AA	3		56	.158
1886	WAS	N	3		44	.138
					101	.149

GLADU, ROLAND EDWIN
B.MAY 10,1913 MONTREAL,QUE.,CAN

YR	CL	LEA	POS	GP	G	REC
1944	BOS	N	3-O		21	.242
		BLTR				

GLAISER, JOHN BURKE
B.JULY 28,1897 YOAKUM,TEX.
D.MAR.7,1959

YR	CL	LEA	POS	GP	G	REC
1920	DET	A	P		9	0- 0
		BLTR				

GLASS, THOMAS JOSEPH
B.APR.29,1902 GREENSBORO,N.C.

YR	CL	LEA	POS	GP	G	REC
1925	PHI	A	P		2	1- 0
		BRTR				

YR	CL	LEA	POS	GP	G	REC

GLASSCOCK, JOHN WESLEY "PEBBLY JACK"
B.JULY 22,1859 WHEELING,W.VA.
D.FEB.24,1947 WHEELING,W.VA.

YR	CL	LEA	POS	GP	G	REC
1879	CLE	N	2-3		80	.209
1880	CLE	N	S		76	.247
1881	CLE	N	2-S		84	.260
1882	CLE	N	S		82	.285
1883	CLE	N	2-S		93	.290
1884	CLE		P-2-S	2	72	0- 0 .249
	CIN	U	2-S		39	.388
1885	STL	N	2-S		111	.280
1886	STL	N	S		121	.325
1887	IND	N	S		121	.349
1888	IND	N	S		112	.269
1889	IND	N	M-S		134	.359
1890	NY	N	S		124	.336
1891	NY	N	S		95	.243
1892	STL	N	S		139	.273
1893	STL	N	S		48	.301
	PIT	N	S		66	.380
1894	PIT	N	S		86	.282
1895	LOU	N	S		18	.373
1895	WAS	N	S		25	.233
	BRTR			2	1726	0- 0 .297

GLAVENICH, LUKE FRANK
B.JAN.17,1894 NEW CHICAGO,CAL.
D.MAY 22,1935

YR	CL	LEA	POS	GP	G	REC
1913	CLE	A	P		1	0- 0

GLAVIANO, THOMAS GIATANO "TOMMY" OR "RABBIT"
B.OCT.26,1923 SACRAMENTO,CAL.

YR	CL	LEA	POS	GP	G	REC
1949	STL	N	2-3		87	.267
1950	STL	N	2-S-O		115	.285
1951	STL	N	2-O		54	.185
1952	STL	N	2-3		80	.241
1953	PHI	N	2-S-3		53	.203
	BRTR				389	.257

GLAZE, DANIEL RALPH
B.MAR.13,1882 DENVER,COL.
D.OCT.31,1968 ATASCADERO,CAL.

YR	CL	LEA	POS	GP	G	REC
1906	BOS	A	P	19	22	4- 6
1907	BOS	A	P		32	9-13
1908	BOS	A	P		10	2- 2
	BRTR			61	64	15-21

GLAZNER, CHARLES FRANKLIN "WHITEY"
B.SEPT.17,1893 SYCAMORE,ALA.

YR	CL	LEA	POS	GP	G	REC
1920	PIT	N	P		2	0- 0
1921	PIT	N	P		36	14- 5
1922	PIT	N	P		33	11-12
1923	PIT	N	P		7	2- 1
	PHI	N	P		28	7-14
1924	PHI	N	P		35	7-16
	BRTR				141	41-48

GLEASON, HARRY GEORGE
B.AUG.17,1882 PHILADELPHIA,PA.
D.OCT.1,1961

YR	CL	LEA	POS	GP	G	REC
1901	BOS	A	3		1	1.000
1902	BOS	A	2-3-O		66	.224
1904	STL	A	S-3		45	.214
1905	STL	A	3		150	.217
	TR				262	.217

GLEASON, JOHN DAY
B.JULY 14,1854 ST.LOUIS,MO.
D.SEPT.4,1944

YR	CL	LEA	POS	GP	G	REC
1877	STL	N	O		1	.250
1882	STL	AA	3-O		78	.262
1883	STL	AA	3-O		9	.205
	LOU	AA	3		84	.276
1884	STL	U	3		77	.312
1885	STL	N	3		2	.143
1886	ATH	AA	3		76	.195
	BRTR				327	.262

GLEASON, JOSEPH PAUL
B.JULY 9,1895 NEW YORK,N.Y.

YR	CL	LEA	POS	GP	G	REC
1920	WAS	A	P		2	0- 0
1922	WAS	A	P		8	2- 2
	BRTR				10	2- 2

GLEASON, ROY WILLIAM
B.APR.9,1943 MELROSE PARK,ILL.

YR	CL	LEA	POS	GP	G	REC
1963	LA	N	H		8	1.000
	BBTR					

GLEASON, WILLIAM
B.1868 CLEVELAND,OHIO
D.DEC.2,1893

YR	CL	LEA	POS	GP	G	REC
1890	CLE	P	P		1	0- 1

GLEASON, WILLIAM G.
B.NOV.12,1858 ST.LOUIS,MO.
D.JULY 21,1932

YR	CL	LEA	POS	GP	G	REC
1882	STL	AA	2-S		79	.286
1883	STL	AA	S		95	.274
1884	STL	AA	S		110	.269
1885	STL	AA	S		112	.253
1886	STL	AA	S		126	.267
1887	STL	AA	S		135	.336
1888	ATH	AA	S		123	.224
1889	LOU	AA	S		15	.216
	BRTR				795	.275

GLEASON, WILLIAM J. "KID"
B.OCT.26,1866 CAMDEN,N.J.
D.JAN.2,1933

YR	CL	LEA	POS	GP	G	REC
1888	PHI	N	P		24	7-17
1889	PHI	N	P	25	28	9-14
1890	PHI	N	P	56	58	39-17
1891	PHI	N	P	50	60	24-26
1892	STL	N	P	44	63	16-24
1893	STL	N	P	46	55	21-25
1894	STL	N	P		10	2- 6
	BAL	N	P		23	15- 6
1895	BAL	N	P-2	4	107	3- 1 .323
1896	NY	N	2		133	.292
1897	NY	N	2		134	.311
1898	NY	N	2		149	.222
1899	NY	N	2		148	.287
1900	NY	N	2		111	.257
1901	DET	A	2		136	.278
1902	DET	A	2		118	.247
1903	PHI	N	2		106	.284
1904	PHI	N	2		153	.274
1905	PHI	N	2		155	.247
1906	PHI	N	2		135	.227
1907	PHI	N	2		35	.143
1908	PHI	N	2-O		2	.000
1912	CHI	A	2		1	.500
	BBTR			282	1944	136-136 .262

NON-PLAYING MANAGER
CHI(A) 1919-23

GLEASON, WILLIAM PATRICK
B.SEPT.8,1893 CHICAGO,ILL.
D.JAN.9,1957

YR	CL	LEA	POS	GP	G	REC
1916	PIT	N	2		1	.000
1917	PIT	N	2		14	.167
1921	STL	A	2		26	.257
	BRTR				41	.220

GLEESON, JAMES JOSEPH "GEE GEE"
B.MAR.5,1912 KANSAS CITY,MO.

YR	CL	LEA	POS	GP	G	REC
1936	CLE	A	O		41	.259
1939	CHI	N	O		111	.223
1940	CHI	N	O		129	.313
1941	CIN	N	O		102	.233
1942	CIN	N	O		9	.200
	BBTR				392	.263

GLEICH, FRANK ELMER "INCH"
B.MAR.7,1901 COLUMBUS,OHIO
D.MAR.27,1949

YR	CL	LEA	POS	GP	G	REC
1919	NY	A	O		4	.333
1920	NY	A	O		24	.122
	BLTR				28	.156

GLENALVIN, ROBERT J.
(REAL NAME ROBERT J. DOWLING)
B.JAN.17,1867 INDIANAPOLIS,IND.
D.MAR.24,1944

YR	CL	LEA	POS	GP	G	REC
1890	CHI	N	2		66	.268
1893	CHI	N	2		16	.400
	TR				82	.294

GLENDON, MARTIN H.
B.1876 CHICAGO,ILL.

YR	CL	LEA	POS	GP	G	REC
1902	CIN	N	P		1	0- 1
1903	CLE	A	P		3	1- 2
					4	1- 3

GLENN, BURDETTE "BOB"
B.JUNE 16,1894 W.SUNBURY,PA.

YR	CL	LEA	POS	GP	G	REC
1920	STL	N	P		2	0- 0

GLENN, EDWARD C. "MOUSE"
B.SEPT.19,1860 RICHMOND,VA.
D.FEB.10,1892

YR	CL	LEA	POS	GP	G	REC
1884	RIC	AA	O		42	.250
1886	PIT	AA	O		71	.182
1888	KC	AA	O		3	.000
1888	BOS	N	O		19	.154
	BRTR				135	.196

GLENN, EDWARD D.
B.1874 LUDLOW,KY.
D.DEC.6,1911 LUDLOW,KY.

YR	CL	LEA	POS	GP	G	REC
1898	NY	N	S		2	.167
1902	CHI	N	S		4	.158

GLENN, HARRY MELVILLE "HUSKY"
B.JUNE 9,1890 SHELBURN,IND.
D.OCT.12,1918

YR	CL	LEA	POS	GP	G	REC
1915	STL	N	C		6	.312
	BRTR					

GLENN, JOHN
B.JULY 10,1928 MOULTRIE,GA.

YR	CL	LEA	POS	GP	G	REC
1960	STL	N	O		32	.258
	BRTR					

GLENN, JOHN W.
B.1849 ROCHESTER,N.Y.
D.NOV.10,1888

YR	CL	LEA	POS	GP	G	REC
1871	OLY	NA	O		25	-
1872	OLY	NA	O		9	.150
	NAT	NA	O		1	.500
1873	NAT	NA	1		39	-
1874	CHI	NA	1-3-O		54	-
1875	CHI	NA	1-O		70	-
1876	CHI	N	1-O		66	.292
1877	CHI	N	1-O		50	.228
	BRTR				314	-

GLENN, JOSEPH CHARLES
(REAL NAME JOSEPH CHARLES GURZENSKY)
B.NOV.19,1908 DICKSON CITY,PA.

YR	CL	LEA	POS	GP	G	REC
1932	NY	A	C		6	.125
1933	NY	A	C		5	.143
1935	NY	A	C		17	.233
1936	NY	A	C		44	.271
1937	NY	A	C		25	.283
1938	NY	A	C		41	.260
1939	STL	A	C		88	.273
1940	BOS	A	C		22	.128
	BRTR				248	.252

GLIATTO, SALVADOR MICHAEL
B.MAY 7,1905 CHICAGO,ILL.

YR	CL	LEA	POS	GP	G	REC
1930	CLE	A	P	8	10	0- 0
	BBTR					

GLOCKSON, NORMAN STANLEY
B.JUNE 15,1894 BLUE ISLAND,ILL.
D.AUG.5,1955 MAYWOOD,ILL.

YR	CL	LEA	POS	GP	G	REC
1914	CIN	N	C		7	.000
	BRTR					

GLOSSOP, ALBAN "AL"
B.JULY 23,1915 CHRISTOPHER,ILL.

YR	CL	LEA	POS	GP	G	REC
1939	NY	N	2		10	.188
1940	NY	N	2		27	.209
	BOS	N	2-S-O		60	.236
1942	PHI	N	2-3		121	.225
1943	BRO	N	2-S-3		87	.171
1946	CHI	N	2-S		4	.000
	BBTR				309	.209

GLYNN, EDWARD PAUL "ED"
B.JUNE 3,1953 FLUSHING,N.Y.

YR	CL	LEA	POS	GP	G	REC
1975	DET	A	P		3	0- 2
1976	DET	A	P		5	1- 3
	BRTL				8	1- 5

GLYNN, WILLIAM VINCENT "BILL"
B.JAN.30,1926 SUSSEX,N.J.

YR	CL	LEA	POS	GP	G	REC
1949	PHI	N	1		8	.200
1952	CLE	A	1		44	.272
1953	CLE	A	1-O		147	.243
1954	CLE	A	1-O		111	.251
	BLTL				310	.249

GOAR, JOSHUA MERCER "JOT"
B.JAN.31,1870 NEW LISBON,IND.
D.APR.4,1947

YR	CL	LEA	POS	GP	G	REC
1896	PIT	N	P		3	0- 0
1898	CIN	N	P		1	0- 0
	BRTR				4	0- 0

YR	CL	LEA	POS	GP	G	REC

GOCHNAUER, JOHN PETER
B.SEPT.12,1875 ALTOONA,PA.
D.SEPT.27,1929

YR	CL	LEA	POS	GP	G	REC
1901	BRO	N	S		3	.363
1902	CLE	A	S		126	.183
1903	CLE	A	S		136	.181
	BRTR				265	.184

GODAR, JOHN MICHAEL
B.OCT.25,1864 CINCINNATI,OHIO
D.JUNE 23,1949

| 1892 | BAL | N | O | | 5 | .333 |

GODBY, DANNY RAY
B.NOV.4,1946 LOGAN,W.VA.

| 1974 | STL | N | O | | 13 | .154 |
| | BRTR | | | | | |

GODDARD, JOSEPH HAROLD "JOE"
B.JULY 23,1950 BECKLEY,W.VA.

| 1972 | SD | N | C | | 12 | .200 |
| | BRTR | | | | | |

GODWIN, JOHN HENRY "BUNNY"
B.MAR.10,1877 E.LIVERPOOL,OHIO
D.MAY 5,1956

1905	BOS	A	3		16	.304
1906	BOS	A	3		66	.187
	BRTR				82	.209

GOEBEL, EDWIN
B.SEPT.1,1899 BROOKLYN,N.Y.

| 1922 | WAS | A | O | | 37 | .271 |
| | BRTR | | | | | |

GOECKEL, WILLIAM JOHN
B.SEPT.3,1871 WILKES-BARRE,PA.
D.NOV.1,1922 PHILADELPHIA,PA.

| 1899 | PHI | N | 1 | | 35 | .283 |
| | BLTL | | | | | |

GOETZ, GEORGE BURT
B.GREENCASTLE,IND.

| 1889 | BAL | AA | P | 1 | 1- 0 | |

GOETZ, JOHN HARDY
B.OCT.24,1937 GOETZVILLE,MICH.

| 1960 | CHI | N | P | 4 | 0- 0 | |
| | BRTR | | | | | |

GOGGIN, CHARLES FRANCIS "CHUCK"
B.JULY 7,1945 POMPANO BEACH,FLA.

1972	PIT	N	2		5	.286
1973	PIT	N	C		1	1.000
	ATL	N	C-2-S-O		64	.289
1974	BOS	A	2		2	.000
	BBTR				72	.293

GOGOLEWSKI, WILLIAM JOSEPH "BILL"
B.OCT.26,1947 OSHKOSH,WIS.

1970	WAS	A	P	8	2- 2	
1971	WAS	A	P	27	6- 5	
1972	TEX	A	P	36	4-11	
1973	TEX	A	P	49	3- 6	
1974	CLE	A	P	5	0- 0	
1975	CHI	A	P	19	0- 0	
	BLTR			144	15-24	

GOLDEN, JAMES EDWARD "JIM"
B.MAR.20,1936 ELDON,MO.

1960	LA	N	P		1	1- 0
1961	LA	N	P		28	1- 1
1962	HOU	N	P	37	43	7-11
1963	HOU	N	P		3	0- 1
	BLTR			69	75	9-13

GOLDEN, MICHAEL HENRY
B.SEPT.11,1851 CHELSEA,MASS.
D.JAN.11,1929

1875	WES	NA	P		13	1-12
	CHI	NA	P-O	14	38	6- 8
						-
1878	MIL	N	P-O	18	54	3-15
						.209
	BRTR			45	105	10-35

GOLDEN, ROY K.
B.JULY 12,1888 CHICAGO,ILL.
D.OCT.4,1961

1910	STL	N	P		7	2- 3
1911	STL	N	P		30	4- 9
	TR				37	6-12

GOLDMAN, JONAH JOHN
B.AUG.29,1906 NEW YORK,N.Y.

1928	CLE	A	S		7	.238
1930	CLE	A	S-3		111	.242
1931	CLE	A	S		30	.129
	BRTR				148	.224

GOLDSBERRY, GORDON FREDERICK
B.AUG.30,1927 SACRAMENTO,CAL.

1949	CHI	A	1		39	.248
1950	CHI	A	1-O		82	.268
1951	CHI	A	1		10	.091
1952	STL	A	1-O		86	.229
	BLTL				217	.241

GOLDSBY, WALTON HUGH
B.DEC.31,1861 LOUISIANA
D.JAN.11,1914

1884	STL	AA	O		5	.211
	WAS	AA	O		6	.375
	RIC	AA	O		10	.222
1886	WAS	N	O		6	.111
1888	BAL	AA	O		44	.227
					71	.233

GOLDSMITH, FRED ERNEST
B.MAY 15,1852 NEW HAVEN,CONN.
D.MAR.28,1939

1879	TRO	N	P-1-	8	9	2- 4
			O			.231
1880	CHI	N	P-1-	25	35	22- 3
			O			.260
1881	CHI	N	P-O	38	40	25-13
						.240
1882	CHI	N	P-1		44	28-16
						.229
1883	CHI	N	P-1-	46	60	28-18
			O			.221
1884	CHI	N	P-O	21	22	8-12
						.135
	BAL	AA	P-1		4	3- 1
						.167
	BRTR			186	214	116-67
						.225

GOLDSMITH, HAROLD EUGENE
B.AUG.18,1898 PECONIC,N.Y.

1926	BOS	N	P		19	5- 7
1927	BOS	N	P		22	1- 3
1928	BOS	N	P		4	0- 0
1929	STL	N	P		2	0- 0.
	BRTR				47	6-10

GOLDSMITH, WALLACE
B.1849 BALTIMORE,MD.

1871	KEK	NA	C-S-3	19	-	
1872	OLY	NA	2-S	9	.225	
1873	MAR	NA	2	1	.000	
1875	WES	NA	3	13	-	
	NH	NA	2	1	-	
				43	-	

GOLDSTEIN, ISADORE
B.JUNE 6,1908 NEW YORK,N.Y.

| 1932 | DET | A | P | 16 | 3- 2 | |
| | BBTR | | | | | |

GOLDSTEIN, LESLIE ELMER "LONNIE"
B.MAY 13,1918 AUSTIN,TEX.

1943	CIN	N	1		5	.200
1946	CIN	N	H		6	.000
	BLTL				11	.100

GOLDY, PURNAL WILLIAM
B.NOV.28,1937 CAMDEN,N.J.

1962	DET	A	O		20	.229
1963	DET	A	H		9	.250
	BRTR				29	.231

GOLETZ, STANLEY "STOSH"
B.MAY 21,1918 CRESENT,OHIO

| 1941 | CHI | A | H | | 5 | .600 |
| | BLTL | | | | | |

GOLIAT, MIKE MITCHELL
B.NOV.5,1925 YATESBORO,PA.

1949	PHI	N	1-2		55	.212
1950	PHI	N	2		145	.234
1951	PHI	N	2-3		41	.225
	STL	A	2		5	.182
1952	STL	A	2		3	.000
	BRTR				249	.225

GOLTZ, DAVID ALLAN "DAVE"
B.JUNE 23,1949 PELICAN RAPIDS, MINN.

1972	MIN	A	P		15	3- 3
1973	MIN	A	P		32	6- 4
1974	MIN	A	P		28	10-10
1975	MIN	A	P		32	14-14
1976	MIN	A	P	36	37	14-14
	BRTR			143	144	47-45

GOLVIN, WALTER GEORGE
B.FEB.1,1894 NORTH PLATTE,NEB.
D.JUNE 11,1973 GARDENA,CAL.

| 1922 | CHI | N | 1 | | 2 | .000 |
| | BLTL | | | | | |

GOMEZ, JOSE LUIS RODRIGUEZ "CHILE"
B.SEPT.23,1910 VILLAUNION,MEX.

1935	PHI	N	2-S		67	.230
1936	PHI	N	2-S		108	.232
1942	WAS	A	2		25	.192
	BRTR				200	.226

GOMEZ, LUIS
B.AUG.19,1951 GUADALAJARA,MEX.

1974	MIN	A	2-S		82	.208
1975	MIN	A	2-S		89	.139
1976	MIN	A	2-S-3-O		38	.193
	BRTR				209	.189

GOMEZ, PEDRO W. (MARTINEZ) "PRESTON"
B.APR.20,1923 CENTRAL PRESTON, CUBA

| 1944 | WAS | A | 2-S | | 8 | .286 |
| | BRTR | | | | | |

NON-PLAYING MANAGER
SD(N) 1969-72, HOU(N) 1974-75

GOMEZ, RUBEN (COLON)
B.JULY 13,1927 ARROYO,P.R.

1953	NY	N	P	29	61	13-11
1954	NY	N	P	37	49	17- 9
1955	NY	N	P	33	42	9-10
1956	NY	N	P-O	40	52	7-17
						.183
1957	NY	N	P-O	38	54	15-13
						.184
1958	SF	N	P	42	48	10-12
1959	PHI	N	P	20	24	3- 8
1960	PHI	N	P		22	0- 3
1962	CLE	A	P	15	16	1- 2
	MIN	A	P		6	1- 1
1967	PHI	N	P		7	0- 0
	BRTR			289	381	76-86
						.199

GOMEZ, VERNON LOUIS "LEFTY"
B.NOV.26,1908 RODEO,CAL.

1930	NY	A	P		15	2- 5
1931	NY	A	P		40	21- 9
1932	NY	A	P		37	24- 7
1933	NY	A	P		35	16-10
1934	NY	A	P		38	26- 5
1935	NY	A	P		34	12-15
1936	NY	A	P		31	13- 7
1937	NY	A	P		34	21-11
1938	NY	A	P		32	18-12
1939	NY	A	P		26	12- 8
1940	NY	A	P		9	3- 3
1941	NY	A	P		23	15- 5
1942	NY	A	P		13	6- 4
1943	WAS	A	P		1	0- 1
	BLTL				368	189-102

GONDER, JESSE LEMAR
B.JAN.20,1936 MONTICELLO,ARK.

1960	NY	A	C		7	.286
1961	NY	A	H		15	.333
1962	CIN	N	H		4	.000
1963	CIN	N	C		31	.313
	NY	N	C		42	.302
1964	NY	N	C		131	.270
1965	NY	N	C		53	.238
	MIL	N	C		31	.151
1966	PIT	N	C		59	.225
1967	PIT	N	C		22	.139
	BLTR				395	.251

GONZALES, EUSEBIO MIGUEL (LOPEZ) "PAPO"
B.JULY 13,1892 HAVANA,CUBA
D.FEB.14,1976 HAVANA,CUBA

| 1918 | BOS | A | S-3 | | 3 | .400 |
| | BRTR | | | | | |

YR   CL LEA POS GP   G   REC

GONZALES, JOE MADRID "SMOKEY"
B.MAR.19,1915 SAN FRANCISCO,CAL
1937 BOS A P   8 1- 2
     BRTR

GONZALES, JULIO ENRIQUE
B.DEC.20,1920 HAVANA,CUBA
1949 WAS A P   13 0- 0
     BRTR

GONZALES, WENCESLAO O'REILLY
B.SEPT.28,1925 QUIVICAN,CUBA
1955 WAS A P   1 0- 0
     BLTL

**GONZALEZ, ANDRES ANTONIO
(GONZALEZ) "TONY"**
B.AUG.28,1936 CAMAGUEY,CUBA
1960 CIN N O   39 .212
     PHI N O   78 .299
1961 PHI N O   126 .277
1962 PHI N O   118 .302
1963 PHI N O   155 .306
1964 PHI N O   131 .278
1965 PHI N O   108 .295
1966 PHI N O   132 .286
1967 PHI N O   149 .339
1968 PHI N O   121 .264
1969 SD N O   53 .225
     ATL N O   89 .294
1970 ATL N O   123 .265
     CAL A O   26 .304
1971 CAL A O   111 .245
     BLTR   1559 .286

**GONZALEZ, JOSE FERNANDO
"FERNANDO"**
B.JUNE 19,1950 ARECIBO,P.R.
1972 PIT N 3   3 .000
1973 PIT N 3   37 .224
1974 KC A 3   9 .143
     NY A 2-S-3   51 .215
     BRTR   100 .207

**GONZALEZ, MIGUEL ANGEL CORDERO
"MIKE"**
B.SEPT.24,1892 HAVANA,CUBA
1912 BOS N C   1 .000
1914 CIN N C   95 .233
1915 STL N C-1   51 .227
1916 STL N C-1   118 .239
1917 STL N C-1   106 .262
1918 STL N C-1-O   117 .252
1919 NY N C-1   58 .190
1920 NY N C   11 .231
1921 NY N C-1   13 .375
1924 STL N C   120 .296
1925 STL N C-1   77 .310
     CHI N C   70 .264
1926 CHI N C   80 .249
1927 CHI N C   39 .241
1928 CHI N C   49 .272
1929 CHI N C   60 .240
1931 STL N C   15 .105
1932 STL N C   17 .143
     BRTR   1042 .254
NON-PLAYING MANAGER
STL(N) 1938 AND 1940

GONZALEZ, ORLANDO EUGENE
B.NOV.15,1951 HAVANA,CUBA
1976 CLE A 1-O   28 .250
     BLTL

GONZALEZ, PEDRO
B.DEC.12,1937 SAN PEDRO DE
MACORIS,D.R.
1963 NY A 2   14 .192
1964 NY 1 1-2-3-O 80 .277
1965 NY A H   7 .400
     CLE A 2-3-O   116 .253
1966 CLE A 2-3-O   110 .233
1967 CLE A 1-2-S-3 80 .228
     BRTR   407 .244

GOOCH, CHARLES FURMAN
B.JUNE 5,1904 SMYRNA,TENN.
1929 WAS A I-S-3   39 .281
     BRTR

GOOCH, JOHN BEVERLY
B.NOV.9,1897 SMYRNA,TENN.
D.MAR.15,1975 NASHVILLE,TENN.
1921 PIT N C   13 .237
1922 PIT N C   105 .328
1923 PIT N C   66 .277
1924 PIT N C   70 .290
1925 PIT N C   79 .298
1926 PIT N C   86 .271
1927 PIT N C   101 .258
1928 PIT N C   31 .238
     BRO N C   42 .317
1929 BRO N H   1 .000
     CIN N H   92 .300
1930 CIN N H   82 .243
1933 BOS A H   37 .182
     BBTR   805 .276

GOOCH, LEE CURRIN
B.FEB.23,1890 OXFORD,N.C.
D.MAY 18,1966
1915 CLE A H   2 .667
1917 PHI A O   17 .288
     BRTR   19 .295

GOOD, EUGENE J.
B.DEC.13,1882 BOSTON,MASS.
D.AUG.6,1947
1906 BOS N O   34 .151

GOOD, RALPH NELSON "HOLY"
B.APR.25,1886 MONTICELLO,ME.
D.NOV.24,1965 WATERVILLE,MAINE
1910 BOS N P   2 0- 0
     BRTR

GOOD, WILBUR DAVID "LEFTY"
B.SEPT.28,1885 JEFFERSON CO.,PA
D.DEC.30,1963 BROOKSVILLE,FLA.
1905 NY A P   5 0- 1
1908 CLE A O   46 .279
1909 CLE A O   94 .214
1910 BOS N O   23 .337
1911 BOS N O   43 .267
     CHI N O   58 .269
1912 CHI N O   39 .143
1913 CHI N O   49 .253
1914 CHI N O   154 .272
1915 CHI N O   128 .253
1916 PHI N O   75 .250
1918 CHI A O   35 .250
     BLTL   5 749 0- 1
                     .258

GOODALL, HERBERT FRANK
B.AUG.10,1866 MANSFIELD,PA.
D.JAN.20,1938
1890 LOU AA P   18 10- 6
     BRTR

GOODELL, JOHN HENRY WILLIAM
B.APR.5,1907 MUSKOGEE,OKLA.
1928 CHI A P   2 0- 0
     BRTL

GOODENOUGH, WILLIAM B.
B.ST.LOUIS,MO.
D.MAY 24,1905
1893 STL N O   10 .178

GOODFELLOW, MICHAEL J.
B.OCT.3,1866 PORT JERVIS,N.Y.
D.FEB.12,1920
1887 STL AA C   1 .000
1888 CLE AA O   69 .250
                     70 .246

GOODMAN, IVAL RICHARD
B.JULY 23,1908 NORTHVIEW,MO.
1935 CIN N O   148 .269
1936 CIN N O   136 .284
1937 CIN N O   147 .273
1938 CIN N O   145 .292
1939 CIN N O   124 .323
1940 CIN N O   136 .258
1941 CIN N O   42 .268
1942 CIN N O   87 .243
1943 CHI N O   80 .320
1944 CHI N O   62 .262
     BLTR   1107 .281

GOODMAN, JACOB
B.SEPT.14,1853 LANCASTER,PA.
D.MAR.9,1890
1878 MIL N 1   59 .246
1882 PIT AA 1   10 .316
                     69 .256

GOODMAN, WILLIAM DALE "BILLY"
B.MAR.22,1926 CONCORD,N.C.
1947 BOS A O   12 .182
1948 BOS A 1-2-3   127 .310
1949 BOS A 1   122 .298
1950 BOS A 1-2-S-3- 110 .354
            O
1951 BOS A 1-2-3-O 141 .297
1952 BOS A 1-2-3-O 138 .306
1953 BOS A 1-2   128 .313
1954 BOS A 1-2-3-O 127 .303
1955 BOS A 1-2-O   149 .294
1956 BOS A 2   105 .293
1957 BOS A H   18 .063
     BAL A 1-2-S   73 .308
1958 CHI A 1-2-S-3 116 .299
1959 CHI A 2-3   104 .250
1960 CHI A 2-3   30 .234
1961 CHI A 1-2-3   41 .255
1962 HOU N 2-3   82 .255
     BLTR   1623 .300

GOODSON, JAMES EDWARD "ED"
B.JAN.25,1948 PULASKI,VA.
1970 SF N 1   7 .273
1971 SF N 1   20 .190
1972 SF N 1   58 .280
1973 SF N 3   102 .302
1974 SF N 1-3   98 .272
1975 SF N 1-3   39 .207
     ATL N 1-3   47 .211
1976 LA N 1-2-3-O 83 .229
     BLTR   454 .265

GOODWIN, ARTHUR INGRAM
B.FEB.27,1876 WHITLEY TWNSP.,PA
D.JUNE 19,1943
1905 NY A P   1 0- 0

GOODWIN, CLAIRE VERNON "PEP"
B.DEC.19,1894 POCATELLO,IDAHO
D.FEB.15,1972 OAKLAND,CAL.
1914 KC F S-3   111 .243
1915 KC F 2-S   81 .235
     BLTR   192 .240

GOODWIN, CLYDE SAMUEL
B.NOV.12,1886 ATHENS CO.,OHIO
1906 WAS A P   3 0- 2
     BRTR

GOODWIN, DANIEL KAY "DANNY"
B.SEPT.2,1953 PEORIA,ILL.
1975 CAL A H   4 .100
     BLTR

GOODWIN, JAMES PATRICK
B.AUG.15,1926 ST.LOUIS,MO.
1948 CHI A P   8 0- 0
     BLTL

GOODWIN, MARVIN MARDO
B.JAN.16,1891 GORDONSVILLE,VA.
D.OCT.21,1925 HOUSTON,TEX.
1916 WAS A P   3 0- 0
1917 STL N P   14 6- 4
1919 STL N P   33 34 11- 9
1920 STL N P   32 3- 8
1921 STL N P   14 1- 2
1922 STL N P   2 0- 0
1925 CIN N P   4 0- 2
     BRTR 102 103 21- 25

GOOLSBY, RAYMOND DANIEL "OX"
B.SEPT.5,1919 FLORALA,ALA.
1946 WAS A O   3 .000
     BRTR

GOOSSEN, GREGORY BRYANT "GREG"
B.DEC.14,1945 LOS ANGELES,CAL.
1965 NY N C   11 .290
1966 NY N C   13 .188
1967 NY N C   37 .159
1968 NY N C-1   38 .208
1969 SEA A 1-O   52 .309
1970 MIL A 1   21 .255
     WAS A 1-O   21 .222
     BRTR   193 .241

GORBOUS, GLEN EDWARD
B.JULY 8,1930 DRUMHELLER,ALT.,
CAN.
1955 CIN N O   8 .333
     PHI N O   91 .237
1956 PHI N O   15 .182
1957 PHI N H   3 .500
     BLTR   117 .238

YR	CL	LEA	POS	GP	G	REC

GORCZYCA, JOHN JOSEPH PERRY
(PLAYED UNDER NAME OF
JOHN JOSEPH PERRY GORSICA)

GORDINIER, RAYMOND CORNELIUS "GORDY"
B.APR.11,1896 ROCHESTER,N.Y.
D.NOV.15,1960 ROCHESTER,N.Y.

YR	CL	LEA	POS	GP	G	REC
1921	BRO	N	P		3	1- 0
1922	BRO	N	P		5	0- 0
	BBTR				8	1- 0

GORDON, JOSEPH LOWELL "JOE" OR "FLASH"
B.FEB.18,1915 LOS ANGELES,CAL.

YR	CL	LEA	POS	G	REC
1938	NY	A	2	127	.255
1939	NY	A	2	151	.284
1940	NY	A	2	155	.281
1941	NY	A	2	156	.276
1942	NY	A	2	147	.322
1943	NY	A	2	152	.249
1946	NY	A	2	112	.210
1947	CLE	A	2	155	.272
1948	CLE	A	2-S	144	.280
1949	CLE	A	2	148	.251
1950	CLE	A	2	119	.236
	BRTR			1566	.268

NON-PLAYING MANAGER
CLE(A) 1958-60, DET(A) 1960,
KC(A) 1961,1969

GORDON, SIDNEY "SID"
B.AUG.13,1918 BROOKLYN,N.Y.
D.JUNE 17,1975 NEW YORK,N.Y.

YR	CL	LEA	POS	G	REC
1941	NY	N	O	9	.258
1942	NY	N	3	6	.316
1943	NY	N	1-2-3-O	131	.251
1946	NY	N	3-O	135	.293
1947	NY	N	O	130	.273
1948	NY	N	3-O	142	.299
1949	NY	N	1-3-O	141	.284
1950	BOS	N	3-O	134	.304
1951	BOS	N	3-O	150	.287
1952	BOS	N	3-O	144	.289
1953	MIL	N	O	140	.274
1954	PIT	N	3-O	131	.306
1955	PIT	N	3-O	16	.170
	NY	N	3-O	66	.243
	BRTR			1475	.283

GORE, GEORGE F. "PIANO LEGS"
B.MAY 3,1852 SACCARAPPA,ME.
D.SEPT.16,1933 UTICA,N.Y.

YR	CL	LEA	POS	G	REC
1879	CHI	N	O	60	.268
1880	CHI	N	1-O	75	.365
1881	CHI	N	1-S-O	73	.297
1882	CHI	N	O	84	.318
1883	CHI	N	O	91	.334
1884	CHI	N	O	101	.316
1885	CHI	N	O	109	.312
1886	CHI	N	O	118	.304
1887	NY	N	O	111	.348
1888	NY	N	O	64	.220
1889	NY	N	O	119	.305
1890	NY	P	O	93	.335
1891	NY	N	O	130	.285
1893	NY	N	O	53	.254
	STL	N	O	20	.200
	BLTR			1301	.308

GORIN, CHARLES PERRY "CHARLEY"
B.FEB.2,1928 WACO,TEX.

YR	CL	LEA	POS	G	REC
1954	MIL	N	P	5	0- 1
1955	MIL	N	P	2	0- 0
	BLTL			7	0- 1

GORMAN, HERBERT ALLEN
B.DEC.18,1925 SAN FRANCISCO,CAL
D.APR.5,1953

YR	CL	LEA	POS	G	REC
1952	STL	N	H	1	.000
	BLTL				

GORMAN, HOWARD PAUL "LEFTY"
B.MAY 14,1913 PITTSBURGH,PA.

YR	CL	LEA	POS	G	REC
1937	PHI	N	O	13	.211
1938	PHI	N	H	1	.000
	BLTL			14	.250

GORMAN, JOHN F. "STOOPING JACK"
B.ST.LOUIS,MO.
D.SEPT.9,1889

YR	CL	LEA	POS	GP	G	REC
1883	STL	AA	C-O		1	.000
1884	KC	U	1-3-O		33	.275
	PIT	AA	P-3-	3	8	1- 2
			O			.133
				3	42	1- 2
						.256

GORMAN, THOMAS ALOYSOIS "TOM"
B.JAN.4,1926 NEW YORK,N.Y.

YR	CL	LEA	POS	G	REC
1952	NY	A	P	12	6- 2
1953	NY	A	P	40	4- 5
1954	NY	A	P	23	0- 0
1955	KC	A	P	57	7- 6
1956	KC	A	P	52	9-10
1957	KC	A	P	38	5- 9
1958	KC	A	P	50	4- 4
1959	KC	A	P	17	1- 0
	BRTR			289	36-36

GORMAN, THOMAS DAVID "TOM"
B.MAR.16,1919 NEW YORK,N.Y.

YR	CL	LEA	POS	G	REC
1939	NY	N	P	4	0- 0
	BRTL				

GORMLEY, JOSEPH
B.DEC.20,1866 SUMMIT HILL,PA.
D.JULY 2,1950 SUMMIT HILL,PA.

YR	CL	LEA	POS	G	REC
1891	PHI	N	P	1	0- 1
	BLTL				

GORNICKI, HENRY FRANK
B.JAN.14,1915 NIAGARA FALLS,N.Y

YR	CL	LEA	POS	G	REC
1941	STL	N	P	4	1- 0
	CHI	N	P	1	0- 0
1942	PIT	N	P	25	5- 6
1943	PIT	N	P	42	9-13
1946	PIT	N	P	7	0- 0
	BRTR			79	15-19

GORSICA, JOHN JOSEPH PERRY
(REAL NAME
JOHN JOSEPH PERRY GORCZYCA)
B.MAR.29,1915 BAYONNE,N.J.

YR	CL	LEA	POS	GP	G	REC
1940	DET	A	P		29	7- 7
1941	DET	A	P		33	9-11
1942	DET	A	P	28	31	3- 2
1943	DET	A	P	35	36	4- 5
1944	DET	A	P	34	40	6-14
1946	DET	A	P		14	0- 0
1947	DET	A	P		31	2- 0
	BRTR			204	214	31-39

GORYL, JOHN ALBERT "JOHNNY"
B.OCT.21,1933 CUMBERLAND,R.I.

YR	CL	LEA	POS	G	REC
1957	CHI	N	3	9	.211
1958	CHI	N	2-3	83	.242
1959	CHI	N	2-3	25	.188
1962	MIN	1	2-S	37	.192
1963	MIN	A	2-S-3	64	.287
1964	MIN	1	2-3	58	.140
	BRTR			276	.225

GOSGER, JAMES CHARLES "JIM"
B.NOV.6,1942 PORT HURON,MICH.

YR	CL	LEA	POS	G	REC
1963	BOS	A	O	19	.063
1965	BOS	A	O	81	.256
1966	BOS	A	O	40	.254
	KC	A	O	88	.224
1967	KC	A	O	134	.242
1968	OAK	A	O	88	.180
1969	SEA	A	O	39	.109
	NY	N	O	10	.133
1970	MON	N	1-O	91	.263
1971	MON	N	1-O	51	.157
1973	NY	N	O	38	.239
1974	NY	N	O	26	.091
	BLTL			705	.226

GOSLIN, LEON ALLEN "GOOSE"
B.OCT.16,1900 SALEM,N.J.
D.MAY 15,1971 BRIDGETON,N.J.

YR	CL	LEA	POS	G	REC
1921	WAS	A	O	14	.260
1922	WAS	A	O	101	.324
1923	WAS	A	O	150	.300
1924	WAS	A	O	154	.344
1925	WAS	A	O	150	.335
1926	WAS	A	O	147	.354
1927	WAS	A	O	148	.334
1928	WAS	A	O	135	.379
1929	WAS	A	O	145	.288
1930	WAS	A	O	47	.270
	STL	A	O	101	.327
1931	STL	A	O	151	.328
1932	STL	A	O	150	.299
1933	WAS	A	O	132	.297
1934	DET	A	O	151	.305
1935	DET	A	O	147	.292
1936	DET	A	O	147	.315
1937	DET	A	O	79	.238
1938	WAS	A	O	38	.158
	BLTR			2287	.316

GOSS, HOWARD WAYNE "HOWIE"
B.NOV.1,1934 WEWOKA,OKLA.

YR	CL	LEA	POS	G	REC
1962	PIT	N	O	89	.243
1963	HOU	N	O	133	.209
	BRTR			222	.216

GOSSAGE, RICHARD MICHAEL "RICH"
B.JULY 5,1951 COLORADO SPRINGS,
COLO.

YR	CL	LEA	POS	GP	G	REC
1972	CHI	A	P		36	7- 1
1973	CHI	A	P	20	21	0- 4
1974	CHI	A	P		39	4- 6
1975	CHI	A	P		62	9- 8
1976	CHI	A	P		31	9-17
	BRTR			188	189	29-36

GOSSETT, JOHN STAR "DICK"
B.AUG.21,1891 DENNISON,OHIO
D.OCT.6,1962

YR	CL	LEA	POS	G	REC
1913	NY	A	C	39	.162
1914	NY	A	C	10	.090
	BRTR			49	.151

GOTAY, JULIO (SANCHEZ)
B.JUNE 9,1939 FAJARDO,P.R.

YR	CL	LEA	POS	G	REC
1960	STL	N	S-3	3	.375
1961	STL	N	S	10	.244
1962	STL	N	2-S-3-O	127	.255
1963	PIT	N	2	4	.500
1964	PIT	N	H	3	.500
1965	CAL	A	2-S-3	40	.247
1966	HOU	N	3	4	.000
1967	HOU	N	2-S-3	77	.282
1968	HOU	N	2-3	75	.248
1969	HOU	N	2-3	46	.259
	BRTR			389	.260

GOULAIT, THEODORE L.
B.1891

YR	CL	LEA	POS	G	REC
1912	NY	N	P	1	0- 0
	BRTR				

GOULD, ALBERT FRANK "PUDGY"
B.JAN.20,1893 MUSCATINE,IOWA

YR	CL	LEA	POS	G	REC
1916	CLE	A	P	30	5- 7
1917	CLE	A	P	27	4- 4
	BRTR			57	9-11

GOULD, CHARLES HARVEY
B.AUG.21,1847 CINCINNATI,OHIO
D.APR.10,1917

YR	CL	LEA	POS	GP	G	REC
1871	BOS	NA	1-O		33	-
1872	BOS	NA	1-O		45	.256
1874	BAL	NA	C-1		33	-
1875	NH	NA	M-1-O		27	-
1876	CIN	N	M-P-	1	61	.246
1877	CIN	N	1-O		24	.275
	BRTR			1	223	0- 0

GOULISH, NICHOLAS EDWARD
B.NOV.13,1917 PUNXSUTAWNEY,PA.

YR	CL	LEA	POS	G	REC
1944	PHI	N	H	1	.000
1945	PHI	N	O	13	.273
	BLTL			14	.250

GOUZZIE, CLAUDE
B.1871 NILES,OHIO
D.SEPT.21,1907 DENVER,COLO.

YR	CL	LEA	POS	G	REC
1903	STL	A	2	1	.000
	BRTR				

GOWDY, HARRY "HANK"
B.AUG.24,1889 COLUMBUS,OHIO
D.AUG.1,1966 COLUMBUS,OHIO

YR	CL	LEA	POS	G	REC
1910	NY	N	1	5	.214
1911	NY	N	1	4	.250
	BOS	N	1	29	.289
1912	BOS	N	C	44	.271
1913	BOS	N	C	3	.600
1914	BOS	N	C	128	.243
1915	BOS	N	C	118	.247
1916	BOS	N	C	118	.252
1917	BOS	N	C	49	.214
1919	BOS	N	C-1	78	.279
1920	BOS	N	C	80	.243
1921	BOS	N	C	64	.299
1922	BOS	N	C-1	92	.316
1923	BOS	N	C	23	.125
	NY	N	C	53	.328
1924	NY	N	C	87	.325
1925	NY	N	C	47	.325
1929	BOS	N	C	10	.438
1930	BOS	N	C	16	.200
	BRTR			1048	.270

NON-PLAYING MANAGER CIN(N) 1946

YR	CL	LEA	POS	GP	G	REC

GOWELL, LAWRENCE CLYDE "LARRY"
B.MAY 2,1948 LEWISTON,ME.
| 1972 | NY | A | P | | 2 | 0- 1 |
| | | | BRTR | | | |

GRABARKEWITZ, BILLY CORDELL
B.JAN.18,1946 LOCKHART,TEX.
1969	LA	N	2-S-3		34	.092
1970	LA	N	2-S-3		156	.289
1971	LA	N	2-S-3		44	.225
1972	LA	N	2-S-3		53	.167
1973	CAL	A	2-S-3-0		61	.163
	PHI	N	2-3-0		25	.288
1974	PHI	N	3-0		34	.133
	CHI	N	2-S-3		53	.248
1975	OAK	A	2		6	.000
			BRTR		466	.236

GRABER, RODNEY BLAINE
B.JUNE 20,1931 MARSHALLVILLE,O.
| 1958 | CLE | A | 0 | | 4 | .125 |
| | | | BLTL | | | |

GRABOWSKI, ALBERT FRANCIS
B.SEPT.6,1903 SYRACUSE,N.Y.
D.OCT.29,1966
1929	STL	N	P		6	3- 2
1930	STL	N	P	33	35	6- 4
			BLTL	39	41	9- 6

GRABOWSKI, JOHN PATRICK "NIG"
B.JAN.7,1900 WARE,MASS.
D.MAY 23,1946
1924	CHI	A	C		20	.250
1925	CHI	A	C		21	.304
1926	CHI	A	C		48	.262
1927	NY	A	C		70	.277
1928	NY	A	C		75	.238
1929	NY	A	L		22	.203
1931	DET	A	C		40	.235
			BRTR		296	.252

GRABOWSKI, REGINALD JOHN
B.JULY 16,1909 SYRACUSE,N.Y.
D.APR.2,1955
1932	PHI	N	P		14	2- 2
1933	PHI	N	P		10	1- 3
1934	PHI	N	P		27	1- 3
			BRTR		51	4- 8

GRACE, JOSEPH LAVERNE "JOE"
B.JAN.5,1914 GORHAM,ILL.
D.SEPT.18,1969 MURPHYSBORO,ILL.
1938	STL	A	0		12	.340
1939	STL	A	0		74	.304
1940	STL	A	C-0		80	.258
1941	STL	A	C-0		115	.309
1946	STL	A	0		48	.230
	WAS	A	0		77	.302
1947	WAS	A	0		78	.248
			BLTR		484	.283

GRACE, ROBERT EARL
B.FEB.24,1907 BARLOW,KY.
1929	CHI	N	C		27	.250
1931	CHI	N	C		7	.111
	PIT	N	C		47	.280
1932	PIT	N	C		115	.274
1933	PIT	N	C		93	.289
1934	PIT	N	C		95	.270
1935	PIT	N	C		77	.263
1936	PIT	N	C		86	.249
1937	PIT	N	C		80	.211
			BLTR		627	.263

GRADY, JOHN J.
B.1860 LOWELL,MASS.
D.JULY 15,1893
| 1884 | ALT | U | 1-0 | | 9 | .289 |

GRADY, MICHAEL WILLIAM
B.DEC.23,1869 KENNETT SQUARE,PA
D.DEC.3,1943
1894	PHI	N	C		50	.363
1895	PHI	N	C		33	.336
1896	PHI	N	C		62	.333
1897	PHI	N	1		4	.154
	STL	N	1		83	.281
1898	NY	N	C-0		83	.293
1899	NY	N	C-3		83	.336
1900	NY	N	C		75	.222
1901	WAS	A	C-1		94	.286
1904	STL	N	C		92	.313
1905	STL	N	C-1		91	.286
1906	STL	N	C-1		92	.250
			BRTR		842	.296

GRAFF, FREDERICK GOTTLEIB
B.AUG.25,1889 CANTON,OHIO
| 1913 | STL | A | 3 | | 4 | .400 |
| | | | BRTR | | | |

GRAFF, JOHN F.
B.PHILADELPHIA,PA.
| 1893 | WAS | N | P | | 2 | 0- 1 |

GRAFF, LOUIS GEORGE
B.1866 PHILADELPHIA,PA.
| 1890 | SYR | AA | C | | 1 | .400 |

GRAFF, MILTON EDWARD "MILT"
B.DEC.30,1930 SAXONBURG,PA.
1957	KC	A	2		56	.181
1958	KC	A	2		5	.000
			BLTR		61	.179

GRAFFEN, S. MASON
B.1845 PHILADELPHIA,PA.
D.NOV.18,1883
NON-PLAYING MANAGER
STL(NA) 1875, STL(N) 1876

**GRAHAM, ARCHIBALD WRIGHT
"MOONLIGHT"**
B.NOV.11,1881 FAYETTEVILLE,N.C.
D.AUG.25,1965
| 1905 | NY | N | 0 | | 1 | .000 |

GRAHAM, ARTHUR WILLIAM "SKINNY"
B.AUG.12,1911 SOMERVILLE,MASS.
D.JULY 10,1967 ARLINGTON,MASS.
1934	BOS	A	0		13	.234
1935	BOS	A	0		8	.300
			BLTR		21	.246

GRAHAM, BARNEY
D.PHILADELPHIA,PA.
D.DEC.31,1896
| 1889 | ATH | AA | 3 | | 4 | .167 |

GRAHAM, BERNARD
B.1858 BELOIT,WIS.
D.OCT.30,1886 MOBILE,ALA.
1884	CHI	U	0		2	.500
	BAL	U	1-0		42	.271
					44	.303

GRAHAM, BERT "B.G."
B.APR.3,1886 TILTON,ILL.
D.JUNE 19,1971 COTTONWOOD,ARIZ.
| 1910 | STL | A | 1-2 | | 8 | .115 |
| | | | BBTR | | | |

GRAHAM, CHARLES HENRY
B.APR.25,1878 SANTA CLARA,CAL.
D.AUG.29,1948
| 1906 | BOS | A | C | | 30 | .233 |
| | | | BRTR | | | |

GRAHAM, DAWSON FRANCIS "TINY"
B.SEPT.9,1892 NASHVILLE,TENN.
D.DEC.29,1962
| 1914 | CHI | N | 1 | | 25 | .230 |
| | | | BRTR | | | |

**GRAHAM, GEORGE FREDERICK
"PEACHES"**
B.MAR.23,1877 ALEDO,ILL.
D.JULY 25,1939
1902	CLE	A	2		2	.333
1903	CHI	N	P		1	0- 1
1908	BOS	N	C		67	.274
1909	BOS	N	C		81	.239
1910	BOS	N	C		91	.282
1911	BOS	N	C		33	.273
	CHI	N	C		36	.239
1912	PHI	N	C		24	.288
			BRTR	1	335	0- 1
						.265

GRAHAM, JOHN BERNARD "JACK"
B.DEC.24,1916 MINNEAPOLIS,MINN.
1946	BRO	N	1		2	.200
	NY	N	1-0		100	.219
1949	STL	A	1		137	.238
			BLTL		239	.231

GRAHAM, KYLE B.
B.AUG.14,1899 BESSEMER,ALA.
D.DEC.1,1973 BESSEMER,ALA.
1924	BOS	N	P		5	0- 4
1925	BOS	N	P		34	7-12
1926	BOS	N	P		15	3- 3
1929	DET	A	P		13	1- 3
			BRTR		67	11-22

GRAHAM, OSCAR M.
B.1877 MANILLA,IOWA
D.SEPT.16,1931
| 1907 | WAS | A | P | 20 | 26 | 4-10 |
| | | | TL | | | |

GRAHAM, ROY VINCENT
B.FEB.22,1899 WAN FRANCISCO,CAL
1922	CHI	A	C		5	.000
1923	CHI	A	C		36	.195
			BRTR		41	.188

GRAHAM, WAYNE LEON
B.APR.6,1937 YOAKUM,TEX.
1963	PHI	N	0		10	.182
1964	NY	N	3		20	.091
			BRTR		30	.127

GRAHAM, WILLIAM
1908	STL	A	P		21	6- 7
1909	STL	A	P		34	8-14
1910	STL	A	P		9	0- 8
			TL		64	14-29

GRAHAM, WILLIAM ALBERT "BILL"
B.JAN.21,1937 FLEMINGSBURG,KY.
1966	DET	A	P		1	0- 0
1967	NY	N	P		5	1- 2
			BRTR		6	1- 2

GRAMLY, BERT THOMAS "TOMMY"
B.APR.19,1945 DALLAS,TEX.
| 1968 | CLE | A | P | 3 | 4 | 0- 1 |
| | | | BRTR | | | |

GRAMMAS, ALEXANDER PETER "ALEX"
B.APR.3,1926 BIRMINGHAM,ALA.
1954	STL	N	S-3		142	.264
1955	STL	N	S		120	.240
1956	STL	N	S		6	.250
	CIN	N	2-S-3		77	.243
1957	CIN	N	2-S-3		73	.303
1958	CIN	N	2-S-3		105	.218
1959	STL	N	S		131	.269
1960	STL	N	2-S-3		102	.245
1961	STL	N	2-S-3		89	.212
1962	STL	N	2-S		21	.111
	CHI	N	2-S-3		23	.233
1963	CHI	N	S		16	.185
			BRTR		913	.247
NON-PLAYING MANAGER
PIT(N) 1969 (INTERIM),
MIL(A) 1976

GRAMPP, HENRY ERCHARDT "HANK"
B.SEPT.28,1903 NEW YORK,N.Y.
1927	CHI	N	P		2	0- 0
1929	CHI	N	P		1	0- 1
			BRTR		3	0- 1

GRANEY, JOHN GLADSTONE "JACK"
B.JUNE 10,1886 ST.THOMAS,ONT.,
CAN.
1908	CLE	A	P		2	0- 0
1910	CLE	A	0		116	.236
1911	CLE	A	0		146	.269
1912	CLE	A	0		78	.242
1913	CLE	A	0		148	.267
1914	CLE	A	0		130	.265
1915	CLE	A	0		116	.260
1916	CLE	A	0		155	.241
1917	CLE	A	0		146	.228
1918	CLE	A	0		70	.237
1919	CLE	A	0		128	.234
1920	CLE	A	0		62	.296
1921	CLE	A	0		68	.299
1922	CLE	A	0		37	.155
			BLTL	2	1402	0- 0
						.250

YR	CL	LEA	POS	GP	G	REC

GRANGER, WAYNE ALLAN
B.MAR.15,1944 SPRINGFIELD,MASS.

YR	CL	LEA	POS	GP	G	REC
1968	STL	N	P		34	4- 2
1969	CIN	N	P		90	9- 6
1970	CIN	N	P-O		67	6- 5
						.100
1971	CIN	N	P		70	7- 6
1972	MIN	A	P		63	4- 6
1973	STL	N	P		33	2- 4
1973	NY	A	P		7	0- 1
1974	CHI	A	P		5	0- 0
1975	HOU	N	P		55	2- 5
1976	MON	N	P		27	1- 0
		BRTR			451	35-35
						.103

GRANT, EDWARD LESLIE "HARVARD EDDIE"
B.MAY 21,1883 FRANKLIN,MASS.
D.OCT.5,1918

YR	CL	LEA	POS	GP	G	REC
1905	CLE	A	2		2	.375
1907	PHI	N	3		74	.243
1908	PHI	N	3		147	.244
1909	PHI	N	3		154	.269
1910	PHI	N	3		152	.268
1911	CIN	N	3		133	.223
1912	CIN	N	S-3		96	.239
1913	CIN	N	3		27	.213
	NY	N	3		27	.200
1914	NY	N	2-S-3		88	.277
1915	NY	N	3		87	.208
		BLTR			987	.249

GRANT, GEORGE ADDISON
B.JAN.6,1903 E.TALLASSEE,ALA.

YR	CL	LEA	POS	GP	G	REC
1923	STL	A	P		4	0- 0
1924	STL	A	P		22	1- 2
1925	STL	A	P		12	0- 2
1927	CLE	A	P		25	4- 6
1928	CLE	A	P	28	29	10- 8
1929	CLE	A	P		12	0- 2
1931	PIT	N	P		11	0- 0
		BRTR		114	115	15-20

GRANT, JAMES CHARLES
B.OCT.6,1918 RACINE,WIS.
D.JULY 8,1970 ROCHESTER,MINN.

YR	CL	LEA	POS	GP	G	REC
1942	CHI	A	3		12	.167
1943	CHI	A	3		58	.259
	CLE	A	3		15	.136
1944	CLE	A	2-3		61	.273
		BLTR			146	.246

GRANT, JAMES RONALD
B.AUG.4,1894 FT.DODGE,IOWA

YR	CL	LEA	POS	GP	G	REC
1923	PHI	N	P		2	0- 0
		BRTL				

GRANT, JAMES TIMOTHY "JIM" OR "MUDCAT"
B.AUG.13,1935 LACOOCHEE,FLA.

YR	CL	LEA	POS	GP	G	REC
1958	CLE	A	P	44	54	10-11
1959	CLE	A	P	38	42	10- 7
1960	CLE	A	P	33	47	9- 8
1961	CLE	A	P	35	48	15- 9
1962	CLE	A	P	26	30	7-10
1963	CLE	A	P	38	53	13-14
1964	CLE	A	P	13	20	3- 4
	MIN	A	P	26	39	11- 9
1965	MIN	A	P	41	50	21- 7
1966	MIN	A	P		35	13-13
1967	MIN	A	P		27	5- 6
1968	LA	N	P	37	43	6- 4
1969	MON	N	P		11	1- 6
	STL	N	P	30	31	7- 5
1970	OAK	A	P		72	6- 2
	PIT	N	P		8	2- 1
1971	PIT	N	P		42	5- 3
	OAK	A	P		15	1- 0
		BRTR		571	667	145-119

GRANTHAM, GEORGE FARLEY "BOOTS"
B.MAY 20,1900 GALENA,KAN.
D.MAR.16,1954 KINGMAN,ARIZ.

YR	CL	LEA	POS	GP	G	REC
1922	CHI	N	3		7	.174
1923	CHI	N	2		152	.281
1924	CHI	N	2-3		127	.316
1925	PIT	N	1		114	.326
1926	PIT	N	1		141	.319
1927	PIT	N	1-2		151	.305
1928	PIT	N	1		124	.323
1929	PIT	N	1-2-0		110	.307
1930	PIT	N	2		146	.324
1931	PIT	N	1-2		127	.305
1932	CIN	N	1-2		126	.292
1933	CIN	N	1-2		87	.204
1934	NY	N	1-3		32	.241
		BLTR			1444	.302

GRASMICK, LOUIS JUNIOR
B.SEPT.11,1924 BALTIMORE,MD.

YR	CL	LEA	POS	GP	G	REC
1948	PHI	N	P		2	0- 0
		BRTR				

GRASSO, NEWTON MICHAEL "MICKEY"
B.MAY 10,1920 NEWARK,N.J.
D.OCT.15,1975 MIAMI,FLA.

YR	CL	LEA	POS	GP	G	REC
1946	NY	N	C		7	.136
1950	WAS	A	C		75	.287
1951	WAS	A	C		52	.206
1952	WAS	A	C		115	.216
1953	WAS	A	C		61	.209
1954	CLE	A	C		4	.333
1955	NY	N	C		8	.000
		BRTR			322	.226

GRATE, DONALD "DON"
B.SEPT.27,1923 GREENFIELD,OHIO

YR	CL	LEA	POS	GP	G	REC
1945	PHI	N	P	4	5	0- 1
1946	PHI	N	P		3	1- 0
		BRTR		7	8	1- 1

GRAULICH, LEWIS
B.CAMDEN,N.J.

YR	CL	LEA	POS	GP	G	REC
1891	PHI	N	C-1		7	.309

GRAVES, FRANK M.
B.NOV.2,1860 CINCINNATI,OHIO

YR	CL	LEA	POS	GP	G	REC
1886	STL	N	C		41	.152

GRAVES, JOSEPH EBENEZER
B.FEB.27,1906 MARBLEHEAD,MASS.

YR	CL	LEA	POS	GP	G	REC
1926	CHI	N	3		2	.000
		BRTR				

GRAVES, SAMUEL SIDNEY "SID"
B.NOV.30,1901 MARBLEHEAD,MASS.

YR	CL	LEA	POS	GP	G	REC
1927	BOS	N	O		7	.250
		BRTR				

GRAY, CHARLES
B.1867 INDIANAPOLIS,IND.

YR	CL	LEA	POS	GP	G	REC
1890	PIT	N	P		5	0- 3

GRAY, DAVID ALEXANDER "DAVE"
B.JAN.7,1943 OGDEN,UTAH

YR	CL	LEA	POS	GP	G	REC
1964	BOS	A	P		9	0- 0
		BRTR				

GRAY, GEORGE EDWARD "CHUMMY"
B.JULY 17,1873 ROCKLAND,ME.
D.AUG.14,1913

YR	CL	LEA	POS	GP	G	REC
1899	PIT	N	P		9	4- 3
		TR				

GRAY, JAMES D. "REDDY"

YR	CL	LEA	POS	GP	G	REC
1890	PIT	P	3		2	.222
	PIT	N	S		1	.000
1893	PIT	N	S		2	.500
					5	.300

GRAY, JAMES W.
B.AUG.7,1862 PITTSBURGH,PA.
D.JAN.31,1938 ALLEGHENY,PA.

YR	CL	LEA	POS	GP	G	REC
1884	PIT	AA	3		1	1.000

GRAY, JOHN LEONARD "JOHNNY"
B.DEC.11,1927 W.PALM BEACH,FLA.

YR	CL	LEA	POS	GP	G	REC
1954	PHI	A	P	18	19	3-12
1955	KC	A	P		8	0- 3
1957	CLE	A	P		7	1- 3
1958	PHI	N	P		15	0- 0
		BRTR		48	49	4-18

GRAY, MILTON MARSHALL
B.FEB.21,1914 LOUISVILLE,KY.
D.JUNE 30,1969 QUINCY,FLA.

YR	CL	LEA	POS	GP	G	REC
1937	WAS	A	C		2	.000
		BRTR				

GRAY, PETER WYSHNER
(REAL NAME PETER WYSHNER)
B.MAR.6,1917 NANTICOKE,PA.

YR	CL	LEA	POS	GP	G	REC
1945	STL	A	O		77	.218
		BLTL				

GRAY, RICHARD BENJAMIN "DICK"
B.JULY 11,1931 JEFFERSON,PA.

YR	CL	LEA	POS	GP	G	REC
1958	LA	N	3		58	.249
1959	LA	N	3		21	.154
	STL	N	2-S-3-O		36	.314
1960	STL	N	2-3		9	.000
		BRTR			124	.240

GRAY, SAMUEL DAVID "DOLLY"
B.OCT.15,1897 VAN ALSTYNE,TEX.
D.APR.16,1953

YR	CL	LEA	POS	GP	G	REC
1924	PHI	A	P		34	8- 7
1925	PHI	A	P		38	11-12
1926	PHI	A	P		32	16- 8
1927	PHI	A	P		37	9- 6
1928	STL	A	P		35	20-12
1929	STL	A	P		43	18-15
1930	STL	A	P		27	4-15
1931	STL	A	P		43	11-24
1932	STL	A	P		52	7-12
1933	STL	A	P		38	7- 4
		BRTR			379	111-115

GRAY, STANLEY
B.SEPT.20,1887 BROONWOOD,TEX.
D.OCT.11,1964

YR	CL	LEA	POS	GP	G	REC
1912	PIT	N	1		7	.250

GRAY, THEODORE GLENN "TED"
B.DEC.31,1924 DETROIT,MICH.

YR	CL	LEA	POS	GP	G	REC
1946	DET	A	P		3	0- 2
1948	DET	A	P		26	6- 2
1949	DET	A	P	34	36	10-10
1950	DET	A	P		27	10- 7
1951	DET	A	P	34	35	7-14
1952	DET	A	P	35	36	12-17
1953	DET	A	P	30	32	10-15
1954	DET	A	P		19	3- 5
1955	CHI	A	P		2	0- 0
	CLE	A	P		2	0- 0
	NY	A	P		1	0- 0
	BAL	A	P		9	1- 2
		BBTL	222	228	59-74
		BR 1946				

GRAY, WILLIAM
B.JAN.4,1872 PITTSBURGH,PA.
D.SEPT.7,1933

YR	CL	LEA	POS	GP	G	REC
1903	PIT	N	O		2	.333

GRAY, WILLIAM DENTON "DOLLY"
B.DEC.4,1878 ISHPEMING,MICH.
D.APR.4,1956

YR	CL	LEA	POS	GP	G	REC
1909	WAS	A	P	36	47	5-19
1910	WAS	A	P	34	35	8-19
1911	WAS	A	P		29	2-12
		BLTL	99	111	15-50

GRBA, ELI
B.AUG.9,1934 CHICAGO,ILL.

YR	CL	LEA	POS	GP	G	REC
1959	NY	A	P		19	2- 5
1960	NY	A	P	24	27	6- 4
1961	LA	A	P	40	42	11-13
1962	LA	A	P	40	42	8- 9
1963	LA	A	P	12	13	1- 2
		BRTR	135	143	28-33

GREASON, WILLIAM HENRY "BILL"
B.SEPT.3,1926 ATLANTA,GA.

YR	CL	LEA	POS	GP	G	REC
1954	STL	N	P		3	0- 1
		BRTR				

GREEN, EDWARD "DANNY"
B.NOV.6,1876 BURLINGTON,N.J.
B.NOV.9,1914

YR	CL	LEA	POS	GP	G	REC
1898	CHI	N	O		47	.328
1899	CHI	N	O		114	.296
1900	CHI	N	O		100	.299
1901	CHI	N	O		132	.317
1902	CHI	A	O		129	.318
1903	CHI	A	O		136	.313
1904	CHI	A	O		148	.266
1905	CHI	A	O		112	.243
		BL			918	.296

YR	CL LEA POS	GP	G	REC

GREEN, EDWARD M.
B.1850 PHILADELPHIA,PA.
D.MAR.22,1917

1890 ATH AA P	39	7-14

GREEN, ELIJAH JERRY "PUMPSIE"
B.OCT.27,1933 OAKLAND,CAL.

1959 BOS A 2-S	50	.233
1960 BOS A 2-S	133	.242
1961 BOS A 2-S	88	.260
1962 BOS A 2-S	56	.231
1963 NY N 3	17	.278
BBTR	344	.246

GREEN, FRED ALLEN
B.SEP.14,1933 TITUSVILLE,N.J.

1959 PIT N P	17	1- 2
1960 PIT N P	45	8- 4
1961 PIT N P	13	0- 0
1962 WAS A P	5	0- 1
1964 PIT N P	8	0- 0
BRTL	88	9- 7

GREEN, GENE LEROY
B.JUNE 26,1933 LOS ANGELES,CAL.

1957 STL N O	6	.200
1958 STL N C-O	137	.281
1959 STL N C-O	30	.189
1960 BAL A O	1	.250
1961 WAS A C-O	110	.280
1962 CLE A 1-O	66	.280
1963 CLE A O	43	.205
CIN N C	15	.226
BRTR	408	.267

GREEN, GEORGE DALLAS "DALLAS"
B.AUG.4,1934 NEWPORT,DEL.

1960 PHI N P	23	24	3- 6
1961 PHI N P		42	2- 4
1962 PHI N P	37	47	6- 6
1963 PHI N P	40	42	7- 5
1964 PHI N P	25	26	2- 1
1965 WAS A P		6	0- 0
1966 NY N P		4	0- 0
1967 PHI N P		8	0- 0
BLTR	185	199	20-22

GREEN, HARVEY G.
B.FEB.9,1915 KENOSHA,WIS.

1935 BRO N P	2	0- 0
BBTR		

GREEN, JAMES R.
B.CLEVELAND,OHIO

1884 WAS U 3-O	10	.139

GREEN, JOSEPH HENRY
(ALSO PLAYED UNDER NAME OF
JOSEPH HENRY GREENE)
B.SEPT.17,1897 PHILADELPHIA,PA.
D.FEB.4,1972 BRYN MAWR,PA.

1924 PHI A H	1	.000
TR		

GREEN, LEONARD CHARLES "LENNY"
B.JAN.6,1933 DETROIT,MICH.

1957 BAL A O	19	.182
1958 BAL A O	69	.231
1959 BAL A O	27	.292
WAS A O	88	.242
1960 WAS A O	127	.294
1961 MIN A O	156	.285
1962 MIN A O	158	.271
1963 MIN A O	145	.239
1964 MIN A O	26	.000
LA A O	39	.250
BAL A O	14	.190
1965 BOS A O	119	.276
1966 BOS A O	85	.241
1967 DET A O	58	.278
1968 DET A O	6	.250
BLTL	1136	.267

GREEN, RICHARD LARRY "DICK"
B.APR.21,1941 SIOUX CITY,IOWA

1963 KC A 2-S	13	.270
1964 KC A 2	130	.264
1965 KC A 2	133	.232
1966 KC A 2-3	140	.250
1967 KC A 1-2-S-3	122	.198
1968 OAK A C-2-3	76	.233
1969 OAK A 2	136	.275
1970 OAK A C-2-3	135	.190
1971 OAK A 2-S	144	.244
1972 OAK A 2	26	.286
1973 OAK A 2-S-3	133	.262
1974 OAK A 2	100	.213
BRTR	1288	.240

GREENBERG, HENRY BENJAMIN "HAMMERIN' HANK"
B.JAN.1,1911 NEW YORK,N.Y.

1930 DET A H	1	.000
1933 DET A 1	117	.301
1934 DET A 1	153	.339
1935 DET A 1	152	.328
1936 DET A 1	12	.348
1937 DET A 1	154	.337
1938 DET A 1	155	.315
1939 DET A 1	138	.312
1940 DET A O	148	.340
1941 DET A O	19	.269
1945 DET A O	78	.311
1946 DET A 1	142	.277
1947 PIT N 1	125	.249
BRTR	1394	.313

GREENE, JOSEPH HENRY
(SEE JOSEPH HENRY GREEN)

GREENE, JULIUS FOUST "JUNE"
B.JUNE 25,1902 GREENSBORO,N.C.
D.1974 SAN CLEMENTE,CAL.

1928 PHI N P	1	11	0- 0
1929 PHI N P	5	21	0- 0
BLTR	6	32	0- 0

GREENE, NELSON GEORGE
B.SEPT.20,1900 PHILADELPHIA,PA.

1924 BRO N P	4	0- 1
1925 BRO N P	11	2- 0
BLTL	15	2- 1

GREENE, PATRICK JOSEPH "PADDY" OR "PATSY"
(PLAYED UNDER NAME OF
PATRICK FOLEY IN 1902)
B.MAR.20,1875 PROVIDENCE,R.I.
D.OCT.20,1934

1902 PHI N 3	19	.188
1903 NY A 3	4	.308
DET A 3	1	.000
BRTR	24	.200

GREENFIELD, KENT
B.JULY 1,1904 GUTHRIE,KY.

1924 NY N P	1	0- 1
1925 NY N P	29	12- 8
1926 NY N P	39	13-12
1927 NY N P	12	2- 2
BOS N P	27	11-14
1928 BOS N P	32	3-11
1929 BOS N P	6	0- 0
BRO N P	7	0- 0
BRTR	152	153	41-48

GREENGRASS, JAMES RAYMOND "JIM"
B.OCT.24,1927 ADDISON,N.Y.

1952 CIN N O	18	.309
1953 CIN N O	154	.285
1954 CIN N O	139	.280
1955 CIN N O	13	.103
PHI N 3-O	94	.272
1956 PHI N 3-O	86	.205
BRTR	504	.269

GREENIG, JOHN A.
(PLAYED UNDER NAME OF
JOHN A. GREENING)

GREENING, JOHN A.
(REAL NAME JOHN A. GREENIG)
B.PHILADELPHIA,PA.

1888 WAS N P	1	0- 1

GREENWOOD, ROBERT CHANDLER "BOB"
B.MAR.13,1928 CANANEA,MEXICO

1954 PHI N P	11	12	1- 2
1955 PHI N P		1	0- 0
BRTR	12	13	1- 2

GREENWOOD, WILLIAM F.
B.1857 PHILADELPHIA,PA.
D.MAY 2,1902

1882 ATH AA 2-O	7	.290
1884 BRO AA 2	92	.220
1887 BAL AA 2	119	.326
1888 BAL AA 2-S	113	.202
1889 COL AA 2	118	.219
1890 ROC AA 2	121	.226
BRTL	570	.246

GREER, EDWARD C.
B.PHILADELPHIA,PA.
D.FEB.4,1890

1885 BAL AA C-O	55	.199
1886 BAL AA C-O	10	.139
ATH AA O	72	.197
1887 ATH AA O	3	.182
BRO AA O	88	.302
BR	228	.237

GREGG, DAVID CHARLES "HIGHPOCKETS"
B.MAR.14,1891 CHEHALIS,WASH.
D.NOV.12,1965

1913 CLE A P	1	0- 0
BRTR		

GREGG, HAROLD DANA "HAL" OR "SKEETS"
B.JULY 11,1921 ANAHEIM,CAL.

1943 BRO N P	5	0- 3
1944 BRO N P	39	42	9-16
1945 BRO N P		42	18-13
1946 BRO N P		26	6- 4
1947 BRO N P		37	4- 5
1948 PIT N P		22	2- 4
1949 PIT N P		8	1- 1
1950 PIT N P		5	0- 1
1952 NY N P		16	0- 1
BRTR	200	203	40-48

GREGG, SYLVEANUS AUGUSTUS "VEAN"
B.OCT.27,1885 CHEHALIS,WASH.
D.JULY 29,1964 ABERDEEN,WAS.

1911 CLE A P	34	23- 7
1912 CLE A P	37	20-13
1913 CLE A P	44	20-13
1914 CLE A P	17	9- 3
BOS A P	12	3- 4
1915 BOS A P	18	5- 3
1916 BOS A P	21	2- 5
1918 PHI A P	30	8-14
1925 WAS A P	26	2- 2
BRTL	239	92-64

GREGORY, FRANK ERNST
B.JULY 25,1888 SPRING VALLEY
TOWNSHIP,OHIO
D.NOV.5,1955 BELOIT,WIS.

1912 CIN N P	4	2- 0
BRTR		

GREGORY, GROVER LEROY "LEE"
B.JUNE 2,1938 BAKERSFIELD,CAL.

1964 CHI N P	11	19	0- 0
BLTL			

GREGORY, HOWARD WATTERSON
B.NOV.18,1886 HANNIBAL,MO.
D.MAY 30,1970 TULSA,OKLA.

1911 STL A P	3	0- 1
BLTR		

GREGORY, PAUL EDWIN
B.JUNE 9,1908 TOMNOLEN,MISS.

1932 CHI A P	33	5- 3
1933 CHI A P	23	4-11
BRTR	56	9-14

```
YR  CL LEA POS GP   G   REC
```

GREIF, WILLIAM BRILEY "BILL"
B.APR.25,1950 FT.STOCKTON,TEX.
```
1971 HOU N P          7   1- 1
1972 SD  N P         34   5-16
1973 SD  N P         36  10-17
1974 SD  N P     43  46   9-19
1975 SD  N P         59   4- 6
1976 SD  N P          5   1- 3
     STL N P         47   1- 5
     BRTR       231 234  31-67
```

GREMMINGER, LORENZO EDWARD "BATTLESHIP"
B.MAR.30,1874 CANTON,OHIO
D.MAY 26,1942
```
1895 CLE N 3     19  .275
1902 BOS N 3    140  .250
1903 BOS N 3    140  .264
1904 DET A 3     82  .215
     TR         381  .249
```

GREMP, LEWIS EDWARD "BUDDY"
B.AUG.5,1919 DENVER,COL.
```
1940 BOS N 1       4  .222
1941 BOS N C-1-2  37  .240
1942 BOS N 1-3    72  .217
     BRTR        113  .224
```

GREVELL, WILLIAM J.
B.MAR.30,1898 WILLIAMSTOWN,N.J.
D.JUNE.21,1923 SPRINGFIELD TOWNSHIP,PA.
```
1919 PHI A P      5   0- 0
```

GREY, WILLIAM TOBIN
B.APR.5,1871 PHILADELPHIA,PA.
D.DEC.8,1932
```
1890 PHI N C     32  .242
1891 PHI N C     18  .264
1895 CIN N 3     47  .301
1896 CIN N 3     35  .216
1898 PIT N 3    137  .232
                269  .246
```

GREYSON
```
1873 NAT NA P     8   1- 7
```

GRICH, ROBERT ANTHONY "BOBBY"
B.JAN.15,1949 MUSKEGON,MICH.
```
1970 BAL A 2-S-3    30  .211
1971 BAL A 2-S       7  .300
1972 BAL A 1-2-S-3 133  .278
1973 BAL A 2       162  .251
1974 BAL A 2       160  .263
1975 BAL A 2       150  .260
1976 BAL A 2-3     144  .266
     BRTR          786  .262
```

GRIESENBECK, CARLOS PHILLIPE TIMOTHY "TIM"
B.DEC.10,1897 SAN ANTONIO,TEX.
D.MAR.25,1953
```
1920 STL N "      5  .331
     BRTR
```

GRIEVE, THOMAS ALAN "TOM"
B.MAR.4,1948 PITTSFIELD,MASS.
```
1970 WAS A O      47  .198
1972 TEX A O      64  .204
1973 TEX A O      66  .309
1974 TEX A 1-O-O  74  .255
1975 TEX A O-O   118  .276
1976 TEX A O-O   149  .255
     BRTR        518  .255
```

GRIFFETH, LEON CLIFFORD
B.MAY 10,1925 CARMEL,N.Y.
```
1946 PHI N O     10   0- 0
     BBTL
```

GRIFFEY, GEORGE KENNETH "KEN"
B.APR.10,1950 DONORA,PA.
```
1973 CIN N O     25  .384
1974 CIN N O     88  .251
1975 CIN N O    132  .305
1976 CIN N O    148  .336
     BLTL       393  .314
```

GRIFFIN, ALFREDO CLAUDINO "AL"
(REAL NAME ALFREDO CLAUDINO BAPTIST (GRIFFIN))
B.OCT.6,1957 SANTO DOMINGO,D.R.
```
1976 CLE A S     12  .250
     BBTR
```

GRIFFIN, DOUGLAS LEE "DOUG"
B.JUNE 4,1947 SOUTH GATE,CAL.
```
1970 CAL A 2-3    18  .127
1971 BOS A 2     125  .244
1972 BOS A 2     129  .260
1973 BOS A 2     113  .255
1974 BOS A 2-S    93  .266
1975 BOS A 2-S   100  .240
1976 BOS A 2      49  .189
     BRTR        627  .246
```

GRIFFIN, FRANCIS ARTHUR "PUG"
B.APR.24,1896 LINCOLN,NEB.
D.OCT.12,1951
```
1917 PHI A 1     18  .200
1920 NY  N O      5  .250
     BRTR        23  .207
```

GRIFFIN, IVY MOORE
B.DEC.25,1897 MOBILE,ALA.
D.AUG.25,1957
```
1919 PHI A 1     17  .294
1920 PHI A 1    129  .238
1921 PHI A 1     39  .321
     BLTR       185  .257
```

GRIFFIN, JAMES LINTON "HANK"
B.1886
D.FEB.11,1950 TERRELL,TEX.
```
1911 CHI N P      1   0- 0
     BOS N P     15   0- 6
1912 BOS N P      3   0- 0
     BRTR        19   0- 6
```

GRIFFIN, MARTIN JOHN
B.SEPT.2,1901 SAN FRANCISCO,CAL
D.NOV.19,1951
```
1928 BOS A P  11 12   0- 3
     BRTR
```

GRIFFIN, MICHAEL JOSEPH
B.MAR.20,1865 UTICA,N.Y.
D.APR.10,1908
```
1887 BAL AA O    136  .368
1888 BAL AA O    137  .261
1889 BAL AA S-O  137  .280
1890 PHI P  O    115  .290
1891 BRO N O     133  .272
1892 BRO N O     129  .276
1893 BRO N O      93  .304
1894 BRO N O     106  .365
1895 BRO N O     132  .335
1896 BRO N O     122  .315
1897 BRO N O     134  .320
1898 BRO N M-O   134  .296
     BLTR       1508  .308
```

GRIFFIN, PATRICK RICHARD
B.MAY 13,1893 NILES,OHIO
D.JUNE 7,1927
```
1914 CIN N P      1   0- 0
     BRTR
```

GRIFFIN, THOMAS W.
B.ROCKFORD,ILL.
```
1884 MIL U 1     11  .295
```

GRIFFIN, TOBIAS CHARLES "SANDY"
B.OCT.24,1860 FAYETTEVILLE,N.Y.
D.JUNE 5,1926
```
1884 NY  N O      15  .164
1890 ROC AA O    107  .305
1891 WAS AA M-O   19  .273
1893 STL N O      23  .204
                 164  .269
```

GRIFFIN, THOMAS JAMES "TOM"
B.FEB.22,1948 LOS ANGELES,CAL.
```
1969 HOU N P      31  11-10
1970 HOU N P      23   3-13
1971 HOU N P      10   0- 6
1972 HOU N P      39   5- 4
1973 HOU N P      25   4- 6
1974 HOU N P  34  37  14-10
1975 HOU N P      17   3- 8
1976 HOU N P      20   5- 3
     SD  N P  11  12   4- 3
     BRTR     210 214  49-63
```

GRIFFITH, BARTHOLOMEW JOSEPH "BERT"
B.MAR.30,1896 ST.LOUIS,MO.
D.MAY 5,1973 BISHOP,CAL.
```
1922 BRO N 1-O   106  .308
1923 BRO N O      79  .294
1924 WAS A O       6  .111
     BRTR        191  .299
```

GRIFFITH, CLARK CALVIN "OLD FOX"
B.NOV.20,1869 CLEAR CREEK,MO.
D.OCT.27,1955 WASHINGTON,D.C.
```
1891 STL AA P      27  11- 8
     BOS AA P       9   3- 1
1893 CHI N  P       3   1- 1
1894 CHI N  P  35  41  20-11
1895 CHI N  P      39  25-14
1896 CHI N  P      36  23-11
1897 CHI N  P  40  46  18-18
1898 CHI N  P      38  25-12
1899 CHI N  P  36  39  21-13
1900 CHI N  P      30  14-13
1901 CHI A  M-P    35  24- 8
1902 CHI A  M-P-28 34  15- 9
            O            .220
1903 NY  A  M-P    24  14-10
1904 NY  A  M-P    16   6- 5
1905 NY  A  M-P    25   6- 5
1906 NY  A  M-P    17   2- 2
1907 NY  A  M-P     5   0- 0
1909 CIN N  M-P     1   0- 1
1910 CIN N  M-H     1    .000
1912 WAS A  M-P     1   0- 0
1913 WAS A  M-P     1   0- 0
1914 WAS A  M-P     1   0- 0
     BRTR      447 469 228-142
                         .233
```
NON-PLAYING MANAGER
NY(A) 1908, CIN(N) 1911,
WAS(A) 1915-20

GRIFFITH, EDWARD
```
1892 CHI N P      1   0- 0
```

GRIFFITH, FRANK WESLEY
B.NOV.18,1872 GILMAN,ILL.
D.DEC.13,1908
```
1894 CLE N P      7   3- 3
```

GRIFFITH, ROBERT DERRELL "DERRELL"
B.DEC.12,1943 ANADARKO,OKLA.
```
1963 LA  N 2       1  .000
1964 LA  N 3-O     78  .290
1965 LA  N O       22  .171
1966 LA  N O       23  .067
     BLTR         124  .260
```

GRIFFITH, THOMAS HERMAN
B.OCT.26,1889 PROSPECT,OHIO
D.APR.13,1967 CINCINNATI,OHIO
```
1913 BOS N O      37  .252
1914 BOS N O      16  .104
1915 CIN N O     160  .307
1916 CIN N O     155  .266
1917 CIN N O     115  .270
1918 CIN N O     118  .265
1919 BRO N O     125  .281
1920 BRO N O      93  .260
1921 BRO N O     129  .312
1922 BRO N O      99  .316
1923 BRO N O     131  .293
1924 BRO N O     140  .251
1925 BRO N O       7  .000
     CHI N O      76  .285
     BLTR       1401  .279
```

GRIGGS, ARTHUR J.
B.JULY 14,1884 TOPEKA,KAN.
D.DEC.19,1938
```
1909 STL A 1      108  .280
1910 STL A 1-2-O  123  .236
1911 CLE A 1       27  .250
1912 CLE A 1       89  .304
1914 BRO F 1       38  .282
1915 BRO F 1       27  .275
1918 DET A 1       28  .364
     BRTR         440  .276
```

GRIGGS, HAROLD LLOYD "HAL"
B.AUG.24,1928 ATLANTA,GA.
```
1956 WAS A P  34  36   1- 6
1957 WAS A P       2   0- 1
1958 WAS A P      32   3-11
1959 WAS A P      37   2- 8
     BRTR     105 107   6-26
```

GRIGSBY, DENVER CLARENCE
B.MAR.25,1901 SAPULPA,OKLA.
D.NOV.10,1973 SAPULPA,OKLA.
```
1923 CHI N O      24  .292
1924 CHI N O     124  .299
1925 CHI N O      51  .255
     BLTR        199  .289
```

YR	CL	LEA	POS	GP	G	REC

GRILLI, GUIDO JOHN
B.JAN.9,1939 MEMPHIS,TENN.
1966 BOS	A	P			6	0- 1
KC	A	P			16	0- 1
		BLTL			22	0- 2

GRILLI, STEPHEN JOSEPH "STEVE"
B.MAY 2,1949 BROOKLYN,N.Y.
1975 DET	A	P			3	0- 0
1976 DET	A	P			36	3- 1
		BRTR			39	3- 1

GRIM, JOHN HELM
B.AUG.9,1867 LEBANON,KY.
D.JULY 28,1961
1888 PHI	N	2			2	.143
1890 ROC	AA	P-C-	2		50	2- 0
		S				.254
1891 MIL	AA	C			28	.233
1892 LOU	N	C			95	.254
1893 LOU	N	C			92	.287
1894 LOU	N	C-2			107	.290
1895 BRO	N	C			90	.288
1896 BRO	N	C			80	.269
1897 BRO	N	C			76	.261
1898 BRO	N	C			50	.275
1899 BRO	N	C			14	.271
		TR	2		684	2- 0
						.272

GRIM, ROBERT ANTON "BOB"
B.MAR.8,1930 NEW YORK,NY.
1954 NY	A	P			37	20- 6
1955 NY	A	P			26	7- 5
1956 NY	A	P			26	6- 1
1957 NY	A	P			46	12- 8
1958 NY	A	P			11	0- 1
KC	A	P			26	7- 6
1959 KC	A	P			40	6-10
1960 CLE	A	P			3	0- 1
CIN	N	P			26	2- 2
STL	N	P			15	1- 0
1962 KC	A	P			12	0- 1
		BRTR			268	61-41

GRIMES, BURLEIGH ARLAND
B.AUG.9,1893 CLEAR LAKE,WIS.
1916 PIT	N	P			6	2- 3
1917 PIT	N	P		37	42	3-16
1918 BRO	N	P			41	19- 9
1919 BRO	N	P		25	26	10-11
1920 BRO	N	P		40	43	23-11
1921 BRO	N	P			37	22-13
1922 BRO	N	P			36	17-14
1923 BRO	N	P		39	40	21-18
1924 BRO	N	P		38	40	22-13
1925 BRO	N	P		33	34	12-19
1926 BRO	N	P		30	31	12-13
1927 NY	N	P			39	19- 8
1928 PIT	N	P			48	25-14
1929 PIT	N	P			33	17- 7
1930 BOS	N	P			11	3- 5
STL	N	P		22	23	13- 6
1931 STL	N	P			29	17- 9
1932 CHI	N	P			30	6-11
1933 CHI	N	P			17	3- 6
STL	N	P			4	0- 1
1934 STL	N	P			4	2- 1
PIT	N	P			8	1- 2
NY	A	P			10	1- 2
		BRTR	617	632	270-212
NON-PLAYING MANAGER
BRO(N) 1937-38

GRIMES, EDWARD ADELBERT
B.SEPT.8,1905 CHICAGO,ILL.
D.OCT.5,1974 CHICAGO,ILL.
1931 STL	A	3			43	.263
1932 STL	A	3			31	.235
		BRTR			74	.248

GRIMES, JOHN C.
B.JULY 7,1876 CLEVELAND,OHIO
D.SEPT.14,1913
| 1897 STL | N | P | | | 3 | 0- 2 |

GRIMES, OSCAR RAY JR.
B.APR.13,1915 MINERVA,OHIO
1938 CLE	A	1-2			4	.200
1939 CLE	A	1-2-S			119	.269
1940 CLE	A	1-3			11	.000
1941 CLE	A	1-2-3			77	.238
1942 CLE	A	1-2-S-3			51	.179
1943 NY	A	1-S			9	.150
1944 NY	A	S-3			116	.279
1945 NY	A	1-3			142	.265
1946 NY	A	2-S			14	.205
PHI	A	2-S-3			59	.262
		BRTR			602	.256

GRIMES, OSCAR RAY SR.
B.SEPT.11,1893 MINERVA,OHIO
D.MAY.25,1953
1920 BOS	A	1			1	.250
1921 CHI	N	1			147	.321
1922 CHI	N	1			138	.354
1923 CHI	N	1			64	.329
1924 CHI	N	1			51	.299
1926 PHI	N	1			32	.297
		BRTR			433	.329

GRIMES, ROY AUSTIN
B.SEPT.11,1893 MINERA,OHIO
D.SEPT.13,1954
| 1920 NY | N | 2 | | | 26 | .158 |
| | | BRTR | | | | |

GRIMM, CHARLES JOHN
"JOLLY CHOLLY"
B.AUG.25,1898 ST.LOUIS,MO.
1916 PHI	A	O			12	.091
1918 STL	N	1-3-0			50	.220
1919 PIT	N	1			14	.318
1920 PIT	N	1			148	.227
1921 PIT	N	1			151	.274
1922 PIT	N	1			154	.292
1923 PIT	N	1			152	.345
1924 PIT	N	1			151	.288
1925 CHI	N	1			141	.306
1926 CHI	N	1			147	.277
1927 CHI	N	1			147	.311
1928 CHI	N	1			147	.294
1929 CHI	N	1			120	.298
1930 CHI	N	1			114	.289
1931 CHI	N	1			146	.331
1932 CHI	N	M-1			149	.307
1933 CHI	N	M-1			107	.247
1934 CHI	N	M-1			75	.296
1935 CHI	N	M-1			2	.000
1936 CHI	N	M-1			39	.250
		BLTL			2166	.290
NON-PLAYING MANAGER
CHI(N) 1937-38, 1944-49,
BOS(N) 1952, MIL(N) 1953-56
CHI(N) 1960

GRIMSHAW, MYRON FREDERICK
"MOOSE"
B.NOV.30,1875 ST.JOHNSVILLE,N.Y
D.DEC.11,1936
1905 BOS	A	1			85	.239
1906 BOS	A	1			110	.290
1907 BOS	A	1-0			64	.204
		BBTR			259	.256

GRIMSLEY, ROSS ALBERT
B.JUNE 4,1924 AMERICUS,GA.
| 1951 CHI | A | P | | | 7 | 0- 0 |
| | | BLTL | | | | |

GRIMSLEY, ROSS ALBERT, II
B.JAN.7,1950 TOPEKA,KAN.
1971 CIN	N	P			26	10- 7
1972 CIN	N	P			30	14- 8
1973 CIN	N	P		38	39	13-10
1974 BAL	A	P			40	18-13
1975 BAL	A	P			35	10-13
1976 BAL	A	P			28	8- 7
		BLTL	197	198	73-58

GRINER, DANIEL DEXTER "RUSTY"
B.MAR.7,1889 CENTERVILLE,TENN.
D.JUNE 3,1950
1912 STL	N	P			12	3- 4
1913 STL	N	P			34	10-22
1914 STL	N	P			37	9-13
1915 STL	N	P		37	39	5-11
1916 STL	N	P			4	0- 0
1918 BRO	N	P			12	1- 5
		BLTR	136	138	28-55

GRISSOM, LEO THEO "LEE"
B.OCT.23,1907 SHERMAN,TEX.
1934 CIN	N	P			4	0- 1
1935 CIN	N	P			3	1- 1
1936 CIN	N	P			6	1- 1
1937 CIN	N	P	50	51	12-17
1938 CIN	N	P			14	2- 3
1939 CIN	N	P			33	9- 7
1940 NY	A	P			5	0- 0
BRO	N	P			14	2- 5
1941 BRO	N	P			4	0- 0
PHI	N	P			29	2-13
		BBTL	162	163	29-48
		BR 1934, 37				

GRISSOM, MARVIN EDWARD "MARV"
B.MAR.31,1918 LOS MOLINOS,CAL.
1946 NY	N	P			4	0- 2
1949 DET	A	P			27	2- 4
1952 CHI	A	P			28	12-10
1953 BOS	A	P			13	2- 6
NY	N	P			21	4- 2
1954 NY	N	P			56	10- 7
1955 NY	N	P			55	5- 4
1956 NY	N	P			43	1- 1
1957 NY	N	P			55	4- 4
1958 SF	N	P			51	7- 5
1959 STL	N	P			3	0- 0
		BRTR			356	47-45

GROAT, RICHARD MORROW "DICK"
B.NOV.4,1930 SWISSVALE,PA.
1952 PIT	N	S			95	.284
1955 PIT	N	S			151	.267
1956 PIT	N	S-3			142	.273
1957 PIT	N	S-3			125	.315
1958 PIT	N	S			151	.300
1959 PIT	N	S			147	.275
1960 PIT	N	S			138	.325
1961 PIT	N	S-3			148	.275
1962 PIT	N	S			161	.294
1963 STL	N	S			158	.319
1964 STL	N	S			161	.292
1965 STL	N	S-3			153	.254
1966 PHI	N	1-S-3			155	.260
1967 PHI	N	S			10	.115
SF	N	2-S			34	.171
		BRTR			1929	.286

GROB, CONRAD GEORGE "CONNIE"
B.NOV.9,1932 CROSS PLAINS,WIS.
| 1956 WAS | A | P | | | 37 | 4- 5 |
| | | BLTR | | | | |

GRODZICKI, JOHN
B.FEB.26,1919 NANTICOKE,PA.
1941 STL	N	P			5	2- 1
1946 STL	N	P			3	0- 0
1947 STL	N	P			16	0- 1
		BRTR			24	2- 2

GROH, HENRY KNIGHT "HEINIE"
B.SEPT.18,1889 ROCHESTER,N.Y.
D.AUG.22,1968 CINCINNATI,OHIO
1912 NY	N	2			27	.271
1913 NY	N	2			4	.000
CIN	N	2			117	.282
1914 CIN	N	2			139	.288
1915 CIN	N	2-3			160	.290
1916 CIN	N	2-S-3			149	.269
1917 CIN	N	3			156	.304
1918 CIN	N	M-3			126	.320
1919 CIN	N	3			122	.310
1920 CIN	N	3			145	.298
1921 CIN	N	3			97	.331
1922 NY	N	3			115	.265
1923 NY	N	3			123	.290
1924 NY	N	3			145	.281
1925 NY	N	2-3			25	.231
1926 NY	N	3			12	.229
1927 PIT	N	3			14	.286
		BRTR			1676	.292

GROH, LEWIS CARL "SILVER"
B.OCT.16,1883 ROCHESTER,N.Y.
B.OCT.20,1960
| 1919 PHI | A | 3 | | | 4 | .000 |
| | | BPTR | | | | |

YR	CL	LEA	POS	GP	G	REC

GROMEK, STEPHEN JOSEPH "STEVE"
B.JAN.15,1920 HAMTRAMCK,MICH.

YR	CL	LEA	POS	GP	G	REC
1941	CLE	A	P		9	1- 1
1942	CLE	A	P		14	2- 0
1943	CLE	A	P		3	0- 0
1944	CLE	A	P	35	44	10- 9
1945	CLE	A	P	33	37	19- 9
1946	CLE	A	P	29	37	5-15
1947	CLE	A	P	29	30	3- 5
1948	CLE	A	P		38	9- 3
1949	CLE	A	P		27	4- 6
1950	CLE	A	P		31	10- 7
1951	CLE	A	P		27	7- 4
1952	CLE	A	P	29	30	7- 7
1953	CLE	A	P		5	1- 1
	DET	A	P		19	6- 8
1954	DET	A	P		36	18-16
1955	DET	A	P		28	13-10
1956	DET	A	P		40	8- 6
1957	DET	A	P		15	0- 1
	BBTR			447	470	123-108

GROOM, ROBERT
B.SEPT.12,1884 BELLEVILLE,ILL.
D.FEB.19,1948

YR	CL	LEA	POS	GP	G	REC
1909	WAS	A	P	44	46	6-26
1910	WAS	A	P		34	12-17
1911	WAS	A	P		38	13-17
1912	WAS	A	P		43	24-13
1913	WAS	A	P		37	15-16
1914	STL	F	P		42	13-20
1915	STL	F	P		37	11-11
1916	STL	A	P		41	13- 9
1917	STL	A	P		38	8-19
1918	CLE	A	P		14	2- 2
	BRTR			368	370	117-150

GROSART, GEORGE ALBERT
B.1879 MEADVILLE,PA.
D.APR.18,1902

YR	CL	LEA	POS	GP	G	REC
1902	BOS	N	O		7	.125

GROSS, DONALD JOHN "DON"
B.JUNE 30,1931 WEIDMAN,MICH.

YR	CL	LEA	POS	GP	G	REC
1955	CIN	N	P		17	4- 5
1956	CIN	N	P		19	3- 0
1957	CIN	N	P		43	7- 9
1958	PIT	N	P		40	5- 7
1959	PIT	N	P		21	1- 1
1960	PIT	N	P		5	0- 0
	BLTL			145		20-22

GROSS, EMIL M.
B.1859 CHICAGO,ILL.

YR	CL	LEA	POS	GP	G	REC
1879	PRO	N	C		30	.379
1880	PRO	N	C		84	.255
1881	PRO	N	C		51	.274
1883	PHI	N	C-O		56	.312
1884	CHI	U	C-O		23	.326
1886	STL	N	C		1	.000
					245	.291

GROSS, EWELL "TURKEY"
B.FEB.21,1896 MESQUITE,TEX.
D.JAN.1,1936 DALLAS,TEX.

YR	CL	LEA	POS	GP	G	REC
1925	BOS	A	S		9	.094
	BRTR					

GROSS, GREGORY EUGENE "GREG"
B.AUG.1,1952 YORK,PA.

YR	CL	LEA	POS	GP	G	REC
1973	HOU	N	O		14	.231
1974	HOU	N	O		156	.314
1975	HOU	N	O		132	.294
1976	HOU	N	O		128	.286
	BLTL			430		.298

GROSS, WAYNE DALE
B.JAN.14,1952 RIVERSIDE,CAL.

YR	CL	LEA	POS	GP	G	REC
1976	OAK	A	1-O		10	.222
	BLTR					

GROSSKLOSS, HOWARD HOFFMAN "HOWDIE"
B.APR.9,1907 PITTSBURGH,PA.

YR	CL	LEA	POS	GP	G	REC
1930	PIT	N	S		2	.333
1931	PIT	N	2		53	.280
1932	PIT	N	S		17	.100
	BRTR				72	.261

GROSSMAN, HARVEY JOSEPH
B.MAY.5,1930 EVANSVILLE,IND.

YR	CL	LEA	POS	GP	G	REC
1952	WAS	A	P		1	0- 0
	BRTR					

GROTE, GERALD WAYNE "JERRY"
B.OCT.6,1942 SAN ANTONIO,TEX.

YR	CL	LEA	POS	GP	G	REC
1963	HOU	N	C		3	.200
1964	HOU	N	C		100	.181
1966	NY	N	C-3		120	.237
1967	NY	N	C		120	.195
1968	NY	N	C		124	.282
1969	NY	N	C		113	.252
1970	NY	N	C		126	.255
1971	NY	N	C		125	.270
1972	NY	N	C-3-O		64	.210
1973	NY	N	C-3		84	.256
1974	NY	N	C		97	.257
1975	NY	N	C		119	.295
1976	NY	N	C-O		101	.272
	BRTR			1296		.250

GROTH, EDWARD JOHN
B.DEC.24,1885 CEDARSBURG,WIS.
D.MAY 23,1950

YR	CL	LEA	POS	GP	G	REC
1904	CHI	N	P		3	0- 2

GROTH, ERNEST WILLIAM
B.MAY 3,1922 BEAVER FALLS,PA.

YR	CL	LEA	POS	GP	G	REC
1947	CLE	A	P		2	0- 0
1948	CLE	A	P	1	2	0- 0
1949	CHI	A	P		3	0- 1
	BRTR			6	7	0- 1

GROTH, JOHN THOMAS "JOHNNY"
B.JULY 23,1926 CHICAGO,ILL.

YR	CL	LEA	POS	GP	G	REC
1946	DET	A	O		4	.000
1947	DET	A	O		2	.357
1948	DET	A	O		6	.471
1949	DET	A	O		103	.293
1950	DET	A	O		157	.306
1951	DET	A	O		118	.299
1952	DET	A	O		141	.284
1953	STL	A	O		141	.253
1954	CHI	A	O		125	.275
1955	CHI	A	O		32	.338
	WAS	A	O		63	.219
1956	KC	A	O		95	.258
1957	KC	A	O		55	.254
	DET	A	O		38	.291
1958	DET	A	O		88	.281
1959	DET	A	O		55	.235
1960	DET	A	O		25	.368
	BRTR			1248		.279

GROVE, ORVAL LEROY
B.AUG.29,1919 MINERAL,KAN.

YR	CL	LEA	POS	GP	G	REC
1940	CHI	A	P		3	0- 0
1941	CHI	A	P		2	0- 0
1942	CHI	A	P		12	4- 6
1943	CHI	A	P		32	15- 9
1944	CHI	A	P		34	14-15
1945	CHI	A	P		33	14-13
1946	CHI	A	P		33	8-13
1947	CHI	A	P		25	6- 8
1948	CHI	A	P		32	2-10
1949	CHI	A	P		1	0- 0
	BRTR			207		63-73

GROVE, ROBERT MOSES "LEFTY"
B.MAR.6,1900 LONACONING,MD.
D.MAY 22,1975 NORWALK,OHIO

YR	CL	LEA	POS	GP	G	REC
1925	PHI	A	P		45	10-12
1926	PHI	A	P		45	13-13
1927	PHI	A	P		51	20-13
1928	PHI	A	P		39	24- 8
1929	PHI	A	P		42	20- 6
1930	PHI	A	P		50	28- 5
1931	PHI	A	P		41	31- 4
1932	PHI	A	P		44	25-10
1933	PHI	A	P		45	24- 8
1934	BOS	A	P		22	8- 8
1935	BOS	A	P		35	20-12
1936	BOS	A	P		35	17-12
1937	BOS	A	P		32	17- 9
1938	BOS	A	P		24	14- 4
1939	BOS	A	P	23	23	15- 4
1940	BOS	A	P	22	23	7- 6
1941	BOS	A	P		21	7- 7
	BLTL			616	619	300-141

GROVER, CHARLES BERT "BUGS"
(BORN CHARLES BYRD GROVER)
B.JUNE 20,1890 HUNTINGTON TOWNSHIP,OHIO
D.MAY 24,1971 EMMETT TOWNSHIP, MICHIGAN

YR	CL	LEA	POS	GP	G	REC
1913	DET	A	P		2	0- 0
	BLTR					

GROVER, ROY ARTHUR
B.JAN.17,1893 SNOHOMISH,WASH.

YR	CL	LEA	POS	GP	G	REC
1916	PHI	A	2		20	.272
1917	PHI	A	2		141	.224
1919	PHI	A	2		22	.232
	WAS	A	2		24	.187
	BRTR			207		.226

GRUBB, HARVEY HARRISON
B.SEPT.18,1890 LEXINGTON,N.C.
D.JAN.25,1970 CORPUS CHRISTI, TEX.

YR	CL	LEA	POS	GP	G	REC
1912	CLE	A	3		1	.000
	BRTR					

GRUBB, JOHN MAYWOOD
B.AUG.4,1948 RICHMOND,VA.

YR	CL	LEA	POS	GP	G	REC
1972	SD	N	O		7	.333
1973	SD	N	3-O		113	.311
1974	SD	N	3-O		140	.286
1975	SD	N	O		144	.269
1976	SD	N	1-3-O		109	.284
	BLTR			513		.286

GRUBBS, THOMAS DILLARD
B.FEB.22,1894 MT.STERLING,KY.

YR	CL	LEA	POS	GP	G	REC
1920	NY	N	P		1	0- 1
	BRTR					

GRUBE, FRANKLIN THOMAS "HANS"
B.JAN.7,1905 EASTON,PA.
D.JULY 2,1945

YR	CL	LEA	POS	GP	G	REC
1931	CHI	A	C		88	.219
1932	CHI	A	C		93	.282
1933	CHI	A	C		85	.230
1934	STL	A	C		65	.288
1935	STL	A	C		3	.333
	CHI	A	C		9	.368
1936	CHI	A	C		33	.161
1941	STL	A	C		18	.154
	BRTR			394		.244

GRUBER, HENRY JOHN
B.DEC.14,1864 NEW HAVEN,CONN.
D.SEPT.26,1932 NEW HAVEN,CONN.

YR	CL	LEA	POS	GP	G	REC
1887	DET	N	P		9	5- 3
1888	DET	N	P		27	11-13
1889	CLE	N	P		23	7-16
1890	CLE	P	P		50	21-20
1891	CLE	N	P		38	16-21
	BRTR			147		60-73

GRUNWALD, ALFRED HENRY "AL"
B.FEB.13,1930 LOS ANGELES,CAL.

YR	CL	LEA	POS	GP	G	REC
1955	PIT	N	P		3	0- 0
1959	KC	A	P	6	7	0- 1
	BLTL			9	10	0- 1

GRYSKA, SIGMUND STANLEY
B.NOV.4,1915 CHICAGO,ILL.

YR	CL	LEA	POS	GP	G	REC
1938	STL	A	S		7	.476
1939	STL	A	S		18	.265
	BRTR			25		.329

GRZENDA, JOSEPH CHARLES "JOE"
B.JUNE 8,1937 SCRANTON,PA.

YR	CL	LEA	POS	GP	G	REC
1961	DET	A	P		4	1- 0
1964	KC	A	P		20	0- 2
1966	KC	A	P		21	0- 2
1967	NY	N	P		11	0- 0
1969	MIN	A	P		38	4- 1
1970	WAS	A	P		49	3- 6
1971	WAS	A	P		46	5- 2
1972	STL	N	P		30	1- 0
	BRTL			219		14-13

GUDAT, MARVIN JOHN "MARV"
B.AUG.27,1905 GOLIAD,TEX.
D.MAR.2,1954

YR	CL	LEA	POS	GP	G	REC
1929	CIN	N	P	7	9	1- 1
1932	CHI	N	P-O	1	60	0- 0
						.255
	BLTL			8	69	1- 1
						.250

YR	CL	LEA	POS	GP	G	REC

GUERRA, FERMIN ROMERO "MIKE"
B.OCT.11,1912 HAVANA,CUBA

1937	WAS	A	C	1		.000
1944	WAS	A	C-O	75		.281
1945	WAS	A	C	56		.210
1946	WAS	A	C	41		.253
1947	PHI	A	C	72		.215
1948	PHI	A	C	53		.211
1949	PHI	A	C	98		.265
1950	PHI	A	C	87		.282
1951	BOS	A	C	10		.156
	WAS	A	C	72		.200
	BRTR			565		.242

GUERRERO, MARIO MIGUEL (ABUD)
B.SEP.28,1949 SANTO DOMINGO,D.R.

1973	BOS	A	2-S	66		.233
1974	BOS	A	S	93		.246
1975	STL	N	S	64		.239
1976	CAL	A	2-S	83		.284
	BRTR			306		.252

GUESE, THEODORE "WHITEY"
B.JAN.23,1873 NEW BREMEN,OHIO
D.APR.8,1951

1901	CIN	N	P	6		1- 4
	BRTR					

GUIDRY, RONALD AMES "RON"
B.AUG.28,1950 LAFAYETTE,LA.

1975	NY	A	P	10		0- 1
1976	NY	A	P	7		0- 0
	BLTL			17		0- 1

GUINDON, ROBERT JOSEPH "BOBBY"
B.SEP.4,1943 BROOKLINE,MASS.

1964	BOS	A	1-O	5		.125
	BLTL					

GUINEY, BENJAMIN FRANKLIN
B.NOV.16,1858 DETROIT,MICH.
D.DEC.5,1930

1883	DET	N	2-O	1		.200
1884	DET	N	O	2		.000
	BBTR			3		.083

GUINN, DRANNON EUGENE "SKIP"
B.OCT.5,1944 ST.CHARLES,MO.

1968	ATL	N	P	3	7	0- 0
1969	HOU	N	P		28	1- 2
1971	HOU	N	P		4	0- 0
	BRTL			35	39	1- 2

GUINTINI, BENJAMIN JOHN "BEN"
B.JAN.13,1920 LOS BANOS,CAL.

1946	PIT	N	O	2		.000
1950	PHI	A	O	3		.000
	BPTR			5		.000

GUISE, WITT ORISON "LEFTY"
B.SEPT.18,1909 DRIGGS,ARK.
D.AUG.13,1968 LITTLE ROCK,ARK.

1940	CIN	N	P	2		0- 0
	BLTL					

GUISTO, LOUIS JOSEPH
B.JAN.16,1894 NAPA,CAL.

1916	CLE	A	1	6		.158
1917	CLE	A	1	73		.185
1921	CLE	A	1	2		.500
1922	CLE	A	1	35		.250
1923	CLE	A	1	40		.181
	BRTR			156		.196

GULLETT, DONALD EDWARD "DON"
B.JAN.6,1951 LYNN,KY.

1970	CIN	N	P		44	5- 2
1971	CIN	N	P	35	40	16- 6
1972	CIN	N	P		31	9-10
1973	CIN	N	P	45	53	18- 8
1974	CIN	N	P	36	39	17-11
1975	CIN	N	P		22	15- 4
1976	CIN	N	P	23	25	11- 3
	BRTL			236	254	91-44

GULLEY, THOMAS JEFFERSON
B.DEC.25,1899 BROOKHAVEN,MISS.
D.NOV.24,1966 ST.CHARLES,ARK.

1923	CLE	A	O	3		.500
1924	CLE	A	O	8		.150
1926	CHI	A	O	16		.229
	BLTR			27		.224

GULLIC, THEODORE JASPER "TED"
B.JAN.2,1907 KOSHKONING,MO.

1930	STL	A	O	92		.250
1933	STL	A	1-3-O	104		.243
	BRTR			196		.247

GUMBERT, ADDISON COURTNEY "AD"
B.OCT.10,1868 PITTSBURGH,PA.
D.APR.23,1925

1888	CHI	N	P		7	3- 3
1889	CHI	N	P	29	49	14-13
1890	BOS	P	P		45	22- 9
1891	CHI	N	P		29	17-10
1892	CHI	N	P	44	48	23-18
1893	PIT	N	P	19	24	13- 6
1894	PIT	N	P	32	33	18-14
1895	BRO	N	P		26	11-15
1896	BRO	N	P		5	0- 4
	PHI	N	P		11	6- 4
	TR			247	277	127-96

GUMPERT, HARRY EDWARD "GUNBOAT"
B.NOV.5,1911 ELIZABETH,PA.

1935	NY	N	P		6	1- 2
1936	NY	N	P		39	11- 3
1937	NY	N	P		34	10-11
1938	NY	N	P	38	40	15-13
1939	NY	N	P	36	37	18-11
1940	NY	N	P		35	12-14
1941	NY	N	P		5	1- 1
	STL	N	P	33	34	11- 5
1942	STL	N	P		38	9- 5
1943	STL	N	P		21	10- 5
1944	STL	N	P		10	4- 2
	CIN	N	P		24	10- 8
1946	CIN	N	P		36	6- 8
1947	CIN	N	P		46	10-10
1948	CIN	N	P		61	10- 8
1949	CIN	N	P		29	4- 3
	PIT	N	P		18	1- 4
1950	PIT	N	P		1	0- 0
	BRTR			508	512	143-113

GUMBERT, WILLIAM SKEEN
B.AUG.8,1865 PITTSBURGH,PA.
D.APR.13,1946

1890	PIT	N	P		10	4- 4
1892	PIT	N	P		7	3- 2
1893	LOU	N	P		1	0- 0
					18	7- 6

GUMPERT, RANDALL PENNINGTON "RANDY"
B.JAN.23,1918 MONOCACY,PA.

1936	PHI	A	P		22	1- 2
1937	PHI	A	P		10	0- 0
1938	PHI	A	P		4	0- 2
1946	NY	A	P		33	11- 3
1947	NY	A	P	24	25	4- 1
1948	NY	A	P		15	1- 0
	CHI	A	P		16	2- 6
1949	CHI	A	P		34	13-16
1950	CHI	A	P	40	41	5-12
1951	CHI	A	P	33	37	9- 8
1952	BOS	A	P		10	1- 0
	WAS	A	P		20	4- 9
	BRTR			261	267	51-59

GUNKEL, WOODWARD WILLIAM "RED"
B.APR.15,1894 SHEFFIELD,ILL.
D.APR.19,1954

1916	CLE	A	P	1		0- 0
	BBTR					

GUNKLE, FREDERICK W.
B.CLEVELAND,OHIO

1879	CLE	N	C-O	1		.000

GUNNING, HYLAND
B.AUG.6,1888 MAPLEWOOD,N.J.
D.MAR.28,1975 TOGUS,ME.

1911	BOS	A	1	4		.111
	BLTR					

GUNNING, THOMAS FRANCIS
B.MAR.4,1862 NEWMARKET,N.H.
D.MAR.17,1931

1884	BOS	N	C	12		.095
1885	BOS	N	C	48		.184
1886	BOS	N	C	27		.224
1887	PHI	N	C	27		.293
1888	ATH	AA	C	23		.217
1889	ATH	AA	C	5		.375
				142		.216

GUNSON, JOSEPH BROOK
B.MAR.23,1863 PHILADELPHIA,PA.
D.NOV.15,1942

1884	WAS	U	C-O	44		.158
1889	KC	AA	C	34		.198
1892	BAL	N	C-O	85		.223
1893	STL	N	C	37		.280
	CLE	N	C	21		.296
	TR			221		.223

GURA, LAWRENCE CYRIL "LARRY"
B.NOV.26,1947 JOLIET,ILL.

1970	CHI	N	P		20	1- 3
1971	CHI	N	P		6	0- 0
1972	CHI	N	P		7	0- 0
1973	CHI	N	P	21	22	2- 4
1974	NY	A	P		8	5- 1
1975	NY	A	P		26	7- 8
1976	KC	A	P		20	4- 0
	BBTL			108	109	19-16
	BR 1970					

GURZENSKY, JOSEPH CHARLES
(PLAYED UNDER NAME OF
JOSEPH CHARLES GLENN)

GUST, ERNEST HERMAN FRANK "RED"
B.JAN.24,1888 BAY CITY,MICH.
D.OCT.26,1945 MAUPIN,ORE.

1911	STL	A	1	3		.000
	BRTR					

GUSTINE, FRANK WILLIAM "FRANKIE"
B.FEB.20,1920 HOOPESTON,ILL.

1939	PIT	N	3	22		.186
1940	PIT	N	2	133		.281
1941	PIT	N	2-3	121		.270
1942	PIT	N	C-2-S-3	115		.229
1943	PIT	N	1-2-S	117		.290
1944	PIT	N	2-S-3	127		.230
1945	PIT	N	C-2-S	128		.280
1946	PIT	N	2-S-3	131		.259
1947	PIT	N	3	156		.297
1948	PIT	N	3	131		.267
1949	CHI	N	2-3	76		.226
1950	STL	A	3	9		.158
	BRTR			1261		.265

GUTH, CHARLES HENRY "BUCKY"
B.AUG.18,1947 BALTIMORE,MD.

1972	MIN	A	S	3		.000
	BRTR					

GUTH, CHARLES J.
B.1856 CHICAGO,ILL.
D.JULY 1883

1880	CHI	N	P	1		1- 0

GUTIERREZ, CESAR DARIO
B.JAN.26,1943 CORO,VENEZ.

1967	SF	N	2-S	18		.143
1969	SF	N	S-3	15		.217
	DET	A	S	17		.245
1970	DET	A	S	135		.243
1971	DET	A	2-S-3	38		.189
	BRTR			223		.235

GUTTERIDGE, DONALD JOSEPH "DON"
B.JUNE 19,1913 PITTSBURG,KAN.

1936	STL	N	3	23		.319
1937	STL	N	3	119		.271
1938	STL	N	S-3	142		.255
1939	STL	N	3	148		.269
1940	STL	N	3	69		.269
1942	STL	A	2-3	147		.255
1943	STL	A	2	132		.273
1944	STL	A	2	148		.245
1945	STL	A	2-O	143		.238
1946	BOS	A	2-3	22		.234
1947	BOS	A	2-3	54		.168
1948	PIT	N	H	4		.000
	BRTR			1151		.256
NON-PLAYING MANAGER
CHI(A) 1969-70

GUZMAN, SANTIAGO DONOVAN
B.JULY 25,1949 SAN PEDRO DE
MACORIS,D.R.

1969	STL	N	P	1		0- 1
1970	STL	N	P	8		1- 1
1971	STL	N	P	2		0- 0
1972	STL	N	P	1		0- 0
	BRTR			12		1- 2

YR	CL	LEA	POS	GP	G	REC

GYSELMAN, RICHARD REYNALD
B.APR.6,1911 SAN FRANCISCO,CAL.

YR	CL	LEA	POS	GP	G	REC
1933	BOS	N	2-S-3		58	.239
1934	BOS	N	3		24	.167
		BRTR			82	.225

HAAS, BERTHOLD JOHN "BERT"
B.FEB.8,1914 NAPERVILLE,ILL.

1937	BRO	N	1		16	.400
1938	BRO	N	H		1	.000
1942	CIN	N	1-3-0		154	.239
1943	CIN	N	1-3-0		101	.262
1946	CIN	N	1-3		140	.264
1947	CIN	N	1-0		135	.286
1948	PHI	N	1-3		95	.282
1949	PHI	N	H		2	.000
	NY	N	1-3		54	.260
1951	CHI	A	1-3-0		23	.163
		BRTR		/	721	.264

HAAS, BRUNO PHILIP "BOON"
B.MAY 5,1891 WORCESTER,MASS.
D.JUNE 5,1952

1915	PHI	A	P		12	0- 2
		BBTL				

HAAS, BRYAN EDMUND "MOOSE"
B.APR.22,1956 BALTIMORE,MD.

1976	MIL	A	P		5	0- 1
		BRTR				

HAAS, GEORGE EDWIN "EDDIE"
B.MAY 26,1935 PADUCAH,KY.

1957	CHI	N	O		14	.208
1958	MIL	N	O		9	.357
1960	MIL	N	O		32	.219
		BLTR			55	.243

HAAS, GEORGE WILLIAM "MULE"
B.OCT.15,1903 MONTCLAIR,N.J.
D.JUNE 30,1974 NEW ORLEANS,LA.

1925	PIT	N	O		4	.000
1928	PHI	A	O		91	.280
1929	PHI	A	O		139	.313
1930	PHI	A	O		132	.299
1931	PHI	A	O		102	.323
1932	PHI	A	O		143	.305
1933	CHI	A	O		146	.287
1934	CHI	A	O		106	.268
1935	CHI	A	O		92	.291
1936	CHI	A	O		119	.284
1937	CHI	A	1		54	.207
1938	PHI	A	O		40	.205
		BLTR			1168	.292

HABENICHT, ROBERT JULIUS "BOB" OR "HOBBY"
B.APR.3,1926 ST.LOUIS,MO.

1951	STL	N	P		3	0- 0
1953	STL	N	P		1	0- 0
		BRTR			4	0- 0

HABERER, EMIL KARL
B.FEB.2,1878 CINCINNATI,OHIO
D.OCT.19,1951

1901	CIN	N	1		6	.167
1903	CIN	N	C		5	.154
1909	CIN	N	C		5	.187
		BRTR			16	.178

HACH, IRVIN "MAJOR"
B.JUNE 6,1873 LOUISVILLE,KY.
D.AUG.13,1936

1897	LOU	N	2-3		15	.163

HACK, STANLEY CAMFIELD "STAN"
B.DEC.6,1909 SACRAMENTO,CAL

1932	CHI	N	3		72	.236
1933	CHI	N	3		20	.350
1934	CHI	N	3		111	.289
1935	CHI	N	1-3		124	.311
1936	CHI	N	3		149	.298
1937	CHI	N	3		154	.297
1938	CHI	N	3		152	.320
1939	CHI	N	3		156	.298
1940	CHI	N	3		149	.317
1941	CHI	N	1-3		151	.317
1942	CHI	N	3		140	.300
1943	CHI	N	3		144	.289
1944	CHI	N	1-3		98	.282
1945	CHI	N	1-3		150	.323
1946	CHI	N	3		92	.285
1947	CHI	N	3		76	.271
		BLTR			1938	.301

NON-PLAYING MANAGER
CHI(N) 1954-56, STL(N) 1958

HACKER, RICHARD WARREN "RICH"
B.OCT.6,1947 BELLEVILLE,ILL.

1971	MON	N	S		16	.121
		BBTR				

HACKER, WARREN LOUIS
B.NOV.21,1924 MARISSA,ILL.

1948	CHI	N	P		3	0- 1
1949	CHI	N	P	30	32	5- 8
1950	CHI	N	P		5	0- 1
1951	CHI	N	P		2	0- 0
1952	CHI	N	P	33	34	15- 9
1953	CHI	N	P	39	42	12-19
1954	CHI	N	P	39	43	6-13
1955	CHI	N	P		35	11-15
1956	CHI	N	P		34	3-13
1957	CIN	N	P		15	3- 2
	PHI	N	P		20	4- 4
1958	PHI	N	P		9	0- 1
1961	CHI	A	P		42	3- 3
		BRTR		306	316	62-89

HACKETT, CHARLES M.
B.HOLYOKE,MASS.
NON-PLAYING MANAGER
CLE(N) 1884, BRO(AA) 1885

HACKETT, JAMES JOSEPH
B.OCT.1,1877 JACKSONVILLE,ILL.
D.MAR.28,1961

1902	STL	N	P-O	4	6	0- 1
						.284
1903	STL	N	P-1	5	96	1- 3
						.228
		BRTR		9	102	1- 4
						.233

HACKETT, MORTIMER MARTIN "MERTIE"
B.NOV.11,1859 CAMBRIDGE,MASS.
D.FEB.22,1938

1883	BOS	N	C-O		46	.234
1884	BOS	N	C-3		68	.203
1885	BOS	N	C		33	.182
1886	KC	N	C		62	.217
1887	IND	N	C		41	.272
		TR			250	.222

HACKETT, WALTER HENRY
B.AUG.15,1857 CAMBRIDGE,MASS.
D.OCT.2,1920

1884	BOS	U	S		102	.248
1885	BOS	N	2-S		35	.184
					137	.233

HADDIX, HARVEY
B.SEP.18,1925 MEDWAY,OHIO

1952	STL	N	P-O	7	9	2- 2
						.214
1953	STL	N	P	36	48	20- 9
1954	STL	N	P	43	61	18-13
1955	STL	N	P		37	12-16
1956	STL	N	P	4	5	1- 0
	PHI	N	P	31	46	12- 8
1957	PHI	N	P	27	41	10-13
1958	CIN	N	P	29	42	8- 7
1959	PIT	N	P		31	12-12
1960	PIT	N	P		29	11-10
1961	PIT	N	P	29	31	10- 6
1962	PIT	N	P		28	9- 6
1963	PIT	N	P	49	50	3- 4
1964	BAL	A	P		49	5- 5
1965	BAL	A	P		24	3- 2
		BLTL		453	531	136-113
						.212

HADDOCK, GEORGE SILAS "GENTLEMAN GEORGE"
B.DEC.25,1866 PORTSMOUTH,N.H.
D.APR.19,1926

1888	WAS	N	P		2	0- 2
1889	WAS	N	P		33	10-19
1890	BUF	P	P-O	35	42	9-26
						.240
1891	BOS	AA	P	52	58	33-11
1892	BRO	N	P		44	31-13
1893	BRO	N	P	18	26	8-10
1894	PHI	N	P		10	4- 3
	WAS	N	P-O	4	5	0- 4
						.250
		TR		198	220	95-88
						.219

HADDOW, JOHN FALCNOR
(PLAYED UNDER NAME OF
JOHN B. BLACK)

HADLEY, IRVING DARIUS "BUMP"
B.JULY 5,1904 LYNN,MASS.
D.FEB.15,1963 LYNN,MASS.

1926	WAS	A	P		1	0- 0
1927	WAS	A	P		30	14- 6
1928	WAS	A	P		33	12-13
1929	WAS	A	P		37	6-16
1930	WAS	A	P		42	15-11
1931	WAS	A	P		55	11-10
1932	CHI	A	P		3	1- 1
	STL	A	P		40	13-20
1933	STL	A	P		45	15-20
1934	STL	A	P		39	10-16
1935	STL	A	P		35	10-15
1936	NY	A	P		31	14- 4
1937	NY	A	P		29	11- 8
1938	NY	A	P		29	9- 8
1939	NY	A	P		26	12- 6
1940	NY	A	O		25	3- 5
1941	NY	N	P		3	1- 0
	PHI	A	P		25	4- 6
		BRTR			528	161-165

HADLEY, KENT WILLIAM
B.DEC.17,1934 POCATELLO,IDAHO

1958	KC	A	1		3	.182
1959	KC	A	1		113	.253
1960	KC	A	1		55	.203
		BLTL			171	.242

HAEFFNER, WILLIAM BERNARD
B.JULY 18,1895 PHILADELPHIA,PA.

1915	PHI	A	C		3	.250
1920	PIT	N	C		54	.194
1928	NY	N	C		2	.000
		BRTR			59	.194

HAEFNER, MILTON ARNOLD "MICKEY"
B.OCT.9,1912 LENZBURG,ILL.

1943	WAS	A	P		36	11- 5
1944	WAS	A	P		31	12-15
1945	WAS	A	P		37	16-14
1946	WAS	A	P		33	14-11
1947	WAS	A	P		31	10-14
1948	WAS	A	P		28	5-13
1949	WAS	A	P	19	20	5- 5
	CHI	A	P		14	4- 6
1950	CHI	A	P		24	1- 6
	BOS	N	P		8	0- 2
		BLTL		261	262	78-91

HAFEY, CHARLES JAMES "CHICK"
B.FEB.12,1903 BERKELEY,CAL.
D.JULY 2,1973 CALISTOGA,CAL.

1924	STL	N	O		24	.253
1925	STL	N	O		93	.302
1926	STL	N	O		78	.271
1927	STL	N	O		103	.330
1928	STL	N	O		138	.337
1929	STL	N	O		134	.339
1930	STL	N	O		120	.336
1931	STL	N	O		122	.349
1932	CIN	N	O		83	.344
1933	CIN	N	O		144	.303
1934	CIN	N	O		140	.293
1935	CIN	N	O		15	.339
1937	CIN	N	O		89	.261
		BRTR			1283	.317

HAFEY, DANIEL ALBERT "BUD"
B.AUG.6,1912 BERKELEY,CAL.

1935	CHI	A	H		2	.000
1936	PIT	N	O		58	.228
					39	.212
1939	CIN	N	O		6	.154
	PHI	N	P-O	2	18	0- 0
						.176
		BRTR		2	123	0- 0
						.213

HAFEY, THOMAS FRANCIS "HEAVE-O"
B.JULY 12,1913 BERKELEY,CAL.

1939	NY	N	3		70	.246
1944	STL	A	1-O		8	.357
		BRTR			78	.248

HAFFORD, LEO EDGAR
B.SEPT.17,1883 SOMERVILLE,MASS.
D.OCT.2,1911

1906	CIN	N	P		3	0- 0

YR	CL	LEA	POS	GP	G	REC

HAGAN, ARTHUR F. "CUT"
B.1863 LONSDALE,R.I.

1883	PHI	N	P	17		1-16
	BUF	N	P-O	2		0- 2
						.000
1884	BUF	N	P	3		1- 2
				22		2-20
						.115

HAGEMAN, KURT R. MORRIS "CASEY"
B.MAY.12,1888 PITTSBURGH,PA.
D.APR.1,1964 NEW BEDFORD,MASS.

1911	BOS	A	P	2		0- 2
1912	BOS	A	P	2		0- 0
1914	STL	N	P	12		2- 4
	CHI	N	P	16		1- 1
		BRTR		32		3- 7

HAGENBUSH, JOHN ALBERT
(PLAYED UNDER NAME OF
JOHN ALBERT PFIESTER)

HAGERMAN, ZERIAH ZEQUIEL "RIP"
B.JUNE 20,1889 LINDEN,KAN.
D.JAN.29,1930

1909	CHI	N	P	13		4- 4
1914	CLE	A	P	37		9-15
1915	CLE	A	P	28		7-13
1916	CLE	A	P	2		0- 0
		BRTR		80		20-32

HAGUE, JOE CLARENCE
B.APR.25,1944 HUNTINGTON,W.VA.

1968	STL	N	1-0	7		.235
1969	STL	N	1-0	40		.170
1970	STL	N	1-0	139		.271
1971	STL	N	1-0	129		.226
1972	STL	N	1-0	27		.237
	CIN	N	1-0	69		.246
1973	CIN	N	1-0	19		.152
		BLTL		430		.239

HAGUE, WILLIAM L.
(REAL NAME WILLIAM L. HAUG)
B.1852 PHILADELPHIA,PA.

1875	STL	NA	1-3	59		.206
1876	LOU	N	3	67		.264
1877	LOU	N	3	59		.267
1878	PRO	N	3	60		.207
1879	PRO	N	3	50		.227
		BRTR		295		.231

HAHN, DONALD ANTONE "DON"
B.NOV.16,1948 SAN FRANCISCO,CAL.

1969	MON	N	O	4		.111
1970	MON	N	O	82		.255
1971	NY	N	O	98		.236
1972	NY	N	O	17		.162
1973	NY	N	O	93		.229
1974	NY	N	O	110		.251
1975	PHI	N	O	9		.000
	STL	N	O	7		.125
	SD	N	O	34		.231
		BRTR		454		.236

HAHN, FRANK GEORGE "NOODLES"
B.APR.29,1879 NASHVILLE,TENN.
D.FEB.6,1960 CANDLER,N.C.

1899	CIN	N	P	38		23- 8
1900	CIN	N	P	40		16-21
1901	CIN	N	P	41		22-19
1902	CIN	N	P-1- 36	37		23-12
			O			.183
1903	CIN	N	P	34		22-12
1904	CIN	N	P	35		15-18
1905	CIN	N	P	12		5- 3
1906	NY	A	P	6		3- 2
		BLTL		242	243	129-95
						.178

HAHN, FREDERICK ALOYS
B.FEB.16,1929 NYACK,N.Y.

| 1952 | STL | N | P | 1 | | 0- 0 |
| | | BRTL | | | | |

HAHN, RICHARD FREDERICK
B.JULY 24,1917 CANTON,OHIO

| 1940 | WAS | A | C | 1 | | .000 |
| | | BRTR | | | | |

HAHN, WILLIAM EDGAR "ED"
B.AUG.27,1875 NEVADA,OHIO
D.NOV.29,1941

1905	NY	A	O	43		.319
1906	NY	A	O	11		.091
	CHI	A	O	130		.227
1907	CHI	A	O	156		.255
1908	CHI	A	O	122		.251
1909	CHI	A	O	76		.182
1910	CHI	A	O	15		.113
		BLTR		553		.237

HAID, HAROLD AUGUSTINE
B.DEC.21,1897 BARBERTON,OHIO
D.AUG.13,1952 LOS ANGELES,CAL.

1919	STL	A	P	1		0- 0
1928	STL	N	P	27		2- 2
1929	STL	N	P	38		9- 9
1930	STL	N	P	20	21	3- 2
1931	BOS	N	P	27		0- 2
1933	CHI	A	P	6		0- 0
		BRTR	119	120		14-15

HAIGH, EDWARD E.
B.FEB.7,1867 PHILADELPHIA,PA.
D.FEB.13,1953

| 1892 | STL | N | O | 1 | | .250 |

HAINES, HENRY LUTHER "HINKEY"
B.DEC.23,1899 RED LION,PA.

| 1923 | NY | A | O | 28 | | .160 |
| | | BRTR | | | | |

HAINES, JESSE JOSEPH "POP"
B.JULY 22,1893 CLAYTON,OHIO

1918	CIN	N	P	1		0 0
1920	STL	N	P	47	48	13-20
1921	STL	N	P	37	39	18-12
1922	STL	N	P-1	29	30	11- 9
						.167
1923	STL	N	P		37	20-13
1924	STL	N	P		35	8-19
1925	STL	N	P		29	13-14
1926	STL	N	P		33	13- 4
1927	STL	N	P		38	24-10
1928	STL	N	P		33	20- 8
1929	STL	N	P		28	13-10
1930	STL	N	P		29	13- 8
1931	STL	N	P		19	12- 3
1932	STL	N	P		20	3- 5
1933	STL	N	P	32	33	9- 6
1934	STL	N	P		37	4- 4
1935	STL	N	P		30	6- 5
1936	STL	N	P		25	7- 5
1937	STL	N	P		16	3- 3
		BRTR	555	560		210-158
						.186

HAIRSTON, JERRY WAYNE
B.FEB.16,1952 BIRMINGHAM,ALA.

1973	CHI	A	1-O	60		.271
1974	CHI	A	O-D	45		.229
1975	CHI	A	O	69		.283
1976	CHI	A	O	44		.227
		BBTR		218		.260

HAIRSTON, JOHN LOUIS "JOHNNY"
B.AUG.29,1945 BIRMINGHAM,ALA.

| 1969 | CHI | N | C-O | 3 | | .250 |
| | | BRTR | | | | |

HAIRSTON, SAMUEL "SAMMY"
B.JAN.20,1925 CRAWFORD,MISS.

| 1951 | CHI | A | C | 4 | | .400 |
| | | BRTR | | | | |

HAISLIP, JAMES CLIFTON "SLIM"
B.AUG.4,1891 FARMERSVILLE,TEX.
D.JAN.22,1970 DALLAS,TEX.

| 1913 | PHI | N | P | 1 | | 0- 0 |
| | | BRTR | | | | |

HAJDUK, CHESTER
B.JULY 21,1919 CHICAGO,ILL.

| 1941 | CHI | A | H | 1 | | .000 |
| | | BRTR | | | | |

HALAS, GEORGE STANLEY
B.FEB.2,1895 CHICAGO,ILL.

| 1919 | NY | A | O | 12 | | .091 |
| | | BBTR | | | | |

HALDEMAN, JOHN AVERY
B.DEC.2,1855 PEE WEE VALLEY,KY.
D.SEPT.17,1899 LOUISVILLE,KY.

| 1877 | LOU | N | 2 | 1 | | .000 |
| | | BLTR | | | | |

**HALE, ARVEL ODELL
"ODELL" OR "BAD NEWS"**
B.AUG.10,1908 HOSSTON,LA.

1931	CLE	A	2-3	25		.283
1933	CLE	A	2-3	98		.276
1934	CLE	A	2	143		.302
1935	CLE	A	2-3	150		.304
1936	CLE	A	3	153		.316
1937	CLE	A	2-3	154		.267
1938	CLE	A	2	130		.278
1939	CLE	A	2	108		.312
1940	CLE	A	3	48		.220
1941	BOS	N	2-3	12		.208
	NY	N	2	41		.196
		BRTR		1062		.289

HALE, GEORGE WAGNER
B.AUG.3,1894 DEXTER,KAN.

1914	STL	A	C	5		.271
1916	STL	A	O	4		.000
1917	STL	A	C	38		.197
1918	STL	A	C	12		.133
		BRTR		59		.184

HALE, JOHN STEVEN
B.AUG.5,1953 FRESNO,CAL.

1974	LA	N	O	4		1.000
1975	LA	N	O	71		.211
1976	LA	N	O	44		.154
		BLTR		119		.204

HALE, ROBERT HOUSTON "BOB"
B.NOV.7,1933 SARASOTA,FLA.

1955	BAL	A	1	67		.357
1956	BAL	A	1	85		.237
1957	BAL	A	1	42		.250
1958	BAL	A	1	19		.350
1959	BAL	A	1	40		.185
1960	CLE	A	1	70		.300
1961	CLE	A	H	42		.167
	NY	A	1	11		.154
		BLTL		376		.273

HALE, ROY L.
B.FEB.18,1880 DOWAGIAC,MICH.
D.FEB.1,1946

1902	BOS	N	P	8		0- 3
	BAL	A	P	3		0- 1
				11		0- 4

HALE, SAMUEL DOUGLAS
B.SEPT.10,1896 GLEN ROSE,TEX.
D.SEPT.6,1974 WHEELER,TEX.

1920	DET	A	3-O	76		.293
1921	DET	A	O	9		.000
1923	PHI	A	3	115		.288
1924	PHI	A	3	80		.318
1925	PHI	A	2-3	110		.345
1926	PHI	A	3	111		.281
1927	PHI	A	3	131		.313
1928	PHI	A	3	88		.309
1929	PHI	A	3	101		.277
1930	STL	A	3	62		.274
		BRTR		883		.302

HALEY, FRED
B.WHEELING,W.VA.

| 1880 | TRO | N | C | 2 | | .000 |

HALEY, RAYMOND TIMOTHY
B.JAN.23,1891 DANBURY,IOWA
D.OCT.8,1973 BRADENTON,FLA.

1915	BOS	A	C	5		.143
1916	BOS	A	C	1		.000
	PHI	A	C	34		.220
1917	PHI	A	C	41		.276
		BRTR		81		.250

HALICKI, EDWARD LOUIS "ED"
B.OCT.4,1950 KEARNY,N.J.

1974	SF	N	P	16		1- 8
1975	SF	N	P	24		9-13
1976	SF	N	P	32		12-14
		BRTR		72		22-35

HALL, ARCHIBALD W. "AL"
B.WORCESTER,MASS.
D.FEB.10,1885

1879	TRO	N	O	66		.255
1880	CLE	N	O	2		.125
1887	MET	AA	O	3		.214
				71		.250

YR	CL	LEA	POS	GP	G	REC

HALL, CHARLES LOUIS "SEA LION"
(REAL NAME CARLOS CLOLO)
B.MAY 6,1888 KERRVILLE,TEX.
D.DEC.6,1943

YR	CL	LEA	POS	GP	G	REC
1906	CIN	N	P		16	3- 6
1907	CIN	N	P		12	4- 3
1909	BOS	A	P		11	6- 4
1910	BOS	A	P	35	47	12- 9
1911	BOS	A	P	32	39	8- 7
1912	BOS	A	P		34	15- 8
1913	BOS	A	P		35	4- 4
1916	STL	N	P		10	0- 4
1918	DET	A	P		6	0- 1
		BRTR		191	210	52-46

HALL, GEORGE W.
B.1849 BROOKLYN,N.Y.

YR	CL	LEA	POS	GP	G	REC
1871	OLY	NA	O		32	-
1872	BAL	NA	1-O		54	.300
1873	BAL	NA	O		35	-
1874	BOS	NA	O		47	.321
1875	ATH	NA	O		77	.298
1876	ATH	N	O		60	.355
1877	LOU	N	O		61	.322
		BL			366	

HALL, HERBERT ERNEST "BERT"
B.OCT.15,1888 PORTLAND,ORE.
D.JULY 18,1948 SEATTLE,WASH.

YR	CL	LEA	POS	GP	G	REC
1911	PHI	N	P		7	0- 1
		BRTR				

HALL, HERBERT SILAS
B.JUNE 5,1893 STEELVILLE,OHIO
D.JULY 1,1970 FRESNO,CAL.

YR	CL	LEA	POS	GP	G	REC
1918	DET	A	O		3	.000
		BBTR				

HALL, IRVIN GLADSTONE
B.OCT.7,1918 ALBERTON,MD.

YR	CL	LEA	POS	GP	G	REC
1943	PHI	A	2-S-3	151		.256
1944	PHI	A	1-2-S	143		.268
1945	PHI	A	2	151		.261
1946	PHI	A	2-S	63		.249
		BRTR		508		.261

HALL, JAMES
D.JAN.30,1886

YR	CL	LEA	POS	GP	G	REC
1872	ATL	NA	2-O	13		.246
1874	ATL	NA	2	2		-
1875	WES	NA	O	1		-
				16		-

HALL, JIMMIE RANDOLPH
B.MAR.17,1938 MT.HOLLY,N.C.

YR	CL	LEA	POS	GP	G	REC
1963	MIN	A	O	156		.260
1964	MIN	A	O	149		.282
1965	MIN	A	O	148		.285
1966	MIN	A	O	120		.239
1967	CAL	A	O	129		.249
1968	CAL	A	O	46		.214
	CLE	A	O	53		.198
1969	CLE	A	O	4		.000
	NY	A	1-O	80		.236
	CHI	N	O	11		.208
1970	CHI	N	O	28		.094
	ATL	N	O	39		.213
		BLTR		963		.254

HALL, JOHN SYLVESTER
B.JAN.9,1924 MUSKOGEE,OKLA.

YR	CL	LEA	POS	GP	G	REC
1948	BRO	N	P		3	0- 0
		BRTR				

HALL, MARCUS
B.AUG.12,1887 JOPLIN,MO.
D.FEB.24,1915

YR	CL	LEA	POS	GP	G	REC
1910	STL	A	P		8	1- 7
1913	DET	A	P		30	9-12
1914	DET	A	P		25	4- 6
		BRTR			63	14-25

HALL, RICHARD WALLACE "DICK"
B.SEP.27,1930 ST.LOUIS,MO.

YR	CL	LEA	POS	GP	G	REC
1952	PIT	N	3-O		26	.138
1953	PIT	N	2		7	.167
1954	PIT	N	O		112	.239
1955	PIT	N	P-O	15	21	6- 6
						.175
1956	PIT	N	P-1	19	33	0- 7
						.345
1957	PIT	N	P		8	10	0- 0
1959	PIT	N	P		2	0- 0
1960	KC	A	P	29	32	8-13
1961	BAL	A	P	29	30	7- 5
1962	BAL	A	P	43	44	6- 6
1963	BAL	A	P	47	48	5- 5
1964	BAL	A	P		45	9- 1
1965	BAL	A	P	48	49	11- 8
1966	BAL	A	P		32	6- 2
1967	PHI	N	P		48	10- 8
1968	PHI	N	P		32	4- 1
1969	BAL	A	P		39	5- 2
1970	BAL	A	P		32	10- 5
1971	BAL	A	P		27	6- 6
		BRTR		495	669	93-75
						.210

HALL, ROBERT LEWIS "BOB"
B.DEC.22,1923 SWISSVALE,PA.

YR	CL	LEA	POS	GP	G	REC
1948	BOS	N	P		31	6- 4
1950	BOS	N	P		21	0- 2
1953	PIT	N	P		37	3-12
		BRTR			89	9-18

HALL, ROBERT PRILL
B.DEC.20,1878 BALTIMORE,MD.
D.DEC.1,1950

YR	CL	LEA	POS	GP	G	REC
1904	PHI	N	S-3		46	.160
1905	NY	N	O		1	.333
	BRO	N	O		52	.236
		TR			99	.203

HALL, ROBERT RUSSELL
B.SEPT.29,1871 SHELBYVILLE,KY.
D.JULY 1,1937

YR	CL	LEA	POS	GP	G	REC
1898	STL	N	S		39	.252
1901	CLE	A	S		1	.500
		TR			40	.259

HALL, TOM EDWARD
B.NOV.23,1947 THOMASVILLE,N.C.

YR	CL	LEA	POS	GP	G	REC
1968	MIN	A	P	8	11	2- 1
1969	MIN	A	P	31	32	8- 7
1970	MIN	A	P	52	53	11- 6
1971	MIN	A	P	48	49	4- 7
1972	CIN	N	P		47	10- 1
1973	CIN	N	P	54	55	8- 5
1974	CIN	N	P		40	3- 1
1975	CIN	N	P		2	0- 0
	NY	N	P	34	35	4- 3
1976	NY	N	P		5	1- 1
	KC	A	P	31	33	1- 1
		BLTL		352	362	52-33

HALL, WILLIAM BERNARD
B.FEB.22,1892 CHARLESTON,W.VA.

YR	CL	LEA	POS	GP	G	REC
1913	BRO	N	P		3	0- 0
		BRTR				

HALL, WILLIAM LEMUEL "BILL"
B.JULY 30,1928 MOULTRIE,GA.

YR	CL	LEA	POS	GP	G	REC
1954	PIT	N	C		5	.000
1956	PIT	N	C		1	.000
1958	PIT	N	C		51	.284
		BLTR			57	.262

HALLA, JOHN ARTHUR
B.MAY 13,1884 ST.LOUIS,MO.
D.SEPT.30,1947 EL SEGUNDO,CAL.

YR	CL	LEA	POS	GP	G	REC
1905	CLE	A	P		3	0- 1
		BLTL				

HALLAHAN, WILLIAM ANTHONY
"WILD BILL"
B.AUG.4,1902 BINGHAMTON,N.Y.

YR	CL	LEA	POS	GP	G	REC
1925	STL	N	P		6	1- 0
1926	STL	N	P		19	1- 4
1929	STL	N	P		20	4- 4
1930	STL	N	P		35	15- 9
1931	STL	N	P		37	19- 9
1932	STL	N	P	25	28	12- 7
1933	STL	N	P	36	37	16-13
1934	STL	N	P		32	8-12
1935	STL	N	P		40	15- 8
1936	STL	N	P		9	2- 2
	CIN	N	P		23	5- 9
1937	CIN	N	P		21	3- 9
1938	PHI	N	P		21	1- 8
		BRTL		324	328	102-94

HALLER, THOMAS FRANK "TOM"
B.JUNE 23,1937 LOCKPORT,ILL.

YR	CL	LEA	POS	GP	G	REC
1961	SF	N	C		30	.145
1962	SF	N	C		99	.261
1963	SF	N	C-O		98	.255
1964	SF	N	C-O		117	.253
1965	SF	N	C		134	.251
1966	SF	N	C-1		142	.240
1967	SF	N	C-O		141	.251
1968	LA	N	C		144	.285
1969	LA	N	C		134	.263
1970	LA	N	C		112	.286
1971	LA	N	C		84	.267
1972	DET	A	C		59	.207
		BLTR		1294		.257

HALLETT, JACK PRICE
B.NOV.13,1913 TOLEDO,OHIO

YR	CL	LEA	POS	GP	G	REC
1940	CHI	A	P		2	1- 1
1941	CHI	A	P		22	5- 5
1942	PIT	N	P		3	0- 1
1943	PIT	N	P		9	1- 2
1946	PIT	N	P		35	5- 7
1948	NY	N	P		2	0- 0
		BRTR			73	12-16

HALLIDAY, NEWTON
B.1897

YR	CL	LEA	POS	GP	G	REC
1916	PIT	N	1		1	.000
		BRTR				

HALLIGAN, WILLIAM E. "JOCKO"
B.DEC.8,1868 AVON,N.Y.
D.FEB.13,1945

YR	CL	LEA	POS	GP	G	REC
1890	BUF	P	C-O		53	.268
1891	CIN	N	O		61	.311
1892	CIN	N	1-O		26	.287
	BAL	N	1-O		44	.269
					184	.287

HALLINAN, EDWARD S.
B.AUG.23,1888 SAN FRANCISCO,CAL
D.AUG.24,1940

YR	CL	LEA	POS	GP	G	REC
1911	STL	A	2-S		52	.207
1912	STL	A	S		27	.221
		BRTR			79	.212

HALLINAN, JAMES H.
B.MAY 27,1849 IRELAND
D.OCT.28,1879

YR	CL	LEA	POS	GP	G	REC
1871	KEK	NA	S		5	-
1875	WES	NA	S		13	-
	MUT	NA	2-S-3		44	-
1876	MUT	N	S		54	.277
1877	CIN	N	2		16	.370
	CHI	N	O		19	.281
1878	CHI	N	2-O		15	.231
	IND	N	O		3	.250
		BLTL			169	-

HALLMAN, WILLIAM HARRY
B.MAR.15,1876 PHILADELPHIA,PA.
D.APR.23,1950

YR	CL	LEA	POS	GP	G	REC
1901	MIL	A	O		139	.256
1903	CHI	A	O		64	.213
1906	PIT	N	O		23	.270
1907	PIT	N	O		84	.222
					310	.240

YR	CL	LEA	POS	GP	G	REC

HALLMAN, WILLIAM WILSON "BILL"
B.MAR.31,1867 PITTSBURGH,PA.
D.SEPT.11,1920

YR	CL	LEA	POS	GP	G	REC
1888	PHI	N	2		16	.206
1889	PHI	N	S		119	.253
1890	PHI	P	C-2-3-O		85	.278
1891	ATH	AA	2		140	.288
1892	PHI	N	2		136	.292
1893	PHI	N	2		132	.328
1894	PHI	N	2		119	.327
1895	PHI	N	2		124	.315
1896	PHI	N	2		120	.318
1897	PHI	N	2		31	.248
	STL	N	M-2		81	.252
1898	BRO	N	2		133	.245
1901	CLE	A	S		5	.211
	PHI	N	2-3		122	.194
1902	PHI	N	3		73	.245
1903	PHI	N	2-3		57	.212
	BRTR				1493	.276

HALLSTROM, CHARLES E.
B.CHICAGO,ILL.

1885	PRO	N	P		1	0- 1

HALPIN, JAMES NATHANIEL
B.OCT.4,1863 ENGLAND
D.JAN.4,1893

1882	WOR	N	3		2	.000
1884	WAS	U	S		44	.182
1885	DET	N	S		15	.129
					61	.163

HALT, ALVA WILLIAM
B.SANDUSKY,OHIO
D.JAN.22,1973 SANDUSKY,OHIO

1914	BRO	F	S		80	.235
1915	BRO	F	S-3		151	.245
1918	CLE	A	3		26	.174
	BRTR				257	.237

HAM, RALPH A.
B.1850 TROY,N.Y.
D.FEB.13,1905

1871	ROK	NA	S-3-O		25	-
1872	MAN	NA	S		1	.333
					26	-

HAMANN, ELMER JOSEPH "DOC"
B.DEC.21,1900 NEW ULM,MINN.
D.JAN.11,1973 MILWAUKEE,WIS.

1922	CLE	A	P		1	0- 0
	BRTR					

HAMBRICK, CHARLES H.
(PLAYED UNDER NAME OF
CHARLES H. HAMBURG)

HAMBRIGHT, ROGER DEE
B.MAR.26,1949 SUNNYSIDE,WASH.

1971	NY	A	P		18	3- 1
	BRTR					

HAMBURG, CHARLES H.
(REAL NAME CHARLES H. HAMBRICK)
B.NOV.22,1863 LOUISVILLE,KY.

1890	LOU	AA	O		134	.265

HAMBY, JAMES SANFORD "CRACKER"
B.JULY 29,1900 WILKESBORO,N.C.

1926	NY	N	C		1	.000
1927	NY	N	C		21	.192
	BRTR				22	.182

HAMILL, JOHN ALEXANDER CHARLES
B.DEC.18,1860 NEW YORK,N.Y.
D.DEC.6,1911

1884	WAS	AA	P		21	2-16
	BRTR					

HAMILTON, DAVID EDWARD "DAVE"
B.DEC.13,1947 SEATTLE,WASH.

1972	OAK	A	P		25	6- 6
1973	OAK	A	P		16	6- 4
1974	OAK	A	P		29	7- 4
1975	OAK	A	P		11	1- 2
	CHI	A	P		30	6- 5
1976	CHI	A	P		45	6- 6
	BLTL				156	32-27

HAMILTON, EARL A.
B.JULY 19,1892 GIBSON CITY,ILL.

1911	STL	A	P		32	5-12
1912	STL	A	P		41	11-14
1913	STL	A	P		31	13-12
1914	STL	A	P		44	16-18
1915	STL	A	P		35	9-17
1916	STL	A	P		20	4- 6
1916	DET	A	P		5	2- 3
1917	STL	A	P		27	0- 9
1918	PIT	N	P		6	6- 0
1919	PIT	N	P		28	8-11
1920	PIT	N	P		39	10-13
1921	PIT	N	P		35	13-15
1922	PIT	N	P		33	11- 7
1923	PIT	N	P		28	7- 9
1924	PHI	N	P		3	0- 1
	BLTL				407	115-147

HAMILTON, THOMAS BALL "TOM"
B.SEPT.29,1925 ALTOONA,KAN.
D.NOV.29,1973 TYLER,TEX.

1952	PHI	A	P		9	.200
1953	PHI	A	1-O		58	.196
	BLTR				67	.197

HAMILTON, JACK EDWIN
B.DEC.25,1938 BURLINGTON,IOWA

1962	PHI	N	P		41	9-12
1963	PHI	N	P		19	2- 1
1964	DET	A	P		5	0- 1
1965	DET	A	P		4	1- 1
1966	NY	N	P		57	6-13
1967	NY	N	P		17	2- 0
	CAL	A	P		26	9- 6
1968	CAL	A	P		21	3- 1
1969	CLE	A	P		20	0- 2
	CHI	A	P		8	0- 3
	BRTR				218	32-40

HAMILTON, STEVE ABSHER
B.NOV.30,1935 COLUMBIA,KY.

1961	CLE	A	P		2	0- 0
1962	WAS	A	P	41	43	3- 8
1963	WAS	A	P		3	0- 1
	NY	A	P		34	5- 1
1964	NY	A	P	30	32	7- 2
1965	NY	A	P		46	3- 1
1966	NY	A	P		44	8- 3
1967	NY	A	P		44	2- 4
1968	NY	A	P		40	2- 2
1969	NY	A	P		38	3- 4
1970	NY	A	P		35	4- 3
	CHI	A	P		3	0- 0
1971	SF	N	P		39	2- 2
1972	CHI	N	P		22	1- 0
	BLTL			421	425	40-31

HAMILTON, WILLIAM ROBERT "SLIDING BILLY"
B.FEB.16,1866 NEWARK,N.J.
D.DEC.16,1940 WORCESTER,MASS.

1888	KC	AA	O		35	.250
1889	KC	AA	O		137	.301
1890	PHI	N	O		123	.324
1891	PHI	N	O		133	.388
1892	PHI	N	O		136	.330
1893	PHI	N	O		82	.395
1894	PHI	N	O		131	.399
1895	PHI	N	O		121	.393
1896	BOS	N	O		131	.363
1897	BOS	N	O		125	.344
1898	BOS	N	O		109	.367
1899	BOS	N	O		81	.306
1900	BOS	N	O		135	.332
1901	BOS	N	O		99	.292
	BLTL				1578	.344

HAMLIN, KENNETH LEE "KEN"
B.MAY 18,1935 DETROIT,MICH.

1957	PIT	N	S		2	.000
1959	PIT	N	S		3	.125
1960	KC	A	S		140	.224
1961	LA	A	S		42	.209
1962	WAS	A	2-S		98	.253
1965	WAS	A	2-S-3		117	.273
1966	WAS	A	2-3		66	.215
	BRTR				468	.241

HAMLIN, LUKE DANIEL "LUKE" OR "HOT POTATO"
B.JULY 3,1906 FERRIS CNTR.,MICH

1933	DET	A	P		3	1- 0
1934	DET	A	P		20	2- 3
1937	BRO	N	P	39	41	11-13
1938	BRO	N	P		44	12-15
1939	BRO	N	P		40	20-13
1940	BRO	N	P	33	35	9- 8
1941	BRO	N	P		30	8- 8
1942	PIT	N	P		23	4- 4
1944	PHI	A	P		29	6-12
	BLTR			261	265	73-76

HAMM, PETER WHITFIELD "PETE"
B.SEP.20,1947 BUFFALO,N.Y.

1970	MIN	A	P		10	0- 2
1971	MIN	A	P		13	2- 4
	BRTR				23	2- 6

HAMMOND, WALTER CHARLES "JACK"
B.FEB.26,1892 AMSTERDAM,N.Y.
D.MAR.4,1942

1915	CLE	A	2		35	.214
1922	CLE	A	2		1	.250
	PIT	N	2		9	.276
	BRTR				45	.232

HAMNER, GRANVILLE WILBUR "GRANNY"
B.APR.26,1927 RICHMOND,VA.

1944	PHI	N	S		21	.247
1945	PHI	N	S		14	.171
1946	PHI	N	S		2	.143
1947	PHI	N	S		2	.286
1948	PHI	N	2-S-3		129	.260
1949	PHI	N	S		154	.263
1950	PHI	N	S		157	.270
1951	PHI	N	S		150	.255
1952	PHI	N	S		151	.275
1953	PHI	N	2-S		154	.276
1954	PHI	N	2-S		152	.299
1955	PHI	N	2-S		104	.257
1956	PHI	N	P-2-	3	122	0- 1
			S			.224
1957	PHI	N	P-2-	1	133	0- 0
			S			.227
1958	PHI	N	2-S-3		35	.301
1959	PHI	N	S-3		21	.297
	CLE	A	2-S-3		27	.164
1962	KC	A	P		3	0- 1
	BRTR			7	1531	0- 2
						.262

HAMNER, RALPH CONANT "BRUZ"
B.SEPT.12,1916 GIBSLAND,LA.

1946	CHI	A	P		25	2- 7
1947	CHI	N	P		3	1- 2
1948	CHI	N	P		27	5- 9
1949	CHI	N	P		6	0- 2
	BRTR				61	8-20

HAMNER, WESLEY GARVIN
B.MAR.18,1924 RICHMOND,VA.

1945	PHI	N	2-S-3		32	.198
	BRTR					

HAMPTON, ISAAC BERNARD "IKE"
B.AUG.22,1951 CAMDEN,S.C.

1974	NY	N	C		4	.000
1975	CAL	A	C-S-3		31	.152
1976	CAL	A	C-S		3	.000
	BBTR				38	.139

HAMRIC, ODBERT HERMAN "BERT"
B.MAR.1,1928 CLARKSBURG,W.VA.

1955	BRO	N	H		2	.000
1958	BAL	A	H		8	.125
	BLTR				10	.111

HAMRICK, RAYMOND BERNARD
B.AUG.1,1921 NASHVILLE,TENN.

1943	PHI	N	2-S		44	.200
1944	PHI	N	S		74	.205
	BRTR				118	.204

HANCKEN, MORRIS MEDLOCK "BUDDY"
B.AUG.30,1914 BIRMINGHAM,ALA.

1940	PHI	A	C		1	.000
	BRTR					

HANCOCK, FRED JAMES
B.AUG.30,1921 ALLENPORT,PA.

1949	CHI	A	S-3-O		39	.135
	BRTR					

HAND, RICHARD ALLEN "RICH"
B.JULY 10,1948 BELLEVUE,WASH.

YR	CL	LEA	POS	GP	G	REC
1970	CLE	A	P		35	6-13
1971	CLE	A	P	15	16	2- 6
1972	TEX	A	P		30	10-14
1973	TEX	A	P		8	2- 3
	CAL	A	P		16	4- 3
	BRTR			104	105	24-39

HANDIBOE, ALOYSIUS JAMES "COALYARD MIKE"
B.JULY 21,1887 WASHINGTON,D.C.
D.JAN.31,1953 SAVANNAH,GA.

YR	CL	LEA	POS	GP	G	REC
1911	NY	A	O		5	.067
	BLTL					

HANDIBOE, JAMES EDWARD
B.JULY 17,1866 COLUMBUS,OHIO
D.NOV.8,1942

YR	CL	LEA	POS	GP	G	REC
1886	PIT	AA	P-O		14	7- 7
						.114

HANDLEY, EUGENE LOUIS "GENE"
B.NOV.25,1914 ST.LOUIS,MO.

YR	CL	LEA	POS	GP	G	REC
1946	PHI	A	2-S-3		89	.251
1947	PHI	A	2-S-3		36	.256
	BRTR				125	.252

HANDLEY, LEE ELMER "JEEP"
B.JULY 31,1913 ST.LOUIS,MO.
D.APR.8,1970 PITTSBURGH,PA.

YR	CL	LEA	POS	GP	G	REC
1936	CIN	N	2		24	.308
1937	PIT	N	2		127	.250
1938	PIT	N	3		139	.268
1939	PIT	N	3		101	.285
1940	PIT	N	2-3		98	.281
1941	PIT	N	3		124	.288
1944	PIT	N	2-S-3		40	.221
1945	PIT	N	3		98	.298
1946	PIT	N	2-3		116	.238
1947	PHI	N	2-S-3		101	.253
	BRTR				968	.269

HANDRAHAN, JAMES VERNON "VERN"
B.NOV.27,1938 CHARLOTTETOWN,
P.E.I.,CANADA

YR	CL	LEA	POS	GP	G	REC
1964	KC	A	P		18	0- 1
1966	KC	A	P		16	0- 1
	BLTR				34	0- 2

HANDS, WILLIAM ALFRED "BILL"
B.MAY.6,1940 HACKENSACK,N.J.

YR	CL	LEA	POS	GP	G	REC
1965	SF	N	P		4	0- 2
1966	CHI	N	P		41	8-13
1967	CHI	N	P		49	7- 8
1968	CHI	N	P		38	16-10
1969	CHI	N	P		41	20-14
1970	CHI	N	P		39	18-15
1971	CHI	N	P		36	12-18
1972	CHI	N	P		32	11- 8
1973	MIN	A	P		39	7-10
1974	MIN	A	P		35	4- 5
	TEX	A	P		2	2- 0
1975	TEX	A	P		18	6- 7
	BRTR				374	111-110

HANEBRINK, HARRY ALOYSIUS
B.NOV.12,1927 ST.LOUIS,MO.

YR	CL	LEA	POS	GP	G	REC
1953	MIL	N	2-3		51	.238
1957	MIL	N	3		6	.286
1958	MIL	N	3-0		63	.188
1959	PHI	N	2-3-0		57	.258
	BLTR				177	.224

HANEY, FRED GIRARD "PUDGE"
B.APR.25,1898 ALBUQUERQUE,N.MEX

YR	CL	LEA	POS	GP	G	REC
1922	DET	A	1-3		81	.352
1923	DET	A	2-S-3		142	.282
1924	DET	A	3		86	.309
1925	DET	A	3		114	.279
1926	BOS	A	3		138	.221
1927	BOS	A	3		47	.276
	CHI	N	H		4	.000
1929	STL	N	3		10	.115
	BRTR				622	.275

NON-PLAYING MANAGER
STL(A) 1939-41, PIT(N) 1953-55,
MIL(N) 1956-59

HANEY, WALLACE LARRY "LARRY"
B.NOV.19,1942 CHARLOTTESVILLE,VA

YR	CL	LEA	POS	GP	G	REC
1966	BAL	A	C		20	.161
1967	BAL	A	C		58	.268
1968	BAL	A	C		38	.236
1969	SEA	A	C		22	.254
	OAK	A	C		53	.151
1970	OAK	A	C		2	.000
1972	OAK	A	C-2		5	.000
1973	OAK	A	C		2	.000
	STL	N	C		2	.000
1974	OAK	A	C-1-3		76	.165
1975	OAK	A	C-3		47	.192
1976	OAK	A	C		88	.226
	BRTR				413	.212

HANFORD, CHARLES JOSEPH
B.JUNE 3,1882 TUNSTALL,ENGLAND
D.JULY 19,1963

YR	CL	LEA	POS	GP	G	REC
1914	BUF	F	O		156	.287
1915	CHI	F	O		74	.239
	BRTR				230	.276

HANIFIN, PATRICK JAMES
B.1868 NOVA SCOTIA,CANADA
D.NOV.5,1908

YR	CL	LEA	POS	GP	G	REC
1897	BRO	N	O		9	.200

HANKINS, DONALD WAYNE
B.FEB.9,1903 PENDLETON,IND.
D.MAY 16,1963 WINSTON-SALEM,N.C

YR	CL	LEA	POS	GP	G	REC
1927	DET	A	P		20	2- 1
	BRTR					

HANKINS, JAY NELSON
B.NOV.7,1935 ST.LOUIS,MO.

YR	CL	LEA	POS	GP	G	REC
1961	KC	A	O		76	.185
1963	KC	A	O		10	.176
	BLTR				86	.184

HANKINSON, FRANK EDWARD
B.1856 NEW YORK,N.Y.
D.APR.5,1911 PALISADES PARK,N.J

YR	CL	LEA	POS	GP	G	REC
1878	CHI	N	P-3	1	57	0- 1
						.268
1879	CHI	N	P-O	24	41	14- 9
						.183
1880	CLE	N	P-3-O	2	68	1- 1
						.209
1881	TRO	N	S-3		84	.196
1883	NY	N	3		91	.221
1884	NY	N	3		101	.235
1885	MET	AA	3		96	.241
1886	MET	AA	3		136	.240
1887	MET	AA	3		127	.315
1888	KC	AA	2		37	.175
	BRTR			27	838	15-11
						.239

HANLEY, JAMES PATRICK
B.OCT.13,1885 PROVIDENCE,R.I.
D.MAY 1,1961 ELMHURST,N.J.

YR	CL	LEA	POS	GP	G	REC
1913	NY	A	P		1	0- 0
	TL					

HANLON, EDWARD HUGH "NED"
B.AUG.22,1857 MONTVILLE,CONN.
D.APR.14,1937

YR	CL	LEA	POS	GP	G	REC
1880	CLE	N	S-3-O		72	.247
1881	DET	N	3-O		75	.278
1882	DET	N	3-O		79	.236
1883	DET	N	2-O		97	.245
1884	DET	N	O		112	.268
1885	DET	N	3-O		106	.301
1886	DET	N	O		126	.234
1887	DET	N	O		118	.316
1888	DET	N	O		108	.265
1889	PIT	N	M-O		115	.238
1890	PIT	P	M-O		119	.284
1891	PIT	N	M-O		115	.274
1892	BAL	N	M-O		8	.233
	BL				1250	.266

NON-PLAYING MANAGER
BAL(N)1893-98, BRO(N)1899-1905,
CIN(N) 1906-07

HANLON, WILLIAM "BIG BILL"
B.CALIFORNIA
D.MAR.18,1951 SACRAMENTO,CAL.

YR	CL	LEA	POS	GP	G	REC
1903	CHI	N	1		8	.045

HANNA, JOHN
B.PHILADELPHIA,PA.

YR	CL	LEA	POS	GP	G	REC
1884	WAS	AA	C-O		24	.113
	RIC	AA	C-S		22	.206
					46	.162

HANNA, PRESTON LEE
B.SEPT.10,1954 PENSACOLA,FLA.

YR	CL	LEA	POS	GP	G	REC
1975	ATL	N	P		4	0- 0
1976	ATL	N	P		5	0- 0
	BRTR				9	0- 0

HANNAH, JAMES HARRISON "TRUCK"
B.JUNE 5,1892 LARIMORE,N.DAK.

YR	CL	LEA	POS	GP	G	REC
1918	NY	A	C		90	.220
1919	NY	A	C		75	.238
1920	NY	A	C		79	.247
	BRTR				244	.235

HANNAHS, GERALD ELLIS "GERRY"
B.MAR.6,1953 BINGHAMTON,N.Y.

YR	CL	LEA	POS	GP	G	REC
1976	MON	N	P		3	2- 0
	BLTL					

HANNAN, JAMES JOHN "JIM"
B.JAN.7,1940 JERSEY CITY,N.J.

YR	CL	LEA	POS	GP	G	REC
1962	WAS	A	P		42	2- 4
1963	WAS	A	P		13	2- 2
1964	WAS	A	P		49	4- 7
1965	WAS	A	P		4	1- 1
1966	WAS	A	P		30	3- 9
1967	WAS	A	P		8	1- 1
1968	WAS	A	P		25	10- 6
1969	WAS	A	P		35	7- 6
1970	WAS	A	P		42	9-11
1971	DET	A	P		7	1- 0
	MIL	A	P		21	1- 1
	BRTR				276	41-48

HANNIFAN, JOHN JOSEPH
B.FEB.25,1883 HOLYOKE,MASS.
D.OCT.27,1945

YR	CL	LEA	POS	GP	G	REC
1906	PHI	A	H		1	.000
	NY	N	S-3		10	.200
1907	NY	N	1-3		49	.228
1908	NY	N	2		1	.000
	BOS	N	3		79	.206
	TR				140	.214

HANNING, LOY VERNON
B.OCT.18,1917 BUNKER,MO.

YR	CL	LEA	POS	GP	G	REC
1939	STL	A	P		4	0- 1
1942	STL	A	P		11	1- 1
	BRTR				15	1- 2

HANSEN, ANDREW VIGGO "ANDY" OR "SWEDE"
B.NOV.12,1924 LAKE WORTH,FLA.

YR	CL	LEA	POS	GP	G	REC
1944	NY	N	P	23	24	3- 3
1945	NY	N	P		23	4- 3
1947	NY	N	P		27	1- 5
1948	NY	N	P		36	5- 3
1949	NY	N	P		33	2- 6
1950	NY	N	P		31	0- 1
1951	PHI	N	P		24	3- 1
1952	PHI	N	P		43	5- 6
1953	PHI	N	P		30	0- 2
	BRTR			270	271	23-30

HANSEN, DOUGLAS WILLIAM
B.DEC.16,1928 LOS ANGELES,CAL.

YR	CL	LEA	POS	GP	G	REC
1951	CLE	A	H		3	.000
	BRTR					

HANSEN, ROBERT JOSEPH "BOB"
B.MAY 26,1948 BOSTON,MASS.

YR	CL	LEA	POS	GP	G	REC
1974	MIL	A	1-O		58	.295
1976	MIL	A	1-O		24	.164
	BLTL				82	.242

HANSEN, RONALD LAVERN "RON"
B.APR.5,1938 OXFORD,NEB.

YR	CL	LEA	POS	GP	G	REC
1958	BAL	A	S		12	.000
1959	BAL	A	S		2	.000
1960	BAL	A	S		153	.255
1961	BAL	A	2-S		155	.248
1962	BAL	A	S		71	.173
1963	CHI	A	S		144	.226
1964	CHI	A	S		158	.261
1965	CHI	A	2-S		162	.235
1966	CHI	A	S		23	.176
1967	CHI	A	S		157	.233
1968	WAS	A	S-3		86	.185
	CHI	A	2-S-3		40	.230
1969	CHI	A	1-2-S-3		85	.259
1970	NY	A	2-S-3		59	.297
1971	NY	A	2-S-3		61	.207
1972	KC	A	2-S-3		16	.133
	BRTR				1384	.234

YR	CL	LEA	POS	GP	G	REC

HANSEN, ROY EMIL "SNIPE"
B.FEB.21,1907 CHICAGO,ILL.

YR	CL	LEA	POS	GP	G	REC
1930	PHI	N	P		22	0- 7
1932	PHI	N	P		39	10-10
1933	PHI	N	P	32	33	6-14
1934	PHI	N	P		50	6-12
1935	PHI	N	P		2	0- 1
	STL	A	P		10	0- 1
	BBTL	155	156	22-45
	BL 1930

HANSEN, ROY INGLOF "ING"
B.MAR.6,1898 BELOIT,WIS.

1918	WAS	A	P		5	1- 0
	BRTR

HANSFORD, F. C.

1898	BRO	N	P		1	0- 1
	TL

HANSKI, DONALD THOMAS
(REAL NAME
DONALD THOMAS HANYZEWSKI)
B.FEB.27,1918 LAPORTE,IND.
D.SEPT.2,1957

1943	CHI	A	P-1	1	9	0- 0
						.238
1944	CHI	A	P		2	0- 0
	BLTL	3	11	0- 0
						.227

HANSON, EARL SYLVESTER "OLLIE"
B.JAN.19,1896 HOLBROOK,MASS.
D.AUG.19,1951 PASSAIC,N.J.

1921	CHI	N	P		2	0- 2
	BRTR

HANSON, JOSEPH
B.ST.LOUIS,MO.

1913	NY	A	C		1	.000
	TR

HANYZEWSKI, DONALD THOMAS
(PLAYED UNDER NAME OF
DONALD THOMAS HANSKI)

HANYZEWSKI, EDWARD MICHAEL
B.SEPT.18,1920 UNION MILLS,IND.

1942	CHI	N	P		6	1- 1
1943	CHI	N	P		33	8- 7
1944	CHI	N	P		14	2- 5
1945	CHI	N	P		2	0- 0
1946	CHI	N	P		3	1- 0
	BRTR				58	12-13

HAPPENNY, JOHN CLIFFORD
B.MAY 18,1901 WALTHAM,MASS.

1923	CHI	A	2		32	.221
	BRTR

HARBIDGE, WILLIAM ARTHUR
"YALLER BILL"
B.MAR.29,1855 PHILADELPHIA,PA.
D.MAR.17,1924

1875	HAR	NA	C-1-2-0	50		-
1876	HAR	N	C-0	30		.211
1877	HAR	N	C-2-0	41		.222
1878	CHI	N	C-0	53		.298
1879	CHI	N	C-0	1		.000
1880	TRO	N	C-0	8		.370
1882	TRO	N	C-1-0	32		.187
1883	PHI	N	C-2-S-3-	73		.221
			O			
1884	CIN	U	O	65		.271
	BLTL			353		-

HARDER, MELVIN LEROY
"MEL" OR "CHIEF"
B.OCT.15,1909 BEEMER,NEB.

1928	CLE	A	P		23	0- 2
1929	CLE	A	P		11	1- 0
1930	CLE	A	P		36	11-10
1931	CLE	A	P		40	13-14
1932	CLE	A	P		39	15-13
1933	CLE	A	P	43	44	15-17
1934	CLE	A	P		44	20-12
1935	CLE	A	P		42	22-11
1936	CLE	A	P		36	15-15
1937	CLE	A	P		38	15-12
1938	CLE	A	P	38	39	17-10
1939	CLE	A	P		29	15- 9
1940	CLE	A	P		31	12-11
1941	CLE	A	P		15	5- 4
1942	CLE	A	P		29	13-14
1943	CLE	A	P		19	8- 7
1944	CLE	A	P		30	12-10
1945	CLE	A	P		11	3- 7
1946	CLE	A	P		13	5- 4
1947	CLE	A	P		15	6- 4
	BRTR	582	584	223-186
NON-PLAYING MANAGER CLE(A) 1961

HARDESTY, SCOTT D.
B.DAYTON,OHIO

1899	NY	N	S		21	.228

HARDIE, LEWIS W.
B.AUG.24,1864 NEW YORK,N.Y.

1884	PHI	N	C		2	.143
1886	CHI	N	C		16	.176
1890	BOS	N	C-0		47	.227
1891	BAL	AA	0		15	.232
					80	.223

HARDIN, JAMES WARREN "JIM"
B.AUG.6,1943 MORRIS CHAPEL,TENN.

1967	BAL	A	P		19	8- 3
1968	BAL	A	P		35	18-13
1969	BAL	A	P		30	6- 7
1970	BAL	A	P		36	6- 5
1971	BAL	A	P		6	0- 0
	NY	A	P		12	0- 2
1972	ATL	N	P		26	5- 2
	BRTR				164	43-32

HARDIN, WILLIAM EDGAR "BUD"
B.JUNE 14,1923 SHELBY,N.C.

1952	CHI	N	2-S		3	.143
	BRTR

HARDING, CHARLES HAROLD
B.JAN.3,1891 NASHVILLE,TENN.
D.OCT.30,1971 BOLD SRPINGS,TENN

1913	DET	A	P		1	0- 0
	BRTR

HARDING, LOUIS EDWARD
B.SAN FRANCISCO,CAL.

1886	STL	AA	C		1	.000

HARDY, CARROLL WILLIAM
B.MAY 18,1933 STURGIS,S.DAK.

1958	CLE	A	0		27	.204
1959	CLE	A	0		32	.208
1960	CLE	A	0		29	.111
	BOS	A	0		73	.234
1961	BOS	A	0		85	.263
1962	BOS	A	0		115	.215
1963	HOU	A	0		15	.227
1964	HOU	A	0		46	.185
1967	MIN	A	0		11	.375
	BRTR				433	.225

HARDY, DAVID ALEXANDER "DOONEY"
B.1877 TORONTO,ONT.,CANADA
D.APR.22,1940

1902	CHI	N	P		4	2- 2
1903	CHI	N	P		3	1- 1
	TL				7	3- 3

HARDY, FRANCIS JOSEPH
B.JAN.6,1923 MARMARTH,N.DAK.

1951	NY	N	P		2	0- 0
	BRTR

HARDY, HARRY
B.NOV.5,1875 STEUBENVILLE,OHIO
D.SEPT.4,1943

1905	WAS	A	P		8	3- 1
1906	WAS	A	P		5	0- 3
					13	3- 4

HARDY, HOWARD LAWRENCE "LARRY"
B.JAN.10,1948 GOOSE CREEK,TEX.

1974	SD	N	P		76	9- 4
1975	SD	N	P		3	0- 0
1976	HOU	N	P		15	0- 0
	BRTR				94	9- 4

HARDY, JOHN DOOLITTLE
B.JANE 23,1880 CLEVELAND,OHIO
D.OCT.20,1921

1903	CLE	A	0		5	.150
1907	WAS	A	C		1	.250
1909	WAS	A	C		10	.167
1910	WAS	A	C		7	.375
	TR				23	.196

HARGAN, STEVEN LOWELL "STEVE"
B.SEP.8,1942 FT.WAYNE,IND.

1965	CLE	A	P		17	4- 3
1966	CLE	A	P		38	13-10
1967	CLE	A	P		30	14-13
1968	CLE	A	P		32	8-15
1969	CLE	A	P	32	34	5-14
1970	CLE	A	P	23	28	11- 3
1971	CLE	A	P		37	1-13
1972	CLE	A	P		12	0- 3
1974	TEX	A	P		37	12- 9
1975	TEX	A	P		33	9-10
1976	TEX	A	P		35	8- 8
	BRTR	326	333	85-100

HARGRAVE, EUGENE FRANKLIN
"BUBBLES"
B.JULY 15,1892 NEW HAVEN,IND.
D.FEB.23,1969 CINCINNATI,OHIO

1913	CHI	N	C		3	.333
1914	CHI	N	C		23	.222
1915	CHI	N	C		15	.158
1921	CIN	N	C		93	.289
1922	CIN	N	C		98	.315
1923	CIN	N	C		118	.333
1924	CIN	N	C		98	.301
1925	CIN	N	C		87	.300
1926	CIN	N	C		105	.353
1927	CIN	N	C		102	.308
1928	CIN	N	C		65	.295
1930	NY	A	C		45	.278
	BRTR				852	.310

HARGRAVE, WILLIAM MCKINLEY
"PINKY"
B.JAN.31,1896 NEW HAVEN,IND.
D.OCT.3,1942

1923	WAS	A	C		33	.288
1924	WAS	A	C		24	.152
1925	WAS	A	C		5	.333
	STL	A	C		67	.284
1926	STL	A	C		92	.275
1928	DET	A	C		121	.275
1929	DET	A	C		76	.330
1930	DET	A	C		55	.286
	WAS	A	C		10	.179
1931	WAS	A	C		40	.325
1932	BOS	N	C		82	.263
1933	BOS	N	C		45	.178
	BBTR				650	.278
	BR 1923-26

HARGREAVES, CHARLES RUSSELL
B.DEC.14,1898 TRENTON,N.J.

1923	BRO	N	C		20	.281
1924	BRO	N	C		15	.407
1925	BRO	N	C-1		45	.277
1926	BRO	N	C		85	.250
1927	BRO	N	C		46	.286
1928	BRO	N	C		20	.197
	PIT	N	C		79	.285
1929	PIT	N	C		102	.268
1930	PIT	N	C		11	.226
	BRTR				423	.270

HARGROVE, DUDLEY MICHAEL "MIKE"
B.OCT.26,1949 PERRYTON,TEX.

1974	TEX	A	1-0-D	131		.323
1975	TEX	A	1-0-D	145		.303
1976	TEX	A	1	151		.287
	BLTL			427		.302

HARGROVE, WILLIAM PATRICK "PAT"
B.MAY 10,1896 PALMYRA COURT
HOUSE,KAN.

1918	CHI	A	H		2	.000
	BRTR

YR	CL	LEA	POS	GP	G	REC

HARKINS, JOHN JOSEPH
B.APR.12,1859 NEWARK,N.J.
D.NOV.20,1940

YR	CL	LEA	POS	GP	G	REC
1884	CLE	N	P-S- 45	60	12-32
			3-0			.205
1885	BRO	AA	P		43	14-21
1886	BRO	AA	P		41	14-16
1887	BRO	AA	P		27	10-14
1888	BAL	AA	P		1	0- 1
		TR		157	172	50-84
						.235

HARKNESS, FREDERICK HARVEY "SPECS"
B.DEC.13,1887 LOS ANGELES,CAL.
D.MAY 16,1952 COMPTON,CAL.

1910	CLE	A	P		26	10- 7
1911	CLE	A	P		12	2- 2
		BRTR			38	12- 9

HARKNESS, THOMAS WILLIAM "TIM"
B.DEC.23,1937 LACHINE,QUE.,CAN.

1961	LA	N	1		5	.000
1962	LA	N	1		92	.258
1963	NY	N	1		123	.211
1964	NY	N	1		39	.282
		BLTL			259	.235

HARLEY, HENRY RISK
B.AUG.18,1874 SPRINGFIELD,OHIO
D.MAY 16,1961

1905	BOS	N	P		7	2- 4
		BRTR				

HARLEY, RICHARD JOSEPH
B.SEPT.25,1872 PHILADELPHIA,PA.
D.APR.3,1952

1897	STL	N	O		89	.288
1898	STL	N	O		142	.248
1899	CLE	N	O		145	.250
1900	CIN	N	O		5	.450
1901	CIN	N	O		133	.268
1902	DET	A	O		124	.276
1903	CHI	N	O		103	.231
		BLTR			741	.261

HARLOW, LARRY DUANE
B.NOV.13,1951 COLORADO SPRINGS, COLO.

1975	BAL	A	O		4	.333
		BLTL				

HARMAN, WILLIAM BELL
B.JAN.2,1919 BRIDGEWATER,VA.

1941	PHI	N	P-C		15	0- 0
						.071
		BRTR				

HARMON, CHARLES BYRON "CHUCK"
B.APR.23,1926 WASHINGTON,IND.

1954	CIN	N	1-3		94	.238
1955	CIN	N	1-3-0		96	.253
1956	CIN	N	1-0		13	.000
	STL	N	1-3-0		20	.000
1957	STL	N	O		9	.333
	PHI	N	1-3-0		57	.256
		BRTR			289	.238

HARMON, ROBERT GREEN
B.OCT.15,1887 LIBERAL,MO.
D.NOV.27,1961

1909	STL	N	P		21	6-11
1910	STL	N	P		43	13-15
1911	STL	N	P		51	23-16
1912	STL	N	P	43	46	18-18
1913	STL	N	P	42	46	8-21
1914	PIT	N	P	37	44	13-17
1915	PIT	N	P	37	42	16-17
1916	PIT	N	P	31	35	8-11
1918	PIT	N	P	17	18	2- 7
		BBTR	322	346	107-133

HARMON, TERRY WALTER
B.APR.12,1944 TOLEDO,OHIO

1967	PHI	N	R		2	.000
1969	PHI	N	2-S-3		87	.239
1970	PHI	N	2-S-3		71	.248
1971	PHI	N	1-2-S-3		79	.204
1972	PHI	N	2-S-3		73	.284
1973	PHI	N	2-S-3		72	.209
1974	PHI	N	2-S		27	.133
1975	PHI	N	2-S-3		48	.181
1976	PHI	N	2-S-3		42	.295
		BRTR			501	.236

HARPER, CHARLES WILLIAM "JACK"
B.APR.2,1878 GALLOWAY,PA.
D.SEPT.30,1950 JAMESTOWN,N.Y.

1899	CLE	N	P		5	1- 4
1900	STL	N	P		1	0- 1
1901	STL	N	P		36	23-13
1902	STL	N	P		29	17-10
1903	CIN	N	P		17	7- 7
1904	CIN	N	P		35	24- 8
1905	CIN	N	P		26	9-14
1906	CIN	N	P		5	0- 3
	CHI	N	P		1	0- 0
		BRTR		155	81-60

HARPER, GEORGE B.
B.AUG.17,1866 MILWAUKEE,WIS.
D.DEC.11,1931

1894	PHI	N	P		12	5- 3
1896	BRO	N	P		16	4- 8
					28	9-11

HARPER, GEORGE WASHINGTON
B.JUNE 24,1892 ARLINGTON,KY.

1916	DET	A	O		44	.161
1917	DET	A	O		47	.205
1918	DET	A	O		69	.243
1922	CIN	N	O		128	.339
1923	CIN	N	O		61	.256
1924	CIN	N	O		28	.270
	PHI	N	O		109	.295
1925	PHI	N	O		132	.349
1926	PHI	N	O		56	.314
1927	NY	N	O		145	.331
1928	NY	N	O		19	.228
	STL	N	O		99	.305
1929	BOS	N	O		136	.291
		BLTR		1073	.303

HARPER, HARRY CLAYTON
B.APR.24,1895 HACKENSACK,N.J.
D.APR.23,1963 LAYTON,N.J.

1913	WAS	A	P		4	0- 0
1914	WAS	A	P		23	2- 1
1915	WAS	A	P		19	5- 4
1916	WAS	A	P		36	15-10
1917	WAS	A	P		31	11-12
1918	WAS	A	P	35	36	11-10
1919	WAS	A	P		35	6-21
1920	BOS	A	P		27	5-14
1921	NY	A	P		8	4- 3
1923	BRO	N	P		1	0- 1
		BLTL	219	220	59-76

HARPER, JOHN WESLEY "JACK"
B.AUG.5,1893 HENDRICKS,W.VA.
D.JUNE 18,1927

1915	PHI	A	P		3	0- 1
		BPTR				

HARPER, TOMMY
B.OCT.14,1940 OAK GROVE,LA.

1962	CIN	N	3		6	.174
1963	CIN	N	3-0		129	.260
1964	CIN	N	3-0		102	.243
1965	CIN	N	2-3-0		159	.257
1966	CIN	N	O		149	.278
1967	CIN	N	O		103	.225
1968	CLE	A	2-0		130	.217
1969	SEA	A	2-3-0		148	.235
1970	MIL	A	2-3-0		154	.296
1971	MIL	A	2-3-0		152	.258
1972	BOS	A	O		144	.254
1973	BOS	A	O		147	.281
1974	BOS	A	O-O		118	.237
1975	CAL	A	1-0-O		89	.239
	OAK	A	1-0-O		34	.319
1976	BAL	A	1-0-O		46	.234
		BRTR		1810	.257

HARPER, WILLIAM HOMER "BLUE SLEEVE"
B.JUNE 14,1889 BERTAND,MO.
D.JUNE 17,1951

1911	STL	A	P		2	0- 0
		BBTR				

HARRAH, COLBERT DALE "TOBY"
B.OCT.26,1948 SISSONVILLE,W.VA.

1969	WAS	A	S		8	.000
1971	WAS	A	S-3		127	.230
1972	TEX	A	S-3		116	.259
1973	TEX	A	S-3		118	.260
1974	TEX	A	S-3		161	.260
1975	TEX	A	2-S-3		151	.293
1976	TEX	A	S-3		155	.260
		BRTR		836	.262

HARRELL, JOHN ROBERT
B.NOV.27,1947 LONG BEACH,CAL.

1969	SF	N	C		2	.500
		BRTR				

HARRELL, OSCAR MARTIN "SLIM"
B.JULY 31,1890 GRANDVIEW,TEX.
D.APR.30,1971 HILLSBORO,TEX.

1912	PHI	A	P		1	0- 0
		BRTR				

HARRELL, RAYMOND JAMES "COWBOY"
B.FEB.16,1912 PETROLIA,TEX.

1935	STL	N	P		11	1- 1
1937	STL	N	P		35	3- 7
1938	STL	N	P		32	2- 3
1939	CHI	N	P		4	0- 2
	PHI	N	P		22	3- 7
1940	PIT	N	P		3	0- 0
1945	NY	N	P		12	0- 0
		BRTR		119	9-20

HARRELL, WILLIAM "BILLY"
B.JULY 18,1928 TROY,N.Y.

1955	CLE	A	S		13	.421
1957	CLE	A	2-S-3		22	.263
1958	CLE	A	2-S-3-0		101	.218
1961	BOS	A	1-S-3		37	.162
		BRTR		173	.231

HARRELSON, DERREL MCKINLEY "BUD"
B.JUNE 6,1944 NILES,CAL.

1965	NY	N	S		19	.108
1966	NY	N	S		33	.222
1967	NY	N	S		151	.254
1968	NY	N	S		111	.219
1969	NY	N	S		123	.248
1970	NY	N	S		157	.243
1971	NY	N	S		142	.252
1972	NY	N	S		115	.215
1973	NY	N	S		106	.258
1974	NY	N	S		106	.227
1975	NY	N	S		34	.219
1976	NY	N	S		118	.234
		BBTR		1215	.238
		BR 1965			

HARRELSON, KENNETH SMITH "KEN"
B.SEP.4,1941 WOODRUFF,S.C.

1963	KC	A	1-0		79	.230
1964	KC	A	1-0		49	.194
1965	KC	A	1-0		150	.238
1966	KC	A	1-0		63	.224
	WAS	A	1		71	.248
1967	WAS	A	1		26	.203
	KC	A	1		61	.305
	BOS	A	1-0		23	.200
1968	BOS	A	1-0		150	.275
1969	BOS	A	1		10	.217
	CLE	A	1-0		149	.222
1970	CLE	A	1		17	.282
1971	CLE	A	1-0		52	.199
		BRTR		900	.239

HARRELSON, WILLIAM CHARLES "BILL"
B.NOV.17,1945 TAHLEQUAH,OKLA.

1968	CAL	A	P		10	1- 6
		BBTR				

HARRINGTON, ANDREW FRANCIS
B.NOV.13,1888 WAKEFIELD,MASS.
D.NOV.12,1938

1913	CIN	N	P		1	0- 0
		BRTR				

HARRINGTON, ANDREW MATTHEW
B.FEB.12,1904 MOUNTAIN VIEW,CAL
D.DEC.12,1938

1925	DET	A	2		1	.000
		BPTR				

HARRINGTON, CHARLES MICHAEL "MIKE"
B.OCT.8,1934 HATTIESBURG,MISS.

1963	PHI	N	R		1	.000
		BRTR				

HARRINGTON, JEREMIAH PETER
B.AUG.12,1869 KEOKUK,IOWA
D.APR.17,1913

1890	CIN	N	C		65	.246
1891	CIN	N	C		90	.229
1892	CIN	N	C		18	.213
1893	LOU	N	C		10	.121
		TR		183	.228

```
YR   CL LEA POS  GP    G    REC
```

HARRINGTON, JOSEPH C.
B.DEC.21,1869 FALL RIVER,MASS.
D.SEPT.13,1933
1895 BOS N 2   18   .299
1896 BOS N 3   53   .203
                    71   .229

HARRINGTON, WILLIAM WOMBLE "BILLY"
B.OCT.3,1927 SANFORD,N.C.
1953 PHI A P   1   0- 0
1955 KC A P   34   3- 3
1956 KC A P   23   2- 2
        BRTR   58   5- 5

HARRIS, ALONZO
B.SEP.17,1947 SELMA,ALA.
1967 HOU N H   6   .000
        BBTR

HARRIS, BENJAMIN F.
B.1889 NASHVILLE,TENN.
1914 KC F P   31   7- 7
1915 KC F P   1   0- 0
        BRTR   32   7- 7

HARRIS, BOYD GAIL "GAIL"
B.OCT.15,1931 ABINGDON,VA.
1955 NY N 1   79   .232
1956 NY N 1   12   .132
1957 NY N 1   90   .240
1958 DET A 1   134   .273
1959 DET A 1   114   .221
1960 DET A 1   8   .000
        BLTL   437   .240

HARRIS, CHALMER LUMAN "LUM"
B.JAN.17,1915
1941 PHI A P   33   4- 4
1942 PHI A P   26 11-15
1943 PHI A P   52   7-21
1944 PHI A P   23 10- 9
1946 PHI A P   34   3-14
1947 WAS A P   3   0- 0
        BRTR   151 35-63
NON-PLAYING MANAGER
BAL(A) 1961, HOU(N) 1964-65,
ATL(N) 1968-72

HARRIS, CHARLES "BUBBA"
B.JAN.17,1925 BIRMINGHAM,ALA.
1948 PHI A P   45   5- 2
1949 PHI A P   37   1- 1
1951 PHI A P   3   0- 0
     CLE A P   2   0- 0
        BRTR   87   6- 3

HARRIS, CHARLES JENKINS
B.OCT.21,1877 MACON,GA.
D.MAR.14,1963
1899 BAL N 3   21   .283

HARRIS, DAVID STANLEY "SHERIFF"
B.JULY 27,1902 GREENSBORO,N.C.
D.SEPT.18,1973 ATLANTA,GA.
1925 BOS N O   92   .265
1928 BOS N O   7   .118
1930 CHI A O   33   .235
     WAS A O   73   .320
1931 WAS A O   77   .312
1932 WAS A O   81   .327
1933 WAS A 1-3-O   82   .260
1934 WAS A O   97   .251
        BRTR   542   .281

HARRIS, FRANK W.
B.NOV.24,1858 PITTSBURGH,PA.
D.NOV.26,1939
1884 ALT U 1-O   24   .242

HARRIS, HERBERT
B.APR.24,1913 WHITING,IND.
1936 PHI A P   4   0- 0
        BLTL

HARRIS, JAMES WILLIAM "BILLY"
B.NOV.24,1943 HAMLET,N.C.
1968 CLE A 2-S-3   38   .213
1969 KC A 2   5   .286
        BLTR   43   .218

HARRIS, JOSEPH "MOON"
B.MAY 30,1892 COULTERS,PA.
D.DEC.10,1959 RENTON,PA.
1914 NY A O   2   .000
1917 CLE A 1   112   .304
1919 CLE A 1   62   .375
1922 BOS A 1-O   119   .316
1923 BOS A O   142   .335
1924 BOS A 1   133   .301
1925 BOS A 1   9   .150
     WAS A 1-O   99   .324
1926 WAS A 1-O   92   .307
1927 PIT N 1   129   .326
1928 PIT N 1   16   .391
     BRO N O   55   .236
        BRTR   970   .317

HARRIS, JOSEPH WHITE
B.FEB.1,1882 MELROSE,MASS.
D.APR.12,1966 MELROSE,MASS.
1935 BOS A P   3   1- 2
1936 BOS A P   30   2-21
1937 BOS A P   12   0- 7
        TR   45   3-30

HARRIS, MAURICE CHARLES "MICKEY"
B.JAN.30,1917 NEW YORK,N.Y.
D.APR.15,1971 FARMINGTON,MICH.
1940 BOS A P   13   4- 2
1941 BOS A P   35   8-14
1946 BOS A P   34 17- 9
1947 BOS A P   15   5- 4
1948 BOS A P   20   7-10
1949 BOS A P   7   2- 3
     WAS A P   23   2-12
1950 WAS A P   53   5- 9
1951 WAS A P   41   6- 8
1952 WAS A P   1   0- 0
     CLE A P   29   3- 0
        BLTL   271 59-71

HARRIS, ROBERT ARTHUR
B.MAY 1,1916 GILLETTE,WYO.
1938 DET A P   3   1- 0
1939 DET A P   5   1- 1
     STL A P   28 29   3-12
1940 STL A P   35 11-15
1941 STL A P   34 12-14
1942 STL A P   6   1- 5
     PHI A P   16   1- 5
        BRTR   127 128 30-52

HARRIS, ROBERT NED
B.JULY 9,1916 AMES,IOWA
1941 DET A O   26   .213
1942 DET A O   121   .271
1943 DET A O   114   .254
1946 DET A H   1   .000
        BLTL   262   .259

HARRIS, SPENCER ANTHONY
B.AUG.12,1900 DULUTH,MINN.
1925 CHI A O   56   .283
1926 CHI A O   80   .252
1929 WAS A O   6   .214
1930 PHI A O   22   .184
        BLTL   164   .250

HARRIS, STANLEY RAYMOND "BUCKY"
B.NOV.8,1896 PORT JERVIS,N.Y.
1919 WAS A 2   8   .214
1920 WAS A 2   137   .300
1921 WAS A 2   154   .289
1922 WAS A 2   154   .269
1923 WAS A 2   145   .282
1924 WAS A M-2   143   .268
1925 WAS A M-2   144   .287
1926 WAS A M-2   141   .283
1927 WAS A M-2   128   .267
1928 WAS A M-2   99   .204
1929 DET A M-2   7   .091
1931 DET A M-2   4   .125
        BRTR   1264   .274
NON-PLAYING MANAGER
DET(A) 1930, 32-33, BOS(A) 1934
WAS(A) 1935-42, PHI(N) 1943,
NY(A) 1947-48, WAS(A) 1950-54,
DET(A) 1955-56

HARRIS, VICTOR LANIER "VIC"
B.MAR.27,1950 LOS ANGELES,CAL.
1972 TEX A 2-S   61   .140
1973 TEX A 2-3-O   152   .249
1974 CHI N 2   62   .195
1975 CHI N 2-3-O   51   .179
1976 STL N 2-S-3-O   97   .228
        BBTR   423   .217

HARRIS, WALTER FRANCIS "BUDDY"
B.DEC.5,1948 PHILADELPHIA,PA.
1970 HOU N P   2   0- 0
1971 HOU N P   20   1- 1
        BRTR   22   1- 1

HARRIS, WILLIAM MILTON
B.JUNE 23,1900 WYLIE,TEX.
D.AUG.21,1965 INDIAN TRAIL,N.C.
1923 CIN N P   22   3- 2
1924 CIN N P   3   0- 0
1931 PIT N P   4   2- 2
1932 PIT N P   37 10- 9
1933 PIT N P   31   4- 4
1934 PIT N P   11   0- 0
1938 BOS A P   13   5- 5
        BRTR   121 24-22

HARRIS, WILLIAM THOMAS
B.DEC.3,1930 MARYSVILLE,N.B., CANADA
1957 BRO N P   1   0- 1
1959 LA N P   1   0- 0
        BLTR   2   0- 1

HARRISON
1875 NH NA C   1   -

HARRISON, CHARLES WILLIAM "CHUCK"
B.APR.25,1941 ABILENE,TEX.
1965 HOU N 1   15   .200
1966 HOU N 1   119   .256
1967 HOU N 1   70   .243
1969 KC A 1   75   .221
1971 KC A 1   49   .217
        BRTR   328   .238

HARRISON, LEO J. "BEN"
1901 WAS A O   1   .000

HARRISON, ROBERT LEE
B.SEPT.22,1930 ST.LOUIS,MO.
1955 BAL A P   1   0- 0
1956 BAL A P   1   0- 0
        BLTR   2   0- 0

HARRISON, RORIC EDWARD
B.SEP.20,1946 LOS ANGELES,CAL.
1972 BAL A P   39   3- 4
1973 ATL N P   38 39 11- 8
1974 ATL N P   20   6-11
1975 ATL N P   15   3- 4
     CLE A P   19   7- 7
        BRTR   131 132 30-34

HARRISON, THOMAS JAMES "TOM"
B.JAN.18,1945 TRAIL,B.C.,CANADA
1965 KC A P   1 2   0- 0
        BRTR

HARRISS, WILLIAM BRYAN "SLIM"
B.DEC.11,1897 BROWNWOOD,TEX.
D.SEPT.19,1963 TEMPLE,TEX.
1920 PHI A P   31   9-14
1921 PHI A P   39 11-16
1922 PHI A P   47   9-20
1923 PHI A P   46 10-16
1924 PHI A P   36   6-10
1925 PHI A P   46 19-12
1926 PHI A P   12   3- 5
     BOS A P   21   6-10
1927 BOS A P   44 14-21
1928 BOS A P   27   8-11
        BRTR   349 95-135

HARRIST, EARL "IRISH"
B.AUG.20,1920 DUBACH,LA.
1945 CIN N P   14   2- 4
1947 CHI A P   33   3- 8
1948 CHI A P   11   1- 3
     WAS A P   23   3- 3
1952 STL A P   36   2- 8
1953 CHI A P   7   1- 0
     DET A P   8   0- 2
        BRTR   132 12-28

YR	CL	LEA	POS	GP	G	REC

HARSHANY, SAMUEL
B.MAY 1,1910 MADISON,ILL.

YR	CL	LEA	POS	GP	G	REC
1937	STL	A	C		5	.091
1938	STL	A	C		11	.292
1939	STL	A	C		42	.241
1940	STL	A	C		3	.000
	BRTR				61	.210

HARSHMAN, JOHN ELVIN "JACK"
B.JULY 12,1927 SAN DIEGO,CAL.

YR	CL	LEA	POS	GP	G	REC
1948	NY	N	1		5	.250
1950	NY	N	1		9	.125
1952	NY	N	P	2	3	0- 2
1954	CHI	A	P-1	35	36	14- 8
						.143
1955	CHI	A	P		32	11- 7
1956	CHI	A	P	34	36	15-11
1957	CHI	A	P		30	8- 8
1958	BAL	A	P-O	34	47	12-15
						.195
1959	BAL	A	P	14	15	0- 6
	BOS	A	P	8	9	2- 3
	CLE	A	P	13	21	5- 1
1960	CLE	A	P		15	2- 4
	BLTL			217	258	69-65
						.179

HARSTAD, OSCAR THEANDER
B.MAY 24,1892 PARKLAND,WASH.

YR	CL	LEA	POS	GP	G	REC
1915	CLE	A	P		32	3- 6

HART, JAMES A.
B.JULY 10,1855 GIRARD,PA.
D.JULY 18,1919
NON-PLAYING MANAGER
LOU(AA) 1885-86, BOS(N) 1889

HART, JAMES HENRY "HUB"
B.FEB.2,1878 EVERETT,MASS.
D.OCT.10,1960

YR	CL	LEA	POS	GP	G	REC
1905	CHI	A	C		11	.125
1906	CHI	A	C		17	.162
1907	CHI	A	C		29	.271
	BLTR				57	.217

HART, JAMES RAY "JIM RAY"
B.OCT.30,1941 HOOKERTOWN,N.C.

YR	CL	LEA	POS	GP	G	REC
1963	SF	N	3		7	.200
1964	SF	N	3-O		153	.286
1965	SF	N	3-O		160	.299
1966	SF	N	3-O		156	.285
1967	SF	N	3-O		158	.289
1968	SF	N	3-O		136	.258
1969	SF	N	3-O		95	.254
1970	SF	N	3-O		76	.282
1971	SF	N	3-O		31	.256
1972	SF	N	3		24	.304
1973	SF	N	3		5	.000
	NY	A	O		114	.254
1974	NY	A	H		10	.053
	BRTR				1125	.278

HART, JOSEPH L.

YR	CL	LEA	POS	GP	G	REC
1890	STL	AA	P		28	12- 9

HART, THOMAS HENRY "BUSHY"
B.JUNE 15,1869 CANAAN,N.Y.
D.SEPT.17,1939

YR	CL	LEA	POS	GP	G	REC
1891	WAS	AA	C-O		8	.130

HART, WARREN F.

YR	CL	LEA	POS	GP	G	REC
1901	BAL	A	1		58	.312

HART, WILLIAM FRANKLIN
B.JULY 19,1865 LOUISVILLE,KY.
D.SEPT.19,1936

YR	CL	LEA	POS	GP	G	REC
1886	ATH	AA	P		23	9-13
1887	ATH	AA	P		3	1- 2
1892	BRO	N	P	25	29	7-10
1895	PIT	N	P		31	14-15
1896	STL	N	P	40	46	13-26
1897	STL	N	P	37	43	9-23
1898	PIT	N	P		15	6- 9
1901	CLE	A	P		20	6-12
				194	210	65-110

HART, WILLIAM WOODROW
B.MAR.4,1915 WICONISCO,PA.
D.JULY 29,1968 LYKENS,PA.

YR	CL	LEA	POS	GP	G	REC
1943	BRO	N	S		8	.158
1944	BRO	N	S-3		29	.178
1945	BRO	N	S-3		58	.230
	BRTR				95	.207

HARTENSTEIN, CHARLES OSCAR "CHUCK"
B.MAY.26,1942 SEGUIN,TEX.

YR	CL	LEA	POS	GP	G	REC
1965	CHI	N	R		1	.000
1966	CHI	N	P		5	0- 0
1967	CHI	N	P		45	9- 5
1968	CHI	N	P		28	2- 4
1969	PIT	N	P		56	5- 4
1970	PIT	N	P		17	1- 1
	STL	N	P		6	0- 0
	BOS	A	P		17	0- 3
	BRTR			174	175	17-17
						.054

HARTER, FRANK PIERCE
B.SEPT.19,1886 KEYESPORT,ILL.
D.APR.14,1959

YR	CL	LEA	POS	GP	G	REC
1912	CIN	N	P		6	1- 2
1913	CIN	N	P		17	1- 1
1914	IND	F	P		6	1- 2
	BPTR				29	3- 5

HARTFORD, BRUCE DANIEL
B.MAY 14,1892 CHICAGO,ILL.
D.MAY 25,1975 LOS ANGELES,CAL.

YR	CL	LEA	POS	GP	G	REC
1914	CLE	A	S		8	.181
	BRTR					

HARTJE, CHRISTIAN HENRY
B.AUG.25,1915 SAN FRANCISCO,CAL
D.JUNE 26,1946

YR	CL	LEA	POS	GP	G	REC
1939	BRO	N	C		9	.313
	BRTR					

HARTLEY, GROVER ALLEN "SLICK"
B.JULY 2,1888 OSGOOD,IND.
D.OCT.19,1964 DAYTONA BEACH,FLA

YR	CL	LEA	POS	GP	G	REC
1911	NY	N	C		10	.222
1912	NY	N	C		25	.235
1913	NY	N	C		23	.316
1914	STL	F	C		86	.286
1915	STL	F	C		117	.271
1916	STL	A	C		89	.225
1917	STL	A	C		19	.231
1924	NY	N	C		4	.286
1925	NY	N	C-1		46	.316
1926	NY	N	C		13	.048
1927	BOS	A	C		103	.275
1929	CLE	A	C		24	.273
1930	CLE	A	C		1	.750
1934	STL	A	C		5	.333
	BRTR				565	.267

HARTLEY, WALTER SCOTT "CHICK"
B.AUG.22,1880 PHILADELPHIA,PA.
D.JULY 18,1948 PHILADELPHIA,PA.

YR	CL	LEA	POS	GP	G	REC
1902	NY	N	O		1	.000
	BRTR					

HARTMAN, CHARLES OTTO
B.AUG.10,1888 LOS ANGELES,CAL.

YR	CL	LEA	POS	GP	G	REC
1908	BOS	A	P		1	0- 0

HARTMAN, FREDERICK ORRIN "DUTCH"
B.APR.25,1868 ALLEGHENY,PA.
D.NOV.11,1938

YR	CL	LEA	POS	GP	G	REC
1894	PIT	N	3		49	.311
1897	STL	N	3		126	.301
1898	NY	N	3		122	.267
1899	NY	N	3		52	.241
1901	CHI	A	3		120	.313
1902	STL	N	1-S-3		112	.221
	TR				581	.278

HARTMAN, J. C. "J.C."
B.APR.15,1934 COTTONTON,ALA.

YR	CL	LEA	POS	GP	G	REC
1962	HOU	N	S		51	.223
1963	HOU	N	S		39	.122
	BRTR				90	.185

HARTMAN, ROBERT LOUIS
B.AUG.28,1937 KENOSHA,WIS.

YR	CL	LEA	POS	GP	G	REC
1959	MIL	N	P		3	0- 0
1962	CLE	A	P		8	0- 1
	BRTL				11	0- 1

HARTNETT, CHARLES LEO "GABBY"
B.DEC.20,1900 WOONSOCKET,R.I.
D.DEC.20,1972 PARK RIDGE,ILL.

YR	CL	LEA	POS	GP	G	REC
1922	CHI	N	C		31	.194
1923	CHI	N	C-1		85	.268
1924	CHI	N	C		111	.299
1925	CHI	N	C		117	.289
1926	CHI	N	C		93	.275
1927	CHI	N	C		127	.294
1928	CHI	N	C		120	.302
1929	CHI	N	C		25	.273
1930	CHI	N	C		141	.339
1931	CHI	N	C		116	.282
1932	CHI	N	C		121	.271
1933	CHI	N	C		140	.276
1934	CHI	N	C		130	.299
1935	CHI	N	C		116	.344
1936	CHI	N	C		121	.307
1937	CHI	N	C		110	.354
1938	CHI	N	M-C		88	.274
1939	CHI	N	M-C		97	.278
1940	CHI	N	M-C-1		37	.266
1941	NY	N	C		64	.300
	BRTR				1990	.298

HARTNETT, PATRICK J. "HAPPY"
B.OCT.20,1863 S.BOSTON,MASS.
D.APR.10,1935

YR	CL	LEA	POS	GP	G	REC
1890	STL	AA	1		13	.200

HARTRANFT, RAYMOND CHARLES
B.SEPT.19,1890 QUAKERTOWN,PA.
D.FEB.10,1955 E.VINCENT
TOWNSHIP,CHESTER CO.,PA.

YR	CL	LEA	POS	GP	G	REC
1913	PHI	N	P		1	0- 0

HARTS, GREGORY RUDOLPH "GREG"
B.APR.21,1950 ATLANTA,GA.

YR	CL	LEA	POS	GP	G	REC
1973	NY	N	H		3	.500
	BLTL					

HARTSEL, TULLOS FREDERICK "TOPSY"
B.JUNE 26,1874 POLK,OHIO
D.OCT.14,1944

YR	CL	LEA	POS	GP	G	REC
1898	LOU	N	O		21	.319
1899	LOU	N	O		20	.261
1900	CIN	N	O		18	.328
1901	CHI	N	O		140	.339
1902	PHI	A	O		137	.286
1903	PHI	A	O		98	.311
1904	PHI	A	O		147	.249
1905	PHI	A	O		148	.276
1906	PHI	A	O		144	.255
1907	PHI	A	O		143	.280
1908	PHI	A	O		129	.243
1909	PHI	A	O		83	.270
1910	PHI	A	O		90	.221
1911	PHI	A	O		25	.237
	BLTL				1343	.276

HARTSFIELD, ROY THOMAS "SPEC"
B.OCT.25,1925 CHATTAHOOCHEE,GA.

YR	CL	LEA	POS	GP	G	REC
1950	BOS	N	2		107	.277
1951	BOS	N	2		120	.271
1952	BOS	N	2		38	.262
	BRTR				265	.273

HARTUNG, CLINTON CLARENCE "FLOPPY"
B.AUG.10,1922 HONDO,TEX.

YR	CL	LEA	POS	GP	G	REC
1947	NY	N	P-O	23	34	9- 7
						.309
1948	NY	N	P	36	43	8- 8
1949	NY	N	P	33	38	9-11
1950	NY	N	P-1- O	20	32	3- 3
						.302
1951	NY	N	O		21	.205
1952	NY	N	O		28	.218
	BRTR			112	196	29-29
						.212

HARTZELL, PAUL FRANKLIN
B.NOV.2,1953 BLOOMSBURG,PA.

YR	CL	LEA	POS	GP	G	REC
1976	CAL	A	P		37	7- 4
	BRTR					

YR	CL	LEA	POS	GP	G	REC

HARTZELL, ROY ALLEN
B.JULY 6,1881 GOLDEN,COLO.
D.NOV.5,1961

YR	CL	LEA	POS	GP	G	REC
1906	STL	A	3		113	.213
1907	STL	A	2-3		60	.236
1908	STL	A	S-O		115	.265
1909	STL	A	O		152	.271
1910	STL	A	S-3-O		151	.218
1911	NY	A	3		144	.296
1912	NY	A	3-O		123	.272
1913	NY	A	2-3-O		141	.259
1914	NY	A	O		137	.233
1915	NY	A	O		119	.251
1916	NY	A	O		33	.187
	BLTR				1288	.252

HARVEL, LUTHER RAYMOND
B.SEPT.30,1905 CAMBRIA,ILL.

YR	CL	LEA	POS	GP	G	REC
1928	CLE	A	O		40	.220
	BRTR					

HARVEY, ERWIN K.
B.JAN.5,1878 SARATOGA,CAL.

YR	CL	LEA	POS	GP	G	REC
1900	CHI	N	P		2	0- 0
1901	CHI	A	P-O	3	17	2- 1
						.256
	CLE	A	P-O	7	44	0- 7
						.351
1902	CLE	A	O		12	.369
				12	75	2- 8
						.336

HASBROUCK, ROBERT LYNDON "ZIGGY"
B.NOV.21,1893 GRUNDY CENTER,IA.
D.FEB.9,1976 GARLAND,TEX.

YR	CL	LEA	POS	GP	G	REC
1916	CHI	A	1		8	.125
1917	CHI	A	2		2	.000
	BRTR				10	.111

HASENMAYER, DONALD IRVIN
B.APR.4,1927 ROSLYN,PA.

YR	CL	LEA	POS	GP	G	REC
1945	PHI	N	2-3		5	.111
1946	PHI	N	3		6	.083
	BRTR				11	.100

HASH, HERBERT HOWARD
B.FEB.13,1912 WOOLWINE,VA.

YR	CL	LEA	POS	GP	G	REC
1940	BOS	A	P	34	35	7- 7
1941	BOS	A	P	4		1- 0
	BRTR			38	39	8- 7

HASLIN, MICHAEL JOSEPH
B.OCT.31,1910 WILKES-BARRE,PA.

YR	CL	LEA	POS	GP	G	REC
1933	PHI	N	2		26	.236
1934	PHI	N	2-3		72	.265
1935	PHI	N	2-S-3		110	.265
1936	PHI	N	2-3		16	.344
	BOS	N	2-3		36	.279
1937	NY	N	2-S-3		27	.190
1938	NY	N	2-3		31	.324
	BRTR				318	.272

HASNEY, PETER JAMES
B.MAY 26,1865 ENGLAND
D.MAY 24,1908

YR	CL	LEA	POS	GP	G	REC
1890	ATH	AA	O		2	.125

HASSAMAER, WILLIAM LOUIS "ROARING BILL"
B.JULY 26,1864 ST.LOUIS,MO.
D.MAY 29,1910

YR	CL	LEA	POS	GP	G	REC
1894	WAS	N	3-O		116	.326
1895	WAS	N	O		89	.278
	LOU	N	1-O		20	.198
1896	LOU	N	1		26	.248
					251	.291

HASSETT, JOHN ALOYSIUS "BUDDY"
B.SEPT.5,1911 NEW YORK,N.Y.

YR	CL	LEA	POS	GP	G	REC
1936	BRO	N	1		156	.310
1937	BRO	N	1		137	.304
1938	BRO	N	O		115	.293
1939	BOS	N	1-O		147	.309
1940	BOS	N	1-O		124	.234
1941	BOS	N	1		118	.296
1942	NY	A	1		132	.284
	BLTL				929	.292

HASSLER, ANDREW EARL "ANDY"
B.OCT.18,1951 TEXAS CITY,TEX.

YR	CL	LEA	POS	GP	G	REC
1971	CAL	A	P		6	0- 3
1973	CAL	A	P		7	0- 4
1974	CAL	A	P		23	7-11
1975	CAL	A	P		30	3-12
1976	CAL	A	P		14	0- 6
	KC	A	P		19	5- 6
	BLTL				99	15-42

HASSLER, JOSEPH FREDERICK
B.APR.7,1905 FT.SMITH,ARK.
D.SEPT.4,1971 DUNCAN,OKLA.

YR	CL	LEA	POS	GP	G	REC
1928	PHI	A	S		28	.265
1929	PHI	A	S		4	.000
1930	STL	A	S		5	.250
	BRTR				37	.239

HASSON, CHARLES EUGENE "GENE"
B.JULY 20,1915 CONNELLSVILLE,PA

YR	CL	LEA	POS	GP	G	REC
1937	PHI	A	1		28	.306
1938	PHI	A	1		19	.275
	BLTL				47	.293

HASTINGS, CHARLES MORTON
B.NOV.11,1870 IRONTON,OHIO
D.AUG.3,1934

YR	CL	LEA	POS	GP	G	REC
1893	CLE	N	P		16	4- 6
1896	PIT	N	P		17	5- 9
1897	PIT	N	P		15	7- 3
1898	PIT	N	P		18	4- 9
					66	20-27

HASTINGS, WINFIELD SCOTT
B.AUG.10,1846 HILLSBORO,OHIO
D.AUG.14,1907

YR	CL	LEA	POS	GP	G	REC
1871	ROK	NA	P-C-2	1	24	0- 1
						-
1872	CLE	NA	M-C-2-O		21	.422
	BAL	NA	C-2		11	.196
1873	BAL	NA	C-1-2-O		31	-
1874	HAR	NA	C-2-O		52	-
1875	CHI	NA	C-2-O		66	-
1876	LOU	N	O		67	.254
1877	CIN	N	C-O		20	.141
	BRTR			1	292	0- 1
						-

HASTY, ROBERT KELLER
B.MAY 3,1896 CANTON,GA.
D.MAY 28,1972 DALLAS,GA.

YR	CL	LEA	POS	GP	G	REC
1919	PHI	A	P		2	0- 2
1920	PHI	A	P		19	1- 3
1921	PHI	A	P		35	5-16
1922	PHI	A	P		28	9-14
1923	PHI	A	P		44	13-15
1924	PHI	A	P		18	1- 3
	BRTR				146	29-53

HATFIELD, FRED JAMES
B.MAR.18,1925 LANETT,ALA.

YR	CL	LEA	POS	GP	G	REC
1950	BOS	A	3		10	.250
1951	BOS	A	3		80	.172
1952	BOS	A	3		20	.286
	DET	A	S-3		111	.237
1953	DET	A	2-S-3		109	.254
1954	DET	A	2-3		81	.294
1955	DET	A	2-S-3		122	.232
1956	DET	A	2		8	.250
	CHI	A	2-S-3		106	.262
1957	CHI	A	3		69	.202
1958	CLE	A	3		3	.125
	CIN	N	2-3		3	.000
	BLTR				722	.241

HATFIELD, GILBERT "COLONEL"
B.JAN.27,1855 HOBOKEN,N.J.
D.MAY 27,1921

YR	CL	LEA	POS	GP	G	REC
1885	BUF	N	2-3		11	.125
1887	NY	N	3		2	.429
1888	NY	N	3		27	.181
1889	NY	N	P-S	6	32	0- 0
						.184
1890	NY	P	S		48	.301
	BOS	P	S		3	.143
	NY	P	P-S- 2		20	0- 0
						.244
1891	WAS	AA	P-S- 2		132	0- 2
			3			.258
1893	BRO	N	3		33	.315
1895	LOU	N	S		5	.196
			TR	10	313	0- 2
						.246

HATFIELD, JOHN VAN BUREN
B.1847
D.FEB.21,1909

YR	CL	LEA	POS	GP	G	REC
1871	MUT	NA	2-3-O		34	-
1872	MUT	NA	2		56	.303
1873	MUT	NA	2-3		53	-
1874	MUT	NA	3-O		64	-
1875	MUT	NA	O		1	-
1876	MUT	N	2		1	.250
					209	-

HATHAWAY, RAY WILSON
B.OCT.13,1919 GREENVILLE,OHIO

YR	CL	LEA	POS	GP	G	REC
1945	BRO	N	P		4	0- 1
	BRTR					

HATTEN, JOSEPH HILARIAN "JOE"
B.NOV.17,1917 BANCROFT,IOWA

YR	CL	LEA	POS	GP	G	REC
1946	BRO	N	P		42	14-11
1947	BRO	N	P		42	17- 8
1948	BRO	N	P	42	43	13-10
1949	BRO	N	P	37	39	12- 8
1950	BRO	N	P	23	27	2- 2
1951	BRO	N	P		11	1- 0
	CHI	N	P		23	2- 6
1952	CHI	N	P	13	17	4- 4
	BRTL			233	244	65-49

HATTER, CLYDE MELNO
B.AUG.7,1908 POPLAR HILL,KY.
D.OCT.16,1937

YR	CL	LEA	POS	GP	G	REC
1935	DET	A	P		8	0- 0
1937	DET	A	P		3	1- 0
	BRTL				11	1- 0

HATTON, GRADY EDGEBERT
B.OCT.7,1922 BEAUMONT,TEX.

YR	CL	LEA	POS	GP	G	REC
1946	CIN	N	3-O		116	.271
1947	CIN	N	3		146	.281
1948	CIN	N	2-S-3-O		133	.240
1949	CIN	N	3		137	.263
1950	CIN	N	2-S-3		130	.260
1951	CIN	N	3-O		96	.254
1952	CIN	N	2		128	.213
1953	CIN	N	1-2-3		83	.233
1954	CIN	N	H		1	.000
	CHI	A	1-3		13	.167
	BOS	A	1-S-3		99	.281
1955	BOS	A	2-3		126	.245
1956	BOS	A	H		5	.400
	STL	N	2-3		44	.247
	BAL	A	2-3		27	.148
1960	CHI	N	2		28	.342
	BLTR				1312	.253

NON-PLAYING MANAGER
HOU(N) 1966-68

HAUG, WILLIAM L.
(PLAYED UNDER NAME OF
WILLIAM L. HAGUE)

HAUGHER, JOHN ARTHUR "ARTHUR"
B.NOV.18,1893 DELHI,OHIO
D.AUG.2,1944 REDWOOD CITY,CAL

YR	CL	LEA	POS	GP	G	REC
1912	CLE	A	O		15	.056
	BLTR					

HAUGHEY, CHRISTOPHER FRANCIS
B.OCT.3,1925 ASTORIA,N.Y.

YR	CL	LEA	POS	GP	G	REC
1943	BRO	N	P		1	0- 1
	BRTR					

HAUGSTAD, PHILIP DONALD "PHIL"
B.FEB.23,1924 BLACK RIVER FALLS
WIS.

YR	CL	LEA	POS	GP	G	REC
1947	BRO	N	P		6	1- 0
1948	BRO	N	P		1	0- 0
1951	BRO	N	P		21	0- 1
1952	CIN	N	P		9	0- 0
	BRTR				37	1- 1

HAUSER, ARNOLD GEORGE "STUB"
B.SEPT.25,1888 CHICAGO,ILL.
D.MAY 22,1966 AURORA,ILL.

YR	CL	LEA	POS	GP	G	REC
1910	STL	N	S		118	.205
1911	STL	N	S		136	.241
1912	STL	N	S		133	.259
1913	STL	N	S		22	.289
1915	CHI	F	S		20	.222
	BRTR				429	.238

YR	CL	LEA	POS	GP	G	REC

HAUSER, JOSEPH JOHN "JOE"
B.JAN.12,1899 MILWAUKEE,WIS.

YR	CL	LEA	POS	GP	G	REC
1922	PHI	A	1		111	.323
1923	PHI	A	1		146	.307
1924	PHI	A	1		149	.288
1926	PHI	A	1		91	.192
1928	PHI	A	1		95	.260
1929	CLE	A	1		37	.250
	BLTL				629	.284

HAUSMAN, THOMAS MATTHEW "TOM"
B.MAR.31,1953 MOBRIDGE,S.D.

YR	CL	LEA	POS	GP	G	REC
1975	MIL	A	P		29	3- 6
1976	MIL	A	P		3	0- 0
	BRTR				32	3- 6

HAUSMANN, CLEMENS RAYMOND
B.AUG.17,1919 HOUSTON,TEX.

YR	CL	LEA	POS	GP	G	REC
1944	BOS	A	P		32	4- 7
1945	BOS	A	P		31	5- 7
1949	PHI	A	P		1	0- 0
	BRTR				64	9-14

HAUSMANN, GEORGE JOHN
B.FEB.11,1917 ST.LOUIS,MO.

YR	CL	LEA	POS	GP	G	REC
1944	NY	N	2		131	.268
1945	NY	N	2		154	.279
1949	NY	N	2		16	.128
	BRTR				301	.268

HAWES, ROY LEE
B.JULY 5,1928 SHILOH,ILL.

YR	CL	LEA	POS	GP	G	REC
1951	WAS	A	1		3	.167
	BLTL					

HAWES, WILLIAM HILDRETH
B.NOV.17,1853 NASHUA,N.H.
D.JUNE 16,1940

YR	CL	LEA	POS	GP	G	REC
1879	BOS	N	O		37	.200
1884	CIN	U	1-O		68	.260
	BRTR				105	.240

HAWK, EDWARD
B.MAY 11,1890 NEOSHO,MO.
D.MAR.26,1936

YR	CL	LEA	POS	GP	G	REC
1911	STL	A	P		5	1- 4
	BLTR					

HAWKE, WILLIAM VICTOR "DICK"
B.APR.28,1870 ELSMERE,DEL.
D.DEC.11,1902 WILMINGTON,DEL.

YR	CL	LEA	POS	GP	G	REC
1892	STL	N	P		15	4- 5
1893	STL	N	P		3	0- 1
	BAL	N	P		28	11-17
1894	BAL	N	P		25	16- 9
	BRTR				71	31-32

HAWKES, THORNDIKE PROCTOR
B.OCT.15,1852 DANVERS,MASS.
D.FEB.3,1929

YR	CL	LEA	POS	GP	G	REC
1879	TRO	N	2		63	.206
1884	WAS	AA	2		38	.256
					101	.226

HAWKINS, WYNN FIRTH
B.FEB.20,1936 E.PALESTINE,OHIO

YR	CL	LEA	POS	GP	G	REC
1960	CLE	A	P		15	4- 4
1961	CLE	A	P		30	7- 9
1962	CLE	A	P		3	1- 0
	BRTR				48	12-13

HAWKS, NELSON LOUIS "CHICKEN"
B.FEB.3,1897 SAN FRANCISCO,CAL.
D.MAY 26,1973 SAN RAFAEL,CAL.

YR	CL	LEA	POS	GP	G	REC
1921	NY	A	O		41	.288
1925	PHI	N	1		105	.322
	BLTL				146	.316

HAWLEY, EMERSON P. "PINK"
B.DEC.5,1872 BEAVER DAM,WIS.
D.SEPT.19,1938

YR	CL	LEA	POS	GP	G	REC
1892	STL	N	P		19	6-13
1893	STL	N	P		33	5-17
1894	STL	N	P		48	18-25
1895	PIT	N	P		53	29-21
1896	PIT	N	P		48	21-21
1897	PIT	N	P		37	18-19
1898	CIN	N	P		42	26-12
1899	CIN	N	P		33	14-17
1900	NY	N	P		39	18-20
1901	MIL	A	P	24	28	7-13
	BLTR			376	380	162-178

HAWLEY, SCOTT

YR	CL	LEA	POS	GP	G	REC
1894	BOS	N	P		1	0- 0

HAWORTH, HOWARD HOMER
B.AUG.27,1895 NEWBERG,ORE.

YR	CL	LEA	POS	GP	G	REC
1915	CLE	A	C		7	.142
	BLTR					

HAYDEL, JOHN HAROLD "HAL"
B.JULY 9,1944 HOUMA,LA.

YR	CL	LEA	POS	GP	G	REC
1970	MIN	A	P		4	2- 0
1971	MIN	A	P		31	4- 2
	BRTR				35	6- 2

HAYDEN, EUGENE FRANKLIN
B.APR.14,1935 SAN FRANCISCO,CAL

YR	CL	LEA	POS	GP	G	REC
1958	CIN	N	P		3	0- 0
	BLTL					

HAYDEN, JOHN FRANCIS
B.OCT.21,1880 BRYN MAWR,PA.
D.AUG.3,1942

YR	CL	LEA	POS	GP	G	REC
1901	PHI	A	O		51	.266
1906	BOS	A	O		85	.248
1908	CHI	N	O		11	.200
					147	.251

HAYES, FRANK WITMAN "BLIMP"
B.OCT.13,1914 JAMESBURG,N.J.
D.JUNE 23,1955

YR	CL	LEA	POS	GP	G	REC
1933	PHI	A	C		3	.000
1934	PHI	A	C		92	.226
1936	PHI	A	C		144	.271
1937	PHI	A	C		60	.261
1938	PHI	A	C		99	.291
1939	PHI	A	C		124	.283
1940	PHI	A	C-1		136	.308
1941	PHI	A	C		126	.280
1942	PHI	A	C		21	.238
	STL	A	C		56	.252
1943	STL	A	C-1		88	.188
1944	PHI	A	C-1		155	.248
1945	PHI	A	C		32	.227
	CLE	A	C		119	.236
1946	CLE	A	C		51	.256
	CHI	A	C		53	.212
1947	BOS	A	C		5	.154
	BRTR				1364	.259

HAYES, JAMES MILLARD
B.FEB.11,1913 MONTEVALLO,ALA.

YR	CL	LEA	POS	GP	G	REC
1935	WAS	A	P		7	2- 4
	BLTR					

HAYES, JOHN J.
B.JUNE 27,1861 BROOKLYN,N.Y.

YR	CL	LEA	POS	GP	G	REC
1882	WOR	N	C-S-3-O		78	.269
1883	PIT	AA	C-2-S-O		83	.263
1884	PIT	AA	C-1-2-O		34	.220
	BRO	AA	C-O		15	.220
1885	BRO	AA	C		42	.132
1886	WAS	N	C		26	.184
1887	BAL	AA	C		8	.143
1890	BRO	P	C		12	.191
	TR				298	.232

HAYES, MICHAEL
B.CLEVELAND,OHIO

YR	CL	LEA	POS	GP	G	REC
1876	MUT	N	O		5	.182

HAYES, MINTER CARNEY "JACKIE"
B.JULY 19,1906 CLANTON,ALA.

YR	CL	LEA	POS	GP	G	REC
1927	WAS	A	S-3		10	.241
1928	WAS	A	2-S		60	.257
1929	WAS	A	2-3		123	.276
1930	WAS	A	2		51	.283
1931	WAS	A	2		38	.222
1932	CHI	A	2-S-3		117	.257
1933	CHI	A	2		138	.258
1934	CHI	A	2		62	.257
1935	CHI	A	2		89	.267
1936	CHI	A	2-S		108	.312
1937	CHI	A	2		143	.229
1938	CHI	A	2		62	.328
1939	CHI	A	2		72	.249
1940	CHI	A	2		18	.195
	BRTR				1091	.265

HAYHURST, ELIAS HICKS
B.1826 PHILADELPHIA,PA.
D.DEC.18,1882 PHILADELPHIA,PA.
NON-PLAYING MANAGER
ATH(AA) 1871-75

HAYNES, JOSEPH WALTON "JOE"
B.SEPT.21,1917 LINCOLNTON,GA.
D.JAN.6,1967 MINNEAPOLIS,MINN.

YR	CL	LEA	POS	GP	G	REC
1939	WAS	A	P		27	8-12
1940	WAS	A	P		22	3- 6
1941	CHI	A	P		8	0- 0
1942	CHI	A	P		40	8- 5
1943	CHI	A	P		35	7- 2
1944	CHI	A	P		33	5- 6
1945	CHI	A	P	14	15	5- 5
1946	CHI	A	P		32	7- 9
1947	CHI	A	P		29	14- 6
1948	CHI	A	P		27	9-10
1949	WAS	A	P		37	2- 9
1950	WAS	A	P		27	7- 5
1951	WAS	A	P		26	1- 4
1952	WAS	A	P		22	0- 3
	BRTR			379	380	76-82

HAYWOOD, WILLIAM KIERNAN "BILL"
B.APR.21,1937 COLON,PANAMA

YR	CL	LEA	POS	GP	G	REC
1968	WAS	A	P		14	0- 0
	BRTR					

HAYWORTH, MYRON CLAUDE "RED"
B.MAY 14,1915 HIGH POINT,N.C.

YR	CL	LEA	POS	GP	G	REC
1944	STL	A	C		89	.223
1945	STL	A	C		56	.194
	BRTR				145	.212

HAYWORTH, RAYMOND HALL
B.JAN.29,1905 HIGH POINT,N.C.

YR	CL	LEA	POS	GP	G	REC
1926	DET	A	C		12	.273
1929	DET	A	C		14	.255
1930	DET	A	C		77	.278
1931	DET	A	C		88	.256
1932	DET	A	C		109	.293
1933	DET	A	C		134	.245
1934	DET	A	C		54	.293
1935	DET	A	C		51	.309
1936	DET	A	C		81	.240
1937	DET	A	C		30	.269
1938	DET	A	C		8	.211
	BRO	N	C		5	.000
1939	BRO	N	C		21	.154
	NY	N	C		5	.231
1942	STL	A	H		1	1.000
1944	BRO	N	C		7	.000
1945	BRO	N	C		2	.000
	BRTR				699	.265

HAZINSKI, STANLEY FRANK
(PLAYED UNDER NAME OF
STANLEY FRANK ROGERS)

HAZLE, ROBERT SIDNEY "BOB"
B.DEC.9,1930 LAURENS,S.C.

YR	CL	LEA	POS	GP	G	REC
1955	CIN	N	O		6	.231
1957	MIL	N	O		41	.403
1958	MIL	N	O		20	.179
	DET	A	O		43	.241
	BLTR				110	.310

HAZLETON, WILLARD CARPENTER "DOC"
B.AUG.28,1876 STRAFFORD,V.T
D.MAR.17,1941

YR	CL	LEA	POS	GP	G	REC
1901	STL	N	1		7	.125
1902	STL	N	1		7	.130
					14	.128

HEAD, EDWARD MARVIN "ED"
B.JAN.25,1920 SELMA,LA.

YR	CL	LEA	POS	GP	G	REC
1940	BRO	N	P	13	14	1- 2
1942	BRO	N	P		36	10- 6
1943	BRO	N	P		47	9-10
1944	BRO	N	P		9	4- 3
1946	BRO	N	P		13	3- 2
	BRTR			118	119	27-23

HEAD, RALPH
B.AUG.30,1894 TALLAPOOSA,GA.
D.OCT.8,1962 MUSCADINE,ALA.

YR	CL	LEA	POS	GP	G	REC
1923	PHI	N	P		35	2- 9
	BRTR					

HEALEY, FRANCIS JEREMIAH
B.JUNE 29,1911 HOLYOKE,MASS.

YR	CL	LEA	POS	GP	G	REC
1930	NY	N	O		7	.000
1931	NY	N	C		6	.143
1932	NY	N	C		14	.250
1934	STL	N	C		15	.308
	BRTR				42	.241

YR	CL LEA POS	GP	G	REC

HEALY, FRANCIS XAVIER "FRAN"
B.SEP.6,1946 HOLYOKE,MASS.

YR	CL LEA POS	GP	G	REC
1969	KC A C		6	.400
1971	SF N C		47	.280
1972	SF N C		45	.152
1973	KC A C		95	.276
1974	KC A C		139	.252
1975	KC A C		56	.255
1976	KC A C		8	.125
	NY A C		46	.267
	BRTR		442	.252

HEALEY, THOMAS
B.1853 CRANSTON,R.I.
D.FEB.6,1891

1878	PRO N P		2	0- 2
	IND N P-O		13	7- 5
				.204
	TR		15	7- 7
				.185

HEALY, JOHN J. "EGYPTIAN"
B.OCT.27,1866 CAIRO,ILL.
D.MAR.16,1899

1885	STL N P		8	1- 7
1886	STL N P	41	42	17-24
1887	IND N P		40	12-28
1888	IND N P		37	12-24
1889	WAS N P		15	1-14
	CHI N P		7	3- 4
1890	TOL AA P		47	22-19
1891	BAL AA P		23	8-12
1892	BAL N P		9	2- 5
	LOU N P		8	1- 1
	BRTR	235	236	79-138

HEALY, THOMAS FITZGERALD
B.OCT.30,1895 ALTOONA,PA.

1915	PHI A 3		23	.221
1916	PHI A 3		6	.261
	BRTR		29	.230

HEARD, CHARLES
B.JAN.30,1872 PHILADELPHIA,PA.
D.FEB.20,1945 PHILADELPHIA,PA.

| 1890 | PIT N P | | 12 | 0- 6 |
| | BRTR | | | |

HEARD, JEHOSIE
B.JAN.17,1925 ATLANTA,GA.

| 1954 | BAL A P | | 2 | 0- 0 |
| | BLTL | | | |

HEARN

| 1872 | OLY NA S-O | | 1 | .333 |

HEARN, BUNN
B.MAY 21,1891 CHAPEL HILL,N.C.
D.OCT.11,1959

1910	STL N P		5	1- 3
1911	STL N P		2	0- 0
1913	NY N P		2	1- 1
1915	PIT F P		29	6-11
1918	BOS N P		17	5- 6
1920	BOS N P		11	0- 3
	BLTL		66	13-24

HEARN, EDMUND
B.SEPT.17,1888 VENDURA,CAL.
D.SEPT.8,1952

| 1910 | BOS A 3 | | 2 | .000 |
| | TR | | | |

HEARN, ELMER LAFAYETTE
B.JAN.13,1904 BROOKLYN,N.Y.
D.MAR.31,1974 VENICE,FLA.

1926	BOS N P		34	4- 9
1927	BOS N P		8	0- 2
1928	BOS N P		7	1- 0
1929	BOS N P		10	2- 0
	BLTL		59	7-11

HEARN, JAMES TOLBERT "JIM"
B.APP.11,1923 ATLANTA,GA.

YR	CL LEA POS	GP	G	REC
1947	STL N P		37	12- 7
1948	STL N P	34	36	8- 6
1949	STL N P		17	1- 3
1950	STL N P		6	0- 1
	NY N P		16	11- 3
1951	NY N P		34	17- 9
1952	NY N P		37	14- 7
1953	NY N P	36	37	9-12
1954	NY N P		29	8- 8
1955	NY N P	39	41	14-16
1956	NY N P	30	32	5-11
1957	PHI N P		36	5- 1
1958	PHI N P		39	5- 3
1959	PHI N P		6	0- 2
	BRTR	396	403	109-89

HEARNE, HUGH JOSEPH "HUGHIE"
B.APR.18,1873 TROY,N.Y.
D.SEPT.22,1932 TROY,N.Y.

1901	BRO N C		2	.500
1902	BRO N C		62	.281
1903	BRO N C		19	.281
	BRTR		83	.284

HEATH, JOHN GEOFFREY "JEFF"
B.APR.1,1916 FT.WILLIAM,ONT.,
CANADA
D.DEC.9,1975 SEATTLE,WASH.

1936	CLE A O		12	.341
1937	CLE A O		20	.230
1938	CLE A O		126	.343
1939	CLE A O		121	.292
1940	CLE A O		100	.219
1941	CLE A O		151	.340
1942	CLE A O		147	.278
1943	CLE A O		118	.274
1944	CLE A O		60	.331
1945	CLE A O		102	.305
1946	WAS A O		48	.283
	STL A O		86	.275
1947	STL A O		141	.251
1948	BOS N O		115	.319
1949	BOS N O		36	.306
	BLTR	1383	.293

HEATH, MINOR WILSON "MICKEY"
B.OCT.30,1903 TOLEDO,OHIO

1931	CIN N 1		7	.269
1932	CIN N 1		39	.201
	BLTL		46	.213

HEATH, SPENCER PAUL
B.NOV.5,1894 CHICAGO,ILL.
D.JAN.25,1930 CHICAGO,ILL.

| 1920 | CHI A P | | 4 | 0- 0 |
| | BBTR | | | |

HEATH, THOMAS GEORGE
B.AUG.18,1913 AKRON,COL.
D.FEB.26,1967 LOS GATOS,CAL.

1935	STL A C		47	.237
1937	STL A C		17	.233
1938	STL A C		70	.227
	BRTR		134	.230

HEATH, WILLIAM CHRIS "BILL"
B.MAR.10,1939 YUBA CITY,CAL.

1965	CHI A H		1	.000
1966	HOU N C		55	.301
1967	HOU N C		9	.091
	DET A C		20	.125
1969	CHI N C		27	.156
	BLTR		112	.236

HEATHCOTE, CLIFTON EARL
B.JAN.24,1898 GLEN ROCK,PA.
D.JAN.19,1939

1918	STL N 1-O		88	.259
1919	STL N 1-O		114	.279
1920	STL N O		133	.284
1921	STL N O		62	.244
1922	STL N O		34	.245
	CHI N O		76	.276
1923	CHI N O		117	.249
1924	CHI N O		113	.309
1925	CHI N O		109	.263
1926	CHI N O		139	.276
1927	CHI N O		83	.294
1928	CHI N O		67	.285
1929	CHI N O		82	.313
1930	CHI N O		70	.260
1931	CIN N O		90	.258
1932	CIN N O		8	.000
	PHI N O		30	.282
	BLTL	1415	.275

HEAVERLO, DAVID WALLACE "DAVE"
B.AUG.25,1950 ELLENSBURG,WASH.

YR	CL LEA POS	GP	G	REC
1975	SF N P		42	3- 1
1976	SF N P		61	4- 4
	BRTR		103	7- 5

HEBERT, WALLACE ANDREW
"PREACHER"
B.AUG.21,1908 LAKE CHARLES,LA.

1931	STL A P		23	6- 7
1932	STL A P		35	1-12
1933	STL A P		33	4- 6
1943	PIT N P	34	35	10-11
	BLTL	125	126	21-36

HEBNER, RICHARD JOSEPH "RICHIE"
B.NOV.26,1947 BOSTON,MASS.

1968	PIT N H		2	.000
1969	PIT N 1-3		129	.301
1970	PIT N 3		120	.290
1971	PIT N 3		112	.271
1972	PIT N 3		124	.300
1973	PIT N 3		144	.271
1974	PIT N 3		146	.291
1975	PIT N 3		128	.246
1976	PIT N 3		132	.249
	BLTR	1037	.277

HECKER, GUY JACKSON
B.APR.3,1856 YOUNGVILLE,PA.
D.DEC.3,1938 WOOSTER,OHIO

1882	LOU AA P-1- 12	78	7- 5
	O			.285
1883	LOU AA P-1- 55	79	28-25
	O			.264
1884	LOU AA P	76	79	52-20
1885	LOU AA P-1	54	72	30-24
				.274
1886	LOU AA P-1	50	84	27-23
				.342
1887	LOU AA P-1	33	91	19-12
				.374
1888	LOU AA P-1	28	55	8-17
				.255
1889	LOU AA P-1	17	82	5-11
				.277
1890	PIT N M-P- 14	86	2-12
	1			.226
	BRTR	339	706	178-149
				.292

HECKINGER, MICHAEL VINCENT
B.FEB.14,1890 CHICAGO,ILL.
D.AUG.13,1967 CHICAGO,ILL.

1912	CHI N C		2	.000
1913	CHI N C		2	.000
	BRO N C		9	.222
	BRTR		13	.143

HEDGEPATH, HARRY MALCOLM
B.SEPT.4,1888 FAYETTEVILLE,N.C.
D.JULY 20,1966 RICHMOND,VA.

| 1913 | WAS A P | | 1 | 0- 0 |
| | BLTL | | | |

HEDLUND, MICHAEL DAVID "MIKE"
B.AUG.11,1946 DALLAS,TEX.

1965	CLE A P		6	0- 0
1968	CLE A P		3	0- 0
1969	KC A P		34	3- 6
1970	KC A P		9	2- 3
1971	KC A P		32	15- 8
1972	KC A P		29	5- 7
	BBTR		113	25-24
	BR 1965, 72			

HEFFNER, DONALD HENRY "JEEP"
B.FEB.8,1911 ROUZERVILLE,PA.

1934	NY A 2		72	.261
1935	NY A 2		10	.306
1936	NY A 2-S-3		19	.229
1937	NY A 2-S		60	.249
1938	STL A 2		141	.245
1939	STL A 2-S		110	.267
1940	STL A 2		126	.236
1941	STL A 2		110	.233
1942	STL A 1-2		19	.167
1943	STL A 1-2		18	.121
	PHI A 1-2		52	.208
1944	DET A 2		6	.211
	BRTR	743	.241
	NON-PLAYING MANAGER CIN(N) 1966			

YR	CL	LEA	POS	GP	G	REC

HEFFNER, ROBERT FREDERICK "BOB"
B.SEP.13,1938 ALLENTOWN,PA.

YR	CL	LEA	POS	GP	G	REC
1963	BOS	A	P	20	21	4- 9
1964	BOS	A	P		55	7- 9
1965	BOS	A	P		27	0- 2
1966	CLE	A	P		5	0- 1
1968	CAL	A	P		7	0- 0
	BRTR			114	115	11-21

HEFLIN, RANDOLPH RUTHERFORD
B.SEPT.11,1919 FREDERICKSBURG, VA.

1945	BOS	A	P		20	4-10
1946	BOS	A	P		5	0- 1
	BLTR				25	4-11

HEGAN, JAMES EDWARD "JIM"
B.AUG.3,1920 LYNN,MASS.

1941	CLE	A	C		16	.319
1942	CLE	A	C		68	.194
1946	CLE	A	C		88	.236
1947	CLE	A	C		135	.249
1948	CLE	A	C		144	.248
1949	CLE	A	C		152	.224
1950	CLE	A	C		131	.219
1951	CLE	A	C		133	.238
1952	CLE	A	C		112	.225
1953	CLE	A	C		112	.217
1954	CLE	A	C		139	.234
1955	CLE	A	C		116	.220
1956	CLE	A	C		122	.222
1957	CLE	A	C		58	.216
1958	DET	A	C		45	.192
	PHI	N	C		25	.220
1959	PHI	N	C		25	.196
	SF	N	C		21	.133
1960	CHI	N	C		24	.209
	BRTR				1666	.228

HEGAN, JAMES MICHAEL "MIKE"
B.JULY 21,1942 CLEVELAND,OHIO

1964	NY	A	1		5	.000
1966	NY	A	1		13	.205
1967	NY	A	1-0		68	.136
1969	SEA	A	1-0		95	.292
1970	MIL	A	1-0		148	.244
1971	MIL	A	1		46	.221
	OAK	A	1-0		65	.236
1972	OAK	A	1-0		98	.329
1973	OAK	A	1-0		75	.183
	NY	A	1		37	.275
1974	NY	A	1		18	.226
	MIL	A	1-0-0		89	.237
1975	MIL	A	1-0		93	.251
1976	MIL	A	1-0-0		80	.248
	BLTL				930	.248

HEHL, HERMAN JACOB "JAKE"
B.DEC.8,1899 BROOKLYN,N.Y.

1918	BRO	N	P		1	0- 0
	BRTR					

HEIDEMANN, JACK SEALE
B.JULY 11,1949 BRENHAM,TEX.

1969	CLE	A	S		3	.000
1970	CLE	A	S		133	.211
1971	CLE	A	S		81	.208
1972	CLE	A	S		10	.150
1974	CLE	A	1-2-S-3		12	.091
	STL	N	S-3		47	.271
1975	NY	N	2-S-3		61	.214
1976	NY	N	2-S		5	.083
	MIL	A	2-S		69	.219
	BRTR				421	.212

HEIDRICK, R. EMMETT "SNAGS"
B.JULY 29,1876 QUEENSTOWN,PA.
D.JAN.20,1916

1898	CLE	N	O		19	.293
1899	STL	N	O		147	.329
1900	STL	N	O		83	.301
1901	STL	N	O		115	.339
1902	STL	A	P-S-3-O	1	110	0- 0 .288
1903	STL	A	O		121	.281
1904	STL	A	O		133	.269
1908	STL	A	O		26	.215
				1	754	0- 0 .299

HEIFER, FRANKLIN "HECK"
B.JAN.18,1854 READING,PA.
D.AUG.29,1893

1875	BOS	NA	1-O		11	.333

HEILBRONER, LOUIS WILBUR
B.JULY 4,1861 FT.WAYNE,IND.
D.DEC.21,1933
NON-PLAYING MANAGER STL(N) 1900

HEILEMAN, JOHN GEORGE "CHINK"
B.AUG.10,1872 CINCINNATI,OHIO
D.JULY 19,1940

1901	CIN	N	3		5	.133
	TR					

HEILMANN, HARRY EDWIN "SLUG"
B.AUG.3,1894 SAN FRANCISCO,CAL.
D.JULY 9,1951 DETROIT,MICH.

1914	DET	A	1-O		67	.225
1916	DET	A	1-O		136	.282
1917	DET	A	1-O		150	.281
1918	DET	A	1-O		79	.276
1919	DET	A	1		140	.320
1920	DET	A	1-O		145	.309
1921	DET	A	O		149	.394
1922	DET	A	O		118	.356
1923	DET	A	O		144	.403
1924	DET	A	O		153	.346
1925	DET	A	O		150	.393
1926	DET	A	O		141	.367
1927	DET	A	O		141	.398
1928	DET	A	1-O		151	.328
1929	DET	A	O		125	.344
1930	CIN	N	1-O		142	.333
1932	CIN	N	1		15	.258
	BRTR				2146	.342

HEIM, VAL RAYMOND
B.NOV.4,1920 PLYMOUTH,WIS.

1942	CHI	A	O		13	.200
	BLTR					

HEIMACH, FRED AMOS "LEFTY"
B.JAN.27,1902 CAMDEN,N.J.
D.JUNE 1,1973 FT.MYERS,FLA.

1920	PHI	A	P		1	0- 1
1921	PHI	A	P		1	1- 0
1922	PHI	A	P		37	7-11
1923	PHI	A	P	40	63	6-12
1924	PHI	A	P	40	58	14-12
1925	PHI	A	P	10	15	0- 1
1926	PHI	A	P	13	14	1- 0
	BOS	A	P	20	26	2- 9
1928	NY	A	P	13	18	2- 3
1929	NY	A	P	35	36	11- 6
1930	BRO	N	P	9	13	0- 2
1931	BRO	N	P	31	39	9- 7
1932	BRO	N	P	36	37	9- 4
1933	BRO	N	P		10	0- 1
	BLTL			296	368	62-69

HEINE, WILLIAM H. "PETE"
B.SEPT.22,1901 ELMIRA,N.Y.

1921	NY	N	2		1	.000
	BLTR					

HEINTZELMAN, KENNETH ALPHONSE "KEN"
B.OCT.14,1915 PERUQUE,MO.

1937	PIT	N	P		1	1- 0
1938	PIT	N	P		1	0- 0
1939	PIT	N	P		17	1- 1
1940	PIT	N	P	39	41	8- 8
1941	PIT	N	P		35	11-11
1942	PIT	N	P		27	8-11
1946	PIT	N	P		32	8-12
1947	PIT	N	P		2	0- 0
	PHI	N	P		24	7-10
1948	PHI	N	P		27	6-11
1949	PHI	N	P		33	17-10
1950	PHI	N	P		23	3- 9
1951	PHI	N	P		35	6-12
1952	PHI	N	P		23	1- 3
	BRTL			319	321	77-98

HEINTZELMAN, THOMAS KENNETH "TOM"
B.NOV.3,1946 ST.CHARLES,MO.

1973	STL	N	2		23	.310
1974	STL	N	2-S-3		38	.230
	BRTR				61	.252

HEINZMAN, JOHN PETER "JACK"
B.SEPT.27,1863 NEW ALBANY,IND.
D.NOV.10,1914 LOUISVILLE,KY.

1886	LOU	AA	1		1	.000
	BRTR					

HEISE, CLARENCE EDWARD "LEFTY"
B.AUG.7,1907 TOPEKA,KAN.

1934	STL	N	P		1	0- 0
	BLTL					

HEISE, JAMES EDWARD
B.SEPT.3,1932 SCOTTDALE,PA.

1957	WAS	A	P		8	0- 3
	BRTR					

HEISE, ROBERT LOWELL "BOB"
B.MAY 12,1947 SAN ANTONIO,TEX.

1967	NY	N	2-S-3		16	.323
1968	NY	N	2-S		6	.217
1969	NY	N	S		4	.300
1970	SF	N	2-S-3		67	.234
1971	SF	N	2-S-3		13	.000
	MIL	A	2-S-3-0		68	.254
1972	MIL	A	2-S-3		95	.266
1973	MIL	A	1-2-S-3		49	.204
1974	STL	N	2		3	.143
	CAL	A	2-S-3		29	.267
1975	BOS	A	1-2-S-3		63	.214
1976	BOS	A	2-S-3		32	.268
	BRTR				445	.247

HEISER, LE ROY BARTON
B.JUNE 22,1942 BALTIMORE,MD.

1961	WAS	A	P		3	0- 0
	BRTR					

HEISMANN, CHRISTIAN ERNEST "CRESE"
B.APR.16,1880 CINCINNATI,OHIO
D.NOV.19,1951

1901	CIN	N	P		3	0- 1
1902	CIN	N	P		5	2- 1
	BAL	A	P		3	0- 3
	BRTL					

HEIST, ALFRED MICHAEL "AL"
B.OCT.5,1927 BROOKLYN,N.Y.

1960	CHI	N	O		41	.275
1961	CHI	N	O		109	.255
1962	HOU	N	O		27	.222
	BRTR				177	.255

HEITMANN, HENRY ANTON
B.OCT.6,1896 ALBANY,N.Y.
D.DEC.15,1958 BROOKLYN,N.Y.

1918	BRO	N	P		1	0- 1
	BRTR					

HEITMULLER, WILLIAM FREDERICK "HEINE"
B.1883 SAN FRANCISCO,CAL.
D.OCT.12,1912

1909	PHI	A	O		64	.286
1910	PHI	A	O		31	.243
					95	.271

HELD, MELVIN NICHOLAS "MEL"
B.APR.12,1929 EDON,OHIO

1956	BAL	A	P		4	0- 0
	BRTR					

HELD, WOODSON GEORGE "WOODY"
B.MAR.25,1932 SACRAMENTO,CAL.

1954	NY	A	S-3		4	.000
1957	NY	A	H		1	.000
	KC	A	O		92	.239
1958	KC	A	S-3-O		47	.214
	CLE	A	S-3-O		67	.194
1959	CLE	A	2-S-3-O		143	.251
1960	CLE	A	S		109	.258
1961	CLE	A	S		146	.267
1962	CLE	A	S-3-O		139	.249
1963	CLE	A	2-S-3-O		133	.248
1964	CLE	A	2-3-O		118	.236
1965	WAS	A	2-S-3-O		122	.247
1966	BAL	A	2-S-3-O		56	.207
1967	BAL	A	2-3-O		26	.146
	CAL	A	2-S-3-O		58	.220
1968	CAL	A	2-S-3-O		33	.111
	CHI	A	2-3-O		40	.167
1969	CHI	A	2-S-3-O		56	.143
	BRTR				1390	.240

HELENIUS, ARTHUR D.
(PLAYED UNDER NAME OF ARTHUR D. DELANEY)

YR	CL LEA POS	GP	G	REC

HELF, HENRY HARTZ
B.AUG.26,1913 AUSTIN,TEX.
1938 CLE A C		6	.077
1940 CLE A C		1	.000
1946 STL A C		71	.192
BRTR		78	.184

HELFRICH, EMORY WILBUR "TY"
B.OCT.9,1890 PLEASANTVILLE,N.J.
D.MAR.18,1955
| 1915 BRO F 2 | | 40 | .245 |
| BRTR | | | |

HELLINGS
| 1875 ATL NA 2 | | 1 | .250 |

HELLMAN, ANTHONY J.
B.1861 CINCINNATI,OHIO
D.MAR.29,1898
| 1886 BAL AA C | | 1 | .000 |

HELMBOLD, HORACE
B.PHILADELPHIA,PA.
| 1890 ATH AA P | | 1 | 1- 0 |

HELMS, TOMMY VANN
B.MAY 5,1941 CHARLOTTE,N.C.
1964 CIN N H		2	.000
1965 CIN N 2-S-3		21	.381
1966 CIN N 2-3		138	.284
1967 CIN N 2-S		137	.274
1968 CIN N 2-S		127	.288
1969 CIN N 2-S		126	.269
1970 CIN N 2-S		150	.237
1971 CIN N 2		150	.258
1972 HOU N 2		139	.259
1973 HOU N 2		146	.287
1974 HOU N 2		137	.279
1975 HOU N 2-S-3		64	.207
1976 PIT N 2-S-3		62	.276
BRTR		1399	.276

HELTZEL, WILLIAM WADE "HEINE"
B.DEC.21,1919 YORK,PA.
1943 BOS N 3		29	.151
1944 PHI N S		11	.182
BRTR		40	.157

HEMAN, RUSSELL FREDERICK "RUSS"
B.FEV.10,1933 OLIVE,CAL.
1961 CLE A P		6	0- 0
LA A P		6	0- 0
BRTR		12	0- 0

HEMINGWAY, EDSON M.
B.MAY 8,1893 SHERIDAN,MICH.
1914 STL A 3		4	.000
1917 NY N 1		7	.320
1918 PHI N 1-2-3		33	.213
BBTR		44	.225

HEMMING, GEORGE EARL
B.DEC.15,1868 CARROLLTON,OHIO
D.JUNE 3,1930
1890 CLE P P		3	0- 3
BRO P P		16	7- 5
1891 BRO N P		22	8-14
1892 CIN N P		1	0- 0
LOU N P		4	2- 1
1893 LOU N P	39	43	18-18
1894 LOU N P		32	11-20
BAL N P		15	5- 0
1895 BAL N P		34	18-12
1896 BAL N P		25	15- 7
1897 LOU N P		8	3- 5
BRTR	199	203	87-85

HEMP, WILLIAM H. "DUCKY"
B.DEC.27,1867 ST.LOUIS,MO.
D.MAR.6,1923
1887 LOU AA O		1	.250
1890 PIT N O		21	.213
SYR AA O		9	.156
		31	.200

HEMPHILL, CHARLES JUDSON
"EAGLE EYE"
B.APR.20,1876 GREENVILLE,MICH.
D.JUNE 22,1953
1899 STL N O		11	.243
CLE N O		51	.280
1901 BOS A O		137	.269
1902 CLE A O		25	.272
STL A O		103	.317
1903 STL A O		106	.238
1904 STL A O		114	.253
1906 STL A O		154	.289
1907 STL A O		153	.259
1908 NY A O		142	.297
1909 NY A O		73	.243
1910 NY A O		102	.239
1911 NY A O		69	.284
BLTL		1240	.271

HEMPHILL, FRANK VERNON
B.MAY 13,1878 GREENVILLE,MICH.
D.NOV.16,1929
1906 CHI A O		13	.075
1909 WAS A O		1	.000
BRTR		14	.070

HEMSLEY, RALSTON BURDETT
"ROLLIE"
B.JUNE 24,1907 SYRACUSE,OHIO
D.JULY 31,1972 WASHINGTON,D.C.
1928 PIT N C		50	.271
1929 PIT N C		88	.289
1930 PIT N C		104	.253
1931 PIT N C		10	.171
CHI N C		66	.309
1932 CHI N C		60	.238
1933 CIN N C		49	.190
STL A C		32	.242
1934 STL A C-O		123	.309
1935 STL A C		144	.290
1936 STL A C		116	.263
1937 STL A C		100	.222
1938 CLE A C		66	.296
1939 CLE A C		107	.263
1940 CLE A C		119	.267
1941 CLE A C		98	.240
1942 CIN N C		36	.113
NY A C		31	.294
1943 NY A C		62	.239
1944 NY A C		81	.268
1946 PHI N C		49	.223
1947 PHI N C		2	.333
BRTR		1593	.262

HEMUS, SOLOMON JOSEPH "SOLLY"
B.APR.17,1924 PHOENIX,ARIZ.
1949 STL N 2		20	.333
1950 STL N 3		11	.133
1951 STL N 2-S		120	.281
1952 STL N S-3		151	.268
1953 STL N 2-S		154	.279
1954 STL N 2-S-3		124	.304
1955 STL N 2-S-3		96	.243
1956 STL N H		8	.200
PHI N 2-3		78	.289
1957 PHI N 2		70	.185
1958 PHI N 2-3		105	.284
1959 STL N M-2-3		24	.235
BLTR		961	.273
NON-PLAYING MANAGER
STL(N) 1960-61

HENDERSON, ALBERT H.
B.BALTIMORE,MD.
NON-PLAYING MANAGER
BAL(NA) 1872-74

HENDERSON, BERNARD "BERNIE"
B.APR.12,1899 DOUGLASSVILLE,TEX
D.JUNE 6,1966 LINDEN,TEX.
| 1921 CLE A P | 2 | 3 | 0- 1 |
| BRTR | | | |

HENDERSON, EDWARD J.
B.1890 NEW YORK,N.Y.
1914 PIT F P		6	0- 3
IND F P		1	1- 0
BLTL		7	1- 3

HENDERSON, JAMES HARDING
"HARDIE"
B.OCT.31,1862 PHILADELPHIA,PA.
D.FEB.6,1903
1883 PHI N P-O	1	2	0- 0
			.250
BAL AA P-S-	45	50	10-30
3-O			.151
1884 BAL AA P	51	54	27-22
1885 BAL AA P		61	26-35
1886 BAL AA P		19	3-16
BRO AA P		14	10- 4
1887 BRO AA P		14	4- 9
1888 PIT N P		5	1- 3
BRTR	210	219	81-119
			.208

HENDERSON, JOSEPH LEE "JOE"
B.JULY 4,1946 LAKE CORMORANT,
MISS.
1974 CHI A P		5	1- 0
1976 CIN N P		4	2- 0
BLTR		9	3- 0

HENDERSON, KENNETH JOSEPH "KEN"
B.JUNE 15,1946 CARROLL,IOWA
1965 SF N O		63	.192
1966 SF N O		11	.310
1967 SF N O		65	.190
1968 SF N O		3	.333
1969 SF N 3-O		113	.225
1970 SF N O		148	.294
1971 SF N 1-O		141	.264
1972 SF N O		130	.257
1973 CHI A O-O		73	.260
1974 CHI A O		162	.292
1975 CHI A O		140	.251
1976 ATL N O		133	.262
BBTR		1182	.262

HENDERSON, WILLIAM C.
NON-PLAYING MANAGER BAL(U) 1884

HENDERSON, WILLIAM MAXWELL
B.NOV.4,1902 PENSACOLA,FLA.
| 1930 NY A P | | 3 | 0- 0 |
| BRTR | | | |

HENDLEY, CHARLES ROBERT "BOB"
B.APR.30,1939 MACON,GA.
1961 MIL N P		19	5- 7
1962 MIL N P	35	36	11-13
1963 MIL N P	41	46	9- 9
1964 SF N P		30	10-11
1965 SF N P		8	0- 0
CHI N P		18	4- 4
1966 CHI N P		43	4- 5
1967 CHI N P		7	2- 0
NY N P		15	3- 3
BRTL	216	222	48-52

HENDRICK, GEORGE ANDREW
B.OCT.18,1949 LOS ANGELES,CAL.
1971 OAK A O		42	.237
1972 OAK A O		58	.182
1973 CLE A O		113	.268
1974 CLE A O		139	.279
1975 CLE A O		145	.258
1976 CLE A O		149	.265
BRTR		646	.261

HENDRICK, HARVEY "GINK"
B.NOV.9,1897 MASON,TENN.
D.OCT.29,1941 COVINGTON,TENN.
1923 NY A O		37	.273
1924 NY A O		40	.263
1925 CLE A 1-O		25	.286
1927 BRO N 1-O		128	.310
1928 BRO N 3-O		126	.318
1929 BRO N 1-O		110	.354
1930 BRO N O		68	.257
1931 BRO N H		1	.000
CIN N 1		137	.315
1932 STL N 3		28	.250
CIN N 1		94	.327
1933 CHI N 1-3-O		69	.291
1934 PHI N O		59	.293
BLTR		922	.308

HENDRICKS, EDWARD
B.1887 BENTON HARBOR,MICH.
D.NOV.28,1930
| 1910 NY N P | | 4 | 0- 1 |

YR	CL	LEA	POS	GP	G	REC

HENDRICKS, ELROD JEROME
B.DEC.22,1940 ST.THOMAS.V.I.

YR	CL	LEA	POS	GP	G	REC
1968	BAL	A	C		79	.202
1969	BAL	A	C-1		105	.244
1970	BAL	A	C		106	.242
1971	BAL	A	C-1		101	.250
1972	BAL	A	C		33	.155
	CHI	N	C		17	.116
1973	BAL	A	C		41	.178
1974	BAL	A	C-1		66	.208
1975	BAL	A	C		85	.215
1976	BAL	A	C		28	.139
	NY	A	C		26	.226
	BLTR				687	.219

HENDRICKS, JOHN CALHOUN
B.APR.9,1876 JOLIET,ILL.
D.MAY 13,1943

1902	NY	N	O		7	.240
	CHI	N	O		2	.500
1903	WAS	A	O		32	.183
	BLTR				41	.211

NON-PLAYING MANAGER
STL(N) 1918, CIN(N) 1924-29

HENDRICKSON, DONALD WILLIAMSON
B.JULY 14,1915 KEWANNA,IND.

1945	BOS	N	P		37	4- 8
1946	BOS	N	P		2	0- 1
	BRTR				39	4- 9

HENDRIX, CLAUDE RAYMOND
B.APR.13,1889 OLATHE,KAN.
D.MAR.22,1944

1911	PIT	N	P		22	4- 6
1912	PIT	N	P		46	24- 9
1913	PIT	N	P	42	53	14-15
1914	CHI	F	P		49	29-10
1915	CHI	F	P	40	46	16-15
1916	CHI	N	P	36	45	8-16
1917	CHI	N	P	40	48	10-12
1918	CHI	N	P	32	35	20- 7
1919	CHI	N	P	33	36	10-14
1920	CHI	N	P	27	34	9-12
	BRTR			367	414	144-116

HENDRYX, TIMOTHY GREEN
B.JAN.31,1891 LEROY,ILL
D.AUG.14,1957

1911	CLE	A	O		3	.285
1912	CLE	A	O		23	.243
1915	NY	A	O		13	.200
1916	NY	A	O		15	.290
1917	NY	A	O		125	.249
1918	STL	A	O		88	.279
1920	BOS	A	O		99	.328
1921	BOS	A	O		49	.241
	BRTR				415	.276

HENGLE, EDWARD S.
B.CHICAGO,ILL.
NON-PLAYING MANAGER CHI(U) 1884

HENGLE, EMORY J. "MOXIE"
B.1858

1884	CHI	U	2		18	.222
	STP	U	2		9	.132
1885	BUF	N	2-O		7	.154
					34	.172

HENION, LAFAYETTE M.
B.1899 SAN DIEGO,CAL.
D.JULY 22,1955 SAN LUIS OBISPO,
CAL.

1919	BRO	N	P		1	0- 0
	BRTR					

HENLEY, GAIL CURTICE
B.OCT.15,1929 WICHITA,KAN.

1954	PIT	N	O		14	.300
	BLTR					

HENLEY, WELDON
B.OCT.25,1880 JASPER,GA.
D.NOV.16,1960

1903	PHI	A	P	29	30	12- 9
1904	PHI	A	P		36	14-16
1905	PHI	A	P		25	4-12
1907	BRO	N	P		7	1- 5
	BRTR			97	98	31-42

HENLINE, WALTER JOHN "BUTCH"
B.DEC.20,1898 FT.WAYNE,IND.
D.OCT.9,1957

1921	NY	N	C	1	.000
	PHI	N	C	33	.306
1922	PHI	N	C	125	.316
1923	PHI	N	C-O	111	.324
1924	PHI	N	C-O	115	.284
1925	PHI	N	C-O	93	.304
1926	PHI	N	C	99	.283
1927	BRO	N	C	67	.266
1928	BRO	N	C	55	.212
1929	BRO	N	C	27	.242
1930	CHI	A	C	3	.125
1931	CHI	A	C	11	.067
	BRTR			740	.291

HENNESSEY, GEORGE "THREE STAR"
B.OCT.28,1907 SLATINGTON,PA.

1937	STL	A	P	5	0- 1
1942	PHI	N	P	5	1- 1
1945	CHI	N	P	2	0- 0
	BRTR			12	1- 2

HENNESSY, LESTER J.
B.DEC.12,1893 LYNN,MASS.

1913	DET	A	2	14	.133
	BRTR				

HENNIGAN, PHILLIP WINSTON "PHIL"
B.APR.10,1946 JASPER,TEX.

1969	CLE	A	P	9	2- 1
1970	CLE	A	P	42	6- 3
1971	CLE	A	P	57	4- 3
1972	CLE	A	P	38	5- 3
1973	NY	N	P	30	0- 4
	BRTR			176	17-14

HENNING, PETER HERMAN
B.DEC.28,1887 CROWN POINT,IND.
D.NOV.9,1939

1914	KC	F	P	28	5- 9
1915	KC	F	P	40	9-15
	BRTR			68	14-24

HENNINGER, RICHARD LEE "RICK"
B.JAN.11,1948 HASTINGS,NEB.

1973	TEX	A	P	6	1- 0
	BRTR				

HENRICH, FRANK WILDE "FRITZ"
B.MAY 8,1899 CINCINNATI,OHIO
D.MAY 1,1959

1924	PHI	N	O	36	.211
	BLTL				

HENRICH, ROBERT EDWARD "BOBBY"
B.DEC.14,1938 LAWRENCE,KAN.

1957	CIN	N	2-S-3-O	29	.200
1958	CIN	N	S	5	.000
1959	CIN	N	S	14	.000
	BRTR			48	.125

HENRICH, THOMAS DAVID
"TOMMY" OR "THE CLUTCH"
B.FEB.20,1913 MASSILLON,OHIO

1937	NY	A	O	67	.320
1938	NY	A	O	131	.270
1939	NY	A	O	99	.277
1940	NY	A	1-O	90	.307
1941	NY	A	O	144	.277
1942	NY	A	1-O	127	.267
1946	NY	A	1-O	150	.251
1947	NY	A	1-O	142	.287
1948	NY	A	1-O	146	.308
1949	NY	A	1-O	115	.287
1950	NY	A	1	73	.272
	BLTL			1284	.282

HENRIKSEN, OLAF "SWEDE"
B.APR.26,1888 KIRKERUP,DENMARK
D.OCT.17,1962

1911	BOS	A	O	27	.366
1912	BOS	A	O	37	.321
1913	BOS	A	O	30	.375
1914	BOS	A	O	61	.253
1915	BOS	A	O	73	.196
1916	BOS	A	O	68	.202
1917	BOS	A	O	15	.083
	BLTL			311	.267

HENRY, EARL CLIFFORD "HOOK"
B.JUNE 10,1917 ROSEVILLE,OHIO

1944	CLE	A	P	2	4	1- 1
1945	CLE	A	P	15	16	0- 3
	BLTL			17	20	1- 4

HENRY, FRANK JOHN "DUTCH"
B.MAY 12,1902 CLEVELAND,OHIO
D.AUG.23,1968 E.CLEVELAND,OHIO

1921	STL	A	P	1	0- 0
1922	STL	A	P	4	0- 0
1923	BRO	N	P	17	4- 6
1924	BRO	N	P	16	1- 2
1927	NY	N	P	45	11- 6
1928	NY	N	P	17	3- 6
1929	NY	N	P	27	5- 6
	CHI	A	P	2	1- 0
1930	CHI	A	P	35	2-17
	BLTL			164	27-43

HENRY, FREDERICK MARSHALL
"SNAKE"
B.JULY 19,1897 RICHMOND,VA.

1922	BOS	N	1	18	.197
1923	BOS	N	1	11	.111
	BLTR			29	.187

HENRY, GEORGE WASHINGTON
B.AUG.10,1863 PHILADELPHIA,PA.
D.DEC.30,1934

1893	CIN	N	O	21	.273
	BRTR				

HENRY, JAMES FRANCIS
B.JUNE 26,1912 DANVILLE,PA.

1936	BOS	A	P	21	22	5- 1
1937	BOS	A	P		3	1- 0
1939	PHI	N	P		9	0- 1
	BRTR			33	34	6- 2

HENRY, JOHN MICHAEL
B.SEPT.2,1863 SPRINGFIELD,MASS.
D.JUNE 11,1939

1884	CLE	N	P-O	5	9	1- 4
						.154
1885	BAL	AA	P-O	9	10	2- 6
						.273
1886	WAS	N	P		4	1- 3
1890	NY	N	O		37	.243
				18	60	4-13
						.241

HENRY, JOHN T.
B.DEC.26,1889 AMHERST,MASS.
D.NOV.24,1941

1910	WAS	A	C	29	.149
1911	WAS	A	C-1	85	.203
1912	WAS	A	C	63	.194
1913	WAS	A	C	96	.226
1914	WAS	A	C	91	.169
1915	WAS	A	C	95	.220
1916	WAS	A	C	117	.190
1917	WAS	A	C	65	.190
1918	BOS	N	C	43	.206
	BRTR			684	.207

HENRY, RONALD BAXTER "RON"
B.AUG.7,1936 CHESTER,PA.

1961	MIN	A	C-1	20	.143
1964	MIN	A	C	22	.122
	BRTR			42	.130

HENRY, WILLIAM FRANCIS "BILL"
B.FEB.15,1942 LONG BEACH,CAL.

1966	NY	A	P	2	0- 0
	BLTL				

HENRY, WILLIAM RODMAN "BILL"
B.OCT.15,1927 ALICE,TEX.

1952	BOS	A	P	13	14	5- 4
1953	BOS	A	P		21	5- 5
1954	BOS	A	P	24	25	3- 7
1955	BOS	A	P		17	2- 4
1958	CHI	N	P		44	5- 4
1959	CHI	N	P		65	9- 8
1960	CIN	N	P		51	1- 5
1961	CIN	N	P	47	48	2- 1
1962	CIN	N	P		40	4- 2
1963	CIN	N	P		47	1- 3
1964	CIN	N	P	37	38	2- 2
1965	CIN	N	P		3	2- 0
	SF	N	P		35	2- 2
1966	SF	N	P		35	1- 1
1967	SF	N	P		28	2- 0
1968	SF	N	P		7	0- 2
	PIT	N	P		10	0- 0
1969	HOU	N	P		3	0- 0
	BLTL			527	531	46-50

YR	CL	LEA	POS	GP	G	REC

HENSHAW, ROY JOHN
B.JULY 29,1911 CHICAGO,ILL.

YR	CL	LEA	POS	GP	G	REC
1933	CHI	N	P		21	2- 1
1935	CHI	N	P		31	13- 5
1936	CHI	N	P		39	6- 5
1937	BRO	N	P	42	43	5-12
1938	STL	N	P		27	5-11
1942	DET	A	P		23	2- 4
1943	DET	A	P		26	0- 2
1944	DET	A	P		7	0- 0
	BRTL			216	217	33-40

HENSIEK, PHILIP FRANK "SID"
B.OCT.13,1901 ST.LOUIS,MO.
D.FEB.21,1972 ST.LOUIS,MO.

YR	CL	LEA	POS	GP	G	REC
1935	WAS	A	P		6	0- 3
	BRTR					

HEPLER, WILLIAM LEWIS "BILL"
B.SEP.25,1945 COVINGTON,VA.

YR	CL	LEA	POS	GP	G	REC
1966	NY	N	P		37	3- 3
	BLTL					

HERBEL, RONALD SAMUEL "RON"
B.JAN.16,1938 DENVER,COLO.

YR	CL	LEA	POS	GP	G	REC
1963	SF	N	P		2	0- 0
1964	SF	N	P	40	41	9- 9
1965	SF	N	P		47	12- 9
1966	SF	N	P		32	4- 5
1967	SF	N	P		42	4- 5
1968	SF	N	P		28	0- 0
1969	SF	N	P		39	4- 1
1970	SD	N	P		64	7- 5
	NY	N	P		12	2- 2
1971	ATL	N	P		25	0- 1
	BRTR			331	332	42-37

HERBERT, ERNIE ALBERT
B.JAN.30,1887 BRECKENRIDGE,MO.
D.JAN.13,1968 DALLAS,TEX.

YR	CL	LEA	POS	GP	G	REC
1913	CIN	N	P		6	0- 0
1914	STL	F	P	19	25	1- 0
1915	STL	F	P	11	12	1- 0
	BRTR			36	43	2- 0

HERBERT, FREDERICK
(REAL NAME
HERBERT FREDERICK KEMMAN)
B.MAR.4,1887 LAGRANGE,ILL.

YR	CL	LEA	POS	GP	G	REC
1915	NY	N	P			1- 1
	BRTR					

HERBERT, RAYMOND ERNEST "RAY"
B.DEC.15,1929 DETROIT,MICH.

YR	CL	LEA	POS	GP	G	REC
1950	DET	A	P		8	1- 2
1951	DET	A	P		5	4- 0
1953	DET	A	P		43	4- 6
1954	DET	A	P		42	3- 6
1955	KC	A	P	23	24	1- 8
1958	KC	A	P		42	8- 8
1959	KC	A	P		37	11-11
1960	KC	A	P		37	14-15
1961	KC	A	P		13	3- 6
	CHI	A	P		21	9- 6
1962	CHI	A	P		35	20- 9
1963	CHI	A	P		33	13-10
1964	CHI	A	P		20	6- 7
1965	PHI	N	P		25	5- 8
1966	PHI	N	P		23	2- 5
	BRTR			407	408	104-107

HERCHENROEDER, NICHOLAS
(PLAYED UNDER NAME OF
NICHOLAS REEDER)

HERMAN, ARTHUR
B.MAY 11,1871 OHIO
D.SEPT.20,1955

YR	CL	LEA	POS	GP	G	REC
1896	LOU	N	P		13	3- 5
1897	LOU	N	P		3	0- 0
					16	3- 5

HERMAN, FLOYD CAVES "BABE"
B.JUNE 26,1903 BUFFALO,N.Y.

YR	CL	LEA	POS	GP	G	REC
1926	BRO	N	1-O		137	.319
1927	BRO	N	1		130	.272
1928	BRO	N	O		134	.340
1929	BRO	N	O		146	.381
1930	BRO	N	O		153	.393
1931	BRO	N	O		151	.313
1932	CIN	N	O		148	.326
1933	CHI	N	O		137	.289
1934	CHI	N	O		125	.304
1935	PIT	N	1-O		26	.235
	CIN	N	1-O		92	.335
1936	CIN	N	1-O		119	.279
1937	DET	A	O		17	.300
1945	BRO	N	O		37	.265
	BLTL				1552	.323

HERMAN, WILLIAM JENNINGS BRYAN "BILLY"
B.JULY 7,1909 NEW ALBANY,IND.

YR	CL	LEA	POS	GP	G	REC
1931	CHI	N	2		25	.327
1932	CHI	N	2		154	.314
1933	CHI	N	2		153	.279
1934	CHI	N	2		113	.303
1935	CHI	N	2		154	.341
1936	CHI	N	2		153	.334
1937	CHI	N	2		138	.335
1938	CHI	N	2		152	.277
1939	CHI	N	2		156	.307
1940	CHI	N	2		135	.292
1941	CHI	N	2		11	.194
	BRO	N	2		133	.291
1942	BRO	N	1-2		155	.256
1943	BRO	N	2-3		153	.330
1946	BRO	N	2-3		47	.288
	BOS	N	1-2-3		75	.306
1947	PIT	N	M-1-2		15	.213
	BRTR				1922	.304
NON-PLAYING MANAGER
BOS(A) 1964-66

HERMANN, ALBERT BARTEL
B.MAR.28,1901 MILLTOWN,N.J.

YR	CL	LEA	POS	GP	G	REC
1923	BOS	N	1-2-3		31	.237
1924	BOS	N	H		1	.000
	BRTR				32	.235

HERMANSKI, EUGENE VICTOR "GENE"
B.MAY 11,1921 PITTSFIELD,MASS.

YR	CL	LEA	POS	GP	G	REC
1943	BRO	N	O		18	.300
1946	BRO	N	O		64	.200
1947	BRO	N	O		79	.275
1948	BRO	N	O		133	.290
1949	BRO	N	O		87	.299
1950	BRO	N	O		94	.298
1951	BRO	N	O		31	.250
	CHI	N	O		75	.282
1952	CHI	N	O		99	.255
1953	CHI	N	O		18	.150
	PIT	N	O		41	.177
	BLTR				739	.272

HERMOSO, ANGEL REMIGIO "REMY"
B.OCT.1,1947 CARACAS,VENEZ.

YR	CL	LEA	POS	GP	G	REC
1967	ATL	N	2-S		11	.308
1969	MON	N	2-S		28	.162
1970	MON	N	2-3		4	.000
1974	CLE	A	2		48	.221
	BRTR				91	.211

HERNAIZ, JESUS RAFAEL (RODRIGUEZ)
B.JAN.8,1948 SANTURCE,P.R.

YR	CL	LEA	POS	GP	G	REC
1974	PHI	N	P		27	2- 3
	BRTR					

HERNANDEZ, ENZO OCTAVIO
B.FEB.12,1949 VALLE DE GUANAPE, VENEZ.

YR	CL	LEA	POS	GP	G	REC
1971	SD	N	S		143	.222
1972	SD	N	S-O		114	.195
1973	SD	N	S		70	.223
1974	SD	N	S		147	.232
1975	SD	N	S		116	.218
1976	SD	N	S		113	.256
	BRTR				703	.225

HERNANDEZ, GREGORIO EVELIO (LOPEZ)
B.DEC.24,1930 GUANABACOA, HAVANA,CUBA

YR	CL	LEA	POS	GP	G	REC
1956	WAS	A	P		4	1- 1
1957	WAS	A	P		14	0- 0
	BRTR				18	1- 1

HERNANDEZ, JACINTO (ZULUETA) "JACKIE"
B.SEP.11,1940 MATANZAS,CUBA

YR	CL	LEA	POS	GP	G	REC
1965	CAL	A	S-3		6	.333
1966	CAL	A	2-S-3-O		58	.043
1967	MIN	A	S-3		29	.143
1968	MIN	A	1-S		83	.176
1969	KC	A	S		145	.222
1970	KC	A	S		83	.231
1971	PIT	N	S-3		88	.206
1972	PIT	N	S-3		72	.188
1973	PIT	N	S		54	.247
	BRTR				618	.208

HERNANDEZ, KEITH
B.OCT.20,1953 SAN FRANCISCO,CAL.

YR	CL	LEA	POS	GP	G	REC
1974	STL	N	1		14	.294
1975	STL	N	1		64	.250
1976	STL	N	1		129	.289
	BLTL				207	.277

HERNANDEZ, RAMON GONZALEZ
B.AUG.31,1940 CAROLINA,P.R.

YR	CL	LEA	POS	GP	G	REC
1967	ATL	N	P		46	0- 2
1968	CHI	N	P		8	0- 0
1971	PIT	N	P		10	0- 1
1972	PIT	N	P		53	5- 0
1973	PIT	N	P		59	4- 5
1974	PIT	N	P		58	5- 2
1975	PIT	N	P		46	7- 2
1976	PIT	N	P		37	2- 2
	CHI	N	P		2	0- 0
	BBTL				319	23-14

HERNANDEZ, RODOFO (ACOSTA) "RUDY"
B.OCT.18,1951 ENPALME,MEXICO

YR	CL	LEA	POS	GP	G	REC
1972	CHI	A	S		8	.190
	BRTR					

HERNANDEZ, RUDOLPH ALBERT
B.DEC.10,1931 SANTIAGO,D.R.

YR	CL	LEA	POS	GP	G	REC
1960	WAS	A	P		24	4- 1
1961	WAS	A	P		7	0- 1
	BRTR				31	4- 2

HERNANDEZ, SALVADOR RAMOS "CHICO"
B.JAN.3,1916 HAVANA,CUBA

YR	CL	LEA	POS	GP	G	REC
1942	CHI	N	C		47	.229
1943	CHI	N	C		43	.270
	BRTR				90	.250

HERNDON, LARRY DARNELL
B.NOV.3,1953 SUNFLOWER,TEX.

YR	CL	LEA	POS	GP	G	REC
1974	STL	N	O		12	1.000
1976	SF	N	O		115	.288
	BRTR				127	.290

HERNON, THOMAS H.
B.NOV.4,1866 E.BRIDGEWATER,MASS
D.FEB.4,1902

YR	CL	LEA	POS	GP	G	REC
1897	CHI	N	O		4	.111
	BRTR					

HEROUX, GEORGE L.
(PLAYED UNDER NAME OF
GEORGE L. WHEELER)

HERR, EDWARD JOSEPH
B.MAY 18,1862 ST.LOUIS,MO.
D.JULY 18,1943

YR	CL	LEA	POS	GP	G	REC
1887	CLE	AA	3		11	.360
1888	STL	AA	S		43	.266
1890	STL	AA	2-O		12	.233
	BRTR				66	.249

HERRELL, WALTER W.
B.WASHINGTON,D.C.

YR	CL	LEA	POS	GP	G	REC
1911	WAS	A	P		1	0- 0

HERRERA, JOSE CONCEPCION (ONTIVEROS)
B.APR.8,1942 SAN LORENZO,VENEZ.

YR	CL	LEA	POS	GP	G	REC
1967	HOU	N	H		5	.250
1968	HOU	N	2-O		27	.240
1969	MON	N	2-3-O		47	.286
1970	MON	N	H		1	.000
	BRTR				80	.264

HERRERA, JUAN FRANCISCO (WILLAVICENCIO)
B.JUNE 16,1934 HAVAN,CUBA

YR	CL	LEA	POS	GP	G	REC
1958	PHI	N	1-3		29	.270
1960	PHI	N	1-2		145	.281
1961	PHI	N	1		126	.258
	BRTR				300	.271

YR	CL LEA POS	GP	G	REC

HERRERA, PROCOPIO RODRIGUEZ
B.JULY 26,1926 NUEVO LAREDO,MEX

1951 STL A P			3	0- 0
BRTR				

HERRERA, RAMON "MIKE"
B.DEC.19,1897 HAVANA,CUBA

1925 BOS A	2		10	.385
1926 BOS A	2-3		74	.257
BRTR			84	.275

HERRIAGE, WILLIAM TROY "TROY"
B.DEC.20,1930 TIPTON,OKLA.

1956 KC A P		31	34	1-13
BRTR				

HERRIN, THOMAS EDWARD "TOM"
B.SEPT.12,1929 SHREVEPORT,LA.

1954 BOS A P			14	1- 2
BRTR				

HERRING, ARTHUR L. "RED"
B.MAR.10,1907 ALTUS,OKLA.

1929 DET A P			4	2- 1
1930 DET A P			23	3- 3
1931 DET A P			35	7-13
1932 DET A P			12	1- 2
1933 DET A P			24	1- 2
1934 BRO N P			14	2- 4
1939 CHI N P			7	0- 0
1944 BRO N P			12	3- 4
1945 BRO N P			23	7- 4
1946 BRO N P			35	7- 2
1947 PIT N P			11	1- 3
BRTR			200	34-38

HERRING, HERBERT LEE
B.JULY 22,1891 DANVILLE,ARK.

1912 WAS A P			1	0- 0
BRTR				

HERRING, SILAS CLARKE "LEFTY"
B.MAR.4,1880 PHILADELPHIA,PA.

1899 WAS N P			2	0- 0
1904 WAS A O			15	.174
BLTL	2	17		0- 0
				.191

HERRING, WILLIAM FRANCIS
B.OCT.31,1893 NEW YORK,N.Y.
D.SEPT.10,1962

1915 BRO F P			3	0- 1

HERRMANN, EDWARD MARTIN "ED"
B.AUG.27,1946 SAN DIEGO,CAL.

1967 CHI A C			2	.667
1969 CHI A C			102	.231
1970 CHI A C			96	.283
1971 CHI A C			101	.214
1972 CHI A C			116	.249
1973 CHI A C			119	.224
1974 CHI A C			107	.259
1975 NY A C-O			80	.255
1976 CAL A C			29	.174
HOU N C			79	.204
BLTR			831	.239

HERRMANN, LEROY GEORGE
B.FEB.27,1906 STEWARD,ILL.
D.JULY 3,1972 LIVERMORE,CAL.

1932 CHI N P			7	2- 1
1933 CHI N P			9	0- 1
1935 CIN N P			29	3- 5
BRTR			45	5- 7

HERRMANN, MARTIN JOHN "LEFTY"
B.JAN.10,1893 OLDENSBURG,IND.
D.SEPT.11,1956 CINCINNATI,OHIO

1918 BRO N P			1	0- 0
BLTL				

HERRSCHER, RICHARD FRANKLIN
B.NOV.3,1931 ST.LOUIS,MO.

1962 NY N 1-S-3-O		35		.220
BRTR				

HERRNSTEIN, JOHN ELLETT
B.MAY 31,1938 HAMPTON,VA.

1962 PHI N O			6	.200
1963 PHI N 1-O			15	.167
1964 PHI N 1-O			125	.234
1965 PHI N 1-O			63	.200
1966 PHI N O			4	.100
CHI N 1-O			9	.176
ATL N O			17	.222
BLTL			239	.220

HERSH, EARL WALTER
B.MAY 21,1932 MANCHESTER,MD.

1956 MIL N O			7	.231
BLTL				

HERSHBERGER, NORMAN MICHAEL "MIKE"
B.OCT.9,1939 MASSILLON,OHIO

1961 CHI A O			15	.309
1962 CHI A O			148	.262
1963 CHI A O			135	.279
1964 CHI A O			141	.230
1965 KC A O			150	.231
1966 KC A O			146	.253
1967 KC A O			142	.254
1968 OAK A O			99	.272
1969 OAK A O			51	.202
1970 MIL A O			49	.235
1971 CHI A O			74	.260
BRTR			1150	.252

HERSHBERGER, WILLARD MC KEE
B.MAY 28,1910 LEMON COVE,CAL.
D.AUG.3,1940

1938 CIN N C-2			49	.275
1939 CIN N C			63	.345
1940 CIN N C			48	.309
BRTR			160	.316

HERSHEY, FRANK
B.SEPT.13,1878 GORHAM,N.Y.

1905 BOS N P			2	0- 1

HERTWECK, NEAL CHARLES
B.NOV.22,1931 ST.LOUIS,MO.

1952 STL N 1			2	.000
BLTL				

\

HERTZ, STEVE ALLAN
B.FEB.26,1945 FAIRFIELD,OHIO

1964 HOU N 3			5	.000
BRTR				

HERZOG, CHARLES LINCOLN "BUCK"
B.JULY 8,1885 BALTIMORE,MD.
D.SEPT.4,1953

1908 NY N 2			59	.300
1909 NY N O			38	.185
1910 BOS N 3			105	.250
1911 BOS N 3			79	.310
NY N 3			69	.267
1912 NY N 3			140	.263
1913 NY N 3			96	.286
1914 CIN N M-S			138	.281
1915 CIN N M-1-S			155	.264
1916 CIN N M-S-3-O			79	.267
NY N 2-S-3			77	.261
1917 NY N 2			114	.235
1918 BOS N 1-2-S			118	.228
1919 BOS N 2			73	.276
CHI N 2			52	.280
1920 CHI N 2-3			91	.193
BRTR			1483	.259

HERZOG, DORREL NORMAN ELVERT "WHITEY"
B.NOV.9,1931 NEW ATHENS,ILL.

1956 WAS A 1-O			117	.245
1957 WAS A O			36	.167
1958 WAS A O			8	.000
KC A 1-O			88	.240
1959 KC A 1-O			38	.293
1960 KC A 1-O			83	.266
1961 BAL A O			113	.291
1962 BAL A O			99	.266
1963 DET A 1-O			52	.151
BLTL			634	.257

NON-PLAYING MANAGER
TEX(A) 1973, CAL(A) 1974
(INTERIM), KC(A) 1975-76

HESLIN, THOMAS
(PLAYED UNDER NAME OF
THOMAS HESS)

HESS, OTTO C.
B.OCT.10,1878 BERNE,SWITZERLAND
D.FEB.25,1926

1902 CLE A P			7	2- 3
1904 CLE A P		21	34	9- 7
1905 CLE A P-O		27	54	10-12
				.251
1906 CLE A P		42	53	20-17
1907 CLE A P		17	19	6- 6
1908 CLE A P-O		4	9	1- 0
				.000
1912 BOS N P			33	12-17
1913 BOS N P		29	35	7-17
1914 BOS N P		14	31	5- 6
1915 BOS N P		4	5	0- 1
BLTL		198	280	72-86
				.214

HESS, THOMAS
(REAL NAME THOMAS HESLIN)
B.AUG.15,1875 BROOKLYN,N.Y.
D.DEC.15,1945

1892 BAL N C			1	.000

HESSELBACHER, GEORGE EDWARD
B.JAN.18,1895 PHILADELPHIA,PA.

1916 PHI A P			6	0- 4
BRTR				

HESTERFER, LAWRENCE
B.JUNE 20,1878 NEWARK,N.J.
D.SEPT.22,1943

1901 NY N P			1	0- 1

HETKI, JOHN EDWARD "JOHNNY"
B.MAY 12,1922 LEAVENWORTH,KAN.

1945 CIN N P			5	1- 2
1946 CIN N P			32	6- 6
1947 CIN N P			37	3- 4
1948 CIN N P			3	0- 1
1950 CIN N P			22	1- 2
1952 STL A P			3	0- 1
1953 PIT N P			54	3- 6
1954 PIT N P			58	4- 4
BRTR			214	18-26

HETLING, AUGUST JULIUS "GUS"
B.NOV.21,1885 ST.LOUIS,MO.
D.OCT.13,1962

1906 DET A 3			2	.143
BRTR				

HEUBEL, GEORGE A.
B.1849 PATERSON,N.J.
D.JAN.22,1896 PHILADELPHIA,PA.

1871 ATH NA 1-O			17	.321
1872 OLY NA O			5	.125
1876 MUT N 1			1	.000
			23	.264

HEUSSER, EDWARD BURLTON "ED"
B.MAY 7,1909 MURRAY,UTAH
D.MAR.1,1956

1935 STL N P			33	5- 5
1936 STL N P			42	7- 3
1938 PHI N P			1	0- 0
1940 PHI A P			41	6-13
1943 CIN N P			26	4- 3
1944 CIN N P			30	13-11
1945 CIN N P			31	11-16
1946 CIN N P			29	7-14
1948 PHI N P			33	3- 2
BBTR			266	56-67
BR 1935-38				

HEVING, JOHN ALOYSIUS
B.APR.29,1898 MENTOR,KY.

1920 STL A C			1	.000
1924 BOS A C			45	.284
1925 BOS A C			45	.168
1928 BOS A C			82	.259
1929 BOS A C			76	.319
1930 BOS A C			75	.277
1931 PHI A C			42	.239
1932 PHI A C			33	.273
BRTR			399	.265

YR	CL	LEA	POS	GP	G	REC

HEVING, JOSEPH WILLIAM "JOE"
B.SEPT.2,1904 COVINGTON,KY.
D.APR.11,1970 COVINGTON,KY.

YR	CL	LEA	POS	GP	G	REC
1930	NY	N	P		41	7- 5
1931	NY	N	P		22	1- 6
1933	CHI	A	P		40	7- 5
1934	CHI	A	P		33	1- 7
1937	CLE	A	P		40	8- 4
1938	CLE	A	P		3	1- 1
	BOS	A	P		16	0- 1
1939	BOS	A	P		46	11- 3
1940	BOS	A	P		39	12- 7
1941	CLE	A	P		27	5- 2
1942	CLE	A	P		27	5- 3
1943	CLE	A	P		30	1- 1
1944	CLE	A	P		63	8- 3
1945	BOS	N	P		3	1- 0
	BRTR				430	76-48

HEWETT, WALTER F.
B.1861 WASHINGTON,D.C.
D.OCT.7,1944 WASHINGTON,D.C.
NON-PLAYING MANAGER WAS(N) 1888

HEWITT, CHARLES JACOB "JAKE"
B.JUNE 6,1871 MAIDSVILLE,W.VA.

YR	CL	LEA	POS	GP	G	REC
1895	PIT	N	P		3	1- 0
	TL					

HEYDEMAN, GREGORY GEORGE "GREG"
B.JAN.2,1952 CARMEL,CAL.

YR	CL	LEA	POS	GP	G	REC
1973	LA	N	P		1	0- 0
	BRTR					

HEYDON, MICHAEL EDWARD "ED"
B.JULY 16,1874 MISSOURI
D.OCT.13,1913

YR	CL	LEA	POS	GP	G	REC
1898	BAL	N	C		3	.111
1899	WAS	N	C		3	.000
1901	STL	N	C		14	.244
1904	CHI	A	C		5	.100
1905	WAS	A	C		71	.192
1906	WAS	A	C		49	.159
1907	WAS	A	C		62	.183
	TR				213	.182

HEYNER, JOHN
B.HYDE PARK,ILL.

YR	CL	LEA	POS	GP	G	REC
1890	PIT	N	P		1	0- 0

HIATT, JACK E.
B.JULY 27,1942 BAKERSFIELD,CAL.

YR	CL	LEA	POS	GP	G	REC
1964	LAX	A	C-1		9	.375
1965	SF	N	C-1		40	.284
1966	SF	N	1		18	.304
1967	SF	N	C-1-0		73	.275
1968	SF	N	C-1		90	.232
1969	SF	N	C-1		69	.196
1970	MON	N	C-1		17	.326
	CHI	N	C-1		66	.242
1971	HOU	N	C-1		69	.276
1972	HOU	N	C		10	.200
	CAL	A	C		22	.289
	BRTR				483	.251

HIBBARD, JOHN DENISON
B.DEC.2,1864 CHICAGO,ILL.
D.NOV.17,1937 HOLLYWOOD,CAL.

YR	CL	LEA	POS	GP	G	REC
1884	CHI	N	P		2	1- 1
	TL					

HIBBS, JAMES KERR "JIM"
B.SEP.10,1944 KLAMATH FALLS,ORE.

YR	CL	LEA	POS	GP	G	REC
1967	CAL	A	H		3	.000
	BRTR					

HICKEY, JAMES ROBERT
B.OCT.22,1920 N.ABINGTON,MASS.

YR	CL	LEA	POS	GP	G	REC
1942	BOS	N	P		1	0- 1
1944	BOS	N	P		8	0- 0
	BRTR				9	0- 1

HICKEY, JOHN W.
B.NOV.3,1881 MINNEAPOLIS,MINN.
D.DEC.28,1941

YR	CL	LEA	POS	GP	G	REC
1904	CLE	A	P		3	0- 3
	BRTR					

HICKEY, MICHAEL EDWARD
B.DEC.25,1871 CHICOPEE,MASS.
D.JUNE 11,1918

YR	CL	LEA	POS	GP	G	REC
1899	BOS	N	2		1	.333
1901	CHI	N	3		10	.176
	BRTR				11	.212

HICKMAN, CHARLES TAYLOR "PIANO LEGS"
B.MAR.4,1876 DUNKIRK,N.Y.
D.APR.19,1934 MORGANTOWN,W.VA.

YR	CL	LEA	POS	GP	G	REC
1897	BOS	N	P		2	0- 0
1898	BOS	N	P		17	2- 2
1899	BOS	N	P		18	7- 0
1900	NY	N	3		125	.313
1901	NY	N	P-S-	8	101	3- 5
			3-O			.287
1902	BOS	A	O		28	.308
	CLE	A	P-1	1	102	0- 1
						.376
1903	CLE	A	1		130	.330
1904	CLE	A	1		85	.415
	DET	A	1		41	.254
1905	DET	A	1-O		59	.221
	WAS	A	2		88	.311
1906	WAS	A	1-O		120	.284
1907	WAS	A	P-1-	1	60	0- 0
			2			.300
	CHI	A	2		21	.226
1908	CLE	A	1-O		65	.234
	BRTR			47	1062	12- 8
						.302

HICKMAN, DAVID JAMES
B.MAY 19,1894 UNION CITY,TENN.

YR	CL	LEA	POS	GP	G	REC
1915	BAL	F	O		20	.210
1916	BRO	N	O		9	.200
1917	BRO	N	O		114	.219
1918	BRO	N	O		53	.234
1919	BRO	N	O		57	.192
	BRTR				253	.218

HICKMAN, ERNEST P.
B.1856 E.ST.LOUIS,ILL.
D.NOV.19,1891

YR	CL	LEA	POS	GP	G	REC
1884	KC	U	P		18	3-13

HICKMAN, JAMES LUCIUS "JIM"
B.MAY 10,1937 HENNING,TENN.

YR	CL	LEA	POS	GP	G	REC
1962	NY	N	O		140	.245
1963	NY	N	3-O		146	.229
1964	NY	N	3-O		139	.257
1965	NY	N	1-3-O		141	.236
1966	NY	N	1-O		58	.238
1967	LA	N	P-	1	65	0- 0
			1-3-O			.163
1968	CHI	N	O		75	.223
1969	CHI	N	O		134	.237
1970	CHI	N	1-O		149	.315
1971	CHI	N	1-O		117	.256
1972	CHI	N	1-O		115	.272
1973	CHI	N	1-O		92	.244
1974	STL	N	1-3		50	.267
	BRTR			1	1421	0- 0
						.252

HICKMAN, JESSE OWENS
B.FEB.18,1939 LECOMPTE,LA.

YR	CL	LEA	POS	GP	G	REC
1965	KC	A	P	12	14	0- 1
1966	KC	A	P	1	1	0- 0
	BRTR			13	15	0- 1

HICKS, CLARENCE WALTER "BUDDY"
B.FEB.15,1927 BELVEDERE,CAL.

YR	CL	LEA	POS	GP	G	REC
1956	DET	A	2-S-3		26	.213
	BBTR					

HICKS, JAMES EDWARD "JIM"
B.MAY 18,1940 EAST CHICAGO,IND.

YR	CL	LEA	POS	GP	G	REC
1964	CHI	A	R		2	.000
1965	CHI	A	O		13	.263
1966	CHI	A	1-O		18	.192
1969	STL	N	O		19	.182
	CAL	A	1-O		37	.083
1970	CAL	A	H		4	.250
	BRTR				93	.163

HICKS, NATHANIEL WOODHULL
B.APR.19,1845 BROOKLYN,N.Y.
D.APR.21,1907

YR	CL	LEA	POS	GP	G	REC
1872	MUT	NA	C-O		56	.308
1873	MUT	NA	C		28	–
1874	PHI	NA	C-O		58	–
1875	MUT	NA	M-C-O		63	–
1876	MUT	N	C		45	.230
1877	CIN	N	C		8	.187
	BRTR				258	–

HICKS, WILLIAM JOSEPH "JOE"
B.APR.7,1933 IVY,VA.

YR	CL	LEA	POS	GP	G	REC
1959	CHI	A	O		6	.429
1960	CHI	A	O		36	.191
1961	WAS	A	O		12	.172
1962	WAS	A	O		102	.224
1963	NY	N	O		56	.226
	BLTR				212	.221

HIGBE, WALTER KIRBY "KIRBY"
B.APR.8,1915 COLUMBIA,S.C.

YR	CL	LEA	POS	GP	G	REC
1937	CHI	N	P		1	1- 0
1938	CHI	N	P		2	0- 0
1939	CHI	N	P		9	2- 1
	PHI	N	P		34	10-14
1940	PHI	N	P		41	14-19
1941	BRO	N	P		48	22- 9
1942	BRO	N	P		38	16-11
1943	BRO	N	P		35	13-10
1946	BRO	N	P		42	17- 8
1947	BRO	N	P		4	2- 0
	PIT	N	P		46	11-17
1948	PIT	N	P		56	8- 7
1949	PIT	N	P		7	0- 2
	NY	N	P		37	2- 0
1950	NY	N	P		18	0- 3
	BRTR				418	118-101

HIGBEE, MAHLON JESSE
B.AUG.16,1901 LOUISVILLE,KY.
D.APR.7,1968 DE PAUW,IND.

YR	CL	LEA	POS	GP	G	REC
1922	NY	N	O		3	.400

HIGBY

YR	CL	LEA	POS	GP	G	REC
1072	ATL	NA	O		1	.000

HIGDON, WILLIAM TRAVIS "BILL"
B.APR.27,1924 CAMP HILL,ALA.

YR	CL	LEA	POS	GP	G	REC
1949	CHI	A	O		11	.304
	BLTR					

HIGGINBOTHAM, IRVING CLINTON
B.APR.26,1882 HOMER,NEB.
D.JUNE 12,1959

YR	CL	LEA	POS	GP	G	REC
1906	STL	N	P		7	1- 6
1908	STL	N	P		19	3- 8
1909	STL	N	P		3	1- 0
	CHI	N	P		19	5- 2
	TR				48	10-16

HIGGINS, DENNIS DEAN
B.AUG.4,1939 JEFFERSON CITY,MO.

YR	CL	LEA	POS	GP	G	REC
1966	CHI	A	P		42	1- 0
1967	CHI	A	P		9	1- 2
1968	WAS	A	P		59	4- 4
1969	WAS	A	P		55	10- 9
1970	CLE	A	P		58	4- 6
1971	STL	N	P		3	1- 0
1972	STL	N	P		15	1- 2
	BRTR				241	22-23

HIGGINS, MICHAEL FRANKLIN "MIKE" OR "PINKEY"
B.MAY 27,1909 RED OAK,TEX.
D.MAR.21,1969 DALLAS,TEX.

YR	CL	LEA	POS	GP	G	REC
1930	PHI	A	2-S-3		14	.250
1933	PHI	A	3		152	.314
1934	PHI	A	3		144	.330
1935	PHI	A	3		133	.296
1936	PHI	A	3		146	.289
1937	BOS	A	3		153	.302
1938	BOS	A	3		139	.303
1939	DET	A	3		132	.276
1940	DET	A	3		131	.271
1941	DET	A	3		147	.298
1942	DET	A	3		143	.267
1943	DET	A	3		138	.277
1944	DET	A	3		148	.297
1946	DET	A	3		18	.217
	BOS	A	3		64	.275
	BRTR				1802	.292
NON-PLAYING MANAGER
BOS(A) 1955-59, 60-62

HIGGINS, ROBERT STONE
B.SEPT.23,1886 FAYETTEVILLE, TENN.
D.MAY 25,1941

YR	CL	LEA	POS	GP	G	REC
1909	CLE	A	C		8	.087
1911	BRO	N	C		4	.300
1912	BRO	N	C		1	.000
	BRTR				13	.143

YR	CL	LEA	POS	GP	G	REC

HIGGINS, THOMAS EDWARD
"EDDIE" OR "IRISH"
B.MAR.18,1889 STREATOR,ILL.
D.FEB.14,1959 ELGIN,ILL.

YR	CL	LEA	POS	GP	G	REC
1909	STL	N	P		16	3- 3
1910	STL	N	P-O		2	0- 1
						.400
	BRTR				18	3- 4
						.231

HIGGINS, WILLIAM H.
B.OCT.3,1862 WILMINGTON,DEL.
D.SEPT.23,1926

YR	CL	LEA	POS	G	REC
1888	BOS	N	2	14	.167
1890	STL	AA	2	64	.251
	SYR	AA	2	1	.250
	TR			79	.236

HIGH, ANDREW AIRD "HANDY ANDY"
B.NOV.21,1897 AVA,ILL.

YR	CL	LEA	POS	G	REC
1922	BRO	N	2-S-3	153	.283
1923	BRO	N	2-S-3	123	.270
1924	BRO	N	2-S-3	144	.328
1925	BRO	N	2-S-3	44	.200
	BOS	N	2-3	60	.288
1926	BOS	N	2-3	130	.296
1927	BOS	N	3	113	.302
1928	STL	N	2-3	111	.285
1929	STL	N	2-3	146	.295
1930	STL	N	3	72	.279
1931	STL	N	2-3	63	.267
1932	CIN	N	2-3	84	.188
1933	CIN	N	2-3	24	.209
1934	PHI	N	3	47	.206
	BLTR			1314	.284

HIGH, CHARLES EDWIN
B.DEC.1,1898 AVA,ILL.
D.SEPT.11,1960

YR	CL	LEA	POS	G	REC
1919	PHI	A	O	11	.077
1920	PHI	A	O	17	.308
	BLTR			28	.242

HIGH, EDWARD T. "LEFTY"
D.FEB.10,1926 BALTIMORE,MD.

YR	CL	LEA	POS	G	REC
1901	DET	A	P	5	3- 2
	TL				

HIGH, HUGH JENKINS "BUNNY"
B.OCT.24,1890 POTTSTOWN,PA.
D.NOV.16,1962

YR	CL	LEA	POS	G	REC
1913	DET	A	O	80	.230
1914	DET	A	O	80	.266
1915	NY	A	O	119	.258
1916	NY	A	O	115	.263
1917	NY	A	O	103	.236
1918	NY	A	O	6	.000
	BLTL			503	.250

HIGHAM, RICHARD
B.1852 ENGLAND
D.MAR.18,1905

YR	CL	LEA	POS	G	REC
1871	MUT	NA	C-2-O	22	-
1872	BAL	NA	C-1-2-3-O	46	.339
1873	MUT	NA	2-O	23	-
	ATL	NA	2	1	-
	MUT	NA	C-3-O	26	-
1874	MUT	NA	M-C-2-O	65	-
1875	CHI	NA	C-2-O	44	-
	MUT	NA	C-1-2-O	14	-
1876	HAR	N	C-O	67	.325
1878	PRO	N	O	60	.315
1880	TRO	N	C-O	1	.200
	BLTR			369	-

HILAND, JOHN W.
B.PHILADELPHIA,PA.

YR	CL	LEA	POS	G	REC
1885	PHI	N	2	3	.000
	TL				

HILCHER, WALTER FRANK "WHITEY"
B.FEB.28,1909 CHICAGO,ILL.

YR	CL	LEA	POS	G	REC
1931	CIN	N	P	2	0- 1
1932	CIN	N	P	11	0- 3
1935	CIN	N	P	4	2- 0
1936	CIN	N	P	14	1- 2
	BRTR			31	3- 6

HILDEBRAND, GEORGE ALBERT
B.SEPT.6,1882 SAN FRANCISCO,CAL
D.MAY 30,1960

YR	CL	LEA	POS	G	REC
1902	BRO	N	O	11	.227

HILDEBRAND, ORAL CLYDE
B.APR.13,1907 INDIANAPOLIS,IND.

YR	CL	LEA	POS	GP	G	REC
1931	CLE	A	P		5	2- 1
1932	CLE	A	P		27	8- 6
1933	CLE	A	P		36	16-11
1934	CLE	A	P		33	11- 9
1935	CLE	A	P		34	9- 8
1936	CLE	A	P		36	10-11
1937	STL	A	P		30	8-17
1938	STL	A	P	23	24	8-10
1939	NY	A	P		21	10- 4
1940	NY	A	P		13	1- 1
	BRTR			258	259	83-78

HILDEBRAND, PALMER MARION
B.DEC.23,1884 SHAUCK,OHIO
D.JAN.25,1960

YR	CL	LEA	POS	G	REC
1913	STL	N	C	26	.164
	BRTR				

HILDEBRAND, R. E.

YR	CL	LEA	POS	G	REC
1902	CHI	N	O	1	.000

HILGENDORF, THOMAS EUGENE "TOM"
B.MAR.10,1942 CLINTON,IOWA

YR	CL	LEA	POS	G	REC
1969	STL	N	P	6	0- 0
1970	STL	N	P	23	0- 4
1972	CLE	A	P	19	3- 1
1973	CLE	A	P	48	5- 3
1974	CLE	A	P	35	4- 3
1975	PHI	N	P	53	7- 3
	BBTL			184	19-14

HILGERINK, WILLIAM EDWARD
(PLAYED UNDER NAME OF
WILLIAM EDWARD HILLY)

HILL, BELDEN L.
B.AUG.24,1863 KEWANEE,ILL.
D.OCT.23,1934

YR	CL	LEA	POS	G	REC
1890	BAL	AA	3	9	.133

HILL, CARMEN PROCTOR "SPECS"
B.OCT.1,1895 ROYALTON,MINN.

YR	CL	LEA	POS	GP	G	REC
1915	PIT	N	P		8	2- 1
1916	PIT	N	P		2	0- 0
1918	PIT	N	P		6	2- 3
1919	PIT	N	P		4	0- 0
1922	NY	N	P		8	2- 1
1926	PIT	N	P		6	3- 3
1927	PIT	N	P	43	44	22-11
1928	PIT	N	P		36	16-10
1929	PIT	N	P		27	2- 3
	STL	N	P		3	0- 0
1930	STL	N	P		4	0- 1
	BRTR			147	148	49-33

HILL, CLIFFORD J. "RED"
B.JAN.25,1894 MARSHALL,TEX.
D.AUG.11,1938 EL PASO,TEX.

YR	CL	LEA	POS	G	REC
1917	PHI	A	P	1	0- 0
	BBTL				

HILL, DAVID BURNHAM
B.NOV.11,1938 MILWAUKEE,WIS.

YR	CL	LEA	POS	G	REC
1957	KC	A	P	2	0- 0
	BRTL				

HILL, GARRY ALTON
B.NOV.3,1946 RUTHERFORDTON,N.C.

YR	CL	LEA	POS	G	REC
1969	ATL	N	P	1	0- 1
	BRTR				

HULL, HERBERT
B.AUG.19,1892 DALLAS,TEX.

YR	CL	LEA	POS	G	REC
1915	CLE	A	P	1	0- 0

HILL, HERMAN ALEXANDER
B.OCT.12,1945 TUSKEGEE,ALA.
D.DEC.14,1970 VALENCIA,VENEZ.

YR	CL	LEA	POS	G	REC
1969	MIN	A	O	16	.000
1970	MIN	A	O	27	.091
	BLTR			43	.083

HILL, HUGH ELLIS
B.JULY 21,1879 RINGGOLD,GA.

YR	CL	LEA	POS	G	REC
1903	CLE	A	H	1	.000
1904	STL	N	O	23	.226
				24	.233

HILL, HUNTER BENJAMIN
B.JUNE 21,1879 AUSTIN,TEX.
D.FEB.22,1959

YR	CL	LEA	POS	G	REC
1903	STL	A	3	86	.249
1904	STL	A	3	58	.220
	WAS	A	3	77	.229
1905	WAS	A	3	103	.209
	TR			324	.219

HILL, JESSE TERRILL
B.JAN.20,1907 YATES,MO.

YR	CL	LEA	POS	G	REC
1935	NY	A	O	107	.293
1936	WAS	A	O	85	.305
1937	WAS	A	O	33	.217
	PHI	A	O	70	.293
	BRTR			295	.289

HILL, JOHN CLINTON
B.OCT.16,1912 POWDER SPRINGS,GA

YR	CL	LEA	POS	G	REC
1939	BOS	N	H	2	.500
	BLTR				

HILL, MARC KEVIN
B.FEB.18,1952 ELSBERRY,MO.

YR	CL	LEA	POS	G	REC
1973	STL	N	C	1	.000
1974	STL	N	C	10	.238
1975	SF	N	C-3	72	.214
1976	SF	N	C-1	54	.183
	BRTR			137	.202

HILL, WILLIAM C. "STILL BILL"
B.AUG.2,1874 CHATTANOOGA,TENN.
D.JAN.28,1938

YR	CL	LEA	POS	G	REC
1896	LOU	N	P	39	10-29
1897	LOU	N	P	26	6-18
1898	CIN	N	P	28	13-15
1899	CLE	N	P-O	11	3- 6
					.121
	BAL	N	P	8	3- 4
	BRO	N	P	1	1- 0
	BLTL			113	36-72
					.166

HILLEBRAND, HOMER HILLER HENRY
B.OCT.10,1879 LEMARS,IOWA
D.JAN.23,1974 ELSINORE,CAL.

YR	CL	LEA	POS	GP	G	REC
1905	PIT	N	P-1	10	36	4- 2
						.236
1906	PIT	N	P		7	3- 2
1908	PIT	N	P		1	0- 0
				18	44	7- 4
						.238

HILLER, CHARLES JOSEPH "CHUCK"
B.OCT.1,1935 JOHNSBURG,ILL.

YR	CL	LEA	POS	G	REC
1961	SF	N	2	70	.238
1962	SF	N	2	161	.276
1963	SF	N	2	111	.223
1964	SF	N	2-3	80	.180
1965	SF	N	2	7	.143
	NY	N	2-3-O	100	.238
1966	NY	N	2-3-O	108	.280
1967	NY	N	2	25	.093
	PHI	N	2	31	.302
1968	PIT	N	2	11	.385
	BLTR			704	.243

HILLER, FRANK WALTER "DUTCH"
B.JULY 13,1920 NEWARK,N.J.

YR	CL	LEA	POS	GP	G	REC
1946	NY	A	P		3	0- 2
1948	NY	A	P		22	5- 2
1949	NY	A	P		4	0- 2
1950	CHI	N	P		38	12- 5
1951	CHI	N	P		24	6-12
1952	CIN	N	P	28	29	5- 8
1953	NY	N	P		19	2- 1
	BRTR			138	139	30-32

HILLER, HARVEY MAX
B.MAY 12,1893 E.MAUCH CHUNK,PA.
D.DEC.27,1956

YR	CL	LEA	POS	G	REC
1920	BOS	A	3	17	.172
1921	BOS	A	O	1	.000
	BRTR			18	.167

YR CL LEA POS GP   G   REC

HILLER, JOHN FREDERICK
B.APR.8,1943 TORONTO,ONT.,CANADA

YR	CL	LEA	POS	GP	G	REC
1965	DET	A	P		5	0- 0
1966	DET	A	P		1	0- 0
1967	DET	A	P		23	4- 3
1968	DET	A	P		39	9- 6
1969	DET	A	P	40	41	4- 4
1970	DET	A	P		47	6- 6
1972	DET	A	P		24	1- 2
1973	DET	A	P		65	10- 5
1974	DET	A	P		59	17-14
1975	DET	A	P		36	2- 3
1976	DET	A	P		56	12- 8
	BRTL			395	396	65-51

HILLEY, EDWARD GARFIELD
B.JUNE 17,1879 CLEVELAND,OHIO
D.NOV.14,1956

YR	CL	LEA	POS	GP	G	REC
1903	PHI	A	3		1	.333
	BRTR					

HILLIS, MALCOLM DAVID "MACK"
B.JULY 23,1901 CAMBRIDGE,MASS.
D.JUNE 16,1961

YR	CL	LEA	POS	GP	G	REC
1922	NY	A	2		1	.000
1928	PIT	N	2		11	.250
	BRTR				12	.243

HILLMAN, DARIUS DUTTON "DAVE"
B.SEPT.14,1927 DUNGANNON,VA.

YR	CL	LEA	POS	GP	G	REC
1955	CHI	N	P	25	26	0- 0
1956	CHI	N	P		2	0- 2
1957	CHI	N	P	32	36	6-11
1958	CHI	N	P	31	32	4- 8
1959	CHI	N	P	39	42	8-11
1960	BOS	A	P	16	0- 3	
1961	BOS	A	P		28	3- 2
1962	CIN	N	P		2	0- 0
	NY	N	P		13	0- 0
	BRTR			188	197	21-37

HILLY, WILLIAM EDWARD
(REAL NAME
WILLIAM EDWARD HILGERINK)
B.FEB.24,1887 FOSTORIA,OHIO
D.JULY 25,1953

YR	CL	LEA	POS	GP	G	REC
1914	PHI	N	O		8	.300
	BRTR					

HILSEY, CHARLES
B.1864 PHILADELPHIA,PA.

YR	CL	LEA	POS	GP	G	REC
1883	PHI	N	P		3	0- 3
1884	ATH	AA	P-O	3	6	2- 1
						.261
				6	9	2- 4
						.235

HILT, BENJAMIN FRANKLIN
B.PHILADELPHIA,PA.
NON-PLAYING MANAGER PHI(P) 1890

HILTON, JOHN DAVID "DAVE"
B.SEP.15,1950 UVALDE,TEX.

YR	CL	LEA	POS	GP	G	REC
1972	SD	N	3		13	.213
1973	SD	N	2-3		70	.197
1974	SD	N	2-3		74	.240
1975	SD	N	3		4	.000
	BRTR				161	.213

HIMES, JOHN H.

YR	CL	LEA	POS	GP	G	REC
1905	STL	N	O		12	.156
1906	STL	N	O		40	.271
					52	.250

HIMSL, AVITUS BERNARD "VEDIE"
B.APR.2,1917 PLEVNA,MONT.
NON-PLAYING MANAGER
CHI(N) 1961-62

HINCHMAN, HARRY SIBLEY
B.AUG.4,1878 PHILADELPHIA,PA.
D.JAN.19,1933

YR	CL	LEA	POS	GP	G	REC
1907	CLE	A	2		15	.216
	BBTR					

HINCHMAN, WILLIAM WHITE
B.APR.4,1883 PROVIDENCE,PA.
D.FEB.21,1963 COLUMBUS,OHIO

YR	CL	LEA	POS	GP	G	REC
1905	CIN	N	O		17	.255
1906	CIN	N	O		16	.204
1907	CLE	A	O		152	.228
1908	CLE	A	S-O		137	.231
1909	CLE	A	O		139	.258
1915	PIT	N	O		156	.307
1916	PIT	N	1-O		152	.315
1917	PIT	N	1-O		69	.189
1918	PIT	N	1-O		50	.234
1920	PIT	N	O		18	.188
	BRTR				906	.261

HINES, HENRY FRED "HUNKIE"
B.SEPT.29,1867 ELGIN,ILL.
D.JAN.2,1928

YR	CL	LEA	POS	GP	G	REC
1895	BRO	N	O		2	.250
	BRTR					

HINES, MICHAEL P.
B.1864 IRELAND
D.MAR.14,1910

YR	CL	LEA	POS	GP	G	REC
1883	BOS	N	C-O		61	.228
1884	BOS	N	C		34	.181
1885	BOS	N	O		14	.250
	BRO	AA	C		2	.167
	PRO	N	C		1	.000
1888	BOS	N	C		3	.167
	TL				115	.213

HINES, PAUL A.
B.MAR.1,1852 WASHINGTON,D.C.
D.JULY 10,1935 HYATTSVILLE,MD.

YR	CL	LEA	POS	GP	G	REC
1872	NAT	NA	1 3		11	.386
1873	NAT	NA	C-2-O		39	—
1874	CHI	NA	2-S-O		59	—
1875	CHI	NA	2-O		69	—
1876	CHI	N	O		64	.330
1877	CHI	N	2-O		60	.280
1878	PRO	N	O		60	.351
1879	PRO	N	O		84	.357
1880	PRO	N	1-2-O		82	.306
1881	PRO	N	2-O		79	.283
1882	PRO	N	1-O		84	.308
1883	PRO	N	1-O		97	.298
1884	PRO	N	P-1- 1		112	0- 0
			O			.304
1885	PRO	N	1-2-S-3-		98	.273
			O			
1886	WAS	N	3-O		121	.312
1887	WAS	N	O		123	.370
1888	IND	N	O		132	.280
1889	IND	N	1		121	.304
1890	PIT	N	1-O		31	.172
	BOS	N	O		69	.266
1891	WAS	AA	O		54	.266
	BRTR			1	1649	0- 0
						—

HINKLE, DANIEL GORDON "GORDIE"
B.APR.3,1905 TORONTO,OHIO
D.MAR.19,1972 HOUSTON,TEX.

YR	CL	LEA	POS	GP	G	REC
1934	BOS	A	C		27	.173
	BRTR					

HINRICHS, PAUL EDWIN
B.AUG.31,1925 MARENGO,IOWA

YR	CL	LEA	POS	GP	G	REC
1951	BOS	A	P		4	0- 0
	BRTR					

HINRICHS, WILLIAM LOUIS "DUTCH"
B.APR.27,1889 ORANGE,CAL.
D.AUG.18,1972 KINGSBURG,CAL.

YR	CL	LEA	POS	GP	G	REC
1910	WAS	A	P		3	0- 1
	BRTR					

HINSLEY, JERRY DEAN
B.APR.9,1944 HUGO,OKLA.

YR	CL	LEA	POS	GP	G	REC
1964	NY	N	P		9	0- 2
1967	NY	N	P		2	0- 0
	BRTR				11	0- 2

HINSON, JAMES PAUL
B.MAY 9,1907 VAN LEER,TENN.

YR	CL	LEA	POS	GP	G	REC
1928	BOS	A	H		3	.000
	BRTR					

HINTON, CHARLES EDWARD "CHUCK"
B.MAY 3,1934 ROCKY MOUNT,N.C.

YR	CL	LEA	POS	GP	G	REC
1961	WAS	A	O		106	.260
1962	WAS	A	2-S-O		151	.310
1963	WAS	A	1-S-3-O		150	.269
1964	WAS	A	3-O		138	.274
1965	CLE	A	1-2-3-O		133	.255
1966	CLE	A	1-2-O		123	.256
1967	CLE	A	2-O		147	.245
1968	CAL	A	1-2-3-O		116	.195
1969	CLE	A	3-O		94	.256
1970	CLE	A	C-1-2-3-		107	.318
			O			
1971	CLE	A	C-1-O		88	.224
	BRTR			1353		.264

HINTON, JOHN R.
B.ALTOONA,PA.

YR	CL	LEA	POS	GP	G	REC
1902	BOS	N	3		4	.071
	TR					

HINTON, RICHARD MICHAEL "RICH"
B.MAY 22,1947 TUCSON,ARIZ.

YR	CL	LEA	POS	GP	G	REC
1971	CHI	A	P	18	3- 4	
1972	NY	A	P	7	1- 0	
	TEX	A	P	5	0- 1	
1975	CHI	A	P	15	1- 0	
1976	CIN	N	P	12	1- 2	
	BLTL			57	6- 7	

HIPPAUF, HERBERT AUGUST "HERB"
B.MAY 9,1940 NEW YORK,N.Y.

YR	CL	LEA	POS	GP	G	REC
1966	ATL	N	P		3	0- 1
	BRTL					

HISER, GENE TAYLOR
B.DEC.11,1948 BALTIMORE,MD.

YR	CL	LEA	POS	GP	G	REC
1971	CHI	N	O		17	.207
1972	CHI	N	O		32	.196
1973	CHI	N	O		100	.174
1974	CHI	N	O		12	.235
1975	CHI	N	1-O		45	.242
	BLTL				206	.202

HISLE, LARRY EUGENE
B.MAY 5,1947 PORTSMOUTH,OHIO

YR	CL	LEA	POS	GP	G	REC
1968	PHI	N	O		7	.364
1969	PHI	N	O		145	.266
1970	PHI	N	O		126	.205
1971	PHI	N	O		36	.197
1973	MIN	A	O		143	.272
1974	MIN	A	O		143	.286
1975	MIN	A	O-D		80	.314
1976	MIN	A	O		155	.272
	BRTR				835	.266

HISNER, HARLEY PARNELL
B.NOV.6,1926 FT.WAYNE,IND.

YR	CL	LEA	POS	GP	G	REC
1951	BOS	A	P		1	0- 1
	BRTR					

HITCHCOCK, JAMES FRANKLIN
B.JUNE 28,1913 INVERNESS,ALA.
D.JUNE 23,1959

YR	CL	LEA	POS	GP	G	REC
1938	BOS	N	S		28	.171
	BRTR					

HITCHCOCK, WILLIAM CLYDE "BILLY"
B.JULY 31,1918 INVERNESS,ALA.

YR	CL	LEA	POS	GP	G	REC
1942	DET	A	S-3		85	.211
1946	DET	A	2		3	.000
	WAS	A	S-3		98	.212
1947	STL	A	1-2-S-3		80	.222
1948	BOS	A	2-3		49	.298
1949	BOS	A	1-2		55	.204
1950	PHI	A	2-S		115	.273
1951	PHI	A	1-2-3		77	.306
1952	PHI	A	1-3		119	.246
1953	DET	A	2-S-3		22	.211
	BRTR				703	.243

NON-PLAYING MANAGER DET(A) 1960
BAL(A) 1961-63, ATL(N) 1966-67

HITT, BRUCE SMITH
B.MAR.14,1898 COMANCHE,TEX.
D.NOV.10,1973 PORTLAND,ORE.

YR	CL	LEA	POS	GP	G	REC
1917	STL	N	P		2	0- 0
	BRTR					

HITT, ROY WESLEY
B.JUNE 22,1884 CARLETON,NEB.
D.FEB.9,1956

YR	CL	LEA	POS	GP	G	REC
1907	CIN	N	P		21	6-10
	TL					

YR	CL	LEA	POS	GP	G	REC

HITTLE, LLOYD ELDON "RED"
B.FEB.21,1924 ACAMPO,CAL.

YR	CL	LEA	POS	GP	G	REC
1949	WAS	A	P		36	5- 7
1950	WAS	A	P		11	2- 4
		BRTL			47	7-11

HOAG, MYRIL OLIVER
B.MAR.8,1908 DAVIS,CAL.
D.JULY 28,1971 HIGH SPRINGS,FLA

1931	NY	A	O		44	.143
1932	NY	A	O		46	.370
1934	NY	A	O		97	.267
1935	NY	A	3-O		48	.255
1936	NY	A	O		45	.301
1937	NY	A	O		106	.301
1938	NY	A	O		85	.277
1939	STL	A	P-O	1	129	0- 0
						.295
1940	STL	A	O		76	.262
1941	STL	A	O		1	.000
	CHI	A	O		106	.255
1942	CHI	A	O		113	.240
1944	CHI	A	O		17	.229
	CLE	A	O		67	.285
1945	CLE	A	P-O	2	40	0- 0
						.211
		BRTR		3	1020	0- 0
						.271

HOAK, DONALD ALBERT "DON"
B.FEB.5,1928 ROULETTE,PA.
D.OCT.9,1969 PITTSBURGH,PA.

1954	BRO	N	3		88	.245
1955	BRO	N	3		94	.240
1956	CHI	N	3		121	.215
1957	CIN	N	2-3		149	.293
1958	CIN	N	S-3		114	.261
1959	PIT	N	3		155	.294
1960	PIT	N	3		155	.282
1961	PIT	N	3		145	.298
1962	PIT	N	3		121	.241
1963	PHI	N	3		115	.231
1964	PHI	N	H		6	.000
		BRTR			1263	.265

HOBAUGH, EDWARD RUSSELL "ED"
B.JUNE 27,1934 KITTANNING,PA.

1961	WAS	A	P	26	27	7- 9
1962	WAS	A	P		26	2- 1
1963	WAS	A	P		9	0- 0
		BRTR		61	62	9-10

HOBBIE, GLEN FREDERICK
B.APR.24,1936 WITT,ILL.

1957	CHI	N	P		2	0- 0
1958	CHI	N	P		55	10- 6
1959	CHI	N	P		46	16-13
1960	CHI	N	P		46	16-20
1961	CHI	N	P		36	7-13
1962	CHI	N	P		42	5-14
1963	CHI	N	P		36	7-10
1964	CHI	N	P		8	0- 3
	STL	N	P		13	1- 2
		BRTR			284	62-81

HOBBS, WILLIAM LEE "SMOKEY"
B.MAY 7,1893 GRANT'S LICK,KY.
D.JAN.5,1945

1913	CIN	N	2		2	.000
1916	CIN	N	S		6	.182
		BRTR			8	.133

HOBLITZEL, RICHARD CARLETON "DOC"
B.OCT.26,1888 WAVERLY,W.VA.
D.NOV.14,1962

1908	CIN	N	1		32	.254
1909	CIN	N	1		142	.308
1910	CIN	N	1		155	.278
1911	CIN	N	1		158	.289
1912	CIN	N	1		148	.294
1913	CIN	N	1		137	.285
1914	CIN	N	1		78	.210
	BOS	A	1		68	.319
1915	BOS	A	1		124	.283
1916	BOS	A	1		130	.259
1917	BOS	A	1		120	.257
1918	BOS	A	1		25	.159
		BRTR			1317	.278

HOBSON, CLELL LAVERN "BUTCH"
B.AUG.17,1951 TUSCALOOSA,ALA.

1975	BOS	A	3		2	.250
1976	BOS	A	3		76	.234
		BRTR			78	.234

HOCH, CYRUS
(PLAYED UNDER NAME OF
WILLIAM E. HOOKER)

HOCH, HARRY KELLER
B.JAN.9,1887 WOODSIDE,DEL.

1908	PHI	N	P		3	2- 1
1914	STL	A	P		15	0- 2
1915	STL	A	P		12	0- 3
		BRTR			30	2- 6

HOCK, EDWARD FRANCIS
B.MAR.27,1900 FRANKLIN FURNACE,
OHIO
D.NOV.21,1963 PORTSMOUTH,OHIO

1920	STL	N	O		1	.000
1923	CIN	N	O		2	.000
1924	CIN	N	O		16	.100
		BLTL			19	.100

HOCKENBERY, CHARLES MARION "CHUCK"
B.DEC.15,1950 LACROSSE,WIS.

1975	CAL	A	P		16	0- 5
		BBTR				

HOCKETT, ORIS LEON "BROWN"
B.SEPT.29,1909 AMBOY,IND.
D.MAR.23,1969 TORRANCE,CAL.

1938	BRO	N	O		21	.329
1939	BRO	N	O		9	.231
1941	CLE	A	O		2	.333
1942	CLE	A	O		148	.250
1943	CLE	A	O		141	.276
1944	CLE	A	O		124	.289
1945	CHI	A	O		106	.293
		BLTR			551	.276

HOCKETTE, GEORGE EDWARD "LEFTY"
B.APR.7,1909 PERTH,MISS.

1934	BOS	A	P		3	2- 1
1935	BOS	A	P		23	2- 3
		BLTL			26	4- 4

HODAPP, URBAN JOHN "JOHNNY"
B.SEPT.26,1905 CINCINNATI,OHIO

1925	CLE	A	3		37	.238
1926	CLE	A	3		3	.200
1927	CLE	A	3		79	.304
1928	CLE	A	1-3		116	.323
1929	CLE	A	2		90	.327
1930	CLE	A	2		154	.354
1931	CLE	A	2		122	.295
1932	CLE	A	H		7	.188
	CHI	A	O		68	.222
1933	BOS	A	1-2		115	.312
		BRTR			791	.311

HODERLEIN, MELVIN ANTHONY "MEL"
B.JUNE 24,1923 MT.CARMEL,OHIO

1951	BOS	A	2-3		9	.357
1952	WAS	A	2		72	.269
1953	WAS	A	2-S		23	.191
1954	WAS	A	2-S		14	.160
		BBTR			118	.252

HODES, CHARLES
B.1848 NEW YORK,N.Y.
D.FEB.14,1875

1871	CHI	NA	C-S-3-O		28	—
1872	TRO	NA	C-S-3-O		13	.231
1874	ATL	NA	2-O		21	—
					62	—

HODGE, CLARENCE CLEMET "SHOVEL"
B.JULY 6,1894 CLAYTON,ALA.

1920	CHI	A	P		4	1- 1
1921	CHI	A	P		36	6- 8
1922	CHI	A	P		35	7- 6
		BLTR			75	14-15

HODGE, EDWARD BURTON "BERT"
B.MAY 25,1918 NEUBERTS,TENN.

1942	PHI	N	3		8	.182
		BLTR				

HODGE, HAROLD MORRIS "GOMER"
B.APR.3,1944 SANTA MONICA,CAL.

1971	CLE	A	1-2-3		80	.205
		BBTR				

HODGES, GILBERT RAYMOND "GIL"
B.APR.4,1924 PRINCETON,IND.
D.APR.2,1972 WEST PALM BEACH,FLA

1943	BRO	N	3		1	.000
1947	BRO	N	C		28	.156
1948	BRO	N	C-1		134	.249
1949	BRO	N	1		156	.285
1950	BRO	N	1		153	.283
1951	BRO	N	1		158	.268
1952	BRO	N	1		153	.254
1953	BRO	N	1-O		141	.302
1954	BRO	N	1		154	.304
1955	BRO	N	1-O		150	.289
1956	BRO	N	C-1-O		153	.265
1957	BRO	N	1-2-3		150	.299
1958	LA	N	C-1-3-O		141	.259
1959	LA	N	1-3		124	.276
1960	LA	N	1-3		101	.198
1961	LA	N	1		109	.242
1962	NY	N	1		54	.252
1963	NY	N	1		11	.227
		BRTR			2071	.273

NON-PLAYING MANAGER
WAS(A) 1963-67, NY(N) 1968-71

HODGES, RONALD WRAY "RON"
B.JUNE 22,1949 ROCKY MOUNT,VA.

1973	NY	N	C		45	.260
1974	NY	N	C		59	.221
1975	NY	N	C		9	.206
1976	NY	N	C		56	.226
		BLTR			169	.232

HODGIN, ELMER RALPH "RALPH"
B.FEB.10,1916 GREENSBORO,N.C.

1939	BOS	N	O		32	.208
1943	CHI	A	3-O		117	.314
1944	CHI	A	3-O		121	.295
1946	CHI	A	O		87	.252
1947	CHI	A	O		59	.294
1948	CHI	A	O		114	.266
		BLTR			530	.285

HOOKEY, ALOYSIUS JOSEPH
B.NOV.3,1918 LORAIN,OHIO

1946	PHI	N	P		2	0- 1
		BLTL				

HODNET, CHARLES
B.ST.LOUIS,MO.

1883	STL	AA	P-O		4	1- 1
						.154
1884	STL	U	P		15	12- 1
					19	13- 2
						.121

HODSON, GEORGE S.
B.1876 HARTFORD,CONN.

1894	BOS	N	P		11	4- 3
1895	PHI	N	P		4	0- 2
					15	4- 5

HOEFT, WILLIAM FREDERICK "BILLY"
B.MAY 17,1932 OSHKOSH,WIS.

1952	DET	A	P		34	2- 7
1953	DET	A	P	29	30	9-14
1954	DET	A	P	34	35	7-15
1955	DET	A	P	32	36	16- 7
1956	DET	A	P	38	42	20-14
1957	DET	A	P	34	42	9-11
1958	DET	A	P	36	43	10- 9
1959	DET	A	P		3	1- 1
	BOS	A	P	5	7	0- 3
	BAL	A	P		16	1- 1
1960	BAL	A	P		19	2- 1
1961	BAL	A	P		35	7- 4
1962	BAL	A	P		57	4- 8
1963	SF	N	P		23	2- 0
1964	MIL	N	P		42	4- 0
1965	CHI	N	P		29	2- 2
1966	CHI	N	P		36	1- 2
	SF	N	P		4	0- 2
		BLTL		505	533	97-101

YR	CL	LEA	POS	GP	G	REC

HOELSKOETTER, ARTHUR
"HOLLEY" OR "HOSS"
(ALSO PLAYED UNDER NAME OF
ARTHUR H. HOSTETTER)
B.SEPT.30,1882 ST.LOUIS,MO.
D.AUG.3,1954

YR	CL	LEA	POS	GP	G	REC
1905	STL	N	P-3	1	24	0- 0
						.241
1906	STL	N	P-S-	1	94	1- 1
			3			.224
1907	STL	N	1-2		118	.247
1908	STL	N	C		45	.232
	BRTR			2	281	1- 1
						.236

HOERNER, JOSEPH WALTER "JOE"
B.NOV.12,1936 DUBUQUE,IOWA

YR	CL	LEA	POS	GP	G	REC
1963	HOU	N	P		1	0- 0
1964	HOU	N	P		7	0- 0
1966	STL	N	P		57	5- 1
1967	STL	N	P		57	4- 4
1968	STL	N	P		47	8- 2
1969	STL	N	P		45	2- 3
1970	PHI	N	P		44	9- 5
1971	PHI	N	P		49	4- 5
1972	PHI	N	P		15	0- 2
	ATL	N	P		25	1- 3
1973	ATL	N	P		20	2- 2
	KC	A	P		22	2- 0
1974	KC	A	P		30	2- 3
1975	PHI	N	P		25	0- 0
1976	TEX	A	P		41	0- 4
	BRTL				485	39-34

HUERNSCHEMETER, LEOPOLD
CHRISTOPHER
(PLAYED UNDER NAME OF
LEE MAGEE)

HOERST, FRANK JOSEPH "LEFTY"
B.AUG.11,1917 PHILADELPHIA,PA.

YR	CL	LEA	POS	GP	G	REC
1940	PHI	N	P		6	1- 0
1941	PHI	N	P		37	3-10
1942	PHI	N	P		33	4-16
1946	PHI	N	P		18	1- 6
1947	PHI	N	P		4	1- 1
	BLTL				98	10-33

HOEY, FREDERICK C.
B.NEW YORK,N.Y.
D.DEC.7,1933
NON-PLAYING MANAGER NY(N) 1899

HOEY, JOHN B.
B.NOV.10,1881 WATERTOWN,MASS.
D.NOV.11,1947 NAGATUCK,CONN.

YR	CL	LEA	POS	GP	G	REC
1906	BOS	A	O		94	.244
1907	BOS	A	O		39	.219
1908	BOS	A	O		13	.139
					146	.230

HOFF, CHESTER CORNELIUS "RED"
B.MAY 8,1891 OSSINING,N.Y.

YR	CL	LEA	POS	GP	G	REC
1911	NY	A	P		5	0- 2
1912	NY	A	P		5	0- 1
1913	NY	A	P		2	0- 0
1915	STL	A	P		11	2- 2
	BLTL				23	2- 5

HOFFER, WILLIAM LEOPOLD "CHICK"
B.NOV.8,1870 CEDAR RAPIDS,IOWA
D.JULY 21,1959

YR	CL	LEA	POS	GP	G	REC
1895	BAL	N	P		38	29- 8
1896	BAL	N	P		35	26- 7
1897	BAL	N	P	34	41	22-10
1898	BAL	N	P-O		5	0- 5
						.235
1899	PIT	N	P		4	3- 0
1901	CLE	A	P		17	6- 7
	BRTR			152	170	94-46
						.230

HOFFERTH, STEWART EDWARD "STEW"
B.JAN.27,1915 LOGANSPORT,IND.

YR	CL	LEA	POS	GP	G	REC
1944	BOS	N	C		66	.200
1945	BOS	N	C		50	.235
1946	BOS	N	C		20	.207
	BRTR				136	.216

HOFFMAN, CLARENCE CASPER "RED"
B.JAN.28,1903 BELLEVILLE,ILL.
D.DEC.6,1962

YR	CL	LEA	POS	GP	G	REC
1929	CHI	A	O		107	.258
	BRTR					

HOFFMAN, DANIEL JOHN
B.MAR.10,1880 CANTON,CONN.
D.MAR.14,1922

YR	CL	LEA	POS	GP	G	REC
1903	PHI	A	O		73	.235
1904	PHI	A	O		53	.305
1905	PHI	A	O		119	.262
1906	PHI	A	O		7	.217
	NY	A	O		100	.257
1907	NY	A	O		136	.253
1908	STL	A	O		99	.251
1909	STL	A	O		110	.269
1910	STL	A	O		106	.237
1911	STL	A	O		24	.210
	BLTL				827	.255

HOFFMAN, EDWARD ADOLPH "TEX"
B.NOV.30,1893 SAN ANTONIO,TEX.
D.MAY 19,1947

YR	CL	LEA	POS	GP	G	REC
1915	CLE	A	3		9	.153
	BLTR					

HOFFMAN, FRANK J.
B.HOUSTON,TEX.

YR	CL	LEA	POS	GP	G	REC
1888	KC	AA	P		12	3- 9

HOFFMAN, HARRY C. "IZZY"
B.JAN.5,1875 BRIDGEPORT,N.J.
D.NOV.13,1942

YR	CL	LEA	POS	GP	G	REC
1904	WAS	A	O		10	.067
1907	BOS	N	O		19	.279
					29	.224

HOFFMAN, JOHN EDWARD
B.OCT.31,1943 ABERDEEN,S.D.

YR	CL	LEA	POS	GP	G	REC
1964	HOU	N	C		6	.067
1965	HOU	N	C		2	.333
	BLTR				8	.143

HOFFMAN, LAWRENCE CHARLES
B.JULY 18,1882 CHICAGO,ILL.
D.DEC.29,1948

YR	CL	LEA	POS	GP	G	REC
1901	CHI	N	3		5	.315
	TR					

HOFFMAN, OTTO CHARLES "HICKEY"
B.OCT.27,1856 CLEVELAND,OHIO
D.OCT.27,1915

YR	CL	LEA	POS	GP	G	REC
1879	CLE	N	C		1	.000

HOFFMAN, RAYMOND LAMONT
B.JUNE 14,1918 DETROIT,MICH.

YR	CL	LEA	POS	GP	G	REC
1942	WAS	A	3		7	.053
	BLTR					

HOFFMAN, WILLIAM JOSEPH
B.MAR.3,1918 PHILADELPHIA,PA.

YR	CL	LEA	POS	GP	G	REC
1939	PHI	N	P		3	0- 0
	BLTL					

HOFFMEISTER, JESSE H.
B.TOLEDO,OHIO

YR	CL	LEA	POS	GP	G	REC
1897	PIT	N	3		47	.312

HOFFNER, WILLIAM
B.DANVILLE,PA.

YR	CL	LEA	POS	GP	G	REC
1888	KC	AA	P		2	0- 2

HOFFORD, JOHN WILLIAM
B.PHILADELPHIA,PA.

YR	CL	LEA	POS	GP	G	REC
1885	PIT	AA	P		3	0- 2
1886	PIT	AA	P		9	3- 6
					12	3- 8

HOFMAN, ARTHUR FREDERICH
"CIRCUS SOLLY"
B.OCT.29,1882 ST.LOUIS,MO.
D.MAR.11,1956

YR	CL	LEA	POS	GP	G	REC
1903	PIT	N	O		3	.000
1904	CHI	N	O		7	.269
1905	CHI	N	2		83	.237
1906	CHI	N	1-O		60	.256
1907	CHI	N	1-S-O		134	.268
1908	CHI	N	1-2-O		116	.243
1909	CHI	N	O		153	.285
1910	CHI	N	1-O		135	.325
1911	CHI	N	1-O		143	.252
1912	CHI	N	O		36	.272
	PIT	N	O		17	.283
1913	PIT	N	O		28	.229
1914	BRO	F	1-2-O		147	.291
1915	BUF	F	O		108	.233
1916	NY	A	O		6	.296
	CHI	N	O		5	.313
	BRTR			1181		.269

HOFMAN, ROBERT GEORGE "BOBBY"
B.OCT.5,1926 ST.LOUIS,MO.

YR	CL	LEA	POS	GP	G	REC
1949	NY	N	2		19	.208
1952	NY	N	1-2-3		32	.286
1953	NY	N	2-3		74	.266
1954	NY	N	1-2-3		71	.224
1955	NY	N	C-1-2-3		96	.266
1956	NY	N	C-1-2-3		47	.179
1957	NY	N	H		2	.000
	BRTR			341		.248

HOFMANN, FRED "BOOT"
D.NOV.19,1964 ST.HELENA,CAL.
D.NOV.19,1964

YR	CL	LEA	POS	GP	G	REC
1919	NY	A	C		1	.000
1920	NY	A	C		15	.292
1921	NY	A	C		23	.177
1922	NY	A	C		37	.297
1923	NY	A	C		72	.290
1924	NY	A	C		62	.175
1925	NY	A	C		3	.000
1927	BOS	A	C		87	.272
1928	BOS	A	C		78	.226
	BRTR			378		.237

HOGAN, GEORGE EMMET
B.SEPT.25,1885 MARION,OHIO
D.FEB.28,1922

YR	CL	LEA	POS	GP	G	REC
1914	KC	F	P		4	3- 1

HOGAN, HARRY S.
B.NOV.1,1875 SYRACUSE,N.Y.
D.JAN.25,1934 SYRACUSE,N.Y.

YR	CL	LEA	POS	GP	G	REC
1901	CLE	A	O		1	.000

HOGAN, JAMES FRANCIS "SHANTY"
B.MAR.21,1906 SOMERVILLE,MASS.
D.APR.7,1967 BOSTON,MASS.

YR	CL	LEA	POS	GP	G	REC
1925	BOS	N	O		9	.286
1926	BOS	N	C		4	.286
1927	BOS	N	C		71	.288
1928	NY	N	C		131	.333
1929	NY	N	C		102	.300
1930	NY	N	C		122	.339
1931	NY	N	C		123	.301
1932	NY	N	C		140	.287
1933	BOS	N	C		96	.253
1934	BOS	N	C		92	.262
1935	BOS	N	C		59	.301
1936	WAS	A	C		19	.323
1937	WAS	A	C		21	.152
	BRTR			989		.295

HOGAN, KENNETH TIMOTHY
B.OCT.9,1902 CLEVELAND,OHIO

YR	CL	LEA	POS	GP	G	REC
1921	CIN	N	O		1	.000
1923	CLE	A	O		1	.000
1924	CLE	A	O		1	.000
	BLTR				3	.000

HOGAN, MARTIN T.
B.OCT.25,1871 WENSBURY,ENGLAND
D.AUG.16,1923

YR	CL	LEA	POS	GP	G	REC
1894	CIN	N	O		6	.174
	STL	N	O		23	.288
1895	STL	N	O		5	.150
					34	.244

HOGAN, ROBERT EDWARD
B.ST.LOUIS,MO.

YR	CL	LEA	POS	GP	G	REC
1882	STL	AA	P		1	0- 1
1884	MIL	U	O		11	.077
1887	MET	AA	O		32	.377
1888	CLE	AA	O		77	.226
	BR			1	121	0- 1
						.277

HOGAN, WILLIAM HENRY "HAPPY"
B.SEPT.14,1884 N.SAN JUAN,CAL.
D.SEPT.28,1974 SAN JOSE,CAL.

YR	CL	LEA	POS	GP	G	REC
1911	PHI	A	O		7	.105
	STL	A	O		123	.260
1912	STL	A	O		107	.214
	BRTR			237		.236

HOGG, CARTER BRADLEY "BRAD"
B.MAR.26,1888 BUENA VISTA,GA.
D.APR.2,1935 BUENA VISTA,GA.

YR	CL	LEA	POS	GP	G	REC
1911	BOS	N	P		8	0- 3
1912	BOS	N	P		10	1- 1
1915	CHI	N	P		2	1- 0
1918	PHI	N	P	30	39	13-13
1919	PHI	N	P	22	25	5-12
	BRTR			72	84	20-29

YR	CL	LEA	POS	GP	G	REC

HOGG, WILBERT GEORGE
B.APR.21,1913 DETROIT,MICH.
| 1934 | BRO | N | 3 | | 2 | .000 |
| | | BRTR | | | | |

HOGG, WILLIAM "BUFFALO BILL"
B.1880 PORT HURON,MICH.
D.DEC.8,1909
1905	NY	A	P		39	9-16
1906	NY	A	P		28	14-13
1907	NY	A	P	26	27	11- 8
1908	NY	A	P		24	4-16
				117	118	38-53

HOGRIEVER, GEORGE C.
B.MAR.17,1869 CINCINNATI,OHIO
D.JAN.26,1961
1895	CIN	N	O		67	.278
1901	MIL	A	O		54	.243
		BRTR			121	.261

HOGSETT, ELON CHESTER "CHIEF"
B.NOV.2,1903 BROWNELL,KAN.
1929	DET	A	P		4	1- 2
1930	DET	A	P		33	9- 8
1931	DET	A	P		22	3- 9
1932	DET	A	P	47	48	11- 9
1933	DET	A	P		45	6-10
1934	DET	A	P		26	3- 2
1935	DET	A	P		40	6- 6
1936	DET	A	P		3	0- 1
	STL	A	P	39	43	13-15
1937	STL	A	P	37	40	6-19
1938	WAS	A	P	31	32	5- 6
1944	DET	A	P		3	0- 0
		BLTL		330	339	63-87

HOGUE, CALVIN GREY "CAL"
B.OCT.24,1927 DAYTON,OHIO
1952	PIT	N	P	19	1- 8
1953	PIT	N	P	3	1- 1
1954	PIT	N	P	3	0- 1
		BRTR		25	2-10

HOGUE, ROBERT CLINTON "BOBBY"
B.APR.5,1921 MIAMI,FLA.
1948	BOS	N	P		40	8- 2
1949	BOS	N	P		33	2- 2
1950	BOS	N	P		36	3- 5
1951	BOS	N	P		3	0- 0
	STL	A	P		18	1- 1
	NY	A	P		7	1- 0
1952	NY	A	P		27	3- 5
	STL	A	P		8	0- 1
		BRTR		172	18-16

HOHMAN, WILLIAM HENRY
B.NOV.27,1903 BALTIMORE,MD.
D.OCT.29,1968 BALTIMORE,MD.
| 1927 | PHI | N | O | | 7 | .278 |
| | | BRTR | | | | |

HOHNHORST, EDWARD HENRY
B.JAN.31,1885 KENTUCKY
D.MAR.28,1916 COVINGTON,KY.
1910	CLE	A	1		17	.323
1912	CLE	A	1		15	.209
		BLTL			32	.267

HOLBERT, WILLIAM H.
B.MAR.14,1855 BALTIMORE,MD.
D.MAR.1,1935
1876	LOU	N	C		12	.256
1878	MIL	N	C-O		44	.184
1879	SYR	N	C-O		57	.199
	TRO	N	C		4	.267
1880	TRO	N	C-O		60	.188
1881	TRO	N	C-O		44	.274
1882	TRO	N	C-1-3-O		68	.186
1883	MET	AA	C-2-O		71	.238
1884	MET	AA	C		65	.208
1885	MET	AA	C		55	.190
1886	MET	AA	C		48	.216
1887	MET	AA	C		70	.252
1888	BRO	AA	C		15	.115
		BRTR			613	.213

HOLBOROW, WALTER ALBERT
B.NOV.30,1913 NEW YORK,N.Y.
1944	WAS	A	P	1	0- 0
1945	WAS	A	P	15	1- 1
1948	PHI	A	P	5	1- 2
		BRTR		21	2- 3

HOLBRIGHTER, EDWARD
B.AUBURN,N.Y.
| 1882 | ATH | AA | P | | 1 | 0- 1 |

HOLBROOK, JAMES MARBURY "SAMMY"
B.JULY 17,1910 MERIDIAN,MISS.
| 1935 | WAS | A | C | | 52 | .259 |
| | | BRTR | | | | |

HOLCOMBE, KENNETH EDWARD "KEN"
B.AUG.23,1918 BURNSVILLE,N.C.
1945	NY	A	P		23	3- 3
1948	CIN	N	P		2	0- 0
1950	CHI	A	P		24	3-10
1951	CHI	A	P		28	11-12
1952	CHI	A	P		7	0- 5
	STL	A	P		12	0- 2
1953	BOS	A	P		3	1- 0
		BRTR			99	18-32

HOLDEN, JOSEPH FRANCIS "SOCKS"
B.JUNE 4,1913 ST.CLAIR,PA.
1934	PHI	N	C		10	.071
1935	PHI	N	C		6	.111
1936	PHI	N	H		1	.000
		BLTR			17	.083

HOLDEN, WILLIAM PAUL
B.OCT.17,1888 ALBANY,GA.
D.SEPT.14,1971 PENSACOLA,FLA.
1913	NY	A	O		18	.302
1914	NY	A	O		50	.182
	CIN	N	O		11	.214
		BRTR			79	.211

HOLDSWORTH, FREDRICK WILLIAM "FRED"
B.MAY 29,1952 DETROIT,MICH.
1972	DET	A	P		2	0- 1
1973	DET	A	P		5	0- 1
1974	DET	A	P		8	0- 3
1976	BAL	A	P		16	4- 1
					31	4- 6

HOLDSWORTH, JAMES "LONG JIM"
B.NEW YORK
1872	CLE	NA	S		21	.321
	ECK	NA	S		2	.250
1873	MUT	NA	S		54	-
1874	PHI	NA	S-3-O		56	-
1875	MUT	NA	S-O		69	-
1876	MUT	N	O		52	.264
1877	HAR	N	O		55	.254
1882	TRO	N	1		1	.000
1884	IND	AA	O		5	.100
		BRTR			315	-

HOLKE, WALTER HENRY "UNION MAN"
B.DEC.25,1892 ST.LOUIS,MO.
D.OCT.12,1954
1914	NY	N	1		2	.333
1916	NY	N	1		34	.351
1917	NY	N	1		153	.277
1918	NY	N	1		88	.252
1919	BOS	N	1		137	.292
1920	BOS	N	1		144	.294
1921	BOS	N	1		150	.261
1922	BOS	N	1		105	.291
1923	PHI	N	P-1	1	147	0- 0
						.311
1924	PHI	N	1		148	.300
1925	PHI	N	1		39	.244
	CIN	N	1		65	.280
		BBTL		1	1212	0- 0
						.287

HOLLAHAN, WILLIAM CHARLES
B.NOV.22,1897 NEW YORK,N.Y.
| 1920 | WAS | A | 3 | | 3 | .167 |
| | | BRTR | | | | |

HOLLAND, HOWARD ARTHUR "MULLIGAN"
B.JAN.6,1903 FRANKLIN,VA.
D.FEB.16,1969 WESTCHESTER,VA.
1926	CIN	N	P		3	0- 0
1927	NY	N	P		2	1- 0
1929	STL	N	P		8	0- 1
		BRTR			13	1- 1

HOLLAND, ROBERT CLYDE "DUTCH"
B.OCT.12,1903 NASHVILLE,N.C.
D.JUNE 16,1967 LUMBERTON,N.C.
1932	BOS	N	O		39	.295
1933	BOS	N	O		13	.258
1934	CLE	A	O		50	.250
		BRTR			102	.273

HOLLAND, WILLARD A.
B.FT.WAYNE,IND.
| 1889 | BAL | AA | S | | 40 | .182 |

HOLLAND, WILLIAM DAVID "DUTCH"
B.JUNE 4,1915 FUQUAY SPRINGS,
N.C.
| 1939 | WAS | A | P | | 3 | 0- 1 |
| | | BLTL | | | | |

HOLLEY, EDWARD EDGAR
B.JULY 23,1901 BENTON,KY.
1928	CHI	N	P		13	0- 0
1932	PHI	N	P		34	11-14
1933	PHI	N	P		30	13-15
1934	PHI	N	P	15	16	1- 8
	PIT	N	P		5	0- 3
		BRTR		97	98	25-40

HOLLIDAY, JAMES WEAR "BUG"
B.FEB.8,1867 ST.LOUIS,MO.
D.FEB.15,1910 CINCINNATI,OHIO
1889	CIN	AA	O		135	.343
1890	CIN	N	O		131	.270
1891	CIN	N	O		110	.318
1892	CIN	N	P-O	1	149	0- 1
						.286
1893	CIN	N	O		122	.332
1894	CIN	N	O		122	.383
1895	CIN	N	O		31	.301
1896	CIN	N	O		22	.346
1897	CIN	N	O		53	.328
1898	CIN	N	O		26	.240
		BRTR		1	901	0- 1
						.319

HOLLING, CARL
B.JULY 9,1896 DANA,CAL.
1921	DET	A	P		35	3- 7
1922	DET	A	P		7	1- 1
		BRTR		40	42	4- 8

**HOLLINGSHEAD, JOHN SAMUEL
(ALSO PLAYED UNDER NAME OF
SAMUEL JOHN HOLLY)**
B.JAN.17,1853 WASHINGTON,D.C.
D.OCT.6,1926
1872	NAT	NA	2		9	.311
1873	NAT	NA	2-O		30	-
1875	NAT	NA	O		17	-
NON-PLAYING MANAGER WAS(AA)1884

HOLLINGSWORTH, ALBERT WAYNE "BOOTS"
B.FEB.25,1908 ST.LOUIS,MO.
1935	CIN	N	P	38	39	6-13
1936	CIN	N	P	29	34	9-10
1937	CIN	N	P	43	46	9-15
1938	CIN	N	P	8	9	2- 2
	PHI	N	P		24	5-16
1939	PHI	N	P		15	1- 9
	BRO	N	P		9	1- 2
1940	WAS	A	P		3	1- 0
1942	STL	A	P	33	36	10- 6
1943	STL	A	P	35	36	6-13
1944	STL	A	P		26	5- 7
1945	STL	A	P	26	28	12- 9
1946	STL	A	P		5	0- 0
	CHI	A	P		21	3- 2
		BLTL		315	331	70-104

HOLLINGSWORTH, JOHN BURNETT
B.DEC.26,1896 KNOXVILLE,TENN.
1922	PIT	N	P		9	0- 0
1923	WAS	A	P		17	3- 7
1924	BRO	N	P		2	1- 0
1928	BOS	N	P		7	0- 2
		BRTR			35	4- 9

HOLLISON, JOHN HENRY
B.MAY 3,1871 CHICAGO,ILL.
| 1892 | CHI | N | P | | 1 | 0- 1 |
| | | TL | | | | |

HOLLMIG, STANLEY ERNEST "STAN"
B.JAN.2,1926 FREDERICKSBURG,TEX
1949	PHI	N	O		81	.255
1950	PHI	N	O		11	.250
1951	PHI	N	H		2	.000
		BRTR			94	.253

YR	CL	LEA	POS	GP	G	REC

HOLLOCHER, CHARLES JACOB
B.JUNE 11,1896 ST.LOUIS,MO.
D.AUG.14,1940 FRONTENAC CO.,MO.

YR	CL	LEA	POS	GP	G	REC
1918	CHI	N	S	131		.316
1919	CHI	N	S	115		.270
1920	CHI	N	S	80		.319
1921	CHI	N	S	140		.289
1922	CHI	N	S	152		.339
1923	CHI	N	S	66		.342
1924	CHI	N	S	76		.245
	BLTR			760		.304

HOLLOMAN, ALVA LEE "BOBO"
B.MAR.7,1926 THOMASTON,GA.

1953	STL	A	P	22		3- 7
	BRTR					

HOLLOWAY, JAMES MADISON
B.SEPT.22,1908 PLAQUEMINE,LA.

1929	PHI	N	P	3		0- 0
	BRTR					

HOLLOWAY, KENNETH EUGENE
B.AUG.8,1897 BARWICK,GA.

1922	DET	A	P	1		0- 0
1923	DET	A	P	42		11-10
1924	DET	A	P	49		14- 6
1925	DET	A	P	38		13- 4
1926	DET	A	P	36		4- 5
1927	DET	A	P	36		11-12
1928	DET	A	P	30		4- 8
1929	CLE	A	P	25		6- 5
1930	CLE	A	P	12		1- 1
	NY	N		16		0- 0
	BRTR			205		64-51

HOLLY, EDWARD WILLIAM
B.JULY 6,1886 CHICAGO,ILL.
D.NOV.27,1973 WILLIAMSPORT,PA.

1906	STL	N	S	9		.067
1907	STL	N	S	150		.229
1914	PIT	F	S	100		.246
1915	PIT	F	S	16		.262
	BRTR			275		.232

HOLLY, SAMUEL JOHN
(ALSO PLAYED UNDER REAL NAME OF
JOHN SAMUEL HOLLINGSHEAD)

HOLM, ROSCOE ALBERT "WATTIE"
B.DEC.28,1901 PETERSON,IOWA
D.MAY 19,1950

1924	STL	N	C-3-O	81		.294
1925	STL	N	O	13		.207
1926	STL	N	O	55		.285
1927	STL	N	O	110		.286
1928	STL	N	3	102		.277
1929	STL	N	O	64		.233
1932	STL	N	O	11		.176
	BRTR			436		.275

HOLM, WILLIAM FREDERICK
B.JULY 21,1912 CHICAGO,ILL.

1943	CHI	N	C	7		.067
1944	CHI	N	C	54		.148
1945	BOS	A	C	58		.185
	BRTR			119		.156

HOLMAN, GARY RICHARD
B.JAN.25,1944 LONG BEACH,CAL.

1968	WAS	A	1-O	75		.294
1969	WAS	A	1-O	41		.161
	BLTL			116		.259

HOLMES, EDWARD M.

1918	PHI	A	P	2		0- 0
	TR					

HOLMES, FREDERICK
B.CHICAGO,ILL.

1903	NY	A	1	1		.000
1904	CHI	N	C	1		.333
	TR			2		.333

HOLMES, HOWARD ELBERT
B.JULY 8,1883 DAYTON,OHIO
D.SEPT.18,1945

1906	STL	N	C	9		.185
	TR					

HOLMES, JAMES SCOTT
B.AUG.2,1882 LAWRENCEBURG,KY.
D.MAR.10,1960 JACKSONVILLE,FLA.

1906	PHI	A	P	3		0- 1
1908	BRO	N	P	13		1- 4
				16		1- 5

HOLMES, JAMES WILLIAM "DUCKY"
B.JAN.28,1869 DES MOINES,IOWA
D.AUG.6,1932

1895	LOU	N	P-O	1	39	1- 0
						.382
1896	LOU	N	P-O	4	37	0- 2
						.276
1897	LOU	N	S		2	.000
	NY	N	O		78	.288
1898	STL	N	O		23	.276
	BAL	N	O		112	.280
1899	BAL	N	O		138	.315
1901	DET	A	O		130	.294
1902	DET	A	O		92	.253
1903	WAS	A	2-3-O		21	.229
	CHI	A	O		86	.279
1904	CHI	A	O		67	.308
1905	CHI	A	O		92	.308
	BLTR			5	917	1- 2
						.283

**HOLMES, THOMAS FRANCIS
"TOMMY" OR "KELLY"**
B.MAR.29,1918 BROOKLYN,N.Y.

1942	BOS	N	O	141		.278
1943	BOS	N	O	152		.270
1944	BOS	N	O	155		.309
1945	BOS	N	O	154		.352
1946	BOS	N	O	149		.310
1947	BOS	N	O	150		.309
1948	BOS	N	O	139		.325
1949	BOS	N	O	117		.266
1950	BOS	N	O	105		.298
1951	BOS	N	M-O	27		.172
1952	BRO	N	O	31		.111
	BLTL			1320		.302

NON-PLAYING MANAGER BOS(N) 1952

HOLSHOUSER, HERMAN ALEXANDER
B.JAN.20,1907 ROCKWELL,N.C.

1930	STL	A	P	25		0- 1
	BRTR					

**HOLT, JAMES EMMETT MADISON
"RED"**
B.JULY 25,1899 DAYTON,TENN.
D.FEB.2,1961

1925	PHI	A	1	27		.273
	BLTL					

HOLT, JAMES WILLIAM "JIM"
B.MAY 27,1944 GRAHAM,N.C.

1968	MIN	A	1-O	70		.208
1969	MIN	A	1-O	12		.357
1970	MIN	A	1-O	142		.266
1971	MIN	A	1-O	126		.259
1972	MIN	A	1-O	10		.444
1973	MIN	A	1-O	132		.297
1974	MIN	A	1-O	79		.254
	OAK	A	1	30		.143
1975	OAK	A	C-1-O	102		.220
1976	OAK	A	H	4		.286
	BLTR			707		.265

HOLTGRAVE, LAVERN GEORGE "VERN"
B.OCT.18,1942 AVISTON,ILL.

1965	DET	A	P	1		0- 0
	BRTR					

HOLTZMAN, KENNETH DALE "KEN"
B.NOV.3,1945 ST.LOUIS,MO.

1965	CHI	N	P	3		0- 0
1966	CHI	N	P	34		11-16
1967	CHI	N	P	12		9- 0
1968	CHI	N	P	34	35	11-14
1969	CHI	N	P		39	17-13
1970	CHI	N	P	39	40	17-11
1971	CHI	N	P		30	9-15
1972	OAK	A	P	39		19-11
1973	OAK	A	P	40		21-13
1974	OAK	A	P		39	19-17
1975	OAK	A	P		39	18-14
1976	BAL	A	P		13	5- 4
	NY	A	P		21	9- 7
	BRTL			382	386	165-135

HONAN, MARTIN
B.CHICAGO,ILL.

1890	CHI	N	C		1	.000
1891	CHI	N	C		5	.167
					6	.133

HOOD, AUBREY LINCOLN "ABE"
B.JAN.31,1903 CUMNOCK,N.C.

1925	BOS	N	2		5	.286
	BLTR					

HOOD, DONALD HARRIS "DON"
B.OCT.16,1949 FLORENCE,S.C.

1973	BAL	A	P		8	3- 2
1974	BAL	A	P	20	25	1- 1
1975	CLE	A	P	29	35	6-10
1976	CLE	A	P	33	34	3- 5
	BLTL			90	102	13-18

HOOD, WALLACE JAMES JR.
B.SEPT.24,1925 LOS ANGELES,CAL.

1949	NY	A	P	2		0- 0
	BRTR					

HOOD, WALLACE JAMES SR.
B.FEB.9,1896 WHITTIER,CAL.
D.MAY 2,1965 HOLLYWOOD,CAL.

1920	BRO	N	O		7	.154
	PIT	N	O		2	.000
1921	BRO	N	O		56	.262
1922	BRO	N	O		2	.000
	BRTR				67	.238

HOOK, JAMES WESLEY "JAY"
B.NOV.18,1936 WAUKEGAN,ILL.

1957	CIN	N	P		3	0- 1
1958	CIN	N	P		1	0- 1
1959	CIN	N	P	17	19	5- 5
1960	CIN	N	P		36	11-18
1961	CIN	N	P		22	1- 3
1962	NY	N	P	37	41	8-19
1963	NY	N	P		41	4-14
1964	NY	N	P		3	0- 1
	BLTR			160	166	29-62

HOOKER, WILLIAM EDWARD "BUCK"
(REAL NAME CYRUS HUCH)
B.AUG.28,1880 RICHMOND,VA.
D.JULY 2,1929 RICHMOND,VA.

1902	CIN	N	P		1	0- 1
1903	CIN	N	P		1	0- 0
					2	0- 1

HOOKS, ALEXANDER MARCUS
B.AUG.29,1908 EDGEWOOD,TEX.

1935	PHI	A	1		15	.227
	BLTL					

HOOPER, HARRY BARTHOLOMEW
B.AUG.24,1887 SANTA CLARA CO.,
CAL.
D.DEC.18,1974 SANTA CRUZ,CAL.

1909	BOS	A	O		81	.282
1910	BOS	A	O		155	.267
1911	BOS	A	O		130	.311
1912	BOS	A	O		147	.242
1913	BOS	A	P-O	1	148	0- 0
						.289
1914	BOS	A	O		141	.258
1915	BOS	A	O		149	.235
1916	BOS	A	O		151	.271
1917	BOS	A	O		151	.256
1918	BOS	A	O		126	.289
1919	BOS	A	O		128	.267
1920	BOS	A	O		139	.312
1921	CHI	A	O		108	.327
1922	CHI	A	O		152	.304
1923	CHI	A	O		145	.288
1924	CHI	A	O		130	.328
1925	CHI	A	O		127	.265
	BLTR			1	2308	0- 0
						.281

HOOPER, MICHAEL H.
B.FEB.7,1850 BALTIMORE,MD.
D.DEC.1,1917 BALTIMORE,MD.

1873	MAR	NA	C-O	3		-

HOOPER, ROBERT NELSON "BOB"
B.MAY 30,1922 LEAMINGTON,ONT.,
CANADA

1950	PHI	A	P	45		15-10
1951	PHI	A	P	38		12-10
1952	PHI	A	P	43		8-15
1953	CLE	A	P	43		5- 4
1954	CLE	A	P	17		0- 0
1955	CIN	N	P	8		0- 2
	BRTR			194		40-41

**HOOTEN, MICHAEL LEON
"LEON"**
B.APR.4,1948 DOWNEY,CAL.

1974	OAK	A	P	6		0- 0
	BRTR					

YR	CL	LEA	POS	GP	G	REC

HOOTON, BURT CARLTON
B.FEB.17,1950 GREENVILLE,TEX.

YR	CL	LEA	POS	GP	G	REC
1971	CHI	N	P		3	2- 0
1972	CHI	N	P		33	11-14
1973	CHI	N	P		42	14-17
1974	CHI	N	P		48	7-11
1975	CHI	N	P		3	0- 2
	LA	N	P		31	18- 7
1976	LA	N	P		33	11-15
		BRTR			193	63-66

HOOVER, CHARLES E.
B.SEPT.21,1865 MOUND CITY,ILL.

1888	KC	AA	C		3	.200
1889	KC	AA	C		71	.247
	TR				74	.245

HOOVER, RICHARD LLOYD
B.DEC.11,1925 COLUMBUS,OHIO

1952	BOS	N	P		2	0- 0
		BLTL				

HOOVER, ROBERT JOSEPH "JOE"
B.APR.15,1916 BRAWLEY,CAL.
D.SEPT.2,1965 LOS ANGELES,CAL.

1943	DET	A	S		144	.243
1944	DET	A	2-S		120	.236
1945	DET	A	S		74	.257
		BRTR			338	.243

HOOVER, WILLIAM J. "BUSTER"
B.1863 PHILADELPHIA,PA.

1884	KEY	U	P-1-	1	61	0- 0
			2-S-0			.355
	PHI	N	O		9	.211
1886	BAL	AA	O		40	.213
1892	CIN	N	O		14	.176
		BRTR		1	124	0- 0
						.285

HOPE, SAMUEL
B.DEC.4,1878 BROOKLYN,N.Y.
D.JUNE 30,1946

1907	PHI	A	P		1	0- 0

HOPKINS, DONALD "DON"
B.JAN.9,1952 WEST POINT,MISS.

1975	OAK	A	P-O-R		82	.167
1976	OAK	A	R		3	.000
		BLTR			85	.167

HOPKINS, GAIL EASON
B.FEB.19,1943 TULSA,OKLA.

1968	CHI	A	1		29	.216
1969	CHI	A	1		124	.265
1970	CHI	A	C-1		116	.286
1971	KC	A	1		103	.278
1972	KC	A	1-3		53	.211
1973	KC	A	1-D		74	.246
1974	LA	N	C-1		15	.222
		BLTR			514	.266

HOPKINS, JOHN WINTON
"BUCK" OR "SIS"
B.JAN.3,1883 GRAFTON,VA.
D.OCT.2,1929 PHOEBUS,VA.

1907	STL	N	O		15	.136
		BRTR				

HOPKINS, MEREDITH HILLIARD
"MARTY"
B.FEB.22,1907 WOLFE CITY,TEX.
D.NOV.20,1963 DALLAS,TEX.

1934	PHI	N	3		10	.120
	CHI	A	3		67	.214
1935	CHI	A	2-3		59	.222
		BRTR			136	.211

HOPKINS, MICHAEL JOSEPH
"SKINNER"
B.NOV.1,1872 GLASGOW,SCOTLAND
D.FEB.5,1952 PITTSBURGH,PA.

1902	PIT	N	C		1	1.000
		BRTR				

HOPKINS, PAUL HENRY
B.SEPT.25,1904 CHESTER,CONN.

1927	WAS	A	P		2	1- 0
1929	WAS	A	P		7	0- 1
	STL	A	P		2	0- 0
		BRTR			11	1- 1

HOPP, JOHN LEONARD "JOHNNY"
B.JULY 18,1916 HASTINGS,NEB.

1939	STL	N	1		6	.500
1940	STL	N	1-O		80	.270
1941	STL	N	1-O		134	.303
1942	STL	N	1		95	.258
1943	STL	N	1-O		91	.224
1944	STL	N	1-O		139	.336
1945	STL	N	1-O		124	.289
1946	BOS	N	1-O		129	.333
1947	BOS	N	O		134	.288
1948	PIT	N	1-O		120	.278
1949	PIT	N	1-O		105	.318
	BRO	N	1-O		8	.000
1950	PIT	N	1-O		106	.240
	NY	A	1-O		19	.333
1951	NY	A	1		46	.206
1952	NY	A	1		15	.160
	DET	A	1-O		42	.217
		BLTL			1393	.296

HOPPER, C. F. "LEFTY"
B.RIDGEWOOD,N.J.

1898	BRO	N	P		2	0- 2
		TL				

HOPPER, JAMES MC DANIEL
B.SEPT.1,1919 CHARLOTTE,N.C.

1946	PIT	N	P		2	0- 1
		BRTR				

HOPPER, WILLIAM BOOTH
"BIRD DOG"
B.OCT.26,1890 JACKSON,TENN.
D.JAN.14,1965

1913	STL	N	P		3	0- 3
1914	STL	N	P		3	0- 0
1915	WAS	A	P		13	0- 1
		BRTR			19	0- 4

HORAN, JOHN J.
B.CHICAGO,ILL.

1884	CHI	U	P-O	11	20	3- 3
						.080

HORAN, JOSEPH PATRICK "SHAGS"
B.SEPT.6,1895 ST.LOUIS,MO.
D.FEB.13,1969 TORRANCE,CAL.

1924	NY	A	O		22	.290
		BRTR				

HORAZDOVSKY, ALBERT
(PLAYED UNDER NAME OF
ALBERT NELSON)

HORLEN, JOEL EDWARD "JOE"
B.AUG.14,1937 SAN ANTONIO,TEX.

1961	CHI	A	P		5	1- 3
1962	CHI	A	P		20	7- 6
1963	CHI	A	P		33	11- 7
1964	CHI	A	P		32	13- 9
1965	CHI	A	P		34	13-13
1966	CHI	A	P	37	64	10-13
1967	CHI	A	P	35	51	19- 7
1968	CHI	A	P	35	41	12-14
1969	CHI	A	P		36	13-16
1970	CHI	A	P		28	6-16
1971	CHI	A	P	34	36	8- 9
1972	OAK	A	P		32	3- 4
		BRTR		361	412	116-117

HORNE, BERLYN DALE "SONNY"
B.APR.12,1899 BACHMAN,OHIO

1929	CHI	N	P		11	1- 1
		BBTR				

HORNER, WILLIAM FRANK "JACK"
B.SEPT.21,1863 BALTIMORE,MD.
D.JULY 14,1910

1894	BAL	N	P		2	0- 1

HORNSBY, ROGERS "RAJAH"
B.APR.27,1896 WINTERS,TEX.
D.JAN.5,1963 CHICAGO,ILL.

1915	STL	N	S		18	.246
1916	STL	N	1-S-3		139	.313
1917	STL	N	S		145	.327
1918	STL	N	S-O		115	.281
1919	STL	N	1-2-S-3		138	.318
1920	STL	N	2		149	.370
1921	STL	N	2		154	.397
1922	STL	N	2		154	.401
1923	STL	N	1-2		107	.384
1924	STL	N	2		143	.424
1925	STL	N	M-2		138	.403
1926	STL	N	M-2		134	.317
1927	NY	N	2		155	.361
1928	BOS	N	M-2		140	.387
1929	CHI	N	2		156	.380
1930	CHI	N	M-2		42	.308
1931	CHI	N	M-2-3		100	.331
1932	CHI	N	M-O		19	.224
1933	STL	N	2		46	.325
	STL	A	M-H		11	.333
1934	STL	A	M-3-O		24	.304
1935	STL	A	M-1-2-3		10	.208
1936	STL	A	M-1		2	.400
1937	STL	A	M-2		20	.321
		BRTR			2259	.358

NON-PLAYING MANAGER
STL(A) 1952, CIN(N) 1952-53

HORNUNG, MICHAEL JOSEPH "UBBO"
B.JUNE 12,1857 CARTHAGE,N.Y.
D.OCT.30,1931

1879	BUF	N	O		78	.266
1880	BUF	N	P-1-	1	82	0- 0
			2-0			.262
1881	BOS	N	O		83	.240
1882	BOS	N	1-O		84	.301
1883	BOS	N	O		98	.278
1884	BOS	N	1-O		110	.266
1885	BOS	N	O		25	.201
1886	BOS	N	O		94	.257
1887	BOS	N	O		97	.299
1888	BOS	N	O		107	.239
1889	BAL	AA	O		135	.227
1890	NY	N	1-O		120	.238
		BRTP		1	1113	0- 0
						.259

HORSEY, HANSON
B.NOV.26,1889 GALENA,MD.
D.DEC.1,1949 MILLINGTON,MD.

1912	CIN	N	P		1	0- 0
		BRTR				

HORSTMAN, OSCAR THEODORE
B.APR.27,1892 ALMA,MO.

1917	STL	N	P		35	9- 4
1918	STL	N	P		9	0- 2
1919	STL	N	P		6	0- 1
		BRTR			50	9- 7

HORTON, ANTHONY DARRIN "TONY"
B.DEC.6,1944 SANTA MONICA,CAL.

1964	BOS	A	1-O		36	.222
1965	BOS	A	1		60	.294
1966	BOS	A	1		6	.136
1967	BOS	A	1		21	.308
	CLE	A	1		106	.281
1968	CLE	A	1		133	.249
1969	CLE	A	1		159	.278
1970	CLE	A	1		115	.269
		BRTR			636	.268

HORTON, ELMER E. "HERKY JERKY"
B.SEPT.4,1869 HAMILTON,OHIO

1896	PIT	N	P		3	0- 2
1898	BRO	N	P		1	0- 1
					4	0- 3

YR	CL	LEA	POS	GP	G	REC

HORTON, WILLIAM WATTISON "WILLIE"
B.OCT.18,1942 ARNO,VA.

YR	CL	LEA	POS	GP	G	REC
1963	DET	A	O		15	.326
1964	DET	A	O		25	.163
1965	DET	A	3-O		143	.273
1966	DET	A	O		146	.262
1967	DET	A	O		122	.274
1968	DET	A	O		143	.285
1969	DET	A	O		141	.262
1970	DET	A	O		96	.305
1971	DET	A	O		119	.289
1972	DET	A	O		108	.231
1973	DET	A	O		111	.316
1974	DET	A	O		72	.298
1975	DET	A	O		159	.275
1976	DET	A	D		114	.262
		BRTR			1514	.276

HOSKINS, DAVID TAYLOR "DAVE"
B.AUG.3,1925 GREENWOOD,MISS.
D.APR.2,1970 FLINT,MICH.

YR	CL	LEA	POS	GP	G	REC
1953	CLE	A	P	26	38	9- 3
1954	CLE	A	P	14	15	0- 1
		BLTR		40	53	9- 4

HOSLEY, TIMOTHY KENNETH "TIM"
B.MAY 10,1947 SPARTANBURG,S.C.

YR	CL	LEA	POS	GP	G	REC
1970	DET	A	C		7	.167
1971	DET	A	C-1		7	.188
1973	OAK	A	C		14	.267
1974	OAK	A	C-1		11	.286
1975	CHI	N	C		62	.255
1976	OAK	A	C		37	.164
	CHI	N	H		1	.000
		BRTR			139	.227

HOST, EUGENE EARL "GENE"
B.JAN.1,1933 LEEPER,PA.

YR	CL	LEA	POS	GP	G	REC
1956	DET	A	P	1		0- 0
1957	KC	A	P	11		0- 2
		BBTL		12		0- 2

HOSTETLER, CHARLES CLOYD
B.SEPT.2,1903 UNIONTOWN,PA.
D.FEB.18,1971 FORT COLLINS,COLO

YR	CL	LEA	POS	GP	G	REC
1944	DET	A	O		90	.298
1945	DET	A	O		42	.159
		BLTR			132	.278

HOSTETTER, ARTHUR
(ALSO PLAYED UNDER NAME OF
ARTHUR HOELSKOETTER)

HOTALING, PETER JAMES "MONKEY"
B.DEC.16,1856 MOHAWK,N.Y.
D.JULY 3,1928

YR	CL	LEA	POS	GP	G	REC
1879	CIN	N	C-2-3-O		80	.278
1880	CLE	N	O		77	.240
1881	WOR	N	C-O		76	.306
1882	BOS	N	O		83	.253
1883	CLE	N	O		97	.255
1884	CLE	N	2-O		101	.242
1885	BRO	AA	O		95	.277
1887	CLE	AA	O		127	.367
1888	CLE	AA	O		97	.250
		BRTR			833	.279

HOTTMAN, KENNETH ROGER "KEN"
B.MAY 7,1948 STOCKTON,CAL.

YR	CL	LEA	POS	GP	G	REC
1971	CHI	A	O		6	.125
		BRTR				

HOUCK, BYRON SIMON
B.AUG.28,1887 PROSPER,MINN.

YR	CL	LEA	POS	GP	G	REC
1912	PHI	A	P	30		8- 8
1913	PHI	A	P	40		15- 6
1914	PHI	A	P	3		0- 0
	BRO	F	P	17		2- 6
1918	STL	A	P	26		2- 4
		BRTR		116		27-24

HOUCK, STEPHEN ARNOLD DOUGLAS "SADIE"
B.1856 WASHINGTON,D.C.

YR	CL	LEA	POS	GP	G	REC
1879	BOS	N	S-O		80	.264
1880	BOS	N	O		12	.170
	PRO	N	O		48	.197
1881	DET	N	S		75	.279
1883	DET	N	S		98	.251
1884	ATH	AA	S		110	.302
1885	ATH	AA	S		92	.259
1886	BAL	AA	S		61	.203
	WAS	N	S		51	.215
1887	MET	AA	S		10	.222
		BRTR			637	.254

HOUGH, CHARLES OLIVER "CHARLIE"
B.JAN.5,1948 HONOLULU,HAWAII

YR	CL	LEA	POS	GP	G	REC
1970	LA	N	P		8	0- 0
1971	LA	N	P		4	0- 0
1972	LA	N	P		2	0- 0
1973	LA	N	P		37	4- 2
1974	LA	N	P		49	9- 4
1975	LA	N	P		38	3- 7
1976	LA	N	P		77	12- 8
		BRTR			215	28-21

HOUK, RALPH GEORGE "MAJOR"
B.AUG.9,1919 LAWRENCE,KAN.

YR	CL	LEA	POS	GP	G	REC
1947	NY	A	C		41	.272
1948	NY	A	C		14	.276
1949	NY	A	C		5	.571
1950	NY	A	C		10	.111
1951	NY	A	C		3	.200
1952	NY	A	C		9	.333
1953	NY	A	C		8	.222
1954	NY	A	H		1	.000
		BRTR			91	.272

NON-PLAYING MANAGER
NY(A) 1961-63, 66-73,
DET(A) 1974-76

HOUSE, HENRY FRANK "PIG"
B.FEB.18,1930 BESSEMER,ALA.

YR	CL	LEA	POS	GP	G	REC
1950	DET	A	C		5	.400
1951	DET	A	C		18	.220
1954	DET	A	C		114	.250
1955	DET	A	C		102	.259
1956	DET	A	C		94	.240
1957	DET	A	C		106	.259
1958	KC	A	C		76	.252
1959	KC	A	L		98	.236
1960	CIN	N	C		23	.179
1961	DET	A	C		17	.227
		BLTR			653	.248

HOUSE, PATRICK LORY "PAT"
B.SEP.1,1940 BOISE,IDAHO

YR	CL	LEA	POS	GP	G	REC
1967	HOU	N	P		6	1- 0
1968	HOU	N	P		18	1- 1
		BLTL			24	2- 1

HOUSE, THOMAS ROSS "TOM"
B.APR.29,1947 SEATTLE,WASH.

YR	CL	LEA	POS	GP	G	REC
1971	ATL	N	P		11	1- 0
1972	ATL	N	P		8	0- 0
1973	ATL	N	P		52	4- 2
1974	ATL	N	P		56	6- 2
1975	ATL	N	P		58	7- 7
1976	BOS	A	P		36	1- 3
		BLTL			221	19-14

HOUSE, WILLARD E.
B.OCT.3,1890 CABOOL,MO.
D.NOV.16,1923 KANSAS CITY,MO.

YR	CL	LEA	POS	GP	G	REC
1913	DET	A	P		19	1- 2
		BRTR				

HOUSEHOLDER, CHARLES F.
B.1856 HARRISBURG,PA.

YR	CL	LEA	POS	GP	G	REC
1884	CHI	U	P-S-	1	64	0- 0
			3-O			.232
	PIT	U	O	1	80	0- 0
						.270
						.240

HOUSEHOLDER, CHARLES W.
B.1856 HARRISBURG,PA.
D.DEC.26,1908

YR	CL	LEA	POS	GP	G	REC
1882	BAL	AA	C-1		73	.244
1884	BRO	AA	C-1		76	.242
		BLTR			149	.243

HOUSEHOLDER, EDWARD H.
B.OCT.12,1869 PITTSBURGH,PA.
D.JULY 3,1924

YR	CL	LEA	POS	GP	G	REC
1903	BRO	N	O		12	.209

HOUSEMAN, FRANK
B.BALTIMORE,MD.

YR	CL	LEA	POS	GP	G	REC
1886	BAL	AA	P		1	0- 1

HOUSEMAN, JOHN FRANKLIN
B.JAN.10,1870 HOLLAND,MICH.
D.NOV.4,1922

YR	CL	LEA	POS	GP	G	REC
1894	CHI	N	S		4	.353
1897	STL	N	2-O		76	.232
					80	.239

HOUSER, BENJAMIN FRANKLIN
B.NOV.30,1883 SHENANDOAH,PA.
D.JAN.15,1952

YR	CL	LEA	POS	GP	G	REC
1910	PHI	A	1		34	.189
1911	BOS	N	1		20	.254
1912	BOS	N	1		108	.286
		BLTL			162	.267

HOUSER, JOSEPH
B.1892 STEUBENVILLE,OHIO

YR	CL	LEA	POS	GP	G	REC
1914	BUF	F	P		8	0- 1
		BLTL				

HOUTTEMAN, ARTHUR JOSEPH "ART"
B.AUG.7,1927 DETROIT,MICH.

YR	CL	LEA	POS	GP	G	REC
1945	DET	A	P		13	0- 2
1946	DET	A	P		1	0- 1
1947	DET	A	P		23	7- 2
1948	DET	A	P		43	2-16
1949	DET	A	P	34	36	15-10
1950	DET	A	P		41	19-12
1952	DET	A	P	35	36	8-20
1953	DET	A	P		16	2- 6
	CLE	A	P	22	23	7- 7
1954	CLE	A	P		32	15- 7
1955	CLE	A	P		35	10- 6
1956	CLE	A	P	22	23	2- 2
1957	CLE	A	P		3	0- 0
	BAL	A	P		5	0- 0
		BRTR		325	330	87-91

HOUTZ, CHARLES
B.ST.LOUIS,MO.

YR	CL	LEA	POS	GP	G	REC
1875	RS	NA	1		19	-
1884	PIT	AA	1-O		9	.226
					28	-

HOUTZ, FRED FRITZ "LEFTY"
B.SEPT.4,1875 CONNERSVILLE,IND.

YR	CL	LEA	POS	GP	G	REC
1899	CIN	N	O		5	.176
		BLTL				

HOVLEY, STEPHEN EUGENE "STEVE"
B.DEC.18,1944 VENTURA,CAL.

YR	CL	LEA	POS	GP	G	REC
1969	SEA	A	O		91	.277
1970	MIL	A	O		40	.281
	OAK	A	O		72	.190
1971	OAK	A	O		24	.111
1972	KC	A	O		105	.270
1973	KC	A	O-O		104	.254
		BLTL			436	.258

HOVLIK, EDWARD C.
B.AUG.10,1891 CLEVELAND,OHIO
D.MAR.23,1955 PAINESVILLE,OHIO

YR	CL	LEA	POS	GP	G	REC
1919	WAS	A	P		3	0- 0
		BRTR			11	2- 1

HOVLIK, JOSEPH
B.AUG.16,1884 CZECHOSLOVAKIA
D.NOV.3,1951

YR	CL	LEA	POS	GP	G	REC
1909	WAS	A	P		3	0- 0
1910	WAS	A	P		1	0- 0
1911	CHI	A	P		12	2- 0
		BRTR			16	2- 0

HOWARD, BRUCE ERNEST
B.MAR.23,1943 SALISBURY,MD.

YR	CL	LEA	POS	GP	G	REC
1963	CHI	A	P		7	2- 1
1964	CHI	A	P		3	2- 1
1965	CHI	A	P		30	9- 8
1966	CHI	A	P		27	9- 5
1967	CHI	A	P		30	3-10
1968	BAL	A	P		10	0- 2
	WAS	A	P		13	1- 4
		BBTR			120	26-31

HOWARD, DAVID AUSTIN
B.MAY 1,1889 WASHINGTON,D.C.
D.JAN.26,1956

YR	CL	LEA	POS	GP	G	REC
1912	WAS	A	H		1	.000
1915	BRO	F	2		20	.222
		BRTR			21	.222

HOWARD, DOUGLAS LYNN "DOUG"
B.FEB.6,1948 SALT LAKE CITY,UTAH

YR	CL	LEA	POS	GP	G	REC
1972	CAL	A	1-3-O		11	.263
1973	CAL	A	1-3-O		8	.095
1974	CAL	A	1-O		22	.231
1975	STL	N	1		17	.207
1976	CLE	A	1-O		39	.211
		BRTR			97	.212

YR	CL	LEA	POS	GP	G	REC

HOWARD, EARL N.
B.JUNE 25,1896 EVERTTT,PA.
D.APR.1937

YR	CL	LEA	POS	GP	G	REC
1918	STL	N	P		1	0- 0
		TR				

HOWARD, ELSTON GENE
B.FEB.23,1929 ST.LOUIS,MO.

YR	CL	LEA	POS	G	REC
1955	NY	A	C-O	97	.290
1956	NY	A	C-O	98	.262
1957	NY	A	C-1-O	110	.253
1958	NY	A	C-1-O	103	.314
1959	NY	A	C-1-O	125	.273
1960	NY	A	C-O	107	.245
1961	NY	A	C-1	129	.348
1962	NY	A	C	136	.279
1963	NY	A	C	135	.287
1964	NY	A	C	150	.313
1965	NY	A	C-1-O	110	.233
1966	NY	A	C-1	126	.256
1967	NY	A	C-1	66	.196
	BOS	A	C	42	.147
1968	BOS	A	C	71	.241
		BRTR		1605	.274

HOWARD, FRANK OLIVER
B.AUG.8,1936 COLUMBUS,OHIO

YR	CL	LEA	POS	G	REC
1958	LA	N	O	8	.241
1959	LA	N	O	9	.143
1960	LA	N	1-O	117	.268
1961	LA	N	1-O	92	.296
1962	LA	N	O	141	.296
1963	LA	N	O	123	.273
1964	LA	N	O	134	.226
1965	WAS	A	O	149	.289
1966	WAS	A	O	146	.278
1967	WAS	A	1-O	149	.256
1968	WAS	A	1-O	158	.274
1969	WAS	A	1-O	161	.296
1970	WAS	A	1-O	161	.283
1971	WAS	A	1-O	153	.279
1972	TEX	A	1-O	95	.244
	DET	A	1-O	14	.242
1973	DET	A	1-O	85	.256
		BRTR		1895	.273

HOWARD, GEORGE ELMER "DEL"
B.DEC.24,1880 KENNEY,ILL.
D.DEC.24,1956

YR	CL	LEA	POS	G	REC
1905	PIT	N	1-O	119	.292
1906	BOS	N	2-O	147	.261
1907	BOS	N	O	48	.273
	CHI	N	1-O	41	.230
1908	CHI	N	1-O	89	.279
1909	CHI	N	1	57	.197
		BLTR		501	.262

HOWARD, IVAN CHESTER
B.OCT.12,1882 KENNEY,ILL.
D.MAR.30,1967 MEDFORD,ORE.

YR	CL	LEA	POS	G	REC
1914	STL	A	1-3	81	.244
1915	STL	A	1-3-O	113	.278
1916	CLE	A	2	81	.187
1917	CLE	A	3	27	.102
		BBTR		302	.233

HOWARD, LAWRENCE RAYFORD "LARRY"
B.JUNE 6,1945 COLUMBUS,OHIO

YR	CL	LEA	POS	G	REC
1970	HOU	N	C-1-O	31	.307
1971	HOU	N	C	24	.234
1972	HOU	N	C-O	54	.223
1973	HOU	N	C	20	.167
	ATL	N	C	4	.125
		BRTR		133	.236

HOWARD, LEE VINCENT
B.NOV.11,1923 STATEN ISLAND,N.Y
DECEASED

YR	CL	LEA	POS	G	REC
1946	PIT	N	P	3	0- 1
1947	PIT	N	P	2	0- 0
		BLTL		5	0- 1

HOWARD, PAUL JOSEPH
B.MAY 20,1884 BOSTON,MASS.

YR	CL	LEA	POS	G	REC
1909	BOS	A	O	6	.230
		BRTR			

HOWARD, WILBUR LEON
B.JAN.8,1949 LOWELL,N.C.

YR	CL	LEA	POS	G	REC
1973	MIL	A	O	16	.205
1974	HOU	N	O	64	.216
1975	HOU	N	O	121	.283
1976	HOU	N	2-O	94	.220
		BBTR		295	.252

HOWARTH, JAMES EUGENE "JIMMY"
B.MAR.7,1947 BILOXI,MISS.

YR	CL	LEA	POS	G	REC
1971	SF	N	O	7	.231
1972	SF	N	1-O	74	.235
1973	SF	N	1-O	65	.200
1974	SF	N	O	6	.000
		BLTL		152	.217

HOWE, ARTHUR HENRY "ART"
B.DEC.15,1946 PITTSBURGH,PA.

YR	CL	LEA	POS	G	REC
1974	PIT	N	S-3	29	.243
1975	PIT	N	S-3	63	.171
1976	HOU	N	2-3	21	.138
		BRTR		113	.189

HOWE, CALVIN EARL
B.NOV.27,1925 ROCK FALLS,ILL.

YR	CL	LEA	POS	G	REC
1952	CHI	N	P	1	0- 0
		BLTL			

HOWE, JOHN "SHORTY"
B.NEW YORK,N.Y.

YR	CL	LEA	POS	G	REC
1890	NY	N	2	17	.172
1893	NY	N	3	1	.500
				18	.203

HOWE, LESTER CURTIS
B.AUG.24,1895 BROOKLYN,N.Y.

YR	CL	LEA	POS	G	REC
1923	BOS	A	P	13	1- 0
1924	BOS	A	P	4	1- 0
		BRTR		17	2- 0

HOWELL, HENRY "HARRY"
B.NOV.14,1876 NEW JERSEY
D.MAY 22,1956

YR	CL	LEA	POS	GP	G	REC
1898	BRO	N	P		2	2- 0
1899	BAL	N	P		28	14- 7
1900	BRO	N	P		21	6- 3
1901	BAL	A	P	38	54	14-21
1902	BAL	A	P-1-	25	96	9-14
			2-S-3-O			.266
1903	NY	A	P	26	41	10- 7
1904	STL	A	P	34	35	13-21
1905	STL	A	P	38	41	14-21
1906	STL	A	P		36	15-13
1907	STL	A	P	42	44	16-15
1908	STL	A	P	40	41	18-18
1909	STL	A	P	10	18	1- 1
1910	STL	A	P		1	0- 0
		BRTR		341	458	132-141
						.217

HOWELL, HOMER ELLIOTT "DIXIE"
B.APR.24,1919 LOUISVILLE,KY.

YR	CL	LEA	POS	G	REC
1947	PIT	N	C	76	.276
1949	CIN	N	C	64	.244
1950	CIN	N	C	82	.223
1951	CIN	N	C	77	.251
1952	CIN	N	C	17	.189
1953	BRO	N	H	1	.000
1955	BRO	N	C	16	.262
1956	BRO	N	C	7	.231
		BRTR		340	.246

HOWELL, MILLARD FILLMORE "DIXIE"
B.JAN.7,1920 BOWMAN,KY.
D.MAR.18,1960

YR	CL	LEA	POS	GP	G	REC
1940	CHI	A	P		3	0- 0
1949	CIN	N	P	5	9	0- 1
1955	CHI	A	P		35	8- 3
1956	CHI	A	P		34	5- 6
1957	CHI	A	P	37	42	6- 5
1958	CHI	A	P		1	0- 0
		BLTR		115	124	19-15

HOWELL, MURRAY DONALD "RED"
B.JAN.29,1909 ATLANTA,GA.
D.OCT.1,1950

YR	CL	LEA	POS	G	REC
1941	CLE	A	H	11	.286
		BRTR			

HOWELL, ROLAND BOATNER
B.JAN.3,1892 NAPOLEONVILLE,LA.

YR	CL	LEA	POS	G	REC
1912	STL	N	P	3	0- 0

HOWELL, ROY LEE
B.DEC.18,1953 LOMPOC,CAL.

YR	CL	LEA	POS	G	REC
1974	TEX	A	3	13	.250
1975	TEX	A	3	125	.251
1976	TEX	A	3	140	.253
		BLTR		278	.252

HOWERTON, WILLIAM RAY "BILL"
B.DEC.12,1921 LOMPOC,CAL.

YR	CL	LEA	POS	G	REC
1949	STL	N	O	9	.308
1950	STL	N	O	110	.281
1951	STL	N	O	24	.262
1951	PIT	N	3-O	80	.274
1952	PIT	N	P	13	.320
	NY	N	O	11	.067
		BLTR		247	.274

HOWLEY, DANIEL PHILIP "HOWLING DAN"
B.OCT.16,1885 E.WEYMOUTH,MASS.
D.MAR.10,1944

YR	CL	LEA	POS	G	REC
1913	PHI	N	C	26	.125
		TR			

NON-PLAYING MANAGER
STL(A) 1927-29, CIN(N) 1930-32

HOWSER, RICHARD DALTON "DICK"
B.MAY 14,1937 MIAMI,FLA.

YR	CL	LEA	POS	G	REC
1961	KC	A	S	158	.280
1962	KC	A	S	83	.238
1963	KC	A	S	15	.195
	CLE	A	S	49	.247
1964	CLE	A	S	162	.256
1965	CLE	A	2-S	107	.235
1966	CLE	A	2-S	67	.229
1967	NY	A	2-S-3	63	.268
1968	NY	A	2-S-3	85	.153
		BRTR		789	.248

HOY, WILLIAM ELLSWORTH "DUMMY"
B.MAY 23,1862 HOUCKSTOWN,OHIO
D.DEC.15,1961 CINCINNATI,OHIO

YR	CL	LEA	POS	G	REC
1888	WAS	N	O	136	.274
1889	WAS	N	O	127	.282
1890	BUF	P	O	122	.299
1891	STL	AA	O	139	.288
1892	WAS	N	O	149	.279
1893	WAS	N	O	130	.259
1894	CIN	N	O	128	.312
1895	CIN	N	O	107	.274
1896	CIN	N	O	121	.296
1897	CIN	N	O	128	.290
1898	LOU	N	O	148	.318
1899	LOU	N	O	155	.306
1901	LOU	A	O	130	.293
1902	CHI	A	O	72	.294
		BLTR		1792	.291

HOYLE, ROLAND EDISON "TEX"
B.JULY 17,1923 CARBONDALE,PA.

YR	CL	LEA	POS	G	REC
1952	PHI	A	P	3	0- 0
		BRTR			

HOYOT, FREDERICK
(PLAYED UNDER NAME OF
FRED JOHN IOTT)

HOYT, WAITE CHARLES "SCHOOLBOY"
B.SEPT.9,1899 BROOKLYN,N.Y.

YR	CL	LEA	POS	G	REC
1918	NY	N	P	1	0- 0
1919	BOS	A	P	13	4- 6
1920	BOS	A	P	22	6- 6
1921	NY	A	P	43	19-13
1922	NY	A	P	37	19-12
1923	NY	A	P	37	17- 9
1924	NY	A	P	46	18-13
1925	NY	A	P	46	11-14
1926	NY	A	P	39	16-12
1927	NY	A	P	36	22- 7
1928	NY	A	P	42	23- 7
1929	NY	A	P	30	10- 9
1930	NY	A	P	8	2- 2
	DET	A	P	26	9- 8
1931	DET	A	P	16	3- 8
	PHI	A	P	16	10- 5
1932	BRO	N	P	8	1- 3
	NY	N	P	18	5- 7
1933	PIT	N	P	36	5- 7
1934	PIT	N	P	48	15- 6
1935	PIT	N	P	39	7-11
1936	PIT	N	P	22	7- 5
1937	PIT	N	P	11	1- 2
	BRO	N	P	27	7- 7
1938	BRO	N	P	6	0- 3
		BRTR		673	237-182

YR	CL	LEA	POS	GP	G	REC

HRABOSKY, ALAN THOMAS "AL"
B.JULY 21,1949 OAKLAND,CAL.

YR	CL	LEA	POS	GP	G	REC
1970	STL	N	P		16	2- 1
1971	STL	N	P		1	0- 0
1972	STL	N	P		5	1- 0
1973	STL	N	P		44	2- 4
1974	STL	N	P	65	66	8- 1
1975	STL	N	P		65	13- 3
1976	STL	N	P		68	8- 6
	BRTL			264	265	34-15

HRINIAK, WALTER JOHN "WALT"
B.MAY 22,1943 NATICK,MASS.

1968	ATL	N	C		9	.346
1969	ATL	N	C		7	.143
	SD	N	C		31	.227
	BLTR				47	.253

HUBBARD, ALLEN
B.DEC.9,1860 WESTFIELD,MASS.
D.DEC.14,1930

1883	ATH	AA	C-S		2	.286

HUBBELL, CARL OWEN "KING CARL"
OR "THE MEAL TICKET"
B.JUNE 22,1903 CARTHAGE,MO.

1928	NY	N	P		20	10- 6
1929	NY	N	P		39	18-11
1930	NY	N	P		37	17-12
1931	NY	N	P		36	14-12
1932	NY	N	P		40	18-11
1933	NY	N	P		45	23-12
1934	NY	N	P		49	21-12
1935	NY	N	P		42	23-12
1936	NY	N	P		42	26- 6
1937	NY	N	P		39	22- 8
1938	NY	N	P		24	13-10
1939	NY	N	P		29	11- 9
1940	NY	N	P		31	11-12
1941	NY	N	P		26	11- 9
1942	NY	N	P		24	11- 8
1943	NY	N	P		12	4- 4
	BRTL			535	253-154
	BB 1928-29,		31-32

HUBBELL, WILBERT WILLIAM
B.JUNE 17,1897 HENDERSON,COLD.

1919	NY	N	P		2	1- 1
1920	NY	N	P		14	0- 1
	PHI	N	P		24	9- 9
1921	PHI	N	P		36	9-16
1922	PHI	N	P		35	7-15
1923	PHI	N	P	22	23	1- 6
1924	PHI	N	P		36	10- 9
1925	PHI	N	P		2	0- 0
	BRO	N	P		33	3- 6
	BRTR			204	205	40-63

HUBBS, KENNETH DOUGLASS "KEN"
B.DEC.23,1941 RIVERSIDE,CAL.
D.FEB.15,1964 PROVO,UTAH

1961	CHI	N	2		10	.179
1962	CHI	N	2		160	.260
1963	CHI	N	2		154	.235
	BRTR				324	.247

HUBER, CLARENCE BILL
B.OCT.27,1897 TYLER,TEX.
D.FEB.22,1965 LAREDO,TEX.

1920	DET	A	3		10	.205
1921	DET	A	3		1	.000
1925	PHI	N	3		124	.284
1926	PHI	N	3		118	.245
	BRTR				253	.266

HUBER, OTTO
B.MAR.12,1917 GARFIELD,N.J.

1939	BOS	N	2-3		11	.273
	BRTR					

HUCKLEBERRY, EARL EUGENE
B.MAY 23,1910 KONAWA,OKLA.

1935	PHI	A	P		1	1- 0
	BRTR					

HUDGENS, JAMES PRICE
B.AUG.24,1902 NEWBURG,MO.

1923	STL	N	1-2		6	.250
1925	CIN	N	1		3	.429
1926	CIN	N	1		17	.250
	BLTR				26	.282

HUDLIN, GEORGE WILLIS "ACE"
B.MAY 23,1906 WAGONER,OKLA.

1926	CLE	A	P		8	1- 3
1927	CLE	A	P		43	18-12
1928	CLE	A	P		42	14-14
1929	CLE	A	P		40	17-15
1930	CLE	A	P		37	13-15
1931	CLE	A	P		44	15-14
1932	CLE	A	P		33	12- 8
1933	CLE	A	P		34	5-13
1934	CLE	A	P		36	15-10
1935	CLE	A	P	36	37	15-11
1936	CLE	A	P		27	1- 5
1937	CLE	A	P		35	12-11
1938	CLE	A	P		29	8- 8
1939	CLE	A	P		27	9-10
1940	CLE	A	P		4	2- 1
	WAS	A	P		8	1- 2
	STL	A	P		6	0- 1
	NY	N	P		1	0- 1
1944	STL	A	P		1	0- 1
	BRTR			491	492	158-156

HUDSON, CHARLES "CHARLIE"
B.AUG.18,1949 ADA,OKLA.

1972	STL	N	P		12	1- 0
1973	TEX	A	P		25	4- 2
1975	CAL	A	P		3	0- 1
	BLTL				40	5- 3

HUDSON, HAL CAMPBELL "BUD"
B.MAY 4,1927 GROSSE POINT,MICH.

1952	STL	A	P		3	0- 0
	CHI	A	P		2	0- 0
1953	CHI	A	P		1	0- 0
	BLTL				6	0- 0

HUDSON, JESSE JAMES
B.JULY 22,1948 MASEFIELD,LA.

1969	NY	N	P		1	0- 0
	BLTL					

HUDSON, JOHN WILSON "MR. CHIPS"
B.JUNE 30,1912 BRYAN,TEX.
D.NOV.7,1970 BRYAN,TEX.

1936	BRO	N	S		6	.167
1937	BRO	N	S		13	.185
1938	BRO	N	2		135	.261
1939	BRO	N	2-S		109	.254
1940	BRO	N	2-S-3		85	.218
1941	CHI	N	2-S-3		50	.202
1945	NY	N	2-3		28	.000
	BRTR				426	.242

HUDSON, NATHANIEL P.
B.JAN.12,1859 CHICAGO,ILL.
D.MAR.14,1928

1886	STL	AA	P	29	40	16-13
1887	STL	AA	P	8	13	3- 5
1888	STL	AA	P	37	55	26-10
1889	STL	AA	P-O	4	13	2- 2
						.245
	TR			78	121	47-30
						.255

HUDSON, REX HAUGHTON
B.AUG.11,1953 TULSA,OKLA.

1974	LA	N	P		1	0- 0
	BBTR					

HUDSON, SIDNEY CHARLES "SID"
B.JAN.3,1917 OLIVER SPRINGS,
TENN.

1940	WAS	A	P		38	17-16
1941	WAS	A	P		33	13-14
1942	WAS	A	P	35	36	10-17
1946	WAS	A	P		31	8-11
1947	WAS	A	P		20	6- 9
1948	WAS	A	P		39	4-16
1949	WAS	A	P		40	8-17
1950	WAS	A	P	30	31	14-14
1951	WAS	A	P	23	24	5-12
1952	WAS	A	P		7	3- 4
	BOS	A	P		21	7- 9
1953	BOS	A	P		30	6- 9
1954	BOS	A	P		33	3- 4
	BRTR			380	383	104-152

HUELSMAN, FRANK ELMER
B.JUNE 5,1874 ST.LOUIS,MO.
D.JUNE 9,1959

1897	STL	N	S		2	.286
1904	CHI	A	O		3	.167
	DET	A	O		4	.333
	CHI	A	H		1	.000
	STL	A	O		20	.221
	WAS	A	O		84	.241
1905	WAS	A	O		121	.271
	BRTR				235	.256

HUENKE, ALBERT JOHN
B.JUNE 26,1891 NEW BREMEN,OHIO

1914	NY	N	P		1	0- 0
	BRTR					

HUFF, GEORGE A. "GEE"
B.JUNE 11,1872 CAHMPAIGN,ILL.
D.OCT.1,1936 CHAMPAIGN,ILL.
NON-PLAYING MANAGER BOS(A) 1907

HUFFMAN, BENJAMIN FRANKLIN
B.JUNE 29,1914 RILEYVILLE,VA.

1937	STL	A	C		76	.273
	BLTR					

HUG, EDWARD AMBROSE
B.JULY 14,1880 FAYETTEVILLE,O.
D.MAY 11,1953

1903	BRO	N	C		1	.000
	BRTR					

HUGGINS, MILLER JAMES
B.MAR.27,1879 CINCINNATI,OHIO
D.SEPT.25,1929 NEW YORK,N.Y.

1904	CIN	N	2		140	.263
1905	CIN	N	2		149	.273
1906	CIN	N	2		146	.292
1907	CIN	N	2		156	.248
1908	CIN	N	2		135	.239
1909	CIN	N	2-3		46	.213
1910	STL	N	2		151	.265
1911	STL	N	2		136	.261
1912	STL	N	2		120	.304
1913	STL	N	M-2		121	.285
1914	STL	N	M-2		148	.263
1915	STL	N	M-2		107	.241
1916	STL	N	M-2		18	.333
	BBTR			1573	.265

NON-PLAYING MANAGER
STL(N) 1917, NY(A) 1918-29

HUGHES, EDWARD

1902	CHI	N	O		1	.000

HUGHES, EDWARD
B.CHICAGO,ILL.

1902	CHI	A	C		1	.250
	TR					

HUGHES, EDWARD H.
B.1880 CHICAGO,ILL.

1905	BOS	A	P		6	3- 0
1906	BOS	A	P		2	0- 0
					8	3- 0

HUGHES, JAMES JAY
B.JAN.22,1874 SACRAMENTO,CAL.
D.JUNE 2,1924

1898	BAL	N	P	35	49	21-11
1899	BRO	N	P		35	25- 5
1901	BRO	N	P		30	17-12
1902	BRO	N	P-O		29	15-11
						.202
				129	143	78-39
						.223

HUGHES, JAMES MICHAEL "JIM"
B.AUG.11,1951 LOS ANGELES,CAL.

1974	MIN	A	P		2	0- 2
1975	MIN	A	P		37	16-14
1976	MIN	A	P		37	9-14
	BRTR				76	25-30

HUGHES, JAMES ROBERT "JIM"
B.MAR.21,1923 CHICAGO,ILL.

1952	BRO	N	P		6	2- 1
1953	BRO	N	P		48	4- 3
1954	BRO	N	P		60	8- 4
1955	BRO	N	P		24	0- 2
1956	BRO	N	P		5	0- 0
	CHI	N	P		25	1- 3
1957	CHI	A	P		4	0- 0
	BRTR				172	15-13

HUGHES, MICHAEL F.
B.OCT.25,1866 NEW YORK,N.Y.
D.APR.10,1931

YR	CL	LEA	POS	GP	G	REC
1888	BRO	AA	P		39	25-13
1889	BRO	AA	P		19	10- 6
1890	BRO	AA	P		8	3- 5
	ATH	AA	P		6	1- 5
	TR				72	39-29

HUGHES, RICHARD HENRY "DICK"
B.FEB.13,1938 STEPHENS,ARK.

YR	CL	LEA	POS	GP	G	REC
1966	STL	N	P		6	2- 1
1967	STL	N	P	37	40	16- 6
1968	STL	N	P		25	2- 2
	BRTR			68	71	20- 9

HUGHES, ROY JOHN "JEEP"
B.JAN.11,1911 CINCINNATI,OHIO

YR	CL	LEA	POS	GP	G	REC
1935	CLE	A	2-S-3		82	.293
1936	CLE	A	2		152	.295
1937	CLE	A	2-3		104	.277
1938	STL	A	2		58	.281
1939	SYL	A	2-S		17	.087
	PHI	N	2		65	.228
1940	PHI	N	2		1	.000
1944	CHI	N	5-3		126	.287
1945	CHI	N	1-2-5-3		69	.261
1946	PHI	N	1-2-5-3		89	.236
	BRTR				763	.273

HUGHES, TERRY WAYNE
B.MAY 13,1949 SPARTANBURG,S.C.

YR	CL	LEA	POS	GP	G	REC
1970	CHI	N	3-0		2	.333
1973	STL	N	1-3		11	.214
1974	BOS	A	3		41	.203
	BRTR				13	.235
	BRTR				54	.209

HUGHES, THOMAS EDWARD
B.SEPT.13,1934 AMCAN,C.Z.,PAN.

YR	CL	LEA	POS	GP	G	REC
1959	STL	N	P		2	0- 2
	BLTR					

HUGHES, THOMAS FRANKLIN
B.AUG.6,1907 EMMET,ARK.

YR	CL	LEA	POS	GP	G	REC
1930	DET	A	O		17	.373
	BLTR					

HUGHES, THOMAS JAMES "LONG TOM"
B.NOV.26,1878 CHICAGO,ILL.
D.FEB.8,1956

YR	CL	LEA	POS	GP	G	REC
1900	CHI	N	P		3	1- 1
1901	CHI	N	P		33	10-23
1902	BAL	A	P		15	7- 8
	BOS	A	P		8	2- 4
1903	BOS	A	P		32	21- 7
1904	NY	A	P		23	7-11
	WAS	A	P		16	2-14
1905	WAS	A	P		39	16-16
1906	WAS	A	P		30	7-17
1907	WAS	A	P	34	36	7-13
1908	WAS	A	P		43	18-15
1909	WAS	A	P		22	4- 8
1911	WAS	A	P		34	11-17
1912	WAS	A	P		31	13-10
1913	WAS	A	P		36	4-12
	TR			399	401	130-176

HUGHES, THOMAS L. "SALIDA TOM"
B.JAN.28,1885 COAL CREEK,COLO.
D.NOV.1,1961

YR	CL	LEA	POS	GP	G	REC
1906	NY	A	P		3	0- 0
1907	NY	A	P		3	2- 1
1909	NY	A	P		25	7- 8
1910	NY	A	P		23	7- 9
1914	BOS	N	P		2	1- 0
1915	BOS	N	P		50	16-14
1916	BOS	N	P		40	16- 3
1917	BOS	N	P	11	13	5- 3
1918	BOS	N	P		3	0- 2
	BRTR			160	162	54-40

HUGHES, THOMAS OWEN
B.OCT.7,1919 WILKES-BARRE,PA.

YR	CL	LEA	POS	GP	G	REC
1941	PHI	N	P	34	37	9-14
1942	PHI	N	P	40	42	12-18
1946	PHI	N	P		29	6- 9
1947	PHI	N	P	29	32	4-11
1948	CIN	N	P		12	0- 4
	BRTR			144	152	31-56

HUGHES, VERNON ALEXANDER
B.APR.15,1893 ETNA,PA.
D.DEC.26,1961

YR	CL	LEA	POS	GP	G	REC
1914	BAL	F	P		3	0- 0
	BLTL					

HUGHES, WILLIAM NESBERT
B.NOV.18,1897 PHILADELPHIA,PA.
D.FEB.25,1963 BIRMINGHAM,ALA.

YR	CL	LEA	POS	GP	G	REC
1921	PIT	N	P		1	0- 0
	BRTR					

HUGHES, WILLIAM R.
B.NOV.25,1866 BLADENSVILLE,ILL.
D.AUG.25,1943 SANTA ANA,CAL.

YR	CL	LEA	POS	GP	G	REC
1884	WAS	U	1-0		14	.122
1885	ATH	AA	P-O	2	4	0- 2
						.188
				2	18	0- 2
						.138

HUGHEY, JAMES ULYSSES "COLDWATER JIM"
B.MAR.8,1869 WAKASHMA,MICH.
D.MAR.29,1945 COLDWATER,MICH.

YR	CL	LEA	POS	GP	G	REC
1891	MIL	AA	P		2	1- 1
1893	CHI	N	P		1	0- 1
1896	PIT	N	P		21	6- 8
1897	PIT	N	P		20	6-13
1898	STL	N	P		34	7-24
1899	CLE	N	P		35	4-29
1900	STL	N	P		20	5- 8
	TR				133	29-84

HUGHSON, CECIL CARLTON "TEX"
B.FEB.9,1916 KYLE,TEX.

YR	CL	LEA	POS	GP	G	REC
1941	BOS	A	P		12	5- 3
1942	BOS	A	P		38	22- 6
1943	BOS	A	P		35	12-15
1944	BOS	A	P		28	18- 5
1946	BOS	A	P		39	20-11
1947	BOS	A	P		29	12-11
1948	BOS	A	P		15	3- 1
1949	BOS	A	P		29	4- 2
	BRTR				225	96-54

HUGHSON, GEORGE H.
B.AUG.1,1834 ERIE CO.,N.Y.
D.AUG.22,1912
NON-PLAYING MANAGER BUF(N) 1885

HUHN, EMIL HUGO
B.MAR.10,1892 NORTH VERNON,IND.
D.SEPT.5,1925

YR	CL	LEA	POS	GP	G	REC
1915	NEW	F	C-1		124	.227
1916	CIN	N	C-1-O		37	.255
1917	CIN	N	C-1		23	.196
	BRTR				184	.229

HULEN, WILLIAM FRANKLIN
B.MAR.12,1869 DIXON,CAL.
D.OCT.2,1947

YR	CL	LEA	POS	GP	G	REC
1896	PHI	N	S		85	.268
1899	WAS	N	S		19	.147
	TL				104	.248

HULIHAN, HARRY JOSEPH
B.APR.18,1899 RUTLAND,VT.

YR	CL	LEA	POS	GP	G	REC
1922	BOS	N	P		7	2- 3
	BRTL					

HULSWITT, RUDOLPH EDWARD
B.FEB.23,1877 NEWPORT,KY.
D.JAN.16,1950

YR	CL	LEA	POS	GP	G	REC
1899	LOU	N	S		1	.000
1902	PHI	N	S-3		128	.272
1903	PHI	N	S		138	.247
1904	PHI	N	S		113	.244
1908	CIN	N	S		119	.228
1909	STL	N	S		77	.280
1910	STL	N	S		32	.248
	BRTR				608	.253

HULVEY, JAMES HENSEL "HANK"
B.JULY 18,1898 MT.SIDNEY,VA.

YR	CL	LEA	POS	GP	G	REC
1923	PHI	A	P		1	0- 1
	BBTR					

HUMMEL, JOHN EDWIN "SILENT JOHN"
B.APR.4,1883 BLOOMSBURG,PA.
D.MAY 18,1959

YR	CL	LEA	POS	GP	G	REC
1905	BRO	N	2		30	.266
1906	BRO	N	1-2-O		86	.199
1907	BRO	N	2-O		97	.234
1908	BRO	N	2-O		154	.241
1909	BRO	N	1-2-S-O		145	.280
1910	BRO	N	2		153	.244
1911	BRO	N	2		133	.270
1912	BRO	N	2-O		122	.282
1913	BRO	N	S-O		67	.242
1914	BRO	N	1-O		73	.264
1915	BRO	N	O		53	.230
1918	NY	A	O		22	.295
	BRTR				1135	.254

HUMPHERIES, ALBERT "BERT"
B.SEPT.21,1880 CALIFORNIA,PA.
D.SEPT.21,1945

YR	CL	LEA	POS	GP	G	REC
1910	PHI	N	P		5	0- 0
1911	PHI	N	P		11	3- 3
	CIN	N	P		14	4- 1
1912	CIN	N	P		30	9-11
1913	CHI	N	P		28	16- 4
1914	CHI	N	P	34	35	10-11
1915	CHI	N	P		31	8-13
				153	154	50-43

HUMPHREY, ALFRED W.
B.FEB.28,1886 ASHTABULA,OHIO
D.MAY 13,1961

YR	CL	LEA	POS	GP	G	REC
1911	BRO	N	O		8	.143
	BLTR					

HUMPHREY, TERRYAL GENE "TERRY"
B.AUG.4,1949 CHICKASHA,OKLA.

YR	CL	LEA	POS	GP	G	REC
1971	MON	N	C		9	.192
1972	MON	N	C		69	.186
1973	MON	N	C		43	.167
1974	MON	N	C		20	.192
1975	DET	A	C		18	.244
1976	CAL	A	C		71	.245
	BRTR				230	.206

HUMPHREYS, ROBERT WILLIAM "BOB"
B.AUG.18,1935 COVINGTON,VA.

YR	CL	LEA	POS	GP	G	REC
1962	DET	A	P		4	0- 1
1963	STL	N	P		9	0- 1
1964	STL	N	P		28	2- 0
1965	CHI	N	P		41	2- 0
1966	WAS	A	P		58	7- 3
1967	WAS	A	P		48	6- 2
1968	WAS	A	P		56	5- 7
1969	WAS	A	P		47	3- 3
1970	WAS	A	P		5	0- 0
	MIL	A	P		23	2- 4
	BRTR				319	27-21

HUMPHREYS, WILLIAM BYRON
B.JUNE 17,1911 VIENNA,MO.

YR	CL	LEA	POS	GP	G	REC
1936	BOS	A	P		2	0- 0
	BRTR					

HUMPHRIES, JOHN HENRY
B.NOV.12,1861 N.GOWER,ONT.,CAN.
D.NOV.29,1933

YR	CL	LEA	POS	GP	G	REC
1883	NY	N	C-O		26	.117
1884	WAS	AA	C-O		48	.178
	NY	N	C		19	.093
	TL				93	.146

HUMPHRIES, JOHN WILLIAM "JOHNNY"
B.JUNE 23,1915 CLIFTON FORGE,VA
D.JUNE 24,1965 NEW ORLEANS,LA.

YR	CL	LEA	POS	GP	G	REC
1938	CLE	A	P		45	9- 8
1939	CLE	A	P		15	2- 4
1940	CLE	A	P		19	0- 2
1941	CHI	A	P		14	4- 2
1942	CHI	A	P		28	12-12
1943	CHI	A	P		28	11-11
1944	CHI	A	P		30	8-10
1945	CHI	A	P		22	6-14
1946	PHI	N	P		10	0- 0
	BRTR				211	52-63

YR	CL	LEA	POS	GP	G	REC

HUNDLEY, CECIL RANDOLPH "RANDY"
B.JUNE 1,1942 MARTINSVILLE,VA.

YR	CL	LEA	POS	GP	G	REC
1964	SF	N	C		2	.000
1965	SF	N	C		6	.067
1966	CHI	N	C		149	.236
1967	CHI	N	C		152	.267
1968	CHI	N	C		160	.226
1969	CHI	N	C		151	.255
1970	CHI	N	C		73	.244
1971	CHI	N	C		9	.333
1972	CHI	N	C		114	.218
1973	CHI	N	C		124	.226
1974	MIN	A	C		32	.193
1975	SD	N	C		74	.206
1976	CHI	N	C		13	.167
		BRTR			1059	.236

HUNGLING, BERNARD HERMAN "BUN"
B.MAR.5,1896 DAYTON,OHIO
D.MAR.30,1968 DAYTON,OHIO

YR	CL	LEA	POS	GP	G	REC
1922	BRO	N	C		39	.255
1923	BRO	N	C		2	.000
1930	STL	A	C		10	.323
		BRTR			51	.241

HUNNEFIELD, WILLIAM FENTON "WILD BILL"
B.JAN.5,1899 DEDHAM,MASS.

YR	CL	LEA	POS	GP	G	REC
1926	CHI	A	2-S-3		131	.274
1927	CHI	A	2-S		112	.285
1928	CHI	A	2		94	.294
1929	CHI	A	2		47	.181
1930	CHI	A	S		31	.272
1931	CLE	A	S		21	.239
	BOS	N	2		11	.286
	NY	N	2		64	.270
		BBTR			511	.272

HUNT, BENJAMIN FRANKLIN "HIGH POCKETS"
B.1888 EUFAULA,OKLA.

YR	CL	LEA	POS	GP	G	REC
1910	BOS	A	P	7	2- 4	
1913	STL	N	P	2	0- 1	
		BLTL		9	2- 5	

HUNT, KENNETH LAWRENCE "KEN"
B.JULY 13,1934 GRAND FORKS,N.DAK

YR	CL	LEA	POS	GP	G	REC
1959	NY	A	O		6	.333
1960	NY	A	O		25	.273
1961	LA	A	2-O		149	.255
1962	LA	A	1		13	.182
1963	LA	A	O		59	.183
	WAS	A	O		7	.200
1964	WAS	A	O		51	.135
		BRTR			310	.226

HUNT, KENNETH RAYMOND
D.DEC.14,1938 OGDEN,UTAH

YR	CL	LEA	POS	GP	G	REC
1961	CIN	N	P	29	9-10	
		BRTR				

HUNT, OLIVER JOEL
B.OCT.11,1905 TEXICO,N.MEX.

YR	CL	LEA	POS	GP	G	REC
1931	STL	N	O		4	.000
1932	STL	N	O		12	.190
		BRTR			16	.182

HUNT, RICHARD M.
B.1847 NEW YORK

YR	CL	LEA	POS	GP	G	REC
1872	ECK	NA	2-O		11	.288

HUNT, RONALD KENNETH "RON"
B.FEB.23,1941 ST.LOUIS,MO.

YR	CL	LEA	POS	GP	G	REC
1963	NY	N	2-3		143	.272
1964	NY	N	2-3		127	.303
1965	NY	N	2-3		57	.240
1966	NY	N	2-S-3		132	.288
1967	LA	A	2-3		110	.263
1968	SF	N	2		148	.250
1969	SF	N	2-3		128	.262
1970	SF	N	2-3		117	.281
1971	MON	N	2-3		152	.279
1972	MON	N	2-3		129	.253
1973	MON	N	2-3		113	.309
1974	MON	N	2-S-3		115	.268
	STL	N	2		12	.174
		BRTR			1483	.273

HUNTER, EDWARD FRANKLIN
B.FEB.6,1907 CINCINNATI,OHIO

YR	CL	LEA	POS	GP	G	REC
1933	CIN	N	3		1	.000
		BRTR				

HUNTER, FREDERICK CREIGHTON "NEWT"
B.JAN.5,1884 CHILLICOTHE,OHIO
D.OCT.26,1963 COLUMBUS,OHIO

YR	CL	LEA	POS	GP	G	REC
1911	PIT	N	1		61	.254
		BRTR				

HUNTER, GEORGE HARRISON
B.JULY 8,1886 BUFFALO,N.Y.
D.JAN.11,1968 DAUPHIN COUNTY,PA

YR	CL	LEA	POS	GP	G	REC
1909	BRO	N	P-O	16	39	4-10
						.228
1910	BRO	N	O		1	.000
	BB			16	40	4-10
						.228

HUNTER, GORDON WILLIAM "BILLY"
B.JUNE 4,1928 PUNXSUTAWNEY,PA.

YR	CL	LEA	POS	GP	G	REC
1953	STL	A	S		154	.219
1954	BAL	A	S		125	.243
1955	NY	A	S		98	.227
1956	NY	A	S-3		39	.280
1957	KC	A	2-S-3		116	.191
1958	KC	A	2-S		22	.155
	CLE	A	S-3		76	.195
		BRTR			630	.219

HUNTER, HAROLD JAMES "BUDDY"
B.AUG.9,1947 OMAHA,NEB.

YR	CL	LEA	POS	GP	G	REC
1971	BOS	A	2		8	.222
1973	BOS	A	2-3		13	.429
1975	BOS	A	2		1	.000
		BRTR			22	.294

HUNTER, HERBERT HARRISON
B.DEC.25,1895 E.BOSTON,MASS.
D.JULY 25,1970 ORLANDO,FLA.

YR	CL	LEA	POS	GP	G	REC
1916	NY	N	3		21	.250
	CHI	N	H		2	.000
1917	CHI	N	2-3		3	.000
1920	BOS	A	O		4	.083
1921	STL	N	1		9	.000
		BLTR			39	.163

HUNTER, JAMES AUGUSTUS "JIM" OR "CATFISH"
B.APR.8,1946 HERTFORD,N.C.

YR	CL	LEA	POS	GP	G	REC
1965	KC	A	P	32	8- 8	
1966	KC	A	P	30	9-11	
1967	KC	A	P-1	35	37	13-17
						.196
1968	OAK	A	P	36	39	13-13
1969	OAK	A	P	38	42	12-15
1970	OAK	A	P	40	43	18-14
1971	OAK	A	P	37	38	21-11
1972	OAK	A	P	38	39	21- 7
1973	OAK	A	P	36	37	21- 5
1974	OAK	A	P		41	25-12
1975	NY	A	P		39	23-14
1976	NY	A	P		36	17-15
		BRTR		438	453	201-142
						.226

HUNTER, ROBERT LEMUEL "LEM"
B.JAN.16,1863 WARREN,OHIO
D.NOV.9,1956

YR	CL	LEA	POS	GP	G	REC
1883	CLE	N	P-O	1	0- 0	
						.250

HUNTER, WILLARD MITCHELL
B.MAR.8,1935 NEWARK,N.J.

YR	CL	LEA	POS	GP	G	REC
1962	LA	N	P	1	10	0- 0
	NY	N	P		27	1- 6
1964	NY	N	P		41	3- 3
		BRTL		69	78	4- 9

HUNTER, WILLIAM ELLSWORTH
B.JULY 8,1886 BUFFALO,N.Y.
D.APR.10,1934

YR	CL	LEA	POS	GP	G	REC
1912	CLE	A	O		21	.165
		BLTL				

HUNTER, WILLIAM ROBERT
B.ST.THOMAS,ONT.,CAN.

YR	CL	LEA	POS	GP	G	REC
1884	LOU	AA	C		2	.429

HUNTZ, STEPHEN MICHAEL "STEVE"
B.DEC.3,1945 CLEVELAND,OHIO

YR	CL	LEA	POS	GP	G	REC
1967	STL	N	2		3	.167
1969	STL	N	2-S-3		71	.194
1970	SD	N	S-3		106	.219
1971	CHI	A	2-S-3		35	.209
1975	SD	N	2-3		22	.151
		BBTR			237	.206

HUNTZINGER, WALTER HENRY
B.FEB.6,1899 POTTSVILLE,PA.

YR	CL	LEA	POS	GP	G	REC
1923	NY	N	P	2	0- 1	
1924	NY	N	P	12	1- 1	
1925	NY	N	P	26	5- 1	
1926	STL	N	P	9	0- 4	
	CHI	N	P	11	1- 1	
		BRTR		60	7- 8	

HURD, THOMAS CARR "TOM"
B.MAY 27,1924 DANVILLE,VA.

YR	CL	LEA	POS	GP	G	REC
1954	BOS	A	P	16	2- 0	
1955	BOS	A	P	43	8- 6	
1956	BOS	A	P	40	3- 4	
		BRTR		99	13-10	

HURLEY, JEREMIAH F.
B.JUNE 15,1864 E.BOSTON,MASS.
D.SEPT.17,1950

YR	CL	LEA	POS	GP	G	REC
1889	BOS	N	C		1	.000
1890	PIT	P	C		8	.273
1891	CIN	AA	C-1-O		26	.220
		TR			35	.227

HURLEY, PATRICK

YR	CL	LEA	POS	GP	G	REC
1901	CIN	N	C		7	.062
1907	BRO	N	C		1	.000
		TR			8	.056

HURLEY, WILLIAM F. "DICK"
B.1847

YR	CL	LEA	POS	GP	G	REC
1872	OLY	NA	O		2	.000

HURST, FRANK O'DONNELL "DON"
B.AUG.17,1906 MAYSVILLE,KY.
D.DEC.6,1952

YR	CL	LEA	POS	GP	G	REC
1928	PHI	N	1		107	.285
1929	PHI	N	1		154	.304
1930	PHI	N	1		119	.327
1931	PHI	N	1		137	.305
1932	PHI	N	1		150	.339
1933	PHI	N	1		147	.267
1934	PHI	N	1		40	.262
	CHI	N	1		51	.199
		BLTL			905	.297

HURST, TIMOTHY CARROLL
B.JUNE 30,1865 ASHLAND,PA.
D.JUNE 4,1915
NON-PLAYING MANAGER STL(N) 1898

HUSTA, CARL LAWRENCE "SOX"
B.APR.8,1902 EGG HARBOR,N.J.
D.NOV.6,1951

YR	CL	LEA	POS	GP	G	REC
1925	PHI	A	S		6	.136
		BRTR				

HUSTED, WILLIAM J.
B.OCT.9,1867 GLOUCESTER,N.J.

YR	CL	LEA	POS	GP	G	REC
1890	PHI	P	P		19	5-10

HUSTING, BERTHOLD JUNEAU "PETE"
B.MAR.6,1878 FOND DU LAC,WIS.
D.SEPT.3,1948

YR	CL	LEA	POS	GP	G	REC
1900	PHI	N	P	2	0- 0	
1901	MIL	A	P	35	9-15	
1902	BOS	A	P	1	0- 1	
	PHI	A	P	32	14- 5	
		BRTR		70	23-21	

HUSTON, HARRY EMANUEL KRESS
B.OCT.14,1883 BELLEFONTAINE,O.
D.OCT.13,1969 BLACKWELL,OKLA.

YR	CL	LEA	POS	GP	G	REC
1906	PHI	N	C		2	.000
		TR				

HUSTON, WARREN LLEWELLYN
B.OCT.31,1913 NEWTON,MASS.

YR	CL	LEA	POS	GP	G	REC
1937	PHI	A	2-S		38	.130
1944	BOS	N	2-S-3		33	.200
		BRTR			71	.165

HUTCHENSON, JAMES F.
B.1863 NEW YORK,N.Y.
D.DEC.24,1941

YR	CL	LEA	POS	GP	G	REC
1884	KC	U	P	2	1- 1	

HUTCHESON, JOSEPH JOHNSON "SLUG"
B.FEB.5,1905 SPRINGTOWN,TEX.

YR	CL	LEA	POS	GP	G	REC
1933	BRO	N	O		55	.234
		BLTR				

YR	CL	LEA	POS	GP	G	REC

HUTCHINGS, JOHN RICHARD JOSEPH
B.APR.14,1916 CHICAGO,ILL.
D.APR.27,1963 INDIANAPOLIS,IND.

YR	CL	LEA	POS	GP	G	REC
1940	CIN	N	P		19	2- 1
1941	CIN	N	P		8	0- 0
1941	BOS	N	P		36	1- 6
1942	BOS	N	P		20	1- 0
1944	BOS	N	P		14	1- 4
1945	BOS	N	P		57	7- 6
1946	BOS	N	P		1	0- 1
	BBTR				155	12-18

HUTCHINSON, EDWARD F.
B.1870 PITTSBURGH,PA.

YR	CL	LEA	POS	GP	G	REC
1890	CHI	N	2		7	.107

HUTCHINSON, FREDERICK CHARLES "FRED"
B.AUG.12,1919 SEATTLE,WASH.
D.NOV.12,1964 BRADENTON,FLA.

YR	CL	LEA	POS	GP	G	REC
1939	DET	A	P		13	3- 6
1940	DET	A	P		17	3- 7
1941	DET	A	H		2	.000
1946	DET	A	P	28	40	14-11
1947	DET	A	P	33	56	18-10
1948	DET	A	P	33	76	13-11
1949	DET	A	P	33	38	15- 7
1950	DET	A	P	39	44	17- 8
1951	DET	A	P	31	47	10-10
1952	DET	A	M-P		17	2- 1
1953	DET	A	M-P-	3	4	0- 0
			1			.167
	BLTR			242	354	95-71
						.263

NON-PLAYING MANAGER DET(A) 1954
STL(N) 1956-58 CIN(N) 1959-64

HUTCHINSON, IRA KENDALL
B.AUG.31,1910 CHICAGO,ILL.
D.AUG.21,1973 CHICAGO,ILL.

YR	CL	LEA	POS	GP	G	REC
1933	CHI	A	P		1	0- 0
1937	BOS	N	P		31	4- 6
1938	BOS	N	P		36	9- 8
1939	BRO	N	P		41	5- 2
1940	STL	N	P		20	4- 2
1941	STL	N	P		29	1- 5
1944	BOS	N	P		40	9- 7
1945	BOS	N	P		11	2- 3
	BRTR				209	34-33

HUTCHINSON, WILLIAM FOREST "WILD BILL"
B.DEC.17,1861 NEW HAVEN,CONN.
D.MAR.19,1926 KANSAS CITY,MO.

YR	CL	LEA	POS	GP	G	REC
1889	CHI	N	P		37	16-17
1890	CHI	N	P		68	42-26
1891	CHI	N	P	63	64	43-19
1892	CHI	N	P		71	37-33
1893	CHI	N	P	40	41	16-24
1894	CHI	N	P		34	16-18
1895	CHI	N	P		34	13-18
1897	STL	N	P		6	1- 4
	TR			353	355	184-159

HUTSON, GEORGE HERBERT "HERB"
B.JULY 17,1949 SAVANNAH,GA.

YR	CL	LEA	POS	GP	G	REC
1974	CHI	N	P		20	0- 2
	BRTR					

HUTSON, ROY LEE
B.FEB.12,1902 SCOTLAND CO.,MO.
D.MAY 20,1957

YR	CL	LEA	POS	GP	G	REC
1925	BRO	N	O		7	.500
	BLTR					

HUTTO, JAMES NEAMON "JIM"
B.OCT.17,1947 NORFOLK,VA.

YR	CL	LEA	POS	GP	G	REC
1970	PHI	N	C-1-3-O	57		.185
1975	BAL	A	C	4		.000
	BRTR			61		.175

HUTTON, THOMAS GEORGE "TOM"
B.APR.20,1946 LOS ANGELES,CAL.

YR	CL	LEA	POS	GP	G	REC
1966	LA	N	1		3	.000
1969	LA	N	1		16	.271
1972	PHI	N	1-O		134	.260
1973	PHI	N	1		106	.263
1974	PHI	N	1-O		96	.240
1975	PHI	N	1-O		113	.248
1976	PHI	N	1-O		95	.202
	BLTL				563	.249

HYATT, ROBERT HAMILTON "HAM"
B.NOV.1,1884 BUNCOMBE CO.,N.C.
D.SEPT.11,1963 LIBERTY LAKE, WASH.

YR	CL	LEA	POS	GP	G	REC
1909	PIT	N	O		49	.299
1910	PIT	N	1		41	.263
1912	PIT	N	O		46	.289
1913	PIT	N	O		63	.333
1914	PIT	N	O		74	.215
1915	STL	N	1-O		106	.268
1918	NY	A	O		53	.229
	BLTR				432	.267

HYDE, RICHARD ELDE "DICK"
B.AUG.3,1928 HINDSBORO,ILL.

YR	CL	LEA	POS	GP	G	REC
1955	WAS	A	P		3	0- 0
1957	WAS	A	P		52	4- 3
1958	WAS	A	P		53	10- 3
1959	WAS	A	P		37	2- 5
1960	WAS	A	P		9	0- 1
1961	BAL	A	P		15	1- 2
	BRTR				169	17-14

HYNDMAN, JAMES WILLIAM
B.1864 KINGSTON,PA.

YR	CL	LEA	POS	GP	G	REC
1886	ATH	AA	P		1	0- 1

HYNES, PATRICK J.
B.MAR.12,1884 ST.LOUIS,MO.
D.MAR.12,1907

YR	CL	LEA	POS	GP	G	REC
1903	STL	N	P		1	0- 1
1904	STL	A	P-O	3	66	1- 0
						.240
				4	67	1- 1
						.237

IBURG, HERMAN EDWARD "HAM"
B.OCT.30,1878 SAN FRANCISCO,CAL

YR	CL	LEA	POS	GP	G	REC
1902	PHI	N	P		30	11-19
	TR					

IGNASIAK, GARY RAYMOND
B.SEP.1,1949 MT.CLEMENS,MICH.

YR	CL	LEA	POS	GP	G	REC
1973	DET	A	P	3		0- 0
	BRTL					

IMLAY, HARRY MILLER "DOC"
B.JAN.12,1889 ALLENTOWN,N.J.
D.OCT.7,1948

YR	CL	LEA	POS	GP	G	REC
1913	PHI	N	P		9	0- 1
	BRTR					

INGERSOLL, ROBERT RANDOLPH
B.JAN.8,1869 RAPID CITY,S.D.
D.JAN.13,1927

YR	CL	LEA	POS	GP	G	REC
1914	CIN	N	P		4	0- 0
	BRTR					

INGERTON, WILLIAM JOHN "SCOTTY"
B.APP.19,1886 PENINSULA,OHIO
D.JUNE 15,1956

YR	CL	LEA	POS	GP	G	REC
1911	BOS	N	3-O		133	.250
	BRTR					

INGRAHAM, CHARLES
B.1860 YOUNGSTOWN,OHIO

YR	CL	LEA	POS	GP	G	REC
1883	BAL	AA	C		1	.250

INGRAM, MELVIN DAVID
B.JULY 4,1904 ASHEVILLE,N.C.

YR	CL	LEA	POS	GP	G	REC
1929	PIT	N	H		3	.000
	BRTR					

INKS, ALBERT PRESTON "BERT"
(REAL NAME ALBERT PRESTON INKSTEIN)
B.JAN.27,1871 LIGONIER,IND.
D.OCT.3,1941

YR	CL	LEA	POS	GP	G	REC
1891	BRO	N	P		13	3- 9
1892	BRO	N	P		9	5- 1
	WAS	N	P		8	2- 4
1894	BAL	N	P		16	8- 5
	LOU	N	P		11	2- 6
1895	LOU	N	P		27	7-19
1896	PHI	N	P		5	0- 1
	CIN	N	P		3	1- 1
	BLTL				92	28-46

INKSTEIN, ALBERT PRESTON
(PLAYED UNDER NAME OF ALBERT PRESTON INKS)

IOTT, CLARENCE EUGENE "HOOKS"
B.DEC.3,1919 MOUNTAIN GROVE,MO.

YR	CL	LEA	POS	GP	G	REC
1941	STL	A	P		2	0- 0
1947	STL	A	P		4	0- 1
	NY	N	P		20	3- 8
	BBTL				26	3- 9

IOTT, FRED JOHN "BIDDO"
(REAL NAME FREDERICK HOYOT)
B.JULY 7,1876 HOULTON,ME.
D.FEB.17,1941 ISLAND FALLS,ME.

YR	CL	LEA	POS	GP	G	REC
1903	CLE	A	O		3	.200
	BRTR					

IRELAN, HAROLD "GRUMP"
B.AUG.5,1890 BURNETTSVILLE,IND.
D.JULY 16,1944 CARMEL,IND.

YR	CL	LEA	POS	GP	G	REC
1914	PHI	N	2		67	.236
	BBTR					

IRVIN, MONTFORD "MONTE"
B.FEB.25,1919 COLUMBIA,ALA.

YR	CL	LEA	POS	GP	G	REC
1949	NY	N	1-3-O		36	.224
1950	NY	N	1-3-O		110	.300
1951	NY	N	1-O		151	.312
1952	NY	N	O		46	.310
1953	NY	N	O		124	.329
1954	NY	N	1-3-O		135	.262
1955	NY	N	O		51	.253
1956	CHI	N	O		111	.271
	BRTR				764	.293

IRVIN, WILLIAM EDWARD "ED"
B.1892 PHILADELPHIA,PA.
D.FEB.18,1916

YR	CL	LEA	POS	GP	G	REC
1912	DET	A	C		1	.667
	TR					

IRWIN, ARTHUR ALBERT "DOC"
B.FEB.14,1858 TORONTO,ONT.,CAN.
D.JULY 16,1921

YR	CL	LEA	POS	GP	G	REC
1880	WOR	N	C-S-3		83	.260
1881	WOR	N	S		49	.266
1882	WOR	N	1-S-3		84	.220
1883	PRO	N	2-S		98	.285
1884	PRO	N	P-S	1	99	0- 0
						.245
1885	PRO	N	2-S		59	.179
1886	PHI	N	S		101	.233
1887	PHI	N	S		99	.339
1888	PHI	N	S		124	.220
1889	PHI	N	S		18	.219
	WAS	N	M-S		85	.233
1890	BOS	P	S		96	.264
1891	BOS	AA	M-S		5	.154
1894	PHI	N	M-S		1	.000
	BLTR			1	1001	0- 0
						.252

NON-PLAYING MANAGER
WAS(N) 1892, PHI(N) 1895,
NY(N) 1896, WAS(N) 1898-99

IRWIN, CHARLES E.
B.FEB.15,1869 SHEFFIELD,ILL.
D.SEPT.21,1925

YR	CL	LEA	POS	GP	G	REC
1893	CHI	N	S		21	.324
1894	CHI	N	S-3		130	.302
1895	CHI	N	S		3	.200
1896	CIN	N	3		127	.295
1897	CIN	N	3		134	.293
1898	CIN	N	3		135	.240
1899	CIN	N	3		87	.231
1900	CIN	N	S-3		85	.271
1901	CIN	N	3		67	.226
	BRO	N	3		64	.223
1902	BRO	N	S-3		131	.273
	BLTR				984	.269

IRWIN, JOHN
B.JULY 21,1861 TORONTO,ONT.,CAN
D.FEB.28,1934

YR	CL	LEA	POS	GP	G	REC
1882	WOR	N	1		1	.000
1884	BOS	U	3		104	.235
1886	ATH	AA	S		2	.333
1887	WAS	N	S		8	.382
1888	WAS	N	3		37	.222
1889	WAS	N	3		58	.289
1890	BUF	P	1-3		77	.220
1891	BOS	AA	3-O		20	.192
	LOU	AA	3		14	.038
1896	BAL	N	2		1	.500
	BLTR				322	.242

IRWIN, THOMAS ANDREW
B.DEC.20,1914 ALTOONA,PA.

YR	CL	LEA	POS	GP	G	REC
1938	CLE	A	S		3	.111
	BRTR					

IRWIN, WALTER KINGSLEY
B.SEPT.23,1897 ALTOONA,PA.
D.AUG.18,1976 SPRING LAKE,MICH.

YR	CL	LEA	POS	GP	G	REC
1921	STL	N	H		4	.000
	BRTR					

IRWIN, WILLIAM FRANKLIN
B.SEPT.17,1859 NEVILLE,OHIO
D.AUG.7,1933

YR	CL	LEA	POS	GP	G	REC
1886	CIN	AA	P		2	0- 2
	BRTR					

ISBELL, WILLIAM FRANK
"BALD EAGLE"
B.AUG.21,1875 DELEVAN,N.Y.
D.JULY 15,1941

YR	CL	LEA	POS	GP	G	REC
1898	CHI	N	P-O	10	41	4- 6
						.235
1901	CHI	A	1		137	.261
1902	CHI	A	P-C-	1	137	1- 0
			1-S			.256
1903	CHI	A	1-3		138	.259
1904	CHI	A	1-2		94	.208
1905	CHI	A	2-O		94	.296
1906	CHI	A	2		143	.279
1907	CHI	A	P-2	1	125	0- 0
						.243
1908	CHI	A	P-1-	1	84	0- 0
			2			.247
1909	CHI	A	1		120	.224
	BLTR			13	1113	5- 6
						.254

IVIE, MICHAEL WILSON "MIKE"
B.AUG.8,1952 ATLANTA,GA.

YR	CL	LEA	POS	GP	G	REC
1971	SD	N	C		6	.471
1974	SD	N	1		12	.088
1975	SD	N	C-1-3		111	.249
1976	SD	N	C-1-3		140	.291
	BRTR				269	.268

IZQUIERDO, ENRIQUE ROBERTO
(VALDEZ) "HANK"
B.MAR.20,1931 MATANZAS,CUBA

YR	CL	LEA	POS	GP	G	REC
1967	MIN	A	C		16	.269
	BRTR					

JABLONOWSKI, PETER WILLIAM
(SEE PETER WILLIAM APPLETON)

JABLONSKI, RAYMOND LEO
"RAY" OR "JABBO"
B.DEC.17,1926 CHICAGO,ILL.

YR	CL	LEA	POS	GP	G	REC
1953	STL	N	3		157	.268
1954	STL	N	1-3		152	.296
1955	CIN	N	3-O		74	.240
1956	CIN	N	2-3		130	.256
1957	NY	N	1-3-O		107	.289
1958	SF	N	3-O		86	.230
1959	STL	N	5-3		60	.253
	KC	A	3		25	.262
1960	KC	A	3		21	.219
	BRTR				812	.268

JACKLITSCH, FREDERICK LAWRENCE
B.MAY 24,1876 BROOKLYN,N.Y.
D.JULY 18,1937

YR	CL	LEA	POS	GP	G	REC
1900	PHI	N	C		5	.181
1901	PHI	N	C		31	.252
1902	PHI	N	C-O		27	.200
1903	BRO	N	C		55	.267
1904	BRO	N	C		23	.234
1905	NY	A	C		1	.000
1907	PHI	N	C		65	.213
1908	PHI	N	C		30	.221
1909	PHI	N	C		19	.310
1910	PHI	N	C		17	.196
1914	BAL	F	C		122	.275
1915	BAL	F	C		48	.237
1917	BOS	N	C		1	.000
	BRTR				444	.243

JACKSON, ALVIN NEIL "AL"
B.DEC.25,1935 WACO,TEX.

YR	CL	LEA	POS	GP	G	REC
1959	PIT	N	P		8	0- 0
1961	PIT	N	P	3	5	1- 0
1962	NY	N	P	36	44	8-20
1963	NY	N	P	37	49	13-17
1964	NY	N	P	40	50	11-16
1965	NY	N	P	37	56	8-20
1966	STL	N	P	36	51	13-15
1967	STL	N	P	38	41	9- 4
1968	NY	N	P	25	27	3- 7
1969	NY	N	P		9	0- 0
	CIN	N	P		33	1- 0
	BLTL			302	373	67-99

JACKSON, CHARLES HERBERT
B.FEB.7,1895 GRANITE CITY,ILL.
D.MAY 27,1968 RADFORD,VA.

YR	CL	LEA	POS	GP	G	REC
1915	CHI	A	H		1	.000
1917	PIT	N	O		41	.240
	BLTL				42	.238

JACKSON, CHARLES W.
B.1882 IOWA

YR	CL	LEA	POS	GP	G	REC
1905	DET	A	P		2	0- 0

JACKSON, GEORGE CHRISTOPHER
"HICKORY"
B.OCT.14,1882 BLUM,TEX.
D.NOV.25,1972 CLEBURNE,TEX.

YR	CL	LEA	POS	GP	G	REC
1911	BOS	N	O		39	.347
1912	BOS	N	O		110	.262
1913	BOS	N	O		3	.300
	BRTR				152	.285

JACKSON, GRANT DWIGHT
B.SEP.28,1942 FOSTORIA,OHIO

YR	CL	LEA	POS	GP	G	REC
1965	PHI	N	P		6	1- 1
1966	PHI	N	P		2	0- 0
1967	PHI	N	P		43	2- 3
1968	PHI	N	P	33	37	1- 6
1969	PHI	N	P	38	40	14-18
1970	PHI	N	P	32	52	5-15
1971	BAL	A	P		29	4- 3
1972	BAL	A	P		32	1- 1
1973	BAL	A	P		45	8- 0
1974	BAL	A	P		49	6- 4
1975	BAL	A	P		41	4- 3
1976	BAL	A	P		13	1- 1
	NY	A	P		21	6- 0
	BLTL			384	410	53-55
	BB 1965-70					

JACKSON, HENRY EVERETT
B.JUNE 23,1861 UNION CITY,IND.
D.SEPT.14,1932

YR	CL	LEA	POS	GP	G	REC
1887	IND	N	1		10	.263
	BRTR					

JACKSON, JAMES BENNER
B.NOV.28,1877 PHILADELPHIA,PA.
D.OCT.9,1955 PHILADELPHIA,PA.

YR	CL	LEA	POS	GP	G	REC
1901	BAL	A	O		97	.254
1902	NY	N	O		35	.193
1905	CLE	A	O		108	.257
1906	CLE	A	O		105	.214
	BRTR				345	.236

JACKSON, JOHN LEWIS
B.JULY 15,1911 WYNNEFIELD,PA.
D.OCT.24,1956

YR	CL	LEA	POS	GP	G	REC
1933	PHI	N	P		10	2- 2
	BRTR					

JACKSON, JOSEPH JEFFERSON
"SHOELESS JOE"
B.JULY 16,1889 BRANDON MILLS,
S.C.
D.DEC.5,1951 GREENVILLE,S.C.

YR	CL	LEA	POS	GP	G	REC
1908	PHI	A	O		5	.131
1909	PHI	A	O		5	.177
1910	CLE	A	O		20	.387
1911	CLE	A	O		147	.408
1912	CLE	A	O		152	.395
1913	CLE	A	O		148	.373
1914	CLE	A	O		122	.338
1915	CLE	A	1-O		82	.326
	CHI	A	O		46	.269
1916	CHI	A	O		155	.341
1917	CHI	A	O		146	.301
1918	CHI	A	O		17	.354
1919	CHI	A	O		139	.351
1920	CHI	A	O		146	.382
	BLTR				1330	.356

JACKSON, LAWRENCE CURTIS "LARRY"
B.JUNE 2,1931 NAMPA,IDAHO

YR	CL	LEA	POS	GP	G	REC
1955	STL	N	P		37	9-14
1956	STL	N	P		51	2- 2
1957	STL	N	P		41	15- 9
1958	STL	N	P	49	50	13-13
1959	STL	N	P	40	54	14-13
1960	STL	N	P	43	52	18-13
1961	STL	N	P	33	34	14-11
1962	STL	N	P		36	16-11
1963	CHI	N	P		37	14-18
1964	CHI	N	P		40	24-11
1965	CHI	N	P	39	49	14-21
1966	CHI	N	P		3	0- 2
	PHI	N	P	35	36	15-13
1967	PHI	N	P	40	42	13-15
1968	PHI	N	P	34	37	13-17
	BRTR			558	599	194-183

JACKSON, LOUIS CLARENCE "LOU"
B.JULY 26,1935 RIVERTON,LA.
D.MAY 27,1969 TOKYO,JAPAN

YR	CL	LEA	POS	GP	G	REC
1958	CHI	N	O		24	.171
1959	CHI	N	H		6	.250
1964	BAL	A	O		4	.375
	BLTR				34	.213

JACKSON, MICHAEL WARREN "MIKE"
B.MAR.27,1946 PATERSON,N.J.

YR	CL	LEA	POS	GP	G	REC
1970	PHI	N	P		5	1- 1
1971	STL	N	P		1	0- 0
1972	KC	A	P		7	1- 2
1973	KC	A	P		9	0- 0
	CLE	A	P		1	0- 0
	BLTL				23	2- 3

JACKSON, RANSOM JOSEPH "RANDY"
B.FEB.10,1926 LITTLE ROCK,ARK.

YR	CL	LEA	POS	GP	G	REC
1950	CHI	N	3		34	.225
1951	CHI	N	3		145	.275
1952	CHI	N	3-O		116	.232
1953	CHI	N	3		139	.285
1954	CHI	N	3		126	.273
1955	CHI	N	3		138	.265
1956	BRO	N	3		101	.274
1957	BRO	N	3		48	.198
1958	LA	N	3		35	.185
	CLE	A	3		29	.242
1959	CLE	A	3		3	.143
	CHI	N	3-O		41	.243
	BRTR				955	.261

JACKSON, REGINALD MARTINEZ
"REGGIE"
B.MAY 18,1946 WYNCOTE,PA.

YR	CL	LEA	POS	GP	G	REC
1967	KC	A	O		35	.178
1968	OAK	A	O		154	.250
1969	OAK	A	O		152	.275
1970	OAK	A	O		149	.237
1971	OAK	A	O		150	.277
1972	OAK	A	O		135	.265
1973	OAK	A	O		151	.293
1974	OAK	A	O-O		148	.289
1975	OAK	A	O		157	.253
1976	BAL	A	O-O		134	.277
	BLTL				1365	.267

JACKSON, ROLAND THOMAS "SONNY"
B.JULY 9,1944 WASHINGTON,D.C.

YR	CL	LEA	POS	GP	G	REC
1963	HOU	N	S		1	.000
1964	HOU	N	S		9	.348
1965	HOU	N	S-3		10	.130
1966	HOU	N	S		150	.292
1967	HOU	N	S		129	.237
1968	ATL	N	S		105	.226
1969	ATL	N	S		98	.239
1970	ATL	N	O		103	.259
1971	ATL	N	O		149	.258
1972	ATL	N	S-3-O'		60	.238
1973	ATL	N	S-O		117	.209
1974	ATL	N	O		5	.429
	BLTR				936	.251

JACKSON, RONALD ALLEN "RON"
B.OCT.22,1933 KALAMAZOO,MICH.

YR	CL	LEA	POS	GP	G	REC
1954	CHI	A	1		40	.280
1955	CHI	A	1		40	.203
1956	CHI	A	1		22	.214
1957	CHI	A	1		13	.317
1958	CHI	A	1		61	.233
1959	CHI	A	1		10	.214
1960	BOS	A	1		10	.226
	BRTR				196	.245

YR	CL	LEA	POS	GP	G	REC

JACKSON, RONNIE "RON"
B.MAY 9,1953 BIRMINGHAM,ALA.

YR	CL	LEA	POS	GP	G	REC
1975	CAL	A	3-0	13		.231
1976	CAL	A	2-3-0	127		.227
		BRTR		140		.227

JACKSON, SAMUEL
B.MAR.24,1849 RIPON,ENGLAND
D.AUG.4,1930

1871	BOS	NA	2-0	16		-
1872	ATL	NA	0	3		.154
		BRTR		19		-

**JACKSON, TRAVIS CALVIN
"STONEWALL"**
B.NOV.2,1903 WALDO,ARK.

1922	NY	N	S	3		.000
1923	NY	N	2-S-3	96		.275
1924	NY	N	S	151		.302
1925	NY	N	S	112		.285
1926	NY	N	S	111		.327
1927	NY	N	S	127		.318
1928	NY	N	S	150		.270
1929	NY	N	S	149		.294
1930	NY	N	S	116		.339
1931	NY	N	S	145		.310
1932	NY	N	S	52		.256
1933	NY	N	S-3	53		.246
1934	NY	N	S	137		.268
1935	NY	N	3	128		.301
1936	NY	N	3	126		.230
		BRTR		1656		.290

JACKSON, WILLIAM RILEY
B.APR.4,1885 PITTSBURGH,PA.
D.SEPT.26,1958

1914	CHI	F	1	17		.040
1915	CHI	F	1	48		.165
		BLTL		65		.139

JACOBS, ANTHONY ROBERT "TONY"
B.AUG.5,1925 DIXMOOR,ILL.

1948	CHI	N	P	1		0- 0
1955	STL	N	P	1		0- 0
		BBTR		2		0- 0

JACOBS, ARTHUR EVAN
B.AUG.28,1903 LUCKEY,OHIO

| 1939 | CIN | N | P | 1 | | 0- 0 |
| | | BLTL | | | | |

**JACOBS, FORREST VANDERGRIFT
"SPOOK"**
B.NOV.4,1925 CHESWOLD,DEL.

1954	PHI	A	2	132		.258
1955	KC	A	2	13		.261
1956	KC	A	2	32		.216
	PIT	N	2	11		.162
		BRTR		188		.247

JACOBS, LAMAR GARY
B.JUNE 9,1937 YOUNGSTOWN,OHIO

1960	WAS	A	H	6		.000
1961	MIN	A	0	4		.250
		BRTR		10		.200

JACOBS, MORRIS ELMORE "MIKE"

| 1902 | CHI | N | S | 5 | | .210 |

JACOBS, NEWTON SMITH "BUCKY"
B.MAR.21,1913 ALTAVISTA,VA.

1937	WAS	A	P	11		1- 1
1939	WAS	A	P	2		0- 0
1940	WAS	A	P	9		0- 1
		BRTR		22		1- 2

JACOBS, OTTO ALBERT
B.APR.19,1889 CHICAGO,ILL.
D.NOV.19,1955

| 1918 | CHI | A | C | 29 | | .205 |
| | | BRTR | | | | |

JACOBS, RAYMOND F.
B.JAN.2,1902 SALT LAKE CITY,
UTAH
D.APR.4,1952

| 1928 | CHI | N | H | 2 | | .000 |
| | | BRTR | | | | |

JACOBS, WILLIAM ELMER
B.AUG.10,1892 SALEM,MO.
D.FEB.10,1958

1916	PHI	N	P	14		1- 3
1916	PIT	N	P	34		6-10
1917	PIT	N	P	38		6-19
1918	PIT	N	P	8		0- 1
	PHI	N	P	18		9- 5
1919	PHI	N	P	17		6-10
1919	STL	N	P	17		3- 6
1920	STL	N	P	23		4- 8
1924	CHI	N	P	38		11-12
1925	CHI	N	P	18		2- 3
1927	CHI	A	P	25		2- 4
		BRTR		250		50-81

JACOBSON, ALBERT L. "BEANY"
B.JUNE 5,1881 PORT WASHINGTON,
WIS.
D.JAN.31,1933

1904	WAS	A	P	33		5-23
1905	WAS	A	P	22		8- 9
1906	STL	A	P	25		9- 9
1907	STL	A	P	7		1- 5
	BOS	A	P	2		0- 0
		TL		89		23-46

**JACOBSON, MERWIN JOHN WILLIAM
"JAKE"**
B.MAR.7,1894 NEW BRITAIN,CONN.

1915	NY	N	0	8		.083
1916	CHI	N	0	4		.231
1926	BRO	N	0	110		.247
1927	BRO	N	0	11		.000
		BLTL		133		.230

**JACOBSON, WILLIAM CHESTER
"BABY DOLL"**
B.AUG.16,1890 CABLE,ILL.

1915	DET	A	0	38		.215
	STL	A	0	33		.209
1917	STL	A	0	148		.248
1919	STL	A	0	120		.323
1920	STL	A	0	154		.355
1921	STL	A	1-0	151		.352
1922	STL	A	0	145		.317
1923	STL	A	0	147		.309
1924	STL	A	0	152		.318
1925	STL	A	0	142		.341
1926	STL	A	0	50		.290
	BOS	A	0	98		.302
1927	BOS	A	0	45		.245
	CLE	A	0	32		.252
	PHI	A	0	17		.229
		BRTR		1472		.311

JACOBUS, STUART LOUIS "LARRY"
B.DEC.13,1896 CINCINNATI,OHIO
D.AUG.19,1965 COLLEGE HILL,OHIO

| 1918 | CIN | N | P | 5 | | 0- 1 |
| | | BBTR | | | | |

JACOBY, HARRY
B.PHILADELPHIA,PA.

1882	BAL	AA	3-0	31		.213
1885	BAL	AA	2	11		.143
				42		.195

JACQUEZ, PATRICK THOMAS "PAT"
B.APR.23,1947 STOCKTON,CAL.

| 1971 | CHI | A | P | 2 | | 0- 0 |
| | | BRTR | | | | |

JAECKEL, PAUL HENRY
B.APR.1,1942 E.LOS ANGELES,CAL.

| 1964 | CHI | N | P | 4 | | 1- 0 |
| | | BRTR | | | | |

JAEGER, CHARLES THOMAS
B.APR.17,1875 OTTAWA,ILL.
D.SEPT.27,1942

| 1904 | DET | A | P | 8 | | 2- 3 |

JAEGER, JOSEPH P.
B.MAR.3,1896 ST.CLOUD,MINN.

| 1920 | CHI | N | P | 2 | | 0- 0 |
| | | BRTR | | | | |

JAHN, ARTHUR CHARLES
B.DEC.2,1895 STRUBLE,LA.
D.JAN.9,1948

1925	CHI	N	0	58		.301
1928	NY	N	0	10		.276
	PHI	N	0	36		.223
		BRTR		104		.278

JAKUCKI, SIGMUND JACK
B.AUG.20,1911 CAMDEN,N.J.

1936	STL	A	P	7		0- 3
1944	STL	A	P	35	36	13- 9
1945	STL	A	P	30		12-10
		BRTR		72	73	25-22

JAMERSON, CHARLES DEWEY "LEFTY"
B.JAN.26,1900 ENFIELD,ILL.

| 1924 | BOS | A | P | 1 | | 0- 0 |
| | | BLTL | | | | |

JAMES, ARTHUR "ART"
B.AUG.2,1952 DETROIT,MICH.

| 1975 | DET | A | 0 | 11 | | .225 |
| | | BLTL | | | | |

JAMES, BERTON HULON "BOB"
B.JULY 7,1886 ADAMSVILLE,KY.

| 1909 | STL | N | 0 | 6 | | .285 |
| | | BLTR | | | | |

JAMES, CHARLES WESLEY "CHARLIE"
B.DEC.22,1937 ST.LOUIS,MO.

1960	STL	N	0	43		.180
1961	STL	N	0	108		.255
1962	STL	N	0	129		.276
1963	STL	N	0	116		.268
1964	STL	N	0	88		.223
1965	CIN	N	0	26		.205
		BRTR		510		.255

JAMES, CLEO JOEL
B.AUG.31,1940 CLARKSDALE,MISS.

1968	LA	N	0	10		.200
1970	CHI	N	0	100		.210
1971	CHI	N	3-0	54		.287
1973	CHI	N	0	44		.111
		BRTR		208		.228

**JAMES, JAMES MC CUTCHEN
(PLAYED UNDER NAME OF
JAMES MC CUTCHEN MC JAMES)**

JAMES, JEFFREY LYNN "JEFF"
B.SEP.29,1941 INDIANAPOLIS,IND.

1968	PHI	N	P	29		4- 4
1969	PHI	N	P	6		2- 2
		BRTR		35		6- 6

JAMES, JOHN PHILLIP "JOHNNY"
B.JULY 23,1933 BONNER'S FERRY,
IDAHO

1958	NY	A	P	1		0- 0
1960	NY	A	P	28		5- 1
1961	NY	A	P	1		0- 0
	LA	A	P	36		0- 2
		BLTR		66	73	5- 3

JAMES, RICHARD LEE "RICK"
B.OCT.11,1947 SHEFFIELD,ALA.

| 1967 | CHI | N | P | 3 | | 0- 1 |
| | | BRTR | | | | |

JAMES, ROBERT BYRNE "BERNIE"
B.SEPT.2,1905 ANGLETON,TEX.

1929	BOS	N	2	46		.307
1930	BOS	N	2	8		.182
1933	NY	N	2-S-3	60		.224
		BBTR		114		.257

JAMES, WILLIAM A. "LEFTY"
B.JULY 1,1890 GLENROY,OHIO
D.MAY 3,1933

1912	CLE	A	P	6		0- 1
1913	CLE	A	P	11		2- 3
1914	CLE	A	P	11		0- 3
		BLTL		28		2- 6

JAMES, WILLIAM HENRY "BIG BILL"
B.JAN.20,1887 DETROIT,MICH.
D.MAY 24,1942

1911	CLE	A	P	8		3- 4
1912	CLE	A	P	3		0- 0
1914	STL	A	P	43		15-14
1915	STL	A	P	34		6-10
	DET	A	P	11		7- 3
1916	DET	A	P	30		7-12
1917	DET	A	P	34		13-10
1918	DET	A	P	19		6-11
1919	DET	A	P	3		3- 0
	BOS	A	P	14		2- 5
	CHI	A	P	5		3- 1
		BBTR		204		65-70

YR	CL	LEA	POS	GP	G	REC

JAMES, WILLIAM LAWRENCE
"SEATTLE BILL"
B.MAR.12,1892 PLACER CO.,CAL.
D.MAR.10,1971 OROVILLE,CAL.

YR	CL	LEA	POS	GP	G	REC
1913	BOS	N	P		24	6-10
1914	BOS	N	P	46	49	26- 7
1915	BOS	N	P	13	14	5- 4
1919	BOS	N	P		1	0- 0
	BRTR			88	37-21

JAMIESON, CHARLES DEVINE
"CHARLEY" OR "CUCKOO"
B.FEB.7,1893 PATERSON,N.J.
D.OCT.27,1969 PATERSON,N.J.

YR	CL	LEA	POS	GP	G	REC
1915	WAS	A	O		17	.279
1916	WAS	A	P-O	1	64	0- 0
						.248
1917	WAS	A	P-O	1	20	0- 0
						.171
	PHI	A	O		85	.267
1918	PHI	A	P-O	5	110	1- 1
						.202
1919	CLE	A	P-O	4	26	0- 0
						.353
1920	CLE	A	O		108	.319
1921	CLE	A	O		140	.310
1922	CLE	A	P-O	2	145	0- 0
						.323
1923	CLE	A	O		152	.345
1924	CLE	A	O		143	.358
1925	CLE	A	O		130	.296
1926	CLE	A	O		143	.299
1927	CLE	A	O		127	.309
1928	CLE	A	O		112	.307
1929	CLE	A	O		102	.291
1930	CLE	A	O		103	.301
1931	CLE	A	O		28	.302
1932	CLE	A	O		16	.063
	BLTL			13	1779	1- 1
						.303

JANESKI, GERALD JOSEPH "JERRY"
B.APR.18,1946 PASADENA,CAL.

YR	CL	LEA	POS	GP	G	REC
1970	CHI	A	P		35	10-17
1971	WAS	A	P		23	1- 5
1972	TEX	A	P		4	0- 1
	BRTR				62	11-23

JANOWICZ, VICTOR FELIX "VIC"
B.FEB.26,1930 ELYRIA,OHIO

YR	CL	LEA	POS	GP	G	REC
1953	PIT	N	C		42	.252
1954	PIT	N	3-O		41	.151
	BRTR				83	.214

JANSEN, LAWRENCE JOSEPH "LARRY"
B.JULY 16,1920 FOREST GROVE,ORE.

YR	CL	LEA	POS	GP	G	REC
1947	NY	N	P		42	21- 5
1948	NY	N	P		42	18-12
1949	NY	N	P		37	15-16
1950	NY	N	P		40	19-13
1951	NY	N	P		39	23-11
1952	NY	N	P		34	11-11
1953	NY	N	P		36	11-16
1954	NY	N	P		13	2- 2
1956	CIN	N	P		8	2- 3
	BRTR				291	122-89

JANSEN, RAYMOND W.
B.1890 ST.LOUIS,MO.

YR	CL	LEA	POS	GP	G	REC
1910	STL	A	3		1	.800
	BRTR					

JANTZEN, WALTER C. "HEINE"
B.1890

YR	CL	LEA	POS	GP	G	REC
1912	STL	A	O		31	.185
	BRTR					

JANVRIN, HAROLD CHANDLER
B.AUG.27,1892 HAVERHILL,MASS.
D.MAR.2,1962

YR	CL	LEA	POS	GP	G	REC
1911	BOS	A	3		10	.153
1913	BOS	A	S-3		86	.206
1914	BOS	A	1-2-S		143	.238
1915	BOS	A	S-3		99	.269
1916	BOS	A	2-S		117	.223
1917	BOS	A	2		55	.197
1919	WAS	A	2		61	.178
	STL	N	2		7	.214
1920	STL	N	1-S-O		87	.274
1921	STL	N	1		18	.281
	BRO	N	1-S		44	.196
1922	BRO	N	1-2-S-3-O		30	.298
	BRTR				757	.232

JARVIS, LEROY GILBERT
B.JUNE 27,1926 OKLAHOMA CITY, OKLA.

YR	CL	LEA	POS	GP	G	REC
1944	BRO	N	C		1	.000
1946	PIT	N	C		2	.250
1947	PIT	N	C		18	.156
	BRTR				21	.160

JARVIS, RAYMOND ARNOLD "RAY"
B.MAY 10,1946 PROVIDENCE,R.I.

YR	CL	LEA	POS	GP	G	REC
1969	BOS	A	P		29	5- 6
1970	BOS	A	P		15	0- 1
	BRTR				44	5- 7

JARVIS, ROBERT PATRICK "PAT"
B.MAR.18,1941 CARLYLE,ILL.

YR	CL	LEA	POS	GP	G	REC
1966	ATL	N	P		10	6- 2
1967	ATL	N	P		32	15-10
1968	ATL	N	P		34	16-12
1969	ATL	N	P		37	13-11
1970	ATL	N	P		36	16-16
1971	ATL	N	P		35	6-14
1972	ATL	N	P		37	11- 7
1973	MON	N	P		28	2- 1
	BRTR				249	85-73

JASPER, HARRY W. "HI"
B.NOV.15,1880 ST.LOUIS,MO.
D.MAY 22,1937 ST.LOUIS,MO.

YR	CL	LEA	POS	GP	G	REC
1914	CHI	A	P		16	1- 0
1915	CHI	A	P		3	1- 1
1916	STL	N	P		21	5- 6
1919	CLE	A	P		12	4- 5
	BRTR				52	11-12

JASTER, LARRY EDWARD
B.JAN.13,1944 MIDLAND,MICH.

YR	CL	LEA	POS	GP	G	REC
1965	STL	N	P		4	3- 0
1966	STL	N	P		26	11- 5
1967	STL	N	P	34	35	9- 7
1968	STL	N	P		31	9-13
1969	MON	N	P		24	1- 6
1970	ATL	N	P		14	1- 1
1972	ATL	N	P		5	1- 1
	BLTL			138	139	35-33

JATA, PAUL
B.SEP.4,1949 ASTORIA,N.Y.

YR	CL	LEA	POS	GP	G	REC
1972	DET	A	C-1-O		32	.230
	BRTR					

JAVERY, ALVA WILLIAM
"BEARTRACKS"
B.JUNE 5,1918 WORCESTER,MASS.

YR	CL	LEA	POS	GP	G	REC
1940	BOS	N	P		29	2- 4
1941	BOS	N	P		34	10-11
1942	BOS	N	P		42	12-16
1943	BOS	N	P		41	17-16
1944	BOS	N	P		40	10-19
1945	BOS	N	P		17	2- 7
1946	BOS	N	P		2	0- 1
	BRTR				205	53-74

JAVIER, IGNACIO ALFRED "AL"
(REAL NAME IGNACIO ALFREDO
WILKES (JAVIER))
B.FEB.4,1954 SAN PEDRO DE
MACORIS,D.R.

YR	CL	LEA	POS	GP	G	REC
1976	HOU	N	O		8	.208
	BRTR					

JAVIER, MANUEL JULIAN (LIRANZO)
"JULIAN"
B.AUG.9,1936 SAN FRANCISCO DE
MACORIS,D.R.

YR	CL	LEA	POS	GP	G	REC
1960	STL	N	2		119	.237
1961	STL	N	2		113	.279
1962	STL	N	2-S		155	.263
1963	STL	N	2		161	.263
1964	STL	N	2		155	.241
1965	STL	N	2		77	.227
1966	STL	N	2		147	.228
1967	STL	N	2		140	.281
1968	STL	N	2		139	.260
1969	STL	N	2		143	.282
1970	STL	N	2		139	.251
1971	STL	N	2-3		90	.259
1972	CIN	N	1-2-3		44	.209
	BRTR				1622	.257

JAY, JOSEPH RICHARD "JOEY"
B.AUG.15,1935 MIDDLETOWN,CONN.

YR	CL	LEA	POS	GP	G	REC
1953	MIL	N	P		3	1- 0
1954	MIL	N	P		15	1- 0
1955	MIL	N	P		12	0- 0
1957	MIL	N	P		1	0- 0
1958	MIL	N	P		18	7- 5
1959	MIL	N	P		34	6-11
1960	MIL	N	P		32	9- 8
1961	CIN	N	P		34	21-10
1962	CIN	N	P		39	21-14
1963	CIN	N	P		30	7-18
1964	CIN	N	P		34	11-11
1965	CIN	N	P		37	9- 8
1966	CIN	N	P		12	6- 2
	ATL	N	P		9	0- 4
	BBTR				310	99-91
	BR 1953					

JEANES, ERNEST LEE "TEX"
B.DEC.19,1900 MAYPEARL,TEX.
D.APR.5,1973 LONGVIEW,TEX.

YR	CL	LEA	POS	GP	G	REC
1921	CLE	A	O		4	.500
1922	CLE	A	P		1	0- 0
1925	WAS	A	O		15	.263
1926	WAS	A	O		21	.233
1927	NY	N	P	1	11	0- 0
	BRTR			2	52	0- 0
						.278

JEFFCOAT, GEORGE EDWARD
B.DEC.24,1913 NEW BROOKLAND,S.C.

YR	CL	LEA	POS	GP	G	REC
1936	BRO	N	P		40	5- 6
1937	BRO	N	P		21	1- 3
1939	BRO	N	P		1	0- 0
1943	BOS	N	P		8	1- 2
	BRTR				70	7-11

JEFFCOAT, HAROLD BENTLY "HAL"
B.SEPT.6,1924 W.COLUMBIA,S.C.

YR	CL	LEA	POS	GP	G	REC
1948	CHI	N	O		134	.279
1949	CHI	N	O		108	.245
1950	CHI	N	O		66	.235
1951	CHI	N	O		113	.273
1952	CHI	N	O		102	.219
1953	CHI	N	O		106	.235
1954	CHI	N	P-O	43	56	5- 6
						.258
1955	CHI	N	P		50	8- 6
1956	CIN	N	P		38	49	8- 2
1957	CIN	N	P		37	53	12-13
1958	CIN	N	P-O	49	50	6- 8
						.556
1959	CIN	N	P		17	0- 1
	STL	N	P	11	12	0- 1
	BRTR			245	918	39-37
						.253

JEFFERSON, JESSE HARRISON
B.MAR.3,1949 MIDLOTHIAN,VA.

YR	CL	LEA	POS	GP	G	REC
1973	BAL	A	P		18	6- 5
1974	BAL	A	P		20	1- 0
1975	BAL	A	P		4	0- 2
	CHI	A	P		22	5- 9
1976	CHI	A	P		19	2- 5
	BRTR				83	14-21

JEFFRIES, IRVINE FRANKLIN
B.SEPT.10,1905 LOUISVILLE,KY.

YR	CL	LEA	POS	GP	G	REC
1930	CHI	A	S-3		40	.237
1931	CHI	A	3		79	.224
1934	PHI	N	2		56	.246
	BRTR				175	.234

JELINICH, FRANK ANTHONY "JELLY"
B.SEPT.3,1919 SAN JOSE,CAL.

YR	CL	LEA	POS	GP	G	REC
1941	CHI	N	O		4	.125
	BRTR					

JENDRUS, GEORGE ANDREW
(PLAYED UNDER NAME OF
GEORGE JENDRUS ANDERSON)

YR	CL	LEA	POS	GP	G	REC

JENKINS, FERGUSON ARTHUR
B.DEC.13,1943 CHATHAM,ONT.,CAN.

YR	CL	LEA	POS	GP	G	REC
1965	PHI	N	P		7	2- 1
1966	PHI	N	P		1	0- 0
	CHI	N	P		60	6- 8
1967	CHI	N	P	38	39	20-13
1968	CHI	N	P		40	20-15
1969	CHI	N	P		43	21-15
1970	CHI	N	P		40	22-16
1971	CHI	N	P		39	24-13
1972	CHI	N	P		36	20-12
1973	CHI	N	P		38	14-16
1974	TEX	A	P		41	25-12
1975	TEX	A	P		37	17-18
1976	BOS	A	P		30	12-11
			BRTR	450	451	203-150

JENKINS, JOHN ROBERT
B.JULY 7,1897 BOSWORTH,MO.
D.AUG.3,1968 COLUMBIA,MO.

1922	CHI	A	2-S		5	.000
			BRTR			

JENKINS, JOSEPH DANIEL
B.OCT.12,1891 SHELBYVILLE,TENN.
D.JUNE 21,1974 FRESNO,CAL.

1914	STL	A	C		19	.125
1917	CHI	A	C		10	.111
1919	CHI	A	C		11	.167
			BRTR		40	.136

JENKINS, THOMAS GRIFFITH "TUT"
B.APR.10,1898 CAMDEN,ALA.

1925	BOS	A	O		15	.297
1926	BOS	A	O		21	.180
	PHI	A	O		6	.174
1929	STL	A	O		21	.182
1930	STL	A	O		2	.250
1931	STL	A	O		81	.265
1932	STL	A	O		25	.323
			BLTR		171	.259

JENKINS, WARREN WASHINGTON "JACK"
B.DEC.22,1942 COVINGTON,VA.

1962	WAS	A	P		3	0- 1
1963	WAS	A	P		4	0- 2
1969	LA	N	P		1	0- 0
			BRTR		8	0- 3

JENNINGS, ALFRED "ALAMAZOO"
B.1851 NEWPORT,KY.
D.NOV.2,1894

1878	MIL	N	C		1	.000

JENNINGS, HUGH AMBROSE "EE-YAH"
B.APR.2,1869 PITTSTON,PA.
D.FEB.1,1928 SCRANTON,PA.

1891	LOU	AA	1-S		87	.286
1892	LOU	N	S		152	.232
1893	LOU	N	S		23	.148
	BAL	N	S		15	.241
1894	BAL	N	S		128	.332
1895	BAL	N	S		131	.386
1896	BAL	N	S		129	.397
1897	BAL	N	S		115	.353
1898	BAL	N	2-S		143	.325
1899	BAL	N	1		10	.200
	BAL	N	2		2	.375
	BRO	N	1-S		51	.320
1900	BRO	N	1		112	.270
1901	PHI	N	1		81	.274
1903	PHI	N	1-2-S		78	.277
	BRO	N	O		6	.235
1907	DET	A	M-S		2	.250
1908	DET	A	,-H		1	.000
1909	DET	A	M-1		2	.500
1912	DET	A	M-H		1	.000
1918	DET	A	M-1		1	.000
			BRTR		1270	.314

NON-PLAYING MANAGER
DET(A) 1910-11, 13-17, 19-20

JENNINGS, WILLIAM LEE
B.SEPT.28,1925 ST.LOUIS,MO.

1951	STL	A	S		64	.179
			BRTR			

JENSEN, FORREST DUCENUS "WOODY"
B.AUG.11,1909 BREMERTON,WASH.

1931	PIT	N	O		73	.243
1932	PIT	N	O		7	.000
1933	PIT	N	O		70	.296
1934	PIT	N	O		88	.290
1935	PIT	N	O		143	.324
1936	PIT	N	O		153	.283
1937	PIT	N	O		124	.279
1938	PIT	N	O		68	.200
1939	PIT	N	O		12	.167
			BLTL		738	.285

JENSEN, JACK EUGENE "JACKIE"
B.MAR.9,1927 SAN FRANCISCO,CAL.

1950	NY	A	O		45	.171
1951	NY	A	O		56	.298
1952	NY	A	O		7	.105
	WAS	A	O		144	.286
1953	WAS	A	O		147	.266
1954	BOS	A	O		152	.276
1955	BOS	A	O		152	.275
1956	BOS	A	O		151	.315
1957	BOS	A	O		145	.281
1958	BOS	A	O		154	.286
1959	BOS	A	O		148	.277
1961	BOS	A	O		137	.263
			BRTR		1438	.279

JENSEN, WILLIAM
B.NOV.23,1888 NEW HAVEN,CONN.

1912	DET	A	P		4	1- 2
1914	PHI	A	P		2	0- 1
			BLTR		6	1- 3

JESSEE, DANIEL EDWARD
B.FEB.22,1901 OLIVE HILL,KY.
D.APR.30,1970

1929	CLE	A	H		1	.000
			BLTR			

JESTADT, GARRY ARTHUR
B.MAR.19,1947 CHICAGO,ILL.

1969	MON	N	S		6	.000
1971	CHI	N	3		3	.000
	SD	N	2-S-3		75	.291
1972	SD	N	2-S-3		92	.246
			BRTR		176	.260

JESTER, VIRGIL MILTON
B.JULY 23,1927 DENVER,COLO.

1952	BOS	N	P		19	3- 5
1953	MIL	N	P		2	0- 0
			BRTR		21	3- 5

JETER, JOHN "JOHNNY"
B.OCT.24,1944 SHREVEPORT,LA.

1969	PIT	N	O		28	.310
1970	PIT	N	O		85	.238
1971	SD	N	O		18	.320
1972	SD	N	O		110	.221
1973	CHI	A	O		89	.241
1974	CLE	A	O		6	.353
			BRTR		336	.244

JETHROE, SAMUEL "SAM" OR "JET"
B.JAN.20,1922 E.ST.LOUIS,ILL.

1950	BOS	N	O		141	.273
1951	BOS	N	O		148	.280
1952	BOS	N	O		151	.232
1954	PIT	N	O		2	.000
			BBTR		442	.261

JEWETT, NATHAN W.
B.1842

1872	ECK	NA	C		2	.125

JIMENEZ, FELIX ELVIO "ELVIO"
B.JAN.6,1943 SAN PEDRO DE MACORIS,D.R.

1964	NY	A	O		1	.333
			BRTR			

JIMENEZ, JUAN ANTONIO (MARTES)
B.MAR.8,1949 LA TORRE,LA VEGA, D.R.

1974	PIT	N	P		4	0- 0
			BRTR			

JIMENEZ, MANUEL EMILIO "MANNY"
B.NOV.19,1938 SAN PEDRO DE MACORIS,D.R.

1962	KC	A	O		139	.301
1963	KC	A	O		60	.280
1964	KC	A	O		95	.225
1966	KC	A	O		13	.114
1967	PIT	N	O		50	.250
1968	PIT	N	O		66	.303
1969	CHI	N	H		6	.167
			BLTR		429	.272

JOHN, THOMAS EDWARD "TOMMY"
B.MAY 22,1943 TERRE HAUTE,IND.

1963	CLE	A	P		6	0- 2
1964	CLE	A	P		25	2- 9
1965	CHI	A	P		39	14- 7
1966	CHI	A	P		34	14-11
1967	CHI	A	P		31	10-13
1968	CHI	A	P		25	10- 5
1969	CHI	A	P		33	9-11
1970	CHI	A	P	37	38	12-17
1971	CHI	A	P		38	13-16
1972	LA	N	P		29	11- 5
1973	LA	N	P		36	16- 7
1974	LA	N	P		22	13- 3
1976	LA	N	P		31	10-10
			BRTL	386	387	134-116

JOHNS, AUGUST FRANCIS
B.SEPT.10,1899 ST.LOUIS,MO.

1926	DET	A	P		35	6- 4
1927	DET	A	P		1	0- 0
			BLTL		36	6- 4

JOHNS, OLIVER TRACY
B.AUG.21,1879 TRENTON,OHIO
D.JUNE 17,1961

1905	CIN	N	P		4	1- 0
			BLTL			

JOHNS, THOMAS P.
B.BALTIMORE,MD.

1873	MAR	NA	O		1	.000

JOHNS, WILLIAM R. "PETE"
B.JAN.17,1889 CLEVELAND,OHIO
D.AUG.9,1964 CLEVELAND,OHIO

1915	CHI	A	3		28	.210
1918	STL	A	1		46	.180
			BRTR		74	.196

JOHNSON, ABRAHAM
B.LONDON,ONT.,CAN.

1893	CHI	N	P		1	0- 0

JOHNSON, ADAM RANKIN JR.
B.MAR.1,1917 HAYDEN,ARIZ.

1941	PHI	A	P		7	1- 0
			BRTR			

JOHNSON, ADAM RANKIN SR. "TEX"
B.FEB.4,1888 BURNET,TEX.
D.JULY 2,1972 WILLIAMSPORT,PA.

1914	BOS	A	P		16	4- 9
	CHI	F	P		16	9- 5
1915	CHI	F	P		11	2- 5
	BAL	F	P		23	7-10
1918	STL	N	P		6	1- 1
			BRTR		72	23-30

JOHNSON, ALBERT J.
B.CHICAGO,ILL.

1896	LOU	N	2		24	.232
1897	LOU	N	2		44	.251
					68	.245

JOHNSON, ALEXANDER "ALEX"
B.DEC.7,1942 HELENA,ARK.

1964	PHI	N	O		43	.303
1965	PHI	N	O		97	.294
1966	STL	N	O		25	.186
1967	STL	N	O		81	.223
1968	CIN	N	O		149	.312
1969	CIN	N	O		139	.315
1970	CAL	A	O		156	.329
1971	CAL	A	O		65	.260
1972	CLE	A	O		108	.239
1973	TEX	A	O-D		158	.287
1974	TEX	A	O-D		114	.291
	NY	A	O		10	.214
1975	NY	A	O-D		52	.261
1976	DET	A	O-D		125	.268
			BRTR		1322	.288

```
YR  CL LEA POS  GP    G   REC        YR  CL LEA POS  GP    G   REC        YR  CL LEA POS  GP    G   REC
```

JOHNSON, ARTHUR GILBERT
B.FEB.15,1901 WARREN,PA.
```
1927 NY  N  P          1    0- 0
     BBTL
```

JOHNSON, ARTHUR HENRY "LEFTY"
B.JULY 16,1916 WINCHESTER,MASS.
```
1940 BOS N  P          2    0- 1
1941 BOS N  P    43    44   7-15
1942 BOS N  P          4    0- 0
     BLTL      49    50   7-16
```

JOHNSON, BENJAMIN FRANKLIN
B.MAY 16,1931 GREENWOOD,S.C.
```
1959 CHI N  P          4    0- 0
1960 CHI N  P         17    2- 1
     BRTR             21    2- 1
```

JOHNSON, CALEB CLARK
B.MAY 23,1844 USTICK TOWNSHIP, ILL.
D.MAR.7,1925
```
1871 CLE NA 2-S-0     16    -
```

JOHNSON, CHARLES CLEVELAND "HOME RUN"
B.MAR.12,1885 SLATINGTON,PA.
D.AUG.28,1940
```
1908 PHI N  O          5   .214
```

JOHNSON, CHESTER LILLIS
B.AUG.1,1918 REDMOND,WASH.
```
1946 STL A  P          5    0- 0
     BLTL
```

JOHNSON, CLAIR BARTH "BART"
B.JAN.3,1950 TORRANCE,CAL.
```
1969 CHI A  P          4    1- 3
1970 CHI A  P         18    4- 7
1971 CHI A  P         53   12-10
1972 CHI A  P          9    0- 3
1973 CHI A  P         22    3- 3
1974 CHI A  P         18   10- 4
1976 CHI A  P         32    9-16
     BRTR            156   39-46
```

JOHNSON, CLIFFORD "CONNIE"
B.DEC.7,1922 STONE MOUNTAIN,GA.
```
1953 CHI A  P    14    15   4- 4
1955 CHI A  P    17    19   7- 4
1956 CHI A  P          5    0- 1
     BAL A  P         26    9-10
1957 BAL A  P         35   14-11
1958 BAL A  P         26    6- 9
     BRTR     123   126   40-39
```

JOHNSON, CLIFFORD "CLIFF"
B.JULY 22,1947 SAN ANTONIO,TEX.
```
1972 HOU N  C          5   .250
1973 HOU N  1          7   .300
1974 HOU N  C-1       83   .228
1975 HOU N  C-1-O    122   .276
1976 HOU N  C-1-O    108   .226
     BRTR            325   .249
```

JOHNSON, DARRELL DEAN
B.AUG.25,1928 ORD,NEB.
```
1952 STL A  C         29   .282
     CHI A  C         22   .108
1957 NY  A  C         21   .217
1958 NY  A  C          5   .250
1960 STL N  C          8   .000
1961 PHI N  C         21   .230
     CIN N  C         20   .315
1962 CIN N  C          2   .000
     BAL A  C          6   .182
     BRTR            134   .234
NON-PLAYING MANAGER
BOS(A) 1974-76
```

JOHNSON, DAVID ALLEN "DAVE"
B.JAN.30,1943 ORLANDO,FLA.
```
1965 BAL A  2-S-3     20   .170
1966 BAL A  2-S      131   .257
1967 BAL A  2-3      148   .247
1968 BAL A  2-S      145   .242
1969 BAL A  2-S      142   .280
1970 BAL A  2-S      149   .281
1971 BAL A  2        142   .282
1972 BAL A  2        118   .221
1973 ATL N  2        157   .270
1974 ATL N  1-2      136   .251
1975 ATL N  H          1  1.000
     BRTR           1289   .260
```

JOHNSON, DAVID CHARLES "DAVE"
B.OCT.4,1948 ABILENE,TEX.
```
1974 BAL A  P         11    2- 2
1975 BAL A  P          6    0- 1
     BRTR             17    2- 3
```

JOHNSON, DERON ROGER
B.JULY 17,1938 SAN DIEGO,CAL.
```
1960 NY  A  3          6   .500
1961 NY  A  3         13   .105
     KC  A  1-3-O     83   .216
1962 KC  A  1-3-O     17   .105
1964 CIN N  1-3-O    140   .273
1965 CIN N  3        159   .287
1966 CIN N  1-3-O    142   .257
1967 CIN N  1-3      108   .224
1968 ATL N  3        127   .208
1969 PHI N  1-3-O    138   .255
1970 PHI N  1-3      159   .256
1971 PHI N  1-3      158   .265
1972 PHI N  1         96   .213
1973 PHI N  1         12   .167
     OAK A  1-D      131   .246
1974 OAK A  D         50   .195
     MIL A  1-D       49   .151
     BOS A  H         11   .120
1975 CHI A  1-D      148   .233
     BOS A  1          3   .600
1976 BOS A  1         15   .132
     BRTR           1765   .244
```

JOHNSON, DONALD ROY "DON"
B.NOV.12,1926 PORTLAND,ORE.
```
1947 NY  A  P         15    4- 3
1950 NY  A  P          8    1- 0
     STL A  P         26    5- 6
1951 STL A  P          6    0- 1
     WAS A  P         21    7-11
1952 WAS A  P         29    0- 5
1954 CHI A  P         46    8- 7
1955 BAL A  P         31    2- 4
1958 SF  N  P         17    0- 1
     BRTR            198   27-38
```

JOHNSON, DONALD SPORI "PEP"
B.DEC.7,1911 CHICAGO,ILL.
```
1943 CHI N  2         10   .190
1944 CHI N  2        154   .278
1945 CHI N  2        138   .302
1946 CHI N  2         83   .242
1947 CHI N  2-3      120   .259
1948 CHI N  2-3        6   .250
     BRTR            511   .268
```

JOHNSON, EARL DOUGLASS "LEFTY"
B.APR.2,1919 REDMOND,WAS.
```
1940 BOS A  P    17    18   6- 2
1941 BOS A  P         17   4- 5
1946 BOS A  P         29   5- 4
1947 BOS A  P    45    46  12-11
1948 BOS A  P         35  10- 4
1949 BOS A  P         19   3- 6
1950 BOS A  P         11   0- 0
1951 DET A  P          6   0- 0
     BLTL     179   181  40-32
```

JOHNSON, EDWIN CYRIL
B.MAR.31,1900 MORGANFIELD,KY.
D.JULY 3,1975 MORGANFIELD,KY.
```
1920 WAS A  1-O        4   .230
     BLTR
```

JOHNSON, ELLIS WATT
B.DEC.8,1892 MINNEAPOLIS,MINN.
```
1912 CHI A  P          5    0- 0
1915 PHI A  P          1    0- 0
1917 PHI A  P          4    0- 2
     BRTR             10    0- 2
```

JOHNSON, ELMER ELLSWORTH
B.JUNE 12,1885 FRANKFORT,IND.
D.OCT.31,1966
```
1914 NY  N  C         11   .166
     BRTR
```

JOHNSON, ERNEST RUDOLPH
B.APR.29,1888 CHICAGO,ILL.
D.MAY 1,1952
```
1912 CHI A  S         18   .262
1915 STL F  S        152   .244
1916 STL A  S         74   .229
1917 STL A  2-S       80   .248
1918 STL A  S         29   .265
1921 CHI A  S        142   .295
1922 STL A  S        145   .254
1923 CHI A  S         12   .189
     NY  A  S         19   .447
1924 NY  A  S         64   .353
1925 NY  A  2-S-3     76   .282
     BLTR            811   .267
```

JOHNSON, ERNEST THORWALD "ERNIE"
B.JUNE 16,1924 BRATTLEBORO,VT.
```
1950 BOS N  P         16    2- 0
1952 BOS N  P         29    6- 3
1953 MIL N  P         36    4- 3
1954 MIL N  P         40    5- 2
1955 MIL N  P         40    5- 7
1956 MIL N  P         36    4- 3
1957 MIL N  P         30    7- 3
1958 MIL N  P         15    3- 1
1959 BAL A  P         31    4- 1
     BRTR            273   40-23
```

JOHNSON, FRANK HERBERT
B.JULY 22,1942 EL PASO,TEX.
```
1966 SF  N  O         15   .219
1967 SF  N  O          8   .300
1968 SF  N  2-S-3-O   67   .190
1969 SF  N  O          7   .100
1970 SF  N  1-O       67   .273
1971 SF  N  1-O       32   .082
     BRTR            196   .211
```

JOHNSON, FREDERICK EDWARD "DEACON"
B.MAR.10,1894 TOLAR,TEX.
D.JUNE 14,1973 KERRVILLE,TEX.
```
1922 NY  N  P          2    0- 2
1923 NY  N  P          3    2- 0
1938 STL A  P         17    3- 7
1939 STL A  P          5    0- 1
     BRTR             27    5-10
```

JOHNSON, GEORGE HOWARD "MURPHY"
B.MAR.30,1886 WINNEBAGO,NEB.
D.JUNE 11,1922
```
1913 CIN N  P         44   14-16
1914 CIN N  P          1    0- 0
     KC  F  P         20    9-10
1915 KC  F  P         45   17-17
     BRTR            110   40-43
```

JOHNSON, HENRY WARD
B.MAY 21,1906 BRADENTON,FLA.
```
1925 NY  A  P         24    1- 3
1926 NY  A  P          1    0- 0
1928 NY  A  P         31   14- 9
1929 NY  A  P    12    13   3- 3
1930 NY  A  P    44    51  14-11
1931 NY  A  P         40   13- 8
1932 NY  A  P     5     6   2- 2
1933 BOS A  P    25    26   8- 6
1934 BOS A  P         31    6- 8
1935 BOS A  P         13    2- 1
1936 PHI A  P          3    0- 2
1939 CIN N  P         20    0- 3
     BRTR     249   259   63-56
     BB 1933
```

JOHNSON, JAMES BRIAN "JIM"
B.NOV.3,1945 MUSKEGON,MICH.
```
1970 SF  N  P          3    1- 0
     BLTL
```

JOHNSON, JERRY MICHAEL
B.DEC.3,1943 MIAMI,FLA.
```
1968 PHI N  P         16    4- 4
1969 PHI N  P         33    6-13
1970 STL N  P          7    2- 0
     SF  N  P         33    3- 4
1971 SF  N  P         67   12- 9
1972 SF  N  P         48    8- 6
1973 CLE A  P         39    5- 6
1974 HOU N  P         34    2- 1
1975 SD  N  P         21    3- 1
1976 SD  N  P         24    1- 3
     BRTR            322   46-47
```

YR	CL LEA POS	GP	G	REC

JOHNSON, JOHN CLIFFORD "SWEDE"
B.SEPT.29,1914 BELMORE,OHIO

YR	CL LEA POS	GP	G	REC
1944	NY A P	22		0- 2
1945	CHI A P	29		3- 0
	BLTL	51		3- 2

JOHNSON, JOHN LOUIS "YOUNGY"
(REAL NAME JOHN LOUIS MERCER)
B.NOV.18,1869 PEKIN,ILL.
D.JAN.28,1941

| 1894 | PHI N P | | 4 | 1- 3 |

JOHNSON, JOHN RALPH "SPUD"
B.1860 CHICAGO,ILL.

1889	COL AA 3-0	117		.285
1890	COL AA 0	137		.354
1891	CLE N 0	80		.263
		334		.307

JOHNSON, KENNETH TRAVIS "KEN"
B.JUNE 16,1933 W.PALM BEACH,FLA.

1958	KC A P	2		0- 0
1959	KC A P	2		1- 1
1960	KC A P	42		5-10
1961	KC A P	6		0- 4
	CIN N P	15		6- 2
1962	HOU N P	33		7-16
1963	HOU N P	37	38	11-17
1964	HOU N P		35	11-16
1965	HOU N P	8		3- 2
	MIL N P	29		13- 8
1966	ATL N P	32		14- 8
1967	ATL N P	29		13- 9
1968	ATL N P	31		5- 8
1969	ATL N P	9		0- 1
	NY A P	12		1- 2
	CHI N P	9		1- 2
1970	MON N P	3		0- 0
	BRTR	334	335	91-106

JOHNSON, KENNETH WANDERSEE
"KEN" OR "HOOK"
B.JAN.14,1923 TOPEKA,KAN.

1947	STL N P		2	1- 0
1948	STL N P	13	20	2- 4
1949	STL N P	14	21	0- 1
1950	STL N P		2	0- 0
	PHI N P	14	21	4- 1
1951	PHI N P	20	36	5- 8
1952	DET A P		9	0- 0
	BLTL	74	111	12-14

JOHNSON, LAMAR
B.SEPT.2,1950 BESSEMER,ALA.

1974	CHI A 1	10		.345
1975	CHI A 1	8		.200
1976	CHI A 1-3-0	82		.320
	BRTR	100		.310

JOHNSON, LARRY DOBY
B.AUG.17,1950 CLEVELAND,OHIO

1972	CLE A C	1		.500
1974	CLE A R	1		.000
1975	MON N C	1		.333
1976	MON N C	6		.154
	BRTR	9		.222

JOHNSON, LLOYD WILLIAM "EPPA"
B.DEC.24,1910 SANTA ROSA,CAL.

| 1934 | PIT N P | | 1 | 0- 0 |
| | BLTL | | | |

JOHNSON, LOUIS BROWN "LOU"
B.SEP.22,1934 LEXINGTON,KY.

1960	CHI N 0	34		.206
1961	LA A 0	1		.000
1962	MIL N 0	61		.282
1965	LA N 0	131		.259
1966	LA N 0	152		.272
1967	LA N 0	104		.270
1968	CHI N 0	62		.244
	CLE A 0	65		.257
1969	CAL A 0	67		.203
	BRTR	677		.258

JOHNSON, MICHAEL NORTON "MIKE"
B.MAR.2,1951 SLAYTON,MINN.

| 1974 | SD N P | 18 | | 0- 2 |
| | BRTR | | | |

JOHNSON, OTIS L.
B.NOV.5,1883 MUNCIE,IND.
D.NOV.9,1915

| 1911 | NY A 2-S | 71 | | .234 |
| | BBTR | | | |

JOHNSON, PAUL OSCAR
B.SEPT.2,1896 N.GROSVENORDALE,
CONN.
D.FEB.14,1973 MC ALLEN,TEX.

1918	BOS N H	1		.000
1920	PHI A 0		18	.208
1921	PHI A 0		48	.315
	BRTR		67	.276

JOHNSON, RICHARD ALLAN
B.FEB.15,1932 DAYTON,OHIO

| 1958 | CHI N H | 8 | | .000 |
| | BLTL | | | |

JOHNSON, ROBERT DALE "BOB"
B.APR.25,1943 AURORA,IND.

1969	NY N P	2		0- 0
1970	KC A P	40		8-13
1971	PIT N P	31		9-10
1972	PIT N P	31		4- 4
1973	PIT N P	50		4- 2
1974	CLE A P	14		3- 4
	BLTR	168		28-33

JOHNSON, ROBERT LEE
"INDIAN BOB"
B.NOV.26,1906 PRYOR,OKLA.

1933	PHI A 0		142	.290
1934	PHI A 0		141	.307
1935	PHI A 0		147	.299
1936	PHI A 2-0		153	.292
1937	PHI A 0		138	.306
1938	PHI A 0		152	.313
1939	PHI A 0		150	.338
1940	PHI A 0		138	.268
1941	PHI A 1-0		149	.275
1942	PHI A 0		149	.291
1943	WAS A 1-3-0		117	.265
1944	BOS A 0		144	.324
1945	BOS A 0		143	.280
	BRTR		1863	.296

JOHNSON, ROBERT WALLACE "BOB"
B.MAR.4,1936 OMAHA,NEB.

1960	KC A 2-S-3	76		.205
1961	WAS A 2-S-3	61		.295
1962	WAS A 2-S-3-0	135		.288
1963	BAL A 1-2-S-3	82		.295
1964	BAL A 1-2-S-3-	93		.248
	0			
1965	BAL A 1-2-S-3	87		.242
1966	BAL A 1-2-3	71		.217
1967	BAL A H	4		.333
	NY N 1-2-S-3	90		.348
1968	CIN N 1-S	16		.267
	ATL N 2-3	59		.262
1969	STL N 1-3	19		.207
	OAK A 1-2	51		.343
1970	OAK A 1-3	30		.174
	BRTR	874		.272

JOHNSON, ROY "HARDROCK"
B.OCT.1,1895 MADILL,OKLA.

| 1918 | PHI A P | 10 | | 1- 5 |
| | BRTR | | | |
| NON-PLAYING MANAGER CHI(N) 1944 |

JOHNSON, ROY CLEVELAND
B.FEB.23,1904 SPAVINAW,OKLA.
D.SEPT.10,1973 TACOMA,WASH.

1929	DET A 0		148	.314
1930	DET A 0		125	.275
1931	DET A 0		151	.279
1932	DET A 0		49	.254
	BOS A 0		94	.296
1933	BOS A 0		133	.313
1934	BOS A 0		143	.320
1935	BOS A 0		145	.315
1936	NY A 0		63	.265
1937	NY A 0		12	.294
	BOS N 0		85	.277
1938	BOS N 0		7	.172
	BLTR		1155	.296

JOHNSON, RUSSELL CONWELL "JING"
B.OCT.9,1894 PARKER FORD,PA.
D.DEC.6,1950

1916	PHI A P		12	2- 9
1917	PHI A P	34	35	9-12
1919	PHI A P	34	35	9-14
1927	PHI A P		17	4- 2
1928	PHI A P		3	0- 0
	BRTR	**100**	**102**	**24-37**

JOHNSON, SILAS KENNETH "SI"
B.OCT.5,1908 MARSEILLES,ILL.

1928	CIN N P	3		0- 0
1929	CIN N P	1		0- 0
1930	CIN N P	35		3- 1
1931	CIN N P	42		11-19
1932	CIN N P	42		13-15
1933	CIN N P	34		7-18
1934	CIN N P	46		7-22
1935	CIN N P	30		5-11
1936	CIN N P	2		0- 0
	STL N P	12		5- 3
1937	STL N P	38		12-12
1938	STL N P	6		0- 3
1940	PHI N P	37		5-14
1941	PHI N P	39		5-12
1942	PHI N P	39		8-19
1943	PHI N P	21		8- 3
1946	PHI N P	1		0- 0
	BOS N P	28		6- 5
1947	BOS N P	36		6- 8
	BRTR	492		101-165

JOHNSON, STANLEY LUCIUS
B.FEB.12,1903 DALLAS,TEX.

1960	CHI A 0	5		.167
1961	KC A 0	3		.000
	BLTL	8		.111

JOHNSON, SYLVESTER W. "SYL"
B.DEC.31,1900 PORTLAND,ORE.

1922	DET A P	29		7- 3
1923	DET A P	37		12- 7
1924	DET A P	29		5- 4
1925	DET A P	6		0- 2
1926	STL N P	19		0- 3
1927	STL N P	2		0- 0
1928	STL N P	34		8- 4
1929	STL N P	42		13- 7
1930	STL N P	32		12-10
1931	STL N P	32		11- 9
1932	STL N P	32		5-14
1933	STL N P	35		3- 3
1934	CIN N P	2		0- 0
	PHI N P	42		5- 9
1935	PHI N P	37		10- 8
1936	PHI N P	39		5- 7
1937	PHI N P	32		4-10
1938	PHI N P	22		2- 7
1939	PHI N P	22		8- 8
1940	PHI N P	17		2- 2
	BRTR	542		112-117

JOHNSON, THOMAS G.
B.SCRANTON,PA.

1897	PHI N P	5		0- 2
1899	NY N P	1		0- 0
		6		0- 2

JOHNSON, THOMAS RAYMOND "TOM"
B.APR.2,1951 ST.PAUL,MINN.

1974	MIN A P	4		2- 0
1975	MIN A P	18		1- 2
1976	MIN A P	18		3- 1
	BRTR	40		6- 3

JOHNSON, TIMOTHY EVALD "TIM"
B.JULY 22,1949 GRAND FORKS,N.D.

1973	MIL A S	136		.213
1974	MIL A 2-S-3-0	93		.245
1975	MIL A 1-2-S-3	38		.141
1976	MIL A 1-2-S-3	105		.275
	BLTR	372		.230

JOHNSON, VICTOR OSCAR "VIC"
B.AUG.3,1920 EAU CLAIRE,WIS.

1944	BOS A P	7		0- 3
1945	BOS A P	26		6- 4
1946	CLE A P	9		0- 1
	BRTL	42		6- 8

YR	CL	LEA	POS	GP	G	REC

JOHNSON, WALTER PERRY "BARNEY"
OR "THE BIG TRAIN"
B.NOV.6,1887 HUMBOLDT,KAN.
D.DEC.10,1946 WASHINGTON,D.C.

1907	WAS	A	P		14	5- 9
1908	WAS	A	P		36	14-14
1909	WAS	A	P		40	13-25
1910	WAS	A	P		45	25-17
1911	WAS	A	P	40	42	23-15
1912	WAS	A	P	50	53	32-12
1913	WAS	A	P	47	51	36- 7
1914	WAS	A	P	50	54	28-18
1915	WAS	A	P	49	64	27-13
1916	WAS	A	P	50	59	25-20
1917	WAS	A	P	48	57	23-16
1918	WAS	A	P	39	65	23-13
1919	WAS	A	P	39	56	20-14
1920	WAS	A	P	21	35	8-10
1921	WAS	A	P	35	38	17-14
1922	WAS	A	P	41	43	15-16
1923	WAS	A	P		42	17-12
1924	WAS	A	P	38	39	23- 7
1925	WAS	A	P	30	36	20- 7
1926	WAS	A	P	33	35	15-16
1927	WAS	A	P	18	26	5- 6
	BRTR			805	930	414-281

NON-PLAYING MANAGER
WAS(A) 1929-32, CLE(A) 1933-35

JOHNSON, WILLIAM LAWRENCE
B.JULY 30,1894 CHICAGO,ILL.
D.NOV.4,1950

1916	PHI	A	O		4	.267
1917	PHI	A	O		48	.174
	BLTR				52	.185

JOHNSON, WILLIAM RUSSELL "BULL"
B.AUG.30,1918 MONTCLAIR,N.J.

1943	NY	A	3		155	.280
1946	NY	A	3		85	.262
1947	NY	A	3		132	.285
1948	NY	A	3		127	.294
1949	NY	A	1-2-3		113	.249
1950	NY	A	1-3		108	.260
1951	NY	A	3		15	.300
	STL	N	3		124	.262
1952	STL	N	3		94	.252
1953	STL	N	3		11	.200
	BRTR				964	.271

JOHNSON, WILLIAM T.
B.CHESTER,PA.
D.1921

1884	KEY	U	O		1	.000
1887	IND	N	O		11	.190
1890	BAL	AA	O		24	.354
1891	BAL	AA	O		127	.269
1892	BAL	N	O		4	.133
	BLTL				167	.264

JOHNSTON, JAMES HARLE
B.DEC.10,1889 CLEVELAND,TENN.
D.FEB.14,1967 CHATTANOOGA,TENN.

1911	CHI	A	O		1	.000
1914	CHI	N	O		50	.228
1916	BRO	N	O		118	.252
1917	BRO	N	O		103	.270
1918	BRO	N	1-2-3-0		123	.281
1919	BRO	N	1-2-S-O		117	.281
1920	BRO	N	3		155	.291
1921	BRO	N	3		152	.325
1922	BRO	N	2-S-3		138	.319
1923	BRO	N	2-S-3		151	.325
1924	BRO	N	1-2-S-3-	86		.298
			O			
1925	BRO	N	1-S-3-O	123		.297
1926	BOS	N	3-O		23	.246
	NY	N	O		37	.232
	BRTR				1377	.294

JOHNSTON, JOHN THOMAS
B.MAR.28,1890 LONGVIEW,TEX.
D.MAR.7,1940

| 1913 | STL | A | O | | 09 | .226 |
| | BLTR | | | | | |

JOHNSTON, REX DAVID
B.NOV.8,1937 COLTON,CAL.

| 1964 | PIT | N | O | | 14 | .000 |
| | BBTR | | | | | |

JOHNSTON, RICHARD FREDERICK
B.APR.6,1863 KINGSTON,N.Y.
D.APR.4,1934

1884	RIC	AA	S-O		39	.286
1885	BOS	N	O		26	.238
1886	BOS	N	O		109	.239
1887	BOS	N	O		124	.283
1888	BOS	N	O		135	.295
1889	BOS	N	O		131	.228
1890	BOS	P	O		2	.111
	NY	P	O		75	.257
1891	CIN	AA	O		99	.219
	BRTR				740	.256

JOHNSTON, WHEELER ROGERS "DOC"
B.SEPT.9,1887 CLEVELAND,TENN.
D.FEB.18,1961

1909	CIN	N	1		3	.000
1912	CLE	A	1		43	.280
1913	CLE	A	1		133	.255
1914	CLE	A	1		103	.244
1915	PIT	N	1		147	.265
1916	PIT	N	1		114	.213
1918	CLE	A	1		74	.227
1919	CLE	A	1		102	.305
1920	CLE	A	1		147	.292
1921	CLE	A	1		118	.297
1922	PHI	A	1		71	.250
	BLTL				1055	.274

JOHNSTON, WILFRED IVEY "RED"
B.JULY 9,1899 CHARLOTTE,N.C.
D.MAY 14,1959 TYLER,TEX.

| 1924 | BRO | N | 2 | | 4 | .250 |
| | BRTR | | | | | |

JOHNSTONE, JOHN WILLIAM "JAY"
B.NOV.20,1945 MANCHESTER,CONN.

1966	CAL	A	O		61	.264
1967	CAL	A	O		79	.209
1968	CAL	A	O		41	.261
1969	CAL	A	O		148	.270
1970	CAL	A	O		119	.238
1971	CHI	A	O		124	.260
1972	CHI	A	O		113	.188
1973	OAK	A	2-O		23	.107
1974	PHI	N	O		64	.295
1975	PHI	N	O		122	.329
1976	PHI	N	1-O		129	.318
	BLTR				1023	.267

JOINER, ROY MERRILL "POP"
B.OCT.30,1907 RED BLUFF,CAL.

1934	CHI	N	P		20	0- 1
1935	CHI	N	P		2	0- 0
1940	NY	N	P		30	3- 2
	BLTL				52	3- 3

JOK, STANLEY EDWARD "STAN"
B.MAY 3,1926 BUFFALO,N.Y.
D.MAR.6,1972 BUFFALO,N.Y.

1954	PHI	N	H		3	.000
	CHI	A	3		3	.167
1955	CHI	A	3-O		6	.250
	BRTR				12	.158

JOLLEY, SMEAD POWELL "GUINEA"
B.JAN.14,1902 EL DORADO,ARK.

1930	CHI	A	O		152	.313
1931	CHI	A	O		54	.300
1932	CHI	A	O		12	.357
	BOS	A	O		137	.309
1933	BOS	A	O		118	.282
	BLTR				473	.305

JOLLY, DAVID "DAVE"
B.OCT.14,1924 STONY POINT,N.C.
D.MAY 27,1963 DURHAM,N.C.

1953	MIL	N	P		24	0- 1
1954	MIL	N	P	47	48	11- 6
1955	MIL	N	P		36	2- 3
1956	MIL	N	P		29	2- 3
1957	MIL	N	P		23	1- 1
	BRTR		159	160	16-14

JONES
B.SYRACUSE,N.Y.

1882	BAL	AA	C-O		4	.067
1884	KEY	U	C-O		4	.154
					8	.107

JONES, ALBERT EDWARD "COWBOY"
B.AUG.23,1874 GOLDEN,COLO.
D.FEB.9,1958

1898	CLE	N	P		8	4- 4
1899	STL	N	P		14	6- 5
1900	STL	N	P		38	13-20
1901	STL	N	P		10	2- 6
	BLTL				70	25-35

JONES, ALEXANDER H.
B.1867 BRADFORD,PA.

1889	PIT	N	P		1	1- 0
1892	LOU	N	P		18	6-12
	WAS	N	P		7	1- 2
1894	PHI	N	P		1	1- 0
1903	DET	A	P		2	0- 2
	TL				29	9-16

JONES, ARTHUR LENOX
B.FEB.7,1907 KERSHAW,S.C.

| 1932 | BRO | N | P | | 1 | 0- 0 |
| | BRTR | | | | | |

JONES, CARROLL ELMER "DEACON"
B.DEC.20,1892 ARCADIA,KAN.
D.DEC.28,1952

1916	DET	A	P		1	0- 0
1917	DET	A	P		24	4- 4
1918	DET	A	P	19	22	2- 2
	BRTR		44	47	6- 6

JONES, CHARLES C. "CASEY"
B.JUNE 2,1876 BUTLER,PA.
D.APR.2,1947

1901	BO3	A	O		10	.119
1904	CHI	A	O		5	.235
1905	WAS	A	O		142	.208
1906	WAS	A	O		131	.241
1907	WAS	A	O		121	.265
1908	STL	A	O		74	.232
	TR				483	.233

JONES, CHARLES F.
B.NEW YORK,N.Y.

1884	BRO	AA	2-3		24	.188
1885	MET	AA	3		1	.250
					25	.191

JONES, CHARLES LEANDER "BUMPUS"
B.JAN.1,1870 CEDARVILLE,OHIO
D.JUNE 25,1938

1892	CIN	N	P		1	1- 0
1893	CIN	N	P		6	1- 3
	NY	N	P		4	0- 1
	BRTR				11	2- 4

JONES, CHARLES WESLEY "BABY"
(REAL NAME
BENJAMIN WESLEY RIPPAY)
B.APR.30,1850 ALAMANCE CO.,N.C.

1873	MAR	NA	O		1	-
1874	BAL	NA	C-O		5	-
1875	WES	NA	O		12	-
	HAR	NA	O		1	.000
1876	CIN	N	O		64	.279
1877	CIN	N	1-O	20		.329
	CHI	N	O		2	.375
	CIN	N	O		35	.330
1878	CIN	N	O		62	.297
1879	BOS	N	O		83	.315
1880	BOS	N	O		64	.297
1883	CIN	AA	O		85	.285
1884	CIN	AA	O		113	.322
1885	CIN	AA	O		112	.327
1886	CIN	AA	O		127	.274
1887	CIN	AA	O		41	.374
	MET	AA	O		63	.302
1888	KC	AA	O		6	.250
	BRTR				896	-

JONES, CLARENCE WOODROW
B.NOV.7,1941 ZANESVILLE,OHIO

1967	CHI	N	1-O		53	.252
1968	CHI	N	1		5	.000
	BLTL				58	.248

YR	CL	LEA	POS	GP	G	REC

JONES, CLEON JOSEPH
B.AUG.4,1942 PLATEAU,ALA.

YR	CL	LEA	POS	GP	G	REC
1963	NY	N	O		6	.133
1965	NY	N	O		30	.149
1966	NY	N	O		139	.275
1967	NY	N	O		129	.246
1968	NY	N	O		147	.297
1969	NY	N	1-O		137	.340
1970	NY	N	O		134	.277
1971	NY	N	O		136	.319
1972	NY	N	1-O		106	.245
1973	NY	N	O		92	.260
1974	NY	N	O		124	.282
1975	NY	N	O		21	.240
1976	CHI	A	O		12	.200
		BRTL			1213	.281

JONES, COBURN DYAS "COBE"
B.AUG.21,1907 DENVER,COLO.
D.JUNE 3,1969 DENVER,COLO.

YR	CL	LEA	POS	GP	G	REC
1928	PIT	N	S		1	.500
1929	PIT	N	S		25	.254
		BBTR			26	.262

JONES, DALE ELDON "NUBS"
B.DEC.17,1918 MARQUETTE,NEB.

YR	CL	LEA	POS	GP	G	REC
1941	PHI	N	P		2	0- 1
		BRTR				

JONES, DANIEL ALBION
"JUMPING JACK"
B.OCT.23,1860 LITCHFIELD,CONN.
D.OCT.19,1936

YR	CL	LEA	POS	GP	G	REC
1883	DET	N	P-O	11	6- 4	
						.243
	ATH	AA	P	7	5- 2	
	TR			18	11- 6	
						.197

JONES, DAVID JEFFERSON
"DAVEY" OR "KANGAROO"
B.JUNE 30,1880 CAMBRIA,WIS.
D.MAR.30,1972 MANKATO,MINN.

YR	CL	LEA	POS	GP	G	REC
1901	MIL	A	O		14	.169
1902	STL	A	O		14	.224
	CHI	N	O		63	.310
1903	CHI	N	O		130	.282
1904	CHI	N	O		97	.244
1906	DET	A	O		84	.260
1907	DET	A	O		126	.273
1908	DET	A	O		56	.207
1909	DET	A	O		69	.279
1910	DET	A	O		113	.265
1911	DET	A	O		98	.273
1912	DET	A	O		97	.294
1913	CHI	A	O		12	.288
1914	PIT	F	O		97	.272
1915	PIT	F	O		14	.327
1918	PIT	A	O		2	.000
		BLTR			1086	.270

JONES, DECATUR POINDEXTER
"DICK"
B.MAY 22,1904 MEADVILLE,MISS.

YR	CL	LEA	POS	GP	G	REC
1926	WAS	A	P	5	2- 1	
1927	WAS	A	P	2	0- 0	
		BLTR		7	2- 1	

JONES, EARL LESLIE "LEFTY"
B.JUNE 11,1919 FRESNO,CAL.

YR	CL	LEA	POS	GP	G	REC
1945	STL	A	P	10	0- 0	
		BLTL				

JONES, ELIJAH ALBERT
B.JAN.27,1882 OXFORD,MICH.
D.APR.28,1943

YR	CL	LEA	POS	GP	G	REC
1907	DET	A	P	4	0- 2	
1909	DET	A	P	2	1- 1	
		BRTR		6	1- 3	

JONES, FIELDER ALLISON
B.AUG.13,1874 SHINGLEHOUSE,PA.
D.MAR.13,1934

YR	CL	LEA	POS	GP	G	REC
1896	BRO	N	O	102		.353
1897	BRO	N	O	135		.322
1898	BRO	N	O	147		.304
1899	BRO	N	O	95		.286
1900	BRO	N	O	136		.309
1901	CHI	A	O	133		.325
1902	CHI	A	O	135		.318
1903	CHI	A	O	137		.304
1904	CHI	A	M-O	150		.245
1905	CHI	A	M-O	153		.245
1906	CHI	A	M-O	144		.230
1907	CHI	A	M-O	154		.261
1908	CHI	A	M-O	149		.253
1914	STL	F	M-H	5		.333
1915	STL	F	M-O	5		.000
		BLTR		1780		.287

NON-PLAYING MANAGER
STL(A) 1916-18

JONES, FRANK M.
B.DULUTH,MINN.

YR	CL	LEA	POS	GP	G	REC
1884	DET	N	2-S-O	34		.209

JONES, GARY HOWELL
B.JUNE 12,1945 HUNTINGTON PARK,
CAL.

YR	CL	LEA	POS	GP	G	REC
1970	NY	A	P	2	0- 0	
1971	NY	A	P	12	0- 0	
		BLTL		14	0- 0	

JONES, GORDON BASSETT
B.APP.2,1930 PORTLAND,ORE.

YR	CL	LEA	POS	GP	G	REC
1954	STL	N	P	11	4- 4	
1955	STL	N	P	15	1- 4	
1956	STL	N	P	5	0- 2	
1957	NY	N	P	10	0- 1	
1958	SF	N	P	11	3- 1	
1959	SF	N	P	31	3- 2	
1960	BAL	A	P	29	1- 1	
1961	BAL	A	P	3	0- 0	
1962	KC	A	P	21	3- 2	
1964	HOU	N	P	34	0- 1	
1965	HOU	N	P	1	0- 0	
		BRTR		171	15-18	

JONES, GROVER WILLIAM "DEACON"
B.APR.18,1934 WHITE PLAINS,N.Y.

YR	CL	LEA	POS	GP	G	REC
1962	CHI	A	1	18		.321
1963	CHI	A	1	17		.188
1966	CHI	A	H	5		.400
		BLTR		40		.286

JONES, HAROLD MARION
B.APR.9,1938 LOUISIANA,MO.

YR	CL	LEA	POS	GP	G	REC
1961	CLE	A	1	12		.171
1962	CLE	A	1	5		.313
		BRTR		17		.216

JONES, HENRY M. "BALDY"
B.CADILLAC,MICH.

YR	CL	LEA	POS	GP	G	REC
1890	PIT	N	P	4	2- 2	

JONES, HOWARD "COTTON"
B.MAR.1,1897 IRWIN,PA.
D.JULY 15,1972 JEANETTE,PA.

YR	CL	LEA	POS	GP	G	REC
1921	STL	N	O	3		.000

JONES, JAMES DALTON
"DALTON"
B.DEC.10,1943 MC COMB,MISS.

YR	CL	LEA	POS	GP	G	REC
1964	BOS	A	2-S-3	118		.230
1965	BOS	A	2-3	112		.270
1966	BOS	A	2-3	115		.234
1967	BOS	A	1-2-3	89		.289
1968	BOS	A	1-2-3	111		.234
1969	BOS	A	1-2-3	111		.220
1970	DET	A	1-2-3	89		.220
1971	DET	A	1-2-3-O	83		.254
1972	DET	A	H	7		.000
	TEX	A	1-2-3-O	72		.159
		BLTR		907		.235

JONES, JAMES MURRELL "JAKE"
B.NOV.23,1920 EPPS,LA.

YR	CL	LEA	POS	GP	G	REC
1941	CHI	A	1	3		.000
1942	CHI	A	1	7		.150
1946	CHI	A	1	24		.266
1947	CHI	A	1	45		.240
	BOS	A	1	109		.235
1948	BOS	A	1	36		.200
		BRTR		224		.229

JONES, JAMES TILFORD "SHERIFF"
B.DEC.25,1878 LONDON,KY.
D.MAY 6,1953

YR	CL	LEA	POS	GP	G	REC
1897	LOU	N	P		2	0- 0
1901	NY	N	P-O	1	21	0- 1
						.209
1902	NY	N	O		65	.236
				3	88	0- 1
						.229

JONES, JESSE FRANK "BROADWAY"
B.NOV.15,1898 MILLSBORO,DEL.

YR	CL	LEA	POS	GP	G	REC
1923	PHI	N	P		3	0- 0
		BRTR				

JONES, JOHN PAUL "ADMIRAL"
B.AUG.25,1892 ARCADIA,LA.

YR	CL	LEA	POS	GP	G	REC
1919	NY	N	P		2	0- 0
1920	BOS	N	P		3	1- 0
		BRTR			5	1- 0

JONES, JOHN WILLIAM
B.JULY 11,1899 ST.LOUIS,MO.
D.MAY 18,1961

YR	CL	LEA	POS	GP	G	REC
1924	BRO	N	S		10	.108
		BRTR				

JONES, JOHN WILLIAM
B.MAY 13,1902 COATESVILLE,PA.
D.NOV.8,1956

YR	CL	LEA	POS	GP	G	REC
1923	PHI	A	O		1	.250
1932	PHI	A	O		4	.167
		BLTL			5	.200

JONES, KENNETH FREDERICK
B.APR.13,1904 DOVER,N.J.

YR	CL	LEA	POS	GP	G	REC
1924	DET	A	P		1	0- 0
1930	BOS	N	P		8	0- 1
		BRTR			9	0- 1

JONES, MACK
B.NOV.6,1938 ALANTA,GA.

YR	CL	LEA	POS	GP	G	REC
1961	MIL	N	O		28	.231
1962	MIL	N	O		91	.255
1963	MIL	N	O		93	.219
1965	MIL	N	O		143	.262
1966	ATL	N	1-O		118	.264
1967	ATL	N	O		140	.253
1968	CIN	N	O		103	.252
1969	MON	N	O		135	.270
1970	MON	N	O		108	.240
1971	MON	N	O		43	.165
		BLTR			1002	.252

JONES, MAURICE MORRIS "RED"
B.NOV.2,1914 TIMPSON,TEX.

YR	CL	LEA	POS	GP	G	REC
1940	STL	N	O		12	.091
		BLTR				

JONES, MICHAEL
B.HAMILTON,ONT.,CANADA
D.MAR.24,1894

YR	CL	LEA	POS	GP	G	REC
1890	LOU	AA	P		4	4- 0

JONES, ODELL
B.JAN.13,1953 TULARE,CAL.

YR	CL	LEA	POS	GP	G	REC
1975	PIT	N	P		2	0- 0
		BRTR				

JONES, OSCAR WINFIELD
"FLIP FLAP"
B.JAN.21,1879 LONDON GROVE,PA.
D.OCT.8,1946

YR	CL	LEA	POS	GP	G	REC
1903	BRO	N	P		38	19-14
1904	BRO	N	P		46	18-26
1905	BRO	N	P	29	30	7-14
		BRTR		113	114	44-54

JONES, PERCY LEE
B.OCT.28,1899 HARWOOD,TEX.

YR	CL	LEA	POS	GP	G	REC
1920	CHI	N	P		4	0- 0
1921	CHI	N	P		32	3- 5
1922	CHI	N	P		44	8- 9
1925	CHI	N	P		28	6- 6
1926	CHI	N	P		30	12- 7
1927	CHI	N	P		30	7- 8
1928	CHI	N	P		39	10- 6
1929	BOS	N	P	35	36	7-15
1930	PIT	N	P		9	0- 1
		BRTL		251	252	53-57

YR	CL	LEA	POS	GP	G	REC

JONES, RANDALL LEO "RANDY"
B.JAN.12,1950 FULLERTON,CAL.

YR	CL	LEA	POS	GP	G	REC
1973	SD	N	P		20	7- 6
1974	SD	N	P	40	46	8-22
1975	SD	N	P	37	40	20-12
1976	SD	N	P		40	22-14
	BRTL			137	146	57-54

JONES, ROBERT OLIVER "BOB"
B.OCT.11,1949 ELKTON,MD.

YR	CL	LEA	POS	GP	G	REC
1974	TEX	A	O		2	.000
1975	TEX	A	O		9	.091
1976	CAL	A	O		78	.211
	BLTL				89	.198

JONES, ROBERT WALTER "DUCKY"
B.DEC.2,1889 CLAYTON,CAL.
D.AUG.30,1964 SAN DIEGO,CAL.

YR	CL	LEA	POS	GP	G	REC
1917	DET	A	2		46	.156
1918	DET	A	3		75	.275
1919	DET	A	3		127	.260
1920	DET	A	3		81	.249
1921	DET	A	3		141	.303
1922	DET	A	3		124	.257
1923	DET	A	3		100	.250
1924	DET	A	3		110	.272
1925	DET	A	3		50	.236
	BLTR				854	.265

JONES, RUPPERT SANDERSON
B.MAR.12,1955 DALLAS,TEX.

YR	CL	LEA	POS	GP	G	REC
1976	KC	A	O		28	.216
	BLTL					

JONES, RYERSON L.
"ANGEL SLEEVES"
B.CINCINNATI,OHIO

YR	CL	LEA	POS	GP	G	REC
1883	LOU	AA	3-O		2	.000
1884	CIN	U	S		55	.265
	TR				57	.258

JONES, SAMUEL "SAM"
B.DEC.14,1925 STEWARTSVILLE,OHIO
D.NOV.5,1971 MORGANTOWN,W.VA.

YR	CL	LEA	POS	GP	G	REC
1951	CLE	A	P		2	0- 1
1952	CLE	A	P		14	2- 3
1955	CHI	N	P		36	14-20
1956	CHI	N	P		33	9-14
1957	STL	N	P		28	12- 9
1958	STL	N	P		35	14-13
1959	SF	N	P		50	21-15
1960	SF	N	P		39	18-14
1961	SF	N	P		37	8- 8
1962	DET	A	P		30	2- 4
1963	STL	N	P		11	2- 0
1964	BAL	A	P		7	0- 0
	BRTR				322	102-101

JONES, SAMUEL POND "SAD SAM"
B.JULY 26,1892 WOODSFIELD,OHIO
D.JULY 6,1966 BARNESVILLE,OHIO

YR	CL	LEA	POS	GP	G	REC
1914	CLE	A	P		1	0- 0
1915	CLE	A	P		48	3- 8
1916	BOS	A	P	12	13	0- 1
1917	BOS	A	P		9	0- 1
1918	BOS	A	P		24	16- 5
1919	BOS	A	P		35	13-20
1920	BOS	A	P	37	44	13-16
1921	BOS	A	P	40	43	23-16
1922	NY	A	P		45	13-13
1923	NY	A	P		39	21- 8
1924	NY	A	P		36	9- 6
1925	NY	A	P-O	43	46	15-21
						.162
1926	NY	A	P	39	44	9- 8
1927	STL	A	P	30	32	8-14
1928	WAS	A	P	30	37	17- 7
1929	WAS	A	P	24	28	9- 9
1930	WAS	A	P	25	30	15- 7
1931	WAS	A	P	25	30	9-10
1932	CHI	A	P	30	39	10-15
1933	CHI	A	P	27	37	10-12
1934	CHI	A	P	27	31	8-12
1935	CHI	A	P	21	22	8- 7
	BRTR			647	713	229-216
						.197

JONES, SHELDON LESLIE
"AVAILABLE"
B.FEB.2,1922 TECUMSEH,NEB.

YR	CL	LEA	POS	GP	G	REC
1946	NY	N	P		6	1- 2
1947	NY	N	P		15	2- 2
1948	NY	N	P		55	16- 8
1949	NY	N	P		42	15-12
1950	NY	N	P		40	13-16
1951	NY	N	P		41	6-11
1952	BOS	N	P		39	1- 4
1953	CHI	N	P		22	0- 2
	BRTR				260	54-57

JONES, SHERMAN JARVIS
"ROADBLOCK"
B.FEB.10,1936 HERTFORD CO.,N.C.

YR	CL	LEA	POS	GP	G	REC
1960	SF	N	P		16	1- 1
1961	CIN	N	P		24	1- 1
1962	NY	N	P		8	0- 4
	BLTR				48	2- 6

JONES, STEVEN HOWELL "STEVE"
B.APR.22,1941 HUNTINGTON PARK,
CAL.

YR	CL	LEA	POS	GP	G	REC
1967	CHI	A	P		11	2- 2
1968	WAS	A	P		7	1- 2
1969	KC	A	P		20	2- 3
	BLTL				38	5- 7

JONES, THOMAS
B.JAN.22,1877 HONESDALE,PA.
D.JUNE 21,1923

YR	CL	LEA	POS	GP	G	REC
1902	BAL	A	1-2		37	.283
1904	STL	A	1-2		156	.241
1905	STL	A	1		135	.242
1906	STL	A	1		144	.252
1907	STL	A	1		155	.250
1908	STL	A	1		155	.248
1909	STL	A	1		97	.254
	DET	A	1		44	.271
1910	DET	A	1		135	.255
	BRTR				1058	.240

JONES, THOMAS FREDRICK "RICK"
B.APR.16,1955 JACKSONVILLE,FLA.

YR	CL	LEA	POS	GP	G	REC
1976	BOS	A	P		24	5- 3
	BLTL					

JONES, VERNAL LEROY "NIPPY"
B.JUNE 29,1925 LOS ANGELES,CAL.

YR	CL	LEA	POS	GP	G	REC
1946	STL	N	2		16	.333
1947	STL	N	2-0		23	.247
1948	STL	N	1		132	.254
1949	STL	N	1		110	.300
1950	STL	N	1		13	.231
1951	STL	N	1		80	.263
1952	PHI	N	1		8	.167
1957	MIL	N	1-0		30	.266
	BRTR				412	.267

JONES, WILLIAM DENNIS "MIDGET"
B.APR.8,1888 HARTLAND,N.B.,CAN.
D.OCT.10,1946

YR	CL	LEA	POS	GP	G	REC
1911	BOS	N	O		18	.216
1912	BOS	N	O		2	.500
	BLTR				20	.226

JONES, WILLIAM RODERICK "TEX"
B.AUG.4,1885 MARION,KAN.
D.FEB.26,1938

YR	CL	LEA	POS	GP	G	REC
1911	CHI	A	1		9	.193
	BRTR					

JONES, WILLIE EDWARD
"PUDDIN' HEAD"
B.AUG.16,1925 DILLON,S.C.

YR	CL	LEA	POS	GP	G	REC
1947	PHI	N	3		18	.226
1948	PHI	N	3		17	.333
1949	PHI	N	3		149	.245
1950	PHI	N	3		157	.267
1951	PHI	N	3		148	.285
1952	PHI	N	3		147	.250
1953	PHI	N	3		149	.225
1954	PHI	N	3		142	.271
1955	PHI	N	3		146	.258
1956	PHI	N	3		149	.277
1957	PHI	N	3		133	.218
1958	PHI	N	1-3		118	.271
1959	PHI	N	3		47	.269
	CLE	A	3		11	.222
	CIN	N	3		72	.249
1960	CIN	N	2-3		79	.268
1961	CIN	N	3		9	.000
	BRTR				1691	.258

JONNARD, CLARENCE JAMES
"BUBBER"
B.NOV.23,1896 NASHVILLE,TENN.

YR	CL	LEA	POS	GP	G	REC
1920	CHI	A	C		2	.000
1922	PIT	N	C		10	.238
1926	PHI	N	C		19	.118
1927	PHI	N	C		53	.294
1929	STL	N	C		18	.097
1935	PHI	N	C		1	.000
	BRTR				103	.230

JONNARD, CLAUDE ALFRED
B.NOV.23,1896 NASHVILLE,TENN.
D.AUG.27,1959

YR	CL	LEA	POS	GP	G	REC
1921	NY	N	P		1	0- 0
1922	NY	N	P		33	6- 1
1923	NY	N	P		45	4- 3
1924	NY	N	P		34	4- 5
1926	STL	A	P		12	0- 2
1929	CHI	N	P		12	0- 1
	BRTR				137	14-12

JOOST, EDWIN DAVID "EDDIE"
B.JUNE 5,1916 SAN FRANCISCO,CAL

YR	CL	LEA	POS	GP	G	REC
1936	CIN	N	2-S		13	.154
1937	CIN	N	2		6	.083
1939	CIN	N	2-S		42	.252
1940	CIN	N	2-S-3		88	.216
1941	CIN	N	1-2-S-3		152	.253
1942	CIN	N	2		142	.224
1943	BOS	N	2-S-3		124	.185
1945	BOS	N	2-3		35	.248
1947	PHI	A	S		151	.206
1948	PHI	A	S		135	.250
1949	PHI	A	S		144	.263
1950	PHI	A	S		131	.233
1951	PHI	A	S		140	.289
1952	PHI	A	S		146	.244
1953	PHI	A	S		51	.249
1954	PHI	A	M-2-S-3		19	.362
1955	BOS	A	2-S-3		55	.193
	BRTR				1574	.239

JORDAN, ADOLF OTTO "DUTCH"
B.JAN.5,1880 PITTSBURGH,PA.
D.DEC.23,1972 W.ALLEGHENY,PA.

YR	CL	LEA	POS	GP	G	REC
1903	BRO	N	2-3		77	.236
1904	BRO	N	2		85	.179
	BRTR				162	.208

JORDAN, BAXTER BYERLY "BUCK"
B.JAN.16,1907 COOLEEMEE,N.C.

YR	CL	LEA	POS	GP	G	REC
1927	NY	N	H		5	.200
1929	NY	N	H		2	.500
1931	WAS	A	1		9	.222
1932	BOS	N	1		49	.321
1933	BOS	N	1		152	.286
1934	BOS	N	1		124	.311
1935	BOS	N	1-3-O		130	.279
1936	BOS	N	1		138	.323
1937	BOS	N	1		8	.250
	CIN	N	1		98	.282
1938	CIN	N	H		9	.286
	PHI	N	1-3		87	.300
	BLTR				811	.299

JORDAN, CHARLES T.
B.OCT.4,1871 BALTIMORE,MD.
D.JUNE 1,1928

YR	CL	LEA	POS	GP	G	REC
1896	PHI	N	P		1	0- 0

JORDAN, HARRY J.
B.TITUSVILLE,PA.

YR	CL	LEA	POS	GP	G	REC
1894	PIT	N	P		1	1- 0
1895	PIT	N	P		2	0- 2
					3	1- 2

JORDAN, JAMES WILLIAM "LORD"
B.JAN.13,1908 TACAPAU,S.C.
D.DEC.4,1957

YR	CL	LEA	POS	GP	G	REC
1933	BRO	N	2-S		70	.256
1934	BRO	N	2-S		97	.266
1935	BRO	N	2-S-3		94	.278
1936	BRO	N	2		115	.234
	BRTR				376	.257

JORDAN, MICHAEL HENRY
B.FEB.7,1863 LAWRENCE,MASS.
D.SEPT.25,1940 LAWRENCE,MASS.

YR	CL	LEA	POS	GP	G	REC
1890	PIT	N	O		37	.096

JORDAN, MILTON MIGNOT
B.MAY 24,1927 MINERAL SPRINGS,
PA.

YR	CL	LEA	POS	GP	G	REC
1953	DET	A	P		8	0- 1
	BRTR					

YR	CL	LEA	POS	GP	G	REC

JORDAN, NILES CHAPMAN
B.DEC.1,1926 LYMAN,WASH.

YR	CL	LEA	POS	GP	G	REC
1951	PHI	N	P		5	2- 3
1952	CIN	N	P		3	0- 1
		BLTL			8	2- 4

JORDAN, RAYMOND WILLIS "RIP"
B.SEPT.28,1889 PORTLAND,ME.
D.JUNE 5,1960

1912	CHI	A	P		4	0- 0
1919	WAS	A	P		1	0- 0
		BLTR			5	0- 0

JORDAN, THOMAS JEFFERSON
B.SEPT.5,1919 LAWTON,OKLA.

1944	CHI	A	C		14	.267
1946	CHI	A	C		10	.267
	CLE	A	C		14	.200
1948	STL	A	H		1	.000
		BRTR			39	.240

JORDAN, TIMOTHY JOSEPH
B.FEB.14,1879 NEW YORK,N.Y.
D.SEPT.13,1949

1901	WAS	A	1		5	.250
	BAL	A	1		1	.000
1902	BAL	A	0		1	.000
1903	NY	A	1		2	.125
1906	BRO	N	1		126	.262
1907	BRO	N	1		143	.274
1908	BRO	N	1		146	.247
1909	BRO	N	1		95	.273
1910	BRO	N	H		5	.200
		BLTR			524	.261

JORGENS, ARNDT LUDWIG "ART"
B.MAY 18,1905 MODUM,NORWAY

1929	NY	A	C		18	.324
1930	NY	A	C		16	.367
1931	NY	A	C		46	.270
1932	NY	A	C		56	.219
1933	NY	A	C		21	.220
1934	NY	A	C		58	.208
1935	NY	A	C		36	.238
1936	NY	A	C		31	.273
1937	NY	A	C		13	.130
1938	NY	A	C		9	.235
1939	NY	A	C		3	.000
		BRTR			307	.238

JORGENS, ORVILLE EDWARD
B.JUNE 4,1909 ROCKFORD,ILL.

1935	PHI	N	P		53	10-15
1936	PHI	N	P		39	8- 8
1937	PHI	N	P		52	3- 4
		BRTR			144	21-27

JORGENSEN, JOHN DONALD "SPIDER"
B.NOV.3,1919 FOLSOM,CAL.

1947	BRO	N	3		129	.274
1948	BRO	N	3		31	.300
1949	BRO	N	3		53	.269
1950	BRO	N	3		2	.000
	NY	N	3		24	.135
1951	NY	N	3-0		28	.235
		BLTR			267	.266

JORGENSEN, MICHAEL "MIKE"
B.AUG.16,1948 PASSAIC,N.J.

1968	NY	N	1		8	.143
1970	NY	N	1-0		76	.195
1971	NY	N	1-0		45	.220
1972	MON	N	1-0		113	.231
1973	MON	N	1-0		138	.230
1974	MON	N	1-0		131	.310
1975	MON	N	1-0		144	.261
1976	MON	N	1-0		125	.254
		BLTL			780	.249

JORGENSON, CARL "PINKY"
B.NOV.21,1916 CORCORAN,CAL.

| 1937 | CIN | N | 0 | | 6 | .286 |
| | | BRTR | | | | |

JOSEPH, RICARDO EMELINO "RICK"
B.AUG.24,1939 SAN PEDRO DE
MACORIS,D.R.

1964	KC	A	1-3		17	.222
1967	PHI	N	1		17	.220
1968	PHI	N	1-3-0		66	.219
1969	PHI	N	1-2-3		99	.273
1970	PHI	N	1-3-0		71	.227
		BRTR			270	.243

JOSEPHS, JOSEPH EMLEY
(SEE JOSEPH EMLEY BORDEN)

JOSEPHSON, DUANE CHARLES
B.JUNE 3,1942 NEW HAMPTON,IOWA

1965	CHI	A	C		4	.111
1966	CHI	A	C		11	.237
1967	CHI	A	C		62	.238
1968	CHI	A	C		128	.247
1969	CHI	A	C		52	.241
1970	CHI	A	C		96	.316
1971	BOS	A	C		91	.245
1972	BOS	A	C-1		26	.268
		BRTR			470	.258

JOSHUA, VON EVERETT
B.MAY 1,1948 OAKLAND,CAL.

1969	LA	N	0		14	.250
1970	LA	N	0		72	.266
1971	LA	N	0		11	.000
1973	LA	N	0		75	.252
1974	LA	N	0		81	.234
1975	SF	N	0		129	.318
1976	SF	N	0		42	.263
	MIL	A	0		107	.267
		BLTL			531	.278

JOSS, ADRIAN "ADDIE"
B.APR.12,1880 JUNEAU,WIS.
D.APR.14,1911

1902	CLE	A	P-1	32	33	17-13
						.116
1903	CLE	A	P	32	34	18-13
1904	CLE	A	P	25	28	14- 8
1905	CLE	A	P	32	34	19-12
1906	CLE	A	P	34	36	21- 9
1907	CLE	A	P		42	27-11
1908	CLE	A	P		42	24-11
1909	CLE	A	P		33	14-13
1910	CLE	A	P		13	5- 5
		BRTR		285	295	159-95
						.145

JOURDAN, THEODORE CHARLES
B.SEPT.5,1895 NEW ORLEANS,LA.
D.SEPT.23,1961

1916	CHI	A	H		3	.000
1917	CHI	A	1		17	.148
1918	CHI	A	1		7	.100
1920	CHI	A	1		48	.240
		BLTL			75	.214

JOY, ALOYSIUS C.
B.JUNE 11,1860 WASHINGTON,D.C.
D.JUNE 28,1937 WASHINGTON,D.C.

| 1884 | WAS | U | 1 | | 35 | .190 |

JOYCE, MICHAEL
(SEE MICHAEL JOYCE O'NEILL)

JOYCE, MICHAEL LEWIS "MIKE"
B.FEB.12,1941 DETROIT,MICH.

1962	CHI	A	P		25	2- 1
1963	CHI	A	P		6	0- 0
		BRTR			31	2- 1

JOYCE, RICHARD EDWARD "DICK"
B.NOV.18,1943 PORTLAND,ME.

| 1965 | KC | A | P | | 5 | 0- 1 |
| | | BLTL | | | | |

JOYCE, ROBERT EMMETT
B.JAN.14,1915 STOCKTON,CAL.

1939	PHI	A	P		30	3- 5
1946	NY	N	P		14	3- 4
		BRTR			44	6- 9

**JOYCE, WILLIAM MICHAEL
"SCRAPPY"**
B.SEPT.21,1865 ST.LOUIS,MO.
D.MAY 8,1941

1890	BRO	P	3		133	.269
1891	BOS	AA	3		65	.317
1892	BRO	N	3		97	.249
1894	WAS	N	3		98	.344
1895	WAS	N	3		128	.308
1896	WAS	N	3		80	.309
	NY	N	M-3		49	.350
1897	NY	N	M-3		110	.305
1898	NY	N	M-1		143	.253
		BLTR			903	.293

JUDD, RALPH WESLEY
B.DEC.7,1901 TOLEDO,OHIO
D.MAY 6,1957 LAPEER,MICH.

1927	WAS	A	P		1	0- 0
1929	NY	N	P		18	3- 0
1930	NY	N	P		2	0- 0
		BLTR			21	3- 0

**JUDD, THOMAS WILLIAM OSCAR
"OSSIE"**
B.FEB.14,1910 LONDON,ONT.,CAN.

1941	BOS	A	P		7	10	0- 0
1942	BOS	A	P		31	36	8-10
1943	BOS	A	P		23	27	11- 6
1944	BOS	A	P		9	10	1- 1
1945	BOS	A	P			2	0- 1
	PHI	N	P		23	27	5- 4
1946	PHI	N	P		30	46	11-12
1947	PHI	N	P		32	44	4-15
1948	PHI	N	P			4	0- 2
		BLTL		161	206	40-51

JUDE, FRANK
B.1884 MINNESOTA
D.MAY 4,1961

| 1906 | CIN | N | 0 | | 80 | .208 |
| | | BRTR | | | | |

JUDGE, JOSEPH IGNATIUS "JOE"
B.MAY 25,1894 BROOKLYN,N.Y.
D.MAR.11,1963 WASHINGTON,D.C.

1915	WAS	A	1		12	.353
1916	WAS	A	1		103	.220
1917	WAS	A	1		102	.285
1918	WAS	A	1		130	.261
1919	WAS	A	1		135	.288
1920	WAS	A	1		126	.333
1921	WAS	A	1		153	.301
1922	WAS	A	1		148	.295
1923	WAS	A	1		113	.314
1924	WAS	A	1		140	.324
1925	WAS	A	1		112	.314
1926	WAS	A	1		134	.291
1927	WAS	A	1		137	.308
1928	WAS	A	1		153	.306
1929	WAS	A	1		143	.315
1930	WAS	A	1		126	.326
1931	WAS	A	1		35	.284
1932	WAS	A	1		82	.258
1933	BRO	N	1		42	.214
	BOS	A	1		34	.288
1934	BOS	A	1		10	.333
		BLTL			2170	.298

**JUDNICH, WALTER FRANKLIN
"WALLY"**
B.JAN.24,1917 SAN FRANCISCO,CAL
D.JULY 12,1971 GLENDALE,CAL.

1940	STL	A	0		137	.303
1941	STL	A	0		146	.284
1942	STL	A	0		132	.313
1946	STL	A	0		142	.262
1947	STL	A	1-0		144	.258
1948	CLE	A	1-0		79	.257
1949	PIT	N	0		10	.229
		BLTL			790	.281

JUDSON, HOWARD KOLLS "HOWIE"
B.FEB.16,1926 HEBRON,ILL.

1948	CHI	A	P		40	41	4- 5
1949	CHI	A	P		26	1-14
1950	CHI	A	P		46	2- 3
1951	CHI	A	P		27	5- 6
1952	CHI	A	P		21	0- 1
1953	CIN	N	P		10	0- 1
1954	CIN	N	P		37	5- 7
		BRTR		207	208	17-37

JUDY, LYLE LEROY
B.NOV.15,1913 LAWRENCEVILLE,ILL

| 1935 | STL | A | 2 | | 8 | .000 |
| | | BRTR | | | | |

JUELICH, JOHN WALTER "RED"
B.SEPT.20,1916 ST.LOUIS,MO.
D.DEC.25,1970 ST.LOUIS,MO.

| 1939 | PIT | N | 2 | | 17 | .239 |
| | | BRTR | | | | |

JUMONVILLE, GEORGE BENEDICT
B.MAY 16,1917 MOBILE,ALA.

1940	PHI	N	S-3		11	.088
1941	PHI	N	2-S		6	.429
		BPTR			17	.146

YR   CL LEA POS GP   G   REC

JUNGELS, KENNETH PETER "CURLY"
B.JUNE 23,1916 AURORA,ILL.
D.SEPT.9,1975 WEST BEND,WIS.
1937	CLE	A	P		2	0- 0
1938	CLE	A	P		9	1- 0
1940	CLE	A	P		2	0- 0
1941	CLE	A	P		6	0- 0
1942	PIT	N	P	6	9	0- 0
	BRTR			25	28	1- 0

JUREWICZ, MICHAEL ALLEN "MIKE"
B.SEP.20,1945 BUFFALO,N.Y.
| 1965 | NY | A | P | | 2 | 0- 0 |
| | BBTL | | | | | |

**JURGES, WILLIAM FREDERICK
"BILLY"**
B.MAY 9,1908 BROOKLYN,N.Y.
1931	CHI	N	2-3	88	.201
1932	CHI	N	S	115	.253
1933	CHI	N	S	143	.269
1934	CHI	N	S	100	.246
1935	CHI	N	S	146	.241
1936	CHI	N	S	118	.280
1937	CHI	N	S	129	.298
1938	CHI	N	S	137	.245
1939	NY	N	S	138	.285
1940	NY	N	S	63	.252
1941	NY	N	S	134	.293
1942	NY	N	S	127	.256
1943	NY	N	S-3	136	.229
1944	NY	N	2-S-3	85	.211
1945	NY	N	S-3	61	.324
1946	CHI	N	2-S-3	82	.222
1947	CHI	N	S	14	.200
	BRTR			1816	.258
NON-PLAYING MANAGER
BOS(A) 1959-60

JURISCH, ALVIN JOSEPH
B.AUG.25,1921 NEW ORLEANS,LA.
1944	STL	N	P	30	7- 9
1945	STL	N	P	27	3- 3
1946	PHI	N	P	13	4- 3
1947	PHI	N	P	34	1- 7
	BRTR			104	15-22

JUST, JOSEPH ERWIN
(REAL NAME
JOSEPH ERWIN JUSZCZAK)
B.JAN.8,1916 MILWAUKEE,WIS.
1944	CIN	N	C	11	.182
1945	CIN	N	C	14	.147
	BRTR			25	.156

JUSTIS, WALTER NEWTON "SMOKE"
B.AUG.17,1883 MOORES HILL,IND.
D.OCT.4,1941 LAWRENCEBURG,IND.
| 1905 | DET | A | P | | 2 | 0- 0 |

JUSZCZAK, JOSEPH ERWIN
(PLAYED UNDER NAME OF
JOSEPH ERWIN JUST)

JUTZE, ALFRED HENRY "SKIP"
B.MAY 28,1946 QUEENS,N.Y.
1972	STL	N	C	21	.239
1973	HOU	N	C	90	.223
1974	HOU	N	C	8	.231
1975	HOU	N	C	51	.226
1976	HOU	N	C	42	.152
	BRTR			212	.214

JUUL, EARL HEROLD "HEROLD"
B.MAY 21,1893 CHICAGO,ILL.
D.JAN.4,1942
| 1914 | BRO | F | P | | 9 | 0- 3 |
| | BRTR | | | | | |

JUUL, HERBERT VICTOR
B.FEB.2,1886 CHICAGO,ILL.
D.NOV.14,1928
| 1911 | CIN | N | P | | 2 | 0- 0 |
| | BLTL | | | | | |

KAAT, JAMES LEE "JIM"
B.NOV.7,1938 ZEELAND,MICH.
1959	WAS	A	P		3	0- 2
1960	WAS	A	P		13	1- 5
1961	MIN	A	P	36	47	9-17
1962	MIN	A	P	39	48	18-14
1963	MIN	A	P	31	36	10-10
1964	MIN	A	P	36	46	17-11
1965	MIN	A	P	45	56	18-11
1966	MIN	A	P	41	47	25-13
1967	MIN	A	P	42	45	16-13
1968	MIN	A	P	30	36	14-12
1969	MIN	A	P	40	43	14-13
1970	MIN	A	P	45	56	14-10
1971	MIN	A	P	39	54	13-14
1972	MIN	A	P	15	24	10- 2
1973	MIN	A	P	29	31	11-12
	CHI	A	P		7	4- 1
1974	CHI	A	P		42	21-13
1975	CHI	A	P		43	20-14
1976	PHI	N	P	38	42	12-14
	BLTL			614	719	247-201

KADING, JOHN FRED
B.NOV.17,1884 WAUKESHA,WIS.
D.JUNE 2,1964
1910	PIT	N	1		8	.304
1914	CHI	F	H		3	.000
					11	.292

KAFORA, FRANK JACOB "JAKE"
B.OCT.16,1888 DETROIT,MICH.
D.MAR.23,1928
1913	PIT	N	C		1	.000
1914	PIT	N	C		21	.130
	BRTR				22	.125

KAHDOT, ISAAC LEONARD
B.OCT.22,1901 SACRED HEART,OKLA
| 1922 | CLE | A | P | | 4 | 0- 0 |
| | BRTR | | | | | |

KAHL, NICHOLAS ALEXANDER
B.APR.10,1879 COULTERVILLE,ILL.
D.JULY 13,1959
| 1905 | CLE | A | 2 | | 38 | .221 |
| | BRTR | | | | | |

KAHLE, ROBERT WAYNE
B.NOV.23,1915 NEWCASTLE,IND.
| 1938 | BOS | N | H | | 8 | .333 |
| | BRTR | | | | | |

KAHLER, GEORGE RANNELS "KRUM"
B.SEPT.6,1889 ATHENS,OHIO
D.FEB.7,1924 BATTLE CREEK,VA.
1910	CLE	A	P	12	6- 4
1911	CLE	A	P	30	9- 8
1912	CLE	A	P	41	12-19
1913	CLE	A	P	24	5-11
1914	CLE	A	P	2	0- 1
	BRTR			109	32-43

KAHN, OWEN EARLE
B.JUNE 11,1905 RICHMOND,VA.
| 1930 | BOS | N | H | | 1 | .000 |
| | BRTR | | | | | |

KAHOE, MICHAEL JOSEPH
B.SEPT.3,1873 YELLOW SPRINGS,O
D.MAY 14,1949 AKRON,OHIO
1895	CIN	N	C		3	.000
1899	CIN	N	C		14	.167
1900	CIN	N	C		49	.186
1901	CIN	N	C		4	.267
	CHI	N	C		65	.215
1902	CHI	N	C-S-3		7	.222
	STL	A	C		54	.251
1903	STL	A	C		74	.188
1904	STL	A	C		71	.215
1905	PHI	N	C		15	.255
1907	CHI	N	C		4	.286
	WAS	A	C		17	.191
1908	WAS	A	C		17	.185
1909	WAS	A	C		4	.125
	BRTR				398	.211

**KAISER, ALFRED EDWARD
"DEERFOOT"**
B.AUG.3,1886 CINCINNATI,OHIO
D.APR.11,1969 CINCINNATI,OHIO
1911	CHI	N	O	26	.250
	BOS	N	O	66	.203
1912	BOS	N	O	4	.000
1914	IND	F	O	59	.226
	BRTR			155	.215

KALINKIEWICZ, FRANK BRUNO
(PLAYED UNDER NAME OF
FRANK BRUNO KALIN)

KALLIO, RUDOLPH
B.DEC.14,1892 PORTLAND,ORE.
1918	DET	A	P	30	31	8-13
1919	DET	A	P	12	0- 0
1925	BOS	A	P	7	1- 4
	BRTR			49	50	9-17

KAISER, CLYDE DONALD "DON"
B.FEB.3,1935 BYNG,OKLA.
1955	CHI	N	P	11	0- 0
1956	CHI	N	P	27	4- 9
1957	CHI	N	P	20	2- 6
	BRTR			58	6-15

KAISER, ROBERT THOMAS "BOB"
B.APR.29,1950 CINCINNATI,OHIO
| 1971 | CLE | A | P | | 5 | 0- 0 |
| | BBTL | | | | | |

KAISERLING, GEORGE
B.AUG.15,1890 STEUBENVILLE,OHIO
D.MAR.2,1918
1914	IND	F	P	37	17-10
1915	NEW	F	P	41	15-16
	BRTR			78	32-26

KALAHAN, JOHN JOSEPH
B.SEPT.30,1878 PHILADELPHIA,PA.
D.JUNE 20,1952
| 1903 | PHI | A | C | | 1 | .000 |
| | TR | | | | | |

KALBFUS, CHARLES HENRY "SKINNY"
B.DEC.28,1864 WASHINGTON,D.C.
D.NOV.18,1941 WASHINGTON,D.C.
| 1884 | WAS | U | O | | 1 | .200 |
| | BRTR | | | | | |

KALFASS, WILLIAM PHILIP
B.MAR.3,1916 NEW YORK,N.Y.
D.SEPT.8,1968 BROOKLYN,N.Y.
| 1937 | PHI | A | P | | 3 | 1- 0 |
| | BRTL | | | | | |

KALIN, FRANK BRUNO "FATS"
(REAL NAME
FRANK BRUNO KALINKIEWICZ)
B.OCT.3,1917 STEUBENVILLIE,OHIO
1940	PIT	N	O		3	.000
1943	CHI	A	H		4	.000
	BRTR				7	.000

KALINE, ALBERT WILLIAM "AL"
B.DEC.19,1934 BALTIMORE,MD.
1953	DET	A	O	30	.250
1954	DET	A	O	138	.276
1955	DET	A	O	152	.340
1956	DET	A	O	153	.314
1957	DET	A	O	149	.295
1958	DET	A	O	146	.313
1959	DET	A	O	136	.327
1960	DET	A	O	147	.278
1961	DET	A	3-O	153	.324
1962	DET	A	O	100	.304
1963	DET	A	O	145	.312
1964	DET	A	O	146	.293
1965	DET	A	3-O	125	.281
1966	DET	A	O	142	.288
1967	DET	A	O	131	.308
1968	DET	A	1-O	102	.287
1969	DET	A	1-O	131	.272
1970	DET	A	1-O	131	.278
1971	DET	A	1-O	133	.294
1972	DET	A	1-O	106	.313
1973	DET	A	1-O	91	.255
1974	DET	A	D	147	.262
	BRTR			2834	.297

KAMM, WILLIAM EDWARD "WILLIE"
B.FEB.2,1900 SAN FRANCISCO,CAL.

YR	CL	LEA	POS	GP	G	REC
1923	CHI	A	3		149	.292
1924	CHI	A	3		147	.254
1925	CHI	A	3		152	.279
1926	CHI	A	3		143	.294
1927	CHI	A	3		148	.270
1928	CHI	A	3		155	.308
1929	CHI	A	3		147	.268
1930	CHI	A	3		111	.269
1931	CHI	A	3		18	.254
	CLE	A	3		114	.295
1932	CLE	A	3		148	.286
1933	CLE	A	3		133	.282
1934	CLE	A	3		121	.269
1935	CLE	A	3		6	.333
		BRTR			1692	.281

KAMP, ALPHONSE FRANCIS "IKE"
B.SEPT.5,1901 ROXBURY,MASS.
D.FEB.26,1955

YR	CL	LEA	POS	GP	G	REC
1924	BOS	N	P		1	0-1
1925	BOS	N	P		24	2-4
		BBTL			25	2-5

KAMPOURIS, ALEXIS WILLIAM
B.NOV.13,1912 SACRAMENTO,CAL.

YR	CL	LEA	POS	GP	G	REC
1934	CIN	N	2		19	.197
1935	CIN	N	2-S		148	.246
1936	CIN	N	2		122	.239
1937	CIN	N	2		146	.249
1938	CIN	N	2		21	.257
	NY	N	2		82	.246
1939	NY	N	2-3		74	.249
1941	BRO	N	2		16	.314
1942	BRO	N	2		10	.238
1943	BRO	N	2		19	.227
	WAS	A	2-3-0		51	.207
		BRTR			708	.243

KANE, FRANCIS THOMAS "SUGAR"
(REAL NAME
FRANCIS THOMAS KILEY)
B.MAR.9,1895 WHITMAN,MASS.
D.DEC.2,1962

YR	CL	LEA	POS	GP	G	REC
1915	BRO	F	O		3	.200
1919	NY	A	O		1	.000
		BLTR			4	.182

KANE, HARRY "KLONDIKE"
(REAL NAME HARRY COHEN)
B.JULY 27,1883 HAMBURG,ARK.
D.SEPT.15,1932

YR	CL	LEA	POS	GP	G	REC
1902	STL	A	P		4	0-1
1903	DET	A	P		3	0-2
1905	PHI	N	P		2	1-1
1906	PHI	N	P		6	1-2
		TL			15	2-6

KANE, JAMES J.
B.NOV.27,1882 SCRANTON,PA.
D.OCT.2,1947

YR	CL	LEA	POS	GP	G	REC
1908	PIT	N	1		40	.241
		BLTL				

KANE, JEREMIAH
B.1867 COLLINSVILLE,ILL.

YR	CL	LEA	POS	GP	G	REC
1890	STL	AA	C-1		8	.160
		BRTR				

KANE, JOHN FRANCIS
B.OCT.24,1883 PITTSBURG,KAN.
D.JAN.28,1934

YR	CL	LEA	POS	GP	G	REC
1907	CIN	N	3-0		75	.248
1908	CIN	N	O		127	.213
1909	CHI	N	1		15	.089
1910	CHI	N	O		30	.242
		BRTR			247	.220

KANE, JOHN FRANCIS
B.FEB.19,1903 CHICAGO,ILL.

YR	CL	LEA	POS	GP	G	REC
1925	CHI	A	2-S		14	.179
		BBTR				

KANE, THOMAS JOSEPH
B.DEC.15,1908 CHICAGO,ILL.

YR	CL	LEA	POS	GP	G	REC
1938	BOS	N	2		2	.000
		BRTR				

KANEHL, RODERICK EDWIN "ROD"
B.APR.1,1934 WICHITA,KAN.

YR	CL	LEA	POS	GP	G	REC
1962	NY	N	1-2-S-3-O		133	.248
1963	NY	N	1-2-3-0		109	.241
1964	NY	N	1-2-3-0		98	.232
		BRTR			340	.241

KANTLEHNER, ERVINE LESTER "PEANUTS"
B.JULY 31,1892 SAN JOSE,CAL.

YR	CL	LEA	POS	GP	G	REC
1914	PIT	N	P		21	3-2
1915	PIT	N	P		29	5-12
1916	PIT	N	P		34	5-15
	PHI	N	P		3	0-0
		BLTL			87	13-29

KAPPEL, HENRY
B.1862 PHILADELPHIA,PA.
D.AUG.27,1905

YR	CL	LEA	POS	GP	G	REC
1887	CIN	AA	2-S-3-0		24	.294
1888	CIN	AA	2-S-3		35	.254
1889	COL	AA	S-3		49	.269
		BRTR			108	.272

KAPPEL, JOSEPH
B.APR.27,1857 PHILADELPHIA,PA.
D.JULY 8,1929

YR	CL	LEA	POS	GP	G	REC
1884	PHI	N	C		4	.067
1890	ATH	AA	S		57	.240
					61	.227

KARDOW, PAUL OTTO "TEX"
B.SEPT.19,1915 HUMBLE,TEX.

YR	CL	LEA	POS	GP	G	REC
1936	CLE	A	P		2	0-0
		BRTR				

KARGER, EDWIN
B.MAY 6,1883 SAN ANGELO,TEX.
D.SEPT.9,1957

YR	CL	LEA	POS	GP	G	REC
1906	PIT	N	P		5	2-3
	STL	N	P		25	5-16
1907	STL	N	P		39	15-19
1908	STL	N	P		22	4-9
1909	CIN	N	P		9	1-3
	BOS	A	P		12	5-2
1910	BOS	A	P		27	11-7
1911	BOS	A	P		25	5-8
		BRTL			164	48-67

KARL, ANTON ANDREW "ANDY"
B.APR.8,1914 MT.VERNON,N.Y.

YR	CL	LEA	POS	GP	G	REC
1943	BOS	A	P		11	1-1
	PHI	N	P	9	11	1-2
1944	PHI	N	P	38	42	3-2
1945	PHI	N	P		67	8-8
1946	PHI	N	P		39	3-7
1947	BOS	N	P		27	2-3
		BRTR		191	197	18-23

KARLON, WILLIAM JOHN "HANK"
B.JAN.21,1909 PALMER,MASS.
D.DEC.7,1964 MONSON,MASS.

YR	CL	LEA	POS	GP	G	REC
1930	NY	A	O		2	.000
		BRTR				

KAROW, MARTIN GREGORY
B.JULY 18,1904 BRADDOCK,PA.

YR	CL	LEA	POS	GP	G	REC
1927	BOS	A	S-3		6	.200
		BRTR				

KARPEL, HERBERT
B.DEC.27,1918 BROOKLYN,N.Y.

YR	CL	LEA	POS	GP	G	REC
1946	NY	A	P		2	0-0
		BLTL				

KARR, BENJAMIN JOYCE "BALDY"
B.NOV.28,1893 MT.PLEASANT,MISS.
D.DEC.8,1968 MEMPHIS,TENN.

YR	CL	LEA	POS	GP	G	REC
1920	BOS	A	P	26	57	3-8
1921	BOS	A	P	26	43	8-7
1922	BOS	A	P	41	65	5-12
1925	CLE	A	P	32	46	11-12
1926	CLE	A	P	30	31	5-6
1927	CLE	A	P		22	3-3
		BLTR		177	265	35-48

KARST, JOHN GOTTLIEB
B.OCT.15,1893 PHILADELPHIA,PA.

YR	CL	LEA	POS	GP	G	REC
1915	BRO	N	3		1	.000
		TR				

KASKO, EDWARD MICHAEL "EDDIE"
B.JUNE 27,1932 LINDEN,N.J.

YR	CL	LEA	POS	GP	G	REC
1957	STL	N	2-S-3		134	.273
1958	STL	N	2-S-3		104	.220
1959	CIN	N	2-S-3		118	.283
1960	CIN	N	2-S-3		126	.292
1961	CIN	N	2-S-3		126	.271
1962	CIN	N	S-3		134	.278
1963	CIN	N	2-S-3		76	.241
1964	HOU	N	S-3		133	.243
1965	HOU	N	S-3		68	.247
1966	BOS	A	2-S-3		58	.213
		BRTR			1077	.264

NON-PLAYING MANAGER
BOS(A) 1970-73

KATOLL, JOHN "BIG JACK"
B.JUNE 24,1872 GERMANY
D.JUNE 18,1955

YR	CL	LEA	POS	GP	G	REC
1898	CHI	N	P		2	0-1
1899	CHI	N	P		3	1-1
1901	CHI	A	P		27	13-12
1902	CHI	A	P		1	0-0
	BAL	A	P-0	13	15	3-10
						.152
		BRTR		46	48	17-24
						.135

KATT, RAYMOND FREDERICK "RAY"
B.MAY 9,1927 NEW BRAUNFELS,TEX.

YR	CL	LEA	POS	GP	G	REC
1952	NY	N	C		9	.222
1953	NY	N	C		8	.172
1954	NY	N	C		86	.255
1955	NY	N	C		124	.215
1956	NY	N	C		37	.228
	STL	N	C		47	.259
1957	NY	N	C		72	.230
1958	STL	N	C		19	.171
1959	STL	N	C		15	.292
		BRTR			417	.232

KATZ, ROBERT CLYDE
B.JAN.30,1911 LANCASTER,PA.

YR	CL	LEA	POS	GP	G	REC
1944	CIN	N	P		6	0-1
		BRTR				

KAUFF, BENJAMIN MICHAEL
B.JAN.5,1891 MIDDLEPORT,OHIO
D.NOV.17,1961

YR	CL	LEA	POS	GP	G	REC
1912	NY	A	O		5	.272
1914	IND	F	O		154	.366
1915	BRO	F	O		136	.344
1916	NY	N	O		154	.264
1917	NY	N	O		153	.308
1918	NY	N	O		67	.315
1919	NY	N	O		135	.277
1920	NY	N	O		55	.274
		BLTL			859	.310

KAUFFMAN, HOWARD RICHARD "DICK"
B.JUNE 22,1888 MILTON,PA.
D.APR.17,1948

YR	CL	LEA	POS	GP	G	REC
1914	STL	A	1		6	.333
1915	STL	A	1		37	.258
		BRTR			43	.266

KAUFMANN, ANTHONY CHARLES
B.DEC.16,1900 CHICAGO,ILL.

YR	CL	LEA	POS	GP	G	REC
1921	CHI	N	P		2	1-0
1922	CHI	N	P	37	38	7-13
1923	CHI	N	P		33	14-10
1924	CHI	N	P	34	35	16-11
1925	CHI	N	P		31	13-13
1926	CHI	N	P	26	30	9-7
1927	CHI	N	P		9	3-3
	PHI	N	P	5	8	0-3
	STL	N	P		1	0-0
1928	STL	N	P	4	5	0-0
1929	NY	N	O		39	.031
1930	STL	N	P		2	0-1
1931	STL	N	P	15	20	1-1
1935	STL	N	P	3	7	0-0
		BRTR		202	260	64-62
						.220

KAVANAGH, CHARLES HUGH "SILK"
B.JUNE 9,1893 CHICAGO,ILL.

YR	CL	LEA	POS	GP	G	REC
1914	CHI	A	O		5	.250
		BRTR				

KAVANAGH, LEO DANIEL
B.AUG.9,1894 CHICAGO,ILL.
D.AUG.10,1950

YR	CL	LEA	POS	GP	G	REC
1914	CHI	F	S		5	.273
		BRTR				

```
YR   CL LEA POS  GP    G    REC
```

KAVANAGH, MARTIN JOSEPH
B.JUNE 13,1891 HARRISON,N.J.
D.JULY 28,1960 ELOISE,MICH.
```
1914 DET A  2         127  .248
1915 DET A  1-2       113  .295
1916 DET A  2          58  .141
     CLE A  2          19  .250
1917 CLE A  2          14  .000
1918 CLE A  1          13  .211
     STL N  2          12  .181
     DET A  1          13  .273
     BRTR             369  .249
```

KAVANAUGH
```
1872 ECK NA 1-0        5   .185
```

KAY, WALTER B. "KING BILL"
B.FEB.14,1878 NEW CASTLE,VA.
D.DEC.3,1945
```
1907 WAS A  0          25  .333
```

KAZAK, EDWARD TERRANCE "EDDIE"
(REAL NAME
EDWARD TERRANCE TKACZUK)
B.JULY 18,1920 STEUBENVILLE,O.
```
1948 STL N  3          6   .273
1949 STL N  2-3        92  .304
1950 STL N  3          93  .256
1951 STL N  3          11  .182
1952 STL N  3          3   .000
     CIN N  1          13  .067
     BRTR             218  .273
```

KAZANSKI, THEODORE STANLEY
B.JAN.25,1934 HAMTRAMCK,MICH.
```
1953 PHI N  S          95  .217
1954 PHI N  S          39  .135
1955 PHI N  S-3        9   .083
1956 PHI N  2-S       117  .211
1957 PHI N  2-S-3      62  .265
1958 PHI N  2-S-3      95  .228
     BRTR             417  .217
```

KEALEY, STEVEN WILLIAM "STEVE"
B.MAY 13,1947 TORRANCE,CAL.
```
1968 CAL A  P          6   0- 1
1969 CAL A  P          15  2- 0
1970 CAL A  P          17  1- 0
1971 CHI A  P          54  2- 2
1972 CHI A  P          40  3- 2
1973 CHI A  P          7   0- 0
     BRTR             139  8- 5
```

KEANE, JOHN JOSEPH "JOHNNY"
B.NOV.3,1911 ST.LOUIS,MO.
D.JAN.6,1967 HOUSTON,TEX.
NON-PLAYING MANAGER
STL(N) 1961-64, NY(A) 1965-66

KEARNS, EDWARD JOSEPH "TED"
B.JAN.1,1900 TRENTON,N.J.
D.DEC.21,1949
```
1924 CHI N  1          4   .250
1925 CHI N  1          3   .500
     BRTR              7   .278
```

KEARNS, THOMAS J. "DASHER"
B.NOV.9,1859 ROCHESTER,N.Y.
D.DEC.7,1938
```
1880 BUF N  C-0        9   .091
1882 DET N  2          4   .308
1884 DET N  2          18  .211
                       31  .188
```

KEARNS, W. A.
B.CHICAGO,ILL.
```
1901 BAL A  P          4   1- 0
```

KEARSE, EDWARD PAUL
B.FEB.23,1918 SAN FRANCISCO,CAL
D.JULY 15,1968 EUREKA,CAL.
```
1942 NY  A  C          11  .192
     BRTR
```

KEAS, EDWARD JAMES
B.FEB.2,1863 DUBUQUE,IOWA
D.JAN.12,1940
```
1888 CLE AA P          6   3- 3
```

KEATING, RAYMOND HERBERT
B.JULY 21,1891 BRIDGEPORT,CONN.
D.DEC.28,1963 SACRAMENTO,CAL.
```
1912 NY  A  P          5   0- 3
1913 NY  A  P          28  6-12
1914 NY  A  P          34  7-11
1915 NY  A  P          11  3- 6
1916 NY  A  P          14  5- 6
1918 NY  A  P          15  2- 2
1919 BOS N  P     22   24  7-11
     BRTR        129  131  30-51
```

KEATING, ROBERT M.
B.SEPT.22,1862 SPRINGFIELD,MASS
D.JAN.19,1922 SPRINGFIELD,MASS.
```
1887 BAL AA P          1   0- 1
     BLTL
```

KEATING, WALTER FRANCIS "CHICK"
B.AUG.8,1891 PHILADELPHIA,PA.
D.JULY 13,1959
```
1913 CHI N  S          2   .200
1914 CHI N  S          20  .100
1915 CHI N  S          4   .000
1926 PHI N  S          4   .000
     BRTR              30  .087
```

KECK, FRANK JOSEPH "CACTUS"
B.JAN.13,1899 ST.LOUIS,MO.
```
1922 CIN N  P          27  7- 6
1923 CIN N  P          35  3- 6
     BRTR              62  10-12
```

KEEFE, DAVID EDWIN
B.JAN.9,1897 WILLISTON,VT.
```
1917 PHI A  P          3   1  0
1918 PHI A  P          1   0- 1
1919 PHI A  P          2   0- 1
1920 PHI A  P     31   32  6- 7
1921 PHI A  P          44  2- 9
1922 CLE A  P          18  0- 0
     BLTR        99   100  9-18
```

KEEFE, GEORGE W.
B.JAN.7,1867 WASHINGTON,D.C.
D.AUG.24,1935 WASHINGTON,D.C.
```
1886 WAS N  P          4   0- 3
1887 WAS N  P          1   0- 1
1888 WAS N  P          13  6- 7
1889 WAS N  P          27  8-18
1890 BUF P  P          25  5-17
1891 WAS AA P          5   0- 5
     BLTL              75  19-51
```

KEEFE, JOHN T.
B.JULY 16,1867 CAMBRIDGE,MASS.
D.AUG.10,1937
```
1890 SYR AA P          44  14-23
```

KEEFE, ROBERT FRANCIS
B.JUNE 16,1882 FOLSOM,CAL.
D.DEC.7,1964 SACRAMENTO,CAL.
```
1907 NY  A  P          19  4- 4
1911 CIN N  P          39  12-13
1912 CIN N  P          17  1- 3
     BRTR              75  17-20
```

KEEFE, TIMOTHY JOHN
"SMILING TIM"
B.JAN.1,1867 CAMBRIDGE,MASS.
D.APR.23,1933 CAMBRIDGE,MASS.
```
1880 TRO N  P          12  6- 6
1881 TRO N  P          46  19-27
1882 TRO N  P-3- 43    51  17-26
         O                 .225
1883 MET AA P-O        70  41-26
                           .220
1884 MET AA P     57   62  35-18
1885 NY  N  P-O   45   46  32-13
                           .162
1886 NY  N  P     63   64  42-20
1887 NY  N  P          56  35-20
1888 NY  N  P     50   51  35-12
1889 NY  N  P          43  30-13
1890 NY  P  P          30  17- 8
     PHI N  P          9   3- 6
1891 NY  N  P          8   2- 5
1892 PHI N  P          36  21-14
1893 PHI N  P          20  10-10
     BRTR        588  604  345-224
                           .199
```

KEEGAN, EDWARD CHARLES "ED"
B.JULY 8,1939 CAMDEN,N.J.
```
1959 PHI N  P          3   0- 3
1961 KC  A  P          6   0- 0
1962 PHI N  P          5   0- 0
     BRTR              14  0- 3
```

KEEGAN, ROBERT CHARLES "BOB"
B.AUG.4,1920 ROCHESTER,N.Y.
```
1953 CHI A  P          22  7- 5
1954 CHI A  P     31   32  16- 9
1955 CHI A  P          18  2- 5
1956 CHI A  P          20  5- 7
1957 CHI A  P          30  10- 8
1958 CHI A  P          14  0- 2
     BRTR        135  136  40-36
```

KEELER, WILLIAM HENRY
"WEE WILLIE"
B.MAR.3,1872 BROOKLYN,N.Y.
D.JAN.1,1923 BROOKLYN,N.Y.
```
1892 NY  N  3          13  .306
1893 NY  N  2-S-O      7   .364
     BRO N  3          19  .340
1894 BAL N  O         128  .367
1895 BAL N  O         131  .394
1896 BAL N  O         127  .392
1897 BAL N  O         128  .432
1898 BAL N  O         128  .379
1899 BRO N  O         143  .376
1900 BRO N  O         137  .366
1901 BRO N  O         136  .355
1902 BRO N  O         132  .342
1903 NY  A  O         132  .318
1904 NY  A  O         143  .343
1905 NY  A  O         149  .302
1906 NY  A  O         152  .304
1907 NY  A  O         107  .234
1908 NY  A  O         91   .263
1909 NY  A  O         99   .264
1910 NY  N  O         17   .300
     BLTL            2119  .345
```

KEELEY, BURTON ELWOOD
B.NOV.2,1888 WILMINGTON,ILL.
D.MAY 4,1952
```
1907 WAS A  P     28   31  6-11
1909 WAS A  P          2   0- 0
     BRTR         30   33  6-11
```

KEELY, ROBERT WILLIAM "BOB"
B.AUG.22,1916 ST.LOUIS,MO.
```
1944 STL N  C          1   .000
1945 STL N  C          1   .000
     BRTR              2   .000
```

KEEN, HOWARD VICTOR "VIC"
B.MAR.16,1900 PHILADELPHIA,PA.
```
1918 PHI A  P          1   1- 0
1921 CHI N  P          5   0- 3
1922 CHI N  P          7   1- 2
1923 CHI N  P          35  12- 8
1924 CHI N  P          40  15-14
1925 CHI N  P          30  2- 6
1926 STL N  P          26  10- 9
1927 STL N  P          21  2- 1
     BRTR             165  43-43
```

KEENAN, HARRY LEON "KID"
B.1875 LOUISVILLE,KY.
D.JUNE 11,1903
```
1891 CIN AA P          1   0- 1
     TR
```

KEENAN, JAMES W.
B.FEB.10,1858 NEW HAVEN,CONN.
D.SEPT.21,1926
```
1875 NH  NA C-3        3    -
1880 BUF N  C          2   .125
1882 PIT AA C-S-O      24  .206
1884 IND AA C-1        68  .305
1885 CIN AA P-C-  1    32  0- 0
            1-0            .282
1886 CIN AA P-C   1    43  0- 0
            1-0            .278
1887 CIN AA C-1        47  .297
1888 CIN AA C-1        84  .229
1889 CIN AA C-1-3      87  .287
1890 CIN N  C          54  .138
1891 CIN N  C-1        75  .203
     BRTR         2   519  0- 0
                            -
```

YR	CL LEA POS	GP	G	REC

KEENAN, JAMES WILLIAM "SPARKPLUG"
B.MAY 25,1889 AVON,N.Y.

1920	PHI N	P		1	0- 0
1921	PHI N	P		15	1- 2
	BLTL			16	1- 2

KEENE, WILLIAM BROWN "REBEL"
B.1891 ATLANTA,GA.

1911	PIT N	1		5	.000
	BRTR				

KEENER, JOSEPH DONALD "JOE"
B.APR.21,1953 SAN PEDRO,CAL.

1976	MON N	P		2	0- 1
	BRTR				

KEENER, JOSHUA HARRY
B.1869 EASTON,PA.
D.MAR.5,1912

1896	PHI N	P		15	2-10

KEERL, GEORGE HENRY
B.APR.10,1847 BALTIMORE,MD.
D.SEPT.9,1923

1875	CHI NA	2		6	-

KEESEY, JAMES WARD
B.OCT.27,1903 PERRYVILLE,MD.
D.SEPT.5,1951

1925	PHI A	1		5	.400
1930	PHI A	1		11	.250
	BRTR			16	.294

KEFFER, C. FRANK
B.PHILADELPHIA,PA.
D.OCT.1,1932

1890	SYR AA	P		1	0- 1

KEHN, CHESTER LAURENCE
B.OCT.30,1921 SAN DIEGO,CAL.

1942	BRO N	P		3	0- 0
	BRTR				

KEIFER, SHERMAN C. "KATIE"
B.1892

1914	IND F	P		1	1- 0
	BBTR				

KEINZIL, WILLIAM
B.PHILADELPHIA,PA.

1882	ATH AA	O		9	.297
1884	KEY U	O		61	.260
	BLTL			70	.265

KEISTER, WILLIAM HOFFMAN "WAGON TONGUE"
B.AUG.17,1874 BALTIMORE,MD.
D.AUG.19,1924

1896	BAL N	2		13	.224
1898	BOS N	2-S		9	.200
1899	BAL N	2-S		134	.331
1900	STL N	2		128	.298
1901	BAL A	S		114	.328
1902	WAS A	2-S-3-O		119	.303
1903	PHI N	O		100	.320
	BLTR			617	.312

KEKICH, MICHAEL DENNIS "MIKE"
B.APR.2,1945 SAN DIEGO,CAL.

1965	LA N	P		5	0- 1
1968	LA N	P		25	2-10
1969	NY A	P		28	4- 6
1970	NY A	P		26	6- 3
1971	NY A	P		37	10- 9
1972	NY A	P		29	10-13
1973	NY A	P		5	1- 1
	CLE A	P	16	19	1- 4
1975	TEX A	P		23	0- 0
	BRTL		194	197	34-47

KELB, GEORGE FRANCIS "PUGGER"
B.JULY 17,1870 TOLEDO,OHIO
D.OCT.20,1936

1898	CLE N	P		3	0- 1
	TL				

KELIHER, MAURICE MICHAEL "MICKEY"
B.JAN.14,1890 WASHINGTON,D.C.
D.SEPT.7,1930 WASHINGTON,D.C.

1911	PIT N	1		3	.000
1912	PIT N	H		2	.000
	BLTL			5	.000

KELL, EVERETT LEE "SKEETER"
B.OCT.11,1929 SWIFTON,ARK.

1952	PHI A	2		75	.221
	BRTR				

KELL, GEORGE CLYDE
B.AUG.23,1922 SWIFTON,ARK.

1943	PHI A	3		1	.200
1944	PHI A	3		139	.268
1945	PHI A	3		147	.272
1946	PHI A	3		26	.299
	DET A	1-3		105	.327
1947	DET A	3		152	.320
1948	DET A	3		92	.304
1949	DET A	3		134	.343
1950	DET A	3		157	.340
1951	DET A	3		147	.319
1952	DET A	3		39	.296
	BOS A	3		75	.319
1953	BOS A	3-O		134	.307
1954	BOS A	3		26	.258
	CHI A	1-3-O		71	.283
1955	CHI A	1-3-O		128	.312
1956	CHI A	1-3		21	.313
	BAL A	1-2-3		102	.261
1957	BAL A	1-3		99	.297
	BRTR			1795	.306

KELLEHER, ALBERT ALOYSIUS "DUKE"
B.SEPT.30,1893 NEW YORK,N.Y.

1916	NY N	C		1	.000
	TR				

KELLEHEP, FRANCIS EUGENE
B.AUG.22,1916 SAN FRANCISCO,CAL

1942	CIN N	P		38	.182
1943	CIN N	O		9	.000
	BRTR			47	.167

KELLEHER, HAROLD JOSEPH
B.JUNE 24,1914 PHILADELPHIA,PA.

1935	PHI N	P		3	2- 0
1936	PHI N	P		14	0- 5
1937	PHI N	P	27	30	2- 4
1938	PHI N	P		6	0- 0
	BRTR			50	53	4- 9

KELLEHER, JOHN PATRICK
B.SEPT.13,1893 BROOKLINE,MASS.
D.AUG.21,1960

1912	STL N	3		6	.363
1916	BRO N	S-3		2	.000
1921	CHI N	2-3		95	.309
1922	CHI N	1-S-3		63	.259
1923	CHI N	1-2-S-3		66	.306
1924	BOS N	3		1	.000
	BRTR			233	.293

KELLEHER, MICHAEL DENNIS "MICK"
B.JULY 25,1947 SEATTLE,WASH.

1972	STL N	S		23	.159
1973	STL N	S		43	.184
1974	HOU N	SS		19	.158
1975	STL N	S		7	.000
1976	CHI N	2-S-3		124	.228
	BRTR			216	.206

KELLER, CHARLES ERNEST "CHARLIE" OR "KING KONG"
B.SEPT.13,1916 MIDDLETOWN,MD.

1939	NY A	O		111	.334
1940	NY A	O		138	.286
1941	NY A	O		140	.298
1942	NY A	O		152	.292
1943	NY A	O		141	.271
1945	NY A	O		44	.301
1946	NY A	O		150	.275
1947	NY A	O		45	.238
1948	NY A	O		83	.267
1949	NY A	O		60	.250
1950	DET A	O		50	.314
1951	DET A	O		54	.258
1952	NY A	O		2	.000
	BLTR			1170	.286

KELLER, HAROLD KEFAUVER "HAL"
B.JULY 7,1927 MIDDLETOWN,MD.

1949	WAS A	H		3	.333
1950	WAS A	C		11	.214
1952	WAS A	C		11	.174
	BLTR			25	.204

KELLEP, RONALD LEE "RON"
B.JUNE 3,1943 INDIANAPOLIS,IND.

1966	MIN A	P		2	3	0- 0
1968	MIN A	P		7	8	0- 1
	BRTR			9	11	0- 1

KELLERT, FRANK WILLIAM
B.JULY 6,1924 OKLAHOMA CITY, OKLA.

1953	STL A	1		2	.000
1954	BAL A	1		10	.206
1955	BRO N	1		39	.325
1956	CHI N	1		71	.186
	BRTR			122	.231

KELLETT, ALFRED HENRY
B.OCT.30,1902 RED BANK,N.J.
D.JULY 14,1960

1923	PHI A	P		5	0- 1
1924	BOS A	P		1	0- 0
				6	0- 1

KELLETT, DONALD STAFFORD "RED"
B.JULY 15,1909 BROOKLYN,N.Y.
D.NOV.3,1970 FT.LAUDERDALE,FLA.

1934	BOS A	2-S-3		9	.000
	BRTR				

KELLEY, HARRY LEROY
B.FEB.13,1906 PARKIN,ARK.
D.MAR.23,1958

1925	WAS A	P		6	1- 1
1926	WAS A	P		7	0- 0
1936	PHI A	P	35	36	15-12
1937	PHI A	P		41	13-21
1938	PHI A	P		4	0- 2
	WAS A	P		38	9- 8
1939	WAS A	P		15	4- 3
	BRTR		146	147	42-47

KELLEY, JOSEPH JAMES "JOE"
B.DEC.9,1871 CAMBRIDGE,MASS.
D.AUG.14,1943 BALTIMORE,MD.

1891	BOS N	O		12	.244
	PIT N	O		2	.143
1892	PIT N	O		56	.245
	BAL N	O		10	.250
1893	BAL N	O		124	.312
1894	BAL N	O		129	.391
1895	BAL N	O		131	.370
1896	BAL N	O		130	.370
1897	BAL N	O		129	.389
1898	BAL N	O		124	.328
1899	BRO N	O		144	.329
1900	BRO N	1-O		118	.318
1901	BRO N	1		120	.309
1902	BAL A	1-3-O		60	.311
	CIN N	M-2-S-3-O		37	.327
1903	CIN N	M-O		104	.316
1904	CIN N	M-1		123	.281
1905	CIN N	M-O		87	.277
1906	CIN N	O		127	.228
1908	BOS N	M-O		62	.259
	BRTR			1829	.321

KELLEY, MICHAEL JOSEPH
B.DEC.2,1875 OTTER RIVER,MASS.
D.JUNE 6,1955

1899	LOU N	1		76	.247

KELLEY, RICHARD ANTHONY "DICK"
B.JAN.8,1940 BOSTON,MASS.

1964	MIL N	P		2	0- 0
1965	MIL N	P	21	22	1- 1
1966	ATL N	P		20	7- 5
1967	ATL N	P		39	2- 9
1968	ATL N	P		31	2- 4
1969	SD N	P		27	4- 8
1971	SD N	P		48	2- 3
	BRTL		188	189	18-30

KELLEY, THOMAS HENRY "TOM"
B.JAN.5,1944 MANCHESTER,CONN.

1964	CLE A	P		6	0- 0
1965	CLE A	P		4	2- 1
1966	CLE A	P		31	4- 8
1967	CLE A	P		1	0- 0
1971	ATL N	P		28	9- 5
1972	ATL N	P		27	5- 7
1973	ATL N	P		7	0- 1
	BRTR			104	20-22

YR	CL	LEA	POS	GP	G	REC

KELLIHER, FRANCIS MORTIMER "YUCKA"
B.MAY 23,1899 SOMERVILLE,MASS.
D.MAR.4,1956

YR	CL	LEA	POS	GP	G	REC
1919	WAS	A	H		1	.000
	BLTL					

KELLNER, ALEXANDER RAYMOND "ALEX"
B.AUG.26,1924 TUCSON,ARIZ.

YR	CL	LEA	POS	GP	G	REC
1948	PHI	A	P		13	0- 0
1949	PHI	A	P		38	20-12
1950	PHI	A	P		36	8-20
1951	PHI	A	P		33	11-14
1952	PHI	A	P		34	12-14
1953	PHI	A	P		25	11-12
1954	PHI	A	P		27	6-17
1955	KC	A	P		30	11- 8
1956	KC	A	P	20	21	7- 4
1957	KC	A	P		28	6- 5
1958	KC	A	P	7	8	0- 2
	CIN	A	P		18	7- 3
1959	STL	N	P		12	2- 1
	BRTL			321	323	101-112

KELLNER, WALTER JOSEPH "WALT"
B.APR.26,1929 TUCSON,ARIZ.

YR	CL	LEA	POS	GP	G	REC
1952	PHI	A	P		1	0- 0
1953	PHI	A	P		2	0- 0
	BRTR				3	0- 0

KELLOGG, ALBERT C.
D.SEPT.1912

YR	CL	LEA	POS	GP	G	REC
1908	PHI	A	P		3	0- 2

KELLOGG, NATHANIEL M.
B.MANCHESTER,N.H.

YR	CL	LEA	POS	GP	G	REC
1885	DET	N	S		5	.118

KELLOGG, RAYMOND NELSON
(PLAYED UNDER NAME OF
RAYMOND N. NELSON)

KELLOGG, WILLIAM DEARSTYNE
B.MAY 25,1884 ALBANY,N.Y.
D.DEC.12,1971 BALTIMORE,MD.

YR	CL	LEA	POS	GP	G	REC
1914	CIN	N	1		71	.175
	BRTR					

KELLUM, WINFORD ANSLEY
B.APR.11,1876 WATERFORD,ONT.,
CANADA
D.AUG.10,1951

YR	CL	LEA	POS	GP	G	REC
1901	BOS	A	P		6	2- 3
1904	CIN	N	P	31	36	16- 8
1905	STL	N	P		11	3- 3
	BBTL			48	53	21-14

KELLY, ALBERT MICHAEL "RED"
B.NOV.15,1884 LIVINGSTON CO.,
ILL.
D.FEB.4,1961

YR	CL	LEA	POS	GP	G	REC
1910	CHI	A	O		14	.155
	TR					

KELLY, CHARLES H.

YR	CL	LEA	POS	GP	G	REC
1883	PHI	N	3		2	.143
1886	ATH	AA	S		1	.000
					3	.100

KELLY, EDWARD L.
B.1890 SPOKANE,WASH.

YR	CL	LEA	POS	GP	G	REC
1914	BOS	A	P		3	0- 0
	BRTR					

KELLY, GEORGE LANGE "HIGH POCKETS"
B.SEP.10,1896 SAN FRANCISCO,CAL

YR	CL	LEA	POS	GP	G	REC
1915	NY	N	1		17	.158
1916	NY	N	1		49	.158
1917	NY	N	P-1-	1	11	1- 0
			O			.000
	PIT	N	1		8	.087
1919	NY	N	1		32	.290
1920	NY	N	1		155	.266
1921	NY	N	1		149	.308
1922	NY	N	1		151	.327
1923	NY	N	1		145	.307
1924	NY	N	1-2-3-O		144	.324
1925	NY	N	1-2-3		147	.309
1926	NY	N	1-2		136	.303
1927	CIN	N	1-2-O		61	.270
1928	CIN	N	1-O		116	.296
1929	CIN	N	1		147	.293
1930	CIN	N	1		51	.288
	CHI	N	1		39	.331
1932	BRO	N	1		64	.243
	BRTR			1	1622	1- 0
						.297

KELLY, HAROLD PATRICK "PAT"
B.JULY 30,1944 PHILADELPHIA,PA.

YR	CL	LEA	POS	GP	G	REC
1967	MIN	A	H		8	.000
1968	MIN	A	O		12	.114
1969	KC	A	O		112	.264
1970	KC	A	O		136	.235
1971	CHI	A	O		67	.291
1972	CHI	A	O		119	.261
1973	CHI	A	O		144	.280
1974	CHI	A	O-D		122	.281
1975	CHI	A	O-D		133	.274
1976	CHI	A	O-D		107	.254
	BLTL				960	.265

KELLY, HERBERT BARRETT "MOKE"
B.JUNE 4,1892 MOBILE,ALA.
D.MAY 18,1973 TORRANCE,CAL.

YR	CL	LEA	POS	GP	G	REC
1914	PIT	N	P		5	0- 2
1915	PIT	N	P		5	1- 1
	BLTL				10	1- 3

KELLY, JAMES ROBERT
(ALSO PLAYED UNDER REAL NAME OF
ROBERT JOHN TAGGART IN 1918)
B.FEB.1,1890 BLOOMFIELD,N.J.

YR	CL	LEA	POS	GP	G	REC
1914	PIT	N	O		32	.227
1915	PIT	F	O		140	.290
1918	BOS	N	O		35	.329
	BLTR				215	.294

KELLY, JAY THOMAS "TOM"
B.AUG.15,1950 GRACEVILLE,MINN.

YR	CL	LEA	POS	GP	G	REC
1975	MIN	A	1-O		49	.181
	BLTL					

KELLY, JOHN

YR	CL	LEA	POS	GP	G	REC
1871	KEK	NA	O		18	-

KELLY, JOHN B.
B.MAR.13,1879 CLIFTON HEIGHTS,
PA.
D.MAR.19,1944 BALTIMORE,MD.

YR	CL	LEA	POS	GP	G	REC
1907	STL	N	O		52	.188

KELLY, JOHN FRANCIS "KICK"
B.1859 PATERSON,N.J.
D.APR.13,1908

YR	CL	LEA	POS	GP	G	REC
1879	SYR	N	C-1		9	.125
1882	CLE	N	C		29	.134
1883	BAL	AA	C-O		46	.224
	PHI	N	O		1	.000
1884	CIN	U	C		39	.253
	WAS	U	C-O		4	.357
	BRTR				128	.211

KELLY, JOHN O. "HONEST JOHN"
B.1856 NEW YORK,N.Y.
D.MAR.27,1926
NON-PLAYING MANAGER LOU(AA)1887

KELLY, JOSEPH HERBERT
B.SEPT.23,1889 WEIR CITY,KAN.

YR	CL	LEA	POS	GP	G	REC
1914	PIT	N	O		141	.222
1916	CHI	N	O		54	.254
1917	BOS	N	O		116	.222
1918	BOS	N	O		47	.232
1919	BOS	N	O		18	.141
	BRTR				376	.224

KELLY, JOSEPH JAMES
B.APR.23,1901 NEW YORK,N.Y.
D.NOV.24,1967 LYNBROOK,N.Y.

YR	CL	LEA	POS	GP	G	REC
1926	CHI	N	O		65	.335
1928	CHI	N	1		32	.212
	BLTL				97	.307

KELLY, MICHAEL J.
B.NOV.9,1902 ST.LOUIS,MO.

YR	CL	LEA	POS	GP	G	REC
1926	PHI	N	P		4	0- 0
	BRTR					

KELLY, MICHAEL JOSEPH "KING"
B.DEC.31,1857 TROY,N.Y.
D.NOV.8,1894 BOSTON,MASS.

YR	CL	LEA	POS	GP	G	REC
1878	CIN	N	C-3-O		61	.281
1879	CIN	N	C-3-O		77	.348
1880	CHI	N	P-C-	1	82	0- 0
			S-3-O			.292
1881	CHI	N	C-3-O		80	.323
1882	CHI	N	C-1-S-3-		84	.305
			O			
1883	CHI	N	P-C-	1	98	0- 0
			2-3-O			.253
1884	CHI	N	P-C-	2	107	0- 0
						.341
1885	CHI	N	C-1-2-3-	107	.287
			C-O			
1886	CHI	N	C-O		118	.388
1887	BOS	N	C-2-O		114	.394
1888	BOS	N	C-O		105	.318
1889	BOS	N	C-O		125	.293
1890	BOS	P	M-C-S		90	.324
1891	CIN	AA	M-P-	3	74	0- 1
			C-1-2-S-			.280
			3-O			
	BOS	AA	C		3	.200
	BOS	N	O		24	.239
1892	BOS	N	C		72	.201
1893	NY	N	C		16	.314
	BRTR			7	1437	0- 1
						.313

KELLY, REYNOLDS CLARENCE
B.NOV.18,1900 SAN FRANCISCO,CAL
D.AUG.24,1963

YR	CL	LEA	POS	GP	G	REC
1923	PHI	A	P		1	0- 0
	BRTR					

KELLY, ROBERT BROWN "SPEED"
B.AUG.19,1887 BRYAN,OHIO
D.MAY 6,1949

YR	CL	LEA	POS	GP	G	REC
1909	WAS	A	3		17	.143
	BRTR					

KELLY, ROBERT EDWARD "BOB"
B.OCT.4,1927 CLEVELAND,OHIO

YR	CL	LEA	POS	GP	G	REC
1951	CHI	N	P		35	7- 4
1952	CHI	N	P		31	4- 9
1953	CHI	N	P		14	0- 1
	CIN	N	P		28	1- 2
1958	CIN	N	P		2	0- 0
	CLE	A	P		13	0- 2
	BRTR				123	12-18

KELLY, VAN HOWARD
B.MAR.18,1946 CHARLOTTE,N.C.

YR	CL	LEA	POS	GP	G	REC
1969	SD	N	2-3		73	.244
1970	SD	N	2-3		38	.169
	BLTR				111	.221

KELLY, WILLIAM HENRY
B.DEC.28,1899 SYRACUSE,N.Y.

YR	CL	LEA	POS	GP	G	REC
1920	PHI	A	1		8	.181
1928	PHI	N	1		23	.169
	BRTR				31	.171

KELLY, WILLIAM JOSEPH
B.MAY 1,1886 BALTIMORE,MD.
D.JUNE 3,1940 DETROIT,MICH.

YR	CL	LEA	POS	GP	G	REC
1910	STL	N	C		2	.000
1911	PIT	N	C		6	.125
1912	PIT	N	C		48	.318
1913	PIT	N	C		48	.268
	BRTR				104	.290

KELSEY, GEORGE W.
B.OHIO

YR	CL	LEA	POS	GP	G	REC
1907	PIT	N	C		2	.400
	TR					

KELSO, WILLIAM EUGENE "BILL"
B.FEB.19,1940 KANSAS CITY,MO.

YR	CL	LEA	POS	GP	G	REC
1964	LA	A	P		10	2- 0
1966	CAL	A	P		5	1- 1
1967	CAL	A	P		69	5- 3
1968	CIN	N	P		35	4- 1
	BRTR				119	12- 5

KELTNER, KENNETH FREDERICK
"KEN" OR "BUTCH"
B.OCT.31,1916 MILWAUKEE,WIS.

YR	CL	LEA	POS	GP	G	REC
1937	CLE	A	3		1	.000
1938	CLE	A	3		149	.276
1939	CLE	A	3		154	.325
1940	CLE	A	3		149	.254
1941	CLE	A	3		149	.269
1942	CLE	A	3		152	.287
1943	CLE	A	3		110	.260
1944	CLE	A	3		149	.295
1946	CLE	A	3		116	.241
1947	CLE	A	3		151	.257
1948	CLE	A	3		153	.297
1949	CLE	A	3		80	.232
1950	CLE	A	1-3		13	.321
	BRTR				1526	.276

KELTY, JOHN E.JOSEPH "CHIEF"
B.1867 JERSEY CITY,N.J.

YR	CL	LEA	POS	GP	G	REC
1890	PIT	N	O		59	.236

KEMMAN, HERBERT FREDERICK
(PLAYED UNDER NAME OF
FREDERICK HERBERT)

KEMMER, WILLIAM E.

YR	CL	LEA	POS	GP	G	REC
1895	LOU	N	3		10	.139

KEMMERER, RUSSELL PAUL "RUSS"
B.NOV.1,1931 PITTSBURGH,PA.

YR	CL	LEA	POS	GP	G	REC
1954	BOS	A	P		19	5- 3
1955	BOS	A	P		7	1- 1
1957	BOS	A	P		1	0- 0
	WAS	A	P		39	7-11
1958	WAS	A	P		40	6-15
1959	WAS	A	P		37	8-17
1960	WAS	A	P		3	0- 2
	CHI	A	P		36	6- 3
1961	CHI	A	P		47	3- 3
1962	CHI	A	P		20	2- 1
	HOU	N	P		36	5- 3
1963	HOU	N	P		17	0- 0
	BRTR				302	43-59

KEMMLER, RUDOLPH
B.CHICAGO,ILL.
D.JUNE 20,1909

YR	CL	LEA	POS	GP	G	REC
1879	PRO	N	C		2	.143
1881	CLE	N	C		1	.000
1882	CIN	AA	C-O		3	.091
	PIT	AA	C-O		25	.218
1883	COL	AA	C-O		85	.202
1884	COL	AA	C		61	.202
1885	PIT	AA	C		18	.191
1886	STL	AA	C		35	.150
1889	COL	AA	C		8	.134
	BRTR				238	.195

KEMNER, HERMAN JOHN "DUTCH"
B.MAR.4,1899 QUINCY,ILL.

YR	CL	LEA	POS	GP	G	REC
1929	CIN	N	P		9	0- 0
	BRTR					

KENDALL, FRED LYN
B.JAN.31,1949 TORRANCE,CAL.

YR	CL	LEA	POS	GP	G	REC
1969	SD	N	C		10	.154
1970	SD	N	C-1-O		4	.000
1971	SD	N	C-1-3		49	.171
1972	SD	N	C-1		91	.216
1973	SD	N	C		145	.282
1974	SD	N	C		141	.231
1975	SD	N	C		103	.199
1976	SD	N	C		146	.246
	BRTR				689	.235

KENDERS, ALBERT DANIEL GEORGE
B.APR.4,1937 BARRINGTON,N.J.

YR	CL	LEA	POS	GP	G	REC
1961	PHI	N	C		10	.174
	BRTR					

KENNA, EDDIE ALOYSIUS
"SCRAP IRON"
B.SEP.19,1897 SAN FRANCISCO,CAL
D.AUG.21,1972 SAN FRANCISCO,CAL

YR	CL	LEA	POS	GP	G	REC
1928	WAS	A	C		41	.297
	BRTR					

KENNA, EDWARD BENNINGHAUS
"POET PITCHER"
B.OCT.17,1877 CHARLESTON,W.VA.
D.MAR.22,1912

YR	CL	LEA	POS	GP	G	REC
1902	PHI	A	P		3	1- 1
	TR					

KENNEDY, CHARLES
B.COHOCTON,N.Y.
D.AUG.19,1897

YR	CL	LEA	POS	GP	G	REC
1884	CIN	U	S-3-O		13	.213
	BRTR					

KENNEDY, EDWARD
B.APR.1,1856 CARBONDALE,PA.
D.MAY 22,1905

YR	CL	LEA	POS	GP	G	REC
1883	MET	AA	O		97	.215
1884	MET	AA	O		103	.184
1885	MET	AA	O		96	.222
1886	BRO	AA	O		6	.181
					302	.209

KENNEDY, JAMES C.
B.1867 NEW YORK,N.Y.
D.APR.20,1904
NON-PLAYING MANAGER BRO(AA)1890

KENNEDY, JAMES EARL "JIM"
B.NOV.1,1946 TULSA,OKLA.

YR	CL	LEA	POS	GP	G	REC
1970	STL	N	2-S		12	.125
	BLTR					

KENNEDY, JOHN EDWARD
B.MAY 29,1941 CHICAGO,ILL.

YR	CL	LEA	POS	GP	G	REC
1962	WAS	A	S-3		14	.262
1963	WAS	A	S-3		36	.177
1964	WAS	A	2-S-3		148	.230
1965	LA	N	S-3		104	.171
1966	LA	N	2-S-3		125	.201
1967	NY	A	2-S-3		78	.196
1969	SEA	A	S-3		61	.234
1970	MIL	A	1-2-S-3		25	.255
	BOS	A	2-3		43	.256
1971	BOS	A	2-S-3		74	.276
1972	BOS	A	2-S-3		71	.245
1973	BOS	A	2-3		67	.181
1974	BOS	A	2-3		10	.133
	BRTR				856	.225

KENNEDY, JOHN IRVIN
B.NOV.23,1934 SUMTER,S.C.

YR	CL	LEA	POS	GP	G	REC
1957	PHI	N	3		5	.000
	BRTR					

KENNEDY, JUNIOR RAYMOND
B.AUG.9,1950 FORT GIBSON,OKLA.

YR	CL	LEA	POS	GP	G	REC
1974	CIN	N	2-3		22	.158
	BRTR					

KENNEDY, LLOYD VERNON "VERN"
B.MAR.20,1907 KANSAS CITY,MO.

YR	CL	LEA	POS	GP	G	REC
1934	CHI	A	P		3	0- 2
1935	CHI	A	P		31	11-11
1936	CHI	A	P	35	36	21- 9
1937	CHI	A	P		32	14-13
1938	DET	A	P	33	37	12- 9
1939	DET	A	P		4	0- 3
	STL	A	P	33	34	9-17
1940	STL	A	P	34	35	12-17
1941	STL	A	P		6	2- 4
	WAS	A	P	17	18	1- 7
1942	CLE	A	P	28	33	4- 8
1943	CLE	A	P	28	38	10- 7
1944	CLE	A	P	12	15	2- 5
	PHI	N	P	12	14	1- 5
1945	PHI	N	P	12	13	0- 3
	CIN	N	P		24	5-12
	BLTR			344	373	104-132

KENNEDY, MICHAEL JOSEPH "DOC"
B.AUG.11,1853 BROOKLYN,N.Y.
D.MAY 23,1920 GROVE,N.Y.

YR	CL	LEA	POS	GP	G	REC
1879	CLE	N	C		47	.285
1880	CLE	N	C		66	.200
1881	CLE	N	C-3-O		38	.313
1882	CLE	N	C		1	.250
1883	BUF	N	C-1-O		5	.286
	BRTR				157	.257

KENNEDY, MONTIA CALVIN "MONTE"
B.MAY 11,1922 AMELIA,VA.

YR	CL	LEA	POS	GP	G	REC
1946	NY	N	P		38	9-10
1947	NY	N	P		34	9-12
1948	NY	N	P	25	26	3- 9
1949	NY	N	P	38	39	12-14
1950	NY	N	P		36	5- 4
1951	NY	N	P		29	1- 2
1952	NY	N	P	31	34	3- 4
1953	NY	N	P	18	19	0- 0
	BRTL			249	255	42-55

KENNEDY, RAYMOND LINCOLN
B.MAY 19,1895 PITTSBURGH,PA.
D.JAN.18,1969 CASSELBERRY,FLA.

YR	CL	LEA	POS	GP	G	REC
1916	STL	A	C		1	.000
	BRTR					

KENNEDY, ROBERT DANIEL "BOB"
B.AUG.18,1920 CHICAGO,ILL.

YR	CL	LEA	POS	GP	G	REC
1939	CHI	A	3		3	.250
1940	CHI	A	3		154	.252
1941	CHI	A	3		76	.206
1942	CHI	A	3-O		113	.231
1946	CHI	A	3-O		113	.258
1947	CHI	A	3-O		115	.262
1948	CHI	A	O		30	.248
	CLE	A	1-2-O		66	.301
1949	CLE	A	3-O		121	.276
1950	CLE	A	O		146	.291
1951	CLE	A	O		108	.246
1952	CLE	A	3-O		22	.300
1953	CLE	A	O		100	.236
1954	CLE	A	O		1	.000
	BAL	A	3-O		106	.251
1955	BAL	A	1-3-O		26	.143
	CHI	A	1-3-O		83	.304
1956	CHI	A	3		8	.077
	DET	A	3-O		69	.232
1957	CHI	A	H		4	.000
	BRO	N	3-O		19	.129
	BRTR				1483	.254

NON-PLAYING MANAGER
CHI(N) 1963-65, OAK(A) 1968

KENNEDY, SHERMAN MONTGOMERY
"SNAPPER"
B.NOV.1,1878 CONNEAUT,OHIO
D.AUG.15,1945 PASADENA,CAL.

YR	CL	LEA	POS	GP	G	REC
1902	CHI	N	O		1	.000
	BBTR					

KENNEDY, THEODORE A.
B.FEB.1865 HENRY,ILL.
D.OCT.31,1907

YR	CL	LEA	POS	GP	G	REC
1885	CHI	N	P-3		9	7- 2
						.065
1886	ATH	AA	P		22	5-15
	LOU	AA	P		4	0- 4
	BL				35	12-21
						.043

KENNEDY, WILLIAM AULTON "LEFTY"
B.MAR.14,1921 CARNESVILLE,GA.

YR	CL	LEA	POS	GP	G	REC
1948	STL	A	P		6	1- 0
1949	STL	A	P		26	7- 8
1950	STL	A	P		48	4-11
1951	STL	A	P		1	0- 0
1952	CHI	A	P		19	1- 5
1953	BOS	A	P		16	0- 0
1956	CIN	N	P		1	0- 0
1957	CIN	N	P		8	0- 2
	BLTL				172	15-28

KENNEDY, WILLIAM GORMAN
B.DEC.22,1918 ALEXANDRIA,VA.

YR	CL	LEA	POS	GP	G	REC
1942	WAS	A	P		8	0- 1
1946	WAS	A	P		21	1- 2
1947	WAS	A	P		2	0- 0
	BLTL				31	1- 3

YR	CL LEA POS	GP	G	REC

KENNEDY, WILLIAM P. "BRICKYARD"
B.OCT.7,1867 BELLAIRE,OHIO
D.SEPT.23,1915 BELLAIRE,OHIO

YR	CL LEA POS	GP	G	REC
1892	BRO N P		22	13- 8
1893	BRO N P		45	25-18
1894	BRO N P		44	24-20
1895	BRO N P		36	19-13
1896	BRO N P		37	15-22
1897	BRO N P	40	42	19-21
1898	BRO N P		38	16-22
1899	BRO N P		37	18- 8
1900	BRO N P		37	22-15
1901	BRO N P		14	3- 5
1902	NY N P		6	1- 4
1903	PIT N P		18	9- 6
	TR	374	376	184-162

KENNEY, GERALD T. "JERRY"
B.JUNE 30,1945 ST.LOUIS,MO.

1967	NY A S		20	.310
1969	NY A S-3-0		130	.257
1970	NY A 2-3		140	.193
1971	NY A 1-S-3		120	.262
1972	NY A S-3		50	.210
1973	CLE A 2		5	.250
	BLTR		465	.237

KENNEY, JOHN

| 1872 | ATL NA 2-0 | | 5 | .000 |

KENNEY, ARTHUR JOSEPH
B.APR.29,1917 MILFORD,MASS.

| 1938 | BOS N P | | 2 | 0- 0 |
| | BLTL | | | |

KENT, EDWARD C.
B.NEW YORK

| 1884 | TOL AA P | | 1 | 0- 1 |
| | TL | | | |

KENT, MAURICE ALLEN
B.SEPT.17,1885 MARSHALLTOWN,IA.
D.APR.19,1966 IOWA CITY,IOWA

1912	BRO N P		20	5- 5
1913	BRO N P		5	0- 0
	BRTR		25	5- 5

KENWORTHY, RICHARD LEE "DICK"
B.APR.1,1941 RED OAK,IOWA

1962	CHI A 2		3	.000
1964	CHI A H		2	.000
1965	CHI A H		3	.000
1966	CHI A 3		9	.200
1967	CHI A 3		50	.227
1968	CHI A 3		58	.221
	BRTR		125	.215

KENWORTHY, WILLIAM JENNINGS "DUKE"
B.JULY 4,1886 CAMBRIDGE,OHIO
D.SEPT.21,1950

1912	WAS A 0		12	.289
1914	KC F 2		146	.316
1915	KC F 2		121	.299
1917	STL A 2		5	.100
	BBTR		284	.305

KENZIE, WALTER H.
B.1859 CHICAGO,ILL.

1882	DET N S		13	.094
1884	CHI N S-3		19	.158
	STL AA 2		2	.125
			34	.133

KEOUGH, JOSEPH WILLIAM "JOE"
B.JAN.7,1946 POMONA,CAL.

1968	OAK A 1-0		34	.214
1969	KC A 1-0		70	.187
1970	KC A 1-0		57	.322
1971	KC A 0		110	.248
1972	KC A 0		56	.249
1973	CHI A H		5	.000
	BLTL		332	.246

KEOUGH, RICHARD MARTIN "MARTY"
B.APR.14,1935 OAKLAND,CAL.

1956	BOS A H		3	.000
1957	BOS A 0		9	.059
1958	BOS A 1-0		68	.220
1959	BOS A 1-0		96	.243
1960	BOS A 0		38	.248
	CLE A 0		65	.248
1961	WAS A 1-0		135	.249
1962	CIN N 1-0		111	.278
1963	CIN N 1-0		95	.227
1964	CIN N 1-0		109	.257
1965	CIN N 1-0		62	.116
1966	ATL N 1-0		17	.059
1966	CHI N 0		33	.231
	BLTL		841	.242

KERIAZAKOS, CONSTANTINE NICHOLAS "GUS"
B.JULY 28,1931 W.ORANGE,N.J.

1950	CHI A P		1	0- 1
1954	WAS A P		22	2- 3
1955	KC A P		5	0- 1
	BRTR		28	2- 5

KERINS, JOHN NELSON
B.JULY 15,1858 INDIANAPOLIS,IND
D.SEPT.8,1919

1884	IND AA 1		93	.210
1885	LOU AA C-1		113	.243
1886	LOU AA C-1		119	.268
1887	LOU AA C-1		112	.360
1888	LOU AA M-C-0		81	.239
1889	LOU AA C-0		2	.333
	BAL AA C-1-S-0		16	.283
1890	STL AA C		19	.136
	BRTR		555	.267

KERKSIECK, WAYMAN WILLIAM
B.DEC.6,1913 ULM,ARK.
D.MAR.11,1970 LITTLE ROCK,ARK.

| 1939 | PHI N P | 23 | 25 | 0- 2 |
| | BRTR | | | |

KERLIN, ORIE MILTON
B.JAN.23,1891 SUMMERFIELD,LA.
D.OCT.29,1974 SHREVEPORT,LA.

| 1915 | PIT F C | | 3 | .000 |
| | TR | | | |

KERN, JAMES LESTER "JIM"
B.MAR.15,1949 GLADWIN,MICH.

1974	CLE A P		4	0- 1
1975	CLE A P		13	1- 2
1976	CLE A P		50	10- 7
	BRTR		67	11-10

KERN, WILLIAM GEORGE
B.FEB.28,1933 COPLAY,PA.

| 1962 | KC A 0 | | 8 | .250 |
| | BRTR | | | |

KERNAN, JOSEPH
B.BALTIMORE,MD.

| 1873 | MAR NA 2-0 | | 2 | - |

KERNEK, GEORGE BOYD
B.JAN.12,1940 HOLDENVILLE,OKLA.

1965	STL N 1		10	.290
1966	STL N 1		20	.240
	BLTL		30	.259

KERNS, DANIEL P.
B.PHILADELPHIA,PA.

| 1920 | PHI N H | | 1 | .000 |

KERNS, RUSSELL ELDON
B.NOV.10,1920 FREMONT,OHIO

| 1945 | DET A H | | 1 | .000 |
| | BLTR | | | |

KERR, JOHN FRANCIS
B.NOV.26,1900 SAN FRANCISCO,CAL

1923	DET A S		19	.214
1924	DET A 3-0		17	.273
1929	CHI A 2		127	.258
1930	CHI A 2-S		70	.289
1931	CHI A 2		128	.268
1932	WAS A 2-S		51	.273
1933	WAS A 2-3		28	.200
1934	WAS A 3		31	.272
	BRTR		471	.266
	BB 1923-24			

KERR, JOHN JONAS "DOC"
B.JAN.17,1882 DEL ROY,OHIO
D.JUNE 9,1937 BALTIMORE,MD.

1914	PIT F C		41	.254
	BAL F C		14	.265
1915	BAL F C		3	.333
	BBTR		58	.260

KERR, JOHN JOSEPH "BUDDY"
B.NOV.6,1922 ASTORIA,N.Y.

1943	NY N S		27	.286
1944	NY N S		150	.267
1945	NY N S		149	.249
1946	NY N S-3		145	.250
1947	NY N S		138	.287
1948	NY N S		144	.240
1949	NY N S		90	.209
1950	BOS N S		155	.227
1951	BOS N 2-S		69	.186
	BRTR		1067	.249

KERR, JOHN MELVILLE "MEL"
B.MAY 22,1904 SOURIS,MANITOBA, CANADA

| 1925 | CHI N H | | 1 | .000 |
| | BLTL | | | |

KERR, RICHARD HENRY "DICKIE"
B.JULY 3,1893 ST.LOUIS,MO.
D.MAY 4,1963 HOUSTON,TEX.

1919	CHI A P		39	13- 8
1920	CHI A P		46	21- 9
1921	CHI A P	44	45	19-17
1925	CHI A P	12	13	0- 1
	BLTL	141	143	53-35

KERRIGAN, JOSEPH THOMAS "JOE"
B.NOV.30,1954 PHILADELPHIA,PA.

| 1976 | MON N P | | 38 | 2- 6 |
| | BRTR | | | |

KERSCHER, WOLFGANG ANDREW
(PLAYED UNDER NAME OF
MICHAEL ANDREW KIRCHER)

KERWIN, DANIEL P.
B.JULY 8,1879 PHILADELPHIA,PA.

| 1903 | CIN N 0 | | 1 | .750 |
| | BLTL | | | |

KESSINGER, DONALD EULON "DON"
B.JULY 17,1942 FORREST CITY,ARK.

1964	CHI N S		4	.167
1965	CHI N S		106	.201
1966	CHI N S		150	.274
1967	CHI N S		145	.231
1968	CHI N S		160	.240
1969	CHI N S		158	.273
1970	CHI N S		154	.266
1971	CHI N S		155	.258
1972	CHI N S		149	.274
1973	CHI N S		160	.262
1974	CHI N S		153	.259
1975	CHI N S-3		154	.243
1976	STL N 2-S-3		145	.239
	BBTR		1793	.254
	BR 1964-65			

KESSLER, HENRY "LUCKY"
B.1847 BROOKLYN,N.Y.
D.JAN.9,1900

1873	ATL NA 1		1	-
1874	ATL NA C-2-3-0		14	-
1875	ATL NA 2-S-0		25	-
1876	CIN N S-3-0		59	.251
1877	CIN N C-1		6	.100
	BRTP		105	-

KESTER, RICHARD LEE "RICK"
B.JULY 7,1946 IOLA,KAN.

1968	ATL N P		5	0- 0
1969	ATL N P		1	0- 0
1970	ATL N P		15	0- 0
	BRTR		21	0- 0

KETCHUM, AUGUSTUS FRANKLIN
B.MAR.21,1897 ROYCE CITY,TEX.

| 1922 | PHI A P | | 6 | 0- 1 |
| | BRTR | | | |

KETCHUM, FREDERICK L.
B.JULY 27,1875 ELMIRA,N.Y.
D.MAR.12,1908

1899	LOU N 0		15	.311
1901	PHI A 0		5	.227
	BLTR		20	.289

YR	CL	LEA	POS	GP	G	REC

KETTER, PHILIP
B.HUTCHINSON,KAN.

YR	CL	LEA	POS	GP	G	REC
1912	STL	A	C		2	.333
	TR					

KEUPPER, HENRY
B.JUNE 24,1887 EGYPT,ILL.
D.AUG.14,1960

| 1914 | STL | F | P | | 42 | 7-20 |
| | BLTL | | | | | |

KIBBIE, HORACE KENT
B.JULY 18,1903 FT.WORTH,TEX.
D.OCT.19,1975 FT.WORTH,TEX.

| 1925 | BOS | N | 2-S | | 11 | .268 |
| | BRTR | | | | | |

KIBBLE, JOHN WESTLY "HAPPY"
B.JAN.2,1892 SEATONVILLE,ILL.

| 1912 | CLE | A | 2-3 | | 5 | .000 |
| | BBTR | | | | | |

KIEFER, JOSEPH WILLIAM
"HARLEM JOE"
B.JULY 19,1899 W.LEYDEN,N.Y.

1920	CHI	A	P		2	0- 1
1925	BOS	A	P		2	0- 2
1926	BOS	A	P		11	0- 3
	BRTR				15	0- 6

KIELY, LEO PATRICK
"LEO" OR "KIKI"
B.NOV.30,1929 HOBOKEN,N.J.

1951	BOS	A	P	17	18	7- 7
1954	BOS	A	P		28	5- 8
1955	BOS	A	P		33	3- 3
1956	BOS	A	P		23	2- 2
1958	BOS	A	P		47	5- 2
1959	BOS	A	P		41	3- 3
1960	KC	A	P		20	1- 2
	BLTL			209	210	26-27

KILDUFF, PETER JOHN
B.APR.4,1894 WEIR CITY,KAN.
D.FEB.14,1930

1917	NY	N	2-S		31	.205
	CHI	N	2-S		56	.277
1918	CHI	N	2		30	.204
1919	CHI	N	2-S-3		31	.273
	BRO	N	2-3		32	.301
1920	BRO	N	2		141	.272
1921	BRO	N	2		107	.288
	BRTR				428	.270

KILEY, FRANCIS THOMAS
(PLAYED UNDER NAME OF
FRANCIS THOMAS KANE)

KILEY, JOHN FREDERICK
B.CAMBRIDGE,MASS.

1884	WAS	AA	O		14	.203
1891	BOS	N	P		1	0- 1
	BLTL			1	15	0- 1
						.197

KILHULLEN, JOSEPH ISADORE "PAT"
B.MAY 3,1888 CARBONDALE,PA.
D.NOV.2,1922

| 1914 | PIT | N | C | | 1 | .000 |
| | TR | | | | | |

KILKENNY, MICHAEL DAVID "MIKE"
B.APR.11,1945 BRADFORD,ONT.,CAN.

1969	DET	A	P		39	8- 6
1970	DET	A	P	36	37	7- 6
1971	DET	A	P		30	4- 5
1972	DET	A	P		1	0- 0
	OAK	A	P		1	0- 0
	SD	N	P		5	0- 0
	CLE	A	P		22	4- 1
1973	CLE	A	P		5	0- 0
	BRTL			139	140	23-18

KILLEBREW, HARMON CLAYTON
B.JUNE 29,1936 PAYETTE,IDAHO

1954	WAS	A	2		9	.308
1955	WAS	A	2-3		38	.200
1956	WAS	A	2-3		44	.222
1957	WAS	A	2-3		9	.290
1958	WAS	A	3		13	.194
1959	WAS	A	3-O		153	.242
1960	WAS	A	1-3		124	.276
1961	MIN	A	1-3-O		150	.288
1962	MIN	A	1-O		155	.243
1963	MIN	A	O		142	.258
1964	MIN	A	O		158	.270
1965	MIN	A	1-3-O		113	.269
1966	MIN	A	1-3-O		162	.281
1967	MIN	A	1-3		163	.269
1968	MIN	A	1-3		100	.210
1969	MIN	A	1-3		162	.276
1970	MIN	A	1-3		157	.271
1971	MIN	A	1-3		147	.254
1972	MIN	A	1		139	.231
1973	MIN	A	1		69	.242
1974	MIN	A	1-O		122	.222
1975	KC	A	1-O		106	.199
	BRTR				2435	.256

KILLEEN, EVANS HENRY
B.FEB.27,1936 ELMONT,N.Y.

| 1959 | KC | A | P | | 4 | 0- 0 |
| | BRTR | | | | | |

KILLEEN, HENRY
B.1871 TROY,N.Y.

| 1891 | CLE | N | P | | 1 | 0- 1 |

KILLEFER, WADE HAMPTON "RED"
B.APR.13,1884 BLOOMINGDALE,MICH
D.SEPT.4,1958

1907	DET	A	O		1	.000
1908	DET	A	2		28	.213
1909	DET	A	2		23	.302
	WAS	A	O		40	.160
1910	WAS	A	2		106	.229
1914	CIN	N	O		42	.277
1915	CIN	N	1-O		155	.272
1916	CIN	N	O		70	.244
	NY	N	H		2	.500
	BRTR				467	.248

KILLEFER, WILLIAM LAVIER
"REINDEER BILL"
B.OCT.10,1888 BLOOMINGDALE,MICH
D.JULY 3,1960 ELSMERE,DEL.

1909	STL	A	C		11	.172
1910	STL	A	C		74	.124
1911	PHI	N	C		6	.188
1912	PHI	N	C		85	.224
1913	PHI	N	C		120	.244
1914	PHI	N	C		98	.234
1915	PHI	N	C		105	.238
1916	PHI	N	C		97	.217
1917	PHI	N	C		125	.274
1918	CHI	N	C		104	.233
1919	CHI	N	C		103	.286
1920	CHI	N	C		62	.200
1921	CHI	N	M-C		45	.323
	BRTR				1035	.239

NON-PLAYING MANAGER
CHI(N) 1922-25, STL(A) 1930-33

KILLEN, FRANK BISSELL "LEFTY"
B.NOV.30,1870 PITTSBURGH,PA.
D.DEC.4,1939

1891	MIL	AA	P		11	8- 3
1892	WAS	N	P		54	29-25
1893	PIT	N	P		47	33-14
1894	PIT	N	P		24	14-10
1895	PIT	N	P		14	7- 6
1896	PIT	N	P		50	31-19
1897	PIT	N	P		41	16-23
1898	PIT	N	P		22	10-12
	WAS	N	P-O		20	7- 9
						.268
1899	WAS	N	P		5	0- 2
	BOS	N	P		12	7- 5
1900	CHI	N	P		6	3- 3
	TL				306	165-131
						.246

KILLIAN, EDWIN HENRY "TWILIGHT"
B.NOV.12,1876 RACINE,WIS.
D.JULY 18,1928

1903	CLE	A	P		10	3- 5
1904	DET	A	P		40	15-20
1905	DET	A	P		39	22-14
1906	DET	A	P		20	9- 6
1907	DET	A	P	42	46	25-13
1908	DET	A	P	27	28	11-10
1909	DET	A	P		25	11- 9
1910	DET	A	P		11	4- 3
	BLTL			214	219	100-80

KILLILAY, JOHN WILLIAM
B.MAY 24,1887 LEAVENWORTH,KAN.
D.OCT.21,1968 TULSA,OKLA.

| 1911 | BOS | A | P | | 14 | 4- 3 |
| | BRTR | | | | | |

KILROY, MATTHEW ALOYSIUS
"MATCHES"
B.JUNE 21,1866 PHILADELPHIA,PA.
D.MAR.2,1940

1886	BAL	AA	P		69	29-34
1887	BAL	AA	P		73	46-20
1888	BAL	AA	P	42	43	16-21
1889	BAL	AA	P	59	65	28-25
1890	BOS	P	P		31	10-13
1891	BOS	AA	P-O	7	8	1- 4
						.190
1892	WAS	N	P		4	1- 1
1893	LOU	N	P		5	3- 2
1894	LOU	N	P		6	0- 6
1898	CHI	N	P		25	6- 6
	TL			321	329	140-132
						.242

KILROY, MICHAEL JOSEPH
B.NOV.4,1872 PHILADELPHIA,PA.
D.OCT.2,1960

1888	BAL	AA	P		1	0- 1
1891	PHI	N	P		3	0- 1
	TR				4	0- 2

KIMBALL, EUGENE B.
B.AUG.31,1850 ROCHESTER,N.Y.
D.AUG.2,1882

| 1871 | CLE | NA | 2-S-O | | 29 | - |

KIMBALL, NEWEL W. "NEWT"
B.MAR.27,1915 LOGAN,UTAH

1937	CHI	N	P		2	0- 0
1938	CHI	N	P		1	0- 0
1940	BRO	N	P		21	3- 1
	STL	N	P		2	1- 0
1941	BRO	N	P		15	3- 1
1942	BRO	N	P		14	2- 0
1943	BRO	N	P		5	1- 1
	PHI	N	P		34	1- 6
	BRTR				94	11- 9

KIMBER, SAMUEL JACKSON
B.OCT.29,1852 PHILADELPHIA,PA.
D.NOV.6,1925

1884	BRO	AA	P		41	18-20
1885	PRO	N	P		1	0- 1
					42	18-21

KIMBERLIN, HARRY LIDDLE
"MULE TRADER"
B.MAR.13,1909 SULLIVAN,MO.

1936	STL	A	P		13	0- 0
1937	STL	A	P		3	0- 2
1938	STL	A	P		1	0- 0
1939	STL	A	P		17	1- 2
	BRTR				34	1- 4

KIMBLE, RICHARD LEWIS
B.JULY 27,1917 BUCHTEL,OHIO

| 1945 | WAS | A | S | | 20 | .245 |
| | BLTR | | | | | |

KIME, HAROLD LEE "LEFTY"
B.MAR.15,1899 W.SALEM,OHIO
D.MAY 16,1939

| 1920 | STL | N | P | | 4 | 0- 0 |
| | BLTL | | | | | |

KIMM, BRUCE EDWARD
B.JUNE 29,1951 CEDAR RAPIDS,IOWA

| 1976 | DET | A | C | | 63 | .263 |
| | BRTR | | | | | |

YR	CL	LEA	POS	GP	G	REC

KIMMICK, WALTER LYONS
B.MAY 30,1898 TURTLE CREEK,PA.
1919	STL	N	S		2	.000
1921	CIN	N	3		3	.167
1922	CIN	N	2-S-3	39		.247
1923	CIN	N	2-S-3	29		.225
1925	PHI	N	2-S-3	70		.305
1926	PHI	N	1-S-3	20		.214
		BRTR		163		.261

KIMSEY, CLYDE ELIAS "CHAD"
B.AUG.6,1905 COPPERHILL,TENN.
D.DEC.3,1942
1929	STL	A	P	24	29	3- 6
1930	STL	A	P	42	60	6-10
1931	STL	A	P	42	47	4- 6
1932	STL	A	P	33	34	4- 2
1933	CHI	A	P		7	1- 1
	CHI	A	P		28	4- 1
1936	DET	A	P		22	2- 3
		BLTR		198	227	24-29

KINDALL, GERALD DONALD "JERRY"
B.MAY 27,1935 ST.PAUL,MINN.
1956	CHI	N	S		32	.164
1957	CHI	N	2-S-3	72		.160
1958	CHI	N	2		3	.167
1960	CHI	N	2-S	89		.240
1961	CHI	N	2-S	96		.242
1962	CLE	A	2	154		.232
1963	CLE	A	1-2-S	86		.205
1964	CLE	A	1	23		.360
	MIN	A	2-S-3	62		.148
1965	MIN	A	2-S-3	125		.196
		BRTR		742		.213
		DB 1960 (PART)				

KINDER, ELLIS RAYMOND
"ELLIS" OR "OLD FOLKS"
B.JULY 26,1914 ATKINS,ARK.
D.OCT.16,1968 JACKSON,TENN.
1946	STL	A	P		33	3- 3
1947	STL	A	P		34	8-15
1948	BOS	A	P		28	10- 7
1949	BOS	A	P		43	23- 6
1950	BOS	A	P		48	14-12
1951	BOS	A	P		63	11- 2
1952	BOS	A	P		23	5- 6
1953	BOS	A	P		69	10- 6
1954	BOS	A	P		48	8- 8
1955	BOS	A	P		43	5- 5
1956	STL	N	P		22	2- 0
	CHI	A	P		29	3- 1
1957	CHI	A	P		1	0- 0
		BRTR		484	102-71

KINER, RALPH MC PHERRAN
B.OCT.27,1922 SANTA RITA,N.MEX.
1946	PIT	N	O		144	.247
1947	PIT	N	O		152	.313
1948	PIT	N	O		156	.265
1949	PIT	N	O		152	.310
1950	PIT	N	O		150	.272
1951	PIT	N	1-O		151	.309
1952	PIT	N	O		149	.244
1953	PIT	N	O		41	.270
	CHI	N	O		117	.283
1954	CHI	N	O		147	.285
1955	CLE	A	O		113	.243
		BRTR		1472		.279

KING, CHARLES FREDERICK
"SILVER"
(REAL NAME
CHARLES FREDERICK KOENIG)
B.JAN.11,1868 ST.LOUIS,MO.
D.MAY 21,1938 ST.LOUIS,MO.
1886	KC	N	P		7	1- 3
1887	STL	AA	P	62	34-11
1888	STL	AA	P	66	44-21
1889	STL	AA	P	54	33-17
1890	CHI	P	P		57	33-20
1891	PIT	N	P		48	17-31
1892	NY	N	P		52	24-24
1893	NY	N	P		15	5- 3
	CIN	N	P		13	7- 6
1896	WAS	N	P		16	10- 6
1897	WAS	N	P		18	9- 9
		BRTR		408	217-151

KING, CHARLES GILBERT
B.NOV.10,1930 PARIS,TENN.
1954	DET	A	O		11	.214
1955	DET	A	O		7	.238
1956	DET	A	O		7	.222
1958	CHI	N	O		8	.250
1959	CHI	N	O		7	.000
	STL	N	O		5	.429
		BRTR		45		.237

KING, CLYDE EDWARD
B.MAY 23,1925 GOLDSBORO,N.C.
1944	BRO	N	P		14	2- 1
1945	BRO	N	P	42	43	5- 5
1947	BRO	N	P		29	6- 5
1948	BRO	N	P		9	0- 1
1951	BRO	N	P		48	14- 7
1952	BRO	N	P		23	2- 0
1953	CIN	N	P		35	3- 6
		BBTR	200	201	32-25
NON-PLAYING MANAGER
SF(N) 1969-70, ATL(N) 1974-75

KING, EDWARD LEE
B.MAR.28,1894 NEW BRITAIN,CONN.
D.SEPT.7,1938
1916	PHI	A	O		42	.188
1919	BOS	N	O		2	.000
		BRTR		44		.186

KING, FREDERICK
(SEE JOHN ALBERT BUTLER)

KING, HAROLD "HAL"
B.FEB.2,1944 OVIEDO,FLA.
1967	HOU	N	C		15	.250
1968	HOU	N	C		27	.145
1970	ATL	N	C		89	.260
1971	ATL	N	C		86	.207
1972	TEX	A	C		50	.180
1973	CIN	N	C		35	.186
1974	CIN	N	C		20	.176
		BLTR		322		.214

KING, JAMES HUBERT "JIM"
B.AUG.27,1932 ELKINS,ARK.
1955	CHI	N	O		113	.256
1956	CHI	N	O		118	.249
1957	STL	N	O		22	.314
1958	SF	N	O		34	.214
1961	WAS	A	C-O		110	.270
1962	WAS	A	O		132	.243
1963	WAS	A	O		136	.231
1964	WAS	A	O		134	.241
1965	WAS	A	O		120	.213
1966	WAS	A	O		117	.248
1967	WAS	A	C-O		47	.210
	CHI	A	O		23	.120
	CLE	A	O		19	.143
		BLTR		1125		.240

KING, LEE
B.DEC.26,1894 FAIRMONT,W.VA.
D.SEPT.16,1967 SHINNSTOWN,W.VA.
1916	PIT	N	O		8	.111
1917	PIT	N	O		111	.249
1918	PIT	N	O		36	.232
1919	NY	N	O		21	.100
1920	NY	N	O		93	.276
1921	NY	N	O		39	.223
	PHI	N	O		64	.269
1922	PHI	N	O		19	.226
	NY	N	1-O		20	.176
		BLTR		411		.247

KING, LYNN PAUL "DIG"
B.NOV.28,1907 VILLISCA,IOWA
D.MAY 11,1972 ATLANTIC,IOWA
1935	STL	N	O		8	.182
1936	STL	N	O		78	.190
1939	STL	N	O		89	.235
		BLTR		175		.208

KING, MARSHAL NEY "MART"
B.1849 TROY,N.Y.
D.OCT.19,1911
1871	CHI	NA	C-S-O	20		-
1872	TRO	NA	O		3	.000
				23		-

KING, NELSON JOSEPH "NELLIE"
B.MAR.15,1928 SHENANDOAH,PA.
1954	PIT	N	P		4	0- 0
1955	PIT	N	P		17	1- 3
1956	PIT	N	P		38	4- 1
1957	PIT	N	P		36	2- 1
		BRTR		95	7- 5

KING, SAMUEL WARREN
B.MAY 17,1852 PEABODY,MASS.
D.OCT.28,1891
1883	PHI	N	C		1	.000
1884	WAS	AA	C		12	.174
				13		.174

KING, STEPHEN F.
B.1845 TROY,N.Y.
D.JULY 8,1895
1871	TRO	NA	O		29	.396
1872	TRO	NA	O		25	.297
1874	PHI	NA	O		12	-
					66	-

KINGDON, WESTCOTT WILLIAM
B.JULY 4,1900 LOS ANGELES,CAL.
D.APR.19,1975 CAPISTRANO,CAL.
| 1932 | WAS | A | S-3 | | 18 | .324 |
| | | BRTR | | | | |

KINGMAN, DAVID ARTHUR "DAVE"
B.DEC.21,1948 PENDLETON,ORE.
1971	SF	N	1-O		41	.278
1972	SF	N	1-3-O		135	.225
1973	SF	N	P-1-3	2	112	0- 0
						.203
1974	SF	N	1-3-O		121	.223
1975	NY	N	1-3-O		134	.231
1976	NY	N	1-O		123	.238
		BRTR	2	666	0- 0
						.229

KINGMAN, HARRY ISES
D.APR.3,1892 POMONA,CAL.
| 1914 | NY | A | 1 | | 4 | .000 |
| | | BLTL | | | | |

KINLOCK, WALTER
B.1878 ST.JOSEPH,MO.
| 1895 | STL | N | 3 | | 1 | .333 |

KINNEY, WALTER WILLIAM
B.SEPT.9,1894 DENISON,TEX.
D.JULY 1,1971 ESCONDIDO,CAL.
1918	BOS	A	P		5	6	0- 0
1919	PHI	A	P	43	57	9-15
1920	PHI	A	P	10	13	2- 4
1923	PHI	A	P		5	0- 1
		BLTL	63	81	11-20

KINSELLA, EDWARD WILLIAM "RUBE"
B.JAN.15,1880 BLOOMINGTON,ILL.
1905	PIT	N	P		3	0- 1
1910	STL	A	P		10	1- 3
		BRTR		13	1- 4

KINSELLA, ROBERT FRANCIS "RED"
B.JAN.5,1899 SPRINGFIELD,ILL.
D.DEC.30,1951 LOS ANGELES,CAL.
1919	NY	N	O		3	.222
1920	NY	N	O		1	.333
		BLTR		4		.250

KINSLER
B.STATEN ISLAND,N.Y.
| 1893 | NY | N | P | | 1 | .000 |

KINSLOW, THOMAS F.
B.JAN.12,1866 WASHINGTON,D.C.
D.FEB.22,1901
1886	WAS	N	C		3	.333
1887	MET	AA	C		2	.000
1890	BRO	P	C		63	.277
1891	BRO	N	C		59	.238
1892	BRO	N	C		63	.309
1893	BRO	N	C		77	.259
1894	BRO	N	C		61	.298
1895	PIT	N	C		17	.230
1896	LOU	N	C		8	2.80
1898	WAS	N	C		3	.111
	STL	N	C		14	.278
		TR		370		.271

KINZY, HARRY HERSEL "SLIM"
B.JULY 19,1910 HALLSVILLE,TEX.
| 1934 | CHI | A | P | | 13 | 0- 1 |

KIPP, FRED LEO
B.OCT.1,1931 PIQUA,KAN.
1957	BRO	N	P		1	0- 0
1958	LA	N	P	40	42	6- 6
1959	LA	N	P		2	0- 0
1960	NY	A	P		4	0- 1
		BLTL	47	49	6- 7

KIPPER, THORNTON JOHN
B.SEPT.27,1928 BAGLEY,WIS.

YR	CL	LEA	POS	GP	G	REC
1953	PHI	N	P		20	3- 3
1954	PHI	N	P		11	0- 0
1955	PHI	N	P		24	0- 1
		BRTR			55	3- 4

KIPPERT, EDWARD AUGUSTUS "KICKAPOO"
B.JAN.3,1880 DETROIT,MICH.
D.JUNE 3,1960

YR	CL	LEA	POS	GP	G	REC
1914	CIN	N	O		2	.000
		BRTR				

KIRBY, CLAYTON LAWS "CLAY"
B.JUNE 25,1948 WASHINGTON,D.C.

YR	CL	LEA	POS	GP	G	REC
1969	SD	N	P		35	7-20
1970	SD	N	P		36	10-16
1971	SD	N	P	38	40	15-13
1972	SD	N	P	34	35	12-14
1973	SD	N	P	34	35	8-18
1974	CIN	N	P		36	12- 9
1975	CIN	N	P		26	10- 6
1976	MON	N	P		22	1- 8
		BRTR		261	265	75-103

KIRBY, JAMES HERSCHEL
B.MAY 5,1923 NASHVILLE,TENN.

YR	CL	LEA	POS	GP	G	REC
1949	CHI	N	H		3	.500
		BRTR				

KIRBY, JOHN F.
B.JAN.13,1865 ST.LOUIS,MO.
D.OCT.6,1931

YR	CL	LEA	POS	GP	G	REC
1884	KC	U	P-O		2	0- 1
						.167
1885	STL	N	P		14	5- 8
1886	STL	N	P	38	41	12-25
1887	IND	N	P-O		8	1- 7
						.138
	CLE	AA	P		5	0- 5
1888	KC	AA	P		6	1- 5
		TR		73	76	19-51
						.108

KIRBY, LARUE V.
B.DEC.30,1889 EUREKA,MICH.
D.JUNE 10,1961

YR	CL	LEA	POS	GP	G	REC
1912	NY	N	P		3	1- 0
1914	STL	F	O		51	.253
1915	STL	F	O		59	.212
		BBTR		3	113	1- 0
						.233

KIRCHER, MICHAEL ANDREW
(REAL NAME
WOLFGANG ANDREW KERSCHER)
B.SEPT.30,1897 ROCHESTER,N.Y.
D.JUNE 26,1972 ROCHESTER,N.Y.

YR	CL	LEA	POS	GP	G	REC
1919	PHI	A	P		2	0- 0
1920	STL	N	P		9	2- 1
1921	STL	N	P		3	0- 1
		BBTR			14	2- 2

KIRK, THOMAS DANIEL
B.SEPT.27,1927 PHILADELPHIA,PA.
D.AUG.1,1974 PHILADELPHIA,PA.

YR	CL	LEA	POS	GP	G	REC
1947	PHI	A	H		1	.000
		BLTL				

KIRK, WILLIAM PARTLEMORE
B.JULY 19,1936 COATESVILLE,PA.

YR	CL	LEA	POS	GP	G	REC
1961	KC	A	P		1	0- 0
		BLTL				

KIRKE, JUDSON FABIAN "JAY"
B.JUNE 16,1888 FLEISCHMANN'S,
N.Y.
D.AUG.31,1968 NEW ORLEANS,LA.

YR	CL	LEA	POS	GP	G	REC
1910	DET	A	2		8	.192
1911	BOS	N	O		20	.360
1912	BOS	N	O		103	.320
1913	BOS	N	O		18	.237
1914	CLE	A	1-O		67	.273
1915	CLE	A	1		87	.310
1918	NY	N	1		17	.250
		BLTR			320	.301

KIRKLAND, WILLIE CHARLES
B.FEB.17,1934 SILURIA,ALA.

YR	CL	LEA	POS	GP	G	REC
1958	SF	N	O		122	.258
1959	SF	N	O		126	.272
1960	SF	N	O		146	.252
1961	CLE	A	O		146	.259
1962	CLE	A	O		137	.200
1963	CLE	A	O		127	.230
1964	BAL	A	O		66	.200
	WAS	A	O		32	.216
1965	WAS	A	O		123	.231
1966	WAS	A	O		124	.190
		BLTR			1149	.240

KIRKPATRICK, EDGAR LEON "ED"
B.OCT.8,1944 SPOKANE,WASH.

YR	CL	LEA	POS	GP	G	REC
1962	LA	A	C		3	.000
1963	LA	A	C-O		34	.195
1964	LA	A	O		75	.242
1965	CAL	A	O		19	.260
1966	CAL	A	1-O		117	.192
1967	CAL	A	C-O		3	.000
1968	CAL	A	C-1-O		89	.230
1969	KC	A	C-1-2-3-O		120	.257
1970	KC	A	C-1-O		134	.229
1971	KC	A	C-O		120	.219
1972	KC	A	C-1		113	.275
1973	KC	A	C-O		126	.263
1974	PIT	N	C-1-O		116	.247
1975	PIT	N	1-O		89	.236
1976	PIT	N	1-3-O		83	.233
		BLTR			1241	.238

KIRKPATRICK, ENOS CLAIRE
B.DEC.8,1885 PITTSBURGH,PA.
D.APR.14,1964 PITTSBURGH,PA.

YR	CL	LEA	POS	GP	G	REC
1912	BRO	N	3		32	.191
1913	BRO	N	2		48	.247
1914	BAL	F	3		55	.259
1915	BAL	F	2-3		60	.241
		BRTR			195	.239

KIRKWOOD, DONALD PAUL "DON"
B.SEPT.24,1949 PONTIAC,MICH.

YR	CL	LEA	POS	GP	G	REC
1974	CAL	A	P		3	0- 0
1975	CAL	A	P	44	45	6- 5
1976	CAL	A	P		28	6-12
		BRTR		75	76	12-17

KIRRENE, JOSEPH JOHN "JOE"
B.OCT.4,1931 SAN FRANCISCO,CAL.

YR	CL	LEA	POS	GP	G	REC
1950	CHI	A	3		1	.250
1954	CHI	A	3		9	.304
		BRTR			10	.296

KIRSCH, HARRY L.
B.OCT.17,1887 PITTSBURGH,PA.
D.DEC.25,1925 OVERBROOK,PA.

YR	CL	LEA	POS	GP	G	REC
1910	CLE	A	P		2	0- 0
		TR				

KISH, ERNEST ALEXANDER
B.FEB.6,1919 WASHINGTON,D.C.

YR	CL	LEA	POS	GP	G	REC
1945	PHI	A	O		43	.245
		BLTR				

KISLEAUSKAS, EDWARD WILLIAM
(PLAYED UNDER NAME OF
EDWARD WILLIAM COLE)

KISON, BRUCE EUGENE
B.FEB.18,1950 PASCO,WASH.

YR	CL	LEA	POS	GP	G	REC
1971	PIT	N	P		18	6- 5
1972	PIT	N	P		32	9- 7
1973	PIT	N	P		7	3- 0
1974	PIT	N	P		40	9- 8
1975	PIT	N	P	33	35	12-11
1976	PIT	N	P		31	14- 9
		BRTR		161	163	53-40

KISSINGER, CHARLES SAMUEL "RUBE"
B.DEC.13,1876 ADRIAN,MICH.
D.JULY 14,1941

YR	CL	LEA	POS	GP	G	REC
1902	DET	A	P		5	1- 4
1903	DET	A	P		16	7- 9
		BRTR			21	8-13

KISSINGER, WILLIAM FRANCIS "SHANG"
B.AUG.15,1871 DAYTON,OHIO
D.APR.20,1929

YR	CL	LEA	POS	GP	G	REC
1895	BAL	N	P		6	1- 1
	STL	N	P	19	23	5-10
1896	STL	N	P		22	2-13
1897	STL	N	P		11	0- 4
		BRTR		58	62	8-28

KITSON, FRANK R.
B.APR.11,1872 HOPKINS,MICH.
D.APR.14,1930

YR	CL	LEA	POS	GP	G	REC
1898	BAL	N	P		23	8- 5
1899	BAL	N	P	38	40	20-16
1900	BRO	N	P	30	33	14-13
1901	BRO	N	P		32	19-11
1902	BRO	N	P		31	19-12
1903	DET	A	P	31	36	15-15
1904	DET	A	P	26	27	10-12
1905	DET	A	P		33	8-17
1906	WAS	A	P	32	33	6-14
1907	WAS	A	P		5	0- 1
	NY	N	P		11	3- 2
		BRTR		292	304	122-118

KITSOS, CHRISTOPHER ANESTOS
B.FEB.2,1929 NEW YORK,N.Y.

YR	CL	LEA	POS	GP	G	REC
1954	CHI	N	S		1	.000
		BBTR				

KITTREDGE, MALACHI J. "JEDEDIAH"
B.OCT.12,1869 CLINTON,MASS.
D.SEPT.12,1927 GARY,IND.

YR	CL	LEA	POS	GP	G	REC
1890	CHI	N	C		96	.201
1891	CHI	N	C		70	.202
1892	CHI	N	C		66	.187
1893	CHI	N	C		67	.245
1894	CHI	N	C		50	.317
1895	CHI	N	C		58	.244
1896	CHI	N	C		61	.223
1897	CHI	N	C		77	.198
1898	LOU	N	C		88	.250
1899	LOU	N	C		46	.174
	WAS	N	C		41	.158
1901	BOS	N	C		113	.247
1902	BOS	N	C		72	.233
1903	BOS	N	C		30	.212
	WAS	A	C		59	.218
1904	WAS	A	M-C		80	.242
1905	WAS	A	C		77	.163
1906	WAS	A	C		22	.191
	CLE	A	C		5	.100
		BRTR			1178	.220

KLAERNER, HUGO EMIL
B.OCT.15,1908 FREDERICKSBURG,
TEX.

YR	CL	LEA	POS	GP	G	REC
1934	CHI	A	P		3	0- 2
		BRTR				

KLAGES, FRED ANTHONY
B.OCT.31,1943 AMBRIDGE,PA.

YR	CL	LEA	POS	GP	G	REC
1966	CHI	A	P		3	1- 0
1967	CHI	A	P	11	12	4- 4
		BRTR		14	15	5- 4

KLAUS, ROBERT FRANCIS "BOBBY"
B.DEC.27,1937 SPRING GROVE,ILL.

YR	CL	LEA	POS	GP	G	REC
1964	CIN	N	2-S-3		40	.183
	NY	N	2-S-3		56	.244
1965	NY	N	2-S-3		119	.191
		BRTR			215	.208

KLAUS, WILLIAM JOSEPH "BILLY"
B.DEC.9,1928 FOX LAKE,ILL.

YR	CL	LEA	POS	GP	G	REC
1952	BOS	N	S		7	.000
1953	MIL	N	H		2	.000
1955	BOS	A	S-3		135	.283
1956	BOS	A	S-3		135	.271
1957	BOS	A	S		127	.252
1958	BOS	A	S		61	.159
1959	BAL	A	2-S-3		104	.249
1960	BAL	A	2-S-3		46	.209
1961	WAS	A	2-S-3-O		91	.227
1962	PHI	N	2-S-3		102	.206
1963	PHI	N	S-3		11	.056
		BLTR			821	.249

KLAWITTER, ALBERT "DUTCH"
B.APR.12,1888 WILKES-BARRE,PA.
D.MAY 2,1950 MILWAUKEE,WIS.

YR	CL	LEA	POS	GP	G	REC
1909	NY	N	P		6	1- 1
1910	NY	N	P		1	0- 0
1913	DET	A	P		6	1- 2
		BRTR			13	2- 3

YR	CL	LEA	POS	GP	G	REC

KLEE, OLLIE CHESTER
B.MAY 20,1900 DAYTON,OHIO
| 1925 | CIN | N | O | | 3 | .000 |
| | | BLTL | | | | |

KLEIN, CHARLES HERBERT "CHUCK"
B.OCT.7,1905 INDIANAPOLIS,IND.
D.MAR.28,1958 INDIANAPOLIS,IND.
1928	PHI	N	O		64	.360
1929	PHI	N	O		149	.356
1930	PHI	N	O		156	.386
1931	PHI	N	O		148	.337
1932	PHI	N	O		154	.348
1933	PHI	N	O		152	.368
1934	CHI	N	O		115	.301
1935	CHI	N	O		119	.293
1936	CHI	N	O		29	.294
	PHI	N	O		117	.309
1937	PHI	N	O		115	.325
1938	PHI	N	O		129	.247
1939	PHI	N	O		25	.191
	PIT	N	O		85	.300
1940	PHI	N	O		116	.218
1941	PHI	N	O		50	.123
1942	PHI	N	H		14	.071
1943	PHI	N	H		12	.100
1944	PHI	N	O		4	.143
		BLTR			1753	.320

KLEIN, LOUIS FRANK "LOU"
B.OCT.22,1918 NEW ORLEANS,LA.
D.JUNE 20,1976 METARIE,LA.
1943	STL	N	2-S		154	.287
1945	STL	N	2-S-3-O		19	.228
1946	STL	N	2		23	.194
1949	STL	N	2-S-3		58	.219
1951	CLE	A	H		2	.000
	PHI	A	2		49	.229
		BRTR			305	.259
NON-PLAYING MANAGER
CHI(N) 1961, 62, 65

KLEINE, HAROLD JOHN
B.JUNE 8,1923 ST.LOUIS,MO.
D.DEC.10,1957
1944	CLE	A	P	11	14	1- 2
1945	CLE	A	P	3	0- 0
		BLTL		14	17	1- 2

KLEINHANS, THEODORE OTTO
B.APR.8,1904 DEER PARK,WIS.
1934	PHI	N	P		5	0- 0
	CIN	N	P	24	25	2- 6
1936	NY	A	P		19	1- 1
1937	CIN	N	P		7	1- 2
1938	CIN	N	P		1	0- 0
		BRTL		56	57	4- 9

KLEINOW, JOHN PETER "RED"
B.JULY 20,1879 MILWAUKEE,WIS.
D.OCT.9,1929
1904	NY	A	C		67	.200
1905	NY	A	C		88	.221
1906	NY	A	C		96	.220
1907	NY	A	C		90	.264
1908	NY	A	C		96	.168
1909	NY	A	C		78	.228
1910	NY	A	C		5	.455
	BOS	A	C		51	.149
1911	BOS	A	C		8	.214
	PHI	N	C		4	.125
		BRTR			583	.212

KLEPFER, EDWARD LLOYD "BIG ED"
B.MAR.17,1888 WARREN,PA.
D.AUG.9,1950
1911	NY	A	P		2	0- 0
1913	NY	A	P		8	0- 1
1915	CHI	A	P		2	0- 0
	CLE	A	P		9	2- 6
1916	CLE	A	P		31	6- 7
1917	CLE	A	P		41	14- 4
1919	CLE	A	P		5	0- 0
		BRTR			98	22-18

KLEVEN, JAY ALLEN
B.DEC.2,1949 OAKLAND,CAL.
| 1976 | NY | N | C | | 2 | .200 |
| | | BRTR | | | | |

KLIEMAN, EDWARD FREDERICK "ED" OR "SPECS"
B.MAR.21,1918 NORWOOD,OHIO
1943	CLE	A	P		1	0- 1
1944	CLE	A	P		47	11-13
1945	CLE	A	P		38	5- 8
1946	CLE	A	P		9	0- 0
1947	CLE	A	P		58	5- 4
1948	CLE	A	P		44	3- 2
1949	WAS	A	P		2	0- 0
	CHI	A	P		18	2- 0
1950	PHI	A	P		5	0- 0
		BRTR		222	26-28

KLIMCHOCK, LOUIS STEPHEN "LOU"
B.OCT.15,1939 HOSTETTER,PA.
1958	KC	A	2		2	.200
1959	KC	A	2		17	.273
1960	KC	A	2		10	.300
1961	KC	A	1-2-3-O		57	.215
1962	MIL	N	H		8	.000
1963	WAS	A	2		9	.143
	MIL	N	1		24	.196
1964	MIL	N	2-3		10	.333
1965	MIL	N	1		34	.077
1966	NY	N	H		5	.000
1968	CLE	A	1-2-3		11	.133
1969	CLE	A	C-2-3		90	.287
1970	CLE	A	1-2		41	.161
		BLTR		318	.232

KLIMKOWSKI, RONALD BERNARD "RON"
B.MAR.1,1944 JERSEY CITY,N.J.
1969	NY	A	P		3	0- 0
1970	NY	A	P		45	6- 7
1971	OAK	A	P		26	2- 2
1972	NY	A	P		16	0- 3
		BRTR			90	8-12

KLINE, JOHN ROBERT
B.JAN.27,1929 ST.PETERSBURG,FLA
1955	WAS	A	P-2-	1	77	0- 0
		S-3				.221
		BRTR				

KLINE, ROBERT GEORGE "JUNIOR"
B.DEC.1,1909 ENTERPRRISE,OHIO
1930	BOS	A	P		1	0- 0
1931	BOS	A	P		28	5- 5
1932	BOS	A	P		47	11-13
1933	BOS	A	P		46	7- 8
1934	PHI	A	P		20	6- 2
	WAS	A	P		6	1- 0
		BRTR		148	30-28

KLINE, RONALD LEE "RON"
B.MAR.9,1932 CALLERY,PA.
1952	PIT	N	P		27	0- 7
1955	PIT	N	P-3	36	37	6-13
						.132
1956	PIT	N	P		44	14-18
1957	PIT	N	P		40	9-16
1958	PIT	N	P	32	33	13-16
1959	PIT	N	P	33	38	11-13
1960	STL	N	P		34	4- 9
1961	LA	N	P		26	3- 6
	DET	A	P		10	5- 3
1962	DET	A	P		36	3- 6
1963	WAS	A	P		62	3- 8
1964	WAS	A	P		61	10- 7
1965	WAS	A	P		74	7- 6
1966	WAS	A	P		63	6- 4
1967	MIN	A	P		54	7- 1
1968	PIT	A	P		56	12- 5
1969	PIT	N	P		20	1- 3
	SF	N	P		7	0- 2
	BOS	A	P		16	0- 1
1970	ATL	N	P		5	0- 0
		BRTR		736	743	114-144
						.092

KLINE, STEVEN JACK "STEVE"
B.OCT.6,1947 WENATCHEE,WASH.
1970	NY	A	P		16	6- 6
1971	NY	A	P		31	12-13
1972	NY	A	P		32	16- 9
1973	NY	A	P		14	4- 7
1974	NY	A	P		4	2- 2
	CLE	A	P		16	3- 8
		BRTR		113	43-45

KLING, JOHN G. "NOISY"
B.NOV.13,1875 KANSAS CITY,MO.
D.JAN.31,1947
1900	CHI	N	C		15	.294
1901	CHI	N	C		70	.266
1902	CHI	N	C-S		113	.286
1903	CHI	N	C		132	.297
1904	CHI	N	C		120	.243
1905	CHI	N	C		110	.218
1906	CHI	N	C		99	.312
1907	CHI	N	C		100	.284
1908	CHI	N	C		125	.276
1910	CHI	N	C		86	.269
1911	CHI	N	C		27	.175
	BOS	N	C		75	.224
1912	BOS	N	M-C		81	.317
1913	CIN	N	M-C		80	.273
		BRTR		1233	.271

KLING, RUDOLPH A.
B.MAR.23,1870 ST.LOUIS,MO.
D.MAR.14,1937
| 1902 | STL | N | S | | 4 | .200 |
| | | TR | | | | |

KLING, WILLIAM
B.JAN.14,1867 KANSAS CITY,MO.
D.AUG.25,1934
1891	PHI	N	P		13	4- 3
1892	BAL	N	P		2	0- 1
1895	LOU	N	P		1	0- 0
		BLTR		16	4- 4

KLINGER, JOSEPH JOHN
B.AUG.2,1902 CANONSBURG,PA.
D.JULY 31,1960
1927	NY	N	O		3	.400
1930	CHI	A	C-1		4	.375
		BRTR		7	.389

KLINGER, ROBERT HAROLD "BOB"
B.JUNE 4,1908 ALLENTON,MO.
1938	PIT	N	P		28	12- 5
1939	PIT	N	P		37	14-17
1940	PIT	N	P		39	8-13
1941	PIT	N	P		35	9- 4
1942	PIT	N	P		37	8-11
1943	PIT	N	P		33	11- 8
1946	BOS	A	P		28	3- 2
1947	BOS	A	P		28	1- 1
		BRTR		265	66-61

KLIPPSTEIN, JOHN CALVIN "JOHNNY"
B.OCT.17,1927 WASHINGTON,D.C.
1950	CHI	N	P	33	35	2- 9
1951	CHI	N	P		35	6- 6
1952	CHI	N	P		41	9-14
1953	CHI	N	P		48	10-11
1954	CHI	N	P		36	4-11
1955	CIN	N	P		39	9-10
1956	CIN	N	P		37	12-11
1957	CIN	N	P		46	8-11
1958	CIN	N	P		12	3- 2
	LA	N	P		45	3- 5
1959	LA	N	P		28	4- 0
1960	CLE	A	P		49	5- 5
1961	WAS	A	P		42	2- 2
1962	CIN	N	P		40	7- 6
1963	PHI	N	P		49	5- 6
1964	PHI	N	P		11	2- 1
	MIN	A	P		33	0- 4
1965	MIN	A	P		56	9- 3
1966	MIN	A	P		26	1- 1
1967	DET	A	P		5	0- 0
		BRTR	711	713	101-118

KLOBEDANZ, FREDERICK AUGUSTUS "DUKE"
B.JUNE 13,1873 WATERBURY,CONN.
D.APR.12,1940
1896	BOS	N	P		11	6- 4
1897	BOS	N	P		38	25- 8
1898	BOS	N	P		32	19-10
1899	BOS	N	P		5	1- 4
1902	BOS	N	P		1	1- 0
		BLTL		87	52-26

KLOPP, STANLEY HAROLD
B.DEC.22,1913 ROBESONIA,PA.
| 1944 | BOS | N | P | | 24 | 1- 2 |
| | | BRTR | | | | |

YR	CL	LEA	POS	GP	G	REC

KLOZA, JOHN CLARENCE "NAP"
B.NOV.2,1904 MILWAUKEE,WIS.
D.JUNE 11,1962

YR	CL	LEA	POS	GP	G	REC
1931	STL	A	O		3	.143
1932	STL	A	O		19	.154
	BRTR				22	.150

KLUGMANN, JOE
B.MAR.26,1895 ST.LOUIS,MO.
D.JULY 18,1951

1921	CHI	N	2		6	.286
1922	CHI	N	2		2	.250
1924	BRO	N	2-S		31	.165
1925	CLE	A	1-2-3		38	.333
	BRTR				77	.251

KLUMPP, ELMER EDWARD
B.AUG.26,1906 ST.LOUIS,MO.

1934	WAS	A	C		12	.133
1937	BRO	N	C		5	.091
	BRTR				17	.115

KLUSMAN, WILLIAM F.
B.MAR.24,1865 CINCINNATI,OHIO
D.JUNE 24,1907

1888	BOS	N	2		28	.168
1890	STL	AA	1		15	.275
	BRTR				43	.206

KLUSZEWSKI, THEODORE BERNARD
"TED"
B.SEPT.10,1924 ARGO,ILL.

1947	CIN	N	1		9	.100
1948	CIN	N	1		113	.275
1949	CIN	N	1		136	.309
1950	CIN	N	1		134	.307
1951	CIN	N	1		154	.259
1952	CIN	N	1		135	.320
1953	CIN	N	1		149	.316
1954	CIN	N	1		149	.326
1955	CIN	N	1		153	.314
1956	CIN	N	1		138	.302
1957	CIN	N	1		69	.268
1958	PIT	N	1		100	.292
1959	PIT	N	1		60	.262
	CHI	A	1		31	.297
1960	CHI	A	1		81	.293
1961	LA	A	1		107	.243
	BLTL				1718	.298

KLUTTS, GENE ELLIS "MICKEY"
B.SEPT.20,1954 MONTEBELLO,CAL.

1976	NY	A	S		2	.000
	BRTR					

KLUTTZ, CLYDE FRANKLIN
B.DEC.12,1918 SALISBURY,N.C.

1942	BOS	N	C		72	.267
1943	BOS	N	C		66	.246
1944	BOS	N	C		81	.279
1945	BOS	N	C		25	.296
	NY	N	C		73	.279
1946	NY	N	C		5	.375
	STL	N	C		52	.265
1947	PIT	N	C		73	.302
1948	PIT	N	C		94	.221
1951	STL	A	C		4	.500
	WAS	A	C		53	.308
1952	WAS	A	C		58	.229
	BRTR				656	.268

KNABE, FRANZ OTTO "DUTCH"
B.JUNE 2,1884 CARRICK,PA.
D.MAY 17,1961

1905	PIT	N	3		3	.300
1907	PHI	N	2		126	.255
1908	PHI	N	2		151	.218
1909	PHI	N	2		111	.234
1910	PHI	N	2		136	.261
1911	PHI	N	2		142	.237
1912	PHI	N	2		126	.282
1913	PHI	N	2		148	.263
1914	BAL	F	M-2		146	.228
1915	BAL	F	M-2		100	.251
1916	PIT	N	2		28	.193
	CHI	N	2		51	.274
	BRTR				1268	.247

KNAPP, ROBERT CHRISTIAN "CHRIS"
B.SEPT.16,1953 CHERRY POINT,N.C.

1975	CHI	A	P		2	0- 0
1976	CHI	A	P		11	3- 1
	BRTR				13	3- 1

KNAUPP, HENRY ANTONE "COTTON"
B.AUG.13,1889 SAN ANTONIO,TEX.
D.JULY 6,1967 NEW ORLEANS,LA.

1910	CLE	A	S		18	.236
1911	CLE	A	S		13	.102
	BRTR				31	.184

KNAUSS, FRANK H.
B.1868 CLEVELAND,OHIO

1890	COL	AA	P	33	21-11
1891	CLE	N	P	3	0- 3
1892	CIN	N	P	1	0- 1
1894	CLE	N	P	2	1- 1
1895	NY	N	P	1	0- 0
	BLTL			40	22-16

KNEISCH, RUDOLPH FRANK
B.APR.10,1900 BALTIMORE,MD.
D.APR.6,1965 BALTIMORE,MD.

1926	DET	A	P		2	0- 1
	BRTL					

KNELL, PHILIP H.
B.1865 MILL VALLEY,CAL.

1888	PIT	N	P		4	1- 2
1890	PHI	P	P		35	20-11
1891	COL	AA	P	58	66	27-27
1892	WAS	N	P		22	9-10
	PHI	N	P		11	4- 6
1894	PIT	N	P		4	0- 0
	LOU	N	P		30	7-22
1895	LOU	N	P		14	0- 6
	CLE	N	P		14	5- 4
	BRTL			192	200	73-88

KNELME, WILLIAM J.
(PLAYED UNDER NAME OF
WILLIAM J. KUEHNE)

KNEPPER, CHARLES
B.FEB.18,1871 ANDERSON,IND.
D.FEB.6,1946

1899	CLE	N	P		27	4-22
	BRTR					

KNEPPER, ROBERT WESLEY "BOB"
B.MAY 25,1954 AKRON,OHIO

1976	SF	N	P		4	1- 2
	BLTL					

KNERR, WALLACE LUTHER "LOU"
B.AUG.21,1921 LANCASTER,PA.

1945	PHI	A	P	21	28	5-11
1946	PHI	A	P		30	3-16
1947	WAS	A	P		6	0- 0
	BRTR			63	64	8-27

KNETZER, ELMER ELLSWORTH
"BARON"
B.JULY 22,1885 CARRICK,PA.
D.OCT.3,1975 PITTSBURGH,PA.

1909	BRO	N	P		5	1- 3
1910	BRO	N	P		20	7- 5
1911	BRO	N	P		35	11-12
1912	BRO	N	P		33	7- 9
1914	PIT	F	P		37	20-12
1915	PIT	F	P		41	18-14
1916	BOS	N	P		2	0- 2
	CIN	N	P	36	37	5-12
1917	CIN	N	P		11	0- 0
	BRTR			220	221	69-69

KNICKERBOCKER, AUSTIN JAY
B.OCT.15,1918 BAGNALL,N.Y.

1947	PHI	A	O		21	.250
	BRTR					

KNICKERBOCKER, WILLIAM HART
B.DEC.29,1911 LOS ANGELES,CAL.

1933	CLE	A	S		80	.226
1934	CLE	A	S		146	.317
1935	CLE	A	S		132	.298
1936	CLE	A	S		155	.294
1937	STL	A	S		121	.261
1938	NY	A	2		46	.250
1939	NY	A	2-S		6	.154
1940	NY	A	S-3		45	.242
1941	CHI	A	2		89	.245
1942	PHI	A	2-S		87	.253
	BRTR				907	.277

KNIGHT, ALONZO P. "LON"
B.JUNE 16,1853 PHILADELPHIA,PA.
D.APR.23,1932

1875	ATH	NA	P		13	6- 5
1876	ATH	N	P-1-	33	55	10-23
			O			.248
1880	WOR	N	O		48	.242
1881	DET	N	1-2-O		83	.270
1882	DET	N	1-O		83	.204
1883	ATH	AA	M-2-3-O		97	.237
1884	ATH	AA	P-O	1	110	0- 1
						.275
1885	ATH	AA	M-O		28	.186
	PRO	N	P-O	1	25	0- 0
						.160
	BRTR			48	542	16-29
						.246

KNIGHT, CHARLES RAY
"RAY"
B.DEC.28,1952 ALBANY,GA.

1974	CIN	N	3		14	.182
	BRTR					

KNIGHT, ELMA RUSSEL "JACK"
B.JAN.12,1895 PITTSBORO,MISS.

1922	STL	N	P		1	0- 0
1925	PHI	N	P	33	40	7- 6
1926	PHI	N	P	35	40	3-12
1927	BOS	N	P		3	0- 0
	BLTR			84	10-18	

KNIGHT, GEORGE HENRY
B.NOV.24,1855 LAKEVILLE,CONN.
D.OCT.4,1912

1875	NH	NA	P		1	1- 0

KNIGHT, JOHN WESLEY "SCHOOLBOY"
B.OCT.6,1886 PHILADELPHIA,PA.
D.DEC.19,1965 WALNUT CREEK,CAL.

1905	PHI	A	S		88	.234
1906	PHI	A	3		74	.194
1907	PHI	A	3		40	.212
	BOS	A	3		98	.215
1909	NY	A	1-2-S		116	.236
1910	NY	A	1-S		117	.312
1911	NY	A	1-2-S		132	.268
1912	WAS	A	2		32	.161
1913	NY	A	1-2		70	.236
	BRTR				767	.239

KNIGHT, JOSEPH WILLIAM
"QUIET JOE"
B.SEPT.28,1859 PORT STANLEY,
ONT.,CANADA
D.OCT.18,1938

1884	PHI	N	P		6	2- 4
1890	CIN	N	O		127	.312
	BLTL	6	133	2- 4	
						.307

KNISELY, PETER C.
B.AUG.11,1887 WAYNESBORO,PA.
D.JULY 1,1948

1912	CIN	N	O		21	.328
1913	CHI	N	O		2	.000
1914	CHI	N	O		37	.130
1915	CHI	N	O		64	.246
	BRTR				124	.235

KNODE, KENNETH THOMSON "MIKE"
B.NOV.8,1895 WESTMINSTER,MD.

1920	STL	N	O		42	.231
	BRTR					

KNODE, ROBERT TROXELL "RAY"
B.JAN.28,1901 WESTMINSTER,MD.

1923	CLE	A	1		22	.289
1924	CLE	A	1		11	.243
1925	CLE	A	1		45	.250
1926	CLE	A	1		31	.333
	BLTL				109	.266

KNOLL, CHARLES ELMER "PUNCH"
B.OCT.7,1881 EVANSVILLE,IND.
D.FEB.7,1960

1905	WAS	A	O		79	.213
	BRTR					

KNOLLS, OSCAR EDWARD "HUB"
B.DEC.18,1883 MEDARYVILLE,IND.
D.JULY 1,1946

1906	BRO	N	P		2	0- 0
	TR					

YR	CL	LEA	POS	GP	G	REC

KNOOP, ROBERT FRANK "BOBBY"
B.OCT.18,1938 SIOUX CITY,IOWA
1964	LA	A	2		162	.216
1965	CAL	A	2		142	.269
1966	CAL	A	2		161	.232
1967	CAL	A	2		159	.245
1968	CAL	A	2		152	.249
1969	CAL	A	2		27	.197
	CHI	A	2		104	.229
1970	CHI	A	2		130	.229
1971	KC	A	2-3		72	.205
1972	KC	A	2-3		44	.237
		BRTR			1153	.236

KNOTHE, GEORGE BERTRAM
B.JAN.12,1900 BAYONNE,N.J.
| 1932 | PHI | N | 2 | | 6 | .083 |
| | | BRTR | | | | |

KNOTHE, WILFRED EDGAR "FRITZ"
B.MAY 1,1904 PASSAIC,N.J.
D.MAR.27,1963 PASSAIC,N.J.
1932	BOS	N	3		89	.238
1933	BOS	N	S-3		44	.228
	PHI	N	2-3		41	.150
		BRTR			174	.220

KNOTT, JOHN HENRY
B.MAR.2,1907 DALLAS,TEX.
1933	STL	A	P		20	1- 8
1934	STL	A	P		45	10- 3
1935	STL	A	P		48	11- 8
1936	STL	A	P		47	9-17
1937	STL	A	P		38	8-18
1938	STL	A	P		7	1- 2
	CHI	A	P		20	5-10
1939	PHI	A	P		25	11- 6
1940	PHI	A	P		25	11- 9
1941	PHI	A	P		27	13-11
1942	PHI	A	P		20	2-10
1946	PHI	A	P		3	0- 1
		BRTR			325	82-103

KNOTTS, JOSEPH
B.BIDDEFORD,ME.
| 1907 | BOS | N | C | | 3 | .000 |
| | | TR | | | | |

KNOUFF, EDWARD
B.1867 PHILADELPHIA,PA.
D.SEPT.14,1900
1885	ATH	AA	P-O		14	7- 6
						.204
1886	BAL	AA	P		1	0- 1
1887	BAL	AA	P		8	0- 6
	STL	AA	P-O	7	16	4- 3
1888	STL	AA	P		9	5- 4
	CLE	AA	P-2		10	6- 4
						.143
1889	ATH	AA	P		3	2- 0
		BRTR		52	61	24-24
						.194

KNOWDELL, JACOB AUGUSTUS
B.BROOKLYN,N.Y.
1874	ATL	NA	C-O		23	-
1875	ATL	NA	C-S-O		42	-
1878	MIL	N	C-O		4	.000
					69	-

KNOWLES, DAROLD DUANE
B.DEC.9,1941 BRUNSWICK,MO.
1965	BAL	A	P		5	0- 1
1966	PHI	N	P		69	6- 5
1967	WAS	A	P		61	6- 8
1968	WAS	A	P		32	1- 1
1969	WAS	A	P		53	9- 2
1971	WAS	A	P		12	2- 2
	OAK	A	P		43	5- 2
1972	OAK	A	P		54	5- 1
1973	OAK	A	P	52	53	6- 8
1974	OAK	A	P		45	3- 3
1975	CHI	N	P		58	6- 9
1976	CHI	N	P		58	5- 7
		BLTL		613	614	56-63

KNOWLES, JAMES "DARBY"
B.1859 TORONTO,ONT.,CANADA
D.MAR.1904
1884	PIT	AA	1		46	.228
	BRO	AA	1-3		41	.237
1886	WAS	N	2-3		115	.212
1887	MET	AA	3		16	.262
1890	ROC	AA	3		124	.281
1892	NY	N	3		15	.169
					357	.240

KNOWLSON, THOMAS H.
B.1895 RIDGWAY,PA.
| 1915 | PHI | A | P | | 18 | 4- 7 |
| | | BBTR | | | | |

KNOWLTON, WILLIAM YOUNG
B.AUG.18,1892 PHILADELPHIA,PA.
D.FEB.25,1944
| 1920 | PHI | A | P | | 1 | 0- 1 |
| | | BRTR | | | | |

KNOX, ANDREW JACKSON "DASHER"
B.JAN.6,1864 PHILADELPHIA,PA.
D.SEPT.14,1940
| 1890 | ATH | AA | 1 | | 21 | .250 |
| | | BRTR | | | | |

KNOX, CLIFFORD H. "BUD"
B.JAN.7,1902 FT.DODGE,IOWA
D.SEPT.24,1965 OSKALOOSA,IOWA
| 1924 | PIT | N | C | | 6 | .222 |
| | | BBTR | | | | |

KNOX, JOHN CLINTON
B.JULY 26,1948 NEWARK,N.J.
1972	DET	A	2		14	.077
1973	DET	A	?		12	.281
1974	DET	A	2-3		55	.307
1975	DET	A	2-3		43	.267
		BLTR			124	.274

KOBACK, NICHOLAS NICHOLIA "NICK"
B.JULY 19,1935 HARTFORD,CONN.
1953	PIT	N	C		7	.125
1954	PIT	N	C		4	.000
1955	PIT	N	C		5	.286
		BRTR			16	.121

KOBEL, KEVIN RICHARD
B.OCT.2,1953 BUFFALO,N.Y.
1973	MIL	A	P		2	0- 1
1974	MIL	A	P		34	6-14
1976	MIL	A	P		3	0- 1
		BRTL			39	6-16

KOCH, ALAN GOODMAN
B.MAR.25,1938 DECATUR,ALA.
1963	DET	A	P	7	8	1- 1
1964	DET	A	P		3	0- 0
	WAS	A	P		32	3-10
		BRTR		42	43	4-11

KOCH, BARNEY
B.MAR.23,1923 CAMPBELL,NEB.
| 1944 | BRO | N | 2-S | | 33 | .219 |
| | | BRTR | | | | |

KOCHER, BRADLEY WILSON
B.JAN.16,1888 WHITE HAVEN,PA.
D.JAN.13,1965 WHITE HAVEN,PA.
1912	DET	A	C		24	.206
1915	NY	N	C		4	.455
1916	NY	N	C		34	.108
		BRTR			62	.179

KOECHER, RICHARD FINLAY "HIGHPOCKETS"
B.MAR.30,1926 PHILADELPHIA,PA.
1946	PHI	N	P		1	0- 1
1947	PHI	N	P		3	0- 2
1948	PHI	N	P		3	0- 1
		BLTL			7	0- 4

KOEGEL, PETER JOHN "PETE"
B.JULY 31,1947 MINEOLA,N.Y.
1970	MIL	A	O		7	.250
1971	MIL	A	1		2	.000
	PHI	N	C-O		12	.231
1972	PHI	N	C-1-3-O		41	.143
		BRTR			62	.174

KOEHLER, BENARD JAMES "BEN"
B.JAN.26,1877 SCHOERNDORN, GERMANY
D.MAY 21,1961
1905	STL	A	O		142	.237
1906	STL	A	O		66	.220
		BRTR			208	.233

KOEHLER, HORACE LEVERING "PIP"
B.JAN.16,1902 GILBERT,PA.
| 1925 | NY | N | O | | 12 | .000 |
| | | BRTR | | | | |

KOENECKE, LEONARD GEORGE
B.JAN.18,1906 BARABOO,WIS.
D.SEPT.17,1935
1932	NY	N	O		42	.255
1934	BRO	N	O		123	.320
1935	BRO	N	O		100	.283
		BLTR			265	.297

KOENIG, CHARLES FREDERICK
(PLAYED UNDER NAME OF
CHARLES FREDERICK KING)

KOENIG, MARK ANTHONY
B.JUL.19,1902 SAN FRANCISCO,CAL
1925	NY	A	S		28	.205
1926	NY	A	S		147	.271
1927	NY	A	S		123	.285
1928	NY	A	S		132	.319
1929	NY	A	S-3		116	.292
1930	NY	A	S		21	.243
	DET	A	P-S	2	76	0- 1
						.236
1931	DET	A	P-2-	3	106	0- 0
						.253
1932	CHI	N	S		33	.353
1933	CHI	N	2-S-3		80	.284
1934	CIN	N	1-2-S-3		151	.272
1935	NY	N	2-S-3		107	.283
1936	NY	N	S		42	.276
		BBTR		5	1162	0- 1
						.279

KUENIGSMARK, WILLIS T.
B.1896
D.JULY 1,1972 WATERLOO,ILL.
| 1919 | STL | N | P | | 1 | 0- 0 |
| | | BRTR | | | | |

KOESTNER, ELMER JOSEPH "BOB"
B.NOV.30,1885 PIPER CITY,ILL.
D.OCT.27,1959
1910	CLE	A	P		27	5-10
1914	CHI	N	P		4	0- 0
	CIN	N	P		5	0- 0
		BRTR			36	5-10

KOHLER, HENRY
B.BALTIMORE,MD.
1871	KEK	NA	1-3		3	.167
1873	MAR	NA	3		6	-
1874	BAL	NA	C-1		5	-
					14	-

KOHLMAN, JOSEPH JAMES "BLACKIE"
B.JAN.28,1913 PHILADELPHIA,PA.
1937	WAS	A	P		2	1- 0
1938	WAS	A	P		7	0- 0
		BRTR			9	1- 0

KOKOS, RICHARD JEROME "DICK"
(REAL NAME
RICHARD JEROME KOKOSZKA)
B.FEB.28,1928 CHICAGO,ILL.
1948	STL	A	O		71	.298
1949	STL	A	O		143	.261
1950	STL	A	O		143	.261
1953	STL	A	O		107	.241
1954	BAL	A	O		11	.200
		BLTL			475	.263

KOKOSZKA, RICHARD JEROME
(PLAYED UNDER NAME OF
RICHARD JEROME KOKOS)

KOLB, EDWARD WILLIAM
B.JULY 20,1880 CINCINNATI,OHIO
| 1899 | CLE | N | P | | 1 | 0- 1 |
| | | BRTR | | | | |

KOLB, GARY ALAN
B.MAR.13,1940 ROCK FALLS,ILL.

YR	CL	LEA	POS	GP	G	REC
1960	STL	N	O		9	.000
1962	STL	N	O		6	.357
1963	STL	N	C-3-O		75	.271
1964	MIL	N	C-2-3-O		36	.188
1965	MIL	N	O		24	.259
	NY	N	1-3-O		40	.167
1968	PIT	N	C-2-3-O		74	.218
1969	PIT	N	C		29	.081
	BLTR				293	.209

KOLLONIGE, JOSEPH EDWARD
(PLAYED UNDER NAME OF
JOSEPH EDWARD COLLINS)

KOLLOWAY, DONALD MARTIN "DON"
B.AUG.4,1918 POSEN,ILL.

YR	CL	LEA	POS	GP	G	REC
1940	CHI	A	2		10	.225
1941	CHI	A	1-2		71	.271
1942	CHI	A	1-2		147	.273
1943	CHI	A	2		85	.216
1946	CHI	A	2-3		123	.280
1947	CHI	A	1-2-3		124	.278
1948	CHI	A	2-3		119	.273
1949	CHI	A	3		4	.000
	DET	A	1-2-3		126	.294
1950	DET	A	1-2		125	.289
1951	DET	A	1		78	.255
1952	DET	A	1-2		65	.243
1953	PHI	A	3		2	.000
	BRTR				1079	.271

KOLP, RAYMOND CARL "JOCKEY"
B.OCT.1,1899 NEW BERLIN,OHIO
D.JULY 29,1967 OHIO

YR	CL	LEA	POS	GP	G	REC
1921	STL	A	P	37	39	8- 7
1922	STL	A	P		32	14- 4
1923	STL	A	P		34	5-12
1924	STL	A	P		25	5- 7
1927	CIN	N	P		24	3- 3
1928	CIN	N	P		44	13-10
1929	CIN	N	P		30	8-10
1930	CIN	N	P		37	7-12
1931	CIN	N	P		30	4- 9
1932	CIN	N	P		32	6-10
1933	CIN	N	P		30	6- 9
1934	CIN	N	P		28	0- 2
	BRTR			383	385	79-95

KOLSETH, KARL DICKEY "KOLEY"
B.DEC.25,1892 CAMBRIDGE,MASS.
D.MAY 3,1956 CUMBERLAND,MD.

YR	CL	LEA	POS	GP	G	REC
1915	BAL	F	1		6	.217
	BLTR					

KOLSTAD, HAROLD EVERETTE "HAL"
B.JUNE 1,1935 RICE LAKE,WIS.

YR	CL	LEA	POS	GP	G	REC
1962	BOS	A	P		27	0- 2
1963	BOS	A	P		7	0- 2
	BRTR				34	0- 4

KOMMERS, FREDERICK RAYMOND
B.MAR.31,1886 CHICAGO,ILL.
D.JUNE 14,1943

YR	CL	LEA	POS	GP	G	REC
1913	PIT	N	O		40	.232
1914	STL	F	O		75	.308
	BAL	F	O		17	.220
	BLTR				132	.271

KONETCHY, EDWARD JOSEPH
"BIG ED"
B.SEPT.3,1885 LACROSSE,WIS.
D.MAY 27,1947

YR	CL	LEA	POS	GP	G	REC
1907	STL	N	1		91	.251
1908	STL	N	1		154	.248
1909	STL	N	1		152	.286
1910	STL	N	P-1	1	144	0- 0
						.302
1911	STL	N	1		158	.289
1912	STL	N	1		143	.314
1913	STL	N	P-1	1	140	1- 0
						.276
1914	PIT	N	1		154	.249
1915	PIT	F	1		152	.310
1916	BOS	N	1		158	.260
1917	BOS	N	1		130	.260
1918	BOS	N	P-1-	1	119	0- 1
			O			.236
1919	BRO	N	1		132	.298
1920	BRO	N	1		131	.308
1921	BRO	N	1		55	.269
	PHI	N	1		72	.321
	BRTR			3	2085	1- 1
						.281

KONIECZNY, DOUGLAS JAMES "DOUG"
B.SEP.27,1951 DETROIT,MICH.

YR	CL	LEA	POS	GP	G	REC
1973	HOU	N	P		2	0- 1
1974	HOU	N	P		6	0- 3
1975	HOU	N	P		32	6-13
	BRTR				40	6-17

KONIKOWSKI, ALEXANDER JAMES
"ALEX" OR "WHITEY"
B.JUNE 8,1928 THROOP,PA.

YR	CL	LEA	POS	GP	G	REC
1948	NY	N	P		22	2- 3
1951	NY	N	P		3	0- 0
1954	NY	N	P		10	0- 0
	BRTR				35	2- 3

KONNICK, MICHAEL ALOYSIUS
B.JAN.13,1889 GLEN LYON,PA.
D.JULY 9,1971 WILKES-BARRE,PA.

YR	CL	LEA	POS	GP	G	REC
1909	CIN	N	C		2	.400
1910	CIN	N	S		1	.000
	BRTR				3	.250

KONOPKA, BRUCE BRUNO
B.SEPT.16,1919 HAMMOND,IND.

YR	CL	LEA	POS	GP	G	REC
1942	PHI	A	1		5	.300
1943	PHI	A	H		2	.000
1946	PHI	A	1-O		38	.237
	BLTL				45	.238

KONSTANTY, CASIMER JAMES "JIM"
B.MAR.2,1917 STRYKERSVILLE,N.Y.
D.JUNE 11,1976 ONEONTA,N.Y.

YR	CL	LEA	POS	GP	G	REC
1944	CIN	N	P		20	6- 4
1946	BOS	N	P		10	0- 1
1948	PHI	N	P		6	1- 0
1949	PHI	N	P		53	9- 5
1950	PHI	N	P		74	16- 7
1951	PHI	N	P		58	4-11
1952	PHI	N	P		42	5- 3
1953	PHI	N	P		48	14-10
1954	PHI	N	P		33	2- 3
	NY	A	P		9	1- 1
1955	NY	A	P		45	7- 2
1956	NY	A	P		8	0- 0
	STL	N	P		27	1- 1
	BRTR				433	66-48

KOOB, ERNEST GERALD
B.SEPT.11,1893 KEELER,MICH.
D.NOV.12,1941 LEMAY,MO.

YR	CL	LEA	POS	GP	G	REC
1915	STL	A	P		28	5- 6
1916	STL	A	P		33	11- 8
1917	STL	A	P		39	6-14
1919	STL	A	P		24	2- 4
	BLTL				124	24-32

KOONCE, CALVIN LEE "CAL"
B.NOV.18,1940 FAYETTEVILLE,N.C.

YR	CL	LEA	POS	GP	G	REC
1962	CHI	N	P		35	10-10
1963	CHI	N	P		21	2- 6
1964	CHI	N	P		6	3- 0
1965	CHI	N	P		38	7- 9
1966	CHI	N	P		45	5- 5
1967	CHI	N	P		34	2- 2
	NY	N	P	11	13	3- 3
1968	NY	N	P		55	6- 4
1969	NY	N	P		40	6- 3
1970	NY	N	P		13	0- 2
	BOS	A	P		23	3- 4
1971	BOS	A	P		13	0- 1
	BRTR			334	336	47-49

KOONS, HARRY M.
B.1863 PHILADELPHIA,PA.

YR	CL	LEA	POS	GP	G	REC
1884	ALT	U	C-3		21	.213
	CHI	U	3		1	.000
					22	.205

KOOSMAN, JEROME MARTIN "JERRY"
B.DEC.23,1942 APPLETON,MINN.

YR	CL	LEA	POS	GP	G	REC
1967	NY	N	P		9	0- 2
1968	NY	N	P		35	19-12
1969	NY	N	P		32	17- 9
1970	NY	N	P		30	12- 7
1971	NY	N	P		26	6-11
1972	NY	N	P		34	11-12
1973	NY	N	P		35	14-15
1974	NY	N	P		35	15-11
1975	NY	N	P		36	14-13
1976	NY	N	P		34	21-10
	BRTL				306	129-101

KOPACZ, GEORGE FELIX
B.FEB.26,1941 CHICAGO,ILL.

YR	CL	LEA	POS	GP	G	REC
1966	ATL	N	1		6	.000
1970	PIT	N	1		10	.188
	BLTL				16	.120

KOPCHIA, JOSEPH
(PLAYED UNDER NAME OF
JOSEPH KOPPE)

KOPF, WALTER HENRY
B.JULY 10,1899 NEW BRITAIN,CONN

YR	CL	LEA	POS	GP	G	REC
1921	NY	N	3		2	.333
	BBTR					

KOPF, WILLIAM LORENZ "LARRY"
(PLAYED UNDER NAME OF
FRED BRADY IN 1913)
B.NOV.3,1890 BRISTOL,CONN.

YR	CL	LEA	POS	GP	G	REC
1913	CLE	A	2-3		6	.300
1914	PHI	A	2		35	.189
1915	PHI	A	S-3		118	.225
1916	CIN	N	S		11	.275
1917	CIN	N	S		148	.255
1919	CIN	N	S		135	.270
1920	CIN	N	2-S-3-O		126	.245
1921	CIN	N	S		107	.218
1922	BOS	N	2-S		126	.266
1923	BOS	N	2-S		39	.275
	BBTR				851	.249

KOPLITZ, HOWARD DEAN "HOWIE"
B.MAY 4,1938 OSHKOSH,WIS.

YR	CL	LEA	POS	GP	G	REC
1961	DET	A	P		4	2- 0
1962	DET	A	P	10	12	3- 0
1964	WAS	A	P		6	0- 0
1965	WAS	A	P		33	4- 7
1966	WAS	A	P		1	0- 0
	BRTR			54	56	9- 7

KOPP, MERLIN H.
B.JAN.2,1892 TOLEDO,OHIO
D.MAY 7,1960

YR	CL	LEA	POS	GP	G	REC
1915	PHI	A	O		16	.250
1918	PHI	A	O		96	.234
1919	PHI	A	O		75	.226
	BBTR				187	.230

KOPPE, GEORGE JOSEPH
(PLAYED UNDER NAME OF
GEORGE JOSEPH CUPPY)

KOPPE, JOSEPH "JOE"
(REAL NAME JOSEPH KOPCHIA)
B.OCT.19,1930 DETROIT,MICH.

YR	CL	LEA	POS	GP	G	REC
1958	MIL	N	S		16	.444
1959	PHI	N	2-S		126	.261
1960	PHI	N	S-3		58	.171
1961	PHI	N	S		6	.000
	LA	A	2-S-3		91	.251
1962	LA	A	2-S-3		128	.227
1963	LA	A	2-S-3-O		76	.210
1964	LA	A	2-S-3		54	.257
1965	CAL	A	2-S-3		23	.212
	BRTR				578	.236

KOPSHAW, GEORGE CHARLES
B.APR.21,1900 PASSAIC,N.J.
D.DEC.26,1934

YR	CL	LEA	POS	GP	G	REC
1923	STL	N	C		2	.200
	BRTR					

KORCHECK, STEPHEN JOSEPH
"STEVE"
B.AUG.11,1932 MC CLELLANDTOWN,
PA.

YR	CL	LEA	POS	GP	G	REC
1954	WAS	A	C		2	.143
1955	WAS	A	C		13	.278
1958	WAS	A	C		21	.078
1959	WAS	A	C		22	.157
	BRTR				58	.159

KORES, ARTHUR EMIL
B.JULY 22,1887 MILWAUKEE,WIS.
D.MAR.26,1974

YR	CL	LEA	POS	GP	G	REC
1915	STL	F	3		60	.229
	BRTR					

KORINCE, GEORGE EUGENE
B.JAN.10,1946 OTTAWA,ONT.,CANADA

YR	CL	LEA	POS	GP	G	REC
1966	DET	A	P		2	0- 0
1967	DET	A	P		9	1- 0
	BRTR				11	1- 0

KORWAN, JAMES "LONG JIM"
B.MAR.4,1874 BROOKLYN,N.Y.
D.AUG.1899

YR	CL	LEA	POS	GP	G	REC
1894	BRO	N	P		1	0- 0
1897	CHI	N	P		5	1- 2
					6	1- 2

YR	CL	LEA	POS	GP	G	REC

KOSCO, ANDREW JOHN "ANDY"
B.OCT.5,1941 YOUNGSTOWN,OHIO
1965	MIN	A	1-0		23	.236
1966	MIN	A	1-0		57	.222
1967	MIN	A	0		9	.143
1968	NY	A	1-0		131	.240
1969	LA	N	1-0		120	.248
1970	LA	N	1-0		74	.228
1971	MIL	A	1-3-0		98	.227
1972	CAL	A	0		49	.239
	BOS	A	0		17	.213
1973	CIN	N	1-0		47	.280
1974	CIN	N	3-0		33	.189
		BRTR		658		.236

KOSHOREK, CLEMENT JOHN "CLEM"
B.JUNE 20,1926 ROYAL OAK,MICH.
1952	PIT	N	2-S-3		98	.261
1953	PIT	N	H		1	.000
		BRTR		99		.260

KOSKI, WILLIAM JOHN
B.FEB.6,1932 MADERA,CAL.
| 1951 | PIT | N | P | | 13 | 0- 1 |
| | | BRTR | | | | |

KOSLO, GEORGE BERNARD "DAVE"
(REAL NAME
GEORGE BERNARD KOSLOWSKI)
B.MAR.31,1920 MENASHA,WIS.
D.DEC.1,1975 MENASHA,WIS.
1941	NY	N	P		4	1- 2
1942	NY	N	P		19	3- 6
1946	NY	N	P	40	41	14-19
1947	NY	N	P		39	15-10
1948	NY	N	P		35	8-10
1949	NY	N	P	38	39	11-14
1950	NY	N	P		40	13-15
1951	NY	N	P		39	10- 9
1952	NY	N	P		41	10- 7
1953	NY	N	P		37	6-12
1954	BAL	A	P		3	0- 1
	MIL	N	P		12	1- 1
1955	MIL	N	P		1	0- 1
		BLTL	348	350		92-107

KOSLOWSKI, GEORGE BERNARD
(PLAYED UNDER NAME OF
GEORGE BERNARD KOSLO)

KOSMAN, MICHAEL THOMAS
B.DEC.10,1917 DETROIT,MICH.
| 1944 | CIN | N | H | | 1 | .000 |
| | | BRTR | | | | |

KOSTAL, JOSEPH
| 1896 | LOU | N | C | | 2 | .000 |

KOSTER, FREDERICK CHARLES "FRITZ"
B.DEC.21,1906 LOUISVILLE,KY.
| 1931 | PHI | N | 0 | | 76 | .225 |
| | | BLTL | | | | |

KOSTRO, FRANK JERRY
B.AUG.4,1937 WINDBER,PA.
1962	DET	A	3		16	.268
1963	DET	A	1-3-0		31	.231
	LA	A	1-3-0		43	.222
1964	MIN	A	1-2-3-0		59	.272
1965	MIN	A	2-3-0		20	.161
1967	MIN	A	3-0		32	.323
1968	MIN	A	1-0		63	.241
1969	MIN	A	H		2	.000
		BRTR		266		.244

KOUFAX, SANFORD "SANDY"
B.DEC.30,1935 BROOKLYN,N.Y.
1955	BRO	N	P		12	2- 2
1956	BRO	N	P		16	2- 4
1957	BRO	N	P		34	5- 4
1958	LA	N	P		40	11-11
1959	LA	N	P		35	8- 6
1960	LA	N	P		37	8-13
1961	LA	N	P		42	18-13
1962	LA	N	P		28	14- 7
1963	LA	N	P		40	25- 5
1964	LA	N	P		29	19- 5
1965	LA	N	P		43	26- 8
1966	LA	N	P		41	27- 9
		BRTL		397		165-87

KOUKALIK, JOSEPH
B.MAR.3,1880 CHICAGO,ILL. ,
D.DEC.27,1945
| 1904 | BRO | N | P | | 1 | 0- 1 |

KOUPAL, LOUIS LADDIE
B.DEC.19,1898 TABOR,S.D.
D.DEC.8,1961
1925	PIT	N	P	6	7	0- 0
1926	PIT	N	P		6	0- 2
1928	BRO	N	P		17	1- 0
1929	BRO	N	P		18	0- 1
	PHI	N	P		15	5- 5
1930	PHI	N	P		13	0- 4
1937	STL	A	P		26	4- 9
		BRTR	101	102		10-21

KOWALEWSKI, HARRY FRANK
(PLAYED UNDER NAME OF
HARRY FRANK COVELESKI)

KOWALEWSKI, STANISLAUS
(PLAYED UNDER NAME OF
STANLEY ANTHONY COVELESKI)

KOWALIK, FABIAN LORENZ
B.APR.22,1909 FALLS CITY,TEX.
D.AUG.14,1954
1932	CHI	N	P	2	6	0- 1
1935	CHI	N	P		20	2- 2
1936	CHI	N	P		6	0- 2
	PHI	N	P	22	42	1- 5
	BOS	N	P	1	2	0- 1
		BBTR	51	76		3-11
		BR 1936				

KOY, ERNEST ANYZ "CHIEF"
B.SEPT.17,1912 SEALY,TEX.
1938	BRO	N	0		142	.299
1939	BRO	N	0		125	.278
1940	BRO	N	0		24	.229
	STL	N	0		93	.310
1941	STL	N	0		13	.200
	CIN	N	0		67	.250
1942	CIN	N	H		3	.000
	PHI	N	0		91	.244
		BRTR		558		.279

KOZAR, ALBERT KENNETH "AL"
B.JULY 5,1922 MCKEE'S ROCKS,PA.
1948	WAS	A	2		150	.250
1949	WAS	A	2		105	.269
1950	WAS	A	2		20	.200
	CHI	A	2-3		10	.300
		BRTR		285		.254

KRACHER, JOSEPH PETER "JUG"
B.NOV.4,1915 PHILADELPHIA,PA.
| 1939 | PHI | N | C | | 5 | .200 |
| | | BRTR | | | | |

KRAFT, CLARENCE OTTO "BIG BOY"
B.JUNE 9,1887 EVANSVILLE,IND.
D.MAR.26,1958
| 1914 | BOS | N | 1-3 | | 3 | .333 |
| | | BRTR | | | | |

KRAKAUSKAS, JOSEPH VICTOR LAWRENCE
B.MAR.28,1916 MONTREAL,QUE.,CAN
D.JULY 8,1960
1937	WAS	A	P		5	4- 1
1938	WAS	A	P		29	7- 5
1939	WAS	A	P		39	11-17
1940	WAS	A	P		32	1- 6
1941	CLE	A	P		12	1- 2
1942	CLE	A	P		3	0- 0
1946	CLE	A	P		29	2- 5
		BLTL		149		26-36

KRALICK, JOHN FRANCIS "JACK"
B.JUNE 1,1935 YOUNGSTOWN,OHIO
1959	WAS	A	P		6	0- 0
1960	WAS	A	P		35	8- 6
1961	MIN	A	P		33	13-11
1962	MIN	A	P		39	12-11
1963	MIN	A	P	5	6	1- 4
	CLE	A	P		28	13- 9
1964	CLE	A	P		30	12- 7
1965	CLE	A	P		30	5-11
1966	CLE	A	P		27	3- 4
1967	CLE	A	P		2	0- 2
		BLTL	235	236		67-65

KRALY, STEVE CHARLES
B.APR.18,1930 WHITING,IND.
| 1953 | NY | A | P | | 5 | 0- 2 |
| | | BLTL | | | | |

KRAMER, JOHN HENRY "JACK"
B.JAN.5,1918 NEW ORLEANS,LA.
1939	STL	A	P		40	9-16
1940	STL	A	P		16	3- 7
1941	STL	A	P		29	4- 3
1943	STL	A	P		3	0- 0
1944	STL	A	P		33	17-13
1945	STL	A	P		29	10-15
1946	STL	A	P		31	13-11
1947	STL	A	P		33	11-16
1948	BOS	A	P		29	18- 5
1949	BOS	A	P		21	6- 8
1950	NY	N	P		35	3- 6
1951	NY	N	P		4	0- 0
	NY	A	P		19	1- 3
		BRTR		322		95-103

KRANEPOOL, EDWARD EMIL "ED"
B.NOV.8,1944 NEW YORK,N.Y.
1962	NY	N	1		3	.167
1963	NY	N	1-0		86	.209
1964	NY	N	1-0		119	.257
1965	NY	N	1		153	.253
1966	NY	N	1-0		146	.254
1967	NY	N	1		141	.269
1968	NY	N	1-0		127	.231
1969	NY	N	1-0		112	.238
1970	NY	N	1		43	.170
1971	NY	N	1-0		122	.280
1972	NY	N	1-0		122	.269
1973	NY	N	1-0		100	.239
1974	NY	N	1-0		94	.300
1975	NY	N	1-0		106	.323
1976	NY	N	1-0		123	.292
		BLTL		1597		.261

KRAPP, EUGENE H. "RUBBER"
B.MAY 12,1887 ROCHESTER,N.Y.
D.APR.13,1923
1911	CLE	A	P	35	36	12- 8
1912	CLE	A	P		9	2- 5
1914	BUF	F	P		37	16-14
1915	BUF	F	P		38	9-19
		BRTR		120		39-46

KRAUS, JOHN WILLIAM "JACK"
B.APR.26,1918 SAN ANTONIO,TEX.
D.JAN.2,1976 SAN ANTONIO,TEX.
1943	PHI	N	P	34	35	9-15
1945	PHI	N	P		19	4- 9
1946	NY	N	P		17	2- 1
		BRTL	70	71		15-25

KRAUSE, HARRY WILLIAM "HAL"
B.JULY 12,1887 SAN FRANCISCO, CAL.
D.OCT.23,1940
1908	PHI	A	P		4	1- 1
1909	PHI	A	P		32	18- 8
1910	PHI	A	P		16	6- 6
1911	PHI	A	P		28	11- 7
1912	PHI	A	P		3	0- 1
	CLE	A	P		3	0- 1
		BBTL		86		36-24

KRAUSSE, LEWIS BERNARD, JR. "LEW"
B.APR.25,1943 MEDIA,PA.
1961	KC	A	P	12	13	2- 5
1964	KC	A	P		5	0- 2
1965	KC	A	P		7	10	2- 4
1966	KC	A	P		36	40	14- 9
1967	KC	A	P		48	49	7-17
1968	OAK	A	P		36	10-11
1969	OAK	A	P		43	7- 7
1970	MIL	A	P	37	38	13-18
1971	MIL	A	P		43	8-12
1972	BOS	A	P		24	1- 3
1973	STL	N	P		1	0- 0
1974	ATL	N	P		29	4- 3
		BRTR	321	334		68-91

KRAUSSE, LEWIS BERNARD, SR.
B.JUNE 8,1912 MEDIA,PA.
1931	PHI	A	P		3	1- 0
1932	PHI	A	P		20	4- 1
		BRTR		23		5- 1

KRAVEC, KENNETH PETER "KEN"
B.JULY 29,1951 CLEVELAND,OHIO
1975	CHI	A	P		2	0- 1
1976	CHI	A	P		9	1- 5
		BBTL		11		1- 6

YR	CL	LEA	POS	GP	G	REC

KRAVITZ, DANIEL "DANNY"
B.DEC.21,1930 LOPEZ,PA.

YR	CL	LEA	POS	GP	G	REC
1956	PIT	N	C-3		32	.265
1957	PIT	N	C		19	.146
1958	PIT	N	C		45	.240
1959	PIT	N	C		52	.253
1960	PIT	N	C		8	.000
	KC	A	C		59	.234
	BLTR				215	.236

KREEVICH, MICHAEL ANDREAS "MIKE"
B.JUNE 10,1910 MT.OLIVE,ILL.

YR	CL	LEA	POS	GP	G	REC
1931	CHI	N	O		5	.167
1935	CHI	A	3		6	.435
1936	CHI	A	O		137	.307
1937	CHI	A	O		144	.302
1938	CHI	A	O		129	.297
1939	CHI	A	O		145	.323
1940	CHI	A	O		144	.265
1941	CHI	A	O		121	.232
1942	PHI	A	O		116	.255
1943	STL	A	O		60	.255
1944	STL	A	O		105	.301
1945	STL	A	O		84	.237
	WAS	A	O		45	.272
	BRTR				1241	.283

KREHMEYER, CHARLES L.
B.JULY 5,1863 ST.LOUIS,MO.
D.FEB.10,1926

YR	CL	LEA	POS	GP	G	REC
1884	STL	AA	C-O		20	.257
1885	LOU	AA	C-1-O		7	.212
	STL	N	C-O		1	.000
					28	.250

KREITNER, ALBERT JOSEPH "MICKEY"
B.OCT.10,1922 NASHVILLE,TENN.

YR	CL	LEA	POS	GP	G	REC
1943	CHI	N	C		3	.375
1944	CHI	N	C		39	.152
	BRTR				42	.172

KREITZ, RALPH WESLEY "RED"
B.NOV.13,1886 PLUM CREEK,NEB.
D.JULY 20,1941

YR	CL	LEA	POS	GP	G	REC
1911	CHI	A	C		7	.176
	BRTR					

KREMER, REMY "RAY"
B.MAR.23,1893 OAKLAND,CAL.
D.FEB.8,1965 PINOLE,CAL.

YR	CL	LEA	POS	GP	G	REC
1924	PIT	N	P	41	42	18-10
1925	PIT	N	P		40	17- 8
1926	PIT	N	P		37	20- 6
1927	PIT	N	P		35	19- 8
1928	PIT	N	P		34	15-13
1929	PIT	N	P		34	18-10
1930	PIT	N	P		39	20-12
1931	PIT	N	P		30	11-15
1932	PIT	N	P		11	4- 3
1933	PIT	N	P		7	1- 0
	BRTR			308	309	143-85

KREMMEL, JAMES LOUIS "JIM"
B.FEB.28,1948 BELLEVILLE,ILL.

YR	CL	LEA	POS	GP	G	REC
1973	TEX	A	P		4	0- 2
1974	CHI	N	P		23	0- 2
	BLTL				27	0- 4

KRESS, CHARLES STEVEN "BUCK"
B.DEC.9,1921 PHILADELPHIA,PA.

YR	CL	LEA	POS	GP	G	REC
1947	CIN	N	1		11	.148
1949	CIN	N	1		27	.207
	CHI	A	1		97	.278
1950	CHI	A	1		3	.000
1954	DET	A	1-O		24	.189
	BRO	N	1		13	.083
	BLTL				175	.249

KRESS, RALPH "RED"
B.JAN.2,1907 COLUMBIA,CAL.
D.NOV.29,1962

YR	CL	LEA	POS	GP	G	REC
1927	STL	A	S		7	.304
1928	STL	A	S		150	.273
1929	STL	A	S		147	.305
1930	STL	A	S-3		154	.313
1931	STL	A	1-S-3-O		150	.311
1932	STL	A	3		14	.191
	CHI	A	S-3-O		135	.283
1933	CHI	A	1-O		129	.248
1934	CHI	A	O		8	.286
	WAS	A	1-O		56	.228
1935	WAS	A	P-1-	3	84	0- 0
			2-S-O			.298
1936	WAS	A	2-S		109	.284
1938	STL	A	S		150	.302
1939	STL	A	S		13	.279
1939	DET	A	S		51	.242
1940	DET	A	S-3		33	.222
1946	NY	N	P		1	0- 0
	BRTR			4	1391	0- 0
						.286

KRETLOW, LOUIS HENRY "LOU" OR "LENA"
B.JUNE 27,1923 APACHE,OKLA.

YR	CL	LEA	POS	GP	G	REC
1946	DET	A	P		1	1- 0
1948	DET	A	P		5	2- 1
1949	DET	A	P		25	3- 2
1950	STL	A	P	9	10	0- 2
	CHI	A	P		11	0- 0
1951	CHI	A	P		26	6- 9
1952	CHI	A	P		19	4- 4
1953	CHI	A	P		9	0- 0
	STL	A	P		22	1- 5
1954	BAL	A	P		32	6-11
1955	BAL	A	P		15	0- 4
1956	KC	A	P		25	4- 9
	BRTR			199	200	27-47

KREUGER, RICHARD ALLEN "RICK"
B.NOV.3,1948 GRAND RAPIDS,MICH.

YR	CL	LEA	POS	GP	G	REC
1975	BOS	A	P		2	0- 0
1976	BOS	A	P		8	2- 1
	B-TL				10	2- 1

KREUTZER, FRANKLIN JAMES "FRANK"
B.FEB.7,1939 BUFFALO,N.Y.

YR	CL	LEA	POS	GP	G	REC
1962	CHI	A	P		1	0- 0
1963	CHI	A	P		1	1- 0
1964	CHI	A	P		17	3- 1
	WAS	A	P		13	2- 6
1965	WAS	A	P		33	2- 6
1966	WAS	A	P		9	0- 5
1969	WAS	A	P		4	0- 0
	BRTL				78	8-18

KRICHELL, PAUL BERNARD
B.DEC.19,1882 NEW YORK,N.Y.
D.JUNE 4,1957

YR	CL	LEA	POS	GP	G	REC
1911	STL	A	C		28	.232
1912	STL	A	C		57	.217
	BRTR				85	.222

KRIEG, WILLIAM FREDERICK
B.JAN.29,1859 PETERSBURG,ILL.
D.MAR.25,1930

YR	CL	LEA	POS	GP	G	REC
1884	CHI	U	C-1-O		59	.231
	PIT	U	C-O		10	.350
1885	CHI	N	C-O		1	.000
	BRO	AA	C		17	.150
1886	WAS	N	1		27	.255
1887	WAS	N	1		24	.304
	BRTR				138	.248

KRIEGER

YR	CL	LEA	POS	GP	G	REC
1884	KC	U	P		1	0- 1

KRIEGER, KURT FERDINAND "DUTCH"
B.SEPT.16,1926 TRAISEN,AUSTRIA
D.AUG.16,1970 ST.LOUIS,MO.

YR	CL	LEA	POS	GP	G	REC
1949	STL	N	P		1	0- 0
1951	STL	N	P		2	0- 0
	BRTR				3	0- 0

KRIST, HOWARD WILBUR "SPUD"
B.FEB.28,1916 W.HENRIETTA,N.Y.

YR	CL	LEA	POS	GP	G	REC
1937	STL	N	P		6	3- 1
1938	STL	N	P		2	0- 0
1941	STL	N	P		37	10- 0
1942	STL	N	P	34	33	13- 3
1943	STL	N	P		34	11- 5
1946	STL	N	P		15	0- 2
	BLTR			128	129	37-11

KROCK, AUGUST H.
B.MAY 9,1866 MILWAUKEE,WIS.
D.MAR.22,1905

YR	CL	LEA	POS	GP	G	REC
1888	CHI	N	P		39	25-14
1889	CHI	N	P		8	4- 4
	IND	N	P		7	5- 2
	WAS	N	P		7	1- 6
1890	BUF	P	P		4	0- 3
	TL				65	35-29

KROH, FLOYD H. "RUBE"
B.AUG.25,1886 FRIENDSHIP,N.Y.
D.MAR.17,1944

YR	CL	LEA	POS	GP	G	REC
1906	BOS	A	P		1	1- 0
1907	BOS	A	P		7	0- 4
1908	CHI	N	P		2	0- 0
1909	CHI	N	P		17	9- 4
1910	CHI	N	P		6	3- 1
1912	BOS	N	P		3	0- 0
	BLTL				36	13- 9

KROLL, GARY MELVIN
B.JULY 8,1941 CULVER CITY,CAL.

YR	CL	LEA	POS	GP	G	REC
1964	PHI	N	P		2	0- 0
	NY	N	P		8	0- 1
1965	NY	N	P		32	6- 6
1966	HOU	N	P		10	0- 0
1969	CLE	A	P		19	0- 0
	BRTR				71	6- 7

KRONER, JOHN HAROLD
B.NOV.13,1908 ST.LOUIS,MO.
D.AUG.26,1968 ST.LOUIS,MO.

YR	CL	LEA	POS	GP	G	REC
1935	BOS	A	3		2	.250
1936	BOS	A	2-S-3		84	.292
1937	CLE	A	2-3		86	.237
1938	CLE	A	2		51	.248
	BRTR				223	.262

KROUSE, WILLIAM
B.AURORA,ILL.

YR	CL	LEA	POS	GP	G	REC
1901	CIN	N	2		1	.250
	TR					

KRSNICH, MICHAEL "MIKE"
B.SEPT.24,1931 W.ALLIS,WIS.

YR	CL	LEA	POS	GP	G	REC
1960	MIL	N	O		4	.333
1962	MIL	N	1-3-O		11	.083
	BRTR				15	.190

KRSNICH, ROCCO PETER "ROCKY"
B.DEC.4,1927 W.ALLIS,WIS.

YR	CL	LEA	POS	GP	G	REC
1949	CHI	A	3		16	.218
1952	CHI	A	3		40	.231
1953	CHI	A	3		64	.202
	BRTR				120	.215

KRUEGER, ERNEST GEORGE
B.DEC.27,1891 CHICAGO,ILL.
D.APR.12,1976 WAUKEGAN,ILL.

YR	CL	LEA	POS	GP	G	REC
1913	CLE	A	C		5	.000
1915	NY	A	C		10	.172
1917	NY	N	C		8	.000
	BRO	N	C		31	.272
1918	BRO	N	C		30	.287
1919	BRO	N	C		80	.248
1920	BRO	N	C		52	.288
1921	BRO	N	C		65	.264
1925	CIN	N	C		37	.307
	BRTR				318	.264

KRUEGER, OOMPAUL ARTHUR
B.SEPT.17,1876 CHICAGO,ILL.
D.FEB.20,1961

YR	CL	LEA	POS	GP	G	REC
1899	CLE	N	3		13	.227
1900	STL	N	2		12	.400
1901	STL	N	3		142	.274
1902	STL	N	S-3		125	.264
1903	PIT	N	S-O		71	.246
1904	PIT	N	S-O		75	.194
1905	PHI	N	P-S	1	30	0- 1
						.184
	BRTR			1	468	0- 1
						.250

KRUG, EVERETT BEN "CHRIS"
B.DEC.25,1939 LOS ANGELES,CAL.

YR	CL	LEA	POS	GP	G	REC
1965	CHI	N	C		60	.201
1966	CHI	N	C		11	.214
1969	SD	N	C		8	.059
	BRTR				79	.192

KRUG, HENRY CHARLES
B.DEC.4,1876 SAN FRANCISCO,CAL.
D.JAN.14,1908

YR	CL	LEA	POS	GP	G	REC
1902	PHI	N	2-S-3-O		53	.225
	TR					

YR	CL	LEA	POS	GP	G	REC

KRUG, MARTIN JOHN
B.SEPT.10,1888 COBLENZ,GERMANY
D.JUNE 27,1966 GLENDALE,CAL.

YR	CL	LEA	POS	GP	G	REC
1912	BOS	A	S		15	.308
1922	CHI	N	2-S-3		127	.275
	BRTR				142	.278

KRUGER, ABRAHAM
B.FEB.14,1886 MORRIS RUN,PA.
D.JULY 14,1962

1908	BRO	N	P		1	0-1

KRUGER, ARTHUR T.
B.MAR.16,1881 SAN ANTONIO,TEX.
D.NOV.28,1949

1907	CIN	N	O		96	.233
1910	CLE	A	O		62	.170
	BOS	N	O		1	.000
1914	KC	F	O		122	.250
1915	KC	F	O		80	.234
	BRTR				361	.228

KRUKOW, MICHAEL EDWARD "MIKE"
B.JAN.21,1952 LONG BEACH,CAL.

1976	CHI	N	P		2	0-0
	BRTR					

KRUMM, ALBERT
B.COLUMBUS,OHIO

1889	PIT	N	P		1	0-1
	TR					

KRYHOSKI, RICHARD DAVID "DICK"
B.MAR.24,1925 LEONIA,N.J.

1949	NY	A	1		54	.294
1950	DET	A	1		53	.219
1951	DET	A	1		119	.287
1952	STL	A	1		111	.243
1953	STL	A	1		104	.278
1954	BAL	A	1		100	.260
1955	KC	A	1		28	.213
	BLTL				569	.264

KUBEK, ANTHONY CHRISTOPHER "TONY"
B.OCT.12,1936 MILWAUKEE,WIS.

1957	NY	A	2-S-3-O		127	.297
1958	NY	A	1-2-S-O		138	.265
1959	NY	A	2-S-3-O		132	.279
1960	NY	A	S-O		147	.273
1961	NY	A	S		153	.276
1962	NY	A	S-O		45	.314
1963	NY	A	S-O		135	.257
1964	NY	A	S		106	.229
1965	NY	A	1-S-O		109	.218
	BLTR				1092	.266

KUBIAK, THEODORE RODGER "TED"
B.MAY 12,1942 NEW BRUNSWICK,N.J.

1967	KC	A	2-S-3		53	.157
1968	OAK	A	2-S		48	.250
1969	OAK	A	2-S		92	.249
1970	MIL	A	2-S		158	.252
1971	MIL	A	2-S		89	.227
	STL	N	2-S		32	.250
1972	TEX	A	2-S-3		46	.224
	OAK	A	2-3		51	.181
1973	OAK	A	2-S-3		106	.220
1974	OAK	A	2-S-3		99	.209
1975	OAK	A	2-S-3		20	.250
	SD	N	1-2-3		87	.224
1976	SD	N	1-2-S-3		96	.236
	BBTR				977	.231

KUBISZYN, JOHN HENRY "JACK"
B.DEC.19,1936 BUFFALO,N.Y.

1961	CLE	A	S-3		25	.214
1962	CLE	A	S-3		25	.169
	BRTR				50	.188

KUCAB, JOHN ALBERT "JOHNNY"
B.DEC.19,1919 OLYPHANT,PA.

1950	PHI	A	P		4	1-1
1951	PHI	A	P		30	4-3
1952	PHI	A	P	25	28	0-1
	BRTR			59	62	5-5

KUCEK, JOHN ANDREW CHARLES "JACK"
B.JUNE 8,1953 WARREN,OHIO

1974	CHI	A	P		9	1-4
1975	CHI	A	P		2	0-0
1976	CHI	A	P		2	0-0
	BRTR				13	1-4

KUCKS, JOHN CHARLES "JOHNNY"
B.JULY 27,1933 HOBOKEN,N.J.

1955	NY	A	P		29	8-7
1956	NY	A	P		34	18-9
1957	NY	A	P		37	8-10
1958	NY	A	P		34	8-8
1959	NY	A	P		9	0-1
	KC	A	P		33	8-11
1960	KC	A	P		31	4-10
	BRTR				207	54-56

KUCZEK, STANISLAW LEO "STEVE"
B.DEC.28,1924 AMSTERDAM,N.Y.

1949	BOS	N	H		1	1.000
	BRTR					

KUCZYNSKI, BERNARD CARL "BERT"
B.JAN.8,1920 PHILADELPHIA,PA.

1943	PHI	A	P		6	0-1
	BRTR					

KUEHL, KARL OTTO
B.SEPT.9,1937 MONTEREY PARK,CAL.
NON-PLAYING MANAGER MON(N) 1976

KUEHNE, WILLIAM J.
(REAL NAME WILLIAM J. KNELME)
B.OCT.24,1863 LEIPZIG,GERMANY
D.OCT.27,1921

1883	COL	AA	2-S-3-O		96	.222
1884	COL	AA	3		110	.238
1885	PIT	AA	3		105	.216
1886	PIT	AA	3-O		117	.211
1887	PIT	N	S		101	.322
1888	PIT	N	S-3		137	.234
1889	PIT	N	3		97	.246
1890	PIT	P	3		126	.243
1891	COL	AA	3		56	.214
	LOU	AA	3		40	.275
1892	LOU	N	3		76	.164
	STL	N	S-3		6	.167
	CIN	N	3		6	.217
	STL	N	3		1	.000
	TR				1074	.236

KUENN, HARVEY EDWARD
B.DEC.4,1930 MILWAUKEE,WIS.

1952	DET	A	S		19	.325
1953	DET	A	S		155	.308
1954	DET	A	S		155	.306
1955	DET	A	S		145	.306
1956	DET	A	S-O		146	.332
1957	DET	A	1-S-3		151	.277
1958	DET	A	O		139	.319
1959	DET	A	O		139	.353
1960	CLE	A	3-O		126	.308
1961	SF	N	S-3-O		131	.265
1962	SF	N	3-O		130	.304
1963	SF	N	3-O		120	.290
1964	SF	N	1-3-O		111	.262
1965	SF	N	1-O		23	.237
	CHI	N	1-O		54	.217
1966	CHI	N	O		3	.333
	PHI	N	1-3-O		86	.296
	BRTR				1833	.303

NON-PLAYING MANAGER MIL(A) 1975 (INTERIM)

KUHEL, JOSEPH ANTHONY "JOE"
B.JUNE 25,1906 CLEVELAND,OHIO

1930	WAS	A	1		18	.286
1931	WAS	A	1		139	.269
1932	WAS	A	1		101	.291
1933	WAS	A	1		153	.322
1934	WAS	A	1		63	.289
1935	WAS	A	1		151	.261
1936	WAS	A	1		149	.321
1937	WAS	A	1		136	.283
1938	WAS	A	1		117	.267
1939	CHI	A	1		139	.300
1940	CHI	A	1		155	.280
1941	CHI	A	1		153	.250
1942	CHI	A	1		115	.249
1943	CHI	A	1		153	.213
1944	WAS	A	1		139	.278
1945	WAS	A	1		142	.285
1946	WAS	A	1		14	.150
	CHI	A	1		64	.273
1947	CHI	A	H		4	.000
	BLTL				2105	.277

NON-PLAYING MANAGER WAS(A) 1948-49

KUHN, BERNARD DANIEL "BUB"
B.OCT.12,1899 VICKSBURG,MICH.
D.NOV.20,1956

1924	CLE	A	P		1	0-1
	BLTR					

KUHN, KENNETH HAROLD "KENNY"
B.MAR.20,1937 LOUISVILLE,KY.

1955	CLE	A	S		4	.333
1956	CLE	A	2-S		27	.273
1957	CLE	A	2-S-3		40	.170
	BLTR				71	.210

KUHN, WALTER CHARLES "RED"
B.FEB.2,1884 FRESNO,CAL.
D.JUNE 14,1935

1912	CHI	A	C		75	.202
1913	CHI	A	C		26	.160
1914	CHI	A	C		17	.275
	BRTR				118	.205

KUHNS, CHARLES B.
B.FREEPORT,PA.
D.JULY 15,1922

1897	PIT	N	3		2	.000
1899	BOS	N	S-3		6	.267
					8	.217

KUIPER, DUANE EUGENE
B.JUNE 19,1950 RACINE,WIS.

1974	CLE	A	2		10	.500
1975	CLE	A	?		90	.292
1976	CLE	A	1-2		135	.263
	BLTR				235	.280

KULL, JOHN A.
B.JUNE 24,1882 SHENANDOAH,PA.
D.MAR.30,1936

1909	PHI	A	P		1	1-0
	TL					

KUME, JOHN MICHAEL
B.MAY 19,1926 PREMIER,W.VA.

1955	KC	A	P		6	0-2
	BRTR					

KUNKEL, WILLIAM GUSTAVE JAMES "BILL"
B.JULY 7,1936 HOBOKEN,N.J.

1961	KC	A	P		58	3-4
1962	KC	A	P		9	0-0
1963	NY	A	P		22	3-2
	BRTR				89	6-6

KUNZ, EARL DEWEY "PINCHES"
B.DEC.25,1899 SACRAMENTO,CAL.
D.APR.14,1963 SACRAMENTO,CAL.

1923	PIT	N	P		21	1-2
	BRTP					

KUROSAKI, RYAN YOSHITOMO
B.JULY 3,1952 HONOLULU,HAWAII

1975	STL	N	P		7	0-0
	BRTR					

KUROWSKI, GEORGE JOHN "WHITEY"
B.APR.19,1918 READING,PA.

1941	STL	N	3		5	.333
1942	STL	N	S-3-O		115	.254
1943	STL	N	S-3		139	.287
1944	STL	N	2-S-3		149	.270
1945	STL	N	S-3		133	.323
1946	STL	N	3		142	.301
1947	STL	N	3		146	.310
1948	STL	N	3		77	.214
1949	STL	N	3		10	.143
	BRTR				916	.286

KURTZ, HAROLD JAMES "HAL"
B.AUG.20,1943 WASHINGTON,D.C.

1968	CLE	A	P	28	30	1-0
	BRTR					

KUSEL, EDWARD
B.FEB.15,1886 CLEVELAND,OHIO
D.OCT.20,1948

1909	STL	A	P		3	0-3

YR	CL	LEA	POS	GP	G	REC

KUSH, EMIL BENEDICT
B.NOV.4,1916 CHICAGO,ILL.
D.NOV.26,1969 RIVER GROVE,ILL.

YR	CL	LEA	POS	GP	G	REC
1941	CHI	N	P		2	0- 0
1942	CHI	N	P		1	0- 0
1946	CHI	N	P		40	9- 2
1947	CHI	N	P		47	8- 3
1948	CHI	N	P		34	1- 4
1949	CHI	N	P		26	3- 3
		BRTR			150	21-12

KUSICK, CRAIG ROBERT
B.SEP.30,1948 MILWAUKEE,WIS.

1973	MIN	A	1-O		15	.250
1974	MIN	A	1		76	.239
1975	MIN	A	1		57	.237
1976	MIN	A	1-D		109	.259
		BRTR			257	.247

KUSNYER, ARTHUR WILLIAM "ART"
B.DEC.19,1945 AKRON,OHIO

1970	CHI	A	C		4	.100
1971	CAL	A	C		6	.154
1972	CAL	A	C		64	.207
1973	CAL	A	C		41	.125
1976	MIL	A	C		15	.118
		BRTR			130	.173

KUSTUS, JULIUS "JOE"
B.DETROIT,MICH.

1909	BRO	N	O		50	.145
		BRTR				

KUTINA, JOSEPH PETER
B.JAN.16,1885 CHICAGO,ILL.
D.APR.13,1945

1911	STL	A	1		26	.259
1912	STL	A	1		67	.205
		BRTR			93	.222

KUTYNA, MARION JOHN "MARTY"
B.NOV.14,1932 PHILADELPHIA,PA.

1959	KC	A	P		4	0- 0
1960	KC	A	P		51	3- 2
1961	WAS	A	P		50	6- 8
1962	WAS	A	P		54	5- 6
		BRTR			159	14-16

KUZAVA, ROBERT LEROY "BOB"
B.MAY 28,1923 WYANDOTTE,MICH.

1946	CLE	A	P		2	1- 0
1947	CLE	A	P		4	1- 1
1949	CHI	A	P		29	10- 6
1950	CHI	A	P		10	1- 3
	WAS	A	P		22	8- 7
1951	WAS	A	P		8	3- 3
	NY	A	P	23	24	8- 4
1952	NY	A	P		28	8- 8
1953	NY	A	P		33	6- 5
1954	NY	A	P		20	1- 3
	BAL	A	P		4	1- 3
1955	BAL	A	P		6	0- 1
	PHI	N	P		17	1- 0
1957	PIT	N	P		4	0- 0
	STL	N	P		3	0- 0
		BBTL		213	214	49-44

KVASNAK, ALEXANDER
B.JAN.11,1921 SAGAMORE,PA.

1942	WAS	A	O		5	.182
		BRTR				

KWIETNIEWSKI, CASIMIR EUGENE
(PLAYED UNDER NAME OF
CASIMIR EUGENE MICHAELS)

KYLE, ANDREW EWING
B.OCT.29,1889 TORONTO,ONT.,CAN.
D.SEPT.6,1971 TORONTO,ONT.,CAN.

1912	CIN	N	O		8	.350
		BLTL				

LAABS, CHESTER PETER "CHET"
B.APR.30,1912 MILWAUKEE,WIS.

1937	DET	A	O		72	.240
1938	DET	A	O		64	.237
1939	DET	A	O		5	.313
	STL	A	O		95	.300
1940	STL	A	O		105	.271
1941	STL	A	O		118	.278
1942	STL	A	O		144	.275
1943	STL	A	O		151	.250
1944	STL	A	O		66	.234
1945	STL	A	O		35	.239
1946	STL	A	O		80	.261
1947	PHI	A	O		15	.219
		BRTR			950	.262

LABINE, CLEMENT WALTER "CLEM"
B.AUG.6,1926 LINCOLN,R.I.

1950	BRO	N	P		1	0- 0
1951	BRO	N	P		14	5- 1
1952	BRO	N	P	25	26	8- 4
1953	BRO	N	P		37	11- 6
1954	BRO	N	P		47	7- 6
1955	BRO	N	P		60	13- 5
1956	BRO	N	P		62	10- 6
1957	BRO	N	P		58	5- 7
1958	LA	N	P		52	6- 6
1959	LA	N	P		56	5-10
1960	LA	N	P		13	0- 1
	DET	A	P		14	0- 3
	PIT	N	P		15	3- 0
1961	PIT	N	P		56	4- 1
1962	NY	N	P		3	0- 0
		BRTR		513	514	77-56

LABOY, JOSE ALBERTO "COCO"
B.JULY 3,1940 PONCE,P.R.

1969	MON	N	3		157	.258
1970	MON	N	2-3		137	.199
1971	MON	N	2-3		76	.252
1972	MON	N	2-S-3		28	.261
1973	MON	N	2-3-O		22	.121
		BRTR			420	.233

LA CHANCE, GEORGE "CANDY"
B.FEB.15,1870 WATERBURY,CONN.
D.AUG.16,1932

1893	BRO	N	C		11	.176
1894	BRO	N	1		65	.329
1895	BRO	N	1		128	.320
1896	BRO	N	1		89	.280
1897	BRO	N	1		125	.308
1898	BRO	N	1-S		135	.243
1899	BAL	N	1		126	.307
1901	CLE	A	1		133	.306
1902	BOS	A	1		138	.275
1903	BOS	A	1		141	.258
1904	BOS	A	1		157	.231
1905	BOS	A	1		12	.128
		BB			1260	.281

LACHEMANN, MARCEL ERNEST
B.JUNE 13,1941 LOS ANGELES,CAL.

1969	OAK	A	P		28	4- 1
1970	OAK	A	P		41	3- 3
1971	OAK	A	P		1	0- 0
		BRTR			70	7- 4

LACHEMANN, RENE GEORGE
B.MAY 4,1945 LOS ANGELES,CAL.

1965	KC	A	C		92	.227
1966	KC	A	C		7	.200
1968	OAK	A	C		19	.150
		BRTR			118	.210

LA CLAIRE, GEORGE L.
B.OCT.18,1886 MILTON,VT.
D.OCT.10,1918 FARNHAM,QUE.,CAN.

1914	PIT	F	P		22	5- 2
1915	PIT	F	P		14	3- 2
	BUF	F	P		1	0- 0
	BAL	F	P		18	0- 6
		TR			55	8-10

LA COCK, RALPH PIERRE "PETER"
B.JAN.17,1952 BURBANK,CAL.

1972	CHI	N	O		5	.500
1973	CHI	N	O		11	.250
1974	CHI	N	1-O		35	.182
1975	CHI	N	1-O		106	.229
1976	CHI	N	1-O		106	.221
		BLTL			263	.221

LA CORTE, FRANK JOSEPH
B.OCT.13,1951 SAN JOSE,CAL.

1975	ATL	N	P		3	0- 3
1976	ATL	N	P	19	21	3-12
		BRTR		22	24	3-15

LACY, LEONDAUS "LEON"
B.APR.10,1948 LONGVIEW,TEX.

1972	LA	N	2		60	.259
1973	LA	N	2		57	.207
1974	LA	N	2-3		48	.282
1975	LA	N	2-S-O		101	.314
1976	LA	N	2-3-O		50	.272
	LA	N	2-3-O		53	.266
		BRTR			369	.273

LACY, OSCEOLA GUY
B.JUNE 12,1897 CLEVELAND,TENN.
D.NOV.19,1953

1926	CLE	A	2		13	.167
		BRTR				

LADD, ARTHUR CLIFFORD HIRAM "HI"
B.FEB.9,1870 WILLIMANTIC,CONN.
D.MAY 7,1948

1898	PIT	N	O		1	.000
	BOS	N	O		1	.000
					2	.000

LADE, DOYLE MARION "PORKY"
B.FEB.17,1921 FAIRBURY,NEB.

1946	CHI	N	P		3	0- 2
1947	CHI	N	P	34	35	11-10
1948	CHI	N	P		19	5- 6
1949	CHI	N	P		36	4- 5
1950	CHI	N	P		34	5- 6
		BRTR		126	127	25-29
		BB 1946-47				

LADEW, STEPHEN
B.ST.LOUIS,MO.

1889	KC	AA	P		2	0- 0

LAFATA, JOSEPH JOSEPH "JOE"
B.AUG.3,1921 DETROIT,MICH.

1947	NY	N	O		62	.221
1948	NY	N	H		1	.000
1949	NY	N	1		64	.236
		BLTL			127	.229

LAFFERTY, FRANK BERNARD "FLIP"
B.MAY 4,1854 SCRANTON,PA.
D.FEB.8,1910

1876	ATH	N	P		1	0- 1
1877	LOU	N	O		4	.059
		TR		1	5	0- 1
						.050

LAFITTE, EDWARD FRANCIS
B.APR.7,1885 NEW ORLEANS,LA.
D.APR.12,1971 JENKINTOWN,PA.

1909	DET	A	P		3	0- 1
1911	DET	A	P	29	31	11- 8
1912	DET	A	P		1	0- 0
1914	BRO	F	P		42	18-15
1915	BRO	F	P		17	7- 9
	BUF	F	P		14	2- 2
		BRTR		106	108	38-35

LA FOREST, BYRON JOSEPH "TY"
B.APR.19,1919 EDMUNDSTON,N.B., CANADA
D.MAY 5,1947 ARLINGTON,MASS.

1945	BOS	A	3-O		52	.250
		BRTR				

LAGGER, EDWIN JOSEPH
B.JULY 14,1912 JOLIET,ILL.

1934	PHI	A	P		8	0- 0
		BRTR				

LA GROW, LERRIN HARRIS
B.JULY 8,1948 PHOENIX,ARIZ.

1970	DET	A	P		10	0- 1
1972	DET	A	P		16	0- 1
1973	DET	A	P		21	1- 5
1974	DET	A	P		37	8-19
1975	DET	A	P		32	7-14
1976	STL	N	P		8	0- 1
		BRTR			124	16-41

LAHOUD, JOSEPH MICHAEL "JOE"
B.APR.14,1947 DANBURY,CONN.

1968	BOS	A	O		29	.192
1969	BOS	A	1-O		101	.188
1970	BOS	A	O		17	.245
1971	BOS	A	O		107	.215
1972	MIL	A	O		111	.237
1973	MIL	A	O-D		96	.204
1974	CAL	A	O-D		127	.271
1975	CAL	A	O-D		76	.214
1976	CAL	A	O		42	.177
	TEX	A	O-D		38	.225
		BLTL			744	.222

LAJESKIE, RICHARD EDWARD
B.JAN.8,1926 PASSAIC,N.J.
D.AUG.15,1976 RAMSEY,N.J.

1946	NY	N	2		6	.200
		BRTR				

YR	CL LEA POS	GP	G	REC

LAJOIE, NAPOLEON
"NAP" OR "LARRY"
B.SEPT.5,1875 WOONSOCKET,R.I.
D.FEB.7,1959 DAYTONA BEACH,FLA.

YR	CL LEA POS	GP	G	REC
1896	PHI N 1		39	.328
1897	PHI N 1-0		126	.363
1898	PHI N 2		147	.328
1899	PHI N 2		72	.379
1900	PHI N 2		102	.346
1901	PHI A 2		131	.422
1902	PHI A 2		1	.200
	CLE A 2		86	.369
1903	CLE A 1-2		126	.355
1904	CLE A 2-S		140	.381
1905	CLE A M-2		65	.329
1906	CLE A M-2-3		152	.355
1907	CLE A M-2		137	.299
1908	CLE A M-2		157	.289
1909	CLE A M-2		128	.324
1910	CLE A 2		159	.384
1911	CLE A 1-2		90	.365
1912	CLE A 1-2		117	.368
1913	CLE A 2		137	.335
1914	CLE A 1-2		121	.258
1915	PHI A 2		129	.280
1916	PHI A 2		113	.246
	BRTR		2475	.339

LAKE, EDWARD ERVING
"EDDIE" OR "SPARKY"
B.MAR.18,1917 ANTIOCH,CAL.

YR	CL LEA POS	GP	G	REC
1939	STL N S		2	.250
1940	STL N 2-S		32	.212
1941	STL N 2-S-3		45	.105
1943	BOS A S		75	.199
1944	BOS A P-2-	6	57	0- 0
	S-3			.206
1945	BOS A S		133	.279
1946	DET A S		155	.254
1947	DET A S		158	.211
1948	DET A 2-3		64	.263
1949	DET A 2-S-3		94	.196
1950	DET A S-3		20	.000
	BRTR	6	835	0- 0
				.231

LAKE, FREDERICK LOVETT
B.OCT.16,1866 NOVA SCOTIA,CAN.
D.NOV.24,1931

YR	CL LEA POS	GP	G	REC
1891	BOS N C		5	.142
1894	LOU N C-2		16	.292
1897	BOS N C		17	.272
1898	PIT N 1		5	.083
1910	PIT N M-H		3	.000
			46	.238

NON-PLAYING MANAGER
BOS(A) 1908-09

LAKE, JOSEPH HENRY
B.JAN.6,1881 BROOKLYN,N.Y.
D.JUNE 30,1950

YR	CL LEA POS	GP	G	REC
1908	NY A P	37	44	9-21
1909	NY A P		32	14-11
1910	STL A P	35	37	11-18
1911	STL A P		30	10-15
1912	STL A P		15	3-10
	DET A P		22	9- 9
1913	DET A P		28	8- 7
	BRTR	199	208	64-91

LAKEMAN, ALBERT WESLEY
"AL" OR "MOOSE"
B.DEC.31,1918 CINCINNATI,OHIO
D.MAY 25,1976 SPARTANBURG,S.C.

YR	CL LEA POS	GP	G	REC
1942	CIN N C		20	.158
1943	CIN N C		22	.255
1944	CIN N H		1	.000
1945	CIN N C		76	.256
1946	CIN N C		23	.133
1947	CIN N H		2	.000
	PHI N C-1		55	.159
1948	PHI N P-C		32	0- 0
				.162
1949	BOS N 1		3	.167
1954	DET A C		5	.000
	BRTR		239	0- 0
				.203

LALLY, DANIEL J. "BUD"
B.AUG.12,1867 JERSEY CITY,N.J.
D.APR.14,1936

YR	CL LEA POS	GP	G	REC
1891	PIT N O		41	.225
1897	STL N O		87	.278
	BRTR		128	.263

LAMABE, JOHN ALEXANDER "JACK"
B.OCT.3,1936 FARMINGDALE,N.Y.

YR	CL LEA POS	GP	G	REC
1962	PIT N P		46	3- 1
1963	BOS A P		65	7- 4
1964	BOS A P		39	9-13
1965	BOS A P		14	0- 3
	HOU N P		3	0- 2
1966	CHI A P		34	7- 9
1967	CHI A P		3	1- 0
	NY N P		16	0- 3
	STL N P		23	3- 4
1968	CHI N P		42	3- 2
	BRTR		285	33-41

LA MACCHIA, ALFRED ANTHONY
B.JULY 22,1921 ST.LOUIS,MO.

YR	CL LEA POS	GP	G	REC
1943	STL A P		1	0- 1
1945	STL A P		5	2- 0
1946	STL A P		8	0- 0
	WAS A P		2	0- 1
	BRTR		16	2- 2

LA MANNA, FRANK
B.AUG.22,1919 WATERTOWN,PA.

YR	CL LEA POS	GP	G	REC
1940	BOS N P		5	1- 0
1941	BOS N P-O	35	47	5- 4
				.281
1942	BOS N P		5	10	0- 1
	BRTR	45	62	6- 5
				.256

LAMANNO, RAYMOND SIMON "RAY"
B.NOV.17,1919 OAKLAND,CAL.

YR	CL LEA POS	GP	G	REC
1941	CIN N C		1	.000
1942	CIN N C		111	.264
1946	CIN N C		85	.243
1947	CIN N C		118	.257
1948	CIN N C		127	.242
	BRTR		442	.252

LAMANSKE, FRANK JAMES
B.SEPT.30,1906 OGLESBY,ILL.
D.AUG.4,1971 OLNEY,ILL.

YR	CL LEA POS	GP	G	REC
1935	BRO N P		2	0- 0
	BLTL			

LAMAR, PIERRE "PETE"
B.1874 HOBOKEN,N.J.
D.OCT.24,1931

YR	CL LEA POS	GP	G	REC
1902	CHI N C		2	.222
1907	CIN N C		1	.000
	TR		3	.182

LAMAR, WILLIAM HARMONG
"GOOD TIME BILL"
B.MAR.21,1897 ROCKVILLE,MD.
D.JULY 19,1970 ROCKPORT,MASS.

YR	CL LEA POS	GP	G	REC
1917	NY A O		11	.244
1918	NY A O		28	.227
1919	NY A O		11	.188
	BOS A O		48	.291
1920	BRO N O		24	.273
1921	BRO N O		3	.333
1924	PHI A O		87	.330
1925	PHI A O		138	.356
1926	PHI A O		116	.284
1927	PHI A O		84	.299
	BLTL		550	.310

LA MASTER, WAYNE LEE
B.FEB.13,1907 SELLERSBURG,IND.

YR	CL LEA POS	GP	G	REC
1937	PHI N P	50	51	15-19
1938	PHI N P		18	4- 7
	BRO N P	3	5	0- 1
	BLTL	71	74	19-27

LAMB, JOHN ANDREW
B.JULY 20,1946 SHARON,CONN.

YR	CL LEA POS	GP	G	REC
1970	PIT N P		23	0- 1
1971	PIT N P		2	0- 0
1973	PIT N P		22	0- 1
	BRTR		47	0- 2

LAMB, LAYMON RAYMOND
B.MAR.17,1895 LINCOLN,NEB.
D.OCT.5,1955 FAYETTEVILLE,ARK.

YR	CL LEA POS	GP	G	REC
1920	STL A O		9	.375
1921	STL A 3		45	.253
	BRTR		54	.272

LAMB, RAYMOND RICHARD "RAY"
B.DEC.23,1944 GLENDALE,CAL.

YR	CL LEA POS	GP	G	REC
1969	LA N P		10	0- 1
1970	LA N P		35	6- 1
1971	CLE A P		43	6-12
1972	CLE A P		34	5- 6
1973	CLE A P		32	3- 3
	BRTR		154	20-23

LAMBERT, CLAYTON PATRICK
B.MAR.26,1917 SUMMITT,ILL.

YR	CL LEA POS	GP	G	REC
1946	CIN N P		23	2- 2
1947	CIN N P		3	0- 0
	BRTR		26	2- 2

LAMBERT, EUGENE MARION
B.APR.26,1921 CRENSHAW,MISS.

YR	CL LEA POS	GP	G	REC
1941	PHI N P		2	0- 1
1942	PHI N P		1	0- 0
	BRTR		3	0- 1

LAMBETH, OTIS SAMUEL
B.MAY 13,1890 BERLIN,KAN.
D.JUNE 5,1976 MORAN,KAN.

YR	CL LEA POS	GP	G	REC
1916	CLE A P	15	16	4- 3
1917	CLE A P		26	7- 6
1918	CLE A P		2	0- 0
	BRTR	43	44	11- 9

LAMLEIN, FREDERICK ARTHUR
(PLAYED UNDER NAME OF
FREDERICK ARTHUR LAMLINE)

LAMLINE, FREDERICK ARTHUR
(REAL NAME
FREDERICK ARTHUR LAMLEIN)
B.AUG.14,1887 PORT HURON,MICH.
D.SEPT.20,1970 PORT HURON,MICH.

YR	CL LEA POS	GP	G	REC
1912	CHI A P		4	0- 0
1915	STL N P		5	0- 0
	BRTR			

LAMONT, GENE WILLIAM
B.DEC.25,1946 ROCKFORD,ILL.

YR	CL LEA POS	GP	G	REC
1970	DET A C		15	.295
1971	DET A C		7	.067
1972	DET A C		1	.000
1974	DET A C		60	.217
1975	DET A C		4	.375
	BLTR		87	.233

LA MOTTE, ROBERT EUGENE
B.FEB.15,1898 SAVANNAH,GA.

YR	CL LEA POS	GP	G	REC
1920	WAS A S		4	.000
1921	WAS A S		16	.195
1922	WAS A 3		68	.252
1925	STL A S-3		97	.273
1926	STL A S		36	.202
	BRTR		221	.253

LAMPARD, CHRISTOPHER KEITH
"KEITH"
B.DEC.20,1945 WARRINGTON,ENGLAND

YR	CL LEA POS	GP	G	REC
1969	HOU N O		9	.250
1970	HOU N 1-O		53	.236
	BLTR		62	.238

LAMPE, HENRY JOSEPH
B.SEPT.19,1872 BOSTON,MASS.
D.SEPT.16,1936

YR	CL LEA POS	GP	G	REC
1894	BOS N P		2	0- 1
1895	PHI N P		7	0- 2
	BRTL		9	0- 3

LANAHAN, RICHARD ANTHONY
B.SEPT.27,1911 WASHINGTON,D.C.

YR	CL LEA POS	GP	G	REC
1935	WAS A P		3	0- 3
1937	WAS A P		6	0- 1
1940	PIT N P		40	6- 8
1941	PIT N P		7	0- 1
	BLTL		56	6-13

LAND, DOC BURRELL
(PLAYED UNDER NAME OF
WILLIAM GILBERT LAND)

LAND, GROVER CLEVELAND
B.SEPT.22,1884 FRANKFORT,KY.
D.JULY 22,1958

YR	CL LEA POS	GP	G	REC
1908	CLE A C		7	.230
1909	CLE A C		1	.500
1910	CLE A C		34	.207
1911	CLE A C		35	.140
1913	CLE A C		17	.235
1914	BRO F C		103	.282
1915	BRO F C		96	.261
	BRTR		293	.247

YR	CL	LEA	POS	GP	G	REC

LAND, WILLIAM GILBERT
(REAL NAME DOC BURRELL LAND)
B.MAY 14,1903 GEIGER,ALA.
1929 WAS A O   1   .000
             BLTL

LANDENBERGER, KENNETH HENRY
"KEN" OR "RED"
B.JULY 29,1928 CLEVELAND,OHIO
D.JULY 28,1960
1952 CHI A 1   2   .200
             BLTL

LANDIS, JAMES HENRY "JIM"
B.MAR.9,1934 FRESNO,CAL.
1957 CHI A O   96   .212
1958 CHI A O   142   .277
1959 CHI A O   149   .272
1960 CHI A O   148   .253
1961 CHI A O   140   .283
1962 CHI A O   149   .228
1963 CHI A O   133   .225
1964 CHI A O   106   .208
1965 KC A O   118   .239
1966 CLE A O   85   .222
1967 DET A O   25   .208
     BOS A O   5   .143
     HOU N O   50   .252
             BRTR   1346   .247

LANDIS, SAMUEL H. "DOC"
B.AUG.16,1854 PHILADELPHIA,PA.
1882 ATH AA P-O   2   3   1- 1
                          .167
     BAL AA P-O 43 51 11-28
                          .160
                 45 54 12-29
                          .161

LANDIS, WILLIAM HENRY "BILL"
B.OCT.8,1942 HANFORD,CAL.
1963 KC A P   1   0- 0
1967 BOS A P   18   21   1- 0
1968 BOS A P   38   3- 3
1969 BOS A P   45   46   5- 5
             BLTL 102 106   9- 8

LANDRETH, LARRY ROBERT
B.MAR.11,1955 STRATFORD,ONT.,CAN
1976 MON N P   3   1- 2
             BRTR

LANDRITH, HOBERT NEAL "HOBIE"
B.MAR.16,1930 DECATUR,ILL.
1950 CIN N C   4   .214
1951 CIN N C   4   .385
1952 CIN N C   15   .260
1953 CIN N C   52   .240
1954 CIN N C   48   .198
1955 CIN N C   43   .253
1956 CHI N C   111   .221
1957 STL N C   75   .243
1958 STL N C   70   .215
1959 SF N C   109   .251
1960 SF N C   71   .242
1961 SF N C   43   .239
1962 NY N C   23   .289
     BAL A C   60   .222
1963 BAL A C   2   .000
     WAS N C   42   .175
             BLTR   772   .233

LANDRUM, DONALD LEROY "DON"
B.FEB.16,1936 SANTA ROSA,CAL.
1957 PHI N O   3   .143
1960 STL N O   13   .245
1961 STL N 2-O   28   .167
1962 STL N O   32   .314
     CHI N O   83   .282
1963 CHI N O   84   .242
1964 CHI N O   11   .000
1965 CHI N O   131   .226
1966 SF N O   72   .186
             BLTR   456   .234

LANDRUM, JESSE GLEN
B.SEPT.11,1912 CROCKETT,TEX.
1938 CHI A 2   4   .000
             BRTR

LANDRUM, JOSEPH BUTLER
B.DEC.13,1928 COLUMBIA,S.C.
1950 BRO N P   7   0- 0
1952 BRO N P   9   1- 3
             BRTR   16   1- 3

LANE, GEORGE M. "CHAPPY"
B.PITTSBURGH,PA.
1882 PIT AA C-1-O   54   .167
1884 TOL AA 1-O   56   .231
                    110   .200

LANE, JAMES HUNTER
B.JULY 20,1900 PULASKI,TENN.
1924 BOS N 2-3   7   .067
             BRTR

LANE, JERALD HAL "JERRY"
B.FEB.7,1926 WINDHAM,N.Y.
1953 WAS A P   20   1- 4
1954 CIN N P   3   1- 0
1955 CIN N P   8   0- 2
             BRTR   31   2- 6

LANE, MARVIN
B.JAN.18,1950 SANDERSVILLE,GA.
1971 DET A O   8   .143
1972 DET A O   8   .000
1973 DET A O   6   .250
1974 DET A O   50   .233
1976 DET A O   18   .188
             BRTR   90   .207

LANE, RICHARD HARRISON "DICK"
B.JUNE 28,1927 DETROIT,MICH.
1949 CHI A O   12   .119

LANFORD, LEWIS GROVER
B.JAN.8,1886 WOODRUFF,S.C.
1907 WAS A P   2   0- 0
             BRTR

LANFRANCONI, WALTER OSWALD
B.NOV.9,1916 BARRE,VT.
1941 CHI N P   2   0- 1
1947 BOS N P   36   37   4- 4
             BRTR   38   39   4- 5

LANG, DONALD CHARLES "DON"
B.MAR.15,1915 SELMA,CAL.
1938 CIN N 2-3   21   .260
1948 STL N 2-3   117   .269
             BRTR   138   .268

LANG, MARTIN JOHN
B.SEPT.27,1907 HOOPER,NEB.
D.JAN.13,1968 LAKEWOOD,COLO.
1930 PIT N P   2   0- 0
             BRTL

LANG, ROBERT DAVID "CHIP"
B.AUG.21,1952 PITTSBURGH,PA.
1975 MON N P   1   0- 0
1976 MON N P   29   1- 3
             BRTR   30   1- 3

LANGE, FRANK M.
B.OCT.28,1883 COLUMBIA,WIS.
D.DEC.26,1945
1910 CHI A P   23   9- 4
1911 CHI A P   29   54   8- 8
1912 CHI A P   31   36   10-10
1913 CHI A P   12   16   1- 4
             BRTR   95 129   28-26

LANGE, ERWIN HENRY
B.APR.12,1887 FOREST PARK,ILL.
D.APR.24,1971 MAYWOOD,ILL.
1914 CHI F P   37   12-11
             BRTR

LANGE, RICHARD OTTO "DICK"
B.SEP.1,1948 HARBOR BEACH,MICH.
1972 CAL A P   2   0- 0
1973 CAL A P   17   2- 1
1974 CAL A P   21   29   3- 8
1975 CAL A P   30   4- 6
             BRTR   70   78   9-15

LANGE, WILLIAM ALEXANDER
"BILL" OR "LITTLE EVA"
B.JUNE 6,1871 SAN FRANCISCO,CAL
D.JULY 23,1950
1893 CHI N 2-O   116   .288
1894 CHI N O   112   .324
1895 CHI N O   122   .388
1896 CHI N O   123   .333
1897 CHI N O   117   .352
1898 CHI N O   111   .332
1899 CHI N O   107   .324
             BRTR   808   .336

LANGFORD, ELTON
B.MAY 21,1900 BRIGGS,TEX.
1926 BOS A O   1   .000
1927 CLE A O   20   .269
1928 CLE A O   110   .276
             BLTR   131   .275

LANGFORD, JAMES RICK "RICK"
B.MAR.20,1952 FARMVILLE,VA.
1976 PIT N P   12   0- 1
             BRTR

LANGSFORD, ROBERT WILLIAM
(REAL NAME
ROBERT HUGO LANKSWERT)
B.AUG.5,1865 LOUISVILLE,KY.
D.JAN.10,1907 LOUISVILLE,KY.
1899 LOU N S   1   .000
             BRTR

LANIER, HAROLD CLIFTON "HAL"
B.JULY 4,1942 DENTON,N.C.
1964 SF N 2-S   98   .274
1965 SF N 2-S   159   .226
1966 SF N 2-S   149   .231
1967 SF N 2-S   151   .213
1968 SF N S   151   .206
1969 SF N S   150   .228
1970 SF N 1-2-S   134   .231
1971 SF N 1-2-S-3 109   .233
1972 NY A 2-S-3   60   .214
1973 NY A 2-S-3   35   .209
             BRTR   1196   .228
             BB 1966-70

LANIER, HUBERT MAX "MAX"
B.AUG.18,1915 DENTON,N.C.
1938 STL N P   18   0- 3
1939 STL N P   7   2- 1
1940 STL N P   35   9- 6
1941 STL N P   35   10- 8
1942 STL N P   34   13- 8
1943 STL N P   32   15- 7
1944 STL N P   33   17-12
1945 STL N P   4   2- 2
1946 STL N P   6   6- 0
1949 STL N P   15   5- 4
1950 STL N P   27   11- 9
1951 STL N P   31   11- 9
1952 NY N P   37   38   7-12
1953 NY N P   3   0- 0
     STL A P   10   0- 1
             BRTL   327 328 108-82

LANIER, LORENZO
B.OCT.19,1948 TUSKEGEE,ALA.
1971 PIT N H   6   .000
             BLTR

LANKSWERT, ROBERT HUGO
(PLAYED UNDER NAME OF
ROBERT WILLIAM LANGSFORD)

LANNING, JOHN YOUNG
"TOBACCO JOHNNY"
B.SEPT.6,1910 ASHEVILLE,N.C.
1936 BOS N P   28   7-11
1937 BOS N P   32   5- 7
1938 BOS N P   32   8- 7
1939 BOS N P   37   5- 6
1940 PIT N P   38   8- 4
1941 PIT N P   34   11-11
1942 PIT N P   34   6- 8
1943 PIT N P   12   4- 1
1945 PIT N P   1   0- 0
1946 PIT N P   27   4- 5
1947 BOS N P   3   0- 0
             BRTR   278   58-60

LANNING, LESTER ALFRED
B.MAY 13,1895 HARVARD,ILL.
D.JUNE 13,1962
1916 PHI A P-O   5 19   0- 3
                          .182
             BLTL

LANNING, THOMAS NEWTON "TOM"
B.APR.22,1909 BILTMORE,N.C.
D.NOV.4,1967 MARIETTA,GA.
1938 PHI N P   3   0- 1
             BLTL

YR	CL	LEA	POS	GP	G	REC

LANSING, EUGENE HEWETT
"GENE" OR "JIGGER"
B.JAN.11,1898 RENNSSELAER,N.Y.
D.JAN.18,1945

YR	CL	LEA	POS	GP	G	REC
1922	BOS	N	P		15	0-1
	BRTR					

LA PALME, PAUL EDMORE
B.DEC.14,1923 SPRINGFIELD,MASS.

YR	CL	LEA	POS	GP	G	REC
1951	PIT	N	P		22	1- 5
1952	PIT	N	P		31	1- 2
1953	PIT	N	P		35	8-16
1954	PIT	N	P		33	4-10
1955	STL	N	P		56	4- 3
1956	STL	N	P		1	0- 0
	CIN	N	P		11	2- 4
	CHI	A	P		29	3- 1
1957	CHI	A	P	35	36	1- 4
	BLTL			253	254	24-45

LAPAN, PETER NELSON
B.JUNE 25,1891 EASTHAMPTON,MASS
D.JAN.5,1953

YR	CL	LEA	POS	GP	G	REC
1922	WAS	A	C		11	.324
1923	WAS	A	C		2	.000
	BRTR				13	.306

LAPIHUSKA, ANDREW "APPLES"
B.NOV.1,1922 LEESBURG,N.J.

YR	CL	LEA	POS	GP	G	REC
1942	PHI	N	P		3	0- 2
1943	PHI	N	P		1	0- 0
	BLTR				4	0- 2

LA POINTE, RALPH JOHN
B.JAN.8,1922 WINOOSKI,VT.
D.SEPT.15,1967 BURLINGTON ,VT.

YR	CL	LEA	POS	GP	G	REC
1947	PHI	N	S		56	.308
1948	STL	N	2-S-3		87	.225
	BRTR				143	.266

LA PORTE, FRANK BREYFOGLE "POT"
B.FEB.6,1880 ULRICHSVILLE,OHIO
D.SEPT.25,1939 NEWCOMERSTOWN,O.

YR	CL	LEA	POS	GP	G	REC
1905	NY	A	2		11	.375
1906	NY	A	3		123	.264
1907	NY	A	3-0		130	.270
1908	BOS	A	2-3		60	.245
	NY	A	2		41	.253
1909	NY	A	2		89	.298
1910	NY	A	2-0		124	.264
1911	STL	A	2		136	.314
1912	STL	A	2		80	.308
	WAS	A	2		39	.316
1913	WAS	A	2-3-0		80	.250
1914	IND	F	2		133	.311
1915	NEW	F	2		148	.251
	BRTR				1194	.281

LAPP, JOHN WALTER "JACK"
B.SEPT.10,1884 FRAZER,PA.
D.FEB.6,1920

YR	CL	LEA	POS	GP	G	REC
1908	PHI	A	C		13	.143
1909	PHI	A	C		21	.336
1910	PHI	A	C		71	.234
1911	PHI	A	C		68	.353
1912	PHI	A	C		90	.292
1913	PHI	A	C		84	.228
1914	PHI	A	C		69	.231
1915	PHI	A	C		112	.272
1916	CHI	A	C		40	.208
	BLTR				568	.263

LA RIVIERE, EDMOND WINGO
(PLAYED UNDER NAME OF
EDMUND WINGO)

LARKER, NORMAN HOWARD "NORM"
B.DEC.27,1930 BEAVER MEADOWS,PA.

YR	CL	LEA	POS	GP	G	REC
1958	LA	N	1-0		99	.277
1959	LA	N	1-0		108	.289
1960	LA	N	1-0		133	.323
1961	LA	N	1-0		97	.270
1962	HOU	N	1-0		147	.263
1963	MIL	N	1		64	.177
	SF	N	1		19	.071
	BLTL				667	.275

LARKIN, EDWARD FRANCIS
B.JULY 1,1885 WYALUSING,PA.
D.MAR.28,1934

YR	CL	LEA	POS	GP	G	REC
1909	PHI	A	C		2	.167
	BRTR					

LARKIN, FRANK "TERRY"
B.NEW YORK,N.Y.

YR	CL	LEA	POS	GP	G	REC
1876	MUT	N	P		1	0- 1
1877	HAR	N	P-2-	56	58	29-25
			3			.228
1878	CHI	N	P	55	57	29-26
1879	CHI	N	P	55	58	30-23
1880	TRO	N	P-S-0		5	0- 5
						.118
1884	WAS	U	3		17	.257
	RIC	AA	2		39	.179
	BRTR			172	235	88-80
						.242

LARKIN, HENRY E. "TED"
B.JAN.12,1860 READING,PA.
D.JAN.31,1942 READING,PA.

YR	CL	LEA	POS	GP	G	REC
1884	ATH	AA	0		87	.296
1885	ATH	AA	0		108	.338
1886	ATH	AA	0		139	.327
1887	ATH	AA	1-0		125	.374
1888	ATH	AA	1		135	.283
1889	ATH	AA	1		133	.324
1890	CLE	P	M-1		125	.327
1891	ATH	AA	1-0		133	.277
1892	WAS	N	1		116	.282
1893	WAS	N	1		81	.322
	BRTR				1182	.313

LARKIN, STEPHEN PATRICK
B.DEC.9,1910 CINCINNATI,OHIO
D.MAY 2,1969 NORRISTOWN,PA.

YR	CL	LEA	POS	GP	G	REC
1934	DET	A	P		2	0- 0
	BRTR					

LARMORE, ROBERT MC KAHAN
B.DEC.6,1896 ANDERSON,IND.
D.JAN.15,1964 ST.LOUIS,MO.

YR	CL	LEA	POS	GP	G	REC
1918	STL	N	S		4	.285
	BRTR					

LA ROCHE, DAVID EUGENE "DAVE"
B.MAY 14,1948 COLORADO SPRINGS,
COLO.

YR	CL	LEA	POS	GP	G	REC
1970	CAL	A	P		38	4- 1
1971	CAL	A	P		56	5- 1
1972	MIN	A	P		62	5- 7
1973	CHI	N	P		45	4- 1
1974	CHI	N	P	49	50	5- 6
1975	CLE	A	P		61	5- 3
1976	CLE	A	P		61	1- 4
	BLTL			372	373	29-23

LA ROQUE, SAMUEL H. J.
B.FEB.26,1864 ST.MATHIAS,QUE.,
CANADA

YR	CL	LEA	POS	GP	G	REC
1888	DET	N	2		2	.444
1890	PIT	N	2-S		111	.242
1891	PIT	N	2		1	.000
	LOU	AA	2		9	.333
					123	.249

LA ROSE, VICTOR RAYMOND "VIC"
B.DEC.23,1944 LOS ANGELES,CAL.

YR	CL	LEA	POS	GP	G	REC
1968	CHI	N	2-S		4	.000
	BRTR					

LA ROSS, HARRY RAYMOND
B.JAN.2,1888 EASTON,PA.
D.MAR.22,1954 HINES,ILL.

YR	CL	LEA	POS	GP	G	REC
1914	CIN	N	0		22	.229

LARSEN, DONALD JAMES "DON"
B.AUG.7,1929 MICHIGAN CITY,IND.

YR	CL	LEA	POS	GP	G	REC
1953	STL	A	P-0	38	50	7-12
						.284
1954	BAL	A	P	29	44	3-21
1955	NY	A	P	19	21	9- 2
1956	NY	A	P	38	45	11- 5
1957	NY	A	P	27	31	10- 4
1958	NY	A	P	19	28	9- 6
1959	NY	A	P	25	29	6- 7
1960	KC	A	P	22	23	1-10
1961	KC	A	P-0	8	18	1- 0
						.300
	CHI	A	P		25	7- 2
1962	SF	N	P	49	52	5- 4
1963	SF	N	P		46	7- 7
1964	SF	N	P		6	0- 1
	HOU	N	P	30	31	4- 8
1965	HOU	N	P		1	0- 0
	BAL	A	P		27	1- 2
1967	CHI	N	P		3	0- 0
	BRTR			412	480	81-91
						.242

LARSEN, ERLING ADELI "SWEDE"
B.NOV.15,1913 JERSEY CITY,N.J.

YR	CL	LEA	POS	GP	G	REC
1936	BOS	N	2		3	.000
	BRTR					

LARSON, DANIEL JAMES "DAN"
B.JULY 4,1954 LOS ANGELES,CAL.

YR	CL	LEA	POS	GP	G	REC
1976	HOU	N	P	13	14	5- 8
	BRTR					

LA RUSSA, ANTHONY "TONY"
B.OCT.4,1944 TAMPA,FLA.

YR	CL	LEA	POS	GP	G	REC
1963	KC	A	2-S		34	.250
1968	OAK	A	H		5	.333
1969	OAK	A	H		8	.000
1970	OAK	A	2		52	.198
1971	OAK	A	2-S-3		23	.000
	ATL	N	2		9	.286
1973	CHI	N	R		1	.000
	BRTR				132	.199

LARY, ALFRED ALLEN "AL"
B.SEPT.26,1929 NORTHPORT,ALA.

YR	CL	LEA	POS	GP	G	REC
1954	CHI	N	P	1	2	0- 0
1955	CHI	N	H		4	.000
1962	CHI	N	P	15	23	0- 1
	BRTR			16	29	0- 1
						.250

LARY, FRANK STRONG
B.APR.10,1930 NORTHPORT,ALA.

YR	CL	LEA	POS	GP	G	REC
1954	DET	A	P		3	0- 0
1955	DET	A	P		36	14-15
1956	DET	A	P		41	21-13
1957	DET	A	P		40	11-16
1958	DET	A	P		39	16-15
1959	DET	A	P		32	17-10
1960	DET	A	P	38	39	15-15
1961	DET	A	P	36	42	23- 9
1962	DET	A	P	17	22	2- 6
1963	DET	A	P		16	4- 9
1964	DET	A	P		6	0- 2
	NY	N	P		13	2- 3
	MIL	N	P		5	1- 0
1965	NY	N	P		14	1- 3
	CHI	A	P		14	1- 0
	BRTR			350	362	128-116

LARY, LYNFORD HOBART
"LYN" OR "BROADWAY"
B.JAN.28,1906 ARMONA,CAL.
D.JAN.9,1973 DOWNEY,CAL.

YR	CL	LEA	POS	GP	G	REC
1929	NY	A	S-3		80	.309
1930	NY	A	S		117	.289
1931	NY	A	S		155	.280
1932	NY	A	S		91	.232
1933	NY	A	1-S-3-0		52	.220
1934	NY	A	S		1	.000
	BOS	A	1-S		129	.241
1935	WAS	A	S		39	.194
	STL	A	S		93	.288
1936	STL	A	S		155	.289
1937	CLE	A	S		156	.290
1938	CLE	A	S		141	.268
1939	CLE	A	S		3	.000
	BRO	N	S-3		29	.161
	STL	N	S		34	.187
1940	STL	A	2-S		27	.056
	BRTR				1302	.269

LASHER, FREDERICK WALTER "FRED"
B.AUG.19,1941 POUGHKEEPSIE,N.Y.

YR	CL	LEA	POS	GP	G	REC
1963	MIN	A	P		11	0- 0
1967	DET	A	P		17	2- 1
1968	DET	A	P		34	5- 1
1969	DET	A	P		32	2- 1
1970	DET	A	P		12	1- 3
	CLE	A	P		43	1- 7
1971	CAL	A	P		2	0- 0
	BRTR				151	11-13

LASLEY, WILLARD ALMOND
B.JULY 13,1902 MARIETTA,OHIO

YR	CL	LEA	POS	GP	G	REC
1924	STL	A	P		2	0- 0
	BBTR					

LA SORDA, THOMAS CHARLES "TOM"
B.SEPT.22,1927 NORRISTOWN,PA.

YR	CL	LEA	POS	GP	G	REC
1954	BRO	N	P		4	0- 0
1955	BRO	N	P		4	0- 0
1956	KC	A	P	18	19	0- 4
	BLTL			26	27	0- 4

NON-PLAYING MANAGER LA N 1976

YR	CL	LEA	POS	GP	G	REC

LASSETTER, DONALD O'NEAL "DON"
B.MAR.27,1933 NEWNAN,GA.
| 1957 | STL | N | O | | 4 | .154 |
| | | BRTR | | | | |

LATHAM, GEORGE WARREN "JUICE"
B.SEPT.6,1852 UTICA,N.Y.
D.MAY 26,1914
1875	BOS	NA	1		16	.320
	NH	NA	1-S-3		20	-
1877	LOU	N	1		59	.290
1882	ATH	AA	1		75	.300
1883	LOU	AA	1-2-S		90	.248
1884	LOU	AA	1		78	.161
		BRTR			338	-

LATHAM, WALTER ARLINGTON "ARLIE"
B.MAR.15,1860 W.LEBANON,N.H.
D.NOV.29,1952
1880	BUF	N	C-S-O		22	.125
1883	STL	AA	3		97	.228
1884	STL	AA	3		110	.276
1885	STL	AA	3		110	.213
1886	STL	AA	3		134	.303
1887	STL	AA	3		136	.307
1888	STL	AA	3		133	.264
1889	STL	AA	3		118	.254
1890	CHI	P	3		52	.241
	CIN	N	3		41	.250
1891	CIN	N	3		135	.271
1892	CIN	N	3		150	.239
1893	CIN	N	3		125	.296
1894	CIN	N	3		130	.313
1895	CIN	N	3		110	.310
1896	STL	N	M-3		8	.229
1899	WAS	N	2		6	.143
1909	NY	N	2		4	.000
		BRTR			1621	.266

LATHERS, CHARLES TEN EYCK "CHICK"
B.OCT.22,1888 DETROIT,MICH.
D.JULY 26,1971 PETOSKEY,MICH.
1910	DET	A	3		41	.232
1911	DET	A	3		29	.222
		BLTR			70	.228

LATHROP, WILLIAM GEORGE
B.AUG.12,1891 HANOVER,WIS.
D.NOV.20,1958
1913	CHI	A	P		6	0- 0
1914	CHI	A	P		19	1- 2
		BRTR			25	1- 2

LATIMER, CLIFFORD WESLEY "TACKS"
B.NOV.30,1877 LOVELAND,OHIO
D.APR.24,1936 LOVELAND,OHIO
1898	NY	N	C		3	.400
1899	LOU	N	C		8	.280
1900	PIT	N	C		4	.333
1901	BAL	A	C		1	.250
1902	BRO	N	C		8	.041
		TR			24	.209

LATMAN, ARNOLD BARRY "BARRY"
B.MAY 21,1936 LOS ANGELES,CAL.
1957	CHI	A	P		7	1- 2
1958	CHI	A	P		13	3- 0
1959	CHI	A	P		37	8- 5
1960	CLE	A	P		31	7- 7
1961	CLE	A	P		45	13- 5
1962	CLE	A	P		45	8-13
1963	CLE	A	P		38	7-12
1964	LA	A	P		40	6-10
1965	CAL	A	P		18	1- 1
1966	HOU	N	P		31	2- 7
1967	HOU	N	P		39	3- 6
		BRTR			344	59-68

LATTEMORE, WILLIAM HERSHEL
B.MAY 25,1884 ROXTON,TEX.
D.OCT.30,1919 COLORADO SPRINGS8
COLO.
| 1908 | CLE | A | P | | 4 | 1- 2 |
| | | BLTL | | | | |

LAU, CHARLES RICHARD "CHARLIE"
B.APR.12,1933 ROMULUS,MICH.
1956	DET	A	C		3	.222
1958	DET	A	C		30	.147
1959	DET	A	C		2	.167
1960	MIL	N	C		21	.189
1961	MIL	N	C		28	.207
	BAL	A	C		17	.170
1962	BAL	A	C		81	.294
1963	BAL	A	C		29	.188
	KC	A	C		62	.294
1964	KC	A	C		43	.271
	BAL	A	C		62	.259
1965	BAL	A	C		68	.295
1966	BAL	A	H		18	.500
1967	BAL	A	H		11	.125
	ATL	N	H		52	.200
		BLTR			527	.255

LAUDER, WILLIAM
B.FEB.23,1874 NEW YORK,N.Y.
D.MAY 20,1933
1898	PHI	N	3		97	.272
1899	PHI	N	3		149	.263
1901	PHI	A	3		2	.125
1902	NY	N	3-O		126	.239
1903	NY	N	3		108	.281
		TR			482	.262

LAUER, JOHN CHARLES "CHUCK"
B.1865 PITTSBURGH,PA.
1884	PIT	AA	P-1-	3	13	0- 2
		O				.109
1889	PIT	N	C		4	.231
1890	CHI	N	C		2	.375
		TR	3	19		0- 2
						.179

LAUGHLIN, BENJAMIN
| 1873 | RES | NA | 2-3 | | 11 | - |

LAUTERBORN, WILLIAM BERNARD
B.JUNE 12,1879 HORNELL,N.Y.
D.APR.19,1965 ANDOVER,N.Y.
1904	BOS	N	2		20	.275
1905	BOS	N	2-3		57	.185
		BRTR			77	.208

LAUZERIQUE, GEORGE ALBERT
B.JULY 22,1947 HAVANA,CUBA
1967	KC	A	P		3	0- 2
1968	OAK	A	P		1	0- 0
1969	CAK	A	P		19	3- 4
1970	MIL	A	P		11	1- 2
		BRTR			34	4- 8

LAVAGETTO, HARRY ARTHUR "COOKIE"
B.DEC.1,1912 OAKLAND,CAL.
1934	PIT	N	2		87	.220
1935	PIT	N	2-3		78	.290
1936	PIT	N	2-3		60	.244
1937	BRO	N	3		149	.282
1938	BRO	N	3		137	.273
1939	BRO	N	3		153	.300
1940	BRO	N	3		118	.257
1941	BRO	N	3		132	.277
1946	BRO	N	3		88	.236
1947	BRO	N	1-3		41	.261
		BRTR			1043	.269
NON-PLAYING MANAGER
WAS(A) 1957-60, MIN(A) 1961

LAVAN, JOHN LEONARD "DOC"
B.OCT.28,1890 GRAND RAPIDS,MICH
D.MAY 29,1952 DETROIT,MICH.
1913	STL	A	S		46	.147
	PHI	A	S		6	.067
1914	STL	A	S		74	.263
1915	STL	A	S		157	.218
1916	STL	A	S		110	.236
1917	STL	A	S		118	.239
1918	WAS	A	S		117	.278
1919	STL	N	S		100	.242
1920	STL	N	S		142	.289
1921	STL	N	S		150	.259
1922	STL	N	S-3		89	.227
1923	STL	N	1-2-S-3		50	.198
1924	STL	N	2-S		4	.000
		BRTR			1163	.246

LAVELLE, GARY ROBERT
B.JAN.3,1949 SCRANTON,PA.
1974	SF	N	P		10	0- 3
1975	SF	N	P		65	6- 3
1976	SF	N	P		65	10- 6
		BBTL			140	16-12

LAVENDER, JAMES SANFORD
B.MAR.26,1885 MONTEZUMA,GA.
D.JAN.12,1960
1912	CHI	N	P		42	16-13
1913	CHI	N	P		40	10-14
1914	CHI	N	P		37	11-11
1915	CHI	N	P		41	10-16
1916	CHI	N	P		36	10-14
1917	PHI	N	P		28	6- 8
		BRTR			224	63-76

LAVIGNE, ARTHUR DAVID
B.JAN.26,1885 WORCESTER,MASS.
D.JULY 18,1950
| 1914 | BUF | F | C | | 45 | .200 |
| | | BRTR | | | | |

LAVIN, JOHN
B.BAY CITY,MICH.
| 1884 | STL | AA | O | | 16 | .204 |

LAW, RONALD DAVID "RON"
B.MAR.14,1946 HAMILTON,ONT.,CAN.
| 1969 | CLE | A | P | | 35 | 3- 4 |
| | | BRTR | | | | |

LAW, VERNON SANDERS "VERN"
B.MAR.12,1930 MERIDIAN,IDAHO
1950	PIT	N	P		27	7- 9
1951	PIT	N	P		28	6- 9
1954	PIT	N	P-O	39	50	9-13
						.231
1955	PIT	N	P	43	44	10-10
1956	PIT	N	P		39	8-16
1957	PIT	N	P	31	34	10- 8
1958	PIT	N	P	35	36	14-12
1959	PIT	N	P	34	38	18- 9
1960	PIT	N	P		35	20- 9
1961	PIT	N	P		11	3- 4
1962	PIT	N	P		23	10- 7
1963	PIT	N	P	18	21	4- 5
1964	PIT	N	P	35	36	12-13
1965	PIT	N	P	29	34	17- 9
1966	PIT	N	P	31	34	12- 8
1967	PIT	N	P	25	26	2- 6
		BRTR		483	516	162-147
						.216

LAWING, GARLAND FREDERICK
B.AUG.29,1919 GASTONIA,N.C.
1946	CIN	N	O		2	.000
	NY	N	O		8	.167
		BRTR			10	.133

LAWLOR, MICHAEL H.
B.MAR.11,1854 TROY,N.Y.
D.AUG.3,1918
1880	TRO	N	C		4	.103
1884	WAS	U	C		2	.000
					6	.059

LAWRENCE, BROOKS ULYSSES "BROOKS" OR "BULL"
B.JAN.30,1925 SPRINGFIELD,OHIO
1954	STL	N	P		35	15- 6
1955	STL	N	P		46	3- 8
1956	CIN	N	P		49	19-10
1957	CIN	N	P		49	16-13
1958	CIN	N	P		46	8-13
1959	CIN	N	P		43	7-12
1960	CIN	N	P		7	1- 0
		BRTR			275	69-62

LAWRENCE, JAMES ROSS "JIM"
B.FEB.12,1939 CALEDONIA,ONT.,CAN
| 1963 | CLE | A | C | | 2 | .000 |
| | | BLTR | | | | |

LAWRENCE, ROBERT ANDREW "LARRY"
B.DEC.14,1899 BROOKLYN,N.Y.
| 1924 | CHI | A | P | | 1 | 0- 0 |
| | | BRTR | | | | |

LAWRENCE, WILLIAM HENRY
B.MAR.11,1906 SAN MATEO,CAL.
| 1932 | DET | A | O | | 25 | .217 |
| | | BRTR | | | | |

LAWRY, OTIS CARROLL
B.NOV.1,1893 FAIRFIELD,ME.
D.OCT.23,1965 CHINA,MAINE
1916	PHI	A	2		41	.203
1917	PHI	A	2		30	.164
		BLTR			71	.191

LAWSON, ALBERT W.
B.BLOOMINGTON,ILL.

YR	CL	LEA	POS	GP	G	REC
1890	BOS	N	P		1	0-1
	PIT	N	P		2	0-1
	BRTR				3	0-2

LAWSON, ALFRED VOYLE "ROXIE"
B.APR.13,1906 DONNELLSON,IOWA

YR	CL	LEA	POS	GP	G	REC
1930	CLE	A	P		7	1-2
1931	CLE	A	P		17	0-2
1933	DET	A	P		4	0-1
1935	DET	A	P		7	3-1
1936	DET	A	P		41	8-6
1937	DET	A	P		37	18-7
1938	DET	A	P		27	8-9
1939	DET	A	P		2	1-1
	STL	A	P	36	37	3-7
1940	STL	A	P		30	5-3
	BRTR			208	209	47-39

LAWSON, ROBERT BAKER
B.AUG.23,1876 BROOKNEAL,VA.
D.OCT.28,1952 CHAPEL HILL,N.C.

YR	CL	LEA	POS	GP	G	REC
1901	BOS	N	P		10	2-2
1902	BAL	A	P		3	0-2
	BRTR				13	2-4

LAWSON, STEVEN GEORGE "STEVE"
B.DEC.28,1950 OAKLAND,CAL.

YR	CL	LEA	POS	GP	G	REC
1972	TEX	A	P		13	0-0
	BRTL					

LAXTON, WILLIAM HARRY "BILL"
B.JAN.5,1948 CAMDEN,N.J.

YR	CL	LEA	POS	GP	G	REC
1970	PHI	N	P		2	0-0
1971	SD	N	P		18	0-2
1974	SD	N	P		30	0-1
1976	DET	A	P		26	0-5
	BLTL				76	0-8

LAYDEN, EUGENE FRANCIS
B.MAR.14,1894 PITTSBURGH,PA.

YR	CL	LEA	POS	GP	G	REC
1915	NY	A	O		3	.286
	BLTL					

LAYDON, PETER JOHN "PETE"
B.DEC.30,1919 DALLAS,TEX.

YR	CL	LEA	POS	GP	G	REC
1948	STL	A	O		41	.250
	BRTR					

LAYNE, HERMAN
B.FEB.13,1901 NEW HAVEN,W.VA.
D.AUG.27,1973 GALLIPOLIS,OHIO

YR	CL	LEA	POS	GP	G	REC
1927	PIT	N	O		11	.000
	BRTR					

LAYNE, IVORIA HILLIS "TONY"
B.FEB.23,1918 WHITWELL,TENN.

YR	CL	LEA	POS	GP	G	REC
1941	WAS	A	3		13	.280
1944	WAS	A	2-3		33	.195
1945	WAS	A	3		61	.299
	BLTR				107	.264

LAYTON, LESTER LEE "LES"
B.NOV.18,1921 NARDIN,OKLA.

YR	CL	LEA	POS	GP	G	REC
1948	NY	N	O		63	.231
	BRTR					

LAZAR, JOHN DANIEL "DANNY"
B.NOV.14,1943 EAST CHICAGO,IND.

YR	CL	LEA	POS	GP	G	REC
1968	CHI	A	P		8	0-1
1969	CHI	A	P		9	0-0
	BLTL				17	0-1

LAZOR, JOHN PAUL "JOHNNY"
B.SEPT.9,1912 TAYLOR,WASH.

YR	CL	LEA	POS	GP	G	REC
1943	BOS	A	O		83	.226
1944	BOS	A	C-O		16	.083
1945	BOS	A	O		101	.310
1946	BOS	A	O		23	.138
	BLTR				223	.263

LAZZERI, ANTHONY MICHAEL
"TONY" OR "POOSH 'EM UP TONY"
B.DEC.6,1903 SAN FRANCISCO,CAL.
D.AUG.6,1948

YR	CL	LEA	POS	GP	G	REC
1926	NY	A	2		155	.275
1927	NY	A	2-S		153	.309
1928	NY	A	2		116	.332
1929	NY	A	2		147	.354
1930	NY	A	2-3		143	.303
1931	NY	A	2-3		135	.267
1932	NY	A	2		142	.300
1933	NY	A	2		139	.294
1934	NY	A	2-3		123	.267
1935	NY	A	2-S		130	.273
1936	NY	A	2		150	.287
1937	NY	A	2		126	.244
1938	CHI	N	S		54	.267
1939	BRO	N	2-3		14	.282
	NY	A	3		13	.295
	BRTR				1740	.292

LEACH, FREDERICK M. "FREDDY"
B.NOV.23,1897 SPRINGFIELD,MO.

YR	CL	LEA	POS	GP	G	REC
1923	PHI	N	O		52	.260
1924	PHI	N	O		8	.464
1925	PHI	N	O		65	.312
1926	PHI	N	O		129	.329
1927	PHI	N	O		140	.306
1928	PHI	N	1-O		145	.304
1929	NY	N	O		113	.290
1930	NY	N	O		126	.327
1931	NY	N	O		129	.309
1932	BOS	N	O		84	.247
	BLTR				991	.307

LEACH, THOMAS WILLIAM "TOMMY"
B.NOV.4,1877 FRENCH CREEK,N.Y.
D.SEPT.29,1969 HAINES CITY,FLA.

YR	CL	LEA	POS	GP	G	REC
1898	LOU	N	3		3	.300
1899	LOU	N	S-3		106	.289
1900	PIT	N	3		45	.215
1901	PIT	N	3		93	.298
1902	PIT	N	3		135	.280
1903	PIT	N	3		127	.298
1904	PIT	N	3		146	.257
1905	PIT	N	3-O		131	.257
1906	PIT	N	3-O		126	.286
1907	PIT	N	3-O		149	.303
1908	PIT	N	3		152	.259
1909	PIT	N	O		151	.261
1910	PIT	N	O		133	.270
1911	PIT	N	O		102	.238
1912	PIT	N	O		28	.299
	CHI	N	O		82	.240
1913	CHI	N	O		131	.287
1914	CHI	N	3-O		153	.263
1915	CIN	N	O		107	.224
1918	PIT	N	S-O		30	.194
	BRTR				2130	.270

LEADLEY, ROBERT H.
B.DETROIT,MICH.
NON-PLAYING MANAGER
DET(N) 1886, CLE(N) 1890-91

LEAHY, DANIEL C.
B.AUG.8,1870 NASHVILLE,TENN.
D.DEC.25,1915

YR	CL	LEA	POS	GP	G	REC
1896	PHI	N	S		2	.333

LEAHY, THOMAS JOSEPH
B.JUNE 2,1869 NEW HAVEN,CONN.
D.JUNE 12,1951

YR	CL	LEA	POS	GP	G	REC
1897	PHI	N	O		23	.242
	WAS	N	C-2-3-O		20	.426
1898	WAS	N	C		15	.182
1901	MIL	A	C		33	.240
	PHI	A	C		3	.294
1905	STL	N	C		29	.227
	TR				123	.256

LEAR, CHARLES BERNARD "KING"
B.JAN.23,1891 GREENCASTLE,PA.

YR	CL	LEA	POS	GP	G	REC
1914	CIN	N	P		17	1-2
1915	CIN	N	P		40	6-10
	BRTR				57	7-12

LEAR, FREDERICK FRANCIS
B.APR.7,1894 NEW YORK,N.Y.
D.OCT.13,1955

YR	CL	LEA	POS	GP	G	REC
1915	PHI	A	3		2	.000
1918	CHI	N	2		2	.000
1919	CHI	N	2		40	.224
1920	NY	N	3		31	.253
	BRTR				75	.235

LEARD, WILLIAM WALLACE
B.OCT.14,1885 ONEIDA,N.Y.
D.JAN.15,1970 SAN FRANCISCO,CAL

YR	CL	LEA	POS	GP	G	REC
1917	BRO	N	2		3	.000
	TR					

LEARY, FRANCIS PATRICK
B.FEB.26,1881 WAYLAND,MASS.
D.OCT.4,1907

YR	CL	LEA	POS	GP	G	REC
1907	CIN	N	P		2	1-1

LEARY, JOHN J.
B.1858 NEW HAVEN,CONN.

YR	CL	LEA	POS	GP	G	REC
1880	BOS	N	P-O		1	0-1
						.000
1881	DET	N	P-O	2	3	0-2
						.273
1882	PIT	AA	P-1-2-3-O	3	61	1-0
						.293
	BAL	AA	P-O	3	4	2-1
						.167
1883	LOU	AA	S		40	.183
	BAL	AA	2		3	.182
1884	ALT	U	P-3-O	3	8	0-3
						.088
	CHI	U	P-2-3-O	2	10	0-0
						.184
				14	130	3-7
						.230

LEARY, JOHN LOUIS "JACK"
B.MAY 2,1891 WALTHAM,MASS.
D.AUG.18,1961

YR	CL	LEA	POS	GP	G	REC
1914	STL	A	1		144	.265
1915	STL	A	1		75	.243
	BRTR				219	.258

LEATHERS, HAROLD LANGFORD
B.DEC.2,1898 LOS ANGELES,CAL.

YR	CL	LEA	POS	GP	G	REC
1920	CHI	N	S		7	.319
	BLTR					

LEBER, EMIL BOHMIEL
B.MAY 15,1881 CLEVELAND,OHIO
D.NOV.6,1924

YR	CL	LEA	POS	GP	G	REC
1905	CLE	A	3		2	.000
	TR					

LE BOURVEAU, DE WITT WILEY
"BEVO"
B.AUG.24,1896 DANA,CAL.
D.DEC.9,1947 NEVADA CITY,CAL.

YR	CL	LEA	POS	GP	G	REC
1919	PHI	N	O		17	.270
1920	PHI	N	O		84	.257
1921	PHI	N	O		93	.295
1922	PHI	N	O		74	.269
1929	PHI	A	O		12	.312
	BLTR				280	.275

LEDBETTER, RALPH OVERTON
B.DEC.8,1894 RUTHERFORD COLLEGE
N.C.
D.FEB.1,1969 W.PALM BEACH,FLA.

YR	CL	LEA	POS	GP	G	REC
1915	DET	A	P		1	0-0
	BRTR					

LEDWITH, MICHAEL
B.BROOKLYN,N.Y.

YR	CL	LEA	POS	GP	G	REC
1874	ATL	NA	C		1	-

LEE, CLIFFORD WALKER
B.AUG.4,1896 LEXINGTON,NEB.

YR	CL	LEA	POS	GP	G	REC
1919	PIT	N	C-O		42	.196
1920	PIT	N	C		37	.237
1921	PHI	N	1-O		88	.308
1922	PHI	N	1-3-O		122	.322
1923	PHI	N	1-O		107	.321
1924	PHI	N	1-O		21	.250
	CIN	N	O		6	.333
1925	CLE	A	O		77	.322
1926	CLE	A	O		21	.175
	BRTR				521	.300

YR	CL	LEA	POS	GP	G	REC

LEE, DONALD EDWARD "DON"
B.FEB.26,1934 GLOBE,ARIZ.

YR	CL	LEA	POS	GP	G	REC
1957	DET	A	P		11	1- 3
1958	DET	A	P		1	0- 0
1960	WAS	A	P		44	8- 7
1961	MIN	A	P		37	3- 6
1962	MIN	A	P		9	3- 3
	LA	A	P		27	8- 8
1963	LA	A	P		40	8-11
1964	LA	A	P		33	5- 4
1965	CAL	A	P		10	0- 1
	HOU	N	P		7	0- 0
1966	HOU	N	P		9	2- 0
	CHI	N	P		16	2- 1
	BRTR				244	40-44

LEE, ERNEST DUDLEY
(PLAYED UNDER NAME OF
ERNEST DUDLEY IN 1920-21)
B.AUG.22,1899 DENVER,COLO.
D.JAN.7,1971 DENVER,COLO.

YR	CL	LEA	POS	GP	G	REC
1920	STL	A	S		1	1.000
1921	STL	A	2-S		72	.167
1924	BOS	A	S		94	.253
1925	BOS	A	S		84	.224
1926	BOS	A	S		2	.143
	BLTR				253	.223

LEE, HAROLD BURNHAM "SHERIFF"
B.FEB.15,1906 LUDLOW,MISS.

YR	CL	LEA	POS	GP	G	REC
1930	BRO	N	O		22	.162
1931	PHI	N	O		44	.221
1932	PHI	N	O		149	.303
1933	PHI	N	O		46	.287
	BOS	N	O		88	.221
1934	BOS	N	O		139	.292
1935	BOS	N	O		112	.303
1936	BOS	N	O		152	.253
	BRTR				752	.275

LEE, LEONIDAS P.
(REAL NAME
LEONIDAS P. FUNKHOUSER)
B.DEC.13,1860 ST.LOUIS,MO.
D.JUNE 11,1912

YR	CL	LEA	POS	GP	G	REC
1877	STL	N	S-O		4	.278

LEE, LE RON
B.MAR.4,1948 BAKERSFIELD,CAL.

YR	CL	LEA	POS	GP	G	REC
1969	STL	N	O		7	.217
1970	STL	N	O		121	.227
1971	STL	N	O		25	.179
	SD	N	O		79	.273
1972	SD	N	O		101	.300
1973	SD	N	O		118	.237
1974	CLE	A	O		79	.233
1975	CLE	A	O		13	.130
	LA	N	O		48	.256
1976	LA	N	O		23	.133
	BLTR				614	.250

LEE, MICHAEL RANDALL "MIKE"
B.MAY 19,1941 BELL,CAL.

YR	CL	LEA	POS	GP	G	REC
1960	CLE	A	P		7	0- 0
1963	LA	A	P		6	1- 1
	BLTL				13	1- 1

LEE, ROBERT DEAN "BOB"
B.NOV.26,1937 OTTUMWA,IOWA

YR	CL	LEA	POS	GP	G	REC
1964	LA	A	P		64	6- 5
1965	CAL	A	P		69	9- 7
1966	CAL	A	P		61	5- 4
1967	LA	N	P		4	0- 0
	CIN	N	P		27	3- 3
1968	CIN	N	P		44	2- 4
	BRTR				269	25-23

LEE, ROY EDWIN
B.SEPT.28,1918 ELMIRA,N.Y.

YR	CL	LEA	POS	GP	G	REC
1945	NY	N	P		3	0- 2
	BLTL					

LEE, THOMAS F.
B.JUNE 9,1862 MILWAUKEE,WIS.
D.MAR.4,1886

YR	CL	LEA	POS	GP	G	REC
1884	CHI	N	P-S	5	6	1- 4
						.125
	BAL	U	P-1-	15	21	5- 8
			S-3-O			.300
				20	27	6-12
						.260

LEE, THORNTON STARR "LEFTY"
B.SEPT.13,1906 SONOMA,CAL.

YR	CL	LEA	POS	GP	G	REC
1933	CLE	A	P		3	1- 1
1934	CLE	A	P		24	1- 1
1935	CLE	A	P		32	7-10
1936	CLE	A	P		43	3- 5
1937	CHI	A	P		30	12-10
1938	CHI	A	P	33	34	13-12
1939	CHI	A	P		33	15-11
1940	CHI	A	P		28	12-13
1941	CHI	A	P		35	22-11
1942	CHI	A	P		11	2- 6
1943	CHI	A	P		19	5- 9
1944	CHI	A	P		15	3- 9
1945	CHI	A	P		29	15-12
1946	CHI	A	P		7	2- 4
1947	CHI	A	P		21	3- 7
1948	NY	A	P		11	1- 3
	BLTL			374	375	117-124

LEE, WILLIAM CRUTCHER
"BIG BILL"
B.OCT.21,1909 PLAQUEMINE,LA.

YR	CL	LEA	POS	GP	G	REC
1934	CHI	N	P	35	40	13-14
1935	CHI	N	P		39	20- 6
1936	CHI	N	P		43	18-11
1937	CHI	N	P		42	14-15
1938	CHI	N	P		44	22- 9
1939	CHI	N	P		37	19-15
1940	CHI	N	P		37	9-17
1941	CHI	N	P		28	8-14
1942	CHI	N	P		32	13-13
1943	CHI	N	P		13	3- 7
	PHI	N	P		13	1- 5
1944	PHI	N	P		31	10-11
1945	PHI	N	P		13	3- 6
	BOS	N	P		16	6- 3
1946	BOS	N	P		25	10- 9
1947	CHI	N	P		14	0- 2
	BRTR			462	467	169-157

LEE, WILLIAM JOSEPH
B.JAN.9,1895 BAYONNE,N.J.

YR	CL	LEA	POS	GP	G	REC
1915	STL	A	3-O		18	.186
1916	STL	A	O		7	.182
	BRTR				25	.186

LEE, WILLIAM FRANCIS "BILL"
B.DEC.28,1946 BURBANK,CAL.

YR	CL	LEA	POS	GP	G	REC
1969	BOS	A	P		20	1- 3
1970	BOS	A	P		11	2- 2
1971	BOS	A	P		47	9- 2
1972	BOS	A	P		47	7- 4
1973	BOS	A	P		38	17-11
1974	BOS	A	P		38	17-15
1975	BOS	A	P		41	17- 9
1976	BOS	A	P	24	26	5- 7
	BLTL			266	268	75-53

LEE, WYATT ARNOLD "WATTY"
B.AUG.12,1879 LYNCH'S STATION,
VA.
D.MAR.6,1936

YR	CL	LEA	POS	GP	G	REC
1901	WAS	A	P	36	42	16-16
1902	WAS	A	P-O	12	108	4- 6
						.261
1903	WAS	A	P-O	23	76	8-13
						.207
1904	PIT	N	P	5	8	1- 2
	TL			76	234	29-37
						.247

LEEK, EUGENE HAROLD "GENE"
B.JULY 15,1937 SAN DIEGO,CAL.

YR	CL	LEA	POS	GP	G	REC
1959	CLE	A	S-3		13	.222
1961	LA	A	S-3-O		57	.226
1962	LA	A	3		7	.143
	BRTR				77	.221

LEES, GEORGE EDWARD
B.FEB.2,1895 BETHLEHEM,PA.

YR	CL	LEA	POS	GP	G	REC
1921	CHI	A	C		20	.214
	BRTR					

LEEVER, SAMUEL W.
"SAM" OR "DEACON"
B.DEC.23,1871 GOSHEN,OHIO
D.MAY 19,1953 GOSHEN,OHIO

YR	CL	LEA	POS	GP	G	REC
1898	PIT	N	P		4	1- 0
1899	PIT	N	P		50	20-23
1900	PIT	N	P		28	15-13
1901	PIT	N	P		19	14- 5
1902	PIT	N	P-O		26	16- 7
						.178
1903	PIT	N	P		36	25- 7
1904	PIT	N	P		34	18-12
1905	PIT	N	P		33	19- 6
1906	PIT	N	P		36	22- 7
1907	PIT	N	P		31	14- 9
1908	PIT	N	P		38	15- 7
1909	PIT	N	P		19	8- 1
1910	PIT	N	P		26	6- 5
	BRTR				380	193-102
						.186

LEFEBVRE, JAMES KENNETH "JIM"
B.JAN.7,1943 INGLEWOOD,CAL.

YR	CL	LEA	POS	GP	G	REC
1965	LA	N	2		157	.250
1966	LA	N	2-3		152	.274
1967	LA	N	1-2-3		136	.261
1968	LA	N	1-2-3-O		84	.241
1969	LA	N	1-2-3		95	.236
1970	LA	N	1-2-3		109	.252
1971	LA	N	2-3		119	.245
1972	LA	N	2-3		70	.201
	BBTR				922	.251

LE FEBVRE, WILFRID HENRY "BILL"
B.NOV.11,1915 NATICK,R.I.

YR	CL	LEA	POS	GP	G	REC
1938	BOS	A	P		1	0- 0
1939	BOS	A	P	5	7	1- 1
1940	WAS	A	P	6	7	2- 0
1944	WAS	A	P-1	24	60	2- 4
						.258
	BLTL			36	75	5- 5
						.276

LE FEVRE, ALFRED MODESTO
B.SEPT.16,1898 NEW YORK,N.Y.

YR	CL	LEA	POS	GP	G	REC
1920	NY	N	2-S		17	.148
	BRTR					

LEFLER, WADE HAMPTON
B.JUNE 5,1897 COOLEEMEE,N.C.

YR	CL	LEA	POS	GP	G	REC
1924	BOS	N	H		1	.000
	WAS	A	O		5	.625
	BL				6	.556

LE FLORE, RONALD "RON"
B.JUNE 16,1948 DETROIT,MICH.

YR	CL	LEA	POS	GP	G	REC
1974	DET	A	O		59	.260
1975	DET	A	O		136	.258
1976	DET	A	O		135	.316
	BRTR				330	.282

LEGETT, LOUIS ALFRED "DOC"
B.JUNE 1,1901 NEW ORLEANS,LA.

YR	CL	LEA	POS	GP	G	REC
1929	BOS	N	C		39	.160
1933	BOS	A	C		8	.200
1934	BOS	A	C		19	.289
1935	BOS	A	H		2	.000
	BRTR				68	.208

LEHANE, MICHAEL PATRICK
B.RHODE ISLAND

YR	CL	LEA	POS	GP	G	REC
1884	WAS	U	S-3		3	.333
1890	COL	AA	1		140	.185
1891	COL	AA	1		137	.217
					280	.204

LEHENY, REGIS FRANCIS
B.JAN.5,1908 PITTSBURGH,PA.

YR	CL	LEA	POS	GP	G	REC
1932	BOS	A	P		2	0- 0
	BLTL					

LEHEW, JAMES ANTHONY "JIM"
B.AUG.19,1937 BALTIMORE,MD.

YR	CL	LEA	POS	GP	G	REC
1961	BAL	A	P		2	0- 0
1962	BAL	A	P		6	0- 0
	BRTR				8	0- 0

LEHMAN, KENNETH KARL "KEN"
B.JUNE 10,1928 SEATTLE,WASH.

YR	CL	LEA	POS	GP	G	REC
1952	BRO	N	P		4	1- 2
1956	BRO	N	P		25	2- 3
1957	BRO	N	P		3	0- 0
	BAL	A	P	30	33	8- 3
1958	BAL	A	P		31	2- 1
1961	PHI	N	P	41	42	1- 1
	BLTL			134	138	14-10

YR	CL	LEA	POS	GP	G	REC

LEHNER, PAUL EUGENE
"PAUL" OR "PEANUTS"
B.JULY 1,1920 DOLOMITE,ALA.
B.DEC.27,1967 BIRMINGHAM,ALA.

YR	CL	LEA	POS	GP	G	REC
1946	STL	A	O		16	.222
1947	STL	A	O		135	.248
1948	STL	A	1-O		103	.276
1949	STL	A	1-O		104	.229
1950	PHI	A	O		114	.309
1951	PHI	A	O		9	.143
	CHI	A	O		23	.208
	STL	A	O		21	.134
	CLE	A	O		12	.231
1952	BOS	A	O		3	.667
	BLTL				540	.257

LEHR, CLARENCE EMANUEL
B.MAY 16,1887 ESCANABA,MICH.
D.JAN.31,1948
| 1911 | PHI | N | 2-S-O | | 12 | .148 |
| | TR | | | | | |

LEHR, NORMAN CARL MICHAEL
B.MAY 28,1901 ROCHESTER,N.Y.
D.JULY 17,1968 CONESUS LAKE,N.Y
| 1926 | CLE | A | P | | 4 | 0- 0 |
| | TR | | | | | |

LEIBER, HENRY EDWARD "HANK"
B.JAN.17,1912 PHOENIX,ARIZ.
1933	NY	N	O		6	.200
1934	NY	N	O		63	.241
1935	NY	N	O		154	.331
1936	NY	N	O		101	.279
1937	NY	N	O		51	.293
1938	NY	N	O		98	.269
1939	CHI	N	O		112	.310
1940	CHI	N	1-O		117	.302
1941	CHI	N	1-O		53	.216
1942	NY	N	P-O	1	58	0- 1
						.218
	BRTR			1	813	0- 1
						.288

LEIBOLD, HARRY LORAN "NEMO"
B.FEB.17,1892 BUTLER,IND.
1913	CLE	A	O		84	.260
1914	CLE	A	O		114	.264
1915	CLE	A	O		56	.246
	CHI	A	O		37	.284
1916	CHI	A	O		45	.244
1917	CHI	A	O		125	.236
1918	CHI	A	O		116	.250
1919	CHI	A	O		122	.302
1920	CHI	A	O		108	.220
1921	BOS	A	O		123	.306
1922	BOS	A	O		81	.258
1923	BOS	A	O		11	.111
	WAS	A	O		96	.305
1924	WAS	A	O		84	.293
1925	WAS	A	3-O		56	.273
	BLTR				1258	.266

LEIFER, ELMER EDWIN
B.MAY 23,1893 CLARINGTON,OHIO
D.SEPT.26,1948
| 1921 | CHI | A | O | | 9 | .300 |
| | BLTR | | | | | |

LEIFIELD, ALBERT PETER "LEFTY"
B.SEPT.5,1883 TRENTON,ILL.
D.OCT.10,1970 ALEXANDRIA,VA.
1905	PIT	N	P		8	5- 2
1906	PIT	N	P		37	18-13
1907	PIT	N	P		40	20-16
1908	PIT	N	P		34	15-14
1909	PIT	N	P		32	19- 8
1910	PIT	N	P		40	15-13
1911	PIT	N	P	42	43	16-16
1912	PIT	N	P		6	1- 2
	CHI	N	P		13	7- 2
1913	CHI	N	P		6	0- 1
1918	STL	A	P		15	2- 6
1919	STL	A	P		19	6- 4
1920	STL	A	P		4	0- 0
	BLTL			296	297	124-97

LEIGHTON, JOHN ATKINSON
B.OCT.4,1861 PEABODY,MASS.
D.OCT.31,1956
| 1890 | SYR | AA | O | | 7 | .266 |

LEINHAUSER, WILLIAM CHARLES
B.NOV.4,1893 PHILADELPHIA,PA.
| 1912 | DET | A | O | | 1 | .000 |

LEIP, EDGAR ELLSWORTH
B.NOV.29,1914 TRENTON,N.J.
1939	WAS	A	2		9	.344
1940	PIT	N	2		3	.200
1941	PIT	N	2-3		15	.200
1942	PIT	N	H		3	.000
	BRTR				30	.274

LEIPER, JOHN HENRY THOMAS
B.DEC.23,1867 CHESTER,PA.
D.AUG.23,1960 WEST GOSHEN,PA.
| 1891 | COL | AA | P | | 6 | 2- 3 |
| | TL | | | | | |

LEITH, WILLIAM "SHADY BILL"
B.MAY 31,1873 MATTEAWAN,N.Y.
D.JULY 16,1940
| 1899 | WAS | N | P | | 1 | 0- 0 |

LEITNER, GEORGE ALOYSIUS "DOC"
B.SEPT.14,1865 PIERMONT,N.Y.
D.MAY 18,1937
| 1887 | IND | N | P | | 9 | 2- 7 |

LEITNER, GEORGE MICHAEL "DUMMY"
B.JUNE 19,1871 BALTIMORE,MD.
D.FEB.20,1960
1901	PHI	A	P		1	0- 0
	NY	N	P		2	0- 2
1902	CLE	A	P		1	0- 1
	CHI	A	P		1	0- 0
					5	0- 3

LEJA, FRANK JOHN
B.FEB.7,1936 HOLYOKE,MASS.
1954	NY	A	1		12	.200
1955	NY	A	1		7	.000
1962	LA	A	1		7	.000
	BLTL				26	.043

LE JEUNE, SHELDON ALDENBERT
"LARRY"
B.JULY 22,1885 CHICAGO,ILL.
D.APR.21,1952
1911	BRO	N	O		6	.157
1915	PIT	N	O		18	.169
					24	.167

LE JOHN, DONALD EVERETT "DON"
B.MAY 13,1934 DAISYTOWN,PA.
| 1965 | LA | N | 3 | | 34 | .256 |
| | BRTR | | | | | |

LELIVELT, JOHN PATRICK "JACK"
B.NOV.14,1885 CHICAGO,ILL.
D.JAN.20,1941
1909	WAS	A	O		91	.292
1910	WAS	A	O		110	.265
1911	WAS	A	O		72	.320
1912	NY	A	O		36	.362
1913	NY	A	O		18	.214
	CLE	A	O		16	.409
1914	CLE	A	O		32	.328
	BLTR				375	.301

LELIVELT, WILLIAM JOHN
B.OCT.21,1886 CHICAGO,ILL.
D.FEB.14,1968 CHICAGO,ILL.
1909	DET	A	P		4	0- 2
1910	DET	A	P		1	0- 1
	BRTR				5	0- 3

LEMANCZYK, DAVID LAWRENCE "DAVE"
B.AUG.17,1950 SYRACUSE,N.Y.
1973	DET	A	P		1	0- 0
1974	DET	A	P		22	2- 1
1975	DET	A	P		26	2- 7
1976	DET	A	P		20	4- 6
	BRTR				69	8-14

LEMASTER, DENVER CLAYTON "DENNY"
B.FEB.25,1939 CORONA,CAL.
1962	MIL	N	P		17	3- 4
1963	MIL	N	P		46	11-14
1964	MIL	N	P		39	17-11
1965	MIL	N	P		32	7-13
1966	ATL	N	P		27	11- 8
1967	ATL	N	P		31	9- 9
1968	HOU	N	P		33	10-15
1969	HOU	N	P		38	13-17
1970	HOU	N	P		39	7-12
1971	HOU	N	P		42	0- 2
1972	MON	N	P		13	2- 0
	BRTL				357	90-105

LE MASTER, JOHNNIE LEE
B.JUNE 19,1954 PORTSMOUTH,OHIO
1975	SF	N	S		22	.189
1976	SF	N	S		33	.210
	BRTR				55	.201

LEMAY, RICHARD PAUL "DICK"
B.AUG.23,1938 CINCINNATI,OHIO
1961	SF	N	P		27	3- 6
1962	SF	N	P		9	0- 1
1963	CHI	N	P		9	0- 1
	BLTL				45	3- 8

LEMBO, STEPHEN NEAL "STEVE"
B.NOV.13,1926 BROOKLYN,N.Y.
1950	BRO	N	C		5	.167
1952	BRO	N	C		2	.200
	BRTR				7	.182

LEMON, CHESTER EARL "CHET"
B.FEB.12,1955 JACKSON,MISS.
1975	CHI	A	3-O		9	.257
1976	CHI	A	O		132	.246
	BRTR				141	.247

LEMON, JAMES ROBERT "JIM"
B.MAR.23,1928 COVINGTON,VA.
1950	CLE	A	O		12	.176
1953	CLE	A	1-O		16	.174
1954	WAS	A	O		37	.234
1955	WAS	A	O		10	.200
1956	WAS	A	O		146	.271
1957	WAS	A	1-O		137	.284
1958	WAS	A	O		142	.246
1959	WAS	A	O		147	.279
1960	WAS	A	O		148	.269
1961	MIN	A	O		129	.258
1962	MIN	A	O		12	.176
1963	MIN	A	O		7	.118
	PHI	N	O		31	.271
	CHI	A	1		36	.200
	BRTR				1010	.262
NON-PLAYING MANAGER WAS(A) 1968						

LEMON, ROBERT GRANVILLE "BOB"
B.SEPT.22,1920 SAN BERNARDINO, CAL.
1941	CLE	A	3		5	.250
1942	CLE	A	3		5	.000
1946	CLE	A	P-O	32	55	4- 5
						.180
1947	CLE	A	P-O	37	47	11- 5
						.321
1948	CLE	A	P	43	52	20-14
1949	CLE	A	P	37	46	22-10
1950	CLE	A	P	44	72	23-11
1951	CLE	A	P	42	56	17-14
1952	CLE	A	P	42	54	22-11
1953	CLE	A	P	41	51	21-15
1954	CLE	A	P	36	40	23- 7
1955	CLE	A	P	35	49	18-10
1956	CLE	A	P	39	43	20-14
1957	CLE	A	P	21	25	6-11
1958	CLE	A	P	11	15	0- 1
	BLTR			460	615	207-128
						.222
NON-PLAYING MANAGER						
KC(A) 1970-72						

LEMONDS, DAVID LEE "DAVE"
B.JULY 5,1948 CHARLOTTE,N.C.
1969	CHI	N	P		2	0- 1
1972	CHI	A	P	31	34	4- 7
	BLTL			33	36	4- 8

LEMONGELLO, MARK
B.JULY 21,1955 JERSEY CITY,N.J.
| 1976 | HOU | N | P | | 4 | 3- 1 |
| | BRTR | | | | | |

LENHARDT, DONALD EUGENE
"DON" OR "FOOTSIE"
B.OCT.4,1922 ALTON,ILL.
1950	STL	A	1-3-O		139	.273
1951	STL	A	1-O		31	.262
	CHI	A	1-O		64	.266
1952	BOS	A	O		30	.295
	DET	A	O		45	.188
	STL	A	1-O		18	.271
1953	STL	A	3-O		97	.317
1954	BAL	A	1-O		13	.152
	BOS	A	3-O		44	.273
	BRTR				481	.271

YR	CL LEA POS	GP	G	REC

LENNON, EDWARD FRANCIS
B.AUG.17,1897 PHILADELPHIA,PA.
D.SEPT.13,1947

| 1928 PHI N | P | | 5 | 0- 0 |
| BRTR | | | | |

LENNON, ROBERT ALBERT "BOB"
B.SEPT.15,1928 BROOKLYN,N.Y.

1954 NY N	H		3	.000
1956 NY N	O		26	.182
1957 CJI N	O		9	.143
BLTL			38	.165

LENNON, WILLIAM F.
B.1848 BROOKLYN,N.Y.

1871 KEK NA	M-C		11	-
1872 NAT NA	C		11	.231
1873 MAR NA	C-1		5	-
			27	-

LENNOX, JAMES EDGAR "EGGIE"
B.NOV.3,1885 CAMDEN,N.J.
D.OCT.26,1939

1906 PHI A	3		6	.059
1909 BRO N	3		121	.262
1910 BRO N	3		100	.259
1912 CHI N	3		27	.235
1914 PIT F	3		124	.317
1915 PIT F	3		55	.321
BRTR			433	.276

LENTZ

| 1872 ECK NA | C | | 4 | .133 |

LEON, EDUARDO ANTONIO "EDDIE"
B.AUG.11,1946 TUCSON,ARIZ.

1968 CLE A	S		6	.000
1969 CLE A	S		64	.239
1970 CLE A	2-S-3		152	.248
1971 CLE A	2-S		131	.261
1972 CLE A	2-S		89	.200
1973 CHI A	2-S		127	.228
1974 CHI A	2-S-3		31	.109
1975 NY A	S		1	.000
BRTR			601	.236

LEON, ISIDORO (BECERRA) "IZZY"
B.JAN.4,1911 CRUCES,LAS VILLAS,
CUBA

| 1945 PHI N | P | | 14 | 0- 4 |
| BRTR | | | | |

LEON, MAXIMINO (MOLINA) "MAX"
B.FEB.4,1950 POZO HONDO, ACULO,
MEXICO

1973 ATL N	P	12	16	2- 2
1974 ATL N	P		34	4- 7
1975 ATL N	P		50	2- 1
1976 ATL N	P		30	2- 4
BRTR		126	130	10-14

LEONARD

| 1892 STL N | O | | 1 | .000 |

LEONARD, ANDREW JACKSON "ANDY"
B.JUNE 1,1846 IRELAND
D.AUG.22,1903

1871 OLY NA	2-S-O		31	-
1872 BOS NA	2-3-O		46	.341
1873 BOS NA	2-S-O		58	.327
1874 BOS NA	2-S-O		71	.342
1875 BOS NA	2-S-3-O		80	.323
1876 BOS N	2-O		64	.277
1877 BOS N	S-O		58	.286
1878 BOS N	O		60	.259
1880 CIN N	2-S-O		33	.210
1882 STL AA	O		1	.250
BRTR			502	-

LEONARD, DENNIS PATRICK
B.MAY 18,1951 BROOKLYN,N.Y.

1974 KC A	P		5	0- 4
1975 KC A	P		32	15- 7
1976 KC A	P		35	17-10
BRTR			72	32-21

LEONARD, ELMER ELLSWORTH
B.NOV.12,1888 NAPA,CAL.

| 1911 PHI A | P | | 5 | 2- 2 |
| BRTR | | | | |

LEONARD, EMIL JOHN "DUTCH"
B.MAR.25,1909 AUBURN,ILL.

1933 BRO N	P		10	2- 3
1934 BRO N	P		44	14-11
1935 BRO N	P		43	2- 9
1936 BRO N	P		16	0- 0
1938 WAS A	P		33	12-15
1939 WAS A	P		34	20- 8
1940 WAS A	P		35	14-19
1941 WAS A	P		34	18-13
1942 WAS A	P		6	2- 2
1943 WAS A	P		31	11-13
1944 WAS A	P		32	14-14
1945 WAS A	P		31	17- 7
1946 WAS A	P		26	10-10
1947 PHI N	P		32	17-12
1948 PHI N	P		34	12-17
1949 CHI N	P		33	7-16
1950 CHI N	P		35	5- 1
1951 CHI N	P		41	10- 6
1952 CHI N	P		45	2- 2
1953 CHI N	P		45	2- 3
BRTR		640	191-181	

LEONARD, HUBERT BENJAMIN "DUTCH"
B.JULY 26,1892 LORAIN CO.,OHIO
D.JULY 11,1952

1913 BOS A	P		42	14-16
1914 BOS A	P		35	19- 5
1915 BOS A	P		32	15- 7
1916 BOS A	P		48	18-12
1917 BOS A	P		37	16-17
1918 BOS A	P		16	8- 6
1919 DET A	P		29	14-13
1920 DET A	P		28	10-17
1921 DET A	P		36	11-13
1924 DET A	P		9	3- 2
1925 DET A	P		18	11- 4
BLTL		330	139-112	

LEONARD, JOSEPH HOWARD
B.NOV.15,1894 W.CHICAGO,ILL.
D.MAY 1,1920

1914 PIT N	3		53	.198
1916 CLE A	3		3	.000
WAS A	3		42	.274
1917 WAS A	1-3		99	.192
1919 WAS A	2-3		71	.258
1920 WAS A	H		1	.000
BLTR			269	.226

LEONHARD, DAVID PAUL "DAVE"
B.JAN.22,1942 ARLINGTON,VA.

1967 BAL A	P		3	0- 0
1968 BAL A	P	28	30	7- 7
1969 BAL A	P	37	38	7- 4
1970 BAL A	P	23	25	0- 0
1971 BAL A	P	12	13	2- 3
1972 BAL A	P	14	16	0- 0
BRTR		117	125	16-14

LEOPOLD, RUDOLPH MATAS
B.JULY 27,1907 GRAND CANE,LA.
D.SEPT.3,1965 BATON ROUGE,LA.

| 1928 CHI A | P | | 2 | 0- 0 |
| BLTL | | | | |

LEOVICH, JOHN JOSEPH
B.MAY 5,1918 PORTLAND,ORE.

| 1941 PHI A | C | | 1 | .500 |
| BRTR | | | | |

LEPCIO, THADDEUS STANLEY "TED"
B.JULY 28,1930 UTICA,N.Y.

1952 BOS A	2-S-3		84	.263
1953 BOS A	2-S-3		66	.236
1954 BOS A	2-S-3		116	.256
1955 BOS A	3		51	.231
1956 BOS A	2-3		83	.261
1957 BOS A	2		79	.241
1958 BOS A	2		50	.199
1959 BOS A	2		3	.333
DET A	2-S-3		76	.279
1960 PHI N	2-S-3		69	.227
1961 CHI A	3		5	.000
MIN A	2-S-3		47	.170
BRTR			729	.245

LEPINE, LOUIS JOSEPH "PETE"
B.SEPT.5,1876 MONTREAL,QUE.,CAN
D.DEC.3,1949

| 1902 DET A | 1-O | | 29 | .202 |
| BLTL | | | | |

LEPPERT, DON EUGENE
B.NOV.20,1930 MEMPHIS,TENN.

| 1955 BAL A | 2 | | 40 | .114 |
| BLTR | | | | |

LEPPERT, DONALD GEORGE "DON"
B.OCT.19,1931 INDIANAPOLIS,IND.

1961 PIT N	C		22	.267
1962 PIT N	C		45	.266
1963 WAS A	C		73	.237
1964 WAS A	C		50	.156
BRTR			190	.229

LERCH, RANDY LOUIS
B.OCT.9,1954 SACRAMENTO,CAL.

1975 PHI N	P		3	0- 0
1976 PHI N	P		1	0- 0
BLTL			4	0- 0

LERCHEN, BERTRAM ROE
B.APR.4,1889 DETROIT,MICH.
D.JAN.7,1962

| 1910 BOS A | S | | 6 | .067 |
| TR | | | | |

LERCHEN, GEORGE EDWARD
B.DEC.1,1922 DETROIT,MICH.

1952 DET A	O		14	.156
1953 CIN N	O		22	.294
BBTR			36	.204
BL 1953				

LERIAN, WALTER IRVIN "PECK"
B.FEB.10,1903 BALTIMORE,MD.
D.OCT.22,1929

1928 PHI N	C		96	.272
1929 PHI N	C		105	.223
BRTR			201	.246

LE ROY, LOUIS PAUL "CHIEF"
B.FEB.18,1879 OMRO VILLAGE,WIS.
D.OCT.10,1944

1905 NY A	P		3	2- 1
1906 NY A	P		11	2- 0
1910 BOS A	P		1	0- 0
BRTR			15	4- 1

LERSCH, BARRY LEE
B.SEP.7,1944 DENVER,COLO.

1969 PHI N	P		10	0- 3
1970 PHI N	P		42	6- 3
1971 PHI N	P	38	44	5-14
1972 PHI N	P	36	37	4- 6
1973 PHI N	P	42	43	3- 6
1974 STL N	P		1	0- 0
BLTR		169	177	18-32
BB 1969-72				

LESHNOCK, DONALD LEE "DON"
B.NOV.25,1946 YOUNGSTOWN,OHIO

| 1972 DET A | P | | 1 | 0- 0 |
| BRTL | | | | |

LESLIE, ROY REID
B.AUG.23,1894 BAILEY,TEX.
D.APR.9,1972 SHERMAN,TEX.

1917 CHI N	1		7	.211
1919 STL N	1		12	.208
1922 PHI N	1		141	.270
BRTR			160	.266

LESLIE, SAMUEL ANDREW "SAMBO"
B.JULY 26,1906 MOSS POINT,MISS.

1929 NY N	O		1	.000
1930 NY N	H		2	.500
1931 NY N	1		53	.302
1932 NY N	1		77	.293
1933 NY N	1		40	.321
BRO N	1		96	.283
1934 BRO N	1		146	.332
1935 BRO N	1		142	.308
1936 NY N	1		117	.295
1937 NY N	1		72	.309
1938 NY N	1		76	.253

LETCHAS, CHARLIE
B.OCT.3,1915 THOMASVILLE,GA.

1939 PHI N	2		12	.227
1941 WAS A	2		2	.125
1944 PHI N	2-S-3		116	.238
1946 PHI N	2		6	.231
BRTR			136	.234

LETCHER, THOMAS F.
B.HARVARD,NEB.

| 1891 MIL AA | O | | 6 | .130 |

YR CL LEA POS GP   G   REC

LEVAN, JESSE ROY
B.JULY 15,1926 READING,PA.
```
1947 PHI N  O          2   .444
1954 WAS A  1-3        7   .300
1955 WAS A  H         16   .188
        BLTL          25   .286
```

LEVERENZ, WALTER FRED "TINY"
B.JULY 21,1887 CHICAGO,ILL.
D.MAR.19,1973 ATASCADERO,CAL.
```
1913 STL A  P         30   6-17
1914 STL A  P     27  28   1-12
1915 STL A  P          5   1- 2
        BLTL      62  63   8-31
```

LEVERETT, GORHAM VANCE "DIXIE"
B.MAR.29,1894 GEORGETOWN,TEX.
D.FEB.20,1957
```
1922 CHI A  P         33  13-10
1923 CHI A  P         38  10-13
1924 CHI A  P         21   2- 3
1926 CHI A  P          6   1- 1
1929 BOS N  P         24   3- 7
        BRTR     122  29-34
```

LEVERETTE, HORACE WILBUR
"LEVY" OR "HOD"
B.FEB.4,1889 SHREVEPORT,LA.
D.APR.10,1958
```
1920 STL A  P          3   0- 2
        BRTR
```

LEVEY, JAMES JULIUS "JIM"
B.SEPT.13,1906 PITTSBURGH,PA.
D.MAR.14,1970 DALLAS,TEX.
```
1930 STL A  S          8   .243
1931 STL A  S        139   .209
1932 STL A  S        152   .280
1933 STL A  S        141   .195
        BBTR         440   .230
        BR 1930-31
```

LEVIS, CHARLES T.
B.ST.LOUIS,MO.
```
1884 BAL U  M-1-3     88   .228
     WAS U  1          1   .000
     IND AA 1          3   .200
1885 BAL AA 1          1   .333
                      93   .226
```

LEVSEN, EMIL HENRY "DUTCH"
B.APR.29,1898 WYOMING,IOWA
D.MAR.12,1972 MINNEAPOLIS,MINN.
```
1923 CLE A  P          3   0- 0
1924 CLE A  P          4   1- 1
1925 CLE A  P          4   1- 2
1926 CLE A  P         33  16-13
1927 CLE A  P         25   3- 7
1928 CLE A  P         11   0- 3
        BRTR          80  21-26
```

LEVY, EDWARD CLARENCE
(REAL NAME
EDWARD CLARENCE WHITNER)
B.OCT.28,1916 BIRMINGHAM,ALA.
```
1940 PHI N  H          1   .000
1942 NY  A  1         13   .122
1944 NY  A  O         40   .242
        BRTR          54   .215
```

LEWALLYN, DENNIS DALE
B.AUG.11,1953 PENSACOLA,FLA.
```
1975 LA  N  P          2   0- 0
1976 LA  N  P          4   1- 1
        BRTR           6   1- 1
```

LEWANDOWSKI, DANIEL WILLIAM
"DAN"
B.JAN.6,1928 BUFFALO,N.Y.
```
1951 STL N  P          2   0- 1
        BRTR
```

LEWIS
B.BROOKLYN,N.Y.
```
1890 BUF P  P          1   0- 0
```

LEWIS, ALLAN SYDNEY
B.DEC.12,1941 COLON,PANAMA
```
1967 KC  A  H-R       34   .167
1968 OAK A  O-R       26   .250
1969 OAK A  H-R       12   .000
1970 OAK A  O-R       25   .250
1972 OAK A  O-R       24   .200
1973 OAK A  O-R       35   .000
        BBTR         156   .207
```

LEWIS, EDWARD MORGAN "PARSON"
B.DEC.25,1872 MACHYNLLETH,WALES
D.MAY 24,1936
```
1896 BOS N  P          6   1- 4
1897 BOS N  P         35  20-12
1898 BOS N  P         34  25- 8
1899 BOS N  P         28  17-11
1900 BOS N  P         26  13-12
1901 BOS A  P         38  17-16
                     167  93-63
```

LEWIS, FREDERICK MILLER
B.OCT.13,1858 BUFFALO,N.Y.
D.JUNE 5,1945
```
1881 BOS N  O         27   .195
1883 PHI N  O         38   .242
     STL AA O         50   .295
1884 STL AA O         72   .322
     STL U  O          8   .281
1885 STL N  O         45   .292
1886 CIN AA O         67   .325
                     307   .296
```

LEWIS, GEORGE EDWARD "DUFFY"
B.APR.18,1888 SAN FRANCISCO,CAL
```
1910 BOS A  O        151   .283
1911 BOS A  O        130   .307
1912 BOS A  O        154   .284
1913 BOS A  P-O   1  149   0- 0
                           .298
1914 BOS A  O        146   .278
1915 BOS A  O        152   .291
1916 BOS A  O        152   .268
1917 BOS A  O        150   .302
1919 NY  A  O        141   .272
1920 NY  A  O        107   .271
1921 WAS A  O         27   .186
        BLTL      1 1459   0- 0
                           .284
```

LEWIS, JOHN D.
B.1888 PITTSBURGH,PA.
```
1911 BOS A  2         18   .271
1914 PIT F  2        117   .234
1915 PIT F  2         77   .268
        BRTR         212   .249
```

LEWIS, JOHN KELLY "BUDDY"
B.AUG.10,1916 GASTONIA,N.C.
```
1935 WAS A  3          8   .107
1936 WAS A  3        143   .291
1937 WAS A  3        156   .314
1938 WAS A  3        151   .296
1939 WAS A  3        140   .319
1940 WAS A  3-O      148   .317
1941 WAS A  3-O      149   .297
1945 WAS A  O         69   .333
1946 WAS A  O        150   .292
1947 WAS A  O        140   .261
1949 WAS A  O         95   .245
        BLTR        1349   .297
```

LEWIS, JOHNNY JOE
B.AUG.10,1939 GREENVILLE,ALA.
```
1964 STL N  O         40   .234
1965 NY  N  O        148   .245
1966 NY  N  O         65   .193
1967 NY  N  O         13   .118
        BLTR         266   .227
```

LEWIS, PHILIP
B.OCT.7,1883 PITTSBURGH,PA.
D.AUG.8,1959
```
1905 BRO N  S        118   .254
1906 BRO N  S        135   .243
1907 BRO N  S        136   .248
1908 BRO N  S        116   .219
        BRTR         505   .242
```

LEWIS, WILLIAM BURTON "BERT"
B.OCT.3,1895 TONAWANDA,N.Y.
D.MAR.24,1950
```
1924 PHI N  P         12   0- 0
        BRTR
```

LEWIS, WILLIAM HENRY
B.OCT.15,1905 RIPLEY,TENN.
```
1933 STL N  C         15   .400
1935 STL N  C          6   .000
1936 BOS N  C         29   .306
        BRTR          50   .327
```

LEY, TERRENCE RICHARD "TERRY"
B.FEB.21,1947 PORTLAND,ORE.
```
1971 NY  A  P          6   0- 0
        BLTL
```

LEZCANO, SIXTO JOAQUIN
(CURRAS)
B.NOV.28,1953 ARECIBO,P.R.
```
1974 MIL A  O         15   .241
1975 MIL A  O        134   .247
1976 MIL A  O        145   .285
        BRTR         294   .266
```

LEZOTTE, ABEL
B.APR.13,1870 LEWISTON,ME.
```
1896 PIT N  1          7   .104
```

LIBBY, STEPHEN AUGUSTUS
B.DEC.8,1853 SCARBOROUGH,ME.
```
1879 BUF N  1          1   .000
```

LIBKE, ALBERT WALTER
B.SEPT.12,1919 TACOMA,WASH.
```
1945 CIN N  P-1- 4  130   0- 0
            O              .283
1946 CIN N  P-O   1  124   0- 0
                           .253
        BLTR      5  254   0- 0
                           .268
```

LIBRAN, FRANCISCO (ROSAS)
"FRANKIE"
B.MAY 6,1948 MAYAGUEZ,P.R.
```
1969 SD  N  S         10   .100
        BRTR
```

LIDDLE, DONALD EUGENE "DON"
B.MAY 25,1926 MT.CARMEL,ILL.
```
1953 MIL N  P         31   7- 6
1954 NY  N  P     28  29   9- 4
1955 NY  N  P         33  10- 4
1956 NY  N  P         11   1- 2
     STL N  P     14  15   1- 2
        BLTL     117 119  28-18
```

LIEBER, CHARLES EDWIN "DUTCH"
B.FEB.1,1909 ALAMEDA,CAL.
D.DEC.31,1961
```
1935 PHI A  P         19   1- 1
1936 PHI A  P          3   0- 1
        BRTR          22   1- 2
```

LIEBHARDT, GLENN IGNATIUS
B.JULY 31,1910 CLEVELAND,OHIO
```
1930 PHI A  P          5   0- 1
1936 STL A  P         24   0- 0
1938 STL A  P          2   0- 0
        BRTR          31   0- 1
```

LIEBHARDT, GLENN JOHN
B.MAR.10,1883 MILTON,IND.
D.JULY 13,1956
```
1906 CLE A  P          2   2- 0
1907 CLE A  P         38  18-14
1908 CLE A  P         38  15-16
1909 CLE A  P         12   1- 5
                      90  36-35
```

LIESE, FREDERICK RICHARD
B.OCT.7,1885 WISCONSIN
D.JUNE 30,1967 LOS ANGELES,CAL.
```
1910 BOS N  P          4   0- 0
```

LIFSIT, HENRY LANDERS
(PLAYED UNDER NAME OF
HENRY LANDERS BOSTICK)

LILLARD, ROBERT EUGENE "GENE"
B.NOV.12,1913 SANTA BARBARA,CAL
```
1936 CHI N  S-3       19   .206
1939 CHI N  P     20  23   3- 5
1940 STL N  P          2   0- 1
        BRTR      22  44   3- 6
                           .182
```

LILLARD, WILLIAM BEVERLY
B.JAN.10,1918 GOLETA,CAL.
```
1939 PHI A  S          7   .316
1940 PHI A  2-S       73   .238
        BRTR          80   .244
```

LILLIE, JAMES J.
B.1862 NEW HAVEN,CONN.
D.NOV.9,1890
```
1883 BUF N  P-2- 1   50   0- 0
            3-O            .231
1884 BUF N  P-C- 1  110   0- 1
            O              .219
1885 BUF N  1-S-O   112   .248
1886 KC  N  O       114   .175
                  2 386   0- 1
                           .217
```

LILLIS, ROBERT PERRY "BOB"
B.JUNE 2,1930 ALTADENA,CAL.

YR	CL	LEA	POS	GP	G	REC
1958	LA	N	S		20	.391
1959	LA	N	S		30	.229
1960	LA	N	2-S-3		48	.267
1961	LA	N	2-S-3		19	.111
	STL	N	2-S		86	.217
1962	HOU	N	2-S-3		129	.249
1963	HOU	N	2-S-3		147	.198
1964	HOU	N	2-S-3		109	.268
1965	HOU	N	2-S-3		124	.221
1966	HOU	N	2-S-3		68	.232
1967	HOU	N	2-S-3		37	.244
	BRTR				817	.236

LIMMER, LOUIS "LOU"
B.MAR.10,1927 NEW YORK,N.Y.

YR	CL	LEA	POS	GP	G	REC
1951	PHI	A	1		94	.159
1954	PHI	A	1		115	.231
	BLTL				209	.202

LINCOLN, EZRA PERRY
B.NOV.17,1868 RAYNHAM,MASS.
D.MAY 7,1951

YR	CL	LEA	POS	GP	G	REC
1890	CLE	N	P		15	3-10
	SYR	AA	P		3	0- 3
	TL				18	3-13

LIND, HENRY CARL "HOOKS"
B.SEPT.19,1903 NEW ORLEANS,LA.
D.AUG.2,1946 NEW YORK,N.Y.

YR	CL	LEA	POS	GP	G	REC
1927	CLE	A	2		12	.135
1928	CLE	A	2		154	.294
1929	CLE	A	2		66	.240
1930	CLE	A	2-S		24	.247
	BRTR				256	.272

LIND, JACKSON HUGH "JACK"
B.JUNE 8,1946 DENVER,COL.

YR	CL	LEA	POS	GP	G	REC
1974	MIL	A	2-S		9	.235
1975	MIL	A	1-S-3		17	.050
	BBTR				26	.135

LINDAMAN, VIVAN ALEXANDER "VIVE"
B.OCT.28,1877 CHARLES CITY,IOWA
D.FEB.13,1927

YR	CL	LEA	POS	GP	G	REC
1906	BOS	N	P		39	12-23
1907	BOS	N	P		34	11-15
1908	BOS	N	P		43	12-16
1909	BOS	N	P		15	1- 6
	BRTR				131	36-60

LINDBECK, EMERIT DESMOND "EM"
B.AUG.27,1935 KEWANEE,ILL.

YR	CL	LEA	POS	GP	G	REC
1960	DET	A	H		2	.000
	BLTR					

LINDBLAD, PAUL AARON
B.AUG.9,1941 CHANUTE,KAN.

YR	CL	LEA	POS	GP	G	REC
1965	KC	A	P		4	0- 1
1966	KC	A	P		38	5-10
1967	KC	A	P	46	48	5- 8
1968	OAK	A	P		47	4- 3
1969	OAK	A	P		60	9- 6
1970	OAK	A	P		62	8- 2
1971	OAK	A	P		8	1- 0
	WAS	A	P		43	6- 4
1972	TEX	A	P		66	5- 8
1973	OAK	A	P		36	1- 5
1974	OAK	A	P		45	4- 4
1975	OAK	A	P		68	9- 1
1976	OAK	A	P		65	6- 5
	BLTL			588	590	63-57

LINDE, LYMAN GILBERT
B.SEPT.20,1920 BEAVER DAM,WIS.

YR	CL	LEA	POS	GP	G	REC
1947	CLE	A	P		1	0- 0
1948	CLE	A	P		3	0- 0
	BRTR				4	0- 0

LINDELL, JOHN HARLAN "JOHNNY"
B.AUG.30,1916 GREELEY,COLO.

YR	CL	LEA	POS	GP	G	REC
1941	NY	A	H		1	.000
1942	NY	A	P	23	27	2- 1
1943	NY	A	O		122	.245
1944	NY	A	O		149	.300
1945	NY	A	O		41	.283
1946	NY	A	1-O		102	.259
1947	NY	A	O		127	.275
1948	NY	A	O		88	.317
1949	NY	A	O		78	.242
1950	NY	A	O		7	.190
	STL	N	O		36	.186
1953	PIT	N	P-1	27	58	5-16
						.286
	PHI	N	P-O	5	11	1- 1
						.389
1954	PHI	N	H		7	.200
	BRTR			55	854	8-18
						.273

LINDEMANN, ERNEST
B.JUNE 10,1883 NEW YORK,N.Y.
D.DEC.27,1951

YR	CL	LEA	POS	GP	G	REC
1907	BOS	N	P		1	0- 0
	BRTR					

LINDEN, WALTER CHARLES
B.MAR.27,1925 CHICAGO,ILL.

YR	CL	LEA	POS	GP	G	REC
1950	BOS	N	C		3	.400
	BRTR					

LINDERMANN, ROBERT J.
B.CHESTER,PA.

YR	CL	LEA	POS	GP	G	REC
1901	PHI	A	O		3	.100
	BRTR					

LINDQUIST, CARL EMIL
B.MAY 9,1920 MORRIS RUN,PA.

YR	CL	LEA	POS	GP	G	REC
1943	BOS	N	P		2	0- 2
1944	BOS	N	P		5	0- 0

LINDSAY, CHRISTIAN H. "PINKY"
B.JULY 21,1878 MONACA,PA.
D.JAN.25,1941

YR	CL	LEA	POS	GP	G	REC
1905	DET	A	1		88	.267
1906	DET	A	1-2		141	.224
	BRTR				229	.240

LINDSAY, WILLIAM GIBBON
B.FEB.24,1887 MADISON,N.C.
D.JULY 14,1963

YR	CL	LEA	POS	GP	G	REC
1911	CLE	A	3		19	.242
	BLTR					

LINDSEY, JAMES KENDRICK "JIM"
B.JAN.24,1900 GREENSBURG,LA.
D.OCT.25,1963 JACKSON,LA.

YR	CL	LEA	POS	GP	G	REC
1922	CLE	A	P		29	4- 5
1924	CLE	A	P		3	0- 0
1929	STL	N	P		2	1- 1
1930	STL	N	P		39	7- 5
1931	STL	N	P		35	6- 4
1932	STL	N	P		33	3- 3
1933	STL	N	P		1	0- 0
1934	CIN	N	P		4	0- 0
	STL	N	P		11	0- 1
1937	BRO	N	P		20	0- 1
	BRTR				177	21-20

LINDSTROM, AXEL OLOF
B.AUG.26,1895 GUSTAFSBERG,
SWEDEN
D.JUNE 24,1940 ASHEVILLE,N.C.

YR	CL	LEA	POS	GP	G	REC
1916	PHI	A	P		1	0- 0
	TR					

LINDSTROM, CHARLES WILLIAM "CHUCK"
B.SEPT.7,1936 CHICAGO,ILL.

YR	CL	LEA	POS	GP	G	REC
1958	CHI	A	C		1	1.000
	BRTR					

LINDSTROM, FREDERICK CHARLES "FREDDY"
B.NOV.21,1905 CHICAGO,ILL.

YR	CL	LEA	POS	GP	G	REC
1924	NY	N	2-3		52	.253
1925	NY	N	2-S-3		104	.287
1926	NY	N	3		140	.302
1927	NY	N	3-O		138	.306
1928	NY	N	3		153	.358
1929	NY	N	3		130	.319
1930	NY	N	3		148	.379
1931	NY	N	O		78	.300
1932	NY	N	3-O		144	.271
1933	PIT	N	O		138	.310
1934	PIT	N	O		97	.290
1935	CHI	N	3-O		90	.275
1936	BRO	N	O		26	.264
	BRTR				1438	.311

LINES, RICHARD GEORGE "DICK"
B.AUG.17,1938 MONTREAL,QUE.,CAN.

YR	CL	LEA	POS	GP	G	REC
1966	WAS	A	P		53	5- 2
1967	WAS	A	P		54	2- 5
	BRTL				107	7- 7

LINHART, CARL JAMES
B.DEC.14,1929 ZBOROV,CZECH.

YR	CL	LEA	POS	GP	G	REC
1952	DET	A	H		3	.000
	BLTR					

LINKE, EDWARD KARL "BABE"
B.NOV.9,1911 CHICAGO,ILL.

YR	CL	LEA	POS	GP	G	REC
1933	WAS	A	P		3	1- 0
1934	WAS	A	P	7	8	2- 2
1935	WAS	A	P		40	11- 7
1936	WAS	A	P		13	1- 5
1937	WAS	A	P	36	37	6- 1
1938	STL	A	P		21	1- 7
	BRTR			120	122	22-22

LINKE, FREDERICK L. "LADDIE"

YR	CL	LEA	POS	GP	G	REC
1910	CLE	A	P		22	5- 6
	STL	A	P		3	0- 0
					25	5- 6

LINT, ROYCE JAMES
B.JAN.1,1921 BIRMINGHAM,ALA.

YR	CL	LEA	POS	GP	G	REC
1954	STL	N	P	30	31	2- 3
	BLTL					

LINTON, CLAUDE C. "BOB"
B.APR.18,1903 EMERSON,ARK.

YR	CL	LEA	POS	GP	G	REC
1929	PIT	N	C		17	.111
	BLTR					

LINTZ, LARRY
B.OCT.10,1949 MARTINEZ,CAL.

YR	CL	LEA	POS	GP	G	REC
1973	MON	N	2-S		52	.250
1974	MON	N	2-S-3		113	.238
1975	MON	N	2-S		46	.197
	STL	N	2-S		27	.278
1976	OAK	A	2-O-R		68	.000
	BBTR				306	.232

LINZ, PHILIP FRANCIS "PHIL"
B.JUNE 4,1939 BALTIMORE,MD.

YR	CL	LEA	POS	GP	G	REC
1962	NY	A	2-S-3-O		71	.287
1963	NY	A	2-S-3-O		72	.269
1964	NY	A	2-S-3-O		112	.250
1965	NY	A	2-S-3-O		99	.207
1966	PHI	N	2-S-3		40	.200
1967	PHI	N	S-3		23	.222
	NY	N	2-S-3-O		24	.207
1968	NY	N	2		78	.209
	BRTR				519	.235

LINZY, FRANK ALFRED
B.SEP.15,1940 FT.GIBSON,OKLA.

YR	CL	LEA	POS	GP	G	REC
1963	SF	N	P		8	0- 0
1965	SF	N	P		57	9- 3
1966	SF	N	P		51	7-11
1967	SF	N	P		57	7- 7
1968	SF	N	P		57	9- 8
1969	SF	N	P		58	14- 9
1970	SF	N	P		20	2- 1
	STL	N	P		47	3- 5
1971	STL	N	P		50	4- 3
1972	MIL	A	P		47	2- 2
1973	MIL	A	P		42	2- 6
1974	PHI	N	P		22	3- 2
	BRTR				516	62-57

LI PETRI, MICHAEL ANGELO "ANGELO"
B.JULY 6,1930 BROOKLYN,N.Y.

YR	CL	LEA	POS	GP	G	REC
1956	PHI	N	P		6	0- 0
1958	PHI	N	P		4	0- 0
	BRTR				10	0- 0

YR	CL	LEA	POS	GP	G	REC

LIPON, JOHN JOSEPH
"JOHNNY" OR "SKIDS"
B.NOV.10,1922 MARTIN'S FERRY,O.

YR	CL	LEA	POS	GP	G	REC
1942	DET	A	S	34		.191
1946	DET	A	S-3	14		.300
1948	DET	A	2-S-3	121		.290
1949	DET	A	S	127		.251
1950	DET	A	S	147		.293
1951	DET	A	S	129		.265
1952	DET	A	S	39		.221
	BOS	A	S-3	79		.205
1953	DET	A	S	60		.214
	STL	A	2-3	7		.222
1954	CIN	N	H	1		.000
			BRTR	758		.259
NON-PLAYING MANAGER CLE(A) 1971

LIPP, THOMAS C.
B.1871 BALTIMORE,MD.

1897	PHI	N	P		1	0- 1

LIPSCOMB, GERARD "NIG"
B.FEB.24,1911 RUTHERFORDTON,N.C.

1937	STL	A	P-2	3	36	0- 0
						.323

LIPSKI, ROBERT PETER "BOB"
B.JULY 7,1938 SCRANTON,PA.

1963	CLE	A	C		2	.000
			BLTR			

LIS, JOSEPH ANTHONY "JOE"
B.AUG.15,1946 SOMERVILLE,N.J.

1970	PHI	N	O		13	.189
1971	PHI	N	O		59	.211
1972	PHI	N	1-O		62	.243
1973	MIN	A	1		103	.245
1974	MIN	A	1		24	.195
	CLE	A	1-3-O		57	.202
1975	CLE	A	1		9	.308
1976	CLE	A	1		20	.314
			BRTR		347	.233

LISENBEE, HORACE MILTON "HOD"
B.SEPT.23,1901 CLARKSVILLE,TENN

1927	WAS	A	P	39		18- 9
1928	WAS	A	P	16		2- 6
1929	BOS	A	P	5		0- 0
1930	BOS	A	P	37		10-17
1931	BOS	A	P	41		5-12
1932	BOS	A	P	19		0- 4
1936	PHI	A	P	19		1- 7
1945	CIN	N	P	31		1- 3
			BRTR	207		37-58

LISKA, ADOLPH JAMES
B.JULY 10,1906 DWIGHT,NEB.

1929	WAS	A	P	24		3- 9
1930	WAS	A	P	32		9- 7
1931	WAS	A	P	2		0- 1
1932	PHI	N	P	8		2- 0
1933	PHI	N	P-O	45	47	3- 1
						.071
			BRTR	111	113	17-18
						.108

LISTER, MORRIS ELMER "PETE"
B.JULY 21,1881 SAVANNA,ILL.
D.MAY 12,1948

1907	CLE	A	1		22	.277
			BRTR			

LITTELL, MARK ALAN
B.JAN.17,1953 CAPE GIRARDEAU,MO.

1973	KC	A	P	8		1- 3
1975	KC	A	P	7		1- 2
1976	KC	A	P	60		8- 4
			BLTR	75		10- 9

LITTLE, GEORGE HARRY
B.ST.LOUIS,MO.
D.JAN.25,1892

1877	STL	N	O		1	.200
	LOU	N	2		1	.000
	STL	N	O		2	.143
			TR		4	.133

LITTLE, WILLIAM ARTHUR "JACK"
B.MAR.12,1891 HART,TEX.
D.JULY 27,1961

1912	NY	N			3	.250
			BRTR			

LITTLEFIELD, RICHARD BERNARD
"DICK"
B.MAR.18,1926 DETROIT,MICH.

1950	BOS	A	P		15	2- 2
1951	CHI	A	P		4	1- 1
1952	DET	A	P		28	0- 3
	STL	A	P		7	2- 3
1953	STL	A	P	36	38	7-12
1954	BAL	A	P		3	0- 0
	PIT	N	P		23	10-11
1955	PIT	N	P		35	5-12
1956	PIT	N	P		6	0- 0
	STL	N	P		3	0- 2
	NY	N	P		31	4- 4
1957	CHI	N	P		48	2- 3
1958	MIL	N	P		4	0- 1
			BLTL	243	245	33-54

LITTLEJOHN, CHARLES CARLISLE
B.OCT.6,1901 IRENE,TEX.

1927	STL	N	P	14	15	3- 1
1928	STL	N	P	12	12	2- 1
			BRTR	26	27	5- 2

LITTRELL, JACK NAPIER
B.JAN.22,1929 LOUISVILLE,KY.

1952	PHI	A	S-3		4	.000
1954	PHI	A	S		9	.300
1955	KC	A	1-2-S		37	.200
1957	CHI	N	2-S-3		61	.190
			BRTR		111	.204

LITWHILER, DANIEL WEBSTER
"DANNY"
B.AUG.31,1917 RINGTOWN,PA.

1940	PHI	N	O		36	.345
1941	PHI	N	O		151	.305
1942	PHI	N	O		151	.271
1943	PHI	N	O		36	.258
	STL	N	O		80	.279
1944	STL	N	O		140	.264
1946	STL	N	H		6	.000
	BOS	N	3-O		79	.292
1947	BOS	N	O		91	.261
1948	BOS	N	O		13	.273
	CIN	N	3-O		106	.275
1949	CIN	N	3-O		102	.291
1950	CIN	N	O		54	.276
1951	CIN	N	O		12	.276
			BRTR		1057	.281

LIVELY, EVERETT ADRIAN "BUDDY"
B.FEB.14,1925 BIRMINGHAM,ALA.

1947	CIN	N	P		38	4- 7
1948	CIN	N	P		10	0- 0
1949	CIN	N	P		31	4- 6
			BRTR		79	8-13

LIVELY, HENRY EVERETT "JACK"
B.MAY 29,1885 JOPPA,ALA.
D.DEC.5,1967 ARAB,ALA.

1911	DET	A	P	18	20	7- 5
			BR			

LIVENGOOD, WESLEY AMOS
B.JULY 18,1911 WINSTON-SALEM,
N.C.

1939	CIN	N	P		5	0- 0
			BRTR			

LIVINGSTON, PATRICK JOSEPH
"PADDY"
B.JAN.14,1880 CLEVELAND,OHIO

1901	CLE	A	C		1	.000
1906	CIN	N	C		47	.158
1909	PHI	A	C		64	.234
1910	PHI	A	C		37	.208
1911	PHI	A	C		27	.239
1912	CLE	A	C		19	.234
1917	STL	N	C		7	.200
			BRTR		202	.208

LIVINGSTON, THOMPSON ORVILLE
"MICKEY"
B.NOV.15,1914 NEWBERRY,S.C.

1938	WAS	A	C		2	.750
1941	PHI	N	C-1		95	.203
1942	PHI	N	C-1		89	.205
1943	PHI	N	C-1		84	.249
	CHI	N	C-1		36	.261
1945	CHI	N	C-1		71	.254
1946	CHI	N	C		66	.256
1947	CHI	N	C		19	.212
	NY	N	C		5	.167
1948	NY	N	C		45	.212
1949	NY	N	C		19	.298
	BOS	N	C		28	.234
1951	BRO	N	C		2	.400
			BRTR		561	.238

LIVINGSTONE, ALBANY
B.NEW YORK
D.JAN.21,1914

1901	NY	N	P		2	0- 2

LLENAS, WINSTON ENRIQUILLO
(DAVILA)
B.SEP.23,1943 SANTIAGO,D.R.

1968	CAL	A	3		16	.128
1969	CAL	A	3		34	.170
1972	CAL	A	2-3-O		64	.266
1973	CAL	A	2-3-O		78	.269
1974	CAL	A	2-3-O-D		72	.261
1975	CAL	A	1-2-3-D		56	.186
			BRTR		300	.230

LLEWELLYN, CLEMENT MANLEY
B.MAR.1,1895 DOBSON,N.C.

1922	NY	A	P		1	1- 0
			BLTR			

LOAN, WILLIAM JOSEPH "MIKE"
B.SEPT.27,1895 PHILADELPHIA,PA.
D.NOV.21,1966

1912	PHI	N	C		1	.500
			TR			

LOANE, ROBERT KENNETH
B.AUG.6,1914 BERKELEY,CAL.

1939	WAS	A	O		3	.000
1940	BOS	N	O		13	.227
			BRTR		16	.161

LOBERT, FRANK JOHN
B.NOV.26,1883 WILLIAMSPORT,PA.
D.MAY 29,1932

1914	BAL	F	3		10	.167
			TR			

LOBERT, JOHN BERNARD "HANS"
B.OCT.18,1881 WILMINGTON,DEL.
D.SEPT.14,1968 PHILADELPHIA,PA.

1903	PIT	N	3		5	.077
1905	CHI	N	3		14	.196
1906	CIN	N	S-3		76	.310
1907	CIN	N	S		147	.246
1908	CIN	N	S-3-O		155	.293
1909	CIN	N	3		122	.212
1910	CIN	N	3		90	.309
1911	PHI	N	3		147	.285
1912	PHI	N	3		65	.327
1913	PHI	N	3		150	.300
1914	PHI	N	3		135	.275
1915	NY	N	3		106	.251
1916	NY	N	3		48	.224
1917	NY	N	3		50	.192
			BRTR		1310	.275
NON-PLAYING MANAGER
PHI(N) 1938, 42

LOCK, DON WILSON
B.JULY 27,1936 WICHITA,KAN.

1962	WAS	A	O		71	.253
1963	WAS	A	O		149	.252
1964	WAS	A	O		152	.248
1965	WAS	A	O		143	.215
1966	WAS	A	O		138	.233
1967	PHI	N	O		112	.252
1968	PHI	N	O		99	.210
1969	PHI	N	O		4	.000
	BOS	A	1-O		53	.224
			BRTR		921	.238

LOCKE, CHARLES EDWARD
B.MAY 5,1932 MALDEN,MO.

1955	BAL	A	P		2	0- 0
			BRTR			

YR	CL	LEA	POS	GP	G	REC

LOCKE, LAWRENCE DONALD "BOBBY"
B.MAR.3,1934 ROWES RUN,PA.

YR	CL	LEA	POS	GP	G	REC
1959	CLE	A	P		24	3- 2
1960	CLE	A	P	32	35	3- 5
1961	CLE	A	P		37	4- 4
1962	STL	N	P		1	0- 0
	PHI	N	P		5	1- 0
1963	PHI	N	P		9	0- 0
1964	PHI	N	P		8	0- 0
1965	CIN	N	P		11	0- 1
1967	CAL	A	P		9	3- 0
1968	CAL	A	P		29	2- 3
	BRTR			165	168	16-15

LOCKE, MARSHALL
B.INDIANAPOLIS,IND.

YR	CL	LEA	POS	GP	G	REC
1874	BAL	NA	S		1	.000
1884	IND	AA	O		7	.241
					8	.233

LOCKE, RONALD THOMAS "RON"
B.APR.4,1942 WAKEFIELD,R.I.

YR	CL	LEA	POS	GP	G	REC
1964	NY	N	P		25	1- 2
	BRTL					

LOCKER, ROBERT AUTRY "BOB"
B.MAR.15,1938 HULL,IOWA

YR	CL	LEA	POS	GP	G	REC
1965	CHI	A	P		51	5- 2
1966	CHI	A	P		56	9- 8
1967	CHI	A	P		77	7- 5
1968	CHI	A	P		70	5- 4
1969	CHI	A	P		17	2- 3
	SEA	A	P		51	3- 3
1970	MIL	A	P		28	0- 1
	OAK	A	P		38	3- 3
1971	OAK	A	P		47	7- 2
1972	OAK	A	P		56	6- 1
1973	CHI	N	P		63	10- 6
1975	CHI	N	P		22	0- 1
	BBTR				576	57-39
	BR 1965-67					

LOCKHEAD, HARRY P.
B.CALIFORNIA

YR	CL	LEA	POS	GP	G	REC
1899	CLE	N	S		146	.223
1901	DET	A	S		1	.500
	PHI	A	S		9	.088
	TR				156	.217

LOCKLEAR, GENE
B.JULY 19,1949 LUMBERTON,N.C.

YR	CL	LEA	POS	GP	G	REC
1973	CIN	N	O		29	.192
	SD	N	O		67	.240
1974	SD	N	O		39	.270
1975	SD	N	O		100	.321
1976	SD	N	O		43	.224
	NY	A	O		13	.219
	BLTR				291	.271

LOCKLIN, STUART CARLTON "STU"
B.JULY 22,1928 APPLETON,WIS.

YR	CL	LEA	POS	GP	G	REC
1955	CLE	A	O		16	.167
1956	CLE	A	O		9	.167
	BLTL				25	.167

LOCKMAN, CARROLL WALTER "WHITEY"
B.JULY 25,1926 LOWELL,N.C.

YR	CL	LEA	POS	GP	G	REC
1945	NY	N	O		32	.341
1947	NY	N	H		2	.500
1948	NY	N	O		146	.286
1949	NY	N	O		151	.301
1950	NY	N	O		129	.295
1951	NY	N	1-O		153	.282
1952	NY	N	1		154	.290
1953	NY	N	1-O		150	.295
1954	NY	N	1-O		148	.251
1955	NY	N	1-O		147	.273
1956	NY	N	1-O		48	.272
	STL	N	1-O		70	.249
1957	NY	N	1-O		133	.248
1958	SF	N	1-2-O		92	.238
1959	BAL	N	1-2-O		38	.217
	CIN	N	1-2-3-O		52	.262
1960	CIN	N	1		21	.200
	BLTR				1666	.279

NON-PLAYING MANAGER
CHI(N) 1972-74

LOCKWOOD, CLAUDE EDWARD "SKIP"
B.AUG.17,1946 BOSTON,MASS.

YR	CL	LEA	POS	GP	G	REC
1965	KC	A	3		42	.121
1969	SEA	A	P		6	0- 1
1970	MIL	A	P		27	5-12
1971	MIL	A	P	33	36	10-15
1972	MIL	A	P	29	31	8-15
1973	MIL	A	P		37	5-12
1974	CAL	A	P		37	2- 5
1975	NY	N	P		24	1- 3
1976	NY	N	P		56	10- 7
	BRTR			249	296	41-70
						.151

LOCKWOOD, MILO HATHAWAY
B.APR.7,1858 CLEVELAND,OHIO
D.OCT.9,1897

YR	CL	LEA	POS	GP	G	REC
1884	WAS	U	P-3-	10	20	1- 9
			O			.209

LODIGIANI, DARIO ANTONIO
B.JUNE 6,1916 SAN FRANCISCO,CAL

YR	CL	LEA	POS	GP	G	REC
1938	PHI	A	2-3		93	.280
1939	PHI	A	2-3		121	.260
1940	PHI	A	H		1	.000
1941	CHI	A	3		87	.239
1942	CHI	A	2-3		59	.280
1946	CHI	A	3		44	.245
	BRTR				405	.260

LOEPP, GEORGE HERBERT
B.SEPT.11,1903 DETROIT,MICH.
D.SEPT.14,1967

YR	CL	LEA	POS	GP	G	REC
1928	BOS	A	O		15	.176
1930	WAS	A	O		50	.276
	BRTR				65	.249

LOES, WILLIAM "BILLY"
B.DEC.13,1929 LONG ISLAND CITY, N.Y.

YR	CL	LEA	POS	GP	G	REC
1950	BRO	N	P		10	0- 0
1952	BRO	N	P	38	39	13- 8
1953	BRO	N	P		32	14- 8
1954	BRO	N	P		28	13- 5
1955	BRO	N	P		22	10- 4
1956	BRO	N	P		1	0- 1
	BAL	A	P		21	2- 7
1957	BAL	A	P		31	12- 7
1958	BAL	A	P		32	3- 9
1959	BAL	A	P		37	4- 7
1960	SF	N	P		37	3- 2
1961	SF	N	P		26	6- 5
	BRTR			315	316	80-63

LOFTUS, FRANCIS PATRICK
B.MAR.10,1900 SCRANTON,PA.

YR	CL	LEA	POS	GP	G	REC
1926	WAS	A	P		1	0- 0
	BRTR					

LOFTUS, RICHARD JOSEPH
B.MAR.7,1901 CONCORD,MASS.
JAN.21,1972 CONCORD,MASS.

YR	CL	LEA	POS	GP	G	REC
1924	BRO	N	1-O		46	.272
1925	BRO	N	O		51	.237
	BLTR				97	.250

LOFTUS, THOMAS JOSEPH
B.NOV.15,1856 ST.LOUIS,MO.
D.APR.16,1910

YR	CL	LEA	POS	GP	G	REC
1877	STL	N	O		3	.182
1883	STL	AA	O		6	.160
					9	.167

NON-PLAYING MANAGER CLE(AA)1888
CLE(N) 1889, CIN(N) 1890-91,
CHI(N) 1900-01, WAS(A) 1902-03

LOGAN, JOHN "JOHNNY"
B.MAR.23,1927 ENDICOTT,N.Y.

YR	CL	LEA	POS	GP	G	REC
1951	BOS	N	S		62	.219
1952	BOS	N	S		117	.283
1953	MIL	N	S		150	.273
1954	MIL	N	S		154	.275
1955	MIL	N	S		154	.297
1956	MIL	N	S		148	.281
1957	MIL	N	S		129	.273
1958	MIL	N	S		145	.226
1959	MIL	N	S		138	.291
1960	MIL	N	S		136	.245
1961	MIL	N	S		18	.105
	PIT	N	S-3		27	.231
1962	PIT	N	3		44	.300
1963	PIT	N	S-3		81	.232
	BRTR				1503	.268

LOGAN, ROBERT DEAN "LEFTY"
B.FEB.8,1910 THOMPSON,NEB.

YR	CL	LEA	POS	GP	G	REC
1935	BRO	N	P		2	0- 1
1937	DET	A	P		1	0- 0
	CHI	N	P		4	0- 0
1938	CHI	N	P		14	0- 2
1941	CIN	N	P		2	0- 1
1945	BOS	N	P		34	7-11
	BRTL				57	7-15

LOHMAN, GEORGE F. "PETE"
B.OCT.21,1864 LAKE ELMO,MINN.
D.NOV.21,1928

YR	CL	LEA	POS	GP	G	REC
1891	WAS	AA	C		32	.200

LOHR, HOWARD SYLVESTER
B.JUNE 3,1892 PHILADELPHIA,PA.

YR	CL	LEA	POS	GP	G	REC
1914	CIN	N	O		18	.213
1916	CLE	A	O		3	.143
	BRTR				21	.204

LOHRKE, JACK WAYNE "LUCKY"
B.FEB.25,1924 LOS ANGELES,CAL.

YR	CL	LEA	POS	GP	G	REC
1947	NY	N	3		112	.240
1948	NY	N	2-3		97	.250
1949	NY	N	2-S-3		55	.267
1950	NY	N	2-3		30	.186
1951	NY	N	S-3		23	.200
1952	PHI	N	2-S-3		25	.207
1953	PHI	N	2-S-3		12	.154
	BRTR				354	.242

LOHRMAN, WILLIAM LE ROY "BILL"
B.MAY 22,1913 BROOKLYN,N.Y.

YR	CL	LEA	POS	GP	G	REC
1934	PHI	N	P		4	0- 1
1937	NY	N	P		2	1- 0
1938	NY	N	P		31	9- 6
1939	NY	N	P		38	12-13
1940	NY	N	P		31	10-15
1941	NY	N	P		33	9-10
1942	STL	N	P		5	1- 1
	NY	N	P		26	13- 4
1943	NY	N	P	17	21	5- 6
	BRO	N	P		6	0- 2
1944	BRO	N	P		3	0- 0
	CIN	N	P		2	0- 1
	BRTR			198	202	60-59

LOLICH, MICHAEL STEPHEN "MICKEY"
B.SEP.12,1940 PORTLAND,ORE.

YR	CL	LEA	POS	GP	G	REC
1963	DET	A	P		33	5- 9
1964	DET	A	P		44	18- 9
1965	DET	A	P		43	15- 9
1966	DET	A	P		40	14-14
1967	DET	A	P	31	32	14-13
1968	DET	A	P	39	41	17- 9
1969	DET	A	P	37	38	19-11
1970	DET	A	P	40	42	14-19
1971	DET	A	P		45	25-14
1972	DET	A	P		41	22-14
1973	DET	A	P		42	16-15
1974	DET	A	P		41	16-21
1975	DET	A	P		32	12-18
1976	NY	N	P		31	8-13
	BBTL			539	545	215-188

LOLICH, RONALD JOHN "RON"
B.SEP.19,1946 PORTLAND,ORE.

YR	CL	LEA	POS	GP	G	REC
1971	CHI	A	O		2	.125
1972	CLE	A	O		24	.188
1973	CLE	A	O-D		61	.229
	BRTR				87	.211

LOLLAR, JOHN SHERMAN "SHERM"
B.AUG.23,1924 DURHAM,ARK.

YR	CL	LEA	POS	GP	G	REC
1946	CLE	A	C		28	.242
1947	NY	A	C		11	.219
1948	NY	A	C		22	.211
1949	STL	A	C		109	.261
1950	STL	A	C		126	.280
1951	STL	A	C-3		98	.252
1952	CHI	A	C		132	.240
1953	CHI	A	C-1		113	.287
1954	CHI	A	C		107	.244
1955	CHI	A	C		138	.261
1956	CHI	A	C		136	.293
1957	CHI	A	C		101	.256
1958	CHI	A	C		127	.273
1959	CHI	A	C-1		140	.265
1960	CHI	A	C		129	.252
1961	CHI	A	C		116	.282
1962	CHI	A	C		84	.268
1963	CHI	A	C-1		35	.233
	BRTR				1752	.264

YR	CL	LEA	POS	GP	G	REC

LOMBARDI, ERNESTO NATALI
"ERNIE" OR "SCHNOZZ"
B.APR.6,1908 OAKLAND,CAL.

1931	BRO	N	C		73	.297
1932	CIN	N	C		118	.303
1933	CIN	N	C		107	.283
1934	CIN	N	C		132	.305
1935	CIN	N	C		120	.343
1936	CIN	N	C		121	.333
1937	CIN	N	C		120	.334
1938	CIN	N	C		129	.342
1939	CIN	N	C		130	.287
1940	CIN	N	C		109	.319
1941	CIN	N	C		117	.264
1942	BOS	N	C		105	.330
1943	NY	N	C		104	.305
1944	NY	N	C		117	.255
1945	NY	N	C		115	.307
1946	NY	N	C		88	.290
1947	NY	N	C		40	.282
			BRTR		1853	.306

LOMBARDI, VICTOR ALVIN "VIC"
B.SEPT.20,1922 BERKELEY,CAL.

1945	BRO	N	P	38	45	10-11
1946	BRO	N	P	41	43	13-10
1947	BRO	N	P	33	36	12-11
1948	PIT	N	P	38	39	10- 9
1949	PIT	N	P	34	43	5- 5
1950	PIT	N	P	39	42	0- 5
			BLTL	223	248	50-51

LOMBARDO, LOUIS
B.NOV.18,1928 CARLSTADT,N.J.

1948	NY	N	P		2	0- 0
			BLTL			

LONBORG, JAMES REYNOLD "JIM"
B.APR.16,1942 SANTA MARIA,CAL.

1965	BOS	A	P		32	9-17
1966	BOS	A	P	45	46	10-10
1967	BOS	A	P		39	22- 9
1968	BOS	A	P		23	6-10
1969	BOS	A	P		29	7-11
1970	BOS	A	P		9	4- 1
1971	BOS	A	P		27	10- 7
1972	MIL	A	P		33	14-12
1973	PHI	N	P		38	13-16
1974	PHI	N	P		39	17-13
1975	PHI	N	P		27	8- 6
1976	PHI	N	P		33	18-10
			BRTR	374	375	138-122

LONERGAN, WALTER E.
B.SEPT.22,1885 S.BOSTON,MASS.
D.JAN.23,1958

1911	BOS	A	2-S-3		9	.269
			BRTR			

LONG, DANIEL W.
B.AUG.27,1867 BOSTON,MASS.
D.APR.30,1929

1888	LOU	AA	O		1	.000
1890	BAL	AA	O		21	.177
					22	.173

LONG, HERMAN C. "GERMANY" OR
"FLYING DUTCHMAN"
B.APR.13,1866 CHICAGO,ILL.
D.SEPT.17,1909 DENVER,COLO.

1889	KC	AA	S		136	.280
1890	BOS	N	S		101	.250
1891	BOS	N	S		139	.287
1892	BOS	N	S		151	.286
1893	BOS	N	S		128	.294
1894	BOS	N	S		103	.324
1895	BOS	N	S		124	.319
1896	BOS	N	S		119	.334
1897	BOS	N	S		106	.327
1898	BOS	N	S		142	.275
1899	BOS	N	S		145	.257
1900	BOS	N	S		124	.256
1901	BOS	N	S		138	.238
1902	BOS	N	2-S		120	.227
1903	NY	A	S		22	.225
	DET	A	2-S		69	.218
1904	PHI	N	2		1	.250
			BLTR	1868		.280

LONG, JAMES ALBERT
B.JUNE 29,1898 FT.DODGE,IOWA
D.SEPT.14,1970 FT.DODGE,IOWA

1922	CHI	A	C		3	.000
			BRTR			

LONG, JAMES M.
B.NOV.15,1862 LOUISVILLE,KY.
D.DEC.12,1932

1891	LOU	AA	O		6	.243
1893	BAL	N	O		55	.225
					61	.227

LONG, JEOFFREY KEITH "JEOFF"
B.OCT.9,1941 COVINGTON,KY.

1963	STL	N	H		5	.200
1964	STL	N	1-O		28	.233
	CHI	N	1-O		23	.143
			BRTR		56	.193

LONG, LESTER
B.JULY 12,1888 SUMMIT,N.J.
D.OCT.21,1958

1911	PHI	A	P		4	0- 0
			BRTR			

LONG, NELSON "RED"
B.SEPT.28,1876 HAMILTON,ONT.,
CANADA
D.AUG.11,1929

1902	BOS	N	P		1	0- 0
			BRTR			

LONG, RICHARD DALE
"DALE"
B.FEB.6,1926 SPRINGFIELD,MO.

1951	PIT	N	1		10	.167
	STL	A	1-O		34	.238
1955	PIT	N	1		131	.291
1956	PIT	N	1		148	.263
1957	PIT	N	1		7	.182
	CHI	N	1		123	.305
1958	CHI	N	C-1		142	.271
1959	CHI	N	1		110	.236
1960	SF	N	1		37	.167
	NY	A	1		26	.366
1961	WAS	A	1		123	.249
1962	WAS	A	1		67	.241
	NY	A	1		41	.298
1963	NY	A	1		14	.200
			BLTL	1013		.267

LONG, THOMAS AUGUSTUS
B.JUNE 1,1890 MITCHUM,ALA.
D.JUNE 15,1972 MOBILE,ALA.

1911	WAS	A	O		14	.208
1912	WAS	A	O		1	.000
1915	STL	N	O		140	.294
1916	STL	N	O		119	.293
1917	STL	N	O		144	.232
			BRTR	418		.269

LONG, THOMAS FRANCIS
"LITTLE HAWK"
B.APR.22,1898 MEMPHIS,TENN.
D.SEPT.16,1973 LOUISVILLE,KY.

1924	BRO	N	P		1	0- 0
			BLTL			

LONNETT, JOSEPH PAUL "JOE"
B.FEB.7,1927 BEAVER FALLS,PA.

1956	PHI	N	C		16	.182
1957	PHI	N	C		67	.169
1958	PHI	N	C		17	.140
1959	PHI	N	C		43	.172
			BRTR		143	.166

LOOK, BRUCE MICHAEL
B.JUNE 9,1943 LANSING,MICH.

1968	MIN	A	C		59	.246
			BLTR			

LOOK, DEAN ZACHARY
B.JULY 23,1937 LANSING,MICH.

1961	CHI	A	O		3	.000
			BRTR			

LOOS, PETER
B.PHILADELPHIA,PA.

1901	PHI	A	P		1	0- 1

LOPAT, EDMUND WALTER "EDDIE"
(REAL NAME
EDMUND WALTER LOPATYNSKI)
B.JUNE 21,1918 NEW YORK,N.Y.

1944	CHI	A	P	27	30	11-10
1945	CHI	A	P	26	32	10-13
1946	CHI	A	P	29	30	13-13
1947	CHI	A	P	31	35	16-13
1948	NY	A	P	33	34	17-11
1949	NY	A	P		31	15-10
1950	NY	A	P	35	36	18- 8
1951	NY	A	P		31	21- 9
1952	NY	A	P		20	10- 5
1953	NY	A	P	25	26	16- 4
1954	NY	A	P		26	12- 4
1955	NY	A	P		16	4- 8
	BAL	A	P		10	3- 4
			BLTL	340	357	166-112

NON-PLAYING MANAGER
KC(A) 1963-64

LOPATA, STANLEY EDWARD
"STAN" OR "STASH"
B.SEPT.12,1925 DELRAY,MICH.

1948	PHI	N	C		6	.133
1949	PHI	N	C		83	.271
1950	PHI	N	C		58	.209
1951	PHI	N	C		3	.000
1952	PHI	N	C		57	.274
1953	PHI	N	C		81	.239
1954	PHI	N	C-1		86	.290
1955	PHI	N	C-1		99	.271
1956	PHI	N	C-1		146	.267
1957	PHI	N	C		116	.237
1958	PHI	N	C		86	.248
1959	MIL	N	C-1		25	.104
1960	MIL	N	C		7	.125
			BRTR	853		.254

LOPATKA, ARTHUR JOSEPH
B.MAY 28,1920 CHICAGO,ILL.

1945	STL	N	P		4	1- 0
1946	PHI	N	P		4	0- 1
			BBTL		8	1- 1

LOPATYNSKI, EDMUND WALTER
(PLAYED UNDER NAME OF
EDMUND WALTER LOPAT)

LOPES, DAVID EARL "DAVEY"
R.MAY 3,1946 E.PROVIDENCE,R.I.

1972	LA	N	2		11	.214
1973	LA	N	2-S-3-O		142	.275
1974	LA	N	2		145	.266
1975	LA	N	2-S-O		155	.262
1976	LA	N	2-O		117	.241
			BRTR	570		.261

LOPEZ, ALFONSO RAMON "AL"
B.AUG.20,1908 TAMPA,FLA.

1928	BRO	N	C		3	.000
1930	BRO	N	C		128	.309
1931	BRO	N	C		111	.269
1932	BRO	N	C		126	.275
1933	BRO	N	C-2		126	.301
1934	BRO	N	C		140	.275
1935	BRO	N	C		128	.251
1936	BOS	N	C		128	.242
1937	BOS	N	C		105	.204
1938	BOS	N	C		71	.267
1939	BOS	N	C		131	.252
1940	BOS	N	C		36	.294
	PIT	N	C		59	.259
1941	PIT	N	C		114	.265
1942	PIT	N	C		103	.256
1943	PIT	N	C-3		118	.263
1944	PIT	N	C-3		115	.230
1945	PIT	N	C-3		91	.218
1946	PIT	N	C-3		56	.307
1947	CLE	A	C-3		61	.262
			BRTR	1950		.261

NON-PLAYING MANAGER
CLE(A) 1951-56,
CHI(A) 1957-65, 68-69

LOPEZ, ARTURO "ART"
B.JUNE 8,1937 MAYAGUEZ,P.R.

1965	NY	A	O		38	.143
			BLTL			

LOPEZ, AURELIO ALEJANDRO (RIOS)
B.SEPT.21,1948 TECAMACHALCO
PUEBLA,MEXICO

1974	KC	A	P		8	0- 0
			BRTR			

```
YR   CL LEA POS  GP    G    REC
```

LOPEZ, CARLOS ANTONIO (MORALES)
B.SEPT.27,1950 MAZATLAN,MEXICO
```
1976 CAL A  O            9   .000
```

LOPEZ, HECTOR HEADLEY
B.JULY 8,1932 COLON,PANAMA
```
1955 KC  A  2-3        128   .290
1956 KC  A  2-S-3-O    151   .273
1957 KC  A  2-3-O      121   .294
1958 KC  A  2-S-3-O    151   .261
1959 KC  A  2           36   .281
     NY  A  3-O        112   .283
1960 NY  A  2-3-O      131   .284
1961 NY  A  O           93   .222
1962 NY  A  2-3-O      106   .275
1963 NY  A  2-O        130   .249
1964 NY  A  3-O        127   .260
1965 NY  A  1-O        111   .261
1966 NY  A  O           54   .214
     BRTR            1451   .269
```

LOPEZ, JOSE RAMON "RAMON"
B.MAY 26,1937 LAS VILLAS,CUBA
```
1966 CAL A  P     4    5   0-1
     BRTR
```

LOPEZ, MARCELINO PONS
B.SEP.23,1943 HAVANA,CUBA
```
1963 PHI N  P     4    5   1-0
1965 CAL A  P    35   52  14-13
1966 CAL A  P    37   55   7-14
1967 CAL A  P     4    7   0-2
     BAL A  P     4    6   1-0
1969 BAL A  P         27   5-3
1970 BAL A  P         25   1-1
1971 MIL A  P    31   34   2-7
1972 CLE A  P     4        0-0
     BRTL  171   215  31-40
```

LORD, BRISTOL ROBOTHAM "BRIS"
B.SEPT.12,1883 UPLAND,PA.
D.NOV.13,1964 ANNAPOLIS,MD.
```
1905 PHI A  O          66   .239
1906 PHI A  P-O   1   118   0-0
                            .233
1907 PHI A  O          57   .182
1909 CLE A  O          69   .269
1910 CLE A  O          57   .226
     PHI A  O          69   .274
1911 PHI A  O         134   .310
1912 PHI A  O          96   .238
1913 BOS N  O          73   .251
     BRTR     1   739   0-0
                            .256
```

LORD, CARLTON
B.JAN.7,1900 PENNSYLVANIA
```
1923 PHI N  3          17   .234
     BRTR
```

LORD, HARRY DONALD
B.MAR.8,1882 PORTER,ME.
D.AUG.9,1948
```
1907 BOS A  3          10   .184
1908 BOS A  3         145   .259
1909 BOS A  3         136   .311
1910 BOS A  3          77   .243
     CHI A  3          44   .310
1911 CHI A  3         141   .321
1912 CHI A  3-O       151   .267
1913 CHI A  3         150   .263
1914 CHI A  3          21   .189
1915 BUF F  M-3        97   .273
     BLTR            972   .278
```

LORENZEN, ADOLPH ANDREAS
B.JAN.12,1893 DAVENPORT,IOWA
D.MAR.5,1963
```
1913 DET A  P     1        0-0
     BLTL
```

LOTZ, JOSEPH PETER "SMOKEY"
B.JAN.2,1891 REMSEN,IOWA
D.JAN.1,1971 CASTRO VALLEY,CAL.
```
1916 STL N  P    12        0-3
     BRTR
```

LOUDELL, ARTHUR
B.1885
```
1910 DET A  P     5        0-1
     BR
```

LOUDEN, WILLIAM "BALDY"
B.AUG.27,1885 PIEDMONT,W.VA.
D.DEC.8,1935
```
1907 NY  A  3           2   .167
1912 DET A  2         121   .241
1913 DET A  2          72   .241
1914 BUF F  S         127   .313
1915 BUF F  2-S-3     137   .280
1916 CIN N  2-S       134   .219
     BRTR            593   .261
```

LOUDENSLAGER, CHARLES E.
B.MAY 21,1881 BALTIMORE,MD.
D.OCT.31,1933 BALTIMORE,MD.
```
1904 BRO N  2           1   .000
     TR
```

LOUGHLIN, LARRY JOHN
B.AUG.16,1941 TACOMA,WASH.
```
1967 PHI N  P     3        0-0
     BLTL
```

LOUGHLIN, WILLIAM H.
B.BALTIMORE,MD.
```
1883 BAL AA O           1   .400
```

LOUGHRAN
B.NEW YORK,N.Y.
```
1884 NY  N  C-O         8   .120
```

LOUN, DONALD NELSON "DON"
B.NOV.9,1940 FREDERICK,MD.
```
1964 WAS A  P     2        1-1
     BRTL
```

LOVE, EDWARD HAUGHTON "SLIM"
B.AUG.1,1890 LOVE,MISS.
D.NOV.30,1942
```
1913 WAS A  P           5   2-0
1916 NY  A  P          20   2-0
1917 NY  A  P          33   6-5
1918 NY  A  P          38  13-12
1919 DET A  P          22   5-4
1920 DET A  P           1   0-0
     BLTL            119  28-21
```

LOVELACE, GROVER THOMAS
B.SEPT.8,1898 WOLFE CITY,TENN.
```
1922 PIT N  O           1   .000
     BRTR
```

LOVENGUTH, LYNN RICHARD
B.NOV.29,1923 CAMDEN,N.Y.
```
1955 PHI N  P          14   0-1
1957 STL N  P     2    3   0-1
     BLTR   16    17   0-2
```

LOVETT, JOHN
B.MAY 6,1877 MONDAY,OHIO
D.DEC.5,1937 MURRAY CITY,OHIO
```
1903 STL N  P     3        0-0
```

LOVETT, LEONARD WALKER
B.JULY 17,1852 LANCASTER CO.,PA
D.NOV.18,1922
```
1873 RES NA P           1   0-1
1875 CEN NA O           5    -
     BRTR   1    6    0-1
                             -
```

LOVETT, MERRITT MARWOOD
B.JUNE 15,1912 CHICAGO,ILL.
```
1933 CHI A  H           1   .000
     BRTR
```

LOVETT, THOMAS JOSEPH
B.DEC.7,1863 PROVIDENCE,R.I.
D.MAR.20,1928
```
1885 ATH AA P          16   7-8
1889 BRO AA P          30  18-10
1890 BRO N  P          44  31-11
1891 BRO N  P          42  24-18
1893 BRO N  P          18   3-6
1894 BOS N  P          15   7-4
     BR             165  90-57
```

LOVITTO, JOSEPH "JOE"
B.JAN.6,1951 SAN PEDRO,CAL.
```
1972 TEX A  O         117   .224
1973 TEX A  3-O        26   .136
1974 TEX A  1-O       113   .223
1975 TEX A  C-1-O      50   .208
     BBTR            306   .216
```

LOVRICH, PETER "PETE"
B.OCT.16,1942 BLUE ISLAND,ILL.
```
1963 KC  A  P          20   1-1
     BRTR
```

LOW, FLETCHER
B.APR.7,1893 ESSEX,MASS.
D.JUNE 6,1973 HANOVER,N.H.
```
1915 BOS N  3           1   .250
     BRTR
```

LOWDERMILK, GROVER CLEVELAND
B.JAN.15,1886 SANBORN,IND.
D.MAR.31,1968 ODIN,ILL.
```
1909 STL N  P           7   0-2
1911 STL N  P          11   0-1
1912 CHI N  P           2   0-1
1915 STL A  P          38   9-18
     DET A  P           7   4-1
1916 DET A  P           2   0-0
     CLE A  P          10   1-5
1917 STL A  P           3   2-1
1918 STL A  P          13   2-6
1919 STL A  P           7   0-0
     CHI A  P          20   5-5
1920 CHI A  P           3   0-0
     BRTR            123  23-40
```

LOWDERMILK, LOUIS BAILEY
B.FEB.23,1887 SANBORN,IND.
D.DEC.27,1975 CENTRALIA,ILL.
```
1911 STL N  P          16   3-4
1912 STL N  P           4   1-1
     BRTL             20   4-5
```

LOWE
```
1884 DET N  C           1   .250
```

LOWE, CHARLES
B.BALTIMORE,MD.
```
1872 ATL NA 2           6   .148
```

LOWE, GEORGE WESLEY
B.APR.25,1895 RIDGEFIELD PARK, N.J.
```
1920 CIN N  P           1   0-0
```

LOWE, ROBERT LINCOLN "BOBBY" OR "LINK"
B.JULY 10,1868 ALLEGHENY,PA.
D.DEC.8,1951
```
1890 BOS N  S-O        52   .280
1891 BOS N  2-O       124   .281
1892 BOS N  O         124   .244
1893 BOS N  2         120   .316
1894 BOS N  2         133   .341
1895 BOS N  2          99   .301
1896 BOS N  2          73   .320
1897 BOS N  2         121   .314
1898 BOS N  2         147   .272
1899 BOS N  2         152   .267
1900 BOS N  2         127   .279
1901 BOS N  2-3       129   .259
1902 CHI N  2-3       121   .260
1903 CHI N  2          28   .267
1904 PIT N  H           1   .000
     DET A  M-2       140   .205
1905 DET A  3-O        58   .193
1906 DET A  2-S        41   .207
1907 DET A  3          17   .243
     BRTR            1807   .275
```

LOWENSTEIN, JOHN LEE
B.JAN.27,1947 WOLF POINT,MONT.
```
1970 CLE A  2-S-3-O    17   .256
1971 CLE A  2-S-O      58   .186
1972 CLE A  1-O        68   .212
1973 CLE A  1-2-3-O    97   .292
1974 CLE A  1-2-3-O   140   .242
1975 CLE A  2-3-O-D    91   .242
1976 CLE A  1-O-D      93   .205
     BLTR            564   .239
```

YR	CL	LEA	POS	GP	G	REC

LOWN, OMAR JOSEPH "TURK"
B.MAY 30,1924 BROOKLYN,N.Y.

YR	CL	LEA	POS	GP	G	REC
1951	CHI	N	P		31	4- 9
1952	CHI	N	P		33	4-11
1953	CHI	N	P		49	8- 7
1954	CHI	N	P	15	16	0- 2
1956	CHI	N	P		61	9- 8
1957	CHI	N	P		67	5- 7
1958	CHI	N	P		4	0- 0
	CIN	N	P		11	0- 2
	CHI	A	P		27	3- 3
1959	CHI	A	P		60	9- 2
1960	CHI	A	P		45	2- 3
1961	CHI	A	P	59	60	7- 5
1962	CHI	A	P		42	4- 2
	BRTR			504	506	55-61

LOWREY, HARRY LEE "PEANUTS"
B.AUG.27,1918 CULVER CITY,CAL.

YR	CL	LEA	POS	GP	G	REC
1942	CHI	N	O		27	.190
1943	CHI	N	2-S-O		130	.292
1945	CHI	N	S-O		143	.283
1946	CHI	N	3-O		144	.257
1947	CHI	N	2-3-O		115	.281
1948	CHI	N	2-S-3-O		129	.294
1949	CHI	N	3-O		38	.270
	CIN	N	O		89	.224
1950	CIN	N	2-O		91	.227
	STL	N	2-3-O		17	.268
1951	STL	N	2-3-O		114	.303
1952	STL	N	3-O		132	.286
1953	STL	N	2-3-O		104	.269
1954	STL	N	O		74	.115
1955	PHI	N	1-2-O		54	.189
	BRTR				1401	.273

LOWRY, JOHN D.
B.BALTIMORE,MD.

YR	CL	LEA	POS	GP	G	REC
1875	NAT	NA	O		6	

LOWRY, SAMUEL JOSEPH
B.MAR.25,1920 PHILADELPHIA,PA.

YR	CL	LEA	POS	GP	G	REC
1942	PHI	A	P	1	0- 0	
1943	PHI	A	P	5	0- 0	
	BRTR			6	0- 0	

LUBY, HUGH MAX "HAL"
B.JUNE 13,1913 BLACKFOOT,IDAHO

YR	CL	LEA	POS	GP	G	REC
1936	PHI	A	2		9	.184
1944	NY	N	1-2-3		111	.254
	BRTR				120	.247

LUBY, JOHN PERKINS "PAT"
B.1868 CHARLESTON,S.C.
D.APR.24,1899

YR	CL	LEA	POS	GP	G	REC
1890	CHI	N	P-1-O		30	20- 8
						.342
1891	CHI	N	P	22	24	10-12
1892	CHI	N	P	30	40	9-21
1895	LOU	N	P		15	1- 5
	TR			97	109	40-46
						.250

LUCADELLO, JOHN "JOHNNY"
B.FEB.22,1919 THURBUR,TEX.

YR	CL	LEA	POS	GP	G	REC
1938	STL	A	3		7	.150
1939	STL	A	2		9	.233
1940	STL	A	2		17	.317
1941	STL	A	2-S-3-O		107	.279
1946	STL	A	2-3		87	.248
1947	NY	A	2		12	.083
	BBTR				239	.264

LUCAS, CHARLES FREDERICK "RED"
B.APR.28,1902 COLUMBIA,TENN.

YR	CL	LEA	POS	GP	G	REC
1923	NY	N	P		3	0- 0
1924	BOS	N	P-3	27	33	1- 4
						.333
1925	BOS	N	2		6	.150
1926	CIN	N	P-2	39	66	8- 5
						.303
1927	CIN	N	P-2-	37	80	18-11
			S-O			.313
1928	CIN	N	P	27	39	13- 9
1929	CIN	N	P	32	76	19-12
1930	CIN	N	P	33	80	14-16
1931	CIN	N	P	29	97	14-13
1932	CIN	N	P	31	76	13-17
1933	CIN	N	P	29	75	10-16
1934	PIT	N	P	29	68	10- 9
1935	PIT	N	P	20	47	8- 6
1936	PIT	N	P	27	69	15- 4
1937	PIT	N	P	20	59	8-10
1938	PIT	N	P	13	33	4- 3
	BLTR			396	907	157-135
						.281

LUCAS, FREDERICK WARRINGTON
B.JAN.19,1905 VINELAND,N.J.

YR	CL	LEA	POS	GP	G	REC
1935	PHI	N	O		20	.265
	BRTR					

LUCAS, HENRY V.
B.SEPT.5,1857 ST.LOUIS,MO.
D.NOV.15,1910
NON-PLAYING MANAGER STL(N) 1885

LUCAS, JOHN CHARLES "BUSTER"
B.FEB.10,1908 GLEN CARBON,ILL.
D.OCT.31,1970 MARYVILLE,ILL.

YR	CL	LEA	POS	GP	G	REC
1931	BOS	A	O		3	.000
1932	BOS	A	O		1	.000
	BRTL				4	.000

LUCAS, J. R. C.
NON-PLAYING MANAGER STL(N) 1877

LUCAS, RAYMOND WESLEY
B.OCT.2,1908 SPRINGFIELD,OHIO
D.OCT.9,1969 HARRISON,MICH.

YR	CL	LEA	POS	GP	G	REC
1929	NY	N	P		3	0- 0
1930	NY	N	P		6	0- 0
1931	NY	N	P		1	0- 0
1933	BRO	N	P		2	0- 0
1934	BRO	N	P		10	1- 1
	BRTR				22	1- 1

LUCE, FRANK EDWARD
B.DEC.6,1896 SPENCER,OHIO
D.FEB.3,1942

YR	CL	LEA	POS	GP	G	REC
1923	PIT	N	O		9	.500
	BLTR					

LUCEY, JOSEPH EARL
B.MAR.27,1900 HOLYOKE,MASS.

YR	CL	LEA	POS	GP	G	REC
1920	NY	A	2		3	.000
1925	BOS	A	P-S	7	10	0- 1
						.133
	BRTR			7	13	0- 1
						.118

LUCCHESI, FRANK JOSEPH
B.APR.24,1927 SAN FRANCISCO,CAL.
NON-PLAYING MANAGER
PHI(N) 1970-72, TEX(A) 1975-76

LUCID, CORNELIUS CONRAD "CON"
B.FEB.24,1869 DUBLIN,IRELAND

YR	CL	LEA	POS	GP	G	REC
1893	LOU	N	P		2	0- 1
1894	BRO	N	P		10	4- 3
1895	BRO	N	P		21	11- 6
	PHI	N	P		10	6- 3
1896	PHI	N	P		5	1- 4
1897	STL	N	P		6	1- 5
					54	23-22

LUCIER, LOUIS JOSEPH
B.MAR.23,1918 NORTHBRIDGE,MASS.

YR	CL	LEA	POS	GP	G	REC
1943	BOS	A	P		16	3- 4
1944	BOS	A	P		3	0- 0
	PHI	N	P		1	0- 0
1945	PHI	N	P		13	0- 1
	BRTR				33	3- 5

LUCKEY, HOWARD J.
B.PHILADELPHIA,PA.

YR	CL	LEA	POS	GP	G	REC
1890	ATH	AA	P		1	0- 0

LUDERUS, FREDERICK WILLIAM "FRED"
B.SEPT.12,1886 MILWAUKEE,WIS.
D.JAN.4,1961

YR	CL	LEA	POS	GP	G	REC
1909	CHI	N	1		11	.305
1910	CHI	N	1		17	.204
	PHI	N	1		19	.294
1911	PHI	N	1		146	.301
1912	PHI	N	1		148	.257
1913	PHI	N	1		155	.262
1914	PHI	N	1		121	.248
1915	PHI	N	1		141	.315
1916	PHI	N	1		146	.281
1917	PHI	N	1		154	.261
1918	PHI	N	1		125	.288
1919	PHI	N	1		138	.293
1920	PHI	N	1		16	.156
	BLTR				1337	.277

LUDOLPH, WILLIAM FRANCIS "WEE WILLIE"
B.JAN.21,1900 SAN FRANCISCO,CAL
D.APR.8,1952

YR	CL	LEA	POS	GP	G	REC
1924	DET	A	P		3	0- 0
	BRTR					

LUDWIG, WILLIAM LAWRENCE
B.MAY 27,1882 LOUISVILLE,KY.
D.SEPT.5,1947

YR	CL	LEA	POS	GP	G	REC
1908	STL	N	C		62	.182
	TR					

LUEBBE, ROY JOHN
B.SEPT.17,1900 PARKERSBURG,IOWA

YR	CL	LEA	POS	GP	G	REC
1925	NY	A	C		8	.000
	BBTR					

LUEBBER, STEPHEN LEE "STEVE"
B.JULY 9,1949 CLINTON,MO.

YR	CL	LEA	POS	GP	G	REC
1971	MIN	A	P	18	19	2- 5
1972	MIN	A	P		2	0- 0
1976	MIN	A	P		38	4- 5
	BRTR				58	6-10

LUEBKE, RICHARD RAYMOND "DICK"
B.APR.8,1935 CHICAGO,ILL.
D.DEC.4,1974 SAN DIEGO,CAL.

YR	CL	LEA	POS	GP	G	REC
1962	BAL	A	P		10	0- 1
	BRTL					

LUFF, HENRY T.
B.SEPT.14,1856 PHILADELPHIA,PA.
D.OCT.11,1916

YR	CL	LEA	POS	GP	G	REC
1875	NH	NA	P-3-	8	38	1- 7
			O			-
1882	DET	N	2-O		3	.273
	CIN	AA	1-O		28	.223
1883	LOU	AA	1-U		6	.174
1884	KEY	U	1-O		24	.266
	KC	U	3-O		5	.053
				8	104	1- 7
						-

LUHRSEN, WILLIAM FERDINAND
B.APR.14,1884 BUCKLEY,ILL.
D.AUG.15,1973 LITTLE ROCK,ARK.

YR	CL	LEA	POS	GP	G	REC
1913	PIT	N	P		5	3- 1
	BRTR					

LUKENS, ALBERT P.
B.1872 VINELAND,N.J.

YR	CL	LEA	POS	GP	G	REC
1894	PHI	N	P		3	0- 1

LUKON, EDWARD PAUL
B.AUG.5,1920 BURGETTSTOWN,PA.

YR	CL	LEA	POS	GP	G	REC
1941	CIN	N	O		23	.267
1945	CIN	N	O		2	.125
1946	CIN	N	O		102	.250
1947	CIN	N	O		86	.205
	BLTL				213	.236

LUM, MICHAEL KEN-WAI "MIKE"
B.OCT.27,1945 HONOLULU,HAWAII

YR	CL	LEA	POS	GP	G	REC
1967	ATL	N	O		9	.231
1968	ATL	N	O		122	.224
1969	ATL	N	O		121	.268
1970	ATL	N	O		123	.254
1971	ATL	N	1-O		145	.269
1972	ATL	N	1-O		123	.228
1973	ATL	N	1-O		138	.294
1974	ATL	N	1-O		106	.233
1975	ATL	N	1-O		124	.228
1976	CIN	N	O		84	.228
	BLTL				1095	.251

LUMENTI, RAPHAEL ANTHONY "RALPH"
B.DEC.21,1936 MILFORD,MASS.

YR	CL	LEA	POS	GP	G	REC
1957	WAS	A	P		3	0- 1
1958	WAS	A	P		8	1- 2
1959	WAS	A	P		2	0- 0
	BLTL				13	1- 3

LUMLEY, HARRY G. "JUDGE"
B.SEPT.29,1880 FOREST CITY,PA.
D.MAY 22,1938

YR	CL	LEA	POS	GP	G	REC
1904	BRO	N	O		150	.279
1905	BRO	N	O		129	.293
1906	BRO	N	O		131	.324
1907	BRO	N	O		118	.267
1908	BRO	N	O		116	.216
1909	BRO	N	M-O		52	.250
1910	BRO	N	O		8	.100
					704	.275

YR	CL	LEA	POS	GP	G	REC

LUMPE, JERRY DEAN
B.JUNE 2,1933 LINCOLN,MO.

YR	CL	LEA	POS	GP	G	REC
1956	NY	A	S-3		20	.258
1957	NY	A	S-3		40	.340
1958	NY	A	S-3		81	.254
1959	NY	A	2-S-3		18	.222
	KC	A	2-S		108	.243
1960	KC	A	2-S		146	.272
1961	KC	A	2		148	.293
1962	KC	A	2-S		156	.301
1963	KC	A	2		157	.271
1964	DET	A	2		158	.256
1965	DET	A	2		145	.257
1966	DET	A	2		113	.231
1967	DET	A	2-3		81	.232
	BLTR			1371		.268

LUNA, GUILLERMO ROMERO "MEMO"
B.JUNE 25,1930 TACUBAYA,MEXICO

1954	STL	N	P		1	0- 1
	BLTL					

LUND, DONALD ANDREW "DON"
B.MAY 18,1923 DETROIT,MICH.

1945	BRO	N	H		4	.000
1947	BRO	N	O		11	.300
1948	BRO	N	O		27	.188
	STL	A	O		63	.248
1949	DET	A	H		2	.000
1952	DET	A	O		8	.304
1953	DET	A	O		131	.257
1954	DET	A	O		35	.130
	BRTR			281		.240

LUND, GORDON THOMAS "GORDY"
B.FEB.23,1941 IRON MOUNTAIN,MICH

1967	CLE	A	S		3	.250
1969	SEA	A	2-S-3		20	.263
	BRTR			23		.261

LUNDBOM, JOHN FREDERICK
B.MAR.10,1877 MANISTEE,MICH.
D.OCT.31,1949

1902	CLE	A	P		8	2- 1
	BRTR					

LUNDGREN, CARL LEONARD
B.FEB.16,1880 MARENGO,ILL.
D.OCT.21,1934 MARENGO,ILL.

1902	CHI	N	P-S	18	19	9- 9
						.106
1903	CHI	N	P		27	11- 9
1904	CHI	N	P		31	17-10
1905	CHI	N	P		23	13- 4
1906	CHI	N	P	27	28	17- 6
1907	CHI	N	P		28	18- 7
1908	CHI	N	P		23	6- 9
1909	CHI	N	P		2	0- 1
	BRTR	179	181	91-55
						.157

LUNDGREN, EBIN DELMAR "DEL"
B.SEPT.21,1900 LINDSBORG,KAN.

1924	PIT	N	P		8	0- 1
1926	BOS	A	P		18	0- 2
1927	BOS	A	P		30	5-12
	BRTR			56		5-15

LUNDSTET, THOMAS ROBERT "TOM"
B.APR.10,1949 DAVENPORT,IOWA

1973	CHI	N	C		4	.000
1974	CHI	N	C		22	.094
1975	MIN	A	C		18	.107
	BBTR			44		.092

LUNTE, HARRY AUGUST
B.SEPT.15,1893 ST.LOUIS,MO.
D.JULY 27,1965 ST.LOUIS,MO.

1919	CLE	A	S		2	.195
1920	CLE	A	S		23	.197

LUPIEN, ULYSSES JOHN "TONY"
B.APR.23,1917 CHELMSFORD,MASS.

1940	BOS	A	1		10	.474
1942	BOS	A	1		128	.281
1943	BOS	A	1		154	.255
1944	PHI	N	1		153	.283
1945	PHI	N	1		15	.315
1948	CHI	A	1		154	.246
	BLTL			614		.268

LUPLOW, ALVIN DAVID "AL"
B.MAR.13,1939 SAGINAW,MICH.

1961	CLE	A	O		5	.056
1962	CLE	A	O		97	.277
1963	CLE	A	O		100	.234
1964	CLE	A	O		19	.111
1965	CLE	A	O		53	.133
1966	NY	N	O		111	.251
1967	NY	N	O		41	.205
	PIT	N	O		55	.184
	BLTR			481		.235

LUQUE, ADOLFO "DOLF"
B.AUG.4,1890 HAVANA,CUBA
D.JULY 3,1957 HAVANA,CUBA

1914	BOS	N	P		2	0- 1
1915	BOS	N	P		2	0- 0
1918	CIN	N	P-O	12	13	6- 3
						.321
1919	CIN	N	P-3	30	31	10- 3
						.125
1920	CIN	N	P		37	13- 9
1921	CIN	N	P	41	42	17-19
1922	CIN	N	P		39	13-23
1923	CIN	N	P	41	43	27- 8
1924	CIN	N	P-O	31	33	10-15
						.178
1925	CIN	N	P	36	37	16-18
1926	CIN	N	P		34	13-16
1927	CIN	N	P		29	13-12
1928	CIN	N	P		33	11-10
1929	CIN	N	P		32	5-16
1930	BRO	N	P		31	14- 8
1931	BRO	N	P		19	7- 6
1932	NY	N	P		38	6- 7
1933	NY	N	P		35	8- 2
1934	NY	N	P		26	4- 3
1935	NY	N	P		2	1- 0
	BRTR	550	558	194-179
						.227

LUSH, ERNEST BENJAMIN
B.OCT.31,1884 BRIDGEPORT,CONN.
D.FEB.26,1937

1910	STL	N	O		1	.000
	TL					

LUSH, JOHN CHARLES
B.OCT.8,1885 WILLIAMSPORT,PA.
D.NOV.18,1946

1904	PHI	N	P-1-	7	102	0- 5
			O			.276
1905	PHI	N	P		6	2- 0
1906	PHI	N	P-O	37	61	18-15
						.264
1907	PHI	N	P		12	5- 6
	STL	N	P		16	5- 9
1908	STL	N	P		38	11-18
1909	STL	N	P	34	45	11-18
1910	STL	N	P		36	14-13
	BLTL	186	316	66-84
						.253

LUSH, WILLIAM LUCAS
B.NOV.10,1873 BRIDGEPORT,CONN.
D.AUG.28,1951

1895	WAS	N	O		5	.210
1896	WAS	N	O		91	.245
1897	WAS	N	O		2	.000
1901	BOS	N	O		7	.185
1902	BOS	N	3-O		118	.231
1903	DET	A	O		117	.278
1904	CLE	A	O		138	.272
	BBTR			478		.254

LUSKEY, CHARLES MELTON
B.APR.6,1876 WASHINGTON,D.C.
D.DEC.20,1962 BETHESDA,MD.

1901	WAS	A	C-O		11	.195

LUTENBERG, CHARLES WILLIAM
B.OCT.4,1864 QUINCY,ILL.
D.DEC.24,1938

1894	LOU	N	1		70	.192

LUTTRELL, LYLE KENNETH
B.FEB.22,1930 BLOOMINGTON,ILL.

1956	WAS	A	S		38	.189
1957	WAS	A	S		19	.200
	BRTR			57		.192

LUTZ, LOUIS WILLIAM "RED"
B.DEC.17,1898 CINCINNATI,OHIO

1922	CIN	N	C		1	1.000
	BRTR					

LUTZ, ROLLIN JOSEPH
B.FEB.18,1925 KEOKUK,IOWA

1951	STL	A	1		14	.167
	BLTL					

LUTZKE, WALTER JOHN "RUBE"
B.NOV.17,1897 MILWAUKEE,WIS.
D.MAR.6,1938 GRANVILLE,WIS.

1923	CLE	A	3		143	.256
1924	CLE	A	3		106	.243
1925	CLE	A	2-3		81	.219
1926	CLE	A	3		142	.261
1927	CLE	A	3		100	.251
	BRTR			572		.249

LUZINSKI, GREGORY MICHAEL "GREG"
B.NOV.22,1950 CHICAGO,ILL.

1970	PHI	N	1		8	.167
1971	PHI	N	1		28	.300
1972	PHI	N	1-O		150	.281
1973	PHI	N	O		161	.285
1974	PHI	N	O		85	.272
1975	PHI	N	O		161	.300
1976	PHI	N	O		149	.304
	BRTR			742		.290

LYLE, ALBERT WALTER "SPARKY"
B.JULY 22,1944 DUBOIS,PA.

1967	BOS	A	P		27	1- 2
1968	BOS	A	P		49	6- 1
1969	BOS	A	P		71	8- 3
1970	BOS	A	P		63	1- 7
1971	BOS	A	P		50	6- 4
1972	NY	A	P		59	9- 5
1973	NY	A	P		51	5- 9
1974	NY	A	P		66	9- 3
1975	NY	A	P		49	5- 7
1976	NY	A	P		64	7- 8
	BLTL			549		57-49

LYLE, JAMES CLAUDE
B.JULY 24,1902 LAKE,MISS.

1925	WAS	A	P		1	0- 0
	BRTR					

LYNCH, ADRIAN RYAN
B.FEB.9,1897 LAURENS,IOWA
D.MAR.16,1934

1920	STL	A	P		5	2- 0
	BRTR					

LYNCH, GERALD THOMAS "JERRY"
B.JULY 17,1930 BAY CITY,MICH.

1954	PIT	N	O		98	.239
1955	PIT	N	C-O		88	.284
1956	PIT	N	O		19	.158
1957	CIN	N	C-O		67	.258
1958	CIN	N	O		122	.312
1959	CIN	N	O		117	.269
1960	CIN	N	O		102	.289
1961	CIN	N	O		96	.315
1962	CIN	N	O		114	.281
1963	CIN	N	O		22	.250
	PIT	N	O		88	.266
1964	PIT	N	O		114	.273
1965	PIT	N	O		73	.281
1966	PIT	N	O		64	.214
	BLTR			1184		.277

LYNCH, HENRY W.
B.1866 WORCESTER,MASS.
D.NOV.23,1925

1893	CHI	N	O		4	.214

LYNCH, JOHN H.
B.FEB.5,1857 NEW YORK,N.Y
D.APR.20,1923

1881	BUF	N	P-O	19	23	10- 9
						.166
1883	MET	AA	P		29	13-16
1884	MET	AA	P		54	39-14
1885	MET	AA	P		45	23-21
1886	MET	AA	P		51	20-30
1887	MET	AA	P		23	7-15
1890	BRO	AA	P		2	0- 2
	BRTR	223	227	112-107
						.151

LYNCH, MATTHEW DANIEL "DUMMY"
B.FEB.7,1927 DALLAS,TEX.

1948	CHI	N	2		7	.286
	BRTR					

LYNCH, MICHAEL JOSEPH
B.SEPT.10,1875 ST.PAUL,MINN.
D.APR.1,1947 JENNINGS LODGE,ORE

1902	CHI	N	O		7	.166

```
YR   CL LEA POS  GP    G    REC
```

LYNCH, MICHAEL JOSEPH
B.JUNE 28,1880 HOLYOKE,MASS.
D.APR.2,1927 GARRISON,N.Y.
```
1904 PIT N  P          27   14-11
1905 PIT N  P          33   17- 7
1906 PIT N  P          18    6- 5
1907 PIT N  P           7    2- 2
     NY  N  P          12    3- 6
     TR               97   42-31
```

LYNCH, THOMAS JAMES
B.APR.3,1860 BENNINGTON,VT.
D.MAR.28,1955
```
1884 CHI N  P-1         5    3- 2
                            .000
     WIL U  C-1-0      16   .281
     PHI N  P-C- 1     12    0- 1
            O               .318
1885 PHI N  2-0       13   .189
     BLTR       6     46    3- 3
                            .256
```

LYNCH, WALTER EDWARD
B.APR.15,1897 BUFFALO,N.Y.
```
1922 BOS A  C          3   .667
     TR
```

LYNN, BYRD "BIRDIE"
B.MAR.13,1889 UNIONVILLE,ILL.
D.FEB.5,1940 NAPA,CAL.
```
1916 CHI A  C         31   .225
1917 CHI A  C         35   .222
1918 CHI A  C          4   .142
1919 CHI A  C         29   .227
1920 CHI A  C         16   .320
     BRTR            115   .237
```

LYNN, FREDRIC MICHAEL "FRED"
B.FEB.3,1952 CHICAGO,ILL.
```
1974 BOS A  O         15   .419
1975 BOS A  O        145   .331
1976 BOS A  O        132   .314
     BLTL            292   .327
```

LYNN, JAPHET MONROE "RED"
B.DEC.27,1913 KENNEY,TEX.
```
1939 DET A  P          4    0- 1
     NY  N  P         26    1- 0
1940 NY  N  P         33    4- 3
1944 CHI N  P         22    5- 4
     BRTR            85   10- 8
```

LYNN, JEROME EDWARD
B.APR.14,1916 SCRANTON,PA.
D.SEPT.25,1972 SCRANTON,PA.
```
1937 WAS A  2          1   .667
     BRTR
```

LYON, RUSSELL MAYO
B.JAN.26,1913 BALL GROUND,GA.
```
1944 CLE A  C          7   .182
     BRTR
```

LYONS, ALBERT HAROLD "AL"
B.JULY 18,1918 ST.JOSEPH,MO.
D.DEC.20,1965 INGLEWOOD,CAL.
```
1944 NY  A  P      11   19   0- 0
1946 NY  A  P             2   0- 1
1947 NY  A  P       6    8   1- 0
     PIT N  P      13   15   1- 2
1948 BOS N  P-O     7   16   1- 0
                            .167
     BRTR          39   60   3- 3
                            .293
```

**LYONS, DENNIS PATRICK ALOYSIUS
"DENNY"**
B.MAR.12,1866 CINCINNATI,OHIO
D.JAN.3,1929 W.COVINGTON,KY.
```
1885 PRO N  3          4   .125
1886 ATH AA 3         32   .226
1887 ATH AA 3        137   .469
1888 ATH AA 3        111   .325
1889 ATH AA 3        131   .327
1890 ATH AA 3         88   .351
1891 STL AA 3        120   .312
1892 NY  N  3        108   .260
1893 PIT N  3        131   .318
1894 PIT N  3         72   .311
1895 STL N  3         33   .290
1896 PIT N  3        116   .306
1897 PIT N  1         36   .206
     BRTR           1119   .325
```

LYONS, EDWARD HOYT "MOUSE"
B.MAY 12,1923 WINSTON-SALEM,N.C
```
1947 WAS A  2          7   .154
     BRTR
```

LYONS, GEORGE TONY
B.JAN.25,1891 BIBLE GROVE,ILL.
```
1920 STL N  P          7    2- 1
1924 STL N  P         26    3- 2
     BRTR            33    5- 3
```

LYONS, HARRY P.
B.1866 CHESTER,PA.
D.JUNE 30,1912
```
1887 PHI N  O          1   .200
     STL AA O          2   .125
1888 STL AA O        123   .190
1889 NY  N  O          5   .100
1890 ROC AA O        132   .264
1892 NY  N  O         96   .245
1893 NY  N  O         46   .272
                     405   .236
```

LYONS, HERSCHEL ENGLEBERT
B.JULY 23,1915 RESNO,CAL.
```
1941 STL N  P          1    0- 0
     BRTR
```

LYONS, PATRICK JERRY
B.1860 CANADA
D.JAN.20,1914
```
1890 CLE N  2         11   .052
```

LYONS, TERENCE HILBERT
B.DEC.14,1908 NEW HOLLAND,OHIO
D.SEPT.9,1959
```
1929 PHI N  1          1   .000
```

LYONS, THEODORE AMAR "TED"
B.DEC.28,1900 LAKE CHARLES,LA.
```
1923 CHI A  P          9    2- 1
1924 CHI A  P         41   12-11
1925 CHI A  P         43   21-11
1926 CHI A  P      39 41   18-16
1927 CHI A  P      39 41   22-14
1928 CHI A  P      39 49   15-14
1929 CHI A  P      37 40   14-20
1930 CHI A  P      42 57   22-15
1931 CHI A  P      22 42    4- 6
1932 CHI A  P      33 49   10-15
1933 CHI A  P      36 51   10-21
1934 CHI A  P      30 50   11-13
1935 CHI A  P      23 29   15- 8
1936 CHI A  P         26   10-13
1937 CHI A  P      22 23   12- 7
1938 CHI A  P      23 24    9-11
1939 CHI A  P         21   14- 6
1940 CHI A  P         22   12- 8
1941 CHI A  P         22   12-10
     CHI A  P         20   14- 4
1946 CHI A  M-P        5    1- 4
     BBTR          594 705 260-230
NON-PLAYING MANAGER
CHI(A) 1947-48
```

LYONS, TOBY A.
B.BOSTON,MASS.
```
1890 SYR AA P          3    1- 2
```

LYSTON, WILLIAM EDWARD
B.1893 NEAR BALTIMORE,MD.
D.AUG 4,1944 BALTIMORE,MD.
```
1891 COL AA P          1    0- 0
1894 CLE N  P          1    0- 1
     TR               2    0- 1
```

LYTLE, EDWARD BENSON "DAD"
B.MAR.10,1862 RACINE,WIS.
D.DEC.21,1950
```
1890 CHI N  O          1   .000
     PIT N  2-O       15   .123
                      16   .115
```

LYTTLE, JAMES LAWRENCE "JIM"
B.MAY 20,1946 HAMILTON,OHIO
```
1969 NY  A  O         28   .181
1970 NY  A  O         87   .310
1971 NY  A  O         49   .198
1972 CHI A  O         44   .232
1973 MON N  O         49   .259
1974 MON N  O         25   .333
1975 MON N  O         44   .273
1976 MON N  O         42   .271
     LA  N  O         23   .221
     BLTR            391   .248
```

MAAS, DUANE FREDRICK "DUKE"
B.JAN.31,1929 UTICA,MICH.
```
1955 DET A  P         18    5- 6
1956 DET A  P         26    0- 7
1957 DET A  P         45   10-14
1958 KC  A  P         10    4- 5
     NY  A  P         22    7- 3
1959 NY  A  P         38   14- 8
1960 NY  A  P         35    5- 1
1961 NY  A  P          1    0- 0
     BRTR            195   45-44
```

MABE, ROBERT LEE "BOB"
B.OCT.8,1929 DANVILLE,VA.
```
1958 STL N  P      31 32    3- 9
1959 CIN N  P         18    4- 2
1960 BAL A  P          2    0- 0
     BRTR       KU   52    7-11
```

MAC CORMACK, FRANK LOUIS
B.SEPT.21,1954 JERSEY CITY,N.J.
```
1976 DET A  P          9    0- 5
     BRTR
```

MAC DONALD, HARVEY FORSYTH
B.MAY 18,1904 NEW YORK,N.Y.
D.OCT.4,1965 MANOA,PA.
```
1928 PHI N  O         13   .250
     BLTL
```

MAC DONALD, WILLIAM PAUL "BILL"
B.MAR.28,1929 ALMEDA,CAL.
```
1950 PIT N  P         32    8-10
1953 PIT N  P          4    0- 1
     BRTR            36    8-11
```

MACE, HARRY L. "JIMMY"
B.WASHINGTON,D.C.
```
1891 WAS AA P          5    0- 4
```

MACEY
B.COLUMBUS,OHIO
```
1890 ATH AA C          1   .000
```

**MAC FAYDEN, DANIEL KNOWLES
"DANNY" OR "DEACON"**
B.JUNE 10,1905 N.TRURO,MASS.
D.AUG.26,1972 BRUNSWICK,ME.
```
1926 BOS A  P          3    0- 1
1927 BOS A  P      35 37    5- 8
1928 BOS A  P      33 35    9-15
1929 BOS A  P         32   10-18
1930 BOS A  P         36   11-14
1931 BOS A  P         35   16-12
1932 BOS A  P         12    1-10
     NY  A  P         16    7- 5
1933 NY  A  P         25    3- 2
1934 NY  A  P         22    4- 3
1935 CIN N  P          7    1- 2
     BOS N  P         28    5-13
1936 BOS N  P         37   17-13
1937 BOS N  P         32   14-14
1938 BOS N  P         29   14- 9
1939 BOS N  P         33    8-14
1940 PIT N  P         35    5- 4
1941 WAS A  P          5    0- 1
1943 BOS N  P         10    2- 1
     BRTR          465 469 132-159
```

MACHA, KENNETH EDWARD "KEN"
B.SEPT.29,1950 MONROEVILLE,PA.
```
1974 PIT N  C          5   .600
     BRTR
```

**MACHEMEHL, CHARLES WALTER
"CHUCK"**
B.APR.20,1947 BRENHAM,TEX.
```
1971 CLE A  P         14    0- 2
     BRTR
```

MACIARZ, JOSEPH JOHN
(PLAYED UNDER NAME OF
JOSEPH JOHN MACK)

YR	CL	LEA	POS	GP	G	REC

MACK, CORNELIUS ALEXANDER
"CONNIE"
(REAL NAME CORNELIUS
ALEXANDER MC GILLICUDDY)
B.DEC.22,1862 E.BROOKFIELD,MASS
D.FEB.8,1956 GERMANTOWN,PA.

1886	WAS	N	C		10	.361
1887	WAS	N	C		80	.220
1888	WAS	N	C		85	.186
1889	WAS	N	C-1-O		97	.292
1890	BUF	P	C		123	.268
1891	PIT	N	C		71	.210
1892	PIT	N	C		86	.257
1893	PIT	N	C		36	.325
1894	PIT	N	M-C		63	.257
1895	PIT	N	M-C		14	.362
1896	PIT	N	M-C-1		30	.207
			BRTR		695	.252

NON-PLAYING MANAGER
PHI(A) 1901-50

MACK, DENNIS JOSEPH
(REAL NAME
DENNIS JOSEPH MC CROHAN)
B.1851 EASTON,PA.
D.APR.10,1888

1871	ROK	NA	P-1-	1	25	0- 1
			S			-
1872	ATH	NA	1-S		46	.247
1873	PHI	NA	1-2-O		45	-
1874	PHI	NA	1		56	-
1876	STL	N	S		48	.204
1880	BUF	N	2-S		17	.203
1882	LOU	AA	2-S-O		72	.193
1883	PIT	AA	1-S		60	.200
			BRTR	1	369	0- 1
						-

MACK, EARLE THADDEUS
B.FEB.1,1890 PHILADELPHIA,PA.
D.FEB.4,1967 UPPER DARBY
TOWNSHIP,PA.

1910	PHI	A	C		1	.500
1911	PHI	A	3		2	.000
1914	PHI	A	1		2	.000
			BLTR		5	.133

MACK, FRANK GEORGE "STUBBY"
B.FEB.2,1900 OKLAHOMA CITY,OKLA.

1922	CHI	A	P		8	2- 2
1923	CHI	A	P		12	0- 1
1925	CHI	A	P		8	0- 0
			BRTR		28	2- 3

MACK, JOSEPH "REDDY"
(REAL NAME JOSEPH MC NAMARA)
B.MAY 2,1866 IRELAND
D.DEC.30,1916

1885	LOU	AA	2		11	.244
1886	LOU	AA	2		137	.244
1887	LOU	AA	2		128	.410
1888	LOU	AA	2		110	.228
1889	BAL	AA	2		136	.236
1890	BAL	AA	2		26	.272
					548	.285

MACK, JOSEPH JOHN
(REAL NAME
JOSEPH JOHN MACIARZ)
B.JULY 4,1915 CHICAGO,ILL.

1945	BOS	N	1		66	.231
			BBTL			

MACK, RAYMOND JAMES "RAY"
(REAL NAME
RAYMOND JAMES MLCKOVSKY)
B.AUG.31,1916 CLEVELAND,OHIO
D.MAY 7,1969 BUCYRUS,OHIO

1938	CLE	A	2		2	.333
1939	CLE	A	2		36	.152
1940	CLE	A	2		146	.283
1941	CLE	A	2		145	.228
1942	CLE	A	2		143	.225
1943	CLE	A	2		153	.220
1944	CLE	A	2		83	.232
1946	CLE	A	2		61	.205
1947	NY	A	H		1	.000
	CHI	N	2		21	.218
			BRTR		791	.232

MACK, WILLIAM FRANCIS
B.FEB.12,1885 ELMIRA,N.Y.
D.SEPT.30,1971 ELMIRA,N.Y.

1908	CHI	N	P		2	0- 0

MACKANIN, PETER "PETE"
B.AUG.1,1951 CHICAGO,ILL.

1973	TEX	A	S-3		44	.100
1974	TEX	A	S		2	.167
1975	MON	N	2-S-3		130	.225
1976	MON	N	2-S-3-O		114	.224
			BRTR		290	.212

MAC KENZIE, ERIC HUGH
B.AUG.29,1932 GLENDON,ALT.,CAN.

1955	KC	A	C		1	.000
			BLTR			

MAC KENZIE, HENRY GORDON
B.JULY 9,1937 ST.PETERSBURG,FLA

1961	KC	A	C		11	.125
			BRTR			

MAC KENZIE, KENNETH PURVIS "KEN"
B.MAR.10,1934 GORE BAY,ONT.,CAN.

1960	MIL	N	P		9	0- 1
1961	MIL	N	P		5	0- 1
1962	NY	N	P		42	5- 4
1963	NY	N	P		34	3- 1
	STL	N	P		8	0- 0
1964	SF	N	P		10	0- 0
1965	HOU	N	P		21	0- 3
			BRTL		129	8-10

MACKIEWICZ, FELIX THADDEUS
B.NOV.20,1917 CHICAGO,ILL.

1941	PHI	A	O		5	.285
1942	PHI	A	O		6	.214
1943	PHI	A	O		9	.063
1945	CLE	A	O		120	.273
1946	CLE	A	O		78	.260
1947	CLE	A	O		2	.000
	WAS	A	O		3	.167
			BRTR		223	.259

MACKINSON, JOHN JOSEPH
B.OCT.29,1923 ORANGE,N.J.

1953	PHI	A	P		1	0- 0
1955	STL	N	P		8	0- 1
			BRTR		9	10	0- 1

MAC LEOD, WILLIAM DANIEL
"BILLY"
B.MAY 13,1942 GLOUCESTER,MASS.

1962	BOS	A	P		2	0- 1
			BLTL			

MACON, MAX CULLEN
B.OCT.14,1915 PENSACOLA,FLA.

1938	STL	N	P	38	46	4-11
1940	BRO	N	P		2	1- 0
1942	BRO	N	P	14	26	5- 5
1943	BRO	N	P-1	25	45	7- 5
						.164
1944	BOS	N	P-1-	1	106	0- 0
			O			.273
1947	BOS	N	P		1	0- 0
			BLTL	81	226	17-19
						.265

MAC PHEE, WALTER SCOTT "WADDY"
B.DEC.23,1902 BROOKLYN,N.Y.

1922	NY	N	3		2	.286
			BRTR			

MAC PHERSON, HARRY WILLIAM
B.JULY 10,1926 N.ANDOVER,MASS.

1944	BOS	N	P		1	0- 0
			BRTR			

MACULLAR, JAMES F. "LITTLE MAC"
B.JAN.6,1855 BOSTON,MASS.
D.APR.8,1924

1879	SYR	N	S-O		63	.231
1882	CIN	AA	O		79	.282
1883	CIN	AA	S-O		14	.151
1884	BAL	AA	S		108	.193
1885	BAL	AA	S		100	.202
1886	BAL	AA	S		76	.227
			BRTL		440	.210

MADDEN
B.PITTSBURGH,PA.

1914	PIT	F	C		2	.500

MADDEN, EUGENE
B.JUNE 5,1892 ELM GROVE,W.VA.
D.APR.6,1949

1916	PIT	N	O		1	.000

MADDEN, LEONARD JOSEPH
B.JULY 2,1890 TOLEDO,OHIO
D.SEPT.9,1949

1912	CHI	N	P		6	0- 1
			BLTL			

MADDEN, MICHAEL JOSEPH "KID"
B.OCT.2,1866 PORTLAND,ME.
D.MAR.16,1896

1887	BOS	N	P		37	22-14
1888	BOS	N	P		19	7-12
1889	BOS	N	P	20	21	10-10
1890	BOS	P	P		14	3- 2
1891	BOS	AA	P		4	0- 2
	BAL	AA	P-O	31	36	14-10
						.257
			TL	125	131	56-50
						.281

MADDEN, THOMAS FRANCIS
B.SEPT.14,1882 BOSTON,MASS.
D.JAN.20,1954

1909	BOS	A	C		12	.168
1910	BOS	A	C		14	.400
1911	BOS	A	C		4	.200
	PHI	N	C		22	.276
			BRTR		52	.285

MADDEN, THOMAS J. "BUNNY"
B.1884

1906	BOS	N	O		4	.267
1910	NY	A	O		1	.000
					5	.250

MADDERN, JAMES CLARENCE
"CLARENCE"
B.SEPT.26,1921 BISBEE,ARIZ.

1946	CHI	N	O		3	.000
1948	CHI	N	O		80	.252
1949	CHI	N	1		10	.333
1951	CLE	A	O		11	.167
			BRTR		104	.248

MADDOX, ELLIOTT
B.DEC.21,1947 EAST ORANGE,N.J.

1970	DET	A	2-S-3-O		109	.248
1971	WAS	A	3-O		128	.217
1972	TEX	A	O		98	.252
1973	TEX	A	3-O		100	.238
1974	NY	A	2-3-O		137	.303
1975	NY	A	2-O		55	.307
1976	NY	A	O		18	.217
			BRTR		645	.265

MADDOX, GARRY LEE
B.SEP.1,1949 CINCINNATI,OHIO

1972	SF	N	O		125	.266
1973	SF	N	O		144	.319
1974	SF	N	O		135	.284
1975	SF	N	O		17	.135
	PHI	N	O		99	.291
1976	PHI	N	O		146	.330
			BRTR		666	.296

MADDOX, NICHOLAS
B.NOV.9,1886 GAVANSTOWN,MD.
D.NOV.27,1954

1907	PIT	N	P		6	5- 1
1908	PIT	N	P		36	23- 8
1909	PIT	N	P		31	13- 8
1910	PIT	N	P		20	2- 3
			TR		93	43-20

MADIGAN, WILLIAM "TICE"
B.1868 WASHINGTON,D.C.
D.DEC.4,1954 WASHINGTON,D.C.

1886	WAS	N	P		14	1-13
			TR			

MADISON, ARTHUR M.
B.JAN.14,1871 CLARKSBURG,MASS.
D.JAN.27,1933

1895	PHI	N	2-S		10	.400
1899	PIT	N	2-S		33	.269
					43	.288

MADISON, DAVID PLEDGER "DAVE"
B.FEB.1,1924 BROOKSVILLE,MISS.

1950	NY	A	P		1	0- 0
1952	STL	A	P		31	4- 2
	DET	A	P		10	1- 1
1953	DET	A	P		32	3- 4
			BRTR		74	8- 7

YR	CL	LEA	POS	GP	G	REC

MADJESKI, EDWARD WILLIAM
(REAL NAME
EDWARD WILLIAM MAJEWSKI)
B.JULY 24,1909 FAR ROCKAWAY,N.Y

YR	CL	LEA	POS	GP	G	REC
1932	PHI	A	C		17	.229
1933	PHI	A	C		51	.282
1934	PHI	A	C		8	.375
	CHI	A	C		85	.221
1937	NY	N	C		5	.200
	BRTR				166	.241

MADLOCK, BILL
B.JAN.2,1951 MEMPHIS,TENN.

1973	TEX	N	3		21	.351
1974	CHI	N	3		128	.313
1975	CHI	N	3		130	.354
1976	CHI	N	3		142	.339
	BRTR				421	.337

MADRID, SALVADOR
B.JUNE 9,1920 EL PASO,TEX.

1947	CHI	N	S		8	.125

MAESTRI, HECTOR ANIBAL
B.APR.19,1935 HAVANA,CUBA

1960	WAS	A	P		1	0- 0
1961	WAS	A	P		1	0- 1
	BRTR				2	0- 1

MAGEE, LEO CHRISTOPHER
(REAL NAME LEOPOLD
CHRISTOPHER HOERNSCHEMEYER)
B.JUNE 4,1889 CINCINNATI,OHIO
D.MAR.14,1966 COLUMBUS,OHIO

1911	STL	N	2		21	.261
1912	STL	N	2-0		128	.290
1913	STL	N	2-0		137	.267
1914	STL	N	1-0		142	.284
1915	BRO	F	M-2		121	.330
1916	NY	A	0		131	.257
1917	NY	A	0		51	.220
	STL	A	0		36	.165
1918	CIN	N	2-3		119	.290
1919	BRO	N	2		45	.238
	CHI	N	2-S-3-0		79	.292
	BBTR				1010	.276

MAGEE, SHERWOOD ROBERT "SHERRY"
B.AUG.6,1884 CLARENDON,PA.
D.MAR.13,1929 PHILADELPHIA,PA.

1904	PHI	N	0		95	.277
1905	PHI	N	0		155	.299
1906	PHI	N	0		154	.282
1907	PHI	N	0		139	.328
1908	PHI	N	0		142	.283
1909	PHI	N	0		143	.270
1910	PHI	N	0		154	.331
1911	PHI	N	0		120	.288
1912	PHI	N	0		132	.306
1913	PHI	N	0		138	.306
1914	PHI	N	1-S-0		146	.314
1915	BOS	N	1-0		156	.280
1916	BOS	N	0		122	.241
1917	BOS	N	0		72	.255
	CIN	N	1-0		45	.324
1918	CIN	N	1-2-0		115	.297
1919	CIN	N	2-3-0		56	.215
	BRTR				2084	.291

MAGEE, WILLIAM M.
B.JAN.11,1868 S.BOSTON,MASS.

1897	LOU	N	P		20	4-13
1898	LOU	N	P		35	16-14
1899	LOU	N	P		11	4- 6
	PHI	N	P		10	3- 5
	WAS	N	P		5	1- 4
1901	STL	N	P		1	0- 1
	NY	N	P		6	0- 3
1902	NY	N	P		3	0- 0
	PHI	N	P		8	2- 4
					99	30-50

MAGGERT, HARL VESS
B.FEB.13,1883 CROMWELL,IND.
D.JAN.7,1963 FRESNO,CAL.

1907	PIT	N	0		3	.000
1912	PHI	A	0		72	.256
	BLTR				75	.250

MAGGERT, HARL WARREN
B.MAY 4,1914 LOS ANGELES,CAL.

1938	BOS	N	0		66	.281
	BRTR					

MAGLIE, SALVATORE ANTHONY
"SAL" OR "THE BARBER"
B.APR.26,1917 NIAGARA FALLS,N.Y

1945	NY	N	P	13	14	5- 4
1950	NY	N	P		47	18- 4
1951	NY	N	P		42	23- 6
1952	NY	N	P		35	18- 8
1953	NY	N	P		27	8- 9
1954	NY	N	P		34	14- 6
1955	NY	N	P		23	9- 5
	CLE	A	P		10	0- 2
1956	CLE	A	P		2	0- 0
	BRO	N	P		28	13- 5
1957	BRO	N	P		19	6- 6
	NY	A	P		6	2- 0
1958	NY	A	P		7	1- 1
	STL	N	P		10	2- 6
	BRTR			303	304	119-62

MAGNER, ESMUND BURKE "STUBBY"
B.FEB.20,1888 KALAMAZOO,MICH.
D.SEPT.6,1956

1911	NY	A	2		12	.194
	BRTR					

MAGNER, WILLIAM JOHN
B.JULY 15,1858 BIRMINGHAM,ENG.
D.JUNE 27,1923

1879	CIN	N	0		1	.000

MAGNUSON, JAMES ROBERT "JIM"
B.AUG.18,1946 MARINETTE,WIS.

1970	CHI	A	P		13	1- 5
1971	CHI	A	P		15	1- 1
1973	NY	A	P		8	0- 1
	BRTL				36	2- 7

MAGOON, GEORGE HENRY "TOPSY"
B.MAY 27,1875 ST.ALBANS,ME.
D.DEC.6,1943

1898	BRO	N	S		93	.227
1899	BAL	N	S		61	.252
	CHI	N	S		59	.235
1901	CIN	N	S		128	.251
1902	CIN	N	2-S		44	.275
1903	CIN	N	2		41	.216
	CHI	A	2		94	.227
	BRTR				520	.240

MAGRINI, PETER ALEXANDER "PETE"
B.JUNE 8,1942 SAN FRANCISCO,CAL.

1966	BOS	A	P		3	0- 1
	BRTR					

MAGUIRE, FREDERICK EDWARD
B.MAY 10,1900 ROXBURY,MASS.
D.NOV.3,1961

1922	NY	N	2		5	.333
1923	NY	N	2-3		41	.200
1928	CHI	N	2		140	.279
1929	BOS	N	2		138	.252
1930	BOS	N	2		146	.267
1931	BOS	N	2		148	.228
	BRTR				618	.252

MAGUIRE, JACK
B.FEB.5,1925 ST.LOUIS,MO.

1950	NY	N	1-0		29	.175
1951	NY	N	0		16	.400
	PIT	N	2-3		8	.000
	STL	A	2-3-0		41	.244
	BRTR				94	.240

MAHADY, JAMES B.
B.APR.22,1902 CORTLAND,N.Y.
D.AUG.9,1936

1921	NY	N	2		1	.000
	BRTR					

MAHAFFEY, ARTHUR "ART"
B.JUNE 4,1938 CINCINNATI,OHIO

1960	PHI	N	P		14	7- 3
1961	PHI	N	P		36	11-19
1962	PHI	N	P	41	42	19-14
1963	PHI	N	P		26	7-10
1964	PHI	N	P		34	12- 9
1965	PHI	N	P		22	2- 5
1966	STL	N	P		12	1- 4
	BRTR			185	186	59-64

MAHAFFEY, LEE ROY "POPEYE"
B.FEB.9,1903 BELTON,S.C.
D.JULY 23,1969 ANDERSON,S.C.

1926	PIT	N	P		4	0- 0
1927	PIT	N	P		2	1- 0
1930	PHI	A	P		33	9- 5
1931	PHI	A	P		30	15- 4
1932	PHI	A	P		37	13-13
1920	DET	A	C		32	.275
1921	DET	A	C		11	.111
1922	DET	A	C		42	.275
1923	DET	A	C		23	.136
1924	DET	A	C		14	.231
1926	DET	A	C		75	.198
1927	DET	A	H		1	.000
1928	STL	A	H		76	.226
1929	STL	A	H		35	.243
1930	STL	A	H		57	.216
1932	CIN	N	H		49	.207
1933	CIN	N	H		36	.167
1934	CIN	N	H		25	.185
	BRTR				476	.218

MANKOWSKI, PHILIP ANTHONY "PHIL"
B.JAN.9,1953 BUFFALO,N.Y.

1976	DET	A	3		24	.271
	BLTR					

MANLOVE, CHARLES HALE
B.OCT.8,1862 PHILADELPHIA,PA.
D.FEB.12,1952

1884	ALT	U	C		1	.750
	NY	N	C		2	.000
	TR				3	.231

MANN, BEN GARTH
B.NOV.6,1918 BRANDON,TEX.

1944	CHI	N	H		1	.000
	BATR					

MANN, FRED I.
B.APR.1,1858 SUTTON,VT.
D.APR.6,1916

1882	WOR	N	1-3		19	.241
	ATH	AA	3		29	.224
1883	COL	AA	1-S-3-0		96	.230
1884	COL	AA	0		99	.276
1885	PIT	AA	0		100	.253
1886	PIT	AA	0		117	.259
1887	CLE	AA	0		64	.375
	ATH	AA	0		55	.310
	BL				579	.277

MANN, JOHN LEO
B.FEB.4,1898 FONTANET,IND.

1928	CHI	A	3		6	.286
	BRTR					

MANN, LESLIE "LES" OR "MAJOR"
B.NOV.18,1893 LINCOLN,NEB.
D.JAN.15,1962

1913	BOS	N	0		120	.253
1914	BOS	N	0		126	.247
1915	CHI	F	0		135	.306
1916	CHI	N	0		127	.272
1917	CHI	N	0		117	.273
1918	CHI	N	0		129	.288
	BOS	N	0		80	.227
1919						
	BOS	N	0		40	.285
1920	BOS	N	0		115	.276
1921	STL	N	0		97	.328
1922	STL	N	0		84	.347
1923	STL	N	0		38	.371
	CIN	N	0		8	.000
1924	BOS	N	0		32	.275
1925	BOS	N	0		60	.342
1926	BOS	N,	0		50	.302
1927	BOS	N	0		29	.258
	NY	N	0		29	.328
1928	NY	N	0		82	.264
	BRTR				1498	.282

MANNING, ERNEST DEVON
B.OCT.9,1890 FLORALA,ALA.
D.APR.28,1973 PENSACOLA,FLA.

1914	STL	A	P		7	0- 0
	BLTR					

MANNING, JAMES BENJAMIN
B.JULY 21,1943 L'ANSE,MICH.

1962	MIN	A	P		5	0- 0
	BRTR					

MANNING, JAMES H.
B.JAN.31,1862 FALL RIVER,MASS.
D.OCT.22,1929 EDINBURG,TEX.

YR	CL	LEA	POS	GP	G	REC
1884	BOS	N	2-S-3-0		84	.241
1885	BOS	N	S-0		84	.206
1885	DET	N	S		20	.269
1886	DET	N	0		26	.185
1887	DET	N	0		13	.250
1889	KC	AA	M-2-0		132	.204
		TR			359	.217

NON-PLAYING MANAGER WAS(A) 1901

MANNING, JOHN E.
B.DEC.20,1853 BRAINTREE,MASS.
D.AUG.15,1929

YR	CL	LEA	POS	GP	G	REC
1873	BOS	NA	1-0		33	.311
1874	BAL	NA	P-2-S	19	42	4-15
	HAR	NA		3	1	-
1875	BOS	NA	P-1-3-0	16	77	14- 2
						.285
1876	BOS	N	P-0	21	70	15- 6
						.258
1877	CIN	N	P-1-2-S-0	9	58	0- 4
						.315
1878	BOS	N	P-0	1	60	1- 0
						.254
1880	CIN	N	1-0		48	.216
1881	BUF	N	0		1	.000
1883	PHI	N	0		97	.265
1884	PHI	N	0		103	.272
1885	PHI	N	0		107	.256
1886	BAL	AA	0		137	.227
		BRTR		66	834	34-27
						-

MANNING, RICHARD EUGENE "RICK"
B.SEPT.2,1954 NIAGARA FALLS,N.Y.

YR	CL	LEA	POS	GP	G	REC
1975	CLE	A	0		120	.285
1976	CLE	A	0		138	.292
		BLTR			258	.289

MANNING, TIMOTHY E.
B.CHICAGO,ILL.

YR	CL	LEA	POS	GP	G	REC
1882	PRO	N	C-S		19	.105
1883	BAL	AA	2		35	.233
1884	BAL	AA	2		91	.207
1885	BAL	AA	2		43	.201
	PRO	N	S		10	.086
					198	.193

MANNING, WALTER S. "RUBE"
B.APR.29,1883 CHAMBERSBURG,PA.
D.AUG.23,1930

YR	CL	LEA	POS	GP	G	REC
1907	NY	A	P		1	0- 1
1908	NY	A	P	42	44	13-16
1909	NY	A	P		26	7-11
1910	NY	A	P		16	2- 4
		TR		85	87	22-32

MANNO, DONALD
B.MAY 4,1918 WILLIAMSPORT,PA.

YR	CL	LEA	POS	GP	G	REC
1940	BOS	N	0		3	.286
1941	BOS	N	1-3-0		22	.167
		BRTR			25	.189

MANSELL, JOHN
B.1861 AUBURN,N.Y.
D.FEB.20,1925

YR	CL	LEA	POS	GP	G	REC
1882	ATH	AA	0		32	.237

MANSELL, MICHAEL R.
B.JAN.15,1859 AUBURN,N.Y.
D.DEC.4,1902

YR	CL	LEA	POS	GP	G	REC
1879	SYR	N	0		66	.211
1880	CIN	N	0		53	.192
1882	PIT	AA	0		73	.283
1883	PIT	AA	0		90	.240
1884	PIT	AA	0		27	.131
	ATH	AA	0		20	.194
	RIC	AA	0		29	.301
		BL			358	.235

MANSELL, THOMAS E. "BRICK"
B.JAN.1,1855 AUBURN,N.Y.
D.OCT.6,1934

YR	CL	LEA	POS	GP	G	REC
1879	TRO	N	0		39	.242
	SYR	N	0		1	.250
1883	DET	N	P-0	1	34	0- 0
						.213
	STL	AA	0		28	.370
1884	CIN	AA	0		65	.244
	COL	AA	0		23	.211
		BL		1	190	0- 0
						.254

MANSKE, LOUIS HUGO
B.JULY 4,1884 MILWAUKEE,WIS.
D.APR.27,1963 MILWAUKEE,WIS.

YR	CL	LEA	POS	GP	G	REC
1906	PIT	N	P		2	0- 0
		BLTL				

MANTILLA, FELIX (LAMELA)
B.JULY 29,1934 ISABELA,P.R.

YR	CL	LEA	POS	GP	G	REC
1956	MIL	N	S-3		35	.283
1957	MIL	N	2-S-3-0		71	.236
1958	MIL	N	2-S-3-0		85	.221
1959	MIL	N	2-S-3-0		103	.215
1960	MIL	N	2-S-0		63	.257
1961	MIL	N	2-S-3-0		45	.215
1962	NY	N	2-S-3		141	.275
1963	BOS	A	2-S-0		66	.315
1964	BOS	A	2-S-3-0		133	.289
1965	BOS	A	1-2-0		150	.275
1966	HOU	N	1-2-3-0		77	.219
		BRTR			969	.261

MANTLE, MICKEY CHARLES
B.OCT.20,1931 SPAVINAW,OKLA.

YR	CL	LEA	POS	GP	G	REC
1951	NY	A	0		96	.267
1952	NY	A	3-0		142	.311
1953	NY	A	S-0		127	.295
1954	NY	A	2-S-0		146	.300
1955	NY	A	S-0		147	.306
1956	NY	A	0		150	.353
1957	NY	A	0		144	.365
1958	NY	A	0		150	.304
1959	NY	A	0		144	.285
1960	NY	A	0		153	.275
1961	NY	A	0		153	.317
1962	NY	A	0		123	.321
1963	NY	A	0		65	.314
1964	NY	A	0		143	.303
1965	NY	A	0		122	.255
1966	NY	A	0		108	.288
1967	NY	A	1		144	.245
1968	NY	A	1		144	.237
		BBTR			2401	.298

MANUEL, CHARLES FUQUA "CHARLIE"
B.JAN.4,1944 NORTH FORK,W.VA.

YR	CL	LEA	POS	GP	G	REC
1969	MIN	A	0		83	.207
1970	MIN	A	0		59	.188
1971	MIN	A	0		18	.125
1972	MIN	A	0		63	.205
1974	LA	N	H		4	.333
1975	LA	N	H		15	.133
		BLTR			242	.198

MANUEL, JERRY
B.DEC.23,1953 HAHIRA,GA.

YR	CL	LEA	POS	GP	G	REC
1975	DET	A	2		6	.056
1976	DET	A	2-S		54	.140
		BBTR			60	.115

MANUEL, MARK GARFIELD "MOXIE"
B.OCT.16,1881 METROPOLIS,ILL.
D.APR.26,1924 MEMPHIS,TENN.

YR	CL	LEA	POS	GP	G	REC
1905	WAS	A	P		3	0- 0
1908	CHI	A	P		17	2- 4
		BRTB			20	2- 4

MANUSH, FRANK BENJAMIN
B.SEPT.18,1886 TUSCUMBIA,ALA.
D.JAN.5,1965 LAGUNA BEACH,CAL.

YR	CL	LEA	POS	GP	G	REC
1908	PHI	A	3		23	.156
		BPTR				

MANUSH, HENRY EMMETT "HEINIE"
B.JULY 20,1901 TUSCUMBIA,ALA.
D.MAY 12,1971 SARASOTA,FLA.

YR	CL	LEA	POS	GP	G	REC
1923	DET	A	0		109	.334
1924	DET	A	0		120	.289
1925	DET	A	0		99	.303
1926	DET	A	0		136	.378
1927	DET	A	0		152	.299
1928	STL	A	0		154	.378
1929	STL	A	0		142	.355
1930	STL	A	0		49	.328
	WAS	A	0		88	.362
1931	WAS	A	0		146	.307
1932	WAS	A	0		149	.342
1933	WAS	A	0		153	.336
1934	WAS	A	0		137	.349
1935	WAS	A	0		119	.273
1936	BOS	A	0		82	.291
1937	BRO	N	0		132	.333
1938	BRO	N	0		17	.235
	PIT	N	0		15	.308
1939	PIT	N	0		10	.000
		BLTL			2009	.331

MANVILLE, RICHARD WESLEY "DICK"
B.DEC.25,1926 DES MOINES,IOWA

YR	CL	LEA	POS	GP	G	REC
1950	BOS	N	P		1	0- 0
1952	CHI	N	P		11	0- 0
		BRTR			12	0- 0

MAPEL, ROLLA HAMILTON
B.MAR.9,1890 LEE'S SUMMITT,MO.
D.APR.6,1966 SAN DIEGO,CAL.

YR	CL	LEA	POS	GP	G	REC
1919	STL	A	P		4	0- 3
		BLTL				

MAPES, CLIFFORD FRANKLIN "CLIFF"
B.MAR.13,1922 SUTHERLAND,NEB.

YR	CL	LEA	POS	GP	G	REC
1948	NY	A	0		53	.250
1949	NY	A	0		111	.247
1950	NY	A	0		108	.247
1951	NY	A	0		45	.216
	STL	A	0		56	.274
1952	DET	A	0		86	.197
		BLTR			459	.242

MAPLE, HOWARD ALBERT "MAPE"
B.JULY 20,1903 AFRIAN,MO.
D.NOV.9,1970 PORTLAND,ORE.

YR	CL	LEA	POS	GP	G	REC
1932	WAS	A	C		44	.244
		BLTR				

MAPPES, GEORGE RICHARD "DICK"
B.DEC.25,1865 ST.LOUIS,MO.
D.FEB.20,1934

YR	CL	LEA	POS	GP	G	REC
1885	BAL	AA	2		6	.211
1886	STL	N	C		6	.143
					12	.182

MARANDA, GEORGES HENRI
B.JAN.15,1932 LEVIS,QUE.,CAN.

YR	CL	LEA	POS	GP	G	REC
1960	SF	N	P		17	1- 4
1962	MIN	A	P		32	1- 3
		BRTR			49	2- 7

MARANVILLE, WALTER JAMES VINCENT "RABBIT"
B.NOV.11,1891 SPRINGFIELD,MASS.
D.JAN.5,1954 NEW YORK,N.Y.

YR	CL	LEA	POS	GP	G	REC
1912	BOS	N	S		26	.209
1913	BOS	N	S		143	.247
1914	BOS	N	S		156	.246
1915	BOS	N	S		149	.244
1916	BOS	N	S		155	.235
1917	BOS	N	S		142	.260
1918	BOS	N	S		11	.316
1919	BOS	N	S		131	.267
1920	BOS	N	S		134	.266
1921	PIT	N	S		153	.294
1922	PIT	N	2-S		155	.294
1923	PIT	N	S		141	.277
1924	PIT	N	2		152	.266
1925	CHI	N	M-2-S		75	.233
1926	BRO	N	2-S		78	.235
1927	STL	N	S		9	.241
1928	STL	N	S		112	.240
1929	BOS	N	S		146	.284
1930	BOS	N	S		142	.281
1931	BOS	N	2-S		145	.260
1932	BOS	N	2		149	.235
1933	BOS	N	2		143	.218
1935	BOS	N	2		23	.149
		BRTR			2670	.258

MARBERRY, FREDERICK "FIRPO"
B.NOV.30,1898 STREETMAN,TEX.
D.AUG.1976 MEXIA,TEX.

YR	CL	LEA	POS	GP	G	REC
1923	WAS	A	P		11	4- 0
1924	WAS	A	P		50	11-12
1925	WAS	A	P		55	8- 6
1926	WAS	A	P		64	11- 7
1927	WAS	A	P		56	10- 7
1928	WAS	A	P		48	13-13
1929	WAS	A	P		49	19-12
1930	WAS	A	P		33	15- 5
1931	WAS	A	P		45	16- 4
1932	WAS	A	P		54	8- 4
1933	DET	A	P		37	16-11
1934	DET	A	P		38	15- 5
1935	DET	A	P		5	0- 1
1936	NY	N	P		1	0- 0
	WAS	A	P		5	0- 2
		BRTR			551	146-89

MARBET, WALTER WILLIAM
B.SEPT.13,1890 PLYMOUTH CO.,IA.
D.SEPT.24,1956

YR	CL	LEA	POS	GP	G	REC
1913	STL	N	P		3	0- 1

YR	CL	LEA	POS	GP	G	REC

MARCANO, JESUS MANUEL (TRILLO)
(SEE JESUS MANUEL
MARCANO TRILLO)

MARCHILDON, PHILIP JOSEPH
"PHIL" OR "BABE"
B.OCT.25,1916 PENETANGUISHENE,
ONT.,CANADA

YR	CL	LEA	POS	GP	G	REC
1940	PHI	A	P		2	0- 2
1941	PHI	A	P		30	10-15
1942	PHI	A	P		38	17-14
1945	PHI	A	P		3	0- 1
1946	PHI	A	P		36	13-16
1947	PHI	A	P		35	19- 9
1948	PHI	A	P		33	9-15
1949	PHI	A	P		7	0- 3
1950	BOS	A	P		1	0- 0
	BRTR				185	68-75

MARCUM, JOHN ALFRED "FOOTSIE"
B.SEPT.9,1908 CAMPBELLSBURG,KY.

YR	CL	LEA	POS	GP	G	REC
1933	PHI	A	P		5	3- 2
1934	PHI	A	P	37	58	14-11
1935	PHI	A	P	39	64	17-12
1936	BOS	A	P	31	48	8-13
1937	BOS	A	P	37	51	13-11
1938	BOS	A	P	15	19	5- 6
1939	STL	A	P	12	16	2- 5
	CHI	A	P	19	38	3- 3
	BLTR			195	299	65-63

MARCZLEWICZ, CHARLES ANTHONY
(PLAYED UNDER NAME OF
CHARLES ANTHONY MARSHALL)

MARENIETTE, LEO JOHN
B.FEB.18,1941 DETROIT,MICH.

YR	CL	LEA	POS	GP	G	REC
1965	DET	A	P		2	0- 0
1969	MON	N	P		3	0- 0
	BRTR				5	0- 0

MARES

YR	CL	LEA	POS	GP	G	REC
1894	LOU	N	O		1	.000

MARGONERI, JOSEPH EMANUEL "JOE"
B.JAN.13,1930 SMITHTON,PA.

YR	CL	LEA	POS	GP	G	REC
1956	NY	N	P		23	6- 6
1957	NY	N	P		13	1- 1
	BLTL				36	7- 7

MARICHAL, JUAN ANTONIO (SANCHEZ)
B.OCT.24,1937 LAGUNA VERDE,D.R.

YR	CL	LEA	POS	GP	G	REC
1960	SF	N	P		11	6- 2
1961	SF	N	P	29	30	13-10
1962	SF	N	P	37	38	18-11
1963	SF	N	P	41	42	25- 8
1964	SF	N	P		33	21- 8
1965	SF	N	P		39	22-13
1966	SF	N	P		37	25- 6
1967	SF	N	P		26	14-10
1968	SF	N	P		38	26- 9
1969	SF	N	P	37	38	21-11
1970	SF	N	P		34	12-10
1971	SF	N	P		37	18-11
1972	SF	N	P		25	6-16
1973	SF	N	P		34	11-15
1974	BOS	A	P		11	5- 1
1975	LA	N	P		2	0- 1
	BRTR			471	475	243-142

MARION, DONALD G. M. "RUBE"
B.1890
D.JAN.19,1933

YR	CL	LEA	POS	GP	G	REC
1914	BRO	F	P		17	3- 3
1915	BRO	F	P		35	12- 9
	BRTR				52	15-12

MARION, JOHN WYETH "RED"
B.MAR.14,1915 RICHBURG,S.C.

YR	CL	LEA	POS	GP	G	REC
1935	WAS	A	O		4	,.182
1943	WAS	A	O		14	.176
	BRTR				18	.179

MARION, MARTIN WHITFORD
"MARTY" OR "SLATS"
B.DEC.1,1917 RICHBURG,S.C.

YR	CL	LEA	POS	GP	G	REC
1940	STL	N	S		125	.278
1941	STL	N	S		155	.252
1942	STL	N	S		147	.276
1943	STL	N	S		129	.280
1944	STL	N	S		144	.267
1945	STL	N	S		123	.277
1946	STL	N	S		146	.233
1947	STL	N	S		149	.272
1948	STL	N	S		144	.252
1949	STL	N	S		134	.272
1950	STL	N	S		106	.247
1952	STL	A	M-S		67	.247
1953	STL	A	M-3		3	.000
	BRTR				1572	.263

NON-PLAYING MANAGER
STL(N) 1951, CHI(A) 1954-56

MARIS, ROGER EUGENE
B.SEP.10,1934 FARGO,MINN.

YR	CL	LEA	POS	GP	G	REC
1957	CLE	A	O		116	.235
1958	CLE	A	O		51	.225
	KC	A	O		99	.247
1959	KC	A	O		122	.273
1960	NY	A	O		136	.283
1961	NY	A	O		161	.269
1962	NY	A	O		157	.256
1963	NY	A	O		90	.269
1964	NY	A	O		141	.281
1965	NY	A	O		46	.239
1966	NY	A	O		119	.233
1967	STL	N	O		125	.261
1968	STL	N	O		100	.255
	BLTR				1463	.260

MARKELL, HARRY DUQUESNE "DUKE"
(REAL NAME
HARRY DUQUESNE MAKOWSKY)
B.AUG.17,1923 PARIS,FRANCE

YR	CL	LEA	POS	GP	G	REC
1951	STL	A	P		5	1- 1
	BRTR					

MARKLAND, CLENETH EUGENE
B.DEC.26,1919 DETROIT,MICH.

YR	CL	LEA	POS	GP	G	REC
1950	PHI	A	2		5	.125
	BRTR					

MARKLE, CLIFFORD MONROE
B.MAY 3,1894 PITTSBURGH,PA.
D.MAY 24,1974 TEMPLE CITY,CAL.

YR	CL	LEA	POS	GP	G	REC
1915	NY	A	P		3	2- 0
1916	NY	A	P		11	4- 3
1921	CIN	N	P		10	2- 6
1922	CIN	N	P		25	4- 5
1924	NY	A	P		7	0- 3
	BRTR				56	12-17

MARLOWE, RICHARD BURTON "DICK"
B.MAY 27,1929 HICKORY,N.C.

YR	CL	LEA	POS	GP	G	REC
1951	DET	A	P		2	0- 1
1952	DET	A	P		4	0- 2
1953	DET	A	P		42	6- 7
1954	DET	A	P		38	5- 4
1955	DET	A	P		4	1- 0
1956	DET	A	P		7	1- 1
	CHI	A	P		1	0- 0
	BRTR				98	13-15

MARNIE, HARRY SYLVESTER
B.JULY 6,1918 PHILADELPHIA,PA.

YR	CL	LEA	POS	GP	G	REC
1940	PHI	N	2		11	.176
1941	PHI	N	2-S-3		61	.241
1942	PHI	N	2-S-3		24	.167
	BRTR				96	.221

MAROLEWSKI, FRED DANIEL
B.OCT.6,1929 CHICAGO,ILL.

YR	CL	LEA	POS	GP	G	REC
1953	STL	N	1		1	.000
	BRTR					

MARONE, LOUIS STEPHEN "LOU"
B.DEC.3,1945 SAN DIEGO,CAL.

YR	CL	LEA	POS	GP	G	REC
1969	PIT	N	P		29	1- 1
1970	PIT	N	P		1	0- 0
	BRTL				30	1- 1

MARONEY, JAMES FRANCIS
B.DEC.4,1883 S.BOSTON,MASS.

YR	CL	LEA	POS	GP	G	REC
1906	BOS	N	P		3	0- 3
1910	CHI	N	P		12	1- 2
1912	CHI	N	P		10	1- 1
	BLTL				25	2- 6

MARQUARD, RICHARD WILLIAM
"RUBE"
B.OCT.9,1889 CLEVELAND,OHIO

YR	CL	LEA	POS	GP	G	REC
1908	NY	N	P		1	0- 1
1909	NY	N	P		29	5-13
1910	NY	N	P		13	4- 4
1911	NY	N	P		45	24- 7
1912	NY	N	P		43	26-11
1913	NY	N	P		42	23-10
1914	NY	N	P		39	12-22
1915	NY	N	P		27	9- 8
	BRO	N	P		6	2- 2
1916	BRO	N	P		36	13- 6
1917	BRO	N	P		37	19-12
1918	BRO	N	P		34	9-18
1919	BRO	N	P		8	3- 3
1920	BRO	N	P		28	10- 7
1921	CIN	N	P		39	17-14
1922	BOS	N	P		39	11-15
1923	BOS	N	P		38	11-14
1924	BOS	N	P		6	1- 2
1925	BOS	N	P		26	2- 8
	BBTL				536	201-177

MARQUARDT, ALBERT LUDWIG
"OLLIE"
B.SEPT.22,1904 TOLEDO,OHIO

YR	CL	LEA	POS	GP	G	REC
1931	BOS	A	2		17	.179
	BRTR					

MARQUEZ, GONZALO ENRIQUE
B.MAR.31,1946 CAUPANO,VENEZ.

YR	CL	LEA	POS	GP	G	REC
1972	OAK	A	1		23	.381
1973	OAK	A	1-2-0		23	.240
	CHI	N	1		19	.224
1974	CHI	N	1		11	.000
	BLTL				76	.235

MARQUEZ, LUIS ANGEL
B.OCT.26,1925 AGUADILLA,P.R.

YR	CL	LEA	POS	GP	G	REC
1951	BOS	N	O		68	.197
1954	CHI	N	O		17	.083
	PIT	N	O		14	.111
	BRTR				99	.182

MARQUIS, JAMES MILBURN
B.NOV.18,1900 YOAKUM,TEX.

YR	CL	LEA	POS	GP	G	REC
1925	NY	A	P		2	0- 0
	BRTR					

MARQUIS, ROBERT RUDOLPH "BOB"
B.DEC.23,1924 OKLAHOMA CITY,
OKLA.

YR	CL	LEA	POS	GP	G	REC
1953	CIN	N	O		40	.273
	BLTL					

MARQUIS, ROGER J.
B.APR.5,1937 HOLYOKE,MASS.

YR	CL	LEA	POS	GP	G	REC
1955	BAL	A	O		1	.000
	BLTL					

MARR, CHARLES W. "LEFTY"
B.SEPT.19,1862 CINCINNATI,OHIO
D.JAN.11,1912

YR	CL	LEA	POS	GP	G	REC
1886	CIN	AA	O		7	.269
1889	COL	AA	S-3-O		139	.303
1890	CIN	N	3-O		130	.299
1891	CIN	N	O		72	.244
	CIN	AA	O		14	.204
	BLTL				362	.289

MARRERO, CONRADO EUGENIO
(RAMOS) "CONNIE"
B.APR.25,1911 LAS VILLAS,CUBA

YR	CL	LEA	POS	GP	G	REC
1950	WAS	A	P		27	6-10
1951	WAS	A	P		25	11- 9
1952	WAS	A	P		22	11- 8
1953	WAS	A	P		22	8- 7
1954	WAS	A	P		22	3- 6
	BRTR				118	39-40

MARRIOTT, WILLIAM EARL
B.APR.18,1894 PRATT,KAN.
D.AUG.11,1969 BERKELEY,CAL.

YR	CL	LEA	POS	GP	G	REC
1917	CHI	N	H		3	.000
1920	CHI	N	2		14	.279
1921	CHI	N	2		30	.316
1925	BOS	N	3-O		103	.268
1926	BRO	N	3		109	.267
1927	BRO	N	3		6	.111
	BLTR				265	.268

YR	CL	LEA	POS	GP	G	REC

MARROW, CHARLES KENNON "BUCK"
B.AUG.29,1909 TARBORO,N.C.
YR	CL	LEA	POS	GP	G	REC
1932	DET	A	P		18	2- 5
1937	BRO	N	P		6	1- 2
1938	BRO	N	P		15	0- 1
		BRTR			39	3- 8

MARS, EDWARD
| 1890 | SYR | AA | P | | 17 | 9- 6 |

MARSANS, ARMANDO
B.OCT.3,1887 MATANZAS,CUBA
1911	CIN	N	O		36	.261
1912	CIN	N	O		110	.317
1913	CIN	N	1-O		118	.297
1914	CIN	N	O		36	.298
	STL	F	2-S		9	.350
1915	STL	F	O		36	.177
1916	STL	A	O		151	.254
1917	STL	A	O		75	.230
	NY	A	O		25	.227
1918	NY	A	O		37	.236
		BRTR			633	.269

MARSH, FRED FRANCIS
B.JAN.5,1924 VALLEY FALLS,KAN.
1949	CLE	A	H		1	.000
1951	STL	A	2-S-3		130	.243
1952	STL	A	2-S		11	.217
	WAS	A	2-O		9	.042
	STL	A	S-3		76	.286
1953	CHI	A	1-2-S-3		67	.200
1954	CHI	A	1-S-3-O		62	.306
1955	BAL	A	2-S-3		89	.218
1956	BAL	A	2-S-3		20	.125
		BRTR			465	.239

MARSHALL, CHARLES ANTHONY
(REAL NAME
CHARLES ANTHONY MARCZLEWICZ)
B.AUG.28,1919 WILMINGTON,DEL.
| 1941 | STL | N | C | | 1 | .000 |
| | | BRTR | | | | |

**MARSHALL, CLARENCE WESTLY
"CUDDLES"**
B.APR.28,1925 BELLINGHAM,WASH.
1946	NY	A	P		23	3- 4
1948	NY	A	P		1	0- 0
1949	NY	A	P		21	3- 0
1950	STL	A	P		28	1- 3
		BRTR			73	7- 7

MARSHALL, DAVID LEWIS "DAVE"
B.JAN.14,1943 ARTESIA,CAL.
1967	SF	N	R		1	.000
1968	SF	N	O		76	.264
1969	SF	N	O		110	.232
1970	NY	N	O		92	.243
1971	NY	N	O		100	.238
1972	NY	N	O		72	.250
1973	SD	N	O		39	.286
		BLTR			490	.246

MARSHALL, EDWARD HERBERT "DOC"
B.JUNE 4,1906 NEW ALBANY,MISS.
1929	NY	N	2		5	.400
1930	NY	N	2-S		78	.309
1931	NY	N	2-S		68	.201
1932	NY	N	S		68	.248
		BRTR			219	.259

MARSHALL, JOSEPH ELMER
B.AUG.22,1875 SAN FRANCISCO,CAL
D.MAY 4,1934 WALLA WALLA,WASH.
1903	PIT	N	2-O		9	.261
1906	STL	N	O		27	.158
		BRTR			36	.178

MARSHALL, KEITH ALAN
B.JULY 2,1951 SAN FRANCISCO,CAL.
| 1973 | KC | A | O | | 8 | .222 |
| | | BRTR | | | | |

MARSHALL, MICHAEL GRANT "MIKE"
B.JAN.15,1943 ADRIAN,MICH.
1967	DET	A	P		37	1- 3
1969	SEA	A	P	20	21	3-10
1970	HOU	N	P		4	0- 1
	MON	N	P		24	3- 7
1971	MON	N	P		66	5- 8
1972	MON	N	P		65	14- 8
1973	MON	N	P		92	14-11
1974	LA	N	P		106	15-12
1975	LA	N	P	57	58	9-14
1976	LA	N	P		30	4- 3
	ATL	N	P		24	2- 1
		BRTR		525	527	70-78

MARSHALL, MILO MAX "MAX"
B.SEPT.18,1913 SHENANDOAH,IOWA
1942	CIN	N	O		131	.255
1943	CIN	N	O		132	.236
1944	CIN	N	O		66	.245
		BLTR			329	.245

MARSHALL, ROY DE VERNE "RUBE"
B.JAN.19,1890 SALINEVILLE,OHIO
1912	PHI	N	P		2	0- 1
1913	PHI	N	P		13	1- 3
1914	PHI	N	P		27	6- 7
1915	BUF	F	P		21	2- 1
		BRTR			63	9-12

MARSHALL, RUFUS JAMES "JIM"
B.MAY 25,1932 DANVILLE,ILL.
1958	BAL	A	1-O		85	.215
	CHI	N	1-O		26	.272
1959	CHI	N	1-O		108	.252
1960	SF	N	1-O		75	.237
1961	SF	N	1-O		44	.222
1962	NY	N	1-O		17	.344
	PIT	N	1		55	.220
		BLTL			410	.242
NON-PLAYING MANAGER
CHI(N) 1974-76

MARSHALL, WILLARD WARREN
B.FEB.8,1921 RICHMOND,VA.
1942	NY	N	O		116	.257
1946	NY	N	O		131	.282
1947	NY	N	O		155	.291
1948	NY	N	O		143	.272
1949	NY	N	O		141	.307
1950	BOS	N	O		105	.235
1951	BOS	N	O		136	.281
1952	BOS	N	O		21	.227
	CIN	N	O		107	.267
1953	CIN	N	O		122	.266
1954	CHI	A	O		47	.254
1955	CHI	A	O		22	.171
		BLTR			1246	.274

MARSHALL, WILLIAM HENRY
B.FEB.14,1909 DORCHESTER,MASS.
1931	BOS	A	H		1	.000
1934	CIN	N	2		6	.125
		BRTR			7	.125

MARSHALL, WILLIAM RIDDLE "DOC"
B.SEPT.22,1875 BUTLER,PA.
D.DEC.11,1959
1904	PHI	N	C		8	.100
	NY	N	C		1	.000
	BOS	N	C		13	.209
	NY	N	H		10	.353
1906	NY	N	C-O		29	.167
	STL	N	C		38	.276
1907	STL	N	C		83	.202
1908	STL	N	C		6	.071
	CHI	N	C		9	.300
1909	BRO	N	C		47	.202
		BRTR			244	.210

MARTEL, LEON ALPHONSE "DOC"
B.JAN.29,1883 BOSTON,MASS.
D.OCT.11,1947
1909	PHI	N	C		24	.268
1910	BOS	N	1		10	.000
		TR			34	.211

MARTIN, ALBERT
(PLAYED UNDER NAME OF
ALBERT MAY)

MARTIN, ALFRED MANUEL "BILLY"
B.MAY 16,1928 BERKELEY,CAL.
1950	NY	A	2-3		34	.250
1951	NY	A	2-S-3-O		51	.259
1952	NY	A	2		109	.267
1953	NY	A	2-S		149	.257
1955	NY	A	2-S		20	.300
1956	NY	A	2-3		121	.264
1957	NY	A	2-3		43	.241
	KC	A	2-S-3		73	.257
1958	DET	A	S-3		131	.255
1959	CLE	A	2-3		73	.260
1960	CIN	N	2		103	.246
1961	MIL	N	H		6	.000
	MIN	A	2-S		108	.246
		BRTR			1021	.257
NON-PLAYING MANAGER
MIN(A) 1969, DET(A) 1971-73
TEX(A) 1973-75, NY(A) 1975-76

MARTIN, ALPHONSE CASE
B.AUG.4,1845 NEW YORK,N.Y.
D.MAY 24,1933
1872	TRO	NA	P-O	3	25	1- 2
						.287
	ECK	NA	P-O	8	18	1- 7
						.183
1873	MUT	NA	P-C-	2	30	0- 2
			O			-
1874	ATL	NA	2-O		7	-
1875	ATL	NA	O		5	-
				13	85	2-11

MARTIN, BARNEY ROBERT
B.MAR.3,1923 COLUMBIA,S.C.
| 1953 | CIN | N | P | | 1 | 0- 0 |
| | | BRTR | | | | |

MARTIN, BORIS MICHAEL "BABE"
(REAL NAME
BORIS MICHAEL MARTINOVICH)
B.MAR.28,1921 SEATTLE,WASH.
1944	STL	A	O		2	.750
1945	STL	A	1-O		54	.200
1946	STL	A	C		3	.222
1948	BOS	A	C		4	.500
1949	BOS	A	C		2	.000
1953	STL	A	C		4	.000
		BRTR			69	.214

MARTIN, ELWOOD GOOD "SPEED"
B.SEPT.15,1893 WAWAWAI,WASH.
1917	STL	A	P	9	10	0- 3
1918	CHI	N	P		9	5- 2
1919	CHI	N	P		35	8- 8
1920	CHI	N	P		35	4-15
1921	CHI	N	P		37	11-15
1922	CHI	N	P		1	1- 0
		BRTR		126	127	29-43

MARTIN, FRANK
B.1877 CHICAGO,ILL.
1897	LOU	N	2		2	.222
1898	CHI	N	2		1	.000
1899	NY	N	2		17	.254
					20	.235

MARTIN, FREDERICK TURNER "FRED"
B.JUNE 27,1915 CAMERON,OKLA.
1946	STL	N	P		6	2- 1
1949	STL	N	P		21	6- 0
1950	STL	N	P	30	31	4- 2
		BRTR		57	58	12- 3

MARTIN, HAROLD WINTHROP "DOC"
B.SEPT.23,1887 ROXBURY,MASS.
D.APR.15,1935 MILTON,MASS.
1908	PHI	A	P		1	0- 1
1911	PHI	A	P		11	1- 3
1912	PHI	A	P		2	0- 0
		BRTR			14	1- 4

MARTIN, HERSHEL RAY
B.SEPT.19,1909 BRIMINGHAM,ALA.
1937	PHI	N	O		141	.283
1938	PHI	N	O		120	.298
1939	PHI	N	O		111	.282
1940	PHI	N	O		33	.253
1944	NY	A	O		85	.302
1945	NY	A	O		117	.267
		BBTR			607	.285

YR	CL	LEA	POS	GP	G	REC

MARTIN, JERRY LINDSEY
B.MAY 11,1949 COLUMBIA,S.C.

YR	CL	LEA	POS	GP	G	REC
1974	PHI	N	O		13	.214
1975	PHI	N	O		57	.212
1976	PHI	N	1-O		130	.248
	BRTR				200	.230

MARTIN, JOHN CHRISTOPHER "JACK"
B.APR.19,1889 PLAINFIELD,N.J.

YR	CL	LEA	POS	GP	G	REC
1913	NY	A	S		69	.225
1914	BOS	N	3		33	.212
	PHI	N	S		83	.253
	BRTR				185	.237

MARTIN, JOHN LEONARD "PEPPER"
B.FEB.29,1904 TEMPLE,OKLA.
D.MAR.5,1965 MC ALESTER,OKLA.

YR	CL	LEA	POS	GP	G	REC
1928	STL	N	O		39	.308
1930	STL	N	O		6	.000
1931	STL	N	O		123	.300
1932	STL	N	3-O		85	.238
1933	STL	N	3		145	.316
1934	STL	N	P-3	1	110	0- 0
						.289
1935	STL	N	3-O		135	.299
1936	STL	N	P-3-O	1	143	0- 0
						.309
1937	STL	N	O		98	.304
1938	STL	N	O		91	.294
1939	STL	N	3-O		88	.306
1940	STL	N	3-O		86	.316
1944	STL	N	O		40	.279
	BRTR			2	1189	0- 0
						.298

MARTIN, JOSEPH CLIFTON "J.C."
B.DEC.13,1936 AXTON,VA.

YR	CL	LEA	POS	GP	G	REC
1959	CHI	A	3		3	.250
1960	CHI	A	1-3		7	.100
1961	CHI	A	1-3		110	.239
1962	CHI	A	C-1-3		18	.077
1963	CHI	A	C-1-3		105	.205
1964	CHI	A	C		122	.197
1965	CHI	A	C-1-3		119	.261
1966	CHI	A	C		67	.255
1967	CHI	A	C-1		101	.234
1968	NY	N	C-1		78	.225
1969	NY	N	C-1		66	.209
1970	CHI	N	C-1		40	.156
1971	CHI	N	C-O		47	.264
1972	CHI	N	C		25	.240
	BLTR				908	.222

MARTIN, JOSEPH SAMUEL
B.JAN.1,1876 HOLLIDAYSBURG,PA.
D.MAY 25,1964 ALTOONA,PA.

YR	CL	LEA	POS	GP	G	REC
1903	WAS	A	2-3-0		36	.208
	STL	A	3-0		44	.231
	BLTR				80	.221

MARTIN, MORRIS WEBSTER
"MORRIE" OR "LEFTY"
B.SEPT.3,1922 DIXON,MO.

YR	CL	LEA	POS	GP	G	REC
1949	BRO	N	P		10	1- 3
1951	PHI	A	P		35	11- 4
1952	PHI	A	P		5	0- 2
1953	PHI	A	P		58	10-12
	CHI	A	P		35	5- 4
1955	CHI	A	P		37	2- 3
1956	CHI	A	P		10	1- 0
	BAL	A	P		9	1- 1
1957	STL	N	P		4	0- 0
1958	STL	N	P		17	3- 1
	CLE	A	P		14	2- 0
1959	CHI	N	P		3	0- 0
	BLTL				250	38-34

MARTIN, PATRICK FRANCIS
B.APR.13,1894 BROOKLYN,N.Y.

YR	CL	LEA	POS	GP	G	REC
1919	PHI	A	P		2	0- 2
1920	PHI	A	P		8	1- 4
	BLTL				10	1- 6

MARTIN, PAUL CHARLES
B.MAR.9,1932 FAYETTE CITY,PA.

YR	CL	LEA	POS	GP	G	REC
1955	PIT	N	P		7	0- 1
	BRTR					

MARTIN, RAYMOND JOSEPH
B.MAR.13,1925 NORWOOD,MASS.

YR	CL	LEA	POS	GP	G	REC
1943	BOS	N	P		2	0- 0
1947	BOS	N	P		1	1- 0
1948	BOS	N	P		2	0- 0
	BRTR				5	1- 0

MARTIN, STUART MC GUIRE
B.NOV.17,1913 RICH SQUARE,N.C.

YR	CL	LEA	POS	GP	G	REC
1936	STL	N	2		92	.298
1937	STL	N	2		90	.260
1938	STL	N	2		114	.278
1939	STL	N	2		120	.268
1940	STL	N	2-3		112	.238
1941	PIT	N	1-2-3		88	.304
1942	PIT	N	1-2-S		42	.225
1943	CHI	N	1-2-3		64	.220
	BLTR				722	.268

MARTIN, THOMAS EUGENE "GENE"
B.JAN.12,1947 AMERICUS,GA.

YR	CL	LEA	POS	GP	G	REC
1968	WAS	A	O		9	.364
	BLTR					

MARTIN, WILLIAM GLOYD "BILLY"
B.FEB.13,1894 WASHINGTON,D.C.
D.SEPT.14,1949 ARLINGTON,VA.

YR	CL	LEA	POS	GP	G	REC
1914	BOS	N	S		1	.000
	BRTR					

MARTIN, WILLIAM JOSEPH
"SMOKEY JOE"
B.JULY 28,1911 SEYMOUR,MO.
D.SEPT.28,1960

YR	CL	LEA	POS	GP	G	REC
1936	NY	N	3		7	.267
1938	CHI	A	H		1	.000
	BRTR				8	.267

MARTINA, JOSEPH JOHN
"OYSTER JOE"
B.JULY 8,1889 NEW ORLEANS,LA.
D.MAR.22,1962

YR	CL	LEA	POS	GP	G	REC
1924	WAS	A	P	24	25	6- 8
	BRTR					

MARTINEZ, FELIX ANTHONY "TIPPY"
B.MAY 31,1950 LAJUNTA,COL.

YR	CL	LEA	POS	GP	G	REC
1974	NY	A	P		10	0- 0
1975	NY	A	P		23	1- 2
1976	NY	A	P		11	2- 0
	BAL	A	P		28	3- 1
	BLTL				72	6- 3

MARTINEZ, GABRIEL ANTONIO (DIAZ)
"TONY"
B.MAR.18,1941 MATANZAS,CUBA

YR	CL	LEA	POS	GP	G	REC
1963	CLE	A	S		43	.156
1964	CLE	A	2-S		9	.214
1965	CLE	A	H		4	.000
1966	CLE	A	2-S		17	.294
	BRTR				73	.171

MARTINEZ, JOHN ALBERT "BUCK"
D.NOV.7,1948 REDDING,CAL.

YR	CL	LEA	POS	GP	G	REC
1969	KC	A	C-O		72	.229
1970	KC	A	C		6	.111
1971	KC	A	L		22	.152
1973	KC	A	L		14	.250
1974	KC	A	L		43	.215
1975	KC	A	L		80	.226
1976	KC	A	C		95	.228
	BRTR				332	.222

MARTINEZ, JOSE (AZCUIZ)
B.JULY 26,1942 CARDENAS,CUBA

YR	CL	LEA	POS	GP	G	REC
1969	PIT	N	2-S-3-0		77	.268
1970	PIT	N	2-S-3		19	.050
	BRTR				96	.245

MARTINEZ, JOSE DENNIS (EMILIA)
"DENNIS"
B.MAY 14,1955 GRANADA,NICARAGUA

YR	CL	LEA	POS	GP	G	REC
1976	BAL	A	P		4	1- 2
	BRTR					

MARTINEZ, ORLANDO (OLIVA)
"MARTY"
B.AUG.23,1941 HAVANA,CUBA

YR	CL	LEA	POS	GP	G	REC
1962	MIN	A	S-3		37	.167
1967	ATL	N	C-1-2-S-		44	.288
1968	ATL	N	C-2-S-3		113	.230
1969	HOU	N	P-C-	1	78	0- 0
			2-S-3-0			.308
1970	HOU	N	C-2-S-3		75	.220
1971	HOU	N	1-2-S-3		32	.258
1972	HOU	N	2-S-3		9	.429
	OAK	A	2-S-3		22	.125
	TEX	A	2-S-3		26	.146
	BBTR			1	436	0- 0
						.243
	BR 1962					

MARTINEZ, ROGELIO (ULLOA)
"LIMONAR"
B.NOV.5,1928 CIDRA,CUBA

YR	CL	LEA	POS	GP	G	REC
1950	WAS	A	P		2	0- 1
	BRTR					

MARTINEZ, RODOLFO HECTOR
"HECTOR"
B.MAY 11,1939 LAS VILLAS,CUBA

YR	CL	LEA	POS	GP	G	REC
1962	KC	A	H		1	.000
1963	KC	A	O		6	.286
	BRTR				7	.267

MARTINEZ, TEODORO NOEL "TED"
B.DEC.10,1947 CENTRAL BARAHONA,
D.R.

YR	CL	LEA	POS	GP	G	REC
1970	NY	N	2-S		4	.063
1971	NY	N	2-S-3-0		38	.288
1972	NY	N	2-S-3-0		103	.224
1973	NY	N	2-S-3-0		92	.255
1974	NY	N	2-S-3-0		116	.219
1975	STL	N	2-S-3-0		16	.190
	OAK	A	2-S-3		86	.172
	BRTR				455	.230
	BB 1973 (PART)					

MARTINI, GUIDO JOE
B.JULY 1,1913 BIRMINGHAM,ALA.
D.OCT.28,1970

YR	CL	LEA	POS	GP	G	REC
1935	PHI	A	P		3	0- 2
	BRTR					

MARTINOVICH, BORIS MICHAEL
(PLAYED UNDER NAME OF
BORIS MICHAEL MARTIN)

MARTY, JOSEPH ANTON "JOE"
B.SEPT.1,1913 SACRAMENTO,CAL.

YR	CL	LEA	POS	GP	G	REC
1937	CHI	N	O		88	.290
1938	CHI	N	O		76	.243
1939	CHI	N	O		23	.132
	PHI	N	P-O	1	91	0- 0
						.254
1940	PHI	N	O		123	.270
1941	PHI	N	O		137	.268
	BRTR			1	538	0- 0
						.261

MARTYN, ROBERT GORDON "BOB"
B.AUG.15,1930 WEISER,IDAHO

YR	CL	LEA	POS	GP	G	REC
1957	KC	A	O		58	.267
1958	KC	A	O		95	.261
1959	KC	A	H		1	.000
	BLTR				154	.263

MARTZ, GARY ARTHUR
B.JAN.10,1951 SPOKANE,WASH.

YR	CL	LEA	POS	GP	G	REC
1975	KC	A	O		1	.000
	BRTR					

MASHORE, CLYDE WAYNE
B.MAY 29,1945 CONCORD,CAL.

YR	CL	LEA	POS	GP	G	REC
1969	CIN	N	H		2	.000
1970	MON	N	O		13	.160
1971	MON	N	3-0		66	.193
1972	MON	N	O		93	.227
1973	MON	N	2-0		67	.204
	BRTR				241	.208

MASI, PHILIP SAMUEL "PHIL"
B.JAN.6,1917 CHICAGO,ILL.

YR	CL	LEA	POS	GP	G	REC
1939	BOS	N	C		46	.254
1940	BOS	N	C		63	.196
1941	BOS	N	C		87	.222
1942	BOS	N	C-O		57	.218
1943	BOS	N	C		80	.273
1944	BOS	N	C-1-3		89	.275
1945	BOS	N	C-1		114	.272
1946	BOS	N	C		133	.267
1947	BOS	N	C		126	.304
1948	BOS	N	C		113	.253
1949	BOS	N	C		37	.210
	PIT	N	C-1		48	.274
1950	CHI	A	C		122	.279
1951	CHI	A	C		84	.271
1952	CHI	A	C		30	.254
	BRTR				1229	.264

MASKREY, HARRY H.
B.DEC.21,1861 MERCER,PA.
D.AUG.17,1930

YR	CL	LEA	POS	GP	G	REC
1882	LOU	AA	O		1	.000

YR	CL	LEA	POS	GP	G	REC
MASKREY, SAMUEL LEECH						
B.FEB.16,1856 MERCER,PA.						
D.APR.1,1922						
1882	LOU	AA	M-2-O		76	.225
1883	LOU	AA	M-S-O		96	.190
1884	LOU	AA	O		107	.247
1885	LOU	AA	O		110	.230
1886	LOU	AA	O		5	.158
	CIN	AA	O		27	.204
					421	.227
MASON, ADELBERT WILLIAM "DEL"						
B.OCT.29,1883 LOCKPORT,N.Y.						
D.DEC.31,1962						
1904	WAS	A	P		5	0- 3
1906	CIN	N	P		2	0- 1
1907	CIN	N	P		25	5-12
		BRTR			32	5-16
MASON, CHARLES E.						
B.JUNE 25,1853 NEW ORLEANS,LA						
D.OCT.21,1936						
1875	CEN	NA	1-O		12	-
	NAT	NA	O		8	-
1883	ATH	AA	M-O		1	.500
		TR			21	-
NON-PLAYING MANAGER						
ATH(AA) 1882, 84-87						
MASON, DONALD STETSON "DON"						
B.DEC.20,1944 BOSTON,MASS.						
1966	SF	N	2		42	.120
1967	SF	N	2		4	.000
1968	SF	N	2-S-3		10	.158
1969	SF	N	2-S-3		104	.228
1970	SF	N	2		46	.139
1971	SD	N	2-3		113	.212
1972	SD	N	2		9	.182
1973	SD	N	2		8	.000
		BLTR			336	.205
MASON, ERNEST						
B.NEW ORLEANS,LA.						
D.AUG.1904						
1894	STL	N	P		4	0- 2
MASON, HENRY						
B.JUNE 19,1931 MARSHALL,MO.						
1958	PHI	N	P		1	0- 0
1960	PHI	N	P		3	0- 0
		BRTR			4	0- 0
MASON, JAMES PERCY "JIM"						
B.AUG.14,1950 MOBILE,ALA.						
1971	WAS	A	S		3	.333
1972	TEX	A	S-3		46	.197
1973	TEX	A	2-S-3		92	.206
1974	NY	A	S		152	.250
1975	NY	A	2-S		94	.152
1976	NY	A	S		93	.180
		BLTR			480	.207
MASSA, GORDON RICHARD						
B.SEPT.2,1935 CINCINNATI,OHIO						
1957	CHI	N	C		6	.467
1958	CHI	N	H		2	.000
		BLTR			8	.412
MASSEY, ROY H.						
B.OCT.9,1892 SEVIERVILLE,TENN.						
D.JUNE 24,1956						
1918	BOS	N	1-S-3-O		66	.291
		BLTR				
MASSEY, WILLIAM HARRY						
"BIG BILL"						
B.JAN.1871 PHILADELPHIA,PA.						
D.OCT.9,1940						
1894	CIN	N	1		13	.294
MASSEY, WILLIAM HERBERT "MIKE"						
B.SEPT.28,1893 GALVESTON,TEX.						
D.OCT.17,1971 SHREVEPORT,LA.						
1917	BOS	N	2		31	.198
		BBTR				
MASTERS, WALTER THOMAS						
B.MAR.28,1907 PEN ARGYL,PA.						
1931	WAS	A	P		3	0- 0
1937	PHI	N	P		1	0- 0
1939	PHI	A	P		4	0- 0
		BRTR			8	0- 0
MASTERSON, PAUL NICKALIS						
B.OCT.16,1915 CHICAGO,ILL.						
1940	PHI	N	P		2	0- 0
1941	PHI	N	P		2	1- 0
1942	PHI	N	P		4	0- 0
		BLTL			8	1- 0
MASTERSON, WALTER EDWARD "WALT"						
B.JUNE 22,1920 PHILADELPHIA,PA.						
1939	WAS	A	P		24	2- 2
1940	WAS	A	P		31	3-13
1941	WAS	A	P		34	4- 3
1942	WAS	A	P	25	26	5- 9
1945	WAS	A	P		4	1- 2
1946	WAS	A	P		29	5- 6
1947	WAS	A	P	35	36	12-16
1948	WAS	A	P		33	8-15
1949	WAS	A	P	10	11	3- 2
	BOS	A	P		18	3- 4
1950	BOS	A	P		33	8- 6
1951	BOS	A	P		30	3- 0
1952	BOS	A	P		5	1- 1
	WAS	A	P		24	9- 8
1953	WAS	A	P		29	10-12
1956	DET	A	P		35	1- 1
		BRTR		399	402	78-100
MATARAZZO, LEONARD						
B.SEPT.12,1928 NEW CASTLE,PA.						
1952	PHI	A	P		1	0- 0
		BRTR				
MATCHICK, JOHN THOMAS "TOMMY"						
B.SEP.7,1943 HAZLETON,PA.						
1967	DET	A	S		8	.167
1968	DET	A	1-2-S		80	.203
1969	DET	A	1-2-S-3		94	.242
1970	BOS	A	2-S-3		10	.071
	KC	A	2-S-3		55	.196
1971	MIL	A	2-3		42	.219
1972	BAL	A	3		3	.222
		BLTR			292	.215
MATHES, JOSEPH JOHN						
B.JULY 28,1891 MILWAUKEE,WIS.						
1912	PHI	A	3		4	.154
1914	STL	F	2		24	.298
1916	BOS	N	2		2	.000
		BBTR			30	.276
MATHEWS, EDWIN LEE "EDDIE"						
B.OCT.13,1931 TEXARKANA,TEX.						
1952	BOS	N	3		145	.242
1953	MIL	N	3		157	.302
1954	MIL	N	3-O		138	.290
1955	MIL	N	3		141	.289
1956	MIL	N	3		151	.272
1957	MIL	N	3		148	.292
1958	MIL	N	3		149	.251
1959	MIL	N	3		148	.306
1960	MIL	N	3		153	.277
1961	MIL	N	3		152	.306
1962	MIL	N	1-3		152	.265
1963	MIL	N	3-O		158	.263
1964	MIL	N	1-3		141	.233
1965	MIL	N	3		156	.251
1966	ATL	N	3		134	.250
1967	HOU	N	1-3		101	.238
	DET	A	1-3		36	.231
1968	DET	A	1-3		31	.212
		BLTR			2391	.271
NON-PLAYING MANAGER						
ATL(N) 1972-74						
MATHEWS, NELSON ELMER						
B.JULY 21,1941 COLUMBIA,ILL.						
1960	CHI	N	O		3	.250
1961	CHI	N	O		3	.111
1962	CHI	N	O		15	.306
1963	CHI	N	O		61	.155
1964	KC	A	O		157	.239
1965	KC	A	O		67	.212
		BRTR			306	.223
MATHEWS, ROBERT T.						
B.NOV.21,1851 BALTIMORE,MD.						
D.APR.17,1898						
1871	KEK	NA	P		19	6-13
1872	BAL	NA	P-2-	42	47	26-16
			O			.229
1873	MUT	NA	P-O	25	26	10-15
						-
	ATL	NA	P		1	1- 0
	MUT	NA	P		26	19- 7
1874	MUT	NA	P		65	42-23
1875	MUT	NA	P		70	29-38
1876	MUT	N	P		56	21-34
1877	CIN	N	P-S-O		15	3-12
						.169
1879	PRO	N	P-O	19	42	11- 5
						.200
1881	PRO	N	P-O	13	15	4- 7
						.155
	BOS	N	P-O	5	19	1- 0
						.169
1882	BOS	N	P-S-	34	45	19-14
			O			.224
1883	ATH	AA	P-O		44	30-14
						.173
1884	ATH	AA	P		49	30-18
1885	ATH	AA	P		48	30-17
1886	ATH	AA	P		23	13- 9
1887	ATH	AA	P		8	3- 5
		BRTR		572	618	298-247
						-
MATHEWS, WILLIAM C.						
B.JAN.12,1878 MAHANOY CITY,PA.						
D.JAN.23,1946						
1909	BOS	A	P		5	0- 0
MATHEWSON, CHRISTOPHER						
"CHRISTY", "MATTY" OR "BIG SIX"						
B.AUG.12,1880 FACTORYVILLE,PA.						
D.OCT.7,1925 SARANAC LAKE,N.Y.						
1900	NY	N	P		6	0- 2
1901	NY	N	P		37	20-16
1902	NY	N	P-1-	34	41	13-18
			O			.200
1903	NY	N	P		45	30-13
1904	NY	N	P		48	33-12
1905	NY	N	P		43	32- 8
1906	NY	N	P		38	22-12
1907	NY	N	P		41	24-12
1908	NY	N	P		56	37-11
1909	NY	N	P		37	25- 6
1910	NY	N	P		38	27- 9
1911	NY	N	P		45	26-13
1912	NY	N	P		43	23-12
1913	NY	N	P		40	25-11
1914	NY	N	P		41	24-13
1915	NY	N	P		27	8-14
1916	NY	N	P		12	3- 4
	CIN	N	M-P		1	1- 0
		BRTR		632	639	373-186
						.214
NON-PLAYING MANAGER						
CIN(N) 1917-18						
MATHEWSON, HENRY						
B.DEC.24,1886 FACTORYVILLE,PA.						
D.JULY 1,1917						
1906	NY	N	P		2	0- 0
1907	NY	N	P		1	0- 0
					3	0- 1
MATHIAS, CARL LYNWOOD						
B.JUNE 13,1936 BECHTELSVILLE,PA						
1960	CLE	A	P		7	0- 1
1961	WAS	A	P		4	0- 1
		BBTL			11	0- 2
MATHISON, I. I.						
1902	BAL	A	S-3		28	.275
MATIAS, JOHN ROY						
B.AUG.15,1944 HONOLULU,HAWAII						
1970	CHI	A	1-O		58	.188
		BLTL				
MATLACK, JONATHAN TRUMPBOUR						
"JON"						
B.JAN.19,1950 WEST CHESTER,PA.						
1971	NY	N	P		7	0- 3
1972	NY	N	P		34	15-10
1973	NY	N	P	34	35	14-16
1974	NY	N	P		34	13-15
1975	NY	N	P		33	16-12
1976	NY	N	P		35	17-10
		BLTL		177	178	75-66

YR	CL LEA POS	GP	G	REC

MATTERN, ALONZO ALBERT
B.JUNE 16,1883 W.RUSH,N.Y.
D.NOV.6,1958

1908	BOS N P		5	1- 2
1909	BOS N P		47	15-21
1910	BOS N P		51	16-19
1911	BOS N P		33	4-15
1912	BOS N P		2	0- 1
	BLTR		138	36-58

MATTERSON, C. V.
B.OHIO

| 1884 | STL U P-O | 1 | 1- 0 |
| | | | .000 |

MATTESON, HENRY EDSON
"EDDIE" OR "MATTY"
B.SEPT.7,1884 GUYS MILLS,PA.
D.SEPT.1,1943 WESTFIELD,N.Y.

1914	PHI N P		15	3- 2
1918	WAS A P		14	5- 3
	BRTR		29	8- 5

MATTHEWS, JAMES VINCENT
B.SEPT.29,1899 BALTIMORE,MD.

| 1922 | BOS N P | | 3 | 0- 1 |
| | BRTL | | | |

MATTHEWS, GARY NATHANIEL
B.JULY 5,1950 SAN FERNANDO,CAL.

1972	SF N O		20	.290
1973	SF N O		148	.300
1974	SF N O		154	.287
1975	SF N O		116	.280
1976	SF N O		156	.279
	BRTR		594	.287

MATTHEWS, ROBERT
B.CAMDEN,N.J.

| 1891 | ATH AA O | 1 | | .333 |

MATTHEWS, WID CURRY
B.OCT.20,1896 RALEIGH,ILL
D.OCT.5,1965 HOLLYWOOD,CAL.

1923	PHI A O		129	.274
1924	WAS A O		53	.302
1925	WAS A O		10	.444
	BLTL		192	.284

MATTHEWSON, DALE WESLEY
B.MAY 15,1923 CATASAUQA,PA.

1943	PHI N P	11	12	0- 3
1944	PHI N P		17	0- 0
	BRTR	28	29	0- 3

MATTHIAS, STEPHEN J.
B.MITCHELLVILLE,MD.

| 1884 | CHI U S | | 35 | .274 |

MATTICK, ROBERT JAMES "BOBBY"
B.DEC.5,1916 SIOUX CITY,IOWA

1938	CIN N S		1	1.000
1939	CIN N S		51	.287
1940	CIN N S-3		128	.218
1941	CIN N 2-S-3		20	.183
1942	CIN N S		6	.200
	BRTR		206	.233

MATTICK, WALTER JOSEPH "CHINK"
B.MAR.12,1887 ST.LOUIS,MO.
D.NOV.5,1968 LOS ALTOS,CAL.

1912	CHI A O		88	.260
1913	CHI A O		68	.188
1918	STL N O		8	.142
	BRTR		164	.227

MATTIMORE, MICHAEL J.
B.1859 RENOVO,PA.
D.APR.29,1931

1887	NY N P		8	3- 4
1888	ATH AA P	26	41	15-10
1889	ATH AA P-O	4	23	2- 2
				.257
	KC AA P-O	2	19	1- 1
				.147
1890	BRO AA P-O	20	33	6-14
				.126
	BLTR	60	124	27-31
				.206

MATTINGLY, LAWRENCE EARL
B.NOV.4,1904 CHARLES CO.,MD.

| 1931 | BRO N P | 8 | | 0- 1 |
| | BRTR | | | |

MATTIS, RALPH L.
B.1891 ST.MARY'S,PA.
D.SEPT.13,1960

| 1914 | PIT F O | | 35 | .247 |
| | BRTR | | | |

MATTOX, CLOY MITCHELL
B.NOV.24,1905 LEESVILLE,VA.

| 1929 | PHI A C | | 3 | .167 |
| | BLTR | | | |

MATTOX, JAMES POWELL
B.DEC.17,1897 LEESVILLE,VA.

1922	PIT N C		29	.294
1923	PIT N C		22	.188
	BLTR		51	.253

MATUZAK, HARRY GEORGE
B.JAN.27,1911 OLMER,MICH.

1934	PHI A P		11	0- 3
1936	PHI A P		6	0- 1
	BRTR		17	0- 4

MAUCH, EUGENE WILLIAM
"GENE" OR "SKIP"
B.NOV.18,1925 SALINA,KAN.

1944	BRO N S		5	.133
1947	PIT N 2-S		16	.300
1948	BRO N 2-S		12	.154
	CHI N 2-S		53	.203
1949	CHI N 2-S-3		72	.247
1950	BOS N 2-S-3		48	.231
1951	BOS N 2-S-3		19	.100
1952	STL N S		7	.000
1956	BOS A 2		7	.320
1957	BOS A 2		65	.270
	BRTR		304	.239

NON-PLAYING MANAGER
PHI(N) 1960-68, MON(N) 1969-75,
MIN(A) 1976

MAUCK, ALFRED MARIS "HAL"
B.MAR.6,1869 PRINCETON,IND.
D.APR.27,1921

| 1893 | CHI N P | | 18 | 8- 9 |

MAUL, ALBERT JOSEPH
"SMILING AL"
B.OCT.9,1866 PHILADELPHIA,PA.
D.MAY 3,1958

1884	KEY U P		1	0- 1
1887	PHI N P	7	16	5- 2
1888	PIT N P-1-	2	73	0- 1
	O			.211
1889	PIT N P-O	6	67	1- 3
				.276
1890	PIT P P-O	32	44	17-11
				.265
1891	PIT N P-O	6	40	1- 2
				.194
1893	WAS N P	34	39	10-23
1894	WAS N P	28	35	11-15
1895	WAS N P	17	20	11- 6
1896	WAS N P		9	5- 2
1897	WAS N P		1	0- 0
	BAL N P		1	0- 0
1898	BAL N P	28	29	20- 7
1899	BRO N P		4	2- 0
1900	PHI N P		5	2- 3
1901	NY N P		3	0- 2
	BRTR	184	387	85-78
				.251

MAULDIN, MARSHALL REESE
B.NOV.5,1914 ATLANTA,GA.

| 1934 | CHI A 3 | | 10 | .263 |
| | BRTR | | | |

MAUN, ERNEST GERALD
B.FEB.3,1901 CLEARWATER,KAN.

1924	NY N P		22	1- 1
1926	PHI N P		14	1- 4
	BLTR		36	2- 5

MAUNEY, RICHARD
B.JAN.26,1920 CONCORD,N.C.
D.FEB.6,1970 ALBERMARLE,N.C.

1945	PHI N P	20	22	6-10
1946	PHI N P	24	25	6- 4
1947	PHI N P	9	15	0- 0
	BRTR	53	62	12-14

MAUPIN, HARRY CARR
B.JULY 11,1872 WELLESVILLE,MO.
D.AUG.23,1952

1898	STL N P		2	0- 2
1899	CLE N P		5	0- 3
			7	0- 5

MAURIELLO, RALPH
B.AUG.25,1934 BROOKLYN,N.Y.

| 1958 | LA N P | | 3 | 1- 1 |
| | BRTR | | | |

MAURO, CARMEN LOUIS
B.NOV.10,1926 ST.PAUL,MINN.

1948	CHI N O		3	.200
1950	CHI N O		62	.227
1951	CHI N O		13	.172
1953	BRO N O		8	.000
	WAS A O		17	.174
	PHI A 3-O		64	.267
	BLTR		167	.231

MAVIS, ROBERT HENRY "BOB"
B.APR.8,1920 MILWAUKEE,WIS.

| 1949 | DET A H | 1 | | .000 |
| | BLTR | | | |

MAXIE, LARRY HANS
B.OCT.10,1940 UPLAND,CAL.

| 1969 | ATL N P | | 2 | 0- 0 |
| | BRTR | | | |

MAXVILL, CHARLES DALLAN "DAL"
B.FEB.18,1939 GRANITE CITY,ILL.

1962	STL N S-3		79	.222
1963	STL N 2-S-3		53	.235
1964	STL N 2-S-3-O		37	.231
1965	STL N 2-S		68	.135
1966	STL N 2-S-O		134	.244
1967	STL N 2-S		152	.227
1968	STL N S		151	.253
1969	STL N S		132	.175
1970	STL N 2-S		152	.201
1971	STL N S		142	.225
1972	STL N 2-S		105	.221
	OAK A 2-S		27	.250
1973	OAK A 2-S-3		29	.211
	PIT N S		74	.189
1974	PIT N S		8	.182
	OAK A 2-S-3		60	.192
1975	OAK A 2-S		20	.200
	BRTR		1423	.217

MAXWELL, CHARLES RICHARD
"CHARLIE"
B.APR.8,1927 LAWTON,MICH.

1950	BOS A O		2	.000
1951	BOS A O		49	.188
1952	BOS A 1-O		8	.067
1954	BOS A O		74	.250
1955	BAL A H		4	.000
	DET A 1-O		55	.266
1956	DET A O		141	.326
1957	DET A O		138	.276
1958	DET A 1-O		131	.272
1959	DET A O		145	.251
1960	DET A O		134	.237
1961	DET A O		79	.229
1962	DET A 1-O		30	.194
	CHI A		69	.296
1963	CHI A 1-O		71	.231
1964	CHI A H		2	.000
	BLTL		1132	.264

MAXWELL, JAMES ALBERT "BERT"
B.OCT.17,1886 TEXARKANA,ARK.
D.DEC.10,1961 BRADY,TEX.

1906	PIT N P		1	0- 1
1908	PHI A P		4	0- 0
1911	NY N P		4	1- 2
1914	BRO F P		12	3- 4
	BBTR		21	4- 7

MAY, ALBERT
(REAL NAME ALBERT MARTIN)

| 1872 | ECK NA 2 | | 4 | .263 |

YP	CL	LEA	POS	GP	G	REC

MAY, CARLOS
B.MAY 17,1948 BIRMINGHAM,ALA.

1968	CHI	A	O		17	.179
1969	CHI	A	O		100	.281
1970	CHI	A	1-O		150	.285
1971	CHI	A	1-O		141	.294
1972	CHI	A	1-O		148	.308
1973	CHI	A	1-O-D		149	.268
1974	CHI	A	O-D		149	.249
1975	CHI	A	1-O-D		128	.271
1976	CHI	A	O		20	.175
1976	NY	A	1-O-D		87	.278
	BLTR				1089	.275

MAY, DAVID LAFRANCE "DAVE"
B.DEC.23,1943 NEW CASTLE,DEL.

1967	BAL	A	O		36	.235
1968	BAL	A	O		84	.191
1969	BAL	A	O		78	.242
1970	BAL	A	O		25	.194
	MIL	A	O		101	.240
1971	MIL	A	O		144	.277
1972	MIL	A	O		143	.238
1973	MIL	A	O		156	.303
1974	MIL	A	O		135	.226
1975	ATL	N	O		82	.276
1976	ATL	N	O		105	.215
	BLTR				1089	.253

MAY, FRANK SPRUIELL "JAKIE"
B.NOV.23,1895 WENDELL,N.C.
D.JUNE 3,1970 WENDELL,N.C.

1917	STL	N	P		15	0- 0
1918	STL	N	P		29	5- 6
1919	STL	N	P		28	3-12
1920	STL	N	P		16	1- 4
1921	STL	N	P		5	1- 3
1924	CIN	N	P		38	3- 3
1925	CIN	N	P		36	8- 9
1926	CIN	N	P		45	13- 9
1927	CIN	N	P		44	15-12
1928	CIN	N	P		21	3- 5
1929	CIN	N	P		41	10-14
1930	CIN	N	P		26	3-11
1931	CHI	N	P		31	5- 5
1932	CHI	N	P		35	2- 2
	BRTL				410	72-95

MAY, JERRY LEE
B.DEC.14,1943 STAUNTON,VA.

1964	PIT	N	C		11	.258
1965	PIT	N	C		4	.500
1966	PIT	N	C		42	.250
1967	PIT	N	C		110	.271
1968	PIT	N	C		137	.219
1969	PIT	N	C		62	.232
1970	PIT	N	C		51	.209
1971	KC	A	C		71	.252
1972	KC	A	C		53	.190
1973	KC	A	C		11	.133
	NY	N	C		4	.250
	BRTR				556	.234

MAY, LEE ANDREW
B.MAR.23,1943 BIRMINGHAM,ALA.

1965	CIN	N	H		5	.000
1966	CIN	N	1		25	.333
1967	CIN	N	1-O		127	.265
1968	CIN	N	1-O		146	.290
1969	CIN	N	1-O		158	.278
1970	CIN	N	1		153	.253
1971	CIN	N	1		147	.278
1972	HOU	N	1		148	.284
1973	HOU	N	1		148	.270
1974	HOU	N	1		152	.268
1975	BAL	A	1		146	.262
1976	BAL	A	1-D		148	.258
	BRTR				1503	.271

MAY, MERRILL GLEND "PINKY"
B.JAN.18,1911 LACONIA,IND.

1939	PHI	N	3		135	.287
1940	PHI	N	S-3		136	.293
1941	PHI	N	3		142	.267
1942	PHI	N	3		115	.238
1943	PHI	N	3		137	.282
	BRTR				665	.275

MAY, MILTON SCOTT "MILT"
B.AUG.1,1950 GARY,IND.

1970	PIT	N	H		5	.500
1971	PIT	N	C		49	.278
1972	PIT	N	C		57	.281
1973	PIT	N	C		101	.269
1974	HOU	N	C		127	.289
1975	HOU	N	C		111	.241
1976	DET	A	C		6	.280
	BLTR				456	.270

MAY, RUDOLPH "RUDY"
B.JULY 18,1944 COFFEYVILLE,KAN.

1965	CAL	A	P		30	4- 9
1969	CAL	A	P	43	44	10-13
1970	CAL	A	P		38	7-13
1971	CAL	A	P		32	11-12
1972	CAL	A	P		35	12-11
1973	CAL	A	P		34	7-17
1974	CAL	A	P		18	0- 1
	NY	A	P		17	8- 4
1975	NY	A	P		32	14-12
1976	NY	A	P		11	4- 3
	BAL	A	P		24	11- 7
	BLTL			314	315	88-101

MAY, WILLIAM HERBERT "BUCKSHOT"
B.DEC.13,1899 BAKERSFIELD,CAL.

1924	PIT	N	P		1	0- 0
	BRTR					

MAYBERRY, JOHN CLAIBORN
B.FEB.18,1950 DETROIT,MICH.

1968	HOU	N	1		4	.000
1969	HOU	N	H		5	.000
1970	HOU	N	1		50	.216
1971	HOU	N	1		46	.182
1972	KC	A	1		149	.298
1973	KC	A	1		152	.278
1974	KC	A	1-O		126	.234
1975	KC	A	1-O		156	.291
1976	KC	A	1		161	.232
	BLTL				849	.259

MAYE, ARTHUR LEE "LEE"
B.DEC.11,1934 TUSCALOOSA,ALA.

1959	MIL	N	O		51	.300
1960	MIL	N	O		41	.301
1961	MIL	N	O		110	.271
1962	MIL	N	O		99	.244
1963	MIL	N	O		124	.271
1964	MIL	N	3-O		153	.304
1965	MIL	N	O		15	.302
	HOU	N	O		108	.251
1966	HOU	N	O		115	.288
1967	CLE	A	2-O		115	.259
1968	CLE	A	1-O		109	.281
1969	CLE	A	O		43	.250
	WAS	A	O		71	.290
1970	WAS	A	3-O		96	.263
	CHI	A	H		6	.167
1971	CHI	A	O		32	.205
	BLTR				1288	.274

MAYER, EDWARD H.
B.AUG.16,1866 MARSHALL,ILL.

1890	PHI	N	3		117	.241
1891	PHI	N	3-O		65	.201
					182	.217

MAYER, EDWIN DAVID
B.NOV.30,1931 SAN FRANCISCO,CAL

1957	CHI	N	P		3	0- 0
1958	CHI	N	P		19	2- 2
	BLTL				22	2- 2

MAYER, ERSKINE JOHN
(REAL NAME JAMES ERSKINE)
B.JAN.16,1889 ATLANTA,GA.
D.MAR.10,1957 LOS ANGELES,CAL.

1912	PHI	N	P		7	0- 1
1913	PHI	N	P		39	9- 9
1914	PHI	N	P		48	21-19
1915	PHI	N	P		43	21-15
1916	PHI	N	P		28	7- 7
1917	PHI	N	P		28	11- 6
1918	PHI	N	P		13	7- 4
	PIT	N	P		15	9- 3
1919	PIT	N	P		18	5- 3
	CHI	A	P		6	1- 3
	BRTR				245	91-70

MAYER, SAMUEL FRANKEL
(REAL NAME
SAMUEL FRANKEL ERSKINE)
B.FEB.28,1893 ATLANTA,GA.
D.JULY 1,1962 ATLANTA,GA.

1915	WAS	A	P-1-	1	11	0- 0
			O			.231
	BRTL					

MAYER, WALTER A.
B.AUG.3,1889 CINCINNATI,OHIO
D.NOV.18,1951

1911	CHI	A	C		1	.000
1912	CHI	A	C		9	.000
1914	CHI	A	C		39	.165
1915	CHI	A	C		22	.222
1917	BOS	A	C		4	.167
1918	BOS	A	C		26	.224
1919	STL	A	C		30	.226
	BRTR				131	.183

MAYES, ADAIR BUSHYHEAD
B.MAR.17,1885 LOCUST GROVE,OKLA
D.MAY 28,1962

1911	PHI	N	O		5	.000
	BLTR					

MAYNARD, JAMES WALTER "BUSTER"
B.MAR.25,1915 HENDERSON,N.C.

1940	NY	N	O		7	.276
1942	NY	N	2-3-O		89	.247
1943	NY	N	3-O		121	.206
1946	NY	N	O		7	.000
	BRTR				224	.221

MAYNARD, LE ROY EVANS "CHICK"
B.NOV.2,1896 TURNERS FALLS,MASS
D.JAN.31,1957

1922	BOS	A	S		12	.125
	TR					

MAYNARD, RICHARD WHEELER
(PLAYED UNDER NAME OF
RICHARD WHEELER)

**MAYO, EDWARD JOSEPH
"EDDIE" OR "HOTSHOT"**
(REAL NAME
EDWARD JOSEPH MAYOSKI)
B.APR.15,1912 HOLYOKE,MASS.

1936	NY	N	3		46	.199
1937	BOS	N	3		65	.227
1938	BOS	N	S-3		8	.214
1943	PHI	A	3		128	.219
1944	DET	A	2-S		154	.249
1945	DET	A	2		134	.285
1946	DET	A	2		51	.252
1947	DET	A	2		142	.279
1948	DET	A	2-3		106	.249
	BLTR				834	.253

MAYO, JOHN LEWIS "JACKIE"
B.JULY 25,1926 LITCHFIELD,ILL.

1948	PHI	N	O		12	.229
1949	PHI	N	O		45	.128
1950	PHI	N	O		18	.222
1951	PHI	N	O		9	.143
1952	PHI	N	1-O		50	.244
1953	PHI	N	O		5	.000
	BLTR				139	.213

MAYOSKI, EDWARD JOSEPH
(PLAYED UNDER NAME OF
EDWARD JOSEPH MAYO)

MAYS, ALBERT C.
B.MAY 17,1865 CANAL DOVER,OHIO
D.MAY 7,1905

1885	LOU	AA	P		17	6-11
1886	MET	AA	P		41	1-27
1887	MET	AA	P		62	17-34
1888	BRO	AA	P		18	9- 9
1889	COL	AA	P		22	9- 9
1890	COL	AA	P		1	0- 1
	BR				161	52-91

YR	CL	LEA	POS	GP	G	REC

MAYS, CARL WILLIAM
B.NOV.1,1891 LIBERTY,KY.
D.APR.4,1971 EL CAJON,CAL.

YR	CL	LEA	POS	GP	G	REC
1915	BOS	A	P		38	4- 6
1916	BOS	A	P	44	48	18-13
1917	BOS	A	P		35	22- 9
1918	BOS	A	P	35	38	21-13
1919	BOS	A	P	21	22	8-12
	NY	A	P		13	5- 2
1920	NY	A	P		45	26-11
1921	NY	A	P	49	51	27- 9
1922	NY	A	P	34	35	12-14
1923	NY	A	P		23	5- 2
1924	CIN	N	P	37	38	20- 9
1925	CIN	N	P		12	3- 5
1926	CIN	N	P		39	19-12
1927	CIN	N	P		14	3- 7
1928	CIN	N	P		14	4- 1
1929	NY	N	P		37	7- 2
	BLTR		490	502	204-127	

MAYS, WILLIE HOWARD
B.MAY 6,1931 WESTFIELD,ALA.

YR	CL	LEA	POS	GP	G	REC
1951	NY	N	O		121	.274
1952	NY	N	O		34	.236
1954	NY	N	O		151	.345
1955	NY	N	O		152	.319
1956	NY	N	O		152	.296
1957	NY	N	O		152	.333
1958	SF	N	O		152	.347
1959	SF	N	O		151	.313
1960	SF	N	O		153	.319
1961	SF	N	O		154	.308
1962	SF	N	O		162	.304
1963	SF	N	S-O		157	.314
1964	SF	N	1-S-3-O		157	.296
1965	SF	N	O		157	.317
1966	SF	N	O		152	.288
1967	SF	N	O		141	.263
1968	SF	N	1-O		148	.289
1969	SF	N	1-O		117	.283
1970	SF	N	1-O		139	.291
1971	SF	N	1-O		136	.271
1972	SF	N	O		19	.184
	NY	N	1-O		69	.267
1973	NY	N	1-O		66	.211
	BRTR			2992	.302	

MAZEROSKI, WILLIAM STANLEY "BILL"
B.SEP.5,1936 WHEELING,W.VA.

YR	CL	LEA	POS	GP	G	REC
1956	PIT	N	2		81	.243
1957	PIT	N	2		148	.283
1958	PIT	N	2		152	.275
1959	PIT	N	2		135	.241
1960	PIT	N	2		151	.273
1961	PIT	N	2		152	.265
1962	PIT	N	2		159	.271
1963	PIT	N	2		142	.245
1964	PIT	N	2		162	.268
1965	PIT	N	2		130	.271
1966	PIT	N	2		162	.262
1967	PIT	N	2		163	.261
1968	PIT	N	2		143	.251
1969	PIT	N	2		67	.229
1970	PIT	N	2		112	.229
1971	PIT	N	2-3		70	.254
1972	PIT	N	2-3		34	.188
	BRTR			2163	.260	

MAZZERA, MELVIN LEONARD "MIKE"
B.JAN.31,1914 STOCKTON,CAL.

YR	CL	LEA	POS	GP	G	REC
1935	STL	A	O		12	.233
1937	STL	A	H		7	.286
1938	STL	A	O		86	.279
1939	STL	A	O		34	.297
1940	PHI	N	1-O		69	.237
	BLTL			208	.268	

MAZZILLI, LEE LOUIS
B.MAR.25,1955 NEW YORK,N.Y.

YR	CL	LEA	POS	GP	G	REC
1976	NY	N	O		24	.195
	BBTR					

MC ADAMS, GEORGE D. JOHN "JACK"
B.DEC.17,1886 BENTON,ARK.
D.MAY 21,1937

YR	CL	LEA	POS	GP	G	REC
1911	STL	N	P		6	0- 0
	BRTR					

MC AFEE, WILLIAM FORT
B.SEPT.7,1907 SMITHVILLE,GA.
D.JULY 8,1958

YR	CL	LEA	POS	GP	G	REC
1930	CHI	N	P		2	0- 0
1931	BOS	N	P		18	0- 1
1932	WAS	A	P		8	6- 1
1933	WAS	A	P-2		27	3- 2
						.267
1934	STL	A	P		28	1- 0
	BRTR			83	10- 4	
						.173

MC ALEER, JAMES ROBERT "LOAFER"
B.JULY 10,1864 YOUNGSTOWN,OHIO
D.APR.29,1931

YR	CL	LEA	POS	GP	G	REC
1889	CLE	N	O		109	.235
1890	CLE	P	O		86	.272
1891	CLE	N	O		135	.246
1892	CLE	N	O		150	.241
1893	CLE	N	O		91	.253
1894	CLE	N	O		64	.298
1895	CLE	N	O		132	.291
1896	CLE	N	O		116	.288
1897	CLE	N	O		23	.224
1898	CLE	N	O		104	.235
1901	CLE	A	M-O		3	.125
1902	STL	A	M-O		2	.167
1907	STL	A	M-H		2	.000
	BRTR			1017	.259	

NON-PLAYING MANAGER
STL(A) 1903-09, WAS(A) 1910-11

MC ALEESE, JOHN JAMES
B.AUG.22,1878 SHARON,PA.
D.NOV.14,1950 NEW YORK,N.Y.

YR	CL	LEA	POS	GP	G	REC
1901	CHI	A	P		1	0- 0
1909	STL	A	O		85	.213
				1	86	0- 0
						.213

MC ALLESTER, WILLIAM LUSK
B.DEC.29,1889 CHATTANOOGA,TENN.
D.MAR.3,1970 CHATTANOOGA,TENN.

YR	CL	LEA	POS	GP	G	REC
1913	STL	A	C		46	.153
	BRTR					

MC ALLISTER, JACK
(SEE ANDREW JAMES COAKLEY)

MC ALLISTER, LEWIS WILLIAM "SPORT"
B.JULY 23,1874 AUSTIN,MISS.
D.JULY 17,1962 WYANDOTTE,MICH.

YR	CL	LEA	POS	GP	G	REC
1896	CLE	N	P-C-	3	7	0- 0
			O			.185
1897	CLE	N	P-O	7	40	2- 3
						.211
1898	CLE	N	P	9	16	3- 3
1899	CLE	N	P-O	1	110	0- 1
						.238
1901	DET	A	C-1		91	.287
1902	DET	A	C-1-2-S-	20		.200
			3-O			
1902	BAL	A	1-2-3		3	.091
	DET	A	C-1-2-S-	44		.209
			3-O			
1903	DET	A	C-S		78	.264
	BBTR		20	409	5- 7	
						.245

MC ANALLY, ERNEST LEE "ERNIE"
B.AUG.15,1946 PITTSBURG,TEX.

YR	CL	LEA	POS	GP	G	REC
1971	MON	N	P		31	11-12
1972	MON	N	P		29	6-15
1973	MON	N	P		27	7- 9
1974	MON	N	P		25	6-13
	BRTR			112	30-49	

MC ANANY, JAMES "JIM"
B.SEPT.4,1936 LOS ANGELES,CAL.

YR	CL	LEA	POS	GP	G	REC
1958	CHI	A	O		5	.000
1959	CHI	A	O		67	.276
1960	CHI	A	H		3	.000
1961	CHI	N	O		11	.300
1962	CHI	N	H		7	.000
	BRTR			93	.253	

MC ANDREW, JAMES CLEMENT "JIM"
B.JAN.11,1944 LOST NATION,IOWA

YR	CL	LEA	POS	GP	G	REC
1968	NY	N	P		12	4- 7
1969	NY	N	P		27	6- 7
1970	NY	N	P		32	10-14
1971	NY	N	P		24	2- 5
1972	NY	N	P		28	11- 8
1973	NY	N	P	23	24	3- 8
1974	SD	N	P		15	1- 4
	BRTR		161	162	37-53	

MC ARTHUR, MALCOLM
B.1862 DETROIT,MICH.

YR	CL	LEA	POS	GP	G	REC
1884	IND	AA	P		6	1- 5
	TR					

MC ARTHUR, OLIVER ALEXANDER "HAPPY"
B.FEB.1,1893 VERNON,ALA.

YR	CL	LEA	POS	GP	G	REC
1914	PIT	N	P		1	0- 0
	BRTR					

MC ATEE, MICHAEL JAMES "BUTCH"
B.1846 LANSINGBURG,N.Y.
D.OCT.18,1876

YR	CL	LEA	POS	GP	G	REC
1871	TRO	NA	1		26	-
1872	TRO	NA	1		25	.209
					51	-

MC AULEY, JAMES EARL "IKE"
B.AUG.19,1893 WICHITA,KAN.
D.APR.6,1928 DES MOINES,IOWA

YR	CL	LEA	POS	GP	G	REC
1914	PIT	N	2-S-3		15	.125
1915	PIT	N	S		5	.133
1916	PIT	N	S		4	.250
1917	STL	N	S		3	.286
1925	CHI	N	S		37	.280
	BRTR			64	.246	

MC AULIFFE, EUGENE LEO
B.FEB.28,1872 RANDOLPH,MASS.
D.APR.29,1913

YR	CL	LEA	POS	GP	G	REC
1904	BOS	N	C		1	.500
	TR					

MC AULIFFE, RICHARD JOHN "DICK"
B.NOV.29,1939 HARTFORD,CONN.

YR	CL	LEA	POS	GP	G	REC
1960	DET	A	S		8	.259
1961	DET	A	S-3		80	.256
1962	DET	A	2-S-3		139	.263
1963	DET	A	S		150	.262
1964	DET	A	S		162	.241
1965	DET	A	S		113	.260
1966	DET	A	S-3		124	.274
1967	DET	A	2-S		153	.239
1968	DET	A	2-S		151	.249
1969	DET	A	2		74	.262
1970	DET	A	2-S-3		146	.234
1971	DET	A	2-S		128	.208
1972	DET	A	2-S-3		122	.240
1973	DET	A	2-S		106	.274
1974	BOS	A	2-S-3		100	.210
1975	BOS	A	3		7	.133
	BLTR			1763	.247	

MC AVOY, GEORGE H.

YR	CL	LEA	POS	GP	G	REC
1914	PHI	N	H		1	.000

MC AVOY, JAMES EUGENE "WICKY"
B.OCT.22,1894 ROCHESTER,N.Y.
D.JULY 5,1973 ROCHESTER,N.Y.

YR	CL	LEA	POS	GP	G	REC
1913	PHI	A	C		4	.111
1914	PHI	A	C		8	.111
1915	PHI	A	C		68	.190
1917	PHI	A	C		10	.250
1918	PHI	A	C		83	.244
1919	PHI	A	C		62	.141
	BRTR			235	.199	

MC AVOY, THOMAS JOHN "TOM"
B.AUG.12,1937 BROOKLYN,N.Y.

YR	CL	LEA	POS	GP	G	REC
1959	WAS	A	P		1	0- 0
	BLTL					

MC BEAN, ALVIN O'NEAL "AL"
B.MAY 15,1938 CHARLOTTE AMALIE, V.I.

YR	CL	LEA	POS	GP	G	REC
1961	PIT	N	P	27	28	3- 2
1962	PIT	N	P	33	34	15-10
1963	PIT	N	P	55	59	13- 3
1964	PIT	N	P		58	8- 3
1965	PIT	N	P-O		62	6- 6
						.222
1966	PIT	N	P	47	50	4- 3
1967	PIT	N	P		51	7- 4
1968	PIT	N	P	36	43	9-12
1969	SD	N	P		1	0- 1
	LA	N	P		31	2- 6
1970	LA	N	P		1	0- 0
	PIT	N	P		7	0- 0
	BRTR		409	425	67-50	
						.197

MC BEE, PRYOR EDWARD
B.JUNE 20,1902 MC ALESTER,OKLA.

YR	CL	LEA	POS	GP	G	REC
1926	CHI	A	P		1	0- 0
	BRTL					

YR	CL	LEA	POS	GP	G	REC

MC BRIDE, ALGERNON BRIGGS
B.MAY.23,1869 MARTINSVILLE,IND.
D.JAN.10,1956

YR	CL	LEA	POS	GP	G	REC
1896	CHI	N	O		9	.233
1898	CIN	N	O		120	.300
1899	CIN	N	O		62	.352
1900	CIN	N	O		109	.277
1901	CIN	N	O		30	.254
	NY	N	O		62	.277
		BLTL			392	.294

MC BRIDE, ARNOLD RAY "BAKE"
B.FEB.3,1949 FULTON,MO.

YR	CL	LEA	POS	GP	G	REC
1973	STL	N	O		40	.302
1974	STL	N	O		150	.309
1975	STL	N	O		116	.300
1976	STL	N	O		72	.335
		BLTR			378	.311

MC BRIDE, GEORGE FLORIAN
B.NOV.20,1880 MILWAUKEE,WIS.
D.JULY 2,1973 MILWAUKEE,WIS.

YR	CL	LEA	POS	GP	G	REC
1901	MIL	A	S		1	.250
1905	PIT	N	S-3		25	.218
	STL	N	S		81	.253
1906	STL	N	S		90	.169
1908	WAS	A	S		155	.232
1909	WAS	A	S		155	.234
1910	WAS	A	S		154	.230
1911	WAS	A	S		154	.236
1912	WAS	A	S		152	.226
1913	WAS	A	S		150	.214
1914	WAS	A	S		156	.203
1915	WAS	A	S		146	.204
1916	WAS	A	S		139	.227
1917	WAS	A	S		50	.192
1918	WAS	A	S		18	.132
1919	WAS	A	S		15	.200
1920	WAS	A	S		14	.219
		BRTR			1655	.218

NON-PLAYING MANAGER WAS(A) 1921

MC BRIDE, JAMES DICKSON "DICK"
B.1845 PHILADELPHIA,PA.
D.OCT.10,1916

YR	CL	LEA	POS	GP	G	REC
1871	ATH	NA	P	25		20- 5
1872	ATH	NA	P	46		31-15
1873	ATH	NA	P-O	48		24-21
						-
1874	ATH	NA	P	55		33-22
1875	ATH	NA	P	59		43-14
1876	BOS	N	P	4		0- 4
		TR		237		151-81
						-

MC BRIDE, JOHN F.

YR	CL	LEA	POS	GP	G	REC
1890	ATH	AA	O		1	.000

MC BRIDE, KENNETH FAYE "KEN"
B.AUG.12,1935 HUNTSVILLE,ALA.

YR	CL	LEA	POS	GP	G	REC
1959	CHI	A	P	11		0- 1
1960	CHI	A	P	5		0- 1
1961	LA	A	P	38	45	12-15
1962	LA	A	P		24	11- 5
1963	LA	A	P	36	38	13-12
1964	LA	A	P		29	4-13
1965	CAL	A	P	8		0- 3
		BRTR		151	160	40-50

MC BRIDE, PETER WILLIAM
B.JULY 9,1875 ADAMS,MASS.
D.JULY 3,1944

YR	CL	LEA	POS	GP	G	REC
1898	CLE	N	P	1		0- 1
1899	STL	N	P	11		2- 5
				12		2- 6

MC BRIDE, THOMAS RAYMOND "TOM"
B.NOV.2,1915 BONHAM,TEX.

YR	CL	LEA	POS	GP	G	REC
1943	BOS	A	O		26	.240
1944	BOS	A	1-O		71	.245
1945	BOS	A	1-O		100	.305
1946	BOS	A	O		61	.301
1947	BOS	A	O		2	.200
	WAS	A	3-O		56	.271
	WAS	A	O		92	.257
		BRTR			408	.275

MC CABE, JAMES ARTHUR "SWAT"
B.NOV.20,1881 TOWANDA,PA.
D.DEC.9,1944

YR	CL	LEA	POS	GP	G	REC
1909	CIN	N	O		4	.461
1910	CIN	N	O		13	.257
		BL			17	.313

MC CABE, JOSEPH ROBERT "JOE"
B.AUG.27,1938 INDIANAPOLIS,IND.

YR	CL	LEA	POS	GP	G	REC
1964	MIN	A	C		14	.158
1965	WAS	A	C		14	.185
		BRTR			28	.174

MC CABE, RALPH HERBERT "MACK"
B.OCT.21,1920 NAPANEE,ONT.,CAN.

YR	CL	LEA	POS	GP	G	REC
1946	CLE	A	P	1		0- 1
		BRTR				

MC CABE, RICHARD JAMES
B.FEB.21,1896 MAMARONECK,N.Y.
D.APR.11,1950

YR	CL	LEA	POS	GP	G	REC
1918	BOS	A	P	3		0- 1
1922	CHI	A	P	3		1- 0
		BRTR		6		1- 1

MC CABE, TIMOTHY
B.OCT.19,1894 GRANITEVILLE,MO.

YR	CL	LEA	POS	GP	G	REC
1915	STL	A	P	7		3- 1
1916	STL	A	P	13		3- 0
1917	STL	A	P	1		0- 0
1918	STL	A	P	2		0- 0
		BRTR		23		6- 1

MC CABE, WILLIAM FRANCIS
B.OCT.28,1894 CHICAGO,ILL.

YR	CL	LEA	POS	GP	G	REC
1918	CHI	N	2-O		29	.178
1919	CHI	N	S-3-O		33	.155
1920	CHI	N	O		3	.500
	BRO	N	O		41	.147
		BBTR			106	.161

BL 1918

MC CAFFERY, HARRY CHARLES
B.NOV.25,1858 ST.LOUIS,MO.
D.APR.19,1928 ST.LOUIS,MO.

YR	CL	LEA	POS	GP	G	REC
1882	STL	AA	1-2-3-O		37	.268
1883	STL	AA	O		5	.053
1885	CIN	AA	P	1		1- 0
		BRTR		1	43	1- 0
						.237

MC CAFFREY, CHARLES P. "SPARROW"
B.PHILADELPHIA,PA.
D.MAY 1894

YR	CL	LEA	POS	GP	G	REC
1889	COL	AA	C		2	.167
1890	ATH	AA	C		1	.250
					3	.200

MC CAHAN, WILLIAM GLENN "BILL"
B.JUNE 7,1921 PHILADELPHIA,PA.

YR	CL	LEA	POS	GP	G	REC
1946	PHI	A	P	4		1- 1
1947	PHI	A	P	29		10- 5
1948	PHI	A	P	17		4- 7
1949	PHI	A	P	7		1- 1
		BRTR		57		16-14

MC CALL, BRIAN ALLEN
B.JAN.25,1943 KENTFIELD,CAL.

YR	CL	LEA	POS	GP	G	REC
1962	CHI	A	O		4	.375
1963	CHI	A	O		3	.000
		BLTL			7	.200

MC CALL, JOHN WILLIAM "WINDY"
B.JUL.18,1925 SAN FRANCISCO,CAL

YR	CL	LEA	POS	GP	G	REC
1948	BOS	A	P	1		0- 1
1949	BOS	A	P	5		0- 0
1950	PIT	N	P	2		0- 0
1954	NY	N	P	33		2- 5
1955	NY	N	P	42		6- 5
1956	NY	N	P	46		3- 4
1957	NY	N	P	5		0- 0
		BLTL		134		11-15

MC CALL, ROBERT LEONARD "DUTCH"
B.DEC.27,1920 COLUMBIA,TENN.

YR	CL	LEA	POS	GP	G	REC
1948	CHI	N	P	30		4-13
		BLTL				

MC CALLISTER, JOHN "JACK"
B.JAN.19,1879 MARIETTA,OHIO
D.OCT.18,1946 COLUMBUS,OHIO
NON-PLAYING MANAGER CLE(A) 1927

MC CANDLESS, JOHN C.
B.1895 PITTSBURGH,PA.

YR	CL	LEA	POS	GP	G	REC
1914	BAL	F	O		11	.258
1915	BAL	F	O		116	.218
		BLTR			127	.221

MC CANN, HENRY EUGENE "MIKE"
B.JUNE 13,1876 BALTIMORE,MD.
D.APR.26,1943

YR	CL	LEA	POS	GP	G	REC
1901	BRO	N	P	6		2- 3
1902	BRO	N	P	3		1- 2
		TR		9		3- 5

MC CANN, ROBERT EMMETT
B.MAR.4,1902 PHILADELPHIA,PA.
D.APR.15,1937

YR	CL	LEA	POS	GP	G	REC
1920	PHI	A	S		10	.286
1921	PHI	A	S		52	.223
1926	BOS	A	S		6	.000
		BRTR			68	.222

MC CARDELL, ROGER MORTON
B.AUG.29,1932 GORSUCH MILLS,MD.

YR	CL	LEA	POS	GP	G	REC
1959	SF	N	C		4	.000
		BRTR				

MC CARREN, WILLIAM JOSEPH
B.NOV.4,1897 FORTENIA,PA.

YR	CL	LEA	POS	GP	G	REC
1923	BRO	N	3-O		69	.245
		BRTR				

MC CARTHY, ALEXANDER GEORGE
B.MAY 12,1888 BRADLEY,ILL.

YR	CL	LEA	POS	GP	G	REC
1910	PIT	N	S		3	.046
1911	PIT	N	S		46	.240
1912	PIT	N	2		111	.277
1913	PIT	N	S		31	.203
1914	PIT	N	3		57	.150
1915	PIT	N	2		21	.204
	CHI	N	2		23	.264
1916	CHI	N	2-S		37	.245
	PIT	N	2-S		50	.197
1917	PIT	N	3		49	.219
		BRTR			428	.229

MC CARTHY, ARCHIBALD J.
B.YPSILANTI,MICH.

YR	CL	LEA	POS	GP	G	REC
1902	DET	A	P	10		1- 7

MC CARTHY, JEROME FRANCIS
B.MAY 23,1923 BROOKLYN,N.Y.
D.OCT.3,1965 OCEANSIDE,N.Y.

YR	CL	LEA	POS	GP	G	REC
1948	STL	A	1		2	.333
		BLTL				

MC CARTHY, JOHN ARTHUR
B.MAR.26,1869 GILBERTVILLE,MASS
D.SEPT.11,1931 CHICAGO,ILL.

YR	CL	LEA	POS	GP	G	REC
1893	CIN	N	O		48	.285
1894	CIN	N	1-O		40	.267
1898	PIT	N	O		137	.289
1899	PIT	N	O		139	.307
1900	CHI	N	O		123	.296
1901	CLE	A	O		86	.314
1902	CLE	A	O		95	.276
1903	CLE	A	O		109	.265
	CHI	N	O		24	.277
1904	CHI	N	O		115	.264
1905	CHI	N	O		43	.276
1906	BRO	N	O		86	.304
1907	BRO	N	O		25	.220
		BLTL			1070	.289

MC CARTHY JOHN JOSEPH "JOHNNY"
B.JAN.7,1913 CHICAGO,ILL.
D.SEPT.13,1973 MUNDELEIN,ILL.

YR	CL	LEA	POS	GP	G	REC
1934	BRO	N	1		17	.179
1935	BRO	N	1		22	.250
1936	NY	N	1		4	.438
1937	NY	N	1		114	.279
1938	NY	N	1		134	.272
1939	NY	N	P-1	1	50	0- 0
						.262
1940	NY	N	1		51	.239
1941	NY	N	1-O		14	.325
1943	BOS	N	1		78	.304
1946	BOS	N	1		2	.143
1948	NY	N	1		56	.263
		BLTL		1	542	0- 0
						.277

MC CARTHY, JOSEPH N.
B.DEC.25,1881 SYRACUSE,N.Y.
D.JAN.12,1937

YR	CL	LEA	POS	GP	G	REC
1905	NY	A	C		1	.000
1906	STL	N	C		14	.237
		TR			15	.225

YR	CL	LEA	POS	GP	G	REC

MC CARTHY, JOSEPH VINCENT
"MARSE JOE"
B.APR.21,1887 PHILADELPHIA,PA.
NON-PLAYING MANAGER
CHI(N) 1926-30, NY(A) 1931-46,
BOS(A) 1948-50

MC CARTHY, THOMAS FRANCIS
MICHAEL "TOMMY"
B.JULY 24,1864 S.BOSTON,MASS.
D.AUG.5,1922 BOSTON,MASS.

1884	BOS	U	P-O	7	53	0- 7
						.218
1885	BOS	N	O		40	.182
1886	PHI	N	O		8	.185
1887	PHI	N	O		18	.208
1888	STL	AA	P-O	1	131	0- 0
						.276
1889	STL	AA	O		139	.297
1890	STL	AA	M-O		133	.332
1891	STL	AA	O		135	.302
1892	BOS	N	O		152	.244
1893	BOS	N	O		116	.360
1894	BOS	N	O		126	.349
1895	BOS	N	O		116	.291
1896	BRO	N	O		101	.253
		BRTR		8	1268	0- 7
						.294

MC CARTHY, THOMAS PATRICK
B.MAY 22,1884 FT.WAYNE,IND.
D.MAR.28,1933

1908	CIN	N	P		1	0- 1
	PIT	N	P		?	0- 0
	BOS	N	P		14	7- 3
1909	BOS	N	P		8	0- 5
					25	7- 9

MC CARTHY, WILLIAM JOHN
B.BOSTON,MASS.

1905	BOS	N	C		1	.000
1907	CIN	N	C		3	.125
		TR			4	.091

MC CARTHY, WILLIAM THOMAS
B.APR.11,1882 ASHLAND,MASS.
D.MAY 29,1939 BOSTON,MASS.

| 1906 | BOS | N | P | | 1 | 0- 0 |
| | | BRTR | | | | |

MC CARTON, FRANK
B.MIDDLETOWN,CONN.

| 1872 | MAN | NA | O | | 19 | .271 |

MC CARTY, GEORGE LEWIS "LEW"
B.NOV.17,1888 MILTON,PA.
D.JUNE 9,1930

1913	BRO	N	C		9	.192
1914	BRO	N	C		90	.254
1915	BRO	N	C		84	.239
1916	BRO	N	C-1		55	.311
	NY	N	C		25	.400
1917	NY	N	C		56	.247
1918	NY	N	C		86	.269
1919	NY	N	C		85	.281
1920	NY	N	C		36	.132
	STL	N	C		5	.286
1921	STL	N	C		1	.000
		BRTR			532	.277

MC CARTY, JOHN A.
B.ST.LOUIS,MO.

| 1889 | KC | AA | P | | 20 | 8- 6 |
| | | TR | | | | |

MC CARVER, JAMES TIMOTHY "TIM"
B.OCT.16,1941 MEMPHIS,TENN.

1959	STL	N	C		8	.167
1960	STL	N	C		10	.200
1961	STL	N	C		22	.239
1963	STL	N	C		127	.289
1964	STL	N	C		143	.288
1965	STL	N	C		113	.276
1966	STL	N	C		150	.274
1967	STL	N	C		138	.295
1968	STL	N	C		128	.253
1969	STL	N	C		138	.260
1970	PHI	N	C		44	.287
1971	PHI	N	C		134	.278
1972	PHI	N	C		45	.237
	MON	N	C-3-O		77	.251
1973	STL	N	C-1		130	.266
1974	STL	N	C-1		74	.217
	BOS	A	C		11	.250
1975	BOS	A	C-1		12	.381
	PHI	N	C-1		47	.254
1976	PHI	N	C-1		90	.277
		BLTR			1641	.271

MC CAULEY, ALLEN B.
B.MAR.4,1863 INDIANAPOLIS,IND.

1884	IND	AA	P-1	9	17	2- 7
						.189
1890	PHI	N	1		112	.244
1891	WAS	AA	1		57	.283
		BLTL		9	186	2- 7
						.262

MC CAULEY, JAMES A.
B.1861 STANLEY,N.Y.

1884	STL	AA	C		1	.000
1885	BUF	N	C-O		24	.205
	CHI	N	C-O		3	.100
1886	BRO	AA	C		10	.233
		BLTR			38	.200

MC CAULEY, PATRICK M.
B.JUNE 10,1870 WARE,MASS.
D.JAN.23,1917

1893	STL	N	C		5	.067
1896	WAS	N	C		21	.247
1903	NY	A	C		6	.096
		TR			32	.200

MC CAULEY, WILLIAM H.

| 1895 | WAS | N | S | | 1 | .000 |

MC CHESNEY, HARRY VINCENT "PUD"
B.JUNE 1,1880 PITTSBURGH,PA.
D.AUG.11,1960

| 1904 | CHI | N | O | | 22 | .261 |
| | | BRTR | | | | |

MC CLAIN, JOSEPH FRED "JOE"
B.MAY 5,1933 JOHNSON CITY,TENN.

1961	WAS	A	P		33	8-18
1962	WAS	A	P		10	0- 4
		BRTR			43	8-22

MC CLANAHAN, PETER
B.OCT.24,1906 COLDSPRING,TEX.

| 1931 | PIT | N | H | | 7 | .500 |
| | | BRTR | | | | |

MC CLELLAN, HERVEY MC DOWELL
"LITTLE MAC"
B.DEC.22,1894 CYNTHIANA,KY.
D.NOV.6,1925

1919	CHI	A	S-3		7	.333
1920	CHI	A	3		10	.300
1921	CHI	A	2-S-O		63	.179
1922	CHI	A	3		91	.226
1923	CHI	A	S		141	.235
1924	CHI	A	S		32	.176
		BRTR			344	.221

MC CLELLAN, WILLIAM HENRY
B.MAR.22,1856 CHICAGO,ILL.
D.JULY 3,1929

1878	CHI	N	2		46	.221
1881	PRO	N	2-S-O		65	.164
1883	PHI	N	S-O		78	.230
1884	PHI	N	S		110	.256
1885	BRO	AA	2-3		113	.251
1886	BRO	AA	2		142	.262
1887	BRO	AA	2		136	.350
1888	BRO	AA	2-O		75	.214
	CLE	AA	2-S-O		22	.222
		BLTL			787	.258

MC CLESKEY, JEFFERSON LAMAR
B.1892 WINDER,GA.
D.MAY 11,1971 AMERICUS,GA.

| 1913 | BOS | N | 3 | | 2 | .000 |
| | | BLTR | | | | |

MC CLOSKEY

| 1875 | NAT | NA | C | | 10 | - |

MC CLOSKEY, JAMES ELLWOOD
B.MAY 26,1910 DANVILLE,PA.
D.AUG.18,1971 JERSEY CITY,N.J.

| 1936 | BOS | N | P | | 4 | 0- 0 |
| | | BLTL | | | | |

MC CLOSKEY, JOHN J.
B.CRIPPLE CREEK,COLO.

1906	PHI	N	P		9	3- 3
1907	PHI	N	P		2	0- 0
					11	3- 3

MC CLOSKEY, JOHN JOSEPH
"HONEST JOHN"
B.APR.4,1862 LOUISVILLE,KY.
D.NOV.17,1940
NON-PLAYING MANAGER
LOU(N) 1895-96, STL(N) 1906-08

MC CLOSKEY, WILLIAM GEORGE
B.PHILADELPHIA,PA.

| 1884 | WIL | U | C-O | | 9 | .133 |

MC CLURE, HAROLD MURRAY
B.AUG.8,1859 LEWISBURG,PA.
D.FEB.19,1919

| 1882 | BOS | N | O | | 2 | .333 |
| | | TR | | | | |

MC CLURE, LAWRENCE LEDWITH
B.OCT.3,1885 WAYNE,W.VA.
D.AUG.31,1949

| 1910 | NY | A | O | | 1 | .000 |
| | | BR | | | | |

MC CLURE, ROBERT CRAIG "BOB"
B.APR.29,1952 OAKLAND,CAL.

1975	KC	A	P		12	1- 0
1976	KC	A	P	8	9	0- 0
		BRTL		20	21	1- 0

MC CLUSKEY, HARRY ROBERTS
B.MAR.26,1893 CLAY CENTER,OHIO
D.JUNE 7,1962

| 1915 | CIN | N | P | | 3 | 0- 0 |
| | | BLTL | | | | |

MC COLL, ALEXANDER BOYD "RED"
B.MAR.29,1896 EAGLEVILLE,OHIO

1933	WAS	A	P		4	1- 0
1934	WAS	A	P		42	3- 4
		BBTR			46	4- 4

MC CONNAUGHEY, RALPH J.
B.AUG.5,1889 PENNSYLVANIA
D.JUNE 4,1966 DETROIT,MICH.

| 1914 | IND | F | P | | 7 | 0- 2 |
| | | BRTR | | | | |

MC CONNELL, AMBROSE MOSES
"AMBY"
B.APR.29,1883 N.POWNAL,VT.
D.MAY 20,1942

1908	BOS	A	2		140	.279
1909	BOS	A	2		121	.238
1910	BOS	A	2		12	.125
	CHI	A	2		32	.296
1911	CHI	A	2		104	.280
		BLTR			409	.264

MC CONNELL, GEORGE NEELY
"SLATS"
B.SEPT.16,1879 SHELBYVILLE,TENN
D.MAY 10,1964 CHATTANOOGA,TENN.

1909	NY	A	P-1	1	13	0- 1
						.209
1912	NY	A	P		23	42	8-12
1913	NY	A	P		35	5-15
1914	CHI	N	P		1	0- 1
1915	CHI	F	P		44	50	25-10
1916	CHI	N	P		28	4-12
		BRTR	132	169	42-51
						.182

MC CONNELL, SAMUEL FAULKNER
B.JUNE 8,1895 PHILADELPHIA,PA.

| 1915 | PHI | A | 3 | | 6 | .191 |
| | | BLTR | | | | |

YR	CL LEA POS	GP	G	REC

MC COOL, WILLIAM JOHN "BILLY"
B.JULY 14,1944 BATESVILLE,IND.

YR	CL LEA POS	GP	G	REC
1964	CIN N P		40	6- 5
1965	CIN N P		62	9-10
1966	CIN N P		57	8- 8
1967	CIN N P		31	3- 7
1968	CIN N P		30	3- 4
1969	SD N P		54	3- 5
1970	STL N P		18	0- 3
	BRTL		292	32-42

MC CORMICK, FRANK ANDREW "BUCK"
B.JUNE 9,1913 NEW YORK,N.Y

YR	CL LEA POS	GP	G	REC
1934	CIN N 1		12	.313
1937	CIN N 1-2-0		24	.325
1938	CIN N 1		151	.326
1939	CIN N 1		156	.332
1940	CIN N 1		155	.309
1941	CIN N 1		154	.269
1942	CIN N 1		145	.277
1943	CIN N 1		126	.303
1944	CIN N 1		153	.305
1945	CIN N 1		152	.276
1946	PHI N 1		135	.284
1947	PHI N 1		15	.225
	BOS N 1		81	.354
1948	BOS N 1		75	.250
	BRTR		1534	.299

MC CORMICK, HARRY ELWOOD "MOOSE"
B.FEB.28,1881 PHILADELPHIA,PA.
D.JULY 9,1962

YR	CL LEA POS	GP	G	REC
1904	NY N O		54	.266
	PIT N O		66	.290
1908	PHI N O		5	.091
	NY N O		65	.302
1909	NY N O		110	.290
1912	NY N O		42	.333
1913	NY N O		57	.275
	TL		399	.285

MC CORMICK, JAMES "JIM"
B.1856 SCOTLAND
D.MAR.10,1918 PATERSON,N.J.

YR	CL LEA POS	GP	G	REC
1878	IND N P	14	15	4- 9
1879	CLE N M-P-	60	75	20-40
	O			.219
1880	CLE N M-P-	73	77	44-29
	O			.250
1881	CLE N M-P-	57	69	26-31
	2-0			.257
1882	CLE N P-O	65	67	35-29
				.216
1883	CLE N M-P-	40	41	27-13
	O			.235
1884	CLE N P-O	41	48	19-22
				.263
	CIN U P-O	26	28	22- 4
				.237
1885	PRO N P		4	1- 3
	CHI N P-O		25	20- 4
				.231
1886	CHI N P		42	31-11
1887	PIT N P		36	13-23
	BRTR	483	527	262-218
				.237

MC CORMICK, JAMES AMBROSE
B.NOV.2,1868 SPENCER,MASS.
D.FEB.1,1948

YR	CL LEA POS	GP	G	REC
1892	STL N 2		2	.000
	BRTR			

MC CORMICK, JOHN "JERRY"
B.PHILADELPHIA,PA.
D.SEPT.19,1905

YR	CL LEA POS	GP	G	REC
1883	BAL AA 3		98	.261
1884	KEY U 2-S-3-0		66	.296
	WAS U S-3		42	.237
			206	.268

MC CORMICK, MICHAEL FRANCIS "MIKE"
B.SEP.29,1938 PASADENA,CAL.

YR	CL LEA POS	GP	G	REC
1956	NY N P		3	0- 1
1957	NY N P		24	3- 1
1958	SF N P		42	11- 8
1959	SF N P		47	12-16
1960	SF N P		40	15-12
1961	SF N P		40	13-16
1962	SF N P	28	29	5- 5
1963	BAL A P		25	6- 8
1964	BAL A P		4	0- 2
1965	WAS A P	44	45	8- 8
1966	WAS A P		41	11-14
1967	SF N P	40	41	22-10
1968	SF N P		38	12-14
1969	SF N P		32	11- 9
1970	SF N P		23	3- 4
	NY A P		9	2- 0
1971	KC A P		4	0- 0
	BLTL	484	487	134-128

MC CORMICK, MICHAEL J. "KID"
B.1883 JERSEY CITY,N.J.
D.NOV.18,1953

YR	CL LEA POS	GP	G	REC
1904	BRO N 3		105	.184
	BRTR			

MC CORMICK, MYRON WINTHROP "MIKE"
B.MAY 6,1917 ANGEL'S CAMP,CAL.
D.APR.14,1976 VENTURA,CAL.

YR	CL LEA POS	GP	G	REC
1940	CIN N O		110	.300
1941	CIN N O		110	.287
1942	CIN N O		40	.237
1943	CIN N O		4	.133
1946	CIN N O		23	.216
	BOS N O		59	.262
1947	BOS N O		92	.285
1948	BOS N O		115	.303
1949	BRO N O		55	.209
1950	NY N H		4	.000
	CHI A O		55	.232
1951	WAS A O		81	.288
	BRTR		748	.275

MC CORMICK, PATRICK HENRY
B.OCT.25,1855 SYRACUSE,N.Y.
D.JUNE 21,1888

YR	CL LEA POS	GP	G	REC
1879	SYR N P	49	55	11-13
1881	WOR N P-O	12	1- 8
				.122
1882	CIN AA P-O	25	26	13-12
				.126
1883	CIN AA P		14	9- 5
	TR	100	107	34-38
				.207

MC CORMICK, WILLIAM J. "BARRY"
B.DEC.25,1874 CINCINNATI,OHIO
D.JAN.28,1956

YR	CL LEA POS	GP	G	REC
1895	LOU N S		3	.273
1896	CHI N 3		45	.219
1897	CHI N S-3		100	.273
1898	CHI N 3		136	.248
1899	CHI N 2		102	.234
1900	CHI N S-3		110	.215
1901	CHI N S		115	.234
1902	STL A S-3-0		139	.246
1903	STL A 2		59	.192
	WAS A 2-3		62	.225
1904	WAS A 2		112	.219
	TR		983	.237

MC CORRY, WILLIAM CHARLES
B.JULY 9,1887 SARANAC LAKE,N.Y.
D.MAR.22,1973 ATLANTA,GA.

YR	CL LEA POS	GP	G	REC
1909	STL A P		2	0- 2
	BLTR			

MC COSKY, WILLIAM BARNEY "BARNEY"
B.APR.11,1918 COAL RUN,PA.

YR	CL LEA POS	GP	G	REC
1939	DET A O		147	.311
1940	DET A O		143	.340
1941	DET A O		127	.324
1942	DET A O		154	.293
1946	DET A O		25	.198
	PHI A O		92	.354
1947	PHI A O		137	.328
1948	PHI A O		135	.326
1950	PHI A O		66	.240
1951	PHI A O		12	.296
	CIN N O		25	.320
	CLE A O		31	.213
1952	CLE A O		54	.213
1953	CLE A H		22	.190
	BLTR		1170	.312

MC COVEY, WILLIE LEE
B.JAN.10,1938 MOBILE,ALA.

YR	CL LEA POS	GP	G	REC
1959	SF N 1		52	.354
1960	SF N 1		101	.238
1961	SF N 1		106	.271
1962	SF N 1-0		91	.293
1963	SF N 1-0		152	.280
1964	SF N 1-0		130	.220
1965	SF N 1		160	.276
1966	SF N 1		150	.295
1967	SF N 1		135	.276
1968	SF N 1		148	.293
1969	SF N 1		149	.320
1970	SF N 1		152	.289
1971	SF N 1		105	.277
1972	SF N 1		81	.213
1973	SF N 1		130	.266
1974	SD N 1		128	.253
1975	SD N 1		122	.252
1976	SD N 1		71	.203
	OAK A H		11	.208
	BLTL		2174	.273

MC COY, A. J.
B.DANVILLE,PA.

YR	CL LEA POS	GP	G	REC
1889	WAS N O		2	.000

MC COY, BENJAMIN JENISON "BENNY"
B.NOV.9,1915 JENISON,MICH.

YR	CL LEA POS	GP	G	REC
1938	DET A 2-3		7	.200
1939	DET A 2-S		55	.302
1940	PHI A 2-3		134	.257
1941	PHI A 2		141	.271
	BLTR		337	.269

MC CRABB, LESTER WILLIAM "BUSTER"
B.NOV.4,1914 FULTON,PA.

YR	CL LEA POS	GP	G	REC
1939	PHI A P		5	1- 2
1940	PHI A P		4	0- 0
1941	PHI A P		26	9-13
1942	PHI A P		1	0- 0
1950	PHI A P		2	0- 0
	BRTR		38	10-15

MC CRAW, TOMMIE LEE
B.NOV.21,1940 MALVERN,ARK.

YR	CL LEA POS	GP	G	REC
1963	CHI A 1		102	.254
1964	CHI A 1-0		125	.261
1965	CHI A 1-0		133	.238
1966	CHI A 1-0		151	.229
1967	CHI A 1-0		125	.236
1968	CHI A 1		136	.235
1969	CHI A 1-0		93	.258
1970	CHI A 1-0		129	.220
1971	WAS A 1-0		122	.213
1972	CLE A 1-0		129	.258
1973	CAL A 1-0		99	.265
1974	CAL A 1-0		56	.286
	CLE A 1-0		45	.304
1975	CLE A 1-0		23	.275
	BLTL		1468	.246

MC CREA, FRANCIS WILLIAM
B.SEPT.6,1898 JERSEY CITY,N.J.

YR	CL LEA POS	GP	G	REC
1925	CLE A C		1	.200
	BRTR			

MC CREEDIE, WALTER HENRY "JUDGE"
B.NOV.29,1876 MANCHESTER,IOWA
D.JULY 29,1934

YR	CL LEA POS	GP	G	REC
1903	BRO N O		56	.324

YR	CL LEA POS	GP	G	REC

MC CREERY, EDWARD P.
B.1891
DECEASED
1914 DET A P   3   1- 0
        BRTR

MC CREERY, THOMAS LEAVENWORTH
B.OCT.19,1874 BEAVER,PA.
D.JULY 3,1941
1895 LOU N P-1- 5   29   3- 2
             O   .336
1896 LOU N P-O   1 110   0- 1
                            .351
1897 LOU N O   89   .283
      NY N 2-O   49   .290
1898 NY N O   34   .198
      PIT N O   51   .304
1899 PIT N O   113   .325
1900 PIT N O   33   .223
1901 BRO N O   84   .302
1902 BRO N 1-O   111   .246
1903 BRO N O   38   .262
      BOS N O   23   .217
        BB   6 764   3- 3
                            .292

MC CRELLIS, MARK
1892 STL N 3   1   .000

MC CROHAN, DENNIS J.
(PLAYED UNDER NAME OF
DENNIS J. MACK)

MC CUE, FRANK ALOYSIUS
B.OCT.4,1900 CHICAGO,ILL.
D.JULY 5,1953
1922 PHI A 3   2   .000
        BBTR

MC CULLOUGH, CHARLES
B.1867 DUBLIN,IRELAND
1890 BRO AA P   24   4-20
      SYR AA P   5   5   2- 2
                     29   6-22

MC CULLOUGH, CLYDE EDWARD
B.MAR.4,1917 NASHVILLE,TENN.
1940 CHI N C   9   .154
1941 CHI N C   125   .227
1942 CHI N C   109   .282
1943 CHI N C   87   .237
1946 CHI N C   95   .287
1947 CHI N C   86   .252
1948 CHI N C   69   .209
1949 PIT N C   91   .237
1950 PIT N C   103   .254
1951 PIT N C   92   .297
1952 PIT N C-1   66   .233
1953 CHI N C   77   .258
1954 CHI N C-3   31   .259
1955 CHI N C   44   .198
1956 CHI N C   14   .211
        BLTR   1098   .252

MC CULLOUGH, PAUL WILLARD
B.JULY 28,1902 NEW CASTLE,PA.
1929 WAS A P   3   0- 0
        BRTR

MC CULLOUGH, PHILIP LAMAR
B.JULY 22,1917 STOCKBRIDGE,GA.
1942 WAS A P   1   0- 0
        BRTR

MC CURDY, HARRY HENRY "HANK"
B.SEPT.15,1899 GREEN BAY,WIS.
D.JULY 21,1972 HOUSTON,TEX.
1922 STL N C-1   13   .196
1923 STL N C   67   .265
1926 CHI A C   44   .326
1927 CHI A C   86   .286
1928 CHI A C   49   .262
1930 PHI N C   80   .331
1931 PHI N C   66   .287
1932 PHI N C   62   .235
1933 PHI N C   73   .278
1934 CIN N 1   3   .000
        BLTR   543   .282

MC DANIEL, LYNDALL DALE "LINDY"
B.DEC.13,1935 HOLLIS,OKLA.
1955 STL N P   4   0- 0
1956 STL N P   39   7- 6
1957 STL N P   30   31 15- 9
1958 STL N P   26   5- 7
1959 STL N P   62 14-12
1960 STL N P   65 12- 4
1961 STL N P   55 10- 6
1962 STL N P   55   3-10
1963 CHI N P   57 13- 7
1964 CHI N P   63   1- 7
1965 CHI N P   71   5- 6
1966 SF N P   64 10- 5
1967 SF N P   41   2- 6
1968 SF N P   12   0- 0
      NY A P   24   4- 1
1969 NY A P   51   5- 6
1970 NY A P   62   9- 5
1971 NY A P   44   5-10
1972 NY A P   37   3- 1
1973 NY A P   47 12- 6
1974 KC A P   38   1- 4
1975 KC A P   40   5- 1
        BRTR   987 988 141-119

MC DANIEL, MAX VON "VON"
B.APR.18,1939 HOLLIS,OKLA.
1957 STL N P   17   7- 5
1958 STL N P   2   0- 0
        BRTR   19   7- 5

MC DERMOTT, FRANK A. "RED"
B.NOV.12,1889 PHILADELPHIA,PA.
D.SEPT.11,1964 PHILADELPHIA,PA.
1912 DET A O   5   .250
        BRTR

MC DERMOTT, JOSEPH
1871 KEK NA O   2   -
1872 ECK NA P   7   0- 7
1873 RES NA S   1   -
                    7   10   0- 7

**MC DERMOTT, MAURICE JOSEPH
"MICKEY"**
B.AUG.29,1928 POUGHKEEPSIE,N.Y.
1948 BOS A P   7   0- 0
1949 BOS A P   12   5- 4
1950 BOS A P   38   39   7- 3
1951 BOS A P   34   43   8- 8
1952 BOS A P   32   45 18-10
1953 BOS A P   30   54   7-15
1954 WAS A P   31   70 10-10
1955 WAS A P   23   2- 6
1956 NY A P   23   46   2- 6
1957 KC A P-1   29   58   1- 4
                            .245
1958 DET N P   2   4   0- 0
1961 STL N P   19   22   1- 0
      KC A P   4   7   0- 0
        BLTL   291 443 69-69
                            .252

MC DERMOTT, MICHAEL JOSEPH
B.SEPT.7,1862 ST.LOUIS,MO.
D.JUNE 30,1943
1889 LOU AA P   9   1- 7
1895 LOU N P   26   4-19
1896 LOU N P   12   2- 7
1897 CLE N P   9   3- 4
      STL N P   7   3- 4
        TR   63 13-41

**MC DERMOTT, TERRENCE MICHAEL
"TERRY"**
B.MAR.20,1951 ROCKVILLE CEN.,N.Y
1972 LA N 1   9   .130
        BRTR

**MC DEVITT, DANIEL EUGENE
"DANNY"**
B.NOV.18,1932 NEW YORK,N.Y.
1957 BRO N P   22   7- 4
1958 LA N P   13   2- 6
1959 LA N P   39 10- 8
1960 LA N P   24   0- 4
1961 NY A P   8   1- 2
      MIN A P   16   1- 0
1962 KC A P   33   0- 3
        BLTL   155 21-27

MC DONALD
1884 WAS U C-O   2   .167

MC DONALD, CHARLES E. "TEX"
(REAL NAME CHARLES C. CRABTREE)
B.JAN.31,1891 FARMERSVILLE,TEX.
D.MAR.31,1943
1912 CIN N S   61   .257
1913 CIN N S   11   .364
      BOS N 3   62   .353
1914 PIT F 2-3   67   .318
      BUF F O   69   .295
1915 BUF F O   87   .271
        BLTR   357   .298

MC DONALD, DANIEL
B.1847 BROOKLYN,N.Y.
D.NOV.23,1880
1872 ATL NA O   14   .214
      ECK NA S   1   .000
                    15   .197

MC DONALD, DAVID BRUCE "DAVE"
B.MAY 20,1943 NEW ALBANY,IND.
1969 NY A 1   9   .217
1971 MON N 1-O   24   .103
        BLTR   33   .145

MC DONALD, EDWARD C.
B.OCT.28,1886 ALBANY,N.Y.
D.MAR.11,1946
1911 BOS N 3   54   .206
1912 BOS N 3   121   .259
1913 CHI N H   1   .000
        BRTR   176   .244

MC DONALD, HENRY M.
B.JAN.16,1911 SANTA MONICA,CAL.
1931 PHI A P   19   2- 4
1933 PHI A P   4   1- 1
      STL A P   25   0- 4
        BRTR   48   3- 9

MC DONALD, JAMES
B.PHILADELPHIA,PA.
1902 NY N O   2   .333

MC DONALD, JAMES A.
B.AUG.6,1860 SAN FRANCISCO,CAL.
D.SEPT.14,1914
1884 PIT AA 3-O   38   .151
1885 BUF N S-O   5   .000
                    43   .138

**MC DONALD, JIMMIE LE ROY
"HOT ROD"**
B.MAY 17,1927 GRANTS PASS,ORE.
1950 BOS A P   9   1- 0
1951 STL A P   16   17   4- 7
1952 NY A P   26   3- 4
1953 NY A P   27   29   9- 7
1954 NY A P   16   4- 1
1955 BAL A P   21   3- 5
1956 CHI A P   8   0- 2
1957 CHI A P   10   0- 1
1958 CHI A P   3   0- 0
        BRTR   136 139 24-27

MC DONALD, JOHN J.
1907 WAS A P   1   0- 0
        TR

MC DONALD, JOSEPH MALCOLM
1910 STL A 3   10   .156

MC DONNELL, JAMES WILLIAM
B.AUG.15,1922 GAGETOWN,MICH.
1943 CLE A C   2   .000
1944 CLE A C   20   .233
1945 CLE A C   28   .196
        BLTR   50   .211

MC DONOUGH, EDWARD
B.SEPT.13,1886 ELGIN,ILL.
D.SEPT.2,1926
1909 PHI N C   1   .000
1910 PHI N C   4   .111
        TR   5   .095

MC DOOLAN
1873 MAR NA P   1   0- 1
1875 RS NA P   1   0- 1
                     2   0- 2

MC DOUGAL, JOHN A.
1895 BRO N P   5   0- 0

YR	CL	LEA	POS	GP	G	REC

MC DOUGAL, JOHN H. "DEWEY"
B.SEPT.19,1871 ALEDO,ILL.
D.APR.28,1936

1895	STL	N	P		15	4-11
1896	STL	N	P		3	0- 1
					18	4-12

MC DOUGALD, GILBERT JAMES "GIL"
B.MAY 19,1928 SAN FRANCISCO,CAL

1951	NY	A	2-3		131	.306
1952	NY	A	2-3		152	.263
1953	NY	A	2-3		141	.285
1954	NY	A	2-3		126	.259
1955	NY	A	2-3		141	.285
1956	NY	A	2-S-3		120	.311
1957	NY	A	2-S-3		141	.289
1958	NY	A	2-S		138	.250
1959	NY	A	2-S-3		127	.251
1960	NY	A	2-3		119	.258
		BRTR			1336	.276

MC DOUGALL, JAMES A. "SANDY"
B.FEB.18,1878 BUFFALO,N.Y.
D.OCT.4,1910

| 1905 | STL | N | P | | 5 | 1- 4 |

MC DOWELL, SAMUEL EDWARD THOMAS "SAM"
B.SEP.21,1942 PITTSBURGH,PA.

1961	CLE	A	P		1	0- 0
1962	CLE	A	P		25	3- 7
1963	CLE	A	P	14	15	3- 5
1964	CLE	A	P		31	11- 6
1965	CLE	A	P	42	43	17-11
1966	CLE	A	P	35	36	9- 8
1967	CLE	A	P		37	13-15
1968	CLE	A	P		38	15-14
1969	CLE	A	P		39	18-14
1970	CLE	A	P-	39	40	20-12
			1-2			.124
1971	CLE	A	P		35	13-17
1972	SF	N	P		28	10- 8
1973	SF	N	P		18	1- 2
	NY	A	P		16	5- 8
1974	NY	A	P		13	1- 6
1975	PIT	N	P		14	2- 1
		BLTL		425	429	141-134
						.154

MC ELROY, JAMES D.
B.SAN FRANCISCO,CAL.
D.FEB.24,1889

1884	PHI	N	P-O		13	1-12
						.136
	WIL	U	P-O		1	0- 1
						.000
					14	1-13
						.131

MC ELVEEN, PRYOR MYNATT "HUMPY"
B.NOV.5,1883 ATLANTA,GA.
D.OCT.27,1951

1909	BRO	N	3		67	.198
1910	BRO	N	3		64	.225
1911	BRO	N	2		16	.193
		TR			147	.209

MC ELWEE, LELAND STANFORD
B.MAY 23,1894 SAN DIEGO,CAL.
D.FEB.6,1957

| 1916 | PHI | A | 3 | | 54 | .265 |
| | | BLTR | | | | |

MC ELYEA, FRANK
B.AUG.4,1918 CARMI,ILL.

| 1942 | BOS | N | O | | 7 | .000 |
| | | BRTR | | | | |

MC ENANEY, WILLIAM HENRY "WILL"
B.FEB.14,1952 SPRINGFIELD,OHIO

1974	CIN	N	P		24	2- 1
1975	CIN	N	P		70	5- 2
1976	CIN	N	P		55	2- 6
		BLTL			149	9- 9

MC EVOY, LOUIS ANTHONY
B.MAY 30,1902 WILLIAMSBURG,KAN.
D.DEC.16,1953

1930	NY	A	P		28	1- 3
1931	NY	A	P		6	0- 0
		BRTR			34	1- 3

MC FADDEN, BERNARD JOSEPH "BARNEY"
B.FEB.22,1874 ECKLEY,PA.
D.APR.28,1924

1901	CIN	N	P		8	3- 4
1902	PHI	N	P		1	0- 1
		BRTR			9	3- 5

MC FADDEN, GUY

| 1895 | STL | N | 1 | | 4 | .200 |

MC FADDEN, LEON
B.APR.26,1944 LITTLE ROCK,ARK.

1968	HOU	N	S		16	.277
1969	HOU	N	S-O		44	.176
1970	HOU	N	R		2	.000
		BRTR			62	.215

MC FARLAN, ALEXANDER SHEPARD
B.OCT.11,1869 ST.LOUIS,MO.
D.MAR.2,1939 PEEWEE VALLEY,KY.

| 1892 | LOU | N | O | | 14 | .162 |

MC FARLAN, ANDERSON DANIEL "DAN"
B.NOV.26,1874 GAINESVILLE,TEX.
D.SEPT.24,1924

1895	LOU	N	P		7	0- 6
1899	BRO	N	P		1	0- 0
	WAS	N	P		29	8-18
					37	8-24

MC FARLAND, CHARLES A. "CHAPPIE"
B.ST.LOUIS,MO.
D.DEC.15,1924

1902	STL	N	P		2	0- 1
1903	STL	N	P		28	9-19
1904	STL	N	P		32	13-18
1905	STL	N	P		31	9-18
1906	STL	N	P		7	3- 4
	PIT	N	P		6	1- 3
	BRO	N	P		1	0- 1
		TR			107	35-64

MC FARLAND, CLAUDE

| 1884 | BAL | U | P-O | 1 | 3 | 0- 1 |
| | | | | | | .286 |

MC FARLAND, EDWARD WILLIAM
B.AUG.3,1874 CLEVELAND,OHIO
D.NOV.28,1959

1893	CLE	N	O		9	.370
1896	STL	N	C		80	.239
1897	STL	N	C-1-2-O		31	.324
	PHI	N	C		36	.221
1898	PHI	N	C		118	.274
1899	PHI	N	C		90	.333
1900	PHI	N	C		90	.307
1901	PHI	N	C		72	.278
1902	CHI	A	C-1-O		71	.231
1903	CHI	A	C		61	.210
1904	CHI	A	C		50	.263
1905	CHI	A	C		80	.280
1906	CHI	A	C		12	.181
1907	CHI	A	C		52	.283
1908	BOS	A	C		19	.208
		BPTR			871	.272

MC FARLAND, HERMAS WALTER
B.MAR.11,1870 DES MOINES,IOWA
D.SEPT.21,1935

1896	LOU	N	O		25	.198
1898	CIN	N	O		15	.286
1901	CHI	A	O		132	.265
1902	CHI	A	O		7	.185
	BAL	A	O		63	.321
1903	NY	A	O		103	.223
		BLTR			345	.257

MC FARLAND, HOWARD ALEXANDER
B.MAR.7,1911 EL RENO,OKLA.

| 1945 | WAS | A | O | | 6 | .091 |
| | | BRTR | | | | |

MC FARLAND, LA MONT A. "MONTE"
B.1871 ILLINOIS
D.NOV.15,1913

1895	CHI	N	P		2	2- 0
1896	CHI	N	P		3	0- 3
					5	2- 3

MC FARLANE, ORLANDO DEJESUS (QUESADA)
B.JUNE 28,1938 ORIENTE,CUBA

1962	PIT	N	C		8	.087
1964	PIT	N	C-O		37	.244
1966	DET	A	C		49	.254
1967	CAL	A	C		12	.227
1968	CAL	A	C		18	.290
		BRTR			124	.240

MC FETRIDGE, JOHN R.
B.AUG.25,1869 PHILADELPHIA,PA.
D.JAN.10,1917

1890	PHI	N	P		1	1- 0
1903	PHI	N	P		14	1-11
					15	2-11

MC GAFFIGAN, MARK ANDREW "PATSY"
B.SEPT.12,1888 CARLYLE,ILL.
D.DEC.22,1940

1917	PHI	N	S		19	.167
1918	PHI	N	2-S		54	.203
		BRTR			73	.194

MC GAH, EDWARD JOSEPH "EDDIE"
B.SEPT.30,1921 OAKLAND,CAL.

1946	BOS	A	C		15	.216
1947	BOS	A	C		9	.000
		BRTR			24	.157

MC GAHA, FRED MELVIN "MEL"
B.SEPT.26,1926 BASTROP,LA.
NON-PLAYING MANAGER
CLE(A) 1962, KC(A) 1964-65

MC GAMWELL, EDWARD M.
B.JAN.10,1878 BUFFALO,N.Y.
D.NOV.1,1950

| 1905 | BRO | N | 1 | | 4 | .267 |

MC GANN, DENNIS LAWRENCE "DAN"
B.JULY 15,1871 SHELBYVILLE,KY.
D.DEC.13,1910

1895	LOU	N	S-3		17	.313
1896	BOS	N	2		42	.315
1898	BAL	N	1		145	.298
1899	BRO	N	1		63	.245
	WAS	N	1		75	.338
1900	STL	N	1		124	.301
1901	STL	N	1		113	.265
1902	BAL	A	1		68	.314
	NY	N	1		61	.301
1903	NY	N	1		129	.270
1904	NY	N	1		141	.286
1905	NY	N	1		136	.299
1906	NY	N	1		133	.237
1907	NY	N	1		81	.298
1908	BOS	N	1		130	.240
		BBTR			1458	.283

MC GARR, JAMES B. "CHIPPY"
B.MAY 10,1863 WORCESTER,MASS.
D.JUNE 6,1904

1884	CHI	U	2		18	.160
1886	ATH	AA	S		72	.271
1887	ATH	AA	S		127	.331
1888	STL	AA	S		35	.187
1889	KC	AA	2-S-3-O		25	.287
	BAL	AA	S		3	.143
1890	BOS	N	3		121	.236
1893	CLE	N	3		63	.309
1894	CLE	N	3		127	.272
1895	CLE	N	3		112	.270
1896	CLE	N	3		111	.266
		BRTR			814	.273

MC GARR, JAMES VINCENT
B.NOV.9,1888 PHILADELPHIA,PA.

| 1912 | DET | A | O | | 1 | .000 |

MC GARVEY, DANIEL

| 1912 | DET | A | O | | 1 | .000 |

MC GEACHY, JOHN CHARLES
B.JAN.23,1861 CLINTON,MASS.
D.APR.5,1930

1886	DET	N	O		7	.333
	STL	N	O		58	.216
1887	IND	N	O		99	.278
1888	IND	N	O		118	.219
1889	IND	N	O		131	.267
1890	BRO	P	O		104	.253
1891	ATH	AA	O		46	.217
	BOS	AA	O		41	.250
		BR			604	.248

MC GEARY, MICHAEL HENRY
B.1851 PHILADELPHIA,PA.

YR	CL	LEA	POS	GP	G	REC
1871	TRO	NA	C-S		29	.244
1872	ATH	NA	C-S-O		46	.344
1873	ATH	NA	C-S		51	-
1874	ATH	NA	C-S-O		54	-
1875	PHI	NA	2-S-3-O		68	.294
1876	STL	N	2		60	.259
1877	STL	N	2-3		57	.253
1879	PRO	N	2-3		84	.276
1880	PRO	N	2-S-3		17	.129
	CLE	N	3-O		31	.233
1881	CLE	N	3		10	.211
1882	DET	N	2-S		33	.149
	BRTR				540	-

MC GEE, DANIEL ALOYSIUS
B.SEPT.29,1913 NEW YORK,N.Y.

YR	CL	LEA	POS	GP	G	REC
1934	BOS	N	S		7	.136
	BRTR					

MC GEE, F.

YR	CL	LEA	POS	GP	G	REC
1874	ATL	NA	2-S-O		16	-
1875	MUT	NA	O		22	-
	ATL	NA	2-3-O		21	-
1884	WAS	U	C-3-O		4	.188
					63	-

MC GEE, FRANCIS D. "TUBBY"
B.APR.28,1899 COLUMBUS,OHIO
D.JAN.30,1934

YR	CL	LEA	POS	GP	G	REC
1925	WAS	A	1		2	.000
	BRTR					

MC GEE, WILLIAM HENRY
"FIDDLER BILL"
B.NOV.16,1911 BATCHTOWN,ILL.

YR	CL	LEA	POS	GP	G	REC
1935	STL	N	P		1	1- 0
1936	STL	N	P		7	1- 1
1937	STL	N	P		4	1- 0
1938	STL	N	P		47	7-12
1939	STL	N	P		43	12- 5
1940	STL	N	P		38	16-10
1941	STL	N	P		4	0- 1
	NY	N	P		22	2- 9
1942	NY	N	P		31	6- 3
	BRTR				197	46-41

MC GEEHAN, CORNELIUS BERNARD
B.OCT.6,1883 DRIFTON,PA.
D.JULY 4,1907

YR	CL	LEA	POS	GP	G	REC
1903	PHI	A	P		6	1- 0

MC GEEHAN, DANIEL DE SALES
B.JUNE 7,1885 DRIFTON,PA.
D.JULY 12,1955

YR	CL	LEA	POS	GP	G	REC
1911	STL	N	2		3	.222
	BRTR					

MC GEHEE, PATRICK HENRY
B.JULY 2,1888 MEADVILLE,MISS.
D.DEC.30,1946

YR	CL	LEA	POS	GP	G	REC
1912	DET	A	P		1	0- 1
	BLTR					

MC GHEE, WARREN EDWARD "ED"
B.SEPT.29,1926 PERRY,ARK.

YR	CL	LEA	POS	GP	G	REC
1950	CHI	A	O		3	.167
1953	CHI	A	O		104	.263
1954	PHI	A	O		21	.208
	CHI	A	O		42	.227
1955	CHI	A	O		26	.077
	BRTR				196	.246

MC GHEE, WILLIAM HARRISON
B.SEPT.5,1908 SHAWMUT,ALA.

YR	CL	LEA	POS	GP	G	REC
1944	PHI	A	1		77	.289
1945	PHI	A	1-O		93	.252
	BLTL				170	.272

MC GILL, WILLIAM JOHN "PARSON"
B.JUNE 29,1880 MC PHERSON,KAN.
D.AUG.9,1959

YR	CL	LEA	POS	GP	G	REC
1907	STL	A	P		2	1- 0
	BRTR					

MC GILL, WILLIAM VANESS "KID"
B.NOV.10,1873 ATLANTA,GA.
D.AUG.29,1944

YR	CL	LEA	POS	GP	G	REC
1890	CLE	P	P		24	11- 9
1891	CIN	AA	P		16	2- 4
	STL	AA	P		28	19- 9
1892	CIN	N	P		3	1- 1
1893	CHI	N	P		35	17-17
1894	CHI	N	P		26	6-19
1895	PHI	N	P		19	10- 8
1896	PHI	N	P		12	4- 4
	TL				163	70-71

MC GILLEN, JOHN JOSEPH
B.AUG.6,1917 EDDYSTONE,PA.

YR	CL	LEA	POS	GP	G	REC
1944	PHI	A	P		2	0- 0
	BLTL					

MC GILLICUDDY, CORNELIUS ALEXANDER
(PLAYED UNDER NAME OF
CORNELIUS ALEXANDER MACK)

MC GILLICUDDY, EARLE
(PLAYED UNDER NAME OF
EARLE MACK)

MC GILVRAY, WILLIAM ALEXANDER
B.APR.29,1883 PORTLAND,ORE.
D.MAY 23,1952

YR	CL	LEA	POS	GP	G	REC
1908	CIN	N	H		2	.000

MC GINLEY, JAMES WILLIAM
B.OCT.2,1878 GROVELAND,MASS.
D.SEPT.20,1961

YR	CL	LEA	POS	GP	G	REC
1904	STL	N	P		3	2- 1
1905	STL	N	P		1	0- 1
					4	2- 2

MC GINLEY, TIMOTHY S.
B.PHILADELPHIA,PA.
D.NOV.2,1899

YR	CL	LEA	POS	GP	G	REC
1875	CEN	NA	C-O		13	-
	NH	NA	C		32	-
1876	BOS	N	C		9	.150
					54	-

MC GINN, DANIEL MICHAEL "DAN"
B.AUG.29,1943 OMAHA,NEB.

YR	CL	LEA	POS	GP	G	REC
1968	CIN	N	P		14	0- 1
1969	MON	N	P		74	7-10
1970	MON	N	P		52	7-10
1971	MON	N	P		28	1- 4
1972	CHI	N	P	42	43	0- 5
	BLTL			210	211	15-30

MC GINN, FRANK J.
B.CINCINNATI,OHIO
D.NOV.19,1897

YR	CL	LEA	POS	GP	G	REC
1890	PIT	N	O		1	.000

MC GINNIS, AUGUST
B.1870 PAINESVILLE,OHIO

YR	CL	LEA	POS	GP	G	REC
1893	CHI	N	P		13	2- 6
	PHI	N	P		5	1- 3
					18	3- 9

MC GINNIS, GEORGE W. "JUMBO"
B.FEB.22,1864 ST.LOUIS,MO.
D.MAY 18,1934

YR	CL	LEA	POS	GP	G	REC
1882	STL	AA	P-2-O	46	51	25-21
						.252
						.227
1883	STL	AA	P-O		44	29-15
						.211
1884	STL	AA	P		40	24-16
1885	STL	AA	P		13	6- 6
1886	STL	AA	P		10	5- 2
	BAL	AA	P		26	11-12
1887	CIN	AA	P		9	3- 6
				188	193	103-78
						.215

MC GINNITY, JOSEPH JEROME
"JOE" OR "IRON MAN"
B.MAR.19,1871 ROCK ISLAND,ILL.
D.NOV.14,1929 BROOKLYN,N.Y.

YR	CL	LEA	POS	GP	G	REC
1899	BAL	N	P	43	47	27-13
1900	BRO	N	P		41	29- 9
1901	BAL	A	P		48	26-19
1902	BAL	A	P-O	26	27	13-10
						.295
	NY	N	P-2-O	16	19	8- 8
						.123
1903	NY	N	P		55	31-20
1904	NY	N	P		51	35- 8
1905	NY	N	P		46	22-16
1906	NY	N	P		45	27-12
1907	NY	N	P		47	18-17
1908	NY	N	P		37	11- 7
	BRTR			455	463	247-139
						.193

MC GLONE, JOHN T.
B.BALTIMORE,MD.

YR	CL	LEA	POS	GP	G	REC
1886	WAS	N	3		3	.091
1887	CLE	AA	3		21	.329
1888	CLE	AA	3		55	.183
					79	.221

MC GLOTHEN, LYNN EVERETT
B.MAR.27,1950 MONROE,LA.

YR	CL	LEA	POS	GP	G	REC
1972	BOS	A	P		22	8- 7
1973	BOS	A	P		6	1- 2
1974	STL	N	P		31	16-12
1975	STL	N	P		35	15-13
1976	STL	N	P		33	13-15
	BLTR				127	53-49

MC GLOTHIN, EZRA MAC "PAT"
B.OCT.27,1922 KNOXVILLE,TENN.

YR	CL	LEA	POS	GP	G	REC
1949	BRO	N	P		7	1- 1
1950	BRO	N	P		1	0- 0
	BLTR				8	1- 1

MC GLOTHLIN, JAMES MILTON "JIM"
B.OCT.6,1943 LOS ANGELES,CAL.
D.DEC.23,1975 UNION,KY.

YR	CL	LEA	POS	GP	G	REC
1965	CAL	A	P		3	0- 3
1966	CAL	A	P		19	3- 1
1967	CAL	A	P		32	12- 8
1968	CAL	A	P		40	10-15
1969	CAL	A	P		37	8-16
1970	CIN	N	P		35	14-10
1971	CIN	N	P		30	8-12
1972	CIN	N	P		31	9- 8
1973	CIN	N	P		24	3- 3
	CHI	A	P		5	0- 1
	BRTR				256	67-77

MC GLYNN, ULYSSES SIMPSON GRANT
"STONEY"
B.MAY 26,1872 LANCASTER,PA.
D.AUG.26,1941

YR	CL	LEA	POS	GP	G	REC
1906	STL	N	P		6	4- 2
1907	STL	N	P		45	14-25
1908	STL	N	P		16	1- 6
					67	19-33

MC GOVERN, ARTHUR JOHN
B.FEB.27,1882 ST.JOHN,N.B.,CAN.
D.NOV.14,1915

YR	CL	LEA	POS	GP	G	REC
1905	BOS	A	C		15	.114

MC GOWAN, FRANK BERNARD
"BEAUTY"
B.NOV.8,1901 BRANFORD,CONN.

YR	CL	LEA	POS	GP	G	REC
1922	PHI	A	O		99	.230
1923	PHI	A	O		95	.254
1928	STL	A	O		47	.363
1929	STL	A	O		125	.254
1937	BOS	N	O		9	.083
	BLTR				375	.262

MC GOWAN, TULLIS EARL "MICKEY"
B.NOV.26,1921 WAYCROSS,GA.

YR	CL	LEA	POS	GP	G	REC
1948	NY	N	P		3	0- 0
	BLTL					

MC GRANER, HOWARD
B.SEPT.11,1889 LUHRIG,OHIO
D.OCT.22,1952

YR	CL	LEA	POS	GP	G	REC
1912	CIN	N	P		2	1- 0
	BLTL					

MC GRAW, JAMES LEO
B.1890
D.NOV.14,1918

YR	CL	LEA	POS	GP	G	REC
1914	BRO	F	P		1	0- 0

YR	CL	LEA	POS	GP	G	REC

MC GRAW, FRANK EDWIN "TUG"
B.AUG.30,1944 MARTINEZ,CAL.

YR	CL	LEA	POS	GP	G	REC
1965	NY	N	P	37	38	2- 7
1966	NY	N	P		15	2- 9
1967	NY	N	P		4	0- 3
1969	NY	N	P	42	43	9- 3
1970	NY	N	P		57	4- 6
1971	NY	N	P		51	11- 4
1972	NY	N	P		54	8- 6
1973	NY	N	P		60	5- 6
1974	NY	N	P		41	6-11
1975	PHI	N	P		56	9- 6
1976	PHI	N	P		58	7- 6
		BRTL		475	477	63-67

MC GRAW, JOHN JOSEPH
"JOHN" OR "LITTLE NAPOLEON"
B.APR.7,1873 TRUXTON,N.Y.
D.FEB.25,1934 NEW ROCHELLE,N.Y.

YR	CL	LEA	POS	GP	G	REC
1891	BAL	AA	S		31	.245
1892	BAL	N	2-O		76	.267
1893	BAL	N	S		127	.328
1894	BAL	N	3		123	.340
1895	BAL	N	3		93	.374
1896	BAL	N	3		19	.356
1897	BAL	N	3		105	.326
1898	BAL	N	3		141	.334
1899	BAL	N	M-3		118	.390
1900	STL	N	3		98	.337
1901	BAL	A	M-3		73	.352
1902	BAL	A	M-3		20	.286
	NY	N	M-S		34	.226
1903	NY	N	M-2		12	.273
1904	NY	N	M-2		3	.300
1905	NY	N	M-O		3	.000
1906	NY	N	M-3		4	.000
		BLTR		1080		.334

NON-PLAYING MANAGER
NY(N) 1907-32

MC GRAW, ROBERT EMMETT
B.APR.10,1895 LA VETA,COLO.

YR	CL	LEA	POS	GP	G	REC
1917	NY	A	P		2	0- 1
1918	NY	A	P		1	0- 1
1919	NY	A	P		6	0- 2
	BOS	A	P		10	1- 0
1920	NY	A	P		15	0- 0
1925	BRO	N	P		2	0- 2
1926	BRO	N	P		33	9-13
1927	BRO	N	P		1	0- 1
	STL	N	P		18	4- 5
1928	PHI	N	P		39	7- 8
1929	PHI	N	P		41	5- 5
		BRTR		168		26-38

MC GREGOR, SCOTT HOUSTON
B.JAN.18,1954 INGLEWOOD,CAL.

YR	CL	LEA	POS	GP	G	REC
1976	BAL	A	P		3	0- 1
		BBTL				

MC GREW, WALTER HOWARD "SLIM"
B.AUG.5,1899 YOAKUM,TEX.
D.AUG.21,1967 PORT ARTHUR,TEX.

YR	CL	LEA	POS	GP	G	REC
1922	WAS	A	P		1	0- 0
1923	WAS	A	P		3	0- 1
1924	WAS	A	P		6	0- 1
		BRTR		10		0- 2

MC GUCKIN, JOSEPH W.
B.1862 PATERSON,N.J.
D.DEC.31,1903

YR	CL	LEA	POS	GP	G	REC
1890	BAL	AA	O		10	.056

MC GUINNESS, JOHN J.

YR	CL	LEA	POS	GP	G	REC
1876	LOU	N	2		1	.000
1879	SYR	N	1		12	.294
1884	KEY	U	1		52	.243
					65	.249

MC GUIRE, JAMES A.
B.FEB.4,1875 DUNKIRK,N.Y.
D.JAN.26,1917

YR	CL	LEA	POS	GP	G	REC
1901	CLE	A	S		18	.232
		TR				

MC GUIRE, JAMES THOMAS "DEACON"
B.NOV.18,1863 YOUNGSTOWN,OHIO
D.OCT.31,1936

YR	CL	LEA	POS	GP	G	REC
1884	TOL	AA	C		45	.184
1885	DET	N	C-O		34	.190
1886	PHI	N	C		48	.197
1887	PHI	N	C		40	.354
1888	PHI	N	C		12	.333
	DET	N	C		3	.000
	CLE	AA	C		25	.207
1890	ROC	AA	C		87	.301
1891	WAS	AA	C		111	.296
1892	WAS	N	C		87	.241
1893	WAS	N	C		59	.262
1894	WAS	N	C		102	.304
1895	WAS	N	C		133	.330
1896	WAS	N	C		95	.325
1897	WAS	N	C		82	.338
1898	WAS	N	M-C-1		128	.273
1899	WAS	N	C		56	.277
	BRO	N	C		43	.338
1900	BRO	N	C		68	.280
1901	BRO	N	C		84	.293
1902	DET	A	C		72	.229
1903	DET	A	C		71	.241
1904	NY	A	C		100	.211
1905	NY	A	C		71	.219
1906	NY	A	C		51	.299
1907	NY	A	H		1	.000
	BOS	A	M-C		6	.500
1908	BOS	A	M-1		1	.000
	CLE	A	C		1	.250
1910	CLE	A	M-C		1	.000
1912	DET	A	C		1	.500
		BBTR		1718		.279

NON-PLAYING MANAGER
CLE(A) 1909, 11

MC GUIRE, MICKEY C.
B.JAN.18,1941 DAYTON,OHIO

YR	CL	LEA	POS	GP	G	REC
1962	BAL	A	S		6	.000
1967	BAL	A	2		10	.235
		BRTR		16		.190

MC GUIRE, MURRAY MASON
B.JAN.19,1872 RICHMOND,VA.
D.SEPT.10,1945

YR	CL	LEA	POS	GP	G	REC
1894	CIN	N	P		1	0- 0

MC GUIRE, THOMAS PATRICK
B.FEB.1,1892 CHICAGO,ILL.
D.DEC.8,1959

YR	CL	LEA	POS	GP	G	REC
1914	CHI	F	P	24	37	5- 6
1919	CHI	A	P		1	0- 0
		BRTR		25	38	5- 6

MC GUNNIGLE, WILLIAM HENRY
"GUNNER"
B.JAN.1,1855 STOUGHTON,MASS.
D.MAR.9,1899

YR	CL	LEA	POS	GP	G	REC
1879	BUF	N	M-P-	13	46	7- 5
			O			.180
1880	BUF	N	M-P-	5	7	2- 3
			O			.174
	WOR	N	P		1	0- 0
1882	CLE	N	O		1	.200
		BRTR		19	55	9- 8
						.177

NON-PLAYING MANAGER
BRO(AA) 1888-89, BRO(N) 1890,
PIT(N) 1891, LOU(N) 1896

MC HALE, JAMES BERNARD
B.DEC.17,1875 MINERS MILLS,PA.
D.JUNE 18,1959

YR	CL	LEA	POS	GP	G	REC
1908	BOS	A	O		21	.224
		BRTR				

MC HALE, JOHN JOSEPH
B.SEPT.21,1921 DETROIT,MICH.

YR	CL	LEA	POS	GP	G	REC
1943	DET	A	H		4	.000
1944	DET	A	H		1	.000
1945	DET	A	1		19	.143
1947	DET	A	1		39	.211
1948	DET	A	H		1	.000
		BLTR		64		.193

MC HALE, MARTIN JOSEPH
B.OCT.30,1888 STONEHAM,MASS.

YR	CL	LEA	POS	GP	G	REC
1910	BOS	A	P		2	0- 2
1911	BOS	A	P		4	0- 0
1913	NY	A	P		7	2- 4
1914	NY	A	P	31	32	7-16
1915	NY	A	P		13	3- 7
1916	BOS	A	P		2	0- 1
	CLE	A	P		5	0- 0
		BRTR		64	65	12-30

MC HALE, ROBERT E. "RABBIT"
B.FEB.7,1870 SACRAMENTO,CAL.

YR	CL	LEA	POS	GP	G	REC
1898	WAS	N	O		10	.171

MC HENRY, AUSTIN BUSH "MAC"
B.SEPT.22,1895 WRIGHTSVILLE,O.
D.NOV.27,1922 JEFFERSON
TOWNSHIP,OHIO

YR	CL	LEA	POS	GP	G	REC
1918	STL	N	O		80	.261
1919	STL	N	2-3-O		110	.286
1920	STL	N	O		137	.282
1921	STL	N	O		152	.350
1922	STL	N	O		64	.303
		BRTR		543		.302

MC ILREE, VANCE ELMER
B.OCT.14,1897 RIVERSIDE,IOWA
D.MAY 6,1959

YR	CL	LEA	POS	GP	G	REC
1921	WAS	A	P		1	0- 0
		BRTR				

MC ILVEEN, HENRY COOKE "IRISH"
B.JULY 27,1880 BELFAST,IRELAND
D.OCT.19,1960

YR	CL	LEA	POS	GP	G	REC
1906	PIT	N	P		5	0- 1
1908	NY	A	O		44	.213
1909	NY	A	H		4	.000
		TL	5	53	0- 1
						.212

MC ILWAIN, STOVER WILLIAM
B.SEPT.22,1939 SANNNAH,GA.
D.JAN.15,1966 BUFFALO,N.Y.

YR	CL	LEA	POS	GP	G	REC
1957	CHI	A	P		1	0- 0
1958	CHI	A	P		1	0- 0
		BRTR			2	0- 0

MC INNIS, JOHN PHAELEN "STUFFY"
B.SEPT.19,1890 GLOUCESTER,MASS.
D.FEB.16,1960 IPSWICH,MASS.

YR	CL	LEA	POS	GP	G	REC
1909	PHI	A	S		19	.239
1910	PHI	A	S		38	.301
1911	PHI	A	1-S		126	.321
1912	PHI	A	1		153	.327
1913	PHI	A	1		148	.326
1914	PHI	A	1		149	.314
1915	PHI	A	1		119	.314
1916	PHI	A	1		140	.295
1917	PHI	A	1		150	.303
1918	BOS	A	1-3		117	.272
1919	BOS	A	1		120	.305
1920	BOS	A	1		148	.297
1921	BOS	A	1		152	.307
1922	CLE	A	1		142	.305
1923	BOS	N	1		154	.315
1924	BOS	N	1		146	.291
1925	PIT	N	1		59	.368
1926	PIT	N	1		47	.299
1927	PHI	N	M-1		1	.000
		BRTR		2128		.308

MC INTIRE, JOHN REID "HARRY"
B.JAN.11,1879 DAYTON,OHIO
D.JAN.9,1949 DAYTONA BEACH,FLA.

YR	CL	LEA	POS	GP	G	REC
1905	BRO	N	P	40	45	9-27
1906	BRO	N	P	39	42	13-21
1907	BRO	N	P		28	7-15
1908	BRO	N	P		40	11-20
1909	BRO	N	P		32	7-17
1910	CHI	N	P		28	13- 9
1911	CHI	N	P		25	11- 7
1912	CHI	N	P		7	1- 2
1913	CIN	N	P		1	0- 1
		BRTR	240	248	72-119

MC INTOSH, JOSEPH ANTHONY "JOE"
B.AUG.4,1951 BILLINGS,MONT.

YR	CL	LEA	POS	GP	G	REC
1974	SD	N	P		10	0- 4
1975	SD	N	P	37	38	8-15
		BBTR	47	48	8-19

MC INTYRE, FRANK W.
D.DETROIT,MICH.

YR	CL	LEA	POS	GP	G	REC
1883	DET	N	P		1	1- 0
	COL	AA	P		2	1- 1
					3	2- 1

YR	CL	LEA	POS	GP	G	REC

MC INTYRE, MATTHEW W.
B.JUNE 12,1880 STONINGTON,CONN.
D.APR.2,1920

1901	PHI	A	O		82	.283
1904	DET	A	O		152	.254
1905	DET	A	O		131	.265
1906	DET	A	O		133	.260
1907	DET	A	O		20	.284
1908	DET	A	O		151	.295
1909	DET	A	O		125	.244
1910	DET	A	O		83	.236
1911	CHI	A	O		146	.323
1912	CHI	A	O		45	.167
		BLTL			1068	.270

MC IVOR, E. OTTO
B.1885 GREENVILLE,TEX.
D.MAY 4,1954

| 1911 | STL | N | O | | 17 | .226 |
| | | BBTL | | | | |

MC JAMES, JAMES MC CUTCHEN
(REAL NAME
JAMES MC CUTCHEN JAMES)
B.AUG.27,1873 WILLIAMSBURG,S.C.
D.SEPT.23,1901

1895	WAS	N	P		3	1- 1
1896	WAS	N	P		34	12-21
1897	WAS	N	P		41	14-24
1898	BAL	N	P		42	27-14
1899	BRO	N	P		33	17-11
1901	BRO	N	P		13	4- 6
		TR			166	75-77

MC KAIN, ARCHIE RICHARD "HAPPY"
B.MAY 12,1911 DELPHOS,KAN.

1937	BOS	A	P	36	38	0- 8
1938	BOS	A	P		37	5- 4
1939	DET	A	P		32	5- 0
1940	DET	A	P		27	5- 0
1941	DET	A	P		15	2- 1
	STL	A	P		8	0- 1
1943	STL	A	P		10	1- 1
		BBTL	165	167	26-21
		BL 1941-43			

MC KAIN, HAROLD LE ROY
B.JULY 10,1906 LOGAN,IOWA
D.JAN.24,1970 SACRAMENTO,CAL.

1927	CLE	A	P		2	0- 1
1929	CHI	A	P		34	6- 9
1930	CHI	A	P	32	33	6- 4
1931	CHI	A	P	27	32	6- 9
1932	CHI	A	P		8	0- 0
		BLTR	.103	109	18-23

MC KAY, DAVID LAWRENCE "DAVE"
B.MAR.14,1950 VANCOUVER,B.C.,CAN

1975	MIN	A	3		33	.256
1976	MIN	A	S-3		45	.203
		BRTR			78	.228

MC KAY, REEVES H.

| 1915 | STL | A | P | | 1 | 0- 0 |

MC KEAN, EDWIN JOHN
B.JUNE 20,1868 CLEVELAND,OHIO
D.AUG.16,1919 CLEVELAND,OHIO

1887	CLE	AA	S		132	.364
1888	CLE	AA	S-O		130	.297
1889	CLE	N	S		123	.302
1890	CLE	N	S		136	.296
1891	CLE	N	S		141	.280
1892	CLE	N	S		128	.269
1893	CLE	N	S		125	.325
1894	CLE	N	S		130	.354
1895	CLE	N	S		132	.344
1896	CLE	N	S		133	.335
1897	CLE	N	S		127	.273
1898	CLE	N	S		151	.285
1899	STL	N	S		67	.281
		BRTR			1655	.311

MC KECHNIE, WILLIAM BOYD
B.AUG.7,1887 WILKINSBURG,PA.
D.OCT.29,1965 BRADENTON,FLA.

1907	PIT	N	2		3	.125
1910	PIT	N	2		60	.217
1911	PIT	N	1-2		92	.227
1912	PIT	N	2-S		24	.247
1913	BOS	N	O		1	.000
	NY	A	2		44	.134
1914	IND	F	3		149	.305
1915	NEW	F	M-3		126	.257
1916	NY	N	M-3		71	.238
	CIN	N	M-3		37	.292
1917	CIN	N	2-S-3		48	.254
1918	PIT	N	3		126	.255
1920	PIT	N	3		40	.218
		BBTR			821	.252

NON-PLAYING MANAGER
PIT(N) 1922-26, STL(N) 1928-29,
BOS(N) 1930-37, CIN(N) 1938-46

MC KEE

| 1884 | WAS | U | C-3-O | | 4 | .188 |

MC KEE, JAMES F.
B.ROCKFORD,ILL.
D.JUNE 26,1912
NON-PLAYING MANAGER MIL(U) 1884

MC KEE, JAMES MARION "JIM"
B.FEB.1,1947 COLUMBUS,OHIO

1972	PIT	N	P		2	1- 0
1973	PIT	N	P		15	0- 1
		BRTR			17	1- 1

MC KEE, RAY "RED"
B.JULY 20,1890 SHAWNEE,OHIO
D.AUG.5,1972 SAGINAW,MICH.

1913	DET	A	C		67	.283
1914	DET	A	C		32	.167
1915	DET	A	C		55	.274
1916	DET	A	C		32	.211
		BLTR			186	.254

MC KEE, ROGERS HORNSBY
B.SEPT.16,1926 SHELBY,N.C.

1943	PHI	N	P		4	1- 0
1944	PHI	N	P		1	0- 0
		BLTL			5	1- 0

MC KEEVER, JAMES
B.APR.19,1861 NEWFOUNDLAND,CAN.
D.AUG.19,1897

| 1884 | BOS | U | C-O | | 16 | .141 |

MC KEITHAN, EMMETT JAMES "TIM"
B.NOV.2,1908 BOSTIC,N.C.
D.AUG.20,1969 FOREST CITY,N.C.

1932	PHI	A	P		4	0- 1
1933	PHI	A	P		3	1- 0
1934	PHI	A	P		3	0- 0
		BRTR			10	1- 1

MC KELVEY, JOHN WELLINGTON
B.AUG.27,1847 ROCHESTER,N.Y.
D.MAY.31,1944

| 1875 | NH | NA | 3-O | | 43 | - |

MC KELVY, RUSSELL ERRETT
B.SEPT.8,1856 MEADVILLE,PA.
D.OCT.30,1915

1878	IND	N	P-O	3	60	0- 0
						.222
1882	PIT	AA	O		1	.000
		TR		3	61	0- 0
						.219

MC KENNA, EDWARD
B.ST.LOUIS,MO.

1874	PHI	NA	1		1	.000
1877	STL	N	O		1	.200
1884	WAS	U	C-O		32	.188
					34	.184

MC KENNA, JAMES WILLIAM "KIT"
B.AUG.19,1873 LYNCHBURG,VA.

1898	BRO	N	P		14	1- 7
1899	BAL	N	P		9	2- 4
					23	3-11

MC KENRY, FRANK GORDON
"BIG PETE"
B.AUG.13,1888 PINEY PLATS,TENN.
D.NOV.1,1956

1915	CIN	N	P		21	5- 5
1916	CIN	N	P		6	1- 1
		BRTR			27	6- 6

MC KEON, JOHN ALOYSIUS "JACK"
B.NOV.23,1930 SOUTH AMBOY,N.J.
NON-PLAYING MANAGER
KC(A) 1973-75

MC KEON, LAWRENCE G.
B.MAR.25,1866 NEW YORK
D.JULY 18,1915 INDIANAPOLIS,IND

1884	IND	AA	P-1	61	70	18-41
						.215
1885	CIN	AA	P-O		33	20-13
						.157
1886	CIN	AA	P-1-	17	18	8- 9
						.250
	KC	N	P		2	0- 2
				113	123	46-65
						.203

MC KEOUGH, DAVID J.
B.1865 UTICA,N.Y.
D.JULY 10,1901

1890	ROC	AA	C		63	.218
1891	ATH	AA	C		15	.278
					78	.231

MC KINNEY, BUCK
B.LOUISVILLE,KY.
NON-PLAYING MANAGER LOU(AA)1889

**MC KINNEY, CHARLES RICHARD
"RICH"**
B.NOV.22,1946 PIQUA,OHIO

1970	CHI	A	S-3		43	.168
1971	CHI	A	2-3-O		114	.271
1972	NY	A	3		37	.215
1973	OAK	A	2-3-O		48	.246
1974	OAK	A	2		5	.143
1975	OAK	A	1		8	.143
		BRTR			255	.230

MC KINNEY, ROBERT FRANCIS
B.OCT.4,1875 MC SHERRYSTOWN,PA.
D.AUG.19,1946

| 1901 | PHI | A | 2 | | 2 | .000 |

MC KINNON, ALEXANDER J.
B.AUG.14,1856 BOSTON,MASS.
D.JULY 24,1887

1884	NY	N	1		112	.275
1885	STL	N	1		100	.270
1886	STL	N	1		122	.301
1887	PIT	N	1		48	.365
					382	.301

MC KNIGHT, HENRY DENNIS "DENNY"
B.1847 PITTSBURGH,PA.
D.MAY 5,1900
NON-PLAYING MANAGER PIT(AA)1884

MC KNIGHT, JAMES ARTHUR "JIM"
B.JUNE 1,1936 BEE BRANCH,ARK.

1960	CHI	N	2-O		3	.333
1962	CHI	N	2-O		60	.224
		BRTR			63	.231

MC LAIN, DENNIS DALE "DENNY"
B.MAR.29,1944 CHICAGO,ILL.

1963	DET	A	P		3	2- 1
1964	DET	A	P	19	20	4- 5
1965	DET	A	P		33	16- 6
1966	DET	A	P		38	20-14
1967	DET	A	P	37	38	17-16
1968	DET	A	P	41	44	31- 6
1969	DET	A	P		42	24- 9
1970	DET	A	P		14	3- 5
1971	WAS	A	P		33	10-22
1972	OAK	A	P		5	1- 2
	ATL	N	P		15	3- 5
		BRTR	280	285	131-91

MC LANE, EDWARD CAMERON
B.AUG.20,1881 WESTON,MASS.

| 1907 | BRO | N | O | | 1 | .000 |

MC LARNEY, ARTHUR JAMES
B.DEC.20,1908 FT.WORDEN,WASH.

| 1932 | NY | N | S | | 9 | .130 |
| | | BBTR | | | | |

MC LARRY, HOWARD ZELL "POLLY"
B.MAR.25,1891 LEONARD,TEX.
D.NOV.4,1971 BONHAM,TEX.

1912	CHI	N	H		2	.000
1915	CHI	N	1-2		68	.197
					70	.194

YR	CL	LEA	POS	GP	G	REC

MC LAUGHLIN, BERNARD
B.1857 IRELAND
D.FEB.13,1921

YR	CL	LEA	POS	GP	G	REC
1882	WOR	N	S-O		15	.207
1884	WAS	U	S		10	.189
	KC	U	P-2-	6	40	0- 4
			O			.218
1887	PHI	N	2		50	.259
1890	SYR	AA	S		81	.260
				6	196	0- 4
						.245

MC LAUGHLIN, FRANCIS EDWARD
B.JUNE 19,1856 LOWELL,MASS.
D.APR.5,1917

YR	CL	LEA	POS	GP	G	REC
1883	PIT	AA	P-2-	1	27	0- 0
			S-O			.200
1884	CIN	U	S		15	.246
	CHI	U	2-S		15	.284
	KC	U	P-2-	4	33	1- 1
			S-3-O			.219
		BRTR		5	90	1- 1
						.235

MC LAUGHLIN, JAMES ANSON "KID"
B.APR.12,1888 RANDOLPH,N.Y.
D.NOV.13,1934

YR	CL	LEA	POS	GP	G	REC
1914	CIN	N	O		3	.000
		BLTR				

MC LAUGHLIN, JAMES C.
B.1860 CLEVELAND,OHIO
D.NOV.16,1895

YR	CL	LEA	POS	GP	G	REC
1884	WAS	U	S-3		10	.194
	BAL	AA	P-O	3	5	1- 2
						.227
		TL		3	15	1- 2
						.207

MC LAUGHLIN, JAMES ROBERT
B.JAN.3,1902 ST.LOUIS,MO.
D.DEC.18,1968 MOUNT VERNON,ILL.

YR	CL	LEA	POS	GP	G	REC
1932	STL	A	3		1	.000
		BRTR				

MC LAUGHLIN, JUSTIN THEODORE
B.MAR.24,1912 ALLSTON,MASS.
D.SEPT.27,1964

YR	CL	LEA	POS	GP	G	REC
1931	BOS	A	P		9	0- 0
1932	BOS	A	P		1	0- 0
1933	BOS	A	P		6	0- 0
		BLTL			16	0- 0

MC LAUGHLIN, MICHAEL DUANE
B.OCT.23,1953 OAKLAND,CAL.

YR	CL	LEA	POS	GP	G	REC
1976	HOU	N	P		17	4- 5
		BRTR				

MC LAUGHLIN, PATRICK ELMER
B.AUG.17,1910 TAYLOR,TEX.

YR	CL	LEA	POS	GP	G	REC
1937	DET	A	P	10	11	0- 2
1940	PHI	A	P		1	0- 0
1945	DET	A	P		1	0- 0
		BRTR		12	13	0- 2

MC LAUGHLIN, THOMAS
B.LOUISVILLE,KY.

YR	CL	LEA	POS	GP	G	REC
1883	LOU	AA	1-2-S-3-		42	.206
			O			
1884	LOU	AA	S		100	.191
1885	LOU	AA	2		113	.215
1886	MET	AA	2		74	.137
1891	WAS	AA	2		14	.250
					343	.198

MC LAUGHLIN, WARREN A.
B.JAN.22,1876 N.PLAINFIELD,N.J.
D.OCT.22,1923

YR	CL	LEA	POS	GP	G	REC
1900	PHI	N	P		1	0- 0
1902	PIT	N	P		3	3- 0
1903	PHI	N	P		3	0- 2
					7	3- 2

MC LAURIN, RALPH EDGAR
B.MAY 23,1885 KISSIMMEE,FLA.
D.FEB.11,1943

YR	CL	LEA	POS	GP	G	REC
1908	STL	N	O		8	.227

MC LEAN, ALBERT ELDON
B.SEPT.20,1912 CHICAGO,ILL.

YR	CL	LEA	POS	GP	G	REC
1935	WAS	A	P		4	0- 0
		BRTR				

MC LEAN, JOHN BANNERMAN "LARRY"
B.JULY 18,1881 CAMBRIDGE,MASS.
D.MAR.24,1921

YR	CL	LEA	POS	GP	G	REC
1901	BOS	A	1		9	.210
1903	CHI	N	C		1	.000
1904	STL	N	C		24	.167
1906	CIN	N	C		12	.191
1907	CIN	N	C		101	.289
1908	CIN	N	C-1		88	.217
1909	CIN	N	C		95	.256
1910	CIN	N	C		119	.298
1911	CIN	N	C		98	.287
1912	CIN	N	C		102	.243
1913	STL	N	C		48	.270
	NY	N	C		30	.320
1914	NY	N	C		79	.260
1915	NY	N	C		13	.152
		BRTR			819	.263

**MC LELAND, WAYNE GAFFNEY
"WAYNE" OR "NUBBIN"**
B.AUG.29,1924 MILTON,IOWA

YR	CL	LEA	POS	GP	G	REC
1951	DET	A	P		6	0- 1
1952	DET	A	P		4	0- 0
		BRTR			10	0- 1

MC LEOD, RALPH ALTON
B.OCT.19,1916 N.QUINCY,MASS.

YR	CL	LEA	POS	GP	G	REC
1938	BOS	N	O		6	.286
		BLTL				

MC LEOD, SOULE JAMES
B.SEPT.12,1909 WILMOT,ARK.

YR	CL	LEA	POS	GP	G	REC
1930	WAS	A	3		18	.265
1932	WAS	A	S		7	.000
1933	PHI	N	3		67	.194
		BRTR			92	.203

**MC LISH, CALVIN COOLIDGE JULIUS
CAESAR TUSKAHOMA "CAL"**
B.DEC.1,1925 ANADARKO,OKLA.

YR	CL	LEA	POS	GP	G	REC
1944	BRO	N	P	23	31	3-10
1946	BRO	N	P		1	0- 0
1947	PIT	N	P		1	0- 0
1948	PIT	N	P	2	3	0- 0
1949	CHI	N	P	8	9	1- 1
1951	CHI	N	P	30	31	4-10
1956	CLE	A	P	37	39	2- 4
1957	CLE	A	P	42	44	9- 7
1958	CLE	A	P		39	16- 8
1959	CLE	A	P		35	19- 8
1960	CIN	N	P		37	4-14
1961	CHI	A	P		31	10-13
1962	PHI	N	P		32	11- 5
1963	PHI	N	P	32	33	13-11
1964	PHI	N	P		2	0- 1
		BBTR		352	368	92-92

MC MACKIN, JOHN WEAVER
B.MAR.6,1878 SPARTANBURG,S.C.
D.SEPT.25,1956

YR	CL	LEA	POS	GP	G	REC
1902	BRO	N	P		4	2- 2
		TR				

MC MACKIN, SAMUEL
B.CLEVELAND,OHIO
D.FEB.11,1903

YR	CL	LEA	POS	GP	G	REC
1902	CHI	A	P		1	0- 0
	DET	A	P		1	0- 0
					2	0- 0

MC MAHAN, JACK WALLY
B.JULY 25,1932 HOT SPRINGS,ARK.

YR	CL	LEA	POS	GP	G	REC
1956	PIT	N	P		11	0- 0
	KC	A	P		23	0- 5
		BRTL			34	0- 5

MC MAHON, DONALD JOHN "DON"
B.JAN.4,1930 BROOKLYN,N.Y.

YR	CL	LEA	POS	GP	G	REC
1957	MIL	N	P		32	2- 3
1958	MIL	N	P		38	7- 2
1959	MIL	N	P		60	5- 3
1960	MIL	N	P		48	3- 6
1961	MIL	N	P		53	6- 4
1962	MIL	N	P		2	0- 1
	HOU	N	P		51	5- 5
1963	HOU	N	P		49	1- 5
1964	CLE	A	P		70	6- 4
1965	CLE	A	P		58	3- 3
1966	CLE	A	P		12	1- 1
	BOS	A	P		49	8- 7
1967	BOS	A	P		11	1- 2
	CHI	A	P		52	5- 0
1968	CHI	A	P		25	2- 1
	DET	A	P		20	3- 1
1969	DET	A	P		34	3- 5
	SF	N	P		13	3- 1
1970	SF	N	P		61	9- 5
1971	SF	N	P		61	10- 6
1972	SF	N	P		44	3- 3
1973	SF	N	P		22	4- 0
1974	SF	N	P		9	0- 0
		BRTR			874	90-68

MC MAHON, HENRY JOHN "DOC"
B.DEC.19,1886 WOBURN,MASS.
D.DEC.12,1929 WOBURN,MASS.

YR	CL	LEA	POS	GP	G	REC
1908	BOS	A	P		1	1- 0

MC MAHON, JOHN HENRY
B.OCT.15,1869 WATERBURY,CONN.
D.DEC.30,1894

YR	CL	LEA	POS	GP	G	REC
1892	NY	N	1		36	.239
1893	NY	N	C		11	.333
		TL			47	.256

MC MAHON, JOHN JOSEPH "SADIE"
B.SEPT.19,1867 WILMINGTON,DEL.
D.FEB.20,1954 DELAWARE CITY,DEL.

YR	CL	LEA	POS	GP	G	REC
1889	ATH	AA	P	29	30	15-11
1890	ATH	AA	P	51		29-17
	BAL	AA	P		12	7- 3
1891	BAL	N	P		60	34-25
1892	BAL	N	P		47	19-28
1893	BAL	N	P		40	23-16
1894	BAL	N	P		34	25- 8
1895	BAL	N	P		15	10- 4
1896	BAL	N	P		21	12- 8
1897	BRO	N	P		9	0- 0
		TR		318	319	174-120

MC MANUS, FRANCIS E.
B.SEPT.21,1875 LAWRENCE,MASS.
D.SEPT.1,1923

YR	CL	LEA	POS	GP	G	REC
1899	WAS	N	C		7	.400
1903	BRO	N	C		2	.000
1904	DET	A	C		1	.000
	NY	A	C		4	.000
		TR			14	.235

MC MANUS, GEORGE
B.1846
D.OCT.2,1918
NON-PLAYING MANAGER STL(N) 1877

MC MANUS, JAMES MICHAEL
B.JULY 20,1936 BROOKLINE,MASS.

YR	CL	LEA	POS	GP	G	REC
1960	KC	A	1		5	.308
		BLTL				

MC MANUS, JOAB LOGAN
B.SEPT.7,1887 PALMYRA,ILL.
D.DEC.23,1955

YR	CL	LEA	POS	GP	G	REC
1913	CIN	N	P		1	0- 0
		BRTR				

YR	CL	LEA	POS	GP	G	REC

MC MANUS, MARTIN JOSEPH "MARTY"
B.MAR.14,1900 CHICAGO,ILL.
D.FEB.18,1966 ST.LOUIS,MO.

1920	STL	A	3		1	.200
1921	STL	A	1-2-3	121		.260
1922	STL	A	2	154		.312
1923	STL	A	1-2	154		.309
1924	STL	A	2	123		.333
1925	STL	A	2	154		.288
1926	STL	A	2-3	149		.284
1927	DET	A	2-S-3	108		.268
1928	DET	A	1-3	139		.288
1929	DET	A	3	154		.280
1930	DET	A	3	132		.320
1931	DET	A	2-3	107		.273
	BOS	A	2-3	17		.276
1932	BOS	A	M-2-3	93		.235
1933	BOS	A	M-1-2-3	106		.284
1934	BOS	N	2-3	119		.276
	BRTR			1831		.289

MC MANUS, P.

| 1879 | TRO | N | P | | 2 | 0- 2 |

MC MATH, JIMMY LEE
B.AUG.10,1949 BIRMINGHAM,ALA.

| 1968 | CHI | N | O | | 6 | .143 |
| | BLTL | | | | | |

MC MILLAN, GEORGE A. "REDDY"
B.EVANSVILLE,IND.

| 1890 | NY | N | O | | 10 | .138 |

MC MILLAN, NORMAN ALEXIS "BUB"
B.OCT.5,1895 LATTA,S.C.
D.SEPT.28,1969 LATTA,S.C.

1922	NY	A	O		33	.256
1923	BOS	A	2-S-3	131		.253
1924	STL	A	2-3	76		.279
1928	CHI	N	2-3	49		.220
1929	CHI	N	3	124		.271
	BRTR			413		.260

MC MILLAN, ROY DAVID
B.JULY 17,1930 BONHAM,TEX.

1951	CIN	N	2-S-3	85		.211
1952	CIN	N	S	154		.244
1953	CIN	N	S	155		.233
1954	CIN	N	S	154		.250
1955	CIN	N	S	151		.268
1956	CIN	N	S	150		.263
1957	CIN	N	S	151		.272
1958	CIN	N	S	145		.229
1959	CIN	N	S	79		.264
1960	CIN	N	2-S	124		.236
1961	MIL	N	S	154		.220
1962	MIL	N	S	137		.246
1963	MIL	N	S	100		.250
1964	MIL	N	S	8		.308
	NY	N	S	113		.211
1965	NY	N	S	157		.242
1966	NY	N	S	76		.214
	BRTR			2093		.243

NON-PLAYING MANAGER
MIL(A) 1972 (INTERIM)
NY(N) 1975

MC MILLAN, THOMAS LAW "RABBIT"
B.APR.17,1887 PITTSTON,PA.
D.JULY 15,1966 ORLANDO,FLA.

1908	BRO	N	S	43		.238
1909	BRO	N	S	108		.212
1910	BRO	N	S	23		.176
	CIN	N	S	82		.185
1912	NY	A	S	41		.228
	BRTR			297		.209

MC MULLEN, GEORGE
B.CALIFORNIA

| 1887 | MET | AA | P | | 3 | 1- 2 |

MC MULLEN, HUGH RAPHAEL
B.DEC.16,1901 LA CYGNE,KAN.

1925	NY	N	C	5		.133
1926	NY	N	C	57		.187
1928	WAS	A	H	1		.000
1929	CIN	N	C	1		.000
	BBTR			64		.176

MC MULLEN, JOHN F. "LEFTY"
B.1849 PHILADELPHIA,PA.
D.APR.11,1881

1871	TRO	NA	P		29	13-15
1872	MUT	NA	P-O	2	54	2- 0
						.231
1873	ATH	NA	P-O	1	51	1- 0
						-
1874	ATH	NA	C-O		55	.387
1875	PHI	NA	P-O	1	53	0- 1
						.249
	BLTL			33	242	16-16

MC MULLEN, KENNETH LEE "KEN"
B.JUNE 1,1942 OXNARD,CAL.

1962	LA	N	O		6	.273
1963	LA	N	2-3-O	79		.236
1964	LA	N	1-3-O	24		.209
1965	WAS	A	1-3-O	150		.263
1966	WAS	A	1-3-O	147		.233
1967	WAS	A	3	146		.245
1968	WAS	A	S-3	151		.248
1969	WAS	A	3	158		.272
1970	WAS	A	3	15		.203
	CAL	A	3	124		.232
1971	CAL	A	3	160		.250
1972	CAL	A	3	137		.269
1973	LA	N	3	42		.247
1974	LA	N	2-3	44		.250
1975	LA	N	1-3	39		.239
1976	OAK	A	1-2-3-O-	98		.220
			O			
	BRTR			1520		.249

MC MULLIN, FREDERICK WILLIAM
B.OCT.13,1891 SCAMMON,KAN.
D.NOV.21,1952

1914	DET	A	S		1	.000
1916	CHI	A	3	68		.257
1917	CHI	A	3	59		.237
1918	CHI	A	3	70		.276
1919	CHI	A	3	60		.294
1920	CHI	A	3	46		.197
	BRTR			304		.256

MC NABB, CARL MAC "SKINNY"
B.JAN.25,1918 STEVENSON,ALA.

| 1945 | DET | A | H | | 1 | .000 |
| | BRTR | | | | | |

MC NABB, EDGAR J. "TEXAS"
B.OCT.24,1865 MT.VERNON,OHIO
D.FEB.28,1894

| 1893 | BAL | N | P | | 17 | 8- 8 |

MC NAIR, DONALD ERIC "BOOB"
B.APR.12,1909 MERIDIAN,MISS.
D.MAR.11,1949

1929	PHI	A	S		4	.500
1930	PHI	A	S-3	70		.266
1931	PHI	A	2-S-3	79		.271
1932	PHI	A	S	135		.285
1933	PHI	A	2-S	89		.261
1934	PHI	A	S	151		.280
1935	PHI	A	1-S-3	137		.270
1936	BOS	A	2-S-3	128		.285
1937	BOS	A	2	126		.292
1938	BOS	A	2-S	46		.156
1939	CHI	A	2-3	129		.324
1940	CHI	A	2-3	66		.227
1941	DET	A	S-3	23		.186
1942	DET	A	S	26		.162
	PHI	A	2-S	34		.243
	BRTR			1251		.274

MC NALLY, DAVID ARTHUR "DAVE"
B.OCT.31,1942 BILLINGS,MONT.

1962	BAL	A	P		1	1- 0
1963	BAL	A	P		29	7- 8
1964	BAL	A	P		30	9-11
1965	BAL	A	P		35	11- 6
1966	BAL	A	P		34	13- 6
1967	BAL	A	P		24	7- 7
1968	BAL	A	P		35	22-10
1969	BAL	A	P		41	20- 7
1970	BAL	A	P	40	41	24- 9
1971	BAL	A	P		30	21- 5
1972	BAL	A	P		36	13-17
1973	BAL	A	P		38	17-17
1974	BAL	A	P		39	16-10
1975	MON	N	P		12	3- 6
	BRTL			424	425	184-119

MC NALLY, MICHAEL JOSEPH "MIKE"
B.SEPT.9,1892 MINOOKA,PA.
D.MAY 29,1965 BETHLEHEM,PA.

1915	BOS	A	3		23	.151
1916	BOS	A	2	87		.171
1917	BOS	A	3	42		.300
1919	BOS	A	3	33		.262
1920	BOS	A	2	93		.256
1921	NY	A	2-3	71		.260
1922	NY	A	3	52		.252
1923	NY	A	2-3	30		.211
1924	NY	A	2-3	49		.247
1925	WAS	A	2-S-3	12		.143
	BRTR			492		.238

MC NAMARA, GEORGE FRANCIS
B.JAN.11,1903 CHICAGO,ILL.

| 1922 | WAS | A | P | | 3 | .272 |
| | BLTR | | | | | |

MC NAMARA, JOHN FRANCIS
B.JUNE 4,1932 SACRAMENTO,CAL.
NON-PLAYING MANAGER
OAK(A) 1969-70, SD(N) 1974-76

MC NAMARA, JOHN RAYMOND "DINNY"
B.SEPT.16,1905 LEXINGTON,MASS.
D.DEC.20,1963 LEXINGTON,MASS.

1927	BOS	N	O		11	.000
1928	BOS	N	O		9	.250
	BLTR			20		.077

MC NAMARA, JOSEPH
(PLAYED UNDER NAME OF
JOSEPH MACK)

MC NAMARA, ROBERT MAXEY
B.SEPT.19,1916 DENVER,COLO.

| 1939 | PHI | A | 3 | | 9 | .222 |
| | BRTR | | | | | |

MC NAMARA, THOMAS HENRY
B.JUNE 19,1894 ROXBURY,MASS.
D.MAY 5,1974 DANVERS,MASS.

| 1922 | PHI | N | H | | 1 | .000 |
| | BR | | | | | |

MC NAMARA, TIMOTHY ALOYSIUS
B.NOV.20,1898 BLACKSTONE,MASS.

1922	BOS	N	P		24	3- 4
1923	BOS	N	P		32	3-13
1924	BOS	N	P		35	8-12
1925	BOS	N	P		1	0- 0
1926	NY	N	P		6	0- 0
	BRTR			98		14-29

MC NAUGHTON, GORDON JOSEPH
B.JULY 31,1910 CHICAGO,ILL.
D.AUG.6,1942

| 1932 | BOS | A | P | | 6 | 0- 1 |
| | BRTR | | | | | |

MC NEAL, JOHN HARLEY "HARRY"
B.AUG.13,1878 IBERIA,OHIO
D.JAN.11,1945

| 1901 | CLE | A | P | | 11 | 5- 6 |
| | BRTR | | | | | |

MC NEELY, GEORGE EARL "EARL"
B.MAY 12,1899 SACRAMENTO,CAL.
D.JULY 16,1971 SACRAMENTO,CAL.

1924	WAS	A	O		43	.330
1925	WAS	A	O	122		.285
1926	WAS	A	O	124		.303
1927	WAS	A	O	73		.276
1928	STL	A	O	127		.236
1929	STL	A	O	69		.243
1930	STL	A	1-O	76		.272
1931	STL	A	O	49		.225
	BRTR			683		.272

MC NEIL, NORMAN FRANCIS
B.OCT.22,1892 CHICAGO,ILL.
D.APR.11,1942

| 1919 | BOS | A | C | | 5 | .273 |
| | BRTR | | | | | |

YR	CL LEA POS	GP	G	REC

MC NERTNEY, GERALD EDWARD "JERRY"
B.AUG.7,1936 BOONE,IOWA

1964	CHI A	C		73	.215
1966	CHI A	C		44	.220
1967	CHI A	C		56	.228
1968	CHI A	C-1		74	.219
1969	SEA A	C		128	.241
1970	MIL A	C-1		111	.243
1971	STL N	C		56	.289
1972	STL N	C		39	.208
1973	PIT N	C		9	.250
	BRTR			590	.237

MC NICHOL, EDWARD
B.WHEELING,W.VA.

1904	BOS N	P		17	2-13

MC NULTY, PATRICK HOWARD
B.MAR.1,1900 CLEVELAND,OHIO
D.MAY 4,1963 HOLLYWOOD,CAL.

1922	CLE A	O		22	.271
1924	CLE A	O		101	.268
1925	CLE A	O		118	.314
1926	CLE A	O		48	.250
1927	CLE A	O		19	.317
	BLTR			308	.290

MC NULTY, WILLIAM FRANCIS "BILL"
B.AUG.29,1946 SACRAMENTO,CAL.

1969	OAK A	O		5	.000
1972	OAK A	3		4	.100
	BRTR			9	.037

MC PARTLIN, FRANK
B.FEB.16,1872 HOOSICK FALLS,N.Y
D.1940

1899	NY N	P		1	0- 0
	TR				

MC PHEE, JOHN ALEXANDER "BID"
B.NOV.1,1859 MASSENA,N.Y.
D.JAN.3,1942 SAN DIEGO,CAL.

1882	CIN AA	2		78	.218
1883	CIN AA	C-2		94	.235
1884	CIN AA	2		113	.292
1885	CIN AA	2		110	.275
1886	CIN AA	2		140	.272
1887	CIN AA	2		129	.354
1888	CIN AA	2		110	.230
1889	CIN AA	2-3		135	.269
1890	CIN N	2		132	.255
1891	CIN N	2		138	.257
1892	CIN N	2		144	.294
1893	CIN N	2		127	.307
1894	CIN N	2		128	.320
1895	CIN N	2		114	.295
1896	CIN N	2		116	.299
1897	CIN N	2		80	.307
1898	CIN N	2		131	.246
1899	CIN N	2		106	.283
	BRTR			2125	.281

NON-PLAYING MANAGER
CIN(N) 1901-02

MC PHERSON, JOHN JACOB
B.MAR.9,1869 EASTON,PA.
D.SEPT.30,1941

1901	PHI A	P		1	0- 1
1904	PHI N	P		15	1- 9
				16	1-10

MC QUAID, HERBERT GEORGE
B.MAR.29,1899 SAN FRANCISCO,CAL
D.APR.4,1966

1923	CIN N	P		12	1- 0
1926	NY A	P		17	1- 0
	BRTR			29	2- 0

MC QUAID, JAMES H.
B.CHICAGO,ILL.

1891	STL AA	2		4	.333
1898	WAS N	O		1	.000
				5	.333

MC QUAIG, GERALD JOSEPH
B.JAN.31,1914 DOUGLAS,GA.

1934	PHI A	O		7	.063
	BRTR				

MC QUEEN, MICHAEL ROBERT "MIKE"
B.AUG.30,1950 OKLAHOMA CITY,OKLA

1969	ATL N	P		1	0- 0
1970	ATL N	P		22	1- 5
1971	ATL N	P		17	4- 1
1972	ATL N	P		23	0- 5
1974	CIN N	P		10	0- 0
	BLTL			73	5-11

MC QUERY, WILLIAM THOMAS "MAX"
B.JUNE 28,1861 GARRARD CO.,KY.
D.JUNE 12,1900

1884	CIN U	1		32	.248
1885	DET N	1		70	.273
1886	KC N	1		122	.247
1890	SYR AA	1		120	.295
1891	WAS AA	1		68	.256
				412	.266

MC QUILLAN, GEORGE WATT
B.MAY 1,1885 BROOKLYN,N.Y.
D.MAR.30,1940

1907	PHI N	P		6	2- 0
1908	PHI N	P		48	23-17
1909	PHI N	P		41	13-16
1910	PHI N	P		24	9- 6
1911	CIN N	P		19	2- 6
1913	PIT N	P		25	8- 6
1914	PIT N	P		45	13-17
1915	PIT N	P		31	8-10
	PHI N	P		9	4- 3
1916	PHI N	P		21	1- 7
1918	CLE A	P		5	0- 1
	BRTR			274	83-89

MC QUILLAN, HUGH A. "HANDSOME HUGH"
B.SEPT.15,1897 NEW YORK,N.Y.
D.AUG.26,1947

1918	BOS N	P		1	1- 0
1919	BOS N	P-O	16	20	2- 3
					.222
1920	BOS N	P		38	11-15
1921	BOS N	P		45	13-17
1922	BOS N	P	28	32	5-10
	NY N	P		15	6- 5
1923	NY N	P	38	41	15-14
1924	NY N	P	27	35	14- 8
1925	NY N	P	14	16	2- 3
1926	NY N	P	33	34	11-10
1927	NY N	P		11	5- 4
	BOS N	P		13	3- 5
	BRTR		279	301	88-94
					.195

MC QUILLEN, GLENN RICHARD "RED"
B.APR.19,1917 STRASBURG,VA.

1938	STL A	O		43	.284
1941	STL A	O		7	.333
1942	STL A	O		100	.283
1946	STL A	O		59	.241
1947	STL A	H		1	.000
	BRTR			210	.274

MC QUINN, GEORGE HARTLEY
B.MAY 29,1909 BALLSTON,VA.

1936	CIN N	1		38	.201
1938	STL A	1		148	.324
1939	STL A	1		154	.316
1940	STL A	1		151	.279
1941	STL A	1		130	.297
1942	STL A	1		145	.262
1943	STL A	1		125	.243
1944	STL A	1		146	.250
1945	STL A	1		139	.277
1946	PHI A	1		136	.225
1947	NY A	1		144	.304
1948	NY A	1		94	.248
	BLTL			1550	.276

MC RAE, HAROLD ABRAHAM "HAL"
B.JULY 10,1946 AVON PARK,FLA.

1968	CIN N	2		17	.196
1970	CIN N	2-3-O		70	.248
1971	CIN N	O		99	.264
1972	CIN N	3-O		61	.278
1973	KC A	3-O-D		106	.234
1974	KC A	3-O-D		148	.310
1975	KC A	3-O-D		126	.306
1976	KC A	O-D		149	.332
	BRTL			776	.290

MC RAE, NORMAN "NORM"
B.SEP.26,1947 ELIZABETH,N.J.

1969	DET A	P		3	0- 0
1970	DET A	P		19	0- 0
	BRTR			22	0- 0

MC REMER

1884	WAS U	P		1	0- 0

MC SHANNIC, PETER ROBERT
B.MAR.20,1864 PITTSBURGH,PA.
D.NOV.30,1946

1888	PIT N	3		26	.194
	BB				

MC SORLEY, JOHN BERNARD "TRICK"
B.DEC.6,1858 ST.LOUIS,MO.
D.FEB.9,1936

1875	RS NA	3-O		13	–
1884	TOL AA	1		21	.249
1885	STL N	3		2	.500
1886	STL AA	5		5	.150
	TR			41	–

MC SWEENEY, PAUL
B.ST.LOUIS,MO.

1891	STL AA	2		3	.250

MC TAMANY, JAMES EDWARD "MAX"
B.JULY 1,1863 PHILADELPHIA,PA.
D.APR.16,1916 LENNI,PA.

1885	BRO AA	O		35	.238
1886	BRO AA	O		113	.248
1887	BRO AA	O		134	.354
1888	KC AA	O		116	.251
1889	COL AA	O		139	.279
1890	COL AA	O		125	.256
1891	COL AA	O		77	.266
	ATH AA	O		53	.209
	BRTR			792	.275

MC TIGUE, WILLIAM PERCY "REBEL"
B.JAN.3,1891 NASHVILLE,TENN.
D.MAY 11,1920

1911	BOS N	P		14	0- 5
1912	BOS N	P		10	2- 0
1913	BOS N	P		1	0- 0
1916	DET A	P		3	0- 1
	BLTL			28	2- 6

MC VEY, CALVIN ALEXANDER "CAL"
B.AUG.30,1850 MONTROSE,IOWA
D.AUG.20,1926

1871	BOS NA	C-O		32	.366
1872	BOS NA	C-O		46	.306
1873	BAL NA	C-1-2-S-3-O		36	–
1874	BOS NA	C-O		70	.385
1875	BOS NA	P-C-1-O	2	82	1- 1
					.352
1876	CHI N	P-1	6	63	6- 0
					.345
1877	CHI N	P-C-1-2-3	17	60	4- 8
					.368
1878	CIN N	M-P-C-3	2	62	1- 0
					.293
1879	CIN N	M-P-C-1-3-O	3	80	0- 2
					.299
	BRTR		30	531	12-11

MC VEY, GEORGE W.
B.1863 COLUMBUS,OHIO
D.MAY 3,1896

1885	BRO AA	C-1		6	.143

MC WEENEY, DOUGLAS LAWRENCE "BUZZ"
B.AUG.17,1896 CHICAGO,ILL.
D.JAN.1,1953

1921	CHI A	P		27	3- 6
1922	CHI A	P		4	0- 1
1924	CHI A	P		13	1- 3
1926	BRO N	P		42	11-13
1927	BRO N	P		34	4- 8
1928	BRO N	P		42	14-14
1929	BRO N	P		36	4-10
1930	CIN N	P		8	0- 2
	BRTR			206	37-57

MC WILLIAMS, WILLIAM HENRY
B.NOV.28,1910 DUBUQUE,IOWA

1931	BOS A	H		2	.000
	BRTR				

MEAD, CHARLES RICHARD
B.APR.9,1921 VERMILION,ALT., CANADA

1943	NY N	O		37	.274
1944	NY N	O		39	.179
1945	NY N	O		11	.270
	BLTR			87	.245

YR	CL	LEA	POS	GP	G	REC

MEADOR, JOHN DAVIS
B.DEC.4,1892 MADISON,N.C.
D.APR.11,1970 WINSTON-SALEM,N.C
1920 PIT N P   12   0- 2
        BRTR

MEADOWS, HENRY LEE "SPECS"
B.JULY 12,1894 OXFORD,N.C.
D.JAN.29,1963 DAYTONA BEACH,FLA
1915 STL N P   39 13-11
1916 STL N P   51 12-23
1917 STL N P   43 15- 9
1918 STL N P   30 31   8-14
1919 STL N P   22   4-10
        PHI N P   18 21   8-10
1920 PHI N P   35 39 16-14
1921 PHI N P   28 11-16
1922 PHI N P   33 12-18
1923 PHI N P   8   1- 3
        PIT N P   31 16-10
1924 PIT N P   36 13-12
1925 PIT N P   35 19-10
1926 PIT N P   36 20- 9
1927 PIT N P   40 19-10
1928 PIT N P   4   1- 1
1929 PIT N P   1   0- 0
        BLTR   490 498 188-180
        BB 1920-21, 26, 28

MEADOWS, RUFUS RIVERS
B.AUG.25,1907 HOPEWELL,VA.
D.MAY 10,1970 WICHITA,KAN.
1926 CIN N P   1   0- 0
        BLTL

MEAKIM, GEORGE CLINTON
B.JULY 11,1865 BROOKLYN,N.Y.
D.FEB.17,1923
1890 LOU AA P   30 10- 8
1891 ATH AA P   6   2- 3
1892 CHI N P   2   0- 1
        CIN N P   3   1- 1
1895 LOU N P   1   0- 0
                        42 13-13

MEANS, HARRY L.
B.JUNE 15,1869 HOPKINSVILLE,KY.
D.FEB.1,1945
NON-PLAYING MANAGER LOU(AA)1889

MEANY, PATRICK
B.1892 PHILADELPHIA,PA.
D.OCT.20,1922
1912 DET A S   1   .000
        TR

MEARA, CHARLES EDWARD
B.APR.16,1891 NEW YORK,N.Y.
1914 NY A P   4   .286
        BLTR

MEDDLEBROOK
1884 BAL U O   1   .667

MEDEIROS, RAY ANTON
B.MAY 9,1926 OAKLAND,CAL.
1945 CIN N H   1   .000
        BRTR

MEDICH, GEORGE FRANCIS "DOC"
B.DEC.9,1948 ALIQUIPPA,PA.
1972 NY A P   1   0- 0
1973 NY A P   34 14- 9
1974 NY A P   38 39 19-15
1975 NY A P   38 16-16
1976 PIT N P   29   8-11
        BRTR   140 141 57-51

MEDLINGER, IRVING JOHN "IRV"
B.NOV.18,1927 CHICAGO,ILL.
D.SEPT.3,1975 WHEELING,ILL.
1949 STL A P   3   0- 0
1951 STL A P   6   0- 0
        BLTL   9   0- 0

MEDWICK, JOSEPH MICHAEL
"JOE" OR "DUCKY"
B.NOV.24,1911 CARTERET,N.J.
D.MAR.21,1975 ST.PETERSBURG,FLA
1932 STL N O   26   .349
1933 STL N O   148   .306
1934 STL N O   149   .319
1935 STL N O   154   .353
1936 STL N O   155   .351
1937 STL N O   156   .374
1938 STL N O   146   .322
1939 STL N O   150   .332
1940 STL N O   37   .304
1940 BRO N O   106   .300
1941 BRO N O   133   .318
1942 BRO N O   142   .300
1943 BRO N O   48   .272
        NY N 1-3   78   .281
1944 NY N O   128   .337
1945 NY N O   26   .304
        BOS N 1-O   66   .284
1946 BRO N 1-O   41   .312
1947 STL N O   75   .307
1948 STL N O   20   .211
        BRTR   1984   .324

MEE, THOMAS WILLIAM
B.MAR.18,1890 CHICAGO,ILL.
1910 STL A S   7   .167
        BRTR

MEEGAN, PETER J. "STEADY PETE"
B.NOV.13,1863 SAN FRANCISCO,CAL
D.MAR.15,1905
1884 RIC AA P-O 22 23   7-12
                             .156
1885 PIT AA P   19   7- 8
                41 42 14-20
                             .156

MEEHAN, WILLIAM THOMAS
B.SEPT.3,1891 OSCEOLA,PA.
1915 PHI A P   1   0- 1

MEEK, FRANK J. "DAD"
B.ST.LOUIS,MO.
D.DEC.26,1922
1889 STL AA C   2   .500
1890 STL AA C   4   .333

MEEKER, CHARLES ROY
B.SEPT.15,1900 LEADMINES,MO.
D.MAR.25,1929
1923 PHI A P   5   3- 0
1924 PHI A P   30   5-12
1926 CIN N P   7   0- 2
        BLTR   42   8-14

MEEKIN, JOUETT
B.FEB.21,1867 NEW ALBANY,IND.
D.DEC.14,1944
1891 LOU AA P   29 33 10-17
1892 LOU N P   25   7-10
        WAS N P   13   2-11
1893 WAS N P   28 29 10-17
1894 NY N P   47 48 36-10
1895 NY N P   30 16-11
1896 NY N P   40 26-13
1897 NY N P   35 38 20-11
1898 NY N P   36 16-20
1899 NY N P   16   5-11
        BOS N P   17   7- 6
1900 PIT N P   2   0- 2
                318 327 155-139

MEEKS, SAMUEL MACK "SAMMY"
B.APR.23,1923 ANDERSON,S.C.
1948 WAS A 2-S   24   .121
1949 CIN N 2-S   16   .306
1950 CIN N S-3   39   .284
1951 CIN N S-3   23   .229
        BRTR   102   .251

MEELER, CHARLES PHILLIP "PHIL"
B.JULY 3,1948 SOUTH BOSTON,VA.
1972 DET A P   7   0- 1
        BRTR

MEERS, RUSSELL HARLAN
B.NOV.27,1919 TILTON,ILL.
1941 CHI N P   1   0- 1
1946 CHI N P   7   1- 2
1947 CHI N P   35   2- 0
        BLTL   43   3- 3

MEIER, ARTHUR ERNST "DUTCH"
B.MAR.30,1879 ST.LOUIS,MO.
D.MAR.23,1948 CHICAGO,ILL.
1906 PIT N S-O   68   .256

MEIKLE, ARTHUR FRANCIS
(PLAYED UNDER NAME OF
ARTHUR FRANCIS NICHOLS)

MEINE, HENRY WILLIAM "HEINIE"
B.MAY 1,1896 ST.LOUIS,MO.
D.MAR.18,1968 ST.LOUIS,MO.
1922 STL A P   1   0- 0
1928 PIT N P   22   7- 6
1930 PIT N P   20   6- 8
1931 PIT N P   36 19-13
1932 PIT N P   28 12- 9
1933 PIT N P   32 15- 8
1934 PIT N P   26   7- 6
        BRTR   165 66-50

MEINERT, WALTER HENRY
B.DEC.11,1890 NEW YORK,N.Y.
D.NOV.9,1958
1913 STL A O   4   .375
        BLTL

MEINKE, FRANK LOUIS
B.OCT.18,1863 CHICAGO,ILL.
D.NOV.8,1931
1884 DET N P-2-3 33 90   8-21
                    S-3   .167
1885 DET N P-O   1   0- 1
                             .000
                    34 91   8-??
                             .166

MEINKE, ROBERT BERNARD
B.JUNE 25,1887 CHICAGO,ILL.
D.DEC.29,1952
1910 CIN N S   2   .000
        BRTR

MEISTER, JOHN F.
B.ALTOONA,PA.
D.JAN.28,1923
1884 TOL AA 3   34   .199
1886 MET AA 2   45   .240
1887 MET AA O   39   .282
                       118   .245

MEISTER, KARL DANIEL
B.MAY 15,1891 MARIETTA,OHIO
D.AUG.15,1967
1913 CIN N O   4   .285
        BRTR

MEIXELL, MERTEN MERRILL "MOXIE"
B.OCT.18,1887 LAKE CRYSTAL,MINN
1912 CLE A O   3   .500
        BLTR

MEJIAS, ROMAN GOMEZ
B.AUG.9,1930 RIO DAMUJI,CUBA
1955 PIT N O   71   .216
1957 PIT N O   58   .275
1958 PIT N O   76   .268
1959 PIT N O   96   .236
1960 PIT N H   3   .000
1961 PIT N O   4   .000
1962 HOU N O   146   .286
1963 BOS A O   111   .227
1964 BOS A O   62   .238
        BRTR   627   .254

MEJIAS, SAMUEL ELIAS "SAM"
B.MAY 9,1952 SANTIAGO,D.R.
1976 STL N O   18   .143
        BRTR

MELE, ALBERT ERNEST "DUTCH"
B.JAN.11,1915 NEW YORK,N.Y.
D.FEB.12,1975 HOLLYWOOD,FLA.
1937 CIN N O   6   .143
        BLTL

YR	CL	LEA	POS	GP	G	REC

MELE, SABATH ANTHONY "SAM"
B.JAN.21,1923 ASTORIA,L.I.,N.Y.

YR	CL	LEA	POS	GP	G	REC
1947	BOS	A	1-O		123	.302
1948	BOS	A	O		66	.233
1949	BOS	A	O		18	.196
	WAS	A	1-O		78	.242
1950	WAS	A	1-O		126	.274
1951	WAS	A	1-O		143	.274
1952	WAS	A	O		9	.429
	CHI	A	1-O		123	.248
1953	CHI	A	1-O		140	.274
1954	BAL	A	O		72	.239
1954	BOS	A	1-O		42	.318
1955	BOS	A	O		14	.129
	CIN	N	1-O		35	.210
1956	CLE	A	1-O		57	.254
			BRTR		1046	.260

NON-PLAYING MANAGER
MIN(A) 1961-67

MELENDEZ, LUIS ANTONIO
B.AUG.11,1949 AIBONITO,P.R.

YR	CL	LEA	POS	GP	G	REC
1970	STL	N	O		21	.300
1971	STL	N	O		88	.225
1972	STL	N	O		118	.238
1973	STL	N	O		121	.267
1974	STL	N	S-O		83	.218
1975	STL	N	O		110	.265
1976	STL	N	O		20	.125
	SD	N	O		72	.244
			BRTR		633	.248

MELILLO, OSCAR DONALD "SKI"
B.AUG.4,1902 PULLMAN,ILL.
D.NOV.14,1963 CHICAGO,ILL.

YR	CL	LEA	POS	GP	G	REC
1926	STL	A	2-3		99	.255
1927	STL	A	2		107	.225
1928	STL	A	2-3		51	.189
1929	STL	A	2		141	.296
1930	STL	A	2		149	.256
1931	STL	A	2		151	.306
1932	STL	A	2		154	.242
1933	STL	A	2		132	.292
1934	STL	A	2		144	.241
1935	STL	A	2		19	.206
	BOS	A	2		106	.261
1936	BOS	A	2		98	.226
1937	BOS	A	2		26	.250
			BRTR		1377	.260

NON-PLAYING MANAGER STL(A) 1938

MELLANA, JOSEPH PETER
B.MAR.11,1905 OAKLAND,CAL.

YR	CL	LEA	POS	GP	G	REC
1927	PHI	A	3		4	.286
			BRTR			

MELLOR, WILLIAM HARPIN
B.JUNE 6,1874 CAMDEN,N.J.
D.NOV.5,1940

YR	CL	LEA	POS	GP	G	REC
1902	BAL	A	1		10	.361
			BRTR			

MELOAN, PAUL B.
B.AUG.23,1888 CLARKSVILLE,MO.
D.FEB.11,1950

YR	CL	LEA	POS	GP	G	REC
1910	CHI	A	O		65	.243
1911	CHI	A	O		1	.333
	STL	A	O		64	.262
			BRTL		130	.253

MELTER, STEPHEN B.

YR	CL	LEA	POS	GP	G	REC
1909	STL	N	P		23	0- 1
			TR			

**MELTON, CLIFFORD GEORGE
"CLIFF" OR "MICKEY MOUSE"**
B.JAN.3,1913 BREVARD,N.C.

YR	CL	LEA	POS	GP	G	REC
1937	NY	N	P	46	20- 9
1938	NY	N	P	36	14-14
1939	NY	N	P	41	12-15
1940	NY	N	P	37	10-11
1941	NY	N	P	42	8-11
1942	NY	N	P	23	11- 5
1943	NY	N	P	34	9-13
1944	NY	N	P	13	2- 2
			BLTL	272	86-80

MELTON, DAVID OLIN "DAVE"
B.OCT.3,1928 PAMPA,TEX.

YR	CL	LEA	POS	GP	G	REC
1956	KC	A	O		3	.333
1958	KC	A	O		9	.000
			BRTR		12	.111

MELTON, REUBEN FRANKLIN "RUBE"
B.FEB.27,1917 CRAMERTON,N.C.
D.SEPT.11,1971 GREER,S.C.

YR	CL	LEA	POS	GP	G	REC
1941	PHI	N	P		25	1- 5
1942	PHI	N	P		42	9-20
1943	BRO	N	P		30	5- 8
1944	BRO	N	P		37	9-13
1946	BRO	N	P		24	6- 3
1947	BRO	N	P		4	0- 1
			BRTR		162	30-50

MELTON, WILLIAM EDWIN "BILL"
B.JULY 7,1945 GULFPORT,MISS.

YR	CL	LEA	POS	GP	G	REC
1968	CHI	A	3		34	.266
1969	CHI	A	3-O		157	.255
1970	CHI	A	3-O		141	.263
1971	CHI	A	3		150	.269
1972	CHI	A	3		57	.245
1973	CHI	A	3		152	.276
1974	CHI	A	3-O		136	.242
1975	CHI	A	3-O		149	.240
1976	CAL	A	1-3-O		118	.208
			BRTR		1094	.253

**MENDOZA, CRISTOBAL RIGOBERTO
"MINNIE"**
B.NOV.16,1933 CEIBA DEL AGUA,
CUBA

YR	CL	LEA	POS	GP	G	REC
1970	MIN	A	2-3		16	.188
			BRTR			

MENDOZA, MARIO (AIZPURU)
B.DEC.26,1950 CHIHUAHUA,MEX.

YR	CL	LEA	POS	GP	G	REC
1974	PIT	N	S		91	.221
1975	PIT	N	S-3		56	.180
1976	PIT	N	2-S-3		50	.185
			BRTR		197	.203

MENEFEE, JOHN "JOCK"
B.JAN.15,1868 WEST VIRGINIA
D.MAR.11,1953 BELLE VERNON,PA.

YR	CL	LEA	POS	GP	G	REC
1892	PIT	N	P		2	0- 0
1893	LOU	N	P	17	21	8- 8
1894	LOU	N	P		34	8-15
	PIT	N	P		13	3- 8
1895	PIT	N	P		2	0- 1
1898	NY	N	P		1	0- 1
1900	CHI	N	P		17	9- 5
1901	CHI	N	P-O	20	46	8-12
						.251
1902	CHI	N	P-1-	22	64	12- 9
			2-3-O			.231
1903	CHI	N	P		22	8-10
			BRTR	148	222	56-69
						.223

MENKE, DENIS JOHN
B.JULY 21,1940 BANCROFT,IOWA

YR	CL	LEA	POS	GP	G	REC
1962	MIL	N	1-2-S-3-O	50	.192
1963	MIL	N	1-2-S-3-O	146	.234
1964	MIL	N	2-S-3	151	.283
1965	MIL	N	1-S-3	71	.243
1966	ATL	N	1-S-3	138	.251
1967	ATL	N	S-3	129	.227
1968	HOU	N	1-2-S-3	150	.249
1969	HOU	N	1-2-S-3	154	.269
1970	HOU	N	1-2-S-3-O	154	.304
1971	HOU	N	1-2-S-3	146	.246
1972	CIN	N	1-3	140	.233
1973	CIN	N	1-2-S-3	139	.191
1974	HOU	N	1-2-S-3	30	.103
			BRTR	1598	.250

**MENOSKY, MICHAEL WILLIAM
"LEAPING MIKE"**
B.OCT.16,1894 FLINT,MICH.

YR	CL	LEA	POS	GP	G	REC
1914	PIT	F	O		60	.260
1915	PIT	F	O		16	.100
1916	WAS	A	O		11	.162
1917	WAS	A	O		114	.258
1919	WAS	A	O		116	.287
1920	BOS	A	O		141	.297
1921	BOS	A	O		133	.300
1922	BOS	A	O		126	.283
1923	BOS	A	O		84	.229
			BLTR		801	.278

**MENSOR, EDWARD E.
"THE MIDGET"**
B.NOV.22,1889 WOODVILLE,ORE.

YR	CL	LEA	POS	GP	G	REC
1912	PIT	N	O		39	.263
1913	PIT	N	O		44	.179
1914	PIT	N	O		44	.202
			BB		127	.221

MENZE, THEODORE CHARLES
B.NOV.4,1897 ST.LOUIS,MO.
D.DEC.23,1969 ST.LOUIS,MO.

YR	CL	LEA	POS	GP	G	REC
1918	STL	N	O		2	.000
			BRTR			

MEOLA, EMILE MICHAEL "MIKE"
B.OCT.19,1908 NEW YORK,N.Y.
D.SEPT.1,1976 FAIR LAWN,N.J.

YR	CL	LEA	POS	GP	G	REC
1933	BOS	A	P		3	0- 0
1936	STL	A	P		9	0- 1
	BOS	A	P		6	0- 2
			BRTR		18	0- 3

MEOLI, RUDOLPH BART "RUDY"
B.MAY 1,1951 TROY,N.Y.

YR	CL	LEA	POS	GP	G	REC
1971	CAL	A	H		7	.000
1973	CAL	A	2-S-3		120	.223
1974	CAL	A	1-2-S-3		36	.244
1975	CAL	A	2-S-3		70	.214
			BLTR		233	.223

MERCANTELLI, EUGENE RUDOLPH
(PLAYED UNDER NAME OF
EUGENE RUDOLPH RYE)

MERCER, GEORGE BARCLAY "WIN"
B.JUNE 20,1874 HARRISVILLE,OHIO
D.JAN.13,1903

YR	CL	LEA	POS	GP	G	REC
1894	WAS	N	P	40	43	16-23
1895	WAS	N	P	38	54	14-24
1896	WAS	N	P		44	25-19
1897	WAS	N	P		24	24-21
1898	WAS	N	P-S-	29	73	12-16
			O			.334
1899	WAS	N	P-3	21	98	7-14
						.303
1900	NY	N	P-3	29	72	13-16
						.308
1901	WAS	A	P	24	50	9-13
1902	DET	A	P		35	15-18
			TR	305	514	135-164
						.293

MERCER, JOHN "JACK"

YR	CL	LEA	POS	GP	G	REC
1910	PIT	N	P		1	0- 0

MERCER, JOHN LOCKE
B.JAN.22,1892 TAYLORTOWN,LA.

YR	CL	LEA	POS	GP	G	REC
1912	STL	N	1		1	.000

MERCER, JOHN LOUIS
(PLAYED UNDER NAME OF
JOHN LOUIS JOHNSON)

MERCHANT, JAMES ANDERSON "ANDY"
B.AUG.30,1950 MOBILE,ALA.

YR	CL	LEA	POS	GP	G	REC
1975	BOS	A	C		1	.500
1976	BOS	A	C		2	.000
			BLTR		3	.333

MERENA, JOHN JOSEPH "SPIKE"
B.NOV.18,1911 PATERSON,N.J.

YR	CL	LEA	POS	GP	G	REC
1934	BOS	A	P		4	1- 2
			BLTL			

MEREWETHER, ARTHUR FRANCIS
B.APR.8,1902 E.PROVIDENCE,R.I.

YR	CL	LEA	POS	GP	G	REC
1922	PIT	N	2		1	.000
			BRTR			

**MERKLE, FREDERICK CHARLES
"FRED"**
B.DEC.20,1888 WATERTOWN,WIS.
D.MAR.2,1956

YR	CL	LEA	POS	GP	G	REC
1907	NY	N	1		15	.255
1908	NY	N	1		18	.268
1909	NY	N	1		71	.191
1910	NY	N	1		144	.292
1911	NY	N	1		148	.283
1912	NY	N	1		129	.309
1913	NY	N	1		153	.261
1914	NY	N	1		146	.258
1915	NY	N	1-O		140	.299
1916	NY	N	1		112	.241
	BRO	N	1		23	.208
1917	BRO	N	1		2	.125
	CHI	N	1		146	.266
1918	CHI	N	1		129	.297
1919	CHI	N	1-2		133	.267
1920	CHI	N	1		92	.285
1925	NY	A	1		7	.385
1926	NY	A	1		1	.000
			BRTR		1609	.273

YR	CL	LEA	POS	GP	G	REC

MERRILL, EDWARD S.
B.1860 CHICAGO,ILL.
1882 WOR	N		3		2	.125
1884 IND	AA		2		54	.183
					56	.181

MERRIMAN, LLOYD ARCHER
B.AUG.2,1924 CLOVIS,CAL.
1949 CIN	N		O		103	.230
1950 CIN	N		O		92	.258
1951 CIN	N		O		114	.242
1954 CIN	N		O		73	.268
1955 CHI	A		H		1	.000
CHI	N		O		72	.214
BLTL					455	.242

MERRITT, GEORGE WASHINGTON
B.APR.14,1880 PATERSON,N.J.
D.FEB.21,1938
1901 PIT	N		P		4	3- 0
1902 PIT	N		P-O	1	2	0- 0
						.333
1903 PIT	N		P		8	0- 0
TR				13	14	3- 0
						.214

MERRITT, HERMAN G.
B.NOV.12,1900 INDEPENDENCE,KAN.
D.MAY 26,1927
1921 DET	A		S		20	.370
BRTR						

MERRITT, JAMES JOSEPH "JIM"
B.DEC.9,1943 ALTADENA,CAL.
1965 MIN	A		P		16	5- 4
1966 MIN	A		P		31	7-14
1967 MIN	A		P		31	13- 7
1968 MIN	A		P		38	12-16
1969 CIN	N		P		42	17- 9
1970 CIN	N		P		35	20-12
1971 CIN	N		P	28	29	1-11
1972 CIN	N		P		4	1- 0
1973 TEX	A		P		35	5-13
1974 TEX	A		P		26	0- 0
1975 TEX	A		P		5	0- 0
BLTL				297	298	81-86

MERRITT, JOHN HOWARD
B.OCT.12,1894 TUPELO,MISS.
D.NOV.3,1955
1913 NY	N		O		1	.000

MERRITT, LLOYD WESLEY
B.APR.8,1933 ST.LOUIS,MO.
1957 STL	N		P		44	1- 2
BRTR						

MERRITT, WILLIAM HENRY
B.JULY 30,1870 LOWELL,MASS.
D.NOV.17,1937
1891 CHI	N		C		11	.218
1892 LOU	N		C		45	.195
1893 BOS	N		C		35	.363
1894 BOS	N		C-O		10	.231
PIT	N		C		26	.300
CIN	N		C-1-3-O		30	.316
1895 CIN	N		C		21	.213
PIT	N		C		66	.273
1896 PIT	N		C		70	.296
1897 PIT	N		C		56	.270
1899 BOS	N		C		1	.000
					371	.274

MERSON
1914 BRO F H   1   .000

MERSON, JOHN WARREN "JACK"
B.JAN.17,1922 ELKRIDGE,MD.
1951 PIT	N		2		13	.360
1952 PIT	N		2-3		111	.246
1953 BOS	A		2		1	.000
BRTR					125	.257

MERTES, SAMUEL BLAIR "SANDOW"
B.AUG.6,1872 SAN FRANCISCO,CAL.
D.MAR.11,1945
1896 PHI	N		O		35	.248
1898 CHI	N		O		70	.304
1899 CHI	N		O		109	.305
1900 CHI	N		1-O		125	.294
1901 CHI	A		2		137	.280
1902 CHI	A		P-C-	1	129	0- 0
			1-2-S-3			.283
1903 NY	N		O		138	.280
1904 NY	N		O		148	.276
1905 NY	N		O		150	.279
1906 NY	N		O		71	.237
STL	N		O		53	.246
BRTR				1	1165	0- 0
						.280

MERTZ, JAMES VERLIN
B.AUG.10,1918 LIMA,OHIO
1943 WAS	N		P		33	5- 7
BRTR						

MERULLO, LEONARD RICHARD "LENNIE"
B.MAY 5,1917 E.BOSTON,MASS.
1941 CHI	N		S		7	.353
1942 CHI	N		S		143	.256
1943 CHI	N		S		129	.254
1944 CHI	N		1-S		66	.212
1945 CHI	N		1-S		121	.239
1946 CHI	N		1-S		65	.151
1947 CHI	N		1-S		108	.241
BRTR					639	.240

MESNER, STEPHAN MATHIAS "STEVE"
B.JAN.13,1918 LOS ANGELES,CAL.
1938 CHI	N		S		2	.250
1939 CHI	N		S		17	.279
1941 STL	N		3		24	.145
1943 CIN	N		3		131	.272
1944 CIN	N		3		121	.242
1945 CIN	N		2-3		150	.254
BRTR					451	.252

MESSENGER, ANDREW WARREN "BUD"
B.FEB.1,1898 GRAND BLANC,MICH.
D.NOV.4,1971 LANSING,MICH.
1924 CLE	N		P		5	2- 0
BRTR						

MESSENGER, CHARLES WALTER
B.MAR.19,1884 BANGOR,ME.
D.JULY 10,1951
1909 CHI	A		O		31	.170
1910 CHI	A		O		9	.185
1911 CHI	A		O		13	.133
1914 STL	A		O		1	.000
BBTR					54	.165

MESSERSMITH, JOHN ALEXANDER "ANDY"
B.AUG.6,1945 TOMS RIVER,N.J.
1968 CAL	A		P	28	29	4- 2
1969 CAL	A		P	40	42	16-11
1970 CAL	A		P	37	38	11-10
1971 CAL	A		P	38	39	20-13
1972 CAL	A		P	25	26	8-11
1973 LA	N		P	33	34	14-10
1974 LA	N		P		39	20- 6
1975 LA	N		P	42	44	19-14
1976 ATL	N		P		29	11-11
BRTR				311	320	123-88

MESSITT, THOMAS JOHN
B.JULY 27,1874 FRANKFORT,PA.
D.SEPT.22,1934
1899 LOU	N		C		2	.125

METCALF, ROBERT
B.BROOKLYN,N.Y.
1875 MUT	NA		S-3-O		7	-

METCALF, THOMAS JOHN "TOM"
B.JULY 16,1940 AMHERST,WIS.
1963 NY	A		P		8	1- 0
BRTR						

METEVIER, GEORGE DEWEY
B.MAY 6,1898 CAMBRIDGE,MASS.
D.MAR.2,1947
1922 CLE	A		P		2	2- 0
1923 CLE	A		P		26	4- 2
1924 CLE	A		P		26	1- 5
BLTR					54	7- 7

METHA, FRANK JOSEPH "SCAT"
B.DEC.13,1913 LOS ANGELES,CAL.
1940 DET	A		2-3		26	.243
BRTR						

METHENY, ARTHUR BEAUREGARD "BUD"
B.JUNE 1,1917 ST.LOUIS,MO.
1943 NY	A		O		103	.261
1944 NY	A		O		137	.239
1945 NY	A		O		133	.248
1946 NY	A		H		3	.000
BLTL					376	.247

METKOVICH, GEORGE MICHAEL "CATFISH"
B.OCT.8,1921 ANGEL'S CAMP,CAL.
1943 BOS	A		1-O		78	.246
1944 BOS	A		1-O		134	.277
1945 BOS	A		1-O		138	.260
1946 BOS	A		O		86	.246
1947 CLE	A		1-O		126	.254
1949 CHI	A		O		93	.237
1951 PIT	N		1-O		120	.293
1952 PIT	N		1-O		125	.271
1953 PIT	N		1-O		26	.146
CHI	N		O		61	.234
1954 MIL	N		1-O		68	.276
BLTL					1055	.261

METPO, CHARLES
(REAL NAME CHARLES MORESKONICH)
B.APR.28,1919 HEILWOOD,PA.
1943 DET	A		O		44	.200
1944 DET	A		O		38	.192
PHI	A		2 3-O		24	.100
1945 PHI	A		O		65	.210
BRTR					171	.193
NON-PLAYING MANAGER
CHI(N) 1962, KC(A) 1970

METZ, LEONARD RAYMOND
B.JULY 6,1899 LAFAYETTE,COLO.
D.FEB.24,1953
1923 PHI	N		2-S		12	.216
1924 PHI	N		S		7	.286
1925 PHI	N		2-S		11	.000
BRTR					30	.169

METZGER, CLARENCE EDWARD "BUTCH"
B.MAY 23,1952 LAFAYETTE,IND.
1974 SF	N		P		10	1- 0
1975 SD	N		P		4	1- 0
1976 SD	N		P		77	11- 4
BRTR					91	13- 4

METZGER, ROGER HENRY
B.OCT.10,1947 FREDERICKSBURG,TEX
1970 CHI	N		S		1	.000
1971 HOU	N		S		150	.235
1972 HOU	N		S		153	.222
1973 HOU	N		S		154	.250
1974 HOU	N		S		143	.253
1975 HOU	N		S		127	.227
1976 HOU	N		2-S		152	.210
BBTR					880	.233
BL 1970						

METZIG, WILLIAM ANDREW
B.DEC.4,1918 FT.DODGE,IOWA
1944 CHI	A		2		5	.125
BRTR						

METZLER, ALEXANDER
B.JAN.4,1903 FRESNO,CAL.
D.NOV.30,1973 FRESNO,CAL.
1925 CHI	N		O		9	.184
1926 PHI	A		O		20	.242
1927 CHI	A		O		134	.319
1928 CHI	A		O		139	.304
1929 CHI	A		O		146	.275
1930 CHI	A		O		56	.176
STL	A		O		56	.261
BLTR					560	.285

YR	CL	LEA	POS	GP	G	REC

MEUSEL, EMIL FREDERICK "IRISH"
B.JUNE 9,1893 OAKLAND,CAL.
D.MAR.1,1963 LONG BEACH,CAL.

YR	CL	LEA	POS	GP	G	REC
1914	WAS	A	O		1	.000
1918	PHI	N	2-O		124	.279
1919	PHI	N	O		135	.305
1920	PHI	N	O		138	.309
1921	PHI	N	O		84	.353
	NY	N	O		62	.329
1922	NY	N	O		154	.330
1923	NY	N	O		146	.297
1924	NY	N	O		139	.310
1925	NY	N	O		135	.328
1926	NY	N	O		129	.292
1927	BRO	N	O		42	.243
		BRTR			1289	.310

MEUSEL, ROBERT WILLIAM "LONG BOB"
B.JULY 19,1896 SAN JOSE,CAL.

YR	CL	LEA	POS	GP	G	REC
1920	NY	A	3-O		119	.328
1921	NY	A	O		149	.318
1922	NY	A	O		121	.319
1923	NY	A	O		132	.313
1924	NY	A	O		143	.325
1925	NY	A	3-O		156	.292
1926	NY	A	O		108	.315
1927	NY	A	O		135	.337
1928	NY	A	O		131	.297
1929	NY	A	O		100	.261
1930	CIN	N	O		113	.289
		BRTR			1407	.309

MEYER, BERNHARD "EARACHE"
B.JAN.1,1888 HEMATITE,MO.
D.FEB.6,1974 FESTUS,MO.

YR	CL	LEA	POS	GP	G	REC
1913	BRO	N	O		38	.195
1914	BAL	F	O		141	.302
1915	BAL	F	O		35	.233
	BUF	F	O		93	.237
1925	PHI	N	2		1	1.000
		BRTR			308	.265

MEYER, DANIEL THOMAS "DAN"
B.AUG.3,1952 HAMILTON,OHIO

YR	CL	LEA	POS	GP	G	REC
1974	DET	A	O		13	.200
1975	DET	A	1-O		122	.236
1976	DET	A	1-O		105	.252
		BLTR			240	.240

MEYER, GEORGE FRANCIS
B.AUG.22,1912 CHICAGO,ILL.

YR	CL	LEA	POS	GP	G	REC
1938	CHI	A	2		24	.296
		BRTR				

MEYER, JOHN ROBERT "JACK"
B.MAR.23,1932 PHILADELPHIA,PA.
D.MAR.9,1967 COLLINGSWOOD,N.J.

YR	CL	LEA	POS	GP	G	REC
1955	PHI	N	P		50	6-11
1956	PHI	N	P		41	7-11
1957	PHI	N	P		19	0- 2
1958	PHI	N	P		37	3- 6
1959	PHI	N	P		47	5- 3
1960	PHI	N	P		7	3- 1
1961	PHI	N	P		1	0- 0
		BRTR			202	24-34

MEYER, LAMBERT DALTON "DUTCH"
B.OCT.6,1915 WACO,TEX.

YR	CL	LEA	POS	GP	G	REC
1937	CHI	N	H		1	.000
1940	DET	A	2		23	.259
1941	DET	A	2		46	.190
1942	DET	A	2		14	.327
1945	CLE	A	2		130	.292
1946	CLE	A	2		72	.232
		BRTR			286	.264

MEYER, LEE

YR	CL	LEA	POS	GP	G	REC
1909	BRO	N	S		7	.130
		TR				

MEYER, ROBERT BERNARD "BOB"
B.AUG.4,1939 TOLEDO,OHIO

YR	CL	LEA	POS	GP	G	REC
1964	NY	A	P		7	0- 3
	LA	A	P		6	1- 1
	KC	A	P	9	12	1- 4
1969	SEA	A	P		6	0- 3
1970	MIL	A	P		10	0- 1
		BRTL		38	41	2-12

MEYER, RUSSELL CHARLES "RUSS" OR "ROWDY"
B.OCT.25,1923 PERU,ILL.

YR	CL	LEA	POS	GP	G	REC
1946	CHI	N	P		4	0- 0
1947	CHI	N	P		23	3- 2
1948	CHI	N	P		29	10-10
1949	PHI	N	P		37	17- 8
1950	PHI	N	P		32	9-11
1951	PHI	N	P		28	8- 9
1952	PHI	N	P		37	13-14
1953	BRO	N	P		34	15- 5
1954	BRO	N	P		36	11- 6
1955	BRO	N	P		18	6- 2
1956	CHI	N	P		20	1- 6
	CIN	N	P		1	0- 0
1957	BOS	A	P		2	0- 0
1959	KC	A	P		18	1- 0
		BBTR			319	94-73

MEYER, WILLIAM ADAM "BILLY"
B.JAN.14,1892 KNOXVILLE,TENN.
D.MAR.31,1957

YR	CL	LEA	POS	GP	G	REC
1913	CHI	A	C		1	1.000
1916	PHI	A	C		50	.232
1917	PHI	A	C		62	.236
		BRTR			113	.236

NON-PLAYING MANAGER
PIT(N) 1948-52

MEYERLE, LEVI SAMUEL "LONG LEVI"
B.1849 PHILADELPHIA,PA.
D.NOV.4,1921

YR	CL	LEA	POS	GP	G	REC
1871	ATH	NA	3		26	.448
1872	ATH	NA	S-3-O		27	.318
1873	PHI	NA	3		47	-
1874	CHI	NA	2-S-3-O		52	-
1875	PHI	NA	1-2-3		67	.314
1876	ATH	N	P-3	2	55	0- 2
						.336
1877	CIN	N	2-S-O		27	.327
1884	KEY	U	1-O		3	.091
		BRTR		2	304	0- 2
						-

MEYERS, JOHN TORTES "CHIEF"
B.JULY 29,1880 RIVERSIDE,CAL.
D.JULY 25,1971 SAN BERNARDINO, CAL.

YR	CL	LEA	POS	GP	G	REC
1909	NY	N	C		64	.277
1910	NY	N	C		117	.285
1911	NY	N	C		128	.332
1912	NY	N	C		126	.358
1913	NY	N	C		120	.312
1914	NY	N	C		134	.286
1915	NY	N	C		110	.232
1916	BRO	N	C		80	.247
1917	BRO	N	C		47	.214
	BOS	N	C		25	.246
		BRTR			951	.291

MEYERS, LEWIS HENRY "CRAZY HORSE"
B.DEC.9,1859 CINCINNATI,OHIO
D.NOV.30,1920

YR	CL	LEA	POS	GP	G	REC
1884	CIN	U	C-O		1	.000
		BRTR				

MICELOTTA, ROBERT PETER "MICKEY"
B.OCT.20,1928 CORONA,L.I.,N.Y.

YR	CL	LEA	POS	GP	G	REC
1954	PHI	N	S		13	.000
1955	PHI	N	S		4	.000
		BRTR			17	.000

MICHAEL, EUGENE RICHARD "GENE"
B.JUNE 2,1938 KENT,OHIO

YR	CL	LEA	POS	GP	G	REC
1966	PIT	N	2-S-3		30	.152
1967	LA	N	S		98	.202
1968	NY	A	P-S	1	61	0- 0
						.198
1969	NY	A	S		119	.272
1970	NY	A	2-S-3		134	.214
1971	NY	A	S		139	.224
1972	NY	A	S		126	.233
1973	NY	A	S		129	.225
1974	NY	A	2-S-3		81	.260
1975	DET	A	2-S-3		56	.214
		BBTR		1	973	0- 0
						.229

MICHAELS, CASIMIR EUGENE "CASS"
(PLAYED UNDER REAL NAME OF CASIMIR EUGENE KWIETNIEWSKI IN 1943)
B.MAR.4,1926 DETROIT,MICH.

YR	CL	LEA	POS	GP	G	REC
1943	CHI	A	3		2	.000
1944	CHI	A	S-3		27	.176
1945	CHI	A	2-S		129	.245
1946	CHI	A	2-S-3		91	.258
1947	CHI	A	2-3		110	.273
1948	CHI	A	2-S-O		145	.248
1949	CHI	A	2		154	.308
1950	CHI	A	2		36	.312
	WAS	A	2		106	.250
1951	WAS	A	2		138	.258
1952	WAS	A	2		22	.233
	STL	A	2-3		55	.265
	PHI	A	2		55	.250
1953	PHI	A	2-3		117	.251
1954	CHI	A	2-3		101	.262
		BRTR			1288	.262

MICHAELS, JOHN JOSEPH
B.JULY 10,1907 BRIDGEPORT,CONN9

YR	CL	LEA	POS	GP	G	REC
1932	BOS	A	P		29	1- 6
		BLTL				

MICHAELS, RALPH JOSEPH
B.MAY 3,1902 ETNA,PA.

YR	CL	LEA	POS	GP	G	REC
1924	CHI	N	S		8	.364
1925	CHI	N	1-2-S-3		22	.280
1926	CHI	N	H		2	.000
		BRTR			32	.295

MICHAELSON, JOHN AUGUST
B.AUG.12,1893 TIVALKOSKI, FINLAND
D.APR.16,1968 WOODRUFF,WIS.

YR	CL	LEA	POS	GP	G	REC
1921	CHI	A	P		2	0- 0
		BRTR				

MICKELSON, EDWARD ALLEN "ED"
B.SEPT.9,1926 OTTAWA,ILL.

YR	CL	LEA	POS	GP	G	REC
1950	STL	N	1		5	.100
1953	STL	A	1		7	.133
1957	CHI	N	1		6	.000
		BRTR			18	.081

MICKENS, GLENN ROGER
B.JULY 26,1930 WILMAR,CAL.

YR	CL	LEA	POS	GP	G	REC
1953	BRO	N	P		4	0- 1
		BRTR				

MIDDLETON, JAMES BLAINE
B.MAY 28,1889 ARGOS,IND.
D.JAN.12,1974 ARGOS,IND.

YR	CL	LEA	POS	GP	G	REC
1917	NY	N	P		13	1- 1
1921	DET	A	P		38	6-11
		BRTR			51	7-12

MIDDLETON, JOHN WAYNE
B.APR.11,1900 MT.CAL4,TEX.

YR	CL	LEA	POS	GP	G	REC
1922	CLE	A	P		2	0- 1
		BLTL				

MIDKIFF, EZRA MILLINGTON
B.NOV.13,1883 SALT ROCK,W.VA.
D.MAR.2,1957

YR	CL	LEA	POS	GP	G	REC
1909	CIN	N	3		1	.000
1912	NY	A	3		21	.244
1913	NY	A	3		68	.215
		BLTR			90	.222

MIDKIFF, RICHARD
B.SEPT.28,1914 GONXALES,TEX.
D.OCT.30,1956

YR	CL	LEA	POS	GP	G	REC
1938	BOS	A	P		13	1- 1
		BRTR				

MIERKOWICZ, EDWARD FRANK "ED" OR "MOUSE"
B.MAR.6,1924 WYANDOTTE,MICH.

YR	CL	LEA	POS	GP	G	REC
1945	DET	A	O		10	.133
1947	DET	A	O		21	.190
1948	DET	A	O		3	.200
1950	STL	N	H		1	.000
		BRTR			35	.175

MIGGINS, LAWRENCE EDWARD "LARRY" OR "IRISH"
B.AUG.20,1925 NEW YORK,N.Y.

YR	CL	LEA	POS	GP	G	REC
1948	STL	N	H		1	.000
1952	STL	N	1-O		42	.229
		BRTR			43	.227

YR	CL	LEA	POS	GP	G	REC

MIHALIC, JOHN
B.NOV.13,1911 CLEVELAND,OHIO

YR	CL	LEA	POS	GP	G	REC
1935	WAS	A	S		6	.227
1936	WAS	A	2		25	.239
1937	WAS	A	2		38	.252
	BRTR				69	.244

MIKKELSEN, PETER JAMES "PETE"
B.OCT.25,1939 STATEN ISLAND,N.Y.

1964	NY	A	P	50	7- 4	
1965	NY	A	P	41	4- 9	
1966	PIT	N	P	71	9- 8	
1967	PIT	N	P	32	1- 2	
	CHI	N	P	7	0- 0	
1968	CHI	N	P	3	0- 0	
	STL	N	P	5	0- 0	
1969	LA	N	P	48	7- 5	
1970	LA	N	P	33	4- 2	
1971	LA	N	P	41	8- 5	
1972	LA	N	P	33	5- 5	
	BRTR			364	45-40	

MIKLOS, JOHN JOSEPH
B.NOV.27,1914 CHICAGO,ILL.

| 1944 | CHI | N | P | | 2 | 0- 0 |
| | BLTL | | | | | |

MIKSIS, EDWARD THOMAS "EDDIE"
B.SEPT.11,1926 BURLINGTON,N.J.

1944	BRO	N	S-3		26	.220
1946	BRO	N	2-3		23	.146
1947	BRO	N	2-S-3-O		45	.267
1948	BRO	N	2-S-3		86	.213
1949	BRO	N	1-2-S-3		50	.221
1950	BRO	N	2-S-3		51	.250
1951	BRO	N	2-3		19	.200
	CHI	N	2		102	.266
1952	CHI	N	2-S		93	.232
1953	CHI	N	2-S		142	.251
1954	CHI	N	2-3-O		38	.202
1955	CHI	N	3-O		131	.235
1956	CHI	N	2-6-O		114	.239
1957	STL	N	O		49	.211
	BAL	A	H		1	.000
1958	BAL	A	S		3	.000
	CIN	N	1-2-S-3-		69	.140
			O			
	BRTR				1042	.236

MILAN, HORACE ROBERT
B.APR.7,1894 LINDEN,TENN.
D.JUNE 29,1955 TEXARKANA,ARK.

1915	WAS	A	O		10	.375
1917	WAS	A	O		31	.288
	BRTR				41	.320

MILAN, JESSE CLYDE "DEERFOOT"
B.MAR.25,1887 LINDEN,TENN.
D.MAR.3,1953 ORLANDO,FLA.

1907	WAS	A	O		48	.279
1908	WAS	A	O		130	.239
1909	WAS	A	O		130	.200
1910	WAS	A	O		142	.279
1911	WAS	A	O		154	.315
1912	WAS	A	O		154	.306
1913	WAS	A	O		154	.299
1914	WAS	A	O		115	.295
1915	WAS	A	O		153	.288
1916	WAS	A	O		150	.273
1917	WAS	A	O		155	.294
1918	WAS	A	O		128	.290
1919	WAS	A	O		88	.287
1920	WAS	A	O		126	.322
1921	WAS	A	O		112	.288
1922	WAS	A	M-O		42	.230
	BLTR				1981	.285

MILBOURNE, LAWRENCE WILLIAM "LARRY"
B.FEB.14,1951 PORT NORRIS,N.J.

1974	HOU	N	2-S-O	112	.279	
1975	HOU	N	2-S	73	.212	
1976	HOU	N	2	59	.248	
	BBTR			244	.245	

MILES, CARL THOMAS
B.MAR.22,1920 TRENTON,MO.

| 1940 | PHI | A | P | | 2 | 0- 0 |
| | BBTL | | | | | |

MILES, DONALD RAY
B.MAR.13,1936 INDIANAPOLIS,IND9

| 1958 | LA | N | | | 8 | .182 |
| | BLTR | | | | | |

MILES, JAMES CHARLIE "JIM"
B.AUG.8,1943 GRENADA,MISS.

1968	WAS	A	P	3	0- 0	
1969	WAS	A	P	10	12	0- 1
	BRTR			13	15	0- 1

MILES, WILSON DANIEL "DEE"
B.FEB.15,1909 KELLERMAN,ALA.

1935	WAS	A	O		60	.264
1936	WAS	A	O		25	.237
1939	PHI	A	O		106	.300
1940	PHI	A	O		88	.301
1941	PHI	A	O		80	.312
1942	PHI	A	O		99	.272
1943	BOS	A	O		45	.215
	BLTR				503	.280

MILEY, MICHAEL WILFRED "MIKE"
B.MAR.30,1953 YAZOO CITY,MISS.

1975	CAL	A	S		70	.174
1976	CAL	A	S		14	.184
	BBTR				84	.176

MILJUS, JOHN KENNETH "JOVO"
B.JUNE 30,1895 PITTSBURGH,PA.
D.FEB.11,1976 POULSON,MONTANA

1915	PIT	F	P		1	0- 0
1917	BRO	N	P		4	0- 1
1920	BRO	N	P	9	10	1- 0
1921	BRO	N	P		28	6- 3
1927	PIT	N	P		19	8- 3
1928	PIT	N	P		21	5- 7
	CLE	A	P		11	1- 4
1929	CLE	A	P		34	8- 8
	BRTR			127	128	29-26

MILLAN, FELIX BERNARDO (MARTINEZ)
B.AUG.21,1943 YABUCOA,P.R.

1966	ATL	N	2-S-3		37	.275
1967	ATL	N	2		41	.235
1968	ATL	N	2		149	.289
1969	ATL	N	2		162	.267
1970	ATL	N	2		142	.310
1971	ATL	N	2		143	.289
1972	ATL	N	2		125	.257
1973	NY	N	2		153	.290
1974	NY	N	2		136	.268
1975	NY	N	2		162	.283
1976	NY	N	2		139	.282
	BRTR				1389	.281

MILLARD, FRANK E.
B.JULY 4,1865 E.ST.LOUIS,ILL.
D.JULY 4,1892

| 1890 | STL | AA | 2 | | 1 | .000 |

MILLER, BERT

| 1897 | PHI | N | 2 | | 3 | .200 |

MILLER, BURT
B.KALAMAZOO,MICH.

| 1897 | LOU | N | P | | 4 | 0- 0 |

MILLER, CHARLES BRADLEY "DUSTY"
B.SEPT.10,1868 OIL CITY,PA.
D.JAN.14,1943 ST.MARTINSVILLE, LA.

1889	BAL	AA	O		11	.125
1890	STL	AA	O		27	.203
1895	CIN	N	O		132	.329
1896	CIN	N	O		125	.318
1897	CIN	N	O		119	.317
1898	CIN	N	O		152	.299
1899	CIN	N	O		80	.260
	STL	N	O		10	.231
	BLTR				656	.299

MILLER, CHARLES BRUCE "BRUCE"
B.MAR.4,1947 FORT WAYNE,IND.

1973	SF	N	2-S-3	12	.143	
1974	SF	N	2-S-3	73	.278	
1975	SF	N	2-S-3	99	.239	
1976	SF	N	2-3	12	.160	
	BRTR			196	.246	

MILLER, CHARLES ELMER
B.JAN.4,1892 WARRENSBURG,MO.
D.APR.12,1972 WARRENSBURG,MO.

| 1912 | STL | A | S | | 1 | .000 |
| | TR | | | | | |

MILLER, CHARLES HESS
B.DEC.30,1877 CONTESTOGA CENTE PA.
D.JAN.13,1951

| 1915 | BAL | F | H | | 1 | .000 |

MILLER, CHARLES MARION "CHUCK"
B.SEPT.18,1889 WOODVILLE,OHIO
D.JUNE 16,1961 HOUSTON,TEX.

1913	STL	N	O		4	.091
1914	STL	N	O		36	.194
	BLTL				40	.170

MILLER, DAKIN E.
B.SEPT.2,1877 MALVERN,IOWA
D.JAN.14,1943

| 1902 | CHI | N | O | | 50 | .225 |

MILLER, DYAR K
B.MAY 29,1946 BATESVILLE,IND.

1975	BAL	A	P		30	6- 3
1976	BAL	A	P		49	2- 4
	BRTR				79	8- 7

MILLER, EDMUND JOHN "BING"
B.AUG.30,1894 VINTON,IOWA
D.MAY 7,1966 PHILADELPHIA,PA.

1921	WAS	A	O		114	.288
1922	PHI	A	O		143	.336
1923	PHI	A	O		123	.299
1924	PHI	A	O		113	.342
1925	PHI	A	1-O		124	.318
1926	PHI	A	O		38	.291
	STL	A	O		94	.331
1927	STL	A	O		144	.325
1928	PHI	A	O		139	.329
1929	PHI	A	O		147	.335
1930	PHI	A	O		154	.303
1931	PHI	A	O		137	.281
1932	PHI	A	O		95	.295
1933	PHI	A	1-O		67	.275
1934	PHI	A	O		81	.243
1935	BOS	A	O		78	.304
1936	BOS	A	O		30	.298
	BRTR				1821	.317

MILLER, EDWARD ROBERT "EPPIE"
B.NOV.26,1916 PITTSBURGH,PA.

1936	CIN	N	S		5	.100
1937	CIN	N	S-3		36	.150
1939	BOS	N	S		77	.267
1940	BOS	N	S		151	.276
1941	BOS	N	S		154	.239
1942	BOS	N	S		142	.244
1943	CIN	N	S		154	.224
1944	CIN	N	S		155	.209
1945	CIN	N	S		115	.238
1946	CIN	N	S		91	.194
1947	CIN	N	S		151	.268
1948	PHI	N	S		130	.246
1950	STL	N	2-S		85	.207
					64	.227
	BRTR				1510	.238

MILLER, EDWIN "BIG ED"
B.NOV.24,1888 ANNVILLE,PA.

1912	STL	A	1-S		12	.155
1914	STL	A	1		34	.138
1918	CLE	A	1		32	.229
	BRTR				78	.195

MILLER, ELMER
B.JULY 28,1890 SANDUSKY,OHIO
D.NOV.28,1944

1912	STL	N	O		12	.189
1915	NY	A	O		26	.145
1916	NY	A	O		43	.224
1917	NY	A	O		114	.251
1918	NY	A	O		67	.243
1921	NY	A	O		56	.298
1922	NY	A	O		51	.286
	BOS	A	O		44	.172
	BRTR				413	.243

MILLER, ELMER LE ROY
B.APR.17,1904 DETROIT,MICH.

| 1929 | PHI | N | P | | 31 | 0- 1 |
| | BLTL | | | | | |

YR	CL	LEA	POS	GP	G	REC

MILLER, FRANK LEE "BULLET"
B.MAY 13,1886 ALLEGAN,MICH.
D.FEB.19,1974 ALLEGAN,MICH.

YR	CL	LEA	POS	GP	G	REC
1913	CHI	A	P		1	0- 1
1916	PIT	N	P		30	7-10
1917	PIT	N	P	38	39	10-19
1918	PIT	N	P		23	11- 8
1919	PIT	N	P		32	13-12
1922	BOS	N	P		31	11-13
1923	BOS	N	P		8	0- 3
	BRTR			163	164	52-66

MILLER, FREDERICK
B.PHILADELPHIA,PA.

1892	WAS	N	S		1	.000

MILLER, FREDERICK HOLMAN "SPEEDY"
B.JUNE 28,1886 FAIRFIELD,IND.
D.MAY 2,1953

1910	BRO	N	P		3	1- 1

MILLER, GEORGE
B.FEB.19,1853 NEWPORT,KY.
D.JULY 24,1929 NORWOOD,OHIO

YR	CL	LEA	POS	GP	G	REC
1877	CIN	N	C		11	.162
1884	CIN	AA	C		6	.250
	BRTR				17	.190

MILLER, GEORGE FREDERICK "FOGHORN"
B.AUG.15,1864 BROOKLYN,N.Y.
D.APR.6,1909

YR	CL	LEA	POS	GP	G	REC
1884	PIT	AA	C-O		88	.222
1885	PIT	AA	C		42	.161
1886	PIT	AA	C		83	.258
1887	PIT	N	C-O		87	.313
1888	PIT	N	C-O		103	.277
1889	PIT	N	C-O		102	.267
1890	PIT	N	3-O		138	.273
1891	PIT	N	C-S-3-O		131	.285
1892	PIT	N	C-S-O		147	.268
1893	PIT	N	C		40	.194
1894	STL	N	M-C-2-3		125	.341
1895	STL	N	C-3-O		123	.290
1896	LOU	N	C-2		84	.273
	BRTR				1293	.274

MILLER, HENRY D.

1892	CHI	N	P		4	1- 2
	TL					

MILLER, HUGH STANLEY "COTTON"
B.DEC.28,1887 ST.LOUIS,MO.
D.DEC.24,1945

YR	CL	LEA	POS	GP	G	REC
1911	PHI	N	H		1	.000
1914	STL	F	1		132	.225
1915	STL	F	1		6	.500
	BRTR				139	.228

MILLER, JACOB GEORGE
B.FEB.5,1897 BALTIMORE,MD.

1922	PIT	N	O		3	.091
	BRTR					

MILLER, JAMES "RABBIT"
B.PITTSBURGH,PA.
D.FEB.8,1937

1901	NY	N	2		18	.136

MILLER, JAMES ELDRIDGE
B.FEB.13,1913 CELESTE,TEX.
D.NOV.21,1966 DALLAS,TEX.

YR	CL	LEA	POS	GP	G	REC
1944	DET	A	C		5	.200
1945	DET	A	C		2	.750
	BRTR				7	.444

MILLER, JOHN ALLEN
B.MAR.14,1944 ALHAMBRA,CAL.

1966	NY	A	1-O		6	.087
1969	LA	N	1-2-3-O		26	.211
	BRTR				32	.164

MILLER, JOHN ANTHONY "OX"
B.MAY 4,1915 GAUSE,TEX.

YR	CL	LEA	POS	GP	G	REC
1943	WAS	A	P		3	0- 0
	STL	A	P		2	0- 0
1945	STL	A	P	4	6	2- 1
1946	STL	A	P		11	1- 3
1947	CHI	N	P		4	1- 2
	BRTR			24	26	4- 6

MILLER, JOHN BARNEY "DOTS"
B.SEPT.9,1886 KEARNY,N.J.
D.SEPT.5,1923

YR	CL	LEA	POS	GP	G	REC
1909	PIT	N	2		150	.279
1910	PIT	N	2		119	.227
1911	PIT	N	2		129	.268
1912	PIT	N	1		148	.275
1913	PIT	N	1		154	.272
1914	STL	N	1-S		155	.290
1915	STL	N	1-2		150	.264
1916	STL	N	1-2-S		143	.238
1917	STL	N	1-2		148	.248
1919	STL	N	1-2		101	.231
1920	PHI	N	2-3		98	.254
1921	PHI	N	1-3		84	.297
	BRTR				1579	.263

MILLER, JOHN ERNEST
B.MAY 30,1941 BALTIMORE,MD.

YR	CL	LEA	POS	GP	G	REC
1962	BAL	A	P		2	1- 1
1963	BAL	A	P		3	1- 1
1965	BAL	A	P		16	6- 4
1966	BAL	A	P		23	4- 8
1967	BAL	A	P		2	0- 0
	BRTR				46	12-14

MILLER, JOSEPH A.
B.FEB.17,1861 BALTIMORE,MD.
D.APR.23,1928 WHEELING,W.V.A

1884	TOL	AA	S		105	.236
1885	LOU	AA	2-S-3		97	.192
					202	.217

MILLER, JOSEPH H. "CYCLONE"
B.SEPT.24,1859 SPRINGFIELD,MASS
D.OCT.13,1916

YR	CL	LEA	POS	GP	G	REC
1884	CHI	U	P		1	0- 0
	PRO	N	P-O		6	2- 4
						.045
	PHI	N	P		1	0- 1
1886	ATH	AA	P		21	10- 9
					29	12-14
						.259

MILLER, JOSEPH WICK
B.JULY 24,1850 GERMANY
D.AUG.30,1891

1872	NAT	NA	M-1		1	.250
1875	WES	NA	2		13	-
	CHI	NA	2-O		16	-
					30	-

MILLER, KENNETH ALBERT
B.MAY 2,1916 ST.LOUIS,MO.

1944	NY	N	P		5	0- 1
	BRTR					

MILLER, L. EDWARD
B.TECUMSEH,MICH.

1884	TOL	AA	O		8	.208

MILLER, LARRY DON
B.JUNE 19,1937 TOPEKA,KAN.

YR	CL	LEA	POS	GP	G	REC
1964	LA	N	P		16	4- 8
1965	NY	N	P		28	1- 4
1966	NY	N	P		4	0- 2
	BLTL				48	5-14

MILLER, LAWRENCE H. "HACK"
B.JAN.1,1894 CHICAGO,ILL.
D.SEPT.17,1971 OAKLAND,CAL.

YR	CL	LEA	POS	GP	G	REC
1916	BRO	N	O		3	.333
1918	BOS	A	O		12	.276
1922	CHI	N	O		122	.351
1923	CHI	N	O		135	.301
1924	CHI	N	O		53	.336
1925	CHI	N	O		24	.279
	BRTR				349	.323

MILLER, LEO ALPHONSO "RED"
B.FEB.11,1897 PHILADELPHIA,PA.

1923	PHI	N	P		1	0- 0
	BRTR					

MILLER, LOWELL OTTO "MOONIE"
B.JUNE 1,1889 MINDEN,NEB.
D.MAR.29,1962

YR	CL	LEA	POS	GP	G	REC
1910	BRO	N	C		28	.197
1911	BRO	N	C		22	.210
1912	BRO	N	C		98	.278
1913	BRO	N	C		104	.272
1914	BRO	N	C		54	.231
1915	BRO	N	C		84	.224
1916	BRO	N	C		73	.255
1917	BRO	N	C		92	.230
1918	BRO	N	C-1		75	.193
1919	BRO	N	C		51	.226
1920	BRO	N	C		90	.289
1921	BRO	N	C		91	.234
1922	BRO	N	C		59	.261
	BRTR				921	.245

MILLER, NORMAN CALVIN "NORM"
B.FEB.5,1946 LOS ANGELES,CAL.

YR	CL	LEA	POS	GP	G	REC
1965	HOU	N	O		11	.200
1966	HOU	N	3-O		11	.147
1967	HOU	N	O		64	.205
1968	HOU	N	O		79	.237
1969	HOU	N	O		119	.264
1970	HOU	N	C-O		90	.239
1971	HOU	N	C-O		45	.257
1972	HOU	N	O		67	.243
1973	HOU	N	O		3	.000
	ATL	N	O		9	.375
1974	ATL	N	O		42	.171
	BLTR				540	.238

MILLER, OTIS LOUIS
B.FEB.2,1901 BELLEVILLE,ILL.
D.JULY 26,1959

YR	CL	LEA	POS	GP	G	REC
1927	STL	A	S-3		51	.224
1930	BOS	A	2-3		112	.286
1931	BOS	A	2-3		107	.272
1932	BOS	A	O		2	.000
	BRTR				272	.273

MILLER, RALPH DARWIN
B.MAR.15,1873 CINCINNATI,OHIO
D.MAY 8,1973 CINCINNATI,OHIO

1898	BRO	N	P	19	21	5-14
1899	BAL	N	P		6	1- 2
	BRTR			25	27	6-16

MILLER, RALPH HENRY "MOOSE"
B.JAN.24,1896 VINTON,IOWA
D.FEB.18,1967

1921	WAS	A	P		1	0- 0
	BRTL					

MILLER, RALPH JOSEPH
B.FEB.29,1896 FT.WAYNE,IND.
D.MAR.18,1939

YR	CL	LEA	POS	GP	G	REC
1920	PHI	N	3		97	.219
1921	PHI	N	S		57	.304
1924	WAS	A	2		9	.133
	BRTR				163	.248

MILLER, RAYMOND PETER
B.FEB.12,1888 ALLEGHENY,PA.
D.APR.7,1927

1917	CLE	A	1		19	.190
	PIT	N	1		6	.148
					25	.188

MILLER, RICHARD ALAN "RICK"
B.APR.19,1948 GRAND RAPIDS,MICH.

YR	CL	LEA	POS	GP	G	REC
1971	BOS	A	O		15	.333
1972	BOS	A	O		89	.214
1973	BOS	A	O		143	.261
1974	BOS	A	O		114	.261
1975	BOS	A	O		77	.194
1976	BOS	A	O		105	.283
	BLTL				543	.258

MILLER, ROBERT GERALD "BOB"
B.JULY 15,1935 CHICAGO,ILL.

YR	CL	LEA	POS	GP	G	REC
1953	DET	A	P		13	1- 2
1954	DET	A	P	32	34	1- 1
1955	DET	A	P	7	9	2- 1
1956	DET	A	P		11	0- 2
1962	CIN	N	P		6	0- 0
	NY	N	P		17	2- 2
	BRTL			86	90	6- 8

YR	CL	LEA	POS	GP	G	REC

MILLER, ROBERT JOHN "BOB"
B.JUNE 16,1926 DETROIT,MICH.

YR	CL	LEA	POS	GP	G	REC
1949	PHI	N	P		3	0- 0
1950	PHI	N	P		35	11- 6
1951	PHI	N	P		17	2- 1
1952	PHI	N	P		3	0- 1
1953	PHI	N	P		35	8- 9
1954	PHI	N	P		30	7- 9
1955	PHI	N	P		40	8- 4
1956	PHI	N	P		49	3- 6
1957	PHI	N	P		32	2- 5
1958	PHI	N	P		17	1- 1
		BRTR			261	42-42

MILLER, ROBERT LANE "BOB"
B.FEB.18,1939 ST.LOUIS,MO.

YR	CL	LEA	POS	GP	G	REC
1957	STL	N	P	5	7	0- 0
1959	STL	N	P		11	4- 3
1960	STL	N	P	15	17	4- 3
1961	STL	N	P	34	35	1- 3
1962	NY	N	P	33	40	1-12
1963	LA	N	P		42	10- 8
1964	LA	N	P		74	7- 7
1965	LA	N	P		61	6- 7
1966	LA	N	P		46	4- 2
1967	LA	N	P		52	2- 9
1968	MIN	A	P		45	0- 3
1969	MIN	A	P		48	5- 5
1970	CLE	A	P		15	2- 2
	CHI	A	P	15	16	4- 6
	CHI	N	P		7	0- 0
1971	CHI	N	P		2	0- 0
	SD	N	P		38	7- 3
	PIT	N	P		16	1- 2
1972	PIT	N	P		36	5- 2
1973	SD	N	P		18	0- 0
	NY	N	P		1	0- 0
	DET	A	P		22	4- 2
1974	NY	N	P		58	2- 2
		BRTR		694	707	69-81

MILLER, ROBERT W.

YR	CL	LEA	POS	GP	G	REC
1890	ROC	AA	P		13	3- 8
1891	WAS	AA	P		7	2- 3
					20	5-11

MILLER, RODNEY CARTER
B.JAN.16,1940 PORTLAND,ORE.

YR	CL	LEA	POS	GP	G	REC
1957	BRO	N	H		1	.000
		BLTR				

MILLER, ROGER WESLEY
B.AUG.1,1954 CONNELLSVILLE,PA.

YR	CL	LEA	POS	GP	G	REC
1974	MIL	A	P		2	0- 0
		BRTR				

MILLER, ROLLAND ARTHUR "RONNIE"
B.AUG.28,1918 MASON CITY,IOWA

YR	CL	LEA	POS	GP	G	REC
1941	WAS	A	P		1	0- 0
		BBTR				

MILLER, ROSCOE CLYDE "RUBBERLEGS"
B.DEC.2,1876 GREENVILLE,IND.
D.APR.18,1913

YR	CL	LEA	POS	GP	G	REC
1901	DET	A	P		39	23-13
1902	DET	A	P		20	6-11
	NY	N	P		10	1- 8
1903	NY	N	P		15	2- 5
1904	PIT	N	P		19	7- 9
					103	39-46

MILLER, ROY OSCAR "DOC"
B.1883 SAN FRANCISCO,CAL.
D.JULY 30,1938

YR	CL	LEA	POS	GP	G	REC
1910	CHI	N	O		1	.000
	BOS	N	O		130	.286
1911	BOS	N	O		146	.333
1912	BOS	N	O		51	.234
	PHI	N	O		67	.288
1913	PHI	N	O		69	.345
1914	CIN	N	O		93	.255
		BLTL			557	.295

MILLER, RUDEL CHARLES
B.JULY 12,1900 KALAMAZOO,MICH.

YR	CL	LEA	POS	GP	G	REC
1929	PHI	A	3		2	.250
		BRTR				

MILLER, RUSSELL LEWIS
B.MAR.25,1900 WAGRAM,OHIO
D.APR.30,1962

YR	CL	LEA	POS	GP	G	REC
1927	PHI	N	P		2	.1- 1
1928	PHI	N	P	33	36	0-12
		BRTR		35	38	1-13

MILLER, STUART LEONARD "STU"
B.DEC.26,1927 NORTHAMPTON,MASS.

YR	CL	LEA	POS	GP	G	REC
1952	STL	N	P		12	6- 3
1953	STL	N	P	40	42	7- 8
1954	STL	N	P	19	20	2- 3
1956	STL	N	P	3	4	0- 1
	PHI	N	P	24	29	5- 8
1957	NY	N	P		38	7- 9
1958	SF	N	P	41	42	6- 9
1959	SF	N	P		59	8- 7
1960	SF	N	P		47	7- 6
1961	SF	N	P	63	64	14- 5
1962	SF	N	P	59	60	5- 8
1963	BAL	A	P		71	5- 8
1964	BAL	A	P		66	7- 7
1965	BAL	A	P		67	14- 7
1966	BAL	A	P		51	9- 4
1967	BAL	A	P		42	3-10
1968	ATL	N	P		2	0- 0
		BRTR		704	716	105-103

MILLER, THOMAS P. "REDDY"
B.PHILADELPHI.,APA.
D.MAY 29,1876

YR	CL	LEA	POS	GP	G	REC
1875	STL	NA	C-3		52	.166

MILLER, THOMAS ROYALL
B.JULY 5,1897 POWHATAN COURT
HOUSE,VA.

YR	CL	LEA	POS	GP	G	REC
1918	BOS	N	H		2	.000
1919	BOS	N	O		7	.333
		BLTR			9	.250

MILLER, WALTER JACOB "JAKE"
B.FEB.28,1897 WAGRAM,OHIO
D.AUG.20,1975 VENICE,FLA.

YR	CL	LEA	POS	GP	G	REC
1924	CLE	A	P		2	0- 1
1925	CLE	A	P		32	10-13
1926	CLE	A	P		18	7- 4
1927	CLE	A	P		34	10- 8
1928	CLE	A	P		25	8- 9
1929	CLE	A	P		29	14-12
1930	CLE	A	P		24	4- 4
1931	CLE	A	P		10	2- 1
1933	CHI	A	P	26	30	5- 6
		BLTL		200	204	60-58

MILLER, WALTER W.
B.OCT.19,1884 GAS CITY,IND.
D.MAR.1,1956

YR	CL	LEA	POS	GP	G	REC
1911	BRO	N	P		3	0- 1
		BRTR				

MILLER, WARD TAYLOR "GRUMP"
B.JULY 5,1885 DIXON,ILL.
D.SEPT.4,1958

YR	CL	LEA	POS	GP	G	REC
1909	PIT	N	O		14	.143
	CIN	N	O		43	.310
1910	CIN	N	O		26	.238
1912	CHI	N	O		86	.307
1913	CHI	N	O		80	.236
1914	STL	F	O		119	.295
1915	STL	F	O		155	.307
1916	STL	A	O		146	.266
1917	STL	A	O		43	.207
		BLTR			712	.278

MILLER, WARREN W.

YR	CL	LEA	POS	GP	G	REC
1909	WAS	A	O		26	.216
1911	WAS	A	O		21	.148
					47	.188

MILLER, WILLIAM
B.CLEVELAND,OHIO

YR	CL	LEA	POS	GP	G	REC
1902	PIT	N	O		1	.200

MILLER, WILLIAM FRANCIS
B.APR.12,1912 HANNIBAL,MO.

YR	CL	LEA	POS	GP	G	REC
1937	STL	A	P		1	0- 1
		BRTR				

MILLER, WILLIAM PAUL "LEFTY"
B.JULY 26,1927 MINERSVILLE,PA.

YR	CL	LEA	POS	GP	G	REC
1952	NY	A	P	21	4- 6	
1953	NY	A	P	13	2- 1	
1954	NY	A	P	2	0- 1	
1955	BAL	A	P	5	0- 1	
		BLTL		41	6- 9	

MILLIES, WALTER LOUIS
B.OCT.18,1908 CHICAGO,ILL.

YR	CL	LEA	POS	GP	G	REC
1934	BRO	N	C		2	.000
1936	WAS	A	C		74	.312
1937	WAS	A	C		59	.223
1939	PHI	N	C		84	.234
1940	PHI	N	C		26	.070
1941	PHI	N	C		1	.000
		BRTR			246	.243

MILLIGAN, JOHN "JOCKO"
B.AUG.8,1861 PHILADELPHIA,PA.
D.AUG.29,1923

YR	CL	LEA	POS	GP	G	REC
1884	ATH	AA	C		66	.295
1885	ATH	AA	C		7	.286
1886	ATH	AA	C-1		76	.249
1887	ATH	AA	C-1		96	.344
1888	STL	AA	C		63	.252
1889	STL	AA	C		72	.370
1890	PHI	P	C		62	.315
1891	ATH	AA	C-1		117	.300
1892	WAS	N	C-1		76	.277
1893	BAL	N	C-1		23	.240
	NY	N	C		40	.243
		BRTR			698	.293

MILLIGAN, JOHN ALEXANDER
B.JAN.22,1904 SCHUYLERSVILLE,
N.Y.
D.MAY 15,1972 FORT PIERCE,FLA.

YR	CL	LEA	POS	GP	G	REC
1928	PHI	N	P		13	2- 5
1929	PHI	N	P		8	0- 1
1930	PHI	N	P		9	1- 2
1931	PHI	N	P		3	0- 0
1934	WAS	A	P		2	0- 0
		BRTL			35	3- 8

MILLIGAN, WILLIAM J.
B.1877 BUFFALO,N.Y.
D.SEPT.3,1928

YR	CL	LEA	POS	GP	G	REC
1901	PHI	A	P		7	0- 3
1904	NY	N	P		5	0- 1
		TL			12	0- 4

MILLIKEN, ROBERT EAGLE "BOBO"
B.AUG.25,1926 MAJORSVILLE,W.VA.

YR	CL	LEA	POS	GP	G	REC
1953	BRO	N	P		37	8- 4
1954	BRO	N	P		24	5- 2
		BRTR			61	13- 6

MILLS, ABBOTT PAIGE "JACK"
B.OCT.23,1889 S.WILLIAMSTOWN,
MASS.
D.JUNE 3,1973 WASHINGTON,D.C.

YR	CL	LEA	POS	GP	G	REC
1911	CLE	A	S		13	.294
		BLTR				

MILLS, ARTHUR GRANT
B.MAR.2,1903 UTICA,N.Y.
D.JULY 23,1975 UTICA,N.Y.

YR	CL	LEA	POS	GP	G	REC
1927	BOS	N	P		15	0- 1
1928	BOS	N	P		4	0- 0
		BRTR			19	0- 1

MILLS, CHARLES
B.BROOKLYN,N.Y.
D.APR.10,1874

YR	CL	LEA	POS	GP	G	REC
1871	MUT	NA	C-O		33	-
1872	MUT	NA	C-3-O		6	.133
					39	-

MILLS, COLONEL BUSTER "BUS"
B.SEPT.16,1908 RANGER,TEX.

YR	CL	LEA	POS	GP	G	REC
1934	STL	N	O		29	.236
1935	BRO	N	O		17	.214
1937	BOS	A	O		123	.295
1938	STL	A	O		123	.285
1940	NY	A	O		34	.397
1942	CLE	A	O		80	.277
1946	CLE	A	O		9	.273
		BRTR			415	.287

NON-PLAYING MANAGER CIN(N) 1953

MILLS, EVERETT
B.1845 NEWARK,N.J.
D.JUNE 22,1908

YR	CL	LEA	POS	GP	G	REC
1871	OLY	NA	1		31	-
1872	BAL	NA	1		53	.274
1873	BAL	NA	1-O		54	-
1874	HAR	NA	1		53	-
1875	HAR	NA	1		78	-
1876	HAR	N	1		63	.259
					332	-

YR	CL LEA POS	GP	G	REC

MILLS, FRANK LE MOYNE
B.MAY 13,1895 KNOXVILLE,OHIO
| 1914 CLE A C | | 4 | .142 |

BLTR

MILLS, HOWARD ROBINSON "LEFTY"
B.MAY 12,1911 DEDHAM,MASS.
1934 STL A P		4	0- 0
1937 STL A P		2	1- 1
1938 STL A P	30		10-12
1939 STL A P	34		4-11
1940 STL A P	26		0- 6
BLTL	96		15-30

MILLS, RICHARD ALAN "DICK"
B.JAN.29,1945 BOSTON,MASS.
| 1970 BOS A P | | 2 | 0- 0 |
BRTR

MILLS, RUPERT FRANK
B.OCT.12,1892 NEWARK,N.J.
D.JULY 20,1929
| 1915 NEW F 1 | 41 | | .205 |
BRTR

MILLS, WILLIAM GRANT
B.AUG.15,1877 SCHENEVUS,N.Y.
D.JULY 5,1914
| 1901 NY N P | | 2 | 0- 2 |

MILLS, WILLIAM HENRY
B.NOV.2,1920 BOSTON,MASS.
| 1944 PHI A C | | 5 | .250 |
BRTR

MILNAR, ALBERT JOSEPH "HAPPY"
B.DEC.26,1913 CLEVELAND,OHIO
1936 CLE A P		4	1- 2
1938 CLE A P	23	24	3- 1
1939 CLE A P	37	41	14-12
1940 CLE A P		37	18-10
1941 CLE A P		35	12-19
1942 CLE A P	28	40	6- 8
1943 CLE A P	16	19	1- 3
STL A P		3	1- 2
1946 STL A P		4	1- 1
PHI N P		1	0- 0
BLTL	188	208	57-58

MILNE, WILLIAM JAMES "PETE"
B.APR.10,1925 MOBILE,ALA.
1948 NY N O		12	.222
1949 NY N O		31	.241
1950 NY N H		4	.250
BLTR		47	.233

MILNER, JOHN DAVID
B.DEC.28,1949 ATLANTA,GA.
1971 NY N O		9	.167
1972 NY N 1-O		117	.238
1973 NY N 1-O		129	.239
1974 NY N 1		137	.252
1975 NY N 1-O		91	.191
1976 NY N 1-O		127	.271
BLTL		610	.243

MILOSEVICH, MICHAEL
B.JAN.13,1915 ZEIGLER,ILL.
D.FEB.3,1966 E.CHICAGO,IND.
1944 NY A S		94	.247
1945 NY A 2-S		30	.217
BRTR		124	.242

MILSTEAD, GEORGE EARL "COWBOY"
B.SEPT.26,1903 CLEBERNE,TEX.
1924 CHI N P	13		1- 1
1925 CHI N P		5	1- 1
1926 CHI N P	18		1- 5
BLTL	36		3- 7

MILTON, S. LAWRENCE "TUG"
B.PITTSBURG,KAN.
| 1903 STL N P | | 1 | 0- 0 |

MINAHAN, DANIEL JOSEPH
B.NOV.28,1865 TROY,N.Y.
D.AUG.8,1929
| 1895 LOU N 3 | | 8 | .361 |
BRTR

MINAHAN, EDMUND JOSEPH "COTTON"
B.DEC.10,1882 SPRINGFIELD,OHIO
D.MAY 20,1958
| 1907 CIN N P | | 2 | 0- 2 |
BRTR

MINARCIN, RUDY ANTHONY
B.MAR.25,1930 N.VANDERGRIFT,PA.
1955 CIN N P		41	5- 9
1956 BOS A P		3	1- 0
1957 BOS A P		26	0- 0
BRTR		70	6- 9

MINCHER, DONALD RAY "DON"
B.JUNE 24,1938 HUNTSVILLE,ALA.
1960 WAS A 1		27	.241
1961 MIN A 1		35	.188
1962 MIN A 1		86	.240
1963 MIN A 1		82	.258
1964 MIN A 1		120	.237
1965 MIN A 1-O		128	.251
1966 MIN A 1		139	.251
1967 CAL A 1-O		147	.273
1968 CAL A 1		120	.236
1969 SEA A 1		140	.246
1970 OAK A 1		140	.246
1971 OAK A 1		28	.239
WAS A 1		100	.291
1972 TEX A 1		61	.236
OAK A 1		47	.148
BLTR		1400	.249

MINCHER, EDWARD JOHN
B.BALTIMORE,MD.
1871 KEK NA O		9	-
1872 NAT NA O		11	.118
		20	-

MINER, RAYMOND THEADORE
B.APR.4,1897 GLENS FALL,SN.Y.
D.SEPT.15,1963
| 1921 PHI A P | | 1 | 0- 0 |
BRTL

MINGORI, STEPHEN BERNARD "STEVE"
B.FEB.29,1944 KANSAS CITY,MO.
1970 CLE A P		21	1- 0
1971 CLE A P		54	1- 2
1972 CLE A P-O	41	42	0- 6
			.125
1973 CLE A P		5	0- 0
KC A P		19	3- 3
1974 KC A P		36	2- 3
1975 KC A P		36	0- 3
1976 KC A P		55	5- 5
BLTL	267	268	12-22
			.167

MINNER, PAUL EDISON "LEFTY"
B.JULY 30,1923 NEW WILMINGTON,
PA.
1946 BRO N P		3	0- 1
1948 BRO N P	28	31	4- 3
1949 BRO N P		27	3- 1
1950 CHI N P	29	43	8-13
1951 CHI N P	33	36	6-17
1952 CHI N P	28	29	14- 9
1953 CHI N P		31	12-15
1954 CHI N P	32	33	11-11
1955 CHI N P		22	9- 9
1956 CHI N P		10	2- 5
BLTL	253	265	69-84

MINNICK, DONALD ATHEY
B.APR.14,1931 LYNCHBURG,VA.
| 1957 WAS A P | | 2 | 0- 1 |
BRTR

**MINOSO, SATURNINO ORESTES
ARRIETA (ARMAS) "MINNIE"**
B.NOV.29,1922 MATANZAS,CUBA
1949 CLE A O		9	.188
1951 CLE A 1		8	.429
CHI A S-3-O		138	.324
1952 CHI A S-3-O		147	.281
1953 CHI A 3-O		151	.313
1954 CHI A 3-O		153	.320
1955 CHI A 3-O		139	.288
1956 CHI A 1-3-O		151	.316
1957 CHI A 3-O		153	.310
1958 CLE A 3-O		149	.302
1959 CLE A O		148	.302
1960 CHI A O		154	.311
1961 CHI A O		152	.280
1962 STL N O		39	.196
1963 WAS A O		109	.229
1964 CHI A O		30	.226
1976 CHI A H		3	.125
BRTR		1833	.298

MINSHALL, JAMES EDWARD "JIM"
B.JULY 4,1947 COVINGTON,KY.
1974 PIT N P		5	0- 1
1975 PIT N P		1	0- 0
BRTR		6	0- 1

MINTON, GREGORY BRIAN "GREG"
B.JULY 29,1951 LUBBOCK,TEX.
1975 SF N P		4	1- 1
1976 SF N P	10	11	0- 3
BBTR	14	15	1- 4

**MIRANDA, GUILLERMO (PEREZ)
"WILLY"**
B.MAY 24,1927 VELASCO,CUBA
1951 WAS A 1-S		7	.444
1952 CHI A 2-S-3		12	.250
STL A S		7	.091
CHI A 2-S-3		58	.218
1953 STL A S-3		17	.167
NY A S		48	.224
1954 NY A 2-S-3		92	.250
1955 BAL A 2-S		153	.255
1956 BAL A S		148	.217
1957 BAL A S		115	.194
1958 BAL A S		102	.201
1959 BAL A 2-S-3		65	.159
BBTR		824	.221

MISSE, JOHN BEVERLY
B.MAY 30,1885 HIGHLAND,KAN.
D.MAR.18,1970 ST.JOSEPH,MO.
| 1914 STL F 2-S | | 97 | .189 |
BRTR

MITCHELL, ALBERT ROY "ROY"
B.APR.19,1885 BELTON,TEX.
D.SEPT.8,1959
1910 STL A P		6	4- 2
1911 STL A P	28	29	4- 8
1912 STL A P		13	3- 4
1913 STL A P		33	13-16
1914 STL A P		28	4- 5
1918 CHI A P		2	0- 1
CIN N P		5	4- 0
1919 CIN N P		7	0- 1
BRTR	122	123	32-37

MITCHELL, CLARENCE ELMER
B.FEB.22,1891 FRANKLIN,NEB.
D.NOV.6,1963 GRAND ISLAND,NEB.
1911 DET A P		5	1- 0
1916 CIN N P-1-	29	56	11-10
O			.239
1917 CIN N P-1-	32	47	9-15
O			.278
1918 BRO N P		10	0- 1
1919 BRO N P	23	34	7- 5
1920 BRO N P	19	55	5- 2
1921 BRO N P-1	37	46	11- 9
			.290
1923 PHI N P	29	53	9-10
1924 PHI N P	29	69	6-13
1925 PHI N P-1	32	52	10-17
			.196
1926 PHI N P	28	39	9-14
1927 PHI N P	13	18	6- 3
1928 PHI N P		3	0- 0
STL N P		19	8- 9
1929 STL N P	25	26	8-11
1930 STL N P		1	1- 0
NY N P		24	10- 3
1931 NY N P		27	13-11
1932 NY N P		8	1- 3
BLTL	390	650	125-139
			.252

MITCHELL, CRAIG SETON
B.APR.14,1954 SANTA ROSA,CAL.
1975 OAK A P		1	0- 1
1976 OAK A P		1	0- 0
BRTR		2	0- 1

YR	CL	LEA	POS	GP	G	REC

MITCHELL, FREDERICK FRANCIS
(REAL NAME
FREDERICK FRANCIS YAPP)
B.JUNE 5,1878 CAMBRIDGE,MASS.
D.OCT.13,1970 NEWTON,MASS.

YR	CL	LEA	POS	GP	G	REC
1901	BOS	A	P		20	6- 9
1902	BOS	A	P		1	0- 1
	PHI	A	P-O	19	20	5- 8
						.184
1903	PHI	N	P		28	11-14
1904	PHI	N	P		25	4- 8
	BRO	N	P		8	2- 4
1905	BRO	N	P		25	3- 7
1910	NY	A	C		68	.230
1913	BOS	N	C		4	.333
	BRTR			126	199	31-51
						.209

NON-PLAYING MANAGER
CHI(N) 1917-20, BOS(N) 1921-23

MITCHELL, JOHN FRANKLIN
B.AUG.9,1894 DETROIT,MICH.
D.NOV.4,1965

YR	CL	LEA	POS	GP	G	REC
1921	NY	A	S		13	.262
1922	NY	A	S		4	.000
	BOS	A	S		59	.251
1923	BOS	A	S		92	.225
1924	BRO	N	S		64	.263
1925	BRO	N	S		97	.250
	BBTR			329		.245

MITCHELL, LOREN DALE "DALE"
B.AUG.23,1921 COLONY,OKLA.

YR	CL	LEA	POS	GP	G	REC
1946	CLE	A	O		11	.432
1947	CLE	A	O		123	.316
1948	CLE	A	O		141	.336
1949	CLE	A	O		149	.317
1950	CLE	A	O		130	.308
1951	CLE	A	O		134	.290
1952	CLF	A	O		134	.323
1953	CLE	A	O		134	.300
1954	CLE	A	1-O		53	.283
1955	CLE	A	1-O		61	.259
1956	CLE	A	O		38	.133
	BRO	N	O		19	.292
	BLTL			1127		.312

MITCHELL, MICHAEL FRANCIS
B.DEC.12,1883 SPRINGFIELD,OHIO
D.JULY 16,1961

YR	CL	LEA	POS	GP	G	REC
1907	CIN	N	O		148	.292
1908	CIN	N	O		119	.222
1909	CIN	N	O		145	.310
1910	CIN	N	O		156	.286
1911	CIN	N	O		140	.291
1912	CIN	N	O		147	.283
1913	CHI	N	O		82	.262
	PIT	N	O		54	.271
1914	PIT	N	O		76	.234
	WAS	A	O		55	.205
	BRTR			1122		.278

MITCHELL, MONROE BARR
B.SEPT.11,1901 STARKVILLE,MISS.

YR	CL	LEA	POS	GP	G	REC
1923	WAS	A	P		10	2- 4
	BRTL					

MITCHELL, PAUL MICHAEL
B.AUG.19,1949 WORCESTER,MASS.

YR	CL	LEA	POS	GP	G	REC
1975	BAL	A	P		11	3- 0
1976	OAK	A	P		26	9- 7
	BRTR			37		12- 7

MITCHELL, ROBERT MC KASHA
B.FEB.6,1856 CINCINNATI,OHIO
D.MAY 1,1933 SPRINGFIELD
TOWNSHIP,OHIO

YR	CL	LEA	POS	GP	G	REC
1877	CIN	N	P-O	12	13	6- 5
						.204
1878	CIN	N	P-S-	9	14	7- 2
			O			.250
1879	CLE	N	P-O	22	30	4-13
						.146
1882	STL	AA	P-O		1	0- 0
						.000
	BLTL			44	58	17-20
						.182

MITCHELL, ROBERT VANCE "BOB"
B.OCT.22,1943 NORRISTOWN,PA.

YR	CL	LEA	POS	GP	G	REC
1970	MIL	A	O		10	.227
1971	MIL	A	O		35	.182
1973	MIL	A	O-D		47	.223
1974	MIL	A	O-D		88	.243
1975	MIL	A	O-D		93	.249
	BRTR			273		.235

MITCHELL, WILLIAM "WILLIE"
B.DEC.1,1889 PLEASANT GROVE,
MISS.
D.NOV.23,1973 SARDIS,MISS.

YR	CL	LEA	POS	GP	G	REC
1909	CLE	A	P		3	1- 2
1910	CLE	A	P		35	12- 8
1911	CLE	A	P	31	32	7-14
1912	CLE	A	P		29	5- 8
1913	CLE	A	P		35	14- 8
1914	CLE	A	P		39	12-17
1915	CLE	A	P		36	11-14
1916	CLE	A	P		11	2- 5
	DET	A	P		24	8- 4
1917	DET	A	P	30	31	12- 8
1918	DET	A	P		1	0- 1
1919	DET	A	P		3	1- 2
	BRTL			277	279	85-91

MITTERLING, RALPH
B.APR.19,1890 FREEBURG,PA.
D.JAN.22,1956

YR	CL	LEA	POS	GP	G	REC
1916	PHI	A	O		13	.154

MITTERWALD, GEORGE EUGENE
B.JUNE 7,1945 BERKELEY,CAL.

YR	CL	LEA	POS	GP	G	REC
1966	MIN	A	C		3	.200
1968	MIN	A	C		11	.206
1969	MIN	A	C-O		69	.257
1970	MIN	A	C		117	.222
1971	MIN	A	C		125	.250
1972	MIN	A	C		64	.184
1973	MIN	A	C		125	.259
1974	CHI	N	C		78	.251
1975	CHI	N	C-1		84	.220
1976	CHI	N	C-1		101	.215
	BRTR			777		.235

MIZE, JOHN ROBERT "JOHNNY"
B.JAN.7,1913 DEMOREST,GA.

YR	CL	LEA	POS	GP	G	REC
1936	STL	N	1		126	.329
1937	STL	N	1		145	.364
1938	STL	N	1		149	.337
1939	STL	N	1		153	.349
1940	STL	N	1		155	.314
1941	STL	N	1		126	.317
1942	NY	N	1		142	.305
1946	NY	N	1		101	.337
1947	NY	N	1		154	.302
1948	NY	N	1		152	.289
1949	NY	N	1		106	.263
	NY	A	1		13	.261
1950	NY	A	1		90	.277
1951	NY	A	1		113	.259
1952	NY	A	1		78	.263
1953	NY	A	1		81	.250
	BLTR			1884		.313

MIZELL, WILMER DAVID
"VINEGAR BEND"
B.AUG.13,1930 LEAKESVILLE,MISS.

YR	CL	LEA	POS	GP	G	REC
1952	STL	N	P		30	10- 8
1953	STL	N	P		33	13-11
1956	STL	N	P		33	14-14
1957	STL	N	P		33	8-10
1958	STL	N	P		30	10-14
1959	STL	N	P		31	13-10
1960	STL	N	P		9	1- 3
	PIT	N	P		23	13- 5
1961	PIT	N	P		25	7-10
1962	PIT	N	P		4	1- 1
	NY	N	P		17	0- 2
	BRTL			268		90-88

MIZEUR, WILLIAM FRANCIS
"BAD BILL"
B.JUNE 22,1900 NOKOMIS,ILL.

YR	CL	LEA	POS	GP	G	REC
1923	STL	A	O		1	.000
1924	STL	A	O		1	.000
	BLTR			2		.000

MLCKOVSKY, RAYMOND JAMES
(PLAYED UNDER NAME OF
RAYMOND JAMES MACK)

MOATES, DAVID ALLAN "DAVE"
B.JAN.30,1948 GREAT LAKES,ILL.

YR	CL	LEA	POS	GP	G	REC
1974	TEX	A	R		1	.000
1975	TEX	A	O		54	.274
1976	TEX	A	O		85	.241
	BLTR			140		.260

MODAK, MICHAEL JOSEPH ALOYSIUS
B.MAY 18,1924 CAMPBELL,OHIO

YR	CL	LEA	POS	GP	G	REC
1945	CIN	N	P		20	1- 2
	BRTR					

MOELLER, DANIEL EDWARD
B.MAR.23,1885 DE WITT,IOWA
D.APR.14,1951

YR	CL	LEA	POS	GP	G	REC
1907	PIT	N	O		11	.285
1908	PIT	N	O		27	.193
1912	WAS	A	O		132	.276
1913	WAS	A	O		153	.236
1914	WAS	A	O		151	.250
1915	WAS	A	O		118	.226
1916	WAS	A	O		78	.245
	CLE	A	O		25	.069
	BBTR			695		.243

MOELLER, JOSEPH DOUGLAS "JOE"
B.FEB.15,1943 CHICAGO,ILL.

YR	CL	LEA	POS	GP	G	REC
1962	LA	N	P		19	6- 5
1964	LA	N	P		27	7-13
1966	LA	N	P		29	2- 4
1967	LA	N	P		6	0- 0
1968	LA	N	P		3	1- 1
1969	LA	N	P		23	1- 0
1970	LA	N	P		31	7- 9
1971	LA	N	P		28	2- 4
	BRTR			166		26-36

MOELLER, RONALD RALPH "RON"
B.OCT.13,1938 CINCINNATI,OHIO

YR	CL	LEA	POS	GP	G	REC
1956	BAL	A	P		4	0- 1
1958	BAL	A	P		4	0- 0
1961	LA	A	P	33	35	4- 8
1963	LA	A	P		3	0- 0
	WAS	A	P		8	2- 0
	BLTL			52	54	6- 9

MOFFETT, JOSEPH W.
B.WHEELING,W.VA.

YR	CL	LEA	POS	GP	G	REC
1884	TOL	AA	1-3		56	.207

MOFFET, SAMUEL R.
B.1857 WHEELING,W.VA.
D.1907

YR	CL	LEA	POS	GP	G	REC
1884	CLE	N	P-1	22	66	3-19
			2-3-O			.179
1887	IND	N	P		11	1- 5
1888	IND	N	P-O	7	10	2- 5
						.114
	TR			40	87	6-29
						.167

MOFFITT, RANDALL JAMES "RANDY"
B.OCT.13,1948 LONG BEACH,CAL.

YR	CL	LEA	POS	GP	G	REC
1972	SF	N	P		40	1- 5
1973	SF	N	P		60	4- 4
1974	SF	N	P		61	5- 7
1975	SF	N	P		55	4- 5
1976	SF	N	P		58	6- 6
	BRTR			274		20-27

MOFORD, HERBERT "HERB"
B.AUG.6,1928 BROOKSVILLE,KY.

YR	CL	LEA	POS	GP	G	REC
1955	STL	N	P		14	1- 1
1958	DET	A	P		25	4- 9
1959	BOS	A	P		4	0- 2
1962	NY	N	P		7	0- 1
	BRTR			50		5-13

MOGRIDGE, GEORGE ANTHONY
B.FEB.18,1889 ROCHESTER,N.Y.
D.MAR.4,1962

YR	CL	LEA	POS	GP	G	REC
1911	CHI	A	P		4	0- 2
1912	CHI	A	P		17	3- 4
1915	NY	A	P		6	2- 3
1916	NY	A	P	30	31	6-12
1917	NY	A	P		29	9-11
1918	NY	A	P	45	48	15-13
1919	NY	A	P		36	10- 8
1920	NY	A	P		26	5- 9
1921	WAS	A	P		38	18-14
1922	WAS	A	P		34	18-13
1923	WAS	A	P		33	13-13
1924	WAS	A	P		30	16-11
1925	WAS	A	P		10	4- 3
	STL	A	P		2	1- 1
1926	BOS	N	P	39	40	6-10
1927	BOS	N	P		20	6- 4
	BLTL			399	404	132-131

MOHARDT, JOHN HENRY
B.JAN.20,1900 PITTSBURGH,PA.
D.NOV.24,1961

YR	CL	LEA	POS	GP	G	REC
1922	DET	A	O		5	1.000

YR	CL	LEA	POS	GP	G	REC

MOHART, GEORGE BENJAMIN
B.MAR.6,1894 BUFFALO,N.Y.
D.OCT.2,1970 SILVER CREEK,N.Y.
1920	BRO	N	P		13	0- 1
1921	BRO	N	P		2	0- 0
	BRTR				15	0- 1

MOHLER, ERNEST FOLLETTE "KID"
B.DEC.13,1874 ONEIDA,ILL.
D.NOV.4,1961
| 1894 | WAS | N | S | | 3 | .125 |

MOISAN, WILLIAM JOSEPH
B.JULY 30,1925 BRADFORD,MASS.
| 1953 | CHI | N | P | | 3 | 0- 0 |
| | BLTR | | | | | |

MOKAN, JOHN LEO
B.SEPT.23,1895 BUFFALO,N.Y.
1921	PIT	N	O		19	.269
1922	PIT	N	O		31	.258
	PHI	N	3-O		47	.252
1923	PHI	N	3-O		113	.313
1924	PHI	N	O		96	.260
1925	PHI	N	O		75	.330
1926	PHI	N	O		127	.303
1927	PHI	N	O		74	.286
	BRTR				582	.291

MOLE, FENTON LE ROY "MUSCLES"
B.JUNE 14,1925 SAN LEANDRO,CAL.
| 1949 | NY | A | 1 | | 10 | .185 |
| | BLTL | | | | | |

MOLESWORTH, CARLTON
B.FEB.15,1876 FREDERICK,MD.
D.JULY 25,1961
| 1895 | WAS | N | P | | 4 | 0- 2 |
| | TL | | | | | |

MOLINARO, ROBERT JOSEPH "BOB"
B.MAY 21,1950 NEWARK,N.J.
| 1975 | DET | A | O | | 6 | .263 |
| | BLTR | | | | | |

MOLLENKAMP, FREDERICK HENRY
B.MAR.15,1890 CINCINNATI,OHIO
D.NOV.1,1948
| 1914 | PHI | N | 1 | | 3 | .125 |

MOLLWITZ, FREDERICK AUGUST "FRITZ"
B.JUNE 6,1891 KOLBERG,GERMANY
D.OCT.3,1967 BRADENTON,FLA.
1913	CHI	N	1		3	.428
1914	CHI	N	1		12	.143
	CIN	N	1		33	.164
1915	CIN	N	1		153	.259
1916	CIN	N	1		65	.224
	CHI	N	1		33	.268
1917	PIT	N	1		36	.257
1918	PIT	N	1		119	.269
1919	PIT	N	1-O		56	.167
	STL	N	1		25	.241
	BRTR				535	.241

MOLONEY, RICHARD HENRY "RICHIE"
B.JUNE 7,1950 BROOKLINE,MASS.
| 1970 | CHI | A | P | | 1 | 0- 0 |
| | BRTR | | | | | |

MOLYNEAUX, VINCENT L.
B.AUG.17,1894 NIAGARA FALLS,N.Y
D.MAY 4,1950
1917	STL	A	P		7	0- 0
1918	BOS	A	P		6	1- 0
	BRTR				13	1- 0

MONACO, BLAS
B.NOV.16,1915 SAN ANTONIO,TEX.
1937	CLE	A	2		5	.286
1946	CLE	A	H		12	.000
	BBTR				17	.154

MONAHAN, EDWARD FRANCIS "RINTY"
B.APR.28,1928 BROOKLYN,N.Y.
| 1953 | PHI | A | P | | 4 | 0- 0 |
| | BRTR | | | | | |

MONBOQUETTE, WILLIAM CHARLES "BILL"
B.AUG.11,1936 MEDFORD,MASS.
1958	BOS	A	P		10	3- 4
1959	BOS	A	P	34	35	7- 7
1960	BOS	A	P	35	38	14-11
1961	BOS	A	P	32	33	14-14
1962	BOS	A	P		35	15-13
1963	BOS	A	P		37	20-10
1964	BOS	A	P	36	39	13-14
1965	BOS	A	P	35	36	10-18
1966	DET	A	P		30	7- 8
1967	DET	A	P		2	0- 0
	NY	A	P		33	6- 5
1968	NY	A	P		17	5- 7
	SF	N	P		7	0- 1
	BRTR			343	352	114-112

MONCEWICZ, FREDERICK ALFRED
B.SEPT.1,1903 BROCKTON,MASS.
D.APR.23,1969 BROCKTON,MASS.
| 1928 | BOS | A | S | | 3 | .000 |
| | BRTR | | | | | |

MONCHAK, ALEX
B.MAR.15,1917 BAYONNE,N.J.
| 1940 | PHI | N | 2-S | | 19 | .143 |
| | BRTR | | | | | |

MONDAY, ROBERT JAMES "RICK"
B.NOV.20,1945 BATESVILLE,ARK.
1966	KC	A	O		17	.098
1967	KC	A	O		124	.251
1968	OAK	A	O		148	.274
1969	OAK	A	O		122	.271
1970	OAK	A	O		112	.290
1971	OAK	A	O		116	.245
1972	CHI	N	O		138	.249
1973	CHI	N	O		149	.267
1974	CHI	N	O		142	.294
1975	CHI	N	O		136	.267
1976	CHI	N	1-O		137	.272
	BLTL				1341	.267

MONEY, DONALD WAYNE "DON"
B.JUNE 7,1947 WASHINGTON,D.C.
1968	PHI	N	S		4	.231
1969	PHI	N	S		127	.229
1970	PHI	N	S-3		120	.295
1971	PHI	N	2-3-O		121	.223
1972	PHI	N	S-3		152	.222
1973	MIL	A	S-3		145	.284
1974	MIL	A	2-3		159	.283
1975	MIL	A	S-3		109	.277
1976	MIL	A	S-3-O		117	.267
	BRTR				1054	.261

MONGE, ISIDRO PEDROZA "SID"
B.APR.11,1951 AGUA PREITA,MEXICO
1975	CAL	A	P		4	0- 2
1976	CAL	A	P		32	6- 7
	BBTL				36	6- 9

MONROE, EDWARD OLIVER
B.FEB.22,1894 LOUISVILLE,KY.
D.APR.29,1969 LOUISVILLE,KY.
1917	NY	A	P		9	1- 0
1918	NY	A	P		1	0- 0
	BRTR				10	1- 0

MONROE, FRANK
B.HAMILTON,OHIO
| 1884 | IND | AA | C | | 1 | .000 |

MONROE, JOHN ALLEN
B.AUG.24,1898 HOUSTON,TEX.
D.JUNE 19,1956
1921	NY	N	2		19	.143
	PHI	N	2		41	.286
	BLTR				60	.266

MONROE, LAWRENCE JAMES "LARRY"
B.JUNE 20,1956 DETROIT,MICH.
| 1976 | CHI | A | P | | 8 | 0- 1 |
| | BRTR | | | | | |

MONROE, ZACHARY CHARLES "ZACH"
B.JULY 8,1931 PEORIA,ILL.
1958	NY	A	P		21	4- 2
1959	NY	A	P		3	0- 0
	BRTR				24	4- 2

MONTAGUE, EDWARD FRANCIS
B.JUL.24,1906 SAN FRANCISCO,CAL
1928	CLE	A	S		32	.235
1930	CLE	A	S-3		58	.263
1931	CLE	A	S		64	.285
1932	CLE	A	S-3		66	.245
	BRTR				220	.262

MONTAGUE, JOHN EVANS
B.SEP.12,1947 NEWPORT NEWS,VA.
1973	MON	N	P		4	0- 0
1974	MON	N	P		46	3- 4
1975	MON	N	P	12	13	0- 1
	PHI	N	P		3	0- 0
	BRTR			65	66	3- 5

MONTANEZ, GUILLERMO "WILLIE"
B.APR.1,1948 CATANO,P.R.
1966	CAL	A	1		8	.000
1970	PHI	N	1-O		18	.240
1971	PHI	N	1-O		158	.255
1972	PHI	N	1-O		147	.247
1973	PHI	N	1-O		146	.263
1974	PHI	N	1-O		143	.304
1975	PHI	N	1		21	.286
	SF	N	1		135	.305
1976	SF	N	1		60	.309
	ATL	N	1		103	.321
	BLTL				939	.282

MONTEAGUDO, AURELIO FAUSTINO (CINTRA)
B.NOV.19,1943 CAIBARIEN,CUBA
1963	KC	A	P		4	0- 0
1964	KC	A	P		11	0- 4
1965	KC	A	P	4	5	0- 0
1966	KC	A	P		6	0- 0
	HOU	N	P		10	0- 0
1967	CHI	A	P		1	0- 1
1970	KC	A	P		21	1- 1
1973	CAL	A	P		15	2- 1
	BRTR			72	73	3- 7

MONTEAGUDO, RENE MIRANDA
B.OCT.12,1915 HAVANA,CUBA
D.SEPT.14,1973 HIALEAH,FLA.
1938	WAS	A	P		5	1 -1
1940	WAS	A	P		27	2- 6
1944	WAS	A	O		10	.289
1945	PHI	N	P-O	14	114	0- 0
						.301
	BLTL			46	156	3- 7
						.289

MONTEFUSCO, JOHN JOSEPH "JOHN" OR "COUNT"
B.MAY 25,1950 LONG BRANCH,N.J.
1974	SF	N	P		7	3- 2
1975	SF	N	P		35	15- 9
1976	SF	N	P	37	38	16-14
	BRTR			79	80	34-25

MONTEJO, MANUEL
B.OCT.16,1936 HAVANA,CUBA
| 1961 | DET | A | P | | 12 | 0- 0 |
| | BRTR | | | | | |

MONTEMAYOR, FELIPE ANGEL
B.FEB.7,1930 MONTERREY,MEXICO
1953	PIT	N	O		28	.109
1955	PIT	N	O		36	.211
	BLTL				64	.173

MONTGOMERY, ALVIN ATLAS
B.JULY 3,1920 LOVING,N.MEX.
D.APR.26,1942
| 1941 | BOS | N | C | | 42 | .192 |
| | BRTR | | | | | |

MONTGOMERY, MONTY BRYSON
B.SEP.1,1946 ALBERMARLE,N.C.
1971	KC	A	P		3	3- 0
1972	KC	A	P		9	3- 3
	BRTR				12	6- 3

MONTGOMERY, ROBERT EDWARD "BOB"
B.APR.16,1944 NASHVILLE,TENN.
1970	BOS	A	C		22	.179
1971	BOS	A	C		67	.239
1972	BOS	A	C		24	.286
1973	BOS	A	C		34	.320
1974	BOS	A	C		88	.252
1975	BOS	A	C-1		62	.226
1976	BOS	A	C		31	.247
	BRTR				328	.250

YR	CL	LEA	POS	GP	G	REC

MONTREUIL, ALLAN ARTHUR "AL"
B.AUG.23,1943 NEW ORLEANS,LA.
1972 CHI N 2   5   .091
     BRTR

MONZANT, RAMON (SEGUNDO)
B.JAN.4,1933 MARACAIBO,VENEZ.
1954 NY N P   6   0- 0
1955 NY N P   28 29   4- 8
1956 NY N P   4   6   1- 0
1957 NY N P   24   3- 2
1958 SF N P   43 44   8-11
1960 SF N P   1   0- 0
     BRTR   106 110 16-21

MONZON, DANIEL FRANCISCO "DAN"
B.MAY 17,1946 BRONX,N.Y.
1972 MIN A 2-S-3-0 55 .273
1973 MIN A 2-3-0   39 .224
     BRTR   94 .244

MOOCK, JOSEPH GEOFFREY "JOE"
B.MAR.12,1944 PLAQUEMINE,LA.
1967 NY N 3   13 .225
     BLTR

MOOLIC, GEORGE HENRY
B.1865 LAWRENCE,MASS.
D.FEB.19,1915
1886 CHI N C   15 .145

MOON, LEO
B.JUNE 22,1899 GRAHAM,N.C.
D.AUG.25,1970 NEW ORLEANS,LA.
1932 CLE A P   1   0- 0
     BRTL

MOON, WALLACE WADE "WALLY"
B.APR.3,1930 BAY,ARK.
1954 STL N O   151 .304
1955 STL N 1-O   152 .295
1956 STL N 1-O   149 .298
1957 STL N O   142 .295
1958 STL N O   108 .238
1959 LA N 1-O   145 .302
1960 LA N O   138 .299
1961 LA N O   134 .328
1962 LA N 1-O   95 .242
1963 LA N O   122 .262
1964 LA N O   68 .220
1965 LA N O   53 .202
     BLTR   1457 .289

MOONEY, JIM IRVING
B.SEPT.4,1906 MOORESBURG,TENN.
1931 NY N P   10   7- 1
1932 NY N P   29   6-10
1933 STL N P   21   2- 5
1934 STL N P   32   2- 4
     BRTL   92 17-20

MOORE, ALBERT JAMES
B.AUG.4,1902 BROOKLYN,N.Y.
D.NOV.29,1974 AT SEA N.Y.TO P.R
1925 NY N O   2   .125
1926 NY N O   28   .222
     BRTR   30   .213

MOORE, ALVIN EARL "JUNIOR"
B.JAN.25,1953 WASKOM,TEX.
1976 ATL N 2-3-O   20   .269
     BRTR

MOORE, ANSELM WINN
B.SEPT.22,1917 DELHI,LA.
1946 DET A O   51   .209
     BLTR

MOORE, ARCHIE FRANCIS
B.AUG.30,1941 UPPER DARBY,PA.
1964 NY A 1-O   31   .174
1965 NY A O   9   .412
     BLTR   40   .275

MOORE, BALOR LILBON
B.JAN.25,1951 SMITHVILLE,TEX.
1970 MON N P   6   0- 2
1972 MON N P   22   9- 9
1973 MON N P   35   7-16
1974 MON N P   8   0- 2
     BLTR   71 16-29

MOORE, CARLOS WITMAN
B.AUG.13,1907 CLINTON,TENN.
D.JULY 2,1958
1930 WAS A P   4   0- 0
     BRTR

MOORE, CHARLES WESLEY
B.DEC.1,1884 JACKSON CO.,IND.
1912 CHI N 2-3   5   .222

MOORE, CHARLES WILLIAM "CHARLIE"
B.JUNE 21,1953 BIRMINGHAM,ALA.
1973 MIL A C   8   .185
1974 MIL A C   72   .245
1975 MIL A C-O   73   .290
1976 MIL A C-3-O   87   .191
     BRTR   240   .240

MOORE, DEE CEE
B.APR.6,1914 AMARILLO,TEX.
1936 CIN N P-C 2   6   0- 0
                         .400
1937 CIN N C   7   .077
1943 BRO N C-3   37   .253
     PHI N C-1-3   37   .239
1946 PHI N C-1   11   .077
     BRTR   2 98   0- 0
                         .232

MOORE, DONNIE RAY
B.FEB.13,1954 LUBBOCK,TEX.
1975 CHI N P   4   0- 0
     BLTR

MOORE, EARL ALONZO "BIG EBBIE"
B.JULY 29,1879 PICKERINGTON,O.
D.NOV.28,1961
1901 CLE A P   31 16-14
1902 CLE A P   36 17-18
1903 CLE A P   29 22- 7
1904 CLE A P   26 13-11
1905 CLE A P   30 16-14
1906 CLE A P   5   1- 1
1907 CLE A P   3   0- 3
     NY A P   12   3- 4
1908 PHI N P   3   2- 1
1909 PHI N P   38 18-12
1910 PHI N P   46 22-15
1911 PHI N P   42 15-19
1912 PHI N P   31   9-14
1913 PHI N P   12   0- 0
     CHI N P   7   1- 1
1914 BUF F P   36 11-15
     BRTR   387 166-149

MOORE, EUEL WALTON "CHIEF"
B.MAY 27,1908 TISHOMINGO,OKLA.
1934 PHI N P   20   5- 7
1935 PHI N P   15   1- 6
     NY N P   6   1- 0
1936 PHI N P   20   2- 3
     BRTR   61   9-16

MOORE, EUGENE JR.
B.AUG.26,1909 LANCASTER,TEX.
1931 CIN N O   4   .143
1933 STL N O   11   .395
1934 STL N O   9   .278
1935 STL N H   3   .000
1936 BOS N O   151   .290
1937 BOS N O   148   .283
1938 BOS N O   54   .272
1939 BRO N O   107   .225
1940 BRO N O   10   .269
     BOS N O   103   .292
1941 BOS N O   129   .272
1942 WAS A O   1   .000
1943 WAS A 1-O   92   .268
1944 STL A 1-O   110   .238
1945 STL A O   110   .260
     BLTL   1042 .270

MOORE, EUGENE SR.
B.NOV.9,1885 LANCASTER,TEX.
D.AUG.31,1938
1909 PIT N P   1   0- 0
1910 PIT N P   4   2- 1
1912 CIN N P   5   0- 1
     BLTL   10   2- 2

MOORE, FERDINAND DEPAGE
B.FEB.21,1896 CAMDEN,N.J.
D.MAY 6,1947
1914 PHI A 1   2   .250

MOORE, GARY DOUGLAS
B.FEB.24,1945 TULSA,OKLA.
1970 LA N 1-O   7   .188
     BRTL

MOORE, GEORGE RAYMOND
B.NOV.25,1872 CAMBRIDGE,MASS.
D.NOV.7,1948 HYANNIS,MASS.
1905 PIT N P   1   0- 0
     BB

MOORE, GRAHAM EDWARD "EDDIE"
B.JAN.18,1899 BARLOW,KY.
D.FEB.10,1976 FT.MYERS,FLA.
1923 PIT N S   6   .269
1924 PIT N 2-3-O   72   .359
1925 PIT N 2-3-O 142   .298
1926 PIT N 2-S-3   43   .227
     BOS N 2-S-3   54   .266
1927 BOS N 2-3-O 112   .302
1928 BOS N O   68   .237
1929 BRO N 2-S   111   .296
1930 BRO N 2-S-O   76   .281
1932 NY N S   37   .264
1934 CLE A 2   27   .154
     BRTR   748   .285

MOORE, GUY W.
B.MAY 29,1899 PINE GROVE,PA.
D.JUNE 14,1957
1922 STL N O   1   .000
     BLTL

MOORE, HARRY S.
1884 WAS U O   107   .337

MOORE, JACKIE SPENCER
B.FEB.19,1939 JAY,FLA.
1965 DET A C   21   .094
     BRTR

MOORE, JAMES STANFORD
B.DEC.14,1903 PRESCOTT,ARK.
D.MAY 18,1973 SEATTLE,WASH.
1928 CLE A P   1   0- 1
1929 CLE A P   2   0- 0
1930 CHI A P   9   2- 1
1931 CHI A P   33   0- 2
1932 CHI A P   1   0- 0
     BRTR   46   2- 4

MOORE, JAMES WILLIAM
B.APR.24,1903 PARIS,TENN.
1930 CHI A O   16   .205
     PHI A O   15   .380
1931 PHI A O   49   .223
     BRTR   80   .254

MOORE, JEREMIAH S.
B.DETROIT,MICH.
1884 ALT U C-O   20   .298
     CLE N C   10   .235
1885 DET N C   5   .200
                    35   .266

MOORE, JOHN FRANCIS
B.MAR.23,1902 WATERVILLE,CONN.
1928 CHI N H   4   .000
1929 CHI N O   37   .286
1931 CHI N O   39   .240
1932 CHI N O   119   .305
1933 CIN N O   135   .263
1934 CIN N O   16   .190
     PHI N O   116   .365
1935 PHI N O   153   .323
1936 PHI N O   124   .328
1937 PHI N O   96   .319
1945 CHI N H   7   .167
     BLTR   846   .308

MOORE, JOSEPH GREGG "JO-JO"
B.DEC.25,1908 GAUSE,TEX.
1930 NY N O   3   .200
1931 NY N O   4   .250
1932 NY N O   86   .305
1933 NY N O   132   .292
1934 NY N O   139   .331
1935 NY N O   155   .295
1936 NY N O   152   .316
1937 NY N O   142   .310
1938 NY N O   125   .302
1939 NY N O   138   .269
1940 NY N O   138   .276
1941 NY N O   121   .273
     BLTR   1335 .298

YR	CL	LEA	POS	GP	G	REC

MOORE, LLOYD ALBERT "WHITEY"
B.JUNE 10,1912 TUSCARAWAS,OHIO

YR	CL	LEA	POS	GP	G	REC
1936	CIN	N	P		1	1- 0
1937	CIN	N	P		13	0- 3
1938	CIN	N	P		19	6- 4
1939	CIN	N	P		42	13-12
1940	CIN	N	P		25	8- 8
1941	CIN	N	P		23	2- 1
1942	CIN	N	P		1	0- 0
	STL	N	P		9	0- 1
		BRTR			133	30-29

MOORE, MAURICE
D.FEB.22,1881

YR	CL	LEA	POS	GP	G	REC
1875	ATL	NA	1-S-3		21	-

MOORE, RANDOLPH EDWARD "RANDY"
B.JUNE 21,1905 NAPLES,TEX.

YR	CL	LEA	POS	GP	G	REC
1927	CHI	A	O		6	.000
1928	CHI	A	O		24	.213
1930	BOS	N	O		83	.288
1931	BOS	N	3-O		83	.260
1932	BOS	N	1-3-O		107	.293
1933	BOS	N	1-O		135	.302
1934	BOS	N	1-O		123	.284
1935	BOS	N	1-O		125	.275
1936	BRO	N	O		42	.239
1937	BRO	N	C		13	.136
	STL	N	O		8	.000
		BLTR			749	.279

MOORE, RAYMOND LEROY "RAY"
B.JUNE 1,1926 MEADOWS,MD.

YR	CL	LEA	POS	GP	G	REC
1952	BRO	N	P		14	1- 2
1953	BRO	N	P		1	0- 0
1955	BAL	A	P		46	10-10
1956	BAL	A	P		32	12- 7
1957	BAL	A	P		34	11-13
1958	CHI	A	P		32	9- 7
1959	CHI	A	P		29	3- 6
1960	CHI	A	P		14	1- 1
	WAS	A	P		37	3- 2
1961	MIN	A	P		46	4- 4
1962	MIN	A	P		49	8- 3
1963	MIN	A	P		31	1- 3
		BRTR			365	63-59

MOORE, ROBERT BARRY "BARRY"
B.APR.3,1943 STATESVILLE,N.C.

YR	CL	LEA	POS	GP	G	REC
1965	WAS	A	P		1	0- 0
1966	WAS	A	P		12	3- 3
1967	WAS	A	P		27	7-11
1968	WAS	A	P	32	34	4- 6
1969	WAS	A	P	31	32	9- 8
1970	CLE	A	P		13	3- 5
	CHI	A	P		24	0- 4
		BLTL		140	143	26-37

MOORE, ROY DANIEL
B.OCT.26,1898 AUSTIN,TEX.

YR	CL	LEA	POS	GP	G	REC
1920	PHI	A	P	24	27	1-13
1921	PHI	A	P	29	33	10-10
1922	PHI	A	P		15	0- 3
	DET	A	P		9	0- 0
1923	DET	A	P	3	4	0- 0
		BBTL		80	86	11-26

MOORE, TERRY BUFORD
B.MAY 27,1912 MEMPHIS,TENN.

YR	CL	LEA	POS	GP	G	REC
1935	STL	N	O		119	.287
1936	STL	N	O		143	.264
1937	STL	N	O		115	.267
1938	STL	N	O		94	.272
1939	STL	N	P-O	1	130	0- 0
						.295
1940	STL	N	O		136	.304
1941	STL	N	O		122	.294
1942	STL	N	3-O		130	.288
1946	STL	N	O		91	.263
1947	STL	N	O		127	.283
1948	STL	N	O		91	.232
		BRTR		1	1298	0- 0
						.281

NON-PLAYING MANAGER PHI(N) 1954

MOORE, TOMMY JOE
B.JULY 7,1948 LYNWOOD,CAL.

YR	CL	LEA	POS	GP	G	REC
1972	NY	N	P		3	0- 0
1973	NY	N	P	3	4	0- 1
1975	STL	N	P		10	0- 0
	TEX	A	P	12	14	0- 2
		BRTR		28	31	0- 3

MOORE, WILLIAM ALLEN "SCRAPPY"
B.DEC.16,1892 ST.LOUIS,MO.
D.OCT.13,1964 LITTLE ROCK,ARK.

YR	CL	LEA	POS	GP	G	REC
1917	STL	A	3		4	.125
		BRTR				

MOORE, WILLIAM AUSTIN "CY"
B.FEB.7,1906 ELBERTON,GA.
D.MAR.28,1972 AUGUSTA,GA.

YR	CL	LEA	POS	GP	G	REC
1929	BRO	N	P		32	3- 3
1930	BRO	N	P		1	0- 0
1931	BRO	N	P		23	1- 2
1932	BRO	N	P	20	21	0- 3
1933	PHI	N	P		36	8- 9
1934	PHI	N	P		35	4- 9
		BRTR		147	148	16-26

MOORE, WILLIAM CHRISTOPHER
B.SEPT.3,1902 CORNING,N.Y.

YR	CL	LEA	POS	GP	G	REC
1925	DET	A	P		1	0- 0
		BRTR				

MOORE, WILLIAM HENRY "WILLIE"
B.DEC.12,1901 KANSAS CITY,MO.
D.MAY 24,1972 KANSAS CITY,MO.

YR	CL	LEA	POS	GP	G	REC
1926	BOS	A	C		5	.167
1927	BOS	A	C		44	.217
		BLTR			49	.207

MOORE, WILLIAM WILCY "CY"
B.MAY.20,1897 BONITA,TEX.
D.MAR.29,1963 HOLLIS,OKLA.

YR	CL	LEA	POS	GP	G	REC
1927	NY	A	P		50	19- 7
1928	NY	A	P		35	4- 4
1929	NY	A	P		41	6- 4
1931	BOS	A	P		53	11-13
1932	BOS	A	P		37	4-10
	NY	A	P		10	2- 0
1933	NY	A	P		35	5- 6
		BRTR			261	51-44

MOORHEAD, CHARLES ROBERT "BOB"
B.JAN.23,1938 CHAMBERSBURG,PA.

YR	CL	LEA	POS	GP	G	REC
1962	NY	N	P		38	0- 2
1965	NY	N	P		9	0- 1
		BRTR			47	0- 3

MOOSE, ROBERT RALPH "BOB"
B.OCT.9,1947 EXPORT,PA.
D.OCT.9,1976 MARTINS FERRY,OHIO

YR	CL	LEA	POS	GP	G	REC
1967	PIT	N	P		2	1- 0
1968	PIT	N	P		38	8-12
1969	PIT	N	P		44	14- 3
1970	PIT	N	P	28	29	11-10
1971	PIT	N	P		30	11- 7
1972	PIT	N	P	31	32	13-10
1973	PIT	N	P	33	37	12-13
1974	PIT	N	P		7	1- 5
1975	PIT	N	P		23	2- 2
1976	PIT	N	P		53	3- 9
		BRTR		289	295	76-71

MOOTY, JACOB T. "JAKE"
B.APR.13,1913 MILSAP,TEX.
D.APR.20,1970 FORT WORTH,TEX.

YR	CL	LEA	POS	GP	G	REC
1936	CIN	N	P		8	0- 0
1937	CIN	N	P	14	15	0- 3
1940	CHI	N	P	20	24	6- 6
1941	CHI	N	P		33	8- 9
1942	CHI	N	P		19	2- 5
1943	CHI	N	P		2	0- 0
1944	DET	A	P		15	0- 0
		BRTR		111	116	16-23

MORA, ANDRES (IBARRA)
B.MAY 25,1955 RIO BRAVO,MEX.

YR	CL	LEA	POS	GP	G	REC
1976	BAL	A	O-D		73	.218
		BRTR				

MORALES, JOSE MANUEL (HERNANDEZ)
B.DEC.30,1944 FREDERIKSTED,V.I.

YR	CL	LEA	POS	GP	G	REC
1973	OAK	A	H		6	.286
	MON	N	H		5	.400
1974	MON	N	C		25	.269
1975	MON	N	C-1-O		93	.301
1976	MON	N	C-1		104	.316
		BRTR			233	.306

MORALES, JULIO RUBEN "JERRY"
B.FEB.18,1949 YABUCAO,P.R.

YR	CL	LEA	POS	GP	G	REC
1969	SD	N	O		19	.195
1970	SD	N	O		28	.155
1971	SD	N	O		12	.118
1972	SD	N	3-O		115	.239
1973	SD	N	O		122	.281
1974	CHI	N	O		151	.273
1975	CHI	N	O		153	.270
1976	CHI	N	O		140	.274
		BRTR			740	.264

MORALES, RICHARD ANGELO "RICH"
B.SEP.20,1943 SAN FRANCISCO,CAL.

YR	CL	LEA	POS	GP	G	REC
1967	CHI	A	S		8	.000
1968	CHI	A	2-S		10	.172
1969	CHI	A	2-S-3		55	.215
1970	CHI	A	2-S-3		62	.161
1971	CHI	A	2-S-3-O		84	.243
1972	CHI	A	2-3		110	.206
1973	CHI	A	2-3		7	.000
	SD	N	2-S		90	.164
1974	SD	N	1-2-S-3		54	.197
		BRTR			480	.195

MORAN, ALBERT THOMAS "HIKER"
B.JUNE 15,1914 ROCHESTER,N.Y.

YR	CL	LEA	POS	GP	G	REC
1938	BOS	N	P		1	0- 0
1939	BOS	N	P		6	1- 1
		BRTR			7	1- 1

MORAN, CARL WILLIAM "BILL"
B.SEPT.26,1950 PORTSMOUTH,VA.

YR	CL	LEA	POS	GP	G	REC
1974	CHI	A	P		15	1- 3
		BRTR				

MORAN, CHARLES BARTHEL "UNCLE CHARLIE"
B.FEB.22,1879 NASHVILLE,TENN.
D.JUNE 13,1949

YR	CL	LEA	POS	GP	G	REC
1903	STL	N	P-S	3	4	0- 1
						.429
1908	STL	N	C		16	.175
		TR		3	20	0- 1
						.221

MORAN, CHARLES VINCENT
B.MAR.26,1879 WASHINGTON,D.C.
D.APR.11,1934

YR	CL	LEA	POS	GP	G	REC
1903	WAS	A	S		98	.232
1904	WAS	A	S		61	.209
	STL	A	3		81	.241
1905	STL	A	2		28	.195
		TR			268	.210

MORAN, HARRY EDWIN
B.APR.2,1889 THAYER,W.VA.
D.NOV.28,1962

YR	CL	LEA	POS	GP	G	REC
1912	DET	A	P		4	0- 2
1914	BUF	F	P		34	10- 7
1915	NEW	F	P		34	13- 9
		BLTL			72	23-18

MORAN, JOHN HERBERT "HERBIE"
B.FEB.16,1884 COSTELLO,PA.
D.SEPT.21,1954 CLARKSON,N.Y.

YR	CL	LEA	POS	GP	G	REC
1908	PHI	A	O		19	.153
	BOS	N	O		8	.266
1909	BOS	N	O		8	.233
1910	BOS	N	O		20	.119
1912	BRO	N	O		130	.276
1913	BRO	N	O		132	.266
1914	CIN	N	O		107	.235
	BOS	N	O		41	.266
1915	BOS	N	O		130	.200
		BLTR			595	.243

MORAN, PATRICK JOSEPH "PAT"
B.FEB.7,1876 FITCHBURG,MASS.
D.MAR.7,1924

YR	CL	LEA	POS	GP	G	REC
1901	BOS	N	C		53	.216
1902	BOS	N	C-1-O		72	.250
1903	BOS	N	C-3		108	.262
1904	BOS	N	C-3		111	.226
1905	BOS	N	C		78	.240
1906	CHI	N	C		61	.250
1907	CHI	N	C		59	.227
1908	CHI	N	C		45	.260
1909	CHI	N	C		74	.219
1910	PHI	N	C		56	.236
1911	PHI	N	C		32	.184
1912	PHI	N	C		13	.115
1913	PHI	N	C		1	.000
1914	PHI	N	C		1	.000
		TR			764	.236

NON-PLAYING MANAGER
PHI(N) 1915-18, CIN(N) 1919-23

YR	CL LEA POS	GP	G	REC

MORAN, RICHARD ALAN "AL"
B.DEC.5,1938 DETROIT,MICH.
1963	NY N S-3		119	.193
1964	NY N S-3		16	.227
	BRTR		135	.195

MORAN, ROY ELLIS
B.SEPT.17,1884 VINCENNES,IND.
D.JULY 1967
| 1912 | WAS A O | | 7 | .077 |
| | BRTR | | | |

MORAN, SAMUEL
B.SEPT.16,1870 ROCHESTER,N.Y.
D.AUG.29,1897
| 1895 | PIT N P | | 10 | 2- 5 |
| | TL | | | |

MORAN, WILLIAM L.
B.OCT.10,1869 JOLIET,ILL.
D.APR.8,1916
1892	STL N C		22	.153
1895	CHI N C		15	.163
			37	.157

MORAN, WILLIAM NELSON "BILLY"
B.NOV.27,1933 MONTGOMERY,ALA.
1958	CLE A 2-S		115	.226
1959	CLE A 2-S		11	.294
1961	LA A 2-S		54	.260
1962	LA A 2		160	.282
1963	LA A 2		153	.275
1964	LA A 2-S-3		50	.268
	CLE A 1-2-3		69	.205
1965	LA A 2-S		22	.125
	BRTR		634	.263

MOPE, FOREST T.
B.SEPT.30,1883 HAYDEN,IND.
1909	STL N P		15	1- 5
	BUS N P		10	1- 5
			25	2-10

MOREHART, RAYMOND ANDERSON
B.DEC.2,1899 KAUFMAN CO.,TEX.
1924	CHI A S		31	.200
1926	CHI A 2		73	.318
1927	NY A 2		73	.256
	BLTR		177	.269

MOREHEAD, DAVID MICHAEL "DAVE"
B.SEP.5,1942 SAN DIEGO,CAL.
1963	BOS A P		29	10-13
1964	BOS A P		32	8-15
1965	BOS A P		34	10-18
1966	BOS A P		12	1- 2
1967	BOS A P		10	5- 4
1968	BOS A P		11	1- 4
1969	KC A P		21	2- 3
1970	KC A P		28	3- 5
	BRTR		177	40-64

MOREHEAD, SETH MARVIN
B.AUG.15,1934 HOUSTON,TEX.
1957	PHI N P		34	1- 1
1958	PHI N P		27	1- 6
1959	PHI N P		3	0- 2
	CHI N P		11	0- 1
1960	CHI N P		45	2- 9
1961	MIL N P		12	1- 0
	BLTL		132	5-19

MOREJON, DANIEL TORRES "DANNY"
B.JULY 21,1930 HAVANA,CUBA
| 1958 | CIN N O | | 12 | .192 |
| | BRTR | | | |

MORELOCK, A. HARRY
B.PHILADELPHIA,PA.
1891	PHI N 3		4	.071
1892	PHI N 3		1	.000
			5	.059

MOREN, LEWIS HOWARD
B.AUG.4,1883 PITTSBURGH,PA.
D.NOV.2,1966 PITTSBURGH,PA.
1903	PIT N P		1	0- 1
1904	PIT N P		1	0- 0
1907	PHI N P		37	11-18
1908	PHI N P		28	8- 9
1909	PHI N P		40	16-15
1910	PHI N P		34	13-14
	TR		141	48-57

MORENO, JULIO GONZALES
B.JAN.28,1921 GUINES,CUBA
1950	WAS A P		4	1- 1
1951	WAS A P		31	5-11
1952	WAS A P		26	9- 9
1953	WAS A P		12	3- 1
	BRTR		73	18-22

MORENO, OMAR RENAN (QUINTERO)
B.OCT.24,1952 PUERTO ARMUELLES,
PANAMA
1975	PIT N O		6	.167
1976	PIT N O		48	.270
	BLTL		54	.266

MORESKONICH, CHARLES
(PLAYED UNDER NAME OF
CHARLES METRO)

MORET, ROGELIO (TORRES)
B.SEP.16,1949 GUAYAMA,P.R.
1970	BOS A P		3	1- 0
1971	BOS A P		13	4- 3
1972	BOS A P		3	0- 0
1973	BOS A P		30	13- 2
1974	BOS A P		31	9-10
1975	BOS A P	36	37	14- 3
1976	ATL N P		27	3- 5
	BBTL	143	144	44-23

MOREY, DAVID BEALE
B.FEB.25,1889 MALDEN,MASS.
| 1913 | PHI A P | | 2 | 0- 0 |
| | BLTR | | | |

MORGAN, CHESTER COLLINS "CHICK"
B.JUNE 6,1910 SKENE,MISS.
1935	DET A O		14	.174
1938	DET A O		74	.284
	BLTR		88	.277

MORGAN, CYRIL ARLON
B.DEC.11,1896 LAKEVILLE,MASS.
D.SEPT.11,1946
1921	BOS N P		17	1- 1
1922	BOS N P		2	0- 0
	BRTR		19	1- 1

MORGAN, EDWARD CARRE "ED"
B.MAY 22,1904 CAIRO,ILL.
1928	CLE A 1-3-O		76	.313
1929	CLE A O		93	.318
1930	CLE A 1 O		150	.350
1931	CLE A 1		131	.351
1932	CLE A 1		144	.293
1933	CLE A 1-O		39	.264
1934	BOS A 1		138	.267
	BRTR		771	.313

MORGAN, EDWIN WILLIS "PEPPER"
B.NOV.19,1914 BRADY LAKE,OHIO
1936	STL N O		8	.278
1937	BRO N O		31	.188
	BLTL		39	.212

MORGAN, HARRY RICHARD "CY"
B.NOV.10,1878 POMERY,OHIO
D.JUNE 28,1962
1903	STL A P		2	0- 2
1904	STL A P		8	0- 2
1905	STL A P		13	2- 6
1907	STL A P		13	2- 5
	BOS A P		13	6- 6
1908	BOS A P		30	13-14
1909	BOS A P		12	3- 9
	PHI A P		27	15- 8
1910	PHI A P		36	18-12
1911	PHI A P		38	15- 7
1912	PHI A P		16	3- 8
1913	CIN N P		1	0- 1
	BRTR		209	77-80

MORGAN, HENRY WILLIAM "BILL"
B.BROOKLYN,N.Y.
1875	RS NA P-3-	5	19	1- 4
				O	-
1878	MIL N 2-3-O		14	.175
1882	PIT AA C-O		16	.279
1883	PIT AA C-2-S-O		30	.167
1884	WAS AA C-2-S-O		44	.181
	RIC AA C-2-O		6	.100
	BAL U C-2-O		2	.250
		5	131	1- 4
					-

MORGAN, JAMES EDWARD "RED"
B.NEOLA,IOWA
DECEASED
| 1906 | BOS A 3 | | 88 | .215 |
| | TR | | | |

MORGAN, JOHN P.
| 1916 | PHI A 3 | | 1 | .250 |
| | TR | | | |

MORGAN, JOSEPH LEONARD "JOE"
B.SEP.19,1943 BONHAM,TEX.
1963	HOU N 2		8	.240
1964	HOU N 2		10	.189
1965	HOU N 2		157	.271
1966	HOU N 2		122	.285
1967	HOU N 2-O		133	.275
1968	HOU N 2-O		10	.250
1969	HOU N 2-O		147	.236
1970	HOU N 2		144	.268
1971	HOU N 2		160	.256
1972	CIN N 2		149	.292
1973	CIN N 2		157	.290
1974	CIN N 2		149	.293
1975	CIN N 2		146	.327
1976	CIN N 2		141	.320
	BLTR		1633	.281

MORGAN, JOSEPH MICHAEL "JOE"
B.NOV.19,1930 WALPOLE,MASS.
1959	MIL N 2		13	.217
	KC A 3		20	.190
1960	PHI N 3		26	.133
	CLE A 3-O		22	.298
1961	CLE A O		4	.200
1964	STL N H		3	.000
	BLTR		88	.193

MORGAN, RAYMOND CARYLL "RAY"
B.JUNE 14,1889 BALTIMORE,MD.
D.FEB.15,1940
1911	WAS A 3		25	.213
1912	WAS A 2		80	.238
1913	WAS A 2		137	.272
1914	WAS A 2		147	.257
1915	WAS A 2		62	.233
1916	WAS A 2		99	.267
1917	WAS A 2		101	.266
1918	WAS A 2		88	.233
	BRTR		739	.254

MORGAN, ROBERT MORRIS "BOBBY"
B.JUNE 29,1926 OKLAHOMA CITY,
OKLA.
1950	BRO N S-3		67	.226
1952	BRO N 2-S-3		67	.236
1953	BRO N S-3		69	.260
1954	PHI N 2-S-3		135	.262
1955	PHI N 1-2-S-3		136	.232
1956	PHI N 2-3		8	.200
	STL N 2-S-3		61	.195
1957	PHI N 2		2	.000
	CHI N 2-3		125	.207
1958	CHI N H		1	.000
	BRTR		671	.233

MORGAN, TOM STEPHEN
B.MAY 20,1930 EL MONTE,CAL.
1951	NY A P		27	9- 3
1952	NY A P		16	5- 4
1954	NY A P		32	11- 5
1955	NY A P		40	7- 3
1956	NY A P		41	6- 7
1957	KC A P		46	9- 7
1958	DET A P		39	2- 5
1959	DET A P		46	1- 4
1960	DET A P		22	3- 2
	WAS A P		14	1- 3
1961	LA A P		59	8- 2
1962	LA A P		48	5- 2
1963	LA A P		13	0- 0
	BRTR		443	67-47

MORGAN, VERNON THOMAS "VERN"
B.AUG.8,1928 EMPORIA,VA.
D.NOV.8,1975 MINNEAPOLIS,MINN.
1954	CHI N 3		24	.234
1955	CHI N 3		7	.143
	BLTR		31	.225

**MORHARDT, MEREDITH GOODWIN
"MOE"**
B.JAN.16,1937 MANCHESTER,CONN.
1961	CHI N 1		7	.278
1962	CHI N H		18	.125
	BLTL		25	.206

YR	CL	LEA	POS	GP	G	REC

MORIARTY, EDWARD JEROME
B.OCT.12,1912 HOLYOKE,MASS.

YR	CL	LEA	POS	GP	G	REC
1935	BOS	N	2		8	.324
1936	BOS	N	H		6	.167
	BRTR				14	.300

MORIARTY, EUGENE JOHN
B.HOLYOKE,MASS.

YR	CL	LEA	POS	GP	G	REC
1884	BOS	N	O		4	.063
	IND	AA	P-3	2	10	0- 2
			O			.216
1885	DET	N	P-S	1	11	0- 0
			3-0			.026
1892	STL	N	O		46	.175
	BL			3	71	0- 2
						.160

MORIARTY, GEORGE JOSEPH
B.JULY 7,1884 CHICAGO,ILL.
D.APR.8,1964 MIAMI,FLA.

YR	CL	LEA	POS	GP	G	REC
1903	CHI	N	3		1	.000
1904	CHI	N	3-0		5	.000
1906	NY	A	3		65	.234
1907	NY	A	1-3		126	.277
1908	NY	A	1-3		101	.236
1909	DET	A	3		133	.273
1910	DET	A	3		136	.251
1911	DET	A	3		130	.243
1912	DET	A	1-3		105	.248
1913	DET	A	3		102	.239
1914	DET	A	3		130	.254
1915	DET	A	3		31	.211
1916	CHI	A	3		7	.200
	TR				1072	.251

NON-PLAYING MANAGER
DET(A) 1927-28

MORIARTY, WILLIAM JOSEPH
B.1883 CHICAGO,ILL.
D.DEC.25,1916 ELGIN,ILL.

YR	CL	LEA	POS	GP	G	REC
1909	CIN	N	S		6	.250
	BRTR					

MORLAN, JOHN GLEN
B.NOV.22,1947 COLUMBUS,OHIO

YR	CL	LEA	POS	GP	G	REC
1973	PIT	N	P		10	2- 2
1974	PIT	N	P		39	0- 3
	BRTR				49	2- 5

MORLEY, WILLIAM M.
B.1890 PORT RICHMOND,S.I.,N.Y.

YR	CL	LEA	POS	GP	G	REC
1913	WAS	A	2		2	.000
	BRTR					

MORRELL, WILLARD BLACKMER
B.APR.9,1900 BOSTON,MASS.
D.AUG.5,1975 BRIMINGHAM,ALA.

YR	CL	LEA	POS	GP	G	REC
1926	WAS	A	P		26	3- 3
1930	NY	N	P		2	0- 0
1931	NY	N	P		20	5- 3
	BRTR				48	8- 6

MORRILL, JOHN FRANCIS
"HONEST JOHN"
B.FEB.19,1855 BOSTON,MASS.
D.APR.2,1932

YR	CL	LEA	POS	GP	G	REC
1876	BOS	N	C-2		66	.260
1877	BOS	N	1-2-3-0		61	.302
1878	BOS	N	1		60	.240
1879	BOS	N	1-3		84	.281
1880	BOS	N	P-1- 3	2	84	0- 0
						.240
1881	BOS	N	P-1- 2-3	1	80	0- 1
						.289
1882	BOS	N	M-P- 1-2-S-3- O	1	82	0- 0
						.289
1883	BOS	N	M-P- 1-2-S-3- O	1	97	1- 0
						.319
1884	BOS	N	M-P- 1-2-3	1	106	1- 0
						.265
1885	BOS	N	M-1-2-3		111	.225
1886	BOS	N	M-1-2-S		117	.246
1887	BOS	N	M-1		124	.331
1888	BOS	N	M-1		134	.197
1889	WAS	N	M-1		44	.185
1890	BOS	P	1-S		2	.143
	BRTR			6	1252	1- 1
						.264

MORRIS, DANNY WALKER
B.JUNE 11,1946 GREENVILLE,KY.

YR	CL	LEA	POS	GP	G	REC
1968	MIN	A	P		3	0- 1
1969	MIN	A	P		3	0- 1
	BRTR				6	0- 2

MORRIS, DOYT THEODORE
B.JULY 15,1916 STANLEY,N.C.

YR	CL	LEA	POS	GP	G	REC
1937	PHI	A	H		6	.154
	BRTR					

MORRIS, E.
B.TRENTON,N.J.

YR	CL	LEA	POS	GP	G	REC
1884	BAL	U	P-O		1	0- 0
						.000

MORRIS, EDWARD "CANNONBALL"
B.SEPT.29,1862 BROOKLYN,N.Y.
D.APR.12,1937

YR	CL	LEA	POS	GP	G	REC
1884	COL	AA	P	49	57	35-13
1885	PIT	AA	P		64	39-24
1886	PIT	AA	P		63	41-20
1887	PIT	N	P		37	14-22
1888	PIT	N	P		54	29-24
1889	PIT	N	P		21	7-14
1890	PIT	P	P		18	8- 6
	BRTL			306	314	173-123

MORRIS, EDWARD "BIG ED"
B.DEC.7,1899 FOSHEE,ALA.
D.MAR.3,1932

YR	CL	LEA	POS	GP	G	REC
1922	CHI	N	P		5	0- 0
1928	BOS	A	P		47	19-15
1929	BOS	A	P		33	14-14
1930	BOS	A	P		18	4- 9
1931	BOS	A	P		37	5- 7
	BRTR				140	42-45

MORRIS, JOHN WALLACE
B.AUG.23,1941 LEWES,DEL.

YR	CL	LEA	POS	GP	G	REC
1966	PHI	N	P		13	1- 1
1968	BAL	A	P		19	2- 0
1969	SEA	A	P		6	0- 0
1970	MIL	A	P		20	4- 3
1971	MIL	A	P		43	2- 2
1972	SF	N	P		7	0- 0
1973	SF	N	P		7	1- 0
1974	SF	N	P		17	1- 1
	BRTL				132	11- 7

MORRIS, JOHN WALTER "WALTER"
B.JAN.31,1880 ROCKWALL,TEX.
D.AUG.2,1961 DALLAS,TEX.

YR	CL	LEA	POS	GP	G	REC
1908	STL	N	S		23	.178
	BRTR					

MORRIS, JOSEPH "BUGS"
(PLAYED UNDER NAME OF
JOSEPH HARLEY BENNETT IN 1918)
B.APR.19,1892 WEIR CITY,KAN.
D.NOV.21,1957

YR	CL	LEA	POS	GP	G	REC
1918	STL	A	P		4	0- 2
1921	STL	A	P		4	0- 4
	STL	A	P		1	0- 0
	BRTR				9	0- 6

MORRIS, P.
B.ROCKFORD,ILL.

YR	CL	LEA	POS	GP	G	REC
1884	WAS	U	S		1	.000

MORRIS, WILLIAM G.
(SEE JOHN L. FLUHRER)

MORRISETTE, WILLIAM LEE
B.JAN.17,1893 BALTIMORE,MD.
D.MAR.25,1966 VIRGINIA BEACH,VA

YR	CL	LEA	POS	GP	G	REC
1915	PHI	A	P		4	2- 0
1916	PHI	A	P		1	0- 0
1920	DET	A	P		8	1- 1
	BRTR				13	3- 1

MORRISON, JOHN DEWEY
"JUGHANDLE JOHNNY"
B.OCT.22,1896 PELLVILLE,KY.
D.MAR.20,1966 LOUISVILLE,KY.

YR	CL	LEA	POS	GP	G	REC
1920	PIT	N	P		2	1- 0
1921	PIT	N	P		21	9- 7
1922	PIT	N	P		45	17-11
1923	PIT	N	P		42	25-13
1924	PIT	N	P		41	11-16
1925	PIT	N	P		44	17-14
1926	PIT	N	P		26	6- 8
1927	PIT	N	P		21	3- 2
1929	BRO	N	P		39	13- 7
1930	BRO	N	P		16	1- 2
	BRTR				297	103-80

MORRISON, JONATHAN W.
B.1859 PORT HURON,MICH.

YR	CL	LEA	POS	GP	G	REC
1884	IND	AA	O		43	.256
1887	MET	AA	O		9	.231
					52	.252

MORRISON, MICHAEL
B.FEB.6,1867 ERIE,PA.
D.JUNE 16,1955

YR	CL	LEA	POS	GP	G	REC
1887	CLE	AA	P		41	15-26
1888	CLE	AA	P		4	1- 3
1890	SYR	AA	P-O	15	32	7- 8
						.238
	BAL	AA	P		4	1- 3
	BRTR			64	81	24-40
						.234

MORRISON, PHILIP MELVIN
B.OCT.18,1894 OWENSBORO,KY.
D.JAN.18,1955

YR	CL	LEA	POS	GP	G	REC
1921	PIT	N	P		1	0- 0
	BBTR					

MORRISON, STEPHEN HENRY "HANK"
B.MAY 22,1866 OLNEYVILLE,R.I.
D.SEPT.30,1927

YR	CL	LEA	POS	GP	G	REC
1887	IND	N	P		8	3- 5
	BRTR					

MORRISON, THOMAS J.
B.1861

YR	CL	LEA	POS	GP	G	REC
1895	LOU	N	S-3		5	.272
1896	LOU	N	3		8	.107
					13	.208

MORRISON, WALTER GUY
B.AUG.29,1895 HINTON,W.VA.
D.AUG.14,1934

YR	CL	LEA	POS	GP	G	REC
1927	BOS	N	P		11	1- 2
1928	BOS	N	P		1	0- 0
	BRTR				12	1- 2

MORRISSEY, FRANK FREDERICK
"DEACON"
B.BALTIMORE,MD.

YR	CL	LEA	POS	GP	G	REC
1901	BOS	A	P		1	0- 0
1902	CHI	N	P-3	5	7	1- 3
						.090
				6	8	1- 3
						.080

MORRISSEY, JOHN ALBERT "KING"
B.MAY 2,1876 LANSING,MICH.
D.OCT.30,1936 LANSING,MICH.

YR	CL	LEA	POS	GP	G	REC
1902	CIN	N	2-0		12	.289
1903	CIN	N	2-S		27	.247
	BBTR				39	.254

MORRISSEY, JOHN H.
B.JANESVILLE,WIS.
D.APR.29,1884

YR	CL	LEA	POS	GP	G	REC
1881	BUF	N	3		12	.191
1882	DET	N	3		2	.286
					14	.204

MORRISSEY, JOSEPH ANSELM
"JO-JO"
B.JAN.16,1904 WARREN,R.I.
D.MAY 2,1950

YR	CL	LEA	POS	GP	G	REC
1932	CIN	N	2-S-3		89	.242
1933	CIN	N	2-S-3		148	.230
1936	CHI	A	2-S-3		17	.184
	BRTR				254	.232

MORRISSEY, THOMAS J.
B.1861 JANESVILLE,WIS.
D.SEPT.23,1941 JANESVILLE,WIS.

YR	CL	LEA	POS	GP	G	REC
1884	MIL	U	3		12	.174

MORROW, ROBERT
B.SEPT.27,1838 ENGLAND
D.FEB.6,1898
NON-PLAYING MANAGER PRO(N) 1881

MORSE, JACOB CHARLES
B.JUNE 7,1860 CONCORD,MASS.
D.APR.12,1937 BROOKLINE,MASS.
NON-PLAYING MANAGER BOS(U) 1884

MORSE, NEWELL OBEDIAH "BUD"
B.SEPT.4,1904 BERKELEY,CAL.

YR	CL	LEA	POS	GP	G	REC
1929	PHI	A	2		8	.074
	BLTR					

MORSE, PETER RAYMOND "PETE"
B.DEC.6,1886 ST.PAUL,MINN.
D.JUNE 19,1974 ST.PAUL,MINN.

YR	CL	LEA	POS	GP	G	REC
1911	STL	N	S-O		4	.000
	TR					

YR	CL	LEA	POS	GP	G	REC

MORTON, CARL WENDLE
B.JAN.18,1944 KANSAS CITY,MD.

YR	CL	LEA	POS	GP	G	REC
1969	MON	N	P		8	0- 3
1970	MON	N	P		43	18-11
1971	MON	N	P		36	10-18
1972	MON	N	P	27	35	7-13
1973	ATL	N	P	38	40	15-10
1974	ATL	N	P		38	16-12
1975	ATL	N	P		39	17-16
1976	ATL	N	P	26	27	4- 9
	BRTR			255	266	87-92

MORTON, CHARLES HAZEN
B.OCT.12,1854 KINGSVILLE,OHIO
D.DEC.9,1921 MASSILLON,OHIO

1882	PIT	AA	2-S-3-O	23		.278
	STL	AA	2-O	9		.059
1884	TOL	AA	M-P-	1	31	0- 1
			3-O			.188
1885	DET	N	M-S-3	22		.177
	TR			1	85	0- 1
						.199

MORTON, GUY JR. "MOOSE"
B.NOV.4,1930 TUSCALOOSA,ALA.

1954	BOS	A	H		1	.000
	BRTR					

MORTON, GUY SR.
B.JUNE 1,1893 VERNON,ALA.
D.OCT.18,1934

1914	CLE	A	P		25	1-13
1915	CLE	A	P		54	15-15
1916	CLE	A	P		27	12- 8
1917	CLE	A	P		35	10-10
1918	CLE	A	P		30	14- 8
1919	CLE	A	P		26	9- 9
1920	CLE	A	P		29	8- 6
1921	CLE	A	P		30	8- 3
1922	CLE	A	P		38	14- 9
1923	CLE	A	P		32	6- 6
1924	CLE	A	P		10	0- 1
	BRTR				317	97-88

MORTON, WILLIAM H. "SPARROW"

1884	PHI	N	P		2	0- 2
	TL					

MORTON, WYCLIFFE NATHANIEL "BUBBA"
B.DEC.13,1931 WASHINGTON,D.C.

1961	DET	A	O		77	.287
1962	DET	A	1-O		90	.262
1963	DET	A	1-O		6	.091
	MIL	N	1-O		15	.179
1966	CAL	A	O		15	.220
1967	CAL	A	O		80	.313
1968	CAL	A	3-O		81	.270
1969	CAL	A	1-O		87	.244
	BRTR				451	.267

MORYN, WALTER JOSEPH "WALT"
B.APR.12,1926 ST.PAUL,MINN.

1954	BRO	N	O		48	.275
1955	BRO	N	O		11	.263
1956	CHI	N	O		147	.285
1957	CHI	N	O		149	.289
1958	CHI	N	O		143	.264
1959	CHI	N	O		117	.234
1960	CHI	N	O		38	.294
	STL	N	O		75	.245
1961	STL	N	O		17	.125
	PIT	N	O		40	.200
	BLTR				785	.266

MOSCHITTO, ROSS ALLEN
B.FEB.15,1945 FRESNO,CAL.

1965	NY	A	O		96	.185
1967	NY	A	O		14	.111
	BRTR				110	.167

MOSELY, EARL VICTOR "VIC"
B.SEPT.7,1884 MIDDLEBURY,OHIO
D.JULY 1,1963 ALLIANCE,OHIO

1913	BOS	A	P		24	9- 5
1914	IND	F	P		43	19-18
1915	NEW	F	P		38	15-15
1916	CIN	N	P		31	7-10
	BRTR				136	50-48

MOSER, ARNOLD ROBERT
B.AUG.9,1915 HOUSTON,TEX.

1937	CIN	N	H		5	.000
	BRTR					

MOSER, WALTER FREDRICK
B.FEB.27,1881 CONCORD,N.C.
D.DEC.10,1946 PHILADELPHIA,PA.

1906	PHI	N	P		6	0- 3
1911	BOS	A	P		6	0- 1
	STL	A	P		2	0- 1
	BRTR				14	0- 5

MOSES, FELIX I.
B.RICHMOND,VA.
NON-PLAYING MANAGER RIC(AA)1884

MOSES, GERALD BRAHEEN "JERRY"
B.AUG.9,1946 YAZOO CITY,MISS.

1965	BOS	A	H		4	.250
1968	BOS	A	C		6	.333
1969	BOS	A	C		53	.304
1970	BOS	A	C-O		92	.263
1971	CAL	A	C-O		69	.227
1972	CAL	A	C-1		52	.220
1973	NY	A	C		20	.254
1974	DET	A	C		74	.237
1975	SD	N	C		13	.158
	CHI	A	1		2	.500
	BRTR				385	.251

MOSES, WALLACE "WALLY"
B.OCT.8,1910 UVALDA,GA.

1935	PHI	A	O		85	.325
1936	PHI	A	O		146	.345
1937	PHI	A	O		154	.320
1938	PHI	A	O		142	.307
1939	PHI	A	O		115	.307
1940	PHI	A	O		142	.309
1941	PHI	A	O		116	.301
1942	CHI	A	O		144	.270
1943	CHI	A	O		150	.245
1944	CHI	A	O		136	.280
1945	CHI	A	O		140	.295
1946	CHI	A	O		56	.274
	BOS	A	O		48	.206
1947	BOS	A	O		90	.275
1948	BOS	A	O		78	.259
1949	PHI	A	O		110	.276
1950	PHI	A	O		88	.264
1951	PHI	A	O		70	.191
	BLTL				2012	.291

MOSKIMAN, WILLIAM BANKHEAD
B.DEC.20,1879 OAKLAND,CAL.
D.JAN.11,1953 SAN LEANDRO,CAL.

1910	BOS	A	P-1-	1	5	0- 0
			O			.111
	BRTR					

MOSOLF, JAMES FREDRICK
B.AUG.21,1907 PULLYAP,WASH.

1929	PIT	N	O		8	.462
1930	PIT	N	P-O	1	40	0- 0
						.333
1931	PIT	N	O		39	.250
1933	CHI	N	O		31	.268
	BLTR			1	118	0- 0
						.295

MOSS, CHARLES CROSBY
B.MAR.20,1911 MERIDIAN,MISS.

1934	PHI	A	C		10	.200
1935	PHI	A	C		4	.333
1936	PHI	A	C		33	.250
	BRTR				47	.246

MOSS, CHARLES MALCOLM "MAL"
B.APR.18,1905 SULLIVAN,IND.

1930	CHI	N	P		12	0- 0
	BRTL					

MOSS, HOWARD GLENN
B.OCT.17,1918 GASTONIA,N.C.

1942	NY	N	O		7	.000
1946	CIN	N	O		7	.192
	CLE	A	3		8	.063
	BRTR				22	.097

MOSS, JOHN LESTER "LES"
B.MAY 14,1925 TULSA,OKLA.

1946	STL	A	C		12	.371
1947	STL	A	C		96	.157
1948	STL	A	C		107	.257
1949	STL	A	C		97	.291
1950	STL	A	C		84	.266
1951	STL	A	C		16	.170
	BOS	A	C		71	.198
1952	STL	A	C		52	.246
1953	STL	A	C		78	.276
1954	BAL	A	C		50	.246
1955	BAL	A	C		29	.339
	CHI	A	C		32	.254
1956	CHI	A	C		56	.244
1957	CHI	A	C		42	.270
1958	CHI	A	H		2	.000
	BRTR				824	.247

NON-PLAYING MANAGER
CHI(A) 1968 (INTERIM)

MOSS, RAYMOND EARL
B.DEC.5,1902 CHATTANOOGA,TENN.

1926	BRO	N	P		1	0- 0
1927	BRO	N	P		1	1- 0
1928	BRO	N	P	22	24	0- 3
1929	BRO	N	P	39	42	11- 6
1930	BRO	N	P		36	9- 6
1931	BRO	N	P		1	0- 0
	BOS	N	P		12	1- 3
	BRTR			112	117	22-18

MOSSI, DONALD LOUIS "DON"
B.JAN.11,1929 ST.HELENA,CAL.

1954	CLE	A	P		40	6- 1
1955	CLE	A	P		57	4- 3
1956	CLE	A	P		48	6- 5
1957	CLE	A	P		36	11-10
1958	CLE	A	P		43	7- 8
1959	DET	A	P	34	36	17- 9
1960	DET	A	P		23	9- 8
1961	DET	A	P		35	15- 7
1962	DET	A	P	35	36	11-13
1963	DET	A	P		24	7- 7
1964	CHI	A	P		34	3- 1
1965	KC	A	P		51	5- 8
	BLTL			460	463	101-80

MOSSOR, EARL DALTON
B.JULY 21,1925 FORBES,TENN.

1951	BRO	N	P		3	0- 0
	BLTR					

MOSTIL, JOHN ANTHONY "JOHNNY"
B.JUNE 1,1896 CHICAGO,ILL.
D.DEC.10,1970 MIDLOTHIAN,ILL.

1918	CHI	A	2		10	.273
1921	CHI	A	O		100	.301
1922	CHI	A	O		132	.304
1923	CHI	A	O		153	.291
1924	CHI	A	O		118	.325
1925	CHI	A	O		153	.299
1926	CHI	A	O		148	.328
1927	CHI	A	O		13	.125
1928	CHI	A	O		133	.270
1929	CHI	A	O		12	.229
	BRTR				972	.301

MOTA, MANUEL RAFAEL (GERONIMO) "MANNY"
B.FEB.18,1938 SANTO DOMINGO,D.R.

1962	SF	N	2-3-O		47	.176
1963	PIT	N	2-O		59	.270
1964	PIT	N	2-3-O		115	.277
1965	PIT	N	O		121	.279
1966	PIT	N	3-O		116	.332
1967	PIT	N	3-O		120	.321
1968	PIT	N	2-3-O		111	.281
1969	MON	N	O		31	.315
	LA	N	O		85	.323
1970	LA	N	3-O		124	.305
1971	LA	N	O		91	.312
1972	LA	N	O		118	.323
1973	LA	N	O		89	.314
1974	LA	N	O		66	.281
1975	LA	N	O		52	.265
1976	LA	N	O		50	.288
	BRTR				1395	.302

MOTT, ELISHA MATTHEW "BITSY"
B.JUNE 12,1920 ARCADIA,FLA.

1945	PHI	N	2-S-3		90	.222
	BRTR					

YR	CL	LEA	POS	GP	G	REC

MOTTON, CURTELL HOWARD "CURT"
B.SEP.24,1940 DARNELL,LA.

YR	CL	LEA	POS	GP	G	REC
1967	BAL	A	O		27	.200
1968	BAL	A	O		83	.198
1969	BAL	A	O		56	.303
1970	BAL	A	O		52	.226
1971	BAL	A	O		38	.189
1972	MIL	A	O		6	.167
	CAL	A	O		42	.154
1973	BAL	A	O		5	.333
1974	BAL	A	O		7	.000
		BRTR			316	.213

MOTZ, FRANK H.
B.OCT.1,1869 FREEBURG,PA.

1890	PHI	N	1		1	.000
1893	CIN	N	1		42	.267
1894	CIN	N	1		18	.204
					61	.244

MOULDER, GLEN HUBERT
B.SEPT.28,1917 CLEVELAND,OKLA.

1946	BRO	N	P		1	0- 0
1947	STL	A	P		32	4- 2
1948	CHI	A	P		33	3- 6
		BRTR			66	7- 8

MOULTON, ALBERT THEODORE "OLLIE"
B.JAN.16,1886 MEDWAY,MASS.

| 1911 | STL | A | 2 | | 4 | .067 |
| | | BRTR | | | | |

MOUNTAIN, FRANK H.
B.MAY 17,1860 FT.EDWARD,N.Y.
D.NOV.19,1939

1880	TRO	N	P		2	1- 1
1881	DET	N	P		7	3- 4
1882	WOR	N	P		5	0- 5
	ATH	AA	P-O	8	9	2- 6
						.308
	WOR	N	P-1-	18	20	2-11
			O			2.16
						.264
1883	COL	AA	P-O	60	71	26-33
						2.16
						.237
1884	COL	AA	P-O	43	58	24-17
						.237
1885	PIT	AA	P		5	1- 4
1886	PIT	AA	P-1	2	18	0- 2
						.148
		TR		150	195	59-83
						.221

MOUNTJOY, WILLIAM R. "MEDICINE BILL"
B.1857 PORT HURON,MICH.
D.MAY 19,1934

1883	CIN	AA	P		1	0- 1
1884	CIN	AA	P-O	32	34	20-12
						.171
1885	CIN	AA	P		17	10- 7
	BAL	AA	P-O	6	7	2- 4
						.063
				56	59	32-24
						.157

MOWE, RAYMOND BENJAMIN
B.JULY 12,1891 ROCHESTER,IND.
D.AUG.14,1968 SARASOTA,FLA.

| 1913 | BRO | N | S | | 5 | .111 |
| | | BLTR | | | | |

MOWREY, HARRY HARLAN "MIKE"
B.MAR.24,1883 CHAMBERSBURG,PA.
D.MAR.20,1947

1905	CIN	N	3		7	.266
1906	CIN	N	3		17	.321
1907	CIN	N	3		138	.252
1908	CIN	N	3		63	.220
1909	CIN	N	3		35	.191
	STL	N	3		8	.241
1910	STL	N	3		141	.282
1911	STL	N	3		135	.267
1912	STL	N	3		114	.255
1913	STL	N	3		132	.260
1914	PIT	N	3		79	.254
1915	PIT	F	3		151	.282
1916	BRO	N	3		144	.244
1917	BRO	N	3		83	.214
		BRTR			1247	.251

MOWRY, JOSEPH ALOYSIUS
B.APR.6,1908 ST.LOUIS,MO.

1933	BOS	N	O		86	.221
1934	BOS	N	O		25	.215
1935	BOS	N	O		81	.265
		BBTR			192	.233

MOYER, CHARLES EDWARD
B.AUG.15,1885 ANDOVER,OHIO

| 1910 | WAS | A | P | | 6 | 0- 3 |

MOYNAHAN, MICHAEL
B.1860 CHICAGO,ILL.

1880	BUF	N	S		27	.296
1881	CLE	N	3-O		33	.223
	DET	N	3		2	.333
1883	ATH	AA	S		93	.283
1884	ATH	AA	S		1	.000
	CLE	N	2-S-O		12	.304
	BL				168	.285

MROZINSKI, RONALD FRANK "RON"
B.SEPT.16,1930 WHITE HAVEN,PA.

1954	PHI	N	P		15	1- 1
1955	PHI	N	P		22	0- 2
		BRTL			37	1- 3

MUDROCK, PHILIP RAY "PHIL"
B.JUNE 12,1937 LOUISVILLE,COLO.

| 1963 | CHI | N | P | | 1 | 0- 0 |
| | | BRTR | | | | |

MUELLER, CLARENCE FRANKLIN "HEINE"
B.SEPT.16,1899 CREVE COEUR,MO.
D.JAN.23,1975 DE SOTO,MO.

1920	STL	N	O		4	.318
1921	STL	N	O		55	.352
1922	STL	N	O		61	.270
1923	STL	N	O		78	.343
1924	STL	N	1-O		92	.264
1925	STL	N	O		78	.313
1926	STL	N	O		52	.267
	NY	N	O		85	.249
1927	NY	N	O		84	.289
1928	BOS	N	O		42	.225
1929	BOS	N	O		46	.204
1935	STL	A	1-O		16	.185
		BLTL			693	.282

MUELLER, DONALD FREDERICK "DON"
B.APR.14,1927 CREVE COEUR,MO.

1948	NY	N	O		36	.358
1949	NY	N	O		51	.232
1950	NY	N	O		132	.291
1951	NY	N	O		122	.277
1952	NY	N	O		126	.281
1953	NY	N	O		131	.333
1954	NY	N	O		153	.342
1955	NY	N	O		147	.306
1956	NY	N	O		138	.269
1957	NY	N	O		135	.258
1958	CHI	A	O		70	.253
1959	CHI	A	H		4	.500
		BLTR			1245	.296

MUELLER, EMMETT JOSEPH
B.JULY 20,1912 ST.LOUIS,MO.

1938	PHI	N	2-3		136	.250
1939	PHI	N	2-3-O		115	.279
1940	PHI	N	1-2-3-O		97	.247
1941	PHI	N	2-3-O		93	.227
		BBTR			441	.253

MUELLER, JOSEPH GORDON "GORDIE"
B.DEC.10,1922 BALTIMORE,MD.

| 1950 | BOS | A | P | | 8 | 0- 0 |
| | | BRTR | | | | |

MUELLER, LESLIE CLYDE
B.MAR.4,1919 BELLEVILLE,ILL.

1941	DET	A	P		4	0- 0
1945	DET	A	P		26	6- 8
		BRTR			30	6- 8

MUELLER, RAY COLEMAN "RAY" OR "IRON MAN"
B.MAR.8,1912 PITTSBURG,KAN.

1935	BOS	N	C		42	.227
1936	BOS	N	C		24	.197
1937	BOS	N	C		64	.251
1938	BOS	N	C		83	.237
1939	PIT	N	C		86	.233
1940	PIT	N	C		4	.333
1943	CIN	N	C		141	.260
1944	CIN	N	C		155	.286
1946	CIN	N	C		114	.254
1947	CIN	N	C		71	.250
1948	CIN	N	C		14	.206
1949	CIN	N	C		32	.274
	NY	N	C		56	.224
1950	NY	N	C		4	.091
	PIT	N	C		67	.269
1951	BOS	N	C		28	.157
		BRTR			985	.252

MUELLER, WALTER JOHN
B.DEC.6,1894 CENTRAL,MO.
D.AUG.16,1971 ST.LOUIS,MO.

1922	PIT	N	O		32	.270
1923	PIT	N	O		40	.306
1924	PIT	N	O		30	.260
1926	PIT	N	O		19	.242
		BRTR			121	.275

MUELLER, WILLIAM LAWRENCE
B.NOV.9,1920 BAY CITY,MICH.

1942	CHI	A	O		26	.165
	CHI	A	O		13	.000
		BRTR			39	.149

MUFFETT, BILLY ARNOLD
B.SEPT.21,1930 HAMMOND,IND.

1957	STL	N	P		23	3- 2
1958	STL	N	P		35	4- 6
1959	SF	N	P		5	0- 0
1960	BOS	A	P		23	6- 4
1961	BOS	A	P		38	3-11
1962	BOS	A	P		1	0- 0
		BRTR			125	16-23

MUICH, IGNATIUS ANDREW "JOE"
B.NOV.27,1904 ST.LOUIS,MO.

| 1924 | BOS | N | P | | 3 | 0- 0 |
| | | BRTR | | | | |

MUIR, JOSEPH ALLEN
B.NOV.26,1922 ORIOLE,MD.

1951	PIT	N	P		9	0- 2
1952	PIT	N	P		12	2- 3
		BLTL			21	2- 5

MULCAHY, HUGH NOYES
B.SEPT.9,1913 BRIGHTON,MASS.

1935	PHI	N	P-O	18	19	1- 5
						.000
1936	PHI	N	P		3	1- 1
1937	PHI	N	P		56	8-18
1938	PHI	N	P	46	47	10-20
1939	PHI	N	P		38	9-16
1940	PHI	N	P	36	37	13-22
1945	PHI	N	P		5	1- 3
1946	PHI	N	P		16	2- 4
1947	PIT	N	P		2	0- 0
		BRTR		220	223	45-89
						.165

MULDOON, MICHAEL
B.HARTFORD,CONN.

1882	CLE	N	O		82	.252
1883	CLE	N	3		95	.224
1884	CLE	N	2-3-O		109	.239
1885	BAL	AA	3		103	.250
1886	BAL	AA	2-3		101	.205
					490	.235

YR	CL	LEA	POS	GP	G	REC

MULLANE, ANTHONY JOHN
"TONY" OR "COUNT"
B.JAN.30,1859 CORK,IRELAND
D.APR.26,1944 CHICAGO,ILL.

YR	CL	LEA	POS	GP	G	REC
1881	DET	N	P		5	1- 4
1882	LOU	AA	P-1-	55	77	31-23
			2-0			.255
1883	STL	AA	P-1-	52	77	35-17
			2-0			.201
1884	TOL	AA	P-1-	66	95	36-26
			0			.276
1886	CIN	AA	P-1-	71	103	31-27
			2-S-0			.228
1887	CIN	AA	P-0	51	61	31-17
						.284
1888	CIN	AA	P-1-	44	51	27-16
			2-0			.251
1889	CIN	AA	P-1-	29	62	11- 8
			3-0			.307
1890	CIN	N	P-3-	22	81	12-10
			0			.276
1891	CIN	N	P	49	61	24-23
1892	CIN	N	P		34	20-14
1893	CIN	N	P		27	7- 7
	BAL	N	P		27	12-15
1894	BAL	N	P		14	7- 6
	CLE	N	P		8	2- 1
	BBTB			554	783	287-214
						.250

BL 1882

MULLEAVY, GREGORY THOMAS "MOE"
B.SEPT.25,1905 DETROIT,MICH.

1930	CHI	A	S		77	.263
1932	CHI	A	2		1	.000
1933	BOS	A	H		1	.000
	BRTR				79	.260

MULLEN

1872	CLE	NA	0		1	.667

MULLEN, CHARLES GEORGE
B.MAR.15,1890 SEATTLE,WASH.
D.JUNE 6,1963 SEATTLE,WASH.

1910	CHI	A	1		41	.195
1911	CHI	A	1		20	.203
1914	NY	A	1		93	.260
1915	NY	A	1		40	.267
1916	NY	A	1-2		59	.247
	BRTR				253	.247

MULLEN, FORD PARKER "MOON"
B.FEB.9,1917 OLYMPIA,WASH.

1944	PHI	N	2-3		118	.267
	BLTR					

MULLEN, WILLIAM JOHN "BILLY"
B.JAN.23,1896 ST.LOUIS,MO.
D.MAY 4,1971 ST.LOUIS,MO.

1920	STL	A	2		2	.000
1921	STL	A	3		4	.000
1923	BRO	N	3		4	.273
1926	DET	A	3		11	.077
1928	STL	A	3		15	.389
	BRTR				36	.220

MULLER

1874	ATH	NA	C		4	-
1876	ATH	N	C		1	.000
	BLTL				5	-

MULLER, FREDERICK WILLIAM
B.DEC.21,1907 NEWARK,CAL.

1933	BOS	A	2		15	.188
1934	BOS	A	2-3		2	.000
	BRTR				17	.184

MULLIGAN

1884	WAS	U	3		1	.000

MULLIGAN, EDWARD JOSEPH
B.AUG.27,1894 ST.LOUIS,MO.

1915	CHI	N	S-3		11	.363
1916	CHI	N	S		58	.153
1921	CHI	A	3		152	.251
1922	CHI	A	3		103	.234
1928	PIT	N	2-3		27	.233
	BRTR				351	.232

MULLIGAN, JOSEPH IGNATIUS
B.JULY 31,1913 E.WEYMOUTH,MASS.

1934	BOS	A	P		14	1- 0
	BRTR					

MULLIGAN, RICHARD CHARLES
B.MAR.18,1918 WILKES-BARRE,PA.

1941	WAS	A	P		1	0- 1
1946	PHI	N	P		19	2- 2
	BOS	N	P		4	1- 0
1947	BOS	N	P		1	0- 0
	BLTL				25	3- 3

MULLIN, GEORGE JOSEPH "WABASH"
B.JULY 4,1880 TOLEDO,OHIO
D.JAN.7,1944 WABASH,IND.

1902	DET	A	P-0	33	37	14-15
						.328
1903	DET	A	P	40	46	19-14
1904	DET	A	P	45	52	16-24
1905	DET	A	P	44	47	22-18
1906	DET	A	P-2	40	50	21-18
			0			.225
1907	DET	A	P-1	47	70	20-20
						.217
1908	DET	A	P	38	55	17-12
1909	DET	A	P	40	52	29- 8
1910	DET	A	P	38	50	21-12
1911	DET	A	P	30	40	18-10
1912	DET	A	P	30	37	12-17
1913	DET	A	P		12	2- 7
	WAS	A	P	6	12	2- 4
1914	IND	F	P	36	40	14-10
1915	NEW	F	P		6	2- 2
	BRTR			485	606	229-191
						.262

MULLIN, HENRY
B.S.BOSTON,MASS.

1884	WAS	AA	0		34	.139
	BOS	U	0		2	.000
					36	.131

MULLIN, JAMES HENRY
B.OCT.16,1883 NEW YORK,N.Y.
D.JAN.24,1925

1904	PHI	A	1		26	.415
	WAS	A	2		26	.168
	PHI	A	2		17	.157
1905	WAS	A	2		49	.190
	TR				118	.197

MULLIN, PATRICK JOSEPH "PAT"
B.NOV.1,1917 TROTTER,PA.

1940	DET	A	0		4	.000
1941	DET	A	0		54	.345
1946	DET	A	0		93	.246
1947	DET	A	0		116	.256
1948	DET	A	0		138	.288
1949	DET	A	0		104	.268
1950	DET	A	0		69	.218
1951	DET	A	0		110	.281
1952	DET	A	0		97	.251
1953	DET	A	0		79	.268
	BLTR				864	.271

MULRENNAN, DOMINICK JOSEPH
B.DEC.18,1894 WOBURN,MASS.
D.JULY 27,1964 MELROSE,MASS.

1921	CHI	A	P		12	2- 8
	TR					

MULRONEY, FRANCIS JOSEPH
B.APR.8,1906 MALLARD,IOWA

1930	BOS	A	P		2	0- 1
	BRTR					

MULVEY, JOSEPH H.
B.OCT.27,1858 PROVIDENCE,R.I.
D.AUG.21,1928

1883	PRO	N	2-S		4	.053
	PHI	N	3		3	.500
1884	PHI	N	3		99	.229
1885	PHI	N	3		106	.268
1886	PHI	N	3		105	.267
1887	PHI	N	3		109	.317
1888	PHI	N	3		99	.215
1889	PHI	N	3		129	.288
1890	PHI	P	3		120	.291
1891	ATH	AA	3		112	.247
1892	PHI	N	3		25	.142
1893	WAS	N	3		55	.242
1895	BRO	N	3		13	.327
	BRTR				979	.266

MUMPHREY, JERRY WAYNE
B.SEPT.9,1952 TYLER,TEX.

1974	STL	N	0		5	.000
1975	STL	N	0		11	.375
1976	STL	N	0		112	.258
	BBTR				128	.261

MUNCE, JOHN "BIG JOHN"
B.PHILADELPHIA,PA.

1884	WIL	U	0		7	.190

MUNCH, JACOB FERDINAND
B.NOV.18,1890 MORTON,PA.
D.JUNE 8,1966 LANSDOWNE,PA.

1918	PHI	A	1		22	.267
	BLTL					

MUNCRIEF, ROBERT CLEVELAND
"BOB"
B.JAN.28,1916 MADILL,OKLA.

1937	STL	A	P		1	0- 0
1939	STL	A	P		2	0- 0
1941	STL	A	P		36	13- 9
1942	STL	A	P		24	6- 8
1943	STL	A	P		35	13-12
1944	STL	A	P		33	13- 8
1945	STL	A	P	27	28	13- 4
1946	STL	A	P		29	3-12
1947	STL	A	P		31	8-14
1948	CLE	A	P		21	5- 4
1949	PIT	N	P		13	1- 5
	CHI	N	P		34	5- 6
1951	NY	A	P		2	0- 0
	BRTR			288	289	80-82

MUNDINGER, GEORGE
B.NEW ORLEANS,LA.

1884	IND	AA	C		3	.200

MUNDY, WILLIAM EDWARD
B.JUNE 28,1889 SALINEVILLE,OHIO
D.SEPT.23,1958

1913	BOS	A	1		17	.255
	BLTL					

MUNGER, GEORGE DAVID "RED"
B.OCT.4,1918 HOUSTON,TEX.

1943	STL	N	P		32	9- 5
1944	STL	N	P		21	11- 3
1946	STL	N	P		10	2- 2
1947	STL	N	P		40	16- 5
1948	STL	N	P		39	10-11
1949	STL	N	P		35	15- 8
1950	STL	N	P		32	7- 8
1951	STL	N	P		23	4- 6
1952	STL	N	P		1	0- 1
	PIT	N	P		5	0- 3
1956	PIT	N	P		35	3- 4
	BRTR				273	77-56

MUNGO, VAN LINGLE
B.JUNE 9,1911 PAGELAND,S.C.

1931	BRO	N	P		5	3- 1
1932	BRO	N	P		39	13-11
1933	BRO	N	P		41	16-15
1934	BRO	N	P	45	46	18-16
1935	BRO	N	P	37	44	16-10
1936	BRO	N	P	45	50	18-19
1937	BRO	N	P	25	28	9-11
1938	BRO	N	P	24	32	4-11
1939	BRO	N	P	14	29	4- 5
1940	BRO	N	P	7	8	1- 0
1941	BRO	N	P		2	0- 0
1942	NY	N	P		9	1- 2
1943	NY	N	P	45	49	3- 7
1945	NY	N	P	26	28	14- 7
	BRTR			364	410	120-115

MUNIZ, MANUEL (RODRIGUEZ)
"MANNY"
B.DEC.31,1947 CAGUAS,P.R.

1971	PHI	N	P		5	0- 1
	BPTR					

MUNN

1875	ATL	NA	2		1	-

MUNNS, LESLIE ERNEST "NEMO"
B.DEC.1,1909 GRAND FORKS,N.DAK.

1934	BRO	N	P	33	34	3- 7
1935	BRO	N	P	21	22	1- 3
1936	STL	N	P	7	8	0- 3
	BRTR			61	64	4-13

MUNSON, CLARENCE HANFORD "RED"
B.JULY 31,1883 CINCINNATI,OHIO
DECEASED

1905	PHI	N	C		9	.222
	TR					

YR	CL	LEA	POS	GP	G	REC

MUNSON, JOSEPH MARTIN NAPOLEON
(REAL NAME
JOSEPH MARTIN NAPOLEON CARLSON)
B.NOV.6,1899 RENOVO,PA.

YR	CL	LEA	POS	GP	G	REC
1925	CHI	N	O		9	.371
1926	CHI	N	O		33	.257
	BLTR				42	.287

MUNSON, THURMAN LEE
B.JUNE 7,1947 AKRON,OHIO

1969	NY	A	C		26	.256
1970	NY	A	C		132	.302
1971	NY	A	C-O		125	.251
1972	NY	A	C		140	.280
1973	NY	A	C		147	.301
1974	NY	A	C		144	.261
1975	NY	A	C-1-O-O		157	.318
1976	NY	A	C-O-O		152	.302
	BRTR				1023	.289

MUNYAN, JOHN B.
B.NOV.14,1860 CHESTER,PA.
D.FEB.18,1945 ENDICOTT,N.Y.

1887	CLE	AA	O		16	.276
1890	COL	AA	O		2	.167
	STL	AA	C		94	.270
1891	STL	AA	C		59	.234
					171	.261

MURAKAMI, MASANORI
B.MAY 6,1944 YAMANASHI,JAPAN

1964	SF	N	P		9	1- 0
1965	SF	N	P		45	4- 1
	BLTL				54	5- 1

MURCER, BOBBY RAY
B.MAY 20,1946 OKLAHOMA CITY,OKLA

1965	NY	A	S		11	.243
1966	NY	A	S		21	.174
1969	NY	A	3-O		152	.259
1970	NY	A	O		159	.251
1971	NY	A	O		146	.331
1972	NY	A	O		153	.292
1973	NY	A	O		160	.304
1974	NY	A	O		156	.274
1975	SF	N	O		147	.298
1976	SF	N	O		147	.259
	BLTR				1252	.281

MURCH, SIMEON T. "SIMMY"
B.NOV.21,1880 CASTINE,ME.
D.JUNE 6,1939

1904	STL	N	2-3		13	.137
1905	STL	N	2-S		4	.111
1908	BRO	N	1		6	.181
	TR				23	.143

MURCHISON, THOMAS MALCOM "TIM"
B.OCT.8,1896 LIBERTY,N.C.
D.OCT.20,1962

1917	STL	N	P		1	0- 0
1920	CLE	A	P		2	0- 0
	BRTL				3	0- 0

MURDOCK, WILBUR E.

| 1908 | STL | N | O | | 16 | .258 |

MURFF, JOHN ROBERT "RED"
B.APR.1,1922 BURLINGTON,TEX.

1956	MIL	N	P		14	0- 0
1957	MIL	N	P		12	2- 2
	BRTR				26	2- 2

MURNANE, TIMOTHY HAYES "TIM"
B.JUNE 4,1852 BRIDGEPORT,CONN.
D.FEB.13,1917

1872	MAN	NA	11		24	.296
1873	ATH	NA	1-2-O		42	-
1874	ATH	NA	1-2-O		19	-
1875	PHI	NA	1-2-O		68	.285
1876	BOS	N	1		69	.275
1877	BOS	N	1-O		35	.279
1878	PRO	N	1-O		48	.245
1884	BOS	U	M-1-O		76	.235
	BLTR				381	-

MURPHY

| 1884 | MET | AA | C | | 1 | .333 |

MURPHY, CLARENCE

| 1886 | LOU | AA | O | | 1 | .000 |

MURPHY, CORNELIUS B. "MONK"
B.OCT.15,1863 WORCESTER,MASS.
D.AUG.1,1914

1884	ALT	U	P		14	4- 6
	PHI	N	P		3	0- 3
1890	BRO	P	P		20	5-10
1890	BRO	AA	P		15	3- 9
	BRO	P	P		2	0- 0
	TR				54	12-28

MURPHY, CORNELIUS DAVID
"STONE FACE"
B.NOV.1,1870 NORTHFIELD,MASS.
D.DEC.14,1945

1893	CIN	N	C		3	.000
1894	CIN	N	C		1	.000
	BLTR				4	.000

MURPHY, DALE BRYAN
B.MAR.12,1956 PORTLAND,ORE.

| 1976 | ATL | N | C | | 19 | .262 |
| | BRTR | | | | | |

MURPHY, DANIEL FRANCIS "DANNY"
B.AUG.11,1876 PHILADELPHIA,PA.
D.NOV.22,1955

1900	NY	N	2		21	.250
1901	NY	N	2		5	.200
1902	PHI	A	2		76	.313
1903	PHI	A	2		133	.275
1904	PHI	A	2		149	.286
1905	PHI	A	2		150	.278
1906	PHI	A	2		119	.301
1907	PHI	A	2		124	.271
1908	PHI	A	2-O		142	.265
1909	PHI	A	O		149	.281
1910	PHI	A	O		151	.300
1911	PHI	A	O		141	.329
1912	PHI	A	O		36	.323
1913	PHI	A	O		40	.322
1914	BRO	F	O		50	.311
1915	BRO	F	O		5	.166
	BRTR				1491	.290

MURPHY, DANIEL FRANCIS "DANNY"
B.AUG.23,1942 BEVERLY,MASS.

1960	CHI	N	O		31	.120
1961	CHI	N	O		4	.385
1962	CHI	N	O		14	.200
1969	CHI	A	P		17	2- 1
1970	CHI	A	P		51	2- 3
	BLTR			68	117	4- 4
						.177

MURPHY, DANIEL JOSEPH
"HANDSOME DAN"
B.SEPT.10,1864 BROOKLYN,N.Y.
D.DEC.14,1915 BROOKLYN,N.Y.

| 1892 | NY | N | C | | 8 | .115 |

MURPHY, DAVID FRANCIS
"DIRTY DAVE"
B.ADAMS,MASS.
D.APR.8,1940 ADAMS,MASS.

| 1905 | BOS | N | S-3 | | 3 | .167 |
| | TR | | | | | |

MURPHY, EDWARD J.
B.JAN.22,1877 AUBURN,N.Y.
D.JAN.29,1935

1898	PHI	N	P		7	1- 3
1901	STL	N	P		20	10- 9
1902	STL	N	P		19	10- 6
1903	STL	N	P	16	24	4- 8
	TR			62	70	25-26

MURPHY, EDWARD JOSEPH
B.AUG.23,1918 JOLIET,ILL.

| 1942 | PHI | N | 1 | | 13 | .250 |
| | BRTR | | | | | |

MURPHY, FRANK MORTON
B.1880 HACKENSACK,N.J.
D.NOV.2,1912

1901	BOS	N	O		45	.271
	NY	N	O		34	.143
					79	.218

MURPHY, HERBERT COURTLAND
"DUMMY"
B.DEC.18,1886 OLNEY,ILL.
D.OCT.10,1962 TALLAHASSEE,FLA.

| 1914 | PHI | N | S | | 9 | .160 |
| | BRTR | | | | | |

MURPHY, HOWARD
B.1882 MILTON,OKLA.
D.SEPT.5,1926

| 1909 | STL | N | O | | 19 | .200 |

MURPHY, JOHN EDWARD "EDDIE"
B.OCT.2,1891 HANCOCK,N.Y.
D.FEB.20,1969 DUMORE,PA.

1912	PHI	A	O		33	.317
1913	PHI	A	O		136	.295
1914	PHI	A	O		148	.272
1915	PHI	A	O		60	.231
	CHI	A	O		78	.315
1916	CHI	A	O		51	.210
1917	CHI	A	O		53	.314
1918	CHI	A	O		91	.297
1919	CHI	A	O		30	.486
1920	CHI	A	O		58	.339
1921	CHI	A	O		6	.200
1926	PIT	N	O		16	.118
	BLTR				760	.287

MURPHY, JOHN H.
B.MAR.8,1867 PHILADELPHIA,PA.

1884	ALT	U	2-O		13	.158
	WIL	U	P-2-	7	10	0- 6
			S-3-O			.065
					23	0- 6
						.133

MURPHY, JOHN JOSEPH "GRANDMA"
B.JULY 14,1908 NEW YORK,N.Y.
D.JAN.14,1970 NEW YORK,N.Y.

1932	NY	A	P		2	0- 0
1934	NY	A	P		40	14-10
1935	NY	A	P		40	10- 5
1936	NY	A	P		27	9- 3
1937	NY	A	P		39	13- 4
1938	NY	A	P		32	8- 2
1939	NY	A	P		38	3- 6
1940	NY	A	P		35	8- 4
1941	NY	A	P		35	8- 3
1942	NY	A	P		31	4-10
1943	NY	A	P		37	12- 4
1946	NY	A	P		27	4- 2
1947	BOS	A	P		32	0- 0
	BRTR				415	93-53

MURPHY, JOHN P. "SOLDIER BOY"
B.1879 NEW HAVEN,CONN.
D.JUNE 1,1914

1902	STL	N	3		1	.600
1903	DET	A	S		5	.182
					6	.240

MURPHY, JOSEPH AKIN
B.SEPT.7,1866 ST.LOUIS,MO.
D.MAR.28,1951

1886	CIN	AA	P		5	2- 3
	STL	N	P		4	0- 4
	STL	AA	P		1	1- 0
1887	STL	AA	P		1	1- 0
					11	4- 7

MURPHY, LAWRENCE PATRICK

| 1891 | WAS | AA | O | | 107 | .255 |
| | BL | | | | | |

MURPHY, LEO JOSEPH
B.JAN.7,1889 TERRE HAUTE,IND.
D.AUG.12,1960

| 1915 | PIT | N | C | | 31 | .098 |
| | BRTR | | | | | |

MURPHY, MICHAEL JEROME
B.AUG.19,1888 FORESTVILLE,PA.
D.OCT.26,1952

1912	STL	N	C		1	.000
1916	PHI	A	C		14	.107
	BRTR				15	.103

MURPHY, MORGAN EDWARD
B.FEB.14,1867 E.PROVIDENCE,R.I.
D.OCT.3,1938

1890	BOS	P	C		60	.238
1891	BOS	AA	C		107	.218
1892	CIN	N	C		69	.192
1893	CIN	N	C		56	.234
1894	CIN	N	C		76	.268
1895	CIN	N	C		22	.272
1896	STL	N	C		48	.251
1897	STL	N	C		55	.177
1898	PIT	N	C		5	.125
	PHI	N	C		25	.202
1900	PHI	N	C		11	.277
1901	PHI	A	C-1		9	.179
	BRTR				543	.221

YR	CL	LEA	POS	GP	G	REC

MURPHY, PATRICK J.
B.JAN.2,1857 AUBURN,MASS.
D.MAY 19,1927

YR	CL	LEA	POS	GP	G	REC
1887	NY	N	C		16	.245
1888	NY	N	C		28	.169
1889	NY	N	C		8	.280
1890	NY	N	C		32	.235
					84	.223

MURPHY, RICHARD LEE
B.OCT.25,1931 CINCINNATI,OHIO

| 1954 | CIN | N | H | | 6 | .000 |
| | | | BLTL | | | |

MURPHY, ROBERT J.
B.DEC.26,1866 DUTCHESS CO.,N.Y.

| 1890 | NY | N | P | | 3 | 1- 1 |

MURPHY, ROBERT R. "BUZZ"
B.APR.26,1895 DENVER,COLO.
D.MAY 11,1938

1918	BOS	N	O		9	.375
1919	WAS	A	O		79	.262
			BLTL		88	.271

MURPHY, THOMAS ANDREW "TOM"
B.DEC.30,1945 CLEVELAND,OHIO

1968	CAL	A	P		15	5- 6
1969	CAL	A	P		36	10-16
1970	CAL	A	P		39	16-13
1971	CAL	A	P		37	6-17
1972	CAL	A	P		6	0- 0
	KC	A	P	18	21	4- 4
1973	STL	N	P		19	3- 7
1974	MIL	A	P		70	10-10
1975	MIL	A	P	52	53	1- 9
1976	MIL	A	P		15	0- 1
	BOS	A	P		37	4- 5
			BRTR	344	348	59-88

MURPHY, WALTER JOSEPH
B.SEPT.27,1907 NEW YORK,N.Y.

| 1931 | BOS | A | P | | 2 | 0- 0 |
| | | | BRTR | | | |

MURPHY, WILLIAM EUGENE "BILLY"
B.MAY 7,1944 PINEVILLE,LA.

| 1966 | NY | N | O | | 84 | .230 |
| | | | BRTR | | | |

MURPHY, WILLIAM HENRY "YALE"
B.NOV.11,1869 SOUTHVILLE,MASS.
D.FEB.14,1906

1894	NY	N	S-O		73	.271
1895	NY	N	O		47	.209
1897	NY	N	S		4	.000
					124	.242

MURPHY, WILLIAM N.
"GENTLE WILLIE"
B.MASSACHUSETTS

1884	CLE	N	S-O		42	.226
	WAS	AA	3-O		5	.454
	BOS	U	C-O		1	.000
					48	.249

MURRAY, ANTHONY JOHN
B.APR.30,1904 CHICAGO,ILL.
D.MAR.19,1974 CHICAGO,ILL.

| 1923 | CHI | N | O | | 2 | .250 |
| | | | BRTR | | | |

MURRAY, DALE ALBERT
B.FEB.2,1950 CUERO,TEX.

1974	MON	N	P		32	1- 1
1975	MON	N	P		63	15- 8
1976	MON	N	P		81	4- 9
			BRTR		176	20-18

MURRAY, EDWARD FRANCIS
B.MAY 12,1896 MYSTIC,CONN.

| 1917 | STL | A | S | | 1 | .000 |
| | | | BRTR | | | |

MURRAY, GEORGE KING "SMILER"
B.SEPT.23,1898 CHARLOTTE,N.C.
D.OCT.18,1955

1922	NY	A	P		22	3- 2
1923	BOS	A	P		39	7-11
1924	BOS	A	P		28	2- 9
1926	WAS	A	P		12	6- 3
1927	WAS	A	P		7	.1- 1
1933	CHI	A	P		2	0- 0
			BRTR		110	19-26

MURRAY, JAMES FRANCIS "BIG JIM"
B.DEC.31,1900 SCRANTON,PA.
D.JULY 15,1973 NEW YORK,N.Y.

| 1922 | BRO | N | P | | 4 | 0- 0 |
| | | | BBTL | | | |

MURRAY, JAMES OSCAR
B.JAN.16,1878 GALVESTON,TEX.
D.APR.25,1945

1902	CHI	N	O		11	.166
1911	STL	A	O		31	.186
1914	BOS	N	O		39	.232
			BRTL		81	.195

MURRAY, JEREMIAH J. "MIAH"
B.JAN.1,1865 BOSTON,MASS.
D.JAN.11,1922

1884	PRO	N	C-1-O		8	.185
1885	LOU	AA	C-1		11	.162
1888	WAS	N	C		12	.098
1891	WAS	AA	C		2	.000
			BRTR		33	.138

MURRAY, JOHN JOSEPH "RED"
B.MAR.4,1884 ARNOT,PA.
D.DEC.4,1958

1906	STL	N	O		41	.257
1907	STL	N	O		131	.262
1908	STL	N	O		154	.282
1909	NY	N	O		149	.263
1910	NY	N	O		148	.277
1911	NY	N	O		131	.291
1912	NY	N	O		143	.277
1913	NY	N	O		147	.267
1914	NY	N	O		86	.223
1915	NY	N	O		65	.320
	CHI	N	O		51	.299
1917	NY	N	O		22	.045
			BRTR		1248	.270

MURRAY, JOSEPH AMBROSE
B.JUNE 4,1913 FALL RIVER,MASS.

| 1936 | BOS | N | P | | 4 | 0- 0 |
| | | | BLTL | | | |

MURRAY, JOSEPH AMBROSE
B.NOV.11,1921 WILKES-BARRE,PA.

| 1950 | PHI | A | P | | 8 | 0- 3 |
| | | | BLTL | | | |

MURRAY, LARRY
B.APR.1,1953 CHICAGO,ILL.

1974	NY	A	O		6	.000
1975	NY	A	O		6	.000
1976	NY	A	O		8	.100
			BBTR		20	.083

MURRAY, PATRICK JOSEPH
B.JULY 18,1897 SCOTTSVILLE,N.Y.

| 1919 | PHI | N | P | | 8 | 0- 2 |
| | | | BRTI | | | |

MURRAY, RAYMOND LEE
"RAY" OR "DEACON"
B.OCT.12,1919 SPRING HOPE,N.C.

1948	CLE	A	H		4	.000
1950	CLE	A	C		55	.273
1951	CLE	A	C		1	1.000
	PHI	A	C		40	.213
1952	PHI	A	C		44	.206
1953	PHI	A	C		84	.284
1954	BAL	A	C		22	.246
			BRTR		250	.252

MURRAY, ROBERT HAYES
B.JULY 4,1898 ST.ALBANS,VT.

| 1923 | WAS | A | 3 | | 10 | .162 |
| | | | TR | | | |

MURRAY, THOMAS
B.1866 SAVANNAH,GA.

| 1894 | PHI | N | S | | 1 | .000 |

MURRAY, WILLIAM ALLENWOOD
B.SEPT.6,1893 VINALHAVEN,ME.
D.SEPT.14,1943 BOSTON,MASS.

| 1917 | WAS | A | 2 | | 8 | .143 |
| | | | BBTR | | | |

MURRAY, WILLIAM JEREMIAH
B.APR.13,1864 PEABODY,MASS.
D.MAR.25,1937
NON-PLAYING MANAGER
PHI(N) 1907-09

MURRELL, IVAN AUGUSTUS
B.APR.24,1945 ALMIRANTE,PANAMA

1963	HOU	N	O		2	.200
1964	HOU	N	O		10	.143
1967	HOU	N	O		10	.310
1968	HOU	N	O		32	.102
1969	SD	N	1-O		111	.255
1970	SD	N	1-O		125	.245
1971	SD	N	O		103	.235
1972	SD	N	O		5	.143
1973	SD	N	1-O		93	.229
1974	ATL	N	1-O		73	.248
			BRTR		564	.236

MURTAUGH, DANIEL EDWARD "DANNY"
B.OCT.8,1917 CHESTER,PA.
D.DEC.2,1976 CHESTER,PA.

1941	PHI	N	2-S		85	.219
1942	PHI	N	2-S-3		144	.241
1943	PHI	N	2		113	.273
1946	PHI	N	2		6	.211
1947	BOS	N	2-3		3	.125
1948	PIT	N	2		146	.290
1949	PIT	N	2		75	.203
1950	PIT	N	2		118	.294
1951	PIT	N	2-3		77	.199
			BRTR		767	.254
NON-PLAYING MANAGER
PIT(N)1957-64, 67, 70-71, 73-76

MUSER, ANTHONY JOSEPH "TONY"
B.AUG.1,1947 VAN NUYS,CAL.

1969	BOS	A	1		2	.111
1971	CHI	A	1		11	.313
1972	CHI	A	1-O		44	.279
1973	CHI	A	1-O-O		109	.285
1974	CHI	A	1-O		103	.291
1975	CHI	A	1		43	.243
1976	BAL	A	1-O-O		136	.227
			BLTL		528	.266

MUSGRAVES, DENNIS EUGENE
B.DEC.25,1943 INDIANAPOLIS,IND.

| 1965 | NY | N | P | | 5 | 0- 0 |
| | | | BRTR | | | |

MUSIAL, STANLEY FRANK
"STAN" OR "STAN THE MAN"
B.NOV.21,1920 DONORA,PA.

1941	STL	N	O		12	.426
1942	STL	N	O		140	.315
1943	STL	N	O		157	.357
1944	STL	N	O		146	.347
1946	STL	N	1-O		156	.365
1947	STL	N	1		149	.312
1948	STL	N	1-O		155	.376
1949	STL	N	1-O		157	.338
1950	STL	N	1-O		146	.346
1951	STL	N	1-O		152	.355
1952	STL	N	P-1-O	1	154	0- 0
						.336
1953	STL	N	O		157	.337
1954	STL	N	1-O		153	.330
1955	STL	N	1-O		154	.319
1956	STL	N	1-O		155	.310
1957	STL	N	1		134	.351
1958	STL	N	1		135	.337
1959	STL	N	1-O		115	.255
1960	STL	N	1-O		116	.275
1961	STL	N	O		123	.288
1962	STL	N	O		135	.330
1963	STL	N	O		124	.255
			BLTL	1	3026	0- 0
						.331

MUSSER, PAUL
B.JUNE 24,1889 MILLHEIM,PA.
D.JULY 7,1973 STATE COLLEGE,PA.

1912	WAS	A	P		8	1- 0
1919	BOS	A	P		5	0- 2
			BRTR		13	1- 2

MUSSER, WILLIAM DANIEL "DANNY"
B.SEPT.5,1906 ZION,PA.

| 1932 | WAS | A | 3 | | 1 | .500 |
| | | | BLTL | | | |

MUSSILL, BERNARD JAMES
B.OCT.1,1920 WOODVILLE,PA.

| 1944 | PHI | N | P | | 16 | 0- 1 |
| | | | BRTL | | | |

YR	CL	LEA	POS	GP	G	REC

MUSTAIKIS, ALEXANDER DOMINICK
B.MAR.26,1909 CHELSEA,MASS.
D.JAN.17,1970 SCRANTON,PA.
1940 BOS A P   6   0- 1
    BRTR

MUTRIE, JAMES J.
"TRUTHFUL JIM"
B.JUNE 13,1851 CHELSEA,MASS.
D.JAN.24,1938
NON-PLAYING MANAGER
MET(AA) 1883-84, NY(N) 1885-91

MYATT, GEORGE EDWARD "MERCURY"
B.JUNE 14,1914 DENVER,COLO.
1938 NY N S-3   43 .306
1939 NY N 3   22 .189
1943 WAS A 2-S-3   42 .245
1944 WAS A 2-S-O 140 .284
1945 WAS A 2-S-3-O 133 .296
1946 WAS A 2-3   15 .235
1947 WAS A 2   12 .000
    BLTR   407 .283
NON-PLAYING MANAGER
PHI(N) 1968-69 (INTERIM)

MYATT, GLENN CALVIN
B.JULY 9,1897 LITTLE ROCK,ARK.
D.AUG.9,1969 HOUSTON,TEX.
1920 PHI A C-O   70 .250
1921 PHI A C   44 .203
1923 CLE A C   92 .286
1924 CLE A C   105 .342
1925 CLE A C-O 106 .271
1926 CLE A C   56 .248
1927 CLE A C   55 .245
1928 CLE A C   58 .288
1929 CLE A C   59 .233
1930 CLE A C   86 .294
1931 CLE A C   65 .247
1932 CLE A C   82 .246
1933 CLE A C   40 .234
1934 CLE A C   36 .318
1935 CLE A C   10 .083
    NY N C   13 .222
1936 DET A C   27 .218
    BLTR   1004 .270

MYER, CHARLES SOLOMON "BUDDY"
B.MAR.16,1904 ELLISVILLE,MISS.
D.OCT.31,1974 BATON ROUGE,LA.
1925 WAS A S   4 .250
1926 WAS A S   132 .304
1927 WAS A S   15 .216
   BOS A S   133 .288
1928 BOS A 3   147 .313
1929 WAS A 2-3 141 .300
1930 WAS A 2   138 .303
1931 WAS A 2   139 .293
1932 WAS A 2   143 .279
1933 WAS A 2   131 .302
1934 WAS A 2   139 .305
1935 WAS A 2   151 .349
1936 WAS A 2   51 .269
1937 WAS A 2   125 .293
1938 WAS A 2   127 .336
1939 WAS A 2   83 .302
1940 WAS A 2   71 .290
1941 WAS A 2   53 .252
    BLTR   1923 .303

MYERS, ALBERT
B.OCT.22,1863 DANVILLE,ILL.
D.DEC.24,1927
1884 MIL U 2   12 .326
1885 PHI N 2   93 .204
1886 KC N 2   118 .276
1887 PHI N 2-S 105 .308
1888 WAS N 2   132 .207
1889 WAS N 2   46 .262
   PHI N 2   75 .269
1890 PHI N 2   117 .277
1891 PHI N 2   134 .238
           832 .255

MYERS, ELMER GLEN
B.MAR.2,1894 YORK SPRINGS,PA.
D.JULY 29,1976 COLLINGSWOOD,N.J
1915 PHI A P   1   1- 0
1916 PHI A P   44   53 14-23
1917 PHI A P   38   9-16
1918 PHI A P   18   4- 8
1919 CLE A P   23   8- 7
1920 CLE A P   16   2- 4
   BOS A P   12   9- 1
1921 BOS A P   30   8-12
1922 BOS A P   3   0- 1
    BRTR   185 194 55-72

MYERS, GEORGE D.
B.1860 BUFFALO,N.Y.
D.JAN.6,1911
1884 BUF N C-O   76 .186
1885 BUF N C-O   89 .205
1886 STL N C   78 .189
1887 IND N C   66 .284
1888 IND N C   66 .238
1889 IND N C-O   39 .194
     BR   414 .219

MYERS, HENRY C.
B.MAY 1858 PHILADELPHIA,PA.
D.APR.18,1895
1881 PRO N S   1 .000
1882 BAL AA M-P- 2   69 0- 2
      S   .223
1884 WIL U 2-S   6 .167
    BRTR   2   76 0- 2
               .216

MYERS, HENRY HARRISON "HI"
B.APR.27,1889 E.LIVERPOOL,OHIO
D.MAY 1,1965 MINERVA,OHIO
1909 BRO N O   6 .227
1911 BRO N O   12 .179
1914 BRO N O   70 .286
1915 BRO N O   153 .248
1916 BRO N O   113 .262
1917 BRO N 1-2-3-O 120 .268
1918 BRO N O   107 .256
1919 BRO N O   133 .307
1920 BRO N O   154 .304
1921 BRO N 2-O 144 .288
1922 BRO N 2-O 153 .317
1923 STL N O   96 .300
1924 STL N 2-3-O   43 .210
1925 STL N O   1 .000
   CIN N O   3 .167
   STL N H   1 1.000
    BRTR   1309 .281

MYERS, HENRY L.
B.1860 PHILADELPHIA,PA.
D.JUNE 28,1898
1890 ATH AA 1-3   5 .167

MYERS, JAMES ALBERT "BERT"
B.WASHINGTON,D.C.
D.OCT.12,1915 WASHINGTON,D.C.
1896 STL N 3   122 .258
1898 WAS N 3   31 .261
1900 PHI N 3   7 .185
           160 .256

MYERS, JOSEPH WILLIAM
B.MAR.18,1862 WILMINGTON,DEL.
D.FEB.11,1956
1909 PHI A P   1   0- 0

MYERS, LYNNWOOD LINCOLN
B.FEB.23,1914 ENOLA,PA.
1938 STL N S   70 .242
1939 STL N S-3   74 .239
    BRTR   144 .241

MYERS, RALPH EDWARD "HAP"
B.AUG.18,1888 SAN FRANCISCO,CAL
D.JUN.30,1967 SAN FRANCISCO,CAL
1910 BOS A C   3 .333
1911 STL A 1   11 .297
   BOS A 1   13 .368
1913 BOS N 1   140 .273
1914 BRO F 1   89 .226
1915 BRO F 1   115 .282
    BRTR   371 .268

MYERS, RICHARD
B.APR.7,1930 SACRAMENTO,CAL.
1956 CHI N H   4 .000
     BR

MYERS, WILLIAM HARRISON "BILLY"
B.AUG.14,1910 ENOLA,PA.
1935 CIN N S   117 .267
1936 CIN N S   98 .269
1937 CIN N 2-S 124 .251
1938 CIN N 2-S 134 .253
1939 CIN N S   151 .281
1940 CIN N S   90 .202
1941 CHI N 2-S   24 .222
    BRTR   738 .257

MYRICK, ROBERT HOWARD "BOB"
B.OCT.1,1952 HATTIESBURG,MISS.
1976 NY N P   21   1- 1
    BRTL

NABORS, JOHN JACKSON
B.NOV.19,1887 PIEDMONT,ALA.
D.OCT.29,1923
1915 PHI A P   10   0- 5
1916 PHI A P   40   1-21
1917 PHI A P   2   0- 0
    BRTR   52   1-26

NAGEL, WILLIAM TAYLOR
B.AUG.19,1915 MEMPHIS,TENN.
1939 PHI A P-2- 1 105   0- 0
        3   .252
1941 PHI N 2-3-O   17 .143
1945 CHI A 1-3   67 .209
    BRTR   1 189   0- 0
               .227

NAGELEISEN, LOUIS MARCELLUS
(PLAYED UNDER NAME OF
LOUIS MARCELLUS NAGELSON)

NAGELSON, LOUIS MARCELLUS
(REAL NAME
LOUIS MARCELLUS NAGELEISEN)
B.JUNE 29,1887 PIQUA,OHIO
D.OCT.22,1965
1912 CLE A C   2 .000
    BRTR

NAGELSON, RUSSELL CHARLES "RUSS"
B.SEP.19,1944 CINCINNATI,OHIO
1968 CLE A H   5 .333
1969 CLE A 1-O   12 .353
1970 CLE A O   17 .125
   DET A 1-O   28 .188
    BLTR   62 .211

NAGLE, THOMAS G.
B.NOV.1,1865 MILWAUKEE,WIS.
D.MAR.9,1946
1890 CHI N C   38 .264
1891 CHI N C   8 .120
            46 .243

NAGLE, WALTER HAROLD "JUDGE"
B.MAR.10,1880 SANTA ROSA,CAL.
D.MAY 27,1971 SANTA ROSA,CAL.
1911 PIT N P   8   4- 2
   BOS A P   5   1- 1
           13   5- 3

NAGY, STEPHEN "STEVE"
B.MAY 28,1920 FRANKLIN,N.J.
1947 PIT N P   6   1- 3
1950 WAS A P   9   15   2- 5
    BLTL   15   21   3- 8

NAGY, MICHAEL TIMOTHY "MIKE"
B.MAR.25,1948 NEW YORK,N.Y.
1969 BOS A P   33   34 12- 2
1970 BOS A P   23   6- 5
1971 BOS A P   12   1- 3
1972 BOS A P   1   0- 0
1973 STL N P   9   0- 2
1974 HOU N P   9   1- 1
    BRTR   87   88 20-13

NAHEM, SAMUEL RALPH
B.OCT.19,1915 NEW YORK,N.Y.
1938 BRO N P   1   1- 0
1941 STL N P   26   5- 2
1942 PHI N P   35   1- 3
1948 PHI N P   28   3- 3
    BRTR   90 10- 8

NAHORODNY, WILLIAM GERARD "BILL"
B.AUG.31,1953 HAMTRAMCK,MICH.
1976 PHI N C   3 .200
    BRTR

YR	CL	LEA	POS	GP	G	REC

NAKTENIS, PETER ERNEST
B.JUNE 12,1914 ABERDEEN,WASH.

YR	CL	LEA	POS	GP	G	REC
1936	PHI	A	P	7		0- 1
1939	CIN	N	P	3		0- 0
	BLTL			10		0- 1

NALEWAY, FRANK "CHICK"
B.JULY 4,1901 CHICAGO,ILL.
D.JAN.28,1949

| 1924 | CHI | A | S | 1 | | .000 |

NANCE, WILLIAM G. "KID"
(REAL NAME WILLIE G. COOPER)
B.AUG.2,1876 FT.WORTH,TEX.
D.MAY 28,1958

1897	LOU	N	O		34	.241
1898	LOU	N	O		22	.329
1901	DET	A	O		133	.290
1904	STL	A	C		1	.333
	BRTR				190	.286

NAPIER, SAMUEL LE ROY "BUDDY"
B.DEC.18,1889 MONTEZUMA,TEX.
D.MAR.29,1968 DALLAS,TEX.

1912	STL	A	P	6		0- 2
1918	CHI	N	P	1		0- 0
1920	CIN	N	P	9		4- 2
1921	CIN	N	P	22		0- 2
	BRTR			38		4- 6

NAPLES, ALOYSIUS FRANCIS
B.AUG.29,1927 ST.GEORGE,S.I.,
N.Y.

| 1949 | STL | A | S | 2 | | .143 |
| | BRTR | | | | | |

NAPOLEON, DANIEL "DANNY"
B.JAN.11,1942 CLAYSBURG,PA.

1965	NY	N	3-O	68		.144
1966	NY	N	O	12		.212
	BRTR			80		.162

NARAGON, HAROLD RICHARD "HAL"
B.OCT.1,1928 ZANESVILLE,OHIO

1951	CLE	A	C	3		.250
1954	CLE	A	C	46		.238
1955	CLE	A	C	57		.323
1956	CLE	A	C	53		.287
1957	CLE	A	C	57		.256
1958	CLE	A	H	9		.333
1959	CLE	A	C	14		.278
	WAS	A	C	71		.241
1960	WAS	A	C	33		.207
1961	MIN	A	C	57		.302
1962	MIN	A	C	24		.229
	BLTR			424		.266

NARANJO, LAZARO RAMON GONZALO "GONZALO"
B.NOV.25,1934 HAVANA,CUBA

| 1956 | PIT | N | P | 17 | | 1- 2 |
| | BLTR | | | | | |

NARLESKI, RAYMOND EDMOND "RAY"
B.NOV.25,1928 CAMDEN,N.J.

1954	CLE	A	P	42		3- 3
1955	CLE	A	P	60		9- 1
1956	CLE	A	P	32		3- 2
1957	CLE	A	P	46		11- 5
1958	CLE	A	P	44		13-10
1959	DET	A	P	42		4-12
	BRTR			266		43-33

NARLESKI, WILLIAM EDWARD "CAP"
B.JUNE 9,1899 KEASBY,N.J.
D.JULY 22,1964 LAUREL SPRINGS,
N.J.

1929	BOS	A	2-S	96		.277
1930	BOS	A	S-3	39		.235
	BRTR			135		.265

NARRON, SAMUEL "SAM"
B.AUG.25,1913 MIDDLESEX,N.C.

1935	STL	N	C	4		.429
1942	STL	N	C	10		.400
1943	STL	N	C	10		.091
	BRTR			24		.286

NARUM, LESLIE FERDINAND "BUSTER"
B.NOV.16,1940 PHILADELPHIA,PA.

1963	BAL	A	P	7		0- 0
1964	WAS	A	P	38		9-15
1965	WAS	A	P	46		4-12
1966	WAS	A	P	3		0- 0
1967	WAS	A	P	2		1- 0
	BRTR			96		14-27

NASH, CHARLES FRANCIS "COTTON"
B.JULY 24,1942 JERSEY CITY,N.J.

1967	CHI	A	1		3	.000
1969	MIN	A	1-O		6	.222
1970	MIN	A	1		4	.250
	BRTR				13	.188

NASH, JAMES EDWIN "JIM"
B.FEB.9,1945 HAWTHORNE,NEV.

1966	KC	A	P		18	12- 1
1967	KC	A	P		37	12-17
1968	OAK	A	P		34	13-13
1969	OAK	A	P		26	8- 8
1970	ATL	N	P		34	13- 9
1971	ATL	N	P	32	33	9- 7
1972	ATL	N	P		11	1- 1
	PHI	N	P		9	0- 8
	BRTR			201	202	68-64

NASH, KENNETH LELAND
(ALSO PLAYED UNDER NAME OF
J. A. COSTELLO)
B.JULY 14,1888 S.WEYMOUTH,MASS.

1912	CLE	A	S		10	.182
1914	STL	N	1-2-S-3		24	.275
	BBTR				34	.247

NASH, WILLIAM MITCHELL
B.JUNE 24,1865 RICHMOND,VA.
D.NOV.15,1929

1884	RIC	AA	3		44	.188
1885	BOS	N	2-3		26	.255
1886	BOS	N	S-3		109	.280
1887	BOS	N	3		118	.368
1888	BOS	N	2-3		135	.283
1889	BOS	N	3		127	.274
1890	BOS	P	3		129	.284
1891	BOS	N	3		139	.276
1892	BOS	N	3		135	.265
1893	BOS	N	3		128	.304
1894	BOS	N	3		132	.294
1895	BOS	N	3		133	.296
1896	PHI	N	M-3		64	.242
1897	PHI	N	S-3		102	.258
1898	PHI	N	3		20	.232
	BRTR				1541	.286

NATON, PETER ALPHONSUS
B.SEPT.9,1931 FLUSHING,L.I.,N.Y

| 1953 | PIT | N | C | | 6 | .167 |
| | BRTR | | | | | |

NAVA, VINCENT P.
(REAL NAME IRWIN SANDY)
B.APR.12,1850 SAN FRANCISCO,CAL
D.JUNE 15,1906

1882	PRO	N	C-O		27	.206
1883	PRO	N	C-O		27	.240
1884	PRO	N	C-2-S-O		32	.089
1885	BAL	AA	C		8	.148
1886	BAL	AA	C-S		2	.200
					96	.176

NAVARRO, JULIO (VENTURA)
B.AUG.8,1936 VIEQUES,P.R.

1962	LA	A	P		9	1- 1
1963	LA	A	P		57	4- 5
1964	LA	A	P		5	0- 0
	DET	A	P		26	2- 1
1965	DET	A	P		15	0- 2
1966	DET	A	P		1	0- 0
1970	ATL	N	P		17	0- 0
	BRTR			130		7- 9

NAYLOR, EARL EUGENE
B.MAY 19,1919 KANSAS CITY,MO.

1942	PHI	N	P-O	20	76	0- 5
						.196
1943	PHI	N	O		33	.175
1946	BRO	N	H		3	.000
	BRTR			20	112	0- 5
						.186

NAYLOR, ROLEINE CECIL "ROLLIE"
B.FEB.4,1892 DENTON,TEX.
D.JUNE 18,1966 FORT WORTH,TEX.

1917	PHI	A	P		5	2- 2
1919	PHI	A	P		31	5-18
1920	PHI	A	P		42	10-23
1921	PHI	A	P	32	33	3-13
1922	PHI	A	P	35	36	10-15
1923	PHI	A	P		26	12- 7
1924	PHI	A	P		10	0- 5
	BRTR			181	183	42-83

NAYMICK, WILLIAM MICHAEL "MIKE"
B.SEPT.4,1917 BERLIN,PA.

1939	CLE	A	P		2	0- 1
1940	CLE	A	P		13	1- 2
1943	CLE	A	P		29	4- 4
1944	CLE	A	P		7	0- 0
	STL	N	P		1	0- 0
	BRTR				52	5- 7

NEAGLE, JOHN HENRY
B.JAN.2,1858 SYRACUSE,N.Y.
D.SEPT.20,1904

1879	PHI	N	P-O	2	3	0- 1
						.167
1883	PHI	N	P-O	8	18	1- 4
						.162
	BAL	AA	P-O	6	9	1- 4
						.270
	PIT	AA	P-O	17	29	3-13
						.168
1884	PIT	AA	P	37	41	11-26
	BRTR			70	100	16-48
						.169

NEAL, CHARLES LENARD "CHARLIE"
B.JAN.30,1931 LONGVIEW,TEX.

1956	BRO	N	2-S		62	.287
1957	BRO	N	2-S-3		128	.270
1958	LA	N	2-3		140	.254
1959	LA	N	2-S		151	.287
1960	LA	N	2-S		139	.256
1961	LA	N	2		108	.235
1962	NY	N	2-S-3		136	.260
1963	NY	N	S-3		72	.225
	CIN	N	2-S-3		34	.156
	BRTR				970	.259

NEAL, JOSEPH H.
B.1865 WADSWORTH,OHIO

1886	LOU	AA	P-O	1	2	0- 1
						.000
					5	0- 4
1887	LOU	AA	P		10	3- 3
1890	STL	AA	P		15	6- 4
1891	STL	AA	P		15	6- 4
	BRTR			31	32	9-12
						.119

NEAL, THEOPHILUS FOUNTAIN "OFFA"
B.JUNE 5,1876 BENTON,ILL.
D.APR.12,1950

| 1905 | NY | N | 2-3 | | 4 | .077 |
| | BLTR | | | | | |

NEALE, ALFRED EARLE "GREASY"
B.NOV.5,1891 PARKERSBURG,W.VA.
D.NOV.2,1973 LAKE WORTH,FLA.

1916	CIN	N	O		138	.262
1917	CIN	N	O		121	.294
1918	CIN	N	O		107	.270
1919	CIN	N	O		139	.242
1920	CIN	N	O		150	.255
1921	PHI	N	O		22	.211
	CIN	N	O		63	.241
1922	CIN	N	O		25	.233
1924	CIN	N	O		3	.000
	BLTR				768	.259

NEALON, JAMES JOSEPH
B.OCT.13,1872 SACRAMENTO,CAL.
D.APR.2,1910

1906	PIT	N	1		154	.255
1907	PIT	N	1		104	.257
					258	.256

NECCIAI, RONALD ANDREW "RON"
B.JUNE 18,1932 MANOWN,PA.

| 1952 | PIT | N | P | | 12 | 1- 6 |
| | BRTR | | | | | |

NEEDHAM, THOMAS J. "DEERFOOT"
B.APR.7,1879 IRELAND
D.DEC.13,1926

1904	BOS	N	C		78	.260
1905	BOS	N	C		82	.218
1906	BOS	N	C		81	.190
1907	BOS	N	C		79	.196
1908	NY	N	C		47	.209
1909	CHI	N	C		10	.200
1910	CHI	N	C		28	.184
1911	CHI	N	C		23	.194
1912	CHI	N	C		33	.178
1913	CHI	N	C		20	.238
1914	CHI	N	C		9	.118
	BRTR				490	.209

YR	CL	LEA	POS	GP	G	REC

NEEMAN, CALVIN AMANDUS "CAL"
B.FEB.18,1929 VALMEYER,ILL.

YR	CL	LEA	POS	GP	G	REC
1957	CHI	N	C		122	.258
1958	CHI	N	C		76	.259
1959	CHI	N	C		44	.162
1960	CHI	N	C		9	.154
	PHI	N	C		59	.181
1961	PHI	N	C		19	.226
1962	PIT	N	C		24	.180
1963	CLE	A	C		9	.000
	WAS	A	C		14	.056
	BRTR				376	.224

NEFF, DOUGLAS WILLIAM
B.OCT.8,1892 HARRISONBURG,VA.
D.MAY 23,1932

YR	CL	LEA	POS	GP	G	REC
1914	WAS	A	S		3	.000
1915	WAS	A	2-S-3		30	.167
	BRTR				33	.159

NEGRAY, RONALD ALVIN "RON"
B.FEB.26,1930 AKRON,OHIO

YR	CL	LEA	POS	GP	G	REC
1952	BRO	N	P		4	0- 0
1955	PHI	N	P		19	4- 3
1956	PHI	N	P		39	2- 3
1958	LA	N	P		4	0- 0
	BRTR				66	6- 6

NEHER, JAMES GILMORE
B.FEB.5,1889 ROCHESTER,N.Y.
D.NOV.11,1951

YR	CL	LEA	POS	GP	G	REC
1912	CLE	A	P		1	0- 0
	BRTR					

NEHF, ARTHUR NEUKOM "ART"
B.JULY 21,1892 TERRE HAUTE,IND.
D.DEC.18,1960 PHOENIX,ARIZ.

YR	CL	LEA	POS	GP	G	REC
1915	BOS	N	P		12	5- 4
1916	BOS	N	P	22	23	7- 5
1917	BOS	N	P		38	17- 8
1918	BOS	N	P-O	32	35	15-15
						.168
1919	BOS	N	P-O	21	22	8- 9
						.197
	NY	N	P		13	9- 2
1920	NY	N	P		40	21-12
1921	NY	N	P	41	42	20-10
1922	NY	N	P		37	19-13
1923	NY	N	P		34	13-10
1924	NY	N	P-O	30	33	14- 4
						.228
1925	NY	N	P	30	33	11- 9
1926	NY	N	P		2	0- 0
	CIN	N	P		7	0- 1
1927	CIN	N	P		21	3- 5
	CHI	N	P		8	1- 1
1928	CHI	N	P		31	13- 7
1929	CHI	N	P		32	8- 5
	BLTL			451	463	184-120
						.211

NEIBAUER, GARY WAYNE
B.OCT.29,1944 BILLINGS,MONT.

YR	CL	LEA	POS	GP	G	REC
1969	ATL	N	P		29	1- 2
1970	ATL	N	P		7	0- 3
1971	ATL	N	P		6	1- 0
1972	ATL	N	P		8	0- 0
	PHI	N	P		9	0- 2
1973	ATL	N	P		16	2- 1
	BRTR				75	4- 8

NEIGER, ALVIN EDWARD
B.MAR.26,1939 WILMINGTON,DEL.

YR	CL	LEA	POS	GP	G	REC
1960	PHI	N	P		6	0- 0
	BLTL					

NEIGHBORS, CYRIL

YR	CL	LEA	POS	GP	G	REC
1908	PIT	N	O		1	.000

NEIGHBORS, ROBERT OTIS
B.NOV.9,1917 TALAHINA,OKLA.
D.AUG.8,1952

YR	CL	LEA	POS	GP	G	REC
1939	STL	A	S		7	.182
	BRTR					

NEILL, THOMAS WHITE
B.NOV.7,1919 HARTSELLE,ALA.

YR	CL	LEA	POS	GP	G	REC
1946	BOS	N	O		13	.267
1947	BOS	N	O		7	.200
	BLTR				20	.255

NEIS, BERNARD EDMUND
B.SEPT.26,1895 BLOOMINGTON,ILL.
D.NOV.29,1972 INVERNESS,FLA.

YR	CL	LEA	POS	GP	G	REC
1920	BRO	N	O		95	.253
1921	BRO	N	O		102	.257
1922	BRO	N	O		61	.229
1923	BRO	N	O		126	.274
1924	BRO	N	O		80	.303
1925	BOS	N	O		106	.285
1926	BOS	N	O		30	.215
1927	CLE	A	O		32	.302
	CHI	A	O		45	.289
	BBTR				677	.272
	BR 1920-21					

NEITZKE, ERNEST FREDERICK
B.NOV.13,1894 TOLEDO,OHIO

YR	CL	LEA	POS	GP	G	REC
1921	BOS	A	P		11	0- 0
	BRTR					

NEKOLA, FRANCIS JOSEPH "BOTS"
B.DEC.10,1907 NEW YORK,N.Y.

YR	CL	LEA	POS	GP	G	REC
1929	NY	A	P		9	0- 0
1933	DET	A	P		2	0- 0
	BLTL				11	0- 0

NELSON, ALBERT FRANCIS "RED"
(REAL NAME
ALBERT F. HORAZDOVSKY)
B.MAY 19,1886 CLEVELAND,OHIO
D.OCT.26,1956

YR	CL	LEA	POS	GP	G	REC
1910	STL	A	P		7	5- 1
1911	STL	A	P		15	3- 9
1912	STL	A	P		8	0- 3
	PHI	N	P		4	2- 0
1913	PHI	N	P		2	0- 0
	CIN	N	P		2	0- 0
	BRTR				38	10-13

NELSON, ANDREW "PEACHES"

YR	CL	LEA	POS	GP	G	REC
1908	CHI	A	P		3	1- 0

NELSON, DAVID EARL "DAVE"
B.JUNE 20,1944 FORT STILL,OKLA.

YR	CL	LEA	POS	GP	G	REC
1968	CLE	A	2-S		88	.233
1969	CLE	A	2-O		52	.203
1970	WAS	A	2		47	.159
1971	WAS	A	2-3		85	.280
1972	TEX	A	3-O		145	.226
1973	TEX	A	2		142	.286
1974	TEX	A	2		121	.236
1975	TEX	A	2		28	.213
1976	KC	A	1-2		78	.235
	BRTR				786	.245
	BB 1968 (PART)					

NELSON, GEORGE EMMETT "RAMROD"
B.FEB.26,1905 VIBORG,S.DAK.

YR	CL	LEA	POS	GP	G	REC
1935	CIN	N	P		19	4- 4
1936	CIN	N	P		6	1- 0
	BRTR				25	5- 4

NELSON, GLENN RICHARD "ROCKY"
B.NOV.18,1924 PORTSMOUTH,OHIO

YR	CL	LEA	POS	GP	G	REC
1949	STL	N	1		82	.221
1950	STL	N	1		76	.247
1951	STL	N	1-O		9	.222
	PIT	N	1-O		71	.267
	CHI	A	H		6	.000
1952	BRO	N	1		37	.256
1954	CLE	A	1		4	.000
1956	BRO	N	1		31	.208
	STL	N	1-O		38	.232
1959	PIT	N	1-O		98	.291
1960	PIT	N	1		93	.300
1961	PIT	N	1		75	.197
	BLTL				620	.249

NELSON, JACKSON W. "CANDY"
B.MAR.14,1849 BROOKLYN,N.Y.
D.SEPT.5,1910

YR	CL	LEA	POS	GP	G	REC
1872	TRO	NA	S-O		4	.368
	ECK	NA	2-3-O		18	.235
1873	MUT	NA	2-3-O		37	-
1874	MUT	NA	2-S		65	-
1875	MUT	NA	2-3-O		70	-
1878	IND	N	S		18	.136
1879	TRO	N	S-O		28	.246
1881	WOR	N	S		23	.275
1883	MET	AA	S		96	.291
1884	MET	AA	S		111	.259
1885	MET	AA	S		107	.251
1886	MET	AA	S-O		109	.230
1887	MET	AA	S-O		68	.361
	NY	N	3		1	.000
1890	BRO	AA	S		60	.234
	BLTR				815	-

NELSON, JAMES LORIN "JIM"
B.JULY 4,1947 BIRMINGHAM,ALA.

YR	CL	LEA	POS	GP	G	REC
1970	PIT	N	P		15	4- 2
1971	PIT	N	P		17	2- 2
	BRTR				32	6- 4

NELSON, LUTHER MARTIN
B.DEC.4,1894 CABLE,ILL.

YR	CL	LEA	POS	GP	G	REC
1919	NY	A	P		9	3- 0
	BRTR					

NELSON, LYNN BERNARD
"LYNN" OR "LINE DRIVE"
B.FEB.24,1905 SHELDON,N.DAK.
D.FEB.15,1955

YR	CL	LEA	POS	GP	G	REC
1930	CHI	N	P		37	3- 2
1933	CHI	N	P	24	29	5- 5
1934	CHI	N	P		2	0- 1
1937	PHI	A	P	30	74	4- 9
1938	PHI	A	P	32	67	10-11
1939	PHI	A	P	35	40	10-13
1940	DET	A	P	6	19	1- 1
	BLTR			166	268	33-42

NELSON, MELVIN FREDERICK "MEL"
B.MAY 30,1936 SAN DIEGO,CAL.

YR	CL	LEA	POS	GP	G	REC
1960	STL	N	P		2	0- 1
1963	LA	A	P	36	39	2- 3
1965	MIN	A	P		28	0- 4
1967	MIN	A	P		1	0- 0
1968	STL	N	P		18	2- 1
1969	STL	N	P		8	0- 1
	BRTL			93	96	4-10

NELSON, RAYMOND "KELL"
(REAL NAME
RAYMOND NELSON KELLOGG)
B.AUG.4,1875 HOLYOKE,MASS.
D.JAN.8,1961 MT.VERNON,N.Y.

YR	CL	LEA	POS	GP	G	REC
1901	NY	N	2		36	.205
	BRTR					

NELSON, ROBERT SIDNEY
B.AUG.7,1936 DALLAS,TEX.

YR	CL	LEA	POS	GP	G	REC
1955	BAL	A	1-O		25	.194
1956	BAL	A	O		39	.206
1957	BAL	A	O		15	.217
	BLTL				79	.205

NELSON, ROGER EUGENE
B.JUNE 7,1944 ALTADENA,CAL.

YR	CL	LEA	POS	GP	G	REC
1967	CHI	A	P		5	0- 1
1968	BAL	A	P		19	4- 3
1969	KC	A	P		29	7-13
1970	KC	A	P		4	0- 2
1971	KC	A	P		13	0- 1
1972	KC	A	P		34	11- 6
1973	CIN	N	P		14	3- 2
1974	CIN	N	P		14	4- 4
1976	KC	A	P		3	0- 0
	BRTR				135	29-32

NELSON, TOM COUSINEAU
B.MAY 1,1917 CHICAGO,ILL.
D.SEPT.24,1973 SAN DIEGO,CAL.

YR	CL	LEA	POS	GP	G	REC
1945	BOS	N	2-3		40	.165
	BRTR					

NELSON, WILLIAM F.
B.SEPT.28,1863 TERRE HAUTE,IND.
D. JUNE 23,1941

YR	CL	LEA	POS	GP	G	REC
1884	PIT	AA	P		3	1- 2
	TR					

NEN, RICHARD LEROY "DICK"
B.SEP.24,1939 SOUTH GATE,CAL.

YR	CL	LEA	POS	GP	G	REC
1963	LA	N	1		7	.125
1965	WAS	A	1		69	.260
1966	WAS	A	1		94	.213
1967	WAS	A	1-O		110	.218
1968	CHI	N	1		81	.181
1970	WAS	A	1		6	.200
	BLTL				367	.224

NESS, JOHN CHARLES
B.NOV.11,1885 CHICAGO,ILL.
D.DEC.3,1957

YR	CL	LEA	POS	GP	G	REC
1911	DET	A	1		12	.161
1916	CHI	A	1		75	.267
	BRTR				87	.248

YR	CL	LEA	POS	GP	G	REC

NETTLES, GRAIG
B.AUG.20,1944 SAN DIEGO,CAL.

YR	CL	LEA	POS	GP	G	REC
1967	MIN	A	H		3	.333
1968	MIN	A	1-3-0		22	.224
1969	MIN	A	3-0		96	.222
1970	CLE	A	3-0		157	.235
1971	CLE	A	3		158	.261
1972	CLE	A	3		150	.253
1973	NY	A	3		160	.234
1974	NY	A	S-3		155	.246
1975	NY	A	3		157	.267
1976	NY	A	3		158	.254
		BLTR			1216	.248

NETTLES, JAMES WILLIAM "JIM"
B.MAR.2,1947 SAN DIEGO,CAL.

YR	CL	LEA	POS	GP	G	REC
1970	MIN	A	O		13	.250
1971	MIN	A	O		70	.250
1972	MIN	A	1-O		102	.204
1974	DET	A	O		43	.227
		BLTL			228	.225

NETTLES, MORRIS
B.JAN.26,1952 LOS ANGELES,CAL.

YR	CL	LEA	POS	GP	G	REC
1974	CAL	A	O		56	.274
1975	CAL	A	O		112	.231
		BLTL			168	.247

NETZEL, MILES A.
B.MAY 12,1887 ELDRED,PA.
D.MAR.18,1938 OXNARD,CAL.

YR	CL	LEA	POS	GP	G	REC
1909	CLE	A	3-0		10	.186
		TR				

NEUBAUER, HAROLD CHARLES
B.MAY 13,1902 HOBOKEN,N.J.
D.SEPT.9,1949

YR	CL	LEA	POS	GP	G	REC
1925	BOS	A	P		7	1- 0
		BRTR				

NEUER, JOHN S. "TACKS"
B.JUNE 0,1877 FREMONT,OHIO
D.JAN.14,1966

YR	CL	LEA	POS	GP	G	REC
1907	NY	A	P		7	4- 2

NEUMEIER, DANIEL GEORGE "DAN"
B.MAR.9,1948 SHAWANO,WIS.

YR	CL	LEA	POS	GP	G	REC
1972	CHI	A	P		3	0- 0
		BRTR				

NEUN, JOHN HENRY "JOHNNY"
B.OCT.28,1900 BALTIMORE,MD.

YR	CL	LEA	POS	GP	G	REC
1925	DET	A	1		60	.266
1926	DET	A	1		97	.298
1927	DET	A	1		79	.323
1928	DET	A	1		36	.213
1930	BOS	N	1		81	.325
1931	BOS	N	1		79	.221
		BBTL			432	.289

NON-PLAYING MANAGER
NY(A) 1946, CIN(N) 1947-48

NEVEL, ERNIE WRYE
B.AUG.17,1919 CHARLESTON,MO.

YR	CL	LEA	POS	GP	G	REC
1950	NY	A	P		3	0- 1
1951	NY	A	P		1	0- 0
1953	CIN	N	P		10	0- 0
		BRTR			14	0- 1

NEVERS, ERNEST ALONZO "ERNIE"
B.JUNE 11,1903 WILLOW RIVER, MINN.
D.MAY 3,1976 SAN RAFAEL,CAL.

YR	CL	LEA	POS	GP	G	REC
1926	STL	A	P	11	12	2- 4
1927	STL	A	P		27	3- 8
1928	STL	A	P		6	1- 0
		BRTR		44	45	6-12

NEVINS

YR	CL	LEA	POS	GP	G	REC
1873	RES	NA	2-3-0		13	-

NEWCOMBE, DONALD "DON"
B.JUNE 14,1926 MADISON,N.J.

YR	CL	LEA	POS	GP	G	REC
1949	BRO	N	P	38	39	17- 8
1950	BRO	N	P		40	19-11
1951	BRO	N	P		40	20- 9
1954	BRO	N	P	29	31	9- 8
1955	BRO	N	P	34	57	20- 5
1956	BRO	N	P	38	52	27- 7
1957	BRO	N	P	28	34	11-12
1958	LA	N	P		11	0- 6
	CIN	N	P	20	39	7- 7
1959	CIN	N	P	30	61	13- 8
1960	CIN	N	P	16	24	4- 6
	CLE	A	P	20	24	2- 3
		BLTR		344	452	149-90

NEWELL, JOHN A.
B.JAN.14,1868 WILMINGTON,DEL.
D.JAN.28,1919

YR	CL	LEA	POS	GP	G	REC
1891	PIT	N	3		5	.111

NEWELL, T. E.
B.ST.LOUIS,MO.

YR	CL	LEA	POS	GP	G	REC
1877	STL	N	S		1	.000

NEWHAUSER, DONALD LOUIS "DON"
B.NOV.7,1947 MIAMI,FLA.

YR	CL	LEA	POS	GP	G	REC
1972	BOS	A	P		31	4- 2
1973	BOS	A	P		9	0- 0
1974	BOS	A	P		2	0- 1
		BRTR			42	4- 3

NEWHOUSER, HAROLD "HAL"
B.MAY 30,1921 DETROIT,MICH.

YR	CL	LEA	POS	GP	G	REC
1939	DET	A	P		1	0- 1
1940	DET	A	P		28	9- 9
1941	DET	A	P		33	9-11
1942	DET	A	P	38	39	8-14
1943	DET	A	P		37	8-17
1944	DET	A	P		47	29- 9
1945	DET	A	P		40	25- 9
1946	DET	A	P		37	26- 9
1947	DET	A	P		40	17-17
1948	DET	A	P		39	21-12
1949	DET	A	P		38	18-11
1950	DET	A	P		35	15-13
1951	DET	A	P	15	17	6- 6
1952	DET	A	P	25	26	9- 9
1953	DET	A	P		7	0- 1
1954	CLE	A	P		26	7- 2
1955	CLE	A	P		2	0- 0
		BLTL		488	492	207-150

NEWKIRK, FLOYD ELMO
B.JULY 16,1908 NORRIS CITY,ILL.

YR	CL	LEA	POS	GP	G	REC
1934	NY	A	P		1	0- 0
		BRTR				

NEWKIRK, JOEL IVAN
B.MAY 1,1896 KYANA,IND.

YR	CL	LEA	POS	GP	G	REC
1919	CHI	N	P		1	0- 0
1920	CHI	N	P		2	0- 1
		BRTR			3	0- 1

NEWLIN, MAURICE MILTON "MICKEY"
B.JUNE 22,1914 BLOOMINGDALE,IND

YR	CL	LEA	POS	GP	G	REC
1940	STL	A	P		1	0- 0
1941	STL	A	P		14	0- 2
		BRTR			15	1- 2

NEWMAN, CHARLES C.
B.INDIANAPOLIS,IND.

YR	CL	LEA	POS	GP	G	REC
1891	STL	AA	C		1	.000
1892	NY	N	O		2	.375
	CHI	N	O		14	.148
					17	.244

NEWMAN, FREDERICK WILLIAM "FRED"
B.FEB.21,1942 BOSTON,MASS.

YR	CL	LEA	POS	GP	G	REC
1962	LA	A	P		4	0- 1
1963	LA	A	P		12	1- 5
1964	LA	A	P	32	39	13-10
1965	CAL	A	P		36	14-16
1966	CAL	A	P		21	4- 7
1967	CAL	A	P		3	1- 0
		BRTR		108	115	33-39

NEWMAN, JEFFREY LYNN "JEFF"
B.SEPT.11,1948 FORT WORTH,TEX.

YR	CL	LEA	POS	GP	G	REC
1976	OAK	A	C		43	.195
		BRTR				

NEWMAN, RAYMOND FRANCIS "RAY"
B.JUNE 20,1945 EVANSVILLE,IND.

YR	CL	LEA	POS	GP	G	REC
1971	CHI	N	P	30	1- 2	
1972	MIL	A	P		4	0- 0
1973	MIL	A	P		11	2- 1
		BLTL			45	3- 3

NEWNAM, PATRICK HENRY
B.DEC.10,1880 HEMPSTEAD,TEX.
D.JUNE 20,1938

YR	CL	LEA	POS	GP	G	REC
1910	STL	A	1		103	.216
1911	STL	A	1		20	.194
		BRTR			123	.213

NEWSOM, LOUIS NORMAN "BOBO"
B.AUG.11,1907 HARTSVILLE,S.C.
D.DEC.7,1962 ORLANDO,FLA.

YR	CL	LEA	POS	GP	G	REC
1929	BRO	N	P		3	0- 3
1930	BRO	N	P		2	0- 0
1932	CHI	N	P		1	0- 0
1934	STL	A	P	47	50	16-20
1935	STL	A	P		7	0- 6
1935	WAS	A	P		28	11-12
1936	WAS	A	P	43	44	17-15
1937	WAS	A	P	11	13	3- 4
	BOS	A	P	30	31	13-10
1938	STL	A	P	44	46	20-16
1939	STL	A	P		6	3- 1
	DET	A	P		35	17-10
1940	DET	A	P		36	21- 5
1941	DET	A	P		43	12-20
1942	WAS	A	P		30	11-17
	BRO	N	P		6	2- 2
1943	BRO	N	P		22	9- 4
	STL	A	P		10	1- 6
	WAS	A	P		6	3- 3
1944	PHI	A	P		37	13-15
1945	PHI	A	P		36	8-20
1946	PHI	A	P		10	3- 5
	WAS	A	P		24	11- 8
1947	WAS	A	P		14	4- 6
	NY	A	P		17	7- 5
1948	NY	A	P		11	0- 4
1952	WAS	A	P		10	1- 1
	PHI	A	P		14	3- 3
1953	PHI	A	P		17	2- 1
		BRTR		600	609	211-222

NEWSOME, ASHBY LAMAR "SKEETER"
B.OCT.18,1910 PHENIX CITY,ALA.

YR	CL	LEA	POS	GP	G	REC
1935	PHI	A	2-S-3-0	59	.207	
1936	PHI	A	S		127	.225
1937	PHI	A	S		122	.253
1938	PHI	A	S		17	.271
1939	PHI	A	S		99	.222
1941	BOS	A	2-S		93	.225
1942	BOS	A	2-S-3		29	.274
1943	BOS	A	S-3		114	.265
1944	BOS	A	2-S-3		136	.242
1945	BOS	A	2-S-3		125	.290
1946	PHI	N	2-S-3		118	.232
1947	PHI	N	2-S-3		95	.229
		BRTR			1128	.245

NEWSOME, HEBER HAMPTON "DICK"
B.DEC.13,1909 AHOSKIE,N.C.
D.DEC.15,1965 AHOSKIE,N.C.

YR	CL	LEA	POS	GP	G	REC
1941	BOS	A	P		36	19-10
1942	BOS	A	P		24	8-10
1943	BOS	A	P		27	8-13
		BRTR			87	35-33

NEWTON, EUSTACE JAMES "DOC"
B.OCT.26,1877 INDIANAPOLIS,IND.
D.MAY 14,1931

YR	CL	LEA	POS	GP	G	REC
1900	CIN	N	P		30	9-14
1901	CIN	N	P		20	4-13
	BRO	N	P		13	7- 5
1902	BRO	N	P-1	30	32	15-14
						.174
1905	NY	A	P		12	2- 4
1906	NY	A	P		21	7- 5
1907	NY	A	P		19	7-10
1908	NY	A	P		23	0- 8
1909	NY	A	P		4	0- 3
		BLTL		172	176	55-73
						.172

NIARHOS, CONSTANTINE GREGORY "GUS"
B.DEC.6,2921 BIRMINGHAM,ALA.

YR	CL	LEA	POS	GP	G	REC
1946	NY	A	C		37	.252
1948	NY	A	C		83	.268
1949	NY	A	C		32	.279
1950	NY	A	H		1	.000
	CHI	A	C		41	.324
1951	CHI	A	C		66	.256
1952	BOS	A	C		29	.103
1953	BOS	A	C		16	.200
1954	PHI	N	C		3	.200
1955	PHI	N	C		7	.111
		BRTR			315	.252

NICE, CHARLES REIFF
B.JULY 1,1870 PHILADELPHIA,PA.
D.MAY 9,1908

YR	CL	LEA	POS	GP	G	REC
1895	BOS	N	S		9	.229

YR	CL	LEA	POS	GP	G	REC

NICHOL, SAMUEL ANDERSON
B.APR.20,1869 IRELAND
D.APR.19,1937

YR	CL	LEA	POS	GP	G	REC
1888	PIT	N	O		8	.045
1890	COL	AA	O		14	.188
					22	.147

NICHOLAS, DONALD LEIGH "DON"
B.OCT.30,1930 PHOENIX,ARIZ.

1952	CHI	A	H		3	.000
1954	CHI	A	H		7	.000
	BLTR				10	.000

NICHOLLS, SIMON BURDETTE
B.JULY 18,1882 GERMANTOWN,MD.
D.MAR.12,1911 BALTIMORE,MD.

1903	DET	A	S		2	.375
1906	PHI	A	S		12	.219
1907	PHI	A	2-S		124	.302
1908	PHI	A	2-S		150	.216
1909	PHI	A	3		21	.211
1910	CLE	A	S		3	.000
	BLTR				312	.252

NICHOLS, ALBERT H.

1875	MUT	N	3		32	-
1876	MUT	N	3		57	.177
1877	LOU	N	1-2-S-3		6	.211
					95	-

NICHOLS, ARTHUR FRANCIS
(REAL NAME
ARTHUR FRANCIS MEIKLE)
B.JULY 14,1871 MANCHESTER,N.H.
D.AUG.9,1945

1898	CHI	N	C		13	.264
1899	CHI	N	C		17	.277
1900	CHI	N	C		8	.208
1901	STL	N	C-O		82	.247
1902	STL	N	C-1-O		69	.272
1903	STL	N	1		33	.192
					222	.248

NICHOLS, CHARLES AUGUSTUS "KID"
B.SEPT.14,1869 MADISON,WIS.
D.APR.11,1953 KANSAS CITY,MO.

1890	BOS	N	P		47	27-19
1891	BOS	N	P		50	30-17
1892	BOS	N	P	53	54	35-16
1893	BOS	N	P	46	47	32-14
1894	BOS	N	P		46	33-13
1895	BOS	N	P		43	27-16
1896	BOS	N	P		45	30-14
1897	BOS	N	P		43	32-11
1898	BOS	N	P		45	33-12
1899	BOS	N	P	38	41	20-18
1900	BOS	N	P		29	13-14
1901	BOS	N	P		46	18-15
1904	STL	N	M-P		36	20-12
1905	STL	N	M-P		8	1- 5
	PHI	N			18	10- 6
1906	PHI	N			4	0- 2
	BBTR			597	602	361-204

NICHOLS, CHESTER RAYMOND JR.
"CHET"
B.FEB.22,1931 PAWTUCKET,R.I.

1951	BOS	N	P		33	11- 8
1954	MIL	N	P		35	9-11
1955	MIL	N	P		34	9- 8
1956	MIL	N	P		2	0- 1
1960	BOS	A	P		6	0- 2
1961	BOS	A	P		26	3- 2
1962	BOS	A	P		29	1- 1
1963	BOS	A	P		21	1- 3
1964	CIN	N	P		3	0- 0
	BBTL				189	34-36

NICHOLS, CHESTER RAYMOND SR.
"NICK"
B.JULY 3,1897 WOONSOCKET,R.I.

1926	PIT	N	P		3	0- 0
1927	PIT	N	P		8	0- 3
1928	NY	N	P		3	0- 0
1930	PHI	N	P	16	26	1- 2
1931	PHI	N	P		3	0- 1
1932	PHI	N	P		11	0- 2
	BRTR			44	54	1- 8

NICHOLS, DOLAN LEVON
B.FEB.28,1930 TISHOMINGO,MISS.

1958	CHI	N	P		24	0- 4
	BRTR					

NICHOLS, FREDERICK C. "TRICKY"
B.BRIDGEPORT,CONN.

1875	NH	NA	P-O	32	33	4-28
						-
1876	BOS	N	P		1	1- 0
1877	STL	N	P-O	42	51	18-23
						.168
1878	PRO	N	P		11	4- 7
1880	WOR	N	P		2	0- 2
1882	BAL	AA	P-O	14	27	1-13
						.154
	BRTP			112	125	28-73
						-

NICHOLS, ROY
B.MAR.3,1921 N.LITTLE ROCK,ARK.

1944	NY	N	2-3		11	.222
	BRTR					

NICHOLSON, DAVID LAWRENCE "DAVE"
B.AUG.29,1939 ST.LOUIS,MO.

1960	BAL	A	O		54	.186
1962	BAL	A	O		97	.173
1963	BAL	A	O		126	.229
1964	BAL	A	O		97	.204
1965	CHI	A	O		54	.153
1966	HOU	N	O		100	.246
1967	ATL	N	O		10	.200
	BRTR				538	.212

NICHOLSON, FRANK COLLINS
B.AUG.29,1889 BERLIN,PA.
D.NOV.10,1972 JERSEY SHORE,PA.

1912	PHI	N	P		2	0- 0
	BRTR					

NICHOLSON, FREDERICK
"SHOEMAKER"
B.SEPT.1,1894 HONEY GROVE,TEX.

1917	DET	A	O		13	.286
1919	PIT	N	1-O		30	.273
1920	PIT	N	O		99	.360
1921	BOS	N	O		83	.327
1922	BOS	N	O		78	.252
	BRTR				303	.311

NICHOLSON, OVID
B.AUG.18,1892 SALEM,IND.
D.MAR.24,1968 SALEM,IND.

1912	PIT	N	O		11	.454
	BLTR					

NICHOLSON, THOMAS C. "PARSON"
B.APR.14,1863 BLAINE,OHIO
D.FEB.28,1917

1888	DET	N	2		24	.259
1890	TOL	AA	2		133	.261
1895	WAS	N	S		10	.184
					167	.256

NICHOLSON, WILLIAM BECK "SWISH"
B.DEC.11,1914 CHESTERTOWN,MD.

1936	PHI	A	O		11	.000
1939	CHI	N	O		58	.295
1940	CHI	N	O		135	.297
1941	CHI	N	O		147	.254
1942	CHI	N	O		152	.294
1943	CHI	N	O		154	.309
1944	CHI	N	O		156	.287
1945	CHI	N	O		151	.243
1946	CHI	N	O		105	.220
1947	CHI	N	O		148	.244
1948	CHI	N	O		143	.261
1949	PHI	N	O		98	.234
1950	PHI	N	O		41	.224
1951	PHI	N	O		85	.241
1952	PHI	N	O		55	.273
1953	PHI	N	O		38	.210
	BLTR				1677	.268

NICKLIN, SAMUEL STRANG
(PLAYED UNDER NAME OF
SAMUEL NICKLIN STRANG)

NICOL, GEORGE EDWARD
B.OCT.17,1870 BARRYMILL.
D.AUG.10,1924

1890	STL	AA	P		4	2- 2
1891	CHI	N	P		3	0- 1
1894	PIT	N	P		9	4- 2
	LOU	N	P-O	6	28	3- 3
						.345
	TL			22	44	9- 8
						.344

NICOL, HUGH N.
B.JAN.1,1858 RAMSEY,SCOTLAND
D.JUNE 27,1921

1881	CHI	N	S-O		26	.203
1882	CHI	N	S-O		47	.198
1883	STL	AA	2-O		85	.263
1884	STL	AA	2-O		110	.270
1885	STL	AA	O		112	.211
1886	STL	AA	O		67	.204
1887	CIN	AA	O		126	.334
1888	CIN	AA	2-S-O		134	.236
1889	CIN	AA	2-3-O		122	.246
1890	CIN	N	O		50	.209
	BRTR				879	.254

NON-PLAYING MANAGER STL(N) 1897

NIEBERGALL, CHARLES ARTHUR
"NIG"
B.MAY 23,1899 NEW YORK,N.Y.

1921	STL	N	C		5	.167
1923	STL	N	C		9	.107
1924	STL	N	C		40	.293
	BRTR				54	.231

NIEHAUS, ALBERT BERNARD
B.JUNE 1,1899 CINCINNATI,OHIO
D.OCT.14,1931

1925	PIT	N	1		17	.219
	CIN	N	1		51	.299
	BRTR				68	.275

NIEHAUS, RICHARD J.
B.OCT.24,1892 COVINGTON,KY.
D.MAR.12,1957

1913	STL	N	P		3	0- 2
1914	STL	N	P		8	1- 0
1915	STL	N	P		15	2- 1
1920	CLE	A	P		19	1- 2
	BLTL				45	4- 5

NIEHOFF, JOHN ALBERT "BERT"
B.MAY 13,1884 LOUISVILLE,KY.
D.DEC.8,1974 INGLEWOOD,CAL.

1913	CIN	N	3		2	.000
1914	CIN	N	3		142	.242
1915	PHI	N	3		148	.238
1916	PHI	N	3		146	.243
1917	PHI	N	3		114	.255
1918	STL	N	3		22	.176
	NY	N	3		7	.261
	BRTR				581	.240

NIEKRO, JOSEPH FRANKLIN "JOE"
B.NOV.7,1944 MARTINS FERRY,OHIO

1967	CHI	N	P		36	10- 7
1968	CHI	N	P		34	14-10
1969	CHI	N	P		4	0- 1
	SD	N	P	37	38	8-17
1970	DET	A	P		38	12-13
1971	DET	A	P	31	32	6- 7
1972	DET	A	P		18	3- 2
1973	ATL	N	P		20	2- 4
1974	ATL	N	P		27	3- 2
1975	HOU	N	P		40	6- 4
1976	HOU	N	P		36	4- 8
	BRTR			321	324	68-75

NIEKRO, PHILIP HENRY "PHIL"
B.APR.1,1939 BLAINE,OHIO

1964	MIL	N	P		10	0- 0
1965	MIL	N	P	41	42	2- 3
1966	ATL	N	P		28	4- 3
1967	ATL	N	P		46	11- 9
1968	ATL	N	P		37	14-12
1969	ATL	N	P		40	23-13
1970	ATL	N	P		34	12-18
1971	ATL	N	P		42	15-14
1972	ATL	N	P		38	16-12
1973	ATL	N	P		42	13-10
1974	ATL	N	P		41	20-13
1975	ATL	N	P		39	15-15
1976	ATL	N	P		38	17-11
	BRTR			476	477	162-133

NIELSEN, MILTON ROBERT
B.FEB.8,1925 TYLER,MINN.

1949	CLE	A	O		3	.111
1951	CLE	A	H		16	.000
	BLTL				19	.067

NIEMAN, ELMER LE ROY "BUTCH"
B.FEB.8,1919 HERKIMER,KAN.

1943	BOS	N	O		101	.251
1944	BOS	N	O		134	.265
1945	BOS	N	O		97	.247
	BLTL				332	.256

YR	CL LEA POS	GP	G	REC

NIEMAN, ROBERT CHARLES "BOB"
B.JAN.26,1927 CINCINNATI,OHIO
1951 STL A	O		12	.372
1952 STL A	O		131	.289
1953 DET A	O		142	.281
1954 DET A	O		91	.263
1955 CHI A	O		99	.283
1956 CHI A	O		14	.300
BAL A	O		114	.322
1957 BAL A	O		129	.276
1958 BAL A	O		105	.325
1959 BAL A	O		118	.292
1960 STL N	O		81	.287
1961 STL N	O		6	.471
CLE A	O		39	.354
1962 CLE A	H		2	.000
SF N	O		30	.300
BRTR			1113	.295

NIEMES, JACOB LELAND
B.OCT.19,1919 CINCINNATI,OHIO
D.MAR.4,1966
| 1943 CIN N | P | | 3 | 0- 0 |
| BRTL | | | | |

NIEMIEC, ALFRED JOSEPH "AL"
B.MAY 18,1911 MERIDEN,CONN.
1934 BOS A	2		9	.219
1936 PHI A	2		69	.197
BRTR			78	.200

NIESON, CHARLES BASSETT "CHUCK"
B.SEP.24,1942 HANFORD,CAL.
| 1964 MIN A | P | | 2 | 0- 0 |
| BRTR | | | | |

NIGGERLING, JOHN ARNOLD "JOHNNY"
B.JULY 10,1905 REMSEN,IOWA
D.SEPT.16,1963 LE MARS,IOWA
1938 BOS N	P		2	1- 0
1939 CIN N	P		10	2- 1
1940 STL A	P		28	7-11
1941 STL A	P		24	7- 9
1942 STL A	P		28	15-11
1943 STL A	P		20	6- 8
WAS A	P		6	4- 2
1944 WAS A	P		24	10- 8
1945 WAS A	P		26	7-12
1946 WAS A	P		8	3- 2
BOS N	P		8	2- 5
BRTR			184	64-69

NILAND, THOMAS JAMES "HONEST TOM"
B.APR.14,1870 LYNN,MASS.
D.APR.30,1950
| 1896 STL N | S-O | | 18 | .162 |
| BRTR | | | | |

NILES, HERBERT CLYDE "HARRY"
B.SEPT.10,1880 BUCHANAN,MICH.
D.APR.18,1953
1906 STL A	3-O		142	.229
1907 STL A	2		120	.289
1908 NY A	2		95	.250
BOS A	2		18	.235
1909 BOS A	O		145	.245
1910 BOS A	O		18	.214
CLE A	O		70	.212
BRTR			608	.246

NILES, WILLIAM A.
B.1869 COVINGTON,KY.
D.JUNE 1,1897
| 1895 PIT N | 3 | | 11 | .205 |

NILL, GEORGE CHARLES "RABBIT"
B.JULY 14,1881 FT.WAYNE,IND.
D.MAY 24,1962
1904 WAS A	2		15	.167
1905 WAS A	2-3		103	.182
1906 WAS A	2-S-O		89	.235
1907 WAS A	2-S-3		66	.218
CLE A	2		12	.286
1908 CLE A	S		11	.215
BRTR			296	.212

NIPPERT, MERLIN LEE
B.SEPT.1,1938 REED,OKLA.
| 1962 BOS A | P | | 4 | 0- 0 |
| BRTR | | | | |

NISCHWITZ, RONALD LEE "RON"
B.JULY 1,1937 DAYTON,OHIO
1961 DET A	P		6	0- 1
1962 DET A	P		48	4- 5
1963 CLE A	P		14	0- 2
1965 DET A	P		20	1- 0
BBTL			88	5- 8

NITCHOLAS, OTHO JAMES
B.SEPT.13,1911 MC KINNEY,TEX.
| 1945 BRO N | P | | 7 | 1- 0 |
| BRTR | | | | |

NIXON, ALBERT RICHARD "HUMPTY DUMPTY"
B.APR.20,1892 ATLANTIC CITY,N.J
D.NOV.9,1960
1915 BRO N	O		14	.231
1916 BRO N	O		1	1.000
1918 BRO N	O		6	.454
1921 BOS N	O		55	.239
1922 BOS N	O		86	.264
1923 BOS N	O		88	.274
1926 PHI N	O		93	.293
1927 PHI N	O		54	.312
1928 PHI N	O		25	.234
BRTL			422	.276

NIXON, RUSSELL EUGENE "RUSS"
B.FEB.19,1935 HARRISON,OHIO
1957 CLE A	C		62	.281
1958 CLE A	C		113	.301
1959 CLE A	C		82	.240
1960 CLE A	C		25	.244
BOS A	C		80	.298
1961 BOS A	C		87	.289
1962 BOS A	C		65	.278
1963 BOS A	C		98	.268
1964 BOS A	C		81	.233
1965 BOS A	C		59	.270
1966 MIN A	C		51	.260
1967 MIN A	C		74	.235
1968 BOS A	C		29	.153
BLTR			906	.268

NIXON, WILLARD LEE
B.JUNE 17,1928 LINDALE,GA.
1950 BOS A	P		22	8- 6
1951 BOS A	P	33	34	7- 4
1952 BOS A	P	23	33	5- 4
1953 BOS A	P		23	4- 8
1954 BOS A	P		31	11-12
1955 BOS A	P		31	12-10
1956 BOS A	P		23	9- 8
1957 BOS A	P	29	32	12-13
1958 BOS A	P		10	1- 7
BLTR	225	239	69-72

NOBLE, RAFAEL MIGUEL "RAY"
B.MAR.15,1922 CENTRAL HATILLO, CUBA
1951 NY N	C		55	.234
1952 NY N	C		6	.000
1953 NY N	C		46	.206
BRTR			107	.218

NOFTSKER, GEORGE W.
| 1884 ALT U | C-O | | 7 | .042 |

NOLAN, EDWARD SYLVESTER "THE ONLY"
B.NOV.7,1858 PATERSON,N.J.
D.MAY 19,1913
1878 IND N	P		35	13-22
1881 CLE N	P-3- 21		40	7-13
	O			.251
1883 PIT AA	P-O		7	0- 6
				.296
1884 WIL U	P-O	5	9	1- 4
				.242
1885 PHI N	P-O		8	1- 7
				.133
BLTR	76	99	22-52
				.247

NOLAN, GARY LYNN
B.MAY 27,1948 HERLONG,CAL.
1967 CIN N	P		33	14- 8
1968 CIN N	P		23	9- 4
1969 CIN N	P	16	17	8- 8
1970 CIN N	P		37	18- 7
1971 CIN N	P		35	12-15
1972 CIN N	P		25	15- 5
1973 CIN N	P		2	0- 1
1975 CIN N	P		32	15- 9
1976 CIN N	P		34	15- 9
BRTR	237	238	106-66

NOLAN, JOSEPH WILLIAM "JOE"
B.MAY 12,1951 ST.LOUIS,MO.
1972 NY N	C		4	.000
1975 ATL N	C		4	.250
BLTR			8	.071

NOLD, RICHARD LEWIS "DICK"
B.MAY 4,1943 SAN FRANCISCO,CAL.
| 1967 WAS A | P | | 7 | 0- 2 |
| BRTR | | | | |

NONNENKAMP, LEO WILLIAM "RED"
B.JULY 7,1911 ST.LOUIS,MO.
1933 PIT N	H		1	.000
1938 BOS A	O		87	.283
1939 BOS A	O		58	.240
1940 BOS A	H		9	.000
BLTL			155	.262

NOONAN, PETER JOHN
B.NOV.24,1881 W.STOCKBRIDGE, MASS.
D.JAN.11,1965 PITTSFIELD,MASS.
1904 PHI A	C		38	.202
1906 CHI N	C		1	.333
STL N	C-1		39	.168
1907 STL N	C		70	.224
BRTR			148	.205

NOPS, JEREMIAH H.
B.JUNE 23,1875 TOLEDO,OHIO
D.MAR.26,1937
1896 PHI N	P		1	1- 0
BAL N	P		3	2- 1
1897 BAL N	P		28	20- 7
1898 BAL N	P		29	19-10
1899 BAL N	P	31	32	16-12
1900 BRO N	P		9	3- 4
1901 BAL A	P		27	11-12
TL	128	129	72-46

NORDBROOK, TIMOTHY CHARLES "TIM"
B.JULY 7,1949 BALTIMORE,MD.
1974 BAL A	2-S		6	.267
1975 BAL A	2-S		40	.118
1976 BAL A	2-S		27	.227
CAL A	2-S		5	.000
BRTR			78	.165

NORDHAGEN, WAYNE OREN
B.JULY 4,1948 THIEF RIVER FALLS, MINN.
| 1976 CHI A | C-O | | 22 | .189 |
| BRTR | | | | |

NORDSTROM, ANDREW ARTHUR
(PLAYED UNDER NAME OF ANDREW ARTHUR CAREY)

NORDYKE, LOUIS ELLIS
B.AUG.7,1876 BRIGHTON,IOWA
D.SEPT.27,1945 LOS ANGELES,CAL.
| 1906 STL A | 1 | | 25 | .245 |

NOREN, IRVING ARNOLD "IRV"
B.NOV.29,1924 JAMESTOWN,N.Y.
1950 WAS A	1-O		138	.295
1951 WAS A	O		129	.279
1952 WAS A	O		12	.245
NY A	1-O		93	.235
1953 NY A	O		109	.267
1954 NY A	1-O		125	.319
1955 NY A	O		132	.253
1956 NY A	1-O		29	.216
1957 KC A	1-O		81	.213
STL N	O		17	.367
1958 STL N	O		117	.264
1959 STL N	1-O		8	.125
CHI N	1-O		65	.321
1960 CHI N	1-O		12	.091
LA N	H		26	.200
BLTL			1093	.275

NORIEGA, JOHN ALAN
B.DEC.20,1943 OGDEN,UTAH
1969 CIN N	P		5	0- 0
1970 CIN N	P		8	0- 0
BRTR			13	0- 0

```
YR   CL LEA POS  GP    G    REC        YR   CL LEA POS  GP    G    REC        YR   CL LEA POS  GP    G    REC

NORMAN, FREDIE HUBERT "FRED"          NORTHEY, SCOTT RICHARD                NOYES, WINFIELD CHARLES "WIN"
B.AUG.20,1942 SAN ANTONIO,TEX.        B.OCT.15,1946 PHILADELPHIA,PA.        B.JUNE 16,1889 PLEASANTON,NEB.
1962 KC  A  P        2   0- 0         1969 KC  A  O       20    .262        D.APR.8,1969 CASHMERE,WASH.
1963 KC  A  P        2   0- 1              BRTR                             1913 BOS N  P       11   0- 0
1964 CHI N  P        8   0- 4                                               1917 PHI A  P       27  10-10
1966 CHI N  P        2   0- 0         NORTHROP, GEORGE HOWARD "JERKY"       1919 PHI A  P       10   1- 5
1967 CHI N  P        1   0- 0         B.JAN.5,1888 LEWISBURG,PA.                 CHI A  P        1   0- 0
1970 LA  N  P       30   2- 0         D.NOV.16,1945                             BRTR           49  11-15
     STL N  P        1   0- 0         1918 BOS N  P        7   5- 1
1971 STL N  P        4   0- 0         1919 BOS N  P       12   1- 5         NUNAMAKER, LESLIE GRANT "LES"
     SD  N  P   20   25   3-12             BLTR           19   6- 6         B.JAN.25,1889 MALCOLM,NEB.
1972 SD  N  P   42   43   9-11                                              D.NOV.14,1938 HASTINGS,NEB.
1973 SD  N  P       12   1- 7         NORTHRUP, JAMES THOMAS "JIM"          1911 BOS A  C       62    .257
     CIN N  P       24  12- 6         B.NOV.24,1939 BRECKENRIDGE,MICH.      1912 BOS A  C       35    .252
1974 CIN N  P       35  13-12         1964 DET A  O        5    .083        1913 BOS A  C       30    .227
1975 CIN N  P       34  12- 4         1965 DET A  O       80    .205        1914 BOS A  C        5    .200
1976 CIN N  P       33  12- 7         1966 DET A  O      123    .265             NY  A  C       86    .265
     BBTL  250  256  64-64            1967 DET A  O      144    .271        1915 NY  A  C       87    .225
     BL 1962-70                       1968 DET A  O      154    .264        1916 NY  A  C       91    .296
                                      1969 DET A  O      148    .295        1917 NY  A  C      104    .261
NORMAN, HENRY WILLIS PATRICK          1970 DET A  O      139    .262        1918 STL A  C       85    .259
"BILL"                                1971 DET A  1-O    136    .270        1919 CLE A  C       26    .256
B.JULY 16,1910 ST.LOUIS,MO.           1972 DET A  1-O    134    .261        1920 CLE A  C       34    .333
D.APR.21,1962                         1973 DET A  O      119    .307        1921 CLE A  C       46    .359
1931 CHI A  O       24    .182        1974 DET A  O       97    .237        1922 CLE A  C       25    .302
1932 CHI A  O       13    .229             MON N  O       21    .241             BRTR          716    .268
     BRTR           37    .204             BAL A  O        8    .571
NON-PLAYING MANAGER                   1975 BAL A  O       84    .273        NUNEZ, GILBERTO TORRES
DET(A) 1958-59                             BLTR         1392    .267        (PLAYED UNDER NAME OF
                                                                           DON GILBERTO TORRES)
NORRIS, LEO JOHN                      NORTON, ELISHA STRONG "LEITER"
B.MAY 17,1908 NEW ORLEANS,LA.         B.AUG.17,1873 CONNEAUT,OHIO          NUNN, HOWARD RALPH "HOWIE"
1936 PHI N  2-S    154    .265        D.MAR.5,1950 ASPINWALL,PA.            B.OCT.18,1935 WESTFIELD,N.C.
1937 PHI N  2-S-3  116    .257        1896 WAS N  P        8   3- 2         1959 STL N  P       16   2- 2
     BRTR          270    .262        1897 WAS N  P        8   1- 1         1961 CIN N  P       24   2- 1
                                           BRTR           16   4- 3         1962 CIN N  P        6   0- 0
NORRIS, MICHAEL KELVIN "MIKE"                                                    BRTR           46   4- 3
B.MAR.19,1955 SAN FRANCISCO,CAL.      NORTON, J. J.
1975 OAK A  P        4   1- 0         (PLAYED UNDER NAME OF                 NUSZ
1976 OAK A  P       24   4- 5         THOMAS JOHN CAREY)                    1884 WAS U  O        1    .000
     BRTR           28   5- 5
                                      NORTON, PETER J.                      NUTTER, EVERETT CLARENCE
NORTH, LOUIS ALEXANDER                B.JUNE 19,1850 WISCONSIN              B.AUG.27,1892 HOCKING CO.,OHIO
B.JUNE 15,1891 ELGIN,ILL.             D.FEB.8,1923                          D.JULY 25,1958
D.MAY 16,1974 SHELTON,CONN.           1871 OLY NA O        1    .000        1919 BOS N  O       18    .212
1913 DET A  1        1   0- 1                                                    BLTR
1917 STL N  1        5   0- 0         NORTON, THOMAS JOHN "TOM"
1920 STL N  1       26   3- 2         B.APR.26,1950 ELYRIA,OHIO             NUXHALL, JOSEPH HENRY "JOE"
1921 STL N  1       40   4- 4         1972 MIN A  P       21   0- 1         B.JULY 30,1928 HAMILTON,OHIO
1922 STL N  1       53  10- 3              BRTR                             1944 CIN N  P        1   0- 0
1923 STL N  1       34   3- 4                                               1952 CIN N  P       37   1- 4
1924 STL N  1        9   0- 0         NOSSEK, JOSEPH RUDOLPH "JOE"          1953 CIN N  P       30   9-11
     BOS N  1        6   1- 2         B.NOV.8,1940 CLEVELAND,OHIO           1954 CIN N  P   35   36  12- 5
     BRTR     172  174  21-16         1964 MIN A  O        7    .000        1955 CIN N  P   50   53  17-12
                                      1965 MIN A  3-O     87    .218        1956 CIN N  P       44  13-11
NORTH, WILLIAM ALEX "BILL"            1966 MIN A  O        4    .000        1957 CIN N  P   39   42  10-10
B.MAY 15,1948 SEATTLE,WASH.                KC  A  3-O     87    .261        1958 CIN N  P       36  12-11
1971 CHI N  O        8    .375        1967 KC  A  O       87    .205        1959 CIN N  P       28   9- 9
1972 CHI N  O       66    .181        1969 OAK A  O       13    .000        1960 CIN N  P   38   39   1- 8
1973 OAK A  O      146    .287             STL N  O        9    .200        1961 KC  A  P   37   56   5- 8
1974 OAK A  O      149    .260        1970 STL N  H        1    .000        1962 LA  A  P        5   0- 0
1975 OAK A  O      140    .273             BRTR          295    .228             CIN A  P       12   5- 0
1976 OAK A  O      154    .276                                              1963 CIN A  P       35  15- 8
     BBTR          663    .270        NOTTEBART, DONALD EDWARD "DON"        1964 CIN A  P   32   34   9- 8
     BR 1971                          B.JAN.23,1936 WEST NEWTON,MASS.       1965 CIN N  P       32  11- 4
                                      1960 MIL N  P        5   1- 0         1966 CIN N  P       35   6- 8
NORTHEN, HUBBARD ELWIN                1961 MIL N  P       38   6- 7              BLTL  526  555 135-117
B.AUG.16,1889 ALTANTA,TEX.            1962 MIL N  P       39   2- 2
D.OCT.1,1947                          1963 HOU N  P       31  11- 8         NYE, OTTO ADAM
1910 STL A  O       26    .198        1964 HOU N  P       28   6-11         B.SEPT.24,1894 SPRINGFIELD,OHIO
1911 CIN N  O        1    .000        1965 HOU N  P       29   4-15         D.SEPT.19,1932
     BRO N  O       19    .316        1966 CIN N  P       59   5- 4         1917 STL A  H        1    .000
1912 BRO N  O      118    .282        1967 CIN N  P       47   0- 3
     BLTL          164    .272        1969 NY  A  P        4   0- 0         NYE, RICHARD RAYMOND "RICH"
                                           CHI N  P       16   1- 1         B.AUG.4,1944 OAKLAND,CAL.
NORTHEY, RONALD JAMES "RON"                BRTR          296  36-51         1966 CHI N  P        3   0- 2
B.APR.26,1920 MAHANOY CITY,PA.                                             1967 CHI N  P       35  13-10
D.APR.16,1971 PITTSBURGH,PA.          NOURSE, CHESTER LINWOOD              1968 CHI N  P       27   7-12
1942 PHI N  O      127    .251        B.AUG.7,1887 IPSWICH,MASS.            1969 CHI N  P   34   36   3- 5
1943 PHI N  O      147    .278        D.APR.20,1958                         1970 STL N  P        8   10   3- 2
1944 PHI N  O      152    .288        1909 BOS A        3   0- 0                 MON N  P        8   10   3- 2
1946 PHI N  O      128    .249                                                  BLTL  113  117  26-31
1947 PHI N  O       13    .255        NOVIKOFF, LOUIS ALEXANDER
     STL N  3-O    110    .293        "LOU" OR "THE MAD RUSSIAN"            NYMAN, GERALD SMITH "JERRY"
1948 STL N  O       96    .321        B.OCT.12,1915 GLENDALE,ARIZ.          B.NOV.23,1942 LOGAN,UTAH
1949 STL N  O       90    .260        D.SEPT.30,1970 LYNWOOD,CAL.           1968 CHI A  P        8   2- 1
1950 CIN N  O       27    .260        1941 CHI N  O       62    .241        1969 CHI A  P   20   21   4- 4
     CHI N  O       53    .281        1942 CHI N  O      128    .300        1970 SD  N  P    2    3   0- 2
1952 CHI N  H        1    .000        1943 CHI N  O       78    .279             BLTL   30   32   6- 7
1955 CHI A  O       14    .357        1944 CHI N  O       71    .281
1956 CHI A  O       53    .354        1946 PHI N  O       17    .304        NYMAN, NILS WALLACE REX
1957 CHI A  H       40    .185             BRTR          356    .282        B.MAR.7,1954 DETROIT,MICH.
     PHI N  H       33    .269                                             1974 CHI A  O        5    .643
     BLTR         1084    .275        NOVOTNEY, RALPH JOSEPH "RUBE"         1975 CHI A  O      106    .226
                                      B.AUG.5,1924 STREATOR,ILL.            1976 CHI A  O        8    .133
                                      1949 CHI N  C       22    .269             BLTR          119    .239
                                           BRTR
```

YR	CL	LEA	POS	GP	G	REC

OAKES, ENNIS TALMADGE "REBEL"
B.DEC.17,1886 HOMER,LA.
D.FEB.28,1948

YR	CL	LEA	POS	GP	G	REC
1909	CIN	N	O		113	.270
1910	STL	N	O		127	.252
1911	STL	N	O		151	.263
1912	STL	N	O		136	.281
1913	STL	N	O		147	.293
1914	PIT	F	M-O		145	.311
1915	PIT	F	M-O		153	.281
	BLTR				972	.280

OANA, HENRY KAUHANE "PRINCE"
B.JAN.22,1910 WAIPAHU,HAWAII
D.JUNE 19,1976 AUSTIN,TEX.

1934	PHI	N	O		6	.238
1943	DET	A	P	10	20	3- 2
1945	DET	A	P		4	0- 0
	BRTR			14	30	3- 2
						.308

OATES, JOHNNY LANE
B.JAN.21,1946 SYLVA,N.C.

1970	BAL	A	C		5	.278
1972	BAL	A	C		85	.261
1973	ATL	N	C		93	.248
1974	ATL	N	C		100	.223
1975	ATL	N	C		8	.222
	PHI	N	C		90	.286
1976	PHI	N	C		37	.253
	BLTR				418	.254

OBERLANDER, HARTMAN LOUIS
B.MAY 12,1864 WAUKEGAN,ILL.
D.NOV.14,1922

1888	CLE	AA	P		3	1- 2

OBERLIN, FRANK RUFUS
B.MAR.26,1876 ELSIE,MICH.
D.JAN.6,1952

1906	BOS	A	P		4	1- 3
1907	BOS	A	P		12	1- 5
	WAS	A	P	11	12	2- 6
1909	WAS	A	P		10	1- 3
1910	WAS	A	P		8	1- 6
	BRTR			45	46	6-23

O'BRIEN, EDWARD JOSEPH "EDDIE"
B.DEC.11,1930 S.AMBOY,N.J.

1953	PIT	N	S		89	.238
1955	PIT	N	S-3-O		75	.233
1956	PIT	N	P-2-	1	63	0- 0
			S-3-O			.264
1957	PIT	N	P		3	1- 0
1958	PIT	N	P		1	0- 0
	BRTR			5	231	1- 0
						.236

O'BRIEN, FRANK ALOYSIUS
"MICKEY"
B.SEPT.13,1894 SAN FRANCISCO,
CAL.
D.NOV.4,1971 MONTEREY PARK,CAL.

1923	PHI	N	C		15	.333
	BRTR					

O'BRIEN, GEORGE JOSEPH
B.NOV.4,1889 CLEVELAND,OHIO
D.MAR.24,1966 COLUMBUS,OHIO

1915	STL	A	C		3	.222
	BRTR					

O'BRIEN, JEREMIAH
B.WORCESTER,MASS.
D.JULY 5,1911

1887	WAS	N	2		1	.000

O'BRIEN, JOHN E.
1884 BAL U O | | 18 | .256

O'BRIEN, JOHN F. "DARBY"
B.APR.15,1867 W.TROY,N.Y.
D.MAR.11,1892 W.TROY,N.Y.

1888	CLE	AA	P	30	31	11-19
1889	CLE	N	P		41	22-17
1890	CLE	N	P		26	.8-16
1891	BOS	AA	P		41	19-13
	BRTR			138	139	60-65

O'BRIEN, JOHN J.
B.JULY 14,1870 ST.JOHN,N.B.,CAN
D.MAY 13,1913

1891	BRO	N	2		43	.251
1893	CHI	N	2		4	.416
1895	LOU	N	2		128	.262
1896	LOU	N	2		49	.333
	WAS	N	2		69	.270
1897	WAS	N	2		84	.242
1899	BAL	N	2		39	.190
	PIT	N	2		76	.223
	BLTR				492	.256

O'BRIEN, JOHN JOSEPH
B.FEB.5,1873 W.TROY,N.Y.
D.JUNE 11,1933

1899	WAS	N	O		121	.279
1901	WAS	A	O		12	.184
	CLE	A	O		91	.286
1903	BOS	A	O		96	.212
					320	.259

O'BRIEN, JOHN K.
(REAL NAME JOHN K. BYRNE)
B.JUNE 12,1860 PHILADELPHIA,PA.
D.NOV.2,1910

1882	ATH	AA	C-1-O		62	.304
1883	ATH	AA	C-1-S-3-		93	.281
			O			
1884	ATH	AA	C-O		38	.300
1885	ATH	AA	C		61	.261
1886	ATH	AA	C-1-3		105	.257
1887	BRO	AA	C		30	.269
1888	BAL	AA	C		57	.224
1890	BAL	AA	1		110	.270
	BRTR				556	.276

O'BRIEN, JOHN THOMAS "JOHNNY"
B.DEC.11,1930 S.AMBOY,N.J.

1953	PIT	N	?-S		89	.247
1955	PIT	N	2		84	.299
1956	PIT	N	P-2-	8	73	1- 0
			S			.173
1957	PIT	N	P-2-	16	34	0- 3
			S			.314
1958	PIT	N	H		3	.000
	STL	N	P-2-	1	12	0- 0
			S			.000
1959	MIL	N	2		44	.198
	BRTR			25	339	1- 3
						.250

O'BRIEN, PETER F.
B.JUNE 16,1868 CHICAGO,ILL.

1890	CHI	N	2		27	.275

O'BRIEN, PETER J.
B.1876 BINGHAMTON,N.Y.
D.JAN.31,1917

1901	CIN	N	2		15	.208
1906	STL	A	2-3		151	.233
1907	CLE	A	3		43	.244
	WAS	A	2		39	.185
	BLTR				248	.231

O'BRIEN, RAYMOND JOSEPH
B.OCT.31,1892 ST.LOUIS,MO.
D.MAR.31,1942

1916	PIT	N	O		16	.211
	BLTL					

O'BRIEN, ROBERT ALLEN "BOB"
B.APR.23,1939 PITTSBURGH,PA.

1971	LA	N	P		14	2- 2
	BLTL					

O'BRIEN, SYDNEY LLOYD "SID"
B.DEC.18,1944 COMPTON,CAL.

1969	BOS	A	2-S-3		100	.243
1970	CHI	A	2-S-3		121	.247
1971	CAL	A	1-2-S-3-		90	.199
			O			
1972	CAL	A	1-2-S-3		36	.179
	MIL	A	2-3		31	.207
	BRTR				378	.230

O'BRIEN, THOMAS EDWARD
B.DEC.19,1918 ANNISTON,ALA.

1943	PIT	N	3-O		89	.310
1944	PIT	N	3-O		85	.250
1945	PIT	N	O		58	.335
1949	BOS	A	O		49	.224
1950	BOS	A	O		9	.129
	WAS	A	O		3	.111
	BRTR				293	.275

O'BRIEN, THOMAS F.
B.FEB.20,1873 VERONA,PA.
D.FEB.4,1901

1897	BAL	N	1		38	.268
1898	BAL	N	O		19	.217
	PIT	N	1-O		104	.259
1899	NY	N	3-O		152	.305
1900	PIT	N	1-O		94	.294
					407	.284

O'BRIEN, THOMAS H.
B.SALEM,MASS.
D.APR.21,1921

1882	WOR	N	2-3-O		22	.202
1883	BAL	AA	2-O		33	.294
1884	BOS	U	2		102	.265
1885	BAL	AA	1-2		8	.182
1887	MET	AA	1		29	.248
1890	ROC	AA	1		73	.181
					267	.239

O'BRIEN, THOMAS JOSEPH "BUCK"
B.MAY 9,1882 BROCKTON,MASS.
D.JULY 25,1959

1911	BOS	A	P		6	5- 1
1912	BOS	A	P		37	18-13
1913	BOS	A	P		15	4- 9
	CHI	A	P		7	0- 3
	BRTR				65	27-26

O'BRIEN, WILLIAM D. "DARBY"
B.SEPT.1,1863 PEORIA,ILL.
D.JUNE 15,1893

1887	MET	AA	O		129	.353
1888	BRO	AA	O		136	.275
1889	BRO	AA	O		136	.312
1890	BRO	N	O		85	.314
1891	BRO	N	O		102	.260
1892	BRO	N	O		121	.245
	BRTR				709	.292

O'BRIEN, WILLIAM SMITH
B.MAR.14,1860 ALBANY,N.Y.
D.MAY 26,1911

1884	STP	U	P-3	3	8	1- 1
						.241
	KC	U	1-3		4	.235
1887	WAS	N	1		113	.310
1888	WAS	N	1		133	.225
1889	WAS	N	1		2	.000
1890	BRO	AA	1		95	.277
	BR			3	355	1- 1
						.266

OCK, HAROLD DAVID "WHITEY"
B.MAR.17,1912 BROOKLYN,N.Y.
D.MAR.18,1975 MT.KISCO,N.Y.

1935	BRO	N	C		1	.000
	BRTR					

OCKEY, WALTER ANDREW
(REAL NAME
WALTER ANDREW OKYPCH)
B.JAN.4,1920 NEW YORK,N.Y.
D.DEC.4,1971 STATEN ISLAND,N.Y.

1944	NY	N	P		2	0- 0
	BRTR					

O'CONNELL, DANIEL FRANCIS
"DANNY"
B.JAN.21,1927 PATERSON,N.J.
D.OCT.2,1969 CLIFTON,N.J.

1950	PIT	N	S-3		79	.292
1953	PIT	N	2-3		149	.294
1954	MIL	N	1-2-S		146	.279
1955	MIL	N	2-S-3		124	.225
1956	MIL	N	2-S-3		139	.239
1957	MIL	N	2		48	.235
	NY	N	2-3		95	.266
1958	SF	N	2-3		107	.232
1959	SF	N	2-3		34	.190
1961	WAS	A	2-3		138	.260
1962	WAS	A	2-3		84	.263
	BRTR				1143	.260

O'CONNELL, JAMES JOSEPH
B.FEB.11,1901 SACRAMENTO,CAL.

1923	NY	N	1-O		87	.250
1924	NY	N	2-O		52	.317
	BLTR				139	.270

O'CONNELL, JOHN CHARLES
B.JUNE 13,1904 PITTSBURGH,PA.

1928	PIT	N	C		1	.000
1929	PIT	N	C		2	.143
	BRTR				3	.125

YR	CL	LEA	POS	GP	G	REC

O'CONNELL, JOHN JOSEPH
B.MAY 16,1872 LAWRENCE,MASS.

1891	BAL	AA	2-S		7	.172
1902	DET	A	1-2		8	.136
					15	.157

O'CONNELL, PATRICK H.
B.JUNE 10,1861 BANGOR,ME.
D.JAN.24,1943

1886	BAL	AA	O		42	.186
1890	BRO	AA	3		11	.237
		BRTR			53	.192

O'CONNOR, ANDREW JAMES
B.SEPT.14,1884 ROXBURY,MASS.

| 1908 | NY | A | P | | 1 | 0- 1 |

O'CONNOR, DANIEL C.
B.AUG.1868 GUELPH,ONT.,CANADA
D.MAR.5,1942

| 1890 | LOU | AA | 1 | | 6 | .480 |

O'CONNOR, FRANK HENRY
B.SEPT.15,1870 KEESEVILLE,N.Y.
D.DEC.26,1913

| 1893 | PHI | N | P | | 3 | 0- 0 |
| | | TL | | | | |

O'CONNOR, JAMES MATTHEW
(PLAYED UNDER NAME OF
JAMES MATTHEW CONNOR)

O'CONNOR, JOHN J.

| 1916 | CHI | N | C | | 1 | .000 |
| | | TR | | | | |

O'CONNOR, JOHN JOSEPH
"ROWDY JACK"
B.JUNE 2,1869 ST.LOUIS,MO.
D.NOV.14,1937

1887	CIN	AA	C-O		12	.133
1888	CIN	AA	C-O		36	.201
1889	COL	AA	C		107	.269
1890	COL	AA	C		118	.341
1891	COL	AA	C-O		56	.260
1892	CLE	N	C-O		139	.253
1893	CLE	N	C-O		93	.309
1894	CLE	N	C-O		80	.324
1895	CLE	N	C-1		88	.293
1896	CLE	N	C		60	.300
1897	CLE	N	1-O		100	.290
1898	CLE	N	C-1		129	.262
1899	STL	N	C-1		79	.261
1900	STL	N	C		10	.219
	PIT	N	C		38	.242
1901	PIT	N	C		56	.200
1902	PIT	N	C-1		45	.292
1903	NY	A	C		64	.197
1904	STL	A	C		13	.178
1906	STL	A	C		58	.190
1907	STL	A	C		25	.157
1910	STL	A	M-C		1	.000
		BRTR			1407	.268

NON-PLAYING MANAGER STL(N) 1909

O'CONNOR, PATRICK FRANCIS
B.AUG.4,1879 WINDSOR LOCKS,CONN
D.AUG.17,1950

1908	PIT	N	C		12	.187
1909	PIT	N	C		9	.312
1910	PIT	N	C		1	.250
1914	STL	N	C		10	.000
1915	PIT	F	C		70	.224
1918	NY	A	C		1	.333
		BRTR			103	.222

O'DAY, HENRY F. "HANK"
B.JULY 8,1863 CHICAGO,ILL.
D.JULY 2,1935

1884	TOL	AA	P-O	40	65	10-29
						.209
1885	PIT	AA	P		14	5- 7
1886	WAS	N	P		6	2- 2
1887	WAS	N	P	30	34	8-19
1888	WAS	N	P		47	16-31
1889	WAS	N	P		13	4- 5
	NY	N	P		15	9- 6
1890	NY	N	P	P		43	22-15
		TR		208	237	76-114
						.198

NON-PLAYING MANAGER
CIN(N) 1912, CHI(N) 1914

O'DEA, JAMES KENNETH "KEN"
B.MAR.16,1913 LIMA,N.Y.

1935	CHI	N	C		76	.257
1936	CHI	N	C		80	.307
1937	CHI	N	C		83	.301
1938	CHI	N	C		86	.263
1939	NY	N	C		52	.175
1940	NY	N	C		48	.240
1941	NY	N	C		59	.213
1942	STL	N	C		58	.234
1943	STL	N	C		71	.281
1944	STL	N	C		85	.249
1945	STL	N	C		100	.254
1946	STL	N	C		22	.123
	BOS	N	C		12	.219
		BLTR			832	.255

O'DEAL, PAUL
B.JULY 3,1920 CLEVELAND,OHIO

1944	CLE	A	P-1	3	76	0- 0
			O			.318
1945	CLE	A	P-O	1	87	0- 0
						.235
		BLTL		4	163	0- 0
						.272

O'DELL, WILLIAM OLIVER "BILLY"
B.FEB.10,1933 WHITMIRE,S.C.

1954	BAL	A	P		7	1- 1
1956	BAL	A	P		4	0- 0
1957	BAL	A	P	35	37	4-10
1958	BAL	A	P	41	42	14-11
1959	BAL	A	P	38	43	10-12
1960	SF	N	P	43	49	8-13
1961	SF	N	P	46	49	7- 5
1962	SF	N	P	43	49	19-14
1963	SF	N	P	36	47	14-10
1964	SF	N	P	36	50	6- 7
1965	MIL	N	P-1		62	10- 6
						.174
1966	ATL	N	P	24	26	2- 3
	PIT	N	P		37	3- 2
1967	PIT	N	P	27	28	5- 6
		BBTL		479	530	105-100
						.125

ODENWALD, THEODORE JOSEPH
B.JAN.4,1902 HUDSON,WIS.
D.OCT.23,1965 SHAKOPEE,MINN.

1921	CLE	A	P		10	1- 0
1922	CLE	A	P		1	0- 0
		BRTL			11	1- 0

ODOM, DAVID EVERETT "BLIMP"
B.JUNE 5,1918 DINUBA,CAL.

| 1943 | BOS | N | P | | 22 | 0- 3 |
| | | BRTR | | | | |

ODOM, HERMAN BOYD "HEINE"
B.OCT.13,1900 RUSK,TEX.
D.AUG.30,1970 RUSK,TEX.

| 1925 | NY | A | 3 | | 1 | 1.000 |
| | | BBTR | | | | |

ODOM, JOHNNY LEE "BLUE MOON"
B.MAY 29,1945 MACON,GA.

1964	KC	A	P		5	1- 2
1965	KC	A	P		1	0- 0
1966	KC	A	P	14	17	5- 5
1967	KC	A	P	29	33	3- 8
1968	OAK	A	P	32	42	16-10
1969	OAK	A	P	32	43	15- 6
1970	OAK	A	P	29	37	9- 8
1971	OAK	A	P	25	37	10-12
1972	OAK	A	P	31	59	15- 6
1973	OAK	A	P	30	51	5-12
1974	OAK	A	P	34	43	1- 5
1975	OAK	A	P	7	8	0- 2
	CLE	A	P		3	1- 0
	ATL	N	P		15	1- 7
1976	CHI	A	P		8	2- 2
		BRTR		295	402	84-85

O'DONNELL

| 1884 | KEY | U | C | | 1 | .250 |

O'DONNELL, EDWARD
(PLAYED UNDER NAME OF
EDWARD DONNELLY)

O'DONNELL, GEORGE DANA
B.MAY 27,1929 JACKSONVILLE,ILL.

| 1954 | PIT | N | P | | 21 | 3- 9 |
| | | BRTR | | | | |

O'DONNELL, HARRY HERMAN "BUTCH"
B.APR.2,1894 PHILADELPHIA,PA.
D.JAN.31,1958

| 1927 | PHI | N | C | | 16 | .063 |
| | | BRTR | | | | |

O'DONOGHUE, JOHN EUGENE
B.OCT.7,1939 KANSAS CITY,MO.

1963	KC	A	P		1	0- 1
1964	KC	A	P	39	40	10-14
1965	KC	A	P	34	39	9-18
1966	CLE	A	P		32	6- 8
1967	CLE	A	P		33	8- 9
1968	BAL	A	P		16	0- 0
1969	SEA	A	P		55	2- 2
1970	MIL	A	P		25	2- 0
	MON	N	P		9	2- 3
1971	MON	N	P		13	0- 0
		BRTL		257	263	39-55

O'DOUL, FRANK JOSEPH "LEFTY"
B.MAR.4,1897 SAN FRANCISCO,CAL.
D.DEC.7,1969 SAN FRANCISCO,CAL.

1919	NY	A	P	3	19	0- 0
1920	NY	A	P	2	13	0- 0
1922	NY	A	P	6	8	0- 0
1923	BOS	A	P	23	36	1- 1
1928	NY	N	O		114	.319
1929	PHI	N	O		154	.398
1930	PHI	N	O		140	.383
1931	BRO	N	O		134	.336
1932	BRO	N	O		148	.368
1933	BRO	N	O		43	.252
	NY	N	O		78	.306
1934	NY	N	O		83	.316
		BLTL		34	970	1- 1
						.349

ODWELL, FREDERICK WILLIAM
B.SEPT.25,1872 DOWNSVILLE,N.Y.
D.AUG.12,1948

1904	CIN	N	O		126	.284
1905	CIN	N	O		126	.241
1906	CIN	N	O		57	.223
1907	CIN	N	O		84	.270
		BLTR		393	.258	

OERTEL, CHARLES FRANK "CHUCK"
B.MAR.12,1931 COFFEYVILLE,KAN.

| 1958 | BAL | A | O | | 14 | .167 |
| | | BLTR | | | | |

OESCHGER, JOSEPH CARL "JOE"
B.MAY 23,1891 GLENDALE,CAL.

1914	PHI	N	P		32	4- 8
1915	PHI	N	P		6	1- 0
1916	PHI	N	P		14	1- 0
1917	PHI	N	P	42	43	15-14
1918	PHI	N	P		30	6-18
1919	PHI	N	P		5	0- 1
	NY	N	P		5	0- 1
	BOS	N	P		7	4- 2
1920	BOS	N	P		38	15-13
1921	BOS	N	P		46	20-14
1922	BOS	N	P		46	6-21
1923	BOS	N	P		44	5-15
1924	NY	N	P		10	2- 0
	PHI	N	P		19	2- 7
1925	BRO	N	P		21	1- 2
		BRTR		365	366	82-116

YR	CL	LEA	POS	GP	G	REC

O'FARRELL, ROBERT ARTHUR "BOB"
B.OCT.19,1896 WAUKEGAN,ILL.

1915	CHI	N	C		2	.667
1916	CHI	N	C		1	.000
1917	CHI	N	C		3	.375
1918	CHI	N	C		52	.283
1919	CHI	N	C		49	.216
1920	CHI	N	C		94	.248
1921	CHI	N	C		96	.250
1922	CHI	N	C		128	.323
1923	CHI	N	C		131	.319
1924	CHI	N	C		71	.241
1925	CHI	N	C		17	.182
	STL	N	C		94	.278
1926	STL	N	C		147	.293
1927	STL	N	M-C		61	.264
1928	STL	N	C		16	.212
	NY	N	C		75	.195
1929	NY	N	C		91	.306
1930	NY	N	C		94	.301
1931	NY	N	C		85	.224
1932	NY	N	C		50	.239
1933	STL	N	C		55	.239
1934	CIN	N	M-C		44	.244
	CHI	N	C		22	.224
1935	STL	N	C		14	.000
	BRTR				1492	.273

OFFICE, ROWLAND JOHNIE
B.OCT.25,1952 SACRAMENTO,CAL.

1972	ATL	N	O		2	.400
1974	ATL	N	O		131	.246
1975	ATL	N	O		126	.290
1976	ATL	N	O		99	.281
	BLTL				358	.276

OGDEN, JOHN MAHLON
B.NOV.5,1897 OGDEN,PA.

1918	NY	N	P		5	0- 0
1928	STL	A	P		38	15-16
1929	STL	A	P		34	4- 8
1931	CIN	N	P	22	23	4- 8
1932	CIN	N	P	24	27	2- 2
	BRTR			123	127	25-34

OGDEN, WARREN HARVEY "CURLY"
B.JAN.24,1901 OGDEN,PA.
D.AUG.6,1964 CHESTER,PA.

1922	PHI	A	P	15	17	1- 4
1923	PHI	A	P	18	19	1- 2
1924	PHI	A	P		5	0- 3
	WAS	A	P	16	17	9- 5
1925	WAS	A	P		17	3- 1
1926	WAS	A	P		22	4- 4
	BRTR			94	97	18-19

OGLESBY, JAMES DORN
B.AUG.10,1915 POLK CO.,MO.
D.SEPT.1,1955

| 1936 | PHI | A | 1 | | 3 | .182 |
| | BLTL | | | | | |

OGLIVIE, BENJAMIN AMBROSIO "BEN"
B.FEB.11,1949 COLON,PANAMA

1971	BOS	A	O		14	.263
1972	BOS	A	O		94	.241
1973	BOS	A	O-D		58	.218
1974	DET	A	1-O		92	.270
1975	DET	A	1-O		100	.286
1976	DET	A	1-O		115	.285
	BLTL				473	.266

OGRODOWSKI, AMBROSE FRANCIS "BRUCE"
B.FEB.17,1913 HOYTVILLE,PA.
D.MAR.5,1956

1936	STL	N	C		94	.228
1937	STL	N	C		90	.233
	BRTR				184	.231

OGRODOWSKI, JOSEPH ANTHONY
B.NOV.30,1906 MORRIS,W.VA.
D.JUNE 24,1959

| 1925 | BOS | N | P | | 1 | 0- 0 |
| | BRTR | | | | | |

O'HAGEN, HARRY P.
B.SEPT.30,1873 WASHINGTON,D.C.
D.JAN.14,1913

1892	WAS	N	C		1	.250
1902	PHI	N	1		33	.188
	NY	N	1		24	.138
	CLE	A	1		3	.384
					61	.177

O'HARA, JAMES FRANCIS "KID"
B.DEC.19,1875 WILKES-BARRE,PA.
D.DEC.1,1954

| 1904 | BOS | N | O | | 8 | .207 |
| | BBTR | | | | | |

O'HARA, THOMAS F.
B.JULY 13,1885 WAVERLY,N.Y.
D.JUNE 8,1954

1906	STL	N	O		14	.321
1907	STL	N	O		47	.237
					61	.257

O'HARA, WILLIAM A.
B.AUG.14,1883 TORONTO,ONT.,CAN.
D.JUNE 15,1931 JERSEY CITY,N.J.

1909	NY	N	O		111	.236
1910	STL	N	P-1-	1	9	0- 0
			O			.150
	BL			1	120	0- 0
						.231

OHL, JOSEPH EARL
B.JAN.10,1888 JOBSTOWN,N.J.
D.DEC.18,1951

| 1909 | WAS | A | P | | 4 | 0- 0 |
| | BLTL | | | | | |

OKRIE, FRANK ANTHONY "LEFTY"
B.OCT.28,1896 DETROIT,MICH.
D.OCT.16,1959

| 1920 | DET | A | P | | 21 | 1- 2 |
| | BLTL | | | | | |

OKRIE, LEONARD JOSEPH "LEN"
B.JULY 16,1924 DETROIT,MICH.

1948	WAS	A	C		19	.238
1950	WAS	A	C		17	.222
1951	WAS	A	C		5	.125
1952	BOS	A	C		1	.000
	BRTR				42	.218

OKYPCH, WALTER ANDREW
(PLAYED UNDER NAME OF
WALTER ANDREW OCKEY)

OLDFIELD, DAVID
B.PHILADELPHIA,PA.

1883	BAL	AA	C		1	.000
1885	BRO	AA	C-O		10	.308
1886	BRO	AA	C		14	.240
	WAS	N	C		19	.158
	TR				44	.211

OLDHAM, JOHN CYRUS "RED"
B.JULY 15,1893 ZION,MO.
D.JAN.28,1961

1914	DET	A	P		9	2- 4
1915	DET	A	P		17	2- 0
1920	DET	A	P		39	8-13
1921	DET	A	P	40	42	11-14
1922	DET	A	P		43	10-13
1925	PIT	N	P		11	3- 2
1926	PIT	N	P		17	2- 2
	BBTL			176	178	38-48
	BL 1922-26					

OLDHAM, JOHN HARDIN
B.NOV.6,1932 SALINAS,CAL.

| 1956 | CIN | N | H | | 1 | .000 |
| | BL | | | | | |

OLDIS, ROBERT CARL "BOB"
B.JAN.5,1928 PRESTON,IOWA

1953	WAS	A	C		7	.250
1954	WAS	A	C-3		11	.333
1955	WAS	A	C		6	.000
1960	PIT	N	C		22	.200
1961	PIT	N	C		4	.000
1962	PHI	N	C		38	.263
1963	PHI	N	C		47	.224
	BRTR				135	.237

OLDRING, REUBEN NOSHIER "RUBE"
B.MAY 30,1884 NEW YORK,N.Y.
D.SEPT.9,1961

1905	NY	N	S		8	.300
1906	PHI	A	3		59	.241
1907	PHI	A	O		117	.286
1908	PHI	A	O		116	.221
1909	PHI	A	O		90	.230
1910	PHI	A	O		134	.308
1911	PHI	A	O		121	.297
1912	PHI	A	O		98	.301
1913	PHI	A	O		136	.283
1914	PHI	A	O		119	.277
1915	PHI	A	O		107	.248
1916	PHI	A	O		40	.247
1916	NY	A	O		43	.234
1918	PHI	A	O		49	.233
	BRTR				1237	.270

O'LEARY, CHARLES TIMOTHY
B.OCT.15,1882 CHICAGO,ILL.
D.JAN.6,1941

1904	DET	A	S		135	.215
1905	DET	A	S		148	.213
1906	DET	A	S		128	.219
1907	DET	A	S		139	.241
1908	DET	A	S		65	.251
1909	DET	A	3		76	.203
1910	DET	A	2-S		65	.242
1911	DET	A	2		74	.266
1912	DET	A	2		3	.200
1913	STL	N	2-S		121	.217
1934	STL	A	H		1	1.000
	BRTR				955	.234

O'LEARY, DANIEL "HUSTLING DAN"
B.OCT.22,1856 DETROIT,MICH.
D.JUNE 24,1922

1879	PRO	N	O		2	.429
1880	BOS	N	O		3	.250
1881	DET	N	O		2	.000
1882	WOR	N	O		6	.167
1884	CIN	U	M-O		27	.252
	BL				40	.235

OLIN, FRANKLIN WALTER
B.JAN.9,1860 WOODFORD,VT.
D.MAY 20,1951

1884	WAS	AA	2-O		21	.386
	WAS	U	O		1	.000
	TOL	AA	O		26	.271
1885	DET	N	3		1	.500
					49	.306

OLIVA, PEDRO (LOPEZ) "TONY"
B.JULY 20,1940 PINAR DEL RIO,
CUBA

1962	MIN	A	O		9	.444
1963	MIN	A	H		7	.429
1964	MIN	A	O		161	.323
1965	MIN	A	O		149	.321
1966	MIN	A	O		159	.307
1967	MIN	A	O		146	.289
1968	MIN	A	O		128	.289
1969	MIN	A	O		153	.309
1970	MIN	A	O		157	.325
1971	MIN	A	O		126	.337
1972	MIN	A	O		10	.321
1973	MIN	A	D		146	.291
1974	MIN	A	D		127	.285
1975	MIN	A	D		131	.270
1976	MIN	A	D		67	.211
	BLTR				1676	.304

OLIVARES, EDWARD (BALZAC)
B.NOV.5,1938 BROOKLYN,N.Y.

1960	STL	N	3		3	.000
1961	STL	N	O		21	.167
	BRTR				24	.143

OLIVER, ALBERT "AL"
B.OCT.14,1946 PORTSMOUTH,OHIO

1968	PIT	N	O		4	.125
1969	PIT	N	1-O		129	.285
1970	PIT	N	1-O		151	.270
1971	PIT	N	1-O		143	.282
1972	PIT	N	1-O		140	.312
1973	PIT	N	1-O		158	.292
1974	PIT	N	1-O		147	.321
1975	PIT	N	1-O		155	.280
1976	PIT	N	1-O		121	.323
	BLTL				1148	.295

YR	CL	LEA	POS	GP	G	REC

OLIVER, EUGENE GEORGE "GENE"
B.MAR.22,1935 MOLINE,ILL.

1959	STL	N	C-1-0	68	.244
1961	STL	N	C-0	22	.269
1962	STL	N	C-1-0	122	.258
1963	STL	N	C	39	.225
	MIL	N	C-1-0	95	.250
1964	MIL	N	C-1	93	.276
1965	MIL	N	C-1-0	122	.270
1966	ATL	N	C-1-0	76	.194
1967	ATL	N	C	17	.196
	PHI	N	C-1	85	.224
1968	BOS	A	C-0	16	.143
	CHI	N	C-1-0	8	.364
1969	CHI	N	C	23	.222
	BRTR			786	.246

**OLIVER, NATHANIEL
"NATE" OR "PEEWEE"**
B.DEC.13,1940 ST.PETERSBURG,FLA.

1963	LA	N	2-S	65	.239
1964	LA	N	2-S	99	.243
1965	LA	N	2	8	1.000
1966	LA	N	2-S-3	80	.193
1967	LA	N	2-S-3	77	.237
1968	SF	N	2-S-3	36	.178
1969	NY	A	H	1	.000
	CHI	N	2	44	.159
	BRTR			410	.226

**OLIVER, RICHARD
(SEE TRACY SOUTER BARRETT)**

OLIVER, ROBERT LEE "BOB"
B.FEB.8,1943 SHREVEPORT,LA.

1965	PIT	N	3		.000
1969	KC	A	1-3-0	118	.254
1970	KC	A	1-3	160	.260
1971	KC	A	1-3-0	128	.244
1972	KC	A	0	16	.270
	CAL	A	1-0	134	.269
1973	CAL	A	1-3-0-D	151	.265
1974	CAL	A	1-3-0	110	.248
	BAL	A	1	9	.150
1975	NY	A	1-3	18	.132
	BRTR			847	.256

OLIVER, THOMAS NOBLE "REBEL"
B.JAN.15,1903 MONTGOMERY,ALA.

1930	BOS	A	0	154	.293
1931	BOS	A	0	148	.276
1932	BOS	A	0	122	.264
1933	BOS	A	0	90	.258
	BPTR			514	.277

**OLIVO, DIOMEDES ANTONIO
(MALDONATO)**
B.JAN.22,1919 GUAYUBIN,D.R.

1960	PIT	N	P	4	0-0
1962	PIT	N	P	62	5-1
1963	STL	N	P	19	0-5
	BLTL			85	5-6

**OLIVO, FEDERICO EMILIO
(MALDONATO) "CHI-CHI"**
B.MAR.18,1928 GUAYUBIN,D.R.

1961	MIL	N	P	3	0-0
1964	MIL	N	P	38	2-1
1965	MIL	N	P	8	0-1
1966	ATL	N	P	47	5-4
	BRTR			96	7-6

OLLOM, JAMES DONALD "JIM"
B.JULY 8,1945 SNOHOMISH,WASH.

1966	MIN	A	P	3	0-0
1967	MIN	A	P	21	0-1
	BRTL			24	0-1

OLMO, LUIS RODRIGUEZ
B.AUG.11,1919 ARECIBO,P.R.

1943	BRO	N	0	57	.303
1944	BRO	N	2-3-0	136	.258
1945	BRO	N	2-3-0	141	.313
1949	BRO	N	0	38	.305
1950	BOS	N	3-0	69	.227
1951	BOS	N	0	21	.196
	BRTR			462	.281

OLMSTED, FREDRICK D.
B.NOV.21,1881 RAVENNA,MICH.
D.JUNE 16,1972 MANISTIQUE,MICH.

1908	CHI	A	P	1	1-0
1909	CHI	A	P	8	3-2
1910	CHI	A	P	32	10-12
1911	CHI	A	P	25	6-6
	BRTR			66	20-20

OLMSTED, HENRY THEODORE
B.JAN.12,1879 SAGINAW BAY,MICH.
D.JAN.6,1969 BRADENTON,FLA.

1905	BOS	A	P	3	1-2

OLSEN, ALBERT WILLIAM
B.MAR.30,1921 SAN DIEGO,CAL.

1943	BOS	A	H	1	.000
	BLTL				

OLSEN, ARTHUR OLE
B.SEPT.12,1896 S.NORWALK,CONN.

1922	DET	A	P	37	39	7-6
1923	DET	A	P		17	1-1
	BRTR			54	56	8-7

OLSEN, BERNARD CHARLES
B.SEPT.11,1919 EVERTT,MASS.

1941	CHI	N	0	24	.288
	BRTR				

OLSEN, VERNON JARL
B.MAR.16,1918 HILLSBORO,ORE.

1939	CHI	N	P	4	1-0
1940	CHI	N	P	34	35	13-9
1941	CHI	N	P		37	10-8
1942	CHI	N	P		32	6-9
1946	CHI	N	P		5	0-0
	BRTL			112	113	30-26

OLSON, IVAN MASSIE "IVY"
B.OCT.14,1885 KANSAS CITY,MO.
D.SEPT.1,1965 INGLEWOOD,CAL.

1911	CLE	A	S	140	.261
1912	CLE	A	S-3	123	.253
1913	CLE	A	1-3	104	.248
1914	CLE	A	2-S-3	89	.242
1915	CIN	N	1-2-3	63	.232
	BRO	N	3	18	.077
1916	BRO	N	3	108	.254
1917	BRO	N	S	139	.269
1918	BRO	N	S	126	.239
1919	BRO	N	S	140	.278
1920	BRO	N	2-S	143	.254
1921	BRO	N	2-S	151	.267
1922	BRO	N	2-S	136	.272
1923	BRO	N	1-2-S-3	82	.260
1924	BRO	N	2-S	10	.222
	BRTR			1572	.267

OLSON, KARL ARTHUR
B.JULY 6,1930 ROSS,CAL.

1951	BOS	A	0	5	.100
1953	BOS	A	0	25	.123
1954	BOS	A	0	101	.260
1955	BOS	A	0	26	.250
1956	WAS	A	0	106	.246
1957	WAS	A	0	8	.167
	DET	A	0	8	.143
	BRTR			279	.235

OLSON, MARVIN CLEMENT
B.MAY 28,1907 GAYVILLE,S.DAK.

1931	BOS	A	2	15	.189
1932	BOS	A	2	115	.248
1933	BOS	A	2	3	.000
	BRTR			133	.241

OLSON, THEODORE OTTO
B.AUG.27,1912 SQUANTUM,MASS.

1936	BOS	A	P	5	1-1
1937	BOS	A	P	11	0-0
1938	BOS	A	P	2	0-0
	BRTR			18	1-1

O'MARA, OLIVER EDWARD
B.MAR.8,1892 ST.LOUIS,MO.

1912	DET	A	S	1	.000
1914	BRO	N	S	67	.263
1915	BRO	N	S	149	.244
1916	BRO	N	S	72	.202
1918	BRO	N	3	121	.213
1919	BRO	N	3	2	.000
	TR			412	.231

O'MEARA, THOMAS EDWARD
B.DEC.12,1872 CHICAGO,ILL.
D.FEB.16,1902

1895	CLE	N	C	1	.000
1896	CLE	N	C	9	.148
				10	.135

O'NEAL

1874	HAR	NA	0	1	.000

O'NEAL, ORAN HERBERT
B.MAY 2,1900 GATEWOOD,MO.

1925	PHI	N	P	11	0-0
1927	PHI	N	P	2	0-0
	BRTR			13	0-0

O'NEIL, DENNIS
B.1861 IRELAND

1893	STL	N	1	7	.120

O'NEIL, EDWARD J.
B.MAR.11,1859 FALL RIVER,MASS.
D.SEPT.30,1892

1890	TOL	AA	P	3	2-1
	ATH	AA	P-3-	8	11	0-8
			0			.176
	TR			11	14	2-9
						.136

O'NEIL, GEORGE MICHAEL "MICKEY"
B.APR.2,1900 ST.LOUIS,MO.
D.APR.8,1964 ST.LOUIS,MO.

1919	BOS	N	C	11	.214
1920	BOS	N	C	112	.283
1921	BOS	N	C	98	.249
1922	BOS	N	C	83	.223
1923	BOS	N	C	96	.212
1924	BOS	N	C	106	.246
1925	BOS	N	C	70	.258
1926	BRO	N	C	75	.209
1927	WAS	A	C	5	.000
	NY	N	C	16	.132
	BRTR			672	.239

O'NEIL, JOHN FRANCIS
B.APR.19,1921 SHELBIANA,KY.

1946	PHI	N	S	46	.266
	BRTR				

O'NEILL
B.BEDFORD,PA.

1875	ATL	NA	P-S-	4	6	0-4
			0			–

O'NEILL, FREDERICK J.
B.1865 LONDON,ONTARIO,CANADA
D.MAR.7,1892

1887	MET	AA	0	5	.391

O'NEILL, HARRY MINK
B.MAY 8,1917 PHILADELPHIA,PA.
D.MAR.6,1945

1939	PHI	A	C	1	.000
	BRTR				

O'NEILL, JAMES EDWARD "TIP"
B.MAY 25,1858 WOODSTOCK,ONT.,
CANADA
D.DEC.31,1915 MONTREAL,QUE.,CAN

1883	NY	N	P-0	20	23	7-13
						.178
1884	STL	AA	P-0	17	77	10-4
						.272
1885	STL	AA	0		51	.342
1886	STL	AA	0		138	.329
1887	STL	AA	0		123	.492
1888	STL	AA	0		130	.332
1889	STL	AA	0		133	.337
1890	CHI	P	0		137	.302
1891	STL	AA	0		127	.321
1892	CIN	N	0		107	.250
	BRTR			37	1046	17-17
						.332

O'NEILL, JAMES LEO
B.FEB.23,1895 MINOOKA,PA.
D.SEPT.5,1976 CHAMBERSBURG,PA.

1920	WAS	A	S	86	.289
1923	WAS	A	2-S	23	.273
	BRTR			109	.287

O'NEILL, JOHN J.
B.NEW YORK,N.Y.

1899	NY	N	C	2	.000
1902	NY	N	C	2	.000
	TR			4	.000

O'NEILL, JOHN JOSEPH
B.JAN.10,1882 GALWAY,IRELAND
D.JUNE 29,1935

1902	STL	N	C	56	.154
1903	STL	N	C	74	.236
1904	CHI	N	C	49	.214
1905	CHI	N	C	50	.198
1906	BOS	N	C	51	.180
	TR			280	.199

YR	CL	LEA	POS	GP	G	REC

O'NEILL, JOSEPH HENRY
B.FEB.1,1897 RIDGETOWN,ONT.,CAN
D.SEPT.5,1969 RIDGETOWN,ONT.,
CAN.

YR	CL	LEA	POS	GP	G	REC
1922	PHI	A	P		1	0- 0
1923	PHI	A	P		3	0- 0
			BRTR		4	0- 0

O'NEILL, MICHAEL JOYCE
(PLAYED UNDER NAME OF
MICHAEL JOYCE IN 1901)
B.SEPT.7,1877 MAAM, COUNTY
GALWAY, IRELAND
D.AUG.12,1959

1901	BUS	A	P		6	2- 2
1902	STL	N	P-O	33	36	16-15
						.318
1903	STL	N	P	19	32	4-13
1904	STL	N	P	25	28	10-14
1907	CIN	N	O		9	.069
			BRTR	83	111	32-44
						.255

**O'NEILL, PHILIP BERNARD
"PEACHES"**
B.AUG.30,1879 ANDERSON,IND.
D.AUG.2,1955

1904	CIN	N	C		8	.267
			TR			

O'NEILL, ROBERT EMMETT "PINKY"
B.JAN.13,1918 SAN MATEO,CAL.

1943	BOS	A	P		11	1- 4
1944	BOS	A	P		28	6-11
1945	BOS	A	P		24	8-11
1946	CHI	A	P		1	0- 0
	CHI	A	P		2	0- 0
			BRTR		66	15-26

**O'NEILL, STEPHEN FRANCIS
"STEVE"**
B.JULY 6,1891 MINOOKA,PA.
D.JAN.26,1962

1911	CLE	A	C		9	.111
1912	CLE	A	C		68	.228
1913	CLE	A	C		78	.295
1914	CLE	A	C		86	.253
1915	CLE	A	C		121	.236
1916	CLE	A	C		130	.235
1917	CLE	A	C		129	.184
1918	CLE	A	C		114	.242
1919	CLE	A	C		125	.289
1920	CLE	A	C		149	.321
1921	CLE	A	C		106	.322
1922	CLE	A	C		133	.311
1923	CLE	A	C		113	.248
1924	BOS	A	C		106	.238
1925	NY	A	C		35	.286
1927	STL	A	C		74	.230
1928	STL	A	C		10	.292
			BRTR		1586	.263

NON-PLAYING MANAGER
CLE(A) 1935-37, DET(A) 1943-48,
BOS(A) 1950-51, PHI(N) 1952-54

O'NEILL, WILLIAM JOHN
B.JAN.12,1880 ST.JOHN,N.B.,CAN.
D.JULY 27,1920

1904	BOS	A	O		18	.192
	WAS	A	O		94	.277
1906	CHI	A	O		94	.248
			BB		206	.242

ONIS, MANUEL RALPH
B.OCT.24,1911 TAMPA,FLA.

1935	BRO	N	C		1	1.000
			BRTR			

ONSLOW, EDWARD JOSEPH "EDDIE"
B.FEB.17,1893 MEADVILLE,PA.

1912	DET	A	1		35	.227
1913	DET	A	1		17	.255
1918	CLE	A	O		2	.200
1927	WAS	A	1		9	.222
			BLTL		63	.232

ONSLOW, JOHN JAMES "JACK"
B.OCT.13,1888 SCOTTDALE,PA.
D.DEC.22,1960

1912	DET	A	C		31	.159
1917	NY	N	C		9	.250
			BRTR		40	.169

NON-PLAYING MANAGER
CHI(A) 1949-50

ONTIVEROS, STEVEN ROBERT "STEVE"
B.OCT.26,1951 BAKERSFIELD,CAL.

1973	SF	N	1-O		24	.242
1974	SF	N	1-3-O		120	.265
1975	SF	N	1-3-O		108	.289
1976	SF	N	1-3-O		59	.176
			BBTR		311	.266

ORAN, THOMAS
D.SEPT.21,1886

1875	RS	NA	O		19	-

ORAVETZ, ERNEST EUGENE "ERNIE"
B.JAN.24,1932 JOHNSTOWN,PA.

1955	WAS	A	O		100	.270
1956	WAS	A	O		88	.248
			BBTL		188	.263

**ORDENNA, ANTONIO (RODRIGUEZ)
"MOSQUITO"**
B.OCT.30,1918 GUANABACOA,
HAVANA,CUBA

1943	PIT	N	S		1	.500
			BRTR			

ORENGO, JOSEPH CHARLES "JOE"
B.NOV.29,1916 SAN FRANCISCO,CAL

1939	STL	N	S		7	.000
1940	STL	N	2-S-3		129	.287
1941	NY	N	2-S-3		77	.214
1943	NY	N	1		83	.218
	BRO	N	3		7	.200
1944	DET	A	1-2-S-3		46	.201
1945	CHI	A	2-3		17	.067
			BRTR		366	.238

O'RILEY, DONALD LEE "DON"
B.MAR.12,1945 TOPEKA,KAN.

1969	KC	A	P	18	19	1- 1
1970	KC	A	P	9	9	0- 0
			BRTR	27	28	1- 1

ORME, GEORGE WILLIAM
B.SEPT.16,1891 LEBANON,IND.
D.MAR.16,1962

1920	BOS	A	O		4	.323
			BRTR			

ORNDORFF, JESSE WALWORK THAYER
B.JAN.15,1881 CHICAGO,ILL.
D.SEPT.28,1960

1907	BOS	N	C		5	.100
			BBTR			

O'ROURKE

1872	ECK	NA	P		1	0- 1

**O'ROURKE, FRANCIS JAMES
"BLACKIE"**
B.NOV.26,1891 HAMILTON,ONT.,CAN

1912	BOS	N	S		61	.122
1917	BRO	N	3		64	.237
1918	BRO	N	2		4	.167
1920	WAS	A	S		14	.277
1921	WAS	A	S		123	.234
1922	BOS	A	S-3		67	.264
1924	DET	A	2		47	.276
1925	DET	A	2-3		124	.293
1926	DET	A	2-S-3		111	.242
1927	STL	A	2-3		140	.268
1928	STL	A	3		99	.263
1929	STL	A	3		154	.251
1930	STL	A	S-3		115	.268
1931	STL	A	1-S		8	.222
			BRTR		1131	.254

**O'ROURKE, JAMES HENRY
"ORATOR JIM"**
B.AUG.24,1852 E.BRIDGEPORT,CONN
D.JAN.8,1919 BRIDGEPORT,CONN.

1872	MAN	NA	S		23	.287
1873	BOS	NA	C-1-O		57	.347
1874	BOS	NA	1		69	.349
1875	BOS	NA	1-3-O		74	.289
1876	BOS	N	O		70	.312
1877	BOS	N	O		61	.362
1878	BOS	N	O		60	.274
1879	PRO	N	1-O		80	.351
1880	BOS	N	C-1-S-3-O		84	.281
1881	BUF	N	M-C-1-S-3-O		83	.301
1882	BUF	N	M-C-S-3-O		84	.281
1883	BUF	N	M-P- 1 C-S-3-O		93	0- 0 .327
1884	BUF	N	M-P- 4 C-1-3-O		104	0- 1 .350
1885	NY	N	C-O		112	.299
1886	NY	N	C-O		104	.309
1887	NY	N	C-3-O		103	.344
1888	NY	N	O		107	.273
1889	NY	N	O		128	.320
1890	NY	P	O		111	.366
1891	NY	N	O		136	.301
1892	NY	N	O		112	.297
1893	WAS	N	M-1-O		129	.305
1904	NY	N	C		1	.250
			BRTR	5	1985	0- 1 .317

O'ROURKE, JAMES PATRICK
B.JUNE 22,1937 WALLA WALLA,WASH

1959	STL	N	H		2	.000
			BRTR			

**O'ROURKE, JAMES STEPHEN
"QUEENIE"**
B.DEC.26,1883 BRIDGEPORT,CONN.

1908	NY	A	2-S-3-O		34	.231
			TR			

O'ROURKE, JOHN
B.BRIDGEPORT,CONN.
D.JUNE 23,1911

1879	BOS	N	O		70	.341
1880	BOS	N	O		78	.282
1883	MET	AA	1-O		79	.256
			BL		227	.299

O'ROURKE, JOSEPH LEO
B.OCT.28,1906 PHILADELPHIA,PA.

1929	PHI	N	H		3	.000
			BLTR			

**O'ROURKE, JOSEPH PATRICK
"PATSY"**
B.APR.13,1884 PHILADELPHIA,PA.
D.APR.18,1956

1908	STL	N	S		53	.195
			TR			

O'ROURKE, MICHAEL J.

1890	BAL	AA	P		9	2- 2

O'ROURKE, THOMAS JOSEPH
B.1863 NEW YORK,N.Y.
D.JULY 19,1929

1887	BOS	N	C		21	.223
1888	BOS	N	C		20	.175
1890	NY	N	C		2	.000
	SYR	AA	C		43	.227
			TR		86	.211

**O'ROURKE, TIMOTHY PATRICK
"VOICELESS TIM"**
B.MAY 18,1864 CHICAGO,ILL.
D.APR.20,1938

1890	SYR	AA	3		82	.288
1891	COL	AA	3		34	.261
1892	BAL	N	S		62	.317
1893	BAL	N	S		31	.379
	LOU	N	S		90	.290
1894	LOU	N	1-3-O		55	.284
	STL	N	1-3-O		18	.274
	WAS	N	1		7	.179
			TR		379	.295

ORR, DAVID
B.SEPT.29,1859 NEW YORK,N.Y.
D.JUNE 3,1915 BROOKLYN,N.Y.

YR	CL	LEA	POS	GP	G	REC
1883	MET	AA	1		1	.250
	NY	N	O		1	.000
	MET	AA	1		12	.326
1884	MET	AA	1		110	.352
1885	MET	AA	1		107	.366
1887	MET	AA	M-1		85	.403
1888	BRO	AA	1		95	.303
1889	COL	AA	1		134	.325
1890	BRO	P	1		107	.387
	BLTR				788	.353

ORR, WILLIAM JOHN "BILLY"
B.APR.22,1891 SAN FRANCISCO,CAL
D.MAR.10,1967 SANTARIUM,CAL.

YR	CL	LEA	POS	GP	G	REC
1913	PHI	A	S		27	.200
1914	PHI	A	S		10	.167
	BRTR				37	.191

ORRELL, FORREST GORDON "JOE"
B.OCT.6,1918 NATIONAL CITY,CAL.

YR	CL	LEA	POS	GP	G	REC
1943	DET	A	P		10	0- 0
1944	DET	A	P		10	2- 1
1945	DET	A	P		12	2- 3
	BRTR				32	4- 4

ORSATTI, ERNEST RALPH "ERNIE"
B.SEPT.18,1902 LOS ANGELES,CAL.
D.SEPT.4,1968 CANOGA PARK,CAL.

YR	CL	LEA	POS	GP	G	REC
1927	STL	N	O		27	.315
1928	STL	N	O		27	.304
1929	STL	N	1-O		113	.332
1930	STL	N	1-O		48	.321
1931	STL	N	O		70	.291
1932	STL	N	O		101	.336
1933	STL	N	1-O		120	.298
1934	STL	N	O		105	.300
1935	STL	N	O		90	.240
	BLTL				701	.306

ORSINO, JOHN JOSEPH
B.APR.22,1938 TEANECK,N.J.

YR	CL	LEA	POS	GP	G	REC
1961	SF	N	C		25	.277
1962	SF	N	C		18	.271
1963	BAL	A	C-1		116	.272
1964	BAL	A	C-1		81	.222
1965	BAL	A	C-1		77	.233
1966	WAS	A	C		14	.174
1967	WAS	A	H		1	.000
	BRTR				332	.249

ORTA, JORGE (NUNEZ)
B.NOV.26,1950 MAZATLAN,MEXICO

YR	CL	LEA	POS	GP	G	REC
1972	CHI	A	2-S-3		51	.202
1973	CHI	A	2-S		128	.266
1974	CHI	A	2-S-O		139	.316
1975	CHI	A	2		140	.304
1976	CHI	A	3-O-O		158	.274
	BLTR				616	.286

ORTEGA, FILOMENO CORONADO "PHIL"
B.OCT.7,1939 GILBERT,ARIZ.

YR	CL	LEA	POS	GP	G	REC
1960	LA	N	P		3	0- 0
1961	LA	N	P		4	0- 2
1962	LA	N	P		24	0- 2
1963	LA	N	P		1	0- 0
1964	LA	N	P	34	35	7- 9
1965	WAS	A	P		35	12-15
1966	WAS	A	P		33	12-12
1967	WAS	A	P		34	10-10
1968	WAS	A	P		31	5-12
1969	CAL	A	P		5	0- 0
	BRTR			204	205	46-62

ORTENZIO, FRANK JOSEPH
B.FEB.24,1951 FRESNO,CAL.

YR	CL	LEA	POS	GP	G	REC
1973	KC	A	1		9	.280
	BRTR					

ORTH, ALBERT LEWIS "SMILING AL"
B.SEPT.5,1872 DANVILLE,IND.
D.OCT.8,1948 LYNCHBURG,VA.

YR	CL	LEA	POS	GP	G	REC
1895	PHI	N	P		11	8- 1
1896	PHI	N	P		24	15- 9
1897	PHI	N	P	33	42	14-19
1898	PHI	N	P	27	32	15-12
1899	PHI	N	P		17	13- 3
1900	PHI	N	P	30	35	14-14
1901	PHI	N	P		35	21-12
1902	WAS	A	P-1-	38	54	19-18
			S-O			.218
1903	WAS	A	P	37	54	10-21
1904	WAS	A	P-O	10	32	3- 4
						.236
	NY	A	P-O	18	24	11- 5
1905	NY	A	P		40	18-18
1906	NY	A	P	45	47	27-17
1907	NY	A	P	37	43	14-21
1908	NY	A	P	21	38	2-13
1909	NY	A	P	1	22	1- 0
	BLTR			424	550	205-187
						.276

ORTIZ, JOSE LUIS (IRIZARRY)
B.JUNE 25,1947 PONCE,P.R.

YR	CL	LEA	POS	GP	G	REC
1969	CHI	N	O		16	.273
1970	CHI	A	O		15	.333
1971	CHI	N	O		36	.295
	BRTR				67	.301

ORTIZ, OLIVERIO NUNEZ "BABY"
B.DEC.5,1919 CAMAGUEY,CUBA

YR	CL	LEA	POS	GP	G	REC
1944	WAS	A	P		2	0- 2
	BRTR					

ORTIZ, ROBERTO GONZALO NUNEZ
B.JUNE 30,1915 SENADO,CUBA
D.SEPT.15,1971 MIAMI,FLA.

YR	CL	LEA	POS	GP	G	REC
1941	WAS	A	O		22	.329
1942	WAS	A	O		20	.167
1943	WAS	A	O		1	.250
1944	WAS	A	O		85	.253
1949	WAS	A	O		40	.279
1950	WAS	A	O		39	.227
	PHI	A	O		6	.071
	BRTR				213	.255

ORWOLL, OSWALD CHRISTIAN
B.NOV.17,1900 PORTLAND,ORE.
D.MAY 8,1967 DECORAH,IOWA

YR	CL	LEA	POS	GP	G	REC
1928	PHI	A	P-1	27	64	6- 5
						.306
1929	PHI	A	P	12	30	0- 2
	BLTL			39	94	6- 7
						.294

OSBORN, DANNY LEON "OZZIE"
B.JUNE 19,1946 SPRINGFIELD,MO.

YR	CL	LEA	POS	GP	G	REC
1975	CHI	A	P		24	3- 0
	BRTR					

OSBORN, FRANK ROBERT
B.APR.17,1903 SAN DIEGO,TEX.

YR	CL	LEA	POS	GP	G	REC
1925	CHI	N	P		1	0- 0
1926	CHI	N	P		31	6- 5
1927	CHI	N	P		24	5- 5
1929	CHI	N	P		3	0- 0
1930	CHI	N	P		35	10- 6
1931	PIT	N	P		27	6- 1
	BRTR				121	27-17

OSBURN, LARRY PATRICK "PAT"
B.MAY 4,1949 MURRAY,KY.

YR	CL	LEA	POS	GP	G	REC
1974	CIN	N	P		6	0- 0
1975	MIL	A	P		6	0- 1
	BLTL				12	0- 1

OSBORN, WILFRED P. "GREEN"
B.NOV.28,1883 SYCAMORE,OHIO
D.SEPT.2,1954

YR	CL	LEA	POS	GP	G	REC
1907	PHI	N	O		37	.276
1908	PHI	N	O		152	.267
1909	PHI	N	O		54	.185
	BLTR				243	.252

OSBORNE, ERNEST PRESTON "TINY"
B.APR.9,1893 COVINGTON,GA.
D.JAN.5,1969 ATLANTA,GA.

YR	CL	LEA	POS	GP	G	REC
1922	CHI	N	P		41	9- 5
1923	CHI	N	P		37	8-15
1924	CHI	N	P		2	0- 0
	BRO	N	P		21	6- 5
1925	BRO	N	P		41	8-15
	BLTR				142	31-40

OSBORNE, FREDERICK W.
B.HAMPTON,IOWA

YR	CL	LEA	POS	GP	G	REC
1890	PIT	N	P-O	6	41	0- 6
						.238

OSBORNE, LAWRENCE SIDNEY "BOBO"
B.OCT.12,1935 CHATTAHOOCHEE,GA.

YR	CL	LEA	POS	GP	G	REC
1957	DET	A	1-O		11	.148
1958	DET	A	H		2	.000
1959	DET	A	1-O		86	.191
1961	DET	A	1-3		71	.215
1962	DET	A	C-1-3		64	.230
1963	WAS	A	1-3		125	.212
	BLTR				359	.206

OSBORNE, WAYNE HAROLD "FISH HOOK"
B.OCT.11,1912 WATSONVILLE,CAL.

YR	CL	LEA	POS	GP	G	REC
1935	PIT	N	P	2	3	0- 0
1936	BOS	N	P		5	1- 1
	BLTR			7	8	1- 1

OSGOOD, CHARLES BENJAMIN
B.NOV.23,1926 SOMERVILLE,MASS.

YR	CL	LEA	POS	GP	G	REC
1944	BRO	N	P		1	0- 0
	BRTR					

O'SHEA, FRANCIS JOSEPH
(PLAYED UNDER NAME OF
FRANCIS JOSEPH SHEA)

OSINSKI, DANIEL "DAN"
B.NOV.17,1933 CHICAGO,ILL.

YR	CL	LEA	POS	GP	G	REC
1962	KC	A	P		4	0- 0
	LA	A	P		33	6- 4
1963	LA	A	P		47	8- 8
1964	LA	A	P		47	3- 3
1965	MIL	N	P		61	0- 3
1966	BOS	A	P		44	4- 3
1967	BOS	A	P		34	3- 1
1969	CHI	A	P		51	5- 5
1970	HOU	N	P		3	0- 1
	BRTR				324	29-28

OSTDIEK, HENRY GIRARD
B.APR.12,1881 OTTUMWA,IOWA
D.MAY 6,1956

YR	CL	LEA	POS	GP	G	REC
1904	CLE	A	C		7	.157
1908	BOS	A	C		1	.000
	BRTR				8	.143

OSTEEN, CLAUDE WILSON
B.AUG.9,1939 CANEY SPRINGS,TENN.

YR	CL	LEA	POS	GP	G	REC
1957	CIN	N	P		3	0- 0
1959	CIN	N	P		2	0- 0
1960	CIN	N	P	20	26	0- 1
1961	CIN	N	P-O	1	6	0- 0
						.000
	WAS	A	P		3	1- 1
1962	WAS	A	P	28	37	8-13
1963	WAS	A	P	40	49	9-14
1964	WAS	A	P	37	40	15-13
1965	LA	N	P	40	42	15-15
1966	LA	N	P		39	17-14
1967	LA	N	P	39	42	17-17
1968	LA	N	P	39	40	12-18
1969	LA	N	P	41	44	20-15
1970	LA	N	P	37	39	16-14
1971	LA	N	P	38	39	14-11
1972	LA	N	P	33	36	20-11
1973	LA	N	P		33	16-11
1974	HOU	N	P		23	9- 9
	STL	N	P		8	0- 2
1975	CHI	A	P		37	7-16
	BLTL			541	588	196-195
						.188

O'STEEN, JAMES CHAMP
B.FEB.24,1877 HENDERSONVILLE, N.C.
D.DEC.14,1962

YR	CL	LEA	POS	GP	G	REC
1903	WAS	A	S		10	.195
1904	NY	A	3		27	.202
1908	STL	N	S		29	.196
1909	STL	N	S		16	.199
	BLTR				82	.199

OSTEEN, MILTON DARRELL "DARREL"
B.FEB.14,1943 OKLAHOMA CITY,OKLA

YR	CL	LEA	POS	GP	G	REC
1965	CIN	N	P		3	0- 0
1966	CIN	N	P	13	16	0- 2
1967	CIN	N	P	10	14	0- 2
1970	OAK	A	P		3	1- 0
	BRTR			29	36	1- 4

```
YR   CL LEA POS  GP    G    REC
```

OSTENDORF, FREDERICK K.
B.1890 BALTIMORE,MD.
D.MAR.9,1965 HAMPTON,VA.
1914 IND F P   1   0- 0
     BLTL

OSTER, WILLIAM CHARLES
B.JAN.2,1933 NEW YORK,N.Y.
1954 PHI A P   8   0- 1
     BLTL

OSTERGARD, ROBERT LUND "RED"
B.MAY 11,1898 GALVESTON,TEX.
1921 CHI A S   12   .364
     BLTR

OSTERHOUT, CHARLES H.
B.1857 SYRACUSE,N.Y.
D.MAY 21,1933
1879 SYR N C-2   2   .000
     TR

OSTERMUELLER, FREDERICK RAYMOND "FRITZ"
B.SEPT.15,1907 QUINCY,ILL.
D.DEC.17,1957
1934 BOS A P   33 10-13
1935 BOS A P   22   7- 8
1936 BOS A P   43 10-16
1937 BOS A P   25   3- 7
1938 BOS A P   31   33 13- 5
1939 BOS A P   34 11- 7
1940 BOS A P   31   33   5- 9
1941 STL A P   15   16   0- 3
1942 STL A P   10   3- 1
1943 STL A P   11   0- 2
     BRO N P   7   8   1- 1
1944 BRO N P   10   11   2- 1
     PIT N P   28   29 11- 7
1945 PIT N P   14   5- 4
1946 PIT N P   27   28 13-10
1947 PIT N P   26 12-10
1948 PIT N P   23   8-11
     BLTL   390 399 114-115

OSTROSSER, BRIAN LEONARD
B.JUNE 17,1949 HAMILTON,ONT.,CAN
1973 NY N S   4   .000
     BLTR

OSTROWSKI, JOHN THEODORE "JOHNNY"
B.OCT.17,1920 CHICAGO,ILL.
1943 CHI N 3-O   10   .207
1944 CHI N O   8   .154
1945 CHI N 3   7   .300
1946 CHI N 2-3   64   .213
1948 BOS A H   1   .000
1949 CHI N 3-O   49   .266
1950 CHI A O   21   .222
     WAS A O   55   .227
     CHI A O   1   .500
     BRTR   216   .234

OSTROWSKI, JOSEPH PAUL "SPECS"
B.AUG.15,1919 W.WYOMING,PA.
1948 STL A P   26   4- 6
1949 STL A P   40   8- 8
1950 STL A P   9   2- 4
     NY A P   21   1- 1
1951 NY A P   34   6- 4
1952 NY A P   20   2- 2
     BLTL   150 23-25

OTERO, REGINO JOSEPH (GOMEZ)
B.SEPT.7,1917 HAVANA,CUBA
1945 CHI N 1   14   .391
     BLTR

OTEY, WILLIAM TILFORD
B.DEC.16,1886 DAYTON,OHIO
D.APR.23,1931
1907 PIT N P   3   0- 1
1910 WAS A P   9   0- 1
1911 WAS A P   12   2- 4
                      24   2- 6

OTIS, AMOS JOSEPH
B.APR.26,1947 MOBILE,ALA.
1967 NY N 3-O   19   .220
1969 NY N 3-O   48   .151
1970 KC A O   159   .284
1971 KC A O   147   .301
1972 KC A O   143   .293
1973 KC A O-D   148   .300
1974 KC A O   146   .284
1975 KC A O   132   .247
1976 KC A O   153   .279
     BRTR   1095   .281

OTIS, HARRY GEORGE
B.OCT.5,1886 W.NEW YORK,N.J.
D.JAN.29,1976 TEANECK,N.J.
1909 CLE A P   5   2- 2
     TL

OTIS, PAUL FRANKLIN
B.DEC.24,1889 SCITUATE,MASS.
1912 NY A O   4   .000

O'TOOLE, DENNIS JOSEPH
B.MAR.13,1949 CHICAGO,ILL.
1969 CHI A P   2   0- 0
1970 CHI A P   3   0- 0
1971 CHI A P   1   0- 0
1972 CHI A P   3   0- 0
1973 CHI A P   6   0- 0
     BRTR   15   0- 0

O'TOOLE, JAMES JEROME "JIM"
B.JAN.10,1937 CHICAGO,ILL.
1958 CIN N P   1   0- 1
1959 CIN N P   28   29   5- 8
1960 CIN N P   34 12-12
1961 CIN N P   39 19- 9
1962 CIN N P   36 16-13
1963 CIN N P   33 17-14
1964 CIN N P   30 17- 7
1965 CIN N P   29   3-10
1966 CIN N P   25   5- 7
1967 CHI A P   15   4- 3
     BBTL   270 271 98-84

O'TOOLE, MARTIN JAMES
B.NOV.27,1888 WM.PENN,PA.
D.FEB.18,1949
1908 CIN N P   3   1- 0
1911 PIT N P   5   3- 2
1912 PIT N P   37 15-17
1913 PIT N P   26   6- 8
1914 PIT N P   19   1- 8
     NY N P   10   1- 1
     BRTR   100 27-36

OTT, MELVIN THOMAS "MEL"
B.MAR.2,1909 GRETNA,LA.
D.NOV.21,1958 NEW ORLEANS,LA.
1926 NY N O   35   .383
1927 NY N O   82   .282
1928 NY N O   124   .322
1929 NY N O   150   .328
1930 NY N O   148   .349
1931 NY N O   138   .292
1932 NY N O   154   .318
1933 NY N O   152   .283
1934 NY N O   153   .326
1935 NY N 3-O   152   .322
1936 NY N O   150   .328
1937 NY N 3-O   151   .294
1938 NY N 3-O   150   .311
1939 NY N 3-O   125   .308
1940 NY N 3-O   151   .289
1941 NY N O   148   .286
1942 NY N M-O   152   .295
1943 NY N M-3-O   125   .234
1944 NY N M-3-O   120   .288
1945 NY N M-O   135   .308
1946 NY N M-O   31   .074
1947 NY N M-H   4   .000
     BLTR   2730   .304
NON-PLAYING MANAGER NY(N) 1948

OTT, NATHAN EDWARD "ED"
B.JULY 11,1951 MUNCY,PA.
1974 PIT N O   7   .000
1975 PIT N C   5   .200
1976 PIT N C   27   .308
     BLTR   39   .265

OTT, WILLIAM JOSEPH "BILLY"
B.NOV.23,1940 NEW YORK,N.Y.
1962 CHI N O   12   .143
1964 CHI N O   20   .179
     BBTR   32   .164

OTTEN JAMES EDWARD "JIM"
B.JULY 1,1951 LEWISTON,MONT.
1974 CHI A P   5   0- 1
1975 CHI A P   2   0- 0
1976 CHI A P   2   0- 0
     BRTR   9   0- 1

OTTEN, JOSEPH G.
B.MURPHYSBORO,ILL.
1895 STL N C   24   .233
     TR

OTTERSON, WILLIAM JOHN
B.MAY 4,1862 ALLEGHENY,PA.
D.SEPT.24,1940
1887 BRO AA S   30   .269
     TR

OULLIBER, JOHN ANDREW
B.FEB.24,1911 NEW ORLEANS,LA.
1933 CLE A O   22   .267
     BRTR

OUTEN, WILLIAM AUSTIN "CHICK"
B.JUNE 17,1905 MT.HOLLY,N.C.
D.SEPT.11,1961
1933 BRO N C   93   .248
     BLTR

OUTLAW, JAMES PAULUS "JIMMY"
B.JAN.20,1913 ORME,TENN.
1937 CIN N 3   49   .273
1938 CIN N H   4   .000
1939 BOS N O   65   .263
1943 DET A O   20   .269
1944 DET A O   139   .273
1945 DET A 3-O   132   .271
1946 DET A 3-O   92   .261
1947 DET A 3-O   70   .228
1948 DET A 3-O   74   .283
1949 DET A H   5   .250
     BRTR   650   .268

OVERALL, ORVAL
B.FEB.2,1881 VISALIA,CAL.
D.JULY 14,1947
1905 CIN N P   42 17-23
1906 CIN N P   13   4- 5
     CHI N P   18 12- 3
1907 CHI N P   36 23- 7
1908 CHI N P   37 15-11
1909 CHI N P   38 20-11
1910 CHI N P   23   24 12- 6
1913 CHI N P   10   4- 5
     BBTR   217 218 107-71

OVERBECK, HENRY A.
B.ST.LOUIS,MO.
1883 PIT AA 1   2   .222
     STL AA O   4   .000
1884 BAL U P-3- 1   33   0- 0
            O   .159
     KC U P-1- 4   26   0- 3
            3-O   .174
                  5   65   0- 3
                            .157

OVERMIRE, FRANK "STUBBY"
B.MAY 16,1919 MOLINE,MICH.
1943 DET A P   29   7- 6
1944 DET A P   32 11-11
1945 DET A P   31   9- 9
1946 DET A P   24   5- 7
1947 DET A P   28 11- 5
1948 DET A P   37   3- 4
1949 DET A P   14   1- 3
1950 STL A P   31   9-12
1951 STL A P   8   1- 6
     NY A P   15   1- 1
1952 STL A P   17   0- 3
     BRTL   266 58-67

OVERY, HARRY MICHAEL "MIKE"
B.JAN.27,1951 CLINTON,ILL.
1976 CAL A P   5   0- 2
     BRTR

OVITZ, ERNEST GAYHEART
B.OCT.7,1885 MINERAL POINT,WIS.
1911 CHI N P   1   0- 0

OWCHINKO, ROBERT DENNIS "BOB"
B.JAN.1,1955 DETROIT,MICH.
1976 SD N P   2   0- 2
     BLTL

YR	CL	LEA	POS	GP	G	REC

OWEN, ARNOLD MALCOLM "MICKEY"
B.APR.4,1916 SPRINGFIELD,MO.

YR	CL	LEA	POS	GP	G	REC
1937	STL	N	C		80	.231
1938	STL	N	C		122	.267
1939	STL	N	C		131	.259
1940	STL	N	C		117	.264
1941	BRO	N	C		128	.231
1942	BRO	N	C		133	.259
1943	BRO	N	C-S		106	.260
1944	BRO	N	C-2		130	.273
1945	BRO	N	C		24	.286
1949	CHI	N	C		62	.273
1950	CHI	N	C		86	.243
1951	CHI	N	C		58	.184
1954	BOS	A	C		32	.235
		BRTR			1209	.255

OWEN, FRANK MALCOLM "YIP"
B.DEC.23,1879 YPSILANTI,MICH.
D.NOV.27,1942

YR	CL	LEA	POS	GP	G	REC
1901	DET	A	P		9	1- 4
1903	CHI	A	P		26	8-11
1904	CHI	A	P		37	21-15
1905	CHI	A	P		42	22-14
1906	CHI	A	P		42	22-13
1907	CHI	A	P		11	2- 3
1908	CHI	A	P		25	6- 7
1909	CHI	A	P		3	1- 1
		TR			195	83-68

OWEN, MARVIN JAMES
"MARV" OR "FRECK"
B.MAR.22,1908 SAN JOSE,CAL.

YR	CL	LEA	POS	GP	G	REC
1931	DET	A	1-S-3		105	.223
1933	DET	A	3		138	.262
1934	DET	A	3		154	.317
1935	DET	A	3		134	.263
1936	DET	A	3		154	.295
1937	DET	A	3		107	.288
1938	CHI	A	3		141	.281
1939	CHI	A	3		58	.237
1940	BOS	A	1-3		20	.211
		BRTR			1011	.275

OWENS, FRANK WALTER
B.JAN.16,1884 TORONTO,ONT.,CAN.
D.JULY 2,1958

YR	CL	LEA	POS	GP	G	REC
1905	BOS	A	C		1	.000
1909	CHI	A	C		64	.201
1914	BRO	F	C		55	.274
1915	BAL	F	C		98	.245
		BRTR			218	.241

OWENS, FURMAN LEE
B.MAY 6,1908 CONVERSE,S.C.
D.NOV.14,1958 GREENVILLE,S.C.

YR	CL	LEA	POS	GP	G	REC
1935	PHI	A	C		2	.250
		BRTR				

OWENS, JAMES PHILIP "JIM"
B.JAN.16,1934 GIFFORD,PA.

YR	CL	LEA	POS	GP	G	REC
1955	PHI	N	P		3	0- 2
1956	PHI	N	P		10	0- 4
1958	PHI	N	P		1	1- 0
1959	PHI	N	P		31	12-12
1960	PHI	N	P		31	4-14
1961	PHI	N	P-O	20	21	5-10
						.074
1962	PHI	N	P		23	2- 4
1963	CIN	N	P		19	0- 2
1964	HOU	N	P		48	8- 7
1965	HOU	N	P		50	6- 5
1966	HOU	N	P		40	4- 7
1967	HOU	N	P		10	0- 1
		BRTR		286	287	42-68
						.101

OWENS, PAUL FRANCIS
B.FEB.7,1924 SALAMANCA,N.Y.
NON-PLAYING MANAGER PHI(N) 1972

OWENS, THOMAS LLEWELLYN "RED"
B.NOV.1,1874 POTTSVILLE,PA.
D.AUG.20,1952

YR	CL	LEA	POS	GP	G	REC
1899	PHI	N	2		8	.045
1905	BRO	N	2		43	.215
		BRTR			51	.196

OXLEY, HENRY HAVELOCK
B.CHARLOTTETOWN,P.E.I.,CANADA

YR	CL	LEA	POS	GP	G	REC
1884	NY	N	C		2	.000
	MET	AA	C		1	.000
					3	.000

OYLER, ANDREW PAUL
B.MAY 5,1880 NEWVILLE,PA.

YR	CL	LEA	POS	GP	G	REC
1902	BAL	A	2-S-3-0		26	.227
		BRTR				

OYLER, RAYMOND FRANCIS "RAY"
B.AUG.4,1938 INDIANAPOLIS,IND.

YR	CL	LEA	POS	GP	G	REC
1965	DET	A	1-2-S-3		82	.186
1966	DET	A	S		71	.171
1967	DET	A	S		148	.207
1968	DET	A	S		111	.135
1969	SEA	A	S		106	.165
1970	CAL	A	S-3		24	.083
		BRTR			542	.175

OZARK, DANIEL LEONARD "DANNY"
B.NOV.26,1923 BUFFALO,N.Y.
NON-PLAYING MANAGER
PHI(N) 1973-76

OZMER, HORACE ROBERT
B.MAY 24,1901 ATLANTA,GA.

YR	CL	LEA	POS	GP	G	REC
1923	PHI	A	P		1	0- 0
		BRTR				

PABOR, CHARLES HENRY
B.SEPT.24,1849 NEW YORK,N.Y.
D.APR.22,1913 NEW HAVEN,CONN.

YR	CL	LEA	POS	GP	G	REC
1871	CLE	NA	M-P-	1	29	0- 1
			O			
1872	CLE	NA	P-O	2	20	1- 1
						.269
1873	ATL	NA	O		55	-
1874	PHI	NA	O		5	-
1875	ATL	NA	M-O		41	-
	NH	NA	O		6	-
		TL		3	156	1- 2
						-

PABST, EDWARD D. A.
B.ST.LOUIS,MO.

YR	CL	LEA	POS	GP	G	REC
1890	ATH	AA	O		8	.345
	STL	AA	O		4	.143
					12	.279

PACK, FRANKIE
B.APR.10,1928 MORRISTOWN,TENN.

YR	CL	LEA	POS	GP	G	REC
1949	STL	A	H		1	.000
		BLTR				

PACKARD, EUGENE MILO
B.JULY 13,1889 COLORADO SPRINGS
COLO.
D.MAY 19,1959

YR	CL	LEA	POS	GP	G	REC
1912	CIN	N	P		1	1- 0
1913	CIN	N	P	39	43	7-11
1914	KC	F	P		42	20-14
1915	KC	F	P		42	20-12
1916	CHI	N	P	37	44	10- 6
1917	CHI	N	P		2	0- 0
	STL	N	P	34	36	9- 6
1918	STL	N	P	30	36	12-12
1919	PHI	N	P	21	27	6- 8
		BLTL		248	273	85-69

PACIOREK, JOHN FRANCIS
B.FEB.11,1945 DETROIT,MICH.

YR	CL	LEA	POS	GP	G	REC
1963	HOU	N	O		1	1.000
		BRTR				

PACIOREK, THOMAS MARIAN "TOM"
B.NOV.2,1946 DETROIT,MICH.

YR	CL	LEA	POS	GP	G	REC
1970	LA	N	O		8	.222
1971	LA	N	O		2	.500
1972	LA	N	1-O		11	.255
1973	LA	N	1-O		96	.262
1974	LA	N	1-O		85	.240
1975	LA	N	O		62	.193
1976	ATL	N	1-3-O		111	.290
		BRTR			375	.256

PACTWA, JOSEPH MARTIN "JOE"
B.JUNE 2,1948 HAMMOND,IND.

YR	CL	LEA	POS	GP	G	REC
1975	CAL	A	P		4	1- 0
		BLTL				

PADDEN, RICHARD JOSEPH "BRAINS"
B.SEPT.17,1870 MARTIN'S FERRY,O
D.OCT.31,1922

YR	CL	LEA	POS	GP	G	REC
1896	PIT	N	2		60	.239
1897	PIT	N	2		135	.281
1898	PIT	N	2		128	.256
1899	WAS	N	2-S		131	.272
1901	STL	N	2		123	.253
1902	STL	A	2		117	.265
1903	STL	A	2		29	.202
1904	STL	A	2		132	.238
1905	STL	A	2		16	.172
		BRTR			871	.256

PADDEN, THOMAS FRANCIS "TOM"
B.OCT.6,1908 MANCHESTER,N.H.
D.JUNE 11,1973 MANCHESTER,N.H.

YR	CL	LEA	POS	GP	G	REC
1932	PIT	N	C		47	.263
1933	PIT	N	C		30	.211
1934	PIT	N	C		82	.321
1935	PIT	N	C		97	.272
1936	PIT	N	C		88	.249
1937	PIT	N	C		35	.286
1943	PHI	N	C		17	.293
	WAS	A	C		3	.000
		BRTR			399	.272

PADDOCK, DELMAR HAROLD
B.JUNE 8,1887 VOLGA,S.DAK.
D.FEB.6,1952 REMER,MINN

YR	CL	LEA	POS	GP	G	REC
1912	CHI	A	H		1	.000
	NY	A	3		45	.287
		BLTR			46	.287

PADGETT, DONALD WILSON "DON"
B.DEC.5,1912 CAROLEEN,N.C.

YR	CL	LEA	POS	GP	G	REC
1937	STL	N	O		123	.314
1938	STL	N	1-O		110	.271
1939	STL	N	C		92	.399
1940	STL	N	C-1		93	.242
1941	STL	N	C-1-O		107	.247
1946	BRO	N	C		19	.167
	BOS	N	C		44	.255
1947	PHI	N	C		75	.316
1948	PHI	N	C		36	.230
		BLTR			699	.288

PADGETT, ERNEST KITCHEN "RED"
B.MAR.1,1899 PHILADELPHIA,PA.
D.APR.15,1957

YR	CL	LEA	POS	GP	G	REC
1923	BOS	N	2-S		4	.182
1924	BOS	N	2-3		138	.255
1925	BOS	N	2-S-3		86	.305
1926	CLE	A	3		36	.210
1927	CLE	A	3		7	.286
		BRTR			271	.266

PAEPKE, DENNIS RAY
B.APR.17,1945 LONG BEACH,CAL.

YR	CL	LEA	POS	GP	G	REC
1969	KC	A	C		12	.111
1971	KC	A	C-O		60	.204
1972	KC	A	C		2	.000
1974	KC	A	C-O		6	.167
		BRTR			80	.183

PAFKO, ANDREW "HANDY ANDY"
B.FEB.25,1921 BOYCEVILLE,WIS.

YR	CL	LEA	POS	GP	G	REC
1943	CHI	N	O		13	.379
1944	CHI	N	O		128	.269
1945	CHI	N	O		144	.298
1946	CHI	N	O		65	.282
1947	CHI	N	O		129	.302
1948	CHI	N	3		142	.312
1949	CHI	N	3-O		144	.281
1950	CHI	N	O		146	.304
1951	CHI	N	O		49	.264
	BRO	N	O		84	.249
1952	BRO	N	3-O		150	.287
1953	MIL	N	O		140	.297
1954	MIL	N	O		138	.286
1955	MIL	N	3-O		86	.266
1956	MIL	N	O		45	.258
1957	MIL	N	O		83	.277
1958	MIL	N	O		95	.238
1959	MIL	N	O		71	.218
		BRTR			1852	.285

PAGAN, DAVID PERCY "DAVE"
B.SEP.15,1949 NIPAWIN,SASK.,CAN.

YR	CL	LEA	POS	GP	G	REC
1973	NY	A	P		4	0- 0
1974	NY	A	P		16	1- 3
1975	NY	A	P		13	0- 0
1976	NY	A	P		7	1- 1
	BAL	A	P		20	1- 4
		BRTR			60	3- 8

YR	CL	LEA	POS	GP	G	REC

PAGAN, JOSE ANTONIO
B.MAY 5,1935 BARCELONETA,P.R.

YR	CL	LEA	POS	GP	G	REC
1959	SF	N	2-S-3	31		.174
1960	SF	N	S-3	18		.286
1961	SF	N	S-0	134		.253
1962	SF	N	S	164		.259
1963	SF	N	2-S-0	148		.234
1964	SF	N	S-0	134		.223
1965	SF	N	S	26		.205
	PIT		S-3	42		.237
1966	PIT	N	2-S-3-0	109		.264
1967	PIT	N	C-2-S-3-0	81		.289
1968	PIT	N	1-2-S-3-0	80		.221
1969	PIT	N	2-3-0	108		.285
1970	PIT	N	1-2-3-0	95		.265
1971	PIT	N	1-3-0	57		.241
1972	PIT	N	3-0	53		.252
1973	PHI	N	1-2-3-0	46		.205
		BRTR		1326		.250

PAGE, JOSEPH FRANCIS
"JOE" OR "FIREMAN"
B.OCT.28,1917 CHERRY VALLEY,PA.

1944	NY	A	P		19	5- 7
1945	NY	A	P		20	6- 3
1946	NY	A	P	31	32	9- 8
1947	NY	A	P		56	14- 8
1948	NY	A	P		55	7- 8
1949	NY	A	P		60	13- 8
1950	NY	A	P		37	3- 7
1954	PIT	N	P		7	0- 0
		BLTL		285	286	57-49

PAGE, MICHAEL RANDY "MIKE"
B.JULY 12,1940 WOODRUFF,S.C.

1968	ATL	N	O		20	.179
		BLTR				

PAGE, PHILIP RAUSAC
B.AUG.23,1905 SPRINGFIELD,MASS.
D.JUNE 26,1958

1928	DET	A	P		3	2- 0
1929	DET	A	P		10	0- 2
1930	DET	A	P		12	0- 1
1934	BRO	N	P		6	1- 0
		BRTL			31	3- 3

PAGE, SAMUEL WALTER
B.FEB.11,1916 WOODRUFF,S.C.

1939	PHI	A	P		4	0- 3
		BLTR				

PAGE, VANCE LINWOOD
B.SEPT.15,1905 ELM CITY,N.C.
D.JULY 14,1951

1938	CHI	N	P		13	5- 4
1939	CHI	N	P		21	7- 7
1940	CHI	N	P	30	31	1- 3
1941	CHI	N	P		25	2- 2
		BRTR		95	96	15-16

PAGLIARONI, JAMES VINCENT "JIM"
B.DEC.8,1937 DEARBORN,MICH.

1955	BOS	A	C		1	.000
1960	BOS	A	C		28	.306
1961	BOS	A	C		120	.242
1962	BOS	A	C		90	.258
1963	PIT	N	C		92	.230
1964	PIT	N	C		97	.295
1965	PIT	N	C		134	.268
1966	PIT	N	C		123	.235
1967	PIT	N	C		44	.200
1968	OAK	A	C		66	.246
1969	OAK	A	C		14	.148
	SEA	A	C-1-0		40	.264
		BRTR			849	.252

PAIGE, GEORGE LYNN "PIGGY"
B.MAY 5,1883 PAW PAW,MICH.
D.JUNE 8,1939 BERLIN,WIS.

1911	CLE	A	P		2	1- 0
		BLTR				

PAIGE, LEROY ROBERT "SATCHEL"
B.JULY 7,1906 MOBILE,ALA.

1948	CLE	A	P		21	6- 1
1949	CLE	A	P		31	4- 7
1951	STL	A	P		23	3- 4
1952	STL	A	P		46	12-10
1953	STL	A	P		57	3- 9
1965	KC	A	P		1	0- 0
		BRTR			179	28-31

PAINE, PHILLIPS STEERE "FLIP"
B.JUNE 8,1930 CHEPACHET,R.I.

1951	BOS	N	P		21	2- 0
1954	MIL	N	P		11	1- 0
1955	MIL	N	P		15	2- 0
1956	MIL	N	P		1	0- 0
1957	MIL	N	P		1	0- 0
1958	STL	N	P		46	5- 1
		BRTR			95	10- 1

PALAGYI, MICHAEL RAYMOND
B.JULY 4,1917 CONNEAUT,OHIO

1939	WAS	A	P		1	0- 0
		BRTR				

PALICA, ERVIN MARTIN "ERV"
(REAL NAME
ERVIN MARTIN PAVLIECIVICH)
B.FEB.9,1928 LOMITA,CAL.

1945	BRO	N	H		2	.000
1947	BRO	N	P		3	0- 1
1948	BRO	N	P	41	45	6- 6
1949	BRO	N	P		49	8- 9
1950	BRO	N	P	43	48	13- 8
1951	BRO	N	P	19	20	2- 6
1953	BRO	N	P		4	0- 0
1954	BRO	N	P	25	28	3- 3
1955	BAL	A	P		33	5-11
1956	BAL	A	P	29	30	4-11
		BRTR		246	262	41-55
						.198

PALM, RICHARD PAUL "MIKE"
B.FEB.13,1925 BOSTON,MASS.

1948	BOS	A	P		3	0- 0
		BRTR				

PALMER
B.ST.LOUIS,MO.

1885	STL	N	P		4	0- 4

PALMER, EDWIN HENRY "BALDY"
B.JUNE 1,1893 PETTY,TEX.

1917	PHI	A	3		16	.212
		BRTR				

PALMER, JAMES ALVIN "JIM"
B.OCT.15,1945 NEW YORK,N.Y.

1965	BAL	A	P	27	29	5- 4
1966	BAL	A	P	30	36	15-10
1967	BAL	A	P		9	3- 1
1969	BAL	A	P	26	27	16- 4
1970	BAL	A	P	39	44	20-10
1971	BAL	A	P	37	38	20- 9
1972	BAL	A	P		36	21-10
1973	BAL	A	P		38	22- 9
1974	BAL	A	P		26	7-12
1975	BAL	A	P		39	23-11
1976	BAL	A	P		40	22-13
		BRTR		347	362	174-93

PALMER, LOWELL RAYMOND
B.AUG.18,1947 SACRAMENTO,CAL.

1969	PHI	N	P		26	2- 8
1970	PHI	N	P		38	1- 2
1971	PHI	N	P		3	0- 0
1972	STL	N	P	16	17	0- 3
	CLE	A	P		1	0- 0
1974	SD	N	P	22	23	2- 5
		BRTR		106	108	5-18

PALMERO, EMILIO ANTONIO "PAL"
B.JUNE 13,1895 HAVANA,CUBA
D.JULY 15,1970 TOLEDO,OHIO

1915	NY	N	P		3	0- 2
1916	NY	N	P		5	0- 3
1921	STL	A	P	24	29	4- 7
1926	WAS	A	P		7	2- 2
1928	BOS	N	P		3	0- 1
		BLTL		42	47	6-15
		BB 1915-16				

PALMISANO, JOSEPH A.
B.NOV.19,1902 WEST POINT,GA.
D.NOV.5,1971 ALBUQUERQUE,N.MEX.

1931	PHI	A	C		19	.227
		BRTR				

PALMQUIST, EDWIN LEE "ED"
B.JUNE 10,1933 LOS ANGELES,CAL.

1960	LA	N	P		22	0- 1
1961	LA	N	P		5	0- 1
	MIN	A	P		9	1- 1
		BRTR			36	1- 3

PALYS, STANLEY FRANCIS "STAN"
B.MAY 1,1930 BLAKELY,PA.

1953	PHI	N	O		2	.000
1954	PHI	N	O		2	.250
1955	PHI	N	O		15	.288
	CIN	N	1-0		79	.230
1956	CIN	N	O		40	.226
		BRTR			138	.237

PANER, GEORGE WASHINGTON
(PLAYED UNDER NAME OF
GEORGE WASHINGTON PAYNTER)

PANTHER, JAMES EDWARD "JIM"
B.MAR.1,1945 BURLINGTON,IOWA

1971	OAK	A	P		4	0- 1
1972	TEX	A	P		58	5- 9
1973	ATL	N	P		23	2- 3
		BRTR			85	7-13

PAOLINELLI, RINALDO ANGELO
(PLAYED UNDER NAME OF
RALPH ARTHUR PINELLI)

PAPA, JOHN PAUL
B.DEC.5,1940 BRIDGEPORT,CONN.

1961	BAL	A	P		2	0- 0
1962	BAL	A	P		1	0- 0
		BRTR			3	0- 0

PAPAI, ALFRED THOMAS "AL"
B.MAY 7,1919 DIVERNON,ILL.

1948	STL	N	P	10	11	0- 1
1949	STL	A	P		42	4-11
1950	BOS	A	P		16	4- 2
	STL	N	P		13	1- 0
1955	CHI	A	P		7	0- 0
		BRTR		88	89	9-14

PAPE, KENNETH WAYNE "KEN"
B.OCT.1,1951 SAN ANTONIO,REX.

1976	TEX	A	2-S-3		21	.217
		BRTR				

PAPE, LAWRENCE ALBERT
R.1883 NORWOOD,OHIO
D.AUG.3,1918

1909	BOS	A	P		11	2- 0
1911	BOS	A	P		27	10- 8
1912	BOS	A	P		13	1- 1
		BRTR			51	13- 9

PAPI, STANLEY GERARD "STAN"
B.FEB.4,1951 FRESNO,CAL.

1974	STL	N	2-S		8	.250
		BRTR				

PAPISH, FRANK RICHARD
B.OCT.21,1917 PUEBLO,COLD.
D.AUG.31,1965 PUEBLO,COLD.

1945	CHI	A	P		19	4- 4
1946	CHI	A	P		31	7- 5
1947	CHI	A	P		38	12-12
1948	CHI	A	P		32	2- 8
1949	CLE	A	P		25	1- 0
1950	PIT	N	P		4	0- 0
		BRTL			149	26-29

PAPPALAU, JOHN JOSEPH
B.APR.3,1875 ALBANY,N.Y.
D.MAY 12,1944

1897	CLE	N	P		2	0- 0

PAPPAS, MILTON STEPHEN "MILT"
B.MAY 11,1939 DETROIT,MICH.

1957	BAL	A	P		4	0- 0
1958	BAL	A	P-2	31	32	10-10
						.143
1959	BAL	A	P		33	15- 9
1960	BAL	A	P		30	15-11
1961	BAL	A	P		26	13- 9
1962	BAL	A	P		35	12-10
1963	BAL	A	P	34	36	16- 9
1964	BAL	A	P		37	16- 7
1965	BAL	A	P		34	13- 9
1966	CIN	N	P	33	36	12-11
1967	CIN	N	P		34	16-13
1968	CIN	N	P	15	16	2- 5
	ATL	N	P		22	10- 8
1969	ATL	N	P		26	6-10
1970	ATL	N	P		11	2- 2
	CHI	N	P		21	10- 8
1971	CHI	N	P		35	17-14
1972	CHI	N	P		29	17- 7
1973	CHI	N	P		30	7-12
		BRTR		520	527	209-164
						.123

YR	CL	LEA	POS	GP	G	REC

PARENT, FREDERICK ALFRED "FRED"
B.NOV.25,1875 BIDDEFORD,ME.
D.NOV.2,1972 SANFORD,MAINE

YR	CL	LEA	POS	GP	G	REC
1899	STL	N	2		2	.125
1901	BOS	A	S		138	.318
1902	BOS	A	S		139	.288
1903	BOS	A	S		139	.304
1904	BOS	A	S		155	.296
1905	BOS	A	S		153	.234
1906	BOS	A	S		149	.235
1907	BOS	A	S-0		114	.276
1908	CHI	A	S		119	.207
1909	CHI	A	S-0		136	.261
1910	CHI	A	S		81	.178
1911	CHI	A	2		3	.444
	BRTR				1328	.265

PARISSE, LOUIS PETER "TONY"
B.JUNE 25,1911 PHILADELPHIA,PA.
D.JUNE 2,1956

YR	CL	LEA	POS	GP	G	REC
1943	PHI	A	C		6	.176
1944	PHI	A	C		4	.000
	BRTR				10	.143

PARK, JAMES
B.NOV.10,1892 RICHMOND,KY.

YR	CL	LEA	POS	GP	G	REC
1915	STL	A	P		3	2- 0
1916	STL	A	P		26	1- 4
1917	STL	A	P		13	1- 1
	BRTR				42	4- 5

PARKER, CLARENCE MC KAY "ACE"
B.MAY 17,1912 PORTSMOUTH,VA.

YR	CL	LEA	POS	GP	G	REC
1937	PHI	A	S		38	.117
1938	PHI	A	S		56	.230
	BRTR				94	.179

PARKER, CLARENCE PERKINS
B.MAY 22,1893 SOMERVILLE,MASS.
D.MAR.21,1967 CLAREMONT,N.H.

YR	CL	LEA	POS	GP	G	REC
1915	STL	A	0		3	.167

PARKER, DAVID GENE "DAVE"
B.JUNE 9,1951 CALHOUN,MISS.

YR	CL	LEA	POS	GP	G	REC
1973	PIT	N	0		54	.288
1974	PIT	N	1-0		73	.282
1975	PIT	N	0		148	.308
1976	PIT	N	0		138	.313
	BLTR				413	.304

PARKER, DOUGLAS WOOLLEY "DIXIE"
B.APR.24,1896 GREEN POND,ALA.
D.MAY 15,1972 TUSCALOOSA,ALA.

YR	CL	LEA	POS	GP	G	REC
1923	PHI	N			4	.200
	BLTR					

PARKER, FRANCIS JAMES "SALTY"
B.JULY 8,1913 E.ST.LOUIS,ILL.

YR	CL	LEA	POS	GP	G	REC
1936	DET	A	1-S		11	.260
	BRTR					

NON-PLAYING MANAGER
NY(N) 1967 (INTERIM),
HOU(N) 1972 (INTERIM)

PARKER, HARLEY PARK "DOC"
B.JUNE 14,1874 THERESA,N.Y.
D.MAR.3,1941

YR	CL	LEA	POS	GP	G	REC
1893	CHI	N	P		1	0- 0
1895	CHI	N	P		7	4- 3
1896	CHI	N	P		10	1- 5
1901	CIN	N	P		1	0- 1
	BRTR				19	5- 9

PARKER, HARRY WILLIAM
B.SEP.14,1947 HIGHLAND,ILL.

YR	CL	LEA	POS	GP	G	REC
1970	STL	N	P		7	1- 1
1971	STL	N	P		4	0- 0
1973	NY	N	P		38	8- 4
1974	NY	N	P		40	4-12
1975	NY	N	P		18	2- 3
	STL	N	P		14	0- 1
1976	CLE	A	P		3	0- 0
	BRTR				124	15-21

PARKER, JAY

YR	CL	LEA	POS	GP	G	REC
1899	PIT	N	P		1	0- 0

PARKER, MAURICE WESLEY "WES"
B.NOV.13,1939 CHICAGO,ILL.

YR	CL	LEA	POS	GP	G	REC
1964	LA	N	1-0		124	.257
1965	LA	N	1-0		154	.238
1966	LA	N	1-0		156	.253
1967	LA	N	1-0		139	.247
1968	LA	N	1-0		135	.239
1969	LA	N	1-0		132	.278
1970	LA	N	1		161	.319
1971	LA	N	1-0		157	.274
1972	LA	N	1-0		130	.279
	BRTL				1288	.267

PARKER, ROY W.
B.1897

YR	CL	LEA	POS	GP	G	REC
1919	STL	N	P		2	0- 0
	BRTR					

PARKER, WILLIAM DAVID "BILLY"
B.JAN.14,1947 HAYNEVILLE,ALA.

YR	CL	LEA	POS	GP	G	REC
1971	CAL	A	2		20	.229
1972	CAL	A	2-S-3-0		36	.213
1973	CAL	A	2-S		38	.225
	BRTR				94	.222

PARKINSON, FRANK JOSEPH
B.MAR.23,1895 DICKSON CITY,N.J.
D.JULY 4,1960 TRENTON,N.J.

YR	CL	LEA	POS	GP	G	REC
1921	PHI	N	S		108	.253
1922	PHI	N	2		141	.275
1923	PHI	N	2-S-3		67	.242
1924	PHI	N	2-S-3		62	.261
	BRTR				378	.256

PARKS, ARTHUR WILLIAM
B.NOV.1,1914 PARIS,ARK.

YR	CL	LEA	POS	GP	G	REC
1937	BRO	N	0		7	.313
1939	BRO	N	0		71	.272
	BLTR				78	.275

PARKS, VERNON HENRY "SLICKER"
B.NOV.10,1897 FOWLER,MICH.

YR	CL	LEA	POS	GP	G	REC
1921	DET	A	P		10	3- 2
	BRTR					

PARKS, WILLIAM ROBERT
B.JUNE 4,1849 EASTON,PA.
D.OCT.10,1911

YR	CL	LEA	POS	GP	G	REC
1875	NAT	NA	P-0	12	25	3- 9
						—
	PHI	NA	0		2	—
1876	BOS	N	0		1	.000
					28	3- 9

PARMELEE, LE ROY EARL "TARZAN"
B.APR.25,1907 LAMBERTVILLE,MICH

YR	CL	LEA	POS	GP	G	REC
1929	NY	N	P		2	1- 0
1930	NY	N	P		11	0- 1
1931	NY	N	P		13	2- 2
1932	NY	N	P		8	0- 3
1933	NY	N	P	32	33	13- 8
1934	NY	N	P		22	10- 6
1935	NY	N	P		34	14-10
1936	STL	N	P		37	11-11
1937	CHI	N	P	33	37	7- 8
1939	PHI	A	P	14	16	1- 6
	BRTR			206	213	59-55

PARNELL, MELVIN LLOYD "MEL" OR "DUSTY"
B.JUNE 13,1922 NEW ORLEANS,LA.

YR	CL	LEA	POS	GP	G	REC
1947	BOS	A	P		15	2- 3
1948	BOS	A	P		35	15- 8
1949	BOS	A	P		39	25- 7
1950	BOS	A	P		40	18-10
1951	BOS	A	P	36	37	18-11
1952	BOS	A	P	33	35	12-12
1953	BOS	A	P		38	21- 8
1954	BOS	A	P		19	3- 7
1955	BOS	A	P	13	14	2- 3
1956	BOS	A	P		21	7- 6
	BLTL			289	293	123-75

PARNHAM, JAMES ARTHUR "RUBE"
B.FEB.1,1896 HEIDELBERG,PA.
D.NOV.25,1963 MC KEESPORT,PA.

YR	CL	LEA	POS	GP	G	REC
1916	PHI	A	P		4	2- 1
1917	PHI	A	P		2	0- 1
	BRTR				6	2- 2

PARRILLA, SAMUEL "SAM"
B.JUNE 12,1943 SANTURCE,P.R.

YR	CL	LEA	POS	GP	G	REC
1970	PHI	N	0		11	.125
	BRTR					

PARRISH, LARRY ALTON
B.NOV.10,1953 WINTER HAVEN,FLA.

YR	CL	LEA	POS	GP	G	REC
1974	MON	N	3		25	.203
1975	MON	N	2-S-3		145	.274
1976	MON	N	3		154	.232
	BRTR				324	.250

PARROTT, THOMAS WILLIAM "TACKS"
B.APR.10,1868 E.PORTLAND,ORE.
D.JAN.1,1932

YR	CL	LEA	POS	GP	G	REC
1893	CHI	N	P		12	0- 4
	CIN	N	P		17	9- 8
1894	CIN	N	P	38	59	19-19
1895	CIN	N	P	31	47	11-20
1896	STL	N	P-0	6	118	1- 1
						.288
	BRTR		104	253	40-52
						.304

PARROTT, WALTER E. "JIGGS"
B.JULY 14,1871 PORTLAND,ORE.
D.APR.14,1898

YR	CL	LEA	POS	GP	G	REC
1892	CHI	N	3		79	.215
1893	CHI	N	3		113	.252
1894	CHI	N	2		126	.244
1895	CHI	N	S		3	.200
					321	.240

PARSON, WILLIAM EDWIN "JIGGS"
B.DEC.27,1886 PARKER,S.DAK.
D.MAY 19,1967 LOS ANGELES,CAL.

YR	CL	LEA	POS	GP	G	REC
1910	BOS	N	P		10	0- 2
1911	BOS	N	P		7	0- 1
	BRTR				17	0- 3

PARSONS, CHARLES J.
B.JULY 18,1863 COVINGTON,PA.
D.APR.1,1936

YR	CL	LEA	POS	GP	G	REC
1886	BOS	N	P		2	0- 2
1887	MET	AA	P		4	1- 1
1890	CLE	N	P		2	0- 1
	TL				8	1- 4

PARSONS, EDWARD DIXON "DIXIE"
B.MAY 12,1916 TALLADEGA,ALA.

YR	CL	LEA	POS	GP	G	REC
1939	DET	A	C		5	.000
1942	DET	A	C		63	.197
1943	DET	A	C		40	.142
	BRTR				108	.176

PARSONS, JOHN S.
B.NAPOLEON,OHIO

YR	CL	LEA	POS	GP	G	REC
1884	CIN	AA	0		1	.000

PARSONS, THOMAS ANTHONY "TOM"
B.SEP.13,1939 LAKEVILLE,CONN.

YR	CL	LEA	POS	GP	G	REC
1963	PIT	N	P		1	0- 1
1964	NY	N	P		4	1- 2
1965	NY	N	P		35	1-10
	BRTR				40	2-13

PARSONS, WILLIAM RAYMOND "BILL"
B.AUG.17,1948 RIVERSIDE,CAL.

YR	CL	LEA	POS	GP	G	REC
1971	MIL	A	P		36	13-17
1972	MIL	A	P		33	13-13
1973	MIL	A	P		20	3- 6
1974	OAK	A	P		4	0- 0
	BRTR				93	29-36

PARTEE, ROY ROBERT
B.SEPT.7,1918 LOS ANGELES,CAL.

YR	CL	LEA	POS	GP	G	REC
1943	BOS	A	C		96	.281
1944	BOS	A	C		89	.243
1946	BOS	A	C		40	.315
1947	BOS	A	C		60	.231
1948	STL	A	C		82	.203
	BRTR				367	.250

PARTENHEIMER, HAROLD PHILIP "STEVE"
B.AUG.30,1891 GREENFIELD,MASS.
D.JUNE 16,1971 MANSFIELD,OHIO

YR	CL	LEA	POS	GP	G	REC
1913	DET	A	3		1	.000
	TR					

PARTENHEIMER, STANWOOD WENDELL
B.OCT.21,1922 CHICOPEE FALLS, MASS.

YR	CL	LEA	POS	GP	G	REC
1944	BOS	A	P		1	0- 0
1945	STL	N	P		8	0- 0
	BBTL				9	0- 0
	BL 1944					

YR	CL LEA POS	GP	G	REC

PARTRIDGE, JAMES BUGG "JAY"
B.NOV.15,1902 MOUNTVILLE,GA.
D.JAN.14,1974 NASHVILLE,TENN.

YR	CL LEA POS	GP	G	REC
1927	BRO N 2		146	.260
1928	BRO N 2		37	.247
	BLTR		183	.259

PASCHAL, BENJAMIN EDWIN "BEN"
B.OCT.13,1895 ENTERPRISE,ALA.
D.NOV.10,1974 CHARLOTTE,N.C.

YR	CL LEA POS	GP	G	REC
1915	CLE A O		9	.111
1920	BOS A O		9	.250
1924	NY A O		4	.272
1925	NY A O		89	.360
1926	NY A O		96	.287
1927	NY A O		50	.317
1928	NY A O		65	.316
1929	NY A O		42	.208
	BRTR		364	.309

PASCUAL, CAMILO ALBERTO
B.JAN.20,1934 HAVANA,CUBA

YR	CL LEA POS	GP	G	REC
1954	WAS A P		48	4- 7
1955	WAS A P		43	2-12
1956	WAS A P	39	43	6-18
1957	WAS A P	29	32	8-17
1958	WAS A P		31	8-12
1959	WAS A P		32	17-10
1960	WAS A P	26	27	12- 8
1961	MIN A P		35	15-16
1962	MIN A P		34	20-11
1963	MIN A P	31	33	21- 9
1964	MIN A P		36	15-12
1965	MIN A P		27	9- 3
1966	MIN A P		21	8- 6
1967	WAS A P		28	12-10
1968	WAS A P		31	13-12
1969	WAS A P	14	17	2- 5
	CIN N P		5	0- 0
1970	LA N P		10	0- 0
1971	CLE A P		9	2- 2
	BRTR	529	542	174-170

PASCUAL, CARLOS LUIS
B.MAR.13,1930 HAVANA,CUBA

YR	CL LEA POS	GP	G	REC
1950	WAS A P		2	1- 1
	BRTR			

PASEK, JOHN PAUL
B.JUNE 26,1906 NIAGARA FALLS,
N.Y.
D.MAR.13,1976 NIAGARA FALLS,N.Y

YR	CL LEA POS	GP	G	REC
1933	DET A C		28	.246
1934	CHI A C		4	.333
	BRTR		32	.257

PASKERT, GEORGE HENRY "DODE"
B.AUG.28,1881 CLEVELAND,OHIO
D.FEB.12,1959

YR	CL LEA POS	GP	G	REC
1907	CIN N O		16	.280
1908	CIN N O		116	.243
1909	CIN N O		88	.251
1910	CIN N O		141	.300
1911	PHI N O		153	.273
1912	PHI N O		145	.315
1913	PHI N O		124	.262
1914	PHI N O		132	.264
1915	PHI N O		109	.244
1916	PHI N O		149	.279
1917	PHI N O		141	.251
1918	CHI N 3-O		127	.286
1919	CHI N O		88	.196
1920	CHI N O		139	.279
1921	CIN N O		27	.174
	BRTR		1695	.268

PASLEY, KEVIN PATRICK
B.JULY 22,1953 BROOKLYN,N.Y.

YR	CL LEA POS	GP	G	REC
1974	LA N C		1	.000
1976	LA N C		23	.231
	BRTR		24	.231

PASQUARIELLO, MICHAEL JOHN
B.NOV.7,1898 PHILADELPHIA,PA.
D.APR.5,1965 BRIDGEPORT,CONN.

YR	CL LEA POS	GP	G	REC
1919	PHI N 1		1	1.000
	STL N H		1	.000
	BRTR		2	.500

PASSEAU, CLAUDE WILLIAM
B.APR.9,1911 WAYNESBORO,MISS.

YR	CL LEA POS	GP	G	REC
1935	PIT N P		1	0- 1
1936	PIT N P	49	50	11-15
1937	PIT N P		50	14-18
1938	PIT N P	44	45	11-18
1939	PIT N P		8	2- 4
	CHI N P	34	35	13- 9
1940	CHI N P		46	20-13
1941	CHI N P		34	14-14
1942	CHI N P		35	19-14
1943	CHI N P		35	15-12
1944	CHI N P		34	15- 9
1945	CHI N P		34	17- 9
1946	CHI N P		21	9- 8
1947	CHI N P		19	2- 6
	BRTR	444	447	162-150

PASTORIUS, JAMES W.
"SUNNY JIM"
B.JULY 12,1881 PITTSBURGH,PA.
D.MAY 10,1941

YR	CL LEA POS	GP	G	REC
1906	BRO N P		29	10-14
1907	BRO N P		28	16-12
1908	BRO N P		28	4-20
1909	BRO N P		12	1- 9
	BLTL		97	31-55

PATE, JOSEPH WILLIAM
B.JUNE 6,1892 ALICE,TEX.
D.DEC.26,1948

YR	CL LEA POS	GP	G	REC
1926	PHI A P		47	9- 0
1927	PHI A P		32	0- 3
	BLTL		79	9- 3

PATEK, FREDERICK JOSEPH "FRED"
B.OCT.9,1944 SEQUIN,TEX.

YR	CL LEA POS	GP	G	REC
1968	PIT N S-3-O	61		.255
1969	PIT N 3	147		.239
1970	PIT N 3	84		.245
1971	KC A S	147		.267
1972	KC A S	136		.212
1973	KC A S	135		.234
1974	KC A S	149		.225
1975	KC A S	136		.228
1976	KC A S	144		.241
	BRTR	1139		.237

PATRICK, ROBERT LEE
B.OCT.27,1917 FT.SMITH,ARK.

YR	CL LEA POS	GP	G	REC
1941	DET A O		5	.286
1942	DET A O		4	.250
	BRTR		9	.267

PATTEE, HARRY ERNEST
B.JAN.17,1882 CHARLESTOWN,MASS.
D.JULY 17,1971 LYNCHBURG,VA.

YR	CL LEA POS	GP	G	REC
1908	BRO N 2		74	.216
	BLTR			

PATTEN, CASE L.
B.MAY 7,1876 WESTPORT,N.Y.
D.MAY 31,1935

YR	CL LEA POS	GP	G	REC
1901	WAS A P		31	18-10
1902	WAS A P-O	36	39	17-17
				.095
1903	WAS A P		35	10-23
1904	WAS A P		44	15-21
1905	WAS A P		43	16-20
1906	WAS A P		38	19-16
1907	WAS A P		36	12-17
1908	WAS A P		5	1- 3
	BOS A P		1	0- 0
1909	BOS A P		1	0- 0
	BBTL	270	273	108-127
				.132

PATTERSON, DANIEL THOMAS
B.1846

YR	CL LEA POS	GP	G	REC
1871	MUT NA O		32	-
1872	ECK NA 1-O		12	.160
1874	MUT NA 1		1	-
1875	ATL NA 2-O		10	-
			55	-

PATTERSON, DARYL ALAN
B.NOV.21,1943 COALINGA,CAL.

YR	CL LEA POS	GP	G	REC
1968	DET A P		38	2- 3
1969	DET A P		18	0- 2
1970	DET A P		43	7- 1
1971	DET A P		12	0- 1
	OAK A P		4	0- 0
	STL N P		13	0- 1
1974	PIT N P		14	2- 1
	BLTR		142	11- 9

PATTERSON, GEORGE

YR	CL LEA POS	GP	G	REC
1884	KEY U O		2	.146

PATTERSON, HAMILTON
B.OCT.13,1877 BELLEVILLE,ILL.
D.NOV.25,1945

YR	CL LEA POS	GP	G	REC
1909	STL A 1-O		17	.204
	CHI A O		1	.000
	TR		18	.192

PATTERSON, HENRY JOSEPH COLQUIT
"HANK"
B.JULY 17,1907 SAN FRANCISCO,
CAL.
D.SEPT.30,1970 PANORAMA CITY,
CAL.

YR	CL LEA POS	GP	G	REC
1932	BOS A C		1	.000
	TR			

PATTERSON, LORENZO CLAIRE
B.OCT.5,1887 ARKANSAS CITY,KAN.
D.MAR.28,1913

YR	CL LEA POS	GP	G	REC
1909	CIN N O		4	.125
	BLTR			

PATTERSON, ROY LEWIS
"BOY WONDER"
B.DEC.17,1877 STODDARD,WIS.
D.APR.14,1953

YR	CL LEA POS	GP	G	REC
1901	CHI A P		40	20-16
1902	CHI A P		34	20-13
1903	CHI A P		34	14-16
1904	CHI A P		22	7- 9
1905	CHI A P		13	4- 5
1906	CHI A P		22	10- 7
1907	CHI A P		19	4- 6
	BRTR		184	79-72

PATTERSON, WILLIAM JENNINGS
BRYAN "PAT"
B.JAN.29,1901 BELLEVILLE,ILL.

YR	CL LEA POS	GP	G	REC
1921	NY N 3		23	.400
	BRTR			

PATTIN, MARTIN WILLIAM "MARTY"
B.APR.6,1943 CHARLESTON,ILL.

YR	CL LEA POS	GP	G	REC
1968	CAL A P		52	4- 4
1969	SEA A P	34	39	7-12
1970	MIL A P	37	43	14-12
1971	MIL A P		36	14-14
1972	BOS A P		38	17-13
1973	BOS A P		34	15-15
1974	KC A P		25	3- 7
1975	KC A P	44	45	10-10
1976	KC A P		44	8-14
	BRTR	344	356	92-101

PATTISON, JAMES WELLS
B.DEC.18,1908 NEW YORK,N.Y.

YR	CL LEA POS	GP	G	REC
1929	BRO N P		6	0- 1
	BLTL			

PATTON, EUGENE TUNNEY
B.JULY 8,1926 COATESVILLE,PA.

YR	CL LEA POS	GP	G	REC
1944	BOS N H		1	.000
	BLTR			

PATTON, GEORGE WILLIAM
B.OCT.7,1912 CORNWALL,PA.

YR	CL LEA POS	GP	G	REC
1935	PHI A C		9	.300
	BRTR			

PATTON, HARRY C.
B.DAVENPORT,IOWA

YR	CL LEA POS	GP	G	REC
1910	STL N P		1	0- 0

PATTON, THOMAS ALLEN
B.SEPT.5,1935 HONEY BROOK,PA.

YR	CL LEA POS	GP	G	REC
1957	BAL A C		1	.000
	BRTR			

PAUL

YR	CL LEA POS	GP	G	REC
1876	ATH N C		3	.167
	BRTR			

YR	CL	LEA	POS	GP	G	REC

PAUL, MICHAEL GEORGE "MIKE"
B.APR.18,1945 DETROIT,MICH.

YR	CL	LEA	POS	GP	G	REC
1968	CLE	A	P-1		36	5- 8
						.167
1969	CLE	A	P		47	5-10
1970	CLE	A	P		30	2- 8
1971	CLE	A	P		17	2- 7
1972	TEX	A	P		49	8- 9
1973	TEX	A	P	36	37	5- 4
	CHI	N	P		11	0- 1
1974	CHI	N	P		2	0- 1
		BLTL		228	229	27-48
						.115

PAULA, CARLOS CONILL
B.NOV.4,1928 HAVANA,CUBA

1954	WAS	A	O		9	.167
1955	WAS	A	O		115	.299
1956	WAS	A	O		33	.183
		BRTR			157	.271

PAULETTE, EUGENE EDWARD "GENE"
B.MAY 26,1891 LITTLE ROCK,ARK.
D.FEB.8,1966

1911	NY	N	1		10	.167
1916	STL	A	H		5	.500
1917	STL	A	1		12	.182
	STL	N	1		95	.265
1918	STL	N	ALL	1	125	0- 0
						.273
1919	STL	N	1-2-S		43	.215
	PHI	N	1-2-O		67	.259
1920	PHI	N	1		143	.288
		BRTR		1	500	0- 0
						.268

PAULSON, PAUL GUILFORD
B.MAR.2,1902 GRAETTINGER,IOWA

1925	STL	N	P		1	0- 0
		BRTR				

PAUXTIS, SIMON FRANCIS
B.JULY 20,1885 W.PITTSTON,PA.
D.MAR.14,1961

1909	CIN	N	C		4	.125
		BRTR				

PAVESKOVICH, JOHN MICHAEL
(PLAYED UNDER NAME OF
JOHN MICHAEL PESKY)

PAVLETICH, DONALD STEPHEN "DON"
B.JULY 13,1938 MILWAUKEE,WIS.

1957	CIN	N	H		1	.000
1959	CIN	N	H		1	.000
1962	CIN	N	C-1		34	.222
1963	CIN	N	C-1		71	.208
1964	CIN	N	C-1		34	.242
1965	CIN	N	C-1		68	.319
1966	CIN	N	C-1		83	.294
1967	CIN	N	C-1-3		74	.238
1968	CIN	N	C-1		46	.286
1969	CHI	A	C-1		78	.245
1970	BOS	A	C-1		32	.138
1971	BOS	A	C		14	.259
		BRTR		536		.254

PAVLIECIVICH, ERVIN MARTIN
(PLAYED UNDER NAME OF
ERVIN MARTIN PALICA)

PAWELEK, THEODORE JOHN
B.AUG.15,1920 CHICAGO HEIGHTS,
ILL.
D.FEB.12,1964 CHICAGO HEIGHTS,
ILL.

1946	CHI	N	C		4	.250
		BLTR				

PAWLOSKI, STANLEY WALTER
B.SEPT.6,1931 WANAMIE,PA.

1955	CLE	A	2		2	.125
		BRTR				

PAYNE, FREDERICK THOMAS
B.SEPT.2,1880 CAMDEN,N.Y.
D.JAN.16,1954

1906	DET	A	C-O		72	.270
1907	DET	A	C		53	.167
1908	DET	A	C		20	.067
1909	CHI	A	C		32	.244
1910	CHI	A	C		91	.222
1911	CHI	A	C		66	.203
		BRTR			334	.215

PAYNE, GEORGE WASHINGTON
B.MAY 23,1894 MT.VERNON,KY.
D.JAN.24,1959

1920	CHI	A	P		12	1- 1
		BRTR				

PAYNE, HARLEY F. "LADY"
B.JAN.9,1868 WINDSOR,OHIO
D.DEC.29,1935

1896	BRO	N	P	31	32	14-13
1897	BRO	N	P	34	39	13-21
1898	BRO	N	P	1	1	1- 0
1899	PIT	N	P		4	1- 3
		TL		70	76	29-37

PAYNTER, GEORGE WASHINGTON
(REAL NAME
GEORGE WASHINGTON PANER)
B.JULY 6,1871 CINCINNATI,OHIO
D.OCT.1,1950

1894	STL	N	O		1	.000

PAZIK, MICHAEL JOSEPH "MIKE"
B.JAN.26,1950 LYNN,MASS.

1975	MIN	A	P		5	0- 4
1976	MIN	A	P		5	0- 0
		BLTL			10	0- 4

PEACOCK, JOHN GASTON "JOHNNY"
B.JAN.10,1910 FREMONT,N.C.

1937	BOS	A	C		9	.313
1938	BOS	A	C		72	.303
1939	BOS	A	C		92	.277
1940	BOS	A	C		63	.282
1941	BOS	A	C		79	.284
1942	BOS	A	C		88	.266
1943	BOS	A	C		48	.202
1944	BOS	A	C		4	.000
	PHI	A	C-2		83	.225
1945	PHI	A	C		33	.203
	BRO	N	C		48	.255
		BLTR			619	.262

PEAK, ELIAS
B.PHILADELPHIA,PA.

1884	BOS	U	O		1	.000
	KEY	U	2-S-O		54	.199
					55	.196

PEAPCE, FRANKLIN THOMAS
B.AUG.31,1905 MIDDLETOWN,KY.
D.SEPT.3,1950 VAN BUREN,IND.

1933	PHI	N	P		20	5- 4
1934	PHI	N	P		7	0- 2
1935	PHI	N	P		5	0- 0
		BRTR			32	5- 6

PEARCE, GEORGE THOMAS "FILBERT"
B.JAN.10,1888 AURORA,ILL.
D.OCT.11,1935

1912	CHI	N	P		3	0- 0
1913	CHI	N	P		25	13- 5
1914	CHI	N	P		30	9-12
1915	CHI	N	P		36	13- 9
1916	CHI	N	P		4	0- 0
1917	STL	N	P		5	1- 1
		BLTL			103	36-27

PEARCE, GRAYSON S. "GRACE"
B.NEW YORK,N.Y.
D.AUG.29,1894

1876	LOU	N	P		1	0- 0
1882	LOU	AA	P		9	.294
	BAL	AA	2-S-O		42	.210
1883	COL	AA	2-O		11	.220
	NY	N	2-O		18	.095
1884	MET	AA	2-O		5	.250
		BRTR		1	86	0- 0
						.200

PEARCE, HARRY JAMES
B.JULY 12,1889 PHILADELPHIA,PA.
D.JAN.8,1942

1917	PHI	N	S		4	.250
1918	PHI	N	1-2-S		60	.244
1919	PHI	N	2-S-3		68	.180
		BRTR			132	.208

PEARCE, JAMES MADISON "JIM"
B.JUNE 9,1925 ZEBULON,N.C.

1949	WAS	A	P		2	0- 1
1950	WAS	A	P		20	2- 1
1953	WAS	A	P		4	0- 1
1954	CIN	N	P		2	1- 0
1955	CIN	N	P		2	0- 1
		BRTR			30	3- 4

PEARCE, RICHARD J. "DICKEY"
B.JAN.2,1836 BROOKLYN,N.Y.
D.SEPT.18,1908

1871	MUT	NA	S		34	-
1872	MUT	NA	M-S-O		43	.188
1873	ATL	NA	S		55	-
1874	ATL	NA	S		36	-
	PHI	NA	S		1	-
	ATL	NA	S-3		20	-
1875	STL	NA	S		67	.256
1876	STL	N	S		25	.200
1877	STL	N	S		8	.172
		BRTR			289	-

PEARCE, WILLIAM C. "DUCKY"
B.MAR.17,1885 CORNING,OHIO
D.MAY 22,1933

1908	CIN	N	C		2	.000
1909	CIN	N	C		2	.000
		BRTR			4	.000

PEARS, FRANK T.
B.ST.LOUIS,MO.

1889	KC	AA	P		3	0- 2
1893	STL	N	P		1	0- 0
		TR			4	0- 2

PEARSON, ALBERT GREGORY "ALBIE"
B.SEP.12,1934 ALHAMBRA,CAL.

1958	WAS	A	O		146	.275
1959	WAS	A	O		25	.188
	BAL	A	O		80	.232
1960	BAL	A	O		48	.244
1961	LA	A	O		144	.288
1962	LA	A	O		160	.261
1963	LA	A	O		154	.304
1964	LA	A	O		107	.223
1965	CAL	A	O		122	.278
1966	CAL	A	O		2	.000
		BLTL			988	.270

PEARSON, ALEXANDER FRANKLIN
B.MAR.7,1877 GREENSBORO,PA.
D.OCT.30,1966 ROCHESTER,PA.

1902	STL	N	P		11	2- 6
1903	CLE	A	P		4	1- 2
		BRTR			15	3- 8

PEARSON, DAVID P.
(REAL NAME DAVID P. PIERSON)
B.AUG.20,1855 WILKES-BARRE,PA.
D.NOV.11,1922 TRENTON,N.J.

1876	CIN	N	P-C-	1	56	0- 1
			O			.235
		BRTR				

PEARSON, ISAAC OVERTON "IKE"
B.MAR.1,1918 GRENADA,MISS.

1939	PHI	N	P	26	27	2-13
1940	PHI	N	P		29	3-14
1941	PHI	N	P		46	4-14
1942	PHI	N	P		35	1- 6
1946	PHI	N	P		5	1- 0
1948	CHI	A	P		23	2- 3
		BRTR		164	165	13-50

PEARSON, MARCELLUS MONTE
"MONTE" OR "HOOT"
B.SEPT.2,1909 OAKLAND,CAL.

1932	CLE	A	P		8	0- 0
1933	CLE	A	P		19	10- 5
1934	CLE	A	P		39	18-13
1935	CLE	A	P		30	8-13
1936	NY	A	P		33	19- 7
1937	NY	A	P		22	9- 3
1938	NY	A	P		28	16- 7
1939	NY	A	P		22	12- 5
1940	NY	A	P		16	7- 6
1941	CIN	N	P	7	8	1- 3
		BRTR		224	225	100-62

PEASLEY, MARVIN WARREN
B.JULY 16,1888 JONESPORT,ME.
D.DEC.27,1948

1910	DET	A	P		2	0- 1
		BLTL				

PECHINEY, GEORGE ADOLPHE
"PISCH"
B.SEPT.20,1861 CINCINNATI,OHIO
D.JULY 14,1943

1885	CIN	AA	P		11	7- 4
1886	CIN	AA	P-O	38	43	17-21
						.221
1887	CLE	AA	P		10	1- 9
		BRTR		59	64	25-34
						.220

YR	CL LEA POS	GP	G	REC

PECHOUS, CHARLES EDWARD
B.OCT.5,1896 CHICAGO,ILL.

1915 CHI F	3		18	.220
1916 CHI N	3		22	.145
1917 CHI N	S		13	.244
BRTR			53	.193

PECK, HAROLD ARTHUR "HAL"
B.APR.20,1917 BIG BEND,WIS.

1943 BRO N	H		1	.000
1944 PHI A	O		2	.250
1945 PHI A	O		112	.276
1946 PHI A	O		48	.247
1947 CLE A	O		114	.293
1948 CLE A	O		45	.286
1949 CLE A	O		33	.310
BLTL			355	.279

PECKINPAUGH, ROGER THORPE
B.FEB.5,1891 WOOSTER,OHIO

1910 CLE A	S		15	.200
1912 CLE A	S		69	.212
1913 CLE A	S		1	.000
NY	A	S	95	.268
1914 NY	A	M-S	157	.223
1915 NY	A	S	142	.220
1916 NY	A	S	142	.255
1917 NY	A	S	148	.260
1918 NY	A	S	122	.231
1919 NY	A	S	122	.305
1920 NY	A	S	139	.270
1921 NY	A	S	149	.288
1922 WAS A	S		147	.254
1923 WAS A	S		154	.264
1924 WAS A	S		155	.272
1925 WAS A	1-S		126	.294
1926 WAS A	S		57	.238
1927 CHI A	S		68	.295
BRTR			2008	.259

NON-PLAYING MANAGER
CLE(A) 1928-33, 41

PEDEN, LESLIE EARL "GOOCH"
B.SEPT.17,1923 AZLE,TEX.

1953 WAS A	C		9	.250
BRTR				

PEDROES, CHARLES P.
B.OCT.27,1869 CHICAGO,ILL.
D.AUG.6,1927 CHICAGO,ILL.

1902 CHI N	O		2	.000

PEEK, STEPHEN GEORGE
B.JULY 30,1914 SPRINGFIELD,MASS

1941 NY	A	P	17	4- 2
BBTR				

PEEL, HOMER HEFNER
B.OCT.10,1902 PORT SULLIVAN,TEX

1927 STL N	O		2	.000
1929 PHI N	O		53	.269
1930 PHI N	O		26	.164
1933 NY	N	O	84	.257
1934 NY	N	O	21	.195
BRTR			186	.238

PEERSON, JACK CHILES
B.AUG.28,1910 BRUNSWICK,GA.

1935 PHI A	S		10	.316
1936 PHI A	2-S		8	.324
BRTR			18	.321

PERRY, GEORGE A. "RED"
B.AUG.15,1906 SANTAQUIN,UTAH

1927 PIT N	P		1	0- 0
1928 BOS N	P	9	10	0- 1
BLTL		10	11	0- 1

PEETE, CHARLES "CHARLEY"
B.FEB.22,1929 FRANKLIN,VA.
D.NOV.27,1956

1956 STL N	O		23	.192
BLTR				

PEFFER, MONTE
B.1891 NEW YORK,N.Y.

1913 PHI A	S		1	.000
BRTR				

PEITZ, HENRY CLEMENT "HEINE"
B.NOV.28,1872 ST.LOUIS,MO.
D.OCT.23,1943 NORWOOD,OHIO

1893 STL N	C		94	.266
1894 STL N	C-1-3		100	.274
1895 STL N	C		90	.288
1896 STL N	C		67	.298
1897 CIN N	C		73	.297
1898 CIN N	C		100	.281
1899 CIN N	C		91	.271
1900 CIN N	C		84	.251
1901 CIN N	C-2		73	.311
1902 CIN N	C-1-2-3		104	.313
1903 CIN N	C		102	.260
1904 CIN N	C-1		82	.243
1905 PIT N	C		88	.223
1906 PIT N	C		38	.240
1913 STL N	C-O		3	.333
BRTR			1189	.274

PEITZ, JOSEPH

1892 STL N	O		1	.000
1894 STL N	O		5	.421
			6	.364

PELLAGRINI, EDWARD CHARLES "EDDIE"
B.MAR.13,1919 BOSTON,MASS.

1946 BOS A	S-3		22	.211
1947 BOS A	S-3		74	.203
1948 STL A	S		105	.238
1949 STL A	S		79	.238
1951 PHI N	2-S-3		86	.234
1952 CIN N	1-2-S-3		46	.170
1953 PIT N	2-S-3		78	.253
1954 PIT N	2-S-3		73	.216
BRTR			563	.226

PELOUZE

1886 STL N	O		1	.000

PELTY, BARNEY
B.SEPT.10,1880 FARMINGTON,MO.
D.MAY 24,1939

1903 STL A	P		8	4- 4
1904 STL A	P		40	14-18
1905 STL A	P		31	13-14
1906 STL A	P		35	17-12
1907 STL A	P		36	12-21
1908 STL A	P	20	21	7- 4
1909 STL A	P	27	37	11-11
1910 STL A	P		27	5-10
1911 STL A	P	28	29	7-15
1912 STL A	P		6	0- 3
WAS A	P		11	2- 6
BRTR		269	281	92-118

PELTZ, JOHN
B.APR.23,1861 NEW ORLEANS,LA.
D.FEB.27,1906

1884 IND AA	O		106	.213
1888 BAL AA	O		1	.250
1890 BRO AA	O		99	.234
SYR AA	O		5	.176
TOL AA	O		18	.227
BRTR			229	.223

PEMBERTON, BROCK
B.NOV.6,1953 TULSA,OKLA.

1974 NY	N	1	11	.182
1975 NY	N	H	2	.000
BBTL			13	.167

PENA, JOSE (GUTIERREZ)
B.DEC.3,1942 JUAREZ,MEXICO

1969 CIN N	P		6	1- 1
1970 LA	N	P	29	4- 3
1971 LA	N	P	21	2- 0
1972 LA	N	P	5	0- 0
BRTR			61	7- 4

PENA, ORLANDO (GUEVARA)
B.NOV.17,1933 VICTORIA DE LAS TUNAS,CUBA

1958 CIN N	P		9	1- 0
1959 CIN N	P		46	5- 9
1960 CIN N	P		4	0- 1
1962 KC	A	P	13	6- 4
1963 KC	A	P	35	12-20
1964 KC	A	P	40	42	12-14
1965 KC	A	P	12	0- 6
DET A	P		30	4- 6
1966 DET A	P		54	4- 2
1967 DET A	P		2	0- 1
CLE A	P		48	0- 3
1970 PIT N	P		23	2- 1
1971 BAL A	P		5	0- 1
1973 BAL A	P		11	1- 1
1973 STL N	P		42	4- 4
1974 STL N	P		42	5- 2
CAL A	P		4	0- 0
1975 CAL A	P		7	0- 2
BRTR		420	429	56-77

PENA, ROBERTO CESAR (RAMIREZ)
B.APR.17,1940 SANTO DOMINGO,D.R.

1965 CHI N	S		51	.218
1966 CHI N	S		6	.176
1968 PHI N	S		138	.260
1969 SD	N	1-2-S-3	139	.250
1970 OAK A	S-3		19	.259
MIL A	1-2-S		121	.238
1971 MIL A	1-2-S-3		113	.237
BRTR			587	.245

PENCE, ELMER CLAIR
B.AUG.17,1900 VALLEY SPRINGS, CAL.

1922 CHI A	O		1	.000
BRTR				

PENCE, RUSSELL WILLIAM "RUSTY"
B.MAR.11,1900 MARINE,ILL.
D.AUG.11,1971 HOT SRPINGS,ARK.

1921 CHI A	P		4	0- 0
BRTR				

PENDLETON, JAMES EDWARD "JIM"
B.JAN.7,1926 ST.CHARLES,MO.

1953 MIL N	S-O		120	.299
1954 MIL N	O		71	.220
1955 MIL N	S-3-O		8	.000
1956 MIL N	1-2-S-3		14	.000
1957 PIT N	S-3-O		46	.305
1958 PIT N	H		3	.333
1959 CIN N	S-3-O		65	.257
1962 HOU N	1-S-3-O		117	.246
BRTR			444	.255

PENNER, WILLIAM KENNETH "KEN"
B.APR.24,1896 FLORENCE,ALA.
D.MAY 28,1959

1916 CLE A	P		4	1- 0
1929 CHI N	P		5	0- 1
BLTR			9	1- 1

PENNINGTON, GEORGE LOUIS "KEWPIE"
B.SEPT.24,1896 NEW YORK,N.Y.

1917 STL A	P		1	0- 0
BRTR				

PENNOCK, HERBERT JEFFERIS
"HERB"
B.FEB.19,1894 KENNETT SQUARE,PA
D.JAN.30,1948 NEW YORK,N.Y.

YR	CL	LEA	POS	GP	G	REC
1912	PHI	A	P		17	1- 2
1913	PHI	A	P		14	4- 1
1914	PHI	A	P		28	11- 4
1915	PHI	A	P		11	3- 5
	BOS	A	P		5	0- 0
1916	BOS	A	P	9	11	0- 2
1917	BOS	A	P		24	5- 5
1919	BOS	A	P		32	17- 8
1920	BOS	A	P	37	38	16-13
1921	BOS	A	P		32	12-14
1922	BOS	A	P		32	10-17
1923	NY	A	P		35	19- 6
1924	NY	A	P		40	21- 9
1925	NY	A	P		47	16-17
1926	NY	A	P		40	23-11
1927	NY	A	P		34	19- 8
1928	NY	A	P		28	17- 6
1929	NY	A	P		27	9-11
1930	NY	A	P		25	11- 7
1931	NY	A	P		25	11- 6
1932	NY	A	P		22	9- 5
1933	NY	A	P		23	7- 4
1934	BOS	A	P		30	2- 0
	BBTL			617	620	243-161

PENSON, PAUL EUGENE
B.JULY 12,1931 KANSAS CITY,KAN.

YR	CL	LEA	POS	GP	G	REC
1954	PHI	N	P		5	1- 1
	BRTR					

PENTZ, EUGENE DAVID "GENE"
B.JUNE 21,1953 JOHNSTOWN,PA.

YR	CL	LEA	POS	GP	G	REC
1975	DET	A	P		13	0- 4
1976	HOU	N	P		40	3- 3
	BRTR				53	3- 7

PEOPLES, JAMES ELLSWORTH
B.OCT.8,1863 BIG BEAVER,MICH.
D.AUG.29,1920 DETROIT,MICH.

YR	CL	LEA	POS	GP	G	REC
1884	CIN	AA	P-C-1-S-3-	70		.180
			O			
1885	CIN	AA	P-C-	2	7	0- 2
			O			.136
	BRO	AA	C		40	.205
1886	BRO	AA	C		94	.221
1887	BRO	AA	C		73	.283
1888	BRO	AA	C		33	.198
1889	COL	AA	C		28	.223
	TR			2	345	0- 2
						.224

PEPITONE, JOSEPH ANTHONY "JOE"
B.OCT.9,1940 BROOKLYN,N.Y.

YR	CL	LEA	POS	GP	G	REC
1962	NY	A	1-O		63	.239
1963	NY	A	1-O		157	.271
1964	NY	A	1-O		160	.251
1965	NY	A	1-O		143	.247
1966	NY	A	1-O		152	.255
1967	NY	A	1-O		133	.251
1968	NY	A	1-O		108	.245
1969	NY	A	1		135	.242
1970	HOU	N	1-O		75	.251
	CHI	N	1-O		56	.268
1971	CHI	N	1-O		115	.307
1972	CHI	N	1		66	.262
1973	CHI	N	1		31	.268
	ATL	N	1		3	.364
	BLTL			1397		.258

PEPLOSKI, HENRY STEPHEN "PEP"
B.SEPT.15,1905 GARLIN,POLAND

YR	CL	LEA	POS	GP	G	REC
1929	BOS	N	3		6	.200
	BLTR					

PEPLOSKI, JOSEPH ALOYSIUS
"PEPPER"
B.SEPT.12,1891 BROOKLYN,N.Y.
DECEASED

YR	CL	LEA	POS	GP	G	REC
1913	DET	A	3		2	.500
	BRTR					

PEPPER, DONALD HOYTE "DON"
B.OCT.8,1943 SARATOGA SPRGS.,N.Y

YR	CL	LEA	POS	GP	G	REC
1966	DET	A	1		4	.000
	BLTR					

PEPPER, HUGH MC LAURIN "LAURIN"
B.JAN.18,1931 VAUGHAN,MISS.

YR	CL	LEA	POS	GP	G	REC
1954	PIT	N	P		14	1- 5
1955	PIT	N	P		14	0- 1
1956	PIT	N	P		11	1- 1
1957	PIT	N	P	5	7	0- 1
	BRTR			44	46	2- 8

PEPPER, RAYMOND WATSON
B.AUG.5,1905 DECATUR,ALA.

YR	CL	LEA	POS	GP	G	REC
1932	STL	A	O		21	.246
1933	STL	A	O		3	.222
1934	STL	A	O		148	.298
1935	STL	A	O		92	.253
1936	STL	A	O		75	.282
	BRTR			339		.281

PEPPER, ROBERT ERNEST
B.MAY 3,1895 ROSSTON,PA.
D.APR.8,1968 FORD CLIFF,PA.

YR	CL	LEA	POS	GP	G	REC
1915	PHI	A	P	1		0- 0
	BRTR					

PEPPER, WILLIAM HARRISON
B.WEBB CITY,MO.

YR	CL	LEA	POS	GP	G	REC
1894	LOU	N	P		2	0- 1

PERAZA, LUIS (RIOS)
B.JUNE 17,1942 RIO PIEDRAS,P.R.

YR	CL	LEA	POS	GP	G	REC
1969	PHI	N	P		8	0- 0
	BRTR					

PERDUE, HUBBARD E. "HUB"
B.JUNE 7,1886 GALLATIN,TENN.
D.OCT.31,1968 GALLATIN,TENN.

YR	CL	LEA	POS	GP	G	REC
1911	BOS	N	P		24	6-10
1912	BOS	N	P		37	13-16
1913	BOS	N	P		38	16-13
1914	BOS	N	P		9	2- 5
	STL	N	P		22	8- 8
1915	STL	N	P		31	6-12
	BRTR			161		51-64

PEREZ, ATANASIO RIGAL "TONY"
B.MAY 14,1942 CIEGO DE AVILA,
CAMAGUEY,CUBA

YR	CL	LEA	POS	GP	G	REC
1964	CIN	N	1		12	.080
1965	CIN	N	1		104	.260
1966	CIN	N	1		99	.265
1967	CIN	N	1-2-3		156	.290
1968	CIN	N	3		160	.282
1969	CIN	N	3		160	.294
1970	CIN	N	1-3		158	.317
1971	CIN	N	1-3		158	.269
1972	CIN	N	1		136	.283
1973	CIN	N	1		151	.314
1974	CIN	N	1		158	.265
1975	CIN	N	1		137	.282
1976	CIN	N	1		139	.260
	BRTR			1728		.283

PEREZ, GEORGE THOMAS
B.DEC.29,1937 SAN FERNANDO,CAL.

YR	CL	LEA	POS	GP	G	REC
1958	PIT	N	P		4	0- 1
	BRTR					

PEREZ, MARTIN ROMAN "MARTY"
B.FEB.28,1947 VISALIA,CAL.

YR	CL	LEA	POS	GP	G	REC
1969	CAL	A	2-S-3		13	.231
1970	CAL	A	S		3	.000
1971	ATL	N	2-S		130	.227
1972	ATL	N	S		141	.228
1973	ATL	N	S		141	.250
1974	ATL	N	2-S-3		127	.260
1975	ATL	N	2-S		120	.275
1976	ATL	N	2-S-3		31	.250
	SF	N	2-S		93	.259
	BRTR			799		.249

PERKINS, CECIL BOYCE
B.DEC.1,1940 BALTIMORE,MD.

YR	CL	LEA	POS	GP	G	REC
1967	NY	A	P		2	0- 1
	BRTR					

PERKINS, CHARLES SULLIVAN
"LEFTY"
B.SEPT.9,1905 BIRMINGHAM,ALA.

YR	CL	LEA	POS	GP	G	REC
1930	PHI	A	P		8	0- 0
1934	BRO	N	P		11	0- 3
	BLTL			19		0- 3

PERKINS, RALPH FOSTER "CY"
B.FEB.27,1896 GLOUCESTER,MASS.
D.OCT.2,1963 PHILADELPHIA,PA.

YR	CL	LEA	POS	GP	G	REC
1915	PHI	A	C		7	.190
1917	PHI	A	C		6	.167
1918	PHI	A	C		68	.188
1919	PHI	A	C		101	.252
1920	PHI	A	C		148	.260
1921	PHI	A	C		141	.288
1922	PHI	A	C		148	.267
1923	PHI	A	C		143	.270
1924	PHI	A	C		128	.242
1925	PHI	A	C-3		65	.307
1926	PHI	A	C		63	.291
1927	PHI	A	C		59	.256
1928	PHI	A	C		19	.172
1929	PHI	A	C		38	.211
1930	PHI	A	C		20	.158
1931	NY	A	C		16	.255
1934	DET	A	H		1	.000
	BRTR			1171		.259

PERKOVICH, JOHN JOSEPH
B.MAR.10,1924 CHICAGO,ILL.

YR	CL	LEA	POS	GP	G	REC
1950	CHI	A	P		1	0- 0
	BRTR					

PERKOWSKI, HARRY WALTER
B.SEPT.6,1922 DANTE,VA.

YR	CL	LEA	POS	GP	G	REC
1947	CIN	N	P		3	0- 0
1949	CIN	N	P		5	1- 1
1950	CIN	N	P	22	32	0- 0
1951	CIN	N	P	35	37	3- 6
1952	CIN	N	P		33	12-10
1953	CIN	N	P		33	12-11
1954	CIN	N	P		28	2- 8
1955	CHI	N	P	25	26	3- 4
	BLTL			184	197	33-40

PERME, LEONARD JOSEPH
B.NOV.25,1918 CLEVELAND,OHIO

YR	CL	LEA	POS	GP	G	REC
1942	CHI	A	P		4	0- 1
1946	CHI	A	P		4	0- 0
	BLTL			8		0- 1

PERNOLL, HENRY HUBBARD "HUB"
B.MAR.14,1888 APPLEGATE,ORE.
D.FEB.18,1944

YR	CL	LEA	POS	GP	G	REC
1910	DET	A	P		11	4- 3
1912	DET	A	P		3	0- 0
	BRTR			14		4- 3

PERRANOSKI, RONALD PETER "RON"
B.APR.1,1936 PATERSON,N.J.

YR	CL	LEA	POS	GP	G	REC
1961	LA	N	P		53	7- 5
1962	LA	N	P		70	6- 6
1963	LA	N	P		69	16- 3
1964	LA	N	P		72	5- 7
1965	LA	N	P		59	6- 6
1966	LA	N	P		55	6- 7
1967	LA	N	P		70	6- 7
1968	MIN	A	P		66	8- 7
1969	MIN	A	P		75	9-10
1970	MIN	A	P		67	7- 8
1971	MIN	A	P		36	1- 4
	DET	A	P		11	0- 1
1972	DET	A	P		17	0- 1
	LA	N	P		9	2- 0
1973	CAL	A	P		8	0- 2
	BLTL			737		79-74

PERRIN, JOHN STEPHENSON
B.FEB.4,1898 ESCANABA,MICH.
D.JUNE 24,1969 DETROIT,MICH.

YR	CL	LEA	POS	GP	G	REC
1921	BOS	A	O		4	.231
	BLTR					

PERRIN, WILLIAM JOSEPH
B.JUNE 23,1911 NEW ORLEANS,LA.
D.JUNE 30,1974 NEW ORLEANS,LA.

YR	CL	LEA	POS	GP	G	REC
1934	CLE	A	P		1	0- 1
	BRTL					

PERRINE, JOHN GROVER "NIG"
B.JAN.14,1885 CLINTON,WIS.
D.AUG.13,1948

YR	CL	LEA	POS	GP	G	REC
1907	WAS	A	2-S		44	.171
	TR					

YR   CL LEA POS GP   G   REC

PERRING, GEORGE WILSON
B.AUG.13,1884 SHARON,WIS.
D.AUG.20,1960
```
1908 CLE A  S-3        89   .216
1909 CLE A  3          88   .223
1910 CLE A  3          39   .221
1914 KC  F  1-3       144   .282
1915 KC  F  1-2-3     153   .257
         BRTR         513   .249
```

PERRITT, WILLIAM DAYTON "POL"
B.AUG.30,1892 ARCADIA,LA.
D.OCT.15,1947
```
1912 STL N  P          6    1- 1
1913 STL N  P         36    6-14
1914 STL N  P         41   16-13
1915 NY  N  P         35   12-18
1916 NY  N  P         40   18-11
1917 NY  N  P         35   17- 7
1918 NY  N  P     35  36   18-13
1919 NY  N  P         11    1- 1
1920 NY  N  P          8    0- 0
1921 NY  N  P          5    2- 0
     DET A  P          4    1- 0
         BRTR    256 257   92-78
```

PERRY, BOYD GLENN
B.MAR.21,1914 SNOW CAMP,N.C.
```
1941 DET A  2-S       36   .181
         BRTR
```

PERRY, CLAYTON SHIELDS
B.DEC.18,1881 CLAYTON,WIS.
D.JAN.13,1954
```
1908 DET A  3          7   .118
         TR
```

PERRY, GAYLORD JACKSON
B.SEP.15,1930 WILLIAMSTON,N.C.
```
1962 SF  N  P         13    3- 1
1963 SF  N  P     31  32    1- 6
1964 SF  N  P     44  46   12-11
1965 SF  N  P     47  49    8-12
1966 SF  N  P         36   21- 8
1967 SF  N  P     39  42   15-17
1968 SF  N  P         39   16-15
1969 SF  N  P         40   19-14
1970 SF  N  P         41   23-13
1971 SF  N  P     37  38   16-12
1972 CLE A  P         41   24-16
1973 CLE A  P         41   19-19
1974 CLE A  P         37   21-13
1975 CLE A  P         15    6- 9
     TEX A  P         22   12- 8
1976 TEX A  P         32   15-14
         BRTR    555 564  231-188
```

PERRY, HERBERT SCOTT "SCOTT"
B.APR.17,1891 DENNISON,TEX.
D.OCT.27,1959
```
1915 STL N  P          1    0- 0
1916 CHI N  P          4    2- 1
1917 CHI N  P          4    0- 0
1918 PHI A  P         44   21-19
1919 PHI A  P         25    4-17
1920 PHI A  P         42   11-25
1921 PHI A  P         12    3- 6
         BRTR        132   41-68
```

PERRY, JAMES EVAN "JIM"
B.OCT.30,1936 WILLIAMSTON,N.C.
```
1959 CLE A  P         44   12-10
1960 CLE A  P     41  42   18-10
1961 CLE A  P         35   10-17
1962 CLE A  P         35   12-12
1963 CLE A  P          5    0- 0
     MIN A  P         35    9- 9
1964 MIN A  P         42    6- 3
1965 MIN A  P         36   12- 7
1966 MIN A  P         33   11- 7
1967 MIN A  P     37  39    8- 7
1968 MIN A  P         32    8- 6
1969 MIN A  P     46  47   20- 6
1970 MIN A  P-O   40  41   24-12
                           .247
1971 MIN A  P         40   17-17
1972 MIN A  P         35   13-16
1973 DET A  P         35   14-13
1974 CLE A  P         36   17-12
1975 CLE A  P          8    1- 6
     OAK A  P         15    3- 4
         BBTR    630 635  215-174
                           .199
```

PERRY, MELVIN GRAY "BOB"
B.SEP.14,1934 NEW BERN,N.C.
```
1963 LA  A  O         61   .253
1964 LA  A  O         70   .276
         BRTR        131   .266
```

PERRY, WILLIAM HENRY "SOCKS"
B.JULY 28,1886 HOWELL,MICH.
D.JULY 18,1956
```
1912 DET A  O         13   .162
         BLTR
```

PERRYMAN, EMMETT KEY "PARSON"
B.OCT.24,1888 EVERETT SPRINGS,
GA.
D.SEPT.12,1966 STARKE,FLA.
```
1915 STL A  P         24    2- 3
         BRTR
```

PERSICO, SALVATORE JOSEPH
(PLAYED UNDER NAME OF
JOSEPH SMITH)

PERTICA, WILLIAM ANDREW
B.AUG.17,1899 SANTA BRABARA,CAL
D.DEC.29,1967 LOS ANGELES,CAL.
```
1918 BOS A  P          1    0- 0
1921 STL N  P         38   14-10
1922 STL N  P-S   34  35    8- 8
                           .181
1923 STL N  P          1    0- 0
         BRTR     74  75   22-18
                           .152
```

PERZANOWSKI, STANLEY "STAN"
B.AUG.25,1950 EAST CHICAGO,ILL.
```
1971 CHI A  P          5    0- 1
1974 CHI A  P          2    0- 0
1975 TEX A  P         12    3- 3
1976 TEX A  P          5    0- 0
         BBTR     24        3- 4
```

PESKY, JOHN MICHAEL "JOHNNY"
(REAL NAME
JOHN MICHAEL PAVESKOVICH)
B.SEPT.27,1919 PORTLAND,ORE.
```
1942 BOS A  S        147   .331
1946 BOS A  S        153   .335
1947 BOS A  S-3      155   .324
1948 BOS A  3        143   .281
1949 BOS A  3        148   .306
1950 BOS A  S-3      127   .312
1951 BOS A  2-S-3    131   .313
1952 BOS A  S-3       25   .149
     DET A  2-S-3     69   .254
1953 DET A  2        103   .292
1954 DET A  H         20   .176
     WAS A  2-S       49   .253
         BLTR       1270   .307
```
NON-PLAYING MANAGER
BOS(A) 1963-64

PETERMAN, WILLIAM DAVID
B.MAR.20,1921 PHILADELPHIA,PA.
```
1942 PHI N  C          1  1.000
         BRTR
```

PETERS, GARY CHARLES
B.APR.21,1937 GROVE CITY,PA.
```
1959 CHI A  P          2    0- 0
1960 CHI A  P          2    0- 0
1961 CHI A  P          3    0- 0
1962 CHI A  P          5    0- 1
1963 CHI A  P     41  50   19- 8
1964 CHI A  P     37  54   20- 8
1965 CHI A  P     33  42   10-12
1966 CHI A  P     30  38   12-10
1967 CHI A  P     38  48   16-11
1968 CHI A  P     31  46    4-13
1969 CHI A  P     36  37   10-15
1970 BOS A  P     34  37   16-11
1971 BOS A  P     34  53   14-11
1972 BOS A  P         33    3- 3
         BLTL    359 450  124-103
```

PETERS, JOHN PAUL
B.APR.8,1850 LOUISIANA,MO.
D.JAN.4,1924
```
1874 CHI NA 2-S-3     54    -
1875 CHI NA 2-S       70    -
1876 CHI N  S         66   .348
1877 CHI N  S         60   .317
1878 MIL N  2-S       54   .311
1879 CHI N  S         79   .254
1880 PRO N  S         83   .230
1881 BUF N  S-O       54   .214
1882 PIT AA 2-S       72   .278
1883 PIT AA S          8   .107
1884 PIT AA S          1   .000
         BRTR        601    -
```

PETERS, JOHN WILLIAM
B.JULY 14,1893 KANSAS CITY,KAN.
D.FEB.21,1932
```
1915 DET A  C          1   .000
1918 CLE A  C          1   .000
1921 PHI N  C         55   .290
1922 PHI N  C         55   .244
         BRTR        112   .265
```

PETERS, OSCAR C. "RUBE"
B.MAR.15,1886 GRAND FORK,ILL.
```
1912 CHI A  P         28    5- 6
1914 BRO F  P         11    1- 1
         BRTR         39    6- 7
```

PETERS, RAYMOND JAMES "RAY"
B.AUG.27,1946 BUFFALO,N.Y.
```
1970 MIL A  P          2    0- 2
         RRTR
```

PETERS, RUSSELL DIXON "RUSTY"
B.DEC.14,1914 ROANOKE,VA.
```
1936 PHI A  S-3       45   .218
1937 PHI A  2-S-3    116   .260
1938 PHI A  S          2   .000
1940 CLE A  1-2-S-3   30   .239
1941 CLE A  2-S-3     29   .206
1942 CLE A  2-S-3     34   .224
1943 CLE A  2-S-3-O   79   .219
1944 CLE A  2-S       88   .223
1946 CLE A  S          9   .206
1947 STL A  2-S       39   .340
         BRTR        471   .236
```

PETERSON, CARL FRANCIS "BUDDY"
B.APR.23,1925 PORTLAND,ORE.
```
1955 CHI A  S          6   .286
1957 BAL A  S          7   .176
         BRTR         13   .237
```

PETERSON, CHARLES ANDREW "CAP"
B.AUG.15,1942 TACOMA,WASH.
```
1962 SF  N  S          4   .167
1963 SF  N  2-S-3-O    22  .259
1964 SF  N  1-2-3-O    66  .203
1965 SF  N  O          63  .248
1966 SF  N  1-O        89  .237
1967 WAS A  O         122  .240
1968 WAS A  O          94  .204
1969 CLE A  3-O        76  .227
         BRTR        536   .230
```

PETERSON, FRED INGELS "FRITZ"
B.FEB.8,1942 CHICAGO,ILL.
```
1966 NY  A  P         34   12-11
1967 NY  A  P         36    8-14
1968 NY  A  P         36   12-11
1969 NY  A  P         37   17-16
1970 NY  A  P         39   20-11
1971 NY  A  P         37   15-13
1972 NY  A  P         35   17-15
1973 NY  A  P         31    8-15
1974 NY  A  P          3    0- 0
     CLE A  P         29    9-14
1975 CLE A  P         25   14- 8
1976 CLE A  P          9    0- 3
     TEX A  P          4    1- 0
         BBTL    355      133-131
```

PETERSON, HARDING WILLIAM
B.OCT.17,1929 PERTH AMBOY,N.J.
```
1955 PIT N  C         32   .247
1957 PIT N  C         30   .301
1958 PIT N  C          2   .333
1959 PIT N  C          2   .000
         BRTR         66   .273
```

YR	CL	LEA	POS	GP	G	REC

PETERSON, JAMES NIELS
B.AUG.18,1908 PHILADELPHIA,PA.
D.APR.8,1975 PALM BEACH,FLA.
1931	PHI	A	P		6	0- 1
1933	PHI	A	P		32	2- 5
1937	BRO	N	P		3	0- 0
	BRTR				41	2- 6

PETERSON, KENT FRANKLIN "PETE"
B.DEC.21,1925 GOSHEN,UTAH
1944	CIN	N	P		1	0- 0
1947	CIN	N	P		37	6-13
1948	CIN	N	P		43	2-15
1949	CIN	N	P		30	4- 5
1950	CIN	N	P		9	0- 3
1951	CIN	N	P		9	1- 1
1952	PHI	N	P		3	0- 0
1953	PHI	N	P		15	0- 1
	BRTL				147	13-38

PETERSON, ROBERT A.
B.PHILADELPHIA,PA.
1906	BOS	A	C		39	.203
1907	BOS	A	C		4	.000
	TR				43	.183

PETERSON, SIDNEY HERBERT
B.JAN.31,1918 HAVELOCK,N.DAK.
| 1943 | STL | A | P | | 3 | 2- 0 |
| | BRTR | | | | | |

PETOSKEY, FREDERICK LEE "TED"
B.JAN.5,1911 ST.CHARLES,MICH.
1934	CIN	N	O		6	.000
1935	CIN	N	O		4	.400
	BRTR				10	.167

PETROCELLI, AMERICO PETER "RICO"
B.JUNE 27,1943 BROOKLYN,N.Y.
1963	BOS	A	S		1	.250
1965	BOS	A	S		103	.232
1966	BOS	A	S-3		139	.238
1967	BOS	A	S		142	.259
1968	BOS	A	1-S		123	.234
1969	BOS	A	S-3		154	.297
1970	BOS	A	S-3		157	.261
1971	BOS	A	3		158	.251
1972	BOS	A	3		147	.240
1973	BOS	A	3		100	.244
1974	BOS	A	3		12	.267
1975	BOS	A	3		115	.239
1976	BOS	A	1-2-S-3		85	.213
	BRTR				1544	.251

PETROSKEY, JAMES
(PLAYED UNDER NAME OF
JAMES CLARK)

PETTEE, PATRICK E.
B.JAN.10,1863 NATICK,MASS.
D.OCT.9,1934
| 1891 | LOU | AA | 2 | | 2 | .167 |
| | TR | | | | | |

PETTIGREW, JIM NED
B.AUG.25,1881 HONEY GROVE,TEX.
D.AUG.20,1952
| 1914 | BUF | F | H | | 2 | .000 |

PETTIT, GEORGE WILLIAM PAUL "PAUL"
B.NOV.29,1931 LOS ANGELES,CAL.
1951	PIT	N	P		2	0- 0
1953	PIT	N	P	10	11	1- 2
	BLTL			12	13	1- 2

PETTIT, LEON ARTHUR "LEFTY"
B.JUNE 23,1902 WAYNESBURG,PA.
D.NOV.21,1974 COLUMBIA,TENN.
1935	WAS	A	P	41	8- 5	
1937	PHI	N	P		3	0- 1
	BLTL				44	8- 6

PETTIT, ROBERT HENRY
B.JULY 19,1861 WILLIAMSTOWN,
MASS.
D.NOV.1,1910
1887	CHI	N	O		32	.301
	CHI	N	O		43	.254
1891	MIL	AA	3		21	.174
					96	.254

PETTY, CHARLES E.
B.JUNE 28,1868 NASHVILLE,TENN.
1889	CIN	AA	P		5	2- 3
1893	NY	N	P		6	5- 2
1894	WAS	N	P		15	3- 8
1894	CLE	N	P		3	0- 2
	TR				32	10-15

PETTY, JESSE LEE
B.NOV.23,1894 ORR,OKLA.
D.OCT.23,1971 MINNEAPOLIS,MINN.
1921	CLE	A	P		4	0- 0
1925	BRO	N	P		28	9- 9
1926	BRO	N	P		38	17-17
1927	BRO	N	P		42	13-18
1928	BRO	N	P		40	15-15
1929	PIT	N	P		36	11-10
1930	PIT	N	P		10	1- 6
	CHI	N	P		9	1- 3
	BRTL				207	67-78

PEZOLD, LORENZ "LARRY"
B.JUNE 22,1893 NEW ORLEANS,LA.
D.OCT.22,1957
| 1914 | CLE | A | 3 | | 23 | .226 |
| | BRTR | | | | | |

PEZZULLO, FRANCESCO STEPHANO
(PLAYED UNDER NAME OF
FRANK L. BODIE)

PEZZULLO, JOHN "PRETZELS"
B.DEC.10,1911 BRIDGEPORT,CONN.
1935	PHI	N	P		41	3- 5
1936	PHI	N	P		1	0- 0
	BLTL				42	3- 5

PFEFFER, EDWARD JOSEPH "JEFF"
B.MAR.4,1888 SEYMOUR,ILL.
D.AUG.15,1972 CHICAGO,ILL.
1911	STL	A	P		2	0- 0
1913	BRO	N	P		5	0- 1
1914	BRO	N	P	43	44	23-12
1915	BRO	N	P		40	19-14
1916	BRO	N	P	41	43	25-11
1917	BRO	N	P	30	31	11-15
1918	BRO	N	P		1	1- 0
1919	BRO	N	P		30	17-13
1920	BRO	N	P		30	16- 9
1921	BRO	N	P		6	1- 5
	STL	N	P		18	9- 3
1922	STL	N	P	44	45	19-12
1923	STL	N	P		26	8- 9
1924	STL	N	P		16	4- 5
	PIT	N	P		15	5- 3
	BRTR			347	352	158-112

PFEFFER, FRANCIS XAVIER "BIG JEFF"
B.MAR.31,1882 CHAMPAIGN,ILL.
D.DEC.19,1954
1905	CHI	N	P		15	5- 5
1906	BOS	N	P	35	50	13-22
1907	BOS	N	P		19	6- 8
1908	BOS	N	P		4	0- 0
1910	BOS	N	P-O	13	14	1- 0
						.158
1911	BOS	N	P	26	30	7- 5
	BRTR			112	132	32-40
						.203

PFEFFER, NATHANIEL FREDERICK "NATE" OR "DANDELION"
B.MAR.17,1860 LOUISVILLE,KY.
D.APR.10,1932
1882	TRO	N	S-3		83	.221
1883	CHI	N	1-2-S-O	96		.234
1884	CHI	N	P-2	1	111	0- 0
						.289
1885	CHI	N	P-2-	4	112	3- 1
			O			.240
1886	CHI	N	2		119	.263
1887	CHI	N	2		123	.325
1888	CHI	N	2		135	.249
1889	CHI	N	2		134	.241
1890	CHI	P	2		123	.268
1891	CHI	N	2		137	.246
1892	LOU	N	M-2		124	.261
1893	LOU	N	2		124	.269
1894	LOU	N	2-S		104	.297
1895	LOU	N	1-2-S		11	.288
1896	NY	N	2		4	.143
	CHI	N	2		95	.244
1897	CHI	N	2		32	.230
	BRTR			5	1667	3- 1
						.262

PFEIL, ROBERT RAYMOND "BOB"
B.NOV.13,1943 PASSAIC,N.J.
1969	NY	N	2-3-O	62	.232	
1971	PHI	N	C-1-2-S-	44	.271	
			3-O			
	BRTR			106	.242	

PFIESTER, JOHN ALBERT
(REAL NAME
JOHN ALBERT HAGENBUSH)
B.MAY 24,1878 CINCINNATI,OHIO
D.SEPT.3,1953 LOVELAND,OHIO
1903	PIT	N	P		3	0- 3
1904	PIT	N	P		3	1- 1
1906	CHI	N	P		31	20- 8
1907	CHI	N	P		30	14- 9
1908	CHI	N	P		33	12-10
1909	CHI	N	P		29	17- 6
1910	CHI	N	P		14	6- 3
1911	CHI	N	P		6	2- 4
	BRTL				149	72-44

PFISTER, DANIEL ALBIN "DAN"
B.DEC.20,1936 PLAINFIELD,N.J.
1961	KC	A	P		2	0- 0
1962	KC	A	P	41	52	4-14
1963	KC	A	P		3	1- 0
1964	KC	A	P		19	20	1- 5
	BRTR			65	78	6-19

PFISTER, GEORGE EDWARD
B.SEPT.4,1918 BOUND BROOK,N.J.
| 1941 | BRO | N | C | | 1 | .000 |
| | BRTR | | | | | |

PFLANN, WILLIAM F.
B.BROOKLYN,N.Y.
| 1894 | CIN | N | P | | 1 | 0- 1 |

PFUND, LE ROY HERBERT
B.OCT.10,1918 OAK PARK,ILL.
| 1946 | BRO | N | P | | 15 | 3- 2 |
| | BRTR | | | | | |

PFYL, MEINHARD CHARLES "MONTE"
B.MAY 11,1886 ST.LOUIS,MO.
D.OCT.18,1945 SAN FRANCISCO,CAL
| 1907 | NY | N | 1 | | 1 | .000 |

PHEBUS, RAYMOND WILLIAM
B.AUG.2,1910 CHERRYVALE,KAN.
1936	WAS	A	P		2	0- 0
1937	WAS	A	P		6	3- 2
1938	WAS	A	P		5	0- 0
	BRTR				13	3- 2

PHELAN, ARTHUR THOMAS
B.AUG.14,1887 NIANTIC,ILL.
D.DEC.27,1964 FT.WORTH,TEX.
1910	CIN	N	3		17	.214
1912	CIN	N	3		130	.243
1913	CHI	N	2-3		91	.249
1914	CHI	N	'S		25	.283
1915	CHI	N	2-3		133	.219
	BRTR				396	.236

PHELAN, DANIEL B.
B.WATERBURY,CONN.
| 1890 | LOU | AA | 1 | | 8 | .250 |

PHELAN, JAMES D. "DICK"
B.DEC.10,1854 TOWANDA,PA.
D.FEB.13,1931
1884	BAL	U	2		97	.254
1885	BUF	N	2		4	.133
	STL	N	3		2	.250
					103	.249

PHELAN, LEWIS G.
NON-PLAYING MANAGER STL(N) 1895

PHELPS, CORNELIUS CARMAN "NEAL"
B.NOV.19,1840 NEW YORK,N.Y.
D.FEB.12,1885
1871	KEK	NA	1		1	.000
1873	MUT	NA	O		1	.000
1874	MUT	NA	O		4	-
1875	MUT	NA	O		2	-
1876	MUT	NA	O		1	.000
	ATH	N	C		1	.000
					10	-

YR	CL	LEA	POS	GP	G	REC

PHELPS, EDWARD JAYKILL "YALLER"
B.MAR.3,1879 ALBANY,N.Y.
D.JAN.31,1942 E.GREENBUSH,N.Y.

YR	CL	LEA	POS	GP	G	REC
1902	PIT	N	C-1		18	.197
1903	PIT	N	C		79	.282
1904	PIT	N	C		92	.242
1905	CIN	N	C		44	.231
1906	CIN	N	C		12	.275
	PIT	N	C		40	.237
1907	PIT	N	C		36	.212
1908	PIT	N	C		20	.234
1909	STL	N	C		83	.248
1910	STL	N	C		80	.263
1912	BRO	N	C		52	.288
1913	BRO	N	C		15	.222
	BRTR				571	.251

PHELPS, ERNEST GORDON "BABE" OR "BLIMP"
B.APR.19,1908 ODENTON,MD.

YR	CL	LEA	POS	GP	G	REC
1931	WAS	A	H		3	.333
1933	CHI	N	C		3	.286
1934	CHI	N	C		44	.286
1935	BRO	N	C		47	.364
1936	BRO	N	C		115	.367
1937	BRO	N	C		121	.313
1938	BRO	N	C		66	.308
1939	BRO	N	C		98	.285
1940	BRO	N	C-1		118	.295
1941	BRO	N	C		16	.233
1942	PIT	N	C		95	.284
	BLTR				726	.310

PHELPS, RAYMOND CLIFFORD
B.DEC.11,1903 DUNLAP,TENN.
D.JULY 7,1971 FORT PIERCE,FLA.

YR	CL	LEA	POS	GP	G	REC
1930	BRO	N	P		36	14- 7
1931	BRO	N	P		28	7- 9
1932	BRO	N	P		20	4- 5
1935	CHI	A	P		27	4- 8
1936	CHI	A	P		15	4- 6
	BRTR				126	33-35

PHILLEY, DAVID EARL "DAVE"
B.MAY 16,1920 PARIS,TEX.

YR	CL	LEA	POS	GP	G	REC
1941	CHI	A	O		7	.222
1946	CHI	A	O		17	.353
1947	CHI	A	3-O		143	.258
1948	CHI	A	O		137	.287
1949	CHI	A	O		146	.286
1950	CHI	A	O		156	.242
1951	CHI	A	O		7	.240
	PHI	A	3-O		125	.263
1952	PHI	A	3-O		151	.263
1953	PHI	A	3-O		157	.303
1954	CLE	A	O		133	.226
	BAL	A	3-O		82	.296
1955	CLE	A	O		44	.306
	BAL	A	3-O		82	.296
1956	DAL	A	3-U		32	.205
	CHI	A	1-O		86	.265
1957	CHI	A	1-O		22	.324
	DET	A	1-3-O		65	.283
1958	PHI	N	1-O		91	.309
1959	PHI	N	1-O		99	.291
1960	PHI	N	1-O		14	.333
	SF	N	3-O		39	.164
	BAL	A	3-O		14	.265
1961	BAL	A	3-O		99	.250
1962	BOS	A	O		38	.143
	BBTR				1904	.270

PHILLIPPE, CHARLES LOUIS "DEACON"
B.MAY 23,1872 RURAL RETREAT,VA.
D.MAR.30,1952 AVALON,PA.

YR	CL	LEA	POS	GP	G	REC
1899	LOU	N	P	39	42	20-17
1900	PIT	N	P		32	18-14
1901	PIT	N	P		34	22-12
1902	PIT	N	P		30	20- 9
1903	PIT	N	P	36	37	25- 9
1904	PIT	N	P		21	10-10
1905	PIT	N	P		38	22-13
1906	PIT	N	P		33	15-10
1907	PIT	N	P		35	14-11
1908	PIT	N	P		5	0- 0
1909	PIT	N	P		22	8- 3
1910	PIT	N	P		31	14- 2
1911	PIT	N	P		3	0- 0
	BRTR			359	363	188-110

PHILLIPS, ADOLFO EMILIO (LOPEZ)
B.DEC.16,1942 PANAMA CITY,PANAMA

YR	CL	LEA	POS	GP	G	REC
1964	PHI	N	O		13	.231
1965	PHI	N	O		41	.230
1966	PHI	N	O		2	.000
	CHI	N	O		116	.262
1967	CHI	N	O		144	.268
1968	CHI	N	O		143	.241
1969	CHI	N	O		28	.224
	MON	N	O		58	.216
1970	MON	N	O		92	.238
1972	CLE	A	O		12	.000
	BRTR				649	.247

PHILLIPS, ALBERT ABERNATHY "BUZZY"
B.MAY 25,1904 NEWTON,N.C.
D.NOV.6,1964 BALTIMORE,MD.

YR	CL	LEA	POS	GP	G	REC
1930	PHI	N	P		14	0- 0
	BRTR					

PHILLIPS, CLARENCE LEMUEL "RED"
B.NOV.3,1911 PAULS VALLEY,OKLA.

YR	CL	LEA	POS	GP	G	REC
1934	DET	A	P		7	2- 0
1936	DET	A	P		22	2- 4
	BRTR				29	4- 4

PHILLIPS, DAMON ROSWELL
B.JUNE 8,1919 CORSICANA,TEX.

YR	CL	LEA	POS	GP	G	REC
1942	CIN	N	S		28	.202
1944	BOS	N	S-3		140	.250
1946	BOS	N	H		2	.500
	BRTR				170	.250

PHILLIPS, EDWARD DAVID
B.FEB.17,1902 WORCESTER,MASS.
D.JAN.26,1968 BUFFALO,N.Y.

YR	CL	LEA	POS	GP	G	REC
1924	BOS	N	C		3	.000
1929	DET	A	C		68	.235
1931	PIT	N	L		106	.232
1932	NY	A	L		9	.290
1934	WAS	A	C		56	.195
1935	CLE	A	C		70	.273
	BRTR				312	.237

PHILLIPS, HAROLD ROSS "LEFTY"
B.JUNE 16,1919 LOS ANGELES,CAL.
D.JUNE 12,1972 FULLERTON,CAL.
NON-PLAYING MANAGER
CAL(A) 1969-71

PHILLIPS, HORACE B.
B.MAY 14,1853 SALEM,OHIO
NON-PLAYING MANAGER COL(AA)1883
PIT(AA) 1884-86; PIT(N) 1887-89

PHILLIPS, HOWARD EDWARD "EDDIE"
B.JULY 8,1931 ST.LOUIS,MO.

YR	CL	LEA	POS	GP	G	REC
1953	STL	N	H		9	.000
	BBTR					

PHILLIPS, JACK DORN "STRETCH"
B.SEPT.6,1921 CLARENCE,N.Y.

YR	CL	LEA	POS	GP	G	REC
1947	NY	A	1		16	.278
1948	NY	A	1		1	.000
1949	NY	A	1		45	.308
	PIT	N	1-3		18	.232
1950	PIT	N	P-1	1	69	0- 0
			3			.293
1951	PIT	N	1-3		70	.237
1952	PIT	N	1		1	.000
1955	DET	A	1-3		55	.316
1956	DET	A	1-2-O		67	.295
1957	DET	A	H		1	.000
	BRTR			1	343	0- 0
						.283

PHILLIPS, JOHN MELVIN "BUBBA"
B.FEB.24,1930 WEST POINT,MISS.

YR	CL	LEA	POS	GP	G	REC
1955	DET	A	3-O		95	.234
1956	CHI	A	3-O		67	.273
1957	CHI	A	3-O		121	.270
1958	CHI	A	3-O		84	.273
1959	CHI	A	3-O		117	.264
1960	CLE	A	S-3-O		113	.207
1961	CLE	A	3		143	.264
1962	CLE	A	2-3-O		148	.258
1963	DET	A	3-O		128	.246
1964	DET	A	3-O		46	.253
	BRTR				1062	.255

PHILLIPS, JOHN STEPHEN "JACK"
B.MAY 21,1919 ST.LOUIS,MO.
D.JUNE 16,1958

YR	CL	LEA	POS	GP	G	REC
1945	NY	N	P		2	0- 0
	BRTR					

PHILLIPS, MARR
B.JUNE 16,1857 PITTSBURGH,PA.
D.APR.1,1928

YR	CL	LEA	POS	GP	G	REC
1884	IND	AA	S		97	.266
1885	DET	N	S		33	.208
	PIT	AA	S		2	.375
1890	ROC	AA	S		65	.196
	NY	N	2-5		197	.235

PHILLIPS, MICHAEL DWAINE "MIKE"
B.AUG.19,1950 BEAUMONT,TEX.

YR	CL	LEA	POS	GP	G	REC
1973	SF	N	2-S-3		63	.240
1974	SF	N	2-S-3		100	.219
1975	SF	N	2-3		10	.194
	NY	N	2-S		116	.256
1976	NY	N	2-S-3		87	.256
	BLTR				376	.243

PHILLIPS, NORMAN EDWIN "ED"
B.SEP.20,1944 ARDMORE,OKLA.

YR	CL	LEA	POS	GP	G	REC
1970	BOS	A	P		18	0- 2
	BRTR					

PHILLIPS, RICHARD EUGENE "DICK"
B.NOV.24,1931 RACINE,WIS.

YR	CL	LEA	POS	GP	G	REC
1962	SF	N	1		5	.000
1963	WAS	A	1-2-3		124	.237
1964	WAS	A	1-3		109	.231
1966	WAS	A	1		25	.162
	BLTR				263	.229

PHILLIPS, THOMAS GERALD
B.APR.5,1889 PHILLIPSBURG,PA.
D.APR.12,1929

YR	CL	LEA	POS	GP	G	REC
1915	STL	A	P		5	1- 3
1919	CLE	A	P		22	3- 2
1921	WAS	A	P		1	1- 0
1922	WAS	A	P		17	3- 7
	BRTR				45	8-12

PHILLIPS, WILLIAM B.
B.1857 ST.JOHN,N.B.,CANADA
D.OCT.7,1900

YR	CL	LEA	POS	GP	G	REC
1879	CLE	N	1		81	.271
1880	CLE	N	1		84	.255
1881	CLE	N	1		84	.270
1882	CLE	N	C-1		76	.266
1883	CLE	N	1		94	.244
1884	CLE	N	1		110	.272
1885	BRO	AA	1		100	.293
1886	BRO	AA	1		142	.281
1887	BRO	AA	1		132	.322
1888	KC	AA	1		129	.235
	BRTR				1032	.273

PHILLIPS, WILLIAM CORCORAN "WHOA BILL"
B.NOV.9,1868 ALLENPORT,PA.
D.OCT.25,1941

YR	CL	LEA	POS	GP	G	REC
1890	PIT	N	P		15	1- 9
1895	CIN	N	P		17	5- 5
1899	CIN	N	P	28	31	17- 8
1900	CIN	N	P	23	27	9-11
1901	CIN	N	P		33	14-18
1902	CIN	N	P		33	16-17
1903	CIN	N	P		16	7- 6
	TR			165	172	69-74

NON-PLAYING MANAGER
IND(F) 1914; NEW(F) 1915

PHILLIPS, WILLIAM TAYLOR "TAYLOR"
B.JUNE 18,1933 ATLANTA,GA.

YR	CL	LEA	POS	GP	G	REC
1956	MIL	N	P		23	5- 3
1957	MIL	N	P		27	3- 2
1958	CHI	N	P		39	7-10
1959	CHI	N	P		7	0- 2
	PHI	N	P		32	1- 4
1960	PHI	N	P		10	0- 1
1963	CHI	A	P		9	0- 0
	BLTL				147	16-22

PHOEBUS, THOMAS HAROLD "TOM"
B.APR.7,1942 BALTIMORE,MD.

YR	CL	LEA	POS	GP	G	REC
1966	BAL	A	P		3	2- 1
1967	BAL	A	P		33	14- 9
1968	BAL	A	P		36	15-15
1969	BAL	A	P		35	14- 7
1970	BAL	A	P		27	5- 5
1971	SD	N	P		29	3-11
1972	SD	N	P		1	0- 1
	CHI	N	P	37	38	3- 3
	BRTR			201	202	56-52

YR	CL	LEA	POS	GP	G	REC

PHYLE, WILLIAM JOSEPH
B.JUNE 25,1875 DULUTH,MINN.
D.AUG.6,1953

YR	CL	LEA	POS	GP	G	REC
1898	CHI	N	P		3	2- 1
1899	CHI	N	P		10	2- 8
1901	NY	N	P		20	7-10
1906	STL	N	3		21	.178
			TR	33	54	11-19
						.176

PIATT, WILEY HARLAN
B.JULY 13,1874 BLUE CREEK,OHIO
D.SEPT.20,1946

1898	PHI	N	P		38	24-14
1899	PHI	N	P		39	23-15
1900	PHI	N	P		19	9- 9
1901	PHI	N	P		18	7-11
	CHI	A	P		8	3- 5
1902	CHI	A	P		31	12-13
1903	BOS	N	P		25	9-15
			BLTL		178	87-82

PICCIUTO, NICHOLAS THOMAS
B.AUG.27,1921 NEWARK,N.J.

| 1945 | PHI | N | 2-3 | | 36 | .135 |
| | | | BRTR | | | |

PICHE, RONALD JACQUES "RON"
B.MAY 22,1935 VERDUN,QUE.,CANADA

1960	MIL	N	P		37	3- 5
1961	MIL	N	P		12	2- 2
1962	MIL	N	P	14	16	3- 2
1963	MIL	N	P		37	1- 1
1965	CAL	N	P		14	0- 3
1966	STL	N	P		20	1- 3
			BRTR	134	136	10-16

PICINICH, VALENTINE JOHN "VAL"
B.APR.1,1889 NEW YORK,N.Y.
D.DEC.5,1942

1916	PHI	A	C		40	.195
1917	PHI	A	C		2	.333
1918	WAS	A	C		47	.230
1919	WAS	A	C		80	.274
1920	WAS	A	C		48	.203
1921	WAS	A	C		45	.277
1922	WAS	A	C		76	.229
1923	BOS	A	C		87	.276
1924	BOS	A	C		69	.273
1925	BOS	A	C-1		90	.255
1926	CIN	N	C		89	.263
1927	CIN	N	C		65	.254
1928	CIN	N	C		96	.302
1929	BRO	N	C		93	.260
1930	BRO	N	C		23	.217
1931	BRO	N	C		24	.267
1932	BRO	N	C		41	.257
1933	BRO	N	C		6	.167
	PIT	N	C		16	.250
			BRTR		1037	.258

PICK, CHARLES THOMAS
B.APR.10,1888 BROOKNEAL,VA.
D.JUNE 26,1954

1914	WAS	A	O		10	.347
1915	WAS	A	H		3	.000
1916	PHI	A	3		121	.241
1918	CHI	N	2-3		29	.326
1919	CHI	N	2-3		75	.231
	BOS	N	1-2-3-0		34	.273
1920	BOS	N	2		95	.274
			BLTR		367	.260

PICK, EDGAR EVERETT
B.MAY 7,1899 PROVIDENCE,R.I.
D.MAY 13,1967 SANTA MONICA,CAL.

1923	CIN	N	O		9	.375
1924	CIN	N	O		3	.000
1927	CHI	N	3		54	.171
			BBTR		66	.178

PICKERING, OLIVER DAN
B.APR.9,1870 OLNEY,ILL.
D.JAN.20,1952

1896	LOU	N	O		45	.303
1897	LOU	N	O		62	.258
	CLE	N	2-O		47	.346
1901	CLE	A	O		138	.308
1902	CLE	A	1-O		60	.259
1903	PHI	A	O		137	.281
1904	PHI	A	O		122	.224
1907	STL	A	O		151	.276
1908	WAS	A	O		113	.225
			BLTR		875	.272

PICKERING, URBANE HENRY "PICK"
B.JUNE 3,1899 HOXIE,KAN.
D.MAY 13,1970 MODESTO,CAL.

1931	BOS	A	2-3		103	.252
1932	BOS	A	3		132	.260
			BRTR		235	.257

PICKETT, CHARLES A.
B.COLUMBUS,OHIO

| 1910 | STL | N | P | | 2 | 0- 0 |

PICKETT, DAVID T.
B.MAY 26,1874 BROOKLINE,MASS.

| 1898 | BOS | N | O | | 14 | .272 |

PICKETT, JOHN THOMAS
B.FEB.20,1866 CHICAGO,ILL.
D.JULY 4,1922

1889	KC	AA	O		41	.223
1890	PHI	P	2		100	.281
1892	BAL	N	2		36	.208
			BRTR		177	.250

PICKREL, CLARENCE DOUGLAS
B.MAR.28,1911 GRENTA,VA.

1933	PHI	N	P		9	1- 0
1934	BOS	N	P		10	0- 0
			BRTR		19	1- 0

PICKUP, CLARENCE WILLIAM
B.OCT.29,1897 PHILADELPHIA,PA.
D.AUG.2,1974 PHILADELPHIA,PA.

| 1918 | PHI | N | O | | 1 | 1.000 |

PICONE, MARIO PETER "BABE"
B.JULY 5,1926 BROOKLYN,N.Y.

1947	NY	N	P		2	0- 0
1952	NY	N	P		2	0- 1
1954	NY	N	P		5	0- 0
	CIN	N	P		4	0- 1
			BRTR		13	0- 2

PICUS, JOHN QUINN
(PLAYED UNDER NAME OF
JOHN PICUS QUINN)

PIECHOTA, ALOYSIUS EDWARD "PIE"
B.JAN.19,1915 CHICAGO,ILL.

1940	BOS	N	P		21	2- 5
1941	BOS	N	P		1	0- 0
			BRTR		22	2- 5

PIEH, EDWIN JOHN "CY"
B.SEPT.29,1886 WAUNAKEE,WIS.
D.SEPT.12,1945

1913	NY	A	P		4	1- 0
1914	NY	A	P		18	4- 4
1915	NY	A	P		21	4- 5
			BRTR		43	9- 9

PIERCE, LAVERN JACK
"JACK"
B.JUNE 2,1948 LAUREL,MISS.

1973	ATL	N	1		11	.050
1974	ATL	N	1		6	.111
1975	DET	A	1		53	.235
			BLTR		70	.211

PIERCE, MAURICE
B.WASHINGTON,D.C.

| 1884 | WAS | U | 3 | | 2 | .143 |

PIERCE, RAYMOND LESTER
B.JUNE 6,1900 EMPORIA,KAN.
D.MAY 4,1963 DENVER,COLO.

1924	CHI	N	P		6	0- 0
1925	PHI	N	P		23	5- 4
1926	PHI	N	P	37	39	2- 7
			BLTL	66	68	7-11

PIERCE, TONY MICHAEL
B.JAN.29,1946 BRUNSWICK,GA.

1967	KC	A	P		49	3- 4
1968	OAK	A	P		17	1- 2
			BRTL		66	4- 6

PIERCE, WALTER WILLIAM "BILLY"
B.APR.2,1927 DETROIT,MICH.

1945	DET	A	P		5	0- 0
1948	DET	A	P		22	3- 0
1949	CHI	A	P	32	39	7-15
1950	CHI	A	P	33	40	12-16
1951	CHI	A	P	37	39	15-14
1952	CHI	A	P	33	35	15-12
1953	CHI	A	P-1	40	42	18-12
						.126
1954	CHI	A	P	36	38	9-10
1955	CHI	A	P	33	34	15-10
1956	CHI	A	P	35	39	20- 9
1957	CHI	A	P	37	41	20-12
1958	CHI	A	P		35	17-11
1959	CHI	A	P		34	14-15
1960	CHI	A	P		32	14- 7
1961	CHI	A	P		39	10- 9
1962	SF	N	P		30	16- 6
1963	SF	N	P		38	3-11
1964	SF	N	P		34	3- 0
			BLTL	585	616	211-169
						.184

PIERCY, ANDREW J.
B.AUG.1856 SAN JOSE,CAL.
D.DEC.27,1932

| 1881 | CHI | N | 2-3 | | 2 | .250 |
| | | | TR | | | |

PIERCY, WILLIAM BENTON
"WILD BILL"
B.MAY 2,1896 EL MONTE,CAL.
D.AUG.28,1951

1917	NY	A	P		1	0- 1
1921	NY	A	P		14	5- 4
1922	BOS	A	P		29	3- 9
1923	BOS	A	P		30	8-17
1924	BOS	A	P		23	5- 7
1926	CHI	N	P		19	6- 5
			BRTR		116	27-43

PIERETTI, MARINO PAUL "CHICK"
B.SEPT.23,1921 MARLIA,ITALY

1945	WAS	A	P		44	14-13
1946	WAS	A	P		30	2- 2
1947	WAS	A	P		23	2- 4
1948	WAS	A	P	8	13	0- 2
	CHI	A	P	21	32	8-10
1949		A	P	39	48	4- 6
1950	CLE	A	P	29	30	0- 1
			BRTR	194	220	30-38

PIEROTTI, ALBERT FELIX
B.OCT.24,1895 BOSTON,MASS.
D.FEB.12,1964 REVERE,MASS.

1920	BOS	N	P		6	1- 1
1921	BOS	N	P		2	0- 1
			BRTR		8	1- 2

PIERRE, RICHARD J.
B.GRAND HAVEN,MICH.

| 1883 | PHI | N | S | | 5 | .158 |

PIERRO, WILLIAM LEONARD "BILL"
B.APR.15,1926 BROOKLYN,N.Y.

| 1950 | PIT | N | P | | 13 | 0- 2 |
| | | | BRTR | | | |

PIERSALL, JAMES ANTHONY "JIM"
B.NOV.14,1929 WATERBURY,CONN.

1950	BOS	A	O		6	.286
1952	BOS	A	S-3-O		56	.267
1953	BOS	A	O		151	.272
1954	BOS	A	O		133	.285
1955	BOS	A	O		149	.283
1956	BOS	A	O		155	.293
1957	BOS	A	O		151	.261
1958	BOS	A	O		130	.237
1959	CLE	A	3-O		100	.246
1960	CLE	A	O		138	.282
1961	CLE	A	O		121	.322
1962	WAS	A	O		135	.244
1963	WAS	A	O		29	.245
	NY	N	O		40	.194
	LA	A	O		20	.308
1964	LA	A	O		87	.314
1965	CAL	A	O		53	.268
1966	CAL	A	O		75	.211
1967	CAL	A	O		5	.000
			BRTR		1734	.272

PIERSON, DAVID P.
(PLAYED UNDER NAME OF
DAVID. P. PEARSON)

YR	CL LEA POS	GP	G	REC

PIERSON, EDMUND DANA
B.1858 NEWARK,N.J.
D.JULY 20,1922 NEWARK,N.Y.

YR	CL LEA POS	GP	G	REC
1885 MET AA 2		3	.091
TR			

PIERSON, WILLIAM MORRIS
B.JUNE 13,1899 ATLANTIC CITY,
N.J.
D.FEB.20,1959

1918 PHI A P		8	0- 1
1919 PHI A P		2	0- 0
1924 PHI A P		1	0- 0
BLTL		11	0- 1

PIET, ANTHONY FRANCIS
(REAL NAME
ANTHONY FRANCIS PIETRUSZKA)
B.DEC.6,1906 BERWICK,PA.

1931 PIT N 2		44	.299
1932 PIT N 2		154	.282
1933 PIT N 2		107	.323
1934 CIN N 2-3		106	.259
1935 CIN N 0		6	.200
CHI A 2-3		77	.298
1936 CHI A 2-3		109	.273
1937 CHI A 2-3		100	.235
1938 DET A 3		41	.213
BRTR		744	.277

PIETRUSZKA, ANTHONY FRANCIS
(PLAYED UNDER NAME OF
ANTHONY FRANCIS PIET)

PIEZ, CHARLES WILLIAM "SANDY"
B.OCT.13,1888 NEW YORK,N.Y.
D.DEC.29,1930

| 1914 NY N 0 | | 35 | .375 |
| BRTR | | | |

PIGNATANU, JÓSÉPH BENJAMIN
"JOE"
B.AUG.4,1929 BROOKLYN,N.Y.

1957 BRO N C		8	.214
1958 LA N C		63	.218
1959 LA N C		52	.237
1960 LA N C		58	.233
1961 KC A C-3		92	.243
1962 SF N C		7	.200
NY N C		27	.232
BRTR		307	.234

PIKE, J.
B.NEW YORK,N.Y.

| 1877 HAR N 0 | | 1 | .250 |

PIKE, JESSE WILLARD
B.JULY 31,1916 DUSTIN,OKLA.

| 1946 NY N 0 | | 16 | .171 |
| BLTR | | | |

PIKE, LIPMAN E.
B.MAY 25,1845 NEW YORK,N.Y.
D.OCT.10,1893

1871 TRO NA M-1-2-0	28	.351
1872 BAL NA 2-3-0	54	.296
1873 BAL NA 2-0	56	-
1874 HAR NA M-2-S-0	52	-
1875 STL NA 2-0	67	.342
1876 STL N 0	63	.314
1877 CIN N M-2-S-0	58	.297
1878 CIN N 0	28	.326
PRO N 2	5	.227
1881 WOR N 0	5	.091
1887 MET AA 0	1	.000
BLTL	417	-

PIKTUZIS, GEORGE RICHARD
B.JAN.3,1932 CHICAGO,ILL.

| 1956 CHI N P | | 2 | 0- 0 |
| BRTL | | | |

PILARCIK, ALFRED JAMES "AL"
B.JULY 3,1930 WHITING,IND.

1956 KC A 0		69	.251
1957 BAL A 0		142	.278
1958 BAL A 0		141	.243
1959 BAL A 0		130	.282
1960 BAL A 0		104	.247
1961 KC A 0		35	.200
CHI A 0		47	.177
BLTL		668	.256

PILLETTE, DUANE XAVIER "DEE"
B.JULY 24,1922 DETROIT,MICH.

1949 NY A P		12	2- 4
1950 NY A P		4	0- 0
STL A P	24	27	3- 5
1951 STL A P	35	41	6-14
1952 STL A P	30	35	10-13
1953 STL A P		31	7-13
1954 BAL A P		25	10-14
1955 BAL A P		7	0- 3
1956 PHI N P		20	0- 0
BRTR	188	202	38-66

PILLETTE, HERMAN POLYCARP
"OLD FOLKS"
B.DEC.26,1895 ST.PAUL,ORE.
D.APR.30,1960

1917 CIN N P		1	0- 0
1922 DET A P		40	19-12
1923 DET A P		47	14-19
1924 DET A P		19	1- 1
BRTR		107	34-32

PILLION, CECIL RANDOLPH "SQUIZ"
B.APR.13,1898 HARTFORD,CONN.
D.SEPT.30,1962

| 1915 PHI A P | | 2 | 0- 0 |
| TL | | | |

PILNEY, ANDREW JAMES
B.JAN.19,1913 FRONTENAC,KAN.

| 1936 BOS N H | | 3 | .000 |

PINA, HORACIO (GARCIA)
B.MAR.12,1945 COAHUILA,MEXICO

1968 CLE A P		12	1- 1
1969 CLE A P		31	4- 2
1970 WAS A P		61	5- 3
1971 WAS A P		56	1- 1
1972 TEX A P		60	2- 7
1973 OAK A P		47	6- 3
1974 CHI N P		34	3- 4
CAL A P		11	1- 2
BRTR		312	23-23

PINELLI, RALPH ARTHUR "BABE"
(REAL NAME
RINALDO ANGELO PAOLINELLI)
B.OCT.18,1895 SAN FRANCISCO,CAL

1918 CHI A 3		24	.231
1920 DET A S-3		102	.229
1922 CIN N 3		156	.305
1923 CIN N 3		117	.277
1924 CIN N 3		144	.306
1925 CIN N S-3		130	.283
1926 CIN N 2-S-3		71	.222
1927 CIN N 2-S-3		30	.197
BRTR		774	.276

PINIELLA, LOUIS VICTOR "LOU"
B.AUG.28,1943 TAMPA,FLA.

1964 BAL A H		4	.000
1968 CLE A 0		6	.000
1969 KC A 0		135	.282
1970 KC A 1-0		144	.301
1971 KC A 0		126	.279
1972 KC A 0		151	.312
1973 KC A 0		144	.250
1974 NY A 1-0		140	.305
1975 NY A 0-D		74	.196
1976 NY A 0-D		100	.281
BRTR		1024	.283

PINKHAM, EDWARD
B.1849 BROOKLYN,N.Y.

1871 CHI NA P-3-	1	24	1- 0
0			-
TL			

PINKNEY, GEORGE BURTON
B.JAN.11,1862 ORANGE PRAIRIE,
ILL.
D.NOV.10,1926

1884 CLE N 2-S		35	.309
1885 BRO AA 2-3		111	.288
1886 BRO AA 3		142	.260
1887 BRO AA 3		138	.326
1888 BRO AA 3		143	.260
1889 BRO AA 3		138	.253
1890 BRO N 3		126	.309
1891 BRO N 3		135	.278
1892 STL N 3		78	.172
1893 LOU N 3		118	.226
BRTR		1164	.272

PINNANCE, EDWARD D. "PEANUTS"
B.OCT.22,1879 WALPOLE ISLAND,
ONT.,CANADA
D.OEC.12,1944

| 1903 PHI A P | | 2 | 0- 1 |
| BLTR | | | |

PINSON, VADA EDWARD
B.AUG.11,1936 MEMPHIS,TENN.

1958 CIN N 0		27	.271
1959 CIN N 0		154	.316
1960 CIN N 0		154	.287
1961 CIN N 0		154	.343
1962 CIN N 0		155	.292
1963 CIN N 0		162	.313
1964 CIN N 0		156	.266
1965 CIN N 0		159	.305
1966 CIN N 0		156	.288
1967 CIN N 0		158	.288
1968 CIN N 0		130	.271
1969 STL N 0		132	.255
1970 CLE A 1-0		148	.286
1971 CLE A 1-0		146	.263
1972 CAL A 1-0		136	.275
1973 CAL A 0		124	.260
1974 KC A 1-0		115	.276
1975 KC A 1-0		103	.223
BLTL		2469	.286

PINTO, WILLIAM LERTON
B.APR.8,1898 CHILLICOTHE,OHIO

1922 PHI N P		9	0- 1
1924 PHI N P		3	0- 0
BLTL		12	0- 1

PIPGRAS, EDWARD JOHN
B.JUNE 15,1905 SCHLESWIG,IOWA
D.APR.13,1964 CURRIE,MINN.

| 1932 BRO N P | | 5 | 0- 1 |
| BRTR | | | |

PIPGRAS, GEORGE WILLIAM
B.DEC.20,1899 DENISON,IOWA

1923 NY A P		8	1- 3
1924 NY A P		9	0- 1
1927 NY A P		29	10- 3
1928 NY A P		46	24-13
1929 NY A P		39	18-12
1930 NY A P		44	15-15
1931 NY A P		36	7- 6
1932 NY A P		32	16- 9
1933 NY A P		4	2- 2
BOS A P		22	9- 8
1934 BOS A P		2	0- 0
1935 BOS A P		5	0- 1
BRTR		276	102-73

PIPP, WALTER CLEMENT "WALLY"
B.FEB.17,1893 CHICAGO,ILL.
D.JAN.11,1965 GRAND RAPIDS,MICH

1913 DET A 1		11	.178
1915 NY A 1		136	.246
1916 NY A 1		151	.262
1917 NY A 1		155	.244
1918 NY A 1		91	.304
1919 NY A 1		138	.275
1920 NY A 1		153	.280
1921 NY A 1		153	.296
1922 NY A 1		152	.329
1923 NY A 1		144	.304
1924 NY A 1		153	.295
1925 NY A 1		62	.230
1926 CIN N 1		155	.291
1927 CIN N 1		122	.260
1928 CIN N 1		95	.283
BLTL		1871	.281

PIPPEN, HENRY HAROLD "COTTON"
B.APR.2,1910 CISCO,TEX.

1936 STL N P		6	0- 2
1939 PHI A P		25	4-11
DET A P		3	0- 1
1940 DET A P		4	1- 2
BRTR		38	5-16

PISONI, JAMES PETE "JIM"
B.AUG.14,1929 ST.LOUIS,MO.

1953 STL A 0		3	.083
1956 KC A 0		10	.267
1957 KC A 0		44	.237
1959 MIL N 0		9	.167
NY A 0		17	.176
1960 NY A 0		20	.111
BRTR		103	.212

YR	CL	LEA	POS	GP	G	REC

PITKO, ALEXANDER "SPUNK"
B.NOV.22,1917 BURLINGTON,N.J.
1938	PHI	N	O		7	.316
1939	WAS	A	O		4	.125
			BRTR		11	.259

PITLER, JACOB ALBERT "JAKE"
B.APR.22,1894 NEW YORK,N.Y.
D.FEB.3,1968 BINGHAMTON,N.Y.
1917	PIT	N	2		109	.233
1918	PIT	N	2		3	.000
			BRTR		112	.232

PITLOCK, LEE PATRICK
B.NOV.6,1947 HILLSIDE,ILL.
1970	SF	N	P		18	5- 5
1974	CHI	A	P		40	3- 3
1975	CHI	A	P		1	0- 0
			BLTL		59	8- 8

PITTINGER, CHARLES RENO "TOGIE"
B.1871 GREENCASTLE,PA.
D.JAN.14,1909
1900	BOS	N	P		18	2- 9
1901	BOS	N	P		32	15-16
1902	BOS	N	P		44	27-15
1903	BOS	N	P		44	18-22
1904	BOS	N	P		38	14-21
1905	PHI	N	P		46	23-16
1906	PHI	N	P		20	8-10
1907	PHI	N	P		16	9- 5
			TR		258	116-114

PITTINGER, CLARKE ALONZO "PINKIE"
B.FEB.24,1899 HUDSON,MICH.
1921	BOS	A	O		40	.198
1922	BOS	A	S-3		66	.259
1923	BOS	A	2		60	.215
1925	CHI	N	S-3		59	.312
1927	CIN	N	2-S-3		31	.274
1928	CIN	N	2-S-3		40	.237
1929	CIN	N	2-S-3		77	.295
			BRTR		373	.252

PITTS, GAYLEN RICHARD
B.JUNE 6,1946 WICHITA,KAN.
1974	OAK	A	1-2-3		18	.244
1975	OAK	A	2-S-3		10	.333
			BRTR		28	.250

PITULA, STANLEY "STAN"
B.MAR.23,1931 HACKENSACK,N.J.
D.AUG.15,1965 HACKENSACK,N.J.
| 1957 | CLE | A | P | 23 | 24 | 2- 2 |
| | | | BRTR | | | |

PITZ, HERMAN
B.JULY 18,1865 BROOKLYN,N.Y.
D.SEPT.3,1924
1890	BRO	AA	C		61	.129
	SYR	AA	C-S-O		29	.216
					90	.155

PIZARRO, JUAN (CORDOVA)
B.FEB.7,1937 SANTURCE,P.R.
1957	MIL	N	P	24	25	5- 6
1958	MIL	N	P		16	6- 4
1959	MIL	N	P		29	6- 2
1960	MIL	N	P	21	23	6- 7
1961	CHI	A	P	39	40	14- 7
1962	CHI	A	P	36	37	12-14
1963	CHI	A	P		32	16- 8
1964	CHI	A	P		33	19- 9
1965	CHI	A	P	18	19	6- 3
1966	CHI	A	P		34	8- 6
1967	PIT	N	P		50	8-10
1968	PIT	N	P	12	13	1- 1
	BOS	A	P	19	20	6- 8
1969	BOS	A	P		6	0- 1
	CLE	A	P		48	3- 3
	OAK	A	P		3	1- 1
1970	CHI	N	P		12	0- 0
1971	CHI	N	P		16	7- 6
1972	CHI	N	P		16	4- 5
1973	CHI	N	P		2	0- 1
	HOU	N	P		15	2- 2
1974	PIT	N	P		7	1- 1
			BLTL	488	496	131-105

PLANETA, EMIL JOSEPH
B.JAN.31,1909 HIGGANUM,CONN.
D.FEB.2,1963 ROCKY HILLS,CONN.
| 1931 | NY | N | P | | 2 | 0- 0 |
| | | | BRTR | | | |

PLANK, EDWARD STEWART "EDDIE"
B.AUG.31,1875 GETTYSBURG,PA.
D.FEB.24,1926 GETTYSBURG,PA.
1901	PHI	A	P		33	16-14
1902	PHI	A	P		36	20-15
1903	PHI	A	P	41	43	23-16
1904	PHI	A	P	44	45	26-15
1905	PHI	A	P		41	26-12
1906	PHI	A	P		26	19- 6
1907	PHI	A	P		43	24-16
1908	PHI	A	P		36	14-16
1909	PHI	A	P	34	35	19-10
1910	PHI	A	P		38	16-10
1911	PHI	A	P		40	22- 8
1912	PHI	A	P		37	26- 6
1913	PHI	A	P		41	17-10
1914	PHI	A	P		34	16- 6
1915	STL	F	P		42	21-11
1916	STL	A	P		37	16-15
1917	STL	A	P		20	5- 6
			BLTL	623	627	326-192

PLARSKI, DONALD JOSEPH "DON"
B.NOV.9,1929 CHICAGO,ILL.
| 1955 | KC | A | O | | 8 | .091 |
| | | | BRTR | | | |

PLASKETT, ELMO ALEXANDER
B.JUNE 27,1938 FREDERIKSTED,V.I.
1962	PIT	N	C		7	.286
1963	PIT	N	C-3		10	.143
			BRTR		17	.200

PLATT, MIZELL GEORGE "WHITEY"
B.AUG.21,1920 W.PALM BEACH,FLA.
D.JULY 27,1970 W.PALM BEACH,FLA
1942	CHI	N	O		4	.063
1943	CHI	N	O		20	.171
1946	CHI	N	O		84	.251
1948	STL	A	O		123	.271
1949	STL	A	1-O		102	.258
			BRTR		333	.255

PLATTE, ALFRED FREDERICK JOSEPH
B.APR.13,1890 GRAND RAPIDS,MICH
D.AUG.29,1976 GRAND RAPIDS,MICH
| 1913 | DET | A | O | | 9 | .111 |
| | | | BLTL | | | |

PLEIS, WILLIAM "BILL"
B.AUG.5,1938 ST.LOUIS,MO.
1961	MIN	A	P		37	4- 2
1962	MIN	A	P		21	2- 5
1963	MIN	A	P		36	6- 2
1964	MIN	A	P		47	4- 1
1965	MIN	A	P		41	4- 4
1966	MIN	A	P		8	1- 2
			BLTL		190	21-16

PLESS, RANCE
B.DEC.6,1925 GREENEVILLE,TENN.
| 1956 | KC | A | 1-3 | | 48 | .271 |
| | | | BRTR | | | |

PLEWS, HERBERT EUGENE "HERB"
B.JUNE 14,1928 HELENA,MONT.
1956	WAS	A	2-S-3		91	.270
1957	WAS	A	2-S-3		110	.271
1958	WAS	A	2-3		111	.258
1959	WAS	A	2		27	.225
	BOS	A	H		13	.083
			BLTR		346	.262

PLITT, NORMAN WILLIAM
B.FEB.21,1893 YORK,PA.
D.FEB.1,1954
1918	BRO	N	P		1	0- 0
1927	BRO	N	P		19	2- 6
	NY	N	P		3	1- 0
			BRTR		23	3- 6

PLOCK, WALTER S.
B.JULY 2,1869 PHILADELPHIA,PA.
D.APR.28,1900
| 1891 | PHI | N | O | | 2 | .400 |

PLODINEC, TIMOTHY ALFRED "TIM"
B.JAN.27,1947 ALIQUIPPA,PA.
| 1972 | STL | N | P | | 1 | 0- 0 |
| | | | BRTR | | | |

PLUMMER, WILLIAM FRANCIS "BILL"
B.MAR.21,1947 ANDERSON,CAL.
1968	CHI	N	C		2	.000
1970	CIN	N	C		4	.125
1971	CIN	N	C-3		10	.000
1972	CIN	N	C-1-3		38	.186
1973	CIN	N	C-3		50	.151
1974	CIN	N	C-3		50	.225
1975	CIN	N	C		65	.182
1976	CIN	N	C		56	.248
			BRTR		275	.194

POAT, RAYMOND WILLIS "RAY"
B.DEC.19,1917 CHICAGO,ILL.
1942	CLE	A	P		4	1- 3
1943	CLE	A	P		17	2- 5
1944	CLE	A	P		36	4- 8
1947	NY	N	P		7	4- 3
1948	NY	N	P		39	11-10
1949	NY	N	P		2	0- 0
	PIT	N	P		11	0- 1
			BRTR		116	22-30

POCOROBA, BIFF
B.JULY 25,1953 BURBANK,CAL.
1975	ATL	N	C		67	.255
1976	ATL	N	C		54	.241
			BBTR		121	.249
			BR 1975 (PART)			

PODBIELAN, CLARENCE ANTHONY "BUD"
B.MAR.6,1924 CURLEW,WASH.
1949	BRO	N	P		7	0- 1
1950	BRO	N	P		20	5- 4
1951	BRO	N	P		27	2- 2
1952	BRO	N	P	3	4	0- 0
	CIN	N	P		24	4- 5
1953	CIN	N	P		36	6-16
1954	CIN	N	P		27	7-10
1955	CIN	N	P		17	1- 2
1957	CIN	N	P		5	0- 1
1959	CLE	A	P		6	0- 1
			BRTR	172	173	25-42

PODGAJNY, JOHN SIGMUND "SPECS"
B.JUNE 10,1920 CHESTER,PA.
D.MAR.2,1971 CHESTER,PA.
1940	PHI	N	P		4	1- 3
1941	PHI	N	P	34	35	9-12
1942	PHI	N	P	43	44	6-14
1943	PHI	N	P		13	4- 4
	PIT	N	P	15	21	0- 4
1946	CLE	A	P		6	0- 0
			BRTR	115	123	20-37

PODRES, JOHN JOSEPH "JOHNNY"
B.SEP.30,1932 WITHERBEE,N.Y.
1953	BRO	N	P	33	34	9- 4
1954	BRO	N	P	29	38	11- 7
1955	BRO	N	P	27	32	9-10
1957	BRO	N	P	31	35	12- 9
1958	LA	N	P	39	42	13-15
1959	LA	N	P		34	14- 9
1960	LA	N	P		34	14-12
1961	LA	N	P		32	18- 5
1962	LA	N	P		40	15-13
1963	LA	N	P		37	14-12
1964	LA	N	P		2	0- 2
1965	LA	N	P		27	7- 6
1966	LA	N	P		1	0- 0
	DET	A	P		36	4- 5
1967	DET	A	P		21	3- 1
1969	SD	N	P		17	5- 6
			BLTL	440	462	148-116

POEPPING, MICHAEL HAROLD "MIKE"
B.AUG.7,1950 LITTLE FALLS,MINN.
| 1975 | MIN | A | O | | 14 | .135 |
| | | | BRTR | | | |

POETZ, JOSEPH FRANK
B.JUNE 22,1900 ST.LOUIS,MO.
D.FEB.7,1942
| 1926 | NY | N | P | | 2 | 0- 1 |
| | | | BRTR | | | |

POFAHL, JAMES WILLARD
B.JUNE 18,1917 FAIRBAULT,MINN.
1940	WAS	A	2-S		119	.234
1941	WAS	A	S		22	.187
1942	WAS	A	2-S-3		84	.208
			BRTR		225	.220

YR	CL	LEA	POS	GP	G	REC

POFFENBERGER, CLETUS ELWOOD "BOOTS"
B.JULY 1,1915 WILLIAMSPORT,MD.

YR	CL	LEA	POS	GP	G	REC
1937	DET	A	P		29	10- 5
1938	DET	A	P		25	6- 7
1939	BRO	N	P		3	0- 0
		BRTR			57	16-12

POHOLSKY, THOMAS GEORGE "TOM"
B.AUG.26,1929 DETROIT,MICH.

1950	STL	N	P		5	0- 0
1951	STL	N	P		38	7-13
1954	STL	N	P		25	5- 7
1955	STL	N	P-O		30	9-11
						.182
1956	STL	N	P		33	9-14
1957	CHI	N	P		28	1- 7
		BRTR			159	31-52
						.171

POINDEXTER, CHESTER JENNINGS "JINX"
B.SEPT.30,1910 PAULS VALLEY, OKLA.

1936	BOS	A	P		3	0- 2
1939	PHI	N	P		11	0- 0
		BLTL			14	0- 2

POINTER, AARON ELTON
B.APR.19,1942 LITTLE ROCK,ARK.

1963	HOU	N	O		2	.200
1966	HOU	N	O		11	.346
1967	HOU	N	O		27	.157
		BRTR			40	.208

POLACHANIN, NICHOLAS JOSEPH
(PLAYED UNDER NAME OF NICHOLAS JOSEPH POLLY)

POLAND, HUGH REID
B.JAN.19,1913 TOMPKINSVILLE,KY.

1943	NY	N	C		4	.083
	BOS	N	C		44	.191
1944	BOS	N	C		8	.130
1946	BOS	N	C		4	.167
1947	PHI	N	C		4	.000
	CIN	N	C		16	.333
1948	CIN	N	H		3	.333
		BLTR			83	.185

POLCHOW, LOUIS WILLIAM
B.MAR.14,1881 MANKATO,MINN.
D.AUG.15,1912 GOOD THUNDER,MINN

1902	CLE	A	P		1	0- 1

POLE, RICHARD HENRY "DICK"
B.OCT.13,1950 TROUT CREEK,MICH.

1973	BOS	A	P		12	3- 2
1974	BOS	A	P		15	1- 1
1975	BOS	A	P		18	4- 6
1976	BOS	A	P		31	6- 5
		BRTR			76	14-14

POLHEMUS, MARK S.
B.OCT.4,1864 BROOKLYN,N.Y.

1887	IND	N	O		19	.259

POLIVKA, KENNETH LYLE "SOUP"
B.JAN.21,1921 CHICAGO,ILL.

1947	CIN	N	P		2	0- 0
		BLTL				

POLLET, HOWARD JOSEPH "HOWIE"
B.JUNE 26,1921 NEW ORLEANS,LA.
D.AUG.8,1974 HOUSTON,TEX.

1941	STL	N	P		9	5- 2
1942	STL	N	P		27	7- 5
1943	STL	N	P		16	8- 4
1946	STL	N	P		40	21-10
1947	STL	N	P		37	9-11
1948	STL	N	P	36	38	13- 8
1949	STL	N	P		39	20- 9
1950	STL	N	P	37	38	14-13
1951	STL	N	P		6	0- 3
	PIT	N	P		21	6-10
1952	PIT	N	P		31	7-16
1953	PIT	N	P		5	1- 1
	CHI	N	P		25	5- 6
1954	CHI	N	P		20	8-10
1955	CHI	N	P		24	.4- 3
1956	CHI	A	P	11	12	3- 1
	PIT	N	P		19	0- 4
		BLTL		403	407	131-116

POLLI, LOUIS AMERICO
B.JULY 9,1903 BARRE,VT.

1932	STL	A	P		5	0- 0
1944	NY	N	P		19	0- 2
		BRTR			24	0- 2

POLLY, NICHOLAS JOSEPH
(REAL NAME
NICHOLAS JOSEPH POLACHANIN)
B.APR.18,1917 CHICAGO,ILL.

1937	BRO	N	3		10	.222
1945	BOS	A	3		4	.143
		BRTR			14	.200

POMORSKI, JOHN LEON
B.DEC.30,1907 BROOKLYN,N.Y.

1934	CHI	A	P		3	0- 0
		BRTR				

POND, ERASMUS ARLINGTON "ARLIE"
B.JAN.19,1872 RUTLAND,VT.
D.SEPT.19,1930

1895	BAL	N	P		7	0- 1
1896	BAL	N	P		24	15- 8
1897	BAL	N	P	27	31	18- 9
1898	BAL	N	P		2	1- 1
		TR		60	64	34-19

POND, RALPH BENJAMIN
B.MAY 4,1888 EAU CLAIRE,WIS.
D.SEPT.8,1947

1910	BOS	A	O		1	.333

PONDER, CHARLES ELMER
B.JUNE 26,1893 MANGUM,OKLA.
D.APR.20,1974 ALBUQUERQUE,N.MEX

1917	PIT	N	P		3	1- 1
1919	PIT	N	P		9	0- 5
1920	PIT	N	P		33	11-15
1921	PIT	N	P		8	2- 0
	CHI	N	P		16	3- 6
		BRTR			69	17-27

POOL, HARLIN WELTY "SAMSON"
B.MAR.13,1908 LAKEPORT,CAL.
D.FEB.15,1963 RODEO,CAL.

1934	CIN	N	O		99	.327
1935	CIN	N	O		28	.176
		BLTR			127	.303

POOLE, EDWARD I.
B.SEPT.7,1877 WHEELING,W.VA.
D.MAR.23,1920

1900	PIT	N	P		2	1- 0
1901	PIT	N	P		23	5- 4
1902	PIT	N	P		1	0- 0
	CIN	N	P		16	12- 4
1903	CIN	N	P		25	8-13
1904	BRO	N	P		24	7-14
		TR			91	33-35

POOLE, JAMES RALPH "EASY"
B.MAY 12,1895 STONY POINT,N.C.
D.JAN.2,1975 HICKORY,N.C.

1925	PHI	A	1		133	.298
1926	PHI	A	1		112	.294
1927	PHI	A	1		38	.222
		BLTR			283	.288

POOLE, RAYMOND HERMAN
B.JAN.16,1920 SALISBURY,N.C.

1941	PHI	A	H		2	.000
1947	PHI	A	H		13	.231
		BLTR			15	.200

POORMAN, THOMAS IVERSON
B.OCT.14,1857 LOCK HAVEN,PA.
D.FEB.18,1905

1880	BUF	N	P-O	11	19	1- 8
						.159
	CHI	N	P-O	2	7	1- 0
						.200
1884	TOL	AA	P-O	1	93	0- 1
						.224
1885	BOS	N	O		55	.241
1886	BOS	N	O		88	.261
1887	ATH	AA	O		135	.316
1888	ATH	AA	O		85	.227
		TR		14	482	2- 9
						.260

POPE, DAVID "DAVE"
B.JUNE 17,1925 TALLADEGA,ALA.

1952	CLE	A	O		12	.294
1954	CLE	A	O		60	.294
1955	CLE	A	O		35	.298
	BAL	A	O		86	.248
1956	BAL	A	O		12	.158
1956	CLE	A	O		25	.243
		BLTR			230	.265

POPOVICH, PAUL EDWARD
B.AUG.18,1940 FLEMINGTON,W.VA.

1964	CHI	N	H		1	1.000
1966	CHI	N	2		2	.000
1967	CHI	N	2-S-3		49	.214
1968	LA	N	2-S-3		134	.232
1969	LA	N	2-S		28	.200
	CHI	N	2-S-3-O		60	.312
1970	CHI	N	2-S-3		78	.253
1971	CHI	N	2-S-3		89	.217
1972	CHI	N	2-S-3		58	.194
1973	CHI	N	2-S-3		99	.236
1974	PIT	N	2-S		59	.217
1975	PIT	N	2-S		25	.200
		BRTR			682	.233
		BR 1964-67				

POPOWSKI, EDWARD JOSEPH "EDDIE"
B.AUG.20,1913 SAYERVILLE,N.J.
NON-PLAYING MANAGER BOS(A)
1969 (INTERIM), 1973 (INTERIM)

POPP, WILLIAM PETER
B.JUNE 7,1877 ST.LOUIS,MO.
D.SEPT.5,1909 ST.LOUIS,MO.

1902	STL	N	P		9	2- 6
		TR				

POPPLEIN, GEORGE J.
B.BALTIMORE,MD.

1873	MAR	NA	O		1	.000

POQUETTE, THOMAS ARTHUR "TOM"
B.OCT.30,1951 EAU CLAIRE,WIS.

1973	KC	A	O		21	.214
1976	KC	A	O		104	.302
		BLTR			125	.296

PORRAY, EDMUND JOSEPH
B.DEC.5,1888 BROOKLYN,N.Y.
D.JULY 13,1954

1914	BUF	F	P		3	0- 1
		BRTR				

PORTER, DANIEL EDWARD
B.OCT.17,1931 DECATUR,ILL.

1951	WAS	A	O		13	.211
		BLTL				

PORTER, DARRELL RAY
B.JAN.17,1952 JOPLIN,MO.

1971	MIL	A	C		22	.214
1972	MIL	A	C		18	.125
1973	MIL	A	C-D		117	.254
1974	MIL	A	C		131	.241
1975	MIL	A	C		130	.232
1976	MIL	A	C		119	.208
		BLTR			537	.229

PORTER, EDWARD S. "NED"
B.MAY 6,1906 APPALACHICOLA,FLA.
D.JUNE 30,1968

1926	NY	N	P		2	0- 0
1927	NY	N	P		1	0- 0
		BRTR			3	0- 0

PORTER, HENRY
B.1857 VERGENNES,VT.
D.DEC.30,1906

1884	KC	U	O		3	.083
	MIL	U	P-1-	6	10	3- 2
			O			.278
1885	BRO	AA	P		55	33-21
1886	BRO	AA	P		48	28-20
1887	BRO	AA	P		40	16-23
1888	KC	AA	P		55	17-37
1889	KC	AA	P		4	0- 3
		BRTR		208	215	97-106
						.189

PORTER, IRVING MARBLE
B.MAY 17,1888 LYNN,MASS.
D.FEB.20,1971 LYNN,MASS.

1914	CHI	A	O		1	.000
		BBTR				

YR	CL	LEA	POS	GP	G	REC

PORTER, J. W. "JAY"
B.JAN.17,1933 SHAWNEE,OKLA.

YR	CL	LEA	POS	GP	G	REC
1952	STL	A	3-O		33	.250
1955	DET	A	C-1-O		24	.236
1956	DET	A	C-O		14	.095
1957	DET	A	C-1-O		58	.250
1958	CLE	A	C-1-3		40	.200
1959	WAS	A	C-1		37	.226
	STL	N	C-1		23	.212
		BRTR			229	.228

PORTER, JAMES
B.BLOOMINGTON,ILL.

| 1902 | PHI | A | P | | 1 | 0- 1 |

PORTER, RICHARD TWILLEY
"DICK" OR "WIGGLES"
B.DEC.30,1901 PRINCESS ANNE,MD.
D.SEPT.24,1974 PHILADELPHIA,PA.

1929	CLE	A	2-O		71	.328
1930	CLE	A	O		119	.350
1931	CLE	A	O		114	.312
1932	CLE	A	O		146	.308
1933	CLE	A	O		132	.267
1934	CLE	A	O		13	.227
	BOS	A	O		80	.302
		BLTR			675	.308

PORTERFIELD, ERWIN COOLIDGE
"BOB"
B.AUG.10,1923 NEWPORT,VA.

1948	NY	A	P		16	5- 3
1949	NY	A	P		12	2- 5
1950	NY	A	P	10	11	1- 1
1951	NY	A	P		2	0- 0
	WAS	A	P		19	9- 8
1952	WAS	A	P		31	13-14
1953	WAS	A	P	34	37	22-10
1954	WAS	A	P		32	13-15
1955	WAS	A	P		30	10-17
1956	BOS	A	P		25	3-12
1957	BOS	A	P		28	4- 4
1958	BOS	A	P		2	0- 0
	PIT	N	P		37	4- 6
1959	PIT	N	P		36	1- 2
	CHI	N	P		4	0- 0
		BRTR		318	322	87-97

PORTO, ALFRED
B.JUNE 27,1927 HEILWOOD,PA.

| 1948 | PHI | N | P | | 3 | 0- 0 |
| | | BLTL | | | | |

PORTOCARRERO, ARNOLD MARIO
"ARNIE"
B.JULY 5,1931 NEW YORK,N.Y.

1954	PHI	A	P		34	9-18
1955	KC	A	P		24	5- 9
1956	KC	A	P		3	0- 1
1957	KC	A	P		33	4- 9
1958	BAL	A	P		32	15-11
1959	BAL	A	P		27	2- 7
1960	BAL	A	P		13	3- 2
		BRTR		166	166	38-57

POSADA, LEOPOLDO (HERNANDEZ)
"LEO"
B.APR.15,1936 HAVANA,CUBA

1960	KC	A	O		10	.361
1961	KC	A	O		116	.253
1962	KC	A	O		29	.196
		BRTR			155	.256

POSEDEL, WILLIAM JOHN
"BARNACLE BILL"
B.AUG.2,1909 SAN FRANCISCO,CAL.

1938	BRO	N	P		33	8- 9
1939	BOS	N	P		33	15-13
1940	BOS	N	P		35	12-17
1941	BOS	N	P		18	4- 4
1946	BOS	N	P		19	2- 0
		BRTR			138	41-43

POSER, JOHN FALK
B.MAR.16,1910 COLUMBUS,WIS.

1932	CHI	A	P	1	5	0- 0
1935	STL	A	P		4	1- 1
		BLTR		5	9	1- 1

POSSEHL, LOUIS THOMAS
B.APR.12,1926 CHICAGO,ILL.

1946	PHI	N	P		4	1- 2
1947	PHI	N	P		2	0- 0
1948	PHI	N	P	3	4	1- 1
1951	PHI	N	P		2	0- 1
1952	PHI	N	P		4	0- 1
		BRTR		15	16	2- 5

POST, SAMUEL GILBERT
B.NOV.17,1896 RICHMOND,VA.
D.MAR.31,1971 PORTSMOUTH,VA.

| 1922 | BRO | N | 1 | | 9 | .280 |
| | | BLTL | | | | |

POST, WALTER CHARLES "WALLY"
B.JULY 9,1929 ST.WENDELIN,OHIO

1949	CIN	N	O		6	.250
1951	CIN	N	O		15	.220
1952	CIN	N	O		19	.155
1953	CIN	N	O		11	.242
1954	CIN	N	O		130	.255
1955	CIN	N	O		154	.309
1956	CIN	N	O		143	.249
1957	CIN	N	O		134	.244
1958	PHI	N	O		110	.282
1959	PHI	N	O		132	.254
1960	PHI	N	O		34	.286
	CIN	N	O		77	.281
1961	CIN	N	O		99	.294
1962	CIN	N	O		109	.263
1963	CIN	N	O		5	.000
	MIN	A	O		21	.191
1964	CLE	A	O		5	.000
		BRTR			1204	.266

POSTE, E.

| 1902 | DET | A | O | | 3 | .083 |

POTT, NELSON ALEXANDER
B.JULY 16,1899 CINCINNATI,OHIO
D.DEC.3,1963 MACK,OHIO

| 1922 | CLE | A | P | | 2 | 0- 0 |
| | | BLTL | | | | |

POTTER, MARYLAND DYKES
B.SEPT.7,1910 ASHLAND,KY.

| 1938 | BRO | N | P | | 2 | 0- 0 |
| | | BRTR | | | | |

POTTER, MICHAEL GARY "MIKE"
B.MAY 16,1951 MONTEBELLO,CAL.

| 1976 | STL | N | O | | 9 | .000 |
| | | BRTR | | | | |

POTTER, NELSON THOMAS "NELLIE"
B.AUG.23,1911 MT.MORRIS,ILL.

1936	STL	N	P		1	0- 0
1938	PHI	A	P	35	38	2-12
1939	PHI	A	P		41	8-12
1940	PHI	A	P		31	9-14
1941	PHI	A	P		10	1- 1
	BOS	A	P		10	2- 0
1943	STL	A	P		33	10- 5
1944	STL	A	P		32	19- 7
1945	STL	A	P		32	15-11
1946	STL	A	P		23	8- 9
1947	STL	A	P		32	4-10
1948	STL	A	P		2	1- 1
	PHI	A	P		8	2- 2
	BOS	N	P		18	5- 2
1949	BOS	N	P		41	6-11
		BLTR		349	352	92-97

POTTER, ROBERT H.
B.MAR.18,1902 FLATWOODS,KY.

| 1923 | WAS | A | P | | 1 | 0- 0 |
| | | BRTR | | | | |

POTTS, DANIEL
B.KENT,OHIO

| 1892 | WAS | N | C | | 1 | .333 |

POTTS, JOHN FREDERICK
B.FEB.6,1887 TROY,OHIO
D.SEPT.5,1962

| 1914 | KC | F | O | | 40 | .287 |
| | | BLTR | | | | |

POULSEN, KEN STERLING
B.AUG.4,1947 VAN NUYS,CAL.

| 1967 | BOS | A | S-3 | | 5 | .200 |
| | | BLTR | | | | |

POUNDS, WILLIAM CHARLES
B.PATERSON,N.J.

1903	CLE	A	P		1	0- 0
	BRO	N	P		1	0- 0
					2	0- 0

POWELL, ALVIN JACOB "JAKE"
B.JULY 15,1908 SILVER SPRING,MD
D.NOV.4,1948

1930	WAS	A	O		3	.000
1934	WAS	A	O		9	.286
1935	WAS	A	2-O		139	.312
1936	WAS	A	O		53	.290
1936	NY	A	O		87	.306
1937	NY	A	O		97	.263
1938	NY	A	O		45	.256
1939	NY	A	O		31	.244
1940	NY	A	O		12	.185
1943	WAS	A	O		37	.265
1944	WAS	A	3-O		96	.240
1945	WAS	A	O		31	.194
	PHI	N	O		48	.231
		BRTR			688	.271

POWELL, CHARLES ABNER "AB"
B.DEC.15,1860 SHENANDOAH,PA.
D.AUG.7,1953

1884	WAS	U	P-2-	19	47	4-12
			3-O			.270
1886	BAL	AA	P-O	7	10	2- 5
						.147
	CIN	AA	P-C-	4	19	0- 1
			S-O			.230
		BRTR		30	76	6-18
						.246

POWELL, GROVER DAVID
B.OCT.10,1940 SAYRE,PA.

| 1963 | NY | N | P | | 20 | 1- 1 |
| | | BLTL | | | | |

POWELL, JAMES E.
B.1859 RICHMOND,VA.

| 1884 | RIC | AA | 1 | | 40 | .243 |

POWELL, JOHN JOSEPH
"JACK" OR "RED"
B.JULY 9,1874 BLOOMINGTON,ILL.
D.OCT.17,1944 CHICAGO,ILL.

1897	STL	N	P	26	28	15- 9
1898	STL	N	P		40	24-15
1899	STL	N	P	44	46	23-21
1900	STL	N	P		37	17-18
1901	STL	N	P		37	19-18
1902	STL	A	P-C-	43	44	22-17
			1-O			.217
1903	STL	A	P	38	39	15-19
1904	NY	A	P		47	23-19
1905	NY	A	P		37	9-11
	STL	A	P		3	2- 1
1906	STL	A	P		29	13-14
1907	STL	A	P		35	13-16
1908	STL	A	P		33	16-13
1909	STL	A	P		34	12-16
1910	STL	A	P		21	7-11
1911	STL	A	P		32	8-19
1912	STL	A	P		32	9-16
		BRTR		568	574	247-253
						.191

POWELL, JOHN WESLEY "BOOG"
B.AUG.17,1941 LAKELAND,FLA.

1961	BAL	A	O		4	.077
1962	BAL	A	1-O		124	.243
1963	BAL	A	1-O		140	.265
1964	BAL	A	1-O		134	.290
1965	BAL	A	1-O		144	.248
1966	BAL	A	1		140	.287
1967	BAL	A	1		125	.234
1968	BAL	A	1		154	.249
1969	BAL	A	1		152	.304
1970	BAL	A	1		154	.297
1971	BAL	A	1		128	.256
1972	BAL	A	1		140	.252
1973	BAL	A	1		114	.265
1974	BAL	A	1		110	.265
1975	CLE	A	1		134	.297
1976	CLE	A	1		95	.215
		BLTR			1992	.266

POWELL, MARTIN J.
B.MAR.25,1856 FITCHBURG,MASS.
D.FEB.5,1888

1881	DET	N	C-1		55	.310
1882	DET	N	1		77	.247
1883	DET	N	1		97	.267
1884	CIN	U	1		45	.314
1885	ATH	AA	1		18	.164
		BL			292	.276

YR	CL	LEA	POS	GP	G	REC

POWELL, PAUL RAY
B.MAR.19,1948 SAN ANGELO,TEX.

YR	CL	LEA	POS	G	REC
1971	MIN	A	O	20	.161
1973	LA	N	O	2	.000
1975	LA	N	C-O	8	.200
	BRTR			30	.167

POWELL, RAYMOND REATH "RABBIT"
B.NOV.20,1888 SILOAM SPRINGS,
ARK.
D.OCT.16,1962

YR	CL	LEA	POS	G	REC
1913	DET	A	O	2	.000
1917	BOS	N	O	88	.272
1918	BOS	N	O	53	.213
1919	BOS	N	O	123	.236
1920	BOS	N	O	147	.225
1921	BOS	N	O	149	.306
1922	BOS	N	O	142	.296
1923	BOS	N	O	97	.302
1924	BOS	N	O	74	.261
	BLTR			875	.271

POWELL, ROBERT LEROY
B.OCT.17,1933 FLINT,MICH.

YR	CL	LEA	POS	G	REC
1955	CHI	A	H	1	.000
1957	CHI	A	H	1	.000
	BRTR			2	.000

POWELL, SAMUEL

YR	CL	LEA	POS	GP	REC
1913	STL	A	P	2	0- 0

POWELL, WILLIAM BURRIS
"BIG BILL"
B.MAY 8,1885 RICHMOND,VA.
D.SEPT.28,1967 E.LIVERPOOL,OHIO

YR	CL	LEA	POS	GP	REC
1909	PIT	N	P	3	0- 1
1910	PIT	N	P	12	4- 6
1912	CHI	N	P	1	0- 0
1913	CIN	N	P	1	0- 1
	BRTR			17	4- 8

POWER, THOMAS E.
B.SAN FRANCISCO,CAL.
D.FEB.25,1898

YR	CL	LEA	POS	G	REC
1890	BAL	AA	1	38	.211

POWERS, ELLIS FOREE "MIKE"
B.MAR.2,1906 CRESTWOOD,KY.

YR	CL	LEA	POS	G	REC
1932	CLE	A	O	14	.182
1933	CLE	A	O	24	.277
	BLTL			38	.238

POWER, VICTOR PELLOT "VIC"
B.NOV.1,1931 ARECIBO,P.R.

YR	CL	LEA	POS	G	REC
1954	PHI	A	1-S-3-O	127	.255
1955	KC	A	1	147	.319
1956	KC	A	1-2-O	127	.309
1957	KC	A	1-2-O	129	.259
1958	KC	A	1-2	52	.302
	CLE	A	1-2-S-3-O	93	.317
1959	CLE	A	1-2-3	147	.289
1960	CLE	A	1-S-3	147	.288
1961	CLE	A	1-2	147	.268
1962	MIN	A	1-2	144	.290
1963	MIN	A	1-2-3	138	.270
1964	MIN	A	1-2	19	.222
	LA	A	1-2-3	68	.249
	PHI	N	1	18	.208
1965	CAL	A	1-2-3	124	.259
	BRTR			1627	.284

POWERS, JAMES T.
B.1868 NEW YORK,N.Y.

YR	CL	LEA	POS	GP	REC
1890	BRO	AA	P	4	1- 2

POWERS, JOHN CALVIN
B.JULY 8,1929 BIRMINGHAM,ALA.

YR	CL	LEA	POS	G	REC
1955	PIT	N	O	2	.250
1956	PIT	N	O	11	.048
1957	PIT	N	O	20	.286
1958	PIT	N	O	57	.183
1959	CIN	N	O	43	.256
1960	BAL	A	O	10	.111
	CAL	A	O	8	.167
	BLTR			151	.195

POWERS, JOHN LLOYD "IKE"
B.MAR.13,1906 HANCOCK,MD.
D.DEC.22,1968 HANCOCK,MD.

YR	CL	LEA	POS	GP	REC
1927	PHI	A	P	11	1- 1
1928	PHI	A	P	9	1- 0
	BRTR			20	2- 1

POWERS, LESLIE EDWIN
B.JAN.20,1912 SEATTLE,WASH.

YR	CL	LEA	POS	G	REC
1938	NY	N	H	2	.000
1939	PHI	N	1	19	.346
	BLTL			21	.327

POWERS, MICHAEL RILEY
B.SEPT.22,1870 PITTSFIELD,MASS.
D.APR.26,1909

YR	CL	LEA	POS	G	REC
1898	LOU	N	C	27	.298
1899	LOU	N	C	41	.211
	WAS	N	C-1	14	.333
1901	PHI	A	C	116	.248
1902	PHI	A	C-1	71	.271
1903	PHI	A	C	74	.227
1904	PHI	A	C	57	.187
1905	PHI	A	C	22	.183
	NY	A	C	11	.083
	PHI	A	C	19	.161
1906	PHI	A	C	58	.157
1907	PHI	A	C	59	.182
1908	PHI	A	C	62	.180
1909	PHI	A	C	1	.250
	BRTR			632	.218

POWERS, PATRICK THOMAS
B.JUNE 27,1860 TRENTON,N.J.
D.AUG.29,1925
NON-PLAYING MANAGER
ROC(AA) 1890, NY(N) 1892

POWERS, PHILLIP J.
"GRANDMOTHER"
B.JULY 26,1854 NEW YORK,N.Y.
D.DEC.22,1914

YR	CL	LEA	POS	G	REC
1878	CHI	N	C-O	9	.140
1880	BOS	N	C-O	35	.148
1881	CLE	N	C-3	6	.143
1882	CIN	AA	C-1-O	15	.212
1883	CIN	AA	C-O	29	.234
1884	CIN	AA	C-1-O	35	.158
1885	CIN	AA	C	15	.267
	BAL	AA	C-O	9	.121
	BRTR			153	.184

POWIS, CARL EDGAR
B.JAN.11,1920 PHILADELPHIA,PA.

YR	CL	LEA	POS	G	REC
1957	BAL	A	O	15	.195
	BRTR				

PRALL, WILFRED ANTHONY "WILLIE"
B.APR.20,1950 HACKENSACK,N.J.

YR	CL	LEA	POS	GP	REC
1975	CHI	N	P	3	0- 2
	BLTL				

PRAMESA, JOHN STEVEN "JOHNNY"
B.AUG.28,1925 BARTON,OHIO

YR	CL	LEA	POS	G	REC
1949	CIN	N	C	17	.240
1950	CIN	N	C	74	.307
1951	CIN	N	C	72	.229
1952	CHI	N	C	22	.283
	BRTR			185	.268

PRATT, ALBERT GEORGE "UNCLE AL"
B.NOV.19,1848 ALLEGHENY,PA.
D.NOV.21,1937

YR	CL	LEA	POS	GP	G	REC
1871	CLE	NA	P-O	28	29	10-18
1872	CLE	NA	P-O	11	15	3- 8
						.261
				39	44	13-26
						-

NON-PLAYING MANAGER
PIT(AA) 1882-83

PRATT, DERRILL BURNHAM "DEL"
B.JAN.10,1888 WALHALLA,S.C.

YR	CL	LEA	POS	G	REC
1912	STL	A	2-S	151	.302
1913	STL	A	2	154	.296
1914	STL	A	2	158	.282
1915	STL	A	2	159	.291
1916	STL	A	2	158	.267
1917	STL	A	2	123	.247
1918	NY	A	2	126	.275
1919	NY	A	2	140	.292
1920	NY	A	2	154	.314
1921	BOS	A	2	135	.324
1922	BOS	A	2	154	.302
1923	DET	A	1-2	101	.310
1924	DET	A	1-2	121	.303
	BRTR			1834	.292

PRATT, FRANCIS BRUCE
B.AUG.24,1897 BLOCTON,ALA.
D.MAR.8,1974 CENTREVILLE,ALA.

YR	CL	LEA	POS	G	REC
1921	CHI	A	H	1	.000
	TR				

PRATT, LESTER JOHN "LARRY"
B.OCT.8,1886 GIBSON CITY,ILL.
D.JAN.8,1969 PEORIA,ILL.

YR	CL	LEA	POS	G	REC
1914	BOS	A	C	5	.000
1915	BRO	F	C	20	.191
	NEW	F	C	5	.500
	BRTR			30	.196

PRATT, THOMAS J.
B.1840 WORCESTER,MASS.
D.SEPT.29,1908

YR	CL	LEA	POS	G	REC
1871	ATH	NA	O	1	-
1884	BAL	AA	O	1	.250
				2	-

NON-PLAYING MANAGER KEY(U) 1884

PREGENZER, JOHN ARTHUR
B.AUG.2,1935 BURLINGTON,WIS.

YR	CL	LEA	POS	GP	REC
1963	SF	N	P	6	0- 0
1964	SF	N	P	13	2- 0
	BRTR			19	2- 0

PREIBISCH, MELVIN ADOLPHUS
"PRIMO"
B.NOV.13,1915 SEALY,TEX.

YR	CL	LEA	POS	G	REC
1940	BOS	N	O	11	.225
1941	BOS	N	O	5	.000
	BRTR			16	.205

PRENDERGAST, JAMES BARTHOLOMEW
"JIM"
B.AUG.23,1917 BROOKLYN,N.Y.

YR	CL	LEA	POS	GP	REC
1948	BOS	N	P	10	1- 1
	BLTL				

PRENDERGAST, MICHAEL THOMAS
B.SEPT.15,1890 APLINGTON,ILL.
D.NOV.18,1967 OMAHA,NEB.

YR	CL	LEA	POS	GP	REC
1914	CHI	F	P	30	5- 9
1915	CHI	F	P	42	14-12
1916	CHI	N	P	35	6-11
1917	CHI	N	P	35	3- 6
1918	PHI	N	P	33	13-14
1919	PHI	N	P	5	0- 1
	BRTR			180	41-53

PRENTISS, GEORGE PEPPER
(PLAYED UNDER NAME OF
GEORGE PEPPER WILSON IN 1901)
B.JUNE 10,1876 WILMINGTON,DEL.
D.SEPT.8,1902

YR	CL	LEA	POS	GP	REC
1901	BOS	A	P	2	1- 0
1902	BOS	A	P	6	2- 2
	BAL	A	P	6	3- 3
	BB			14	6- 5

PRESCOTT, GEORGE BERTRAND
"BOBBY"
B.MAR.27,1931 COLON,PANAMA

YR	CL	LEA	POS	G	REC
1961	KC	A	O	10	.083
	BRTR				

PRESKO, JOSEPH EDWARD "JOE"
B.OCT.7,1928 KANSAS CITY,MO.

YR	CL	LEA	POS	GP	G	REC
1951	STL	N	P		15	7- 4
1952	STL	N	P		28	7-10
1953	STL	N	P	34	35	6-13
1954	STL	N	P	37	38	4- 9
1957	DET	A	P		7	1- 1
1958	DET	A	P		7	0- 0
	BRTR			128	130	25-37

PRESSNELL, FOREST CHARLES "TOT"
B.AUG.8,1907 FINDLAY,OHIO

YR	CL	LEA	POS	GP	REC
1938	BRO	N	P	43	11-14
1939	BRO	N	P	31	9- 7
1940	BRO	N	P	24	6- 5
1941	CHI	N	P	29	5- 3
1942	CHI	N	P	27	1- 1

PRESTON, WALTER B.
B.1871 GALVESTON,TEX.

YR	CL	LEA	POS	G	REC
1895	LOU	N	3-O	49	.292
	BLTR				

PRICE, JAMES L.
NON-PLAYING MANAGER NY(N) 1884

PRICE, JIMMIE WILLIAM
B.OCT.13,1941 HARRISBURG,PA.

YR	CL	LEA	POS	G	REC
1967	DET	A	C	44	.261
1968	DET	A	C	64	.174
1969	DET	A	C	72	.234
1970	DET	A	C	52	.182
1971	DET	A	C	29	.241
	BRTR			261	.214

YR	CL	LEA	POS	GP	G	REC

PRICE, JOHN THOMAS REID
"JACKIE"
B.NOV.13,1913 WINBORN,MISS.
D.OCT.2,1967 SAN FRANCISCO,CAL.
1946 CLE A S   7   .231
     BLTR

PRICE, JOSEPH PRESTON
B.AUG.10,1897 MILLIGAN COLLEGE,
TENN.
D.JAN.15,1961
1928 NY N O   1   .000
     BRTR

PRICE, WILLIAM
B.PHILADELPHIA,PA.
1890 ATH AA P   1   1- 0

PRICHARD, ROBERT ALEXANDER
B.OCT.21,1917 PARIS,TEX.
1939 WAS A 1   26   .235
     BLTL

PRIDDY, GERALD EDWARD "JERRY"
B.NOV.9,1919 LOS ANGELES,CAL.
1941 NY A 1-2-3   56   .213
1942 NY A 1-2-5-3 59   .280
1943 WAS A 2-S-3   149   .271
1946 WAS A 2   138   .254
1947 WAS A 2   147   .214
1948 STL A 2   151   .296
1949 STL A 2   145   .290
1950 DET A 2   157   .277
1951 DET A 2-S   154   .260
1952 DET A 2   75   .283
1953 DET A 1-2-3   65   .235
     BRTR   1296   .265

PRIDDY, ROBERT SIMPSON "BOB"
B.DEC.10,1939 PITTSBURGH,PA.
1962 PIT N P   2   1- 0
1964 PIT N P   19   1- 2
1965 SF N P   8   9   1- 0
1966 SF N P   38 39   6- 3
1967 WAS A P   46 49   3- 7
1968 CHI A P   35 42   3-11
1969 CHI A P   4   0- 0
     CAL A P   15   0- 1
     ATL N P   1   0- 0
1970 ATL N P   41   5- 5
1971 ATL N P   40   4- 9
     BRTR   249 261 24-38

PRIEST, JOHN GOODING
B.JUNE 23,1891 ST.JOSEPH,MO.
1911 NY A 2   8   .142
1912 NY A H   2   .500
     BRTR   10   .174

PRIM, RAYMOND LEE "POP"
B.DEC.30,1906 SALITPA,ALA.
1933 WAS A P   2   0- 1
1934 WAS A P   8   0- 2
1935 PHI N P   29   3- 4
1943 CHI N P   29   4- 3
1945 CHI N P   34 13- 8
1946 CHI N P   14   2- 3
     BRTL   116 22-21

PRINCE, DONALD MARK
B.APR.5,1938 CLARKTON,N.C.
1962 CHI N P   1   0- 0
     BRTR

PRINCE, WALTER F.
B.1860 N.ANDOVER,MASS.
D.MAR.2,1938
1883 LOU AA 1-S-O   4   .182
1884 DET N O   7   .130
     WAS AA 1   43   .211
     WAS U 1   1   .250
                    55   .200

PRITCHARD, HAROLD WILLIAM
"BUDDY"
B.JAN.25,1936 SOUTH GATE,CAL.
1957 PIT N S-O   23   .091
     BRTR

PROCTOR, JAMES ARTHUR
B.SEPT.9,1935 BRANDYWINE,MD.
1959 DET A P   2   0- 1
     BRTR

PROCTOR, L.
1912 STL A H   1   .000

PROCTOR, NOAH RICHARD
B.OCT.27,1900 WILLIAMSBURG,VA.
D.DEC.17,1954
1923 CHI A P   2   0- 0
     BRTR

PROESER, GEORGE "YATZ"
B.MAY 30,1864 CINCINNATI,OHIO
D.OCT.13,1941
1888 CLE AA P   7   3- 4
1890 SYR AA O   13   .264
     BLTL   7   20   3- 4
                         .276

PROLY, MICHAEL JAMES "MIKE"
B.DEC.15,1950 JAMAICA,N.Y.
1976 STL N P   14   1- 0
     BRTR

PROPST, WILLIAM JACOB "JAKE"
B.MAR.10,1895 KENNEDY,ALA.
D.FEB.24,1967 COLUMBUS,MISS.
1923 WAS A H   1   .000

PROTHRO, JAMES THOMSON "DOC"
B.JULY 20,1893 MEMPHIS,TENN.
D.OCT.14,1971 MEMPHIS,TENN.
1920 WAS A S   6   .385
1923 WAS A 3   6   .250
1924 WAS A 3   46   .333
1925 BOS A S-3   119   .313
1926 CIN N 3   3   .200
     BRTR   180   .319
NON-PLAYING MANAGER
PHI(N) 1939-41

PROUGH, HERSCHEL CLINTON
B.NOV.28,1897 MARKLE,IND.
D.DEC.29,1936 RICHMOND,IND.
1912 CIN N P   1   0- 0
     BRTR

PRUDHOMME, JOHN OLGUS
B.NOV.20,1902 FRIERSON,LA.
1929 DET A P   34   1- 6
     BRTR

PRUESS, EARL HENRY
B.APR.2,1895 CHICAGO,ILL.
1920 STL A O   1   .000
     BPTR

PRUETT, HUBERT SHELBY "SHUCKS"
B.SEPT.1,1900 HIGGINSVILLE,KY.
1922 STL A P   39   7- 7
1923 STL A P   32   4- 7
1924 STL A P   33   3- 4
1927 PHI N P   31   7-17
1928 PHI N P   13   2- 4
1930 NY N P   45   5- 4
1932 BOS N P   18   1- 5
     BLTL   211 29-48

PRUETT, JAMES CALVIN
B.DEC.16,1918 NASHVILLE,TENN.
1944 PHI A C   3   .250
1945 PHI A C   6   .222
     BRTR   9   .231

PRUIETT, CHARLES LE ROY "TEX"
B.APR.10,1883 OSGOOD,IND.
D.MAR.6,1953
1907 BOS A P   35   3-11
1908 BOS A P   13   1- 7
     BLTL   48   4-18

PRUITT, RONALD RALPH "RON"
B.OCT.21,1951 FLINT,MICH.
1975 TEX A C-O   14   .176
1976 CLE A C-1-3-O 47   .267
     BRTR   61   .252

PRYOR, GREGORY RUSSELL "GREG"
B.OCT.2,1949 MARIETTA,OHIO
1976 TEX A 2-S-3   5   .375
     BRTR

PUCCINELLI, GEORGE LAWRENCE
"POOCH" OR "COUNT"
B.JUNE 22,1907 SAN FRANCISCO,
CAL.
D.APR.16,1956
1930 STL N O   11   .563
1932 STL N O   31   .278
1934 STL N O   10   .231
1936 PHI A O   135   .278
     BRTR   187   .283

PUCKETT, TROY LEVI
B.DEC.10,1889 WINCHESTER,IND.
D.APR.13,1971 WINCHESTER,IND.
1911 PHI N P   1   0- 0
     BLTR

PUENTE, MIGUEL ANTONIO
B.MAY 8,1948 SAN LUIS POTOSI,MEX
1970 SF N P   6   1- 3
     BRTR

PUHL, JOHN G.
B.1875 BAYONNE,N.J.
D.AUG.24,1900
1898 NY N 3   2   .250
1899 NY N 3   1   .000
                     3   .200

PUIG, RICHARD GERALD "RICK"
B.MAR.16,1953 TAMPA,FLA.
1974 NY N 2-3   4   .000
     BLTR

PUMPELLY, SPENCER ARMSTRONG
B.APR.11,1893 OWEGO,N.Y.
D.DEC.5,1973 SAYRE,PA.
1925 WAS A P   1   0- 0

PURCELL, WILLIAM ALOYSIUS
"BLONDY"
B.PATERSON,N.J.
D.1905
1879 SYR N P-C- 22 62   4-14
            O   .265
     CIN N P-O   2   12   0- 2
                           .231
1880 CIN N P-S- 26 76   3-16
            O   .283
1881 CLE N O   20   .165
     BUF N P-O   9   30   4- 1
                           .267
1882 BUF N P-O   4   84   2- 2
                           .276
1883 PHI N P-S- 10 96   2- 8
            3-O   .270
1884 PHI N P-O   7 102   2- 5
                           .244
1885 ATH AA P-O   1   66   0- 1
                           .298
     BOS N O   21   2.18
1886 BAL AA O   27   .224
1887 BAL AA O   140   .305
1888 BAL AA O   101   .233
     ATH AA 3-O   18   .167
1889 ATH AA O   130   .306
1890 ATH AA O   106   .287
                 81 1091 17-49
                           .272

PURDIN, JOHN NOLAN
B.JULY 16,1942 DAYTON,OHIO
1964 LA N P   3   2- 0
1965 LA N P   11   2- 1
1968 LA N P   35 36   2- 3
1969 LA N P   9   0- 0
     BRTR   58 59   6- 4

PURDY, EVERETT VIRGIL "PID"
B.JUNE 15,1904 BEATRICE,NEB.
D.JAN.16,1951
1926 CHI A O   11   *182
1927 CIN N O   18   .355
1928 CIN N O   70   .309
1929 CIN N O   82   .271
     BLTR   181   .293

YR	CL	LEA	POS	GP	G	REC

PURKEY, ROBERT THOMAS "BOB"
B.JULY 14,1929 PITTSBURGH,PA.

YR	CL	LEA	POS	GP	G	REC
1954	PIT	N	P		36	3- 8
1955	PIT	N	P		14	2- 7
1956	PIT	N	P		2	0- 0
1957	PIT	N	P		48	11-14
1958	CIN	N	P		37	17-11
1959	CIN	N	P		38	13-18
1960	CIN	N	P		41	17-11
1961	CIN	N	P		36	16-12
1962	CIN	N	P		37	23- 5
1963	CIN	N	P		21	6-10
1964	CIN	N	P		34	11- 9
1965	STL	N	P		32	10- 9
1966	PIT	N	P	10	11	0- 1
		BRTR		386	387	129-115

PURNELL, JESSE RHOADES
B.MAY 11,1879 EDGE HILL,PA.
D.JULY 4,1966

| 1904 | PHI | N | 3 | | 7 | .105 |

PURNER, OSCAR E.

| 1895 | WAS | N | P | | 1 | 0- 0 |

PURTELL, WILLIAM PATRICK
B.JAN.6,1886 COLUMBUS,OHIO
D.MAR.17,1962

1908	CHI	A	3		26	.130
1909	CHI	A	2-3		103	.258
1910	CHI	A	3		102	.222
	BOS	A	3		49	.211
1911	BOS	A	3		27	.280
		BRTR			333	.227

PUTNAM, AUGUSTUS
B.NOV.21,1817 HARTFORD,CONN.
D.JAN.13,1890
NON-PLAYING MANAGER MAN(NA)1872

PUTNAM, EDDY WILLIAM "ED"
B.SEPT.25,1953 LOS ANGELES,CAL.

| 1976 | CHI | N | C-1 | | 5 | .429 |
| | | BRTR | | | | |

PUTTMANN, AMBROSE NICHOLAS "PUTT"
B.SEPT.9,1880 CINCINNATI,OHIO
D.JUNE 21,1936 JAMAICA,N.Y.

1903	NY	A	P		3	2- 0
1904	NY	A	P		10	2- 0
1905	NY	A	P		17	3- 7
1906	STL	N	P		4	2- 2
		TL			34	9- 9

PYBURN, JAMES EDWARD "JIM"
B.NOV.1,1932 FAIRFIELD,ALA.

1955	BAL	A	3-0		39	.204
1956	BAL	A	0		84	.173
1957	BAL	A	C-0		35	.225
		BRTR			158	.190

PYECHA, JOHN NICHOLAS
B.NOV.25,1931 ALIQUIPPA,PA.

| 1954 | CHI | N | P | | 1 | 0- 1 |
| | | BRTR | | | | |

PYLE, HARLAN ALBERT
B.JAN.31,1905 LIBERTY,NEB.

| 1928 | CIN | N | P | | 2 | 0- 0 |

PYLE, HARRY THOMAS "SHADOW"
B.OCT.30,1861 READING,PA.
D.NOV.26,1908

1884	PHI	N	P		1	0- 1
1887	CHI	N	P		4	1- 3
					5	1- 4

PYLE, HERBERT EWALD "LEFTY"
B.AUG.27,1913 ST.LOUIS,MO.

1939	STL	A	P		6	0- 2
1942	STL	A	P		2	0- 0
1943	WAS	A	P		18	4- 8
1944	NY	N	P		31	7-10
1945	NY	N	P		6	0- 0
	BOS	N	P		4	0- 1
		BLTL			67	11-21

PYTLAK, FRANK ANTHONY
B.JULY 30,1908 BUFFALO,N.Y.

1932	CLE	A	C		12	.241
1933	CLE	A	C		80	.310
1934	CLE	A	C		91	.260
1935	CLE	A	C		55	.295
1936	CLE	A	C		75	.321
1937	CLE	A	C		125	.315
1938	CLE	A	C		113	.308
1939	CLE	A	C		63	.268
1940	CLE	A	C-0		62	.141
1941	BOS	A	C		106	.271
1945	BOS	A	C		9	.118
1946	BOS	A	C		4	.143
		BRTR			795	.282

QUALLS, JAMES ROBERT "JIM"
B.OCT.9,1946 EXETER,CAL.

1969	CHI	N	2-0		43	.250
1970	MON	N	2-0		9	.111
1972	CHI	A	0		11	.000
		BBTR			63	.223

QUALTERS, THOMAS FRANCIS "TOM"
B.APR.1,1935 MC KEESPORT,PA.

1953	PHI	N	P		1	0- 0
1957	PHI	N	P		6	0- 0
1958	PHI	N	P		1	0- 0
	CHI	A	P		26	0- 0
		BRTR			34	0- 0

QUARLES, WILLIAM H.
B.1869 PETERSBURG,VA.
D.MAR.25,1897

1891	WAS	AA	P		4	2- 2
1893	BOS	N	P		4	2- 2
					8	4- 4

QUEEN, MELVIN DOUGLAS "MEL"
B.MAR.26,1942 JOHNSON CITY,N.Y.

1964	CIN	N	0		48	.200
1965	CIN	N	0		5	.000
1966	CIN	N	P-0	7	56	0- 0
						.127
1967	CIN	N	P	31	49	14- 8
1968	CIN	N	P	5	10	0- 1
1969	CIN	N	P		2	1- 0
1970	CAL	A	P	34	37	3- 6
1971	CAL	A	P	44	45	2- 2
1972	CAL	A	P		17	0- 0
		BLTR		140	269	20-17
						.179

QUEEN, MELVIN JOSEPH "MEL"
B.MAR.4,1918 MAXWELL,PA.

1942	NY	A	P		4	1- 0
1944	NY	A	P		10	6- 3
1946	NY	A	P		14	1- 1
1947	NY	A	P		5	0- 0
	PIT	N	P		14	5- 7
1948	PIT	N	P		25	4- 4
1950	PIT	N	P		33	5-14
1951	PIT	N	P		39	7- 9
1952	PIT	N	P		2	0- 2
		BRTR			146	27-40

QUEEN, WILLIAM EDDLEMAN "BILLY"
B.NOV.28,1928 GASTONIA,N.C.

| 1954 | MIL | N | 0 | | 3 | .000 |
| | | BRTR | | | | |

QUELLICH, GEORGE WILLIAM
B.FEB.10,1903 JOHNSVILLE,CAL.
D.AUG.31,1958

| 1931 | DET | A | 0 | | 13 | .222 |
| | | BRTR | | | | |

QUEST, JOSEPH L.
B.1852 NEW CASTLE,PA.

1871	CLE	NA	2-S		3	—
1878	IND	N	2		59	.213
1879	CHI	N	2		79	.220
1880	CHI	N	2-S		80	.245
1881	CHI	N	2		77	.249
1882	CHI	N	2		42	.201
1883	DET	N	2		36	.204
	STL	AA	2		20	.253
1884	STL	AA	2		81	.200
	PIT	AA	2-S		12	.209
1885	DET	N	2-S		55	.195
1886	ATH	AA	S		41	.200
		BRTR			585	—

QUICK, EDWIN S.
B.BALTIMORE,MD.

| 1903 | NY | A | P | | 1 | 0- 1 |

QUICK, JAMES HAROLD
B.OCT.4,1919 ROME,GA.

| 1939 | WAS | A | S | | 12 | .244 |
| | | BRTR | | | | |

QUILICI, FRANK RALPH
B.MAY 11,1939 CHICAGO,ILL.

1965	MIN	A	2-S		56	.208
1967	MIN	A	2-S-3		23	.105
1968	MIN	A	1-2-S-3		97	.245
1969	MIN	A	2-S-3		118	.174
1970	MIN	A	2-S-3		111	.227
		BRTR			405	.214

NON-PLAYING MANAGER
MIN(A) 1972-75

QUILLEN, LEE A.
B.MAY 5,1882 NORTH BRANCH,MINN.
D.MAY 14,1965 ST.PAUL,MINN.

1906	CHI	A	S		3	.111
1907	CHI	A	3		49	.192
		TR			52	.186

QUINLAN

| 1874 | PHI | NA | S | | 1 | .000 |

QUINLAN, LAWRENCE A.
B.MARLBORO,MASS.

| 1891 | BOS | AA | C | | 2 | .000 |

QUINLAN, THOMAS FINNERS
B.OCT.21,1887 SCRANTON,PA.
D.FEB.17,1966 SCRANTON,PA.

1913	STL	N	0		13	.160
1915	CHI	A	U		42	.193
		BLTL			55	.183

QUINN, CLARENCE C.

1902	PHI	A	P		1	0- 1
1903	PHI	A	P		2	0- 0
					3	0- 1

QUINN, FRANK J.
B.GRAND RAPIDS,MICH.
D.FEB.17,1920

| 1899 | CHI | N | 0 | | 12 | .181 |

QUINN, FRANK WILLIAM
B.NOV.27,1927 SPRINGFIELD,MASS.

1949	BOS	A	P		8	0- 0
1950	BOS	A	P		1	0- 0
		BRTR			9	0- 0

QUINN, JOHN EDWARD PICK
B.SEPT.12,1885 FRAMINGHAM,MASS.
D.APR.9,1956

| 1911 | PHI | N | C | | 1 | .000 |
| | | TR | | | | |

QUINN, JOHN PICUS "JACK"
(REAL NAME JOHN QUINN PICUS)
B.JULY 5,1884 HAZLETON,PA.
D.APR.17,1946 POTTSVILLE,PA.

1909	NY	A	P		22	9- 5
1910	NY	A	P		35	18-12
1911	NY	A	P		39	8- 9
1912	NY	A	P		18	5- 7
1913	BOS	N	P		8	4- 3
1914	BAL	F	P	45	48	26-14
1915	BAL	F	P	44	54	9-22
1918	CHI	A	P		6	5- 1
1919	NY	A	P		38	15-14
1920	NY	A	P		41	18-10
1921	NY	A	P		33	8- 7
1922	BOS	A	P		40	13-15
1923	BOS	A	P		42	13-17
1924	BOS	A	P		44	12-13
1925	BOS	A	P		19	7- 8
	PHI	A	P		18	6- 3
1926	PHI	A	P		31	10-11
1927	PHI	A	P		34	15-10
1928	PHI	A	P		31	18- 7
1929	PHI	A	P		35	11- 9
1930	PHI	A	P		35	9- 7
1931	BRO	N	P		39	5- 4
1932	BRO	N	P		42	3- 7
1933	CIN	N	P		14	0- 1
		BRTR		754	766	247-216

QUINN, JOSEPH C.
B.1851 CHICAGO,ILL.
D.JAN.2,1909

YR	CL	LEA	POS	GP	G	REC
1871	KEK	NA	C		4	-
1875	WES	NA	C-O		11	-
	HAR	NA	C-O		4	-
	CHI	NA	C-O		16	-
1881	BOS	N	1		1	.000
	WOR	N	C		2	.125
					38	-

QUINN, JOSEPH J.
B.DEC.25,1864 SYDNEY,AUSTRALIA
D.NOV.12,1940

YR	CL	LEA	POS	GP	G	REC
1884	STL	U	1		82	.261
1885	STL	N	1-3-O		97	.212
1886	STL	N	2-O		75	.232
1888	BOS	N	·2		38	.201
1889	BOS	N	2-S		111	.261
1890	BOS	P	2		129	.296
1891	BOS	N	2		123	.247
1892	BOS	N	2		142	.219
1893	STL	N	2		135	.241
1894	STL	N	2		106	.274
1895	STL	N	M-2		134	.309
1896	STL	N	2		48	.231
	BAL	N	2		20	.295
1897	BAL	N	S-3		71	.264
1898	BAL	N	2-3-O		11	.281
	STL	N	2		99	.250
1899	CLE	N	M-2		146	.292
1900	STL	N	2-S-3		22	.259
	CIN	N	2		72	.279
1901	WAS	A	2		66	.251
	BRTR				1727	.262

QUINN, PATRICK
B.BOSTON,MASS.
D.MAR.1893

YR	CL	LEA	POS	GP	G	REC
1873	RES	NA	C		1	-
1875	ATL	NA	3-O		2	-
1877	CHI	N	O		4	.071
					7	-

QUINN, THOMAS G.
B.APR.25,1864 ANNAPOLIS,MD.
D.JULY 24,1932

YR	CL	LEA	POS	GP	G	REC
1886	PIT	AA	C		3	.000
1889	BAL	AA	C		54	.174
1890	PIT	P	C		56	.207
					113	.181

QUINN, WELLINGTON HUNT "WIMPY"
B.MAY 12,1918 BIRMINGHAM,ALA.
D.SEPT.1,1954 SANTA MONICA,CAL.

YR	CL	LEA	POS	GP	G	REC
1941	CHI	N	P		3	0- 0
	BRTR					

QUINTANA, LUIS JOAQUIN (SANTOS)
B.DEC.25,1951 VEGA BAJA,P.R.

YR	CL	LEA	POS	GP	G	REC
1974	CAL	A	P		18	2- 1
1975	CAL	A	P		4	0- 2
	BLTL				22	2- 3

QUINTON, MARSHALL J.
B.PHILADELPHIA,PA.

YR	CL	LEA	POS	GP	G	REC
1884	RIC	AA	C-O		26	.231
1885	ATH	AA	C		7	.207
					33	.226

QUIRK, ARTHUR LINCOLN "ART"
B.APR.11,1938 PROVIDENCE,R.I.

YR	CL	LEA	POS	GP	G	REC
1962	BAL	A	P		7	2- 2
1963	WAS	A	P		7	1- 0
	BRTL				14	3- 2

QUIRK, JAMES PATRICK "JAMIE"
B.OCT.22,1954 WHITTIER,CAL.

YR	CL	LEA	POS	GP	G	REC
1975	KC	A	3-O		14	.256
1976	KC	A	1-S-3-O		64	.246
	BLTR				78	.248

RABBITT, JOSEPH PATRICK
B.JAN.16,1900 FRONTENAC,KAN.
D.DEC.5,1969 NORWALK,CONN.

YR	CL	LEA	POS	GP	G	REC
1922	CLE	A	O		2	.333
	BLTR					

RABE, CHARLES HENRY "CHARLIE"
B.MAY 6,1932 BOYCE,TEX.

YR	CL	LEA	POS	GP	G	REC
1957	CIN	N	P		2	0- 1
1958	CIN	N	P		9	0- 3
	BLTL				11	0- 4

RACHUNOK, STEPHEN STEPANOVICH
B.DEC.5,1916 RITTMAN,OHIO

YR	CL	LEA	POS	GP	G	REC
1940	BRO	N	P		2	0- 1
	BRTR					

RACKLEY, MARVIN EUGENE "MARV"
B.JULY 25,1921 SENECA,S.C.

YR	CL	LEA	POS	GP	G	REC
1947	BRO	N	O		18	.222
1948	BRO	N	O		88	.327
1949	BRO	N	O		9	.444
	PIT	N	O		11	.314
	BRO	N	O		54	.291
1950	CIN	N	H		5	.500
	BLTL				185	.317

RADATZ, RICHARD RAYMOND "DICK"
B.APR.2,1937 DETROIT,MICH.

YR	CL	LEA	POS	GP	G	REC
1962	BOS	A	P		62	9- 6
1963	BOS	A	P		66	15- 6
1964	BOS	A	P		79	16- 9
1965	BOS	A	P		63	9-11
1966	BOS	A	P		16	0- 2
	CLE	A	P		39	0- 3
1967	CLE	A	P		3	0- 0
	CHI	N	P		20	1- 0
1969	DET	A	P		11	2- 2
	MON	N	P		22	0- 4
	BRTR				381	52-43

RADBOURN, CHARLES "OLD HOSS"
B.DEC.9,1853 ROCHESTER,N.Y.
D.FEB.5,1897 BLOOMINGTON,ILL.

YR	CL	LEA	POS	GP	G	REC
1880	BUF	N	2-O		6	.143
1881	PRO	N	P-2-	37	70	25-12
			S-O			.221
1882	PRO	N	P-S-	54	83	33-19
			O			.239
1883	PRO	N	P-1-	72	89	44-23
						.283
1884	PRO	N	P-1-	72	85	60-12
			2-S-3-O			.233
1885	PRO	N	P-2-	49	65	28-21
			O			.232
1886	BOS	N	P	58	66	27-31
1887	BOS	N	P		48	24-23
1888	BOS	N	P		24	7-16
1889	BOS	N	P	32	35	20-11
1890	BOS	P	P		43	26-12
1891	CIN	N	P	25	27	12-12
	BRTR			514	641	306-192
						.241

RADBOURN, GEORGE
B.APR.8,1856 BLOOMINGTON,ILL.
D.JAN.1,1904

YR	CL	LEA	POS	GP	G	REC
1883	DET	N	P-O		3	1- 1
						.154

RADCLIFF, JOHN J.
B.1846 CAMDEN,N.J.
D.JULY 26,1911

YR	CL	LEA	POS	GP	G	REC
1871	ATH	NA	S		28	.333
1872	BAL	NA	2-S-3		54	.283
1873	BAL	NA	2-S-3-O		45	-
1874	PHI	NA	1-2-S-3-O		22	-
1875	CEN	NA	S		5	-
					154	-

RADCLIFF, RAYMOND ALLEN "RIP"
B.JAN.19,1906 KIOWA,OKLA.
D.MAY 23,1962 ENID,OKLA.

YR	CL	LEA	POS	GP	G	REC
1934	CHI	A	O		14	.268
1935	CHI	A	O		146	.286
1936	CHI	A	O		138	.335
1937	CHI	A	O		144	.325
1938	CHI	A	1-O		129	.330
1939	CHI	A	1-O		113	.264
1940	STL	A	1-O		150	.342
1941	STL	A	O		19	.282
	DET	A	O		96	.317
1942	DET	A	1-O		62	.250
1943	DET	A	1-O		70	.261
	BLTL				1081	.311

RADEBAUGH, ROY
B.FEB.22,1884 CHAMPAIGN,ILL.
D.JAN.17,1945

YR	CL	LEA	POS	GP	G	REC
1911	STL	N	P		2	0- 0
	BRTR					

RADER, DAVID MARTIN "DAVE"
B.DEC.26,1948 CLAREMORE,OKLA.

YR	CL	LEA	POS	GP	G	REC
1971	SF	N	C		3	.000
1972	SF	N	C		133	.259
1973	SF	N	C		148	.229
1974	SF	N	C		113	.291
1975	SF	N	C		98	.291
1976	SF	N	C		88	.263
	BLTR				583	.262

RADER, DONALD R.
B.SEPT.5,1894 WOLCOTT,IND.

YR	CL	LEA	POS	GP	G	REC
1913	CHI	A	3-O		4	.333
1921	PHI	N	S		9	.281
	BRTR				13	.286

RADER, DOUGLAS LEE "DOUG"
B.JULY 30,1944 CHICAGO,ILL.

YR	CL	LEA	POS	GP	G	REC
1967	HOU	N	1-3		47	.333
1968	HOU	N	1-3		98	.267
1969	HOU	N	1-3		155	.246
1970	HOU	N	1-3		156	.252
1971	HOU	N	3		135	.244
1972	HOU	N	3		152	.237
1973	HOU	N	3		154	.254
1974	HOU	N	3		152	.257
1975	HOU	N	S-3		129	.223
1976	SD	N	3		139	.257
	BRTR				1317	.251

RADER, DREW LEON
B.AUG.19,1901 ELMIRA,N.Y.
D.JUNE 5,1975

YR	CL	LEA	POS	GP	G	REC
1921	PIT	N	P		1	0- 0
	BRTL					

RADFORD, PAUL REVERE "SHORTY"
B.OCT.14,1861 ROXBURY,MASS.
D.FEB.21,1945

YR	CL	LEA	POS	GP	G	REC
1883	BOS	N	O		71	.205
1884	PRO	N	P-1-	2	96	0- 0
			S-O			.202
1885	PRO	N	P-S-	2	105	0- 1
			O			.242
1886	KC	N	S-O		122	.229
1887	MET	AA	S-O		128	.404
1888	BRO	AA	O		91	.224
1889	CLE	N	O		136	.238
1890	CLE	P	S-O		122	.292
1891	BOS	AA	S		133	.257
1892	WAS	N	S-3-O		134	.254
1893	WAS	N	O		124	.228
1894	WAS	N	2-S-O		93	.233
	BRTR			4	1355	0- 1
						.259

RADTKE, JACK WILLIAM
B.APR.14,1913 DENVER,COLO.

YR	CL	LEA	POS	GP	G	REC
1936	BRO	N	2		33	.097
	BBTR					

RAETHER, HAROLD HERMAN "HAL"
B.OCT.10,1932 LAKE MILLS,WIS.

YR	CL	LEA	POS	GP	G	REC
1954	PHI	A	P		1	0- 0
1957	KC	A	P		1	0- 0
	BRTR				2	0- 0

RAFFENSBERGER, KENNETH DAVID "KEN"
B.AUG.8,1917 YORK,PA.

YR	CL	LEA	POS	GP	G	REC
1939	STL	N	P		1	0- 0
1940	CHI	N	P		43	7- 9
1941	CHI	N	P		10	0- 1
1943	PHI	N	P		1	0- 1
1944	PHI	N	P	37	38	13-20
1945	PHI	N	P		5	0- 3
1946	PHI	N	P		39	8-15
1947	PHI	N	P		10	2- 6
	CIN	N	P		19	6- 5
1948	CIN	N	P		40	11-12
1949	CIN	N	P		41	18-17
1950	CIN	N	P		38	14-19
1951	CIN	N	P		42	16-17
1952	CIN	N	P		38	17-13
1953	CIN	N	P		26	7-14
1954	CIN	N	P		6	0- 2
	BRTL			396	397	119-154

RAFFO, ALBERT MARTIN "AL"
B.NOV.27,1941 SAN FRANCISCO,CAL.

YR	CL	LEA	POS	GP	G	REC
1969	PHI	N	P		45	1- 3
	BRTR					

YR	CL LEA POS	GP	G	REC

RAFTER, JOHN CORNELIUS
B.FEB.20,1875 LANSINGBURG,N.Y.
D.JAN.5,1943

YR	CL LEA POS	GP	G	REC
1904 PIT N C		1	.000
TR			

RAFTERY, THOMAS FRANCIS
B.OCT.5,1881 BOSTON,MASS.
D.DEC.31,1954 BOSTON,MASS.

| 1909 CLE A O | | 8 | .269 |

RAGAN, DON CARLOS PATRICK "PAT"
B.NOV.15,1888 BLANCHARD,IOWA
D.SEPT.4,1956

1909 CIN N P	2	1- 0
CHI N P	2	0- 0
1911 BRO N P	22	4- 3
1912 BRO N P	36	7-18
1913 BRO N P	44	15-18
1914 BRO N P	38	10-15
1915 BRO N P	4	1- 0
BOS N P	34	16-12
1916 BOS N P	31	9- 9
1917 BOS N P	30	6- 9
1918 BOS N P	30	8-17
1919 BOS N P	4	0- 2
NY N P	7	1- 0
CHI A P	1	0- 0
1923 PHI N P	1	0- 0
BRTR	286	77-104

PAGLAND, FRANK ROLAND
B.MAY 26,1905 PARIS,MISS.
D.JULY 28,1959

1932 WAS A P	12	1- 0
1933 PHI N P	11	0- 4
BRTR	23	1- 4

RAGLAND, THOMAS "TOM"
B.JUNE 16,1946 TALLADEGA,ALA.

1971 WAS A 2	10	.174
1972 TEX A 2-S-3	25	.172
1973 CLE A 2-S	66	.257
BRTR	101	.231

RAICH, ERIC JAMES
B.NOV.1,1951 DETROIT,MICH.

1975 CLE A P	18	7- 8
1976 CLE A P	1	0- 0
BRTR	19	7- 8

RAINES, LAWRENCE GLENN "LARRY"
B.MAR.2,1930 CINCINNATI,OHIO

1957 CLE A 2-S-3-0	96	.262
1958 CLE A 2	7	.000
BRTR	103	.253

RAINEY, JOHN PAUL
B.JULY 26,1864 BIRMINGHAM,MICH.
D.NOV.11,1912

1887 NY N 3	17	.349
1890 BUF P O	42	.248
BLTR	59	.276

RAKOW, EDWARD CHARLES "ED"
B.MAY 30,1936 PITTSBURGH,PA.

1960 LA N P	9	0- 1
1961 KC A P	45	2- 8
1962 KC A P	42	14-17
1963 KC A P	34	9-10
1964 DET A P	42	8- 9
1965 DET A P	6	0- 0
1967 ATL N P	17	3- 2
BBTR	195	36-47
BR 1960-61		

RALEIGH, JOHN AUSTIN
B.APR.21,1889 ELKHORN,WIS.
D.AUG.24,1955

1909 STL N P	15	1-10
1910 STL N P	3	0- 0
BRTL	18	1-10

RALSTON, SAMUEL BERYL "DOC"
B.AUG.3,1885 PIERPONT,OHIO

| 1910 WAS A O | 22 | .205 |
| BRTR | | |

RAMAZZOTTI, ROBERT LOUIS "BOB"
B.JAN.16,1919 ELANORA,PA.

1946 BRO N 2-3	62	.208
1948 BRO N 2	4	.000
1949 BRO N 3	5	.154
CHI N 2-S-3	65	.179
1950 CHI N 2-S-3	61	.262
1951 CHI N 2-S-3	73	.247
1952 CHI N 2	50	.284
1953 CHI N 2	26	.154
BRTR	346	.230

RAMBERT, ELMER DONALD "PEP"
B.AUG.1,1917 CLEVELAND,OHIO

1939 PIT N P	2	0- 0
1940 PIT N P	3	0- 1
BR	5	0- 1

RAMBO, WARREN DAWSON
B.NOV.1,1906 THOROUGHFARE,N.J.

| 1926 PHI N P | 1 | 0- 0 |
| BRTR | | |

RAMIREZ, MILTON (BARBOZA)
"MILT"
B.APR.2,1950 MAYAGUEZ,P.R.

1970 STL N S-3	62	.190
1971 STL N S	4	.273
BRTR	66	.200

RAMIREZ, ORLANDO (LEAL)
B.DEC.18,1951 CARTAGENA,COLOMBIA

1974 CAL A S	31	.163
1975 CAL A S	44	.240
1976 CAL A S	30	.200
BRTR	105	.203

RAMOS, JESUS MANUEL GARCIA
"CHUCHO"
B.APR.17,1919 MATURIN,VENEZ.

| 1944 CIN N O | 4 | .500 |
| BRTL | | |

RAMOS, PEDRO
B.MAR.28,1935 PINAR DEL RIO,CUBA

1955 WAS A P	45	59	5-11
1956 WAS A P	37	56	12-10
1957 WAS A P	43	56	12-16
1958 WAS A P	43	53	14-18
1959 WAS A P	37	45	13-19
1960 WAS A P	43	53	11-18
1961 MIN A P	42	53	11-20
1962 CLE A P	37	39	10-12
1963 CLE A P	36	54	9- 8
1964 CLE A P	36	44	7-10
NY A P		13	1- 0
1965 NY A P		65	5- 5
1966 NY A P		52	3- 9
1967 PHI N P		6	0- 0
1969 PIT N P		5	0- 1
CIN N P		38	4- 3
1970 WAS A P	4	5	0- 0
BBTR	582	696	117-160
BR 1955-59			

RAMSDELL, JAMES WILLARD
"WILLIE" OR "THE KNUCK"
B.APR.18,1918 WILLIAMSBURG,KAN.
D.OCT.8,1969 WICHITA,KAN.

1947 BRO N P	2	1- 1
1948 BRO N P	27	4- 4
1950 BRO N P	5	1- 2
CIN N P	27	7-12
1951 CIN N P	31	9-17
1952 CHI N P	19	2- 3
BRTR	111	24-39

RAMSEY, THOMAS A. "TOAD"
B.AUG.8,1864 INDIANAPOLIS,IND.
D.MAR.27,1906

1885 LOU AA P		9	3- 4
1886 LOU AA P		66	37-27
1887 LOU AA P		66	39-27
1888 LOU AA P	38	41	8-30
1889 LOU AA P		20	2-18
STL AA P		6	4- 2
1890 STL AA P		44	22-14
BRTL	249	252	115-122

RAMSEY, WILLIAM THRACE
B.FEB.20,1921 OSCEOLA,ARK.

| 1945 BOS N O | 78 | .292 |
| BRTR | | |

RAND, RICHARD HILTON "DICK"
B.MAR.7,1931 SOUTH GATE,CAL.

1953 STL N C	9	.290
1955 STL N C	3	.300
1957 PIT N C	60	.219
BRTP	72	.240

RANDALL, NEWTON J.
B.FEB.3,1881 NEW LOWELL,ONT.,
CANADA
D.MAY 3,1955

1907 CHI N O	21	.205
BOS N O	73	.213
	94	.211

RANDALL, ROBERT LEE "BOB"
B.JUNE 6,1948 NORTON,KAN.

| 1976 MIN A 2 | 153 | .267 |
| BRTR | | |

RANDLE, LEONARD SHENOFF "LEN"
B.FEB.12,1949 LONG BEACH,CAL.

1971 WAS A 2	75	.219
1972 TEX A 2-S-0	74	.193
1973 TEX A 2-0	10	.207
1974 TEX A 2-S-3-0	151	.302
1975 TEX A C-2-S-3-	156	.276
	O		
1976 TEX A 2-3-0	142	.224
BBTR	608	.253
BR 1971		

RANDOLPH, WILLIE LARRY
B.JULY 6,1954 HOLLY HILL,S.C.

1975 PIT N 2-3	30	.164
1976 NY A 2	125	.267
BRTR	155	.255

RANEW, MERRITT THOMAS
B.MAY 10,1938 ALBANY,GA.

1962 HOU N C	71	.234
1963 CHI N C-1	78	.338
1964 CHI N C	16	.091
MIL N C	9	.118
1965 CAL A C	41	.209
1969 SEA A C-3-0	54	.247
BLTR	269	.247

RANEY, FRANK ROBERT "RIBS"
(REAL NAME
FRANK ROBERT RANISZEWSKI)
B.FEB.16,1923 DETROIT,MICH.

1949 STL A P	3	1- 2
1950 STL A P	1	0- 1
BRTR	4	1- 3

RANISZEWSKI, FRANK ROBERT
(PLAYED UNDER NAME OF
FRANK ROBERT RANEY)

RAPP, EARL WELLINGTON
B.MAY 20,1921 CORUNNA,MICH.

1949 DET A H	1	.000
CHI A O	19	.259
1951 NY N H	13	.091
STL A O	26	.327
1952 STL A O	30	.143
WAS A O	46	.284
BLTR	135	.262

RAPP, JOSEPH ALOYSIUS "GOLDIE"
B.FEB.6,1892 CINCINNATI,OHIO

1921 NY N 3	58	.215
PHI N 3	52	.277
1922 PHI N S-3	119	.253
1923 PHI N 3	47	.263
BBTR	276	.253

RARIDEN, WILLIAM ANGEL "BILL"
B.FEB.5,1888 BEDFORD,IND.
D.AUG.28,1942

1909 BOS N C	13	.167
1910 BOS N C	49	.226
1911 BOS N C	69	.228
1912 BOS N C	79	.223
1913 BOS N C	95	.236
1914 IND F C	132	.236
1915 NEW F C	142	.278
1916 NY N C	120	.222
1917 NY N C	101	.271
1918 NY N C	69	.224
1919 CIN N C	74	.216
1920 CIN N C	39	.248
BRTR	982	.239

YR	CL	LEA	POS	GP	G	REC

RASCHI, VICTOR ANGELO JOHN "VIC"
B.MAR.28,1919 W.SPRINGFIELD, MASS.

YR	CL	LEA	POS	GP	G	REC
1946	NY	A	P	2	2- 0	
1947	NY	A	P	15	7- 2	
1948	NY	A	P	36	19- 8	
1949	NY	A	P	38	21-10	
1950	NY	A	P	33	21- 8	
1951	NY	A	P	35	21-10	
1952	NY	A	P	31	16- 6	
1953	NY	A	P	28	13- 6	
1954	STL	N	P	30	8- 9	
1955	STL	N	P	1	0- 1	
	KC	A	P	20	4- 6	
		BRTR		269	132-66	

RASMUSSEN, HAROLD RALPH "HARRY"
B.MAR.22,1952 RACINE,WIS.

YR	CL	LEA	POS	GP	G	REC
1975	STL	N	P	14	5- 5	
1976	STL	N	P	43	6-12	
		BRTR		57	11-17	

RASMUSSEN, HENRY
B.1893 CHICAGO,ILL.

YR	CL	LEA	POS	GP	G	REC
1915	CHI	F	P	2	0- 0	

RATH, FRED HELSHER
B.SEP.1,1943 LITTLE ROCK,ARK.

YR	CL	LEA	POS	GP	G	REC
1968	CHI	A	P	5	0- 0	
1969	CHI	A	P	3	0- 2	
		BPTR		8	0- 2	

RATH, MORRIS CHARLES
B.DEC.25,1886 MOBETTIE,TEX.
D.NOV.18,1945 UPPER DARBY,PA.

YR	CL	LEA	POS	GP	G	REC
1909	PHI	A	S-3	7	.269	
1910	PHI	A	3	15	.160	
	CLE	A	3	27	.191	
1912	CHI	A	2	157	.272	
1913	CHI	A	2	90	.197	
1919	CIN	N	2	138	.264	
1920	CIN	N	2-3-0	129	.267	
		BLTR		563	.254	

RATLIFF, KELLY EUGENE "GENE"
B.SEP.28,1945 MACON,GA.

YR	CL	LEA	POS	GP	G	REC
1965	HOU	N	H	4	.000	
		BRTR				

RATLIFF, PAUL HAWTHORNE
B.JAN.23,1944 SAN DIEGO,CAL.

YR	CL	LEA	POS	GP	G	REC
1963	MIN	A	C	10	.190	
1970	MIN	A	C	69	.268	
1971	MIN	A	C	21	.159	
	MIL	A	C	23	.171	
1972	MIL	A	C	22	.071	
		BLTR		145	.205	

RAU, DOUGLAS JAMES "DOUG"
B.DEC.15,1948 COLUMBUS,TEX.

YR	CL	LEA	POS	GP	G	REC
1972	LA	N	P	7	2- 2	
1973	LA	N	P	31	4- 2	
1974	LA	N	P	36	13-11	
1975	LA	N	P	38	15- 9	
1976	LA	N	P	34	16-12	
		BLTL		146	50-36	

RAUB, THOMAS JEFFERSON
B.MAY 7,1875 PATERSON,N.J.
D.FEB.16,1949

YR	CL	LEA	POS	GP	G	REC
1903	CHI	N	C	27	.226	
1906	STL	N	C	22	.282	
	TR			49	.253	

RAUCH, ROBERT JOHN "BOB"
B.JUNE 16,1949 BROOKINGS,S.D.

YR	CL	LEA	POS	GP	G	REC
1972	NY	N	P	19	0- 1	
		BRTR				

RAUDMAN, ROBERT JOYCE "BOB"
B.MAR.14,1942 ERIE,PA.

YR	CL	LEA	POS	GP	G	REC
1966	CHI	N	O	8	.241	
1967	CHI	N	O	8	.154	
		BLTL		16	.200	

RAWLINGS, JOHN WILLIAM "RED"
B.AUG.17,1892 BLOOMFIELD,IOWA
D.OCT.16,1972 INGLEWOOD,CAL.

YR	CL	LEA	POS	GP	G	REC
1914	CIN	N	3	33	.217	
	KC	F	S	61	.209	
1915	KC	F	S	120	.213	
1917	BOS	N	2-S	122	.256	
1918	BOS	N	2-S-0	111	.207	
1919	BOS	N	2-S-0	77	.255	
1920	BOS	N	2	5	.000	
	PHI	N	2	98	.234	
1921	PHI	N	2	60	.291	
1921	NY	N	2	86	.267	
1922	NY	N	2-3	88	.282	
1923	PIT	N	2	119	.284	
1924	PIT	N	H	3	.333	
1925	PIT	N	2	36	.282	
1926	PIT	N	2	61	.232	
		BRTR		1080	.249	

RAY, CARL GRADY
B.1893 GREENSBORO,N.C.
D.APR.3,1970 WALNUT COVE,N.C.

YR	CL	LEA	POS	GP	G	REC
1915	PHI	A	P	2	0- 1	
1916	PHI	A	P	3	0- 1	
		BLTL		5	0- 2	

RAY, IRVING BURTON "STUBBY"
B.JAN.22,1864 HARRINGTON,ME.
D.FEB.21,1948 HARRINGTON,ME.

YR	CL	LEA	POS	GP	G	REC
1888	BOS	N	S	50	.247	
1889	BOS	N	S	9	.312	
	BAL	AA	S	27	.330	
1890	BAL	AA	S	38	.347	
1891	BAL	AA	S-O	103	.277	
	TL			227	.290	

RAY, JAMES FRANCIS "JIM"
B.DEC.1,1944 ROCK HILL,S.C.

YR	CL	LEA	POS	GP	G	REC
1965	HOU	N	P	3	0- 2	
1966	HOU	N	P	1	0- 0	
1968	HOU	N	P	41	42	2- 3
1969	HOU	N	P	40	8- 2	
1970	HOU	N	P	52	6- 3	
1971	HOU	N	P	47	10- 4	
1972	HOU	N	P	54	10- 9	
1973	HOU	N	P	42	6- 4	
1974	DET	A	P	28	1- 3	
		BRTR		308	309	43-30

RAY, ROBERT HENRY "FARMER"
B.SEPT.17,1886 FT.LYON,COLO.
D.MAR.11,1963 ELECTRA,TEX.

YR	CL	LEA	POS	GP	G	REC
1910	STL	A	P	21	4-10	
		BLTR				

RAYDON, CURTIS LOWELL "CURT"
B.NOV.18,1933 BLOOMINGTON,ILL.

YR	CL	LEA	POS	GP	G	REC
1958	PIT	N	P	31	8- 4	
		BRTR				

RAYMER, FREDERICK CHARLES
B.NOV.12,1875 LEAVENWORTH,KAN.
D.JUNE 11,1957 LOS ANGELES,CAL.

YR	CL	LEA	POS	GP	G	REC
1901	CIN	N	S-3	118	.235	
1904	BOS	N	2	114	.210	
1905	BOS	N	2	136	.211	
	TR			368	.218	

RAYMOND, ARTHUR LAWRENCE "BUGS"
B.FEB.24,1882 CHICAGO,ILL.
D.SEPT.7,1912

YR	CL	LEA	POS	GP	G	REC
1904	DET	A	P	5	0- 1	
1907	STL	N	P	10	3- 4	
1908	STL	N	P	48	15-25	
1909	NY	N	P	39	18-12	
1910	NY	N	P	19	4-11	
1911	NY	N	P	17	6- 4	
		BRTR		138	46-57	

RAYMOND, HARRY H.
(REAL NAME HARRY H. TRUMAN)
B.FEB.20,1866 UTICA,N.Y.

YR	CL	LEA	POS	GP	G	REC
1888	LOU	AA	3	32	.208	
1889	LOU	AA	P-3	1	130	0- 0
					.241	
1890	LOU	AA	3	122	.280	
1891	LOU	AA	S	14	.207	
1892	PIT	N	3	11	.083	
	WAS	N	3	4	.067	
				1	313	0- 0
					.247	

RAYMOND, JOSEPH CLAUDE MARC "CLAUDE"
B.MAY 7,1937 ST.JEAN,QUE.,CANADA

YR	CL	LEA	POS	GP	G	REC
1959	CHI	A	P	3	0- 0	
1961	MIL	N	P	13	1- 0	
1962	MIL	N	P	26	5- 5	
1963	MIL	N	P	45	4- 6	
1964	HOU	N	P	38	41	5- 5
1965	HOU	N	P	33	34	7- 4
1966	HOU	N	P	62	7- 5	
1967	HOU	N	P	21	0- 4	
	ATL	N	P	28	4- 1	
1968	ATL	N	P	36	3- 5	
1969	ATL	N	P	33	2- 2	
	MON	N	P	15	1- 2	
1970	MON	N	P	59	6- 7	
1971	MON	N	P	37	1- 7	
		BRTR		449	453	46-53

RAYMOND, LOUIS ANTHONY
B.DEC.11,1894 BUFFALO,N.Y.

YR	CL	LEA	POS	GP	G	REC
1919	PHI	N	2	1	.500	

RAZIANO, BARRY JOHN
B.FEB.5,1947 NEW ORLEANS,LA.

YR	CL	LEA	POS	GP	G	REC
1973	KC	A	P	2	0- 0	
1974	CAL	A	P	13	1- 2	
		BBTR		15	1- 2	

REACH, ALFRED JAMES
B.MAY 25,1840 LONDON,ENGLAND
D.JAN.14,1928

YR	CL	LEA	POS	GP	G	REC
1871	ATH	NA	2	26	.371	
1872	ATH	NA	1-O	23	.191	
1873	ATH	NA	2	12	-	
1874	ATH	NA	O	14	-	
1875	ATH	NA	2-O	5	-	
	TL			80	-	

REACH, ROBERT
B.AUG.28,1843 WILLIAMSBURG,N.Y.
D.MAY 9,1922

YR	CL	LEA	POS	GP	G	REC
1872	OLY	NA	S	1	.200	
1873	NAT	NA	S	1	-	
				2	-	

REAGAN, ARTHUR "RIP"
B.1882 FT.SCOTT,KAN.

YR	CL	LEA	POS	GP	G	REC
1903	CIN	N	P	3	0- 2	
		BRTR				

REAGAN, J.

YR	CL	LEA	POS	GP	G	REC
1898	NY	N	O	2	.200	

REAMS, LEROY
B.AUG.11,1943 PINE BLUFF,ARK.

YR	CL	LEA	POS	GP	G	REC
1969	PHI	N	H	1	.000	
		BLTR				

REARDON, JAMES MATTHEW
B.1866 HOOSICK FALLS,N.Y.
D.FEB.25,1891

YR	CL	LEA	POS	GP	G	REC
1886	STL	N	P	1	0- 1	
	CIN	AA	P-O	1	0- 1	
					.000	
				2	0- 2	
					.143	

REARDON, PHILIP MICHAEL
B.OCT.3,1883 BROOKLYN,N.Y.
D.SEPT.28,1920

YR	CL	LEA	POS	GP	G	REC
1906	BRO	N	O	5	.071	
		BPTR				

REBEL, ARTHUR ANTHONY
B.MAR.4,1915 CINCINNATI,OHIO

YR	CL	LEA	POS	GP	G	REC
1938	PHI	N	O	7	.222	
1945	STL	N	O	26	.347	
		BLTL		33	.333	

REBERGER, FRANK BEALL
B.JUNE 7,1944 CALDWELL,IDAHO

YR	CL	LEA	POS	GP	G	REC
1968	CHI	N	P	3	0- 1	
1969	SD	N	P	67	1- 2	
1970	SF	N	P	45	48	7- 8
1971	SF	N	P	13	16	3- 0
1972	SF	N	P	20	22	3- 4
		BLTR		148	156	14-15

RECCIUS, J. WILLIAM "BILL"
B.1847 FRANKFURT-ON-MAIN, GERMANY
D.JAN.25,1911
NON-PLAYING MANAGER
LOU(AA) 1882-83

YR CL LEA POS GP   G   REC

RECCIUS, JOHN
B.JUNE 7,1862 LOUISVILLE,KY.
D.SEPT.1,1930
1882 LOU AA P-O 14 73   4- 6
                         .216
1883 LOU AA P-O 1 17   0- 0
                         .154
               15 90   4- 6
                         .205

RECCIUS, PHILLIP
B.JUNE 7,1862 LOUISVILLE,KY.
D.FEB.15,1903 LOUISVILLE,KY.
1882 LOU AA O   3 .091
1883 LOU AA O   1 .333
1884 LOU AA P-S- 13   75   5- 7
         3   .249
1885 LOU AA P-3 5 105   0- 5
                       .240
1886 LOU AA P-O 1   5   0- 1
                       .267
1887 LOU AA S-O   11 .341
     CLE A 3   62 .295
1888 LOU AA 3   2 .223
1890 ROC AA O   1 .000
          19 265   5-13
                   .243

REDDING, PHILIP HAYDEN
B.JAN.25,1890 CRYSTAL SPRINGS,
MISS.
D.MAR.31,1928
1912 STL N P   3 2- 1
1913 STL N P   1 0- 0
     BLTR   4 2- 1

REDER, JOHN ANTHONY
B.SEPT.24,1909 LUBLIN,POLAND
1932 BOS A 1   17 .135
     BRTR

REDFERN, GEORGE HOWARD "BUCK"
B.APR.7,1902 ASHEVILLE,N.C.
D.SEPT.8,1964 ASHEVILLE,N.C.
1928 CHI A 2-S   86 .234
1929 CHI A 2   21 .130
     BRTR   107 .218

REDFERN, PETER IRVINE "PETE"
B.AUG.25,1954 GLENDALE,CAL.
1976 MIN A P   23 8- 8
     BRTR

REDMON, GLENN VINCENT
B.JAN.11,1948 DETROIT,MICH.
1974 SF N 2   7 .235
     BRTR

REDMOND, HARRY JOHN
B.SEPT.13,1887 CLEVELAND,OHIO
D.JULY 10,1960
1909 BRO N 2   6 .100
     TR

**REDMOND, HOWARD WAYNE
"WAYNE"**
B.NOV.25,1945 ATHENS,ALA.
1965 DET A O   4 .000
1969 DET A H   5 .000
     BRTR   9 .000

**REDMOND, JACKSON MC KITTRICK
"RED"**
B.SEPT.3,1910 FLORENCE,ARIZ.
D.JULY 27,1968 GARLAND,TEX.
1935 WAS A C   22 .176
     BLTR

REDMOND, WILLIAM T.
B.ST.LOUIS,MO.
1875 RS NA S-3   19   -
1877 CIN N S   3 .250
1878 MIL N S-O   47 .229
     BLTL   69   -

REED
1874 BAL NA O   1 .000

REED, HOWARD DEAN "HOWIE"
B.DEC.21,1936 DALLAS,TEX.
1958 KC A P   3 1- 0
1959 KC A P   6 0- 3
1960 KC A P   1 0- 0
1964 LA N P   26 3- 4
1965 LA N P   38 7- 5
1966 LA N P   1 0- 0
     CAL A P   19 0- 1
1967 HOU N P   4 1- 1
1969 MON N P   31 6- 7
1970 MON N P   57 6- 5
1971 MON N P   43 2- 3
     BRTR   229 26-29

REED, JOHN BURWELL "JACK"
B.FEB.2,1933 SILVER CITY,MISS.
1961 NY A O   28 .154
1962 NY A O   88 .302
1963 NY A O   106 .205
     BRTR   222 .233

REED, MILTON D.
B.JULY 4,1890 ATLANTA,GA.
D.JULY 27,1938 ATLANTA,GA.
1911 STL N H   1 .000
1913 PHI N 2-S   13 .240
1914 PHI N S   44 .206
1915 BRO F 2   10 .290
     BLTR   68 .224

REED, RALPH EDWIN "TED"
B.OCT.18,1890 BEAVER,PA.
D.FEB.16,1959
1915 NEW F 3   20 .247
     BRTR

REED, ROBERT EDWARD "BOB"
B.JAN.12,1945 BOSTON,MASS.
1969 DET A P   8   0- 0
1970 DET A P 16 17   2- 4
     BRTR   24 25   2- 4

REED, RONALD LEE "RON"
B.NOV.2,1942 LAPORTE,IND.
1966 ATL N P   2 1- 1
1967 ATL N P   3 1- 1
1968 ATL N P   35 11-10
1969 ATL N P 36 37 18-10
1970 ATL N P 21 22 7-10
1971 ATL N P   32 13-14
1972 ATL N P   31 11-15
1973 ATL N P 20 21 4-11
1974 ATL N P   28 10-11
1975 ATL N P   10 4- 5
     STL N P   24 9- 8
1976 PHI N P   59 8- 7
     BRTR   301 304 97-102

REED, WILLIAM JOSEPH "BILL"
B.NOV.12,1922 SHAWANO,WIS.
1952 BOS N 2   15 .250
     BLTR

REEDER, JAMES EDWARD "ICICLE"
B.1865 CINCINNATI,OHIO
1884 CIN AA O   3 .143
     WAS U O   3 .167
               6 .154

**REEDER, NICHOLAS
(REAL NAME
NICHOLAS HERCHENROEDER)**
B.MAR.22,1867 LOUISVILLE,KY.
D.SEPT.26,1894
1891 LOU AA 3   1 .000
     BRTR

REEDER, WILLIAM EDGAR
B.FEB.20,1922 DIKE,TEXAS
1949 STL N P   21 1- 1
     BRTR

REES, STANLEY MILTON "NELLIE"
B.FEB.25,1899 CYNTHIANA,KY.
D.AUG.30,1937 LEXINGTON,KY.
1918 WAS A P   2 1- 0
     BLTL

REESE, ANDREW JACKSON
B.FEB.7,1904 TUPELO,MISS.
D.JAN.10,1966 TUPELO,MISS.
1927 NY N 3-O   97 .265
1928 NY N 2-O   109 .308
1929 NY N 2   58 .263
1930 NY N 3-O   67 .278
     BRTR   331 .281

REESE, HAROLD HENRY "PEEWEE"
B.JULY 23,1919 EKRON,KY.
1940 BRO N S   84 .272
1941 BRO N S   152 .228
1942 BRO N S   151 .255
1946 BRO N S   152 .284
1947 BRO N S   142 .284
1948 BRO N S   151 .274
1949 BRO N S   155 .279
1950 BRO N S-3   141 .260
1952 BRO N S   154 .286
     BRO N S   149 .272
1953 BRO N S   140 .271
1954 BRO N S   141 .309
1955 BRO N S   145 .282
1956 BRO N S-3   147 .257
1957 BRO N S   103 .224
1958 LA N S-3   59 .224
     BRTR   2166 .269

**REESE, JAMES HERMAN
(REAL NAME
JAMES HERMAN SOLOMON)**
B.OCT.1,1905 LOS ANGELES,CAL.
1930 NY A 2   77 .346
1931 NY A 2   65 .241
1932 STL N 2   90 .265
     BLTR   232 .278

REESE, RICHARD BENJAMIN "RICH"
B.SEP.29,1941 LEIPSIC,OHIO
1964 MIN A 1   10 .000
1965 MIN A 1-O   18 .296
1966 MIN A H   3 .000
1967 MIN A 1-O   95 .248
1968 MIN A 1-O   126 .259
1969 MIN A 1-O   132 .322
1970 MIN A 1   153 .261
1971 MIN A 1-O   120 .219
1972 MIN A 1-O   132 .218
1973 DET A 1-O   59 .137
     MIN A 1   22 .174
     BLTL   866 .253

REEVES, ROBERT EDWIN "GUNNER"
B.JUNE 24,1904 CHATTANOOGA,TENN
1926 WAS A 3   20 .224
1927 WAS A S-3   112 .255
1928 WAS A 2-S   102 .303
1929 BOS A 3   140 .248
1930 BOS A 2-S-3 92 .217
1931 BOS A P-2 1 36 0- 0
                      .167
     BRTR   1 502 0- 0
                      .252

**REGALADO, RUDOLPH VALENTINO
"RUDY"**
B.OCT.1,1930 LOS ANGELES,CAL.
1954 CLE A 2-3   65 .250
1955 CLE A 2-3   10 .240
1956 CLE A 1-3   16 .234
     BRTR   91 .246

REGAN, MICHAEL JOSEPH
B.NOV.19,1888 PHOENIX,N.Y.
D.MAY 23,1961
1917 CIN N P 22 33 11-10
1918 CIN N P 22 23 5- 5
1919 CIN N P   1 0- 0
     BRTR   55 57 16-15

REGAN, PHILIP RAYMOND "PHIL"
B.APR.6,1937 OTSEGO,MICH.
1960 DET A P   17 0- 4
1961 DET A P 32 33 10- 7
1962 DET A P   35 11- 9
1963 DET A P   38 15- 9
1964 DET A P 32 33 5-10
1965 DET A P   16 1- 5
1966 LA N P   65 14- 1
1967 LA N P   55 6- 9
1968 LA N P   5 2- 0
     CHI N P   68 10- 5
1969 CHI N P   71 12- 6
1970 CHI N P   54 5- 9
1971 CHI N P   48 5- 5
1972 CHI N P   5 0- 1
     CHI A P   10 0- 1
     BRTR   551 553 96-81

YR	CL	LEA	POS	GP	G	REC

REGAN, WILLIAM WRIGHT
B.JAN.23,1899 PITTSBURGH,PA.
D.JUNE 11,1968 PITTSBURGH,PA.

1926	BOS	A	2		108	.263
1927	BOS	A	2		129	.274
1928	BOS	A	2		138	.264
1929	BOS	A	2-3		104	.288
1930	BOS	A	2		134	.266
1931	PIT	N	2		28	.202
		BRTR			641	.267

REGO, ANTONE "TONY"
(REAL NAME ANTONE DO REGO)
B.OCT.31,1897 WAILUKU,HAWAII

1924	STL	A	C		24	.220
1925	STL	A	C		20	.406
		BRTR			44	.286

REHG, WALTER PHILLIP
B.AUG.31,1888 SUMMERFIELD,ILL.
D.APR.5,1946

1912	PIT	N	O		7	.000
1913	BOS	A	O		30	.277
1914	BOS	A	O		84	.218
1915	BOS	A	O		5	.200
1917	BOS	N	O		87	.270
1918	BOS	N	O		40	.241
1919	CIN	N	O		5	.167
		BRTR			258	.251

REIBER, FRANK BERNARD
B.SEPT.19,1909 HUNTINGTON,W.VA.

1933	DET	A	C		13	.278
1934	DET	A	H		3	.000
1935	DET	A	C		8	.273
1936	DET	A	C		20	.273
		BRTR			44	.271

REICH, HERMAN CHARLES
B.NOV.23,1918 LOS ANGELES,CAL.

1949	WAS	A	H		2	.000
	CLE	A	O		1	.500
	CHI	N	1-O		108	.280
		BRTL			111	.279

REICHARDT, FREDERIC CARL "RICK"
B.MAR.16,1943 MADISON,WIS.

1964	LA	A	O		11	.162
1965	CAL	A	O		20	.267
1966	CAL	A	O		89	.288
1967	CAL	A	O		146	.265
1968	CAL	A	O		151	.255
1969	CAL	A	1-O		137	.254
1970	CAL	A	O		9	.167
	WAS	A	3-O		107	.253
1971	CHI	A	1-O		138	.278
1972	CHI	A	O		101	.251
1973	CHI	A	O		46	.275
	KC	A	0-O		41	.220
1974	KC	A	H		1	1.000
		BRTR			997	.261

REICHLE, RICHARD WENDELL
B.NOV.23,1897 LINCOLN,ILL.
D.JUNE 13,1967 ST.LOUIS,MO.

1922	BOS	A	O		6	.250
1923	BOS	A	O		122	.258
		BLTR			128	.257

REID, EARL PERCY
B.JUNE 8,1915 HOLLY POND,ALA.

1946	BOS	N	P		2	1- 0
		BLTR				

REID, SCOTT DONALD
B.JAN.7,1947 CHICAGO,ILL.

1969	PHI	N	O		13	.211
1970	PHI	N	O		25	.122
		BLTR			38	.147

REID, WILLIAM ALEXANDER "SANDY"
B.MAY 17,1857 LONDON,ONT.,CAN.
D.JUNE 26,1940 LONDON,ONT.,CAN.

1883	BAL	AA	2-S		16·	.285
1884	PIT	AA	O		19	.246
					35	.269

REIDY, WILLIAM JOSEPH
B.OCT.9,1873 CLEVELAND,OHIO
D.OCT.14,1915

1896	NY	N	P		2	0- 1
1899	BRO	N	P		2	0- 0
1901	MIL	A	P		36	15-18
1902	STL	A	P-O	11	13	3- 5
						.195
1903	STL	A	P		6	1- 5
	BRO	N	P		15	6- 7
1904	BRO	N	P-2	6	11	0- 4
						.196
		TR		78	85	25-40
						.150

REILLEY, ALEXANDER ALOYSIUS "DUKE"
B.AUG.25,1884 CHICAGO,ILL.
D.MAR.4,1968 INDIANAPOLIS,IND.

1909	CLE	A	O		20	.210
		BRTR				

REILLEY, CHARLES E.
B.1856 MASSACHUSETTS
D.1888

1879	TRO	N	C-1		61	.232
1880	CIN	N	C-3-O		29	.204
1881	DET	N	C-1-S-3-		18	.179
			O			
1881	WOR	N	C		2	.375
1882	PRO	N	C		3	.182
		TR			113	.214

REILLY, ARCHER E.
B.FEB.18,1893 HUNTINGTON,W.VA.
D.NOV.29,1963 COLUMBUS,OHIO

1917	PIT	N	3		1	.000
		BRTR				

REILLY, BERNARD EUGENE "BARNEY"
B.FEB.7,1884 BROCKTON,MASS.
D.NOV.15,1934

1909	CHI	A	2		12	.120
		BRTR				

REILLY, CHARLES "JOSH"
B.1868 SAN FRANCISCO,CAL.
D.JUNE 13,1938

1896	CHI	N	2		9	.205

REILLY, CHARLES THOMAS "PRINCETON"
B.JUNE 24,1855 PRINCETON,N.J.
D.DEC.16,1937

1889	COL	AA	3		6	.478
1890	COL	AA	3		137	.270
1891	PIT	N	3		110	.211
1892	PHI	N	3		81	.201
1893	PHI	N	3		104	.252
1894	PHI	N	3		36	.272
1895	PHI	N	S		44	.267
1897	WAS	N	3		101	.275
		BBTR			619	.250

REILLY, HAROLD J.
B.

1919	CHI	N	O		1	.000

REILLY, JOHN GOOD "LONG JOHN"
B.OCT.5,1858 TUSCULM,OHIO
D.MAY 31,1937

1880	CIN	N	1-O		72	.195
1883	CIN	AA	1		97	.289
1884	CIN	AA	1-S-O		106	.339
1885	CIN	AA	1-O		106	.308
1886	CIN	AA	1-O		115	.270
1887	CIN	AA	1-O		134	.334
1888	CIN	AA	1-O		126	.324
1889	CIN	AA	1-O		111	.261
1890	CIN	N	1		133	.300
1891	CIN	N	1-O		133	.200
		BRTR			1133	.284

REILLY, JOSEPH J.
B.NEW YORK,N.Y.

1884	BOS	U	3-O		3	.000
1885	MET	AA	2-3		10	.122
					13	.096

REILLY, THOMAS HENRY
B.AUG.3,1884 ST.LOUIS,MO.
D.OCT.19,1918 NEW ORLEANS,LA.

1908	STL	N	S		29	.173
1909	STL	N	S		4	.167
1914	CLE	A	H		1	.000
		BPTR			34	.170

REINBACH, MICHAEL WAYNE "MIKE"
B.AUG.6,1949 SAN DIEGO,CAL.

1974	BAL	A	O		12	.250
		BLTR				

REINHART, ARTHUR CONRAD
B.MAY 29,1899 ACKLEY,IOWA
D.NOV.11,1946

1919	STL	N	P		1	0- 0
1925	STL	N	P	20	28	11- 5
1926	STL	N	P	27	40	10- 5
1927	STL	N	P	21	27	5- 2
1928	STL	N	P	23	27	4- 6
		BLTL		92	123	30-18

REINHOLZ, ARTHUR AUGUST
B.JAN.27,1903 DETROIT,MICH.

1928	CLE	A	3		2	.333
		BRTR				

REINICKER, WALTER
(REAL NAME WALTER SMITH)

1915	BAL	F	3		3	.125
		TR				

REIPSCHLAGER, CHRISTOPHER FREDERICK "RIP"
B.JUNE 11,1862 NEW YORK,N.Y.
D.SEPT.19,1910

1883	MET	AA	C-O		35	.189
1884	MET	AA	C		59	.236
1885	MET	AA	C		72	.234
1886	MET	AA	C		66	.221
1887	CLE	AA	C		63	.248
		BRTR			295	.229

REIS, HARRIE CRANE "JACK"
B.JUNE 14,1890 CINCINNATI,OHIO
D.JULY 20,1939

1911	STL	N	P		3	0- 0
		BRTR				

REIS, LAWRENCE P.

1877	CHI	N	P		4	3- 1
1878	CHI	N	P-O	4	5	1- 3
						.150
		BRTR		8	9	4- 4
						.140

REIS, ROBERT JOSEPH THOMAS
B.JAN.2,1909 WOODSIDE,N.Y.
D.MAY 1,1973 ST.PAUL,MINN.

1931	BRO	N	2-3		6	.294
1932	BRO	N	3		1	.250
1935	BRO	N	P-1-	14	52	3- 2
			2-3-O			.247
1936	BOS	N	P	35	37	6- 5
1937	BOS	N	P-O	4	45	0- 0
						.244
1938	BOS	N	P-O	16	34	1- 6
						.184
		BRTR		69	175	10-13
						.233

REIS, THOMAS EDWARD
B.AUG.6,1915 NEWPORT,KY.

1938	PHI	N	P		4	0- 1
	BOS	N	P		4	0- 0
		BRTR			8	0- 1

REISER, HAROLD PATRICK "PETE"
B.MAR.17,1919 ST.LOUIS,MO.

1940	BRO	N	S-3-O		58	.293
1941	BRO	N	O		137	.343
1942	BRO	N	O		125	.310
1946	BRO	N	3-O		122	.277
1947	BRO	N	O		110	.309
1948	BRO	N	O		64	.236
1949	BOS	N	3-O		84	.272
1950	BOS	N	3-O		53	.205
1951	PIT	N	3-O		74	.271
1952	CLE	A	O		34	.136
		BLTR			861	.295

REISGL, JACOB "BUGS"
B.DEC.12,1887 BROOKLYN,N.Y.
D.FEB.24,1957 AMSTERDAM,N.Y.

1911	CLE	A	P		2	0- 1
		BRTR				

REISING, CHARLES

1884	IND	AA	O		1	.000

REISLING, FRANK CARL "DOC"
B.JULY 25,1874 MARTINS FERRY,O.
D.MAR.4,1955 TULSA,OKLA.

YR	CL	LEA	POS	GP	G	REC
1904	BRO	N	P		7	3- 3
1905	BRO	N	P		2	0- 0
1909	WAS	A	P	10	12	2- 4
1910	WAS	A	P	30	31	9-10
	BRTR			49	52	14-17

REISS, ALBERT ALLEN
B.JAN.8,1909 ELIZABETH,N.J.

YR	CL	LEA	POS	GP	G	REC
1932	PHI	A	S		9	.200
	BBTR					

REITZ, HENRY P. "HEINE"
B.JUNE 29,1867 CHICAGO,ILL.
D.NOV.10,1914

YR	CL	LEA	POS	GP	G	REC
1893	BAL	N	2		130	.297
1894	BAL	N	2		109	.306
1895	BAL	N	2-3		63	.281
1896	BAL	N	2		119	.283
1897	BAL	N	2		127	.289
1898	WAS	N	2		132	.302
1899	PIT	N	2		35	.263
	TR				715	.293

REITZ, KENNETH JOHN "KEN"
B.JUNE 24,1951 SAN FRANCISCO,CAL

YR	CL	LEA	POS	GP	G	REC
1972	STL	N	3		21	.359
1973	STL	N	S-3		147	.235
1974	STL	N	2-S-3		154	.271
1975	STL	N	3		161	.269
1976	SF	N	S-3		155	.267
	BRTR				638	.266

REMENTER, WILLIS J. "BUTCH"
B.PHILADELPHIA,PA.

YR	CL	LEA	POS	GP	G	REC
1904	PHI	N	C		1	.000
	TR					

REMNEAS, ALEXANDER NORMAN
B.FEB.21,1886
D.AUG.27,1975 PHOENIX,ARIZ.

YR	CL	LEA	POS	GP	G	REC
1912	DET	A	P		1	0- 0
1915	STL	A	P		2	0- 0
	BRTR				3	0- 0

REMSEN, JOHN RAY
B.1851 BROOKLYN,N.Y.

YR	CL	LEA	POS	GP	G	REC
1872	ATL	NA	O		35	.205
1873	ATL	NA	O		51	-
1874	MUT	NA	O		64	-
1875	HAR	NA	O		85	-
1876	HAR	N	O		69	.274
1877	STL	N	O		33	.260
1878	CHI	N	O		55	.233
1879	CHI	N	1-O		39	.248
1881	CLE	N	O		48	.174
1884	BRO	AA	O		10	.222
	BRO	AA	O		81	.238
	BR				570	-

REMY, GERALD PETER "JERRY"
B.NOV.8,1952 FALL RIVER,MASS.

YR	CL	LEA	POS	GP	G	REC
1975	CAL	A	2		147	.258
1976	CAL	A	2		143	.263
	BLTR				290	.261

RENFER, ERWIN ARTHUR
B.DEC.11,1895 ELGIN,ILL.
D.OCT.26,1958

YR	CL	LEA	POS	GP	G	REC
1913	DET	A	P		1	0- 1
	BRTR					

RENFROE, MARSHALL DANIEL
B.MAY 25,1936 CENTURY,FLA.

YR	CL	LEA	POS	GP	G	REC
1959	SF	N	P		1	0- 0
	BLTL					

RENICK, WARREN RICHARD "RICK"
B.MAR.16,1944 LONDON,OHIO

YR	CL	LEA	POS	GP	G	REC
1968	MIN	A	S		42	.216
1969	MIN	A	S-3-O		71	.245
1970	MIN	A	S-3-O		81	.229
1971	MIN	A	3-O		27	.222
1972	MIN	A	1-S-3-O		55	.172
	BRTR				276	.221

RENIFF, HAROLD EUGENE "HAL"
B.JULY 2,1938 WARREN,OHIO

YR	CL	LEA	POS	GP	G	REC
1961	NY	A	P		25	2- 0
1962	NY	A	P		2	0- 0
1963	NY	A	P		48	4- 3
1964	NY	A	P	41	44	5- 4
1965	NY	A	P		51	3- 4
1966	NY	A	P		56	3- 7
1967	NY	A	P		24	0- 2
	NY	N	P		29	3- 3
	BRTR			276	279	21-23

RENINGER, JAMES DAVID
B.MAR.7,1916 AURORA,ILL.

YR	CL	LEA	POS	GP	G	REC
1938	PHI	A	P		4	0- 2
1939	PHI	A	P		4	0- 2
	BRTR				8	0- 4

RENKO, STEVEN "STEVE"
B.DEC.10,1944 KANSAS CITY,KAN.

YR	CL	LEA	POS	GP	G	REC
1969	MON	N	P		18	6- 7
1970	MON	N	P		41	13-11
1971	MON	N	P	40	41	15-14
1972	MON	N	P-1	30	32	1-10
						.292
1973	MON	N	P	36	41	15-11
1974	MON	N	P		37	12-16
1975	MON	N	P	31	33	6-12
1976	MON	N	P		5	0- 1
	CHI	N	P	28	29	8-11
	BRTR			266	277	76-93
						.216

RENNA, WILLIAM DENEDITTO "BILL"
B.OCT.14,1924 HANFORD,CAL.

YR	CL	LEA	POS	GP	G	REC
1953	NY	A	O		61	.314
1954	PHI	A	O		123	.232
1955	KC	A	O		100	.213
1956	KC	A	O		33	.271
1958	DDS	A	O		39	.268
1959	BOS	A	O		14	.091
	BRTR				370	.239

RENSA, GEORGE ANTHONY "PUG"
B.SEPT.29,1901 PARSONS,PA.

YR	CL	LEA	POS	GP	G	REC
1930	DET	A	C		20	.270
	PHI	N	C		54	.285
1931	PHI	N	C		19	.103
1933	NY	A	C		8	.310
1937	CHI	A	C		26	.298
1938	CHI	A	C		59	.248
1939	CHI	A	C		14	.200
	BPTR				200	.261

REPASS, ROBERT WILLIS
B.NOV.6,1917 W.PITTSTON,PA.

YR	CL	LEA	POS	GP	G	REC
1939	STL	N	2		3	.333
1942	WAS	A	2-S-3		81	.239
	BRTR				84	.242

REPOZ, ROGER ALLEN
B.AUG.3,1940 BELLINGHAM,WASH.

YR	CL	LEA	POS	GP	G	REC
1964	NY	A	O		11	.000
1965	NY	A	O		79	.220
1966	NY	A	O		37	.349
	KC	A	1-O		101	.216
1967	KC	A	O		40	.241
	CAL	A	O		74	.250
1968	CAL	A	O		133	.240
1969	CAL	A	1-O		103	.164
1970	CAL	A	1-O		137	.238
1971	CAL	A	1-O		113	.199
1972	CAL	A	H		3	.333
	BLTL				831	.224

REPULSKI, ELDON JOHN "RIP"
B.OCT.4,1927 SAUK RAPIDS,MINN.

YR	CL	LEA	POS	GP	G	REC
1953	STL	N	O		153	.275
1954	STL	N	O		152	.283
1955	STL	N	O		147	.270
1956	STL	N	O		112	.277
1957	PHI	N	O		134	.260
1958	PHI	N	O		85	.244
1959	LA	N	O		53	.255
1960	LA	N	O		4	.200
	BOS	A	O		73	.243
1961	BOS	A	O		15	.284
	BRTR				928	.269

RESCIGNO, XAVIER FREDERICK "MR. X."
B.OCT.13,1913 NEW YORK,N.Y.

YR	CL	LEA	POS	GP	G	REC
1943	PIT	N	P		37	6- 9
1944	PIT	N	P		48	10- 8
1945	PIT	N	P		44	3- 5
	BRTR				129	19-22

RESSLER, LAWRENCE P.

YR	CL	LEA	POS	GP	G	REC
1875	NAT	NA	2-O		25	-

RESTELLI, DINO PAUL "DINGO"
B.SEPT.23,1924 ST.LOUIS,MO.

YR	CL	LEA	POS	GP	G	REC
1949	PIT	N	1-O		72	.250
1951	PIT	N	O		21	.184
	BRTR				93	.241

RETTENMUND, MERVIN WELDON "MERV"
B.JUNE 6,1943 FLINT,MICH.

YR	CL	LEA	POS	GP	G	REC
1968	BAL	A	O		31	.297
1969	BAL	A	O		95	.247
1970	BAL	A	O		106	.322
1971	BAL	A	O		141	.318
1972	BAL	A	O		102	.233
1973	BAL	A	O		95	.262
1974	CIN	N	O		80	.216
1975	CIN	N	3-O		93	.239
1976	SD	N	O		86	.229
	BRTR				829	.271

RETTGER, GEORGE EDWARD
B.JULY 29,1868 CLEVELAND,OHIO
D.JUNE 5,1921

YR	CL	LEA	POS	GP	G	REC
1891	STL	AA	P		15	10- 3
1892	CLE	N	P		6	1- 4
	CIN	N	P-O	1	2	1- 0
						.125
	TR			22	23	12- 7
						.092

RETTIG, ADOLPH JOHN "OTTO"
B.JAN.29,1894 NEW YORK,N.Y.

YR	CL	LEA	POS	GP	G	REC
1922	PHI	A	P		4	1- 2
	BRTR					

RETZER, KENNETH LEO "KEN"
B.APR.30,1934 WOOD RIVER,ILL.

YR	CL	LEA	POS	GP	G	REC
1961	WAS	A	C		16	.340
1962	WAS	A	C		109	.285
1963	WAS	A	C		95	.242
1964	WAS	A	C		17	.094
	BLTR				237	.264

REULBACH, EDWARD MARVIN "BIG ED"
B.DEC.1,1882 DETROIT,MICH.
D.JULY 17,1961

YR	CL	LEA	POS	GP	G	REC
1905	CHI	N	P		34	17-13
1906	CHI	N	P	33	34	19- 4
1907	CHI	N	P		27	17- 4
1908	CHI	N	P		46	24- 7
1909	CHI	N	P		35	19-10
1910	CHI	N	P		24	12- 8
1911	CHI	N	P		33	16- 9
1912	CHI	N	P		39	10- 6
1913	CHI	N	P		9	1- 3
	BRO	N	P		16	7- 6
1914	BRO	N	P		44	11-18
1915	NEW	F	P		33	21-10
1916	BOS	N	P		21	7- 6
1917	BOS	N	P		5	0- 1
	BRTR			399	400	181-105

REUSCHEL, PAUL RICHARD
B.JAN.12,1947 QUINCY,ILL.

YR	CL	LEA	POS	GP	G	REC
1975	CHI	N	P		28	1- 3
1976	CHI	N	P		50	4- 2
	BRTR				78	5- 5

REUSCHEL, RICKEY EUGENE "RICK"
B.MAY 16,1949 QUINCY,ILL.

YR	CL	LEA	POS	GP	G	REC
1972	CHI	N	P		21	10- 8
1973	CHI	N	P		36	14-15
1974	CHI	N	P		41	13-12
1975	CHI	N	P		38	11-17
1976	CHI	N	P		38	14-12
	BRTR				174	62-64

REUSS, JERRY
B.JUNE 19,1949 ST.LOUIS,MO.

YR	CL	LEA	POS	GP	G	REC
1969	STL	N	P		1	1- 0
1970	STL	N	P		20	7- 8
1971	STL	N	P		36	14-14
1972	HOU	N	P		33	9-13
1973	HOU	N	P	41	42	16-13
1974	PIT	N	P		35	16-11
1975	PIT	N	P		32	18-11
1976	PIT	N	P		31	14- 9
	BLTL			229	230	95-79

REVELS

YR	CL	LEA	POS	GP	G	REC
1874	BAL	NA	O		1	.000

YR	CL LEA POS	GP	G	REC

REXTER
| 1875 ATL NA O | | 1 | .000 |

REYES, NAPOLEON AGUILERA
B.NOV.24,1919 ORIENTE PROVINCE CUBA

1943 NY N 1-3		40	.256
1944 NY N 1-3-O		116	.289
1945 NY N 1-3		122	.288
1950 NY N 1		1	.000
BRTR		279	.284

PEYNOLDS, ALLIE PIERCE
B.FEB.10,1915 BETHANY,OKLA.

1942 CLE A P		2	0- 0
1943 CLE A P	34	39	11-12
1944 CLE A P	28	41	11- 8
1945 CLE A P		44	18-12
1946 CLE A P	31	35	11-15
1947 NY A P	34	38	19- 8
1948 NY A P	39	41	16- 7
1949 NY A P	35	37	17- 6
1950 NY A P	35	36	16-12
1951 NY A P	40	43	17- 8
1952 NY A P	35	41	20- 8
1953 NY A P	41	42	13- 7
1954 NY A P		36	13- 4
BRTR	434	475	182-107

REYNOLDS, ARCHIE EDWARD
B.JAN.3,1946 GLENDALE,CAL.

1968 CHI N P		7	0- 1
1969 CHI N P		2	0- 1
1970 CHI N P		7	0- 2
1971 CAL A P		15	0- 3
1972 MIL A P		5	0- 1
BRTR		36	0- 8

REYNOLDS, CARL NETTLES
B.FEB.1,1903 LA RUE,TEX.

1927 CHI A O		14	.214
1928 CHI A O		84	.323
1929 CHI A O		131	.317
1930 CHI A O		138	.359
1931 CHI A O		118	.290
1932 WAS A O		102	.305
1933 STL A O		135	.286
1934 BOS A O		113	.303
1935 BOS A O		78	.270
1936 WAS A O		89	.276
1937 CHI N O		7	.273
1938 CHI N O		125	.302
1939 CHI N O		88	.246
BRTR		1222	.302

REYNOLDS, CHARLES E.
B.JULY 31,1857 ALLEGANY,N.Y.
D.MAY 1,1913

| 1882 ATH AA P-O | | 2 | 1- 1 |
| | | | .125 |

REYNOLDS, CHARLES L.
B.MAY 1,1865 WILLIAMSBURGH,IND.

1889 KC AA C		1	.250
BRO AA C		11	.222
		12	.225

REYNOLDS, DANIEL VANCE "SQUIRREL"
B.NOV.27,1919 STONY POINT,N.C.

| 1945 CHI A 2-S | | 29 | .167 |
| BRTR | | | |

REYNOLDS, E. ROSS
B.AUG.20,1889 EDWARDS CO.,TEX.

1914 DET A P		26/	5- 3
1915 DET A P		4	0- 1
BRTR		30	5- 4

REYNOLDS, GORDON CRAIG "CRAIG"
B.DEC.27,1952 HOUSTON,TEX.

1975 PIT N S		31	.224
1976 PIT N 2-S		7	.250
BLTR		38	.225

REYNOLDS, KENNETH LEE "KEN"
B.JAN.4,1947 TREVOSE,PA.

1970 PHI N P		4	0- 0
1971 PHI N P	35	36	5- 9
1972 PHI N P	33	48	2-15
1973 MIL A P		2	0- 1
1975 STL N P		10	0- 1
1976 SD N P		19	0- 3
BLTL	103	119	7-29

REYNOLDS, ROBERT ALLEN "BOB"
B.JAN.21,1947 SEATTLE,WASH.

1969 MON N P		1	0- 0
1971 STL N P		4	0- 0
MIL A P		3	0- 1
1972 BAL A P		3	0- 0
1973 BAL A P		42	7- 5
1974 BAL A P		54	7- 5
1975 BAL A P		7	0- 1
DET A P		21	0- 2
CLE A P		5	0- 2
BRTR		140	14-16

REYNOLDS, TOMMIE D.
B.AUG.15,1941 ARIZONA,LA.

1963 KC A O		8	.053
1964 KC A 3-O		31	.202
1965 KC A 3-O		90	.237
1967 NY N C-3-O		101	.206
1969 OAK A O		107	.257
1970 CAL A 3-O		59	.250
1971 CAL A 3-O		45	.186
1972 MIL A 1-3-O		72	.200
BBTR		513	.226
BB 1967 (PART)			

REYNOLDS, WILLIAM DEE
B.AUG.14,1884 EASTLAND,TEX.
D.JUNE 5,1924 CARNEGIE,OKLA.

1913 NY A C		5	.000
1914 NY A C		4	.400
BRTR		9	.200

RHAWN, ROBERT JOHN "ROCKY"
B.FEB.13,1919 CATAWISSA,PA.

1947 NY N 2-3		13	.311
1948 NY N S-3		36	.273
1949 NY N 2		14	.172
PIT N 3		3	.143
CHI A S-3		24	.205
BRTR		90	.237

RHEAM, KENNETH JOHNSTON "CY"
B.SEPT.28,1893 PITTSBURGH,PA.
D.OCT.23,1947

1914 PIT F 1		72	.209
1915 PIT F O		27	.174
BRTR		99	.201

RHEM, CHARLES FLINT "FLINT"
B.JAN.24,1901 RHEMS,S.C.
D.JULY 30,1969 COLUMBIA,S.C.

1924 STL N P		6	2- 2
1925 STL N P		30	8-13
1926 STL N P		34	20- 7
1927 STL N P		27	10-12
1928 STL N P		28	11- 8
1930 STL N P		26	12- 8
1931 STL N P		33	11-10
1932 STL N P		6	4- 2
PHI N P		26	11- 7
1933 PHI N P		28	5-14
1934 STL N P		5	1- 0
BOS N P		25	8- 8
1935 BOS N P		10	0- 5
1936 STL N P		10	2- 1
BRTR		294	105-97

RHIEL, WILLIAM JOSEPH
B.SEPT.30,1901 YOUNGSTOWN,OHIO
D.AUG.16,1946

1929 BRO N 2		76	.278
1930 BOS N 3		20	.170
1932 DET A 1-3		85	.280
1933 DET A O		19	.176
BRTR		200	.266

RHINES, WILLIAM PEARL "BUNKER"
B.MAR.14,1869 RIDGWAY,PA.
D.JAN.30,1922

1890 CIN N P		45	28-17
1891 CIN N P		43	16-27
1892 CIN N P		12	3- 4
1893 LOU N P		5	1- 3
1895 CIN N P		32	20-12
1896 CIN N P		17	10- 7
1897 CIN N P		36	19-15
1898 PIT N P		31	12-15
1899 PIT N P		10	4- 3
		231	113-103

RHOADES, ROBERT BRUCE "DUSTY"
B.OCT.4,1879 WOOSTER,OHIO
D.FEB.12,1967 SAN BERNARDINO, CAL.

1902 CHI N P		16	4- 7
1903 STL N P	17	18	5- 8
CLE A P		5	2- 3
1904 CLE A P	22	29	11- 9
1905 CLE A P	29	33	17-12
1906 CLE A P		38	22-10
1907 CLE A P		35	15-14
1908 CLE A P		37	18-12
1909 CLE A P		20	5- 9
TR	219	231	99-84

RHODEN, RICHARD ALAN "RICK"
B.MAY 16,1953 BOYNTON BEACH,FLA.

1974 LA N P		4	1- 0
1975 LA N P		26	3- 3
1976 LA N P		27	12- 3
BRTR		57	16- 6

RHODES, CHARLES ANDERSON "DUSTY"
B.APR.7,1885 CANEY,KAN.
D.OCT.26,1918 CANEY,KAN.

1906 STL N P		9	4- 5
1908 CIN N P		1	0- 0
STL N P		4	1- 2
1909 STL N P		12	3- 5
BRTR		26	8-12

RHODES, JAMES LAMAR "DUSTY"
B.MAY 13,1927 MATHEWS,ALA.

1952 NY N O		67	.250
1953 NY N O		76	.233
1954 NY N O		82	.341
1955 NY N O		94	.305
1956 NY N O		111	.217
1957 NY N O		92	.205
1959 SF N H		54	.188
BLTR		576	.253

RHODES, JOHN GORDON "DUSTY"
B.AUG.11,1907 SALT LAKE CITY, UTAH
D.MAR.22,1960

1929 NY A P		10	0- 4
1930 NY A P		3	0- 0
1931 NY A P		18	6- 3
1932 NY A P		10	1- 2
BOS A P		12	1- 8
1933 BOS A P	34	35	12-15
1934 BOS A P		44	12-12
1935 BOS A P	34	36	2-10
1936 PHI A P		35	9-20
BRTR	200	203	43-74

RHODES, WILLIAM CLARENCE
B.POTTSTOWN,PA.

| 1893 LOU N P | | 17 | 5-12 |

RHYNE, HAROLD
B.MAR.30,1899 SAN JOSE,CAL.
D.JAN.7,1971 ORANGEVILLE,CAL.

1926 PIT N 2-S		109	.251
1927 PIT N 2-3		62	.274
1929 BOS A S		120	.252
1930 BOS A S		107	.203
1931 BOS A S		147	.273
1932 BOS A S		71	.227
1933 CHI A 2-S-3		39	.265
BRTR		655	.250

RIBANT, DENNIS JOSEPH
B.SEP.20,1941 DETROIT,MICH.

1964 NY N P	14	17	1- 5
1965 NY N P		19	1- 3
1966 NY N P	39	40	11- 9
1967 PIT N P	38	47	9- 8
1968 DET A P	14	16	2- 2
CHI A P		17	0- 2
1969 STL N P	1	2	0- 0
CIN N P		7	0- 0
BRTR	149	165	24-29

RICCELLI, FRANK JOSEPH
B.FEB.24,1953 SYRACUSE,N.Y.

| 1976 SF N P | | 4 | 1- 1 |
| BLTL | | | |

```
YR   CL LEA POS  GP     G   REC
```

RICE, DELBERT W. "DEL"
B.OCT.27,1922 PORTSMOUTH,OHIO
```
1945 STL N C         83  .261
1946 STL N C         55  .273
1947 STL N C         97  .218
1948 STL N C        100  .197
1949 STL N C         92  .236
1950 STL N C        130  .244
1951 STL N C        122  .251
1952 STL N C        147  .259
1953 STL N C        135  .236
1954 STL N C         56  .252
1955 STL N C         20  .203
     MIL N C         27  .197
1956 MIL N C         71  .213
1957 MIL N C         54  .229
1958 MIL N C         43  .223
1959 MIL N C         13  .207
1960 CHI N C         18  .231
     STL N C          1  .000
     BAL A C          1  .000
1961 LA  A C         44  .241
     BRTR          1309  .237
```
NON-PLAYING MANAGER CAL(A) 1972

RICE, EDGAR CHARLES "SAM"
B.FEB.20,1892 MOROCCO,IND.
D.OCT.13,1974 ROSSMOR,MD.
```
1915 WAS A P          4   1- 0
1916 WAS A P-O   5   58   0- 1
                         .299
1917 WAS A O        155  .302
1918 WAS A O          7  .348
1919 WAS A O        141  .321
1920 WAS A O        153  .338
1921 WAS A O        143  .330
1922 WAS A O        154  .295
1923 WAS A O        148  .316
1924 WAS A O        154  .334
1925 WAS A O        152  .350
1926 WAS A O        152  .337
1927 WAS A O        142  .297
1928 WAS A O        148  .328
1929 WAS A O        150  .323
1930 WAS A O        147  .349
1931 WAS A O        120  .310
1932 WAS A O        106  .323
1933 WAS A O         73  .294
1934 CLE A O         97  .293
     BLTR     9   2404   1- 1
                         .322
```

RICE, HAROLD HOUSTEN "HOOT"
B.FEB.11,1924 MORGANETTE,W.VA.
```
1948 STL N O          8  .323
1949 STL N O         40  .196
1950 STL N O         44  .211
1951 STL N O         69  .254
1952 STL N O         98  .288
1953 STL N H          8  .250
     PIT N O         78  .311
1954 PIT N O         28  .173
     CHI N O         51  .153
     BLTR           424  .260
```

RICE, HARRY FRANCIS
B.NOV.22,1900 ANNA,ILL.
D.JAN.1,1971 PORTLAND,ORE.
```
1923 STL A H          4  .000
1924 STL A 3         44  .279
1925 STL A C-1-2-3- 103  .359
           O
1926 STL A O        148  .313
1927 STL A O        137  .287
1928 DET A O        131  .302
1929 DET A O        130  .304
1930 DET A O         37  .305
     NY  A O        100  .298
1931 WAS A O         47  .265
1933 CIN N 3-O      143  .261
     BLTR          1024  .299
```

RICE, JAMES EDWARD "JIM"
B.MAR.8,1953 ANDERSON,S.C.
```
1974 BOS A O-D       24  .269
1975 BOS A O-D      144  .309
1976 BOS A O-D      153  .282
     BRTR           321  .294
```

RICE, LEONARD OLIVER
B.SEPT.2,1918 LEAD,S.DAK.
```
1944 CIN N O         10  .000
1945 CHI N C         32  .232
     BRTR            42  .223
```

RICE, ROBERT TURNBULL
B.MAY 28,1900 PHILADELPHIA,PA.
```
1926 PHI N 3         19  .148
     BRTR
```

RICH, WOODROW EARL "WOODY"
B.MAR.9,1917 MORGANTON,N.C.
```
1939 BOS A P         21   4- 3
1940 BOS A P          3   1- 0
1941 BOS A P          2   0- 0
1944 BOS N P          7   1- 1
     BLTR            33   6- 4
```

RICHARD, JAMES RODNEY "J.R."
B.MAR.7,1950 VIENNA,LA.
```
1971 HOU N P          4   2- 1
1972 HOU N P          4   1- 0
1973 HOU N P         16   6- 2
1974 HOU N P         15   2- 3
1975 HOU N P         33  12-10
1976 HOU N P         39  20-15
     BRTR           111  43-31
```

RICHARD, LEE EDWARD "BEEBEE"
B.SEP.18,1948 LAFAYETTE,LA.
```
1971 CHI A S-O       87  .231
1972 CHI A S-O       11  .241
1974 CHI A 2-S-3-O   32  .164
1975 CHI A 2-S-3     43  .200
1976 STL N 2-S-3     66  .176
     BRTR           239  .209
     BB 1975
```

RICHARDS, DUANE LEE
B.DEC.16,1936 RANDOLPH CO.,IND.
```
1960 CIN N P          2   0- 0
     BRTR
```

RICHARDS, FRED CHARLES
B.NOV.3,1927 WARREN,OHIO
```
1951 CIN N 1         10  .296
     BLTL
```

RICHARDS, PAUL RAPIER
B.NOV.21,1908 WAXAHACHIE,TEX.
```
1932 BRO N C          3  .000
1933 NY  N C         51  .195
1934 NY  N C         42  .160
1935 NY  N C          7  .250
     PHI A C         85  .245
1943 DET A C        100  .220
1944 DET A C         95  .237
1945 DET A C         83  .256
1946 DET A C         57  .201
     BRTR           523  .227
```
NON-PLAYING MANAGER
CHI(A) 1951-54, BAL(A) 1955-61,
CHI(A) 1976

RICHARDSON
```
1804 CHI U 2          1  .000
```

RICHARDSON, ARTHUR HARDING "HARDY"
B.APR.21,1855 PAULSBORO,N.J.
D.JAN.14,1931
```
1879 BUF N 3         78  .278
1880 BUF N C-3       80  .252
1881 BUF N 2-S-O     83  .290
1882 BUF N 2         83  .271
1883 BUF N 2         90  .310
1884 BUF N 1-2-3-O   98  .301
1885 BUF N P-2-  1   96   0- 0
           S-O           .319
1886 DET N 2-O      125  .351
1887 DET N 2-O      120  .363
1888 DET N 2         57  .289
1889 BOS N 2-O      132  .304
1890 BOS P O        130  .332
1891 BOS AA O        74  .264
1892 WAS N 2-O        9  .114
     NY  N 2-O       61  .223
     BRTR     1   1316   0- 0
                         .302
```

RICHARDSON, CLIFFORD NOLEN
B.JAN.18,1903 CHATTANOOGA,TENN.
D.SEPT.25,1951
```
1929 DET A S         13  .190
1931 DET A 3         38  .270
1932 DET A 3         69  .219
1935 NY  A S         12  .217
1938 CIN N S         35  .290
1939 CIN N S          1  .000
     BRTR           168  .247
```

RICHARDSON, DANIEL "DENNY"
B.JAN.25,1863 ELMIRA,N.Y.
D.SEPT.15,1926
```
1884 NY  N S-O       70  .259
1885 NY  N P-3-  9   48   5- 1
           O             .262
1886 NY  N P-O   1   64   0- 1
                         .232
1887 NY  N 2        122  .332
1888 NY  N 2        135  .226
1889 NY  N 2        124  .279
1890 NY  P 2-S      123  .258
1891 NY  N 2        123  .262
1892 WAS N M-2-S    142  .240
1893 BRO N 2         51  .246
1894 LOU N S        116  .255
     BRTR     10  1118   5- 2
                         .261
```

RICHARDSON, GORDON CLARK "GORDY"
B.JULY 19,1938 COLQUITT,GA.
```
1964 STL N P         19   4- 2
1965 NY  N P         35   2- 2
1966 NY  N P         15   0- 2
     BRTL            69   6- 6
```

RICHARDSON, JOHN WILLIAM
B.OCT.3,1891 CENTRAL CITY,ILL.
D.JAN.18,1970 MARION,ILL.
```
1915 PHI A P          3   0- 1
1916 PHI A P          1   0- 0
     BBTR             4   0- 1
```

RICHARDSON, KENNETH FRANKLIN
B.MAY 2,1915 ORLEANS,IND.
```
1942 PHI A 1-3-O      6  .067
1946 PHI N 2          6  .150
     BRTR            12  .114
```

RICHARDSON, ROBERT CLINTON "BOBBY"
B.AUG.19,1935 SUMTER,S.C.
```
1955 NY  A 2-S       11  .154
1956 NY  A 2          5  .143
1957 NY  A 2         97  .256
1958 NY  A 2-S-3     73  .247
1959 NY  A 2-S-3    134  .301
1960 NY  A 2-3      150  .252
1961 NY  A 2        162  .261
1962 NY  A 2        161  .302
1963 NY  A 2        151  .265
1964 NY  A 2-S      159  .267
1965 NY  A 2        160  .247
1966 NY  A 2-3      149  .251
     BRTR          1412  .266
```

RICHARDSON, THOMAS MITCHELL
B.AUG.7,1883 LOUISVILLE,ILL.
D.NOV.15,1939
```
1917 STL A H          1  .000
     BRTR
```

RICHARDSON, WILLIAM H.
B.LEAVENWORTH,KAN.
D.APR.11,1954
```
1901 STL N 1         15  .211
```

RICHBOURG, LANCELOT CLAYTON "LANCE"
B.DEC.18,1897 DE FUNIAK SPRINGS
FLA.
D.SEPT.10,1975 CRESTVIEW,FLA.
```
1921 PHI N 2         10  .200
1924 WAS A O         15  .281
1927 BOS N O        115  .309
1928 BOS N O        148  .337
1929 BOS N O        139  .305
1930 BOS N O        130  .304
1931 BOS N O         97  .287
1932 CHI N O         44  .257
     BLTR           698  .308
```

YR	CL	LEA	POS	GP	G	REC

RICHERT, PETER GERARD "PETE"
B.OCT.29,1939 FLORAL PARK,N.Y.

1962	LA	N	P		19	5- 4
1963	LA	N	P		20	5- 3
1964	LA	N	P		8	2- 3
1965	WAS	A	P	34	42	15-12
1966	WAS	A	P	36	43	14-14
1967	WAS	A	P	11	12	2- 6
	BAL	A	P	26	27	7-10
1968	BAL	A	P		36	6- 3
1969	BAL	A	P		44	7- 4
1970	BAL	A	P		50	7- 2
1971	BAL	A	P		35	3- 5
1972	LA	N	P		37	2- 3
1973	LA	N	P		39	3- 3
1974	STL	N	P		13	0- 0
1974	PHI	N	P		21	2- 1
	BLTL			429	446	80-73

RICHIE, LEWIS A.
B.AUG.23,1883 AMBLER,PA.
D.AUG.15,1936

1906	PHI	N	P		33	9-11
1907	PHI	N	P		25	6- 6
1908	PHI	N	P		25	7-10
1909	PHI	N	P		11	1- 1
	BOS	N	P		25	7- 7
1910	BOS	N	P		4	0- 3
	CHI	N	P		28	11- 4
1911	CHI	N	P		36	15-11
1912	CHI	N	P		39	16- 8
1913	CHI	N	P		16	2- 4
	BRTR				242	74-65

RICHMOND, BERYL JUSTICE
B.AUG.24,1908 GLEN EASTON,W.VA.

1933	CHI	N	P		5	0- 0
1934	CHI	N	P		6	1- 2
	BBTL				11	1- 2
	BR 1933					

RICHMOND, DONALD LESTER "DON"
B.OCT.27,1919 GILLETT,PA.

1941	PHI	A	3		9	.200
1946	PHI	A	3		16	.290
1947	PHI	A	2-3		19	.190
1951	STL	N	3		12	.088
	BLTR				56	.211

RICHMOND, JOHN H.
B.PHILADELPHIA,PA.

1875	ATH	NA	C-2-0		27	.213
1879	SYR	N	S-0		61	.211
1880	BOS	N	S-0		31	.248
1881	BOS	N	S-0		26	.275
1882	CLE	N	0		39	.154
	ATH	AA	0		19	.173
1883	COL	AA	S		91	.274
1884	COL	AA	S		105	.237
1885	PIT	AA	S		34	.206
	TR				433	.231

RICHMOND, JOHN LEE
B.MAY 5,1857 SHEFFIELD,OHIO
D.SEPT.30,1929

1879	BOS	N	P		1	1- 0
1880	WOR	N	P-0	67	75	31-33
						.224
1881	WOR	N	P-0	52	60	25-27
						.251
1882	WOR	N	P-0	47	55	14-33
						.280
1883	PRO	N	P-0	11	48	3- 8
						.283
1886	CIN	AA	P-0	3	8	0- 1
						.260
	TL			181	247	74-102
						.258

RICHMOND, RAYMOND S.
B.JUNE 5,1896 FILLMORE,ILL.

1920	STL	A	P		2	2- 0
1921	STL	A	P		6	0- 1
	BRTR				8	2- 1

RICHTER, ALLEN GORDON "AL"
B.FEB.7,1928 NORFOLK,VA.

1951	BOS	A	S		5	.091
1953	BOS	A	S		1	.000
	BRTR				6	.091

RICHTER, EMIL HENRY "REGGIE"
B.SEPT.14,1889 DUSSELDORF,
GERMANY
D.AUG.3,1934

| 1911 | CHI | N | P | | 22 | 1- 3 |
| | BRTR | | | | | |

RICHTER, JOHN M.
B.LOUISVILLE,KY.

| 1898 | LOU | N | 3 | | 3 | .154 |

RICKERT, JOSEPH FRANCIS
B.DEC.12,1876 LONDON,OHIO
D.OCT.15,1943

1898	PIT	N	0		2	.167
1901	BOS	N	0		13	.175
					15	.174

RICKERT, MARVIN AUGUST "MARV"
B.JAN.8,1921 LONG BRANCH,WAHS.

1942	CHI	N	0		8	.269
1946	CHI	N	0		111	.263
1947	CHI	N	1-0		71	.146
1948	CIN	N	H		8	.167
	BOS	N	0		3	.231
1949	BOS	N	1-0		100	.292
1950	PIT	N	0		17	.150
	CHI	A	1-0		84	.237
	BLTR				402	.247

RICKETTS, DAVID WILLIAM "DAVE"
B.JULY 12,1935 POTTSTOWN,PA.

1963	STL	N	C		3	.250
1965	STL	N	C		11	.241
1967	STL	N	C		52	.273
1968	STL	N	C		20	.136
1969	STL	N	C		30	.273
1970	PIT	N	C		14	.182
	BBTR				130	.249

RICKETTS, RICHARD JAMES "DICK"
B.DEC.4,1933 POTTSTOWN,PA.

| 1959 | STL | N | P | | 12 | 1- 6 |
| | BLTR | | | | | |

**RICKEY, WESLEY BRANCH
"BRANCH"**
B.DEC.20,1881 LUCASVILLE,OHIO
D.DEC.9,1965 COLUMBIA,MO.

1905	STL	A	C		1	.000
1906	STL	A	C		64	.284
1907	NY	A	C-0		52	.182
1914	STL	A	M-H		2	.000
	BLTR				119	.239

NON-PLAYING MANAGER
STL(A) 1913-15, STL(N) 1919-25

RICKLEY, CHRISTOPHER
B.PHILADELPHIA,PA.

| 1884 | KEY | U | S | | 7 | .207 |

RICKS, JOHN

1891	STL	AA	3		5	.158
1894	STL	N	3		1	.000
					6	.150

RICO, ALFREDO (CRUZ) "FRED"
B.JULY 4,1944 JEROME,ARIZ.

| 1969 | KC | A | 3-0 | | 12 | .231 |
| | BRTR | | | | | |

RICO, ARTHUR RAYMOND
B.JULY 23,1896 ROXBURY,MASS.
D.JAN.6,1919

1916	BOS	N	C		4	.000
1917	BOS	N	C		13	.286
	BRTR				17	.222

RICONDA, HARRY PAUL
B.MAR.17,1897 NEW YORK,N.Y.
D.NOV.15,1958

1923	PHI	A	3		55	.263
1924	PHI	A	3		83	.253
1926	BOS	N	3		4	.167
1928	BRO	N	2-S-3		92	.224
1929	PIT	N	S		8	.467
1930	CIN	N	H		1	.000
	BRTR				243	.243

RIDDLE, ELMER RAY
B.JULY 31,1914 COLUMBUS,GA.

1939	CIN	N	P		1	0- 0
1940	CIN	N	P		15	1- 2
1941	CIN	N	P		33	19- 4
1942	CIN	N	P		29	7-11
1943	CIN	N	P		36	21-11
1944	CIN	N	P		4	2- 2
1945	CIN	N	P		12	1- 4
1947	CIN	N	P		16	1- 0
1948	PIT	N	P	28	29	12-10
1949	PIT	N	P		16	1- 8
	BRTR			190	191	65-52

RIDDLE, JOHN H.
B.PHILADELPHIA,PA.

1889	WAS	N	C		11	.210
1890	ATH	AA	C-0		25	.115
					36	.147

RIDDLE, JOHN LUDY "MUTT"
B.OCT.3,1905 CLINTON,S.C.

1930	CHI	A	C		25	.241
1937	WAS	A	C		8	.269
	BOS	N	C		2	.000
1938	BOS	N	C		19	.281
1941	CIN	N	C		10	.300
1944	CIN	N	C		1	.000
1945	CIN	N	C		23	.178
1948	PIT	N	C		10	.200
	BRTR				98	.238

RIDDLEBERGER, DENNIS MICHAEL
B.NOV.22,1945 CLIFTON FORGE,VA.

1970	WAS	A	P		8	0- 0
1971	WAS	A	P		57	3- 1
1972	CLE	A	P		38	1- 3
	BRTL				103	4- 4

RIDDLEMOSER, DORSEY LEE
B.MAR.25,1875 FREDERICK,MD.
D.MAY 11,1954 FREDERICK,MD.

| 1899 | WAS | N | P | | 1 | 0- 0 |
| | BRTR | | | | | |

RIDGEWAY, JOHN A.
B.1891 PHILADELPHIA,PA.

| 1914 | BAL | F | P | | 4 | 0- 0 |
| | BLTR | | | | | |

RIDZIK, STEPHEN GEORGE "STEVE"
B.APR.29,1929 YONKERS,N.Y.

1950	PHI	N	P		1	0- 0
1952	PHI	N	P		24	4- 2
1953	PHI	N	P		42	9- 6
1954	PHI	N	P		35	4- 5
1955	PHI	N	P		3	0- 1
	CIN	N	P		13	0- 3
1956	CIN	N	P	41	44	6- 2
1957	CIN	N	P	15	16	0- 2
1958	CLE	A	P		6	0- 2
1963	WAS	A	P		20	5- 6
1964	WAS	A	P		49	5- 5
1965	WAS	A	P		63	6- 4
1966	PHI	N	P		2	0- 0
	BRTR			314	318	39-38

RIEBE, HARVEY DONALD "HANK"
B.OCT.10,1921 EUCLID,OHIO

1942	DET	A	C		11	.314
1947	DET	A	C		8	.000
1948	DET	A	C		25	.194
1949	DET	A	C		17	.182
	BRTR				61	.212

RIEGER, ELMER JAY
B.FEB.25,1889 PERRIS,CAL.
D.OCT.21,1959

| 1910 | STL | N | P | | 13 | 0- 2 |
| | BBTR | | | | | |

RIGGERT, JOSEPH ALOYSIUS
B.DEC.11,1886 JANESVILLE,WIS.
D.DEC.10,1973 KANSAS CITY,MO.

1911	BOS	A	0		50	.212
1914	BRO	N	0		27	.190
	STL	N	0		34	.216
1919	BOS	N	0		63	.283
	BRTR				174	.240

RIGGS, LEWIS SIDNEY
B.APR.22,1910 MEBANE,N.C.
D.AUG.12,1975 DURHAM,N.C.

1934	STL	N	H		2	.000
1935	CIN	N	3		142	.278
1936	CIN	N	3		141	.257
1937	CIN	N	2-S-3		122	.242
1938	CIN	N	3		142	.252
1939	CIN	N	3		22	.158
1940	CIN	N	3		41	.292
1941	BRO	N	1-2-3		77	.305
1942	BRO	N	1-3		70	.278
1946	BRO	N	3		1	.000
	BLTR				760	.262

YR	CL	LEA	POS	GP	G	REC

RIGNEY, EMORY ELMO "TOPPER"
B.JAN.7,1897 GROVETON,TEX.
D.JUNE 16,1972 SAN ANTONIO,TEX.

YR	CL	LEA	POS	GP	G	REC
1922	DET	A	S		155	.300
1923	DET	A	S		129	.315
1924	DET	A	S		147	.289
1925	DET	A	S-3		62	.247
1926	BOS	A	S		148	.270
1927	BOS	A	3		7	.118
	WAS	A	S-3		46	.271
	BRTR				694	.288

RIGNEY, JOHN DUNGAN "JOHNNY"
B.OCT.28,1914 OAK PARK,ILL.

1937	CHI	A	P		22	2- 5
1938	CHI	A	P		38	9- 9
1939	CHI	A	P		35	15- 8
1940	CHI	A	P	39	40	15-18
1941	CHI	A	P		30	13-13
1942	CHI	A	P		7	3- 3
1946	CHI	A	P		15	5- 5
1947	CHI	A	P		11	2- 3
	BRTR			197	198	64-64

RIGNEY, WILLIAM JOSEPH
"BILL" OR "SPECS"
B.JAN.29,1918 ALAMEDA,CAL.

1946	NY	N	S-3		110	.236
1947	NY	N	2-S-3		130	.267
1948	NY	N	2-S		113	.264
1949	NY	N	2-S-3		122	.278
1950	NY	N	2-3		56	.181
1951	NY	N	2-3		44	.232
1952	NY	N	1-2-S-3		60	.300
1953	NY	N	2-3		19	.250
	BRTR				654	.259

NON-PLAYING MANAGER
NY(N) 1956-57, SF(N) 1958-60,
LA(A) 1963-65, CAL(A) 1966-69,
MIN(A) 1970-72, SF(N) 1976

RIKARD, CULLEY
B.MAY 9,1915 OXFORD,MISS.

1941	PIT	N	O		6	.200
1942	PIT	N	O		38	.192
1947	PIT	N	O		109	.287
	BLTR				153	.270

RILEY, JAMES JOSEPH
B.NOV.10,1886 BUFFALO,N.Y.
D.MAR.25,1949

| 1910 | BOS | N | O | | 1 | .000 |
| | TR | | | | | |

RILEY, JAMES NORMAN
B.MAY 25,1897 BAYFIELD,N.B.,CAN
D.MAY 25,1969 SEGUIN,TEX.

1921	STL	A	3		4	.000
1923	WAS	A	1		2	.000
	BLTR				6	.000

RILEY, LEON FRANCIS
B.AUG.20,1906 PRINCETON,NEB.
D.SEPT.13,1970 SCHENECTADY,N.Y.

| 1944 | PHI | N | O | | 4 | .083 |
| | BLTR | | | | | |

RILEY, WILLIAM J. "PIGTAIL"
B.NOV.1853 PHILADELPHIA,PA.
D.NOV.9,1887

1875	WES	NA	O		8	-
1879	CLE	N	O		43	.142
					51	-

RING, JAMES JOSEPH "JIMMY"
B.FEB.15,1895 BROOKLYN,N.Y.
D.JULY 2,1965 NEW YORK,N.Y.

1917	CIN	N	P		24	3- 7
1918	CIN	N	P		21	9- 5
1919	CIN	N	P		32	10- 9
1920	CIN	N	P		42	17-16
1921	PHI	N	P		34	10-19
1922	PHI	N	P		40	12-18
1923	PHI	N	P	39	41	18-16
1924	PHI	N	P		32	10-12
1925	PHI	N	P		38	14-16
1926	NY	N	P		39	11-10
1927	STL	N	P		13	0- 4
1928	PHI	N	P		35	4-17
	BRTR			389	391	118-149

RINGO, FRANK C.
B.OCT.12,1861 LIBERTY,MO.
D.APR.12,1889

1883	PHI	N	C-2-S-3-O		57	.183
1884	PHI	N	C		25	.132
	ATH	AA	C		2	.000
1885	DET	N	C-3-O		16	.246
	PIT	AA	C		3	.182
1886	PIT	AA	C-1		16	.241
	KC	N	C		16	.232
					135	.193

RINKER, ROBERT JOHN
B.APR.21,1923 AUDENRIED,PA.

| 1950 | PHI | A | C | | 3 | .333 |
| | BRTR | | | | | |

RIOS, JUAN O. (VELEZ)
B.JULY 14,1945 MAYAGUEZ,P.R.

| 1969 | KC | A | 2-S-3 | | 87 | .224 |
| | BRTR | | | | | |

RIPLEY, WALTER FRANKLIN
B.NOV.26,1916 WORCESTER,MASS.

| 1935 | BOS | A | P | | 2 | 0- 0 |
| | BRTR | | | | | |

RIPPAY, BENJAMIN WESLEY
(PLAYED UNDER NAME OF
CHARLES WESLEY JONES)

RIPPELMEYER, RAYMOND
B.JULY 9,1933 VALMEYER,ILL.

| 1962 | WAS | A | P | | 18 | 1- 2 |
| | BRTR | | | | | |

RIPPLE, CHARLES DAWSON
B.DEC.1,1921 BOLTON,N.C.

1944	PHI	N	P		1	0- 0
1945	PHI	N	P		4	0- 1
1946	PHI	N	P		6	1- 0
	BLTL				11	1- 1

RIPPLE, JAMES ALBERT "JIMMY"
B.OCT.14,1909 EXPORT,PA.
D.JULY 16,1959

1936	NY	N	O		96	.305
1937	NY	N	O		121	.317
1938	NY	N	O		134	.261
1939	NY	N	O		66	.228
	BRO	N	O		28	.330
1940	BRO	N	O		7	.231
	CIN	N	O		32	.307
1941	CIN	N	O		38	.216
1943	PHI	A	O		32	.238
	BLTR				554	.282

RISBERG, CHARLES AUGUST "SWEDE"
B.OCT.13,1894 SAN FRANCISCO,CAL
D.OCT.13,1975 RED BLUFF,CAL.

1917	CHI	A	S		149	.203
1918	CHI	A	2-S-3		82	.256
1919	CHI	A	1-S		119	.256
1920	CHI	A	S		126	.266
	BRTR				476	.243

RISING, PERRY SUMNER "POP"
B.INDUSTRY,PA.

| 1905 | BOS | A | O | | 11 | .100 |

RITCHEY, CLAUDE CASSIUS
B.OCT.5,1873 EMIENTON,PA.
D.NOV.8,1951

1897	CIN	N	S-O		100	.288
1898	LOU	N	2-S		152	.259
1899	LOU	N	2		147	.309
1900	PIT	N	2		123	.295
1901	PIT	N	2		140	.298
1902	PIT	N	2-O		114	.275
1903	PIT	N	2		137	.287
1904	PIT	N	2		156	.263
1905	PIT	N	2		153	.255
1906	PIT	N	2		151	.269
1907	BOS	N	2		144	.255
1908	BOS	N	2		120	.273
1909	BOS	N	2		25	.172
	BBTR				1662	.276

RITCHIE, JAY SEAY
B.NOV.20,1936 SALISBURY,N.C.

1964	BOS	A	P		21	1- 1
1965	BOS	A	P		44	1- 2
1966	ATL	N	P		22	0- 1
1967	ATL	N	P		52	4- 6
1968	CIN	N	P		28	2- 3
	BRTR				167	8-13

RITTER

| 1885 | BUF | N | 2 | | 2 | .167 |

RITTER, FLOYD ALEXANDER
B.JUNE 1,1870 DORSET,OHIO
D.FEB.7,1943

| 1890 | TOL | AA | C | | 1 | .000 |

RITTER, LOUIS ELMER "OLD DOG"
B.SEPT.7,1875 LIBERPOOL,PA.
D.MAY 27,1952

1902	BRO	N	C		16	.250
1903	BRO	N	C		75	.236
1904	BRO	N	C		63	.248
1905	BRO	N	C		90	.219
1906	BRO	N	C		67	.208
1907	BRO	N	C		89	.203
1908	BRO	N	C		37	.192
	TR				437	.221

RITTER, WILLIAM HERBERT "HANK"
B.OCT.12,1893 MC COYSVILLE,PA.
D.SEPT.3,1964 AKRON,OHIO

1912	PHI	N	P		3	0- 0
1914	NY	N	P		1	1- 0
1915	NY	N	P		22	2- 1
1916	NY	N	P		3	1- 0
	BRTR				29	4- 1

RITTERSON, E. W.

| 1876 | ATH | N | C | | 15 | .250 |

RITTWAGE, JAMES MICHAEL "JIM"
B.OCT.23,1944 CLEVELAND,OHIO

1970	CLE	A	P-3		8	1- 1
						.375
	BRTR					

RITZ, JAMES L.
B.1874 PITTSBURGH,PA.
D.NOV.10,1896

| 1894 | PIT | N | 3 | | 1 | .000 |

RIVERA, JESUS MANUEL (TORRES)
"BOMBO"
B.AUG.2,1952 PONCE,PR.

1975	MON	N	O		5	.111
1976	MON	N	O		68	.276
	BRTR				73	.268

RIVERA, MANUEL JOSEPH "JIM"
OR "JUNGLE JIM"
B.JULY 22,1922 BROOKLYN,N.Y.

1952	STL	A	O		97	.256
	CHI	A	O		53	.249
1953	CHI	A	O		156	.259
1954	CHI	A	O		145	.286
1955	CHI	A	O		147	.264
1956	CHI	A	O		139	.255
1957	CHI	A	1-O		125	.256
1958	CHI	A	O		116	.225
1959	CHI	A	O		80	.220
1960	CHI	A	O		48	.294
1961	CHI	A	H		1	.000
	KC	A	O		64	.241
	BLTL				1171	.256

RIVIERE, ARTHUR BERNARD "TINK"
B.AUG.2,1899 LIBERTY,TEX.
D.SEPT.27,1965 LIBERTY,TEX.

1921	STL	N	P		18	1- 0
1925	CHI	A	P		3	0- 0
	BRTR				21	1- 0

RIVERS, JOHN MILTON "MICKEY"
B.OCT.31,1948 MIAMI,FLA.

1970	CAL	A	O		17	.320
1971	CAL	A	O		78	.265
1972	CAL	A	O		58	.214
1973	CAL	A	O		30	.349
1974	CAL	A	O		118	.285
1975	CAL	A	O		155	.284
1976	NY	A	O		137	.312
	BLTL				593	.289

RIXEY, EPPA "JEPTHA"
B.MAY 3,1891 CULPEPER,VA.
D.FEB.28,1963 CINCINNATI,OHIO

YR	CL	LEA	POS	GP	G	REC
1912	PHI	N	P		23	10-10
1913	PHI	N	P		35	9- 5
1914	PHI	N	P		24	2-11
1915	PHI	N	P		29	11-12
1916	PHI	N	P		38	22-10
1917	PHI	N	P		39	16-21
1919	PHI	N	P		23	6-12
1920	PHI	N	P	41	43	11-22
1921	CIN	N	P		40	19-18
1922	CIN	N	P		40	25-13
1923	CIN	N	P		42	20-15
1924	CIN	N	P		35	15-14
1925	CIN	N	P		39	21-11
1926	CIN	N	P		37	14- 8
1927	CIN	N	P		34	12-10
1928	CIN	N	P		43	19-18
1929	CIN	N	P		35	10-13
1930	CIN	N	P		32	9-13
1931	CIN	N	P		22	4- 7
1932	CIN	N	P		25	5- 5
1933	CIN	N	P		16	6- 3
	BRTL			692	694	266-251

RIZZO, JOHN COSTA
B.JULY 30,1912 HOUSTON,TEX.

YR	CL	LEA	POS	GP	G	REC
1938	PIT	N	O		143	.301
1939	PIT	N	O		94	.261
1940	PIT	N	O		9	.179
	CIN	N	O		31	.282
	PHI	N	3-O		103	.292
1941	PHI	N	3-O		99	.217
1942	BRO	N	O		78	.230
	BRTR				557	.270

RIZZUTO, PHILIP FRANCIS
"PHIL" OR "SCOOTER"
B.SEPT.25,1917 BROOKLYN,N.Y.

YR	CL	LEA	POS	GP	G	REC
1941	NY	A	S		133	.307
1942	NY	A	S		144	.284
1946	NY	A	S		126	.257
1947	NY	A	S		153	.273
1948	NY	A	S		128	.252
1949	NY	A	S		153	.275
1950	NY	A	S		155	.324
1951	NY	A	S		144	.274
1952	NY	A	S		152	.254
1953	NY	A	S		134	.271
1954	NY	A	2-S		127	.195
1955	NY	A	2-S		81	.259
1956	NY	A	S		31	.231
	BRTR				1661	.273

ROACH, JAMES MICHAEL "MIKE"
B.1876 NEW YORK,N.Y.
D.NOV.12,1916

YR	CL	LEA	POS	GP	G	REC
1899	WAS	N	C		21	.237

ROACH, JOHN F.
B.ATHENS,PA.
D.MAR.1,1915

YR	CL	LEA	POS	GP	G	REC
1887	NY	N	P		1	0- 1
	TL					

ROACH, MELVIN EARL "MEL"
B.JAN.25,1933 RICHMOND,VA.

YR	CL	LEA	POS	GP	G	REC
1953	MIL	N	2		5	.000
1954	MIL	N	1		3	.000
1957	MIL	N	2		7	.167
1958	MIL	N	1-2-O		44	.309
1959	MIL	N	2-3-O		19	.097
1960	MIL	N	1-2-3-O		48	.300
1961	MIL	N	1-O		13	.167
	CHI	N	1-2		23	.128
1962	PHI	N	1-2-3-O		65	.190
	BRTR				227	.239

ROACH, SKEL
(REAL NAME
RUDOLPH C. WEICHBRODT)
B.OCT.20,1871 GERMANY
D.MAR.9,1958

YR	CL	LEA	POS	GP	G	REC
1899	CHI	N	P		1	1- 0

ROACH, WILBUR CHARLES "ROXEY"
B.NOV.28,1882 ANITA,PA.
D.DEC.26,1947

YR	CL	LEA	POS	GP	G	REC
1910	NY	A	S		70	.214
1911	NY	A	S		12	.250
1912	WAS	A	S		2	.500
1915	BUF	F	S		92	.270
	BRTR				176	.249

ROARKE, MICHAEL THOMAS "MIKE"
B.NOV.8,1930 WEST WARWICK,R.I.

YR	CL	LEA	POS	GP	G	REC
1961	DET	A	C		86	.223
1962	DET	A	C		56	.213
1963	DET	A	C		23	.318
1964	DET	A	C		29	.232
	BRTR				194	.230

BOAT, FREDERICK
B.FEB.10,1868 OREGON,ILL.

YR	CL	LEA	POS	GP	G	REC
1890	PIT	N	3		57	.223
1892	CHI	N	2		8	.200
					65	.220

ROBELLO, THOMAS VARDASCO
B.FEB.9,1913 OAKLAND,CAL.

YR	CL	LEA	POS	GP	G	REC
1933	CIN	N	2-3		14	.233
1934	CIN	N	H		2	.000
	BRTR				16	.219

ROBERGE, JOSEPH ALBERT ARMAND
"SKIPPY"
B.MAY 19,1917 LOWELL,MASS.

YR	CL	LEA	POS	GP	G	REC
1941	BOS	N	2-S-3		55	.216
1942	BOS	N	2-3		74	.215
1946	BOS	N	3		48	.231
	BRTR				177	.220

ROBERSON, JOHN HENRY
(PLAYED UNDER NAME OF
JOHN HENRY ROBINSON)

ROBERTS, CHARLES EMORY "RED"
B.AUG.8,1918 CARROLLTON,GA.

YR	CL	LEA	POS	GP	G	REC
1943	WAS	A	S-3		9	.261
	BRTR					

ROBERTS, CLARENCE ASHLEY
"SKIPPER"
B.JAN.11,1888 KELLOGG,IDAHO
D.DEC.24,1963

YR	CL	LEA	POS	GP	G	REC
1913	STL	N	C		26	.146
1914	PIT	F	C		32	.226
	CHI	F	C		4	.333
	PIT	F	C		18	.228
	BLTR				80	.210

ROBERTS, CURTIS BENJAMIN "CURT"
B.AUG.16,1929 PINELAND,TEX.

YR	CL	LEA	POS	GP	G	REC
1954	PIT	N	2		134	.232
1955	PIT	N	2		6	.118
1956	PIT	N	2		31	.177
	BRTR				171	.223

ROBERTS, DALE
B.APR.12,1942 OWENTON,KY.

YR	CL	LEA	POS	GP	G	REC
1967	NY	A	P		2	0- 0
	BRTL					

ROBERTS, DAVID ARTHUR "DAVE"
B.SEP.11,1944 GALLIPOLIS,OHIO

YR	CL	LEA	POS	GP	G	REC
1969	SD	N	P	22	23	0- 3
1970	SD	N	P		43	8-14
1971	SD	N	P	37	38	14-17
1972	HOU	N	P		35	12- 7
1973	HOU	N	P	39	41	17-11
1974	HOU	N	P	34	35	10-12
1975	HOU	N	P		32	8-14
1976	DET	A	P		36	16-17
	BLTL			278	283	85-95

ROBERTS, DAVID LEONARD "DAVE"
B.JUNE 30,1933 PANAMA CITY,PAN.

YR	CL	LEA	POS	GP	G	REC
1962	HOU	N	1-O		16	.245
1964	HOU	N	1-O		61	.184
1966	PIT	N	1		14	.125
	BLTL				91	.196

ROBERTS, DAVID WAYNE "DAVE"
B.FEB.17,1951 LEBANON,ORE.

YR	CL	LEA	POS	GP	G	REC
1972	SD	N	C-2-S-3		100	.244
1973	SD	N	2-3		127	.286
1974	SD	N	S-3-O		113	.167
1975	SD	N	2-3		33	.283
	BRTR				373	.244

ROBERTS, JAMES NEWSOM
B.OCT.13,1895 ARTESIA,MISS.

YR	CL	LEA	POS	GP	G	REC
1924	BRO	N	P		11	0- 3
1925	BRO	N	P		1	0- 0
	BRTR				12	0- 3

ROBERTS, LEON KAUFFMAN
B.JAN.22,1951 VICKSBURG,MICH.

YR	CL	LEA	POS	GP	G	REC
1974	DET	A	O		17	.270
1975	DET	A	O		129	.257
1976	HOU	N	O		87	.289
	BRTR				233	.268

ROBERTS, RAYMOND
B.AUG.25,1896 CRUGER,MISS.
D.JAN.30,1962

YR	CL	LEA	POS	GP	G	REC
1919	PHI	A	P		3	0- 2
	BLTR					

ROBERTS, ROBIN EVAN
B.SEP.30,1926 SPRINGFIELD,ILL.

YR	CL	LEA	POS	GP	G	REC
1948	PHI	N	P	20	21	7- 9
1949	PHI	N	P		43	15-15
1950	PHI	N	P		40	20-11
1951	PHI	N	P		44	21-15
1952	PHI	N	P		39	28- 7
1953	PHI	N	P		44	23-16
1954	PHI	N	P		45	23-15
1955	PHI	N	P	41	51	23-14
1956	PHI	N	P		43	19-18
1957	PHI	N	P		39	10-22
1958	PHI	N	P	35	36	17-14
1959	PHI	N	P		35	15-17
1960	PHI	N	P		35	12-16
1961	PHI	N	P		26	1-10
1962	BAL	A	P		27	10- 9
1963	BAL	A	P		35	14-13
1964	BAL	A	P		31	13- 7
1965	BAL	A	P		20	5- 7
	HOU	N	P		10	5- 2
1966	HOU	N	P		13	3- 5
	CHI	N	P		11	2- 3
	BRTR			676	688	286-245
	BR 1948-52					

ROBERTS, THOMAS
B.BALTIMORE,MD.

YR	CL	LEA	POS	GP	G	REC
1874	ATL	NA	O		1	.000

ROBERTSON, ALFRED JAMES "JIM"
B.JAN.29,1928 CHICAGO,ILL.

YR	CL	LEA	POS	GP	G	REC
1954	PHI	A	C		63	.184
1955	KC	A	C		6	.250
	BRTR				69	.187

ROBERTSON, CHARLES CULBERTSON
B.JAN.31,1897 SHERMAN,TEX.

YR	CL	LEA	POS	GP	G	REC
1919	CHI	A	P		1	0- 1
1922	CHI	A	P		37	14-15
1923	CHI	A	P		38	13-18
1924	CHI	A	P		17	4-10
1925	CHI	A	P		24	8-12
1926	STL	A	P		8	1- 2
1927	BOS	N	P		28	7-17
1928	BOS	N	P		13	2- 5
	BLTR				166	49-80

ROBERTSON, DARYL BERDENE
B.JAN.5,1936 CRIPPLE CREEK,COLO

YR	CL	LEA	POS	GP	G	REC
1962	CHI	N	S-3		9	.105
	BRTR					

ROBERTSON, DAVIS AYDELOTTE
"DAVE"
B.JUNE 10,1889 NORFOLK,VA.
D.NOV.5,1970 VIRGINIA BEACH,VA.

YR	CL	LEA	POS	GP	G	REC
1912	NY	N	1-O		3	.000
1914	NY	N	O		82	.266
1915	NY	N	O		141	.294
1916	NY	N	O		150	.307
1917	NY	N	O		142	.259
1919	NY	N	O		1	.000
	CHI	N	O		27	.208
1920	CHI	N	O		134	.300
1921	CHI	N	O		22	.222
	PIT	N	O		60	.322
1922	NY	N	O		42	.276
	BLTL				804	.287

ROBERTSON, DONALD ALEXANDER
B.OCT.15,1930 HARVEY,ILL.

YR	CL	LEA	POS	GP	G	REC
1954	CHI	N	O		14	.000
	BLTL					

YR	CL	LEA	POS	GP	G	REC

ROBERTSON, EUGENE EDWARD
B.DEC.25,1899 ST.LOUIS,MO.

YR	CL	LEA	POS	GP	G	REC
1919	STL	A	S		5	.143
1922	STL	A	S-3		18	.296
1923	STL	A	3		78	.247
1924	STL	A	3		121	.319
1925	STL	A	S-3		154	.271
1926	STL	A	S-3		78	.251
1928	NY	A	3		83	.291
1929	NY	A	3		90	.298
1929	BOS	N	3		8	.286
1930	BOS	N	3		21	.186
		BLTR			656	.280

ROBERTSON, JERRY LEE
B.OCT.13,1943 WINCHESTER,KAN.

YR	CL	LEA	POS	GP	G	REC
1969	MON	N	P		38	5-16
1970	DET	A	P		11	0- 0
		BBTR			49	5-16

ROBERTSON, RICHARD J.
B.1891 WASHINGTON,D.C.

YR	CL	LEA	POS	GP	G	REC
1913	CIN	N	P		2	0- 1
1918	BRO	N	P	13	14	3- 6
1919	WAS	A	P		7	0- 2
		BRTR		22	23	3- 9

ROBERTSON, RICHARD PAUL "RICH"
B.OCT.14,1944 ALBANY,CAL.

YR	CL	LEA	POS	GP	G	REC
1966	SF	N	P	1	0- 0	
1967	SF	N	P	1	0- 0	
1968	SF	N	P	3	2- 0	
1969	SF	N	P	17	1- 3	
1970	SF	N	P	41	8- 9	
1971	SF	N	P	23	2- 2	
		BRTR		86	13-14	

ROBERTSON, ROBERT EUGENE "BOB"
B.OCT.2,1946 FROSTBURG,MD.

YR	CL	LEA	POS	GP	G	REC
1967	PIT	N	1		9	.171
1969	PIT	N	1		32	.208
1970	PIT	N	1-3-0		117	.287
1971	PIT	N	1		131	.271
1972	PIT	N	1-3-0		115	.193
1973	PIT	N	1		119	.239
1974	PIT	N	1		91	.229
1975	PIT	N	1		75	.274
1976	PIT	N	1		61	.217
		BRTR			750	.245

ROBERTSON, SHERRARD ALEXANDER "SHERRY"
B.JAN.1,1919 MONTREAL,QUE.,CAN.
D.OCT.23,1970 HOUGHTON,S.DAK.

YR	CL	LEA	POS	GP	G	REC
1940	WAS	A	S		10	.212
1941	WAS	A	3		1	.000
1943	WAS	A	S-3		59	.217
1946	WAS	A	2-S-3-0		74	.200
1947	WAS	A	2-3-0		95	.233
1948	WAS	A	0		71	.246
1949	WAS	A	2-3-0		110	.251
1950	WAS	A	2-3-0		71	.260
1951	WAS	A	0		62	.189
1952	WAS	A	H		1	.000
	PHI	A	2-3-0		43	.200
		BLTR			597	.230

ROBINSON, AARON ANDREW
B.JUNE 23,1916 LANCASTER,S.C.
D.MAR.9,1966 LANCASTER,S.C.

YR	CL	LEA	POS	GP	G	REC
1943	NY	A	H		1	.000
1945	NY	A	H		50	.281
1946	NY	A	H		100	.297
1947	NY	A	H		82	.270
1948	CHI	A	H		98	.252
1949	DET	A	H		110	.269
1950	DET	A	H		107	.226
1951	DET	A	H		36	.207
	BOS	A	H		26	.203
		BLTR			610	.260

ROBINSON, ALFRED V.

YR	CL	LEA	POS	GP	G	REC
1872	OLY	NA	0		7	.188

ROBINSON, BROOKS CALBERT
B.MAY 18,1937 LITTLE ROCK,ARK.

YR	CL	LEA	POS	GP	G	REC
1955	BAL	A	3		6	.091
1956	BAL	A	2-3		15	.227
1957	BAL	A	3		50	.239
1958	BAL	A	2-3		145	.238
1959	BAL	A	2-3		88	.284
1960	BAL	A	2-3		152	.294
1961	BAL	A	2-S-3		163	.287
1962	BAL	A	2-S-3		162	.303
1963	BAL	A	S-3		161	.251
1964	BAL	A	3		163	.317
1965	BAL	A	3		144	.297
1966	BAL	A	3		157	.269
1967	BAL	A	3		158	.269
1968	BAL	A	3		162	.253
1969	BAL	A	3		156	.234
1970	BAL	A	3		158	.276
1971	BAL	A	3		156	.272
1972	BAL	A	3		153	.250
1973	BAL	A	3		155	.256
1974	BAL	A	3		153	.288
1975	BAL	A	3		144	.201
1976	BAL	A	3		71	.211
		BRTR			2872	.268

ROBINSON, CHARLES HENRY
B.JULY 27,1856 WESTERLY,R.I.
D.MAY 18,1913

YR	CL	LEA	POS	GP	G	REC
1884	IND	AA	C-S-0		19	.286
1885	BRO	AA	C		12	.143
					31	.241

ROBINSON, CLYDE "RABBIT"
B.ASHTABULA,OHIO
D.APR.16,1915

YR	CL	LEA	POS	GP	G	REC
1903	WAS	A	2-S-0		103	.219
1904	DET	A	2-S-3-0		97	.204
1910	CIN	N	3		2	.000
		TR			202	.210

ROBINSON, CRAIG GEORGE
B.AUG.21,1948 ABINGTON,PA.

YR	CL	LEA	POS	GP	G	REC
1972	PHI	N	S		5	.200
1973	PHI	N	2-S		46	.226
1974	ATL	N	S		145	.230
1975	ATL	N	S		10	.059
	SF	N	2-S		29	.069
1976	SF	N	2-S-3		15	.308
	ATL	N	2-S-3		15	.235
		BRTR			265	.219

ROBINSON, DAVID TANNER "DAVE"
B.MAY 22,1946 MINNEAPOLIS,MINN.

YR	CL	LEA	POS	GP	G	REC
1970	SD	N	P		15	.316
1971	SD	N	H		7	.000
		BBTL			22	.273

ROBINSON, EARL JOHN
B.NOV.3,1936 NEW ORLEANS,LA.

YR	CL	LEA	POS	GP	G	REC
1958	LA	N	3		8	.200
1961	BAL	A	0		96	.266
1962	BAL	A	0		29	.286
1964	BAL	A	0		37	.273
		BRTR			170	.268

ROBINSON, FLOYD ANDREW
B.MAY 9,1936 PRESCOTT,ARK.

YR	CL	LEA	POS	GP	G	REC
1960	CHI	A	0		22	.283
1961	CHI	A	0		132	.310
1962	CHI	A	0		156	.312
1963	CHI	A	0		146	.283
1964	CHI	A	0		141	.301
1965	CHI	A	0		156	.265
1966	CHI	A	0		127	.237
1967	CIN	N	0		55	.238
1968	OAK	A	0		53	.247
	BOS	A	0		24	.125
		BLTR			1012	.283

ROBINSON, FRANK
B.AUG.31,1935 BEAUMONT,TEX.

YR	CL	LEA	POS	GP	G	REC
1956	CIN	N	0		152	.290
1957	CIN	N	1-0		150	.322
1958	CIN	N	3-0		148	.269
1959	CIN	N	1-0		146	.311
1960	CIN	N	1-3-0		139	.297
1961	CIN	N	3-0		153	.323
1962	CIN	N	0		162	.342
1963	CIN	N	1-0		140	.259
1964	CIN	N	0		156	.306
1965	CIN	N	0		156	.296
1966	BAL	A	1-0		155	.316
1967	BAL	A	1-0		129	.311
1968	BAL	A	1-0		130	.268
1969	BAL	A	1-0		148	.308
1970	BAL	A	1-0		132	.306
1971	BAL	A	1-0		133	.281
1972	LA	N	0		103	.251
1973	CAL	A	0-D		147	.266
1974	CAL	A	0-D		129	.251
	CLE	A	1-D		15	.200
1975	CLE	A	D		49	.237
1976	CLE	A	1-0-D		36	.224
		BRTR			2808	.294
NON-PLAYING MANAGER
CLE(A) 1975-76

ROBINSON, FREDERIC HENRY
B.JULY 6,1856 SOUTH ACTON,MASS.
D.DEC.18,1933

YR	CL	LEA	POS	GP	G	REC
1884	CIN	U	2		3	.231
		BRTR				

ROBINSON, HUMBERTO VALENTINO
B.JUNE 25,1930 COLON,PANAMA

YR	CL	LEA	POS	GP	G	REC
1955	MIL	N	P		13	3- 1
1956	MIL	N	P		1	0- 0
1958	MIL	N	P		19	2- 0
1959	CLE	A	P		5	1- 0
	PHI	N	P		31	2- 4
1960	PHI	N	P		33	0- 4
		BRTR			102	8-13

ROBINSON, JACK ROOSEVELT "JACKIE"
B.JAN.31,1919 CAIRO,GA.
D.OCT.24,1972 STAMFORD,CONN.

YR	CL	LEA	POS	GP	G	REC
1947	BRO	N	1		151	.296
1948	BRO	N	1-2		147	.296
1949	BRO	N	2		156	.342
1950	BRO	N	2		144	.328
1951	BRO	N	2		153	.338
1952	BRO	N	2		149	.308
1953	BRO	N	1-2-S-3-0		136	.329
1954	BRO	N	2-3-0		124	.311
1955	DRO	N	1-2-3-0		105	.256
1956	BRO	N	1-2-3-0		117	.275
		BRTR			1382	.311

ROBINSON, JOHN "BRIDGEPORT"
B.E.GREENWICH,CONN.

YR	CL	LEA	POS	GP	G	REC
1902	NY	N	C		4	.000
		TR				

ROBINSON, JOHN EDWARD
B.FEB.20,1921 ORANGE,N.J.

YR	CL	LEA	POS	GP	G	REC
1949	BOS	A	P		3	0- 0
		BRTR				

ROBINSON, JOHN HENRY "HANK"
(REAL NAME
JOHN HENRY ROBERSON)
B.AUG.16,1889 FLOYD,ARK.
D.JULY 3,1965 N.LITTLE ROCK,ARK

YR	CL	LEA	POS	GP	G	REC
1911	PIT	N	P		5	0- 1
1912	PIT	N	P		33	12- 7
1913	PIT	N	P		43	14- 9
1914	STL	N	P		26	7- 8
1915	STL	N	P		32	7- 8
1918	NY	A	P		11	2- 4
		BRTL			150	42-37

YR	CL	LEA	POS	GP	G	REC

ROBINSON, WILBERT
"UNCLE ROBBY"
B.JUNE 29,1864 BOLTON,MASS.
D.AUG.8,1934 ATLANTA,GA.

YR	CL	LEA	POS	GP	G	REC
1886	ATH	AA	C-1		87	.205
1887	ATH	AA	C		68	.286
1888	ATH	AA	C		67	.268
1889	ATH	AA	C		69	.242
1890	ATH	AA	C		83	.236
	BAL	AA	C-1		14	.271
1891	BAL	AA	C		93	.222
1892	BAL	N	C		83	.270
1893	BAL	N	C		91	.338
1894	BAL	N	C		106	.348
1895	BAL	N	C		74	.264
1896	BAL	N	C		66	.354
1897	BAL	N	C		47	.313
1898	BAL	N	C		77	.276
1899	BAL	N	C		105	.284
1900	STL	N	C		56	.255
1901	BAL	A	C		71	.298
1902	BAL	A	M-C		90	.292
			BRTR		1347	.286

NON-PLAYING MANAGER
BRO(N) 1914-31

ROBINSON, WILLIAM EDWARD
"EDDIE"
B.DEC.15,1920 PARIS,TEX.

YR	CL	LEA	POS	GP	G	REC
1942	CLE	A	1		8	.125
1946	CLE	A	1		7	.467
1947	CLE	A	1		95	.245
1948	CLE	A	1		134	.254
1949	WAS	A	1		143	.294
1950	WAS	A	1		36	.240
	CHI	A	1		119	.311
1951	CHI	A	1		151	.282
1952	CHI	A	1		155	.296
1953	PHI	A	1		156	.247
1954	NY	A	1		85	.261
1955	NY	A	1		88	.208
1956	NY	A	1		26	.222
	KC	A	1		75	.198
1957	DET	A	H		13	.000
	CLE	A	1		19	.222
	BAL	A	H		4	.000
			BLTR		1314	.268

ROBINSON, WILLIAM H. "YANK"
B.SEPT.19,1859 PHILADELPHIA,PA.
D.AUG.25,1894 ST.LOUIS,MO.

YR	CL	LEA	POS	GP	G	REC
1882	DET	N	P-S-	1	11	0- 0
			O			.162
1884	BAL	U	P-C-	6	98	2- 3
			S-3			.269
1885	STL	AA	C-2-0		78	.259
1886	STL	AA	P-2	1	133	0- 1
						.279
1887	STL	AA	2		124	.426
1888	STL	AA	2-S		134	.231
1889	STL	AA	2		132	.210
1890	PIT	P	2		98	.239
1891	CIN	AA	2-S		97	.178
1892	WAS	N	3		64	.180
			BRTR	8	969	2- 4
						.262

ROBINSON, WILLIAM HENRY "BILL"
B.JUNE 26,1943 MCKEESPORT,PA.

YR	CL	LEA	POS	GP	G	REC
1966	ATL	N	O		6	.273
1967	NY	A	O		116	.196
1968	NY	A	O		107	.240
1969	NY	A	1-O		87	.171
1972	PHI	N	O		82	.239
1973	PHI	N	3-O		124	.288
1974	PHI	N	O		100	.236
1975	PIT	N	O		92	.280
1976	PIT	N	1-3-O		122	.303
			BRTR		836	.249

ROBISON, MATTHEW STANLEY
B.1857 DUBUQUE,IOWA
D.MAR.24,1911
NON-PLAYING MANAGER STL(N) 1905

ROBITAILLE, JOSEPH ANTHONY
"CHICK"
B.MAR.2,1879 WHITEHALL,N.Y.
D.JULY 30,1947

YR	CL	LEA	POS	GP	G	REC
1904	PIT	N	P		9	5- 3
1905	PIT	N	P		17	7- 6
					26	12- 9

ROBLE, RAFAEL (BATISTA)
(SEE RAFAEL BATISTA)

ROBLES, RAFAEL ORLANDO (NATERA)
B.OCT.20,1947 SAN PEDRO DE
MACORIS,D.R.

YR	CL	LEA	POS	GP	G	REC
1969	SD	N	S		6	.100
1970	SD	N	S		23	.213
1972	SD	N	S-3		18	.167
			BRTR		47	.188

ROBLES, SERGIO (VALENZUELA)
B.APR.16,1946 MAGDALENA,MEXICO

YR	CL	LEA	POS	GP	G	REC
1972	BAL	A	C		2	.200
1973	BAL	A	C		8	.077
1976	LA	N	C		6	.000
			BRTR		16	.095

ROBSON, THOMAS JAMES "TOM"
B.JAN.15,1946 ROCHESTER,N.Y.

YR	CL	LEA	POS	GP	G	REC
1974	TEX	A	1		6	.231
1975	TEX	A	1		17	.200
			BRTR		23	.208

ROCAP, ADAM
B.1854 PHILADELPHIA,PA.
D.MAR.29,1892

YR	CL	LEA	POS	GP	G	REC
1875	ATH	NA	2-O		13	.186

ROCCO, MICHAEL DOMINIC "MIKE"
B.MAR.2,1916 ST.PAUL,MINN.

YR	CL	LEA	POS	GP	G	REC
1943	CLE	A	1		108	.240
1944	CLE	A	1		155	.266
1945	CLE	A	1		143	.264
1946	CLE	A	1		34	.245
			BLTL		440	.258

ROCHE, ARMANDO BAEZ
B.DEC.7,1926 HAVANA,CUBA

YR	CL	LEA	POS	GP	G	REC
1945	WAS	A	P		2	0- 0
			BRTR			

ROCHE, JOHN JOSEPH "RED"
B.NOV.22,1890 LOS ANGELES,CAL.

YR	CL	LEA	POS	GP	G	REC
1914	STL	N	C		12	.667
1915	STL	N	C		46	.205
1917	STL	N	C		1	.000
			BRTR		59	.286

ROCHEFORT, BENNETT HAROLD
(REAL NAME BENNETT
HAROLD ROCHEFORT GILBERT)
B.AUG.15,1896 CAMDEN,N.J.

YR	CL	LEA	POS	GP	G	REC
1914	PHI	A	1		1	.500
			BLTR			

ROCHELLI, LOUIS JOSEPH
B.JAN.11,1919 WILLIAMSON,ILL.

YR	CL	LEA	POS	GP	G	REC
1944	BRO	N	2		5	.176
			BRTR			

ROCK, LESTER HENRY
(REAL NAME
LESTER HENRY SCHWARZROCK)
B.AUG.19,1912 SPRINGFIELD,MINN.

YR	CL	LEA	POS	GP	G	REC
1936	CHI	A	1		2	.000
			BLTR			

ROCKENFIELD, ISSAC B.
B.NOV.3,1876 OMAHA,NEB.
D.FEB.21,1927 SAN DIEGO,CAL.

YR	CL	LEA	POS	GP	G	REC
1905	STL	A	2		95	.217
1906	STL	A	2		27	.239
	TR				122	.222

ROCKETT, PATRICK EDWARD "PAT"
B.JAN.9,1955 SAN ANTONIO,TEX.

YR	CL	LEA	POS	GP	G	REC
1976	ATL	N	S		4	.200
			BRTR			

RODGERS, KENNETH ANDRE IAN
"ANDRE"
B.DEC.2,1934 NASSAU,BAHAMAS

YR	CL	LEA	POS	GP	G	REC
1957	NY	N	S-3		32	.244
1958	SF	N	S		22	.206
1959	SF	N	S		71	.250
1960	SF	N	1-S-3-O		81	.244
1961	CHI	N	1-2-S-O		73	.266
1962	CHI	N	1-S		138	.278
1963	CHI	N	S		150	.229
1964	CHI	N	S		129	.239
1965	PIT	N	1-2-S-3		75	.287
1966	PIT	N	1-S-3-O		36	.184
1967	PIT	N	1-2-S-3		47	.230
			BRTR		854	.249

RODGERS, ROBERT LEROY "BOB"
B.AUG.16,1938 DELAWARE,OHIO

YR	CL	LEA	POS	GP	G	REC
1961	LA	A	C		16	.321
1962	LA	A	C		155	.258
1963	LA	A	C		100	.233
1964	LA	A	C		148	.243
1965	CAL	A	C		132	.210
1966	CAL	A	C		133	.236
1967	CAL	A	C-O		139	.219
1968	CAL	A	C		91	.190
1969	CAL	A	C		18	.196
			BBTR		932	.232

RODGERS, WILBUR KINCAID
"RAWMEAT BILL"
B.APR.18,1887 AMBERLY VILLAGE,O

YR	CL	LEA	POS	GP	G	REC
1915	CLE	A	2		16	.298
	BOS	A	2		11	.000
	CIN	N	2-S-3-O		72	.239
1916	CIN	N	2-S		3	.000
			BLTR		102	.243

RODGERS, WILLIAM SHERMAN
B.DEC.5,1922 HARRISBURG,PA.

YR	CL	LEA	POS	GP	G	REC
1944	PIT	N	O		2	.250
1945	PIT	N	H		1	1.000
			BLTL		3	.400

RODIN, ERIC CHAPMAN
B.FEB.5,1930 ORANGE,N.J.

YR	CL	LEA	POS	GP	G	REC
1954	NY	N	O		5	.000
			BRTR			

RODRIGUEZ, ANTONIO ORDENANA
(PLAYED UNDER NAME OF
ANTONIO ORDENANA)

RODRIGUEZ, AURELIO (ITUARTE)
B.DEC.28,1947 CANANEA,MEXICO

YR	CL	LEA	POS	GP	G	REC
1967	CAL	A	3		29	.238
1968	CAL	A	2-3		76	.242
1969	CAL	A	3		159	.232
1970	CAL	A	3		17	.270
	WAS	A	S-3		142	.247
1971	DET	A	S-3		154	.253
1972	DET	A	S-3		153	.236
1973	DET	A	S-3		160	.222
1974	DET	A	3		159	.222
1975	DET	A	3		151	.245
1976	DET	A	3		128	.240
			BRTR		1328	.238

RODRIGUEZ, EDUARDO (REYES)
B.MAR.6,1952 BARCELONETA,P.R.

YR	CL	LEA	POS	GP	G	REC
1973	MIL	A	P		30	9- 7
1974	MIL	A	P		43	7- 4
1975	MIL	A	P		43	7- 0
1976	MIL	A	P		45	5-13
			BRTR		161	28-24

RODRIGUEZ, ELISEO (DELGADO)
"ELLIE"
B.MAY 24,1946 FAJARDO,P.R.

YR	CL	LEA	POS	GP	G	REC
1968	NY	A	C		9	.208
1969	KC	A	C		95	.236
1970	KC	A	C		80	.225
1971	MIL	A	C		115	.210
1972	MIL	A	C		116	.285
1973	MIL	A	C-D		94	.269
1974	CAL	A	C		140	.253
1975	CAL	A	C		90	.235
1976	LA	N	C		36	.212
			BRTR		775	.245

RODRIGUEZ, FERNANDO PEDRO
B.APR.29,1920 HAVANA,CUBA

YR	CL	LEA	POS	GP	G	REC
1958	CHI	N	P		7	0- 0
1959	PHI	N	P		1	0- 0
			BRTR		8	0- 0

RODRIGUEZ, HECTOR ANTONIO
B.JUNE 13,1921 ALQUIZAR,CUBA

YR	CL	LEA	POS	GP	G	REC
1952	CHI	A	3		124	.265
			BRTR			

RODRIGUEZ, JOSE
"EL HOMBRE GOMA"
B.FEB.23,1894 HAVANA,CUBA
D.JAN.21,1953 HAVANA,CUBA

YR	CL	LEA	POS	GP	G	REC
1916	NY	N	H		1	.000
1917	NY	N	1		7	.200
1918	NY	N	1-2-3		50	.160
			BRTR		58	.166

YR	CL	LEA	POS	GP	G	REC

RODRIGUEZ, ROBERTO MUNOZ
B.NOV.29,1943 CARACAS,VENEZ.

1967	KC	A	P		15	1- 1
1970	OAK	A	P		6	0- 0
	SD	N	P		10	0- 0
	CHI	N	P		26	3- 2
		BRTR			57	4- 3

ROE, ELWIN CHARLES "PREACHER"
B.FEB.26,1915 ASH FLAT,ARK.

1938	STL	N	P		1	0- 0
1944	PIT	N	P		39	13-11
1945	PIT	N	P		33	14-13
1946	PIT	N	P		21	3- 8
1947	PIT	N	P		38	4-15
1948	BRO	N	P		34	12- 8
1949	BRO	N	P		30	15- 6
1950	BRO	N	P		36	19-11
1951	BRO	N	P		34	22- 3
1952	BRO	N	P		27	11- 2
1953	BRO	N	P		25	11- 3
1954	BRO	N	P		15	3- 4
		BRTL			333	127-84

ROE, JAMES CLAY "LEFTY"
B.JAN.7,1904 GREENBRIAR,TENN.
D.APR.4,1956 CLEVELAND,MISS.

| 1923 | WAS | A | P | | 1 | 0- 1 |
| | | BLTL | | | | |

ROEBUCK, EDWARD JACK "ED"
B.JULY 3,1931 EAST MILLSBORO,PA.

1955	BRO	N	P		47	5- 6
1956	BRO	N	P		43	5- 6
1957	BRO	N	P		44	8- 2
1958	LA	N	P		32	0- 1
1960	LA	N	P		58	8- 3
1961	LA	N	P		5	2- 0
1962	LA	N	P		64	10- 2
1963	LA	N	P		29	2- 4
	WAS	A	P		26	2- 1
1964	WAS	A	P		2	0- 0
	PHI	N	P		60	5- 3
1965	PHI	N	P		44	5- 3
1966	PHI	N	P		6	0- 2
		BRTR			460	52-31

ROENICKE, GARY STEVEN
B.DEC.5,1954 COVINA,CAL.

| 1976 | MON | N | O | | 29 | .222 |
| | | BRTR | | | | |

**ROETTGER, OSCAR FREDERICK LOUIS
"OKKIE"**
B.FEB.19,1900 ST.LOUIS,MO.

1923	NY	A	P		5	0- 0
1924	NY	A	P		1	0- 0
1927	BRO	N	O		5	.000
1932	PHI	A	1		26	.233
		BRTR		6	37	0- 0
						.212

ROETTGER, WALTER HENRY
B.AUG.28,1902 ST.LOUIS,MO.
D.SEPT.14,1951

1927	STL	N	O		5	.000
1928	STL	N	O		68	.341
1929	STL	N	O		79	.253
1930	NY	N	O		121	.283
1931	CIN	N	O		44	.351
	STL	N	O		45	.285
1932	CIN	N	O		106	.277
1933	CIN	N	O		84	.239
1934	PIT	N	O		47	.245
		BRTR			599	.285

ROETZ, EDWARD BERNARD
B.SEPT.6,1905 PHILADELPHIA,PA.
D.MAR.16,1965 PHILADELPHIA,PA.

| 1929 | STL | A | 1-2-3 | | 16 | .244 |
| | | BRTR | | | | |

ROGALSKI, JOSEPH ANTHONY
B.JULY 15,1912 ASHLAND,WIS.
D.NOV.20,1951

| 1938 | DET | A | P | | 2 | 0- 0 |
| | | BRTR | | | | |

ROGELL, WILLIAM GEORGE "BILLY"
B.NOV.24,1904 SPRINGFIELD,ILL.

1925	BOS	A	2-S		58	.195
1927	BOS	A	3		82	.266
1928	BOS	A	2-S		102	.233
1930	DET	A	S-3		54	.166
1931	DET	A	S		48	.303
1932	DET	A	S		144	.271
1933	DET	A	S		155	.295
1934	DET	A	S		154	.296
1935	DET	A	S		150	.275
1936	DET	A	S		146	.274
1937	DET	A	S		146	.276
1938	DET	A	S		136	.259
1939	DET	A	S-3		74	.230
1940	CHI	N	2-S-3		33	.136
		BBTR			1482	.267

ROGERS, EMMETT
B.1868 ROME,N.Y.

| 1890 | TOL | AA | C | | 35 | .184 |

ROGERS, FRALEY W.
B.BROOKLYN,N.Y.
D.MAY 10,1881

| 1872 | BOS | NA | 1-O | | 46 | .294 |

ROGERS, JAMES F.
B.APR.9,1872 HARTFORD,CONN.

1896	WAS	N	2-3-O		38	.279
	LOU	N	2		74	.256
1897	LOU	N	M-2		40	.148
					152	.235

ROGERS, JAY LEWIS
B.AUG.3,1888 SANDUSKY,N.Y.
D.JULY 1,1964

| 1914 | NY | A | C | | 5 | .000 |
| | | BRTR | | | | |

ROGERS, LEE OTIS "BUCK"
B.OCT.8,1913 TUSCALOOSA,ALA.

1938	BOS	A	P		14	1- 1
	BRO	N	P	12	14	0- 2
		BRTL		26	28	1- 3

ROGERS, ORLIN WOODROW "BUCK"
B.NOV.5,1912 SPRING GARDEN,VA.

| 1935 | WAS | A | P | | 2 | 0- 1 |
| | | BRTL | | | | |

ROGERS, STANLEY FRANK "PACKY"
(REAL NAME
STANLEY FRANK HAZINSKI)
B.APR.26,1914 SWOYERSVILLE,PA.

| 1938 | BRO | N | 2-S-3 | | 23 | .189 |
| | | BRTR | | | | |

ROGERS, STEPHEN DOUGLAS "STEVE"
B.OCT.26,1949 JEFFERSON CITY,MO.

1973	MON	N	P		17	10- 5
1974	MON	N	P		38	15-22
1975	MON	N	P		35	11-12
1976	MON	N	P	33	35	7-17
		BRTR		123	125	43-56

ROGERS, THOMAS ANDREW "SHOTGUN"
B.FEB.12,1892 WHITE CO.,TENN.
D.MAR.7,1936 NASHVILLE,TENN.

1917	STL	A	P		24	3- 6
1918	STL	A	P		29	8-10
1919	STL	A	P		2	0- 1
	PHI	A	P		23	4-12
1921	NY	A	P	5	6	0- 1
		BRTR		83	84	15-30

ROGGE, FRANCIS CLINTON
B.JULY 19,1889 MEMPHIS,MICH.
D.JAN.6,1969 MT.CLEMENS,MICH.

1915	PIT	F	P		37	17-11
1921	CIN	N	P		6	1- 2
		BLTR			43	18-13

ROGGENBURK, GARRY EARL
B.APR.16,1940 CLEVELAND,OHIO

1963	MIN	A	P		36	2- 4
1965	MIN	A	P		12	1- 0
1966	MIN	A	P		12	1- 2
	BOS	A	P		1	0- 0
1968	BOS	A	P		4	0- 0
1969	BOS	A	P		7	0- 1
	SEA	A	P		7	2- 2
		BRTL			79	6- 9

**ROGODZINSKI, MICHAEL GEORGE
"MIKE"**
B.FEB.22,1948 EVANSTON,ILL.

1973	PHI	N	O		66	.238
1974	PHI	N	O		17	.067
1975	PHI	N	O		16	.263
		BLTR			99	.219

ROGOVIN, SAUL WALTER
B.OCT.10,1922 BROOKLYN,N.Y.

1949	DET	A	P		5	0- 1
1950	DET	A	P		11	2- 1
1951	DET	A	P		5	1- 1
	CHI	A	P	22	24	11- 7
1952	CHI	A	P		33	14- 9
1953	CHI	A	P		22	7-12
1955	BAL	A	P	14	15	1- 8
	PHI	N	P	12	13	5- 3
1956	PHI	N	P		22	7- 6
1957	PHI	N	P		4	0- 0
		BRTR		150	154	48-48

ROHE, GEORGE ANTHONY
B.SEPT.15,1875 CINCINNATI,OHIO
D.JUNE 10,1957

1901	BAL	A	3		14	.294
1905	CHI	A	2-3		34	.212
1906	CHI	A	3		74	.258
1907	CHI	A	2-S-3		144	.213
		BRTR			266	.227

ROHR, LESLIE NORVIN "LES"
B.MAR.5,1946 LOWESTOFT,ENGLAND

1967	NY	N	P		3	2- 1
1968	NY	N	P		2	0- 2
1969	NY	N	P		1	0- 0
		BLTL			6	2- 3

ROHR, WILLIAM JOSEPH "BILLY"
B.JULY 1,1945 SAN DIEGO,CAL.

1967	BOS	A	P		10	2- 3
1968	CLE	A	P		17	1- 0
		BLTL			27	3- 3

ROHWER, RAY
B.JUNE 5,1895 DIXON,CAL.

1921	PIT	N	O		30	.250
1922	PIT	N	O		53	.294
		BLTL			83	.284

ROIG, ANTON AMBROSE "TONY"
B.DEC.23,1927 NEW ORLEANS,LA.

1953	WAS	A	2		3	.125
1955	WAS	A	2-3		29	.228
1956	WAS	A	2-S		44	.210
		BRTR			76	.212

ROJAS, FELIPE (ALOU)
(SEE FELIPE ROJAS ALOU)

ROJAS, JESUS MARIA (ALOU)
(SEE JESUS MARIA ROJAS ALOU)

ROJAS, MATEO (ALOU)
(SEE MATEO ROJAS ALOU)

**ROJAS, MINERVINO ALEJANDRO
(LANDIN) "MINNIE"**
B.NOV.23,1938 LAS VILLAS,CUBA

1966	CAL	A	P		47	7- 4
1967	CAL	A	P		72	12- 9
1968	CAL	A	P		38	4- 3
		BRTR			157	23-16

ROJAS, OCTAVIO (RIVAS) "COOKIE"
B.MAR.6,1939 HAVANA,CUBA

1962	CIN	N	2-3		39	.221
1963	PHI	N	2-O		64	.221
1964	PHI	N	C-2-S-3-O		109	.291
1965	PHI	N	C-1-2-S-O		142	.303
1966	PHI	N	2-S-O		156	.268
1967	PHI	N	P-C-1-2-S-3-O		147	0- 0 .259
1968	PHI	N	C-2		152	.232
1969	PHI	N	2-O		110	.228
1970	STL	N	2-S-O		23	.106
	KC	A	2		98	.260
1971	KC	A	2-S-O		115	.300
1972	KC	A	2-S-3		137	.261
1973	KC	A	2		139	.276
1974	KC	A	2		144	.271
1975	KC	A	2		120	.254
1976	KC	A	1-2-3		63	.242
		BRTR		1	1758	0- 0 .263

YR	CL LEA POS	GP	G	REC

ROJEK, STANLEY ANDREW "STAN"
B.APR.21,1919 N.TONAWANDA,N.Y.

YR	CL LEA POS	GP	G	REC
1942	BRO N H		1	.000
1946	BRO N 2-S-3		45	.277
1947	BRO N 2-S-3		32	.263
1948	PIT N S		156	.290
1949	PIT N S		144	.244
1950	PIT N 2-S		76	.257
1951	PIT N S		8	.188
	STL N S		51	.274
1952	STL A 2-S		9	.143
	BRTR		522	.266

ROLAND, JAMES IVAN "JIM"
B.DEC.14,1942 FRANKLIN,N.C.

YR	CL LEA POS	GP	G	REC
1962	MIN A P		1	0- 0
1963	MIN A P		10	4- 1
1964	MIN A P		30	2- 6
1966	MIN A P		1	0- 0
1967	MIN A P		25	0- 1
1968	MIN A P	28	29	4- 1
1969	OAK A P		39	5- 1
1970	OAK A P		28	3- 3
1971	OAK A P		31	1- 3
1972	OAK A P		2	0- 0
	NY A P		16	0- 1
	TEX A P		5	0- 0
	BRTL	216	217	19-17

ROLFE, ROBERT ABIAL "RED"
B.OCT.17,1908 PENACOOK,N.H.
D.JULY 8,1969 GUILFORD,N.H.

YR	CL LEA POS	GP	G	REC
1931	NY A S		1	.000
1934	NY A S-3		89	.287
1935	NY A S-3		149	.300
1936	NY A 3		135	.319
1937	NY A 3		154	.276
1938	NY A 3		151	.311
1939	NY A 3		152	.329
1940	NY A 3		139	.250
1941	NY A 3		136	.264
1942	NY A 3		69	.219
	BLTR		1175	.289

NON-PLAYING MANAGER
DET(A) 1949-52

ROLLING, RAYMOND COPELAND
B.SEPT.8,1896 ST.LOUIS,MO.
D.AUG.25,1966 MAHTOMEDI,MINN.

YR	CL LEA POS	GP	G	REC
1912	STL N 2		5	.200
	BRTR			

ROLLINGS, WILLIAM RUSSELL "RED"
B.MAR.21,1904 MOBILE,ALA.
D.DEC.31,1964 MOBILE,ALA.

YR	CL LEA POS	GP	G	REC
1927	BOS A 1-3		82	.266
1928	BOS A 1-2-3		50	.229
1930	BOS N 2-3		52	.236
	BLTR		184	.251

ROLLINS, RICHARD JOHN "RICH"
B.APR.16,1938 MOUNT PLEASANT,PA.

YR	CL LEA POS	GP	G	REC
1961	MIN A 2-3		13	.294
1962	MIN A S-3		159	.298
1963	MIN A 2-3		136	.307
1964	MIN A 3		148	.270
1965	MIN A 2-3		140	.249
1966	MIN A 2-3-0		90	.245
1967	MIN A 3		109	.245
1968	MIN A 3		93	.241
1969	SEA A S-3		58	.225
1970	MIN A 3		14	.200
	CLE A 3		42	.233
	BRTR		1002	.269

ROLLINSON

YR	CL LEA POS	GP	G	REC
1884	WAS U C		1	.000

ROMAN, WILLIAM ANTHONY "BILL"
B.OCT.11,1938 DETROIT,MICH.

YR	CL LEA POS	GP	G	REC
1964	DET A 1		3	.375
1965	DET A 1		21	.074
	BLTL		24	.143

ROMANO, JAMES KING
B.APR.6,1927 BROOKLYN,N.Y.

YR	CL LEA POS	GP	G	REC
1950	BRO N P		3	0- 0
	BRTR			

ROMANO, JOHN ANTHONY
B.AUG.23,1934 HOBOKEN,N.J.

YR	CL LEA POS	GP	G	REC
1958	CHI A C		4	.286
1959	CHI A C		53	.294
1960	CLE A C		108	.272
1961	CLE A C		142	.299
1962	CLE A C		135	.261
1963	CLE A C-0		89	.216
1964	CLE A C-1		106	.241
1965	CHI A C-1-0		122	.242
1966	CHI A C		122	.231
1967	STL N C		24	.121
	BRTR		905	.255

ROMBERGER, ALLEN IRVING "DUTCH"
B.MAY 26,1927 KLONGERTOWN,PA.

YR	CL LEA POS	GP	G	REC
1954	PHI A P		10	1- 1
	BRTR			

ROMMEL, EDWIN AMERICUS "EDDIE"
B.SEPT.13,1897 BALTIMORE,MD.
D.AUG.26,1970 BALTIMORE,MD.

YR	CL LEA POS	GP	G	REC
1920	PHI A P	33	34	7- 7
1921	PHI A P		46	16-23
1922	PHI A P		51	27-13
1923	PHI A P		56	18-19
1924	PHI A P	43	45	18-15
1925	PHI A P		52	21-10
1926	PHI A P		37	11-11
1927	PHI A P		30	11- 3
1928	PHI A P		43	13- 5
1929	PHI A P		32	12- 2
1930	PHI A P		35	9- 4
1931	PHI A P	25	29	7- 5
1932	PHI A P		17	1- 2
	BRTR	500	507	171-119

ROMO, VICENTE (NAVARRO)
B.MAY 21,1943 SANTA ROSALIA,MEX.

YR	CL LEA POS	GP	G	REC
1968	LA N P		1	0- 0
	CLE A P		40	5- 3
1969	CLE A P		3	1- 1
	BOS A P		52	7- 9
1970	BOS A P		48	7- 3
1971	CHI A P		45	1- 7
1972	CHI A P		28	3- 0
1973	SD N P		49	2- 3
1974	SD N P		54	5- 5
	BRTR		320	31-31

ROMONOSKY, JOHN
B.JULY 7,1929 HARRISBURG,ILL.

YR	CL LEA POS	GP	G	REC
1953	STL N P		2	0- 0
1958	WAS A P	18	27	2- 4
1959	WAS A P	12	20	1- 0
	BRTR	32	49	3- 4

RONDEAU, HENRI JOSEPH
B.MAY 7,1887 DANIELSON,CONN.
D.MAY 28,1943

YR	CL LEA POS	GP	G	REC
1913	DET A C-1		35	.186
1915	WAS A 0		14	.154
1916	WAS A 0		50	.222
	BRTR		99	.203

RONDON, GILBERT
B.NOV.18,1953 BRONX,N.Y.

YR	CL LEA POS	GP	G	REC
1976	HOU N P		19	2- 2
	BRTR			

ROOF, PHILLIP ANTHONY "PHIL"
B.MAR.5,1941 PADUCAH,KY.

YR	CL LEA POS	GP	G	REC
1961	MIL N C		1	.000
1964	MIL N C		1	.000
1965	CAL A C		9	.136
	CLE A C		43	.173
1966	KC A C-1		127	.209
1967	KC A C		114	.205
1968	OAK A C		34	.188
1969	OAK A C		106	.235
1970	MIL A C-1		110	.227
1971	MIL A C		41	.193
	MIN A C		31	.241
1972	MIN A C		61	.205
1973	MIN A C		47	.197
1974	MIN A C		44	.196
1975	MIN A C		63	.302
1976	MIN A C		18	.217
	CHI A C		4	.111
	BRTR		854	.216

ROOKER, JAMES PHILLIP "JIM"
B.SEP.23,1941 LAKEVIEW,ORE.

YR	CL LEA POS	GP	G	REC
1968	DET A P		2	0- 0
1969	KC A P	28	34	4-16
1970	KC A P-0	38	41	10-15
				.200
1971	KC A P	20	21	2- 7
1972	KC A P		18	5- 6
1973	PIT N P	41	42	10- 6
1974	PIT N P		33	15-11
1975	PIT N P		28	13-11
1976	PIT N P	30	33	15- 8
	BRTL	238	252	74-80
				.216

ROOKS, GEORGE BRINTON MC CLELLAN
(REAL NAME GEORGE
BRINTON MC CLELLAN RUCKSER)
B.OCT.21,1863 CHICAGO,ILL.
D.MAR.11,1935

YR	CL LEA POS	GP	G	REC
1891	BOS N 0		5	.125

ROONEY, FRANK L.

YR	CL LEA POS	GP	G	REC
1914	IND F 1		12	.212

ROOT, CHARLES HENRY "CHARLEY"
B.MAR.17,1899 MIDDLETOWN,OHIO
D.NOV.5,1970 HOLLISTER,CAL.

YR	CL LEA POS	GP	G	REC
1923	STL A P		1	0- 4
1926	CHI N P		42	18-17
1927	CHI N P		48	26-15
1928	CHI N P		40	14-18
1929	CHI N P		43	19- 6
1930	CHI N P		37	16-14
1931	CHI N P		39	17-14
1932	CHI N P		39	15-10
1933	CHI N P		35	15-10
1934	CHI N P		34	4- 7
1935	CHI N P		38	15- 8
1936	CHI N P		33	3- 6
1937	CHI N P		43	13- 5
1938	CHI N P		44	8- 7
1939	CHI N P		35	8- 8
1940	CHI N P		36	2- 4
1941	CHI N P		19	8- 7
	BRTR		632	201-160

ROQUE, JORGE
B.APR.28,1950 PONCE,P.R.

YR	CL LEA POS	GP	G	REC
1970	STL N 0		5	.000
1971	STL N 0		3	.300
1972	STL N 0		32	.104
1973	MON N 0		25	.148
	BRTR		65	.137

ROSAR, WARREN VINCENT "BUDDY"
B.JULY 3,1914 BUFFALO,N.Y.

YR	CL LEA POS	GP	G	REC
1939	NY A C		43	.276
1940	NY A C		73	.298
1941	NY A C		67	.287
1942	NY A C		69	.230
1943	CLE A C		115	.283
1944	CLE A C		99	.263
1945	PHI A C		92	.210
1946	PHI A C		121	.283
1947	PHI A C		102	.259
1948	PHI A C		90	.255
1949	PHI A C		32	.200
1950	BOS A C		27	.298
1951	BOS A C		58	.229
	BRTR		988	.261

ROSARIO, ANGEL RAMON "JIM"
B.MAY 5,1945 BAYAMON,P.R.

YR	CL LEA POS	GP	G	REC
1971	SF N 0		92	.224
1972	SF N 0		7	.000
1976	MIL A 0		15	.189
	BBTR		114	.216

ROSARIO, SANTIAGO
B.JULY 25,1939 GUAYANILLA,P.R.

YR	CL LEA POS	GP	G	REC
1965	KC A 1-0		81	.235
	BLTL			

ROSE, CHARLES ALFRED
B.SEPT.1,1885 MACON,MO.
D.AUG.4,1961

YR	CL LEA POS	GP	G	REC
1909	STL A P		3	1- 2
	BLTL			

ROSE, DONALD GARY "DON"
B.MAR.19,1947 COVINA,CAL.

YR	CL LEA POS	GP	G	REC
1971	NY N P		1	0- 0
1972	CAL A P		16	1- 4
1974	SF N P		2	0- 0
	BRTR		19	1- 4

YR	CL	LEA	POS	GP	G	REC

ROSE, PETER EDWARD "PETE"
B.APR.14,1941 CINCINNATI,OHIO

YR	CL	LEA	POS	GP	G	REC
1963	CIN	N	2-0		157	.273
1964	CIN	N	2		136	.269
1965	CIN	N	2		162	.312
1966	CIN	N	2-3		156	.313
1967	CIN	N	2-0		148	.301
1968	CIN	N	1-2-0		149	.335
1969	CIN	N	2-0		156	.348
1970	CIN	N	0		159	.316
1971	CIN	N	0		160	.304
1972	CIN	N	0		154	.307
1973	CIN	N	0		160	.338
1974	CIN	N	0		163	.284
1975	CIN	N	3-0		162	.317
1976	CIN	N	3-0		162	.323
		BBTR			2184	.311

ROSEBORO, JOHN
B.MAY 13,1933 ASHLAND,OHIO

YR	CL	LEA	POS	GP	G	REC
1957	BRO	N	C-1		35	.145
1958	LA	N	C-0		114	.271
1959	LA	N	C		118	.232
1960	LA	N	C-1-3		103	.213
1961	LA	N	C		128	.251
1962	LA	N	C		128	.249
1963	LA	N	C		135	.236
1964	LA	N	C		134	.287
1965	LA	N	C-3		136	.233
1966	LA	N	C		142	.276
1967	LA	N	C		116	.272
1968	MIN	A	C		135	.216
1969	MIN	A	C		115	.263
1970	WAS	A	C		46	.233
		BLTR			1585	.249

ROSEBROUGH, E. E. "ZEKE"
B.CHARLESTON,ILL.

YR	CL	LEA	POS	GP	G	REC
1898	PIT	N	P		4	0- 2
1899	PIT	N	P		2	0- 1
					6	0- 3

ROSELLI, ROBERT EDWARD "BOB"
B.DEC.10,1931 SAN FRANCISCO,CAL

YR	CL	LEA	POS	GP	G	REC
1955	MIL	N	C		6	.222
1956	MIL	N	C		4	.500
1958	MIL	N	H		1	.000
1961	CHI	A	C		22	.263
1962	CHI	A	C		35	.188
		BRTR			68	.219

ROSELLO, DAVID (RODRIGUEZ) "DAVE"
B.JUNE 26,1950 MAYAGUEZ,P.R.

YR	CL	LEA	POS	GP	G	REC
1972	CHI	N	S		5	.250
1973	CHI	N	2-S		16	.263
1974	CHI	N	2-S		62	.203
1975	CHI	N	S		19	.259
1976	CHI	N	2-S		91	.242
		BRTR			193	.234

ROSEMAN, JAMES J. "CHIEF"
B.1856 NEW YORK,N.Y.

YR	CL	LEA	POS	GP	G	REC
1882	TRO	N	0		80	.236
1883	MET	AA	1-0		93	.260
1884	MET	AA	0		107	.295
1885	MET	AA	P-0	1	101	0- 1
						.284
1886	MET	AA	0		134	.228
1887	ATH	AA	0		21	.325
	MET	AA	0		59	.281
	BRO	AA	0		1	.250
1890	STL	AA	M-0		80	.322
	LOU	AA	0		2	.250
				1	678	0- 1
						.271

ROSEN, ALBERT LEONARD "FLIP"
B.FEB.29,1924 SPARTANBURG,S.C.

YR	CL	LEA	POS	GP	G	REC
1947	CLE	A	3-0		7	.111
1948	CLE	A	3		5	.200
1949	CLE	A	3		23	.159
1950	CLE	A	3		155	.287
1951	CLE	A	3		154	.265
1952	CLE	A	1-S-3		148	.302
1953	CLE	A	1-S-3		155	.336
1954	CLE	A	1-2-S-3		137	.300
1955	CLE	A	1-3		139	.244
1956	CLE	A	3		121	.267
		BRTR			1044	.285

ROSEN, GOODWIN GEORGE "GOODY"
B.AUG.28,1913 TORONTO,ONT.,CAN.
CAL.

YR	CL	LEA	POS	GP	G	REC
1937	BRO	N	0		22	.312
1938	BRO	N	0		138	.281
1939	BRO	N	0		54	.251
1944	BRO	N	0		89	.261
1945	BRO	N	0		145	.325
1946	BRO	N	0		3	.333
	NY	N	0		100	.281
		BLTL			551	.291

ROSENBERG, HARRY
B.JUNE 22,1909 SAN FRANCISCO,

YR	CL	LEA	POS	GP	G	REC
1930	NY	N	0		9	.000
		BRTR				

ROSENBERG, LOUIS
B.MAR.5,1903 SAN FRANCISCO,CAL.

YR	CL	LEA	POS	GP	G	REC
1923	CHI	A	2-0		3	.250
		BRTR				

ROSENFELD, MAX
B.DEC.23,1902 NEW YORK,N.Y.
D.MAR.10,1969 MIAMI,FLA.

YR	CL	LEA	POS	GP	G	REC
1931	BRO	N	0		3	.222
1932	BRO	N	0		34	.359
1933	BRO	N	0		5	.111
		BRTR			42	.298

ROSENTHAL, LAWRENCE JOHN
B.MAY 21,1912 ST.PAUL,MINN.

YR	CL	LEA	POS	GP	G	REC
1936	CHI	A	0		85	.281
1937	CHI	A	0		58	.289
1938	CHI	A	0		61	.286
1939	CHI	A	0		107	.265
1940	CHI	A	0		107	.301
1941	CHI	A	0		20	.237
	CLE	A	1-0		45	.187
1944	NY	A	0		36	.198
	PHI	A	U		32	.204
1945	PHI	A	0		28	.200
		BLTL			579	.263

ROSENTHAL, SIMON "SI"
B.NOV.13,1903 BOSTON,MASS.
D.APR.7,1969 BOSTON,MASS.

YR	CL	LEA	POS	GP	G	REC
1925	BOS	A	0		19	.264
1926	BOS	A	0		104	.267
		BLTL			123	.266

ROSER, EMERSON COREY "STEVE"
B.JAN.25,1918 ROME,N.Y.

YR	CL	LEA	POS	GP	G	REC
1944	NY	A	P		16	4- 3
1945	NY	A	P		11	0- 0
1946	NY	A	P		4	1- 1
	BOS	N	P		14	1- 1
		BRTR			45	6- 5

ROSER, JOHN JOSEPH
B.NOV.15,1901 ST.LOUIS,MO.

YR	CL	LEA	POS	GP	G	REC
1922	BOS	N	0		32	.239
		BLTL				

ROSS, CHESTER FRANKLIN "BUSTER"
B.MAR.11,1904 MAYFIELD,KY.

YR	CL	LEA	POS	GP	G	REC
1924	BOS	A	P		30	4- 3
1925	BOS	A	P		33	3- 8
1926	BOS	A	P		1	0- 1
		BLTL			64	7-12

ROSS, CHESTER JAMES "CHET"
B.APR.1,1918 BUFFALO,N.Y.

YR	CL	LEA	POS	GP	G	REC
1939	BOS	N	0		11	.323
1940	BOS	N	0		149	.281
1941	BOS	N	0		29	.120
1942	BOS	N	0		76	.195
1943	BOS	N	0		94	.218
1944	BOS	N	0		54	.227
		BRTR			413	.241

ROSS, CLIFFORD DAVID
B.AUG.3,1928 PHILADELPHIA,PA.

YR	CL	LEA	POS	GP	G	REC
1954	CIN	N	P		4	0- 0
		BLTL				

ROSS, DONALD RAYMOND "DON"
B.JULY 16,1915 PASADENA,CAL.

YR	CL	LEA	POS	GP	G	REC
1938	DET	A	3		77	.260
1940	BRO	N	3		10	.289
1942	DET	A	3-0		87	.274
1943	DET	A	2-S-3-0		89	.267
1944	DET	A	1-0		66	.210
1945	DET	A	3		8	.379
	CLE	A	3		106	.262
1946	CLE	A	3-0		55	.268
		BRTR			498	.262

ROSS, EBEN B.
B.GANANOQUE,ONT.,CAN.

YR	CL	LEA	POS	GP	G	REC
1902	BAL	A	P		2	1- 1

ROSS, FLOYD ROBERT
B.NOV.2,1928 FULLERTON,CAL.

YR	CL	LEA	POS	GP	G	REC
1950	WAS	A	P		6	0- 1
1951	WAS	A	P		11	0- 1
1956	PHI	N	P		3	0- 0
		BRTL			20	0- 2

ROSS, GARY DOUGLAS
B.SEP.16,1947 MCKEESPORT,PA.

YR	CL	LEA	POS	GP	G	REC
1968	CHI	N	P		13	1- 1
1969	CHI	N	P		2	0- 0
	SD	N	P		46	3-12
1970	SD	N	P		33	2- 3
1971	SD	N	P		13	1- 3
1972	SD	N	P		60	4- 3
1973	SD	N	P		58	4- 4
1974	SD	N	P		9	0- 0
1975	CAL	A	P		1	0- 1
1976	CAL	A	P		34	8-16
		BRTR			269	23-43

ROSS, GEORGE SIDNEY
B.JUNE 28,1893 SAN RAFAEL,CAL.
D.APR.22,1935

YR	CL	LEA	POS	GP	G	REC
1918	NY	N	P		1	0- 0
		BLTL				

ROSS, LEE RAVEN "BUCK"
B.FEB.3,1915 NORWOOD,N.C.

YR	CL	LEA	POS	GP	G	REC
1936	PHI	A	P		30	9-14
1937	PHI	A	P		28	5-10
1938	PHI	A	P		29	9-16
1939	PHI	A	P		29	6-14
1940	PHI	A	P		24	5-10
1941	PHI	A	P		1	0- 1
	CHI	A	P		20	3- 8
1942	CHI	A	P		22	5- 7
1943	CHI	A	P		21	11- 7
1944	CHI	A	P		20	2- 7
1945	CHI	A	P		13	1- 5
		BRTR			237	56-95

ROSSI, JOSEPH ANTHONY "JOE"
B.MAR.13,1923 OAKLAND,CAL.

YR	CL	LEA	POS	GP	G	REC
1952	CIN	N	C		55	.221
		BRTR				

ROSSMAN, CLAUDE R.
B.JUNE 17,1881 PHILMONT,N.Y.
D.JAN.16,1928

YR	CL	LEA	POS	GP	G	REC
1904	CLE	A	0		18	.190
1906	CLE	A	1		118	.308
1907	DET	A	1		153	.277
1908	DET	A	1		138	.294
1909	DET	A	1		80	.246
	STL	A	1		4	.467
		BLTL			511	.282

ROSSO, FRANCIS JAMES
B.MAR.1,1921 AGAWAM,MASS.

YR	CL	LEA	POS	GP	G	REC
1944	NY	N	P		3	0- 0
		BRTR				

ROTBLATT, MARVIN JOSEPH "MARV"
B.OCT.18,1927 CHICAGO,ILL.

YR	CL	LEA	POS	GP	G	REC
1948	CHI	A	P		7	0- 1
1950	CHI	A	P		2	0- 0
1951	CHI	A	P		26	4- 2
		BBTL			35	4- 3

ROTH, FRANK CHARLES
B.OCT.11,1878 BURLINGTON,WIS.
D.MAR.27,1955

YR	CL	LEA	POS	GP	G	REC
1903	PHI	N	C		61	.273
1904	PHI	N	C		68	.258
1905	STL	A	C		35	.262
1906	CHI	A	C		16	.196
1909	CIN	N	C		52	.238
1910	CIN	N	C		27	.200
		BRTR			259	.248

YR	CL	LEA	POS	GP	G	REC

ROTH, ROBERT FRANK "BRAGGO"
B.AUG.28,1892 BURLINGTON,WIS.
D.SEPT.11,1936

1914	CHI	A	O		34	.294
1915	CHI	A	3-O		69	.257
	CLE	A	O		40	.287
1916	CLE	A	O		125	.286
1917	CLE	A	O		145	.285
1918	CLE	A	O		106	.283
1919	PHI	A	O		48	.323
	BOS	A	O		63	.256
1920	WAS	A	O		138	.290
1921	NY	A	O		43	.283
		BRTR			811	.284

ROTHEL, BOBERT BURTON
B.SEPT.17,1923 COLUMBIA STATION
OHIO

| 1945 | CLE | A | 3 | | 4 | .200 |
| | | BRTR | | | | |

ROTHERMEL, EDWARD HILL "BOBBY"
B.DEC.18,1870 FLEETWOOD,PA.
D.FEB.11,1927 DETROIT,MICH.

| 1899 | BAL | N | 2 | | 10 | .095 |

ROTHFUSS, JOHN ALBERT
B.1872 IRVINGTON,N.J.
D.APR.20,1947

| 1897 | PIT | N | 1 | | 31 | .348 |

ROTHGEB, CLAUDE JAMES
B.JAN.1,1880 MILFORD,ILL.
D.JULY 5,1944

| 1905 | WAS | A | O | | 6 | .133 |
| | | BB | | | | |

ROTHROCK, JOHN HUSTON "JACK"
B.MAR.14,1905 LONG BEACH,CAL.

1925	BOS	A	S		22	.345
1926	BOS	A	S		15	.294
1927	BOS	A	1-2-S-3	117		.264
1928	BOS	A	P-1-	1	117	0- 0
			S-3-O			.267
1929	BOS	A	O		143	.300
1930	BOS	A	3-O		45	.277
1931	BOS	A	2-O		133	.278
1932	BOS	A	O		12	.208
	CHI	A	O		39	.188
1934	STL	N	O		154	.284
1935	STL	N	O		129	.273
1937	PHI	A	O		88	.267
		BBTR		1	1014	0- 0
						.276

ROUNSAVILLE, VIRLE GENE "GENE"
B.SEP.27,1944 KONAWA,OKLA.

| 1970 | CHI | A | P | | 8 | 0- 1 |
| | | BRTR | | | | |

ROUSH, EDD J.
B.MAY 8,1893 OAKLAND CITY,IND.

1913	CHI	A	O		9	.100
1914	IND	F	O		74	.333
1915	NEW	F	O		145	.298
1916	NY	N	O		39	.188
	CIN	N	O		69	.287
1917	CIN	N	O		136	.341
1918	CIN	N	O		113	.333
1919	CIN	N	O		133	.321
1920	CIN	N	1-2-O		149	.339
1921	CIN	N	O		112	.352
1922	CIN	N	O		49	.351
1923	CIN	N	O		138	.351
1924	CIN	N	O		121	.348
1925	CIN	N	O		134	.339
1926	CIN	N	1-O		144	.323
1927	NY	N	O		140	.304
1928	NY	N	O		46	.252
1929	NY	N	O		115	.324
1931	CIN	N	O		101	.271
		BLTL			1967	.323

ROUTCLIFFE, PHILIP J. "CHICKEN"
B.OCT.24,1870 OSWEGO,N.Y.
D.OCT.4,1918

| 1890 | PIT | N | O | | 1 | .250 |

ROWAN, DAVID
(REAL NAME DAVID DROHAN)
B.DEC.6,1882 ELORA,ONT.,CANADA
D.JULY 30,1955 TORONTO,ONT.,CAN

| 1911 | STL | A | 1 | | 18 | .384 |
| | | BLTL | | | | |

ROWAN, JOHN ARTHUR
B.JUNE 16,1886 NEW CASTLE,PA.
D.SEPT.29,1966

1906	DET	A	P		1	0- 1
1908	CIN	N	P		8	3- 3
1909	CIN	N	P		38	11-12
1910	CIN	N	P		42	14-13
1911	PHI	N	P		12	3- 4
	CHI	N	P		1	0- 0
1913	CIN	N	P		5	0- 4
1914	CIN	N	P		12	1- 3
		BRTR			119	32-40

ROWE, DAVID E.
B.JACKSONVILLE,ILL.
D.OCT.12,1918

1877	CHI	N	P-O	1	2	0- 1
						.286
1882	CLE	N	P-O	1	23	0- 1
						.247
1883	BAL	AA	P-1-	1	59	0- 0
			S-O			.297
1884	STL	U	P-S-	1	87	1- 0
			O			.292
1885	STL	N	O		16	.161
1886	KC	N	M-O		105	.249
1888	KC	AA	M-O		32	.195
		BR		4	324	1- 2
						.257

ROWE, DONALD HOWARD "DON"
B.APR.3,1936 BRAWLEY,CAL.

| 1963 | NY | N | P | | 26 | 0- 0 |
| | | BLTL | | | | |

ROWE, HARLAND STIMSON
B.APR.20,1896 SPRINGVALE,ME.
D.MAY 26,1969 SPRINGVALE,MAINE

| 1916 | PHI | A | 3 | | 17 | .139 |
| | | BLTR | | | | |

ROWE, JOHN CHARLES
B.DEC.8,1857 HARRISBURG,PA.
D.APR.26,1911

1879	BUF	N	C-O		8	.382
1880	BUF	N	C-3-O		77	.256
1881	BUF	N	C-S-3-O		61	.333
1882	BUF	N	C-S-3-O		75	.266
1883	BUF	N	C-S-3-O		86	.275
1884	BUF	N	C-S-O		91	.310
1885	BUF	N	C-S-O		98	.289
1886	DET	N	S		111	.303
1887	DET	N	S		123	.363
1888	DET	N	S		105	.277
1889	PIT	N	S		74	.258
1890	BUF	P	M-S		125	.250
		BLTR			1034	.292

ROWE, KENNETH DARRELL "KEN"
B.DEC.31,1933 FERNDALE,MICH.

1963	LA	N	P		14	1- 1
1964	BAL	A	P		6	1- 0
1965	BAL	A	P		6	0- 0
		BRTR			26	2- 1

ROWE, LYNWOOD THOMAS "SCHOOLBOY"
B.JAN.11,1912 WACO,TEX.
D.JAN.8,1961

1933	DET	A	P	19	21	7- 4
1934	DET	A	P	45	51	24- 8
1935	DET	A	P	42	45	19-13
1936	DET	A	P	41	45	19-10
1937	DET	A	P		10	1- 4
1938	DET	A	P		4	0- 2
1939	DET	A	P	28	31	10-12
1940	DET	A	P		27	16- 3
1941	DET	A	P	27	32	8- 6
1942	DET	A	P		2	1- 0
	BRO	N	P	9	14	1- 0
1943	PHI	N	P	27	82	14- 8
1946	PHI	N	P	17	30	11- 4
1947	PHI	N	P	31	43	14-10
1948	PHI	N	P	30	31	10-10
1949	PHI	N	P		23	3- 7
		BRTR		382	491	158-101

ROWELL, CARVEL WILLIAM "BAMA"
B.JAN.13,1917 CITRONELLE,ALA.

1939	BOS	N	O		21	.186
1940	BOS	N	2-O		130	.305
1941	BOS	N	2-3-O		138	.267
1946	BOS	N	O		95	.280
1947	BOS	N	2-3-O		113	.276
1948	PHI	N	2-3-O		77	.240
		BLTR			574	.275

ROWEN, W. EDWARD "ED"
B.OCT.22,1857 BRIDGEPORT,CONN.
D.FEB.22,1892

1882	BOS	N	C-S-3-O		82	.245
1883	ATH	AA	C-2-3-O		49	.227
1884	ATH	AA	C		4	.400
					135	.243

ROWLAND, CHARLES LELAND
B.JULY 23,1899 HENDERSON,N.C.

| 1923 | PHI | A | C | | 6 | .000 |
| | | BRTR | | | | |

ROWLAND, CLARENCE HENRY "PANTS"
B.FEB.12,1879 PLATTEVILLE,WIS.
D.MAY 17,1969 CHICAGO,ILL.
NON-PLAYING MANAGER
CHI(A) 1915-18

ROXBOUGH, JAMES A.
B.SAN FRANCISCO,CAL.

1884	BAL	AA	C		2	.333
1887	ATH	AA	C		2	.125
		BRTR			4	.214

ROY, CHARLES ROBERT
B.JUNE 22,1884 BEAULIEU,MINN.
D.FEB.10,1950 BLACKFOOT,IDAHO

| 1906 | PHI | N | P | | 8 | 0- 1 |

ROY, EMILE ARTHUR
B.MAY 26,1907 BRIGHTON,MASS.

| 1933 | PHI | A | P | | 1 | 0- 1 |
| | | BRTR | | | | |

ROY, JEAN PIERRE
B.JUNE 26,1920 MONTREAL,QOE.,CAN.

| 1946 | BRO | N | P | | 3 | 0- 0 |
| | | BRTR | | | | |

ROY, LUTHER FRANKLIN
B.JULY 29,1902 DALTENAH,TENN.
D.JULY 24,1963 GRAND RAPIDS,MICH.

1924	CLE	A	P		16	0- 5
1925	CLE	A	P		6	0- 0
1927	CHI	N	P		11	3- 1
1929	PHI	N	P		21	3- 6
	BRO	N	P		2	0- 0
		BRTR			56	6-12

ROY, NORMAN BROOKS "NORMIE"
B.NOV.15,1928 NEWTON,MASS.

| 1950 | BOS | N | P | | 19 | 4- 3 |
| | | BRTR | | | | |

ROYSTER, JERON KENNIS "JERRY"
B.OCT.18,1952 SACRAMENTO,CAL.

1973	LA	N	2-3		10	.211
1974	LA	N	2-3-O		6	.000
1975	LA	N	2-S-3-O		13	.250
1976	ATL	N	S-3		149	.248
		BRTR			178	.247

ROZEK, RICHARD LOUIS "DICK"
B.MAR.27,1927 CEDAR RAPIDS,IOWS

1950	CLE	A	P		12	0- 0
1951	CLE	A	P		7	0- 0
1952	CLE	A	P		10	1- 0
1953	PHI	A	P		2	0- 0
1954	PHI	A	P		2	0- 0
		BLTL			33	1- 0

ROZNOVSKY, VICTOR JOSEPH "VIC"
B.OCT.19,1938 SHINER,TEX.

1964	CHI	N	C		35	.197
1965	CHI	N	C		71	.221
1966	BAL	A	C		41	.237
1967	BAL	A	C		45	.206
1969	PHI	N	C		13	.231
		BLTR			205	.218

RUBELING, ALBERT WILLIAM
B.MAY 10,1914 PARKVILLE,MD.

1940	PHI	A	2-3		108	.245
1941	PHI	A	3		6	.263
1943	PIT	N	2-3		47	.262
1944	PIT	N	2-3-O		92	.245
		BRTR			253	.249

RUBERTO, JOHN EDWARD
B.JAN.2,1946 STATEN ISLAND,N.Y.

1969	SD	N	C		19	.143
1972	CIN	N	C		2	.000
		BRTR			21	.125

YR	CL LEA POS	GP	G	REC

RUBIO, JORGE JESUS
B.APR.23,1945 MEXICALI,MEXICO

YR	CL LEA POS	GP	G	REC
1966	CAL A P		7	2- 1
1967	CAL A P		3	0- 2
	BRTR		10	2- 3

RUBLE, WILLIAM ARTHUR "ART"
B.MAR.11,1903 KNOXVILLE,TENN.

1927	DET A O		56	.165
1934	PHI A O		19	.278
	BLTR		75	.207

RUCKER, GEORGE NAPOLEON "NAP"
B.SEPT.30,1884 CRABAPPLE,GA.
D.DEC.19,1970 ALPHARETTA,GA.

1907	BRO N P		37	15-13
1908	BRO N P		42	17-19
1909	BRO N P		38	13-19
1910	BRO N P		41	17-18
1911	BRO N P		48	22-18
1912	BRO N P		45	18-21
1913	BRO N P		41	14-15
1914	BRO N P		16	7- 6
1915	BRO N P		19	9- 4
1916	BRO N P		9	2- 1
	BRTL		336	134-134

RUCKER, JOHN JOEL "JOHNNY"
B.JAN.15,1917 CRABAPPLE,GA.

1940	NY N O		86	.296
1941	NY N O		143	.288
1943	NY N O		132	.273
1944	NY N O		144	.244
1945	NY N O		105	.373
1946	NY N O		95	.264
	BLTR		705	.272

RUCKSER, GEORGE BRINTON
MC CLELLAN
(PLAYED UNDER NAME OF GEORGE
BRINTON MC CLELLAN ROOKS)

RUDDERHAM, JOHN EDMUND
B.AUG.30,1863 QUINCY,MASS.
D.APR.3,1942

| 1884 | BOS U O | | 1 | .250 |
| | BRTR | | | |

RUDI, JOSEPH ODEN "JOE"
B.SEP.7,1946 MODESTO,CAL.

1967	KC A 1-O		19	.186
1968	OAK A O		68	.177
1969	OAK A 1-O		35	.189
1970	OAK A 1-O		106	.309
1971	OAK A 1-O		127	.267
1972	OAK A 3-O		147	.305
1973	OAK A 1-O		120	.270
1974	OAK A 1-O		158	.293
1975	OAK A 1-O		126	.278
1976	OAK A 1-O		130	.270
	BRTR		1036	.275

RUDOLPH, ERNEST WILLIAM
B.FEB.13,1913 BLACK RIVER FALLS
WIS.

| 1945 | BRO N P | | 7 | 1- 0 |
| | BLTR | | | |

RUDOLPH, FREDERICK DONALD "DON"
B.AUG.16,1931 BALTIMORE,MD.
D.SEP.12,1968 ENCINO,CAL.

1957	CHI A P		5	1- 0
1958	CHI A P		7	1- 0
1959	CHI A P		4	0- 0
	CIN N P		5	0- 0
1962	CLE A P		1	0- 0
	WAS A P		37	8-10
1963	WAS A P		37	7-19
1964	WAS A P		28	1- 3
	BLTL		124	18-32

RUDOLPH, JOHN HERMAN
B.JULY 10,1882 NATRONA,PA.
D.APR.17,1967 ALLEGHENY VALLEY,
PA.

1903	PHI N H		1	.000
1904	CHI N O		2	.250
			3	.200

RUDOLPH, KENNETH VICTOR "KEN"
B.DEC.29,1946 ROCKFORD,ILL.

1969	CHI N C-O		27	.206
1970	CHI N C		20	.100
1971	CHI N C		25	.197
1972	CHI N C		42	.236
1973	CHI N C		64	.206
1974	SF N C		57	.259
1975	STL N C		44	.200
1976	STL N C		27	.160
	BRTR		306	.211

RUDOLPH, RICHARD
"DICK" OR "BALDY"
B.AUG.25,1887 NEW YORK,N.Y.
D.OCT.20,1949

1910	NY N P		3	0- 1
1911	NY N P		1	0- 0
1913	BOS N P	33	35	14-13
1914	BOS N P	42	43	27-10
1915	BOS N P	44	45	22-19
1916	BOS N P		41	19-12
1917	BOS N P	31	32	13-13
1918	BOS N P		21	9-10
1919	BOS N P		37	13-18
1920	BOS N P		18	4- 8
1922	BOS N P		3	0- 2
1923	BOS N P		4	1- 2
1927	BOS N P		1	0- 0
	BRTR	279	284	122-108
	BB 1919-27			

RUEL, HEROLD DOMINIC "MUDDY"
B.FEB.20,1896 ST.LOUIS,MO.
D.NOV.13,1963 PALO ALTO,CAL.

1915	STL A C		10	.000
1917	NY A C		6	.118
1918	NY A C		3	.333
1919	NY A C		81	.240
1920	NY A C		82	.268
1921	BOS A C		113	.277
1922	BOS A C		114	.256
1923	WAS A C		136	.316
1924	WAS A C		149	.283
1925	WAS A C-1		127	.310
1926	WAS A C		117	.299
1927	WAS A C		131	.308
1928	WAS A C		108	.257
1929	WAS A C		69	.245
1930	WAS A C		66	.253
1931	BOS A C		33	.301
	DET A C		14	.120
1932	DET A C		51	.235
1933	STL A C		36	.190
1934	CHI A C		22	.211
	BRTR		1470	.276

NON-PLAYING MANAGER STL(A) 1947

RUETHER, WALTER HENRY "DUTCH"
B.SEPT.13,1893 ALAMEDA,CAL.
D.MAY 16,1970 PHOENIX,ARIZ.

1917	CIN N P	10	31	2- 0
	CIN N P	7	19	1- 2
1918	CIN N P		2	0- 1
1919	CIN N P	33	42	19- 6
1920	CIN N P	37	45	16-12
1921	BRO N P	36	49	10-13
1922	BRO N P	35	67	21-12
1923	BRO N P-1	34	49	15-14
				.274
1924	BRO N P	30	33	8-13
1925	WAS A P-1	30	55	18- 7
				.333
1926	WAS A P	23	47	13- 6
	NY A P	5	13	2- 3
1927	NY A P	27	35	13- 6
	BLTL	309	487	138-95
				.258

RUFER, RUDOLPH JOSEPH "RUDY"
B.OCT.28,1926 NEW YORK,N.Y.

1949	NY N S		7	.067
1950	NY N S		15	.091
	BRTR		22	.077

RUFFING, CHARLES HERBERT "RED"
B.MAY 3,1904 GRANVILLE,ILL.

1924	BOS A P		8	0- 0
1925	BOS A P		37	9-18
1926	BOS A P		37	6-15
1927	BOS A P	26	29	5-13
1928	BOS A P	42	60	10-25
1929	BOS A P	35	60	9-22
1930	BOS A P	4	6	0- 3
	NY A P	34	52	15- 5
1931	NY A P	37	48	16-14
1932	NY A P	35	55	18- 7
1933	NY A P	35	55	9-14
1934	NY A P	36	45	19-11
1935	NY A P	30	50	16-11
1936	NY A P	33	53	20-12
1937	NY A P	31	54	20- 7
1938	NY A P	31	45	21- 7
1939	NY A P	28	44	21- 7
1940	NY A P	30	33	15-12
1941	NY A P	23	38	15- 6
1942	NY A P	24	30	14- 7
1945	NY A P	11	21	7- 3
1946	NY A P		8	5- 1
1947	CHI A P	9	14	3- 5
	BRTR	624	882	273-225
				.269

RUHLE, VERNON GERALD "VERN"
B.JAN.25,1951 COLEMAN,MICH.

1974	DET A P		5	2- 0
1975	DET A P		32	11-12
1976	DET A P		32	9-12
	BRTR		69	22-24

RUIZ, HIRALDO SABLON "CHICO"
B.DEC.5,1938 SANTO DOMINGO,CUBA
D.FEB.9,1972 SAN DIEGO,CAL.

1964	CIN N 2-3		77	.244
1965	CIN N S-3		29	.111
1966	CIN N S-3-O		82	.255
1967	CIN N 2-S-3-O		105	.220
1968	CIN N 1-2-S-3		85	.259
1969	CIN N 1-2-S-3-O		88	.245
1970	CAL A C-1-2-S-3		68	.243
1971	CAL A 2-3		31	.263
	BBTR		565	.240

RULLO, JOSEPH VINCENT
B.JUNE 16,1916 NEW YORK,N.Y.
D.OCT.28,1969 PHILADELPHIA,PA.

1943	PHI A 2		16	.291
1944	PHI A 1-2		35	.167
	BRTR		51	.212

RUMLER, WILLIAM GEORGE
B.MAR.27,1892 MILFORD,NEB.
D.MAY 26,1966 LINCOLN,NEB.

1914	STL A C		33	.174
1916	STL A O		27	.324
1917	STL A O		78	.261
	BRTR		138	.251

RUNNELS, JAMES EDWARD "PETE"
B.JAN.28,1928 LUFKIN,TEX.

1951	WAS A S		78	.278
1952	WAS A 2-S		152	.285
1953	WAS A 2-S		137	.257
1954	WAS A 2-S-O		139	.268
1955	WAS A 2-S		134	.284
1956	WAS A 1-2-S		147	.310
1957	WAS A 1-2-3		134	.230
1958	BOS A 1-2		147	.322
1959	BOS A 1-2-S		147	.314
1960	BOS A 1-2-3		143	.320
1961	BOS A 1-2-S-3		143	.317
1962	BOS A 1		152	.326
1963	HOU N 1-2-3		124	.253
1964	HOU N 1		22	.196
	BLTR		1799	.291

NON-PLAYING MANAGER
BOS (A) 1966 (INTERIM)

RUSH, JESS HOWARD "ANDY"
B.DEC.26,1896 NEW HAVEN,W.VA.
D.MAR.16,1969 FRESNO,CAL.

| 1925 | BRO N P | | 4 | 0- 1 |
| | BRTR | | | |

YR	CL	LEA	POS	GP	G	REC

RUSH, ROBERT RANSOM "BOB"
B.DEC.21,1925 BATTLE CREEK,MICH

YR	CL	LEA	POS	GP	G	REC
1948	CHI	N	P	36	38	5-11
1949	CHI	N	P		35	10-18
1950	CHI	N	P	39	40	13-20
1951	CHI	N	P		37	11-12
1952	CHI	N	P		34	17-13
1953	CHI	N	P		29	9-14
1954	CHI	N	P		33	13-15
1955	CHI	N	P		33	13-11
1956	CHI	N	P		32	13-10
1957	CHI	N	P		31	6-16
1958	MIL	N	P		28	10- 6
1959	MIL	N	P		31	5- 6
1960	MIL	N	P		10	2- 0
	CHI	A	P		9	0- 0
	BRTR			417	420	127-152

RUSIE, AMOS WILSON
B.MAY 30,1871 MOORESVILLE,IND.
D.DEC.6,1942 SEATTLE,WASH.

YR	CL	LEA	POS	GP	G	REC
1889	IND	N	P		26	11-11
1890	NY	N	P	64	73	28-33
1891	NY	N	P		56	34-20
1892	NY	N	P	62	65	32-28
1893	NY	N	P	54	55	33-21
1894	NY	N	P		50	36-13
1895	NY	N	P		47	23-22
1897	NY	N	P		37	28- 8
1898	NY	N	P	35	36	20-11
1901	CIN	N	P		3	0- 1
	BRTR			434	448	245-168

RUSSELL, ALLAN E. "RUBBERARM"
B.JULY 31,1893 BALTIMORE,MS.

YR	CL	LEA	POS	GP	G	REC
1915	NY	A	P		5	1- 2
1916	NY	A	P	34	35	6-10
1917	NY	A	P	25	30	7- 8
1918	NY	A	P	27	29	8-11
1919	NY	A	P		23	9- 4
	BOS	A	P		21	8- 5
1920	BOS	A	P	16	17	5- 6
1921	BOS	A	P		39	7-11
1922	BOS	A	P		34	6- 7
1923	WAS	A	P	52	54	10- 7
1924	WAS	A	P		37	5- 1
1925	WAS	A	P		32	2- 4
	BBTR			345	356	74-76

RUSSELL, BENJAMIN PAUL
B.1870 READING,PA.

YR	CL	LEA	POS	GP	G	REC
1894	STL	N	O		3	.100

RUSSELL, CLARENCE DICKSON "LEFTY"
B.JULY 18,1890 BALTIMORE,MD.
D.JAN.22,1962

YR	CL	LEA	POS	GP	G	REC
1910	PHI	A	P		1	1- 0
1911	PHI	A	P		7	0- 2
1912	PHI	A	P		3	0- 2
	BLTL			11	1- 4	

RUSSELL, EWELL ALBERT "REB"
B.APR.12,1889 JACKSON,MISS.
D.SEPT.30,1973 INDIANAPOLIS,IND

YR	CL	LEA	POS	GP	G	REC
1913	CHI	A	P	51	52	22-16
1914	CHI	A	P	38	39	8-12
1915	CHI	A	P	41	45	11-12
1916	CHI	A	P		56	18-11
1917	CHI	A	P	35	39	15- 5
1918	CHI	A	P	19	27	6- 5
1919	CHI	A	P		1	0- 0
1922	PIT	N	O		60	.368
1923	PIT	N	O		94	.289
	BLTL			241	413	80-61
						.269

RUSSELL, GLEN DAVID "RIP"
B.JAN.26,1915 LOS ANGELES,CAL.
D.SEPT.26,1976 LOS ALAMITOS,CAL

YR	CL	LEA	POS	GP	G	REC
1939	CHI	N	1		143	.273
1940	CHI	N	1-3		68	.247
1941	CHI	N	1		6	.294
1942	CHI	N	1-2-3-O	102	.242	
1946	BOS	A	2-3		80	.208
1947	BOS	A	3		26	.154
	BRTR			425	.255	

RUSSELL, HARVEY HOLMES
B.JAN.10,1887 MARSHALL,VA.

YR	CL	LEA	POS	GP	G	REC
1914	BAL	F	C		79	.247
1915	BAL	F	C		52	.243
	BLTR			131	.246	

RUSSELL, JACK ERWIN
B.OCT.24,1905 PARIS,TEX.

YR	CL	LEA	POS	GP	G	REC
1926	BOS	A	P		37	0- 5
1927	BOS	A	P	34	35	4- 9
1928	BOS	A	P	32	35	11-14
1929	BOS	A	P	35	37	6-18
1930	BOS	A	P	35	41	9-20
1931	BOS	A	P	36	41	10-18
1932	BOS	A	P		11	1- 7
	CLE	A	P	18	20	5- 7
1933	WAS	A	P		50	12- 6
1934	WAS	A	P		54	5-10
1935	WAS	A	P		43	4- 9
1936	WAS	A	P		18	3- 2
	BOS	A	P		23	0- 3
1937	DET	A	P		25	2- 5
1938	CHI	N	P		42	6- 1
1939	CHI	N	P	39	43	4- 3
1940	STL	N	P		26	3- 4
	BRTR			558	581	85-141

RUSSELL, JAMES WILLIAM "JIM"
B.OCT.1,1919 FAYETTE CITY,PA.

YR	CL	LEA	POS	GP	G	REC
1942	PIT	N	O		5	.071
1943	PIT	N	1-O	146	.259	
1944	PIT	N	O		152	.312
1945	PIT	N	O		146	.284
1946	PIT	N	1-O	146	.277	
1947	PIT	N	O		128	.253
1948	BOS	N	O		89	.264
1949	BOS	N	O		130	.231
1950	BRO	N	O		77	.229
1951	BRO	N	O		16	.000
	BBTR			1035	.267	

RUSSELL, JOHN ALBERT
B.OCT.20,1895 SAN MATEO,CAL.
D.NOV.20,1930

YR	CL	LEA	POS	GP	G	REC
1917	BRO	N	P		5	0- 1
1918	BRO	N	P		1	0- 0
1921	CHI	A	P		11	2- 5
1922	CHI	A	P		5	0- 1
	BLTL			22	2- 7	

RUSSELL, LLOYD OPAL
B.APR.10,1915 ADA,OKLA
D.MAY 24,1968

YR	CL	LEA	POS	GP	G	REC
1938	CLE	A	H		2	.000
	BRTR					

RUSSELL, WILLIAM ELLIS "BILL"
B.OCT.21,1948 PITTSBURG,KAN.

YR	CL	LEA	POS	GP	G	REC
1969	LA	N	O		98	.226
1970	LA	N	S-O		81	.259
1971	LA	N	2-S-O		91	.227
1972	LA	N	S-O		129	.272
1973	LA	N	S		162	.265
1974	LA	N	S-O		160	.269
1975	LA	N	S		84	.206
1976	LA	N	S		149	.274
	BRTR			954	.258	
	BB 1971					

RUSSO, MARIUS UGO "LEFTY"
B.JULY 19,1914 BROOKLYN,N.Y.

YR	CL	LEA	POS	GP	G	REC
1939	NY	A	P		21	8- 3
1940	NY	A	P		30	14- 8
1941	NY	A	P		28	14-10
1942	NY	A	P		9	4- 1
1943	NY	A	P		24	5-10
1946	NY	A	P	8	10	0- 2
	BRTL			120	122	45-34

RUST
B.LOUISVILLE,KY.

YR	CL	LEA	POS	GP	G	REC
1882	BAL	AA	P-O		1	0- 0
						.333

RUSTECK, RICHARD FRANK "DICK"
B.JULY 12,1941 CHICAGO,ILL.

YR	CL	LEA	POS	GP	G	REC
1966	NY	N	P		8	1- 2
	BRTL					

RUSZKOWSKI, HENRY ALEXANDER
B.NOV.10,1925 CLEVELAND,OHIO

YR	CL	LEA	POS	GP	G	REC
1944	CLE	A	C		3	.375
1945	CLE	A	C		14	.204
1947	CLE	A	C		23	.259
	BRTR			40	.238	

RUTH, GEORGE HERMAN "BABE"
"THE BAMBINO" OR
"THE SULTAN OF SWAT"
B.FEB.6,1895 BALTIMORE,MD.
D.AUG.16,1948 NEW YORK,N.Y.

YR	CL	LEA	POS	GP	G	REC
1914	BOS	A	P	4	5	2- 1
1915	BOS	A	P	32	42	18- 6
1916	BOS	A	P	44	67	23-12
1917	BOS	A	P	41	52	24-13
1918	BOS	A	P-1-	20	95	13- 7
			O			.300
1919	BOS	A	P-O	17	130	8- 5
						.322
1920	NY	A	P-O	1	142	1- 0
						.376
1921	NY	A	P-O	2	152	2- 0
						.378
1922	NY	A	O		110	.315
1923	NY	A	O		152	.393
1924	NY	A	O		153	.378
1925	NY	A	O		98	.290
1926	NY	A	O		152	.372
1927	NY	A	O		151	.356
1928	NY	A	O		154	.323
1929	NY	A	O		135	.345
1930	NY	A	P-O	1	145	1- 0
						.359
1931	NY	A	O		145	.373
1932	NY	A	O		133	.341
1933	NY	A	P-O	1	137	1- 0
						.301
1934	NY	A	O		125	.288
1935	BOS	N	O		28	.181
	BLTL			163	2503	93-44
						.342

RUTHERFORD, JAMES HOLLIS
B.SEPT.26,1886 STILLWATER,MICH.
D.SEPT.18,1956

YR	CL	LEA	POS	GP	G	REC
1910	CLE	A	O		1	.500

RUTHERFORD, JOHN WILLIAM
B.MAY 5,1926 BELLEVILLE,ONT.,
CANADA

YR	CL	LEA	POS	GP	G	REC
1952	BRO	N	P		22	7- 7
	BLTR					

RUTHVEN, RICHARD DAVID "DICK"
B.MAR.27,1951 SACRAMENTO,CAL.

YR	CL	LEA	POS	GP	G	REC
1973	PHI	N	P	25	27	6- 9
1974	PHI	N	P		35	9-13
1975	PHI	N	P	11	12	2- 2
1976	ATL	N	P	36	37	14-17
	BRTR			107	111	31-41

RUTNER, MILTON MICKEY
B.MAR.18,1920 HEMPSTEAD,N.Y.

YR	CL	LEA	POS	GP	G	REC
1947	PHI	A	3		12	.250
	BRTR					

RYAN, CORNELIUS JOSEPH "CONNIE"
B.FEB.27,1920 NEW ORLEANS,LA.

YR	CL	LEA	POS	GP	G	REC
1942	NY	N	2		11	.185
1943	BOS	N	2-3		132	.212
1944	BOS	N	2		88	.295
1946	BOS	N	2-3		143	.241
1947	BOS	N	2-S		150	.265
1948	BOS	N	2-3		51	.213
1949	BOS	N	1-2-S-3	85	.250	
1950	BOS	N	2		20	.194
	CIN	N	2		106	.259
1951	CIN	N	1-2-3-O	136	.237	
1952	PHI	N	2		154	.241
1953	PHI	N	1-2		90	.296
	CHI	A	3		17	.222
1954	CIN	N	H		1	.000
	BRTR			1184	.248	
NON-PLAYING MANAGER
ATL(N) 1975 (INTERIM)

RYAN, DANIEL R. "CYCLONE"
B.1866 ERIE,PA.
D.JAN.30,1917

YR	CL	LEA	POS	GP	G	REC
1887	MET	AA	1		8	.285
1891	BOS	N	P	1	0- 0	
				9	0- 0	
						.278

RYAN, J.

YR	CL	LEA	POS	GP	G	REC
1895	STL	N	3		2	.000

YR CL LEA POS GP G REC

RYAN, JACK "GULFPORT"
B.SEPT.19,1884 LAWRENCEVILLE, ILL.
D.OCT.16,1949
```
1908 CLE A  P        8   1- 0
1909 BOS A  P   13  14   4- 3
1911 BRO N  P        3   0- 1
          TR   24  25   5- 4
```

RYAN, JAMES E. "JIMMY"
B.FEB.11,1863 CLINTON,MASS.
D.OCT.26,1923 CHICAGO,ILL.
```
1885 CHI N  S-O        3   .462
1886 CHI N  O         84   .306
1887 CHI N  P-O   1  126   0- 0
                           .355
1888 CHI N  P-O   4  130   3- 1
                           .331
1889 CHI N  S-O      135   .324
1890 CHI P  O        118   .330
1891 CHI N  O        118   .289
1892 CHI N  O        127   .289
1893 CHI N  O         82   .304
1894 CHI N  O        108   .359
1895 CHI N  O        108   .322
1896 CHI N  O        127   .312
1897 CHI N  O        135   .309
1898 CHI N  O        143   .322
1899 CHI N  O        124   .301
1900 CHI N  O        106   .276
1902 WAS A  O        120   .317
1903 WAS A  O        114   .245
         BRTL   5 2008   3- 1
                           .314
```

RYAN, JOHN A.
(PLAYED 1 GAME UNDER REAL NAME OF DANIEL SHEEHAN)
B.BIRMINGHAM,MICH.
```
1884 BAL U  P-O   6   3- 2
                      .095
```

RYAN, JOHN BENNETT
B.NOV.12,1868 HAVERILL,MASS.
```
1889 LOU AA C          21   .163
1890 LOU AA C          94   .219
1891 LOU AA C          75   .212
1894 BOS N  C          49   .271
1895 BOS N  C          49   .295
1896 BOS N  C           8   .094
1898 BRO N  C          82   .189
1899 BAL N  C           2   .500
1901 STL N  C          80   .196
1902 STL N  C-1-2-S-   74   .177
              3
1903 STL N  C-1        66   .238
1912 WAS A  3           1   .000
1913 WAS A  C           1   .000
         BRTR         602   .216
```

RYAN, JOHN BUDD "BUD"
B.OCT.6,1885 KANSAS
D.JULY 9,1956 SACRAMENTO,CAL.
```
1912 CLE A  O    93   .271
1913 CLE A  O    73   .296
         BLTR   166   .282
```

RYAN, JOHN COLLINS "BLONDY"
B.JAN.4,1906 LYNN,MASS
D.NOV.28,1959
```
1930 CHI A  3       28   .207
1933 NY N   S      146   .238
1934 NY N   2-S-3  110   .242
1935 PHI N  2-S-3   39   .264
     NY A   S        30   .238
1937 NY N   S        21   .240
1938 NY N   2-S-3   12   .208
         BRTR       386   .239
```

RYAN, JOHN FRANCIS
B.MAY 5,1905 KANSAS CITY,KAN.
D.SEPT.2,1967 ROCHESTER,MINN.
```
1929 BOS A  S-O   2   .000
         BRTR
```

RYAN, JOHN JOSEPH
B.PHILADELPHIA,PA.
D.MAR.22,1902
```
1873 PHI NA 1           1    -
1874 BAL NA O          47    -
1875 NH  NA P-C-   6   37   1- 5
            S-3-O           -
1876 LOU N  O          65   .247
1877 CIN N  O           6   .154
                6  156   1- 5
                           -
```

RYAN, JOHN M.
B.HAMILTON,OHIO
```
1884 WAS U  3-0   7   .143
     WIL U  O     2   .167
                  9   .147
```

RYAN, LYNN NOLAN "NOLAN"
B.JAN.31,1947 REFUGIO,TEX.
```
1966 NY N   P      2    0- 1
1968 NY N   P     21    6- 9
1969 NY N   P     25    6- 3
1970 NY N   P     27    7-11
1971 NY N   P     30   10-14
1972 CAL A  P     39   19-16
1973 CAL A  P     41   21-16
1974 CAL A  P     42   22-16
1975 CAL A  P     28   14-12
1976 CAL A  P     39   17-18
         BRTR    294  122-115
```

RYAN, MICHAEL JAMES "MIKE"
B.NOV.25,1941 HAVERILL,MASS.
```
1964 BOS A  C      1   .333
1965 BOS A  C     33   .159
1966 BOS A  C    116   .214
1967 BOS A  C     79   .199
1968 PHI N  C     96   .179
1969 PHI N  C    133   .204
1970 PHI N  C     46   .179
1971 PHI N  C     43   .164
1972 PHI N  C     46   .179
1973 PHI N  C     28   .232
1974 PIT N  C     15   .100
         BRTR    636   .193
```

RYAN, WILFRED PATRICK DOLAN "ROSY"
B.MAR.15,1898 WORCESTER,MASS.
```
1919 NY N   P          4    1- 2
1920 NY N   P          3    0- 1
1921 NY N   P         36    7-10
1923 NY N   P         45   16- 5
1924 NY N   P         37    8- 6
1925 BOS N  P   37    38    2- 8
1926 BOS N  P          7    0- 2
1928 NY A   P          3    0- 0
1933 BRO N  P         30    1- 1
         BLTR  248   249   52-47
```

RYBA, DOMINIC JOSEPH "MIKE"
B.JUNE 9,1903 DE LANCEY,PA.
D.DEC.13,1971 BROOKLINE STATION MO.
```
1935 STL N  P            2    1- 1
1936 STL N  P    14    18    5- 1
1937 STL N  P    38    41    9- 6
1938 STL N  P           3    1- 1
1941 BOS A  P          40    7- 3
1942 BOS A  P-C  18    21    3- 3
                             .294
1943 BOS A  P          40    7- 5
1944 BOS A  P          42   12- 7
1945 BOS A  P          34    7- 6
1946 BOS A  P           9    0- 1
         BRTR   240   250   52-34
                             .214
```

RYDER, THOMAS
```
1884 STL U  O   8   .214
```

RYE, EUGENE RUDOLPH "HALF-PINT"
(REAL NAME
EUGENE RUDOLPH MERCANTELLI)
B.NOV.15,1906 CHICAGO,ILL.
```
1931 BOS A  O   17   .179
         BLTR
```

RYERSON, GARY LAWRENCE
B.JUNE 7,1948 LOS ANGELES,CAL.
```
1972 MIL A  P   20   3- 8
1973 MIL A  P    9   0- 1
         BRTL   29   3- 9
```

SABO, ALEXANDER "GIZ"
(REAL NAME ALEXANDER SZABO)
B.FEB.14,1910 NEW BRUNSWICK,N.J
```
1936 WAS A  C   4   .375
1937 WAS A  C   1   .000
         BRTR   5   .375
```

SACKA, FRANK
B.AUG.30,1924 ROMULUS,MICH.
```
1951 WAS A  C    7   .250
1953 WAS A  C    7   .278
         BRTR   14   .265
```

SADECKI, RAYMOND MICHAEL "RAY"
B.DEC.26,1940 KANSAS CITY,KAN.
```
1960 STL N  P   26   29    9- 9
1961 STL N  P   31   36   14-10
1962 STL N  P   22   24    6- 8
1963 STL N  P   36   39   10-10
1964 STL N  P   37   39   20-11
1965 STL N  P        36    6-15
1966 STL N  P    5    6    2- 1
     SF N   P        26    3- 7
1967 SF N   P   35   37   12- 6
1968 SF N   P   38   43   12-18
1969 SF N   P   29   30    5- 8
1970 NY N   P        28    8- 4
1971 NY N   P        34    7- 7
1972 NY N   P        34    2- 1
1973 NY N   P        31    5- 4
1974 NY N   P        34    8- 8
1975 STL N  P         8    1- 0
     KC A   P        25    2- 3
     KC A   P         5    1- 0
1976 KC A   P         3    0- 0
     MIL A  P        36    2- 0
         BLTL  559  583  135-130
```

SADEK, MICHAEL GEORGE "MIKE"
B.MAY 30,1946 MINNEAPOLIS,MINN.
```
1973 SF N   C    39   .167
1975 SF N   C    42   .236
1976 SF N   C    55   .204
         BRTR   136   .208
```

SADOWSKI, EDWARD ROMAN "ED"
B.JAN.19,1932 PITTSBURGH,PA.
```
1960 BOS A  C    38   .215
1961 LA A   C    69   .232
1962 LA A   C    27   .200
1963 LA A   C    80   .172
1966 ATL N  C     3   .111
         BRTR   217   .202
```

SADOWSKI, JAMES MICHAEL "JIM"
B.AUG.7,1951 PITTSBURGH,PA.
```
1974 PIT N  P   4   0- 1
         BRTR
```

SADOWSKI, ROBERT "BOB"
B.FEB.19,1938 PITTSBURGH,PA.
```
1963 MIL N  P    19    5- 7
1964 MIL N  P    51    9-10
1965 MIL N  P    34    5- 9
1966 BOS A  P    11    1- 1
         BRTR   115   20-27
```

SADOWSKI, ROBERT FRANK "BOB"
B.JAN.15,1937 ST.LOUIS,MO.
```
1960 STL N  2      1   .000
1961 PHI N  3     16   .130
1962 CHI A  2-3   79   .231
1963 LA A   2-3-0 88   .250
         BLTR    184   .222
```

SADOWSKI, THEODORE "TED"
B.APR.1,1936 PITTSBURGH,PA.
```
1960 WAS A  P    9   1- 0
1961 MIN A  P   15   0- 2
1962 MIN A  P   19   1- 1
         BRTR   43   2- 3
```

SAFFELL, THOMAS JUDSON "TOM"
B.JULY 26,1922 ETOWAH,TENN.
```
1949 PIT N  O    73   .322
1950 PIT N  O    67   .203
1951 PIT N  O    49   .200
1955 PIT N  O    73   .168
     KC A   O     9   .216
         BLTR   271   .238
```

SAGE, HENRY
B.MAR.16,1864 ROCK ISLAND,ILL.
D.MAY 27,1947
```
1890 TOL AA P-C   1   58   0- 1
                          .139
          BR
```

SAGER, SAMUEL B. "PONY"
B.1847 MARSHALLTOWN,IOWA
```
1871 ROK NA S-O   8    -
```

YR	CL	LEA	POS	GP	G	REC

SAIER, VICTOR SYLVESTER "VIC"
B.MAY 4,1891 LANSING,MICH.
D.MAY 14,1967 E.LANSING,MICH.

YR	CL	LEA	POS	GP	G	REC
1911	CHI	N	1		73	.259
1912	CHI	N	1		122	.288
1913	CHI	N	1		149	.289
1914	CHI	N	1		153	.240
1915	CHI	N	1		144	.264
1916	CHI	N	1		147	.253
1917	CHI	N	1		6	.238
1919	PIT	N	1		58	.223
		BLTR			852	.262

SAIN, JOHN FRANKLIN "JOHNNY"
B.SEPT.25,1917 HAVANA,ARK.

YR	CL	LEA	POS	GP	G	REC
1942	BOS	N	`P		40	4- 7
1946	BOS	N	P	37	40	20-14
1947	BOS	N	P	38	40	21-12
1948	BOS	N	P	42	43	24-15
1949	BOS	N	P	37	39	10-17
1950	BOS	N	P		37	20-13
1951	BOS	N	P		26	5-13
	NY	A	P		7	2- 1
1952	NY	A	P	35	41	11- 6
1953	NY	A	P	40	41	14- 7
1954	NY	A	P		45	6- 6
1955	NY	A	P		3	0- 0
	KC	A	P		25	2- 5
		BRTR		412	433	139-116

ST.CLAIRE, EDWARD JOSEPH "EBBA"
B.AUG.5,1921 WHITEHALL,N.Y.

YR	CL	LEA	POS	GP	G	REC
1951	BOS	N	C		72	.282
1952	BOS	N	C		39	.213
1953	MIL	N	C		33	.200
1954	NY	N	C		20	.262
		BBTR			164	.249

ST.VRAIN, JAMES H.
B.JUNE 6,1883 MONROE CO.,MO.
D.JUNE 12,1937

YR	CL	LEA	POS	GP	G	REC
1902	CHI	N	P		12	5- 6
		BRTL				

SALE, FREDERICK LINK
B.MAY 2,1902 CHESTER,S.C.
D.MAY 27,1956

YR	CL	LEA	POS	GP	G	REC
1924	PIT	N	P		1	0- 0
		BRTR				

SALES, EDWARD A.
B.1861 HARRISBURG,PA.
D.AUG.10,1912

YR	CL	LEA	POS	GP	G	REC
1890	PIT	N	S		51	.228
		TR				

SALISBURY, HENRY H.
B.MAY 15,1855 PROVIDENCE,R.I.
D.MAR.29,1933

YR	CL	LEA	POS	GP	G	REC
1879	TRO	N	P-O	10	4- 6	
					.056	
1882	PIT	AA	P-O	39	20-19	
					.152	
				49	24-25	
					.143	

SALISBURY, WILLIAM A.
B.1876 IOWA

YR	CL	LEA	POS	GP	G	REC
1902	PHI	N	P		2	0- 0

SALKELD, WILLIAM FRANKLIN "BILL"
B.MAR.8,1917 POCATELLO,IDAHO
D.APR.22,1967 LOS ANGELES,CAL.

YR	CL	LEA	POS	GP	G	REC
1945	PIT	N	C		95	.311
1946	PIT	N	C		69	.294
1947	PIT	N	C		47	.213
1948	BOS	N	C		78	.242
1949	BOS	N	C		66	.255
1950	CHI	A	C		1	.000
		BLTR			356	.273

SALLEE, HARRY FRANKLIN "SLIM"
B.FEB.3,1885 HIGGINSPORT,OHIO
D.MAR.22,1950 HIGGINSPORT,OHIO

YR	CL	LEA	POS	GP	G	REC
1908	STL	N	P		25	3- 8
1909	STL	N	P		32	10-11
1910	STL	N	P		18	7- 8
1911	STL	N	P		36	15- 9
1912	STL	N	P		48	16-17
1913	STL	N	P		50	19-15
1914	STL	N	P		46	18-17
1915	STL	N	P		46	13-17
1916	STL	N	P		16	5- 5
	NY	N	P		15	9- 4
1917	NY	N	P		34	18- 7
1918	NY	N	P		18	8- 8
1919	CIN	N	P		29	21- 7
1920	CIN	N	P		21	5- 6
	NY	N	P		5	1- 0
1921	NY	N	P		37	6- 4
		BLTL			476	174-143

SALMON, ROGER ELLIOTT
B.MAY 11,1891 NEWARK,N.J.
D.JUNE 17,1974 BELFAST,ME.

YR	CL	LEA	POS	GP	G	REC
1912	PHI	A	P		1	1- 0
		BLTL				

SALMON, RUTHFORD EDUARDO "CHICO"
B.DEC.2,1940 COLON,PANAMA

YR	CL	LEA	POS	GP	G	REC
1964	CLE	A	1-2-O		86	.307
1965	CLE	A	1-2-3-O		79	.242
1966	CLE	A	1-2-S-3-O		126	.256
1967	CLE	A	1-2-S-3-O		90	.227
1968	CLE	A	1-2-S-3-O		103	.214
1969	BAL	A	1-2-S-3-O		52	.297
1970	BAL	A	1-2-S-3		63	.250
1971	BAL	A	1-2-S-3		42	.179
1972	BAL	A	1-3		17	.063
		BRTR			658	.249

SALTZGAVER, OTTO HAMLIN "JACK"
B.JAN.23,1903 CROTON,IOWA

YR	CL	LEA	POS	GP	G	REC
1932	NY	A	2		20	.128
1934	NY	A	1-3		94	.271
1935	NY	A	1-2-3		61	.262
1936	NY	A	3		34	.211
1937	NY	A	1		17	.182
1945	PIT	N	2-3		52	.325
		BLTR			278	.260

SALVE, AUGUSTUS WILLIAM "GUS"
B.DEC.29,1885 BOSTON,MASS.
D.MAR.29,1971 PROVIDENCE,R.I.

YR	CL	LEA	POS	GP	G	REC
1908	PHI	A	P		2	0- 1
		TL				

SALVESON, JOHN THEODORE "JACK"
B.JAN.5,1914 FULLERTON,CAL.
D.DEC.28,1974 NORWALK,CAL.

YR	CL	LEA	POS	GP	G	REC
1933	NY	N	P		8	0- 2
1934	NY	N	P	12	13	3- 1
1935	PIT	N	P		5	0- 1
	CHI	A	P		20	1- 2
1943	CLE	A	P		23	5- 3
1945	CLE	A	P		19	0- 0
		BRTR		87	88	9- 9

SALVO, MANUEL "GYP"
B.JUNE 30,1913 SACRAMENTO,CAL.

YR	CL	LEA	POS	GP	G	REC
1939	NY	N	P		32	4-10
1940	BOS	N	P		21	10- 9
1941	BOS	N	P		35	7-16
1942	BOS	N	P		25	7- 8
1943	BOS	N	P		1	0- 0
	PHI	N	P		1	0- 0
	BOS	N	P		20	5- 7
		BRTR			135	33-50

SAMBITO, JOSEPH CHARLES "JOE"
B.JUNE 28,1952 BROOKLYN,N.Y.

YR	CL	LEA	POS	GP	G	REC
1976	HOU	N	P		20	3- 2
		BLTL				

SAMCOFF, EDWARD WILLIAM "ED"
B.SEPT.1,1924 SACRAMENTO,CAL.

YR	CL	LEA	POS	GP	G	REC
1951	PHI	A	2		4	.000
		BRTR				

SAMFORD, RONALD EDWARD "RON"
B.FEB.28,1930 DALLAS,TEX.

YR	CL	LEA	POS	GP	G	REC
1954	NY	N	2		12	.000
1955	DET	A	S		1	.000
1957	DET	A	2-S-3		54	.220
1959	WAS	A	2-S		91	.224
		BRTR			158	.219

SAMUEL, AMADO RUPERTO
B.DEC.6,1938 SAN PEDRO DE MACORIS,D.R.

YR	CL	LEA	POS	GP	G	REC
1962	MIL	N	2-S-3		76	.206
1963	MIL	N	2-S		15	.176
1964	NY	N	2-S-3		53	.232
		BRTR			144	.215

SAMUELS, JOSEPH JONAS
B.MAR.21,1908 SCRANTON,PA.

YR	CL	LEA	POS	GP	G	REC
1930	DET	A	3		22	.186
		BRTR				

SAMUELS, SAMUEL EARL "IKE"
B.FEB.20,1876 CHICAGO,ILL.

YR	CL	LEA	POS	GP	G	REC
1895	STL	N	3		22	.186
		BRTR				

SANBERG, GUSTAVE E.
B.FEB.23,1896 LONG ISLAND CITY,N.Y.
D.FEB.3,1930

YR	CL	LEA	POS	GP	G	REC
1923	CIN	N	C		7	.176
1924	CIN	N	C		24	.173
		BRTR			31	.174

SANCHEZ, CELERINO (PEREZ)
B.FEB.3,1944 VERACRUZ,MEXICO

YR	CL	LEA	POS	GP	G	REC
1972	NY	A	3		71	.248
1973	NY	A	S-3-O-D		34	.219
		BRTR			105	.242

SANCHEZ, RAUL GUADALUPE (RODRIGUEZ)
B.DEC.12,1930 MARIANAO,CUBA

YR	CL	LEA	POS	GP	G	REC
1952	WAS	A	P		3	1- 1
1957	CIN	N	P		38	3- 2
1960	CIN	N	P		8	1- 0
		BRTR			49	5- 3

SAND, JOHN HENRY "HEINE"
B.JULY 3,1897 SAN FRANCISCO,CAL.
D.NOV.3,1958

YR	CL	LEA	POS	GP	G	REC
1923	PHI	N	S-3		132	.228
1924	PHI	N	S		137	.245
1925	PHI	N	S		148	.278
1926	PHI	N	S		149	.272
1927	PHI	N	S-3		141	.299
1928	PHI	N	S		141	.211
		BRTR			848	.258

SANDERS, ALEXANDER BENJAMIN "BEN"
B.FEB.16,1865 CARPATHEN,VA.
D.AUG.29,1930

YR	CL	LEA	POS	GP	G	REC
1888	PHI	N	P-O	31	57	19-10
						.245
1889	PHI	N	P	40	41	19-17
1890	PHI	P	P	4	44	21-19
1891	ATH	AA	P-O	21	41	12- 7
						.253
1892	LOU	N	P-1	31	53	12-17
						.267
		BRTR		167	236	83-70
						.267

SANDERS, DEE WILMA
B.APR.8,1921 QUITMAN,TEX.

YR	CL	LEA	POS	GP	G	REC
1945	STL	A	P		2	0- 0
		BRTR				

SANDERS, JOHN FRANK
B.NOV.20,1945 GRAND ISLAND,NEB.

YR	CL	LEA	POS	GP	G	REC
1965	KC	A	R		1	.000
		BRTR				

YR	CL	LEA	POS	GP	G	REC

SANDERS, KENNETH GEORGE "KEN"
B.JULY 8,1941 ST.LOUIS,MO.

YR	CL	LEA	POS	GP	G	REC
1964	KC	A	P		21	0- 2
1966	BOS	A	P		24	3- 6
	KC		A	P	38	3- 4
1968	OAK	A	P		7	0- 1
1970	MIL	A	P		50	5- 2
1971	MIL	A	P		83	7-12
1972	MIL	A	P		62	2- 9
1973	MIN	A	P		27	2- 4
	CLE	A	P		15	5- 1
1974	CLE	A	P		9	0- 1
	CAL	A	P		9	0- 0
1975	NY	N	P	29	30	1- 1
1976	NY	N	P		31	1- 2
	KC		A	P	3	0- 0
	BRTR			408	409	29-45

SANDERS, RAYMOND FLOYD "RAY"
B.DEC.4,1917 BONNE TERRE,MO.

YR	CL	LEA	POS	GP	G	REC
1942	STL	N	1		95	.252
1943	STL	N	1		144	.280
1944	STL	N	1		154	.295
1945	STL	N	1		143	.276
1946	BOS	N	1		80	.243
1948	BOS	N	H		5	.250
1949	BOS	N	1		9	.143
	BLTR				630	.275

SANDERS, REGINALD JEROME "REGGIE"
B.SEPT.9,1949 BIRMINGHAM,ALA.

YR	CL	LEA	POS	GP	G	REC
1974	DET	A	1		26	.273
	BRTR					

SANDERS, ROY GARVIN "PEP"
B.AUG.1,1893 STAFFORD,KAN.
D.JAN.17,1950

YR	CL	LEA	POS	GP	G	REC
1917	CIN	N	P	2	3	0- 1
1918	PIT	N	P		28	7- 9
	BRTR			30	31	7-10

SANDERS, ROY L. "SIMON"
B.1894

YR	CL	LEA	POS	GP	G	REC
1918	NY	A	P		6	0- 2
1920	STL	A	P		8	1- 1
	BRTR				14	1- 3

SANDERS, WARREN WILLIAMS
B.AUG.2,1877 MAYNARDVILLE,TENN.
D.AUG.3,1962

YR	CL	LEA	POS	GP	G	REC
1903	STL	N	P		8	1- 6
1904	STL	N	P		4	1- 2
	BLTL				12	2- 8

SANDLOCK, MICHAEL JOSEPH "MIKE"
B.OCT.17,1916 OLD GREENWICH, CONN.

YR	CL	LEA	POS	GP	G	REC
1942	BOS	N	S		2	1.000
1944	BOS	N	S-3		30	.100
1945	BRO	N	C-2-S-3		80	.282
1946	BRO	N	C-3		19	.147
1953	PIT	N	C		64	.231
	BBTR				195	.240
	BL 1944					

SANDS, CHARLES DUANE "CHARLIE"
B.DEC.17,1947 NEWPORT NEWS,VA.

YR	CL	LEA	POS	GP	G	REC
1967	NY	A	H		1	.000
1971	PIT	N	C		28	.200
1972	PIT	N	H		1	.000
1973	CAL	A	C		17	.273
1974	CAL	A	C-O		43	.193
1975	OAK	A	H		3	.500
	BLTR				93	.214

SANDT, THOMAS JAMES "TOMMY"
B.DEC.22,1950 BROOKLYN,N.Y.

YR	CL	LEA	POS	GP	G	REC
1975	OAK	A	2		1	.000
1976	OAK	A	2-S-3		41	.209
	BRTR				42	.209

SANDY, IRWIN
(PLAYED UNDER NAME OF VINCENT NAVA)

SANFORD, JOHN DOWARD
B.JUNE 23,1917 CHATHAM,VA.

YR	CL	LEA	POS	GP	G	REC
1940	WAS	A	1		34	.197
1941	WAS	A	1		3	.400
1946	WAS	A	1		10	.231
	BRTR				47	.209

SANFORD, JOHN FREDERICK "FRED"
B.AUG.9,1919 SALT LAKE CITY, UTAH

YR	CL	LEA	POS	GP	G	REC
1943	STL	A	P		3	0- 0
1946	STL	A	P		3	2- 1
1947	STL	A	P		34	7-16
1948	STL	A	P	42	43	12-21
1949	NY	A	P		29	7- 3
1950	NY	A	P		26	5- 4
1951	NY	A	P		11	0- 3
	WAS	A	P		7	2- 3
	STL	A	P		9	2- 4
	BBTR			164	165	37-55
	BR 1948					

SANFORD, JOHN STANLEY "JACK"
B.MAY 18,1929 WELLESLEY HILLS, MASS.

YR	CL	LEA	POS	GP	G	REC
1956	PHI	N	P		3	1- 0
1957	PHI	N	P		33	19- 8
1958	PHI	N	P		38	10-13
1959	SF	N	P		36	15-12
1960	SF	N	P		37	12-14
1961	SF	N	P	38	39	13- 9
1962	SF	N	P		39	24- 7
1963	SF	N	P	42	45	16-13
1964	SF	N	P	18	19	5- 7
1965	SF	N	P		23	4- 5
	CAL	A	P		9	1- 2
1966	CAL	A	P		50	13- 7
1967	CAL	A	P		12	3- 2
	KC	A	P		10	1- 2
	BRTR			388	393	137-101

SANGUILLEN, MANUEL DEJESUS "MANNY"
B.MAR.21,1944 COLON,PANAMA

YR	CL	LEA	POS	GP	G	REC
1967	PIT	N	C		30	.271
1969	PIT	N	C		129	.303
1970	PIT	N	C		128	.325
1971	PIT	N	C		138	.319
1972	PIT	N	C-O		136	.298
1973	PIT	N	C-O		149	.282
1974	PIT	N	C		151	.287
1975	PIT	N	C		133	.328
1976	PIT	N	C		114	.290
	BRTR				1108	.303

SANICKI, EDWARD ROBERT "BUTCH"
B.JULY 7,1924 WALLINGTON,N.J.

YR	CL	LEA	POS	GP	G	REC
1949	PHI	N	O		7	.231
1951	PHI	N	O		13	.500
	BRTR				20	.294

SANKEY, BENJAMIN TURNER
B.SEPT.2,1907 NAUVOO,ALA.

YR	CL	LEA	POS	GP	G	REC
1929	PIT	N	S		2	.143
1930	PIT	N	2-S		13	.167
1931	PIT	N	S		57	.227
	BRTR				72	.213

SANTIAGO, JOSE GUILLERMO
B.APR.9,1929 COAMO,P.R.

YR	CL	LEA	POS	GP	G	REC
1954	CLE	A	P		1	0- 0
1955	CLE	A	P		17	2- 0
1956	KC	A	P		9	1- 2
	BRTR				27	3- 2

SANTIAGO, JOSE RAFAEL (ALFONSO)
B.AUG.15,1940 JUANA DIAZ,P.R.

YR	CL	LEA	POS	GP	G	REC
1963	KC	A	P		4	1- 0
1964	KC	A	P		34	0- 6
1965	KC	A	P		4	0- 0
1966	BOS	A	P	35	38	12-13
1967	BOS	A	P		50	12- 4
1968	BOS	A	P	18	23	9- 4
1969	BOS	A	P		10	0- 1
1970	BOS	A	P	8	9	0- 2
	BRTR			163	172	34-29

SANTO, RONALD EDWARD "RON"
B.FEB.25,1940 SEATTLE,WASH.

YR	CL	LEA	POS	GP	G	REC
1960	CHI	N	3		95	.251
1961	CHI	N	3		154	.284
1962	CHI	N	S-3		162	.227
1963	CHI	N	3		162	.297
1964	CHI	N	3		161	.313
1965	CHI	N	3		164	.285
1966	CHI	N	S-3		155	.312
1967	CHI	N	3		161	.300
1968	CHI	N	3		162	.246
1969	CHI	N	3		160	.289
1970	CHI	N	3-0		154	.267
1971	CHI	N	3-0		154	.267
1972	CHI	N	2-S-3-0		133	.302
1973	CHI	N	3		149	.267
1974	CHI	A	1-2-S-3-D		117	.221
	BRTR				2243	.277

SANTORINI, ALAN JOEL "AL"
B.MAY 19,1948 IRVINGTON,N.J.

YR	CL	LEA	POS	GP	G	REC
1968	ATL	N	P		1	0- 1
1969	SD	N	P		32	8-14
1970	SD	N	P		21	1- 8
1971	SD	N	P		18	0- 2
	STL	N	P		19	0- 2
1972	STL	N	P		30	8-11
1973	STL	N	P		6	0- 0
	BRTR				127	17-38

SANTRY, EDWARD
B.CHICAGO,ILL.

YR	CL	LEA	POS	GP	G	REC
1884	DET	N	2-S		6	.174

SARGENT, JOSEPH ALEXANDER
B.SEPT.24,1893 ROCHESTER,N.Y.
D.JULY 5,1950

YR	CL	LEA	POS	GP	G	REC
1921	DET	A	2-S-3		66	.253
	BRTR					

SARMIENTO, MANUEL EDUARDO (APONTE) "MANNY"
B.FEB.2,1956 CAGUA,VENEZ.

YR	CL	LEA	POS	GP	G	REC
1976	CIN	N	P		22	5- 1
	BRTR					

SARNI, WILLIAM F. "BILL"
B.SEPT.19,1927 LOS ANGELES,CAL.

YR	CL	LEA	POS	GP	G	REC
1951	STL	N	C		36	.174
1952	STL	N	C		3	.200
1954	STL	N	C		123	.300
1955	STL	N	C		107	.256
1956	STL	N	C		43	.291
	NY	N	C		78	.231
	BRTR				390	.263

SATRIANO, THOMAS VICTOR "TOM"
B.AUG.28,1940 PITTSBURGH,PA.

YR	CL	LEA	POS	GP	G	REC
1961	LA	A	2-S-3		35	.198
1962	LA	A	3		10	.421
1963	LA	A	C-1-3		23	.180
1964	LA	A	C-1-2-S-3		108	.200
1965	CAL	A	C-1-2-3		47	.165
1966	CAL	A	C-1-2-3		103	.239
1967	CAL	A	C-1-2-3		90	.224
1968	CAL	A	C-1-2-3		111	.253
1969	CAL	A	C-1-2		41	.259
	BOS	A	C		47	.189
1970	BOS	A	C		59	.236
	BLTR				674	.225

SAUCIER, FRANCIS FIELD "FRANK"
B.MAY 28,1927 LESLIE,MO.

YR	CL	LEA	POS	GP	G	REC
1951	STL	A	O		18	.071
	BLTR					

SAUER, EDWARD "EDDIE" OR "HORN"
B.JAN.3,1920 PITTSBURGH,PA.

YR	CL	LEA	POS	GP	G	REC
1943	CHI	N	O		14	.273
1944	CHI	N	O		23	.220
1945	CHI	N	O		49	.258
1949	STL	N	H		24	.222
	BOS	N	O		79	.266
	BRTR				189	.256

YR	CL	LEA	POS	GP	G	REC

SAUER, HENRY JOHN "HANK"
B.MAR.17,1919 PITTSBURGH,PA.

YR	CL	LEA	POS	GP	G	REC
1941	CIN	N	O		9	.303
1942	CIN	N	1		7	.250
1945	CIN	N	1-O		31	.293
1948	CIN	N	1-O		145	.260
1949	CIN	N	1-O		42	.237
	CHI	N	O		96	.291
1950	CHI	N	1-O		145	.274
1951	CHI	N	O		141	.263
1952	CHI	N	O		151	.270
1953	CHI	N	O		108	.263
1954	CHI	N	O		142	.288
1955	CHI	N	O		79	.211
1956	STL	N	O		75	.298
1957	NY	N	O		127	.259
1958	SF	N	O		88	.250
1959	SF	N	O		13	.067
	BRTR				1399	.266

SAUNDERS, DENNIS JAMES
B.JAN.4,1949 ALHAMBRA,CAL.

YR	CL	LEA	POS	GP	G	REC
1970	DET	N	P		8	1- 1
	BBTR					

SAUNDERS, RUSSELL COLLIER
B.MAR.12,1906 TRENTON,N.J.

YR	CL	LEA	POS	GP	G	REC
1927	PHI	A	O		5	.133
	BRTR					

SAUTERS, AL
B.PHILADELPHIA,PA.

YR	CL	LEA	POS	GP	G	REC
1890	ATH	AA	3		14	.098

SAVAGE, DONALD ANTHONY
B.MAR.5,1919 BLOOMFIELD,N.J.
D.DEC.25,1961

YR	CL	LEA	POS	GP	G	REC
1944	NY	A	3		71	.264
1945	NY	A	3-O		34	.224
	BRTR				105	.256

SAVAGE, HAROLD JAMES
B.BRIDGEPORT,CONN.
D.JUNE 26,1940 NEW CASTLE,PA.

YR	CL	LEA	POS	GP	G	REC
1912	PHI	N	2		2	.000
1914	PIT	F	3-O		132	.285
1915	PIT	F	O		14	.150
	BLTR				148	.280

SAVAGE, JOHN ROBERT "BOB"
B.DEC.1,1921 MANCHESTER,N.H.

YR	CL	LEA	POS	GP	G	REC
1942	PHI	A	P		8	0- 1
1946	PHI	A	P		40	3-15
1947	PHI	A	P		44	8-10
1948	PHI	A	P		33	5- 1
1949	STL	A	P		4	0- 0
	BRTR				129	16-27

SAVAGE, THEODORE E. "TED"
(BORN EPHESIAN SAVAGE)
B.FEB.21,1937 VENICE,ILL.

YR	CL	LEA	POS	GP	G	REC
1962	PHI	N	O		127	.266
1963	PIT	N	O		85	.195
1965	STL	N	O		30	.159
1966	STL	N	O		16	.172
1967	STL	N	H		9	.125
	CHI	N	3-O		96	.218
1968	CHI	N	O		3	.250
	LA	N	O		61	.206
1969	CIN	N	2-O		68	.227
1970	MIL	A	1-O		114	.279
1971	MIL	A	O		14	.176
	KC	A	O		19	.172
	BRTR				642	.233

SAVERINE, ROBERT PAUL "BOB"
B.JUNE 2,1941 NORWALK,CONN.

YR	CL	LEA	POS	GP	G	REC
1959	BAL	A	R		1	.000
1962	BAL	A	2		8	.238
1963	BAL	A	2-S-O		115	.234
1964	BAL	A	S-O		46	.147
1966	WAS	A	2-S-3-O		120	.251
1967	WAS	A	2-S-3-O		89	.236
	BBTR				379	.239

SAVIDGE, DONALD SNYDER
B.AUG.28,1908 BERWICK,PA.

YR	CL	LEA	POS	GP	G	REC
1929	WAS	A	3		3	0- 0
	BRTR					

SAVIDGE, RALPH AUSTIN
B.FEB.3,1879 BERWICK,PA.
D.JULY 22,1959

YR	CL	LEA	POS	GP	G	REC
1908	CIN	N	P		4	0- 1
1909	CIN	N	P		1	0- 0
	BRTR				5	0- 1

SAVRANSKY, MORRIS "MOE"
B.JAN.13,1929 CLEVELAND,OHIO

YR	CL	LEA	POS	GP	G	REC
1954	CIN	N	P		16	0- 2
	BLTL					

SAWATSKI, CARL ERNEST
B.NOV.4,1927 SHICKSHINNY,PA.

YR	CL	LEA	POS	GP	G	REC
1948	CHI	N	H		2	.000
1950	CHI	N	C		38	.175
1953	CHI	N	C		43	.220
1954	CHI	A	C		43	.183
1957	MIL	N	C		58	.238
1958	MIL	N	C		10	.100
	PHI	N	C		60	.230
1959	PHI	N	C		74	.293
1960	STL	N	C		78	.229
1961	STL	N	C-O		86	.299
1962	STL	N	C		85	.252
1963	STL	N	C		56	.238
	BLTR				633	.242

SAWYER, CARL EVERETT "HUCK"
B.OCT.19,1890 SEATTLE,WASH.
D.JAN.17,1957 LOS ANGELES,CAL.

YR	CL	LEA	POS	GP	G	REC
1915	WAS	A	2		10	.117
1916	WAS	A	2		16	.194
	BRTR				26	.190

SAWYER, EDWIN MILBY "EDDIE"
B.SEPT.10,1910 WESTERLY,R.I.
NON-PLAYING MANAGER
PHI(N) 1948-52, 58-60

SAWYER, RICHARD CLYDE "RICK"
B.APR.7,1948 BAKERSFIELD,CAL.

YR	CL	LEA	POS	GP	G	REC
1974	NY	A	P		1	0- 0
1975	NY	A	P		4	0- 0
1976	SD	N	P		13	5- 3
	BRTR				18	5- 3

SAWYER, WILLARD NEWTON
B.JULY 29,1864 BRIMFIELD,OHIO
D.JAN.5,1936 KENT,OHIO

YR	CL	LEA	POS	GP	G	REC
1883	CLE	N	P		17	4-10
	BLTL					

SAX, ERIK OLIVER "OLLIE"
B.NOV.5,1906 BRANFORD,CONN.

YR	CL	LEA	POS	GP	G	REC
1928	STL	A	3		16	.176
	BRTR					

SAY, JAMES I.
B.1862 BALTIMORE,MD.
D.JUNE 23,1894

YR	CL	LEA	POS	GP	G	REC
1882	LOU	AA	3		1	.500
	ATH	AA	S		1	.500
1884	WIL	U	3		16	.220
	KC	U	3		2	.250
1887	CLE	AA	3		15	.367
					35	.304

SAY, LEWIS I.
B.FEB.4,1854 BALTIMORE,MD.
D.JUNE 5,1930

YR	CL	LEA	POS	GP	G	REC
1873	MAR	NA	S-O		3	–
1874	BAL	NA	S		18	–
1875	NAT	NA	2-S-O		9	–
1880	CIN	N	S		47	.202
1882	ATH	AA	S		71	.221
1883	BAL	AA	S		84	.260
1884	BAL	U	S		79	.236
	KC	U	2-S		17	.217
	BRTR				328	–

SAYLES, WILLIAM NISBETH
B.JULY 27,1917 PORTLAND,ORE.

YR	CL	LEA	POS	GP	G	REC
1939	BOS	A	P		5	0- 0
1943	NY	N	P	18	19	1- 3
	BRO	N	P	5	6	0- 0
	BRTR			28	30	1- 3

SAYLOR, PHILIP ANDREW "LEFTY"
B.JAN.2,1871 VAN WERT CO.,OHIO
D.JULY 23,1937

YR	CL	LEA	POS	GP	G	REC
1891	PHI	N	P		1	0- 0
	TL					

SCALA, GERARD DANIEL "JERRY"
B.SEPT.27,1926 BAYONNE,N.J.

YR	CL	LEA	POS	GP	G	REC
1948	CHI	A	O		3	.000
1949	CHI	A	O		37	.250
1950	CHI	A	O		40	.194
	BLTR				80	.223

SCALZI, FRANK JOHN "SKEETER"
B.JUNE 16,1915 LAFFERTY,OHIO

YR	CL	LEA	POS	GP	G	REC
1939	NY	N	S-3		11	.333
	BRTR					

SCALZI, JOHN ANTHONY
B.MAR.22,1907 STAMFORD,CONN.
D.SEPT.27,1962 PORT CHESTER,N.Y

YR	CL	LEA	POS	GP	G	REC
1931	BOS	N	H		2	.000
	BRTR					

SCANLAN, FRANK ALOYSIUS
B.APR.28,1890 SYRACUSE,N.Y.

YR	CL	LEA	POS	GP	G	REC
1909	PHI	N	P		6	0- 0

SCANLAN, WILLIAM DENNIS "DOC"
B.MAR.7,1881 SYRACUSE,N.Y.
D.MAY 29,1949

YR	CL	LEA	POS	GP	G	REC
1903	PIT	N	P		1	0- 1
1904	PIT	N	P		4	1- 2
	BRO	N	P		14	7- 7
1905	BRO	N	P		33	15-11
1906	BRO	N	P		38	18-13
1907	BRO	N	P		17	8- 8
1909	BRO	N	P		19	8- 7
1910	BRO	N	P		34	9-11
1911	BRO	N	P		22	3-10
	BLTR				182	67-70

SCANLON, JAMES PATRICK "PAT"
B.SEPT.23,1952 MINNEAPOLIS,MINN.

YR	CL	LEA	POS	GP	G	REC
1974	MON	N	3		2	.250
1975	MON	N	1-3		60	.183
1976	MON	N	1-3		11	.185
	BLTR				73	.186

SCANLON, M. J.
B.CHICAGO,ILL.

YR	CL	LEA	POS	GP	G	REC
1890	NY	N	1		3	.000

SCANLON, MICHAEL B.
B.1847 CORK,IRELAND
D.JAN.18,1929
NON-PLAYING MANAGER
WAS(U) 1884, WAS(N) 1886

SCANNELL, JOHN J.
B.1864 BOS U O

YR	CL	LEA	POS	GP	G	REC
1884	BOS	U	O		6	.304

SCANTLEBURY, PATRICO ATHELSTAN "PAT"
B.NOV.11,1925 PANAMA CITY,PAN.

YR	CL	LEA	POS	GP	G	REC
1956	CIN	N	P		8	0- 1
	BLTL					

SCARBOROUGH, RAY WILSON
B.JULY 23,1917 MT.GILEAD,N.C.

YR	CL	LEA	POS	GP	G	REC
1942	WAS	A	P		17	2- 1
1943	WAS	A	P		24	4- 4
1946	WAS	A	P		32	7-11
1947	WAS	A	P		33	6-13
1948	WAS	A	P		31	15- 8
1949	WAS	A	P		34	13-11
1950	WAS	A	P		8	3- 5
	CHI	A	P		27	10-13
1951	BOS	A	P		37	12- 9
1952	BOS	A	P		28	1- 5
	NY	A	P		9	5- 1
1953	NY	A	P		25	2- 2
	DET	A	P		13	0- 2
	BRTR				318	80-85

SCARCE, GUERRANT MC CURDY "MAC"
B.APR.8,1949 DANVILLE,VA.

YR	CL	LEA	POS	GP	G	REC
1972	PHI	N	P		31	1- 2
1973	PHI	N	P		52	1- 8
1974	PHI	N	P		58	3- 8
1975	NY	N	P		1	0- 0
	BLTL				142	5-18

SCARRITT, RUSSELL MALLORY
B.JAN.14,1903 PENSACOLA,FLA.

YR	CL	LEA	POS	GP	G	REC
1929	BOS	A	O		151	.296
1930	BOS	A	O		113	.289
1931	BOS	A	O		10	.154
1932	PHI	N	O		11	.182
	BLTR				285	.285

SCARSELLA, LESLIE GEORGE "LES"
B.NOV.23,1913 SANTA CRUZ,CAL.
D.DEC.17,1958

YR	CL	LEA	POS	GP	G	REC
1935	CIN	N	1		6	.200
1936	CIN	N	1		115	.313
1937	CIN	N	1-O		110	.246
1939	CIN	N	N		16	.143
1940	BOS	N	1		18	.300
	BLTL				265	.285

SCHAAL, PAUL
B.MAR.3,1943 PITTSBURGH,PA.

YR	CL	LEA	POS	GP	G	REC
1964	LA	A	2-3		17	.125
1965	CAL	A	2-3		155	.224
1966	CAL	A	3		138	.244
1967	CAL	A	2-S-3		99	.188
1968	CAL	A	3		60	.210
1969	KC	A	2-S-3		61	.263
1970	KC	A	2-S-3		124	.268
1971	KC	A	3		161	.274
1972	KC	A	S-3		127	.228
1973	KC	A	3		121	.288
1974	KC	A	3		12	.176
	CAL	A	3		53	.248
	BRTR				1128	.244

SCHACHT, ALEXANDER "AL"
B.NOV.11,1892 NEW YORK,N.Y.

YR	CL	LEA	POS	GP	G	REC
1919	WAS	A	P		2	2- 0
1920	WAS	A	P		22	6- 4
1921	WAS	A	P		30	6- 6
	BRTR				54	14-10

SCHACHT, SIDNEY "SID"
B.FEB.3,1924 BOGOTA,N.J.

YR	CL	LEA	POS	GP	G	REC
1950	STL	A	P		9	0- 0
1951	STL	A	P		6	0- 0
	BOS	N	P		5	0- 2
	BRTR				20	0- 2

SCHACKER, HAROLD
B.APR.6,1925 BROOKLYN,N.Y.

YR	CL	LEA	POS	GP	G	REC
1945	BOS	N	P		6	0- 1
	BRTR					

SCHAEFER, HERMAN A. "GERMANY"
B.FEB.4,1877 CHICAGO,ILL.
D.MAY 16,1919 SARANAC LAKE,N.Y.

YR	CL	LEA	POS	GP	G	REC
1901	CHI	N	2		2	.375
1902	CHI	N	1-3-0		80	.188
1905	DET	A	2		153	.244
1906	DET	A	2		124	.238
1907	DET	A	2-S		109	.258
1908	DET	A	2-S-3		153	.259
1909	DET	A	2		87	.250
	WAS	A	2		37	.155
1910	WAS	A	2-0		74	.275
1911	WAS	A	1		125	.334
1912	WAS	A	1-2-0		60	.247
1913	WAS	A	P-2	1	52	0- 0
						.320
1914	WAS	A	2		25	.241
1915	NEW	F	O		58	.214
1916	NY	A	O		1	.000
1918	CLE	A	2		1	.000
	BRTR			1	1141	0- 0
						.256

SCHAEFFER, HARRY EDWARD
B.JUNE 23,1925 READING,PA.

YR	CL	LEA	POS	GP	G	REC
1952	NY	A	P		5	0- 1
	BLTL					

**SCHAFER, HARRY C.
"SILK STOCKING"**
B.AUG.14,1846 PHILADELPHIA,PA.
D.FEB.28,1935

YR	CL	LEA	POS	GP	G	REC
1871	BOS	NA	3		33	-
1872	BOS	NA	3-0		48	.262
1873	BOS	NA	3-0		60	.284
1874	BOS	NA	3		71	.275
1875	BOS	NA	3		51	.295
1876	BOS	N	3		70	.248
1877	BOS	N	S-3-0		33	.277
1878	BOS	N	O		4	.235
1879	CIN	N	S		1	1.000
	BRTR				371	-

SCHAFER, JOHN W.
B.LOCK HAVEN,PA.

YR	CL	LEA	POS	GP	G	REC
1886	MET	AA	P		8	5- 3
1887	MET	AA	P		13	2-11
					21	7-14

SCHAEFFER, MARK PHILIP
B.JUNE 5,1948 SANTA MONICA,CAL.

YR	CL	LEA	POS	GP	G	REC
1972	SD	N	P		41	2- 0
	BLTL					

SCHAFFER, JIMMIE RONALD
B.APR.5,1936 LIMEPORT,PA.

YR	CL	LEA	POS	GP	G	REC
1961	STL	N	C		68	.255
1962	STL	N	C		70	.242
1963	CHI	N	C		57	.239
1964	CHI	N	C		54	.205
1965	CHI	A	C		17	.194
	NY	N	C		24	.135
1966	PHI	N	C		8	.133
1967	PHI	N	C		2	.000
1968	CIN	N	C		4	.167
	BRTR				304	.223

**SCHAFFERNOTH, JOSEPH ARTHUR
"JOE"**
B.AUG.6,1937 SPRINGFIELD,N.J.

YR	CL	LEA	POS	GP	G	REC
1959	CHI	N	P		5	1- 0
1960	CHI	N	P		33	2- 3
1961	CHI	N	P		21	0- 4
	CLE	A	P		15	0- 1
	BRTR				74	3- 8

SCHAIVE, JOHN EDWARD "JOHNNY"
B.FEB.25,1934 SPRINGFIELD,ILL.

YR	CL	LEA	POS	GP	G	REC
1958	WAS	A	H		7	.250
1959	WAS	A	2		16	.153
1960	WAS	A	2		6	.250
1962	WAS	A	2-3		82	.253
1963	WAS	A	H		3	.000
	BRTR				114	.232

SCHALK, LE ROY JOHN
B.NOV.9,1908 CHICAGO,ILL.

YR	CL	LEA	POS	GP	G	REC
1932	NY	A	2		3	.250
1944	CHI	A	2-S		146	.220
1945	CHI	A	2		133	.248
	BRTR				282	.233

**SCHALK, RAYMOND WILLIAM
"RAY" OR "CRACKER"**
B.AUG.12,1892 HARVEL,ILL.
D.MAY 19,1970 CHICAGO,ILL.

YR	CL	LEA	POS	GP	G	REC
1912	CHI	A	C		23	.286
1913	CHI	A	C		128	.244
1914	CHI	A	C		135	.270
1915	CHI	A	C		135	.266
1916	CHI	A	C		129	.232
1917	CHI	A	C		140	.227
1918	CHI	A	C		108	.219
1919	CHI	A	C		131	.282
1920	CHI	A	C		151	.270
1921	CHI	A	C		128	.252
1922	CHI	A	C		142	.281
1923	CHI	A	C		123	.228
1924	CHI	A	C		57	.196
1925	CHI	A	C		125	.274
1926	CHI	A	C		82	.265
1927	CHI	A	M-C		16	.231
1928	CHI	A	M-C		2	1.000
1929	NY	N	C		5	.000
	BRTR				1760	.253

SCHALLER, WALTER "BIFF"
B.SEPT.23,1889 CHICAGO,ILL.
D.OCT.9,1939

YR	CL	LEA	POS	GP	G	REC
1911	DET	A	O		40	.133
1913	CHI	A	O		34	.219
	BLTR				74	.186

SCHALLICK, AUGUST
(PLAYED UNDER NAME OF
AUGUST SHALLIX)

**SCHALLOCK, ARTHUR LAWRENCE
"ART"**
B.APR.25,1925 MILL VALLEY,CAL.

YR	CL	LEA	POS	GP	G	REC
1951	NY	A	P		11	3- 1
1952	NY	A	P		2	0- 0
1953	NY	A	P		7	0- 0
1954	NY	A	P		6	0- 1
1955	NY	A	P		2	0- 0
	BAL	A	P		30	3- 5
	BLTL				58	6- 7

SCHANG, ROBERT MARTIN
B.DEC.7,1891 S.WALES,N.Y.
D.AUG.29,1966 SACRAMENTO,CAL.

YR	CL	LEA	POS	GP	G	REC
1914	PIT	N	C		10	.250
1915	PIT	N	C		56	.184
	NY	N	C		12	.143
1927	STL	N	C		3	.200
	BRTR				81	.188

SCHANG, WALTER HENRY "WALLY"
B.AUG.22,1889 S.WALES,N.Y.
D.MAR.6,1965 ST.LOUIS,MO.

YR	CL	LEA	POS	GP	G	REC
1913	PHI	A	C		77	.266
1914	PHI	A	C		107	.287
1915	PHI	A	C-3-0		116	.248
1916	PHI	A	C-0		110	.266
1917	PHI	A	C		118	.285
1918	BOS	A	C-0		88	.245
1919	BOS	A	C-0		113	.306
1920	BOS	A	C-0		122	.305
1921	NY	A	C		134	.316
1922	NY	A	C		124	.319
1923	NY	A	C		84	.276
1924	NY	A	C		114	.292
1925	NY	A	C		73	.240
1926	STL	A	C		103	.330
1927	STL	A	C		97	.319
1928	STL	A	C		91	.285
1929	STL	A	C		94	.237
1930	PHI	A	C		45	.174
1931	DET	A	C		30	.184
	BBTR				1840	.284

SCHANZ, CHARLEY MURRELL
B.JUNE 8,1919 ANACORTES,WASH.

YR	CL	LEA	POS	GP	G	REC
1944	PHI	N	P		40	13-16
1945	PHI	N	P		35	4-15
1946	PHI	N	P		32	6- 6
1947	PHI	N	P		34	2- 4
1950	BOS	A	P		14	3- 2
	BRTR				155	28-43

SCHAPPERT, JOHN
B.BROOKLYN,N.Y.
D.JULY 29,1916

YR	CL	LEA	POS	GP	G	REC
1882	STL	AA	P-O		15	8- 7
						.173

SCHARDT, WILBUR
B.JAN.20,1886 CLEVELAND,OHIO
D.JULY 20,1964 VERMILION,OHIO

YR	CL	LEA	POS	GP	G	REC
1911	BRO	N	P		39	5-15
1912	BRO	N	P		7	0- 1
	BRTR				46	5-16

SCHAREIN, ARTHUR OTTO "SCOOP"
B.JUNE 30,1905 DECATUR,ILL.
D.JULY 3,1969 SAN ANTONIO,TEX.

YR	CL	LEA	POS	GP	G	REC
1932	STL	A	3		81	.304
1933	STL	A	2-S-3		123	.204
1934	STL	A	H		1	.500
	BRTR				205	.244

SCHAREIN, GEORGE ALBERT "TOM"
B.NOV.21,1914 DECATUR,ILL.

YR	CL	LEA	POS	GP	G	REC
1937	PHI	N	S		146	.241
1938	PHI	N	2-5		117	.238
1939	PHI	N	S		118	.238
1940	PHI	N	S		7	.294
	BRTR				388	.240

SCHARF, EDWARD T.
B.BALTIMORE,MD.
D.MAY 12,1937

YR	CL	LEA	POS	GP	G	REC
1882	BAL	AA	3-0		10	.243
1883	BAL	AA	S		3	.143
					13	.216

SCHAUER, ALEXANDER JOHN "RUBE"
(REAL NAME
DIMITRI IVANOVICH DIMITRIHOFF)
B.MAR.19,1892 ODESSA,RUSSIA
D.APR.15,1957

YR	CL	LEA	POS	GP	G	REC
1913	NY	N	P		3	0- 1
1914	NY	N	P		6	0- 0
1915	NY	N	P		32	2- 8
1916	NY	N	P		19	1- 4
1917	PHI	A	P		33	7-16
	BRTR				93	10-29

SCHEER, ALLAN G.
B.OCT.21,1888 DAYTON,OHIO
D.MAY 6,1959

YR	CL	LEA	POS	GP	G	REC
1913	BRO	N	O		6	.272
1914	IND	F	O		117	.309
1915	NEW	F	O		155	.269
	BLTR				278	.283

SCHEER, HENRY WILLIAM "HEINE"
B.JULY 31,1900 NEW YORK,N.Y.
D.MAR.21,1976 NEW HAVEN,CONN.

YR	CL	LEA	POS	GP	G	REC
1922	PHI	A	2-3		51	.171
1923	PHI	A	2		69	.238
	BRTR				120	.212

SCHEEREN, FREDERICK "FRITZ"
B.SEPT.8,1891 FORD CITY,PA.
D.JUNE 17,1973 OIL CITY,PA.

YR	CL LEA POS	GP	G	REC
1914 PIT N O			11	.267
1915 PIT N O			4	.000
BRTR			15	.243

SCHEETZ, OWEN FRANKLIN
B.DEC.24,1913 NEW BEDFORD,OHIO

YR	CL LEA POS	GP	G	REC
1943 WAS A P			6	0- 0
BRTR				

SCHEFFING, ROBERT BODEN "BOB"
B.AUG.11,1915 OVERLAND,MO.

YR	CL LEA POS	GP	G	REC
1941 CHI N C			51	.242
1942 CHI N C			44	.196
1946 CHI N C			63	.278
1947 CHI N C			110	.264
1948 CHI N C			102	.300
1949 CHI N C			55	.268
1950 CHI N C			12	.188
CIN N C			21	.277
1951 CIN N C			47	.254
STL N C			12	.111
BRTR			517	.263

NON-PLAYING MANAGER
CHI(N) 1957-59, DET(A) 1961-63

SCHEFFLER, THEODORE J.
B.NEW YORK,N.Y.

YR	CL LEA POS	GP	G	REC
1888 DET N O			27	.202
1890 ROC AA O			117	.239
			144	.233

SCHEGG, "LEFTY"

YR	CL LEA POS	GP	G	REC
1912 WAS A P			2	0- 0
TL				

SCHEIB, CARL ALVIN
B.JAN.1,1927 GRATZ,PA.

YR	CL LEA POS	GP	G	REC
1943 PHI A P			6	0- 1
1944 PHI A P			15	0- 0
1945 PHI A P			4	0- 0
1947 PHI A P	21	22	4- 6
1948 PHI A P-O	32	52	14- 8
				.298
1949 PHI A P	38	47	9-12
1950 PHI A P	43	50	3-10
1951 PHI A P	46	48	1-12
1952 PHI A P	30	44	11- 7
1953 PHI A P	28	35	3- 7
1954 PHI A P		1	0- 1
STL N P		3	0- 1
BRTR	267	327	45-65
				.250

SCHEIBECK, FRANK
B.JUNE 28,1865 DETROIT,MICH.
D.OCT.22,1956

YR	CL LEA POS	GP	G	REC
1887 CLE AA P-3	1	3	0- 0
				.364
1888 DET N S		1	.000
1890 TOL AA S		134	.234
1894 PIT N 2-S-3-O		26	.347
WAS N S		49	.238
1895 WAS N S		48	.182
1899 WAS N S		27	.287
1901 CLE A S		93	.217
1906 DET A 2		3	.125
BRTR	1	384	0- 0
				.243

SCHEIBLE, JOHN G. "JACK"
B.FEB.16,1866 YOUNGSTOWN,OHIO
D.AUG.9,1897

YR	CL LEA POS	GP	G	REC
1893 CLE N P		3	1- 1
1894 PHI N P		1	0- 1
TL		4	1- 2

SCHEINBLUM, RICHARD ALAN "RICHIE"
B.NOV.5,1942 NEW YORK,N.Y.

YR	CL LEA POS	GP	G	REC
1965 CLE A H			4	.000
1967 CLE A O			18	.318
1968 CLE A O			19	.218
1969 CLE A O			102	.186
1971 WAS A O			27	.143
1972 KC A O			134	.300
1973 CIN N O			29	.222
CAL A O			77	.328
1974 CAL A O			10	.154
KC A O-D			36	.181
STL N H			6	.333
BBTR			462	.263

SCHELL, CLYDE DANIEL "DANNY"
B.DEC.26,1927 FOSTORIA,MICH.
D.MAY 11,1972 MAYVILLE,MICH.

YR	CL LEA POS	GP	G	REC
1954 PHI N O			92	.283
1955 PHI N H			2	.000
BRTR			94	.281

SCHELLE, GERALD ANTHONY "JIM"
B.APR.13,1917 BALTIMORE,MD.

YR	CL LEA POS	GP	G	REC
1939 PHI A P			1	0- 0
BRTR				

SCHELLHASSE, ALBERT HERMAN
B.MAR.22,1864 EVANSVILLE,IND.
D.JAN.4,1919

YR	CL LEA POS	GP	G	REC
1890 BOS N C-O			9	.096
1891 LOU AA C			6	.156
TR			15	.120

SCHEMANSKE, FREDERICK GEORGE
B.APR.28,1903 DETROIT,MICH.
D.FEB.18,1960

YR	CL LEA POS	GP	G	REC
1923 WAS A P			2	0- 0

SCHEMER, MICHAEL
B.NOV.20,1917 BALTIMORE,MD.

YR	CL LEA POS	GP	G	REC
1945 NY N 1			31	.333
1946 NY N H			1	.000
BLTL			32	.330

SCHENCK, WILLIAM G.
B.BROOKLYN,N.Y.

YR	CL LEA POS	GP	G	REC
1882 LOU AA P-S-	3	59	1- 0
3-O				.265
1884 RIC AA 2-S		41	.218
1885 BRO AA 3		1	.000
	1	101	1- 0
				.237

SCHENEBERG, JOHN B.
B.SEPT.15,1890 GUYANDOTTE,W.VA.
D.SEPT.7,1950

YR	CL LEA POS	GP	G	REC
1913 PIT N P		1	0- 1
1920 STL A P		1	0- 0
BBTR		2	0- 1

SCHENZ, HENRY LEONARD "HANK"
B.APR.11,1921 NEW RICHMOND,OHIO

YR	CL LEA POS	GP	G	REC
1946 CHI N 3			6	.182
1947 CHI N 3			7	.071
1948 CHI N 2-3			96	.261
1949 CHI N 3			7	.429
1950 PIT N 2-S-3			58	.228
1951 PIT N 2-3			25	.213
NY N H			8	.000
BRTR			207	.247

SCHEPNER, JOSEPH MARTIN
B.AUG.10,1895 ALIQUIPPA,PA.
D.JULY 25,1959

YR	CL LEA POS	GP	G	REC
1919 STL A 3			14	.212
BRTR				

SCHERBARTH, ROBERT ELMER "BOB"
B.JAN.18,1926 MILWAUKEE,WIS.

YR	CL LEA POS	GP	G	REC
1950 BOS A C			1	.000
BRTR				

SCHERER, HARRY

YR	CL LEA POS	GP	G	REC
1889 LOU AA O			1	.333

SCHERMAN, FREDERICK JOHN "FRED"
B.JULY 25,1944 DAYTON,OHIO

YR	CL LEA POS	GP	G	REC
1969 DET A P		4	1- 0
1970 DET A P		48	4- 4
1971 DET A P		69	11- 6
1972 DET A P		57	7- 3
1973 DET A P	34	35	2- 2
1974 HOU N P		53	2- 5
1975 HOU N P		16	0- 1
MON N P		34	4- 3
1976 MON N P		31	2- 2
BLTL	346	347	33-26

SCHESLER, CHARLES "DUTCH"
B.JUNE 1,1900 FRANKFORT,GERMANY
D.NOV.19,1953

YR	CL LEA POS	GP	G	REC
1931 PHI N P			17	0- 0
BRTR				

SCHETTLER, LOUIS MARTIN
B.JUNE 12,1886 PITTSBURGH,PA.
D.MAY 1,1960 YOUNGSTOWN,OHIO

YR	CL LEA POS	GP	G	REC
1910 PHI N P			27	2- 6
BRTR				

SCHIAPPACASSE, LOUIS JOSEPH
B.MAR.29,1881 ANN ARBOR,MICH.
D.SEPT.20,1910

YR	CL LEA POS	GP	G	REC
1902 DET A O			2	.000

SCHICK, MAURICE FRANCIS
B.APR.17,1895 CHICAGO,ILL.

YR	CL LEA POS	GP	G	REC
1917 CHI N O			14	.147
BRTR				

SCHILLING, CHARLES THOMAS "CHUCK"
B.OCT.25,1937 BROOKLYN,N.Y.

YR	CL LEA POS	GP	G	REC
1961 BOS A 2			158	.259
1962 BOS A 2			119	.230
1963 BOS A 2			146	.234
1964 BOS A 2			47	.196
1965 BOS A 2			71	.240
BRTR			541	.235

SCHILLINGS, ELBERT ISAIAH "RED.
B.MAR.29,1900 DEPORT,TEX.
D.JAN.7,1954

YR	CL LEA POS	GP	G	REC
1922 PHI A P			4	0- 0
BRTR				

SCHINDLER, WILLIAM GIBBONS
B.JULY 10,1896 PERRYVILLE,MO.

YR	CL LEA POS	GP	G	REC
1920 STL N C			1	.000
BRTR				

SCHIRICK, HARRY ERNEST "DUTCH"
B.JUNE 15,1890 RUBY,N.Y.
D.NOV.12,1968

YR	CL LEA POS	GP	G	REC
1914 STL A H			1	.000
BRTR				

SCHLAFLY, HARRY LINTON "LARRY"
B.SEPT.20,1878 PORT WASHINGTON, OHIO
D.JUNE 27,1919 BEACH CITY,OHIO

YR	CL LEA POS	GP	G	REC
1902 CHI N 2-S-3-O			10	.333
1906 WAS A 2			123	.246
1907 WAS A 2			24	.135
1914 BUF F M-2			52	.254
BPTR			209	.239

NON-PLAYING MANAGER BUF(F) 1915

SCHLEI, GEORGE HENRY "ADMIRAL"
B.JAN.12,1882 CINCINNATI,OHIO
D.JAN.24,1958

YR	CL LEA POS	GP	G	REC
1904 CIN N C			88	.237
1905 CIN N C			95	.226
1906 CIN N C-1			112	.245
1907 CIN N C			72	.272
1908 CIN N C			88	.220
1909 NY N C			89	.244
1910 NY N C			49	.192
1911 NY N C			1	.000
BRTR			594	.237

SCHLEIBNER, FREDERICK PAUL "DUTCH"
B.MAY 19,1894 BERLIN,GERMANY
D.APR.15,1975 TOLEDO,OHIO

YR	CL LEA POS	GP	G	REC
1923 BRO N 1			19	.250
STL A 1			127	.275
BRTR			146	.271

SCHLESINGER, WILLIAM CORDES "BILL"
B.NOV.5,1941 CINCINNATI,OHIO

YR	CL LEA POS	GP	G	REC
1965 BOS A H			1	.000
BRTR				

SCHLITZER, VICTOR JOSEPH "BIFF"
B.DEC.4,1884 ROCHESTER,N.Y.
D.JAN.4,1948

YR	CL LEA POS	GP	G	REC
1908 PHI A P			23	6- 8
1909 PHI A P			9	2- 6
BOS A P			9	2- 2
1914 BUF F P			3	0- 0
BRTR			44	10-16

SCHLUETER, JAY D.
B.JULY 31,1949 PHOENIX,ARIZ.

YR	CL LEA POS	GP	G	REC
1971 HOU N O			7	.333
BRTR				

SCHLUETER, NORMAN JOHN "DUKE"
B.SEPT.25,1917 BELLEVILLE,ILL.

YR	CL LEA POS	GP	G	REC
1938 CHI A C			35	.229
1939 CHI A C			34	.232
1944 CLE A C			49	.123
BRTR			118	.186

YR	CL	LEA	POS	GP	G	REC

SCHMANDT, RAYMOND HENRY
B.JAN.25,1896 ST.LOUIS,MO.
D.FEB.1,1969 ST.LOUIS,MO.

YR	CL	LEA	POS	GP	G	REC
1915	STL	A	1		2	.000
1918	BRO	N	2		34	.307
1919	BRO	N	1-2-3		47	.165
1920	BRO	N	1		28	.238
1921	BRO	N	1		95	.306
1922	BRO	N	1		110	.267
	BRTR				316	.269

SCHMEES, GEORGE EDWARD
B.SEPT.6,1924 CINCINNATI,OHIO

YR	CL	LEA	POS	GP	G	REC
1952	STL	A	1-0		34	.131
	BOS	A	P-1-	2	42	0- 0
			O			.203
	BLTL			2	76	0- 0
						.168

SCHMELZ, ALAN GEORGE "AL"
B.NOV.12,1943 WHITTIER,CAL.

YR	CL	LEA	POS	GP	G	REC
1967	NY	N	P		2	0- 0
	BRTR					

SCHMELZ, GUSTAVIUS HEINRICH
B.SEPT.26,1850 COLUMBUS,OHIO
D.OCT.13,1925 COLUMBUS,OHIO
NON-PLAYING MANAGER
COL(AA) 1884, STL(N) 1886,
CIN(AA) 1887-89, CLE(N) 1890
COL(AA) 1890-91, WAS(N) 1894-97

SCHMIDT, CHARLES "BOSS"
B.SEPT.12,1880 LONDON,ARK.
D.NOV.14,1932

YR	CL	LEA	POS	GP	G	REC
1906	DET	A	C		68	.218
1907	DET	A	C		104	.244
1908	DET	A	C		122	.265
1909	DET	A	C		84	.209
1910	DET	A	C		71	.259
1911	DET	A	C		28	.283
	BBTR				477	.243

SCHMIDT, CHARLES JOHN "BUTCH"
B.JULY 19,1886 BALTIMORE,MD.
D.SEPT.4,1952 BALTIMORE,MD.

YR	CL	LEA	POS	GP	G	REC
1909	NY	A	1		1	0- 0
1913	BOS	N	1		22	.308
1914	BOS	N	1		147	.285
1915	BOS	N	1		127	.251
	BLTL			1	297	0- 0
						.272

SCHMIDT, FRANK ELMER
(PLAYED UNDER NAME OF
FRANK ELMER SMITH)

SCHMIDT, FREDERICK "CRAZY"
B.FEB.13,1868 CHICAGO,ILL.
D.OCT.5,1940

YR	CL	LEA	POS	GP	G	REC
1890	PIT	N	P		11	1- 9
1892	BAL	N	P		7	1- 4
1893	BAL	N	P		9	3- 2
	NY	N	P		4	0- 2
1899	CLE	N	P	19	21	2-17
1901	BAL	A	P		4	0- 2
	BLTL			54	56	7-36

SCHMIDT, FREDERICK ALBERT
B.FEB.9,1916 HARTFORD,CONN.

YR	CL	LEA	POS	GP	G	REC
1944	STL	N	P		37	7- 3
1946	STL	N	P		16	1- 0
1947	STL	N	P		2	0- 0
	PHI	N	P		29	5- 8
	CHI	N	P		1	0- 0
	BRTR				85	13-11

SCHMIDT, HENRY M.
B.JUNE 26,1873 BROWNSVILLE,TEX.
D.APR.23,1926

YR	CL	LEA	POS	GP	G	REC
1903	BRO	N	P	40	41	22-13

SCHMIDT, HERMAN "PETE"
B.ST.LOUIS,MO.

YR	CL	LEA	POS	GP	G	REC
1913	STL	A	P		1	0- 0

SCHMIDT, MICHAEL JACK "MIKE"
B.SEP.27,1949 DAYTON,OHIO

YR	CL	LEA	POS	GP	G	REC
1972	PHI	N	2-3		13	.206
1973	PHI	N	1-2-S-3		132	.196
1974	PHI	N	3		162	.282
1975	PHI	N	S-3		158	.249
1976	PHI	N	3		160	.262
	BRTR				625	.252

SCHMIDT, ROBERT BENJAMIN "BOB"
B.APR.22,1933 ST.LOUIS,MO.

YR	CL	LEA	POS	GP	G	REC
1958	SF	N	C		127	.244
1959	SF	N	C		71	.243
1960	SF	N	C		110	.267
1961	SF	N	C		2	.167
	CIN	N	C		27	.129
1962	WAS	A	C		88	.242
1963	WAS	A	C		9	.200
1965	NY	A	C		20	.250
	BRTR				454	.243

SCHMIDT, WALTER JOSEPH
B.MAR.20,1887 COAL HILL,ARK.
D.JULY 4,1973 CERES,CAL.

YR	CL	LEA	POS	GP	G	REC
1916	PIT	N	C		64	.190
1917	PIT	N	C		72	.246
1918	PIT	N	C		105	.238
1919	PIT	N	C		85	.251
1920	PIT	N	C		94	.277
1921	PIT	N	C		114	.282
1922	PIT	N	C		40	.328
1923	PIT	N	C		97	.248
1924	PIT	N	C		58	.243
1925	STL	N	C		37	.253
	BRTR				766	.257

SCHMIDT, WILLARD RAYMOND
B.MAY 29,1929 HAYS,KAN.

YR	CL	LEA	POS	GP	G	REC
1952	STL	N	P		18	2- 3
1953	STL	N	P		6	0- 2
1955	STL	N	P		20	7- 6
1956	STL	N	P		33	6- 8
1957	STL	N	P		40	10- 3
1958	CIN	N	P		41	3- 5
1959	CIN	N	P		36	3- 2
	BRTR				194	31-29

SCHMITZ, JOHN ALBERT
"JOHNNY" OR "BEAR TRACKS"
B.NOV.27,1920 WAUSAU,WIS.

YR	CL	LEA	POS	GP	G	REC
1941	CHI	N	P		6	2- 0
1942	CHI	N	P		23	3- 7
1946	CHI	N	P		42	11-11
1947	CHI	N	P		38	13-18
1948	CHI	N	P		34	18-13
1949	CHI	N	P		36	11-13
1950	CHI	N	P		39	10-16
1951	CHI	N	P		8	1- 2
	BRO	N	P		16	1- 4
1952	BRO	N	P		10	1- 1
	NY	N	P		5	1- 1
	CIN	N	P		3	1- 0
1953	NY	A	P		3	0- 0
	WAS	A	P		24	2- 7
1954	WAS	A	P		29	11- 8
1955	WAS	A	P		32	7-10
1956	BOS	A	P		2	0- 0
	BAL	A	P		18	0- 3
	BRTL				368	93-114

SCHMULBACH, HENRY ALPHUES
B.JAN.17,1925 E.ST.LOUIS,ILL.

YR	CL	LEA	POS	GP	G	REC
1943	STL	A	H		1	.000
	BLTR					

SCHMUTZ, CHARLES OTTO "KING"
B.JAN.1,1890 SAN DIEGO,CAL.
D.JUNE 27,1962 SEATTLE,WASH.

YR	CL	LEA	POS	GP	G	REC
1914	BRO	N	P		18	1- 3
1915	BRO	N	P		1	0- 0
	BRTR				19	1- 3

SCHNECK, DAVID LEE "DAVE"
B.JUNE 18,1949 ALLENTOWN,PA.

YR	CL	LEA	POS	GP	G	REC
1972	NY	N	O		37	.187
1973	NY	N	O		13	.194
1974	NY	N	O		93	.205
	BLTL				143	.199

SCHNEIBERG, FRANK FREDERICK
B.MAR.12,1882 MILWAUKEE,WIS.
D.MAY 18,1948

YR	CL	LEA	POS	GP	G	REC
1910	BRO	N	P		1	0- 0

SCHNEIDER, DANIEL LOUIS "DAN"
B.AUG.29,1942 EVANSVILLE,IND.

YR	CL	LEA	POS	GP	G	REC
1963	MIL	N	P		30	1- 0
1964	MIL	N	P	13	14	1- 2
1966	ATL	N	P		14	0- 0
1967	HOU	N	P	54	55	0- 2
1969	HOU	N	P		6	0- 1
	BLTL			117	119	2- 5

SCHNEIDER, EMANUEL SEBASTIAN
(PLAYED UNDER NAME OF
EMANUEL SEBASTIAN SNYDER)

SCHNEIDER, PETER JOSEPH "PETE"
B.AUG.20,1895 LOS ANGELES,CAL.
D.JUNE 1,1957

YR	CL	LEA	POS	GP	G	REC
1914	CIN	N	P	29	31	5-13
1915	CIN	N	P		48	14-19
1916	CIN	N	P	44	49	10-19
1917	CIN	N	P	46	49	20-19
1918	CIN	N	P	33	36	10-15
1919	NY	A	P		7	0- 1
	BRTR			207	220	59-86

SCHNELL, KARL OTTO
B.SEPT.20,1899 LOS ANGELES,CAL.

YR	CL	LEA	POS	GP	G	REC
1922	CIN	N	P		10	0- 0
1923	CIN	N	P		1	0- 0
	BRTR				11	0- 0

SCHOEN, GERALD THOMAS "JERRY"
B.JAN.20,1947 NEW ORLEANS,LA.

YR	CL	LEA	POS	GP	G	REC
1968	WAS	A	P		1	0- 1
	BRTR					

SCHOENDIENST, ALBERT FRED "RED"
B.FEB.2,1923 GERMANTOWN,ILL.

YR	CL	LEA	POS	GP	G	REC
1945	STL	N	2-S-O		137	.278
1946	STL	N	2-S-3		142	.281
1947	STL	N	2-3-O		151	.253
1948	STL	N	2		119	.272
1949	STL	N	2-S-3-O		151	.297
1950	STL	N	2-S-3		153	.276
1951	STL	N	2-3		135	.289
1952	STL	N	2-S-3		152	.303
1953	STL	N	2		146	.342
1954	STL	N	2		148	.315
1955	STL	N	2		145	.268
1956	STL	N	2		40	.314
	NY	N	2		92	.296
1957	NY	N	2		57	.307
	MIL	N	2-O		93	.310
1958	MIL	N	2		106	.262
1959	MIL	N	2		5	.000
1960	MIL	N	2		68	.257
1961	STL	N	2		72	.300
1962	STL	N	2-3		98	.301
1963	STL	N	H		6	.000
	BBTR				2216	.289

NON-PLAYING MANAGER
STL(N) 1965-76

SCHOENICK, LEWIS N. "JUMBO"
B.1862 CHICAGO,ILL.

YR	CL	LEA	POS	GP	G	REC
1884	CHI	U	1-O		70	.315
	PIT	U	1		18	.276
	BAL	U	1		16	.283
1888	IND	N	1		48	.237
1889	IND	N	1		16	.242
	TR				168	.280

SCHOFIELD, JOHN RICHARD "DICK"
B.JAN.7,1935 SPRINGFIELD,ILL.

YR	CL	LEA	POS	GP	G	REC
1953	STL	N	S		33	.179
1954	STL	N	S		43	.143
1955	STL	N	S		12	.000
1956	STL	N	S		16	.100
1957	STL	N	S		65	.161
1958	STL	N	S		39	.213
	PIT	N	S		26	.148
1959	PIT	N	2-S-O		81	.234
1960	PIT	N	2-S-3		65	.333
1961	PIT	N	2-S-3-O		60	.192
1962	PIT	N	2-S-3		54	.288
1963	PIT	N	S		138	.246
1964	PIT	N	S		121	.246
1965	PIT	N	S		31	.229
	SF	N	S		101	.203
1966	SF	N	S		11	.063
	NY	A	S		25	.155
	LA	N	S-3		20	.257
1967	LA	N	2-S-3		84	.216
1968	STL	N	2-S		69	.220
1969	BOS	A	2-S-3-O		94	.257
1970	BOS	A	2-S-3		76	.187
1971	MIL	A	2-S-3		23	.107
	STL	N	2-S-3		34	.217
	BBTR				1321	.227

YR	CL	LEA	POS	GP	G	REC

SCHOMBERG, OTTO H.
(REAL NAME
OTTO H. SHAMBRICK)
B.NOV.14,1864 MILWAUKEE,WIS.
D.MAY 3,1927

YR	CL	LEA	POS	GP	G	REC
1886	PIT	AA	1		72	.295
1887	IND	N	1		112	.389
1888	IND	N	1		29	.214
		TL			213	.329

SCHOONMAKER, JERALD LEE "JERRY"
B.DEC.14,1933 SEYMOUR,MO.

1955	WAS	A	O		20	.152
1957	WAS	A	O		30	.087
	BRTR				50	.130

SCHORR, EDWARD WALTER
B.FEB.16,1891 BREMEN,OHIO
D.SEPT.12,1969 ATLANTIC CITY,
N.J.

| 1915 | CHI | N | P | | 2 | 0-0 |
| | BRTR | | | | | |

SCHOTT, EUGENE ARTHUR "GENE"
B.JULY 14,1913 BATAVIA,OHIO

1935	CIN	N	P	33	36	8-11
1936	CIN	N	P	31	39	11-11
1937	CIN	N	P	37	50	4-13
1938	CIN	N	P		31	5- 5
1939	PHI	N	P	4	8	0- 1
	BRO	N	R		1	.000
	BRTR			136	165	28-41
						.211

SCHRAMKA, PAUL EDWARD
B.MAR.22,1928 MILWAUKEE,WIS.

| 1953 | CHI | N | O | | 2 | .000 |
| | BLTL | | | | | |

SCHRECKENGOST, OSSEE FREEMAN
(ALSO PLAYED UNDER NAME
OF OSSEE SCHRECK)
B.APR.11,1875 FAIRMONT CITY,PA.
D.JULY 9,1914

1897	LOU	N	C		1	.000
1898	CLE	N	C		5	.367
1899	STL	N	1-O		6	.000
	CLE	N	C-1-S-O	43		.315
	STL	N	C		60	.306
1901	BOS	A	C		83	.320
1902	CLE	A	1	18		.338
	PHI	A	C-1-O	78		.312
1903	PHI	A	C		91	.222
1904	PHI	A	C		94	.189
1905	PHI	A	C		114	.274
1906	PHI	A	C		98	.284
1907	PHI	A	C		101	.272
1908	PHI	A	C		71	.222
	CHI	A	C		6	.188
	BRTR				869	.272

SCHREIBER, DAVID "BARNEY"
B.MAY 8,1882 WAVERLY,OHIO
D.OCT.6,1964 CHILLICOTHE,OHIO

| 1911 | CIN | N | P | | 3 | 0- 1 |
| | BLTL | | | | | |

SCHREIBER, HENRY WARD "HANK"
B.JULY 13,1893 CLEVELAND,OHIO
D.FEB.23,1968 INDIANAPOLIS,IND.

1914	CHI	A	O		1	.000
1917	BOS	N	S-3		2	.286
1919	CIN	N	S-3		19	.224
1921	NY	N	2-S		4	.167
1926	CHI	N	2-S-3		10	.056
	NRTR				36	.187

SCHREIBER, PAUL FREDERICK
B.OCT.8,1902 JACKSONVILLE,FLA.

1922	BRO	N	P		1	0- 0
1923	BRO	N	P		9	0- 0
1945	NY	A	P		2	0- 0
	BRTR				12	0- 0

SCHREIBER, THEODORE HENRY "TED"
B.JULY 11,1938 BROOKLYN,N.Y.

| 1963 | NY | N | 2-S-3 | | 39 | .160 |
| | BRTR | | | | | |

**SCHRIVER, WILLIAM FREDERICK
"POP"**
B.JULY 11,1865 BROOKLYN,N.Y.
D.DEC.27,1932

1886	BRO	AA	C-O		9	.040
1888	PHI	N	C		39	.194
1889	PHI	N	C		55	.265
1890	PHI	N	C		57	.273
1891	CHI	N	C		25	.311
1892	CHI	N	C		89	.222
1893	CHI	N	C		59	.295
1894	CHI	N	C		94	.269
1895	NY	N	C		24	.290
1897	CIN	N	C		52	.310
1898	PIT	N	C		93	.227
1899	PIT	N	C		84	.297
1900	PIT	N	C		23	.317
1901	STL	N	C-1		44	.286
	BRTR				747	.263

SCHRODER, ROBERT JAMES "BOB"
B.DEC.30,1944 RIDGEFIELD,N.J.

1965	SF	N	2-3	31		.222
1966	SF	N	S	10		.242
1967	SF	N	2-3	62		.230
1968	SF	N	2-S-3	35		.159
	BLTR			138		.217

SCHROLL ALBERT BRINGHURST "AL"
B.MAR.22,1932 NEW ORLEANS,LA.

1958	BOS	A	P		5	0- 0
1959	PHI	N	P		3	1- 1
	BOS	A	P		14	1- 4
1960	CHI	N	P		2	0- 0
1961	MIN	A	P		11	4- 4
	BRTR				35	6- 9

SCHUBLE, HENRY GEORGE "HEINE"
B.NOV.1,1906 HOUSTON,TEX.

1927	STL	N	S	65		.257
1929	DET	A	S	92		.233
1932	DET	A	S-3	102		.271
1933	DET	A	2-S-3	49		.219
1934	DET	A	2-S-3	11		.267
1935	DET	A	2-3	11		.250
1936	STL	N	3	2		.000
	BRTR			332		.251

SCHUELER, RONALD RICHARD "RON"
B.APR.14,1948 CATHERINE,KAN.

1972	ATL	N	P		37	5- 8
1973	ATL	N	P		39	8- 7
1974	PHI	N	P		44	11-16
1975	PHI	N	P		46	4- 4
1976	PHI	N	P		35	1- 0
	BRTR				201	29-35

SCHUERHOLZ, FRED PETER
(PLAYED UNDER NAME OF
FRED PETER SHERRY)

**SCHULMERICH, EDWARD WESLEY
"WES"**
B.APR.21,1902 HILLSBORO,ORE.

1931	BOS	N	O		95	.309
1932	BOS	N	O		119	.260
1933	BOS	N	O		29	.247
	PHI	N	O		97	.334
1934	PHI	N	O		15	.250
	CIN	N	O		74	.263
	BRTR				429	.289

SCHULT, ARTHUR WILLIAM "DUTCH"
B.JUNE 20,1928 BROOKLYN,N.Y.

1953	NY	A	H		7	.000
1956	CIN	N	O		5	.429
1957	CIN	N	O		21	.265
	WAS	A	1-O		77	.263
1959	CHI	N	1-O		42	.271
1960	CHI	N	1-O		12	.133
	BRTR				164	.264

SCHULT, FRED WILLIAM
(PLAYED UNDER NAME OF
FRED WILLIAM SCHULTE)

SCHULTE, FRANK "WILDFIRE"
B.SEPT.17,1882 COHOCTON,N.Y.
D.OCT.2,1949

1904	CHI	N	O		20	.286
1905	CHI	N	O		123	.274
1906	CHI	N	O		146	.281
1907	CHI	N	O		92	.287
1908	CHI	N	O		102	.236
1909	CHI	N	O		140	.264
1910	CHI	N	O		150	.301
1911	CHI	N	O		154	.300
1912	CHI	N	O		139	.264
1913	CHI	N	O		132	.278
1914	CHI	N	O		137	.241
1915	CHI	N	O		151	.249
1916	CHI	N	O		72	.305
	PIT	N	O		55	.241
1917	PIT	N	O		30	.216
	PHI	N	O		64	.213
1918	WAS	A	O		93	.288
	BLTR				1800	.270

SCHULTE, FRED WILLIAM
(REAL NAME
FRED WILLIAM SCHULT)
B.JAN.13,1904 BELVIDERE,ILL.

1927	STL	A	O		60	.317
1928	STL	A	O		146	.286
1929	STL	A	O		121	.307
1930	STL	A	O		113	.278
1931	STL	A	O		134	.304
1932	STL	A	O		146	.294
1933	WAS	A	O		144	.295
1934	WAS	A	O		136	.298
1935	WAS	A	O		75	.268
1936	PIT	N	O		74	.261
1937	PIT	N	O		29	.100
	BRTR				1178	.292

SCHULTE, HERMAN JOSEPH "HAM"
(REAL NAME
HERMAN JOSEPH SCHULTEHENRICH)
B.SEPT.1,1913 ST.CHARLES,MO.

| 1940 | PHI | N | 2-S | | 120 | .236 |
| | BRTR | | | | | |

SCHULTE, JOHN CLEMENT
B.SEPT.8,1897 FREDERICKTOWN,MO.

1923	STL	A	C		7	.000
1927	STL	N	C		64	.288
1928	PHI	N	C		65	.248
1929	CHI	N	C		31	.261
1932	STL	A	C		15	.208
	BOS	N	C		10	.222
	BLTR				192	.261

**SCHULTE, JOHN HERMAN FRANK
"JACK"**
B.NOV.15,1881 CINCINNATI,OHIO
D.AUG.17,1975 ROSEVILLE,MICH.

| 1906 | BOS | N | S | | 2 | .000 |
| | BRTR | | | | | |

SCHULTE, LEONARD WILLIAM
(REAL NAME
LEONARD WILLIAM SCHULTEHENRICH)
B.DEC.6,1917 ST.CHARLES,MO.

1944	STL	A	H		1	.000
1945	STL	A	2-S-3		119	.247
1946	STL	A	2-3		4	.400
	BRTR				124	.248

SCHULTEHENRICH, HERMAN JOSEPH
(PLAYED UNDER NAME OF
HERMAN JOSEPH SCHULTE)

SCHULTEHENRICH, LEONARD WILLIAM
(PLAYED UNDER NAME OF
LEONARD WILLIAM SCHULTE)

SCHULTZ, CHARLES BUDD "BUDDY"
B.SEPT.19,1950 CLEVELAND,OHIO

1975	CHI	N	P		6	2- 0
1976	CHI	N	P		29	1- 1
	BRTL				35	3- 1

SCHULTZ, GEORGE WARREN "BARNEY"
B.AUG.15,1926 BEVERLY,N.J.

1955	STL	N	P		19	1- 2
1959	DET	A	P		13	1- 2
1961	CHI	N	P		41	7- 6
1962	CHI	N	P		51	5- 5
1963	CHI	N	P		15	1- 0
	STL	N	P		24	2- 0
1964	STL	N	P		30	1- 3
1965	STL	N	P		34	2- 2
	BRTR				227	20-20

YR	CL LEA POS	GP	G	REC

SCHULTZ, HOWARD HENRY "STRETCH"
B.JULY 3,1922 ST.PAUL,MINN.
1943	BRO N	1		45	.269
1944	BRO N	1	138		.255
1945	BRO N	1	39		.239
1946	BRO N	1	90		.253
1947	BRO N	1	2		.000
	PHI N	1	114		.223
1948	PHI N	1	6		.077
	CIN N	1	36		.167
	BRTR		470		.241

SCHULTZ, JOHN
B.ST.LOUIS,MO.
| 1891 | STL AA C | 1 | | .000 |

SCHULTZ, JOSEPH CHARLES JR. "DODE"
B.AUG.29,1918 CHICAGO,ILL.
1939	PIT N	C	4		.286
1940	PIT N	C	16		.194
1941	PIT N	C	2		.500
1943	STL A	C	46		.239
1944	STL A	C	3		.250
1945	STL A	C	41		.295
1946	STL A	C	42		.386
1947	STL A	H	43		.184
1948	STL A	H	43		.189
	BLTR		240		.259
NON-PLAYING MANAGER
SEA(A) 1969, DET(A) 1973

SCHULTZ, JOSEPH CHARLES SR. "GERMANY"
B.JULY 24,1893 PITTSBURGH,PA.
D.APR.13,1941
1912	BOS N	2	4		.250
1913	BOS N	O	8		.222
1915	BRO N	3	56		.292
	CHI N	3	7		.250
1916	PIT N	2-3	77		.260
1919	STL N	O	88		.253
1920	STL N	O	99		.263
1921	STL N	O	92		.309
1922	STL N	O	112		.313
1923	STL N	O	2		.286
1924	STL N	O	12		.167
	PHI N	O	88		.285
1925	PHI N	O	24		.344
	CIN N	2-O	33		.323
	BRTR		702		.285

SCHULTZ, ROBERT DUFFY "BILL"
B.NOV.27,1925 LOUISVILLE,KY.
1951	CHI N	P	17	3- 6
1952	CHI N	P	29	6- 3
1953	CHI N	P	7	0- 2
	PIT N	P	11	0- 2
1955	DET A	P	1	0- 0
	BRTL		65	9-13

SCHULTZ, WEBB CARL
B.JAN.31,1898 WAUTOMA,WIS.
| 1924 | CHI A | P | 1 | 0- 0 |
| | BRTR | | | |

SCHULTZ, WILLIAM MICHAEL "MIKE"
B.DEC.17,1920 SYRACUSE,N.Y.
| 1947 | CIN N | P | 1 | 0- 0 |
| | BLTL | | | |

SCHULTZE, JOHN F.
B.BURLINGTON,N.J.
| 1891 | PHI N | P | 6 | 0- 3 |

SCHULZ, ALBERT C. "LEFTY"
B.MAY 12,1889 TOLEDO,OHIO
D.DEC.14,1931
1912	NY A	P	3	1- 0
1913	NY A	P	38	8-14
1914	NY A	P	4	1- 3
	BUF F	P	27	9-12
1915	BUF F	P	42	21-14
1916	CIN N	P	44	8-19
	BRTL		158	48-62

SCHULZ, WALTER FREDERICK
B.APR.16,1900 ST.LOUIS,MO.
D.FEB.27,1928
| 1920 | STL N | P | 2 | 0- 0 |
| | BRTR | | | |

SCHUMACHER, HAROLD HENRY "PRINCE HAL"
B.NOV.23,1910 HINCKLEY,N.Y.
1931	NY N	P		8	1- 1
1932	NY N	P	27	30	5- 6
1933	NY N	P	35	39	19-12
1934	NY N	P	41	44	23-10
1935	NY N	P	33	38	19- 9
1936	NY N	P	35	46	11-13
1937	NY N	P	38	45	13-12
1938	NY N	P	28	36	13- 8
1939	NY N	P	29	30	13-10
1940	NY N	P	34	35	13-13
1941	NY N	P-O	30	38	12-10
					.152
1942	NY N	P	29	37	12-13
1946	NY N	P		24	4- 4
	BRTR		391	450	158-121
					.202

SCHUMANN, CARL J. "HACK"
B.AUG.13,1884 BUFFALO,N.Y.
D.MAR.25,1946
| 1906 | PHI A | P | 4 | 0- 2 |
| | TR | | | |

SCHUPP, FERDINAND MAURICE
B.JAN.16,1891 LOUISVILLE,KY.
D.DEC.16,1971 LOS ANGELES,CAL.
1913	NY N	P		5	0- 0
1914	NY N	P		8	0- 0
1915	NY N	P		23	1- 0
1916	NY N	P		30	9- 3
1917	NY N	P		36	21- 7
1918	NY N	P		10	0- 1
1919	NY N	P		9	1- 3
	STL N	P		10	4- 4
1920	STL N	P	38	39	16-13
1921	STL N	P		9	2- 0
	BRO N	P		20	3- 4
1922	CHI A	P		18	4- 4
	BRTR		216	217	61-39

SCHURR, WAYNE ALLEN
B.AUG.6,1937 GARRETT,IND.
| 1964 | CHI N | P | 26 | 0- 0 |
| | BRTR | | | |

SCHUSTER, WILLIAM CHARLES "BROADWAY BILL"
B.AUG.4,1912 BUFFALO,N.Y.
1937	PIT N	S	3		.500
1939	BOS N	S-3	2		.000
1943	CHI N	S	13		.294
1944	CHI N	2-S	60		.221
1945	CHI N	2-S-3	45		.191
	BRTR		123		.234

SCHWALL, DONALD BERNARD "DON"
B.MAR.2,1936 WILKES-BARRE,PA.
1961	BOS A	P	25	27	15- 7
1962	BOS A	P	33	34	9-15
1963	PIT N	P		33	6-12
1964	PIT N	P	15	16	4- 3
1965	PIT N	P		43	9- 6
1966	PIT N	P		11	3- 2
	ATL N	P		11	3- 3
1967	ATL N	P		1	0- 0
	BRTR		172	176	49-48

SCHWAMB, RALPH RICHARD "BLACKIE"
B.AUG.6,1926 LOS ANGELES,CAL.
| 1948 | STL A | P | 12 | 1- 1 |
| | BRTR | | | |

SCHWARTZ, DOUGLAS RANDALL "RANDY"
B.FEB.9,1944 LOS ANGELES,CAL.
1965	KC A	1	6		.286
1966	KC A	1	10		.091
	BLTL		16		.167

SCHWARTZ, WILLIAM AUGUST "SCOOPER BILL"
B.APR.3,1864 JAMESTOWN,KY.
D.DEC.22,1940
1883	COL AA	C-1	2		.250
1884	CIN U	C	24		.263
	BRTR		26		.262

SCHWARTZ, WILLIAM CHARLES
B.APR.22,1884 CLEVELAND,OHIO
D.AUG.29,1961
| 1904 | CLE A | 1 | 24 | | .151 |
| | TR | | | |

SCHWARTZ, WILLIAM DWIGHT
B.JAN.30,1891 BIRMINGHAM,ALA.
D.JUNE 24,1969
| 1914 | NY A | C | 1 | | .000 |
| | TR | | | |

SCHWARZROCK, LESTER HENRY
(PLAYED UNDER NAME OF LESTER HENRY ROCK)

SCHWEITZER, ALBERT CASPAR
B.DEC.1882 CLEVELAND,OHIO
D.JAN.27,1969 NEWARK,OHIO
1908	STL A	O	64		.291
1909	STL A	O	27		.224
1910	STL A	O	113		.230
1911	STL A	O	76		.215
	BRTR		280		.238

SCHWENCK, HAROLD EDWARD
B.AUG.23,1890 SCHUYLKILL HAVEN, PA.
D.SEPT.3,1955
| 1913 | STL A | P | 1 | 1- 0 |
| | BLTL | | | |

SCHWENCK, RUDOLPH C. "RUBY"
B.APR.6,1884 LOUISVILLE,KY.
D.NOV.27,1941
| 1909 | CHI N | P | 3 | 1- 1 |

SCHWERT, PIUS LOUIS "PI"
B.NOV.22,1892 ANGOLA,N.Y.
D.MAR.11,1941 WASHINGTON,D.C.
1914	NY A	C	2		.000
1915	NY A	C	9		.278
	BRTR		11		.208

SCHWIND, ARTHUR E.
B.1892 OTTAWA,ONT.,CANADA
| 1912 | BOS N | 3 | 1 | | .000 |
| | BRTR | | | |

SCHYPINSKI, GERALD ALBERT "GERRY"
B.SEPT.16,1931 DETROIT,MICH.
| 1955 | KC A | 2-S | 22 | | .217 |
| | BLTR | | | |

SCOFFIC, LOUIS "WEASER"
B.MAY 20,1914 HERRIN,ILL.
| 1936 | STL N | O | 4 | | .429 |
| | BRTR | | | |

SCORE, HERBERT JUDE "HERB"
B.JUNE 7,1933 ROSEDALE,N.Y.
1955	CLE A	P	33	16-10
1956	CLE A	P	35	20- 9
1957	CLE A	P	5	2- 1
1958	CLE A	P	12	2- 3
1959	CLE A	P	30	9-11
1960	CHI A	P	23	5-10
1961	CHI A	P	8	1- 2
1962	CHI A	P	4	0- 0
	BLTL		150	55-46

SCOTT
| 1884 | BAL U | 3-O | 13 | | .226 |

SCOTT, AMOS RICHARD "DICK"
B.FEB.5,1882 BETHEL,OHIO
D.APR.11,1911
| 1901 | CIN N | P | 3 | 0- 2 |
| | BRTR | | | |

SCOTT, ANTHONY "TONY"
B.SEP.18,1951 CINCINNATI,OHIO
1973	MON N	O	11		.000
1974	MON N	O	19		.286
1975	MON N	O	92		.182
	BBTR		122		.185

SCOTT, EDWARD
B.AUG.12,1870 WALBRIDGE,OHIO
D.NOV.1,1933 TOLEDO,OHIO
1900	CIN N	P	39	17-20
1901	CLE A	P	16	7- 6
	BRTR		55	24-26

SCOTT, FLOYD JOHN "PETE"
B.DEC.21,1898 WOODLAND,CAL.
D.MAY 3,1953
1926	CHI N	O	77		.286
1927	CHI N	O	71		.314
1928	PIT N	O	60		.311
	BRTR		208		.303

YR	CL	LEA	POS	GP	G	REC

SCOTT, GEORGE CHARLES
B.MAR.23,1944 GREENVILLE,MISS.

YR	CL	LEA	POS	GP	G	REC
1966	BOS	A	1-3		162	.245
1967	BOS	A	1-3		159	.303
1968	BOS	A	1-3		124	.171
1969	BOS	A	1-3		152	.253
1970	BOS	A	1-3		127	.296
1971	BOS	A	1		146	.263
1972	MIL	A	1-3		152	.266
1973	MIL	A	1		158	.306
1974	MIL	A	1		158	.281
1975	MIL	A	1-3-0		158	.285
1976	MIL	A	1		156	.274
		BRTR			1652	.271

SCOTT, GEORGE WILLIAM
B.NOV.17,1896 TRENTON,MO.

YR	CL	LEA	POS	GP	G	REC
1920	STL	N · P			2	0- 0
		BRTR				

SCOTT, JAMES "DEATH VALLEY"
B.APR.23,1888 DEADWOOD,S.DAK.
D.APR.7,1957

YR	CL	LEA	POS	GP	G	REC
1909	CHI	A	P		36	12-12
1910	CHI	A	P		40	8-18
1911	CHI	A	P		39	14-11
1912	CHI	A	P		5	2- 2
1913	CHI	A	P		48	20-20
1914	CHI	A	P		43	14-18
1915	CHI	A	P		48	24-11
1916	CHI	A	P		32	7-14
1917	CHI	A	P		24	6- 7
		BRTR			315	107-113

SCOTT, JAMES WALTER
B.SEPT.22,1888 SHENANDOAH,PA.
D.MAY 12,1972 S.PASADENA,FLA.

YR	CL	LEA	POS	GP	G	REC
1914	PIT	F	S		8	.250
		BRTR				

SCOTT, JOHN HENRY
B.JAN.24,1952 JACKSON,MISS.

YR	CL	LEA	POS	GP	G	REC
1974	SD	N	O		14	.067
1975	SD	N	O		25	.000
		BRTR			39	.042

SCOTT, JOHN WILLIAM "JACK"
B.APR.18,1892 RIDGEWAY,N.C.
D.NOV.30,1959 DURHAM,N.C.

YR	CL	LEA	POS	GP	G	REC
1916	PIT	N	P		3	0- 0
1917	BOS	N	P		7	1- 2
1919	BOS	N	P-O	19	24	6- 6
						.185
1920	BOS	N	P		44	10-21
1921	BOS	N	P	47	51	15-13
1922	CIN	N	P		1	0- 0
	NY	N	P		17	8- 2
1923	NY	N	P		40	16- 7
1925	NY	N	P	36	41	14-15
1926	NY	N	P	50	51	13-15
1927	PHI	N	P	48	83	9-21
1928	NY	N	P		16	4- 1
1929	NY	N	P		30	7- 6
		BLTR		358	408	103-109
						.275

SCOTT, LEGRAND EDWARD
B.JULY 25,1911 CLEVELAND,OHIO

YR	CL	LEA	POS	GP	G	REC
1939	PHI	N	O		78	.280
		BLTL				

SCOTT, LEWIS EVERETT "DEACON"
B.NOV.19,1892 BLUFFTON,IND.
D.NOV.2,1960

YR	CL	LEA	POS	GP	G	REC
1914	BOS	A	S		144	.239
1915	BOS	A	S		100	.201
1916	BOS	A	S		123	.323
1917	BOS	A	S		157	.241
1918	BOS	A	S		126	.221
1919	BOS	A	S		138	.278
1920	BOS	A	S		154	.269
1921	BOS	A	S		154	.262
1922	NY	A	S		154	.269
1923	NY	A	S		152	.246
1924	NY	A	S		153	.250
1925	NY	A	S		22	.217
	WAS	A	S		33	.272
1926	CHI	A	S		40	.252
	CIN	N	S		4	.667
		BRTR			1654	.249

SCOTT, MARSHALL "LEFTY"
B.JULY 15,1915 ROSWELL,N.MEX.
D.MAR.3,1964 HOUSTON,TEX.

YR	CL	LEA	POS	GP	G	REC
1945	PHI	N	P		8	0- 2
		BRTL				

SCOTT, MILTON PARKER
B.JAN.17,1866 CHICAGO,ILL.
D.NOV.3,1938

YR	CL	LEA	POS	GP	G	REC
1882	CHI	N	1		1	.400
1884	DET	N	1		108	.249
1885	DET	N	1		38	.263
	PIT	AA	1		55	.241
1886	BAL	AA	1		137	.192
					339	.232

SCOTT, RALPH ROBERT "MICKEY"
B.JULY 25,1947 WEIMAR,GERMANY

YR	CL	LEA	POS	GP	G	REC
1972	BAL	A	P		15	0- 1
1973	BAL	A	P		1	0- 0
	MON	N	P		22	1- 2
1975	CAL	A	P		50	4- 2
1976	CAL	A	P	33	35	3- 0
		BLTL		121	123	8- 5

SCOTT, RICHARD LEWIS "DICK"
B.MAR.15,1943 PORTSMOUTH,N.H.

YR	CL	LEA	POS	GP	G	REC
1963	LA	N	P		9	0- 0
1964	CHI	N	P		3	0- 0
		BRTL			12	0- 0

SCOTT, RODNEY DARRELL "ROD"
B.OCT.16,1953 INDIANAPOLIS,CAL.

YR	CL	LEA	POS	GP	G	REC
1975	KC	A	2-S-R		48	.067
1976	MON	N	2-S		7	.400
		BRTR			55	.200

SCRIVENER, WAYNE ALLISON "CHUCK"
B.OCT.3,1947 ALEXANDRIA,VA.

YR	CL	LEA	POS	GP	G	REC
1975	DET	A	S-3		4	.250
1976	DET	A	2-S-3		80	.221
		BRTR			84	.223

SCROGGINS, JAMES LYNN
B.1893

YR	CL	LEA	POS	GP	G	REC
1913	CHI	A	P		1	0- 0
		BLTL				

SCZEPKOWSKI, THEODORE WALTER
(PLAYED UNDER NAME OF
THEODORE WALTER SEPKOWSKI)

SEALE, JOHNNY RAY
B.NOV.13,1948 EDGEWATER,COLO.

YR	CL	LEA	POS	GP	G	REC
1964	DET	A	P		4	1- 0
1965	DET	A	P		4	0- 0
		BLTL			8	1- 0

SEARS, KENNETH EUGENE "ZIGGY"
B.JULY 6,1917 STREATOR,ILL.

YR	CL	LEA	POS	GP	G	REC
1943	NY	A	C		60	.278
1946	STL	A	C		7	.333
		BLTR			67	.282

SEATON, THOMAS GORDON
B.AUG.30,1887 BLAIR,NEB.
D.APR.10,1940

YR	CL	LEA	POS	GP	G	REC
1912	PHI	N	P		44	16-12
1913	PHI	N	P		52	27-12
1914	BRO	F	P		44	25-14
1915	BRO	F	P		26	7- 7
	NEW	F	P		18	7-10
1916	CHI	N	P		31	6- 6
1917	CHI	N	P		16	5- 4
		BBTR			231	93-65

SEATS, THOMAS EDWARD
B.SEPT.24,1912 FARMINGTON,N.C.

YR	CL	LEA	POS	GP	G	REC
1940	DET	A	P		26	2- 2
1945	BRO	N	P		31	10- 7
		BBTL			57	12- 9
		BR 1945				

SEAVER, GEORGE THOMAS "TOM"
B.NOV.17,1944 FRESNO,CAL.

YR	CL	LEA	POS	GP	G	REC
1967	NY	N	P	35	36	16-13
1968	NY	N	P	36	38	16-12
1969	NY	N	P	36	39	25- 7
1970	NY	N	P	37	42	18-12
1971	NY	N	P	36	39	20-10
1972	NY	N	P	35	36	21-12
1973	NY	N	P	36	39	19-10
1974	NY	N	P		32	11-11
1975	NY	N	P	36	37	22- 9
1976	NY	N	P		35	14-11
		BRTR		354	373	182-106

SEBRING, JAMES DENNISON
B.MAR.22,1882 WILLIAMSPORT,PA.
D.DEC.22,1909

YR	CL	LEA	POS	GP	G	REC
1902	PIT	N	O		19	.338
1903	PIT	N	O		124	.277
1904	PIT	N	O		80	.269
	CIN	N	O		56	.225
1905	CIN	N	O		56	.286
1909	BRO	N	O		25	.099
	WAS	A	O		1	.000
		BLTL			361	.262

SECHRIST, THEODORE O'HARA "DOC"
B.FEB.10,1876 WILLIAMSTOWN,KY.
D.APR.2,1950

YR	CL	LEA	POS	GP	G	REC
1899	NY	N	P		1	0- 0
		BRTR				

SECORY, FRANK EDWARD
B.AUG.24,1912 MASON CITY,IOWA

YR	CL	LEA	POS	GP	G	REC
1940	DET	A	H		1	.000
1942	CIN	N	O		2	.000
1944	CIN	N	O		22	.321
1945	CHI	N	O		35	.158
1946	CHI	N	O		33	.233
		BRTR			93	.228

SECRIST, DONALD LAVERNE "DON"
B.FEB.26,1944 SEATTLE,WASH.

YR	CL	LEA	POS	GP	G	REC
1969	CHI	A	P		19	0- 1
1970	CHI	A	P		9	0- 0
		BLTL			28	0- 1

SEDGWICK, HENRY KENNETH "DUKE"
B.JUNE 1,1899 MARTINS FERRY,O.

YR	CL	LEA	POS	GP	G	REC
1921	PHI	N	P		16	1- 3
1923	WAS	A	P		5	0- 1
		BRTR			21	1- 4

SEE, CHARLES HENRY "CHAD"
B.OCT.13,1897 PLEASANTVILLE,N.Y
D.JULY 19,1948

YR	CL	LEA	POS	GP	G	REC
1919	CIN	N	O		8	.286
1920	CIN	N	P-O	1	47	0- 0
						.305
1921	CIN	N	O		37	.245
		BLTR		1	92	0- 0
						.267

SEEDS, ROBERT IRA
"SUITCASE BOB"
B.FEB.24,1907 RINGGOLD,TEX.

YR	CL	LEA	POS	GP	G	REC
1930	CLE	A	O		85	.285
1931	CLE	A	O		48	.306
1932	CLE	A	O		2	.000
	CHI	A	O		116	.291
1933	BOS	A	1-O		82	.243
1934	BOS	A	O		8	.167
	CLE	A	O		61	.247
1936	NY	A	O		13	.262
1938	NY	N	O		81	.291
1939	NY	N	O		63	.266
1940	NY	N	O		56	.290
		BRTR			615	.277

SEELBACH, CHARLES FREDERICK
"CHUCK"
B.MAR.20,1948 LAKEWOOD,OHIO

YR	CL	LEA	POS	GP	G	REC
1971	DET	A	P		5	0- 0
1972	DET	A	P		61	9- 8
1973	DET	A	P		5	1- 0
1974	DET	A	P		4	0- 0
		BRTR			75	10- 8

SEEREY, JAMES PATRICK "PAT"
B.MAR.17,1923 WILBURTON,OKLA.

YR	CL	LEA	POS	GP	G	REC
1943	CLE	A	O		26	.222
1944	CLE	A	O		101	.234
1945	CLE	A	O		126	.237
1946	CLE	A	O		117	.225
1947	CLE	A	O		82	.171
1948	CLE	A	O		10	.261
	CHI	A	O		95	.229
1949	CHI	A	O		4	.000
		BRTR			561	.224

YR	CL	LEA	POS	GP	G	REC

SEERY, JOHN EMMETT
B.FEB.13,1861 PRINCEVILLE,ILL.

YR	CL	LEA	POS	GP	G	REC
1884	BAL	U	C-3-O	107		.309
	KC	U	O	1		.400
1885	STL	N	3-O	58		.162
1886	STL	N	3-O	126		.238
1887	IND	N	3-O	122		.326
1888	IND	N	3-O	133		.220
1889	IND	N	3-O	127		.313
1890	BRO	P	3-O	104		.222
1891	CIN	AA	3-O	97		.282
1892	LOU	N	3-O	42		.194
		BLTR		917		.266

SEGRIST, KAL HILL
B.APR.14,1931 GREENVILLE,TEX.

YR	CL	LEA	POS	GP	G	REC
1952	NY	A	2-3	13		.043
1955	BAL	A	1-2-3	7		.333
		BRTR		20		.125

SEGUI, DIEGO PABLO (GONZALEZ)
B.AUG.17,1938 HOLGUIN,CUBA

YR	CL	LEA	POS	GP	G	REC
1962	KC	A	P		37	8- 5
1963	KC	A	P		38	9- 6
1964	KC	A	P		40	8-17
1965	KC	A	P	40	41	5-15
1966	WAS	A	P		21	3- 7
1967	KC	A	P		36	3- 4
1968	OAK	A	P		52	6- 5
1969	SEA	A	P		66	12- 6
1970	OAK	A	P		47	10-10
1971	OAK	A	P		26	10- 8
1972	OAK	A	P		7	0- 1
	STL	N	P		33	3- 1
1973	STL	N	P		65	7- 6
1974	BOS	A	P		58	6- 8
1975	BOS	A	P		33	2- 5
		BRTR		599	600	92-104

SEIBOLD, HARRY "SOCKS"
B.APR.3,1896 PHILADELPHIA,PA.
D.SEPT.21,1965 PHILADELPHIA,PA.

YR	CL	LEA	POS	GP	G	REC
1915	PHI	A	S		10	.115
1916	PHI	A	P		5	1- 2
1917	PHI	A	P	32	36	4-16
1919	PHI	A	P	14	15	2- 3
1929	BOS	N	P		33	12-17
1930	BOS	N	P		36	15-16
1931	BOS	N	P		33	10-18
1932	BOS	N	P		28	3-10
1933	BOS	N	P		11	1- 4
		BRTR		192	207	48-86
						.196

SELBACH, ALBERT KARL "KIP"
B.MAR.24,1872 COLUMBUS,OHIO
D.FEB.17,1956 COLUMBUS,OHIO

YR	CL	LEA	POS	GP	G	REC
1894	WAS	N	S-O	96		.300
1895	WAS	N	O	129		.324
1896	WAS	N	O	121		.316
1897	WAS	N	O	126		.317
1898	WAS	N	O	131		.302
1899	CIN	N	O	139		.302
1900	NY	N	O	141		.345
1901	NY	N	O	125		.292
1902	BAL	A	O	128		.321
1903	WAS	A	O	141		.252
1904	WAS	A	O	48		.264
	BOS	A	O	98		.258
1905	BOS	A	O	115		.246
1906	BOS	A	O	60		.211
		BRTR		1598		.296

SELEE, FRANK GIBSON
B.OCT.26,1859 AMHERST,N.Y.
D.JULY 5,1909
NON-PLAYING MANAGER
BOS(N)1890-1901, CHI(N)1902-05

SELKIRK, GEORGE ALEXANDER
"TWINKLETOES"
B.JAN.4,1899 HUNTSVILLE,ONT.,
CANADA

YR	CL	LEA	POS	GP	G	REC
1934	NY	A	O		46	.313
1935	NY	A	O		128	.312
1936	NY	A	O		137	.308
1937	NY	A	O		78	.328
1938	NY	A	O		99	.254
1939	NY	A	O		128	.306
1940	NY	A	O		118	.269
1941	NY	A	O		70	.220
1942	NY	A	O		42	.192
		BLTR			846	.290

SELL, LESTER ELWOOD "EPP"
B.APR.26,1897 LLEWELLYN,PA.
D.FEB.20,1961

YR	CL	LEA	POS	GP	G	REC
1922	STL	N	P		7	4- 2
1923	STL	N	P		5	0- 1
		BRTR			12	4- 3

SELLERS, OLIVER
B.MAR.7,1881 HOMEVILLE,PA.
D.JAN.14,1952

YR	CL	LEA	POS	GP	G	REC
1910	BOS	N	O		12	.156
		BRTR				

SELLS, DAVID WAYNE "DAVE"
B.SEP.18,1946 VACAVILLE,CAL.

YR	CL	LEA	POS	GP	G	REC
1972	CAL	A	P		10	2- 0
1973	CAL	A	P		51	7- 2
1974	CAL	A	P		20	2- 3
1975	CAL	A	P		4	0- 0
	LA	N	P		5	0- 2
		BRTR			90	11- 7

SELMA, RICHARD JAY "DICK"
B.NOV.4,1943 SANTA ANA,CAL.

YR	CL	LEA	POS	GP	G	REC
1965	NY	N	P	4	7	2- 1
1966	NY	N	P	30	31	4- 6
1967	NY	N	P	38	43	2- 4
1968	NY	N	P	33	39	9-10
1969	SD	N	P		4	2- 2
	CHI	N	P		36	10- 8
1970	PHI	N	P-1-3		73	8- 9
						.150
1971	PHI	N	P	17	18	0- 2
1972	PHI	N	P	46	47	2- 9
1973	PHI	N	P		6	1- 1
1974	CAL	A	P		18	2- 2
	MIL	A	P		2	0- 0
		BRTR		307	324	42-54
						.172

BB 1966 (PART)

SELMAN, FRANK C.
(ALSO PLAYED UNDER NAME OF
FRANK C. WILLIAMS)
B.BALTIMORE,MD.
D.OCT.14,1890

YR	CL	LEA	POS	GP	G	REC
1871	KEK	NA	C-3		14	-
1872	OLY	NA	C-3		8	.275
1873	MAR	NA	P		1	0- 1
1874	BAL	NA	C-S-O		12	-
1875	NAT	NA	1		1	-
					1	36	0- 1
						-

SELPH, CAREY ISOM
B.DEC.5,1902 DONALDSON,ARK.
D.FEB.24,1976 HOUSTON,TEX.

YR	CL	LEA	POS	GP	G	REC
1929	STL	N	2		25	.235
1932	CHI	A	3		116	.283
		BRTR			141	.277

SEMBERA, CARROLL WILLIAM
B.JULY 26,1941 SHINER,TEX.

YR	CL	LEA	POS	GP	G	REC
1965	HOU	N	P		2	0- 1
1966	HOU	N	P		24	1- 2
1967	HOU	N	P		45	2- 6
1969	MON	N	P		23	0- 2
1970	MON	N	P		5	0- 0
		BRTR			99	3-11

SEMINICK, ANDREW WASIL "ANDY"
B.SEPT.12,1920 PIERCE,W.VA.

YR	CL	LEA	POS	GP	G	REC
1943	PHI	N	C		22	.181
1944	PHI	N	C-O		22	.222
1945	PHI	N	C-3-O		80	.239
1946	PHI	N	C		124	.264
1947	PHI	N	C		111	.252
1948	PHI	N	C		125	.225
1949	PHI	N	C		109	.243
1950	PHI	N	C		130	.288
1951	PHI	N	C		101	.227
1952	CIN	N	C		108	.256
1953	CIN	N	C		119	.235
1954	CIN	N	C		86	.235
1955	CIN	N	C		6	.133
	PHI	N	C		93	.246
1956	PHI	N	C		60	.199
1957	PHI	N	C		8	.091
		BRTR			1304	.243

SEMPROCH, ROMAN ANTHONY
B.JAN.7,1931 CLEVELAND,OHIO

YR	CL	LEA	POS	GP	G	REC
1958	PHI	N	P		36	13-11
1959	PHI	N	P		30	3-10
1960	DET	A	P		17	3- 0
1961	LA	A	P		2	0- 0
		BRTR			85	19-21

SENERCHIA, EMANUEL ROBERT
"SONNY"
B.APR.8,1931 NEWARK,N.J.

YR	CL	LEA	POS	GP	G	REC
1952	PIT	N	3		29	.220
		BRTR				

SENSENDERFER, JOHN PHILLIPS
JENKINS
B.DEC.28,1847 PHILADELPHIA,PA.
D.MAY 3,1903

YR	CL	LEA	POS	GP	G	REC
1871	ATH	NA	O		25	.371
1872	ATH	NA	O		1	.400
1873	ATH	NA	O		19	-
1874	ATH	NA	O		4	-
					49	-

SENTELL, LEOPOLD THEODORE
"PAUL"
B.AUG.27,1879 NEW ORLEANS,LA.
D.APR.27,1923

YR	CL	LEA	POS	GP	G	REC
1906	PHI	N	2-3		55	.229
1907	PHI	N	S		3	.000
		TR			58	.226

SEPKOWSKI, THEODORE WALTER
(REAL NAME
THEODORE WALTER SCZEPKOWSKI)
B.NOV.9,1923 BALTIMORE,MD.

YR	CL	LEA	POS	GP	G	REC
1942	CLE	A	2		5	.100
1946	CLE	A	3		2	.500
1947	CLE	A	O		10	.125
	NY	A	H		2	.000
		BLTR			19	.231

SERAD, WILLIAM I.
B.1863 PHILADELPHIA,PA.
D.NOV.1,1925

YR	CL	LEA	POS	GP	G	REC
1884	BUF	N	P-O		38	17-21
						.175
1885	BUF	N	P		29	8-21
1887	CIN	AA	P-O		22	11-11
						.278
1888	CIN	AA	P		6	1- 3
		BRTR			95	37-56
						.183

SERAFIN, JOSEPH STANLEY
(PLAYED UNDER NAME OF
JOSEPH STANLEY COBB)

SERENA, WILLIAM ROBERT "BILL"
B.OCT.2,1924 ALMEDA,CAL.

YR	CL	LEA	POS	GP	G	REC
1949	CHI	N	3		12	.216
1950	CHI	N	3		127	.239
1951	CHI	N	3		13	.333
1952	CHI	N	2-3		122	.274
1953	CHI	N	2-3		93	.251
1954	CHI	N	2-3		41	.159
		BRTR			408	.251

SESSI, WALTER ANTHONY
B.JULY 23,1918 FINLEYVILLE,PA.

YR	CL	LEA	POS	GP	G	REC
1941	STL	N	O		5	.000
1946	STL	N	H		15	.143
		BLTL			20	.074

SETTLEMIRE, EDGAR MERLE "LEFTY"
B.JAN.19,1903 SANTA FE,OHIO

YR	CL	LEA	POS	GP	G	REC
1928	BOS	A	P		33	0- 6
		BLTL				

SEVCIK, JOHN JOSEPH
B.JULY 11,1942 OAK PARK,ILL.

YR	CL	LEA	POS	GP	G	REC
1965	MIN	A	C		12	.063
		BRTR				

SEVEREID, HENRY LEVAI "HANK"
B.JUNE 1,1891 STORY CITY,IOWA
D.DEC.17,1968 SAN ANTONIO,TEX.

YR	CL	LEA	POS	GP	G	REC
1911	CIN	N	C		22	.304
1912	CIN	N	C		50	.237
1913	CIN	N	C		8	.200
1915	STL	A	C		80	.222
1916	STL	A	C		100	.273
1917	STL	A	C		143	.265
1918	STL	A	C		51	.256
1919	STL	A	C		112	.248
1920	STL	A	C		123	.277
1921	STL	A	C		143	.324
1922	STL	A	C		137	.321
1923	STL	A	C		122	.308
1924	STL	A	C		137	.308
1925	STL	A	C		34	.358
	WAS	A	C		50	.364
1926	WAS	A	C		22	.212
	NY	A	C		41	.266
		BRTR			1375	.289

YR	CL	LEA	POS	GP	G	REC

SEVERINSEN, ALBERT HENRY "AL"
B.NOV.9,1944 BROOKLYN,N.Y.

YR	CL	LEA	POS	GP	G	REC
1969	BAL	A	P		12	1- 1
1971	SD	N	P		59	2- 5
1972	SD	N	P		17	0- 1
		BRTR			88	3- 7

SEVERSON, RICHARD ALLEN "RICH"
B.JAN.18,1945 ARTESIA,CAL.

YR	CL	LEA	POS	GP	G	REC
1970	KC	A	2-S		77	.250
1971	KC	A	2-S-3		16	.300
		BBTR			93	.256

SEWARD, EDWARD WILLIAM
(REAL NAME EDWARD W. SEWER)
B.JUNE 29,1867 CLEVELAND,OHIO
D.JULY 30,1947

YR	CL	LEA	POS	GP	G	REC
1885	PRO	N	P		1	0- 1
1887	ATH	AA	P	55	75	25-24
1888	ATH	AA	P	57	64	34-19
1889	ATH	AA	P	38	45	21-16
1890	ATH	AA	P	21	27	6-13
1891	CLE	N	P		7	1- 0
		TR		179	219	87-73

SEWARD, FRANK MARTIN
B.APR.7,1922 PENSAUKEN,N.J.

YR	CL	LEA	POS	GP	G	REC
1943	NY	N	P		1	0- 1
1944	NY	N	P		25	3- 2
		BRTR			26	3- 3

SEWARD, GEORGE E.
B.ST.LOUIS,MO.

YR	CL	LEA	POS	GP	G	REC
1875	STL	NA	C-2-O		23	.210
1876	MUT	N	2		1	.000
1882	STL	AA	C-O		38	.195
					62	.198

SEWELL, JAMES LUTHER "LUKE"
B.JAN.15,1901 TITUS,ALA.

YR	CL	LEA	POS	GP	G	REC
1921	CLE	A	C		3	.000
1922	CLE	A	C		41	.264
1923	CLE	A	C		10	.200
1924	CLE	A	C		63	.291
1925	CLE	A	C-O		74	.232
1926	CLE	A	C		126	.238
1927	CLE	A	C		128	.293
1928	CLE	A	C		122	.270
1929	CLE	A	C		124	.236
1930	CLE	A	C		76	.257
1931	CLE	A	C		108	.275
1932	CLE	A	C		87	.253
1933	WAS	A	C		141	.264
1934	WAS	A	C-1-2-3-O		72	.237
1935	CHI	A	C		118	.285
1936	CHI	A	C		128	.251
1937	CHI	A	C		122	.269
1938	CHI	A	C		65	.213
1939	CLE	A	C		16	.150
1942	STL	A	M-C		6	.083
		BRTR			1630	.259

NON-PLAYING MANAGER STL(A)
1941, 43-46, CIN(N) 1949-52

SEWELL, JOSEPH WHEELER "JOE"
B.OCT.9,1898 TITUS,ALA.

YR	CL	LEA	POS	GP	G	REC
1920	CLE	A	S		22	.329
1921	CLE	A	S		154	.318
1922	CLE	A	2-S		153	.299
1923	CLE	A	S		153	.353
1924	CLE	A	S		153	.316
1925	CLE	A	2-S		155	.335
1926	CLE	A	S		154	.324
1927	CLE	A	S		153	.316
1928	CLE	A	S-3		155	.323
1929	CLE	A	3		152	.315
1930	CLE	A	3		109	.289
1931	NY	A	3		130	.302
1932	NY	A	3		125	.272
1933	NY	A	3		135	.273
		BLTR			1903	.312

SEWELL, THOMAS WESLEY
B.APR.16,1906 TITUS,ALA.
D.JULY 30,1956

YR	CL	LEA	POS	GP	G	REC
1927	CHI	N	H		1	.000
		BLTR				

SEWELL, TRUETT BANKS "RIP"
B.MAY 11,1908 DECATUR,ALA.

YR	CL	LEA	POS	GP	G	REC
1932	DET	A	P		5	0- 0
1938	PIT	N	P		17	0- 1
1939	PIT	N	P		52	10- 9
1940	PIT	N	P	33	47	16- 5
1941	PIT	N	P	39	42	14-17
1942	PIT	N	P	40	41	17-15
1943	PIT	N	P	35	41	21- 9
1944	PIT	N	P	38	44	21-12
1945	PIT	N	P	33	35	11- 9
1946	PIT	N	P	25	26	8-12
1947	PIT	N	P		24	6- 4
1948	PIT	N	P		21	13- 3
1949	PIT	N	P		28	6- 1
		BLTR		390	423	143-97

SEWER, EDWARD W.
(PLAYED UNDER NAME OF
EDWARD W. SEWARD)

SEXAUER, ELMER GEORGE
B.MAY 21,1926 ST.LOUIS CO.,MO.

YR	CL	LEA	POS	GP	G	REC
1948	BRO	N	P		2	0- 0
		BRTR				

SEXTON, FRANK JOSEPH
B.JULY 8,1872 BROCKTON,MASS.
D.JAN.4,1938

YR	CL	LEA	POS	GP	G	REC
1895	BOS	N	P		10	1- 4

SEXTON, THOMAS W.
B.MAR.14,1865 ROCK ISLAND,ILL.
D.FEB.8,1934

YR	CL	LEA	POS	GP	G	REC
1884	MIL	U	S		12	.229

SEYBOLD, RALPH ORLANDO "SOCKS"
B.NOV.23,1870 WASHINGTONVILLE,O
D.DEC.22,1921

YR	CL	LEA	POS	GP	G	REC
1899	CIN	N	O		22	.221
1901	PHI	A	1-O		114	.332
1902	PHI	A	O		137	.317
1903	PHI	A	1-O		137	.299
1904	PHI	A	O		143	.282
1905	PHI	A	O		132	.271
1906	PHI	A	O		116	.316
1907	PHI	A	O		147	.271
1908	PHI	A	O		48	.215
		BRTR			996	.293

SEYFRIED, GORDON CLAY
B.JULY 4,1937 LONG BEACH,CAL.

YR	CL	LEA	POS	GP	G	REC
1963	CLE	A	P		3	0- 1
1964	CLE	A	P		2	0- 0
		BRTR			5	0- 1

SEYMOUR, JOHN BENTLEY "CY"
B.DEC.9,1872 ALBANY,N.Y.
D.SEPT.20,1919 NEW YORK,N.Y.

YR	CL	LEA	POS	GP	G	REC
1896	NY	N	P		12	2- 4
1897	NY	N	P	34	41	20-14
1898	NY	N	P-O	44	78	25-17
						.273
1899	NY	N	P	33	45	13-18
1900	NY	N	P		21	2- 2
1901	BAL	A	O		137	.302
1902	BAL	A	O		72	.278
	CIN	N	P-3-O	1	60	0- 0
						.349
1903	CIN	N	O		135	.342
1904	CIN	N	O		130	.312
1905	CIN	N	O		149	.377
1906	CIN	N	O		79	.257
	NY	N	O		72	.320
1907	NY	N	O		126	.294
1908	NY	N	O		155	.267
1909	NY	N	O		73	.310
1910	NY	N	O		76	.265
1913	BOS	N	O		39	.178
		BLTL		145	1500	62-55
						.307

SEYMOUR, THOMAS
B.1858 PITTSBURGH,PA.
D.FEB.17,1916

YR	CL	LEA	POS	GP	G	REC
1882	PIT	AA	P		1	0- 1

SHAFER, ARTHUR JOSEPH "TILLIE"
B.MAR.22,1889 LOS ANGELES,CAL.
D.JAN.10,1962

YR	CL	LEA	POS	GP	G	REC
1909	NY	N	3		31	.179
1910	NY	N	3		27	.182
1912	NY	N	S		78	.288
1913	NY	N	2-S-3-O		138	.287
		BBTR			274	.273

SHAFER, RALPH NEWTON
B.MAR.17,1894 CINCINNATI,OHIO
D.FEB.5,1950

YR	CL	LEA	POS	GP	G	REC
1914	PIT	N	H		1	.000

SHAFFER

YR	CL	LEA	POS	GP	G	REC
1875	ATL	NA	O		1	.000

SHAFFER, FRANK

YR	CL	LEA	POS	GP	G	REC
1884	ALT	U	C-3-O		19	.284
	KC	U	C-2-S-3-O		43	.172
	BAL	U	O		3	.077
					65	.200

SHAFFER, GEORGE "ORATOR"
B.1852 PHILADELPHIA,PA.

YR	CL	LEA	POS	GP	G	REC
1874	HAR	NA	O		9	-
	MUT	NA	O		1	-
1875	PHI	NA	10-OO		16	.262
1877	LOU	N	1-O		61	.285
1878	IND	N	O		60	.344
1879	CHI	N	O		70	.319
1880	CLE	N	O		82	.265
1881	CLE	N	O		84	.257
1882	CLE	N	O		82	.218
1883	BUF	N	O		94	.292
1884	STL	U	O		89	.354
1885	STL	N	O		69	.194
	ATH	AA	O		2	.222
1886	ATH	AA	O		21	.344
1890	ATH	AA	O		106	.286
		BLTR			846	-

SHAFFER, TAYLOR
B.PHILADELPHIA,PA.

YR	CL	LEA	POS	GP	G	REC
1890	ATH	AA	2		70	.178

SHALLIX, AUGUST
(REAL NAME AUGUST SCHALLIX)
B.MAR.29,1858 PADERBORN,
WESTPHALIA,GERMANY
D.OCT.28,1937 CINCINNATI,OHIO

YR	CL	LEA	POS	GP	G	REC
1884	CIN	AA	P		23	11-10
1885	CIN	AA	P-O		13	7- 4
						.128
		BRTR			36	18-14
						.085

SHAMBRICK, OTTO H.
(PLAYED UNDER NAME OF
OTTO H. SCHOMBERG)

SHAMSKY, ARTHUR LOUIS "ART"
B.OCT.14,1941 ST.LOUIS,MO.

YR	CL	LEA	POS	GP	G	REC
1965	CIN	N	1-O		64	.260
1966	CIN	N	O		96	.231
1967	CIN	N	O		76	.197
1968	NY	N	1-O		116	.238
1969	NY	N	1-O		100	.300
1970	NY	N	1-O		122	.293
1971	NY	N	1-O		68	.185
1972	CHI	N	1		15	.125
	OAK	A	H		8	.000
		BLTL			665	.253

SHANABROOK, WARREN H.
B.NOV.30,1880 MASSILLON,OHIO

YR	CL	LEA	POS	GP	G	REC
1906	WAS	A	3		1	.000
		TR				

SHANAHAN, PAUL GREGORY "GREG"
B.DEC.11,1947 EUREKA,CAL.

YR	CL	LEA	POS	GP	G	REC
1973	LA	N	P		7	0- 0
1974	LA	N	P		4	0- 0
		BRTR			11	0- 0

SHANDLEY, JAMES J.
B.NEW YORK
D.NOV.7,1904

YR	CL	LEA	POS	GP	G	REC
1876	MUT	N	O		2	.125

SHANER, WALTER DEDAKER "SKINNY"
B.MAY 24,1901 LYNCHBURG,VA.

YR	CL	LEA	POS	GP	G	REC
1923	CLE	A	3		3	.250
1926	BOS	A	O		69	.283
1927	BOS	A	O		122	.273
1929	CIN	N	1-O		13	.321
		BRTR			207	.278

SHANK, HARVEY TILLMAN
B.JULY 29,1946 TORONTO,ONT.,CAN.

YR	CL	LEA	POS	GP	G	REC
1970	CAL	A	P		1	0- 0
		BRTR				

YR	CL	LEA	POS	GP	G	REC

SHANKS, HOWARD SAMUEL "HANK"
B.JULY 21,1890 CHICAGO,ILL.
D.JULY 30,1941

YR	CL	LEA	POS	GP	G	REC
1912	WAS	A	O		115	.236
1913	WAS	A	O		109	.254
1914	WAS	A	O		143	.224
1915	WAS	A	3-O		141	.250
1916	WAS	A	3-O		140	.253
1917	WAS	A	S-O		126	.202
1918	WAS	A	2-O		120	.257
1919	WAS	A	2-S		135	.248
1920	WAS	A	1-3-O		128	.268
1921	WAS	A	3		154	.302
1922	WAS	A	3-O		84	.283
1923	BOS	A	2-3		131	.259
1924	BOS	A	S-3		72	.259
1925	NY	A	2-3-O		66	.258
		BRTR			1664	.253

SHANLEY, HENRY ROAT "DOC"
B.JAN.30,1889 CHICAGO,ILL.
D.DEC.14,1934

YR	CL	LEA	POS	GP	G	REC
1912	STL	A	S		5	.000
		BRTR				

SHANNER, W. W.

YR	CL	LEA	POS	GP	G	REC
1920	PHI	A	P		1	0- 0

SHANNON, DANIEL W.
B.MAR.23,1865 BRIDGEPORT,CONN.
D.OCT.25,1913

YR	CL	LEA	POS	GP	G	REC
1889	LOU	AA	M-2		120	.262
1890	PHI	P	2		18	.260
	NY	P	2-S-3		83	.230
1891	WAS	AA	M-S		19	.118
					240	.238

SHANNON, FRANK E. "TOD"
B.DEC.3,1873 SAN FRANCISCO,CAL.

YR	CL	LEA	POS	GP	G	REC
1892	WAS	N	S		1	.200
1895	WAS	N	S		1	.200
1896	LOU	N	3		31	.161
					33	.163

SHANNON, JOSEPH ALOYSIUS
B.FEB.11,1895 JERSEY CITY,N.J.
D.JULY 28,1955

YR	CL	LEA	POS	GP	G	REC
1915	BOS	N	O		5	.200
		BRTR				

SHANNON, MAURICE JOSEPH "RED"
B.FEB.11,1895 JERSEY CITY,N.J.
D.APR.12,1970 JERSEY CITY,N.J.

YR	CL	LEA	POS	GP	G	REC
1915	BOS	N	S		1	.000
1917	PHI	A	S		11	.257
1918	PHI	A	2-S		72	.240
1919	PHI	A	2		39	.271
	BOS	A	2		80	.259
1920	WAS	A	S		63	.288
	PHI	A	S		24	.167
1921	PHI	A	H		1	.000
1926	CHI	N	S		19	.333
		BBTR			310	.257

SHANNON, THOMAS MICHAEL "MIKE"
B.JULY 5,1939 ST.LOUIS,MO.

YR	CL	LEA	POS	GP	G	REC
1962	STL	N	O		10	.133
1963	STL	N	O		32	.308
1964	STL	N	O		88	.261
1965	STL	N	C-O		124	.221
1966	STL	N	C-O		137	.288
1967	STL	N	3-O		130	.245
1968	STL	N	3		156	.266
1969	STL	N	3		150	.254
1970	STL	N	3		55	.213
		BRTR			882	.255

SHANNON, OWEN DENNIS IGNATIUS
B.DEC.22,1885 OMAHA,NEB.
D.APR.10,1918

YR	CL	LEA	POS	GP	G	REC
1903	STL	A	C		8	.200
1907	WAS	A	C		4	.143
		BRTR			12	.188

SHANNON, WALTER CHARLES "WALLY"
B.JAN.23,1934 CLEVELAND,OHIO

YR	CL	LEA	POS	GP	G	REC
1959	STL	N	2-S		47	.284
1960	STL	N	2-S		18	.174
		BLTR			65	.263

SHANNON, WILLIAM PORTER "SPIKE"
B.FEB.7,1878 PITTSBURGH,PA.
D.MAY 16,1940

YR	CL	LEA	POS	GP	G	REC
1904	STL	N	O		133	.280
1905	STL	N	O		140	.268
1906	STL	N	O		80	.258
	NY	N	O		76	.254
1907	NY	N	O		155	.265
1908	NY	N	O		74	.224
	PIT	N	O		32	.197
		BBTR			690	.259

SHANTZ, ROBERT CLAYTON "BOBBY"
B.SEP.26,1925 POTTSTOWN,PA.

YR	CL	LEA	POS	GP	G	REC
1949	PHI	A	P		33	6- 8
1950	PHI	A	P	36	37	8-14
1951	PHI	A	P	32	36	18-10
1952	PHI	A	P	33	34	24- 7
1953	PHI	A	P	16	21	5- 9
1954	PHI	A	P	2	7	1- 0
1955	KC	A	P	23	26	5-10
1956	KC	A	P	45	51	2- 7
1957	NY	A	P	30	33	11- 5
1958	NY	A	P-O		33	7- 6
						.229
1959	NY	A	P	33	40	7- 3
1960	NY	A	P	42	43	5- 4
1961	PIT	N	P	43	44	6- 3
1962	HOU	N	P	3	7	1- 1
	STL	N	P		28	5- 3
1963	STL	N	P		55	6- 4
1964	STL	N	P		16	1- 3
	CHI	N	P		20	0- 1
	PHI	N	P		14	1- 1
		BRTL		537	578	119-99
						.195

SHANTZ, WILMER EBERT "BILLY"
B.JULY 31,1927 POTTSTOWN,PA.

YR	CL	LEA	POS	GP	G	REC
1954	PHI	A	C		51	.256
1955	KC	A	C		79	.258
1960	NY	A	C		1	.000
		BRTR			131	.257

SHARMAN, RALPH EDWARD "BALLY"
B.APR.11,1895 CLEVELAND,OHIO
D.MAY 24,1918 CAMP SHERIDAN,ALA

YR	CL	LEA	POS	GP	G	REC
1917	PHI	A	O		13	.297
		BRTR				

SHARON, RICHARD LOUIS "DICK"
B.APR.15,1950 SAN MATEO,CAL.

YR	CL	LEA	POS	GP	G	REC
1973	DET	A	O		91	.242
1974	DET	A	O		60	.217
1975	SD	N	O		91	.194
		BRTR			242	.218

SHARP, WILLIAM HOWARD "BILL"
B.JAN.18,1950 LIMA,OHIO

YR	CL	LEA	POS	GP	G	REC
1973	CHI	A	O		76	.276
1974	CHI	A	O		100	.253
1975	CHI	A	O		18	.200
	MIL	A	O		125	.255
1976	MIL	A	O		78	.244
		BLTL			397	.255

SHARPE, BAYARD HESTON "BUD"
B.AUG.6,1881 WEST CHESTER,PA.
D.MAY 31,1916

YR	CL	LEA	POS	GP	G	REC
1905	BOS	N	O		45	.182
1910	BOS	N	1		113	.239
	PIT	N	1		4	.188
		BLTR			162	.222

SHARROTT, GEORGE OSCAR
B.NOV.2,1869 W.NEW BRIGHTON,
S.I.,N.Y.
D.JAN.6,1932

YR	CL	LEA	POS	GP	G	REC
1893	BRO	N	P		11	4- 7
1894	BRO	N	P		3	1- 1
		TL			14	5- 8

SHARROTT, JOHN HENRY
B.AUG.13,1869 BANGOR,ME.
D.DEC.31,1927

YR	CL	LEA	POS	GP	G	REC
1890	NY	N	P	23	29	11- 9
1891	NY	N	P	10	4- 3	
1892	NY	N	P-O	1	5	0- 1
						.000
1893	PHI	N	P-O	8	30	2- 3
						.254
				42	74	17-16
						.236

SHARSIG, WILLIAM A.
B.1855 PHILADELPHIA,PA.
D.FEB.1,1902 PHILADELPHIA,PA.
NON-PLAYING MANAGER
ATH(AA) 1882-91

SHAUGHNESSY, FRANCIS JOSEPH "SHAG"
B.APR.8,1885 S.AMBOY,ILL.
D.MAY 15,1969 MONTREAL,QUE.,CAN

YR	CL	LEA	POS	GP	G	REC
1905	WAS	A	O		1	.000
1908	PHI	A	O		8	.321
		BRTR			9	.290

SHAUTE, JOSEPH BENJAMIN "LEFTY"
B.AUG.1,1899 PECKVILLE,PA.
D.FEB.21,1970 SCRANTON,PA.

YR	CL	LEA	POS	GP	G	REC
1922	CLE	A	P	2	5	0- 0
1923	CLE	A	P	33	34	10- 8
1924	CLE	A	P		46	20-17
1925	CLE	A	P	26	29	4-12
1926	CLE	A	P		34	14-10
1927	CLE	A	P		45	9-16
1928	CLE	A	P		36	13-17
1929	CLE	A	P		26	8- 8
1930	CLE	A	P		4	0- 0
1931	BRO	N	P		25	11- 8
1932	BRO	N	P	34	35	7- 7
1933	BRO	N	P		41	3- 4
1934	CIN	N	P		8	0- 2
		BLTL		360	368	99-109

SHAW, ALBERT SIMPSON
B.MAR.1,1881 TOLEDO,ILL.
D.DEC.30,1974 DANVILLE,ILL.

YR	CL	LEA	POS	GP	G	REC
1907	STL	N	O		8	.303
1908	STL	N	O		96	.264
1909	STL	N	O		92	.248
1914	BRO	F	O		110	.321
1915	KC	F	O		132	.279
		BLTR			438	.279

SHAW, ALFRED "SHODDY"
B.MAY 22,1874 BURSLEM,ENGLAND
D.MAR.25,1958 ULRICHSVILLE,OHIO

YR	CL	LEA	POS	GP	G	REC
1901	DET	A	C		57	.275
1907	BOS	A	C		76	.192
1908	CHI	A	C		32	.082
1909	BOS	N	C		18	.100
		BRTR			183	.207

SHAW, BENAJMIN NATHANIEL
B.MAR.16,1896 LA CENTER,KY.
D.MAR.16,1959

YR	CL	LEA	POS	GP	G	REC
1917	PIT	N	O		2	.000
1918	PIT	N	O		21	.194
		BRTR			23	.184

SHAW, DONALD WELLINGTON "DON"
B.FEB.23,1944 PITTSBURGH,PA.

YR	CL	LEA	POS	GP	G	REC
1967	NY	N	P		40	4- 5
1968	NY	N	P		7	0- 0
1969	MON	N	P		35	2- 5
1971	STL	N	P		45	7- 2
1972	STL	N	P		8	0- 1
	OAK	A	P		3	0- 1
		BLTL			138	13-14

SHAW, FREDERICK LANDER "DUPEE"
B.MAY 31,1859 CHARLESTOWN,MASS.
D.JUNE 11,1938

YR	CL	LEA	POS	GP	G	REC
1883	DET	N	P-O	29	38	11-18
						.189
1884	DET	N	P-O	26	36	8-18
						.191
	BOS	U	P-O	39	44	22-15
						.235
1885	PRO	N	P-O		49	23-26
						.133
1886	WAS	N	P		45	14-31
1887	WAS	N	P		21	7-14
1888	WAS	N	P		3	0- 3
		TL		212	236	85-125
						.174

YR	CL	LEA	POS	GP	G	REC

SHAW, JAMES ALOYSIUS
"GRUNTING JIM"
B.AUG.19,1893 PITTSBURGH,PA.
D.JAN.27,1962

YR	CL	LEA	POS	GP	G	REC
1913	WAS	A	P		2	0- 1
1914	WAS	A	P		48	15-17
1915	WAS	A	P		25	5-12
1916	WAS	A	P		26	3- 8
1917	WAS	A	P		47	15-14
1918	WAS	A	P		41	16-12
1919	WAS	A	P		45	16-17
1920	WAS	A	P		38	11-18
1921	WAS	A	P		15	1- 0
		BRTR			287	82-99

SHAW, ROBERT JOHN "BOB"
B.JUNE 29,1933 BRONX,N.Y.

1957	DET	A	P		7	0- 1
1958	DET	A	P	11	12	1- 2
	CHI	A	P		29	4- 2
1959	CHI	A	P		47	18- 6
1960	CHI	A	P		36	13-13
1961	CHI	A	P		14	3- 4
	KC	A	P	26	28	9-10
1962	MIL	N	P		38	15- 9
1963	MIL	N	P		48	7-11
1964	SF	N	P		61	7- 6
1965	SF	N	P		42	16- 9
1966	SF	N	P		13	1- 4
	NY	N	P		26	11-10
1967	NY	N	P		23	3- 9
	CHI	N	P		9	0- 2
		BRTR		430	433	108-98

SHAW, ROYAL N. "HUNKY"
B.SEPT.29,1884 N.YAKIMA,WASH.
D.JULY 3,1969 YAKIMA,WASH.

1908	PIT	N	O		1	.000
1909	PIT	N	H		1	.000
		BBTR			2	.000

SHAW, SAMUEL E.
B.1863 BALTIMORE,MD.

1888	BAL	AA	P		6	2- 4
1893	CHI	N	P		2	1- 0
		BRTR			8	3- 4

SHAWKEY, JAMES ROBERT "BOB"
B.DEC.4,1890 SIGEL,PA.

1913	PHI	A	P		18	7- 5
1914	PHI	A	P		38	16- 8
1915	PHI	A	P		17	6- 5
	NY	A	P		16	4- 8
1916	NY	A	P		53	24-14
1917	NY	A	P		32	13-15
1918	NY	A	P		3	1- 1
1919	NY	A	P		41	20-11
1920	NY	A	P		38	20-13
1921	NY	A	P		38	18-12
1922	NY	A	P		39	20-12
1923	NY	A	P		36	16-11
1924	NY	A	P		38	16-11
1925	NY	A	P		32	6-14
1926	NY	A	P		29	8- 7
1927	NY	A	P		19	2- 3
		BRTR		487		197-150
NON-PLAYING MANAGER NY(A) 1930						

SHAY, ARTHUR JOSEPH "MARTY"
B.APR.25,1898 BOSTON,MASS.
D.FEB.20,1951

1916	CHI	N	2		2	.286
1924	CHI	N	2-S		19	.235
		BRTR			21	.240

SHAY, DANIEL C.
B.NOV.8,1876 SPRINGFIELD,OHIO
D.DEC.1,1927

1901	CLE	A	S		19	.226
1904	STL	N	S		98	.256
1905	STL	N	2-S		78	.238
1907	NY	N	S		24	.190
		TR			219	.240

SHEA, FRANCIS JOSEPH "SPEC"
(REAL NAME
FRANCIS JOSEPH O'SHEA)
B.OCT.2,1922 NAUGATUCK,CONN.

1947	NY	A	P		27	14- 5
1948	NY	A	P		28	9-10
1949	NY	A	P		20	1- 1
1951	NY	A	P		25	5- 5
1952	WAS	A	P		22	11- 7
1953	WAS	A	P		23	12- 7
1954	WAS	A	P		23	2- 9
1955	WAS	A	P		27	2- 2
		BRTR			195	56-46

SHEA, GERALD J.
B.JULY 26,1881 ST.LOUIS,MO.
D.MAY 3,1964 BERKELEY,MD.

| 1905 | STL | N | C | | 2 | .333 |
| | | TR | | | | |

SHEA, JOHN EDWARD "NAPOLEON"
B.MAY 23,1878 WARE,MASS.
D.JULY 8,1956 WARE,MASS.

| 1902 | PHI | N | C | | 3 | .111 |
| | | BRTR | | | | |

SHEA, JOHN MICHAEL JOSEPH
"LEFTY"
B.DEC.27,1904 EVERETT,MASS.
D.NOV.30,1956 MALDEN,MASS.

| 1928 | BOS | A | P | | 1 | 0- 0 |
| | | BLTL | | | | |

SHEA, MERVYN DAVID JOHN "MERV"
B.SEPT.5,1900 SAN FRANCISCO,CAL
D.JAN.27,1953

1927	DET	A	C		34	.176
1928	DET	A	C		39	.236
1929	DET	A	C		50	.290
1933	BOS	A	C		16	.143
	STL	A	C		94	.262
1934	CHI	A	C		62	.159
1935	CHI	A	C		46	.230
1936	CHI	A	C		14	.125
1937	CHI	A	C		25	.211
1938	BRO	N	C		48	.183
1939	DET	A	C		4	.000
1944	PHI	N	C		7	.267
		BRTR			439	.220

SHEA, MICHAEL J.
B.MAR.10,1867 NEW ORLEANS,LA.

| 1887 | CIN | AA | P | | 2 | 1- 1 |

SHEA, PATRICK HENRY "RED"
B.NOV.29,1898 WARE,MASS.

1918	PHI	A	P		3	0- 0
1921	NY	N	P		9	5- 2
1922	NY	N	P		11	0- 3
		BRTR			23	5- 5

SHEA, STEVEN FRANCIS "STEVE"
B.DEC.5,1942 WORCESTER,MASS.

1968	HOU	N	P		30	4- 4
1969	MON	N	P		10	0- 0
		BRTR			40	4- 4

SHEALY, ALBERT BERLEY
B.MAR.24,1902 CHAPIN,S.C.
D.MAR.7,1967 HAGERSTOWN,MD.

1928	NY	A	P		23	8- 6
1930	CHI	N	P		24	0- 0
		BRTR			47	8- 6

SHEAN, DAVID WILLIAM
B.JULY 9,1883 ARLINGTON,MASS.
D.MAY 22,1963 BOSTON,MASS.

1906	PHI	A	2		22	.213
1908	PHI	N	S		14	.106
1909	PHI	N	2		29	.232
	BOS	N	2		72	.241
1910	BOS	N	2		148	.239
1911	CHI	N	2-S		43	.193
1912	BOS	N	S		2	.400
1917	CIN	N	2		131	.210
1918	BOS	A	2		115	.264
1919	BOS	A	2		29	.140
		BRTR			605	.228

SHEARER, RAY SOLOMON
B.SEPT.19,1929 JACOBUS,PA.

| 1957 | MIL | N | O | | 2 | .500 |
| | | BRTR | | | | |

SHEARON, JOHN M.
B.1870 PITTSBURGH,PA.

1891	CLE	N	P-O	6	30	1- 4
						.234
1896	CLE	N	O		15	.174
				6	45	1- 4
						.214

SHEARS, GEORGE PENFIELD
B.APR.13,1890 MARSHALL,MO.

| 1912 | NY | A | P | | 4 | 0- 0 |
| | | BRTL | | | | |

SHECKARD, SAMUEL JAMES TILDEN
"JIMMY"
B.NOV.23,1878 UPPER CHANCEFORD,
PA.
D.JAN.15,1947 LANCASTER,PA.

1897	BRO	N	S-O		13	.326
1898	BRO	N	O		105	.290
1899	BAL	N	O		147	.298
1900	BRO	N	O		75	.305
1901	BRO	N	O		133	.353
1902	BAL	A	O		4	.266
	BRO	N	O		122	.273
1903	BRO	N	O		139	.332
1904	BRO	N	O		143	.239
1905	BRO	N	O		129	.292
1906	CHI	N	O		149	.262
1907	CHI	N	O		142	.267
1908	CHI	N	O		115	.231
1909	CHI	N	O		148	.255
1910	CHI	N	O		143	.256
1911	CHI	N	O		156	.276
1912	CHI	N	O		146	.245
1913	STL	N	O		52	.199
	CIN	N	O		47	.190
		BLTR			2108	.276

SHEEHAN, DANIEL
(SEE JOHN J. RYAN)

SHEEHAN, DANIEL
B.GLENVILLE,OHIO

| 1900 | NY | N | S | | 1 | .000 |

SHEEHAN, JAMES THOMAS
B.JUNE 3,1915 NEW HAVEN,CONN.

| 1936 | NY | N | C | | 1 | .000 |
| | | BRTR | | | | |

SHEEHAN, JOHN THOMAS
B.APR.15,1894 CHICAGO,ILL.

1920	BRO	N	3		4	.400
1921	BRO	N	3		5	.000
		BBTR			9	.176

SHEEHAN, THOMAS CLANCY
B.MAR.31,1894 OTTAWA,ILL.

1915	PHI	A	P		15	4- 8
1916	PHI	A	P		38	1-15
1921	NY	A	P		12	1- 0
1924	CIN	N	P	39	41	9-11
1925	CIN	N	P		10	1- 0
	PIT	N	P	23	24	1- 1
1926	PIT	N	P		9	0- 2
		BRTR		146	149	17-37
NON-PLAYING MANAGER SF(N) 1960						

SHEEHAN, THOMAS H.
B.NOV.6,1877 SACRAMENTO,CAL.
D.MAY 22,1959

1906	PIT	N	3		90	.241
1907	PIT	N	3		67	.274
1908	BRO	N	3		145	.214
		TR			302	.236

SHEEHAN, TIMOTHY JAMES
B.FEB.13,1868 HARTFORD,CONN.
D.OCT.21,1923

1895	STL	N	O		49	.324
1896	STL	N	O		5	.133
					54	.309

SHEELY, EARL HOMER "WHITEY"
B.FEB.12,1893 BUSHNELL,ILL.
D.SEPT.16,1952

1921	CHI	A	1		154	.304
1922	CHI	A	1		149	.317
1923	CHI	A	1		156	.296
1924	CHI	A	1		146	.320
1925	CHI	A	1		153	.315
1926	CHI	A	1		145	.299
1927	CHI	A	1		45	.209
1929	PIT	N	1		139	.293
1931	BOS	N	1		147	.273
		BRTR			1234	.300

SHEELY, HOLLIS KIMBALL
B.NOV.26,1920 SPOKANE,WASH.

1951	CHI	A	C		34	.180
1952	CHI	A	C		36	.240
1953	CHI	A	C		31	.217
		BLTR			101	.210

SHEERIN, CHARLES JOSEPH "CHUCK"
B.APR.17,1909 BROOKLYN,N.Y.

| 1936 | PHI | N | 2-3 | | 39 | .264 |
| | | BRTR | | | | |

YR	CL	LEA	POS	GP	G	REC

SHELDON, BOB MITCHELL
B.NOV.27,1950 MONTEBELLO,CAL.

YR	CL	LEA	POS	GP	G	REC
1974	MIL	A	2		10	.118
1975	MIL	A	2		53	.287
	BLTR				63	.273

SHELDON, ROLAND FRANK "ROLLIE"
B.DEC.17,1936 PUTNAM,CONN.

YR	CL	LEA	POS	GP	G	REC
1961	NY	A	P	35	36	11- 5
1962	NY	A	P		34	7- 8
1964	NY	A	P		19	5- 2
1965	NY	A	P		3	0- 0
	KC	A	P		32	10- 8
1966	KC	A	P		14	4- 7
	BOS	A	P		23	1- 6
	BRTR			160	161	38-36

SHELLENBACK, FRANK VICTOR
B.DEC.16,1898 JOPLIN,MO.
D.AUG.17,1969 NEWTON,MASS.

YR	CL	LEA	POS	GP	G	REC
1918	CHI	A	P	28	29	10-12
1919	CHI	A	P		8	1- 3
	BRTR			36	37	11-15

SHELLENBACK, JAMES PHILIP "JIM"
B.NOV.18,1943 RIVERSIDE,CAL.

YR	CL	LEA	POS	GP	G	REC
1966	PIT	N	P		2	0- 0
1967	PIT	N	P		6	1- 1
1969	PIT	N	P		8	0- 0
	WAS	A	P		30	4- 7
1970	WAS	A	P	39	40	6- 7
1971	WAS	A	P		40	3-11
1972	TEX	A	P		22	2- 4
1973	TEX	A	P		2	0- 0
1974	TEX	A	P		11	0- 0
	BLTL			160	161	16-30

SHELLEY, HUBERT LENEIRRE "HUGH"
B.OCT.26,1910 ROGERS,TEX.

YR	CL	LEA	POS	GP	G	REC
1935	DET	A	O		7	.250
	BRTR					

SHELTON, ANDREW KEMPER "SKEETER"
B.JUNE 29,1888 HUNTINGTON,W.VA.
D.JAN.9,1954

YR	CL	LEA	POS	GP	G	REC
1915	NY	A	O		10	.025
	BRTR					

SHEMO, STEPHEN STANLEY
B.APR.9,1917 SWOYERSVILLE,PA.

YR	CL	LEA	POS	GP	G	REC
1944	BOS	N	2-3		18	.290
1945	BOS	N	2-S-3		17	.239
	BRTR				35	.260

SHEPARD, BERT ROBERT
B.JUNE 29,1920 DANA,IND.

YR	CL	LEA	POS	GP	G	REC
1945	WAS	A	P		1	0- 0
	BLTL					

SHEPARD, JACK LEROY
B.MAY 13,1932 CLOVIS,CAL.

YR	CL	LEA	POS	GP	G	REC
1953	PIT	N	C		2	.250
1954	PIT	N	C		82	.304
1955	PIT	N	C		94	.239
1956	PIT	N	C-1		100	.242
	BRTR				278	.260

SHEPARD, LAWRENCE WILLIAM "LARRY"
B.APR.3,1919 LAKEWOOD,OHIO
NON-PLAYING MANAGER
PIT(N) 1968-69

SHEPARDSON, RAYMOND FRANCIS
B.MAY 3,1897 LITTLE FALLS,N.Y.
D.NOV.8,1975 LITTLE FALLS,N.Y.

YR	CL	LEA	POS	GP	G	REC
1924	STL	N	C		3	.000
	BRTR					

SHEPPARD, JOHN
B.BALTIMORE,MD.

YR	CL	LEA	POS	GP	G	REC
1873	MAR	NA	C-O		3	.000

SHERDEL, WILLIAM HENRY "WEE WILLIE"
B.AUG.15,1896 HANOVER,PA.
D.NOV.14,1968 MC SHERRYSTOWN,PA

YR	CL	LEA	POS	GP	G	REC
1918	STL	N	P		35	6-12
1919	STL	N	P	36	40	5- 9
1920	STL	N	P	43	49	11-10
1921	STL	N	P	38	39	9- 8
1922	STL	N	P	47	48	17-13
1923	STL	N	P	39	45	15-13
1924	STL	N	P-O	35	49	8- 9
						.200
1925	STL	N	P	32	33	15- 6
1926	STL	N	P	34	36	16-12
1927	STL	N	P		39	17-12
1928	STL	N	P		38	21-10
1929	STL	N	P		33	10-15
1930	STL	N	P		13	3- 2
	BOS	N	P		21	6- 5
1931	BOS	N	P		27	6-10
1932	BOS	N	P		1	0- 0
	STL	N	P		3	0- 0
	BLTL			514	549	165-146
						.223

SHERID, ROY RICHARD
B.JAN.25,1908 NORRISTOWN,PA.

YR	CL	LEA	POS	GP	G	REC
1929	NY	A	P		33	6- 6
1930	NY	A	P		37	12-13
1931	NY	A	P		17	5- 5
	BRTR				87	23-24

SHERIDAN

YR	CL	LEA	POS	GP	G	REC
1875	ATL	NA	O		1	.000

SHERIDAN, EUGENE ANTHONY "RED"
B.NOV.14,1896 BROOKLYN,N.Y.
D.NOV.25,1975 QUEENS VILLAGE, N.Y.

YR	CL	LEA	POS	GP	G	REC
1918	BRO	N	2		2	.250
1920	BRO	N	S		2	.000
	BRTR				4	.167

SHERIDAN, NEILL RAWLINS
B.NOV.20,1921 SACRAMENTO,CAL.

YR	CL	LEA	POS	GP	G	REC
1948	BOS	A	H		2	.000
	BRTR					

SHERLING, EDWARD CREECH
B.JULY 18,1897 COALBURG,ALA.
D.NOV.16,1965

YR	CL	LEA	POS	GP	G	REC
1924	PHI	A	H		4	.500
	BPTR					

SHERLOCK, JOHN CLINTON "MONK"
B.OCT.26,1904 DUFFALO,N.Y.

YR	CL	LEA	POS	GP	G	REC
1930	PHI	N	1		92	.324
	BRTR					

SHERLOCK, VINCENT THOMAS "BALDY"
B.MAR.27,1909 BUFFALO,N.Y.

YR	CL	LEA	POS	GP	G	REC
1935	BRO	N	2		9	.462
	BRTR					

SHERMAN, DANIEL L. "BABE"
B.1892 CONNECTICUT

YR	CL	LEA	POS	GP	G	REC
1914	CHI	F	P		1	0- 1
	BRTR					

SHERMAN, JOEL POWERS
B.NOV.14,1890 YARMOUTH,MASS.

YR	CL	LEA	POS	GP	G	REC
1915	PHI	A	P		2	1- 0
	BRTR					

SHERRY, FRED PETER
(REAL NAME
FRED PETER SCHUERHOLZ)
B.JAN.13,1889 HONESDALE,PA.
D.JULY 27,1975 HONESDALE,PA.

YR	CL	LEA	POS	GP	G	REC
1911	WAS	A	P		10	0- 4
	BRTR					

SHERRY, LAWRENCE "LARRY"
B.JULY 25,1935 LOS ANGELES,CAL.

YR	CL	LEA	POS	GP	G	REC
1958	LA	N	P		5	0- 0
1959	LA	N	P		23	7- 2
1960	LA	N	P		57	14-10
1961	LA	N	P		53	4- 4
1962	LA	N	P		58	7- 3
1963	LA	N	P		36	2- 6
1964	DET	A	P		38	7- 5
1965	DET	A	P		39	3- 6
1966	DET	A	P		55	8- 5
1967	DET	A	P		20	0- 1
	HOU	N	P		29	1- 2
1968	CAL	A	P		3	0- 0
	BRTR			416		53-44

SHERRY, NORMAN BURT "NORM"
B.JULY 16,1931 NEW YORK,N.Y.

YR	CL	LEA	POS	GP	G	REC
1959	LA	N	C		2	.333
1960	LA	N	C		47	.283
1961	LA	N	C		47	.256
1962	LA	N	C		35	.182
1963	NY	N	C		63	.136
	BRTR				194	.215

NON-PLAYING MANAGER CAL(A) 1976

SHETRONE, BARRY STEVAN
B.JULY 6,1938 BALTIMORE,MD.

YR	CL	LEA	POS	GP	G	REC
1959	BAL	A	O		33	.203
1960	BAL	A	R		1	.000
1961	BAL	A	O		3	.143
1962	BAL	A	O		21	.250
1963	WAS	A	H		2	.000
	BLTR				60	.205

SHETTSLINE, WILLIAM JOSEPH
B.OCT.25,1863 PHILADELPHIA,PA.
D.FEB.22,1933
NON-PLAYING MANAGER
PHI(N) 1898-1902

SHETZLINE, JOHN HENRY
B.1850 PHILADELPHIA,PA.
D.DEC.15,1892

YR	CL	LEA	POS	GP	G	REC
1882	BAL	AA	2-S-3-O		76	.226

SHEVLIN, JAMES CORNELIUS
B.JULY 9,1909 CINCINNATI,OHIO
D.OCT.30,1974 FT.LAUDERDALE,FLA

YR	CL	LEA	POS	GP	G	REC
1930	DET	A	1		28	.143
1932	CIN	N	1		7	.208
1934	CIN	N	1		18	.308
	BLTL				53	.247

SHIELDS, BENJAMIN COWAN "LEFTY"
B.JUNE 17,1903 HUNTERSVILLE,N.C

YR	CL	LEA	POS	GP	G	REC
1924	NY	A	P		2	0- 0
1925	NY	A	P		4	3- 0
1930	BOS	A	P		3	0- 0
1931	PHI	N	P		4	1- 0
	BBTL				13	4- 0

SHIELDS, CHARLES S.
B.DEC.10,1879 JACKSON,TENN.
D.AUG.27,1953

YR	CL	LEA	POS	GP	G	REC
1902	BAL	A	P-O		23	3- 9
						.163
	STL	A	P		4	3- 0
1907	STL	N	P		3	0- 3
	BLTL				30	6-12
						.219

SHIELDS, FRANCIS LEROY "PETE"
B.SEPT.21,1891 SWIFTWATER,MISS.
D.FEB.11,1961

YR	CL	LEA	POS	GP	G	REC
1915	CLE	A	1		23	.208
	BRTR					

SHIELDS, WILLIAM WILLIAM
B.NOV.18,1902 FREDERICTON,N.B.,
CANADA
D.OCT.17,1952

YR	CL	LEA	POS	GP	G	REC
1924	STL	N	P		3	1- 1
	BLTL					

SHIFFLETT, GARLAND JESSIE
B.MAR.28,1935 ELKTON,VA.

YR	CL	LEA	POS	GP	G	REC
1957	WAS	A	P		6	0- 0
1964	MIN	A	P		10	0- 2
	BRTR				16	0- 2

SHILLING, JAMES ROBERT
B.MAY 14,1915 TULSA,OKLA.

YR	CL	LEA	POS	GP	G	REC
1939	CLE	A	2		31	.276
	PHI	N	2-S-3		11	.303
	BRTR				42	.282

SHINAULT, ENOCH ERSKINE "GINGER"
B.SEPT.7,1892 BENTON,ARK.
D.DEC.29,1930 DENVER,COLO.

YR	CL	LEA	POS	GP	G	REC
1921	CLE	A	C		22	.378
1922	CLE	A	C		13	.133
	BRTR				35	.295

SHINDLE, WILLIAM
B.DEC.5,1863 GLOUCESTER,N.J.

YR	CL	LEA	POS	GP	G	REC
1886	DET	N	S		5	.333
1887	DET	N	3		20	.340
1888	BAL	AA	3		135	.216
1889	BAL	AA	3		138	.315
1890	PHI	P	S		132	.236
1891	PHI	N	3		103	.210
1892	BAL	N	3		143	.253
1893	BAL	N	3		125	.259
1894	BRO	N	3		117	.300
1895	BRO	N	3		118	.278
1896	BRO	N	3		131	.281
1897	BRO	N	3		134	.289
1898	BRO	N	3		120	.228
	TR				1421	.271

SHINNERS, RALPH PETER
B.OCT.4,1897 MILWAUKEE,WIS.
D.JULY 23,1962

YR	CL	LEA	POS	GP	G	REC
1922	NY	N	O		56	.251
1923	NY	N	O		33	.154
1925	STL	N	O		74	.295
	BRTR				163	.276

SHINNICK, TIMOTHY JAMES "DANDY"
B.NOV.6,1867 EXETER,N.H.
D.MAY 18,1944

YR	CL	LEA	POS	GP	G	REC
1890	LOU	AA	2		133	.267
1891	LOU	AA	2		135	.225
	BBTR				268	.244

SHIPKE, WILLIAM MARTIN "TONY"
(REAL NAME
WILLIAM MARTIN SHIPKRETHAVER)
B.NOV.18,1882 ST.LOUIS,MO.
D.SEPT.10,1940 OMAHA,NEB.

YR	CL	LEA	POS	GP	G	REC
1906	CLE	A	3		2	.000
1907	WAS	A	3		64	.196
1908	WAS	A	3		111	.208
1909	WAS	A	3		8	.154
	TR				185	.200

SHIPKRETHAVER, WILLIAM MARTIN
(PLAYED UNDER NAME OF
WILLIAM MARTIN SHIPKE)

SHIPLEY, JOSEPH CLARK "JOE"
B.MAY 9,1935 MORRISTOWN,TENN.

YR	CL	LEA	POS	GP	G	REC
1958	SF	N	P		1	0- 0
1959	SF	N	P		10	0- 0
1960	SF	N	P		15	0- 0
1963	CHI	A	P		3	0- 1
	BRTR				29	0- 1

SHIRES, CHARLES ARTHUR "THE GREAT"
B.AUG.13,1907 ITALY,TEX.
D.JULY 13,1967 ITALY,TEX.

YR	CL	LEA	POS	GP	G	REC
1928	CHI	A	1		33	.341
1929	CHI	A	1		100	.312
1930	CHI	A	1		37	.260
	WAS	A	1		38	.365
1932	BOS	N	1		82	.238
	BLTR				290	.291

SHIREY, CLAIR LEE "DUKE"
B.1899 HAGERSTOWN,MD.
D.SEPT.1,1962

YR	CL	LEA	POS	GP	G	REC
1920	WAS	A	P		2	0- 1
	BR					

SHIRLEY, ALVIS NEWMAN "TEX"
B.APR.25,1918 BIRTHRIGHT,TEX.

YR	CL	LEA	POS	GP	G	REC
1941	PHI	A	P		5	0- 1
1942	PHI	A	P		15	0- 1
1944	STL	A	P	23	30	5- 4
1945	STL	A	P	32	43	8-12
1946	STL	A	P	27	35	6-12
	BBTR			102	128	19-30
	BR 1941-42					

SHIRLEY, BARTON ARVIN "BART"
B.JAN.4,1940 CORPUS CHRISTI,TEX.

YR	CL	LEA	POS	GP	G	REC
1964	LA	N	S-3		18	.274
1966	LA	N	S		12	.200
1967	NY	N	2		6	.000
1968	LA	N	2-S		39	.181
	BRTR				75	.204

SHIRLEY, ERNEST RAEFORD "MULE"
B.MAY 24,1901 SNOW HILL,N.C.
D.AUG.4,1955

YR	CL	LEA	POS	GP	G	REC
1924	WAS	A	1		30	.234
1925	WAS	A	1		14	.130
	BLTL				44	.210

SHIVER, IVEY MERWIN "CHICK"
B.JAN.22,1907 SYLVESTER,GA.
D.AUG.31,1972 SAVANNAH,GA.

YR	CL	LEA	POS	GP	G	REC
1931	DET	A	O		2	.111
1934	CIN	N	O		19	.203
	BRTR				21	.191

SHOCH, GEORGE QUINTUS
B.JAN.6,1859 PHILADELPHIA,PA.
D.SEPT.30,1937

YR	CL	LEA	POS	GP	G	REC
1886	WAS	N	O		26	.294
1887	WAS	N	O		69	.294
1888	WAS	N	S-O		90	.183
1889	WAS	N	O		30	.238
1891	MIL	AA	2-S		34	.299
1892	BAL	N	S		75	.279
1893	BRO	N	3-O		93	.276
1894	BRO	N	O		63	.320
1895	BRO	N	O		58	.263
1896	BRO	N	2		75	.278
1897	BRO	N	2		79	.290
	BRTR				692	.271

SHOCKCOR, URBAIN JACQUES
(PLAYED UNDER NAME OF
URBAN JAMES SHOCKER)

SHOCKER, URBAN JAMES
(REAL NAME
URBAIN JACQUES SHOCKCOR)
B.AUG.22,1890 CLEVELAND,OHIO
D.SEPT.9,1928 DENVER,COLO.

YR	CL	LEA	POS	GP	G	REC
1916	NY	A	P		12	4- 3
1917	NY	A	P		26	8- 5
1918	STL	A	P		14	6- 5
1919	STL	A	P		30	13-11
1920	STL	A	P		38	20-10
1921	STL	A	P		47	27-12
1922	STL	A	P		48	24-17
1923	STL	A	P		43	20-12
1924	STL	A	P		40	16-13
1925	NY	A	P		41	12-12
1926	NY	A	P		41	19-11
1927	NY	A	P		31	18- 6
1928	NY	A	P		1	0- 0
	BRTR				412	187-117

SHOCKLEY, JOHN COSTEN "COSTEN"
B.FEB.8,1942 GEORGETOWN,DEL.

YR	CL	LEA	POS	GP	G	REC
1964	PHI	N	1		11	.229
1965	CAL	A	1-O		40	.187
	BLTL				51	.197

SHOEMAKER, CHARLES LANDIS "CHARLIE"
B.AUG.10,1939 LOS ANGELES,CAL.

YR	CL	LEA	POS	GP	G	REC
1961	KC	A	2		7	.385
1962	KC	A	2		5	.182
1964	KC	A	2		16	.212
	BLTR				28	.258

SHOFFNER, MILBURN JAMES "MILT"
B.NOV.13,1905 SHERMAN,TEX.

YR	CL	LEA	POS	GP	G	REC
1929	CLE	A	P		11	2- 3
1930	CLE	A	P		24	3- 4
1931	CLE	A	P		12	2- 3
1937	BOS	N	P		6	3- 1
1938	BOS	N	P	26	27	8- 7
1939	BOS	N	P		25	4- 6
	CIN	N	P		10	2- 2
1940	CIN	N	P		20	1- 0
	BLTL			134	135	25-26

SHOFNER, FRANK STRICKLAND "STRICK"
B.JULY 23,1919 CRAWFORD,TEX.

YR	CL	LEA	POS	GP	G	REC
1947	BOS	A	3		5	.154
	BLTR					

SHOKES, EDWARD CHRISTOPHER
B.JAN.27,1920 CHARLESTON,S.C.

YR	CL	LEA	POS	GP	G	REC
1941	CIN	N	H		1	.000
1946	CIN	N	1		31	.120
	BLTL				32	.119

SHOOK, RAYMOND CURTIS
B.NOV.18,1889 PERRY,OHIO
D.SEPT.16,1970 SOUTH BEND,IND.

YR	CL	LEA	POS	GP	G	REC
1916	CHI	A	H		1	.000
	BRTR					

SHOOP, RONALD LEE "RON"
B.SEPT.19,1932 RURAL VALLEY,PA.

YR	CL	LEA	POS	GP	G	REC
1959	DET	A	C		3	.143
	BRTR					

SHOPAY, THOMAS MICHAEL "TOM"
B.FEB.21,1945 BRISTOL,CONN.

YR	CL	LEA	POS	GP	G	REC
1967	NY	A	O		8	.296
1969	NY	A	O		28	.083
1971	BAL	A	O		47	.257
1972	BAL	A	O		49	.225
1975	BAL	A	C-O		40	.161
1976	BAL	A	C-O		14	.200
	BLTR				186	.204

SHORE, ERNEST GRADY "ERNIE"
B.MAR.24,1891 EAST BEND,N.C.

YR	CL	LEA	POS	GP	G	REC
1912	NY	N	P		1	0- 0
1914	BOS	A	P		19	10- 4
1915	BOS	A	P		38	19- 7
1916	BOS	A	P		38	16-10
1917	BOS	A	P		29	13-10
1919	NY	A	P		20	5- 8
1920	NY	A	P		14	2- 2
	BRTR				159	65-41

SHORE, RAYMOND EVERETT "RAY"
B.JUNE 9,1921 CINCINNATI,OHIO

YR	CL	LEA	POS	GP	G	REC
1946	STL	A	P		1	0- 0
1948	STL	A	P		17	1- 2
1949	STL	A	P		13	0- 1
	BRTR				31	1- 3

SHORES, WILLIAM DAVID
B.MAY 26,1904 ABILENE,TEX.

YR	CL	LEA	POS	GP	G	REC
1928	PHI	A	P		3	1- 1
1929	PHI	A	P		39	11- 6
1930	PHI	A	P		31	12- 4
1931	PHI	A	P		6	0- 3
1933	NY	N	P		8	2- 1
1936	CHI	A	P		9	0- 0
	BRTR				96	26-15

SHORT, CHRISTOPHER JOSEPH "CHRIS"
B.SEP.19,1937 MILFORD,DEL.

YR	CL	LEA	POS	GP	G	REC
1959	PHI	N	P		3	0- 0
1960	PHI	N	P		42	6- 9
1961	PHI	N	P-C	39	40	6-12
						-.162
1962	PHI	N	P	47	48	11- 9
1963	PHI	N	P		38	9-12
1964	PHI	N	P	42	44	17- 9
1965	PHI	N	P		47	18-11
1966	PHI	N	P		42	20-10
1967	PHI	N	P		29	9-11
1968	PHI	N	P	42	43	19-13
1969	PHI	N	P		2	0- 0
1970	PHI	N	P		36	9-16
1971	PHI	N	P		31	7-14
1972	PHI	N	P		19	1- 1
1973	MIL	N	P		42	3- 5
	BRTL			501	506	135-132
						.126
	BB 1970-71					

SHORT, DAVID ORVIS
B.MAY 11,1917 MAGNOLIA,ARK.

YR	CL	LEA	POS	GP	G	REC
1940	CHI	A	O		4	.333
1941	CHI	A	O		3	.000
	BLTR				7	.091

SHORT, WILLIAM ROSS "BILL"
B.NOV.27,1937 KINGSTON,N.Y.

YR	CL	LEA	POS	GP	G	REC
1960	NY	A	P		10	3- 5
1962	BAL	A	P		5	0- 0
1966	BAL	A	P		6	2- 3
	BOS	A	P		8	0- 0
1967	PIT	N	P		6	0- 0
1968	NY	N	P		34	0- 3
1969	CIN	N	P		4	0- 0
	BLTL				73	5-11

YR	CL	LEA	POS	GP	G	REC

SHORTEN, CHARLES HENRY "CHICK"
B.APR.19,1893 SCRANTON,PA.
D.OCT.23,1965 SCRANTON,PA.

YR	CL	LEA	POS	GP	G	REC
1915	BOS	A	O		6	.214
1916	BOS	A	O		53	.295
1917	BOS	A	O		69	.179
1919	DET	A	O		95	.315
1920	DET	A	O		116	.288
1921	DET	A	O		92	.272
1922	STL	A	O		55	.275
1924	CIN	N	O		41	.275
	BLTL				527	.275

SHOTTON, BURTON EDWIN "BARNEY"
B.OCT.18,1884 BROWNHELM,OHIO
D.JULY 29,1962

YR	CL	LEA	POS	GP	G	REC
1909	STL	A	O		17	.262
1911	STL	A	O		139	.255
1912	STL	A	O		154	.290
1913	STL	A	O		149	.293
1914	STL	A	O		154	.269
1915	STL	A	O		156	.283
1916	STL	A	O		157	.282
1917	STL	A	O		118	.224
1918	WAS	A	O		126	.261
1919	STL	N	O		85	.285
1920	STL	N	O		62	.228
1921	STL	N	O		38	.250
1922	STL	N	O		34	.200
1923	STL	N	O		1	.000
	BLTR				1390	.270

NON-PLAYING MANAGER
PHI(N) 1928-33, CIN(N) 1934,
BRO(N) 1947, 48-50

SHOUN, CLYDE MITCHELL "HARDROCK"
B.MAR.20,1915 MOUNTAIN CITY,
TENN.
D.MAR.20,1968 MOUNTAIN HOME,
TENN.

YR	CL	LEA	POS	GP	G	REC
1935	CHI	N	P		5	1- 0
1936	CHI	N	P		4	0- 0
1937	CHI	N	P		37	7- 7
1938	STL	N	P		40	6- 6
1939	STL	N	P		53	3- 1
1940	STL	N	P		54	13-11
1941	STL	N	P		26	3- 5
1942	STL	N	P		2	0- 0
	CIN	N	P		34	1- 3
1943	CIN	N	P		45	14- 5
1944	CIN	N	P		38	13-10
1946	CIN	N	P		27	1- 6
1947	CIN	N	P		10	0- 0
	BOS	N	P		26	5- 3
1948	BOS	N	P		36	5- 1
1949	BOS	N	P		1	0- 0
	CHI	N	P		16	1- 1
	BLTL				454	73-59

SHOUP, JOHN F.
B.SEPT.30,1851 CINCINNATI,OHIO
D.FEB.13,1920

YR	CL	LEA	POS	GP	G	REC
1879	TRO	N	S		10	.097
1882	STL	AA	2		2	.000
1884	WAS	U	O		1	.750
	TL				13	.135

SHOVELIN, JOHN JOSEPH
B.JULY 19,1892 DRIFTON,PA.
D.FEB.16,1976 BETHESDA,MD.

YR	CL	LEA	POS	GP	G	REC
1911	PIT	N	H		2	.000
1919	STL	A	2		9	.212
1920	STL	A	2		7	.286
	BRTR				18	.220

SHREVE, LOUIS LEONARD "LEDELL"
B.LOUISVILLE,KY.

YR	CL	LEA	POS	GP	G	REC
1887	BAL	AA	P		6	2- 1
	IND	N	P		15	5-10
1888	IND	N	P	35	36	11-24
1889	IND	N	P		3	0- 3
	TR			59	60	18-38

SHRIVER, HARRY GRAYDON
B.SEPT.2,1896 WADESTOWN,W.VA.
D.JAN.21,1970 MORGANTOWN,W.VA.

YR	CL	LEA	POS	GP	G	REC
1922	BRO	N	P		25	6- 6
1923	BRO	N	P		1	0- 0
	BRTR				26	4- 6

SHUBA, GEORGE THOMAS "SHOTGUN"
B.DEC.13,1924 YOUNGSTOWN,OHIO

YR	CL	LEA	POS	GP	G	REC
1948	BRO	N	O		63	.267
1949	BRO	N	H		1	.000
1950	BRO	N	O		34	.207
1952	BRO	N	O		94	.305
1953	BRO	N	O		74	.254
1954	BRO	N	O		45	.154
1955	BRO	N	O		44	.275
	BLTR				355	.259

SHUGART, WILLIAM FRANK
B.1867 CHICAGO,ILL.

YR	CL	LEA	POS	GP	G	REC
1890	CHI	P	S		29	.177
1891	PIT	N	S		75	.285
1892	PIT	N	S		137	.276
1893	PIT	N	S-O		52	.274
	STL	N	S-O		57	.297
1894	STL	N	O		133	.285
1895	LOU	N	S-O		112	.256
1897	PHI	N	S		40	.251
1901	CHI	A	S		107	.251
	BLTR				742	.268

SHULTZ, WALLACE LUTHER
B.OCT.10,1888 MC KEESPORT,PA.
D.JAN.30,1959

YR	CL	LEA	POS	GP	G	REC
1911	PHI	N	P		5	0- 3
1912	PHI	N	P	22	23	1- 4
	BRTR			27	28	1- 7

SHUMAN, HARRY
B.MAR.5,1916 PHILADELPHIA,PA.

YR	CL	LEA	POS	GP	G	REC
1942	PIT	N	P		1	0- 0
1943	PIT	N	P		11	0- 0
1944	PHI	N	P		18	0- 0
	BRTR				30	0- 0

SHUPE, VINCENT WILLIAM
B.SEPT.5,1921 E.CANTON,OHIO
D.APR.5,1962

YR	CL	LEA	POS	GP	G	REC
1945	BOS	N	1		78	.269
	BLTL					

SICKING, EDWARD JOSEPH
B.MAR.30,1897 ST.BERNARD,OHIO

YR	CL	LEA	POS	GP	G	REC
1916	CHI	N	3		1	.000
1918	NY	N	2-S-3		46	.250
1919	NY	N	2-S		6	.333
	PHI	N	2-S-3		61	.216
1920	NY	N	3		46	.172
	CIN	N	2-S-3		37	.266
1927	PIT	N	2		6	.143
	BRTR				203	.226

SIEBERN, NORMAN LEROY "NORM"
B.JULY 26,1933 ST.LOUIS,MO.

YR	CL	LEA	POS	GP	G	REC
1956	NY	A	O		54	.204
1958	NY	A	O		136	.300
1959	NY	A	1-O		120	.271
1960	KC	A	1-O		144	.279
1961	KC	A	1-O		153	.296
1962	KC	A	1		162	.308
1963	KC	A	1-O		152	.272
1964	BAL	A	1		150	.245
1965	BAL	A	1		106	.256
1966	CAL	A	1		125	.247
1967	SF	N	1-O		46	.155
	BOS	A	1-O		33	.205
1968	BOS	A	1-O		27	.067
	BLTR				1408	.272

SIEBERT, PAUL EDWARD
B.JUNE 5,1953 MINNEAPOLIS,MINN.

YR	CL	LEA	POS	GP	G	REC
1974	HOU	N	P		5	1- 1
1975	HOU	N	P		7	0- 2
1976	HOU	N	P		19	0- 2
	BLTL				31	1- 5

SIEBERT, RICHARD WALTHER "DICK"
B.FEB.19,1912 FALL RIVER,MASS.

YR	CL	LEA	POS	GP	G	REC
1932	BRO	N	1		6	.286
1936	BRO	N	O		2	.000
1937	STL	N	1		22	.184
1938	STL	N	H		1	1.000
	PHI	A	1		48	.284
1939	PHI	A	1		101	.294
1940	PHI	A	1		154	.286
1941	PHI	A	1		123	.334
1942	PHI	A	1		153	.260
1943	PHI	A	1		146	.251
1944	PHI	A	1-O		132	.306
1945	PHI	A	1		147	.267
	BLTL				1035	.282

SIEBERT, WILFRED CHARLES "SONNY"
B.JAN.14,1937 ST.MARY'S,MO.

YR	CL	LEA	POS	GP	G	REC
1964	CLE	A	P	41	42	7- 9
1965	CLE	A	P	39	40	16- 8
1966	CLE	A	P		34	16- 8
1967	CLE	A	P		34	10-12
1968	CLE	A	P	31	33	12-10
1969	CLE	A	P		2	0- 1
	BOS	A	P		43	14-10
1970	BOS	A	P		33	15- 8
1971	BOS	A	P		32	16-10
1972	BOS	A	P	32	33	12-12
1973	BOS	A	P		2	0- 1
	TEX	A	P		25	7-11
1974	STL	N	P		28	8- 8
1975	SD	N	P	6	7	3- 2
	OAK	A	P		17	4- 4
	BRTR			399	405	140-114

SIEBLER, DWIGHT LEROY
B.AUG.5,1937 COLUMBUS,NEB.

YR	CL	LEA	POS	GP	G	REC
1963	MIN	A	P		7	2- 1
1964	MIN	A	P		9	0- 0
1965	MIN	A	P		7	0- 0
1966	MIN	A	P		23	2- 2
1967	MIN	A	P		2	0- 0
	BRTR				48	4- 3

SIEFKE, FREDERICK EDWIN
B.MAR.27,1870 NEW YORK,N.Y.
D.APR.18,1893

YR	CL	LEA	POS	GP	G	REC
1890	BRO	AA	3		16	.137

SIEGEL, JOHN
B.YORK,PA.

YR	CL	LEA	POS	GP	G	REC
1884	KEY	U	3		8	.226

SIEGLE, JOHN HERBERT
B.JULY 8,1874 URBANA,OHIO
D.FEB.12,1968 URBANA,OHIO

YR	CL	LEA	POS	GP	G	REC
1905	CIN	N	O		16	.304
1906	CIN	N	O		21	.118
	BRTR				37	.202

SIEMER, OSCAR SYLVESTER
B.AUG.14,1902 ST.LOUIS,MO.
D.DEC.5,1959

YR	CL	LEA	POS	GP	G	REC
1925	BOS	N	C		16	.304
1926	BOS	N	C		31	.205
	BRTR				47	.244

SIEVER, EDWARD T.
B.APR.2,1878 LEWISTOWN,ILL.
D.FEB.5,1920

YR	CL	LEA	POS	GP	G	REC
1901	DET	A	P		37	18-11
1902	DET	A	P		25	8-13
1903	STL	A	P		32	14-15
1904	STL	A	P		30	11-16
1906	DET	A	P		29	14-10
1907	DET	A	P		38	19-10
1908	DET	A	P		11	2- 6
	TL				202	86-81

SIEVERS, ROY EDWARD
B.NOV.18,1926 ST.LOUIS,MO.

YR	CL	LEA	POS	GP	G	REC
1949	STL	A	3-O		140	.306
1950	STL	A	3-O		113	.238
1951	STL	A	O		31	.225
1952	STL	A	1		11	.200
1953	STL	A	1		92	.270
1954	WAS	A	1-O		145	.232
1955	WAS	A	1-3-O		144	.271
1956	WAS	A	1-O		152	.253
1957	WAS	A	1-O		152	.301
1958	WAS	A	1-O		148	.295
1959	WAS	A	1-O		115	.242
1960	CHI	A	1-O		127	.295
1961	CHI	A	1		141	.295
1962	PHI	N	1-O		144	.262
1963	PHI	N	1		138	.240
1964	PHI	N	1		49	.183
	WAS	A	1		33	.172
1965	WAS	A	1		12	.190
	BRTR				1887	.267

SIFFEL, FRANK
B.PHILADELPHIA,PA.

YR	CL	LEA	POS	GP	G	REC
1884	ATH	AA	C		7	.143
1885	ATH	AA	C-O		3	.100
					10	.129

SIGAFOOS, FRANCIS LEONARD
B.MAR.21,1904 EASTON,PA.
D.APR.12,1968 INDIANAPOLIS,IND.

YR	CL	LEA	POS	GP	G	REC
1926	PHI	A	S		13	.255
1929	DET	A	2-S-3		14	.174
	CHI	A	H		7	.333
1931	CIN	N	S-3		21	.169
	BRTR				55	.201

SIGLIN, WESLEY PETER "PADDY"
B.SEPT.24,1891 AURELIA,IOWA
D.AUG.5,1956

YR	CL	LEA	POS	GP	G	REC
1914	PIT	N	2		14	.154
1915	PIT	N	2		6	.285
1916	PIT	N	2		3	.250
	BRTR				23	.180

SIGMAN, WESLEY TRIPP "TRIP"
B.JAN.17,1899 MOORESVILLE,N.C.
D.MAR.8,1971 AUGUSTA,GA.

YR	CL	LEA	POS	GP	G	REC
1929	PHI	N	O		10	.517
1930	PHI	N	O		52	.270
	BLTR				62	.325

SIGNER, WALTER DONALD ALOYSIUS
B.OCT.12,1910 NEW YORK,N.Y.
D.JULY 23,1974 GREENWICH,CONN.

YR	CL	LEA	POS	GP	G	REC
1943	CHI	N	P	4	2- 1	
1945	CHI	N	P	6	0- 0	
	BRTR			10	2- 1	

SIGSBY, SETH DEWITT
B.TROY,N.Y.

YR	CL	LEA	POS	GP	G	REC
1893	NY	N	P	1	0- 0	

SILBER, EDWARD JAMES
B.JUNE 8,1915 PHILADELPHIA,PA.

YR	CL	LEA	POS	GP	G	REC
1937	STL	A	O		22	.313
1939	STL	A	H		1	.000
	BRTR				23	.310

SILCH, EDWARD "BALDY"
B.FEB.22,1865 ST.LOUIS,MO.
D.JAN.15,1895

YR	CL	LEA	POS	GP	G	REC
1888	BRO	AA	O		13	.260
	TR					

SILVA, DANIEL JAMES
B.OCT.5,1899 EVERETT,MASS.
D.APR.4,1974 HYANNIS,MASS.

YR	CL	LEA	POS	GP	G	REC
1919	WAS	A	3		1	.250
	BRTR					

SILVERA, AARON ALBERT
B.AUG.26,1935 SAN DIEGO,CAL.

YR	CL	LEA	POS	GP	G	REC
1955	CIN	N	O		13	.143
1956	CIN	N	O		1	.000
	BRTR				14	.143

SILVERA, CHARLES ANTHONY RYAN "CHARLIE" OR "SWEDE"
B.OCT.13,1924 SAN FRANCISCO,CAL.

YR	CL	LEA	POS	GP	G	REC
1948	NY	A	C		4	.571
1949	NY	A	C		58	.315
1950	NY	A	C		18	.160
1951	NY	A	C		18	.275
1952	NY	A	C		20	.327
1953	NY	A	C-3		42	.280
1954	NY	A	C		20	.270
1955	NY	A	C		14	.192
1956	NY	A	C		7	.222
1957	CHI	N	C		26	.208
	BRTR				227	.282

SILVERIO, TOMAS ROBERTO "TOM"
B.OCT.14,1945 SANTIAGO,D.R.

YR	CL	LEA	POS	GP	G	REC
1970	CAL	A	1-O		15	.000
1971	CAL	A	O		3	.333
1972	CAL	A	O		13	.167
	BLTL				31	.100

SILVERMAN, MICHAEL
(PLAYED UNDER NAME OF
JESSE BAKER)

SILVESTRI, KENNETH JOSEPH
B.MAY 3,1916 CHICAGO,ILL.

YR	CL	LEA	POS	GP	G	REC
1939	CHI	A	C		22	.173
1940	CHI	A	C		28	.250
1941	NY	A	C		17	.250
1946	NY	A	C		13	.286
1947	NY	A	C		3	.200
1949	PHI	N	C-2-S		4	.000
1950	PHI	N	C		11	.250
1951	PHI	N	C-2		4	.222
	BBTR				102	.217

NON-PLAYING MANAGER
ATL(N) 1967 (INTERIM)

SIMA, ALBERT "AL"
B.OCT.7,1921 MAHWAH,N.J.

YR	CL	LEA	POS	GP	G	REC
1950	WAS	A	P	17	4- 5	
1951	WAS	A	P	18	3- 7	
1953	WAS	A	P	31	2- 3	
1954	CHI	A	P	5	0- 1	
	PHI	A	P	29	2- 5	
	BRTL			100	11-21	

SIMMONS, ALOYSIUS HARRY "AL" OR "BUCKETFOOT" (REAL NAME ALOIS SZYMANSKI)
B.MAY 22,1902 MILWAUKEE,WIS.
D.MAY 26,1956 MILWAUKEE,WIS.

YR	CL	LEA	POS	GP	G	REC
1924	PHI	A	O		152	.308
1925	PHI	A	O		153	.386
1926	PHI	A	O		147	.343
1927	PHI	A	O		106	.392
1928	PHI	A	O		119	.351
1929	PHI	A	O		143	.365
1930	PHI	A	O		138	.381
1931	PHI	A	O		128	.390
1932	PHI	A	O		154	.322
1933	CHI	A	O		146	.331
1934	CHI	A	O		138	.344
1935	CHI	A	O		128	.267
1936	DET	A	O		143	.327
1937	WAS	A	O		103	.279
1938	WAS	A	O		125	.302
1939	BOS	N	O		93	.282
	CIN	N	O		9	.143
1940	PHI	A	O		37	.309
1941	PHI	A	O		9	.125
1943	BOS	A	O		40	.203
1944	PHI	A	O		4	.500
	BRTR				2215	.334

SIMMONS, CURTIS THOMAS "CURT"
B.MAY.19,1929 EGYPT,PA.

YR	CL	LEA	POS	GP	G	REC
1947	PHI	N	P		1	1- 0
1948	PHI	N	P		31	7-13
1949	PHI	N	P	38	39	4-10
1950	PHI	N	P	31	34	17- 8
1952	PHI	N	P		28	14- 8
1953	PHI	N	P		32	16-13
1954	PHI	N	P	34	38	14-15
1955	PHI	N	P	25	27	8- 8
1956	PHI	N	P	33	39	15-10
1957	PHI	N	P	32	38	12-11
1958	PHI	N	P	29	38	7-14
1959	PHI	N	P	7	8	0- 0
1960	PHI	N	P		4	0- 0
	STL	N	P	23	29	7- 4
1961	STL	N	P	30	32	9-10
1962	STL	N	P		31	10-10
1963	STL	N	P		32	15- 9
1964	STL	N	P		34	18- 9
1965	STL	N	P		34	9-15
1966	STL	N	P		10	1- 1
	CHI	N	P		19	4- 7
1967	CHI	N	P		17	3- 7
	CAL	A	P		14	2- 1
	BLTL			569	609	193-183

SIMMONS, GEORGE WASHINGTON "HACK"
B.JAN.29,1885 BROOKLYN,N.Y.
D.APR.26,1942

YR	CL	LEA	POS	GP	G	REC
1910	DET	A	1		42	.191
1912	NY	A	2		110	.239
1914	BAL	F	2-O		113	.269
1915	BAL	F	O		39	.205
	BRTR				304	.242

SIMMONS, JOHN EARL
B.JULY 7,1924 BIRMINGHAM,ALA.

YR	CL	LEA	POS	GP	G	REC
1949	WAS	A	O		62	.215
	BRTR					

SIMMONS, JOSEPH S.
B.JUNE 13,1845 NEW YORK,N.Y.
D.DEC.10,1888

YR	CL	LEA	POS	GP	G	REC
1871	CHI	NA	1-O		27	-
1872	CLE	NA	1-O		17	.230
1875	WES	NA	1-O		13	-
					57	-

NON-PLAYING MANAGER WIL(U) 1884

SIMMONS, LEWIS
B.AUG.27,1838 NEW CASTLE,PA.
D.SEPT.2,1911
NON-PLAYING MANAGER ATH(AA)1886

SIMMONS, PATRICK CLEMENT
B.NOV.29,1908 WATERVLIET,N.Y.
D.JULY 3,1968

YR	CL	LEA	POS	GP	G	REC
1928	BOS	A	P		31	0- 2
1929	BOS	A	P		2	0- 0
	BRTR				33	0- 2

SIMMONS, TED LYLE
B.AUG.9,1949 HIGHLAND PARK,MICH.

YR	CL	LEA	POS	GP	G	REC
1968	STL	N	C		2	.333
1969	STL	N	C		5	.214
1970	STL	N	C		82	.243
1971	STL	N	C		133	.304
1972	STL	N	C-1		152	.303
1973	STL	N	C-1-O		161	.310
1974	STL	N	C-1		152	.272
1975	STL	N	C-1-O		157	.332
1976	STL	N	C-1-3-O		150	.291
	BBTR				994	.297

SIMON, HENRY JOSEPH "HANK"
B.AUG.25,1862 HAWKINSVILLE,N.Y.
D.JAN.1,1925 ALBANY,N.Y.

YR	CL	LEA	POS	GP	G	REC
1887	CLE	AA	O		3	.100
1890	BRO	AA	O		90	.248
	SYR	AA	O		37	.294
	BRTR				130	.257

SIMON, MICHAEL EDWARD
B.APR.13,1883 N.VERNON,IND.

YR	CL	LEA	POS	GP	G	REC
1909	PIT	N	C		12	.167
1910	PIT	N	C		20	.213
1911	PIT	N	C		68	.228
1912	PIT	N	C		42	.301
1913	PIT	N	C		92	.247
1914	STL	F	C		93	.219
1915	BRO	F	C		47	.175
	BRTR				374	.229

SIMON, SYLVESTER ADAM "SAMMY"
B.DEC.14,1897 EVANSVILLE,IND.
D.FEB.28,1973 CHANDLER,IND.

YR	CL	LEA	POS	GP	G	REC
1923	STL	A	H		1	.000
1924	STL	A	S-3		23	.250
	BRTR				24	.242

SIMONS, MELBERN ELLIS "BUTCH"
B.JULY 1,1902 CARLYLE,ILL.
D.NOV.10,1974 PADUCAH,KY.

YR	CL	LEA	POS	GP	G	REC
1931	CHI	A	O		68	.275
1932	CHI	A	O		7	.000
	BLTR				75	.268

SIMPSON, HARRY LEON "SUITCASE"
B.DEC.3,1925 ATLANTA,GA.

YR	CL	LEA	POS	GP	G	REC
1951	CLE	A	1-O		122	.229
1952	CLE	A	1-O		146	.266
1953	CLE	A	1-O		82	.227
1955	CLE	A	H		3	.000
	KC	A	1-O		112	.301
1956	KC	A	1-O		141	.293
1957	KC	A	1-O		50	.296
	NY	A	1-O		75	.250
1958	NY	A	O		24	.216
	KC	A	1-O		78	.264
1959	KC	A	1		8	.286
	CHI	A	1-O		38	.187
	PIT	N	O		9	.267
	BLTR				888	.266

SIMPSON, JOE ALLEN
B.DEC.31,1951 PURCELL,OKLA.

YR	CL	LEA	POS	GP	G	REC
1975	LA	N	O		9	.333
1976	LA	N	O		23	.133
	BLTL				32	.167

SIMPSON, MARTIN
B.BALTIMORE,MD.

YR	CL	LEA	POS	GP	G	REC
1873	MAR	NA	C-2		4	-

YR	CL	LEA	POS	GP	G	REC

SIMPSON, RICHARD CHARLES "DICK"
B.JULY 28,1943 WASHINGTON,D.C.

YR	CL	LEA	POS	GP	G	REC
1962	LA	A	O		6	.250
1964	LA	A	O		21	.140
1965	CAL	A	O		8	.222
1966	CIN	N	O		92	.238
1967	CIN	N	O		44	.259
1968	STL	N	O		26	.232
	HOU	N	O		59	.186
1969	NY	A	O		6	.273
	SEA	A	O		26	.176
	BRTR				288	.207

SIMPSON, STEVEN EDWARD "STEVE"
B.AUG.30,1948 ST.JOSEPH,MO.

YR	CL	LEA	POS	GP	G	REC
1972	SD	N	P		9	0- 2
	BRTR					

SIMPSON, THOMAS LEO "DUKE"
B.SEPT.15,1927 COLUMBUS,OHIO

YR	CL	LEA	POS	GP	G	REC
1953	CHI	N	P		30	1- 2
	BRTR					

SIMPSON, WAYNE KIRBY
B.DEC.2,1948 LOS ANGELES,CAL.

YR	CL	LEA	POS	GP	G	REC
1970	CIN	N	P	26	27	14- 3
1971	CIN	N	P		22	4- 7
1972	CIN	N	P		24	8- 5
1973	KC	A	P		16	3- 4
1975	PHI	N	P		7	1- 0
	BRTR			95	96	30-19

SIMS, CLARENCE
B.1892
D.DEC.2,1968 DALLAS,TEX.

YR	CL	LEA	POS	GP	G	REC
1915	STL	A	P		3	1- 0
	BRTR					

SIMS, DUANE B. "DUKE"
B.JUNE 5,1941 SALT LAKE CITY,UT.

YR	CL	LEA	POS	GP	G	REC
1964	CLE	A	C		2	.000
1965	CLE	A	C		48	.178
1966	CLE	A	C		52	.263
1967	CLE	A	C		88	.202
1968	CLE	A	C-1-O		122	.249
1969	CLE	A	C-1-O		114	.236
1970	CLE	A	C-1-O		110	.264
1971	LA	N	C		90	.274
1972	LA	N	C		51	.192
	DET	A	C-O		38	.316
1973	DET	A	C-O		80	.242
	NY	A	C		4	.333
1974	NY	A	C		5	.133
	TEX	A	C		39	.208
	BLTR				843	.239

SIMS, GREGORY EMMETT "GREG"
B.JUNE 28,1946 SAN FRANCISCO,CAL

YR	CL	LEA	POS	GP	G	REC
1966	HOU	N	O		7	.167
	BBTR					

SINCOCK, HEBRET SYLVESTER
B.SEPT.8,1887 BARKERSVILLE,B.C.
CANADA
D.AUG.1,1946

YR	CL	LEA	POS	GP	G	REC
1908	CIN	N	P		1	0- 0

SINER, HOSEA JOHN
B.MAR.20,1885 SHELBURN,IND.
D.JUNE 11,1948

YR	CL	LEA	POS	GP	G	REC
1909	BOS	N	3		10	.130
	TR					

SINGER, WILLIAM ROBERT "BILL"
B.APR.24,1944 LOS ANGELES,CAL.

YR	CL	LEA	POS	GP	G	REC
1964	LA	N	P		2	0- 1
1965	LA	N	P		2	0- 0
1966	LA	N	P		3	0- 0
1967	LA	N	P	32	34	12- 8
1968	LA	N	P		37	13-17
1969	LA	N	P		41	20-12
1970	LA	N	P		16	8- 5
1971	LA	N	P		31	10-17
1972	LA	N	P		26	6-16
1973	CAL	A	P		40	20-14
1974	CAL	A	P		14	7- 4
1975	CAL	A	P		29	7-15
1976	TEX	A	P		10	4- 1
	MIN	A	P		26	9- 9
	BRTR			309	311	116-119

SINGLETON, BERT ELMER "SMOKY"
B.JUNE 26,1920 OGDEN,UTAH

YR	CL	LEA	POS	GP	G	REC
1945	BOS	N	P		7	1- 4
1946	BOS	N	P	15	16	0- 1
1947	PIT	N	P	36	41	2- 2
1948	PIT	N	P		38	4- 6
1950	WAS	A	P		21	1- 2
1957	CHI	N	P	5	6	0- 1
1958	CHI	N	P		2	1- 0
1959	CHI	N	P		21	2- 1
	BRTR			145	152	11-17
	BB 1957-58					

SINGLETON, JOHN EDWARD
B.NOV.27,1896 GALLOPLUS,OHIO
D.OCT.23,1937

YR	CL	LEA	POS	GP	G	REC
1922	PHI	N	P		22	1-10
	BRTR					

SINGLETON, KENNETH WAYNE "KEN"
B.JUNE 10,1947 NEW YORK,N.Y.

YR	CL	LEA	POS	GP	G	REC
1970	NY	N	O		69	.263
1971	NY	N	O		115	.245
1972	MON	N	O		142	.274
1973	MON	N	O		162	.302
1974	MON	N	O		148	.276
1975	BAL	A	O		155	.300
1976	BAL	A	O-D		154	.278
	BBTR				945	.281

SINGTON, FREDERIC WILLIAM
B.FEB.24,1910 BRIMINGHAM,ALA.

YR	CL	LEA	POS	GP	G	REC
1934	WAS	A	O		9	.286
1935	WAS	A	O		20	.182
1936	WAS	A	O		25	.319
1937	WAS	A	O		78	.237
1938	BRO	N	O		17	.358
1939	BRO	N	O		32	.274
	BRTR				181	.273

SIPEK, RICHARD FRANCIS
B.JAN.16,1923 CHICAGO,ILL.

YR	CL	LEA	POS	GP	G	REC
1945	CIN	N	O		82	.244
	BLTR					

SIPIN, JOHN WHITE
B.AUG.29,1946 WATSONVILLE,CAL.

YR	CL	LEA	POS	GP	G	REC
1969	SD	N	2		68	.223
	BRTR					

SISK, TOMMIE WAYNE
B.APR.12,1942 ARDMORE,OKLA.

YR	CL	LEA	POS	GP	G	REC
1962	PIT	N	P		5	0- 2
1963	PIT	N	P		57	1- 3
1964	PIT	N	P		42	1- 4
1965	PIT	N	P	38	39	7- 3
1966	PIT	N	P		34	10- 5
1967	PIT	N	P		37	13-13
1968	PIT	N	P		33	5- 5
1969	SD	N	P		53	2-13
1970	CHI	A	P		17	1- 1
	BRTR			316	317	40-49

SISLER, DAVID MICHAEL "DAVE"
B.OCT.16,1931 ST.LOUIS,MO.

YR	CL	LEA	POS	GP	G	REC
1956	BOS	A	P		39	9- 8
1957	BOS	A	P		22	7- 8
1958	BOS	A	P		30	8- 9
1959	BOS	A	P		3	0- 0
	DET	A	P		32	1- 3
1960	DET	A	P		41	7- 5
1961	WAS	A	P		45	2- 8
1962	CIN	N	P		35	4- 3
	BRTR				247	38-44

SISLER, GEORGE HAROLD "GEORGEOUS GEORGE"
B.MAR.24,1893 MANCHESTER,OHIO
D.MAR.26,1973 ST.LOUIS,MO.

YR	CL	LEA	POS	GP	G	REC
1915	STL	A	P-1-O	15	81	4- 4
						.285
1916	STL	A	P-1-3	3	151	1- 2
						.305
1917	STL	A	1-2		135	.353
1918	STL	A	P-1	2	114	0- 0
						.341
1919	STL	A	1		132	.352
1920	STL	A	P-1	1	154	0- 0
						.407
1921	STL	A	1		138	.371
1922	STL	A	1		142	.420
1924	STL	A	M-1		151	.305
1925	STL	A	M-P-1	1	150	0- 0
						.345
1926	STL	A	M-P-1	1	150	0- 0
						.289
1927	STL	A	1		149	.327
1928	WAS	A	1-O		20	.245
1928	BOS	N	P-1	1	118	0- 0
						.340
1929	BOS	N	1		154	.326
1930	BOS	N	1		116	.309
	BLTL			24	2055	5- 6
						.340

SISLER, RICHARD ALLAN "DICK"
B.NOV.2,1920 ST.LOUIS,MO.

YR	CL	LEA	POS	GP	G	REC
1946	STL	N	1-O		83	.260
1947	STL	N	1-O		46	.203
1948	PHI	N	1		121	.274
1949	PHI	N	1		121	.289
1950	PHI	N	O		141	.296
1951	PHI	N	O		125	.287
1952	CIN	N	O		11	.185
	STL	N	1		119	.261
1953	STL	N	1		32	.256
	BLTR				799	.276

NON-PLAYING MANAGER
CIN(N) 1964-65

SISTI, SEBASTIAN DANIEL "SIBBY"
B.JULY 26,1920 BUFFALO,N.Y.

YR	CL	LEA	POS	GP	G	REC
1939	BOS	N	2-S-3		63	.226
1940	BOS	N	2-3		123	.251
1941	BOS	N	2-S-3		140	.259
1942	BOS	N	2-O		129	.211
1946	BOS	N	3		1	.000
1947	BOS	N	2-S		56	.281
1948	BOS	N	2-S		83	.244
1949	BOS	N	2-S-3		101	.257
1950	BOS	N	1-2-S-3-O		69	.171
1951	BOS	N	1-2-S-3-O		114	.279
1952	BOS	N	2-S-3-O		90	.212
1953	MIL	N	2-S-3		38	.217
1954	MIL	N	H		9	.000
	BRTR				1016	.244

SITTON, CARL VETTER
B.SEPT.22,1882 PENDLETON,S.C.
D.SEPT.11,1931

YR	CL	LEA	POS	GP	G	REC
1909	CLE	A	P		14	3- 2
	TR					

SIVESS, PETER
B.SEPT.23,1913 SOUTH RIVER,N.J.

YR	CL	LEA	POS	GP	G	REC
1936	PHI	N	P		17	3- 4
1937	PHI	N	P		6	1- 1
1938	PHI	N	P		39	3- 6
	BRTR				62	7-11

SIXSMITH, EDWARD
B.FEB.26,1863 PHILADELPHIA,PA.
D.DEC.12,1926 PHILADELPHIA,PA.

YR	CL	LEA	POS	GP	G	REC
1884	PHI	N	C		1	.000
	BRTR					

SIZEMORE, TED CRAWFORD
B.APR.15,1945 GADSDEN,ALA.

YR	CL	LEA	POS	GP	G	REC
1969	LA	N	2-S-O		159	.271
1970	LA	N	2-S-O		96	.306
1971	STL	N	2-S-3-O		135	.264
1972	STL	N	2		120	.264
1973	STL	N	2-3		142	.282
1974	STL	N	2-S-O		129	.250
1975	STL	N	2		153	.264
1976	LA	N	C-2-3		84	.241
	BRTR				1018	.264

YR	CL LEA POS	GP	G	REC

SKAFF, FRANCIS MICHAEL "FRANK"
B.SEPT.30,1913 LA CROSSE,WIS.

YR	CL LEA POS	GP	G	REC
1935 BRO N	3		6	.545
1943 PHI A	1-S-3		32	.281
BRTR			38	.320

NON-PLAYING MANAGER DET(A) 1966

SKAUGSTAD, DAVID WENDELL
B.JAN.10,1940 ALGONA,IOWA

1957 CIN N	P		2	0- 0
BLTL				

SKEELS, DAVID
B.DEC.29,1892 WASHINGTON STATE
D.DEC.2,1926 SPOKANE,WASH.

1910 DET A	P		1	0- 0
BLTR				

SKETCHLEY, HARRY CLEMENT
B.MAR.30,1920 VIRDEN,MAN.,CAN.

1942 CHI A	0		13	.194
BLTL				

SKIDMORE, ROBERT ROE "BOB"
B.OCT.30,1945 DECATUR,ILL.

1970 CHI N	H		1	1.000
BRTR				

SKIFF, WILLIAM FRANKLIN
B.OCT.16,1895 NEW ROCHELLE,N.Y.

1921 PIT N	C		16	.289
1926 NY A	C		6	.099
BRTR			22	.250

SKINNER

1884 BAL U	0		1	.333
CHI U	0		1	.333
			2	.333

SKINNER, ELISHA HARRISON CAMP
B.JUNE 25,1900 DOUGLASVILLE,GA.
D.AUG.4,1944

1922 NY A	0		27	.182
1923 BOS A	0		7	.230
BLTR			34	.196

SKINNER, ROBERT RALPH "BOB"
B.OCT.3,1931 LAJOLLA,CAL.

1954 PIT N	1-0		132	.249
1956 PIT N	1-3-0		113	.202
1957 PIT N	1-3-0		126	.305
1958 PIT N	0		144	.321
1959 PIT N	1-0		143	.280
1960 PIT N	0		145	.273
1961 PIT N	0		119	.268
1962 PIT N	0		144	.302
1963 PIT N	0		34	.270
CIN N	0		72	.253
1964 CIN N	0		25	.220
STL N	0		55	.271
1965 STL N	0		80	.309
1966 STL N	H		49	.156
BLTR			1381	.277

NON-PLAYING MANAGER
PHI(N) 1968-69

SKIZAS, LOUIS PETER "LOU"
B.JUNE 2,1932 CHICAGO,ILL.

1956 NY A	H		6	.167
KC A	0		83	.316
1957 KC A	3-0		119	.245
1958 DET A	3-0		23	.242
1959 CHI A	0		8	.077
BRTR			239	.270

SKOK, CRAIG RICHARD
B.SEP.1,1947 DOBBS FERRY,N.Y.

1973 BOS A	P		11	0- 1
1976 TEX A	P		9	0- 1
BRTL			20	0- 2

SKOPEC, JOHN "BUCKSHOT"
B.CHICAGO,ILL.

1901 CHI A	P		10	6- 4
1903 DET A	P		6	2- 2
TL			16	8- 6

**SKOWRON, WILLIAM JOSEPH
"BILL" OR "MOOSE"**
B.DEC.18,1930 CHICAGO,ILL.

1954 NY A	1-2-3		87	.340
1955 NY A	1-3		108	.319
1956 NY A	1-3		134	.308
1957 NY A	1		122	.304
1958 NY A	1-3		126	.273
1959 NY A	1		74	.298
1960 NY A	1		146	.309
1961 NY A	1		150	.267
1962 NY A	1		140	.270
1963 LA N	1-3		89	.203
1964 WAS A	1		73	.271
CHI A	1		73	.293
1965 CHI A	1		146	.274
1966 CHI A	1		120	.249
1967 CHI A	H		8	.000
CAL A	1		62	.220
BRTR			1658	.282

SLADE, GORDON LEIGH "OSKIE"
B.OCT.9,1904 SALT LAKE CITY,
UTAH
D.JAN.2,1974 LONG BEACH,CAL.

1930 BRO N	S		25	.216
1931 BRO N	S		85	.239
1932 BRO N	S-3		79	.240
1933 STL N	2-S		39	.113
1934 CIN N	2-S		138	.285
1935 CIN N	2-S-3-0		71	.281
BRTR			437	.257

SLADEN, ARTHUR
B.LOWELL,MASS.

1884 BOS U	0		2	.000

SLAGLE, JAMES FRANKLIN "SHORTY"
B.JULY 11,1873 WORTHVILLE,PA.
D.MAY 10,1956

1899 WAS N	0		146	.273
1900 PHI N	0		141	.299
1901 PHI N	0		48	.189
BOS N	0		65	.278
1902 CHI N	0		114	.313
1903 CHI N	0		139	.298
1904 CHI N	0		120	.260
1905 CHI N	0		155	.269
1906 CHI N	0		127	.239
1907 CHI N	0		136	.258
1908 CHI N	0		101	.222
BLTR			1292	.269

SLAGLE, JOHN A.
B.LAWRENCE,IND.

1891 CIN AA	P		1	0- 0

SLAGLE, WALTER JENNINGS
B.DEC.15,1878 KENTON,OHIO
D.JUNE 17,1974 SAN GABRIEL,CAL.

1910 CIN N	P		1	0- 0
BBTR				

SLAPNICKA, CYRIL CHARLES "CY"
B.MAR.23,1886 CEDAR RAPIDS,IOWA

1911 CHI N	P		3	0- 2
1918 PIT N	P		7	1- 4
BBTR			10	1- 6

SLAPPEY, JOHN HENRY
B.AUG.8,1898 ALBANY,GA.
D.JUNE 10,1957

1920 PHI A	P		3	0- 1
BLTL				

SLATON, JAMES MICHAEL "JIM"
B.JUNE 19,1950 LONG BEACH,CAL.

1971 MIL A	P		26	10- 8
1972 MIL A	P		9	1- 6
1973 MIL A	P		38	13-15
1974 MIL A	P		40	13-16
1975 MIL A	P		37	11-18
1976 MIL A	P		38	14-15
BRTR			188	62-78

SLATTERY, JOHN THOMAS
B.JAN.6,1878 S.BOSTON,MASS.
D.JULY 17,1949

1901 BOS A	C		1	.500
1903 CLE A	1		4	.000
CHI A	C-1		61	.231
1906 STL N	C		2	.000
1909 WAS A	C		32	.214
TR			100	.221

NON-PLAYING MANAGER BOS(N) 1928

SLATTERY, MICHAEL J.
B.OCT.28,1865 S.BOSTON,MASS.
D.OCT.16,1904

1884 BOS U	0		105	.208
1888 NY N	n		103	.245
1889 NY N	0		12	.286
1890 NY P	0		97	.290
1891 CIN N	0		41	.221
WAS AA	0		15	.283
BLTL			373	.249

SLATTERY, PHILIP RICHARD
B.FEB.25,1894 HARPER,IOWA
D.MAR.2,1968 LONG BEACH,CAL.

1915 PIT N	P		3	0- 0
BRTL				

**SLAUGHTER, BYRON ATKINS
"BARNEY"**
B.OCT.6,1884 SMYRNA,DEL.
D.MAY 17,1961

1910 PHI N	P		8	0- 1
BRTR				

**SLAUGHTER, ENOS BRADSHER
"COUNTRY"**
B.APR.27,1916 ROXBORO,N.C.

1938 STL N	0		112	.276
1939 STL N	0		149	.320
1940 STL N	0		140	.306
1941 STL N	0		113	.311
1942 STL N	0		152	.318
1946 STL N	0		156	.300
1947 STL N	0		147	.294
1948 STL N	0		146	.321
1949 STL N	0		151	.336
1950 STL N	0		148	.290
1951 STL N	0		123	.281
1952 STL N	0		140	.300
1953 STL N	0		143	.291
1954 NY A	0		69	.248
1955 NY A	H		10	.111
KC A	0		108	.322
1956 KC A	0		91	.278
NY A	0		24	.289
1957 NY A	0		96	.254
1958 NY A	0		77	.304
1959 NY A	0		74	.172
MIL N	0		11	.167
BLTR			2380	.300

SLAUGHTER, STERLING F.
B.NOV.18,1941 DANVILLE,ILL.

1964 CHI N	P		20	2- 4
BRTR				

SLAYBACK, ELBERT
B.MAY 12,1902 PADUCAH,KY.

1926 NY N	2		2	.000
BRTR				

SLAYBACK, WILLIAM GROVER "BILL"
B.FEB.21,1948 HOLLYWOOD,CAL.

1972 DET A	P		23	5- 6
1973 DET A	P		3	0- 0
1974 DET A	P		16	1- 3
BRTR			42	6- 9

SLAYTON, FOSTER HERBERT "STEVE"
B.APR.26,1902 BARRE,VT.

1928 BOS A	P		3	0- 0
BRTR				

SLEATER, LOUIS MORTIMER "LOU"
B.SEPT.8,1927 ST.LOUIS,MO.

1950 STL A	P		1	0- 0
1951 STL A	P	20	25	1- 9
1952 STL A	P		4	0- 1
WAS A	P	14	15	4- 2
1955 KC A	P	16	21	1- 1
1956 MIL N			25	2- 2
1957 DET A	P		41	3- 3
1958 DET A	P		4	0- 0
BAL A	P	6	9	1- 0
BLTL		131	145	12-18

SLOAN, BRUCE ADAMS
B.OCT.4,1914 MC ALESTER,OKLA.
D.SEPT.24,1973 OKLAHOMA CITY,
OKLA.

1944 NY N	0		59	.269
BLTL				

```
YR   CL LEA POS  GP    G    REC
```

SLOAN, YALE YEASTMAN
B.DEC.24,1891 MADISONVILLE,TENN
D.SEPT.12,1956
```
1913 STL A  O          7   .269
1917 STL A  O        109   .230
1919 STL A  O         27   .238
     BLTR            143   .234
```

SLOAT, DWAIN CLIFFORD "LEFTY"
B.DEC.1,1918 NOKOMIS,ILL.
```
1948 BRO N  P          4   0- 1
1949 CHI N  P          5   0- 0
     BRTL              9   0- 1
```

SLOCUM, RONALD REECE "RON"
B.JULY 2,1945 MODESTO,CAL.
```
1969 SD  N  2-S-3     13   .292
1970 SD  N  C-2-S-3   60   .141
1971 SD  N  3          7   .000
     BRTR             80   .150
```

SMADT, JAN
(PLAYED UNDER NAME OF
JOHN W. SMITH)

SMALL, CHARLES ALBERT
B.OCT.24,1905 AUBURN,ME.
D.JAN.14,1953 AUBURN,ME.
```
1930 BOS A  O         25   .167
     BLTR
```

SMALL, JAMES ARTHUR "JIM"
B.MAR.28,1937 PORTLAND,ORE.
```
1955 DET A  O         12   .000
1956 DET A  O         58   .319
1957 DET A  O         36   .214
1958 KC  A  O          2   .000
     BLTL            108   .270
```

SMALLEY, ROY FREDERICK JR.
B.OCT.25,1952 LOS ANGELES,CAL.
```
1975 TEX A  C-2-S     70   .228
1976 TEX A  2-S       41   .225
     MIN A  S        103   .271
     BBTR            222   .249
```

SMALLEY, ROY FREDERICK SR.
B.JUNE 9,1926 SPRINGFIELD,MO.
```
1948 CHI N  S        124   .216
1949 CHI N  S        135   .245
1950 CHI N  S        154   .230
1951 CHI N  S         79   .231
1952 CHI N  S         87   .222
1953 CHI N  S         82   .249
1954 MIL N  1-2-S     25   .222
1955 PHI N  2-S-3     92   .196
1956 PHI N  S         65   .226
1957 PHI N  S         28   .161
1958 PHI N  S          1   .000
     BRTR            872   .227
```

SMALLEY, WILLIAM D. "DEACON"
B.JUNE 27,1871 OAKLAND,CAL.
D.OCT.11,1891
```
1890 CLE N  3        136   .213
1891 WAS AA 3          9   .171
     BRTR            145   .208
```

SMALLWOOD, WALTER CLAYTON
B.APR.24,1895 BROOKVILLE,MD.
D.APR.29,1967 BALTIMORE,MD.
```
1917 NY  A  P          2   0- 0
1919 NY  A  P          6   0- 0
     BRTR              8   0- 0
```

SMAZA, JOSEPH PAUL
B.JULY 7,1923 DETROIT,MICH.
```
1946 CHI A  O          2   .200
     BLTL
```

SMILEY, WILLIAM B.
B.1856 BALTIMORE,MD.
D.JULY 11,1884
```
1874 BAL NA 3          2    -
1882 SLT AA 2-S-O     58   .208
     BAL AA 2-S       16   .113
                      76    -
```

SMITH, ALBERT EDGAR
B.OCT.15,1860 NORTH HAVEN,CONN.
```
1883 BOS N  O         29   .217
```

SMITH, ALEXANDER BENJAMIN
"BROADWAY"
B.1871 NEW YORK,N.Y.
D.JULY 9,1919
```
1897 BRO N  C-O       61   .309
1898 BRO N  C-O       48   .260
1899 BRO N  C         16   .164
     BAL N  C-1-O     41   .383
1900 BRO N  C-3        7   .240
1901 NY  N  P-C    1  29   0- 1
                          .168
1902 BAL A  C-1-2-3- 40   .234
            O  2
1903 BOS A  C         12   .333
1904 CHI N  C-1       10   .173
1906 NY  N  C-1       14   .185
     TR            1 278   0- 1
                          .263
```

SMITH, ALEXANDER CHARLES
B.SEPT.12,1855 TROY,N.Y.
D.MAR.29,1932
```
1882 TRO N  1         34   .236
     WOR N  1         19   .216
                      53   .230
```

SMITH, ALFRED JOHN "AL"
B.OCT.12,1908 BELLEVILLE,ILL.
```
1934 NY  N  P         30   3- 5
1935 NY  N  P         40   10- 8
1936 NY  N  P         43   14-13
1937 NY  N  P         33   5- 4
1938 PHI N  P         37   1- 4
1939 PHI N  P          5   0- 0
1940 CLE A  P         31   15- 7
1941 CLE A  P     29  30   12-13
1942 CLE A  P         30   10 15
1943 CLE A  P     29  30   17- 7
1944 CLE A  P         28   7-13
1945 CLF A  P     21  22   5-12
     BLTL        356 359   99-101
```

SMITH, ALFRED KENDRICKS
B.DEC.13,1903 NORRISTOWN,PA.
```
1926 NY  N  P      1       0- 0
     BRTR
```

SMITH, ALPHONSE EUGENE "AL"
B.FEB.7,1928 KIRKWOOD,MO.
```
1953 CLE A  3-O       47   .240
1954 CLE A  3-S-O    131   .281
1955 CLE A  2-S-3-O  154   .306
1956 CLE A  2-3-O    141   .274
1957 CLE A  3-O      135   .247
1958 CHI A  3-O      139   .252
1959 CHI A  3-O      129   .237
1960 CHI A  O        142   .315
1961 CHI A  3-O      147   .278
1962 CHI A  S-O      142   .292
1963 BAL A  O        120   .272
1964 CLE A  3-O       61   .162
     BOS A  3-O       29   .216
     BRTR           1517   .272
```

SMITH, ANTHONY "TONY"
B.MAY 14,1884 CHICAGO,ILL.
D.FEB.27,1964 GALVESTON,TEX.
```
1907 WAS A  S        51   .187
1910 BRO N  S       106   .181
1911 BRO N  S        12   .138
     BRTR           169   .180
```

SMITH, ARMSTRONG FREDERICK
"KLONDIKE"
B.JAN.4,1887 LONDON,ENGLAND
D.NOV.15,1959 SPRINGFIELD,MASS.
```
1912 NY  A  P         7   .185
     BLTL
```

SMITH, ARTHUR LAIRD
B.JUNE 21,1906 BOSTON,MASS.
```
1932 CHI A  P         3   0- 1
     BRTR
```

SMITH, BILLY EDWARD
B.JULY 14,1953 HODGE,LA.
```
1975 CAL A  S-3      59   .203
1976 CAL A  S        13   .375
     BBTR            72   .212
```

SMITH, BOBBY GENE
"BOBBY GENE"
B.MAY 28,1934 HOOD RIVER,ORE.
```
1957 STL N  O         93   .211
1958 STL N  O         28   .284
1959 STL N  O         43   .217
1960 PHI N  3-O       98   .286
1961 PHI N  O         79   .253
1962 NY  N  O          8   .136
     CHI N  O         13   .172
     STL N  O         91   .231
1965 CAL A  O         23   .228
     BRTR            476   .243
```

SMITH, CALVIN BERNARD "BERNIE"
B.SEP.4,1941 PONCHATOULA,LA.
```
1970 MIL A  O         44   .276
1971 MIL A  O         15   .139
     BRTR             59   .232
```

SMITH, CARL REGINALD "REGGIE"
B.APR.2,1945 SHREVEPORT,LA.
```
1966 BOS A  O          6   .154
1967 BOS A  2-O      158   .246
1968 BOS A  O        155   .265
1969 BOS A  O        143   .309
1970 BOS A  O        147   .303
1971 BOS A  O        159   .283
1972 BOS A  O        131   .270
1973 BOS A  1-O      115   .303
1974 STL N  1-O      143   .309
1975 STL N  1-3-O    135   .302
1976 STL N  1-3-O     47   .218
     LA  N  3-O       65   .280
     BBTR           1404   .284
```

SMITH, CARR E.
B.APR.8,1901 KERNERSVILLE,N.C.
```
1923 WAS A  O          5   .111
1924 WAS A  O          6   .191
     BRTR             11   .150
```

SMITH, CHARLES F.
B.APR.20,1880 CLEVELAND,OHIO
D.JAN.3,1929
```
1902 CLE A  P          3   0- 1
1906 WAS A  P         33   9-16
1907 WAS A  P     36  37   11-21
1908 WAS A  P     26  30   9-13
1909 WAS A  P         21   2-12
     BOS A  P          5   4- 0
1910 BOS A  P         23   11- 6
1911 BOS A  P          1   0- 0
     CHI N  P          7   3- 2
1912 CHI N  P         21   7- 4
1913 CHI N  P         20   7- 9
1914 CHI N  P         16   2- 4
     BRTR         212 217   65-88
```

SMITH, CHARLES J.
B.DEC.11,1840 BROOKLYN,N.Y.
D.NOV.15,1897
```
1871 MUT NA 2-3       15    -
```

SMITH, CHARLES MARVIN "POP"
B.OCT.12,1856 WINDSOR,N.S.,CAN.
D.APR.18,1927
```
1880 CIN N  2-O       82   .199
1881 CLE N  3         10   .118
     WOR N  2-O       11   .068
     BUF N  2          3   .000
1882 ATH AA 2-S-3-O   20   .090
     BAL AA O          3   .090
     LOU AA S          3   .182
1883 COL AA P-2-   2  96   0- 0
            3             .258
1884 COL AA 2        108   .240
1885 PIT AA 2        106   .258
1886 PIT N  2-S      126   .223
1887 PIT N  2-S      122   .263
1888 PIT N  2-S      130   .207
1889 PIT N  S         72   .210
     BOS N  S         59   .257
1890 BOS N  2        134   .229
1891 WAS AA 2         27   .161
     BRTR          2 1110   0- 0
                          .228
```

YR	CL	LEA	POS	GP	G	REC

SMITH, CHARLES WILLIAM "CHARLIE"
B.SEP.15,1937 CHARLESTON,S.C.

1960	LA	N	3		18	.167
1961	LA	N	S-3		9	.250
	PHI	N	S-3		112	.248
1962	CHI	A	3		65	.207
1963	CHI	A	S		4	.286
1964	CHI	A	3		2	.143
	NY	N	S-3-O		127	.239
1965	NY	N	2-S-3		135	.244
1966	STL	N	S-3		116	.266
1967	NY	A	3		135	.224
1968	NY	A	3		46	.229
1969	CHI	N	H		2	.000
			BRTR		771	.239

SMITH, CLARENCE OSSIE "POP-BOY"
B.MAY 23,1892 NEWPORT,TENN.
D.FEB.12,1924

1913	CHI	A	P		15	0- 1
1916	CLE	A	P		5	1- 3
1917	CLE	A	P		6	0- 1
			BRTR		26	1- 5

SMITH, CLAY JAMIESON
B.SEPT.11,1914 CAMBRIDGE,KAN.

1938	CLE	A	P		4	0- 0
1940	DET	A	P		14	1- 1
			BRTR		18	1- 1

SMITH, DAVID MERWIN
B.DEC.17,1914 SELLERS,S.C.

1938	PHI	A	P		21	2- 1
1939	PHI	A	P		1	0- 0
			BRTR		22	2- 1

SMITH, DOUGLAS WELDON
B.MAY 25,1892 MILLERS FALLS,
MASS.
D.SEPT.18,1973 GREENFIELD,MASS.

| 1912 | BOS | A | P | | 1 | 0- 0 |
| | | | BLTL | | | |

SMITH, E. J.

| 1890 | BUF | P | 1 | | 1 | .000 |

SMITH, EARL CALVIN
B.MAR.14,1928 SUNNYSIDE,WASH.

| 1955 | PIT | N | O | | 5 | .063 |
| | | | BRTR | | | |

SMITH, EARL LEONARD "SHERIFF"
B.JAN.20,1891 OAK HILL,OHIO
D.MAR.14,1943

1916	CHI	N	O		14	.259
1917	STL	A	O		52	.281
1918	STL	A	O		89	.269
1919	STL	A	O		88	.250
1920	STL	A	3-O		103	.306
1921	STL	A	3-O		25	.333
	WAS	A	O		59	.217
1922	WAS	A	O		65	.259
			BBTR		495	.271

SMITH, EARL SUTTON "OIL"
B.FEB.14,1897 HOT SPRINGS,ARK.
D.JUNE 9,1963 LITTLE ROCK,ARK.

1919	NY	N	C		21	.250
1920	NY	N	C		91	.294
1921	NY	N	C		89	.336
1922	NY	N	C		90	.277
1923	NY	N	C		24	.206
	BOS	N	C		72	.288
1924	BOS	N	C		33	.271
	PIT	N	C		39	.369
1925	PIT	N	C		109	.313
1926	PIT	N	C		105	.346
1927	PIT	N	C		66	.270
1928	PIT	N	C		32	.247
	STL	N	C		24	.224
1929	STL	N	C		57	.345
1930	STL	N	C		8	.000
			BLTR		860	.303

SMITH, EDGAR
B.DEC.14,1913 COLUMBUS,N.J.

1936	PHI	A	P		2	1- 1
1937	PHI	A	P	38	40	4-17
1938	PHI	A	P		43	3-10
1939	PHI	A	P		3	1- 0
	CHI	A	P		29	9-11
1940	CHI	A	P		32	14- 9
1941	CHI	A	P		34	13-17
1942	CHI	A	P		29	7-20
1943	CHI	A	P		25	11-11
1946	CHI	A	P		24	8-11
1947	CHI	A	P		15	1- 3
	BOS	A	P		8	1- 3
			BBTL	282	284	73-113

SMITH, EDGAR E.
B.1862 PROVIDENCE,R.I.

1883	PRO	N	1-O		2	.222
	PHI	N	P-O		1	0- 1
						.750
1884	WAS	AA	P-O	3	14	0- 2
						.089
1885	PRO	N	P		1	1- 0
1890	CLE	N	P		7	1- 4
			BRTR	14	25	2- 7
						.173

SMITH, EDWARD MAYO "MAYO"
B.JAN.17,1915 NEW LONDON,MO.

| 1945 | PHI | A | O | | 73 | .212 |
| | | | BLTR | | | |

NON-PLAYING MANAGER
PHI(N) 1955-58, CIN(N) 1959,
DET(A) 1967-70

SMITH, ELMER ELLSWORTH "MIKE"
B.MAR.23,1868 ALLEGHENY,PA.
D.NOV.5,1945 PITTSBURGH,PA.

1886	CIN	AA	P-O		9	4- 5
						.308
1887	CIN	AA	P-O	51	52	33-18
						.288
1888	CIN	AA	P-O	39	40	22-17
						.220
1889	CIN	AA	P		29	10-12
1892	PIT	N	P-O	13	136	7- 6
						.282
1893	PIT	N	O		128	.366
1894	PIT	N	O		125	.352
1895	PIT	N	O		124	.296
1896	PIT	N	O		120	.358
1897	PIT	N	O		122	.311
1898	CIN	N	O		122	.344
1899	CIN	N	O		87	.295
1900	CIN	N	O		29	.270
	NY	N	O		87	.274
1901	PIT	N	O		4	.000
	BOS	N	O		18	.240
			BLTL	141	1232	76-58
						.314

SMITH, ELMER JOHN
B.SEPT.21,1892 SANDUSKY,OHIO

1914	CLE	A	O		13	.333
	CLE	A	O		144	.248
1916	CLE	A	O		79	.277
	WAS	A	O		45	.214
1917	WAS	A	O		35	.222
	CLE	A	O		64	.261
1919	CLE	A	O		114	.278
1920	CLE	A	O		129	.316
	CLE	A	O		129	.290
1922	BOS	A	O		73	.282
	NY	A	O		21	.208
1923	NY	A	O		70	.306
1925	CIN	N	O		96	.271
			BLTR		1012	.277

SMITH, ELWOOD HOPE
B.NOV.16,1904 S.NORFOLK,VA.

| 1926 | NY | N | O | | 4 | .143 |
| | | | BLTR | | | |

**SMITH, ERNEST HENRY
"KANSAS CITY KID"**
B.OCT.11,1899 TOTOWA,N.J.
D.APR.6,1973 BROOKLYN,N.Y.

| 1930 | CHI | A | S | | 24 | .241 |
| | | | BRTR | | | |

SMITH, FRANK ELMER "NIG"
(REAL NAME FRANK ELMER SCHMIDT)
B.OCT.28,1879 PITTSBURGH,PA.
D.NOV.3,1952

1904	CHI	A	P		26	16-10
1905	CHI	A	P		39	19-12
1906	CHI	A	P		20	5- 5
1907	CHI	A	P	41	42	22-11
1908	CHI	A	P	41	43	16-17
1909	CHI	A	P	51	53	25-17
1910	CHI	A	P	19	24	4-10
	BOS	A	P		4	1- 1
1911	BOS	A	P		1	0- 0
	CIN	N	P		34	10-14
1912	CIN	N	P		8	1- 1
1914	BAL	F	P		39	10- 8
1915	BAL	F	P		17	4- 6
	BRO	F	P		15	5- 0
			BRTR	355	365	138-112

SMITH, FRANK L.
B.1857 CANANDAIGUA,N.H.

| 1884 | PIT | AA | C-O | | 10 | .263 |

SMITH, FRANK THOMAS
B.APR.4,1928 PIERREPONT MANOR,
N.Y.

1950	CIN	N	P		38	2- 7
1951	CIN	N	P		50	5- 5
1952	CIN	N	P		53	12-11
1953	CIN	N	P		50	8- 1
1954	CIN	N	P		50	5- 8
1955	STL	N	P		28	3- 1
1956	CIN	N	P		2	0- 0
			BRTR		271	35-33

SMITH, FREDERICK
B.NOV.24,1878 NEW DIGGINS,WIS.
D.FEB.4,1964 LOS ANGELES,CAL.

| 1907 | CIN | N | P | | 18 | 2- 7 |
| | | | BLTR | | | |

SMITH, FREDERICK C.
B.1863

| 1890 | TOL | AA | P | | 37 | 19-14 |
| | | | BLTR | | | |

SMITH, FREDERICK VINCENT
B.JULY 29,1891 CLEVELAND,OHIO
D.MAY 28,1961 CLEVELAND,OHIO

1913	BOS	N	3		92	.228
1914	BUF	F	S-3		146	.222
1915	BUF	F	S		35	.220
	BRO	F	S		109	.245
1917	STL	N	3		56	.182
			BRTR		438	.225

**SMITH, GEORGE ALLEN
"COLUMBIA GEORGE"**
B.MAY 31,1892 E.PORT CHESTER,
CONN.
D.JAN.7,1965 GREENWICH,CONN.

1916	NY	N	P		9	3- 0
1917	NY	N	P		14	0- 3
1918	CIN	N	P		10	2- 3
	NY	N	P		5	2- 3
	BRO	N	P		8	4- 1
1919	NY	N	P		3	0- 2
	PHI	N	P		31	5-11
1920	PHI	N	P		43	13-18
1921	PHI	N	P		39	4-20
1922	PHI	N	P		42	5-14
1923	BRO	N	P		25	3- 6
			BRTR		229	41-81

SMITH, GEORGE CORNELIUS
B.JULY 7,1938 ST.PETERSBURG,FLA.

1963	DET	A	2		52	.216
1964	DET	A	2		5	.286
1965	DET	A	2-S-3		32	.094
1966	BOS	A	2-S		128	.213
			BRTR		217	.205

SMITH, GEORGE HENRY "HEINIE"
B.MAR.4,1873 PITTSBURGH,PA.
D.JUNE 25,1939

1897	LOU	N	2		21	.280
1898	LOU	N	2		31	.207
1899	PIT	N	2		15	.264
1902	NY	N	M-2		140	.248
1903	DET	A	2		93	.222
			BRTR		300	.239

YR	CL LEA POS	GP	G	REC

SMITH, GEORGE J. "GERMANY"
B.APR.21,1863 PITTSBURGH,PA.
D.DEC.1,1927

1884 ALT U P-S	1	25	0- 0
			.307
CLE N 2-S		71	.258
1885 BRO AA S		109	.256
1886 BRO AA S		117	.249
1887 BRO AA S		104	.307
1888 BRO AA S		103	.214
1889 BRO AA S		121	.233
1890 BRO N S		129	.191
1891 CIN N S		138	.205
1892 CIN N S		138	.248
1893 CIN N S		130	.244
1894 CIN N S		128	.266
1895 CIN N S		127	.297
1896 CIN N S		119	.282
1897 BRO N S		113	.207
1898 STL N S		51	.156
BRTR	1	1723	0- 0
			.245

SMITH, GEORGE L.
NON-PLAYING MANAGER SYR(N) 1879

SMITH, GEORGE SHELBY
B.OCT.27,1901 LOUISVILLE,KY.

1926 DET A P		23	1- 2
1927 DET A P		30	4- 1
1928 DET A P		39	1- 1
1929 DET A P		14	3- 2
1930 BOS A P	27	29	1- 2
BRTR	133	135	10- 8

SMITH, HAROLD LAVERNE
B.JUNE 30,1905 CRESTON,IOWA

1932 PIT N P		2	1- 0
1933 PIT N P		28	8- 7
1934 PIT N P		20	3- 4
1935 PIT N P		1	0- 0
BRTR		51	12-11

SMITH, HAROLD RAYMOND "HAL"
B.JUNE 1,1931 BARLING,ARK.

1956 STL N C		75	.282
1957 STL N C		100	.279
1958 STL N C		77	.227
1959 STL N C		142	.270
1960 STL N C		127	.228
1961 STL N C		45	.248
1965 PIT N C		4	.000
BRTR		570	.258

SMITH, HAROLD WAYNE "HAL"
B.DEC.30,1930 WEST FRANKFORT,ILL

1955 BAL A C		135	.271
1956 BAL A C		78	.262
KC A C		36	.275
1957 KC A C		107	.303
1958 KC A C-1-3		99	.273
1959 KC A C-3		108	.288
1960 PIT N C		77	.295
1961 PIT N C		67	.223
1962 HOU N C-1-3		109	.235
1963 HOU N C		31	.241
1964 CIN N C		32	.121
BRTR		879	.267

SMITH, HARRISON M.
B.AUG.15,1889 AVOCA,NEB.
D.JULY 26,1964

| 1912 CHI A P | | 1 | 1- 0 |
| BRTR | | | |

SMITH, HARRY THOMAS
B.OCT.31,1874 YORKSHIRE,ENGLAND
D.FEB.17,1933

1901 PHI A C		11	.308
1902 PIT N C		49	.187
1903 PIT N C		61	.175
1904 PIT N C		47	.248
1905 PIT N C		1	.000
1906 PIT N C		1	.000
1907 PIT N C		18	.263
1908 BOS N C		38	.246
1909 BOS N M-C		31	.168
1910 BOS N C		38	.238
BRTR		295	.212

SMITH, HARRY W.
B.FEB.5,1856 N.VERNON,IND.
D.JUNE 4,1898

1877 CHI N 2-O		24	.202
CIN N C-2-O		9	.241
1889 LOU N		1	1.000
BRTR		34	.228

SMITH, HARVEY FETTERHOFF
B.JULY 24,1871 DAUPHIN CO.,PA.
D.NOV.12,1962

| 1896 WAS N 3 | | 34 | .288 |
| BLTR | | | |

SMITH, HENRY JOSEPH "HAPPY"
B.JULY 14,1883 COQUILLE,ORE.

| 1910 BRO N O | | 16 | .237 |
| BLTR | | | |

SMITH, JACK HATFIELD
B.NOV.15,1935 PINEVILLE,KY.

1962 LA N P		8	0- 0
1963 LA N P		4	0- 0
1964 MIL N P		22	2- 2
BRTR		34	2- 2

SMITH, JACOB G.
B.DUBOIS,PA.

| 1911 PHI N P | | 2 | 0- 0 |

SMITH, JAMES A. "STUB"
B.NOV.26,1876 ELMWOOD,ILL.

| 1898 BOS N S | | 3 | .100 |

SMITH, JAMES CARLISLE "RED"
B.APR.6,1890 ATLANTA,GA.
D.OCT.11,1966 ATLANTA,GA.

1911 BRO N 3		28	.261
1912 BRO N 3		128	.286
1913 BRO N 3		151	.296
1914 BRO N 3		90	.245
BOS N 3		60	.314
1915 BOS N 3		157	.264
1916 BOS N 3		150	.259
1917 BOS N 3		147	.295
1918 BOS N 3		119	.298
1919 BOS N 3-O		87	.245
BRTR		1117	.278

SMITH, JAMES HARRY
B.MAY 15,1890 BALTIMORE,MD.
D.APR.1,1922

1914 NY N C		5	.428
1915 NY N C		21	.125
BRO F C		25	.215
1917 CIN N C		8	.118
1918 CIN N C		13	.185
BRTR		72	.189

SMITH, JAMES LAWRENCE
"GREENFIELD JIMMY"
B.MAY 15,1895 PITTSBURGH,PA.
D.JAN.1,1974 PITTSBURGH,PA.

1914 CHI F S		3	.500
1915 CHI F S		94	.217
BAL F S		33	.191
1916 PIT N S		36	.188
1917 NY N 2		36	.229
1918 BOS N 2-S-3-O		34	.225
1919 CIN N 2-S-3-O		28	.275
1921 PHI N 2		67	.231
1922 PHI N 2-S-3		38	.219
BBTR		369	.221
BR 1914			

SMITH, JOHN
B.BALTIMORE,MD.

1873 MAR NA S-O		5	-
1874 BAL NA S		5	-
1875 NH NA S		1	-
		11	-

SMITH, JOHN "JACK"
B.JUNE 23,1895 CHICAGO,ILL.
D.MAY 2,1972 WESTCHESTER,ILL.

1915 STL N O		4	.187
1916 STL N O		130	.244
1917 STL N O		137	.297
1918 STL N O		42	.211
1919 STL N O		119	.223
1920 STL N O		91	.332
1921 STL N O		116	.328
1922 STL N O		143	.309
1923 STL N O		124	.310
1924 STL N O		124	.283
1925 STL N O		80	.251
1926 STL N O		1	.000
BOS N O		96	.311
1927 BOS N O		84	.317
1928 BOS N O		96	.280
1929 BOS N O		19	.250
BLTL		1406	.287

SMITH, JOHN FRANCIS
"PHENOMENAL"
(REAL NAME JOHN FRANCIS GAMMON)
B.DEC.12,1864 PHILADELPHIA,PA.
D.APR.3,1952

1884 BAL U P-O	8	10	3- 5
			.158
ATH AA P		1	0- 1
PIT AA P		1	0- 1
1885 BRO AA P		1	0- 1
ATH AA P		1	0- 1
1886 DET N P		3	1- 1
1887 BAL AA P		62	29-29
1888 BAL AA P		35	15-20
ATH AA P		3	2- 0
1889 PHI N P		4	1- 3
1890 PHI N P		22	7-15
PIT N P		5	2- 3
1891 PHI N P		3	1- 2
BLTL	149	151	61-82
			.279

SMITH, JOHN MARSHALL
B.SEPT.27,1906 WASHINGTON,D.C.

| 1931 BOS A 1 | | 4 | .133 |
| BBTR | | | |

SMITH, JOHN W. "CHICK"
(REAL NAME JAN SMADT)
B.DEC.2,1892 DAYTON,KY.
D.OCT.11,1935

| 1913 CIN N P | | 5 | 0- 1 |
| BLTL | | | |

SMITH, JOSEPH
(REAL NAME
SALVATORE JOSEPH PERSICO)
B.DEC.29,1893 NEW YORK,N.Y.

| 1913 NY N C | | 14 | .161 |
| BRTR | | | |

SMITH, JUDSON GRANT
B.JAN.13,1869 GREEN OAK,MICH.
D.DEC.7,1947

1893 CIN N S-3-O		16	.233
STL N 3		4	.067
1896 PIT N 3		4	.333
1898 WAS N 3		65	.302
1901 PIT N 3		6	.130
BRTR		95	.275

SMITH, LAWRENCE PATRICK "PADDY"
B.MAY 10,1894 NEW ROCHELLE,N.Y.

| 1920 BOS A C | | 2 | .000 |
| BLTR | | | |

SMITH, LEO H.
B.MAY 13,1863 BROOKLYN,N.Y.

| 1890 ROC AA S | | 35 | .190 |

SMITH, LOUIS O. "BULL"

1904 PIT N O		13	.142
1906 CHI N H		1	.000
1911 WAS A H		1	.000
TR		15	.140

SMITH, MARVIN HAROLD "RED"
B.JULY 17,1900 ASHLEY,ILL.
D.FEB.19,1961

| 1925 PHI A S-3 | | 20 | .286 |
| BLTR | | | |

SMITH, MILTON "MILT"
B.MAR.27,1929 COLUMBUS,GA.

| 1955 CIN N 2-3 | | 36 | .196 |
| BRTR | | | |

SMITH, NATHANIEL BEVERLY
B.APR.26,1935 CHICAGO,ILL.

| 1962 BAL A C | | 5 | .222 |
| BRTR | | | |

SMITH, OLIVER H.
B.1868 MT.VERNON,OHIO

| 1894 LOU N O | | 89 | .288 |

SMITH, PAUL LESLIE
B.MAR.19,1931 NEW CASTLE,PA.

1953 PIT N 1-O		118	.283
1957 PIT N 1-O		81	.253
1958 PIT N H		6	.333
CHI N 1		18	.150
BLTL		223	.270

SMITH, PAUL STONER
B.MAY 7,1888 MT.ZION,ILL.
D.JULY 3,1958

YR	CL	LEA	POS	GP	G	REC
1916	CIN	N	O		10	.227
	BLTR					

SMITH, PETER LUKE "PETE"
B.MAR.19,1940 NATICK,MASS.

YR	CL	LEA	POS	GP	G	REC
1962	BOS	A	P		1	0- 1
1963	BOS	A	P		6	0- 0
	BRTR				7	0- 1

SMITH, REGINALD
B.LOUISVILLE,KY.

YR	CL	LEA	POS	GP	G	REC
1886	ATH	AA	P		1	0- 1

SMITH, RHESA EDWARD
B.FEB.21,1879 MENTONE,IND.
D.MAR.20,1955 TARPON SPRINGS,
FLA.

YR	CL	LEA	POS	GP	G	REC
1906	STL	A	P		19	7-10
	BRTR					

SMITH, RICHARD ARTHUR "DICK"
B.MAY 17,1939 LEBANON,ORE.

YR	CL	LEA	POS	GP	G	REC
1963	NY	N	1-O		20	.238
1964	NY	N	1-O		46	.223
1965	LA	N	O		10	.000
	BRTR				76	.218

SMITH, RICHARD HARRISON "DICK"
B.JULY 21,1927 BLANDBURG,PA.

YR	CL	LEA	POS	GP	G	REC
1951	PIT	N	3		12	.174
1952	PIT	N	2-S-3		29	.106
1953	PIT	N	S		13	.163
1954	PIT	N	3		12	.097
1955	PIT	N	S		4	.000
	BRTR				70	.134

SMITH, RICHARD KELLY "DICK"
B.AUG.25,1944 LINCOLNTON,N.C.

YR	CL	LEA	POS	GP	G	REC
1969	WAS	A	O		21	.107
	BRTR					

SMITH, RICHARD PAUL
B.MAY 18,1904 BROKOW,WIS.

YR	CL	LEA	POS	GP	G	REC
1927	NY	N	C		1	.000
	BRTR					

SMITH, ROBERT A.
B.1892

YR	CL	LEA	POS	GP	G	REC
1913	CHI	A	P		1	0- 0
1915	BUF	F	P		1	0- 0
	BRTR				2	0- 0

SMITH, ROBERT ELDRIDGE
B.APR.22,1898 ROGERSVILLE,TENN.

YR	CL	LEA	POS	GP	G	REC
1923	BOS	N	2-S		115	.251
1924	BOS	N	S-3		106	.228
1925	BOS	N	P-2-	13	58	5- 3
			S-O			.282
1926	BOS	N	P	33	40	10-13
1927	BOS	N	P	41	54	10-18
1928	BOS	N	P	38	39	13-17
1929	BOS	N	P	34	39	11-17
1930	BOS	N	P	38	39	10-14
1931	CHI	N	P		36	15-12
1932	CHI	N	P	34	36	4- 3
1933	CIN	N	P-S	16	23	4- 4
						.200
	BOS	N	P		14	4- 3
1934	BOS	N	P	39	42	6- 9
1935	BOS	N	P	46	47	8-18
1936	BOS	N	P		35	6- 7
1937	BOS	N	P	18	19	0- 1
	BRTR			435	742	106-139
						.242

SMITH, ROBERT GILCHRIST "BOB"
B.FEB.1,1931 WOODSVILLE,N.H.

YR	CL	LEA	POS	GP	G	REC
1955	BOS	A	P		1	0- 0
1957	STL	N	P		6	0- 0
	PIT	N	P		20	2- 4
1958	PIT	N	P		35	2- 2
1959	PIT	N	P		20	0- 0
	DET	A	P		9	0- 3
	BRTL				91	4- 9

SMITH, ROBERT WALKAY "BOB"
B.MAY 13,1928 CLARENCE,MO.

YR	CL	LEA	POS	GP	G	REC
1958	BOS	A	P		17	4- 3
1959	CHI	N	P		1	0- 0
	CLE	A	P		12	0- 1
	BBTL				30	4- 4
	BL 1958					

SMITH, RUFUS FRAZIER "SHIRT"
B.JAN.24,1905 GUILFORD COLLEGE,
N.C.

YR	CL	LEA	POS	GP	G	REC
1927	DET	A	P		1	0- 0
	BRTL					

SMITH, SAMUEL
B.1857 BALTIMORE,MD.

YR	CL	LEA	POS	GP	G	REC
1888	LOU	AA	1		56	.246
	BR					

SMITH, SHERROD MALONE "SHERRY"
B.FEB.18,1891 MANSFIELD,GA.
D.SEPT.12,1949

YR	CL	LEA	POS	GP	G	REC
1911	PIT	N	P		1	0- 0
1912	PIT	N	P		3	0- 0
1915	BRO	N	P		29	14- 8
1916	BRO	N	P	36	38	14-10
1917	BRO	N	P	38	43	12-12
1919	BRO	N	P		30	7-12
1920	BRO	N	P		33	11- 9
1921	BRO	N	P		35	7-11
1922	BRO	N	P		28	4- 8
	CLE	A	P		2	1- 0
1923	CLE	A	P		30	9- 6
1924	CLE	A	P	39	40	12-14
1925	CLE	A	P		31	11-14
1926	CLE	A	P		27	11-10
1927	CLE	A	P		11	1- 4
	BRTL			373	381	114-118

SMITH, SYDNEY
B.AUG.31,1883 CAMDEN,S.C.
D.JUNE 5,1961

YR	CL	LEA	POS	GP	G	REC
1908	PHI	A	C		45	.205
	STL	A	C		28	.182
1910	CLE	A	C		9	.346
1911	CLE	A	C		58	.299
1914	PIT	N	C		4	.300
1915	PIT	N	H		1	.000
	BRTR				145	.247

SMITH, THOMAS E.
B.DEC.5,1871 S.BOSTON,MASS.
D.MAR.2,1929

YR	CL	LEA	POS	GP	G	REC
1894	BOS	N	P		2	0- 0
1895	PHI	N	P		11	3- 3
1896	LOU	N	P		14	1- 5
1898	STL	N	P		1	0- 1
					28	4- 9

SMITH, THOMAS N.
B.BALTIMORE,MD.

YR	CL	LEA	POS	GP	G	REC
1875	ATL	NA	2		3	-

SMITH, TOMMY ALEXANDER
B.AUG.1,1948 ALBERMARLE,N.C.

YR	CL	LEA	POS	GP	G	REC
1973	CLE	A	O		14	.244
1974	CLE	A	O		23	.097
1975	CLE	A	1-O		8	.125
1976	CLE	A	O		55	.256
	BRTL				100	.230

SMITH, VINCENT AMBROSE
B.DEC.7,1916 RICHMOND,VA.

YR	CL	LEA	POS	GP	G	REC
1941	PIT	N	C		9	.303
1946	PIT	N	C		7	.190
	BRTR				16	.259

SMITH, WALLACE H.
B.MAR.13,1889 PHILADELPHIA,PA.

YR	CL	LEA	POS	GP	G	REC
1911	STL	N	S-3		60	.216
1912	STL	N	S-3		75	.256
1914	WAS	A	2		45	.196
	BRTR				180	.229

SMITH, WALTER
(PLAYED UNDER NAME OF
WALTER REINICKER)

SMITH, WILBUR FLOYD "WIB"
B.AUG.30,1886 EVART,MICH.
D.NOV.18,1959

YR	CL	LEA	POS	GP	G	REC
1909	STL	A	C		17	.190
	BLTR					

SMITH, WILLARD JEHU "RED"
B.APR.11,1892 LOGANSPORT,IND.
D.JULY 17,1972 NOBLESVILLE,IND.

YR	CL	LEA	POS	GP	G	REC
1917	PIT	N	C		11	.143
1918	PIT	N	C		15	.167
	BRTR				26	.156

SMITH, WILLIAM
D.OCT.28,1897

YR	CL	LEA	POS	GP	G	REC
1886	DET	N	P		10	5- 4

SMITH, WILLIAM E.
B.E.LIVERPOOL,OHIO

YR	CL	LEA	POS	GP	G	REC
1884	CLE	N	O		1	.000

SMITH, WILLIAM GARLAND
B.JUNE 8,1934 WASHINGTON,D.C.

YR	CL	LEA	POS	GP	G	REC
1958	STL	N	P		2	0- 1
1959	STL	N	P		6	0- 0
1962	PHI	N	P		24	1- 5
	BLTL				32	1- 6

SMITH, WILLIAM J.
B.BALTIMORE,MD.
D.AUG.9,1886

YR	CL	LEA	POS	GP	G	REC
1873	MAR	NA	M-C-2-O		6	-

SMITH, WILLIE
B.FEB.11,1939 ANNISTON,ALA.

YR	CL	LEA	POS	GP	G	REC
1963	DET	A	P	11	17	1- 0
1964	LA	A	P-O	15	118	1- 4
						.301
1965	CAL	A	1-O		136	.261
1966	CAL	A	O		90	.185
1967	CLE	A	1-O		21	.219
1968	CLE	A	P-1-O 2		33	0- 0
						.143
	CHI	N	P-1-O 1		55	0- 0
						.275
1969	CHI	N	1-O		103	.246
1970	CHI	N	1-O		87	.216
1971	CIN	N	1		31	.164
	BLTL			29	691	2- 4
						.248

SMOLL, CLYDE HETRICK "LEFTY"
B.APR.17,1915 QUAKERTOWN,PA.

YR	CL	LEA	POS	GP	G	REC
1940	PHI	N	P		33	2- 8
	BBTL					

SMOOT, HOMER VERNON "DOC"
B.MAR.26,1878 GALESTOWN,MD.
D.MAR.25,1928

YR	CL	LEA	POS	GP	G	REC
1902	STL	N	O		129	.310
1903	STL	N	O		129	.296
1904	STL	N	O		137	.281
1905	STL	N	O		138	.311
1906	STL	N	O		86	.248
	CIN	N	O		59	.259
	BLTR				678	.290

SMOYER, HENRY NEITZ
B.APR.25,1890 FREDERICKSBURG,PA
D.FEB.28,1958 DUBOIS,PA.

YR	CL	LEA	POS	GP	G	REC
1912	STL	A	S-3		6	.214
	TR					

SMYKAL, FRANK JOHN
B.OCT.13,1889 CHICAGO,ILL.
D.AUG.11,1950

YR	CL	LEA	POS	GP	G	REC
1916	PIT	N	S		6	.300
	BRTR					

**SMYRES, CLARENCE MELVIN
"CLANCY"**
B.MAY 24,1922 CULVER CITY,CAL.

YR	CL	LEA	POS	GP	G	REC
1944	BRO	N	H		5	.000
	BBTR					

SMYTH, JAMES DANIEL "RED"
B.JAN.30,1893 HOLLY SPRINGS,
MISS.
D.APR.14,1958

YR	CL	LEA	POS	GP	G	REC
1915	BRO	N	O		19	.136
1916	BRO	N	O		2	.000
1917	BRO	N	O		29	.120
	STL	N	O		38	.211
1918	STL	N	2-O		40	.212
	BLTR				128	.193

SMYTHE, WILLIAM HARRY
B.OCT.24,1904 AUGUSTA,GA.

YR	CL	LEA	POS	GP	G	REC
1929	PHI	N	P	19	20	4- 6
1930	PHI	N	R		25	0- 3
1934	NY	A	P		8	0- 2
	BRO	N	P	8	10	1- 1
	BLTL				63	5-12

SNEED, JOHN L.
B.COLUMBUS,OHIO
D.JAN.4,1899

YR	CL	LEA	POS	GP	G	REC
1884	IND	AA	O		27	.105
1890	TOL	AA	O		9	.167
	COL	AA	O		128	.309
1891	COL	AA	O		99	.261
					263	.267

YR	CL	LEA	POS	GP	G	REC

SNELL, CHARLES A.
B.NOV.29,1893 READING,PA.

YR	CL	LEA	POS	GP	G	REC
1912	STL	A	C		8	.222
	BRTR					

SNELL, WALTER HENRY "DOC"
B.MAY 19,1889 W.BRIDGEWATER,
MASS.

YR	CL	LEA	POS	GP	G	REC
1913	BOS	A	C		6	.250
	BRTR					

SNIDER, EDWIN DONALD "DUKE"
B.SEP.19,1926 LOS ANGELES,CAL.

YR	CL	LEA	POS	GP	G	REC
1947	BRO	N	O		40	.241
1948	BRO	N	O		53	.244
1949	BRO	N	O		146	.292
1950	BRO	N	O		152	.321
1951	BRO	N	O		150	.277
1952	BRO	N	O		144	.303
1953	BRO	N	O		153	.336
1954	BRO	N	O		149	.341
1955	BRO	N	O		148	.309
1956	BRO	N	O		151	.292
1957	BRO	N	O		139	.274
1958	LA	N	O		106	.312
1959	LA	N	O		126	.308
1960	LA	N	O		101	.243
1961	LA	N	O		85	.296
1962	LA	N	O		80	.278
1963	NY	N	O		129	.243
1964	SF	N	O		91	.210
	BLTR				2143	.295

SNIPES, WYATT EURE "ROXY"
B.OCT.26,1896 MARION,S.C.
D.MAY 1,1941

YR	CL	LEA	POS	GP	G	REC
1923	CHI	A	H		1	.000
	BLTR					

SNODGRASS, FRED CARLISLE
B.OCT.19,1887 VENTURA,CAL.
D.APR.5,1974 VENTURA,CAL.

YR	CL	LEA	POS	GP	G	REC
1908	NY	N	C		5	.250
1909	NY	N	O		22	.300
1910	NY	N	O		112	.321
1911	NY	N	O		151	.294
1912	NY	N	1-O		146	.269
1913	NY	N	O		141	.291
1914	NY	N	O		113	.263
1915	NY	N	O		80	.151
	BOS	N	O		23	.278
1916	BOS	N	O		112	.249
	BRTR				905	.275

SNODGRASS, WALTER AMZI
B.SPRINGFIELD,OHIO

YR	CL	LEA	POS	GP	G	REC
1901	BAL	A	O		2	.100

SNOOK, FRANK WALTER
B.MAR.28,1949 SOMERVILLE,N.J.

YR	CL	LEA	POS	GP	G	REC
1973	SD	N	P		18	0- 2
	BRTR					

SNOVER, COLONEL LESTER
B.MAY 16,1896 HALLSTEAD,PA.
D.APR.30,1969 ROCHESTER,N.Y.

YR	CL	LEA	POS	GP	G	REC
1919	NY	N	P		2	0- 1
	BLTL					

SNOW
B.BOSTON,MASS.

YR	CL	LEA	POS	GP	G	REC
1874	ATL	NA	O		1	.000

SNYDER, BERNARD AUSTIN
B.AUG.25,1913 PHILADELPHIA,PA.

YR	CL	LEA	POS	GP	G	REC
1935	PHI	A	2-S		10	.344
	BRTR					

SNYDER, CHARLES
B.CAMDEN,N.J.
D.MAR.10,1901

YR	CL	LEA	POS	GP	G	REC
1890	ATH	AA	C-O		9	.419

SNYDER, CHARLES N. "POP"
B.OCT.6,1854 WASHINGTON,D.C.
D.OCT.29,1924

YR	CL	LEA	POS	GP	G	REC
1873	NAT	NA	C-O		28	-
1874	BAL	NA	C		34	-
1875	PHI	NA	C		65	.233
1876	LOU	N	C		56	.195
1877	LOU	N	C-S-O		61	.258
1878	BOS	N	C		60	.212
1879	BOS	N	C		81	.234
1880	BOS	N	C-2-S-O		60	.228
1882	CIN	AA	C-1-O		72	.289
1883	CIN	AA	M-C-S		58	.245
1884	CIN	AA	M-C-1-O		68	.284
1885	CIN	AA	C-1		38	.250
1886	CIN	AA	C-1-O		52	.195
1887	CLE	AA	C		73	.276
1888	CLE	AA	C		63	.216
1889	CLE	N	C		21	.192
1890	CLE	P	C		12	.183
1891	WAS	AA	M-C		8	.179
	BRTR				910	-

**SNYDER, EMANUEL SEBASTIAN
"REDLEG"
(REAL NAME
EMANUEL SEBASTIAN SCHNEIDER)**
B.DEC.12,1853 CAMDEN,N.J.
D.NOV.11,1933

YR	CL	LEA	POS	GP	G	REC
1876	CIN	N	O		55	.150
1884	WIL	U	1-O		17	.192
	BRTR					

SNYDER, EUGENE WALTER
B.MAR.31,1931 YORK,PA.

YR	CL	LEA	POS	GP	G	REC
1959	LA	N	P		11	1- 1
	BRTL					

SNYDER, FRANK C. "COONEY"
B.LONDON,ONT.,CANADA
D.MAR.9,1917

YR	CL	LEA	POS	GP	G	REC
1898	LOU	N	C		15	.169

SNYDER, FRANK J. "PANCHO"
B.MAY 27,1893 SAN ANTONIO,TEX.
D.JAN.5,1962

YR	CL	LEA	POS	GP	G	REC
1912	STL	N	C		11	.111
1913	STL	N	C		7	.190
1914	STL	N	C		100	.230
1915	STL	N	C		144	.298
1916	STL	N	C-1		132	.259
1917	STL	N	C		115	.237
1918	STL	N	C-1		39	.250
1919	STL	N	C-1		50	.182
	NY	N	C		32	.228
1920	NY	N	C		87	.250
1921	NY	N	C		108	.320
1922	NY	N	C		104	.343
1923	NY	N	C		120	.256
1924	NY	N	C		118	.302
1925	NY	N	C		107	.240
1926	NY	N	C		55	.216
1927	STL	N	C		63	.258
	BRTR				1392	.265

SNYDER, GEORGE T.
B.1849 PHILADELPHIA,PA.
D.AUG.2,1905

YR	CL	LEA	POS	GP	G	REC
1882	ATH	AA	P		1	1- 0

SNYDER, JAMES
B.1851 NEW YORK
D.1881

YR	CL	LEA	POS	GP	G	REC
1872	ECK	NA	C-S-O		26	.275

SNYDER, JAMES ROBERT "JIM"
B.AUG.15,1932 DEARBON,MICH.

YR	CL	LEA	POS	GP	G	REC
1961	MIN	A	2		3	.000
1962	MIN	A	1-2		12	.100
1964	MIN	A	2		26	.155
	BRTR				41	.140

SNYDER, JERRY GEORGE
B.JULY 21,1929 JENKS,OKLA.

YR	CL	LEA	POS	GP	G	REC
1952	WAS	A	2-S		36	.158
1953	WAS	A	2-S		29	.339
1954	WAS	A	2-S		64	.234
1955	WAS	A	2-S		46	.224
1956	WAS	A	2-S		43	.270
1957	WAS	A	2-S-3		42	.151
1958	WAS	A	2-S		6	.111
	BRTR				266	.230

SNYDER, JOHN WILLIAM
B.1892 ALLEGHENY CO.,PA.

YR	CL	LEA	POS	GP	G	REC
1914	BUF	F	C		1	.000
1917	BRO	N	C		7	.273
	BRTR				8	.273

SNYDER, JOSHUA
D.1881

YR	CL	LEA	POS	GP	G	REC
1872	ECK	NA	O		9	.171

SNYDER, RUSSELL HENRY "RUSS"
B.JUNE 22,1934 OAK,NEB.

YR	CL	LEA	POS	GP	G	REC
1959	KC	A	O		73	.313
1960	KC	A	O		125	.260
1961	BAL	A	O		115	.292
1962	BAL	A	O		139	.305
1963	BAL	A	O		148	.256
1964	BAL	A	O		56	.290
1965	BAL	A	O		132	.270
1966	BAL	A	O		117	.306
1967	BAL	A	O		108	.236
1968	CHI	A	O		38	.134
	CLE	A	1-O		68	.281
1969	CLE	A	O		122	.248
1970	MIL	A	O		124	.232
	BLTR				1365	.271

SNYDER, WILLIAM NICHOLS
B.JAN.28,1898 MANSFIELD,OHIO
D.OCT.8,1934

YR	CL	LEA	POS	GP	G	REC
1919	WAS	A	P		2	0- 1
1920	WAS	A	P		16	2- 1
	BRTR				18	2- 2

SOCKALEXIS, LEWIS M. "CHIEF"
B.OCT.24,1873 OLD TOWN,ME.
D.DEC.24,1913

YR	CL	LEA	POS	GP	G	REC
1897	CLE	N	O		66	.331
1898	CLE	N	O		20	.222
1899	CLE	N	O		7	.252
	BLTR				93	.307

SODD, WILLIAM
B.SEPT.18,1914 FT.WORTH,TEX.

YR	CL	LEA	POS	GP	G	REC
1937	CLE	A	H		1	.000
	BRTR					

SODERHOLM, ERIC THANE
B.SEP.24,1948 CORTLAND,N.Y.

YR	CL	LEA	POS	GP	G	REC
1971	MIN	A	3		21	.156
1972	MIN	A	3		93	.188
1973	MIN	A	S-3		35	.297
1974	MIN	A	S-3		141	.276
1975	MIN	A	3		117	.286
	BRTR				407	.257

SOLAITA, TOLIA "TONY"
B.JAN.15,1947 TUTUILA,AMER.SAMOA

YR	CL	LEA	POS	GP	G	REC
1968	NY	A	1		1	.000
1974	KC	A	1-O-D		96	.268
1975	KC	A	1-O		93	.260
1976	KC	A	1-O		31	.235
	CAL	A	1		63	.270
	BLTL				284	.263

SOLIS, MARCELINO
B.JULY 19,1930 SAN LUIS POTOSI,
MEXICO

YR	CL	LEA	POS	GP	G	REC
1958	CHI	N	P		15	3- 3
	BLTL					

SOLOMON, EDDIE
B.FEB.9,1951 PERRY,GA.

YR	CL	LEA	POS	GP	G	REC
1973	LA	N	P		4	0- 0
1974	LA	N	P		4	0- 0
1975	CHI	N	P		6	0- 0
1976	STL	N	P		26	1- 1
	BRTR				40	1- 1

**SOLOMON, JAMES HERMAN
(PLAYED UNDER NAME OF
JAMES HERMAN REESE)**

SOLOMON, MOSES "HICKORY"
B.DEC.8,1900 NEW YORK,N.Y.
D.JUNE 25,1966 MIAMI,FLA.

YR	CL	LEA	POS	GP	G	REC
1923	NY	N	O		2	.375
	BLTL					

YR	CL	LEA	POS	GP	G	REC

SOLTERS, JULIUS JOSEPH "MOOSE"
(REAL NAME
JULIUS JOSEPH SOLTESZ)
B.MAR.22,1906 PITTSBURGH,PA.
D.SEPT.28,1975

YR	CL	LEA	POS	GP	G	REC
1934	BOS	A	O		101	.299
1935	BOS	A	O		24	.241
	STL	A	O		127	.330
1936	STL	A	O		152	.291
1937	CLE	A	O		152	.323
1938	CLE	A	O		67	.201
1939	CLE	A	O		41	.275
	STL	A	O		40	.206
1940	CHI	A	O		116	.308
1941	CHI	A	O		76	.259
1943	CHI	A	O		42	.155
		BRTR			938	.289

SOLTESZ, JULIUS JOSEPH
(PLAYED UNDER NAME OF
JULIUS JOSEPH SOLTERS)

SOMERLOTT, JOHN WESLEY
B.OCT.26,1882 FLINT,IND.
D.APR.21,1965

1910	WAS	A	1		16	.222
1911	WAS	A	1		13	.175
	TR				29	.204

SOMERVILLE, EDWARD
D.SEPT,1877

1875	CEN	NA	2-3		14	-
	NH	NA	1-2-S-3		33	-
1876	LOU	N	2		64	.187
		BRTR			111	-

SOMMER, JOSEPH JOHN
B.APR.3,1853 COVINGTON,KY.
D.JAN.16,1938

1880	CIN	N	S-3-O		20	.182
1882	CIN	AA	O		80	.280
1883	CIN	AA	P-3-	1	97	0- 0
			O			.281
1884	BAL	AA	3-O		107	.272
1885	BAL	AA	O		110	.250
1886	BAL	AA	2-O		139	.215
1887	BAL	AA	O		131	.355
1888	BAL	AA	S-O		79	.215
1889	BAL	AA	O		106	.224
1890	CLE	N	P-O	1	9	0- 1
						.294
	BAL	AA	O		38	.239
		BRTR		2	916	0- 1
						.262

SOMMERS, JOSEPH ANDREW "PETE"
B.OCT.26,1866 CLEVELAND,OHIO
D.JULY 22,1908

1887	MET	AA	C		32	.219
1888	BOS	N	C		4	.231
1889	CHI	N	C		12	.239
	IND	N	C		19	.241
1890	NY	N	C-1-O		17	.070
	CLE	N	C-O		8	.192
		BR			92	.209

SOMMERS, RUDOLPH
B.OCT.30,1888 CINCINNATI,OHIO
D.MAR.18,1949

1912	CHI	N	P		1	0- 1
1914	BRO	F	P		23	2- 7
1926	BOS	A	P		2	0- 0
1927	BOS	A	P		7	0- 0
		BBTL			33	2- 8

SOMMERS, WILLIAM "KID"
B.TORONTO,ONT.,CANADA
D.OCT.16,1895

1889	CLE	N	C		2	.000
1893	STL	N	C		2	.000
	TR				4	.000

SOMMERS, WILLIAM DUNN "BILL"
B.FEB.17,1923 BROOKLYN,N.Y.

| 1950 | STL | A | 2-3 | | 65 | .255 |
| | | BRTR | | | | |

SOMMERVILLE, ANDREW
(REAL NAME
HENRY TRAVERS SUMMERSGILL)
B.FEB.6,1876 BROOKLYN,N.Y.
D.JUNE 16,1931

| 1894 | BRO | N | P | | 1 | 0- 1 |

SONGER, DONALD C.
B.JAN.31,1900 WALNUT,KAN.
D.OCT.3,1962

1924	PIT	N	P		4	0- 0
1925	PIT	N	P		8	0- 1
1926	PIT	N	P		35	7- 8
1927	PIT	N	P		2	0- 0
	NY	N	P		22	3- 5
		BLTL			71	10-14

SORRELL, VICTOR GARLAND "VIC"
B.APR.9,1901 MORRISVILLE,N.C.
D.MAY 4,1972 RALEIGH,N.C.

1928	DET	A	P		29	8-11
1929	DET	A	P		36	14-15
1930	DET	A	P		35	16-11
1931	DET	A	P		35	13-14
1932	DET	A	P	32	33	14-14
1933	DET	A	P		36	11-15
1934	DET	A	P		28	6- 9
1935	DET	A	P		12	4- 3
1936	DET	A	P		30	6- 7
1937	DET	A	P		7	0- 2
		BRTR		280	281	92-101

SORRELL, WILLIAM "BILL"
B.OCT.14,1940 MOREHEAD,KY.

1965	PHI	N	3		10	.385
1967	SF	N	O		18	.176
1970	KC	A	1-3-O		57	.267
		BLTR			85	.267

SORRELLS, RAYMOND EDWIN "CHICK"
B.JULY 31,1898 ROYSE CITY,TEX.

| 1922 | CLE | A | S | | 2 | .000 |
| | | BRTR | | | | |

SOSA, ELIAS (MARTINEZ)
B.JUNE 10,1950 LA VEGA,D.R.

1972	SF	N	P		8	0- 1
1973	SF	N	P		71	10- 4
1974	SF	N	P		68	9- 7
1975	STL	N	P		14	0- 3
	ATL	N	P		43	2- 2
1976	ATL	N	P		21	4- 4
	LA	N	P		24	2- 4
		BRTR			249	27-25

SOSA, JOSE YNOCENCIO
B.DEC.28,1952 SANTO DOMINGO,D.R.

1975	HOU	N	P	25	26	1- 3
1976	HOU	N	P		9	0- 0
		BRTR		34	35	1- 3

SOTHERN, DENNIS ELWOOD
B.JAN.20,1904 WASHINGTON,D.C.

1926	PHI	N	O		14	.245
1928	PHI	N	O		161	.285
1929	PHI	N	O		76	.306
1930	PHI	N	O		90	.280
	PIT	N	O		17	.176
1931	BRO	N	O		19	.161
		BRTR			357	.280

SOTHORON, ALLAN SUTTON
B.APR.27,1893 BRADFORD,OHIO
D.JUNE 17,1939

1914	STL	A	P		1	0- 0
1915	STL	A	P		3	0- 1
1917	STL	A	P		49	14-19
1918	STL	A	P		29	13-12
1919	STL	A	P		39	20-12
1920	STL	A	P		36	8-15
1921	STL	A	P		5	1- 2
	BOS	A	P		2	0- 2
	CLE	A	P		22	12- 4
1922	CLE	A	P		6	1- 3
1924	STL	N	P		29	10-16
1925	STL	N	P		28	10-10
1926	STL	N	P		15	3- 3
		BBTR		264	92-99
NON-PLAYING MANAGER STL(A) 1933						
		BR 1924-26				

SOUCHOCK, STEPHEN "BUD"
B.MAR.3,1919 YATESBORO,PA.

1946	NY	A	1		47	.302
1948	NY	A	1		44	.203
1949	CHI	A	1-O		84	.234
1951	DET	A	1-2-3-O		91	.245
1952	DET	A	1-3-O		92	.249
1953	DET	A	1-O		89	.302
1954	DET	A	3-O		25	.179
1955	DET	A	H		1	1.000
		BRTR			473	.255

SOUTHWICK, CLYDE AUBRA
B.NOV.3,1886 MAXWELL,IOWA
D.OCT.14,1961

| 1911 | STL | A | C | | 4 | .250 |
| | | BLTR | | | | |

SOUTHWORTH, WILLIAM FREDERICK
"BILL"
B.NOV.10,1945 MADISON,WIS.

| 1964 | MIL | N | 3 | | 3 | .286 |
| | | BRTR | | | | |

SOUTHWORTH, WILLIAM HARRISON
"BILLY"
B.MAR.9,1893 HARVARD,NEB.
D.NOV.15,1969 COLUMBUS,OHIO

1913	CLE	A	O		1	.000
1915	CLE	A	O		60	.220
1918	PIT	N	O		64	.341
1919	PIT	N	O		121	.280
1920	PIT	N	O		146	.284
1921	BOS	N	O		141	.308
1922	BOS	N	O		43	.322
1923	BOS	N	2-O		153	.319
1924	NY	N	O		94	.256
1925	NY	N	O		123	.292
1926	NY	N	O		36	.328
	STL	N	O		99	.317
1927	STL	N	O		92	.301
1929	STL	N	M-O		19	.188
		BLTR			1192	.298
NON-PLAYING MANAGER						
STL(N) 1940-45, BOS(N) 1946-51						

SOWDERS, JOHN
B.DEC.10,1866 LOUISVILLE,KY.
D.JULY 29,1908

1887	IND	N	P		1	0- 0
1889	KC	AA	P		28	6-16
1890	BRO	P	P		40	18-16
		BRTL			69	24-32

SOWDERS, LEONARD
B.JUNE 29,1861 LOUISVILLE,KY.
D.NOV.19,1888

| 1886 | BAL | AA | O | | 23 | .267 |

SOWDERS, WILLIAM JEFFERSON
"LITTLE BILL"
B.NOV.29,1864 LOUISVILLE,KY.
D.FEB.2,1951

1888	BOS	N	P		35	19-15
1889	BOS	N	P		4	2- 2
	PIT	N	P-O	12	14	5- 4
						.256
1890	PIT	N	P		17	3- 7
		BRTR		68	70	29-28
						.189

SPADE, ROBERT
B.JAN.4,1877 AKRON,OHIO
D.SEPT.7,1924

1907	CIN	N	P		3	1- 1
1908	CIN	N	P		35	17-12
1909	CIN	N	P		14	5- 5
1910	CIN	N	P		3	1- 2
	STL	A	P		7	1- 3
		BRTR			62	25-23

SPAHN, WARREN EDWARD
B.APR.23,1921 BUFFALO,N.Y.

1942	BOS	N	P		4	0- 0
1946	BOS	N	P		24	8- 5
1947	BOS	N	P	40	41	21-10
1948	BOS	N	P		36	15-12
1949	BOS	N	P	38	40	21-14
1950	BOS	N	P		41	21-17
1951	BOS	N	P	39	42	22-14
1952	BOS	N	P	40	52	14-19
1953	MIL	N	P	35	38	23- 7
1954	MIL	N	P	39	41	21-12
1955	MIL	N	P	39	40	17-14
1956	MIL	N	P		39	20-11
1957	MIL	N	P		39	21-11
1958	MIL	N	P	38	41	22-11
1959	MIL	N	P		40	21-15
1960	MIL	N	P		40	21-10
1961	MIL	N	P	38	39	21-13
1962	MIL	N	P	34	36	18-14
1963	MIL	N	P		33	23- 7
1964	MIL	N	P	38	39	6-13
1965	NY	N	P	20	21	4-12
	SF	N	P		16	3- 4
		BLTL		750	782	363-245

YR	CL	LEA	POS	GP	G	REC

SPALDING, ALBERT GOODWILL
B.SEPT.2,1850 BYRON,ILL.
D.SEPT.9,1915 POINT LOMA,CAL.

YR	CL	LEA	POS	GP	G	REC
1871	BOS	NA	P		33	21-10
1872	BOS	NA	P-O		48	36- 8
						.338
1873	BOS	NA	P-O		60	41-15
						.359
1874	BOS	NA	P		71	52-18
1875	BOS	NA	P-1- 66	66	74	56- 5
			O			.318
1876	CHI	N	M-P- 60		66	46-14
			O			.306
1877	CHI	N	M-P- 4		60	0- 0
			1-2-3			.256
1878	CHI	N	2		1	.500
	BRTR		342		413	252-70
						-

SPALDING, CHARLES HARRY "DICK"
B.OCT.13,1897 PHILADELPHIA,PA.
D.FEB.6,1950

YR	CL	LEA	POS	GP	G	REC
1927	PHI	N	O		115	.296
1928	WAS	A	O		16	.348
	BLTL				131	.299

SPANGLER, ALBERT DONALD "AL"
B.JULY 8,1933 PHILADELPHIA,PA.

YR	CL	LEA	POS	GP	G	REC
1959	MIL	N	O		6	.417
1960	MIL	N	O		101	.267
1961	MIL	N	U		88	.266
1962	HOU	N	O		129	.285
1963	HOU	N	O		120	.281
1964	HOU	N	O		135	.245
1965	HOU	N	O		38	.214
	CAL	A	O		51	.260
1966	CAL	A	O		6	.667
1967	CHI	N	O		62	.254
1968	CHI	N	O		88	.271
1969	CHI	N	O		82	.211
1970	CHI	N	O		21	.143
1971	CHI	N	H		5	.400
	BLTL				912	.262

SPANSWICK, WILLIAM HENRY "BILL"
B.JULY 8,1938 SPRINGFIELD,MASS.

YR	CL	LEA	POS	GP	G	REC
1964	BOS	A	P		29	2- 3
	BLTR					

SPARKS, TULLY FRANK
B.APR.18,1877 MONROE,LA.
D.JULY 15,1937

YR	CL	LEA	POS	GP	G	REC
1897	PHI	N	P		1	0- 1
1899	PIT	N	P		25	9- 7
1901	MIL	A	P		30	6-17
1902	NY	N	P		15	4-11
	BOS	A	P		17	7- 8
1903	PHI	N	P		28	11-15
1904	PHI	N	P		26	9-16
1905	PHI	N	P		34	13-11
1906	PHI	N	P		42	19-16
1907	PHI	N	P		33	22- 8
1908	PHI	N	P		33	16-15
1909	PHI	N	P		24	6-11
1910	PHI	N	P		3	0- 2
	BRTR				311	122-138

SPARMA, JOSEPH BLASE "JOE"
B.FEB.4,1942 MASSILLON,OHIO

YR	CL	LEA	POS	GP	G	REC
1964	DET	A	P	21	23	5- 6
1965	DET	A	P		30	13- 8
1966	DET	A	P		29	2- 7
1967	DET	A	P		37	16- 9
1968	DET	A	P		34	10-10
1969	DET	A	P		23	6- 8
1970	MON	N	P		9	0- 4
	BRTR		183		185	52-52

SPEAKE, ROBERT CHARLES "BOB"
B.AUG.22,1930 SPRINGFIELD,MO.

YR	CL	LEA	POS	GP	G	REC
1955	CHI	N	1-O		95	.218
1957	CHI	N	1-O		129	.232
1958	SF	N	O		66	.211
1959	SF	N	H		15	.091
	BLTL				305	.223

SPEAKER, TRISTRAM E. "TRIS"
B.APR.4,1888 HUBBARD,TEX.
D.DEC.8,1958 LAKE WHITNEY,TEX.

YR	CL	LEA	POS	GP	G	REC
1907	BOS	A	O		7	.158
1908	BOS	A	O		31	.220
1909	BOS	A	O		143	.309
1910	BOS	A	O		141	.340
1911	BOS	A	O		141	.327
1912	BOS	A	O		153	.383
1913	BOS	A	O		141	.366
1914	BOS	A	P-O	1	158	0- 0
						.338
1915	BOS	A	O		150	.322
1916	CLE	A	O		151	.386
1917	CLE	A	O		142	.352
1918	CLE	A	O		127	.319
1919	CLE	A	M-O		134	.296
1920	CLE	A	M-O		150	.388
1921	CLE	A	M-O		132	.362
1922	CLE	A	M-O		131	.378
1923	CLE	A	M-O		150	.380
1924	CLE	A	M-O		135	.344
1925	CLE	A	M-O		117	.389
1926	CLE	A	M-O		150	.304
1927	WAS	A	1-O		141	.327
1928	PHI	A	O		64	.267
	BLTL		1		2789	0- 0
						.344

SPEECE, BYRON FRANKLIN
B.JAN.6,1897 WEST BADEN,IND.
D.SEPT.29,1974 ELGIN,ORE.

YR	CL	LEA	POS	GP	G	REC
1924	WAS	A	P		21	2- 1
1925	CLE	A	P		28	3- 5
1926	CLE	A	P		7	0- 0
1930	PHI	N	P		11	0- 0
	BRTR				62	5- 6

SPEED, HORACE ARTHUR
B.OCT.4,1951 LOS ANGELES,CAL.

YR	CL	LEA	POS	GP	G	REC
1975	SF	N	O		17	.133
	BRTR					

SPEER, FLOYD VERNIE
B.JAN.27,1914 BOONEVILLE,ARK.

YR	CL	LEA	POS	GP	G	REC
1943	CHI	A	P		1	0- 0
1944	CHI	A	P		2	0- 0
	BRTR				3	0- 0

SPEER, GEORGE NATHAN "KID"
B.JUNE 16,1886 CORNING,MO.
D.JAN.13,1946

YR	CL	LEA	POS	GP	G	REC
1909	DET	A	P		13	4- 4
	BLTL					

SPEIER, CHRIS EDWARD
B.JUNE 28,1950 ALAMEDA,CAL.

YR	CL	LEA	POS	GP	G	REC
1971	SF	N	S		157	.235
1972	SF	N	S		150	.269
1973	SF	N	2-S		153	.249
1974	SF	N	2-S		141	.250
1975	SF	N	S-3		141	.271
1976	SF	N	1-2-S-3		145	.226
	BRTR				887	.250

SPENCE, HARRISON L.
B.JUNE.22,1856 NEW YORK,N.Y.
D.MAY 19,1908
NON-PLAYING MANAGER IND(N) 1888

SPENCE, ROBERT JOHN "BOB"
B.FEB.10,1946 SAN DIEGO,CAL.

YR	CL	LEA	POS	GP	G	REC
1969	CHI	A	1		12	.154
1970	CHI	A	1		46	.223
1971	CHI	A	1		14	.148
	BLTR				72	.202

SPENCE, STANLEY ORVILLE "STAN"
B.MAR.20,1915 S.PORTSMOUTH,KY.

YR	CL	LEA	POS	GP	G	REC
1940	BOS	A	O		51	.279
1941	BOS	A	1-O		86	.232
1942	WAS	A	O		149	.323
1943	WAS	A	O		149	.267
1944	WAS	A	1-O		153	.313
1946	WAS	A	O		152	.292
1947	WAS	A	O		147	.279
1948	BOS	A	1-O		114	.235
1949	BOS	A	O		7	.150
	STL	A	1-O		104	.245
	BLTL				1112	.282

SPENCER

YR	CL	LEA	POS	GP	G	REC
1872	NAT	NA	S		2	.200

SPENCER, CHESTER ARTHUR
B.MAR.4,1883 PORTSMOUTH,OHIO
D.NOV.10,1938

YR	CL	LEA	POS	GP	G	REC
1906	BOS	N	O		7	.148
	BLTR					

SPENCER, DARYL DEAN
B.JULY 13,1929 WICHITA,KAN.

YR	CL	LEA	POS	GP	G	REC
1952	NY	N	S-3		7	.294
1953	NY	N	2-S-3		118	.208
1956	NY	N	2-S-3		146	.221
1957	NY	N	2-S-3		148	.249
1958	SF	N	2-S		148	.256
1959	SF	N	2-S		152	.265
1960	STL	N	2-S		148	.258
1961	STL	N	S		37	.254
	LA	N	S-3		60	.243
1962	LA	N	S-3		77	.236
1963	LA	N	3		7	.111
	CIN	N	3		50	.239
	BRTR				1098	.244

SPENCER, EDWARD RUSSELL "TUBBY"
B.JAN.26,1884 OIL CITY,PA.
D.FEB.1,1945

YR	CL	LEA	POS	GP	G	REC
1905	STL	A	C		35	.235
1906	STL	A	C		58	.176
1907	STL	A	C		71	.265
1908	STL	A	C		91	.210
1909	BOS	A	C		28	.162
1911	PHI	N	C		11	.156
1916	DET	A	L		19	.370
1917	DET	A	C		70	.239
1918	DET	A	C		66	.219
	BRTR				469	.225

SPENCER, FRANK G.
B.1886

YR	CL	LEA	POS	GP	G	REC
1912	STL	A	P		1	0- 0
	BRTR					

SPENCER, GEORGE ELWELL
B.JULY 7,1926 COLUMBUS,OHIO

YR	CL	LEA	POS	GP	G	REC
1950	NY	N	P		10	1- 0
1951	NY	N	P		57	10- 4
1952	NY	N	P		35	3- 5
1953	NY	N	P		1	0- 0
1954	NY	N	P		6	1- 0
1955	NY	N	P		1	0- 0
1958	DET	A	P		7	1- 0
1960	DET	A	P		5	0- 1
	BRTR				122	16-10

SPENCER, GLENN EDWARD
B.SEPT.11,1905 CORNING,N.Y.
D.DEC.30,1958

YR	CL	LEA	POS	GP	G	REC
1928	PIT	N	P		4	0- 0
1930	PIT	N	P		41	8- 9
1931	PIT	N	P		38	11-12
1932	PIT	N	P		39	4- 8
1933	NY	N	P		17	0- 2
	BRTR				139	23-31

SPENCER, JAMES LLOYD "JIM"
B.JULY 30,1947 HANOVER,PA.

YR	CL	LEA	POS	GP	G	REC
1968	CAL	A	1		19	.191
1969	CAL	A	1		113	.254
1970	CAL	A	1		146	.274
1971	CAL	A	1		148	.237
1972	CAL	A	1-O		82	.222
1973	CAL	A	1		29	.241
	TEX	A	1		102	.267
1974	TEX	A	1-O		118	.278
1975	TEX	A	1-O		132	.266
1976	CHI	A	1		150	.253
	BLTR				1039	.256

SPENCER, L. BENJAMIN "BEN"
B.1890

YR	CL	LEA	POS	GP	G	REC
1913	WAS	A	O		8	.300
	BLTL					

YR	CL	LEA	POS	GP	G	REC

SPENCER, ROY HAMPTON
B.FEB.22,1900 SCRANTON,N.C.
D.FEB.8,1973 PORT CHARLOTTE,FLA

YR	CL	LEA	POS	GP	G	REC
1925	PIT	N	C		14	.214
1926	PIT	N	C		28	.395
1927	PIT	N	C		38	.283
1929	WAS	A	C		50	.155
1930	WAS	A	C		93	.255
1931	WAS	A	C		145	.275
1932	WAS	A	C		102	.246
1933	CLE	A	C		75	.203
1934	CLE	A	C		5	.143
1936	NY	N	C		19	.278
1937	BRO	N	C		51	.205
1938	BRO	N	C		16	.267
		BRTR			636	.247

SPENCER, VERNON MURRAY
B.FEB.23,1896 WIXOM,MICH.

1920	NY	N	O		45	.200
		BLTR				

SPERAW, PAUL BACHMAN
B.OCT.5,1896 ANNVILLE,PA.
D.FEB.22,1962

1920	STL	A	3		1	.000
		BRTR				

SPERBER, EDWIN GEORGE
B.JAN.21,1897 CINCINNATI,OHIO

1924	BOS	N	O		24	.288
1925	BOS	N	O		2	.000
		BLTL			26	.279

SPERRING, ROBERT WALTER "ROB"
B.OCT.10,1949 SAN FRANCISCO,CAL.

1974	CHI	N	2-S		42	.206
1975	CHI	N	2-S-3-O		65	.208
1976	CHI	N	2-S-3-O		43	.258
		BRTR			150	.221

SPERRY, STANLEY KENNETH
B.JUNE.19,1914 EVANSVILLE,WIS.
D.SEPT.27,1962

1936	PHI	N	2		20	.135
1937	PHI	A	2		60	.273
		BLTR			80	.255

SPICER, ROBERT OBERTON "BOB"
B.APR.11,1925 RICHMOND,VA.

1955	KC	A	P		2	0- 0
1956	KC	A	P		2	0- 0
		BLTR			4	0- 0

SPIES, HENRY "HARRY"
B.JUNE 12,1866 NEW ORLEANS,LA.
D.JULY 7,1942

1895	CIN	N	C		14	.200
	LOU	N	C		69	.268
					83	.257

SPIEZIO, EDWARD WAYNE "ED"
B.OCT.31,1941 JOLIET,ILL.

1964	STL	N	H		12	.333
1965	STL	N	3		10	.167
1966	STL	N	3		26	.219
1967	STL	N	3-O		55	.210
1968	STL	N	3-O		29	.157
1969	SD	N	3-O		121	.234
1970	SD	N	3		110	.285
1971	SD	N	3-O		97	.231
1972	SD	N	3		20	.138
	CHI	A	3		74	.238
		BRTR			554	.238

SPIKES, LESLIE CHARLES "CHARLIE"
B.JAN.23,1951 BOGALUSA,LA.

1972	NY	A	O		14	.147
1973	CLE	A	O-O		140	.237
1974	CLE	A	O		155	.271
1975	CLE	A	O		111	.229
1976	CLE	A	O		101	.237
		BRTR			521	.245

SPILLNER, DANIEL RAY "DAN"
B.NOV.27,1951 CASPER,WYO.

1974	SD	N	P		30	9-11
1975	SD	N	P		37	5-13
1976	SD	N	P	32	33	2-11
		BRTR		99	100	16-35

SPINDEL, HAROLD STEWART
B.MAY 27,1913 CHANDLER,OKLA.

1939	STL	A	C		48	.269
1945	PHI	N	C		36	.230
1946	PHI	N	C		1	.333
		BRTR			85	.254

SPINKS, SCIPIO RONALD
B.JULY 12,1947 CHICAGO,ILL.

1969	HOU	N	P		1	0- 0
1970	HOU	N	P	5	6	0- 1
1971	HOU	N	P		5	1- 0
1972	STL	N	P	16	21	5- 5
1973	STL	N	P		8	1- 5
		BRTR		35	41	7-11

SPLITTORFF, PAUL WILLIAM
B.OCT.8,1946 EVANSVILLE,IND.

1970	KC	A	P		2	0- 1
1971	KC	A	P		22	8- 9
1972	KC	A	P		35	12-12
1973	KC	A	P		38	20-11
1974	KC	A	P	36	37	13-19
1975	KC	A	P		35	9-10
1976	KC	A	P		26	11- 8
		BLTL		194	195	73-70

SPOGNARDI, ANDREW ETTORE
B.OCT.18,1908 BOSTON,MASS.

1932	BOS	A	2-S-3		17	.294
		BRTR				

SPOHRER, ALFRED R. "AL"
B.DEC.3,1902 PHILADELPHIA,PA.
D.JULY 17,1972 PLYMOUTH,N.H.

1928	NY	N	C		2	.000
	BOS	N	C		51	.218
1929	BOS	N	C		114	.272
1930	BOS	N	C		112	.317
1931	BOS	N	C		114	.240
1932	BOS	N	C		104	.269
1933	BOS	N	C		67	.250
1934	BOS	N	C		100	.223
1935	BOS	N	C		92	.242
		BRTR			756	.259

SPONGBERG, CARL GUSTAV "SPONY"
B.JUNE 21,1884 PARIS,IDAHO
D.JUNE 20,1938 LOS ANGELES,CAL.

1908	CHI	N	P		1	0- 0
		BRTR				

SPOONER, KARL BENAJMIN
B.JUNE 23,1931 ORISKANY FALLS,
N.Y.

1954	BRO	N	P		2	2- 0
1955	BRO	N	P		29	8- 6
		BRTL			31	10- 6

SPOTTS, JAMES RUSSELL
B.APR.12,1909 HONEY BROOK,PA.
D.JUNE 30,1964

1930	PHI	N	C		3	.000
		BRTR				

SPRAGINS, HOMER FRANKLIN
B.NOV.9,1920 MINTER CITY,MISS.

1947	PHI	N	P		4	0- 0
		BRTR				

SPRAGUE, CHARLES WELLINGTON
B.OCT.10,1864 CLEVELAND,OHIO
D.DEC.31,1912

1887	CHI	N	P		3	1- 1
1889	CLE	N	P		3	0- 3
1890	TOL	AA	P-O	14	51	6- 7
						.245
				20	57	7-11
						.236

SPRAGUE, EDWARD NELSON "ED"
B.SEP.16,1945 BOSTON,MASS.

1968	OAK	A	P		47	3- 4
1969	OAK	A	P		27	1- 1
1971	CIN	N	P		7	1- 0
1972	CIN	N	P		33	3- 3
1973	CIN	N	P		28	1- 3
	STL	N	P		8	0- 0
1974	MIL	A	P		7	0- 1
1975	MIL	A	P		20	7- 2
1976	MIL	A	P		18	1- 7
	MIL	A	P		3	0- 2
		BRTR			198	17-23

SPRATT, HENRY LEE
B.JULY 10,1888 MASON,VA.
D.JULY 3,1969 WASHINGTON,D.C.

1911	BOS	N	S		41	.240
1912	BOS	N	S		27	.258
		BLTR			68	.247

SPRIGGS, GEORGE HERMAN
B.MAY 22,1941 LOTHIAN,MD.

1965	PIT	N	O		9	.500
1966	PIT	N	H		9	.143
1967	PIT	N	O		38	.175
1969	KC	A	O		23	.138
1970	KC	A	O		51	.208
		BLTR			130	.191

SPRING, JACK RUSSELL
B.MAR.11,1933 SPOKANE,WASH.

1955	PHI	N	P		2	0- 1
1957	BOS	A	P		1	0- 0
1958	WAS	A	P		3	0- 0
1961	LA	A	P		18	3- 0
1962	LA	A	P		57	4- 2
1963	LA	A	P		45	3- 0
1964	LA	A	P		6	1- 0
	CHI	N	P		7	0- 0
	STL	N	P		2	0- 0
1965	CLE	A	P		14	1- 2
		BRTL			155	12- 5

SPRINGER, BRADFORD LOUIS
B.MAY 9,1904 DETROIT,MICH.
D.JAN.4,1970 BIRMINGHAM,MICH.

1925	STL	A	P		2	0- 0
1926	CIN	N	P		1	0- 0
		BLTL			3	0- 0

SPRINGER, EDWARD E.
B.DETROIT,MICH.

1889	LOU	AA	P		1	0- 1

SPRINZ, JOSEPH CONRAD
B.AUG.3,1902 ST.LOUIS,MO.

1930	CLE	A	C		17	.178
1931	CLE	A	C		1	.000
1933	STL	N	C		3	.200
		BRTP			21	.170

SPROULL, CHARLES WILLIAM
B.JAN.9,1919 TAYLORSVILLE,GA.

1945	PHI	N	P		34	4-10
		BRTR				

SPROUT, ROBERT SAMUEL
B.DEC.5,1941 FLORIN,PA.

1961	LA	A	P		1	0- 0
		BLTL				

SPURGEON, FREDDIE
B.OCT.9,1900 WABASH,IND.
D.NOV.5,1970 KALAMAZOO,MICH.

1924	CLE	A	2		2	.167
1925	CLE	A	2-S-3		107	.287
1926	CLE	A	2		149	.294
1927	CLE	A	2		57	.252
		BRTR			315	.285

SPURNEY, EDWARD FREDERICK
B.JAN.9,1872 CLEVELAND,OHIO
D.OCT.12,1932

1891	PIT	N	S		3	.285

SQUIRES, MICHAEL LYNN "MIKE"
B.MAR.5,1952 KALAMAZOO,MICH.

1975	CHI	A	1		20	.231
		BLTL				

STACK, WILLIAM EDWARD "EDDIE"
B.OCT.24,1887 CHICAGO,ILL.
D.AUG.28,1958

1910	PHI	N	P		20	6- 7
1911	PHI	N	P		12	5- 5
1912	BRO	N	P		28	7- 5
1913	BRO	N	P		23	4- 4
	CHI	N	P		11	4- 2
1914	CHI	N	P		6	0- 1
		BRTR			100	26-24

STAEHLE, MARVIN GUSTAVE "MARV"
B.MAR.13,1942 OAK PARK,ILL.

1964	CHI	A	H		6	.400
1965	CHI	A	H		7	.429
1966	CHI	A	2		8	.133
1967	CHI	A	2-S		32	.111
1969	MON	N	2		6	.412
1970	MON	N	2-S		104	.218
1971	ATL	N	2-3		22	.111
		BLTR			185	.207

YR	CL	LEA	POS	GP	G	REC

STAFFORD, HENRY ALEXANDER "HEINE"
B.NOV.1,1891 ORLEANS,VT.
D.JAN.12,1972 LAKE WORTH,FLA.
1916 NY N H 1 .000
TR

STAFFORD, JAMES JOSEPH "JAMSEY"
B.JULY 9,1868 WEBSTER,MASS.
D.SEPT.11,1923 WORCESTER,MASS.
1890 BUF P P 15 3- 9
1893 NY N O 67 .301
1894 NY N 3 11 .229
1895 NY N 2 123 .293
1896 NY N O 59 .282
1897 NY N S-O 7 .091
LOU N S 112 .280
1898 LOU N O 42 .312
BOS N 1-O 37 .270
1899 BOS N O 50 .313
WAS N 2-S-3 30 .243
BRTR 15 553 3- 9
.284

STAFFORD, JOHN HENRY "DOC"
B.APR.8,1870 DUDLEY,MASS.
D.JULY 3,1940 WORCESTER,MASS.
1893 CLE N P 2 0- 0
BRTR

STAFFORD, ROBERT LEE
1890 ATH AA O 1 .000

STAFFORD, WILLIAM CHARLES "BILL"
B.AUG.13,1939 CATSKILL,N.Y.
1960 NY A P 11 12 3- 1
1961 NY A P 36 14- 9
1962 NY A P 35 14- 9
1963 NY A P 28 4- 8
1964 NY A P 31 5- 0
1965 NY A P 22 3- 8
1966 KC A P 9 0- 4
1967 KC A P 14 0- 1
BRTR 186 187 43-40

STAHL, CHARLES SYLVESTER "CHICK"
B.JAN.10,1873 FT.WAYNE,IND.
D.MAR.28,1907 W.BADEN SPRINGS, FLA.
1897 BOS N O 111 .359
1898 BOS N O 125 .311
1899 BOS N O 148 .348
1900 BOS N O 134 .293
1901 BOS A O 130 .310
1902 BOS A O 127 .318
1903 BOS A O 78 .279
1904 BOS A O 157 .300
1905 BOS A O 134 .258
1906 BOS A M-O 155 .286
BLTL 1299 .306

STAHL, GARLAND "JAKE"
B.APR.13,1879 ELKHART,ILL.
D.SEPT.18,1922
1903 BOS A C 38 .239
1904 WAS A 1-O 141 .261
1905 WAS A M-1 140 .250
1906 WAS A M-1 137 .222
1908 NY A 1-O 74 .259
BOS A 1 79 .240
1909 BOS A 1 127 .294
1910 BOS A 1 144 .271
1912 BOS A M-1 95 .301
1913 BOS A M-1 1 .000
BRTR 976 .260

STAHL, LARRY FLOYD
B.JUNE 29,1941 BELLEVILLE,ILL.
1964 KC A O 15 .261
1965 KC A O 28 .198
1966 KC A O 119 .250
1967 NY N O 71 .239
1968 NY N 1-O 53 .235
1969 SD N 1-O 95 .198
1970 SD N O 52 .182
1971 SD N 1-O 114 .253
1972 SD N 1-O 107 .226
1973 CIN N 1-O 76 .225
BLTL 730 .232

STAIGER, ROY JOSEPH
B.JAN.6,1950 TULSA,OKLA.
1975 NY N 3 13 .158
1976 NY N S-3 95 .220
BRTR 108 .217

STAINBACK, GEORGE TUCKER "TUCK"
B.AUG.4,1910 LOS ANGELES,CAL.
1934 CHI N O 104 .306
1935 CHI N O 47 .255
1936 CHI N O 44 .173
1937 CHI N O 72 .231
1938 STL N O 6 .000
PHI N O 30 .259
BRO N O 35 .327
1939 BRO N O 68 .269
1940 DET A O 15 .225
1941 DET A O 94 .245
1942 NY A O 15 .200
1943 NY A O 71 .260
1944 NY A O 30 .218
1945 NY A O 95 .257
1946 PHI A O 91 .244
BRTR 817 .258

STALBERGER, WILLIAM
B.DETROIT,MICH.
1885 PRO N P 1 0- 1

STALEY, GALE
B.MAY 2,1903 OSHKOSH,WIS.
1925 CHI N 2 7 .423
BLTR

STALEY, GERALD LEE "GERRY"
B.AUG.21,1920 BRUSH PRAIRIE, WASH.
1947 STL N P 18 1- 0
1948 STL N P 31 4- 4
1949 STL N P 45 10-10
1950 STL N P 42 13-13
1951 STL N P 42 19-13
1952 STL N P 35 17-14
1953 STL N P 40 18- 9
1954 STL N P 18 7-13
1955 CIN N P 30 5- 8
NY A P 2 0- 0
1956 NY A P 1 0- 0
CHI A P 26 8- 3
1957 CHI A P 47 5- 1
1958 CHI A P 50 4- 5
1959 CHI A P 67 8- 5
1960 CHI A P 64 13- 8
1961 CHI A P 16 0- 3
KC A P 23 1- 1
DET A P 13 1- 1
BRTR 640 134-111

STALEY, HENRY E.
B.MAY 2,1866 JACKSONVILLE,ILL.
D.JAN.12,1910
1888 PIT N P 24 12-12
1889 PIT N P 48 49 21-26
1890 PIT P P 47 21-23
1891 PIT N P 9 2- 4
BOS N P 27 19- 8
1892 BOS N P 35 24-11
1893 BOS N P 32 19-10
1894 BOS N P 27 13-14
1895 STL N P 18 5-13
BRTR 267 268 136-121

STALLARD, EVAN TRACY "TRACY"
B.AUG.31,1937 COEBURN,VA.
1960 BOS A P 4 0- 0
1961 BOS A P 43 2- 7
1962 BOS A P 1 0- 0
1963 NY N P 39 6-17
1964 NY N P 36 10-20
1965 STL N P 40 11- 8
1966 STL N P 20 1- 5
BRTR 183 30-57

STALLCUP, THOMAS VIRGIL "RED"
B.JAN.3,1922 RAVENSFORD,N.C.
1947 CIN N S 8 .000
1948 CIN N S 149 .228
1949 CIN N S 141 .254
1950 CIN N S 136 .251
1951 CIN N S 121 .241
1952 CIN N S 2 .000
STL N S 29 .129
1953 STL N H 1 .000
BRTR 587 .241

STALLER, GEORGE WALBORN
B.APR.1,1916 RUTHERFORD HEIGHTS PA
1943 PHI A O 21 .271
BLTL

STALLINGS, GEORGE TWEEDY
B.NOV.17,1867 AUGUSTA,GA.
D.MAY 13,1929
1890 BRO N C 4 .000
1897 PHI N M-1 1 .400
BRTR 5 .100
NON-PLAYING MANAGER
PHI(N) 1898, DET(A) 1901,
NY(A) 1909-10, BOS(N) 1913-20

STANAGE, OSCAR HARLAND
B.MAR.17,1883 TULARE,CAL.
D.NOV.11,1964 DETROIT,MICH.
1906 CIN N C 1 1.000
1909 DET A C 77 .262
1910 DET A C 88 .207
1911 DET A C 141 .264
1912 DET A C 119 .261
1913 DET A C 80 .224
1914 DET A C 122 .193
1915 DET A C 100 .223
1916 DET A C 94 .237
1917 DET A C 99 .205
1918 DET A C 54 .253
1919 DET A C 38 .242
1920 DET A C 78 .231
1925 DET A C 3 .200
BRTR 1094 .234

STANCEAU, CHARLES
B.JAN.9,1916 CANTON,OHIO
D.APR.3,1969 CANTON,OHIO
1941 NY A P 22 3- 3
1946 NY A P 3 0- 0
PHI N P 14 2- 4
BRTR 39 5- 7

STANDAERT, JEROME JOHN
B.NOV.2,1901 CHICAGO,ILL.
D.AUG.4,1964 CHICAGO,ILL.
1925 BRO N H 1 .000
1926 BRO N 2-3 66 .345
1929 BOS A 1 19 .167
BRTR 86 .318

STANDRIDGE, ALFRED PETER "PETE"
B.APR.25,1891 BLACK DIAMOND, WASH.
D.AUG.?,1963 SAN FRANCISCO,CAL.
1911 STL N P 2 0- 0
1915 CHI N P 29 30 4- 1
BRTR 31 32 4- 1

STANEK, ALBERT WILFRED "AL"
B.DEC.24,1943 SPRINGFIELD,MASS.
1963 SF N P 11 0- 0

STANGE, ALBERT LEE "LEE"
B.OCT.27,1936 CHICAGO,ILL.
1961 MIN A P 7 1- 0
1962 MIN A P 44 4- 3
1963 MIN A P 32 12- 5
1964 MIN A P 14 3- 6
CLE A P 23 24 4- 8
1965 CLE A P 41 8- 4
1966 CLE A P 8 1- 0
BOS A P 28 7- 9
1967 BOS A P 35 8-10
1968 BOS A P 50 5- 5
1969 BOS A P 41 6- 9
1970 BOS A P 20 2- 2
CHI A P 16 1- 0
BRTR 359 360 62-61

STANHOUSE, DONALD JOSEPH "DON"
B.FEB.12,1951 DU QUOIN,ILL.
1972 TEX A P 24 26 2- 9
1973 TEX A P 21 23 1- 7
1974 TEX A P 18 1- 1
1975 MON N P 4 0- 0
1976 MON N P 34 9-12
BRTR 101 105 13-29

STANKA, JOE DONALD
B.JULY 23,1931 HAMMON,OKLA.
1959 CHI A P 2 1- 0

STANKARD, THOMAS FRANCIS
B.MAR.20,1882 WALTHAM,MASS.
D.JUNE 13,1958
1904 PIT N 3 2 .000
BRTR

YR	CL	LEA	POS	GP	G	REC

STANKY, EDWARD RAYMOND
"EDDIE" OR "THE BRAT"
B.SEPT.3,1916 PHILADELPHIA,PA.

YR	CL	LEA	POS	GP	G	REC
1943	CHI	N	2-S-3		142	.245
1944	CHI	N	2-S-3		13	.240
	BRO	N	2-S-3		89	.276
1945	BRO	N	2-S		153	.258
1946	BRO	N	2		144	.273
1947	BRO	N	2		146	.252
1948	BOS	N	2		67	.320
1949	BOS	N	2		138	.285
1950	NY	N	2		152	.300
1951	NY	N	2		145	.247
1952	STL	N	M-2		53	.229
1953	STL	N	M-2		17	.267
	BRTR				1259	.268

NON-PLAYING MANAGER
STL(N) 1954-55, CHI(A) 1966-68

STANLEY, FREDERICK BLAIR "FRED"
B.AUG.13,1947 FARNHAMVILLE,IOWA

YR	CL	LEA	POS	GP	G	REC
1969	SEA	A	2-S		17	.279
1970	MIL	A	2		6	.000
1971	CLE	A	S		60	.225
1972	CLE	A	2-S		6	.167
	SD	N	2-S-3		39	.200
1973	NY	A	2-S		26	.212
1974	NY	A	2-0		33	.184
1975	NY	A	2-S-3		117	.222
1976	NY	A	2-S		110	.238
	BRTR				414	.225
	BB	1969-71				

STANLEY, JAMES F.
B.1889

YR	CL	LEA	POS	GP	G	REC
1914	CHI	F	S		46	.206

STANLEY, JOHN LEONARD "BUCK"
B.NOV.13,1889 WASHINGTON,D.C.
D.AUG.13,1940

YR	CL	LEA	POS	GP	G	REC
1911	PHI	N	P		4	0- 1
	BLTL					

STANLEY, JOSEPH
B.NEW JERSEY

YR	CL	LEA	POS	GP	G	REC
1884	BAL	U	0		5	.217

STANLEY, JOSEPH BERNARD
B.APR.2,1881 WASHINGTON,D.C.
D.SEPT.13,1967 DETROIT,MICH.

YR	CL	LEA	POS	GP	G	REC
1897	WAS	N	P		1	0- 0
1902	WAS	A	0		3	.333
1903	BOS	N	P-0	1	79	0- 0
						.250
1904	BOS	N	0		3	.000
1905	WAS	A	0		28	.261
1906	WAS	A	0		73	.163
1909	CHI	N	0		16	.135
	BBTR			2	203	0- 0
						.213

STANLEY, MITCHELL JACK "MICKEY"
B.JULY 20,1942 GRAND RAPIDS,MICH

YR	CL	LEA	POS	GP	G	REC
1964	DET	A	0		4	.273
1965	DET	A	0		30	.239
1966	DET	A	0		92	.289
1967	DET	A	1-0		145	.210
1968	DET	A	1-2-S-0		153	.259
1969	DET	A	1-S-0		149	.235
1970	DET	A	0		142	.252
1971	DET	A	0		139	.292
1972	DET	A	0		142	.234
1973	DET	A	0		157	.244
1974	DET	A	1-2-S		99	.221
1975	DET	A	1-3-0		52	.256
1976	DET	A	1-2-S-3-0		84	.257
	BRTR				1388	.248

STANSBURY, JOHN JAMES
B.DEC.6,1888 PHILLIPSBURG,N.J.
D.DEC.26,1970 EASTON,PA.

YR	CL	LEA	POS	GP	G	REC
1918	BOS	A	3		20	.128
	BRTR					

STANTON, GEORGE WASHINGTON
"BUCK"
B.JUNE 19,1906 STANTONSBURG,N.C

YR	CL	LEA	POS	GP	G	REC
1931	STL	A	0		13	.200
	BLTL					

STANTON, HARRY ANDREW
B.ST.LOUIS,MO.

YR	CL	LEA	POS	GP	G	REC
1900	STL	N	C		1	.000
1904	CHI	N	C		1	.000
	TR				2	.000

STANTON, LEROY BOBBY
B.APR.10,1946 LATTA,S.C.

YR	CL	LEA	POS	GP	G	REC
1970	NY	N	0		4	.250
1971	NY	N	0		5	.190
1972	CAL	A	0		127	.251
1973	CAL	A	0		119	.235
1974	CAL	A	0		118	.267
1975	CAL	A	0		137	.261
1976	CAL	A	0		93	.190
	BRTR				603	.246

STANTON, MICHAEL THOMAS "MIKE"
B.SEPT.25,1952 PHENIX CITY,ALA.

YR	CL	LEA	POS	GP	G	REC
1975	HOU	N	P		7	0- 2
	BRTR					

STAPLES, JOSEPH F.
B.BUFFALO,N.Y.

YR	CL	LEA	POS	GP	G	REC
1885	BUF	N	2-0		7	.045

STARGELL, WILVER DORNEL "WILLIE"
B.MAR.6,1940 EARLSBORO,OKLA.

YR	CL	LEA	POS	GP	G	REC
1962	PIT	N	0		10	.290
1963	PIT	N	1-0		108	.243
1964	PIT	N	1-0		117	.273
1965	PIT	N	1-0		144	.272
1966	PIT	N	1-0		140	.315
1967	PIT	N	1-0		134	.271
1968	PIT	N	1-0		128	.237
1969	PIT	N	1-0		145	.307
1970	PIT	N	1-0		136	.264
1971	PIT	N	0		141	.295
1972	PIT	N	0		138	.293
1973	PIT	N	0		148	.299
1974	PIT	N	1-0		140	.301
1975	PIT	N	1		124	.295
1976	PIT	N	1		117	.257
	BLTL				1870	.282

STARK, MONROE RANDOLPH
B.JAN.19,1885 RIPLEY,MASS.
D.DEC.1,1924

YR	CL	LEA	POS	GP	G	REC
1909	CLE	A	S		19	.200
1910	BRO	N	S		30	.165
1911	BRO	N	2-S		55	.295
1912	BRO	N	S		8	.182
	BRTR				112	.238

STARKEL, CONRAD
B.NOV.16,1880 GERMANY
D.JAN.12,1933 TACOMA,WASH.

YR	CL	LEA	POS	GP	G	REC
1906	WAS	A	P		1	0- 0
	TR					

STARNAGLE, GEORGE HENRY
(REAL NAME
GEORGE HENRY STEUERNAGEL)
B.OCT.6,1873 BELLEVILLE,ILL.
D.FEB.15,1946 BELLEVILLE,ILL.

YR	CL	LEA	POS	GP	G	REC
1902	CLE	A	C		1	.000
	BRTR					

STARR, CHARLES WATKIN
B.AUG.30,1878 PIKE CO.,OHIO
D.OCT.18,1937

YR	CL	LEA	POS	GP	G	REC
1905	STL	A	2		24	.206
1908	PIT	N	S		19	.186
1909	BOS	N	2		61	.222
	PHI	N	2		3	.000
	TR				107	.211

STARR, RAYMOND FRANCIS "RAY"
B.APR.23,1906 NOWATA,OKLA.
D.FEB.9,1963 BAYLISS,ILL.

YR	CL	LEA	POS	GP	G	REC
1932	STL	N	P		3	1- 1
1933	NY	N	P		6	0- 1
	BOS	N	P		9	0- 1
1941	CIN	N	P		7	3- 2
1942	CIN	N	P		37	15-13
1943	CIN	N	P		36	11-10
1944	PIT	N	P		27	6- 5
1945	PIT	N	P		4	0- 2
	CHI	N	P		9	1- 0
	BRTR				138	37-35

STARR, RICHARD EUGENE "DICK"
B.MAR.2,1921 KITTANNING,PA.

YR	CL	LEA	POS	GP	G	REC
1947	NY	A	P		4	1- 0
1948	NY	A	P		1	0- 0
1949	STL	A	P		30	1- 7
1950	STL	A	P	32	33	7- 5
1951	STL	A	P		15	2- 5
	WAS	A	P		11	1- 7
	BRTR		.0		94	12-24

STARR, WILLIAM "CHICK"
B.FEB.16,1911 BROOKLYN,N.Y.

YR	CL	LEA	POS	GP	G	REC
1935	WAS	A	C		12	.208
1936	WAS	A	C		1	.000
	BRTR				13	.208

STARRETTE, HERMAN PAUL
B.NOV.20,1938 STATESVILLE,N.C.

YR	CL	LEA	POS	GP	G	REC
1963	BAL	A	P		18	0- 1
1964	BAL	A	P		5	1- 0
1965	BAL	A	P		4	0- 0
	BRTR				27	1- 1

START, JOSEPH "ROCKS"
B.OCT.14,1843 NEW YORK,N.Y.
D.MAR.27,1927

YR	CL	LEA	POS	GP	G	REC
1871	MUT	NA	1		34	–
1872	MUT	NA	1		55	.274
1873	MUT	NA	1		54	–
1874	MUT	NA	1		64	–
1875	MUT	NA	1		69	.210
1876	MUT	N	1		56	.276
1877	HAR	N	1		60	.332
1878	CHI	N	1		60	.345
1879	PRO	N	1		65	.318
1880	PRO	N	1		79	.280
1881	PRO	N	1		79	.327
1882	PRO	N	1		82	.328
1883	PRO	N	1		87	.283
1884	PRO	N	1		90	.273
1885	PRO	N	1		99	.275
1886	WAS	N	1		29	.229
	BLTL				1062	–

STATON, JOSEPH "JOE"
B.MAR.8,1948 SEATTLE,WASH.

YR	CL	LEA	POS	GP	G	REC
1972	DET	A	1		6	.000
1973	DET	A	1		9	.235
	BLTL				15	.211

STATZ, ARNOLD JOHN "JIGGER"
B.OCT.20,1897 WAUKEGAN,ILL.

YR	CL	LEA	POS	GP	G	REC
1919	NY	N	2-0		21	.300
1920	NY	N	0		16	.133
	BOS	A	0		2	.000
1922	CHI	N	0		110	.297
1923	CHI	N	0		154	.319
1924	CHI	N	2-0		135	.277
1925	CHI	N	0		38	.257
1927	BRO	N	0		130	.274
1928	BRO	N	0		77	.234
	BRTR				683	.285
	BB	1922 (PART)				

STAUB, DANIEL JOSEPH "RUSTY"
B.APR.1,1944 NEW ORLEANS,LA.

YR	CL	LEA	POS	GP	G	REC
1963	HOU	N	1-0		150	.224
1964	HOU	N	1-0		89	.216
1965	HOU	N	1-0		131	.256
1966	HOU	N	1-0		153	.280
1967	HOU	N	0		149	.333
1968	HOU	N	1-0		161	.291
1969	MON	N	0		158	.302
1970	MON	N	0		160	.274
1971	MON	N	0		162	.311
1972	NY	N	0		66	.293
1973	NY	N	0		152	.279
1974	NY	N	0		151	.258
1975	NY	N	0		155	.282
1976	DET	A	0-0		161	.299
	BLTR				1998	.281

STAUFFER, CHARLES EDWARD
B.JAN.10,1898 EMSWORTH,PA.

YR	CL	LEA	POS	GP	G	REC
1923	CIN	N	P		1	0- 0
1925	STL	A	P		20	0- 1
	BRTR				21	0- 1

STEARNS, DANIEL ECKFORD
B.OCT.18,1861 BUFFALO,N.Y.
D.JUNE 28,1944

YR	CL	LEA	POS	GP	G	REC
1880	BUF	N	C-2-S-3-		21	.232
			0			
1881	DET	N	S		3	.100
1882	CIN	AA	1-2-S-0		49	.302
1883	BAL	AA	1-0		94	.248
1884	BAL	AA	1		101	.241
1885	BAL	AA	1		67	.186
	BUF	N	C-1-S		30	.200
1889	KC	AA	1		139	.288
	BLTR				504	.252

YR	CL	LEA	POS	GP	G	REC

STEARNS, JOHN HARDIN
B.AUG.21,1951 DENVER,COL.

YR	CL	LEA	POS	GP	G	REC
1974	PHI	N	C		1	.500
1975	NY	N	C		59	.189
1976	NY	N	C		32	.262
	BRTR				92	.219

STEARNS, WILLIAM

1871	OLY	NA	P		2	2- 0
1872	NAT	NA	P		11	0-10
1873	NAT	NA	P		31	7-24
1874	HAR	NA	P-O	18	32	2-16
						-
1875	NAT	NA	P-O	14	19	2-12
						-
				76	95	13-62
						-

STECHER, CHARLES
B.BORDENTOWN,N.J.

1890	ATH	AA	P		10	0- 7

STEDROUSKE
B.TROY,N.Y.

1879	CHI	N	2-3		4	.083

STEELE, ELMER RAE
B.MAY 17,1886 MUITEZSKILL,N.Y.
D.MAR.9,1966 RHINEBECK,N.Y.

1907	BOS	A	P		4	0- 1
1908	BOS	A	P		16	5- 7
1909	BOS	A	P		15	4- 2
1910	PIT	N	P		3	0- 3
1911	PIT	N	P		31	9- 9
	BRO	N	P		5	0- 0
	BBTR				74	18-22

STEELE, ROBERT WESLEY
B.JAN.5,1895 VANKLEEK HILL,ONT.
CANADA
D.JAN.27,1962

1916	STL	N	P		29	5-15
1917	STL	N	P		12	1- 3
	PIT	N	P	27	33	5-11
1918	PIT	N	P		10	2- 3
	NY	N	P		12	3- 5
1919	NY	N	P		1	0- 1
	BBTL			91	97	16-38

STEELE, WILLIAM MITCHELL
"BIG BILL"
B.OCT.5,1885 MILFORD,PA.
D.OCT.19,1949

1910	STL	N	P		9	4- 4
1911	STL	N	P		43	18-19
1912	STL	N	P	40	41	9-13
1913	STL	N	P		12	4- 4
1914	STL	N	P		17	1- 2
	BRO	N	P		8	1- 1
	BRTR			129	130	37-43

STEELMAN, MORRIS JAMES
"FARMER"
B.JUNE 29,1875 MILLVILLE,N.J.
D.SEPT.16,1944

1899	LOU	N	C		5	.062
1900	BRO	N	C		1	.000
1901	BRO	N	C		1	.333
	PHI	A	C		27	.267
1902	PHI	A	C-O		10	.187
	TR				44	.220

STEEN, WILLIAM JOHN
B.NOV.11,1887 PITTSBURGH,PA.

1912	CLE	A	P		26	9- 8
1913	CLE	A	P		22	4- 5
1914	CLE	A	P		30	9-14
1915	CLE	A	P		10	0- 4
	DET	A	P		20	6- 1
	BRTR				108	28-32

STEENGRAFE, MILTON HENRY
B.MAY 26,1900 SAN FRANCISCO,CAL

1924	CHI	A	P		3	0- 0
1926	CHI	A	P		13	1- 2
	BRTR				16	1- 2

STEERE, FRED EUGENE
B.AUG.16,1872 S.SCITUATE,R.I.
D.MAR.13,1942

1894	PIT	N	S		10	.184

STEEVENS, MORRIS DALE
B.OCT.7,1940 SALEM,ILL.

1962	CHI	N	P		12	0- 1
1964	PHI	N	P		4	0- 0
1965	PHI	N	P		6	0- 1
	BLTL				22	0- 2

STEIN, EDWARD F.
B.SEPT.5,1869 DETROIT,MICH.
D.MAY 10,1928

1890	CHI	N	P		18	11- 6
1891	CHI	N	P		13	6- 6
1892	BRO	N	P		45	27-18
1893	BRO	N	P		35	19-14
1894	BRO	N	P		41	26-14
1895	BRO	N	P		28	15-13
1896	BRO	N	P		17	3- 7
1898	BRO	N	P		3	0- 2
					200	107-80

STEIN, IRVIN MICHAEL
B.MAY 21,1911 MADISONVILLE,LA.

1932	PHI	A	P		1	0- 0
	BRTR					

STEIN, JUSTIN MARION
B.AUG.9,1913 ST.LOUIS,MO.

1938	PHI	N	2-3		11	.256
	CIN	N	2-S		11	.333
	BRTR				22	.281

STEIN, WILLIAM ALLEN "BILL"
B.JAN.21,1947 BATTLE CREEK,MICH.

1972	STL	N	3-O		14	.314
1973	STL	N	1-3-O		32	.218
1974	CHI	A	3		13	.279
1975	CHI	A	2-3-O-D		76	.270
1976	CHI	A	1-2-S-3-O		117	.268
	BRTR				252	.268

STEINBACHER, HENRY JOHN
B.MAR.22,1913 SACRAMENTO,CAL.

1937	CHI	A	O		26	.260
1938	CHI	A	O		106	.331
1939	CHI	A	O		71	.171
	BLTR				203	.292

STEINBRENNER, EUGENE GASS
B.NOV.16,1892 PITTSBURGH,PA.
D.APR.25,1970 PITTSBURGH,PA.

1912	PHI	N	2		3	.100
	TR					

STEINECKE, WILLIAM ROBERT
B.FEB.7,1907 CINCINNATI,OHIO

1931	PIT	N	C		4	.000
	BRTR					

STEINEDER, RAYMOND J.
B.FEB.25,1897 VINELAND,N.J.

1923	PIT	N	P		15	2- 0
1924	PIT	N	P		5	0- 1
	PHI	N	P		9	1- 1
	BRTR				29	3- 2

STEINER, BENAJMIN SAUNDERS
"BEN"
B.JULY 28,1922 ALEXANDRIA,VA.

1945	BOS	A	2		78	.257
1946	BOS	A	3		3	.250
1947	DET	A	H		1	.000
	BLTR				82	.256

STEINER, JAMES HARRY "RED"
B.JAN.7,1915 LOS ANGELES,CAL.

1945	CLE	A	C		12	.143
	BOS	A	C		26	.207
	BLTR				38	.190

STEINFELDT, HARRY M.
B.SEPT.29,1877 ST.LOUIS,MO.
D.AUG.17,1914

1898	CIN	N	2-O		83	.289
1899	CIN	N	2-3		107	.242
1900	CIN	N	2-3		136	.247
1901	CIN	N	2-3		105	.250
1902	CIN	N	S-3-O		128	.276
1903	CIN	N	3		118	.312
1904	CIN	N	3		98	.244
1905	CIN	N	3		106	.271
1906	CHI	N	3		151	.327
1907	CHI	N	3		151	.266
1908	CHI	N	3		150	.241
1909	CHI	N	3		151	.252
1910	CHI	N	3		128	.252
1911	BOS	N	3		19	.254
	BRTR				1631	.267

STELLBAUER, WILLIAM JENNINGS
B.MAR.20,1894 BREMOND,TEX.
D.FEB.16,1974 HOUSTON,TEX.

1916	PHI	A	O		25	.270
	BRTR					

STELZLE, JACOB C.
(PLAYED UNDER NAME OF
JACOB C. STENZEL)

STELMASZEK, RICHARD FRANCIS
"RICH"
B.OCT.8,1948 CHICAGO,ILL.

1971	WAS	A	C		6	.000
1973	TEX	A	C		7	.111
	CAL	A	C		21	.154
1974	CHI	N	C		25	.227
	BLTR				59	.170

STEM, FREDERICK BOOTHE
B.SEPT.22,1885 OXFORD,N.C.
D.SEPT.5,1964 DARLINGTON,S.C.

1908	BOS	N	1		19	.278
1909	BOS	N	1		68	.208
	BLTR				87	.224

STEMMEYER, WILLIAM
"CANNON BALL"
B.MAY 6,1864 CLEVELAND,OHIO
D.MAY 4,1945

1885	BOS	N	P		2	1- 1
1886	BOS	N	P		41	22-18
1887	BOS	N	P		14	6- 8
1888	CLE	AA	P		3	0- 2
	BRTR				60	29-29

STENGEL, CHARLES DILLON "CASEY"
B.JULY 30,1890 KANSAS CITY,MO.
D.SEPT.29,1975 GLENDALE,CAL.

1912	BRO	N	O		17	.316
1913	BRO	N	O		124	.272
1914	BRO	N	O		126	.316
1915	BRO	N	O		132	.237
1916	BRO	N	O		127	.279
1917	BRO	N	O		150	.257
1918	PIT	N	O		39	.246
1919	PIT	N	O		89	.293
1920	PHI	N	O		129	.292
1921	PHI	N	O		24	.305
	NY	N	O		18	.227
1922	NY	N	O		84	.368
1923	NY	N	O		75	.339
1924	BOS	N	O		131	.280
1925	BOS	N	O		12	.077
	BLTL				1277	.284

NON-PLAYING MANAGER
BRO(N) 1934-36, BOS(N) 1938-43,
NY(A) 1949-60, NY(N) 1962-65

STENHOUSE, DAVID ROTCHFORD
"DAVE"
B.SEP.12,1933 WESTERLY,R.I.

1962	WAS	A	P		34	11-12
1963	WAS	A	P		16	3- 9
1964	WAS	A	P		26	2- 7
	BRTR				76	16-28

STENNETT, RENALDO ANTONIO
"RENNIE"
B.APR.5,1951 COLON,PANAMA

1971	PIT	N	2		50	.353
1972	PIT	N	2-S-O		109	.286
1973	PIT	N	2-S-O		128	.242
1974	PIT	N	2-O		157	.291
1975	PIT	N	2		148	.286
1976	PIT	N	2-S		157	.257
	BRTR				749	.277

YR	CL	LEA	POS	GP	G	REC

STENZEL, JACOB C.
(REAL NAME JACOB C. STELZLE)
B.JUNE 24,1867 CINCINNATI,OHIO
D.JAN.6,1919

YR	CL	LEA	POS	GP	G	REC
1890	CHI	N	C-O		11	.209
1893	PIT	N	O		2	.000
	PIT	N	O		51	.409
1894	PIT	N	O		131	.351
1895	PIT	N	O		131	.384
1896	PIT	N	O		112	.366
1897	BAL	N	O		131	.351
1898	STL	N	O		35	.254
	STL	N	O		105	.287
1899	STL	N	O		32	.270
	CIN	N	O		9	.321
	BRTR				750	.344

STEPHEN, LOUIS ROBERTS "LOU"
B.JULY 13,1944 PORTERVILLE,CAL.

YR	CL	LEA	POS	GP	G	REC
1968	MIN	A	P	2	1- 1	
	BRTR					

STEPHENS, BRYAN MARIS
B.JULY 14,1920 FAYETTEVILLE,ARK

YR	CL	LEA	POS	GP	G	REC
1947	CLE	A	P	31	5-10	
1948	STL	A	P	43	3- 6	
	BRTR			74	8-16	

STEPHENS, CLARENCE WRIGHT
B.AUG.19,1863 CINCINNATI,OHIO
D.FEB.28,1945

YR	CL	LEA	POS	GP	G	REC
1886	CIN	AA	P	1	1- 0	
1891	CIN	N	P	1	0- 1	
1892	CIN	N	P	2	0- 1	
	TR			4	1- 2	

STEPHENS, GEORGE BENAJMIN
B.SEPT.28,1867 ROMEO,MICH.
D.AUG.5,1896 ARMADA,MICH.

YR	CL	LEA	POS	GP	G	REC
1892	BAL	N	P	5	1- 0	
1893	WAS	N	P	9	1- 6	
1894	WAS	N	P	3	0- 3	
				17	2- 9	

STEPHENS, GLEN EUGENE "GENE"
B.JAN.20,1933 GRAVETTE,ARK.

YR	CL	LEA	POS	GP	G	REC
1952	BOS	A	O		21	.226
1953	BOS	A	O		78	.204
1955	BOS	A	O		109	.293
1956	BOS	A	O		104	.270
1957	BOS	A	O		120	.266
1958	BOS	A	O		134	.219
1959	BOS	A	O		92	.278
1960	BOS	A	O		35	.229
	BAL	A	O		84	.238
1961	BAL	A	O		32	.190
	KC	A	O		62	.208
1962	KC	A	H		5	.000
1963	CHI	A	O		6	.389
1964	CHI	A	O		82	.234
	BLTR				964	.240

STEPHENS, JAMES WALTER
B.DEC.10,1883 SALINEVILLE,OHIO
D.JAN.2,1965 OXFORD,ALA.

YR	CL	LEA	POS	GP	G	REC
1907	STL	A	C		58	.202
1908	STL	A	C		47	.200
1909	STL	A	C		79	.220
1910	STL	A	C		99	.241
1911	STL	A	C		70	.231
1912	STL	A	C		74	.249
	BRTR				427	.227

STEPHENS, VERNON DECATUR
"VERN" OR "JUNIOR"
B.OCT.23,1920 MC ALISTER,N.MEX.
D.NOV.4,1968 LONG BEACH,CAL.

YR	CL	LEA	POS	GP	G	REC
1941	STL	A	S		3	.500
1942	STL	A	S		145	.294
1943	STL	A	S-O		137	.289
1944	STL	A	S		145	.293
1945	STL	A	S-3		149	.289
1946	STL	A	S		115	.307
1947	STL	A	S		150	.279
1948	BOS	A	S		155	.269
1949	BOS	A	S		155	.290
1950	BOS	A	S		149	.295
1951	BOS	A	S-3		109	.300
1952	BOS	A	S-3		92	.254
1953	CHI	A	S-3		44	.186
	STL	A	3		46	.321
1954	BAL	A	3		101	.285
1955	BAL	A	3		3	.167
	CHI	A	3		22	.250
	BRTR				1720	.286

STEPHENSON, CHESTER EARL
"EARL"
B.JULY 31,1947 BENSON,N.C.

YR	CL	LEA	POS	GP	G	REC
1971	CHI	N	P	16	1- 0	
1972	MIL	A	P	35	3- 5	
	BLTL			51	4- 5	

STEPHENSON, JACKSON RIGGS
"RIGGS" OR "OLD HOSS"
B.JAN.5,1898 AKRON,ALA.

YR	CL	LEA	POS	GP	G	REC
1921	CLE	A	2		65	.330
1922	CLE	A	2-3		86	.339
1923	CLE	A	2		91	.319
1924	CLE	A	2		71	.371
1925	CLE	A	O		19	.296
1926	CHI	N	O		82	.338
1927	CHI	N	O		152	.344
1928	CHI	N	O		137	.324
1929	CHI	N	O		136	.362
1930	CHI	N	O		109	.367
1931	CHI	N	O		80	.319
1932	CHI	N	O		147	.324
1933	CHI	N	O		97	.329
1934	CHI	N	O		38	.216
	BRTR				1310	.336

STEPHENSON, JERRY JOSEPH
B.OCT.6,1943 DETROIT,MICH.

YR	CL	LEA	POS	GP	G	REC
1963	BOS	A	P	1	0- 0	
1965	BOS	A	P	15	1- 5	
1966	BOS	A	P	15	2- 5	
1967	BOS	A	P	8	3- 1	
1968	BOS	A	P	23	2- 8	
1969	SEA	A	P	2	0- 0	
1970	LA	N	P	3	0- 0	
	BLTR			67	8-19	

STEPHENSON, JOHN HERMAN
B.APP.13,1941 S.PORTSMOUTH,KY.

YR	CL	LEA	POS	GP	G	REC
1964	NY	N	3-O		37	.158
1965	NY	N	C-O		62	.215
1966	NY	N	C-O		63	.196
1967	CHI	N	C		18	.224
1968	CHI	N	H		2	.000
1969	SF	N	C-3		22	.222
1970	SF	N	C-O		23	.070
1971	CAL	A	C		98	.219
1972	CAL	A	C		66	.274
1973	CAL	A	C		60	.246
	BLTR				451	.216

STEPHENSON, JOSEPH CHESTER
B.JUNE 30,1921 DETROIT,MICH.

YR	CL	LEA	POS	GP	G	REC
1943	NY	N	C		9	.250
1944	CHI	N	C		4	.125
1947	CHI	A	C		16	.143
	BRTR				29	.179

STEPHENSON, REUBEN CRANDOL
"DUMMY"
B.SEPT.22,1869 PETERSBURG,N.J.
D.DEC.1,1924 TRENTON,N.J.

YR	CL	LEA	POS	GP	G	REC
1892	PHI	N	O		8	.277

STEPHENSON, ROBERT LOYD "BOBBY"
B.AUG.11,1928 BLAIR,OKLA.

YR	CL	LEA	POS	GP	G	REC
1955	STL	N	2-S-3		67	.243
	BRTR					

STEPHENSON, WALTER MC QUEEN
"TARZAN"
B.MAR.27,1913 SALUDA,N.C.

YR	CL	LEA	POS	GP	G	REC
1935	CHI	N	C		16	.385
1936	CHI	N	C		6	.083
1937	PHI	N	C		10	.261
	BRTR				32	.279

STERLING, JOHN A.
B.PHILADELPHIA,PA.

YR	CL	LEA	POS	GP	G	REC
1890	ATH	AA	P	1	0- 1	

STERLING, RANDALL WAYNE "RANDY"
B.APR.21,1951 KEY WEST,FLA.

YR	CL	LEA	POS	GP	G	REC
1974	NY	N	P	3	1- 1	
	BBTR					

STERRETT, CHARLES HURLBUT
"DUTCH"
B.OCT.1,1889 MILROY,PA.
D.DEC.9,1965 GLYNDON,MD.

YR	CL	LEA	POS	GP	G	REC
1912	NY	A	1-O		66	.265
1913	NY	A	C		21	.171
	BRTR				87	.253

STEUERNAGEL, GEORGE HENRY
(PLAYED UNDER NAME OF
GEORGE HENRY STARNAGLE)

STEVENS, CHARLES AUGUSTUS
"CHUCK"
B.JULY 10,1918 VAN HOUTEN,N.MEX

YR	CL	LEA	POS	GP	G	REC
1941	STL	A	1		4	.154
1946	STL	A	1		122	.248
1948	STL	A	1		85	.260
	BBTL				211	.251

STEVENS, EDWARD LEE "ED"
B.JAN.12,1925 GALVESTON,TEX.

YR	CL	LEA	POS	GP	G	REC
1945	BRO	N	1		55	.274
1946	BRO	N	1		103	.242
1947	BRO	N	1		5	.154
1948	PIT	N	1		128	.254
1949	PIT	N	1		67	.262
1950	PIT	N	1		17	.196
	BLTL				375	.252

STEVENS, JAMES ARTHUR
B.AUG.25,1889 WILLIAMSBURG,MD.
D.SEPT.25,1966 BALTIMORE,MD.

YR	CL	LEA	POS	GP	G	REC
1914	WAS	A	P	2	0- 0	
	BRTR					

STEVENS, R. C.
B.JULY 22,1934 MOULTRIE,GA.

YR	CL	LEA	POS	GP	G	REC
1958	PIT	N	1		59	.267
1959	PIT	N	1		3	.286
1960	PIT	N	1		9	.000
1961	WAS	A	1		33	.129
	BLTR				104	.210

STEVENS, ROBERT JORDAN
B.APR.17,1910 CHEVY CHASE,MD.

YR	CL	LEA	POS	GP	G	REC
1931	PHI	N	S		12	.343
	BLTR					

STEWART, ASA "ACE"
B.FEB.14,1869 TERRE HAUTE,IND.
D.APR.17,1912

YR	CL	LEA	POS	GP	G	REC
1895	CHI	N	2		97	.244
	BRTR					

STEWART, CHARLES EUGENE "TUFFY"
B.JULY 31,1883 CHICAGO,ILL.
D.NOV.18,1934

YR	CL	LEA	POS	GP	G	REC
1913	CHI	N	O		9	.125
1914	CHI	N	H		1	.000
	BLTL				10	.111

STEWART, EDWARD PERRY "BUD"
B.JUNE 15,1916 SACRAMENTO,CAL.

YR	CL	LEA	POS	GP	G	REC
1941	PIT	N	O		73	.267
1942	PIT	N	2-3-O		82	.219
1948	NY	A	H		6	.000
	WAS	A	O		118	.279
1949	WAS	A	O		118	.284
1950	WAS	A	O		118	.267
1951	CHI	A	O		95	.276
1952	CHI	A	O		92	.267
1953	CHI	A	O		53	.271
1954	CHI	A	O		18	.077
	BLTR				773	.268

STEWART, FRANK
B.SEPT.8,1906 MINNEAPOLIS,MINN.

YR	CL	LEA	POS	GP	G	REC
1927	CHI	A	P	1	0- 1	
	BRTR					

STEWART, GLEN WELDON "GABBY"
B.SEPT.29,1914 TULLAHOMA,TENN.

YR	CL	LEA	POS	GP	G	REC
1940	NY	N	S-3		15	.138
1943	PHI	N	C-1-2-S		110	.211
1944	PHI	N	2-S-3		118	.220
	BRTR				243	.213

STEWART, JAMES FRANKLIN "JIMMY"
B.JUNE 11,1939 OPELIKA,ALA.

YR	CL	LEA	POS	GP	G	REC
1963	CHI	N	2-S		13	.297
1964	CHI	N	2-S-3-O		132	.253
1965	CHI	N	S-O		116	.223
1966	CHI	N	2-S-3-O		57	.178
1967	CHI	N	H		6	.167
	CHI	A	2-S-O		24	.167
1969	CIN	N	2-S-3-O		119	.253
1970	CIN	N	C-1-2-S-O		101	.267
1971	CIN	N	2-3-O		80	.232
1972	HOU	N	1-2-3-O		68	.219
1973	HOU	N	2-3-O		61	.191
	BBTR				777	.237

YR	CL LEA POS	GP	G	REC

STEWART, JOHN FRANKLIN "STUFFY"
B.JAN.31,1896 LAKE CITY,FLA.

YR	CL LEA POS	GP	G	REC
1916	STL N 2		9	.176
1917	STL N 2		13	.000
1921	STL A H		3	.333
1922	PIT N 2		3	.154
1923	BRO N 2		4	.364
1925	WAS A 2-3		7	.353
1926	WAS A 2		62	.270
1927	WAS A 2		56	.240
1929	WAS A 2		22	.000
	BRTR		179	.238

STEWART, JOSEPH LAWRENCE "ACE"
B.MAR.11,1879 MONROE,N.C.
D.FEB.9,1913 YOUNGSTOWN,OHIO

1904	BOS N P		2	0- 0
	TR			

STEWART, MARK
B.OCT.11,1889 PARIS,TENN.
D.JAN.17,1932

1913	CIN N C		1	.000
	BLTR			

STEWART, VESTON GOFF "BUNKY"
B.JAN.7,1931 NEW BERN,N.C.

1952	WAS A P		1	0- 0
1953	WAS A P		2	0- 2
1954	WAS A P		29	0- 2
1955	WAS A P		7	0- 0
1956	WAS A P	33	34	5- 7
	BLTL	72	73	5-11

STEWART, WALTER CLEVELAND "LEFTY"
B.SEPT.23,1900 SPARTA,TENN.
D.SEPT.26,1974 KNOXVILLE,TENN.

1921	DET A P		3	0- 0
1927	STL A P	27	28	8-11
1928	STL A P		29	7- 9
1929	STL A P		23	9- 6
1930	STL A P		35	20-12
1931	STL A P		36	14-17
1932	STL A P		41	15-19
1933	WAS A P-2	34	35	15- 6
				.143
1934	WAS A P	24	25	7-11
1935	STL A P		1	0- 1
	CLE A P		24	6- 6
	BRTL	279	282	101-98
				.204

STEWART, WALTER NESBITT "NEB"
B.MAY 21,1918 S.CHARLESTON,OHIO

1940	PHI N P		10	.129
	BBTR			

STEWART, WILLIAM MACKLIN "MACK"
B.SEPT.23,1913 STEVENSON,ALA.
D.MAR.21,1960 MACON,GA.

1944	CHI N P		8	0- 0
1945	CHI N P		16	0- 1
	BRTR		24	0- 1

STEWART, WILLIAM WAYNE "BILL"
B.APR.15,1929 BAY CITY,MICH.

1955	KC A A		11	.111
	BRTR			

STIELY, FREDERICK WARREN
B.JUNE 1,1901 VALLEY VIEW,PA.

1929	STL A P		1	1- 0
1930	STL A P	4	5	0- 1
1931	STL A P		4	0- 0
	BLTL	9	10	1- 1

STIGMAN, RICHARD LEWIS "DICK"
B.JAN.24,1936 NIMROD,MINN.

1960	CLE A P		41	5-11
1961	CLE A P		22	2- 5
1962	MIN A P		40	12- 5
1963	MIN A P		33	15-15
1964	MIN A P		32	6-15
1965	MIN A P		33	4- 2
1966	BOS A P		34	2- 1
	BRTL		235	46-54

STILES, ROLLAND MAYS "LENA"
B.NOV.17,1906 RATCLIFF,ARK.

1930	STL A P		20	3- 6
1931	STL A P		34	3- 1
1933	STL A P		31	3- 7
	BRTR		85	9-14

STILLMAN, ROYLE ELDEN
B.JAN.2,1951 SANTA MONICA,CAL.

1975	BAL A D		13	.429
1976	BAL A 1		20	.091
	BLTL		33	.222

STILLWELL, RONALD ROY "RON"
B.DEC.3,1939 LOS ANGELES,CAL.

1961	WAS A S		8	.125
1962	WAS A 2-S		6	.273
	BRTR		14	.211

STIMMEL, ARCHIBALD MAY "LUMBAGO"
B.MAY 30,1873 WOODSBORO,MD.
D.AUG.18,1958

1900	CIN N P		2	1- 1
1901	CIN N P		20	4-14
1902	CIN N P		4	0- 4
	BRTR		26	5-19

STIMSON, CARL REMUS
B.JULY 18,1894 HAMBURG,IOWA
D.NOV.9,1939

1923	BOS A P		2	0- 0
	BBTR			

STINE, HARRY C.
B.FEB.20,1864 SHENANDOAH,PA.
D.JUNE 5,1924

1890	ATH AA P		1	0- 1

STINE, LEE ELBERT
B.NOV.17,1913 STILLWATER,OKLA.

1934	CHI A P		4	0- 0
1935	CHI A P		1	0- 0
1936	CIN N P		40	3- 8
1938	NY A P		4	0- 0
	BRTR		49	3- 8

STINSON, GORRELL ROBERT "BOB"
B.OCT.11,1945 ELKIN,N.C.

1969	LA N C		4	.375
1970	LA N C		4	.000
1971	STL N C-O		17	.211
1972	HOU N C-O		27	.171
1973	MON N C-3		48	.261
1974	MON N C		38	.172
1975	KC A C-1-2-O		63	.265
1976	KC A C		79	.263
	BBTR		280	.244
	BR 1969			

STIRES, GARRETT
B.OCT.13,1849 HUNTERDON CO.,N.J
D.JUNE 13,1933

1871	ROK NA O		25	-

STIRNWEISS, GEORGE HENRY "SNUFFY"
B.OCT.26,1919 NEW YORK,N.Y.
D.SEPT.15,1958

1943	NY A 2-S		83	.219
1944	NY A 2		154	.319
1945	NY A 2		152	.309
1946	NY A 2-S-3		129	.251
1947	NY A 2		148	.256
1948	NY A 2		141	.252
1949	NY A 2-3		70	.261
1950	NY A 2		7	.000
	STL A 2-S-3		93	.218
1951	CLE A 2-3		50	.216
1952	CLE A 3		1	.000
	BRTR		1028	.268

STIVETTS, JOHN ELMER "HAPPY JACK"
B.MAR.31,1868 ASHLAND,PA.
D.APR.18,1930 ASHLAND,PA.

1889	STL AA P	25	26	12- 7
1890	STL AA P	49	67	31-20
1891	STL AA P-O	66	85	31-21
				.305
1892	BOS N P-O	47	64	33-14
				.300
1893	BOS N P	33	41	21-12
1894	BOS N P	41	57	25-14
1895	BOS N P	34	38	16-16
1896	BOS N P	39	59	22-13
1897	BOS N P-O	26	49	12- 4
				.388
1898	BOS N P-O	1	27	0- 1
				.252
1899	CLE N P	6	18	0- 4
	BRTR	367	531	203-126
				.305

STOBBS, CHARLES KLEIN "CHUCK"
B.JULY 2,1929 WHEELING,W.VA.

1947	BOS A P		4	0- 1
1948	BOS A P		6	0- 0
1949	BOS A P		26	11- 6
1950	BOS A P		32	12- 7
1951	BOS A P		34	10- 9
1952	CHI A P		38	7-12
1953	WAS A P		27	11- 8
1955	WAS A P		31	11-11
	WAS A P		4	4-14
1956	WAS A P	37	38	15-15
1957	WAS A P		42	8-20
1958	WAS A P		19	2- 6
	STL N P		17	1- 3
1959	WAS A P		41	1- 8
1960	WAS A P		40	12- 7
1961	MIN A P		24	2- 3
	BLTL	459	460	107-130

STOCK, MILTON JOSEPH "MILT"
B.JULY 11,1893 CHICAGO,ILL.

1913	NY N S		7	.176
1914	NY N 3		115	.263
1915	PHI N 3		69	.260
1916	PHI N S-3		132	.281
1917	PHI N S-3		150	.264
1918	PHI N 3		123	.274
1919	STL N 2-3		135	.307
1920	STL N 3		155	.319
1921	STL N 3		149	.307
1922	STL N S-3		151	.304
1923	STL N 2-3		151	.289
1924	BRO N 3		142	.242
1925	BRO N 2-3		146	.328
1926	BRO N 2		3	.000
	BRTR		1628	.289

STOCK, WESLEY GAY "WES"
B.APR.10,1934 LONGVIEW,WASH.

1959	BAL A P		7	0- 0
1960	BAL A P		17	2- 2
1961	BAL A P		35	5- 0
1962	BAL A P		53	3- 2
1963	BAL A P		47	7- 0
1964	BAL A P		14	2- 0
	KC A P		50	6- 3
1965	KC A P		62	0- 4
1966	KC A P		35	2- 2
1967	KC A P		1	0- 0
	BRTR		321	27-13

STOCKSDALE, OTIS H.
B.AUG.7,1871 CARROLL CO.,MD.

1893	WAS N P		12	2- 8
1894	WAS N P	16	19	5- 8
1895	WAS N P		20	5-10
	BOS N P-1	7	8	2- 2
				.308
1896	BAL N P		2	0- 0
	BRTR		57	61	14-28
				.323

STOCKWELL, LEONARD C.
B.AUG.25,1859 CORDOVA,ILL.
D.SEPT.15,1904

1879	CLE N O		2	.000
1884	LOU AA C-O		2	.111
1890	CLE N O		2	.286
	TR		6	.136

STODDARD

1875	ATL NA O		2	-

STODDARD, TIMOTHY PAUL "TIM"
B.JAN.24,1953 E.CHICAGO,IND.

1975	CHI A P		1	0- 0
	BRTR			

STOKES, ALBERT JOHN
B.JAN.1,1900 CHICAGO,ILL.

1925	BOS A C		17	.212
1926	BOS A C		30	.163
	BRTR		47	.181

STOKES, ARTHUR MELTON
B.SEPT.13,1897 EMMITSBURG,MD.
D.JUNE 3,1962

1925	PHI A P		12	1- 1
	BRTR			

STONE, CHARLES RICHARD "DICK"
B.DEC.5,1911 OKLAHOMA CITY,OKLA

1945	WAS A P		3	0- 0
	BLTL			

YR	CL	LEA	POS	GP	G	REC

STONE, DARRAH DEAN
"DEAN"
B.SEP.1,1930 MOLINE,ILL.

1953	WAS	A	P		3	0- 1
1954	WAS	A	P		31	12-10
1955	WAS	A	P		43	6-13
1956	WAS	A	P	41	42	5- 7
1957	WAS	A	P		3	0- 0
	BOS	A	P		17	1- 3
1959	STL	N	P		18	0- 1
1962	HOU	N	P		15	3- 2
	CHI	A	P		27	1- 0
1963	BAL	A	P		17	1- 2
	BLTL	215	216	29-39

STONE, DWIGHT ELY
B.AUG.2,1886 HOLT CO.,NEB.

1913	STL	A	P		18	2- 6
1914	KC	F	P		39	7-14
	BRTR			57	9-20

STONE, EDWIN ARNOLD
B.OCT.9,1897 HUDSON FALLS,N.Y.
D.JULY 29,1948

1923	PIT	N	P		9	0- 1
1924	PIT	N	P		26	4- 2
	BRTL			35	4- 3

STONE, EUGENE DANIEL "GENE"
B.JAN.16,1944 BURBANK,CAL.

| 1969 | PHI | N | 1 | | 18 | .214 |
| | BLTL | | | | | |

STONE, GEORGE HEARD
B.JULY 9,1946 RUSTON,LA.

1967	ATL	N	P		2	0- 0
1968	ATL	N	P		17	7- 4
1969	ATL	N	P		36	13-10
1970	ATL	N	P		35	11-11
1971	ATL	N	P	27	30	6- 8
1972	ATL	N	P	31	33	6-11
1973	NY	N	P	27	28	12- 3
1974	NY	N	P		15	2- 7
1975	NY	N	P		13	3- 3
	BLTL	203	209	60-57

STONE, GEORGE ROBERT
B.SEP.3,1876 CLINTON,IOWA
D.JAN.5,1945

1903	BOS	A	H		2	.000
1905	STL	A	O		154	.296
1906	STL	A	O		154	.358
1907	STL	A	O		155	.320
1908	STL	A	O		148	.281
1909	STL	A	O		83	.287
1910	STL	A	O		152	.256
	BLTL			848	.301

STONE, HARRY RONALD "RON"
B.SEP.9,1942 CORNING,CAL.

1966	KC	A	1-O		26	.273
1969	PHI	N	O		103	.239
1970	PHI	N	1-O		123	.262
1971	PHI	N	1-O		95	.227
1972	PHI	N	O		41	.167
	BLTL			388	.241

STONE, JOHN VERNON "ROCKY"
B.AUG.23,1918 REDDING,CAL.

| 1943 | CIN | N | P | | 13 | 0- 1 |
| | BRTR | | | | | |

STONE, JOHN THOMAS "JONATHAN"
B.OCT.10,1905 MULBERRY,TENN.
D.NOV.30,1955 SHELBYVILLE,TENN.

1928	DET	A	O		26	.354
1929	DET	A	O		51	.260
1930	DET	A	O		126	.313
1931	DET	A	O		147	.327
1932	DET	A	O		145	.297
1933	DET	A	O		148	.280
1934	WAS	A	O		113	.315
1935	WAS	A	O		125	.315
1936	WAS	A	O		123	.341
1937	WAS	A	O		139	.330
1938	WAS	A	O		56	.244
	BLTR			1199	.314

STONE, STEVEN MICHAEL "STEVE"
B.JULY 14,1947 EUCLID,OHIO

1971	SF	N	P		24	5- 9
1972	SF	N	P		27	6- 8
1973	CHI	A	P	36	39	6-11
1974	CHI	N	P	38	42	8- 6
1975	CHI	N	P	33	34	12- 8
1976	CHI	N	P		17	3- 6
	BRTR	175	183	40-48

STONE, WILLIAM ARTHUR "TIGE"
B.SEPT.18,1901 MACON,GA.
D.JAN.1,1960

| 1923 | STL | N | P-O | 1 | 5 | 0- 0 |
| | | | | | | 1.000 |

STONEHAM, JOHN ANDREW
B.NOV.8,1908 WOOD RIVER,ILL.

| 1933 | CHI | A | O | | 10 | .120 |
| | BLTR | | | | | |

STONEMAN, WILLIAM HAMBLY "BILL"
B.APR.7,1944 OAK PARK,ILL.

1967	CHI	N	P		28	2- 4
1968	CHI	N	P		18	0- 1
1969	MON	N	P		42	11-19
1970	MON	N	P	40	42	7-15
1971	MON	N	P	39	41	17-16
1972	MON	N	P	36	40	12-14
1973	MON	N	P		29	4- 8
1974	CAL	A	P		13	1- 8
	BRTR	245	253	54-85

STONER, ULYSSES SIMPSON GRANT
"LIL"
B.FEB.28,1899 BOWIE,TEX.
D.JUNE 26,1966 ENID,OKLA.

1922	DET	A	P		17	4- 4
1924	DET	A	P	36	37	11-11
1925	DET	A	P		34	10- 9
1926	DET	A	P		32	7-10
1927	DET	A	P		38	10-13
1928	DET	A	P		36	5- 8
1929	DET	A	P		24	3- 3
1930	PIT	N	P		5	0- 0
1931	PHI	N	P		7	0- 0
	BRTR	229	230	50-58

STORIE, HOWARD EDWARD "SPONGE"
B.MAY 15,1911 PITTSFIELD,MASS.
D.JULY 27,1968 PITTSFIELD,MASS.

1931	BOS	A	C		6	.118
1932	BOS	A	C		6	.375
	BRTR			12	.200

STORKE, ALAN MARSHALL
B.SEPT.27,1884 AUBURN,N.Y.
D.MAR.18,1910

1906	PIT	N	S-3		5	.250
1907	PIT	N	1-3		102	.258
1908	PIT	N	1		56	.252
1909	PIT	N	1		32	.254
	STL	N	S		48	.282
	TR			243	.260

STORTI, LINDO IVAN
B.DEC.5,1906 SANTA MONICA,CAL.

1930	STL	A	2		7	.321
1931	STL	A	3		86	.220
1932	STL	A	3		53	.259
1933	STL	A	2-3		70	.195
	BBTR	216			.227

STOTTLEMYRE, MELVIN LEON "MEL"
B.NOV.13,1941 HAZELTON,MO.

1964	NY	A	P	13	14	9- 3
1965	NY	A	P		37	20- 9
1966	NY	A	P		37	12-20
1967	NY	A	P		36	15-15
1968	NY	A	P		36	21-12
1969	NY	A	P		39	20-14
1970	NY	A	P	37	38	15-13
1971	NY	A	P		35	16-12
1972	NY	A	P	36	37	14-18
1973	NY	A	P		38	16-16
1974	NY	A	P	16	19	6- 7
	BRTR	360	366	164-139

STOUCH, THOMAS C.
B.PHILADELPHIA,PA.
D.OCT.7,1956

| 1898 | LOU | N | 2 | | 4 | .377 |

STOUT, ALLYN MC CLELLAND
"FISH HOOK"
B.OCT.31,1904 PEORIA,ILL.
D.DEC.22,1974 SIKESTOWN,MO.

1931	STL	N	P		30	6- 0
1932	STL	N	P		36	4- 5
1933	STL	N	P		1	0- 0
	CIN	N	P		23	2- 3
1934	CIN	N	P		41	6- 8
1935	NY	N	P		40	1- 4
1943	BOS	N	P		9	1- 0
	BRTR			180	20-20

STOVALL, GEORGE THOMAS
"FIREBRAND"
B.NOV.23,1878 INDEPENDENCE,MO.
D.NOV.5,1951

1904	CLE	A	1		51	.297
1905	CLE	A	1-2		111	.272
1906	CLE	A	1-2-3		116	.270
1907	CLE	A	1		124	.236
1908	CLE	A	1		138	.292
1909	CLE	A	1		145	.246
1910	CLE	A	1		142	.261
1911	CLE	A	M-1		126	.271
1912	STL	A	M-1		115	.254
1913	STL	A	M-1		89	.287
1914	KC	F	M-1		122	.270
1915	KC	F	M-1		130	.233
	BRTR			1409	.264

STOVALL, JESSE CRAMER "SCOUT"
B.JULY 24,1875 INDEPENDENCE,MO.
D.JULY 12,1955

1903	CLE	A	P		6	5- 1
1904	DET	A	P	21	23	2-13
	BLTR	27	29	7-14

STOVEY, HARRY DUFFIELD
(REAL NAME
HARRY DIFFIELD STOWE)
B.DEC.26,1856 PHILADELPHIA,PA.
D.SEPT.20,1937 NEW BEDFORD,MASS

1880	WOR	N	P-1	1	81	0- 0
			O			.258
1881	WOR	N	1-O		74	.270
1882	WOR	N	1-O		84	.288
1883	ATH	AA	P-C-	1	93	0- 0
			1-O			.318
1884	ATH	AA	1-O		106	.404
1885	ATH	AA	1-O		112	.342
1886	ATH	AA	1-O		123	.317
1887	ATH	AA	1-O		124	.402
1888	ATH	AA	O		130	.318
1889	ATH	AA	O		138	.330
1890	BOS	P	O		118	.308
1891	BOS	N	O		133	.279
1892	BOS	N	O		38	.171
	BAL	N	O		74	.374
1893	BAL	N	O		8	.167
	BRO	N	O		45	.266
	BRTR	2	1481	0- 0
						.320

STOVIAK, RAYMOND THOMAS
B.JUNE 7,1915 SCOTTDALE,PA.

| 1938 | PHI | N | O | | 10 | .000 |
| | BLTL | | | | | |

STOWE, HAROLD RUDOLPH "HAL"
B.AUG.29,1937 GASTONIA,N.C.

| 1960 | NY | A | P | | 1 | 0- 0 |
| | BLTL | | | | | |

STOWE, HARRY DUFFIELD
(PLAYED UNDER NAME OF
HARRY DUFFIELD STOVEY)

STRAHLER, MICHAEL WAYNE "MIKE"
B.MAR.14,1947 CHICAGO,ILL.

1970	LA	N	P		6	1- 1
1971	LA	N	P		6	0- 0
1972	LA	N	P		19	1- 2
1973	DET	A	P		22	4- 5
	BRTR			53	6- 8

STRAHS, RICHARD BERNARD "DICK"
B.DEC.4,1926 EVANSTON,ILL.

| 1954 | CHI | A | P | | 9 | 0- 0 |
| | BLTR | | | | | |

STRAMPE, ROBERT EDWIN "BOB"
B.JUNE 13,1950 JANESVILLE,WIS.

| 1972 | DET | A | P | | 7 | 0- 0 |
| | BBTR | | | | | |

STRAND, PAUL EDWARD
B.DEC.19,1894 CARBONADO,WASH.
D.JULY 2,1974 SALT LAKE CITY,
UTAH

1913	BOS	N	P		7	0- 0
1914	BOS	N	P	16	18	6- 2
1915	BOS	N	P	6	24	1- 1
1924	PHI	A	O		47	.228
	BRTL	29	96	7- 3
						.215

YR	CL	LEA	POS	GP	G	REC

STRANDS, JOHN LAWRENCE "LARRY"
B.1889 CHICAGO,ILL.
D.JAN.19,1957

YR	CL	LEA	POS	GP	G	REC
1915	NEW	F	2-3		34	.187
	BRTR					

STRANDS, LEWIS

| 1915 | CHI | F | 2 | | 1 | .000 |

STRANG, SMAUEL NICKLIN
(REAL NAME
SAMUEL STRANG NICKLIN)
B.DEC.16,1876 CHATTANOOGA,TENN.
D.MAR.13,1932

YR	CL	LEA	POS	GP	G	REC
1896	LOU	N	S		14	.222
1900	CHI	N	3		25	.276
1901	NY	N	2-3		135	.291
1902	CHI	A	3		137	.273
	CHI	N	2-3		3	.363
1903	BRO	N	3		135	.272
1904	BRO	N	2		76	.192
1905	NY	N	2-0		96	.259
1906	NY	N	2-0		104	.319
1907	NY	N	0		95	.252
1908	NY	N	3		22	.094
	BBTR				842	.266

STRANGE, ALAN COCHRANE "INKY"
B.NOV.7,1909 PHILADELPHIA,PA.

YR	CL	LEA	POS	GP	G	REC
1934	STL	A	S		127	.233
1935	STL	A	S		49	.231
	WAS	A	S		20	.185
1940	STL	A	2-0		54	.186
1941	STL	A	1-S-3		45	.232
1942	STL	A	2-S-3		19	.270
	BRTR				314	.223

STRATTON, ASA EVANS
B.FEB.10,1853 GRAFTON,MASS.
D.AUG.14,1925

| 1881 | WOR | N | S | | 1 | .250 |

STRATTON, C. SCOTT
B.OCT.2,1869 CAMPELLSBURG,KY.
D.MAR.6,1939

YR	CL	LEA	POS	GP	G	REC
1888	LOU	AA	P-O	34	65	10-17
						.266
1889	LOU	AA	P-O	19	62	3-14
						.280
1890	LOU	AA	P		54	34-15
1891	PIT	N	P	3		0- 2
	LOU	AA	P	22	33	6-12
1892	LOU	N	P	41	60	21-20
1893	LOU	N	P	38	58	12-24
						.252
1894	LOU	N	P-O	7	13	1- 3
						.202
	CHI	N	P	15	20	9- 6
1895	CHI	N	P	8		2- 3
	TR			241	376	98-116
						.280

STRATTON, EDWARD
B.BALTIMORE,MD.

| 1873 | MAR | NA | P-O | 3 | 4 | 0- 3 |
| | | | | | | - |

STRATTON, MONTY FRANKLIN PIERCE
B.MAY 21,1912 CELESTE,TEX.

YR	CL	LEA	POS	GP	G	REC
1934	CHI	A	P		1	0- 0
1935	CHI	A	P		5	1- 2
1936	CHI	A	P		16	5- 7
1937	CHI	A	P		22	15- 5
1938	CHI	A	P	26	27	15- 9
	BRTR			70	71	36-23

STRAUB, JOSEPH
B.JAN.19,1858 MILWAUKEE,WIS.

YR	CL	LEA	POS	GP	G	REC
1880	TRO	N	C		3	.231
1882	ATH	AA	C-O		8	.188
1883	COL	AA	C-1-0		27	.135
					38	.152

STRAUSS, JOSEPH
B.1844 HUNGARY
D.JUNE 25,1906

YR	CL	LEA	POS	GP	G	REC
1884	KC	U	C-2-3-0		15	.208
1885	LOU	AA	C-O		12	.167
1886	LOU	AA	C-O		77	.210
	BRO	AA	C-O		9	.235
	TR				103	.213

STREAKER, JOHN A.
(PLAYED UNDER NAME OF
JOHN A. STRICKER)

STREET, CHARLES EVARD "GABBY"
B.SEPT.30,1882 HUNTSVILLE,ALA.
D.FEB.6,1951

YR	CL	LEA	POS	GP	G	REC
1904	CIN	N	C		11	.121
1905	CIN	N	C		2	.000
	BOS	N	C		3	.167
	CIN	N	C		27	.247
1908	WAS	A	C		131	.206
1909	WAS	A	C		137	.211
1910	WAS	A	C		89	.203
1911	WAS	A	C		72	.222
1912	NY	A	C		28	.182
1931	STL	N	M-C		1	.000
	BRTR				501	.208

NON-PLAYING MANAGER
STL(N) 1930, 32-33, STL(A) 1938

STREIT, OSCAR W.
B.JULY 7,1873 FLORENCE,ALA.
D.OCT.10,1935

YR	CL	LEA	POS	GP	G	REC
1899	BOS	N	P		2	1- 0
1902	CLE	A	P		8	0- 7
					10	1- 7

STRELECKI, EDWARD HAROLD
B.APR.10,1905 NEWARK,N.J.
D.JAN.9,1968 NEWARK,N.J.

YR	CL	LEA	POS	GP	G	REC
1928	STL	A	P		22	0- 2
1929	STL	A	P		7	1- 1
1931	CIN	N	P		13	0- 0
	BRTR				42	1- 3

STREMMEL, PHILIP
B.APR.16,1880 ZANESVILLE,OHIO
D.DEC.26,1947

YR	CL	LEA	POS	GP	G	REC
1909	STL	A	P		2	0- 2
1910	STL	A	P		5	0- 3
					7	0- 5

STREULI, WALTER HERBERT "WALT"
B.SEPT.26,1935 MEMPHIS,TENN.

YR	CL	LEA	POS	GP	G	REC
1954	DET	A	C		1	.000
1955	DET	A	C		2	.250
1956	DET	A	C		3	.250
	BRTR				6	.250

STRICKER, JOHN A. "CUB"
(REAL NAME JOHN A. STREAKER)
B.JUNE 8,1859 PHILADELPHIA,PA.

YR	CL	LEA	POS	GP	G	REC
1882	ATH	AA	P-2-1	1	74	1- 0
			0			
						.203
1883	ATH	AA	C-2-3		89	.254
1884	ATH	AA	2		109	.236
1885	ATH	AA	2		106	.211
1887	CLE	AA	2		131	.333
1888	CLE	AA	2		126	.231
1889	CLE	N	2		136	.251
1890	CLE	P	2		127	.248
1891	BOS	AA	2		139	.225
1892	STL	N	2-S		28	.206
	BAL	N	2		72	.275
1893	WAS	N	2		59	.181
	BRTR			1	1196	1- 0
						.240

STRICKLAND, GEORGE BEVAN "BO"
B.JAN.10,1926 NEW ORLEANS,LA.

YR	CL	LEA	POS	GP	G	REC
1950	PIT	N	S-3		23	.111
1951	PIT	N	2-S		138	.216
1952	PIT	N	1-2-S-3		76	.177
	CLE	A	2-S		31	.216
1953	CLE	A	1-S		123	.284
1954	CLE	A	S		112	.213
1955	CLE	A	S		130	.209
1956	CLE	A	2-S-3		85	.211
1957	CLE	A	2-S-3		89	.234
1959	CLE	A	2-S-3		132	.238
1960	CLE	A	2-S-3		32	.167
	BRTR				971	.224

NON-PLAYING MANAGER
CLE(A) 1966

STRICKLAND, JAMES MICHAEL "JIM"
B.JUNE 12,1946 LOS ANGELES,CAL.

YR	CL	LEA	POS	GP	G	REC
1971	MIN	A	P		24	1- 0
1972	MIN	A	P		25	3- 1
1973	MIN	A	P		7	0- 1
1975	CLE	A	P		4	0- 0
	BLTL				60	4- 2

STRICKLAND, WILLIAM GOSS
B.MAR.29,1911 NASHVILLE,GA.

| 1937 | STL | A | P | | 9 | 0- 0 |
| | BRTR | | | | | |

STRICKLETT, ELMER GRIFFIN
"SPITBALL"
B.AUG.29,1876 GLASCO,KAN.
D.JUNE 7,1964 SANTZ CRUZ,CAL.

YR	CL	LEA	POS	GP	G	REC
1904	CHI	A	P		1	0- 1
1905	BRO	N	P		33	8-20
1906	BRO	N	P		41	14-18
1907	BRO	N	P	29	30	12-14
	TR			104	105	34-53

STRIEF, GEORGE ANDREW
B.OCT.16,1856 CINCINNATI,OHIO
D.APR.1,1946

YR	CL	LEA	POS	GP	G	REC
1879	CLE	N	2-0		71	.174
1882	PIT	AA	2-S		73	.202
1883	STL	AA	2-0		78	.211
1884	STL	AA	0		47	.193
	KC	U	2		14	.094
	PIT	U	2		15	.182
	CLE	N	3-0		8	.241
1885	ATH	AA	2-S-3		44	.270
					350	.197

STRIKE, JOHN
B.PHILADELPHIA,PA.

YR	CL	LEA	POS	GP	G	REC
1882	LOU	AA	C-1-2-S-		33	.142
			0			
1886	PHI	N	P		2	1- 1
				2	35	1- 1
						.134

STRIKER, WILBUR SCOTT "JAKE"
B.OCT.23,1933 CRANBERRY TWP.,O.

YR	CL	LEA	POS	GP	G	REC
1959	CLE	A	P		1	1- 0
1960	CHI	A	P		2	0- 0
	BLTL				3	1- 0

STRINCEVICH, NICHOLAS
MIHAILOVICH "NICK"
B.MAR.1,1916 GARY,IND.

YR	CL	LEA	POS	GP	G	REC
1940	BOS	N	P	32	33	4- 8
1941	BOS	N	P		3	0- 0
	PIT	N	P		12	1- 2
1942	PIT	N	P		7	0- 0
1944	PIT	N	P		40	14- 7
1945	PIT	N	P		36	16-10
1946	PIT	N	P		32	10-15
1947	PIT	N	P		32	1- 6
1948	PIT	N	P		3	0- 0
	PHI	N	P		6	0- 1
	BRTR			203	204	46-49

STRINGER, LOUIS BERNARD "LOU"
B.MAY 13,1917 GRAND RAPIDS,MICH

YR	CL	LEA	POS	GP	G	REC
1941	CHI	N	2-S		145	.246
1942	CHI	N	2-3		121	.236
1946	CHI	N	2-S-3		80	.244
1948	BOS	A	2		4	.091
1949	BOS	A	2		35	.268
1950	BOS	A	2-S-3		24	.294
	BRTR				409	.242

STRIPP, JOSEPH VALENTINE
"JERSEY JOE"
B.FEB.3,1903 HARRISON,N.J.

YR	CL	LEA	POS	GP	G	REC
1928	CIN	N	S-3-0		42	.288
1929	CIN	N	2-3		64	.214
1930	CIN	N	1-3		130	.306
1931	CIN	N	1-3		105	.324
1932	BRO	N	1-3		138	.303
1933	BRO	N	3		141	.277
1934	BRO	N	3		104	.315
1935	BRO	N	1-3-0		109	.306
1936	BRO	N	3		110	.317
1937	BRO	N	1-3		90	.243
1938	STL	N	3		54	.286
	BOS	A	3		59	.275
	BRTR				1146	.294

STROBEL, ALBERT IRVING "ALLIE"
B.JUNE 11,1884 BOSTON,MASS.
D.FEB.10,1955 HOLLYWOOD,FLA.

YR	CL	LEA	POS	GP	G	REC
1905	BOS	N	3-0		5	.105
1906	BOS	N	2		99	.202
	TR				104	.196

STROHMAYER, JOHN EMERY
B.OCT.13,1946 BELLE FOURCHE,S.D.

YR	CL	LEA	POS	GP	G	REC
1970	MON	N	P		42	3- 1
1971	MON	N	P		27	7- 5
1972	MON	N	P		48	1- 2
1973	MON	N	P		17	0- 1
	NY	N	P		7	0- 0
1974	NY	N	P		1	0- 0
	BRTR				142	11- 9

YR	CL	LEA	POS	GP	G	REC

STROM, BRENT TERRY
B.OCT.14,1948 SAN DIEGO,CAL.

YR	CL	LEA	POS	GP	G	REC
1972	NY	N	P		11	0- 3
1973	CLE	A	P		27	2-10
1975	SD	N	P		18	8- 8
1976	SD	N	P	36	38	12-16
	BRTL			92	94	22-37

STROMME, FLOYD MARVIN "ROCK"
B.AUG.1,1916 COPPERSTOWN,N.DAK.

1939	CLE	A	P		5	0- 1
	BRTR					

STRONER, JAMES M.
B.MAY 29,1904 CHICAGO,ILL.

1929	PIT	N	3		6	.375
	BRTR					

STROUD, EDWIN MARVIN "ED"
B.OCT.31,1939 LAPINE,ALA.

1966	CHI	A	O		12	.167
1967	CHI	A	O		20	.296
	WAS	A	O		87	.201
1968	WAS	A	O		105	.239
1969	WAS	A	O		123	.252
1970	WAS	A	O		129	.266
1971	CHI	A	O		53	.177
	BLTR				529	.237

STROUD, RALPH VIVIAN "SAILOR"
B.MAY 15,1885 IRONIA,N.J.

1910	DET	A	P		28	5- 9
1915	NY	N	P		32	12- 9
1916	NY	N	P		10	3- 2
	BRTR				70	20-20

STRUNK, AMOS AARON
B.NOV.22,1889 PHILADELPHIA,PA.

1908	PHI	A	O		12	.222
1909	PHI	A	O		11	.114
1910	PHI	A	O		16	.333
1911	PHI	A	O		74	.256
1912	PHI	A	O		120	.289
1913	PHI	A	O		93	.305
1914	PHI	A	O		122	.275
1915	PHI	A	1-O		132	.297
1916	PHI	A	O		150	.316
1917	PHI	A	O		148	.281
1918	BOS	A	O		114	.256
1919	BOS	A	O		48	.271
	PHI	A	O		60	.211
1920	PHI	A	O		57	.307
	CHI	A	O		52	.220
1921	CHI	A	O		121	.332
1922	CHI	A	O		92	.289
1923	CHI	A	O		54	.315
1924	CHI	A	O		1	.000
	PHI	A	O		30	.143
	BLTL				1507	.283

STRUSS, CLARENCE HERBERT "STEAMBOAT"
B.FEB.24,1912 CHICAGO,ILL.

1934	PIT	N	P		2	0- 1
	BRTR					

STRYKER, STERLING ALBERT "DUTCH"
B.JULY 29,1896 ATLANTIC
HIGHLANDS,N.J.
D.NOV.5,1964 RED BANK,N.J.

1924	BOS	N	P		20	3- 8
1926	BRO	N	P		2	0- 0
	BRTR				22	3- 8

STUART, JOHN DAVIS
B.APR.27,1901 CLINTON,TENN.
D.MAY 13,1970 CHARLESTON,W.VA.

1922	STL	N	P		2	0- 0
1923	STL	N	P		37	9- 5
1924	STL	N	P-3	28	30	9-11
						.204
1925	STL	N	P		15	2- 2
	BRTR			82	84	20-18
						.228

STUART, LUTHER LANE "LUKE"
B.MAY 23,1892 ALAMANCE CO.,N.C.
D.JUNE 15,1947 WINSTON-SALEM,
N.C.

1921	STL	A	2		3	.333
	BRTR					

STUART, MARLIN HENRY
B.AUG.8,1918 PARAGOULD,ARK.

1949	DET	A	P	14	15	0- 2
1950	DET	A	P		19	3- 1
1951	DET	A	P		29	4- 6
1952	DET	A	P		30	3- 2
	STL	A	P		12	1- 2
1953	STL	A	P		60	8- 2
1954	BAL	A	P		22	1- 2
	NY	A	P		10	3- 0
	BLTR			196	197	23-17

STUART, RICHARD LEE "DICK"
B.NOV.7,1932 SAN FRANCISCO,CAL.

1958	PIT	N	1		67	.268
1959	PIT	N	1-O		118	.297
1960	PIT	N	1		122	.260
1961	PIT	N	1-O		138	.301
1962	PIT	N	1		114	.228
1963	BOS	A	1		157	.261
1964	BOS	A	1		156	.279
1965	PHI	N	1-3		149	.234
1966	NY	N	1		31	.218
	LA	N	1		38	.264
1969	CAL	A	1		22	.157
	BRTR				1112	.264

STUART, WILLIAM ALEXANDER "CHAUNCEY"
B.DONORA,PA.

1895	PIT	N	S		19	.259
1899	NY	N	2		1	.000
					20	.250

STUBING, LAWRENCE GEORGE "LARRY"
B.MAR.31,1938 NEW YORK,N.Y.

1967	CAL	A	H		5	.000
	BLTL					

STUDLEY, SEYMOUR L. "WARHORSE"
B.WASHINGTON,D.C.
D.1874

1872	NAT	NA	O		5	.136

STUELAND, GEORGE ANTON
B.MAR.2,1899 RENWICK,IOWA

1921	CHI	N	P		2	0- 1
1922	CHI	N	P		35	9- 4
1923	CHI	N	P		6	0- 1
1925	CHI	N	P		2	0- 0
	BBTR				45	9- 6

STUFFEL, PAUL HARRINGTON
B.MAR.22,1927 CANTON,OHIO

1950	PHI	N	P		3	0- 0
1952	PHI	N	P		2	1- 0
1953	PHI	N	P		2	0- 0
	BRTR				7	1- 0

STULTZ, GEORGE IRVIN
B.JUNE 30,1873 LOUISVILLE,KY.

1894	BOS	N	P		1	1- 0

STUMP, JAMES GILBERT "JIM"
B.FEB.10,1932 LANSING,MICH.

1957	DET	A	P		6	1- 0
1959	DET	A	P		5	0- 0
	BRTR				11	1- 0

STUMPF, GEORGE FREDERICK
B.DEC.15,1910 NEW ORLEANS,LA.

1931	BOS	A	O		7	.250
1932	BOS	A	O		79	.201
1933	BOS	A	O		22	.341
1936	CHI	A	O		10	.273
	BLTL				118	.235

STUMPF, WILLIAM FREDERICK
B.MAR.21,1892 BALTIMORE,MD.
D.FEB.14,1966

1912	NY	A	S		40	.240
1913	NY	A	S		12	.207
	BRTR				52	.236

STURDIVANT, THOMAS VIRGIL "TOM"
B.APR.28,1930 GORDON,KAN.

1955	NY	A	P		33	1- 3
1956	NY	A	P		32	16- 8
1957	NY	A	P		28	16- 6
1958	NY	A	P		15	3- 6
1959	NY	A	P		7	0- 2
	KC	A	P	36	37	2- 6
1960	BOS	A	P		40	3- 3
1961	WAS	A	P		15	2- 6
	PIT	N	P		13	5- 2
1962	PIT	N	P		49	9- 5
1963	PIT	N	P		3	0- 0
	DET	A	P		28	1- 2
	KC	A	P		17	1- 2
1964	KC	A	P		3	0- 0
	NY	N	P		16	0- 0
	BLTR			335	336	59-51

STURDY, GUY A.
B.AUG.7,1899 SHERMAN,TEX.
D.MAY 4,1965 MARSHALL,TEX.

1927	STL	A	1		5	.429
1928	STL	A	1		54	.222
	BLTL				59	.288

STURGEON, ROBERT HARWOOD "BOB"
B.AUG.6,1920 CLINTON,IND.

1940	CHI	N	S		7	.190
1941	CHI	N	2-S-3		129	.245
1942	CHI	N	2-S-3		63	.247
1946	CHI	N	2-S		100	.296
1947	CHI	N	2-S-3		87	.254
1948	BOS	N	2-S-3		34	.218
	BPTR				420	.257

STURGIS, DEAN DONNELL
B.DEC.1,1893 UNIONTOWN,PA.
D.JUNE 4,1950

1914	PHI	A	C		4	.250
	BRTR					

STURM JOHN PETER JOSEPH
B.JAN.23,1916 ST.LOUIS,MO.

1941	NY	A	1		124	.239
	BLTL					

STUTZ, GEORGE "SATAN"
B.FEB.12,1893 PHILADELPHIA,PA.
D.DEC.29,1930

1926	PHI	N	S		6	.000
	BRTR					

STYLES, WILLIAM GRAVES "LENA"
B.NOV.27,1897 GURLEY,ALA.
D.MAR.14,1956

1919	PHI	A	C		8	.273
1920	PHI	A	C		24	.260
1921	PHI	A	C		4	.200
1930	CIN	N	C-1		7	.250
1931	CIN	N	C		34	.241
	BRTR				77	.249

STYNES, CORNELIUS W.
B.1869 ARLINGTON,MASS.
D.MAR.26,1944

1890	CLE	P	C		2	.000

SUAREZ, KENNETH RAYMOND "KEN"
B.APR.12,1943 TAMPA,FLA.

1966	KC	A	C		35	.145
1967	KC	A	C		39	.238
1968	CLE	A	C-2-3-O		17	.100
1969	CLE	A	O		36	.294
1971	CLE	A	C		50	.203
1972	TEX	A	C		25	.152
1973	TEX	A	C		93	.248
	BPTR				295	.227

SUAREZ, LUIS ABELARDO
B.AUG.24,1916 ALTO SONGO,CUBA

1944	WAS	A	3		1	.000
	BRTR					

SUCH, RICHARD STANLEY "DICK"
B.OCT.15,1944 SANFORD,N.C.

1970	WAS	A	P	21	22	1- 5
	BLTR					

SUCHE, CHARLES MORRIS
B.AUG.5,1915 SAN ANTONIO,TEX.

1938	CLE	A	P		1	0- 0
	BRTL					

YR	CL LEA POS	GP	G	REC

SUCHECKI, JAMES JOSEPH "JIM"
B.AUG.25,1927 CHICAGO,ILL.
1950	BOS A	P		4	0- 0
1951	STL A	P		29	0- 6
1952	PIT N	P		5	0- 0
	BRTR			38	0- 6

SUCK, ANTHONY
B.JUNE 11,1858 CHICAGO,ILL.
D.JAN.29,1895
1883	BUF N	C-O		2	.000
1884	CHI U	C-S-3-O		43	.149
	PIT U	C		10	.182
	BAL U	C		3	.300
				58	.156

SUDAKIS, WILLIAM PAUL "BILL"
B.MAR.27,1946 JOLIET,ILL.
1968	LA N	3		24	.276
1969	LA N	3		132	.234
1970	LA N	C-1-3-O		94	.264
1971	LA N	C-1-3-O		41	.193
1972	NY N	C-1		18	.143
1973	TEX N	C-1-3-O		82	.255
1974	NY A	C-1-3-O		89	.232
1975	CAL A	C-1-O		30	.121
	CLE N	C-1		20	.196
	BBTR			530	.234

SUDER, PETER "PETE" OR "PECKY"
B.APR.16,1916 ALIQUIPPA,PA.
1941	PHI A	2-S-3		139	.245
1942	PHI A	2-S-3		128	.256
1943	PHI A	2-S-3		131	.221
1946	PHI A	1-2-S-3-O		128	.281
1947	PHI A	2-S-3		145	.241
1948	PHI A	2		148	.241
1949	PHI A	2-S-3		118	.267
1950	PHI A	1-2-S-3		77	.246
1951	PHI A	2-S-3		123	.245
1952	PHI A	2-S-3		74	.241
1953	PHI A	2-S-3		115	.286
1954	PHI A	2-S-3		69	.200
1955	KC A	2		26	.210
	BRTR			1421	.249

SUDHOFF, JOHN WILLIAM "WEE WILLIE"
B.SEPT.17,1874 ST.LOUIS,MO.
D.MAY 25,1917
1897	STL N	P		11	1- 8
1898	STL N	P		38	11-26
1899	CLE N	P		22	3- 8
	STL N	P		22	12-10
1900	STL N	P	16	32	6- 8
1901	STL N	P		33	17-11
1902	STL A	P-O		31	11-13
					.171
1903	STL A	P	38	41	21-16
1904	STL A	P		29	7-14
1905	STL A	P		32	10-20
1906	WAS A	P		8	0- 2
	TR		280	299	99-136
					.180

SUGDEN, JOSEPH
B.JULY 31,1870 PHILADELPHIA,PA.
D.JUNE 28,1959
1893	PIT N	C		25	.273
1894	PIT N	C		39	.333
1895	PIT N	C		45	.310
1896	PIT N	C		77	.298
1897	PIT N	C		83	.219
1898	STL N	C		80	.259
1899	CLE N	C		78	.281
1901	CHI A	C		48	.283
1902	STL A	P-C-	1	69	0- 0
		1-O			.231
1903	STL A	C		79	.214
1904	STL A	C-1		104	.262
1905	STL A	P-C	1	91	0- 1
					.173
1912	DET A	1		1	..333
	BBTR		2	819	0- 1
					.255

SUGGS, GEORGE FRANKLIN
B.JULY 7,1883 KINSTON,N.C.
D.APR.4,1949
1908	DET A	P		6	1- 0
1909	DET A	P		9	1- 3
1910	CIN N	P		35	20-12
1911	CIN N	P		36	15-13
1912	CIN N	P		42	19-16
1913	CIN N	P		36	8-15
1914	BAL F	P		46	24-14
1915	BAL F	P		35	11-17
	BRTR			245	99-90

SUHR, AUGUST RICHARD "GUS"
B.JAN.3,1907 SAN FRANCISCO,CAL.
1930	PIT N	1		151	.286
1931	PIT N	1		87	.211
1932	PIT N	1		154	.263
1933	PIT N	1		154	.267
1934	PIT N	1		151	.283
1935	PIT N	1-O		153	.272
1936	PIT N	1		156	.312
1937	PIT N	1		151	.278
1938	PIT N	1		145	.294
1939	PIT N	1		63	.289
	PHI N	1		60	.318
1940	PHI N	1		10	.160
	BLTR			1435	.281

SUKEFORTH, CLYDE LEROY
B.NOV.30,1901 WASHINGTON,ME.
1926	CIN N	H		1	.000
1927	CIN N	C		38	.190
1928	CIN N	C		33	.132
1929	CIN N	C		84	.354
1930	CIN N	C		94	.284
1931	CIN N	C		112	.256
1932	BRO N	C		59	.234
1933	BRO N	C		20	.056
1934	BRO N	C		27	.103
1945	BRO N	C		18	.294
	BLTR			486	.264
NON-PLAYING MANAGER BRO(N) 1947

SUKLA, EDWARD ANTHONY "ED"
B.MAR.3,1943 LONG BEACH,CAL.
1964	LA A	P		2	0- 1
1965	CAL A	P		25	2- 3
1966	CAL A	P		12	1- 1
	BRTR			39	3- 5

SULIK, ERNEST RICHARD "DAVE"
B.JULY 7,1910 SAN FRANCISCO, CAL.
D.MAY 31,1963 OAKLAND,CAL.
| 1936 | PHI N | O | | 122 | .287 |
| | BLTL | | | | |

SULLIVAN
?875 NH NA O | 2 | - |

SULLIVAN, ANDREW R.
B.AUG.30,1884 SOUTHBOROUGH,MASS
D.FEB.14,1920
| 1904 | BOS N | S | | 1 | .000 |
| | TR | | | | |

SULLIVAN, CARL MANCEL "JACKIE"
B.FEB.22,1918 PRINCETON,TEX.
| 1944 | DET A | 2 | | 1 | .000 |
| | BRTR | | | | |

SULLIVAN, CHARLES EDWARD
B.MAY 23,1903 YADKIN VALLEY,N.C
D.MAY 28,1935
1928	DET A	P		3	0- 2
1930	DET A	P		40	1- 5
1931	DET A	P		31	3- 2
	BLTR			74	4- 9

SULLIVAN, DANIEL C. "LINK"
B.MAY 9,1857 PROVIDENCE,R.I.
D.OCT.26,1893
1882	LOU AA	C-S-3-O		67	.284
1883	LOU AA	C-S-3-O		36	.225
1884	LOU AA	C		64	.245
1885	LOU AA	C		13	.156
	STL AA	C		17	.138
1886	PIT AA	C		1	.000
	TR			198	.242

SULLIVAN, DENNIS J.
B.1854 BOSTON,MASS.
1879	PRO N	C		5	.250
1880	BOS N	C		1	.250
				6	.250

SULLIVAN, DENNIS WILLIAM
B.SEPT.28,1882 HILLSBORO,WIS.
D.JUNE 2,1956 W.LOS ANGELES,CAL
1905	WAS A	O		3	.000
1907	BOS A	O		144	.245
1908	BOS A	O		100	.241
	CLE A	O		4	.000
1909	CLE A	O		3	.667
	BLTR			254	.239

SULLIVAN, EDWARD TROWBRIDGE
(SEE
EDWARD TROWBRIDGE COLLINS SR)

SULLIVAN, FLORENCE P.
B.1862 E.ST.LOUIS,ILL.
D.FEB.15,1897
| 1884 | PIT AA | P | 51 | 54 | 16-35 |

SULLIVAN, FRANKLIN LEAL "FRANK"
B.JAN.23,1930 HOLLYWOOD,CAL.
1953	BOS A	P		14	1- 1
1954	BOS A	P		36	15-12
1955	BOS A	P		35	18-13
1956	BOS A	P		34	14- 7
1957	BOS A	P		31	14-11
1958	BOS A	P		32	13- 9
1959	BOS A	P		30	9-11
1960	BOS A	P		40	6-16
1961	PHI N	P		49	3-16
1962	PHI N	P		19	0- 2
	MIN A	P		21	4- 1
1963	MIN A	P		10	0- 1
	BRTR			351	97-100

SULLIVAN, HARRY ANDREW
B.APR.12,1888 ROCKFORD,ILL.
D.SEPT.22,1919
| 1909 | STL N | P | | 2 | 0- 0 |
| | BLTL | | | | |

SULLIVAN, HAYWOOD COOPER
B.DEC.15,1930 DONALSONVILLE,GA.
1955	BOS A	C		2	.000
1957	BOS A	C		2	.000
1959	BOS A	C		4	.000
1960	BOS A	C		52	.161
1961	KC A	C-1-O		117	.242
1962	KC A	C-1		95	.248
1963	KC A	C		40	.212
	BRTR			312	.226
NON-PLAYING MANAGER KC(A) 1965

SULLIVAN, JAMES E.
B.APR.25,1869 CHARLESTOWN,MASS.
D.DEC.2,1901
1891	BOS N	P		1	0- 0
	COL AA	P		1	0- 1
1895	BOS N	P	25	26	11- 9
1896	BOS N	P		24	11-13
1897	BOS N	P		13	4- 4
				64	26-27

SULLIVAN, JAMES P.
D.MAY 22,1898
NON-PLAYING MANAGER COL(AA)1890

SULLIVAN, JAMES RICHARD
B.APR.5,1894 MINE RUN,VA.
D.FEB.12,1972 BURTONSVILLE,MD.
1921	PHI A	P		2	0- 2
1922	PHI A	P		20	0- 2
1923	CLE A	P		3	0- 1
	BRTR			25	0- 5

SULLIVAN, JOHN EUGENE
B.FEB.16,1873 ILLINOIS
D.JUNE 5,1924
1905	DET A	C		13	.176
1908	PIT N	C		1	.000
	TR			14	.171

SULLIVAN, JOHN FRANK "CHUBB"
B.JAN.12,1859 BOSTON,MASS.
D.SEPT.12,1881
1877	CIN N	1		8	.250
1878	CIN N	1		62	.255
1880	WOR N	1		42	.267
	BRTR			112	.262

SULLIVAN, JOHN JEREMIAH
B.MAY 31,1896 CHICAGO,ILL.
D.JULY 7,1958
| 1919 | CHI A | P | | 4 | 0- 1 |
| | BLTL | | | | |

YR	CL	LEA	POS	GP	G	REC

SULLIVAN, JOHN LAWRENCE
B.MAR.21,1893 WILLIAMSPORT,PA.
D.APR.1,1966 KENTON TOWNSHIP,
UNION COUNTY,PA.

YR	CL	LEA	POS	GP	G	REC
1920	BOS	N	O		81	.296
1921	BOS	N	O		5	.000
	CHI	N	O		76	.329
	BRTR				162	.309

SULLIVAN, JOHN PATRICK
B.NOV.2,1920 CHICAGO,ILL.

1942	WAS	A	S		94	.235
1943	WAS	A	S		134	.208
1944	WAS	A	S		138	.251
1947	WAS	A	2-S		49	.256
1948	WAS	A	2-S		85	.208
1949	STL	A	2-S-3		105	.226
	BRTR				605	.230

SULLIVAN, JOHN PETER
B.JAN.3,1941 SOMERVILLE,N.J.

1963	DET	A	C		3	.000
1964	DET	A	C		2	.000
1965	DET	A	C		34	.267
1967	NY	N	C		65	.218
1968	PHI	N	C		12	.222
	BLTR				116	.228

SULLIVAN, JOE
B.SEPT.26,1910 MASON CITY,ILL.

1935	DET	A	P		25	6- 6
1936	DET	A	P		26	2- 5
1939	BOS	N	P	31	33	6- 9
1940	BOS	N	P		36	10-14
1941	BOS	N	P		16	2- 2
	PIT	N	P		16	4- 1
	BLTL	150	152	30-37

SULLIVAN, JOSEPH DANIEL
B.JAN.6,1870 CHARLESTOWN,MASS.
D.NOV.2,1897

1893	WAS	N	S		127	.271
1894	WAS	N	2-S-3		17	.239
	PHI	N	S		76	.358
1895	PHI	N	S		91	.340
1896	PHI	N	3-O		38	.269
	STL	N	O		60	.287
					409	.304

SULLIVAN, MARTIN J.
B.OCT.20,1862 LOWELL,MASS.
D.JAN.5,1894

1887	CHI	N	O		115	.334
1888	CHI	N	O		75	.235
1889	IND	N	O		69	.285
1890	BOS	N	O		121	.285
1891	BOS	N	O		17	.224
	CLE	N	O		1	.250
	BRTR				398	.288

SULLIVAN, MICHAEL JOSEPH
B.JUNE 10,1860 WEBSTER,MASS.
D.MAR.21,1929 WEBSTER,MASS.

| 1888 | ATH | AA | 3-O | | 28 | .277 |
| | BRTR | | | | | |

SULLIVAN, MICHAEL J. "BIG MIKE"
B.OCT.23,1866 S.BOSTON,MASS.
D.JUNE 14,1906

1889	WAS	N	P	9	0- 3
1890	CHI	N	P	12	5- 6
1891	ATH	AA	P	2	0- 2
	NY	N	P	3	1- 2
1892	CIN	N	P	18	12- 6
1893	CIN	N	P	22	7-13
1894	WAS	N	P	14	2-10
	CLE	N	P	12	6- 4
1895	CLE	N	P	5	1- 4
1896	NY	N	P	23	10-12
1897	NY	N	P	21	8- 7
1898	BOS	N	P	3	0- 2
1899	BOS	N	P	1	1- 0
	BL			145	53-71

SULLIVAN, PATRICK
B.DEC.23,1862 MILWAUKEE,WIS.
D.MAR.29,1886

1884	KC	U	P-C-	1	31	0- 1
			3-O			.193
	TR					

SULLIVAN, PAUL THOMAS "LEFTY"
B.SEPT.7,1916 NASHVILLE,TENN.

| 1939 | CLE | A | P | | 7 | 0- 1 |
| | BLTL | | | | | |

SULLIVAN, RUSSELL GUY "RUSS"
B.FEB.19,1923 FREDERICKSBURG,VA

1951	DET	A	O		7	.192
1952	DET	A	O		15	.327
1953	DET	A	O		23	.250
	BLTR				45	.267

SULLIVAN, SUTER G.
B.1872 BALTIMORE,MD.

1898	STL	N	S		40	.225
1899	CLE	N	3-O		126	.250
					166	.245

SULLIVAN, THOMAS
B.MAR.1,1860 NEW YORK,N.Y.
D.APR.12,1947

1884	COL	AA	P	4	2- 2
1886	LOU	AA	P	9	2- 7
1888	KC	AA	P-O	24	28	8-16
						.109
1889	KC	AA	P	10	2- 8
				47	51	14-33
						.116

SULLIVAN, THOMAS A.
B.OCT.18,1897 BOSTON,MASS.

| 1922 | PHI | N | P | | 3 | 0- 0 |
| | BLTL | | | | | |

SULLIVAN, THOMAS BRANDON
B.DEC.19,1906 NOME,ALASKA
D.AUG.16,1944

| 1925 | CIN | N | S | | 1 | .000 |
| | BRTR | | | | | |

**SULLIVAN, THOMAS JEFFERSON
"SLEEPER"**
B.ST.LOUIS,MO.
D.SEPT.25,1899

1881	BUF	N	C-O		31	.190
1882	STL	AA	C		51	.182
1883	STL	AA	C-O		8	.148
1884	STL	U	P-C	1	2	1- 0
						.167
	TR		1	92	1- 0
						.185

SULLIVAN, TIMOTHY PAUL "TED"
B.1851 COUNTY CLARE,IRELAND
D.JULY 5,1929 WASHINGTON,D.C.

| 1884 | KC | U | M-S-O | 3 | .333 |

NON-PLAYING MANAGER
STL(A) 1882-83, STL(U) 1884,
WAS(N) 1888

SULLIVAN, WILLIAM
B.JULY 4,1854 IRELAND
D.NOV.13,1884

| 1878 | CHI | N | O | | 2 | .000 |

SULLIVAN, WILLIAM JOSEPH JR.
B.OCT.23,1910 CHICAGO,ILL.

1931	CHI	A	3		92	.275
1932	CHI	A	1-3		93	.316
1933	CHI	A	C-1		54	.192
1935	CIN	N	1-2-3		85	.266
1936	CLE	A	C		93	.351
1937	CLE	A	C		72	.286
1938	STL	A	C		111	.277
1939	STL	A	C-O		118	.289
1940	DET	A	C-3		78	.309
1941	DET	A	C		85	.282
1942	BRO	N	C		43	.267
1947	PIT	N	C		38	.255
	BLTR				962	.289

SULLIVAN, WILLIAM JOSEPH SR.
B.FEB.1,1875 OAKLAND,WIS.
D.JAN.28,1965 NEWBERG,ORE.

1899	BOS	N	C		22	.284
1900	BOS	N	C		66	.267
1901	CHI	A	C		98	.245
1902	CHI	A	C-1-O		78	.151
1903	CHI	A	C		32	.188
1904	CHI	A	C		108	.235
1905	CHI	A	C		98	.201
1906	CHI	A	C		118	.214
1907	CHI	A	C		112	.179
1908	CHI	A	C		137	.191
1909	CHI	A	M-C		97	.162
1910	CHI	A	M-C		45	.183
1911	CHI	A	M-C		89	.215
1912	CHI	A	M-C		39	.209
1914	CHI	A	M-C		1	.000
1916	DET	A	M-C		1	.000
	BRTR				1141	.213

SULLIVAN, WILLIAM T.

| 1890 | SYR | AA | P | | 6 | 2- 4 |

SUMMA, HOMER WAYNE
B.NOV.3,1899 GENTRY,MO.
D.JAN.29,1966 LOS ANGELES,CAL.

1920	PIT	N	O		10	.318
1922	CLE	A	O		12	.348
1923	CLE	A	O		137	.328
1924	CLE	A	O		111	.290
1925	CLE	A	3-O		75	.330
1926	CLE	A	O		154	.308
1927	CLE	A	O		145	.286
1928	CLE	A	O		134	.284
1929	PHI	A	O		37	.272
1930	PHI	A	O		25	.278
	BLTR				840	.301

SUMMERS, JOHN JUNIOR "CHAMP"
B.JUNE 15,1946 BREMERTON,WASH.

1974	OAK	A	O		20	.125
1975	CHI	N	O		76	.231
1976	CHI	N	C-1-O		83	.206
	BLTR				179	.207

**SUMMERS, OREN EDGAR
"KICKAPOO ED"**
B.DEC.5,1884 LADOGA,IND.
D.MAY 12,1953

1908	DET	A	P		40	24-12
1909	DET	A	P		35	19- 9
1910	DET	A	P		30	13-12
1911	DET	A	P		30	11-11
1912	DET	A	P		3	2- 1
	BBTR				138	69-45

**SUMMERSGILL, HENRY TRAVERS
(PLAYED UNDER NAME OF
ANDREW SOMMERVILLE)**

SUMNER, CARL RINGDAHL "LEFTY"
B.SEPT.28,1908 CAMBRIDGE,MASS.

| 1928 | BOS | A | O | | 16 | .276 |
| | BLTR | | | | | |

**SUNDAY, ARTHUR
(REAL NAME AUGUST WACHER)**
B.JAN.21,1862 SPRINGFIELD,OHIO

| 1890 | BRO | P | O | | 24 | .292 |

**SUNDAY, WILLIAM ASHLEY
"BILLY" OR "PARSON"**
B.NOV.9,1862 AMES,IOWA
D.NOV.6,1935

1883	CHI	N	O		15	.259
1884	CHI	N	O		43	.221
1885	CHI	N	O		42	.255
1886	CHI	N	O		25	.242
1887	CHI	N	O		48	.359
1888	PIT	N	O		119	.233
1889	PIT	N	O		80	.239
1890	PIT	N	O		85	.268
	PHI	N	O		31	.256
	BL				488	.258

SUNDBERG, JAMES HOWARD "JIM"
B.MAY 18,1951 GALESBURG,ILL.

1974	TEX	A	C		132	.247
1975	TEX	A	C		155	.199
1976	TEX	A	C		140	.228
	BRTR				427	.223

SUNDIN, GORDON VINCENT
B.OCT.10,1937 MINNEAPOLIS,MINN.

| 1956 | BAL | A | P | | 1 | 0- 0 |
| | BRTR | | | | | |

**SUNDRA, STEPHEN RICHARD
"STEVE" OR "SMOKEY"**
B.MAR.27,1910 LUXOR,PA.
D.MAR.23,1952

1936	NY	A	P		1	0- 0
1938	NY	A	P		25	6- 4
1939	NY	A	P		24	11- 1
1940	NY	A	P		27	4- 6
1941	WAS	A	P		28	9-13
1942	WAS	A	P		6	1- 3
	STL	A	P		20	8- 3
1943	STL	A	P		32	15-11
1944	STL	A	P		3	2- 0
1946	STL	A	P		2	0- 0
	BBTR				168	56-41
	BR 1941-43					

YR	CL	LEA	POS	GP	G	REC

SUNKEL, THOMAS JACOB "LEFTY"
B.AUG.9,1912 PARIS,ILL.

YR	CL	LEA	POS	GP	G	REC
1937	STL	N	P	9		0- 0
1939	STL	N	P	20		4- 4
1941	NY	N	P	2		1- 1
1942	NY	N	P	19		3- 6
1943	NY	N	P	1		0- 1
1944	BRO	N	P	12		1- 3
	BLTL			63		9-15

SURKONT, MAXIM CONSTANTINE "MAX"
B.JUNE 16,1922 CENTRAL FALLS, R.I.

1949	CHI	A	P	44		3- 5
1950	BOS	N	P	9		5- 2
1951	BOS	N	P	37		12-16
1952	BOS	N	P	31		12-13
1953	MIL	N	P	28		11- 5
1954	PIT	N	P	33		9-18
1955	PIT	N	P	35		7-14
1956	PIT	N	P	1		0- 0
	STL	N	P	5		0- 0
	NY	N	P	8		2- 2
1957	NY	N	P	5		0- 1
	BRTR			236		61-76

SUSCE, GEORGE CYRIL METHODIUS "GOOD KID"
B.AUG.13,1908 PITTSBURGH,PA.

1929	PHI	N	C	17		.294
1932	DET	A	C	2		.000
1939	PIT	N	C	31		.227
1940	STL	A	C	61		.212
1941	CLE	A	C	1		.000
1942	CLE	A	C	2		1.000
1943	CLE	A	C	3		.000
1944	CLE	A	C	29		.230
	BRTR			146		.228

SUSCE, GEORGE DANIEL
B.SEPT.13,1931 PITTSBURGH,PA.

1955	BOS	A	P	29		9- 7
1956	BOS	A	P	21		2- 4
1957	BOS	A	P	29		7- 3
1958	BOS	A	P	2		0- 0
	DET	A	P	27		4- 3
1959	DET	A	P	9		0- 0
	BRTR			117		22-17

SUSKO, PETER JOHN
B.JULY 20,1904 LAURA,OHIO

1934	WAS	A	1	58		.286
	BLTL					

SUTCLIFFE, CHARLES INIGO
B.JULY 22,1915 FALL RIVER,MASS.

1938	BOS	N	C	4		.250

SUTCLIFFE, EDWARD ELMER "SY"
B.APR.15,1863 WHEATON,ILL.
D.FEB.18,1893

1884	CHI	N	N	4		.200
1885	CHI	N	C-O	11		.195
	STL	N	C-O	15		.140
1888	DET	N	S	49		.257
1889	CLE	N	C	65		.248
1890	CLE	P	C-O	99		.329
1891	WAS	AA	C-O	51		.365
1892	BAL	N	1	66		.275
	BL			360		.273

SUTCLIFFE, RICHARD LEE "RICK"
B.JUNE 21,1956 INDEPENDENCE,MO.

1976	LA	N	P	1		0- 0
	BLTR					

SUTER, HARRY RICHARD "HANDSOME HARRY"
B.SEPT.15,1867 INDEPENDENCE,MO.
D.JULY 24,1971 TOPEKA,KAN.

1909	CHI	A	P	18		2- 3
	BLTL					

SUTHERLAND, DARRELL WAYNE
B.NOV.14,1941 GLENDALE,CAL.

1964	NY	N	P	10		0- 3
1965	NY	N	P	18		3- 1
1966	NY	N	P	31		2- 0
1968	CLE	A	P	3		0- 0
	BRTR			62		5- 4

SUTHERLAND, GARY LYNN
B.SEP.27,1944 GLENDALE,CAL.

1966	PHI	N	S	3		.000
1967	PHI	N	S-O	103		.247
1968	PHI	N	2-S-3-O	67		.275
1969	MON	N	2-S-O	141		.239
1970	MON	N	2-S-3	116		.206
1971	MON	N	2-S-3-O	111		.257
1972	HOU	N	2-3	5		.125
1973	HOU	N	2-S	16		.259
1974	DET	A	2-S-3	149		.254
1975	DET	A	2	129		.258
1976	DET	A	2	42		.205
	MIL	A	1-2	59		.217
	BRTR			941		.243

SUTHERLAND, HARVEY S. "SUDS"
B.FEB.20,1896 COBURG,ORE.

1921	DET	A	P	13	17	6- 2
	BRTR					

SUTHERLAND, HOWARD ALVIN "DIZZY"
B.APR.9,1923 WASHINGTON,D.C.

1949	WAS	A	P	1		0- 1
	BLTL					

SUTTER, HOWARD BRUCE "BRUCE"
B.JAN.8,1953 LANCASTER,PA.

1976	CHI	N	P	52		6- 3
	BRTR					

SUTTHOFF, JOHN GERHARD "SUNNY JACK"
B.JUNE 29,1873 CINCINNATI,OHIO
D.AUG.3,1942

1898	WAS	N	P	2		0- 2
1899	STL	N	P	2		1- 1
1901	CIN	N	P-O	10	11	1- 6
						.121
1903	CIN	N	P	30		16-11
1904	CIN	N	P	12		3- 3
	PHI	N	P	19		4-13
1905	PHI	N	P	13		3- 3
	BLTR			88	89	28-39
						.149

SUTTON, DONALD HOWARD "DON"
B.APR.2,1945 CLIO,ALA.

1966	LA	N	P	37	38	12-12
1967	LA	N	P	37	43	11-15
1968	LA	N	P	35	36	11-15
1969	LA	N	P		41	17-18
1970	LA	N	P	38	40	15-13
1971	LA	N	P	38	39	17-12
1972	LA	N	P		33	19- 9
1973	LA	N	P		33	10-10
1974	LA	N	P		40	19- 9
1975	LA	N	P		35	16-13
1976	LA	N	P		35	21-10
	BRTR			402	413	176-136

SUTTON, EZRA BALLOU
B.SEPT.17,1850 SENECA,N.Y.
D.JUNE 20,1907

1871	CLE	NA	3	29		-
1872	CLE	NA	3	21		.282
1873	ATH	NA	2-S-3	50		-
1874	ATH	NA	S-3	55		-
1875	ATH	NA	1-3-O	75		.328
1876	ATH	N	1-2-3	54		.293
1877	BOS	N	S-3	58		.292
1878	BOS	N	3	60		.226
1879	BOS	N	S-3	84		.248
1880	BOS	N	S-3	74		.250
1881	BOS	N	S-3	83		.291
1882	BOS	N	S-3	80		.255
1883	BOS	N	S-3-O	94		.323
1884	BOS	N	3	106		.349
1885	BOS	N	1-S-3	108		.312
1886	BOS	N	2-S-3-O	116		.276
1887	BOS	N	S-O	74		.327
1888	BOS	N	3	28		.218
	BRTR			1249		-

SWABACH, WILLIAM

1887	NY	N	P	2		0- 1

SWACINA, HARRY J. "SWATS"
B.1881 ST.LOUIS,MO.
D.JUNE 21,1944

1907	PIT	N	1	26		.200
1908	PIT	N	1	50		.216
1914	BAL	F	1	158		.276
1915	BAL	F	1	85		.247
	BRTR			319		.254

SWAIM, JOHN HILLARY "CY"
B.MAR.11,1874 CADWALADER,OHIO
D.NOV.8,1918

1897	WAS	N	P	24		5-12
1898	WAS	N	P	15		3-11
				39		8-23

SWAN, ALBERT D.
B.MAY 11,1845 TWEKSBURY,MASS.
D.AUG.27,1885

1884	WAS	AA	1-3	5		.143
	RIC	AA	1	3		.500
				8		.258

SWAN, CRAIG STEVEN
B.NOV.30,1950 VAN NUYS,CAL.

1973	NY	N	P	3		0- 1
1974	NY	N	P	7		1- 3
1975	NY	N	P	6		1- 3
1976	NY	N	P	23		6- 9
	BRTR			39		8-16

SWANDELL, JOHN MARTIN "MARTY"
B.1845 NEW YORK

1872	ECK	NA	1-2-3-O	14		.207
1873	RES	NA	1	2		-
				16		-

SWANDER, EDWARD C. "PINKY"
B.JULY 4,1880 PORTSMOUTH,OHIO
D.OCT.24,1944

1903	STL	A	O	14		.250
1904	STL	A	O	1		.000
				15		.245

SWANN, HENRY "DUCKY"
B.1892

1914	KC	F	P	1		0- 1
	BRTR					

SWANSON, ARTHUR LEONARD
B.OCT.15,1936 BATON ROUGE,LA.

1955	PIT	N	P	1		0- 0
1956	PIT	N	P	9	10	0- 0
1957	PIT	N	P	32		3- 3
	BPTR			42	43	3- 3

SWANSON, ERNEST EVAR "EVAR"
B.OCT.15,1902 DE KALB,ILL.
D.JULY 17,1973 GALESBURG,ILL.

1929	CIN	N	O	148		.300
1930	CIN	N	O	95		.309
1932	CHI	A	O	14		.308
1933	CHI	A	O	144		.306
1934	CHI	A	O	117		.298
	BRTR			518		.303

SWANSON, KARL EDWARD
B.DEC.17,1903 MOLINE,ILL.

1928	CHI	A	2	22		.141
1929	CHI	A	H	2		.000
	BLTR			24		.138

SWANSON, STANLEY LAWRENCE "STAN"
B.MAY 19,1944 YUBA CITY,CAL.

1971	MON	N	O	49		.245
	BRTR					

SWANSON, WILLIAM ANDREW
B.OCT.12,1888 NEW YORK,N.Y.
D.OCT.14,1954 NEW YORK,N.Y.

1914	BOS	A	2	11		.211
	BBTR					

SWARTWOOD, CYRUS EDWARD
B.JAN.12,1859 ROCKFORD,ILL.
D.MAY 10,1924

1881	BUF	N	O	1		.250
1882	PIT	AA	1-O	71		.319
1883	PIT	AA	C-1-O	95		.369
1884	PIT	AA	1-O	102		.330
1885	BRO	AA	O	100		.242
1886	BRO	AA	O	123		.262
1887	BRO	AA	O	91		.344
1890	TOL	AA	O	126		.309
1892	PIT	N	O	12		.263
	TR			721		.309

SWARTZ, MONROE
B.JAN.1,1897 FARMERSVILLE,OHIO

1920	CIN	N	P	1		0- 1
	BRTR					

SWARTZ, SHERWIN MERLE "BUD"
B.JUNE 13,1929 TULSA,OKLA.

1947	STL	A	P	5		0- 0
	BLTL					

YR	CL	LEA	POS	GP	G	REC

SWARTZEL, PARK B.
B.NOV.21,1865 KNIGHTSTOWN,IND.
D.JAN.3,1940 LOS ANGELES,CAL.

| 1889 | KC | AA | P | 48 | 52 | 19-26 |
| | | BRTR | | | | |

SWASEY, CHARLES JAMES
(PLAYED UNDER NAME OF
CHARLES JAMES SWEAZY)

SWEAZY, CHARLES JAMES
(REAL NAME
CHARLES JAMES SWASEY)
B.SEPT.3,1847 HVAERHILL,N.H.
D.MAR.30,1908

1871	OLY	NA	2		4	-
1872	CLE	NA	2-0		11	.222
1873	BOS	NA	2		1	-
1874	BAL	NA	2-0		8	-
	ATL	NA	2		10	-
1875	RS	NA	M-2		19	-
1876	CIN	N	2-0		56	.203
1878	PRO	N	2		54	.178
		BRTR			163	-

SWEENEY

| 1914 | PHI | A | 0 | | 1 | .000 |

SWEENEY, CHARLES J.
B.APR.13,1863 SAN FRANCISCO,CAL
D.APR.4,1902

1882	ATH	AA	P-0	21	24	8-11
						.175
	PRO	N	0		1	.000
1883	PRO	N	P-1-0		21	11- 9
						.218
1884	PRO	N	P-1-	25	40	17- 7
			0			.302
	STL	U	P-1-	34	46	24- 8
			0			.307
1885	STL	N	P-0	38	73	12-20
						.207
1886	STL	N	P		17	5- 6
1887	CLE	AA	P-1	3	36	0- 3
						.329
				142	258	77-64
						.259

SWEENEY, DANIEL J.
B.JAN.28,1868 PHILADELPHIA,PA.
D.JULY 13,1913

| 1895 | LOU | N | 0 | | 21 | .279 |

SWEENEY, EDWARD FRANCIS
"BIG ED"
B.JULY 19,1888 CHICAGO,ILL.
D.JULY 4,1947

1908	NY	A	C		32	.146
1909	NY	A	C		67	.267
1910	NY	A	C		78	.200
1911	NY	A	C		83	.231
1912	NY	A	C		110	.268
1913	NY	A	C		117	.265
1914	NY	A	C		87	.213
1915	NY	A	C		53	.190
1919	PIT	N	C		17	.095
		BRTR			644	.232

SWEENEY, HENRY LEON
B.DEC.26,1917 FRANKLIN,TENN.

| 1944 | PIT | N | 1 | | 1 | .000 |
| | | BLTL | | | | |

SWEENEY, JEREMIAH H.
B.1860 BOSTON,MASS.
D.AUG.25,1891

| 1884 | KC | U | 1 | | 30 | .260 |

SWEENEY, JOHN J. "ROONEY"
B.1860
D.AUG.10,1886

1883	BAL	AA	C-2-0		25	.232
1884	BAL	U	C-0		43	.239
1885	STL	N	C-0		3	.091
					71	.231

SWEENEY, PETER JAY
B.DEC.31,1863 CALIFORNIA
D.AUG.22,1901

1888	WAS	N	3		11	.181
1889	WAS	N	3		49	.228
	STL	AA	3		9	.310
1890	STL	AA	3		49	.162
	LOU	AA	3		2	.143
	ATH	AA	3		14	.157
		BRTR			134	.202

SWEENEY, WILLIAM J.
B.1858 PHILADELPHIA,PA.
D.AUG.2,1903

| 1884 | BAL | U | P | | 83 | 40-21 |

SWEENEY, WILLIAM JOHN
B.MAR.6,1886 COVINGTON,KY.
D.MAY 26,1948

1907	CHI	N	3		3	.100
	BOS	N	S-3		57	.262
1908	BOS	N	3		127	.244
1909	BOS	N	S-3		138	.243
1910	BOS	N	1-S-3		147	.267
1911	BOS	N	2		136	.314
1912	BOS	N	2		153	.344
1913	BOS	N	2		139	.257
1914	CHI	N	2		134	.218
		BRTR			1034	.272

SWEENEY, WILLIAM JOSEPH
B.DEC.29,1904 CLEVELAND,OHIO
D.APR.18,1957

1928	DET	A	1		89	.252
1930	BOS	A	1		88	.309
1931	BOS	A	1		131	.295
		BRTR			308	.286

SWEETLAND, LESTER LEO
(BORN LEO SWEETLAND)
B.AUG.15,1901 ST.IGNACE,MICH.
D.MAR.4,1974 MELBOURNE,FLA.

1927	PHI	N	P	21	25	2-10
1928	PHI	N	P	37	41	3-15
1929	PHI	N	P	43	53	13-11
1930	PHI	N	P	34	35	7-15
1932	CHI	N	P	26	29	8- 7
		BBTL		161	183	33-58
		BR 1927-29				

SWEIGERT

| 1890 | ATH | AA | 0 | | 1 | .000 |

SWENTOR, AUGUST WALTER
B.DEC.13,1902 ROCKFORD,ILL.

| 1922 | CHI | A | 3 | | 1 | .000 |
| | | BRTR | | | | |

SWETONIC, STEPHEN ALBERT
B.AUG.13,1904 MT.PLEASANT,PA.
D.APR.22,1974 CANONSBURG,PA.

1929	PIT	N	P	41	42	8-10
1930	PIT	N	P		23	6- 6
1931	PIT	N	P		14	0- 2
1932	PIT	N	P		24	11- 6
1933	PIT	N	P		31	12-12
1935	PIT	N	R		1	.000
		BRTR		133	135	37-36
						.170

SWETT, CHARLES A. "POP"
B.APR.15,1868 SAN FRANCISCO,CAL

| 1890 | BOS | P | C | | 37 | .193 |

SWIFT, ROBERT VIRGIL "BOB"
B.MAR.6,1915 SALINA,KAN.
D.OCT.17,1966 DETROIT,MICH.

1940	STL	A	C		130	.244
1941	STL	A	C		63	.259
1942	STL	A	C		29	.187
	PHI	A	C		60	.229
1943	PHI	A	C		77	.192
1944	DET	A	C		80	.255
1945	DET	A	C		95	.233
1946	DET	A	C		42	.234
1947	DET	A	C		97	.251
1948	DET	A	C		113	.223
1949	DET	A	C		74	.238
1950	DET	A	C		67	.227
1951	DET	A	C		44	.192
1952	DET	A	C		28	.138
1953	DET	A	C		2	.333
		BRTR			1001	.231
NON-PLAYING MANAGER DET(A) 1966						

SWIFT, WILLIAM VINCENT "BILL"
B.JAN.10,1908 ELMIRA,N.Y.
D.FEB.23,1969 BARTOW,FLA.

1932	PIT	N	P		39	14-10
1933	PIT	N	P		37	14-10
1934	PIT	N	P		37	11-13
1935	PIT	N	P		39	15- 8
1936	PIT	N	P		45	16-16
1937	PIT	N	P		36	9-10
1938	PIT	N	P		36	7- 5
1939	PIT	N	P		36	5- 7
1940	BOS	N	P		4	1- 1
1941	BRO	N	P		9	3- 0
1943	CHI	A	P		18	0- 2
		BRTR			336	95-82

SWIGART, OADIS VAUGHN
B.FEB.13,1916 ARCHIE,MO.

1939	PIT	N	P		3	1- 1
1940	PIT	N	P		7	0- 2
		BLTR			10	1- 3

SWIGLER, ADAM WILLIAM "DOC"
B.SEPT.21,1895 PHILADELPHIA,PA.
D.FEB.5,1975 PHILADELPHIA,PA.

| 1917 | NY | N | P | | 1 | 0- 1 |

SWINDELL, CHARLES JAY
B.OCT.26,1877 ROCKFORD,ILL.
D.JULY 22,1940

| 1904 | STL | N | C | | 3 | .125 |
| | | TR | | | | |

SWINDELL, JOSHUA ERNEST
B.JULY 5,1885 ROSE HILL,KAN.
D.MAR.19,1969 FRUITA,COLO.

1911	CLE	A	P		4	0- 1
1913	CLE	A	H		1	.000
		TR		4	5	0- 1
						.200

SWISHER, STEVEN EUGENE "STEVE"
B.AUG.9,1951 PARKERSBURG,W.VA.

1974	CHI	N	C		90	.214
1975	CHI	N	C		93	.213
1976	CHI	N	C		109	.236
		BRTR			292	.223

SWOBODA, RONALD ALAN "RON"
B.JUNE 30,1944 BALTIMORE,MD.

1965	NY	N	0		135	.228
1966	NY	N	0		112	.222
1967	NY	N	1-0		134	.281
1968	NY	N	0		132	.242
1969	NY	N	0		109	.235
1970	NY	N	0		115	.233
1971	MON	N	0		39	.253
	NY	A	0		54	.261
1972	NY	A	1-0		63	.248
1973	NY	A	0		34	.116
		BRTR			927	.242

SWORMSTEDT, LEONARD B.
B.CINCINNATI,OHIO

1901	CIN	N	P		4	2- 1
1902	CIN	N	P		2	0- 1
1906	BOS	A	P		3	1- 1
		BRTR			9	3- 3

SYLVESTER, LOUIS J.
B.FEB.14,1855 SPRINGFIELD,ILL.

1884	CIN	U	P-0	2	70	0- 2
						.264
1886	LOU	AA	0		54	.227
	CIN	AA	0		14	.156
1887	STL	AA	0		28	.298
		BRTR		2	166	0- 2
						.253

SZABO, ALEXANDER
(PLAYED UNDER NAME OF
ALEXANDER SABO)

SZEKELY, JOSEPH
B.FEB.2,1926 CLEVELAND,OHIO

| 1953 | CIN | N | 0 | | 5 | .077 |
| | | BRTR | | | | |

SZOTKIEWICZ, KENNETH JOHN "KEN"
B.FEB.25,1947 WILMINGTON,DEL.

| 1970 | DET | A | S | | 47 | .107 |
| | | BLTR | | | | |

SZYMANSKI, ALOIS
(PLAYED UNDER NAME OF
ALOYSIUS HARRY SIMMONS)

YR CL LEA POS GP   G   REC

TABB, JERRY LYNN
B.MAR.17,1952 ALTUS,OKLA.
1976 CHI N 1   11   .292
     BLTR

TABER, EDWARD TIMOTHY "LEFTY"
B.JAN.11,1902 ROCK ISLAND,ILL.
1926 PHI N P   6   0- 0
1927 PHI N P   3   0- 1
     BLTL   9   0- 1

TABER, JOHN PARDON
B.JUNE 28,1868 ACUSHNET,MASS.
D.FEB.21,1940
1890 BOS N P   2   0- 1

TABOR, JAMES REUBIN "JIM"
B.NOV.5,1916 OWENS CROSSROADS,
ALA.
D.AUG.22,1953
1938 BOS A 3   19   .316
1939 BOS A 3   149   .289
1940 BOS A 3   120   .285
1941 BOS A 3   126   .279
1942 BOS A 3   139   .252
1943 BOS A 3-0   137   .242
1944 BOS A 3   116   .285
1946 PHI N 3   124   .268
1947 PHI N 3   75   .235
     BRTR   1005   .270

TAFF, JOHN G.
B.1890
D.MAY 15,1961 HOUSTON,TEX.
1913 PHI A P   5   0- 1
     BRTR

TAGGART, ROBERT JOHN
(SEE JAMES KELLY)

TAITT, DOUGLAS JOHN "POCO"
B.AUG.3,1903 BAY CITY,MICH.
D.DEC.12,1970 PORTLAND,ORE.
1928 BOS A P-O 1   143   0- 0
                           .299
1929 BOS A O   26   .281
     CHI A O   47   .168
1931 PHI N O   38   .225
1932 PHI N H   4   .000
     BLTR   1   258   0- 0
                           .263

TALBOT, FRED LEALAND
B.JUNE 28,1941 WASHINGTON,D.C.
1963 CHI A P   1   0- 0
1964 CHI A P   17   18   4- 5
1965 KC A P   39   47 10-12
1966 KC A P   11   4- 4
     NY A P   23   7- 7
1967 NY A P   29   30   6- 8
1968 NY A P   29   1- 9
1969 NY A P   8   0- 0
     SEA A P   25   27   5- 8
     OAK A P   12   1- 2
1970 OAK A P   1   0- 1
     BRTR   195 207 38-56

TALBOT, ROBERT DALE "BOB"
B.JUNE 6,1941 VISALIA,CAL.
1953 CHI N O   8   .333
1954 CHI N O   114   .241
     BRTR   122   .247

TALCOTT, LE ROY EVERETT
B.JAN.16,1921 BOSTON,MASS.
1943 BOS N P   1   0- 0
     BRTR

TALTON, MARION LEE "TIM"
B.JAN.14,1939 PIKEVILLE,N.C.
1966 KC A C-1   37   .340
1967 KC A C-1   46   .254
     BLTR   83   .295

TAMARGO, JOHN FELIX
B.NOV.7,1951 TAMPA,FLA.
1976 STL N C   10   .300
     BBTR

TAMULIS, VITAUTAS CASIMIRUS "VITO"
B.JULY 11,1911 CAMBRIDGE,MASS.
D.MAY 5,1974 NASHVILLE,TENN.
1934 NY A P   1   1- 0
1935 NY A P   30 10- 5
1938 STL A P   3   0- 3
     BRO N P   38   39 12- 6
1939 BRO N P   39   9- 8
1940 BRO N P-1 41   42   8- 5
                           .130
1941 PHI N P   6   0- 1
     BRO N P   12   0- 0
     BLTL   170 172 40-28
                           .175

TANANA, FRANK DARYL
B.JULY 3,1953 DETROIT,MICH.
1973 CAL A P   4   2- 2
1974 CAL A P   39 14-19
1975 CAL A P   34 16- 9
1976 CAL A P   34   35 19-10
     BLTL   111 112 51-40

TANKERSLEY, LAWRENCE WILLIAM "LEO"
B.JUNE 8,1901 TERRELL,TEX.
1925 CHI A C   1   .000
     BRTR

TANNEHILL, JESSE NILES "POWDER"
B.JULY 14,1874 DAYTON,KY.
D.SEPT.22,1956 DAYTON,KY.
1894 CIN N P   5   1- 1
1897 PIT N P-O 17   53   8- 8
                           .266
1898 PIT N P   38   45 24-14
1899 PIT N P   38   40 23-14
1900 PIT N P   28   32 20- 7
1901 PIT N P   32   40 18-10
1902 PIT N P-O 27   41 20- 6
                           .289
1903 NY A P   32   39 15-15
1904 BOS A P   33   45 20-10
1905 BOS A P   37 23-10
1906 BOS A P   26   31 13-11
1907 BOS A P   18   21   6- 7
1908 BOS A P   1   1- 0
     WAS A P   10   26   1- 4
1909 WAS A P   3   16   1- 1
1911 CIN N P   1   0- 0
     BBTL   346 473 194-118
                           .261

BL 1903

TANNEHILL, LEE FORD
B.OCT.26,1880 DAYTON,KY.
D.FEB.16,1938
1903 CHI A S   136   .220
1904 CHI A 3   153   .226
1905 CHI A 3   142   .200
1906 CHI A S-3   112   .175
1907 CHI A 3   33   .241
1908 CHI A 3   141   .216
1909 CHI A S-3   155   .222
1910 CHI A 1-S   67   .222
1911 CHI A 2-S   141   .254
1912 CHI A 3   2   .000
     BRTR   1082   .219

TANNER, CHARLES WILLIAM "CHUCK"
B.JULY 4,1929 NEW CASTLE,PA.
1955 MIL N O   97   .247
1956 MIL N O   60   .238
1957 MIL N O   22   .246
     CHI N O   95   .286
1958 CHI N O   73   .262
1959 CLE A O   14   .250
1960 CLE A O   21   .280
1961 LA A O   7   .125
1962 LA A O   7   .125
     BLTL   396   .261
NON-PLAYING MANAGER
CHI(A) 1970-75, OAK(A) 1976

TAPPAN, WALTER VAN DORN "TAP"
B.OCT.8,1890 CARLINVILLE,ILL.
D.DEC.19,1967 LYNWOOD,CAL.
1914 KC F 3   18   .200
     BRTR

TAPPE, ELVIN WALTER
B.MAY 21,1929 QUINCY,ILL.
1954 CHI N C   46   .185
1955 CHI N C   2   .000
1956 CHI N C   3   .000
1958 CHI N C   17   .214
1960 CHI N C   51   .233
1962 CHI N M-C   26   .208
     BRTR   145   .207
NON-PLAYING MANAGER CHI(N) 1961

TAPPE, THEODORE NASH "TED"
B.FEB.2,1931 SEATTLE,WASH.
1950 CIN N H   7   .200
1951 CIN N H   4   .333
1955 CIN N O   23   .260
     BLTR   34   .259

TARBERT, WILBUR ARLINGTON "ARLIE"
B.SEPT.10,1904 CLEVELAND,OHIO
D.NOV.27,1946
1927 BOS A O   33   .189
1928 BOS A O   6   .176
     BRTR   39   .186

TARTABULL, JOSE (MILAGES)
B.NOV.27,1938 CIENFUEGOS,CUBA
1962 KC A O   107   .277
1963 KC A O   79   .240
1964 KC A O   104   .200
1965 KC A O   68   .312
1966 KC A O   37   .236
     BOS A O   68   .277
1967 BOS A O   115   .223
1968 BOS A O   72   .281
1969 OAK A O   75   .267
1970 OAK A O   24   .231
     BLTL   749   .261

TASBY, WILLIE
B.JAN.8,1933 SHREVEPORT,LA.
1958 BAL A O   18   .200
1959 BAL A O   142   .250
1960 BAL A O   39   .212
     BOS A O   105   .281
1961 WAS A O   141   .251
1962 WAS A O   11   .206
     CLE A 3-O   75   .241
1963 CLE A 2-O   52   .224
     BRTR   583   .250

TATE, ALVIN ELROY
B.JULY 1,1919 COLEMAN,OKLA.
1946 PIT N P   2   0- 1
     BRTR

TATE, EDWARD CHRISTOPHER "POP"
B.DEC.22,1860 RICHMOND,VA.
D.JUNE 25,1932
1885 BOS N C   4   .167
1886 BOS N C   31   .226
1887 BOS N C   55   .271
1888 BOS N C   40   .229
1889 BAL AA C   72   .178
1890 BAL AA C   20   .219
     BRTL   222   .225

TATE, HENRY BENNETT "BENNIE"
B.DEC.3,1901 WHITWELL,TENN.
D.OCT.27,1973 W.FRANKFURT,ILL.
1924 WAS A C   21   .302
1925 WAS A C   16   .481
1926 WAS A C   59   .267
1927 WAS A C   61   .313
1928 WAS A C   57   .246
1929 WAS A C   81   .294
1930 WAS A C   14   .231
     CHI A C   72   .326
1931 CHI A C   89   .267
1932 CHI A C   4   .100
     BOS A C   81   .245
1934 CHI A C   11   .125
     BLTR   566   .279

TATE, HUGH HENRY
B.MAY 19,1880 EVERETT,PA.
D.AUG.7,1956
1905 WAS A O   4   .230
     BRTR

TATE, LEE WILLIE
B.MAR.18,1932 BLACK ROCK,ARK.
1958 STL N S   10   .200
1959 STL N 2-S-3   41   .140
     BRTR   51   .165

TATE, RANDALL LEE "RANDY"
B.OCT.23,1952 FLORENCE,ALA.

YR	CL	LEA	POS	GP	G	REC
1975	NY	N	P		26	5-13
		BRTR				

TATUM, JARVIS
B.OCT.11,1946 FRESNO,CAL.

YR	CL	LEA	POS	GP	G	REC
1968	CAL	A	O		17	.176
1969	CAL	A	O		10	.318
1970	CAL	A	O		75	.238
		BRTR			102	.232

TATUM, KENNETH RAY "KEN"
B.APR.25,1944 ALEXANDRIA,LA.

YR	CL	LEA	POS	GP	G	REC
1969	CAL	A	P		45	7- 2
1970	CAL	A	P		62	7- 4
1971	BOS	A	P		36	2- 4
1972	BOS	A	P		22	0- 2
1973	BOS	A	P		1	0- 0
1974	CHI	A	P		10	0- 0
		BRTR			176	16-12

TATUM, THOMAS VEE TEE
B.JULY 16,1919 BOYD,TEX.
D.AUG.7,1956

YR	CL	LEA	POS	GP	G	REC
1941	BRO	N	O		8	.167
1947	BRO	N	O		4	.000
	CIN	N	2-O		69	.273
		BRTR			81	.258

TAUBENSEE, FRED JOSEPH
(PLAYED UNDER NAME OF
FRED JOSEPH TAUBY)

TAUBY, FRED JOSEPH
(REAL NAME
FRED JOSEPH TAUBENSEE)
B.MAR.27,1906 CANTON,OHIO
D.NOV.23,1955

YR	CL	LEA	POS	GP	G	REC
1935	CHI	A	O		13	.125
1937	PHI	N	O		11	.000
		BRTR			24	.077

TAUSCHER, WALTER EDWARD
B.NOV.22,1903 LA SALLE,ILL.

YR	CL	LEA	POS	GP	G	REC
1928	PIT	N	P		17	0- 0
1931	WAS	A	P		6	1- 0
		BRTR			23	1- 0

TAUSSIG, DONALD FRANKLIN "DON"
B.FEB.19,1932 NEW YORK,N.Y.

YR	CL	LEA	POS	GP	G	REC
1958	SF	N	O		39	.200
1961	STL	N	O		98	.287
1962	HOU	N	O		16	.200
		BRTR			153	.262

TAVENER, JOHN ADAM "RABBIT"
B.DEC.27,1897 CELINA,OHIO
D.SEPT.14,1969 FORT WORTH,TEX.

YR	CL	LEA	POS	GP	G	REC
1921	DET	A	S		2	.000
1925	DET	A	S		134	.245
1926	DET	A	S		156	.265
1927	DET	A	S		116	.274
1928	DET	A	S		132	.260
1929	CLE	A	S		92	.212
		BLTR			632	.255

**TAVERAS, ALEJANDRO ANTONIO
(BETANCES) "ALEX"**
B.OCT.9,1955 SANTIAGO,D.R.

YR	CL	LEA	POS	GP	G	REC
1976	HOU	N	2-S		14	.217
		BRTR				

**TAVERAS, FRANK CRISOSTOMO
(FABIAN)**
B.DEC.24,1949 LAS MATAS DE
SANTA CRUZ,D.R.

YR	CL	LEA	POS	GP	G	REC
1971	PIT	N	R		1	.000
1972	PIT	N	S		4	.000
1974	PIT	N	S		126	.246
1975	PIT	N	S		134	.212
1976	PIT	N	S		144	.258
		BRTR			409	.240

**TAYLOR, ANTONIO NEMESIO
(SANCHEZ) "TONY"**
B.DEC.19,1935 MATANZAS,CUBA

YR	CL	LEA	POS	GP	G	REC
1958	CHI	N	2-3		140	.235
1959	CHI	N	2-S		150	.280
1960	CHI	N	2		19	.263
	PHI	N	2-3		127	.287
1961	PHI	N	2-3		106	.250
1962	PHI	N	2-S		152	.259
1963	PHI	N	2-3		157	.281
1964	PHI	N	2		154	.251
1965	PHI	N	2-3		106	.229
1966	PHI	N	2-3		125	.242
1967	PHI	N	1-2-S-3		132	.238
1968	PHI	N	1-2-3		145	.250
1969	PHI	N	1-2-3		138	.262
1970	PHI	N	2-S-3-O		124	.301
1971	PHI	N	1-2-3		36	.261
	DET	A	2-3		55	.287
1972	DET	N	1-2-3		78	.303
1973	DET	A	1-2-3-O		84	.229
1974	PHI	N	1-2-3		62	.328
1975	PHI	N	1-2-3		79	.243
1976	PHI	N	2-3		26	.261
		BRTR			2195	.261

TAYLOR, ARLISS W.
B.CLEARFIELD,PA.

YR	CL	LEA	POS	GP	G	REC
1921	PHI	A	P		1	0- 1

TAYLOR, BENJAMIN

YR	CL	LEA	POS	GP	G	REC
1912	CIN	N	P		2	0- 0
		TR				

TAYLOR, BENJAMIN EUGENE "BEN"
B.SEPT.30,1927 METROPOLIS,ILL.

YR	CL	LEA	POS	GP	G	REC
1951	STL	A	1		33	.258
1952	DET	A	1		7	.167
1955	MIL	N	1		12	.100
		BLTL			52	.231

TAYLOR, C. L. "CHINK"
B.FEB.9,1898 BURNET,TEX.

YR	CL	LEA	POS	GP	G	REC
1925	CHI	N	O		8	.000
		BRTR				

TAYLOR, CARL MEANS
B.JAN.20,1944 SARASOTA,FLA.

YR	CL	LEA	POS	GP	G	REC
1968	PIT	N	C-O		44	.211
1969	PIT	N	1-O		104	.348
1970	STL	N	1-3-O		104	.249
1971	PIT	N	O		7	.167
	KC	A	O		20	.179
1972	KC	A	C-1-3-O		63	.265
1973	KC	A	C-1		69	.228
		BRTR			411	.266

TAYLOR, CHARLES GILBERT "CHUCK"
B.APR.18,1942 SHELBYVILLE,TENN.

YR	CL	LEA	POS	GP	G	REC
1969	STL	N	P		27	7- 5
1970	STL	N	P		56	6- 7
1971	STL	N	P		43	3- 1
1972	NY	N	P		20	0- 0
	MIL	A	P		5	0- 0
1973	MON	N	P		8	2- 0
1974	MON	N	P		61	6- 2
1975	MON	N	P		54	2- 2
1976	MON	N	P		31	2- 3
		BRTR			305	28-20

TAYLOR, DANIEL TURNEY
B.DEC.23,1900 LASH,PA.
D.OCT.11,1972 LATROBE,PA.

YR	CL	LEA	POS	GP	G	REC
1926	WAS	A	O		21	.300
1929	CHI	N	O		2	.000
1930	CHI	N	O		74	.283
1931	CHI	N	O		88	.300
1932	CHI	N	O		6	.227
	BRO	N	O		105	.324
1933	BRO	N	O		103	.285
1934	BRO	N	O		120	.299
1935	BRO	N	O		112	.290
1936	BRO	N	O		43	.293
		BRTR			674	.297

TAYLOR, EDWARD

YR	CL	LEA	POS	GP	G	REC
1903	STL	N	P		1	0- 0

TAYLOR, EDWARD JAMES
B.NOV.17,1902 CHICAGO,ILL.

YR	CL	LEA	POS	GP	G	REC
1926	BOS	N	S-3		92	.268
		BRTR				

TAYLOR, FREDERICK RANKIN
B.DEC.3,1926 ZANESVILLE,OHIO

YR	CL	LEA	POS	GP	G	REC
1950	WAS	A	1		6	.125
1951	WAS	A	1		6	.167
1952	WAS	A	1		10	.263
		BLTR			22	.191

TAYLOR, GARY WILLIAM
B.OCT.19,1945 DETROIT,MICH.

YR	CL	LEA	POS	GP	G	REC
1969	DET	A	P		7	0- 1
		BRTR				

TAYLOR, GEORGE EDWARD
B.FEB.3,1855 BELFAST,ME.
D.FEB.19,1888

YR	CL	LEA	POS	GP	G	REC
1884	PIT	AA	O		41	.202

TAYLOR, GEORGE J.
B.NOV.22,1853 NEW YORK
NON-PLAYING MANAGER BRO(AA)1884

TAYLOR, HARRY EVANS
B.DEC.2,1934 SAN ANGELO,TEX.

YR	CL	LEA	POS	GP	G	REC
1957	KC	A	P		2	0- 0
		BRTR				

TAYLOR, HARRY LEONARD
B.APR.14,1866 HALSEY VALLEY,N.Y
D.JULY 12,1955

YR	CL	LEA	POS	GP	G	REC
1890	LOU	AA	1		134	.279
1891	LOU	AA	1		91	.289
1892	LOU	N	1-O		123	.274
1893	BAL	N	1		88	.294
		BL			436	.283

TAYLOR, HARRY WARREN
B.DEC.26,1908 MC KEESPORT,PA.
D.APR.27,1969 TOLEDO,OHIO

YR	CL	LEA	POS	GP	G	REC
1932	CHI	N	1		10	.125
		BLTL				

TAYLOR, JAMES HARRY "HARRY"
B.MAY 20,1919 E.GLENN,IND.

YR	CL	LEA	POS	GP	G	REC
1946	BRO	N	P		4	0- 0
1947	BRO	N	P		33	10- 5
1948	BRO	N	P		17	2- 7
1950	BOS	A	P		3	2- 0
1951	BOS	A	P		31	4- 9
1952	BOS	A	P		2	1- 0
		BRTR			90	19-21

TAYLOR, JAMES WREN "ZACK"
B.JULY 27,1898 YULEE,FLA.
D.SEPT.19,1974 ORLANDO,FLA.

YR	CL	LEA	POS	GP	G	REC
1920	BRO	N	C		5	.167
1921	BRO	N	C		30	.196
1922	BRO	N	C		7	.214
1923	BRO	N	C		96	.288
1924	BRO	N	C		99	.290
1925	BRO	N	C		109	.310
1926	BOS	N	C		125	.255
1927	BOS	N	C		30	.240
	NY	N	C		83	.233
1928	BOS	N	C		125	.251
1929	BOS	N	C		34	.248
	CHI	N	C		64	.274
1930	CHI	N	C		32	.232
1931	CHI	N	C		8	.250
1932	CHI	N	C		21	.200
1933	CHI	N	C		16	.000
1934	NY	A	C		4	.143
1935	BRO	N	C		26	.130
		BRTR			914	.261

NON-PLAYING MANAGER
STL(A) 1946, 48-51

TAYLOR, JOE CEPHUS
B.MAR.2,1926 CHAPMAN,ALA.

YR	CL	LEA	POS	GP	G	REC
1954	PHI	A	O		18	.224
1957	CIN	N	O		33	.262
1958	STL	N	O		18	.304
	BAL	A	O		36	.273
1959	BAL	A	O		14	.156
		BRTR			119	.249

YR	CL LEA POS	GP	G	REC

TAYLOR, JOHN BUDD "BREWERY"
B.MAY 27,1873 W.NEW BBRIGHTON,
S.I.,N.Y.
D.FEB.7,1900

YR	CL LEA POS	GP	G	REC
1891	NY N P		1	0- 1
1892	PHI N P		3	2- 0
1893	PHI N P	17	19	8- 8
1894	PHI N P		34	24-10
1895	PHI N P		40	26-13
1896	PHI N P		44	21-20
1897	PHI N P	36	37	18-18
1898	STL N P	47	49	16-31
1899	CIN N P		24	8-10
			246	251 123-111

TAYLOR, JOHN W. "JACK"
B.JAN.14,1874 NEW
STRAIGHTSVILLE,OHIO
D.MAR.4,1938

1898	CHI N P		5	5- 0
1899	CHI N P	41	42	18-22
1900	CHI N P		27	9-17
1901	CHI N P		33	13-19
1902	CHI N P-1-	38	53	22-11
	2-3-O			.239
1903	CHI N P	37	39	21-14
1904	STL N P		41	22-19
1905	STL N P	37	39	15-20
1906	STL N P		17	8- 9
	CHI N P		17	12- 3
1907	CHI N P	18	18	7- 5
	BRTR	309	331	152-139
				.222

TAYLOR, LEO THOMAS
B.MAY 13,1903 WALLA WALLA,WASH.

1923	CHI A H		1	.000
	BRTR			

TAYLOR, LUTHER HADEN "DUMMY"
B.FEB.21,1876 OLATHE,KAN.
D.AUG.22,1958

1900	NY N P		11	4- 3
1901	NY N P		45	18-27
1902	CLE A P		4	1- 3
	NY N P		23	8-15
1903	NY N P		33	13-13
1904	NY N P		37	21-15
1905	NY N P		32	16- 9
1906	NY N P		31	17- 9
1907	NY N P	28	29	11- 7
1908	NY N P		27	8- 5
	BRTR	271	272	117-106

TAYLOR, ROBERT DALE "HAWK"
B.APR.3,1939 METROPOLIS,Ill.

1957	MIL N C		7	.000
1958	MIL N O		4	.125
1961	MIL N C-O		20	.192
1962	MIL N O		20	.255
1963	MIL N O		16	.069
1964	NY N C-O		92	.240
1965	NY N C-1		25	.152
1966	NY N C-1		53	.174
1967	NY N C		13	.243
	CAL A C		23	.308
1969	KC N C-O		64	.270
1970	KC N C-1		57	.164
	BRTR		394	.218

TAYLOR, ROBERT LEE "BOB"
B.MAR.20,1944 LELAND,MISS.

1970	SF N C-O		63	.190
	BLTR			

TAYLOR, RONALD WESLEY "RON"
B.DEC.13,1937 TORONTO,ONT.,CAN.

1962	CLE A P	8	2- 2
1963	STL N P	54	9- 7
1964	STL N P	63	8- 4
1965	STL N P	25	2- 1
	HOU N P	32	1- 5
1966	HOU N P	36	2- 3
1967	NY N P	50	4- 6
1968	NY N P	58	1- 5
1969	NY N P	59	9- 4
1970	NY N P	57	5- 4
1971	NY N P	45	2- 2
1972	SD N P	4	0- 0
	BRTR	491	45-43

TAYLOR, SAMUEL DOUGLAS "SAMMY"
B.FEB.27,1933 WOODRUFF,S.C.

1958	CHI N C	96	.259
1959	CHI N C	110	.269
1960	CHI N C	74	.207
1961	CHI N C	89	.238
1962	CHI N C	7	.133
1962	NY N C	68	.222
1963	NY N C	22	.257
	CIN N C	3	.000
	CLE A C	4	.300
	BLTR	473	.245

**TAYLOR, THOMAS LIVINGSTONE
CARLTON**
B.SEPT.17,1895 MEXIA,TEX.
D.APR.5,1956

1924	WAS A 3	26	.260
	BRTR		

TAYLOR, VERNON CHARLES "PETE"
B.NOV.26,1927 SEVERN,MD.

1952	STL A P	1	0- 0
	BRTR		

TAYLOR, WALLACE NAPOLEON
B.1872 PITTSBURGH,PA.
D.SEPT.13,1905

1898	LOU N 3	9	.200

TAYLOR, WILEY
B.MAR.18,1888 WAMEGO,KAN.
D.JULY 9,1954

1911	DET A P	3	0- 2
1912	CHI A P	3	0- 1
1913	STL A P	5	0- 2
1914	STL A P	16	2- 5
	BRTR	27	2-10

**TAYLOR, WILLIAM HENRY
"BOLLICKY BILL"**
B.1855 WASHINGTON,D.C.
D.MAY 14,1900

1874	BAL NA 1		12	
1877	HAR N O		2	.375
1879	TRO N O		24	.214
1881	WOR N P-O	1	6	0- 1
				.111
	DET N 3		1	.500
	CLE N P-3-	1	25	0- 0
	O			.222
1882	PIT AA P-C-	1	65	0- 0
	1-3-O			.286
1883	PIT AA P-C-	11	83	3- 8
	1-O			.259
1884	STL U P-1-	31	42	24- 2
	O			.371
	ATH AA P		32	18-12
1885	ATH AA P		6	1- 5
1886	BAL AA P-O	7	10	1- 6
				.333
1887	ATH AA P		1	1- 0
	TR	91	309	48-34
				-

TEACHOUT, ARTHUR JOHN "BUD"
B.FEB.27,1904 LOS ANGELES,CAL.

1930	CHI N P	40	42	11- 4
1931	CHI N P	27	37	1- 2
1932	STL N P		1	0- 0
	BRTL	68	80	12- 6

**TEBBETTS, GEORGE ROBERT
"BIRDIE"**
B.NOV.10,1912 BURLINGTON,VT.

1936	DET A C	10	.303
1937	DET A C	50	.191
1938	DET A C	53	.294
1939	DET A C	106	.261
1940	DET A C	111	.296
1941	DET A C	110	.284
1942	DET A C	99	.247
1946	DET A C	87	.243
1947	DET A C	20	.094
	BOS A C	90	.299
1948	BOS A C	128	.280
1949	BOS A C	122	.270
1950	BOS A C	79	.310
1951	CLE A C	55	.263
1952	CLE A C	42	.248
	BRTR	1162	.270

NON-PLAYING MANAGER
CIN(N) 1954-58, MIL(N) 1961-62,
CLE(A) 1963-66

TEBEAU, C. A.

1895	CLE N O	2	.500

TEBEAU, GEORGE E. "WHITE WINGS"
B.DEC.26,1861 ST.LOUIS,MO.
D.FEB.4,1923 DENVER,COLO.

1887	CIN AA P-O	1	88	0- 0
				.361
1888	CIN AA O		121	.228
1889	CIN AA 1-O		135	.255
1890	TOL AA O		96	.261
1894	WAS N O		60	.226
	CLE N O		45	.316
1895	CLE N 1-O		87	.323
	BRTR	1	632	0- 0
				.284

TEBEAU, OLIVER WENDELL "PATSY"
B.DEC.5,1866 ST LOUIS,MO
D.MAY 15,1918

1887	CHI N 3	20	.208
1889	CLE N 3	136	.282
1890	CLE P M-3	108	.292
1891	CLE N M-3	61	.261
1892	CLE N M-3	84	.246
1893	CLE N M-1-3	115	.359
1894	CLE N M-1	110	.305
1895	CLE N M-1	66	.329
1896	CLE N M-1	132	.271
1897	CLE N M-1-2	111	.267
1898	CLE N M-1-2	130	.254
1899	STL N M-1	76	.253
1900	STL N M-1	1	.000

TEDROW, ALLEN SEYMOUR
B.DEC.14,1891 WESTERVILLE,OHIO
D.JAN.23,1958

1914	CLE A P	4	1- 2
	BRTL		

TEED, RICHARD LEROY "DICK"
B.MAR.8,1926 SPRINGFIELD,MASS.

1953	BRO N H	1	.000
	BBTR		

TEKULVE, KENTON CHARLES "KENT"
B.MAR.5,1947 CINCINNATI,OHIO

1974	PIT N P	8	1- 1
1975	PIT N P	34	1- 2
1976	PIT N P	64	5- 3
	BRTR	106	7- 6

TEMPLE, JOHN ELLIS "JOHNNY"
B.AUG.8,1928 LEXINGTON,N.C.

1952	CIN N 2	30	.196
1953	CIN N 2	63	.264
1954	CIN N 2	146	.307
1955	CIN N 2-S	150	.281
1956	CIN N 2-O	154	.285
1957	CIN N 2	145	.284
1958	CIN N 1-2	141	.306
1959	CIN N 2	149	.311
1960	CLE A 2-3	98	.268
1961	CLE A 2	129	.276
1962	BAL A 2	78	.263
	HOU N 2-3	31	.263
1963	HOU N 2-3	100	.264
1964	CIN N H	6	.000
	BRTR	1420	.284

YR CL LEA POS GP G REC

TEMPLETON, CHARLES SHERMAN "CHUCK"
B.JUNE 1,1932 DETROIT,MICH.
1955	BRO	N	P		4	0- 1
1956	BRO	N	P		6	0- 1
	BRTL				10	0- 2

TEMPLETON, GARRY LEWIS
B.MAR.24,1956 LOCKEY,TEX.
| 1976 | STL | N | S | | 53 | .291 |
| | BBTR | | | | | |

TENER, JOHN KINLEY
B.JULY 25,1863 TYRONE CO.,
IRELAND
D.MAY 19,1946
1885	BAL	AA	O		1	.000
1888	CHI	N	P		14	7- 5
1889	CHI	N	P	31	38	14-15
1890	PIT	P	P		19	3-13
	BRTR			65	72	24-33
						.235

TENACE, FURY GENE "GENE"
B.OCT.10,1946 RUSSELTON,PA.
1969	OAK	A	C		16	.158
1970	OAK	A	C		38	.305
1971	OAK	A	C-O		65	.274
1972	OAK	A	C-1-2-3- O		82	.225
1973	OAK	A	C-1-2		160	.258
1974	OAK	A	C-1-2		158	.211
1975	OAK	A	C-1		158	.255
1976	OAK	A	C-1		128	.249
	BRTR				805	.245

TENNANT, JAMES MC DONNELL
B.MAR.3,1907 SHEPHERDSTOWN,W.VA
D.APR.16,1967 TRUMBULL,CONN.
| 1929 | NY | N | P | | 1 | 0- 0 |
| | BRTR | | | | | |

TENNANT, THOMAS FRANCIS
B.JULY 3,1882 MONROE,WIS.
D.FEB.16,1955
| 1912 | STL | A | H | | 2 | .000 |
| | BLTL | | | | | |

TENNEY, FREDERICK "FRED"
B.NOV.26,1871 GEORGETOWN,MASS.
D.JULY 3,1952 BOSTON,MASS.
1894	BOS	N	C		24	.387
1895	BOS	N	C-O		42	.276
1896	BOS	N	C-O		86	.342
1897	BOS	N	1		131	.325
1898	BOS	N	1		117	.335
1899	BOS	N	1		150	.350
1900	BOS	N	1		111	.284
1901	BOS	N	1		113	.278
1902	BOS	N	1		134	.314
1903	BOS	N	1		122	.313
1904	BOS	N	1		147	.270
1905	BOS	N	M-1		148	.288
1906	BOS	N	M-1		143	.283
1907	BOS	N	M-1		149	.273
1908	NY	N	1		156	.256
1909	NY	N	1		98	.235
1911	BOS	N	M-1		98	.263
	BLTL				1969	.295

TENNEY, FREDERICK CLAY
B.JUNE 9,1859 MARLBORO,N.H.
1884	WAS	U	1-O		30	.236
	BOS	U	P		5	4- 1
	WIL	U	P		1	0- 1
				6	36	4- 2
						.217

TEPEDINO, FRANK RONALD
B.NOV.23,1947 BROOKLYN,N.Y.
1967	NY	A	1		9	.400
1969	NY	A	O		13	.231
1970	NY	A	1-O		16	.316
1971	NY	A	O		6	.000
	MIL	A	1		53	.198
1972	NY	A	H		8	.000
1973	ATL	N	1		74	.304
1974	ATL	N	1		78	.231
1975	ATL	N	H		8	.000
	BLTL				265	.241

TEPSIC, JOSEPH JOHN
B.SEPT.18,1923 SOLVAN,PA.
| 1946 | BRO | N | O | | 15 | .000 |
| | BRTR | | | | | |

TERLECKI, ROBERT JOSEPH "BOB"
B.FEB.14,1945 TRENTON,N.J.
| 1972 | PHI | N | P | | 9 | 0- 0 |
| | BRTR | | | | | |

TERLECKY, GREGORY JOHN "GREG"
B.MAR.20,1952 CULVER CITY,CAL.
| 1975 | STL | N | P | | 20 | 0- 1 |
| | BRTR | | | | | |

TERPKO, JEFFREY MICHAEL "JEFF"
B.OCT.16,1950 SAYRE,PA.
1974	TEX	A	P		3	0- 0
1976	TEX	A	P		32	3- 3
	BRTR				35	3- 3

TERRELL, JERRY WAYNE
B.JULY 13,1946 WASECA,MINN.
1973	MIN	A	2-S-3-O		124	.265
1974	MIN	A	1-2-S-3- O-D		116	.245
1975	MIN	A	1-2-S-3-O O		108	.286
1976	MIN	A	2-S-3-O		89	.246
	BRTR				437	.265
	BB 1974 (PART)					

TERRELL, THOMAS
B.LOUISVILLE,KY.
D.JULY 1893
| 1886 | LOU | AA | C | | 1 | .250 |

TERRY
| 1875 | NAT | NA | 1-O | | 5 | - |

TERRY, JOHN
B.ST.LOUIS,MO.
1902	DET	A	P		1	0- 1
1903	STL	A	P		3	1- 0
					4	1- 1

TERRY, LANCELOT YANK "YANK"
B.FEB.11,1911 BEDFORD,IND.
1940	BOS	A	P		4	1- 0
1942	BOS	A	P		20	6- 5
1943	BOS	A	P		30	7- 9
1944	BOS	A	P		27	6-10
1945	BOS	A	P		12	0- 4
	BRTR				93	20-28

TERRY, RALPH WILLARD
B.JAN.9,1936 BIG CABIN,OKLA.
1956	NY	A	P		3	1- 2
1957	NY	A	P		7	1- 1
	KC	A	P	21	22	4-11
1958	KC	A	P		40	11-13
1959	KC	A	P		9	2- 4
	NY	A	P		24	3- 7
1960	NY	A	P		35	10- 8
1961	NY	A	P		31	16- 3
1962	NY	A	P		43	23-12
1963	NY	A	P		40	17-15
1964	NY	A	P		27	7-11
1965	CLE	A	P		30	11- 6
1966	KC	A	P		15	1- 5
	NY	N	P		11	0- 1
1967	NY	N	P		2	0- 0
	BRTR			338	339	107-99

TERRY, WILLIAM HAROLD "MEMPHIS BILL"
B.OCT.30,1898 ATLANTA,GA.
1923	NY	N	1		3	.143
1924	NY	N	1		77	.239
1925	NY	N	1		133	.319
1926	NY	N	1-O		98	.289
1927	NY	N	1		150	.326
1928	NY	N	1		149	.326
1929	NY	N	1		150	.372
1930	NY	N	1		154	.401
1931	NY	N	1		153	.349
1932	NY	N	M-1		154	.350
1933	NY	N	M-1		123	.322
1934	NY	N	M-1		153	.354
1935	NY	N	M-1		145	.341
1936	NY	N	M-1		79	.310
	BLTL				1721	.341
NON-PLAYING MANAGER
NY(N) 1937-41

TERRY, WILLIAM H. "ADONIS"
B.AUG.7,1864 WESTFIELD,MASS.
D.FEB.24,1914 MILWAUKEE,WIS.
1884	BRO	AA	P-O	55	57	19-35
						.235
1885	BRO	AA	P-O	25	70	6-16
						.162
1886	BRO	AA	P-O	33	75	18-15
						.250
1887	BRO	AA	P-O	40	86	17-16
						.335
1888	BRO	AA	P	24	30	13- 8
1889	BRO	AA	P	40	48	21-16
1890	BRO	N	P-O	44	99	26-15
						.278
1891	BRO	N	P	23	25	6-15
1892	BAL	N	P		6	1- 1
	PIT	N	P		27	20- 7
1893	PIT	N	P		21	12- 7
1894	PIT	N	P		6	0- 1
	CHI	N	P		24	4-12
1895	CHI	N	P	37	39	21-14
1896	CHI	N	P		29	14-15
1897	CHI	N	P		1	0- 0
	BRTR			435	653	198-193
						.271

TERRY, ZEBULON ALEXANDER "ZEB"
B.JUNE 17,1891 DENISON,TEX.
1916	CHI	A	S		94	.190
1917	CHI	A	S		2	.100
1918	BOS	N	S		28	.305
1919	PIT	N	S		129	.227
1920	CHI	N	2-S		133	.280
1921	CHI	N	2		123	.275
1922	CHI	N	2-S-3		131	.286
	BRTR				640	.260

TERWILLIGER, RICHARD MARTIN
B.JUNE 27,1906 SAND LAKE,MICH.
D.JAN.21,1969 GREENVILLE,MICH.
| 1932 | STL | N | P | | 1 | 0- 0 |
| | BRTR | | | | | |

TERWILLIGER, WILLARD WAYNE "WAYNE" OR "TWIG"
B.JUNE 27,1925 CLARE,MICH.
1949	CHI	N	2		36	.223
1950	CHI	N	1-2-3-O		133	.242
1951	CHI	N	2		50	.214
	BRO	N	2-3		37	.280
1953	WAS	A	2		134	.252
1954	WAS	A	2-S-3		106	.208
1955	NY	N	2-S-3		80	.257
1956	NY	N	2		14	.222
1959	KC	A	2-S-3		74	.267
1960	KC	A	2		2	.000
	BRTR				666	.240

TESCH, ALBERT JOHN
B.JAN.27,1891 JERSEY CITY,N.J.
D.AUG.3,1947
| 1915 | BRO | F | 2 | | 7 | .286 |
| | BBTR | | | | | |

TESREAU, CHARLES MONROE "JEFF"
B.MAR.5,1889 IRONTON,MO.
D.SEPT.24,1946
1912	NY	N	P		36	17- 7
1913	NY	N	P		41	22-13
1914	NY	N	P		42	26-10
1915	NY	N	P		43	19-16
1916	NY	N	P	40	41	14-14
1917	NY	N	P		33	13- 8
1918	NY	N	P		12	4- 4
	BRTR			247	248	115-72

TESTA, NICHOLAS "NICK"
B.JUNE 29,1928 NEW YORK,N.Y.
| 1958 | SF | N | C | | 1 | .000 |
| | BRTR | | | | | |

TETTELBACH, RICHARD MORLEY "DICK"
B.JUNE 26,1929 NEW HAVEN,CONN.
1955	NY	A	O		2	.000
1956	WAS	A	O		18	.156
1957	WAS	A	O		9	.182
	BRTR				29	.150

TEXTOR, GEORGE B.
B.DEC.27,1889 NEWPORT,KY.
D.MAR.11,1954
1914	IND	F	C		20	.179
1915	NEW	F	C		3	.333
	BBTR				23	.194

YR	CL	LEA	POS	GP	G	REC

THACKER, MORRIS BENTON "MOE"
B.MAY 21,1934 LOUISVILLE,KY.

YR	CL	LEA	POS	GP	G	REC
1958	CHI	N	C		11	.250
1960	CHI	N	C		54	.156
1961	CHI	N	C		25	.171
1962	CHI	N	C		65	.187
1963	STL	N	C		3	.000
	BRTR				158	.177

THAKE, ALBERT
B.1847 NEW YORK,N.Y.
D.SEPT.1,1872

| 1872 | ATL | NA | 2-0 | | 17 | .274 |

THATCHER, ULYSSES GRANT
B.FEB.23,1877 MAYTOWN,PA.
D.MAR.17,1936

1903	BRO	N	P		4	3- 1
1904	BRO	N	P		1	1- 0
	TR				5	4- 1

THAYER, EDWARD L.
B.MECHANIC FALLS,ME.

| 1876 | MUT | N | 2 | | 1 | .000 |

THEIS, JOHN LEWIS
B.JULY 23,1891 GEORGETOWN,OHIO
D.JULY 6,1941

| 1920 | CIN | N | P | | 1 | 0- 0 |
| | BRTR | | | | | |

THEOBALD, RONALD MERRILL "RON"
B.JULY 28,1943 OAKLAND,CAL.

1971	MIL	A	2-S-3		126	.276
1972	MIL	A	2		125	.220
	BRTR				251	.248

THEODORE, GEORGE BASIL
B.NOV.13,1947 SALT LAKE CITY,UT.

1973	NY	N	1-0		45	.259
1974	NY	N	1-0		60	.158
	BRTR				105	.219

THESENGA, ARNOLD JOSEPH "JUG"
B.APR.27,1914 JEFFERSON,S.DAK.

| 1944 | WAS | A | P | | 5 | 0- 0 |
| | BRTR | | | | | |

THEVENOW, THOMAS JOSEPH "TOMMY"
B.SEPT.6,1903 MADISON,IND.
D.JULY 28,1957

1924	STL	N	S		23	.202
1925	STL	N	S		50	.269
1926	STL	N	S		156	.256
1927	STL	N	S		59	.194
1928	STL	N	S		69	.205
1929	PHI	N	S		90	.227
1930	PHI	N	S		156	.286
1931	PIT	N	S		120	.213
1932	PIT	N	S-3		59	.237
1933	PIT	N	2-S-3		73	.312
1934	PIT	N	2-3		122	.271
1935	PIT	N	2-S-3		110	.238
1936	CIN	N	2-S-3		106	.234
1937	BOS	N	S		21	.118
1938	PIT	N	2-S-3		15	.200
	BRTR				1229	.248

THIEL, MAYNARD BERT "BERT"
B.MAY 4,1926 MARION,WIS.

| 1952 | BOS | N | P | | 4 | 1- 1 |
| | BRTR | | | | | |

THIELMAN, HENRY JOSEPH
B.OCT.18,1880 ST.CLOUD,MINN.
D.SEPT.2,1942

1902	NY	N	P-0	5	6	0- 1
						.111
	CIN	N	P		29	9-15
1903	BRO	N	P		8	0- 3
	BRTR			42	43	9-19
						.121

THIELMAN, JOHN PETER "JAKE"
B.MAR.30,1879 ST.CLOUD,MINN.
D.JAN.28,1928

1905	STL	N	P	32	33	15-16
1906	STL	N	P		3	0- 3
1907	CLE	A	P	20	21	11- 8
1908	CLE	A	P		11	3- 3
	BOS	A	P		1	1- 0
				67	69	30-30

THIES, DAVID ROBERT "DAVE"
B.MAR.21,1938 MINNEAPOLIS,MINN.

| 1963 | KC | A | P | | 9 | 0- 1 |
| | BRTR | | | | | |

THIES, VERNON ARTHUR "JAKE"
B.APR.1,1928 ST.LOUIS,MO.

1954	PIT	N	P		33	3- 9
1955	PIT	N	P		1	0- 0
	BRTR				34	3-10

THOENEN, RICHARD CRISPIN "DICK"
B.JAN.9,1944 MEXICO,MO.

| 1967 | PHI | N | P | | 1 | 0- 0 |
| | BRTR | | | | | |

THOENY, JOHN
(PLAYED UNDER NAME OF
JOHN THONEY)

THOMAS, ALPHONSE THOMAS "TOMMY"
B.DEC.23,1899 BALTIMORE,MD.

1926	CHI	A	P		44	15-12
1927	CHI	A	P		40	19-16
1928	CHI	A	P		36	17-16
1929	CHI	A	P	36	37	14-18
1930	CHI	A	P		34	5-13
1931	CHI	A	P		43	10-14
1932	CHI	A	P		12	3- 3
	WAS	A	P		18	8- 7
1933	WAS	A	P		35	7- 7
1934	WAS	A	P		33	8- 9
1935	WAS	A	P		1	0- 0
	PHI	N	P		4	0- 1
1936	STL	A	P		36	11- 9
1937	STL	A	P		17	0- 1
	BOS	A	P		9	0- 2
	BRTR			398	399	117-128

THOMAS, BLAINE M.
B.1888 PAYSON,ARIZ.
D.AUG.21,1915

| 1911 | BOS | A | P | | 2 | 0- 0 |
| | BRTR | | | | | |

THOMAS, CARL LESLIE
B.MAY 28,1932 MINNEAPOLIS,MINN.

| 1960 | CLE | A | P | | 5 | 1- 0 |
| | BRTR | | | | | |

THOMAS, CHESTER DAVID "PINCH"
B.JAN.24,1888 CAMP POINT,ILL.
D.DEC.24,1953

1912	BOS	A	C		13	.194
1913	BOS	A	C		37	.286
1914	BOS	A	C		63	.192
1915	BOS	A	C		86	.236
1916	BOS	A	C		99	.264
1917	BOS	A	C		83	.238
1918	CLE	A	C		32	.247
1919	CLE	A	C		34	.109
1920	CLE	A	C		7	.333
1921	CLE	A	C		21	.257
	BLTR				475	.237

THOMAS, CLARENCE FLETCHER "LEFTY"
B.OCT.4,1903 GLADE SPPINGS,VA.
D.MAR.21,1952 CHARLOTTESVILLE, VA.

1925	WAS	A	P		2	0- 2
1926	WAS	A	P		6	0- 0
	BRTL				8	0- 2

THOMAS, CLAUDE ALFRED
B.MAY 15,1890 STANBERRY,MO.
D.MAR.6,1946

| 1916 | WAS | A | P | | 7 | 0- 3 |
| | BLTL | | | | | |

THOMAS, DANNY LEE "DAN"
B.MAY 9,1951 BIRMINGHAM,ALA.

| 1976 | MIL | A | 0 | | 32 | .276 |
| | BRTR | | | | | |

THOMAS, DERRELL OSBON
B.JAN.14,1951 LOS ANGELES,CAL.

1971	HOU	N	2		5	.000
1972	SD	N	2-S-0		130	.230
1973	SD	N	2-S		113	.238
1974	SD	N	2-S-3-0		141	.247
1975	SF	N	2-0		144	.276
1976	SF	N	2-S-3-0		81	.232
	BBTR				614	.246

THOMAS, FAY WESLEY "SCOW"
B.OCT.10,1904 WICHITA,KAN.

1927	NY	N	P		9	0- 0
1931	CLE	A	P		16	2- 4
1932	BRO	N	P		7	0- 1
1935	STL	A	P		49	7-15
	BRTR				81	9-20

THOMAS, FORREST "FROSTY"
B.MAY 23,1883 BUCHANAN CO.,MO.
D.MAR.18,1970 ST.JOSEPH,MO.

| 1905 | DET | A | P | | 2 | 0- 2 |
| | BRTR | | | | | |

THOMAS, FRANK JOSEPH
B.JUNE 11,1929 PITTSBURGH,PA.

1951	PIT	N	0		39	.264
1952	PIT	N	0		6	.095
1953	PIT	N	0		128	.255
1954	PIT	N	0		153	.298
1955	PIT	N	0		142	.245
1956	PIT	N	2-3-0		157	.282
1957	PIT	N	1-3-0		151	.290
1958	PIT	N	1-3-0		149	.281
1959	CIN	N	1-3-0		108	.225
1960	CHI	N	1-3-0		135	.238
1961	CHI	N	1-0		15	.260
	MIL	N	1-0		124	.284
1962	NY	N	1-3-0		156	.266
1963	NY	N	1-3-0		126	.260
1964	NY	N	1-3-0		60	.254
	PHI	N	1		39	.294
1965	PHI	N	1-3-0		35	.260
	HOU	N	1-3-0		23	.172
	MIL	N	1-0		15	.212
1966	CHI	N	H		5	.000
	BRTR				1766	.266

THOMAS, FRED HARVEY "TOMMY"
B.DEC.19,1892 MILWAUKEE,WIS.

1918	BOS	A	3		44	.257
1919	PHI	A	3		124	.212
1920	PHI	A	3		77	.233
	WAS	A	3		2	.000

THOMAS, FREDERICK L.
D.INDIANA
NON-PLAYING MANAGER IND(N) 1887

THOMAS, GEORGE EDWARD
B.NOV.29,1937 MINNEAPOLIS,MINN.

1957	DET	A	3		1	.000
1958	DET	A	0		1	.000
1961	DET	A	S-0		17	.000
	LA	A	3-0		79	.280
1962	LA	A	0		56	.238
1963	LA	A	1-3-0		53	.210
	DET	A	2-0		49	.239
1964	DET	A	3-0		105	.286
1965	DET	A	2-0		79	.213
1966	BOS	A	C-1-3-0		69	.237
1967	BOS	A	C-1-0		65	.213
1968	BOS	A	0		12	.200
1969	BOS	A	C-1-3-0		29	.353
1970	BOS	A	3-0		38	.343
1971	BOS	A	0		9	.077
	MIN	A	1-3-0		23	.267
	BRTR				685	.255

THOMAS, HERBERT MARK
B.MAR.26,1902 SAMPSON CITY,FLA.

1924	BOS	N	0		32	.220
1925	BOS	N	2		5	.235
1927	BOS	N	2		24	.230
	NY	N	0		13	.176
	BRTR				74	.221

THOMAS, IRA FELIX
B.JAN.22,1881 BALLSTON SPA,N.Y.
D.OCT.11,1958

1906	NY	A	C		44	.200
1907	NY	A	C		80	.192
1908	DET	A	C		40	.307
1909	PHI	A	C		84	.223
1910	PHI	A	C		60	.277
1911	PHI	A	C		103	.273
1912	PHI	A	C		46	.216
1913	PHI	A	C		21	.283
1914	PHI	A	C		2	.000
1915	PHI	A	C		1	.000
	BRTR				481	.242

THOMAS, JAMES GORMAN "GORMAN"
B.DEC.12,1950 CHARLESTON,S.C.

1973	MIL	A	3-0		59	.187
1974	MIL	A	0		17	.261
1975	MIL	A	0		121	.179
1976	MIL	A	3-0		99	.198
	BRTR				296	.193

YR	CL	LEA	POS	GP	G	REC

THOMAS, JAMES LEROY "LEE"
B.FEB.5,1936 PEORIA,ILL.

YR	CL	LEA	POS	GP	G	REC
1961	NY	A	H		2	.500
	LA	A	1-O	ƚ30		.284
1962	LA	A	1-O	160		.290
1963	LA	A	1-O	149		.220
1964	LA	A	1-O	47		.273
	BOS	A	1-O	107		.257
1965	BOS	A	1-O	151		.271
1966	ATL	N	1	39		.198
	CHI	N	1-O	75		.242
1967	CHI	N	1-O	77		.220
1968	HOU	N	1-O	90		.194
	BLTR			1027		.255

THOMAS, JOHN TILLMAN "BUD"
B.MAR.10,1929 SEDALIA,MO.

| 1951 | STL | A | -S | | 14 | .350 |

THOMAS, KEITH MARSHALL "KITE"
B.APR.27,1924 KANSAS CITY,KAN.

1952	PHI	A	O		75	.250
1953	PHI	A	O		24	.122
	WAS	A	C-O		38	.293
	BRTR				137	.233

THOMAS, LEO RAYMOND
B.JULY 26,1923 TURLOCK,CAL.

1950	STL	A	3		35	.198
1952	STL	A	2-S-3		41	.234
	CHI	A	3		19	.167
	BRTR				95	.212

THOMAS, LUTHER BAXTER "BUD"
B.SEPT.6,1910 N.GARDEN,VA.

1932	WAS	A	P		2	0- 0
1933	WAS	A	P		2	0- 0
1937	PHI	A	P		35	8-15
1938	PHI	A	P		42	9-14
1939	PHI	A	P		2	0- 1
	WAS	A	P		4	0- 0
	DET	A	P		27	7- 0
1940	DET	A	P		3	0- 1
1941	DET	A	P		26	1- 3
	BRTR				143	25-34

THOMAS, MYLES LEWIS
B.OCT.22,1899 STATE COLLEGE,PA.
D.DEC.12,1963 TOLEDO,OHIO

1926	NY	A	P		33	6- 6
1927	NY	A	P		21	7- 4
1928	NY	A	P	12	13	1- 0
1929	NY	A	P		5	0- 2
	WAS	A	P		22	7- 8
1930	WAS	A	P	12	14	2- 2
	BRTR			105	108	23-22

THOMAS, RAYMOND JOSEPH
B.JULY 9,1910 DOVER,N.H.

| 1938 | BRO | N | C | | 1 | .333 |

THOMAS, ROBERT WILLIAM "RED"
B.APR.25,1899 HARGROVE,ALA.
D.MAR.29,1962

| 1921 | CHI | N | O | | 8 | .267 |
| | BRTR | | | | | |

THOMAS, ROY ALLEN
B.MAR.24,1874 NORRISTOWN,PA.
D.NOV.20,1959

1899	PHI	N	O		148	.324
1900	PHI	N	P-O	1	139	0- 0
						.325
1901	PHI	N	O		128	.305
1902	PHI	N	O		138	.292
1903	PHI	N	O		130	.327
1904	PHI	N	O		139	.290
1905	PHI	N	O		147	.317
1906	PHI	N	O		142	.254
1907	PHI	N	O		121	.243
1908	PHI	N	O		6	.167
	PIT	N	O		101	.256
1909	BOS	N	O		77	.263
1910	PHI	N	O		20	.183
1911	PHI	N	O		21	.133
	BLTL			1	1457	0- 0
						.291

THOMAS, STANLEY BROWN "STAN"
B.JULY 11,1949 RUMFORD,ME.

1974	TEX	A	P		12	0- 0
1975	TEX	A	P		46	4- 4
1976	CLE	A	P		37	4- 4
	BRTR				95	8- 8

THOMAS, THOMAS W.
B.DEC.27,1873 SHAWNEE,OHIO
D.SEPT.22,1942

1899	STL	N	P		4	1- 1
1900	STL	N	P		5	1- 0
					9	2- 1

THOMAS, VALMY
B.OCT.21,1928 SANTURCE,P.R.

1957	NY	N	C		88	.249
1958	SF	N	C		63	.259
1959	PHI	N	C-3		66	.200
1960	BAL	A	C		8	.063
1961	CLE	A	C		27	.209
	BRTR				252	.230

THOMAS, WALTER W.

| 1908 | BOS | N | S | | 5 | .154 |
| | TR | | | | | |

THOMAS, WILLIAM MISKEY
B.DEC.8,1877 NORRISTOWN,PA.
D.JAN.14,1950

| 1902 | PHI | N | 1-2-O | | 6 | .176 |
| | TR | | | | | |

THOMASEN, ARTHUR WILSON
B.SEPT.9,1884 LIBERTY,MO.
D.MAY 2,1944

| 1910 | CLE | A | O | | 17 | .158 |

THOMASON, MELVIN ERSKINE "ERSKINE"
B.AUG.13,1948 LAURENS,S.C.

| 1974 | PHI | N | P | | 1 | 0- 0 |
| | BRTR | | | | | |

THOMASSON, GARY LEAH
B.JULY 29,1951 SAN DIEGO,CAL.

1972	SF	N	1-O		10	.333
1973	SF	N	1-O		112	.285
1974	SF	N	1-O		120	.244
1975	SF	N	1-O		114	.227
1976	SF	N	1-O		103	.259
	BLTL				459	.253

THOMPSON, A. M.
B.ST.PAUL,MINN.

1875	NAT	NA	C-O		10	-
	ATL	NA	O		1	-
					11	-

NON-PLAYING MANAGER STP(U) 1884

THOMPSON, ARTHUR J.

| 1884 | WAS | U | P | | 1 | 0- 1 |

THOMPSON, CHARLES LEMOINE "TIM"
B.MAR.1,1926 COALPORT,PA.

1954	BRO	N	C		10	.154
1956	KC	A	C		92	.272
1957	KC	A	C		81	.204
1958	DET	A	C		4	.167
	BLTR				187	.238

THOMPSON, DANNY LEON
B.FEB.1,1947 WICHITA,KAN.
D.DEC.10,1976 ROCHESTER,MINN.

1970	MIN	A	2-S-3		96	.219
1971	MIN	A	2-S-3		48	.263
1972	MIN	A	S		144	.276
1973	MIN	A	S-3		99	.225
1974	MIN	A	S-3		97	.250
1975	MIN	A	2-S-3		112	.270
1976	MIN	A	S		34	.234
	TEX	A	2-S-3		64	.214
	BRTR				694	.248

THOMPSON, DAVID FORREST
B.MAR.3,1918 MOORESVILLE,N.C.

1948	WAS	A	P		46	6-10
1949	WAS	A	P	9	10	1- 3
	BLTL			55	56	7-13

THOMPSON, DONALD NEWLIN "DON"
B.DEC.28,1923 SWEPSONVILLE,N.C.

1949	BOS	N	O		7	.182
1951	BRO	N	O		80	.229
1953	BRO	N	O		96	.242
1954	BRO	N	O		34	.040
	BLTL				217	.218

THOMPSON, EUGENE EARL "JUNIOR"
B.JUNE 7,1917 LATHAM,ILL.

1939	CIN	N	P		42	13- 5
1940	CIN	N	P		33	16- 9
1941	CIN	N	P		27	6- 6
1942	CIN	N	P		29	4- 7
1946	NY	N	P		39	4- 6
1947	NY	N	P		15	4- 2
	BRTR				185	47-35

THOMPSON, FRANK E.
B.JULY 4,1893 SPRINGFIELD,MO.
D.JUNE 27,1940 MINERAL TWSP.,MO

| 1920 | STL | A | 3 | | 22 | .170 |
| | BRTR | | | | | |

THOMPSON, FULLER WEIDNER
B.MAY 1,1889 LOS ANGELES,CAL.
D.FEB.19,1972 LOS ANGELES,CAL.

| 1911 | BOS | N | P | | 3 | 0- 0 |
| | BRTR | | | | | |

THOMPSON, HARRY
B.MAR.25,1893 NANTICOKE,PA.
D.FEB.14,1951

1919	WAS	A	P	12	18	0- 3
	PHI	A	P	3	5	0- 1
	BLTL			15	23	0- 4

THOMPSON, HENRY CURTIS "HANK"
B.DEC.8,1925 OKLAHOMA CITY,OKLA
D.SEPT.30,1969 FRESNO,CAL.

1947	STL	A	2		27	.256
1949	NY	N	2-3		75	.280
1950	NY	N	3-O		148	.289
1951	NY	N	3		87	.235
1952	NY	N	2-3-O		128	.260
1953	NY	N	2-3-O		114	.302
1954	NY	N	2-3-O		136	.263
1955	NY	N	2-S-3		135	.245
1956	NY	N	2-3-O		83	.235
	BLTR				933	.267

THOMPSON, JAMES ALFRED "SHAG"
B.APR.29,1893 HAW RIVER,N.C.

1914	PHI	A	O		16	.172
1915	PHI	A	O		17	.333
1916	PHI	A	O		15	.000
	BLTR				48	.203

THOMPSON, JASON DOLPH
B.JULY 6,1954 HOLLYWOOD,CAL.

| 1976 | DET | A | 1 | | 123 | .218 |
| | BLTL | | | | | |

THOMPSON, JOHN DUDLEY "LEE"
B.FEB.26,1898 SMITHFIELD,UTAH
D.FEB.17,1963 SANTA BARBARA,CAL

| 1921 | CHI | A | P | | 4 | 0- 3 |
| | BLTR | | | | | |

THOMPSON, JOHN GUS
B.JUNE 22,1877 HUMBOLDT,IOWA
D.MAR.28,1958

1903	PIT	N	P		5	2- 2
1906	STL	N	P		17	2-11
					22	4-13

THOMPSON, JOHN P. F. "TUG"
B.INDIANAPOLIS,IND.

1882	CIN	AA	O		1	.200
1884	IND	AA	C-O		24	.204
					25	.204

THOMPSON, JOHN SAMUEL "JOCKO"
B.JAN.17,1920 BEVERLY,MASS.

1948	PHI	N	P		2	1- 0
1949	PHI	N	P	8	9	1- 3
1950	PHI	N	P		2	0- 0
1951	PHI	N	P	29	30	4- 8
	BLTL			41	43	6-11

THOMPSON, LAFAYETTE FRESCO "FRESCO"
B.JUNE 6,1903 CENTERVILLE,ALA.
D.NOV.20,1968 FULLERTON,CAL.

1925	PIT	N	2		14	.243
1926	NY	N	2		2	.625
1927	PHI	N	2		153	.303
1928	PHI	N	2		152	.287
1929	PHI	N	2		148	.324
1930	PHI	N	2		122	.282
1931	BRO	N	2-S		74	.265
1932	BRO	N	H		3	.000
1934	NY	N	H		1	.000
	BRTR				669	.298

YR	CL	LEA	POS	GP	G	REC

THOMPSON, MICHAEL WAYNE "MIKE"
B.SEP.6,1949 DENVER,COLO.

YR	CL	LEA	POS	GP	G	REC
1971	WAS	A	P		16	1- 6
1973	STL	N	P		2	0- 0
1974	STL	N	P		19	0- 3
	ATL	N	P		1	0- 0
1975	ATL	N	P		16	0- 6
	BRTR				54	1-15

THOMPSON, RUPERT LOCKHART "TOMMY"
B.MAY 19,1910 ELKHART,ILL.
D.MAY 24,1971 AUBURN,CAL.

YR	CL	LEA	POS	GP	G	REC
1933	BOS	N	O		24	.186
1934	BOS	N	O		105	.265
1935	BOS	N	O		112	.273
1936	BOS	N	1-O		106	.286
1938	CHI	A	1		19	.111
1939	CHI	A	O		1	.000
	STL	A	O		30	.302
	BLTR				397	.266

THOMPSON, SAMUEL L. "BIG SAM"
B.MAR.5,1860 DANVILLE,IND.
D.NOV.7,1922 DETROIT,MICH.

YR	CL	LEA	POS	GP	G	REC
1885	DET	N	O		63	.303
1886	DET	N	O		122	.310
1887	DET	N	O		127	.406
1888	DET	N	O		55	.281
1889	PHI	N	O		128	.296
1890	PHI	N	O		132	.313
1891	PHI	N	O		133	.295
1892	PHI	N	O		151	.303
1893	PHI	N	O		130	.377
1894	PHI	N	O		102	.403
1895	PHI	N	O		118	.394
1896	PHI	N	O		119	.305
1897	PHI	N	O		3	.250
1898	PHI	N	O		14	.365
1906	DET	A	O		8	.225
	BLTL				1405	.336

THOMPSON, THOMAS CARL
B.NOV.7,1889 SPRING CITY,TENN.
D.JAN.16,1963 LA JOLLA,CAL.

YR	CL	LEA	POS	GP	G	REC
1912	NY	A	P		8	0- 2
	BRTR					

THOMPSON, THOMAS HOMER "HOMER"
B.JUNE 1,1892 SPRING CITY,TENN.

YR	CL	LEA	POS	GP	G	REC
1912	NY	A	C		1	.000
	BRTR					

THOMPSON, WILL MC LAIN
B.AUG.30,1870 PITTSBURGH,PA.

YR	CL	LEA	POS	GP	G	REC
1892	PIT	N	P		1	0- 1

THOMSON, ROBERT BROWN "BOBBY"
B.OCT.25,1923 GLASGOW,SCOTLAND

YR	CL	LEA	POS	GP	G	REC
1946	NY	N	3		18	.315
1947	NY	N	2-O		138	.283
1948	NY	N	O		138	.248
1949	NY	N	O		156	.309
1950	NY	N	O		149	.252
1951	NY	N	3-O		148	.294
1952	NY	N	3-O		153	.270
1953	NY	N	O		154	.288
1954	MIL	N	O		43	.232
1955	MIL	N	O		101	.257
1956	MIL	N	3-O		142	.235
1957	MIL	N	O		41	.236
	NY	N	3-O		81	.242
1958	CHI	N	3-O		152	.283
1959	CHI	N	O		122	.259
1960	BOS	A	1-O		40	.263
	BAL	A	O		3	.000
	BRTR				1779	.270

THONEY, JOHN "BULLET JOHN"
(REAL NAME JOHN THOENY)
B.DEC.8,1879 FT.THOMAS,KY.
D.OCT.24,1948

YR	CL	LEA	POS	GP	G	REC
1902	CLE	A	2-S-O		28	.291
	BAL	A	3		3	.000
1903	CLE	A	O		32	.213
1904	WAS	A	O		17	.300
	NY	A	3-O		35	.231
1908	BOS	A	O		109	.255
1909	BOS	A	O		14	.184
1911	BOS	A	O		26	.250
	BRTR				264	.235

THORMAHLEN, HERBERT EHLER "HERB" OR "LEFTY"
B.JULY 5,1896 JERSEY CITY,N.J.
D.FEB.6,1955

YR	CL	LEA	POS	GP	G	REC
1917	NY	A	P		1	0- 1
1918	NY	A	P		16	7- 3
1919	NY	A	P		30	13- 9
1920	NY	A	P		29	9- 6
1921	BOS	A	P		23	1- 7
1925	BRO	N	P		5	0- 3
	BLTL				104	30-29

THORNTON, ANDRE "ANDY"
B.AUG.13,1949 TUSKEGEE,ALA.

YR	CL	LEA	POS	GP	G	REC
1973	CHI	N	1		17	.200
1974	CHI	N	1-3		107	.261
1975	CHI	N	1-3		120	.293
1976	CHI	N	1		27	.200
	MON	N	1-O		69	.191
	BRTR				340	.253

THORNTON, JOHN
B.1870 WASHINGTON,D.C.
D.AUG.31,1893

YR	CL	LEA	POS	GP	G	REC
1889	WAS	N	P		1	0- 1
1891	PHI	N	P		30	15-11
1892	PHI	N	P-O	3	5	0- 1
						.385
	STL	N	O		1	.000
				34	37	15-13
						.157

THORNTON, OTIS BENJAMIN
B.JUNE 30,1945 DOCENA,ALA.

YR	CL	LEA	POS	GP	G	REC
1973	HOU	N	C		2	.000
	BRTR					

THORNTON, WALTER MILLER
B.FEB.18,1875 PEORIA,ILL.
D.JULY 14,1960

YR	CL	LEA	POS	GP	G	REC
1895	CHI	N	P		9	3- 2
1896	CHI	N	P		9	2- 1
1897	CHI	N	P-O	16	71	6- 9
						.329
1898	CHI	N	P-O	24	56	12- 9
						.283
	TL			58	145	23-21
						.313

THORPE, BENJAMIN ROBERT "BOB"
B.NOV.19,1926 CARYVILLE,FLA.

YR	CL	LEA	POS	GP	G	REC
1951	BOS	N	H		2	.500
1952	BOS	N	O		81	.260
1953	MIL	N	O		27	.162
	BRTR				110	.251

THORPE, JAMES FRANCIS "JIM"
B.MAY 28,1886 PRAGUE,OKLA.
D.MAR.28,1953

YR	CL	LEA	POS	GP	G	REC
1913	NY	N	O		19	.143
1914	NY	N	O		30	.194
1915	NY	N	O		17	.231
1917	CIN	N	O		77	.247
	NY	N	O		26	.200
1918	NY	N	O		58	.248
1919	NY	N	O		2	.333
	BOS	N	1-O		60	.327
	BRTR				289	.252

THORPE, ROBERT JOSEPH "BOB"
B.JAN.12,1935 SAN DIEGO,CAL.
D.MAR.17,1960

YR	CL	LEA	POS	GP	G	REC
1955	CHI	N	P		2	0- 0
	BRTR					

THRASHER, FRANK EDWARD "BUCK"
B.AUG.9,1889 WATKINSVILLE,GA.
D.JUNE 12,1938

YR	CL	LEA	POS	GP	G	REC
1916	PHI	A	O		7	.310
1917	PHI	A	O		23	.234
	BLTR				30	.255

THRONEBERRY, MARVIN EUGENE "MARV"
B.SEP.2,1933 SHELBY COUNTY,TENN.

YR	CL	LEA	POS	GP	G	REC
1955	NY	A	1		1	1.000
1958	NY	A	1-O		60	.227
1959	NY	A	1-O		80	.240
1960	KC	A	1		104	.250
1961	KC	A	1-O		40	.238
	BAL	A	1-O		56	.208
1962	BAL	A	O		9	.000
	NY	N	1		116	.244
1963	NY	N	1		14	.143
	BLTL				480	.237

THRONEBERRY, MAYNARD FAYE "FAYE"
B.JUNE 22,1931 MEMPHIS,TENN.

YR	CL	LEA	POS	GP	G	REC
1952	BOS	A	O		98	.258
1955	BOS	A	O		60	.257
1956	BOS	A	O		24	.220
1957	BOS	A	H		1	.000
	WAS	A	O		68	.185
1958	WAS	A	O		44	.184
1959	WAS	A	O		117	.251
1960	WAS	A	O		85	.248
1961	LA	A	O		24	.194
	BLTR				521	.236

THROOP, GEORGE LYNFORD
B.NOV.24,1950 PASADENA,CAL.

YR	CL	LEA	POS	GP	G	REC
1975	KC	A	P		7	0- 0
	BRTR					

THUMAN, LOUIS CHARLES FRANK
B.DEC.13,1916 BALTIMORE,MD.

YR	CL	LEA	POS	GP	G	REC
1939	WAS	A	P		3	0- 0
1940	WAS	A	P		2	0- 1
	BRTR				5	0- 1

THURMAN, ROBERT BURNS "BOB"
B.MAY 14,1923 WICHITA,KAN.

YR	CL	LEA	POS	GP	G	REC
1955	CIN	N	O		82	.217
1956	CIN	N	O		80	.295
1957	CIN	N	O		74	.247
1958	CIN	N	O		94	.230
1959	CIN	N	H		4	.250
	BLTL				334	.246

THURSTON, HOLLIS JOHN "SLOPPY"
B.JUNE 2,1899 FREMONT,NEB.
D.SEPT.14,1973 LOS ANGELES,CAL.

YR	CL	LEA	POS	GP	G	REC
1923	STL	A	P		2	0- 0
	CHI	A	P	44	45	7- 8
1924	CHI	A	P	38	51	20-16
1925	CHI	A	P	36	44	10-14
1926	CHI	A	P	31	38	6- 8
1927	WAS	A	P	29	42	13-13
1930	BRO	N	P	24	36	6- 4
1931	BRO	N	P		24	9- 9
1932	BRO	N	P	28	29	12- 8
1933	BRO	N	P		32	6- 8
	BRTR			288	343	89-86

TIANT, LUIS CLEMENTE (VEGA)
B.NOV.23,1940 HAVANA,CUBA

YR	CL	LEA	POS	GP	G	REC
1964	CLE	A	P		19	10- 4
1965	CLE	A	P		41	11-11
1966	CLE	A	P		46	12-11
1967	CLE	A	P		33	12- 9
1968	CLE	A	P		34	21- 9
1969	CLE	A	P		38	9-20
1970	MIN	A	P		18	7- 3
1971	BOS	A	P		21	1- 7
1972	BOS	A	P		43	15- 6
1973	BOS	A	P		35	20-13
1974	BOS	A	P		38	22-13
1975	BOS	A	P		35	18-14
1976	BOS	A	P		38	21-12
	BRTR				439	179-132

TIDROW, RICHARD WILLIAM "DICK"
B.MAY 14,1947 SAN FRANCISCO,CAL.

YR	CL	LEA	POS	GP	G	REC
1972	CLE	A	P		39	14-15
1973	CLE	A	P		42	14-16
1974	CLE	A	P		4	1- 3
	NY	A	P		33	11- 9
1975	NY	A	P		37	6- 3
1976	NY	A	P		47	4- 5
	BRTR				202	50-51

TIEFENAUER, BOBBY GENE
B.OCT.10,1929 DESLOGE,MO.

YR	CL	LEA	POS	GP	G	REC
1952	STL	N	P		6	0- 0
1955	STL	N	P		18	1- 4
1960	CLE	A	P		6	0- 1
1961	STL	N	P		3	0- 0
1962	HOU	N	P		43	2- 4
1963	MIL	N	P		12	1- 1
1964	MIL	N	P		46	4- 6
1965	MIL	N	P		6	0- 1
	NY	A	P		10	1- 1
	CLE	A	P		15	0- 5
1967	CLE	A	P		5	0- 1
1968	CHI	N	P		9	0- 1
	BRTR				179	9-25

TIEFENTHALER, VERLE MATHEW
B.JULY 11,1937 BREDA,IOWA

YR	CL	LEA	POS	GP	G	REC
1962	CHI	A	P		3	0- 0
	BLTR					

YR	CL LEA POS	GP	G	REC

TIEMEYER, EDWARD CARL
B.MAY 9,1885 CINCINNATI,OHIO
D.SEPT.27,1946 CINCINNATI,OHIO

YR	CL LEA POS	GP	G	REC
1906	CIN N P-3	1	5	0- 0
				.181
1907	CIN N H		1	.000
1909	NY A 1		4	.363
	BRTR	1	10	0- 0
				.273

TIERNAN, MICHAEL JOSEPH
"SILENT MIKE"
B.JAN.21,1867 TRENTON,N.J.
D.NOV.9,1918 NEW YORK,N.Y.

YR	CL LEA POS	GP	G	REC
1887	NY N O		103	.340
1888	NY N O		113	.293
1889	NY N O		122	.334
1890	NY N O		133	.303
1891	NY N O		133	.303
1892	NY N O		114	.297
1893	NY N O		124	.327
1894	NY N O		112	.282
1895	NY N O		119	.354
1896	NY N O		133	.361
1897	NY N O		129	.331
1898	NY N O		103	.286
1899	NY N O		36	.250
	BLTL		1474	.318

TIERNAY, WILLIAM J.
B.MAY 14,1858 WASHINGTON,D.C.
D.SEPT.21,1898

YR	CL LEA POS	GP	G	REC
1882	CIN AA 1		1	.000
1884	BAL U O		1	.333
			2	.125

TIERNEY, JAMES ARTHUR "COTTON"
B.FEB.10,1894 KANSAS CITY,KAN.
D.APR.18,1953

YR	CL LEA POS	GP	G	REC
1920	PIT N 2		12	.260
1921	PIT N 2-3		117	.299
1922	PIT N 2-3-0		122	.345
1923	PIT N 2		29	.292
	PHI N 2-3-0		121	.317
1924	BOS N 2-3		136	.259
1925	BRO N 1-2-3		93	.257
	BRTR		630	.296

TIETJE, LESLIE WILLIAM "TOOTS"
B.SEPT.11,1911 SUMNER,IOWA

YR	CL LEA POS	GP	G	REC
1933	CHI A P		3	2- 0
1934	CHI A P		34	5-14
1935	CHI A P,		30	9-15
1936	CHI A P		2	0- 0
	STL A P	14	16	3- 5
1937	STL A P		5	1- 2
1938	STL A P		18	2- 5
	BRTR	106	108	22-41

TIFT, RAYMOND FRANK
B.JUNE 21,1884 FITCHBURG,MASS.
D.MAR.29,1945

YR	CL LEA POS	GP	G	REC
1907	NY A P		4	0- 0
	TR			

TIGHE, JOHN THOMAS "JACK"
B.AUG.9,1913 KEARNY,N.J.
NON-PLAYING MANAGER
DET(A) 1957-58

TILLEY, JOHN C.
B.1856 NEW YORK,N.Y.

YR	CL LEA POS	GP	G	REC
1882	CLE N O		15	.089
1884	TOL AA O		17	.182
	STP U O		9	.148
			41	.138

TILLMAN, JOHN L. "DUCKY"
B.OCT.6,1898 BRIDGEPORT,CONN.
D.APR.7,1964 HARRISBURG,PA.

YR	CL LEA POS	GP	G	REC
1915	STL A P		2	0- 0
	BBTR			

TILLMAN, JOHN ROBERT "BOB"
B.MAR.24,1937 NASHVILLE,TENN.

YR	CL LEA POS	GP	G	REC
1962	BOS A C		81	.229
1963	BOS A C		96	.225
1964	BOS A C		131	.278
1965	BOS A C		111	.215
1966	BOS A C		78	.230
1967	BOS A C		30	.188
	NY A C		22	.254
1968	ATL N C		86	.220
1969	ATL N C		69	.195
1970	ATL N C		71	.238
	BRTR		775	.232

TILLOTSON, THADDEUS ASA "THAD"
B.DEC.20,1940 MERCED,CAL.

YR	CL LEA POS	GP	G	REC
1967	NY A P		43	3- 9
1968	NY A P		7	1- 0
	BRTR		50	4- 9

TIMBERLAKE, GARY DALE
B.AUG.8,1948 LACONIA,IND.

YR	CL LEA POS	GP	G	REC
1969	SEA A P		2	0- 0
	BRTL			

TIMMERMAN, THOMAS HENRY "TOM"
B.MAY 12,1940 BREESE,ILL.

YR	CL LEA POS	GP	G	REC
1969	DET A P		31	4- 3
1970	DET A P		61	6- 7
1971	DET A P		52	7- 6
1972	DET A P	34	35	8-10
1973	DET A P		17	1- 1
	CLE A P		29	8- 7
1974	CLE A P		4	1- 1
	BRTR	228	229	35-35

TINCUP, AUSTIN BEN "BEN"
B.DEC.14,1890 SHERMAN,TEX.

YR	CL LEA POS	GP	G	REC
1914	PHI N P	28	31	8-10
1915	PHI N P		11	0- 0
1916	PHI N P		1	0- 0
1918	PHI N P	8	11	0- 1
1920	CHI N P		2	0- 0
	BLTR	50	56	8-11

TINKER, JOSEPH BERT "JOE"
B.JULY 27,1880 MUSCOTAH,KAN.
D.JULY 27,1948 ORLANDO,FLA.

YR	CL LEA POS	GP	G	REC
1902	CHI N S-3		133	.273
1903	CHI N S-3		124	.291
1904	CHI N S		141	.221
1905	CHI N S		149	.247
1906	CHI N S		148	.233
1907	CHI N S		113	.221
1908	CHI N S		157	.266
1909	CHI N S		143	.256
1910	CHI N S		132	.288
1911	CHI N S		143	.278
1912	CHI N S		142	.282
1913	CIN N M-S		110	.317
1914	CHI F M-S		127	.259
1915	CHI F M-S		30	.275
1916	CHI F M-2		7	.100
	BRTR		1799	.263

TINNING, LYLE FORREST "BUD"
B.MAR.12,1907 PILGER,NEB.
D.JAN.17,1961

YR	CL LEA POS	GP	G	REC
1932	CHI N P		24	5- 3
1933	CHI N P		32	13- 6
1934	CHI N P		39	4- 6
1935	STL N P		4	0- 0
	BBTR		99	22-15
	BR 1934-35			

TIPPER, JAMES
B.JUNE 18,1849 MIDDLETOWN,CONN.
D.APR.19,1895

YR	CL LEA POS	GP	G	REC
1872	MAN NA 3-0		24	.264
1874	HAR NA O		45	-
1875	NH NA O		41	-
			110	-

TIPPLE, DANIEL E. "BIG DAN"
B.FEB.13,1892 ROCKFORD,ILL.
D.MAR.26,1960

YR	CL LEA POS	GP	G	REC
1915	NY A P		3	1- 1
	BRTR			

TIPTON, ERIC GORDON "THE RED"
B.APR.20,1915 PETERSBURG,VA.

YR	CL LEA POS	GP	G	REC
1939	PHI A O		47	.231
1940	PHI A O		2	.125
1941	PHI A O		1	.500
1942	CIN N O		63	.222
1943	CIN N O		140	.288
1944	CIN N O		140	.301
1945	CIN N O		108	.242
	BRTR		501	.270

TIPTON, JOSEPH JOHN "JOE"
B.FEB.18,1923 COPPERHILL,TENN.

YR	CL LEA POS	GP	G	REC
1948	CLE A C		47	.289
1949	CHI A C		67	.204
1950	PHI A C		64	.266
1951	PHI A C		72	.239
1952	PHI A C		23	.191
	CLE A C		43	.248
1953	CLE A C		47	.229
1954	WAS A C		54	.223
	BRTR		417	.236

TISCHINSKI, THOMAS ARTHUR "TOM"
B.JULY 12,1944 KANSAS CITY,MO.

YR	CL LEA POS	GP	G	REC
1969	MIN A C		37	.191
1970	MIN A C		24	.196
1971	MIN A C		21	.130
	BRTR		82	.181

TISING, JOHN JOSEPH
B.OCT.9,1903 HIGH POINT,MO.
D.SEPT.5,1967 LEADVILLE,OHIO

YR	CL LEA POS	GP	G	REC
1936	PIT N P		10	1- 3
	BLTR			

TITCOMB, LEDELL "CANNONBALL"
B.AUG.21,1866 W.BALDWIN,ME.
D.JUNE 8,1950

YR	CL LEA POS	GP	G	REC
1886	PHI N P		5	0- 5
1887	ATH AA P		3	1- 2
	NY N P		9	4- 3
1888	NY N P		23	14- 8
1889	NY N P		4	2- 2
1890	ROC AA P		21	9- 8
	BLTL		65	30-28

TITUS, JOHN FRANKLIN
"SILENT JOHN"
B.FEB.21,1876 ST.CLAIR,PA.
D.JAN.8,1943

YR	CL LEA POS	GP	G	REC
1903	PHI N O		72	.286
1904	PHI N O		140	.294
1905	PHI N O		147	.308
1906	PHI N O		142	.267
	PHI N O		142	.275
1908	PHI N O		149	.286
1909	PHI N O		149	.270
1910	PHI N O		142	.241
1911	PHI N O		60	.284
1912	PHI N O		45	.274
	BOS N O		96	.325
1913	BOS N O		87	.297
	BLTL		1371	.282

TKACZUK, EDWARD TERRANCE
(PLAYED UNDER NAME OF
EDWARD TERRANCE KAZAK)

TOBIN, JAMES ANTHONY
"JIM" OR "ABBA DABBA"
B.DEC.27,1912 OAKLAND,CAL.
D.MAY 19,1969 OAKLAND,CAL.

YR	CL LEA POS	GP	G	REC
1937	PIT N P	20	21	6- 3
1938	PIT N P	40	56	14-12
1939	PIT N P	25	43	9- 9
1940	BOS N P	15	20	7- 3
1941	BOS N P	33	43	12-12
1942	BOS N P	37	47	12-21
1943	BOS N P-1	33	46	14-14
				.280
1944	BOS N P	43	62	18-19
1945	BOS N P	27	41	9-14
	DET A P	14	17	4- 5
	BRTR	287	396	105-112
				.230

TOBIN, JOHN MARTIN
B.SEPT.15,1908 JAMAICA PLAIN,
MASS.

YR	CL LEA POS	GP	G	REC
1932	NY N H		1	.000
	BRTR			

TOBIN, JOHN PATRICK
B.JAN.8,1921 OAKLAND,CAL.

YR	CL LEA POS	GP	G	REC
1945	BOS A 2-3-O		84	.252
	BLTR			

TOBIN, JOHN THOMAS "JACK"
B.MAY 4,1892 ST.LOUIS,MO.
D.DEC.10,1969 ST.LOUIS,MO.

YR	CL LEA POS	GP	G	REC
1914	STL F O		135	.270
1915	STL F O		158	.299
1916	STL A O		77	.213
1918	STL A O		122	.277
1919	STL A O		127	.327
1920	STL A O		147	.340
1921	STL A O		150	.352
1922	STL A O		146	.331
1923	STL A O		151	.317
1924	STL A O		136	.299
1925	STL A 1-O		77	.301
1926	WAS A O		27	.212
	BOS A O		51	.273
1927	BOS A O		111	.310
	BLTL		1615	.309

YR	CL	LEA	POS	GP	G	REC

TOBIN, MARION BROOKS "PAT"
B.JAN.28,1916 HERMITAGE,ARK.
D.JAN.21,1975 SHREVEPORT,LA.

YR	CL	LEA	POS	GP	G	REC
1941	PHI	A	P		1	0- 0
	BRTR					

TOBIN, WILLIAM
B.FEB.6,1859 HARTFORD,CONN.
D.OCT.10,1912

1880	WOR	N	1		5	.125
	TRO	N	1		32	.152
					37	.142

TODD, ALFRED CHESTER
B.JAN.7,1902 TROY,N.Y.

1932	PHI	N	C		33	.229
1933	PHI	N	C-O		73	.206
1934	PHI	N	C		91	.318
1935	PHI	N	C		107	.290
1936	PIT	N	C		76	.273
1937	PIT	N	C		133	.307
1938	PIT	N	C		133	.265
1939	BRO	N	C		86	.277
1940	CHI	N	C		104	.255
1941	CHI	N	H		6	.167
1943	CHI	N	C		21	.133
	BRTR				863	.276

TODD, FRANK
B.ABERDEEN,MD.

1898	LOU	N	P		3	0- 3
	TL					

TODD, JAMES RICHARD "JIM"
B.SEPT.21,1947 LAMCASTER,PA.

1974	CHI	N	P		43	4- 2
1975	OAK	A	P		58	8- 3
1976	OAK	A	P		49	7- 8
	BLTR				49	7- 8

TODT, PHILIP JULIUS "HOOK"
B.AUG.9,1901 ST.LOUIS,MO.
D.NOV.15,1973 ST.LOUIS,MO.

1924	BOS	A	1		52	.262
1925	BOS	A	1		141	.278
1926	BOS	A	1		154	.255
1927	BOS	A	1		140	.236
1928	BOS	A	1		144	.252
1929	BOS	A	1		153	.262
1930	BOS	A	1		111	.269
1931	PHI	A	1		62	.244

TOENES, WILLIAM HARRELL "HAL"
B.OCT.8,1917 MOBILE,ALA.

1947	WAS	A	P		3	0- 1
	BRTR					

TOLAN, ROBERT "BOBBY"
B.NOV.19,1945 LOS ANGELES,CAL.

1965	STL	N	O		17	.188
1966	STL	N	1-O		43	.172
1967	STL	N	1-O		110	.253
1968	STL	N	1-O		92	.230
1969	CIN	N	O		152	.305
1970	CIN	N	O		152	.316
1972	CIN	N	O		149	.283
1973	CIN	N	O		129	.206
1974	SD	N	O		95	.266
1975	SD	N	1-O		147	.255
1976	PHI	N	1-O		110	.261
	BLTL				1196	.267

TOLSON, CHARLES JULIUS "CHICK"
B.NOV.6,1901 WASHINGTON,D.C.

1925	CLE	A	1		3	.250
1926	CHI	N	1		57	.313
1927	CHI	N	1		39	.296
1929	CHI	N	1		32	.257
1930	CHI	N	1		13	.300
	BRTR				144	.284

TOMANEK, RICHARD CARL "DICK" OR "BONES"
B.JAN.6,1931 AVON LAKE,OHIO

1953	CLE	A	P		1	1- 0
1954	CLE	A	P		1	0- 0
1957	CLE	A	P		34	2- 1
1958	CLE	A	P	18	20	2- 3
	KC	A	P		36	5- 5
1959	KC	A	P		16	0- 1
	BLTL				108	10-10

TOMASIC, ANDREW JOHN
B.DEC.10,1919 HOKENDAUQUA,PA.

1949	NY	N	P		2	0- 1
	BRTR					

TOMER, GEORGE CLARENCE
B.NOV.26,1895 PERRY,IOWA

1913	STL	A	H		1	.000
	BLTR					

TOMLIN, DAVID ALLEN "DAVE"
B.JUNE 22,1949 MAYSVILLE,KY.

1972	CIN	N	P		3	0- 0
1973	CIN	N	P		16	1- 2
1974	SD	N	P		47	2- 0
1975	SD	N	P		67	4- 2
1976	SD	N	P		49	0- 1
	BLTL				182	7- 5

TOMNEY, PHILIP HOWARD "BUSTER"
B.JULY 17,1863 READING,PA.
D.MAR.18,1892 READING,PA.

1888	LOU	AA	S		34	.149
1889	LOU	AA	S		112	.215
1890	LOU	AA	S		110	.264
	BRTR				256	.229

TOMPKINS, CHARLES HERBERT
B.SEPT.1,1889 PRESCOTT,ARK.
D.SEPT.20,1975 PRESCOTT,ARK.

1912	CIN	N	P		1	0- 0
	BRTR					

TOMPKINS, RONALD EVERETT "RON"
B.NOV.27,1944 SAN DIEGO,CAL.

1965	KC	A	P		5	0- 0
1971	CHI	N	P		35	0- 2
	BRTR				40	0- 2

TOMS, THOMAS HOWARD "TOMMY"
B.OCT.15,1951 CHARLOTTESVILLE,VA

1975	SF	N	P		7	0- 1
1976	SF	N	P		7	0- 1
	BNTR				14	0- 2

TONEY, FREDERICK ARTHUR "FRED"
B.DEC.11,1887 NASHVILLE,TENN.
D.MAR.11,1953

1911	CHI	N	P		18	1- 1
1912	CHI	N	P		9	1- 2
1913	CHI	N	P		7	2- 2
1915	CIN	N	P		36	17- 6
1916	CIN	N	P		41	14-17
1917	CIN	N	P		43	24-16
1918	CIN	N	P		22	6-10
	NY	N	P		11	6- 2
1919	NY	N	P		24	13- 6
1920	NY	N	P		42	21-11
1921	NY	N	P		42	18-11
1922	NY	N	P		13	5- 6
1923	STL	N	P		29	11-12
	BRTR				337	139-102

TONKIN, HARRY GLENVILLE "DOC"
B.AUG.11,1881 CONCORD,N.H.
D.MAY 30,1959

1907	WAS	A	P		1	0- 0
	BLTL					

TONNEMAN, CHARLES RICHARD
B.SEPT.10,1881 CHICAGO,ILL.
D.AUG.7,1951

1911	BOS	A	C		2	.200
	BRTR					

TOOLE, STEPHEN J.
B.1862 NEW ORLEANS,LA.

1886	BRO	AA	P		13	6- 6
1887	BRO	AA	P		26	13-10
1888	KC	AA	P		13	4- 6
1890	BRO	AA	P		6	2- 4
	BRTL				58	25-26

TOOLEY, ALBERT R. "BERT"
B.AUG.30,1886 HOWELL,MICH.
D.AUG.17,1976 MARSHALL,MICH.

1911	BRO	N	S		114	.206
1912	BRO	N	S		77	.234
	BRTR				191	.216

TORPORCER, GEORGE "SPECS"
B.FEB.9,1899 NEW YORK,N.Y.

1921	STL	N	2		22	.264
1922	STL	N	2-S-3-O		116	.323
1923	STL	N	1-2-S-3		97	.254
1924	STL	N	2-S-3		70	.313
1925	STL	N	2-S		83	.284
1926	STL	N	2		64	.250
1927	STL	N	S-3		86	.248
1928	STL	N	1-2		8	.000
	BLTR				546	.279

TOPPIN, RUPERTO
B.DEC.7,1941 PANAMA CITY,PANAMA

1962	KC	A	P		2	0- 0
	BPTR					

TORBORG, JEFFREY ALLEN "JEFF"
B.NOV.26,1941 PLAINFIELD,N.J.

1964	LA	N	C		28	.233
1965	LA	N	C		56	.240
1966	LA	N	C		46	.225
1967	LA	N	C		76	.214
1968	LA	N	C		37	.161
1969	LA	N	C		51	.185
1970	LA	N	C		64	.231
1971	CAL	A	C		55	.203
1972	CAL	A	C		59	.209
1973	CAL	A	C		102	.220
	BRTR				574	.214

TORGESON, CLIFFORD EARL "EARL"
B.JAN.1,1924 SNOHOMISH,WASH.

1947	BOS	N	1		128	.281
1948	BOS	N	1		134	.253
1949	BOS	N	1		25	.260
1950	BOS	N	1		156	.290
1951	BOS	N	1		155	.263
1952	BOS	N	1-O		122	.230
1953	PHI	N	1		111	.274
1954	PHI	N	1		135	.271
1955	PHI	N	1		47	.267
	DET	A	1		89	.283
1956	DET	A	1		117	.264
1957	DET	A	1		30	.240
	CHI	A	1-O		86	.295
1958	CHI	A	1		96	.266
1959	CHI	A	1		127	.220
1960	CHI	A	1		68	.263
1961	CHI	A	1		20	.067
	NY	A	1		22	.111
	BLTL				1668	.265

TORKELSON, CHESTER LEROY "RED"
B.MAR.19,1894 CHICAGO,ILL.
D.SEPT.22,1964

1917	CLE	A	P		4	2- 1
	BRTR					

TORPHY, WALTER ANTHONY "RED"
B.NOV.6,1898 FALL RIVER,MASS.

1920	BOS	N	1		3	.200
	BRTR					

TORRE, FRANK JOSEPH
B.DEC.30,1931 BROOKLYN,N.Y.

1956	MIL	N	1		111	.258
1957	MIL	N	1		129	.272
1958	MIL	N	1		138	.309
1959	MIL	N	1		115	.228
1960	MIL	N	1		21	.205
1962	PHI	N	1		108	.310
1963	PHI	N	1		92	.250
	BLTL				714	.273

TORRE, JOSEPH PAUL "JOE"
B.JULY 18,1940 BROOKLYN,N.Y.

1960	MIL	N	H		2	.500
1961	MIL	N	C		113	.278
1962	MIL	N	C		80	.282
1963	MIL	N	C-1-O		142	.293
1964	MIL	N	C-1		154	.321
1965	MIL	N	C-1		148	.291
1966	ATL	N	C-1		148	.315
1967	ATL	N	C-1		135	.277
1968	ATL	N	C-1		115	.271
1969	STL	N	C-1		159	.289
1970	STL	N	C-1-3		161	.325
1971	STL	N	3		161	.363
1972	STL	N	1-3		149	.289
1973	STL	N	1-3		141	.287
1974	STL	N	1-3		147	.282
1975	NY	N	1-3		114	.247
1976	NY	N	1-3		114	.306
	BRTR				2183	.298

TORREALBA, PABLO ARNOLDO (TORREALBA)
B.APR.28,1948 BARQUISIMENTO,VEN.

1975	ATL	N	P		6	0- 1
1976	ATL	N	P		36	0- 2
	BLTL				42	0- 3

YR	CL	LEA	POS	GP	G	REC

TORRES, DON GILBERTO NUNEZ "GIL"
(REAL NAME
GILBERTO TORRES NUNEZ)
B.AUG.23,1915 REGLA,CUBA

YR	CL	LEA	POS	GP	G	REC
1940	WAS	A	P		2	0- 0
1944	WAS	A	1-2-3		134	.267
1945	WAS	A	S-3		147	.237
1946	WAS	A	P-2-	3	63	0- 0
			S-3			.254
		BRTR		5	346	0- 0
						.252

TORRES, FELIX (SANCHEZ)
B.MAY 1,1932 PONCE,P.R.

1962	LA	A	3		127	.259
1963	LA	A	1-3		138	.261
1964	LA	A	1-3		100	.231
		BRTR			365	.254

TORRES, HECTOR EPITACIO (MARROQUIN)
B.SEP.16,1945 MONTERREY,MEXICO

1968	HOU	N	2-S		128	.223
1969	HOU	N	S		34	.159
1970	HOU	N	2-S		31	.246
1971	CHI	N	2-S		31	.224
1972	MON	N	1	83	0- 0
			2-S-3-0			.155
1973	HOU	N	2-S		38	.091
1975	SD	N	2-S-3		112	.259
1976	SD	N	2-S-3		74	.195
		BRTR		1	531	0- 0
						.211

TORRES, RICARDO J.
B.1894 CUBA

1920	WAS	A	C-1		16	.333
1921	WAS	A	C		2	.333
1922	WAS	A	C		4	.000
		BRTR			22	.297

TORRES, ROSENDO ANTONIO "RUSTY"
B.SEP.30,1948 AQUADILLA,P.R.

1971	NY	A	O		9	.385
1972	NY	A	O		80	.211
1973	CLE	A	O		121	.205
1974	CLE	A	O		108	.187
1976	CAL	A	3-0		120	.205
		BBTR			438	.208

TORREZ, MICHAEL AUGUSTINE "MIKE"
B.AUG.28,1946 TOPEKA,KAN.

1967	STL	N	P		3	0- 1
1968	STL	N	P		5	2- 1
1969	STL	N	P		24	10- 4
1970	STL	N	P		30	8-10
1971	STL	N	P		9	1- 2
	MON	N	P		1	0- 0
1972	MON	N	P		34	16-12
1973	MON	N	P		36	9-12
1974	MON	N	P	32	36	15- 8
1975	BAL	A	P		36	20- 9
1976	OAK	A	P		39	16-12
		BRTR		249	253	97-71

TOST, LOUIS EUGENE
B.DEC.1,1914 ENUMCLAW,WASH.
D.FEB.22,1967 SANTA CLARA,CAL.

1942	BOS	N	P		35	10-10
1943	BOS	N	P		3	0- 1
1947	PIT	N	P		1	0- 0
		BLTL			39	10-11

TOTH, PAUL LOUIS
B.JUNE 30,1935 MCROBERTS,KY.

1962	STL	N	P		6	1- 0
	CHI	N	P		6	3- 1
1963	CHI	N	P		27	5- 9
1964	CHI	N	P		4	0- 2
		BRTR			43	9-12

TOUCHSTONE, CLAYLAND MAFFITT
B.JAN.24,1903 MOORE,PA.
D.APR.28,1949

1918	BOS	N	P		5	0- 0
1919	BOS	N	P		1	0- 0
1945	CHI	A	P		6	0- 0
		BRTR			12	0- 0

TOVAR, CESAR LEONARDO
B.JULY 3,1940 CARACAS,VENEZ.

1965	MIN	A	2-S-3-0		18	.200
1966	MIN	A	2-S-0		134	.260
1967	MIN	A	2-S-3-0		164	.267
1968	MIN	A	ALL	1	157	0- 0
						.272
1969	MIN	A	2-3-0		158	.288
1970	MIN	A	2-3-0		161	.300
1971	MIN	A	2-3-0		157	.311
1972	MIN	A	O		141	.265
1973	PHI	N	2-3-0		97	.268
1974	TEX	A	O		138	.292
1975	TEX	A	2-0-0		102	.258
	OAK	A	2-S-3		19	.231
1976	OAK	A	O		29	.178
	NY	A	2		13	.154
		BRTR		1	1488	0- 0
						.278

TOWNE, JAY KING "BABE"
B.MAR.12,1880 COON RAPID,IOWA
D.OCT.29,1938

1906	CHI	A	C		13	.290
		BLTR				

TOWNSEND, GEORGE H. "SLEEPY"
B.JUNE 4,1868 HARTSDALE,N.Y.
D.MAR.15,1930

1887	ATH	AA	C		34	.217
1888	ATH	AA	C		43	.150
1890	BAL	AA	C		19	.214
1891	BAL	AA	C		59	.178
		BRTR			155	.186

TOWNSEND, IRA DANCE
B.JAN.9,1897 WEIMAR,TEX.
D.JULY 21,1965 SCHULENBERG,TEX.

1920	BOS	N	P		4	0- 0
1921	BOS	N	P		4	0- 0
		BRTR			8	0- 0

TOWNSEND, JOHN "HAPPY"
B.APR.9,1883 TOWNSEND,DEL.
D.DEC.21,1963 WILMINGTON,DEL.

1901	PHI	N	P		18	9- 6
1902	WAS	A	P		27	9-16
1903	WAS	A	P		20	2-11
1904	WAS	A	P	36	38	5-27
1905	WAS	A	P		34	6-17
1906	CLE	A	P		16	3- 7
		BRTR		151	153	34-84

TOWNSEND, LEO ALPHONSE
B.JAN.15,1891 MOBILE,ALA.

1920	BOS	N	P		7	2- 2
1921	BOS	N	P		1	0- 1
		BLTL			8	2- 3

TOY, JAMES MADISON
B.FEB.20,1858 BEAVER FALLS,PA.
D.MAR.13,1919

1887	CLE	AA	1		109	.239
1890	BRO	AA	C		43	.172
					152	.218

TOZIER, WILLIAM RALPH
B.JULY 3,1882 ST.LOUIS,MO.
D.FEB.23,1955

1908	CIN	N	P		4	0- 0
		BRTR				

TRACEWSKI, RICHARD JOSEPH "DICK"
B.FEB.3,1935 EYNON,PA.

1962	LA	N	S		15	.000
1963	LA	N	2-S		104	.226
1964	LA	N	2-S-3		106	.247
1965	LA	N	2-S-3		78	.215
1966	DET	A	2-S		81	.194
1967	DET	A	2-S-3		74	.280
1968	DET	A	2-S-3		90	.156
1969	DET	A	2-S-3		66	.139
		BRTR			614	.213

TRAFFLEY, JOHN
B.1862 CHICAGO,ILL.
D.JULY 17,1900 BALTIMORE,MD.

1889	LOU	AA	O		1	.500

TRAFFLEY, WILLIAM F.
B.DEC.21,1859 STATEN ISLAND,N.Y
D.JUNE 24,1908

1878	CHI	N	C		2	.111
1883	CIN	AA	C-2-S		29	.200
1884	BAL	AA	C-O		54	.186
1885	BAL	AA	C		70	.156
1886	BAL	AA	C		25	.224
		BRTR			180	.181

TRAGESSER, WALTER JOSEPH
B.JUNE 14,1887 LAFAYETTE,IND.
D.DEC.14,1970 LAFAYETTE,IND.

1913	BOS	N	C		1	.000
1915	BOS	N	C		7	.000
1916	BOS	N	C		41	.204
1917	BOS	N	C		98	.222
1918	BOS	N	C		7	.000
1919	BOS	N	C		20	.272
	PHI	N	C		35	.164
1920	PHI	N	C		62	.210
		BRTR			271	.215

TRAMBACK, STEPHEN JOSEPH "RED"
B.OCT.1,1918 ISELIN,PA.

1940	NY	N	O		2	.250
		BLTL				

TRAUTMAN, FREDERICK ORLANDO
B.MAR.24,1892 BUCYRUS,OHIO
D.FEB.15,1964

1915	NEW	F	P		1	0- 0
		BRTR				

TRAVERS, ALOYSIUS JOSEPH "JOE"
B.MAY 7,1892 PHILADELPHIA,PA.
D.APR.19,1968 PHILADELPHIA,PA.

1912	DET	A	P		1	0- 1
		BRTR				

TRAVERS, WILLIAM EDWARD "BILL"
B.OCT.27,1952 NORWOOD,MASS.

1974	MIL	A	P		23	2- 3
1975	MIL	A	P		28	6-11
1976	MIL	A	P		34	15-16
		BLTL			85	23-30

TRAVIS, CECIL HOWEL
B.AUG.8,1913 RIVERDALE,GA.

1933	WAS	A	3		18	.302
1934	WAS	A	3		109	.319
1935	WAS	A	3-0		138	.318
1936	WAS	A	S-0		138	.317
1937	WAS	A	S		135	.344
1938	WAS	A	S		146	.335
1939	WAS	A	S		130	.292
1940	WAS	A	S-3		136	.322
1941	WAS	A	S-3		152	.359
1945	WAS	A	3		15	.241
1946	WAS	A	S-3		137	.252
1947	WAS	A	S-3		74	.216
		BLTR			1328	.313

TRAY, JAMES
B.1860 JACKSON,MICH.

1884	IND	AA	C-1		6	.261

TRAYNOR, HAROLD JOSEPH "PIE"
B.NOV.11,1899 FRAMINGHAM,MASS.
D.MAR.16,1972 PITTSBURGH,PA.

1920	PIT	N	S		17	.212
1921	PIT	N	3		7	.263
1922	PIT	N	S-3		142	.281
1923	PIT	N	3		153	.338
1924	PIT	N	3		142	.294
1925	PIT	N	S-3		150	.320
1926	PIT	N	3		152	.317
1927	PIT	N	3		149	.342
1928	PIT	N	3		144	.337
1929	PIT	N	3		130	.356
1930	PIT	N	3		130	.366
1931	PIT	N	3		155	.298
1932	PIT	N	3		135	.329
1933	PIT	N	3		154	.304
1934	PIT	N	M-3		119	.309
1935	PIT	N	M-1-3		57	.279
1937	PIT	N	M-3		5	.167
		BRTR			1941	.320

NON-PLAYING MANAGER
PIT(N) 1936, 38-39

YR	CL LEA POS	GP	G	REC

TREACEY, FREDERICK
B.1847 BROOKLYN,N.Y.

1871 CHI NA O	25	-
1872 ATH NA O	46	.256
1873 PHI NA O	51	-
1874 CHI NA O	35	-
1875 CEN NA O	11	-
1875 PHI NA O	42	-
1876 MUT N O	57	.210
	267	-

TREACY, P.
B.1852 BROOKLYN,N.Y.

1876 MUT N S	2	.167

TREADAWAY, EDGAR RAYMOND "RAY"
B.OCT.31,1907 RAGLAND,ALA.
D.OCT.12,1935

1930 WAS A 3	6	.211
BLTR		

TREADWAY, GEORGE B.
B.NOV.11,1866 GREENUP CO.,KY.
D.NOV.17,1928

1893 BAL N O	114	.268
1894 BRO N O	122	.336
1895 BRO N O	85	.262
1896 LOU N O	2	.143
BL	323	.292

TREADWAY, THADFORD LEON "RED"
B.APR.28,1920 ATHALON,N.C.

1944 NY N O	50	.300
1945 NY N O	88	.241
BLTR	138	.267

TRECHOCK, FRANK ADAM
B.DEC.24,1915 WINDBER,PA.

1937 WAS A S	1	.500
BRTR		

TREKELL, HARRY R.
B.1893

1913 STL N P	7	0- 1
BRTR		

TREMARK, NICHOLAS JOSEPH
B.OCT.15,1912 YONKERS,N.Y.

1934 BRO N O	17	.250
1935 BRO N O	10	.231
1936 BRO N O	8	.250
BLTL	35	.247

TREMBLY, EDWARD J.
(PLAYED UNDER NAME OF
EDWARD J. TRUMBULL)

TREMEL, WILLIAM LEONARD "BILL"
B.JULY 4,1929 LILLY,PA.

1954 CHI N P	33	1- 2
1955 CHI N P	23	3- 0
1956 CHI N P	1	0- 0
BRTR	57	4- 2

TREMPER, CARLTON OVERTON
B.MAR.22,1906 BROOKLYN,N.Y.

1927 BRO N O	26	.233
1928 BRO N O	10	.194
BRTR	36	.220

TRENWITH, GEORGE
D.FEB.1,1890

1875 CEN NA 3	10	-
NH NA 3	6	-
	16	-

TRESH, MICHAEL "MIKE"
B.FEB.23,1914 HAZELTON,PA.
D.OCT.4,1966 DETROIT,MICH.

1938 CHI A C	10	.241
1939 CHI A C	119	.259
1940 CHI A C	135	.281
1941 CHI A C	115	.251
1942 CHI A C	72	.232
1943 CHI A C	86	.215
1944 CHI A C	93	.260
1945 CHI A C	150	.249
1946 CHI A C	80	.217
1947 CHI A C	90	.241
1948 CHI A C	39	.250
1949 CLE A C	38	.216
BRTR	1027	.249

TRESH, THOMAS MICHAEL "TOM"
B.SEP.20,1937 DETROIT,MICH.

1961 NY A S	9	.250
1962 NY A S-O	157	.286
1963 NY A O	145	.269
1964 NY A O	153	.246
1965 NY A O	156	.279
1966 NY A 3-O	151	.233
1967 NY A O	130	.219
1968 NY A S-O	152	.195
1969 NY A S	45	.182
DET A S-3-O	94	.224
BBTR	1192	.245

TREVINO, CARLOS "BOBBY"
B.JULY 11,1946 MONTERREY,MEXICO

1968 CAL A O	17	.225
BRTR		

TRIANDOS, GUS
B.JULY 30,1930 SAN FRANCISCO,CAL

1953 NY A C-1	18	.157
1954 NY A C	2	.000
1955 BAL A C-1-3	140	.277
1956 BAL A C-1	131	.279
1957 BAL A C	129	.254
1958 BAL A C	137	.245
1959 BAL A C	126	.216
1960 BAL A C	109	.269
1961 BAL A C	115	.244
1962 BAL A C	66	.159
1963 DET A C	106	.239
1964 PHI A C-1	73	.250
1965 PHI N C	30	.171
HOU N C	24	.181
BRTR	1206	.244

TRICE, ROBERT LEE "BOB"
B.AUG.28,1928 NEWTON,GA.

1953 PHI A P	3	2- 1
1954 PHI A P	19	20	7- 8
1955 KC A P	4	0- 0
BRTR	26	27	9- 9

TRIEBEL, GEORGE W.
(PLAYED UNDER NAME OF
GEORGE W. CREAMER)

TRILLO, JESUS MANUEL MARCANO "MANNY"
(REAL NAME
JESUS MANUEL MARCANO (TRILLO))
B.DEC.25,1950 CARIPITO,VEN.

1973 OAK A 2	17	.250
1974 OAK A 2	21	.152
1975 CHI N 2-S	154	.248
1976 CHI N 2-S	158	.239
BRTR	350	.241

TRIMBLE, JOSEPH GERARD "JOE"
B.OCT.12,1930 PROVIDENCE,R.I.

1955 BOS A P	2	0- 0
1957 PIT N P	5	0- 2
BRTR	7	0- 2

TRIMBLE, WILLIAM T.
D.JULY 29,1927 COLUMBUS,OHIO
NON-PLAYING MANAGER WES(NA)1875

TRINKLE, KENNETH WAYNE "KEN"
B.DEC.15,1919 PAOLI,IND.

1943 NY N P	11	1- 5
1946 NY N P	48	7-14
1947 NY N P	62	8- 4
1948 NY N P	53	4- 5
1949 PHI N P	42	1- 1
BRTR	216	21-29

TRIPLETT, HERMAN COAKER "COAKER"
B.DEC.18,1914 BOONE,N.C.

1938 CHI N O	12	.250
1941 STL N O	76	.286
1942 STL N O	64	.273
1943 STL N O	9	.080
PHI N O	105	.272
1944 PHI N O	84	.234
1945 PHI N O	120	.240
BRTR	470	.256

TROEDSON, RICHARD LA MONTE "RICH"
B.MAY 1,1950 PALO ALTO,CAL.

1973 SD N P	50	7- 9
1974 SD N P	15	1- 1
BLTL	65	8-10

TROSKY, HAROLD ARTHUR JR. "HAL"
(REAL NAME
HAROLD ARTHUR TROYAVESKY JR.)
B.SEPT.29,1936 CLEVELAND,OHIO

1958 CHI A P	2	1- 0
BRTR		

TROSKY, HAROLD ARTHUR SR. "HAL"
(REAL NAME
HAROLD ARTHUR TROYAVESKY SR.)
B.NOV.11,1912 NORWAY,IOWA

1933 CLE A 1	11	.295
1934 CLE A 1	154	.330
1935 CLE A 1	154	.271
1936 CLE A 1	151	.343
1937 CLE A 1	153	.298
1938 CLE A 1	150	.334
1939 CLE A 1	122	.335
1940 CLE A 1	140	.295
1941 CLE A 1	89	.294
1944 CHI A 1	135	.241
1946 CHI A 1	88	.254
BLTR	1347	.302

TROST, MICHAEL J.
B.1866 PHILADELPHIA,PA.
D.MAR.24,1901

1890 STL AA C	17	.250
1895 LOU N 1	2	.111
	19	.217

TROTT, SAMUEL W.
B.1858 WASHINGTON,D.C.
D.JUNE 5,1925 CATONSVILLE,MD.

1880 BOS N C-O	38	.197
1881 DET N C	6	.192
1882 DET N C-1-2-S-	30	.246
	O	
1883 DET N C-1-2-O	73	.233
1884 BAL AA C	72	.254
1885 BAL AA C	20	.289
1887 BAL AA C	85	.302
1888 BAL AA C	31	.275
BLTR	355	.258
NON-PLAYING MANAGER WAS(AA)1891

TROTTER, WILLIAM FELIX "BILL"
B.AUG.10,1908 CISNE,ILL.

1937 STL A P	34	2- 9
1938 STL A P	1	0- 1
1939 STL A P	41	6-13
1940 STL A P	36	7- 6
1941 STL A P	29	4- 2
1942 STL A P	3	0- 1
WAS A P	17	3- 1
1944 STL N P	2	0- 1
BRTR	163	22-34

TROUPE, QUINCY THOMAS
B.DEC.25,1922 ST.LOUIS,MO.

1952 CLE A C	6	.100
BBTR		

TROUT, PAUL HOWARD "DIZZY"
B.JUNE 29,1915 SANDICUT,IND.
D.FEB.28,1972 HARVEY,ILL.

1939 DET A P	33	35	9-10
1940 DET A P	33	3- 7
1941 DET A P	37	40	9- 9
1942 DET A P	35	36	12-18
1943 DET A P	44	45	20-12
1944 DET A P	49	51	27-14
1945 DET A P	41	42	18-15
1946 DET A P	38	40	17-13
1947 DET A P	32	34	10-11
1948 DET A P	32	10-14
1949 DET A P	33	3- 6
1950 DET A P	34	13- 5
1951 DET A P	42	9-14
1952 DET A P	10	1- 5
BOS A P	26	9- 8
1957 BAL A P	2	0- 0
BRTR	521	535	170-161

TROWBRIDGE, ROBERT "BOB"
B.JUNE 27,1930 HUDSON,N.Y.

1956 MIL N P	19	3- 2
1957 MIL N P	32	7- 5
1958 MIL N P	27	1- 3
1959 MIL N P	16	1- 0
1960 KC A P	22	1- 3
BRTR	116	13-13

YR	CL LEA POS	GP	G	REC

TROY, JOHN JOSEPH "DASHER"
B.MAY 8,1856 NEW YORK,N.Y.
D.MAR.30,1938

1881 DET N	2-3		11	.304
1882 DET N	2-S		39	.232
1882 PRO N	S		4	.235
1883 NY N	2-S		82	.216
1884 MET AA	2		107	.264
1885 MET AA	2		46	.225
	BRTR		289	.242

TROY, ROBERT
B.AUG.22,1888 GERMANY
D.OCT.7,1918

| 1912 DET A | P | | 1 | 0- 1 |
| | BRTR | | | |

TROYAVESKY, HAROLD ARTHUR JR.
(PLAYED UNDER NAME OF
HAROLD ARTHUR TROSKY JR.)

TROYAVESKY, HAROLD ARTHUR SR.
(PLAYED UNDER NAME OF
HAROLD ARTHUR TROSKY SR.)

TRUAX, FREDERICK W.
1890 PIT N   O   1   .333

TRUBY, HARRY GARVIN "BIRD EYE"
B.MAY 12,1870 IRONTON,OHIO
D.MAR.21,1953

1895 CHI N	2		33	.339
1896 CHI N	2		27	.266
PIT N	2		8	.156
	TR		68	.286

TRUCKS, VIRGIL OLIVER "FIRE"
B.APR.26,1919 BIRMINGHAM,ALA.

1941 DET A	P		1	0- 0
1942 DET A	P		28	14- 8
1943 DET A	P		33	16-10
1945 DET A	P		1	0- 0
1946 DET A	P		32	14- 9
1947 DET A	P		36	10-12
1948 DET A	P		43	14-13
1949 DET A	P		41	19-11
1950 DET A	P		7	3- 1
1951 DET A	P		37	13- 8
1952 DET A	P		35	5-19
1953 STL A	P		16	5- 4
CHI A	P		24	15- 6
1954 CHI A	P		40	19-12
1955 CHI A	P		32	13- 8
1956 DET A	P		22	6- 5
1957 KC A	P		48	9- 7
1958 KC A	P		16	0- 1
NY A	P		25	2- 1
	BRTR		517	177-135

TRUESDALE, FRANK D.
B.DEC.12,1885 KIRKWOOD,MO.

1910 STL A	2		123	.219
1911 STL A	2		1	.000
1914 NY A	2		77	.212
1918 BOS A	2		15	.278
	BBTR		216	.220

TRUMAN, HARRY H.
(PLAYED UNDER NAME OF
HARRY H. RAYMOND)

TRUMBULL, EDWARD J.
(REAL NAME EDWARD J. TREMBLY)
B.NOV.3,1860 CHICOPEE FALLS,
MASS.

| 1884 WAS AA | P-O | 10 | 24 | 1- 9 |
| | | | | .109 |

TSITOURIS, JOHN PHILIP
B.MAY 4,1936 MONROE,N.C.

1957 DET A	P		2	1- 0
1958 KC A	P		1	0- 0
1959 KC A	P		24	4- 3
1960 KC A	P		14	0- 2
1962 CIN N	P		4	1- 0
1963 CIN N	P		30	12- 8
1964 CIN N	P		37	9-13
1965 CIN N	P		31	6- 9
1966 CIN N	P		1	0- 0
1967 CIN N	P		2	1- 0
1968 CIN N	P		3	0- 3
	BRTR		149	34-38

TUCKER, OLIVER DINWIDDIE
"OLLIE"
B.JAN.27,1902 RADIANT,VA.
D.JULY 13,1940 RADIANT,VA.

1927 WAS A	O		20	.208
1928 CLE A	O		14	.128
	BLTR		34	.155

TUCKER, THOMAS JOSEPH "FOGHORN"
B.OCT.28,1863 HOLYOKE,MASS.
D.OCT.22,1935 MONTAGUE,MASS.

1887 BAL AA	1		136	.315
1888 BAL AA	1		136	.291
1889 BAL AA	1		134	.375
1890 BOS N	1		132	.295
1891 BOS N	1		140	.272
1892 BOS N	1		148	.281
1893 BOS N	1		121	.299
1894 BOS N	1		122	.328
1895 BOS N	1		126	.254
1896 BOS N	1		122	.304
1897 BOS N	1		2	.143
WAS N	1		96	.333
1898 BRO N	1		73	.278
STL N	1		72	.238
1899 CLE N	1		126	.237
	BBTR		1686	.295

TUCKER, THURMAN LOWELL "JOE E."
B.SEPT.26,1917 GORDON,TEX.

1942 CHI A	O		7	.125
1943 CHI A	O		139	.235
1944 CHI A	O		124	.287
1946 CHI A	O		121	.288
1947 CHI A	O		89	.236
1948 CLE A	O		83	.260
1949 CLE A	O		80	.244
1950 CLE A	O		57	.178
1951 CLE A	H		1	.000
	BLTR		701	.255

TUCKER, THOMAS H.
"TABASCO TOM"
B.BIRMINGHAM, ENGLAND
D.OCT.17,1950 NEW YORK,N.Y.

| 1908 BOS N | P | | 8 | 3- 3 |
| 1909 BOS N | P | | 17 | 0- 9 |

TUERO, OSCAR MONZON
B.DEC.17,1892 HAVANA,CUBA

1918 STL N	P	11	12	1- 2
1919 STL N	P		45	5- 7
1920 STL N	P		2	0- 0
	BRTR	58	59	6- 9

TURBEVILLE, GEORGE EDWARD
B.AUG.24,1916 TURBEVILLE,S.C.

1935 PHI A	P		19	0- 3
1936 PHI A	P		12	2- 5
1937 PHI A	P		31	0- 4
	BRTL		62	2-12

TURBIDY, JEREMIAH
B.JULY 4,1852 DUDLEY,MASS.
D.SEPT.5,1920

| 1884 KC U | S | | 12 | .279 |

TURCHIN, EDWARD LAWRENCE
B.FEB.10,1917 NEW YORK,N.Y.

| 1943 CLE A | S-3 | | 11 | .231 |
| | BRTR | | | |

TURGEON, EUGENE JOSEPH "PETE"
B.JAN.3,1898 MINNEAPOLIS,MINN.

| 1923 CHI N | S | | 3 | .167 |
| | BRTR | | | |

TURK, LUCAS NEWTON "HARLEM"
B.MAY 2,1898 HOMER,GA.

| 1922 WAS A | P | | 5 | 0- 0 |
| | BRTR | | | |

TURLEY, ROBERT LEE "BOB"
OR "BULLET BOB"
B.SEP.19,1930 TROY,ILL.

1951 STL A	P		1	0- 1
1953 STL A	P		10	2- 6
1954 BAL A	P		35	14-15
1955 NY A	P		36	17-13
1956 NY A	P		27	8- 4
1957 NY A	P		32	13- 6
1958 NY A	P		33	21- 7
1959 NY A	P		33	8-11
1960 NY A	P		34	9- 3
1961 NY A	P		15	3- 5
1962 NY A	P		24	3- 3
1963 LA A	P		19	2- 7
BOS A	P		11	1- 4
	BRTR		310	101-85

TURNER, EARL EDWIN
B.MAY 6,1923 PITTSFIELD,MASS.

1948 PIT N	C		2	.000
1950 PIT N	C		40	.243
	BRTR		42	.240

TURNER, GEORGE A. "TUCK"
B.1870 W.NEW BRIGHTON,S.I.,,N.Y.

1893 PHI N	O		35	.324
1894 PHI N	O		77	.423
1895 PHI N	O		48	.388
1896 PHI N	O		11	.231
STL N	O		48	.255
1897 STL N	O		102	.289
1898 STL N	O		34	.210
	BL		355	.325

TURNER, JAMES RILEY "MILKMAN"
B.AUG.6,1904 ANTIOCH,TENN.

1937 BOS N	P	33	39	20-11
1938 BOS N	P		35	14-18
1939 BOS N	P		25	4-11
1940 CIN N	P	24	25	14- 7
1941 CIN N	P		23	6- 4
1942 CIN N	P		3	0- 0
NY A	P		5	1- 1
1943 NY A	P		18	3- 0
1944 NY A	P		35	4- 4
1945 NY A	P		30	3- 4
	BLTR		231 238	69-60

TURNER, JOHN WEBBER "JERRY"
B.JAN.17,1954 TEXARKANA,ARK.

1974 SD N	O		17	.292
1975 SD N	O		11	.273
1976 SD N	O		105	.267
	BLTL		133	.271

TURNER, KENNETH CHARLES "KEN"
B.AUG.17,1943 FRAMINGHAM,MASS.

| 1967 CAL A | P | | 13 | 1- 2 |
| | BRTL | | | |

TURNER, TERRENCE LAMONT
"TERRY" OR "COTTON"
B.FEB.28,1881 SANDY LAKE,PA.
D.JULY 18,1960

1901 PIT N	3		2	.428
1904 CLE A	S		111	.236
1905 CLE A	S		154	.263
1906 CLE A	S		147	.291
1907 CLE A	S		142	.242
1908 CLE A	S-O		60	.239
1909 CLE A	2-S		53	.250
1910 CLE A	S-3		150	.230
1911 CLE A	3		117	.252
1912 CLE A	3		103	.308
1913 CLE A	2-S-3		120	.248
1914 CLE A	2-3		120	.245
1915 CLE A	2-3		75	.252
1916 CLE A	2-3		124	.262
1917 CLE A	2-3		69	.205
1918 CLE A	2-3		74	.249
1919 PHI A	S		38	.189
	BRTR		1659	.256

TURNER, THEODORE HOLTOP
B.MAY 4,1892 LOUISVILLE,KY.
D.FEB.4,1958

| 1920 CHI N | P | | 1 | 0- 0 |
| | BRTR | | | |

TURNER, THOMAS LOVATT "TINK"
B.FEB.20,1890 PHILADELPHIA,PA.
D.FEB.25,1962

| 1915 PHI A | P | | 1 | 0- 1 |
| | BRTR | | | |

YR CL LEA POS GP G REC

TURNER, THOMAS RICHARD
B.SEPT.8,1916 CUSTER CO.,OKLA.
1940 CHI A C 37 .208
1941 CHI A C 38 .238
1942 CHI A C 56 .242
1943 CHI A C 51 .240
1944 CHI A C 36 .230
STL A C 15 .320
BRTR 233 .237

TUTTLE, WILLIAM ROBERT "BILL"
B.JULY 4,1929 ELMWOOD,ILL.
1952 DET A O 7 .240
1954 DET A O 147 .266
1955 DET A O 154 .279
1956 DET A O 140 .253
1957 DET A O 133 .251
1958 KC A O 148 .231
1959 KC A O 126 .300
1960 KC A O 151 .256
1961 KC A O 25 .262
MIN A 2-3-O 113 .246
1962 MIN A O 110 .210
1963 MIN A O 16 .000
BRTR 1270 .259

TUTWEILER, ELMER S.
B.NOV.19,1905 CARBON HILL,ALA.
1928 PIT N P 2 0- 0
BRTR

TUTWEILER, GUY ISBELL
B.JULY 17,1889 COALBURG,ALA.
D.AUG.15,1930
1911 DET A 2-0 13 .186
1913 DET A 1 14 .191
BLTR 27 .190

TWINEHAM, ARTHUR W. "OLD HOSS"
B.NOV.26,1866 GALESBURG,ILL.
1893 STL N C 14 .325
1894 STL N C 31 .314
BLTR 45 .317

TWINING, HOWARD EARLE "DOC"
B.MAY 30,1894 HORSHAM,PA.
D.JUNE 14,1973 LANSDALE,PA.
1916 CIN N P 1 0- 0
BRTR

TWITCHELL, LAWRENCE GRANT
B.FEB.18,1864 CLEVELAND,OHIO
D.APR.23,1930
1886 DET N P 4 2- 2
1887 DET N P-O 11 63 10- 1
.352
1888 DET N O 130 .244
1889 CLE N O 134 .275
1890 CLE P P-O 3 56 0- 0
.224
BUF P P-O 12 44 5- 7
.216
1891 COL AA P-O 2 57 1- 1
.275
1892 WAS N O 51 .221
1893 LOU N O 45 .331
1894 LOU N O 51 .265
BRTR 32 635 18-11
.266

TWITCHELL, WAYNE LEE
B.MAR.10,1948 PORTLAND,ORE.
1970 MIL N P 2 0- 0
1971 PHI N P 6 1- 0
1972 PHI N P 49 5- 9
1973 PHI N P 34 13- 9
1974 PHI N P 25 6- 9
1975 PHI N P 36 5-10
1976 PHI N P 26 3- 1
BRTR 178 33-38

TWOMBLY, CLARENCE EDWARD
B.JAN.18,1896 JAMAICA PLAIN,
MASS.
D.NOV.23,1974 SAN CLEMENTE,CAL.
1920 CHI N O 78 .235
1921 CHI N O 87 .377
BLTR 165 .304

TWOMBLY, EDWIN PARKER "CY"
B.JUNE 14,1897 GROVELAND,MASS.
D.DEC.3,1974 SAVANNAH,GA.
1921 CHI A P 7 1- 2
BLTL

TWOMBLY, GEORGE FREDERICK
B.JUNE 4,1892 BOSTON,MASS.
D.FEB.17,1975 LEXINGTON,MASS.
1914 CIN N O 68 .233
1915 CIN N O 46 .197
1916 CIN N O 3 .000
1917 BOS N O 32 .186
1919 WAS A O 1 .000
BRTR 150 .211

TYACK, JAMES FREDERICK
B.JAN.9,1911 FLORENCE,MONT.
1943 PHI A O 54 .258
BLTR

TYLER, FREDERICK FRANKLIN
"CLANCY"
B.DEC.16,1891 DERRY,N.H.
D.OCT.14,1945 DERRY,N.H.
1914 BOS N C 6 .105
TR

TYLER, GEORGE ALBERT "LEFTY"
B.DEC.14,1889 DERRY,N.H.
D.SEPT.29,1953
1910 BOS N P 4 0- 0
1911 BOS N P 28 7-10
1912 BOS N P 42 12-22
1913 BOS N P 39 43 16-17
1914 BOS N P 38 16-14
1915 BOS N P 32 45 10- 9
1916 BOS N P 34 39 17-10
1917 BOS N P 32 61 14-12
1918 CHI N P 33 38 19- 8
1919 CHI N P 6 2- 2
1920 CHI N P 27 29 11-12
1921 CHI N P 10 19 5- 2
BLTL 325 392 127-118

TYLER, JOHN ANTHONY "KATZ"
(REAL NAME JOHN TYLKA)
B.JULY 30,1906 MT.PLEASANT,PA.
D.JULY 11,1972 MT.PLEASANT,PA.
1934 BOS N O 3 .167
1935 BOS N O 13 .340
BBTR 16 .321

TYLKA, JOHN
(PLAYED UNDER NAME OF
JOHN ANTHONY TYLER)

TYNG, JAMES ALEXANDER
B.MAY 27,1856 PHILADELPHIA,PA.
D.OCT.30,1931
1879 BOS N P 3 1- 2
1888 PHI N P 1 0- 0
4 1- 2

TYREE, EARL CARLTON "TY"
B.MAR.4,1890 RUSHVILLE,ILL.
D.MAY 17,1954
1914 CHI N C 1 .000
BRTR

TYRIVER, DAVID BURTON
B.OCT.31,1937 OSHKOSH,WIS.
1962 CLE A P 4 0- 0
BRTR

TYRONE, JAMES VERNON "JIM"
B.JAN.29,1949 ALICE,TEX.
1972 CHI N O 13 .000
1974 CHI N 3-O 57 .185
1975 CHI N O 11 .227
BRTR 81 .180

TYRONE, OSCAR WAYNE "WAYNE"
B.AUG.1,1950 ALICE,TEX.
1976 CHI N 1-3-O 30 .228
BRTR

TYSON, ALBERT THOMAS "TY"
B.JUNE 1,1897 WILKES-BARRE,PA.
D.AUG.16,1953
1926 NY N O 97 .293
1927 NY N O 43 .264
1928 BRO N O 59 .271
BRTR 199 .280

TYSON, CECIL WASHINGTON "SLIM"
B.DEC.6,1914 ELM CITY,N.C.
1944 PHI N H 1 .000
BLTR

TYSON, MICHAEL RAY "MIKE"
B.JAN.13,1950 ROCKY MOUNT,N.C.
1972 STL N 2-S 13 .189
1973 STL N 2-S 144 .243
1974 STL N 2-S 151 .223
1975 STL N 2-S-3 122 .266
1976 STL N 2 76 .286
BRTR 506 .249
BB 1972

UCHRINSCKO, JAMES EMERSON
B.OCT.20,1902 W.NEWTON,PA.
1926 WAS A P 3 0- 0
BLTR

UECKER, ROBERT GEORGE "BOB"
B.JAN.26,1935 MILWAUKEE,WIS.
1962 MIL N C 33 .250
1963 MIL N C 13 .250
1964 STL N C 40 .198
1965 STL N C 53 .228
1966 PHI N C 78 .208
1967 PHI N C 18 .171
ATL N C 62 .146
BRTR 297 .200

UHALT, BERNARD BARTHOLOMEW
"FRENCHY"
B.APR.27,1910 BAKERSFIELD,CAL.
1934 CHI A O 57 .242
BLTR

UHLAENDER, THEODORE OTTO "TED"
B.OCT.21,1939 MCALLEN,TEX.
1965 MIN A O 13 .182
1966 MIN A O 105 .226
1967 MIN A O 133 .258
1968 MIN A O 140 .283
1969 MIN A O 152 .273
1970 CLE A O 161 .268
1971 CLE A O 141 .288
1972 CIN N O 73 .159
BLTR 898 .263

UHLE, GEORGE ERNEST "THE BULL"
B.SEPT.18,1898 CLEVELAND,OHIO
1919 CLE A P 26 10- 5
1920 CLE A P 27 4- 5
1921 CLE A P 41 48 16-13
1922 CLE A P 50 56 22-16
1923 CLE A P 54 58 26-16
1924 CLE A P 28 59 9-15
1925 CLE A P 29 55 13-11
1926 CLE A P 39 50 27-11
1927 CLE A P 25 43 8- 9
1928 CLE A P 31 55 12-17
1929 DET A P 32 40 15-11
1930 DET A P 33 59 12-12
1931 DET A P 29 53 11-12
1932 DET A P 33 38 6- 6
1933 DET A P 1 0- 0
NY N P 6 8 1- 1
NY A P 12 6- 1
1934 NY A P 10 2- 4
1936 CLE A P 7 24 0- 1
BRTR 513 722 200-166
.288

UHLE, ROBERT ELWOOD
B.SEPT.17,1914 SAN FRANCISCO,
CAL.
1938 CHI A P 1 0- 0
1940 DET A P 1 0- 0
BBTL 2 0- 0

UHLER, MAURICE W.
B.DEC.14,1886 PIKESVILLE,MD.
D.MAY 4,1918
1914 CIN N O 46 .214
BRTR

UHLIR, CHARLES
B.JULY 30,1912 CHICAGO,ILL.
1934 CHI A O 14 .148
BLTL

ULATOWSKI, CLEMENT LAMBERT
(PLAYED UNDER NAME OF
CLEMENT LAMBERT CLEMENS)

ULISNEY, MICHAEL EDWARD
B.SEPT.28,1917 GREENWALL,PA.
1945 BOS N C 11 .389
BRTR

YR	CL	LEA	POS	GP	G	REC

ULLRICH, CARLOS SANTIAGO CASTELLO "SANDY"
B.JULY 25,1922 HAVANA,CUBA

YR	CL	LEA	POS	GP	G	REC
1944 WAS	A	P			3	0- 0
1945 WAS	A	P			28	3- 3
BRTR					31	3- 3

ULRICH, FRANK W. "DUTCH"
B.NOV.18,1899 BALTIMORE,MD.
D.FEB.11,1929

1925 PHI	N	P			21	3- 3
1926 PHI	N	P			45	8-13
1927 PHI	N	P			32	8-11
BRTR					98	19-27

ULRICH, GEORGE F.
B.PHILADELPHIA,PA.

1892 WAS	N	S			6	.291
1893 CIN	N	O			1	.000
1896 NY	N	O			14	.178
					21	.208

UMBACH, ARNOLD WILLAIM
B.DEC.6,1942 WILLIAMSBURG,VA.

1964 MIL	N	P		1	1- 0
1966 ATL	N	P		22	0- 2
BRTR				23	1- 2

UMBARGER, JAMES HAROLD "JIM"
B.FEB.17,1953 BURBANK,CAL.

1975 TEX	A	P			56	8- 7
1976 TEX	A	P			30	10-12
BLTL					86	18-19

UMBRICHT, JAMES "JIM"
B.SEP.17,1930 CHICAGO,ILL.
D.APR.8,1964 HOUSTON,TEX.

1959 PIT	N	P			1	0- 0
1960 PIT	N	P			17	1- 2
1961 PIT	N	P			1	0- 0
1962 HOU	N	P			34	4- 0
1963 HOU	N	P			35	4- 3
BRTR					88	9- 5

UMPHLETT, THOMAS MULLEN "TOM"
B.MAY 1,1930 SCOTLAND NECK,N.C.

1953 BOS	A	O			137	.283
1954 WAS	A	1-O			114	.219
1955 WAS	A	O			110	.217
BRTR					361	.246

UNDERHILL, WILLIE VERN
B.SEPT.6,1904 YOWELL,TEX.

1927 CLE	A	P		4	0- 2
1928 CLE	A	P		11	1- 2
BRTR				15	1- 4

UNDERWOOD, FRED G.
B.1869 KANSAS
D.JAN.26,1906

1894 BRO	N	P			7	2- 3

UNDERWOOD, THOMAS GERALD "TOM"
B.DEC.22,1953 KOKOMO,IND.

1974 PHI	N	P			7	1- 0
1975 PHI	N	P		35	14-13
1976 PHI	N	P	33	34	10- 5
BRTL			75	76	25-18

UNGLAUB, ROBERT ALEXANDER
B.JULY 31,1881 BALTIMORE,MD.
D.NOV.29,1916

1904 NY	A	3			6	.211
BOS	A	3			7	.182
1905 BOS	A	3			43	.223
1907 BOS	A	M-1			139	.255
1908 BOS	A	1			72	.262
WAS	A	1			72	.307
1909 WAS	A	1-2-O			130	.264
1910 WAS	A	1			124	.234
BRTR					593	.258

UNSER, ALBERT BERNARD "AL"
B.OCT.21,1914 MORRISVILLE,ILL.

1942 DET	A	C			4	.375
1943 DET	A	C			38	.248
1944 DET	A	C-2			11	.120
1945 CIN	N	O			67	.265
BRTR					120	.252

UNSER, DELBERT BERNARD "DEL"
B.DEC.9,1944 DECATUR,ILL.

1968 WAS	A	1-O			156	.230
1969 WAS	A	O			153	.286
1970 WAS	A	O			119	.258
1971 WAS	A	O			153	.255
1972 CLE	A	O			132	.238
1973 PHI	N	O			136	.289
1974 PHI	N	O			142	.264
1975 NY	N	O			147	.294
1976 NY	N	O			77	.228
MON	N	O			69	.227
BLTL					1284	.260

UPCHURCH, JEFFERSON WOODROW "WOODY"
B.APR.13,1911 BUIES CREEK,N.C.
D.OCT.23,1971 BUIES CREEK,N.C.

1935 PHI	A	P			3	0- 2
1936 PHI	A	P			7	0- 2
BRTL					10	0- 4

UPHAM, JOHN LESLIE
B.DEC.29,1941 WINDSOR,ONT.,CAN.

1967 CHI	N	P	5	8	0- 1
1968 CHI	N	P-O	2	13	0- 0
					.200
BLTL	7	21	0- 1
					.308

UPHAM, WILLIAM LAWRENCE
B.APR.4,1888 AKRON,OHIO
D.SEPT.14,1959 NEWARK,N.J.

1915 BRO	F	P			33	6- 8
1918 BOS	N	P			3	1- 1
BBTR					36	7- 9

UPP, GEORGE HENRY "JERRY"
B.DEC.10,1883 SANDUSKY,OHIO
D.JUNE 30,1937

1909 CLE	A	P			7	2- 1
TL						

UPRIGHT, R. T. "DIXIE"
B.MAY 30,1926 CABARRUS CO.,N.C.

1953 STL	A	H			9	.250
BLTL						

UPSHAW, CECIL LEE
B.OCT.22,1942 SPEARSVILLE,LA.

1966 ATL	N	P			1	0- 0
1967 ATL	N	P			30	2- 3
1968 ATL	N	P			52	8- 7
1969 ATL	N	P			62	6- 4
1971 ATL	N	P			49	11- 6
1972 ATL	N	P			42	3- 5
1973 ATL	N	P			5	0- 1
HOU	N	P			35	2- 3
1974 CLE	A	P			7	0- 1
NY	A	P			36	1- 5
1975 CHI	A	P			29	1- 1
BRTR					348	34-36

UPTON, THOMAS HERBERT "TOM" OR "MUSCLES"
B.DEC.29,1926 ESTER,MO.

1950 STL	A	2-S-3			124	.237
1951 STL	A	S			52	.198
1952 WAS	A	S			5	.000
BRTR					181	.225

UPTON, WILLIAM RAY
B.JULY 18,1929 ESTER,MO.

1954 PHI	A	P			2	0- 0
BRTR						

URBAN, JACK ELMER
B.DEC.5,1928 OMAHA,NEB.

1957 KC	A	P	31	37	7- 4
1958 KC	A	P	30	31	8-11
1959 STL	N	P		8	0- 0
BRTR		69	76	15-15

URBAN, LOUIS JOHN "LUKE"
B.MAR.20,1898 FALL RIVER,MASS.

1927 BOS	N	C			35	.288
1928 BOS	N	C			15	.176
BRTR					50	.273

URBANSKI, WILLIAM MICHAEL "BILLY"
B.JUNE 15,1903 LINDLEUMVILLE, S.I.,N.Y.
D.JULY 12,1973 PERTH AMBOY,N.J.

1931 BOS	N	S-3			82	.238
1932 BOS	N	S			136	.272
1933 BOS	N	S			144	.251
1934 BOS	N	S			146	.293
1935 BOS	N	S			132	.229
1936 BOS	N	S-3			122	.261
1937 BOS	N	H			1	.000
BRTR					763	.260

URY, LOUIS
B.FT.SMITH,ARK.

1903 STL	N	1			2	.142
TR						

USHER, ROBERT ROYCE "BOB"
B.MAR.1,1925 SAN DIEGO,CAL.

1946 CIN	N	3-O			92	.204
1947 CIN	N	O			9	.182
1950 CIN	N	O			106	.259
1951 CIN	N	O			114	.208
1952 CHI	N	H			1	.000
1957 CLE	A	3-O			10	.125
WAS	A	O			96	.261
BRTR					428	.235

USSAT, WILLIAM AUGUST
B.APR.11,1904 DAYTON,OHIO
D.MAY 29,1959

1925 CLE	A	2			1	.000
1927 CLE	A	3			4	.187
BRTR					5	.187

VACHE, ERNEST LEWIS "TEX"
B.NOV.17,1895 SANTA MONICA,CAL.
D.JUNE 11,1953

1925 BOS	A	O			110	.313
BRTR						

VADEBONCOEUR, EUGENE F.
B.SYRACUSE,N.Y.
D.OCT.16,1935

1884 PHI	N	C			4	.214

VAIL, MICHAEL LEWIS "MIKE"
B.NOV.10,1951 SAN FRANCISCO,CAL.

1975 NY	N	O			38	.302
1976 NY	N	O			53	.217
BRTR					91	.217

VAIL, ROBERT GARFIELD "DOC"
B.1882 HODGDON,ME.

1908 PIT	N	P			4	1- 2

VALDES, ARMANDO VIERA
B.MAY 2,1922 CARDENAS,CUBA

1944 WAS	A	H			1	.000
BRTR						

VALDES, RENE (GUTIERREZ)
B.JUNE 2,1929 GUANABACOA,CUBA

1957 BRO	N	P			5	1- 1
BRTR						

VALDESPINO, HILARIO (BORROTO) "SANDY"
B.JAN.14,1939 HAVANA,CUBA

1965 MIN	A	O			108	.261
1966 MIN	A	O			52	.176
1967 MIN	A	O			99	.165
1968 ATL	N	O			36	.233
1969 HOU	N	O			41	.244
SEA	A	O			20	.211
1970 MIL	A	O			8	.000
1971 KC	A	O			18	.317
BLTL					382	.230

VALDIVIELSO, JOSE (LOPEZ)
B.MAY 22,1934 MATANZAS,CUBA

1955 WAS	A	S			94	.221
1956 WAS	A	S			90	.236
1959 WAS	A	S			24	.286
1960 WAS	A	S-3			117	.213
1961 MIN	A	2-S-3			76	.195
BRTR					401	.219

VALENTINE, ELLIS CLARENCE
B.JULY 30,1954 HELENA,ARK.

1975 MON	N	O			12	.364
1976 MON	N	O			94	.279
BRTR					106	.287

YR	CL	LEA	POS	GP	G	REC

VALENTINE, FRED LEE
B.JAN.19,1935 CLARKSDALE,MISS.
1959	BAL	A	O		12	.316
1963	BAL	A	O		26	.268
1964	WAS	A	O		102	.226
1965	WAS	A	O		12	.241
1966	WAS	A	1-O		146	.276
1967	WAS	A	O		151	.234
1968	WAS	A	O		37	.238
	BAL	A	O		47	.187
	BBTR				533	.247

VALENTINE, HAROLD LEWIS "CORKY"
B.JAN.4,1930 TROY,OHIO
1954	CIN	N	P		36	12-11
1955	CIN	N	P		10	2- 1
	BRTR				46	14-12

VALENTINE, JOHN G.
B.NOV.21,1855 BROOKLYN,N.Y.
| 1883 | COL | AA | P-O | | 15 | 2- 9 |
| | | | | | | .294 |

VALENTINE, ROBERT
| 1876 | MUT | N | C | | 1 | .000 |

VALENTINE, ROBERT JOHN "BOBBY"
B.MAY 13,1950 STAMFORD,CONN.
1969	LA	N	R		5	.000
1971	LA	N	2-S-3-O	101	.249
1972	LA	N	2-S-3-O	119	.274
1973	CAL	A	S-O		32	.302
1974	CAL	A	2-S-3-O	117	.261
1975	CAL	A	1-3-O-O	26	.281
	SD	N	O		7	.133
1976	SD	N	1-O		15	.367
	BRTR				422	.270

VALENTINETTI, VITO JOHN
B.SEPT.16,1929 W.NEW YORK,N.J.
1954	CHI	A	P		1	0- 0
1956	CHI	N	P		42	6- 4
1957	CHI	N	P		9	0- 0
	CLE	A	P		11	2- 7
1958	DET	A	P		15	1- 0
	WAS	A	P		23	4- 6
1959	WAS	A	P		7	0- 2
	BRTR				108	13-14

VALENZUELA, BENJAMIN BELTRAN
B.JUNE 2,1933 LOS MOCHIS,MEXICO
| 1958 | STL | N | 3 | | 10 | .214 |
| | BRTR | | | | | |

VALLE, HECTOR JOSE
B.OCT.27,1940 VEGA BAJA,P.R.
| 1965 | LA | N | C | | 9 | .308 |
| | BRTR | | | | | |

VALO, ELMER WILLIAM
B.MAR.5,1921 RIBNIK,CZECH.
1940	PHI	A	O		6	.548
1941	PHI	A	O		15	.420
1942	PHI	A	O		133	.251
1943	PHI	A	O		77	.221
1946	PHI	A	O		108	.307
1947	PHI	A	O		112	.300
1948	PHI	A	O		113	.305
1949	PHI	A	O		150	.283
1950	PHI	A	O		129	.280
1951	PHI	A	O		123	.302
1952	PHI	A	O		129	.281
1953	PHI	A	O		50	.224
1954	PHI	A	O		95	.214
1955	KC	A	O		112	.364
1956	KC	A	O		9	.222
	PHI	N	O		98	.289
1957	BRO	N	O		81	.273
1958	LA	N	O		65	.248
1959	CLE	A	O		34	.292
1960	NY	A	O		8	.000
	WAS	A	O		76	.281
1961	MIN	A	O		33	.156
	PHI	N	O		50	.186
	BLTR				1806	.282

VAN ALSTYNE, CLAYTON EMORY "SPIKE"
B.MAY 24,1900 STUYVESANT,N.Y.
D.JAN.5,1960
1927	WAS	A	P		2	0- 0
1928	WAS	A	P		4	0- 0
	BRTR				6	0- 0

VAN ATTA, RUSSELL "SHERIFF"
B.JUNE 21,1906 AUGUSTA,N.J.
1933	NY	A	P		26	12- 4
1934	NY	A	P		28	3- 5
1935	NY	A	P		5	0- 0
	STL	A	P		53	9-16
1936	STL	A	P	52	53	4- 7
1937	STL	A	P		16	1- 2
1938	STL	A	P		25	4- 7
1939	STL	A	P		2	0- 0
	BLTL			207	208	33-41

VAN BRABANT, CAMILLE OSCAR "OSSIE"
B.SEPT.28,1928 BERKLEY,MICH.
1954	PHI	A	P		9	0- 2
1955	KC	A	P		2	0- 0
	BRTR				11	0- 2

VAN BUREN, EDWARD EUGENE "DEACON"
B.DEC.14,1870 LA SALLE CO.,ILL.
D.JUNE 29,1957
1904	BRO	N	O		1	1.000
	PHI	N	O		12	.233
					13	.250

VAN CAMP, ALBERT JOSEPH
B.SEPT.7,1904 MOLINE,ILL.
1928	CLE	A	1		5	.235
1931	BOS	A	1-O	101	.275
1932	BOS	A	1		34	.223
	BRTR				140	.261

VANCE, CLARENCE ARTHUR "DAZZY"
B.MAR.4,1891 ORIENT,IOWA
D.FEB.16,1961 HOMOSASSA SPRINGS FLA
1915	PIT	N	P		1	0- 1
	NY	A	P		8	0- 3
1918	NY	A	P		2	0- 0
1922	BRO	N	P		36	18-12
1923	BRO	N	P		37	18-15
1924	BRO	N	P		35	28- 6
1925	BRO	N	P		31	22- 9
1926	BRO	N	P		22	9-10
1927	BRO	N	P		34	16-15
1928	BRO	N	P		38	22-10
1929	BRO	N	P		31	14-13
1930	BRO	N	P		35	17-15
1931	BRO	N	P		30	11-13
1932	BRO	N	P		27	12-11
1933	STL	N	P		28	6- 2
1934	CIN	N	P		6	0- 2
	STL	N	P		19	1- 1
1935	BRO	N	P		20	3- 2
	BRTR				440	197-140

VANCE, GENE COVINGTON "SANDY"
B.JAN.5,1947 LAMAR,COLO.
1970	LA	N	P		20	7- 7
1971	LA	N	P		10	2- 1
	BRTR				30	9- 8

VANCE, JOSEPH ALBERT "SANDY"
B.SEPT.16,1905 DEVINE,TEX.
1935	CHI	A	P		10	2- 2
1937	NY	A	P		2	1- 0
1938	NY	A	P	3	4	0- 0
	BRTR			15	16	3- 2

VAN CUYK, CHRISTIAN GERALD "CHRIS"
B.MAR.1,1927 KIMBERLY,WIS.
1950	BRO	N	P		12	1- 3
1951	BRO	N	P		9	1- 2
1952	BRO	N	P		23	5- 6
	BLTL				44	7-11

VAN CUYK, JOHN HENRY "JOHNNY"
B.JULY 7,1921 LITTLE CHUTE,WIS.
1947	BRO	N	P		2	0- 0
1948	BRO	N	P		3	0- 0
1949	BRO	N	P		2	0- 0
	BLTL				7	0- 0

VANDAGRIFT, CARL WILLIAM
B.APR.22,1883 CENTRALIA,ILL.
D.OCT.9,1920
| 1914 | IND | F | 2 | | 42 | .246 |
| | BRTR | | | | | |

VANDEMANN, FREDERICK H.
(PLAYED UNDER NAME OF FREDERICK H. ABBOTT)

VANDENBERG, HAROLD HARRIS "HY"
B.MAR.17,1909 ABILENE,KAN.
1935	BOS	A	P		3	0- 0
1937	NY	N	P		1	0- 1
1938	NY	N	P		6	0- 1
1939	NY	N	P		2	0- 0
1940	NY	N	P		13	1- 1
1944	CHI	N	P		35	7- 4
1945	CHI	N	P		30	7- 3
	BRTR				90	15-10

VANDER MEER, JOHN SAMUEL "JOHNNY"
B.NOV.2,1914 PROSPECT PARK,N.J.
1937	CIN	N	P	19	21	3- 5
1938	CIN	N	P	32	33	15-10
1939	CIN	N	P		30	5- 9
1940	CIN	N	P	10	12	3- 1
1941	CIN	N	P	33	35	16-13
1942	CIN	N	P	33	37	18-12
1943	CIN	N	P	36	40	15-16
1946	CIN	N	P	29	33	10-12
1947	CIN	N	P	30	31	9-14
1948	CIN	N	P	33	41	17-14
1949	CIN	N	P	28	33	5-10
1950	CHI	N	P	32	35	3- 4
1951	CLE	A	P		1	0- 1
	BBTL			346	382	119-121

VAN DUSEN, FREDERICK WILLIAM "FRED"
B.JULY 31,1937 JACKSON HEIGHTS, N.Y.
| 1955 | PHI | N | H | | 1 | .000 |
| | BL | | | | | |

VAN DYKE, BENJAMIN HARRISON
B.AUG.15,1888 CLINTONVILLE,PA.
D.OCT.22,1973 SARASOTA,FLA.
1909	PHI	N	P		2	0- 0
1912	BOS	A	P		3	1- 0
	BRTL				5	1- 0

VAN DYKE, WILLIAM JENNINGS
B.DEC.15,1863 PARIS,ILL.
D.MAY 5,1933
1890	TOL	AA	O		128	.266
1892	STL	N	O		3	.000
1893	BOS	N	O		3	.250
	BRTR				134	.262

VANGILDER, ELAM RUSSELL
B.APR.23,1896 CAPE GIRARDEAU,MO
1919	STL	A	P		3	1- 0
1920	STL	A	P		24	3- 8
1921	STL	A	P		31	11-12
1922	STL	A	P	43	45	19-13
1923	STL	A	P	41	45	16-17
1924	STL	A	P		43	5-10
1925	STL	A	P		52	14- 8
1926	STL	A	P		42	9-11
1927	STL	A	P		44	10-12
1928	DET	A	P		38	11-10
1929	DET	A	P		6	0- 1
	BRTR			367	373	99-102

YR	CL	LEA	POS	GP	G	REC

VAN HALTREN, GEORGE E. "RIP"
B.MAR.30,1866 ST.LOUIS,MO.
D.OCT.1,1945 OAKLAND,CAL.
```
1887 CHI N   P-O   19    44   12- 7
                                .278
1888 CHI N   P-O   27    81   13-11
                                .283
1889 CHI N   O           134    .322
1890 BRO P   P-O   26    92   15-10
                                .346
1891 BAL AA  M-P-   6   136    0- 1
             S-O                .316
1892 BAL N   M-P-   4   135    0- 0
             O                  .304
     PIT N   O            13    .212
1893 PIT N   O           123    .350
1894 NY  N   O           139    .333
1895 NY  N   P-O    1   131    0- 0
                                .338
1896 NY  N   P-O    2   133    1- 0
                                .353
1897 NY  N   O           131    .332
1898 NY  N   O           155    .315
1899 NY  N   O           153    .301
1900 NY  N   P-O    1   141    0- 0
                                .319
1901 NY  N   P-O    1   133    0- 1
                                .342
1902 NY  N   O            26    .250
1903 NY  N   O            75    .257
     BLTL          87  1975   41-30
                                .322
```

VANN, JOHN SILAS
B.JUNE 7,1893 FAIRLAND,OKLA.
D.JUNE 10,1958
```
1913 STL N   H            1   .000
     BRTR
```

VAN NOY, JAY LOWELL
B.NOV.4,1928 GARLAND,UTAH
```
1951 STL N   O            6   .000
     BLTR
```

VAN ROBAYS, MAURICE RENE "BOMBER"
B.NOV.15,1914 DETROIT,MICH.
D.MAR.1,1965 DETROIT,MICH.
```
1939 PIT N   O           27    .314
1940 PIT N   1-O        145    .273
1941 PIT N   O          129    .282
1942 PIT N   O          100    .232
1943 PIT N   O           69    .288
1946 PIT N   1-O         59    .212
     BRTR               529    .267
```

VAN ZANDT, CHARLES ISAAC "IKE"
B.1877 BROOKLYN,N.Y.
D.SEPT.14,1908
```
1901 NY  N   P            3    0- 0
1904 CHI N   O            3    .000
1905 STL A   O           94    .233
                    3   100    0- 0
                                .224
```

VAN ZANT, RICHARD
```
1888 CLE AA  3           10    .187
```

VARENHORST, H.
B.ST.LOUIS,MO.
```
1904 STL A   H            1    .000
```

VARGA, ANDREW WILLIAM "ANDY"
B.DEC.11,1930 CHICAGO,ILL.
```
1950 CHI N   P            1    0- 0
1951 CHI N   P            2    0- 0
     BRTL                 3    0- 0
```

VARGAS, ROBERTO ENRIQUE
B.MAY 29,1929 SANTURCE,P.R.
```
1955 MIL N   P           25    0- 0
     BLTL
```

VARGUS, WILLIAM FAY
B.NOV.11,1900 N.SCITUATE,MASS.
```
1925 BOS N   P           11    1- 1
1926 BOS N   P            4    0- 0
     BLTL                15    1- 1
```

VARNER, GLEN GANN "BUCK"
B.AUG.17,1930 HIXON,TENN.
```
1952 WAS A   O            2    .000
     BLTR
```

VARNEY, LAWRENCE DELANO "DIKE"
B.AUG.9,1880 DOVER,N.H.
D.APR.23,1950
```
1902 CLE A   P            3    2- 1
     TL
```

VARNEY, RICHARD FRED "PETE"
B.APR.10,1949 ROXBURY,MASS.
```
1973 CHI A   C            5    .000
1974 CHI A   C            9    .250
1975 CHI A   C           36    .271
1976 CHI A   C           14    .244
     ATL A   C            5    .100
     BRTR                69    .247
```

VASBINDER, MOSES CALHOUN
B.JULY 19,1880 SCIO,OHIO
D.DEC.22,1950
```
1902 CLE A   P            2    0- 0
     BRTR
```

VAUGHAN, CECIL PORTER
B.MAY 11,1919 STEVENSVILLE,VA.
```
1940 PHI A   P           18    2- 9
1941 PHI A   P            5    0- 2
1946 PHI A   P            1    0- 0
     BRTL                24    2-11
```

VAUGHAN, CHARLES WAYNE "CHARLIE"
B.OCT.6,1947 MERCEDES,TEX.
```
1966 ATL N   P            1    1- 0
1969 ATL N   P            1    0- 0
     BRTL                 2    1- 0
```

VAUGHAN, GLENN EDWARD
B.FEB.15,1944 COMPTON,CAL.
```
1963 HOU N   S-3         9    .167
     BBTR
```

VAUGHAN, JOSEPH FLOYD "ARKY"
B.MAR.9,1912 CLIFTY,ARK.
D.AUG.30,1952 EAGLEVILLE,CAL.
```
1932 PIT N   S          129    .318
1933 PIT N   S          152    .314
1934 PIT N   S          149    .333
1935 PIT N   S          137    .385
1936 PIT N   S          156    .335
1937 PIT N   S-O        126    .322
1938 PIT N   S          148    .322
1939 PIT N   S          152    .306
1940 PIT N   S-3        156    .300
1941 PIT N   S-3        106    .316
1942 BRO N   2-S-3      128    .277
1943 BRO N   S-3        149    .305
1947 BRO N   3-O         64    .325
1948 BRO N   3-O         65    .244
     BLTR              1817    .318
```

VAUGHN, CLARENCE LEROY
B.SEPT.4,1911 SEDALIA,MO.
D.MAR.1,1937 MARTINSVILLE,VA.
```
1934 PHI A   P            2    0- 0
     BBTR
```

VAUGHN, FREDERICK THOMAS
B.OCT.18,1918 COALINGA,CAL.
D.MAR.3,1964 LAKE WALES,FLA.
```
1944 WAS A   2-3         30    .257
1945 WAS A   2-S         80    .235
     BRTR               110    .242
```

VAUGHN, HARRY FRANCIS "FARMER"
B.MAR.1,1864 RURAL,OHIO
D.FEB.21,1914
```
1886 CIN AA  C            1    .000
1888 LOU AA  C-O         49    .203
1889 LOU AA  C           90    .233
1890 NY  P   C           45    .248
1891 CIN AA  P-C-   1    45    0- 0
             1-3-O              .255
     MIL AA  C-1         24    .330
1892 CIN N   C           85    .257
1893 CIN N   C-1-O      119    .299
1894 CIN N   C           67    .309
1895 CIN N   C           88    .305
1896 CIN N   C-1        113    .297
1897 CIN N   1           50    .305
1898 CIN N   C-1         73    .303
1899 CIN N   1           28    .178
     BRTR           1   877    0- 0
                                .276
```

VAUGHN, JAMES LESLIE "HIPPO"
B.APR.9,1888 WEATHERFORD,TEX.
D.MAY 29,1966 CHICAGO,ILL.
```
1908 NY  A   P            2    0- 0
1910 NY  A   P           29   13-11
1911 NY  A   P           26    8-10
1912 NY  A   P           15    2- 8
     WAS A   P           12    4- 3
1913 CHI N   P            7    5- 1
1914 CHI N   P           42   21-13
1915 CHI N   P      41   43   20-12
1916 CHI N   P           44   17-15
1917 CHI N   P           41   23-13
1918 CHI N   P           35   22-10
1919 CHI N   P           38   21-14
1920 CHI N   P           40   19-16
1921 CHI N   P           17    3-11
     BBTL         389   391  178-137
```

VAUGHN, ROBERT
B.JUNE 4,1885 STAMFORD,N.Y.
D.APR.11,1965
```
1909 NY  A   2            5    .143
1915 STL F   2          144    .274
     BRTR               149    .271
```

VEACH, ALVIS LINDELL
B.AUG.6,1911 MAYLENE,ALA.
```
1935 PHI A   P            2    0- 2
     BRTR
```

VEACH, ROBERT HAYES "BOBBY"
B.JUNE 29,1888 ST.CHARLES,KY.
D.AUG.7,1945 DETROIT,MICH.
```
1912 DET A   O           23    .342
1913 DET A   O          138    .269
1914 DET A   O          149    .275
1915 DET A   O          152    .313
1916 DET A   O          150    .306
1917 DET A   O          154    .319
1918 DET A   P-O    1   127    0- 0
                                .279
1919 DET A   O          139    .355
1920 DET A   O          154    .307
1921 DET A   O          150    .338
1922 DET A   O          155    .327
1923 DET A   O          114    .321
1924 BOS A   O          142    .295
1925 BOS A   O            1    .200
     NY  A   O           56    .353
     WAS A   O           18    .243
     BLTR          1  1822    0- 0
                                .310
```

VEACH, WILLIAM WALTER "PEAK-A-BOO"
B.JUNE 15,1862 INDIANAPOLIS,IND
D.NOV.12,1937
```
1884 KC  U   P-O   14    27    2- 9
                                .127
1887 LOU AA  P            1    0- 1
1890 CLE N   1           62    .237
     PIT N   1            8    .300
                   15    98    2-10
                                .216
```

VEAL, ORVILLE INMAN "COOT"
B.JULY 9,1932 SANDERSVILLE,GA.
```
1958 DET A   S           58    .256
1959 DET A   S           77    .202
1960 DET A   2-S-3       27    .297
1961 WAS A   S           69    .202
1962 PIT N   H            1    .000
1963 DET A   S           15    .219
     BRTR               247    .231
```

VEALE, ROBERT ANDREW "BOB"
B.OCT.28,1935 BIRMINGHAM,ALA.
```
1962 PIT N   P           11    2- 2
1963 PIT N   P      34   35    5- 2
1964 PIT N   P      40   41   18-12
1965 PIT N   P           39   17-12
1966 PIT N   P           38   16-12
1967 PIT N   P           33   16- 8
1968 PIT N   P           36   13-14
1969 PIT N   P           34   13-14
1970 PIT N   P           34   10-15
1971 PIT N   P           37    6- 0
1972 PIT N   P            5    0- 0
     BOS A   P            6    2- 0
1973 BOS A   P           32    2- 3
1974 BOS A   P           18    0- 1
     BBTR         397   399  120-95
```

YR	CL	LEA	POS	GP	G	REC

VEDDER, LOUIS EDWARD
B.APR.20,1897 OAKVILLE,MICH.
| 1920 DET | A | P | | 1 | 0- 0 |
| | | BRTR | | | |

VEIGEL, ALLEN FRANCIS
B.JAN.30,1917 TUSCARAWAS,OHIO
| 1939 BOS | N | P | | 2 | 0- 1 |
| | | BRTR | | | |

VEIL, FREDERICK WILLIAM "BUCKY"
B.AUG.2,1881 TYRONE,PA.
D.APR.16,1931 ALTOONA,PA.
1903 PIT	N	P		12	5- 3
1904 PIT	N	P		1	0- 0
		TR		13	5- 3

VELAZQUEZ, CARLOS (QUINONES)
B.MAR.22,1948 LOIZA,P.R.
| 1973 MIL | A | P | | 18 | 2- 2 |
| | | BRTR | | | |

VELAZQUEZ, FEDERICO ANTONIO "FREDDIE"
B.DEC.6,1937 SANTO DOMINGO,D.R.
1969 SEA	A	C		6	.125
1973 ATL	N	C		15	.348
		BRTR		21	.256

VELEZ, OTONIEL (FRANCESCHI) "OTTO"
B.NOV.29,1950 PONCE,P.R.
1973 NY	A	O		23	.195
1974 NY	A	1-3-O		27	.209
1975 NY	A	1		6	.250
1976 NY	A	1-3-O		49	.266
		BRTR		105	.228

VELTMAN, ARTHUR PATRICK "PAT"
B.MAR.24,1906 MOBILE,ALA.
1926 CHI	A	U		4	.000
1928 NY	N	O		1	.333
1929 NY	N	C		2	.000
1931 BOS	N	H		1	.000
1932 NY	N	H		2	.000
1934 PIT	N	C		12	.107
		BRTR		22	.132

VENTURA, VINCENT
B.APR.18,1917 NEW YORK,N.Y.
| 1945 WAS | A | O | | 18 | .207 |
| | | BRTR | | | |

VERBAN, EMIL MATTHEW "ANTELOPE"
B.AUG.27,1915 LINCOLN,ILL.
1944 STL	N	2		146	.257
1945 STL	N	2		155	.278
1946 STL	N	2		1	.000
PHI	N	2		138	.275
1947 PHI	N	2		155	.285
1948 PHI	N	2		55	.231
CHI	N	2		56	.295
1949 CHI	N	2		98	.289
1950 CHI	N	2-S-3-O		45	.108
BOS	N	2		4	.000
		BRTR		853	.272

VERBANIC, JOSEPH MICHAEL "JOE"
B.APR.24,1943 WASHINGTON,PA.
1966 PHI	N	P		17	1- 1
1967 NY	A	P		28	4- 3
1968 NY	A	P		40	6- 7
1970 NY	A	P		7	1- 0
		BRTR		92	12-11

VERBLE, GENE KERMIT
B.JUNE 29,1928 CONCORD,N.C.
1951 WAS	A	2-S-3		68	.203
1953 WAS	A	S		13	.190
		BRTR		81	.202

VERDEL, ALFRED ALFRED
B.JUNE 10,1921 PUNXSUTAWNEY,PA.
| 1944 PHI | N | P | | 1 | 0- 0 |
| | | BRTR | | | |

VERDI, FRANK MICHAEL
B.JUNE 2,1926 BROOKLYN,N.Y.
| 1953 NY | A | S | | 1 | .000 |
| | | BRTR | | | |

VEREKER, THOMAS
| 1915 BAL | F | P | | 2 | 0- 0 |

VERGEZ, JOHN LOUIS
B.JULY 9,1906 OAKLAND,CAL.
1931 NY	N	3		152	.278
1932 NY	N	3		118	.261
1933 NY	N	3		123	.271
1934 NY	N	3		108	.200
1935 PHI	N	S-3		148	.249
1936 PHI	N	3		15	.275
STL	N	3		8	.167
		BRTR		672	.255

VERHOEVEN, JOHN C
B.JULY 3,1953 LONG BEACH,CAL.
| 1976 CAL | A | P | | 21 | 0- 2 |
| | | BRTR | | | |

VERNON, JAMES BARTON "MICKEY"
B.APR.22,1918 MARCUS HOOK,PA.
1939 WAS	A	1		76	.257
1940 WAS	A	1		5	.158
1941 WAS	A	1		138	.299
1942 WAS	A	1		151	.271
1943 WAS	A	1		145	.268
1946 WAS	A	1		148	.353
1947 WAS	A	1		154	.265
1948 WAS	A	1		150	.242
1949 CLE	A	1		153	.291
1950 CLE	A	1		28	.189
WAS	A	1		90	.306
1951 WAS	A	1		141	.293
1952 WAS	A	1		154	.251
1953 WAS	A	1		152	.337
1954 WAS	A	1		151	.290
1955 WAS	A	1		150	.301
1956 BOS	A	1		119	.310
1957 BOS	A	1		102	.241
1958 CLE	A	1		119	.293
1959 MIL	N	1-O		74	.220
1960 PIT	N	H		9	.125
		BLTL		2409	.286
NON-PLAYING MANAGER
WAS(A) 1961-63

VERNON, JOSEPH HENRY
B.NOV.25,1889 MANSFIELD,MASS.
D.MAR.13,1955
1912 CHI	N	P		1	0- 0
1914 BRO	F	P		1	0- 0
		BRTR		2	0- 0

VERSALLES, ZOILO (RODRIGUEZ)
B.DEC.18,1939 HAVANA,CUBA
1959 WAS	A	S		29	.153
1960 WAS	A	S		15	.133
1961 MIN	A	S		129	.280
1962 MIN	A	S		160	.241
1963 MIN	A	S		159	.261
1964 MIN	A	S		160	.259
1965 MIN	A	S		160	.273
1966 MIN	A	S		137	.249
1967 MIN	A	S		160	.200
1968 LA	N	S		122	.196
1969 CLE	A	2-S-3		72	.226
WAS	A	2-S-3		31	.267
1971 ATL	N	2-S-3		66	.191
		BRTR		1400	.242

VERYZER, THOMAS MARTIN "TOM"
B.FEB.11,1953 PORT JEFFERSON,N.Y
1973 DET	A	S		18	.300
1974 DET	A	S		22	.236
1975 DET	A	S		128	.252
1976 DET	A	S		97	.234
		BRTR		265	.245

VIAU, LEON
B.JULY 5,1866 CORINTH,VT.
D.DEC.31,1947
1888 CIN	AA	P-O		41	27-14
					.085
1889 CIN	AA	P		47	21-19
1890 CIN	N	P		12	7- 3
CLE	N	P		14	4-10
1891 CLE	N	P		39	18-20
1892 CLE	N	P		1	1- 0
LOU	N	P	15	20	4-11
BOS	N	P		2	1- 0
		BRTR	171	176	83-77
					.141

VICK, HENRY ARTHUR "ERNIE"
B.JULY 2,1900 TOLEDO,OHIO
1922 STL	N	C		3	.333
1924 STL	N	C		16	.348
1925 STL	N	C		14	.188
1926 STL	N	C		24	.196
		BRTR		57	.232

VICK, SAMUEL BRUCE
B.APR.12,1895 CENTRAL ACADEMY, MISS.
1917 NY	A	O		10	.278
1918 NY	A	O		2	.667
1919 NY	A	O		106	.248
1920 NY	A	O		51	.220
1921 BOS	A	O		44	.260
		BRTR		213	.248

VICKERS, HARRY PORTER "RUBE"
B.MAY 17,1878 PITTSFORD,MICH.
D.DEC.9,1958
1902 CIN	N	P-C		3	4	0- 3
						.363
1903 BRO	N	P-O		2	3	0- 1
						.000
1907 PHI	A	P			10	2- 2
1908 PHI	A	P			53	18-19
1909 PHI	A	P			18	2- 2
		BLTR		86	88	22-27
						.167

VICKERY, THOMAS GILL "VINEGAR TOM"
B.MAY 5,1867 MILFORD,MASS.
D.MAR.21,1921
1890 PHI	N	P		45	24-18
1891 CHI	N	P		14	6- 5
1892 BAL	N	P		19	8-11
1893 PHI	N	P		14	5- 5
				92	43-39

VICO, GEORGE STEVE "SAM"
B.AUG.9,1923 SAN FRANCISCO,CAL.
1948 DET	A	1		144	.267
1949 DET	A	1		67	.190
		BLTR		211	.250

VIDAL, JOSE (NICOLAS)
B.APR.3,1940 BATEY LECHUGAS,D.R.
1966 CLE	A	O		17	.188
1967 CLE	A	O		16	.118
1968 CLE	A	1-O		37	.167
1969 SEA	A	O		18	.192
		BRTR		88	.164

VINES, ROBERT EARL
B.FEB.25,1898 WAXAHACHIE,TEX.
1924 STL	N	P		2	0- 0
1925 PHI	N	P		3	0- 0
		BRTR		5	0- 0

VINEYARD, DAVID KENT "DAVE"
B.FEB.25,1941 CLAY,W.VA.
| 1964 BAL | A | P | | 19 | 2- 5 |
| | | BRTR | | | |

VINSON, CHARLES ANTHONY "CHARLIE"
B.JAN.5,1944 WASHINGTON,D.C.
| 1966 CAL | A | 1 | | 13 | .182 |
| | | BLTL | | | |

VINSON, ERNEST AUGUSTUS "RUBE"
B.MAR.20,1879 DOVER,DEL.
D.OCT.12,1951
1904 CLE	A	O		15	.269
1905 CLE	A	O		38	.195
1906 CHI	A	O		10	.250
				63	.220

VINTON, WILLIAM MILLER
B.APR.27,1865 WINTHROP,MASS.
D.SEPT.3,1893
1884 PHI	N	P		21	9- 8
1885 PHI	N	P		9	3- 6
ATH	AA	P-O		7	4- 3
					.192
		BRTR		37	16-17
					.119

VIOX, JAMES HARRY
B.DEC.30,1890 LOCKLAND,OHIO
D.JAN.6,1969 ERLANGER,KY.
1912 PIT	N	3		33	.186
1913 PIT	N	2		137	.317
1914 PIT	N	2		143	.265
1915 PIT	N	2		150	.256
1916 PIT	N	2		43	.250
		BRTR		506	.272

YR	CL	LEA	POS	GP	G	REC

VIRDON, WILLIAM CHARLES "BILL"
B.JUNE 9,1931 HAZEL PARK,MICH.

1955	STL	N	O		144	.281
1956	STL	N	O		24	.211
	PIT	N	O		133	.334
1957	PIT	N	O		144	.251
1958	PIT	N	O		144	.267
1959	PIT	N	O		144	.254
1960	PIT	N	O		120	.264
1961	PIT	N	O		146	.260
1962	PIT	N	O		156	.247
1963	PIT	N	O		142	.269
1964	PIT	N	O		145	.243
1965	PIT	N	O		135	.279
1968	PIT	N	O		6	.333
	BLTR				1583	.267

NON-PLAYING MANAGER
PIT(N) 1972-73, NY(A) 1974-75,
HOU(N) 1975-76

VIRGIL, OSVALDO JOSE "OSSIE"
B.MAY 17,1933 CORPUS CHRISTI,D.R

1956	NY	N	3		3	.417
1957	NY	N	S-3-O		96	.235
1958	DET	A	3		49	.244
1960	DET	A	C-2-S-3		62	.227
1961	DET	A	C-2-S-3		20	.133
	KC	A	C-3		11	.143
1962	BAL	A	H		1	.000
1965	PIT	N	C-2-3		39	.265
1966	SF	N	C-1-2-3-O		42	.213
1969	SF	N	H		1	.000
	BRTR				324	.231

VIRTUE, JACOB KITCHLINE "GUESSES"
B.MAR.2,1865 PHILADELPHIA,PA.
D.FEB.3,1943

1890	CLE	N	1		62	.305
1891	CLE	N	1		139	.262
1892	CLE	N	1		147	.282
1893	CLE	N	1		95	.287
1894	CLE	N	O		23	.270
	BB				466	.282

VISNER, JOSEPH P.
B.SEPT.27,1862 MINNEAPOLIS,MINN

1885	BAL	AA	O		4	.214
1889	BRO	AA	C-O		80	.249
1890	PIT	P	O		127	.265
1891	WAS	AA	O		13	.229
	STL	AA	O		5	.136
	BLTR				229	.258

VITELLI, JOSEPH ANTHONY
B.APR.12,1911 MCKEE'S ROCKS,PA.
D.FEB.7,1967

1944	PIT	N	P	4		0- 0
1945	PIT	N	H	1		.000
	BRTR			4	5	0- 0
						.000

VITT, OSCAR JOSEPH "OSSIE"
B.JAN.4,1890 SAN FRANCISCO,CAL.
D.JAN.31,1963 OAKLAND,CAL.

1912	DET	A	2-3-O		73	.245
1913	DET	A	2-3		99	.240
1914	DET	A	2-3		66	.251
1915	DET	A	3		152	.250
1916	DET	A	3		153	.226
1917	DET	A	2		140	.254
1918	DET	A	3		81	.239
1919	BOS	A	3		133	.243
1920	BOS	A	2-3		87	.220
1921	BOS	A	3		78	.190
	BRTR				1062	.240

NON-PLAYING MANAGER
CLE(A) 1938-40

VOGEL, OTTO HENRY
B.OCT.26,1899 DAVENPORT,IOWA
D.JULY 19,1969 IOWA CITY,IOWA

1923	CHI	N	3-O		41	.210
1924	CHI	N	O		70	.267
	BRTR				111	.249

VOIGHT, OLEN EDWARD "ODE"
B.JAN.21,1899 WHEATON,ILL.
D.APR.7,1970 SCOTTSDALE,ARIZ.

| 1924 | STL | A | P | | 8 | 1- 0 |
| | BLTR | | | | | |

VOISELLE, WILLIAM SYMMES "BIG BILL"
B.JAN.29,1919 GREENWOOD,S.C.

1942	NY	N	P		2	0- 1
1943	NY	N	P		4	1- 2
1944	NY	N	P	43	44	21-16
1945	NY	N	P		41	14-14
1946	NY	N	P		36	9-15
1947	NY	N	P		11	1- 4
	BOS	N	P		22	8- 7
1948	BOS	N	P		37	13-13
1949	BOS	N	P		30	7- 8
1950	CHI	N	P		19	0- 4
	BRTR			245	246	74-84

VOLLMER, CLYDE FREDERICK
B.SEPT.24,1921 CINCINNATI,OHIO

1942	CIN	N	O		12	.093
1946	CIN	N	O		9	.182
1947	CIN	N	O		78	.219
1948	CIN	N	O		7	.111
	WAS	A	O		1	.400
1949	WAS	A	O		129	.253
1950	WAS	A	O		6	.286
	BOS	A	O		57	.284
1951	BOS	A	O		115	.251
1952	BOS	A	O		90	.264
1953	BOS	A	H		1	.000
	WAS	A	O		118	.260
1954	WAS	A	O		62	.256
	BRTR				685	.251

VOLZ, JACOB PHILLIP
B.APR.4,1878 SAN ANTONIO,TEX.
D.AUG.11,1962

1901	BOS	A	P		1	1- 0
1905	BOS	N	P		3	0- 2
1908	CIN	N	P		7	1- 2
	BRTR				11	2- 4

VON DER AHE, CHRISTIAN FREDERICK WILHELM "CHRIS"
B.NOV.7,1851 HILLE,GERMANY
D.JUNE 7,1913
NON-PLAYING MANAGER
STL(AA) 1884, STL(N) 1892,95,97

VON FRICKEN, ANTHONY "HON"
B.1870 BROOKLYN,N.Y.
D.MAR.22,1947 TROY,N.Y.

| 1890 | BOS | N | P | | 1 | 0- 1 |

VON HOFF, BRUCE FREDERICK
B.NOV.17,1943 OAKLAND,CAL.

1965	HOU	N	P		3	0- 0
1967	HOU	N	P		10	0- 3
	BRTR				13	0- 3

VON KOLNITZ, ALFRED HOLMES "FRITZ"
B.MAY 20,1893 CHARLESTON,S.C.
D.MAR.18,1948

1914	CIN	N	3		41	.221
1915	CIN	N	C-1-S-3-O		50	.192
1916	CHI	A	3		24	.227
	BRTR				115	.212

VORHEES, HENRY BERT "CY"
B.SEPT.30,1874 LODI,OHIO
D.FEB.8,1910 PERRY TOWNSHIP,O.

1902	PHI	N	P		10	3- 2
	WAS	A	P		1	0- 1
					11	3·· 3

VOSMIK, JOSEPH FRANKLIN "JOE"
B.APR.4,1910 CLEVELAND,OHIO
D.JAN.27,1962 CLEVELAND,OHIO

1930	CLE	A	O		9	.231
1931	CLE	A	O		149	.320
1932	CLE	A	O		153	.312
1933	CLE	A	O		119	.263
1934	CLE	A	O		104	.341
1935	CLE	A	O		152	.348
1936	CLE	A	O		138	.287
1937	STL	A	O		144	.325
1938	BOS	A	O		146	.324
1939	BOS	A	O		145	.276
1940	BRO	N	O		116	.282
1941	BRO	N	O		25	.196
1944	WAS	A	O		14	.194
	BRTR				1414	.307

VOSS, ALEXANDER
B.1855 ATLANTA,GA.
D.AUG.31,1906

1884	WAS	U	P-1-	26	63	7-14
			S-3-O			.190
	KC	U	P-O	8	14	1- 7
						.089
	BRTR			34	77	8-21
						.173

VOSS, WILLIAM EDWARD "BILL"
B.OCT.31,1945 GLENDALE,CAL.

1965	CHI	A	O		11	.182
1966	CHI	A	O		2	.000
1967	CHI	A	O		13	.091
1968	CHI	A	O		61	.156
1969	CAL	A	1-O		133	.261
1970	CAL	A	O		80	.243
1971	MIL	A	O		97	.251
1972	MIL	A	O		27	.083
	OAK	A	O		40	.227
	STL	N	O		11	.267
	BLTL				475	.227

VOWINKEL, JOHN HENRY "RIP"
B.NOV.18,1884 OSWEGO,N.Y.
D.JULY 13,1966 OSWEGO,N.Y.

| 1905 | CIN | N | P | | 6 | 3- 3 |
| | BPTR | | | | | |

VOYLES, PHILIP VANCE
B.MAY 12,1900 MURPHY,N.C.
D.NOV.3,1972 MARLBORO,MASS.

| 1929 | BOS | N | O | | 20 | .235 |
| | BLTL | | | | | |

VUCKOVICH, PETER DENNIS "PETE"
B.OCT.27,1952 JOHNSTOWN,PA.

1975	CHI	A	P		4	0- 1
1976	CHI	A	P		33	7- 4
	BRTR				37	7- 5

VUKOVICH, JOHN CHRISTOPHER
B.JULY 31,1947 SACRAMENTO,CAL.

1970	PHI	N	S-3		3	.125
1971	PHI	N	3		74	.166
1973	MIL	A	1-S-3		55	.125
1974	MIL	A	1-2-S-3		38	.188
1975	CIN	N	3		31	.211
1976	PHI	N	1-3		4	.125
	BRTR				205	.161

WACHER, AUGUST
(PLAYED UNDER NAME OF
ARTHUR SUNDAY)

WACHTEL, PAUL HORINE
B.APR.30,1893 MYERSVILLE,MD.
D.DEC.15,1964 SAN ANTONIO,TEX.

| 1917 | BRO | N | P | | 2 | 0- 0 |
| | BRTR | | | | | |

WACKER, CHARLES
B.NEW ALBANY,IND.

| 1909 | PIT | N | P | | 1 | 0- 0 |
| | BRTR | | | | | |

WADDELL, GEORGE EDWARD "RUBE"
B.OCT.13,1876 BRADFORD,PA.
D.APR.1,1914 SAN ANTONIO,TEX.

1897	LOU	N	P		2	0- 1
1899	LOU	N	P		10	7- 2
1900	PIT	N	P	29	30	10-10
1901	PIT	N	P		2	0- 2
	CHI	N	P		31	14-14
1902	PHI	A	P		33	24- 7
1903	PHI	A	P		38	22-16
1904	PHI	A	P		46	26-17
1905	PHI	A	P		46	26-11
1906	PHI	A	P		41	16-16
1907	PHI	A	P		43	19-13
1908	STL	A	P		43	19-14
1909	STL	A	P		31	11-14
1910	STL	A	P		10	3- 1
	BRTL			405	406	197-138

WADDEY, FRANK ORUM
B.AUG.21,1905 MEMPHIS,TENN.

| 1931 | STL | A | O | | 14 | .273 |
| | BLTL | | | | | |

WADE, ABRAHAM LINCOLN
B.DEC.20,1880 SPRING CITY,PA.
D.JULY 21,1968 RIVERSIDE
TOWNSHIP,N.J.

| 1907 | NY | N | O | | 1 | .000 |
| | BRTR | | | | | |

YR	CL LEA POS	GP	G	REC

WADE, BENJAMIN STYRON "BEN"
B.NOV.26,1922 MOREHEAD CITY,N.C
1948	CHI N P		2	0- 1
1952	BRO N P		37	11- 9
1953	BRO N P		32	7- 5
1954	BRO N P		23	1- 1
	STL N P		13	0- 0
1955	PIT N P		11	0- 1
	BRTR		118	19-17

WADE, GALEARD LEE "GALE"
B.JAN.20,1929 HOLLISTER,MO.
1955	CHI N O		9	.182
1956	CHI N O		10	.000
	BLTR		19	.133

WADE, JACOB FIELDS
"WHISTLING JAKE"
B.APR.1,1912 MOREHEAD CITY,N.C.
1936	DET A P		13	4- 5
1937	DET A P		33	7-10
1938	DET A P		27	3- 2
1939	BOS A P		20	1- 4
	STL A P		4	0- 2
1942	CHI A P		15	5- 5
1943	CHI A P		21	3- 7
1944	CHI A P		19	2- 4
1946	NY A P		13	2- 1
	WAS A P		6	0- 0
	BLTL		171	27-40

WADE, RICHARD FRANK "RIP"
B.JAN.12,1898 DULUTH,MINN.
D.JUNE 15,1957
| 1923 | WAS A O | | 33 | .232 |
| | BLTR | | | |

WADSWORTH, JOHN L. "JACK"
B.DEC.16,1868 WELLINGTON,OHIO
D.JULY 8,1941 ELYRIA,OHIO
1890	CLE N P		20	2-15
1893	BAL N P		3	0- 2
1894	LOU N P		23	4-17
1895	LOU N P		2	0- 1
	BLTR		48	6-35

WAGENHURST, ELWOOD OTTO
B.JUNE 3,1863 KUTZTOWN,PA.
D.FEB.12,1946
| 1888 | PHI N 3 | | 2 | .125 |

WAGNER, ALBERT "BUTZ"
B.SEPT.17,1869 CARNEGIE,PA.
D.NOV.26,1928
1898	WAS N 3		57	.232
	BRO N 3		11	.237
			68	.233

WAGNER, CHARLES F. "HEINIE"
B.SEPT.23,1880 NEW YORK,N.Y.
D.MAR.20,1943
1902	NY N S		17	.214
1906	BOS A 2		9	.250
1907	BOS A S		111	.213
1908	BOS A S		153	.247
1909	BOS A S		124	.256
1910	BOS A S		142	.273
1911	BOS A 2-S		80	.257
1912	BOS A S		144	.274
1913	BOS A S		109	.226
1915	BOS A 2		84	.239
1916	BOS A S		4	.500
1918	BOS A 2		3	.125
	BRTR		980	.249
NON-PLAYING MANAGER BOS(A) 1930

WAGNER, CHARLES THOMAS
"CHARLIE" OR "BROADWAY"
B.DEC.3,1912 READING,PA.
1938	BOS A P		13	1- 3
1939	BOS A P	9	11	3- 1
1940	BOS A P	12	13	1- 0
1941	BOS A P		29	12- 8
1942	BOS A P		29	14-11
1946	BOS A P		8	1- 0
	BRTR	100	103	32-23

WAGNER, GARY EDWARD
B.JUNE 28,1940 BRIDGEPORT,ILL.
1965	PHI N P		59	7- 7
1966	PHI N P		5	0- 1
1967	PHI N P		1	0- 0
1968	PHI N P		44	4- 4
1969	PHI N P		9	0- 3
	BOS A P		6	1- 3
1970	BOS A P		38	3- 1
	BRTR		162	15-19

WAGNER, HAROLD EDWARD "HAL"
B.JULY 2,1915 RIVERTON,N.J.
1937	PHI A C		1	.000
1938	PHI A C		33	.227
1939	PHI A C		5	.125
1940	PHI A C		34	.253
1941	PHI A C		46	.221
1942	PHI A C		104	.236
1943	PHI A C		111	.239
1944	PHI A C		5	.250
	BOS A C		66	.332
1946	BOS A C		117	.230
1947	BOS A C		21	.231
	DET A C		71	.288
1948	DET A C		54	.202
	PHI N C		3	.000
1949	PHI N C		1	.000
	BLTR		672	.248

WAGNER, JACOB EARLE
B.NOV.6,1861 YORK,PA.
D.NOV.10,1943
NON-PLAYING MANAGER
WAS(N) 1892-93

WAGNER, JOHN PETER "HONUS"
B.FEB.24,1874 CARNEGIE,PA.
D.DEC.6,1955 CARNEGIE,PA.
1897	LOU N O		61	.344
1898	LOU N 1-3		148	.305
1899	LOU N 3-O		144	.359
1900	PIT N O		134	.381
1901	PIT N S-3-O		141	.352
1902	PIT N P-1-	1	137	0- 0
	2-S-O			.329
1903	PIT N S		129	.355
1904	PIT N S		132	.349
1905	PIT N S		147	.363
1906	PIT N S		140	.339
1907	PIT N S		142	.350
1908	PIT N S		151	.354
1909	PIT N S		137	.339
1910	PIT N 1-S		150	.320
1911	PIT N 1-S		130	.334
1912	PIT N S		145	.324
1913	PIT N S		114	.300
1914	PIT N S-3		150	.252
1915	PIT N S		156	.274
1916	PIT N 1-S		123	.287
1917	PIT N M-1-3		74	.265
	BRTR	1	2785	0- 0
				.329

WAGNER, JOSEPH BERNARD
B.APR.24,1889 NEW YORK,N.Y.
D.NOV.15,1948
| 1915 | CIN N 2-S-3-O | | 75 | .178 |

WAGNER, LEON LAMAR
B.MAY 13,1934 CHATTANOOGA,TENN.
1958	SF N O		74	.317
1959	SF N O		87	.225
1960	STL N O		39	.214
1961	LA A O		133	.280
1962	LA A O		160	.268
1963	LA A O		149	.291
1964	CLE A O		163	.253
1965	CLE A O		144	.294
1966	CLE A O		150	.279
1967	CLE A O		135	.242
1968	CLE A O		38	.184
	CHI A O		69	.284
1969	SF N O		11	.333
	BLTR		1352	.272

WAGNER, MARK DUANE
B.MAR.4,1954 CONNEAUT,OHIO
| 1976 | DET A S | | 39 | .261 |
| | BRTR | | | |

WAGNER, WILLIAM GEORGE "BULL"
B.JAN.1,1887 LILLIE,MICH.
D.OCT.2,1967
1913	BRO N P		18	4- 2
1914	BRO N P		6	0- 1
	BRTR		24	4- 3

WAGNER, WILLIAM JOSEPH
B.JAN.2,1894 JESSUP,IOWA
D.JAN.11,1951
1914	PIT N C		3	.000
1915	PIT N C		5	.000
1916	PIT N C		19	.237
1917	PIT N C		53	.205
1918	BOS N C		13	.213
	BRTR		93	.207

WAHL, KERMIT EMERSON
B.NOV.18,1922 COLUMBIA,S.DAK.
1944	CIN N 3		4	.000
1945	CIN N 2-S-3		71	.201
1947	CIN N 2-S-3		39	.173
1950	PHI A 2-S-3		89	.257
1951	PHI A 3		20	.186
	STL A 3		8	.333
	BRTR		231	.226

WAITKUS, EDWARD STEPHEN "EDDIE"
B.SEPT.4,1919 CAMBRIDGE,MASS.
D.SEPT.15,1972 BOSTON,MASS.
1941	CHI N 1		12	.179
1946	CHI N 1		113	.304
1947	CHI N 1		130	.292
1948	CHI N 1-O		139	.296
1949	PHI N 1		54	.306
1950	PHI N 1		154	.284
1951	PHI N 1		145	.257
1952	PHI N 1		146	.289
1953	PHI N 1		81	.291
1954	BAL A 1		95	.283
1955	BAL A 1		38	.259
	PHI N 1		33	.280
	BLTL		1140	.285

WAITS, MICHAEL RICHARD "RICKY"
B.MAY 15,1952 ATLANTA,GA.
1973	TEX A P		1	0- 0
1975	CLE A P		16	6- 2
1976	CLE A P	26	36	7- 9
	BLTR	43	53	13-11

WAITT, CHARLES C.
B.OCT.14,1853 HALLOWELL,ME.
1875	STL NA O		30	.211
1877	CHI N O		10	.098
1882	BAL AA O		72	.154
1883	PHI N O		1	.333
			113	.167

WAKEFIELD, HOWARD JOHN
B.APR.2,1884 BUCYRUS,OHIO
D.APR.16,1941
1905	CLE A C		10	.111
1906	WAS A C		77	.280
1907	CLE A C		26	.135
	BRTR		113	.248

WAKEFIELD, RICHARD CUMMINGS
"DICK"
B.MAY 6,1921 CHICAGO,ILL.
1941	DET A O		7	.143
1943	DET A O		155	.316
1944	DET A O		78	.355
1946	DET A O		111	.268
1947	DET A O		112	.283
1948	DET A O		110	.276
1949	DET A O		59	.206
1950	NY A H		3	.500
1952	NY N H		3	.000
	BLTR		638	.293

WAKEFIELD, WILLIAM SUMNER "BILL"
B.MAY 24,1941 KANSAS CITY,MO.
| 1964 | NY N P | | 62 | 3- 5 |
| | BRTR | | | |

WALBERG, GEORGE ELVIN "RUBE"
B.JULY 27,1896 PINE CITY,MINN.
1923	NY N P		2	0- 0
	PHI A P		26	4- 8
1924	PHI A P		6	0- 0
1925	PHI A P		53	8-14
1926	PHI A P		40	12-10
1927	PHI A P	46	47	16-12
1928	PHI A P		38	17-12
1929	PHI A P		40	18-11
1930	PHI A P		38	13-12
1931	PHI A P	44	45	20-12
1932	PHI A P		41	17-10
1933	PHI A P	40	41	9-13
1934	BOS A P		30	6- 7
1935	BOS A P		44	5- 9
1936	BOS A P		24	5- 4
1937	BOS A P		32	5- 7
	BLTL	544	547	155-141

WALCZAK, EDWIN JOSEPH
B.SEPT.21,1918 JEWETT CITY,CONN
| 1945 | PHI N 2-S | | 20 | .211 |
| | BRTR | | | |

YR	CL	LEA	POS	GP	G	REC

WALDBAUER, ALBERT CHARLES "DOC"
B.FEB.22,1892 RICHMOND,VA.
D.JULY 16,1969 YAKIMA,WASH.

| 1917 | WAS | A | P | | 2 | 0- 0 |
| | | BRTR | | | | |

WALDEN, THOMAS FRED
B.JUNE 25,1890 FAYETTE,MO.
D.SEPT.27,1955 JEFFERSON
BARRACKS,MO.

| 1912 | STL | A | C | | 1 | .000 |
| | | BRTR | | | | |

WALDO, HIRAM HUNGERFORD
B.NOV.23,1827 ELBA,N.Y.
D.APR.26,1912
NON-PLAYING MANAGER ROK(NA)1871

WALDRON, IRVING
B.JAN.21,1876 HILLSIDE,N.Y.
D.JULY 22,1944

1901	MIL	A	O		62	.288
	WAS	A	O		79	.321
		BRTR			141	.306

WALENTOSKI, NORMAN EDWARD
(PLAYED UNDER NAME OF
NORMAN EDWARD WALLEN)

WALKER, ALBERT BLUFORD "RUBE"
B.MAY 16,1926 LENOIR,N.C.

1948	CHI	N	C		79	.275
1949	CHI	N	C		56	.244
1950	CHI	N	C		74	.230
1951	CHI	N	C		37	.234
	BRO	N	C		36	.243
1952	BRO	N	C		46	.259
1953	BRO	N	C		43	.242
1954	BRO	N	C		50	.181
1955	BRO	N	C		48	.252
1956	BRO	N	C		54	.212
1957	BRO	N	C		60	.181
1958	LA	N	C		25	.114
		BLTR			608	.227

WALKER, CHARLES FRANKLIN "FRANK"
B.SEPT.22,1894 ENOREE,S.C.
D.SEPT.16,1974 BRISTOL,TENN.

1917	DET	A	O		2	.000
1918	DET	A	O		55	.198
1920	PHI	A	O		24	.231
1921	PHI	A	O		19	.227
1925	NY	N	O		39	.222
		BRTR			139	.214

WALKER, CLARENCE WILLIAM "TILLY"
B.SEPT.4,1887 TELFORD,TENN.
D.SEPT.21,1959 UNICOI,TENN.

1911	WAS	A	O		98	.278
1912	WAS	A	O		36	.273
1913	STL	A	O		23	.294
1914	STL	A	O		151	.298
1915	STL	A	O		144	.269
1916	BOS	A	O		128	.265
1917	BOS	A	O		106	.246
1918	PHI	A	O		114	.294
1919	PHI	A	O		125	.292
1920	PHI	A	O		149	.268
1921	PHI	A	O		142	.304
1922	PHI	A	O		153	.283
1923	PHI	A	O		52	.275
		BRTR			1421	.281

WALKER, EDWARD HARRISON
B.AUG.11,1874 CAMBOIS,ENGLAND
D.SEPT.30,1947

1902	CLE	A	P		1	0- 1
1903	CLE	A	P		3	0- 0
		TL			4	0- 1

WALKER, ERNEST ROBERT
B.SEPT.15,1890 BLOSSBURG,PA.
D.APR.1,1965 PELL CITY,ALA.

1913	STL	A	O		7	.214
1914	STL	A	O		71	.298
1915	STL	A	O		50	.211
		BLTR			128	.256

WALKER, EWART GLADSTONE "DIXIE"
B.JUNE 1,1887 BROWNSVILLE,PA.
D.NOV.14,1965 LEEDS,ALA.

1909	WAS	A	P		4	3- 1
1910	WAS	A	P		29	11-11
1911	WAS	A	P	32	34	8-13
1912	WAS	A	P		9	3- 6
		BLTR		74	76	25-31

WALKER, FRED "DIXIE"
B.SEPT.24,1910 VILLA RICA,GA.

1931	NY	A	O		2	.300
1933	NY	A	O		98	.274
1934	NY	A	O		17	.118
1935	NY	A	O		8	.154
1936	NY	A	O		6	.350
	CHI	A	O		26	.271
1937	CHI	A	O		154	.302
1938	DET	A	O		127	.308
1939	DET	A	O		43	.305
	BRO	N	O		61	.280
1940	BRO	N	3		143	.308
1941	BRO	N	O		148	.311
1942	BRO	N	O		118	.290
1943	BRO	N	O		138	.302
1944	BRO	N	O		147	.357
1945	BRO	N	O		154	.300
1946	BRO	N	O		150	.319
1947	BRO	N	O		148	.306
1948	PIT	N	O		129	.316
1949	PIT	N	1-O		88	.282
		BLTR			1905	.306

WALKER, FREDERICK MITCHELL "MYSTERIOUS"
B.MAR.21,1884 UTICA,NEB.
D.FEB.1,1958

1910	CIN	N	P		1	0- 0
1913	BRO	N	P		10	1- 3
1914	PIT	F	P		35	4-16
1915	BRO	F	P		13	2- 4
		BRTR			59	7-23

WALKER, GEORGE A.
B.HAMILTON,ONT.,CANADA

| 1888 | BAL | AA | P | | 4 | 1- 3 |

WALKER, GERALD HOLMES "GEE"
B.MAR.19,1908 GULFPORT,MISS.

1931	DET	A	O		59	.296
1932	DET	A	O		127	.323
1933	DET	A	O		127	.280
1934	DET	A	O		98	.300
1935	DET	A	O		98	.301
1936	DET	A	O		134	.353
1937	DET	A	O		151	.335
1938	CHI	A	O		120	.305
1939	CHI	A	O		149	.291
1940	WAS	A	O		140	.294
1941	CLE	A	O		121	.283
1942	CIN	N	O		119	.230
1943	CIN	N	O		114	.245
1944	CIN	N	O		121	.278
1945	CIN	N	3-O		106	.253
		BRTR			1784	.294

WALKER, HARRY WILLIAM "THE HAT"
B.OCT.22,1918 PASCAGOULA,MISS.

1940	STL	N	O		7	.185
1941	STL	N	O		7	.267
1942	STL	N	2-O		74	.314
1943	STL	N	2-O		148	.295
1946	STL	N	1-O		112	.237
1947	STL	N	O		10	.200
	PHI	N	1-O		130	.371
1948	PHI	N	1-3-O		112	.292
1949	CHI	N	O		42	.264
	CIN	N	O		86	.318
1950	STL	N	1-O		60	.207
1951	STL	N	1-O		8	.308
1955	STL	N	M-O		11	.357
		BLTR			807	.296

NON-PLAYING MANAGER
PIT(N) 1965-67, HOU(N) 1968-72

WALKER, HARVEY WILLOS "HUB"
B.AUG.17,1906 GULFPORT,MISS.

1931	DET	A	O		90	.286
1935	DET	A	O		9	.160
1936	CIN	N	C-1-O		92	.275
1937	CIN	N	2-O		78	.249
1945	DET	A	O		28	.130
		BLTR			297	.263

WALKER, JAMES LUKE "LUKE"
B.SEP.2,1943 DEKALB,TEX.

1965	PIT	N	P		2	0- 0
1966	PIT	N	P		10	0- 1
1968	PIT	N	P		39	0- 3
1969	PIT	N	P		31	4- 6
1970	PIT	N	P		42	15- 6
1971	PIT	N	P		28	10- 8
1972	PIT	N	P		26	4- 6
1973	PIT	N	P		37	7-12
1974	DET	A	P		28	5- 5
		BLTL			243	45-47

WALKER, JAMES ROY
B.MAR.12,1893 LAWRENCEBURG,TENN
D.FEB.10,1962

1912	CLE	A	P		2	0- 0
1915	CLE	A	P		25	5- 9
1917	CHI	N	P		2	0- 1
1918	CHI	N	P		13	1- 3
1921	STL	N	P		38	11-12
1922	STL	N	P		12	1- 2
		BBTR			92	18-27

BR 1912-15, 21

WALKER, JERRY ALLEN
B.FEB.12,1939 ADA,OKLA.

1957	BAL	A	P		13	1- 0
1958	BAL	A	P		6	0- 0
1959	BAL	A	P	30	31	11-10
1960	BAL	A	P	29	35	3- 4
1961	KC	A	P	36	45	8-14
1962	KC	A	P	31	36	8- 9
1963	CLE	A	P		39	6- 6
1964	CLE	A	P		6	0- 1
		BBTR	190	211	37-44

BR 1963-64

WALKER, JOHN MILES
B.DEC.4,1896 TOULON,ILL.

1919	PHI	A	C		3	.000
1920	PHI	A	C		6	.235
1921	PHI	A	1		113	.258
1922	PHI	A	C		2	.000
		BRTR			124	.252

WALKER, JOSEPH RICHARD
B.JAN.23,1901 MUNHALL,PA.

| 1923 | STL | N | 2 | | 2 | .286 |
| | | BRTR | | | | |

WALKER, MARTIN VAN BUREN
B.MAR.27,1903 PHILADELPHIA,PA.

| 1928 | PHI | N | P | | 1 | 0- 1 |
| | | BLTL | | | | |

WALKER, MOSES FLEETWOOD "FLEET"
B.OCT.7,1857 MT.PLEASANT,OHIO
D.MAY 11,1924

| 1884 | TOL | AA | C | | 41 | .251 |
| | | BRTR | | | | |

WALKER, OSCAR
B.MAR.18,1854 BROOKLYN,N.Y.
D.MAY 20,1889

1875	ATL	NA	O		1	.000
1879	BUF	N	1		70	.266
1880	BUF	N	1		33	.230
1882	STL	AA	1-2-O		76	.233
1884	BRO	AA	1-O		95	.268
		BL			275	.253

WALKER, ROBERT THOMAS "TOM"
B.NOV.7,1948 TAMPA,FLA.

1972	MON	N	P		46	2- 2
1973	MON	N	P		54	7- 5
1974	MON	N	P		33	4- 5
1975	DET	A	P		36	3- 8
1976	STL	N	P		10	1- 2
		BRTR			179	17-22

WALKER, THOMAS WILLIAM
B.AUG.1,1881 PHILADELPHIA,PA.
D.JULY 10,1944

1902	PHI	A	P		1	0- 1
1904	CIN	N	P		25	15-10
1905	CIN	N	P		23	10- 6
		BRTR			49	25-17

WALKER, WALTER S.
B.IONIA,MICH.

1884	DET	N	C		1	.250
1885	BAL	AA	O		3	.000
					4	.077

YR	CL	LEA	POS	GP	G	REC

WALKER, WELDAY WILBERFORCE
B.JUNE 1859 STEUBENVILLE,OHIO
D.NOV.23,1937

YR	CL	LEA	POS	GP	G	REC
1884	TOL	AA	O		5	.222

WALKER, WILLIAM CURTIS "CURT"
B.JULY 3,1896 BEEVILLE,TEX.
D.DEC.9,1955 BEEVILLE,TEX.

YR	CL	LEA	POS	GP	G	REC
1919	NY	A	H		1	.000
1920	NY	N	O		8	.000
1921	NY	N	O		64	.286
	PHI	N	O		21	.338
1922	PHI	N	O		148	.337
1923	PHI	N	1-O		140	.281
1924	PHI	N	1-O		24	.296
	CIN	N	1-O		109	.300
1925	CIN	N	1-O		145	.318
1926	CIN	N	1-O		155	.306
1927	CIN	N	1-O		146	.292
1928	CIN	N	1-O		123	.279
1929	CIN	N	1-O		141	.313
1930	CIN	N	1-O		134	.307
	BLTR				1359	.304

WALKER, WILLIAM HENRY "BILL"
B.OCT.7,1903 E.ST.LOUIS,ILL.
D.JUNE 14,1966 E.ST.LOUIS,ILL.

YR	CL	LEA	POS	GP	G	REC
1927	NY	N	P		3	0- 0
1928	NY	N	P		22	3- 6
1929	NY	N	P		29	14- 7
1930	NY	N	P	39	40	17-15
1931	NY	N	P		37	16- 9
1932	NY	N	P		31	8-12
1933	STL	N	P		29	9-10
1934	STL	N	P		24	12- 4
1935	STL	N	P	37	38	13- 8
1936	STL	N	P	21	22	5- 6
	BRTL			272	275	97-77

WALKUP, JAMES ELTON "JIM"
B.DEC.14,1911 HAVANA,ARK.

YR	CL	LEA	POS	GP	G	REC
1934	STL	A	P		3	0- 0
1935	STL	A	P		55	6- 9
1936	STL	A	P		5	0- 3
1937	STL	A	P		27	9-12
1938	STL	A	P		18	1-12
1939	STL	A	P		1	0- 1
	DET	A	P		7	0- 1
	BRTR				116	16-38

WALKUP, JAMES HUEY "JIM"
B.NOV.3,1895 HAVANA,ARK.

YR	CL	LEA	POS	GP	G	REC
1927	DET	A	P		2	0- 0
	BRTL					

WALL
1873 NAT NA S 1 -

WALL, JOSEPH FRANCIS "GUMMY"
B.JULY 24,1873 BROOKLYN,N.Y.
D.JULY 17,1936

YR	CL	LEA	POS	GP	G	REC
1901	NY	N	O		3	.286
1902	NY	N	O		6	.357
	BRO	N	C		5	.176
	BLTL				14	.282

WALL, MURRAY WESLEY
B.SEPT.19,1926 DALLAS,TEX.
D.OCT.8,1971 LONE OAK,TEX.

YR	CL	LEA	POS	GP	G	REC
1950	BOS	N	P		1	0- 0
1957	BOS	A	P		11	3- 0
1958	BOS	A	P		52	8- 9
1959	BOS	A	P		15	1- 4
	WAS	A	P		1	0- 0
	BOS	A	P		11	1- 1
	BRTR				91	13-14

WALL, STANLEY ARTHUR "STAN"
B.JUNE 16,1951 BUTLER,MO.

YR	CL	LEA	POS	GP	G	REC
1975	LA	N	P		10	0- 1
1976	LA	N	P		31	2- 2
	BLTL				41	2- 3

WALLACE, C. E. "JACK"
B.1891

YR	CL	LEA	POS	GP	G	REC
1915	CHI	N	C		2	.285
	BRTR					

WALLACE, DAVID WILLIAM "DAVE"
B.SEP.7,1947 WATERBURY,CONN.

YR	CL	LEA	POS	GP	G	REC
1973	PHI	N	P		4	0- 0
1974	PHI	N	P		3	0- 1
	BRTR				7	0- 1

WALLACE, DONALD ALLEN "DON"
B.AUG.25,1940 SAPULPA,OKLA.

YR	CL	LEA	POS	GP	G	REC
1967	CAL	A	1-2-3		23	.000
	BLTR					

WALLACE, FREDERICK RENSHAW "JESSE"
B.SEPT.30,1893 CHURCH HILL,MD.
D.DEC.31,1964

YR	CL	LEA	POS	GP	G	REC
1919	PHI	N	S		2	.200
	TR					

WALLACE, HARRY CLINTON "LEFTY"
B.JULY 23,1882 RICHMOND,IND.
D.JULY 9,1951

YR	CL	LEA	POS	GP	G	REC
1912	PHI	N	P		4	0- 0
	BLTL					

WALLACE, JAMES HAROLD "LEFTY"
B.AUG.12,1921 EVANSVILLE,IND.

YR	CL	LEA	POS	GP	G	REC
1942	BOS	N	P		19	1- 3
1945	BOS	N	P	5	6	1- 0
1946	BOS	N	P		27	3- 3
	BLTL			51	52	5- 6

WALLACE, JAMES L.
B.NOV.14,1881 S.BOSTON,MASS.
D.MAY 16,1953

YR	CL	LEA	POS	GP	G	REC
1905	PIT	N	O		7	.214
	BLTL					

WALLACE, MICHAEL SHERMAN "MIKE"
B.FEB.3,1951 GASTONIA,N.C.

YR	CL	LEA	POS	GP	G	REC
1973	PHI	N	P		20	1- 1
1974	PHI	N	P		8	1- 0
	NY	A	P		23	6- 0
1975	NY	A	P		3	0- 0
	STL	N	P		9	0- 0
1976	STL	N	P		49	3- 2
	BLTL				112	11- 3

WALLACE, RHODERICK JOHN "BOBBY"
B.NOV.4,1873 PITTSBURGH,PA.
D.NOV.3,1960 TORRANCE,CAL.

YR	CL	LEA	POS	GP	G	REC
1894	CLE	N	P		4	2- 2
1895	CLE	N	P		27	14-10
1896	CLE	N	P	15	33	9- 6
1897	CLE	N	3		131	.339
1898	CLE	N	3		153	.269
1899	STL	N	S-3		151	.302
1900	STL	N	S		129	.272
1901	STL	N	S		135	.322
1902	STL	A	P-S-	1	133	0- 0
			O			.287
1903	STL	A	S		136	.245
1904	STL	A	S		139	.273
1905	STL	A	S		156	.271
1906	STL	A	S		139	.258
1907	STL	A	S		147	.257
1908	STL	A	S		137	.253
1909	STL	A	S-3		116	.238
1910	STL	A	S-3		138	.258
1911	STL	A	M-S		125	.232
1912	STL	A	M-S		99	.241
1913	STL	A	S		52	.211
1914	STL	A	S		26	.219
1915	STL	A	S		9	.231
1916	STL	A	S-3		14	.278
1917	STL	N	S		8	.100
1918	STL	N	2-S-3		32	.153
	BRTR			47	2369	25-18
						.268

NON-PLAYING MANAGER CIN(N) 1937

WALLAESA, JOHN "JACK"
B.AUG.31,1919 EASTON,PA.

YR	CL	LEA	POS	GP	G	REC
1940	PHI	A	S		6	.150
1942	PHI	A	S		36	.256
1946	PHI	A	S		63	.196
1947	CHI	A	S-3-O		81	.195
1948	CHI	A	S-O		33	.188
	BBTR				219	.205
	BR	1940				

WALLEN, NORMAN EDWARD
(REAL NAME
NORMAN EDWARD WALENTOSKI)
B.FEB.13,1917 MILWAUKEE,WIS.

YR	CL	LEA	POS	GP	G	REC
1945	BOS	N	3		4	.133
	BRTR					

WALLER, JOHN FRANCIS "RED"
B.1883 WASHINGTON,D.C.
D.FEB.9,1915

YR	CL	LEA	POS	GP	G	REC
1909	NY	N	P		1	0- 0

WALLING, DENNIS MARTIN
B.APR.17,1954 NEPTUNE,N.J.

YR	CL	LEA	POS	GP	G	REC
1975	OAK	A	O		6	.125
1976	OAK	A	O		3	.273
	BLTR				9	.211

WALLIS, HAROLD JOSEPH "JOE"
B.JAN.9,1952 E.ST.LOUIS,ILL.

YR	CL	LEA	POS	GP	G	REC
1975	CHI	N	O		16	.286
1976	CHI	N	O		121	.254
	BBTR				137	.259

WALLS, RAY LEE "LEE"
B.JAN.6,1933 SAN DIEGO,CAL.

YR	CL	LEA	POS	GP	G	REC
1952	PIT	N	O		32	.188
1956	PIT	N	O		143	.274
1957	PIT	N	O		8	.182
	CHI	N	3-O		117	.240
1958	CHI	N	O		136	.304
1959	CHI	N	O		120	.257
1960	CIN	N	1-O		29	.274
	PHI	N	1-3-O		65	.199
1961	PHI	N	1-3-O		91	.280
1962	LA	N	1-3-O		60	.266
1963	LA	N	1-3-O		64	.233
1964	LA	N	C-O		37	.179
	BRTR				902	.262

WALSH, AUGUST S.
B.AUG.9,1904 WILMINGTON,DEL.

YR	CL	LEA	POS	GP	G	REC
1927	PHI	N	P		1	0- 1
1928	PHI	N	P	38	39	4- 9
	BRTR			39	40	4-10

WALSH, AUSTIN
B.1892

YR	CL	LEA	POS	GP	G	REC
1914	CHI	F	O		52	.235
	BLTL					

WALSH, CORNELIUS R.
B.APR.23,1882 ST.LOUIS,MO.
D.APR.5,1953

YR	CL	LEA	POS	GP	G	REC
1907	PIT	N	P		1	0- 0

WALSH, EDWARD ARTHUR
B.FEB.11,1905 MERIDEN,CONN.
D.OCT.31,1937

YR	CL	LEA	POS	GP	G	REC
1928	CHI	A	P		14	4- 7
1929	CHI	A	P	24	25	6-11
1930	CHI	A	P	37	39	1- 4
1932	CHI	A	P		4	0- 2
	BRTR			79	82	11-24

WALSH, EDWARD AUGUSTIN "BIG ED"
B.MAY 14,1881 PLAINS,PA.
D.MAY 26,1959 POMPANO BEACH,FLA

YR	CL	LEA	POS	GP	G	REC
1904	CHI	A	P		18	5- 5
1905	CHI	A	P	22	29	8- 5
1906	CHI	A	P	41	42	17-13
1907	CHI	A	P	56	57	24-18
1908	CHI	A	P		66	40-15
1909	CHI	A	P	31	32	15-11
1910	CHI	A	P	45	52	18-20
1911	CHI	A	P	55	62	27-18
1912	CHI	A	P		62	27-17
1913	CHI	A	P		16	8- 3
1914	CHI	A	P	9	11	2- 3
1915	CHI	A	P	3	5	3- 0
1916	CHI	A	P		2	0- 1
1917	BOS	N	P		4	0- 1
	BRTR			430	458	194-130

WALSH, JAMES CHARLES
B.SEPT.22,1885 CONNEAUGHT,
IRELAND
D.JULY 3,1962

YR	CL	LEA	POS	GP	G	REC
1912	PHI	A	O		31	.252
1913	PHI	A	O		94	.255
1914	NY	A	O		43	.207
	PHI	A	O		67	.226
1915	PHI	A	O		117	.206
1916	PHI	A	O		112	.222
	BOS	A	O		15	.348
1917	BOS	A	O		57	.265
	BRTR				536	.231

WALSH, JAMES GERALD "JUNIOR"
B.MAR.7,1920 NEWARK,N.J.

YR	CL	LEA	POS	GP	G	REC
1946	PIT	N	P		4	0- 1
1948	PIT	N	P		2	1- 0
1949	PIT	N	P		9	1- 4
1950	PIT	N	P		38	1- 1
1951	PIT	N	P		36	1- 4
	BRTR				89	4-10

YR	CL LEA POS	GP	G	REC

WALSH, JAMES THOMAS
B.JULY 10,1894 BOSTON,MASS.
1921 DET A P   3   0- 0
　　 TL

WALSH, JOHN
B.WILKES-BARRE,PA.
1903 PHI N 3   1   .000
　　 TR

WALSH, JOSEPH A. "REDDY"
B.NOV.1865 CHICAGO,ILL.
1891 BAL AA 2-S   25   .189

WALSH, JOSEPH FRANCIS
B.OCT.14,1887 WATERBURY,CONN.
D.JAN.6,1967 NEW YORK,N.Y.
1910 NY A 'C   2   .333
1911 NY A C   4   .222
　　 BRTR   6   .267

WALSH, JOSEPH PATRICK "TWEET"
B.MAR.13,1917 ROXBURY,MASS.
1938 BOS N S   4   .000
　　 BRTR

WALSH, LEO THOMAS "DEE"
B.MAR.28,1890 ST.LOUIS,MO.
D.JULY 14,1971 ST.LOUIS,MO.
1913 STL A S   23   .170
1914 STL A S   7   .087
1915 STL A P-O 1 59   0- 0
　　　　　　　　　 .220
　　 BBTR   89   0- 0
　　　　　　　　　 .195

WALSH, MICHAEL F.
B.1852 COVINGTON,KY.
NON-PLAYING MANAGER LOU(AA)1884

WALSH, MICHAEL TIMOTHY "RUNT"
B.MAR.25,1887 LIMA,OHIO
D.JAN.21,1947
1910 PHI N 2-O   67   .248
1911 PHI N ALL   1 84   0- 0
　　　　　　　　　 .270
1912 PHI N 2   51   .267
1913 PHI N 2   26   .333
1914 BAL F 3   117   .310
1915 BAL F 3   109   .304
　　 STL F 3   14   .200
　　 BRTR   1 468   0- 0
　　　　　　　　　 .269

WALSH, THOMAS JOSEPH
B.FEB.28,1886 DAVENPORT,IOWA
D.MAR.16,1963
1906 CHI N C   2   .000
　　 TR

WALSH, WALTER WILLIAM
B.APR.30,1897 NEWARK,N.J.
1920 PHI N H   1   .000
　　 BRTR

WALTER, JAMES BERNARD
B.AUG.15,1908 DOVER,TENN.
1930 PIT N P   1   0- 0
　　 BRTR

WALTERS, ALFRED JOHN "ROXY"
B.NOV.5,1892 SAN FRANCISCO,CAL.
D.JUNE 6,1956
1915 NY A C   2   .333
1916 NY A C   66   .266
1917 NY A C   61   .263
1918 NY A C   64   .199
1919 BOS A C   48   .193
1920 BOS A C   88   .198
1921 BOS A C   54   .201
1922 BOS A C   38   .194
1923 BOS A C   40   .250
1924 CLE A C   32   .257
1925 CLE A C   5   .200
　　 BRTR   498   .222

**WALTERS, CHARLES LEONARD
"CHARLIE"**
B.FEB.21,1947 MINNEAPOLIS,MINN.
1969 MIN A P   6   0- 0
　　 BRTR

WALTERS, JAMES FREDERICK
B.SEPT.4,1912 LAUREL,MISS.
1945 BOS A C   40   .172
　　 BRTR

WALTERS, KENNETH ROGERS "KEN"
B.NOV.11,1933 FRESNO,CAL.
1960 PHI N O   124   .239
1961 PHI N 1-3-O   86   .228
1963 CIN N 1-O   49   .187
　　 BRTR   259   .231

WALTERS, WILLIAM HENRY "BUCKY"
B.APR.19,1909 PHILADELPHIA,PA.
1931 BOS N 2-3   9   .211
1932 BOS N 3   22   .187
1933 BOS A 2-3   52   .256
1934 BOS A 3   23   .216
　　 PHI N P-3   2 83   0- 0
　　　　　　　　　 .260
1935 PHI N P-2- 24 49   9- 9
　　　　　 3-O   .250
1936 PHI N P   40 64 11-21
1937 PHI N P   37 56 14-15
1938 PHI N P   12 15   4- 8
　　 CIN N P   27 36 11- 6
1939 CIN N P   39 40 27-11
1940 CIN N P   36 37 22-10
1941 CIN N P   37 39 19-15
1942 CIN N P-O 34 40 15-14
　　　　　　　　　 .242
1943 CIN N P   34 37 15-15
1944 CIN N P   34 37 23- 8
1945 CIN N P   22 24 10-10
1946 CIN N P   22 24 10- 7
1947 CIN N P   20   8- 8
1948 CIN N M-P   7   0- 3
1950 BOS N P   1   0- 0
　　 BRTR   428 715 198-160
　　　　　　　　　 .242
NON-PLAYING MANAGER CIN(N) 1949

WALTON, DANIEL JAMES "DANNY"
B.JULY 14,1947 LOS ANGELES,CAL.
1968 HOU N H   2   .000
1969 SEA A O   23   .217
1970 MIL A O   117   .257
1971 MIL A 3-O   30   .203
　　 NY A O   5   .143
1973 MIN A 3-O-D   37   .177
1975 MIN A C-1   42   .175
1976 LA N H   18   .133
　　 BRTR   274   .225
　　 BB 1975

WALTON, ZACH
(SEE JONATHAN
THOMPSON WALTON ZACHARY)

WALTZ, JOHN J.
NON-PLAYING MANAGER BAL(N) 1892

WAMBSGANSS, WILLIAM ADOLPH
B.MAR.19,1894 CLEVELAND,OHIO
1914 CLE A S   43   .217
1915 CLE A 2-3   121   .195
1916 CLE A 2-S-3   136   .246
1917 CLE A 2   141   .255
1918 CLE A 2   87   .295
1919 CLE A 2   139   .278
1920 CLE A 2   153   .244
1921 CLE A 2   107   .285
1922 CLE A 2-S   143   .262
1923 CLE A 2   101   .290
1924 BOS A 2   155   .275
1925 BOS A 1-2   111   .231
1926 PHI A S   54   .352
　　 BRTR   1491   .259

**WANER, LLOYD JAMES
"LITTLE POISON"**
B.MAR.16,1906 HARRAH,OKLA.
1927 PIT N O   150   .355
1928 PIT N O   152   .335
1929 PIT N O   151   .353
1930 PIT N O   68   .362
1931 PIT N O   154   .314
1932 PIT N O   134   .333
1933 PIT N O   121   .276
1934 PIT N O   140   .283
1935 PIT N O   122   .309
1936 PIT N O   106   .321
1937 PIT N O   129   .330
1938 PIT N O   147   .313
1939 PIT N O   112   .285
1940 PIT N O   72   .259
1941 PIT N O   3   .250
　　 BOS N O   19   .412
　　 CIN N O   55   .256
1942 PHI N O   101   .261
1944 BRO N O   15   .286
　　 PIT N O   19   .357
1945 PIT N O   23   .263
　　 BLTR   1993   .316

WANER, PAUL GLEE "BIG POISON"
B.APR.16,1903 HARRAH,OKLA.
D.AUG.29,1965 SARASOTA,FLA.
1926 PIT N O   144   .336
1927 PIT N 1-O   155   .380
1928 PIT N 1-O   152   .370
1929 PIT N O   151   .336
1930 PIT N O   145   .368
1931 PIT N 1-O   150   .322
1932 PIT N O   154   .341
1933 PIT N O   154   .309
1934 PIT N O   146   .362
1935 PIT N O   139   .321
1936 PIT N O   148   .373
1937 PIT N O   154   .354
1938 PIT N O   148   .280
1939 PIT N O   125   .328
1940 PIT N 1-O   89   .290
　　 BOS N 1-O   95   .279
1942 BOS N O   114   .258
1943 BRO N O   82   .311
1944 BRO N O   83   .287
　　 NY A O   9   .143
1945 NY A O   1   .000
　　 BLTL   2549   .333

**WANNER, CLARENCE CURTIS
"JOHNNY"**
B.NOV.29,1885 GENESEO,ILL.
D.MAY 28,1919 GENESEO,ILL.
1909 NY A S   3   .125
　　 BRTR

WANNINGER, PAUL LOUIS "PEE-WEE"
B.DEC.12,1904 BIRMINGHAM,ALA.
1925 NY A 2-S-3   117   .236
1927 BOS A S   18   .200
　　 CIN N S   28   .247
　　 BLTR   163   .234

WANTZ, RICHARD CARTER "DICK"
B.APR.11,1940 SOUTH GATE,CAL.
D.MAY 13,1965 INGLEWOOD,CAL.
1965 CAL A P   1   0- 0
　　 BRTR

WARD, "HAP"
1912 DET A O   1   .000

WARD, AARON LEE
B.AUG.28,1896 BOONEVILLE,ARK.
D.JAN.30,1961
1917 NY A S   8   .115
1918 NY A S   20   .125
1919 NY A 1-S   27   .205
1920 NY A 3   127   .256
1921 NY A 2-3   153   .306
1922 NY A 2   154   .267
1923 NY A 2   152   .284
1924 NY A 2   120   .253
1925 NY A 2-3   125   .246
1926 NY A 1   22   .323
1927 CHI A 2   145   .270
1928 CLE A 2-S-3   6   .111
　　 BRTR   1059   .268

YR	CL	LEA	POS	GP	G	REC

WARD, CHARLES WILLIAM "CHUCK"
B.JULY 31,1893 ST.LOUIS,MO.
D.APR.4,1969 ST.PETERSBURG,FLA.

YR	CL	LEA	POS	GP	G	REC
1917	PIT	N	S		125	.236
1918	BRO	N	S		2	.333
1919	BRO	N	3		45	.233
1920	BRO	N	S		19	.155
1921	BRO	N	S		12	.071
1922	BRO	N	S		33	.274
		BRTR			236	.228

WARD, CHRIS GILBERT
B.MAY 18,1949 OAKLAND,CAL.

1972	CHI	N	H		1	.000
1974	CHI	N	1-O		92	.204
		BLTL			93	.203

WARD, E. JOHN
B.WASHINGTON,D.C.

1884	WAS	U	O		1	.250
1885	PRO	N	P		1	0- 1
				1	2	0- 1
						.143

WARD, FRANK GRAY "PIGGY"
B.APR.16,1867 CHAMBERSBURG,PA.
D.OCT.24,1912

1883	PHI	N	3		1	.000
1889	PHI	N	2		7	.160
1891	PIT	N	O		5	.333
1892	BAL	N	O		53	.282
1893	BAL	N	O		11	.250
	CIN	N	O		38	.281
1894	WAS	N	2		89	.303
					204	.286

WARD, JAMES H. H.
B.MAR.1855 BOSTON,MASS.
D.JUNE 4,1906

| 1876 | ATH | N | C | | 1 | .500 |

WARD, JOHN A. "RUBE"
B.WASHINGTON COURT HOUSE,OHIO

| 1902 | BRO | N | O | | 13 | .290 |

WARD, JOHN FRANCIS "JAY"
B.SEP.9,1938 BROOKFIELD,MO.

1963	MIN	A	3-O		9	.067
1964	MIN	A	2-O		12	.226
1970	CIN	N	1-2-3		6	.000
		BRTR			27	.163

WARD, JOHN MONTGOMERY "MONTE"
B.MAR.3,1860 BELLEFONTE,PA.
D.MAR.4,1925 AUGUSTA,GA.

1878	PRO	N	P		35	22-13
1879	PRO	N	P-3	65	82	44-18
						.287
1880	PRO	N	P-3-	63	82	40-23
			O			.226
1881	PRO	N	P-S-	36	83	18-18
			O			.241
1882	PRO	N	P-S-	32	83	19-13
			O			.245
1883	NY	N	P-2-	33	88	12-14
			S-3-O			.258
1884	NY	N	P-2-	9	109	3- 3
			O			.249
1885	NY	N	S		111	.226
1886	NY	N	S		122	.273
1887	NY	N	S		129	.371
1888	NY	N	S		122	.251
1889	NY	N	S		114	.298
1890	BRO	P	M-S		128	.371
1891	BRO	N	M-2		104	.287
1892	BRO	N	M-2		148	.273
1893	NY	N	M-2		134	.348
1894	NY	N	M-2		136	.262
		BLTR		273	1810	158-102
						.284
		BB 1888				

WARD, JOSEPH A.
B.SEPT.1,1884 PHILADELPHIA,PA.
D.AUG.11,1934

1906	PHI	N	3		30	.295
1909	NY	A	2		9	.179
	PHI	N	2		63	.266
1910	PHI	N	1		33	.145
		TR			135	.237

WARD, PETER THOMAS "PETE"
B.JULY 26,1939 MONTREAL,QUE.,CAN

1962	BAL	A	O		8	.143
1963	CHI	A	2-S-3	157		.295
1964	CHI	A	3	144		.282
1965	CHI	A	2-3	138		.247
1966	CHI	A	1-3-O	84		.219
1967	CHI	A	1-3-O	146		.233
1968	CHI	A	1-3-O	125		.216
1969	CHI	A	1-3-O	105		.246
1970	NY	A	1		66	.260
		BLTR		973		.254

WARD, PRESTON MEYER
B.JULY 24,1927 COLUMBIA,MO.

1948	BRO	N	1		42	.260
1950	CHI	N	1		80	.253
1953	CHI	N	1-O		33	.230
	PIT	N	1		88	.210
1954	PIT	N	1-3-O		117	.269
1955	PIT	N	1-O		84	.212
1956	PIT	N	3-O		16	.333
	CLE	A	O		87	.253
1957	CLE	A	1		10	.182
1958	CLE	A	1-3-O		48	.338
	KC	A	1-3-O		81	.254
1959	KC	A	1-O		58	.248
		BLTR		744		.253

WARD, RICHARD O.
B.MAY 21,1911 KENNEBEC,S.DAK.
D.MAY 30,1966 FREELAND,WASH.

1934	CHI	N	P		3	0- 0
1935	STL	N	P		1	0- 0
		BRTR			4	0- 0

WARDEN, JONATHAN EDGAR "JON"
B.OCT.1,1946 COLUMBUS,OHIO

| 1968 | DET | A | P | | 28 | 4- 1 |
| | | BBTL | | | | |

WARE, GEORGE
NON-PLAYING MANAGER PRO(N) 1878

WARES, CLYDE ELLSWORTH "BUZZY"
B.MAR.23,1886 NEWBURG TOWNSHIP,
MICH.
D.MAY 26,1964 SOUTH BEND,IND.

1913	STL	A	S		10	.286
1914	STL	A	S		81	.209
		BRTR			91	.220

WARHOP, JOHN MILTON "CHIEF"
(REAL NAME JOHN MILTON WAUHOP)
B.JULY 4,1884 HINTON,W.VA.
D.OCT.4,1960

1908	NY	A	P		5	1- 3
1909	NY	A	P		36	13-15
1910	NY	A	P		37	14-14
1911	NY	A	P	30	32	12-13
1912	NY	A	P		39	10-19
1913	NY	A	P		15	4- 4
1914	NY	A	P		37	8-15
1915	NY	A	P		21	7- 9
		BRTR		220	222	69-92

WARMOTH, WALLACE WALTER "CY"
B.FEB.2,1893 MT.CARMEL,ILL.
D.JUNE 20,1957

1916	STL	N	P		3	0- 0
1922	WAS	A	P		5	1- 0
1923	WAS	A	P		21	7- 4
		BLTL			29	8- 4

WARNEKE, LONNIE "LON"
OR "THE ARKANSAS HUMMINGBIRD"
B.MAR.28,1909 MT.IDA,ARK.
D.JUNE 23,1976 HOT SPRINGS,ARK.

1930	CHI	N	P		1	0- 0
1931	CHI	N	P		20	2- 4
1932	CHI	N	P		35	22- 6
1933	CHI	N	P	36	39	18-13
1934	CHI	N	P	43	52	22-10
1935	CHI	N	P	42	44	20-13
1936	CHI	N	P		40	16-13
1937	STL	N	P		38	18-11
1938	STL	N	P		31	13- 8
1939	STL	N	P		34	13- 7
1940	STL	N	P		33	16-10
1941	STL	N	P		37	17- 9
1942	STL	N	P		12	6- 4
	CHI	N	P		15	5- 7
1943	CHI	N	P		21	4- 5
1945	CHI	N	P		9	0- 1
		BRTR		445	459	192-121

WARNER, EDWARD EMORY
B.DEC.29,1888 FITCHBURG,MASS.
D.FEB.2,1954

| 1912 | PIT | N | P | | 11 | 1- 1 |
| | | BRTL | | | | |

WARNER, FREDERICK JOHN RODNEY
B.1855 PHILADELPHIA,PA.
D.FEB.13,1886

1875	CEN	NA	O		14	-
1876	ATH	N	O		1	.000
1878	IND	N	S		41	.243
1879	CLE	N	3-O		76	.243
1883	PHI	N	3		38	.233
1884	BRO	AA	3		85	.212
					255	-

WARNER, GEORGE HOKE "HOOKS"
B.MAY 22,1894 PITTSBURGH,PA.
D.FEB.19,1947

1916	PIT	N	3		44	.238
1917	PIT	N	3		3	.200
1919	PIT	N	3		6	.125
1921	CHI	N	3		14	.211
		BLTR			67	.228

WARNER, JACK DYER
B.JULY 12,1940 BRANDYWINE,W.VA.

1962	CHI	N	P		7	0- 0
1963	CHI	N	P		8	0- 1
1964	CHI	N	P		7	0- 0
1965	CHI	N	P		11	0- 1
		BRTR			33	0- 2

WARNER, JOHN JOSEPH
B.AUG.15,1872 NEW YORK,N.Y.
D.DEC.21,1943

1895	BOS	N	C		3	.143
	LOU	N	C		60	.263
1896	LOU	N	C-1		33	.209
	NY	N	C		16	.264
1897	NY	N	C		110	.274
1898	NY	N	C		108	.259
1899	NY	N	C		83	.271
1900	NY	N	C		31	.269
1901	NY	N	C		77	.239
1902	BOS	A	C		64	.234
1903	NY	N	C		85	.284
1904	NY	N	C		86	.199
1905	STL	N	C		41	.255
	DET	A	C		36	.202
1906	DET	A	C		49	.242
	WAS	A	C		33	.204
1907	WAS	A	C		72	.256
1908	WAS	A	C		51	.241
		TR		1038		.250

WARNER, JOHN JOSEPH "JACKIE"
B.AUG.1,1943 MONROVIA,CAL.

| 1966 | CAL | A | O | | 45 | .211 |
| | | BRTR | | | | |

WARNER, JOHN RALPH
B.AUG.29,1903 EVANSVILLE,IND.

1925	DET	A	3		10	.333
1926	DET	A	3		100	.251
1927	DET	A	3		139	.267
1928	DET	A	3		75	.214
1929	BRO	N	S		17	.274
1930	BRO	N	3		21	.320
1931	BRO	N	S-3		9	.500
1933	PHI	N	2-S-3		107	.224
		BRTR		478		.250

WARNOCK, HAROLD CHARLES
B.JAN.6,1912 NEW YORK,N.Y.

| 1935 | STL | A | O | | 6 | .286 |
| | | BLTR | | | | |

WARREN, BENJAMIN LOUIS "BENNIE"
B.MAR.1,1913 ELK CITY,OKLA.

1939	PHI	N	C		18	.232
1940	PHI	N	C-1		106	.246
1941	PHI	N	C		121	.215
1942	PHI	N	C-1		90	.209
1946	NY	N	C		39	.159
1947	NY	N	C		3	.200
		BRTR			377	.219

WARREN, THOMAS GENTRY
B.JULY 5,1917 TULSA,OKLA.
D.JAN.2,1968 TULSA,OKLA.

| 1944 | BRO | N | P | 22 | 41 | 1- 4 |
| | | BBTL | | | | |

YR	CL	LEA	POS	GP	G	REC

WARREN, WILLIAM
(SEE WILLIAM WARREN WHITE)

WARREN, WILLIAM H.
B.FEB.11,1887 CAIRO,ILL.
1914 IND	F	C			23	.239
1915 NEW	F	C			5	.333
	BLTR				28	.245

WARSTLER, HAROLD BURTON
"RABBIT"
B.SEPT.13,1907 N.CANTON,OHIO
D.MAY 31,1964 N.CANTON,OHIO
1930 BOS	A	S			54	.185
1931 BOS	A	2-S			66	.243
1932 BOS	A	S			115	.211
1933 BOS	A	S			92	.217
1934 PHI	A	2			117	.236
1935 PHI	A	2-3			138	.250
1936 PHI	A	2			66	.250
BOS	N	S			74	.211
1937 BOS	N	S			149	.223
1938 BOS	N	S			142	.231
1939 BOS	N	2-S-3			114	.243
1940 BOS	N	2			33	.211
CHI	N	2-S			45	.226
	BRTR				1205	.229

WARTHEN, DANIEL DEAN "DAN"
B.DEC.1,1952 OMAHA,NEB.
1975 MON	N	P		40	8- 6	
1976 MON	N	P		23	2-10	
	BBTL			63	10-16	

WARWICK, CARL WAYNE
B.FEB.27,1937 DALLAS,TEX.
1961 LA	N	O			19	.091
STL	N	O			55	.250
1962 STL	N	O			13	.348
HOU	N	O			130	.260
1963 HOU	N	1-O			150	.254
1964 STL	N	O			88	.259
1965 STL	N	1-O			50	.156
BAL	A	O			9	.000
1966 CHI	N	O			16	.227
	BRTR				530	.248

WARWICK, FIRMIN NEWTON "BILL"
B.NOV.26,1898 PHILADELPHIA,PA.
1921 PIT	N	C			1	.000
1925 STL	N	C			13	.293
1926 STL	N	C			9	.357
	BRTR				23	.304

WASDELL, JAMES CHARLES "JIMMY"
B.MAY 15,1915 CLEVELAND,OHIO
1937 WAS	A	1			32	.255
1938 WAS	A	1			53	.236
1939 WAS	A	1			29	.303
1940 WAS	A	1			10	.086
BRO	N	1-O			77	.278
1941 BRO	N	O			94	.299
1942 PIT	N	1-O			122	.259
1943 PIT	N	H			4	.500
PHI	N	1-O			141	.261
1944 PHI	N	1-O			133	.277
1945 PHI	N	1-O			134	.300
1946 PHI	N	1-O			26	.255
CLE	A	1-O			32	.268
1947 CLE	A	H			1	.000
	BLTL				888	.273

WASEM, LINCOLN WILLIAM
B.JAN.30,1911 BIRMINGHAM,OHIO
1937 BOS	N	C			2	.000
	BRTR					

WASHBURN, GEORGE EDWARD
B.OCT.6,1914 SOLON,ME.
1941 NY	A	P		1	0- 1	
	BLTR					

WASHBURN, GREGORY JAMES "GREG"
B.DEC.3,1946 COAL CITY,ILL.
1969 CAL	A	P		8	0- 2	
	BRTR					

WASHBURN, LIBEUS "LIBE"
B.JUNE 16,1874 LYME,N.H.
D.MAR.22,1940 MALONE,N.Y.
1902 NY	N	O			6	.444
1903 PHI	N	P		4	8	0- 4
	BBTL			4	14	0- 4
						.286

WASHBURN, RAY CLARK
B.MAY 31,1938 PASCO,WASH.
1961 STL	N	P		3	1- 1	
1962 STL	N	P		34	12- 9	
1963 STL	N	P		11	5- 3	
1964 STL	N	P		15	3- 4	
1965 STL	N	P		28	9-11	
1966 STL	N	P		27	11- 9	
1967 STL	N	P		27	10- 7	
1968 STL	N	P		31	14- 8	
1969 STL	N	P		28	3- 8	
1970 CIN	N	P		35	4- 4	
	BRTR			239	72-64	

WASHER, WILLIAM "BUCK"
B.OCT.11,1882 AKRON,OHIO
D.DEC.8,1955
1905 PHI	N	P		1	0- 0	
	TR					

WASHINGTON, CLAUDELL
B.AUG.31,1954 LOS ANGELES,CAL.
1974 OAK	A	O-D			73	.285
1975 OAK	A	O			148	.308
1976 OAK	A	O			134	.257
	BLTL				355	.285

WASHINGTON, HERBERT LEE "HERB"
B.NOV.16,1950 FLINT,MICH.
1974 OAK	A	R			92	.000
1975 OAK	A	R			13	.000
	BRTR				105	.000

WASHINGTON, SLOANE VERNON
"VERN"
B.JUNE 4,1908 LINDEN,TEX.
1935 CHI	A	O			108	.288
1936 CHI	A	O			20	.163
	BLTR				128	.268

WASLEWSKI, GARY LEE
B.JULY 21,1941 MERIDEN,CONN.
1967 BOS	A	P		12	2- 2	
1968 BOS	A	P	34	39	4- 7	
1969 STL	N	P		12	0- 0	
MON	N	P		30	3- 7	
1970 MON	N	P		6	0- 2	
NY	A	P		26	2- 2	
1971 NY	A	P		24	0- 1	
1972 OAK	A	P		8	0- 3	
	BRTR		152	157	11-26	

WATERBURY, STEVEN CRAIG "STEVE"
B.APR.6,1952 CARBONDALE,ILL.
1976 STL	N	P		5	0- 0	
	BRTR					

WATERMAN, FREDERICK A.
B.1846 NEW YORK,N.Y.
D.DEC.16,1899
1871 OLY	NA	C-3			32	–
1872 OLY	NA	C-3			9	.400
1873 NAT	NA	S-3-O			15	–
1875 CHI	NA	2-3			4	–
					60	–

WATERS, FRED WARREN
B.JAN.3,1928 BENTON,MISS.
1955 PIT	N	P		2	0- 0	
1956 PIT	N	P		23	2- 2	
	BLTL			25	2- 2	

WATHAN, JOHN DAVID
B.OCT.4,1949 CEDAR RAPIDS,IOWA
1976 KC	A	C-1			27	.286
	BRTR					

WATKINS, DAVID ROGER "DAVE"
B.MAR.15,1944 OWENSBORO,KY.
1969 PHI	N	C-3-O			69	.176
	BRTR					

WATKINS, EDWARD
1902 PHI	N	O			1	.000

WATKINS, GEORGE ARCHIBALD
B.JUNE 4,1902 PALESTINE,TEX.
D.JUNE 1,1970 HOUSTON,TEX.
1930 STL	N	1-O			119	.373
1931 STL	N	O			131	.288
1932 STL	N	O			127	.312
1933 STL	N	O			138	.278
1934 NY	N	O			105	.247
1935 PHI	N	O			150	.270
1936 PHI	N	O			19	.243
BRO	N	O			105	.256
	BLTR				894	.288

WATKINS, HARVEY L.
NON-PLAYING MANAGER NY(N) 1895

WATKINS, ROBERT CECIL "BOB"
B.MAR.12,1948 SAN FRANCISCO,CAL.
1969 HOU	N	P		5	0- 0	
	BRTR					

WATKINS, WILLIAM HENRY
B.MAY 5,1858 BRANTFORD,ONT.,CAN
D.JUNE 9,1937
1884 IND	AA	M-2-3			34	.211
NON-PLAYING MANAGER
DET(N) 1885-88, KC(AA) 1888-89,
STL(N) 1893, PIT(N) 1898-99

WATLINGTON, JULIUS NEAL
B.DEC.25,1925 YANCEYVILLE,N.C.
1953 PHI	A	C			21	.159
	BLTR					

WATSON, ARTHUR "DOC"
B.1886 LOUISVILLE,KY.
1914 BRO	F	C			19	.289
1915 BRO	F	C			8	.294
BUF	F	C			21	.452
	BLTR				48	.344

WATSON, CHARLES J.
B.1889
1913 CHI	N	P		1	1- 0	
1914 CHI	F	P		26	9- 8	
STL	F	P		9	3- 4	
1915 STL	F	P		33	9- 9	
	BRTL			69	22-21	

WATSON, JOHN REEVES "MULE"
B.OCT.15,1896 HOMER,LA.
D.AUG.25,1949
1918 PHI	A	P		21	6-10	
1919 PHI	A	P		4	0- 1	
1920 BOS	N	P		13	5- 4	
PIT	N	P		5	0- 0	
1921 BOS	N	P		44	14-13	
1922 BOS	N	P		41	8-14	
1923 BOS	N	P		11	1- 2	
NY	N	P		17	8- 5	
1924 NY	N	P		22	7- 4	
	BRTR			178	49-53	

WATSON, JOHN THOMAS
B.JAN.16,1909 TAZEWELL,VA.
D.APR.29,1965 HUNTINGTON,W.VA.
1930 DET	A	S			4	.250
	BLTR					

WATSON, MILTON W.
B.1893 TEXAS
1916 STL	N	P		18	4- 6	
1917 STL	N	P		41	10-13	
1918 PHI	N	P		23	5- 7	
1919 PHI	N	P		8	2- 4	
	BRTR			90	21-30	

WATSON, ROBERT JOSE "BOB"
B.APR.10,1946 LOS ANGELES,CAL.
1966 HOU	N	H			1	.000
1967 HOU	N	1			6	.214
1968 HOU	N	O			45	.229
1969 HOU	N	C-1-O			20	.275
1970 HOU	N	C-1-O			97	.272
1971 HOU	N	1-O			129	.288
1972 HOU	N	1-O			147	.312
1973 HOU	N	C-1-O			158	.312
1974 HOU	N	1-O			150	.298
1975 HOU	N	1-O			132	.324
1976 HOU	N	1			157	.313
	BRTR				1042	.301

WATSON, WALTER L. "MOTHER"
B.JAN.27,1865 MIDDLEPORT,OHIO
D.NOV.23,1898
1887 CIN	AA	P-O		2	1- 1	
						.222

WATT, ALBERT BAILEY
B.DEC.12,1899 WASHINGTON,D.C.
D.MAR.15,1968 NORFOLK,VA.
1920 WAS	A	2			1	1.000
	BRTR					

YR	CL	LEA	POS	GP	G	REC

WATT, EDWARD DEAN "EDDIE"
B.APR.4,1942 LAMONI,IOWA

YR	CL	LEA	POS	G	REC
1966	BAL	A	P	43	9- 7
1967	BAL	A	P	49	3- 5
1968	BAL	A	P	59	5- 5
1969	BAL	A	P	56	5- 2
1970	BAL	A	P	53	7- 7
1971	BAL	A	P	35	3- 1
1972	BAL	A	P	38	2- 3
1973	BAL	A	P	30	3- 4
1974	PHI	N	P	42	1- 1
1975	CHI	N	P	6	0- 1
	BRTR			411	38-36

WATT, FRANK MARION "KILO"
B.DEC.15,1902 WASHINGTON,D.C.
D.AUG.30,1956

YR	CL	LEA	POS	G	REC
1931	PHI	N	P	38	5- 5
	BRTR				

WATWOOD, JOHN CLIFFORD
B.AUG.17,1906 ALEXANDER CITY, ALA.

YR	CL	LEA	POS	G	REC
1929	CHI	A	O	85	.302
1930	CHI	A	1-O	133	.302
1931	CHI	A	O	128	.283
1932	CHI	A	O	13	.296
	BOS	A	1-O	95	.249
1933	BOS	A	O	13	.133
1939	PHI	N	1	2	.167
	BLTL			469	.283

WAUGH, JAMES ELDEN "JIM"
B.NOV.25,1933 LANCASTER,OHIO

YR	CL	LEA	POS	G	REC
1952	PIT	N	P	17	1- 6
1953	PIT	N	P	29	4- 5
	BRTR			46	5-11

WAUHOP, JOHN MILTON
(PLAYED UNDER NAME OF JOHN MILTON WARHOP)

WAY, ROBERT CLINTON
B.APR.2,1906 EMLENTOH,PA.
D.JUNE 20,1974 PITTSBURGH,PA.

YR	CL	LEA	POS	G	REC
1927	CHI	A	2	5	.333
	BRTR				

WAYENBURG, FRANK
B.AUG.27,1900 FLEMING,KAN.
D.APR.16,1975 ZANESVILLE,OHIO

YR	CL	LEA	POS	G	REC
1924	CLE	N	P	2	0- 0
	BRTR				

WEAFER, KENNETH ALBERT "AL"
B.FEB.6,1914 WOBURN,MASS.

YR	CL	LEA	POS	G	REC
1936	BOS	N	P	1	0- 0
	BRTR				

WEATHERLY, CYRIL ROY "ROY" OR "STORMY"
B.FEB.25,1915 WARREN,TEX.

YR	CL	LEA	POS	G	REC
1936	CLE	A	O	84	.335
1937	CLE	A	O	53	.201
1938	CLE	A	O	83	.262
1939	CLE	A	O	95	.310
1940	CLE	A	O	135	.303
1941	CLE	A	O	102	.289
1942	CLE	A	O	128	.258
1943	NY	A	O	77	.264
1946	NY	A	H	2	.500
1950	NY	N	O	52	.261
	BLTR			811	.286

WEAVER, ARTHUR COGGSHALL "SIX O'CLOCK"
B.APR.7,1879 WICHITA,KAN.
D.MAR.23,1917

YR	CL	LEA	POS	G	REC
1902	STL	N	C	11	.171
1903	STL	N	C	16	.245
	PIT	N	C	15	.239
1905	STL	A	C	28	.120
1908	CHI	A	C	15	.200
	TR			85	.184

WEAVER, DAVID FLOYD "FLOYD"
B.MAY 12,1941 BEN FRANKLIN,TEX.

YR	CL	LEA	POS	G	REC
1962	CLE	A	P	1	1- 0
1965	CLE	A	P	32	2- 2
1970	CHI	A	P	31	1- 2
1971	MIL	A	P	21	0- 1
	BRTR			85	4- 5

WEAVER, EARL SIDNEY
B.AUG.14,1930 ST.LOUIS,MO.
NON-PLAYING MANAGER
BAL(A) 1968-76

WEAVER, GEORGE DAVIS "BUCK"
B.AUG.18,1890 STOWE,PA.
D.JAN.31,1956

YR	CL	LEA	POS	G	REC
1912	CHI	A	S	147	.224
1913	CHI	A	S	151	.272
1914	CHI	A	S	136	.246
1915	CHI	A	S	148	.268
1916	CHI	A	S-3	151	.227
1917	CHI	A	S-3	118	.284
1918	CHI	A	S-3	112	.300
1919	CHI	A	S-3	140	.296
1920	CHI	A	S-3	151	.333
	BBTR			1254	.272

WEAVER, HARRY A.
B.FEB.26,1895 CLARENDON,PA.

YR	CL	LEA	POS	G	REC
1915	PHI	A	P	2	0- 2
1916	PHI	A	P	3	0- 0
1917	CHI	N	P	4	1- 1
1918	CHI	N	P	8	2- 2
1919	CHI	N	P	2	0- 1
	BRTR			19	3- 6

WEAVER, JAMES BRIAN "JIM"
B.FEB.19,1939 LANCASTER,PA.

YR	CL	LEA	POS	G	REC
1967	CAL	A	P	13	3- 0
1968	CAL	A	P	14	0- 1
	BLTL			27	3- 1

WEAVER, JAMES DEMENT "BIG JIM"
B.NOV.25,1904 FULTON,KY.

YR	CL	LEA	POS	G	REC
1928	WAS	A	P	3	0- 0
1931	NY	A	P	17	2- 1
1934	STL	A	P	5	2- 0
	CHI	N	P	27	11- 9
1935	PIT	N	P	33	14- 8
1936	PIT	N	P	38	14- 8
1937	PIT	N	P	32	8- 5
1938	STL	A	P	1	0- 1
	CIN	N	P	30	6- 4
1939	CIN	N	P	3	0- 0
	BRTR			189	57-36

WEAVER, MONTGOMERY MORTON "MONTE" OR "PROF"
B.JUNE 15,1906 HELTON,N.C.

YR	CL	LEA	POS	GP	G	REC
1931	WAS	A	P		3	1- 0
1932	WAS	A	P	43	44	22-10
1933	WAS	A	P		23	10- 5
1934	WAS	A	P		31	11-15
1935	WAS	A	P		5	1- 1
1936	WAS	A	P		26	6- 4
1937	WAS	A	P		30	12- 9
1938	WAS	A	P		31	7- 6
1939	BOS	A	P		9	1- 0
	BLTR			201	202	71-50

WEAVER, ORLIE FOREST "BUCK"
B.JUNE 4,1886 NEWPORT,KY.
D.NOV.28,1970 NEW ORLEANS,LA.

YR	CL	LEA	POS	G	REC
1910	CHI	N	P	7	1- 1
1911	CHI	N	P	6	2- 2
	BOS	N	P	27	3-12
	BRTR			40	6-15

WEAVER, SAMUEL H.
B.JULY 20,1855 PHIADELPHIA,PA.
D.FEB.1,1914

YR	CL	LEA	POS	GP	G	REC
1875	PHI	NA	P		1	1- 0
1878	MIL	N	P	42	47	12-30
1882	ATH	AA	P-O	41	42	26-15
						.240
1883	LOU	AA	P-1	46	50	24-20
						.195
1884	KEY	U	P		20	5-12
1886	ATH	AA	P		2	0- 2
	BRTR			152	162	68-79
						.211

WEAVER, WILLIAM B. "FARMER"
B.MAR.23,1865 PARKERSBURG,W.VA.
D.JAN.25,1943

YR	CL	LEA	POS	G	REC
1886	BRO	AA	C	1	.000
1888	LOU	AA	O	26	.274
1889	LOU	AA	O	124	.290
1890	LOU	AA	O	130	.292
1891	LOU	AA	O	133	.284
1892	LOU	N	O	136	.268
1893	LOU	N	C-O	104	.309
1894	LOU	N	C	60	.206
	PIT	N	C-S-3-O	30	.352
				744	.285

WEBB, CLEON EARL
B.MAR.1,1885 MT.GILEAD,OHIO
D.JAN.12,1958

YR	CL	LEA	POS	G	REC
1910	PIT	N	P	7	2- 1
	BBTL				

WEBB, EARL WILLIAM
B.SEPT.17,1899 RAVENSCROFT,TENN
D.MAY 23,1965 JAMESTOWN,TENN.

YR	CL	LEA	POS	G	REC
1925	NY	N	O	4	.000
1927	CHI	N	O	102	.301
1928	CHI	N	O	62	.250
1930	BOS	A	O	127	.323
1931	BOS	A	O	151	.333
1932	BOS	A	O	52	.281
	DET	A	O	88	.287
1933	DET	A	O	6	.273
	CHI	A	O	58	.308
	BLTR			650	.306

WEBB, HENRY GAYLON MATTHEW "HANK"
B.MAY 21,1950 COPIAGUE,N.Y.

YR	CL	LEA	POS	GP	G	REC
1972	NY	N	P		6	0- 0
1973	NY	N	P		2	0- 0
1974	NY	N	P		3	0- 2
1975	NY	N	P	29	31	7- 6
1976	NY	N	P		8	0- 1
	BRTR			48	50	7- 9

WEBB, JAMES LEVERNE "SKEETER"
B.NOV.4,1911 MERIDIAN,MISS.

YR	CL	LEA	POS	G	REC
1932	STL	N	S	1	.000
1938	CLE	A	S	20	.276
1939	CLE	A	S	81	.264
1940	CHI	A	2-S-3	84	.237
1941	CHI	A	2-S-3	29	.190
1942	CHI	A	2	32	.170
1943	CHI	A	2	58	.235
1944	CHI	A	2-S	139	.311
1945	DET	A	2-S	118	.199
1946	DET	A	2-S	64	.219
1947	DET	A	2-S	50	.203
1948	PHI	A	2-S	23	.148
	BRTR			699	.219

WEBB, SAMUEL HENRY "RED"
B.SEPT.25,1924 WASHINGTON,D.C.

YR	CL	LEA	POS	G	REC
1948	NY	N	P	5	2- 1
1949	NY	N	P	20	1- 1
	BLTR			25	3- 2

WEBB, WILLIAM FREDERICK
B.DEC.12,1917 ATLANTA,GA.

YR	CL	LEA	POS	G	REC
1943	PHI	N	P	1	0- 0
	BRTR				

WEBB, WILLIAM JOSEPH
B.JUNE 25,1896 CHICAGO,ILL.
D.JAN.12,1943

YR	CL	LEA	POS	G	REC
1917	PIT	N	2-S	5	.200
	BRTR				

WEBBER, JOSEPH EDWARD
B.1861 HAMILTON,ONT.,CANADA
D.DEC.15,1921 HAMILTON,ONT.,CAN

YR	CL	LEA	POS	G	REC
1884	IND	AA	C	3	.000

WEBBER, LESTER ELMER
B.MAY 6,1917 SANTA MARIA,CAL.

YR	CL	LEA	POS	G	REC
1942	BRO	N	P	19	3- 2
1943	BRO	N	P	54	7- 2
1944	BRO	N	P	48	7- 8
1945	BRO	N	P	17	7- 3
1946	BRO	N	P	11	3- 3
	CLE	A	P	4	1- 1
1948	CLE	A	P	1	0- 0

WEBER, CHARLES P. "COUNT"
B.OCT.22,1868 CINCINNATI,OHIO
D.JUNE 13,1914

YR	CL	LEA	POS	G	REC
1898	WAS	N	P	1	0- 2

WEBER, HARRY
B.INDIANAPOLIS,IND.

YR	CL	LEA	POS	G	REC
1884	DET	N	O	2	.000

WEBSTER, RAMON ALBERTO "RAY"
B.AUG.31,1942 COLON,PANAMA

YR	CL	LEA	POS	G	REC
1967	KC	A	1-O	122	.256
1968	OAK	A	1	66	.214
1969	OAK	A	1	64	.260
1970	SD	N	1-O	95	.259
1971	SD	N	H	10	.125
	OAK	A	1	7	.000
	CHI	N	1	16	.313
	BLTL			380	.244

YR	CL	LEA	POS	GP	G	REC

WEBSTER, RAYMOND GEORGE "RAY"
B.NOV.15,1937 GRASS VALLEY,CAL.

1959	CLE	A	2-3		40	.203
1960	BOS	A	2		7	.000
		BRTR			47	.195

WECKBECKER, PETER
B.AUG.30,1864 BUTLER,PA.
D.MAY 16,1935

1889	IND	N	C		1	.000
1890	LOU	AA	C		30	.234
					31	.232

WEEDEN, CHARLES ALBERT "BERT"
B.DEC.21,1882 NORTHWOOD,N.H.
D.JAN.7,1939 NORTHWOOD,N.H.

| 1911 | BOS | N | H | | 1 | .000 |
| | | BLTL | | | | |

WEEKLY, JOHNNY
B.JUNE 14,1937 WATERPROOF,LA.
D.NOV.24,1974 WALNUT CREEK,CAL.

1962	HOU	N	O		13	.192
1963	HOU	N	O		34	.225
1964	HOU	N	O		6	.133
		BRTR			53	.207

WEGENER, MICHAEL DENIS "MIKE"
B.OCT.8,1946 DENVER,COLO.

1969	MON	N	P		32	5-14
1970	MON	N	P		25	3- 6
		BRTR			57	8-20

WEHDE, WILBUR "BIGGS"
B.NOV.23,1906 HOLSTEIN,IOWA
D.SEPT.21,1970 SIOUX FALLS,
S.DAK.

1930	CHI	A	P		4	0- 0
1931	CHI	A	P		8	1- 0
		BRTR			12	1- 0

WEHMEIER, HERMAN RALPH "HERM"
B.FEB.18,1927 CINCINNATI,OHIO
D.MAY 21,1973 DALLAS,TEX.

1945	CIN	N	P	2	3	0- 1
1947	CIN	N	P	1	1	0- 0
1948	CIN	N	P	33	36	11- 8
1949	CIN	N	P	33	36	11-12
1950	CIN	N	P	41	54	10-18
1951	CIN	N	P	39	46	7-10
1952	CIN	N	P	33	41	9-11
1953	CIN	N	P	28	29	1- 6
1954	CIN	N	P	12	13	0- 3
	PHI	N	P		25	10- 8
1955	PHI	N	P	31	34	10-12
1956	PHI	N	P		3	0- 2
	STL	N	P	34	42	12- 9
1957	STL	N	P	36	40	10- 7
1958	STL	N	P		3	0- 1
	DET	A	P		7	1- 0
		BRTR		361	413	92-108

WEHRMEISTER, DAVID THOMAS "DAVE"
B.NOV.9,1952 BERWYN,ILL.

| 1976 | SD | N | P | | 7 | 0- 4 |
| | | BRTR | | | | |

WEICHBRODT, RUDOLPH C.
(PLAYED UNDER NAME OF
SKEL ROACH)

WEIDMAN, GEORGE E. "STUMP"
B.FEB.17,1861 ROCHESTER,N.H.
D.MAR.3,1905

1880	BUF	N	P-O	17	23	0-10
						.100
1881	DET	N	P		13	8- 5
1882	DET	N	P-S-	46	50	26-20
			O			.217
1883	DET	N	P-2-	45	76	19-23
			O			.173
1884	DET	N	P-2-	27	79	5-22
			S-O			.162
1885	DET	N	P-O	38	43	14-23
						.156
1886	KC	N	P	49	51	12-37
1887	DET	N	P		21	13- 6
	MET	AA	P-O	12	14	4- 8
						.229
	NY	N	P		2	0- 2
1888	NY	N	P		2	1- 1
		BRTR		272	374	102-157
						.177

WEIGEL, RALPH RICHARD
B.OCT.2,1921 MERCER CO.,OHIO

1946	CLE	A	C		6	.167
1948	CHI	A	C-O	66		.233
1949	WAS	A	C		34	.233
		BRTR			106	.230

WEIHE, JOHN GARIBALDI "PODGE"
B.NOV.13,1862 CINCINNATI,OHIO
D.APR.15,1914

1883	CIN	AA	O		1	.250
1884	IND	AA	O		64	.261
		BRTR			65	.260

WEIK, RICHARD HENRY
"DICK" OR "LEGS"
B.NOV.17,1927 WATERLOO,IOWA

1948	WAS	A	P		3	1- 2
1949	WAS	A	P	27	28	3-12
1950	WAS	A	P		14	1- 3
	CLE	A	P		11	1- 3
1953	CLE	A	R		1	.000
	DET	A	P		12	0- 1
1954	DET	A	P		9	0- 1
		BRTR		76	78	6-22
						.226

WEILAND, EDWIN NICHOLAS
B.NOV.26,1914 EVANSTON,ILL.
D.JULY 12,1971 CHICAGO,ILL.

1940	CHI	A	P		5	0- 0
1942	CHI	A	P		5	0- 0
		BLTR			10	0- 0

WEILAND, ROBERT GEORGE "LEFTY"
B.DEC.14,1905 CHICAGO,ILL.

1928	CHI	A	P	1	1- 0
1929	CHI	A	P	15	2- 4
1930	CHI	A	P	14	0- 4
1931	CHI	A	P	15	2- 7
1932	BOS	A	P	43	6-16
1933	BOS	A	P	39	8-14
1934	BOS	A	P	11	1- 5
	CLE	A	P	16	1- 5
1935	STL	A	P	14	0- 2
1937	STL	N	P	41	15-14
1938	STL	N	P	35	16-11
1939	STL	N	P	32	10-12
1940	STL	N	P	1	0- 0
		BLTL		277	62-94

WEILENMANN, CARL WOOLWORTH
(PLAYED UNDER NAME OF
CARL WOOLWORTH WEILMAN)

WEILMAN, CARL WOOLWORTH "ZEKE"
(REAL NAME
CARL WOOLWORTH WEILENMANN)
B.NOV.29,1889 HAMILTON,OHIO
D.MAY 26,1924

1912	STL	A	P		9	2- 4
1913	STL	A	P		39	10-20
1914	STL	A	P		45	19-13
1915	STL	A	P		47	18-18
1916	STL	A	P		46	17-18
1917	STL	A	P		5	1- 2
1919	STL	A	P		20	10- 6
1920	STL	A	P		30	9-13
		BLTL			241	86-94

WEIMER, JOHN WILLIAM "JAKE"
B.NOV.13,1883 READING,PA.
D.NOV.30,1944

1903	CHI	N	P		35	20- 8
1904	CHI	N	P		37	20-13
1905	CHI	N	P		33	18-13
1906	CIN	N	P		41	20-14
1907	CIN	N	P		29	11-14
1908	CIN	N	P		15	8- 7
1909	NY	N	P		1	0- 0
		BRTL			191	97-69

WEINERT, PHILLIP WALTER "LEFTY"
B.APR.21,1900 PHILADELPHIA,PA.
D.APR.17,1973 ROCKLEDGE,FLA.

1919	PHI	N	P		1	0- 0
1920	PHI	N	P		10	1- 1
1921	PHI	N	P		8	1- 0
1922	PHI	N	P		34	8-11
1923	PHI	N	P	38	39	4-17
1924	PHI	N	P		8	0- 1
1927	CHI	N	P		5	1- 1
1928	CHI	N	P		10	1- 0
1931	NY	A	P		17	2- 2
		BLTL		131	132	18-33

WEINGARTNER, ELMER WILLIAM
B.AUG.13,1918 CLEVELAND,OHIO

| 1945 | CLE | A | S | | 20 | .231 |
| | | BRTR | | | | |

WEINTRAUB, PHILIP "MICKEY"
B.OCT.12,1907 CHICAGO,ILL.

1933	NY	N	O		8	.200
1934	NY	N	O		31	.351
1935	NY	N	1-O		64	.241
1937	CIN	N	O		49	.271
	NY	N	O		6	.333
1938	PHI	N	1		100	.311
1944	NY	N	1		104	.316
1945	NY	N	1		82	.272
		BLTL			444	.295

WEIR, WILLIAM FRANKLIN
B.FEB.25,1913 PORTLAND,ME.

1936	BOS	N	P	12	13	4- 3
1937	BOS	N	P		10	1- 1
1938	BOS	N	P		5	1- 0
1939	BOS	N	P		2	0- 0
		BLTL		29	30	6- 4

WEIS, ALBERT JOHN "AL"
B.APR.2,1938 FRANKLIN SQUARE,N.Y

1962	CHI	A	2-S-3		7	.083
1963	CHI	A	2-S-3		99	.271
1964	CHI	A	2-S-O		133	.247
1965	CHI	A	2-S-3-O		103	.296
1966	CHI	A	2-S		129	.155
1967	CHI	A	2-S		50	.245
1968	NY	N	2-S-3		90	.172
1969	NY	N	2-S-3		103	.215
1970	NY	N	2-S		75	.207
1971	NY	N	2-3		11	.000
		BBTR			800	.219
		BR 1969-71				

WEIS, ARTHUR JOHN "BUTCH"
B.MAR.2,1903 ST.LOUIS,MO.

1922	CHI	N	O		2	.500
1923	CHI	N	O		22	.231
1924	CHI	N	O		37	.278
1925	CHI	N	O		67	.267
		BLTL			128	.270

WEISER, HARRY BUDSON "BUD"
B.JAN.8,1891 SHAMOKIN,PA.
D.JULY 31,1961

1915	PHI	N	O		37	.141
1916	PHI	N	O		4	.300
		BRTR			41	.162

WEISS, JOSEPH HAROLD
B.JAN.27,1894 CHICAGO,ILL.

| 1915 | CHI | F | 1 | | 29 | .239 |
| | | BRTR | | | | |

WELAJ, JOHN LUDWIG
B.MAY 27,1915 MOSS CREEK,PA.

1939	WAS	A	O		63	.274
1940	WAS	A	O		88	.256
1941	WAS	A	O		49	.208
1943	PHI	A	O		93	.242
		BRTR			293	.250

WELCH, CURTIS BENTON
B.FEB.11,1862 E.LIVERPOOL,OHIO
D.AUG.29,1896

1884	TOL	AA	O		109	.224
1885	STL	AA	O		112	.266
1886	STL	AA	O		138	.285
1887	STL	AA	O		131	.307
1888	ATH	AA	O		136	.291
1889	ATH	AA	O		125	.273
1890	ATH	AA	O		106	.283
	BAL	AA	1-O		19	.122
1891	BAL	AA	O		130	.278
1892	BAL	N	O		63	.233
	CIN	N	O		24	.220
1893	LOU	N	O		14	.181
		BR			1107	.269

YR	CL	LEA	POS	GP	G	REC

WELCH, FRANK "BOOGER"
B.AUG.10,1897 BIRMINGHAM,ALA.
D.JULY 25,1957

YR	CL	LEA	POS	GP	G	REC
1919	PHI	A	O		15	.167
1920	PHI	A	O		100	.258
1921	PHI	A	O		115	.285
1922	PHI	A	O		114	.259
1923	PHI	A	O		125	.297
1924	PHI	A	O		94	.290
1925	PHI	A	O		85	.277
1926	PHI	A	O		75	.281
1927	BOS	A	O		15	.179
	BRTR				738	.284

WELCH, HERBERT M. "DUTCH"
B.OCT.19,1900 DYERSBURG,TENN.
D.APR.15,1967 DYERSBURG,TENN.

YR	CL	LEA	POS	GP	G	REC
1925	BOS	A	S		13	.289

WELCH, JOHN VERNON
B.DEC.2,1906 WASHINGTON,D.C.
D.SEPT.2,1940

YR	CL	LEA	POS	GP	G	REC
1926	CHI	N	P		3	0- 0
1927	CHI	N	P		1	0- 0
1928	CHI	N	P		3	0- 0
1931	CHI	N	P		8	2- 1
1932	BOS	A	P	20	23	4- 6
1933	BOS	A	P		47	4- 9
1934	BOS	A	P		41	13-15
1935	BOS	A	P		31	10- 9
1936	BOS	A	P		9	2- 1
	PIT	N	P		9	0- 0
	BLTR			172	175	35-41

WELCH, MICHAEL FRANCIS "SMILING MICKEY"
B.JULY 4,1859 BROOKLYN,N.Y.
D.JULY 30,1941 NASHUA,N.H.

YR	CL	LEA	POS	GP	G	REC
1880	TRO	N	P-O	64	66	34-30
						.286
1881	TRO	N	P		39	20-18
1882	TRO	N	P-O	30	37	14-16
						.248
1883	NY	N	P-O	48	81	27-21
						.239
1884	NY	N	P-O	60	67	39-21
						.256
1885	NY	N	P-O		58	47-11
						.206
1886	NY	N	P	58	59	33-23
1887	NY	N	P		40	23-15
1888	NY	N	P		47	26-19
1889	NY	N	P		41	28-12
1890	NY	N	P		35	18-13
1891	NY	N	P	18	19	5-11
1892	NY	N	P		2	1- 1
	BRTR			540	591	315-211
						.229

WELCH, MILTON EDWARD
B.JULY 26,1924 FARMERSVILLE,ILL

YR	CL	LEA	POS	GP	G	REC
1945	DET	A	C		1	.000
	BRTR					

WELCH, THEODORE
B.1893

YR	CL	LEA	POS	GP	G	REC
1914	STL	F	P		3	0- 0
	BLTR					

WELCHONCE, HARRY MONROE
B.NOV.20,1888 NORTH POINT,PA.

YR	CL	LEA	POS	GP	G	REC
1911	PHI	N	O		17	.212
	BLTR					

WELDAY, LYNDON EARL "MIKE"
B.DEC.19,1879 CONWAY,IOWA
D.MAY 28,1942

YR	CL	LEA	POS	GP	G	REC
1907	CHI	A	O		24	.229
1909	CHI	A	O		29	.189
	BLTL				53	.202

WELF, OLIVER HENRY
B.JAN.17,1889 CLEVELAND,OHIO
D.JUNE 15,1967 CUYAHOGA,OHIO

YR	CL	LEA	POS	GP	G	REC
1916	CLE	A	H		1	.000

WELLMAN, ROBERT JOSEPH
B.JULY 15,1925 NORWOOD,OHIO

YR	CL	LEA	POS	GP	G	REC
1948	PHI	A	1-O		4	.200
1950	PHI	A	O		11	.333
	BRTR				15	.280

WELLS, EDWIN LEE "SATCHELFOOT"
B.JUNE 7,1900 ASHLAND,OHIO

YR	CL	LEA	POS	GP	G	REC
1923	DET	A	P		7	1- 0
1924	DET	A	P		29	6- 8
1925	DET	A	P		35	6- 9
1926	DET	A	P		36	12-10
1927	DET	A	P		8	0- 1
1929	NY	A	P		31	13- 9
1930	NY	A	P	27	29	12- 3
1931	NY	A	P	27	28	9- 5
1932	NY	A	P	22	24	3- 3
1933	STL	A	P	36	38	6-14
1934	STL	A	P		33	1- 7
	BLTL			291	298	69-69

WELLS, JACOB
B.AUG.9,1863 MEMPHIS,TENN.
D.MAR.16,1927

YR	CL	LEA	POS	GP	G	REC
1888	DET	N	C		16	.157
1890	STL	AA	C		28	.238
	BRTR				44	.210

WELLS, JOHN FREDERICK
B.NOV.25,1922 JUNCTION CITY,KAN

YR	CL	LEA	POS	GP	G	REC
1944	BRO	N	P		4	0- 2
	BRTR					

WELLS, LEO DONALD
B.JAN.18,1917 KANSAS CITY,KAN.

YR	CL	LEA	POS	GP	G	REC
1942	CHI	A	S		35	.194
1946	CHI	A	S-3		45	.189
	BRTR				80	.190

WELSH, JAMES D.
B.OCT.9,1903 DENVER,COLO.

YR	CL	LEA	POS	GP	G	REC
1925	BOS	N	2-O		122	.312
1926	BOS	N	O		134	.278
1927	BOS	N	O		131	.288
1928	NY	N	O		124	.307
1929	NY	N	O		39	.349
	BOS	N	O		53	.290
1930	BOS	N	O		113	.275
	BLTR				715	.290

WELSH, JAMES J. "TUB"
B.JULY 3,1866 ST.LOUIS,MO.

YR	CL	LEA	POS	GP	G	REC
1890	TOL	AA	C		33	.263
1895	LOU	N	C-1		39	.224
					72	.241

WELTEROTH, RICHARD JOHN "DICK"
B.AUG.3,1927 WILLIAMSPORT,PA.

YR	CL	LEA	POS	GP	G	REC
1948	WAS	A	P		33	2- 1
1949	WAS	A	P		52	2- 5
1950	WAS	A	P		5	0- 0
	BRTR				90	4- 6

WELZER, TONY FRANK
B.APR.5,1899 GERMANY
D.MAR.18,1971 MILWAUKEE,WIS.

YR	CL	LEA	POS	GP	G	REC
1926	BOS	A	P		40	4- 2
1927	BOS	A	P		37	6-11
	BRTR				77	10-13

WENDELL, LEWIS CHARLES
B.MAR.22,1892 NEW YORK,N.Y.
D.JULY 11,1953

YR	CL	LEA	POS	GP	G	REC
1915	NY	N	C		20	.222
1916	NY	N	C		2	.000
1924	PHI	N	C		21	.250
1925	PHI	N	C		18	.077
1926	PHI	N	C		1	.000
	BRTR				62	.180

WENSLOFF, CHARLES WILLIAM "BUTCH"
B.DEC.3,1915 SAUSALITO,CAL.

YR	CL	LEA	POS	GP	G	REC
1943	NY	A	P		29	13-11
1947	NY	A	P		11	3- 1
1948	CLE	A	P		1	0- 1
	BRTR				41	16-13

WENTZ, JOHN GEORGE
(REAL NAME JOHN GEORGE WERNZ)
B.MAR.4,1863 LOUISVILLE,KY.
D.SEPT.14,1907

YR	CL	LEA	POS	GP	G	REC
1891	LOU	AA	2		1	.250

WENTZEL, STANLEY AARON
B.JAN.13,1917 EXETER TOWNSHIP, PA.

YR	CL	LEA	POS	GP	G	REC
1945	BOS	N	O		4	.211
	BRTR					

WENZ, FREDERICK CHARLES "FRED"
B.AUG.26,1941 BOUND BROOK,N.J.

YR	CL	LEA	POS	GP	G	REC
1968	BOS	A	P		1	0- 0
1969	BOS	A	P		8	1- 0
1970	PHI	N	P		22	2- 0
	BRTR				31	3- 0

WERA, JULIAN VALENTINE "JULES"
B.FEB.9,1902 WINONA,MINN.
D.DEC.12,1975 ROCHESTER,MINN.

YR	CL	LEA	POS	GP	G	REC
1927	NY	A	3		38	.239
1929	NY	A	3		5	.417
	BRTR				43	.259

WERBER, WILLIAM MURRAY "BILLY"
B.JUNE 20,1908 BERWYN,MD.

YR	CL	LEA	POS	GP	G	REC
1930	NY	A	S-3		4	.286
1933	NY	A	H		3	.000
	BOS	A	S-3		108	.258
1934	BOS	A	S-3		152	.321
1935	BOS	A	3		124	.255
1936	BOS	A	3-O		145	.275
1937	PHI	A	3		128	.292
1938	PHI	A	3		134	.259
1939	CIN	N	3		147	.289
1940	CIN	N	3		143	.277
1941	CIN	N	3		109	.239
1942	NY	N	3		98	.205
	BRTR				1295	.271

WERDEN, PERCIVAL WHERITT "PERRY"
B.JULY 21,1865 ST.LOUIS,MO.
D.JAN.9,1934

YR	CL	LEA	POS	GP	G	REC
1884	STL	U	P-O	15	18	11- 1
						.237
1888	WAS	N	O		3	.500
1890	TOL	AA	O		129	.283
1891	BAL	AA	O		137	.292
1892	STL	N	O		148	.255
1893	STL	N	O		124	.284
1897	LOU	N	O		134	.301
	BRTR			15	693	11- 1
						.283

WERHAS, JOHN CHARLES "JOHNNY"
B.FEB.7,1938 HIGHLAND PARK,MICH.

YR	CL	LEA	POS	GP	G	REC
1964	LA	N	3		29	.193
1965	LA	N	1		4	.000
1967	LA	N	H		7	.143
	CAL	A	1-3-O		49	.160
	BRTR				89	.173

WERLE, WILLIAM GEORGE "BILL" OR "BUGS"
B.DEC.21,1920 OAKLAND,CAL.

YR	CL	LEA	POS	GP	G	REC
1949	PIT	N	P		35	12-13
1950	PIT	N	P		48	8-16
1951	PIT	N	P		59	8- 6
1952	PIT	N	P		5	0- 0
	STL	N	P		19	1- 2
1953	BOS	A	P		5	0- 1
1954	BOS	A	P		14	0- 1
	BLTL				185	29-39

WERLEY, GEORGE WILLIAM
B.SEPT.8,1938 ST.LOUIS,MO.

YR	CL	LEA	POS	GP	G	REC
1956	BAL	A	P		1	0- 0
	BRTR					

WERNER, DONALD PAUL "DON"
B.MAR.8,1953 APPLETON,WIS.

YR	CL	LEA	POS	GP	G	REC
1975	CIN	N	C		7	.125
1976	CIN	N	C		3	.500
	BRTR				10	.250

WERNZ, JOHN GEORGE
(PLAYED UNDER NAME OF JOHN GEORGE WENTZ)

WERRICK, JOSEPH ABRAHAM
B.OCT.25,1861 ST.PAUL,MINN.
D.MAY 10,1943

YR	CL	LEA	POS	GP	G	REC
1884	STP	U	S		9	.071
1886	LOU	AA	3		136	.250
1887	LOU	AA	3		136	.333
1888	LOU	AA	3		109	.210
	TR				390	.266

YR	CL	LEA	POS	GP	G	REC

WERT, DONALD RALPH "DON"
B.JULY 29,1938 STRASBURG,PA.

YR	CL	LEA	POS	GP	G	REC
1963	DET	A	2-S-3		78	.259
1964	DET	A	S-3		148	.257
1965	DET	A	2-S-3		162	.261
1966	DET	A	3		150	.268
1967	DET	A	S-3		142	.257
1968	DET	A	S-3		150	.200
1969	DET	A	3		132	.225
1970	DET	A	2-3		128	.218
1971	WAS	A	2-S-3		20	.050
		BRTR			1110	.242

WERTZ, DWIGHT LEWIS "DEL"
B.1891

YR	CL	LEA	POS	GP	G	REC
1914	BUF	F	S		3	.000
		BRTR				

WERTZ, HENRY LEVI
B.APR.20,1901 POMARIA,S.C.

YR	CL	LEA	POS	GP	G	REC
1926	BOS	N	P	32		11- 9
1927	BOS	N	P	42		4-10
1928	BOS	N	P	10		0- 2
1929	BOS	N	P	4		0- 0
		BRTR		88		15-21

WERTZ, VICTOR WOODROW "VIC"
B.FEB.9,1925 YORK,PA.

YR	CL	LEA	POS	GP	G	REC
1947	DET	A	O		102	.288
1948	DET	A	O		119	.248
1949	DET	A	O		155	.304
1950	DET	A	O		149	.308
1951	DET	A	O		136	.285
1952	DET	A	O		85	.246
	STL	A	O		37	.346
1953	STL	A	O		128	.268
1954	BAL	A	O		29	.202
	CLE	A	1-O		94	.275
1955	CLE	A	1-O		74	.253
1956	CLE	A	1		136	.264
1957	CLE	A	1		144	.282
1958	CLE	A	1		25	.279
1959	BOS	A	1		94	.275
1960	BOS	A	1		131	.282
1961	BOS	A	1		99	.262
	DET	A	H		8	.167
1962	DET	A	1		74	.324
1963	DET	A	H		6	.000
	MIN	A	1		35	.136
		BLTR			1860	.277

WEST, FRANK
B.1873 WILMERDING,PA.

YR	CL	LEA	POS	GP	G	REC
1894	BOS	N	P	1		0- 0

WEST, JAMES "HI"
B.AUG.8,1884 ROSEVILLE,ILL.
D.MAY 25,1963 LOS ANGELES,CAL.

YR	CL	LEA	POS	GP	G	REC
1905	CLE	A	P	6		2- 2
1911	CLE	A	P	13		2- 4
		BRTR		19		4- 6

WEST, MAX EDWARD
B.NOV.28,1916 DEXTER,MO.

YR	CL	LEA	POS	GP	G	REC
1938	BOS	N	O		123	.234
1939	BOS	N	O		130	.285
1940	BOS	N	1-O		139	.261
1941	BOS	N	O		138	.277
1942	BOS	N	1-O		134	.255
1946	BOS	N	1		1	.000
	CIN	N	O		72	.213
1948	PIT	N	1-O		87	.178
		BLTR			824	.254

WEST, MILTON DOUGLASS "BUCK"
B.AUG.29,1860 SPRING MILL,OHIO
D.JAN.13,1929

YR	CL	LEA	POS	GP	G	REC
1884	CIN	AA	O		33	.292
1890	CLE	N	O		37	.245
		BRTR			70	.265

WEST, RICHARD THOMAS
B.NOV.24,1917 LOUISVILLE,KY.

YR	CL	LEA	POS	GP	G	REC
1938	CIN	N	H		1	.000
1939	CIN	N	C-O		8	.211
1940	CIN	N	C		7	.393
1941	CIN	N	C		67	.215
1942	CIN	N	C-O		33	.177
1943	CIN	N	H		3	.000
		BRTR			119	.221

WEST, SAMUEL FILMORE "SAM"
B.OCT.5,1904 LONGVIEW,TEX.

YR	CL	LEA	POS	GP	G	REC
1927	WAS	A	O		38	.239
1928	WAS	A	O		125	.301
1929	WAS	A	O		142	.267
1930	WAS	A	O		120	.328
1931	WAS	A	O		132	.333
1932	WAS	A	O		146	.287
1933	STL	A	O		133	.300
1934	STL	A	O		122	.326
1935	STL	A	O		138	.300
1936	STL	A	O		152	.278
1937	STL	A	O		122	.328
1938	STL	A	O		44	.309
	WAS	A	O		92	.302
1939	WAS	A	1-O		115	.282
1940	WAS	A	1-O		57	.253
1941	WAS	A	O		26	.270
1942	CHI	A	O		49	.232
		BLTL			1753	.283

WEST, WALTER MAXWELL "MAX"
B.JULY 14,1904 SUNSET,TEX.
D.APR.25,1971 HOUSTON,TEX.

YR	CL	LEA	POS	GP	G	REC
1928	BRO	N	O		7	.286
1929	BRO	N	O		5	.250
		BRTR			12	.276

WEST, WELDON EDISON
B.SEPT.3,1915 GIBSONVILLE,N.C.

YR	CL	LEA	POS	GP	G	REC
1944	STL	A	P	11		0- 0
1945	STL	A	P	24		3- 4
		BRTL		35		3- 4

WEST, WILLIAM NELSON
B.AUG.21,1840 PHILADELPHIA,PA.
D.AUG.18,1891

YR	CL	LEA	POS	GP	G	REC
1874	ATL	NA	2	10		-
1876	MUT	N	2	1		.000
				11		-

WESTERBERG, OSCAR W.
B.1882
D.APR.17,1909 W.ALAMEDA CO.,CAL

YR	CL	LEA	POS	GP	G	REC
1907	BOS	N	S	3		.222
		TR				

WESTERVELT, HUYLER
B.OCT.1,1870 PIERMONT,N.Y.

YR	CL	LEA	POS	GP	G	REC
1894	NY	N	P	18		7- 9

WESTLAKE, JAMES PATRICK "JIM"
B.JULY 3,1930 SACRAMENTO,CAL.

YR	CL	LEA	POS	GP	G	REC
1955	PHI	N	H	1		.000
		BLTL				

WESTLAKE, WALDON THOMAS "WALLY"
B.NOV.8,1920 GRIDLEY,CAL.

YR	CL	LEA	POS	GP	G	REC
1947	PIT	N	O		112	.273
1948	PIT	N	O		132	.285
1949	PIT	N	O		147	.282
1950	PIT	N	O		139	.285
1951	PIT	N	3-O		50	.282
	STL	N	O		73	.255
1952	STL	N	O		21	.216
	CIN	N	O		59	.202
	CLE	A	O		29	.232
1953	CLE	A	O		82	.330
1954	CLE	A	O		85	.263
1955	CLE	A	O		16	.250
	BAL	A	O		8	.125
1956	PHI	N	H		5	.000
		BRTR			958	.272

WESTON, ALFRED JOHN
B.DEC.17,1905 LYNN,MASS.

YR	CL	LEA	POS	GP	G	REC
1929	BOS	N	H	3		.000
		BRTR				

WESTRUM, WESLEY NOREEN "WES"
B.NOV.28,1922 CLEARBROOK,MINN.

YR	CL	LEA	POS	GP	G	REC
1947	NY	N	C		6	.417
1948	NY	N	C		66	.160
1949	NY	N	C		64	.243
1950	NY	N	C		140	.236
1951	NY	N	C		124	.219
1952	NY	N	C		114	.221
1953	NY	N	C-3		107	.224
1954	NY	N	C		98	.187
1955	NY	N	C		69	.212
1956	NY	N	C		68	.220
1957	NY	N	C		63	.165
		BRTR			919	.217

NON-PLAYING MANAGER
NY(N) 1965-67, SF(N) 1974-75

WETZEL, CHARLES EDWARD "BUZZ"
B.AUG.25,1894 JAY,OKLA.
D.MAR.7,1941 GLOBE,ARIZ.

YR	CL	LEA	POS	GP	G	REC
1927	PHI	A	P	2		0- 0
		BRTR				

WETZEL, FRANKLIN BURTON "BUZZ"
B.JULY 7,1893 COLUMBUS,IND.
D.MAR.5,1942

YR	CL	LEA	POS	GP	G	REC
1920	STL	A	O		7	.428
1921	STL	A	O		61	.210
		BRTR			68	.243

WETZEL, GEORGE WILLIAM "SHORTY"
B.1868 PHILADELPHIA,PA.
D.FEB.25,1899

YR	CL	LEA	POS	GP	G	REC
1885	BAL	AA	P	2		0- 2

WEYHING, AUGUST "CANNONBALL"
B.SEPT.29,1866 LOUISVILLE,KY.
D.SEPT.4,1955 LOUISVILLE,KY.

YR	CL	LEA	POS	GP	G	REC
1887	ATH	AA	P		55	27-27
1888	ATH	AA	P	48	49	29-18
1889	ATH	AA	P		53	30-20
1890	BRO	P	P		49	31-15
1891	ATH	AA	P	53	54	31-20
1892	PHI	N	P	53	54	28-23
1893	PHI	N	P	40	41	24-16
1894	PHI	N	P		36	17-14
1895	PHI	N	P		2	0- 2
	PIT	N	P		3	1- 0
	LOU	N	P		27	8-19
1896	LOU	N	P		6	2- 3
1898	WAS	N	P		43	15-26
1899	WAS	N	P		40	16-21
1900	STL	N	P		7	3- 4
	BRO	N	P		8	3- 2
1901	CLE	A	P		2	0- 0
	CIN	N	P		1	0- 1
		BRTR		526	530	265-231

WEYHING, JOHN
B.JUNE 24,1869 LOUISVILLE,KY.
D.JUNE 20,1890

YR	CL	LEA	POS	GP	G	REC
1888	CIN	AA	P		8	3- 4
1889	COL	AA	P		1	0- 0
		BLTL			9	3- 4

WHALEY, WILLIAM CARL
B.FEB.10,1899 INDIANAPOLIS,IND.
D.MAR.3,1943

YR	CL	LEA	POS	GP	G	REC
1923	STL	A	O		23	.240
		BRTR				

WHALING, ALBERT "BERT"
B.JUNE 25,1890 LOS ANGELES,CAL.
D.JAN.21,1965 LOS ANGELES,CAL.

YR	CL	LEA	POS	GP	G	REC
1913	BOS	N	C		79	.242
1914	BOS	N	C		60	.209
1915	BOS	N	C		72	.221
		BRTR			211	.225

WHEAT, LEROY WILLIAM "LEE"
B.SEPT.15,1929 EDWARDSVILLE,ILL

YR	CL	LEA	POS	GP	G	REC
1954	PHI	A	P	8		0- 2
1955	KC	A	P	3		0- 0
		BRTR		11		0- 2

WHEAT, MC KINLEY DAVID "MACK"
B.JUNE 9,1893 POLO,MO.

YR	CL	LEA	POS	GP	G	REC
1915	BRO	N	C		8	.071
1916	BRO	N	C		2	.000
1917	BRO	N	C		29	.133
1918	BRO	N	C-O		57	.217
1919	BRO	N	C		41	.205
1920	PHI	N	C		78	.226
1921	PHI	N	C		10	.185
		BRTR			225	.204

YR	CL	LEA	POS	GP	G	REC

WHEAT, ZACHARY DAVIS "ZACK"
B.MAY 23,1888 HAMILTON,MO.
D.MAR.11,1972 SEDALIA,MO.

1909	BRO	N	O		26	.304
1910	BRO	N	O		156	.284
1911	BRO	N	O		136	.287
1912	BRO	N	O		123	.305
1913	BRO	N	O		138	.301
1914	BRO	N	O		145	.319
1915	BRO	N	O		146	.258
1916	BRO	N	O		149	.312
1917	BRO	N	O		109	.312
1918	BRO	N	O		105	.335
1919	BRO	N	O		137	.297
1920	BRO	N	O		148	.328
1921	BRO	N	O		148	.320
1922	BRO	N	O		152	.335
1923	BRO	N	O		98	.375
1924	BRO	N	O		141	.375
1925	BRO	N	O		150	.359
1926	BRO	N	O		111	.290
1927	PHI	A	O		88	.324
	BLTR				2406	.317

WEATLEY, CHARLES
B.JUNE 27,1893 ROSEDALE,KAN.

| 1912 | DET | A | P | | 5 | 0- 4 |
| | BRTR | | | | | |

WHEATON, ELWOOD PIERCE "WOODY"
B.OCT.3,1915 PHILADELPHIA,PA.

1943	PHI	A	O		7	.200
1944	PHI	A	P-O	11	30	0- 1
						.186
	BLTL			11	37	0- 1
						.191

WHEELER, DONALD WESLEY
B.SEPT.29,1922 MINNEAPOLIS,MINN

| 1949 | CHI | A | C | | 67 | .240 |
| | BRTR | | | | | |

WHEELER, EDWARD L.
B.JUNE 15,1878 SHERMAN,MICH.
D.AUG.15,1960 FT.WORTH,TEX.

| 1902 | BRO | N | 2-S-3 | | 24 | .127 |
| | BBTR | | | | | |

WHEELER, EDWARD RAYMOND
B.MAY 24,1917 LOS ANGELES,CAL.

| 1945 | CLE | A | 2-S-3 | | 46 | .194 |
| | BRTR | | | | | |

WHEELER, FLOYD CLARK "RIP"
B.MAR.2,1898 MARION,KY.

1921	PIT	N	P		1	0- 0
1922	PIT	N	P		1	0- 0
1923	CHI	N	P		3	1- 2
1924	CHI	N	P		29	3- 6
	BRTR				34	4- 8

WHEELER, GEORGE HARRISON "HEAVY"
B.NOV.10,1881 SHELBURN,IND.
D.JUNE 14,1918

| 1910 | CIN | N | O | | 3 | .000 |
| | BLTR | | | | | |

WHEELER, GEORGE L.
(REAL NAME GEORGE L. HEROUX)
B.AUG.3,1869 METHEUN,MASS.
D.MAY 23,1946

1896	PHI	N	P		3	1- 1
1897	PHI	N	P		25	10-10
1898	PHI	N	P		15	6- 9
1899	PHI	N	P		5	3- 2
					48	20-22

WHEELER, HARRY EUGENE
B.MAR.3,1858 VERSAILLES,IND.
D.OCT.9,1900

1878	PRO	N	P		7	6- 1
1879	CIN	N	P-O		1	0- 1
						.000
1880	CLE	N	O		1	.250
	CIN	N	3-O		17	.108
1882	CIN	AA	P-1-	3	75	1- 2
			O			.250
1883	COL	AA	P-O	1	83	0- 1
						.225
1884	STL	AA	O		5	.200
	KC	U	P-O	1	14	0- 1
						.246
	CHI	U	O		19	.241
	PIT	U	O		17	.236
	BAL	U	O		17	.254
	BRTR			13	256	7- 6
						.225

WHEELER, RICHARD
(REAL NAME
RICHARD WHEELER MAYNARD)
B.JAN.14,1898 KEENE,N.H.
D.FEB.12,1962 LEXINGTON,MASS.

| 1918 | STL | N | O | | 5 | .000 |
| | BRTR | | | | | |

WHEELOCK, GARY RICHARD
B.NOV.29,1951 BAKERSFIELD,CAL.

| 1976 | CAL | A | P | | 2 | 0- 0 |
| | BRTR | | | | | |

WHEELOCK, WARREN H. "BOBBY"
B.AUG.6,1864 CHARLESTOWN,MASS.
D.MAR.13,1928

1887	BOS	N	S-O		44	.314
1890	COL	AA	S		59	.267
1891	COL	AA	E		136	.230
	BRTR				239	.257

WHELAN, JAMES FRANK
B.1890

| 1913 | STL | N | O | | 1 | .000 |
| | BRTR | | | | | |

WHELAN, THOMAS JOSEPH
B.JAN.3,1894 LYNN,MASS.
D.JUNE 26,1957

| 1920 | BOS | N | 1 | | 1 | .000 |
| | BRTR | | | | | |

WHICKER, KEMP CASWELL
(PLAYED UNDER NAME OF
KEMP CASWELL WICKER)

WHILLOCK, JACK FRANKLIN
B.NOV.4,1942 CLINTON,ARK.

| 1971 | DET | A | P | | 7 | 0- 2 |
| | BRTR | | | | | |

WHISENANT, THOMAS PETER "PETE"
B.DEC.14,1929 ASHEVILLE,N.C.

1952	BOS	N	O		24	.192
1955	STL	N	O		58	.191
1956	CHI	N	O		103	.239
1957	CIN	N	O		67	.211
1958	CIN	N	2-O		85	.236
1959	CIN	N	O		36	.239
1960	CIN	N	H		1	.000
	CLE	A	O		7	.167
	WAS	A	O		58	.226
1962	MIN	A	O		10	.000
	CIN	N	C-3-O		26	.200
	BRTR				475	.224

WHISTLER, LEWIS
(REAL NAME LEWIS WISSLER)
B.MAR.10,1868 ST.LOUIS,MO.
D.DEC.30,1959

1890	NY	N	1		45	.288
1891	NY	N	S-O		71	.245
1892	BAL	N	1		52	.227
	LOU	N	1		80	.252
1893	LOU	N	1		13	.222
	STL	N	1		10	.243
					271	.250

WHITAKER, STEPHEN EDWARD "STEVE"
B.MAY 7,1943 TACOMA,WASH.

1966	NY	A	O		31	.246
1967	NY	A	O		122	.243
1968	NY	A	O		28	.117
1969	SEA	A	O		69	.250
1970	SF	N	O		16	.111
	BLTR				266	.230

WHITAKER, WALTER ELTON
B.JUNE 27,1884 CHELSEA,MASS.
D.AUG.9,1965 PEMBROKE,MASS.

| 1916 | PHI | A | P | | 1 | 0- 0 |

WHITAKER, WILLIAM H.
B.1865 ST.LOUIS,MO.

1888	BAL	AA	P		2	1- 1
1889	BAL	AA	P		1	1- 0
	TR				3	2- 1

WHITBY, WILLIAM EDWARD "BILL"
B.JULY 29,1943 CREWE,VA.

| 1964 | MIN | A | P | | 4 | 0- 0 |
| | BRTR | | | | | |

WHITCHER, ROBERT ARTHUR
B.APR.29,1919 BERLIN,N.H.

| 1945 | BOS | N | P | | 9 | 0- 2 |
| | BLTL | | | | | |

WHITE, ADELL ABE
B.MAY 16,1906 BRASELTONS,GA.

| 1937 | STL | N | P | | 5 | 0- 1 |
| | BRTL | | | | | |

WHITE, ALBERT EUGENE "FUZZ"
B.JUNE 27,1919 SPRINGFIELD,MO.

1940	STL	A	H		2	.000
1947	NY	N	H		7	.231
	BLTR				9	.200

WHITE, C B.
B.WAKEMAN,OHIO

| 1883 | PHI | N | 3 | | 1 | .000 |

WHITE, CHARLES "CHARLIE"
D.AUG.12,1928 KINSTON,N.C.

1954	MIL	N	C		50	.237
1955	MIL	N	C		12	.233
	BLTR				62	.236

WHITE, DONALD WILLIAM "DON"
B.JAN.8,1919 EVERETT,WASH.

1948	PHI	A	3-O		86	.245
1949	PHI	A	3-O		57	.213
	BRTR				143	.232

WHITE, EDWARD PERRY "ED"
B.APR.6,1926 ANNISTON,ALA.

| 1955 | CHI | A | O | | 3 | .500 |
| | BRTR | | | | | |

WHITE, ELDER LAFAYETTE
B.DEC.23,1934 COLERAIN,N.C.

| 1962 | CHI | N | 2-S | | 23 | .151 |
| | BRTR | | | | | |

WHITE, ELMER
B.MAY 23,1850 CATON,N.Y.
D.JULY 19,1938

| 1871 | CLE | NA | C-O | | 16 | - |

WHITE, ERNEST DANIEL "ERNIE"
B.SEPT.5,1916 PACOLET MILLS,S.C
D.MAY 22,1974 AUGUSTA,GA.

1940	STL	N	P		8	9	1- 1
1941	STL	N	P		32	33	17- 7
1942	STL	N	P		26	27	7- 5
1943	STL	N	P		14	21	5- 5
1946	BOS	N	P		12	14	0- 1
1947	BOS	N	P			1	0- 0
1948	BOS	N	P		15	16	0- 2
	BRTL				108	121	30-21

WHITE, FRANK
B.SEP.4,1950 GREENVILLE,MISS.

1973	KC	A	2-S		50	.223
1974	KC	A	2-S-3		99	.221
1975	KC	A	C-2-S-3		111	.250
1976	KC	A	2-S		152	.229
	BRTR				412	.232

WHITE, GEORGE FREDERICK "DEKE"
B.SEPT.8,1872 ALBANY,N.Y.
D.NOV.27,1957

| 1895 | PHI | N | P | | 3 | 1- 0 |
| | BBTL | | | | | |

YR	CL	LEA	POS	GP	G	REC

WHITE, GUY HARRIS "DOC"
B.APR.9,1879 WASHINGTON,D.C.
D.FEB.17,1969 SILVER SPRING,MD.

YR	CL	LEA	POS	GP	G	REC
1901	PHI	N	P		28	14-13
1902	PHI	N	P-O	36	50	16-20
						.274
1903	CHI	A	P		38	17-16
1904	CHI	A	P		30	16-10
1905	CHI	A	P		34	18-14
1906	CHI	A	P		28	18- 6
1907	CHI	A	P	47	48	27-13
1908	CHI	A	P	41	51	19-13
1909	CHI	A	P-O	23	71	10- 9
						.238
1910	CHI	A	P	33	56	15-13
1911	CHI	A	P	34	39	10-14
1912	CHI	A	P		32	8-10
1913	CHI	A	P	19	20	2- 4
		BLTL		423	525	190-155
						.217

WHITE, HAROLD GEORGE "HAL"
B.MAR.18,1919 UTICA,N.Y.

YR	CL	LEA	POS	GP	G	REC
1941	DET	A	P		4	0- 0
1942	DET	A	P		34	12-12
1943	DET	A	P		32	7-12
1946	DET	A	P		11	1- 1
1947	DET	A	P		35	4- 5
1948	DET	A	P		27	2- 1
1949	DET	A	P		10	1- 0
1950	DET	A	P		42	9- 6
1951	DET	A	P		38	3- 4
1952	DET	A	P		41	1- 8
1953	DET	A	P	9	10	0- 0
	STL	N	P		49	6- 5
1954	STL	N	P		4	0- 0
		BRTR		336	337	46-54

WHITE, JAMES LAURIE "DEACON"
B.DEC.2,1847 CATON,N.Y.
D.JULY 7,1939 AURORA,ILL.

YR	CL	LEA	POS	GP	G	REC
1871	CLE	NA	C-2-O		29	-
1872	CLE	NA	C-2-O		21	.336
1873	BOS	NA	C-O		60	.389
1874	BOS	NA	C-1-O		68	.326
1875	BOS	NA	C-O		80	.355
1876	CHI	N	C		66	.335
1877	BOS	N	C-1-O		59	.387
1878	CIN	N	C-3-O		60	.313
1879	CIN	N	M-C-1-O		77	.330
1880	CIN	N	1-2-O		34	.302
1881	BUF	N	C-1-2-3-O	78		.310
1882	BUF	N	C-3		83	.281
1883	BUF	N	C-3		93	.289
1884	BUF	N	C-3		106	.325
1885	BUF	N	3		98	.292
1886	DET	N	3		124	.289
1887	DET	N	3		111	.341
1888	DET	N	3		125	.298
1889	PIT	N	3		55	.253
1890	BUF	P	P-1-3	1	122	0- 1
						.264
		BLTR		1	1549	0- 1
						-

WHITE, JEROME CARDELL "JERRY"
B.AUG.23,1952 SHIRLEY,MASS.

YR	CL	LEA	POS	GP	G	REC
1974	MON	N	O		9	.400
1975	MON	N	O		39	.299
1976	MON	N	O		114	.245
		BBTR			162	.262

WHITE, JOHN F.
B.NOV.20,1876 INDIANAPOLIS,IND.

YR	CL	LEA	POS	GP	G	REC
1904	BOS	N	O		1	.000
		BL				

WHITE, JOHN PETER
B.AUG.31,1905 NEW YORK,N.Y.
D.JUNE 19,1971 FLUSHING,N.Y.

YR	CL	LEA	POS	GP	G	REC
1927	CIN	N	2-S		5	.000
1928	CIN	N	2		1	.000
		BBTR			6	.000

WHITE, JOYNER CLIFFORD "JO-JO"
B.JUNE 1,1909 RED OAK,GA.

YR	CL	LEA	POS	GP	G	REC
1932	DET	A	O	80		.260
1933	DET	A	O	91		.252
1934	DET	A	O	115		.313
1935	DET	A	O	114		.240
1936	DET	A	O	58		.275
1937	DET	A	O	94		.246
1938	DET	A	O	78		.262
1943	PHI	A	O	139		.248
1944	PHI	A	S-O	85		.221
	CIN	N	O	24		.235
		BLTR		878		.256

NON-PLAYING MANAGER
CLE(A) 1960 (INTERIM)

WHITE, JOYNER MICHAEL "MIKE"
B.DEC.18,1938 DETROIT,MICH.

YR	CL	LEA	POS	GP	G	REC
1963	HOU	N	2		3	.286
1964	HOU	N	2-3-O	89		.271
1965	HOU	N	3		8	.000
		BRTR		100		.264

WHITE, KIRBY "RED"
B.JAN.3,1884 HILLSBORO,OHIO
D.APR.22,1943

YR	CL	LEA	POS	GP	G	REC
1909	BOS	N	P		23	6-13
1910	BOS	N	P		3	1- 2
	PIT	N	P		30	10- 9
1911	PIT	N	P		2	0- 1
		TR			58	17-25

WHITE, ROY HILTON
B.DEC.27,1943 LOS ANGELES,CAL.

YR	CL	LEA	POS	GP	G	REC
1965	NY	A	2-O		14	.333
1966	NY	A	2-O	115		.225
1967	NY	A	3-O	70		.224
1968	NY	A	O	159		.267
1969	NY	A	O	130		.290
1970	NY	A	O	162		.296
1971	NY	A	O	147		.292
1972	NY	A	O	155		.270
1973	NY	A	O	162		.246
1974	NY	A	O-O	136		.275
1975	NY	A	1-O	148		.290
1976	NY	A	O	156		.286
		BBTR		1554		.274

WHITE, SAMUEL
B.1895

YR	CL	LEA	POS	GP	G	REC
1919	BOS	N	C		1	.000
		BRTR				

WHITE, SAMUEL CHARLES "SAMMY"
B.JULY 7,1928 WENATCHEE,WASH.

YR	CL	LEA	POS	GP	G	REC
1951	BOS	A	C		4	.182
1952	BOS	A	C	115		.281
1953	BOS	A	C	136		.273
1954	BOS	A	C	137		.282
1955	BOS	A	C	143		.261
1956	BOS	A	C	114		.245
1957	BOS	A	C	111		.215
1958	BOS	A	C	102		.259
1959	BOS	A	C	119		.284
1961	MIL	N	C		21	.222
1962	PHI	N	C		41	.216
		BRTR		1043		.262

WHITE, STEPHEN VINCENT
B.DEC.21,1884 DORCHESTER,MASS.
D.JAN.29,1975 BRAINTREE,MASS.

YR	CL	LEA	POS	GP	G	REC
1912	WAS	A	P		1	0- 0
	BOS	N	P		3	0- 0
		BRTR			4	0- 0

WHITE, WILLIAM BARNEY
B.JUNE 25,1924 PARIS,TEX.

YR	CL	LEA	POS	GP	G	REC
1945	BRO	N	S-3		4	.000
		BRTR				

WHITE, WILLIAM DEKOVA "BILL"
B.JAN.28,1934 LAKEWOOD,FLA.

YR	CL	LEA	POS	GP	G	REC
1956	NY	N	1-O	138		.256
1958	SF	N	1-O	26		.241
1959	STL	N	1-O	138		.302
1960	STL	N	1-O	144		.283
1961	STL	N	1	153		.286
1962	STL	N	1-O	159		.324
1963	STL	N	1	162		.304
1964	STL	N	1	160		.303
1965	STL	N	1	148		.289
1966	PHI	N	1	159		.276
1967	PHI	N	1	110		.250
1968	PHI	N	1	127		.239
1969	STL	N	1	49		.211
		BLTL		1673		.286

WHITE, WILLIAM DIGHTON
B.MAY 1,1860 BRIDGEPORT,OHIO
D.DEC.29,1924 BELLAIRE,OHIO

YR	CL	LEA	POS	GP	G	REC
1884	PIT	AA	S-3		74	.219
1886	LOU	AA	S	135		.262
1887	LOU	AA	S	132		.311
1888	LOU	AA	S-3	49		.283
	STL	AA	S		60	.176
					450	.259

WHITE, WILLIAM EDWARD
B.MILNER,GA.

YR	CL	LEA	POS	GP	G	REC
1879	PRO	N	1		1	.250

WHITE, WILLIAM HENRY "WILL"
B.OCT.11,1854 CATON,N.Y.
D.AUG.31,1911 FORT COLLIER,ONT.
CAN.

YR	CL	LEA	POS	GP	G	REC
1877	BOS	N	P		3	2- 1
1878	CIN	N	P-O	51		29-21
						.132
1879	CIN	N	P	75		38-30
1880	CIN	N	P-O	61		18-43
						.165
1881	DET	N	P		2	0- 2
1882	CIN	AA	P-1-O	54		40-12
						.264
1883	CIN	AA	P	65		43-22
1884	CIN	AA	M-P	54		34-18
1885	CIN	AA	P	35		17-15
1886	CIN	AA	P		3	1- 2
		BBTR		403		222-166
						.185

WHITE, WILLIAM WARREN
(ALSO PLAYED UNDER NAME OF
WILLIAM WARREN)
D.MAR.3,1898

YR	CL	LEA	POS	GP	G	REC
1871	OLY	NA	2		1	.000
1872	NAT	NA	S-3		10	.318
1873	NAT	NA	S-3		39	-
1874	BAL	NA	3		45	-
1875	CHI	NA	2-S-3-O		70	-
1884	WAS	U	2-3		2	.000
					167	-

WHITEHEAD, BURGESS URQUHART
B.JUNE 29,1910 TARBORO,N.C.

YR	CL	LEA	POS	GP	G	REC
1933	STL	N	2-S		12	.286
1934	STL	N	2-S-3	100		.277
1935	STL	N	2-S-3	107		.263
1936	NY	N	2	154		.278
1937	NY	N	2	152		.286
1939	NY	N	2	95		.239
1940	NY	N	2-S-3	133		.282
1941	NY	N	2-3	116		.228
1946	PIT	N	2-S-3	55		.220
		BRTR		924		.263

**WHITEHEAD, JOHN HENDERSON
"SILENT JOHN"**
B.APR.27,1900 COLEMAN,TEX.
D.OCT.20,1964 BONHAM,TEX.

YR	CL	LEA	POS	GP	G	REC
1935	CHI	A	P		28	13-13
1936	CHI	A	P		34	13-13
1937	CHI	A	P		26	11- 8
1938	CHI	A	P		32	10-11
1939	CHI	A	P		7	0- 3
	STL	A	P		26	1- 3
1940	STL	A	P		15	1- 3
1942	STL	A	P		4	0- 0
		BPTR		172		49-54

WHITEHEAD, MILTON P.

YR	CL	LEA	POS	GP	G	REC
1884	STL	U	P-2	1	100	0- 1
			S-3-O			.225
	KC	U	2-S-3		5	.150
				1	105	0- 1
						.222

YR	CL	LEA	POS	GP	G	REC

WHITEHILL, EARL OLIVER
B.FEB.7,1900 CEDAR RAPIDS,IOWA
D.OCT.22,1954 OMAHA,NEB.

YR	CL	LEA	POS	GP	G	REC
1923	DET	A	P		8	2- 0
1924	DET	A	P	35	37	17- 9
1925	DET	A	P	35	36	11-11
1926	DET	A	P		36	16-13
1927	DET	A	P		41	16-14
1928	DET	A	P		31	11-16
1929	DET	A	P		38	14-15
1930	DET	A	P		34	17-13
1931	DET	A	P		34	13-16
1932	DET	A	P		33	16-12
1933	WAS	A	P-O	39	40	22- 8
						.222
1934	WAS	A	P	32	35	14-11
1935	WAS	A	P		34	14-13
1936	WAS	A	P		28	14-11
1937	CLE	A	P		33	8- 8
1938	CLE	A	P		26	9- 8
1939	CHI	N	P		24	4- 7
	BBTL			541	548	218-185

WHITEHOUSE, CHARLES EVIS
B.JULY 9,1894 MATTOON,ILL.
D.JULY 19,1960

YR	CL	LEA	POS	GP	G	REC
1914	IND	F	P		8	2- 0
1915	NEW	F	P		11	2- 2
1919	WAS	A	P		6	0- 1
	BBTL				25	4- 3

WHITEHOUSE, GILBERT ARTHUR
B.OCT.15,1893 SOMERVILLE,MASS.
D.FEB.14,1926 BREWER,ME.

YR	CL	LEA	POS	GP	G	REC
1912	BOS	N	C		1	.000
1915	NEW	F	O		35	.217
	BBTR				36	.211

WHITEHORN, LEE
(PLAYED UNDER NAME OF
ARTHUR LEE DANEY)

WHITELY, GURDON
B.OCT.5,1859 ASHAWAY,R.I.
D.NOV.24,1924

YR	CL	LEA	POS	GP	G	REC
1884	CLE	N	O		8	.147
1885	BOS	N	C-O		33	.185
					41	.178

WHITEMAN, GEORGE "LUCKY"
B.DEC.23,1882 PEORIA,ILL.
D.FEB.10,1947

YR	CL	LEA	POS	GP	G	REC
1907	BOS	A	O		4	.167
1913	NY	A	O		11	.343
1918	BOS	A	O		71	.267
	BRTR				86	.271

WHITFIELD, FRED DWIGHT
B.JAN.7,1938 VANDIVER,ALA.

YR	CL	LEA	POS	GP	G	REC
1962	STL	N	1		73	.266
1963	CLE	A	1		109	.251
1964	CLE	A	1		101	.270
1965	CLE	A	1		132	.293
1966	CLE	A	1		137	.241
1967	CLE	A	1		100	.218
1968	CIN	N	1		87	.257
1969	CIN	N	1		74	.149
1970	MON	N	1		4	.067
	BLTL				817	.253

WHITFIELD, TERRY BERTLAND
B.JAN.12,1953 BLYTHE,CAL.

YR	CL	LEA	POS	GP	G	REC
1974	NY	A	O		2	.200
1975	NY	A	O		28	.272
1976	NY	A	O		1	.000
	BLTR				31	.267

WHITING, EDWARD C.
(ALSO PLAYED UNDER NAME OF
HARRY ZIEBER)
B.PHILADELPHIA,PA.

YR	CL	LEA	POS	GP	G	REC
1882	BAL	AA	C-1-O		73	.267
1883	LOU	AA	C-1-3-O		55	.295
1884	LOU	AA	C		42	.220
1886	WAS	N	C		6	.000
	BLTR				176	.254

WHITING, JESSE W.

YR	CL	LEA	POS	GP	G	REC
1902	PHI	N	P		1	0- 1
1906	BRO	N	P		3	,1- 1
1907	BRO	N	P		2	0- 0
					6	1- 2

WHITMAN, DICK CORWIN
B.NOV.9,1920 WOODBURN,ORE.

YR	CL	LEA	POS	GP	G	REC
1946	BRO	N	O		104	.260
1947	BRO	N	O		4	.400
1948	BRO	N	O		60	.291
1949	BRO	N	O		23	.184
1950	PHI	N	O		75	.250
1951	PHI	N	O		19	.118
	BLTR				285	.259

WHITMAN, WALTER FRANKLIN "HOOKER"
B.AUG.15,1924 MARENGO,IND.

YR	CL	LEA	POS	GP	G	REC
1946	CHI	A	1-2-S		17	.063
1948	CHI	A	S		3	.000
	BRTR				20	.045

WHITNER, EDWARD CLARENCE
(PLAYED UNDER NAME OF
EDWARD CLARENCE LEVY)

WHITNEY, ARTHUR CARTER "PINKEY"
B.JAN.2,1906 SAN ANTONIO,TEX.

YR	CL	LEA	POS	GP	G	REC
1928	PHI	N	3		151	.301
1929	PHI	N	3		154	.327
1930	PHI	N	3		149	.342
1931	PHI	N	3		130	.287
1932	PHI	N	3		154	.298
1933	PHI	N	3		31	.264
	BOS	N	2-3		100	.246
1934	BOS	N	2-3		146	.259
1935	BOS	N	2-3		126	.273
1936	BOS	N	3		10	.175
	PHI	N	3		114	.294
1937	PHI	N	3		138	.341
1938	PHI	N	3		102	.277
1939	PHI	N	3		34	.187
	BRTR				1539	.295

WHITNEY, ARTHUR WILSON
B.JAN.16,1858 BROCKTON,MASS.
D.AUG.15,1943

YR	CL	LEA	POS	GP	G	REC
1880	WOR	N	3		75	.222
1881	DET	N	3		58	.182
1882	PRO	N	S		11	.071
	DET	N	P-S- 3	3	30	0- 1
			3			.177
1884	PIT	AA	3		22	.299
1885	PIT	AA	S		90	.227
1886	PIT	AA	S-3		136	.225
1887	PIT	N	3		119	.343
1888	NY	N	3		90	.219
1889	NY	N	3		129	.217
1890	NY	N	P-S-3		119	.212
	STL	AA	S-3		2	.000
1891	CIN	AA	S-3		86	.200
	BRTR			3	967	0- 1
						.235

WHITNEY, FRANK THOMAS
B.FEB.18,1856 BROCKTON,MASS.
D.OCT.30,1943

YR	CL	LEA	POS	GP	G	REC
1876	BOS	N	O		34	.236
	BRTR					

WHITNEY, JAMES E. "GRASSHOPPER"
B.1856 BINGHAMTON,N.Y.
D.MAY 21,1891

YR	CL	LEA	POS	GP	G	REC
1881	BOS	N	P-1-	64	74	31-33
			O			.255
1882	BOS	N	P-1-	46	60	24-22
			O			.325
1883	BOS	N	P-1-	62	96	38-22
			O			.282
1884	BOS	N	P-1-	48	62	31-17
			3-O			.260
1885	BOS	N	P-1-	50	72	17-32
			O			.234
1886	KC	N	P-O	40	67	12-32
						.239
1887	WAS	N	P	46	52	24-21
1888	WAS	N	M-P	40	42	19-21
1889	IND	N	P	10		2- 7
1890	ATH	AA	P	7		2- 3
	BLTR			419	542	200-210
						.266

WHITROCK, WILLIAM FRANKLIN
B.MAR.4,1870 CINCINNATI,OHIO
D.JULY 26,1935

YR	CL	LEA	POS	GP	G	REC
1890	STL	AA	P		13	6- 7
1893	LOU	N	P		8	2- 4
1894	LOU	N	P		2	0- 1
	CIN	N	P		17	2- 5
1896	PHI	N	P		2	0- 1
	TR				42	10-18

WHITT, LEO ERNEST "ERNIE"
B.JUNE 13,1952 DETROIT,MICH.

YR	CL	LEA	POS	GP	G	REC
1976	BOS	A	C		8	.222
	BLTR					

WHITTED, GEORGE BOSTIC "POSSUM"
B.FEB.4,1891 DURHAM,N.C.
D.OCT.16,1962

YR	CL	LEA	POS	GP	G	REC
1912	STL	N	3		12	.282
1913	STL	N	S-3-O		123	.220
1914	STL	N	O		20	.129
	BOS	N	O		66	.216
1915	PHI	N	O		128	.281
1916	PHI	N	1-O		147	.281
1917	PHI	N	O		149	.280
1918	PHI	N	O		24	.244
1919	PHI	N	2		78	.249
	PIT	N	3-O		35	.398
1920	PIT	N	3		134	.261
1921	PIT	N	O		108	.280
1922	BRO	N	O		1	.000
	BRTR				1025	.270

WICKER, FLOYD EULISS
B.SEP.12,1943 BURLINGTON,N.C.

YR	CL	LEA	POS	GP	G	REC
1968	STL	N	H		5	.500
1969	MON	N	O		41	.103
1970	MIL	A	C		15	.195
1971	MIL	A	H		11	.125
	SF	N	O		9	.143
	BLTR				81	.159

WICKER, KEMP CASWELL
(REAL NAME
KEMP CASWELL WHICKER)
B.AUG.13,1906 KERNERSVILLE,N.C.
D.JUNE 11,1973 KERNERSVILLE,N.C.

YR	CL	LEA	POS	GP	G	REC
1936	NY	A	P		7	1- 2
1937	NY	A	P		14	7- 3
1938	NY	A	P		1	1- 0
1941	BRO	N	P		16	1- 2
	BRTL				40	10- 7

WICKER, ROBERT KITRIDGE
B.MAY 25,1878 LAWRENCE CO.,IND.
D.JAN.22,1955

YR	CL	LEA	POS	GP	G	REC
1901	STL	N	P		3	0- 0
1902	STL	N	P-O	19	22	5-11
						.234
1903	STL	N	P		1	0- 0
	CHI	N	P		32	20- 9
1904	CHI	N	P-O	30	50	17-10
						.219
1905	CHI	N	P	22	25	13- 7
1906	CHI	N	P		10	3- 5
	CIN	N	P		20	6-11
	BRTR			137	163	64-53
						.206

WICKERSHAM, DAVID CLIFFORD "DAVE"
B.SEP.27,1935 ERIE,PA.

YR	CL	LEA	POS	GP	G	REC
1960	KC	A	P		5	0- 0
1961	KC	A	P		17	2- 1
1962	KC	A	P		30	11- 4
1963	KC	A	P		38	12-15
1964	DET	A	P		40	19-12
1965	DET	A	P		34	9-14
1966	DET	A	P		38	8- 3
1967	DET	A	P		36	4- 5
1968	PIT	N	P		11	1- 0
1969	KC	A	P		34	2- 3
	BRTR				283	68-57

WICKLAND, ALBERT
B.JAN.27,1890 CHICAGO,ILL.

YR	CL	LEA	POS	GP	G	REC
1913	CIN	N	O		26	.215
1914	CHI	F	O		158	.288
1915	CHI	F	O		30	.235
	PIT	F	O		110	.303
1918	BOS	N	O		95	.262
1919	NY	A	O		26	.152
	BLTL				445	.275

WIDMAR, ALBERT JOSEPH "AL"
B.MAR.20,1925 CLEVELAND,OHIO

YR	CL	LEA	POS	GP	G	REC
1947	BOS	A	P		2	0- 0
1948	STL	A	P		49	2- 6
1950	STL	A	P		36	7-15
1951	STL	A	P		26	4- 9
1952	CHI	A	P		1	0- 0
	BRTR				114	13-30

YR	CL	LEA	POS	GP	G	REC

WIDNER, WILLIAM WATERFIELD "WILD BILL"
B.JUNE 3,1867 CUMMINSVILLE,OHIO
D.DEC.10,1908

YR	CL	LEA	POS	GP	G	REC
1887	CIN	AA	P		1	1- 0
1888	WAS	N	P		15	4- 7
1889	COL	AA	P		40	13-22
1890	COL	AA	P		13	4- 8
1891	CIN	AA	P		1	0- 1
		BRTR			70	22-38

WIEAND, FRANKLIN DELANO ROOSEVELT "TED"
B.APR.4,1933 WALNUTPORT,PA.

YR	CL	LEA	POS	GP	G	REC
1958	CIN	N	P		1	0- 0
1960	CIN	N	P		5	0- 1
		BRTR			6	0- 1

WIEDEMEYER, CHARLES JOHN
B.JAN.31,1915 CHICAGO,ILL.

YR	CL	LEA	POS	GP	G	REC
1934	CHI	N	P		4	0- 0
		BRTL				

WIENECKE, JOHN
B.MAR.10,1894 SALTZBURG,PA.
D.MAR.16,1933

YR	CL	LEA	POS	GP	G	REC
1921	CHI	A	P		10	0- 1
		BRTL				

WIESLER, ROBERT GEORGE "BOB"
B.AUG.13,1930 ST.LOUIS,MO.

YR	CL	LEA	POS	GP	G	REC
1951	NY	A	P		4	0- 2
1954	NY	A	P		6	3- 2
1955	NY	A	P		16	0- 2
1956	WAS	A	P	37	38	3-12
1957	WAS	A	P		3	1- 1
1958	WAS	A	P		4	0- 0
		BBTL		70	71	7-19

WIETELMANN, WILLIAM FREDERICK "WHITEY"
B.MAR.15,1920 ZANESVILLE,OHIO

YR	CL	LEA	POS	GP	G	REC
1939	BOS	N	S		23	.203
1940	BOS	N	2-S-3		35	.195
1941	BOS	N	2-S-3		16	.091
1942	BOS	N	2-S		13	.206
1943	BOS	N	S		153	.215
1944	BOS	N	2-S-3		125	.240
1945	BOS	N	P-2-	1	123	0- 0
			S-3			.271
1946	BOS	N	P-2-	3	44	0- 0
			S-3			.205
1947	PIT	N	1-2-S-3		48	.234
		BBTR		4	580	0- 0
						.232
		BR 1939-41				

WIGGS, JAMES ALVIN
B.SEPT.1,1879 TRONDHEIM,NORWAY
D.JAN.20,1963 XENIA,OHIO

YR	CL	LEA	POS	GP	G	REC
1903	CIN	N	P		2	0- 1
1905	DET	A	P		6	3- 3
1906	DET	A	P		4	1- 1
		BBTR			12	4- 5

WIGHT, WILLIAM ROBERT "BILL" OR "LEFTY"
B.APR.12,1922 RIO VISTA,CAL.

YR	CL	LEA	POS	GP	G	REC
1946	NY	A	P		14	2- 2
1947	NY	A	P		1	1- 0
1948	CHI	A	P		34	9-20
1949	CHI	A	P		35	15-13
1950	CHI	A	P		30	10-16
1951	BOS	A	P		34	7- 7
1952	BOS	A	P		10	2- 1
	DET	A	P		23	5- 9
1953	DET	A	P		13	0- 3
	CLE	A	P		20	2- 1
1955	CLE	A	P		17	0- 0
	BAL	A	P-1		19	6- 8
						.083
1956	BAL	A	P		35	9-12
1957	BAL	A	P		27	6- 6
1958	CIN	N	P		7	0- 1
	STL	N	P		28	3- 0
		BLTL			347	77-99
						.115

WIGINTON, FREDERICK THOMAS
B.DEC.16,1899 SCHUYLER,NEB.

YR	CL	LEA	POS	GP	G	REC
1923	STL	N	P		4	0- 0
		BRTR				

WILBER, DELBERT QUENTIN "DEL" OR "BABE"
B.FEB.24,1919 LINCOLN PARK,MICH

YR	CL	LEA	POS	GP	G	REC
1946	STL	N	C		4	.000
1947	STL	N	C		51	.232
1948	STL	N	C		27	.190
1949	STL	N	C		2	.250
1951	PHI	N	C		84	.278
1952	PHI	N	H		2	.000
	BOS	A	H		47	.267
1953	BOS	A	C-1		58	.241
1954	BOS	A	C		24	.131
		BRTR			299	.242

NON-PLAYING MANAGER
TEX(A) 1973 (INTERIM)

WILBORN, CLAUDE EDWARD
B.SEPT.1,1912 DENNISTON,VA.

YR	CL	LEA	POS	GP	G	REC
1940	BOS	N	O		5	.000
		BLTR				

WILCOX, MILTON EDWARD "MILT"
B.APR.20,1950 HONOLULU,HAWAII

YR	CL	LEA	POS	GP	G	REC
1970	CIN	N	P		5	3- 1
1971	CIN	N	P		18	2- 2
1972	CLE	A	P		32	7-14
1973	CLE	A	P	26	27	8-10
1974	CLE	A	P		41	2- 2
1975	CHI	N	P		25	0- 1
		BRTR		147	148	22-30

WILEY

YR	CL	LEA	POS	GP	G	REC
1884	WAS	U	3-0		1	.000

WILEY, MARK EUGENE
B.FEB.28,1948 NATIONAL CITY,CAL.

YR	CL	LEA	POS	GP	G	REC
1975	MIN	A	P		15	1- 3
		BRTR				

WILHELM, CHARLES ERNEST
B.MAY 23,1929 BALTIMORE,MD.

YR	CL	LEA	POS	GP	G	REC
1953	PHI	A	S		7	.286
		BRTR				

WILHELM, HARRY LESTER
B.APR.7,1874 UNIONTOWN,PA.
D.FEB.20,1944 REPUBLIC,PA.

YR	CL	LEA	POS	GP	G	REC
1899	LOU	N	P		4	1- 1

WILHELM, IRVING KEY "KAISER"
B.JAN.26,1878 WOOSTER,OHIO
D.MAY 21,1936

YR	CL	LEA	POS	GP	G	REC
1903	PIT	N	P		13	5- 3
1904	BOS	N	P		39	15-21
1905	BOS	N	P	34	38	4-25
1908	BOS	N	P		42	16-22
1909	BOS	N	P		22	3-13
1910	BOS	N	P		15	3- 7
1914	BAL	F	P		47	12-17
1915	BAL	F	P		1	0- 0
1921	PHI	N	M-P		4	0- 0
		BRTR		217	221	58-108

NON-PLAYING MANAGER PHI(N) 1922

WILHELM, JAMES HOYT "HOYT"
B.JULY 26,1923 HUNTERSVILLE,N.C.

YR	CL	LEA	POS	GP	G	REC
1952	NY	N	P		71	15- 3
1953	NY	N	P		68	7- 8
1954	NY	N	P		57	12- 4
1955	NY	N	P		59	4- 1
1956	NY	N	P		64	4- 9
1957	STL	N	P		40	1- 4
	CLE	A	P		2	1- 0
1958	CLE	A	P		30	2- 7
	BAL	A	P		9	1- 3
1959	BAL	A	P		32	15-11
1960	BAL	A	P		41	11- 8
1961	BAL	A	P		51	9- 7
1962	BAL	A	P		52	7-10
1963	CHI	A	P		55	5- 8
1964	CHI	A	P		73	12- 9
1965	CHI	A	P		66	7- 7
1966	CHI	A	P		46	5- 2
1967	CHI	A	P		49	8- 3
1968	CHI	A	P		72	4- 4
1969	CAL	A	P		44	5- 7
	ATL	N	P		8	2- 0
1970	ATL	N	P		50	6- 4
	CHI	N	P		3	0- 1
1971	ATL	N	P		3	0- 0
	LA	N	P		9	0- 1
1972	LA	N	P		16	0- 1
		BRTR		1070		143-122

WILHOIT, JOSEPH WILLIAM
B.DEC.20,1891 HIAWATHA,KAN.
D.SEPT.25,1930

YR	CL	LEA	POS	GP	G	REC
1916	BOS	N	O		116	.230
1917	BOS	N	O		54	.280
	PIT	N	O		9	.200
	NY	N	O		34	.320
1918	NY	N	O		64	.274
1919	BOS	A	O		6	.333
		BLTR			283	.257

WILIE, DENNEY EARNEST
B.SEPT.22,1890 WACO,TEX.
D.JUNE 20,1966 HAYWARD,CAL.

YR	CL	LEA	POS	GP	G	REC
1911	STL	N	O		15	.235
1912	STL	N	O		30	.229
1915	CLE	A	O		45	.252
		BLTL			90	.243

WILKE, HARRY JOSEPH
B.DEC.14,1901 CINCINNATI,OHIO

YR	CL	LEA	POS	GP	G	REC
1927	CHI	N	3		3	.000
		BRTR				

WILKES, IGNACIO ALFREDO (JAVIER)
(SEE IGNACIO ALFREDO JAVIER)

WILKIE, ALDON JAY
B.OCT.30,1915 ZEALANDIA,SASK., CANADA

YR	CL	LEA	POS	GP	G	REC
1941	PIT	N	P		26	2- 4
1942	PIT	N	P	35	36	6- 7
1946	PIT	N	P		7	0- 0
		BLTL		68	69	8-11

WILKINS, ROBERT LINWOOD
B.AUG.11,1922 NORFOLK,VA.

YR	CL	LEA	POS	GP	G	REC
1944	PHI	A	S		24	.240
1945	PHI	A	S-O		62	.260
		BRTR			86	.257

WILKINSON, EDWARD E.
B.1890 SAN FRANCISCO,CAL.

YR	CL	LEA	POS	GP	G	REC
1911	NY	A	O		10	.231
		BRTR				

WILKINSON, ROY HAMILTON
B.MAY 8,1894 CANANDAIGUA,N.Y.

YR	CL	LEA	POS	GP	G	REC
1918	CLE	A	P		1	0- 0
1919	CHI	A	P		4	1- 1
1920	CHI	A	P		34	7- 9
1921	CHI	A	P		36	4-19
1922	CHI	A	P		4	0- 1
		BRTR			79	12-30

WILKS, THEODORE "TED" OR "CORK"
B.NOV.13,1915 FULTON,N.Y.

YR	CL	LEA	POS	GP	G	REC
1944	STL	N	P		36	17- 4
1945	STL	N	P		18	4- 7
1946	STL	N	P		40	8- 0
1947	STL	N	P		37	4- 0
1948	STL	N	P		57	6- 6
1949	STL	N	P		59	10- 3
1950	STL	N	P		18	2- 0
1951	STL	N	P		17	0- 0
	PIT	N	P		48	3- 5
1952	PIT	N	P		44	5- 5
	CLE	A	P		7	0- 0
1953	CLE	A	P		4	0- 0
		BRTR			385	59-30

WILL, ROBERT LEE "BOB"
B.JULY 15,1931 BERWYN,ILL.

YR	CL	LEA	POS	GP	G	REC
1957	CHI	N	O		70	.223
1958	CHI	N	O		6	.250
1960	CHI	N	O		138	.255
1961	CHI	N	1-O		86	.257
1962	CHI	N	O		87	.239
1963	CHI	N	1		23	.174
		BLTR			410	.247

WILLETT, ROBERT EDGAR "ED"
B.MAR.7,1884 NORFOLK,VA.
D.MAY 10,1934

YR	CL	LEA	POS	GP	G	REC
1906	DET	A	P		4	0- 3
1907	DET	A	P		9	1- 5
1908	DET	A	P		30	15- 9
1909	DET	A	P	40	41	22- 9
1910	DET	A	P		38	16-11
1911	DET	A	P		39	13-14
1912	DET	A	P		37	17-15
1913	DET	A	P	33	34	13-14
1914	STL	F	P		27	4-16
1915	STL	F	P		17	2- 3
		BRTR		274	276	103-99

YR	CL	LEA	POS	GP	G	REC

WILLEY, CARLTON FRANCIS "CARL"
B.JUNE 6,1931 CHERRYFIELD,ME.

1958	MIL	N	P		23	9- 7
1959	MIL	N	P		26	5- 9
1960	MIL	N	P		28	6- 7
1961	MIL	N	P		35	6-12
1962	MIL	N	P		30	2- 5
1963	NY	N	P		30	9-14
1964	NY	N	P		14	0- 2
1965	NY	N	P		13	1- 2
		BRTR			199	38-58

WILLHITE, JON NICHOLAS "NICK"
B.JAN.27,1941 TULSA,OKLA.

1963	LA	N	P		8	2- 3
1964	LA	N	P		10	2- 4
1965	WAS	A	P		5	0- 0
	LA	N	P		15	2- 2
1966	LA	N	P		6	0- 0
1967	CAL	A	P		10	0- 2
	NY	N	P		4	0- 1
		BLTL			58	6-12

WILLIAMS, ALMON EDWARD
B.MAY 11,1914 HARTSELLE,ALA.
D.JULY 19,1969 JEFFERSON,TEX.

1937	PHI	A	P		16	4- 1
1938	PHI	A	P		30	0- 7
		BRTR			46	4- 8

WILLIAMS, ALVA MITCHEL "RIP"
B.JAN.31,1882 CARTHAGE,ILL.
D.JULY 23,1933

1911	BOS	A	C-1		95	.239
1912	WAS	A	C		56	.318
1913	WAS	A	C		64	.283
1914	WAS	A	C		81	.278
1915	WAS	A	C-1		91	.244
1916	WAS	A	C-1		76	.267
1918	CLE	A	1		28	.239
		BRTR			491	.265

WILLIAMS, ARTHUR FRANKLIN
B.AUG.26,1877 SOMERVILLE,MASS.
D.MAY 16,1941 ARLINGTON,VA.

| 1902 | CHI | N | 1-O | | 49 | .232 |
| | | TR | | | | |

WILLIAMS, AUGUST JOSEPH "GLOOMY GUS"
B.MAR.20,1887 NEW JERSEY
D.APR.16,1964 STERLING,ILL.

1911	STL	A	O		9	.269
1912	STL	A	O		64	.290
1913	STL	A	O		149	.273
1914	STL	A	O		143	.253
1915	STL	A	O		45	.202
		BLTL			410	.263

WILLIAMS, AUGUSTINE H.
B.1870 NEW YORK,N.Y.
D.OCT.14,1890

| 1890 | BRO | AA | P | | 2 | 1- 1 |

WILLIAMS, BERNARD "BERNIE"
B.OCT.8,1948 ALAMEDA,CAL.

1970	SF	N	O		7	.313
1971	SF	N	O		35	.178
1972	SF	N	O		46	.191
1974	SD	N	O		14	.133
		BRTR			102	.192

WILLIAMS, BILLY LEO
B.JUNE 15,1938 WHISTLER,ALA.

1959	CHI	N	O		18	.152
1960	CHI	N	O		12	.277
1961	CHI	N	O		146	.278
1962	CHI	N	O		159	.298
1963	CHI	N	O		161	.286
1964	CHI	N	O		162	.312
1965	CHI	N	O		164	.315
1966	CHI	N	O		162	.276
1967	CHI	N	O		162	.278
1968	CHI	N	O		163	.288
1969	CHI	N	O		163	.293
1970	CHI	N	O		161	.322
1971	CHI	N	O		157	.301
1972	CHI	N	1-O		150	.333
1973	CHI	N	1-O		156	.288
1974	CHI	N	1-O		117	.280
1975	OAK	A	1-O		155	.244
1976	OAK	A	O-D		120	.211
		BLTR			2488	.290

WILLIAMS, CHARLES PROSEK "CHARLIE"
B.OCT.11,1947 FLUSHING,N.Y.

1971	NY	N	P		31	5- 6
1972	SF	N	P		3	0- 2
1973	SF	N	P		12	3- 0
1974	SF	N	P		39	1- 3
1975	SF	N	P		55	5- 3
1976	SF	N	P		48	2- 0
		BRTR			188	16-14

WILLIAMS, CLAUDE PRESTON
B.MAR.9,1893 AURORA,MO.
D.NOV.4,1959

1913	DET	A	P		4	0- 1
1914	DET	A	P		3	0- 0
1916	CHI	A	P		43	13- 7
1917	CHI	A	P		45	17- 8
1918	CHI	A	P		15	6- 4
1919	CHI	A	P		41	23-11
1920	CHI	A	P		39	22-14
		BRTL			190	81-45

WILLIAMS, DAVID CARLOUS "DAVEY"
B.NOV.2,1928 DALLAS,TEX.

1949	NY	N	2		13	.240
1951	NY	N	2		30	.266
1952	NY	N	2		138	.254
1953	NY	N	2		112	.297
1954	NY	N	2		142	.222
1955	NY	N	2		82	.251
		BRTR			517	.252

WILLIAMS, DAVID CARTER "MUTT"
B.JULY 31,1891 OZARK,ARK.
D.MAR.30,1962 FAYETTEVILLE,ARK.

1913	WAS	A	P		1	1- 0
1914	WAS	A	P		5	0- 0
		BRTR			6	1- 0

WILLIAMS, DAVID D.
B.SCRANTON,PA.

| 1902 | BOS | A | P | | 3 | 0- 0 |
| | | TL | | | | |

WILLIAMS, DEWEY EDGAR "DEE"
B.FEB.5,1916 DURHAM,N.C.

1944	CHI	N	C		79	.240
1945	CHI	N	C		59	.280
1946	CHI	N	C		4	.200
1947	CHI	N	C		3	.000
1948	CIN	N	C		48	.168
		BRTR			193	.233

WILLIAMS, DONALD FRED "DON"
B.SEPT.14,1931 FLOYD,VA.

1958	PIT	N	P		2	0- 0
1959	PIT	N	P		6	0- 0
1962	KC	A	P		3	0- 0
		BRTR			11	0- 0

WILLIAMS, DONALD REID "DON"
B.SEP.2,1935 LOS ANGELES,CAL.

| 1963 | MIN | A | P | | 3 | 0- 0 |
| | | BRTR | | | | |

WILLIAMS, EARL BAXTER
B.JAN.27,1903 CUMBERLAND GAP, TENN.
D.MAR.10,1958

| 1928 | BOS | N | C | | 3 | .000 |
| | | BRTR | | | | |

WILLIAMS, EARL CRAIG
B.JULY 14,1948 NEWARK,N.J.

1970	ATL	N	1-3		10	.368
1971	ATL	N	C-1-3		145	.260
1972	ATL	N	C-1-3		151	.258
1973	BAL	A	C-1		132	.237
1974	BAL	A	C-1		118	.254
1975	BAL	A	C-1		111	.240
1976	ATL	N	C-1		61	.212
	MON	N	C-1		61	.237
		BRTR			789	.248

WILLIAMS, EDWIN DIBRELL "DIB"
B.JAN.19,1910 GREENBRIER,ARK.

1930	PHI	A	2-S		67	.262
1931	PHI	A	2-S		86	.269
1932	PHI	A	2		62	.251
1933	PHI	A	2-S		115	.289
1934	PHI	A	2		66	.273
1935	PHI	A	2-S		4	.100
	BOS	A	2-S-3		75	.211
		BRTR			475	.267

WILLIAMS, ELISHA ALPHONSO "DALE"
B.OCT.6,1855 LUDLOW,KY.
D.OCT.22,1939

| 1876 | CIN | N | P | | 9 | 1- 8 |
| | | BRTR | | | | |

WILLIAMS, EVON DANIEL "DENNY"
B.DEC.13,1899 PORTLAND,ORE.
D.MAR.24,1929

1921	CIN	N	O		10	.000
1924	BOS	A	O		25	.365
1925	BOS	A	O		68	.229
1928	BOS	A	O		16	.222
		BLTR			119	.259

WILLIAMS, FRANK C.
(SEE FRANK C. SELMAN)

WILLIAMS, FREDERICK "CY"
B.DEC.21,1888 WADENA,IND.
D.APR.23,1974 EAGLE RIVER,WIS.

1912	CHI	N	O		28	.242
1913	CHI	N	O		49	.224
1914	CHI	N	O		55	.202
1915	CHI	N	O		151	.257
1916	CHI	N	O		118	.279
1917	CHI	N	O		138	.241
1918	PHI	N	O		94	.276
1919	PHI	N	O		109	.278
1920	PHI	N	O		148	.325
1921	PHI	N	O		146	.320
1922	PHI	N	O		151	.308
1923	PHI	N	O		136	.293
1924	PHI	N	O		148	.328
1925	PHI	N	O		107	.331
1926	PHI	N	O		107	.345
1927	PHI	N	O		131	.274
1928	PHI	N	O		99	.256
1929	PHI	N	O		66	.202
1930	PHI	N	O		21	.471
		BLTL			2002	.292

WILLIAMS, FREDERICK "PAP"
B.JULY 17,1913 MERIDIAN,MISS.

| 1945 | CLE | A | 1 | | 19 | .211 |
| | | BRTR | | | | |

WILLIAMS, GEORGE
B.OCT.23,1939 DETROIT,MICH.

1961	PHI	N	2		17	.250
1962	HOU	N	2		5	.375
1964	KC	A	2-S-3-O		37	.209
		BRTR			59	.230

WILLIAMS, HARRY PETER
B.JUNE 23,1890 OMAHA,NEB.
D.DEC.21,1963 HUNTINGTON PARK, CAL.

| 1913 | NY | A | 1 | | 27 | .256 |
| | | BRTR | | | | |

WILLIAMS, JAMES A.
B.JAN.3,1848 COLUMBUS,OHIO
D.OCT.24,1918
NON-PLAYING MANAGER
STL(AA) 1884, CLE(AA) 1887-88

WILLIAMS, JAMES ALFRED "JIM"
B.APR.29,1947 ZACHARY,LA.

1969	SD	N	O		13	.280
1970	SD	N	O		11	.286
		BRTR			24	.282

WILLIAMS, JAMES FRANCIS "JIM"
B.OCT.4,1943 SANTA MARIA,CAL.

1966	STL	N	2-S		13	.273
1967	STL	N	S		1	.000
		BRTR			14	.231

WILLIAMS, JAMES THOMAS WILLIAMS
B.DEC.20,1876 ST.LUUIS,MO.
D.JAN.16,1965 ST.PETERSBURG,FLA

1899	PIT	N	3		153	.352
1900	PIT	N	3		106	.266
1901	BAL	A	3		131	.321
1902	BAL	A	1-2-3		125	.311
1903	NY	A	2		132	.281
1904	NY	A	2		146	.259
1905	NY	A	2		129	.228
1906	NY	A	2		139	.277
1907	NY	A	2		139	.270
1908	STL	A	2		148	.236
1909	STL	A	2		110	.195
		BRTR			1458	.276

YR	CL	LEA	POS	GP	G	REC

WILLIAMS, JOHN BRODIE
B.JULY 16,1889 HONOLULU,HAWAII
D.SEPT.8,1963 LONG BEACH,CAL.
1914 DET A P   4 0- 3
BRTR

WILLIAMS, KENNETH ROY "KEN"
B.JUNE 28,1890 GRANT'S PASS,ORE
D.JAN.22,1959 GRANT'S PASS,ORE.
1915 CIN N O   71 .242
1916 CIN N O   10 .111
1918 STL A O   2 .000
1919 STL A O   65 .300
1920 STL A O   141 .307
1921 STL A O   146 .347
1922 STL A O   153 .332
1923 STL A O   147 .357
1924 STL A O   114 .324
1925 STL A O   102 .331
1926 STL A O   108 .280
1927 STL A O   131 .323
1928 BOS A O   133 .303
1929 BOS A O   74 .346
BLTR   1397 .319

WILLIAMS, LEON THEO "LEFTY"
B.DEC.2,1905 MACON,GA.
1926 BRO N P   8 12 0- 0
BLTL

WILLIAMS, MARSHALL MC DIARMID "MARSH"
B.FEB.21,1893 FAISON,N.C.
D.FEB.22,1935 TUCSON,ARIZ.
1916 PHI A P   10 0- 6
BRTR

WILLIAMS, OTTO GEORGE
B.NOV.2,1877 NEWARK,N.J.
D.MAR.19,1937
1902 STL N S   2 .400
1903 STL N S   53 .203
     CHI N S   37 .223
1904 CHI N 1-O   54 .200
1906 WAS A 2   20 .137
BRTR   166 .202

WILLIAMS, REES GEPPERT "STEAMBOAT"
B.JAN.31,1892 CASCADE,MONT.
1914 STL N P   6 0- 1
1916 STL N P   36 6- 7
BLTR   42 6- 8

WILLIAMS, RICHARD HIRSHFELD "DICK"
B.MAY 7,1928 ST.LOUIS,MO.
1951 BRO N O   23 .200
1952 BRO N 1-3-O   36 .309
1953 BRO N O   30 .218
1954 BRO N O   16 .147
1956 BRO N H   7 .286
     BAL A 1-2-3-O 87 .286
1957 BAL A 1-3-O   47 .234
     CLE A 3-O   67 .283
1958 BAL A 1-2-3-O 128 .276
1959 KC A 1-2-3-O 130 .266
1960 KC A 1-3-O   127 .288
1961 BAL A 1-3-O   103 .206
1962 BAL A 1-3-O   82 .247
1963 BOS A 1-3-O   79 .257
1964 BOS A 1-3-O   61 .159
BRTR   1023 .260
NON-PLAYING MANAGER
BOS(A) 1967-69, OAK(A) 1971-73,
CAL(A) 1974-76

WILLIAMS, RINALDO LEWIS
B.DEC.18,1893 SANTA CRUZ,CAL.
D.APR.24,1966
1914 BRO F 3   4 .207
BLTR

WILLIAMS, ROBERT ELIAS
B.APR.27,1884 MONDAY,OHIO
D.AUG.6,1962
1911 NY A C   20 .191
1912 NY A C   20 .136
1913 NY A C   6 .158
1914 NY A 1   59 .163
BRTR   105 .163

WILLIAMS, ROBERT FULTON "ACE"
B.MAR.18,1918 MONTCLAIR,N.J.
1940 BOS N P   5 0- 0
1946 BOS N P   1 0- 0
BRTL   6 0- 0

WILLIAMS, STANLEY WILSON "STAN"
B.SEP.14,1936 ENFIELD,N.H.
1958 LA N P   27 9- 7
1959 LA N P   35 5- 5
1960 LA N P   38 14-10
1961 LA N P   41 15-12
1962 LA N P   40 14-12
1963 NY A P   29 9- 8
1964 NY A P   21 22 1- 5
1965 CLE A P   3 0- 0
1967 CLE A P   16 6- 4
1968 CLE A P   44 13-11
1969 CLE A P   61 6-14
1970 MIN A P   68 10- 1
1971 MIN A P   46 4- 5
     STL N P   10 3- 0
1972 BOS A P   3 0- 0
BRTR   482 483 109-94

WILLIAMS, THEODORE SAMUEL "TED", "THE KID" OR "THE SPLENDID SPLINTER"
B.AUG.30,1918 SAN DIEGO,CAL.
1939 BOS A O   149 .327
1940 BOS A P-O 1 144 0- 0
                        .344
1941 BOS A O   143 .406
1942 BOS A O   150 .356
1946 BOS A O   150 .342
1947 BOS A O   156 .343
1948 BOS A O   137 .369
1949 BOS A O   155 .343
1950 BOS A O   89 .317
1951 BOS A O   148 .318
1952 BOS A O   6 .400
1953 BOS A O   37 .407
1954 BOS A O   117 .345
1955 BOS A O   98 .356
1956 BOS A O   136 .345
1957 BOS A O   132 .388
1958 BOS A O   129 .328
1959 BOS A O   103 .254
1960 BOS A O   113 .316
BLTR   1 2292 0- 0
                        .344
NON-PLAYING MANAGER
WAS(A) 1969-71, TEX(A) 1972

WILLIAMS, THOMAS C.
B.AUG.19,1870 POMEROY,OHIO
1892 CLE N P   3 1- 0
1893 CLE N P   8 1- 1
                    11 2- 1

WILLIAMS, WALTER ALLEN "WALT"
B.DEC.19,1943 BROWNWOOD,TEX.
1964 HOU N O   10 .000
1967 CHI A O   104 .240
1968 CHI A O   63 .241
1969 CHI A O   135 .304
1970 CHI A O   110 .251
1971 CHI A 3-O   114 .294
1972 CHI A 3-O   77 .249
1973 CLE A O-D   104 .289
1974 NY A O   43 .113
1975 NY A 2-O-D   82 .281
BRTR   842 .270

WILLIAMS, WALTER MERRILL "POP"
B.MAY 19,1874 BOWNDOINHAM,ME.
D.AUG.4,1959
1898 WAS N P   2 0- 2
1902 CHI N P-O 31 32 11-15
                        .194
1903 CHI N P   2 0- 1
     PHI N P   3 1- 2
     BOS N P   14 4- 5
BLTL   52 53 16-25
                        .217

WILLIAMS, WASHINGTON J.
B.PHILADELPHIA,PA.
D.AUG.9,1892
1884 RIC AA O   2 .250
1885 CHI N P-O   1 0- 0
                        .250
                  1 3 0- 0
                        .250

WILLIAMS, WILLIAM "BILLY"
B.JUNE 13,1933 NEWBERRY,S.C.
1969 SEA A O   4 .000
BLTR

WILLIAMS, WOODROW WILSON "WOODY"
B.AUG.22,1912 PAMPLIA,VA.
1938 BRO N S   20 .333
1943 CIN N 2-S-3   30 .377
1944 CIN N 2   155 .240
1945 CIN N 2   133 .237
BRTR   338 .250

WILLIAMSON, EDWARD NAGLE "NED"
B.OCT.24,1857 PHILADELPHIA,PA.
D.MAR.3,1894
1878 IND N 3   60 .223
1879 CHI N 3   77 .299
1880 CHI N C-2-3   74 .255
1881 CHI N P-2- 1 82 0- 1
               S-3   .268
1882 CHI N P-3 1 82 0- 0
                        .281
1883 CHI N P-C- 1 98 0- 0
               3   .276
1884 CHI N P-C- 1 106 0- 0
               3   .278
1885 CHI N P-C- 2 112 0- 0
               3   .238
1886 CHI N S   121 .216
1887 CHI N S   127 .371
1888 CHI N S   132 .250
1889 CHI N S   47 .237
1890 CHI P S-3   73 .204
BRTR   6 1191 0- 1
                        .267

WILLIAMSON, NATHANIEL HOWARD "HOWIE"
B.DEC.23,1904 LITTLE ROCK,ARK.
1928 STL N H   10 .222
BLTL

WILLIAMSON, SILAS ALBERT
B.FEB.20,1903 BUCKVILLE,ARK.
1928 CHI A P   1 0- 0
BRTR

WILLIGROD, JULIUS
B.CALIFORNIA
1882 DET N S-O   2 .286
     CLE N O   9 .114
                    10 .143

WILLINGHAM, THOMAS HUGH
B.MAY 30,1908 DALHART,TEX.
1930 CHI A 2   3 .250
1931 PHI N 1-S-3   23 .257
1932 PHI N H   4 .000
1933 PHI N H   1 .000
BRTR   31 .233

WILLIS, CHARLES WILLIAM "LEFTY"
B.NOV.4,1905 LEETOWN,W.VA.
D.MAY 10,1962
1925 PHI A P   3 0- 0
1926 PHI A P   13 0- 0
1927 PHI A P   14 3- 1
BLTL   30 3- 1

WILLIS, DALE JEROME
B.MAY 29,1938 CALHOUN,GA.
1963 KC A P   25 26 0- 2
BRTR

WILLIS, JAMES GLADDEN
B.MAR.30,1927 DOYLINE,LA.
1953 CHI N P   13 2- 1
1954 CHI N P   14 0- 1
BLTR   27 2- 2

WILLIS, JOSEPH
B.APR.9,1892 ORONTON,OHIO
D.DEC.4,1966
1911 STL A P   1 0- 0
     STL N P   2 0- 1
1912 STL N P   31 4- 9
1913 STL N P   2 0- 0
BRTL   36 4-10

WILLIS, LESTER EVANS "WIMPY"
B.JAN.17,1911 NAGADOCHES,TEX.
1947 CLE A P   22 0- 2
BLTL

YR	CL LEA POS	GP	G	REC

WILLIS, RONALD EARL "RON"
B.JULY 12,1943 NEWBERN,TENN.

1966 STL N P		4	0- 0
1967 STL N P		65	6- 5
1968 STL N P		48	2- 3
1969 STL N P		26	1- 2
HOU N P		3	0- 0
1970 SD N P		42	2- 2
BRTR		188	11-12

WILLIS, VICTOR GAZAWAY "VIC"
B.APR.12,1876 WILMINGTON,DEL.
D.AUG.3,1947 ELKTON,MD.

1898 BOS N P		38	23-12
1899 BOS N P	38	40	27- 9
1900 BOS N P		28	9-16
1901 BOS N P		36	18-17
1902 BOS N P		51	27-19
1903 BOS N P	33	39	12-19
1904 BOS N P	43	49	18-25
1905 BOS N P		41	10-29
1906 PIT N P		41	23-13
1907 PIT N P		39	21-11
1908 PIT N P		41	23-11
1909 PIT N P		39	22-11
1910 STL N P		33	9-12
BRTR	501	515	242-204

WILLOUGHBY, CLAUDE WILLIAM "FLUNKY"
B.NOV.14,1898 FREDONIA,KAN.
D.AUG.14,1973 MC PHERSON,KAN.

1925 PHI N P		3	2- 1
1926 PHI N P		47	8-12
1927 PHI N P		35	3- 7
1928 PHI N P		35	6- 5
1929 PHI N P		49	15-14
1930 PHI N P		41	4-17
1931 PIT N P		9	0- 2
DRTR	219		38-58

WILLOUGHBY, JAMES ARTHUR "JIM"
B.JAN.31,1949 SALINAS,CAL.

1971 SF N P		2	0- 1
1972 SF N P		11	6- 4
1973 SF N P	39	41	4- 5
1974 SF N P	18	20	1- 4
1975 BOS A P		24	5- 2
1976 BOS A P		54	3-12
BRTR	148	152	19-28

WILLS

1884 WAS AA O		4	.133
KC U O		5	.150
		9	.143

WILLS, DAVIS BOWLES "DAVE"
B.JAN.26,1877 CHARLOTTESVILLE, VA.
D.OCT.12,1959 WASHINGTON,D.C.

| 1899 LOU N 1 | | 24 | .255 |
| BLTL | | | |

WILLS, MAURICE MORNING "MAURY"
B.OCT.2,1932 WASHINGTON,D.C.

1959 LA N S		83	.260
1960 LA N S		148	.295
1961 LA N S		148	.282
1962 LA N S		165	.299
1963 LA N S-3		134	.302
1964 LA N S-3		158	.275
1965 LA N S		158	.286
1966 LA N S-3		143	.273
1967 PIT N S-3		149	.302
1968 PIT N S-3		153	.278
1969 MON N 2-S		47	.222
LA N S		104	.297
1970 LA N S-3		132	.270
1971 LA N S-3		149	.281
1972 LA N S-3		71	.129
BBTR	1942		.281

WILLS, THEODORE CARL "TED"
B.FEB.9,1934 FRESNO,CAL.

1959 BOS A P		9	2- 6
1960 BOS A P	15	16	1- 1
1961 BOS A P		17	3- 2
1962 BOS A P		1	0- 0
CIN N P		26	0- 2
1965 CHI A P		15	2- 0
BLTL	83	84	8-11

WILLSON, FRANK HOXIE
B.NOV.3,1896 BLOOMINGTON,NEB.
D.APR.17,1964 UNION GAP,WAS.

1918 CHI A H		4	.000
1927 CHI A O		7	.100
BLTL		11	.091

WILMOT, WALTER ROBERT
B.OCT.18,1863 PLOVER,WIS.
D.FEB.1,1929 CHICAGO,ILL.

1888 WAS N O		119	.224
1889 WAS N O		107	.301
1890 CHI N O		139	.278
1891 CHI N O		120	.285
1892 CHI N O		92	.220
1893 CHI N O		93	.318
1894 CHI N O		135	.331
1895 CHI N O		108	.299
1897 NY N O		13	.242
1898 NY N O		34	.246

WILSHERE, VERNON SPRAGUE "WHITEY"
B.AUG.3,1912 SKANEATELES,N.Y.

1934 PHI A P		9	0- 1
1935 PHI A P		27	9- 9
1936 PHI A P		5	1- 2
BLTL		41	10-12

WILSHUSEN, TERRY WAYNE
B.MAR.22,1949 ATASCADERO,CAL.

| 1973 CAL A P | | 1 | 0- 0 |
| BRTR | | | |

WILSON, ARCHIE CLIFTON
B.NOV.25,1923 LOS ANGELES,CAL.

1951 NY A O		6	.000
1952 NY A H		3	.500
WAS A O		26	.208
BOS A O		18	.263
BRTR		51	.221

WILSON, ARTHUR EARL
B.DEC.11,1885 MACON,ILL.
D.JUNE 12,1960

1908 NY N C		1	.000
1909 NY N C		17	.238
1910 NY N C		26	.269
1911 NY N C		64	.302
1912 NY N C		65	.289
1913 NY N C		54	.190
1914 CHI F C		138	.287
1915 CHI F C		96	.309
1916 PIT N C		53	.258
CHI N C		36	.193
1917 CHI N C		81	.213
1918 BOS N C		89	.211
1919 BOS N C-1		71	.257
1920 BOS N O		16	.053
1921 CLE A C		2	.000
BRTR		809	.258

WILSON, ARTHUR LEE
B.OCT.28,1920 SPRINGFIELD,ALA.

| 1951 NY N 1-2-S | | 19 | .182 |
| BLTL | | | |

WILSON, A. PARKE
B.OCT.26,1867 KEITHSBURG,ILL.
D.DEC.20,1934

1893 NY N C		29	.280
1894 NY N C		45	.329
1895 NY N C		62	.243
1896 NY N C		69	.230
1897 NY N C		44	.310
1898 NY N O		1	.000
1899 NY N C-1		93	.268
		343	.270

WILSON, A. PETER "PETE"

1908 NY A P		7	3- 3
1909 NY A P		14	5- 6
TL		21	8- 9

WILSON, CHARLES MAX "MAXIE"
B.JUNE 3,1916 HAW RIVER,N.C.

1940 PHI N P		3	0- 0
1946 WAS A P		9	0- 1
BLTL		12	0- 1

WILSON, CHARLES WOODROW
B.JAN.13,1906 CLINTON,S.C.
D.DEC.19,1970 ROCHESTER,N.Y.

1931 BOS N 3		16	.190
1932 STL N S		24	.198
1933 STL N S		1	.000
1935 STL N 3		16	.323
BBTR		57	.215

WILSON, DONALD EDWARD "DON"
B.FEB.15,1945 MONROE,LA.
D.JAN.5,1975 HOUSTON,TEX.

1966 HOU N P		1	1- 0
1967 HOU N P		31	10- 9
1968 HOU N P	33	34	13-16
1969 HOU N P		34	16-12
1970 HOU N P	29	30	11- 6
1971 HOU N P		35	16-10
1972 HOU N P		33	15-10
1973 HOU N P		37	11-16
1974 HOU N P		33	11-13
BRTR	266	268	104-92

WILSON, DUANE LEWIS
B.JUNE 29,1934 WICHITA,KAN.

| 1958 BOS A P | | 2 | 0- 0 |
| BLTL | | | |

WILSON, EDWARD FRANCIS
B.SEPT.7,1910 NEW HAVEN,CONN.

1936 BRO N O		52	.347
1937 BRO N O		36	.222
BLTL		88	.317

WILSON, FINIS ELBERT
B.DEC.9,1889 EAST FORK,KY.
D.MAR.9,1959 CORAL GABLES,FLA.

1914 BRO F P		2	0- 1
1915 BRO F P		18	1- 8
BLTL		20	1- 9

WILSON, FRANCIS EDWARD "SQUASH"
B.APR.19,1901 MALDEN,MASS.
D.NOV.25,1974 LEICESTER,MASS.

1924 BOS N O		61	.237
1925 BOS N O		12	.419
1926 BOS N O		87	.237
1928 CLE A H		2	.000
STL A O		6	.000
BLTR		168	.246

WILSON, FRANK EALTON "ZEKE"
B.DEC.24,1869 BENTON,ALA.
D.APR.26,1928

1895 BOS N P		6	2- 4
CLE N P		11	5- 2
1896 CLE N P		29	17-10
1897 CLE N P	29	35	14-14
1898 CLE N P	32	34	13-18
1899 STL N P		5	1- 1
	112	120	52-49

WILSON, GEORGE ARCHIBALD W. "HICKIE"
B.BROOKLYN,N.Y.

| 1884 BPO AA C-O | | 24 | .214 |

WILSON, GEORGE FRANK "SQUANTO"
B.MAR.29,1889 OLD TOWN,ME.
D.MAR.26,1967 WINTHROP,MAINE

1911 DET A C		5	.187
1914 BOS A 1		1	.000
BBTR		6	.187

WILSON, GEORGE PEACOCK "ICE HOUSE"
B.SEPT.14,1912 MARICOPA,CAL.
D.OCT.13,1973 BERKELEY,CAL.

| 1934 DET A H | | 1 | .000 |
| BR | | | |

WILSON, GEORGE PEPPER "GARRY"
(SEE GEORGE PEPPER PRENTISS)

WILSON, GEORGE WASHINGTON "TEDDY"
B.AUG.30,1925 CHEPRYVILLE,N.C.
D.OCT.29,1974 GASTONIA,N.C.

1952 CHI A O		8	.111
NY N 1-O		62	.241
1953 NY N H		11	.125
1956 NY N O		53	.132
NY A O		11	.167
BLTR		145	.191

YR CL LEA POS GP G REC

WILSON, GOMER RUSSELL "TEX"
B.JULY 8,1902 TRENTON,TEX.
D.SEPT.15,1946
1924 BRO N P   2   0- 0
       BRTL

WILSON, GRADY HERBERT
B.NOV.23,1922 COLUMBUS,GA.
1948 PIT N S   12   .100
       BRTR

WILSON, HENRY C.
B.BALTIMORE,MD.
1898 BAL N C   1   .000

WILSON, HOWARD P. "HIGHBALL"
B.PHILADELPHIA,PA.
1899 CLE N P   1   0- 1
1902 PHI A P   13   7- 4
1903 WAS A P   31 32   8-18
1904 WAS A P   3   4   0- 3
       TR   48 50 15-26

WILSON, HOWARD WILLIAM "CHINK"
1906 WAS A P   1   0- 1

WILSON, JAMES "JIMMIE"
B.JULY 23,1900 PHILADELPHIA,PA.
D.JUNE 1,1947
1923 PHI N C-O   85   .262
1924 PHI N C-1-O   95   .279
1925 PHI N C-O   108   .328
1926 PHI N C-O   90   .305
1927 PHI N C-O   128   .275
1928 PHI N C-O   21   .300
     STL N C-O   120   .258
1929 PHI N C-O   120   .325
1930 STL N C-O   107   .318
1931 STL N C-O   115   .274
1932 STL N C-O   92   .248
1933 STL N C-O   113   .255
1934 STL N M-C   91   .292
1935 STL N M-C-2   93   .279
1936 STL N M-C   85   .278
1937 STL N M-C   39   .276
1938 STL N M-C   3   .000
1939 CIN N C   4   .333
1940 CIN N C   16   .243
       BRTR   1525   .284
NON-PLAYING MANAGER
CHI(N) 1941-44

WILSON, JAMES ALGER "JIM"
B.FEB.20,1922 SAN DIEGO,CAL.
1945 BOS A P   23 25   6- 8
1946 BOS A P   1   0- 0
1948 STL A P   4   0- 0
1949 PHI A P   2   0- 0
1951 BOS N P   20   7- 7
1952 BOS N P   33 12-14
1953 MIL N P   20   4- 9
1954 MIL N P   27   8- 2
1955 BAL A P   34 12-18
1956 BAL A P   7   4- 2
     CHI A P   28   9-12
1957 CHI A P   30 31 15- 8
1958 CHI A P   28   9- 9
       BRTR 257 260 86-89

WILSON, JAMES GARRETT "GARY"
B.JAN.12,1878 BALTIMORE,MD.
1902 BOS A 2   3   .181
       TR

WILSON, JOHN FRANCIS
"BLACK JACK"
B.APR.12,1912 PORTLAND,ORE.
1934 PHI A P   2   0- 1
     BOS A P   23   3- 4
1936 BOS A P   43 44   6- 8
1937 BOS A P   51 16-10
1938 BOS A P   37 15-15
1939 BOS A P   36 37 11-11
1940 BOS A P   41 12- 6
1941 BOS A P   27   4-13
1942 WAS A P   12   1- 4
     DET A P   9   0- 0
       BRTR 281 283 68-72

WILSON, JOHN NICODEMUS
B.JUNE 15,1890 BOONSBORO,MD.
D.SEPT.23,1954 ANNAPOLIS,MD.
1913 WAS A P   3   0- 0

WILSON, JOHN OWEN "CHIEF"
B.AUG.21,1883 AUSTIN,TEX.
D.FEB.22,1954
1908 PIT N O   144   .227
1909 PIT N O   154   .273
1910 PIT N O   146   .276
1911 PIT N O   146   .300
1912 PIT N O   152   .300
1913 PIT N O   155   .266
1914 STL N O   154   .259
1915 STL N O   107   .276
1916 STL N O   120   .239
       BLTR   1278   .268

WILSON, JOHN SAMUEL
B.APR.25,1905 COAL CITY,ALA.
1927 BOS A P   5   0- 2
1928 BOS A P   2   0- 0
       BRTR   7   0- 2

WILSON, LESTER WILBUR
B.JULY 15,1885 EDMONDS,WASH.
1911 BOS A O   4   .000
       BLTR

WILSON, LEWIS ROBERT "HACK"
B.APR.26,1900 ELLWOOD CITY,PA.
D.NOV.23,1948 BALTIMORE,MD.
1923 NY N O   3   .200
1924 NY N O   107   .295
1925 NY N O   62   .239
1926 CHI N O   142   .321
1927 CHI N O   146   .318
1928 CHI N O   145   .313
1929 CHI N O   150   .345
1930 CHI N O   155   .356
1931 CHI N O   112   .261
1932 BRO N O   135   .297
1933 BRO N 2-O   117   .267
1934 BRO N O   67   .262
     PHI N O   7   .100
       BRTR   1348   .307

WILSON, ROBERT
B.FEB.22,1928 MEXIA,TEX.
1958 LA N O   3   .200
       BRTR

WILSON, ROBERT EARL
"EARL"
(NAME CHANGED FROM
WILSON, EARL LAWRENCE)
B.OCT.2,1935 PONCHATOULA,LA.
1959 BOS A P   9   1- 1
1960 BOS A P   13 15   3- 2
1962 BOS A P   31 35 12- 8
1963 BOS A P   37 38 11-16
1964 BOS A P   33 54 11-12
1965 BOS A P   36 47 13-14
1966 BOS A P   15 18   5- 5
     DET A P   23 27 13- 6
1967 DET A P   39 52 22-11
1968 DET A P   34 40 13-12
1969 DET A P   35 37 12-10
1970 DET A P   18   4- 6
     SD N P   15   1- 6
       BRTR 338 405 121-109

WILSON, ROBERT JAMES "RED"
B.MAR.7,1929 MILWAUKEE,WIS.
1951 CHI A C   4   .273
1952 CHI A C   2   .000
1953 CHI A C   71   .250
1954 CHI A C   8   .200
     DET A C   54   .282
1955 DET A C   78   .220
1956 DET A C   78   .289
1957 DET A C   59   .242
1958 DET A C   103   .299
1959 DET A C   67   .263
1960 DET A C   45   .216
     CLE A C   32   .216
       BRTR   601   .258

WILSON, ROY EDWARD
B.SEPT.13,1896 FOSTER,IOWA
1928 CHI A P   1   0- 0
       BLTL

WILSON, SAMUEL MARSHALL "MIKE"
B.DEC.2,1896 GLENSIDE,PA.
1921 PIT N C   5   .000
       BRTR

WILSON, SAMUEL O'NEIL
B.JUNE 14,1935 LEXINGTON,TENN.
1960 SF N C   6   .000
       BLTR

WILSON, THOMAS C.
B.1889
1914 WAS A C   1   .000
       BRTR

WILSON, WALTER WOOD
B.NOV.24,1913 GLENN,GA.
1945 DET A P   25   1- 3
       BLTR

WILSON, WILLIAM
B.OCT.28,1867 HANNIBAL,MO.
1890 PIT N C-1-O   83   .213
1897 LOU N C   106   .218
1898 LOU N C   30   .182
                  219   .211

WILSON, WILLIAM CLARENCE "LANK"
B.JULY 20,1896 KISER,N.C.
D.AUG.31,1962
1920 DET A P   3   1- 1
       BRTR

WILSON, WILLIAM DONALD "BILL"
B.NOV.6,1928 CENTRAL CITY,NEB.
1950 CHI A O   3   .000
1953 CHI A O   9   .059
1954 CHI A O   20   .171
     PHI A O   94   .238
1955 KC A P-O   1 98   0- 0
                        .223
       BRTR   1 224   0- 0
                        .222

WILSON, WILLIAM HARLAN "BILL"
B.SEP.21,1942 POMEROY,OHIO
1969 PHI N P   37   2- 5
1970 PHI N P   37   1- 0
1971 PHI N P-3   38   4- 6
                        .100
1972 PHI N P   23   1- 1
1973 PHI N P   44   1- 3
       BRTR   179   9-15
                        .083

WILSON, WILLIE JAMES
B.JULY 9,1955 MONTGOMERY,ALA.
1976 KC A O   12   .167
       BRTR

WILSONHOLM
1883 PHI N C-O   3   .091

WILTSE, GEORGE LEROY "HOOKS"
B.SEPT.8,1880 HAMILTON,N.Y.
D.JAN.21,1959
1904 NY N P   25 13- 3
1906 NY N P   32 33 14- 7
1907 NY N P   38 38 16-11
1908 NY N P   33 34 13-12
1909 NY N P   44 23-14
1910 NY N P   37 20-11
1911 NY N P   36 14-12
1912 NY N P   30 12- 9
1913 NY N P   17 28   9- 6
1914 NY N P   20 20   0- 0
1915 BRO F P   18 19   3- 5
       BRTL 358 367 138-91

WILTSE, HAROLD JAMES "WHITEY"
B.AUG.6,1903 CLAY CITY,ILL.
1926 BOS A P   37   8-15
1927 BOS A P   36 10-18
1928 BOS A P   2   0- 2
     STL A P   26   2- 5
1931 PHI N P   1   0- 0
       BLTL   102 20-40

WILTSE, LEWIS DE WITT "SNAKE"
B.DEC.5,1871 BOUCKVILLE,N.Y.
D.AUG.25,1928
1901 PHI N P   7   1- 4
     PHI A P   19 14- 5
1902 PHI A P   20   8- 8
     BAL A P-1- 16 35   7- 9
            2-O   .296
1903 NY A P   4   0- 3
       BRTL   66 85 30-29
                        .276

YR	CL	LEA	POS	GP	G	REC

WINCENIAK, EDWARD JOSEPH "ED"
B.APR.16,1929 CHICAGO,ILL.

YR	CL	LEA	POS	GP	G	REC
1956	CHI	N	2-3		15	.118
1957	CHI	N	2-S-3		17	.240
	BRTR				32	.209

WINCHELL, FREDERICK RUSSELL
(REAL NAME FREDERICK COOK)
B.JAN.23,1882 ARLINGTON,MASS.
D.AUG.8,1958 TORONTO,ONT.,CAN.

YR	CL	LEA	POS	GP	G	REC
1909	CLE	A	P		4	0- 3

WINDHORN, GORDON RAY "GORDIE"
B.DEC.19,1933 WATSEKA,ILL.

YR	CL	LEA	POS	GP	G	REC
1959	NY	A	O		7	.000
1961	LA	N	O		34	.242
1962	KC	A	O		14	.158
	LA	A	O		40	.178
	BRTR				95	.176

WINDLE, WILLIS BREWER
B.DEC.13,1905 GALENA,KAN.

YR	CL	LEA	POS	GP	G	REC
1928	PIT	N	1		1	1.000
1929	PIT	N	1		2	.000
	BLTL				3	.500

WINE, ROBERT PAUL "BOBBY"
B.SEP.17,1938 NEW YORK,N.Y.

YR	CL	LEA	POS	GP	G	REC
1960	PHI	N	S		4	.143
1962	PHI	N	S-3		112	.244
1963	PHI	N	S-3		142	.215
1964	PHI	N	S-3		126	.212
1965	PHI	N	1-S		139	.228
1966	PHI	N	S-O		46	.236
1967	PHI	N	1-S		135	.190
1968	PHI	N	S-3		27	.169
1969	MON	N	1=S+3		121	.200
1970	MON	N	S		159	.232
1971	MON	N	S		119	.200
1972	MON	N	2-S-3		34	.222
	BRTR				1164	.215

WINCAPPLE, EDWARD "LEFTY"
B.AUG.10,1906 SALEM,MASS.

YR	CL	LEA	POS	GP	G	REC
1929	WAS	A	P		1	0- 0
	BLIL					

WINEGARNER, RALPH LEE
B.OCT.29,1909 BENTON,KAN.

YR	CL	LEA	POS	GP	G	REC
1930	CLE	A	3		5	.455
1932	CLE	A	P	5	7	1- 0
1934	CLE	A	P-O	22	32	5- 4
						.196
1935	CLE	A	P-1-3-O	25	65	2- 2
						.310
1936	CLE	A	P	9	18	0- 0
1949	STL	A	P		9	0- 0
	BRTR			70	136	8- 6
						.276

WINFIELD, DAVID MARK "DAVE"
B.OCT.3,1951 ST.PAUL,MINN.

YR	CL	LEA	POS	GP	G	REC
1973	SD	N	1-O		56	.277
1974	SD	N	O		145	.265
1975	SD	N	O		143	.267
1976	SD	N	O		137	.283
	BRTR				481	.272

WINFORD, JAMES HAROLD "COWBOY"
B.OCT.9,1909 SHELBYVILLE,TENN.

YR	CL	LEA	POS	GP	G	REC
1932	STL	N	P		4	1- 3
1934	STL	N	P		5	0- 2
1935	STL	N	P		2	0- 0
1936	STL	N	P		39	11-10
1937	STL	N	P		16	2- 4
1938	BRO	N	P		2	0- 1
	BRTR				68	14-18

WINGARD, ERNEST JAMES "JIM"
B.OCT.17,1900 PRATTVILLE,ALA.

YR	CL	LEA	POS	GP	G	REC
1924	STL	A	P	36	37	13-12
1925	STL	A	P-O	32	34	9-10
						.288
1926	STL	A	P	39	42	5- 8
1927	STL	A	P	38	42	2-13
	BLTL			145	155	29-43
						.232

WINGFIELD, FREDERICK DAVIS "TED"
B.AUG.7,1899 BEDFORD,VA.
D.JULY 18,1975 JOHNSON CITY, TENN.

YR	CL	LEA	POS	GP	G	REC
1923	WAS	A	P		1	0- 0
1924	WAS	A	P		4	0- 0
	BOS	A	P		4	0- 2
1925	BOS	A	P		41	12-19
1926	BOS	A	P		43	11-16
1927	BOS	A	P	20	22	1- 7
	BRTR			113	115	24-44

WINGO, ABSALOM HOLBROOK "RED"
B.MAY 6,1898 NORCORSS,GA.
D.OCT.9,1964 DETROIT,MICH.

YR	CL	LEA	POS	GP	G	REC
1919	PHI	A	O		15	.305
1924	DET	A	O		78	.287
1925	DET	A	O		130	.370
1926	DET	A	O		108	.282
1927	DET	A	O		75	.234
1928	DET	A	O		87	.285
	BLTR				493	.308

WINGO, EDMUND
(REAL NAME EDMOND LA RIVIERE)
B.OCT.3,1895 ST.ANNE DE BELLEVUE,QUE.,CANADA
D.DEC.6,1964

YR	CL	LEA	POS	GP	G	REC
1920	PHI	A	C		1	.250
	BRTR					

WINGO, IVY BROWN
B.JULY 8,1890 NORCROSS,GA.
D.MAR.1,1941

YR	CL	LEA	POS	GP	G	REC
1911	STL	N	C		18	.211
1912	STL	N	C		100	.265
1913	STL	N	C		112	.254
1914	STL	N	C		80	.300
1915	CIN	N	C-O		119	.221
1916	CIN	N	M-C		119	.245
1917	CIN	N	C		121	.266
1918	CIN	N	C-O		100	.254
1919	CIN	N	C		76	.273
1920	CIN	N	C-2		108	.264
1921	CIN	N	C		97	.268
1922	CIN	N	C		80	.284
1923	CIN	N	C		61	.263
1924	CIN	N	C-1		66	.286
1925	CIN	N	C		55	.205
1926	CIN	N	C		7	.200
1929	CIN	N	C		1	.000
	BLTL				1320	.260

WINHAM, LAFAYETTE SHARKEY "LEFTY LAVE"
B.OCT.23,1881 BROOKLYN,N.Y.
D.SEPT.11,1951 BROOKLYN,N.Y.

YR	CL	LEA	POS	GP	G	REC
1902	BRO	N	P		1	0- 0
1903	PIT	N	P		5	3- 1
	BLTL				6	3- 1

WINKELMAN

YR	CL	LEA	POS	GP	G	REC
1886	WAS	N	P		1	0- 1
	BLTL					

WINKELMAN, GEORGE EDWARD
B.FEB.18,1865 WASHINGTON,D.C.
D.MAY 19,1960 WASHINGTON,D.C.

YR	CL	LEA	POS	GP	G	REC
1883	LOU	AA	O		4	.000

WINKLES, BOBBY BROOKS
B.MAR.11,1930 TUCKERMAN,ARK.
NON-PLAYING MANAGER
CAL(A) 1973-74

WINN, GEORGE BENJAMIN
B.OCT.26,1897 PERRY,GA.

YR	CL	LEA	POS	GP	G	REC
1919	BOS	A	P		3	0- 0
1922	CLE	A	P		8	1- 2
1923	CLE	A	P		1	0- 0
	BLTL				12	1- 2

WINSETT, JOHN THOMAS "LONG TOM"
B.NOV.24,1909 MC KENZIE,TENN.

YR	CL	LEA	POS	GP	G	REC
1930	BOS	A	H		1	.000
1931	BOS	A	O		64	.198
1933	BOS	A	O		6	.083
1935	STL	N	O		7	.500
1936	BRO	N	O		22	.235
1937	BRO	N	P-O	1	118	0- 0
						.237
1938	BRO	N	O		12	.300
	BLTR			1	230	0- 0
						.237

WINSTON, HENRY RUDOLPH
B.JUNE 15,1909 YOUNGVILLE,N.C.
D.FEB.4,1974 JACKSONVILLE,FLA.

YR	CL	LEA	POS	GP	G	REC
1933	PHI	A	P		1	0- 0
1936	BRO	N	P		14	1- 3
	BLTR				15	1- 3

WINTER, GEORGE LOVINGTON "SASSAFRAS"
B.APR.27,1878 NEW PROVIDENCE,PA
D.MAY 26,1951

YR	CL	LEA	POS	GP	G	REC
1901	BOS	A	P		28	17-10
1902	BOS	A	P		20	11- 9
1903	BOS	A	P		23	10- 8
1904	BOS	A	P		20	8- 4
1905	BOS	A	P		34	14-16
1906	BOS	A	P		29	6-18
1907	BOS	A	P		35	12-15
1908	BOS	A	P		22	3-14
	DET	A	P		7	2- 5
	TR				218	83-99

WINTERS, CLARENCE JESSE
B.SEPT.7,1900 DETROIT,MICH.
D.JUNE 29,1945

YR	CL	LEA	POS	GP	G	REC
1924	BOS	A	P		4	0- 1

WINTERS, JESSE FRANKLIN "BUCK"
B.DEC.22,1895 ABILENE,TEX.

YR	CL	LEA	POS	GP	G	REC
1919	NY	N	P		16	1- 2
1920	NY	N	P		21	0- 0
1921	PHI	N	P		18	5-10
1922	PHI	N	P		34	6- 6
1923	PHI	N	P		21	1- 6
	BRTR				110	13-24

WIRTS, ELWOOD VERNON "KETTLE"
B.OCT.30,1897 SACRAMENTO,CAL.
D.JULY 12,1968 SACRAMENTO,CAL.

YR	CL	LEA	POS	GP	G	REC
1921	CHI	N	C		7	.182
1922	CHI	N	C		31	.172
1923	CHI	N	C		5	.200
1924	CHI	A	C		5	.083
	BRTR				48	.165

WISE, ARCHIBALD EDWIN
B.JULY 31,1912 WAXAHACHIE,TEX.

YR	CL	LEA	POS	GP	G	REC
1932	CHI	A	P		3	0- 0
	BRTR					

WISE, HUGH EDWARD
B.MAR.9,1906 CAMPBELLSVILLE,KY.

YR	CL	LEA	POS	GP	G	REC
1930	DET	A	C		2	.333
	BBTR					

WISE, KENDALL COLE "CASEY"
B.SEPT.8,1932 LAFAYETTE,IND.

YR	CL	LEA	POS	GP	G	REC
1957	CHI	N	2-S		43	.179
1958	MIL	N	2-S-3		31	.197
1959	MIL	N	2-S		22	.171
1960	DET	A	2-S-3		30	.147
	BBTR				126	.175

WISE, NICHOLAS JOSEPH
B.JUNE 15,1867 BOSTON,MASS.
D.JAN.15,1923

YR	CL	LEA	POS	GP	G	REC
1888	BOS	N	C		1	.000
	BRTR					

WISE, RICHARD CHARLES "RICK"
B.SEP.13,1945 JACKSON,MICH.

YR	CL	LEA	POS	GP	G	REC
1964	PHI	N	P		25	5- 3
1966	PHI	N	P	22	23	5- 6
1967	PHI	N	P		36	11-11
1968	PHI	N	P		30	9-15
1969	PHI	N	P		33	15-13
1970	PHI	N	P	35	37	13-14
1971	PHI	N	P	38	39	17-14
1972	STL	N	P		35	16-16
1973	STL	N	P		35	16-12
1974	BOS	A	P		9	3- 4
1975	BOS	A	P		35	19-12
1976	BOS	A	P		34	14-11
	BRTR			367	371	143-131

WISE, ROY OGDEN
B.NOV.18,1924 SPRINGFIELD,ILL.

YR	CL	LEA	POS	GP	G	REC
1944	PIT	N	P		2	0- 0
	BBTR					

YR	CL	LEA	POS	GP	G	REC

WISE, SAMUEL WASHINGTON "MODOC"
B.AUG.18,1857 AKRON,OHIO
D.JAN.22,1910 AKRON,OHIO

YR	CL	LEA	POS	GP	G	REC
1881	DET	N	3		1	.500
1882	BOS	N	S-3		77	.225
1883	BOS	N	S		95	.270
1884	BOS	N	2-S		109	.220
1885	BOS	N	2-S-O		107	.283
1886	BOS	N	1-2-S		96	.289
1887	BOS	N	S-O		110	.380
	BOS	N	S		104	.239
1889	WAS	N	2-S		120	.250
1890	BUF	P	2		119	.295
1891	BAL	AA	2		103	.250
1893	WAS	N	2-3		121	.317
	TR				1162	.285

WISE, WILLIAM E.
B.MAR.15,1861 WASHINGTON,D.C.
D.MAY 5,1940 WASHINGTON,D.C.

YR	CL	LEA	POS	GP	G	REC
1882	BAL	AA	P-O	3	5	1- 1
						.150
1884	WAS	U	P-O	44	78	23-20
						.233
1886	WAS	N	P		1	0- 1
				48	84	24-22
						.224

WISNER, JOHN HENRY
B.NOV.5,1899 GRAND RAPIDS,MICH.

YR	CL	LEA	POS	GP	G	REC
1919	PIT	N	P		4	1- 0
1920	PIT	N	P		17	1- 3
1925	NY	N	P		24	0- 0
1926	NY	N	P		5	2- 2
	BR	TR			50	4- 5

WISNER, PHILIP N.
B.WASHINGTON,D.C.

YR	CL	LEA	POS	GP	G	REC
1895	WAS	N	S		1	.000
	TR					

WISSLER, LEWIS
(PLAYED UNDER NAME OF
LEWIS WHISTLER)

WISSMAN, DAVID ALVIN "DAVE"
B.FEB.17,1941 GREENFIELD,MASS.

YR	CL	LEA	POS	GP	G	REC
1964	PIT	N	O		16	.148
	BLTR					

WISTERT, FRANCIS MICHAEL "WHITEY"
B.FEB.2,1912 CHICAGO,ILL.

YR	CL	LEA	POS	GP	G	REC
1934	CIN	N	P	2	3	0- 1
	BRTR					

WISTERZIL, GEORGE J. "TEX"
B.MAR.7,1891 DETROIT,MICH.
D.JUNE 27,1964 SAN ANTONIO,TEX.

YR	CL	LEA	POS	GP	G	REC
1914	BRO	F	3		149	.253
1915	BRO	F	3		36	.311
	CHI	F	3		7	.250
	STL	F	3		50	.240
	BRTR				242	.258

WITEK, NICHOLAS JOSEPH "MICKEY"
B.DEC.19,1915 LUZERNE,PA.

YR	CL	LEA	POS	GP	G	REC
1940	NY	N	2-S		119	.256
1941	NY	N	2		26	.362
1942	NY	N	2		148	.260
1943	NY	N	2		153	.314
1946	NY	N	2-3		82	.264
1947	NY	N	2		51	.219
1949	NY	A	H		1	1.000
	BRTR				580	.277

WITHERUP, LE ROY FOSTER
B.JULY 26,1887 N.WASHINGTON,PA.
D.DEC.23,1941

YR	CL	LEA	POS	GP	G	REC
1906	BOS	N	P		8	0- 3
1908	WAS	A	P		6	2- 4
1909	WAS	A	P		12	2- 6
					26	4-13

WITHROW, FRANK BLAINE
B.JUNE 14,1892 GREENWOOD,MO.
D.SEPT.5,1966

YR	CL	LEA	POS	GP	G	REC
1920	PHI	N	C		48	.182
1922	PHI	N	C		10	.333
	BRTR				58	.208

WITHROW, RAYMOND WALLACE "CORKY"
B.NOV.28,1937 HIGH COAL,W.VA.

YR	CL	LEA	POS	GP	G	REC
1963	STL	N	O		6	.000
	BRTR					

WITT, GEORGE ADRIAN
B.NOV.9,1933 LONG BEACH,CAL.

YR	CL	LEA	POS	GP	G	REC
1957	PIT	N	P		1	0- 1
1958	PIT	N	P		18	9- 2
1959	PIT	N	P		15	0- 7
1960	PIT	N	P		10	1- 2
1961	PIT	A	P		9	0- 1
1962	LA	A	P		5	1- 1
	HOU	N	P		8	0- 2
	BRTR				66	11-16

WITT, LAWTON WALTER "WHITEY"
(REAL NAME
LADISLAW WALDEMAR WITTKOWSKI)
B.SEPT.28,1895 ORANGE,MASS.

YR	CL	LEA	POS	GP	G	REC
1916	PHI	A	S		143	.245
1917	PHI	A	S		128	.252
1919	PHI	A	2-O		122	.267
1920	PHI	A	O		65	.321
1921	PHI	A	O		154	.315
1922	NY	A	O		140	.297
1923	NY	A	O		146	.314
1924	NY	A	O		147	.297
1925	NY	A	O		31	.200
1926	BRO	N	O		63	.259
	BLTR				1139	.287

WITTE, JEROME CHARLES
B.JULY 30,1917 ST.LOUIS,MO.

YR	CL	LEA	POS	GP	G	REC
1946	STL	A	1		18	.192
1947	STL	A	1		34	.141
	BRTR				52	.159

WITTIG, JOHN CARL "JOHNNY"
B.JUNE 16,1914 BALTIMORE,MD.

YR	CL	LEA	POS	GP	G	REC
1938	NY	N	P		13	2- 3
1939	NY	N	P		5	0- 2
1941	NY	N	P		25	3- 5
1943	NY	N	P		40	5-15
1949	BOS	A	P		1	0- 0
	BRTR				84	10-25

WITTKOWSKI, LADISLAW WALDEMAR
(PLAYED UNDER NAME OF
LAWTON WALTER WITT)

WOCKENFUSS, JOHNNY BILTON "JOHN"
B.FEB.27,1949 WELCH,W.VA.

YR	CL	LEA	POS	GP	G	REC
1974	DET	A	C		13	.138
1975	DET	A	C		35	.229
1976	DET	A	C		60	.222
					108	.216

WOEHR, ANDREW EMIL
B.FEB.4,1898 FT.WAYNE,IND.

YR	CL	LEA	POS	GP	G	REC
1923	PHI	N	3		13	3341
1924	PHI	N	2-3		50	.217
	BRTR				63	.244

WOERLIN
B.ST.LOUIS,MO.

YR	CL	LEA	POS	GP	G	REC
1895	WAS	N	S		1	.333

WOHLFORD, JAMES EUGENE "JIM"
B.FEB.28,1951 VISALIA,CAL.

YR	CL	LEA	POS	GP	G	REC
1972	KC	A	2		15	.240
1973	KC	A	O-D		45	.266
1974	KC	A	O		143	.271
1975	KC	A	O		116	.255
1976	KC	A	2-O		107	.249
	BRTR				426	.261

WOJCIK, JOHN JOSEPH
B.APR.6,1942 OLEAN,N.Y.

YR	CL	LEA	POS	GP	G	REC
1962	KC	A	O		16	.302
1963	KC	A	O		19	.186
1964	KC	A	O		6	.136
	BLTR				41	.218

WOJEY, PETER PAUL "PETE"
B.DEC.1,1922 STOWE,PA.

YR	CL	LEA	POS	GP	G	REC
1954	BRO	N	P		14	1- 1
1956	DET	A	P		2	0- 0
1957	DET	A	P		2	0- 0
	BRTR				18	1- 1

WOLF, EMIL
B.1890

YR	CL	LEA	POS	GP	G	REC
1912	CLE	A	P		1	0- 0

WOLF, RAYMOND BERNARD "GRANDPA"
B.JULY 15,1904 CHICAGO,ILL.

YR	CL	LEA	POS	GP	G	REC
1927	CIN	N	1		1	.000

WOLF, WALTER BECK "WALLY"
B.JAN.5,1942 SOUTH GATE,CAL.

YR	CL	LEA	POS	GP	G	REC
1969	CAL	A	P		2	0- 0
1970	CAL	A	P		4	0- 0
	BRTR				6	0- 0

WOLF, WALTER FRANCIS
B.JUNE 10,1900 HARTFORD,CONN.
D.SEPT.25,1971 NEW ORLEANS,LA.

YR	CL	LEA	POS	GP	G	REC
1921	PHI	A	P		9	0- 0
	BRTL					

WOLF, WILLIAM V. "CHICKEN"
B.MAY 12,1862 LOUISVILLE,KY.
D.MAY 16,1903

YR	CL	LEA	POS	GP	G	REC
1882	LOU	AA	P-1-	1	78	0- 0
			S-3-O			.294
1883	LOU	AA	C-2-S-O		88	.250
1884	LOU	AA	C-O		112	.303
1885	LOU	AA	O		113	.288
1886	LOU	AA	O		129	.274
1887	LOU	AA	O		137	.324
1888	LOU	AA	S-O		127	.298
1889	LOU	AA	M-O		130	.291
1890	LOU	AA	M-O		134	.366
1891	LOU	AA	M-O		136	.250
1892	STL	N	M-O		4	.220
	BR			1	1188	0- 0
						.296

WOLFE, CHARLES HUNT
B.FEB.15,1899 WOLDSBURG,PA.
D.NOV.27,1957

YR	CL	LEA	POS	GP	G	REC
1923	PHI	A	P		3	0- 0
	BLTR					

WOLFE, EDWARD ANTHONY
B.JAN.2,1929 LOS ANGELES,CAL.

YR	CL	LEA	POS	GP	G	REC
1952	PIT	N	P		3	0- 0
	BRTR					

WOLFE, HARRY
B.JULY 7,1893 CLEVELAND,OHIO

YR	CL	LEA	POS	GP	G	REC
1917	CHI	N	S		5	.333
	PIT	N	2		2	.000
	BRTR				7	.200

WOLFE, ROY CHAMBERLAIN "POLLY"
B.SEPT.1,1888 KNOXVILLE,ILL.
D.NOV.21,1938

YR	CL	LEA	POS	GP	G	REC
1912	CHI	A	O		1	.000
1914	CHI	A	O		8	.214
	BLTR				9	.207

WOLFE, WILLIAM
B.JERSEY CITY,N.J.

YR	CL	LEA	POS	GP	G	REC
1902	PHI	N	P		1	0- 1

WOLFE, WILLIAM O.
B.JAN.7,1876 INDEPENDENCE,PA.
D.FEB.27,1953

YR	CL	LEA	POS	GP	G	REC
1903	NY	A	P		20	6- 9
1904	NY	A	P		7	0- 3
	WAS	A	P		18	6- 9
1905	WAS	A	P		27	9-14
1906	WAS	A	P		4	0- 3
	BRTR				76	21-38

WOLFF, ROGER FRANCIS
B.APR.10,1911 EVANSVILLE,ILL.

YR	CL	LEA	POS	GP	G	REC
1941	PHI	A	P		2	0- 2
1942	PHI	A	P		32	12-15
1943	PHI	A	P		41	10-15
1944	WAS	A	P		33	4-15
1945	WAS	A	P		33	20-10
1946	WAS	A	P		21	5- 8
1947	CLE	A	P		7	0- 0
	PIT	N	P		13	1- 4
	BRTR				182	52-69

WOLFGANG, MELDON JOHN
B.MAR.20,1880 ALBANY,N.Y.
D.JUNE 30,1947

YR	CL	LEA	POS	GP	G	REC
1914	CHI	A	P		24	9- 5
1915	CHI	A	P		17	2- 2
1916	CHI	A	P		28	4- 6
1917	CHI	A	P		5	0- 0
1918	CHI	A	P		5	0- 1
	BRTR				79	15-14

```
YR   CL LEA POS  GP   G   REC        YR   CL LEA POS  GP   G   REC        YR   CL LEA POS  GP   G   REC
```

WOLTER, HARRY MEIGS
B.JULY 11,1884 MONTEREY,CAL.
D.JULY 7,1970 PALO ALTO,CAL.
```
1907 CIN N  O             4  .133
     PIT N  P        1     0- 0
     STL N  P     3  12    0- 0
1909 BOS A  P-1  10  54    4- 3
                             .244
1910 NY  A  O           135  .267
1911 NY  A  O           122  .304
1912 NY  A  O            11  .393
1913 NY  A  O           127  .256
1917 CHI N  O           117  .249
     BLTL        14 583    4- 3
                             .270
```

WOLTERS, REINDERS ALBERTIS
"RINIE"
B.DEC.18,1842 SCHAANTZ,HOLLAND
D.JAN.3,1917
```
1871 MUT NA P            32 15-16
1872 CLE NA P-O   8  15   2- 6
                             .221
1873 RES NA P        1    0- 1
                 41  48  17-23
```

WOLVERTON, HARRY STERLING
"FIGHTING HARRY"
B.DEC.6,1873 MT.VERNON,OHIO
D.FEB.4,1937
```
1898 CHI N  3            13  .327
1899 CHI N  3            99  .295
1900 CHI N  3             3  .182
     PHI N  3            98  .280
1901 PHI N  3            92  .308
1902 WAS A  3            59  .257
     PHI N  3            54  .284
1903 PHI N  3           123  .308
1904 PHI N  3           102  .266
1905 BOS N  3           177  .225
1912 NY  A  M-O          33  .300
     TR                778  .279
```

WOMACK, HORACE GUY "DOOLEY"
B.AUG.25,1939 COLUMBIA,S.C.
```
1966 NY  A  P           42   7- 3
1967 NY  A  P           65   5- 6
1968 NY  A  P           45   3- 7
1969 HOU N  P           30   2- 1
     SEA A  P            9   2- 1
1970 OAK A  P            2   0- 0
     BLTR              193  19-18
```

WOMACK, SIDNEY KIRK
B.OCT.2,1897 GREENSBURG,LA.
D.AUG.8,1958
```
1926 BOS N  C            1  .000
     BRTR
```

WOOD, CHARLES ASHER "SPADES"
B.JAN.13,1909 SPARTANBURG,S.C.
```
1930 PIT N  P            9   4- 3
1931 PIT N  P           15   2- 6
     BLTL               24   6- 9
```

WOOD, CHARLES SPENCER "DOC"
B.FEB.28,1900 BATESVILLE,MISS.
D.NOV.3,1974 NEW ORLEANS,LA.
```
1923 PHI A  S            3  .333
     BRTR
```

WOOD, FRED S.
B.1863 HAMILTON,ONT.,CANADA
D.AUG.23,1933
```
1884 DET N  P-C-  1  28   0- 1
          S-O                .221
1885 BUF N  C            1  .250
                  1  29   0- 1
                             .222
```

WOOD, GEORGE A. "DANDY"
B.NOV.9,1858 BOSTON,MASS.
D.APR.4,1924
```
1880 WOR N  1-O          79  .243
1881 DET N  O            80  .296
1882 DET N  O            81  .263
1883 DET N  P-O   1      96  0- 0
                             .295
1884 DET N  3-O         112  .251
1885 DET N  P-S-  1      82  0- 0
          3-O                .290
1886 PHI N  O           106  .273
1887 PHI N  O           113  .342
1888 PHI N  O           105  .230
1889 PHI N  O            97  .251
     BAL AA O             3  .200
1890 PHI P  O           132  .304
1891 ATH AA M-O         131  .302
1892 BAL N  O            20  .183
     CIN N  O            30  .210
     BLTR        2 1267   0- 0
                             .278
```

WOOD, HARRY
B.BALTIMORE,MD.
```
1903 CIN N  O            2  .000
     BLTR
```

WOOD, JACOB "JAKE"
B.JUNE 22,1937 ELIZABETH,N.J.
```
1961 DET A  2          162  .258
1962 DET A  2          111  .226
1963 DET A  2-3         85  .271
1964 DET A  1-2-3-O     64  .232
1965 DET A  1-2-S-3     58  .288
1966 DET A  1-2-3       98  .252
1967 DET A  1-2         14  .050
     CIN N  O           16  .118
     BRTR             608  .250
```

WOOD, JAMES BURR
B.DEC.1,1844 BROOKLYN,N.Y.
D.NOV.30,1886
```
1871 CHI NA 2           28   -
1872 TRO NA M-2         25  .322
     ECK NA M-2          7  .176
1873 BAL NA 2           41   -
1874 BAL NA 2            1  .000
                       102   -
NON-PLAYING MANAGER
CHI(NA) 1874-75
```

WOOD, JOHN B.
```
1896 STL N  P           1   0- 0
```

WOOD, JOSEPH "SMOKEY JOE"
B.OCT.25,1889 KANSAS CITY,MO.
```
1908 BOS A  P            6   1- 1
1909 BOS A  P           24  11- 7
1910 BOS A  P           35  12-13
1911 BOS A  P           44  23-17
1912 BOS A  P           43  34- 5
1913 BOS A  P    22  23  11- 5
1914 BOS A  P    18  20   9- 3
1915 BOS A  P    25  29  14- 5
1917 CLE A  P     5  10   0- 1
1918 CLE A  2-O        119  .296
1919 CLE A  P-O   1  72   0- 0
                             .255
1920 CLE A  P-O   1  61   0- 0
                             .270
1921 CLE A  O           66  .366
1922 CLE A  O          142  .297
     BRTR       224 694 115-57
                             .284
```

WOOD, JOSEPH FRANK
B.MAY 20,1916 PIKE CO.,PA.
```
1944 BOS A  P           3   0- 1
     BRTR
```

WOOD, JOSEPH PERRY
B.OCT.3,1919 HOUSTON,TEX.
```
1943 DET A  2-3         60  .323
     BRTR
```

WOOD, KENNETH LANIER "KEN"
B.JULY 1,1924 LINCOLNTON,N.C.
```
1948 STL A  O           10  .083
1949 STL A  O            7  .000
1950 STL A  O          128  .225
1951 STL A  O          109  .237
1952 BOS A  O           15  .100
     WAS A  O           61  .238
1953 WAS A  O           12  .212
     BRTR             342  .224
```

WOOD, PETER BURKE
B.FEB.1,1857 HAMILTON,ONT.,CAN.
D.MAR.15,1923
```
1885 BUF N  P-1- 23  28   8-15
          O                  .212
1889 PHI N  P           3   1- 1
          TR     26  31   9-16
                             .205
```

WOOD, ROBERT LYNN
B.JULY 28,1865 THORN HILL,OHIO
D.MAY 22,1943 CHURCHILL,OHIO
```
1898 CIN N  C           30  .280
1899 CIN N  C           58  .317
1900 CIN N  C-3         34  .264
1901 CLE A  C           96  .289
1902 CLE A  C-1-2-3-    81  .286
          O
1904 DET A  C           49  .244
1905 DET A  C            8  .125
     BRTR             356 2280
```

WOOD, ROY WINTON
B.MAY 5,1893 LITTLE ROCK,ARK.
D.APR.6,1974 FAYETTEVILLE,ARK.
```
1913 PHI N  O           14  .285
1914 CLE A  1-O         72  .236
1915 CLE A  1           33  .193
     BRTR             119  .231
```

WOOD, WILBUR FORRESTER
B.OCT.22,1941 CAMBRIDGE,MASS.
```
1961 BOS A  P           6   0- 0
1962 BOS A  P           1   0- 0
1963 BOS A  P          25   0- 5
1964 BOS A  P           4   0- 0
     PIT N  P           3   0- 2
1965 PIT N  P          34   1- 1
1967 CHI A  P          51   4- 2
1968 CHI A  P          88  13-12
1969 CHI A  P          76  10-11
1970 CHI A  P          77   9-13
1971 CHI A  P          44  22-13
1972 CHI A  P          49  24-17
1973 CHI A  P          49  24-20
1974 CHI A  P          42  20-19
1975 CHI A  P          43  16-20
1976 CHI A  P           7   4- 3
     BRTL             599 147-138
```

WOODALL, CHARLES LAWRENCE
"LARRY"
B.JULY 26,1894 STAUNTON,VA.
D.MAY 6,1963 NEWTON,MASS.
```
1920 DET A  C           18  .245
1921 DET A  C           46  .363
1922 DET A  C           50  .344
1923 DET A  C           71  .277
1924 DET A  C           67  .309
1925 DET A  C           75  .205
1926 DET A  C           67  .233
1927 DET A  C           88  .280
1928 DET A  C           65  .210
1929 DET A  H            1  .000
     BRTR             548  .268
```

WOODBURN, EUGENE STEWART
B.AUG.20,1886 BLAIR,OHIO
D.JAN.18,1961 SANDUSKY,OHIO
```
1911 STL N  P          11   1- 5
1912 STL N  P          20   1- 4
     BRTR              31   2- 9
```

WOODCOCK, FRED WAYLAND
B.MAY 17,1868 WINCHENDON,MASS.
D.AUG.11,1943 ASHBURNHAM,MASS.
```
1892 PIT N  P           7   1- 3
     BLTL
```

WOODEND, GEORGE ANTHONY
B.DEC.9,1917 HARTFORD,CONN.
```
1944 BOS N  P           3   0- 0
     BRTR
```

```
YR  CL LEA POS   GP    G    REC
```

WOODESHICK, HAROLD JOSEPH "HAL"
B.AUG.24,1932 WILKES-BARRE,PA.
```
1956 DET A  P              2    0- 2
1958 CLE A  P             14    6- 6
1959 WAS A  P       31    32    2- 4
1960 WAS A  P             41    4- 5
1961 WAS A  P              7    3- 2
     DET A  P             12    1- 1
1962 HOU N  P             31    5-16
1963 HOU N  P             55   11- 9
1964 HOU N  P             61    2- 9
1965 HOU N  P             27    3- 4
     STL N  P             51    3- 2
1966 STL N  P             59    2- 1
1967 STL N  P             36    2- 1
     BRTL       427     428   44-62
```

WOODHEAD, JAMES "RED"
B.1851 ENGLAND
D.1881
```
1873 MAR NA S             1    .000
1879 SYR N  3            34    .169
                        35    .168
```

WOODLING, EUGENE RICHARD "GENE"
B.AUG.16,1922 AKRON,OHIO
```
1943 CLE A  O              8    .320
1946 CLE A  O             61    .188
1947 PIT N  O             22    .266
1949 NY  A  O            112    .270
1950 NY  A  O            122    .283
1951 NY  A  O            120    .281
1952 NY  A  O            122    .309
1953 NY  A  O            125    .306
1954 NY  A  O             97    .250
1955 BAL A  O             47    .221
     CLE A  O             79    .278
1956 CLE A  O            100    .262
1957 CLE A  O            133    .321
1958 BAL A  O            133    .276
1959 BAL A  O            140    .300
1960 BAL A  O            140    .283
1961 WAS A  O            110    .313
1962 WAS A  O             44    .280
     NY  N  O             81    .274
     BLTR              1796    .284
```

WOODMAN, DANIEL COURTNEY "COCOA"
B.JULY 8,1893 DANVERS,MASS.
D.DEC.14,1962
```
1914 BUF F  P             13    0- 0
1915 BUF F  P              6    0- 0
     BR                  19    0- 0
```

WOODRUFF, ORVILLE FRANCIS "SAM"
B.DEC.27,1876 CHILO,OHIO
D.JULY 22,1937
```
1899 NY  N  O             20    .246
1901 CLE A  O              1    .250
1904 CIN N  2-3          87    .190
1910 CIN N  3            21    .148
     BRTR               129    .192
```

WOODS, CLARENCE COFIELD
B.JUNE 11,1892 OHIO CO.,IND.
D.JULY 2,1969 RISING SUN,IND.
```
1914 IND F  P              2    0- 0
     BRTR
```

WOODS, GARY LEE
B.JULY 20,1954 SANTA BARBARA,CAL
```
1976 OAK A  O              6    .125
     BRTR
```

WOODS, GEORGE ROWLAND "PINKY"
B.MAY 22,1920 WATERBURY,CONN.
```
1943 BOS A  P             23    5- 6
1944 BOS A  P             38    4- 8
1945 BOS A  P             24    4- 7
     BRTR                85   13-21
```

WOODS, JAMES JEROME
B.SEPT.17,1939 CHICAGO,ILL.
```
1957 CHI N  H              2    .000
1960 PHI N  3             11    .176
1961 PHI N  3             23    .229
     BRTR                36    .207
```

WOODS, JOHN FULTON
B.JAN.18,1901 PRINCETON,W.VA.
D.OCT.4,1946
```
1924 BOS A  P              1    0- 0
     BRTR
```

WOODS, RONALD LAWRENCE "RON"
B.FEB.1,1943 HAMILTON,OHIO
```
1969 DET A  O             17    .267
     NY  A  O             72    .175
1970 NY  A  O             95    .227
1971 NY  A  O             25    .250
     MON N  O             51    .297
1972 MON N  O             97    .258
1973 MON N  O            135    .230
1974 MON N  O             90    .205
     BRTR               582    .233
```

WOODS, WALTER SYDNEY
B.APR.28,1875 RYE,N.H.
D.OCT.30,1951
```
1898 CHI N  P       22    41    9-13
1899 LOU N  P       22    40    8-13
1900 PIT N  P              1    0- 0
                    45    82   17-26
```

WOODSON, RICHARD LEE "DICK"
B.MAR.30,1945 OELWEIN,IOWA
```
1969 MIN A  P             44    7- 5
1970 MIN A  P             21    1- 2
1972 MIN A  P             36   14-14
1973 MIN A  P             23   10- 8
1974 MIN A  P              5    1- 1
     NY  A  P              8    1- 2
     BRTR               137   34-32
```

WOODWARD, FRANK RUSSELL
B.MAY 17,1896 NEW HAVEN,CONN.
D.JUNE 11,1961
```
1918 PHI N  P              2    0- 0
1919 PHI N  P             17    6- 9
     STL N  P             17    3- 5
1921 WAS A  P              3    0- 0
1922 WAS A  P              1    0- 0
1923 CHI A  P              2    0- 1
     BRTR                42    9-15
```

WOODWARD, WILLIAM FREDERICK "WOODY"
B.SEP.23,1942 MIAMI,FLA.
```
1963 MIL N  S             10    .000
1964 MIL N  1-2-S-3       77    .209
1965 MIL N  2-S          112    .208
1966 ATL N  2-S          144    .264
1967 ATL N  2-S          136    .226
1968 ATL N  2-S-3         12    .167
     CIN N  1-2-S         56    .244
1969 CIN N  2-S           97    .261
1970 CIN N  1-2-S-3      100    .223
1971 CIN N  2-S-3        136    .242
     BRTR               880    .236
```

WOOLDRIDGE, FLOYD LEWIS
B.AUG.25,1928 JERICO SPRINGS,MO
```
1955 STL N  P             18    2- 4
     BRTR
```

WOOTEN, EARL HAZELL "JINIOR"
B.JAN.16,1924 PELZER,S.C.
```
1947 WAS A  O              6    .083
1948 WAS A  P-1     1     88    0- 0
           O                   .256
     BRTL       1     94    0- 0
                             .241
```

WORDEN, FRED
```
1914 PHI A  P              1    0- 0
```

WORDSWORTH, FAVEL PERRY
B.JAN.1851 NEW YORK,N.Y.
D.AUG.2,1888
```
1873 RES NA S            10    -
```

WORKMAN, CHARLES THOMAS
B.JAN.6,1915 LEETON,MO.
D.JAN.3,1953
```
1938 CLE A  O              2    .400
1941 CLE A  H              9    .000
1943 BOS N  1-3-O        153    .249
1944 BOS N  3-O          140    .208
1945 BOS N  3-O          139    .274
1946 BOS N  O             25    .167
     PIT N  3-O           58    .221
     BLTR               526    .242
```

WORKMAN, HARRY HALL "HOGE"
B.SEPT.25,1899 HUNTINGTON,W.VA.
D.MAY 20,1972 FT.MYERS,FLA.
```
1924 BOS A  P             11    0- 0
     BRTR
```

WORKMAN, HENRY KILGARIFF "HANK"
B.FEB.5,1926 LOS ANGELES,CAL.
```
1950 NY  A  1              2    .200
     BLTR
```

WORKS, RALPH TALMADGE "JUDGE"
B.MAR.16,1888 PAYSON,ILL.
D.AUG.8,1941
```
1909 DET A  P             16    3- 1
1910 DET A  P             18    3- 6
1911 DET A  P             31   11- 5
1912 DET A  P             27    5-10
     CIN N  P              3    1- 1
1913 CIN N  P              4    0- 1
     BRTR                99   23-24
```

WORTH, HERBERT
```
1872 ATL NA O             1    .167
```

WORTHINGTON, ALLAN FULTON "AL" OR "RED"
B.FEB.5,1929 BIRMINGHAM,ALA.
```
1953 NY  N  P             20    4- 8
1954 NY  N  P             10    0- 2
1956 NY  N  P             28    7-14
1957 NY  N  P             55    8-11
1958 SF  N  P             54   11- 7
1959 SF  N  P             42    2- 3
1960 BOS A  P              6    0- 1
     CHI A  P              4    1- 1
1963 CIN N  P             50    4- 4
1964 CIN N  P              6    1- 0
     MIN A  P             41    5- 6
1965 MIN A  P             62   10- 7
1966 MIN A  P             65    6- 3
1967 MIN A  P             59    8- 9
1968 MIN A  P             54    4- 5
1969 MIN A  P             46    4- 1
     BRTR               602   75-82
```

WORTHINGTON, ROBERT LEE "RED"
B.APR.24,1906 ALHAMBRA,CAL.
D.DEC.8,1963 LOS ANGELES,CAL.
```
1931 BOS N  O            128    .291
1932 BOS N  O            105    .303
1933 BOS N  O             17    .156
1934 BOS N  O             41    .246
     STL N  H              1    .000
     BRTR               292    .287
```

WORTMAN, WILLIAM LEWIS "CHUCK"
B.JAN.5,1892 BALTIMORE,MD.
```
1916 CHI N  S             69    .201
1917 CHI N  S             75    .174
1918 CHI N  2-S           17    .118
     BRTR               161    .163
```

WOULFFE, JAMES JOSEPH
B.NOV.25,1859 NEW ORLEANS,LA.
D.DEC.20,1924
```
1884 CIN AA 3-O           8    .118
     PIT AA O            16    .127
     TR                  24    .124
```

WRIGHT, ALBERT EDGAR "A-1"
B.NOV.11,1912 SAN FRANCISCO,CAL
```
1933 BOS N  2              4   1.000
     BRTR
```

WRIGHT, ALBERT OWEN "AB"
B.NOV.16,1909 TERLTON,OKLA.
```
1935 CLE A  O             67    .238
1944 BOS N  O             71    .256
     BRTR               138    .248
```

WRIGHT, ALFRED L. H.
B.MAR.30,1842 CEDAR GROVE,N.J.
D.APR.20,1905
NON-PLAYING MANAGER ATH(N) 1876

WRIGHT, CLARENCE EUGENE
B.DEC.11,1878 CLEVELAND,OHIO
D.OCT.29,1930
```
1901 BRO N  P              1    1- 0
1902 CLE A  P-1     22    24    7- 9
                             .143
1903 CLE A  P             15    2- 7
     STL A  P              8    2- 4
1904 STL A  P              1    0- 1
     BRTR        47    49   12-21
                             .165
```

YR	CL	LEA	POS	GP	G	REC

WRIGHT, CLYDE
B.FEB.20,1943 JEFFERSON CITY, TENN.

YR	CL	LEA	POS	GP	G	REC
1966	CAL	A	P	20	24	4- 7
1967	CAL	A	P	20	23	5- 5
1968	CAL	A	P	41	51	10- 6
1969	CAL	A	P	37	40	1- 8
1970	CAL	A	P	39	47	22-12
1971	CAL	A	P	37	40	16-17
1972	CAL	A	P		35	18-11
1973	CAL	A	P		37	11-19
1974	MIL	A	P		38	9-20
1975	TEX	A	P		25	4- 6
	BRTL			329	360	100-111

WRIGHT, DAVID WILLIAM
B.AUG.27,1875 DENNISON,OHIO
D.JAN.18,1946

1895	PIT	N	P		1	0- 0
1897	CHI	N	P		1	1- 0
	BRTR				2	1- 0

WRIGHT, EDWARD YATMAN

1916	CHI	A	S		8	.000
	BLTR					

WRIGHT, FOREST GLENN
"GLENN" OR "BUCKSHOT"
B.FEB.6,1901 ARCHIE,MO.

1924	PIT	N	S		153	.287
1925	PIT	N	S-3		153	.308
1926	PIT	N	S		119	.308
1927	PIT	N	S		143	.281
1928	PIT	N	S		108	.310
1929	BRO	N	S		24	.200
1930	BRO	N	S		135	.321
1931	BRO	N	S		77	.284
1932	BRO	N	S		127	.274
1933	BRO	N	1-S-3		71	.255
1935	CHI	A	2		9	.120
	BRTR				1119	.294

WRIGHT, GEORGE
B.JAN.28,1847 NEW YORK,N.Y.
D.AUG.21,1937 BOSTON,MASS.

1871	BOS	NA	1-S		17	.387
1872	BOS	NA	S		48	.336
1873	BOS	NA	S		59	.378
1874	BOS	NA	S		60	.344
1875	BOS	NA	S		79	.337
1876	BOS	N	S		70	.292
1877	BOS	N	2-S		61	.276
1878	BOS	N	S		59	.224
1879	PRO	N	M-S		84	.281
1880	BOS	N	S		1	.250
1881	BOS	N	S		7	.179
1882	PRO	N	S		45	.162
	BRTR				590	.303

WRIGHT, HENDERSON EDWARD "ED"
B.MAY 15,1919 DYERSBURG,TENN.

1945	BOS	N	P		15	8- 3
1946	BOS	N	P		36	12- 9
1947	BOS	N	P		23	3- 3
1948	BOS	N	P		3	0- 0
1952	PHI	A	P		24	2- 1
	BRTR				101	25-16

WRIGHT, JAMES "JIGGS"
B.SEPT.19,1900 HYDE,ENGLAND
D.APR.12,1963 OAKLAND,CAL.

1927	STL	A	P		2	1- 0
1928	STL	A	P		2	0- 0
	BRTR				4	1- 0

WRIGHT, JOSEPH
B.PITTSBURGH,PA.

1895	LOU	N	O		59	.289
1896	LOU	N	O		2	.143
	PIT	N	O		15	.308
	BL				76	.279

WRIGHT, KENNETH WARREN "KEN"
B.SEP.4,1946 PENSACOLA,FLA.

1970	KC	A	P		47	1- 2
1971	KC	A	P		21	3- 6
1972	KC	A	P		17	1- 2
1973	KC	A	P		25	6- 5
1974	NY	A	P		3	0- 0
	BRTR				113	11-15

WRIGHT, MELVIN JAMES "MEL"
B.MAY 11,1929 MANILA,ARK.

1954	STL	N	P		9	0- 0
1955	STL	N	P		29	2- 2
1960	CHI	N	P		9	0- 1
1961	CHI	N	P		11	0- 1
	BRTR				58	2- 4

WRIGHT, PATRICK W.
B.JULY 5,1868 POTTSVILLE,PA.

1890	CHI	N	2		1	.000
1893	BAL	N	2		1	.500
					2	.250

WRIGHT, ROBERT CASSIUS
B.DEC.18,1891 GREENSBURG,IND.

1915	CHI	N	P		2	0- 0
	BRTR					

WRIGHT, ROY EARL
B.SEPT.26,1933 BUCHTEL,OHIO

1956	NY	N	P		1	0- 1
	BRTR					

WRIGHT, SAMUEL
B.NOV.25,1848 BOSTON,MASS.
D.MAY 6,1928

1875	NH	NA	S		33	-
1876	BOS	N	S		2	.125
1880	CIN	N	S		9	.058
1881	BOS	N	S		1	.250
					45	-

WRIGHT, TAFT SHEDRON "TAFFY"
B.AUG.10,1913 TABOR CITY,N.C.

1938	WAS	A	O		100	.350
1939	WAS	A	3		129	.309
1940	CHI	A	O		147	.337
1941	CHI	A	O		136	.322
1942	CHI	A	O		85	.333
1946	CHI	A	O		115	.275
1947	CHI	A	O		124	.324
1948	CHI	A	O		134	.279
1949	PHI	A	O		59	.235
	BLTR				1029	.311

WRIGHT, THOMAS EVERETT "TOM"
B.SEPT.22,1923 RUTHERFORD CO., N.C.

1948	BOS	A	H		3	.500
1949	BOS	A	H		5	.250
1950	BOS	A	O		54	.318
1951	BOS	A	O		28	.222
1952	STL	A	O		29	.242
	CHI	A	O		60	.258
1953	CHI	A	O		77	.250
1954	WAS	A	O		76	.246
1955	WAS	A	H		7	.000
1956	WAS	A	H		2	.000
	BLTR				341	.255

WRIGHT, WAYNE BROMLEY "RASTY"
B.NOV.5,1895 CEREDO,W.VA.
D.JUNE 12,1948

1917	STL	A	P		16	0- 0
	STL	A	P		18	8- 2
1919	STL	A	P		24	0- 5
1922	STL	A	P		31	9- 7
1923	STL	A	P		20	7- 4
	BRTR				109	24-18

WRIGHT, WILLARD JAMES "DICK"
B.MAY 5,1890 WORCESTER,N.Y.
D.JAN.25,1952

1915	BRO	F	C		4	.000
	TR					

WRIGHT, WILLIAM H.

1887	WAS	N	C		1	.667

WRIGHT, WILLIAM HENRY "HARRY"
B.JAN.10,1835 SHEFFIELD,ENGLAND
D.OCT.3,1895 ATLANTIC CITY,N.J.

1871	BOS	NA	M-S-O		33	.300
1872	BOS	NA	M-P-	2	48	2- 0
			O			.261
1873	BOS	NA	M-P-	3	58	2- 1
			O			.260
1874	BOS	NA	M-C-O		41	.310
1875	BOS	NA	M-O		1	.250
1876	BOS	N	M-O		1	.000
1877	BOS	N	M-O		1	.000
1878	BOS	N	M-O		1	.000
	BRTR			5	184	4- 1
						.278

NON-PLAYING MANAGER
BOS(N) 1879-81, PRO(N) 1882-83, PHI(N) 1884-93

WRIGHT, WILLIAM S. "RASTY"
B.JAN.31,1863 BIRMINGHAM,MICH.
D.OCT.14,1922

1890	SYR	AA	O		89	.285
	CLE	N	O		13	.106
					102	.265

WRIGHT, WILLIAM SIMMONS "LUCKY"
B.FEB.21,1880 TONTOGANY,OHIO
D.JULY 8,1941

1909	CLE	A	P		5	0- 4

WRIGHTSTONE, RUSSELL GUY "RUSS"
B.MAR.18,1893 BOWMANSDALE,PA.
D.MAR.1,1969 HARRISBURG,PA.

1920	PHI	N	3		76	.262
1921	PHI	N	3-O		109	.296
1922	PHI	N	1-S-3		99	.305
1923	PHI	N	2-S-3		119	.273
1924	PHI	N	2-S-3-O		118	.307
1925	PHI	N	1-2-S-3-	O	92	.346
1926	PHI	N	1-2-3		112	.307
1927	PHI	N	1		141	.306
1928	PHI	N	O		33	.209
	NY	N	H		30	.160
	BLTR				929	.297

WRIGLEY, GEORGE WATSON "ZEKE"
B.JAN.18,1874 PHILADELPHIA,PA.
D.SEPT.28,1952

1896	WAS	N	2		5	.100
1897	WAS	N	S-3-O		102	.284
1898	WAS	N	S		111	.245
1899	NY	N	3		4	.133
	BRO	N	S		15	.229
					237	.258

WUESTING, GEORGE "YATS"
B.OCT.18,1903 ST.LOUIS,MO.
D.APR.26,1970 ST.LOUIS,MO.

1929	DET	A	S		54	.200
1930	DET	A	S		4	.000
	NY	A	S		25	.190
	BRTR				83	.189

WURN, FRANK JAMES
B.APR.27,1924 SALEM,N.Y.

1944	BRO	N	P		1	0- 0
	BBTL					

WYATT, JOHN THOMAS
B.APR.19,1935 CHICAGO,ILL.

1961	KC	A	P		5	0- 0
1962	KC	A	P		59	10- 7
1963	KC	A	P		63	6- 4
1964	KC	A	P		81	9- 8
1965	KC	A	P		65	2- 6
1966	KC	A	P		19	0- 3
	BOS	A	P		42	3- 4
1967	BOS	A	P		60	10- 7
1968	BOS	A	P		8	1- 2
	NY	A	P		7	0- 2
	DET	A	P		22	1- 0
1969	OAK	A	P		4	0- 1
	BRTR				435	42-44

YR	CL	LEA	POS	GP	G	REC

WYATT, JOHN WHITLOW "WHIT"
B.SEPT.27,1907 EKNSINGTON,GA.

YR	CL	LEA	POS	GP	G	REC
1929	DET	A	P		4	0- 1
1930	DET	A	P	21	22	4- 5
1931	DET	A	P		4	0- 2
1932	DET	A	P		43	9-13
1933	DET	A	P		10	0- 1
	CHI	A	P		26	3- 4
1934	CHI	A	P		23	4-11
1935	CHI	A	P		30	4- 3
1936	CHI	A	P		3	0- 0
1937	CLE	A	P		29	2- 3
1939	BRO	N	P		16	8- 3
1940	BRO	N	P		37	15-14
1941	BRO	N	P	38	40	22-10
1942	BRO	N	P		31	19- 7
1943	BRO	N	P	26	27	14- 5
1944	BRO	N	P	9	11	2- 6
1945	PHI	N	P		10	0- 7
	BRTR			360	366	106-95

WYATT, LORAL JOHN "JOE"
B.APR.6,1900 PETERSBURG,IND.
D.DEC.5,1970 OBLONG,ILL.

YR	CL	LEA	POS	GP	G	REC
1924	CLE	A	O		4	.166
	BRTR					

WYCKOFF, JOHN WELDON
B.FEB.19,1892 WILLIAMSPORT,PA.
D.MAY 8,1961

YR	CL	LEA	POS	GP	G	REC
1913	PHI	A	P		17	3- 4
1914	PHI	A	P		32	11- 8
1915	PHI	A	P	43	45	10-22
1916	PHI	A	P		8	0- 1
	BOS	A	P		8	0- 0
1917	BOS	A	P		1	0- 0
1918	BOS	A	P		1	0- 0
	BRTR		110	112	24-35	

WYLIE, JAMES RENWICK
B.DEC.14,1861 ELIZABETH,PA.
D.AUG.17,1951

YR	CL	LEA	POS	GP	G	REC
1882	PIT	AA	O		1	.000

WYMAN, FRANK C.
B.MAY 10,1862 HAVERILL,MASS.

YR	CL	LEA	POS	GP	G	REC
1884	KC	U	P-1-	3	30	0- 2
			3-0			.203
	CHI	U	1		2	.375
				3	32	0- 2
						.214

WYNEGAR, HAROLD DELANO "BUTCH"
B.MAR.14,1956 YORK,PA.

YR	CL	LEA	POS	GP	G	REC
1976	MIN	A	C-D		149	.260
	BBTR					

WYNN, EARLY
B.JAN.6,1920 HARTFORD,ALA.

YR	CL	LEA	POS	GP	G	REC
1939	WAS	A	P		3	0- 2
1941	WAS	A	P		5	3- 1
1942	WAS	A	P		30	10-16
1943	WAS	A	P	37	38	18-12
1944	WAS	A	P	33	43	8-17
1946	WAS	A	P	17	25	8- 5
1947	WAS	A	P	33	54	17-15
1948	WAS	A	P	33	73	8-19
1949	CLE	A	P	26	35	11- 7
1950	CLE	A	P	32	39	18- 8
1951	CLE	A	P	37	41	20-13
1952	CLE	A	P	42	44	23-12
1953	CLE	A	P	36	37	17-12
1954	CLE	A	P		40	23-11
1955	CLE	A	P	32	34	17-11
1956	CLE	A	P		38	20- 9
1957	CLE	A	P		40	14-17
1958	CHI	A	P		40	14-16
1959	CHI	A	P		37	22-10
1960	CHI	A	P		36	13-12
1961	CHI	A	P		17	8- 2
1962	CHI	A	P		27	7-15
1963	CLE	A	P		20	1- 2
	BBTR	691	796	300-244		
	BR 1941-44					

WYNN, JAMES SHERMAN "JIM"
B.MAR.12,1942 CINCINNATI,OHIO

YR	CL	LEA	POS	GP	G	REC
1963	HOU	N	S-3-O		70	.244
1964	HOU	N	O		67	.224
1965	HOU	N	O		157	.275
1966	HOU	N	O		105	.256
1967	HOU	N	O		158	.249
1968	HOU	N	O		156	.269
1969	HOU	N	O		149	.269
1970	HOU	N	O		157	.282
1971	HOU	N	O		123	.203
1972	HOU	N	O		145	.273
1973	HOU	N	O		139	.220
1974	LA	N	O		150	.271
1975	LA	N	O		130	.248
1976	ATL	N	O		148	.207
	BRTR	1854	.253			

WYNNE, BILLY VERNON
B.JULY 31,1943 WILLIAMSTON,N.C.

YR	CL	LEA	POS	GP	G	REC
1967	NY	N	P		6	0- 0
1968	CHI	A	P		1	0- 0
1969	CHI	A	P		20	7- 7
1970	CHI	A	P		12	1- 4
1971	CAL	A	P		3	0- 0
	BLTR				42	8-11

WYNNE, WILLIAM AVERY
B.MAR.27,1869 NEUSE,N.C.
D.AUG.7,1951

YR	CL	LEA	POS	GP	G	REC
1894	WAS	N	P		1	0- 1

WYROSTEK, JOHN BARNEY "JOHNNY"
B.JULY 12,1919 FAIRMONT CITY,
ILL.

YR	CL	LEA	POS	GP	G	REC
1942	PIT	N	O		9	.114
1943	PIT	N	1-2-3-O	51	.152	
1946	PHI	N	O		145	.281
1947	PHI	N	O		128	.273
1948	CIN	N	O		136	.273
1949	CIN	N	O		134	.249
1950	CIN	N	1-O		131	.285
1951	CIN	N	O		142	.311
1952	CIN	N	1-O		30	.236
	CHI	N	O		98	.274
1953	CHI	N	O		125	.271
1954	CHI	N	1-O		92	.239
	BLTR	1221	.271			

WYSE, HENRY WASHINGTON "HANK"
B.MAR.1,1918 LUNSFORD,ARK.

YR	CL	LEA	POS	GP	G	REC
1942	CHI	N	P		4	2- 1
1943	CHI	N	P	38	40	9- 7
1944	CHI	N	P		41	16-15
1945	CHI	N	P		38	22-10
1946	CHI	N	P		40	14-12
1947	CHI	N	P		37	6- 9
1950	PHI	A	P		41	9-14
1951	PHI	A	P		9	1- 2
	WAS	A	P		3	0- 0
	BRTR	251	253	79-70		

WYSHNER, PETER
(PLAYED UNDER NAME OF
PETER GRAY)

WYSONG, HARLAN "BILL"
B.APR.13,1905 CLARKSVILLE,OHIO
D.AUG.8,1951

YR	CL	LEA	POS	GP	G	REC
1930	CIN	N	P		1	0- 1
1931	CIN	N	P		12	0- 2
1932	CIN	N	P		7	1- 0
	BLTL			20	1- 3	

YAIK, HENRY
B.DETROIT,MICH.

YR	CL	LEA	POS	GP	G	REC
1888	PIT	N	C		2	.333

YALE, WILLIAM M. "AD"
B.APR.17,1870 BRISTOL,CONN.
D.APR.27,1948

YR	CL	LEA	POS	GP	G	REC
1905	BRO	N	1		4	.076

YANCY, HUGH
B.OCT.16,1950 SARASOTA,FLA.

YR	CL	LEA	POS	GP	G	REC
1972	CHI	A	3		3	.111
1974	CHI	A	H		1	.000
1976	CHI	A	2		3	.100
	BRTR				7	.105

YANKOWSKI, GEORGE EDWARD
B.NOV.19,1922 CAMBRIDGE,MASS.

YR	CL	LEA	POS	GP	G	REC
1942	PHI	A	C		6	.154
1949	CHI	A	C		12	.167
	BRTR				18	.161

YANTZ, GEORGE WEBB
B.JULY 27,1886 LOUISVILLE,KY.
D.FEB.26,1967 LOUISVILLE,KY.

YR	CL	LEA	POS	GP	G	REC
1912	CHI	N	C		1	1.000
	BRTR					

YAPP, FREDERICK FRANCIS
(PLAYED UNDER NAME OF
FREDERICK FRANCIS MITCHELL)

YARNELL, WALDO WILLIAM "RUSTY"
B.OCT.22,1902 MAYSVILLE,KY.
D.MAR.22,1934

YR	CL	LEA	POS	GP	G	REC
1926	PHI	N	P		1	0- 1
	BRTR					

YARRISON, BYRON WORDSWORTH "RUBE"
B.MAR.9,1896 MONTGOMERY,PA.

YR	CL	LEA	POS	GP	G	REC
1922	PHI	A	P		18	1- 2
1924	BRO	N	P		3	0- 2
	BRTR				21	1- 4

YARYAN, CLARENCE EVERETT "YAM"
B.NOV.5,1893 KNOWITON,IOWA
D.NOV.16,1964 BIRMINGHAM,ALA.

YR	CL	LEA	POS	GP	G	REC
1921	CHI	A	C		45	.304
1922	CHI	A	C		36	.197
	BRTR				81	.260

YASTRZEMSKI, CARL MICHAEL
B.AUG.22,1939 SOUTHAMPTON,N.Y.

YR	CL	LEA	POS	GP	G	REC
1961	BOS	A	O		148	.266
1962	BOS	A	O		160	.296
1963	BOS	A	O		151	.321
1964	BOS	A	3-O		151	.289
1965	BOS	A	O		133	.312
1966	BOS	A	O		160	.278
1967	BOS	A	O		161	.326
1968	BOS	A	1-O		157	.301
1969	BOS	A	1-O		162	.255
1970	BOS	A	1-O		161	.329
1971	BOS	A	O		148	.254
1972	BOS	A	1-O		125	.264
1973	BOS	A	1-3-O		152	.296
1974	BOS	A	1-O		148	.301
1975	BOS	A	1-O		149	.269
1976	BOS	A	1-O-D		155	.267
	BLTR	2421	.289			

YATES, ALBERT ARTHUR "AL"
B.MAY 26,1945 JERSEY CITY,N.J.

YR	CL	LEA	POS	GP	G	REC
1971	MIL	A	O		24	.277
	BRTR					

YDE, EMIL OGDEN
B.JAN.28,1900 GREAT LAKES,ILL.
D.DEC.4,1968 LEESBURG,FLA.

YR	CL	LEA	POS	GP	G	REC
1924	PIT	N	P	33	50	16- 3
1925	PIT	N	P	33	47	17- 9
1926	PIT	N	P	37	43	8- 7
1927	PIT	N	P	9	23	1- 3
1929	DET	A	P	29	46	7- 3
	BBTL	141	209	49-25		

YEABSLEY, ROBERT WATSON "BERT"
B.DEC.17,1894 PHILADELPHIA,PA.
D.FEB.8,1961

YR	CL	LEA	POS	GP	G	REC
1919	PHI	N	H		2	.000
	TR					

YEAGER, GEORGE E. "ABE"
B.JUNE 4,1873 CINCINNATI,OHIO

YR	CL	LEA	POS	GP	G	REC
1896	BOS	N	1		2	.167
1897	BOS	N	C		26	.239
1898	BOS	N	C		57	.263
1899	BOS	N	C		2	.000
1901	CLE	A	C		39	.226
	PIT	N	C		24	.267
1902	NY	N	C-1-O		29	.194
	BAL	A	C		11	.184
	TR				190	.236

YR	CL	LEA	POS	GP	G	REC

YEAGER, JOSEPH F. "LITTLE JOE"
B.AUG.28,1875 PHILADELPHIA,PA.
D.JULY 2,1937

1898	BRO	N	P	33	36	13-20
1899	BRO	N	P	10	15	3- 2
1900	BRO	N	P-3	2	3	1- 1
						.333
1901	DET	A	P	26	37	12-12
1902	DET	A	P-2-	19	48	5-12
			S-3-O			.231
1903	DET	A	3		109	.259
1905	NY	A	S-3		115	.267
1906	NY	A	S		57	.301
1907	STL	A	2-3		123	.239
1908	STL	A	2		10	.352
		TR		90	553	34-47
						.254

YEAGER, STEPHEN WAYNE "STEVE"
B.NOV.24,1948 HUNTINGTON,W.VA.

1972	LA	N	C		35	.274
1973	LA	N	C		54	.254
1974	LA	N	C		94	.266
1975	LA	N	C		135	.228
1976	LA	N	C		117	.214
		BRTR			435	.239

YEARGIN, JAMES ALMOND "AL"
B.OCT.16,1901 MAULDIN,S.C.
D.MAY 8,1937 GREENVILLE,S.C.

1922	BOS	N	P	1		0- 1
1924	BOS	N	P		32	1-11
		BRTR			33	1-12

YEATMAN, WILLIAM SUTER
B.1859 ALEXANDRIA,VA.
D.APR.20,1901 YORK,PA.

| 1872 | NAT | NA | O | | 1 | .000 |

YELLE, ARCHIE JOSEPH
B.JUNE 11,1892 SAGINAW,MICH.

1917	DET	A	C		25	.137
1918	DET	A	C		56	.174
1919	DET	A	C		6	.000
		BRTR			87	.166

YELLEN, LAWRENCE ALAN "LARRY"
B.JAN.4,1943 BROOKLYN,N.Y.

1963	HOU	N	P		1	0- 0
1964	HOU	N	P		13	0- 0
		BRTR			14	0- 0

YELLOWHORSE, MOSES J. "CHIEF"
B.MAR.28,1900 PAWNEE,OKLA.
D.APR.10,1964 PAWNEE,OKLA.

1921	PIT	N	P		10	5- 3
1922	PIT	N	P		28	3- 1
		BRTR			38	8- 4

YERKES, CHARLES CARROLL
B.JUNE 13,1903 MC SHERRYSTOWN,
PA.
D.DEC.20,1950

1927	PHI	A	P		1	0- 0
1928	PHI	A	P		2	0- 1
1929	PHI	A	P		19	1- 0
1932	CHI	N	P		2	0- 0
1933	CHI	N	P		1	0- 0
		BRTL			25	1- 1

YERKES, STANLEY LEWIS "YANK"
B.NOV.28,1874 CHELTENHAM,PA.
D.JULY 28,1940 BOSTON,MASS.

1901	BAL	A	P		1	0- 1
		STL	N	P	4	3- 1
1902	STL	N	P		36	12-21
1903	STL	N	P		1	0- 1
					42	15-24

YERKES, STEPHEN DOUGLAS
B.FEB.19,1888 HATBORO,PA.
D.JAN.31,1971 LANSDALE,PA.

1909	BOS	A	S		5	.286
1911	BOS	A	S		142	.279
1912	BOS	A	2		131	.252
1913	BOS	A	2		137	.267
1914	BOS	A	2		92	.218
		PIT	F	S		39	.333
1915	PIT	F	2		121	.286
1916	CHI	N	2		44	.263
		BRTR			711	.267

YERRICK, WILLIAM J.
(PLAYED UNDER NAME OF
WILLIAM J. BANKS)

YEWCIC, THOMAS "TOM"
B.MAY 9,1932 CONEMAUGH,PA.

| 1957 | DET | A | C | | 1 | .000 |
| | | BRTR | | | | |

YEWELL, EDWIN LEONARD
B.AUG.22,1872 WASHINGTON,D.C.
D.SEPT.15,1940 WASHINGTON,D.C.

1884	WAS	AA	2-3		35	.258
		WAS	U	3		1	.000
					36	.247

YINGLING, EARL HERSHEY "CHINK"
B.OCT.29,1888 CHILLICOTHE,OHIO
D.OCT.2,1962

1911	CLE	A	P		6	2- 1
1912	BRO	N	P		25	6-11
1913	BRO	N	P	26	40	8- 8
1914	CIN	N	P	34	61	9-13
1918	WAS	A	P		8	1- 2
		BLTL		99	140	26-35

YINGLING, JOSEPH
B.1864 BALTIMORE,MD.

1886	WAS	N	P	1		0- 1
1894	PHI	N	S	1		.333
				1	2	0- 1
						.200

YOCHIM, LEONARD JOSEPH "LEN"
B.OCT.16,1928 NEW ORLEANS,LA.

1951	PIT	N	P		2	1- 1
1954	PIT	N	P		10	0- 1
		BLTL			12	1- 2

**YOCHIM, RAYMOND AUSTIN ALOYSIUS
"RAY"**
B.JULY 19,1922 NEW ORLEANS,LA.

1948	3TL	N	P		1	0- 0
1949	STL	N	P		3	0- 0
		BRTR			4	0- 0

YOHE, WILLIAM F.
B.SEPT.2,1879 MATOON,ILL.

| 1909 | WAS | A | 3 | | 21 | .208 |
| | | TR | | | | |

YORK, ANTHONY BATTON
B.NOV.27,1912 IRENE,TEX.

| 1944 | CHI | N | S-3 | | 28 | .235 |
| | | BRTR | | | | |

YORK, JAMES E. "LEFTY"
B.NOV.1,1895 TUSKEGEE,ALA.
D.APR.9,1961 YORK,PA.

1919	PHI	A	P		2	0- 2
1921	CHI	N	P		40	5- 9
		BRTL			42	5-11

YORK, JAMES HARLAN "JIM"
B.AUG.27,1947 MAYWOOD,CAL.

1970	KC	A	P		4	1- 1
1971	KC	A	P		53	5- 5
1972	HOU	N	P		26	0- 1
1973	HOU	N	P		41	3- 4
1974	HOU	N	P		28	2- 2
1975	HOU	N	P		19	4- 4
1976	NY	A	P		3	1- 0
		BRTR			174	16-17

YORK, PRESTON RUDOLPH "RUDY"
B.AUG.17,1913 RAGLAND,ALA.
D.FEB.5,1970 ROME,GA.

1934	DET	A	C		3	.167
1937	DET	A	C-3		104	.307
1938	DET	A	C-O		135	.298
1939	DET	A	C-1		102	.307
1940	DET	A	1		155	.316
1941	DET	A	1		155	.259
1942	DET	A	1		153	.260
1943	DET	A	1		155	.271
1944	DET	A	1		151	.276
1945	DET	A	1		155	.264
1946	BOS	A	1		154	.276
1947	BOS	A	1		48	.212
		CHI	A	1		102	.243
1948	PHI	A	1		31	.157
		BRTR			1603	.275

NON-PLAYING MANAGER
BOS(A) 1959 (INTERIM)

YORK, THOMAS J.
B.JULY 13,1850 BROOKLYN,N.Y.
D.FEB.17,1936

1871	TRO	NA	O		29	.218
1872	BAL	NA	O		49	.269
1873	BAL	NA	P-O	1	57	1- 0
						-
1874	PHI	NA	O		50	-
1875	HAR	NA	O		85	-
1876	HAR	N	O		67	.249
1877	HAR	N	O		56	.283
1878	PRO	N	O		60	.302
1879	PRO	N	O		80	.307
1880	PRO	N	O		50	.211
1881	PRO	N	O		84	.304
1882	PRO	N	O		81	.267
1883	CLE	N	O		97	.255
1884	BAL	AA	O		84	.228
1885	BAL	AA	O		22	.271
		BL		1	951	1- 0
						-

YOST, EDWARD FREDERICK "EDDIE"
B.OCT.13,1926 BROOKLYN,N.Y.

1944	WAS	A	S-3		7	.143
1946	WAS	A	3		8	.080
1947	WAS	A	3		115	.238
1948	WAS	A	3		145	.249
1949	WAS	A	3		124	.253
1950	WAS	A	3		155	.295
1951	WAS	A	3-O		154	.283
1952	WAS	A	3		157	.233
1953	WAS	A	3		152	.272
1954	WAS	A	3		155	.256
1955	WAS	A	3		122	.243
1956	WAS	A	3-O		152	.231
1957	WAS	A	3		110	.251
1958	WAS	A	1-2-3-O		136	.224
1959	DET	A	2-3		148	.278
1960	DET	A	3		143	.260
1961	LA	A	3		76	.202
1962	LA	A	1-3		52	.240
		BRTR			2109	.254

YOST, GUS

| 1893 | CHI | N | P | | 1 | 1- 0 |

YOTER, ELMER ELSWORTH
B.JUNE 26,1900 CARLISLE,PA.
D.JULY 26,1966 CAMP HILL,PA.

1921	PHI	A	H		2	.000
1924	CLE	A	3		19	.273
1927	CHI	N	3		13	.222
1928	CHI	N	3		1	.000

YOUNG, CHARLES V.
B.1894 TRENTON,N.J.

| 1915 | BAL | F | P | | 9 | 2- 3 |
| | | BBTR | | | | |

YOUNG, DAVID
B.OCT.6,1872 PHILADELPHIA,PA.
D.OCT.25,1924

| 1895 | STL | N | 3 | | 1 | .400 |

YOUNG, DELMAR JOHN
B.OCT.24,1888 MACON,MO.
D.DEC.17,1959

1909	CIN	N	O		2	.286
1914	BUF	F	O		79	.278
1915	BUF	F	O		12	.133
		BLTR			93	.268

YOUNG, DELMER EDWARD "DEL"
B.MAR.11,1912 CLEVELAND,OHIO

1937	PHI	N	2		109	.194
1938	PHI	N	2-S		108	.229
1939	PHI	N	2-S		77	.263
1940	PHI	N	2-S		15	.242
		BBTR			309	.224

YR	CL	LEA	POS	GP	G	REC

YOUNG, DENTON TRUE "CY"
B.MAR.29,1867 GILMORE,OHIO
D.NOV.4,1955 NEWCOMERSTOWN,OHIO

YR	CL	LEA	POS	GP	G	REC
1890	CLE	N	P		17	9- 7
1891	CLE	N	P		50	28-20
1892	CLE	N	P		49	36-11
1893	CLE	N	P		51	34-17
1894	CLE	N	P	47	48	25-21
1895	CLE	N	P	45	46	33-10
1896	CLE	N	P	47	48	29-14
1897	CLE	N	P	40	45	21-18
1898	CLE	N	P	41	44	24-15
1899	STL	N	P	42	43	26-14
1900	STL	N	P		39	20-16
1901	BOS	A	P	42	45	31-10
1902	BOS	A	P		45	32-11
1903	BOS	A	P	40	41	28- 9
1904	BOS	A	P		43	26-16
1905	BOS	A	P		38	16-18
1906	BOS	A	P	39	40	13-21
1907	BOS	A	M-P	44	45	22-15
1908	CLE	A	P		36	21-11
1909	CLE	A	P		34	19-15
1910	CLE	A	P		21	7-10
1911	CLE	A	P		7	3- 4
	BOS	N	P	10	11	4- 5
	BRTR			867	886	507-308

YOUNG, DONALD WAYNE "DON"
B.OCT.18,1945 HOUSTON,TEX.

1965	CHI	N	O		11	.057
1969	CHI	N	O		101	.239
	BBTR				112	.218

YOUNG, GEORGE JOSEPH
B.APR.1,1890 BROOKLYN,N.Y.
D.MAR.13,1950 BRIGHTWATERS,N.Y.

1913	CLE	A	H		2	.000
	BLTR					

YOUNG, GEORGE W.
NON-PLAYING MANAGER
PHI(NA) 1873, 75

YOUNG, HARLEY E.
B.KANSAS

1908	PIT	N	P		8	0- 2
	BOS	N	P		6	0- 1
	TL				14	0- 3

YOUNG, HERMAN JOHN
B.APR.14,1886 BOSTON,MASS.
D.DEC.13,1966 IPSWICH,MASS.

1911	BOS	N	S-3		9	.230
	BRTR					

YOUNG, IRVING MELROSE
"YOUNG CY"
B.JULY 21,1876 COLUMBIA FALLS,
ME.
D.JAN.14,1935

1905	BOS	N	P		43	20-21
1906	BOS	N	P		43	16-25
1907	BOS	N	P		40	10-23
1908	BOS	N	P		16	4- 9
	PIT	N	P		16	4- 3
1910	CHI	A	P		27	4- 8
1911	CHI	A	P		24	5- 6
	BRTL				209	63-95

YOUNG, J. D.
B.MT.CARMEL,PA.

1892	STL	N	P		1	0- 0

YOUNG, JOHN THOMAS
B.FEB.9,1949 LOS ANGELES,CAL.

1971	DET	A	1		2	.500
	BLTL					

YOUNG, LEMUEL FLOYD "PEP"
B.AUG.29,1907 JAMESTOWN,N.C.
D.JAN.14,1962

1933	PIT	N	2-S		25	.300
1934	PIT	N	2-S		19	.235
1935	PIT	N	2-S-3-O	128		.265
1936	PIT	N	2		125	.248
1937	PIT	N	2-S-3		113	.260
1938	PIT	N	2		149	.278
1939	PIT	N	2		84	.276
1940	PIT	N	2-S-3		54	.250
1941	CIN	N	3		4	.167
	STL	N	H		2	.000
1945	STL	N	2-S-3		27	.149
	BRTR				730	.262

YOUNG, NICHOLAS EPHRAIM
B.SEPT.12,1840 AMSTERDAM,N.Y.
D.OCT.31,1916 WASHINGTON,D.C.
NON-PLAYING MANAGER
OLY(NA) 1871-72, NAT(NA) 1873

YOUNG, NORMAN ROBERT "BABE"
B.JULY 1,1915 ASTORIA,N.Y.

1936	NY	N	1		1	.000
1939	NY	N	1		22	.307
1940	NY	N	1		149	.286
1941	NY	N	1		152	.265
1942	NY	N	1-O		101	.279
1946	NY	N	1-O		104	.278
1947	NY	N	H		14	.071
	CIN	N	1		95	.283
1948	CIN	N	1-O		49	.231
	STL	N	1		41	.243
	BLTL				728	.274

YOUNG, RALPH STUART
B.SEPT.19,1890 PHILADELPHIA,PA.
D.JAN.24,1965 PHILADELPHIA,PA.

1913	NY	A	S		7	.067
1915	DET	A	2		123	.244
1916	DET	A	2		153	.263
1917	DET	A	2		141	.231
1918	DET	A	2		91	.188
1919	DET	A	2		125	.210
1920	DET	A	2		150	.291
1921	DET	A	2		107	.299
1922	PHI	A	2		125	.223
	BBTR				1022	.247

YOUNG, RICHARD ENNIS "DICK"
B.JUNE 3,1928 SEATTLE,WASH.

1951	PHI	N	2		15	.235
1952	PHI	N	2		5	.222
	BBTR				20	.234
	BL 1951					

YOUNG, ROBERT GEORGE "BOBBY"
B.JAN.22,1925 GRANITE,MD.

1948	STL	N	3		3	.000
1951	STL	A	2		147	.260
1952	STL	A	2		149	.247
1953	STL	A	2		148	.255
1954	BAL	A	2		130	.245
1955	BAL	A	2		59	.199
	CLE	A	2-3		18	.311
1956	CLE	A	H		1	.000
1958	PHI	N	2		32	.233
	BLTR				687	.249

YOUNG, RUSSELL CHARLES
B.SEPT.15,1903 BRYAN,OHIO

1931	STL	A	C		16	.118
	BBTR					

YOUNGBLOOD, ALBERT CLYDE
"CHIEF"
B.JUNE 13,1900 HILLSBORO,TEX.
D.JULY 6,1968 AMARILLO,TEX.

1922	WAS	A	P		2	0- 0
	BLTR					

YOUNGBLOOD, JOEL RANDOLPH
B.AUG.28,1951 HOUSTON,TEX.

1976	CIN	N	C-2-3-O	55		.193
	BRTR					

YOUNGMAN, HENRY
B.1865 INDIANA,PA.
D.JAN.24,1936

1890	PIT	N	2-3		13	.167

YOUNGS, ROSS MIDDLEBROOK
(REAL NAME
ROYCE MIDDLEBROOK YOUNGS)
B.APR.10,1897 SHINER,TEX.
D.OCT.22,1927 SAN ANTONIO,TEX.

1917	NY	N	O		7	.346
1918	NY	N	2-O		121	.302
1919	NY	N	O		130	.311
1920	NY	N	O		153	.351
1921	NY	N	O		141	.327
1922	NY	N	O		149	.330
1923	NY	N	O		152	.336
1924	NY	N	2-O		133	.355
1925	NY	N	2-O		130	.264
1926	NY	N	O		95	.306
	BLTR				1211	.322

YOUNGS, ROYCE MIDDLEBROOK
(PLAYED UNDER NAME OF
ROSS MIDDLEBROOK YOUNGS)

YOUNT, FLOYD EDWIN "EDDIE"
B.DEC.19,1916 NEWTON,N.C.
D.OCT.26,1973 NEWTON,N.C.

1937	PHI	A	H		4	.286
1939	PIT	N	O		2	.000
	BRTR				6	.222

YOUNT, HERBERT MACON "DUCKY"
B.DEC.7,1885 IREDELL CO.,N.C.
D.MAY 9,1970 WINSTON-SALEM,N.C.

1914	BAL	F	P		14	1- 1
	BRTR					

YOUNT, LAWRENCE KING "LARRY"
B.FEB.15,1950 HOUSTON,TEX.

1971	HOU	N	P		1	0- 0
	BRTR					

YOUNT, ROBIN R
B.SEPT.16,1955 DANVILLE,ILL.

1974	MIL	A	S		107	.250
1975	MIL	A	S		147	.267
1976	MIL	A	S-O		161	.252
	BRTR				415	.257

YOWELL, CARL COLUMBUS
B.DEC.20,1903 MADISON,VA.

1924	CLE	A	P		4	1- 1
1925	CLE	A	P		12	2- 3
	BLTL				16	3- 4

YUHAS, JOHN EDWARD "EDDIE"
B.AUG.5,1924 YOUNGSTOWN,OHIO

1952	STL	N	P		54	12- 2
1953	STL	N	P		2	0- 0
	BRTR				56	12- 2

YVARS, SALVADOR ANTHONY "SAL"
B.FEB.20,1924 NEW YORK,N.Y.

1947	NY	N	C		1	.200
1948	NY	N	C		15	.211
1949	NY	N	C		3	.000
1950	NY	N	C		9	.143
1951	NY	N	C		25	.317
1952	NY	N	C		66	.245
1953	NY	N	C		23	.277
	STL	N	C		30	.246
1954	STL	N	C		38	.246
	BRTR				210	.244

ZABALA, ADRIAN RODRIGUEZ
B.AUG.26,1916 SAN ANTONIO
DE LOS BANOS,CUBA

1945	NY	N	P		11	2- 4
1949	NY	N	P		15	2- 3
	BLTL				26	4- 7

ZABEL, GEORGE WASHINGTON "ZIP"
B.FEB.18,1891 WETMORE,KAN.
D.MAY 31,1970 BELOIT,WIS.

1913	CHI	N	P		1	1- 0
1914	CHI	N	P		29	4- 4
1915	CHI	N	P	36	37	7-10
	BRTR			66	67	12-14

ZACHARY, ALBERT MYRON "CHINK"
B.OCT.19,1917 BROOKLYN,N.Y.

1944	BRO	N	P		4	0- 2
	BRTR					

ZACHARY, JONATHAN THOMPSON WALTON "TOM"
(PLAYED UNDER NAME OF ZACH WALTON IN 1918)
B.MAY 7,1896 GRAHAM,N.C.
D.JAN.24,1969 GRAHAM,N.C.

YR	CL	LEA	POS	GP	G	REC
1918	PHI	A	P		2	2- 0
1919	WAS	A	P		17	1- 5
1920	WAS	A	P	44	51	15-16
1921	WAS	A	P		38	18-16
1922	WAS	A	P		32	15-10
1923	WAS	A	P		35	10-16
1924	WAS	A	P		32	15- 9
1925	WAS	A	P		38	12-15
1926	STL	A	P		34	14-15
1927	STL	A	P		13	4- 6
	WAS	A	P		15	4- 7
1928	WAS	A	P		20	6- 9
	NY	A	P		7	3- 3
1929	NY	A	P		26	12- 0
1930	NY	A	P		3	1- 1
	BOS	N	P	24	25	11- 5
1931	BOS	N	P		33	11-15
1932	BOS	N	P	32	33	12-11
1933	BOS	N	P	26	27	7- 9
1934	BOS	N	P		5	1- 2
	BRO	N	P	22	24	5- 6
1935	BRO	N	P		25	7-12
1936	BRO	N	P		1	0- 0
	PHI	N	P	7	8	0- 3
	BLTL			531	544	186-191

ZACHARY, WILLIAM CHRIS "CHRIS"
B.FEB.19,1944 KNOXVILLE,TENN.

YR	CL	LEA	POS	GP	G	REC
1963	HOU	N	P		22	2- 2
1964	HOU	N	P		1	0- 1
1965	HOU	N	P		4	0- 2
1966	HOU	N	P		10	3- 5
1967	HOU	N	P	9	10	1- 6
1969	KC	A	P		8	0- 1
1971	STL	N	P	23	24	3-10
1972	DET	A	P		25	1- 1
1973	PIT	N	P		6	0- 1
	BLTR			108	110	10-29

ZACHER, ELMER HENRY "SILVER"
B.SEPT.17,1883 BUFFALO,N.Y.
D.DEC.20,1944

YR	CL	LEA	POS	G	REC
1910	NY	N	O	1	.000
	STL	N	O	38	.212
	BRTR			39	.212

ZACHRY, PATRICK PAUL "PAT"
B.APR.24,1952 RICHMOND,TEX.

YR	CL	LEA	POS	G	REC
1976	CIN	N	P	38	14- 7
	BRTR				

ZACKERT, GEORGE
B.1885 MISSOURI

YR	CL	LEA	POS	G	REC
1911	STL	N	P	4	0- 2
1912	STL	N	P	1	0- 0
	BLTL			5	0- 2

ZAHN, GEOFFREY CLAYTON "JEFF"
B.DEC.19,1945 BALTIMORE,MD.

YR	CL	LEA	POS	G	REC
1973	LA	N	P	6	1- 0
1974	LA	N	P	21	3- 5
1975	LA	N	P	2	0- 1
	CHI	N	P	16	2- 7
1976	CHI	N	P	3	0- 1
	BLTL			48	6-14

ZAHNER, FREDERICK JOSEPH
B.JUNE 5,1870 LOUISVILLE,KY.
D.JULY 24,1900

YR	CL	LEA	POS	G	REC
1894	LOU	N	C	14	.204
1895	LOU	N	C	18	.234
				32	.218

ZAHNISER, PAUL VERNON
B.SEPT.6,1896 SAC CITY,IOWA
D.SEPT.26,1964

YR	CL	LEA	POS	G	REC
1923	WAS	A	P	33	9-10
1924	WAS	A	P	23	5- 7
1925	BOS	A	P	38	5-12
1926	BOS	A	P	30	6-18
1929	CIN	N	P	1	0- 0
	BRTR			125	25-47

ZAK, FRANK TOM
B.FEB.23,1923 PASSAIC,N.J.
D.FEB.6,1972 PASSAIC,N.J.

YR	CL	LEA	POS	G	REC
1944	PIT	N	S	87	.300
1945	PIT	N	2-S	15	.143
1946	PIT	N	S	21	.200
	BRTR			123	.269

ZALUSKY, JOHN FRANCIS
B.JUNE 22,1879 MINNEAPOLIS,MINN
D.AUG.11,1935

YR	CL	LEA	POS	G	REC
1903	NY	A	C	6	.267
	BRTR				

ZAMLOCH, CARL EUGENE
B.OCT.6,1890 OAKLAND,CAL.
D.AUG.19,1963 SANTA BARBARA,CAL

YR	CL	LEA	POS	G	REC
1913	DET	A	P	17	1- 6
	BRTR				

ZAMORA, OSCAR JOSE (SOSA)
B.SEPT.23,1944 CAMAGUEY,CUBA

YR	CL	LEA	POS	G	REC
1974	CHI	N	P	56	3- 9
1975	CHI	N	P	52	5- 2
1976	CHI	N	P	40	5- 3
	BRTR			148	13-14

ZANNI, DOMINICK THOMAS "DOM"
B.MAR.1,1932 NEW YORK,N.Y.

YR	CL	LEA	POS	G	REC
1958	SF	N	P	1	1- 0
1959	SF	N	P	9	0- 0
1961	SF	N	P	8	1- 0
1962	CHI	A	P	44	6- 5
1963	CHI	A	P	5	0- 0
	CIN	N	P	31	1- 1
1965	CIN	N	P	8	0- 0
1966	CIN	N	P	5	0- 0
	BRTR			111	9- 6

ZAPUSTAS, JOSEPH JOHN
B.JULY 25,1911 S.BOSTON,MASS.

YR	CL	LEA	POS	G	REC
1933	PHI	A	O	2	.200
	BRTR				

ZARDON, JOSE ANTONIO (VALDES) "GUINEO"
B.MAY 20,1923 HAVANA,CUBA

YR	CL	LEA	POS	G	REC
1945	WAS	A	O	54	.290
	BRTR				

ZARILLA, ALLEN LEE "ZEKE"
B.MAY 1,1919 LOS ANGELES,CAL.

YR	CL	LEA	POS	G	REC
1943	STL	A	O	70	.254
1944	STL	A	O	100	.299
1946	STL	A	O	125	.259
1947	STL	A	O	127	.224
1948	STL	A	O	144	.329
1949	STL	A	O	15	.250
	BOS	A	O	124	.285
1950	BOS	A	O	130	.325
1951	CHI	A	O	120	.257
1952	CHI	A	O	39	.232
	STL	A	O	48	.238
	BOS	A	O	21	.183
1953	BOS	A	O	57	.194
	BLTR			1120	.277

ZAUCHIN, NORBERT HENRY "NORM"
B.NOV.17,1929 DETROIT,MICH.

YR	CL	LEA	POS	G	REC
1951	BOS	A	1	5	.167
1955	BOS	A	1	130	.239
1956	BOS	A	1	44	.214
1957	BOS	A	1	52	.264
1958	WAS	A	1	96	.228
1959	WAS	A	1	19	.211
	BRTR			346	.233

ZAY

YR	CL	LEA	POS	G	REC
1886	BAL	AA	P	1	0- 1

ZEARFOSS, DAVID WILLIAM TILDEN
B.JAN.1,1868 SCHENECTADY,N.Y.
D.SEPT.12,1945

YR	CL	LEA	POS	G	REC
1896	NY	N	C	16	.220
1897	NY	N	C	5	.363
1898	NY	N	C	1	1.000
1904	STL	N	C	25	.213
1905	STL	N	C	19	.157
	TR			66	.208

ZEIDER, ROLLIE HUBERT "BUNIONS"
B.NOV.16,1883 AUBURN,IND.
D.SEPT.12,1967 AUBURN,IND.

YR	CL	LEA	POS	G	REC
1910	CHI	A	2-S	136	.217
1911	CHI	A	1-S	73	.254
1912	CHI	A	1-3	129	.245
1913	CHI	A	2	15	.438
	NY	A	2-S	46	.227
1914	CHI	F	3	120	.263
1915	CHI	F	2-S-3	130	.233
1916	CHI	N	2-3	98	.235
1917	CHI	N	2-S-3	108	.243
1918	CHI	N	1-2-3	82	.223
	BRTR			937	.239

ZEISER, MATTHEW J.
B.SEPT.25,1888 CHICAGO,ILL.

YR	CL	LEA	POS	G	REC
1914	BOS	A	P	2	0- 0
	BRTR				

ZELLER, BARTON WALLACE "BART"
B.JULY 22,1941 CHICAGO HEIGHTS, ILL.

YR	CL	LEA	POS	G	REC
1970	STL	N	C	1	.000
	BRTR				

ZEPP, WILLIAM CLINTON "BILL"
B.JULY 22,1946 DETROIT,MICH.

YR	CL	LEA	POS	G	REC
1969	MIN	A	P	4	0- 0
1970	MIN	A	P	43	9- 4
1971	DET	A	P	16	1- 1
	BRTR			63	10- 5

ZERNIAL, GUS EDWARD "OZARK IKE"
B.JUNE 27,1923 BEAUMONT,TEX.

YR	CL	LEA	POS	G	REC
1949	CHI	A	O	73	.318
1950	CHI	A	O	143	.280
1951	CHI	A	O	4	.105
	PHI	A	O	139	.274
1952	PHI	A	O	145	.262
1953	PHI	A	O	147	.284
1954	PHI	A	1-O	97	.250
1955	KC	A	1-O	120	.254
1956	KC	A	1-O	109	.224
1957	KC	A	1-O	131	.236
1958	DET	A	O	66	.323
1959	DET	A	1-O	60	.227
	BRTR			1234	.265

ZETTLEIN, GEORGE "CHARMER"
B.JULY 18,1844 BROOKLYN,N.Y.
D.MAY 23,1905

YR	CL	LEA	POS	GP	G	REC
1871	CHI	NA	P-O	24	25	17- 7
	MUT	NA	P		1	0- 1
	CHI	NA	P		3	1- 2
1872	TRO	NA	P-O	22	25	14- 8
						.248
	ECK	NA	P-U	8	9	1- 7
						.059
1873	PHI	NA	P		49	35-14
1874	CHI	NA	P		57	27-30
1875	CHI	NA	P		33	18-15
	PHI	NA	P	20	21	11- 9
1876	ATH	N	P-1	25	32	4-19
						.211
	BRTR			242	255	128-112

ZICK, ROBERT GEORGE
B.APR.26,1927 CHICAGO,ILL.

YR	CL	LEA	POS	G	REC
1954	CHI	N	P	10	0- 0
	BLTR				

ZIEBER, HARRY
(SEE EDWARD C. WHITING)

ZIEGLER, CHARLES W.
B.FEB.2,1875 CANTON,OHIO
D.MAR.16,1904

YR	CL	LEA	POS	G	REC
1899	CLE	N	2-S	2	.250
1900	PHI	N	3	3	.273
				5	.263

ZIEGLER, GEORGE J.
B.1872 CHICAGO,ILL.
D.JULY 22,1916

YR	CL	LEA	POS	G	REC
1890	PIT	N	P	1	0- 0

ZIENTARA, BENEDICT JOSEPH
B.FEB.14,1920 CHICAGO,ILL.

YR	CL	LEA	POS	G	REC
1941	CIN	N	2	9	.286
1946	CIN	N	2-3	78	.289
1947	CIN	N	2-3	117	.258
1948	CIN	N	2-3-S	74	.187
	BRTR			278	.254

ZIES, WILLIAM

YR	CL	LEA	POS	G	REC
1891	STL	AA	C	1	.000

YR	CL	LEA	POS	GP	G	REC

ZIMMER, CHARLES LOUIS "CHIEF"
B.NOV.23,1860 MARIETTA,OHIO
D.AUG.22,1949

YR	CL	LEA	POS	GP	G	REC
1884	DET	N	C-O		8	.071
1886	MET	AA	C		5	.187
1887	CLE	AA	C		14	.321
1888	CLE	AA	C		63	.250
1889	CLE	N	C		80	.258
1890	CLE	N	C		125	.214
1891	CLE	N	C		116	.261
1892	CLE	N	C		111	.268
1893	CLE	N	C		55	.309
1894	CLE	N	C		88	.285
1895	CLE	N	C		83	.336
1896	CLE	N	C		89	.273
1897	CLE	N	C		81	.314
1898	CLE	N	C		18	.250
1899	CLE	N	C		20	.342
	LOU	N	C		74	.299
1900	PIT	N	C		80	.298
1901	PIT	N	C		67	.222
1902	PIT	N	C-1		40	.268
1903	PHI	N	M-C		35	.220
	BRTR				1252	.272

ZIMMER, DONALD WILLIAM "DON"
B.JAN.17,1931 CINCINNATI,OHIO

YR	CL	LEA	POS	GP	G	REC
1954	BRO	N	S		24	.182
1955	BRO	N	2-S-3		88	.239
1956	BRO	N	2-S-3		17	.300
1957	BRO	N	2-S-3		84	.219
1958	LA	N	2-S-3		127	.262
1959	LA	N	2-S-3		97	.165
1960	CHI	N	2-S-3-O		132	.258
1961	CHI	N	2-3-O		128	.252
1962	NY	N	3		14	.077
	CIN	N	2-S-3		63	.250
1963	LA	N	2-S-3		22	.217
	WAS	A	2-3		83	.248
1964	WAS	A	C-2-3-O		121	.246
1965	WAS	A	C-2-3		95	.199
	BRTR				1095	.235

NON-PLAYING MANAGER
SD(N) 1972-73, BOS(A) 1976

ZIMMERMAN, EDWARD DESMOND
B.JAN.4,1883 OCEANIC,N.J.
D.MAY 6,1945

YR	CL	LEA	POS	GP	G	REC
1906	STL	N	3		5	.213
1911	BRO	N	3		122	.185
	BRTR				127	.186

ZIMMERMAN, GERALD ROBERT "JERRY"
B.SEP.21,1934 OMAHA,NEB.

YR	CL	LEA	POS	GP	G	REC
1961	CIN	N	C		76	.206
1962	MIN	A	C		34	.274
1963	MIN	A	C		39	.232
1964	MIN	A	C		63	.200
1965	MIN	A	C		83	.214
1966	MIN	A	C		60	.252
1967	MIN	A	C		104	.167
1968	MIN	A	C		24	.111
	BRTR				483	.204

ZIMMERMAN, HENRY "HEINE"
B.FEB.9,1887 NEW YORK,N.Y.
D.MAR.14,1969 NEW YORK,N.Y.

YR	CL	LEA	POS	GP	G	REC
1907	CHI	N	2		3	.142
1908	CHI	N	2		30	.292
1909	CHI	N	2		47	.273
1910	CHI	N	2-S-3		86	.284
1911	CHI	N	2-3		139	.307
1912	CHI	N	1-3		145	.372
1913	CHI	N	3		127	.313
1914	CHI	N	S-3		146	.296
1915	CHI	N	2-3		139	.265
1916	CHI	N	2-3		107	.294
	NY	N	2-3		40	.265
1917	NY	N	3		150	.297
1918	NY	N	1-3		121	.272
1919	NY	N	3		123	.255
	BRTR				1403	.295

ZIMMERMAN, ROY FRANKLIN
B.SEPT.13,1916 PINE GROVE,PA.

YR	CL	LEA	POS	GP	G	REC
1945	NY	N	1-O		27	.276
	BLTL					

ZIMMERMAN, WILLIAM H.
B.JAN.20,1889 KENGEN,GERMANY
D.OCT.4,1952

YR	CL	LEA	POS	GP	G	REC
1915	BRO	N	O		22	.281
	BRTR					

ZINK, WALTER CYRUS
B.NOV.21,1898 PITTSFIELD,MASS.
D.JUNE 14,1964

YR	CL	LEA	POS	GP	G	REC
1921	NY	N	P		2	0- 0
	BRTR					

ZINN, FRANK
B.1865 PHILADELPHIA,PA.

YR	CL	LEA	POS	GP	G	REC
1888	ATH	AA	C		2	.000

ZINN, GUY
B.FEB.13,1887 RICHIE CO.,W.VA.
D.OCT.6,1949

YR	CL	LEA	POS	GP	G	REC
1911	NY	A	O		9	.148
1912	NY	A	O		106	.264
1913	BOS	N	O		36	.297
1914	BAL	F	O		61	.277
1915	BAL	F	O		100	.269
	BLTR				312	.270

ZINN, JAMES EDWARD
B.JAN.31,1897 BENTON,ARK.

YR	CL	LEA	POS	GP	G	REC
1919	PHI	A	P	5	10	1- 3
1920	PIT	N	P	6	8	1- 1
1921	PIT	N	P	32	33	7- 6
1922	PIT	N	P		5	0- 0
1929	CLE	A	P	18	20	4- 6
	BLTR			66	76	13-16

ZINSER, WILLIAM FRANCIS
B.JAN.6,1918 ASTORIA,N.Y.

YR	CL	LEA	POS	GP	G	REC
1944	WAS	A	P		2	0- 0
	BRTR					

ZIPFEL, MARION SYLVESTER "BUD"
B.NOV.18,1938 BELLEVILLE,ILL.

YR	CL	LEA	POS	GP	G	REC
1961	WAS	A	1		50	.200
1962	WAS	A	1-O		68	.239
	BLTR				118	.220

ZISK, RICHARD WALTER "RICHIE"
B.FEB.6,1949 BROOKLYN,N.Y.

YR	CL	LEA	POS	GP	G	REC
1971	PIT	N	O		7	.200
1972	PIT	N	O		17	.189
1973	PIT	N	O		103	.324
1974	PIT	N	O		149	.313
1975	PIT	N	O		147	.290
1976	PIT	N	O		155	.289
	BRTR				578	.299

ZITZMANN, WILLIAM ARTHUR
B.NOV.19,1897 LONG ISLAND CITY, N.Y.

YR	CL	LEA	POS	GP	G	REC
1919	PIT	N	O		11	.192
	CIN	N	O		2	.000
1925	CIN	N	S-O		104	.252
1926	CIN	N	O		53	.245
1927	CIN	N	S-3-O		88	.284
1928	CIN	N	3-O		101	.297
1929	CIN	N	1-O		47	.226
	BRTR				406	.267

ZMICH, EDWARD A.
B.1882

YR	CL	LEA	POS	GP	G	REC
1910	STL	N	P		9	0- 5
1911	STL	N	P		4	1- 0
	BLTL				13	1- 5

ZOLDAK, SAMUEL WALTER "SAD SAM"
B.DEC.8,1919 BROOKLYN,N.Y.
D.AUG.25,1966 MINEOLA,N.Y.

YR	CL	LEA	POS	GP	G	REC
1944	STL	A	P		18	0- 0
1945	STL	A	P	26	27	3- 2
1946	STL	A	P		35	9-11
1947	STL	A	P		35	9-10
1948	STL	A	P		11	2- 4
	CLE	A	P		23	9- 6
1949	CLE	A	P		27	1- 2
1950	CLE	A	P		33	4- 2
1951	PHI	A	P		26	6-10
1952	PHI	A	P		16	0- 6
	BLTL			250	251	43-53

ZUBER, WILLIAM HENRY "BILL" OR "GOOBER"
B.MAR.26,1913 AMANA,IOWA

YR	CL	LEA	POS	GP	G	REC
1936	CLE	A	P		2	1- 1
1938	CLE	A	P		15	0- 3
1939	CLE	A	P		16	2- 0
1940	CLE	A	P		17	1- 1
1941	WAS	A	P		36	6- 4
1942	WAS	A	P		37	9- 9
1943	NY	A	P		20	8- 4
1944	NY	A	P		22	5- 7
1945	NY	A	P		21	5-11
1946	NY	A	P		3	0- 1
	BOS	A	P		15	5- 1
1947	BOS	A	P		20	1- 0
	BRTR				224	43-42

ZUPO, FRANK JOSEPH
B.AUG.29,1939 SAN FRANCISCO,CAL

YR	CL	LEA	POS	GP	G	REC
1957	BAL	A	C		10	.083
1958	BAL	A	C		1	.000
1961	BAL	A	C		5	.500
	BLTR				16	.167

ZUVERINK, GEORGE
B.AUG.20,1924 HOLLAND,MICH.

YR	CL	LEA	POS	GP	G	REC
1951	CLE	A	P		16	0- 0
1952	CLE	A	P	1	2	0- 0
1954	CIN	N	P		2	0- 0
	DET	A	P		35	9-13
1955	DET	A	P		14	0- 5
	BAL	A	P		28	4- 3
1956	BAL	A	P		62	7- 6
1957	BAL	A	P		56	10- 6
1958	BAL	A	P		45	2- 2
1959	BAL	A	P		6	0- 1
	BRTR		265	266	32-36

ZWILLING, EDWARD HARRISON "DUTCH"
B.NOV.2,1888 ST.LOUIS,MO.

YR	CL	LEA	POS	GP	G	REC
1910	CHI	A	O		27	.184
1914	CHI	F	O		155	.308
1915	CHI	F	O		150	.291
1916	CHI	N	O		35	.113
	BLTL				367	.284

THE LAST OF HIS KIND

Connie Mack, baseball's most revered figure, died February 8, 1956, in German-town, Pa., at the age of 93. His career spanned two centuries as player, manager and clubowner, and for the first 50 years of the American League he was the Phila-delphia Athletics' only manager. In 1886 (left) the thin New England shoe factory hand started as a catcher with Washington of the National League. This is how he looked (right), 70 years later, only three months before he was to die.

IV WORLD SERIES

America's most discussed and popular sporting event is the World Series which annually pits the championship teams of the two major leagues against each other.

The Series is a logical, lucrative and legendary climax to every baseball season. After five months of campaigning, each club strictly within its own league, two teams survive as the fittest. What better than a post-season play-off to determine a single undisputed champion? Yet the World Series did not always extend in an unbroken skein through professional baseball history. League snobbishness of one sort or another has kept pennant winners apart in certain years rather than let the question of league superiority be settled on the ball field.

In those seasons when the majors consisted of only one league, no World Series was necessary. Still, it is interesting to note that the craving for some sort of post-season playoff was so strong that for several years there was an artificial "championship" set played each Autumn between the first and second place finishers for the Temple Cup.

Herewith are the highlights, scoring summary, winning and losing pitchers, homers and attendance figures of all past World Series games:

1882

At the end of the American Association's first season, the champion Cincinnati club challenged Chicago's NL winners. Bespectacled Will White blanked Chicago in the opener. Larry Corcoran retaliated in the next game. With honors all even, the series came to an untimely end. AA president Denny McKnight, enraged at player raids and other shabby treatment during the season from the NL, wired the Reds that they would be expelled if they continued the series. Cincinnati was ready to defy McKnight, but Chicago player-manager Cap Anson decided to abandon further play for the best interest of all concerned.

Result: Chicago NL won 1; Cincinnati AA, 1.

```
1st Game, at Cincinnati, Oct 6            R.  H.  E.
Chicago (NL)       000  000  000   ---    0   7   3
Cincinnati (AA)    000  004  00x   ---    4  10   2
   Pitchers--GOLDSMITH vs. WHITE. Attendance--2,700.

2nd Game, at Cincinnati, Oct. 7
Chicago (NL)       200  000  000   ---    2   4   0
Cincinnati (AA)    000  000  000   ---    0   3   3
   Pitchers--CORCORAN vs. WHITE. Attendance--4,500.
```

1884

With league quarrels ironed out by now, the pennant winners met in a fully sanctioned playoff. Hardly tired after pitching 60 victories for Providence in NL competition, Old Hoss Radbourn went on to conquer New York's Mets, pride of the AA, three times in as many days. He topped Tim Keefe's fine flinging the first two games. Keefe turned umpire for the third game, and when it began to turn into a rout he mercifully called a halt because of alleged darkness at the end of six innings.

Result: Providence NL won 3; Mets AA, 0.

```
1st Game, at New York, Oct. 23            R.  H.  E.
Metropolitan(AA) 000  000  000     ---    0   2   1
Providence (NL)  201  000  30x     ---    6   5   3
   Pitchers--KEEFE vs. RADBOURN. Attend.--1,800.

2nd Game, at New York, Oct. 24
Providence (NL)  000  030  0       ---    3   5   3
Metropolitan(AA) 000  010  0       ---    1   3   0
          (called, end of seventh: darkness)
   Pitchers -- RADBOURN vs. KEEFE. Homer -- Denny
(Pro.). Attendance--1,000.

3rd Game, at New York, Oct. 25
Providence (NL) 120  144         ---   12  13   4
Metropolitan(AA) 000  011        ---    2   5   2
          (called, end of sixth: darkness)
   Pitchers--RADBOURN vs. BECANNON. Att.--300.
```

1885

In the sixth inning of the second game of this bitter rivalry, manager-captain-first baseman Charlie Comiskey pulled his St. Louis AA club off the field in protest against a decision by umpire Dan Sullivan. The game was declared forfeit to Chicago NL, but the Browns won a moral victory since Sullivan did not officiate thereafter. Animosity lingered long after the series, which ended in a tie. St. Louis counted itself the champion, insisting that the forfeited second game should not count in the records. Most people agreed with Cap Anson that his White Stockings were co-champions. Anson hit safely in every game, batting .423. Comiskey, first to field his position away from first base, was outstanding on defense during an erratic series which totaled more errors than hits.

Result: Chicago NL won 3; St. Louis AA, 3; 1 tie.

```
1st Game, at Chicago, Oct. 14          R.  H.  E.
St. Louis (AA)   010  400  00    ---   5   7   4
Chicago (NL)     000  100  04    ---   5   6  11
         (called, end of 8th: darkness)
Pitchers -- Caruthers vs. Clarkson. Homer -- Pfeffer
(Chi.). Attendance -- 3,000.

2nd Game, at St. Louis, Oct. 15
Chicago (NL)     110  003       ---   5   6   5
St. Louis (AA)   300  10x       ---   4   2   4
         (Game forfeited to Chicago, 9-0)
Pitchers--McCORMICK vs. FOUTZ. Attendance--2,000.

3rd Game, at St. Louis, Oct. 16
Chicago (NL)     111  000  001   ---  4   8  12
St. Louis (AA)   500  002  00x   ---  7   8   4
    Pitchers--CLARKSON vs. CARUTHERS. Att.--3,000.

4th Game, at St. Louis, Oct. 17
Chicago (NL)     000  020  000   ---  2   8   3
St. Louis (AA)   001  000  02x   ---  3   6   7
Pitchers--McCORMICK vs. FOUTZ. Homer--Dalrymple
(Chi.). Attendance--3,000.

5th Game, at Pittsburgh, Oct. 22
Chicago (NL)     400  110  3     ---  9   7   1
St. Louis (AA)   010  000  1     ---  2   4   7
         (called, end of 7th: darkness)
Pitchers--CLARKSON vs. FOUTZ. Attendance--500.

6th Game, at Cincinnati, Oct. 23
Chicago (NL)     200  111  040   ---  9  11  10
St. Louis (AA)   002  000  000   ---  2   2   7
Pitchers--McCORMICK vs. CARUTHERS. Att.--1,500.

7th Game, at Cincinnati, Oct. 24
Chicago (NL)     200  020  00    ---  4   9  17
St. Louis (AA)   004  621  0x    ---  13  12  10
         (called in 8th: darkness)
Pitchers--McCORMICK vs. FOUTZ. Attend.--1,200.
```

1886

Renewing their feud of the previous Fall, the Browns and White Stockings met on a winner-take-all basis. St. Louis won only one of the first three games in Chicago, but swept all three at home to make their colorful club-owner, Chris Von der Ahe, gloat over "my poys, champeens of the world." The series ended on a dramatic note. Curt Welch, Brown centerfielder, was on third base in the 10th inning of the last game when King Kelly signaled for a pitchout. Welch daringly streaked for home and made it when Kelly momentarily bobbled the pitch in his mitt. This play was dubbed "Welch's fifteen thousand dollar slide," as a rough estimate of how much it meant to the winners.

Result: St. Louis AA won 4; Chicago NL, 2.

```
1st Game, at Chicago, Oct. 18          R.  H.  E.
St. Louis (AA)   000  000  000   ---   0   5   7
Chicago (NL)     200  001  03x   ---   6  10   5
    Pitchers--FOUTZ vs. CLARKSON. Attend.--6,000.

2nd Game, at Chicago, Oct. 19
St. Louis (AA)   200  230  50    ---  12  13   5
Chicago (NL)     000  000  00    ---   0   2  13
         (called, end of 8th: darkness)
Pitchers--CARUTHERS vs. McCORMICK. Homers --
O'Neill (St. L.) 2. Attendance--3,000.

3rd Game, at Chicago, Oct. 20
Chicago (NL)     200  112  32    ---  11  11   7
St. Louis (AA)   010  002  01    ---   4   9   7
         (called, end of 8th: darkness)
Pitchers--CLARKSON, Williamson (8) vs. CARUTHERS.
Homers--Kelly (Chi.), Gore (Chi.). Attendance--6,000.

4th Game, at St. Louis, Oct. 21
Chicago (NL)     300  002  0     ---   5   6   4
St. Louis (AA)   011  033  x     ---   8   7   4
         (called in 7th: darkness)
Pitchers--CLARKSON vs. FOUTZ. Attendance--8,000.

5th Game, at St. Louis, Oct. 22
Chicago (NL)     011  100  00    ---   3   3   3
St. Louis (AA)   214  003  0x    ---  10  11   3
         (called in 8th: darkness)
Pitchers--WILLIAMSON, Ryan (2) vs. HUDSON. At-
tendance--10,000.

6th Game, at St. Louis, Oct. 23
Chicago (NL)     010  101  000  0  ---  3   6   2
St. Louis (AA)   000  000  030  1  ---  4   5   3
Pitchers--CLARKSON vs. CARUTHERS. Homer--
Pfeffer (Chi.). Attendance--8,000.
```

1887

Behind its famed "Big Four" of Dan Brouthers, Deacon White, Hardy Richardson and Jack Rowe, Detroit NL trounced St. Louis AA in a 15-game traveling circus played in 10 different cities. Pitchers Charles Getzein and Lady Baldwin each won four for the new champions, while Ned Hanlon gained a reputation for

his fine field direction from center-field. Arlie Latham stole a dozen bases for the losers, acted as pivot-man in a triple play and hit .333.

Result: Detroit NL won 10; St. Louis AA, 5.

1st Game, at St. Louis, Oct. 10
				R.	H.	E.
St. Louis (AA)	200 040 000	---		6	16	0
Detroit (NL)	000 000 001	---		1	5	5

Pitchers--CARUTHERS vs. GETZEIN. Attend.--4,208.

2nd Game, at St. Louis, Oct. 11
Detroit (NL)	022 000 100	---		5	12	2
St. Louis (AA)	000 000 120	---		3	10	7

Pitchers--CONWAY vs. FOUTZ. Attendance--6,408.

3rd Game, at Detroit, Oct. 12
St. Louis (AA)	010 000 000 000 0	---	1	13	7
Detroit (NL)	000 000 010 000 1	---	2	7	1

Pitchers--CARUTHERS vs. GETZEIN. Attend.--4,509.

4th Game, at Pittsburgh, Oct. 13
Detroit (NL)	410 012 000	---		8	12	1
St. Louis (AA)	000 000 000	---		0	5	6

Pitchers--BALDWIN vs. KING. Attendance--2,447.

5th Game, at Brooklyn, Oct. 14
St. Louis (AA)	200 002 100	---		5	7	4
Detroit (NL)	000 020 000	---		2	8	5

Pitchers--CARUTHERS vs. CONWAY. Att.--6,796.

6th Game, at New York, Oct. 15
Detroit (NL)	330 000 003	---		9	15	1
St. Louis (AA)	000 000 000	---		0	5	8

Pitchers--GETZEN vs. FOUTZ. Attendance--5,797.

7th Game, at Philadelphia, Oct. 17
St. Louis (AA)	000 000 001	---		1	10	1
Detroit (NL)	030 000 00x	---		3	7	2

Pitchers--CARUTHERS vs. BALDWIN. Homer--O'Neill (St. L.). Attendance--6,478.

8th Game, at Boston, Oct. 18
Detroit (NL)	031 003 200	---		9	17	2
St. Louis (AA)	100 001 000	---		2	12	5

Pitchers -- GETZEIN vs. CARUTHERS. Homers -- Thompson (Det.) 2. Attendance--2,891.

9th Game, at Philadelphia, Oct. 19
St. Louis (AA)	000 101 000	---		2	9	2
Detroit (NL)	000 100 21x	---		4	6	3

Pitchers--KING vs. CONWAY. Attendance--2,389.

10th Game, at Washington, Oct. 21 (AM)
Detroit (NL)	200 010 001	---		4	9	3
St. Louis (AA)	200 031 41x	---		11	19	5

Pitchers--GETZEIN vs. CARUTHERS. Homers--Latham (St. L.), Welch (St. L.), Richardson (Det.). Attendance--1,261.

11th Game, at Baltimore, Oct. 21 (PM)
St. Louis (AA)	110 010 000	---		3	13	7
Detroit (NL)	100 344 10x	---		13	18	7

Pitchers -- FOUTZ vs. BALDWIN. Homer -- Twitchell (Det.). Attendance--2,707.

12th Game, at Brooklyn, Oct. 22
Detroit (NL)	000 010 0	---		1	5	3
St. Louis (AA)	410 000 x	---		5	10	2

(called in 7th: darkness)
Pitchers--CONWAY vs. KING. Attendance--1,138.

13th Game, at Detroit, Oct. 24
Detroit (NL)	020 100 120	---		6	14	3
St. Louis (AA)	100 010 001	---		3	5	5

Pitchers--BALDWIN vs. CARUTHERS. Attend.--3,389.

14th Game, at Chicago, Oct. 25
St. Louis (AA)	000 002 100	---		3	10	5
Detroit (NL)	300 010 00x	---		4	4	4

Pitchers--KING vs. GETZEIN. Attendance--378.

15th Game, at St. Louis, Oct. 26
St. Louis (AA)	340 110	---		9	11	4
Detroit (NL)	011 000	---		2	10	7

(called, end of 6th: cold)
Pitchers--CARUTHERS vs. BALDWIN. Att.--689.

1888

Though St. Louis sold five regulars after losing the previous series, the Browns won the AA pennant for the fourth straight year... only to lose to their NL rivals again. It was decided to play a best-six-out-of-ten series. The New York Giants clinched it in eight games, then tossed away the last two by sending home their big stars: Tim Keefe, Buck Ewing and John Montgomery Ward. Keefe fast-balled four victories. Ewing hit hard and, in an era of stolen bases and passed balls galore, stood out as the colossus of catchers. Ward was such a superb all-around player that one newspaperman wrote that the Browns would have won the series if Ward had shortstopped for them instead.

Result: New York NL won 6; St. Louis AA, 4.

1st Game, at New York, Oct. 16
				R.	H.	E.
St. Louis (AA)	001 000 000	---		1	3	5
New York (NL)	011 000 00x	---		2	3	4

Pitchers--KING vs. KEEFE. Attendance--4,876.

2nd Game, at New York, Oct. 17
St. Louis (AA)	010 000 002	---		3	7	4
New York (NL)	000 000 000	---		0	6	1

Pitchers--CHAMBERLAIN vs. WELCH. Att.--5,575.

3rd Game, at New York, Oct. 18
St. Louis (AA)	000 000 011	---		2	5	5
New York (NL)	200 100 10x	---		4	5	2

Pitchers--KING vs. KEEFE. Attendance--5,780.

4th Game, at Brooklyn, Oct. 19
New York (NL)	104 010 000	---		6	8	2
St. Louis (AA)	001 000 020	---		3	6	4

Pitchers--CRANE vs. CHAMBERLAIN. Att.--3,062.

5th Game, at New York, Oct. 20
St. Louis (AA)	003 001 00	---		4	5	5
New York (NL)	100 000 05	---		6	9	2

(called, end of 8th: darkness)
Pitchers--KING vs. KEEFE. Attendance--9,124.

6th Game, at Philadelphia, Oct. 22
New York (NL)	000 103 35	---		12	13	5
St. Louis (AA)	301 000 01	---		5	3	7

(called, end of 8th: darkness)
Pitchers--WELCH vs. CHAMBERLAIN. Att.--3,281.

7th Game, at St. Louis, Oct. 24
New York (NL)	030 002 00	---		5	11	3
St. Louis (AA)	000 300 04	---		7	8	3

(called, end of 8th: darkness)
Pitchers--CRANE vs. KING. Attendance--4,624.

8th Game, at St. Louis, Oct. 25
New York (NL)	103 100 006	---		11	12	2
St. Louis (AA)	000 100 110	---		3	5	6

Pitchers--KEEFE vs. CHAMBERLAIN. Homers--Ewing (N.Y.), Tiernan (N.Y.). Attendance--4,865.

9th Game, at St. Louis, Oct. 26
St. Louis (AA)	140 020 202 3	---	14	15	4
New York (NL)	035 000 120 0	---	11	14	5

Pitchers--KING, DEVLIN (4) vs. GEORGE. Homer--O'Neill (St. L.). Attendance--711.

10th Game, at St. Louis, Oct. 27
St. Louis (AA)	010 505 421	---		18	17	3
New York (NL)	310 000 021	---		7	13	8

Pitchers--CHAMBERLAIN vs. TITCOMB (5). Homers--George (N.Y.), O'Neill (St. L.), McCarthy (St. L.). Attendance--412.

1889

Manager Jim Mutrie wore his stovepipe hat with regal pride when his Giants repeated as world champions. Cannonball Ed Crane won four games and Hank O'Day, later a famous umpire, won two others. John Ward hit .417 and shortstopped wonderfully. Brooklyn won three of the first four games, only to lose the next five straight.

Result: New York NL won 6; Brooklyn AA, 3.

```
1st Game, at New York, Oct. 18              R.  H.  E.
New York (NL)  020  210  50    ---   10  11   3
Brooklyn (AA)  510  000  24    ---   12  14   6
          (called, end of 8th: darkness)
   Pitchers--KEEFE vs. TERRY. Homer--Collins (Bklyn.).
Attendance--8,848.

2nd Game, at Brooklyn, Oct. 19
New York (NL)  111  120  000   ---    6   9   4
Brooklyn (AA)  110  000  000   ---    2   3   8
   Pitchers--CRANE vs. CARUTHERS. Attend.--16,172.

3rd Game, at New York, Oct. 22
New York (NL)  200  032  00    ---    7  15   2
Brooklyn (AA)  033  120  00    ---    8  11   3
          (called, end of 8th: darkness)
   Pitchers--WELCH, O'Day (6) vs. HUGHES, Caruthers (8).
Homers--Corkhill (Bklyn.), O'Rourke (N.Y.). Attendance--
5,181.

4th Game, at Brooklyn, Oct. 23
New York (NL)  001  105        ---    7   9   8
Brooklyn (AA)  202  033        ---   10   7   1
          (called end of sixth: darkness)
   Pitchers--CRANE vs. TERRY. Homer--Burns (Bklyn.).
Attendance--3,045.

5th Game, at Brooklyn, Oct. 24
New York (NL)  004  040  021   ---   11  12   2
Brooklyn (AA)  000  111  000   ---    3   8   2
   Pitchers--CRANE vs. CARUTHERS. Homers--Brown
(N.Y.), Richardson (N.Y.), Crane (N.Y.). Attendance--2,901.

6th Game, at New York, Oct. 25
Brooklyn (AA)  010  000  000  00 --- 1   6   4
New York (NL)  000  000  001  01 --- 2   6   1
   Pitchers--TERRY vs O'DAY. Attendance--2,556.

7th Game, at New York, Oct. 26
Brooklyn (AA)  004  030  000   ---    7   5   3
New York (NL)  180  001  10x   ---   11  14   4
   Pitchers--LOVETT, Caruthers (4) vs. CRANE, Keefe
(5). Homers--Richardson (N.Y.), O'Rourke (N.Y.). Attend-
ance--3,312.

8th Game, at Brooklyn, Oct. 28
New York (NL)  541  203  001   ---   16  15   4
Brooklyn (AA)  200  000  023   ---    7   5   4
   Pitchers--CRANE vs. TERRY, Foutz (5). Homers--
Foutz (Bklyn.), Tiernan (N.Y.). Attendance--2,584.

9th Game, at New York, Oct. 29
Brooklyn (AA)  200  000  000   ---    2   4   2
New York (NL)  100  001  10x   ---    3   8   5
   Pitchers--TERRY vs. O'DAY. Attendance--3,067.
```

1890

Brooklyn's AA kingpins of 1889 jumped to the NL in 1890 and won the pennant. In the AA, Louisville rose from last to first in one season. However, much of the top talent had switched to the Players League, so the public couldn't cotton to the alleged "world championship" playoff between the NL and AA leaders. Miserable weather further plagued the series. After seven games, the whole thing was called off. By then, each team had won three and one was tied, so, appropriately enough, there was no clear-cut champion.

Result: Brooklyn NL won 3; Louisville AA, 3; 1 tie.

```
1st Game, at Louisville, Oct. 17            R.  H.  E.
Brooklyn (NL)  300  030  30    ---    9  11   1
Louisville (AA) 000  000  00   ---    0   2   6
          (called, end of 8th: darkness)
   Pitchers--TERRY vs. STRATTON. Attendance--5,600.

2nd Game, at Louisville, Oct. 18
Brooklyn (NL)  020  201  000   ---    5   5   3
Louisville (AA) 101  000  001  ---    3   6   5
   Pitchers--LOVETT vs. DAILY. Attendance--2,860.

3rd Game, at Louisville, Oct. 20
Brooklyn (NL)  020  130  10    ---    7  10   2
Louisville (AA) 001  102  03   ---    7  11   3
          (called, end of 8th: darkness)
   Pitchers--Terry vs Stratton, Meakim (4). Attendance
--2,500.

4th Game, at Louisville, Oct. 21
Brooklyn (NL)  031  000  000   ---    4   7   2
Louisville (AA) 301  000  10x  ---    5   9   2
   Pitchers--LOVETT vs. EHRET. Attendance--1,050.

5th Game, at Brooklyn, Oct. 25
Louisville (AA) 010  010  000  ---    2   5   6
Brooklyn (NL)  210  200  20x   ---    7   7   0
   Pitchers--DAILY vs. LOVETT. Homer--Burns (Bklyn.).
Attendance--1,000.

6th Game, at Brooklyn, Oct. 27
Louisville (AA) 012  101  220  ---    9  13   3
Brooklyn (NL)  100  004  030   ---    8  12   3
   Pitchers--STRATTON, Ehret (7) vs. TERRY. Attend-
ance--600.

7th Game, at Brooklyn, Oct. 28
Louisville (AA) 103  000  020  ---    6   8   3
Brooklyn (NL)  200  000  000   ---    2   4   1
   Pitchers--EHRET vs. LOVETT. Attendance--300.
```

1892

Interleague bitterness over player raids prevented an AA-NL playoff in 1891. By the next year, the majors had amalgamated into one league, the 12-club NL. They used an artificial "split season" to create a "world series," but the experiment was dropped after one trial. Cleveland's Spiders won the first-half pennant.

Boston won the second-half, and also had the best full-season record. The opening playoff game was a memorable 11-inning scoreless tie between two pitchers now in the Hall of Fame, Cy Young and Kid Nichols. Boston won the next five straight. No line scores are listed for this spurious World Series, nor for the similar Temple Cup games of the '90s.

Result: Boston NL won 5, Cleveland NL, 0; 1 tie.

1894

William C. Temple, a Pittsburgh sportsman, donated an expensive cup as prize for a post-season series between the NL champion and runner-up. Ned Hanlon's colorful, scrappy Baltimore Orioles refused to take this series seriously after winning the pennant. They didn't bother keeping in shape, and fell easy prey to the second place Giants.

Result: New York NL won 4; Baltimore NL, 0.

1895

Ned Hanlon's Orioles, still regarding the Temple Cub play as post-season exhibition games, bowed again as the runnerup Spiders cleaned up in five games.

Result: Cleveland NL won 4; Baltimore NL, 1.

1896

Stung by taunts of fans who wouldn't let them forget two straight playoff beatings, the Orioles captured their third straight pennant and then entered the Temple Cup set with calculated fury. Third baseman John McGraw and the rest of Baltimore's champions worked into tiptop shape for the October series. They perfected new strategy, including the notable cutoff play. Then they tore into Cleveland for vengeful 7-1, 7-2, 6-2 and 5-0 trouncings.

Result: Baltimore NL won 4; Cleveland NL, 0.

1897

Baltimore barely lost to Boston in the regular season, but the Orioles proved too strong in post-season play, with 54 runs in five games. Since the Temple Cup was one-sided for the fourth straight year, the event lost its flavor, so the league returned the cup to its donor with thanks and ended the unprofitable playoffs.

Result: Baltimore NL won 4; Boston NL, 1.

1903

Marking the end of AL-NL warfare, presidents of the pennant-winning clubs arranged a best five-out-of nine Series. Pittsburgh had just won its third straight NL flag, but untimely injuries reduced the Pirate pitching staff to one effective operator, Deacon Phillippe. The Deacon pitched 44 innings and won three games, but couldn't carry the load alone. Boston lost three of the first four games, then won four straight to bring the crown to the new league. Bill Dinneen pitched three victories and Cy Young two for Boston.

Result: Boston AL won 5; Pittsburgh NL, 3.

```
1st Game, at Boston, Oct. 1                     R.  H.  E.
Pittsburgh (NL)  401   100   100   ---    7   12   2
Boston (AL)      000   000   201   ---    3    6   4
  Pitchers -- PHILLIPPE vs. YOUNG. Homer -- Sebring
(Pitt.). Attendance--16,242.

2nd Game, at Boston, Oct. 2
Pittsburgh (NL)  000   000   000   ---    0    3   2
Boston (AL)      200   001   00x   ---    3    9   0
  Pitchers--LEEVER. Vail (2) vs. DINNEEN. Homers--
Dougherty (Bos.) 2. Attendance--9,415.

3rd Game, at Boston, Oct. 3
Pittsburgh (NL)  012   000   010   ---    4    7   0
Boston (AL)      000   100   010   ---    2    4   2
  Pitchers--PHILLIPPE vs. HUGHES, Young (3). Attend-
ance--18,801.

4th Game, at Pittsburgh, Oct. 6
Boston (AL)      000   010   030   ---    4    9   1
Pittsburgh (NL)  100   010   30x   ---    5   12   1
  Pitchers--DINNEEN vs. PHILLIPPE. Attend.--7,600.

5th Game, at Pittsburgh, Oct. 7
Boston (AL)      000   006   410   ---   11   14   2
Pittsburgh (NL)  000   000   020   ---    2    6   4
  Pitchers--YOUNG vs. KENNEDY, Thompson (8). At-
tendance--12,322.
```

6th Game, at Pittsburgh, Oct. 8

					R.	H.	E.
Boston (AL)	003	020	100	---	6	10	1
Pittsburgh (NL)	000	000	300	--	3	10	3

Pitchers--DINEEN vs. LEEVER. Attendance--11,556.

7th Game, at Pittsburgh, Oct. 10

					R.	H.	E.
Boston (NL)	200	202	010	---	7	11	4
Pittsburgh (NL)	000	101	001	---	3	10	3

Pitchers--YOUNG vs. PHILLIPPE. Attend.--17,038.

8th Game, at Boston, Oct. 13

					R.	H.	E.
Pittsburgh (NL)	000	000	000	---	0	4	3
Boston (AL)	000	201	00x	---	3	8	0

Pitchers--PHILLIPPE vs. DINEEN. Attend.--7,455.

1905

Owner John T. Brush and manager John J. McGraw of the Giants felt such personal bitterness toward the "upstart" American League that they refused to let their 1904 NL champions meet Boston's repeating AL winners. Giant players petitioned in vain to have the series played. However, fans and writers criticized Brush so severely that he later drew up the Brush Rules to govern annual post-season playoffs. These regulations are the same ones that are used today, with few exceptions. Brush's Giants happened to repeat in 1905, so they became the first NL team to play under the modern code. Connie Mack's Athletics furnished poor opposition, since Rube Waddell was sidelined with a lame arm. All five games ended in shutouts, with young Christy Mathewson wielding three of them.

Result: New York NL won 4; Philadelphia AL, 1.

1st Game, at Philadelphia, Oct. 9

					R.	H.	E.
New York (NL)	000	020	001	---	3	10	1
Philadelphia(AL)	000	000	000	---	0	4	0

Pitchers--MATHEWSON vs. PLANK. Attend.--17,955.

2nd Game, at New York, Oct. 10

					R.	H.	E.
Philadelphia(AL)	001	000	020	---	3	6	2
New York (NL)	000	000	000	---	0	4	2

Pitchers--BENDER vs. McGINNITY, Ames (9). Attendance--24,922.

3rd Game, at Philadelphia, Oct. 12

					R.	H.	E.
New York (NL)	200	050	002	---	9	9	1
Philadelphia(AL)	000	000	000	---	0	4	5

Pitchers--MATHEWSON vs. COAKLEY. Att.--10,991.

4th Game, at New York, Oct. 13

					R.	H.	E.
Philadelphia(AL)	000	000	000	---	0	5	2
New York (NL)	000	100	00x	---	1	4	1

Pitchers--PLANK vs. McGINNITY. Att.--13,598.

5th Game, at New York, Oct. 14

					R.	H.	E.
Philadelphia (AL)	000	000	000	---	0	6	0
New York (NL)	000	010	01x	---	2	5	1

Pitchers--BENDER vs. MATHEWSON. Attend.--24,187.

1906

No upset in World Series history ever matched the one in this first intracity battle. The Cubs were favored after having won a record number of 116 games that gave them the NL flag by a margin of 20 games. The White Sox, mired in the second division at midseason, finished first only by virtue of a 19-game winning streak in the last month. The "Hitless Wonders" owned a season batting average of .228, ranking next to last in the majors. Yet outfielder-manager Fielder Jones' White Sox won the series in six games. A lowly substitute named George Rohe decided two games for them with triples, and hit .333. Ed Reulbach pitched a one-hitter and Three-Fingered Brown a two-hitter for the only Cub victories.

Result: Chicago AL won 4; Chicago NL, 2.

1st Game, at West Side Park, Chi., Oct. 9

					R.	H.	E.
Chicago (AL)	000	011	000	---	2	4	1
Chicago (NL)	000	001	000	---	1	4	2

Pitchers--ALTROCK vs. BROWN. Attendance--12,693.

2nd Game, at Comiskey Park, Chi., Oct. 10

					R.	H.	E.
Chicago (AL)	031	001	020	---	7	10	2
Chicago (AL)	000	010	000	---	1	1	2

Pitchers--REULBACH vs. WHITE, Owen. Att.--12,595.

3rd Game, at West Side Park, Chi., Oct. 11

					R.	H.	E.
Chicago (AL)	000	003	000	---	3	4	1
Chicago (NL)	000	000	000	---	0	2	2

Pitchers--WALSH vs. PFEISTER. Attendance--13,750.

4th Game, at Comiskey Park, Chi., Oct. 12

					R.	H.	E.
Chicago (NL)	000	000	100	---	1	7	1
Chicago (AL)	000	000	000	---	0	2	1

Pitchers--BROWN vs. ALTROCK. Attendance--18,385.

5th Game, at West Side Park, Chi., Oct. 13

					R.	H.	E.
Chicago (AL)	102	401	000	---	8	12	6
Chicago (NL)	300	102	000	---	6	6	0

Pitchers--WALSH, White (7) vs. Reulbach, PFEISTER (3), Overall (4). Attendance--23,257.

6th Game, at Comiskey Park, Chi., Oct. 14

					R.	H.	E.
Chicago (NL)	100	010	001	---	3	7	0
Chicago (AL)	340	000	01x	---	8	14	3

Pitchers--BROWN, Overall (2) vs. WHITE. Att.--19,249.

1907

Though a 20-year-old thunderbolt named Ty Cobb had just won his first of a dozen batting crowns, he was a .200 bust in the series, and his Tiger teammates collapsed with him. Hit-

ting hero with a .470 average was Harry Steinfeldt, underrated third baseman of the Cubs' legendary Tinker-Evers-Chance double play combination. Detroit would have won the opener if catcher Charley Schmidt hadn't muffed a third strike with two out in the ninth. Chicago capitalized with the two tying runs, and the game ended in a 12-inning deadlock. The Cubs easily bagged the next four games.

Result: Chicago NL won 4; Detroit AL, 0; 1 tie.

						R.	H.	E.
1st Game, at Chicago, Oct. 8								
Detroit (AL)	000	000	030	000	---	3	9	3
Chicago (NL)	000	100	002	000	---	3	10	5

(called, end of 12th: darkness)
Pitchers--Donovan vs. Overall, Reulbach (10). Attendance--24,377.

2nd Game, at Chicago, Oct. 9							
Detroit (AL)	010	000	000	---	1	9	1
Chicago (NL)	010	200	00x	---	3	9	1

Pitchers--MULLIN vs. PFEISTER. Attend.--21,901.

3rd Game, at Chicago, Oct. 10							
Detroit (AL)	000	001	000	---	1	6	1
Chicago (NL)	010	310	00x	---	5	10	1

Pitchers--SIEVER, Killian (5) vs. REULBACH. Attendance--13,114.

4th Game, at Detroit, Oct. 11							
Chicago (NL)	000	020	301	---	6	7	2
Detroit (AL)	000	100	000	---	1	5	2

Pitchers--OVERALL vs. DONOVAN. Attend.--11,306.

5th Game, at Detroit, Oct. 12							
Chicago (NL)	110	000	000	---	2	7	1
Detroit (AL)	000	000	000	---	0	7	2

Pitchers--BROWN vs. MULLIN. Attendance--7,370.

1908

After winning the pennant on the last day of the season, the Tigers ran into their series nemesis and lost again in five games. Manager-first baseman Frank Chance, whose Cubs clinched the pennant in a playoff of the "Merkle Boner" game with the Giants, led his team with a .421 batting average and five stolen bases. Orvie Overall and Three-Fingered Brown each pitched a shutout and won one other decision.

Result: Chicago NL won 4; Detroit AL, 1.

				R.	H.	E.
1st Game, at Detroit, Oct. 10						
Chicago (NL)	004	000	105	---	10	14	2
Detroit (AL)	100	000	320	---	6	10	4

Pitchers--Reulbach, Overall (7), BROWN (8) vs. Killian, SUMMERS (3). Attendance--10,812.

2nd Game, at Chicago, Oct. 11						
Detroit (AL)	000	000	001	---	1	4	1
Chicago (NL)	000	000	06x	---	6	7	1

Pitchers--DONOVAN vs. OVERALL. Homer--Tinker (Chi.). Attendance--17,760.

						R	H	E
3rd Game, at Chicago, Oct. 12								
Detroit (AL)	100	005	020	---	8	11	4
Chicago (NL)	000	300	000	---	3	7	2

Pitchers--MULLIN vs. PFEISTER, Reulbach (9). Attendance--14,543.

4th Game, at Detroit, Oct. 13						
Chicago (NL)	002	000	001	---	3	10	0
Detroit (AL)	000	000	000	---	0	4	1

Pitchers--BROWN vs. SUMMERS, Winter (9). Attendance--12,907.

5th Game, at Detroit, Oct. 14						
Chicago (NL)	100	010	000	---	2	10	0
Detroit (AL)	000	000	000	---	0	3	0

Pitchers--OVERALL vs. DONOVAN. Attend.--6,210.

1909

After winning 66 games for Pittsburgh in the regular season, Howie Camnitz, Vic Willis and Lefty Leifield failed to take a series game. But freshman righthander Charles (Babe) Adams whipped the Tigers three times. In the only direct offensive duel between those diamond immortals, Honus Wagner of Pittsburgh surpassed Ty Cobb. Wagner hit .333 stole six bases. Cobb hit only .231 and stole one base, a daring dash home which helped win the second game.

Result: Pittsburgh NL won 4; Detroit AL, 3.

				R.	H.	E.
1st Game, at Pittsburgh, Oct. 8						
Detroit (AL)	100	000	000	---	1	6	4
Pittsburgh (NL)	000	121	00x	---	4	5	0

Pitchers--MULLIN vs. ADAMS. Homer--Clarke (Pitt.). Attendance--29,264.

2nd Game, at Pittsburgh, Oct. 9						
Detroit (AL)	023	020	000	---	7	9	3
Pittsburgh (NL)	200	000	000	---	2	5	1

Pitchers--DONOVAN vs. CAMNITZ, Willis (3). Attendance--30,915.

3rd Game, at Detroit, Oct. 11						
Pittsburgh (NL)	510	000	002	---	8	10	3
Detroit (AL)	000	000	402	---	6	10	5

Pitchers--MADDOX vs. SUMMERS, Willett (1), Works (8). Attendance--18,277.

4th Game, at Detroit, Oct. 12						
Pittsburgh (NL)	000	000	000	---	0	5	6
Detroit (AL)	020	300	00x	---	5	8	0

Pitchers--LEIFIELD, Phillippe (5) vs. MULLIN. Attendance--17,036.

5th Game, at Pittsburgh, Oct 13						
Detroit (AL)	100	002	010	---	4	6	1
Pittsburgh (NL)	111	000	41x	---	8	10	2

Pitchers--SUMMERS, Willett (8) vs. ADAMS. Homers--D. Jones (Det.), Crawford (Det.), Clarke (Pitts.). Attendance--21,706.

6th Game, at Detroit, Oct. 14						
Pittsburgh (NL)	300	000	001	---	4	7	3
Detroit (AL)	100	211	00x	---	5	10	3

Pitchers--WILLIS, Camnitz (6), Phillippe (7) vs. MULLIN. Attendance--10,535.

7th Game, at Detroit, Oct. 16						
Pittsburgh (NL)	020	203	010	---	8	7	0
Detroit (AL)	000	000	000	---	0	6	3

Pitchers--ADAMS vs. DONOVAN, Mullin (4). Attendance--17,562.

1910

After winning the pennant for the fourth time in five years, the veteran Cubs ran into a series ambush by the young Athletics and were thrashed in five games. Philadelphia averaged seven runs a game and feasted on Cub hurling for a .317 average. Jack Coombs posted three victories and Eddie Collins hit .429.

Result: Philadelphia AL won 4; Chicago NL, 1.

1st Game, at Philadelphia, Oct. 17				R.	H.	E.
Chicago (NL)	000	000	001	---	1	3	1
Philadelphia(AL)	021	000	01x	---	4	7	2

Pitchers--OVERALL, McIntire (4) vs. BENDER. Attendance--26,891.

2nd Game, at Philadelphia, Oct. 18						
Chicago (NL)	100	000	101	---	3	8	3
Philadelphia(AL)	002	010	60x	---	9	14	4

Pitchers--BROWN, Richie (8) vs. COOMBS, Attendance--24,597.

3rd Game, at Chicago, Oct. 20						
Philadelphia(AL)	125	000	400	---	12	15	1
Chicago (NL)	120	000	020	---	5	6	5

Pitchers -- COOMBS vs. Reulbach, McINTIRE (3), Pfeister (3). Homer -- Murphy (Phila.). Attend.--26,210.

4th Game, at Chicago, Oct. 22						
Philadelphia(AL)	001	200	000	0	---	3	11	3
Chicago (NL)	100	100	001	1	---	4	9	1

Pitchers--BENDER vs. Cole, BROWN (9). Attendance--19,150.

5th Game, at Chicago, Oct. 23						
Philadelphia(AL)	100	010	050	---	7	9	1
Chicago (NL)	010	000	010	---	2	9	2

Pitchers--COOMBS vs. BROWN. Attendance--27,374.

1911

John Franklin Baker, third baseman for the A's, earned the nickname "Home Run" in this series. His four-base blasts beat Rube Marquard in the second game and Christy Mathewson in the third. Though the Giants had stolen 347 bases from NL rivals, they took no such liberties against A's catching. Every game was a pitching duel till the finale, when the A's hammered three hurlers for 13 hits and 13 runs that brought Chief Bender an easy decision. Giant cleanup hitter Jack Murray went 21-for-0 at the plate.

Result: Philadelphia AL won 4; New York NL, 2.

1st Game, at New York, Oct. 14				R.	H.	E.
Philadelphia(AL)	010	000	000	---	1	6	2
New York (NL)	000	100	10x	---	2	5	0

Pitchers--BENDER vs. MATHEWSON. Att.--38,281.

2nd Game, at Philadelphia, Oct. 16						
New York (NL)	010	000	000	---	1	5	3
Philadelphia(AL)	100	002	00x	---	3	4	0

Pitchers--MARQUARD, Crandall (8) vs. PLANK. Homer--Baker (Phil.). Attendance--26,286.

3rd Game, at New York, Oct. 17						
Philadelphia(AL)	000	000	001	02	---	3	9	2
New York (NL)	001	000	000	01	---	2	3	5

Pitchers--COOMBS vs. MATHEWSON. Homer--Baker (Phil.). Attendance--37,216.

4th Game, at Philadelphia, Oct. 24						
New York (NL)	200	000	000	---	2	7	3
Philadelphia(AL)	000	310	00x	---	4	11	1

Pitchers--MATHEWSON, Wiltse (8) vs. BENDER. Attendance--24,355.

5th Game, at New York, Oct. 25						
Philadelphia(AL)	003	000	000	0	---	3	7	1
New York (NL)	000	000	102	1	---	4	9	2

Pitchers--Coombs, PLANK (10) vs. Marquard, Ames (4), CRANDALL (8). Homer--Oldring (Phil.). Attendance--33,228.

6th Game, at Philadelphia, Oct. 26						
New York (NL)	100	000	001	---	2	4	3
Philadelphia(AL)	001	401	70x	---	13	13	5

Pitchers--AMES, Wiltse (5), Marquard (7) vs. BENDER. Attendance--20,485.

1912

Behind, three games to one, the Giants rallied to win the next two and practically clinched the title with a 2-1 lead behind Matty in the 10th inning of the last game. In the fateful last half, outfielder Fred Snodgrass muffed a lazy fly by Clyde Engle, Red Sox pinch hitter. On the next play, Snodgrass speared Harry Hooper's deep drive. Steve Yerkes walked. Tris Speaker's simple foul fell between Chief Meyers and Fred Merkle, though either could have caught the ball while shaking hands with the other. Speaker then lined a single to score Engle with the tying run. Duffy Lewis was passed intentionally, and Larry Gardner flied to Josh Devore in deep right, Yerkes scoring after the catch for the winning tally. This marked the third victory of the series for Smoky Joe Wood, who had posted a phenomenal 34-5 season mark for the Sox.

Result: Boston AL won 4; New York NL, 3; 1 tie.

1st Game, at New York, Oct. 8				R.	H.	E.
Boston (AL)	000	001	300	---	4	6	1
New York (NL)	020	000	001	---	3	8	1

Pitchers--WOOD vs. TESREAU, Crandall (8). Attendance--35,730.

2nd Game, at Boston, Oct. 9
```
New York (NL)   010  100  030  10  ---   6  11  5
Boston (AL)     300  010  010  10  ---   6  10  1
```
(called, end of 11th: darkness)
Pitchers--Mathewson vs. Collins, Hall (8). Bedient (11). Attendance--30,148.

3rd Game, at Boston, Oct. 10
```
New York (NL)   010  010  000  ---   2  7  1
Boston (AL)     000  000  001  ---   1  7  0
```
Pitchers--MARQUARD vs. O'BRIEN, Bedient (9). Attendance--36,624.

4th Game, at New York, Oct. 11
```
Boston (AL)     010  100  001  ---   3  8  1
New York (NL)   000  000  100  ---   1  9  1
```
Pitchers--WOOD vs. TESREAU, Ames (8). Attendance --36,502.

5th Game, at Boston, Oct. 12
```
New York (NL)   000  000  100  ---   1  3  1
Boston (AL)     002  000  00x  ---   2  5  1
```
Pitchers--MATHEWSON vs. BEDIENT. Att.--34,683.

6th Game, at New York, Oct. 14
```
Boston (AL)     020  000  000  ---   2  7  2
New York (NL)   500  000  00x  ---   5  11  2
```
Pitchers--O'BRIEN, Collins (2) vs. MARQUARD. Attendance--30,622.

7th Game, at Boston, Oct. 15
```
New York (NL)   610  002  101  ---  11  16  4
Boston (AL)     010  000  210  ---   4   9  3
```
Pitchers--TESREAU vs. WOOD, Hall (2). Homers--Doyle (N. Y.), Gardner (Bos.). Attendance--32,694.

8th Game, at Boston, Oct. 16
```
New York (NL)   001  000  000  1  ---   2  9  2
Boston (AL)     000  000  100  2  ---   3  8  5
```
Pitchers--MATHEWSON vs. Bedient, WOOD (8). Attendance--17,034.

1913

A series of injuries ruined Giant chances. Their only victory was a 10-inning shutout by Mathewson. The A's really romped, with another home run for Baker, who hit .450, plus a .421 average for Eddie Collins. Chief Bender won two; Eddie Plank pitched a two-hitter to top his rival of college days, Matty, and 20-year-old Bullet Joe Bush won his only start handily.

Result: Philadelphia AL won 4; New York NL, 1.

1st Game, at New York, Oct. 7
```
                                         R.  H.  E.
Philadelphia(AL) 000  320  010  ---   6  11  1
New York (NL)    001  030  000  ---   4  11  0
```
Pitchers--BENDER vs. MARQUARD, Crandall (6), Tesreau (8). Homer--Baker (Phil.). Attend.--36,291.

2nd Game, at Philadelphia, Oct. 8
```
New York (NL)    000  000  000  3  ---   3  7  2
Philadelphia(AL) 000  000  000  0  ---   0  8  2
```
Pitchers--MATHEWSON vs. PLANK. Attend.--20,563.

3rd Game, at New York, Oct. 9
```
Philadelphia(AL) 320  000  210  ---   8  12  1
New York (NL)    010  010  100  ---   2   5  1
```
Pitchers--BUSH vs. TESREAU, Crandall (7). Homer--Schang (Phil.). Attendance--36,896.

4th Game, at Philadelphia, Oct. 10
```
New York (NL)    000  000  320  ---   5  8  2
Philadelphia(AL) 010  320  00x  ---   6  9  0
```
Pitchers--MARQUARD vs. BENDER. Homer--Merkle (N. Y.). Attendance--20,568.

5th Game, at New York, Oct. 11
```
Philadelphia(AL) 102  000  000  ---   3  6  1
New York (NL)    000  010  000  ---   1  2  2
```
Pitchers--PLANK vs. MATHEWSON. Attend.--36,682.

1914

Rising from the cellar in mid-July to the pennant in September, the Boston Braves "Miracle Team" kept their magic touch through the Fall classic. They swept the vaunted A's, $100,000 infield and all. Connie Mack was so shocked that he broke up his star-studded squad the next season. Boston's dependable mound trio of Dick Rudolph, Bill James and George Tyler held the A's to a collective BA of .172. Hank Gowdy went on a .545 hitting rampage for Boston with five walks, a single, three doubles, a triple and homer.

Result: Boston NL won 4; Philadelphia AL, 0.

1st Game, at Philadelphia, Oct. 9
```
                                        R.  H.  E.
Boston (NL)      020  013  010  ---   7  11  2
Philadelphia(AL) 010  000  000  ---   1   5  0
```
Pitchers--RUDOLPH vs. BENDER, Wyckoff (6). Attendance--20,562.

2nd Game, at Philadelphia, Oct. 10
```
Boston (NL)      000  000  001  ---   1  7  1
Philadelphia(AL) 000  000  000  ---   0  2  1
```
Pitchers--JAMES vs. PLANK. Attendance--20,562.

3rd Game, at Boston, Oct. 12
```
Philadelphia(AL) 100  100  000  200  ---   4  8  2
Boston (NL)      010  000  000  201  ---   5  9  1
```
Pitchers--BUSH vs. Tyler, JAMES (11). Homer--Gowdy (Bos.). Attendance--35,520.

4th Game, at Boston, Oct. 13
```
Philadelphia(AL) 000  010  000  ---   1  7  0
Boston (NL)      000  120  .00x  ---   3  6  0
```
Pitchers--SHAWKEY, Pennock (6) vs. RUDOLPH. Attend. --34,365.

1915

Grover Alexander's 31 victories earned the Phils their first pennant. Alex proceeded to shade Ernie Shore of the Red Sox in the series opener. But Boston bounced back to win the next four, each by one run. Woodrow Wilson, first U. S. President to attend a World Series, threw out the first ball in the second game. A rookie named George Herman Ruth had led the AL with a won-lost of 18-6, but manager Bill Carrigan wouldn't risk him in series competition beyond one unsuccessful pinch-hitting appearance.

Result: Boston AL won 4; Philadelphia NL, 1.

```
1st Game, at Philadelphia, Oct. 8        R.  H.  E.
Boston (AL)      000   000   010  ---    1   8   1
Philadelphia(NL) 000   100   02x  ---    3   5   1
   Pitchers--SHORE vs. ALEXANDER. Attend.--19,343.
```

```
2nd Game at Philadelphia, Oct. 9
Boston (AL)      100   000   001  ---    2  10   0
Philadelphia(NL) 000   010   000  ---    1   3   1
   Pitchers--FOSTER vs. MAYER. Attendance--20,306.
```

```
3rd Game, at Boston, Oct. 11
Philadelphia(NL) 001   000   000  ---    1   3   0
Boston (AL)      000   100   001  ---    2   6   1
   Pitchers--ALEXANDER vs. LEONARD. Att.--42,300.
```

```
4th Game, at Boston, Oct. 12
Philadelphia(NL) 000   000   010  ---    1   7   0
Boston (AL)      001   001   00x  ---    2   8   1
   Pitchers--CHALMERS vs. SHORE. Attendance--41,096.
```

```
5th Game, at Philadelphia, Oct. 13
Boston (AL)      011   000   021  ---    5  10   1
Philadelphia(NL) 200   200   000  ---    4   9   1
   Pitchers--FOSTER vs. Mayer, RIXEY (3). Homers--
Hooper (Bos.) 2, Lewis (Bos.), Luderus (Phil.). At.--20,306.
```

1916

Brooklyn's plan to beat the Red Sox with southpaws failed. The only Dodger victory was notched by Jack Coombs, the old AL castoff, who thereby won his fifth series game while never being beaten. Duffy Lewis led the Boston batters and Casey Stengel was Brooklyn's hardest hitter. The second game turned out to be the longest in series history, 14 innings, with Babe Ruth blanking the Brooks after a first-inning homer by Hi Myers. Babe drove in the tying run two innings later. Boston won in the 14th when pinch-runner Mike McNally scored from first on a pinch double by Del Gainer.

Result: Boston AL won 4; Brooklyn NL, 1.

```
1st Game, at Boston, Oct. 7             R.  H.  E.
Brooklyn (NL)    000   100   004  ---   5  10   4
Boston (AL)      001   010   31x  ---   6   8   1
   Pitchers--MARQUARD, Pfeffer (8) vs. SHORE, Mays (9).
Attendance--36,117.
```

```
2nd Game at Boston, Oct. 9
Brooklyn (NL) 100  000  000 000 00 --  1   6   2
Boston (AL)   001  000  000 000 01 --  2   7   1
   Pitchers--SMITH vs. RUTH. Homer--H. Myers (Bklyn.).
Attendance--41,373.
```

```
3rd Game, at Brooklyn, Oct. 10
Boston (AL)      000   002   100  ---   3   7   1
Brooklyn (NL)    001   120   00x  ---   4  10   0
   Pitchers--MAYS, Foster (6) vs. COOMBS, Pfeffer (7).
Homer--Gardner (Bos.). Attendance--21,087.
```

```
4th Game, at Brooklyn, Oct. 11
Boston (AL)      030   110   100  ---   6  10   1
Brooklyn (NL)    200   000   000  ---   2   5   4
   Pitchers--LEONARD vs. MARQUARD, Cheney (5),
Rucker (8). Homer--Gardner (Bos.). Attendance--21,662.
```

```
5th Game, at Boston, Oct. 12
Brooklyn (NL)    010   000   000  ---   1   3   3
Boston (AL)      012   010   00x  ---   4   7   2
   Pitchers--PFEFFER, Dell (8) vs. SHORE. Attendance--
42,620.
```

1917

This was a series of heroes and goats. Sometimes the same man was cheered and jeered. Urban Faber tried to steal second base with the bag already occupied, yet more than compensated for the boner by beating the Giants three times. Dave Robertson made a costly muff in the last game, yet the Giant right fielder led both teams with 11 for 22, or an even .500 batting average. Ferdie Schupp, knocked out of the box by the White Sox in less than two innings of the second game, came back to hurl a shutout in the fourth. Third baseman Heinie Zimmerman of the Giants was unjustly ridiculed for chasing Eddie Collins home with the deciding run of the last game, but the real goats were the catcher and first baseman, who had left the plate uncovered in the rundown play. Collins led the victorious Sox with a BA of .409.

Result: Chicago AL won 4; New York NL, 2.

```
1st Game, at Chicago, Oct. 6           R.  H.  E.
New York (NL)    000   010   000  ---   1   7   1
Chicago (AL)     001   100   00x  ---   2   7   1
   Pitchers -- SALLEE vs. CICOTTE. Homer -- Felsch
(Chi.). Attendance--32,000.
```

```
2nd Game, at Chicago, Oct. 7
New York (NL)    020   000   000  ---   2   8   1
Chicago (AL)     020   500   00x  ---   7  14   1
   Pitchers--Schupp, ANDERSON (2), Perritt (4), Tesreau
(8) vs. FABER. Attendance--32,000.
```

```
3rd Game, at New York, Oct. 10
Chicago (AL)     000   000   000  ---   0   5   3
New York (NL)    000   200   00x  ---   2   8   2
   Pitchers--CICOTTE vs. BENTON. Attendance--33,616.
```

```
4th Game, at New York, Oct. 11
Chicago (AL)     000   000   000  ---   0   7   0
New York (NL)    000   110   12x  ---   5  10   1
   Pitchers--FABER, Danforth (8) vs. SCHUPP. Homers--
Kauff (N.Y.) 2. Attendance--27,746.
```

```
5th Game, at Chicago, Oct. 13
New York (NL)    200   200   100  ---   5  12   3
Chicago (AL)     001   001   33x  ---   8  14   6
   Pitchers--SALLEE, Perritt (8) vs. Russell, Cicotte (1),
Williams (7), FABER (8). Attendance--27,323.
```

```
6th Game, at New York, Oct. 15
Chicago (AL)     000   300   001  ---   4   7   1
New York (NL)    000   020   000  ---   2   6   3
   Pitchers--FABER vs. BENTON, Perritt (6). Attendance
--33,969.
```

1918

In this war-curtailed season, the World Series continued only through special permission from the government. Many topnotch stars were in

the Service. George Whiteman, a wartime replacement, helped the Red Sox beat Chicago with five timely hits and several crucial catches. Babe Ruth and Carl Mays each won twice, with Babe extending his streak to an all-time record that still stands—29 consecutive scoreless innings. Ruth was held to only one hit in the series, but it was a triple that drove in two runs of a 3-2 decision in the fourth game. The start of the fifth game was delayed an hour by an unsuccessful player "strike" for a higher share of the receipts.

Result: Boston AL won 4; Chicago NL, 2.

1st Game, at Chicago, Sept. 5					R.	H.	E.
Boston (AL)	000	100	000	---	1	5	0
Chicago (NL)	000	000	000	---	0	6	0

Pitchers--RUTH vs. VAUGHN. Attendance--19,274.

2nd Game, at Chicago, Sept. 6							
Boston (AL)	000	000	001	---	1	6	1
Chicago (NL)	030	000	00x	---	3	7	1

Pitchers--BUSH vs. TYLER. Attendance--20,040.

3rd Game, at Chicago, Sept. 7							
Boston (AL)	000	200	000	---	2	7	0
Chicago (NL)	000	010	000	---	1	7	1

Pitchers--MAYS vs. VAUGHN. Attendance--27,054.

4th Game, at Boston, Sept. 9							
Chicago (NL)	000	000	020	---	2	7	1
Boston (AL)	000	200	01x	---	3	4	0

Pitchers--Tyler, DOUGLASS (8) vs. RUTH, Bush (9). Attendance--22,183.

5th Game, at Boston, Sept. 10							
Chicago (NL)	001	000	002	---	3	7	0
Boston (AL)	000	000	000	---	0	5	0

Pitchers--VAUGHN vs. JONES. Attendance--24,694.

6th Game, at Boston, Sept. 11							
Chicago (NL)	000	100	000	---	1	3	2
Boston (AL)	002	000	00x	---	2	5	0

Pitchers--TYLER, Hendrix (8) vs. MAYS. Attendance--15,238.

1919

Post-war interest in baseball was so high that the series was stretched to best-five-out-of-nine. Chicago's White Sox and the Cincinnati Reds had outclassed their league rivals completely. What should have been a memorable struggle between champions turned out to be one of the most shameful events in sports history, because eight players of the favored Sox "sold out" to gamblers. Ed Cicotte, one of the notorious "Black Sox" later dropped by organized baseball, was knocked out of the box in the opening game. Little Dickie

Kerr bravely tried to hold off the Reds and won twice. But Chicago was ruined by the conspirators and lost in eight games. Strangely, Shoeless Joe Jackson led his team with a .375 average even though he was in on the shady deal. Earle (Greasy) Neale, later a famous football coach, led the Reds with .357.

Result: Cincinnati NL won 5; Chicago AL, 3.

1st Game, at Cincinnati, Oct. 1					R.	H.	E.
Chicago (AL)	010	000	000	---	1	6	1
Cincinnati (NL)	100	500	21x	---	9	14	1

Pitchers--CICOTTE, Wilkinson (4), Lowdermilk (8) vs. RUETHER. Attendance--30,511.

2nd Game, at Cincinnati, Oct. 2							
Chicago (AL)	000	000	200	---	2	10	1
Cincinnati (NL)	000	301	00x	---	4	4	2

Pitchers--WILLIAMS vs. SALLEE. Attend.--29,690.

3rd Game, at Chicago, Oct. 3							
Cincinnati (NL)	000	000	000	---	0	3	1
Chicago (AL)	020	100	00x	---	3	7	0

Pitchers--FISHER, Luque (8) vs. KERR. Att.--29,126.

4th Game, at Chicago, Oct. 4							
Cincinnati (NL)	000	020	000	---	2	5	2
Chicago (AL)	000	000	000	---	0	3	2

Pitchers--RING vs. CICOTTE. Attendance--34,363.

5th Game, at Chicago, Oct. 6							
Cincinnati (NL)	000	004	001	---	5	4	0
Chicago (AL)	000	000	000	---	0	3	3

Pitchers--ELLER vs. WILLIAMS, Mayer (9). Attendance--34,379.

6th Game, at Cincinnati, Oct. 7							
Chicago (AL)	000	013	000	1 ---	5	10	3
Cincinnati (NL)	000	100	000	0 ---	4	11	0

Pitchers--KERR vs. Ruether, RING (6). Att.--32,006.

7th Game, at Cincinnati, Oct. 8							
Chicago (AL)	101	020	000	---	4	10	1
Cincinnati (NL)	000	001	000	---	1	7	4

Pitchers--CICOTTE vs. SALLEE, Fisher (5), Luque (6). Attendance--13,923.

8th Game, at Chicago, Oct. 9							
Cincinnati (NL)	410	013	010	---	10	16	2
Chicago (AL)	001	000	040	---	5	10	1

Pitchers--ELLER vs. WILLIAMS, James (1), Wilkinson (6). Homer--Jackson (Chi.). Attendance--32,930.

1920

Player-manager Tris Speaker reached his greatest glory by leading the Indians to the world championship over the Dodgers. Cleveland's conquest was featured by that sturdy battery of former coal miners from Pennsylvania: spitball pitcher Stanley Coveleski, who pitched three complete-game victories and allowed exactly five hits each time, and catcher Steve O'Neill, who hit .333. Walter Mails, a Dodger castoff, hurled a three-hitter to shade Brooklyn's ace, Sherry Smith, 1-0. In the weird fifth

game, Brooklyn outhit Cleveland, yet lost, 8-1; Elmer Smith hit a grand slam homer, and Indian second baseman Bill Wambsganns executed an unassisted triple play.

Result: Cleveland AL won 5; Brooklyn NL, 2.

1st Game, at Brooklyn, Oct. 5

				R.	H.	E.
Cleveland (AL)	020	100	000	--- 3	5	0
Brooklyn (NL)	000	000	100	--- 1	5	1

Pitchers--COVELESKI vs. MARQUARD, Mamaux (7). Cadore (9). Attendance--23,573.

2nd Game, at Brooklyn, Oct. 6

Cleveland (AL)	000	000	000	--- 0	7	1
Brooklyn (NL)	101	010	00x	--- 3	7	0

Pitchers--BAGBY, Uhle (7) vs. GRIMES. Att.--22,559.

3rd Game, at Brooklyn, Oct. 7

Cleveland (AL)	000	100	000	--- 1	3	1
Brooklyn (NL)	200	000	00x	--- 2	6	1

Pitchers--CALDWELL, Mails (1), Uhle (8) vs. SMITH. Attendance--25,088.

4th Game, at Cleveland, Oct. 9

Brooklyn (NL)	000	100	000	--- 1	5	1
Cleveland (AL)	202	001	00x	--- 5	12	2

Pitchers--CADORE, Mamaux (2), Marquard (3), Pfeffer (6) vs. COVELESKI. Attendance--25,734.

5th Game, at Cleveland, Oct. 10

Brooklyn (NL)	000	000	001	--- 1	13	1
Cleveland (AL)	400	310	00x	--- 8	12	2

Pitchers--GRIMES, Mitchell (4) vs BAGBY. Homers--E. Smith (Clev.), Bagby (Clev.). Attendance--26,884.

6th Game, at Cleveland, Oct. 11

Brooklyn (NL)	000	000	000	--- 0	3	0
Cleveland (AL)	000	001	00x	--- 1	7	3

Pitchers--SMITH vs. MAILS. Attendance--27,194.

7th Game, at Cleveland, Oct. 12

Brooklyn (NL)	000	000	000	--- 0	5	2
Cleveland (AL)	000	110	10x	--- 3	7	3

Pitchers--GRIMES, Mamaux (8) vs. COVELESKI. Attendance--27,525.

1921

The Yankees, later to dominate the World Series scene, won their first league title but failed to beat the Giants in an all-New York series. Successive shutouts by Carl Mays and Waite Hoyt gave the Yankees a two-game edge. Then the Giants found their batting eye and evened up the series. Hoyt won the fifth game, too, but Babe Ruth wrenched his knee and was lost to the Yanks. The Giants rallied to capture the next three games and the title. Hoyt, who hurled 27 innings in this series without an earned run, lost a 1-0 duel with Art Nehf in the finale.

Result: New York NL won 5; New York AL, 3.

1st Game, at Polo Grounds, N. Y., Oct. 5

				R.	H.	E.
New York (AL)	100	011	000	--- 3	7	0
New York (NL)	000	000	000	--- 0	5	0

Pitchers--MAYS vs. DOUGLAS, Barnes (9). Attendance --30,202.

2nd Game, at Polo Grounds, N. Y., Oct. 6

New York (NL)	000	000	000	--- 0	2	3
New York (AL)	000	100	02x	--- 3	3	0

Pitchers--NEHF vs. HOYT. Attendance--34,939.

3rd Game, at Polo Grounds, N. Y., Oct. 7

New York (AL)	004	000	010	--- 5	8	0
New York (NL)	004	000	81x	--- 13	20	0

Pitchers--Shawkey, QUINN (3), Collins (7), Rogers (8) vs. Toney, BARNES (3). Attendance--36,509.

4th Game, at Polo Grounds, N. Y., Oct. 9

New York (NL)	000	000	031	--- 4	9	1
New York (AL)	000	010	001	--- 2	7	1

Pitchers--DOUGLAS vs. MAYS. Homer--Ruth (AL). Attendance--36,372.

5th Game, at Polo Grounds, N. Y., Oct. 10

New York (AL)	001	200	000	--- 3	6	1
New York (NL)	100	000	000	--- 1	10	1

Pitchers--HOYT vs. NEHF. Attendance--35,758.

6th Game, at Polo Grounds, N. Y., Oct. 11

New York (NL)	030	401	000	--- 8	13	0
New York (AL)	320	000	000	--- 5	7	2

Pitchers--Toney, BARNES (1) vs. Harper, SHAWKEY (2), Piercy (9). Homers--E. Meusel (NL), Snyder (NL), Fewster (AL). Attendance--34,283.

7th Game, at Polo Grounds, N. Y., Oct. 12

New York (AL)	010	000	000	--- 1	8	1
New York (NL)	100	000	10x	--- 2	6	0

Pitchers--MAYS vs. DOUGLAS. Attendance--36,503.

8th Game, at Polo Grounds, N. Y., Oct. 13

New York (NL)	100	000	000	--- 1	6	0
New York (AL)	000	000	000	--- 0	4	1

Pitchers--NEHF vs. HOYT. Attendance--25,410.

1922

Giant pitchers held the Yankees to a .203 batting average, Babe Ruth himself being shackled at .118. Poor baserunning further hampered the Yanks, and the best they could do was tie one game. The second match was called at 3-3 after 10 innings because of "darkness." Since there was still half an hour of daylight left, fans booed the game's untimely ending so heavily that Commissioner Landis ordered the gate receipts that day, about $120,000, turned over to charity. Heavy Giant hitting was paced by Heinie Groh's .474 and Frankie Frisch's .471.

Result: New York NL won 4; New York AL, 0; 1 tie.

1st Game, at Polo Grounds, N. Y., Oct. 4

				R.	H.	E.
New York (AL)	000	001	100	--- 2	7	0
New York (NL)	000	000	03x	--- 3	11	3

Pitchers--BUSH, Hoyt (8) vs. Nehf, RYAN (8). Attendance--36,514.

2nd Game, at Polo Grounds, N. Y., Oct. 5

New York (NL)	300	000	000	0 --- 3	8	1
New York (AL)	100	100	010	0 --- 3	8	0

(called, end of 10th: darkness)
Pitchers--Barnes vs. Shawkey. Homers--E. Meusel (NL), Ward (AL). Attendance--37,020.

3rd Game, at Polo Grounds, N. Y., Oct. 6

New York (AL)	000	000	000	--- 0	4	1
New York (NL)	002	000	10x	--- 3	12	1

Pitchers--HOYT, Jones (8) vs. J. SCOTT. Att.--37,620.

4th Game, at Polo Grounds, N. Y., Oct. 7
```
New York (NL)   000  040  000   ---    4   9  1
New York (AL)   200  000  100   ---    3   8  0
```
Pitchers--McQUILLAN vs. MAYS, Jones (9). Homer--Ward (AL). Attendance--36,242.

5th Game, at Polo Grounds, N. Y., Oct. 8
```
New York (AL)   100  010  100   ---    3   5  0
New York (AL)   010  000  03x   ---    5  10  0
```
Pitchers--BUSH vs. NEHF. Attendance--38,551.

1923

The same rivals met for the third straight Fall, but this time there was a new setting and a different result. The Yankees now had their own Stadium and proceeded to bring it their first world championship banner. Outfielder Casey Stengel of the Giants, destined for fame as manager of Yankee champions more than a quarter century later, accounted for the only two NL victories with timely homers. Herb Pennock pitched two complete game victories and saved another for the Yanks in relief. Babe Ruth featured this first million-dollar Series with three homers, a triple, a double, three singles and eight walks.

Result: New York AL won 4; New York NL, 2.

1st Game, at Yankee Stadium, N. Y., Oct. 10 R. H. E.
```
New York (NL)   004  000  001   ---    5   8  0
New York (AL)   120  000  100   ---    4  12  1
```
Pitchers--Watson, RYAN (3) vs. Hoyt, BUSH (3). Homer--Stengel (NL). Attendance--55,307.

2nd Game, at Polo Grounds, N. Y., Oct. 11
```
New York (AL)   010  210  000   ---    4  10  0
New York (NL)   010  001  000   ---    2   9  2
```
Pitchers -- PENNOCK vs. McQUILLAN, Bentley (4). Homers--Ward (AL), E. Meusel (NL), Ruth (AL) 2. Attendance--40,402.

3rd Game, at Yankee Stadium, N. Y., Oct. 12
```
New York (NL)   000  000  100   ---    1   4  0
New York (AL)   000  000  000   ---    0   6  1
```
Pitchers--NEHF vs. JONES, Bush (8). Homer--Stengel (NL). Attendance--62,430.

4th Game, at Polo Grounds, N. Y., Oct. 13
```
New York (AL)   061  100  000   ---    8  13  1
New York (NL)   000  000  031   ---    4  13  1
```
Pitchers--SHAWKEY, Pennock (8) vs. J. SCOTT, Ryan (2), McQuillan (3), Jonnard (8), Barnes (9). Homer--Youngs (NL). Attendance--46,302.

5th Game, at Yankee Stadium, N. Y., Oct. 14
```
New York (NL)   010  000  000   ---    1   3  2
New York (AL)   340  100  00x   ---    8  14  0
```
Pitchers--BENTLEY, J. Scott (2), Barnes (4), Jonnard (8) vs. BUSH. Homer--Dugan (AL). Attendance--62,817.

6th Game, at Polo Grounds, N. Y., Oct. 15
```
New York (AL)   100  000  050   ---    6   5  0
New York (NL)   100  111  000   ---    4  10  1
```
Pitchers--PENNOCK, Jones (8) vs. NEHF, Ryan (8). Homers--Ruth (AL), Snyder (NL). Attendance--34,172.

1924

Second baseman Bucky Harris was only 27, and in his first year as manager, when he brought Washington its first flag. In the Series he conquered John McGraw's last pennant club by the barest margin. The opener went to the Giants, 4-3, with old Walter Johnson bowing to Art Nehf in 12 innings. The seventh and deciding game also was a 12-inning, 4-3 affair, but this time Johnson, appearing in his first World Series after 18 seasons with the Senators, was the winner. The last game saw the Giants suffer three bad breaks: in the eighth, Harris' grounder took a sudden hop over the head of the substitute third baseman Fred Lindstrom, allowing the two tying runs to score; in the 12th, Giant catcher Hank Gowdy dropped a foul fly when he accidentally stepped on his mask, and on the last play of the series Earl McNeely's grounder took a sharp bounce over Lindstrom's head to send in the winning run.

Result: Washington AL won 4; New York NL, 3.

1st Game, at Washington, Oct. 4   R. H. E.
```
New York (NL)   010  100  000  002  ---    4  14  1
Washington (AL) 000  001  001  001  ---    3  10  1
```
Pitchers--NEHF vs. JOHNSON. Homers--Kelly (N.Y.), Terry (N.Y.). Attendance--35,760.

2nd Game, at Washington, Oct. 5
```
New York (NL)   000  000  102   ---    3   6  0
Washington (AL) 200  010  001   ---    4   6  1
```
Pitchers--BENTLEY vs. ZACHARY, Marberry (9). Homers--Goslin (Wash.), Harris (Wash.). Attend.--35,922.

3rd Game, at New York, Oct. 6
```
Washington (AL) 000  200  011   ---    4   9  2
New York (NL)   021  101  01x   ---    6  12  0
```
Pitchers--MARBERRY, Russell (4), Martina (7), Speece (8) vs. McQuillan, RYAN (4), Jonnard (9), Watson (9). Homer--Ryan (N.Y.). Attendance--47,608.

4th Game, at New York, Oct. 7
```
Washington (AL) 003  020  020   ---    7  13  3
New York (NL)   100  011  ---    4   6  1
```
Pitchers--MOGRIDGE, Marberry (8) vs. BARNES, Baldwin (6), Dean (8). Homer--Goslin (Wash.). Att.--49,243.

5th Game, at New York, Oct. 8
```
Washington (AL) 000  100  010   ---    2   9  1
New York (NL)   001  020  03x   ---    6  13  0
```
Pitchers--JOHNSON vs. BENTLEY, McQuillan (8). Homers--Bentley (N.Y.), Goslin (Wash.). Attend.--49,211.

6th Game, at Washington, Oct. 9
```
New York (NL)   100  000  000   ---    1   7  1
Washington (AL) 000  020  00x   ---    2   4  0
```
Pitchers--NEHF, Ryan (8) vs. ZACHARY. Attendance--34,254.

7th Game, at Washington, Oct. 10
```
New York (NL)   000  003  000  000  ---    3   8  3
Washington (AL) 000  100  020  001  ---    4  10  4
```
Pitchers--Barnes, McQuillan (8), Nehf (10), BENTLEY (11) vs. Ogden, Mogridge (1), Marberry (6), JOHNSON (9). Homer--Harris (Wash.). Attendance--31,667.

1925

On the verge of extinction several times, Pittsburgh rallied to upset Washington in seven games. Walter Johnson won the opener. His shutout in the fourth gave the Senators a 3-1 edge. But Pittsburgh swept the next three, with Johnson the subject of a sad form reversal in the finale. The gallant righthander couldn't put his usual stuff on the wet ball, this final rainy afternoon, so that the seven Senator runs were not enough. Kiki Cuyler doubled off him with bases loaded in the eighth to drive in the tying and winning runs. Roger Peckinpaugh was the Washington "goat" with eight errors.

Result: Pittsburgh NL won 4; Washington AL, 3.

```
1st Game, at Pittsburgh, Oct. 7          R.  H.  E.
Washington (AL) 010   020   001   ---    4   8   1
Pittsburgh (NL) 000   010   000   ---    1   5   0
   Pitchers--JOHNSON vs. MEADOWS, Morrison (9). Hom-
ers--J. Harris (Wash.), Traynor (Pitt.). Att.--41,723.

2nd Game, at Pittsburgh, Oct. 8
Washington (AL) 010   000   001   ---    2   8   2
Pittsburgh (NL) 000   100   02x   ---    3   7   0
   Pitchers -- COVELESKIE vs. ALDRIDGE. Homers --
Judge (Wash.), Wright (Pitt.), Cuyler (Pitt.). Att.--43,364.

3rd Game, at Washington, Oct. 10
Pittsburgh (NL) 010   101   000   ---    3   8   3
Washington (AL) 001   001   20x   ---    4   10  1
   Pitchers -- KREMER vs. FERGUSON, Marberry (8).
Homer--Goslin (Wash.). Attendance--36,495.

4th Game, at Washington, Oct. 11
Pittsburgh (NL) 000   000   000   ---    0   6   1
Washington (AL) 004   000   00x   ---    4   12  0
   Pitchers--YDE, Morrison (3) Adams (8) vs. JOHNSON.
Homers--Goslin (Wash.), J. Harris (Wash.). Att.--38,701.

5th Game, at Washington, Oct. 12
Pittsburgh (NL) 002   000   211   ---    6   13  0
Washington (AL) 100   100   100   ---    3   8   0
   Pitchers--ALDRIDGE vs. COVELESKIE, Ballou (7),
Zachary (8), Marberry (9). Homer--J. Harris (Wash.). At-
tendance--35,899.

6th Game, at Pittsburgh, Oct. 13
Washington (AL) 110   000   000   ---    2   6   2
Pittsburgh (NL) 002   010   00x   ---    3   7   1
   Pitchers--FERGUSON, Ballou (8) vs. KREMER. Homers
--Goslin (Wash.), Moore (Pitt.). Attendance--43,810.

7th Game, at Pittsburgh, Oct. 15
Washington (AL) 400   200   010   ---    7   7   2
Pittsburgh (NL) 003   010   23x   ---    9   15  2
   Pitchers--JOHNSON vs. Aldridge, Morrison (1) KREMER
(5), Oldham (9). Homer--Peckinpaugh (Wash.). Attendance--
42,856.
```

1926

Led by Rogers Hornsby, St. Louis won its first NL pennant and upset the Yankees in the Series. Babe Ruth blasted four homers, three of them in one game, but 39-year-old Grover Alexander emerged as the legendary hero of this battle. Alex won the second and sixth games, then ambled out of the bullpen in the seventh inning of the seventh game to strike out Tony Lazzeri with bases loaded. He added two more hitless innings to seal the triumph.

Result: St. Louis NL won 4; New York AL, 3.

```
1st Game, at New York, Oct. 2            R.  H.  E.
St. Louis (NL)  100   000   000   ---    1   3   1
New York (AL)   100   001   00x   ---    2   6   0
   Pitchers--SHERDEL, Haines (8) vs. PENNOCK. At-
tendance--61,658.

2nd Game, at New York, Oct. 3
St. Louis (NL)  002   000   301   ---    6   12  1
New York (AL)   020   000   000   ---    2   4   0
   Pitchers--HOYT vs. SHOCKER, Shawkey (8),
Jones (9). Homers--Southworth (St. L.), Thevenow (St. L.).
Attendance--63,600.

3rd Game, at St. Louis, Oct. 5
New York (AL)   000   000   000   ---    0   5   1
St. Louis (NL)  000   310   00x   ---    4   8   0
   Pitchers--RUETHER, Shawkey (5), Thomas (8) vs.
HAINES. Homer--Haines (St. L.). Attendance--37,708.

4th Game, at St. Louis, Oct. 6
New York (AL)   101   142   100   ---    10  14  1
St. Louis (NL)  100   300   001   ---    5   14  0
   Pitchers--HOYT vs. Rhem, REINHART (5), H. Bell (5),
Hallahan (7), Keen (9). Homers--Ruth (N.Y.) 3. Attendance--
38,825.

5th Game, at St. Louis, Oct. 7
New York (AL)   000   001   001   1   ---   3   9   1
St. Louis (NL)  000   100   100   0   ---   2   7   1
   Pitchers--PENNOCK vs. SHERDEL. Att.--39,552.

6th Game, at New York, Oct. 9
St. Louis (NL)  300   010   501   ---    10  13  2
New York (AL)   000   100   100   ---    2   8   1
   Pitchers--ALEXANDER vs. SHAWKEY, Shocker (7),
Thomas (8). Homer--L. Bell (St. L.). Attend.--48,615.

7th Game, at New York, Oct. 10
St. Louis (NL)  000   300   000   ---    3   8   0
New York (AL)   001   001   000   ---    2   8   3
   Pitchers--HAINES, Alexander (7) vs. HOYT, Pennock
(7). Homer--Ruth (N.Y.). Attendance--38,093.
```

1927

Regarded by many experts as the greatest team of all time, the 1927 Yankees set a league record with 110 victories and went on to sink the Pirates in four straight. Ruth added two Series homers to his season's bag of 60. Relief specialist Cy Moore started the last game for the Yanks and won when John Miljus wild-pitched home the winning run with two out in the ninth. Though he had hit .309 in the regular season, Kiki Cuyler, hero of the 1925 series, was kept on the Pirate bench throughout

these four games because of a grudge held by manager Donie Bush.

Result: New York AL won 4; Pittsburgh NL, 0.

1st Game, at Pittsburgh, Oct 5				R.	H.	E.
New York (AL)	103	010	000	---	5	6	1
Pittsburgh (NL)	101	010	010	---	4	9	2

Pitchers--HOYT, Moore (8) vs. KREMER, Miljus (6). Attendance--41,567.

2nd Game, at Pittsburgh, Oct. 6					R.	H.	E.
New York (AL)	003	000	030	---	6	11	0
Pittsburgh (NL)	100	000	010	---	2	7	2

Pitchers--PIPGRAS vs. ALDRIDGE, Cvengros (8), Dawson (9). Attendance--41,634.

3rd Game, at New York, Oct. 7					R.	H.	E.
Pittsburgh (NL)	000	000	010	---	1	3	1
New York (AL)	200	000	60x	---	8	9	0

Pitchers -- MEADOWS, Cvengros (7) vs. PENNOCK. Homer--Ruth (N.Y.). Attendance--60,695.

4th Game, at New York, Oct. 8					R.	H.	E.
Pittsburgh (NL)	100	000	200	---	3	10	1
New York (AL)	100	020	001	---	4	12	2

Pitchers--Hill, MILJUS (7) vs. MOORE. Homer--Ruth (N.Y.). Attendance--57,909.

1928

Though riddled by injuries to four regulars, the Yankees revenged their 1926 upset by mowing down the Cardinals in four straight. Ruth, lame ankle and all, murdered St. Louis pitching for a .625 average, highest in series history. He topped off the fourth game with three homers. Waite Hoyt won the first and last games. Lou Gehrig, middle man in the Yankee "Murderers' Row", had six passes and six hits for the four games, including four homers.

Result: New York AL won 4; St. Louis NL, 0.

1st Game, at New York, Oct. 4					R.	H.	E.
St. Louis (NL)	000	000	100	---	1	3	1
New York (AL)	100	200	01x	---	4	7	0

Pitchers--SHERDEL, Johnson (8) vs. HOYT. Homers--Meusel (N.Y.), Bottomley (St. L.). Attendance--61,425.

2nd Game, at New York, Oct. 5					R.	H.	E.
St. Louis (NL)	030	000	000	---	3	4	1
New york (AL)	314	000	10x	---	9	8	2

Pitchers--ALEXANDER, Mitchell (3) vs. PIPGRAS. Homer--Gehrig (N.Y.). Attendance--60,714.

3rd Game, at St. Louis, Oct. 7					R.	H.	E.
New York (AL)	010	203	100	---	7	7	2
St. Louis (NL)	200	010	000	---	3	9	3

Pitchers -- ZACHARY vs. HAINES, Johnson (7), Rhem (8). Homers--Gehrig (N.Y.) 2. Attendance--39,602.

4th Game, at St. Louis, Oct. 9					R.	H.	E.
New York (AL)	000	100	420	---	7	15	2
St. Louis (NL)	001	100	001	---	3	11	0

Pitchers--HOYT vs. SHERDEL, Alexander (7). Homers--Ruth (NY.) 3, Durst (N.Y.), Gehrig (N.Y.). Att.--37,331.

1929

The A's trounced the Cubs by unleashing two of the greatest surprises in World Series history. Connie Mack's pitching choice in the opener was aged Howard Ehmke, who had worked only 55 innings in the regular season. The sidearmer struck out 13, a new Series record, to trim Cub ace Charlie Root. The next thunderbolt came in the seventh inning of the fourth game. With Chicago leading, 8-0, Philadelphia suddenly tore into four pitchers with a record 10-run rally. The ill-starred Cubs had a 2-0 lead in the last inning of the fifth game, with one out and bases empty, when the A's exploded for three runs that wound up the Series.

Result: Philadelphia AL won 4; Chicago NL, 1.

1st Game, at Chicago, Oct. 8					R.	H.	E
Philadelphia(AL)	000	000	102	---	3	6	1
Chicago (NL)	000	000	001	---	1	8	2

Pitchers--EHMKE vs. ROOT, Bush (8). Homer--Foxx (Phil.). Attendance--50,740.

2nd Game, at Chicago, Oct. 9					R.	H.	E
Philadelphia(AL)	003	300	120	---	9	12	0
Chicago (NL)	000	030	000	---	3	11	1

Pitchers--EARNSHAW, Grove (5) vs. MALONE, Blake (4), Carlson (6), Nehf (9). Homers--Simmons (Phil.), Foxx (Phil.). Attendance--49,987.

3rd Game, at Philadelphia, Oct. 11					R.	H.	E
Chicago (NL)	000	003	000	---	3	6	1
Philadelphia(AL)	000	010	000	---	1	9	1

Pitchers--BUSH vs. EARNSHAW. Attendance--29,991.

4th Game, at Philadelphia, Oct. 12					R.	H.	E
Chicago (NL)	000	205	100	---	8	10	2
Philadelphia(AL)	000	000	(10)0x	---	10	15	2

Pitchers--Root, Nehf (7), BLAKE (7), Malone (7), Carlson (8) vs. Quinn, Walberg (6), ROMMEL (7), Grove (8). Homers--Grimm (Chi.), Haas (Phil.), Simmons (Phil.). Attendance--29,991.

5th Game, at Philadelphia, Oct. 14					R.	H.	E
Chicago (NL)	002	000	000	---	2	8	1
Philadelphia(AL)	000	000	003	---	3	6	0

Pitchers--MALONE vs. Ehmke, WALBERG (4). Homer--Haas (Phil.). Attendance--29,991.

1930

Connie Mack piloted his fifth world championship team, his A's trumping the Cards in a well-pitched Series. Philadelphia won the first two at home and lost the next two in St. Louis. The fifth game was a scoreless tie until the ninth inning, when Jimmy Foxx cracked a two-run homer off Burleigh Grimes. George Earnshaw notched his second complete-game victory in the sixth game to end the struggle.

Result: Philadelphia AL won 4; St. Louis NL, 2.

1st Game, at Philadelphia, Oct. 1
                                R. H. E.
St. Louis (NL)   002 000 000 --- 2 9 0
Philadelphia(AL) 010 101 11x --- 5 5 0
  Pitchers -- GRIMES vs. GROVE. Homers -- Cochrane (Phil.), Simmons (Phil.). Attendance--32,295.

2nd Game, at Philadelphia, Oct. 2
St. Louis (NL)   010 000 000 --- 1 6 2
Philadelphia(AL) 202 -200 00x --- 6 7 2
  Pitchers--RHEM, Lindsey (4), Johnson (7) vs. EARN-SHAW. Homers--Cochrane (Phil.), Watkins (St. L.). Attendance--32,295.

3rd Game, at St. Louis, Oct. 4
Philadelphia(AL) 000 000 000 --- 0 7 0
St. Louis (NL)   000 110 21x --- 5 10 0
  Pitchers--WALBERG, Shores (5), Quinn (7) vs. HALLA-HAN. Homer--Douthit (St. L.). Attendance--36,944.

4th Game, at St. Louis, Oct. 5
Philadelphia(AL) 100 000 000 --- 1 4 1
St. Louis (NL)   001 200 00x --- 3 5 1
  Pitchers--GROVE vs. HAINES. Attendance--39,946.

5th Game, at St. Louis, Oct. 6
Philadelphia(AL) 000 000 002 --- 2 5 0
St. Louis (NL)   000 000 000 --- 0 3 1
  Pitchers--Earnshaw, GROVE (8) vs. GRIMES. Homer--Foxx (Phil.). Attendance--38,844.

6th Game, at Philadelphia, Oct. 8
St. Louis (NL)   000 000 001 --- 1 5 1
Philadelphia(AL) 201 211 00x --- 7 7 0
  Pitchers--HALLAHAN, Johnson (3), Lindsey (6), Bell (8) vs. EARNSHAW. Homers -- Dykes (Phil.), Simmons (Phil.). Attendance--32,295.

1931

Pepper Martin, a brash rookie, ran wild for the Cardinals to thwart a star-studded A's team. Martin batted .500, with a homer, four doubles, seven singles, five runs scored and five runs batted in. Hardboiled Burleigh Grimes and lefthander Bill Hallahan each won a pair. Hallahan beat Earnshaw with a shutout in the second game, yielded only one run while beating Waite Hoyt in the fifth and came back in the seventh and last game to save Grimes' victory by stifling a ninth-inning rally.

Result: St. Louis NL won 4; Philadelphia AL, 3.

1st Game, at St. Louis, Oct. 1
                                R. H. E.
Philadelphia(AL) 004 000 200 --- 6 11 0
St. Louis (NL)   200 000 000 --- 2 12 0
  Pitchers--GROVE vs. DERRINGER, Johnson (8). Homer--Simmons (Phil.). Attendance--38,529.

2nd Game, at St. Louis, Oct. 2
Philadelphia(AL) 000 000 000 --- 0 3 0
St. Louis (NL)   010 000 10x --- 2 6 1
  Pitchers--EARNSHAW vs. HALLAHAN. Att.--35,947.

3rd Game, at Philadelphia, Oct. 5
St. Louis (NL)   020 200 001 --- 5 12 0
Philadelphia(AL) 000 000 002 --- 2 2 0
  Pitchers--GRIMES vs. GROVE, Mahaffey (9). Homer--Simmons (Phil.). Attendance--32,295.

4th Game, at Philadelphia, Oct. 6
St. Louis (NL)   000 000 000 --- 0 2 1
Philadelphia(AL) 100 002 00x --- 3 10 0
  Pitchers--JOHNSON, Lindsey (6) vs. EARNSHAW. Homer--Foxx (Phil.). Attendance--32,295.

5th Game, at Philadelphia, Oct. 7
                                R. H. E.
St. Louis (NL)   100 002 011 --- 5 12 0
Philadelphia(AL) 000 000 100 --- 1 9 0
  Pitchers--HALLAHAN vs. HOYT, Walberg (7), Rommel (9). Homers--Martin (St. L.), Watkins (St. L.). Attendance--32,295.

6th Game, at St. Louis, Oct. 9
Philadelphia(AL) 000 040 400 --- 8 8 1
St. Louis (NL)   000 001 000 --- 1 5 2
  Pitchers--GROVE vs. DERRINGER, Johnson (5), Lindsey (7), Rhem (9). Attendance--39,401.

7th Game, at St. Louis, Oct. 10
Philadelphia(AL) 000 000 002 --- 2 7 1
St. Louis (NL)   202 000 00x --- 4 5 0
  Pitchers--EARNSHAW, Walberg (8) vs. GRIMES, Hallahan (9). Attendance--20,805.

1932

The old Yankee habit of winning in four straight victimized the Cubs this time. It was sweet revenge for Yank manager Joe McCarthy, who had been fired as Cub manager two years earlier. Playing in his last World Series, Ruth poled two homers, including his blast into the bleachers right after fabulously pointing there. Though less dramatic than Babe, Gehrig was even more effective with three homers, a double, five singles, two passes, nine runs scored and eight runs batted in.

Result: New York AL won 4; Chicago NL, 0.

1st Game, at New York, Sept. 28
                             R. H. E.
Chicago (NL) 200 000 220 --- 6 10 1
New York (AL) 000 305 31x --- 12 8 2
  Pitchers--BUSH, Grimes (6), Smith (8) vs. RUFFING. Homer--Gehrig (N.Y.). Attendance--41,459.

2nd Game, at New York, Sept. 29
Chicago (NL) 101 000 000 --- 2 9 0
New York (AL) 202 010 00x --- 5 10 1
  Pitchers--WARNEKE vs. GOMEZ. Attendance--50,709.

3rd Game, at Chicago, Oct. 1
New York (AL) 301 020 001 --- 7 8 1
Chicago (NL) 102 100 001 --- 5 9 4
  Pitchers--PIPGRAS, Pennock (9) vs. ROOT, Malone (5), May (7), Tinning (9). Homers--Ruth (N.Y.) 2, Gehrig (N.Y.) 2, Cuyler (Chi.), Hartnett (Chi.). Attendance--49,986.

4th Game, at Chicago, Oct. 2
New York (AL) 102 002 404 --- 13 19 4
Chicago (NL) 400 001 001 --- 6 9 1
  Pitchers--Allen, MOORE (1), Pennock (7) vs. Bush, Warneke (1), MAY (4), Tinning (9), Grimes (9). Homers--Demaree (Chi.), Lazzeri (N.Y.) 2, Combs (N.Y.). Attendance--49,844.

1933

Player-manager Bill Terry's strategy, sterling Giant pitching and strong stickwork by Mel Ott repulsed the Senators in five games. Earl

Whitehill prevented a sweep by blanking the Giants in the third game. Carl Hubbell won twice, including an 11-inning struggle in the fourth game. The fifth game also went into extra innings. Ott homered in the 10th, and Dolph Luque stemmed a Senator surge in the last half to end the Series.

Result: New York NL won 4; Washington AL, 1.

```
1st Game, at New York, Oct. 3              R.   H.   E.
Washington (AL) 000  100  001   ---   2    5    3
New York (NL)   202  000  00x   ---   4   10    2
  Pitchers--STEWART, Russell (3), Thomas (8) vs. HUB-
BELL. Homer--Ott (N.Y.). Attendance--46,672.

2nd Game, at New York, Oct. 4
Washington (AL) 001  000  000   ---   1    5    0
New York (NL)   000  006  00x   ---   6   10    0
  Pitchers--CROWDER, Thomas (6), McColl (7) vs. SCHU-
MACHER. Homer--Goslin (Wash.). Attend.--35,461.

3rd Game, at Washington, Oct. 5
New York (NL)   000  000  000   ---   0    5    0
Washington (AL) 210  000  10x   ---   4    9    1
  Pitchers--FITZSIMMONS, Bell (8) vs. WHITEHILL.
Attendance--25,727.

4th Game, at Washington, Oct. 6
New York (NL)   000  000  000  01  ---  2  11   1
Washington (AL) 000  000  100  00  ---  1   8   0
  Pitchers--HUBBELL vs. WEAVER, Russell (11). Homer
--Terry (N.Y.). Attendance--27,762.

5th Game, at Washington, Oct. 7
New York (NL)   020  001  000  1   ---  4  11   1
Washington (AL) 000  003  000  0   ---  3  10   0
  Pitchers--Schumacher, LUQUE (6) vs. Crowder, RUS-
SELL (6). Homers--Schulte (Wash.), Ott (N.Y.). Attendance
--28,454.
```

1934

Coming from behind to capture the NL flag on the last day of the season, the swashbuckling Gashouse Gang then tamed the Tigers. Dizzy Dean, with 30 victories in the regular season, stole the spotlight with two more against Detroit. Brother Paul (nicknamed Daffy) also won a pair. Dizzy was beaned while pinch running in the fourth game, and had to be carried off the field, yet returned to pitch the next day. The roisterous seventh game was an 11-0 triumph for Dizzy, who contributed two of the 17 hits off half a dozen Detroit pitchers. St. Louis slugging star Ducky Medwick bowled over third baseman Owen with a slashing slide in the seventh inning of the finale. When Medwick went to his position in left field, the fans showered him with fruit, vegetables and assorted missiles, so

Commissioner Landis ordered Medwick benched to end the ruckus.

Result: St. Louis NL won 4; Detroit AL, 3.

```
1st Game, at Detroit, Oct. 3              R.   H.   E.
St. Louis (NL)  021  014  000   ---   8   13    2
Detroit (AL)    001  001  010   ---   3    8    5
  Pitchers--J. DEAN vs. CROWDER, Marberry (6) Hogsett
(6). Homers--Medwick (St. L.), Greenberg (Det.). Attend-
ance--42,505.

2nd Game, at Detroit, Oct. 4
St. Louis (NL)  011  000  000  000  ---  2   7   3
Detroit (AL)    000  100  001  ---  3   7   0
  Pitchers--Hallahan, W. WALKER (9) vs. ROWE. At-
tendance--43,451.

3rd Game, at St. Louis, Oct. 5
Detroit (AL)    000  000  001   ---   1    8    2
St. Louis (NL)  110  020  00x   ---   4    9    1
  Pitchers--BRIDGES, Hogsett (5) vs. P. DEAN. Attend-
ance--34,073.

4th Game, at St. Louis, Oct. 6
Detroit (AL)    003  100  150   ---  10   13   1
St. Louis (NL)  011  200  000   ---   4   10   5
  Pitchers--AUKER vs. Carleton, Vance (3), W. WALKER
(5), Haines (8), Mooney (9). Attendance--37,492.

5th Game, at St. Louis, Oct. 7
Detroit (AL)    010  002  000   ---   3    7    0
St. Louis (NL)  000  000  100   ---   1    7    1
  Pitchers--BRIDGES vs. J. DEAN, Carleton (9). Homers
--Gehringer (Det.), Delancey (St. L.). Attendance--38,536.

6th Game, at Detroit, Oct. 8
St. Louis (NL)  100  020  100   ---   4   10    2
Detroit (AL)    001  002  000   ---   3    7    1
  Pitchers--P. DEAN vs. ROWE. Attendance--44,551.

7th Game, at Detroit, Oct. 9
St. Louis (NL)  007  002  200   ---  11   17    1
Detroit (AL)    000  000  000   ---   0    6    3
  Pitchers--J. DEAN vs. AUKER, Rowe (3), Hogsett (3),
Bridges (4), Marberry (8), Crowder (9). Attendance--40,-
902.
```

1935

Detroit lost its heavy hitting first baseman, Hank Greenberg, with a broken wrist in the third game, but still managed to stop the Cubs in six games. Tommy Bridges curve-balled two decisions for Detroit and Lon Warneke won Chicago's pair. With the score tied in the last inning of the sixth game, and the Cubs needing a victory to square the series, Stan Hack led off for them with a triple. However, he was stranded as Bridges retired the next three batters. In the Tiger half, catcher-manager Mickey Cochrane singled, advanced on an infield out and scored the deciding run on Goose Goslin's single.

Result: Detroit AL won 4; Chicago NL, 2.

```
1st Game, at Detroit, Oct. 2              R.   H.   E.
Chicago (NL)    200  000  001   ---   3    7    0
Detroit (AL)    000  000  000   ---   0    4    3
  Pitchers -- WARNEKE vs. ROWE. Homer -- Demaree
(Chi.). Attendance--47,391.
```

2nd Game, at Detroit, Oct. 3
Chicago (NL)   000 010 200   ---   3   6   1
Detroit (AL)   400 300 10x   ---   8   9   2
Pitchers--ROOT, Henshaw (1) Kowalik (4) vs. BRIDGES.
Homer--Greenberg (Det.). Attendance--46,742.

3rd Game, at Chicago, Oct. 4
Detroit (AL)   000 001 040 01 ---   6   12   2
Chicago (NL)   020 010 002 00 ---   5   10   3
Pitchers--Auker, Hogsett (7), ROWE (8) vs. Lee, War-
neke (8), FRENCH (10). Homer--Demaree. Attendance--
45,532.

4th Game, at Chicago, Oct. 5
Detroit (AL)   001 001 000   ---   2   7   0
Chicago (NL)   010 000 000   ---   1   5   2
Pitchers--CROWDER vs. CARLETON, Root (8). Homer
--Hartnett (Chi.). Attendance--49,350.

5th Game, at Chicago, Oct. 6
Detroit (AL)   000 000 001   ---   1   7   1
Chicago (NL)   002 000 10x   ---   3   8   0
Pitchers--ROWE vs. WARNEKE, Lee (7). Homer--Klein
(Chi.). Attendance--49,237.

6th Game, at Detroit, Oct. 7
Chicago (NL)   001 020 000   ---   3   12   0
Detroit (AL)   100 101 001   ---   4   12   1
Pitchers -- FRENCH vs. BRIDGES. Homer -- Herman
(Chi.). Attendance--48,420.

1936

Carl Hubbell closed the NL season with 16 straight victories and opened the Series with a 6-1 triumph for the Giants. But the Yanks bounced back to bag four of the next five. Lefty Gomez was winning pitcher in a record 18-4 drubbing and a 13-5 whipping that each featured a seven-run inning. Contrasted with his ignoble bases-loaded strikeout of 1926, Tony Lazzeri cleaned the sacks with a homer in the second game. Leading Yank sluggers included Jake Powell (.455), Red Rolfe and rookie Joe DiMaggio.

Result: New York AL won 4; New York NL, 2.

1st Game, at Polo Grounds, N. Y., Sept. 30 R. H. E.
New York (AL)   001 000 000   ---   1   7   2
New York (NL)   000 011 04x   ---   6   9   1
Pitchers--RUFFING vs. HUBBELL. Homers--Bartell
(NL), Selkirk (AL). Attendance--39,419.

2nd Game, at Polo Grounds, N. Y., Oct. 2
New York (AL)   207 001 206   ---   18   17   0
New York (NL)   010 300 000   ---   4   6   1
Pitchers--GOMEZ vs. SCHUMACHER, Smith (3), Coff-
man (3), Gabler (5), Gumbert (9). Homers--Dickey (AL),
Lazzeri (AL). Attendance--43,543.

3rd Game, at Yankee Stadium, N. Y., Oct. 3
New York (NL)   000 010 000   ---   1   11   0
New York (AL)   010 000 01x   ---   2   4   0
Pitchers--FITZSIMMONS vs. HADLEY, Malone (9).
Homers--Gehrig (AL), Ripple (NL). Attendance--64,842.

4th Game, at Yankee Stadium, N. Y., Oct. 4
New York (NL)   000 100 010   ---   2   7   1
New York (AL)   013 000 00x   ---   5   10   1
Pitchers--HUBBELL, Gabler (8) vs. PEARSON. Homer
--Gehrig (AL). Attendance--66,669.

5th Game, at Yankee Stadium, N. Y., Oct. 5
New York (NL)   300 001 000 1 ---   5   8   3
New York (AL)   011 002 000 0 ---   4   9   0
Pitchers--SCHUMACHER vs. Ruffing, MALONE (7).
Homer--Selkirk (AL). Attendance--50,024.

6th Game, at Polo Grounds, N. Y., Oct. 6
New York (AL)   021 200 017   ---   13   17   2
New York (NL)   200 010 110   ---   5   9   1
Pitchers--GOMEZ, Murphy (7) vs. FITZSIMMONS, Cas-
tleman (4), Coffman (9), Gumbert (9). Homers--Moore (NL),
Ott (NL), Powell (AL). Attendance--38,427.

1937

Interrupted only by Hubbell's victory in the fourth game, the Yanks easily drove through the Giants. Hubbell was the opening-game victim of a typical Yank "big inning" as the AL sluggers scored seven runs in the sixth inning. Lazzeri hit safely in every game and led the batters with .400. Gomez again won twice.

Result: New York AL won 4; New York NL, 1.

1st Game, at Yankee Stadium, N. Y., Oct. 6 R. H. E.
New York (NL)   000 010 000   ---   1   6   2
New York (AL)   000 007 01x   ---   8   7   0
Pitchers--HUBBELL, Gumbert (6), Coffman (6), Smith
(8) vs. GOMEZ. Homer--Lazzeri (AL). Attend.--60,573.

2nd Game, at Yankee Stadium, N. Y., Oct. 7
New York (NL)   100 000 000   ---   1   7   0
New York (AL)   000 024 20x   ---   8   12   0
Pitchers--MELTON, Gumbert (6), Coffman (6) vs. RUF-
FING. Attendance--57,675.

3rd Game, at Polo Grounds, N. Y., Oct. 8
New York (AL)   012 110 000   ---   5   9   0
New York (NL)   000 000 100   ---   1   3   4
Pitchers--PEARSON, Murphy (9) vs. SCHUMACHER,
Melton (7), Brennan (9). Attendance--37,395.

4th Game, at Polo Grounds, N. Y., Oct. 9
New York (AL)   101 000 001   ---   3   6   0
New York (NL)   060 000 10x   ---   7   12   3
Pitchers--HADLEY, Andrews (2), Wicker (8) vs. HUB-
BELL. Homer--Gehrig (AL). Attendance--44,293.

5th Game, at Polo Grounds, N. Y., Oct. 10
New York (AL)   011 020 000   ---   4   8   0
New York (NL)   002 000 000   ---   2   10   0
Pitchers--GOMEZ vs. MELTON, Smith (6), Brennan (8).
Homers--DiMaggio (AL), Hoag (AL), Ott (NL). Att.--38,-
216.

1938

Manager Joe McCarthy again beat his former Cub club in four straight games. Big Bill Lee, who won 22 while leading Chicago to the pennant, lost both his starts to the Yanks. Dizzy Dean's fireball was gone, but his slick sidearm stuff stopped the Bombers for seven innings. Diz lost when Frank Crosetti and Joe DiMaggio poked two-run homers in the last two innings. Veteran catcher Bill Dickey and rookie infielder Joe Gordon each hit .400 for the Yanks.

Result: New York AL won 4; Chicago NL, 0.

1st Game, at Chicago, Oct. 5
```
                           R.  H.  E.
New York (AL)  020  000  100   ---   3  12   1
Chicago (NL)   001  000  000   ---   1   9   1
```
    Pitchers--RUFFING vs. LEE, Russell (9). Attendance
--43,642.

2nd Game, at Chicago, Oct. 6
```
New York (AL)  020  000  022   ---   6   7   2
Chicago (NL)   102  000  000   ---   3  11   0
```
    Pitchers--GOMEZ, Murphy (8) vs. J. DEAN, French (9).
Homers--Crosetti (N.Y.), DiMaggio (N.Y.). Att.--42,108.

3rd Game, at New York, Oct. 8
```
Chicago (NL)   000  010  010   ---   2   5   1
New York (AL)  000  022  01x   ---   5   7   2
```
    Pitchers--BRYANT, Russell (6), French (7) vs. PEAR-
SON. Homers--Dickey (N.Y.), Gordon (N.Y.), Marty (Chi.).
Attendance--55,236.

4th Game, at New York, Oct. 9
```
Chicago (NL)   000  100  020   ---   3   8   1
New York (AL)  030  001  04x   ---   8  11   1
```
    Pitchers--LEE, Root (4), Page (7), French (8), Carleton
(8), Dean (8) vs. RUFFING. Homers--Henrich (N.Y.), O'Dea
(Chi.). Attendance--59,847.

1939

Alert and able to cash in on every
break, the Yankees snuffed out the
Reds in four straight games to become the first team to win four
straight world championships. Monte
Pearson's two-hitter in the second
game was backed by the timely hitting
of Babe Dahlgren, who filled in at
first base for non-playing captain
Lou Gehrig. Yankee rookie Charlie
Keller hit hardest in the Series. Enjoying a 4-2 lead in the ninth inning
of the fourth game, the Reds suddenly
snapped their Series streak of errorless ball with four costly bobbles in
two innings, including catcher Ernie
Lombardi's famous "snooze" at home
plate (when he was understandably
stunned in a collision with King Kong
Keller).

Result: New York AL won 4; Cincinnati NL, 0.

1st Game, at New York, Oct. 4
```
                           R.  H.  E.
Cincinnati (NL)  000  100  000   ---   1   4   0
New York (AL)    000  010  001   ---   2   6   0
```
    Pitchers--DERRINGER vs. RUFFING. Attend.--58,541.

2nd Game, at New York, Oct. 5
```
Cincinnati (NL)  000  000  000   ---   0   2   0
New York (AL)    003  100  00x   ---   4   9   0
```
    Pitchers--WALTERS vs. PEARSON. Homer--Dahlgren
(N.Y.). Attendance--59,791.

3rd Game, at Cincinnati, Oct. 7
```
New York (AL)    202  030  000   ---   7   5   1
Cincinnati (NL)  120  000  000   ---   3  10   0
```
    Pitchers--Gomez, HADLEY (2) vs. THOMPSON, Gris-
som (5), Moore (7). Homers--Keller (N.Y.) 2, DiMaggio
(N.Y.), Dickey (N.Y.). Attendance--32,723.

4th Game, at Cincinnati, Oct. 8
```
New York (AL)    000  000  202   3 ---   7   7   1
Cincinnati (NL)  000  000  310   0 ---   4  11   4
```
    Pitchers--Hildebrand, Sundra (5), MURPHY (7) vs.
Derringer, WALTERS (8). Homers--Keller (N.Y.), Dickey
(N.Y.). Attendance--32,794.

1940

No longer having to face the terri-
fying Yankees, the NL returned to the
peak. Cincinnati nipped Detroit's
team of oldsters in an airtight series.
Bobo Newsom won the opener, but
his father, up from South Carolina to
watch him, died of a heart attack
several hours after the game. Newsom pitched a shutout "for dad" in
his next start. Newsom's two decisions were matched by each of two
Reds, Bucky Walters and Paul Derringer. Derringer beat Newsom in the
finale, when each yielded only seven
hits, as slow fielding by Detroit enabled Cincy to score an extra run.
Forty-year-old Jimmy Wilson, filling
in behind the bat for lame Ernie
Lombardi in six games, hit .353 and
stole the only base of the Series.

Result: Cincinnati NL won 4; Detroit AL, 3.

1st Game, at Cincinnati, Oct. 2
```
                           R.  H.  E.
Detroit (AL)     050  020  000   ---   7  10   1
Cincinnati (NL)  000  100  010   ---   2   8   3
```
    Pitchers--NEWSOM vs. DERRINGER, Moore (2), Riddle
(9). Homer--Campbell (Det.). Attendance--31,793.

2nd Game, at Cincinnati, Oct. 3
```
Detroit (AL)     200  001  000   ---   3   3   1
Cincinnati (NL)  022  100  00x   ---   5   9   0
```
    Pitchers--ROWE, Gorsica (4) vs. WALTERS. Homer--
Ripple (Cin.). Attendance--30,640.

3rd Game, at Detroit, Oct. 4
```
Cincinnati (NL)  100  000  012   ---   4  10   1
Detroit (AL)     000  100  42x   ---   7  13   1
```
    Pitchers--TURNER, Moore (7), Beggs (8) vs. BRIDGES.
Homers--York (Det.), Higgins (Det.). Attend.--52,877.

4th Game, at Detroit, Oct. 5
```
Cincinnati (NL)  201  100  010   ---   5  11   1
Detroit (AL)     001  001  000   ---   2   5   1
```
    Pitchers--DERRINGER vs. TROUT, Smith (3), McKain
(7). Attendance--54,093.

5th Game, at Detroit, Oct. 6
```
Cincinnati (NL)  000  000  000   ---   0   3   0
Detroit (AL)     003  400  01x   ---   8  13   0
```
    Pitchers--THOMPSON, Moore (4), Vander Meer (5),
Hutchings (8), vs. NEWSOM. Homer--Greenberg (Det.).
Attendance--55,189.

6th Game, at Cincinnati, Oct. 7
```
Detroit (AL)     000  000  000   ---   0   5   0
Cincinnati (NL)  200  001  01x   ---   4  10   2
```
    Pitchers--ROWE, Gorsica (1), Hutchinson (8) vs. WAL-
TERS. Homer--Walters (Cin.). Attendance--30,481.

7th Game, at Cincinnati, Oct. 8
```
Detroit (AL)     001  000  000   ---   1   7   0
Cincinnati (NL)  000  000  20x   ---   2   7   1
```
    Pitchers--NEWSOM vs. DERRINGER. Att.--26,854.

1941

Brooklyn bowed to the Yankees in
five games that had some bizarre
highlights. Joe Gordon, who hit an

even .500, backed Red Ruffing's pitching with the deciding runs in the opener. This marked 10 consecutive Series games won by the Bronx Bombers. Whitlow Wyatt severed the proud streak the next day. Fred Fitzsimmons was locked in a scoreless hill duel with Marius Russo in the third game when Russo lined a seventh-inning drive off Fitz kneecap, sending him to the hospital. Sloppy fielding by relief pitcher Hugh Casey opened the gate for the two crucial Yank runs in the eighth. Next day, Casey struck out Tom Henrich for what should have been the last out of the game. But catcher Mickey Owen muffed the pitch too. Henrich raced to first to ignite a four-run rally that won for the Yanks, 7-4.

Result: New York AL won 4; Brooklyn NL, 1.

1st Game, at New York, Oct. 1   R. H. E.
Brooklyn (NL)   000   010   100   ---   2   6   0
New York (AL)   010   101   00x   ---   3   6   1
  Pitchers--DAVIS, Casey (6), Allen (7) vs. RUFFING.
Homer--Gordon (N.Y.). Attendance--68,540.

2nd Game, at New York, Oct. 2
Brooklyn (NL)   000   021   000   ---   3   6   2
New York (AL)   011   000   000   ---   2   9   1
  Pitchers--WYATT vs. CHANDLER, Murphy (6). Attendance--66,248.

3rd Game, at Brooklyn, Oct. 4
New York (AL)   000   000   020   ---   2   8   0
Brooklyn (NL)   000   000   010   ---   1   4   0
  Pitchers--RUSSO vs. Fitzsimmons, CASEY (8), French (8), Allen (9). Attendance--33,100.

4th Game, at Brooklyn, Oct. 5
New York (AL)   100   200   004   ---   7   12   0
Brooklyn (NL)   000   220   000   ---   4   9   1
  Pitchers--Donald, Breuer (5), MURPHY (8) vs. Higbe, French (4), Allen (5), CASEY (5). Homer--Reiser (Bklyn.). Attendance--33,813.

5th Game, Brooklyn, Oct. 6
New York (AL)   020   010   000   ---   3   6   0
Brooklyn (NL)   001   000   000   ---   1   4   1
  Pitchers -- BONHAM vs. WYATT. Homer -- Henrich (N.Y.). Attendance--34,072.

1942

A youthful, speedy and nervy Cardinal crew exploded a baseball bombshell by winning the pennant after trailing the Dodgers by 10 1/2 games in August. The Redbirds followed with even a more astounding assault, beating the awesome Yankees four straight after dropping the Series opener to Red Ruffing. St. Louis went winging with such freshman phenoms

as third baseman Whitey Kurowski, pitcher John Beazley and outfielder Stan Musial. Kurowski's triple in the eighth inning of the second game and last-inning homer in the finale brought victory to Beazley each time. Rival centerfielders Terry Moore and Joe DiMaggio dazzled on defense.

Result: St. Louis NL won 4; New York AL, 1.

1st Game, at St. Louis, Sept. 30   R. H. E.
New York (AL)   000   110   032   ---   7   11   0
St. Louis (NL)   000   000   004   ---   4   7   4
  Pitchers--RUFFING, Chandler (9) vs. M. COOPER, Gumbert (8), Lanier (9). Attendance--34,385.

2nd Game, at St. Louis, Oct. 1
New York (AL)   000   000   030   ---   3   10   2
St. Louis (NL)   200   000   110   ---   4   6   0
  Pitchers -- BONHAM vs. BEAZLEY. Homer -- Keller (N.Y.). Attendance--34,255.

3rd Game, at New York, Oct. 2
St. Louis (NL)   001   000   001   ---   2   5   1
New York (AL)   000   000   000   ---   0   6   1
  Pitchers--WHITE vs. CHANDLER, Breuer (9), Turner (9). Attendance--69,123.

4th Game, at New York, Oct. 4
St. Louis (NL)   000   600   201   ---   9   12   1
New York (AL)   100   005   000   ---   6   10   1
  Pitchers--M. Cooper, Gumbert (6), Pollet (6), LANIER (7) vs. Borowy, DONALD (4), Bonham (7). Homer--Keller (N.Y.). Attendance--69,902.

5th Game, at New York, Oct. 5
St. Louis (NL)   000   101   002   ---   4   9   4
New York (AL)   100   100   000   ---   2   7   1
  Pitchers--BEAZLEY vs. RUFFING. Homers--Rizzuto (N.Y.), Slaughter (St. L.), Kurowski (St. L.). Att.--69,052.

1943

This one was a reverse of 1942, with the Yanks whipping the Cards in five games. Spud Chandler won the opener and closer. Though his father died the morning of the second game, Morton Cooper pitched to brother Walker, and they brought St. Louis its only decision. Two Card errors in the eighth inning of the third game opened the gates for the winning four-run rally. Marius Russo pitched and batted his way to a 2-1 victory in the next game. Bill Dickey's homer with one aboard accounted for all the runs in the finale, which also saw Cooper strike out the first five Yank batters.

Result: New York AL won 4; St. Louis NL, 1.

1st Game, at New York, Oct. 5   R. H. E.
St. Louis (NL)   010   010   000   ---   2   7   2
New York (AL)   000   202   00x   ---   4   8   2
  Pitchers--LANIER vs. CHANDLER. Homer--Gordon (N.Y.). Attendance--68,676.

2nd Game, at New York, Oct. 6

| St. Louis (NL) | 001 | 300 | 000 | --- | 4 | 7 | 2 |
| New York (AL) | 000 | 100 | 002 | --- | 3 | 6 | 0 |

Pitchers--M. COOPER vs. BONHAM, Murphy (9). Homers--Marion (St. L.), Sanders (St. L.). Att.--68,578.

3rd Game, at New York, Oct. 7

| St. Louis (NL) | 000 | 200 | 000 | --- | 2 | 6 | 4 |
| New York (AL) | 000 | 001 | 05x | --- | 6 | 8 | 0 |

Pitchers--BRAZLE, Krist (8), Brecheen (8) vs. BOROWY, Murphy (9). Attendance--69,990.

4th Game, at St. Louis, Oct. 10

| New York (AL) | 000 | 100 | 010 | --- | 2 | 6 | 2 |
| St. Louis (NL) | 000 | 000 | 100 | --- | 1 | 7 | 1 |

Pitchers--RUSSO vs. Lanier, BRECHEEN (8). Attendance--36,196.

5th Game, at St. Louis, Oct. 11

| New York (AL) | 000 | 002 | 000 | --- | 2 | 7 | 1 |
| St. Louis (NL) | 000 | 000 | 000 | --- | 0 | 10 | 1 |

Pitchers--CHANDLER vs. M. COOPER, Lanier (8), Dickson (9). Homer--Dickey (N.Y.). Attendance--33,872.

1944

The city of St. Louis enjoyed a "Trolley Series," with the NL entry twice coming from behind to beat the only Brownie team ever to win the AL flag. Of 10 Brown errors, seven came in scoring innings. Mort Cooper lost the opener despite a two-hitter, as George McQuinn blasted a two-run homer. Ken O'Dea's pinch single in the 10th won the next for the Cards. Jack Kramer tamed the Cards the next day, but they snapped back with three straight pitching gems to capture the crown.

Result: St. Louis NL won 4; St. Louis AL, 2.

1st Game, at Sportsman's Park, Oct. 4

					R.	H.	E.
St. Louis (AL)	000	200	000	---	2	2	0
St. Louis (NL)	000	000	001	---	1	7	0

Pitchers--GALEHOUSE vs. M. COOPER, Donnelly (8). Homer--McQuinn (AL). Attendance--33,242.

2nd Game, at Sportsman's Park, Oct. 5

| St. Louis (AL) | 000 | 002 | 000 | 0 --- | 2 | 7 | 4 |
| St. Louis (NL) | 001 | 100 | 000 | 1 --- | 3 | 7 | 0 |

Pitchers--Potter, MUNCRIEF (7) vs. Lanier, DONNELLY (8). Attendance--35,076.

3rd Game, at Sportsman's Park, Oct. 6

| St. Louis (NL) | 100 | 000 | 100 | --- | 2 | 7 | 0 |
| St. Louis (AL) | 004 | 000 | 20x | --- | 6 | 8 | 2 |

Pitchers--WILKS, Schmidt (3), Jurisich (7), Byerly (7) vs. KRAMER. Attendance--34,737.

4th Game, at Sportsman's Park, Oct. 7

| St. Louis (NL) | 202 | 001 | 000 | --- | 5 | 12 | 0 |
| St. Louis (AL) | 000 | 000 | 010 | --- | 1 | 9 | 1 |

Pitchers--BRECHEEN vs. JAKUCKI, Hollingsworth (4), Shirley (8). Homer--Musial (NL). Attendance--35,455.

5th Game, at Sportsman's Park, Oct. 8

| St. Louis (NL) | 000 | 001 | 010 | --- | 2 | 6 | 1 |
| St. Louis (AL) | 000 | 000 | 000 | --- | 0 | 7 | 1 |

Pitchers--M. COOPER vs. GALEHOUSE. Homers--Sanders (NL), Litwhiler (NL). Attendance--36,568.

6th Game, at Sportsman's Park, Oct. 9

| St. Louis (AL) | 010 | 000 | 000 | --- | 1 | 3 | 2 |
| St. Louis (NL) | 000 | 300 | 00x | --- | 3 | 10 | 0 |

Pitchers--POTTER, Muncrief (4), Kramer (7) vs. LANIER, Wilks (6). Attendance--31,630.

1945

Returned from war service in midseason, Hank Greenberg hit a grandslam homer on the last day of the season to put Detroit into the Series. He continued his timely hitting to help beat the Cubs, though he couldn't match the 11 hits each by Doc Cramer, Stan Hack and Phil Cavarretta. Hank Borowy, waived out of the AL in midseason, blanked Detroit in the opener. Only 10 days out of the Navy, Virgil Trucks cuffed the Cubs in the next. Then came Claude Passeau's historic one-hitter, fine flinging jobs by Detroit's Dizzy Trout and Hal Newhouser and a weird overtime Cub victory. That put it up to Newhouser vs. Borowy in the finale, and lefty Hal won decisively as he extended his strikeout total for the Series to 22, a new record.

Result: Detroit AL won 4; Chicago NL, 3.

1st Game, at Detroit, Oct. 3

					R.	H.	E.
Chicago (NL)	403	000	200	---	9	13	0
Detroit (AL)	000	000	000	---	0	6	0

Pitchers--BOROWY vs. NEWHOUSER, Benton (3), Tobin (5), Mueller (8). Homer--Cavarretta (Chi.). Attendance--54,637.

2nd Game, at Detroit, Oct. 4

| Chicago (NL) | 000 | 100 | 000 | --- | 1 | 7 | 0 |
| Detroit (AL) | 000 | 040 | 00x | --- | 4 | 7 | 0 |

Pitchers--WYSE, Erickson (7) vs. TRUCKS. Homer--Greenberg (Det.). Attendance--53,636.

3rd Game, at Detroit, Oct. 5

| Chicago (NL) | 000 | 200 | 100 | --- | 3 | 8 | 0 |
| Detroit (AL) | 000 | 000 | 000 | --- | 0 | 1 | 2 |

Pitchers--PASSEAU vs. OVERMIRE, Benton (7). Attendance--55,500.

4th Game, at Chicago, Oct. 6

| Detroit (AL) | 000 | 400 | 000 | --- | 4 | 7 | 1 |
| Chicago (NL) | 000 | 001 | 000 | --- | 1 | 5 | 1 |

Pitchers--TROUT vs. PRIM, Derringer (4), Vandenberg (6), Erickson (8). Attendance--42,923.

5th Game, at Chicago, Oct. 7

| Detroit (AL) | 001 | 004 | 102 | --- | 8 | 11 | 0 |
| Chicago (NL) | 001 | 000 | 201 | --- | 4 | 7 | 2 |

Pitchers--NEWHOUSER vs. BOROWY, Vandenberg (6), Chipman (6), Derringer (7), Erickson (9). Attend.--43,463.

6th Game, at Chicago, Oct. 8

| Detroit (AL) | 010 | 000 | 240 | 000 | --- | 7 | 13 | 1 |
| Chicago (NL) | 000 | 041 | 200 | 001 | --- | 8 | 15 | 3 |

Pitchers--Trucks, Caster (5), Bridges (6), Benton (7), TROUT (8) vs. Passeau, Wyse (7), Prim (8), BOROWY (9). Homer--Greenberg (Det.). Attendance--41,708.

7th Game, at Chicago, Oct. 10

| Detroit (AL) | 510 | 000 | 120 | --- | 9 | 9 | 1 |
| Chicago (NL) | 100 | 100 | 010 | --- | 3 | 10 | 0 |

Pitchers--NEWHOUSER vs. BOROWY, Derringer (1), Vandenberg (2), Erickson (6), Passeau (8), Wyse (9). Attendance--41,590.

1946

Freshman manager Eddie Dyer guided the Cards to victory in the

first pennant playoff in major league history, to break a tie with Brooklyn. Then his underdog team went on to topple the mighty Red Sox in the Series. Hero laurels went to Harry Brecheen for his three victories. Ted Williams earned the "goat horns" for figuratively beating his head against the stonewall "Boudreau defense" throughout the Series. Only once did he deliberately slice a bunt against the overshifted defense, and he reached base easily. Otherwise he pulled as hard as ever and collected only four other hits, all singles, for a .200 average. With two out and the score tied in the eighth inning of the last game, Enos Slaughter scored all the way from first on Harry Walker's hit over the shortstop's head.

Result: St. Louis NL won 4; Boston AL, 3.

1st Game, at St. Louis, Oct. 6

				R.	H.	E.
Boston (AL)	010	000	001	1 ---	3	9	2
St. Louis (NL)	000	001	010	0 ---	2	7	0

Pitchers--Hughson, JOHNSON (9) vs. POLLET. Homer--York (Bos.). Attendance--36,218.

2nd Game, at St. Louis, Oct. 7

					R.	H.	E.
Boston (AL)	000	000	000	---	0	4	1
St. Louis (NL)	001	020	00x	---	3	6	0

Pitchers--HARRIS, Dobson (8) vs. BRECHEEN. Attendance--35,815.

3rd Game, at Boston, Oct. 9

					R.	H.	E.
St. Louis (NL)	000	000	000	---	0	6	1
Boston (AL)	300	000	01x	---	4	8	0

Pitchers--DICKSON, Wilks (8) vs. FERRISS. Homer--York (Bos.). Attendance--34,500.

4th Game, at Boston, Oct. 10

					R.	H.	E.
St. Louis (NL)	033	010	104	---	12	20	1
Boston (AL)	000	100	020	---	3	9	4

Pitchers--MUNGER vs. HUGHSON, Bagby (3), Zuber (6), Brown (8), Ryba (9), Dreisewerd (9). Homers--Slaughter (St. L.), Doerr (Bos.). Attendance--35,645.

5th Game, at Boston, Oct. 11

					R.	H.	E.
St. Louis (NL)	010	000	002	---	3	4	1
Boston (AL)	110	001	30x	---	6	11	3

Pitchers--Pollet, BRAZLE (1), Beazley (8) vs DOBSON. Homer--Culberson (Bos.). Attendance--35,982.

6th Game, at St. Louis, Oct. 13

					R.	H.	E.
Boston (AL)	000	000	100	---	1	7	0
St. Louis (NL)	003	000	01x	---	4	8	0

Pitchers--HARRIS, Hughson (3), Johnson (8) vs. BRECHEEN. Attendance--35,768.

7th Game, at St. Louis, Oct. 15

					R.	H.	E.
Boston (AL)	100	000	020	---	3	8	0
St. Louis (NL)	010	020	01x	---	4	9	1

Pitchers--Ferriss, Dobson (5), KLINGER (8), Johnson (8) vs. Dickson, BRECHEEN (8). Attendance--36,143.

1947

Despite the lack of a single route-going pitcher, the Dodgers forced the Yanks to the full seven games before

bowing. This two-million-dollar series was a duel between two of the greatest relief artists in history, with Joe Page surpassing Hugh Casey. In the memorable fourth game, Bill Bevens was one out away from an unprecedented no-hitter when pinch hitter Cookie Lavagetto suddenly doubled home the tying and winning runs for Brooklyn. The sixth game was a three-hour, 19-minute marathon highlighted by Al Gionfriddo's miraculous stab of Joe DiMaggio's 415-foot drive to the bullpen gate. Page pitched five scoreless innings of relief to sew up the finale.

Result: New York AL won 4; Brooklyn NL, 3.

1st Game, at New York, Sept. 30

					R.	H.	E.
Brooklyn (NL)	100	001	100	---	3	6	0
New York (AL)	000	050	00x	---	5	4	0

Pitchers--BRANCA, Behrman (5), Casey (7) vs. SHEA, Page (6). Attendance--73,365.

2nd Game, at New York, Oct. 1

					R.	H.	E.
Brooklyn (NL)	001	100	001	---	3	9	2
New York (AL)	101	121	40x	---	10	15	1

Pitchers--LOMBARDI, Gregg (5), Behrman (7), Barney (7) vs. REYNOLDS. Homers--Walker (Bklyn.), Henrich (N.Y.). Attendance--69,865.

3rd Game, at Brooklyn, Oct. 2

					R.	H.	E.
New York (AL)	002	221	100	---	8	13	0
Brooklyn (NL)	061	200	00x	---	9	13	1

Pitchers--NEWSOM, Raschi (2), Drews (3), Chandler (4), Page (6). vs. Hatten, Branca (5), CASEY (7). Homers--DiMaggio (N.Y.), Berra (N.Y.). Attendance--33,098.

4th Game, at Brooklyn, Oct. 3

					R.	H.	E.
New York (AL)	100	100	000	---	2	8	1
Brooklyn (NL)	000	010	002	---	3	1	3

Pitchers--BEVENS vs. Taylor, Gregg (1), Behrman (8), CASEY (9). Attendance--33,443.

5th Game, at Brooklyn, Oct. 4

					R.	H.	E.
New York (AL)	000	110	000	---	2	5	0
Brooklyn (NL)	000	000	000	---	1	4	1

Pitchers--SHEA vs. BARNEY, Hatten (5), Behrman (7), Casey (8). Homer--DiMaggio (N.Y.). Attendance--34,379.

6th Game, at New York, Oct. 5

					R.	H.	E.
Brooklyn (NL)	202	004	000	---	8	12	1
New York (AL)	004	100	001	---	6	15	2

Pitchers--Lombardi, BRANCA (3), Hatten (6), Casey (9) vs. Reynolds, Drews (3), PAGE (5), Newsom (6), Raschi (7), Wensloff (8). Attendance--74,065.

7th Game, at New York, Oct. 6

					R.	H.	E.
Brooklyn (NL)	020	000	000	---	2	7	0
New York (AL)	010	201	10x	---	5	7	0

Pitchers--GREGG, Behrman (4), Hatten (6), Barney (6), Casey (7) vs. Shea, Bevens (2), PAGE (5). Att.--71,548.

1948

Player-manager Lou Boudreau cracked four-for-four to beat Boston for Cleveland in the first playoff in AL annals. But Gene Bearden, a wounded war veteran, was the hurling hero of that extra game, and the

rookie southpaw proved the main difference in the Series, too. Bob Feller lost the opener to the Braves despite a two-hitter. Bob Lemon, a converted outfielder; Bearden, via shutout, and second-stringer Steve Gromek pitched the Indians to victory in the next three games. Boston won an 11-5 slugfest before the largest crowd in baseball history: 86,288 paid. Lemon started folding late in the sixth game, so tireless Bearden came out of the bullpen for a relief job that clinched the championship.

Result: Cleveland AL won 4; Boston NL, 2.

```
1st Game, at Boston, Oct. 6              R.  H.  E.
Cleveland (AL)  000  000  000   ---     0   4   0
Boston (NL)     000  000  01x   ---     1   2   2
    Pitchers--FELLER vs. SAIN. Attendance--40,135.

2nd Game, at Boston, Oct. 7
Cleveland (AL)  000  210  001   ---     4   8   1
Boston (NL)     100  000  000   ---     1   8   3
    Pitchers--LEMON vs. SPAHN, Barrett (5), Potter (8).
Attendance--39,633.

3rd Game, at Cleveland, Oct. 8
Boston (NL)     000  000  000   ---     0   5   1
Cleveland (AL)  001  100  00x   ---     2   5   0
    Pitchers--BICKFORD, Voiselle (4), Barrett (8) vs.
BEARDEN. Attendance--70,306.

4th Game, at Cleveland, Oct. 9
Boston (NL)     000  000  100   ---     1   7   0
Cleveland (AL)  101  000  00x   ---     2   5   0
    Pitchers--SAIN vs. GROMEK. Homers--Doby (Cle.),
Rickert (Bost.). Attendance--81,897.

5th Game, at Cleveland, Oct. 10
Boston (NL)     301  001  600   ---    11  12   0
Cleveland (AL)  100  400  000   ---     5   6   2
    Pitchers--Potter, SPAHN (4) vs. FELLER, Klieman (7),
Christopher (7), Paige (7), Muncrief (8). Homers--Elliott
(Bost.) 2, Mitchell (Cle.), Hegan (Cle.), Salkeld (Bost.). At-
tendance--86,288.

6th Game, at Boston, Oct. 11
Cleveland (AL)  001  002  010   ---     4  10   0
Boston (NL)     000  100  020   ---     3   9   0
    Pitchers--LEMON, Bearden (8) vs. VOISELLE, Spahn
(8). Homer--Gordon (Cle.). Attendance--40,103.
```

1949

Conquering the Dodgers for the third time in less than a decade, the Yankees kept coming up with the right man in the right spot to win in five games. Don Newcombe struck out 11 Yanks in eight innings, only to lose his first game scoreless duel with Allie Reynolds as Tom Henrich opened the home ninth with a homer. Preacher Roe evened it up with a 1-0 job the next day. However, Brooklyn was ruined in the three remaining games by an old nemesis, Bobby Brown, a part-time third baseman and medical student. Brown blasted six hits in those three games and accounted for the deciding margin in all three. Fireman Joe Page contributed more of his incomparable relief to seal the Yankee triumph.

Result: New York AL won 4; Brooklyn NL, 1.

```
1st Game, at New York, Oct. 5           R.  H.  E.
Brooklyn (NL)   000  000  000   ---     0   2   0
New York (AL)   000  000  001   ---     1   5   1
    Pitchers -- NEWCOMBE vs. REYNOLDS. Homer --
Henrich (N.Y.). Attendance--66,224.

2nd Game, at New York, Oct. 6
Brooklyn (NL)   010  000  000   ---     1   7   2
New York (AL)   000  000  000   ---     0   6   1
    Pitchers--ROE vs. RASCHI. Attendance--70,053.

3rd Game, at Brooklyn, Oct. 7
New York (AL)   001  000  003   ---     4   5   0
Brooklyn (NL)   000  100  002   ---     3   5   0
    Pitchers--Byrne, PAGE (4) vs. BRANCA, Banta (9).
Homers -- Reese (Bkly.), Olmo (Bkly.), Campanella
(Bkly.). Attendance--32,788.

4th Game, at Brooklyn, Oct. 8
New York (AL)   000  330  000   ---     6  10   0
Brooklyn (NL)   000  004  000   ---     4   9   1
    Pitchers--LOPAT, Reynolds (6) vs. NEWCOMBE, Hat-
ten (4), Erskine (6), Banta (7). Attendance--33,934.

5th Game, at Brooklyn, Oct. 9
New York (AL)   203  113  000   ---    10  11   1
Brooklyn (NL)   001  001  400   ---     6  11   2
    Pitchers--RASCHI, Page (7) vs. BARNEY, Banta (3),
Erskine (6), Hatten (6), Palica (7), Minner (9). Homers--
DiMaggio (N.Y.), Hodges (Bkly.). Attendance--33,711.
```

1950

After winning the pennant in the 10th inning of the last day of the season, the Philadelphia "Whiz Kids" suffered a severe letdown in the World Series, losing four straight to the Yankees. A daring gamble almost paid off for the NL entry. Manager Ed Sawyer named Jim Konstanty to open the Series, though the bullpen denizen had broken the all-time season record with 74 relief appearances (and no starts!). Konstanty dropped a 1-0 duel to Vic Raschi, who spun a two-hitter. Locked in a .222 batting slump, the Yankees relied on further fine pitching by Allie Reynolds, Ed Lopat, Tom Ferrick and rookie Ed Ford to sweep the rest of the series for their 13th title. Joe DiMaggio blasted a 10th-inning homer into the upper deck of Shibe Park to win the second game.

Result: New York AL won 4; Philadelphia NL, 0.

1st Game, at Philadelphia, Oct. 4   R.   H.   E.
New York (AL)   000   100   000   ---   1   5   0
Philadelphia(NL) 000   000   000   ---   0   2   1
    Pitchers--RASCHI vs. KONSTANTY, Meyer (9). Attendance--30,746.

2nd Game, at Philadelphia, Oct. 5
New York (AL)   010   000   000   1   ---   2   10   0
Philadelphia(NL) 000   010   000   0   ---   1   7   0
    Pitchers--REYNOLDS vs. ROBERTS. Homer--DiMaggio (N.Y.). Attendance--32,660.

3rd Game, at New York, Oct. 6
Philadelphia(NL) 000   001   100   ---   2   10   2
New York (AL)   001   000   011   ---   3   7   0
    Pitchers--Heintzelman, Konstanty (8). MEYER (9) vs. Lopat, FERRICK (9). Attendance--64,505.

4th Game, at NewYork, Oct. 7
Philadelphia(NL) 000   000   002   ---   2   7   1
New York (AL)   200   003   00x   ---   5   8   2
    Pitchers--MILLER, Konstanty (1), Roberts(8)vs. FORD, Reynolds (9). Homer--Berra (N.Y.). Att.--68,098.

1951

The red-hot New York Giants, who had made a sensational late season drive to haul in the NL pennant, were cooled off in the series by a rainy day and resurgent Yankee bats. The Giants had taken a 2-1 lead in games when rain postponed the fourth contest and gave Yankee pitching ace Allie Reynolds an additional day of rest. The Giants were unable to win a game after play resumed. Monte Irvin's theft of home—first in fall competition since 1928—and lefty Dave Koslo's strong hurling job got the Giants off in front in the opener. After Lopat whipped the Giants in the second clash Jim Hearn put the NL one-up the following day. Then came the rain which washed out the Giant chances. McDougald's bases-loaded homer in the fourth battle, Lopat's second win in the fifth and Bob Kuzava's strong relief bit and Hank Bauer's game-saving catch in the sixth game featured the Yankees' next three victories. Irvin slammed 11 hits to tie a record for most safeties in a six-game set, and paced all series hitters with a .458 figure. The series also was marked by the famous "drop kick" incident when Ed Stanky kicked the ball from Phil Rizzuto's hand as the Yankee shortstop was about to tag out the fiery Giant infielder who was attempting to slide into second base on a hit and run play which backfired. Rizzuto dropped the ball and the Giants went on to score

five runs in the inning, a vital factor in their third game triumph.

Result: New York AL won 4; New York NL, 2.

1st Game, at Yankee Stadium, N.Y., Oct. 4   R.   H.   E.
New York (NL)   200   003   000   ---   5   10   1
New York (AL)   010   000   000   ---   1   7   1
    Pitchers--KOSLO vs. REYNOLDS, Hogue (7), Morgan (8). Homer--Dark (NL). Attendance--65,673.

2nd Game, at Yankee Stadium, N.Y., Oct. 5
New York (NL)   000   000   100   ---   1   5   1
New York (AL)   110   000   01x   ---   3   6   0
    Pitchers--JANSEN, Spencer (7) vs. LOPAT. Homer--Collins (AL). Attendance--66,018.

3rd Game, at Polo Grounds, N.Y., Oct. 6
New York (AL)   000   000   011   ---   2   5   2
New York (NL)   010   050   00x   ---   6   7   2
    Pitchers--RASCHI, Hogue (5), Ostrowski (7)vs.HEARN, Jones (8). Homers--Lockman (NL), Woodling (AL). Attendance--52,035.

4th Game, at Polo Grounds, N.Y., Oct. 8
New York (AL)   010   120   200   ---   6   12   0
New York (NL)   100   000   001   ---   2   8   2
    Pitchers--REYNOLDS vs. MAGLIE, Jones (6), Kennedy (9). Homer--DiMaggio (AL). Attendance--49,010.

5th Game, at Polo Grounds, N.Y., Oct. 9
New York (AL)   005   202   400   ---   13   12   1
New York (NL)   100   000   000   ---   1   5   3
    Pitchers--LOPAT vs. JANSEN, Kennedy (4), Spencer (6), Corwin (7), Konikowski (9). Homers--McDougald (AL), Rizzuto (AL). Attendance--47,530.

6th Game, at Yankee Stadium, N.Y., Oct. 10
New York (NL)   000   010   002   ---   3   11   1
New York (AL)   100   003   00x   ---   4   7   0
    Pitchers--KOSLO, Hearn (7), Jansen (8) vs. RASCHI, Sain (7), Kuzava (9). Attendance--61,711.

1952

Casey Stengel tied the world's championship record of four straight titles as he guided the Yankees through a successful seven-game set against the Brooklyn Dodgers. It equaled the mark established by the Bombers of Joe McCarthy vintage who nailed down titles in 1936, '37, '38 and '39. The Yankees did it the hard way, coming from behind to defeat the Dodgers in the last two games played at the National Leaguers' park. Dodger manager Charley Dressen started ace relief artist Joe Black in the opening game and the big right hander responded with a 4-2 victory. It was the first series pitching triumph ever turned in by a Negro. The teams alternated in winning the next four games before the Yankees thundered back to take the last two. Perhaps the most exciting game of the set was the 11-inning thriller won by Brooklyn, 6-5, which gave the Dodgers their three-two edge. Carl Erskine pitched

the distance for the Dodgers, allowing all Yankee runs in the fifth inning. The most dramatic moment of the series was reserved for the seventh inning of the final game. Jackie Robinson popped up a wind-blown fly ball with two out and bases-loaded. With all the runners dashing plate-ward, second baseman Billy Martin circled for the catch. When it appeared as if the ball would drop safely, he just managed to grab it with a last second lunge. Duke Snider slammed four homers for the Dodgers.

Result: New York AL won 4; Brooklyn NL, 3.

1st Game, at Brooklyn, Oct. 1			R.	H.	E.
New York (AL)	010 000 010	---	2	6	2
Brooklyn (NL)	010 002 01x	---	4	6	0

Pitchers--REYNOLDS, Scarborough (8) vs. BLACK. Homers--Robinson (Bklyn.), Snider (Bklyn.), Reese (Bklyn.), McDougald (N.Y.). Attendance--34,861.

2nd Game, at Brooklyn, Oct. 2					
New York (AL)	000 115 000	---	7	10	0
Brooklyn (NL)	001 000 000	---	1	3	1

Pitchers--RASCHI vs. ERSKINE, Loes (6), Lehman (8). Homer--Martin (N.Y.). Attendance--33,792.

3rd Game, at New York, Oct. 3					
Brooklyn (NL)	001 010 012	---	5	11	0
New York (AL)	010 000 010	---	3	6	2

Pitchers--ROE vs. LOPAT, Gorman (9). Homers--Berra (N.Y.), Mize (N.Y.). Attendance--66,698.

4th Game, at New York, Oct. 4					
Brooklyn (NL)	000 000 000	---	0	4	1
New York (AL)	000 100 01x	---	2	4	1

Pitchers -- BLACK, Rutherford (8) vs. REYNOLDS. Homer--Mize (N.Y.). Attendance--71,787.

5th Game, at New York, Oct. 5					
Brooklyn (NL)	010 030 100 01	---	6	10	0
New York (AL)	000 050 000 00	---	5	5	1

Pitchers--ERSKINE vs. Blackwell, SAIN (6). Homers--Snider (Bklyn.), Mize (N.Y.). Attendance--70,536.

6th Game, at Brooklyn, Oct. 6					
New York (AL)	000 000 210	---	3	9	0
Brooklyn (NL)	000 001 010	---	2	8	1

Pitchers--RASCHI, Reynolds (8) vs. LOES, Roe (9). Homers--Snider (Bklyn.) 2, Berra (N.Y.), Mantle (N.Y.). Attendance--30,037.

7th Game, at Brooklyn, Oct. 7					
New York (AL)	000 111 100	---	4	10	4
Brooklyn (NL)	001 110 000	---	2	8	1

Pitchers--Lopat, REYNOLDS (4), Raschi (7), Kuzava (7) vs. BLACK, Roe (6), Erskine (8). Homers--Woodling (N.Y.), Mantle (N.Y.). Attendance--33,195.

1953

The Yankees became the first team in history to win five straight world championships as they again tamed Brooklyn, this time in six games. The Yankees won the first two games; the Dodgers rallied to cop the next two but the Yankees, with Mickey Mantle driving a grandslammer in the third inning of game No. 5, took the next two clashes. Erskine es-

tablished an all-time series mark by striking out 14 batters to give Brooklyn its first victory, a brilliant 3-2 effort which wasn't decided until catcher Roy Campanella clouted an eighth inning home run. Billy Loes got Brooklyn even the following day with a nine-hit triumph before the Yankees recovered to sail through the next two games. Carl Furillo's two-on ninth-inning homer tied the score in the sixth game but Billy Martin, brilliant at bat and in the field throughout, delivered the payoff poke, a game-winning single in the Bombers' half. It was Martin's 12th hit—a new record for a six game series—and he wound up with a .500 batting average.

Result: New York AL won 4; Brooklyn NL, 2.

1st Game, at New York, Sept. 30			R.	H.	E.
Brooklyn (NL)	000 013 100	---	5	12	2
New York (AL)	400 010 13x	---	9	12	0

Pitchers--Erskine, Hughes (2), LABINE (6), Wade (8) vs. Reynolds, SAIN (6). Homers--Gilliam (Bklyn.), Hodges (Bklyn.), Shuba (Bklyn.), Berra (N.Y.), Collins (N.Y.). Attendance--69,374.

2nd Game, at New York, Oct. 1					
Brooklyn (NL)	000 200 000	---	2	9	1
New York (AL)	100 000 12x	---	4	5	0

Pitchers--ROE vs. LOPAT. Homers--Martin (N.Y.), Mantle (N.Y.). Attendance--66,786.

3rd Game, at Brooklyn, Oct. 2					
New York (AL)	000 010 010	---	2	6	0
Brooklyn (NL)	000 011 ,01x	---	3	9	0

Pitchers--RASCHI vs. ERSKINE. Homer--Campanella (Bklyn.). Attendance--35,270.

4th Game, at Brooklyn, Oct. 3					
New York (AL)	000 020 001	---	3	9	0
Brooklyn (NL)	300 102 10x	---	7	12	0

Pitchers--FORD, Gorman (2), Sain (5), Schallock (7) vs. LOES, Labine (6). Homers--McDougald (N.Y.), Snider (Bklyn.). Attendance--36,775.

5th Game, at Brooklyn, Oct. 4					
New York (AL)	105 000 311	---	11	11	1
Brooklyn (NL)	010 010 041	---	7	14	1

Pitchers--MCDONALD, Kuzava (8), Reynolds (9), vs. PODRES, Meyer (3), Wade (8), Black (9). Homers--Woodling (N.Y.), Mantle (N.Y.), Martin (N.Y.), McDougald (N.Y.), Cox (Bklyn.), Gilliam (Bklyn.). Attendance--36,665.

6th Game, at New York, Oct. 5					
Brooklyn (NL)	000 001 002	---	3	8	3
New York (AL)	210 000 001	---	4	13	0

Pitchers--Erskine, Milliken (5), LABINE (7) vs. Ford, REYNOLDS (8). Homer--Furillo (Bklyn.). Attendance--62,370.

1954

The irrepressible Giants waved their magic wand known as Dusty Rhodes to blot out Cleveland four straight times and smash a seven-year monopoly held by the AL in

post-season conflict. It was the first time since 1946 that the AL had lost a series and only the second time in the history of the classic that the NL had swept a series, the miracle Boston Braves first performing the trick on the Philadelphia Athletics in 1914. A Cleveland team which had established a new standard for league victories with 111 was no match for Leo Durocher's surprises after the first two games. The Indians seemed on their way to victory in the eighth inning of the opener only to see outfielder Willie Mays snatch it from their grasp at the base of the centerfield wall. His incredible catch of Vic Wertz' long bid for a triple with two aboard will remain as one of the series' most historic fielding plays. It prevented the Tribe from nailing down the verdict and allowed Rhodes, pinch hitter extraordinary, to drive a three-run, game-winning homer which barely reached the right field stands in the 10th inning. Pitcher Early Wynn failed the following day, as his opponent, Johnny Antonelli, drove in what proved to be the winning tally and Rhodes once again belted a home run. Cleveland's famed hurling staff came apart in the third and fourth frays and the Giants didn't have to resort to heroics to clinch victories in both of them. Rhodes, in six official times at bat, drove in seven runs; Al Dark hit .412 to top the New York batters; Giant third baseman Hank Thompson coaxed seven bases on balls, a new record for a four-game series. But Wertz, the bald-headed outfielder-first baseman, hit for a .500 average to lead both clubs.

Result: New York NL won 4; Cleveland AL, 0.

1st Game, at New York, Sept. 29   R. H. E.
Cleveland (AL) 200 000 000 0 ---   2   8   0
New York (NL)   002 000 000 .3 ---   5   9   0
   Pitchers--LEMON vs. Maglie, Liddle (8), GRISSOM (8). Homer--Rhodes (N.Y.). Attendance--52,751

2nd Game, at New York, Sept. 30
Cleveland (AL) 100 000 000   ---   1   8   0
New York (NL)   000 020 10x   ---   3   4   0
   Pitchers--WYNN, Mossi (8) vs. ANTONELLI. Homers--Smith (Cleve), Rhodes (N.Y.). Attendance--49,099.

3rd Game, at Cleveland, Oct. 1
New York (NL)   103 011 000   ---   6 10   1
Cleveland (AL) 000 000 110   ---   2   4   2
   Pitchers--GOMEZ, Wilhelm (7) vs. GARCIA, Houtteman (4), Narleski (6), Mossi (9). Homer -- Wertz (Cleve). Attendance--71,555.

4th Game, at Cleveland, Oct. 2
New York (NL)   021 040 000   ---   7 10   3
Cleveland (AL) 000 030 100   ---   4   6   2
   Pitchers -- LIDDLE, Wilhelm (7), Antonelli (8) vs. LEMON, Newhouser (5), Narleski (5), Mossi (6), Garcia (8). Homer--Majeski (Cleve.). Attendance--78,102.

1955

This became the "next year" Brooklyn fans had waited for since their American Association champs of 1889 began the habit of losing post-season series. Fittingly enough, the Dodgers, who made a complete shambles of the NL race, victimized the Yankees, a team which had thwarted their last five series bids. Moreover, Walter Alston's boys broke an old series jinx by becoming the first club to take a seven-game set after losing the first two games. Hero of the victory was a 23-year old southpaw, Johnny Podres, who twice befuddled the Yankee sluggers with his tantalizing change-up, winning the third game, 8-3, and then taking the decisive seventh contest, 2-0. In that last one, Gil Hodges, goat of so many past Dodger series setbacks, batted in both runs with a single and a sacrifice fly, while Sandy Amoros made a game-saving catch on Yogi Berra's slice down the left field line and turned it into a double play to kill the Yanks' sixth inning rally. Casey Stengel had defied the "no-southpaws-against-Brooklyn" tradition to win the first two games at Yankee Stadium behind Whitey Ford and Tommy Byrne, the pitchers who had enabled New York to win a close AL pennant race from Cleveland, Chicago and Boston. But the Dodgers came back to take three at Ebbets Field on the pitching of Podres and Clem Labine and the home runs of Duke Snider and Roy Campanella. Alston passed up 20-game winner Don Newcombe to start rookie Karl Spooner in the sixth game, but he was blasted in a five-run first inning, featuring Bill Skowron's three-run homer, and Ford had his first complete game series win. This left it to Podres and Byrne in the finale, with the young southpaw from up-

state New York edging the hero of 1955's biggest baseball comeback story. Snider's four homers raised his NL series record to nine, one back of Lou Gehrig, six behind Babe Ruth.

Result: Brooklyn NL won 4; New York AL, 3.

1st game, at New York, Sept. 28

					R.	H.	E.
Brooklyn (NL)	021	000	020	---	5	10	0
New York (AL)	021	102	00x	---	6	9	1

Pitchers--NEWCOMBE, Bessent (6), Labine (8) vs. FORD, Grim (9). Homers--Furillo (Bklyn), Snider (Bklyn), Howard (N.Y.), Collins (N.Y.) 2. Attendance--63,869.

2nd game, at New York, Sept. 29

Brooklyn (NL)	000	110	000	---	2	5	2
New York (AL)	000	400	00x	---	4	8	0

Pitchers--LOES, Bessent (4), Spooner (5), Labine (8) vs BYRNE. Attendance--64,707.

3rd game, at Brooklyn, Sept. 30

New York (AL)	020	000	100	---	3	7	0
Brooklyn (NL)	220	200	20x	---	8	11	1

Pitchers--TURLEY, Morgan (2), Kucks (5), Sturdivant (7) vs PODRES. Homers--Campanella (Bklyn), Mantle (N.Y.). Attendance--34,209.

4th game, at Brooklyn, Oct. 1

New York (AL)	110	102	000	---	5	9	0
Brooklyn (NL)	001	330	10x	---	8	14	0

Pitchers--LARSEN, Kucks (5), R. Coleman (6), Morgan (7), Sturdivant (8) vs Erskine, Bessent (4), LABINE (5). Homers--McDougald (N.Y.), Campanella (Bklyn), Hodges (Bklyn), Snider (Bklyn). Attendance--36,242.

5th game, at Brooklyn, Oct. 2

New York (AL)	000	100	110	---	3	6	0
Brooklyn (NL)	021	010	01x	---	5	9	2

Pitchers--GRIM, Turley (7) vs CRAIG, Labine (7). Homers--Cerv (N.Y.), Berra (N.Y.), Amoros (Bklyn), Snider (Bklyn) 2. Attendance--36,796.

6th game, at New York, Oct. 3

Brooklyn (NL)	000	100	000	---	1	4	1
New York (AL)	000	500	00x	---	5	8	0

Pitchers--SPOONER, Meyer (1), Roebuck (7) vs FORD. Homer--Skowron (N.Y.). Attendance--64,022.

7th game, at New York, Oct. 4

Brooklyn (NL)	000	101	000	---	2	5	0
New York (AL)	000	000	000	---	0	8	1

Pitchers--PODRES vs BYRNE, Grim (6), Turley (8). Attendance--62,465.

Pitcher Don Larsen is greeted jubilantly by Catcher Yogi Berra after final out of the fifth game in the 1956 World Series. Larsen retired 27 Dodgers in order for the first perfectly pitched game in Series history. (Wide World Photo)

1956

Don Larsen, who in 1954 had lost 21 games while pitching for Baltimore, made history by pitching the only perfect game (27 batters retired consecutively) in Series history when he turned back the Dodgers in the fifth game, 2-0. Form took a complete reversal of the Series played between these two clubs the previous year. This time the Dodgers started fast with victories in the first two games, only to see the Yankees sweep the next three. Clem Labine then outdueled Bob Turley in a 10-inning, 1-0 duel to tie the set at three games apiece before the Yankees blasted Don Newcombe in the decisive contest, 9-0, behind the three-hit pitching of Johnny Kucks. Yogi Berra slammed two homers in the finale and his .360 average was tops for the classic. The Yankee catcher established a new Series mark when he drove in ten runs. Duke Snider's tenth homer put him in a second-place tie with Lou Gehrig for most homers in Series competition. The Yankees established two undistinguished records for futility in the second game when they (1) paraded seven pitchers to the mound (2) who issued a total of 11 bases on balls. But the next five Yankee starters went the distance as the American Leaguers won their 17th title and sixth over their most persistent post-season challengers. Larsen's perfect game, in which Mickey Mantle's homer and Hank Bauer's sacrifice fly accounted for both Yank runs, and Labine's sixth game shutout were the top pitching performances of the Series. Jackie Robinson's left field single tied up the Series in game No. 6.

Result: New York AL won 4; Brooklyn NL, 3.

1st Game, at Brooklyn, Oct. 3

					R.	H.	E.
New York (AL)	200	100	000	---	3	9	1
Brooklyn (NL)	023	100	00x	---	6	9	0

Pitchers--FORD, Kucks (4), Morgan (6) vs. MAGLIE. Homers--Mantle (N.Y.), Robinson (Bklyn.), Hodges (Bklyn.). Martin (N.Y.). Attendance--34,479.

2nd Game, at Brooklyn, Oct. 5

New York (AL)	150	100	001	---	8	12	2
Brooklyn (NL)	061	220	02x	---	13	12	0

Pitchers--Larsen. Kucks (2). Byrne (2), Sturdivant (3). MORGAN (3), Turley (5), McDermott (6) vs. Newcombe. Roebuck (2). BESSENT (3). Homers--Berra (N.Y.), Snider (Bklyn.). Attendance--36,217.

3rd Game, at New York, Oct. 6

Brooklyn (NL)	010	001	100	---	3	8	1
New York (AL)	010	003	01x	---	5	8	1

Pitchers--CRAIG. Labine (7) vs. FORD   Homers--Martin (N.Y.). Slaughter (N.Y.). Attendance--73,977.

4th Game, at New York, Oct. 7

Brooklyn (NL)	000	100	001	---	2	6	0
New York (AL)	000	100	20x	---	6	7	2

Pitchers--ERSKINE. Roebuck (5). Drysdale (7) vs. STURDIVANT. Homers--Mantle (N.Y.). Bauer (N.Y.). Attendance--69,705.

5th Game, at New York, Oct. 8

Brooklyn (NL)	000	000	000	---	0	0	0
New York (AL)	000	101	00x	---	2	5	0

Pitchers--MAGLIE vs. LARSEN. Homer -- Mantle (N.Y.). Attendance--64,519.

6th Game, at Brooklyn, Oct. 9

New York (AL)	000	000	000	0----	0	7	0
Brooklyn (NL)	000	000	000	1----	1	4	0

Pitchers--TURLEY vs. LABINE. Attendance--33,224.

7th Game, at Brooklyn, Oct. 10

New York (AL)	202	100	400	---	9	10	0
Brooklyn (NL)	000	000	000	---	0	3	1

Pitchers--KUCKS vs. NEWCOMBE. Bessent (4). Craig (7). Roebuck (7). Erskine (9). Homers--Berra (N.Y.) 2. Howard (N.Y.). Skowron (N.Y.). Attendance--33,782.

1957

Lew Burdette, who was brought up to the big leagues by the Yankees, turned on his old mates with the most superb one-man pitching performance since Christy Mathewson of the Giants shut out the Philadelphia Athletics three times in the 1905 Series. The tall righthander who had been suspected—but never convicted—of firing the outlawed spit ball during the season, turned in three complete game triumphs as Milwaukee won its first post-season classic. Warren Spahn, the lefthander who hooked up with Burdette to pace the Braves to the pennant, was the other winner—a 10-inning, 7—5 thriller which Eddie Mathews decided with a one-on homer. Burdette began his mastery of the Yankees in the second game, and concluded the Series with a second shutout, 5-0, at Yankee Stadium. Whitey Ford, Don Larsen and Bob Turley were the winning Yankee hurlers. Milwaukee's Hank Aaron hit safely in every game and his .393 average led both clubs. The Yankees were below par physically due to Mickey Mantle's

leg injury and Bill Skowron's back injury. The Braves played without Bill Bruton, their regular center-fielder. The Series established two historic records—most attendance (394,712) and total receipts ($5,475,-978.94). The net gate receipts were $2,475,978.94 but an additional three million dollars from a new TV-radio contract was added to the kitty to help establish a new financial high.

Result: Milwaukee NL won 4; New York AL, 3.

```
1st Game, at New York, Oct. 2           R.  H.  E.
Milwaukee (NL)  000  000  100  ---   1   5   0
New York (AL)   000  012  00x  ---   3   9   1
   Pitchers--SPAHN, Johnson (6), McMahon (7) vs. FORD.
Attendance--69,476.

2nd Game, at New York, Oct. 3
Milwaukee (NL)  011  200  000  ---   4   8   0
New York (AL)   011  000  000  ---   2   7   2
   Pitchers--BURDETTE vs. SHANTZ, Ditmar (4), Grim
(8). Homers--Logan (Mil.), Bauer (N.Y.). Attendance--
65,202.

3rd Game, at Milwaukee, Oct. 5
New York (AL)   302  200  500  ---  12   9   0
Milwaukee (NL)  010  020  000  ---   3   8   1
   Pitchers--Turley, LARSEN (2) vs. BUHL, Pizarro (1),
Conley (3), Johnson (5), Trowbridge (7), McMahon (8).
Homers--Kubek (N.Y.) 2, Mantle (N.Y.), Aaron (Mil.).
Attendance--45,804.

4th Game, at Milwaukee, Oct. 6
New York (AL)   100  000  003  1  ---   5  11   0
Milwaukee (NL)  000  400  000  3  ---   7   7   0
   Pitchers--Sturdivant, Shantz (5), Kucks (8), Byrne (8),
GRIM (10) vs. SPAHN. Homers--Aaron (Mil.), Torre (Mil.),
Howard (N.Y.), Mathews (Mil.). Attendance--45,804.

5th Game, at Milwaukee, Oct. 7
New York (AL)   000  000  000  ---   0   7   0
Milwaukee (NL)  000  001  00x  ---   1   6   1
   Pitchers--FORD, Turley (8) vs. BURDETTE. Attend-
ance--45,811.

6th Game, at New York, Oct. 9
Milwaukee (NL)  000  010  100  ---   2   4   0
New York (AL)   002  000  10x  ---   3   7   0
   Pitchers--Buhl, JOHNSON (3), McMahon (8) vs.
TURLEY. Homers--Berra (N.Y.), Torre (Mil.), Aaron
(Mil.), Bauer (N.Y.). Attendance--61,408.

7th Game, at New York, Oct. 10
Milwaukee (NL)  004  000  010  ---   5   9   1
New York (AL)   000  000  000  ---   0   7   3
   Pitchers--BURDETTE vs. LARSEN, Shantz (3), Ditmar
(4), Sturdivant (6), Byrne (8). Homer--Crandall (Mil.). At-
tendance--61,207.
```

1958

The New York Yankees, down three games to one, staged a magnificent comeback to whip the Milwaukee Braves in the fourth straight Series to go the legal limit of seven games.

Only once before—when Pittsburgh upset Washington in 1925—had a team come from so far behind to take the classic. It was the 18th championship for the Yankees in 24 attempts and their seventh in nine tries under the guidance of Casey Stengel who settled his personal score with Milwaukee manager Fred Haney. The Braves, behind Warren Spahn and Lew Burdette, took the first two games at Milwaukee. Don Larsen and Ryne Duren combined to halt the Braves in the third contest but Spahn's sparkling two-hit shutout in the fourth game gave the National Leaguers a commanding 3-1 lead and almost assured them of their second straight title. However, the Yankees, with brilliant pitching, refused to fold. Bob Turley hurled a five-hit shutout in the fifth game and stout relief pitching by Art Ditmar, Duren and Turley overcame Spahn's heroic effort in the 4-3 sixth contest which went ten innings. Larsen and Burdette started the decisive battle but big Don left in the third inning after the Yanks had taken a 2-1 lead. Del Crandall's sixth-inning homer tied the game and it was 2-2 as the eighth inning started. After Burdette retired the first two batters, the American Leaguers exploded. Yogi Berra doubled to right and scored on Elston Howard's single through the middle. Andy Carey then beat out an infield hit and Bill Skowron delivered the clincher with a three-run homer. It was the end of the road for Burdette and the Braves. Hank Bauer tied a Series record with four home runs. Milwaukee's Ed Mathews established a new individual mark for futility with eleven strikeouts.

Result: New York AL won 4; Milwaukee NL, 3.

```
1st Game, at Milwaukee, Oct. 1           R.  H.  E.
New York (AL)   000  120  000  0  ---   3   8   1
Milwaukee (NL)  000  200  010  1  ---   4  10   0
   Pitchers -- Ford, DUREN (8) vs. SPAHN. Homers--
Skowron (N.Y.), Bauer (N.Y.). Attendance--46,367.

2nd Game, at Milwaukee, Oct. 2
New York (AL)   100  100  003  ---   5   7   0
Milwaukee (NL)  710  000  23x  ---  13  15   1
   Pitchers -- TURLEY, Maas (1), Kucks (1), Dickson (5).
Monroe (8) vs. BURDETTE. Homers--Bruton (Mil.), Bur-
dette (Mil.), Mantle (N.Y.) 2, Bauer (N.Y.). Attendance--
46,367.
```

3rd Game, at New York, Oct. 4
Milwaukee (NL)   000 000 000   ---   0   6   0
New York (AL)   000 020 20x   ---   4   4   0
    Pitchers--RUSH, McMahon (7) vs. LARSEN, Duren (8).
Homer--Bauer (N.Y.). Attendance--71,599.

4th Game, at New York, Oct. 5
Milwaukee (NL)   000 001 110   ---   3   9   0
New York (AL)   000 000 000   ---.   0   2   0
    Pitchers--SPAHN vs. FORD, Kucks (8), Dickson (9).
Attendance--71,563.

5th Game, at New York, Oct. 6
Milwaukee (NL)   000 000 000   ---   0   5   0
New York (AL)   001 006 00x   ---   7   10   0
    Pitchers--BURDETTE, Pizarro (6), Willey (8) vs.
TURLEY. Homer--McDougald (N.Y.). Attendance--65,279.

6th Game, at Milwaukee, Oct. 8
New York (AL)   100 001 000 2   ---   4   10   1
Milwaukee (NL)   110 000 000 1   ---   3   10   4
    Pitchers--Ford, Ditmar (2), DUREN (6), Turley (10) vs.
SPAHN, McMahon (10). Homers--Bauer (N.Y.), McDougald
(N.Y.). Attendance--46,367.

7th Game, at Milwaukee, Oct. 9
New York (AL)   020 000 040   ---   6   8   0
Milwaukee (NL)   100 001 000   ---   2   5   2
    Pitchers--Larsen, TURLEY (3) vs. BURDETTE,
McMahon (8). Homers--Crandall (Mil.), Skowron (N.Y.).
Attendance--46,367.

1959

After eight failures in nine attempts, the rejuvenated Dodgers, now transplanted to the West Coast, beat Al Lopez' Chicago White Sox, in six games in the fifty-sixth fall classic. For attendance, receipts and size of players' shares, the series broke all existing records thanks to the enormous seating capacity of the Los Angeles Memorial Coliseum. The three games at Los Angeles drew 92,394; 92,650, and 92,700 respectively. Including the TV and radio rights the receipts totaled $5,628,809.44. Each winning Dodger received $11,231.18 while the losing White Sox each received $7,275.17, also a record. Opening the Series in Chicago Early Wynn, mainstay of the White Sox staff, had little trouble in white-washing the Dodgers 11-0. The Dodgers played badly with Duke Snider booting two chances in the same inning for a Series record. In the third inning the Dodgers collapsed completely when the Go-Go Sox scored seven runs climaxed by Ted Kluszewski's first homer with two aboard. Big Klu repeated with another powerful clout with Landis aboard in the fourth. The Dodgers eked out a victory in the second game on two homers by Charley Neal and another by pinch-hitter Chuck Essegian. Larry Sherry, coming to the aid of Johnny Podres, did a masterful relief job. In the third game the Sox lacked the punch and scored only one run although they got 12 hits, 4 walks, and Billy Goodman was hit by a pitched ball. Don Drysdale gained the victory, although Larry Sherry again had to be called in from the bull pen. The fourth game was a different story to Wynn who gave up 8 hits in 2-2/3 innings and had to give way to Turk Lown when the Dodgers jumped on him in the third for five hits and four runs. The Sox came to life in the seventh and tied the score when Sherm Lollar hammered one over the left field screen scoring Fox and Big Klu, who had singled. Gil Hodges homer in the eighth was the deciding blow as the Dodgers picked up the marbles 5-4. The fifth game was a thriller as Shaw and Donovan stifled the Dodger bats and allowed only one extra-base hit, a triple, by Hodges. In the seventh inning Rivera went to right field and made a sensational running catch of Neal's hard drive with runners on second and third. Fox scored the only run of the game when he led off the fourth inning with a single, advanced to third on Landis' one-bagger, and scored when Lollar hit into a double play. The Dodgers made 13 hits including homers by Snider, Moon, and Essegian to smother the Sox 9-3 in the sixth and deciding game. Wynn, making his third start, was the victim of the savage Dodger attack and left the game in the fourth when the Dodgers scored six runs to put the game and the series on ice.

Result: Los Angeles NL won 4; Chicago AL, 2.

1959

1st Game, at Chicago, Oct. 1st			R	H	E
Los Angeles (NL)	000	000 000	---	0	8	3
Chicago (AL)	207	200 00X	---	11	11	0

Pitchers—CRAIG, Churn (3), Labine (4), Koufax (5), Klippstein (2) vs. WYNN, Staley (8). Homers—Kluszewski (Chi.) 2. Attendance—48,013.

2nd Game, at Chicago, Oct. 2nd			R	H	E
Los Angeles (NL)	000	010 300	---	4	9	1
Chicago (AL)	200	000 010	---	3	8	0

Pitchers—PODRES, Sherry (7) vs. SHAW, Lown (7). Homers—Neal (LA) 2, Essegian (LA). Attendance—47,368.

3rd Game, at Los Angeles, Oct. 4th			R	H	E
Chicago (AL)	000	000 010	---	1	12	0
Los Angeles (NL)	000	000 21X	---	3	5	0

Pitchers—DONOVAN, Staley (7) vs. DRYSDALE, Sherry (8). Attendance—92,394.

4th Game, at Los Angeles, Oct. 5th			R	H	E
Chicago, (AL)	000	000 400	---	4	10	3
Los Angeles (NL)	004	000 01X	---	5	9	0

Pitchers—Wynn, Lown (3), Pierce (4), STALEY (7) vs. Craig, SHERRY (8). Homers—Lollar, (Chi), Hodges (LA). Attendance—92,650.

5th Game, at Los Angeles, Oct. 6th			R	H	E
Chicago (AL)	000	100 000	---	1	5	0
Los Angeles (NL)	000	000 000	---	0	9	0

Pitchers—SHAW, Pierce (7), Donovan (8) vs. KOUFAX, Williams (8). Attendance—92,706.

6th Game, at Chicago, Oct. 8th			R	H	E
Los Angeles (NL)	002	600 001	---	9	13	0
Chicago (AL)	000	300 000	---	3	6	1

Pitchers—Podres, SHERRY (4) vs. WYNN, Donovan (4), Staley (5), Pierce (8), Moore (9). Homers—Snider (LA), Moon (LA), Kluszewski (Chi), Essegian (LA). Attendance—47,653.

1960

    The 57th World Series was most peculiar due to the fact that the New York Yankees set many amazing records but were defeated by the Pirates four games to three. Among the World Series records set by the Yanks were: highest batting average (.338), most runs (55), most hits (91), most total bases (142) and most runs batted in (54). The Pirates' ability to come from behind was demonstrated in the first game when Maris homered with two out in the first inning. In their half, the Pirates bounced back with three runs and managed to stay ahead for the rest of the game with Bill Mazeroski, who later clouted the homer that beat the Yanks in the final game, weighing in with his first four-bagger. The second game was a breeze for the Yanks who belted six Pirate pitchers for 16 runs on 19 hits including two homers by Mickey Mantle for a 16-3 win behind Bullet Bob Turley. Resuming the series in Yankee Stadium on Oct. 8th, the Yanks again powdered the ball, winning 10-0 on 16 hits and Whitey Ford's fine four-hit pitching performance. In this game, Bobby Richardson, Yank second-sacker who hit only one home run during the entire season, hit a grand-slam homer in the first inning and batted in a record-breaking six runs during the game. In the fourth game Vern Law and Elroy Face combined to stifle the Yankee bats aided by a remarkable circus catch by Bill Virdon of a liner off Bob Cerv's bat. From that point Face went on to save a 3-2 decision for Law. The Yankee drouth continued into the fifth game despite Maris' second home run of the series. They could do little with Harvey Haddix and when they did threaten the Pirate's lead in the seventh, Face again put out the fire in his accustomed fashion. The sixth game was almost a repetition of the fourth with Whitey Ford returning to the mound. He allowed only seven hits and one walk, shutting out the Pirates by a 12-0 score. In this game the Yank bats again exploded for 17 hits including two triples by Richardson. With the series all even at three games apiece the do-or-die Pirates went to work on Turley and Stafford by scoring four times in the first two innings. Skowron's homer in the fifth gave the Yanks their first run. They scored four more in the sixth which was featured by Yogi Berra's three-run homer. They went ahead 7-4 by continuing the assault on reliefer Elroy Face. Coming to bat in their half of the eighth with their backs to the wall, the Pirates

found themselves in familiar surroundings and proceeded to blast out five runs capped by catcher Hal Smith's mighty three-run homer over the left field wall giving them a 9-7 lead. Murtaugh then sent Friend in to protect the 2-run lead but the Yanks tied it all up at 9-9 on three singles and a force. Mazeroski, the lead-off batter for the Pirates in the bottom of the ninth, clobbered Ralph Terry's second pitch over the left field wall and the Corsairs wrapped up their first World Championship since 1925.

Result: Pittsburgh NL won 4; New York AL, 3.

1960

```
1st Game, at Pittsburgh, Oct. 5th        R   H   E
New York (AL)   100  100  002    ---     4  13   2
Pittsburgh (NL) 300  201  00X    ---     6   8   0
Pitchers—DITMAR, Coates (1), Maas (5), Duren (7)
vs. LAW, Face (8). Homers—Maris (NY), Mazeroski (Pit),
Howard (NY). Attendance—36,676.
```

```
2nd Game, at Pittsburgh, Oct. 6th        R   H   E
New York (AL)   002  127  301    ---    16  19   1
Pittsburgh (NL) 000  100  002    ---     3  13   1
    Pitchers - - TURLEY, Shantz  (9)  vs.
FRIEND, Green (5), Labine (6), Witt (6),
Gibbon (7), Cheney (9). Homers - - Mantle
(NY) 2. Attendance - - 37,308.
```

```
3rd Game, at New York, Oct. 8th          R   H   E
Pittsburgh (NL) 000  000  000    ---     0   4   0
New York (AL)   600  400  00X    ---    10  16   1
Pitchers—MIZELL, Labine (1), Green (1), Witt (4),
Cheney (6), Gibbon (8) vs. FORD. Homers—Richardson
(NY), Mantle (NY). Attendance—70,001.
```

```
4th Game, at New York, Oct. 9th          R   H   E
Pittsburgh (NL) 000  030  000    ---     3   7   0
New York (AL)   000  100  100    ---     2   8   0
Pitchers—LAW, Face (7), vs. TERRY, Shantz (7),
Coates (8). Homers—Skowron (NY). Attendance—67,812.
```

```
5th Game, at New York, Oct. 10th         R   H   E
Pittsburgh (NL) 031  000  001    ---     5  10   2
New York (AL)   011  000  000    ---     2   5   2
Pitchers—HADDIX, Face (7), vs. DITMAR, Arroyo (2),
Stafford (3), Duren (8). Homers—Maris (NY). Attend-
ance—62,753.
```

```
6th Game, at Pittsburgh, Oct. 12th       R   H   E
New York (AL)   015  002  220    ---    12  17   1
Pittsburgh (NL) 000  000  000    ---     0   7   1
Pitchers—FORD vs. FRIEND, Cheney (3), Mizell (4),
Green (6), Labine (6), Witt (9). Attendance--38,580.
```

```
7th Game, at Pittsburgh, Oct. 13th       R   H   E
New York (AL)   000  014  022    ---     9  13   1
Pittsburgh (NL) 220  000  051    ---    10  11   0
Pitchers—Turley, Stafford (2), Shantz (3), Coates (8),
TERRY (8) vs. Law, Face (6), Friend (9), HADDIX (9).
Homers—Nelson (Pit), Skowron (NY), Berra (NY), Smith
(Pit), Mazeroski (Pit). Attendance—36,683.
```

1961

The Yankees returned to their winning ways in the 1961 series, having no trouble in disposing of the jittery Cincinnati Reds in five games. In the first game, the peerless Whitey Ford set the Reds down on two measley singles for a 2-0 shutout, striking out six and allowing only one base on balls. Elston Howard and Bill Skowron supplied the punch—each with a homer. Bobby Richardson, batting star of the 1960 series, smacked three singles in four trips to the plate. The Reds turned the tables in the second game, thanks to Joey Jay's 4-hit pitching, and beat the Yanks by a score of 6-2. Scoring two runs in the fourth on an error by Boyer followed by Gordon Coleman's homer, they scored one in each the fifth and sixth and added a couple more in the eighth for good measure. The third game in Cincinnati was a thriller featured by a Yankee attack in the last three innings which overcame a two-run deficit. Roger Maris, who had gone hitless until he came up in the ninth, supplied the clincher when he homered off Bob Purkey. It was all Whitey Ford in the fourth game when he handed out another string of goose-eggs to the Reds allowing only five singles until he retired in the sixth with an ankle injury suffered earlier in the game. In pitching five scoreless frames Ford broke Babe Ruth's record of 29-2/3 consecutive scoreless inning which had stood since 1918. Richardson was again a thorn

in the Reds side as he made three more hits. The fifth game resulted in a complete rout of the Reds, the Yanks scoring 13 runs of eight Red pitchers. It set a new record for the number of pitchers used in one World Series game. The Yanks lost no time when nine batters paraded to the plate in the first inning—five of them scoring. Another 5-run blast in the fourth topped by Hector Lopez' homer over the center field fence put the game entirely out of reach of the hapless Reds.

Result: New York AL won 4; Cincinnati NL, 1.

1st Game, at New York, Oct. 4th
				R	H	E
Cincinnati (NL)	000	000	000	---	0	2	0
New York (AL)	000	101	00X	---	2	6	0

Pitchers—O'TOOLE, Brosnan (8), vs. FORD. Homers—Howard (NY), Skowron (NY). Attendance—62,397.

2nd Game, at New York, Oct. 5th
				R	H	E
Cincinnati (NL)	000	211	020	---	6	9	0
New York (AL)	000	200	000	---	2	4	3

Pitchers—JAY vs. TERRY, Arroyo (8). Homers—Coleman (Cin.), Berra (NY). Attendance—63,083.

3rd Game, at Cincinnati, Oct. 7th
				R	H	E
New York (AL)	000	000	111	---	3	6	1
Cincinnati (NL)	001	000	100	---	2	8	0

Pitchers—Stafford, Daley (7), ARROYO (8) vs. PURKEY. Homers—Blanchard (NY), Maris (NY). Attendance—32,589.

4th Game, at Cincinnati, Oct. 8th
				R	H	E
New York (AL)	000	112	300	---	7	11	0
Cincinnati (NL)	000	000	000	---	0	5	1

Pitchers—FORD, Coates (6), vs. O'TOOLE, Brosnan (6), Henry (9). Attendance—32,589.

5th Game, at Cincinnati, Oct. 9th
				R	H	E
New York (AL)	510	502	000	---	13	15	1
Cincinnati (NL)	003	020	000	---	5	11	3

Pitchers—Terry, DALEY (3), vs. JAY, Maloney (1), K. Johnson (2), Henry (3), Jones (4), Purkey (5), Brosnan (7), Hunt (9). Homers—Blanchard (NY), Robinson (Cin.), Lopez (NY), Post (Cin.). Attendance—32,589.

1962

Rainstorms, first in New York and then in San Francisco, produced the most elongated World Series in history. Beginning in New York, the first game was played on October 4th and the final or 7th game finally was completed on October 16th. As usual, the Yankee ace, Whitey Ford, got the Yanks off to a flying start by setting the Giants down by a score of 6 to 2. It was his fifth consecutive victory in World Series play and his 10th World Series win. The game was even at 2-2 until the Yanks finally broke through with one run in the 7th, two in the 8th and another one for good measure in the ninth. Clete Boyer really iced the game in the 7th when he clouted a homer over the left field fence. The Giants evened it up in the second game with a classy 3-hit performance by Jack Sanford who throttled the Yanks completely, shutting them out by a score of 2-0. Sanford allowed only one extra base hit to Mickey Mantle in pitching his masterpiece. Willie McCovey hit a tremendous homer over the right field barrier for the insurance run. The see-saw action continued in the third game when Roger Maris singled sharply to right-center driving in Tresh and Mantle who had singles before him. Ed Bailey's two-run homer in the ninth was the Giants only scoring threat. The game was well pitched on both sides with Stafford and Pierce in a scoreless duel until the 7th. Pierce allowed the Yanks 5 hits to Stafford's 4 for the Giants. The Giants evened it up again in game Number 4. The go-ahead runs were produced by Chuck Hiller's grand slam homer in the seventh inning. It was the first grand-slammer ever hit by a National League player in a World Series. The Giants used four pitchers in this game and the Yanks three. Whitey Ford was going along with a 2-2 tie when he was lifted for Jim Coates in the seventh. Coates had walked Jim Davenport and Haller had struck out when Matty Alou, batting for Pagan doubled to left. Houk then sent in Bridges and with two down, Hiller lined his homer into the right field seats. As in the previous game, game Number 5 was all tied up at 2-2 in the eighth when Rookie Tom Tresh connected with one of Jack Sanford's serves and the Yankees went ahead to stay. Moving to San

Francisco after the 5th game, the series was delayed five days by rain and
it was not until October 15th that the sixth game was played. This time it
was all Billy Pierce. Bouncing back after his loss in game Number 3, Billy
was master of the situation all the way allowing the powerful Yanks only 3
hits and winning by a score of 5-2. With the Giants ahead 3-0, Roger Maris
hammered one over the right field fence. The only other extra base blow
was Clete Boyer's double in the eighth. However the Yanks were not to be
denied and in the final game they rallied behind Ralph Terry's 4-hit shutout
to eke out a narrow 1-0 victory and the series. It was a heart-breaker for
Jack Sanford who allowed the Yanks only 7 hits. The lone run was scored in
the 5th when Bill Skowron and Clete Boyer singled, Terry walked when Sanford temporarily lost control and Skowron scored as Kubek bounced into a
double play. The pitching in the series on the part of both clubs was outstanding especially the Giants corps which held the vaunted power of the
Yanks to a meager team average of .199.

Result: New York AL won 4; San Francisco NL, 3.

1962

```
1st Game, at San Francisco, Oct. 4th      R   H   E
New York (AL)    200  000  121   ---      6   11  0
San Francisco
     (NL)        011  000  000   ---      2   10  0
  Pitchers—FORD vs. O'DELL, Larson (7), Miller (1).
Homer  Boyer (NY).  Attendance—43,852.
```

```
2nd Game, at San Francisco, Oct. 5th      R   H   E
New York (AL)    000  000  000   ---      0   3   1
San Francisco
     (NL)        100  000  10X   ---      2   6   0
  Pitchers—TERRY, Daley (8) vs. SANFORD. Homer—
McCovey (SF)  Attendance—43,910.
```

```
3rd Game, at New York, Oct. 7th           R   H   E
San Francisco
     (NL)        000  000  002   ---      2   4   3
New York (AL)    000  000  30X   ---      3   5   1
  Pitchers—PIERCE, Larsen (7), Bolin (8) vs. STAF-
FORD. Homer—Bailey (SF). Attendance—71,434.
```

```
4th Game, at New York, Oct. 8th           R   H   E
San Francisco
     (NL)        020  000  401   ---      7   9   1
New York (AL)    000  002  001   ---      3   9   1
  Pitchers—Marichal, Bolin (5), LARSEN (6), O'Dell (7)
vs. Ford, COATES (7), Bridges (7). Homers—Haller (SF),
Hiller (SF). Attendance—66,607.
```

```
5th Game, at New York, Oct. 10th          R   H   E
San Francisco
     (NL)        001  010  001   ---      3   8   2
New York (AL)    000  101  03X   ---      5   6   0
  Pitchers SANFORD, Miller (8) vs. TERRY. Homers—
Pagan (SF), Tresh (NY). Attendance—63,165.
```

```
6th Game, at San Francisco, Oct. 15th     R   H   E
New York (AL)    000  000  000   ---      2   3   2
San Francisco
     (NL)        000  320  00X   ---      5   10  1
  Pitchers—FORD, Coates (5), Bridges (8) vs. PIERCE.
Homer—Maris (NY). Attendance—43,948.
```

```
7th Game, at San Francisco, Oct. 16th     R   H   E
New York (AL)    000  010  000   ---      1   7   0
San Francisco
     (NL)        000  000  000   ---      0   4   1
  Pitchers—TERRY vs. SANFORD, O'Dell (8). Attend-
ance—43,948.
```

1963

Stung by the caustic remarks of their followers when they booted away the 1962
pennant to their arch-rivals, the Giants, in a play-off, the surprising Dodgers performed the incredible feat of whipping the vaunted Yanks four straight games to
win the Series in 1963. It was the first time that the Yanks had been shut out in a
World Series since the Giants turned the trick in 1922.

MVP Sandy Koufax was the big gun of the Series when he won the opener 5-2
and repeated in the fourth game by a score of 2-1. Money pitcher Johnny Podres
did his usual excellent pressure job in the second game with a little help from ace reliever Ron Perranoski. The pitching gem of the Series, however, was Don Drysdale's
1-0 victory in the third game. In his three-hit masterpiece, Big Don mowed down
the Yanks with monotonous regularity, facing only the minimum three batters per
inning in six of the nine innings.

Whitey Ford turned in a fine 2-hit performance in the fourth and final game but
had the misfortune to run into Koufax again. This game was a nip and tuck affair

with a 1-1 tie due to homers by Frank Howard and Mickey Mantle when an error by Joe Pepitone on a throw by third baseman Clete Boyer gave a life to Jim Gilliam who raced all the way to third and scored the deciding run on a fly to deep center by Willie Davis. It was a dramatic victory for the Dodgers and one of the greatest upsets in World Series history.

Result: Los Angeles NL won 4; New York AL, 0.

1st Game, at New York, Oct. 2nd   R H E
Los Angeles (NL) 041 000 000   5 9 0
New York (AL)   000 000 020   2 6 0
    Pitchers—KOUFAX vs. FORD, Williams (6),
Hamilton (9). Homers—Roseboro (LA) Tresh (NY).
Attendance—69,000.

2nd Game, at New York, Oct. 3rd   R H   E
Los Angeles (NL) 200 100 010   4 10 1
New York (AL)   000 000 001   1 7   0
    Pitchers—PODRES, Perranoski (9) vs. DOWN-
ING, Terry (6), Reniff (9). Homer—Skowron (LA).
Attendance—66,455.

3rd Game, at Los Angeles, Oct. 5th   R H E
New York (AL)   000 000 000   0 3 0
Los Angeles (NL) 100 000 00x   1 4 1
    Pitchers—BOUTON, Reniff (8) vs. DRYSDALE.
Attendance—55,912.

4th Game, at Los Angeles, Oct. 6th   R H E
New York (AL)   000 000 100   1 6 1
Los Angeles (NL) 000 010 10x   2 2 1
    Pitchers—FORD, Reniff (8) vs. KOUFAX.
Homers—F. Howard (LA), Mantle (NY). Attendance
—55,912.

1964

The Cardinals, who finished fast to win the National League pennant on the final day, continued their winning ways by defeating the Yankees in the World Series, four games to three. It marked the first time since 1921-22 that the Bronx Bombers lost two consecutive Series. Surprisingly, the Bombers had most of the batting and pitching stars. Mickey Mantle unloaded three prodigious home runs to raise his record total to 18, and set several other marks besides. Bobby Richardson broke another Series record by collecting 13 hits and Joe Pepitone hit a grand slam home run, still something of a Series rarity. In pitching, Jim Bouton posted two victories and youthful Mel Stottlemyre one, although he did well enough to have won more often. The Cards roared into the Series by taking the opener, 9-5, overcoming a 4-2 deficit to do it. The Yanks squared it the next day, 8-3, behind Stottlemyre, who tossed a 7-hitter. Card ace Bob Gibson was the loser, no less. Mantle's dramatic ninth-inning homer off reliever Barney Schultz provided the Bombers with the third game, 2-1. Bouton held the Redbirds to six hits and the Yankees managed only four off St. Louis starter Curt Simmons through eight. Ken Boyer's fifth-inning bases-filled homer accounted for all the runs in the Cards' 4-3 triumph in Game No. 4. The Yanks chased 20-game winner Ray Sadecki in the first, scoring three runs on five hits, but Roger Craig and Ron Taylor limited them to one safety the rest of the way. Another home run, this one by catcher Tim McCarver in the 10th inning, decided the fifth game in St. Louis' favor, 5-2. Gibson, who struck out 13, appeared headed for a 2-0 victory, but Tom Tresh's two-run circuit in the ninth tied it. McCarver's clout came with two aboard. New York had the big bats in the sixth game as Roger Maris and Mantle stroked back-to-back homers on consecutive pitches and Pepitone hit his 'slam' for an 8-3 verdict. Gibson came back in the seventh game for St. Louis and, although he was touched for homers by Mantle, Clete Boyer and Phil Linz, was around at the finish which saw a 7-5 Cardinal victory. Gibson eclipsed a Series mark with 31 strikeouts and was generally considered to be the Classic's most valuable player.

Result: St. Louis NL won 4; New York AL, 3.

1st Game, at St. Louis, Oct. 7th   R H   E
New York (AL) 030 010 010   5 12 2
St. Louis (NL) 110 004 03x   9 12 0
    Pitchers—FORD, Downing (6), Sheldon (8),
Mikkelsen (9) vs. SADECKI, Schultz (7). Homers—
Tresh (NY), Shannon (St. L.). Attendance—30,805.

2nd Game, at St. Louis, Oct. 8th   R H   E
New York (AL) 000 101 204   8 12 0
St. Louis (NL) 001 000 011   3 7   0
    Pitchers—STOTTLEMYRE vs. GIBSON, Schultz
(9), Richardson (9), Craig (9). Homer—Linz (NY).
Attendance—30,805.

3rd Game, at New York, Oct. 10th   R H E
St. Louis (NL) 000 010 000   1 6 0
New York (AL) 010 000 001   2 5 2
    Pitchers—Simmons, SCHULTZ (9) vs. BOUTON.
Homer—Mantle (NY). Attendance—67,101.

4th Game, at New York, Oct. 11th   R H E
St. Louis (NL) 000 004 000   4 6 1
New York (AL) 300 000 000   3 6 1
    Pitchers—Sadecki, CRAIG (1), Taylor (6) vs.
DOWNING, Mikkelsen (7), Terry (8). Homer—K.
Boyer (St. L.). Attendance—66,312.

5th Game, at New York, Oct. 12th   R H   E
St. Louis (NL) 000 020 000 3   5 10 1
New York (AL) 000 000 002 0   2 6   2
    Pitchers—GIBSON vs. Stottlemyre, Reniff (8),
MIKKELSEN (8). Homers—Tresh (NY), McCarver
(St. L.). Attendance—65,633.

6th Game, at St. Louis, Oct. 14th   R H   E
New York (AL) 000 012 050   8 10 0
St. Louis (NL) 100 000 011   3 10 1
    Pitchers—BOUTON, Hamilton (9) vs. SIM-
MONS, Taylor (7), Schultz (8), Richardson (8),
Humphreys (9). Homers—Maris (NY), Mantle (NY),
Pepitone (NY). Attendance—30,805.

7th Game, at St. Louis, Oct. 15th   R   H   E
New York (AL)   000 003 002 5   9   2
St. Louis (NL)   000 330 10x 7   10   1
    Pitchers—STOTTLEMYRE, Downing (5), Sheldon (5), Hamilton (7), Mikkelsen (8) vs. GIBSON. Homers—Brock (St. L.), Mantle (NY), K. Boyer (St. L.), C. Boyer (NY), Linz (NY). Attendance—30,346.

1965

The National League triumphed for the eighth time in 12 years and won its third straight as Los Angeles defeated Minnesota in a seven-game thriller. Again, it was the superior Dodger pitching that told the story. The great Sandy Koufax, who lost his initial start although surrendering only one earned run, came back with shutouts in the fifth and seventh games to give the Dodgers their fourth world title. And both Don Drysdale and Claude Osteen pitched creditably. The Twins, however, chased Drysdale in the opener with a six-run third inning and went on to an 8-2 triumph. Zoilo Versalles and Don Mincher hit round-trippers for Minnesota, which had often used the home run to advantage during the regular season. The Twins took a 2-0 lead in the classic by defeating Koufax, 5-1, as Jim Kaat checked the Dodgers on 7 hits. Leftfielder Bob Allison made a brilliant catch of Jim Lefebvre's sinking liner in the fifth to prevent a Dodger run. The Series shifted to Dodger Stadium for Game Three, and the Dodgers did an about-face, taking the next three games. Osteen, who had been obtained from the lowly Washington Senators in the off-season, got them started with a nifty 5-hit, 4-0 win. Drysdale followed with another 5-hitter and a 7-2 triumph as Los Angeles squared the Series. There were four homers in the game, two by each side, but two Twin errors helped to put the win in the Dodger column. Koufax scattered four singles in Game Five as L.A. rolled to a 7-0 decision. He was helped by Maury Wills' record-tying four hits. The Twins weren't through, though, as Jim (Mudcat) Grant pitched and batted them to a Series-tying 5-1 win. Grant allowed six hits and smashed a three-run homer in the sixth inning. But the invincible Koufax came back with a sparkling 2-0 three-hitter in the decisive seventh game. Sandy struck out 10, giving him 29 for three games. Lou Johnson, minor league retread, gave him all the runs he needed when he led off the fourth inning with his second homer of the Series.

Result: Los Angeles NL won 4; Minnesota AL, 3.

1st Game, at Minnesota, Oct. 6th   R   H   E
Los Angeles (NL) 010 000 001 2   10   1
Minnesota (AL)   016 001 00x 8   10   0
    Pitchers—DRYSDALE, Reed (3), Brewer (5), Perranoski (7) vs. GRANT. Homers—Fairly (LA), Mincher (M), Versalles (M). Attendance—47,797.

2nd Game, at Minnesota, Oct. 7th   R   H   E
Los Angeles (NL) 000 000 100 1   7   3
Minnesota (AL)   000 002 12x 5   9   0
    Pitchers—KOUFAX, Perranoski (7), Miller (8) vs. KAAT. Attendance—48,700.

3rd Game, at Los Angeles, Oct. 9th   R   H   E
Minnesota (AL)   000 000 000 0   5   0
Los Angeles (NL) 000 211 00x 4   10   1
    Pitchers—PASCUAL, Merritt (6), Klippstein (8) vs. OSTEEN. Attendance—55,934.

4th Game, at Los Angeles, Oct. 10th   R   H   E
Minnesota (AL)   000 101 000 2   5   2
Los Angeles (NL) 110 103 01x 7   10   0
    Pitchers—GRANT, Worthington (6), Pleis (8) vs. DRYSDALE. Homers—Killebrew (M), Parker (LA), Oliva (M), Johnson (LA). Attendance—55,920.

5th Game, at Los Angeles, Oct. 11th   R   H   E
Minnesota (AL)   000 000 000 0   4   1
Los Angeles (NL) 202 100 20x 7   14   0
    Pitchers—KAAT, Boswell (3), Perry (6) vs. KOUFAX. Attendance—55,801.

6th Game, at Minnesota, Oct. 13th   R   H   E
Los Angeles (NL) 000 000 100 1   6   1
Minnesota (AL)   000 203 00x 5   6   1
    Pitchers—OSTEEN, Reed (6), Miller (8) vs. GRANT. Homers—Allison (M), Grant (M), Fairly (LA). Attendance—49,578.

7th Game, at Minnesota, Oct. 14th   R   H   E
Los Angeles (NL) 000 200 000 2   7   0
Minnesota (AL)   000 000 000 0   3   1
    Pitchers—KOUFAX vs. KAAT, Worthington (4), Klippstein (6), Merritt (7), Perry (9). Homer—Johnson (LA). Attendance—50,596.

1966

The Dodgers set new lows for futility as Baltimore rolled to a four-game sweep. The Orioles pitching, suspect during the season, held Los Angeles to two runs and 17 hits for a .142 batting average climaxed by 33 consecutive scoreless innings. One would have to go back to 1905, when the Giants blanked Philadelphia for 28 straight innings, to find something comparable. Never before had the Dodgers, either in

Brooklyn or Los Angeles, been swept in a World Series; never before had Baltimore even participated in one. The Baltimore heroes were, naturally, its pitchers: Jim Palmer, 20, Wally Bunker, 21, Dave McNally, 23, and Moe Drabowsky, a 31-year-old castoff. Drabowski relieved McNally in the third inning of the opener and proceeded to hurl 6⅔ innings of one-hit, 11-strikeout relief as the Orioles posted a 5-2 triumph. Six of his strikeouts were consecutive, tying Hod Eller's mark with the 1919 Cincinnati Reds. The Robinsons, Frank and Brooks, unloaded successive home runs, the former with one man on, off Dodger starter Don Drysdale in the first inning for a quick 3-0 lead. Jim Lefebvre's homer in the second and a bases-filled walk to Jim Gilliam — and by Drabowsky, no less — in the third produced the only Dodger runs of the game — and Series. Palmer's 4-hit pitching combined with a faulty Dodger defense gave the second game to Baltimore, 4-0. Dodger star Sandy Koufax was the victim of five miscues, including three on two successive plays by center-fielder Willie Davis in the fifth when the Orioles scored three times. There was a sixth Dodger error in the eighth as Baltimore scored twice. Bunker dazzled the Dodgers on six hits in Game Three at Baltimore in outdueling Claude Osteen, 1-0. Osteen permitted only three hits, but one was a home run by Paul Blair, and that was all the Orioles needed. Baltimore completed the sweep the next day, 1-0, behind the 4-hit twirling of McNally. Drysdale pitched well this time, also giving up four hits, but, as in Osteen's case, one was a homer. Frank Robinson was the culprit. Boog Powell, whose .357 average led both teams, had a potential home run taken away by Davis' brilliant leaping catch in dead center in the sixth. Except for the first game, the Los Angeles pitching was nearly as effective as the Orioles' holding the American League champs to a .200 average.

Result: Baltimore AL won 4; Los Angeles NL, 0.

1st Game, at Los Angeles, Oct. 5th

	R	H	E
Baltimore (AL) 310 100 000	5	9	0
Los Angeles (NL) 011 000 000	2	3	0

Pitchers--McNally, DRABOWSKY (3) vs. DRYSDALE, Moeller (3), Miller (5), Perranoski (8). Homers--F. Robinson (B), B. Robinson (B), Lefebvre (LA). Attendance--55,941.

2nd Game, at Los Angeles, Oct. 6th

	R	H	E
Baltimore (AL) 000 031 020	6	8	0
Los Angeles (NL) 000 000 000	0	4	6

Pitchers—PALMER vs. KOUFAX, Perranoski (7), Regan (8), Brewer (9). Attendance—55,947.

3rd Game, at Baltimore, Oct. 8th

	R	H	E
Los Angeles (NL) 000 000 000	0	6	0
Baltimore (AL) 000 010 000	1	3	0

Pitchers—OSTEEN, Regan (8) vs. BUNKER. Homer—Blair (B). Attendance—54,445.

4th Game, at Baltimore, Oct. 9th

	R	H	E
Los Angeles (NL) 000 000 000	0	4	0
Baltimore (AL) 000 100 000	1	4	0

Pitchers—DRYSDALE vs. McNALLY. Homer—F. Robinson (B). Attendance—54,458.

1967

The 64th World Series almost was a case of Bob Gibson vs. Jim Lonborg. Gibson, the Cardinal fireballer, tied a record last equalled by Lew Burdette in 1957 by winning three games, including the decisive seventh. Lonborg, 22-game winner of the surprising Boston Red Sox, who won the American League flag on the final day, breezed to two triumphs before being shelled in the finale after coming back with only two days rest. St. Louis, long the National League's best in these autumn classics, won its eighth World Series in 11 tries with some slugging help from veteran Roger Maris and some record base-stealing by fleet Lou Brock. Maris batted in seven runs, high for both sides, and hit .385, second to Brock's .414. The latter's 12 hits came within one of tying a record, but his seven stolen bases eclipsed by one Honus Wagner's record in the 1909 classic. Boston's Triple Crown Winner, Carl Yastrzemski, also enjoyed a fine Series with three home runs and a .400 batting average. St. Louis took the opener, 2-1, behind Gibson's 6-hit pitching and the four hits of Brock, who became the 32nd player to achieve this feat. Boston's run was supplied by losing pitcher Jose Santiago, who homered in the third inning. Lonborg pitched a masterly 1-hitter — a two-out double by Julian Javier in the eighth — as Boston squared the Series with a 5-0 win. Gentleman Jim had a perfect game going for 6⅔ innings. Yastrzemski provided the punch with two round-trippers, good for four RBIs. The third game went to St. Louis, 5-2, behind the steady 7-hit pitching of Nelson Briles, and the Cards went two up, 6-0, as Gibson shackled the Bosox on 5 hits in Game Four. It was up to Lonborg to keep the Sox in the Series, and he responded with a 3-hit, 3-1 victory. Maris' homer in the ninth deprived him of his second straight shutout. A home run barrage, including a record three in the fourth inning, put the sixth game

in the Boston win column, 8-4, and evened the Series again. Shortstop Rico Petrocelli smashed two and Yastrzemski and rookie Reggie Smith one apiece. This left it up to Gibson and Lonborg in the seventh game, but the latter, who had pitched just two days previously, was tired and wasn't his old self. St. Louis cuffed him for all of its 10 hits and seven runs the first six innings and coasted to a 7-2 triumph behind Gibson's 3-hitter. Gibson even homered in the fifth and Javier supplied the death blow with a three-run wallop in the sixth. Brock swiped three bases in the finale to break Wagner's record.

Result: St. Louis NL won 4; Boston AL, 3.

1st Game, at Boston, Oct. 4th	R	H	E
St. Louis (NL)	001 000 100	2	10	0
Boston (AL)	001 000 000	1	6	0

Pitchers—GIBSON vs. SANTIAGO, Wyatt (8). Homer—Santiago (B). Attendance—34,796.

2nd Game, at Boston, Oct. 5th	R	H	E
St. Louis (NL)	000 000 000	0	1	1
Boston (AL)	000 101 30x	5	9	0

Pitchers—HUGHES, Willis (6), Hoerner (7), Lamabe (7) vs. LONBORG. Home runs—Yastrzemski (B) 2. Attendance—35,188.

3rd Game, at St. Louis, Oct. 7th	R	H	E
Boston (AL)	000 001 100	2	7	1
St. Louis (NL)	120 000 01x	5	10	0

Pitchers—BELL, Waslewski (3), Stange (6), Osinski (8) vs. BRILES. Home runs—Shannon (St. L.), Smith (B). Attendance—54,575.

4th Game, at St. Louis, Oct. 8th	R	H	E
Boston (AL)	000 000 000	0	5	0
St. Louis (NL)	402 000 00x	6	9	0

Pitchers—SANTIAGO, Bell (1). Stephenson (3), Morehead (5), Brett (8) vs. GIBSON. Attendance—54,575.

5th Game, at St. Louis, Oct. 9th	R	H	E
Boston (AL)	001 000 002	3	6	1
St. Louis (NL)	000 000 001	1	3	2

Pitchers—LONBORG vs. CARLTON, Washburn (7), Willis (9), Lamabe (9). Home runs—Maris (St. L.). Attendance—54,575.

6th Game, at Boston, Oct. 11th	R	H	E
St. Louis (NL)	002 000 200	4	8	0
Boston (AL)	010 300 40x	8	12	1

Pitchers—Hughes, Willis (4), Briles (5),, LAMABE (7), Hoerner (7), Jaster (7), Washburn (7), Woodeshick (8) vs. Waslewski, WYATT (6), Bell (8). Home runs—Petrocelli (B) 2, Yastrzemski (B), Smith (B), Brock (St. L.). Attendance—35,188.

7th Game, at Boston, Oct. 12th	R	H	E
St. Louis (NL)	002 023 000	7	10	1
Boston (AL)	000 010 010	2	3	1

Pitchers—GIBSON vs. LONBORG, Santiago (6), Morehead (9), Osinski (9), Brett (9). Home runs—Gibson (St. L.), Javier (St. L.). Attendance—35,188.

1968

Mickey Lolich, a portly lefthander, equalled the World Series record by pitching three complete-game victories as Detroit overcame the Cardinals' 3-1 edge in games to post its first Series triumph since 1945. Bob Gibson, St. Louis' brilliant righthander, won two games, which gave him seven career victories in these fall classics, but dropped the decisive seventh game to Lolich, 4-1. Bob set a Series record of 17 strikeouts in the opener as he handcuffed the Motor City team on five hits, 4-0. Detroit bounced back the next day, 8-1, on Lolich's 6-hitter, and Mickey was one of three Tigers to crash home runs. But St. Louis took the next two for a commanding 3-1 lead. The Cards collected 13 hits en route to a 7-3 win in Game Four and Gibson and swift Lou Brock combined talents in a 10-1 Redbird rout in Game Five. Bob scattered five hits as he became the first pitcher to win seven Series games in a row; his fourth-inning homer made him the only hurler with two Series round-trippers. Brock homered, tripled and doubled and stole his seventh base—which tied his own one-Series record established the previous year. His career total of 14 SBs tied Eddie Collins' long-standing mark. But it was Detroit the rest of the way. Lolich survived St. Louis' three-run outburst in the first inning of Game Five for a 5-3 win and Denny McLain, a 31-game winner during the season but twice a loser in the classic, squared things in the sixth contest with a one-sided 13-1 decision. The Tigers put it away early by scoring 10 runs in the third inning, the big blow being Jim Northrup's grand-slam homer. For the third time in five years, the Cards left it up to Gibson in the finale. Bob blanked the Tigers for six innings, but the Bengals erupted for three runs in the seventh, two of them scoring on Northrup's triple which was misplayed by centerfielder Curt Flood. The Tigers added another tally in the ninth as Lolich responded with a 5-hit, 4-1 victory. Mike Shannon's homer in the ninth spoiled his shutout but little else.

Result: Detroit AL won 4; St. Louis NL, 3.

1st Game, at St. Louis, Oct. 2   R H E
Detroit (AL)   000 000 000   0   5   3
St. Louis (NL)   000 300 10x   4   6   0
   Pitchers—McLAIN, Dobson (8), McMahon
(8) vs. GIBSON. Homers—Brock (St. L.). At-
tendance—54,692.

2nd Game, at St. Louis, Oct. 3   R H E
Detroit (AL)   011 003 102   8 13   1
St. Louis (NL)   000 001 000   1   6   1
   Pitchers—LOLICH vs. BRILES, Carlton (6),
Willis (7), Hoerner (9). Homers—Horton
(D), Lolich (D), Cash (D). Attendance—
54,692.

3rd Game, at Detroit, Oct. 5   R H E
St. Louis (NL)   000 040 300   7 13   0
Detroit (AL)   002 010 000   3   4   0
   Pitchers—WASHBURN, Hoerner (6) vs.
WILSON, Dobson (5), McMahon (6), Patter-
son (7), Hiller (8). Homers—Kaline (D), Mc-
Carver (St. L.), McAuliffe (D), Cepeda (St.
L.). Attendance—53,634.

4th Game, at Detroit, Oct. 6   R H E
St. Louis (NL)   202 200 040   10 13   0
Detroit (AL)   000 100 000   1   5   4
   Pitchers—GIBSON vs. McLAIN, Sparma (3),
Patterson (4), Lasher (6), Hiller (8), Dob-
son (8). Homers—Brock (St. L.), Gibson (St.
L.), Northrup (D). Attendance—53,634.

5th Game, at Detroit, Oct. 7   R H E
St. Louis (NL)   300 000 000   3   9   0
Detroit (AL)   000 200 30x   5   9   1
   Pitchers—Briles, HOERNER (7), Willis (7)
vs. LOLICH. Homers—Cepeda (St. L.). At-
tendance—53,634.

6th Game, at St. Louis, Oct. 9   R H E
Detroit (AL)   02 10 010 000   13 12   1
St. Louis (NL)   00 0 000 001   1   9   1
   Pitchers—McLAIN vs. WASHBURN, Jaster
(3), Willis (3), Hughes (3), Carlton (4),
Granger (7), Nelson (9). Homers—Northrup
(D), Kaline (D). Attendance—54,692.

7th Game, at St. Louis, Oct. 10   R H E
Detroit (AL)   000 000 301   4   8   1
St. Louis (NL)   000 000 001   1   5   0
   Pitchers—LOLICH vs. GIBSON. Homers—
Shannon (St. L.). Attendance—54,692.

1969

This was the year of the cinderella club. The New York Mets, after having languished in ninth and tenth place for the first eight years of its existence, finally reached the pinacle. Winning four consecutive games after losing the opener to the American League champion Baltimore Orioles was a feat last performed in 1942. Baltimore took the opener for the eighth consecutive post-season success after eliminating the Los Angeles Dodgers in the 1966 Series by four games and the Minnesota Twins in three games in the American League playoff to qualify for the 1969 Series. The single run by the NL champs in the seventh inning of the first game broke a streak of 39 consecutive Series shutout innings by the Orioles. Don Buford's home run·gave him the distinction of being the eighth player to hit for the circuit on his first trip to the plate in World Series competition. In the same inning, Brooks Robinson made a spectacular third base play bare-handed to stop the Mets most serious threat of the day. Oriole pitcher Mike Cuellar, in winning his six-hitter, became the second Cuban to win a Series game. In the second game of the Series, Jerry Koosman, N.Y. pitcher, achieved a brilliant two-hitter that even spotlight fielding from both teams could not diminish. The third game was exceptional for Met outfielder Tommie Agee with fingertip catches. The National League champs again triumphed in ten innings of the fourth game by a throwing error. Pinch hitter J. C. Martin of the Mets was struck on the wrist after Oriole pitcher Pete Richert picked up Martin's bunt and threw toward first base. The ball struck Martin and lurched toward second, bringing in the winning run standing up. It wasn't until the sixth inning of the fifth game before the Mets got on the scoreboard. The Orioles were enjoying a 3–0 lead when Cleon Jones, New York outfielder, jumped to get out of the way of a low pitched curve. A black

smudge of shoe polish proved Jones was struck, as he had claimed, and was waved on first. Donn Clendenon slammed a scorcher to the scoreboard making the score 3–2. That homer was No. 3 for Clendenon in the Series. Al Weis drove the tying run home over the 371-foot mark in left field. Weis' homer brought his batting average for the Series to .455 for eleven trips to the plate. Cleon Jones scored the go-ahead run when Ron Swoboda lined to left field. Swoboda scored the fifth and final run with a bobbled ball and error.

Result: New York NL won 4; Baltimore AL, 1.

1st Game, at Baltimore, Oct. 11th   R H E
New York (NL)   000 000 100   1 6 1
Baltimore (AL)   100 300 00x   4 6 0
Pitchers–SEAVER, Cardwell (6), Taylor (7) vs. CUELLAR. Home runs—Buford (Bal.). Attendance—50,429.

2nd Game, at Baltimore, Oct. 12th   R H E
New York (NL)   000 100 001   2 6 0
Baltimore (AL)   000 000 100   1 2 0
Pitchers—KOOSMAN, Taylor (9) vs. McNALLY. Home runs—Clendenon (N.Y.). Attendance—50,850.

3rd Game, at New York, Oct. 14th   R H E
Baltimore (AL)   000 000 000   0 4 1
New York (NL)   120 001 01x   5 6 0
Pitchers—PALMER, Leonhard (7) vs. GENTRY, Ryan (7). Home runs—Agee (N.Y.), Kranepool (N.Y.), Attendance 56,335.

4th Game, at New York, Oct. 15th   R H E
Baltimore (AL)   000 000 001 0   1 6 1
New York (NL)   010 000 000 1   2 10 1
Pitchers - - Cuellar, Watt (8), HALL (10), Richert (10) vs. SEAVER. Homer - - Clendenon (N.Y.). Attendance - - 57,367.

5th Game, at New York, Oct. 16th   R H E
Baltimore (AL)   003 000 000   3 5 2
New York (NL)   000 002 12x   5 7 0
Pitchers—McNally, WATT (8) vs. KOOSMAN. Home runs—McNally (Bal.), F. Robinson (Bal.), Clendenon (N.Y.), Weis (N.Y.). Attendance—57,397.

1970

The Baltimore Orioles easily whipped the Cincinnati Reds, four games to one. Brooks Robinson led the Orioles to their triumph, although many players contributed to the balanced attack which featured superior hitting, fielding and pitching. Brooks slugged at an .810 clip and handled 23 chances in the field, coming up with fine plays time after time. The Reds were weakened by injuries to their pitching staff. Reliever Clay Carroll hurled eight shutout innings in four games and saved the only contest Cincinnati could win. Lee May was the lone Red regular to hit well, slugging at a .833 rate. The Orioles repeatedly came from behind to win, rallying from 3–0 deficits in the first, second and fifth games. These comebacks were often sparked by home runs. Three circuit clouts decided the first game, a two-run job by Boog Powell and solo blasts by Elrod Hendricks and Brooks Robinson. Brooks contributed a defensive gem off May in the 6th inning. Later that inning Bernie Carbo was called out at home in a disputed play when he unexpectedly attempted to score on a chopper in front of the plate. Photos afterwards showed that Carbo had been safe. The Birds won 4–3. Hendricks stroked a key double to lead the Baltimore team to their second game rally and a 6–5 victory. The third game was won easily 9–3, as pitcher Dave McNally slugged a grand slam home run. Cincinnati's only win came next by a 6–5 score, as May clouted a three-run homer in the 8th to overcome a 5–3 Oriole lead. Carroll fashioned 3⅔ innings of scoreless relief. Baltimore stormed back quickly in the fifth game to take the series. The 9–3 victory was sparked by Frank Robinson's two-run homer in the first and Paul Blair struck the eventual winning blow, a single in the second. Mike Cuellar allowed only two hits and no runs after the first inning to pick up the win.

Result: Baltimore AL won 4; Cincinnati NL, 1.

1st Game, at Cincinnati, Oct. 10th R H E
Baltimore (AL)   000 210 100 4 7 2
Cincinnati (NL)   102 000 000 3 5 0
    Pitchers - - PALMER, Richert (9) vs. NOLAN, Carroll (7). Home runs - - May (Cin), Powell (Bal), Hendricks (Bal), B. Robinson (Bal). Attendance - - 51,531.

2nd Game, at Cincinnati, Oct. 11th R H E
Baltimore (AL)   000 150 000 6 10 2
Cincinnati (NL)   301 001 000 5 7 0
    Pitchers—Cuellar, PHOEBUS (3), Drabowsky (5), Lopez (7), Hall (7) vs. McGlothlin, WILCOX (5), Carroll (5), Gullett (8). Home runs—Tolan (Cin), Powell (Bal), Bench (Cin). Attendance—51,531.

3rd Game, at Baltimore, Oct. 13th R H E
Cincinnati (NL)   010 000 200 3 9 0
Baltimore (AL)   201 014 10x 9 10 1
    Pitchers—CLONINGER, Granger (6), Gullett (7) vs. McNALLY. Home runs—F. Robinson (Bal), Buford (Bal), McNally (Bal). Attendance—51,773.

4th Game, at Baltimore, Oct. 14th R H E
Cincinnati (NL)   011 010 030 6 8 3
Baltimore (AL)   013 001 000 5 8 0
    Pitchers—Nolan, Gullett (3), CARROLL (6) vs. Palmer, WATT (8), Drabowsky (9). Home runs—B. Robinson (Bal), Rose (Cin.), May (Cin). Attendance—53,007.

5th Game, at Baltimore, Oct. 15th R H E
Cincinnati (NL)   300 000 000 3 6 0
Baltimore (AL)   222 010 02x 9 15 0
    Pitchers—MERRITT, Granger (2), Wilcox (3), Cloninger (5), Washburn (7), Carroll (8) vs. CUELLAR. Home runs—F. Robinson (Bal), Rettenmund (Bal). Attendance—45,341.

1971

    Roberto Clemente excelled as the Pittsburgh Pirates took a close decision from the Baltimore Orioles in seven games. Clemente topped all hitters with a .414 mark, hit safely in every game and played superb right field. Steve Blass won his two starts, allowing only seven hits and two runs. The Orioles won the first two games rather easily. After a shaky defense gave the Pirates three unearned runs, the Birds came back with three homers—solo blasts by Frank Robinson and Don Buford sandwiched around a three-run shot by Merv Rettenmund. Dave McNally threw a three-hitter as the Orioles won, 5–3. The Bucs next fell 11–3, as Brooks Robinson drove in three runs and got on base five times. Blass started the Pirate comeback in Game Three, firing a three-hitter. Bob Robertson supplied the power with a three-run homer after missing a bunt sign. The pivotal fourth game went to Pittsburgh, 4–3. Young Bruce Kison slammed the door on the Birds, relieving after a three-run first and allowing the Pirates to get back into the game. Al Oliver drove in two runs and then Milt May delivered a tie-breaking pinch single. Nelson Briles weaved a two-hit shutout in the next game, a 4–0 verdict which gave Pittsburgh the series lead for the first time. Hustle by Frank Robinson capped the Orioles' 3–2 squeaker in ten innings in Game Six. Frank walked in the tenth, sped to third on Rettenmund's single and scored on a short sacrifice fly by Brooks. This set the stage for the dramatic seventh game. Clemente had an early homer, but the deciding blow was a double by Jose Pagan to score Willie Stargell in the 8th. Blass allowed only four hits and was at his best in the bottom of the 8th when Baltimore made their final bid. With runners on second and third and only one out, Steve escaped with a single run being scored, winning 2–1.
    Result: Pittsburgh NL won 4; Baltimore AL, 3.

1st Game, at Baltimore, Oct. 9th   R H E
Pittsburgh (NL)   030 000 000   3 3 0
Baltimore (AL)   013 010 00x   5 10 3
  Pitchers—ELLIS, Moose (3), Miller (7) vs.
McNALLY. Home runs—F. Robinson (Bal),
Rettenmund (Bal), Buford (Bal). Attendance
—53,229.

2nd Game, at Baltimore, Oct. 11th   R H E
Pittsburgh (NL)   000 000 030   3 8 1
Baltimore (AL)   010 361 00x 11 14 1
  Pitchers - - R. JOHNSON, Kison (4), Moose
(4), Veale (5), Miller (6), Giusti (8) vs.
PALMER, Hall (9). Homerun - - Hebner (Pit).
Attendance - - 53,239.

3rd Game, at Pittsburgh, Oct. 12th   R H E
Baltimore (AL)   000 000 100   1 3 3
Pittsburgh (NL)   100 001 30x   5 7 0
  Pitchers—CUELLAR, Dukes (7), Watt (8)
vs. BLASS. Home runs—F. Robinson (Bal),
Robertson (Pit). Attendance—50,403.

4th Game, at Pittsburgh, Oct. 13th   R H E
Baltimore (AL)   300 000 000   3 4 1
Pittsburgh (NL)   201 000 10x   4 14 0
  Pitchers—Dobson, Jackson (6), WATT (7),
Richert (8) vs. Walker, KISON (1), Giusti
(8). Attendance—51,378.

5th Game, at Pittsburgh, Oct. 14th   R H E
Baltimore (AL)   000 000 000   0 2 1
Pittsburgh (NL)   021 010 00x   4 9 0
  Pitchers—McNALLY, Leonard (5), Dukes
(6) vs. BRILES. Home run—Robertson (Pit).
Attendance—51,377.

6th Game, at Baltimore, Oct. 16th   R H E
Pittsburgh (NL)   000 000 000   2 9 1
Baltimore (AL)   000 001 1001   3 8 0
  Pitchers—Moose, R. Johnson (6), Giusti (7),
MILLER (10) vs. Palmer, Dobson (10), Mc-
NALLY (10). Home runs—Clemente (Pit),
Buford (Bal). Attendance—44,174.

7th Game, at Baltimore, Oct. 17th   R H E
Pittsburgh (NL)   000 100 010   2 6 1
Baltimore (AL)   000 000 010   1 4 0
  Pitchers—BLASS vs. CUELLAR, Dobson (9),
McNally (9). Home run—Clemente (Pit). At-
tendance—47,291

1972

    The Oakland A's edged the big red machine from Cincinnati in the closest series ever. All but one of the seven games were decided by a single run. The hero was unquestionably Gene Tenace, who had hit only .225 as a utility man for the A's during the season. He banged out four homers, drove in nine runs, hit .348 and slugged .913 in the series. Tenace hit home runs his first two times up in Game One, knocking in all runs for a 3–2 triumph. He also had a key hit in a rally that won the fourth game, clouted a three-run homer in a losing cause in the fifth contest, and contributed an important double in the final game. A's pilot Dick Williams and Reds' skipper Sparky Anderson used innumerable pinch hitters, pinch runners, and relief pitchers throughout the series. Rollie Fingers appeared in six games for Oakland, winning one and saving two, while Tom Hall hurled 8⅓ shutout innings for the Reds in four games. Ross Grimsley picked up two wins in relief for Cincinnati. Jim Hunter won two games for the Athletics and Jack Billingham did not allow an earned run for the Reds in 13⅔ innings. Joe Rudi led the A's to a 2–1 win in the second game, whacking a homer to break a 1–1 tie and making a game-saving miraculous catch in the ninth. Billingham shut out Oakland in Game Three, 1–0, as Cesar Geronimo drove in the only run. The A's took the apparent series-tieing game out of the Reds' hands in the last inning of game number four. Three pinch hits were sandwiched around Tenace's single, as Angel Mangual scored Gene with the winning run, 3–2. The Cincinnati club rallied to win the next two games, one on a ninth-inning tie-breaking outburst sparked by Pete Rose and the next in the only runaway game in the series, 8–1, truly a team effort. The final game reverted to the nip-and-tuck pattern, as the A's triumphed 3–2. Tenace's double knocked across the second run. His pinch runner, Allan Lewis, who was

used in six of the seven games, scored the winner on a double by Sal Bando. Result: Oakland AL won 4; Cincinnati NL, 3.

1st Game, at Cincinnati, Oct. 14th   R H E
Oakland (AL)   020 010 000   3 4 0
Cincinnati (NL)   010 100 000   2 7 0
Pitchers—HOLTZMAN, Fingers (6), Blue (7) vs. NOLAN, Borbon (7), Carroll (8). Homers—Tenace (Oak) 2. Attendance—52,918.

2nd Game, at Cincinnati, Oct. 15th   R H E
Oakland (AL)   011 000 000   2 9 2
Cincinnati (NL)   000 000 000   1 6 0
Pitchers—HUNTER, Fingers (9) vs. GRIMS-LEY, Borbon (6), Hall (8). Homer—Rudi (Oak). Attendance—53,224.

3rd Game, at Oakland, Oct. 18th   R H E
Cincinnati (NL)   000 000 100   1 4 2
Oakland (AL)   000 000 000   0 3 2
Pitchers—BILLINGHAM, Carroll (9) vs. ODOM, Blue (8), Fingers (8). Attendance—49,410.

4th Game, at Oakland, Oct. 19th   R H E
Cincinnati (NL)   000 000 020   2 7 1
Oakland (AL)   000 010 002   3 10 1
Pitchers—Gullett, Borbon (8), CARROLL (9) vs. Holtzman, Blue (8), FINGERS (9). Homer—Tenace (Oak). Attendance—49,410.

5th Game, at Oakland, Oct. 20th   R H E
Cincinnati (NL)   100 110 011   5 8 0
Oakland (AL)   030 100 000   4 7 2
Pitchers—McGlothlin, Borbon (4), Hall (5), Carroll (7), GRIMSLEY, Billingham (9) vs. Hunter, FINGERS (5), Hamilton (9). Homers—Rose (Cin), Tenace (Oak), Menke (Cin). Attendance—49,410.

6th Game, at Cincinnati, Oct. 21st   R H E
Oakland (AL)   000 010 000   1 7 1
Cincinnati (NL)   000 111 50x   8 10 0
Pitchers—BLUE, Locker (6), Hamilton (7), Horlen (7) vs. Nolan, GRIMSLEY (5), Borbon (6), Hall (7). Homer—Bench (Cin). Attendance—52,737.

7th Game, at Cincinnati, Oct. 22nd   R H E
Oakland (AL)   100 002 000   3 6 1
Cincinnati (NL)   000 010 010   2 4 2
Pitchers—Odom, HUNTER (5), Holtzman (8), Fingers (8) vs. Billingham, BORBON (6), Carroll (6), Grimsley (7), Hall (8). Attendance—56,040.

1973

Oakland nipped the amazing New York Mets in seven games in what had to be the most hectic series in history. On and off field developments vied for the limelight daily. There were many heroes. Reggie Jackson was the key man in the A's rally which gave them the final two games. Darold Knowles appeared in all seven games and saved two, while Rollie Fingers matched the two saves in one less game. Ken Holtzman won the first and last games. Bert Campaneris and Joe Rudi sparkled both at the plate and in the field. The Mets were led by Rusty Staub, who gave a marvelous performance. With a shoulder so sore he could barely throw, Rusty led all hitters with a .423 mark. Jon Matlack allowed no earned runs in his first two starts and reliever Tug McGraw appeared in five games, winning one and saving one. Bud Harrelson excelled at shortstop. Holtzman pitched the A's to the first game win, 2–1. He also rapped a doubled which keyed the two-run third, as Felix Millan made a damaging error that inning. The second game was a wild 10–7 victory for the Mets in 12 innings. Willie Mays drove in the lead run for the New Yorkers and Oakland's Mike Andrews made two errors that led to three more runs. The A's, who had rallied to score two in the 9th for a 6–6 tie, came back with one in the bottom of the 12th. After the game, Andrews was placed on the disabled list by owner Finley, resulting in a revolt by the Oakland players. Leaders were Sal Bando and Jackson, who asked to be traded. Commissioner Kuhn ordered Andrews reinstated and Mike received a standing ovation from the Met fans when he appeared in Game Four. Manager Dick Williams, who had been opposed to Finley's action, announced to his players that he would resign after the series, a fact that later leaked out and was con-

firmed before the seventh game had begun. Oakland settled down to win the third game, 3–2, also in extra innings. Campaneris scored the tieing run in the 8th and knocked in the winner in the 10th. In the only runaway game of the series, the Mets evened things up in the fourth game, 6–1. Staub banged out four hits and drove in five runs to back fine pitching by Matlack. The Mets won again the following day, 2–0, as runs were knocked in by John Milner and Don Hahn. Jerry Koosman and McGraw combined for the whitewash. Then Jackson took over, twice doubling in runs and later scoring the third to help Hunter to a 3–1 verdict, and matching Campaneris with a two-run homer in the 5–2 finale. The last out was made with the Mets having the tieing run at the plate. After the series, Jackson revealed that a threat had been made on his life and that he had been under FBI guard since the final weeks of the season.

Result: Oakland AL won 4, New York NL, 3.

1st Game, at Oakland, Oct. 13th R H E
New York (NL)   000 100 000   1 7 2
Oakland (AL)   002 000 00x   2 4 0
Pitchers—MATLACK, McGraw (7) vs. HOLTZMAN, Fingers (6), Knowles, (9). Attendance—46,021.

2nd Game, at Oakland, Oct. 14th R H E
New York (NL) 011 004 000 004 10 15 1
Oakland (AL) 210 000 102 001 7 13 5
Pitchers—Koosman, Sadecki (3), Parker (5), McGRAW (6), Stone (12) vs. Blue, Pina (6), Knowles (6), Odom (8), FINGERS (10), Lindblad (12). Homers—Jones (NY), Garrett (NY). Attendance—49,151.

3rd Game, at New York, Oct. 16th R H E
Oakland (AL)   000 001 010 01 3 10 1
New York (NL) 200 000 000 00 2 10 2
Pitchers—Hunter, Knowles (7), LINDBLAD (9), Fingers (11) vs. Seaver, Sadecki (9), McGraw (9), PARKER (11). Homer—Garrett (NY). Attendance—54,817.

4th Game, at New York, Oct. 17th R H E
Oakland (AL)   000 100 000   1 5 1
New York (NL) 300 300 00x   6 13 1
Pitchers—HOLTZMAN, Odom (1), Knowles (4), Pina (5), Lindblad (8) vs. MATLACK, Sadecki (9). Homer—Staub (NY). Attendance—54,817.

5th Game, at New York, Oct. 18th R H E
Oakland (AL)   000 000 000   0 3 1
New York (NL) 010 001 00x   2 7 1
Pitchers—BLUE, Knowles (6), Fingers (7) vs. KOOSMAN, McGraw (7). Attendance—54,817.

6th Game, at Oakland, Oct. 20th R H E
New York (NL) 000 000 010   1 6 2
Oakland (AL)   101 000 01x   3 7 0
Pitchers—SEAVER, McGraw (8) vs. HUNTER, Knowles (8), Fingers (8). Attendance—49,333.

7th Game, at Oakland, Oct. 21st R H E
New York (NL) 000 001 001   2 8 1
Oakland (AL)   004 010 00x   5 9 1
Pitchers—MATLACK, Parker (3), Sadecki (5), Stone (7) vs. HOLTZMAN, Fingers (6), Knowles (9). Homers—Campaneris (Oak), Jackson (Oak). Attendance—49,333.

1974

Oakland won their third straight series, beating Los Angeles in five games. This was the first time since 1953 that any team had managed this feat, and it was the third longest streak in history. As in recent years, the games were close, with four of the five being decided by 3–2 scores. A major contributor for the A's was Ken Holtzman, who pitched four scoreless innings and smacked a double in the first game, which Oakland won, 3–2. He also hit a homer and got credit for the win in Game Four. Steve Garvey was the top Dodger, hitting .381 in the series. Joe Ferguson, who had made a fine throw from the outfield

in the first game, clubbed a two-run homer in Game Two, as the Dodgers came back to win, 3-2, behind Don Sutton. Bert Campaneris, who scored the winning run in the first game, drove in the deciding marker in the A's 3-2 victory in Game Three. Campy hit .353 overall. It looked like the Dodgers were on their way to tieing the series in Game Four, building a 2-1 lead on Bill Russell's two-run triple. But Oakland turned the series around with a four-run rally in the sixth. After the A's had tied the score, pinch-hitter Jim Holt cracked out a two-run single which led to a 5-2 win. The final game was another nip-and-tuck affair. Los Angeles came back to cancel a two-run Oakland lead in the sixth. But in the next inning, after a six-min-ute delay to remove debris thrown on the field for no apparent reason by the A's fans, Oakland struck again. Joe Rudi, a .333 hitter for the series, clouted Mike Marshall's first pitch into the left field seats. The game ended with no further scoring. Bill Buckner led off the eighth with a single for the Dodgers, and went to second as the ball got by the outfield. But when he tried to go all the way to third, he was thrown out by a fine relay from Reggie Jackson to Dick Green to Sal Bando. Green, who went hitless in the series, was still a factor due to his superior fielding throughout. Rollie Fingers, who had picked up a win in the first game, preserved Athletic victories in the final three games.

Result: Oakland AL won 4; Los Angeles NL, 1.

1st Game, at Los Angeles, Oct. 12th R H E
Oakland (AL)   0 1 0 0 1 0 0 1 0   3 6 2
Los Angeles (NL) 0 0 0 0 1 0 0 0 1   2 11 1
Pitchers—Holtzman, FINGERS (5), Hunter (9) vs. MESSERSMITH, Marshall (9). Homers—Jackson (Oak), Wynn (LA). Attendance—55,974.

2nd Game, at Los Angeles, Oct. 13 R H E
Oakland (AL)   0 0 0 0 0 0 0 0 2   2 6 0
Los Angeles (NL) 0 1 0 0 0 2 0 0 x   3 6 1
Pitchers—BLUE, Odom (8) vs. SUTTON, Marshall (9). Homer—Ferguson (LA). Attendance—55,989.

3rd Game at Oakland, Oct. 15th   R H E
Los Angeles (NL) 0 0 0 0 0 0 0 1 1   2 7 2
Oakland (AL)   0 0 2 1 0 0 0 0 x   3 5 2
Pitchers—DOWNING, Brewer (4), Hough (5), Marshall (7) vs. HUNTER, Fingers (8). Homers—Buckner (LA), Crawford (LA). Attendance—49,347.

4th Game, at Oakland, Oct. 16th   R H E
Los Angeles (NL) 0 0 0 2 0 0 0 0 0   2 7 1
Oakland (AL)   0 0 1 0 0 4 0 0 x   5 7 0
Pitchers—MESSERSMITH, Marshall (7) vs. HOLTZMAN, Fingers (8). Homer—Holtzman (Oak). Atttendance—49,347.

5th Game, at Oakland, Oct. 17th   R H E
Los Angeles (NL) 0 0 0 0 0 2 0 0 0   2 5 1
Oakland (AL)   1 1 0 0 0 0 1 0 x   3 6 1
Pitchers—Sutton, MARSHALL (6) vs. Blue, ODOM (7), Fingers (8). Homers—Fosse (Oak), Rudi (Oak). Attendance—49,347.

1975

The Cincinnati Reds outlasted the Boston Red Sox in seven games in a series whose sixth game was one of the classics in history. Virtually every player on both teams contributed a key play during the series. Pete Rose, who hit .370, led the Reds, along with young reliever Rawly Eastwick, who won two games

and saved a third. Luis Tiant, who won two games for Boston, started the series with a masterful five-hit shutout. All runs were scored in a six-run seventh-inning rally by the Sox, sparked by a two-run single by Rico Petrocelli. Cincinnati came back to win Game Two, 3-2, with a two-out ninth inning rally. Dave Concepcion sent a perfectly-placed bouncer up the middle to score Johnny Bench with the tieing run, then stole second and came home on Ken Griffey's double. The third game also went to the Reds with a last-inning rally, this time in the tenth on a controversial play. Boston had come from a 5-1 deficit to tie the score, thanks to homers by Bernie Carbo and Dwight Evans. Cesar Geronimo started the tenth with a single and Ed Armbrister attempted to bunt him along. Sox catcher Carlton Fisk collided with Armbrister while fielding the ball, and then made a hurried throw past second. This gave the Reds runners on second and third with none out. Boston argued that interference had taken place, but were denied. Joe Morgan's single then won the game. Tiant came back in Game Four to win 5-4, as the Sox scored five in the fourth, keyed by Evans' two-run triple. Cincinnati went ahead in the series, winning the fifth game 6-2, as Tony Perez hit two home runs good for four runs. Boston then won the sixth game in truly dramatic fashion. Super rookie Fred Lynn gave the Sox an early lead with a three-run homer in the first, but the Reds came back to tie in the fifth with a three-run rally. A double by George Foster and homer by Cesar Geronimo gave Cincinnati a 6-3 lead off Tiant going into the last of the eighth. But Bernie Carbo struck a towering homer to center with two on to tie the score. The Sox loaded the bases with none out in the ninth, but were unable to score, as Foster made a fine catch and throw which resulted in a double play at the plate. Then in the eleventh, it looked like the Reds' turn, as Morgan sent a screaming liner to right with Griffey on first. But Evans came up with a terrific catch to save the game, doubling up Griffey. Carlton Fisk then won the game with a smash off the foul pole in the twelfth. The seventh game was an anti-climax, as both clubs seemed spent. Boston got an early 3-0 lead thanks to Cincinnati wildness, but the Reds picked away and finally won in the top of the ninth, 4-3, on a bloop single by Joe Morgan.

Result: Cincinnati NL won 4; Boston AL 3.

1st Game, at Boston, Oct. 11th

	R	H	E
Cincinnati (NL) 000 000 000	0	5	0
Boston (AL) 000 000 60x	6	12	0

Pitchers—GULLETT, Carroll (7), McEnaney (7) vs. TIANT. Attendance—35,205.

2nd Game, at Boston, Oct 12th

	R	H	E
Cincinnatti (NL) 000 100 002	3	7	1
Boston (AL) 100 001 000	2	7	0

Pitchers—Billingham, Borbon (6), McEnaney (7), EASTWICK (8) vs. Lee, DRAGO (9). Attendance—35,205.

3rd Game, at Cincinnati, Oct. 14th

	R	H	E
Boston (AL) 010 001 102 0	5	10	2
Cincinnati (NL) 000 230 000 1	6	7	0

Pitchers—Wise, Burton (5), Cleveland (5), WILLOUGHBY (7), Moret (10) vs. Nolan, Darcy (5), Carroll (7), McEnaney (7), EASTWICK (9). Homers—Fisk (Bos), Bench (Cin), Concepcion (Cin), Geronimo (Cin), Carbo (Bos), Evans (Bos). Attendance—55,392.

4th Game, at Cincinnati, Oct. 15th R H E
Boston (AL)   000 500 000   5 11 1
Cincinnati (NL) 200 200 000   4 9 1
Pitchers——TIANT vs. NORMAN, Borbon (4), Carroll (5), Eastwick (7). Attendance—55,667.

5th Game, at Cincinnati, Oct. 16th R H E
Boston (AL)   100 000 001   2 5 0
Cincinnati (NL) 000 113 01x   6 8 0
Pitchers—CLEVELAND, Willoughby (6), Pole (8), Segui (8) vs. GULLETT, Eastwick (9). Homers—Perez (Cin) 2. Attendance—56,393.

6th Game, at Boston, Oct. 21st   R H E
Cincinnati (NL) 000 030 210 000   6 14 0
Boston (AL)   300 000 030 001   7 10 1
Pitchers—Nolan, Norman (3), Billingham (3), Carroll (5), Borbon (6), Eastwick (8), McEnaney (9), DARCY (10) vs. Tiant, Moret (8), Drago (9), WISE (12). Homers—Lynn (Bos), Geronimo (Cin), Carbo (Bos), Fisk (Bos). Attendance—35, 205.

7th Game, at Boston, Oct. 22nd   R H E
Cincinnati (NL) 000 002 101   4 9 0
Boston (AL)   003 000 000   3 5 2
Pitchers—Gullett, Billingham (5), CARROLL (7), McEnaney (9) vs. Lee, Moret (7), Willoughby (7), BURTON (9), Cleveland (9). Homer—Perez (Cin). Attendance—35,205.

1976

The Cincinati Reds swept aside the New York Yankees in four straight games, thus becoming the first NL club since 1922 to win back-to-back championships. The Reds trailed only for three innings at the start of the third game and became the first team to win seven post-season games in a row. Johnny Bench, who had been hampered with injuries during the regular season, batted .533 in the series and drove in six runs with seventeen total bases in fifteen at bats. Six other Reds went over the .300 mark, including George Foster at .429, and the club as a unit compiled a .313 mark. The AL's designated hitter rule was in force in the series for the first time. Cincinnati's Dan Driessen hit .357, while a combination of Yankee DH's managed an anemic .063. The first game went to the Reds 5–1, but starter Don Gullett dislocated his ankle and was lost for the rest of the series. The Yankees' only threat towards a victory came in the next game, as Catfish Hunter settled down after allowing three runs in the second and the New Yorkers pecked away to tie. The Reds rose to the challenge, however, with Tony Perez driving in the winning run in the last of the ninth. Game Three was another clear Cincinnati victory. Bench nailed the coffin shut in the final game, clouting two home runs. The first was a two-run blast in the fourth that gave the Reds the lead and the second went for three runs in the ninth. Roy White made a gallant effort to keep the ball out of the stands. The Reds' superb relief crew was led by Will McEnaney with two saves. A tower of strength for New York was Thurman Munson, who batted .529, after a .435 mark in the championship series. Chris Chambliss, whose dramatic homer won the final game with Kansas City, hit .524 in that set and .313 in the World Series.

Result: Cincinnati NL won 4; New York AL, 0.

1st Game, at Cincinnati, Oct. 16th R H E
New York (AL)   010 000 000   1 5 1
Cincinnati (NL) 101 000 12x   5 10 1
Pitchers—ALEXANDER, Lyle (7), vs. GULLETT, Borbon (8). Homers—Morgan (Cin). Attendance—54,826.

2nd Game, at Cincinnati, Oct. 17th R H E
New York (AL)   000 100 200   3 9 1
Cincinnati (NL) 030 000 001   4 10 0
Pitchers—HUNTER vs. Norman, BILLINGHAM (7). Attendance—54,816.

3rd Game, at New York, Oct. 19th. R H E
Cincinnati (NL) 030 100 020   6 13 2
New York (AL)   000 100 100   2 8 0
Pitchers—ZACHRY, McEnaney (7) vs. ELLIS, Jackson (4), Tidrow (8). Homers—Driessen (Cin), Mason (NY). Attendance—56,667.

4th Game, at New York, Oct. 21st. R H E
Cincinnati (NL) 000 300 004   7 9 2
New York (AL)   100 010 000   2 8 0
Pitchers—NOLAN, McEnaney (7) vs. FIGUEROA, Tidrow (9), Lyle (9). Homers—Bench (Cin) 2. Attendance—56,700.

Year	National League	American League (or AA).	Games W-L	Attendance	Receipts	Winning Player's Share	Losing Player's Share
1882	Chicago	Cincinnati(AA)	1-1	7,200	$ 2,000.00	$ 0	$ 0
1884	*Providence	Metropolitans(AA)	3-0	3,100	850.00	100.00	0
1885	Chicago	St. Louis(AA)	3-3a	14,200	3,000.00	0	0
1886	Chicago	*St. Louis(AA)	2-4	43,000	14.000.00	855.00	0
1887	*Detroit	St. Louis(AA)	10-5	51,455	41,050.00	500.00	0
1888	*New York	St. Louis(AA)	6-4	42,270	24,362.10	450.00	0
1889	*New York	Brooklyn (AA)	6-3	47,256	24,262.10	380.15	389.29
1890	Brooklyn	Louisville (AA)	3-3a	13,910	6,000.00	100.00	100.00
1903	Pittsburgh	*Boston	3-5	100,429	55,500.00	1,316.25	1,182.00
1905	*New York	Philadelphia	4-1	91,723	68,437.00	1,142.00	833.75
1906	Chicago	*Chicago	2-4	99,845	106.550.00	1,874.63	439.50
1907	*Chicago	Detroit	4-0a	78,068	101,728.50	2,142.85	1,945.96
1908	*Chicago	Detroit	4-1	62,232	94,975.50	1,317.58	870.00
1909	*Pittsburgh	Detroit	4-3	145,295	188,302.50	1,825.22	1,274.76
1910	Chicago	*Philadelphia	1-4	124,222	173,980.00	2,062.79	1,375.16
1911	New York	*Philadelphia	2-4	179,851	342,164.50	3,654.58	2,436.39
1912	New York	*Boston	3-4a	252,037	490,449.00	4,024.68	2,566.47
1913	New York	*Philadelphia	1-4	151,000	325,980.00	3,246.36	2,164.22
1914	*Boston	Philadelphia	4-0	111,009	225,739.00	2,812.28	2,031.65
1915	Philadelphia	*Boston	1-4	143,351	320,361.50	3,780.25	2,520.17
1916	Brooklyn	*Boston	1-4	162,859	385,590.50	3,910.26	2,834.82
1917	New York	*Chicago	2-4	186,654	425,878.00	3,669.32	2,442.61
1918	Chicago	*Boston	2-4	128,483	179,619.00	1,102.51	671.09
1919	*Cincinnati	Chicago	5-3	236,928	722,414.00	5,207.01	3,254.36
1920	Brooklyn	*Cleveland	2-5	178,737	564,800.00	4,168.00	2,419.60
1921	*New York	New York	5-3	269,976	900,233.00	5,265.00	3,510.00
1922	*New York	New York	4-0a	185,947	605,475.00	4,470.00	3,225.00
1923	New York	*New York	2-4	301,430	1,063,815.00	6,143.49	4,112.89
1924	New York	*Washington	3-4	283,665	1,093,104.00	5,969.64	3,820.29
1925	*Pittsburgh	Washington	4-3	282,848	1,182,854.00	5,332.72	3,734.60
1926	*St. Louis	New York	4-3	328,051	1,207,864.00	5,584.51	3,417.75
1927	Pittsburgh	*New York	0-4	201,705	783,217.00	5,592.17	3,728.10
1928	St. Louis	*New York	0-4	199,072	777,290.00	5,531.91	4,197.37
1929	Chicago	*Philadelphia	1-4	190,490	859,494.00	5,620.57	3,782.01
1930	St. Louis	*Philadelphia	2-4	212,619	953,772.00	5,785.00	3,875.00
1931	*St. Louis	Philadelphia	4-3	231,567	1,030,723.00	4,467.59	3,032.09
1932	Chicago	*New York	0-4	191,998	713,377.00	5,231.77	4,244.60
1933	*New York	Washington	4-1	163,076	679,365.00	4,256.72	3,019.86
1934	*St. Louis	Detroit	4-3	281,510	1,031,341.00	5,389.57	3,354.57
1935	Chicago	*Detroit	2-4	286,672	1,073,794.00	6,544.76	4,198.53
1936	New York	*New York	2-4	302,924	1,204,399.00	6,430.55	4,655.58
1937	New York	*New York	1-4	238,142	985,994.00	6,471.10	4,489.05
1938	Chicago	*New York	0-4	200,833	851,166.00	5,782.76	4,674.87
1939	Cincinnati	*New York	0-4	183,849	745,329.00	5,614.26	4,282.58
1940	*Cincinnati	Detroit	4-3	281,927	1,222,328.21	5,803.62	3,531.81
1941	Brooklyn	*New York	1-4	235,773	1,007,762.00	5,943.31	4,829.40
1942	*St. Louis	New York	4-1	277,101	1,105,249.00	5,573.78	3,018.77
1943	St. Louis	*New York	1-4	277,312	1,105,784.00	6,139.46	4,321.96
1944	*St. Louis	St. Louis	4-2	206,708	906,122.00	4,626.01	2,743.79
1945	Chicago	*Detroit	3-4	333,457	1,492,454.00	6,443.34	3,930.22
1946	*St. Louis	Boston	4-3	250,071	1,052,900.00	3,742.34	2,140.89
1947	Brooklyn	*New York	3-4	389,763	1,781,348.92	5,830.03	4,081.19
1948	Boston	*Cleveland	2-4	358,362	1,633,685.56	6,772.05	4,651.51
1949	Brooklyn	*New York	1-4	236,710	1,129,627.88	5,665.54	4,272.73
1950	Philadelphia	*New York	0-4	196,009	953,669.03	5,737.95	4,081.34
1951	New York	*New York	2-4	341,977	1,633,457.47	6,446.09	4,951.03
1952	Brooklyn	*New York	3-4	340,906	1,622,753.01	5,982.65	4,200.64
1953	Brooklyn	*New York	2-4	307,350	1,779,269.44	8,280.68	6,178.42
1954	*New York	Cleveland	4-0	251,507	1,566,203.38	11,147.90	6,712.50
1955	*Brooklyn	New York	4-3	362,310	2,337,515.34	9,768.00	5,598.00
1956	Brooklyn	*New York	3-4	345,903	2,183,254.59	8,714.76	6,934.34
1957	*Milwaukee	New York	4-3	394,712	2,475,978.94	8,924.36	5,606.06
1958	Milwaukee	*New York	3-4	393,909	2,397,223.03	8,759.10	5,896.09

Year	National League	American League	Games W-L	Attendance	Receipts	Winning Player's Share	Losing Player's Share
1959	*Los Angeles	Chicago	4–2	420,784	2,628,809.44	11,231.18	7,257,17
1960	*Pittsburgh	New York	4–3	349,813	2,230,627.88	8,417.94	5,214.64
1961	Cincinnati	*New York	1–4	223,247	1,480,059.95	7,389.13	5,356.37
1962	San Francisco	*New York	3–4	376,864	2,878,891.11	9,882.74	7,291.49
1963	*Los Angeles	New York	4–0	247,279	1,995,189.09	12,794.00	7,874.32
1964	*St. Louis	New York	4–3	321,807	2,243,187.96	8,622.19	5,309.29
1965	*Los Angeles	Minnesota	4–3	364,326	2,975,041.60	10,297.43	6,634.36
1966	Los Angeles	*Baltimore	0–4	220,791	2,047,142.46	11,683.04	8,189.36
1967	*St. Louis	Boston	4–3	304,085	2,350,607.10	8,314.81	5,115.23
1968	St. Louis	*Detroit	3–4	379,670	3,018,113.40	10,936.66	7,078.71
1969	*New York	Baltimore	4–1	272,378	2,857,782.78	18,338.18	14,904.21
1970	Cincinnati	*Baltimore	1–4	253,183	2,599,170.26	18,215.78	13,687.59
1971	*Pittsburgh	Baltimore	4–3	351,091	3,049,803.46	18,164.58	13,906.46
1972	Cincinnati	*Oakland	3–4	363,149	3,954,542.99	20,705.01	15,080.25
1973	New York	*Oakland	3–4	358,289	3,923,968.37	24,617.57	14,950.17
1974	Los Angeles	*Oakland	1–4	260,004	3,007,194.00	22,219.09	15,703.97
1975	*Cincinnati	Boston	4–3	308,272	3,380,579.61	19,060.46	13,325.87
1976	*Cincinnati	New York	4–0	223,009	2,498,416.53	26,366.68	19,935.48

Note: Player's shares for 1969 to date include League Championship Series

* indicates winning team
a indicates one game tied

TEAM RECAPITULATION (1903–1975)

(Figure after team indicates number of Series participated in; figures in parentheses indicate number of Series won and lost; figures following parentheses indicate number of Series games won and lost.)

NATIONAL LEAGUE
Boston, 2 (1–1) 6–4
Brooklyn, 9 (1–8) 20–36
Chicago, 10 (2–8) 19–33
Cincinnati, 8 (4–4) 22–25
Los Angeles, 5 (3–2) 13–13
Milwaukee, 2 (1–1) 7–7
Philadelphia, 2 (0–2) 1–8
Pittsburgh, 6 (4–2) 19–21
New York Giants, 14 (5–9) 39–41
New York Mets, 2 (1–1) 7–5
San Francisco, 1 (0–1) 3–4
St. Louis, 12 (8–4) 38–37

AMERICAN LEAGUE
Baltimore, 4 (2–2) 12–9
Boston, 8 (5–3) 30–22
Chicago, 4 (2–2) 13–13
Cleveland, 3 (2–1) 9–8
Detroit, 8 (3–5) 22–28
Minnesota, 1 (0–1) 3–4
New York, 30 (20–10) 99–69
Oakland, 3 (3–0) 12–7
Philadelphia, 8 (5–3) 24–19
St. Louis, 1 (0–1) 2–4
Washington, 3 (1–2) 8–11

YR	CL	LEA	POS	GP	G	REC

AARON, HENRY LOUIS

1957	MIL	N	O		7	.393
1958	MIL	N	O		7	.333
					14	.364

ABBATICCHIO, EDWARD JAMES

| 1909 | PIT | N | H | | 1 | .000 |

ABSTEIN, WILLIAM HENRY

| 1909 | PIT | N | 1 | | 7 | .231 |

ADAIR, KENNETH JERRY

| 1967 | BOS | A | 2 | | 5 | .125 |

ADAMS, CHARLES BENJAMIN

1909	PIT	N	P		3	3- 0
1925	PIT	N	P		1	0- 0
					4	3- 0

ADAMS, EARL JOHN

1930	STL	N	3		6	.143
1931	STL	N	3		2	.250
					8	.160

ADAMS, SPENCER DEWEY

1925	WAS	A	2		2	.000
1926	NY	A	H		2	.000
					4	.000

ADCOCK, JOSEPH WILBUR

1957	MIL	N	1		5	.200
1958	MIL	N	1		4	.308
					9	.250

AGEE, TOMMIE LEE

| 1969 | NY | N | O | | 5 | .167 |

AGNEW, SAMUEL LESTER

| 1918 | BOS | A | C | | 4 | .000 |

ALDRIDGE, VICTOR E.

1925	PIT	N	P		3	2- 0
1927	PIT	N	P		1	0- 1
					4	2- 1

ALEXANDER, DOYLE LAFAYETTE

| 1976 | NY | A | P | | 1 | 0- 1 |

ALEXANDER, GROVER CLEVELAND

1915	PHI	N	P		2	1- 1
1926	STL	N	P		3	2- 0
1928	STL	N	P		2	0- 1
					7	3- 2

ALLEN, JOHN THOMAS

1932	NY	A	P		1	0- 0
1941	BRO	N	P		3	0- 0
					4	0- 0

ALLEY, LEONARD EUGENE

| 1971 | PIT | N | S | | 2 | .000 |

ALLISON, WILLIAM ROBERT

| 1965 | MIN | A | O | | 5 | .125 |

ALOU, FELIPE ROJAS

| 1962 | SF | N | O | | 7 | .269 |

ALOU, JESUS MARIA ROJAS

1973	OAK	A	O		7	.158
1974	OAK	A	H		1	.000
					8	.150

ALOU, MATEO ROJAS

1962	SF	N	O		6	.333
1972	OAK	A	O		7	.042
					13	.139

ALTROCK, NICHOLAS

| 1906 | CHI | A | P | | 2 | 1- 1 |

AMES, LEON KESSLING

1905	NY	N	P		1	0- 0
1911	NY	N	P		2	0- 1
1912	NY	N	P		1	0- 0
					4	0- 1

AMOROS, EDMUNDO ISASI

1952	BRO	N	H		1	.000
1955	BRO	N	O		5	.333
1956	BRO	N	O		6	.053
					12	.161

ANDERSON, JOHN FREDERICK

| 1917 | NY | N | P | | 1 | 0- 1 |

ANDREWS, IVY PAUL

| 1937 | NY | A | P | | 1 | 0- 0 |

ANDREWS, MICHAEL JAY

1967	BOS	A	2		5	.308
1973	OAK	A	2		2	.000
					7	.250

ANTONELLI, JOHN AUGUST

| 1954 | NY | N | P | | 2 | 1- 0 |

APARICIO, LUIS ERNESTO

1959	CHI	A	S		6	.308
1966	BAL	A	S		4	.250
					10	.286

ARCHER, JAMES PATRICK

1907	DET	A	C		1	.000
1910	CHI	N	C-1		3	.182
					4	.143

ARMBRISTER, EDISON ROSANDA

| 1975 | CIN | N | H | | 4 | .000 |

ARNOVICH, MORRIS

| 1940 | CIN | N | O | | 1 | .000 |

ARROYO, LUIS ENRIQUE

1960	NY	A	P		1	0- 0
1961	NY	A	P		2	1- 0
					3	1- 0

ASHBURN, RICHIE

| 1950 | PHI | N | O | | 4 | .176 |

AUERBACH, FREDERICK STEVEN

| 1974 | LA | N | R | | 1 | .000 |

AUKER, ELDON LEROY

1934	DET	A	P		2	1- 1
1935	DET	A	P		1	0- 0
					3	1- 1

AVERILL, HOWARD EARL

| 1940 | DET | A | H | | 3 | .000 |

AVILA, ROBERTO FRANCISCO

| 1954 | CLE | A | 2 | | 4 | .133 |

BAGBY, JAMES CHARLES JR.

| 1946 | BOS | A | P | | 1 | 0- 0 |

BAGBY, JAMES CHARLES SR.

| 1920 | CLE | A | P | | 2 | 1- 1 |

BAILEY, LONAS EDGAR

| 1962 | SF | N | C | | 6 | .071 |

BAKER, EUGENE WALTER

| 1960 | PIT | N | H | | 3 | .000 |

BAKER, FLOYD WILSON

| 1944 | STL | A | 2 | | 2 | .000 |

BAKER, JOHN FRANKLIN

1910	PHI	A	3		5	.409
1911	PHI	A	3		6	.375
1913	PHI	A	3		5	.450
1914	PHI	A	3		4	.250
1921	NY	A	3		4	.250
1922	NY	A	H		1	.000
					25	.363

BAKER, WILLIAM PRESLEY

| 1940 | CIN | N | C | | 3 | .250 |

BALDWIN, HOWARD EDWARD

| 1924 | NY | N | P | | 1 | 0- 0 |

BALL, CORNELIUS

| 1912 | BOS | A | H | | 1 | .000 |

BALLOU, NOBLE WINFRED

| 1925 | WAS | A | P | | 2 | 0- 0 |

BANCROFT, DAVID JAMES

1915	PHI	N	S		5	.294
1921	NY	N	S		8	.152
1922	NY	N	S		5	.211
1923	NY	N	S		6	.083
					24	.172

BANDO, SALVATORE LEONARD

1972	OAK	A	3		7	.269
1973	OAK	A	3		7	.231
1974	OAK	A	3		5	.063
					19	.206

BANKHEAD, DANIEL ROBERT

| 1947 | BRO | N | R | | 1 | .000 |

BANTA, JOHN KAY

| 1949 | BRO | N | P | | 3 | 0- 0 |

BARBER, TYRUS TURNER

| 1918 | CHI | N | H | | 3 | .000 |

BARBIERI, JAMES PATRICK

| 1966 | LA | N | H | | 1 | .000 |

BARNES, JESSE LAWRENCE

1921	NY	N	P		3	2- 0
1922	NY	N	P		1	0- 0
					4	2- 0

BARNES, VIRGIL JENNINGS

1923	NY	N	P		2	0- 0
1924	NY	N	P		2	0- 1
					4	0- 1

BARNEY, REX EDWARD

1947	BRO	N	P		3	0- 1
1949	BRO	N	P		1	0- 1
					4	0- 2

BARNHART, CLYDE LEE

1925	PIT	N	O		7	.250
1927	PIT	N	O		4	.313
					11	.273

BARRETT, CHARLES HENRY

| 1948 | BOS | N | P | | 2 | 0- 0 |

BARRY, JOHN JOSEPH

1910	PHI	A	S		5	.235
1911	PHI	A	S		6	.368
1913	PHI	A	S		5	.300
1914	PHI	A	S		4	.071
1915	BOS	A	2		5	.176
					25	.241

BARTELL, RICHARD WILLIAM

1936	NY	N	S		6	.381
1937	NY	N	S		5	.238
1940	DET	A	S		7	.269
					18	.294

BATTEY, EARL JESSE

| 1965 | MIN | A | C | | 7 | .120 |

BAUER, HENRY ALBERT

1949	NY	A	O		3	.167
1950	NY	A	O		4	.133
1951	NY	A	O		6	.167
1952	NY	A	O		7	.056
1953	NY	A	O		6	.261
1955	NY	A	O		6	.429
1956	NY	A	O		7	.281
1957	NY	A	O		7	.258
1958	NY	A	O		7	.323
					53	.245

BEARDEN, HENRY EUGENE

| 1948 | CLE | A | P | | 2 | 1- 0 |

BEAUCHAMP, JAMES EDWARD

| 1973 | NY | N | H | | 4 | .000 |

BEAUMONT, CLARENCE HOWETH

1903	PIT	N	O		8	.265
1910	CHI	N	O		3	.000
					11	.250

BEAZLEY, JOHN ANDREW

1942	STL	N	P		2	2- 0
1946	STL	N	P		1	0- 0
					3	2- 0

BECKER, BEALS

1911	NY	N	H		3	.000
1912	NY	N	O		2	.000
1915	PHI	N	O		2	.000
					7	.000

BECKER, HEINZ RICHARD

| 1945 | CHI | N | H | | 3 | .500 |

BEDIENT, HUGH CARPENTER

| 1912 | BOS | A | P | | 4 | 1- 0 |

BEGGS, JOSEPH STANLEY

| 1940 | CIN | N | P | | 1 | 0- 0 |

BEHRMAN, HENRY BERNARD

YR	CL	LEA	POS	GP	G	REC
1947	BRO	N	P		5	0- 0

BELANGER, MARK HENRY

YR	CL	LEA	POS	GP	G	REC
1969	BAL	A	S		5	.200
1970	BAL	A	S		5	.105
1971	BAL	A	S		7	.238
					17	.182

BELARDI, CARROLL WAYNE

YR	CL	LEA	POS	GP	G	REC
1953	BRO	N	H		2	.000

BELL, DAVID RUSSELL

YR	CL	LEA	POS	GP	G	REC
1961	CIN	N	H		3	.000

BELL, GARY

YR	CL	LEA	POS	GP	G	REC
1967	BOS	A	P		3	0- 1

BELL, HERMAN S.

YR	CL	LEA	POS	GP	G	REC
1926	STL	N	P		1	0- 0
1930	STL	N	P		1	0- 0
1933	NY	N	P		1	0- 0
					3	0- 0

BELL, LESTER ROWLAND

YR	CL	LEA	POS	GP	G	REC
1926	STL	N	3		7	.259

BENCH, JOHNNY LEE

YR	CL	LEA	POS	GP	G	REC
1970	CIN	N	C		5	.211
1972	CIN	N	C		7	.261
1975	CIN	N	C		7	.207
1976	CIN	N	C		4	.533
					23	.279

BENDER, CHARLES ALBERT

YR	CL	LEA	POS	GP	G	REC
1905	PHI	A	P		2	1- 1
1910	PHI	A	P		2	1- 1
1911	PHI	A	P		3	2- 1
1913	PHI	A	P		2	2- 0
1914	PHI	A	P		1	0- 1
					10	6- 4

BENGOUGH, BERNARD OLIVER

YR	CL	LEA	POS	GP	G	REC
1927	NY	A	C		2	.000
1928	NY	A	C		4	.231
					6	.176

BENIQUEZ, JUAN JOSE

YR	CL	LEA	POS	GP	G	REC
1975	BOS	A	O		3	.125

BENTLEY, JOHN NEEDLES

YR	CL	LEA	POS	GP	G	REC
1923	NY	N	P	2	5	0- 1
1924	NY	N	P	3	5	1- 2
				5	10	1- 3

BENTON, JOHN ALTON

YR	CL	LEA	POS	GP	G	REC
1945	DET	A	P		3	0- 0

BENTON, JOHN CLEVELAND

YR	CL	LEA	POS	GP	G	REC
1917	NY	N	P		2	1- 1

BERGAMO, AUGUST SAMUEL

YR	CL	LEA	POS	GP	G	REC
1944	STL	N	O		3	.000

BERGER, WALTER ANTON

YR	CL	LEA	POS	GP	G	REC
1937	NY	N	H		3	.000
1939	CIN	N	O		4	.000
					7	.000

BERRA, LAWRENCE PETER

YR	CL	LEA	POS	GP	G	REC
1947	NY	A	C-O		6	.158
1949	NY	A	C		4	.063
1950	NY	A	C		4	.200
1951	NY	A	C		6	.261
1952	NY	A	C		7	.214
1953	NY	A	C		6	.429
1955	NY	A	C		7	.417
1956	NY	A	C		7	.360
1957	NY	A	C		7	.320
1958	NY	A	C		7	.222
1960	NY	A	C-O		7	.318
1961	NY	A	O		4	.273
1962	NY	A	C		2	.000
1963	NY	A	H		1	.000
					75	.274

BESSENT, FRED DONALD

YR	CL	LEA	POS	GP	G	REC
1955	BRO	N	P		3	0- 0
1956	BRO	N	P		2	1- 0
					5	1- 0

BEVENS, FLOYD CLIFFORD

YR	CL	LEA	POS	GP	G	REC
1947	NY	A	P		2	0- 1

BICKFORD, VERNON EDGELL

YR	CL	LEA	POS	GP	G	REC
1948	BOS	N	P		1	0- 1

BIGBEE, CARSON LEE

YR	CL	LEA	POS	GP	G	REC
1925	PIT	N	O		4	.333

BILLINGHAM, JOHN EUGENE

YR	CL	LEA	POS	GP	G	REC
1972	CIN	N	P		3	1- 0
1975	CIN	N	P		3	0- 0
1976	CIN	N	P		1	1- 0
					7	2- 0

BISHOP, MAX FREDERICK

YR	CL	LEA	POS	GP	G	REC
1929	PHI	A	2		5	.190
1930	PHI	A	2		6	.222
1931	PHI	A	2		7	.148
					18	.182

BLACK, JOSEPH

YR	CL	LEA	POS	GP	G	REC
1952	BRO	N	P		3	1- 2
1953	BRO	N	P		1	0- 0
					4	1- 2

BLACKWELL, EWELL

YR	CL	LEA	POS	GP	G	REC
1952	NY	A	P		1	0- 0

BLADES, FRANCIS RAYMOND

YR	CL	LEA	POS	GP	G	REC
1928	STL	N	H		1	.000
1930	STL	N	O		5	.111
1931	STL	N	H		2	.000
					8	.083

BLAIR, CLARENCE VICK

YR	CL	LEA	POS	GP	G	REC
1929	CHI	N	H		1	.000

BLAIR, PAUL L. D.

YR	CL	LEA	POS	GP	G	REC
1966	BAL	A	O		4	.167
1969	BAL	A	O		5	.100
1970	BAL	A	O		5	.474
1971	BAL	A	O		4	.333
					18	.278

BLAKE, JOHN FREDERICK

YR	CL	LEA	POS	GP	G	REC
1929	CHI	N	P		2	0- 1

BLANCHARD, JOHN EDWIN

YR	CL	LEA	POS	GP	G	REC
1960	NY	A	C		5	.455
1961	NY	A	O		4	.400
1962	NY	A	H		1	.000
1963	NY	A	O		1	.000
1964	NY	A	H		4	.250
					15	.345

BLASINGAME, DONALD LEE

YR	CL	LEA	POS	GP	G	REC
1961	CIN	N	2		3	.143

BLASS, STEPHEN ROBERT

YR	CL	LEA	POS	GP	G	REC
1971	PIT	N	P		2	2- 0

BLEFARY, CURTIS LEROY

YR	CL	LEA	POS	GP	G	REC
1966	BAL	A	O		4	.077

BLOCK, SEYMOUR

YR	CL	LEA	POS	GP	G	REC
1945	CHI	N	R		1	.000

BLOODWORTH, JAMES HENRY

YR	CL	LEA	POS	GP	G	REC
1950	PHI	N	2		1	.000

BLUE, VIDA ROCHELLE

YR	CL	LEA	POS	GP	G	REC
1972	OAK	A	P		4	0- 1
1973	OAK	A	P		2	0- 1
1974	OAK	A	P		2	0- 1
					8	0- 3

BLUEGE, OSWALD LOUIS

YR	CL	LEA	POS	GP	G	REC
1924	WAS	A	S-3		7	.192
1925	WAS	A	3		5	.278
1933	WAS	A	3		5	.125
					17	.200

BOLEY, JOHN PETER

YR	CL	LEA	POS	GP	G	REC
1929	PHI	A	S		5	.235
1930	PHI	A	S		6	.095
1931	PHI	A	H		1	.000
					12	.154

BOLIN, BOBBY DONALD

YR	CL	LEA	POS	GP	G	REC
1962	SF	N	P		2	0- 0

BOLLWEG, DONALD RAYMOND

YR	CL	LEA	POS	GP	G	REC
1953	NY	A	1		3	.000

BOLTON, WILLIAM CLIFTON

YR	CL	LEA	POS	GP	G	REC
1933	WAS	A	H		2	.000

BONGIOVANNI, ANTHONY THOMAS

YR	CL	LEA	POS	GP	G	REC
1939	CIN	N	H		1	.000

BONHAM, ERNEST EDWARD

YR	CL	LEA	POS	GP	G	REC
1941	NY	A	P		1	1- 0
1942	NY	A	P		2	0- 1
1943	NY	A	P		1	0- 1
					4	1- 2

BOONE, RAYMOND OTIS

YR	CL	LEA	POS	GP	G	REC
1948	CLE	A	H		1	.000

BORBON, PEDRO

YR	CL	LEA	POS	GP	G	REC
1972	CIN	N	P		6	0 -1
1975	CIN	N	P		3	0- 0
1976	CIN	N	P		1	0- 0
					10	0- 1

BORDAGARAY, STANLEY GEORGE

YR	CL	LEA	POS	GP	G	REC
1939	CIN	N	R		2	.000
1941	NY	A	R		1	.000
					3	.000

BOROM, EDWARD JONES

YR	CL	LEA	POS	GP	G	REC
1945	DET	A	H		2	.000

BOROWY, HENRY LUDWIG

YR	CL	LEA	POS	GP	G	REC
1942	NY	A	P		1	0- 0
1943	NY	A	P		1	1- 0
1945	CHI	N	P		4	2- 2
					6	3- 2

BOSWELL, DAVID WILSON

YR	CL	LEA	POS	GP	G	REC
1965	MIN	A	P		1	1- 0

BOSWELL, KENNETH GEORGE

YR	CL	LEA	POS	GP	G	REC
1969	NY	N	2		1	.333
1973	NY	N	2		3	1.000
					4	.667

BOTTOMLEY, JAMES LEROY

YR	CL	LEA	POS	GP	G	REC
1926	STL	N	1		7	.345
1928	STL	N	1		4	.214
1930	STL	N	1		6	.045
1931	STL	N	1		7	.160
					24	.200

BOUDREAU, LOUIS

YR	CL	LEA	POS	GP	G	REC
1948	CLE	A	S		6	.273

BOURQUE, PATRICK DANIEL

YR	CL	LEA	POS	GP	G	REC
1973	OAK	A	1		2	.500

BOUTON, JAMES ALAN

YR	CL	LEA	POS	GP	G	REC
1963	NY	A	P		1	0- 1
1964	NY	A	P		2	2- 0

BOWMAN, ERNEST FERRELL

YR	CL	LEA	POS	GP	G	REC
1962	SF	N	S		2	.000

BOYER, CLETIS LEROY

YR	CL	LEA	POS	GP	G	REC
1960	NY	A	S-3		4	.250
1961	NY	A	3		5	.267
1962	NY	A	3		7	.318
1963	NY	A	3		4	.077
1964	NY	A	3		7	.208
					27	.233

BOYER, KENTON LLOYD

YR	CL	LEA	POS	GP	G	REC
1964	STL	N	3		7	.222

BRAGAN, ROBERT RANDALL

YR	CL	LEA	POS	GP	G	REC
1947	BRO	N	H		1	1.000

BRANCA, RALPH THEODORE JOSEPH

YR	CL	LEA	POS	GP	G	REC
1947	BRO	N	P		3	1- 1
1949	BRO	N	P		1	0- 1
					4	1- 2

BRANSFIELD, WILLIAM EDWARD

YR	CL	LEA	POS	GP	G	REC
1903	PIT	N	1		8	.207

BRAVO, ANGEL

YR	CL	LEA	POS	GP	G	REC
1970	CIN	N	H		4	.000

BRAZLE, ALPHA EUGENE

YR	CL	LEA	POS	GP	G	REC
1943	STL	N	P		1	0- 1
1946	STL	N	P		1	0- 1
					2	0- 2

BRECHEEN, HARRY DAVID

YR	CL	LEA	POS	GP	G	REC
1943	STL	N	P		3	0- 1
1944	STL	N	P		1	1- 0
1946	STL	N	P		3	3- 0
					7	4- 1

```
YR  CL LEA POS  GP   G    REC
```

BRENNAN, JAMES DONALD
1937 NY N P   2   0- 0

BRESNAHAN, ROGER PATRICK
1905 NY N C   5   .313

BRESSOUD, EDWARD FRANCIS
1967 STL N S   2   .000

BRETT, KENNETH ALVEN
1967 BOS A P   2   0- 0

BREUER, MARVIN HOWARD
1941 NY A P   1   0- 0
1942 NY A P   1   0- 0
                   2   0- 0

BREWER, JAMES THOMAS
1965 LA N P   1   0- 0
1966 LA N P   1   0- 0
1974 LA N P   1   0- 0
                   3   0- 0

BRICKELL, GEORGE FREDERICK
1927 PIT N H   2   .000

BRIDGES, MARSHALL
1962 NY A P   2   0- 0

BRIDGES, THOMAS JEFFERSON DAVIS
1934 DET A P   3   1- 1
1935 DET A P   2   2- 0
1940 DET A P   1   1- 0
1945 DET A P   1   0- 0
                   7   4- 1

BRIGHT, HARRY JAMES
1963 NY A H   ?   .000

BRILES, NELSON KELLEY
1967 STL N P   2   1- 0
1968 STL N P   2   0- 1
1971 PIT N P   1   1- 0
                   5   2- 1

BROCK, LOUIS CLARK
1964 STL N O   7   .300
1967 STL N O   7   .414
1968 STL N O   7   .464
                      21   .391

BROSNAN, JAMES PATRICK
1961 CIN N P   0- 0

BROWN, JAMES ROBERSON
1942 STL N 2   5   .300

BROWN, MACE STANLEY
1946 BOS A P   1   0- 0

BROWN, MORDECAI PETER
1906 CHI N P   3   1- 2
1907 CHI N P   1   1- 0
1908 CHI N P   2   2- 0
1910 CHI N P   3   1- 2
                   9   5- 4

BROWN, ROBERT WILLIAM
1947 NY A H   4   1.000
1949 NY A 3   4   .500
1950 NY A 3   4   .333
1951 NY A 3   5   .357
                      17   .439

BROWN, THOMAS MICHAEL
1949 BRO N H   2   .000

BROWN, WILLIAM JAMES
1968 DET A H   1   .000

BROWNE, GEORGE E.
1905 NY N O   5   .182

BRUTON, WILLIAM HARON
1958 MIL N O   7   .412

BRYANT, CLAIBORNE HENRY
1938 CHI N P   1   0- 1

BUCHEK, GERALD PETER
1964 STL N 2   4   1.000

BUCKNER, WILLIAM JOSEPH
1974 LA N O   5   .250

BUFORD, DONALD ALVIN
1969 BAL A O   5   .100
1970 BAL A O   4   .267
1971 BAL A O   6   .261
                      15   .207

BUHL, ROBERT RAY
1957 MIL N P   2   0- 1

BUNKER, WALLACE EDWARD
1966 BAL A P   1   1- 0

BURDETTE, SELVA LEWIS
1957 MIL N P   3   3- 0
1958 MIL N P   3   1- 2
                       6   4- 2

BURGESS, FORREST HARRILL
1960 PIT N C   5   .333

BURLESON, RICHARD PAUL
1975 BOS A S   7   .292

BURNS, EDWARD JAMES
1915 PHI N C   5   .188

BURNS, GEORGE HENRY
1920 CLE A 1   5   .300
1929 PHI A H   1   .000
                       6   .250

BURNS, GEORGE JOSEPH
1913 NY N O   5   .158
1917 NY N O   6   .227
1921 NY N O   8   .333
                      19   .257

BURTON, JIM SCOTT
1975 BOS A P   2   0- 1

BUSH, GUY TERRELL
1929 CHI N P   2   1- 0
1932 CHI N P   2   0- 1
                       4   1- 1

BUSH, LESLIE AMBROSE
1913 PHI A P   1   1- 0
1914 PHI A P   1   0- 1
1918 BOS A P   2   0- 1
1922 NY A P   2   0- 2
1923 NY A P   3 4   1- 1
                9 10   2- 5

BUSH, OWEN JOSEPH
1909 DET A S   7   .261

BYERLY, ELDRED WILLIAM
1944 STL N P   1   0- 0

BYRD, SAMUEL DEWEY
1932 NY A O   1   .000

BYRNE, ROBERT MATHEW
1909 PIT N 3   7   .250
1915 PHI N H   1   .000
                       8   .240

BYRNE, THOMAS JOSEPH
1949 NY A P   1   0- 0
1955 NY A P   2 3   1- 1
1956 NY A P   1 2   0- 0
1957 NY A P   2   0- 0
                6 8   1- 1

BYRNES, MILTON JOHN
1944 STL A H   3   .000

CABALLERO, RALPH JOSEPH
1950 PHI N H   3   .000

CADORE, LEON JOSEPH
1920 BRO N P   2   0- 1

CADY, FORREST LEROY
1912 BOS A C   7   .136
1915 BOS A C   4   .333
1916 BOS A C   2   .250
                      13   .188

CALDWELL, RAYMOND BENJAMIN
1920 CLE A P   1   0- 1

CAMILLI, ADOLPH LOUIS
1941 BRO N 1   5   .167

CAMNITZ, SAMUEL HOWARD
1909 PIT N P   2   0- 1

CAMPANELLA, ROY
1949 BRO N C   5   .267
1952 BRO N C   7   .214
1953 BRO N C   6   .273
1955 BRO N C   7   .259
1956 BRO N C   7   .182
                      32   .237

CAMPANERIS, DAGOBERTO
1972 OAK A S   7   .179
1973 OAK A S   7   .290
1974 OAK A S   5   .353
                      19   .263

CAMPBELL, BRUCE DOUGLAS
1940 DET A O   7   .360

CAMPBELL, PAUL MC LAUGHLIN
1946 BOS A R   1   .000

CARBO, BERNARDO
1970 CIN N O   4   .000
1975 BOS A O   4   .429
                       8   .200

CARDENAS, LEONARDO ALFONSO
1961 CIN N H   3   .333

CARDWELL, DONALD EUGENE
1969 NY N P   1   0- 0

CAREY, ANDREW ARTHUR
1955 NY A H   2   .500
1956 NY A 3   7   .158
1957 NY A 3   2   .286
1958 NY A 3   5   .083
                      16   .175

CAREY, MAX GEORGE
1925 PIT N O   7   .458

CARLETON, JAMES OTTO
1934 STL N P   2   0- 0
1935 CHI N P   1   0- 1
1938 CHI N P   1   0- 0
                       4   0- 1

CARLSON, HAROLD GUST
1929 CHI N P   2   0- 0

CARLTON, STEVEN NORMAN
1967 STL N P   1   0- 1
1968 STL N P   2   0- 0
                   3   0- 1

CARRIGAN, WILLIAM FRANCIS
1912 BOS A C   2   .000
1915 BOS A C   1   .000
1916 BOS A C   1   .667
                       4   .167

CARROLL, CLAY PALMER
1970 CIN N P   4   1- 0
1972 CIN N P   5   0- 1
1975 CIN N P   5   1- 0
                      14   2- 1

CARROLL, THOMAS EDWARD
1955 NY A R   2   .000

CASEY, HUGH THOMAS
1941 BRO N P   3   0- 2
1947 BRO N P   6   2- 0
                       9   2- 2

CASH, DAVID
1971 PIT N 2   7   .133

CASH, NORMAN DALTON
1959 CHI A H   4   .000
1968 DET A 1   7   .385
                      11   .333

CASTER, GEORGE JASPER
1945 DET A P   1   0- 0

CASTLEMAN, CLYDELL
1936 NY N P   1   0- 0

CATHER, THEODORE P.
1914 BOS N O   1   .000

YR	CL	LEA	POS	GP	G	REC

CAVARETTA, PHILIP JOSEPH

YR	CL	LEA	POS	GP	G	REC
1935	CHI	N	1		6	.125
1938	CHI	N	O		4	.462
1945	CHI	N	1		7	.423
					17	.317

CEPEDA, ORLANDO MANUEL

1962	SF	N	1		5	.158
1967	STL	N	1		7	.103
1968	STL	N	1		7	.250
					19	.171

CERV, ROBERT HENRY

1955	NY	A	O		5	.125
1956	NY	A	H		1	1.000
1960	NY	A	O		4	.357
					10	.258

CEY, RONALD CHARLES

| 1974 | LA | N | 3 | | 5 | .176 |

CHACON, ELIO RODRIGUEZ

| 1961 | CIN | N | 2 | | 4 | .250 |

CHALMERS, GEORGE W.

| 1915 | PHI | N | P | 1 | 0- 1 | |

CHAMBLISS, CARROLL CHRISTOPHER

| 1976 | NY | A | 1 | | 4 | .313 |

CHANCE, FRANK LEROY

1906	CHI	N	1		6	.238
1907	CHI	N	1		4	.214
1908	CHI	N	1		5	.421
1910	CHI	N	1		5	.353
					20	.310

CHANDLER, SPURGEON FERDINAND

1941	NY	A	P	1	0- 1	
1942	NY	A	P	2	0- 1	
1943	NY	A	P	2	2- 0	
1947	NY	A	P	1	0- 0	
				6	2- 2	

CHANEY, DARREL LEE

1970	CIN	N	S		3	.000
1972	CIN	N	S		4	.000
1975	CIN	N	H		2	.000
					9	.000

CHAPMAN, WILLIAM BENJAMIN

| 1932 | NY | A | O | | 4 | .294 |

CHARLES, EDWIN DOUGLAS

| 1969 | NY | N | 3 | | 4 | .133 |

CHARTAK, MICHAEL GEORGE

| 1944 | STL | A | H | | 2 | .000 |

CHENEY, LAWRENCE RUSSELL

| 1916 | BRO | N | P | 1 | 0- 0 | |

CHENEY, THOMAS EDGAR

| 1960 | PIT | N | P | 3 | 0- 0 | |

CHIOZZA, LOUIS PEO

| 1937 | NY | N | O | | 2 | .286 |

CHIPMAN, ROBERT HOWARD

| 1945 | CHI | N | P | 1 | 0- 0 | |

CHRISTMAN, MARQUETTE JOSEPH

| 1944 | STL | A | 3 | | 6 | .091 |

CHRISTOPHER, JOSEPH O'NEAL

| 1960 | PIT | N | H | | 3 | .000 |

CHRISTOPHER, RUSSELL ORMAND

| 1948 | CLE | A | P | 1 | 0- 0 | |

CHURN, CLARENCE NOTTINGHAM

| 1959 | LA | N | P | 1 | 0- 0 | |

CICOTTE, EDWARD VICTOR

1917	CHI	A	P	3	1- 1	
1919	CHI	A	P	3	1- 2	
				6	2- 3	

CIMOLI, GINO NICHOLAS

1956	BRO	N	O		1	.000
1960	PIT	N	O		7	.250
					8	.250

CLARK, ALFRED ALOYSIUS

1947	NY	A	O		3	.500
1948	CLE	A	O		1	.000
					4	.200

CLARKE, FREDERICK CLIFFORD

1903	PIT	N	O		8	.265
1909	PIT	N	O		7	.211
					15	.245

CLARY, ELLIS

| 1944 | STL | A | H | | 1 | .000 |

CLEMENTE, ROBERTO WALKER

1960	PIT	N	O		7	.310
1971	PIT	N	O		7	.414
					14	.362

CLENDENON, DONN ALVIN

| 1969 | NY | N | 1 | | 4 | .357 |

CLEVELAND, REGINALD LESLIE

| 1975 | BOS | A | P | 3 | 0- 1 | |

CLIFTON, HERMAN EARL

| 1935 | DET | A | 3 | | 4 | .000 |

CLINE, TYRONE ALEXANDER

| 1970 | CIN | N | H | | 3 | .333 |

CLINES, EUGENE

| 1971 | PIT | N | O | | 3 | .091 |

CLONINGER, TONY LEE

| 1970 | CIN | N | P | 2 | 0- 1 | |

COAKLEY, ANDREW JAMES

| 1905 | PHI | A | P | 1 | 0- 1 | |

COATES, JAMES ALTON

1960	NY	A	P	3	0- 0	
1961	NY	A	P	1	0- 0	
1962	NY	A	P	2	0- 1	
				6	0- 1	

COBB, TYRUS RAYMOND

1907	DET	A	O		5	.200
1908	DET	A	O		5	.368
1909	DET	A	O		7	.231
					17	.262

COCHRANE, GORDON STANLEY

1929	PHI	A	C		5	.400
1930	PHI	A	C		6	.222
1931	PHI	A	C		7	.160
1934	DET	A	C		7	.214
1935	DET	A	C		6	.292
					31	.245

COFFMAN, SAMUEL RICHARD

1936	NY	N	P	2	0- 0	
1937	NY	N	P	2	0- 0	
				4	0- 0	

COLE, LEONARD LESLIE

| 1910 | CHI | N | P | 1 | 0- 0 | |

COLEMAN, GERALD FRANCIS

1949	NY	A	2		5	.250
1950	NY	A	2		4	.286
1951	NY	A	2		5	.250
1955	NY	A	S		3	.000
1956	NY	A	2		2	.000
1957	NY	A	2		7	.364
					26	.275

COLEMAN, GORDON CALVIN

| 1961 | CIN | N | 1 | | 5 | .250 |

COLEMAN, WALTER GARY

| 1955 | NY | A | P | 1 | 0- 0 | |

COLLINS, EDWARD TROWBRIDGE

1910	PHI	A	2		5	.429
1911	PHI	A	2		6	.286
1913	PHI	A	2		5	.421
1914	PHI	A	2		4	.214
1917	CHI	A	2		6	.409
1919	CHI	A	2		8	.226
					34	.328

COLLINS, HARRY WARREN

| 1921 | NY | A | P | 1 | 0- 0 | |

COLLINS, JAMES ANTHONY

1931	STL	N	H		2	.000
1934	STL	N	1		7	.367
1938	CHI	N	1		4	.133
					13	.277

COLLINS, JAMES JOSEPH

| 1903 | BOS | A | 3 | | 8 | .250 |

COLLINS, JOHN FRANCIS

1917	CHI	A	O		6	.286
1919	CHI	A	O		4	.250
					10	.270

COLLINS, JOSEPH EDWARD

1950	NY	A	1		1	.000
1951	NY	A	1-O		6	.222
1952	NY	A	1		6	.000
1953	NY	A	1		6	.167
1955	NY	A	1-O		5	.167
1956	NY	A	1		6	.238
1957	NY	A	1		6	.000
					36	.163

COLLINS, RAYMOND WILLISTON

| 1912 | BOS | A | P | 2 | 0- 0 | |

COLLINS, THARON PATRICK

1926	NY	A	C		3	.000
1927	NY	A	C		2	.600
1928	NY	A	C		1	1.000
					6	.500

COMBS, EARLE BRYAN

1926	NY	A	O		7	.357
1927	NY	A	O		4	.313
1928	NY	A	H		1	.000
1932	NY	A	O		4	.375
					16	.350

COMER, HARRY WAYNE

| 1968 | DET | A | H | | 1 | 1.000 |

CONATSER, CLINTON ASTOR

| 1948 | BOS | N | O | | 2 | .000 |

CONCEPCION, DAVID ISMAEL

1970	CIN	N	S		3	.333
1972	CIN	N	S		6	.308
1975	CIN	N	S		7	.179
1976	CIN	N	S		4	.357
					20	.266

CONIGLIARO, WILLIAM MICHAEL

| 1973 | OAK | A | H | | 3 | .000 |

CONLEY, DONALD EUGENE

| 1957 | MIL | N | P | 1 | 0- 0 | |

CONNOLLY, JOSEPH ALOYSIUS

| 1914 | BOS | N | O | | 3 | .111 |

COOMBS, JOHN WESLEY

1910	PHI	A	P	3	3- 0	
1911	PHI	A	P	2	1- 0	
1916	BRO	N	P	1	1- 0	
				6	5- 0	

COOPER, CECIL CELESTER

| 1975 | BOS | A | 1 | | 5 | .053 |

COOPER, CLAUDE

| 1913 | NY | N | R | | 2 | .000 |

COOPER, MORTON CECIL

1942	STL	N	P	2	0- 1	
1943	STL	N	P	2	1- 1	
1944	STL	N	P	2	1- 1	
				6	2- 3	

COOPER, WILLIAM WALKER

1942	STL	N	C		5	.286
1943	STL	N	C		5	.294
1944	STL	N	C		6	.318
					16	.300

CORRALÈS, PATRICK

| 1970 | CIN | N | H | | 1 | .000 |

CORWIN, ELMER NATHAN

| 1951 | NY | N | P | 1 | 0- 0 | |

COSCARART, PETER JOSEPH

| 1941 | BRO | N | 2 | | 3 | .000 |

COUGHLIN, WILLIAM PAUL

1907	DET	A	3		5	.250
1908	DET	A	3		3	.125
					8	.214

YR	CL LEA POS	GP	G	REC

COVELESKI, STANLEY
1920 CLE A	P		3	3- 0
1925 WAS A	P		2	0- 2
			5	3- 2

COVINGTON, JOHN WESLEY
1957 MIL N	O		7	.208
1958 MIL N	O		7	.269
1966 LA N	H		1	.000
			15	.235

COX, WILLIAM RICHARD
1949 BRO N	3		2	.333
1952 BRO N	3		7	.296
1953 BRO N	3		6	.304
			15	.302

CRAFT, HARRY FRANCIS
1939 CIN N	O		4	.091
1940 CIN N	H		1	.000
			5	.083

CRAIG, ROGER LEE
1955 BRO N	P		1	1- 0
1956 BRO N	P		2	0- 1
1959 LA N	P		2	0- 1
1964 STL N	P		2	1- 0
			7	2- 2

CRAMER, ROGER MAXWELL
1931 PHI A	H		2	.500
1945 DET A	O		7	.379
			9	.387

CRANDALL, DELMAR WESLEY
1957 MIL N	C		6	.211
1958 MIL N	C		7	.240
			13	.227

CRANDALL, JAMES OTIS
1911 NY N	P	2	3	1- 0
1912 NY N	P		1	0- 0
1913 NY N	P	2	4	0- 0
			5	8	1- 0

CRAVATH, CLIFFORD CARLTON
| 1915 PHI N | O | | 5 | .125 |

CRAWFORD, CLIFFORD RANKIN
| 1934 STL N | H | | 3 | .000 |

CRAWFORD, SAMUEL EARL
1907 DET A	O		5	.238
1908 DET A	O		5	.238
1909 DET A	1-O		7	.250
			17	.243

CRAWFORD, WILLIE MURPHY
1965 LA N	H		2	.500
1974 LA N	O		3	.333
			5	.375

CRESPI, FRANK ANGELO JOHN
| 1942 STL N | R | | 1 | .000 |

CRIGER, LOUIS
| 1903 BOS A | C | | 8 | .231 |

CRITZ, HUGH MELVILLE
| 1933 NY N | 2 | | 5 | .136 |

CRONIN, JOSEPH EDWARD
| 1933 WAS A | S | | 5 | .318 |

CROSETTI, FRANK PETER JOSEPH
1932 NY A	S		4	.133
1936 NY A	S		6	.269
1937 NY A	S		5	.048
1938 NY A	S		4	.250
1939 NY A	S		4	.063
1942 NY A	3		1	.000
1943 NY A	S		5	.278
			29	.174

CROSS, LAVE NAPOLEON
| 1905 PHI A | 3 | | 5 | .105 |

CROSS, MONTFORD MONTGOMERY
| 1905 PHI A | S | | 5 | .176 |

CROUCHER, FRANK DONALD
| 1940 DET A | S | | 1 | .000 |

CROWDER, ALVIN FLOYD
1933 WAS A	P		2	0- 1
1934 DET A	P		2	0- 1
1935 DET A	P		1	1- 0
			5	1- 2

CROWLEY, TERRENCE MICHAEL
1970 BAL A	H		1	.000
1975 CIN N	H		2	.500
			3	.333

CUELLAR, MIGUEL ANGEL
1969 BAL A	P		2	1- 0
1970 BAL A	P		2	1- 0
1971 BAL A	P		2	0- 2
			6	2- 2

CULBERSON, DELBERT LEON
| 1946 BOS A | O | | 5 | .222 |

CULLENBINE, ROY JOSEPH
1942 NY A	O		5	.263
1945 DET A	O		7	.227
			12	.244

CUNNINGHAM, WILLIAM ALOYSIUS
1922 NY N	O		4	.200
1923 NY N	O		4	.143
			8	.176

CUTSHAW, GEORGE WILLIAM
| 1916 BRO N | 2 | | 5 | .105 |

CUYLER, HAZEN SHIRLEY
1925 PIT N	O		7	.269
1929 CHI N	O		5	.300
1932 CHI N	O		4	.278
			16	.281

CVENGROS, MICHAEL JOHN
| 1927 PIT N | P | | 2 | 0- 0 |

DAHLEN, WILLIAM FREDERICK
| 1905 NY N | S | | 5 | .000 |

DAHLGREN, ELLSWORTH TENNEY
| 1939 NY A | 1 | | 4 | .214 |

DALEY, LEAVITT LEO
1961 NY A	P		1	1- 0
1962 NY A	P		1	0- 0
			3	1- 0

DALRYMPLE, CLAYTON ERROL
| 1969 BAL A | H | | 2 | 1.000 |

DANFORTH, DAVID CHARLES
| 1917 CHI A | P | | 1 | 0- 0 |

DANNING, HARRY
1936 NY N	C		2	.000
1937 NY N	C		3	.250
			5	.214

DARCY, PATRICK LEONARD
| 1975 CIN N | P | | 2 | 0- 1 |

DARK, ALVIN RALPH
1948 BOS N	S		6	.167
1951 NY N	S		6	.417
1954 NY N	S		4	.412
			16	.323

DAUBERT, JACOB ELLSWORTH
1916 BRO N	1		4	.176
1919 CIN N	1		8	.241
			12	.217

DAVALILLO, VICTOR JOSE
1971 PIT N	O		3	.333
1973 OAK A	1-O		6	.091
			9	.143

DAVENPORT, JAMES HOUSTON
| 1962 SF N | 3 | | 7 | .136 |

DAVIS, CURTIS BENTON
| 1941 BRO N | P | | 1 | 0- 1 |

DAVIS, GEORGE STACEY
| 1906 CHI A | S | | 3 | .308 |

DAVIS, GEORGE WILLIS
1933 NY N	O		5	.368
1936 NY N	H		4	.500
			9	.381

DAVIS, HARRY H.
1905 PHI A	1		5	.200
1910 PHI A	1		5	.353
1911 PHI A	1		6	.208
			16	.246

DAVIS, HERMAN THOMAS
1963 LA N	O		4	.400
1966 LA N	O		4	.250
			8	.348

DAVIS, RONALD EVERETTE
| 1968 STL N | O | | 2 | .000 |

DAVIS, VIRGIL LAWRENCE
| 1934 STL N | H | | 2 | 1.000 |

DAVIS, WILLIAM HENRY
1963 LA N	O		4	.167
1965 LA N	O		7	.231
1966 LA N	O		4	.063
			15	.167

DAWSON, RALPH FENTON
| 1927 PIT N | P | | 1 | 0- 0 |

DEAL, CHARLES ALBERT
1914 BOS N	3		4	.125
1918 CHI N	3		6	.176
			10	.152

DEAN, JAY HANNA
1934 STL N	P	3	4	2- 1
1938 CHI N	P		2	0- 1
			5	6	2- 2

DEAN, PAUL DEE
| 1934 STL N | P | | 2 | 2- 0 |

DEAN, WAYLAND OGDEN
| 1924 NY N | P | | 1 | 0- 0 |

DELAHANTY, JAMES CHRISTOPHER
| 1909 DET A | 2 | | 7 | .346 |

DE LANCEY, WILLIAM PINKNEY
| 1934 STL N | C | | 7 | .172 |

DELL, WEISER GEORGE
| 1916 BRO N | P | | 1 | 0- 0 |

DE MAESTRI, JOSEPH PAUL
| 1960 NY A | S | | 4 | .500 |

DEMAREE, ALBERT WENTWORTH
| 1913 NY N | P | | 1 | 0- 1 |

DEMAREE, JOSEPH FRANKLIN
1932 CHI N	O		2	.286
1935 CHI N	O		6	.250
1938 CHI N	O		3	.100
1943 STL N	H		1	.000
			12	.214

DE MERIT, JOHN STEPHEN
| 1957 MIL N | R | | 1 | .000 |

DEMETER, DONALD LEE
| 1959 LA N | O | | 6 | .250 |

DENTE, SAMUEL JOSEPH
| 1954 CLE A | S | | 3 | .000 |

DERRINGER, SAMUEL PAUL
1931 STL N	P		3	0- 2
1939 CIN N	P		2	0- 1
1940 CIN N	P		3	2- 1
1945 CHI N	P		3	0- 0
			11	2- 4

DEVLIN, ARTHUR MC ARTHUR
| 1905 NY N | 3 | | 5 | .250 |

DEVORE, JOSHUA D.
1911 NY N	O		6	.167
1912 NY N	O		7	.250
1914 BOS N	H		1	.000
			14	.204

DE VORMER, ALBERT E.
| 1921 NY A | C | | 2 | .000 |

YR	CL	LEA	POS	GP	G	REC
DICKEY, WILLIAM MALCOLM						
1932 NY	A		C		4	.438
1936 NY	A		C		6	.120
1937 NY	A		C		5	.211
1938 NY	A		C		4	.400
1939 NY	A		C		4	.267
1941 NY	A		C		5	.167
1942 NY	A		C		5	.263
1943 NY	A		C		5	.278
					38	.255
DICKSON, MURRY MONROE						
1943 STL	N		P	1		0- 0
1946 STL	N		P	2		0- 1
1958 NY	A		P	2		0- 0
				5		0- 1
DI MAGGIO, DOMINIC PAUL						
1946 BOS	A		O		7	.259
DI MAGGIO, JOSEPH PAUL						
1936 NY	A		O		6	.346
1937 NY	A		O		5	.273
1938 NY	A		O		4	.267
1939 NY	A		O		4	.313
1941 NY	A		O		5	.263
1942 NY	A		O		5	.333
1947 NY	A		O		7	.231
1949 NY	A		O		5	.111
1950 NY	A		O		4	.308
1951 NY	A		O		6	.261
					51	.271
DINNEEN, WILLIAM HENRY						
1903 BOS	A		P	4		3- 1
DITMAR, ARTHUR JOHN						
1957 NY	A		P	2		0- 0
1958 NY	A		P	1		0- 0
1960 NY	A		P	2		0- 2
				5		0- 2
DOBSON, JOSEPH GORDON						
1946 BOS	A		P	3		1- 0
DOBSON, PATRICK EDWARD						
1968 DET	A		P	3		0- 0
1971 BAL	A		P	3		0- 0
				6		0- 0
DOBY, LAWRENCE EUGENE						
1948 CLE	A		O		6	.318
1954 CLE	A		O		4	.125
					10	.237
DOERR, ROBERT PERSHING						
1946 BOS	A		2		6	.409
DOLJACK, FRANK JOSEPH						
1934 DET	A		O		2	.000
DONAHUE, JOHN AUGUSTUS						
1906 CHI	A		1		6	.333
DONALD, RICHARD ATLEY						
1941 NY	A		P	1		0- 0
1942 NY	A		P	1		0- 1
				2		0- 1
DONLIN, MICHAEL JOSEPH						
1905 NY	N		O		5	.263
DONNELLY, SYLVESTER URBAN						
1944 STL	N		P	2		1- 0
DONOVAN, RICHARD EDWARD						
1959 CHI	A		P	3		0- 1
DONOVAN, WILLIAM EDWARD						
1907 DET	A		P	2		0- 1
1908 DET	A		P	2		0- 2
1909 DET	A		P	2		1- 1
				6		1- 4
DOUGHERTY, PATRICK HENRY						
1903 BOS	A		O		8	.235
1906 CHI	A		O		6	.100
					14	.185
DOUGLAS, PHILIP BROOKS						
1918 CHI	N		P	1		0- 1
1921 NY	N		P	3		2- 1
				4		2- 2

YR	CL	LEA	POS	GP	G	REC
DOUTHIT, TAYLOR LEE						
1926 STL	N		O		4	.267
1928 STL	N		O		3	.091
1930 STL	N		O		6	.083
					13	.140
DOWNING, ALPHONSO ERWIN						
1963 NY	A		P	1		0- 1
1964 NY	A		P	3		0- 1
1974 LA	N		P	1		0- 1
				5		0- 3
DOWNS, JEROME WILLIS						
1908 DET	A		2		2	.167
DOYLE, LAWRENCE JOSEPH						
1911 NY	N		2		6	.304
1912 NY	N		2		8	.242
1913 NY	N		2		5	.150
					19	.237
DOYLE, ROBERT DENNIS						
1975 BOS	A		2		7	.267
DRABOWSKY, MYRON WALTER						
1966 BAL	A		P	1		1- 0
1970 BAL	A		P	2		0- 0
				3		1- 0
DRAGO, RICHARD ANTHONY						
1975 BOS	A		P	2		0- 1
DREISEWERD, CLEMENT JOHN						
1946 BOS	A		P	1		0- 0
DREWS, KARL AUGUST						
1947 NY	A		P	2		0- 0
DRIESSEN, DANIEL						
1975 CIN	N		H	2		.000
1976 CIN	N		O	4		.357
				6		.312
DRYSDALE, DONALD SCOTT						
1956 BRO	N		P	1		0- 0
1959 LA	N		P	1		1- 0
1963 LA	N		P	1		1- 0
1965 LA	N		P	2	3	1- 1
1966 LA	N		P	2		0- 2
				7	8	3- 3
DUBUC, JEAN ARTHUR						
1918 BOS	A		H	1		.000
DUGAN, JOSEPH ANTHONY						
1922 NY	A		3		5	.250
1923 NY	A		3		6	.280
1926 NY	A		3		7	.333
1927 NY	A		3		4	.200
1928 NY	A		3		3	.167
					25	.267
DUGEY, OSCAR JOSEPH						
1915 PHI	N		R		2	.000
DUKES, THOMAS EARL						
1971 BAL	A		P	2		0- 0
DUNCAN, DAVID EDWIN						
1972 OAK	A		C		3	.200
DUNCAN, LOUIS BAIRD						
1919 CIN	N		O		8	.269
DUREN, RINOLD GEORGE						
1958 NY	A		P	3		1- 1
1960 NY	A		P	2		0- 0
				5		1- 1
DUROCHER, LEO ERNEST						
1928 NY	A		2		4	.000
1934 STL	N		S		7	.259
					11	.241
DURST, CEDRIC MONTGOMERY						
1927 NY	A		H		1	.000
1928 NY	A		O		4	.375
					5	.333
DUSAK, ERVIN FRANK						
1946 STL	N		O		4	.250
DYER, DON ROBERT						
1969 NY	N		H	1		.000

YR	CL	LEA	POS	GP	G	REC
DYKES, JAMES JOSEPH						
1929 PHI	A		3		5	.421
1930 PHI	A		3		6	.222
1931 PHI	A		3		7	.227
					18	.288
EARNSHAW, GEORGE LIVINGSTON						
1929 PHI	A		P	2		1- 1
1930 PHI	A		P	3		2- 0
1931 PHI	A		P	3		1- 2
				8		4- 3
EASTWICK, RAWLINS JACKSON						
1975 CIN	N		P	5		2- 0
EATON, ZEBULON VANCE						
1945 DET	A		H	1		.000
EDWARDS, CHARLES BRUCE						
1947 BRO	N		C		7	.222
1949 BRO	N		H		2	.500
					9	.241
EDWARDS, JOHN ALBAN						
1961 CIN	N		C		3	.364
1968 STL	N		H		1	.000
					4	.333
EHMKE, HOWARD JOHN						
1929 PHI	A		P	2		1- 0
ELLER, HORACE OWEN						
1919 CIN	N		P	2		2- 0
ELLIOTT, ROBERT IRVING						
1948 BOS	N		3		6	.333
ELLIS, DOCK PHILLIP						
1971 PIT	N		P	1		0- 1
1976 NY	A		P	1		0- 1
				2		0- 2
ENGLE, ARTHUR CLYDE						
1912 BOS	A		H		3	.333
ENGLISH, ELWOOD GEORGE						
1929 CHI	N		S		5	.190
1932 CHI	N		3		4	.176
					9	.184
ENNIS, DELMER						
1950 PHI	N		O		4	.143
EPSTEIN, MICHAEL PETER						
1972 OAK	A		1		6	.000
ERICKSON, PAUL WAKEFIELD						
1945 CHI	N		P	4		0- 0
ERSKINE, CARL DANIEL						
1949 BRO	N		P	2		0- 0
1952 BRO	N		P	3		1- 1
1953 BRO	N		P	3		1- 0
1955 BRO	N		P	1		0- 0
1956 BRO	N		P	2		0- 1
				11		2- 2
ESPOSITO, SAMUEL						
1959 CHI	A		3		2	.000
ESSEGIAN, CHARLES ABRAHAM						
1959 LA	N		H		4	.667
ETCHEBARREN, ANDREW AUGUSTE						
1966 BAL	A		C		4	.083
1969 BAL	A		C		2	.000
1970 BAL	A		C		2	.143
1971 BAL	A		C		1	.000
					9	.075
ETTEN, NICHOLAS RAYMOND THOMAS						
1943 NY	A		1		5	.105
EVANS, DWIGHT MICHAEL						
1975 BOS	A		O		7	.292
EVANS, JOSEPH PATTON						
1920 CLE	A		O		4	.308
EVERS, JOHN JOSEPH						
1906 CHI	N		2		6	.150
1907 CHI	N		2-S		5	.350
1908 CHI	N		2		5	.350
1914 BOS	N		2		4	.438
					20	.316

```
YR   CL LEA POS  GP   G    REC
```

FABER, URBAN CHARLES
1917 CHI A P   4   3- 1

FACE, ELROY LEON
1960 PIT N P   4   0- 0

FAIRLY, RONALD RAY
1959 LA N O   6   .000
1963 LA N O   4   .000
1965 LA N O   7   .379
1966 LA N 1-O   3   .143
                     20   .300

FALLON, GEORGE DECATUR
1944 STL N 2   2   .000

FARRELL, CHARLES ANDREW
1903 BOS A H   2   .000

FELLER, ROBERT WILLIAM ANDREW
1948 CLE A P   2   0- 2

FELSCH, OSCAR EMIL
1917 CHI A O   6   .273
1919 CHI A O   8   .192
                     14   .229

FERGUSON, JAMES ALEXANDER
1925 WAS A P   2   1- 1

FERGUSON, JOSEPH VANCE
1974 LA N C-O   5   .125

FERRARA, ALFRED JOHN
1966 LA N H   1   1.000

FERRICK, THOMAS JEROME
1950 NY A P   1   1- 0

FERRIS, ALBERT SAYLES
1903 BOS A 2   8   .290

FERRISS, DAVID MEADOW
1946 BOS A P   2   1- 0

FEWSTER, WILSON LLOYD
1921 NY A O   4   .200

FIGUEROA, EDUARDO
1976 NY A P   1   0- 1

FINGERS, ROLAND GLEN
1972 OAK A P   6   1- 1
1973 OAK A P   6   0- 1
1974 OAK A P   4   1- 0
                     16   2- 2

FISHER, GEORGE ALOYS
1930 STL N H   2   .500

FISHER, RAYMOND LYLE
1919 CIN N P   2   0- 1

FISK, CARLTON ERNEST
1975 BOS A C   7   .240

FITZSIMMONS, FREDERICK LANDIS
1933 NY N P   1   0- 1
1936 NY N P   2   0- 2
1941 BRO N P   1   0- 0
                      4   0- 3

FLACK, MAX JOHN
1918 CHI N O   6   .263

FLETCHER, ARTHUR
1911 NY N S   6   .130
1912 NY N S   8   .179
1913 NY N S   5   .278
1917 NY N S   6   .200
                     25   .191

FLOOD, CURTIS CHARLES
1964 STL N O   7   .200
1967 STL N O   7   .179
1968 STL N O   7   .286
                     21   .221

FLOWERS, D'ARCY RAYMOND
1926 STL N H   3   .000
1931 STL N 3   5   1091
                      8   .071

FORD, EDWARD CHARLES
1950 NY A P   1   1- 0
1953 NY A P   2   0- 1
1955 NY A P   2   2- 0
1956 NY A P   2   1- 1
1957 NY A P   2   1- 1
1958 NY A P   3   0- 1
1960 NY A P   2   2- 0
1961 NY A P   2   2- 0
1962 NY A P   3   1- 1
1963 NY A P   2   0- 2
1964 NY A P   1   0- 1
                     22 10- 8

FOSSE, RAYMOND EARL
1973 OAK A C   7   .158
1974 OAK A C   5   .143
                     12   .152

FOSTER, GEORGE
1915 BOS A P   2   2- 0
1916 BOS A P   1   0- 0
                      3   2- 0

FOSTER, GEORGE ARTHUR
1972 CIN N O   2   .000
1975 CIN N O   7   .276
1976 CIN N O   4   .429
                     13   .326

FOX, ERVIN
1934 DET A O   7   .286
1935 DET A O   6   .385
1940 DET A H   1   .000
                     14   .327

FOX, JACOB NELSON
1959 CHI A 2   6   .375

FOXX, JAMES EMORY
1929 PHI A 1   5   .350
1930 PHI A 1   6   .333
1931 PHI A 1   7   .348
                     18   .344

FOY, JOSEPH ANTHONY
1967 BOS A 3   6   .133

FRANKS, HERMAN LOUIS
1941 BRO N C   1   .000

FREEHAN, WILLIAM ASHLEY
1968 DET A C   7   .083

FREEMAN, JOHN F.
1903 BOS A O   8   .281

FREESE, EUGENE LEWIS
1961 CIN N 3   5   .063

FRENCH, LAWRENCE HERBERT
1935 CHI N P   2   0- 2
1938 CHI N P   3   0- 0
1941 BRO N P   2   0- 0
                      7   0- 2

FRENCH, WALTER EDWARD
1929 PHI A H   1   .000

FREY, LINUS REINHARD
1939 CIN N 2   4   .000
1940 CIN N H   3   .000
1947 NY A H   1   .000
                      8   .000

FRIEND, ROBERT BARTMESS
1960 PIT N P   3   0- 2

FRISCH, FRANK FRANCIS
1921 NY N 3   8   .300
1922 NY N 2   5   .471
1923 NY N 2   6   .400
1924 NY N 2-3   7   .333
1928 STL N 2   4   .231
1930 STL N 2   6   .208
1931 STL N 2   7   .259
1934 STL N 2   7   .194
                     50   .294

FULLIS, CHARLES PHILIP
1934 STL N O   3   .400

FURILLO, CARL ANTHONY
1947 BRO N O   6   .353
1949 BRO N O   3   .125
1952 BRO N O   7   .174
1953 BRO N O   6   .333
1955 BRO N O   7   .296
1956 BRO N O   7   .240
1959 LA N O   4   .250
                     40   .266

GABLER, FRANK HAROLD
1936 NY N P   2   0- 0

GAGLIANO, PHILIP JOSEPH
1967 STL N H   1   .000
1968 STL N H   3   .000
                      4   .000

GAINER, DELLOS CHARLES
1915 BOS A 1   1   .333
1916 BOS A H   1   1.000
                      2   .500

GALAN, AUGUST JOHN
1935 CHI N O   6   .160
1938 CHI N H   2   .000
1941 BRO N H   2   .000
                     10   .138

GALEHOUSE, DENNIS WARD
1944 STL A P   2   1- 1

GAMBLE, LEE JESSE
1939 CIN N H   1   .000

GAMBLE, OSCAR CHARLES
1976 NY A O   3   .125

GANDIL, CHARLES ARNOLD
1917 CHI A 1   6   .261
1919 CHI A 1   8   .233
                     14   .245

GARAGIOLA, JOSEPH HENRY
1946 STL N C   5   .316

GARCIA, EDWARD MICHAEL
1954 CLE A P   2   0- 1

GARDNER, WILLIAM FREDERICK
1961 NY A H   1   .000

GARDNER, WILLIAM LAWRENCE
1912 BOS A 3   8   .179
1915 BOS A 3   5   .235
1916 BOS A 3   5   .176
1920 CLE A 3   7   .208
                     25   .198

GARMS, DEBS C.
1943 STL N O   2   .000
1944 STL N H   2   .000
                      4   .000

GARRETT, RONALD WAYNE
1969 NY N 3   2   .000
1973 NY N 3   7   .167
                      9   .161

GARVEY, STEVEN PATRICK
1974 LA N 1   5   .381

GASPAR, RODNEY EARL
1969 NY N O   3   .000

GAZELLA, MICHAEL
1926 NY A 3   1   .000

GEARIN, DENNIS JOHN
1923 NY N R   1   .000

GEHRIG, HENRY LOUIS
1926 NY A 1   7   .348
1927 NY A 1   4   .308
1928 NY A 1   4   .545
1932 NY A 1   4   .529
1936 NY A 1   6   .292
1937 NY A 1   5   .294
1938 NY A 1   4   .286
                     34   .361

GEHRINGER, CHARLES LEONARD
1934 DET A 2   7   .379
1935 DET A 2   6   .375
1940 DET A 2   7   .214
                     20   .321

YR	CL LEA POS	GP	G	REC
GELBERT, CHARLES MAGNUS				
1930 STL N S		6		.353
1931 STL N S		7		.261
		13		.360
GENTRY, GARY EDWARD				
1969 NY N P		1	1- 0	
GERNERT, RICHARD EDWARD				
1961 CIN N H		4		.000
GERONIMO, CESAR FRANCISCO				
1972 CIN N O		7		.158
1975 CIN N O		7		.280
1976 CIN N O		4		.308
		18		.246
GESSLER, HARRY HOMER				
1906 CHI N H		2		.000
GETZ, GUSTAVE				
1916 BRO N H		1		.000
GIBBON, JOSEPH CHARLES				
1960 PIT N P		2	0- 0	
GIBSON, GEORGE				
1909 PIT N C		7		.240
GIBSON, JOHN RUSSELL				
1967 BOS A C		2		.000
GIBSON, ROBERT				
1964 STL N P		3	2- 1	
1967 STL N P		3	3- 0	
1968 STL N P		3	2- 1	
		9	7- 2	
GILBERT, LAWRENCE WILLIAM				
1914 BOS N H		1		.000
GILBERT, WILLIAM OLIVER				
1905 NY N 2		5		.235
GILLESPIE, PAUL ALLEN				
1945 CHI N C		3		.000
GILLIAM, JAMES WILLIAM				
1953 BRO N 2		6		.296
1955 BRO N 2-O		7		.292
1956 BRO N 2-O		7		.083
1959 LA N 3		6		.240
1963 LA N 3		4		.154
1965 LA N 3		7		.214
1966 LA N 3		2		.000
		39		.211
GIONFRIDDO, ALBERT FRANCIS				
1947 BRO N O		4		.000
GIUSTI, DAVID JOHN				
1971 PIT N P		3	0- 0	
GLYNN, WILLIAM VINCENT				
1954 CLE A 1		2		.500
GOLIAT, MIKE MITCHELL				
1950 PHI N 2		4		.214
GOMEZ, RUBEN				
1954 NY N P		1	1- 0	
GOMEZ, VERNON LOUIS				
1932 NY A P		1	1- 0	
1936 NY A P		2	2- 0	
1937 NY A P		2	2- 0	
1938 NY A P		1	1- 0	
1939 NY A P		1	0- 0	
		7	6- 0	
GONZALEZ, MIGUEL ANGEL CORDERO				
1929 CHI N C		2		.000
GONZALEZ, PEDRO				
1964 NY A 3		1		.000
GOOCH, JOHN BEVERLY				
1925 PIT N C		3		.000
1927 PIT N C		3		.000
		6		.000
GOODMAN, IVAL RICHARD				
1939 CIN N O		4		.333
1940 CIN N O		7		.276
		11		.295

YR	CL LEA POS	GP	G	REC
GOODMAN, WILLIAM DALE				
1959 CHI A 3		5		.231
GORDON, JOSEPH LOWELL				
1938 NY A 2		4		.400
1939 NY A 2		4		.143
1941 NY A 2		5		.500
1942 NY A 2		5		.095
1943 NY A 2		5		.235
1948 CLE A 2		6		.182
		29		.243
GORMAN, THOMAS ALOYSIUS				
1952 NY A P		1	0- 0	
1953 NY A P		1	0- 0	
		2	0- 0	
GORSICA, JOHN JOSEPH PERRY				
1940 DET A P		2	0- 0	
GOSLIN, LEON ALLEN				
1924 WAS A O		7		.344
1925 WAS A O		7		.308
1933 WAS A O		5		.250
1934 DET A O		7		.241
1935 DET A O		6		.273
		32		.287
GOWDY, HARRY				
1914 BOS N C		4		.545
1923 NY N C		3		.000
1924 NY N C		7		.259
		14		.310
GRABOWSKI, JOHN PATRICK				
1927 NY A C		1		.000
GRANEY, JOHN GLADSTONE				
1920 CLE A O		3		.000
GRANGER, WAYNE ALLAN				
1968 STL N P		1	0- 0	
1970 CIN N P		2	0- 0	
		3	0- 0	
GRANT, EDWARD LESLIE				
1913 NY N H		2		.000
GRANT, JAMES TIMOTHY				
1965 MIN A P		3	2- 1	
GRANTHAM, GEORGE FARLEY				
1925 PIT N 1		5		.133
1927 PIT N 2		3		.364
		8		.231
GRASSO, NEWTON MICHAEL				
1954 CLE A C		1		.000
GRBA, ELI				
1960 NY A R		1		.000
GREEN, FRED ALLEN				
1960 PIT N P		3	0- 0	
GREEN, RICHARD LARRY				
1972 OAK A 2		7		.333
1973 OAK A 2		7		.063
1974 OAK A 2		5		.000
		19		.149
GREENBERG, HENRY BENJAMIN				
1934 DET A 1		7		.321
1935 DET A 1		2		.167
1940 DET A O		7		.357
1945 DET A O		7		.304
		23		.318
GREGG, HAROLD DANA				
1947 BRO N P		3	0- 1	
GRIFFEY, GEORGE KENNETH				
1975 CIN N O		7		.269
1976 CIN N O		4		.059
		11		.186
GRIFFIN, DOUGLAS LEE				
1975 BOS A H		1		.000
GRIFFITH, THOMAS HERMAN				
1920 BRO N O		7		.190
GRIM, ROBERT ANTON				
1955 NY A P		3	0- 1	
1957 NY A P		2	0- 1	
		5	0- 2	

YR	CL LEA POS	GP	G	REC
GRIMES, BURLEIGH ARLAND				
1920 BRO N P		3	1- 2	
1930 STL N P		2	0- 2	
1931 STL N P		2	2- 0	
1932 CHI N P		2	0- 0	
		9	3- 4	
GRIMM, CHARLES JOHN				
1929 CHI N 1		5		.389
1932 CHI N 1		4		.333
		9		.364
GRIMSLEY, ROSS ALBERT II				
1972 CIN N P		4	2- 1	
GRISSOM, LEO THEO				
1939 CIN N P		1	0- 0	
GRISSOM, MARVIN EDWARD				
1954 NY N P		1	1- 0	
GROAT, RICHARD MORROW				
1960 PIT N S		7		.214
1964 STL N S		7		.192
		14		.204
GROH, HENRY KNIGHT				
1919 CIN N 3		8		.172
1922 NY N 3		5		.474
1923 NY N 3		6		.182
1924 NY N H		1		1.000
1927 PIT N H		1		.000
		21		.264
GROMEK, STEPHEN JOSEPH				
1948 CLE A P		1	1- 0	
GROTE, GERALD WAYNE				
1969 NY N C		5		.211
1973 NY N C		7		.267
		12		.245
GROVE, ROBERT MOSES				
1929 PHI A P		2	0- 0	
1930 PHI A P		3	2- 1	
1931 PHI A P		3	2- 1	
		8	4- 2	
GUDAT, MARVIN JOHN				
1932 CHI N H		2		.000
GULLETT, DONALD EDWARD				
1970 CIN N P		3	0- 0	
1972 CIN N P		1	0- 0	
1975 CIN N P		3	1- 1	
1976 CIN N P		1	1- 0	
		8	2- 1	
GUMBERT, HARRY EDWARD				
1936 NY N P		2	0- 0	
1937 NY N P		2	0- 0	
1942 STL N P		2	0- 0	
		6	0- 0	
GUTTERIDGE, DONALD JOSEPH				
1944 STL A 2		6		.143
1946 BOS A 2		3		.400
		9		.192
HAAS, GEORGE WILLIAM				
1929 PHI A O		5		.238
1930 PHI A O		6		.111
1931 PHI A O		7		.130
		18		.161
HACK, STANLEY CAMFIELD				
1932 CHI N H		1		.000
1935 CHI N S-3		6		.227
1938 CHI N 3		4		.471
1945 CHI N 3		7		.367
		18		.348
HADDIX, HARVEY				
1960 PIT N P		2	2- 0	
HADLEY, IRVING DARIUS				
1936 NY A P		1	1- 0	
1937 NY A P		1	0- 1	
1939 NY A P		1	1- 0	
		3	2- 1	
HAFEY, CHARLES JAMES				
1926 STL N O		7		.185
1928 STL N O		4		.200
1930 STL N O		6		.273
1931 STL N O		6		.167
		23		.205

YR	CL LEA POS	GP	G	REC

HAGUE, JOE CLARENCE
1972 CIN N O   3 .000

HAHN, DONALD ANTONE
1973 NY N O   7 .241

HAHN, EDGAR WILLIAM
1906 CHI A O   6 .273

HAINES, HENRY LUTHER
1923 NY A O   2 .000

HAINES, JESSE JOSEPH
1926 STL N P   3 2- 0
1928 STL N P   1 0- 1
1930 STL N P   1 1- 0
1934 STL N P   1 0- 0
          6 3- 1

HALL, CHARLES LOUIS
1912 BOS A P   2 0- 0

HALL, JAMES RANDOLPH
1965 MIN A O   2 .143

HALL, RICHARD WALLACE
1969 BAL A P   1 0- 1
1970 BAL A P   1 0- 0
1971 BAL A P   1 0- 0
          3 0- 1

HALL, TOM EDWARD
1972 CIN N P   4 0- 0

HALLAHAN, WILLIAM ANTHONY
1926 STL N P   1 0- 0
1930 STL N P   2 1- 1
1931 STL N P   3 2- 0
1934 STL N P   1 0- 0
          7 3- 1

HALLER, THOMAS FRANK
1962 SF N C   4 .206

HAMILTON, DAVID EDWARD
1972 OAK A P   2 0- 0

HAMILTON, STEVE ABSHER
1963 NY A P   1 0- 0
1964 NY A P   2 0- 0
          3 0= 0

HAMNER, GRANVILLE WILBUR
1950 PHI N S   4 .429

HANEBRINK, HARRY ALOYSIUS
1958 MIL N H   2 .000

HANEY, WALLACE LARRY
1974 OAK A C   2 .000

HARPER, GEORGE WASHINGTON
1928 STL N O   3 .111

HARPER, HARRY CLAYTON
1921 NY A P   1 0- 0

HARRELSON, DERREL MC KINLEY
1969 NY N S   5 .176
1973 NY N S   7 .250
          12 .220

HARRELSON, KENNETH SMITH
1967 BOS A O   4 .077

HARRIS, DAVID STANLEY
1933 WAS A O   3 .000

HARRIS, JOSEPH
1925 WAS A O   7 .440
1927 PIT N 1   4 .200
          11 .350

HARRIS, MAURICE CHARLES
1946 BOS A P   2 0- 2

HARRIS, STANLEY RAYMOND
1924 WAS A 2   7 .333
1925 WAS A 2   7 .087
          14 .232

HARTNETT, CHARLES LEO
1929 CHI N H   3 .000
1932 CHI N C   4 .313
1935 CHI N C   6 .292
1938 CHI N C   3 .091
          16 .241

HARTSEL, TULLOS FREDERICK
1905 PHI A O   5 .294
1910 PHI A O   1 .200
          6 .273

HARTUNG, CLINTON CLARENCE
1951 NY N O   2 .000

HASSETT, JOHN ALOYSIUS
1942 NY A 1   3 .333

HATTEN, JOSEPH HILARIAN
1947 BRO N P   4 0- 0
1949 BRO N P   2 0- 0
          6 0- 0

HAYWORTH, MYRON CLAUDE
1944 STL A C   6 .118

HAYWORTH, RAYMOND HALL
1934 DET A C   1 .000

HAZLE, ROBERT SIDNEY
1957 MIL N O   4 .154

HEARN, JAMES TOLBERT
1951 NY N P   2 1- 0

HEATHCOTE, CLIFTON EARL
1929 CHI N H   2 .000

HEBNER, RICHARD JOSEPH
1971 PIT N 3   3 .167

HEGAN, JAMES EDWARD
1948 CLE A C   6 .211
1954 CLE A C   4 .154
          10 .188

HEGAN, JAMES MICHAEL
1964 NY A H   3 .000
1972 OAK A 1   6 .200
          9 .167

HEINTZELMAN, KENNETH ALPHONSE
1950 PHI N P   1 0- 0

HELMS, TOMMY VANN
1970 CIN N 2   5 .222

HEMSLEY, RALSTON BURDETT
1932 CHI N C   3 .000

HENDRICK, GEORGE ANDREW
1972 OAK A O   5 .133

HENDRICK, HARVEY
1923 NY A H   1 .000

HENDRICKS, ELROD JEROME
1969 BAL A C   3 .100
1970 BAL A C   3 .364
1971 BAL A C   6 .263
1976 NY A H   2 .000
          14 .238

HENDRIX, CLAUDE RAYMOND
1918 CHI N P   1 2 0- 0

HENRICH, THOMAS DAVID
1938 NY A O   4 .250
1941 NY A O   5 .167
1947 NY A O   7 .323
1949 NY A 1   5 .263
          21 .262

HENRICKSEN, OLAF
1912 BOS A H   2 1.000
1915 BOS A H   2 .000
1916 BOS A H   1 .000
          5 .333

HENRY, WILLIAM RODMAN
1961 CIN N P   2 0- 0

HENSHAW, ROY JOHN
1935 CHI N P   1 0- 0

HERMAN, WILLIAM JENNINGS BRYAN
1932 CHI N 2   4 .222
1935 CHI N 2   6 .333
1938 CHI N 2   4 .188
1941 BRO N 2   4 .125
          18 .242

HERMANSKI, EUGENE VICTOR
1947 BRO N O   7 .158
1949 BRO N O   4 .308
          11 .219

HERNANDEZ, JACINTO
1971 PIT N S   7 .222

HERSHBERGER, WILLARD MC KEE
1939 CIN N C   3 .500

HERZOG, CHARLES LINCOLN
1911 NY N 3   6 .190
1912 NY N 3   8 .400
1913 NY N 3   5 .053
1917 NY N 2   6 .250
          25 .245

HEVING, JOHN ALOYSIUS
1931 PHI A H   1 .000

HIGBE, WALTER KIRBY
1941 BRO N P   1 0- 0

HIGGINS, MICHAEL FRANCIS
1940 DET A 3   7 .333
1946 BOS A 3   7 .208
          14 .271

HIGH, ANDREW AIRD
1928 STL N 3   4 .294
1930 STL N 3   1 .500
1931 STL N 3   4 .267
          9 .294

HILDEBRAND, ORAL CLYDE
1939 NY A P   1 0- 0

HILL, CARMEN PROCTOR
1927 PIT N P   1 0- 0

HILLER, CHARLES JOSEPH
1962 SF N 2   7 .269

HILLER, JOHN FREDERICK
1968 DET A P   2 0- 0

HOAG, MYRIL OLIVER
1932 NY A H   1 .000
1937 NY A O   5 .300
1938 NY A O   2 .400
          8 .320

HOAK, DONALD ALBERT
1955 BRO N 3   3 .333
1960 PIT N 3   7 .217
          10 .231

HOBLITZEL, RICHARD CARLETON
1915 BOS A 1   5 .313
1916 BOS A 1   5 .235
          10 .273

HODGES, GILBERT RAYMOND
1947 BRO N H   1 .000
1949 BRO N 1   5 .235
1952 BRO N 1   7 .000
1953 BRO N 1   6 .364
1955 BRO N 1   7 .292
1956 BRO N 1   7 .304
1959 LA N 1   6 .391
          39 .267

HODGES, RONALD WRAY
1973 NY N H   1 .000

HOERNER, JOSEPH WALTER
1967 STL N P   2 0- 0
1968 STL N P   3 0- 1
          5 0- 1

HOFFMAN, DANIEL JOHN
1905 PHI A H   1 .000

HOFMAN, ARTHUR FREDERICK
1906 CHI N O   6 .304
1908 CHI N O   5 .316
1910 CHI N O   5 .267
          16 .298

HOFMAN, FRED
1923 NY A H   2 .000

HOGSETT, ELON CHESTER
1934 DET A P   3 0- 0
1935 DET A P   1 0- 0
          4 0- 0

YR	CL	LEA	POS	GP	G	REC

HOGUE, ROBERT CLINTON
| 1951 | NY | A | P | 2 | | 0- 0 |

HOLKE, WALTER HENRY
| 1917 | NY | N | 1 | 6 | | .286 |

HOLLINGSWORTH, ALBERT WAYNE
| 1944 | STL | A | P | 1 | | 0- 0 |

HOLLOCHER, CHARLES JACOB
| 1918 | CHI | N | S | 6 | | .190 |

HOLM, ROSCOE ALBERT
1926	STL	N	O	5		.125
1928	STL	N	O	3		.167
				8		.136

HOLMES, THOMAS FRANCIS
1948	BOS	N	O	6		.192
1952	BRO	N	O	3		.000
				9		.185

HOLT, JAMES WILLIAM
| 1974 | OAK | A | 1 | 4 | | .667 |

HOLTZMAN, KENNETH DALE
1972	OAK	A	P	3		1- 0
1973	OAK	A	P	3		2- 1
1974	OAK	A	P	2		1- 0
				8		4- 1

HOOPER, HARRY BARTHOLOMEW
1912	BOS	A	O	8		.290
1915	BOS	A	O	5		.350
1916	BOS	A	O	5		.333
1918	BOS	A	O	6		.200
				24		.293

HOOVER, ROBERT JOSEPH
| 1945 | DET | A | S | 1 | | .333 |

HOPP, JOHN LEONARD
1942	STL	N	1	5		.176
1943	STL	N	O	1		.000
1944	STL	N	O	6		.185
1950	NY	A	1	3		.000
1951	NY	A	H	1		.000
				16		.160

HORLEN, JOEL EDWARD
| 1972 | OAK | A | P | 1 | | 0- 0 |

HORNSBY, ROGERS
1926	STL	N	2	7		.250
1929	CHI	N	2	5		.238
				12		.245

HORTON, WILLIAM WATTISON
| 1968 | DET | A | O | 7 | | .304 |

HOSTETLER, CHARLES CLOYD
| 1945 | DET | A | H | 3 | | .000 |

HOUGH, CHARLES OLIVER
| 1974 | LA | N | P | 1 | | 0- 0 |

HOUK, RALPH GEORGE
1947	NY	A	H	1		1.000
1952	NY	A	H	1		.000
				2		.500

HOUTTEMAN, ARTHUR JOSEPH
| 1954 | CLE | A | P | 1 | | 0- 0 |

HOWARD, ELSTON GENE
1955	NY	A	O	7		.192
1956	NY	A	O	1		.400
1957	NY	A	O	6		.273
1958	NY	A	O	6		.222
1960	NY	A	C	5		.462
1961	NY	A	C	5		.250
1962	NY	A	C	6		.143
1963	NY	A	C	4		.333
1964	NY	A	C	7		.292
1967	BOS	A	C	7		.111
				54		.246

HOWARD, FRANK OLIVER
| 1963 | LA | N | O | 3 | | .300 |

HOWARD, GEORGE ELMER
1907	CHI	N	1	2		.200
1908	CHI	N	H	1		.000
				3		.167

HOYT, WAITE CHARLES
1921	NY	A	P	3		2- 1
1922	NY	A	P	2		0- 1
1923	NY	A	P	1		0- 0
1926	NY	A	P	2		1- 1
1927	NY	A	P	1		1- 0
1928	NY	A	P	2		2- 0
1931	PHI	A	P	1		0- 1
				12		6- 4

HUBBELL, CARL OWEN
1933	NY	N	P	2		2- 0
1936	NY	N	P	2		1- 1
1937	NY	N	P	2		1- 1
				6		4- 2

HUGHES, JAMES ROBERT
| 1953 | BRO | N | P | 1 | | 0- 0 |

HUGHES, RICHARD HENRY
1967	STL	N	P	2		0- 1
1968	STL	N	P	1		0- 0
				3		0- 1

HUGHES, ROY JOHN
| 1945 | CHI | N | S | 6 | | .294 |

HUGHES, THOMAS JAMES
| 1903 | BOS | A | P | 1 | | 0- 1 |

HUGHSON, CECIL CARLTON
| 1946 | BOS | A | P | 3 | | 0- 1 |

HUMPHREYS, ROBERT WILLIAM
| 1964 | STL | N | P | 1 | | 0- 0 |

HUNT, KENNETH RAYMOND
| 1961 | CIN | N | P | 1 | | 0- 0 |

HUNTER, JAMES AUGUSTUS
1972	OAK	A	P	3		2- 0
1973	OAK	A	P	2		1- 0
1974	OAK	A	P	2		1- 0
1976	NY	A	P	1		0- 1
				8		4- 1

HUTCHINGS, JOHN RICHARD JOSEPH
| 1940 | CIN | N | P | 1 | | 0- 0 |

HUTCHINSON, FREDERICK CHARLES
| 1940 | DET | A | P | 1 | | 0- 0 |

HYATT, ROBERT HAMILTON
| 1909 | PIT | N | O | 2 | | .000 |

IRVIN, MONFORD
1951	NY	N	O	6		.458
1954	NY	N	O	4		.222
				10		.394

ISBELL, WILLIAM FRANK
| 1906 | CHI | A | 2 | 6 | | .308 |

JACKSON, GRANT DWIGHT
1971	BAL	A	P	1		0- 0
1976	NY	A	P	1		0- 0
				2		0- 0

JACKSON, JOSEPH JEFFERSON
1917	CHI	A	O	6		.304
1919	CHI	A	O	8		.375
				14		.345

JACKSON, RANSOM JOSEPH
| 1956 | BRO | N | H | 3 | | .000 |

JACKSON, REGINALD MARTINEZ
1973	OAK	A	O	7		.310
1974	OAK	A	O	5		.286
				12		.302

JACKSON, TRAVIS CALVIN
1923	NY	N	H	1		.000
1924	NY	N	S	7		.074
1933	NY	N	3	5		.222
1936	NY	N	3	6		.190
				19		.149

JAKUCKI, SIGMUND JACK
| 1944 | STL | A | P | 1 | | 0- 1 |

JAMES, CHARLES WESLEY
| 1964 | STL | N | H | 3 | | .000 |

JAMES, WILLIAM HENRY
| 1919 | CHI | A | P | 1 | | 0- 0 |

JAMES, WILLIAM LAWRENCE
| 1914 | BOS | N | P | 2 | | 2- 0 |

JAMIESON, CHARLES DEVINE
| 1920 | CLE | A | O | 6 | | .333 |

JANSEN, LAWRENCE JOSEPH
| 1951 | NY | N | P | 3 | | 0- 2 |

JANVRIN, HAROLD CHANDLER
1915	BOS	A	S	1		.000
1916	BOS	A	2	5		.217
				6		.208

JASTER, LARRY EDWARD
1967	STL	N	P	1		0- 0
1968	STL	N	P	1		0- 0
				2		0- 0

JAVIER, MANUEL JULIAN
1964	STL	N	2	1		.000
1967	STL	N	2	7		.360
1968	STL	N	2	7		.333
1972	CIN	N	H	4		.000
				19		.333

JAY, JOSEPH RICHARD
| 1961 | CIN | N | P | 2 | | 1- 1 |

JENSEN, JACK EUGENE
| 1950 | NY | A | R | | | .000 |

JOHNSON, DARRELL DEAN
| 1961 | CIN | N | C | 2 | | .500 |

JOHNSON, DAVID ALLEN
1966	BAL	A	2	4		.286
1969	BAL	A	2	5		.063
1970	BAL	A	2	5		.313
1971	BAL	A	2	7		.148
				21		.192

JOHNSON, DERON ROGER
| 1973 | OAK | A | 1 | 6 | | .300 |

JOHNSON, DONALD SPORE
| 1945 | CHI | N | 2 | 7 | | .172 |

JOHNSON, EARL DOUGLASS
| 1946 | BOS | A | P | 3 | | 1- 0 |

JOHNSON, ERNEST RUDOLPH
| 1923 | NY | A | S | 2 | | .000 |

JOHNSON, ERNEST THORWALD
| 1957 | MIL | N | P | 3 | | 0- 1 |

JOHNSON, KENNETH TRAVIS
| 1961 | CIN | N | P | 1 | | 0- 0 |

JOHNSON, KENNETH WANDERSEE
| 1950 | PHI | N | R | 1 | | .000 |

JOHNSON, LOUIS BROWN
1965	LA	N	O	7		.296
1966	LA	N	O	4		.267
				11		.286

JOHNSON, ROY CLEVELAND
| 1936 | NY | A | H | 2 | | .000 |

JOHNSON, ROBERT DALE
| 1971 | PIT | N | P | 2 | | 0- 1 |

JOHNSON, SYLVESTER W.
1928	STL	N	P	2		0- 0
1930	STL	N	P	2		0- 0
1931	STL	N	P	3		0- 1
				7		0- 1

JOHNSON, WALTER PERRY
1924	WAS	A	P	3		1- 2
1925	WAS	A	P	3		2- 1
				6		3- 3

JOHNSON, WILLIAM RUSSELL
1943	NY	A	3	5		.300
1947	NY	A	3	7		.269
1949	NY	A	3	2		.143
1950	NY	A	3	4		.000
				18		.237

YR	CL	LEA	POS	GP	G	REC
JOHNSTON, JAMES HARLE						
1916	BRO	N	O		3	.300
1920	BRO	N	3		4	.214
					7	.250
JOHNSTON, WHEELER ROGERS						
1920	CLE	A	1		5	.273
JONES, CLEON JOSEPH						
1969	NY	N	O		5	.158
1973	NY	N	O		7	.286
					12	.234
JONES, DAVID JEFFERSON						
1907	DET	A	O		5	.353
1908	DET	A	H		3	.000
1909	DET	A	O		7	.233
					15	.265
JONES, FIELDER ALLISON						
1906	CHI	A	O		6	.095
JONES, JAMES DALTON						
1967	BOS	A	3		6	.389
JONES, SAMUEL POND						
1918	BOS	A	P	1		0- 1
1922	NY	A	P	2		0- 0
1923	NY	A	P	2		0- 1
1926	NY	A	P	1		0- 0
				6		0- 2
JONES, SHELDON LESLIE						
1951	NY	N	P	2		0- 0
JONES, SHERMAN JARVIS						
1961	CIN	N	P	1		0- 0
JONES, THOMAS						
1909	DET	A	1		7	.250
JONES, VERNAL LEROY						
1946	STL	N	H		1	.000
1957	MIL	N	H		3	.000
					4	.000
JONES, WILLIE EDWARD						
1950	PHI	N	3		4	.286
JUNNARD, CLAUDE ALFRED						
1923	NY	N	P	2		0- 0
1924	NY	N	P	1		0- 0
				3		0- 0
JOOST, EDWIN DAVID						
1940	CIN	N	2		7	.200
JORGENSEN, JOHN DONALD						
1947	BRO	N	3		7	.200
1949	BRO	N	3		4	.182
					11	.194
JOSHUA, VON EVERETT						
1974	LA	N	H		4	.000
JUDGE, JOSEPH IGNATIUS						
1924	WAS	A	1		7	.385
1925	WAS	A	1		7	.174
					14	.286
JUDNICH, WALTER FRANKLIN						
1948	CLE	A	O		4	.077
JURGES, WILLIAM FREDERICK						
1932	CHI	N	S		3	.364
1935	CHI	N	S		6	.250
1938	CHI	N	S		4	.231
					13	.275
JURISICH, ALVIN JOSEPH						
1944	STL	N	P	1		0- 0
KAAT, JAMES LEE						
1965	MIN	A	P	3		1- 2
KALINE, ALBERT WILLIAM						
1968	DET	A	O		7	.379
KANE, JOHN FRANCIS						
1910	CHI	N	R		1	.000
KASKO, EDWARD MICHAEL						
1961	CIN	N	S		5	.318
KAUFF, BENJAMIN MICHAEL						
1917	NY	N	O		6	.160
KEEN, HOWARD VICTOR						
1926	STL	N	P	1		0- 0
KELLER, CHARLES ERNEST						
1939	NY	A	O		4	.438
1941	NY	A	O		5	.389
1942	NY	A	O		5	.200
1943	NY	A	O		5	.222
					19	.306
KELLERT, FRANK WILLIAM						
1955	BRO	N	H		3	.333
KELLY, GEORGE LANGE						
1921	NY	N	1		8	.233
1922	NY	N	1		5	.278
1923	NY	N	1		6	.182
1924	NY	N	1-2-7		7	.290
					26	.248
KELTNER, KENNETH FREDERICK						
1948	CLE	A	3		6	.095
KENNEDY, JOHN EDWARD						
1965	LA	N	3		4	.000
1966	LA	N	3		2	.200
					6	.167
KENNEDY, MONTIA CALVIN						
1951	NY	N	P	2		0- 0
KENNEDY, ROBERT DANIEL						
1948	CLE	A	O		3	.500
KENNEDY, WILLIAM P.						
1903	PIT	N	P	1		0- 1
KERR, JOHN FRANCIS						
1933	WAS	A	R	1		.000
KERR, RICHARD HENRY						
1919	CHI	A	P	2		2- 0
KILDUFF, PETER JOHN						
1920	BRO	N	2		7	.095
KILLEBREW, HARMON CLAYTON						
1965	MIN	A	3		7	.286
KILLEFER, WILLIAM LAVIER						
1915	PHI	N	H		1	.000
1918	CHI	N	C		6	.118
					7	.111
KILLIAN, EDWIN HENRY						
1907	DET	A	P	1		0- 0
1908	DET	A	P	1		0- 0
				2		0- 0
KING, LEE						
1922	NY	N	O		2	1.000
KISON, BRUCE EUGENE						
1971	PIT	N	P	2		1- 0
KLEIN, CHARLES HERBERT						
1935	CHI	N	O		5	.333
KLEIN, LOUIS FRANK						
1943	STL	N	2		5	.136
KLIEMAN, EDWARD FREDERICK						
1948	CLE	A	P	1		0- 0
KLING, JOHN G.						
1906	CHI	N	C		6	.176
1907	CHI	N	C		5	.211
1908	CHI	N	C		5	.250
1910	CHI	N	C		5	.077
					21	.185
KLINGER, ROBERT HAROLD						
1946	BOS	A	P	1		0- 1
KLIPPSTEIN, JOHN CALVIN						
1959	LA	N	P	1		0- 0
1965	MIN	A	P	2		0- 0
				3		0- 0
KLUSZEWSKI, THEODORE BERNARD						
1959	CHI	A	1		6	.391
KNOWLES, DAROLD DUANE						
1973	OAK	A	P	7		0- 0
KOENIG, MARK ANTHONY						
1926	NY	A	S		7	.125
1927	NY	A	S		4	.500
1928	NY	A	S		4	.158
1932	CHI	N	S		2	.250
1936	NY	N	2		3	.333
					20	.237
KONETCHY, EDWARD JOSEPH						
1920	BRO	N	1		7	.174
KONIKOWSKI, ALEXANDER JAMES						
1951	NY	N	P	1		0- 0
KONSTANTY, CASIMER JAMES						
1950	PHI	N	P	3		0- 1
KOOSMAN, JERRY MARTIN						
1969	NY	N	P	2		2- 0
1973	NY	N	P	2		1- 0
				4		3- 0
KOPF, WILLIAM LORENZ						
1919	CIN	N	S		8	.222
KOSLO, GEORGE BERNARD						
1951	NY	N	P	2		1- 1
KOUFAX, SANFORD						
1959	LA	N	P	2		0- 1
1963	LA	N	P	2		2- 0
1965	LA	N	P	3		2- 1
1966	LA	N	P	1		0- 1
				8		4- 3
KOWALIK, FABIAN LORENZ						
1935	CHI	N	P	1		0- 0
KRAMER, JOHN HENRY						
1944	STL	A	P	2		1- 0
KRANEPOOL, EDWARD EMIL						
1969	NY	N	1		1	.250
1973	NY	N	H		4	.000
					5	.143
KREEVICH, MICHAEL ANDREAS						
1944	STL	A	O		6	.231
KREMER, REMY						
1925	PIT	N	P	3		2 -1
1927	PIT	N	P	1		0- 1
				4		2- 2
KRIST, HOWARD WILBUR						
1943	STL	N	P	1		0- 0
KRUEGER, ERNEST GEORGE						
1920	BRO	N	C		4	.167
KUBEK, ANTHONY CHRISTOPHER						
1957	NY	A	3-O		7	.286
1958	NY	A	S		7	.048
1960	NY	A	S-O		7	.333
1961	NY	A	S		5	.227
1962	NY	A	S		7	.276
1963	NY	A	S		4	.188
					37	.240
KUBIAK, THEODORE RODGER						
1972	OAK	A	2		4	.333
1973	OAK	A	2		4	.000
					8	.167
KUCKS, JOHN CHARLES						
1955	NY	A	P	2		0- 0
1956	NY	A	P	3		1- 0
1957	NY	A	P	1		0- 0
1958	NY	A	P	2		0- 0
				8		1- 0
KUENN, HARVEY EDWARD						
1962	SF	N	O		4	.083
KUHEL, JOSEPH ANTHONY						
1933	WAS	A	1		5	.150
KUROWSKI, GEORGE JOHN						
1942	STL	N	3		5	.267
1943	STL	N	3		5	.222
1944	STL	N	3		6	.217
1946	STL	N	3		7	.296
					23	.253

```
YR   CL LEA POS  GP    G    REC

KUZAVA, ROBERT LEROY
1951 NY   A   P         1    0- 0
1952 NY   A   P         1    0- 0
1953 NY   A   P         1    0- 0
                        3    0- 0

LAABS, CHESTER PETER
1944 STL  A   O         5    .200

LABINE, CLEMENT WALTER
1953 BRO  N   P         3    0- 2
1955 BRO  N   P         4    1- 0
1956 BRO  N   P         2    1- 0
1959 LA   N   P         1    0- 0
1960 PIT  N   P         3    0- 0
                       13    2- 2

LA CHANCE, GEORGE
1903 BOS  A   1         8    .222

LACY, LEONDAUS
1974 LA   N   H         1    .000

LAMABE, JOHN ALEXANDER
1967 STL  N   P         3    0- 1

LAMAR, WILLIAM HARMONG
1920 BRO  N   H         3    .000

LANDIS, JOHN HENRY
1959 CHI  A   O         6    .292

LANIER, HUBERT MAX
1942 STL  N   P         2    1- 0
1943 STL  N   P         3    0- 1
1944 STL  N   P         2    1- 0
                        7    2- 1

LAPP, JOHN WALKER
1910 PHI  A   C         1    .250
1911 PHI  A   C         2    .250
1913 PHI  A   C         1    .250
1914 PHI  A   C         1    .000
                        5    .235

LARKER, NORMAN HOWARD
1959 LA   N   O         6    .188

LARSEN, DONALD JAMES
1955 NY   A   P         1    0- 1
1956 NY   A   P         2    1- 0
1957 NY   A   P         2    1- 1
1958 NY   A   P         2    1- 0
1962 SF   N   P         3    1- 0
                       10    4- 2

LASHER, FREDERICK WALTER
1968 DET  A   P         1    0- 0

LAVAGETTO, HARRY ARTHUR
1941 BRO  N   3         3    .100
1947 BRO  N   3         5    .143
                        8    .118

LAW, VERNON SANDERS
1960 PIT  N   P         3    2- 0

LAZZERI, ANTHONY MICHAEL
1926 NY   A   2         7    .192
1927 NY   A   2         4    .267
1928 NY   A   2         4    .250
1932 NY   A   2         4    .294
1936 NY   A   2         6    .250
1937 NY   A   2         5    .400
1938 CHI  N   H         2    .000
                       32    .262

LEACH, THOMAS WILLIAM
1903 PIT  N   3         8    .273
1909 PIT  N   3-O       7    .320
                       15    .293

LEE, WILLIAM CRUTCHER
1935 CHI  N   P         2    0- 0
1938 CHI  N   P         2    0- 2
                        4    0- 2

LEE, WILLIAM FRANCIS
1975 BOS  A   P         2    0- 0

LEEVER, SAMUEL W.
1903 PIT  N   P         2    0- 2

LEFEBVRE, JAMES KENNETH
1965 LA   N   2         3    .400
1966 LA   N   2         4    .167
                        7    .273


LEHMAN, KENNETH KARL
1952 BRO  N   P         1    0- 0

LEIBER, HENRY EDWARD
1936 NY   N   O         2    .000
1937 NY   N   O         3    .364
                        5    .235

LEIBOLD, HARRY LORAN
1917 CHI  A   O         2    .400
1919 CHI  A   O         5    .056
1924 WAS  A   O         3    .167
1925 WAS  A   H         3    .500
                       13    .161

LEIFIELD, ALBERT PETER
1909 PIT  N   P         1    0- 1

LE JOHN, DONALD EVERETT
1965 LA   N   H         1    .000

LEMON, ROBERT GRANVILLE
1948 CLE  A   P         2    2- 0
1954 CLE  A   P     2   3    0- 2
                    4   5    2- 2

LEONARD, HUBERT BENJAMIN
1915 BOS  A   P         1    1- 0
1916 BOS  A   P         1    1- 0
                        2    2- 0

LEONHARD, DAVID PAUL
1969 BAL  A   P         1    0- 0
1971 BAL  A   P         1    0- 0
                        2    0- 0

LESLIE, SAMUEL ANDREW
1936 NY   N   H         3    .667
1937 NY   N   H         2    .000
                        5    .500

LEWIS, ALLAN SYDNEY
1972 OAK  A   R         6    .000
1973 OAK  A   R         3    .000
                        9    .000

LEWIS, GEORGE EDWARD
1912 BOS  A   O         8    .156
1915 BOS  A   O         5    .444
1916 BOS  A   O         5    .353
                       18    .284

LIDDLE, DONALD EUGENE
1954 NY   N   P         2    1- 0

LINDBLAD, PAUL AARON
1973 OAK  A   P         3    1- 0

LINDELL, JOHN HARLAN
1943 NY   A   O         4    .111
1947 NY   A   O         6    .500
1949 NY   A   O         2    .143
                       12    .324

LINDSEY, JAMES KENDRICK
1930 STL  N   P         2    0- 0
1931 STL  N   P         2    0- 0
                        4    0- 0

LINDSTROM, FREDERICK CHARLES
1924 NY   N   3         7    .333
1935 CHI  N   3-O       4    .200
                       11    .289

LINZ, PHILIP FRANCIS
1963 NY   A   H         3    .333
1964 NY   A   S         7    .226
                       10    .235

LITWHILER, DANIEL WEBSTER
1943 STL  N   O         5    .267
1944 STL  N   O         5    .200
                       10    .229

LIVINGSTON, THOMPSON ORVILLE
1945 CHI  N   C         6    .364

LOCKER, ROBERT AUTRY
1972 OAK  A   P         1    0- 0

LOCKMAN, CARROLL WALTER
1951 NY   N   1         6    .240
1954 NY   N   1         4    .111
                       10    .186


LOES, WILLIAM
1952 BRO  N   P         2    0- 1
1953 BRO  N   P         1    1- 0
1955 BRO  N   P         1    0- 1
                        4    1- 2

LOGAN, JOHN
1957 MIL  N   S         7    .185
1958 MIL  N   S         7    .120
                       14    .154

LOHRKE, JACK WAYNE
1951 NY   N   H         2    .000

LOLICH, MICHAEL STEVEN
1968 DET  A   P         3    3- 0

LOLLAR, JOHN SHERMAN
1947 NY   A   C         2    .750
1959 CHI  A   C         6    .227
                        8    .308

LOMBARDI, ERNESTO NATALI
1939 CIN  N   C         4    .214
1940 CIN  N   C         2    .333
                        6    .235

LOMBARDI, VICTOR ALVIN
1947 BRO  N   P     2   3    0- 1

LONBORG, JAMES REYNOLD
1967 BOS  A   P         3    2- 1

LONG, RICHARD DALE
1960 NY   A   H         3    .333
1962 NY   A   1         2    .200
                        5    .250

LOPAT, EDMUND WALTER
1949 NY   A   P         1    1- 0
1950 NY   A   P         1    0- 0
1951 NY   A   P         2    2- 0
1952 NY   A   P         2    0- 1
1953 NY   A   P         1    1- 0
                        7    4- 1

LOPATA, STANLEY EDWARD
1950 PHI  N   C         2    .000

LOPES, DAVID EARL
1974 LA   N   2         5    .111

LOPEZ, HECTOR HEADLEY
1960 NY   A   O         3    .429
1961 NY   A   O         4    .333
1962 NY   A   H         2    .000
1963 NY   A   O         3    .250
1964 NY   A   O         3    .000
                       15    .286

LOPEZ, MARCELINO PONS
1970 BAL  A   P         1    0- 0

LORD, BRISTOL ROBOTHAM
1905 PHI  A   O         5    .100
1910 PHI  A   O         5    .182
1911 PHI  A   O         6    .185
                       16    .159

LOWDERMILK, GROVER CLEVELAND
1919 CHI  A   P         1    0- 0

LOWERY, HARRY LEE
1945 CHI  N   O         7    .310

LOWN, OMAR JOSEPH
1959 CHI  A   P         3    0- 0

LUDERUS, FREDERICK WILLIAM
1915 PHI  N   1         5    .438

LUMPE, JERRY DEAN
1957 NY   A   3         6    .286
1958 NY   A   S-3       6    .167
                       12    .231

LUNTE, HARRY AUGUST
1920 CLE  A   2         1    .000

LUQUE, ADOLFO
1919 CIN  N   P         2    0- 0
1933 NY   N   P         1    1- 0
                        3    1- 0
```

YR	CL	LEA	POS	GP	G	REC

LYLE, ALBERT WALTER
1976 NY A P 2 0- 0

LYNCH, GERALD THOMAS
1961 CIN N H 4 .000

LYNN, BYRD
1917 CHI A H 1 .000
1919 CHI A C 1 .000
2 .000

LYNN, FREDRIC MICHAEL
1975 BOS A O 7 .280

MAAS, DUANE FREDRICK
1958 NY A P 1 0- 0
1960 NY A P 1 0- 0
2 0- 0

MADDOX, ELLIOTT
1976 NY A O-D 2 .200

MADDOX, NICHOLAS
1909 PIT N P 1 1- 0

MAGEE, SHERWOOD ROBERT
1919 CIN N H 2 .500

MAGLIE, SALVATORE ANTHONY
1951 NY N P 1 0- 1
1954 NY N P 1 0- 0
1956 BRO N P 2 1- 1
4 1- 2

MAGUIRE, FREDERICK EDWARD
1923 NY N R 2 .000

MAHAFFEY, LEE ROY
1931 PHI A P 1 0- 0

MAIER, ROBERT PHILIP
1945 DET A H 1 1.000

MAILS, JOHN WALTER
1920 CLE A P 2 1- 0

MAJESKI, HENRY
1954 CLE A 3 4 .167

MALONE, PERCE LEIGH
1929 CHI N P 3 0- 2
1932 CHI N P 1 0- 0
1936 NY A P 2 0- 1
6 0- 3

MALONEY, JAMES WILLIAM
1961 CIN N P 1 0- 0

MAMAUX, ALBERT LEON
1920 BRO N P 3 0- 0

MANCUSO, AUGUST RODNEY
1930 STL N C 2 .286
1931 STL N C 2 .000
1933 NY N C 5 .118
1936 NY N C 6 .263
1937 NY N C 3 .000
18 .173

MANCUSO, FRANK OCTAVIUS
1944 STL A C 2 .667

MANGUAL, ANGEL LUIS
1972 OAK A O 4 .300
1973 OAK A O 5 .000
1974 OAK A H 1 .000
10 .176

MANN, LESLIE
1914 BOS N O 3 .286
1918 CHI N O 6 .227
9 .241

MANTILLA, FELIX
1957 MIL N 2 4 .000
1958 MIL N S 4 .000
8 .000

MANTLE, MICKEY CHARLES
1951 NY A O 2 .200
1952 NY A O 7 .345
1953 NY A O 6 .208
1955 NY A O 3 .200
1956 NY A O 7 .250
1957 NY A O 6 .263
1958 NY A O 7 .250
1960 NY A O 7 .400
1961 NY A O 2 .167
1962 NY A O 7 .120
1963 NY A O 4 .133
1964 NY A O 7 .333
65 .257

MANUSH, HENRY EMMETT
1933 WAS A O 5 .111

MAPES, CLIFFORD FRANKLIN
1949 NY A O 4 .100
1950 NY A O 1 .000
5 .071

MARANVILLE, WALTER JAMES VINCENT
1914 BOS N S 4 .308
1928 STL N S 4 .308
8 .308

MARBERRY, FREDERICK
1924 WAS A P 4 0- 1
1925 WAS A P 2 0- 0
1934 DET A P 2 0- 0
8 0- 1

MARICHAL, JUAN ANTONIO
1962 SF N P 1 0- 0

MARION, MARTIN WHITFORD
1942 STL N S 5 .111
1943 STL N S 5 .357
1944 STL N S 6 .227
1946 STL N S 7 .250
23 .231

MARIS, ROGER EUGENE
1960 NY A O 7 .267
1961 NY A O 5 .105
1962 NY A O 7 .174
1963 NY A O 2 .000
1964 NY A O 7 .200
1967 STL N O 7 .385
1968 STL N O 6 .158
41 .217

MARQUARD, RICHARD WILLIAM
1911 NY N P 3 0- 1
1912 NY N P 2 2- 0
1913 NY N P 2 0- 1
1916 BRO N P 2 0- 2
1920 BRO N P 2 0- 1
11 2- 5

MARQUEZ, GONZALO ENRIQUE
1972 OAK A H 5 .600

MARSHALL, MICHAEL GRANT
1974 LA N P 5 0- 1

MARTIN, ALFRED MANUEL
1951 NY A H 1 .000
1952 NY A 2 7 .217
1953 NY A 2 6 .500
1955 NY A 2 7 .320
1956 NY A 2-3 7 .296
28 .333

MARTIN, JOHN LEONARD
1928 STL N R 1 .000
1931 STL N O 7 .500
1934 STL N 3 7 .355
15 .418

MARTIN, JOSEPH CLIFTON
1969 NY N H 1 .000

MARTINA, JOSEPH JOHN
1924 WAS A P 1 0- 0

MARTINEZ, TEODORO NOEL
1973 NY N R 2 .000

MARTY, JOSEPH ANTON
1938 CHI N O 3 .500

MASI, PHILIP SAMUEL
1948 BOS N C 5 .125

MASON, JAMES PERCY
1976 NY A S 3 1.000

MATCHICK, JOHN THOMAS
1968 DET A H 3 .000

MATHEWS, EDWIN LEE
1957 MIL N 3 7 .227
1958 MIL N 3 7 .160
1968 DET A 3 2 .333
16 .200

MATHEWSON, CHRISTOPHER
1905 NY N P 3 3- 0
1911 NY N P 3 1- 2
1912 NY N P 3 0- 2
1913 NY N P 2 1- 1
11 5- 5

MATLACK, JONATHAN TRUMPBOUR
1973 NY N P 3 1- 2

MAXVILL, CHARLES DALLAN
1964 STL N 2 7 .200
1967 STL N S 7 .158
1968 STL N S 7 .000
1974 OAK A 2 2 .000
23 .115

MAY, CARLOS
1976 NY A O 4 .000

MAY, DAVID LA FRANCE
1969 BAL A H 2 .000

MAY, FRANK SPRUIELL
1932 CHI N P 2 0- 1

MAY, LEE ANDREW
1970 CIN N 1 5 .389

MAY, MILTON SCOTT
1971 PIT N P 2 .500

MAYER, ERSKINE JOHN
1915 PHI N P 2 0- 1
1919 CHI A P 1 0- 0
3 0- 1

MAYO, EDWARD JOSEPH
1936 NY N 3 1 .000
1945 DET A 2 7 .250
8 .241

MAYO, JOHN LEWIS
1950 PHI N O 3 .000

MAYS, CARL WILLIAM
1916 BOS A P 2 0- 1
1918 BOS A P 2 2- 0
1921 NY A P 3 1- 2
1922 NY A P 1 0- 1
8 3- 4

MAYS, WILLIE HOWARD
1951 NY N O 6 .182
1954 NY N O 4 .286
1962 SF N O 7 .250
1973 NY N O 3 .286
20 .239

MAZEROSKI, WILLIAM STANLEY
1960 PIT N 2 7 .320
1971 PIT N H 1 .000
8 .308

MC ANANY, JAMES
1959 CHI A O 3 .000

MC AULIFFE, RICHARD JOHN
1968 DET A 2 7 .222

MC BRIDE, THOMAS RAYMOND
1946 BOS A O 5 .167

MC CABE, WILLIAM FRANCIS
1918 CHI N H 3 .000
1920 BRO N R 1 .000
4 .000

MC CARTHY, JOHN JOSEPH
1937 NY N 1 5 .211

```
YR  CL LEA POS  GP   G   REC

MC CARTY, GEORGE LEWIS
1917 NY  N   C         3   .400

MC CARVER, JAMES TIMOTHY
1964 STL N   C         7   .478
1967 STL N   C         7   .125
1968 STL N   C         7   .333
                      21   .311

MC COLL, ALEXANDER BOYD
1933 WAS A   P         1   0- 0

MC CORMICK, FRANK ANDREW
1939 CIN N   1         4   .400
1940 CIN N   1         7   .214
1948 BOS N   1         3   .200
                      14   .271

MC CORMICK, HARRY ELWOOD
1912 NY  N   H         5   .250
1913 NY  N   H         2   .500
                       7   .333

MC CORMICK, MYRON WINTHROP
1940 CIN N   O         7   .310
1948 BOS N   O         6   .261
1949 BRO N   O         1   .000
                      14   .288

MC COSKY, WILLIAM BARNEY
1940 DET A   O         7   .304

MC COVEY, WILLIE LEE
1962 SF  N  1-0        4   .200

MC CULLOUGH, CLYDE EDWARD
1945 CHI N   H         1   .000

MC DERMOTT, MAURICE JOSEPH
1956 NY  A   P         1   0- 0

MC DONALD, JIMMIE LE ROY
1953 NY  A   P         1   1- 0

MC DOUGALD, GILBERT JAMES
1951 NY  A  2-3        6   .261
1952 NY  A   3         7   .200
1953 NY  A   3         6   .167
1955 NY  A   3         7   .259
1956 NY  A   S         7   .143
1957 NY  A   S         7   .250
1958 NY  A   2         7   .321
1960 NY  A   3         6   .278
                      53   .237

MC ENANEY, WILLIAM HENRY
1975 CIN N   P         5   0- 0
1976 CIN N   P         2   0- 0
                       7   0- 0

MC FARLAND, EDWARD WILLIAM
1906 CHI A   H         1   .000

MC GANN, DENNIS LAWRENCE
1905 NY  N   1         5   .235

MC GINNITY, JOSEPH JEROME
1905 NY  N   P         2   1- 1

MC GLOTHLIN, JAMES MILTON
1970 CIN N   P         1   0- 0
1972 CIN N   P         1   0- 0
                       2   0- 0

MC GRAW, FRANK EDWIN
1973 NY  N   P         5   1- 0

MC HALE, JOHN JOSEPH
1945 DET A   H         3   .000

MC INNIS, JOHN PHAELEN
1911 PHI A   1         1   .000
1913 PHI A   1         5   .118
1914 PHI A   1         4   .143
1918 BOS A   1         6   .250
1925 PIT N   1         4   .286
                      20   .200

MC INTIRE, JOHN REID
1910 CHI N   P         2   0- 1

MC INTYRE, MATTHEW W.
1908 DET A   O         5   .222
1909 DET A   O         4   .000
                       9   .190


MC KAIN, ARCHIE RICHARD
1940 DET A   P         1   0- 0

MC LAIN, DENNIS DALE
1968 DET A   P         3   1- 2

MC LEAN, JOHN BANNERMAN
1913 NY  N   C         5   .500

MC MAHON, DONALD JOHN
1957 MIL N   P         3   0- 0
1958 MIL N   P         3   0- 0
1968 DET A   P         2   0- 0
                       8   0- 0

MC MILLAN, NORMAN ALEXIS
1922 NY  A   O         1   .000
1929 CHI N   3         5   .100
                       6   .091

MC MULLIN, FREDERICK WILLIAM
1917 CHI A   3         6   .125
1919 CHI A   H         2   .500
                       8   .154

MC NAIR, DONALD ERIC
1930 PHI A   H         1   .000
1931 PHI A   2         2   .000
                       3   .000

NC NALLY, DAVID ARTHUR
1966 BAL A   P         2   1- 0
1969 BAL A   P         2   0- 1
1970 BAL A   P         1   1- 0
1971 BAL A   P         4   2- 1
                       9   4- 2

MC NALLY, MICHAEL JOSEPH
1916 BOS A   H         1   .000
1921 NY  A   3         7   .200
1922 NY  A   2         1   .000
                       9   .200

MC NEELY, GEORGE EARL
1924 WAS A   O         7   .222
1925 WAS A   O         4   .000
                      11   .222

MC QUILLAN, HUGH A.
1922 NY  N   P         1   1- 0
1923 NY  N   P         2   0- 1
1924 NY  N   P         3   0- 0
                       6   1- 1

MC QUINN, GEORGE HARTLEY
1944 STL A   1         6   .438
1947 NY  A   1         7   .130
                      13   .256

MC RAE, HAROLD ABRAHAM
1970 CIN N   O         3   .455
1972 CIN N   O         5   .444
                       8   .450

MEADOWS, HENRY LEE
1925 PIT N   P         1   0- 1
1927 PIT N   P         1   0- 1
                       2   0- 2

MEDWICK, JOSEPH MICHAEL
1934 STL N   O         7   .379
1941 BRO N   O         5   .235
                      12   .326

MELTON, CLIFFORD GEORGE
1937 NY  N   P         3   0- 2

MENKE, DENIS JOHN
1972 CIN N   3         7   .083

MERKLE, FREDERICK CHARLES
1911 NY  N   1         6   .150
1912 NY  N   1         8   .273
1913 NY  N   1         4   .231
1916 BRO N   1         3   .250
1918 CHI N   1         6   .278
                      27   .239

MERRITT, JAMES JOSEPH
1965 MIN A   P         2   0- 0
1970 CIN N   P         1   0- 1
                       3   0- 1

MERTES, SAMUEL BLAIR
1905 NY  N   O         5   .176


MERULLO, LEONARD RICHARD
1945 CHI N   S         3   .000

MESSERSMITH, JOHN ALEXANDER
1974 LA  N   P         2   0- 2

METHENY, ARTHUR BEAUREGARD
1943 NY  A   O         2   .125

METKOVICH, GEORGE MICHAEL
1946 BOS A   H         2   .500

MEUSEL, EMIL FREDERICK
1921 NY  N   O         8   .345
1922 NY  N   O         5   .250
1923 NY  N   O         6   .280
1924 NY  N   O         4   .154
                      23   .276

MEUSEL, ROBERT WILLIAM
1921 NY  A   O         8   .200
1922 NY  A   O         5   .300
1923 NY  A   C         6   .269
1926 NY  A   O         7   .238
1927 NY  A   O         4   .118
1928 NY  A   O         4   .200
                      34   .225

MEYER, RUSSELL CHARLES
1950 PHI N   P         2   0- 1
1953 BRO N   P         1   0- 0
1955 BRO N   P         1   0- 0
                       4   0- 1

MEYERS, JOHN TORTES
1911 NY  N   C         6   .300
1912 NY  N   C         8   .357
1913 NY  N   C         1   .000
1916 BRO N   C         3   .200
                      18   .290

MIERKOWICZ, EDWARD FRANK
1945 DET A   O         1   .000

MIKKELSEN, PETER JAMES
1964 NY  A   P         4   0- 1

MIKSIS, EDWARD THOMAS
1947 BRO N  2-0        5   .250
1949 BRO N   3         3   .286
                       8   .273

MILJUS, JOHN KENNETH
1927 PIT N   P         2   0- 1

MILLAN, FELIX BERNARDO
1973 NY  N   2         7   .187

MILLER, EDMUND JOHN
1929 PHI A   O         5   .368
1930 PHI A   O         6   .143
1931 PHI A   O         6   .269
                      18   .258

MILLER, ELMER
1921 NY  A   O         8   .161

MILLER, JOHN BARNEY
1909 PIT N   2         7   .250

MILLER, LAWRENCE H.
1918 BOS A   H         1   .000

MILLER, LOWELL OTTO
1916 BRO N   C         2   .125
1920 BRO N   C         6   .143
                       8   .136

MILLER, RALPH JOSEPH
1924 WAS A   3         4   .182

MILLER, RICHARD ALAN
1975 BOS A   O         3   .000

MILLER, ROBERT JOHN
1950 PHI N   P         1   0- 1

MILLER, ROBERT LANE
1965 LA  N   P         2   0- 0
1966 LA  N   P         1   0- 0
1971 PIT N   P         3   0- 1
                       6   0- 1

MILLER, STUART LEONARD
1962 SF  N   P         2   0- 0
```

YR	CL LEA POS	GP	G	REC

MILLIKEN, ROBERT FOGLE
1953 BRO N P   1   0- 0

MILNER, JOHN DAVID
1973 NY N 1   7   .296

MINCHER, DONALD RAY
1965 MIN A 1   7   .130
1972 OAK A H   3   1.000
              10   .167

MINNER, PAUL EDISON
1949 BRO N P   1   0- 0

MITCHELL, CLARENCE ELMER
1920 BRO N P   1   2   0- 0
1928 STL N P   1   0- 0
           2   3   0- 0

MITCHELL, LOREN DALE
1948 CLE A O   6   .174
1954 CLE A H   3   .000
1956 BRO N H   4   .000
              13   .138

MIZE, JOHN ROBERT
1949 NY A H   2   1.000
1950 NY A 1   4   .133
1951 NY A 1   4   .286
1952 NY A 1   5   .400
1953 NY A H   3   .000
              18   .286

MIZELL, WILMER DAVID
1960 PIT N P   2   0- 1

MOELLER, JOSEPH DOUGLAS
1966 LA N P   1   0- 0

MOGRIDGE, GEORGE ANTHONY
1924 WAS A P   2   1- 0

MONROE, ZACHARY CHARLES
1958 NY A P   1   0- 0

MONTGOMERY, ROBERT EDWARD
1975 BOS A H   1   .000

MOON, WALLACE WADE
1959 LA N O   6   .261
1965 LA N H   2   .000
             8   .240

MOONEY, JIM IRVING
1934 STL N P   1   0- 0

MOORE, EUGENE JR.
1944 STL A O   6   .182

MOORE, GRAHAM EDWARD
1925 PIT N 2   7   .231

MOORE, JAMES WILLIAM
1930 PHI A O   3   .333
1931 PHI A O   2   .333
             5   .333

MOORE, JOHN FRANCIS
1932 CHI N O   2   .000

MOORE, JOSEPH GREGG
1933 NY N O   5   .227
1936 NY N O   6   .214
1937 NY N O   5   .391
             16   .274

MOORE, LLOYD ALBERT
1939 CIN N P   1   0- 0
1940 CIN N P   3   0- 0
             4   0- 0

MOORE, RAYMOND LEROY
1959 CHI A P   1   0- 0

MOORE, TERRY BUFORD
1942 STL N O   5   .294
1946 STL N O   7   .148
             12   .205

MOORE, WILLIAM WILCY
1927 NY A P   2   1- 0
1932 NY A P   1   1- 0
             3   2- 0

MOOSE, ROBERT RALPH
1971 PIT N P   3   0- 0

MORAN, JOSEPH HERBERT
1914 BOS N O   3   .077

MORAN, PATRICK JOSEPH
1906 CHI N H   2   .000
1907 CHI N H   1   .000
             3   .000

MOREHEAD, DAVID MICHAEL
1967 BOS A P   2   0- 0

MORET, ROGELIO
1975 BOS A P   3   0- 0

MORGAN, JOSEPH LEONARD
1972 CIN N 2   7   .125
1975 CIN N 2   7   .259
1976 CIN N 2   4   .333
             18   .227

MORGAN, ROBERT MORRIS
1952 BRO N 3   2   .000
1953 BRO N H   1   .000
             3   .000

MORGAN, TOM STEPHEN
1951 NY A P   1   0- 0
1955 NY A P   2   0- 0
1956 NY A P   2   0- 1
             5   0- 1

MORIARTY, GEORGE JOSEPH
1909 DET A 3   7   .273

MORRISON, JOHN DEWEY
1925 PIT N P   3   0- 0

MOSES, WALLACE
1946 BOS A O   4   .417

MOSSI, DONALD LOUIS
1954 CLE A P   3   0- 0

MOTTON, CURTELL HOWARD
1969 BAL A H   1   .000

MOWERY, HARRY HARLAN
1916 BRO N 3   5   .176

MUELLER, DONALD FREDERICK
1954 NY N O   4   .389

MUELLER, LESLIE CLYDE
1945 DET A P   1   0- 0

MULLIN, GEORGE JOSEPH
1907 DET A P   2   0- 2
1908 DET A P   1   1- 0
1909 DET A P   4   6   2- 1
           7   9   3- 3

MUNCRIEF, ROBERT CLEVELAND
1944 STL A P   2   0- 1
1948 CLE A P   1   0- 0
             3   0- 1

MUNGER, GEORGE DAVID
1946 STL N P   1   1- 0

MUNSON, THURMAN LEE
1976 NY A C   4   .529

MURPHY, DANIEL FRANCIS
1905 PHI A 2   5   .188
1910 PHI A O   5   .350
1911 PHI A O   6   .304
             16   .288

MURPHY, JOHN JOSEPH
1936 NY A P   1   0- 0
1937 NY A P   1   0- 0
1938 NY A P   1   0- 0
1939 NY A P   1   1- 0
1941 NY A P   2   1- 0
1943 NY A P   2   0- 0
             8   2- 0

MURPHY, JOSEPH EDWARD
1913 PHI A O   5   .227
1914 PHI A O   4   .188
1919 CHI A H   3   .000
             12   .200

MURRAY, JOHN JOSEPH
1911 NY N O   6   .000
1912 NY N O   8   .323
1913 NY N O   5   .250
             19   .206

MUSIAL, STANLEY FRANK
1942 STL N O   5   .222
1943 STL N O   5   .278
1944 STL N O   6   .304
1946 STL N 1   7   .222
             23   .256

MYER, CHARLES SOLOMON
1925 WAS A 3   3   .250
1933 WAS A 2   5   .300
             8   .286

MYERS, HENRY HARRISON
1916 BRO N O   5   .182
1920 BRO N O   7   .231
             12   .208

MYERS, WILLIAM HARRISON
1939 CIN N S   4   .333
1940 CIN N S   7   .130
             11   .200

NARAGON, HAROLD RICHARD
1954 CLE A C   1   .000

NARLESKI, RAYMOND EDMOND
1954 CLE A P   2   0- 0

NAPRON, SAMUEL
1943 STL N H   1   .000

NEAL, CHARLES LENARD
1956 BRO N 2   1   .000
1959 LA N 2   6   .370
             7   .323

NEALE, ALFRED EARLE
1919 CIN N O   8   .357

NEEDHAM, THOMAS J.
1910 CHI N H   1   .000

NEHF, ARTHUR NEUKOM
1921 NY N P   3   1- 2
1922 NY N P   2   1- 0
1923 NY N P   2   1- 1
1924 NY N P   3   1- 1
1929 CHI N P   2   0- 0
             12   4- 4

NEIS, BERNARD EDMUND
1920 BRO N O   4   .000

NELSON, GLENN RICHARD
1952 BRO N H   4   .000
1960 PIT N 1   4   .333
             8   .250

NELSON, MELVIN FREDERICK
1968 STL N P   1   0- 0

NETTLES, GRAIG
1976 NY A 3   4   .250

NEWCOMBE, DONALD
1949 BRO N P   2   0- 2
1955 BRO N P   1   0- 1
1956 BRO N P   2   0- 1
             5   0- 4

NEWHOUSER, HAROLD
1945 DET A P   3   2- 1
1954 CLE A P   1   0- 0
             4   2- 1

NEWSOM, LOUIS NORMAN
1940 DET A P   3   2- 1
1947 NY A P   2   0- 1
             5   2- 2

NIARHOS, CONSTANTINE GREGORY
1949 NY A C   1   .000

NICHOLSON, WILLIAM BECK
1945 CHI N O   7   .214

NIEHOFF, JOHN ALBERT
1915 PHI N 2   5   .063

YR	CL	LEA	POS	GP	G	REC
NIEMAN, ROBERT CHARLES						
1962 SF	N		H		1	.000
NOBLE, RAFAEL MIGUEL						
1951 NY	N		C		2	.000
NOLAN, GARY LYNN						
1970 CIN	N		P		2	0-1
1972 CIN	N		P		2	0-1
1975 CIN	N		P		2	0-0
1976 CIN	N		P		1	1-0
					7	1-2
NOREN, IRVING ARNOLD						
1952 NY	A		O		4	.300
1953 NY	A		H		2	.000
1955 NY	A		O		5	.063
					11	.148
NORMAN, FREDIE HUBERT						
1975 CIN	N		P		2	0-1
1976 CIN	N		P		1	0-0
					3	0-1
NORTH, WILLIAM ALEXANDER						
1974 OAK	A		O		5	.059
NORTHRUP, JAMES THOMAS						
1968 DET	A		O		7	.250
NOSSEK, JOSEPH RUDOLPH						
1965 MIN	A		O		6	.200
NUNAMAKER, LESLIE GRANT						
1920 CLE	A		C		2	.500
O'BRIEN, JOHN JOSEPH						
1903 BOS	A		H		2	.000
O'BRIEN, THOMAS JOSEPH						
1912 BOS	A		P		2	0-2
O'CONNELL, JAMES JOSEPH						
1923 NY	N		H		2	.000
O'CONNOR, PATRICK FRANCIS						
1909 PIT	N		H		1	.000
O'DEA, JAMES KENNETH						
1935 CHI	N		H		1	1.000
1938 CHI	N		C		3	.200
1942 STL	N		H		1	1.000
1943 STL	N		C		2	.667
1944 STL	N		H		3	.333
					10	.462
O'DELL, WILLIAM OLIVER						
1962 SF	N		P		3	0-1
ODOM, JOHNNY LEE						
1972 OAK	A		P	2	4	0-1
O'DOUL, FRANK JOSEPH						
1973 OAK	A		P	2	3	0-0
1974 OAK	A		P	2	2	1-0
				6	9	1-1
1933 NY	N		H		1	1.000
O'FARRELL, ROBERT ARTHUR						
1918 CHI	N		C		3	.000
1926 STL	N		C		7	.304
					10	.269
OGDEN, WARREN HARVEY						
1924 WAS	A		P		1	0-0
OLDHAM, JOHN CYRUS						
1925 PIT	N		P		1	0-0
OLDIS, ROBERT CARL						
1960 PIT	N		C		2	.000
OLDRING, REUBEN NOSHIER						
1911 PHI	A		O		6	.200
1913 PHI	A		O		5	.273
1914 PHI	A		O		4	.067
					15	.194
O'LEARY, CHARLES TIMOTHY						
1907 DET	A		S		5	.059
1908 DET	A		S		5	.158
1909 DET	A		3		1	.000
					11	.103

YR	CL	LEA	POS	GP	G	REC
OLIVA, PEDRO						
1965 MIN	A		O		7	.192
OLIVER, ALBERT						
1971 PIT	N		O		5	.211
OLIVER, NATHANIEL						
1966 LA	N		R		1	.000
OLMO, LUIS RODRIGUEZ						
1949 BRO	N		O		4	.273
OLSON, IVAN MASSIE						
1916 BRO	N		S		5	.250
1920 BRO	N		S		7	.320
					12	.293
O'MARA, OLIVER EDWARD						
1916 BRO	N		H		1	.000
O'NEILL, STEPHEN FRANCIS						
1920 CLE	A		C		7	.333
O'NEILL, WILLIAM JOHN						
1906 CHI	A		O		1	.000
ORSATTI, ERNEST RALPH						
1928 STL	N		O		4	.286
1930 STL	N		H		1	.000
1931 STL	N		C		1	.000
1934 STL	N		O		7	.318
					13	.273
ORSINO, JOHN JOSEPH						
1962 SF	N		C		1	.000
OSINSKI, DANIEL						
1967 BOS	A		P		2	0-0
OSTEEN, CLAUDE WILSON						
1965 LA	N		P		2	1-1
1966 LA	N		P		1	0-1
					3	1-2
OSTROWSKI, JOSEPH PAUL						
1951 NY	A		P		1	0-0
O'TOOLE, JAMES JEROME						
1961 CIN	N		P		2	0-2
OTT, MELVIN THOMAS						
1933 NY	N		O		5	.389
1936 NY	N		O		6	.304
1937 NY	N		3		5	.200
					16	.295
OUTLAW, JAMES PAULUS						
1945 DET	A		3		7	.179
OVERALL, ORVAL						
1906 CHI	N		P		2	0-0
1907 CHI	N		P		2	1-0
1908 CHI	N		P		3	2-0
1910 CHI	N		P		1	0-1
					8	3-1
OVERMIRE, FRANK						
1945 DET	A		P		1	0-1
OWEN, ARNOLD MALCOLM						
1941 BRO	N		C		5	.167
OWEN, FRANK MALCOLM						
1906 CHI	A		P		1	0-0
OWEN, MARVIN JAMES						
1934 DET	A		3		7	.069
1935 DET	A		1-3		6	.050
					13	.061
OYLER, RAYMOND FRANCIS						
1968 DET	A		S			.000
PACIOREK, THOMAS MARION						
1974 LA	N		H		3	.500
PAFKO, ANDREW						
1945 CHI	N		O		7	.214
1952 BRO	N		O		7	.190
1957 MIL	N		O		6	.214
1958 MIL	N		O		4	.333
					24	.222
PAGAN, JOSE ANTONIO						
1962 SF	N		S		7	.368
1971 PIT	N		3		4	.267
					11	.324

YR	CL	LEA	POS	GP	G	REC
PAGE, JOSEPH FRANCIS						
1947 NY	A		P		4	1-1
1949 NY	A		P		3	1-0
					7	2-1
PAGE, VANCE LINWOOD						
1938 CHI	N		P		1	0-0
PAIGE, LEROY ROBERT						
1948 CLE	A		P		1	0-0
PALICA, ERWIN MARTIN						
1949 BRO	N		P		1	0-0
PALMER, JAMES ALVIN						
1966 BAL	A		P		1	1-0
1969 BAL	A		P		1	0-1
1970 BAL	A		P		2	1-0
1971 BAL	A		P		2	1-0
					6	3-1
PARENT, FREDERICK ALFRED						
1903 BOS	A		S		8	.281
PARKER, HARRY WILLIAM						
1973 NY	N		P		3	0-1
PARKER, MAURICE WESLEY						
1965 LA	N		1		7	.304
1966 LA	N		1		4	.231
					11	.278
PARTEE, ROY ROBERT						
1946 BOS	A		C		5	.100
PASCHAL, BENJAMIN EDWIN						
1926 NY	A		H		5	.250
1928 NY	A		O		3	.200
					8	.214
PASCUAL, CAMILO ALBERTO						
1965 MIN	A		P		1	0-1
PASKERT, GEORGE HENRY						
1915 PHI	N		O		5	.158
1918 CHI	N		O		6	.190
					11	.175
PASSEAU, CLAUDE WILLIAM						
1945 CHI	N		P		3	1-0
PATTERSON, DARYL ALAN						
1968 DET	A		P		2	0-0
PAYNE, FREDERICK THOMAS						
1907 DET	A		C		2	.250
PEARSON, MARCELLUS MONTE						
1936 NY	A		P		1	1-0
1937 NY	A		P		1	1-0
1938 NY	A		P		1	1-0
1939 NY	A		P		1	1-0
					4	4-0
PECK, HAROLD ARTHUR						
1948 CLE	A		O		1	.000
PECKINPAUGH, ROGER THORPE						
1921 NY	A		S		8	.179
1924 WAS	A		S		4	.417
1925 WAS	A		S		7	.250
					19	.250
PEEL, HOMER HEFNER						
1933 NY	N		O		2	.500
PENNOCK, HERBERT JEFFRIES						
1914 PHI	A		P		1	0-0
1923 NY	A		P		3	2-0
1926 NY	A		P		3	2-0
1927 NY	A		P		1	1-0
1932 NY	A		P		2	0-0
					10	5-0
PEPITONE, JOSEPH ANTHONY						
1963 NY	A		1		4	.154
1964 NY	A		1		7	.154
					11	.154
PEREZ, ATANASIO RIGAL						
1970 CIN	N		3		5	.056
1972 CIN	N		1		7	.435
1975 CIN	N		1		7	.179
1976 CIN	N		1		4	.313
					23	.247

YR	CL	LEA	POS	GP	G	REC

PERRANOSKI, RONALD PETER
1963	LA	N	P		1	0- 0
1965	LA	N	P		2	0- 0
1966	LA	N	P		2	0- 0
					5	0- 0

PERRITT, WILLIAM DAYTON
| 1917 | NY | N | P | | 3 | 0- 0 |

PERRY, JAMES EVAN
| 1965 | MIN | A | P | | 2 | 0- 0 |

PESKY, JOHN MICHAEL
| 1946 | BOS | A | S | | 7 | .233 |

PETROCELLI, AMERICO PETER
1967	BOS	A	S		7	.200
1975	BOS	A	3		7	.308
					14	.261

PFEFFER, EDWARD JOSEPH
1916	BRO	N	P	3	4	0- 1
1920	BRO	N	P		1	0- 0
				4	5	0- 1

PFIESTER, JOHN ALBERT
1906	CHI	N	P		2	0- 2
1907	CHI	N	P		1	1- 0
1908	CHI	N	P		1	0- 1
1910	CHI	N	P		1	0- 0
					5	1- 3

PHELPS, EDWARD JOSEPH
| 1903 | PIT | N | C | | 8 | .231 |

PHILLEY, DAVID EARL
| 1954 | CLE | A | O | | 4 | .125 |

PHILLIPPE, CHARLES LOUIS
1903	PIT	N	P		5	3- 2
1909	PIT	N	P		2	0- 0
					7	3- 2

PHILLIPS, JACK DORN
| 1947 | NY | A | 1 | | 2 | .000 |

PHILLIPS, JOHN MELVIN
| 1959 | CHI | A | 3-O | | 3 | .300 |

PHOEBUS, THOMAS HAROLD
| 1970 | BAL | A | P | | 1 | 1- 0 |

PICK, CHARLES THOMAS
| 1918 | CHI | N | 2 | | 6 | .389 |

PIERCE, WALTER WILLIAM
1959	CHI	A	P		3	0- 0
1962	SF	N	P		2	1- 1
					5	1- 1

PIERCY, WILLIAM BENTON
| 1921 | NY | A | P | | 1 | 0- 0 |

PIGNATANO, JOSEPH BENJAMIN
| 1959 | LA | N | C | | 1 | .000 |

PINA, HORACIO
| 1973 | OAK | A | P | | 2 | 0- 0 |

PINIELLA, LOUIS VICTOR
| 1976 | NY | A | O-D | | 4 | .333 |

PINSON, VADA EDWARD
| 1961 | CIN | N | O | | 5 | .091 |

PIPGRAS, GEORGE WILLIAM
1927	NY	A	P		1	1- 0
1928	NY	A	P		1	1- 0
1932	NY	A	P		1	1- 0
					3	3- 0

PIPP, WALTER CLEMENT
1921	NY	A	1		8	.154
1922	NY	A	1		5	.286
1923	NY	A	1		6	.250
					19	.224

PIZARRO, JUAN
1957	MIL	N	P		1	`0- 0
1958	MIL	N	P		1	0- 0
					2	0- 0

PLANK, EDWARD STEWART
1905	PHI	A	P		2	0- 2
1911	PHI	A	P		2	1- 1
1913	PHI	A	P		2	1- 1
1914	PHI	A	P		1	0- 1
					7	2- 5

PLEIS, WILLIAM
| 1965 | MIN | A | P | | 1 | 0- 0 |

PODRES, JOHN JOSEPH
1953	BRO	N	P		1	0- 1
1955	BRO	N	P		2	2- 0
1959	LA	N	P	2	3	1- 0
1963	LA	N	P		1	1- 0
				6	7	4- 1

POLE, RICHARD HENRY
| 1975 | BOS | A | P | | 1 | 0- 0 |

POLLET, HOWARD JOSEPH
1942	STL	N	P		1	0- 0
1946	STL	N	P		2	0- 1
					3	0- 1

POPE, DAVID
| 1954 | CLE | A | O | | 3 | .000 |

POST, WALTER CHARLES
| 1961 | CIN | N | O | | 5 | .333 |

POTTER, NELSON THOMAS
1944	STL	A	P		2	0- 1
1948	BOS	N	P		2	0- 0
					4	0- 1

POWELL, ALVIN JACOB
1936	NY	A	O		6	.455
1937	NY	A	H		1	.000
1938	NY	A	O		1	.000
					8	.435

POWELL, JOHN WESLEY
1966	BAL	A	1		4	.357
1969	BAL	A	1		5	.263
1970	BAL	A	1		5	.294
1971	BAL	A	1		7	.111
					21	.234

POWERS, MICHAEL RILEY
| 1905 | PHI | A | C | | 3 | .143 |

PRICE, JAMES WILLIAM
| 1968 | DET | A | H | | 2 | .000 |

PRIDDY, GERALD EDWARD
| 1942 | NY | A | 1-3 | | 3 | .100 |

PRIM, RAYMOND LEE
| 1945 | CHI | N | P | | 2 | 0- 1 |

PUCCINELLI, GEORGE LAWRENCE
| 1930 | STL | N | H | | 1 | .000 |

PURKEY, ROBERT THOMAS
| 1961 | CIN | N | P | | 2 | 0- 1 |

QUILICI, FRANK RALPH
| 1965 | MIN | A | 2 | | 7 | .200 |

QUINN, JOHN PICUS
1921	NY	A	P		1	0- 1
1929	PHI	A	P		1	0- 0
1930	PHI	A	P		1	0- 0
					3	0- 1

RACKLEY, MARVIN EUGENE
| 1949 | BRO | N | O | | 2 | .000 |

RANDOLPH, WILLIE LARRY
| 1976 | NY | A | 2 | | 4 | .071 |

RARIDEN, WILLIAM ANGEL
1917	NY	N	C		5	.385
1919	CIN	N	C		5	.211
					10	.281

RASCHI, VICTOR ANGELO JOHN
1947	NY	A	P		2	0- 0
1949	NY	A	P		2	1- 1
1950	NY	A	P		1	1- 0
1951	NY	A	P		2	1- 1
1952	NY	A	P		3	2- 0
1953	NY	A	P		1	0- 1
					11	5- 3

RATH, MORRIS CHARLES
| 1919 | CIN | N | 2 | | 8 | .226 |

RAWLINGS, JOHN WILLIAM
| 1921 | NY | N | 2 | | 8 | .333 |

REED, HOWARD DEAN
| 1965 | LA | N | P | | 2 | 0- 0 |

REED, JOHN BURWELL
| 1961 | NY | A | O | | 3 | .000 |

REESE, HAROLD HENRY
1941	BRO	N	S		5	.200
1947	BRO	N	S		7	.304
1949	BRO	N	S		5	.316
1952	BRO	N	S		7	.345
1953	BRO	N	S		6	.208
1955	BRO	N	S		7	.296
1956	BRO	N	S		7	.222
					44	.272

REGALADO, RUDOLPH VALENTINO
| 1954 | CLE | A | H | | 4 | .333 |

REGAN, PHILIP RAYMOND
| 1966 | LA | N | P | | 2 | 0- 0 |

REINHART, ARTHUR CONRAD
| 1926 | STL | N | P | | 1 | 0- 1 |

REISER, HAROLD PATRICK
1941	BRO	N	O		5	.200
1947	BRO	N	O		5	.250
					10	.214

RENIFF, HAROLD EUGENE
1963	NY	A	P		3	0- 0
1964	NY	A	P		1	0- 0
					4	0- 0

REPULSKI, ELDON JOHN
| 1959 | LA | N | O | | 1 | .000 |

RETTENMUND, MERVIN WELDON
1969	BAL	A	R		1	.000
1970	BAL	A	O		2	.400
1971	BAL	A	O		7	.185
1975	CIN	N	H		3	.000
					13	.200

REULBACH, EDWARD MARVIN
1906	CHI	N	P		2	1- 0
1907	CHI	N	P		2	1- 0
1908	CHI	N	P		2	0- 0
1910	CHI	N	P		1	0- 0
					7	2- 0

REYNOLDS, ALLIE PIERCE
1947	NY	A	P		2	1- 0
1949	NY	A	P		2	1- 0
1950	NY	A	P		2	1- 0
1951	NY	A	P		2	1- 1
1952	NY	A	P		4	2- 1
1953	NY	A	P		3	1- 0
					15	7- 2

REYNOLDS, CARL NETTLES
| 1938 | CHI | N | O | | 4 | .000 |

RHEM, CHARLES FLINT
1926	STL	N	P		1	0- 0
1928	STL	N	P		1	0- 0
1930	STL	N	P		1	0- 1
1931	STL	N	P		1	0- 0
					4	0- 1

RHODES, JAMES LAMAR
| 1954 | NY | N | O | | 3 | .667 |

RHYNE, HAROLD
| 1927 | PIT | N | 2 | | 1 | .000 |

RICE, DELBERT W.
1946	STL	N	C		3	.500
1957	MIL	N	C		2	.167
					5	.333

RICE, EDGAR CHARLES
1924	WAS	A	O		7	.207
1925	WAS	A	O		7	.364
1933	WAS	A	H		1	1.000
					15	.302

RICHARDS, PAUL RAPIER

YR	CL	LEA	POS	GP	G	REC
1945	DET	A	C		7	.211

RICHARDSON, GORDON CLARK

YR	CL	LEA	POS	GP	G	REC
1964	STL	N	P		2	0- 0

RICHARDSON, ROBERT CLINTON

YR	CL	LEA	POS	GP	G	REC
1957	NY	A	2		2	.000
1958	NY	A	3		4	.000
1960	NY	A	2		7	.367
1961	NY	A	2		5	.391
1962	NY	A	2		7	.148
1963	NY	A	2		4	.214
1964	NY	A	2		7	.406
					36	.305

RICHERT, PETER GERARD

YR	CL	LEA	POS	GP	G	REC
1969	BAL	A	.P		1	0- 0
1970	BAL	A	P		1	0- 0
1971	BAL	A	P		1	0- 0
					3	0- 0

RICHIE, LEWIS A.

YR	CL	LEA	POS	GP	G	REC
1910	CHI	N	P		1	0- 0

RICKERT, MARVIN AUGUST

YR	CL	LEA	POS	GP	G	REC
1948	BOS	N	O		5	.211

RICKETTS, DAVID WILLIAM

YR	CL	LEA	POS	GP	G	REC
1967	STL	N	H		3	.000
1968	STL	N	H		1	1.000
					4	.250

RIDDLE, ELMER RAY

YR	CL	LEA	POS	GP	G	REC
1940	CIN	N	P		1	0- 0

RIGGS, LEWIS SIDNEY

YR	CL	LEA	POS	GP	G	REC
1940	CIN	N	H		3	.000
1941	BRO	N	3		3	.250
					6	.182

RIGNEY, WILLIAM JOSEPH

YR	CL	LEA	POS	GP	G	REC
1951	NY	N	H		4	.250

RING, JAMES JOSEPH

YR	CL	LEA	POS	GP	G	REC
1919	CIN	N	P		2	1- 1

RIPPLE, JAMES ALBERT

YR	CL	LEA	POS	GP	G	REC
1936	NY	N	O		5	.333
1937	NY	N	O		5	.294
1940	CIN	N	O		7	.333
					17	.320

RISBERG, CHARLES AUGUST

YR	CL	LEA	POS	GP	G	REC
1917	CHI	A	H		2	.500
1919	CHI	A	S		8	.080
					10	.111

RITCHEY, CLAUDE CASSIUS

YR	CL	LEA	POS	GP	G	REC
1903	PIT	N	2		8	.111

RIVERA, MANUEL JOSEPH

YR	CL	LEA	POS	GP	G	REC
1959	CHI	A	O		5	.000

RIVERS, JOHN MILTON

YR	CL	LEA	POS	GP	G	REC
1976	NY	A	O		4	.167

RIXEY, EPPA

YR	CL	LEA	POS	GP	G	REC
1915	PHI	N	P		1	0- 1

RIZZUTO, PHILIP FRANCIS

YR	CL	LEA	POS	GP	G	REC
1941	NY	A	S		5	.111
1942	NY	A	S		5	.381
1947	NY	A	S		7	.308
1949	NY	A	S		5	.167
1950	NY	A	S		4	.143
1951	NY	A	S		6	.320
1952	NY	A	S		7	.148
1953	NY	A	S		6	.316
1955	NY	A	S		7	.267
					52	.246

ROBERTS, ROBIN EVAN

YR	CL	LEA	POS	GP	G	REC
1950	PHI	N	P		2	0- 1

ROBERTSON, DAVIS AYDELOTTE

YR	CL	LEA	POS	GP	G	REC
1917	NY	N	O		6	.500

ROBERTSON, EUGENE EDWARD

YR	CL	LEA	POS	GP	G	REC
1928	NY	A	3		3	.125

ROBERTSON, ROBERT EUGENE

YR	CL	LEA	POS	GP	G	REC
1971	PIT	N	1		7	.240

ROBINSON, AARON ANDREW

YR	CL	LEA	POS	GP	G	REC
1947	NY	A	C		3	.200

ROBINSON, BROOKS CALBERT

YR	CL	LEA	POS	GP	G	REC
1966	BAL	A	3		4	.214
1969	BAL	A	3		5	.053
1970	BAL	A	3		5	.429
1971	BAL	A	3		7	.318
					21	.263

ROBINSON, FRANK

YR	CL	LEA	POS	GP	G	REC
1961	CIN	N	O		5	.200
1966	BAL	A	O		4	.286
1969	BAL	A	O		5	.188
1970	BAL	A	O		5	.273
1971	BAL	A	O		7	.280
					26	.250

ROBINSON, JACK ROOSEVELT

YR	CL	LEA	POS	GP	G	REC
1947	BRO	N	1		7	.259
1949	BRO	N	2		5	.188
1952	BRO	N	2		7	.174
1953	BRO	N	O		6	.320
1955	BRO	N	3		6	.182
1956	BRO	N	3		7	.250
					38	.234

ROBINSON, WILLIAM EDWARD

YR	CL	LEA	POS	GP	G	REC
1948	CLE	N	1		6	.300
1955	NY	A	1		4	.667
					10	.348

ROE, ELWIN CHARLES

YR	CL	LEA	POS	GP	G	REC
1949	BRO	N	P		1	1- 0
1952	BRO	N	P		3	1- 0
1953	BRO	N	P		1	0- 1
					5	2- 1

ROEBUCK, EDWARD JACK

YR	CL	LEA	POS	GP	G	REC
1955	BRO	N	P		1	0- 0
1956	BRO	N	P		3	0- 0
					4	0- 0

ROETTGER, WALTER HENRY

YR	CL	LEA	POS	GP	G	REC
1931	STL	N	O		3	.286

ROGELL, WILLIAM GEORGE

YR	CL	LEA	POS	GP	G	REC
1934	DET	A	S		7	.276
1935	DET	A	S		6	.292
					13	.283

ROGERS, THOMAS ANDREW

YR	CL	LEA	POS	GP	G	REC
1921	NY	A	P		1	0- 0

ROHE, GEORGE ANTHONY

YR	CL	LEA	POS	GP	G	REC
1906	CHI	A	3		6	.333

ROLFE, ROBERT ABAIL

YR	CL	LEA	POS	GP	G	REC
1936	NY	A	3		6	.400
1937	NY	A	3		5	.300
1938	NY	A	3		4	.167
1939	NY	A	3		4	.125
1941	NY	A	3		5	.300
1942	NY	A	3		4	.353
					28	.284

ROLLINS, RICHARD JOHN

YR	CL	LEA	POS	GP	G	REC
1965	MIN	A	H		3	.000

ROMANO, JOHN ANTHONY

YR	CL	LEA	POS	GP	G	REC
1959	CHI	A	H		1	.000

ROMMEL, EDWIN AMERICUS

YR	CL	LEA	POS	GP	G	REC
1929	PHI	A	P		1	1- 0
1931	PHI	A	P		1	0- 0
					2	1- 0

ROOT, CHARLES HENRY

YR	CL	LEA	POS	GP	G	REC
1929	CHI	N	P		2	0- 1
1932	CHI	N	P		1	0- 1
1935	CHI	N	P		2	0- 1
1938	CHI	N	P		1	0- 0
					6	0- 3

ROSAR, WARREN VINCENT

YR	CL	LEA	POS	GP	G	REC
1941	NY	A	C		1	.000
1942	NY	A	H		1	1.000
					2	1.000

ROSE, PETER EDWARD

YR	CL	LEA	POS	GP	G	REC
1970	CIN	N	O		5	.250
1972	CIN	N	O		7	.214
1975	CIN	N	3		7	.370
1976	CIN	N	3		4	.188
					23	.264

ROSEBORO, JOHN

YR	CL	LEA	POS	GP	G	REC
1959	LA	N	C		6	.095
1963	LA	N	C		4	.143
1965	LA	N	C		7	.286
1966	LA	N	C		4	.071
					21	.157

ROSEN, ALBERT LEONARD

YR	CL	LEA	POS	GP	G	REC
1948	CLE	A	H		1	.000
1954	CLE	A	3		3	.250
					4	.231

ROSSMAN, CLAUDE R.

YR	CL	LEA	POS	GP	G	REC
1907	DET	A	1		5	.400
1908	DET	A	1		5	.211
					10	.308

ROTHROCK, JOHN HUSTON

YR	CL	LEA	POS	GP	G	REC
1934	STL	N	O		7	.233

ROUSH, EDD J.

YR	CL	LEA	POS	GP	G	REC
1919	CIN	N	O		8	.214

ROWE, LYNWOOD THOMAS

YR	CL	LEA	POS	GP	G	REC
1934	DET	A	P		3	1- 1
1935	DET	A	P		3	1- 2
1940	DET	A	P		2	0- 2
					8	2- 5

RUCKER, GEORGE NAPOLEON

YR	CL	LEA	POS	GP	G	REC
1916	BRO	N	P		1	0- 0

RUDI, JOSEPH ODEN

YR	CL	LEA	POS	GP	G	REC
1972	OAK	A	O		7	.240
1973	OAK	A	O		7	.333
1974	OAK	A	O		5	.333
					19	.300

RUDOLPH, RICHARD

YR	CL	LEA	POS	GP	G	REC
1914	BOS	N	P		2	2- 0

RUEL, HEROLD DOMINIC

YR	CL	LEA	POS	GP	G	REC
1924	WAS	A	C		7	.095
1925	WAS	A	C		7	.316
					14	.200

RUETHER, WALTER HENRY

YR	CL	LEA	POS	GP	G	REC
1919	CIN	N	P	2	3	1- 0
1925	WAS	A	H		1	.000
1926	NY	A	P	1	3	0- 1
				3	7	1- 1
						.364

RUFFING, CHARLES HERBERT

YR	CL	LEA	POS	GP	G	REC
1932	NY	A	P	1	2	1- 0
1936	NY	A	P	2	3	0- 1
1937	NY	A	P		1	1- 0
1938	NY	A	P		2	2- 0
1939	NY	A	P		1	1- 0
1941	NY	A	P		1	1- 0
1942	NY	A	P	2	4	1- 1
				10	14	7- 2

RUSH, ROBERT RANSOM

YR	CL	LEA	POS	GP	G	REC
1958	MIL	N	P		1	0- 1

RUSSELL, ALLAN E.

YR	CL	LEA	POS	GP	G	REC
1924	WAS	A	P		1	0- 0

RUSSELL, EWELL ALBERT

YR	CL	LEA	POS	GP	G	REC
1917	CHI	A	P		1	0- 0

RUSSELL, GLEN DAVID

YR	CL	LEA	POS	GP	G	REC
1946	BOS	A	3		2	1.000

RUSSELL, JACK ERWIN

YR	CL	LEA	POS	GP	G	REC
1933	WAS	A	P		3	0- 1
1938	CHI	N	P		2	0- 0
					5	0- 1

RUSSELL, WILLIAM ELLIS

YR	CL	LEA	POS	GP	G	REC
1974	LA	N	S		5	.222

RUSSO, MARIUS UGO

YR	CL	LEA	POS	GP	G	REC
1941	NY	A	P		1	1- 0
1943	NY	A	P		1	1- 0
					2	2- 0

YR	CL	LEA	POS	GP	G	REC

RUTH, GEORGE HERMAN

YR	CL	LEA	POS	GP	G	REC
1915	BOS	A	H		1	.000
1916	BOS	A	P		1	1- 0
1918	BOS	A	P-O	2	3	2- 0
						.200
1921	NY	A	O		6	.313
1922	NY	A	O		5	.118
1923	NY	A	1-O		6	.368
1926	NY	A	O		7	.300
1927	NY	A	O		4	.400
1928	NY	A	O		4	.625
1932	NY	A	O		4	.333
				3	41	3- 0
						.326.

RUTHERFORD, JOHN WILLIAM

1952	BRO	N	P		1	0- 0

RYAN, CORNELIUS JOSEPH

1948	BOS	N	H		2	.000

RYAN, JOHN COLLINS

1933	NY	N	S		5	.278
1937	NY	N	H		1	.000
					6	.263

RYAN, LYNN NOLAN

1969	NY	N	P		1	0- 0

RYAN, MICHAEL JAMES

1967	BOS	A	C		1	.000

RYAN, WILFRED PATRICK DOLAN

1922	NY	N	P		1	1- 0
1923	NY	N	P		3	1- 0
1924	NY	N	P		2	1- 0
					6	3- 0

RYBA, DOMINIC JOSEPH

1946	BOS	A	P		1	0- 0

SADECKI, RAYMOND MICHAEL

1964	STL	N	P		2	1- 0
1973	NY	N	P		4	0- 0
					6	1- 0

SAIN, JOHN FRANKLIN

1948	BOS	N	P		2	1- 1
1951	NY	A	P		1	0- 0
1952	NY	A	P	1	2	0- 1
1953	NY	A	P		2	1- 0
				6	7	2- 2

SALKELD, WILLIAM FRANKLIN

1948	BOS	N	C		5	.222

SALLEE, HARRY FRANKLIN

1917	NY	N	P		2	0- 2
1919	CIN	N	P		2	1- 1
					4	1- 3

SALMON, RUTHFORD EDUARDO

1969	BAL	A	R		2	.000
1970	BAL	A	H		1	1.000
					3	1.000

SANDERS, RAYMOND FLOYD

1942	STL	N	H		2	.000
1943	STL	N	1		5	.294
1944	STL	N	1		6	.286
1948	BOS	N	H		1	.000
					14	.275

SANDS, CHARLES DUANE

1971	PIT	N	H		1	.000

SANFORD, JOHN STANLEY

1962	SF	N	P		3	1- 2

SANGUILLEN, MANUEL DE JESUS

1971	PIT	N	C		7	.379

SANTIAGO, JOSE RAFAEL

1967	BOS	A	P		3	0- 2

SAUER, EDWARD

1945	CHI	N	H		2	.000

SAWATSKI, CARL ERNEST

1957	MIL	N	H		2	.000

SCARBOROUGH, RAY WILSON

1952	NY	A	P		1	0- 0

SCHAEFER, HERMAN A.

1907	DET	A	2		5	.143
1908	DET	A	2-3		5	.125
					10	.135

SCHALK, RAYMOND WILLIAM

1917	CHI	A	C		6	.263
1919	CHI	A	C		8	.304
					14	.286

SCHALLOCK, ARTHUR LAWRENCE

1953	NY	A	P		1	0- 0

SCHANG, WALTER HENRY

1913	PHI	A	C		4	.357
1914	PHI	A	C		4	.167
1918	BOS	A	C		5	.444
1921	NY	A	C		8	.286
1922	NY	A	C		5	.188
1923	NY	A	C		6	.318
					32	.287

SCHENZ, HENRY LEONARD

1951	NY	N	R		1	.000

SCHMANDT, RAYMOND HENRY

1920	BRO	N	H		1	.000

SCHMIDT, CHARLES

1907	DET	A	C		4	.167
1908	DET	A	C		4	.071
1909	DET	A	C		6	.222
					14	.159

SCHMIDT, CHARLES JOHN

1914	BOS	N	1		4	.294

SCHMIDT, FREDERICK ALBERT

1944	STL	N	P		1	0- 0

SCHOENDIENST, ALBERT FRED

1946	STL	N	2		7	.233
1957	MIL	N	2		5	.278
1958	MIL	N	2		7	.300
					19	.269

SCHOFIELD, JOHN RICHARD

1960	PIT	N	S		3	.333
1968	STL	N	S		2	.000
					5	.333

SCHRECKENGOST, OSSEE FREEMAN

1905	PHI	A	C		3	.222

SCHULTE, FRANK

1906	CHI	N	O		6	.269
1907	CHI	N	O		5	.250
1908	CHI	N	O		5	.389
1910	CHI	N	O		5	.353
					21	.309

SCHULTE, FRED WILLIAM

1933	WAS	A	O		5	.333

SCHULTZ, GEORGE WARREN

1964	STL	N	P		4	0- 1

SCHUMACHER, HAROLD HENRY

1933	NY	N	P		2	1- 0
1936	NY	N	P		2	1- 1
1937	NY	N	P		1	0- 1
					5	2- 2

SCHUPP, FERDINAND MAURICE

1917	NY	N	P		2	1- 0

SCHUSTER, WILLIAM CHARLES

1945	CHI	N	S		2	.000

SCOTT, GEORGE CHARLES

1967	BOS	A	1		7	.231

SCOTT, JOHN WILLIAM

1922	NY	N	P		1	1- 0
1923	NY	N	P		2	0- 1
					3	1- 1

SCOTT, LEWIS EVERETT

1915	BOS	A	S		5	.056
1916	BOS	A	S		5	.125
1918	BOS	A	S		6	.095
1922	NY	A	S		5	.143
1923	NY	A	S		6	.318
					27	.156

SEAVER, GEORGE THOMAS

1969	NY	N	P		2	1- 1
1973	NY	N	P		2	0- 1
					4	1- 2

SEBRING, JAMES DENNISON

1903	PIT	N	O		8	.367

SECORY, FRANK EDWARD

1945	CHI	N	H		5	.400

SEEDS, ROBERT IRA

1936	NY	A	R		1	.000

SEGUI, DIEGO PABLO

1975	BOS	A	P		1	0- 0

SELKIRK, GEORGE ALEXANDER

1936	NY	A	O		6	.333
1937	NY	A	O		5	.263
1938	NY	A	O		3	.200
1939	NY	A	O		4	.167
1941	NY	A	H		2	.500
1942	NY	A	H		1	.000
					21	.265

SEMINICK, ANDREW WASIL

1950	PHI	N	C		4	.182

SEVEREID, HENRY LEVAI

1925	WAS	A	C		1	.333
1926	NY	A	C		7	.273
					8	.280

SEWELL, JAMES LUTHER

1933	WAS	A	C		5	.176

SEWELL, JOSEPH WHEELER

1920	CLE	A	S		7	.174
1932	NY	A	3		4	.333
					11	.207

SEYBOLD, RALPH ORLANDO

1905	PHI	A	O		5	.125

SHAFER, ARTHUR JOSEPH

1912	NY	N	S		3	.000
1913	NY	N	3-O		5	.158
					8	.158

SHAMSKY, ARTHUR LOUIS

1969	NY	N	O		3	.000

SHANNON, THOMAS MICHAEL

1964	STL	N	O		7	.214
1967	STL	N	3		7	.208
1968	STL	N	3		7	.276
					21	.235

SHANTZ, ROBERT CLAYTON

1957	NY	A	P		3	0- 1
1960	NY	A	P		3	0- 0
					6	0- 1

SHAW, ROBERT JOHN

1959	CHI	A	P		2	1- 1

SHAWKEY, JAMES ROBERT

1914	PHI	A	P		1	0- 1
1921	NY	A	P		2	0- 1
1922	NY	A	P		1	0- 0
1923	NY	A	P		1	1- 0
1926	NY	A	P		3	0- 1
					8	1- 3

SHEA, FRANCIS JOSEPH

1947	NY	A	P		3	2- 0

SHEAN, DAVID WILLIAM

1918	BOS	A	2		6	.211

SHECKARD, SAMUEL JAMES TILDEN

1906	CHI	N	O		6	.000
1907	CHI	N	O		5	.238
1908	CHI	N	O		5	.238
1910	CHI	N	O		5	.286
					21	.182

SHEEHAN, JOHN THOMAS

1920	BRO	N	3		3	.182

SHELDON, ROLAND FRANK

1964	NY	A	P		2	0- 0

YR	CL LEA POS	GP	G	REC

SHERDEL, WILLIAM HENRY

1926 STL N P		2	0- 2
1928 STL N P		2	0- 2
		4	0- 4

SHERRY, LAWRENCE

| 1959 LA N P | 4 | 5 | 2- 0 |

SHIRLEY, ALVIS NEWMAN

| 1944 STL A P | | 2 | 0- 0 |

SHIRLEY, ERNEST RAEFORD

| 1924 WAS A H | | 3 | .500 |

SHOCKER, URBAN JAMES

| 1926 NY A P | | 2 | 0- 1 |

SHOPAY, THOMAS MICHAEL

| 1971 BAL A H | | 5 | .000 |

SHORE, ERNEST GRADY

1915 BOS A P		2	1- 1
1916 BOS A P		2	2- 0
		4	3- 1

SHORES, WILLIAM DAVID

| 1930 PHI A P | | 1 | 0- 0 |

SHORTEN, CHARLES HENRY

| 1916 BOS A U | | 2 | .571 |

SHUBA, GEORGE THOMAS

1952 BRO N O		4	.300
1953 BRO N H		2	1.000
1955 BRO N H		1	.000
		7	.333

SIEBERN, NORMAN LEROY

1956 NY A H		1	.000
1958 NY A O		3	.125
1967 BOS A O		3	.333
		7	.167

SIEVER, EDWARD T.

| 1907 DET A P | | 1 | 0- 1 |

SILVERA, CHARLES ANTHONY RYAN

| 1949 NY A C | | 1 | .000 |

SILVESTRI, KENNETH JOSEPH

| 1950 PHI N C | | 1 | .000 |

SIMMONS, ALOYSIUS HARRY

1929 PHI A O		5	.300
1930 PHI A O		6	.364
1931 PHI A O		7	.333
1939 CIN N O		1	.250
		19	.329

SIMMONS, CURTIS THOMAS

| 1964 STL N P | | 2 | 0- 1 |

SIMPSON, HARRY LEON

| 1957 NY A 1 | | 5 | .083 |

SISLER, RICHARD ALLAN

1946 STL N H		2	.000
1950 PHI N O		4	.059
		6	.053

SISTI, SEBASTIAN DANIEL

| 1948 BOS N 2 | | 2 | .000 |

SKINNER, ROBERT RALPH

1960 PIT N O		2	.200
1964 STL N H		4	.667
		6	.375

SKOWRON, WILLIAM JOSEPH

1955 NY A 1		5	.333
1956 NY A 1		3	.100
1957 NY A 1		2	.000
1958 NY A 1		7	.259
1960 NY A 1		7	.375
1961 NY A 1		5	.353
1962 NY A 1		6	.222
1963 LA N 1		4	.385
		39	.293

SLAGLE, JAMES JULIUS

| 1907 CHI N O | | 5 | .273 |

SLAUGHTER, ENOS BRADSHEAR

1942 STL N O		5	.263
1946 STL N O		7	.320
1956 NY A O		6	.350
1957 NY A O		5	.250
1958 NY A H		4	.000
		27	.291

SMITH, ALFRED JOHN

1936 NY N P		1	0- 0
1937 NY N P		2	0- 0
		3	0- 0

SMITH, ALPHONSE EUGENE

1954 CLE A O		4	.214
1959 CHI A O		6	.250
		10	.235

SMITH, CARL REGINALD

| 1967 BOS A O | | 7 | .250 |

SMITH, CLAY JAMIESON

| 1940 DET A P | | 1 | 0- 0 |

SMITH, EARL SUTTON

1921 NY N C		3	.000
1922 NY N C		4	.143
1925 PIT N C		6	.350
1927 PIT N C		3	.000
1928 STL N C		1	.750
		17	.239

SMITH, ELMER JOHN

1920 CLE A O		5	308
1922 NY A H		2	.000
		7	.267

SMITH, HAROLD WAYNE

| 1960 PIT N C | | 3 | .375 |

SMITH, HARRY THOMAS

| 1903 PIT N C | | 1 | .000 |

SMITH, JAMES LAWRENCE

| 1919 CIN N R | | 1 | .000 |

SMITH, ROBERT ELDRIDGE

| 1932 CHI N P | | 1 | 0- 0 |

SMITH, SHERROD MALONE

1916 BRO N P		1	0- 1
1920 BRO N P		2	1- 1
		3	1- 2

SNIDER, EDWIN DONALD

1949 BRO N O		5	.143
1952 BRO N O		7	.345
1953 BRO N O		6	.320
1955 BRO N O		7	.320
1956 BRO N O		7	.304
1959 LA N O		4	.200
		36	.286

SNODGRASS, FRED CARLISLE

1911 NY N O		6	.105
1912 NY N O		8	.212
1913 NY N 1-O		2	.333
		16	.182

SNYDER, FRANK J.

1921 NY N C		7	.364
1922 NY N C		4	.333
1923 NY N C		5	.118
1924 NY N H		1	.000
		17	.273

SNYDER, RUSSELL HENRY

| 1966 BAL A O | | 3 | .167 |

SOUTHWORTH, WILLIAM HARRISON

1924 NY N O		5	.000
1926 STL N O		7	.345
		12	.333

SPAHN, WARREN EDWARD

1948 BOS N P		3	1- 1
1957 MIL N P		2	1- 1
1958 MIL N P		3	2- 1
		8	4- 3

SPARMA, JOSEPH BLASE

| 1968 DET A P | | 1 | 0- 0 |

SPEAKER, TRISTRAM E.

1912 BOS A O		8	.300
1915 BOS A O		5	.294
1920 CLE A O		7	.320
		20	.306

SPEECE, BYRON FRANKLIN

| 1924 WAS A P | | 1 | 0- 0 |

SPENCER, GEORGE ELWELL

| 1951 NY N P | | 2 | 0- 0 |

SPENCER, ROY HAMPTON

| 1927 PIT N C | | 1 | .000 |

SPIEZIO, EDWARD WAYNE

1967 STL N H		1	.000
1968 STL N H		1	1.000
		2	.500

SPOONER, KARL BENJAMIN

| 1955 BRO N P | | 2 | 0- 1 |

STAFFORD, WILLIAM CHARLES

1960 NY A P		2	0- 0
1961 NY A P		1	0- 0
1962 NY A P		1	1- 0
		4	1- 0

STAHL, CHARLES SYLVESTER

| 1903 BOS A O | | 8 | .303 |

STAHL, GARLAND

| 1912 BOS A 1 | | 8 | .281 |

STAINBACK, GEORGE TUCKER

1942 NY A H		2	.000
1943 NY A O		5	.176
		7	.176

STALEY, GERALD LEE

| 1959 CHI A P | | 4 | 0- 1 |

STANAGE, OSCAR HARLAND

| 1909 DET A C | | 2 | .200 |

STANGE, ALBERT LEE

| 1967 BOS A P | | 1 | 0- 0 |

STANKY, EDWARD RAYMOND

1947 BRO N 2		7	.240
1948 BOS N 2		6	.286
1951 NY N 2		6	.136
		19	.213

STANLEY, FREDERICK BLAIR

| 1976 NY A S | | 4 | .167 |

STANLEY, MITCHELL JACK

| 1968 DET A S-O | | 7 | .214 |

STARGELL, WILVER DORNEL

| 1971 PIT N O | | 7 | .208 |

STAUB, DANIEL JOSEPH

| 1973 NY N O | | 7 | .423 |

STEINFELDT, HARRY M.

1906 CHI N 3		6	.250
1907 CHI N 3		5	.471
1908 CHI N 3		5	.250
1910 CHI N 3		5	.100
		21	.260

STENGEL, CHARLES DILLON

1916 BRO N O		4	.364
1922 NY N O		2	.400
1923 NY N O		6	.417
		12	.393

STEPHENS, VERNON DECATUR

| 1944 STL A S | | 6 | .227 |

STEPHENSON, JACKSON RIGGS

1929 CHI N O		5	.316
1932 CHI N O		4	.444
		9	.378

STEPHENSON, JERRY JOSEPH

| 1967 BOS A P | | 1 | 0- 0 |

STEPHENSON, WALTER MC QUEEN

| 1935 CHI N H | | 1 | .000 |

```
YR   CL LEA POS  GP    G    REC          YR   CL LEA POS  GP    G    REC          YR   CL LEA POS  GP    G    REC

STEWART, JAMES FRANKLIN                  TAYLOR, THOMAS LIVINGSTONE              TINKER, JOSEPH BERT
1970 CIN N  H          2    .000         CARLTON                                 1906 CHI N  S          6    .167
                                         1924 WAS A  3          3    .000         1907 CHI N  S          5    .154
STEWART, WALTER CLEVELAND                                                        1908 CHI N  S          5    .263
1933 WAS A  P          1    0- 1         TEBBETTS, GEORGE ROBERT                 1910 CHI N  S          5    .333
                                         1940 DET A  C          4    .000                               21   .235
STIRNWEISS, GEORGE HENRY
1943 NY  A  H          1    .000         TENACE, FURY GENE                       TINNING, LYLE FORREST
1947 NY  A  2          7    .259         1972 OAK A  C-1        7    .348         1932 CHI N  P          2    0- 0
1949 NY  A  H          1    .000         1973 OAK A  C-1        7    .158
                       9    .250         1974 OAK A  1          5    .222         TIPTON, JOSEPH JOHN
                                                                19   .255         1948 CLE A  H          1    .000
STOCK, MILTON JOSEPH
1915 PHI N  3          5    .118         TERRY, RALPH WILLARD                    TOBIN, JAMES ANTHONY
                                         1960 NY  A  P          2    0- 2         1945 DET A  P          1    0- 0
STONE, GEORGE HEARD                      1961 NY  A  P          2    0- 1
1973 NY  N  P          2    0- 0         1962 NY  A  P          3    2- 1         TODT, PHILIP JULIUS
                                         1963 NY  A  P          1    0- 0         1931 PHI A  H          1    .000
STOTTLEMYRE, MELVIN LEON                 1964 NY  A  P          1    0- 0
1964 NY  A  P          3    1- 1                                9    2- 4         TOLAN, ROBERT
                                                                                 1967 STL N  H          3    .000
STRANG, SAMUEL NICKLIN                   TERRY, WILLIAM HAROLD                   1968 STL N  H          1    .000
1905 NY  N  H          1    .000         1924 NY  N  1          5    .429         1970 CIN N  O          5    .211
                                         1933 NY  N  1          5    .273         1972 CIN N  O          7    .269
STRICKLAND, GEORGE BEVAN                 1936 NY  N  1          6    .240                               16   .229
1954 CLE A  S          3    .000                                16   .295
                                                                                 TOLSON, CHARLES JULIUS
STRUNK, AMOS AARON                       TESREAU, CHARLES MONROE                 1929 CHI N  H          1    .000
1910 PHI A  O          4    .278         1912 NY  N  P          3    1- 2
1911 PHI A  H          1    .000         1913 NY  N  P          2    0- 1         TONEY, FREDERICK ARTHUR
1913 PHI A  O          5    .118         1917 NY  N  P          1    0- 0         1921 NY  N  P          2    0- 0
1914 PHI A  O          2    .286                                6    1- 3
1918 BOS A  O          6    .174                                                 TORPORCER, GEORGE
                       18   .200         THEODORE, GEORGE BASIL                  1926 STL N  H          1    .000
                                         1973 NY  N  O          2    .000
STUART, RICHARD LEE                                                              TORGESON, CLIFFORD EARL
1960 PIT N  1          5    .150         THEVENOW, THOMAS JOSEPH                 1948 BOS N  1          5    .389
1966 LA  A  H          2    .000         1926 STL N  S          7    .417         1959 CHI A  1          3    .000
                       7    .136         1928 STL N  S          1    .000                               8    .368
                                                                8    .417
STURDIVANT, THOMAS VIRGIL                                                        TORRE, FRANK JOSEPH
1955 NY  A  P          2    0- 0         THOMAS, ALPHONSE THOMAS                 1957 MIL N  1          7    .300
1956 NY  A  P          2    1- 0         1932 WAS A  P          2    0- 0         1958 MIL N  1          7    .176
1957 NY  A  P          2    0- 0                                                                        14   .222
                       6    1- 0         THOMAS, CHESTER DAVID
                                         1915 BOS A  C          2    .200         TOWNE, JAY KING
STURM, JOHN PETER JOSEPH                 1916 BOS A  C          3    .143         1906 CHI N  H          1    .000
1941 NY  A  1          5    .286         1920 CLE A  C          1    .000
                                                                6    .167         TRACEWSKI, RICHARD JOSEPH
SULLIVAN, WILLIAM JOSEPH JR.                                                     1963 LA  N  2          4    .154
1940 DET A  C          5    .154         THOMAS, FREDERICK HARVEY                1965 LA  N  2          6    .118
                                         1918 BOS A  3          6    .125         1968 DET A  3          2    .000
SULLIVAN, WILLIAM JOSEPH SR.                                                                            12   .133
1906 CHI A  C          6    .000         THOMAS, GEORGE EDWARD
                                         1967 BOS A  O          2    .000         TRAYNOR, HAROLD JOSEPH
SUMMA, HOMER WAYNE                                                               1925 PIT N  3          7    .346
1929 PHI A  H          1    .000         THOMAS, IRA FELIX                       1927 PIT N  3          4    .200
                                         1908 DET A  C          2    .500                               11   .293
SUMMERS, OREN EDGAR                      1910 PHI A  C          4    .250
1908 DET A  P          2    0- 2         1911 PHI A  C          4    .083         TRESH, THOMAS MICHAEL
1909 DET A  P          2    0- 2                                10   .214         1962 NY  A  O          7    .321
                       4    0- 4                                                 1963 NY  A  O          4    .200
                                         THOMAS, MYLES LEWIS                     1964 NY  A  O          7    .273
SUNDRA, STEPHEN RICHARD                  1926 NY  A  P          2    0- 0                               18   .277
1939 NY  A  P          1    0- 0
                                         THOMPSON, DONALD NEWLIN                 TROUT, PAUL HOWARD
SUTTON, DONALD HOWARD                    1953 BRO N  O          2    .000         1940 DET A  P          1    0- 1
1974 LA  N  P          2    1- 0                                                 1945 DET A  P          2    1- 1
                                         THOMPSON, EUGENE EARL                                          3    1- 2
SWIFT, ROBERT VIRGIL                     1939 CIN N  P          1    0- 1
1945 DET A  C          3    .250         1940 CIN N  P          1    0- 1         TROWBRIDGE, ROBERT
                                                                2    0- 2         1957 MIL N  P          1    0- 0
SWOBODA, RONALD ALAN
1969 NY  N  O          4    .400         THOMPSON, HENRY CURTIS                  TRUCKS, VIRGIL OLIVER
                                         1951 NY  N  O          5    .143         1945 DET A  P          2    1- 0
TANNEHILL, LEE FORD                      1954 NY  N  3          4    .364
1906 CHI A  S          3    .111                                9    .240         TUCKER, THURMAN LOWELL
                                                                                 1948 CLE A  O          1    .333
TARTABULL, JOSE                          THOMPSON, JOHN GUS
1967 BOS A  O          7    .154         1903 PIT N  P          1    0- 0         TURLEY, ROBERT LEE
                                                                                 1955 NY  A  P          3    0- 1
TATE, HENRY BENNETT                      THOMSON, ROBERT BROWN                   1956 NY  A  P          3    0- 1
1924 WAS A  H          3    .000         1951 NY  N  3          6    .237         1957 NY  A  P          3    1- 0
                                                                                 1958 NY  A  P          4    2- 1
TAYLOR, JAMES HARRY                      THORPE, JAMES FRANCIS                   1960 NY  A  P          2    1- 0
1947 BRO N  P          1    0- 0         1917 NY  N  O          1    .000                               15   4- 3

TAYLOR, JAMES WREN                       THRONEBERRY, MARVIN EUGENE             TURNER, JAMES RILEY
1929 CHI N  C          5    .176         1958 NY  A  H          1    .000         1940 CIN N  P          1    0- 1
                                                                                 1942 NY  A  P          1    0- 0
TAYLOR, RONALD WESLEY                    TIANT, LUIS CLEMENTE                                            2    0- 1
1964 STL N  P          2    0- 0         1975 BOS A  P          3    2- 0
1969 NY  N  P          2    0- 0                                                 TURNER, THOMAS RICHARD
                       4    0- 0         TIDROW, RICHARD WILLIAM                 1944 STL A  H          1    .000
                                         1976 NY  A  P          2    0- 0
```

YR	CL LEA POS	GP	G	REC

TYLER, GEORGE ALBERT
1914 BOS N	P	1	0- 0	
1918 CHI N	P	3	1- 1	
		4	1- 1	

UHLAENDER, THEODORE OTTO
| 1972 CIN N | H | 4 | | .250 |

UHLE, GEORGE ERNEST
| 1920 CLE A | P | 2 | 0- 0 | |

VALDESPINO, HILARIO
| 1965 MIN A | O | 5 | | .273 |

VANCE, CLARENCE ARTHUR
| 1934 STL N | P | 1 | 0- 0 | |

VANDENBERG, HAROLD HARRIS
| 1945 CHI N | P | 3 | 0- 0 | |

VANDER MEER, JOHN SAMUEL
| 1940 CIN N | P | 1 | 0- 0 | |

VAUGHAN, JOSEPH FLOYD
| 1947 BRO N | H | 3 | | .500 |

VAUGHN, JAMES LESLIE
| 1918 CHI N | P | 3 | 1- 2 | |

VEACH, ROBERT HENRY
| 1925 WAS A | H | 2 | | .000 |

VEALE, ROBERT ANDREW
| 1971 PIT N | P | 1 | 0- 0 | |

VERBAN, EMIL MATTHEW
| 1944 STL N | 2 | 6 | | .412 |

VEIL, FREDERICK WILLIAM
| 1903 PIT N | P | 1 | 0- 0 | |

VELEZ, OTONIEL
| 1976 NY A | H | 3 | | .000 |

VERSALLES, ZOILO
| 1965 MIN A | S | 7 | | .286 |

VIRDON, WILLIAM CHARLES
| 1960 PIT N | O | 7 | | .241 |

VOISELLE, WILLIAM SYMMES
| 1948 BOS N | P | 2 | 0- 1 | |

WADE, BENJAMIN STYRON
| 1953 BRO N | P | 2 | 0- 0 | |

WAGNER, CHARLES F.
| 1912 BOS A | S | 8 | | .167 |

WAGNER, HAROLD EDWARD
| 1946 BOS A | C | 5 | | .000 |

WAGNER, JOHN PETER
1903 PIT N	S	8		.222
1909 PIT N	S	7		.333
		15		.275

WAITKUS, EDWARD STEPHEN
| 1950 PHI N | 1 | 4 | | .267 |

WALBERG, GEORGE ELVIN
1929 PHI A	P	2	1- 0	
1930 PHI A	P	1	0- 1	
1931 PHI A	P	2	0- 0	
		5	1- 1	

WALKER, ALFRED BLUFORD
| 1956 BRO N | H | 2 | | .000 |

WALKER, CLARENCE WILLIAM
| 1916 BOS A | O | 3 | | .273 |

WALKER, FRED
1941 BRO N	O	5		.222
1947 BRO N	O	7		.222
		12		.222

WALKER, GERALD HOLMES
1934 DET A	H	3		.333
1935 DET A	O	3		.250
		6		.286

WALKER, HARRY WILLIAM
1942 STL N	H	1		.000
1943 STL N	O	5		.167
1946 STL N	O	7		.412
		13		.278

WALKER, HARVEY WILLOS
| 1945 DET A | H | 2 | | .500 |

WALKER, JAMES LUKE
| 1971 PIT N | P | 1 | 0- 0 | |

WALKER, WILLIAM HENRY
| 1934 STL N | P | 2 | 0- 2 | |

WALSH, EDWARD AUGUSTIN
| 1906 CHI A | P | 2 | 2- 0 | |

WALSH, JAMES CHARLES
1914 PHI A	O	3		.333
1916 BOS A	O	1		.000
		4		.222

WALTERS, WILLIAM HENRY
1939 CIN N	P	2	0- 2	
1940 CIN N	P	2	2- 0	
		4	2- 2	

WAMBGANSS, WILLIAM ADOLPH
| 1920 CLE A | 2 | 7 | | .154 |

WANER, LLOYD JAMES
| 1927 PIT N | O | 4 | | .400 |

WANER, PAUL GLEE
| 1927 PIT N | O | 4 | | .333 |

WARD, AARON LEE
1921 NY A	2	8		.231
1922 NY A	2	5		.154
1923 NY A	2	6		.417
		19		.286

WARNEKE, LONNIE
1932 CHI N	P	2	0- 1	
1935 CHI N	P	3	2- 0	
		5	2- 1	

WARWICK, CARL WAYNE
| 1964 STL N | H | 5 | | .750 |

WASDELL, JAMES CHARLES
| 1941 BRO N | O | 3 | | .200 |

WASHBURN, RAY CLARK
1967 STL N	P	2	0- 0	
1968 STL N	P	2	1- 1	
1970 CIN N	P	1	0- 0	
		5	1- 1	

WASHINGTON, CLAUDELL
| 1974 OAK A | O | 5 | | .571 |

WASHINGTON, HERBERT LEE
| 1974 OAK A | R | 3 | | .000 |

WASLEWSKI, GARY LEE
| 1967 BOS A | P | 2 | 0- 0 | |

WATKINS, GEORGE ARCHIBALD
1930 STL N	O	4		.167
1931 STL N	O	5		.286
		9		.231

WATSON, JOHN REEVES
1923 NY N	P	1	0- 0	
1924 NY N	P	1	0- 0	
		2	0- 0	

WATT, EDWARD DEAN
1969 BAL A	P	2	0- 1	
1970 BAL A	P	1	0- 1	
1971 BAL A	P	2	0- 1	
		5	0- 3	

WEATHERLY, CYRIL ROY
| 1943 NY A | H | 1 | | .000 |

WEAVER, GEORGE DAVIS
1917 CHI A	S	6		.333
1919 CHI A	3	8		.324
		14		.327

WEAVER, MONTGOMERY MORTON
| 1933 WAS A | P | 1 | 0- 1 | |

WEBB, JAMES LEVERNE
| 1945 DET A | S | 7 | | .185 |

WEIS, ALBERT JOHN
| 1969 NY N | 2 | 5 | | .455 |

WENSLOFF, CHARLES WILLIAM
| 1947 NY A | P | 1 | 0- 0 | |

WERBER, WILLIAM MURRAY
1939 CIN N	3	4		.250
1940 CIN N	3	7		.370
		11		.326

WERT, DONALD RALPH
| 1968 DET A | 3 | 6 | | .118 |

WERTZ, VICTOR WOODROW
| 1954 CLE A | 1 | 4 | | .500 |

WESTLAKE, WALDON THOMAS
| 1954 CLE A | O | 2 | | .143 |

WESTRUM, WESLEY NOREEN
1951 NY N	C	6		.235
1954 NY N	C	4		.273
		10		.250

WHEAT, ZACHARY DAVIS
1916 BRO N	O	5		.211
1920 BRO N	O	7		.333
		12		.283

WHITE, ERNEST DANIEL
1942 STL N	P	1	1- 0	
1943 STL N	R	1	0- 0	
		2	1- 0	
				.000

WHITE, GUY HARRIS
| 1906 CHI A | P | 3 | 1- 1 | |

WHITER, JOYNER CLIFFORD
1934 DET A	O	7		.130
1935 DET A	O	5		.263
		12		.190

WHITE, ROY HILTON
| 1976 NY A | O | 4 | | .133 |

WHITE, WILLIAM DEKOVA
| 1964 STL N | 1 | 7 | | .111 |

WHITEHEAD, BURGESS URQUHART
1934 STL N	S	1		.000
1936 NY N	2	6		.048
1937 NY N	2	5		.250
		12		.135

WHITEHILL, EARL OLIVER
| 1933 WAS A | P | 1 | 1- 0 | |

WHITEMAN, GEORGE
| 1918 BOS A | O | 6 | | .250 |

WHITMAN, DICK CORWIN
1949 BRO N	H	1		.000
1950 PHI N	H	3		.000
		4		.000

WHITTED, GEORGE BOSTIC
1914 BOS N	O	4		.214
1915 PHI N	1-O	5		.067
		9		.138

WICKER, KEMP CASWELL
| 1937 NY A | P | 1 | 0- 0 | |

WILCOX, MILTON EDWARD
| 1970 CIN N | P | 2 | 0- 1 | |

WILHELM, JAMES HOYT
| 1954 NY N | P | 2 | 0- 0 | |

WILHOIT, JOSEPH WILLIAM
| 1917 NY N | H | 2 | | .000 |

WILKINSON, ROY HAMILTON
| 1919 CHI A | P | 2 | 0- 0 | |

WILKS, THEODORE
1944 STL N	P	2	0- 1	
1946 STL N	P	1	0- 0	
		3	0- 1	

WILLETT, ROBERT EDGAR
| 1909 DET A | P | 2 | 0- 0 | |

WILLEY, CARLTON FRANCIS
| 1958 MIL N | P | 1 | 0- 0 | |

YR	CL	LEA	POS	GP	G	REC

WILLIAMS, CLAUDE PRESTON
1917	CHI	A	P	1		0- 0
1919	CHI	A	P	3		0- 3
				4		0- 3

WILLIAMS, DAVID CARLOUS
1951	NY	N	H	2		.000
1954	NY	N	2	4		.000
				6		.000

WILLIAMS, DEWEY EDGAR
| 1945 | CHI | N | C | 2 | | .000 |

WILLIAMS, EDWIN DIBRELL
| 1931 | PHI | A | S | 7 | | .320 |

WILLIAMS, RICHARD HIRSHFELD
| 1953 | BRO | N | H | 3 | | .500 |

WILLIAMS, STANLEY WILSON
1959	LA	N	P	1		0- 0
1963	NY	A	P	1		0- 0
				2		0- 0

WILLIAMS, THEODORE SAMUEL
| 1946 | BOS | A | O | 7 | | .200 |

WILLIS, RONALD EARL
1967	STL	N	P	3		0- 0
1968	STL	N	P	3		0- 0
				6		0- 0

WILLIS, VICTOR GAZAWAY
| 1909 | PIT | N | P | 2 | | 0- 1 |

WILLOUGHBY, JAMES ARTHUR
| 1975 | BOS | A | P | 3 | | 0- 1 |

WILLS, MAURICE MORNING
1959	LA	N	S	6		.250
1963	LA	N	S	4		.133
1965	LA	N	S	7		.367
1966	LA	N	S	4		.077
				21		.244

WILSON, ARTHUR EARL
1911	NY	N	C	1		.000
1912	NY	N	C	2		1.000
1913	NY	N	C	3		.000
				6		.200

WILSON, GEORGE WASHINGTON
| 1956 | NY | A | H | 1 | | .000 |

WILSON, JAMES
1928	STL	N	C	3		.091
1930	STL	N	C	4		.267
1931	STL	N	C	7		.217
1940	CIN	N	C	6		.353
				20		.242

WILSON, JOHN OWEN
| 1909 | PIT | N | O | 7 | | .154 |

WILSON, LEWIS ROBERT
1924	NY	N	O	7		.233
1929	CHI	N	O	5		.471
				12		.319

WILSON, ROBERT EARL
| 1968 | DET | A | P | 1 | | 0- 1 |

WILTSE, GEORGE LE ROY
1911	NY	N	P	2		0- 0
1913	NY	N	R	2		.000
				2	4	0- 0
						.000

WINGO, IVY BROWN
| 1919 | CIN | N | C | 3 | | .571 |

WINTER, GEORGE LOVINGTON
| 1908 | DET | A | P | 1 | 2 | 0- 0 |

WISE, KENDALL COLE
| 1958 | MIL | N | H | 2 | | .000 |

WISE, RICHARD CHARLES
| 1975 | BOS | A | P | 2 | | 1- 0 |

WITT, GEORGE ADRIAN
| 1960 | PIT | N | P | 3 | | 0- 0 |

WITT, LAWTON WALTER
1922	NY	A	O	5		.222
1923	NY	A	O	6		.240
				11		.233

WOOD, JOSEPH
1912	BOS	A	P	4		3- 1
1920	CLE	A	O	4		.200
				4	8	3- 1
						.235

WOODESHICK, HAROLD JOSEPH
| 1967 | STL | N | P | 1 | | 0- 0 |

WOODLING, EUGENE RICHARD
1949	NY	A	O	3		.400
1950	NY	A	O	4		.429
1951	NY	A	O	6		.167
1952	NY	A	O	7		.348
1953	NY	A	O	6		.300
				26		.318

WOODWARD, WILLIAM FREDERICK
| 1970 | CIN | N | S | | | .200 |

WORKS, RALPH TALMADGE
| 1909 | DET | A | P | 1 | | 0- 0 |

WORTHINGTON, ALLAN FULTON
| 1965 | MIN | A | P | 2 | | 0- 0 |

WORTMAN, WILLIAM LEWIS
| 1918 | CHI | N | 2 | 1 | | .000 |

WRIGHT, FORREST GLENN
1925	PIT	N	S	7		.185
1927	PIT	N	S	4		.154
				11		.175

WYATT, JOHN THOMAS
| 1967 | BOS | A | P | 2 | | 1- 0 |

WYATT, JOHN WHITLOW
| 1941 | BRO | N | P | 2 | | 1- 1 |

WYCKOFF, JOHN WELDON
| 1914 | PHI | A | P | 1 | | 0- 0 |

WYNN, EARLY
1954	CLE	A	P	1		0- 1
1959	CHI	A	P	3		1- 1
				4		1- 2

WYNN, JAMES SHERMAN
| 1974 | LA | N | O | 5 | | .188 |

WYSE, HENRY WASHINGTON
| 1945 | CHI | N | P | 3 | | 0- 1 |

YASTRZEMSKI, CARL MICHAEL
1967	BOS	A	O	7		.400
1975	BOS	A	1-O	7		.310
				14		.352

YDE, EMIL OGDEN
1925	PIT	N	P	1	2	0- 1
1927	PIT	N	R		1	.000
				1	3	0- 1
						.000

YEAGER, STEPHEN WAYNE
| 1974 | LA | N | C | 4 | | .364 |

YERKES, STEPHEN DOUGLAS
| 1912 | BOS | A | 2 | | 8 | .250 |

YORK, PRESTON RUDOLPH
1940	DET	A	1	7		.231
1945	DET	A	1	7		.179
1946	BOS	A	1	7		.261
				21		.221

YOUNG, DENTON TRUE
| 1903 | BOS | A | P | 4 | | 2- 1 |

YOUNG, ROSS MIDDLEBROOK
1921	NY	N	O	8		.280
1922	NY	N	O	5		.375
1923	NY	N	O	6		.348
1924	NY	N	O	7		.185
				26		.285

YVARS, SALVADOR ANTHONY
| 1951 | NY | N | H | 1 | | .000 |

ZACHARY, JONATHAN THOMPSON WALTON
1924	WAS	A	P	2		2- 0
1925	WAS	A	P	1		0- 0
1928	NY	A	P	1		1- 0
				4		3- 0

ZACHRY, PATRICK PAUL
| 1976 | CIN | N | P | 1 | | 1- 0 |

ZARILLA, ALLEN LEE
| 1944 | STL | A | O | 4 | | .100 |

ZEIDER, ROLLA HUBERT
| 1918 | CHI | N | 3 | 2 | | .000 |

ZIMMER, DONALD WILLIAM
1955	BRO	N	2	4		.222
1959	LA	N	S	1		.000
				5		.200

ZIMMERMAN, GERALD ROBERT
1961	CIN	N	C	2		.000
1965	MIN	A	C	2		.000
				4		.000

ZIMMERMAN, HENRY
1907	CHI	N	2	1		.000
1910	CHI	N	2	5		.235
1917	NY	N	3	6		.120
				12		.163

ZUBER, WILLIAM HENRY
| 1946 | BOS | A | P | 1 | | 0- 0 |

V BEST LIFETIME MARKS

MANAGERIAL LEADERS
(Top Five in Each Classification)

SEASONS MANAGED —Connie Mack 53, John McGraw 34, Bucky Harris 29, Bill McKechnie 25, Casey Stengel 25.

PENNANTS WON —McGraw 10, Stengel 10, Mack 9, Joe McCarthy 9, Walter Alston 7, Miller Huggins 6, Harry Wright 6.

WORLD SERIES WON—McCarthy 7, Stengel 7, Mack 5, Alston 4, McGraw 3, Huggins 3.

THREE THOUSAND HITTERS
(Players Who Have Amassed 3,000 or More Hits in the Majors)

	YEARS	GAMES	HITS		YEARS	GAMES	HITS
Ty Cobb	24	3,033	4,191	Willie Mays	22	2,992	3,283
Stan Musial	21	3,026	3,630	Nap Lajoie	21	2,475	3,251
Cap Anson	27	2,509	3,516	Paul Waner	20	2,549	3,152
Tris Speaker	22	2,789	3,515	Al Kaline	22	2,834	3,007
Hank Aaron	23	3,298	3,771	Roberto			
Honus Wagner	21	2,785	3,430	Clemente	18	2,433	3,000
Eddie Collins	25	2,826	3,313				

THREE HUNDRED VICTORIES
(Pitchers Who Have Won 300 or More Games in the Majors)

		Games				Games	
	Years	Pitched	Won		Years	Pitched	Won
Cy Young	22	867	507	Tim Keefe	14	588	345
Walter Johnson	21	805	414	John Clarkson	12	523	327
Grover Alexander	20	696	373	Ed Plank	17	605	326
Christy Mathewson	17	632	373	Mike Welch	13	540	315
Warren Spahn	21	750	363	Hoss Radbourn	11	514	306
Jim Galvin	15	682	362	Lefty Grove	17	616	300
Kid Nichols	15	597	361	Early Wynn	23	691	300

FIFTY HOMERS A SEASON
(Players Who Have Hit 50 or More Homers in a Season)

	YEAR	HOMERS		YEAR	HOMERS
Roger Maris	1961	61	Mickey Mantle	1961	54
Babe Ruth	1927	60	Ralph Kiner	1949	54
Babe Ruth	1921	59	Mickey Mantle	1956	52
Hank Greenberg	1938	58	Willie Mays	1965	52
Jimmy Foxx	1932	58	Ralph Kiner	1947	51
Hack Wilson	1930	56	Willie Mays	1955	51
Babe Ruth	1920	54	Johnny Mize	1947	51
Babe Ruth	1928	54	Jimmy Foxx	1938	50

FOUR HUNDRED HOMER HITTERS
(Players Who Have Hit 400 or More Homers in the Majors)

	YEARS	HOMERS		YEARS	HOMERS
Hank Aaron	23	755	Eddie Mathews	17	512
Babe Ruth	22	714	Ernie Banks	19	512
Willie Mays	22	660	Mel Ott	22	511
Frank Robinson	21	586	Lou Gehrig	17	493
Harmon Killebrew	22	573	Stan Musial	22	475
Mickey Mantle	18	536	Willie McCovey	18	465
Jimmy Foxx	20	534	Billy Williams	18	426
Ted Williams	19	521	Duke Snider	18	407

TRIPLE PLAY UNASSISTED

Neal Ball (shortstop), Cleveland AL vs. Boston, July 19, 1909.
George H. Burns (first base), Boston AL vs. Cleveland, Sept. 14, 1923.
Ernest K. Padgett (shortstop), Boston NL vs. Philadelphia, Oct. 6, 1923.
Forest Glenn Wright (shortstop), Pittsburgh NL vs. St. Louis, May 7, 1925.
James E. Cooney (shortstop), Chicago NL at Pittsburgh, May 30, 1927.
John H. Neun (first base), Detroit AL vs. Cleveland, May 31, 1927.
Ronald L. Hansen (shortstop), Washington AL at Cleveland, July 30, 1968

NOTE: William A. Wambganss (second base), Cleveland AL vs. Brooklyn NL, Oct. 10, 1920 (World Series).

FOUR HUNDRED BATTERS
(Players Who Have Hit .400 or More per Season, at Least 100 Games)

	YEAR	B.A.		YEAR	B.A.
Hugh Duffy	1894	.438	Tip O'Neill	1887	.492
Willie Keeler	1897	.432	Pete Browning	1887	.471
Rogers Hornsby	1924	.424	Denny Lyons	1887	.469
Jesse Burkett	1895	.423	Yank Robinson	1887	.426
Nap Lajoie	1901	.422	Cap Anson	1887	.421
Ty Cobb	1911	.420	Dan Brouthers	1887	.419
George Sisler	1922	.420	Reddy Mack	1887	.410
Jesse Burkett	1896	.410	Sam Thompson	1887	.406
Ty Cobb	1912	.410	Paul Radford	1887	.404
Dude Esterbrook	1884	.408	Harry Stovey	1887	.402
Ed Delahanty	1899	.408	Tom Burns	1887	.401
Joe Jackson	1911	.408			
George Sisler	1920	.407			
Fred Clarke	1897	.406	NOTE: In 1887, Walks counted as		
Ted Williams	1941	.406	Hits; if walks were not		
Harry Stovey	1884	.404	counted as hits, only three		
Sam Thompson	1894	.403	players would have hit over		
Harry Heilmann	1923	.403	.400		
Rogers Hornsby	1925	.403			
Jesse Burkett	1899	.402	Tip O'Neill	1887	.442
Ty Cobb	1922	.401	Denny Lyons	1887	.425
Rogers Hornsby	1922	.401	Pete Browning	1887	.418
Bill Terry	1930	.401			
Ed Delahanty	1894	.400			

HIGHEST LIFETIME BATTERS
(Players Whose Lifetime Average is .340 or Better)

	YEARS	B.A.		YEARS	B.A.
Ty Cobb	24	.367	Tris Speaker	22	.344
Rogers Hornsby	23	.358	Ted Williams	19	.344
Joe Jackson	13	.356	Babe Ruth	22	.342
Pete Browning	13	.355	Jesse Burkett	16	.342
Lefty O'Doul	11	.349	Harry Heilmann	17	.342
Dan Brouthers	19	.348	Bill Terry	14	.341
Ed Delahanty	16	.346	George Sisler	15	.340
Willie Keeler	19	.345	Lou Gehrig	17	.340
Billy Hamilton	14	.344			

SEVEN HUNDRED SLUGGERS
(Players who have Slugged .700 or more per Season, at least 100 Games,
Slugging Percentage equals Total Bases divided by At Bats)

	YEAR	S.A.		YEAR	S.A.
Babe Ruth	1920	.847	Hack Wilson	1930	.723
Babe Ruth	1921	.846	Rogers Hornsby	1922	.722
Babe Ruth	1927	.772	Lou Gehrig	1930	.721
Lou Gehrig	1927	.765	Babe Ruth	1928	.709
Babe Ruth	1923	.764	Al Simmons	1930	.708
Rogers Hornsby	1925	.756	Lou Gehrig	1934	.706
Jimmie Foxx	1932	.749	Mickey Mantle	1956	.705
Babe Ruth	1924	.739	Jimmie Foxx	1938	.704
Babe Ruth	1926	.737	Jimmie Foxx	1933	.703
Ted Williams	1941	.735	Stan Musial	1948	.702
Babe Ruth	1930	.732	Babe Ruth	1931	.700
Ted Williams	1957	.731			

HIGHEST LIFETIME SLUGGERS
(Players whose Lifetime Slugging Average is .520 or better)

	YEARS	S.A.		YEARS	S.A.
Babe Ruth	22	.690	Hack Wilson	12	.545
Ted Williams	19	.634	Chuck Klein	17	.543
Lou Gehrig	17	.632	Duke Snider	18	.540
Jimmie Foxx	20	.609	Dick Allen	14	.539
Hank Greenberg	13	.605	Frank Robinson	21	.537
Joe DiMaggio	13	.579	Mel Ott	22	.533
Rogers Hornsby	23	.577	Earl Averill	13	.533
Johnny Mize	15	.562	Babe Herman	15	.532
Stan Musial	22	.559	Ken Williams	14	.531
Willie Mays	22	.557	Willie McCovey	18	.531
Mickey Mantle	18	.557	Willie Stargell	15	.529
Hank Aaron	23	.555	Chick Hafey	13	.526
Ralph Kiner	10	.548	Hal Trosky	11	.522

HIGHEST SEASON ON-BASE AVERAGE
(Players with .490 or better On-Base Average per season, at least 100 games,
On-Base Average counts walks and hit-by-pitch as base hits)

	YEAR	OBA		YEAR	OBA
Ted Williams	1941	.551	Joe Kelley	1894	.501
John McGraw	1899	.545	Hugh Duffy	1894	.500
Babe Ruth	1923	.545	Ted Williams	1942	.499
Babe Ruth	1920	.530	Ted Williams	1947	.499
Ted Williams	1957	.528	Rogers Hornsby	1928	.498
Billy Hamilton	1894	.516	Ted Williams	1946	.497
Ted Williams	1954	.516	Ed Delahanty	1895	.496
Babe Ruth	1926	.516	Billy Hamilton	1896	.494
Mickey Mantle	1957	.515	Babe Ruth	1931	.494
Babe Ruth	1924	.513	Babe Ruth	1930	.493
Babe Ruth	1921	.512	Arky Vaughan	1935	.492
Rogers Hornsby	1924	.507	Tip O'Neill	1887	.492

HIGHEST LIFETIME ON-BASE AVERAGE
(Players whose Lifetime On-Base Average is .410 or better)

	YEARS	OBA		YEARS	OBA
Ted Williams	19	.483	Mickey Mantle	18	.423
Babe Ruth	22	.474	Clarence Childs	13	.421
John McGraw	16	.464	Denny Lyons	13	.419
Billy Hamilton	14	.457	Mickey Cochrane	13	.419
Lou Gehrig	17	.447	Stan Musial	22	.418
Rogers Hornsby	23	.434	Jesse Burkett	16	.418
Ty Cobb	24	.433	Mel Ott	22	.414
Jimmie Foxx	20	.430	Ed Delahanty	16	.412
Tris Speaker	22	.427	Hank Greenberg	13	.412
Ferris Fain	9	.425	Roy Thomas	13	.411
Dan Brouthers	19	.424	Charley Keller	13	.410
Eddie Collins	25	.424	Eddie Stanky	11	.410
Joe Jackson	13	.423	Jackie Robinson	10	.410
Max Bishop	12	.423	Harry Heilmann	17	.410

CONSECUTIVE RECORD STREAKS

(1) CLUB CONSECUTIVE MARKS

World Series Won—
5, New York AL (1949–53)
4, New York AL (1936–39)
3, Oakland AL (1972–75)

Pennants Won—
5, New York AL (1949–53)
5, New York AL (1960–64)
4, Boston NA (1872–75)
4, St. Louis AA (1885–88)
4, New York NL (1921–24)
4, New York AL (1936–39)
4, New York AL (1955–58)

Games Won—
26, New York NL (1916)
26, Boston NA (1875)
21, Chicago NL (1880)
21, Chicago NL (1935)
20, St. Louis UA (1884)
20, Providence NL (1884)
19, Chicago AL (1906)
19, New York AL (1947)

Games Lost—
26, Louisville AA (1889)
24, Cleveland NL (1899)
23, Philadelphia NL (1961)
23, Pittsburgh NL (1890)
22, Philadelphia AA (1890)
20, Boston AL (1906)
20, Philadelphia AL (1916)
20, Philadelphia AL (1943)
20, Louisville NL (1894)
20, Montreal NL (1969)

Games without being shut out—
308, New York AL (1931–33)
196, Athletics AA (1886–88)
182, Philadelphia NL (1893–95)

Innings shut out opponents—
56, Pittsburgh NL (1903)
47, Cleveland AL (1948)

Innings shut out by opponents—
48, Philadelphia AL (1906)
48, Chicago NL (1968)

Games in which homers were hit—
25, New York AL (1941)
24, Brooklyn NL (1953)

Errorless games—
15, Cincinnati NL (1975)
12, Detroit AL (1963)

(2) BATTING STREAKS
Games played—
2,130 H. L. Gehrig AL (1925–39)
1,117 B. L. Williams NL (1963–70)

Games scoring runs—
24, W. R. Hamilton NL (1894)
18, R. A. Rolfe AL (1939)
17, T. B. Kluszewski NL (1954)

Games hit safely—
56, J. P. DiMaggio AL (1941)
44, W. H. Keeler NL (1897)
37, T. F. Holmes NL (1945)

Games hit homer—
8, R. D. Long NL (1956)
6, K. R. Williams AL (1922)
6, H. L. Gehrig AL (1931)
6, R. E. Sievers AL (1957)
6, R. E. Maris AL (1961)
6, F. O. Howard AL (1968)
6, R. M. Jackson AL (1976)
Hits—
12, M. F. Higgins AL (1938)
12, W. Dropo AL (1952)
10, E. J. Delahanty NL (1897)
10, J. J.Gettman NL (1897)
10, E. J. Konetchy NL (1919)
10, H. S. Cuyler NL (1925)
10, C. J. Hafey NL (1929)
10, J. M. Medwick NL (1936)
10, W. W. Williams NL (1943)

Bases on balls—
7, W. G. Rogell AL (1938)
7, M. T. Ott NL (1943)
7, E. R. Stanky NL (1950)

Strikeouts—
14, W. A. Hands NL (1968)
13, J. J. Hannan AL (1968)

(3) FIELDING STREAKS
Games caught—
312, F. W. Hayes AL (1943–46)
233, R. C. Mueller NL (1943–46)

Catcher's chances without error—
950, L. P. Berra AL (1957–59)
805, J. A. Edwards NL (1970–71)

Catcher's games without error—
148, L. P. Berra AL (1957–59)
138, J. A. Edwards NL (1970–71)

Pitcher's chances without error—
273, C. W. Passeau NL (1941–46)
159, T. A. Lyons AL (1934–38)

Pitcher's games without error—
385, P. A. Lindblad AL (1966–74)
225, L. D. McDaniel NL (1964–68)

First baseman's chances without error—
1625, J. P. McInnis AL (1921–22)
1337, F. A. McCormick NL (1945–46)

First baseman's games without error—
178, J. M. Hegan AL (1970–73)
(Note: Hegan was used as a late-inning
defensive replacement in many of the
178 games)
163, J. P. McInnis AL (1921–22)
138, F. A. McCormick NL (1945–46)

Second baseman's chances without error—
458, K. J. Adair AL (1964–65)
418, K. D. Hubbs NL (1962)

Second baseman's games without error—
89, K. J. Adair AL (1964–65)
85, K. G. Boswell NL (1970)

Shortstop's chances without error—
383, J. J. Kerr NL (1946–47)
331, E. A. Brinkman AL (1972)

Shortstop's games without error—
72, E. A. Brinkman AL (1972)
68, J. J. Kerr NL (1946–47)

Third baseman's chances without error—
261, D. W. Money AL (1973–74)
209, J. H. Davenport NL (1966–68)

Third baseman's games without error—
97, J. H. Davenport NL (1966–68)
88, D. W. Money AL (1973–74)

Outfielder's chances without error—
568, C. C. Flood NL (1965–67)
439, L. E. Doby AL (1954–55)

Outfielder's games without error—
266, D. L. Demeter NL-AL (1962–65)
242, A. W. Kaline AL (1970–72)
226, C. C. Flood NL (1965–67)

(4) PITCHING STREAKS
Innings without relief—
1727, J. W. Taylor NL (1901–06)
337, W.H. Dineen AL (1904)

Games won—
24, C. O. Hubbell NL (1936–37)
24, A. G. Spalding NA (1875)
19, T. J. Keefe NL (1888)
19, R. W. Marquard NL (1912)
17, J. T. Allen AL (1936–37)
17, D. A. McNally AL (1968–69)
16, W. P. Johnson AL (1912)
16, J. Wood AL (1912)
16, R. M. Grove AL (1931)
16, L. T. Rowe AL (1934)

Games lost—
23, C. G. Curtis NL (1910–11)
19, R. Groom AL (1909)
19, J. H. Nabors AL (1916)
18, C. G. Curtis NL (1910)
18, R. L. Craig NL (1963)

Shut out games—
6, D. S. Drysdale NL (1968)
5, G. H. White AL (1904)

Shut out innings—
  58 2/3, D. S. Drysdale NL (1968)
  56, W. P. Johnson AL (1913)

Strikeouts—
  10, G. T. Seaver NL (1970)
  9, M. F. Welch NL (1884)
  8, C. G. Buffington NL (1885)
  8, E. L. Cushman AA (1885)
  8, M. G. Surkont NL (1953)
  8, J. J. Podres NL (1962)
  8, J. W. Maloney NL (1963)
  8, D. E. Wilson NL (1968)
  8, L. N. Ryan AL (1972, 1973)

Bases on balls—
  7, W. D. Gray AL (1909)
  6, W. H. Kennedy NL (1900)

Innings without base on balls—
  84 1/3, W. C. Fischer AL (1962)
  68, C. Mathewson NL (1913)
  68, R. L. Jones NL (1976)

LIFETIME MARKS
Season, Game, Inning

"Many" shows that the record is held jointly by more than two players or teams.

Number in parenthesis, following apostrophe, shows year in which record was made.

ML—Major Leagues, NL—National League, MNL—Modern National League (1900 to date), AL—American League, AA—American Association, PL—Players League, UA—Union Association

INDIVIDUAL BATTING RECORDS

Seasons
27 Anson, A. C., ML
26 McGuire, J. T., ML
25 Collins, E. T., AL
25 Wallace, R. J., ML
24 Cobb, T. R., AL
23 Maranville, W. J., NL
23 Hornsby, R., ML
23 Aaron, H. L., ML

Games—Lifetime
3298 Aaron, H. L., ML
3033 Cobb, T. R., AL
3026 Musial, S. F., NL
2992 Mays, W. H., NL
2826 Collins, E. T., AL
(3076 Aaron, H. L., NL)
Season (162-game schedule)
165 Wills, M. M., NL (1962)
165 Tovar, C. L., AL (1967)
Season (154-game schedule)
162 Barrett, J. E., AL (1904)
160 Groh, H. K., NL (1915)
Griffith, T. H., NL (1915)

At bats—Lifetime
12364 Aaron, H. L., ML
11429 Cobb, T. R., AL
10972 Musial, S. F., NL
10881 Mays, W. H., NL
10427 Wagner, J.P., NL
(11628 Aaron, H. L., NL)
Season (162-game schedule)
699 Cash, D., NL (1975)
692 Richardson, R. C., AL (1962)
Season (154-game schedule)
696 Jensen, F. D., AL (1936)
679 Kuenn, H. E., AL (1953)
Game (extra innings)
11 Many, NL/AL
Game (nine innings)
8 Many, NL
7 Many, MNL/AL
Inning
3 Many, NL/AL

Runs—Lifetime
2244 Cobb, T. R., AL
2174 Ruth, G. H., ML
2174 Aaron, H. L., ML
2062 Mays, W. H., NL
1969 Anson, A. C., ML
(2107 Aaron, H. L., NL)
Season
196 Hamilton, W. R., NL (1894)
177 Ruth, G. H., AL (1921)
158 Klein, C. H., MNL (1930)
Game
7 Hecker, G. J., AA (1886)
6 Pesky, J. M., AL (1946)
6 Many, NL
6 Ott, M. T., MNL (1934 and 1944)
Torre, F. J., (1957)

Inning
3 Burns, T. E., NL (1883)
Williamson, E. N., NL (1883)
3 White, S. C., AL (1953)
2 Many, MNL
Hits—Lifetime
4191 Cobb, T. R., AL
3771 Aaron, H. L., ML
3630 Musial, S. F., NL
3516 Anson, A. C., ML
3515 Speaker, T. E., AL
Season
257 Sisler, G. H., AL (1920)
254 O'Doul, F. J., NL (1929)
Terry, W. H. (1930)
Game (extra innings)
9 Burnett, J. H., AL (1932)
Game (nine innings)
7 Robinson, W., NL (1892)
7 Stennett, R. A. NL (1975)
6 Many, AL
Inning
3 Burns, T. E., NL (1883)
Williamson, E. N., NL (1883)
3 Stephens, G. E., AL (1953)
2 Many, MNL
Total Bases—Lifetime
6856 Aaron, H. L., ML
6134 Musial, S. F., NL
6066 Mays, W. H., NL
5863 Cobb, T. R., AL
5793 Ruth, G. H., ML
(6591 Aaron, H. L., NL)
Season
457 Ruth, G. H., AL (1921)
450 Hornsby, R., NL (1922)
Game (nine innings)
18 Adcock, J. W., NL (1954)
16 Cobb, T. R., AL (1925)
Gehrig, H. L., AL (1932)
Colavito, R. D., AL (1959)
Lynn, F. M., AL (1975)
Game (extra innings)
16 Seerey, J. P., AL (1948)
Foxx, J. E., AL (1932)
Inning
8 Many, NL/AL
Times on Base—Lifetime
5531 Cobb, T. R., AL
5282 Musial, S. F., NL
5107 Aaron, H. L., ML
4998 Speaker, T. E., AL
4971 Ruth, G. H., ML
Season
379 Ruth, G. H., AL (1923)
358 Hamilton, W. R., NL (1894)
334 O'Doul, F. J., MNL (1929)
Singles—Lifetime
3052 Cobb, T. R., AL
2650 Anson, A. C., ML
2641 Collins, E. T., AL

2534 Keeler, W. H., ML
2426 Wagner, J. P., NL
(2253 Musial, S. F., MNL)
Season
202 Keeler, W. H., NL (1898)
198 Waner, L. J., MNL (1927)
182 Rice, E. C., AL (1925)
Game (extra innings)
7 Burnett, J. H., AL (1932)
Game (nine innings)
6 Many, NL/AL
Inning
2 Many, NL/AL

Doubles—Lifetime
793 Speaker, T. E., AL
725 Musial, S. F., NL
724 Cobb, T. R., AL
651 Wagner, J. P., NL
650 Lajoie, N., ML
Season
67 Webb, E. W., AL (1931)
64 Medwick, J. M., NL (1936)
Game
(four doubles in a game)
4 Larkin, H. E., AA (1885)
  Milligan, J., AA (1886)
4 O'Rourke, J., NL (1880)
  Anson, A. C., NL (1883)
  Dalrymple, A. F., NL (1883)
  Tucker, T. J., NL (1893)
  Bonner, F. J., NL (1894)
  Kelley, J. J., NL (1894)
  Delahanty, E. J., NL (1899)
  Cravath, C. C., NL (1915)
  Sothern, D. E., NL (1930)
  Waner, P. G., NL (1932)
  Bartell, R. W., NL (1933)
  Lombardi, E. N., NL (1935)
  Medwick, J. M., NL (1937)
  Werber, W. M., NL (1940)
  Jones, W. E., NL (1949)
  Greengrass, J. R., NL (1954)
  Williams, B. L., NL (1969)
4 Dillon, F. E., AL (1901)
  Werber, W. M., AL (1935)
  Hayes, F. W., AL (1936)
  Kreevich, M. A., AL (1937)
  Owen, M. J., AL (1939)
  Lindell, J. H., AL (1944)
  Boudreau, L., AL· (1946)
  Zarilla, A. L., AL (1950)
  Wertz, V. W., AL (1956)
  Lau, C. R., AL (1962)
  Bruton, W. H., AL (1963)
  Cepeda, O. M., AL (1973)
  Mason, J. P., AL (1974)
  Duncan, D. E., AL (1975)
Inning
2 Many, NL/AL

Triples—Lifetime
312 Crawford, S. E., ML
297 Cobb, T. R., AL
252 Wagner, J. P., NL
246 Beckley, J. P., ML
227 Connor, R., ML
(231 Wagner, J. P., MNL)
Season
36 Wilson, J. O., NL (1912)
26 Jackson, J. J., AL (1912)
   Crawford, S. E., AL (1914)

Game
4 Strief, G. A., AA (1885)
4 Joyce, W. M., NL (1897)

(three triples since 1900)

3 Wolverton, H. S., MNL (1900)
  Sheckard, J. T., MNL (1901)
  Donlin, M. J., MNL (1903)
  Huggins, M. J., MNL (1904)
  Brain, D. L., MNL (1905 twice)
  Moran, P. J., MNL (1905)
  Wilson, J. O., MNL (1911)
  Youngs, R. M., MNL (1920)
  Powell, R. R., MNL (1921)
  Hollocher, C. J., MNL (1922)
  Bottomley, J. L., MNL (1923 and 1927)
  Bell, L. R., MNL (1926)
  Richbourg, L. C., MNL (1929)
  Bernier, C. R., MNL (1953)
  O'Connell, D. F., MNL (1956)
  Clemente, R. W., MNL (1958)
  Mays, W. H., MNL (1960)
  Banks, E., MNL (1966)
3 Flick, E. H., AL (1902)
  Bradley, W. J., AL (1903)
  Dougherty, P. H., AL (1903)
  Lush, W. L., AL (1903)
  Lajoie, N., AL (1904)
  Chase, H. H., AL (1906)
  Jackson, J. J., AL (1912)
  Williams, A. R., AL (1913)
  Jacobson, W. C., AL (1922)
  Judge, J. I., AL (1921)
  Tavener, J. A., AL (1925)
  Combs, E. B., AL (1927)
  Gehringer, C. L., AL (1929)
  Kuhel, J. A., AL (1937)
  DiMaggio, J. P., AL (1938)
  Chapman, W. B., AL (1939)
  Campaneris, D. B., AL (1967)
  Bumbry, A. B., AL (1973)

Inning
2 Wheeler, H. E., AA (1882)
  Stovey, H. D., AA (1884)
2 Hornung, M. J., NL (1882)
  Pietz, H. C., NL (1895)
  Freeman, J. B., NL (1900)
  Dahlen, W. F., NL (1900)
  Walker, W. C., NL (1926)
2 Zarilla, A. L., AL (1946)
  Coan, G. F., AL (1951)

Home Runs—Lifetime
755 Aaron, H. L., ML
714 Ruth, G. H., ML
660 Mays, W. H., NL
586 Robinson, F., ML
573 Killebrew, H. C., AL
(733 Aaron, H. L., NL)·
(708 Ruth, G. H., AL)
Season (162-game schedule)
61 Maris, R. E., AL (1961)
Season (154-game schedule)
60 Ruth, G. H., AL (1927)
56 Wilson, L. R., NL (1930)
Game (extra innings)
4 Seerey, J. P., AL (1948)
4 Klein, C. H., NL (1936)
Game (nine innings)
4 Lowe, R. L., NL (1894)
  Delahanty, E. J., NL (1896)

Hodges, G. R., NL (1950)
Adcock, J. W., NL (1954)
Mays, W. H., NL (1961)
Schmidt, M. J., NL (1976)
4 Gehrig, H. L., AL (1932)
Colavito, R. D., AL (1959)
Inning
2 Many, NL/AL

Runs Batted In—Lifetime
2297 Aaron, H. L., ML
2205 Ruth, G. H., ML
1990 Gehrig, H. L., AL
1954 Cobb, T. R., AL
1951 Musial, S. F., NL
(2202 Aaron, H. L., NL)
(2193 Ruth, G. H., AL)
Season
190 Wilson, L. R., NL (1930)
184 Gehrig, H. L., AL (1931)
Game
12 Bottomley, J. L., NL (1924)
11 Lazzeri, A. M., AL (1936)
Inning
7 Cartwright, E. H., AA (1890)
6 Many, NL/AL

Batting Average—Lifetime
.367 Cobb, T. R., AL
.358 Hornsby, R., ML
.356 Jackson, J. J., AL
.355 Browning, L. R., ML
.349 O'Doul, F. J., ML
(.359 Hornsby, R., NL)
Season
.438 Duffy, H., NL (1894)
.424 Hornsby, R., MNL (1924)
.422 Lajoie, N., AL (1901)

Slugging Average—Lifetime
.690 Ruth, G. H., ML
.634 Williams, T. S., AL
.632 Gehrig, H. L., AL
.609 Foxx, J. E., ML
.605 Greenberg, H. B., AL
(.692 Ruth, G. H., AL)
.578 Hornsby, R., NL)
Season
.847 Ruth, G. H., AL (1920)
.756 Hornsby, R., NL (1925)

On-Base Average—Lifetime
.483 Williams, T.S., AL
.474 Ruth, G. H., ML
.464 McGraw, J. J., NL
.457 Hamilton, W. R., ML
.447 Gehrig, H. L., AL
(.434 Hornsby, R., MNL)
Season
.551 Williams, T. S., AL (1941)
.545 McGraw, J. J., NL (1899)
.507 Hornsby, R., MNL (1924)

Bases on Balls—Lifetime
2057 Ruth, G. H., ML
2018 Williams, T. S., AL
1734 Mantle, M. C., AL
1708 Ott, M. T., NL
1614 Yost, E. F., AL
(2036 Ruth, G. H., AL)
Season (154-game schedule)
170 Ruth, G. H., AL (1923)
148 Stanky, E. R., NL (1945)

Season (162-game schedule)
148 Wynn, J. S., NL (1969)
Game
6 Wilmot, W. R., NL (1891)
6 Foxx, J. E., AL (1938)
5 Many, MNL
Inning
2 Many, NL/AL

Strikeouts—Lifetime
1710 Mantle, M. C., AL
1699 Killebrew, H. C., AL
1598 Stargell, W. D., NL
1584 Brock, L. C., NL
1532 Robinson, F., ML
Season (162-game schedule)
189 Bonds, B. L., NL (1970)
175 Nicholson, D. L., AL (1963)
Season (154-game schedule)
138 Lemon, J. R., AL (1956)
136 Herrera, J. F., NL (1960)
Game (extra innings)
6 Many, NL/AL
Game (nine innings)
5 Many, NL/AL
Inning
2 Many, NL/AL

Hit by Pitch—Lifetime (1887–date)
260 Jennings, H. A., ML
250 Tucker, T. J., ML
243 Hunt, R. K., NL
198 Robinson, F., ML
192 Minoso, O. A., ML
(250 Jennings, H. A., NL)
189 Minoso, O. A., AL)
Season
51 Jennings, H. A., NL (1896)
50 Hunt, R. K., MNL (1971)
25 Elberfeld, N. A., AL (1911)
Game
3 Many, NL/AL
Inning
2 Schmidt, W. R., NL (1959)
Thomas, F. J., NL (1959)
1 Many, AL

Note: Hit by pitch first in effect 1887.

Sacrifice Hits—Lifetime (1894–date)
511 Collins, E. T., AL
392 Daubert, J. E., NL
383 McInnis, J. P., ML
372 Keeler, W. H., ML
340 Chapman, R. J., AL
Season (including sacrifice flies)
67 Chapman, R. J., AL (1917)
46 Sheckard, J. T., NL (1909)
Season (no sacrifice flies)
46 Bradley, W. J., AL (1907)
43 Gleason, W. J., NL (1905)
Game
4 Killefer, W. H., AL (1910)
Barry, J. J., AL (1916)
Chapman, R. J., AL (1919)
4 Daubert, J. E., NL (1914)
Inning
2 Benton, J. A., AL (1941)
1 Many, NL

Note: Sacrifice hits were first recorded in 1889. They were credited to batters for advancing runners on any out and at-bats were charged. In 1894 the rule was changed so that only bunts were counted as sacrifices with no at-bats charged. A sacrifice fly was tabulated with no time at bat for scoring a runner with a fly ball out from 1908 to 1930, 1939 and 1954 to the present. In addition from 1926–1930 a sacrifice fly was counted for advancing any runner with a fly ball out.

Stolen Bases—Lifetime (1886–date)
  937 Hamilton, W. R., ML
  892 Cobb, T. R., AL
  865 Brock, L. C., NL
  791 Latham, W. A., ML
  744 Stovey, H. D., ML
Season (162-game schedule)
  118 Brock, L. C., NL (1974)
Season (154-game schedule)
  156 Stovey, H. D., AA (1888)
  115 Hamilton, W. R., NL (1891)
   96 Cobb, T. R., AL (1915)
   80 Bescher, R. H., MNL (1911)
Game
   7 Gore, G. F., NL (1881)
     Hamilton, W. R., NL (1894)
   6 Collins, E. T., AL (1912 twice)
   5 McGann, D. L., MNL (1904)
     Lopes, D. E., MNL (1974)

Inning
  3 Many, NL/AL

Note: Stolen bases were first recorded in 1886. They were credited to runners for any extra bases taken on pitches or hits. In 1898 the rule was changed so that only bases stolen on pitches without errors were counted as stolen bases. Gore's game record in 1881 was established before official tabulation but was documented in newspaper accounts.

INDIVIDUAL PITCHING RECORDS

Seasons
  28 Quinn, J. P., ML
  23 Wynn, E., AL
  22 Young, D. T., ML
  22 Pennock, H. J., AL
  22 Jones, S. P., AL
  22 Ruffing, C. H., AL
  (21 Spahn, W. E., NL
  21 Rixey, E., NL)

Games—Lifetime
  1070 Wilhelm, J. H., ML
  987 McDaniel, L. D., ML
  867 Young, D. T., ML
  865 McMahon, D. J., ML
  848 Face, E. L., ML
  (846 Face, E. L., NL
  805 Johnson, W. P., AL)
Season (162-game schedule)
  106 Marshall, M. G., NL (1974)
   88 Wood, W. F., AL (1968)

Season (154-game schedule)
  75 White, W. H., NL (1879)
  74 Konstanty, C. J., MNL (1950)
  70 Fornieles, J. M., AL (1960)

Innings Pitched—Lifetime
  7377 Young, D. T., ML
  5959 Galvin, J. F., ML
  5925 Johnson, W. P., AL
  5246 Spahn, W. E., NL
  5189 Alexander, G. C., NL
Season
  683 White, W. H., NL (1879)
  464 Walsh, E. A., AL (1908)
  434 McGinnity, J. J., MNL (1903)
Game (extra innings)
  26 Oeschger, J. C., NL (1920)
     Cadore, L. L., NL (1920)
  24 Coombs, J. W., AL (1906)
     Harris, J. W., AL (1906)

Complete Games—Lifetime
  751 Young, D. T., ML
  639 Galvin, J. F., ML
  555 Keefe, T. J., ML
  531 Johnson, W. P., AL
  530 Nichols, C. A., NL
  (560 Galvin, J. F., NL
  437 Alexander, G. C., MNL)
Season
  74 White, W. H., NL (1879)
  48 Chesbro, J. D., AL (1904)
  45 Willis, V. G., MNL (1902)
Games Won—Lifetime
  507 Young, D. T., ML
  414 Johnson, W. P., AL
  373 Mathewson, C., NL
  373 Alexander, G. C., NL
  363 Spahn, W. E., NL
Season
  60 Radbourn, C. G., NL (1884)
  41 Chesbro, J. D., AL (1904)
  40 Walsh, E. A., AL (1908)
  37 Mathewson, C., MNL (1908)

Games Lost—Lifetime
  308 Galvin, J. F., ML
  308 Young, D. T., ML
  281 Johnson, W. P., AL
  253 Powell, J. J., ML
  251 Rixey, E., NL
Season
  48 Coleman, J. F., NL (1883)
  29 Willis, V. G., MNL (1905)
  27 Townsend, J., AL (1904)

Shutouts—Lifetime
  113 Johnson, W. P., AL
   90 Alexander, G. C., NL
   83 Mathewson, C., NL
   77 Young, D. T., ML
   70 Plank, E. S., ML
Season
  16 Bradley, G. W., NL (1876)
     Alexander, G. C., NL (1916)
  13 Coombs, J. W., AL (1910)

Runs Allowed—Lifetime
  3168 Young, D. T., ML
  2117 Ruffing, C. H., AL
  2033 Grimes, B. A., MNL

Season
544 Coleman, J. F., NL (1883)
211 McGinnity, J. J., AL (1901)
196 Pittinger, C. R., MNL (1903)
Game
35 Rowe, D. E., NL (1882)
24 Travers, A. J., AL (1912)
21 Parker, H. P., MNL (1901)
Inning
16 Mullane, A. J., NL (1894)
13 O'Doul, F. J., AL (1923)
12 Kelleher, H. J., MNL (1938)

Hits Allowed—Lifetime
7078 Young, D. T., ML
6334 Galvin, J. F., ML
4920 Johnson, W. P., AL
4868 Alexander. G. C., MNL
4854 Nichols, C A., NL
(5490 Galvin, J. F., NL)
Season
809 Coleman, J. F., NL (1883)
401 McGinnity, J. J., AL (1901)
393 Pittinger, C. R., MNL (1903)
Game
36 Wadsworth, W. J., NL (1894)
26 Lisenbee, H. M., AL (1936)
26 Parker, H. P., MNL (1901)
Inning
13 Weidman, G. E., NL (1883)
12 Adkins, M. T., AL (1902)
11 Grabowski, R. J., MNL (1934)

Strikeouts—Lifetime
3508 Johnson, W. P., AL
3117 Gibson, R. NL
2855 Bunning, J. P., ML
2819 Young, D. T., ML
2799 Lolich, M. S., ML .
Season (162-game schedule)
383 Ryan, L. N., AL (1973)
382 Koufax, S., MNL (1965)
Season (154-game schedule)
505 Kilroy, M. A., AA (1886)
411 Radbourn, C. G., NL (1884)
349 Waddell, G. E., AL (1904)
269 Koufax, S., MNL (1961)
Game (extra innings)
21 Cheney, T. E., AL (1962)
Game (nine innings)
19 Sweeney, C. J., NL (1884)
Carlton, S. N., NL (1969)
Seaver, G. T., NL (1970)
19 Daly, H. I., UA (1884)
19 Ryan, L. N., AL (1974)
Inning
4 Many, NL/AL
Bases on Balls—Lifetime
1775 Wynn, E., AL
1637 Rusie, A. W., NL
1434 Spahn, W. E., MNL
Season
276 Rusie, A. W., NL (1890)
208 Feller, R. W. A., AL (1938)
185 Jones, S., MNL (1955)
Game
16 George, W. M., NL (1887)
VanHaltren, G. E., NL (1887)
16 Gruber, H. J., PL (1890)
16 Haas, B. P., AL (1915)
14 Mathewson, H., MNL (1906)

Inning
8 Gray, W. D., AL (1909)
7 Mullane, A. J., NL (1894)
Ewing, G. L., NL (1902)

Hit Batsmen (1887–date)
217 Fraser, C. C., ML
206 Johnson, W. P., AL
205 Hawley, E. P., ML
(195 Hawley, E. P., NL
154 Drysdale, D. S., MNL)
Season
54 Knell, P. H., AA (1891)
41 McGinnity, J. J., NL (1900)
32 Fraser, C. C., AL (1901)
Game
6 Knouff, E., AA (1887)
5 Shaw, S., NL (1893)
Hawley, E. P., NL (1896)
Bates, F. C., NL (1899)
4 Many, MNL/AL
Inning
3 Many, NL/AL

Homers Allowed—Lifetime
502 Roberts, R. E., ML
434 Spahn, W. E., NL
335 Wynn, E., AL
Season
56 Roberts, R. E., NL (1956)
43 Ramos, P., AL (1957)
Game
6 Benton, L. J., NL (1930)
Thurston, H. J., NL (1932)
Kerksieck, W. W., NL (1939)
6 Thomas, A. T., AL (1936)
Caster, G. J., AL (1940)
Inning
4 Many, NL/AL

Wild Pitches
Season
64 Stemmeyer, W., NL (1886)
30 Ames, L. K., MNL (1905)
21 Johnson, W. P., AL (1910)
Wilson, R. E., AL (1963)
Game
10 Ryan, J. J., NL (1876)
5 Wheatley, C., AL (1912)
5 Cheney, L. D., MNL (1918)
Inning
6 Cunningham, E. E., PL (1890)
4 Johnson, W. P., AL (1914)
3 Many, NL
Balks
Season
8 Shaw, R. J., NL (1963)
Bonham, W. G., NL (1974)
6 Boehling, J. J., AL (1915)
Raschi, V. A., AL (1950)
Game
5 Shaw, R. J., NL (1963)
4 Raschi, V. A., AL (1950)
Inning
3 Shoffner, M. J., AL (1930)
3 Shaw, R. J., NL (1963)
Owens, J. P., NL (1963)

Earned Run Average (Lowest)
Season
1.01 Leonard, H. B., AL (1914)

1.12 Gibson, R., NL (1968)

Note: Earned run average first recorded in 1912 for the NL and 1913 for the AL.

TEAM BATTING RECORDS

At Bats
Season (162-game schedule)
  5767 Cincinnati, NL (1968)
  5705 New York, AL (1964)
Season (154-game schedule)
  5667 Philadelphia, NL (1930)
  5646 Cleveland, AL (1936)
Game (extra innings)
  85 New York, AL (1962)
  89 New York, NL (1974)
Game (nine innings)
  66 Chicago, NL (1883)
  58 New York, MNL (1925 and 1931)
  56 New York, AL (1939)
Batters faced pitcher—inning
  23 Chicago, NL (1883)
  23 Boston, AL (1953)
  21 Brooklyn, MNL (1952)

Runs
Season
  1221 Boston, NL (1894)
  1067 New York, AL (1931)
  1004 St. Louis, MNL (1930)
Game
  36 Chicago, NL (1897)
  29 Boston, AL (1950)
     Chicago, AL (1955)
  28 St. Louis, MNL (1929)
Inning
  18 Chicago, NL (1883)
  17 Boston, AL (1953)
  15 Brooklyn, MNL (1952)

Hits
Season
  1783 Philadelphia, NL (1930)
  1724 Detroit, AL (1921)
Game (extra innings)
  33 Cleveland, AL (1932)
Game (nine innings)
  36 Philadelphia, NL (1894)
  31 New York, MNL (1901)
  30 New York, AL (1923)
Inning
  18 Chicago, NL (1883)
  14 Boston, AL (1953)
  12 St. Louis, MNL (1925)

Total bases
Season
  2703 New York, AL (1936)
  2684 Chicago, NL (1930)
Game
  60 Boston, AL (1950)
  55 Cincinnati, NL (1893)
  50 San Francisco, MNL (1958)
Inning
  29 Chicago, NL (1883)
  27 San Francisco, MNL (1961)
  25 Boston, AL (1940)

Batting Average
Season
  .343 Philadelphia, NL (1894)
  .319 New York, MNL (1930)
  .316 Detroit, AL (1921)

Note: In 1887 when walks counted as hits, Detroit NL hit .347.

Singles
Season
  1338 Philadelphia, NL (1894)
  1298 Detroit, AL (1921)
  1297 Pittsburgh, MNL (1922)
Game
  28 Philadelphia, NL (1894)
     Boston, NL (1896)
  28 Cleveland, AL (1928)
     Boston, AL (1953)
  23 New York, MNL (1931)
Inning
  11 St. Louis, NL (1925)
  11 Boston, AL (1953)

Doubles
Season
  373 St. Louis, NL (1930)
  358 Cleveland, AL (1930)
Game
  14 Chicago, NL (1883)
  13 St. Louis, MNL (1931)
  11 Detroit, AL (1934)
Inning
  7 Boston, NL (1936)
  6 Washington, AL (1934)

Triples
Season
  153 Baltimore, NL (1894)
  129 Pittsburgh, MNL (1912)
  112 Baltimore, AL (1901)
      Boston, AL (1903)
Game
  9 Baltimore, NL (1894)
  8 Pittsburgh, MNL (1925)
  6 Chicago, AL (1901 and 1920)
     Detroit, AL (1922)
Inning
  5 Chicago, AL (1901)
  4 Boston, NL (1882)
     Baltimore, NL (1892)
     St. Louis, NL (1895)
     Chicago, NL (1899)
     Brooklyn, NL (1902)
     Cincinnati, NL (1926)
     New York, NL (1936)

Homers
Season (162-game schedule)
  240 New York, AL (1961)
Season (154-game schedule)
  221 New York, NL (1947)
      Cincinnati, NL (1956)
  190 New York, AL (1960)
Game
  8 New York, AL (1939)
     Minnesota, AL (1963)
  8 Milwaukee, NL (1953)
     Cincinnati, NL (1956)
     San Francisco, NL (1961)

Inning
  5 New York, NL (1939)
    Philadelphia, NL (1949)
    San Francisco, NL (1961)
  5 Minnesota, AL (1966)

Bases on Balls
  Season
    835 Boston, AL (1949)
    732 Brooklyn, NL (1947)
  Game (extra innings)
    20 Boston, AL (1920)
  Game (nine innings)
    19 Louisville, AA (1887)
    18 Detroit, AL (1916)
       Cleveland, AL (1948)
    17 Chicago, NL (1887)
       Brooklyn, NL (1903)
       New York, NL (1944)
  Inning
    11 New York, AL (1949)
     9 Cincinnati, NL (1957)

Strikeouts
  Season (162-game schedule)
    1203 New York, NL (1968)
    1125 Washington, AL (1965)
  Season (154-game schedule)
    1054 Philadelphia, NL (1960)
     883 Washington, AL (1960)
  Game (extra innings)
    26 California, AL (1971)
    22 New York, NL (1964)
       Cincinnati, NL (1972)
  Game (nine innings)
    19 Boston, NL (1884)
       New York, NL (1969)
       San Diego, NL (1970)
    19 Boston, UA (1884)
    19 Detroit, AL (1966)
  Inning
     4 Many, NL/AL

Hit Batsmen
  Season (162-game schedule)
    78 Montreal, MNL (1971)
  Season (154-game schedule)
    151 Baltimore, NL (1898)
     80 Washington, AL (1911)
     78 St. Louis, MNL (1910)
  Game
     6 Brooklyn, AA (1887)
     6 New York, NL (1893)
     6 New York, AL (1913)
     5 Atlanta, MNL (1969)
  Inning
     3 Many, MNL/AL

Sacrifice Hits (1894–date)
  Season (including sacrifice flies)
    310 Boston, AL (1917)
    270 Chicago, NL (1908)
  Season (no sacrifice flies)
    231 Chicago, NL (1906)
    207 Chicago, AL (1906)
  Game
     8 New York, AL (1918)
       Chicago, AL (1927)
       St. Louis, AL (1928)
     8 Cincinnati, NL (1926)

Inning
  3 Cleveland, AL (1949)
    Detroit, AL (1970)
  3 Chicago, NL (1962)
    Philadelphia, NL (1967)
    Los Angeles, NL (1972)

Stolen Bases (1886–date)
  Season
    638 Philadelphia, AA (1887)
    426 New York, NL (1893)
    347 New York, MNL (1911)
    341 Oakland AL (1976)
  Game
    19 Philadelphia, AA (1890)
    17 New York, NL (1890)
    15 New York, AL (1911)
    11 New York, MNL (1912)
       St. Louis, MNL (1916)

Left on Base
  Season (162-game schedule)
    1328 Cincinnati NL (1976)
  Season (154-game schedule)
    1334 St. Louis, AL (1941)
    1278 Brooklyn, NL (1947)
  Game (extra innings)
    27 Atlanta, NL (1973)
    24 Cleveland, AL (1932)
  Game (nine innings)
    20 New York, AL (1956)
    18 Baltimore, AA (1891)
    18 Many, NL

Runs scored at home
  Season
    625 Boston, AL (1950)
    543 Philadelphia, NL (1930)

Runs scored on road
  Season
    591 New York, AL (1930)
    492 Chicago, NL (1929)

Runs allowed at home
  Season
    644 Philadelphia, NL (1930)
    561 St. Louis, AL (1939)

Runs allowed on road
  Season
    555 Philadelphia, NL (1930)
    523 Philadelphia, AL (1940)

TEAM FIELDING RECORDS

Putouts
  Season (162-game schedule)
    4520 New York, AL (1964)
    4473 Los Angeles, NL (1973)
  Season (154-game schedule)
    4396 Cleveland, AL (1910)
    4359 Philadelphia, NL (1913)

Assists
  Season
    2446 Chicago, AL (1907)
    2293 St. Louis, NL (1917)
  Game (extra innings)
    41 Boston, NL (1920)

38 Detroit, AL (1945)
   Washington, AL (1967)
Game (nine innings)
   28 Pittsburgh, NL (1911)
   27 St. Louis, AL (1919)
Inning
   10 Cleveland, AL, 1921)
      Boston, AL (1952)
    8 Boston, NL (1911)

Errors
   Season
      867 Washington, NL (1886)
      425 Detroit, AL (1901)
      408 Brooklyn, MNL (1905)
   Game
      24 Boston, NL (1876)
      12 Detroit, AL (1901)
         Chicago, AL (1903)
      11 St. Louis, MNL (1902 and 1909)
         Boston, MNL (1906)
   Inning
      7 Cleveland, AL (1905)
      6 Pittsburgh, MNL (1903)

Double Plays
   Season (162-game schedule)
      215 Pittsburgh, NL (1966)
   Season (154-game schedule)
      217 Philadelphia, AL (1949)
      198 Los Angeles, NL (1958)
   Game
      7 New York, AL (1942)
      7 Houston, NL (1969)

Triple Plays
   Season
      3 Cincinnati, AA (1882)
        Rochester, AA (1890)
      3 Detroit, AL (1911)
        Boston, AL (1924)
      3 Philadelphia, NL (1964)
        Chicago, NL (1965)

Fielding Average
   Season
      .9847 Baltimore, AL (1964)
      .9837 Cincinnati NL (1975)

GENERAL TEAM RECORDS

World Series Won
   20 New York, AL
    8 St Louis, NL
Pennants Won
   29 New York, AL
   17 New York Giants, NL
   16 New York Giants, MNL
Note: The Giants also won one pennant in
   San Francisco.

Games Won —Season
   116 Chicago, NL (1906)
   111 Cleveland, AL (1954)
Games Lost
   Season (162-game schedule)
      120 New York, MNL (1962)
   Season (154-game schedule)
      134 Cleveland, NL (1899)
      117 Philadelphia, AL (1916)
      115 Boston, MNL (1935)
Shutouts Won—Season
   32 Chicago, NL (1907 and 1909)
   30 Chicago, AL (1906)
Shutouts Lost—Season
   33 St. Louis, NL (1908)
   29 Washington, AL (1909)

Longest Game (innings)
   26 Bro. vs. Bos., NL (1920)
   24 Phi. vs. Bos., AL (1906)
      Det. vs. Phi., AL (1945)
Longest Game (time) extra innings
   7:23 S.F. vs. N.Y., NL (1964)
   7:00 N.Y., vs. Det., AL (1962)
Longest Game (time) nine innings
   4:18 L.A. vs. S.F., NL (1962)
   3:54 Det. vs. K.C., AL (1961)
Shortest Game (time) nine innings
   0:51 N.Y. vs. Phi., NL (1919)
   0:55 St.L. vs. N.Y., AL (1926)
Players Used
   Season (162-game schedule)
      54 New York, NL (1967)
   Season (154-game schedule)
      56 Philadelphia, AL (1915)
      53 Brooklyn, NL (1944)
   Game (extra innings)
      30 Oakland, AL (1972)
      27 Philadelphia NL (1974)
   Game (nine innings)
      27 Kansas City, AL (1969)
      25 St. Louis, NL (1959)
         Milwaukee, NL (1964)
Pitchers Used
   Season (162-game schedule)
      27 New York, NL (1967)
   Season (154-game schedule)
      27 Philadelphia, AL (1915)
         Kansas City, AL (1955)
      24 Cincinnati, NL (1912)
         Philadelphia, NL (1946)
   Game (extra innings)
      9 Los Angeles, AL (1963)
         Minnesota, AL (1964)
         Washington, AL (1971)
         Cleveland, AL (1971)
      9 Cincinnati, NL (1962)
   Game (nine innings)
      9 St. Louis, AL (1949)
      8 Many, NL

VI LEAGUE LEADERS

YEAR	LG	BATTING		RUNS		HITS		DOUBLES		TRIPLES	
1876	N	BARNES CHI	.404	BARNES CHI	126	BARNES CHI	138	BARNES CHI	23	HALL,ATH PIKE,STL	12
1877	N	J.WHITE BOS	.387	J.WHITE BOS	39	O'ROURKE BOS	89	ANSON CHI	20	JONES CIN	10
1878	N	DALRYMPLE MIL	.356	HIGHAM,PRO START,CHI	58	START CHI	97	BURDOCK BOS	17	HIGHAM PRO	16
1879	N	ANSON CHI	.407	JONES BOS	85	HINES PRO	145	EDEN CLE	26	DICKERSON CIN	14
1880	N	GORE CHI	.365	DALRYMPLE CHI	90	DALRYMPLE CHI	123	WILLIAMSON CHI	29	STOVEY WOR	13
1881	N	ANSON CHI	.399	GORE CHI	86	ANSON CHI	137	KELLY CHI	27	ROWE BUF	11
1882	N	BROUTHERS BUF	.367	GORE CHI	99	BROUTHERS BUF	129	KELLY CHI	34	CONNOR TRO	17
	AA	BROWNING LOU	.382	SWARTWOOD PIT	93	CARPENTER CIN	125	BROWNING LOU	18	TAYLOR PIT	12
1883	N	BROUTHERS BUF	.371	HORNUNG BOS	106	BROUTHERS BUF	156	WILLIAMSON CHI	50	BROUTHERS BUF	11
	AA	SWARTWOOD PIT	.369	STOVEY ATH	110	SWARTWOOD PIT	149	STOVEY ATH	30	SMITH COL	18
1884	N	O'ROURKE BUF	.350	KELLY CHI	120	DALRYMPLE CHI	160	HINES PRO	34	EWING NY	18
	AA	ESTERBROOK MET	.408	STOVEY ATH	126	ESTERBROOK MET	185	BARKLEY TOL	39	STOVEY ATH	25
	U	DUNLAP STL	.420	DUNLAP STL	157	DUNLAP STL	178	SHAFFER STL	38	ROWE STL	13
1885	N	CONNOR NY	.371	KELLY CHI	124	CONNOR NY	169	ANSON CHI	35	O'ROURKE NY	16
	AA	BROWNING LOU	.367	STOVEY ATH	128	BROWNING LOU	176	LARKIN ATH	40	KUEHNE PIT	20
1886	N	KELLY CHI	.388	KELLY CHI	155	RICHARDSON DET	189	BROUTHERS DET	38	CONNOR NY	20
	AA	ORR MET	.346	LATHAM STL	153	ORR MET	196	LARKIN ATH	34	ORR MET	33
1887	N	ANSON CHI	.421	BROUTHERS DET	153	BROUTHERS DET	239	BROUTHERS DET	33	CONNOR NY	24
	AA	O'NEILL STL	.492	O'NEILL STL	170	LYONS ATH	284	O'NEILL STL	46	O'NEILL STL	24
1888	N	ANSON CHI	.343	BROUTHERS DET	118	RYAN CHI	182	RYAN CHI	36	CONNOR NY	17
	AA	O'NEILL STL	.332	PINCKNEY BRO	133	O'NEILL STL	176	REILLY CIN	33	STOVEY ATH	21
1889	N	BROUTHERS BOS	.373	TIERNAN NY	146	GLASSCOCK IND	209	KELLY BOS	40	WILMOT WAS	18
	AA	TUCKER BAL	.375	STOVEY ATH	154	TUCKER BAL	198	WELCH ATH	38	HAMILTON KC	15
1890	N	GLASSCOCK NY	.336	COLLINS BRO	148	GLASSCOCK,NY THOMPSON,PH	172	THOMPSON PHI	38	REILLY CIN	26
	AA	WOLF LOU	.366	MC CARTHY STL	134	WOLF LOU	200	CHILDS SYR	32	JOHNSON,COL WERDEN,TOL	19
	P	BROWNING CLE	.391	DUFFY CHI	161	DUFFY CHI	194	BROWNING,CLE BECKLEY,PIT	41	SHINDLE PHI	25
1891	N	HAMILTON PHI	.338	HAMILTON PHI	142	HAMILTON PHI	179	GRIFFIN BRO	44	STOVEY BOS	22
	AA	BROUTHERS BOS	.352	BROWN BOS	170	BROUTHERS BOS	160	BROWN BOS	35	BROWN BOS	22
1892	N	CHILDS CLE	.335	CHILDS CLE	135	BROUTHERS BRO	197	CONNOR PHI	29	SHINDLE BAL	14
1893	N	DUFFY BOS	.378	LONG,BOS DUFFY,BOS	149	THOMPSON PHI	220	THOMPSON PHI	38	WERDEN STL	28
1894	N	DUFFY BOS	.438	HAMILTON PHI	196	DUFFY BOS	236	DUFFY BOS	46	THOMPSON,PHI REITZ,BAL	28
1895	N	BURKETT CLE	.423	HAMILTON PHI	166	BURKETT CLE	235	DELAHANTY PHI	49	THOMPSON,PHI COOLEY,STL	21
1896	N	BURKETT CLE	.410	BURKETT CLE	159	BURKETT CLE	240	MILLER CIN	35	DAHLEN CHI	21

HOME RUNS	RUNS BATTED IN	STOLEN BASES	STRIKEOUTS	WON-LOST PCT.	EARNED RUN AVE.
HALL ATH 5			SPALDING CHI 115	SPALDING CHI 46-14	76
PIKE CIN 4			BOND BOS 123	BOND BOS 40-17	77
MC KELVY IND 9			BOND BOS 177	BOND BOS 40-19	78
JONES BOS 9			WARD PRO 271	WARD PRO 44-18	79
O'ROURKE,BOS STOVEY,WOR 6			GOLDSMITH CHI 178	GOLDSMITH CHI 22- 3	80
BROUTHERS BUF 8			CORCORAN CHI 252	CORCORAN CHI 31-14	81
WOOD DET 7			KEEFE TRO 289	CORCORAN CHI 27-13	82
WALKER STL 7			MULLANE LOU 281	WHITE CIN 40-12	
EWING NY 9			WHITNEY BOS 308	MC CORMICK CLE 27-13	83
STOVEY ATH 14			KEEFE MET 360	MATHEWS ATH 30-14	
WILLIAMSON CHI 27			RADBOURN PRO 411	RADBOURN PRO 60-12	84
STOVEY,ATH REILLY,CIN 11			HECKER LOU 368	LYNCH MET 39-14	
DUNLAP,STL CRANE,BOS 13			DALY CHI-PIT 464	TAYLOR STL 24- 2	
DALRYMPLE CHI 11			CLARKSON CHI 333	WELCH NY 47-11	85
STOVEY ATH 13			MORRIS PIT 303	CARUTHERS STL 40-13	
RICHARDSON DET 11		ANDREWS PHI 56	BALDWIN DET 340	FLYNN CHI 24- 6	86
MC PHEE CIN 8		STOVEY ATH 96	KILROY BAL 505	FOUTZ STL 41-16	
W.O'BRIEN WAS 19		WARD NY 111	CLARKSON CHI 227	GETZEIN DET 29-13	87
O'NEILL STL 13		STOVEY ATH 143	RAMSEY LOU 348	CARUTHERS STL 29- 9	
RYAN CHI 16		HOY WAS 82	KEEFE NY 334	KEEFE NY 35-12	88
REILLY CIN 12		STOVEY ATH 156	SEWARD ATH 219	HUDSON STL 26-10	
THOMPSON,PHI DENNY,IND 17		FOGARTY PHI 99	CLARKSON BOS 292	CLARKSON BOS 48-19	89
HOLLIDAY,CIN STOVEY,ATH 19		HAMILTON KC 117	BALDWIN COL 368	CARUTHERS BRO 40-12	
TIERNAN NY 14		HAMILTON PHI 102	RUSIE NY 345	LOVETT BRO 31-11	90
CAMPAU STL 9		WELCH ATH-BAL 95	RAMSEY STL 234	STRATTON LOU 34-15	
RICHARDSON,BOS CONNOR,NY 13		BROWN BOS 87	BALDWIN CHI 200	GUMBERT BOS 22- 9	
STOVEY,BOS TIERNAN,NY 16		HAMILTON PHI 115	RUSIE NY 321	HUTCHINSON CHI 43-19	91
FARRELL BOS 12		BROWN BOS 110	STIVETTS STL 232	BUFFINGTON BOS 27- 9 HADDOCK BOS 33-11	
HOLLIDAY CIN 9		WARD BRO 94	RUSIE NY 303	YOUNG CLE 36-11	92
DELAHANTY PHI 19		WARD NY 72	RUSIE NY 208	GASTRIGHT PIT-BOS 15- 6	93
DUFFY BOS 18		HAMILTON PHI 99	RUSIE NY 204	MEEKIN NY 36-10	94
THOMPSON PHI 18		HAMILTON PHI 95	RUSIE NY 199	HOFFER BAL 29- 8	95
DELAHANTY PHI 13		LANGE CHI 100	YOUNG CLE 137	HOFFER BAL 26- 7	96

YEAR	LG	BATTING		RUNS		HITS		DOUBLES		TRIPLES	
1897	N	KEELER BAL	.432	HAMILTON BOS	153	KEELER BAL	243	BECKLEY CIN	38	DAVIS PIT	28
1898	N	KEELER BAL	.379	MC GRAW BAL	142	BURKETT CLE	215	LAJOIE PHI	43	ANDERSON BRO	20
1899	N	DELAHANTY PHI	.408	KEELER BRO	141	DELAHANTY PHI	234	DELAHANTY PHI	56	WILLIAMS PIT	27
1900	N	WAGNER PIT	.381	THOMAS PHI	131	VAN HALTREN NY	181	WAGNER PIT	45	WAGNER PIT	22
1901	N	BURKETT STL	.382	BURKETT STL	139	BURKETT STL	228	BECKLEY CIN	39	SHECKARD BRO	21
	A	LAJOIE PHI	.422	LAJOIE PHI	145	LAJOIE PHI	229	LAJOIE PHI	48	WILLIAMS BAL	22
1902	N	BEAUMONT PIT	.357	WAGNER PIT	105	BEAUMONT PIT	194	WAGNER PIT	32	CRAWFORD CIN	23
	A	DELAHANTY WAS	.376	FULTZ PHI	110	HICKMAN CLE	194	DAVIS PHI	43	WILLIAMS BAL	23
1903	N	WAGNER PIT	.355	BEAUMONT PIT	137	BEAUMONT PIT	209	STEINFELDT,CIN CLARKE,PIT MERTES,NY	32	WAGNER PIT	19
	A	LAJOIE CLE	.355	DOUGHERTY BOS	108	DOUGHERTY BOS	195	SEYBOLD PHI	43	CRAWFORD DET	25
1904	N	WAGNER PIT	.349	BROWNE NY	99	BECKLEY STL	179	WAGNER PIT	44	LUMLEY BRO	18
	A	LAJOIE CLE	.381	DOUGHERTY BOS-NY	113	LAJOIE CLE	211	LAJOIE CLE	50	STAHL BOS	22
1905	N	SEYMOUR CIN	.377	DONLIN NY	124	SEYMOUR CIN	219	SEYMOUR CIN	40	SEYMOUR CIN	21
	A	FLICK CLE	.306	DAVIS PHI	92	STONE STL	187	DAVIS PHI	47	FLICK CLE	19
1906	N	WAGNER PIT	.339	CHANCE,CHI WAGNER,PIT	103	STEINFELDT CHI	176	WAGNER PIT	38	CLARKE,PIT SCHULTE,CHI	13
	A	STONE STL	.358	FLICK CLE	98	LAJOIE CLE	214	LAJOIE CLE	49	FLICK CLE	22
1907	N	WAGNER PIT	.350	SHANNON NY	104	BEAUMONT BOS	187	WAGNER PIT	38	ALPERMAN,BRO GANZEL,CIN	16
	A	COBB DET	.350	CRAWFORD DET	102	COBB DET	212	DAVIS PHI	37	FLICK CLE	18
1908	N	WAGNER PIT	.354	TENNEY NY	101	WAGNER PIT	201	WAGNER PIT	39	WAGNER PIT	19
	A	COBB DET	.324	MC INTYRE DET	105	COBB DET	188	COBB DET	36	COBB DET	20
1909	N	WAGNER PIT	.339	LEACH PIT	126	DOYLE NY	172	WAGNER PIT	39	MITCHELL CIN	17
	A	COBB DET	.377	COBB DET	116	COBB DET	216	CRAWFORD DET	35	BAKER PHI	19
1910	N	MAGEE PHI	.331	MAGEE PHI	110	BYRNE,PIT WAGNER,PIT	178	BYRNE PIT	43	MITCHELL CIN	18
	A	COBB DET	.385	COBB DET	106	LAJOIE CLE	227	LAJOIE CLE	51	CRAWFORD DET	19
1911	N	WAGNER PIT	.334	SHECKARD CHI	121	MILLER BOS	192	KONETCHY STL	38	DOYLE NY	25
	A	COBB DET	.420	COBB DET	147	COBB DET	248	COBB DET	47	COBB DET	24
1912	N	ZIMMERMAN CHI	.372	BESCHER CIN	120	ZIMMERMAN CHI	207	ZIMMERMAN CHI	41	WILSON PIT	36
	A	COBB DET	.410	COLLINS PHI	137	COBB DET	227	SPEAKER BOS	53	JACKSON CLE	26
1913	N	DAUBERT BRO	.350	CAREY,PIT LEACH,PIT	99	CRAVATH PHI	179	SMITH BRO	40	SAIER CHI	21
	A	COBB DET	.390	COLLINS PHI	125	JACKSON CLE	197	JACKSON CLE	39	CRAWFORD DET	23
1914	N	DAUBERT BRO	.329	BURNS NY	100	MAGEE PHI	171	MAGEE PHI	39	CAREY PIT	17
	A	COBB DET	.368	COLLINS PHI	122	SPEAKER BOS	193	SPEAKER BOS	46	CRAWFORD DET	26
	F	KAUFF IND	.366	KAUFF IND	118	KAUFF IND	210	KAUFF IND	45	EVANS BRO	15

HOME RUNS	RUNS BATTED IN	STOLEN BASES	STRIKEOUTS	WON-LOST PCT.	EARNED RUN AVE.	
DELAHANTY PHI 29		LANGE CHI 83	MC JAMES WAS 161	RUSIE NY 28- 8		97
COLLINS BOS 15		F.CLARKE LOU 66	SEYMOUR NY 249	LEWIS BOS 25- 8		98
FREEMAN WAS 25		SHECKARD BAL 78	HAHN CIN 147	HUGHES BRO 25- 5		99
LONG BOS 12		BARRETT CIN 46	WADDELL PIT 133	MC GINNITY BRO 29- 9		00
CRAWFORD CIN 16		WAGNER PIT 48	HAHN CIN 237	CHESBRO PIT 21- 9		01
LAJOIE PHI 13		ISBELL CHI 48	YOUNG BOS 163	YOUNG BOS 31-10		
LEACH PIT 6		WAGNER PIT 43	WILLIS BOS 219	CHESBRO PIT 27- 6		02
SEYBOLD PHI 16		HARTSEL PHI 54	WADDELL PHI 210	WADDELL PHI 24- 7		
SHECKARD BRO 9		SHECKARD,BRO CHANCE,CHI 67	MATHEWSON NY 267	LEEVER PIT 25- 7		03
FREEMAN BOS 13		BAY CLE 46	WADDELL PHI 301	MOORE CLE 22- 7		
LUMLEY BRO 9		WAGNER PIT 53	MATHEWSON NY 212	MC GINNITY NY 35- 8		04
DAVIS ' PHI 10		FLICK CLE 42	WADDELL PHI 349	CHESBRO NY 41-13		
ODWELL CIN 9		MALONEY,CHI DEVLIN,NY 59	MATHEWSON NY 206	MATHEWSON NY 32- 8		05
DAVIS PHI 8		HOFFMAN PHI 46	WADDELL PHI 286	COAKLEY PHI 20- 8		
JORDAN BRO 12		CHANCE CHI 57	BEEBE CHI-STL 171	REULBACH CHI 19- 4		06
DAVIS PHI 12		ANDERSON,WAS FLICK,CLE 39	WADDELL PHI 203	PLANK PHI 19- 6		
BRAIN BOS 10	WAGNER PIT 91	WAGNER PIT 61	MATHEWSON NY 178	REULBACH CHI 17- 4		07
DAVIS PHI 8	COBB DET 116	COBB DET 49	WADDELL PHI 226	DONOVAN DET 25- 4		
JORDAN BRO 12	WAGNER PIT 106	WAGNER PIT 53	MATHEWSON NY 259	REULBACH CHI 24- 7		08
CRAWFORD DET 7	COBB DET 101	DOUGHERTY CHI 47	WALSH CHI 269	WALSH CHI 40-15		
MURRAY NY 7	WAGNER PIT 102	BESCHER CIN 54	OVERALL CHI 205	MATHEWSON,NY S.CAMNITZ 25- 6 PIT		09
COBB DET 9	COBB DET 115	COBB DET 76	SMITH CHI 177	MULLIN DET 29- 8		
BECK,BOS SCHULTE,CHI 10	MAGEE PHI 116	BESCHER CIN 70	MOORE PHI 185	COLE CHI 20- 4		10
STAHL BOS 10	CRAWFORD DET 115	COLLINS PHI 81	JOHNSON WAS 313	BENDER PHI 23- 5		
SCHULTE CHI 21	SCHULTE CHI 121	BESCHER CIN 80	MARQUARD NY 237	MARQUARD NY 24- 7		11
BAKER PHI 9	COBB DET 144	COBB DET 83	WALSH CHI 255	BENDER PHI 17- 5		
ZIMMERMAN CHI 14	ZIMMERMAN CHI 106	BESCHER CIN 67	ALEXANDER PHI 195	HENDRIX PIT 24- 9	TESREAU NY 1.96	12
BAKER PHI 10	BAKER PHI 133	MILAN WAS 88	JOHNSON WAS 303	WOOD BOS 34- 5		
CRAVATH PHI 19	CRAVATH PHI 129	CAREY PIT 61	SEATON PHI 168	HUMPHRIES CHI 16- 4	MATHEWSON NY 2.06	13
BAKER PHI 12	BAKER PHI 126	MILAN WAS 74	JOHNSON WAS 243	JOHNSON WAS 36- 7	JOHNSON WAS 1.09	
CRAVATH PHI 19	MAGEE PHI 101	BURNS NY 62	ALEXANDER PHI 214	JAMES BOS 26- 7	DOAK STL 1.72	14
CRAWFORD,DET BAKER,PHI 8	CRAWFORD DET 112	MAISEL NY 74	JOHNSON WAS 225	BENDER PHI 17- 3	LEONARD BOS 1.01	
ZWILLING CHI 16		KAUFF IND 75	FALKENBERG IND 245	FORD BUF 21- 6	KRAPP BUF 1.19	

YEAR	LG	BATTING		RUNS		HITS		DOUBLES		TRIPLES	
1915	N	DOYLE NY	.320	CRAVATH PHI	89	DOYLE NY	189	DOYLE NY	40	LONG STL	25
	A	COBB DET	.370	COBB DET	144	COBB DET	208	VEACH DET	40	CRAWFORD DET	19
	F	KAUFF BRO	.344	BORTON STL	99	TOBIN STL	186	CHASE BUF	33	KELLY,PIT MANN,CHI	19
1916	N	CHASE CIN	.339	BURNS NY	105	CHASE CIN	184	NIEHOFF PHI	42	HINCHMAN PIT	16
	A	SPEAKER CLE	.386	COBB DET	113	SPEAKER CLE	211	GRANEY,CLE SPEAKER,CLE	41	JACKSON CHI	21
1917	N	ROUSH CIN	.341	BURNS NY	103	GROH CIN	182	GROH CIN	39	HORNSBY STL	17
	A	COBB DET	.383	BUSH DET	112	COBB DET	225	COBB DET	44	COBB DET	23
1918	N	WHEAT BRO	.335	GROH CIN	88	HOLLOCHER CHI	161	GROH CIN	28	DAUBERT BRO	15
	A	COBB DET	.382	CHAPMAN CLE	84	BURNS PHI	178	SPEAKER CLE	33	COBB DET	14
1919	N	ROUSH CIN	.321	BURNS NY	86	OLSON BRO	164	YOUNGS NY	31	SOUTHWORTH,PIT MYERS,BRO	14
	A	COBB DET	.384	RUTH BOS	103	COBB,DET VEACH,DET	191	VEACH DET	45	VEACH DET	17
1920	N	HORNSBY STL	.370	BURNS NY	115	HORNSBY STL	218	HORNSBY STL	44	MYERS BRO	22
	A	SISLER STL	.407	RUTH NY	158	SISLER STL	257	SPEAKER CLE	50	JACKSON CHI	20
1921	N	HORNSBY STL	.397	HORNSBY STL	131	HORNSBY STL	235	HORNSBY STL	44	HORNSBY,STL POWELL,BOS	18
	A	HEILMANN DET	.394	RUTH NY	177	HEILMANN DET	237	SPEAKER CLE	52	SHANKS WAS	19
1922	N	HORNSBY STL	.401	HORNSBY STL	141	HORNSBY STL	250	HORNSBY STL	46	DAUBERT CIN	22
	A	SISLER STL	.420	SISLER STL	134	SISLER STL	246	SPEAKER CLE	48	SISLER STL	18
1923	N	HORNSBY STL	.384	YOUNGS NY	121	FRISCH NY	223	ROUSH CIN	41	TRAYNOR,PIT CAREY,PIT	19
	A	HEILMANN DET	.403	RUTH NY	151	JAMIESON CLE	222	SPEAKER CLE	59	GOSLIN,WAS RICE,WAS	18
1924	N	HORNSBY STL	.424	HORNSBY,STL FRISCH,NY	121	HORNSBY STL	227	HORNSBY STL	43	ROUSH CIN	21
	A	RUTH NY	.378	RUTH NY	143	RICE WAS	216	HEILMANN,DET J.SEWELL CLE	43	PIPP NY	19
1925	N	HORNSBY STL	.403	CUYLER PIT	144	BOTTOMLEY STL	227	BOTTOMLEY STL	44	CUYLER PIT	26
	A	HEILMANN DET	.393	MOSTIL CHI	135	SIMMONS PHI	253	MC MANUS STL	44	GOSLIN WAS	20
1926	N	HARGRAVE CIN	.353	CUYLER PIT	113	BROWN BOS	201	BOTTOMLEY STL	40	P.WANER PIT	22
	A	MANUSH DET	.378	RUTH NY	139	BURNS,CLE RICE,WAS	216	BURNS CLE	64	GEHRIG NY	20
1927	N	P.WANER PIT	.380	L.WANER,PIT HORNSBY,NY	133	P.WANER PIT	237	STEPHENSON CHI	46	P.WANER PIT	17
	A	HEILMANN DET	.398	RUTH NY	158	COMBS NY	231	GEHRIG NY	52	COMBS NY	23
1928	N	HORNSBY BOS	.387	P.WANER PIT	142	LINDSTROM NY	231	P.WANER PIT	50	BOTTOMLEY STL	20
	A	GOSLIN WAS	.379	RUTH NY	163	MANUSH STL	241	MANUSH,STL GEHRIG,NY	47	COMBS NY	21
1929	N	O'DOUL PHI	.398	HORNSBY CHI	156	O'DOUL PHI	254	FREDERICK BRO	52	L.WANER PIT	20
	A	FONSECA CLE	.369	GEHRINGER DET	131	ALEXANDER,DET GEHRINGER,DET	215	GEHRINGER,DET MANUSH,STL JOHNSON,DET	45	GEHRINGER DET	19
1930	N	TERRY NY	.401	KLEIN PHI	158	TERRY NY	254	KLEIN PHI	59	COMOROSKY PIT	23
	A	SIMMONS PHI	.381	SIMMONS PHI	152	HODAPP CLE	225	HODAPP CLE	51	COMBS NY	22

HOME RUNS	RUNS BATTED IN	STOLEN BASES	STRIKEOUTS	WON-LOST PCT.	EARNED RUN AVE.	
CRAVATH PHI 24	CRAVATH PHI 118	CAREY PIT 36	ALEXANDER PHI 241	ALEXANDER PHI 31-10	ALEXANDER PHI 1.22	15
ROTH CHI-CLE 7	CRAWFORD DET 116	COBB DET 96	JOHNSON WAS 203	RUTH BOS 18-6	WOOD BOS 1.49	
CHASE BUF 17		KAUFF BRO 54	DAVENPORT STL 228	MC CONNELL CHI 25-10	PLANK STL 2.01	
ROBERTSON,NY WILLIAMS,CH 12	CHASE CIN 84	CAREY PIT 63	ALEXANDER PHI 167	HUGHES BOS 16-3	ALEXANDER PHI 1.55	16
PIPP NY 12	PIPP NY 99	COBB DET 68	JOHNSON WAS 228	CICOTTE CHI 15-7	RUTH BOS 1.75	
ROBERTSON,NY CRAVATH,PHI 12	ZIMMERMAN NY 100	CAREY PIT 46	ALEXANDER PHI 201	SCHUPP NY 21-7	ALEXANDER PHI 1.85	17
PIPP NY 9	VEACH DET 115	COBB DET 55	JOHNSON WAS 185	RUSSELL CHI 15-5	CICOTTE CHI 1.53	
CRAVATH PHI 8	MERKLE CHI 71	CAREY PIT 58	VAUGHN CHI 148	HENDRIX CHI 20-7	VAUGHN CHI 1.74	18
RUTH,BOS WALKER,PHI 11	BURNS,PHI VEACH,DET 74	SISLER STL 45	JOHNSON WAS 162	JONES BOS 16-5	JOHNSON WAS 1.28	
CRAVATH PHI 12	MYERS BRO 72	BURNS NY 40	VAUGHN CHI 141	RUETHER CIN 19-6	ALEXANDER PHI 1.72	19
RUTH BOS 29	RUTH BOS 112	E.COLLINS CHI 33	JOHNSON WAS 147	CICOTTE CHI 29-7	JOHNSON WAS 1.49	
WILLIAMS PHI 15	HORNSBY,STL KELLY,NY 94	CAREY PIT 52	ALEXANDER CHI 173	GRIMES BRO 23-11	ALEXANDER CHI 1.91	20
RUTH NY 54	RUTH NY 137	RICE WAS 62	COVELESKI CLE 133	BAGBY CLE 31-12	SHAWKEY NY 2.46	
KELLY NY 23	HORNSBY STL 126	FRISCH NY 49	GRIMES BRO 136	DOAK STL 15-6	DOAK STL 2.58	21
RUTH NY 59	RUTH NY 171	SISLER STL 35	JOHNSON WAS 143	MAYS NY 27-9	FABER CHI 2.48	
HORNSBY STL 42	HORNSBY STL 152	CAREY PIT 51	VANCE BRO 134	DONOHUE CIN 18-9	RYAN NY 3.00	22
WILLIAMS STL 39	WILLIAMS STL 155	SISLER STL 51	SHOCKER STL 149	BUSH NY 26-7	FABER CHI 2.81	
WILLIAMS PHI 41	MEUSEL NY 125	CAREY PIT 51	VANCE BRO 197	LUQUE CIN 27-8	LUQUE CIN 1.93	23
RUTH NY 41	RUTH NY 131	COLLINS CHI 49	JOHNSON WAS 126	PENNOCK NY 19-6	COVELESKI CLE 2.76	
FOURNIER BRO 27	KELLY NY 136	CAREY PIT 49	VANCE BRO 262	YDE PIT 16-3	VANCE BRO 2.16	24
RUTH NY 46	GOSLIN WAS 129	COLLINS CHI 42	JOHNSON WAS 158	JOHNSON WAS 23-7	JOHNSON WAS 2.72	
HORNSBY STL 39	HORNSBY STL 143	CAREY PIT 46	VANCE BRO 221	SHERDEL STL 15-6	LUQUE CIN 2.63	25
MEUSEL NY 33	MEUSEL NY 138	MOSTIL CHI 43	GROVE PHI 116	COVELESKI WAS 20-5	COVELESKI WAS 2.84	
WILSON CHI 21	BOTTOMLEY STL 120	CUYLER PIT 35	VANCE BRO 140	KREMER PIT 20-6	KREMER PIT 2.61	26
RUTH NY 47	RUTH NY 145	MOSTIL CHI 35	GROVE PHI 194	UHLE CLE 27-11	GROVE PHI 2.51	
WILLIAMS,PHI WILSON,CHI 30	P.WANER PIT 131	FRISCH STL 48	VANCE BRO 184	BENTON BOS 17-7	KREMER PIT 2.47	27
RUTH NY 60	GEHRIG NY 175	SISLER STL 27	GROVE PHI 174	HOYT NY 22-7	MOORE NY 2.28	
BOTTOMLEY,STL WILSON,CHI 31	BOTTOMLEY STL 136	CUYLER CHI 37	VANCE BRO 200	BENTON NY 25-9	VANCE BRO 2.09	28
RUTH NY 54	GEHRIG,NY RUTH,NY 142	MYER BOS 30	GROVE PHI 183	CROWDER STL 21-5	BRAXTON WAS 2.52	
KLEIN PHI 43	WILSON CHI 159	CUYLER CHI 43	MALONE CHI 166	ROOT CHI 19-6	WALKER NY 3.08	29
RUTH NY 46	SIMMONS PHI 157	GEHRINGER DET 27	GROVE PHI 170	GROVE PHI 20-6	ZACHARY NY 2.47	
WILSON CHI 56	WILSON CHI 190	CUYLER CHI 37	HALLAHAN STL 177	FITZSIMMONS NY 19-7	VANCE BRO 2.61	30
RUTH NY 49	GEHRIG NY 174	MC MANUS DET 23	GROVE PHI 209	GROVE PHI 28-5	GROVE PHI 2.54	

YEAR	LG	BATTING		RUNS		HITS		DOUBLES		TRIPLES	
1931	N	HAFEY STL	.349	KLEIN,PHI TERRY,NY	121	L.WANER PIT	214	ADAMS STL	46	TERRY NY	20
	A	SIMMONS PHI	.390	GEHRIG NY	163	GEHRIG NY	211	WEBB BOS	67	JOHNSON DET	19
1932	N	O'DOUL BRO	.368	KLEIN PHI	152	KLEIN PHI	226	P.WANER PIT	62	HERMAN CIN	19
	A	ALEXANDER DET-BOS	.367	FOXX PHI	151	SIMMONS PHI	216	MC NAIR PHI	47	CRONIN WAS	18
1933	N	KLEIN PHI	.368	MARTIN STL	122	KLEIN PHI	223	KLEIN PHI	44	VAUGHAN PIT	19
	A	FOXX PHI	.356	GEHRIG NY	138	MANUSH WAS	221	CRONIN WAS	45	MANUSH WAS	17
1934	N	P.WANER PIT	.362	P.WANER PIT	122	P.WANER PIT	217	CUYLER,CHI ALLEN,PHI	42	MEDWICK STL	18
	A	GEHRIG NY	.363	GEHRINGER DET	134	GEHRINGER DET	214	GREENBERG DET	63	CHAPMAN NY	13
1935	N	VAUGHAN PIT	.385	GALAN CHI	133	HERMAN CHI	227	HERMAN CHI	57	GOODMAN CIN	18
	A	MYER WAS	.349	GEHRIG NY	125	VOSMIK CLE	216	VOSMIK CLE	47	VOSMIK CLE	20
1936	N	P.WANER PIT	.373	VAUGHAN PIT	122	MEDWICK STL	223	MEDWICK STL	64	GOODMAN CIN	14
	A	APPLING CHI	.388	GEHRIG NY	167	AVERILL CLE	232	GEHRINGER DET	60	DI MAGGIO,NY ROLFE,NY AVERILL,CLE	15
1937	N	MEDWICK STL	.374	MEDWICK STL	111	MEDWICK STL	237	MEDWICK STL	56	VAUGHAN PIT	17
	A	GEHRINGER DET	.371	DI MAGGIO NY	151	BELL STL	218	BELL STL	51	KREEVICH,CHI WALKER,CHI	16
1938	N	LOMBARDI CIN	.342	OTT NY	116	MC CORMICK CIN	209	MEDWICK STL	47	MIZE STL	16
	A	FOXX BOS	.349	GREENBERG DET	144	VOSMIK BOS	201	CRONIN BOS	51	HEATH CLE	18
1939	N	MIZE STL	.349	WERBER CIN	115	MC CORMICK CIN	209	SLAUGHTER STL	52	HERMAN CHI	18
	A	DI MAGGIO NY	.381	ROLFE NY	139	ROLFE NY	213	ROLFE NY	46	LEWIS WAS	16
1940	N	GARMS PIT	.355	VAUGHAN PIT	113	MC CORMICK,CIN HACK,CHI	191	F.MC CORMICK CIN	44	VAUGHAN PIT	15
	A	DI MAGGIO NY	.352	WILLIAMS BOS	134	MC COSKY,DET CRAMER,BOS RADCLIFF,STL	200	GREENBERG DET	50	MC COSKY DET	19
1941	N	REISER BRO	.343	REISER BRO	117	HACK CHI	186	REISER,BRO MIZE,STL	39	REISER BRO	17
	A	WILLIAMS BOS	.406	WILLIAMS BOS	135	TRAVIS WAS	218	BOUDREAU CLE	45	HEATH CLE	20
1942	N	LOMBARDI BOS	.330	OTT NY	118	SLAUGHTER STL	188	MARION STL	38	SLAUGHTER STL	17
	A	WILLIAMS BOS	.356	WILLIAMS BOS	141	PESKY BOS	205	KOLLOWAY CHI	40	SPENCE WAS	15
1943	N	MUSIAL STL	.357	VAUGHAN BRO	112	MUSIAL STL	220	MUSIAL STL	48	MUSIAL STL	20
	A	APPLING CHI	.328	CASE WAS	102	WAKEFIELD DET	200	WAKEFIELD DET	38	LINDELL,NY MOSES,CHI	12
1944	N	WALKER BRO	.357	NICHOLSON CHI	116	CAVARETTA,CHI MUSIAL,STL	197	MUSIAL STL	51	BARRETT PIT	19
	A	BOUDREAU CLE	.327	STIRNWEISS NY	125	STIRNWEISS NY	205	BOUDREAU CLE	45	STIRNWEISS,NY LINDELL,NY	16
1945	N	CAVARETTA CHI	.355	STANKY BRO	128	HOLMES BOS	224	HOLMES BOS	47	OLMO BRO	13
	A	STIRNWEISS NY	.309	STIRNWEISS NY	107	STIRNWEISS NY	195	MOSES CHI	35	STIRNWEISS NY	22
1946	N	MUSIAL STL	.365	MUSIAL STL	124	MUSIAL STL	228	MUSIAL STL	50	MUSIAL STL	20
	A	VERNON WAS	.353	WILLIAMS BOS	142	PESKY BOS	208	VERNON WAS	51	EDWARDS CLE	16

	HOME RUNS	RUNS BATTED IN	STOLEN BASES	STRIKEOUTS	WON-LOST PCT.	EARNED RUN AVE.
31	KLEIN PHI 31	KLEIN PHI 121	FRISCH STL 28	HALLAHAN STL 159	DERRINGER STL 18-8	WALKER NY 2.26
	GEHRIG,NY RUTH,NY 46	GEHRIG NY 184	CHAPMAN NY 61	GROVE PHI 175	GROVE PHI 31-4	GROVE PHI 2.05
32	KLEIN,PHI OTT,NY 38	HURST PHI 143	KLEIN PHI 20	DEAN STL 191	WARNEKE CHI 22-6	WARNEKE CHI 2.37
	FOXX PHI 58	FOXX PHI 169	CHAPMAN NY 38	RUFFING NY 190	ALLEN NY 17-4	GROVE PHI 2.84
33	KLEIN PHI 28	KLEIN PHI 120	MARTIN STL 26	DEAN STL 199	CANTWELL BOS 20-10	HUBBELL NY 1.66
	FOXX PHI 48	FOXX PHI 163	CHAPMAN NY 27	GOMEZ NY 163	GROVE PHI 24-8	PEARSON CLE 2.35
34	COLLINS,STL OTT,NY 35	OTT NY 135	MARTIN STL 23	J.DEAN STL 195	J.DEAN STL 30-7	HUBBELL NY 2.30
	GEHRIG NY 49	GEHRIG NY 165	WERBER BOS 40	GOMEZ NY 158	GOMEZ NY 26-5	GOMEZ NY 2.33
35	BERGER BOS 34	BERGER BOS 130	GALAN CHI 22	J.DEAN STL 182	LEE CHI 20-6	BLANTON PIT 2.59
	GREENBERG,DET FOXX,PHI 36	GREENBERG DET 170	WERBER BOS 29	BRIDGES DET 163	AUKER DET 18-7	GROVE BOS 2.70
36	OTT NY 33	MEDWICK STL 138	J.MARTIN STL 23	MUNGO BRO 238	HUBBELL NY 26-6	HUBBELL NY 2.31
	GEHRIG NY 49	TROSKY CLE 162	LARY STL 37	BRIDGES DET 175	PEARSON NY 19-7	GROVE BOS 2.81
37	MEDWICK,STL OTT,NY 31	MEDWICK STL 154	GALAN CHI 23	HUBBELL NY 159	HUBBELL NY 22-8	TURNER BOS 2.38
	DI MAGGIO NY 46	GREENBERG DET 183	CHAPMAN,WAS-BOS WERBER,PHI 35	GOMEZ NY 194	ALLEN CLE 15-1	GOMEZ NY 2.33
38	OTT NY 36	MEDWICK STL 122	HACK CHI 16	BRYANT CHI 135	LEE CHI 22-9	LEE CHI 2.66
	GREENBERG DET 58	FOXX BOS 175	CROSETTI NY 27	FELLER CLE 240	RUFFING NY 21-7	GROVE BOS 3.07
39	MIZE STL 28	MC CORMICK CIN 128	HANDLEY,PIT HACK,CHI 17	PASSEAU,PHI-CHI WALTERS CIN 137	DERRINGER CIN 25-7	WALTERS CIN 2.29
	FOXX BOS 35	WILLIAMS BOS 145	CASE WAS 51	FELLER CLE 246	GROVE BOS 15-4	GROVE BOS 2.54
40	MIZE STL 43	MIZE STL 137	FREY CIN 22	HIGBE PHI 137	FITZSIMMONS BRO 16-2	WALTERS CIN 2.48
	GREENBERG DET 41	GREENBERG DET 150	CASE WAS 35	FELLER CLE 261	ROWE DET 16-3	FELLER CLE 2.62
41	CAMILLI BRO 34	CAMILLI BRO 120	MURTAUGH PHI 18	VANDER MEER CIN 202	E.RIDDLE CIN 19-4	E.RIDDLE CIN 2.24
	WILLIAMS BOS 37	DI MAGGIO NY 125	CASE WAS 33	FELLER CLE 260	GOMEZ NY 15-5	LEE CHI 2.37
42	OTT NY 30	MIZE NY 110	REISER BRO 20	VANDER MEER CIN 186	FRENCH BRO 15-4	M.COOPER STL 1.77
	WILLIAMS BOS 36	WILLIAMS BOS 137	CASE WAS 44	HUGHSON,BOS NEWSOM,WAS 113	BONHAM NY 21-5	LYONS CHI 2.10
43	NICHOLSON CHI 29	NICHOLSON CHI 128	VAUGHAN BRO 20	VANDER MEER CIN 174	M.COOPER STL 21-8	POLLET STL 1.75
	YORK DET 34	YORK DET 118	CASE WAS 61	REYNOLDS CLE 151	CHANDLER NY 20-4	CHANDLER NY 1.64
44	NICHOLSON CHI 33	NICHOLSON CHI 122	BARRETT PIT 28	VOISELLE NY 161	WILKS STL 17-4	HEUSSER CIN 2.38
	ETTEN NY 22	STEPHENS STL 109	STIRNWEISS NY 55	NEWHOUSER DET 187	HUGHSON BOS 18-5	TROUT DET 2.12
45	HOLMES BOS 28	WALKER BRO 124	SCHOENDIENST STL 26	ROE PIT 148	BRECHEEN STL 15-4	BOROWY CHI 2.14
	STEPHENS STL 24	ETTEN NY 111	STIRNWEISS NY 33	NEWHOUSER DET 212	NEWHOUSER DET 25-9	NEWHOUSER DET 1.81
46	KINER PIT 23	SLAUGHTER STL 130	REISER BRO 34	SCHMITZ CHI 135	DICKSON STL 15-6	POLLET STL 2.10
	GREENBERG DET 44	GREENBERG DET 127	CASE CLE 28	FELLER CLE 348	FERRISS BOS 25-6	NEWHOUSER DET 1.94

YEAR	LG	BATTING		RUNS		HITS		DOUBLES		TRIPLES	
1947	N	WALKER STL-PHI	.363	MIZE NY	137	HOLMES BOS	191	MILLER CIN	38	WALKER STL-PHI	16
	A	WILLIAMS BOS	.343	WILLIAMS BOS	125	PESKY BOS	207	BOUDREAU CLE	45	HENRICH NY	13
1948	N	MUSIAL STL	.376	MUSIAL STL	135	MUSIAL STL	230	MUSIAL STL	46	MUSIAL STL	18
	A	WILLIAMS BOS	.369	HENRICH NY	138	DILLINGER STL	207	WILLIAMS BOS	44	HENRICH NY	14
1949	N	ROBINSON BRO	.342	REESE BRO	132	MUSIAL STL	207	MUSIAL STL	41	SLAUGHTER,STL MUSIAL,STL	13
	A	KELL DET	.343	WILLIAMS BOS	150	MITCHELL CLE	203	WILLIAMS BOS	39	MITCHELL CLE	23
1950	N	MUSIAL STL	.346	TORGESON BOS	120	SNIDER BRO	199	SCHOENDIENST STL	43	ASHBURN PHI	14
	A	GOODMAN BOS	.354	DI MAGGIO BOS	131	KELL DET	218	KELL DET	56	DI MAGGIO,BOS DOERR,BOS EVERS,DET	11
1951	N	MUSIAL STL	.355	MUSIAL,STL KINER,PIT	124	ASHBURN PHI	221	DARK NY	41	MUSIAL,STL BELL,PIT	12
	A	FAIN PHI	.344	DI MAGGIO BOS	113	KELL DET	191	KELL,DET MELE,WAS YOST,WAS	48	MINOSO CLE-CHI	14
1952	N	MUSIAL STL	.336	MUSIAL,STL HEMUS,STL	105	MUSIAL STL	194	MUSIAL STL	42	THOMSON NY	14
	A	FAIN PHI	.327	DOBY CLE	104	FOX CHI	192	FAIN PHI	43	AVILA CLE	11
1953	N	FURILLO BRO	.344	SNIDER BRO	132	ASHBURN PHI	205	MUSIAL STL	53	GILLIAM BRO	17
	A	VERNON WAS	.337	ROSEN CLE	115	KUENN DET	209	VERNON WAS	43	RIVERA CHI	16
1954	N	MAYS NY	.345	MUSIAL,STL SNIDER,BRO	120	MUELLER NY	212	MUSIAL STL	41	MAYS NY	13
	A	AVILA CLE	.341	MANTLE NY	129	KUENN,DET FOX,CHI	201	VERNON WAS	33	MINOSO CHI	18
1955	N	ASHBURN PHI	.338	SNIDER BRO	126	KLUSZEWSKI CIN	192	LOGAN,MIL AARON,MIL	37	MAYS,NY LONG,PIT	13
	A	KALINE DET	.340	SMITH CLE	123	KALINE DET	200	KUENN DET	38	MANTLE,NY CAREY,NY	11
1956	N	AARON MIL	.328	ROBINSON CIN	122	AARON MIL	200	AARON MIL	34	BRUTON MIL	15
	A	MANTLE NY	.353	MANTLE NY	132	KUENN DET	196	PIERSALL BOS	40	JENSEN,BOS LEMON,WAS MINOSO,CHI SIMPSON,KC	11
1957	N	MUSIAL STL	.351	AARON MIL	118	SCHOENDIENST NY-MIL	200	HOAK CIN	39	MAYS NY	20
	A	WILLIAMS BOS	.388	MANTLE NY	121	FOX CHI	196	GARDNER,BAL MINOSO,CHI	36	MC DOUGALD,NY BAUER,NY SIMPSON KC-NY	9
1958	N	ASHBURN PHI	.350	MAYS SF	121	ASHBURN PHI	215	CEPEDA SF	38	ASHBURN PHI	13
	A	WILLIAMS BOS	.328	MANTLE NY	127	FOX CHI	187	KUENN DET	39	POWER KC-CLE	10
1959	N	AARON MIL	.355	PINSON CIN	131	AARON MIL	223	PINSON CIN	47	MOON,LA NEAL,LA	11
	A	KUENN DET	.353	YOST DET	115	KUENN DET	198	KUENN DET	42	ALLISON WAS	9
1960	N	GROAT PIT	.325	BRUTON MIL	112	MAYS SF	190	PINSON CIN	37	BRUTON MIL	13
	A	RUNNELS BOS	.320	MANTLE NY	119	MINOSO CHI	184	FRANCONA CLE	36	FOX CHI	10
1961	N	CLEMENTE PIT	.351	MAYS SF	129	PINSON CIN	208	AARON MIL	39	ALTMAN CHI	12
	A	CASH DET	.361	MANTLE,NY MARIS,NY	132	CASH DET	193	KALINE DET	41	WOOD DET	14

HOME RUNS	RUNS BATTED IN	STOLEN BASES	STRIKEOUTS	WON-LOST PCT.	EARNED RUN AVE.	
KINER,PIT MIZE,NY 51	MIZE NY 138	ROBINSON BRO 29	BLACKWELL CIN 193	JANSEN NY 21- 5	SPAHN BOS 2.33	47
WILLIAMS BOS 32	WILLIAMS BOS 114	DILLINGER STL 34	FELLER CLE 196	REYNOLDS NY 19- 8	HAYNES CHI 2.42	
KINER,PIT MIZE,NY 40	MUSIAL STL 131	ASHBURN PHI 32	BRECHEEN STL 149	BRECHEEN STL 20- 7	BRECHEEN STL 2.24	48
DI MAGGIO NY 39	DI MAGGIO NY 155	DILLINGER STL 28	FELLER CLE 164	KRAMER BOS 18- 5	BEARDEN CLE 2.43	
KINER PIT 54	KINER PIT 127	ROBINSON BRO 37	SPAHN BOS 151	ROE BRO 15- 6	KOSLO NY 2.50	49
WILLIAMS BOS 43	STEPHENS,BOS WILLIAMS,BO 159	DILLINGER STL 20	TRUCKS DET 153	KINDER BOS 23- 6	PARNELL BOS 2.78	
KINER PIT 47	ENNIS PHI 126	JETHROE BOS 35	SPAHN BOS 191	MAGLIE NY 18- 4	HEARN STL-NY 2.49	50
ROSEN CLE 37	STEPHENS,BOS DROPO,BOS 144	DI MAGGIO BOS 15	LEMON CLE 170	RASCHI NY 21- 8	WYNN CLE 3.20	
KINER PIT 42	IRVIN NY 121	JETHROE BOS 35	NEWCOMBE,BRO SPAHN,BOS 164	ROE BRO 22- 3	NICHOLS BOS 2.88	51
ZERNIAL CHI-PHI 33	ZERNIAL CHI-PHI 129	MINOSO CLE-CHI 31	RASCHI NY 164	FELLER CLE 22- 8	ROGOVIN DET-CHI 2.78	
KINER,PIT SAUER,CHI 37	SAUER CHI 121	REESE BRO 30	SPAHN BOS 183	WILHELM NY 15- 3	WILHELM NY 2.43	52
DOBY CLE 32	ROSEN CLE 105	MINOSO CHI 22	REYNOLDS NY 160	SHANTZ PHI 24- 7	REYNOLDS NY 2.07	
MATHEWS MIL 47	CAMPANELLA BRO 142	BRUTON MIL 26	ROBERTS PHI 198	ERSKINE BRO 20- 6	SPAHN MIL 2.10	53
ROSEN CLE 43	ROSEN CLE 145	MINOSO CHI 25	PIERCE CHI 186	LOPAT NY 16- 4	LOPAT NY 2.43	
KLUSZEWSKI CIN 49	KLUSZEWSKI CIN 141	BRUTON MIL 34	ROBERTS PHI 185	ANTONELLI NY 21- 7	ANTONELLI NY 2.29	54
DOBY CLE 32	DOBY CLE 126	JENSEN BOS 22	TURLEY BAL 185	CONSUEGRA CHI 16- 3	GARCIA CLE 2.64	
MAYS NY 51	SNIDER BRO 136	BRUTON MIL 25	JONES CHI 198	NEWCOMBE BRO 20- 5	FRIEND PIT 2.84	55
MANTLE NY 37	JENSEN,BOS BOONE,DET 116	RIVERA CHI 25	SCORE CLE 245	BYRNE NY 16- 5	PIERCE CHI 1.97	
SNIDER BRO 43	MUSIAL STL 109	MAYS NY 40	JONES CHI 176	NEWCOMBE BRO 27- 7	BURDETTE MIL 2.71	56
MANTLE NY 52	MANTLE NY 130	APARICIO CHI 21	SCORE CLE 263	FORD NY 19- 6	FORD NY 2.46	
AARON MIL 44	AARON MIL 132	MAYS SF 38	SANFORD PHI 188	BUHL MIL 18- 7	PODRES BRO 2.66	57
SIEVERS WAS 42	SIEVERS WAS 114	APARICIO CHI 28	WYNN CLE 184	STURDIVANT,NY DONOVAN CHI 16- 6	SHANTZ NY 2.45	
BANKS CHI 47	BANKS CHI 129	MAYS SF 31	JONES STL 225	BURDETTE MIL 20-10 SPAHN MIL 22-11	MILLER SF 2.47	58
MANTLE NY 42	JENSEN BOS 122	APARICIO CHI 29	WYNN CHI 179	TURLEY NY 21- 7	FORD NY 2.01	
MATHEWS MIL 46	BANKS CHI 143	MAYS SF 27	DRYSDALE LA 242	FACE PIT 18- 1	JONES SF 2.82	59
KILLEBREW,WAS COLAVITO CLE 42	JENSEN BOS 112	APARICIO CHI 56	BUNNING DET 201	WYNN CHI 22-10	WILHELM BAL 2.19	
BANKS CHI 41	AARON MIL 126	WILLS LA 50	DRYSDALE LA 246	BROGLIO STL 21- 9	MC CORMICK SF 2.70	60
MANTLE NY 40	MARIS NY 112	APARICIO CHI 51	BUNNING DET 201	J.PERRY CLE 18-10	BAUMANN CHI 2.68	
CEPEDA SF 46	CEPEDA SF 142	WILLS LA 35	KOUFAX LA 269	PODRES LA 18- 5	SPAHN MIL 3.01	61
MARIS NY 61	MARIS NY 142	APARICIO CHI 53	PASCUAL MIN 221	FORD NY 25- 4	DONOVAN WAS 2.40	

YEAR	LG	BATTING			RUNS			HITS			DOUBLES			TRIPLES		
1962	N	H.DAVIS	BRO	.346	ROBINSON	CIN	134	H.DAVIS	BRO	230	ROBINSON	CIN	51	CALLISON,PHI WILLS,LA W.DAVIS,LA VIRDON,PIT		10
	A	RUNNELS	BOS	.326	PEARSON	LA	115	RICHARDSON	NY	209	F.ROBINSON	CHI	45	CIMOLI	KC	15
1963	N	H.DAVIS	BRO	.326	H.AARON	MIL	121	PINSON	CIN	204	GROAT	STL	43	PINSON	CIN	14
	A	YASTRZEMSKI	BOS	.321	ALLISON	MIN	99	YASTRZEMSKI	BOS	183	YASTRZEMSKI	BOS	40	VERSALLES	MIN	13
1964	N	CLEMENTE	PIT	.339	ALLEN	PHI	125	CLEMENTE,PIT FLOOD,STL		211	MAYE	MIL	44	ALLEN,PHI SANTO,CHI		13
	A	OLIVA	MIN	.323	OLIVA	MIN	109	OLIVA	MIN	217	OLIVA	MIN	43	ROLLINS,MINN VERSALLES	MIN	10
1965	N	CLEMENTE	PIT	.329	HARPER	CIN	126	ROSE	CIN	209	H.AARON	MIL	40	CALLISON	PHI	16
	A	OLIVA	MIN	.321	VERSALLES	MIN	126	OLIVA	MIN	185	YASTRZEMSKI,BOS VERSALLES	MIN	45	CAMPANERIS,KC VERSALLES	MIN	12
1966	N	M.ALOU	PIT	.342	F.ALOU	ATL	122	F.ALOU	ATL	218	CALLISON	PHI	40	MC CARVER	STL	13
	A	F.ROBINSON	BAL	.326	F.ROBINSON	BAL	122	OLIVA	MIN	191	YASTRZEMSKI	BOS	39	KNOOP	CAL	11
1967	N	CLEMENTE	PIT	.357	AARON,ATL BROCK,STL		113	CLEMENTE	PIT	209	STAUB	HOU	44	PINSON	CIN	13
	A	YASTRZEMSKI	BOS	.326	YASTRZEMSKI	BOS	112	YASTRZEMSKI	BOS	189	OLIVA	MIN	34	BLAIR	BAL	12
1968	N	ROSE	CIN	.335	BECKERT	CHI	98	F.ALOU,ATL ROSE,CIN		210	BROCK	STL	46	BROCK	STL	14
	A	YASTRZEMSKI	BOS	.301	MC AULIFFE	DET	95	CAMPANERIS	OAK	177	SMITH	BOS	37	FREGOSI	CAL	13
1969	N	ROSE	CIN	.348	ROSE,CIN BONDS,SF		120	M.ALOU	PIT	231	M.ALOU	PIT	41	CLEMENTE	PIT	12
	A	CAREW	MIN	.332	JACKSON	OAK	123	OLIVA	MIN	197	OLIVA	MIN	39	UNSER	WAS	8
1970	N	CARTY	ATL	.366	WILLIAMS	CHI	137	WILLIAMS,CHI ROSE,CIN		205	PARKER	LA	47	DAVIS	LA	16
	A	JOHNSON	CAL	.329	YASTRZEMSKI	BOS	125	OLIVA	MIN	204	OLIVA,MIN OTIS,KC TOVAR,MINN		36	TOVAR	MIN	13
1971	N	TORRE	STL	.363	BROCK	STL	126	TORRE	STL	230	CEDENO	HOU	40	METZGER,HOU MORGAN,HOU		11
	A	OLIVA	MIN	.337	BUFORD	BAL	99	TOVAR	MIN	204	SMITH	BOS	33	PATEK	KC	11
1972	N	WILLIAMS	CHI	.333	MORGAN	CIN	122	ROSE	CIN	198	MONTANEZ,PHI CEDENO,HOU		39	BOWA	PHI	13
	A	CAREW	MIN	.318	MURCER	NY	102	RUDI	OAK	181	PINIELLA	KC	33	FISK,BOS RUDI,OAK		9
1973	N	ROSE	CIN	.338	BONDS	SF	131	ROSE	CIN	230	STARGELL	PIT	43	METZGER	HOU	14
	A	CAREW	MIN	.350	JACKSON	OAK	99	CAREW	MIN	203	BANDO,OAK GARCIA,MIL		32	BUMBRY,BAL CAREW,MIN		11
1974	N	GARR	ATL	.353	ROSE	CIN	110	GARR	ATL	214	ROSE	CIN	45	GARR	ATL	17
	A	CAREW	MIN	.364	YASTRZEMSKI	BOS	93	CAREW	MIN	218	RUDI	OAK	39	RIVERS	CAL	11
1975	N	MADLOCK	CHI	.354	ROSE	CIN	112	CASH	PHI	213	ROSE	CIN	47	GARR	ATL	11
	A	CAREW	MIN	.359	LYNN	BOS	103	BRETT	KC	195	LYNN	BOS	47	RIVERS,CAL BRETT,KC		13
1976	N	MADLOCK	CHI	.339	ROSE	CIN	130	ROSE	CIN	215	ROSE	CIN	42	CASH	PHI	12
	A	BRETT	KC	.333	WHITE	NY	104	BRETT	KC	215	OTIS	KC	40	BRETT	KC	14

HOME RUNS	RUNS BATTED IN	STOLEN BASES	STRIKEOUTS	WON-LOST PCT.	EARNED RUN AVE.	
MAYS SF 49	H.DAVIS LA 153	WILLS LA 104	DRYSDALE LA 232	PURKEY CIN 23-5	KOUFAX LA 2.54	62
KILLEBREW MIN 48	KILLEBREW MIN 126	APARICIO CHI 31	PASCUAL MIN 206	HERBERT CHI 20-9	AGUIRRE DET 2.21	
MC COVEY,SF H.AARON,MIL 44	H.AARON MIL 130	WILLS LA 40	KOUFAX LA 306	PERRANOSKI LA 16-3	KOUFAX LA 1.88	63
KILLEBREW MIN 45	STUART BOS 118	APARICIO BAL 40	PASCUAL MIN 202	FORD NY 24-7	PETERS CHI 2.33	
MAYS SF 47	BOYER STL 119	WILLS LA 53	VEALE PIT 250	KOUFAX LA 19-5	KOUFAX LA 1.74	64
KILLEBREW MIN 49	B.ROBINSON BAL 118	APARICIO BAL 57	DOWNING NY 217	BUNKER BAL 19-5	CHANCE LA 1.65	
MAYS SF 52	JOHNSON CIN 130	WILLS LA 94	KOUFAX LA 382	KOUFAX LA 26-8	KOUFAX LA 2.04	65
CONIGLIARO BOS 32	COLAVITO CLE 108	CAMPANERIS LC 51	MC DOWELL CLE 325	GRANT MIN 21-7	MC DOWELL CLE 2.18	
H.AARON ATL 44	H.AARON ATL 127	BROCK STL 74	KOUFAX LA 317	MARICHAL SF 25-6	KOUFAX LA 1.73	66
F.ROBINSON BAL 49	F.ROBINSON BAL 122	CAMPANERIS KC 52	MC DOWELL CLE 225	SIEBERT CLE 16-8	PETERS CHI 1.98	
H.AARON ATL 39	CEPEDA SF 111	BROCK STL 52	BUNNING PHI 253	HUGHES STL 16-6	P.NIEKRO ATL 1.87	67
YASTRZEMSKI,BOS KILLEBREW MIN 44	YASTRZEMSKI BOS 121	CAMPANERIS KC 55	LONBORG BOS 246	HORLEN CHI 19-7	HORLEN CHI 2.06	
MC COVEY SF 36	MC COVEY SF 105	BROCK STL 62	GIBSON STL 268	BLASS PIT 18-6	GIBSON STL 1.12	68
HOWARD WAS 44	HARRELSON BOS 109	CAMPANERIS OAK 62	MC DOWELL CLE 283	MC LAIN DET 31-6	TIANT CLE 1.60	
MC COVEY SF 45	MC COVEY SF 126	BROCK STL 53	JENKINS CHI 273	SEAVER NY 25-7	MARICHAL SF 2.10	69
KILLEBREW MIN 49	KILLEBREW MIN 140	HARPER SEA 73	MC DOWELL CLE 279	PALMER BAL 16-4	BOSMAN WAS 2.19	
BENCH CIN 45	BENCH CIN 148	TOLAN CIN 57	SEAVER NY 283	GIBSON STL 23-7	SEAVER NY 2.81	70
HOWARD WAS 44	HOWARD WAS 126	CAMPANERIS OAK 42	MC DOWELL CLE 304	CUELLAR BAL 24-8	SEGUI OAK 2.56	
STARGELL PIT 48	TORRE STL 137	BROCK STL 64	SEAVER NY 289	GULLETT CIN 16-6	SEAVER NY 1.76	71
MELTON CHI 33	KILLEBREW MIN 119	OTIS KC 52	LOLICH DET 308	MC NALLY BAL 21-5	BLUE OAK 1.82	
BENCH CIN 40	BENCH CIN 125	BROCK STL 63	CARLTON PHI 310	NOLAN CIN 15-5	CARLTON PHI 1.98	72
R.ALLEN CHI 37	R.ALLEN CHI 113	CAMPANERIS OAK 52	RYAN CAL 329	HUNTER OAK 21-7	TIANT BOS 1.91	
STARGELL PIT 44	STARGELL PIT 119	BROCK STL 70	SEAVER NY 251	JOHN LA 16-7	SEAVER NY 2.08	73
JACKSON OAK 32	JACKSON OAK 117	HARPER BOS 54	RYAN CAL 383	HUNTER OAK 21-5	PALMER BAL 2.40	
SCHMIDT PHI 36	BENCH CIN 129	BROCK STL 118	CARLTON PHI 240	MESSERSMITH LA 20-6	CAPRA ATL 2.28	74
ALLEN CHI 32	BURROUGHS TEX 118	NORTH OAK 54	RYAN CAL 367	CUELLAR BAL 22-10	HUNTER OAK 2.49	
SCHMIDT PHI 38	LUZINSKI PHI 120	LOPES LA 77	SEAVER NY 243	GULLETT CIN 15-4	JONES SD 2.24	75
JACKSON,OAK SCOTT,MIL 36	SCOTT MIL 109	RIVERS CAL 70	TANANA CAL 269	TORREZ BAL 20-9	PALMER BAL 2.09	
SCHMIDT PHI 38	FOSTER CIN 121	LOPES LA 63	SEAVER NY 235	CARLTON PHI 20-7	DENNY STL 2.52	76
NETTLES NY 32	MAY BAL 109	NORTH OAK 75	RYAN CAL 327	CAMPBELL MIN 17-5	FIDRYCH DET 2.34	

CLUB LEADERS—INDIVIDUAL LIFETIME

AMERICAN ASSOCIATION

CLUB	BATTING	REC.	PITCHING	W–L	REC.
Athletics	Dennis Lyons (1887)	.469	Bob Matthews (1883)	30–14	.682
Baltimore	Tommy Burns (1887)	.401	Mat Kilroy (1887)	46–20	.697
Boston	Dan Brouthers (1891)	.352	Charles Buffinton (1891)	27–9	.750
			George Haddock (1891)	33–11	.750
Brooklyn	Jim McTamany (1887)	.354	Bob Caruthers (1889)	40–12	.769
Cincinnati	Frank Fennelly (1887)	.368	Will White (1882)	40–12	.769
Cleveland	Pete Hotaling (1887)	.367	Ed Bakely (1888)	25–33	.417
Columbus	John Johnson (1890)	.354	Ed Morris (1884)	35–13	.729
Indianapolis	Jim Keenan (1884)	.305	Larry McKeon (1884)	18–41	.305
Kansas City	Jim Burns (1889)	.303	Jim Conway (1889)	18–19	.486
Louisville	Pete Browning (1887)	.471	Guy Hecker (1884)	52–20	.722
Metropolitans	Dude Esterbrook (1884)	.408	John Lynch (1884)	39–14	.736
Milwaukee	Harry Vaughn (1891)	.330	Frank Killen (1891)	8–3	.727
Pittsburgh	Cy Swartwood (1883)	.369	Ed Morris (1886)	41–20	.672
Richmond	Mike Mansell (1884)	.301	Pete Meegan (1884)	7–12	.368
Rochester	Sandy Griffin (1890)	.305	Bill Calihan (1890)	18–13	.581
St. Louis	Tip O'Neill (1887)	.492	Silver King (1887)	34–11	.756
Syracuse	Cupid Childs (1890)	.344	Ed Mars (1890)	9–6	.600
Toledo	Cy Swartwood (1890)	.309	Tony Mullane (1884)	36–26	.581
Washington	Jim McGuire (1891)	.296	Frank Foreman (1891)	22–22	.500

AMERICAN LEAGUE

CLUB	BATTING	REC.	PITCHING	W–L	REC.
Baltimore					
1901–02	Mike Donlin (1901)	.340	Joe McGinnity (1901)	26–19	.578
1954–	Bob Nieman (1956)	.322	Dave McNally (1971)	21–5	.808
Boston	Ted Williams (1941)	.406	Joe Wood (1912)	34–5	.872
California	Alex Johnson (1970)	.329	Dean Chance (1964)	20–9	.690
Chicago	Luke Appling (1936)	.388	Sandy Consuegra (1954)	16–3	.842
Cleveland	Joe Jackson (1911)	.408	Johnny Allen (1937)	15–1	.938
Detroit	Ty Cobb (1911)	.420	Bill Donovan (1907)	25–4	.862
Kansas City					
1955–67	Vic Power (1955)	.319	Bud Daley (1959)	16–13	.522
1969–	George Brett (1976)	.333	Dennis Leonard (1975)	15–7	.682
Milwaukee					
1901	John Anderson (1901)	.339	Bill Reidy (1901)	15–18	.455
1970–	George Scott (1973)	.306	Jim Colborn (1973)	20–12	.625
Minnesota	Rod Carew (1974)	.364	Bill Campbell (1976)	17–5	.773
New York	Babe Ruth (1923)	.393	Whitey Ford (1961)	25–4	.862
Oakland	Joe Rudi (1970)	.309	Jim Hunter (1973)	21–5	.808
Philadelphia	Nap Lajoie (1901)	.422	Lefty Grove (1931)	31–4	.886
St. Louis	George Sisler (1922)	.420	General Crowder (1928)	21–5	.808
Seattle	Tommy Davis (1969)	.271	Diego Segui (1969)	12–6	.667
Texas	Mike Hargrove (1975)	.303	Ferguson Jenkins (1974)	25–12	.676
Washington					
1901–60	Goose Goslin (1928)	.379	Walter Johnson (1913)	36–7	.837
1961–71	Chuck Hinton (1962)	.310	Dick Bosman (1970)	16–12	.571

FEDERAL LEAGUE

CLUB	BATTING	REC.	PITCHING	W–L	REC.
Baltimore	Steve Evans (1915)	.319	Jack Quinn (1914)	26–14	.650
Brooklyn	Steve Evans (1914)	.355	Tom Seaton (1914)	25–14	.641
Buffalo	Hal Chase (1914)	.354	Russ Ford (1914)	21–6	.778
Chicago	Bill Fischer (1915)	.326	Claude Hendrix (1914)	29–10	.744
Indianapolis	Bennie Kauff (1914)	.366	George Kaiserling (1914)	17–10	.630
Kansas City	Ted Easterly (1914)	.331	Nick Cullop (1915)	22–11	.667
Newark	Vin Campbell (1915)	.314	Ed Reulbach (1915)	21–10	.677
Pittsburgh	Eggie Lennox (1914)	.317	Frank Allen (1915)	23–13	.639
St. Louis	Doc Crandall (1914)	.312	Mordecai Brown (1914)	11–5	.684

NATIONAL ASSOCIATION

Due to the fact that the records of this first major league are largely incomplete and that some box scores are missing, it is therefore impossible to compute the club leaders in batting and pitching for the National Association.

NATIONAL LEAGUE (1876–1899)

CLUB	BATTING	REC.	PITCHING	W–L	REC.
Athletics	George Hall (1876)	.355	Lon Knight (1876)	10–23	.303
Baltimore	Willie Keeler (1897)	.432	Bill Hoffer (1896)	26–7	.788
Boston	Hugh Duffy (1894)	.438	Fred Klobedanz (1897)	25–8	.758
			Parson Lewis (1898)	25–8	.758
Brooklyn	Willie Keeler (1899)	.376	Jim Hughes (1899)	25–5	.833
Buffalo	Dan Brouthers (1883)	.371	Jim Galvin (1884)	46–21	.687
Chicago	Cap Anson (1887)	.421	Fred Goldsmith (1880)	22–3	.880
Cincinnati	Bug Holliday (1894)	.383	Noodles Hahn (1899)	23–8	.742
Cleveland	Jess Burkett (1895)	.423	Cy Young (1895)	33–10	.767
Detroit	Dan Brouthers (1887)	.419	Lady Baldwin (1886)	31–11	.764
Hartford	John Cassidy (1877)	.378	Tommy Bond (1876)	32–13	.711
Indianapolis	Otto Shomberg (1887)	.389	Bill Burdick (1888)	10–10	.500
			Amos Rusie (1889)	11–11	.500
Kansas City	Al Myers (1886)	.276	Grasshopper Whitney (1886)	12–32	.273
Louisville	Fred Clarke (1897)	.406	Ellsworth Cunningham (1898)	28–15	.651
Milwaukee	Abner Dalrymple (1878)	.356	Sam Weaver (1878)	12–30	.286
Mutuals	Jim Hallinan (1876)	.277	Bob Mathews (1876)	21–34	.382
New York	Roger Connor (1887)	.382	Mickey Welch (1885)	47–11	.810
Philadelphia	Ed Delahanty (1899)	.408	Al Orth (1899)	13–3	.813
Pittsburgh	Jake Stenzel (1895)	.384	Adonis Terry (1892)	20–7	.741
Providence	Paul Hines (1879)	.357	Hoss Radbourn (1884)	60–12	.833
St. Louis	Jess Burkett (1899)	.402	George Bradley (1876)	45–19	.703
Syracuse	John Farrell (1879)	.304	Pat McCormick (1879)	11–13	.458
Troy	Roger Connor (1880)	.332	Mickey Welch (1880)	34–30	.531
Washington	Paul Hines (1887)	.370	Al Maul (1895)	11–6	.647
Worcester	Lewis Dickerson (1881)	.316	Fred Corey (1880)	9–8	.529

NATIONAL LEAGUE (1900–1973)

CLUB	BATTING	REC.	PITCHING	W–L	REC.
Atlanta	Rico Carty (1970)	.366	Ron Reed (1969)	18–8	.643
Boston	Rogers Hornsby (1928)	.387	Tom Hughes (1916)	16–3	.842
Brooklyn	Babe Herman (1930)	.393	Fred Fitzsimmons (1940)	16–2	.889
Chicago	Rogers Hornsby (1929)	.380	King Cole (1910)	20–4	.833
Cincinnati	Cy Seymour (1905)	.377	Elmer Riddle (1941)	19–4	.826
Houston	Rusty Staub (1967)	.333	Larry Dierker (1972)	15–8	.652
Los Angeles	Tommy Davis (1962)	.346	Ron Perranoski (1963)	16–3	.842
Milwaukee	Hank Aaron (1959)	.355	Warren Spahn (1953, 63)	23–7	.767
			Mike Torrez (1974)	15–8	.652
Montreal	Rusty Staub (1971)	.311	Dale Murray (1975)	15–8	.652
N. Y. Giants	Bill Terry (1930)	.401	Hoyt Wilhelm (1952)	15–3	.833
N. Y. Mets	Cleon Jones (1969)	.340	Tom Seaver (1969)	25–7	.781
Philadelphia	Lefty O'Doul (1929)	.398	Robin Roberts (1952)	28–7	.800
Pittsburgh	Arky Vaughan (1935)	.385	Elroy Face (1959)	18–1	.947
St. Louis	Rogers Hornsby (1924)	.424	Dizzy Dean (1934)	30–7	.811
San Diego	Clarence Gaston (1970)	.318	Randy Jones (1975)	20–12	.625
San Francisco	Willie Mays (1958)	.347	Juan Marichal (1966)	25–6	.806

PLAYER'S LEAGUE

CLUB	BATTING	REC.	PITCHING	W–L	REC.
Boston	Dan Brouthers (1890)	.345	Ad Gumbert (1890)	22–9	.710
Brooklyn	Dave Orr (1890)	.387	Gus Weyhing (1890)	31–15	.674
Buffalo	Ed Beecher (1890)	.357	Bert Cunningham (1890)	10–15	.400
Chicago	Jimmy Ryan (1890)	.330	Silver King (1890)	33–20	.623
Cleveland	Pete Browning (1890)	.391	Billy McGill (1890)	11–9	.550
New York	Roger Connor (1890)	.372	Tim Keefe (1890)	17–8	.680
Philadelphia	George Wood (1890)	.304	Philip Knell (1890)	20–11	.645
Pittsburgh	Jake Beckley (1890)	.325	Al Maul (1890)	17–11	.607

UNION ASSOCIATION

CLUB	BATTING	REC.	PITCHING	W–L	REC.
Altoona	Germany Smith (1884)	.307	Connie Murphy (1884)	4–6	.400
Baltimore	John Seery (1884)	.309	Bill Sweeney (1884)	40–21	.656
Boston	Ed Crane (1884)	.304	Dupee Shaw (1884)	22–15	.595
Chicago	Lew Shoenick (1884)	.315	One-Arm Daly (1884)	22–25	.468
Cincinnati	Dick Burns (1884)	.315	Jim McCormick (1884)	22–4	.846
Kansas City	Jack Gorman (1884)	.275	Ernest Hickman (1884)	3–13	.188
Keystone	Bill Hoover (1884)	.355	Enoch Bakely (1884)	14–24	.368
Milwaukee	Al Myers (1884)	.326	Ed Cushman (1884)	4–0	1.000
Pittsburgh	Lew Shoenick (1884)	.276	One-Arm Daly (1884)	5–4	.556
St. Louis	Fred Dunlap (1884)	.420	Charles Hodnet (1884)	12–1	.923
			Bill Taylor (1884)	24–2	.923
St. Paul	Jimmy Brown (1884)	.313	Bill O'Brien (1884)	1–1	.500
Washington	Harry Moore (1884)	.337	Charles Gagus (1884)	11–9	.550
Wilmington	Tom Lynch (1884)	.281	Dan Casey (1884)	1–1	.500

SPECIAL AWARDS

(Chosen by Baseball Writers' Association)

MOST VALUABLE PLAYER

*unanimous selection

Year	AMERICAN LEAGUE — Player Club	NATIONAL LEAGUE — Player Club
1931	Robert Grove, Philadelphia, p	Frank Frisch, St. Louis, 2b
1932	James Foxx, Philadelphia, 1b	Charles Klein, Philadelphia, of
1933	James Foxx, Philadelphia, 1b	Carl Hubbell, New York, p
1934	Gordon Cochrane, Detroit, c	Jerome Dean, St. Louis, p
1935	Henry Greenberg, Detroit, 1b*	Charles Hartnett, Chicago, c
1936	H. Louis Gehrig, New York, 1b	Carl Hubbell, New York, p
1937	Charles Gehringer, Detroit, 2b	Joseph Medwick, St. Louis, of
1938	James Foxx, Boston, 1b	Ernest Lombardi, Cinncinnati, c
1939	Joseph DiMaggio, N. York, of	William Walters, Cincinnati, p
1940	Henry Greenberg, Detroit, of	Frank McCormick, Cincinnati, 1b
1941	Joseph DiMaggio, N. York, of	Adolph Camilli, Brooklyn, 1b
1942	Joseph Gordon, New York, 2b	Morton Cooper, St. Louis, p
1943	Spurgeon Chandler, N. Y., p	Stanley Musial, St. Louis, of
1944	Harold Newhouser, Detroit, p	Martin Marion, St. Louis, ss
1945	Harold Newhouser, Detroit, p	Philip Cavarretta, Chicago, 1b
1946	Theodore Williams, Boston, of	Stanley Musial, St. Louis, 1b
1947	Joseph DiMaggio, N. York, of	Robert Elliott, Boston, 3b
1948	Louis Boudreau, Cleveland, ss	Stanley Musial, St. Louis, of
1949	Theodore Williams, Boston, of	Jack Robinson, Brooklyn, 2b
1950	Philip Rizzuto, New York, ss	C. James Konstanty, Philadelphia, p
1951	Lawrence Berra, New York, c	Roy Campanella, Brooklyn, c
1952	Robert Shantz, Philadelphia, p	Henry Sauer, Chicago, of
1953	Albert Rosen, Cleveland, 3b*	Roy Campanella, Brooklyn, c
1954	Lawrence Berra, New York, c	Willie Mays, New York, of
1955	Lawrence Berra, New York, c	Roy Campanella, Brooklyn, c
1956	Mickey Mantle, New York, of*	Donald Newcombe, Brooklyn, p
1957	Mickey Mantle, New York, of	Henry Aaron, Milwaukee, of
1958	Jack Jensen, Boston, of	Ernest Banks, Chicago, ss
1959	J. Nelson Fox, Chicago, 2b	Ernest Banks, Chicago, ss
1960	Roger Maris, New York, of	Richard Groat, Pittsburgh, ss
1961	Roger Maris, New York, of	Frank Robinson, Cincinnati, of
1962	Mickey Mantle, New York, of	Maurice Wills, Los Angeles, ss
1963	Elston Howard, New York, c	Sanford Koufax, Los Angeles, p
1964	Brooks Robinson, Baltimore, 3b	Kenton Boyer, St. Louis, 3b
1965	Zoilo Versalles, Minn., ss	Willie Mays, San Francisco, of
1966	Frank Robinson, Baltimore, of*	Roberto Clemente, Pittsburgh, of
1967	Carl Yastrzemski, Boston, of	Orlando Cepeda, St. Louis, 1b*
1968	Dennis McLain, Detroit, p*	Robert Gibson, St. Louis, p
1969	Harmon Killebrew, Minn., 1-3b	Willie McCovey, San Francisco, 1b
1970	John Powell, Baltimore, 1b	Johnny Bench, Cincinnati, c
1971	Vida Blue, Oakland, p	Joe Torre, St. Louis, 1-c
1972	Richard Allen, Chicago 1b	Johnny Bench, Cincinnati, c
1973	Reginald Jackson, Oakland, of	Peter Rose, Cincinnati, of
1974	Jeffrey Burroughs, Texas, of	Steven Garvey, Los Angeles, 1b
1975	Fredric Lynn, Boston, of	Joseph Morgan, Cincinnati, 2b
1976	Thurman Munson, New York, c	Joseph Morgan, Cincinnati, 2b

ROOKIE OF THE YEAR

1947—Combined selection—Jack Robinson, Brooklyn, 1b
1948—Combined selection—Alvin Dark, Boston, N. L., ss

AMERICAN LEAGUE	NATIONAL LEAGUE
Year Player Club	Player Club
1949—Roy Sievers, St. Louis, of	Donald Newcombe, Brooklyn, p
1950—Walter Dropo, Boston, 1b	Samuel Jethroe, Boston, of
1951—Gilbert McDougald, N. Y., 3b	Willie Mays, New York, of
1952—Harry Byrd, Philadelphia, p	Joseph Black, Brooklyn, p
1953—Harvey Kuenn, Detroit, ss	James Gilliam, Brooklyn, 2b
1954—Robert Grim, New York, p	Wallace Moon, St. Louis, of
1955—Herbert Score, Cleveland, p	William Virdon, St. Louis, of
1956—Louis Aparicio, Chicago, ss	Frank Robinson, Cincinnati, of•
1957—Anthony Kubek, N. Y., inf.-of	John Sanford, Philadelphia, p
1958—Albert Pearson, Washington, of	Orlando Cepeda, San Francisco, 1b•
1959—W. Robert Allison, Wash., of	Willie McCovey, San Francisco, 1b•
1960—Ronald Hansen, Baltimore, ss	Frank Howard, Los Angeles, of
1961—Donald Schwall, Boston, p	Billy Williams, Chicago, of
1962—Thomas Tresh, New York, of-ss	Kenneth Hubbs, Chicago, 2b
1963—Gary Peters, Chicago, p	Peter Rose, Cincinnati, 2b
1964—Pedro (Tony) Oliva, Minn., of	Richard Allen, Philadelphia, 3b
1965—Curtis Blefary, Baltimore, of	James Lefebvre, Los Angeles, 2b
1966—Tommic Agee, Chicago, of	Tommy Helms, Cincinnati, 3b
1967—Rod Carew, Minnesota, 2b	Tom Seaver, New York, p
1968—Stan Bahnsen, New York, p	Johnny Bench, Cincinnati, c
1969—Lou Piniella, Kansas City, of	Ted Sizemore, Los Angeles, 2b
1970—Thurman Munson, New York, c	Carl Morton, Montreal, p
1971—Chris Chambliss, Cleveland, 1b	Earl Williams, Atlanta, 3b
1972—Carlton Fisk, Boston, c	Jonathan Matlack, New York, p
1973—Alonza Bumbry, Baltimore, of	Gary Matthews, San Francisco, of
1974—D. Michael Hargrove, Texas, 1b	Arnold McBride, St. Louis, of
1975—Fredric Lynn, Boston, of	John Montefusco, San Francisco, p
1976—Mark Fidrych, Detroit, p	Clarence Metzger, San Diego, p (tie)
	Patrick Zachry, Cincinnati, p (tie)

CY YOUNG MEMORIAL AWARD

Year   Pitcher   Club
1956—Donald Newcombe, Brooklyn
1957—Warren Spahn, Milwaukee
1958—Robert Turley, N. Y., A. L.
1959—Early Wynn, Chicago, A. L.
1960—Vernon Law, Pittsburgh
1961—Edward Ford, N. Y., A. L.
1962—Donald Drysdale, L. A., N. L.
1963—Sanford Koufax, L. A., N. L.•
1964—Dean Chance, L. A., A. L.
1965—Sanford Koufax, L. A., N. L.•
1966—Sanford Koufax, L. A., N. L.•
1967—A. L.—Jim Lonborg, Boston
      N. L.—Michael McCormick, San Francisco
1968—A. L.—Dennis McLain, Detroit•
      N. L.—Bob Gibson, St Louis•
1969—A. L.—Dennis McLain, Detroit
          Mike Cuellar, Baltimore
      N. L.—Tom Seaver, New York
1970—A. L.—Jim Perry, Minn.
      N. L.—Bob Gibson, St. Louis
1971—A. L.—Vida Blue, Oakland
      N. L.—Ferguson Jenkins, Chicago
1972—A. L.—Gaylord Perry, Cleveland
      N. L.—Steven Carlton, Philadelphia•
1973—A. L.—James Palmer, Baltimore
      N. L.—G. Thomas Seaver, New York
1974—A. L.—James Hunter, Oakland
      N. L.—Michael Marshall, Los Angeles
1975—A. L.—James Palmer, Baltimore
      N. L.—G. Thomas Seaver, New York
1976—A. L.—James Palmer, Baltimore
      N. L.—Randall Jones, San Diego

VII SPECIAL RECORDS

VANDY'S DOUBLE NO-HITTER

In 1938 a 23-year-old Cincinnati lefthander put together baseball's most unusual pitching feat—no-hit, no-run games back-to-back.

Johnny Vander Meer earned the distinction of being called "Double No-Hitter" by pitching 18 consecutive hitless inning in two complete games, perhaps the most phenomenal of all single season pitching records.

Vandy was in his second season in the National League when lightning struck twice for him. It started on June 11 at Cincinnati where the southpaw whipped the Boston Bees, 3-0. Losing pitcher Danny MacFayden allowed only six hits but gave up a run in the fourth inning and a one-on home run to Ernie Lombardi in the sixth. Vandy's initial no-hitter was fashioned in one hour and 48 minutes, and only his three passes prevented a perfect performance.

On June 15, four days after he became a national figure, Vandy turned in his second successive no-hit, no-run job under more dramatic circumstances. The game marked the first night contest at Brooklyn's Ebbets Field and a capacity crowd watched the Reds' lefty blank the Dodgers, 6-0. Losing pitcher Max Butcher, Tot Pressnell, Luke Hamlin and Vito Tamulis were the Brooklyn hurlers but the center of attraction was the visitors' moundsman.

Four runs in the third inning all but assured Cincinnati of victory but the fans stayed to watch Vander Meer's bid for his double no-hitter. When he recorded the 27th out—his 54th straight without a hit—he had established a personal pitching record which may never be equaled in baseball history.

GIANTS' RECORD STREAKS

The New York Giants of 1916 ran off a remarkable winning streak of 26 games, modern baseball's longest victory string. However, unlike other teams which used long winning runs to make their push for a pennant a bit easier, the Giants of that year finished no higher than fourth.

The streaky Giants actually played that 1916 season in two parts: the first one being another victory string of 17 straight, the second a run of 26. Of the 86 games won by the New Yorkers that season, 43 were accomplished in unusual fashion. The 17 straight victories were all made while the Giants were the visiting club; the streak of 26 was compiled in the last month of the season, all at the Polo Grounds, home grounds for the Giants.

Here are the dates and scores of the two streaks:

ABROAD (17 straight)			HOME (26 straight)	
May 9:	13—Pittsburgh 5.		September 7:	4—Brooklyn 1.
May 10:	7—Pittsburgh 1.		September 8:	9—Philadelphia 3.
May 11:	3—Pittsburgh 2.		September 9:	3—Philadelphia 1.
May 12:	3—Pittsburgh 2.		September 9:	3—Philadelphia 0.
May 14:	6—Chicago 4.		September 10:	9—Philadelphia 4.
May 15:	3—Chicago 2.		September 12:	3—Cincinnati 2.
May 17:	9—St. Louis 3.		September 13:	3—Cincinnati 0.
May 18:	3—St. Louis 0.		September 13:	6—Cincinnati 4.
May 19:	5—St. Louis 4.		September 14:	3—Cincinnati 1.
May 20:	4—St. Louis 1.		September 16:	8—Pittsburgh 2.
May 21:	11—Cincinnati 1.		September 16:	4—Pittsburgh 3.
May 23:	4—Cincinnati 3.		September 18:	2—Pittsburgh 0.
May 24:	6—Cincinnati 1.		September 18:	1—Pittsburgh 1 (tie)
May 26:	12—Boston 1.		September 19:	9—Pittsburgh 2.
May 27:	4—Boston 3.		September 19:	5—Pittsburgh 1.
May 27:	2—Boston 1.		September 20:	4—Chicago 2.
May 29:	3—Boston 0.		September 21:	4—Chicago 0.
			September 22:	5—Chicago 0.
			September 23:	6—St. Louis 1.
			September 23:	3—St. Louis 0.
			September 25:	1—St. Louis 0.
			September 25:	6—St. Louis 2.
			September 26:	6—St. Louis 1.
			September 27:	3—St. Louis 2.
			September 28:	2—Boston 0.
			September 28:	6—Boston 0.
			September 30:	4—Boston 0.

DIMAGGIO'S 56

Baseball's most amazing single season hitting streak is the one performed by Joe DiMaggio in 1941 when he hit safely in 56 straight games. The graceful New York Yankee outfielder started his incredible string on May 15 and continued it through July 16, a two-month period during which he hit for a .408 average.

On his way to this all-time standard DiMag early passed the National League mark of 33 made by Rogers Hornsby and eclipsed the then existing American League record of 41 set by George Sisler. Three games later, the previous record run of 44 established by Willie Keeler in 1897 was by the boards.

Here is the statistical story of the DiMaggio streak, from start to finish:

Date	Club—Pitchers	AB	R	H	2B	3B	HR	RBI
May 15	Chi—Smith	4	—	1	—	—	—	1
16	Chi—Lee	4	2	2	—	1	1	1
17	Chi—Rigney	3	1	1	—	—	—	—
18	St. L—Harris (2 hits), Niggeling (1)	3	3	3	1	—	—	1
19	St. L—Galehouse	3	—	1	1	—	—	—
20	St. L—Auker	5	1	1	—	—	—	1
21	Det—Rowe (1), Benton (1)	5	—	2	—	—	—	1
22	Det—McKain	4	—	1	—	—	—	1
23	Bos—Newsom	5	—	1	—	—	—	2
24	Bos—Johnson	4	2	1	—	—	—	2
25	Bos—Grove	4	—	1	—	—	--	—
27	Was—Chase (1), Anderson (2), Carrasquel (1)	5	3	4	—	-	1	3
(Night) 28	Was—Hudson	4	1	1	—	1	—	—
29	Was—Sundra	3	1	1	—	-	—	—
30	Bos—Johnson	2	1	1	—	-	—	—
30	Bos—Harris	3	—	1	1	-	—	—
June 1	Cle—Milnar	4	1	1	—	-	—	—
1	Cle—Harder	4	—	1	—	-	—	—
2	Cle—Feller	4	2	2	1	-	—	—
3	Det—Trout	4	1	1	—	-	1	1
5	Det—Newhouser	5	1	1	—	1	—	1
7	St. L—Muncrief (1), Allen (1), Caster (1)	5	2	3	—	-	—	1
8	St. L—Auker	4	3	2	—	-	2	4
8	St. L—Caster (1), Kramer (1)	4	1	2	1	-	1	3
10	Chi—Rigney	5	1	1	—	-	—	—
(Night) 12	Chi—Lee	4	1	2	—	-	1	1
14	Cle—Feller	2	—	1	1	-	—	1
15	Cle—Bagby	3	1	1	—	-	1	1
16	Cle—Milnar	5	—	1	1	-	—	—
17	Chi—Rigney	4	1	1	—	-	—	—
18	Chi—Lee	3	—	1	—	-	—	—
19	Chi—Smith (1), Ross (2)	3	2	3	—	-	1	2
20	Det—Newsom (2), McKain (2)	5	3	4	1	-	—	1
21	Det—Trout	4	—	1	—	-	—	1
22	Det—Newhouser (1), Newsom (1)	5	1	2	1	-	1	2
24	St. L—Muncrief	4	1	1	—	-	—	—
25	St. L—Galehouse	4	1	1	—	-	1	3
26	St. L—Auker	4	—	1	1	-	—	1
27	Phi—Dean	3	1	2	—	-	1	2
28	Phi—Babich (1), Harris (1)	5	1	2	1	-	—	—
29	Was—Leonard	4	1	1	1	-	—	—
29	Was—Anderson	5	1	1	—	-	—	1
July 1	Bos—Harris (1), Ryba (1)	4	—	2	—	-	—	1
1	Bos—Wilson	3	1	1	—	-	—	1
2	Bos—Newsom	5	1	1	—	-	1	3
5	Phi—Marchildon	4	2	1	—	-	1	2
6	Phi—Babich (1), Hadley (3)	5	2	4	1	-	—	2
6	Phi—Knott	4	—	2	1	-	—	2
(Night) 10	St. L—Niggeling	2	—	1	—	-	—	—
11	St. L—Harris (3), Kramer (1)	5	1	4	—	-	1	2
12	St. L—Auker (1), Muncrief (1)	5	1	2	1	-	—	1
13	Chi—Lyons (2), Hallett (1)	4	2	3	—	-	—	—
13	Chi—Lee	4	—	1	—	-	—	—
14	Chi—Rigney	3	—	1	—	-	—	—
15	Chi—Smith	4	1	2	1	-	—	2
16	Cle—Milnar (2), Krakauskas (1)	4	3	3	1	-	—	—
	Totals for 56 games	223	56	91	16	4	15	55

Streak stopped in Cleveland night game, July 17, by Smith and Bagby. Batting average for this streak, .408.

Numbers in parenthesis indicate number of hits off each pitcher if there was more than one in game.

RUTH'S 60 Quick, now! Which is baseball's most remembered number? Why 60, of course, the total number of home runs hit by Babe Ruth in 1927.

It's true that when Ruth reached the magic figure of 60 in 1927 a ball which bounced from the field into the stands was scored as a home run. Under today's rules, this is scored as a two base hit. However, those fortunate enough to see Ruth in all his majesty cannot recall when any of the home runs he drove in his record-making year first struck the playing field before bouncing into the stands.

The Babe, who was the creator of all the home run standards in the ledgers of baseball, hit his 60th homer in the last game of the season. Previous record-holder? Babe Ruth, with 59 in 1921.

The Significant Sixty smashed by Ruth, only 28 of which were hit at his home grounds, the Yankee Stadium.

HR No.	Game No. Date	Opposing Pitcher and Club	Where Made	HR No.	Game No. Date	Opposing Pitcher and Club	Where Made
	April			42.	125	28--Wingard, (L), St. L . . .	St.L.
1.	4	15--Ehmke, (R), Phi	N.Y.	43.	127	31--Welzer, (R), Bos	N.Y.
2.	11	23--Walberg, (L), Phi	Phi.		September		
3.	12	24--Thurston, (R), Was . .	Was.	44.	128	2--Walberg, (L), Phi	Phi.
4.	14	29--Harriss, (R), Bos . . .	Bos.	45.	132	6--Welzer, (R), Bos	Bos.
	May			46.	132	6--Welzer, (R), Bos	Bos.
5.	16	1 Quinn, (R), Phi	N.Y.	47.	133	6--Russell, (R), Bos	Bos.
6.	16	1--Walberg, (L), Phi . . .	N.Y.	48.	134	7--MacFayden, (R), Bos. .	Bos.
7.	24	10--Gaston, (R), St. L	St.L.	49.	134	7--Harriss, (R), Bos	Bos.
8.	25	11--Nevers, (R), St.L	St.L.	50.	138	11--Gaston, (R), St. L	N.Y.
9.	29	17--Collins, (R), Det. . . .	Det.	51.	139	13--Hudlin, (R), Cle	N.Y.
10.	33	22--Karr, (R), Cle	Cle.	52.	140	13--Shaute, (L), Cle	N.Y.
11.	34	23--Thurston, (R), Was. . .	Was.	53.	143	16--Blankenship, (R), Chi .	N.Y.
12.	37	28--Thurston, (R), Was. . .	N.Y.	54.	147	18--Lyons, (R), Chi	N.Y.
13.	39	29--MacFayden, (R), Bos .	N.Y.	55.	148	21--Gibson, (R), Det	N.Y.
14.	41	30--Walberg, (L), Phi . . .	Phi.	56.	149	22--Holloway, (R), Det . . .	N.Y.
15.	42	31--Ehmke, (R), Phi.	Phi.	57.	152	27--Grove, (L), Phi	N.Y.
16.	43	31--Quinn, (R), Phi	Phi.	58.	153	29--Lisenbee, (R), Was . . .	N.Y.
	June			59.	153	29--Hopkins, (R), Was . . .	N.Y.
17.	47	5--Whitehill, (L), Det . . .	N.Y.	60.	154	30--Zachary, (L), Was . . .	N.Y.
18.	48	7--Thomas, (R), Chi	N.Y.				
19.	52	11--Buckeye, (L), Cle. . . .	N.Y.				
20.	52	11--Buckeye, (L), Cle. . . .	N.Y.				
21.	53	12--Uhle, (R), Cle	N.Y.				
22.	55	16--Zachary, (L), St.L . . .	N.Y.				
23.	60	22--Wiltse, (L), Bos	Bos.				
24.	60	22--Wiltse, (L), Bos	Bos.				
25.	70	30--Harriss, (R), Bos	N.Y.				
	July						
26.	73	3--Lisenbee, (R), Was . . .	Was.				
27.	78	8--Whitehill, (L), Det . . .	Det.				
28.	79	9--Holloway, (R), Det . . .	Det.				
29.	79	9--Holloway, (R), Det . . .	Det.				
30.	83	12--Shaute, (L), Cle	Cle.				
31.	94	24--Thomas, (R), Chi	Chi.				
32.	95	26--Gaston, (R), St. L . . .	N.Y.				
33.	95	26--Gaston, (R), St. L	N.Y.				
34.	98	28--Stewart, (L), St. L . . .	N.Y.				
	August						
35.	106	5--G. Smith, (R), Det . . .	N.Y.				
36.	110	10--Zachary, (L), Was . . .	Was.				
37.	114	16--Thomas, (R), Chi	Chi.				
38.	115	17--Connally, (R), Chi. . . .	Chi.				
39.	118	20--Miller, (L), Cle	Cle.				
40.	120	22--Shaute, (L), Cle	Cle.				
41.	124	27--Nevers, (R), St. L. . . .	St.L.				

MARIS' 61 Ever since Babe Ruth hit his 60 home runs in 1927 fans have argued about the chances of his record being broken. These arguments were revived in 1930 when Hack Wilson of the Chicago Cubs walloped 56, and again in 1932 and 1938 when first Jimmy Foxx and then Hammerin' Hank Greenberg smacked 58. It took an elongated season of 162 games and Roger Maris' booming bat to best the Babe's record. Like the Babe, Roger socked his record-breaking homer in the last game of the season. Maris, however, hit 30 homers at the Yankee Stadium whereas Babe hit only 28 on his home grounds.

HR No.	Game No.	Date	Opposing Pitcher and Club	Where Made
		April		
1.	10	26--	Foytack, (R), Det	Det.
		May		
2.	16	3--	Ramos, (R), Min.	Min.
3.	19	6--	Grba, (R), L.A.	L.A.
4.	28	17--	Burnside (L), Was . . .	N.Y.
5.	29	19--	Perry (R), Cle.	Cle.
6.	30	20--	Bell, (R), Cle	Cle.
7.	31	21--	Estrada, (R), Bal	N.Y.
8.	34	24--	Conley (R), Bos	N.Y.
9.	37	28--	McLish, (R), Chi	N.Y.
10.	39	30--	Conley (R), Bos	Bos.
11.	39	30--	Fornieles (R), Bos . . .	Bos.
12.	40	31--	Muffett (R), Bos	Bos.
		June		
13.	42	2--	McLish (R), Chi.	Chi.
14.	43	3--	Shaw (R), Chi	Chi.
15.	44	4--	Kemmerer (R), Chi. . .	Chi.
16.	47	6--	Palmquist, (R), Min . .	N.Y.
17.	48	7--	Ramos, (R), Min.	N.Y.
18.	51	9--	Herbert, (R), K.C . . .	N.Y.
19.	54	11--	Grba, (R), L.A.	N.Y.
20.	54	11--	James, (R), L.A.	N.Y.
21.	56	13--	Perry, (R), Cle	Cle.
22.	57	14--	Bell, (R), Cle	Cle.
23.	60	17--	Mossi, (L), Det	Det.
24.	61	18--	Casale, (R), Det	Det.
25.	62	19--	Archer, (L), K.C	K.C.
26.	63	20--	Nuxhall, (L), K.C	K.C.
27.	65	22--	Bass, (R), K.C	K.C.
		July		
28.	73	1--	Sisler, (R), Was	N.Y.
29.	74	2--	Burnside, (L), Was . . .	N.Y.
30.	74	2--	Klippstein, (R), Was . .	N.Y.
31.	76	4--	Lary, (R), Det	N.Y.
32.	77	5--	Funk, (R), Cle	N.Y.
33.	81	9--	Monbouquette, (R), Bos	N.Y.
34.	83	13--	Wynn, (R), Chi.	Chi.
		July		
35.	85	15--	Herbert, (R), Chi	Chi.
36.	91	21--	Monbouquette, (R), Bos.	Bos.
37.	94	25--	Baumann, (L), Chi . . .	N.Y.
38.	94	25--	Larsen, (R), Chi.	N.Y.
39.	95	25--	Kemmerer, (R), Chi . .	N.Y.
40.	95	25--	Hacker, (R), Chi.	N.Y.
		August		
41.	105	4--	Pascual, (R), Min	N.Y.
42.	113	11--	Burnside, (L), Was . . .	Was.
43.	114	12--	Donovan, (R), Was . . .	Was.
44.	115	13--	Daniels, (R), Was	Was.
45.	116	13--	Kutyna, (R), Was	Was.
46.	117	15--	Pizarro, (L), Chi	N.Y.
47.	118	16--	Pierce, (L), Chi.	N.Y.
48.	118	16--	Pierce, (L), Chi.	N.Y.
49.	122	20--	Perry, (R), Cle	Cle.
50.	124	22--	McBride, (R), L.A . . .	L.A.
51.	128	26--	Walker, (R), K.C	K.C.
		September		
52.	134	2--	Lary, (R), Det	N.Y.
53.	134	2--	Aguirre, (L), Det	N.Y.
54.	139	6--	Cheney, (R), Was	N.Y.
55.	140	7--	Stigman, (L), Cle	N.Y.
56.	142	9--	Grant, (R), Cle.	N.Y.
57.	150	16--	Lary, (R), Det	Det.
58.	151	17--	Fox, (R), Det	Det.
59.	154	20--	Pappas, (R), Bal.	Bal.
60.	158	26--	Fisher, (R), Bal	N.Y.
		October		
61.	162	1--	Stallard, (R), Bos	N.Y.

19 STRAIGHT WINS

Two more remarkable pitching performances were those recorded by two New York Giants under different pitching standards. Tim Keefe and Rube Marquard each pitched 19 straight victories, Keefe's coming in 1888 when the pitching distance to the plate was a mere 50 feet. Lefthander Marquard managed his record in 1912 under present day pitching requirements. The victory-by-victory tables of baseball's best season winning streaks:

TIM KEEFE, NEW YORK, N. L., 1888

50 feet; 5½ × 4 Box. High or Low Ball abolished.

DATE	OPPOSING CLUB	DATE	OPPOSING CLUB
June 23 -- Keefe, 7;	Philadelphia, 6	July 20 -- Keefe, 7;	Philadelphia, 6
June 26 -- Keefe, 4;	Philadelphia, 1	July 23 -- Keefe, 2;	Boston, 0
June 29 -- Keefe, 8;	Washington, 3	July 25 -- Keefe, 5;	Boston, 1
July 2 -- Keefe, 6;	Washington, 2	July 28 -- Keefe, 4;	Philadelphia, 2
July 4 -- Keefe, 4;	Detroit, 1	Aug. 1 -- Keefe, 5;	Washington, 4
July 7 -- Keefe, 6;	Pittsburgh, 4	Aug. 3 -- Keefe, 9;	Boston, 6
July 11 -- Keefe, 5;	Indianapolis, 2	Aug. 6 -- Keefe, 3;	Indianapolis, 2
July 13 -- Keefe, 4;	Indianapolis, 0	Aug. 8 -- Keefe, 4;	Indianapolis, 1
July 16 -- Keefe, 12;	Chicago, 4	Aug. 10 -- Keefe, 2;	Pittsburgh, 1
July 17 -- Keefe, 7;	Chicago, 4		

RUBE MARQUARD, NEW YORK, N. L., 1912

60 feet, 5 inches; 24-inch Slab; One Step.

DATE	OPPOSING CLUB	DATE	OPPOSING CLUB
April 11 -- Marquard, 18;	Brooklyn, 3	June 3 -- Marquard, 8;	St. Louis, 3
April 16 -- Marquard, 8;	Boston, 2	June 8 -- Marquard, 6;	Cincinnati, 2
April 24 -- Marquard, 11;	Philadelphia, 4	June 12 -- Marquard, 3;	Chicago, 2
May 1 -- Marquard, 11;	Philadelphia, 4	June 17 -- Marquard, 5;	Pittsburgh, 4
May 7 -- Marquard, 6;	St. Louis, 2	June 19 -- Marquard, 6;	Boston, 5
May 11 -- Marquard, 10;	Chicago, 3	June 21 -- Marquard, 5;	Boston, 2
May 16 -- Marquard, 4;	Pittsburgh, 1	June 25 -- Marquard, 2;	Philadelphia, 1
May 20 -- Marquard, 3;	Cincinnati, 0	June 29 -- Marquard, 8;	Boston, 6
May 24 -- Marquard, 6;	Brooklyn, 3	July 3 — Marquard, 2;	Brooklyn, 1
May 30 -- Marquard, 7;	Philadelphia, 1		

VIII   HONORED PLAYERS

HALL OF FAME   Baseball has produced giants in all departments of play
since the National Association was born in 1871, and
it was inevitable that the deeds of these greats would
someday be enshrined in a permanent vault which would
make imperishable their all-time credentials.

Thirty-two years before the National Baseball Hall of Fame was established in Cooperstown, New York, on June 12, 1939 the administrators of baseball had set into motion the machinery which was to result in the recognition of this small central New York State village as the cradle of the game.

A special investigating committee appointed by Albert G. Spalding was entrusted with the historical task of discovering the original spot on which baseball was played in America. This committee, headed by A. G. Mills, a former National League president, reported on December 30, 1907 that "the first scheme for playing baseball, according to best obtainable evidence, was devised by Abner Doubleday at Cooperstown, New York, in 1839."

No committee was ever so far from the facts. Doubleday, who may have played at some form of baseball, and in the very village which borders picturesque Lake Otsego, was a student at West Point in the very year he was supposed to have "devised his scheme." Evidently Mills and his committee never bothered to investigate the authenticity of a report which in later years was proved to be without any circumstantial foundation by recognized historians.

But baseball deserves a shrine, and since the natives of Cooperstown have provided a mecca worthy of the pastime just where and when the game was started no longer is an issue of bitter and major controversy. Now at last the game was granted its own permanent museum and display case and dedication came on June 12, 1939. The Museum, Hall of Fame and Doubleday Field, which used to be Farmer Phinney's pasture when Doubleday, later to become a Union Major General in the Civil War, romped as a schoolboy, were all officially launched in impressive ceremonies, the most dramatic of which was the spectacle of the game's greatest heroes taking their appointed places with immortality.

In the National Baseball Museum is housed the world's most complete collection of the game's memorabilia: the largest baseball library in the world; priceless relics such as the first catcher's mitt and the bat with which Ruth clouted his 60th homer in 1927; sculptures, paintings, photographs and drawings that form a classic and graphic history of the colorful long-ago.

Enshrined in The Hall of Fame wing of the Museum are the bronze plaques of the pastime's immortals, placed there by a vote of outstanding experts who have been selected to choose the greats of the diamond. The method of selection is simple: A special committee of baseball officials, picked because of their deep knowledge and service to the game, is entrusted with the honor of choosing players who performed more than a quarter of century ago. All players whose careers began 30 years before and ended five years prior to the election are eligible to gain entrance into the Hall of Fame by a ballot system. Only members of the Baseball Writers' Association of America for at

least ten years are eligible to vote, and the successful player must receive at least 75 percent of all votes cast to gain admission.

Since the first group was chosen in 1936 the annual balloting system has been frequently under attack by those who claim sectional and personal favoritism occasionally is the basis for a writer's ballot. However few will deny the qualities of the giants who have been so honored. Their selection has met with an almost unanimous approval from the fans.

A special committee also votes on candidates for Veterans Hall of Fame plaque awards. To be eligible for admission an oldtime player must be retired for at least 30 years prior to election; managers and umpires, retired from their capacities for at least five years, are also eligible.

THE SELECT FIVE

To start its huge family in 1936 the baseball writers of that era chose five players whose performances have stamped them as the greatest of them all by more people than any others. The Select Five to acquire more than 75 percent on the first balloting for Hall of Fame entrance consisted of Ty Cobb, Babe Ruth, Christy Mathewson, Honus Wagner and Walter Johnson, all selected in that order.

It's only fitting that the man to establish more records than any other spiked hero would receive the greatest number of votes. That would be Cobb, the Georgia Peach, son of an educator, who in 24 years in the American League played 3,033 games as if each one was the final clash of a World Series.

What qualities did Cobb possess which made him the first of a heroic group? What abilities did this comet from the South bring to the diamond which enabled him to create records which will forever withstand assault?

TY COBB First, and always, in the trigger-mind of Cobb was the idea that in competition there must be a loser, and he wanted to be in that role as seldom as possible. Cobb made himself learn to beat his opponent through the simple method of studying his every move and habit. He punished himself to the point of perfection, creating new tricks and ideas which would always keep him far removed, and above, from the rest. He knew the habits of every player he faced, their weaknesses and strengths, and he learned to strike at their most vulnerable points with a fiery spirit, constant study and an unquenchable desire for victory. His education paid off handsomely. He stole 892 bases, compiled 4,191 hits, scored 2,244 runs and amassed a batting average of .367—the most imposing individual lifetime marks ever established in the majors.

Cobb just didn't play at baseball, he lived it—on and off the field. For 12 seasons he paced the league in batting, nine of them in a row. He batted .400 or better three times, and belted .420 in 1911 and .410 the following season.

A lefthanded hitter who gripped his bat with his left hand four inches above his right, Cobb subscribed to the theory that this was the best method with which to strike at a pitched ball. Although the unorthodox grip nullified some of his power, Ty could belt them long when the situation called for it. However, he proved that this grip was adaptable to the drag bunt, at which he was a master, and perfect to pull a pitch to right field, slice it to left or smash straight through the middle of the diamond.

A centerfielder by choice Ty also played the other outfield positions, filled in at second and first base and even pitched. For 24 years he was baseball's dominant figure, the scourge of rival pitchers and opponents' stratagems. Just once did he fail to reach the .300 level—in his freshman season in 1905 when he was an 18-year-old stripling.

Ty was the game's fiercest competitor. He baited rivals, umpires and teammates—but always for a purpose. He claimed, and the records bear him out, that all of this was calculated psychology designed to upset the opposition and inspire his teammates. Cobb's methods must have been successful, his name leads all others in the Hall of Fame.

Cobb helped the Tigers to three pennants; he managed Detroit from 1921 to 1926 and closed out his career with the Philadelphia Athletics, batting .323 in his final season when he was 41 years old. He was truly the game's most dynamic competitor.

BABE RUTH

If Ty Cobb was the most dynamic figure in the history of baseball then George Herman Ruth must have been the most fabulous. Babe Ruth, a snub-nosed, moon-faced man captured the imagination of a nation with a mincing walk, a pair of pipe-stem legs and the most explosive bat ever carried. For 20 years he held the interest of millions merely by swinging a 42-ounce bat which propelled 714 home runs, more than any player in history.

No other sports figure fired the emotion as did the Babe. Whatever he did—slam a home run or strike out—was accomplished with dramatic overtones. He was a giant of a figure who did everything with gargantuan effects.

Ruth's early boyhood was passed in a Baltimore orphanage while his father eked out a livelihood as a bartender in one of the city's less swanky districts. It was in such a setting that one of America's most legendary sports figures began an education which would elevate him to a position befitting presidents, kings and emperors.

It was as a pitcher that Ruth started his diamond career, and in that role he made his first entrance into the record books. The Boston Red Sox purchased his contract from the Baltimore Orioles of the International League and baseball's most amazing Odyssey was about to be written.

Babe became an outstanding hurler with the Sox, leading the league on two occasions in earned run averages. He also established a World Series record for consecutive scoreless innings by stringing together 29 in the 1916 and 1918 classics. Ruth was quite a pitcher but he was already evidencing prowess at the plate and his manager, Ed Barrow, decided that Ruth as an everyday performer would be more valuable than as an occasional pitcher.

In 1919, playing the outfield when he wasn't occupied on the mound, Ruth shattered all previous home run marks with an insignificant total of 29. The following winter he was sold to the New York Yankees in baseball's biggest deal, the Red Sox receiving $125,000 for their slugging pitcher-outfielder, and an additional $350,000 loan to pay off debts. Ruth's pitching days were now at an end, except for an occasional chore at season's end.

Recognizing the gate attraction of the Bambino's homeric slams, the magnates quickly agreed to introduce the lively ball. It brought fame and fortune to Ruth who crashed 59 homers in 1921 and bettered this standard with an output of 60 in 1927.

His booming bat brought showmanship and busy turnstiles to the game and helped the Yankees erect the Yankee Stadium in 1923, referred to as The House That Ruth Built. The Babe was baseball and he demanded, and received, top dollar for his achievements which included record salaries of

$85,000 in 1930 and 1931, years which will be recalled as the peak of a severe depression.

Ruth was more than just a home run slugger. It was said that he never made a bad play. As a pitcher, he constantly kept the hitters guessing; as an outfielder, he was invariably in the proper position and runners seldom dared to take liberties with one of the game's most powerful and accurate throwing arms; as a base runner, he knew exactly when to try for an extra base.

The Babe retired in 1935 but, like the true showman, reserved one of his most spectacular hitting performances for his last appearance. He slammed three homers in this farewell to baseball at Pittsburgh's spacious Forbes Field, one of which is still regarded as the longest blow ever struck in that city. So closed 22 years by the game's greatest power hitter.

Everything the Babe did was majestic. He commanded the largest tax-free baseball salary, hit the most homers, drew the biggest fine ($5,000) and brought baseball its most lush period. Even in death the Bambino played to an SRO crowd. Thousands filed past to view the idol of millions as his body lay in kingly state in, appropriately enough, The House that He Had Built.

There will always be controversy as to who was better, Cobb or Ruth. Each was superb in his field—Cobb for hitting and base running and aggressive play, Ruth for power, pitching and crowd appeal.

CHRISTY MATHEWSON

Perhaps the first prototype of the All-American boy to enter the majors was Christopher Mathewson, Bucknell University football hero who pitched 373 victories in the National League from 1900 to 1916, a 20th century all-time yearly high average of 23 triumphs.

Matty was cut from a slightly different mold than most of the players of his era and this quality plus his amazing World Series performance in 1905 was to make him the idol of the sports world. Although a member of the New York Giants, one of baseball's most truculent teams of the time, Matty managed to remain above the rest of a hurly-burly cast. His gentle manner and casual aloofness stamped him as an individual who definitely didn't fit in with the pattern of his era.

Mathewson was a model of perfection in all departments. He was more than a pitcher, and frequently served as a fill-in in the outfield and first base replacement, and occasionally was called upon as a pinch-hitter. But Matty was essentially a pitcher, perhaps the finest in the modern annals of the National League and certainly a champion performer in crucial contests.

Perhaps his most sensational stint was the World Series of 1905 when he hurled three victories, all shutouts. He helped the Giants defeat the Philadelphia Athletics by yielding a total of 14 hits in his three shutout triumphs, an unparalleled performance. This was Matty's greatest pitching hour.

Before he concluded his career as manager of the Cincinnati Reds, Matty was to win 30 or more games for three seasons and 20 or more for 12 straight years. He was the greatest exponent of control in the game, and in 1908 walked but 42 batters in 416 innings with a pitch known as the fadeaway. today's version of the screwball. He didn't require the normal four days' rest between assignments and was always ready to pitch an important contest.

Matty was anathema to most of the hitters in the league, but to the weak-hitting Joe Tinker he was just another pitcher. It was the Chicago shortstop who assaulted Matty for the game-winning blows in the memorable 1908 "playoff" contest which gave the pennant to the Cubs.

The loosely-written amateur rules of Matty's day enabled him to embark on a major league career almost immediately after leaving college. While at Bucknell he pitched in the New England League, and was soon moved to the Virginia League where he won 21 games for Norfolk. This earned him a chance with the Giants in 1900 but, after losing three games, he was sent back to the minors. Cincinnati drafted him for the 1901 season, but traded him to the Giants before the opening game. Matty's freshman year was a success and he won 20 games, one of which was a no-hitter. He was to lead New York to four pennants and strike out 2,499, an all-time league standard, in 17 seasons.

Big Six, as he was called, after a famous New York fire engine, had his career—and life—curtailed as a result of World War I. He was gassed while on active duty and fought a losing battle with tuberculosis. When he died in 1925, Matty was president of the Boston Braves.

Beneath the centerfield stands of New York's Polo Grounds a bronze tablet was erected to the memory of Christopher Mathewson. The walk which leads to the campus of Bucknell University also reveres Matty's memory. Baseball, too, hasn't forgotten --and justifiably so. Matty was touched with immortality, enough of it to qualify for The Select Five.

HONUS WAGNER

John McGraw, the famed New York Giant manager, and Ed Barrow, who helped create the New York Yankee dynasty, were regarded as the shrewdest judges of diamond talent of their day. Whenever they were asked to name the best all-around player either ever saw, the answer would always be the same: Honus Wagner.

John Peter Wagner was more than a myth, he was baseball's best shortstop, his league's best hitter, one of its fleetest runners and his league's top record maker. An ungainly man who carried most of his 200 pounds on a ponderous chest and in his gorilla-like arms, Wagner had sheer power and an eagerness for competition which clearly placed him in a class by himself.

His brute strength also lay in a huge pair of hands which were as deft and certain as any that ever pounced on a ground ball. Wagner just didn't scoop up ground balls, he excavated them, digging up large portions of loose dirt and stones. His throws were swift and powerful, and somehow the first baseman could always pluck the ball from the hail of debris aimed at him by Wagner. Very few hits skipped by Honus, and very few runners took their time getting down to first base when he cocked his muscular arm to throw.

Honus' first hero was his brother Al who was something of a semipro star, but it was young John who got to the majors first. However, Honus couldn't quite make up his mind as to whether he was a pitcher, outfielder or infielder, and it wasn't until 1901, his fifth National League season, that he was shifted to shortstop on a permanent basis. It didn't make too much difference where he played, as long as he was allowed to get up to the plate. Honus was at home immediately in his freshman year at Louisville where he carved out a .344 figure. He was to hit better than .300 for the next 16 seasons, play every position but catcher, and finish a brilliant 21-year career with a .329 lifetime average, most of it compiled against a ball as lively as a spool of cotton. After three seasons at Louisville, Wagner was to spend the rest of a remarkable span in Pittsburgh.

Ed Barrow was chiefly responsible for getting Honus started on his baseball career, but only because Ed was out scouting brother Al. Barrow was told he could find the elder Wagner around the railroad tracks outside of Mansfield, Ohio, "throwing stones." So Barrow headed for the tracks. A bowlegged, broad-shouldered youngster was tossing stones faster—and far-

ther—than the others and Barrow was immediately impressed by the boy's marksmanship and strength. It was the wrong Wagner, but Barrow made no mistake. Two seasons of minor league ball and the Flying Dutchman was ready for a career which would see him lead the league eight times in batting, appear in 2,785 games and get 3,430 hits.

In death as in the record-making department, Wagner has proved to be second best and about as imperishable. Matty, Walter Johnson and Babe Ruth preceded the Flying Dutchman to Valhalla. Cobb remained the last stubborn holdout to the inevitable.

WALTER JOHNSON

Of all the nicknames bestowed upon ball players since Adrian Constantine (Cap) Anson came down the pike, perhaps none was more appropriate than the tag placed on Walter Perry (Barney) Johnson. The Big Train he was called, and he was the fastest express of them all.

Johnson was a man, and a pitcher, completely without guile. Born on a farm in Humboldt, Kansas, he never attempted to act the part of a sophisticated cavalier. On the mound, he remained in character. Speed was his forte, and he never resorted to other artful devices to deceive the batter. Johnson was completely honest at all times—a simple, sincere man; a pitcher of enormous strength who made the ball whistle past the plate like bird shot. It is said that his announced appearance on the mound created more sick cases than the common cold, batters suddenly becoming indisposed when Johnson began his pregame warmup session. But he never took advantage of his exalted position, and none who ever batted against him can recall Johnson deliberately using his tremendous speed to drive batters away from the plate.

From the day he began a fabled career with Washington in 1907, until 1927, when he pitched the last of his 416 victories for the Senators, Walter wasn't heavily blessed with diamond fortune. During his finest years when his arm was strong and his fast ball resembled a blue darter, Washington bore slight resemblance to a baseball team. But in the mid-twenties, when the Senators were chronic challengers and two-time pennant winners, The Big Train was about to be shunted on to a siding.

Johnson's total victories are more than any ever put together in the modern era. His strikeouts (3,508), innings pitched (5,924), complete games (531) and shutouts (113) are other all-time modern marks which are far beyond the grasp of any current competitor. And all of these incredible figures were achieved while he was surrounded by mediocrity and lack of talent. Yet Barney never complained of his lot. He was happy in Washington, and Washington was more than pleased with Walter.

Johnson may never have scaled the peak of pitching pinnacles if it wasn't for the persistence of a cigar salesman who saw him pitch a semipro game in 1906 in Weiser, Idaho. The salesman saw in Walter a potential star, but Joe Cantillon, Washington manager, paid no heed when the salesman wrote him of his Idaho discovery. More letters came to Cantillon, so detailed, that Cantillon no longer could ignore them. Finally Cantillon dispatched an aide to look over Johnson, who reported that everything the salesman said was true.

After three mediocre seasons, Johnson finally caught fire, but not before he blanked the New York Highlanders three times in four days in 1908. Walter's first big season was 1910 when he won 25 games; he was to win 20 or more 11 more times, and twice went over the 30-won mark. During this span he averaged fewer than 2.00 earned runs per season 6 times; won 16

straight in 1912; 14 straight in 1913 and 13 in 1914. In 1913 he pitched 56 consecutive scoreless innings.

Walter, so rich in talent as a pitcher, closed his major league career as an unsuccessful manager. He led his beloved Senators from 1929 through '32 and piloted Cleveland from 1933 to '35. However, these lack-lustre campaigns as a field leader never dulled his brilliant playing record, the finest ever assembled by a pitcher, after the turn of the century.

Gentle in spirit, indomitable in competition, Walter Perry Johnson made baseball much richer by his performances.

HALL OF FAME MEMBERS

Pilgrimages to Cooperstown always reach the Hall of Fame wing of the Museum. Here are enshrined the real immortals of the game, titans all. With an eminently qualified Hall of Fame Committee selecting a core of oldtimers, and baseball writers of at least 10 years' standing choosing the modern players (by 75% vote), a true cross-section of the sport's greats has been elected. Plaques with suitable inscriptions hang in the Hall of Fame honoring the following:

Members	Year Elected	Members	Year Elected
GROVER CLEVELAND ALEXANDER	1938	ED. DELAHANTY	1945
ADRIAN CONSTANTINE ANSON	1939	WILLIAM DICKEY	1954
LUCIUS APPLING	1964	JOSEPH P. DiMAGGIO	1955
H. EARL AVERILL	1975	HUGH DUFFY	1945
J. FRANKLIN (HOME RUN) BAKER	1955	WILLIAM G. EVANS	1973
DAVID J. BANCROFT	1971	JOHN JOSEPH EVERS	1946
EDWARD G. BARROW	1953	WM. B. (BUCK) EWING	1939
JACOB P. BECKLEY	1971	URBAN C. FABER	1964
JAMES (COOL PAPA) BELL	1974	ROBERT W. FELLER	1962
CHARLES (CHIEF) BENDER	1953	ELMER H. FLICK	1963
LAWRENCE P. (YOGI) BERRA	1972	EDWARD C. (WHITEY) FORD	1974
JAMES L. BOTTOMLEY	1974	JAMES E. FOXX	1951
LOUIS BOUDREAU	1970	FORD FRICK	1970
ROGER BRESNAHAN	1945	FRANK FRISCH	1947
DAN BROUTHERS	1945	JAMES F. GALVIN	1965
MORDECAI PETER BROWN	1949	HENRY LOUIS GEHRIG	1939
HON. MORGAN G. BULKELEY	1937	CHARLES GEHRINGER	1949
JESSE C. BURKETT	1946	JOSHUA GIBSON	1972
ROY CAMPANELLA	1969	VERNON L. (LEFTY) GOMEZ	1972
MAX G. CAREY	1961	HENRY GREENBERG	1956
ALEXANDER JOY CARTWRIGHT, JR.	1938	CLARK C. GRIFFITH	1946
HENRY CHADWICK	1938	LEON A. GOSLIN	1968
FRANK LEROY CHANCE	1946	BURLEIGH A. GRIMES	1964
OSCAR CHARLESTON	1976	ROBERT MOSES GROVE	1947
JOHN DWIGHT CHESBRO	1946	CHARLES J. (CHIC) HAFEY	1971
FRED CLARKE	1945	JESSE J. HAINES	1970
JOHN G. CLARKSON	1963	WILLIAM R. HAMILTON	1961
ROBERTO W. CLEMENTE	1973	WILLIAM HARRIDGE	1972
TYRUS RAYMOND COBB	1936	STANLEY R. (BUCKY) HARRIS	1975
GORDON (MICKEY) COCHRANE	1947	CHARLES LEO (GABBY) HARTNETT	1955
EDWARD TROWBRIDGE COLLINS	1939	HARRY HEILMANN	1952
JAMES COLLINS	1945	WILLIAM J. B. HERMAN	1975
EARLE B. COMBS	1970	HARRY B. HOOPER	1971
CHARLES A. COMISKEY	1939	ROGERS HORNSBY	1942
JOHN B. (JOCKO) CONLAN	1974	WAITE C. HOYT	1969
THOMAS H. CONNOLLY	1953	R. CAL HUBBARD	1976
ROGER CONNOR	1976	CARL HUBBELL	1947
STANLEY A. COVELESKI	1969	MILLER J. HUGGINS	1964
SAM CRAWFORD	1957	MONFORD M. IRVIN	1973
JOSEPH CRONIN	1956	HUGHIE JENNINGS	1945
W. A. (CANDY) CUMMINGS	1939	BYRON BANCROFT JOHNSON	1937
HAZEN S. CUYLER	1968	WALTER PERRY JOHNSON	1936
JAY HANNA (DIZZY) DEAN	1953	WILLIAM J. (JUDY) JOHNSON	1975

Members	Year Elected	Members	Year Elected
TIMOTHY J. KEEFE	1964	WESLEY BRANCH RICKEY	1967
WILLIE KEELER	1939	EPPA RIXEY	1963
JOSEPH JAMES KELLEY	1971	ROBIN E. ROBERTS	1976
GEORGE L. KELLY	1973	WILBERT ROBINSON	1945
MIKE J. (KING) KELLY	1945	JACK ROBINSON	1962
RALPH M. KINER	1975	EDD J. ROUSH	1962
WILLIAM J. KLEM	1953	CHARLES H. RUFFING	1967
SANFORD KOUFAX	1972	GEORGE HERMAN (BABE) RUTH	1936
NAPOLEON (LARRY) LAJOIE	1937	RAY SCHALK	1955
KENESAW MOUNTAIN LANDIS	1944	AL SIMMONS	1953
ROBERT G. LEMON	1976	GEORGE HAROLD SISLER	1939
WALTER F. (BUCK) LEONARD	1972	WARREN E. SPAHN	1973
FREDERICK C. LINDSTROM	1976	ALBERT GOODWILL SPALDING	1939
THEODORE LYONS	1955	TRISTRAM E. (TRIS) SPEAKER	1937
CONNIE MACK	1937	CHARLES D. STENGEL	1966
MICKEY C. MANTLE	1974	WILLIAM H. TERRY	1954
HENRY E. MANUSH	1964	SAMUEL L. THOMPSON	1974
WALTER (RABBIT) MARANVILLE	1954	JOSEPH B. TINKER	1946
RICHARD W. (RUBE) MARQUARD	1971	HAROLD J. (PIE) TRAYNOR	1948
CHRISTY MATHEWSON	1936	C. ARTHUR (DAZZY) VANCE	1955
JOSEPH V. McCARTHY	1957	GEORGE EDWARD WADDELL	1946
THOMAS F. McCARTHY	1946	HONUS WAGNER	1936
JOSEPH JEROME McGINNITY	1946	RODERICK (BOBBY) WALLACE	1953
JOHN J. McGRAW	1937	EDWARD ARTHUR WALSH	1946
WILLIAM B. MC KECHNIE	1962	LLOYD J. WANER	1967
JOSEPH M. MEDWICK	1968	PAUL WANER	1952
STANLEY F. MUSIAL	1969	JOHN MONTGOMERY WARD	1964
CHARLES A. (KID) NICHOLS	1949	GEORGE M. WEISS	1971
JAMES H. O'ROURKE	1945	MICHAEL F. WELCH	1973
MELVIN T. OTT	1951	ZACK WHEAT	1959
LEROY R. (SATCHEL) PAIGE	1971	THEODORE S. WIILLIAMS	1966
HERBERT J. PENNOCK	1948	GEORGE WRIGHT	1937
EDWARD S. PLANK	1946	HARRY WRIGHT	1953
CHARLIE RADBOURN	1939	EARLY WYNN	1972
EDGAR C. RICE	1963	DENTON T. (CY) YOUNG	1937
		ROSS M. YOUNGS	1972

NO-HIT GAMES

Quite distinct from baseball's Hall of Fame is its "hall of fame." The capital difference comes down to this—meritorious service for a long period of years leads to candidacy for an actual plaque in Cooperstown's honored corridors, whereas anybody can make the lower-case "hall of fame" simply by pitching a no-hit game.

Many mediocrities have found the magic formula for one unhittable afternoon, pitchers who landed back in the minors a scant year or two after their headline-making masterpiece. "It's like catching lightning in a bottle," says one veteran manager. Though this simile exaggerates the factor of luck involved, still it can't be a matter of sheer skill, speed and stamina, because fully half the pitchers in the upper-strata, upper-case Hall of Fame never notched no-hitters.

When no batter can reach base—whether by hit, walk, error, hit-by-pitched-ball or plain black magic—then the pitcher has earned a "perfect game." Seven such paragons adorn the no-hit roster, though some statistical purists still challenge Ernie Shore's right to rank up there.

On June 23, 1917, Shore shuffled out of the Red Sox bullpen to relieve Babe Ruth, who had just been ordered out of the game for squawking too boisterously after pitching a fourth ball to the first Washington batter, Ray Morgan. With Shore on the mound, Morgan was thrown out trying to steal second base. Shore proceeded to retire the remaining 26 batters in order.

Far more controversial than Shore's game are two other entries on the all-time. no-hit honor roll, which made the grade only when the official scorer changed his mind after having announced a "hit" earlier in the game. Some record books also omit the early no-hitters, because all pitching was underhand until 1884, while the pitching distance was only 45 feet until 1881, 50 feet until 1893 and 60½ feet thereafter.

Here is the complete chronological collection of major league no-hit performances over the first nine innings of a game. An asterisk (*) marks "perfect game." Each line shows the date, pitcher, his club and league, opposing club and final score. All games were played in the home park of the no-hit hurler, except when "at" appears just before the name of the victimized club.

July   28, 1875 - Joseph E. Borden, Philadelphia NA vs. Chicago   4-0
July   15, 1876 - George W. Bradley, St. Louis NL vs. Hartford   2-0
June   12, 1880 - John L. Richmond, Worcester NL vs. Cleveland........   1-0*
June   17, 1880 - John M. Ward, Providence NL vs. Buffalo (AM) 5-0*
Aug.   19, 1880 - Lawrence J. Corcoran, Chicago NL vs. Boston   6-0
Aug.   20, 1880 - James F. Galvin, Buffalo NL at Worcester   1-0
Sept. 11, 1882 - Antoine J. Mullane, Louisville AA at Cincinnati   2-0
Sept. 19, 1882 - Guy J. Hecker, Louisville AA at Pittsburgh   3-1
Sept. 20, 1882 - Lawrence J. Corcoran, Chicago NL vs. Worcester   5-0
July   25, 1883 - Charles G. Radbourn, Providence NL at Cleveland....   8-0
Sept. 13, 1883 - Hugh I. Daly, Cleveland NL at Philadelphia   1-0
May   24, 1884 - Albert W. Atkisson, Philadelphia AA at Pittsburgh.... 10-1
May   29, 1884 - Edward Morris, Columbus AA at Pittsburgh   5-0
June   5, 1884 - Frank H. Mountain, Columbus AA at Washington 12-0
June   27, 1884 - Lawrence J. Corcoran, Chicago NL vs. Providence ...   6-0
Aug.   4, 1884 - James F. Galvin, Buffalo NL at Detroit 18-0
Aug.   26, 1884 - Richard S. Burns, Cincinnati UA at Kansas City   3-1
Sept. 28, 1884 - Edward L. Cushman, Milwaukee UA vs. Washington...   5-0
Oct.   4, 1884 - Samuel J. Kimber, Brooklyn AA at Toledo (10
                  innings)..   0-0
July   27, 1885 - John G. Clarkson, Chicago NL at Providence...........   4-0
Aug.   29, 1885 - Charles J. Ferguson, Philadelphia NL vs. Providence   1-0
May   1, 1886 - Albert W. Atkisson, Philadelphia AA vs. New York ...   3-2
July   24, 1886 - William J. Terry, Brooklyn AA vs. St. Louis............   1-0
Oct.   6, 1886 - Matthew A. Kilroy, Baltimore AA at Pittsburgh   6-0
May   27, 1888 - William J. Terry, Brooklyn AA vs. Louisville   4-0
June   6, 1888 - Henry Porter, Kansas City AA at Baltimore.............   4-0
July   26, 1888 - Edward W. Seward, Philadelphia AA vs. Cincinnati ... 12-2
July   31, 1888 - August P. Weyhing, Philadelphia AA vs. Kansas City   4-0
Sept. 15, 1890 - Ledell Titcomb, Rochester AA vs. Syracuse.............   7-0
June   22, 1891 - Thomas J. Lovett, Brooklyn NL vs. New York   4-0
July   31, 1891 - Amos W. Rusie, New York NL vs. Brooklyn   6-0
Oct.   4, 1891 - Theodore P. Breitenstein, St. Louis AA vs. Louisville   8-0
Aug.   6, 1892 - John C. Stivetts, Boston NL at Brooklyn 11-0
Aug.   22, 1892 - Alexander B. Sanders, Louisville NL vs. Baltimore...   6-2
Oct.   15, 1892 - Charles L. Jones, Cincinnati NL vs. Pittsburgh   7-1
Aug.   16, 1893 - William V. Hawke, Baltimore NL at Washington........   5-0
Sept. 18, 1897 - Denton T. Young, Cleveland NL vs. Cincinnati   6-0
Apr.   22, 1398 - Theodore P. Breitenstein, Cincinnati NL vs. Pitts-
                  burgh 11-0
Apr.   22, 1898 - James J. Hughes, Baltimore NL vs. Boston..............   8-0

July   8, 1898 - Francis R. Donahue, Philadelphia NL vs. Boston....... 5-0
Aug. 21, 1898 - Walter M. Thornton, Chicago NL vs. Brooklyn.......... 2-0
May   25, 1899 - Charles L. Phillippe, Louisville NL vs. New York..... 7-0
Aug.   7, 1899 - Victor G. Willis, Boston NL vs. Washington............ 7-1
July 12, 1900 - Frank G. Hahn, Cincinnati NL vs. Philadelphia........ 4-0
May   9, 1901 - Earl L. Moore, Cleveland AL vs. Chicago (9 in-
                 nings, lost 10th)..................................... 2-4
July 15, 1901 - Christopher Mathewson, New York NL at St. Louis.... 5-0
Sept. 20, 1902 - James J. Callahan, Chicago AL vs. Detroit (1st game) 3-0
Sept. 18, 1903 - Charles C. Fraser, Philadelphia NL at Chicago....... 10-0
May   5, 1904 - Denton T. Young, Boston AL vs. Philadelphia.......... 3-0*
June 11, 1904 - Robert K. Wicker, Chicago NL vs. New York (9 in-
                 nings, won in 12th).................................. 1-0
Aug. 17, 1904 - Jesse N. Tannehill, Boston AL at Chicago............. 6-0
June 13, 1905 - Christopher Mathewson, New York NL at Chicago..... 1-0
July 22, 1905 - Weldon Henley, Philadelphia AL at St. Louis (1st game) 6-0
Sept. 6, 1905 - Frank E. Smith, Chicago AL at Detroit (2nd game).... 15-0
Sept. 27, 1905 - William H. Dinneen, Boston AL vs. Chicago (1st game) 2-0
May   1, 1906 - John C. Lush, Philadelphia NL at Brooklyn.............. 1-0
July 20, 1906 - Malcolm W. Eason, Brooklyn NL at St. Louis........... 2-0
Aug.   1, 1906 - Harry M. McIntire, Brooklyn NL vs. Pittsburgh (10
                 innings, lost in 13th)............................... 0-1
May   8, 1907 - Francis X. Pfeffer, Boston NL vs. Cincinnati.......... 6-0
Sept. 20, 1907 - Nicholas Maddox, Pittsburgh NL vs. Brooklyn.......... 2-1
June 30, 1908 - Denton T. Young, Boston AL at New York 8-0
July   4, 1908 - George L. Wiltse, New York NL vs. Philadelphia (10
                 innings) (AM).. 1-0
Sept. 5, 1908 - George N. Rucker, Brooklyn NL vs. Boston (2nd
                 game).. 6-0
Sept. 18, 1908 - Robert B. Rhoades, Cleveland AL vs. Boston............ 2-1
Sept. 20, 1908 - Frank E. Smith, Chicago AL vs. Philadelphia.......... 1-0
Oct.   2, 1908 - Adrian C. Joss, Cleveland AL vs. Chicago............... 1-0*
Apr. 15, 1909 - Leon K. Ames, New York NL vs. Brooklyn (9 in-
                 nings, lost in 13th)................................. 0-3
Apr. 20, 1910 - Adrian C. Joss, Cleveland AL at Chicago............... 1-0
May   12, 1910 - Charles A. Bender, Philadelphia AL vs. Cleveland.... 4-0
Aug. 30, 1910 - Thomas L. Hughes, New York AL vs. Cleveland (9
                 innings, lost in 11th)............................... 0-5
July 29, 1911 - Joe Wood, Boston AL vs. St. Louis (1st game).......... 5-0
Aug. 27, 1911 - Edward A. Walsh, Chicago AL vs. Boston................ 5-0
July   4, 1912 - George E. Mullin, Detroit AL vs. St. Louis (PM)....... 7-0
Aug. 30, 1912 - Earl A. Hamilton, St. Louis AL at Detroit............. 5-1
Sept. 6, 1912 - Charles M. Tesreau, New York NL at Philadelphia
                 (1st game)... 3-0
May   14, 1914 - James Scott, Chicago AL at Washington (9 innings,
                 lost in 10th).. 0-1
May   31, 1914 - Joseph L. Benz, Chicago AL vs. Cleveland 6-1
Sept. 9, 1914 - George A. Davis, Boston NL vs. Philadelphia (2nd
                 game).. 7-0
Sept. 19, 1914 - Edward F. LaFitte, Brooklyn FL vs. Kansas City
                 (1st game)... 6-2
Apr. 15, 1915 - Richard W. Marquard, New York NL vs. Brooklyn 2-0
Apr. 24, 1915 - Frank L. Allen, Pittsburgh FL at St. Louis............. 2-0
May   15, 1915 - Claude R. Hendrix, Chicago FL at Pittsburgh.......... 10-0

Aug. 16, 1915 - Miles G. Main, Kansas City FL at Buffalo............... 5-0
Aug. 31, 1915 - James S. Lavender, Chicago NL at New York (1st game).. 2-0
Sept. 7, 1915 - Arthur D. Davenport, St. Louis FL vs. Chicago (1st game).. 3-0
June 16, 1916 - Thomas L. Hughes, Boston NL vs. Pittsburgh............ 2-0
June 21, 1916 - George Foster, Boston AL vs. New York................. 2-0
Aug. 26, 1916 - Leslie J. Bush, Philadelphia AL vs. Cleveland.......... 5-0
Aug. 30, 1916 - Hubert B. Leonard, Boston AL vs. St. Louis............. 4-0
Apr. 14, 1917 - Edward V. Cicotte, Chicago AL at St. Louis............. 11-0
Apr. 24, 1917 - George A. Mogridge, New York AL at Boston........... 2-1
May   2, 1917 - Frederick A. Toney, Cincinnati NL at Chicago (10 innings)... 1-0
May   2, 1917 - James L. Vaughn, Chicago NL vs. Cincinnati (9 innings, lost in 10th) 0-1
May   5, 1917 - Ernest G. Koob, St. Louis AL vs. Chicago............... 1-0
May   6, 1917 - Robert Groom, St. Louis AL vs. Chicago (2nd game).. 3-0
June 23, 1917 - Ernest G. Shore, Boston· AL vs. Washington (1st game).. 4-0*
June 3, 1918 - Hubert B. Leonard, Boston AL at Detroit 5-0
May 11, 1919 - Horace O. Eller, Cincinnati NL vs. St. Louis........... 6-0
Sept. 10, 1919 - Raymond B. Caldwell, Cleveland AL at New York (1st game)........ 3-0
July   1, 1920 - Walter P. Johnson, Washington AL at Boston........... 1-0
Apr. 30, 1922 - Charles C. Robertson, Chicago AL at Detroit........... 2-0*
May   7, 1922 - Jesse L. Barnes, New York NL vs. Philadelphia....... 6-0
Sept. 4, 1923 - Samuel P. Jones, New York AL at Philadelphia......... 2-0
Sept. 7, 1923 - Howard J. Ehmke, Boston AL at Philadelphia........... 4-0
July 17, 1924 - Jesse J. Haines, St. Louis NL vs. Boston 5-0
Sept. 13, 1925 - Arthur C. Vance, Brooklyn NL vs. Philadelphia (1st game).. 10-1
Aug. 21, 1926 - Theodore A. Lyons, Chicago AL at Boston.............. 6-0
May   8, 1929 - Carl O. Hubbell, New York NL vs. Pittsburgh........... 11-0
Apr. 29, 1931 - Wesley C. Ferrell, Cleveland AL vs. St. Louis......... 9-0
Aug. 8, 1931 - Robert J. Burke, Washington AL vs. Boston............. 5-0
Sept. 18, 1934 - Louis N. Newsom, St. Louis AL vs. Boston (9 innings, lost 10th).. 1-2
Sept. 21, 1934 - Paul D. Dean, St. Louis NL at Brooklyn (2nd game)... 3-0
Aug. 31, 1935 - Lloyd V. Kennedy, Chicago AL vs. Cleveland........... 5-0
June 1, 1937 - William J. Dietrich, Chicago AL vs. St. Louis.......... 8-0
June 11, 1938 - John S. Vander Meer, Cincinnati NL vs. Boston........ 3-0
June 15, 1938 - John S. Vander Meer, Cincinnati NL vs. Brooklyn (night) 6-0
Aug. 27, 1938 - Marcellus M. Pearson, New York AL vs. Cleveland (2nd game)... 13-0
Apr. 16, 1940 - Robert W. Feller, Cleveland AL at Chicago.............. 1-0
Apr. 30, 1940 - James O. Carleton, Brooklyn NL at Cincinnati.......... 3-0
Aug. 30, 1941 - Lonnie Warneke, St. Louis NL at Cincinnati............ 2-0
Apr. 27, 1944 - James A. Tobin, Boston NL vs. Brooklyn 2-0
May 15, 1944 - Clyde M. Shoun, Cincinnati NL vs. Boston 1-0
Sept. 9, 1945 - Richard J. Fowler, Philadelphia AL vs. St. Louis (2nd game).. 1-0
Apr. 23, 1946 - Edward M. Head, Brooklyn NL vs. Boston................ 5-0

Apr. 30, 1946	Robert W. Feller, Cleveland AL at New York	1-0
June 18, 1947	Ewell Blackwell, Cincinnati NL vs. Boston (night)	6-0
July 10, 1947	Donald P. Black, Cleveland AL vs. Philadelphia (twilight)	3-0
Sept. 3, 1947	William G. McCahan, Philadelphia AL vs. Washington	3-0
June 30, 1948	Robert G. Lemon, Cleveland AL at Detroit (night)	2-0
Sept. 9, 1948	Rex E. Barney, Brooklyn NL at New York (night)	2-0
Aug. 11, 1950	Vernon E. Bickford, Boston NL vs. Brooklyn (night) ..	7-0
May 6, 1951	Clifford D. Chambers, Pittsburgh NL at Boston (2nd game)...	3-0
July 1, 1951	Robert W. Feller, Cleveland AL vs. Detroit (1st game)..	2-1
July 12, 1951	Allie P. Reynolds, New York AL at Cleveland (night)	1-0
Sept. 28, 1951	Allie P. Reynolds, New York AL vs. Boston (1st game)...	8-0
May 15, 1952	Virgil O. Trucks, Detroit AL vs. Washington	1-0
June 19, 1952	Carl D. Erskine, Brooklyn NL vs. Chicago	5-0
Aug. 25, 1952	Virgil O. Trucks, Detroit AL at New York	1-0
May 6, 1953	Alva L. Holloman, St. Louis AL vs. Philadelphia (night)	6-0
June 12, 1954	James A. Wilson, Milwaukee NL vs. Philadelphia	2-0
May 12, 1955	Sam Jones, Chicago NL vs. Pittsburgh	4-0
May 12, 1956	Carl D. Erskine, Brooklyn NL vs. New York	3-0
July 14, 1956	Melvin L. Parnell, Boston AL vs. Chicago	4-0
Sept. 25, 1956	Salvatore A. Maglie, Brooklyn NL vs. Philadelphia ...	5-0
Oct. 8, 1956	Donald J. Larsen, New York AL vs. Brooklyn NL (World Series)	2-0*
Aug. 20, 1957	Robert C. Keegan, Chicago AL vs. Washington (2nd game, night)	6-0
July 20, 1958	James Bunning, Detroit AL at Boston (1st game)	3-0
Sept. 20, 1958	Hoyt Wilhelm, Baltimore AL vs. New York	1-0
May 26, 1959	Harvey Haddix, Pittsburgh NL at Milwaukee (night)	0-1
May 15, 1960	Donald Cardwell, Chicago NL vs. St. Louis (2nd game)	4-0
Aug. 18, 1960	S. Lewis Burdette, Milwaukee NL vs. Philadelphia (night)	1-0
Sept. 16, 1960	Warren E. Spahn, Milwaukee NL vs. Philadelphia (night)	4-0
April 28, 1961	Warren E. Spahn, Milwaukee NL vs. San Francisco (night)	1-0
May 5, 1962	Robert Belinsky, Los Angeles AL vs. Baltimore (night)	2-0
June 26, 1962	Earl L. Wilson, Boston AL vs. Los Angeles (night) ..	2-0
June 30, 1962	Sandy Koufax, Los Angeles NL vs. New York (night) ..	5-0
Aug. 1, 1962	William Monbouquette, Boston AL at Chicago (night)	1-0
Aug. 26, 1962	Jack Kralick, Minnesota AL vs. Kansas City	1-0
May 11, 1963	Sandy Koufax, Los Angeles NL vs. San Francisco (night)	8-0
May 17, 1963	Donald Nottebart, Houston NL vs. Philadelphia (night)	4-1
June 15, 1963	Juan Marichal, San Francisco NL vs. Houston	1-0
April 23, 1964	Kenneth T. Johnson, Houston NL vs. Cincinnati (night)	0-1
June 4, 1964	Sandy Koufax, Los Angeles NL at Philadelphia (night)	3-0
June 21, 1964	James Bunning, Philadelphia NL at New York (1st game)	6-0*
June 14, 1965	James W. Maloney, Cincinnati NL vs. New York (night) (10 innings, lost in 11th)	0-1
Aug. 19, 1965	James W. Maloney, Cincinnati NL at Chicago (1st game, 10 innings)	1-0
Sept. 9, 1965	Sandy Koufax, Los Angeles NL vs. Chicago (night) ..	1-0*
Sept. 16, 1965	David M. Morehead, Boston AL vs. Cleveland	2-0
June 10, 1966	Wilfred C. Siebert, Cleveland AL vs. Washington (night)	3-0
June 18, 1967	Donald E. Wilson, Houston NL vs. Atlanta	2-0
Aug. 25, 1967	W. Dean Chance, Minnesota AL at Cleveland (2nd game, night)	2-1

Sept. 10, 1967—Joel E. Horlen, Chicago AL vs. Detroit (1st game) ...   6-0
April 27, 1968—Thomas H. Phoebus, Baltimore AL vs. Boston   6-0
May   8, 1968—James A. Hunter, Oakland AL at Minnesota (night) ..   4-0*
July 29, 1968—George R. Culver, Cincinnati NL at Philadelphia (2nd
              game, night)   6-1
Sept. 17, 1968—Gaylord Perry, San Francisco NL vs. St. Louis (night) .   1-0
Sept. 18, 1968—Ray C. Washburn, St. Louis NL at San Francisco   2-0
April 17, 1969—William H. Stoneman, Montreal NL at Philadelphia
              (night)   7-0
April 30, 1969—James W. Maloney, Cincinnati NL vs. Houston (night)   10-0
May   1, 1969—Donald E. Wilson, Houston NL at Cincinnati (night)   4-0
Aug. 13, 1969—James A. Palmer, Baltimore AL vs. Oakland (night) ..   8-0
Aug. 19, 1969—Kenneth Holtzman, Chicago NL vs. Atlanta   3-0
Sept. 20, 1969—Robert R. Moose, Pittsburgh NL at New York   4-0
June 12, 1970—Dock Ellis, Pittsburgh NL at San Diego (1st game) ..   2-0
July   3, 1970—Clyde Wright, California AL vs. Oakland (night)   4-0
July 20, 1970—William Singer, Los Angeles NL vs. Philadelphia   5-0
Sept. 21, 1970—Vida Blue, Oakland AL vs. Minnesota (night)   6-0
June   3, 1971—Kenneth Holtzman, Chicago NL at Cincinnati (night) ..   1-0
June 23, 1971—Richard Wise, Philadelphia NL at Cincinnati (night) ..   4-0
Aug. 14, 1971—Robert Gibson, St. Louis NL at Pittsburgh (night)   11-0
April 16, 1972—Burt Hooton, Chicago NL vs. Philadelphia   4-0
Sept. 2, 1972—Milton Pappas, Chicago NL vs. San Diego   8-0
Oct.   2, 1972—William Stoneman, Montreal NL vs. New York (1st game,
              twilight)   7-0
April 27, 1973—Steven Busby, Kansas City AL at Detroit (night)   3-0
May   15, 1973—L. Nolan Ryan, California AL at Kansas City (night)   3-0
July 15, 1973—L. Nolan Ryan, California AL at Detroit   6-0
July 30, 1973—James Bibby, Texas AL at Oakland (night)   6-0
Aug.   5, 1973—Philip Niekro, Atlanta NL vs. San Diego   9-0
June 19, 1974—Steven Busby, Kansas City AL at Milwaukee (night)   2-0
July 19, 1974—Richard Bosman, Cleveland AL vs. Oakland (night)   4-0
Sept. 28, 1974—L. Nolan Ryan, California AL vs. Minnesota (night) ..   4-0
June   1, 1975—L. Nolan Ryan, California AL vs. Baltimore   1-0
Aug. 24, 1975—Edward Halicki, San Francisco NL vs. New York (2nd g)   6-0
July   9, 1976—Lawrence Dierker, Houston NL vs. Montreal (night) ..   6-0
Aug.   9, 1976—John Candelaria, Pittsburgh NL vs. Los Angeles (night) ..   2-0
Sept. 29, 1976—John Montefusco, San Francisco NL at Atlanta (night) ..   9-0

ALL-STAR GAMES

For sheer spectacle, the All-Star Game is perhaps baseball's greatest one-day show for the fans. The idea, conceived by the late Arch Ward, sports editor of the *Chicago Tribune,* was originally planned to add a baseball flavor to the Chicago Century of Progress exposition in 1933. However, the success of the initial contest made Ward envision an annual affair between the two leagues in which the best players from each circuit would play.

For a time the fans selected the makeup of the two teams through the use of ballots. However, baseball decided that it would be the best judge of playing talent, and the squads were chosen by the rival managers. When the fans expressed nation-wide dissatisfaction with this system, the game was placed back into their hands. Only the pitchers are now chosen by the rival managers, who qualify for their posts by virtue of winning the pennant in the previous season.

HIGHLIGHTS, THROUGH THE YEARS: 1933, Babe Ruth's line drive homer with one aboard brought the AL triumph. Two of baseball's most famous managers were selected to guide their respective leagues, Connie Mack and John McGraw. . . . 1934, Carl Hubbell, although pitching for the losing NL, gained immortality by striking out Babe Ruth, Lou Gehrig, Jimmy Foxx, Al Simmons and Joe Cronin in succession with his incredible screwball. . . . 1935, Lefty Gomez and Mel Harder hurled flawlessly for the winning AL. . . . 1936, Joe DiMaggio, baseball's highly-touted rookie, played poorly as Augie Galan's foul-pole homer gave NL its first triumph. . . . 1937, President Roosevelt watched Dizzy Dean receive a broken toe which was to hasten the end of his meteoric career. . . . 1938, Double no-hit hero Johnny Vander Meer hurled NL to victory. . . . 1939, Bob Feller, in relief role, helped Yankee-dominated AL. . . . 1940, Max West's first inning homer with two aboard clinched triumph for NL. . . . 1941, Ted Williams drove circuit over right field roof with two on and two out in ninth inning to give AL dramatic come-from-behind verdict. . . . 1942, Twilight game marked by pair of first inning AL homers. . . . 1943, Bobby Doerr drove in three runs for victorious AL. . . . 1944, NL coasted as Phil Cavarretta reached base five times. . . . 1945, Game suspended in order to comply with wartime restrictions on travel curtailment. . . . 1946, Two homers by Ted Williams gave AL its most one-sided triumph. . . . 1947, Pitching dominated in slickly-played AL verdict. . . . 1948, Underdog AL, riddled by injuries, prevailed. . . . 1949, Hitters held sway as AL won slugfest. . . . 1950, Red Schoendienst's 14th inning homer gave NL victory behind brilliant pitching. . . . 1951, Four homers helped NL. . . . 1952, Rain-curtailed contest decided by NL circuit clouts. . . . 1953, Strong NL pitching kept AL hitters at bay. . . . 1954, Nellie Fox's eighth-inning bloop single gave AL decision in homer-punctuated thriller. . . . 1955, Stan Musial cracked game-winning homer in 12th inning as NL overcame five-run deficit. . . . 1956, Timely hitting and sparkling third-base play by Ken Boyer helped NL to victory. . . . 1957, Early AL lead barely held off late NL rally. . . . 1958, Superb relief hurling by Billy O'Dell featured AL triumph. . . . 1959, Increased to two games to increase player's pension fund. A pitching duel climaxed by Willie Mays' triple enabled the Nationals to win 5–4. The AL won the second tilt 5–3. The big blows were a homer by Berra, two errors and a single by Nellie Fox. . . . 1960, Again a double feature with NL winning both games. Mays' triple and Banks' homer featured the NL attack in the first game. The second game featured four home runs by Mathews, Mays, Musial and Boyer; the Nationals winning 6–0. . . . 1961, Two games again featured the 1961 All-Star games. The Nationals won the first game and the second ended in a 1–1 tie. Most of the action in the first game was concentrated in the 9th

and 10th innings when the Giants relief artist, little Stu Miller was almost blown off the mound for a costly balk from the gales blowing in Candlestick Park. The gale was also responsible for the 7 errors committed in the game. George Altman of the Cubs entered the game as a pinch hitter in the 8th inning and slammed a home run. The second game marked the first tie game in All-Star history when the rains washed it out after nine innings of play. Rocky Colavito of the Tigers connected with one of Bob Purkey's pitches for a homer in the first inning and the Nationals tied it up in the sixth, filling the bases and then scoring the lone run on an infield hit by Bill White. . . . 1962, In the first game played in Washington's new park Maury Wills of the Dodgers put on a base-running exhibition by stealing second as a pinch runner for Stan Musial who had singled and again in the eighth, this time on his own, he thrilled the crowd by stealing third on a single to left when Colavito momentarily held the ball and then scoring on a short fly to right field. The Nationals triumphed 3–1 to win their fifth victory in seven games and to come within one game of tying the Americans. However the American League recovered to take the second game which was played in Wrigley Field, Chicago by a score of 9 to 4. The AL won this one by relying on their old weapon, the home run. Pete Runnels, Leon Wagner and Rocky Colavito slammed the round-trippers for the Americans. The game was also featured by the excellent pitching of the White Sox' Ray Herbert who entered the game in the third and faced only 10 batters until relieved by Hank Aguirre of the Tigers at the start of the sixth inning. . . . 1963—Reverting to the single All-Star Game for the first time since 1958, the NL won the 34th game of the All-Star Classic by a score of 5–3. Willie Mays was the outstanding star of this one when he stole two bases and played his usual brilliant game in the field. Tommy Davis scored the deciding run. . . . 1964—Johnny Callison's dramatic three-run homer in the bottom of the ninth provided the NL with a 7–4 victory in the 35th game. Billy Williams and Ken Boyer also cracked round-trippers for the Nationals, who squared the series at 17 games apiece with one tie. . . . 1965—Mays, who has made the All-Star game his private showcase, homered, walked twice, scored the deciding run and starred afield as the NL posted a 6–5 triumph and took the lead in the series for the first time, 18 to 17. Joe Torre and Willie Stargell also connected for the senior circuit while Dick McAuliffe and Harmon Killebrew poled circuits for the AL. . . . 1966—The 37th All-Star game was the fourth to go into extra innings, and for the third time a member of the St. Louis Cardinals scored the winning run. Redbird catcher Tim McCarver opened the 10th with a sharp single, moved to second on Ron Hunts' perfect sacrifice bunt and tallied on Maury Wills' single to short right, the NL prevailing by a 2–1 count. Brooks Robinson, Baltimore's crack third baseman, punched out three hits, scored the Americans' only run and set a record for third sackers by handling eight chances, several of an eye-catching nature. . . . 1967—Home runs accounted for all the scoring and, as has become the habit in recent games, the NL had the edge. Richie Allen connected in the second inning and Tony Perez hit one out in the 15th to win the 38th classic, 2–1. Brooks Robinson homered in the sixth for the AL. . . . 1968—The NL extended its winning streak to six and its over-all advantage to 21–17 with a narrow 1–0 victory in Houston's Astrodome. Pitchers stole the spotlight as the winning NL managed only five hits, the losing AL three. Willie Mays scored the lone run on a double play. . . . 1969—The hitters finally broke loose, after three pitching-dominated games, with the NL romping to a 9–3 win for its seventh straight triumph. San Francisco's Willie McCovey slammed a pair of homers and Cincinnati catcher John Bench hit one to lead the Nationals' onslaught. Frank Howard and Bill Freehan tagged solo homers for the AL.

. . . 1970—After 13 years, balloting for players was again given to the fans. The NL won their eighth straight game, 5–4 in 12 innings. Jim Hickman singled in Pete Rose, who bowled over catcher Ray Fosse, with the winning run. The NL had rallied from a 4–1 deficit to tie the game in the ninth. . . . 1971—The AL won their first game in nine years, thanks to two-run homers by Frank Robinson, Reggie Jackson, and Harmon Killebrew. All runs for both teams in the 6–4 triumph resulted from the record-tying six home runs. . . . 1972—Joe Morgan scored Nate Colbert from second in the last of the tenth to give the NL a 4–3 verdict. The Nationals had to come from behind in the ninth to tie after Hank Aaron and Cookie Rojas exchanged two-run homers earlier. . . . 1973—Bobby Bonds cracked out a double and two-run homer to lead the NL to a 7–1 romp. Johnny Bench and Willie Davis also homered for the Nationals, who now stand 25–18 in 44 games. Willie Mays tied Stan Musial's mark of 24 games played. . . . 1974—Steve Garvey contributed a double, single and a key defensive play as the NL took another victory, 7–2. Reggie Smith added a homer. . . . 1975— The National League took advantage of sloppy fielding to score three runs in the 9th, giving them a 6–3 win, their 12th in the last 13 games, and 27 of 45 overall. Carl Yastrzemski had previously cancelled an early NL lead with a pinch 3-run homer in the 6th. Hank Aaron played in his 24th game, tying Musial and Mays. . . . 1976—George Foster led the National League to still another All-Star win, driving in three runs. Foster was one of five Cincinnati players voted into the starting lineup.

1st game, at Chicago (AL), July 6, 1933   R. H. E.

					R.	H.	E.
National	000	002	000	---	2	8	0
American	012	001	00x	---	4	9	1

Pitchers--HALLAHAN, Warneke (3), Hubbell (7) vs. GOMEZ, Crowder (4), Grove (7). Homers--Ruth (AL), Frisch (NL). Attendance--49,200. Receipts--$56,378.50.

2nd game, at New York (NL), July 10, 1934

American	000	261	000	---	9	14	1
National	103	030	000	---	7	8	1

Pitchers--Gomez, Ruffing (4), HARDER (7) vs. Hubbell, Warneke (4), MUNGO (5), J. Dean (6), Frankhouse (9). Homers--Frisch (NL), Medwick (NL). Attendance--48,363 Receipts--$52,982.

3rd game, at Cleveland (AL), July 8, 1935

National	000	100	000	---	1	4	1
American	210	010	00x	---	4	8	0

Pitchers--WALKER, Schumacher (3), Derringer (7), J. Dean (8) vs. GOMEZ, Harder (7). Homer--Foxx (AL). Attendance- 69,812. Receipts--$82,179.12.

4th game, at Boston (NL), July 7, 1936

American	000	000	300	---	3	7	1
National	020	020	00x	---	4	9	0

Pitchers--GROVE, Rowe (4), Harder (7) vs. J. DEAN, Hubbell (4), C. Davis (7), Warneke (7). Homers--Gehrig (AL), Galan (NL). Attendance--25,534. Receipts--$24,588.-80.

5th game, at Washington (AL), July 7, 1937

National	000	111	000	---	3	13	0
American	002	312	00x	---	8	13	2

Pitchers--J. DEAN, Hubbell (4), Blanton (4), Grissom (5), Mungo (6), Walters (8) vs. GOMEZ, Bridges (4), Harder (7). Homer--Gehrig (AL). Attendance--31,391. Receipts--$28,475.18.

6th game, at Cincinnati (NL), July 6, 1938

American	000	000	001	---	1	7	4
National	100	100	20x	---	4	8	0

Pitchers--GOMEZ, Allen (4), Grove (7) vs. VANDER MEER, Lee (4), Brown (7). Homers--None. Attendance--27,607. Receipts--$38,469.05.

7th game, at New York (AL), July 11, 1939

National	001	000	000	---	1	7	1
American	000	210	00x	---	3	6	1

Pitchers--Derringer, LEE (4), Fette (7) vs. Ruffing, BRIDGES (4), Feller (6). Homer--J. DiMaggio (AL). Attendance--62,892. Receipts--$75,701.

8th game, at St. Louis (NL), July 9, 1940

American	000	000	000	---	0	3	1
National	300	000	01x	---	4	7	0

Pitchers--RUFFING, Newsom (4), Feller (7) vs. DERRINGER, Walters (3), Wyatt (5), French (7), Hubbell (9). Homer--West (NL). Attendance--32,373. Receipts--$36,-723.03.

9th game, at Detroit (AL), July 8, 1941

National	000	001	220	---	5	10	2
American	000	101	014	---	7	11	3

Pitchers--Wyatt, Derringer (3), Walters (5), PASSEAU (7) vs. Feller, Lee (4), Hudson (7), SMITH (8). Homers--Vaughan (NL) 2, Williams (AL). Attendance--54,675. Receipts--$63,267.08.

10th game, at New York (NL), July 6, 1942

American	300	000	000	---	3	7	0
National	000	000	010	---	1	6	1

Pitchers--CHANDLER, Benton (5), vs. M. COOPER, Vander Meer (4), Passeau (7), Walters (9). Homers--Boudreau (AL), York (AL), Owen (NL). Attendance--33,694. Receipts--$86,102.98.

11th game, at Philadelphia (AL), July 13, 1943

National	100	000	101	---	3	10	1
American	031	010	00x	---	5	8	2

Pitchers--M. COOPER, Vander Meer (3), Sewell (6), Javery (7) vs. LEONARD, Newhouser (4), Hughson (7). Homers--Doerr (AL), V. DiMaggio (NL). Attendance--31,938. Receipts--$65,674.

12th game, at Pittsburgh (NL), July 11, 1944

American	010	000	000	---	1	6	3
National	000	040	21x	---	7	12	1

Pitchers--Borowy, HUGHSON (4), Muncrief (5), Newhouser (7), Newsom (8) vs. Walters, RAFFENSBERGER (4), Sewell (6), Tobin (9). Homers--None. Attendance--29,589. Receipts--$81,275.

(NO GAME IN 1945)   R. H. E.

13th game, at Boston (AL), July 9, 1946

National	000	000	000	---	0	3	0
American	200	130	24x	---	12	14	1

Pitchers--PASSEAU, Higbe (4), Blackwell (5), Sewell (8) vs. FELLER, Newhouser (4), Kramer (7). Homers- Williams (AL) 2, Keller (AL). Attendance--34,906. Receipts--$89,071.

14th game, at Chicago (NL), July 8, 1947

American	000	001	100	---	2	8	0
National	000	100	000	---	1	5	1

Pitchers--Newhouser, SHEA (4), Masterson (7), Page (8) vs. Blackwell, Brecheen (4), SAIN (7), Spahn (8). Homer Mize (NL). Attendance--41,123. Receipts--$105,314.90.

15th game, at St. Louis (AL), July 13, 1948

National	200	000	000	---	2	8	0
American	011	300	00x	---	5	6	0

Pitchers--Branca, SCHMITZ (4), Sain (4), Blackwell (6) vs. Masterson, RASCHI (4), Coleman (7). Homers--Musial (NL), Evers (AL). Attendance--34,009. Receipts--$93,447.07.

16th game, at Brooklyn (NL), July 12, 1949

American	400	202	300	---	11	13	1
National	212	002	000	---	7	12	5

Pitchers--Parnell, TRUCKS (2), Brissie (4), Raschi (7) vs. Spahn, NEWCOMBE (2), Munger (5), Bickford (6), Pollet (7), Blackwell (8), Roe (9). Homers- Musial (NL), Kiner (AL). Attendance--32,577. Receipts--$79,225.02.

17th game, at Chicago (AL), July 11, 1950

National	020	000	001 000 01	--	4	10	0
American	020	000	000 00	--	3	8	1

Pitchers--Roberts, Newcombe (4), Konstanty (6), Jansen (7), BLACKWELL (12) vs. Raschi, Lemon (4), Houtteman (7), Reynolds (10), GRAY (13), Feller (14). Homers--Kiner (NL), Schoendienst (NL). Attendance- 46,127. Receipts--$126,179.51.

18th game, at Detroit (AL), July 10, 1951

National	100	302	110	---	8	12	1
American	010	110	000	---	3	10	2

Pitchers--Roberts, MAGLIE (3). Newcombe (6), Blackwell (9) vs. Garver, LOPAT (4), Hutchinson (5), Parnell (8), Lemon (9). Homers--Musial (NL), Elliott (NL), Hodges (NL), Kiner (NL), Wertz (AL), Kell (AL). Attendance--52,075. Receipts--$124,294.07.

19th game, at Philadelphia (NL), July 8, 1952

American	000	20	---	2	5	0
National	100	20	---	3	3	0

Pitchers--Raschi, LEMON (3), Shantz (5) vs. Simmons, RUSH (4). Homers--Robinson (NL), Sauer (NL). Attendance--32,785. Receipts--$108,762.40.

20th game, at Cincinnati (NL), July 14, 1953

American	000	000	001	---	1	5	0
National	000	020	12x	---	5	10	0

Pitchers--Pierce, REYNOLDS (4), Garcia (6), Paige (8) vs. Roberts, SPAHN (4), Simmons, Dickson (8). Attendance--30,846. Receipts--$155,654.

21st game, at Cleveland (AL), July 13, 1954

National	000	520	020	---	9	14	0
American	004	121	03x	---	11	17	1

Roberts, Antonelli (4), Spahn (5), Grissom (6), CONLEY (8), Erskin (8) vs. Ford, Consuegra (4), Lemon (4), Porterfield (5), Keegan (8), STONE (8), Trucks (9). Homers--Rosen (AL) 2, Boone (AL), Doby (AL), Kluszewski (NL), Bell (NL). Attendance--68,751. Receipts--$292,678.

22nd game, at Milwaukee (NL), July 12, 1955

American	400	001	000 000	---	5	10	2
National	000	000	230 001	---	6	13	1

Pierce, Wynn (4), Ford (7), SULLIVAN (8) vs. Roberts, Haddix (4), Newcombe (7), Jones (8), Nuxhall (8), CONLEY (12). Homers--Mantle (AL), Musial (NL). Attendance--45,314. Receipts--$179,545.50.

23rd Game, at Washington (AL), July 10, 1956

National	001	211	200	---	7 11 0
American	000	003	000	---	3 11 0

FRIEND, Spahn (4), Antonelli (6) vs. PIERCE, Ford (4), Wilson (5), Brewer (6), Score (8), Wynn (9). Homers--Mays (NL), Musial (NL), Williams (AL), Mantle (AL). Attendance--28,843. Receipts--$105,928.50.

24th game, at St. Louis (NL), July 9, 1957

American	020	001	003	---	6 10 0
National	000	000	203	---	5 9 1

BUNNING, Loes (4), Wynn (7), Pierce (7), Moss (9), Grim (9) vs. SIMMONS, Burdette (2), Sanford (6), Jackson (7), Labine (9). Attendance--30,693. Receipts--$122,027.

25th game, at Baltimore (AL), July 8, 1958

National	210	000	000	---	3 4 2
American	110	011	00x	---	4 9 2

Spahn, FRIEND (4), Jackson (6), Farrell (7) vs. Turley, Narleski (2), WYNN (6), O'Dell (7). Attendance--48,829. Receipts--$202,492.

26th game, at Pittsburgh (NL), July 7, 1959 (1st game)

American	000	100	030	---	4 8 4
National	100	000	22X	---	5 9 1

Pitchers--Wynn, Duren (4), Bunning (7), FORD (8), Daley (8) vs Drysdale, Burdette (4), Face (7), ANTONELLI (8), Elston (9). Homers--Mathews (NL), Kaline (AL). Attendance--35,277. Receipts--$229,636.

27th game, at Los Angeles (NL), August 3, 1959 (2nd game)

American	012	000	110	---	5 6 0
National	100	010	100	---	3 6 3

Pitchers--WALKER, Wynn (4), Wilhelm (6), O'Dell (7), McLish (8) vs DRYSDALE, Conley (4), Jones (6), Face (8). Homers--Malzone (AL), Berra (AL), Robinson (NL), Gilliam (NL), Colavito (AL). Attendance--55,105. Receipts--$283,120.

28th game, at Kansas City (AL), July 11, 1960 (1st game)

National	311	000	000	---	5 12 4
American	000	001	020	---	3 6 1

Pitchers--FRIEND, McCormick (4), Face (6), Buhl (8), Law (9) vs MONBOUQUETTE, Estrada (3), Coates (4), Bell (6), Lary (8), Daley (9). Homers--Banks (NL), Crandall (NL), Kaline (AL) 2, Fox (AL). Attendance--30,619. Receipts--$151,238.38 (net).

29th game, at New York (AL), July 13, 1960 (2nd game)

National	021	000	102	---	6 10 0
American	000	000	000	---	0 8 0

Pitchers--LAW, Podres (3), S. Williams (5), Jackson (7), Henry (8), McDaniel (9) vs FORD, Wynn (4), Staley (6), Lary (8), Bell (9). Homers--Mathews (NL), Mays (NL), Musial (NL), Boyer (NL). Attendance--38,362. Receipts--$177,688.57 (net).

30th game, at San Francisco (NL), July 11, 1961 (1st game)

American	**000**	**001**	**002**	**1**	**.... 4 4 2**
National	**010**	**100**	**010**	**2**	**.... 5 11 5**

Pitchers--Ford, Lary (4), Donovan (4), Bunning (6), Fornieles (8), WILHELM (8) vs Spahn, Purkey (4), McCormick (6), Face (9), Koufax (9), MILLER (9). Homers--Killebrew (AL), Altman (NL). Attendance--44,115. Receipts--$259,230.81 (net).

31st game, at Boston (AL), July 31, 1961 (2nd game)

National	000	001	000	---	1 5 1
American	100	000	000	---	1 4 0

Pitchers--Bunning, Schwall (4), Pascual (7) vs Purkey, Mahaffey (3), Koufax (5), Miller (7). Homer--Colavito (AL). Attendance--31,851. Receipts--$172,298.19 (net).

32nd Game, at Washington (AL), July 10, 1962 (1st Game)

					R. H. E.
National	000	002	010	---	3 8 0
American	000	001	000	---	1 4 0

Pitchers--Bunning, PASCUAL (4), Donovan (7), Pappas (9) vs Drysdale, MARICHAL (4), Purkey (6), Shaw (8). Attendance--45,480. Receipts--$228,082.21.

33rd game, at Chicago (NL), July 30, 1962 (2nd game)

American	001	201	302	---	9 10 0
National	010	000	111	---	4 10 4

Pitchers--Stenhouse, HERBERT (3), Aguirre (6), Pappas (9) vs Podres, MAHAFFEY (3), Gibson (5), Farrell (7), Marichal (8). Homers--Runnels (AL), Wagner (AL), Colavito (AL). Roseboro (NL). Attendance--38,359. Receipts--$216,908.71.

34th game, at Cleveland (AL) July 9, 1963

American	012	000	000	......	3 11 1
National	012	010	010		5 6 0

Pitchers--O'Toole, JACKSON (3), Culp (5), Woodeshick (6), Drysdale (8) vs. McBride, BUNNING (4), Bouton (6), Pizarro (7), Radatz (8). Attendance--44,160. Receipts--$250,584.59 (net).

35th game, at New York (NL) July 7, 1964

American	100	002	100		4 9 1
National	000	210	004		7 8 0

Pitchers--Chance, Wyatt (4), Pascual (5), RADATZ (7) vs. Drysdale, Bunning (4), Short (6), Farrell (7), MARICHAL (9). Homers--Williams (NL), Boyer (NL), Callison (NL). Attendance--50,850. Receipts--$215,801.85 (net).

36th game, at Minnesota (AL) July 13, 1965

American	000	140	000		5 8 0
National	320	000	100		6 11 0

Pitchers--Marichal, Maloney (4), Drysdale (5), KOUFAX (6), Farrell (7), Gibson (8) vs. Pappas, Grant (2), Richert (4), McDOWELL (6), Fisher (8). Homers--Mays (NL), Torre (NL), Stargell (NL), McAuliffe (AL), Killebrew (AL). Attendance-- 46,706. Receipts--$284,949.31 (net).

37th game, at St. Louis (N) July 12, 1966

American	010	000	000	......	1 6 0
National	000	100	000	1	2 6 0

Pitchers--McLain, Kaat (4), Stottlemyre (6), Siebert (8), RICHERT (10) vs. Koufax, Bunning (4), Marichal (6), PERRY (9). Attendance--49,936. Receipts--$284,949.31 (net).

38th game, at California (A) July 11, 1967

National	010	000	000	000 001	.... 2 9 0
American	000	001	000	000 000	.... 1 8 0

Pitchers--Marichal, Jenkins (4), Gibson (7), Short (9), Cuellar (11), DRYSDALE (13), Seaver (15) vs. Chance, McGlothlin (4), Peters (6), Downing (9), HUNTER (11). Homers--Allen (NL), B. Robinson (AL), Perez (NL). Attendance--46,309. Receipts--$324,428 (gross).

39th game, at Houston (N) July 9, 1968

American	000	000	000	....	0 3 1
National	100	000	00x	....	1 5 0

Pitchers--TIANT, Odom (3), McLain (5), McDowell (7), Stottlemyre (8), John (8) vs. DRYSDALE, Marichal (4), Carlton (6), Seaver (7), Reed (9), Koosman (9). Attendance--48,321.

40th game, at Washington (AL) July 23, 1969

National	125	100	000	....	9 11 0
American	011	100	000	....	3 6 2

Pitchers--CARLTON, Gibson (4), Singer (5), Koosman (7), Dierker (8), P. Niekro (9) vs. STOTTLEMYRE, Odom (3), Knowles (3), McLain (4), McNally (5), McDowell (7), Culp (9). Homers--Bench (NL), Howard (AL), McCovey 2 (NL), Freehan (AL). Attendance--45,259.

41st Game, at Cincinnati (NL), July 14, 1970

```
                                R. H. E.
American       000 001 120 000— 4 12  0
National       000 000 103 001— 5 10  0
```
Pitchers—Palmer, McDowell (4), J. Perry (7), Hunter (9), Peterson (9), Stottlemyre (9), WRIGHT (11) vs. Seaver, Merritt (4), G. Perry (6), Gibson (8), OSTEEN (10). Homer—Dietz (NL). Attendance—51,838.

42nd Game, at Detroit (AL), July 13, 1971

```
                                R. H. E.
National       021   000   010— 4   5  0
American       004   002   00X— 6   7  0
```
Pitcher—ELLIS, Marichal (4), Jenkins (6), Wilson (7) vs. BLUE, Palmer (4), Cuellar (6), Lolich (8). Homers—Bench (NL), Aaron (NL), Jackson (AL), F. Robinson (AL), Killebrew (AL), Clemente (NL). Attendance —53,559.

43rd Game, at Atlanta (NL), July 25, 1972

```
                                R  H  E
American       001 000 020 0— 3  6  0
National       000 002 001 1— 4  8  0
```
Pitchers—Palmer, Lolich (4), G. Perry (6), Wood (8), McNALLY (10) vs. Gibson, Blass (3), Sutton (4), Carlton (6), Stoneman (7), McGRAW (9). Homers—Aaron (NL), Rojas (AL). Attendance—53,107.

44th Game, at Kansas City (AL), July 24, 1973

```
                                 R  H  E
National       002 122 000—7 10  0
American       010 000 000—1  5  0
```
Pitchers—WISE, Osteen (3), Sutton (5), Twitchell (6), Giusti (7), Seaver (8), Brewer (9) vs. Hunter, Holtzman (2), BLYLEVEN (3), Singer (4), Ryan (6), Lyle (8), Fingers (9). Homers—Bench (NL), Bonds (NL), W. Davis (NL). Attendance—40,849.

45th Game, at Pittsburgh (NL), July 23, 1974

```
                                 R. H. E.
American       002 000 000—2  4  1
National       010 210 12x—7 10  1
```
Pitchers—Perry, TIANT (6), Hunter (6), Fingers (8) vs. Messersmith, BRETT (4), Matlack (6), McGlothen (7), Marshall (8). Homer—Smith (NL). Attendance—50,706.

46th Game, at Milwaukee (AL), July 15, 1975

```
                                 R. H. E.
National       021 000 003—6 13  1
American       000 003 000—3 10  1
```
Pitchers—Reuss, Sutton (4), Seaver (6), MATLACK (7), Jones (9) vs. Blue, Busby (3), Kaat (5), HUNTER (7), Gossage (9). Homers—Garvey (NL), Wynn (NL), Yastrzemski (AL). Attendance—51,480.

47th Game, at Philadelphia (NL), July 13, 1976

```
                                 R  H  E
American       000 100 000—1  5  0
National       202 000 03x—7 10  0
```
Pitchers—FIDRYCH, Hunter (3), Tiant (5), Tanana (7) vs. JONES, Seaver (4), Montefusco (6), Rhoden (8), Forsch (9). Homers—Foster (NL), Lynn (AL), Cedeno (NL). Attendance—63,974.

IX UMPIRES

"Please Do Not Shoot the Umpire; he is Doing the Best he Can."
This was the inspiring prose which greeted the durable man in blue who umpired a game during the 1886 National League season in the Kansas City park. On the outfield barrier, for all to see, was this ode to the umpire which was not too far removed from the emotion of the day's fan and player.

Between baseball's earliest days and his present-day standing of absolute autocracy on the field of play, the umpire passed through one of the diamond's roughest and rowdiest eras. He could do no right in the eyes of the fan, the player, the owner, the press; he was wrong, blind, lame, incompetent and crooked, accusations which were hurled ceaselessly and shamefully. But in the long history of the sport it is interesting to note that the umpire—not the player—has been far removed from suspicion. Only one umpire has been expelled because of dishonesty: Richard Higham, in 1882, who committed the unpardonable sin of announcing to certain people the probable winners of games in which he was to officiate. But Higham's offense never may have occurred if the owners had the foresight to hire extra umpires and spread their work a bit more around the rest of the league.

Higham's high-handed tactics were suspected by William G. Thompson, president of the Detroit team, who thought his club was losing too many games in which Higham served as arbiter. Higham officiated 26 of the first 29 games played by Detroit, and private detectives learned the umpire's work was not always beyond reproach. They produced evidence in the form of a letter Higham allegedly had written in which he tipped off eventual winners of games in which he was to work, enough to expel baseball's only dishonest umpire.

In baseball's earliest days, before the start of the major leagues, the position of the umpire was dignified. He donned a Prince Albert coat, silk hat and cane. Stationed just outside the foul line between home and first, he was given a stool on which to rest one foot as he viewed the game. In those days of long-flowing whiskers, he gave his decisions deliberately.

Between the patriarchal overseer of the early 19th century and the nimble, forceful man-in-blue of the present, the umpiring profession has weathered many storms. "Kill the umpire!" once was more than a euphemism. Clarence (Brick) Owens got his nickname from the object thrown at him in a game. Minor league umpires have been tarred and feathered. Police protection used to be standard equipment for a long time even in the big leagues.

Founding fathers of professional baseball recognized the need for investing the umpire with real authority. For that reason they stated in the first set of pro rules, 1871, that there can be no appeal from a decision involving the umpire's judgment (fair or foul, safe or out, etc.). Protests can be based only on interpretation of the rules. This fundamental principle has not been changed since.

Hoping to insure the integrity of the umpire, league officials forbade any pay for working the game. The visiting club would submit three names as prospective umpires for the game, and the home team would select one. The system sagged so badly, the day's umpire often had to be picked from a volunteer in the stands.

Back in the pioneering National Association, a part-time prize fighter from

Philadelphia, William B. McLean, quickly established himself as "King of Umpires." He ran the games so competently that clubs gladly paid his expenses for road trips, and he became the first umpire to officiate in every city.

McLean was responsible for another innovation. He commanded a fee of $5 a game. In the first two years of the National League, rules-makers tried to stick to the amateur tradition, but by 1878 it became obvious that capable officials could be obtained only by proper pay, and the McLean standard of $5 a game was written into the rules.

At first, the visiting club was required to pay the $5, while the home club paid all other expenses. Later, the home club became responsible for all umpiring costs.

In 1883, the American Association decided to pay the umpires out of the league treasury at the rate of $140 per month "plus traveling expenses and hotel bills, not to exceed $3 a day." Umpires by now were technically members of the league staff. They no longer could be removed in the middle of a game merely by agreement of the rival captains. Yet league headquarters still failed to back up the umpires in disputes with players. Fines didn't stick. Suspensions were easily rescinded.

Until the end of the 19th century, and well into the 20th, league games were handled by a single umpire. While the harassed official behind the plate ran part of the way down the baseline to judge a drive near the foul line in right field, baserunners would cut inside second base en route from first to third. In the boisterous 90's, fights often broke out because the third baseman would slyly grab the belt of the baserunner and restrain him while the lone umpire was busy watching the relay from the outfield.

In the early 1900's, a second umpire finally came into general use. It wasn't till 1910 that the rules spoke of an Umpire-in-Chief (plate umpire) and Field Umpire (for baseline decisions). Thirty years later, a third umpire became a regular sight. By now, it is taken for granted that there will be four umpires at all important games, with six being used at the World Series (one for each base, and one at each foul pole to decide between home runs and foul balls).

Leagues have always tried various stratagems to bolster the respect of umpires. The old AA ruled that no umpire while in uniform could enter a poolroom or saloon, under penalty of fine by the league president. They also halted the "undignified practice" of allowing the umpire to take testimony from spectators in case of doubt over whether a ball had left the field fair or foul, or whether a fair catch had been made in the outfield. The National League in the 1890's even wrote into the rules that the players must address him as "Mr. Umpire!"

Yet all these dodges to compel respect for the umpires faded when the belligerent players were allowed to intimidate the officials without reprisal from the league's top echelon. One of the main reasons the American League became soundly established at the start of this century was that its founder, Byron Bancroft (Ban) Johnson, removed rowdyism from the game by carefully selecting a staff of umpires and by completely backing every one of their field rulings, a wise move which put to an end the endless debates between the umpires and outraged players.

John McGraw, bred in the boisterous Old Oriole days, found himself practically manacled in the new AL, so he jumped into the NL.

For a few years, McGraw had a picnic with the arbiters. Then he crossed the path of a spunky little newcomer named Bill Klem. Ordered out of a game by Klem, the Little Napoleon raged, "I'll have your job for this!"

"If it's possible for you to take my job," answered Klem coldly, "then I don't want it."

Largely through the insistence of Klem, who was to earn an immortal niche as "The Old Arbitrator," the NL began raising its umpiring standards to meet the Americans. Through Klem's campaigning, World Series pay rose from $400 to $2,500. Umpires were provided with a separate clubhouse, so they no longer had to retreat to an old peanut shed or storage bin after a game, to use a sponge and fire bucket to swab the day's dust from their body.

Klem umpired in 18 World Series, a record. He brought dignity, respect and authority to the job. In 1949, the fans honored him with a special "Day" at the Polo Grounds. Sports writers awarded him a plaque for meritorious service to baseball over a long period of years, and in his brief but dramatic acceptance speech he announced his credo, "Baseball is more than a game to me—it's a religion!"

Klem started the practice of "getting on the ball" by crouching to judge each pitch from right over the catcher's shoulder. Cy Rigler was the one who started the sensible custom of raising the right arm to denote a strike. There are some 60,000 in the umpiring population of the United States, counting high school and sandlot games. The leagues have an elaborate scouting system to bring up the best. They look for a man with keen eyesight, knowledge of the rules, ability to get into the right position quickly, poise, decisiveness, impartiality (meaning an imperviousness to the hoots of a home crowd, which tries to sway decisions toward the home team), psychology of handling men and a flair for the game.

For his salary of about $20,000 to cover the six-month season, the big league umpire is a lonely man. He may not fraternize with the players on the field, nor can he travel in the same train or stay at the same hotel as the players. His future assignments are never made more than a week ahead, so his family life is practically nil during the season.

Umpires have a host of duties, besides the obvious ball-and-strike decisions (more than 200 of these a game for the plate umpire), safe-or-out and fair-or-foul. He administers rules as to equipment, conditions of the grounds, etc. He is the sole judge over whether to end a game because of climatic conditions or other circumstances.

Still, there are many decisions which an umpire is not allowed to make unless there is a direct protest. These are "appeal plays," and include declaring a runner out for failing to tag a bag. Klem once admitted that the deciding run of the fifth game of the 1911 World Series was scored by Larry Doyle, who slid half a foot wide of the plate to avoid a tag that never was made. Doyle brushed himself off, trotted to the clubhouse and Klem had no way of declaring him out, since the catcher also walked away.

Besides the aforementioned McLean, Rigler and Klem, there have been many famous umpires of long service, like Honest John Kelly, John Gaffney, Hank O'Day, Silk O'Loughlin, Tom Connolly, Bill Dinneen, Charles Moran, Billy Evans and many others. Bill McGowan set the Iron man mark by umpiring 2,541 consecutive AL games in 16½ seasons without missing an inning.

John K. Tener, who later became Governor of the state of Pennsylvania, umpired one season in the NL. On June 26, 1897 in Washington, Thomas J. Lynch umpired the first Giant game and John A. Heydler umpired the second. Lynch and Heydler later became presidents of the league.

Baseball management was confronted with an umpire strike threat in the spring of 1969 by the newly formed Association of Major League Umpires. Umpires of both leagues formed one union on September 30, 1968, and at that time agreed to stage a general strike the following spring unless umpires Al Salerno and Bill Valentine were reinstated by American League President Joe Cronin.

Both Valentine and Salerno had been released by Cronin for imcompetence and their contracts not renewed for the 1969 season. A charge of unfair labor practice was brought against the American League by Salerno and Valentine as they insisted they were fired because of their activities in unionizing their fellow A.L. umpires. Attorney Jack Reynolds, administrator and league counsel for the N.L. umpires, began bargaining procedures with Cronin. Eventually an economic agreement was announced with umpires in both leagues advised to sign their contracts. The law suit would be handled separately.

The Salerno and Valentine case was dismissed by the National Labor Relations Board on July 13, 1970, for lack of sufficient evidence. Attorneys for the umpires appealed to higher courts, even the Supreme Court in January, 1971, with the same verdict. The case was then returned to the NLRB in Washington for final arbitration. The umpires charges were finally dismissed on April 2, 1972.

A one-day strike on Oct. 3, 1970, prompted re-opening of contract negotiations between baseball commissioner Bowie Kuhn, league presidents Chub Feeney and Joe Cronin, and Jack Reynolds, attorney for the Association of Major League Umpires. The playoffs proceeded as usual using minor league umps. Agreement provided increased wages for senior umpires along with new pension benefits and championship playoffs, World Series and All-Star Games raises.

ALL-TIME REGISTER

NATIONAL LEAGUE

Abbey, Charles S., 1897
Abbot, 1905
Adams, James, 1897
Allen, Hezekiah, 1876
Anderson, William, 1890
Andrews, George E., 1889, 1893, 1895, 1898-99
Arundel, John T., 1888
Ayers, 1876
Baker, Charles, 1884
Baker, Philip, 1889
Baldwin, Marcus E., 1892
Ballanfant, Edward L., 1936-57
Bannon, James H., 1894
Barker, Alfred L., 1876, 1880-81
Barlick, Albert J., 1940-43, 46-55, 58-71
Barnie, William S., 1882, 1892
Barr, George M., 1931-49
Barton, 1876
Bates, 1877
Battin, Joseph V., 1882, 1889, 1891, 1895-96
Bausewine, George, 1908
Beard, Oliver P., 1894
Becannon, James M., 1885
Beck, Erwin T., 1902
Beckley, Jacob P., 1906
Beebe, Fred L., 1907
Behle, Frank, 1895-96, 1901
Berger, Frederick, 1886
Berger, John H., 1891
Betts, William G., 1893-96, 1898-99
Bigelow, 1877
Bittman, Henry, 1892-95, 1897
Blakiston, Robert J., 1884
Blodgett, C. W., 1876
Boggess, Lynton, 1944-48, 50-62
Boles, Charles, 1877
Bond, Thomas H., 1883, 1885
Bonner, Frank J., 1894
Boston, K. K., 1878
Boyle, Henry J., 1886
Boyle, John A., 1892, 1897
Bradley, George H., 1877, 1879-83
Brady, 1877
Brady, Jackson, 1887
Bransfield, William E., 1917
Bredburg, George W., 1877, 1879
Breitenstein, Theodore P., 1900
Brennan, John E., 1887, 1899
Brennan, William T., 1909, 1913, 1921
Briody, Charles F., 1882
Brockway, John, 1877, 1879
Brown, Samuel W., 1907
Brown, Thomas T., 1891, 1898-99, 1901-02
Brunton, Thomas H., 1879
Buckenberger, Alfred C., 1890
Budding, 1877
Buelow, Frederick W., 1901

Buffinton, Charles G., 1883, 1888-89, 1892
Bullymore, Charles L., 1882
Bunce, Joshua, 1877
Burke, 1892
Burkhart, William Kenneth, 1957-73
Burlingame, Frank A., 1878
Burnham, George W., 1883, 1886-87, 1889, 1893, 1895
Burns, John S., 1884
Burns, Thomas E., 1892
Burns, Thomas P., 1895, 1899
Burtis, D. W., 1876-77
Bush, Garner C., 1911-12
Bushong, Albert J., 1880, 1890
Butler, Richard H., 1897
Byron, William J., 1913-19
Callahan, Edward J., 1881
Campbell, Al., 1886
Campbell, Daniel, 1893-97
Campbell, William M., 1939-40
Cantillon, Joseph D., 1902
Carey, S., 1870
Carey, Thomas J., 1881-82
Carpenter, William B., 1897, 1904, 1906-07
Carrick, William M., 1900
Carroll, Frederick H., 1887
Carsey, Wilfred, 1894, 1896, 1901
Caruthers, Robert L., 1886, 1891, 1893
Casey, Daniel M., 1888
Caskin, Edward J., 1884
Cassidy, John P., 1882
Chamberlain, Elton P., 1894
Chance, Frank L., 1902
Chandler, Moses E., 1877
Chaplin, Harry, 1886
Chapman, John C., 1876, 1880, 1882-83, 1885
Chapman, John, 1880
Chill, Oliver P., 1916
Chipper, 1876
Clack, Robert H., 1876, 1897
Clark, Arthur F., 1890
Clarke, Robert M., 1930-31
Clarke, William J., 1893-94, 1896
Clarkson, Arthur H., 1892-96
Clarkson, John G., 1888, 1892-93

Cockill, George W., 1915
Cohen, 1893
Coleman, John F., 1884
Colgan, Harry W., 1899, 1901, 1903
Collins, Daniel T., 1876
Colosi, Nicholas, 1968-76
Cone, J. F., 1876-77
Conlan, John, 1941-64
Connell, Terence G., 1885, 1887
Connolly, John M., 1886-87, 1892-93

Connolly, Thomas H., 1898-1900
Conahan, 1896
Conway, John H., 1906
Coogan, Daniel G., 1895
Crandall, Robert, 1876-78
Crane, Edward N., 1892-93
Crane, Samuel N., 1886-87, 1890
Crawford, Henry C., 1956-75
Cray, 1893
Crolius, Frederick J., 1901
Cronin, John J., 1902-03
Cross, John A., 1876, 1878-79
Cross, Lafayette N., 1892
Cunningham, Elmer E., 1896-97, 1900-01
Cuppy, George M., 1894
Curren, Peter, 1876
Curry, Wesley, 1885-86, 1889-90, 1898
Cusack, Stephen P., 1909
Cushman, Carles H., 1884-85, 1894, 1898
Cusick, Andrew, 1886-87
Daily, Cornelius F., 1886, 1891, 1894, 1896
Dailey, John J., 1882
Dale, Jerry P., 1970-76
Daly, Thomas P., 1901
Daniels, Charles F., 1876-80, 1887-88
Darling, Dell C., 1887
Dascoli, Frank, 1948-62
Davidson, David L., 1969-76
Davis, C. E., 1880
Day, 1879
Dealey, Patrick E., 1886
Deane, Henry C., 1876, 1878
Decker, Stewart M., 1883-85, 1888
Delmore, Victor, 1956-59
Devinney, Daniel, 1876-77
Dexter, Charles D., 1896-97
Dezelan, Frank J., 1966-70
Dixon, Hal, 1953-59
Donahue, Francis R., 1897
Donahue, Timothy C., 1895-96
Donatelli, August J., 1950-73
Donlin, Michael J., 1900
Donnelly, Charles H., 1931-32
Donnelly, James B., 1896
Donohue, Michael R., 1930
Donovan, Timothy H., 1882
Donovan, William E., 1902
Dooin, Charles S., 1904
Doscher, John H., 1879-82, 1887
Douglass, William B., 1903
Dowse, Thomas J., 1890
Doyle, John J., 1911
Draper, John H., 1877
Ducharme, 1876-77
Duggleby, William J., 1905
Dunlap, Frederick C., 1879
Dunn, John, 1879
Dunn, Thomas P., 1939-46

Dunnigan, Joseph, 1881-82
Dwyer, John F., 1889, 1893-97, 1899, 1901
Dyler, John F., 1892, 1897
Eagan, John J., 1878, 1886
Earle, William M., 1892, 1894
Eason, Malcolm W., 1901-02, 1910-15
Ehret, Philip S., 1892, 1895-97
Ellick, Joseph J., 1886
Emslie, Robert D., 1891-1924
Engel, Robert A., 1965-76
Engeln, William R., 1952-56
English, John W., 1876
Evans, Jacob, 1886
Farrell, Charles A., 1901-02
Feber, Fred W., 1879
Fenno, Norman, 1876
Ferguson, Robert V., 1879, 1884-85
Fessenden, Wallace C., 1889-90
Finch, R. B., 1880
Finneran, William E., 1911-12
Fisher, William C., 1876
Flaherty, Patrick J., 1904-1907
Flynn, John A., 1893
Force, David W., 1881
Foreman, Frank I., 1895
Foreman, John D., 1896
Forman, Allen, 1962-65
Foster, Clarence F., 1900
Fountain, Edward G., 1879
Fouser, William C., 1876
Frary, Robert, 1911
Freeman, John F., 1900
Froemming, Bruce N., 1971-76
Fulmer, Charles J., 1881, 1886
Furlong, William E., 1877-80, 1882-84, 1888
Gaffney, John H., 1884-95
Galvin, James F., 1886-87, 1889, 1893, 1895
Ganzel, Charles W., 1901
Gardner, James A., 1899
Geer, William H., 1879
George, William M., 1889
German, Lester S., 1895
Getzein, Charles N., 1890
Gifford, James H., 1881
Gill, Thomas H., 1886
Gillean, Thomas, 1879-81
Gleason, John D., 1877
Gleason, William G., 1877
Gleason, William J., 1890, 1892
Glenn, John W., 1880
Goetz, Lawrence J., 1936-57
Goldsmith, Frederick E., 1886
Gore, Arthur J., 1947-56
Gorman, Thomas D., 1951-76
Grady, Michael W., 1895
Graves, Frank M., 1886, 1895
Griffith, Clark C., 1894
Grim, John H., 1892, 1895-96
Gross, Edward M., 1881
Gruber, Henry J., 1889
Guglielmo, Angelo, 1952
Guinney, Daniel, 1882-83
Gumbert, Addison C., 1892-1895
Gunning, Thomas F., 1884-85, 1887
Gunson, Joseph B., 1892

Guthrie, William J., 1913-1915
Hackett, Merton M., 1886
Haddock, George S., 1889
Haley, Ed., 1876
Hallman, William W., 1903
Hanlon, Edward H., 1892
Hardie, Louis W., 1887
Harrison, Peter A., 1916-20
Hart, Eugene F., 1920-29
Hart, William F., 1896-97, 1914-15
Hartley, John. 1894
Harvey, H. Douglas, 1962-76
Hastings, Winfield S., 1877
Hatfield, Gilbert, 1889
Hatfield, John V. B., 1876
Hawes, William A., 1881-82
Healy, John J., 1887
Hegeman, William H., 1881
Hemming, George E., 1895-96
Henderson, James H., 1895-96
Hengle, Edward S., 1887
Henline, Walter J., 1945-48
Hernon, Thomas H., 1894
Heuble, George A., 1876
Heydler, John A., 1895-98
Hickey, James L., 1882
Higham, Richard, 1881-82
Hiller, George J., 1881
Hines, Michael P., 1884
Hoagland, Willard A., 1894
Hodges, A. D., 1876-77, 1879
Hoffer, William L., 1896
Hogan, 1897
Hogriever, George C., 1893
Holland, John A., 1887
Holliday, James W., 1897, 1903
Hornung, Joseph M., 1892-93, 1896
Houtz, Charles, 1876, 1879
Howard, C. F., 1884
Howe, John, 1890
Hunt, John T., 1893, 1895, 1898-99
Hurst, Timothy C., 1891-98, 1900, 1903-04
Hyatt, Robert H., 1912
Irwin, Arthur A., 1881, 1902
Jacklitsch, Fred L., 1901
Jackowski, William, 1952-68
Jeffers, W. W., 1881
Jennings, Hugh A., 1893, 1900
Jevne, Frederick, 1892-95
Johnson, Harry S., 1914
Johnstone, James E., 1903-12
Jones, Henry M., 1890
Jones, Nicholas L., 1944-49
Jorda, Louis D., 1927-31, 1940-52
Jose, 1889
Joyce, C. E., 1879
Julian, Joseph O., 1878
Kahle, 1905
Kane, Stephen J., 1906, 1909-10
Karger, Edwin, 1906
Kecher, W. H., 1910
Keefe, Timothy J., 1880, 1882-85, 1887, 1892-96
Keenan, James W., 1881, 1890, 1893
Kelley, Joseph J., 1892, 1904

Kelley, W. W., 1877
Kellum, Winford A., 1905
Kelly, John O., 1882, 1884-85, 1888. 1897
Kelly, Michael J., 1893
Kelly, S., 1880
Kennedy, Charles, 1904
Kennedy, Michael J., 1884
Kenney, John, 1876-77
Kerins, John A., 1888
Kibler, John W., 1963-76
Killen, Frank B., 1896-97
Kinslow, Thomas F., 1892
Kipp, Eden, 1881
Kitson, Frank R., 1902
Klem, William J., 1905-41
Kling, John G., 1901
Klusman, William F., 1892-93
Knell, Philip H., 1895
Knight, Alonzo P., 1876, 1888-89
Knowles, James, 1892
Krieg, William F., 1887
Kunkel, William G., 1968-73
Lally, Daniel J., 1891-94, 1896
Landes, Stanley A., 1955-72
Lane, Frank, 1883
Laney, B., 1884
Lanigan, Charles, 1908
Latham, Walter A., 1899-1900, 1902
Laughlin, 1876
Lavers, George W., 1882
Lawler, Michael H., 1882
Leever, Samuel W., 1900, 1904
Libby, Stephen A., 1880
Lincoln, Frederick H., 1914, 1917
Lindeman, Vivian A., 1907
Long, William H., 1893, 1895, 1897
Lowell, William, 1882
Luciano, Ron M., 1969-73
Lundgren, Carl L., 1905-06
Lynch, J. T., 1880
Lynch, Thomas J., 1888-99, 1902
Macullar, John F., 1892
Maddox, Charles, 1882
Magee, Sherwood R., 1928
Magerkurth, George L., 1929-47
Mahoney, Michael J., 1892
Malone, Ferguson G., 1884, 1892
Maloney, George P., 1969-73
Maloney, William A., 1902
Manassau, Alfred S., 1899
Manning, James H., 1886, 1893
Mapledoram, Blake A., 1886
Martin, Alphonse C., 1876
Mason, Charles E., 1876
Mathews, Robert T., 1876, 1880, 1882
Mathewson, Christopher, 1901, 1907
Mayer, 1893
McAllister, Louis W., 1899
McCaffrey, Harry, 1885, 86
McCarthy, Thomas F. M., 1896
McCauley, Patrick M., 1896
McCauley, Allen B., 1890

McCormick, James, 1885
McCormick, William J., 1919-29
McCoy, Larry S., 1970–73
McCrum, 1892
McDermott, Michael J., 1890, 1897
McDonald, James F., 1895, 1897-99
McDowell, 1893
McElwee, Harvey, 1877
McFarland, Edward W., 1896
McFarland, Horace, 1896-97
McGann, Dennis L., 1903
McGarr, James B., 1895, 1899
McGee, 1876
McGinnis, 1910
McGinnity, Joseph J., 1900
McGinty, 1897
McGrew, Harry T., 1930-31, 1933-34
McGuire, James T., 1886-87, 1894, 1896-97, 1901
McGunnigle, Edward, 1888
McKinley, William F., 1946-65
McLaughlin, Edward J., 1929
McLaughlin, Michael, 1893
McLaughlin, Peter J., 1924-26
McLean, William B., 1876-80, 1882-84
McLeod, 1895
McMahon, John H., 1893
McMater, 1877
McMullen, John F., 1876
McQuaid, John H., 1889-95
McSherry, John P., 1971–76
Meagher, John, 1877
Mears, Charles W., 1894
Medart, William, 1876-77
Meekin, Jouette, 1895-96
Megrue, Cliff, 1876
Mertes, Samuel B., 1903-05
Miller, George E., 1879
Miller, George F., 1893, 1896
Miller, Joseph H., 1884
Mills, Abraham G., 1877
Mitchell, Charles, 1892
Montague, 1877
Montague, Edward M., 1976
Moran, 1894
Moran, August, 1903–04, 1910–11, 1918
Moran, Charles B., 1917-39
Moran, Patrick J., 1901
Morrill, John F., 1891, 1896
Morris, Edward, 1895, 1897
Morris, John S., 1876
Muir, Thomas, 1876
Mullane, Anthony J., 1893, 1897
Mullen, Peter C., 1893
Mullin, John, 1909
Mulvey, Joseph H., 1895
Murnane, Timothy H., 1886
Murphy, Henry, 1880
Murphy, Morgan E., 1893, 1896, 1898
Murphy, Martin W., 1886
Murphy, William H., 1895, 1897
Murray, Jeremiah J., 1893-95, 1900, 1905, 1910
Myers, George D., 1886

Myers, Henry C., 1890
Napp, Larry A., 1951–73
Nash, William M., 1901
Needham, Thomas J., 1904, 1907
Neudecker, Jerome A., 1966–73
Newton, Eustace J., 1902
Nichols, Charles A., 1900-01
Nickerson, S. W., 1880
Nicol, Hugh N., 1894
Nolan, Edward S., 1881
Noonan, Peter J., 1906-07
O'Brien, John F., 1889
O'Brien, William, 1876
O'Connor, Arthur, 1914
O'Connor, John J., 1893-1901
O'Day, Henry F., 1888-89, 1893, 1895-1911, 1913, 1915-27
Odlin, Albert F., 1883
Odom, James C., 1965–73
O'Hara, 1915
O'Leary, Daniel, 1879
Olsen, Andrew H., 1968–76
O'Neill, Michael J., 1904
O'Rourke, James H., 1893-94
Orth, Albert L., 1901, 1912-17
Osborne, William, 1876
O'Sullivan, John J., 1922
Overall, Orval, 1905, 1910
Owens, Clarence B., 1908, 1912-13
Paparella, Joseph J., 1946–65
Parker, George L., 1936-38
Pearce, Grayson S., 1886-87, 1892
Pearce, Richard J., 1878, 1882
Pears, Frank, 1897
Peitz, Henry C., 1901, 1906
Pelekoudas, Chris G., 1960–75
Pfeffer, Nathaniel F., 1897
Pfirman, Charles H., 1922-36
Phelan, 1896
Phelps, Edward J., 1912
Phillippe, Charles L., 1903
Phillips, David R., 1971–73
Pierce, 1893
Pike, Lipman E., 1890
Pinelli, Ralph A., 1935-56
Powell, Jack, 1923-24, 1933
Power, Charles B., 1893, 1895, 1902
Power, Thomas E., 1887-88, 1894-95
Powers, James T., 1895
Powers, Philip J., 1881, 1886-91
Pratt, Albert G., 1879-80, 1887
Pratt, Thomas J., 1886
Pryor, J. Paul, 1961–76
Pulli, Frank V., 1972–76
Quest, Joseph L., 1886-87
Quick, James E., 1976
Quigley, Ernest C., 1913-37
Quinn, Joseph C., 1881-82
Quinn, Joseph J., 1889, 1894, 1896
Quinn, P. J., 1876
Quinn, William H., 1887
Reardon, John E., 1926-49
Redheffer, 1893, 1895
Reid, William A., 1882
Reilly, Charles T., 1892-95
Reilly, William, 1880
Reitz, Henry P., 1895

Remsen, John J., 1880
Rennert, Lawrence H., 1973–76
Rhines, William P., 1891, 1896
Rhodes, Eugene A., 1887
Rice, John L., 1955–73
Richardson, Arthur H., 1887, 1892
Richmond, John L., 1883
Rigler, Charles, 1905-22, 1924-35
Riley, William J., 1880
Ritchie, F., 1876
Robb, Douglas W., 1948-52
Roberts, Lew, 1953-55
Robinson, Wilbert, 1898
Rocap, Adam, 1876
Roll, 1876
Rudderham, Francis F., 1907
Rudderham, John E., 1908
Runge, Edward, 1954–70
Runge, Paul E., 1973–76
Ryan, James E., 1892
Ryan, Walter, 1946
Sanders, Alexander B., 1889
Schew, Augustus, 1880-81
Schmidt, Henry M., 1903
Schofield, J. W., 1880
Schriver, William F., 1901
Schurer, 1896
Scott, James, 1930-31
Sears, John W., 1934-45
Secory, Frank, 1952-70
Sentelle, Leopold T., 1922-23
Serad, William T., 1884
Seward, Edward W., 1892-93
Seward, George E., 1876-79
Sheridan, John F., 1892-93, 1896-97
Simons, J., 1876
Skinner, S. A., 1886
Smith, 1876
Smith, Charles M., 1881-82
Smith, Edward E., 1890
Smith, George H., 1901
Smith, Vincent, 1957-65
Smith, William A., 1960–65
Smith, William E., 1886
Smith, William W., 1898-99
Sneeden, 1895
Snyder, Charles N., 1892-95, 1898, 1901
Soar, Albert H., 1950–72
Sommers, Joseph A., 1889, 1893
Springstead, Martin J., 1966–73
Stafford, John H., 1906
Stage, Charles W., 1893-95
Staley, Harry E., 1892, 1895
Stambaugh, Calvin G., 1876-79
Stark, Albert D., 1928-35, 1937-39, 1942
Stearns, Daniel E., 1880-81
Stein, Edward F., 1890, 1894, 1896
Steiner, Melvin J., 1961–72
Steinfeldt, Henry M., 1905
Stello, Richard J., 1968–76
Sternburg, 1909
Stevens, John, 1948–71
Stewart, Robert, 1959–70
Stewart, William J., 1933-54
Stivetts, John C., 1894
Stockdale, M. J., 1915

1945-53
Pears, Frank, 1903
Perrine, Fred, 1909-12
Phillips, David R., 1971-76
Pipgras, George W., 1938-46
Quigley, Ernest C., 1906
Quinn, John A., 1935-42
Rice, John L., 1955-73
Robb, Douglas W., 1952-53
Rodriguez, Armando H., 1974-75
Rommel, Edwin A., 1938-59
Rowland, Clarence H., 1923-27
Rue, Joseph W., 1938-47

Runge, Edward P., 1954-70
Salerno, Al, 1961-68
Schwarts, Harry C., 1960-62
Sheridan, John F., 1901-14
Smith, William A., 1960-65
Soar, Albert H., 1950-73
Springstead, Martin J., 1966-76
Stafford, John H., 1907
Stevens, John W., 1948-71
Stewart, Ernest D., 1941-45
Stewart, Robert W., 1959-70
Summers, William R., 1933-59

Tabacchi, Frank, 1956-59
Umont, Frank W., 1954-73
Van Graflan, Roy, 1927-33
Wallace, Roderick J., 1915-16
Walsh, Edward A., 1922
Weafer, Harold L., 1943-47
Westervelt, Frederick E., 1911-12
Wilson, John A., 1887
Wilson, Parke A., 1894-96, 1899
Wilson, Frank, 1921-22
Valentine, William, 1963-68

X BASEBALL ADMINISTRATION

Baseball's first professional league, the National Association, folded because its forthright player-president, Bob Ferguson, had a blustering type of ballfield leadership that did not carry over into sorely needed executive diplomacy. NA directors ignored his roars for sorely needed reform. Suave, magnetic and dynamic William A. Hulbert proved perfect for establishing the National League on a permanent basis.

Col. A. G. Mills, an uncompromising administrator in the Hulbert mold, ruled the NL for two years before the iron-handed "Bismarck of Baseball" resigned when the league refused his demand to crack down on players who had jumped to the "outlaw" Union Association in 1884.

That brought kindly, honest and conciliatory Nicholas E. Young into power in 1885. Uncle Nick was so unaggressive that clubowners' cliques virtually ruled the sprawling 12-club NL in the Gay Nineties. Umpires were kicked and choked. The rowdy Baltimore Orioles were a law unto themselves. Young's timidity gave reign to excesses that eventually wrecked his administration and led to the establishment of the AL.

After two years of ruinous war between the leagues, genial and expansive Garry Herrmann, president of the Cincinnati Reds, engineered peace in January, 1903. For his valuable services, Herrmann was rewarded with the chairmanship of a new three-man National Commission which was to rule baseball for almost two full decades. The other Commission members were the league presidents, Ban Johnson and Harry Pulliam.

Baseball's triumvirate started disintegrating in the wake of the Browns vs. Pirates battle over title to George Sisler. When Herrmann cast the deciding vote with the AL club, Barney Dreyfuss of the Pirates howled at Herrmann's "treason" to his own league. He accused Herrmann of being under the influence of his old friend, AL president Johnson. Dreyfuss had pamphlets printed which intended to discredit Herrmann's decision. This insurrection died down, but the three-man Commission had lost face, and Dreyfuss at least succeeded in starting a snowballing drive to name a single Commissioner with no stake in baseball.

Johnson had trouble in his own league. The Yankees overruled him with a court injunction on the Carl Mays case, then drew support from the Red Sox and White Sox in a secession move aimed at switching to the NL. Meanwhile, NL president John A. Heydler felt the pressure of anti-Herrmann propaganda, and refused to vote to return the Reds' chief to the Commission in 1920. Since Johnson and Heydler couldn't agree on Herrmann's successor, baseball was without an actual chief in 1920, leaving the two presidents to settle their own league controversies.

On September 28, the Black Sox scandal exploded in a Chicago courtroom. Eight Chicago players were exposed as having agreed to lose the 1919 World Series to Cincinnati. The sports world was especially bitter that this crisis in baseball history should .come at a time when there was no real governing head. In the nation's press, on the floor of Congress and from pulpits came cries to clean up the game for its very salvation.

Commissioner's Office

Against this turbulent backdrop, Federal Judge K. M. Landis was ushered into baseball's throne room. The white-maned jurist had earned the gratitude of organized ball in 1915 by his deft handling of the dangerous lawsuit brought by the "outlaw" Federal League. He also had a reputation as a racket-buster, having fined Standard Oil Company $29,240,000 in a rebate case in 1907.

Though Landis was earning only $7,500 on the Federal bench, he didn't indicate immediate enthusiasm at baseball's offer of a seven-year contract at $50,000 per. He demanded and immediately was granted carte blanche in any matter he deemed "detrimental to baseball." Under this sweeping provision he wielded the big stick, often autocratically, yet with such crusading zeal that he restored the good name of the game.

The new Czar risked his crown that very first year when he fined Babe Ruth and suspended him for breaking the post-season barnstorming rule of 1921. Babe's immeasurable popularity caused the public to grumble over the drastic decree; but the complaints were tinged with a growing respect for this inflexible disciple of law and order.

In a quarter century as administrator, Landis became known as the "ballplayer's friend." He fought for extension of the annual draft to all minor leagues. He regarded the "farm system" as a similar stratagem to cover up capable players in the bushes, and in two earthquaking edicts the Great Emancipator freed 127 Cardinal farmhands in 1938 and 91 Tiger chattels in 1940. Other player petitions resulted in free agency for Tommy Henrich, Rick Ferrell, Phil Todt, Claude Jonnard and dozens of others.

Landis never compromised with even the slightest tint of gambling or dishonesty. He forced Giant owner Charles Stoneham and manager John McGraw to sell their interests in the Havana racetrack. He expelled Bill Cox, president of the Phillies, for betting on a game. Though the courts failed to convict the Black Sox, Landis blacklisted them from baseball for life: Joe Jackson, Ed Cicotte, Chick Gandil, Swede Risberg, Happy Felsch, Buck Weaver, Claude Williams and Fred McMullin. He also threw his dreaded black book in later years at players Benny Kauff, Cozy Dolan, Phil Douglas and Jim O'Connell. However, he exonerated Ty Cobb and Tris Speaker after Hubert (Dutch) Leonard had charged them in 1926 with collusion on a 1919 game.

Judge Landis died November 25, 1944. His assistant, Leslie O'Connor, took charge of affairs until U. S. Senator Albert Benjamin (Happy) Chandler was elected on April 24, 1945 for a seven-year term at $50,000 a year (later raised to $65,000). The former Class D ballplayer headed the game through its most prosperous years, but he met his share of administrative headaches.

Early in 1946, the free-spending Mexican League raided the majors. Chandler stemmed the tide by announcing a five-year ban against jumping players. Three years later, after the Jorge Pasquel-bankrolled league collapsed, Chandler declared general amnesty. However, Danny Gardella, former outfielder who had broken only the reserve clause of his Giant contract to take the "Mexican holiday" pressed a lawsuit against organized baseball's alleged monopoly. When this case received a favorable vote in the New York State Supreme Court, Chandler suddenly effected an out-of-court settlement with Gardella who, incidentally, was represented by Chandler's former classmate at Harvard Law School, Frederic A. Johnson.

In 1947, Chandler suspended Dodger manager Lippy Leo Durocher for a year, citing an accumulation of "incidents." Lippy took his medicine and returned the next year.

The Commissioner's vigilant administration of the rule against signing high school players brought him into head-on battle with Leslie O'Conner, former Acting Commissioner, who was fined as White Sox general manager for signing a schoolboy. O'Connor claimed Chandler was overstepping his authority, and even threatened to go to court. Chandler held firm. Sox owners finally paid the fine and released O'Connor.

Seeking a renewal of his contract in December, 1950, Chandler received a majority vote, but not the required two-thirds. Clubowners then decided on a committee to select a new Commissioner "as soon as practicable." Chandler, whose contract ran to April, 1952, was voted out of office before his contract expired.

Ford C. Frick, who had advanced to the presidency of the National League after serving as a sportswriter on a New York newspaper, radio sportscaster and manager of the National League Service Bureau, became baseball's third commissioner on September 20, 1951. He signed a seven-year contract at a salary of $65,000 per year. In 1957, Frick signed his second seven-year contract.

Financially, the Commissioner's office is supported solely by the World Series. Fifteen percent of all net receipts of each game are set aside for the expenses (salaries, travel and overhead) involved in conducting the normal business of the office.

Frick announced his intentions to retire in 1965 and finally, on November 17, after a year-long search, William Dole Eckert, a retired Air Force lieutenant-general, was named the game's fourth commissioner. Eckert, 56, was elected to a seven-year term with an annual salary of $65,000, the same as Frick received.

Most fans and even the news media were surprised at Eckert's selection. He had had, for example, no previous connection with baseball. Although his name appeared among the original 156 nominees, it was never mentioned publicly. He was not included when the list was reduced to 15 in July, but was subsequently restored to the list and reportly was the only man to whom the job was offered.

William Eckert resigned as Commissioner of Baseball on the final day of the winter meeting in San Francisco of 1968, effective with the appointment of his successor. Removal from office, after serving only three years of his seven-year contract, was urged by owners who wanted reconstruction of the game to combat upcoming professional football.

By the end of December there were four candidates named. Deadlocked meetings brought about a compromise candidate; a Wall Street lawyer active in baseball legislation since 1950. Bowie Kuhn was selected protem commissioner by unanimous consent of the Executive Committee in February, 1969, and then given a firm seven-year contract shortly thereafter.

One of his first acts as Commissioner was the settlement of a pension dispute between club owners and the Major League Baseball Players' Association to prevent baseball's first general player strike. Major league players were threatening a boycott of spring training unless a satisfactory method was found of splitting the revenue from games in the playoff system about to be established for the World Series.

Kuhn faced many crises as his term progressed. He ironed out retirement problems with Donn Clendenon and Ken Harrelson in 1969, Tony Conigliaro and Clete Boyer in 1971 and Vida Blue in 1972. He dealt suspensions to Denny McLain in 1969 and 1970. He was sued by Curt Flood in 1969 in a test of the reserve clause. Flood's final appeal was denied by the Supreme Court in 1972. He chastised Jim Bouton about his writings in 1970. He was unable to avert the 1972 player strike, which resulted in one week of unplayed games and an improved pension plan for the players. He ruled that Charley Finley had to

reinstate Mike Andrews during the 1973 World Series and later fined Finley $7000 and placed him on probation for his conduct in the matter.

Finley and Kuhn clashed again in 1976. Faced with the likely defection of his stars after the season, Charley peddled Vida Blue to the Yankees for $1.5 million, and Joe Rudi and Rollie Fingers to the Red Sox for $1 million each in June. However, Kuhn voided the sales, stating that they were not in the best interests of baseball.

League Agreements

Organized Baseball has five main documents: Major League Agreement, Major League Rules, Major-Minor League Agreements, Major-Minor League Rules and the National Association Rules.

Top man is the Commissioner. As specified in the Major League Agreement, and underwritten in the Major-Minor pact, his functions may be summarized as follows:

(a) To investigate any act detrimental to baseball.

(b) To decide on punitive action.

(c) To decide any interleague dispute brought to him by either league president.

(d) To determine any dispute involving a player.

(e) To formulate rules of procedure in cases under his control.

In case "detrimental conduct" originates outside of organized baseball, Article I, Section 4 says he "may pursue appropriate legal remedies, advocate remedial legislation and take such other steps as he may deem necessary and proper to the interests and morale of the players and the honor of the game."

Another important article in the Major League Agreement stipulates that all contracts between clubs and their officers, players and other employers shall contain a clause binding the parties to submit to the discipline of the Commissioner.

Baseball's legislative arm is the joint meeting of major leagues. In interleague affairs, majority rules within each circuit, and then each league votes as a unit. In case of a tie, the Commissioner casts the deciding vote.

In the interim between league meetings, the majors are guided by an Executive Council. It consists of the Commissioner, both league presidents and one member elected by each of the leagues. However, in matters dealing with players' grievances, two active players are added to this Council, with majority to rule and all decisions binding and final.

Except in cases of critical clashes, the Major League Agreement is not as important as the Major League Rules. The latter is a lengthy covenant completely regulating league, club, player and umpire rights and responsibilities. The Commissioner is obliged to enforce these rules, and has no power to abrogate any of them on "detrimental to baseball" grounds. Any amendment passed by the majors, which affect the Major-Minor Agreement, must be submitted to a mail vote of all the minor leagues.

The Major-Minor League Agreement places the minors under jurisdiction of the Commissioner either in cases of "detrimental conduct" or in major-minor disputes. It also sets up a Major-Minor Executive Council for interim rule, and fixes the scale of payments in the annual player draft.

Major-Minor League Rules deal with protection of franchises, player limits, reserve lists, drafting, optional agreements, stock ownership, etc. As for the fifth charter of baseball's government, the National Association Agreement details a method of operation for the minors.

OFFICIAL PLAYER'S CONTRACT

PARTIES. Between .... herein called the Club, and .... of ...., herein called the Player.

RECITAL. The Club is a member of the American League of Professional Baseball Clubs, a voluntary association of eight member clubs which has subscribed to the Major League Rules with the National League of Professional Baseball Clubs and its constituent clubs and to the Major-Minor League Rules with that League and the National Association of Baseball Leagues. The purpose of those rules is to insure the public wholesome and high-class professional baseball by defining the relations between the Club and Player, between club and club, between league and league, and by vesting in a designated Commissioner broad powers of control and discipline, and of decision in case of disputes.

AGREEMENT. In consideration of the facts above recited and of the promises of each to the other, the parties agree as follows:

EMPLOYMENT. 1. The Club hereby employs the Player to render, and the Player agrees to render, skilled services as a baseball player during the year ....196... including the Club's training season, the Club's exhibition games, the Club's playing season, and the World Series (or any other official series in which the Club may participate and in any receipts of which the player may be entitled to share).

PAYMENT. 2. For performance of the Player's services and promises hereunder the Club will pay the Player the sum of $............................... ...., as follows:

In semi-monthly installments after the commencement of the playing season covered by this contract, unless the Player is "abroad" with the Club for the purpose of playing games, in which event the amount then due shall be paid on the first week-day after the return "home" of the Club, the terms "home" and "abroad" meaning respectively at and away from the city in which the Club has its baseball field.

If a monthly rate of payment is stipulated above, it shall begin with the commencement of the Club's playing season (or such subsequent date as the Player's services may commence) and end with the termination of the Club's scheduled playing season, and shall be payable in semi-monthly installments as above provided.

If the player is in the service of the Club for part of the playing season only, he shall receive such proportion of the sum above mentioned, as the number of days of his actual employment in the Club's playing season bears to the number of days in said season.

Notwithstanding the rate of payment stipulated above, the minimum rate of payment to the Player for each day of service on a Major League Club shall be at the rate of $6,000 per year; except that such minimum rate of payment shall be at the rate of $7,000 per year retroactive to the beginning of the season if the Player is on a Major League Club's roster on June 15 and shall be at the rate of $7,000 per year if the Player physically joins a Major League Club between June 15 and August 31. If a player physically joins a Major League Club on or after September 1, the minimum rate of payment shall be at the rate of $6,000 per year for each day of service with such Major League Club.

LOYALTY. 3. (a) The Player agrees to perform his services hereunder diligently and faithfully, to keep himself in first class physical condition and to obey the Club's training rules, and pledges himself to the American public and to the Club to conform to high standards of personal conduct, fair play and good sportsmanship.

BASEBALL PROMOTION. (b) In addition to his services in connection with the actual playing of baseball, the Player agrees to cooperate with the Club and participate in any and all promotional activities of the Club and its League, which, in the opinion of the Club, will promote the welfare of the Club or professional baseball, and to observe and comply with all requirements of the Club respecting conduct and service of its team and its players, at all times whether on or off the field.

PICTURES AND PUBLIC APPEARANCES. (c) The Player agrees that his picture may be taken for still photographs, motion pictures or television at such times as the Club may designate and agrees that all rights in such pictures shall belong to the Club and may be used by the Club for publicity purposes in any manner it desires. The Player further agrees that during the playing season he will not make public appearances, participate in radio or television programs or permit his picture to be taken or write or sponsor newspaper or magazine articles or sponsor commercial products without the written consent of the Club, which shall not be withheld except in the reasonable interests of the Club or professional baseball.

PLAYER REPRESENTATIONS

ABILITY. 4. (a) The Player represents and agrees that he has exceptional and unique skill and ability as a baseball player; that his services to be rendered hereunder are of a special unusual and extraordinary character which gives them peculiar value which cannot be reasonably or adequately compensated for in damages at law, and that the Player's breach of this contract will cause the Club great and irreparable injury and damage. The Player agrees that, in addition to other remedies, the Club shall be entitled to injunctive and other equitable relief to prevent a breach of this contract by the Player, including, among others, the right to enjoin the Player from playing baseball for any other person or organization during the term of this contract.

CONDITION (b) The Player represents that he has no physical or mental defects, known to him, which would prevent or impair performance of his services.

INTEREST IN CLUB (c) The Player represents that he does not, directly or indirectly, own stock or have any financial interest in the ownership or earnings of any Major League club, except as hereinafter expressly set forth, and covenants that he will not hereafter, while connected with any Major League club, acquire or hold any such stock or interest except in accordance with Major League Rule 20 (e).

SERVICE 5. (a) The Player agrees that, while under contract, and prior to expiration of the Club's right to renew this contract, he will not play baseball otherwise than for the Club, except that the Player may participate in post-season games under the conditions prescribed in the Major League Rules. [Reference is made here to Major League Rule 18(b); see page 500.]

OTHER SPORTS (b) The Player and the Club recognize and agree that the Player's participation in other sports may impair or destroy his ability and skill as a baseball player. Accordingly the Player agrees that he will not engage in professional boxing or wrestling; and that, except with the written consent of the Club, he will not engage in any game or exhibition of football, basketball, hockey or other athletic sport.

ASSIGNMENT

6. (a) The Player agrees that this contract may be assigned by the Club (and reassigned by any assignee Club) to any other club in accordance with the Major League Rules and the Professional Baseball Rules.

NO SALARY REDUCTION (b) The amount stated in paragraph 2 hereof which is payable to the Player for the period stated in paragraph 1 hereof shall not be diminished by any such assignment, except for failure to report as provided in the next sub-paragraph (c).

REPORTING (c) The Player shall report to the assignee Club promptly (as provided in the Regulations) upon receipt of written notice from the Club of the assignment of this contract. If the Player fails so to report, he shall not be entitled to any payment for the period from the date he receives written notice of assignment until he reports to the assignee Club.

OBLIGATIONS OF ASSIGNOR AND ASSIGNEE CLUBS (d) Upon and after such assignment, all rights and obligations of the assignor Club hereunder shall become the rights and obligations of the assignee Club; provided, however, that

(1) The assignee Club shall be liable to the Player for payments accruing only from the date of assignment and shall not be liable (but the assignor shall remain liable) for payments accrued prior to that date.

(2) If at any time the assignee is a Major League Club, it shall be liable to pay the Player at the full rate stipulated in paragraph 2 hereof for the remainder of the period stated in paragraph 1 hereof and all prior assignors and assignees shall be relieved of liability for any payment for such period.

(3) Unless the assignor and assignee clubs agree otherwise, if the assignee Club is a National Association Club, the assignee Club shall be liable only to pay the Player at the rate usually paid by said assignee Club to other players of similar skill and ability in its classification and the assignor Club shall be liable to pay the difference for the remainder of the period stated in paragraph 1 hereof between an amount computed at the rate stipulated in paragraph 2 hereof and the amount so payable by the assignee Club.

MOVING EXPENSES (e) If this contract is assigned by a Major League Club to another Major League Club during the playing season, the assignor Club shall pay the Player, for all moving and other expenses resulting from such assignment, the sum of $300 if the contract is assigned between Clubs in the same zone; the sum of $600 if the contract is assigned between a Club in the Eastern Zone and a Club in the Central Zone; the sum of $900 if the contract is assigned between a Club in the Central Zone and a Club in the Western Zone; and the sum of $1,200 if the contract is assigned between a Club in the Eastern Zone and a Club in the Western Zone. The Eastern Zone shall include the Philadelphia and Pittsburgh Clubs in the National League and the Baltimore, Boston, New York and Washington Clubs in the American League; the Central Zone shall include the Chicago, Cincinnati, Milwaukee and St. Louis Clubs in the National League and the Chicago, Cleveland, Detroit and Kansas City Clubs in the American League; the Western Zone shall include the Los Angeles and San Francisco Clubs in the National League.

If this contract is assigned by a Major League Club to a National Association Club during the playing season, the assignor Club shall pay the Player his reasonable and actual moving expenses resulting from such assignment and shall reimburse the Player for up to one month's rental payments for living quarters in the city of the assignor Club for which he is legally obliged after the date of such assignment and for which he is not otherwise reimbursed.

"CLUB" (f) All references in other paragraphs of this contract to "the Club" shall be deemed to mean and include any assignee of this contract.

TERMINATION

BY PLAYER 7. (a) The Player may terminate this contract, upon written notice to the Club, if the Club shall default in the payments to the Player provided for in paragraph 2 hereof or shall fail to perform any other obligation agreed to be performed by the Club hereunder and if the Club shall fail to remedy such default within ten (10) days after the receipt by the Club of written notice of such default. The Player may also terminate this contract as provided in sub-paragraph (f) (4) of this paragraph 7.

BY CLUB (b) The Club may terminate this contract upon written notice to the Player (but only after requesting and obtaining waivers of this contract from all other Major League Clubs) if the Player shall at any time:

(1) fail, refuse or neglect to conform his personal conduct to the standards of good citizenship and good sportsmanship or to keep himself in first class physical condition or to obey the Club's training rules; or

(2) fail, in the opinion of the Club's management, to exhibit sufficient skill or competitive ability to qualify or continue as a member of the Club's team; or

(3) fail, refuse or neglect to render his services hereunder or in any other manner materially breach this contract.

(c) If this contract is terminated by the Club by reason of the Player's failure to render his services hereunder due to disability resulting directly from injury sustained in the course and within the scope of his employment hereunder and written notice of such injury is given by the Player as provided in the Regulations, the Player shall be entitled to receive his full salary for the season in which the injury was sustained, less all workmen's compensation payments paid or payable by reason of said injury.

(d) If this contract is terminated by the Club during the training season, payment by the Club of the Player's board, lodging and expense allowance during the training season to the date of termination and of the reasonable traveling expenses of the Player to his home city and the expert training and coaching provided by the Club to the Player during the training season shall be full payment to the Player.

(e) If this contract is terminated by the Club during the playing season, then, except in the case provided for in sub-paragraph (c) of this paragraph 7, the Player shall be entitled to receive as full payment hereunder such portion of the amount stipulated in paragraph 2 hereof as the number of days of his actual employment in the Club's playing season bears to the total number of days in said season, provided, however, that if this contract is terminated under sub-paragraph (b) (2) of this paragraph 7 for failure to exhibit sufficient skill or competitive ability, the Player shall be entitled to an additional amount equal to thirty (30) days payment at the rate stipulated in paragraph 2 hereof and the reasonable traveling expenses of the Player to his home.

PROCEDURE (f) If the Club proposes to terminate this contract in accordance with sub-paragraph (b) of this paragraph 7, the procedure shall be as follows:

(1) The Club shall request waivers from all other Major League clubs. Such waiver request must state that it is for the purpose of terminating this contract and it may not be withdrawn.

(2) Upon receipt of the waiver request, any other Major League club may claim assignment of this contract at a waiver price of $1.00, the priority of claims to be determined in accordance with the Major League Rules.

(3) If this contract is so claimed, the Club shall, promptly and before any assignment, notify the Player that it had requested waivers for the purpose of terminating this contract and that the contract had been claimed.

(4) Within 5 days after receipt of notice of such claim, the Player shall be entitled, by written notice to the Club, to terminate this contract on the date of his notice of termination. If the Player fails so to notify the Club, this contract shall be assigned to the claiming club.

(5) If the contract is not claimed, the Club shall promptly deliver written notice of termination to the Player at the expiration of the waiver period.

(g) Upon any termination of this contract by the Player, all obligations of both parties hereunder shall cease on the date of termination, except the obligation of the Club to pay the Player's compensation to said date.

REGULATIONS 8. The Player accepts as part of this contract the Regulations [reference is made here to the contract page on which the Regulations are printed; see page 499 of this book].

RULES 9. (a) The Club and the Player agree to accept, abide by and comply with all provisions of the Major League Rules and the Professional Baseball Rules which concern player conduct and player-club relationships and with all decisions of the Commissioner and the President of the Club's League, pursuant thereto.

DISPUTES (b) In case of dispute between the Player and the Club, the same shall be referred to the Commissioner as an arbitrator, and his decision shall be accepted by all parties as final; and the Club and the Player agree than any such dispute, or any claim or complaint by either party against the other, shall be presented to the Commissioner within one year from the date it arose.

PUBLICATION (c) The Club, the League President and the Commissioner, or any of them, may make public the findings, decision and record of any inquiry, investigation or hearing held or conducted, including in such record all evidence or information, given, received or obtained in connection therewith.

RENEWAL 10. (a) On or before January 15th (or if a Sunday, then the next preceding business day) of the year next following the last playing season covered by this contract, the Club may tender to the Player a contract for the term of that year by mailing the same to the Player at his address following his signature hereto, or if none be given, then at his last address of record with the Club. If prior to the March 1 next succeeding said January 15, the Player and the Club have not agreed upon the terms of such contract, then on or before 10 days after said March 1, the Club shall have the right by written notice to the Player at said address to renew this contract for the period of one year on the same terms, except that the amount payable to the Player shall be such as the Club shall fix in said notice; provided, however, that said amount, if fixed by a Major League Club, shall be an amount payable at a rate not less than 75% of the rate stipulated for the preceding year.

(b) The Club's right to renew this contract, as provided in sub-paragraph (a) of this paragraph 10, and the promise of the Player not to play otherwise than with the Club have been taken into consideration in determining the amount payable under paragraph 2 hereof.

11. This contract is subject to federal or state legislation, regulations, executive or other official orders or other governmental action, now or hereafter in effect respecting military, naval, air or other governmental service, which may directly or indirectly affect the Player, Club or the League and subject also to the right of the Commissioner to suspend the operation of this contract during any national emergency.

COMMISSIONER 12. The term "Commissioner" wherever used in this contract shall be deemed to mean the Commissioner designated under the Major League Agreement, or in the case of a vacancy in the office of Commissioner, the Executive Council or such other body or person or persons as shall be designated in the Major League Agreement to exercise the powers and duties of the Commissioner during such vacancy.

SUPPLEMENTAL AGREEMENTS The Club and the Player covenant that this contract fully sets forth all understandings and agreements between them, and agree that no other understandings or agreements, whether heretofore or hereafter made, shall be valid, recognizable, or of any effect whatsoever, unless expressly set forth in a new or supplemental contract executed by the Player and the Club (acting by its president, or such other officer as shall have been thereunto duly authorized by the president or Board of Directors, as evidenced by a certificate filed of record with the League President and Commissioner) and complying with the Major League Rules and the Professional Baseball Rules.

SPECIAL COVENANTS (Space is provided for the insertion here of special terms which may be appended to the contract, such as bonuses based on attendance, further Player restrictions or privileges, etc.)

APPROVAL This contract or any supplement hereto shall not be valid or effective unless and until approved by the League President.

Signed in duplicate this .... day of ...., A. D. 196 .....

....
          (Player)   (Club)
....   By ....
  (Home address of Player)   (Authorized Signature)
Social Security No. ....
Approved ...., 196...,
....
President, American League of Professional Baseball Clubs

REGULATIONS

1. The Club's playing season for each year covered by this contract and all renewals hereof shall be as fixed by the American League of Professional Baseball Clubs, or if this contract shall be assigned to a Club in another league, then by the league of which such assignee is a member.

2. The Player, when requested by the Club, must submit to a complete physical examination at the expense of the Club, and if necessary to treatment by a regular physician or dentist in good standing. Upon refusal of the Player to submit to a complete medical or dental examination the Club may consider such refusal a violation of this regulation and may take such action as it deems advisable under Regulation 5 of this contract. Disability directly resulting from injury sustained in the course and within the scope of his employment under this contract shall not impair the right of the Player to receive his full salary for the period of such disability or for the season in which the injury was sustained (whichever period is shorter), together with the reasonable medical and hospital expenses incurred by reason of the injury and during the term of this contract, less all workmen's compensation payments paid or payable by reason of said injury; but only upon the express prerequisite conditions that (a) written notice of such injury, including the time, place, cause and nature of the injury, is served upon and received by the Club within twenty days of the sustaining of said injury and (b) the Club shall have the right to designate the doctors and hospitals furnishing such medical and hospital services. Any other disability may be grounds for suspending or terminating this contract at the discretion of the Club.

3. The Club will furnish the Player with two complete uniforms, exclusive of shoes, the Player making a deposit of $30 therefor, which deposit will be returned to him at the end of the season or upon the termination of this contract, upon the surrender of the uniforms by him to the Club.

4. The Club will pay all proper and necessary traveling expenses of the Player while "abroad," or traveling with the Club in other cities, including board, lodging, Pullman accommodations, if available, and during the training season, an allowance of $25 per week, payable in advance, to cover other training trip expenses. The Club will also pay the reasonable traveling expenses of the Player to his home at the end of the season.

5. For violation by the Player of any regulation or other provision of this contract, the Club may impose a reasonable fine and deduct the amount thereof from the Player's salary or may suspend the Player without salary for a period not exceeding thirty days, or both, at the discretion of the Club. Written notice of the fine or suspension or both and of the reasons therefor shall in every case be given to the Player.

6. In order to enable the Player to fit himself for his duties under this contract, the Club may require the Player to report for practice at such places as the Club may designate and to participate in such exhibition contests as may be arranged by the Club for a period beginning not earlier than February 15 in 1947 and not earlier than March 1 in 1948 and subsequent years without any other compensation than that herein elsewhere provided, the Club, however, to pay the necessary traveling expenses, including Pullman accommodations, if available, and meals en route, of the Player from his home city to the training place of the Club, whether he be ordered to go there direct or by way of the home city of the Club. In the event of the failure of the Player to report for practice or to participate in the exhibition games, as provided for, he shall be required to get in playing condition to the satisfaction of the Club's team manager, and at the Player's own expense, before his salary shall commence.

7. In case of assignment of this contract the Player shall report promptly to the assignee club within 72 hours from the date he receives written notice from the Club of such assignment, if the Player is then not more than 1600 miles by most direct available railroad route from the assignee Club, plus an additional 24 hours for each additional 800 miles.

Post-Season Exhibition Games. Major League Rule 18 (b) provides:

Exhibition Games. (b) No Player shall participate in any exhibition game played during the period between the close of the Major League championship season and the following training season; except that a Player, with the written consent of the Commissioner, may participate in exhibition games which are played within thirty days after the close of the Major League championship season and which are approved by the Commissioner. Player conduct, on and off the field, in connection with such post-season exhibition games shall be subject to the discipline of the Commissioner. The Commissioner shall not approve more than three Players of any one Club on the same team. No Player shall participate in any exhibition game with or against any team which, during the current season or within one year, has had any ineligible player or which is or has been during the current season or within one year, managed and controlled by an ineligible player or by any person who has listed an ineligible player under an assumed name or who otherwise has violated, or attempted to violate, any exhibition game contract; or with or against any team which, during said season or within one year, has played against teams containing such ineligible players, or so managed or controlled. Any player violating this rule shall be fined not less than fifty dollars ($50) nor more than five hundred dollars ($500), except that in no event shall such fine be less than the consideration received by such player for participating in such game.

(Editor's note: The foregoing Official Contract is the standard form used in the American League. A similar document is used in the National League, since both major leagues observe the same basic guarantees and requirements. League presidents may impose additional restrictions, such as forbidding players to pose while wearing uniform in advertisements for beer or cigarettes.)

XI BASEBALL AUXILIARIES

It is true that the vast popularity of baseball is due to its national, year-round publicity in the form of box scores, daily reports, feature stories, notes, columns, etc., all dutifully reported in every newspaper in the land.

The morning-after straight result story of the game is eagerly absorbed by the fan for information and discussion with his neighbor and fellow-worker. The box score is as important a way of life as the normal functions of the day. The afternoon paper carries the whys and hows of the previous day's game and the "confidential" information on how it was won or lost. This is called a "p.m." story and is usually composed from a so-called "angle" in which the writer is permitted more latitude of expression than his colleague on a morning paper. However, both types of stories have their vast audiences who, because of business and family duties, are forced to follow their favorites only through the words of an on-the-scene observer.

Writers

Baseball writing is probably as old as baseball playing. Ex-Senator William Cauldwell, editor of the *New York Mercury*, wrote baseball news in his paper as far back as 1853. Three years later, British-born Henry Chadwick became the first professional baseball writer. This is the same "Father Chadwick" who guided the development of official rules, edited annuals, crusaded for fundamental baseball reforms and served as the sport's "Chief Justice" for half a century.

Then came a string of other famous chroniclers of the sport: Charles Peverelly, who wrote the first history of the game; Mike Kelly, who introduced the short-hand system of scoring in 1861; the Rankin brothers of New York, W. M. Spink of St. Louis and many more. Among the earliest baseball scribes was Walt Whitman of the *Brooklyn Eagle*, whose stilted reporting ("Mr. Johnson struck the ball well in the seventh innings.") gave no portent of his classic poetry to come.

After the 1887 season, major league baseball writers banded into the first national organization, with George Munson of St. Louis as president. It was called the National Base Ball Reporters' Association and had a short but useful life. This group suggested a number of changes in the playing and scoring rules which were subsequently adopted. However, it broke up in 1890, when the Brotherhood war split baseball into two hostile camps.

The second attempt at a scribes' association grew out of the 1908 World Series, which climaxed endless hardships and indignities suffered by the working press. In Detroit, the press box could be reached only by climbing a rickety ladder. In Chicago, the press box was as wide open as a Barbary saloon, "crashed" by assorted actors, politicians, jockeys and pals of the club officials.

When Hugh Fullerton reached his press seat in the Cub ballpark, he found it already occupied by Louis Mann, the famous actor. Mann refused to vacate. So Fullerton plunked himself down in Mann's lap and covered the entire World Series game from that bizarre perch.

That did it. On October 10, 1908, the writers formed a temporary organization. A permanent union was formed two months later in New York, with 125 members, and Joe Jackson of Detroit as president. The first constitution

of the Base Ball Writers' Association of America set up its objectives as (1) Better accommodations in press boxes, (2) More uniformity in scoring, and (3) Conferences with the majors' rules committee regarding playing rules.

The BBWAA has made great strides since that humble beginning. It now controls every major league press box, and even the clubowner is not allowed to enter his press box without permission of the scribes. It has been woven into the fabric of the big leagues to the extent of handling the official scoring for all games, picking the Most Valuable Players as well as Rookie for the Year, naming players to the Hall of Fame and serving on the joint major leagues' committee on playing rules.

Radio and Television

Modern electronics have brought baseball its greatest popularity in history. Through the magic lantern of the television tube and the all-reaching sound of radio, a major league game can be seen and/or heard by just about everyone in the country. Whether this is good for the future profit growth of the game is something the clubowners must still decide.

The daily chatter of the radio play-by-play announcer and the casual flick of a TV dial can bring a major league contest into any room in an American home. The game is no longer isolated to its point of origin and the characteristics, performances and personal statistics of all the players are known to millions who have yet to see a "live" major league game.

Over the years, these lusty and lucrative wireless media have converted countless millions of new fans to baseball . . . brought over a hundred million dollars from sponsors into the coffers of the clubs . . . and, in a vital service that is too easily overlooked, brightened the lives of hospitalized veterans and other shut-ins.

It all started back in 1921, when Graham McNamee sat in front of a pie-sized microphone at the Polo Grounds and broadcast the eight games of the Yank-Giant World Series. Subsequent Series were aired, too, but it was not until 1934 that a sponsor moved in: Henry Ford signed a four-year contract at $100,000 per. Eventually the All-Star Game came into radio "gravy" too.

It was a big step from broadcasting special events to transmitting every game in the regular season. The first station to venture into daily baseball broadcasts directly from the ballpark was Chicago's WMAQ, with Hal Totten describing the games in 1924. This custom eventually blanketed practically every club in organized ball.

By 1959, more than a thousand radio stations were saturating the country with play-by-play, costing sponsors about $40,000,000. The Mutual Broadcasting System sent a "live" account of its cooperatively-sponsored Game of the Day through about 500 stations all over the nation. Television, too, with two major networks beaming big league baseball into non-major league areas, was on a coast-to-coast weekly schedule and creating vast problems for those minor league teams which played games in those cities where the fans could stay at home and watch a major league game via television.

A major headache arose when minor league clubs claimed that "invasion" of their territory by big league broadcasts was ruining their gate. The majors were eager to help, but feared placing any restraint on the all-engulfing networks lest organized baseball be hauled into court and sued on the touchy issue of "monopolistic practice in interstate commerce." As a compromise a 50-mile area of protection was set up to screen minor league games, but this couldn't

be enforced, and the leagues had to set up special committees to handle radio and TV problems.

Television cameras were focussed on major league teams in action for the first time at Ebbets Field on August 26, 1939, at a Dodger-Red doubleheader. Though only a handful of TV sets existed in the entire metropolitan area at the time, National Broadcasting Company engineers moved their experimental equipment into Ebbets Field. Walter L. (Red) Barber, already famous as a radio broadcaster, gave this pioneering effort the full treatment by announcing the plays. Between games, Barber brought Bucky Walters and Dolph Camilli to the field cameras, for closeups that showed how Bucky gripped the ball for a curve and how Dolph kept his hand in the first baseman's mitt. The telecast went out over station W2XBS, atop the Empire State Building.

Bold and imaginative Larry MacPhail, Dodger president, encouraged the telecasters, and through 1940–41 on the average of one game a week was screened at Ebbets Field. The war put a quietus on TV activity, but when MacPhail headed the Yankees in 1946, he sold the first commercial rights. Metropolitan New York had fewer than 500 sets at the time, but Dumont paid $75,000 for season rights to Yankee games.

Video fees multiplied so rapidly that by 1950 Dumont was able to pay sportscaster Dizzy Dean $30,000, or more than he had ever gotten as a star pitcher with the Cards and Cubs. Since then the number one telecaster in areas like New York and Chicago has been handsomely rewarded by the sponsors and the ball clubs. In 1950 Commissioner A. B. Chandler closed a deal bringing baseball $6,000,000 for the TV rights alone to the World Series covering 1951–56. An even juicier deal for World Series TV-radio privileges was made with the start of the 1957 World Series. The sponsors (The Gillette Safety Razor Company) paid $3,000,000 annually for the exclusive TV-radio rights, or approximately $15,000,000 for the period from 1957 through 1962. This bonanza just about guaranteed the success of the costly ballplayers' pension fund.

Most of the outstanding sportscasters like Barber, Russ Hodges, Mel Allen, Jim Britt, Bob Elson, etc., cut their eyeteeth in this profession. However, there are many former major league ballplayers who stepped right into sportscasting and made an instant hit.

With the increasing coverage of baseball by television and radio, many of the sportscasters became household names and their faces and voices became as familiar as those of the players.

In May of 1971, the Major Leagues signed a new 4-year contract with NBC increasing the number of night games, especially in 1972. The World Series had one night game, with plans for three games in 1972. The financial details were not made public due to the Major League Players Association pact with the major league teams concerning property rights for its pension fund.

Sources indicated that the contract was worth around $70 million for 1972 through 1975. Divided between 24 teams, it would amount to over two million dollars plus what each team receives from local radio-tv packages, an average of $1 million more.

Statisticians

Baseball statisticians are a breed apart. Strange but admirable, they pursue Truth in the shape of cold, hard numbers. Never compromising, never relaxing, these busy beavers compile the totals and averages that form the only possible unbiased evaluation of a ballplayer.

Most amateur statisticians are like Thomas Gray's "Many a flower is born

to blush unseen, and waste its sweetness on the desert air." Notable exception is John A. Heydler, a Washington linotype operator who kept exhaustive baseball records as a hobby. When Harry Pulliam became National League president in 1903 and found the league statistics in terrible shape, he hired Heydler as secretary and statistician. Honest John soon became the league's secretary-treasurer and eventually president.

Newspaper, wire service and radio/TV demand nowadays for quick, accurate daily statistics during the season would put too great a strain on the league offices, so the figure-tending is farmed out to pros: Elias Sports Bureau (New York City) for the NL, Sports Information Center (Boston) for the AL. The American League went to a computerized system of record-keeping in 1973. Daily score sheets are sent across phone lines and up-to-date figures are returned to each club in time for the next game. The Howe News Bureau (Chicago), which previously handled the AL work, and William J. Weiss (San Mateo, California) do most of the minor league work and derive further income from club officials who want complete up-to-the-minute averages of the minor leagues— either to check on their farmhands' progress or to scout other prospects.

During the baseball season, the Howe and Elias offices employ a dozen or more figure filberts for such jobs as entering data in a master ledger from the official score sheets (which are large, detailed pages sent in by newspapermen designated by the league as official scorers); figuring out the five leading players in each department, for use in daily newspaper "boxes"; compiling full league averages for use in weekend editions; writing "leads," or short descriptive articles, to interpret and accompany the averages issued to papers and radio or TV stations; filing, mimeographing, checking, etc.

Someone once figured out that of the myriad statistics issued all season long, these bureaus err about once in every 3,500 figures. However, after some 7,057,600 "live" figures on file are quadruple-checked for official release each winter, they prove to be 99.9996 correct!

Irwin Howe founded his bureau in 1911, and Al Munro Elias started his a few years later. These baseball mills are now run respectively by John Phillips and Seymour Siwoff, who also edits the oldest and most famous annual of "best" records, The Little Red Book, which was first compiled by Charlie White and John B. Foster.

Both bureaus are antedated by the Heilbroner Baseball Bureau, founded in 1909 at Fort Wayne, Indiana, by ex-St. Louis Cardinal manager Louis Heilbroner. The HBB, a service bureau for all pro baseball, keeps personal cards and transaction records to cover every organized league. Ever since 1910, it has issued the annual Baseball Blue Book, the most complete and authentic directory of the game. Earle Halstead is the Heilbroner chief.

The tremendous burden of daily, up-to-the game statistical information has placed greater emphasis on the figure filbert. Many clubs now carry full-time statisticians to record the inning-by-inning report of all games. Radio and TV announcers have added a season-long statistician to their staffs to prepare the latest in figures for their audiences.

Concessionaires

"The hot dog is king," a Chicago Club official once explained. "For every dollar we get in paid admissions, our total cost of operating the club is $1.06. If we didn't have extra income from concessions in the ballpark, we'd have to lock our gates."

To save all the headaches that go with the catering business, practically all ball clubs lease the food-and-drink privileges at their park to established concessionaires like the Stevens family, Blake Harper, Jacobs Brothers, etc. The result is substantial revenue and no risk. Vending rights can prove quite lucrative, as when the all-time record was set at a Chicago White Sox doubleheader in 1950, averaging $1.05 spent per fan.

The royal family of sports caterers is the Stevens clan. Operating under the corporate title of Harry Mosley Stevens, Inc., the founder's four sons and several grandsons boomed the business beyond even the fabulous pace of old Harry M., who died a multi-millionaire 55 years after arriving here in 1879 from England, down to his last pound ($5). The Stevens concession empire embraces ballparks and racetracks stretching, as their letterhead proudly boasts, "From the Hudson to the Rio Grande."

"Columbus, 1492" may be the famous date for schoolboys, but "Columbus, 1887" is the memorable milestone in concession history. On a summer day in 1887, Harry M. Stevens went to a ballgame in Columbus, Ohio. He bought a scorecard, but couldn't decipher its garbled list of players. Soon after the last putout, he was in the club's front office, offering $700 for the privilege of printing and selling a decent scorecard in the park. Improving the design and selling space on his scorecard, Harry quickly recouped his initial investment and started operating in the black. To this day, the Stevens brothers still publish scorecards for the several ballparks in which they have catering rights.

Shortly after his scorecard success, Harry M. branched into the peanuts-and soda-pop line. He reached the big leagues for good in 1894, moving into the Polo Grounds. A few years later, at a cold and windy Giant game, he noticed his soft drinks sales lagging. So he rushed his vendors to buy up all the frankfurters and rolls in the neighborhood. He boiled the franks, split the rolls to form a natural bed for them and sold them to the chilled spectators, with the slogan that still rings up sales to this very day, "Get 'em while they're hot!"

Frankfurter sales proved popular from the first. Sports cartoonist Tad Dorgan liked to caricature the dachshund-shaped delicacy as animated dogs, but despite the whimsical "libel" on the beef ingredients, customers consumed the "hot dogs" in ever increasing numbers. Soon the item became world famous.

The Stevens business kept growing until now it employs almost 3,500 people on an average summer day. The Jacobs Brothers and other baseball concessionaires hire thousands of others.

The vendor in the ballpark is paid on salary plus commission. He (or she, since some concessionaires employ women to sell) usually has a minimum guarantee of $3 per day and averages from $16 to $20 daily, if the attendance is of normal size. A top vendor can make as much as $50 at a capacity crowd.

In the average big league ballpark, the total yearly consumption by fans includes 700,000 bottles of pop, 800,000 hot dogs, 500,000 slabs of ice cream and 400,000 bags of peanuts.

Fans

Professional implies "for pay." Pay means money, money comes from the cash customer . . . and so, quite obviously, the most important factor in professional baseball is the fan. Everybody connected with sports recognizes this axiom. In fact, even the caustic newspaperman is treated graciously by the ball club, only because he represents a link with the thousands (or millions) of fans who read his story daily.

Rabid fans, who worship the baseball headliner, aren't adverse to making headlines themselves. There was the Dodger fan who shot a Giant rooter to death for making cynical cracks. En route to the electric chair, the murderer asked the chaplain, "Did the Bums beat the Giants today?" Then there was the Cleveland flagpole sitter who vowed not to leave his perch till the Indians returned to first place . . . the fan who climbed out of the Ebbets Field grandstand to assault umpire George Magerkurth . . . and the psychotic girl who shot Eddie Waitkus to prove her intense love for the Philly first baseman.

In the "old faithful" class, Arthur Felsch of Milwaukee rates notice because every year he parks outside the bleacher entrance about a week before the start of the World Series, and lives in a cardboard crate . . . just so he can have the honor of being the first one admitted to the park. However, the long-term rooters are usually more reserved and rarely make even a single line in the papers all their lives. In this latter category are such veterans as George Doerzbach, who saw 55 consecutive season opening games at Cleveland; Lou Schulte, who missed only seven Cincinnati home games in 24 years, and Hyman Pearlstone, who made at least one road trip a season with the defunct Philadelphia Athletics for 44 years.

Every ballpark abounds in favorite grandstand "characters." St. Louis had Mary Ott for many years, distracting enemy players with her penetrating whinny; Pittsburgh had a coal dealer who barked like a wounded seal; Cincinnati had Harry Thobe, retired bricklayer, who danced on the dugout roof while holding a red umbrella and wearing a red-banded straw hat. The "daffy Dodgers", as might be expected, always led the way in quaint customers: the late Shorty Laurice and his catch-as-catch-can Sym-phoney Band; Hilda Chester and her cowbell; Eddie Bettan with his tin whistle and explorer's helmet; Jack Pearce and his gas-filled balloons, etc.

The Hollywood influence has invaded baseball in recent years, and "fan clubs" seem to be the rage, numbering most of its membership among teenage girls.

Brooklyn still recalls Abie the Iceman, who would hitch his ice wagon just outside Ebbets Field every afternoon and go in to jeer at the Dodgers. "Ya bums, ya!" he'd rasp. One day, manager Wilbert Robinson came up to Abie and said, "Wouldn't you like a season pass, so you can see the games free instead of having to pay every day? Here, take this. Just stop yelling at my boys. You make them nervous."

Abie accepted the pass joyfully. But a week later he knocked on the clubhouse door, came up to Uncle Robbie and said, "I can't stand it any more. Here's back your pass. I gotta yell—'cause they ARE bums!"

Patsy O'Toole, a Navin Field and then Briggs Stadium fixture, was Detroit's most prominent rooter. He would roar "you're a faker!" at opposing players and his bellow could be heard throughout the stands.

Cleveland once honored one of its patrons with a Special Fan's Night, showering the lucky fan with a number of gifts for his loyalty to the Indians.

XII FEATURES

Famous Families

When a man wants his son to inherit his money, he writes a will. But all the penmanship and planning in the world cannot guarantee that a boy will inherit the skill, the strength or the spiritual drive of his father. Baseball immortals like Ty Cobb and Walter Johnson were frustrated when their sons showed no special aptitude or preference for the sport. Yet there are enough examples of father-and-son or brothers who made the majors to conclude that playing talent can run in a family.

Of all the great baseball clans, none could match the six Cleveland-born sons of Irish immigrants James Delahanty and Bridget Croke. Five of their boys made the majors. A sixth, Willie, starred in the minors and was drafted by the Dodgers—but before he could report for National League duty, he was hit in the head by a pitched ball at Waterbury, Connecticut, and he had to give up the game soon afterward.

Big Ed Delahanty, eldest of the baseball tribe, is the only person ever to lead both the National and American Leagues in batting, with .408 for Philadelphia NL in 1899 and .376 for Washington AL in 1902. A prodigious slugger, he once hit four homers in one game and added a single for good measure. Jim Delahanty led the World Series hitters of 1909 with an average of .346. Brother Joe was the main prop for St. Louis NL at one time. Tom and Frank both played for Cleveland.

Another clan of shillelagh swingers de luxe was the O'Neill quartet of brothers, Mike, Steve, Jack and Jim. Brother trios include the families Allen, Alou, Boyer, Clarkson, Cross, Cruz, DiMaggio, High, Mansell, Reccius, Sadowski, Sewell, Sowders and Wright.

Here is a comprehensive list of the major leagues' famous families:

Father and Son

ADAMS—Robert H., R. Michael
ARAGON—Angel, Angel Jr.
AVERILL—Howard E., Earl D.
BAGBY—James C., James C., Jr.
BARNHART—Clyde L., Victor D.
BELL—David R., David G.
BERRY—Charles J., Charles F.
BERRY—Joseph H., Joseph H., Jr.
BOONE—Raymond O., Robert R.
BRICKELL—Frederick B., Fritz D.
BRUCKER—Earle F., Earle F., Jr.
CAMILLI—Adolph L., Douglas J.
CAMPANIS—Alexander S., James A.
COLEMAN—Joseph P., Joseph H.
COLLINS—Edward T., Edward T., Jr.
CONNOLLY—Edward J., Edward J., Jr.

COONEY—James J., James E. & John W.
CORRIDEN—John M., John M., Jr.
CROUCH—William H., William E.
DOSCHER—John H., John H., Jr.
ESCHEN—James G., Lawrence E.
GABRIELSON—Leonard H., Leonard G.
GANZEL—Charles W., Foster P.
GILBERT—Lawrence W., Charles M. & Harold J.
GRAHAM—George F., John B.
GRIMES—Oscar R., Oscar R., Jr.
GRIMSLEY—Ross A., Ross A., II
HAIRSTON—Samuel, John L. & Jerry
HEGAN—James E., James M.
HEINTZELMAN—Kenneth A., Thomas K.

HOOD—Wallace J., Wallace J., Jr.
JOHNSON—Adam R., Adam R., Jr.
JOHNSON—Edward W., James B.
JOHNSON—Ernest R., Donald S.
KRAUSSE—Lewis B., Lewis B., Jr.
LANIER—Hubert M., Harold C.
LEE—Thornton S., Donald E.
LERCHEN—Bertram R., George E.
LIEBHARDT—Glenn J., Glenn I.
LINDSTROM—Frederick C.,
    Charles W.
LIVELY—Henry E., Everett A.
MACK—Cornelius, Earle T.
MAGGERT—Harl V., Harl W.
MALAY—Charles F., Joseph C.
MATTICK—Walter J., Robert J.
MAY—Merrill G., Milton S.
MEINKE—Frank L., Robert B.
MILLS—William G., Arthur G.
MONTEAGUDO—Rene M.,
    Aurelio F.
MOORE—Eugene, Eugene Jr.
MORTON—Guy, Guy Jr.
MUELLER—Walter J., Donald F.
NARLESKI—William E., Raymond E.
NICHOLS—Chester R., Chester R., Jr.
NORTHEY—Ronald J., Scott R.
OKRIE—Frank A., Leonard J.
O'ROURKE—James H., James S.

O'ROURKE—Joseph P., Joseph L.
OSBORNE—Ernest P., Lawrence S.
PARTENHEIMER—Harold P.,
    Stanwood W.
PILLETTE—Herman P., Duane X.
QUEEN—Melvin J., Melvin D.
SAVIDGE—Ralph A., Donald S.
SCHULTZ—Joseph C., Joseph C., Jr.
SHEELY—Earl H., Hollis K.
SIEBERT—Richard W., Paul E.
SISLER—George H., David M.
    & Richard A.
SMALLEY—Roy F., Roy F., Jr.
STEPHENSON—Joseph C., Jerry J.
SULLIVAN—William J., William J.,
    Jr.
SUSCE—George C. M., George D.
TORRES—Ricardo J., Don G.
TRESH—Michael, Thomas Michael
TROSKY—Harold A., Harold A., Jr.
UNSER—Albert B., Delbert B.
WAKEFIELD—Howard J., Richard C.
WALKER—Ewart G., Fred
    & Harry W.
WALSH—Edward A., Edward A., Jr.
WHITE—Joyner C., Joyner M.
WOOD—Joseph, Joseph F.
YOUNG—Delmar J., Delmar E.

Brothers

AARON—Henry L., Tommie L.
ACOSTA—Balmadero M., Jose
ADAMS—Richard L., Robert H.
ALLEN—(3) Harold A., Richard A.,
    & Ronald F.
ALLISON—Arthur A., Douglass L.
ALOU—Felipe R., Mateo R., Jesus M.
ANDREWS—Michael J., Robert P.
ASPROMONTE—Kenneth J.,
    Robert T.
BAILEY—James H., Lonas E.
BANNON—James H., Thomas E.
BARNES—Jesse L., Virgil J.
BAXES—Dimitrios S., Michael
BELL—Charles C., Frank G.
BENNETT—David H., Dennis J.
BERGEN—Martin, William A.
BIGBEE—Carson L., Lyle R.
BLANKENSHIP—Homer, Theodore
BLUEGE—Oswald L., Otto A.

BOLLING—Frank E., Milton J.
BOONE—Isaac M., James A.
BOYER—(3) Cletus L., Cloyd V.
    & Kenton L.
BOYLE—Edward J., John A.
BOYLE—James J., Ralph F.
BRASHEAR—Robert N., Roy P.
BREEDEN—Danny R., Harold N.
BRETT—George H., Kenneth A.
BRINKMAN—Charles, Edwin A.
BROWN—Jackie G., Paul
BROWN—Larry L., Richard E.
BROWN—Ollie L., Oscar L.
CAMNITZ—R. Harry, Samuel H.
CAMP—Llewellyn R., Winfield S.
CAMPBELL—Hugh, Michael
CANTWELL—Michael J., Thomas A.
CARLYLE—Hiram C., Roy E.
CASEY—Daniel M., Dennis P.
CHAPMAN—Calvin L., Edwin V.

CHIOZZA—Dino J., Louis P.
CHRISTOPHER—Loyd E., Russell O.
CLAPP—Aaron B., John E.
CLARKE—Fred C., Joshua B.
CLARKE—Rufus R., Sumpter E.
CLARKSON—(3) Arthur H., John G.
& Walter H.
COFFMAN—George D., Samuel R.
COHEN—Andrew H., Sydney H.
CONIGLIARO—Anthony R.,
William M.
CONNELL—Eugene J., Joseph B.
CONNOR—Joseph F., Roger
CONWAY—James P., Peter J.
CONWAY—Richard B., William F.
COONEY—James E., John W.
COOPER—Morton C., William W.
CORCORAN—Lawrence J., M.
COSCARART—Joseph M., Peter J.
COVELESKI—Harry F., Stanley A.
COVINGTON—Clarence C.,
William W.
CROSS—(3) Amos C., Frank A.
& Lafayette N.
CRUZ—(3) Cirilo, Hector, Jose
CUCCINELLO—Alfred E.,
Anthony F.
DAILY—Cornelius F., Edward M.
DALY—Joseph J., Thomas P.
DANNING—Harry, Ike
DARINGER—Clifford C., Rolla H.
DAVALILLO—Pompeyo R., Victor J.
DAVENPORT—Arthur D., Claude E.
DEAN—Jay H., Paul D.
DEASLEY—James, Thomas H.
DELAHANTY—(5) Edward J., Frank
G., James C., Joseph N., Thomas J.
DeMONTREVILLE—Eugene N.,
Leon
DICKEY—George W., William M.
DiMAGGIO—(3) Dominic P., Joseph
P. & Vincent P.
DONAHUE—John A., Patrick W.
DONOVAN—Jeremiah F., Thomas J.
DONOVAN—Patrick J., William E.
DORGAN—Jeremiah F., Michael C.
DOYLE—Cornelius J., John J.
DRAKE—Samuel H., Solomon L.
DUGAN—Edward J., William E.
EGGLER—David D., John
ENS—Anton, Jewel W.
ERAUTT—Edward L. S., Joseph M.
EVERS—John J., Joseph F.

EWING—John, William
FALK—Bibb A., Chester E.
FERRELL—Richard B., Wesley C.
FERRY—Alfred J., John F.
FINNEY—Harold W., Louis K.
FISHER—Chauncey B., Thomas C.
FISHER—Newton, Robert T.
FOGARTY—James G., Joseph J.
FOLEY—Thomas J., William B.
FORD—Eugene W., Russell W.
FOREMAN—Francis I., John D.
FORSCH—Kenneth R., Robert H.
FREESE—Eugene L., George W.
FRIEL—Patrick H., William E.
FULLER—Henry W., William B.
GAGLIANO—Philip J., Ralph M.
GARRETT—Henry A., Ronald W.
GALVIN—James F., Louis
GANZEL—Charles W., John H.
GARBARK—Nathaniel M.,
Robert M.
GARDELLA—Alfred S., Daniel L.
GASTON—Alexander N.,
Nathaniel M.
GETTINGER—Charles H.,
Thomas L.
GILBERT—Charles M., Harold J.
GILBERT—Harry, John G.
GLEASON—Harry G., William J.
GLEASON—John D., William G.
GRABOWSKI—Albert F., Reginald J.
GRAVES—Joseph E., Samuel S.
GREGG—David C., Sylveanus A.
GRIMES—(Twins) Oscar R., Roy A.
GRISSOM—Leo T., Marvin E.
GROH—Henry K., Lewis C.
GUMBERT—Addison C., William S.
HACKETT—Mortimer M., Walter H.
HAFEY—Daniel A., Thomas F.
HAIRSTON—Jerry, John L.
HALL—George W., James
HAMNER—Granville W., Wesley G.
HANDLEY—Eugene L., Lee E.
HARGARVE—Eugene F., William M.
HARRINGTON—Andrew F.,
Joseph C.
HATFIELD—Gilbert, John V.
HAYWORTH—Myron C.,
Raymond H.
HEMPHILL—Charles J., Frank V.
HENGLE—Edward S., Emory J.
HEVING—John A., Joseph W.
HIGH—(3) Andrew A., Charles E.
& Hugh J.

HILL—Hugh E., William C.
HINCHMAN—Harry S., William W.
HITCHCOCK—James F., William C.
HOVLIK—Edward C., Joseph
HOWARD—George E., Ivan C.
HUGHES—Edward H., Thomas J.
HUGHES—James J., Michael F.
HUNTER—(Twins) George H.,
    William E.
IRWIN—Arhur A., John
JEFFCOAT—George E., Harold B.
JIMENEZ—Felix E., Manuel E.
JOHNSON—Chester L., Earl D.
JOHNSON—Robert L., Roy C.
JOHNSTON—James H., Wheeler R.
JONES—Gary H., Steven H.
JONNARD—(Twins) Clarence J.,
    Claude A.
JORGENS—Arndt L., Orville E.
KAPPEL—Henry, Joseph
KELL—Everett L., George C.
KELLER—Charles E., Howard K.
KELLNER—Alexander R., Walter J.
KELLY—George L., Reynolds C.
KENNEDY—James E., Junior R.
KEOUGH—Richard M., Joseph
KILLEFER—Wade H., William L.
KILROY—Matthew A., Michael J.
KING—Marshall N., Stephen F.
KLAUS—William J., Robert F.
KLING—John G., William
KNODE—Kenneth T., Robert T.
KNOTHE—George B., Wilfred E.
KOPF—William L., Walter H.
KRSNICH—Michael, Rocco P.
LACHEMANN—Marcel E., Rene G.
LARY—Alfred A., Frank S.
LELIVELT—John F., William J.
LILLARD—Robert E., William B.
LOBERT—Frank J., John B.
LOOK—Dean Z., Bruce M.
LOWDERMILK—Grover C., Louis B.
LUSH—Ernest B., William L.
MAHER—F., Thomas
MAISEL—Frederick C., George J.
MANCUSO—August R., Frank O.
MANGUAL—Angel L., Jose M.
MANSELL—(3) John, Michael R.
    & Thomas E.
MANUSH—Frank B., Henry E.
MARION—John W., Martin W.
MASKREY—Harry H., Samuel L.
MATHEWSON—Christopher, Henry

MATTOX—Cloy M., James P.
MAY—Carlos, Lee A.
MAYER—James E., Samuel F.
McDANIEL—Lyndall D., Max V.
McFARLAN—Alexander S.,
    Anderson D.
McFARLAND—Charles E., Lamont A.
McGEEHAN—Cornelius B., Daniel D.
McLAUGHLIN—Bernard, Francis M.
MEUSEL—Emil F., Robert W.
MEYER—Benjamin, Lee
MILAN—Horace R., Jesse C.
MILLER—Edmund J., Ralph H.
MILLER—Russell L., Walter J.
MOFFET—Joseph W., Samuel R.
MORIARTY—George J., William J.
MORRISON—John D., Philip M.
MORRISSEY—John H., Thomas J.
MUELLER—Clarence F., Walter J.
MYERS—Lynn, William H.
NETTLES—Graig, James W.
NIEKRO—Joseph, Philip H.
O'BRIEN—(Twins) Edward J.,
    John T.
OGDEN—John M., Warren H.
OLIVO—Diomedes Antonio,
    Fred Emilio
O'NEILL—(4) James L., John J.,
    Stephen F., Michael J.
ONSLOW—Edward J., John J.
O'ROURKE—James H., John
ORTIZ—Oliverio N., Roberto G.
O'TOOLE—Dennis J., James
PACIOREK—John F., Thomas M.
PARKER—Harley P., Jay
PARROTT—Thomas W., Walter E.
PASCUAL—Camilo A., Carlos L.
PATTERSON—Hamilton, William
    J. B.
PEITZ—Henry C., Joseph
PEPLOSKI—Henry S., Joseph A.
PERRY—Gaylord J., James E.
PFEFFER—Edward J., Francis X.
PIERSON—Donald P., Edmund D.
PIKE—J., Lipman E.
PIPGRAS—Edward J., George W.
RECCIUS—(3) J. William, (Twins)
    Philip, John
REUSCHEL—Paul R., Rickey E.
RICKETTS—David W., Richard J.
RIDDLE—Elmer R., John L.
ROBINSON—Frederic H., Wilbert
ROETTGER—Oscar F., Walter H.

ROSENBERG—Harry, Louis
ROTH—Frank C., Robert F.
ROWE—David E., John C.
ROY—Charles R., Luther F.
RUSSELL—Allen E., Clarence D.
SADOWSKI—Edward R., Robert, Theodore
SAUER—Edward, Henry J.
SAY—James I., Lewis I.
SCANLAN—Frank A., William D.
SCHAFFER—George, Taylor
SCHANG—Robert M., Walter H.
SCHAREIN—Arthur O., George A.
SCHMIDT—Charles, Walter J.
SCHULTE—Herman J., Leonard W.
SEWELL—(3) James L., Joseph W. & Thomas W.
SHAFFER—(3) Frank, George, Taylor
SHANNON—(Twins) Joseph A., Maurice
SHANTZ—Robert C., Wilmer E.
SHERLOCK—John C., Vincent T.
SHERRY—Lawrence, Norman B.
SISLER—David M., Richard A.
SMITH—Charles E., Frederick V.
SNYDER—James, Joshua
SOWDERS—(3) John, Leonard, & William J.
STAFFORD—James J., John J.
STAHL—Charles S., Garland
STANLEY—John L., Joseph B.
STOVALL—George T., Jesse C.
SUTHERLAND—Darrell W., Gary L.
TANNEHILL—Jesse N., Lee F.
TEBEAU—George E., Oliver W.

THIELMAN—Henry J., John P.
THOMAS—Roy A., William M.
THOMPSON—Homer, Thomas C.
THRONEBERRY—Marvin E., Maynard F.
TOBIN—James A., John P.
TORRE—Frank J., Joseph P.
TRAFFLEY—John, William F.
TREACEY—Frederick, P.
TWOMBLY—Clarence E., George F.
TYLER—Frederick F., George A.
TYRONE—James V., O. Wayne
VAN CUYK—Christian G., John H.
WADE—Benjamin S., Jacob F.
WAGNER—Albert, John P.
WALKER—Ernest R., Ewart G.
WALKER—Fred, Harry W.
WALKER—Gerald H., Harvey W.
WALKER—Moses F., Welday W.
WANER—Lloyd J., Paul G.
WATT—Albert B., Frank M.
WEILAND—Edwin N., Robert G.
WESTLAKE—James P., Waldon T.
WEYHING—August, John
WHEAT—McKinley D., Zachary D.
WHITE—James L., William H.
WHITNEY—Arthur W., Frank T.
WILLIAMS—August R., Harry P.
WILTSE—George L., Lewis D.
WINGO—Absalom H., Ivy B.
WOOD—Fred S., Peter B.
WRIGHT—(3) George, Samuel, & William H.
YOCHIM—Leonard J., Raymond A.
YOUNT—Lawrence K., Robin R.

Grandfather and Grandson

COLLINS—John F., and GALLAGHER, Robert C.
HERRMANN—Martin J., Edward M.
SPENCER—L. Benjamin, James L.

Night Baseball

There's nothing new under the sun—nor under electric lights either. Though night baseball has been called the saviour of the modern game, it actually dates back to September, 1880. Two amateur teams tangled at Nantasket Beach, Massachusetts, and with the aid of arclights strung along the field they were able to complete nine full innings between 8 and 9:30 P.M.

The next night game of record was June 2, 1883, when the Quincys of Illinois beat a picked team of home players at Fort Wayne, Indiana, 19–11. Other 19th-century games at night were strictly exhibitions, too. Baltimore played at Hartford, Connecticut, on July 23, 1890. Manager Ed Barrow arranged a game for his Paterson, New Jersey, team (boasting Honus Wagner at shortstop) on the night of July 4, 1896 at Wilmington, Delaware.

E. Lee Keyser boldly announced at the National Association meeting in the winter of 1929 that his Des Moines club would be the first in organized baseball to play a league game at night. However, Des Moines opened the season on the road, and Keyser, after having spent $19,000 to install lights, was robbed of the distinction when promoters at Independence, Kansas—a rival club in the Western Association—hastily posted some arclights and played against Muskogee on the night of April 28, 1930. Four days afterward, Des Moines staged its gala arclight affair.

Two seasons later, Larry MacPhail, as general manager of the Columbus Redbirds of the American Association, installed high-level lighting in his stadium. In 1935, as leader of Cincinnati, he introduced night ball to the majors, with President Roosevelt in the White House pressing a button that first turned on the Crosley Field lights. Later, as president of the Dodgers and Yanks, MacPhail put lights in Ebbets Field and Yankee Stadium. Now every team in the majors except Chicago's Wrigley Field NL has lights at home.

Originally, the big leagues limited each team to seven home night games a season. In 1942, ostensibly to cater to the defense worker, the limit was raised to 14, with Washington insisting on 21. Since the summer sun makes a blast furnace of the Kansas City, Los Angeles, Washington and St. Louis ballparks at mid-day, these cities now play practically all their mid-season games in the cooler evening air.

Introduced into organized ball strictly as a novelty, night baseball proved such an immediate success that it saved dozens of minor leagues in the depression years of the 1930's. It also wrought financial miracles for poorer major league clubs.

Modern engineering has made night baseball enjoyable for the players as well as fans. Boston's Fenway Park, for instance, is bathed in 10 times as much light as the average person gets while reading under his living room lamp. Scientific angling of the individual floodlights—and even specialized styles of mowing the grass—add up to optimum visibility. The owners don't stint, either, for Tiger Stadium's 1,386 floodlights are 1,500 watts each . . . enough power to light a city of 10,000 people!

In 1971, the fourth game of the World Series came under the lights for the first time. With an estimated 61,000,000 TV-viewing audience, all weekday games were played at night, starting in 1972. In 1976, the Sunday game was played at night.

Spring Training

With scattered exceptions, 19th-century ballplayers trained at home. They would report to their home park a week or two before the season started, then shiver through a crude training period. In case of rain or snow, they would pitch, catch, bunt and run under the stands.

Today every team travels to a tropical clime for leisurely and luxurious spring training. Why? Certainly not in chase of the almighty dollar. The hard fact is that practically every club loses money in the venture . . . as much as $30,000 each spring. Yet they all indulge, for two compelling reasons:

(1) Conditioning. After five months of loafing, players would strain many more tendons and muscles if they had to work into regular season form in a chilly week or two.

(2) Publicity. When big league heroes cavort under the palms of Florida, and California, a full contingent of newspapermen, sportscasters and photographers are on hand to report daily progress to the baseball-hungry fans at home.

Whetting the customers' appetite by furnishing accounts of spring training, instead of letting the fans watch it first hand, is such valid psychology that even the minor league clubs of Southern cities train at distant bases. Clubowners have found it better salesmanship to bring in their club, fresh and unseen, for the opening of the championship season.

Once the teams got the spring wanderlust, even this country's boundaries couldn't contain them. The Yanks of 1911 were the first to leave the U. S. They trained on Bermuda's coral strand. The touring custom has become so prevalent in recent years that New York fans hardly batted an eye in 1947 when their three home teams trained and played spring exhibitions in such faraway places as Puerto Rico, Venezuela, Cuba, Panama and Hawaii.

As far back as 1884, the Boston Nationals played some spring games in New Orleans. However, the inaugural year of spring training is generally accepted as 1886, when Harry Wright brought his Phillies to Charleston, South Carolina, and Cap Anson took a dozen of his Chicago regulars for conditioning at Hot Springs, Arkansas.

These early "luxury" trips were hardly joyrides. Connie Mack tells of going South with the Washington club in '88: "It took us three nights and two days to reach Jacksonville, Florida. At night we'd travel Pullman, with two players sleeping in each berth, and by day we'd switch to coaches. The first hotel we tried wouldn't even register us. Manager Ted Sullivan scoured the town before he finally found us lodgings—though the hotel clerk made the strict stipulation that the ballplayers would not mingle with the other guests or eat in the same dining room."

By contrast, even the swankiest hotels nowadays vie for patronage by the ball clubs. Many a Chamber of Commerce lies awake nights thinking up ways to lure big league teams to their town as a training base, mindful of the priceless publicity and lucrative business that accrues.

Nicknames

Americans dote on nicknames. This habit is so ingrained, that in time a person's real name becomes obscured. Not many baseball fans, for instance, know the correct first names of Babe Ruth, Jake Flowers, Kiki Cuyler, Honus Wagner, Ping Bodie, Zack Taylor or Arky Vaughan. (Answers: George, D'Arcy, Hazen, John, Frank, James and Joseph).

A minor victim of this custom was Jeff Tesreau. While he was coaching Dartmouth's baseball team, townsfolk persuaded him to run for public office. He lost the race . . . only because local rules specified that a man's legal name must be written on the ballot in order for it to be valid. To the baseball public, which means most of America, the former Giant pitching hero was always "Jeff." Few ever knew him as Charles Monroe Tesreau!

Baseball players often resort to the direct approach, either by tagging someone for the color of his hair (Whitey Lockman, Red Ruffing, Blondy Ryan) or for some other obvious physical characteristic: Lefty Grove, Slim Sallee, Stubby Overmire, Fatty Fothergill, etc. On the other hand, they sometimes become whimsical, calling big fellows "Babe" (Phelps) or "Tiny" (Bonham).

No stick-in-the-muds, baseball folks keep 'em guessing by applying the same nickname for different reasons. Harold Reese is "Pee Wee" because he once was a champion at marbles (which are also known as "pee wees"); Peewee Wanninger, on the other hand simply was a little fellow. Spec Meadows, for his specs (spectacles); Spec Shea, because he's freckled . . . speckled.

Odell Hale was "Bad News" in tribute to his troubling enemy pitchers. However, Jim Galloway had the same nickname for another reason. The star infielder was a telegrapher before he came into pro ball. In order to break away from work for semipro games, he'd have a crony in another office fake a message to him that some relative was sick and had to see him. So many of these "bad news" wires came during the season that he soon acquired that nickname.

Among other appelations serving double duty are Birdie (Tebbetts, because he chirps like a bird; Cree, because he once played under the assumed name of Burdee) . . . Zack (Taylor, because of a famous general by that name; Wheat, because his first name is Zachary)' . . . Spud (Chandler, to abbreviate his first name, Spurgeon; Davis, because he liked "spuds," or potatoes) . . . Crab (Burkett, because of his crabby disposition; Evers, because of the sure way he clawed the ball) . . . Cy (Young, shorted from "cyclone"; Williams, a rustic appelation for the hayseed-looking rookie).

Baseball dips heavily into the animal kingdom for nicknames indicating a resemblance: Ducky Medwick, Rabbit Maranville, Skeeter Newsome, Goose Goslin, Moose McCormick, Old Hoss Radbourn, Flea Clifton, Spider Jorgenson, Bullfrog Dietrich, Mule Haas, Ox Eckhardt, Hippo Vaughn, Monk Dubiel, Harry (The Cat) Brecheen, etc.

Loquaciousness is never overlooked. Hence Lippy Durocher, Gabby Hartnett, Dizzy Dean, Goofy Gomez, Buzzy Wares, Orator O'Rourke, Foghorn Kennedy.

Since comic strips have always been among the favorite reading matter of ballplayers, many nicknames are derived from that source, including Wimpy Quinn, Flash Gordon, Bing Miller, Skinny Shaner, Boob McNair, Li'l Abner Erickson, Nemo Liebold, Muggsy McGraw, Pinky Whitney, Dusty Rhodes, Buster Brown, Moon Mullen, Stinky Davis, Jeep Handley, Tarzan Parmelee, Popeye Mahaffey, Available Jones. Hack Wilson was tagged in honor of his physique, which resembled the great wrestler, Hackenschmidt; Firpo Marberry and Jeff Tesreau were nicknamed after the famous heavyweights, and Packy Rogers earned his tag for being as scrappy as Packy McFarland.

Since Mickey Cochrane was such a great catcher, subsequent receivers of any promise were called Mickey, too, even though their correct names happened to be Arnold Owen, Thompson Livingston and Newton Grasso. The ironic part of it all is that Mickey isn't even Cochrane's legitimate tag. His first name is Gordon, and he was called Mickey only because Bostonians thought he had a real Irish face, and "Mickey" is the catch-name for Irishmen, the way "Hans"

is used for a German or "Ivan" for a Russian.

Some players are stuck with infant mispronunciations. When Harold Gilbert at the age of 2 said "Tookie" instead of rookie, the family never let him live it down. Players who had difficulty in saying "brother" as tots, wound up in the majors as Bubba Harris, Boo Ferriss and Bruz Hammer.

Predilections for certain foods got these fellows their nicknames: Nap Rucker, Pie Traynor, Salty Parker, Lemons Solters, Pretzels Pezzullo, Candy Cummings. Geographical handles include Dixie Walker, Tex Carleton, Bama Rowell and Arky Vaughan, the last two coming from Alabama and Arkansas.

Nationalities enter the picture, too, as in the cases of Greek George, Frenchy Bordagaray, Swede Hansen, Dutch Leonard, Jap Barbeau, Chink Mattick. Dapper dressers included Broadway Smith, Dude Esterbrook, Beau Bell and Count Mullane. Staid, sedate fellows earned appropriate soubriquets: Deacon Phillippe, Parson Nicholson and Preacher Roe.

Other interesting derivations: Casey Stengel, because he comes from Kansas City (KC) ; Grandma Murphy, for his rocking-chair motion when winding up; Satchel Paige, whose feet seemed as big as suitcases; Bruno Betzel, from the name of the dog that was his inseparable pal in boyhood; Beauty Bancroft, for yelling that word invariably when a teammate made a nice play; Wish Egan, shortened from his baptismal name of Aloysius; Suitcase Seeds, always seemed en route from one club to another; Pants Rowland, once tore his trousers sliding home; Cracker Schalk, whose rear view was square and small like a cracker when he squatted behind the plate.

More recent players have continued the tradition of having colorful nicknames. Yogi Berra reversed the normal procedure by having a cartoon character named after him. Hair color gave Whitey Ford, Red Schoendienst and Rusty Staub their nicknames. Boog Powell's name was the result of a childhood word for one that gets into mischief. The Oakland Athletics at one time had a pitching staff that included Mudcat Grant, Blue Moon Odom and Catfish Hunter (Jim, John, and Jim respectively) .

FAMOUS FIRSTS

1845—First code of playing rules, by A. J. Cartwright.

1846—First match game, N.Y. Knickerbockers losing to New York Club, 23-1.

1849—First playing uniform, Knickerbockers' blue and white.

1853—First box score appeared in N.Y. *Clipper*.

1856—First regular baseball reporter, Henry Chadwick.

1857—First official rulebook published and edited by Chadwick...First baseball league: National Association of Baseball Players.

1858—First admission charged, 50 cents, All-Star N. Y. vs. Brooklyn, at Fashion Race Course, L. I.

1859—First college game, Amherst beat Williams.

1862—First enclosed ballpark, Union Grounds, Brooklyn.

1863—First calling of balls and strikes.

1864—First professional player, A. J. Reach, paid $1,000 for season by Philadelphia.

1865—First stolen base, Ed Cuthbert of Keystones.

1866—First slide to steal a base, Bob Addy of Rockford; Dicky Pearce of Atlantics first to lay down bunt.

1867—First prominent use of curve ball, W. A. Cummings.

1869—First salaried team, Cincinnati Red Stockings, who were also first team to wear short trousers.

1870—First demonstration at Brooklyn by Fred Goldsmith (Aug. 16) that a baseball really curves.

1871—First professional league, NA.

1873—First time two games played in one day. Resolutes at Boston, July 4.

1874—First foreign tour, Athletics and Boston to England.

1875—First mask, worn by Jim Tyng as invented by Harvard teammate Fred Thayer . . . . First glove, by Charles Waite.... First major league 1-0 game, Chicago beating St. Louis.

1876—First year of NL... First major team to play twice in one day, Cincinnati.

1877—First minor league organized, International Association.

1878—First turnstiles.

1879—First use of reserve clause in player contract.

1882—First salaried staff of umpires paid by league, AA, and adopted by NL the next year. . . First interleague playoff (World Series). . . First doubleheader Sept. 25 (Providence vs. Worcester) NL.

1884—First organization of a third "major league", UA.

1885—First use of chest protectors for catchers and umpires.

1886—First use of two umpires in one game, World Series. . . First Players' union recognized, "Brotherhood of Ball Players"...First spring training trip, Chicago NL at Hot Springs, Ark.

1887—First catcher to work continuously behind bat, Charles Zimmer.

1888—First round-the-world tour by baseball teams.

1892—First Sunday games permitted in NL.

1894—First player to hit four homers in one game, Bobby Lowe.

1901—First American League game, Chicago vs. Cleveland.

1902—First organization of minor leagues, National Association.

1903—First NL-AL World Series.

1907—First shin guards for catcher introduced by Roger Bresnahan.

1909—First unassisted triple play in majors, Neal Ball... First U.S. President at opening game, W. H. Taft.

1910—First use of cork center in baseball.

1913—First round-world tour by two major league teams, Giants and White Sox.

1919—First Sunday game allowed in New York.

1921—First baseball commissioner takes office, K. M. Landis. . First radio broadcast of World Series.

1926—First amplifiers used, Polo Grounds.

1933—First All-Star Game.

1935—First major league night game, at Cincinnati. . . First major league team to fly, Cincinnati.

1936—First players elected to Hall of Fame: Cobb, Ruth, Mathewson, Wagner and Johnson.

1939—First use of yellow baseball, Pittsburgh vs. Brooklyn. . . First telecast of game, in Brooklyn.

1941—First team to wear helmets at bat, Brooklyn.

1946—First Negro player in modern pro ball, Jackie Robinson at Montreal. . . First playoff in NL, St. Louis beating Brooklyn in two straight games.

1947—First Negro player in NL, Robinson; first in AL, Larry Doby.

1953—First franchise shift of modern times, Boston NL moves to Milwaukee.

1956—First World Series no-hitter and perfect game, Don Larsen, New York AL vs. Brooklyn.

1958—First major league franchises on West Coast, Brooklyn NL and New York NL shift to Los Angeles and San Francisco, respectively.

1961—First expansion of modern times, American League adds Los Angeles and Washington (with former Washington club shifting to Minnesota).

1962—First Negro elected to Hall of Fame, Jackie Robinson.

1965—First domed stadium, the "Astrodome" in Houston, also first stadium with artificial turf.

1968—First expansion of NL to cross international borders, awarding Montreal along with San Diego franchises to begin participation in 1969.

1971—First night World Series game played.

1973—First permanent pinch-hitter for pitcher—American League designated hitter.

1975—First black manager—Frank Robinson, Cleveland AL

THE AMERICAN LEAGUE
DESIGNATED HITTER FOR THE PITCHER

A hitter may be designated to bat for the starting pitcher and all subsequent pitchers in any game without otherwise affecting the status of the pitcher(s) in the game. A Designated Hitter for the pitcher must be selected prior to the game and must be included in the lineup cards presented to the umpire-in-chief.

It is not mandatory that a club designate a hitter for the pitcher, but failure to do so prior to the game precludes the use of a Designated Hitter for that game.

Pinch hitters for a Designated Hitter may be used. Any substitute hitter for a Designated Hitter himself becomes a Designated Hitter. A replaced Designated Hitter shall not re-enter the game in any capacity.

The Designated Hitter may be used defensively, continuing to bat in the same position in the batting order, but the pitcher must then bat in the place of the substituted defensive player, unless more than one substitution is made, and the manager then must designate their spots in the batting order.

A runner may be substituted for the Designated Hitter and the runner assumes the role of Designated Hitter.

A Designated Hitter is "locked" into the batting order. No multiple substitutions may be made that will alter the batting rotation of the Designated Hitter.

Once the game pitcher is switched from the mound to a defensive position this move shall terminate the Designated Hitter role for the remainder of the game.

Once a pinch hitter bats for any player in the batting order and then enters the game to pitch, this move shall terminate the Designated Hitter role for the remainder of the game.

Once the game pitcher bats for the Designated Hitter this move shall terminate the Designated Hitter role for the remainder of the game. (The game pitcher may only pinch-hit for the Designated Hitter.)

Once a Designated Hitter assumes a defensive position this move shall terminate the Designated Hitter role for the remainder of the game.

ONE-DAY MAJOR LEAGUERS

Every young man who has ever played high school or college baseball harbors dreams of someday becoming a major leaguer. Such vision rarely becomes reality but Ty Cobb, unwittingly, made it so for eight awe-struck St. Joseph's (Philadelphia) College players on May 18, 1912.

The truculent Detroit Tigers came to Philadelphia on that date to play a scheduled game with the world champion Athletics, but Cobb was not allowed to play. A fracas in New York three days before when he climbed into the stands to chase down a heckler resulted in a suspension for the fiery Georgia Peach, league action by president Ban Johnson which the Tiger players considered unjust.

His teammates stood by Cobb. "If Ty doesn't play," they agreed, "neither do we. We'll strike." Reminded by manager Hugh Jennings that a forfeiture would result in a $5,000 fine, the players still remained adamant.

Athletics' manager Connie Mack, informed of the Tiger players' stand, approached Jennings and suggested he hire, for the one game, a group of collegians. Mack's idea made sense to Jennings who was worried lest he would be unable to place a team on the field. The Tiger pilot wasted no time. He had contracts drawn up and they were signed by Jack Coffey, Aloysius Travers, Pat Meany, Hap Ward, Billy Maharg, Jim McGarr, Dan McGarvey and Bill Leinhauser. The dream was realized for eight St. Joseph's collegians—they were to be Kings for a Day! Ed Irwin, a sandlotter, also was added to the day's Detroit roster.

The game itself was a travesty, but Detroit saved $5,000. Travers, later to be ordained a Catholic priest, pitched for the Tigers and established an all-time single game mark which still stands—most runs allowed in one game. The 20-year-old Travers was belted by 24-2, nine errors by his mates allowing 10 unearned runs.

Of the four hits collected by the Tigers two were obtained by the sandlotter, Irwin. He cracked two triples in three times at bat for a lifetime batting average of .667.

Of the nine one-day fill-ins only Maharg, later to become a professional boxer, was to play again. Four years later he appeared in the outfield of the Philadelphia Phillies, another one-day stand.

Perhaps the proudest of the collegians was Leinhauser, the wearer of Cobb's uniform. Eventually it was through Leinhauser, who was to become a Philadelphia police officer, that S. C. Thompson, co-author of THE OFFICIAL ENCYCLOPEDIA OF BASEBALL, was able to track down the full names and birth data on the one-shot big leaguers who saved the Detroit club $5,000.

Moses F. Walker, 1884 Toledo A.A. (Courtesy of Ralph Lin Weber, Baseball Research Bureau.)

Negro Players

Cap Anson, the giant of his day and one of the pillars of organized baseball, may have been one of the factors which mitigated against the Negro player in the early days of the majors. During the first 73 years of the majors only two Negro players managed to get into a big league box score before Jackie Robinson.

In 1884 the Walker brothers—Welday and Moses—played for Toledo of the American Association, a recognized major league at the time. Both quickly faded into oblivion although Moses was above average as a catcher.

Anson indicated his sentiments toward the Negro player when he brought his Chicago White Stockings to Newark, New Jersey in 1884 for an exhibition game with the local minor leaguers. George Stovey, artful Negro hurler, was scheduled to pitch against the big leaguers. When Anson discovered that his team would face the fast slants of a Negro, he refused to have his men play the Newark club unless Stovey was removed from the lineup. So the management kept Stovey out of the game.

Anson continued to crusade against the entrance of Negro players into the National League, because of their color not their ability.

Between the Walkers' brief tenure at Toledo, and Jackie Robinson's epochal entrance into Brooklyn in 1947, there were several Negro players in organized ball—all of them in the 19th century minor leagues. They included such standouts as shortstop Clarence Matthews, second baseman Frank Grant, first baseman Charles Kelly and second baseman J. W. (Bud) Fowler.

The first team of paid Negro players was a group of fellow waiters Frank Thompson recruited in 1885 at the Argyle Hotel, Babylon, Long Island. They played 10 games that summer against white teams on Long Island, then went on tour billed as the Cuban Giants. Thompson hoped to ease the social barriers by passing his team off as Cubans, and a few players furthered the illusion by chattering in a rapid Spanish-sounding gibberish on the field. Thompson

added the nickname Giants because it was a popular team in the majors at that time. It remained a good tag, and later Negro teams were known as the Lincoln Giants, Chicago American Giants, Bacharach Giants, Brooklyn Royal Giants, etc.

None of these troupes could establish a stable league setup till 1920, when the Negro National League was formed in Kansas City. The next year a Negro Eastern League arose, and they started a regular World Series in 1924.

These leagues collapsed in the depression depths of 1932. Several years later, the Negro American and National Leagues opened shop, followed by a host of lesser leagues in the South. Player incomes were rounded out by winter ball in Mexico, Cuba and Venezuela, which had no color lines.

Between World Wars I and II, Negro baseball boasted such legendary heroes as shortstop John Henry Lloyd, catcher Josh Gibson, pitchers Cyclone Joe Williams and Cannonball Dick Redding, outfielder Oscar Charleston, etc. Only one of the fabled figures of this lost chapter in baseball history managed to benefit through modern emancipation: Leroy (Satchel) Paige, though well past 40 at the time, joined the Indians and helped pitch them to the pennant in 1948.

A special committee was set up in 1971 to enshrine the best players from the Negro Leagues in the Hall of Fame.

Spitball Pitchers

The spitball pitcher—legally—is as extinct as the American buffalo. When Burleigh Grimes tossed his last dewy pitch in 1934, it marked the end of a hurling breed which was declared null and void as far back as 1920 when the game's administrators outlawed the pitch.

The 17 pitchers in the majors at the time the pitch was outlawed were permitted to continue their salivary trade, but no other hurler was allowed to introduce it if it wasn't already part of his mound repertoire.

There are still occasional squawks from the batters that they have been slipped a spitball every now and then, but the umpires are vigilant and have instructions to eject from the game any pitcher they detect resorting to the outlawed pitch.

Here is the list of spitball hurlers in action at the time the 1920 ban was imposed (showing first and last season of major league action):

NATIONAL	AMERICAN
Bill Doak (1912–29)	Yancey Ayers (1913–21)
Phil Douglas (1912–22)	Ray Caldwell (1910–21)
Dana Fillingim (1915–25)	Stan Coveleskie (1912–28)
Ray Fisher (1910–20)	Urban Faber (1914–33)
Marvin Goodwin (1916–25)	Hub Leonard (1913–25)
Burleigh Grimes (1916–34)	Jack Quinn (1909–33)
Clarence Mitchell (1911–32)	Allan Russell (1915–25)
Dick Rudolph (1910–27)	Urban Shocker (1916–28)
	Allen Sothoron (1914–26)

Handicaps

The bespectacled major league no longer is a novelty, and the nickname "specs," first applied to a player who wore glasses, has long since passed into limbo. However, baseball has known players who have played creditably despite the handicap of the loss of a leg, arm or eye.

A one-legged player was Bert Shepard, who lost his right limb as the result of an Army crash. Shepard had been a fair minor league prospect and was determined to make the majors, finally realizing his ambition in 1945 when he hurled for the Washington Senators.

Perhaps the most remarkable of all physically handicapped ball players was a pitcher, Hugh (One-Arm) Daly, who won 72 games in his career. Daly, who also played second base and shortstop, recorded a no-hit, no-run triumph and struck out 19 players in a game, still the all-time mark.

A handicap worked in favor of Mordecai Brown, the famous Chicago Cub pitcher of the early century, who didn't possess all the fingers on his pitching hand. The crippled digits on Brown's hand enabled him to grip the ball in such a manner that his curve was actually more effective.

Pete Gray, who had one arm, played the outfield for the 1945 St. Louis Browns and the loss of several toes didn't hamper pitcher Charley Ruffing and outfielder Hal Peck.

Harry Jasper lost the sight of an eye when hit by a batted ball, but he played several seasons of major league ball after the accident. Few knew Tom Sunkel's left eye was blinded by a cataract throughout his big league career. Still another one-eyed pitcher was Bill Irwin of the old Cincinnati club.

So much for one-eyed players. How about the "four-eyes" . . . the eyeglass brigade? A bespectacled player used to be a rare spectacle indeed, with Will White of Cincinnati the lone lens wearer in the first 44 years of organized baseball. But recent generations produced dozens of examples to refute the saying, "Baseball doesn't make passes at players who wear glasses."

Trying to explain the eyeglass evolution, veteran Arlie Latham always insisted, "Back in the '80s, the diamond was laid out east to west, from batter to pitcher, so that the afternoon sun shone only in the batter's eyes. Nowadays the fields are turned around so that the sinking sun slants steadily into the fielders' faces. That's what ruins the players' eyes and that's why so many of them have to wear glasses."

A more likely explanation is that common sense has replaced common vanity. When people need glasses to correct their vision nowadays, they wear them.

Foreign Tours

The Boston and Athletics teams, only ones to win pennants in the old National Association, made the first foreign baseball trip in 1874. They played in 14 baseball games and seven cricket matches in England and Ireland. Five years later Frank Bancroft took a barnstorming team to Havana, but it was a financial failure. The A's and Phillies had better results when they visited Cuba in 1886.

The first globe-circling ambassadors of the game were the 20 players headed by A. G. Spalding, who made a notable tour in 1888–89. The Chicago NL team played a picked club of league rivals, tagged the All-American nine, in such places as Auckland, New Zealand; Sydney and Melbourne, Australia; Ceylon; Egypt; Rome, Naples and Florence, Italy; Paris, several English cities and Dublin, Ireland. Though expenses ran to $50,000, the trip proved profitable.

The Reach All-America team toured Japan in 1908, and a year later the University of Wisconsin played a series of games there. But the first big league teams to show as units in that baseball-loving land were the Giants and White Sox, who toured the world in 1913–14 under the guidance of John McGraw and Charlie Comiskey. From here, the teams went on to play in Shanghai, Hong Kong, Manila, Australia, Ceylon, Egypt, Italy, France and Great Britain . . . 31 games in all, with Bill Klem as umpire.

McGraw and Comiskey planned a similar tour in 1924, but had to quit after playing in England, Ireland and France. The reason: poor attendances. However, baseball was at fever pitch in Japan, and a 1922 tour by major league barnstormers was quite successful. Herb Hunter, who organized the 1922 trip, rounded up another with the help of sportswriter Fred Lieb in 1931, using many World Series players. Four games in Tokyo drew 250,000! Soon after this, the Japanese developed professional teams for the first time.

Lefty O'Doul, one of the players on that 1931 junket to Japan, returned to that isle five times in later years, and became the second greatest sports idol over there. Lefty was overshadowed only by the immortal Babe Ruth, who headed Connie Mack's team of American Leaguers that whipped the best available Japanese competition in an 18-game series in 1934.

Since 1953, a major league club has visited Japan every few years. In 1962 an agreement was reached between the respective commissioners—Ford Frick and Yushi Uchimura concerning the honoring of each other's player contracts. Approximately twenty players from the U. S. play in the Japanese leagues each season, many of them ex-major leaguers.

Baseball Ballads

Since every game is a new adventure, every season a new saga, baseball lends itself well to song and story. Even daily newspaper sportswriters sometimes attempt Homeric prose in praise of their latest hero. Sentiment runs so high, baseball odes don't have to be epics to capture popular appeal. Still, the game has inspired some gusty classics . . . like "Casey At The Bat," which, even if it doesn't rate as full-blown literature, must be accorded everlasting tribute for rescuing the horde of fading vaudevillians who recited "Casey" as a last prop against unemployment.

Back in 1869, when Cincinnati's Red Stockings were riding high through an unbeaten season, the players had their own theme song. It was written to the tune of "Bonnie Blue Flag." Just before each game, the mustachioed Reds would line up near home plate, hat in hand, to serenade the grandstand with:

We are a band of baseball players
From Cincinnati city.
We come to toss the ball around
And sing to you our ditty.

And if you listen to our song
We are about to sing,
We'll tell you all about baseball
And make the welkin ring.

Hurrah, hurrah,
For the noble game, hurrah.
Red Stockings all will toss the ball
And shout our loud hurrah.

Baseball polkas and poems turned up as frequently as pennant winners in those early years. Yet none of the 19th-century compositions had the flair and flavor of that fictional opus written in 1888, and popularized by the masterful recitations of De Wolf Hopper, to wit:

CASEY AT THE BAT
By Ernest L. Thayer

The outlook wasn't brilliant for the Mudville nine that day;
The score stood four to two with but one inning more to play.
And then when Cooney died at first, and Barrows did the same,
A sickly silence fell upon the patrons of the game.

A straggling few got up to go in deep despair. The rest
Clung to that hope which springs eternal in the human breast.
They thought if only Casey could but get a whack at that—
We'd put up even money now with Casey at the bat.

But Flynn preceded Casey, as did also Jimmy Blake,
And the former was a lulu and the latter was a cake;
So upon the stricken multitude grim melancholy sat,
For there seemed but little chance of Casey's getting to the bat.

But Flynn let drive a single, to the wonderment of all,
And Blake, the much despised, tore the cover off the ball;
And when the dust had lifted and the men saw what had occurred,
There was Johnny safe at second and Flynn a-hugging third.

Then from 5,000 throats and more there rose a lusty yell;
It rambled through the valley, it rattled in the dell;
It knocked upon the mountain and recoiled upon the flat,
For Casey, mighty Casey, was advancing to the bat.

There was ease in Casey's manner as he stepped into his place;
There was pride in Casey's bearing and a smile on Casey's face.
And when, responding to the cheers, he lightly doffed his hat,
No stranger in the crowd could doubt 'twas Casey at the bat.

Ten thousand eyes were on him as he rubbed his hands with dirt;
Five thousand tongues applauded when he wiped them on his shirt.
Then while the writhing pitcher ground the ball into his hip,
Defiance gleamed in Casey's eye, a sneer curled Casey's lip.

And now the leather-covered sphere came hurtling through the air,
And Casey stood a-watching it in haughty grandeur there.
Close by the sturdy batsman the ball unheeded sped—
"That ain't my style," said Casey. "Strike one," the umpire said.

From the benches, black with people, there went up a muffled roar,
Like the beating of the storm waves on a stern and distant shore.
"Kill him! Kill the umpire!" shouted some one in the stand,
And it's likely they'd have killed him had not Casey raised his hand.

With a smile of Christian charity great Casey's visage shone;
He stilled the rising tumult, he bade the game go on;
He signaled to the pitcher, and once more the spheroid flew;
But Casey still ignored it, and the umpire said, "Strike two."

"Fraud!" cried the maddened thousands, and the echo answered "Fraud!"
But one scornful look from Casey and the audience was awed.
They saw his face grow stern and cold, they saw his muscles strain,
And they knew that Casey wouldn't let that ball go by again.

The sneer is gone from Casey's lip, his teeth are clenched in hate;
He pounds with cruel violence his bat upon the plate.
And now the pitcher holds the ball, and now he lets it go,
And now the air is shattered by the force of Casey's blow.

Oh! somewhere in this favored land the sun is shining bright;
The band is playing somewhere, and somewhere hearts are light.
And somewhere men are laughing, and somewhere children shout;
But there is no joy in Mudville—mighty Casey has struck out.

But the American public, notorious in its constant clamor for a "winner," wouldn't settle for a discredited Casey. In the very nature of baseball's campaign, "there is always another game tomorrow," so mighty Casey had to have his revenge. It remained for a proud young Southerner to redeem the fallen hero by composing this ode in 1906:

CASEY'S REVENGE
By James Wilson

There were saddened hearts in Mudville for a week or even more;
There were mutterd oaths and curses—every fan in town was sore.
"Just think," said one, "how soft it looked with Casey at the bat,
And to think he'd go and spring a bush league trick like that."

All his past fame was forgotten—he was now a hopeless "shine"—
They called him "Strike-out Casey" from the Mayor down the line;
And as he came to bat each day his bosom heaved a sigh,
While a look of hopeless fury shone in Casey's eye.

He soon began to sulk and loaf—his batting eye went lame;
No home runs on the score card now were chalked against his name.
The fans without exception gave the manager no peace,
For one and all kept clamoring for Casey's quick release.

The lane is long, some one has said, that never turns again,
And Fate, though fickle, often gives another chance to men;
And Casey smiled—his rugged face no longer wore a frown—
The pitcher who had started all the trouble came to town.

All Mudville had assembled—ten thousand fans had come
To see the twirler who had put big Casey on the bum;
And when he stepped into the box the multitude went wild.
He doffed his cap in proud disdain—but Casey only smiled.

"Play ball!" the umpire's voice rang out—and then the game began;
But in that throng of thousands there was not a single fan
Who thought that Mudville had a chance, and with the setting sun
Their hopes sank low—the rival team was leading "four to one."

The last half of the ninth came round with no change in the score,
But when the first man up hit safe the crowd began to roar;
The din increased—the echo of ten thousand shouts was heard
When the pitcher hit the second and gave "four balls" to the third.

Three men on base—nobody out—three runs to tie the game!
A triple meant the highest niche in Mudville's hall of fame;
But here the rally ended and the gloom was deep as night,
When the fourth one "fouled to catcher" and the fifth "flew out to right."

A dismal, groaning chorus came—a scowl was on each face—
When Casey walked up, bat in hand, and slowly took his place.
His bloodshot eyes in fury gleamed—his teeth were clenched in hate;
He gave his cap a vicious hook and pounded on the plate.

The pitcher smiled and cut one loose—across the plate it sped—
Another hiss—another groan—"Strike one," the umpire said.
Zip! Like a shot the second curve broke just below his knee—
"Strike two!" the umpire roared aloud—but Casey made no plea.

No roasting for the umpire now—his was an easy lot;
But here the pitcher whirled again—was that a rifle shot?
A whack—a crack—and out through space the leather pellet flew:
A blot against the distant sky—a speck against the blue.

Above the fence in centre field in rapid whirling flight
The sphere sailed on—the blot grew dim and then was lost to sight;
Ten thousand hats were thrown in air—ten thousand threw a fit—
But no one ever found the ball that mighty Casey hit.

Oh! somewhere in this favored land dark clouds may hide the sun,
And somewhere bands no longer play and children have no fun;
And somewhere over blighted loves there hangs a heavy pall;
But Mudville hearts are happy now—for Casey hit the ball

———

Around this same period, Jack Norworth and Albert Von Tilzer wrote a song that is destined to live as long as the game itself, "Take Me Out To The Ball Game." Norworth sang it in the Follies with his wife, the beauteous Nora Bayes. Almost overnight, it became the game's national anthem, and today it's as popular as ever.

Another lilting rhythm that became baseball legend was "Tinker to Evers to Chance," an eight-line lament penned by Franklin P. Adams of the old *New York Evening Mail*. Though this double play combination of the Cubs was not the greatest of all time, it was the most dreaded of its day. As F.P.A. versified:

These are the saddest of possible words:
"Tinker to Evers to Chance."
Trio of bear Cubs and fleeter than birds,
"Tinker to Evers to Chance."
Ruthlessly pricking our gonfalon bubble,
Making a Giant hit into a double—
Words that are heavy with nothing but trouble:
"Tinker to Evers to Chance."

But baseball isn't all romance and poetry. The characters and situations rife in the sport are ripe material for literate wits; so it's no wonder that a sports-minded genius like Ring Lardner was able to weave such classic comedy as his "You Know Me Al" series. First a comic strip and later a series of short stories, this literary effort excels all the plays, books and movies written about the national pastime.

In recent years, baseball's best ballads have evolved from the writers' annual winter banquets held in the big cities. With tabs ranging up to $25 per plate, and guests numbering 1,500, they serve tender steaks . . . but not half so tender as the "hams", meaning the baseball writers disporting on the stage in hour-long topical revues. If the acting is sometimes punk, the lyrics never are. The scribes really outdo themselves with songs ranging from sentimental ballads to pungent parodies.

Manufacture of a Bat

Bats are made of ash, hackberry and hickory, but ash is preferred because of superior resiliency or "drive." The best white ash comes from Northeastern United States. Special bat timber experts determine which trees are suitable, and these are felled, cut into logs about 40 inches long and hauled to the timber mill. There they are sawed into either square or round billets before being sent to the bat factory.

Upon arrival at the yards of the factory, the billets are inspected, graded and then stacked loosely—so that air can circulate freely—for 10 to 18 months of seasoning. More than 3,000,000 billets are in the process of drying this way at any one time.

Billets which have split during seasoning are thrown out and the others hauled to the factory to go through a turning process that brings them into the approximate shape of a bat. They are then weighed and graded to see for which models they will best be suitable. The bat is then placed on a lathe alongside the original model and cut down to the same shape. The turner weighs and measures for fractional accuracy, then sands the embryo bat, which is finally stained and branded.

Manufacture of a Baseball

Harassed pitchers may swear there's a live jackrabbit inside the ball, but according to A. G. Spalding Bros. Inc.—which manufactures all the official American and National League baseballs in its plant at Chicopee, Massachusetts —actually the core consists of a cork composition containing a small percentage of rubber. This core is 13/16 of an inch in diameter.

Two black rubber shells, each approximately 5/32 of an inch thick, are wrapped around the core, with a thin cushion of red rubber between the edges of the hemispherical black rubber shells. Next comes a red rubber wrapping 3/32 of an inch thick. The entire "pill" is molded perfectly round to 4 1/8 inches circumference.

Wool is wound around the pill under precise humidity and tension control in three operations: first application, 121 yards of four-ply gray woolen yarn, brings size to 7 3/4 inches circumference; second winding, 45 yards of three-ply white woolen yarn, increases it to 8 3/16 inches circumference; third winding, 53 yards of three-ply gray woolen yarn, makes size of ball 8 3/4 inches circumference. Next comes 150 yards of fine cotton winding, coated with a layer of latex (rubber cement) to prevent unraveling. By now the overall circumference is 8 7/8 inches.

The covers, of selected horsehide leather between .050–.055 of an inch thick, are cut on a machine into the pattern of "a swollen figure 8," with 108 stitch-holes bordering each cover. Two such pieces are used to cover a baseball. After dampening the horsehide to make it pliable, the covers are hand-stitched with red cotton thread. Any pinching that occurs when the cover shrinks back tight is eliminated by rolling the balls. By now the circumference is the regulation 9–9 1/4 inches circumference and weighs between 5–5 1/4 ounces.

All the balls head for either of two stamping machines. One, for American League baseball, stamps the "Reach" trademark plus the AL president's autograph on the cover. The other, for official NL balls, registers the "Spalding" symbol as well as the league president's signature. Aside from the printing on the cover, the balls of both leagues are absolutely identical.

Manufacture of a Glove

Leather for baseball gloves comes from hides of native cows. Animals slaughtered in late May and early November (called Summer Hides) are preferred. The tanned leather is then taken to die-cutting machines.

Next step is stamping. This is done by applying heat and pressure while the glove palm is laid out flat. Fielders' gloves are then sewn inside out with finest quality cotton thread. More expensive gloves have an extra row of stitches around the thumb, sewed with wax linen thread. After sewing, gloves are turned and then stretched over a form heated to about 210 degrees Fahrenheit. They remain there long enough to set the shape, the operation ironing all the seams evenly and giving the glove a well-tailored appearance.

Sewed linings are then inserted, followed by binding, wrist eyeletting and lacing. The gloves are then oiled, with warm oil rubbed in by hand. This water-proofs the leather and gives the glove a good feel and fine color.

The gloves are then "laid off" over another hot form. This consists of pulling the heel into position, ironing all wrinkles out of the lining, forming the pocket and putting a further set in the leather. One more inspection, and then they're ready for shipment.

Care of Equipment

Bats—Hit with the "label up," since batting against the grain invites breakage. Never hit the bat against sole of the shoe to dislodge mud or dirt, as chipping may result. Bats should not be left in dew-covered grass. In the offseason, rub the bat with linseed oil or tung oil, or with any good lubricant, like vaseline. Keep the bat in a dry place, but not near any excessive heat, lest it dry out. Many players advise bone-rubbing the bat as a further preservative.

Baseballs—Even a single broken stitch should be repaired immediately. Covers should be cleaned and kept dry.

Gloves—High temperatures and excessive moisture are the most common sources of trouble. In order to prevent green mold rot, keep the glove in a cool dry place. When wet, dry the glove immediately, but the action should not be forced. It should be dried at normal room temperature without use of artificial heat. If repeated wetting occurs, harshness in the leather may develop, but this can be counter-acted by applying neat's-foot oil or light paraffin (mineral) oil. Leather that has become soiled should be cleaned with saddle soap only. Use a moist cloth to work up a cream by rubbing over the soap. Rub the cloth over the leather until the lather works loose the dirt. Dirty lather should then be wiped off with a clean cloth, and the leather briskly rubbed with a clean cloth.

Shoes—Oil or other lubricant should be used often on uppers to maintain softness and strength. Since night games causes shoes to be soaked in dew, use treatment recommended in preceding paragraph for repeated wetting of gloves.

XIII PLAYING HINTS

HOW TO HIT
BY TY COBB

The first item in scientific hitting is selection of bat. For a swing hitter (one who starts his bat far back and completes his swing with a full follow-through) I suggest a bat with the feel on the light side. For the one with a shorter, more compact swing, the bat should feel slightly heavy.

Next comes position. Never copy a batter with an exaggerated crouch. The best hitters stand up and have the look of a good hitter. In case your normal stance becomes uncomfortable while awaiting the delivery, breaking of the knees (a dip or slight squat) will relieve this. But of course you must always come back to the position first assumed.

The space between feet should be measured by how well balanced you feel. This will measure about 14 inches for players of average height. But don't think of this kind of thing in inches. Just stand so you feel balanced, and can step either into the pitch or away.

If you are able to put a little extra weight on the front foot and still feel balanced to step either way, so much the better. The ability to do this will assure proper stride and, when swinging, will bring the body and arms up to the ball more automatically. I emphasize the value of proper striding because over-striding is fatal. It causes uppercutting and fly balls, upsets coordination and costs freedom to step in or out.

A righthanded batter attempting to hit the ball to right, or opposite (from normal), field should use the closed stance. That means the left foot is about 4 inches closer to the plate than the right. Hitting to left field, his front foot is about 4 inches further away, or in open stance. The straightaway hitter lines up both feet with the line of the pitch.

I always had trouble hitting lefthanded pitching, especially curve ballers, until I went to the back line of the batter's box. That gave me the benefit of the extra inches from the pitcher, and the split-second extra time in which to judge the pitch.

Keep your arms, particularly the elbows, away from the body. This insures freedom of swing. I also recommend the elbow nearer the pitcher be raised and exaggerated. This, plus a slight bending of the body from the waist up, will give you better body balance, insures automatically hitting the ball out in front and brings your eyes in better focusing position.

Do all your "fixing" as to grip and stance before delivery, then forget about your swing. Watch the pitcher's every move and never let your eye leave the ball. Many batters are thrown out by a half-step, so once you've hit the ball, run with all the speed you have, no matter where the ball goes.

(Condensed from "Famous Slugger Year Book," Copyright 1950 by Hillerich & Bradsby Co., Louisville, Ky.)

HOW TO PITCH
BY CARL HUBBELL

Pitching is the most important single factor in any game...as much as 70%, according to some deep thinkers. I would like to offer these "ten commandments" for pitching aspirants:

1: A limber arm. 2: A rugged physique, or, as an alternative, wiriness. 3: A repertoire, meaning a fast ball and at least one breaking ball, preferably

a curve. 4: Control. 5: Competitive courage. 6: Endurance. 7: Intelligence. 8: The ability to size up a hitter. 9: Confidence. 10: Fielding skill.

Note that the list emphasizes developed skills over natural endowment. Development of these "extras" will give a pitcher the advantage over those relying entirely on physical assets.

Of course, the arm must be the primary consideration. Unless a boy can throw hard, or a "live" ball with reasonable speed, his pitching future can only be limited. Tricky deliveries may succeed on the sandlots, but as a pitcher moves into faster company, conditions eventually demand that he overpower a good hitter.

Pitching mechanics are important, too. A smooth, easy delivery, perfected by attention to detail, is an aid to control. Faulty form beats pitchers more often than opposing hitters, and often explains arm ailments.

The pitching delivery can be broken down and analyzed to reveal six distinct actions: Windup, Stretch, Leg Lift, Stride, Body Pivot and Follow Through.

The Windup promotes rhythm, so each pitcher can best judge his own style. It's usual to start with hands brought forward and then upward over the head. The Stretch brings the pitching arm behind the head. The Leg Lift gets drive into the motion, while the Stride is an important element for control. Most young pitchers tend to over-stride, thereby losing power and accuracy.

The weight shifts from rear to front foot in the Body Pivot. Follow Through enables the pitcher to get his body into the pitch and is also a control element. A pitcher constantly throwing the ball too high generally is failing to follow through properly.

To deliver a fast ball, the pitcher should grip it tightly, with index and middle fingers on top of the ball, and the thumb underneath. The fingers are usually placed across the seams, but if along them, then at the place where the seams are closest together. When pitched, the ball rolls from under the fingers. This reverse rotation gives the ball back-spin, causing it to "hop."

The grip for the curve is the same as for the fast ball. With the pitch, the ball rolls over the fingers as the wrist is snapped sharply to provide forward spin for the ball. The thumb does its work as it comes over with the wrist snap. The wrist snap should be sharp. . . the sharper the snap, the sharper the curve. All curves should be thrown low to a batter. The ball takes more spin that way, breaks away from the batter and is harder to hit.

The change of pace differs from the fast ball only in the manner in which it is held. Where the fast ball is gripped tightly, the change of pace is only lightly held by the fingers on top. Some pitchers lift these guiding fingers slightly as they let the ball go.

HOW TO CATCH BY BILL DICKEY

Since a catcher's job requires endurance, he should be sturdy rather than fast afoot. Yet he has to be nimble to pounce on bunts and waste no time or steps chasing pop fouls. He must also have a good arm.

Brain-power must come with stamina in this job. The catcher mentally catalogues the batting strength and weakness of every player in the league. He needs fine judgment to mix up the pitches he calls for, in such a way as to pace the pitcher and baffle the hitter. He must decide when to call for a pitchout, when to throw to a base, and also directs the throw of teammates who field bunts or slow rollers with men on base.

To give signals, the catcher squats on his haunches, feet comfortably apart about six inches, with the weight balanced on the ball of each foot. Signs come from the fingers of the right hand, which is held well up the thigh. The mitt helps shield the fingered signal from enemy coaches.

Just before the delivery, the catcher shifts into a quarter-crouch, with the left foot slightly forward and the legs slightly farther apart. The full face of his mitt is presented toward the pitcher, making a good target. By playing as close as possible to the batter, the catcher is less likely to miss foul tips, gets into best position to throw on steals, is best situated to catch low pitches in the strike zone and is poised to break for a bunt.

The right hand should be relaxed, while awaiting the pitch, with fingers loosely closed around the thumb. This avoids broken fingers on foul tips. As the ball thuds into the mitt, the mitt hand rolls over and traps the ball in the pocket, fingers automatically encircling the ball in correct throwing position.

If the pitch is above the belt, catch it with the fingers of the mitt pointed upward; if below, hold the fingers down. Don't just reach for a wide pitch—step in that direction, too. If the pitch is too low, drop your knees into the dirt to block it with a man on base.

Immediately after receiving the pitch, snap into a good throwing position by pivoting with the weight on the right foot, striding forward with the left, and throwing the ball overhand...especially for basestealers. The weight shifts from right foot to left as the throw is made, thus putting body and shoulders behind it. To nab a base-stealer, throw in a low trajectory. Bluff throws to keep runners close to the bag.

In fielding a bunt, use one hand only if the ball has stopped dead. If the bunt is rolling, place your mitt in front of it and scoop the ball into the mitt with your bare hand. Never take your eye off the ball, or try to throw it, before you actually have it.

Other tips: On pop fouls, flip off your mask immediately and toss it in opposite direction from ball...Tag with both hands when possible...With a man on first, hurry to cover third on a sacrifice bunt...Back up throws to first with none on...Practice exhaustively on catching high fouls, because the ball has terrific spin as it hits the mitt...Keep the mitt in a flat plane when catching pop-ups.

HOW TO PLAY FIRST BASE
BY GEORGE SISLER

Everything else being equal, the tall left-hander has the edge as a first baseman. He can reach farther for high, wide or late throws, and he can throw more easily to the other bases. However, there have been smaller righthanded fielders who were good on defense.

When fielding a ball hit to him, the first baseman should, as the pitch is made, have his weight come over on the ball of each foot. Don't ever be back on your heels. If possible, advance toward the ball, judging the hop as it comes. A good fielder is one who can judge a bounce well. A long hop or short pickup is easiest to catch. The long pickup (sometimes called a short hop) is hardest, and should be avoided if possible. Catch the ball in front of you and "give" with the catch. Keep your eye on the grounder from the time it leaves the bat. Never be caught with your chin up in the air.

When not guarding the bag to keep the runner from taking too big a lead, the first baseman should play 20 to 25 feet back of the base and as far away from the foul line as the type of hitter would justify. On the hit to another infielder, go quickly to first base and find the bag with your left foot. Then turn to take the throw, shifting feet if necessary. I am against straddling the bag and kicking back to tag the base as the catch is made, because the first

baseman would not have time for these actions if he were playing at his maximum depth to start with.

Here are some important tips on first base play:

(1) When the play is close and the ball is thrown into the runner, the left-handed first baseman must keep his left foot on the base, right foot forward, and make a one-handed, backhand catch of the ball.

(2) On close plays, stretch forward as far as possible to catch the ball as soon as possible. The last portion of the foot to touch the bag is the toe, and not the heel, because if you try to stretch with only the heel on the bag, it certainly will come off.

(3) Catch the ball with two hands if possible.

(4) Make long throws to third base overhanded.

(5) If the throw to you is bad, and you see you will not be able to stick on the bag while reaching the ball, then by all means leave the bag and make the catch. That will prevent the runner from taking an extra base.

(6) Shifting should be done with a little natural hop from side to side. Practice this a lot.

(7) Do not reach for a runner in tagging Make him come to you. Be able to cover every portion of the bag with your tagging hand.

(8) If you are no longer needed at first base, move around and back up bases or go out for relays. Make yourself generally useful. Learn your role for cut-off plays.

(9) Catch all pop flies that are in your territory.

(10) When fielding a ball in such a way that the pitcher has to cover first, throw the ball to him underhanded and while moving toward him. Aim the toss chest-high and never conceal the ball from him.

HOW TO PLAY
SECOND BASE
BY ROGERS HORNSBY

The second baseman has many responsibilities that require not only skill but mental alertness. There are many things to do besides field ground balls and throw to first base . . . but as he has to field and throw many times in an average game, it is important that he reach the highest point of efficiency in these departments. That means hours and hours of practice.

Be set to make a quick start either to the left or right for a grounder. Be prepared to dash in for a slow, dribbling grounder or to turn around and run back for a short fly into the shallow outfield.

Do not overlook your training in mastering the art of catching a pop fly.

Proper position on the diamond is not fixed. Shift according to whether the batter is left or right handed, whether he is a notorious pull hitter or straight-away or slicer. Play the left handed pull hitter a bit deeper, say on the edge of the outfield grass, and closer to first than usual. If he is a very fast runner, however, you can't afford to play him quite that deep.

When expecting a sacrifice bunt, play closer to the batter and far enough toward first so you can cover that bag should the first baseman go in for a bunt. Be sure, however, not to leave your position too soon, or the batter may double-cross you by hitting through the vacant spot, or by dragging a bunt in that direction.

Also be alert in case the ball is bunted past the pitcher. In this case you have to field it and try for the putout at first.

When a double play is hoped for, then, regardless of whether a right or left-handed batter is at the plate, you must move toward second base so as to be in position to cover that bag in time for the double play. In order to pivot

correctly, always try to touch the bag with your right foot, then step with the left foot in toward the pitcher's mound and make the throw to first.

In running to cover second, it is wise to straddle the bag, so that in case of a wide throw you can touch the bag with either foot for a forceout.

When runners on first and third try a double steal, the second baseman is important in breaking it up. In case of a pitchout, the second baseman runs to a spot 10 feet in front of the bag while the shortstop goes right to the bag. If the runner on third starts for home, the second baseman should cut off the throw from the catcher and return the ball to the plate. When the double steal is attempted without a pitchout, the bag is covered as in the usual manner with only a man on first, and the man who takes the throw at second base never waits for the tag but instead fires the ball right back to the catcher.

When a ball is hit to right or right center for extra bases, the second baseman should run out to take the relay throw. Make up your mind as you dash out whether the ball will be good for three bases or a homer, and you'll know where to relay the ball. If the ball should not be good for more than a double, then the second baseman should break for second to be in position for the throw. With the ball hit to left field, the shortstop takes the throw at second, with the second baseman backing him up in case of a wild throw.

(*Condensed from "How to Play," Copyright* 1951 *by The Sporting News, St. Louis*)

HOW TO PLAY
SHORTSTOP
BY HONUS WAGNER

A shortstop must have a good arm as the prime requisite. Next, he must be fast, able to shift his feet and ready to move in any direction. Keep trying. Don't be afraid of making an error. Seek the advice of older players, the coaches and manager. Above all, never lose sight of the ball.

Always keep in mind the number of outs, which bases are occupied and the score. Study each hitter. On a fast runner, you must handle the ball cleanly and hurry the throw. Shift for each batter, according to where he is most likely to hit.

Think out each play before it happens. If you boot the ball, think where you're going to throw it even before you pick it up, so no time is lost.

The hardest play for a shortstop to make is going to his right for a deep hit ball. Set yourself when you get your hands on the ball, and be in a position to throw to first. Another tough play is the slowly hit ball coming right at you, especially with a fast batter. Play this on your barehanded side so as to get the ball away quickly, picking the ball up and throwing it without hesitation in virtually a single motion.

In starting a double play, remember it is wiser to make sure of one out than lose two. Grab the ball and feed it to the second baseman letter-high. If the ball goes to your right, or deep, put something on the throw to second. If it's a grounder near second, flip it underhand to the second baseman.

When pivoting in a double play, be in motion when receiving the ball, step on second base with the right foot and remain on balance by stepping forward with the left before finally throwing to first.

With a runner on first, the shortstop covers second on a bunt. With runners on first and second, keep the runner as close to second as possible by feinting him back. To pick a runner off second, stand about five feet behind the line and slowly work your way up close behind him. Break for the bag when the runner is leaning toward the next base, so as to catch him off balance.

The shortstop takes most of the relays on long hits to the outfield; otherwise, he directs the player who does take the relay, as to where the throw should go.

With a runner on first and a hit to right field, the shortstop stands about 25 feet in front of third base, on the grass, awaiting and guiding the throw from the outfielder. If there is a chance for the third baseman to catch the runner coming from first, he yells to the shortstop, "Let it go!" The shortstop bluffs the catch, to discourage the batter from advancing during the ensuing play, but lets the ball go through to the third baseman.

Other tips: Shortstop gets pitching signs from catcher and relays them to outfielders by hand or voice signal...Whether short or second baseman covers base on attempted steal depends on batter and type of pitch. . .Tag a runner with almost the same motion you get the ball, then get rid of the ball as fast as you can. . . Size up a pop fly and yell for it as soon as you feel sure you can get it; otherwise yell for either the left or center fielder to take it.

(Condensed from "How to Play Shortstop," by Honus Wagner, in April 13, 1949 issue of The Sporting News, St. Louis)

HOW TO PLAY THIRD BASE BY PIE TRAYNOR

Like any other player on the field, the third baseman must always make up his mind—before each pitch—exactly what to do with the ball if it is hit to him. The number of men on base, the score, the inning, the number of outs, the speed afoot of batter and baserunners. . . all figure in the decision. But, like a woman's mind and the cost of living, that decision is subject to change without notice. A reckless baserunner may break, or a grounder may take a bad hop and the "correct" play becomes something entirely different from the preconceived strategy. Split-second thinking in such situations is not completely a matter of intuition. Experience counts!

Position play depends on the tactical situation of the game and the type of hitter. In general it is best to play behind the line. Move up against a lefthanded batter or notorious bunter. In any case, the third baseman must have a trained reflex to spring toward the plate the moment a bunt develops. When the batter snaps into the flatfooted, square-facing bunt posture, the third baseman should be charging in even before the pitch reaches the plate.

Hard-hit balls are the true test of a third baseman. If he can't field them, or at least block them, extra-base hits result. It takes more courage than skill to stop those smashes.

The swinging bunt, or topped dribbler by a batter taking full cut, is really tough. Since he can't get the jump on such a play, the third baseman reaches the ball late. To make up for lost time, the baseman must charge in, while keeping his eyes glued to the ball, scoop it up barehanded and make the throw to first with the same motion.

Many hard smashes reach the third baseman before the hitter has broken out of the batter's box. That leaves plenty of time for the throw. The baseman should straighten his body, take aim, cock his arm and coordinate his throw with the stride.

Many valuable putouts are made even when the third baseman can only knock down the ball. A quick recovery and immediate throw will turn the trick. The baseman should practice throwing from any position, since he must get rid of the ball as soon as possible, and he should cock his arm only for throws on which he has plenty of time.

Other hints for third basemen:

Straddle the bag to receive a throw. If the play is not close, leave the bag to take the throw.

Practice exhaustively on catching high pop fouls.

Range as far as possible on grounders to your left.

When fielding a grounder with less than two out and men on first and second, make the double play relay via second base. Never start the play be stepping on third, unless the act of fielding the ball brings you toward the bag.

Handle squeeze bunts with a barehanded scoop-up and underhand throw.

Never let the runner on third take a long lead. Feint him back.

If the pitcher fields a bunt with a man on base, direct his throw and hurry back to cover third base.

HOW TO PLAY THE OUTFIELD BY JOE DiMAGGIO

To be an outfielder in the majors today, a player must be a good, consistent hitter, exceptionally fast if he isn't a long-ball hitter, and a first-rate flychaser and thrower. A team is far better off with an outfielder who piles up errors trying for hard catches than with one who handles perfectly every ball hit to him but doesn't go after the tough ones.

Before every play, size up the possibilities. Know the hitter and where he is likely to hit certain types of pitches. Get the sign from the shortstop as to what type of pitch is coming, so you will know in which direction to break "with the crack of the bat." Curve balls are more likely to be pulled than fast balls. Pregame practice will familiarize you with ground conditions (whether the bounce is likely to be hard or soft), wind, background, fences, etc. However, wind currents are tricky, so check occasionally with flags flying around the stands.

Make every catch in the best possible position from which to throw. I prefer to take fly balls with my hands above my head, left foot toward the plate, so as to save time making the throw. On ground balls, there is rarely any choice; when you catch up with it, the ball is usually hugging the ground. If it happens to be a bouncing ball, charge it in order to field it at the top of the hop, leaving you in good throwing position.

It is easier to catch a ball when standing still than on the dead run. Still, an outfielder who has a good jump on the ball may slow down in order to take the ball deliberately on the run to increase the force of his throw to beat a runner to the plate.

With a man on base, make up your mind in advance where you will throw, but be ready to react instantly to any change in circumstances. The safest rule to follow is: throw ahead of the runner. On throws to all bases, it is better to throw on one hop than on the fly. A bounding throw is more accurate and easier for a fielder to handle. Also, low throws set up cutoffs plays. Exception to the bounce-throw rule is when the ground is soft because of recent rain, and only when the outfielder is close enough to reach the base on the fly.

All outfielders should wear sunglasses. Never stare into the sun. Even with sunglasses, no outfielder can take a ball coming out of the sun. The sun-fielder should try to gauge the ball by getting a sidewise glimpse and shielding his eyes with his glove.

No outfielder is a real workman unless he can turn his back on the ball, run his legs off and take the catch over his shoulder. Practice this play till you are sure of it. Backpedalling outfielders get nowhere.

Other outfielding tips: Never gamble with a shoestring or diving catch unless a single would send in the tying or winning run. . .Use both hands for a catch, except where extra reach is necessary. . .Remember that balls hit wide of the centerfielder tend to swerve toward the nearer foul line. . .There are some advantages to playing shallow, but in these days of the lively ball it is dangerous

. . .Outfielders should back each other up and also back up the infield whenever possible. A "bluff catch" of a Texas Leaguer often keeps a runner from advancing an extra base.

(Condensed from "Baseball for Everyone," Copyright 1948 by Whittlesey House, N.Y.)

HOW TO UMPIRE
BY BILLY EVANS

Umpiring is a mixture of good physique, good eyes, plenty of courage, pride in your work, a knowledge of the rules, getting the right angle, a respect for the ability of others—managers, players and umpires—plus plenty of common sense. There is no greater asset than common sense properly applied.

Anticipation is an umpire's greatest trouble-maker. It is invariably the source of calling plays too quickly. Instead of anticipating the play, let it happen, follow it intently to its completion before reaching a decision.

There is considerably more to umpiring than the mere calling of ball or strike—out or safe—fair or foul. True, they are six basic operations in the life of an umpire, but many other things are equally important.

Umpires are human—all opinions to the contrary—hence, they err. In all the 25 years that I umpired, I have never tried to prove infallibility. Rather, I have very forcefully stated that I called the play as I saw it, and that made the decision arrived at "official." Even when positive I had not erred. I always regarded it as diplomacy to listen to the player's side of the argument. It is far easier to reason with the player who has let off steam rather than one who is burning up over an adverse decision and finds no one willing to listen. It is then that he goes berserk.

Never try to alibi your error. That makes two mistakes out of one. Umpires dislike ball players who alibi. In like manner, ball players have no particular use for the umpire who always has an alibi.

Don't work your thumb overtime, pointing the way to the clubhouse. Baseball is played on the field, not under the showers. Eject players from the game only as a last resort. Constantly work for some other solution. However, there are times when nothing but a nice cold shower will cool off a protesting player.

"Run your ball game, but don't overrun it."

Umpiring is largely a matter of angles. There is a best angle or spot for every play. Be in the right spot and you reduce the chances to err to a minimum.

The right way on the bases is always to be on top of the play. If you are over the play and miss it, you are far more liable to get away with an incorrect ruling than if you rendered the same decision fifteen or twenty feet away from the play. Ball players like umpires who hustle.

In getting over a play, I think it helps the umpire's judgment if he comes to a stop as he focuses on the play rather than rendering the decision while on the run.

Never lose sight of the ball. If you know where the ball is at all times, it will keep you out of a lot of trouble. Nothing shows up an umpire more than not to see the hidden ball trick. It makes the umpire look far worse than the player who was trapped.

Keep your eye on the ball to the completion of every play. Never turn your head or run by a play after you have given a decision. A lot of things can happen to the ball while you are looking in some other direction after making final ruling.

(Condensed from "Umpiring from the Inside," Copyright 1947 by Wm. G. Evans.)

BALL PARKS
American League

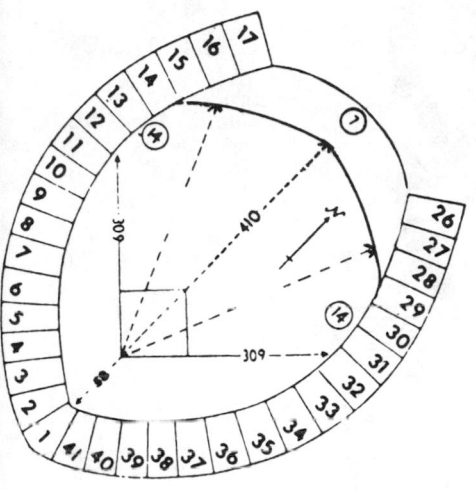

MEMORIAL STADIUM

MEMORIAL STADIUM
Home of:
   Baltimore Orioles AL
Seating Capacity: 52,137

FENWAY PARK

FENWAY PARK
Home of:
   Boston Red Sox AL
Seating Capacity: 33,437

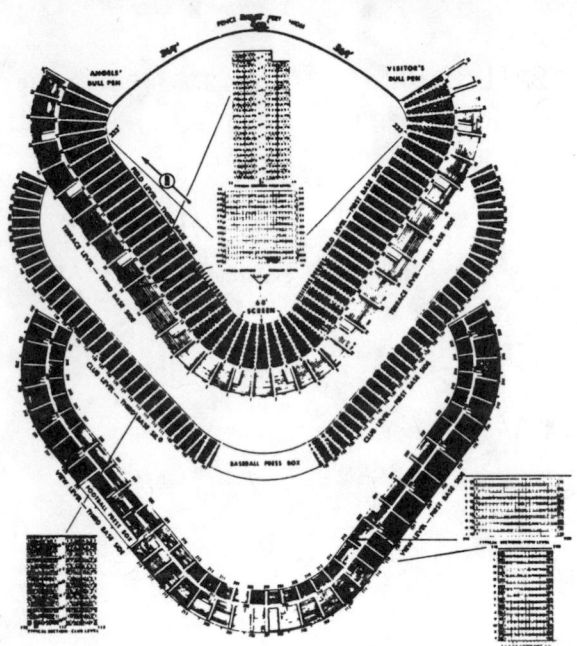

ANAHEIM STADIUM

Home of:
 California Angels AL
Seating Capacity: 43,204

COMISKEY PARK
Home of:
 Chicago White Sox AL
Seating Capacity: 44,492

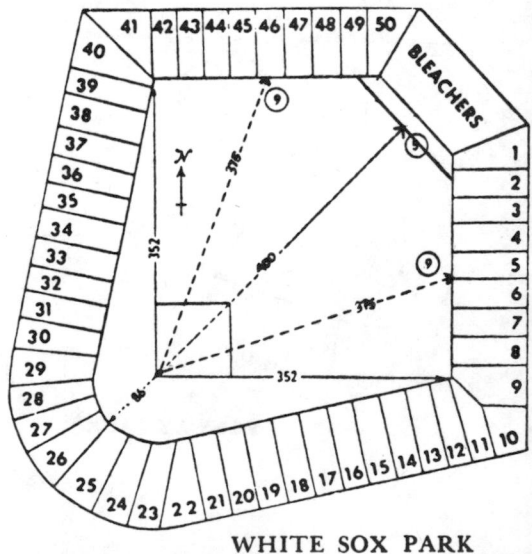

WHITE SOX PARK

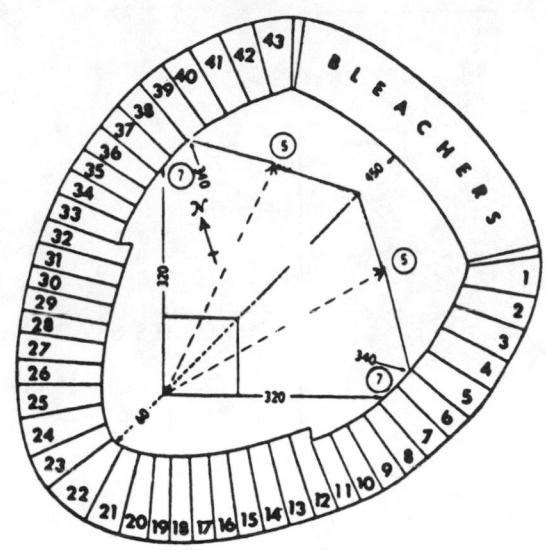

MUNICIPAL STADIUM

Home of:
Cleveland Indians AL
Seating Capacity, 76,713

MUNICIPAL STADIUM

TIGER STADIUM

Home of:
Detroit Tigers AL
Seating Capacity: 54,226

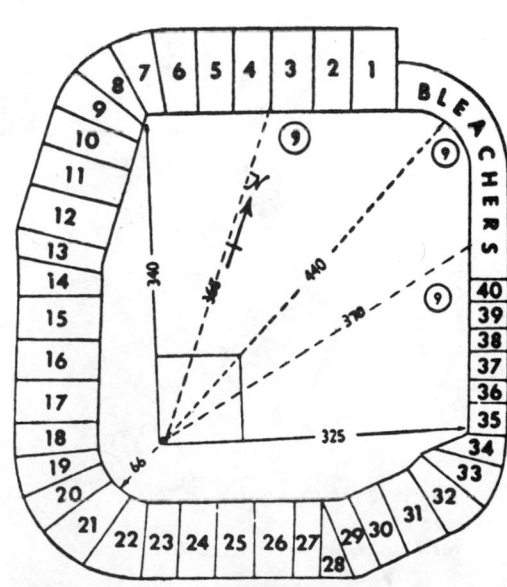

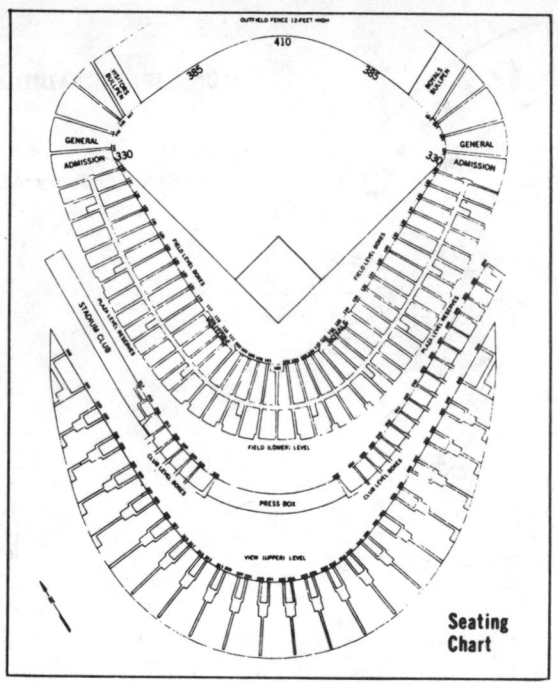

ROYALS STADIUM
Home of:
   Kansas City Royals A
Seating Capacity: 40,767

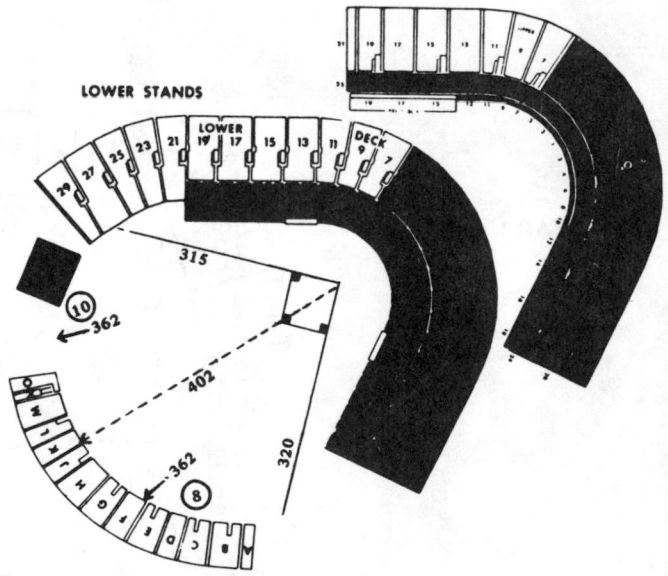

COUNTY STADIUM
Home of:
   Milwaukee Brewers AL
Seating Capacity: 52,198

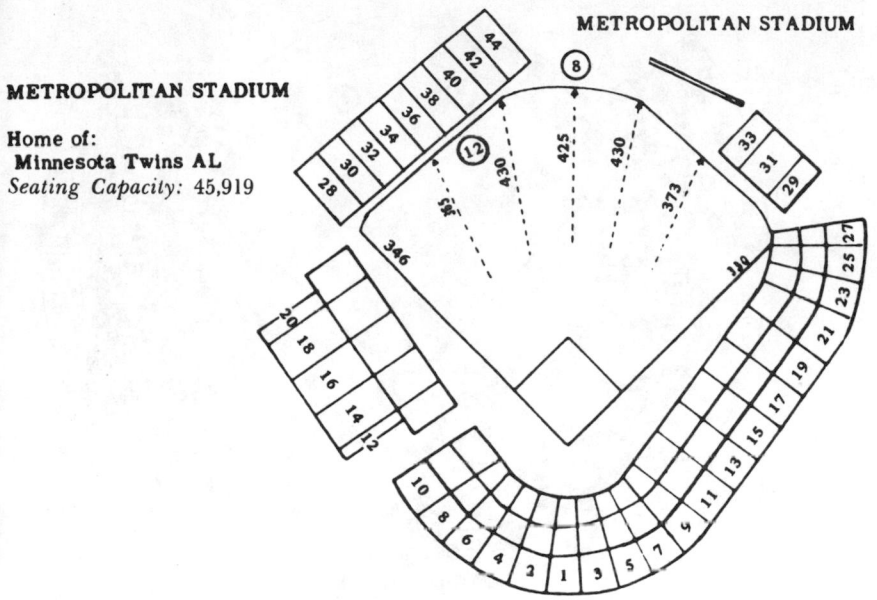

METROPOLITAN STADIUM

Home of:
 Minnesota Twins AL
Seating Capacity: 45,919

METROPOLITAN STADIUM

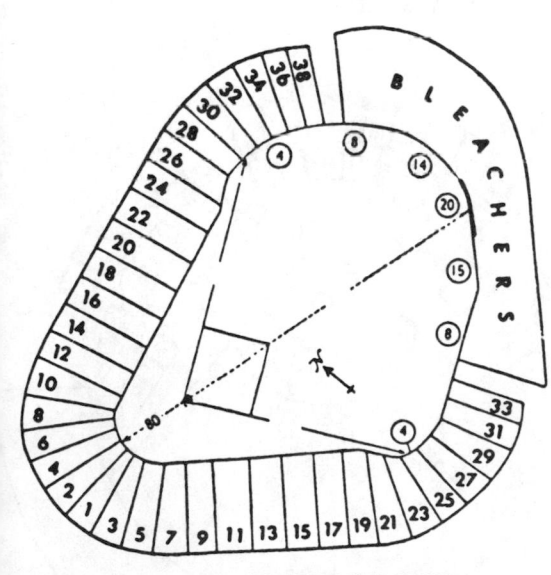

YANKEE STADIUM
Home of:
 New York Yankees AL
Seating Capacity: 54,028

YANKEE STADIUM

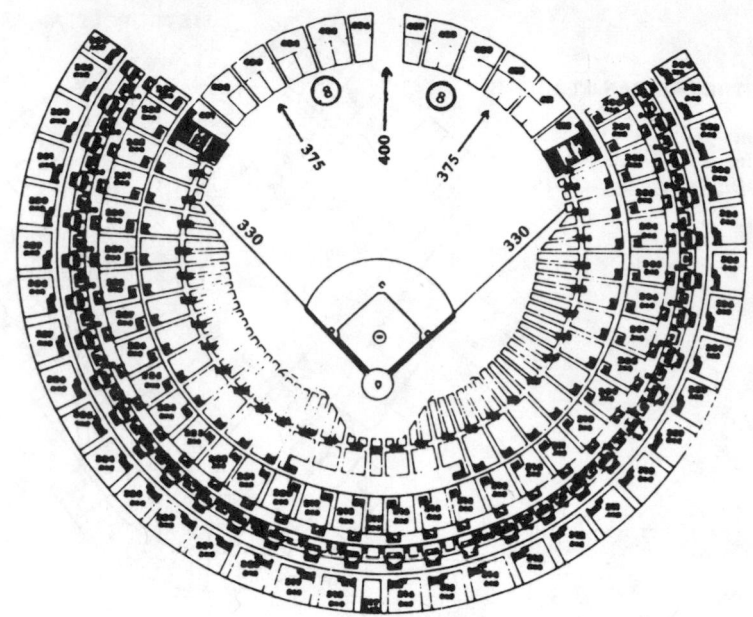

OAKLAND-ALAMEDA COUNTY STADIUM

Home of:
   Oakland Athletics AL
Seating Capacity: 50,000

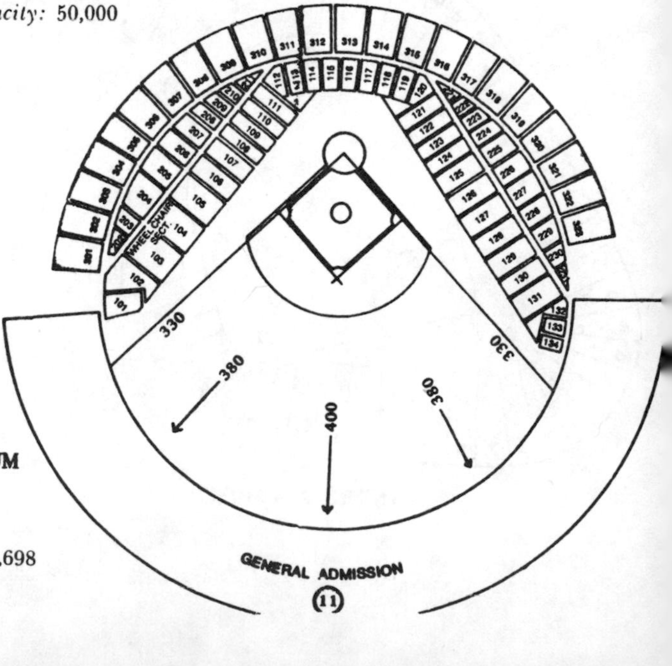

ARLINGTON STADIUM

Home of:
   Texas Rangers AL
Seating Capacity: 35,698

ATLANTA STADIUM

Home of:
Atlanta Braves NL
Seating Capacity: 52,744

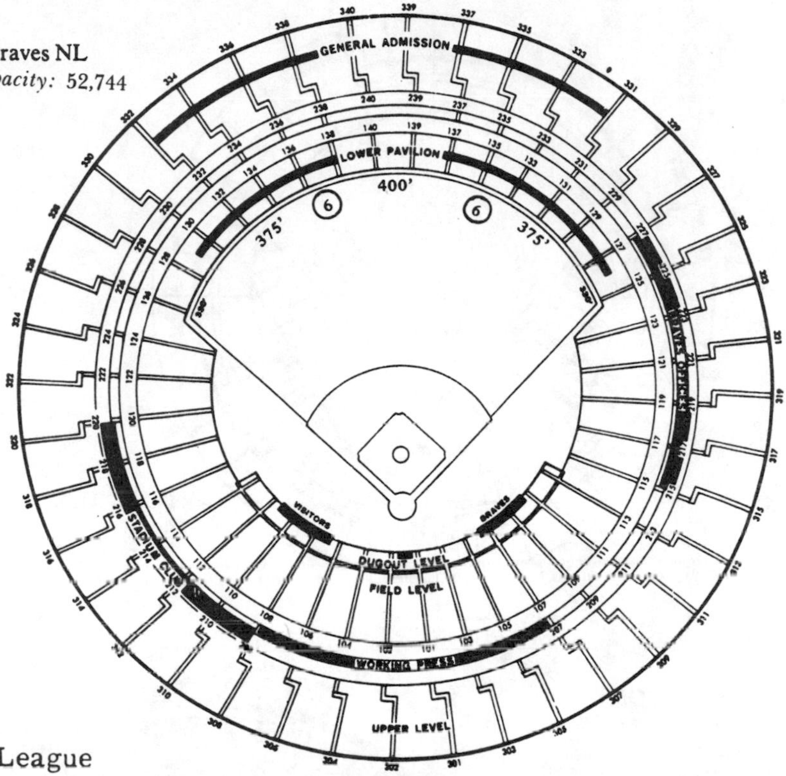

GENERAL ADMISSION
LOWER PAVILION
400'
375'
375'
6
6
VISITORS
BRAVES
DUGOUT LEVEL
FIELD LEVEL
WORKING PRESS
UPPER LEVEL
STADIUM CLUB
BRAVES OFFICES

National League

WRIGLEY FIELD

Home of:
Chicago Cubs NL
Seating Capacity: 37,741

BLEACHERS
357
368
355
400
368
363
353
12
12
12
1
30
37
43
50
57
7
80
90
96
110
120
127

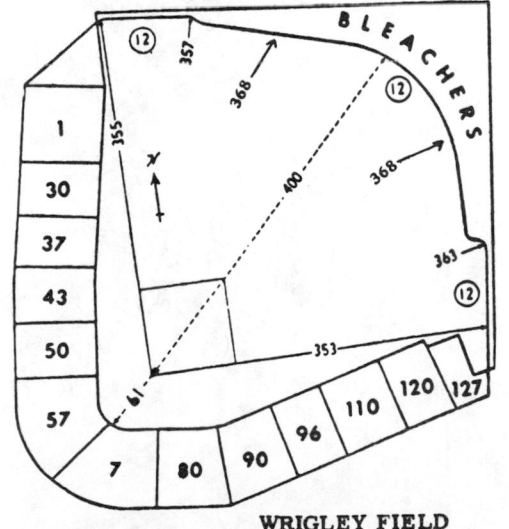

WRIGLEY FIELD

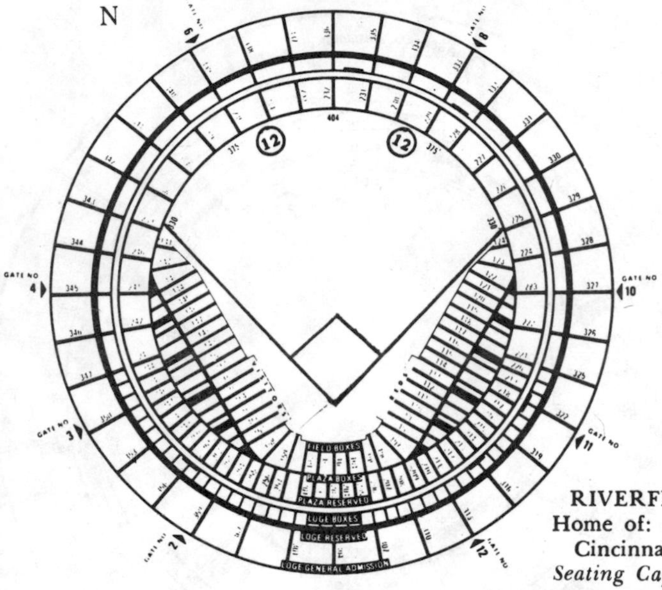

RIVERFRONT STADIUM
Home of:
   Cincinnati Reds NL
Seating Capacity: 51,786

ASTRODOME

Home of:
   Houston Astros NL
Seating Capacity: 45,000

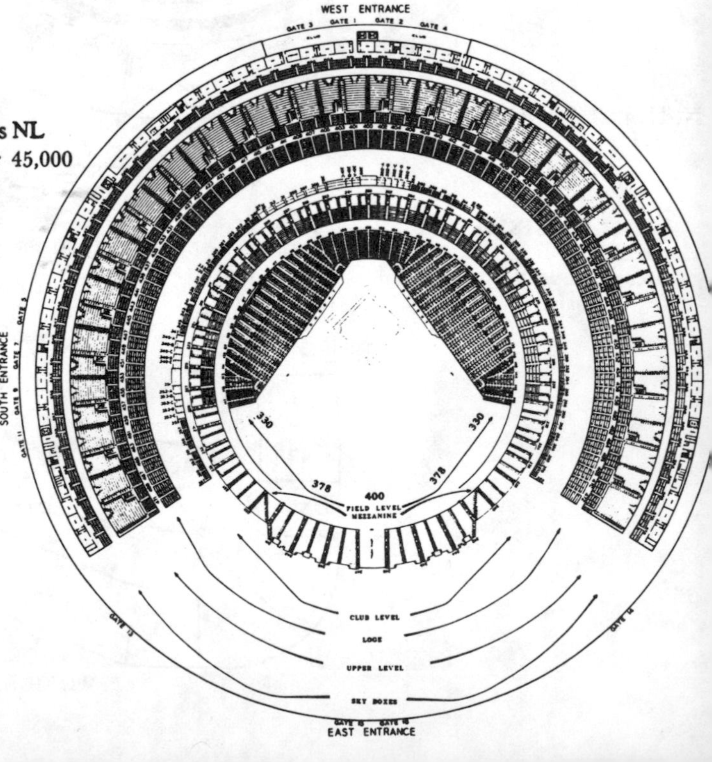

DODGER STADIUM

Home of:
Los Angeles Dodgers NL
Seating Capacity: 56,000

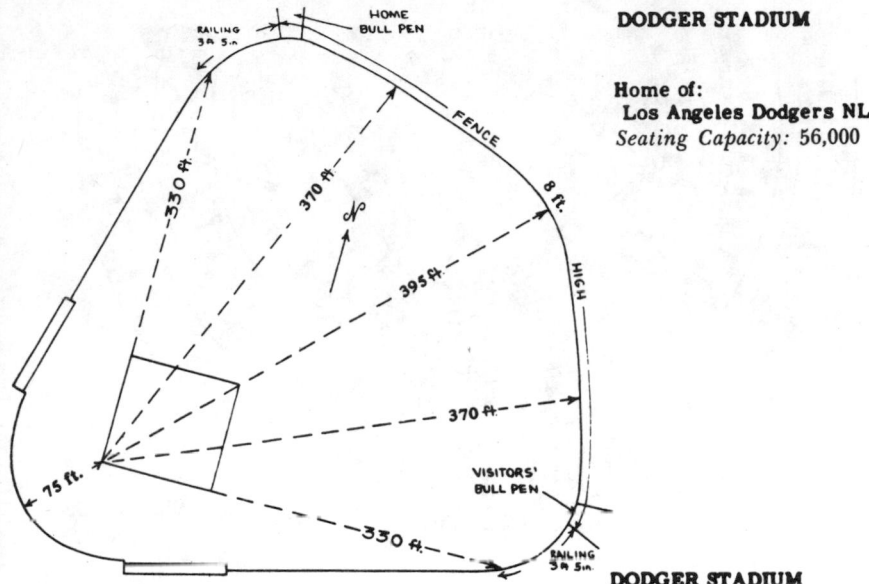

DODGER STADIUM

SHEA STADIUM

Home of:
New York Mets NL
Seating Capacity: 55,300

VETERANS STADIUM
Home of:
Philadelphia Phillies NL
Seating Capacity: 56,581

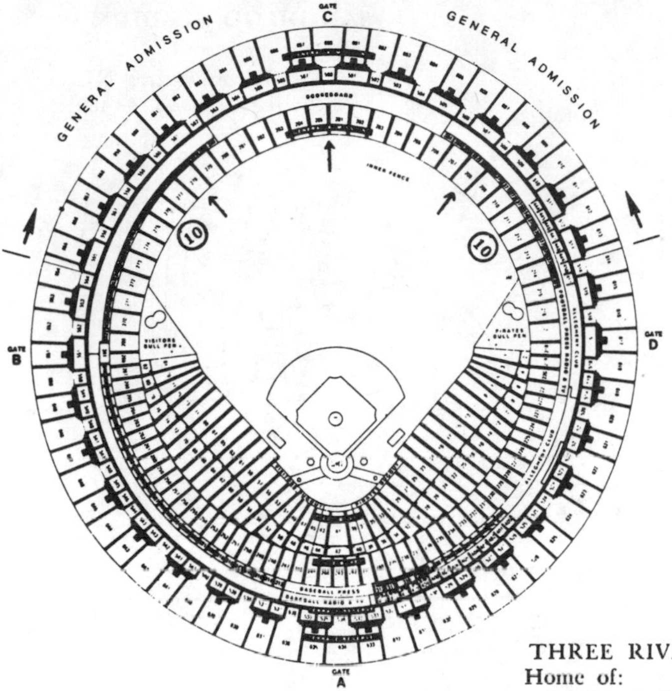

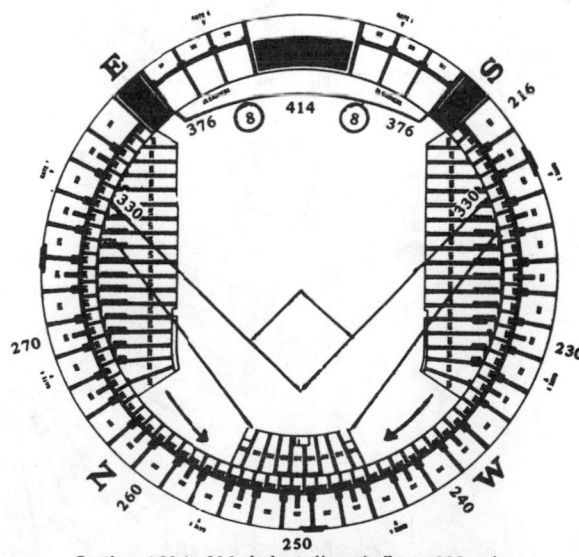

THREE RIVERS STADIUM
Home of:
Pittsburgh Pirates NL
Seating Capacity: **50,230**

BUSCH MEMORIAL STADIUM

Home of:
St. Louis Cardinals NL
Seating Capacity: 50,100

Sections 301 to 396 circle stadium similar to 200 series.

SAN DIEGO STADIUM
Home of
San Diego Padres NL
Seating Capacity: 48,460

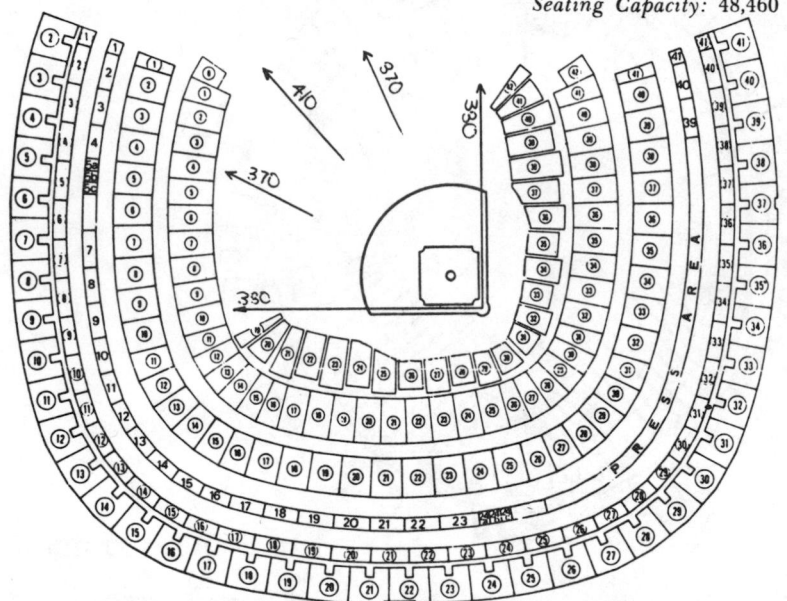

CANDLESTICK PARK

Home of:
San Francisco Giants NL
Seating Capacity: 58,000

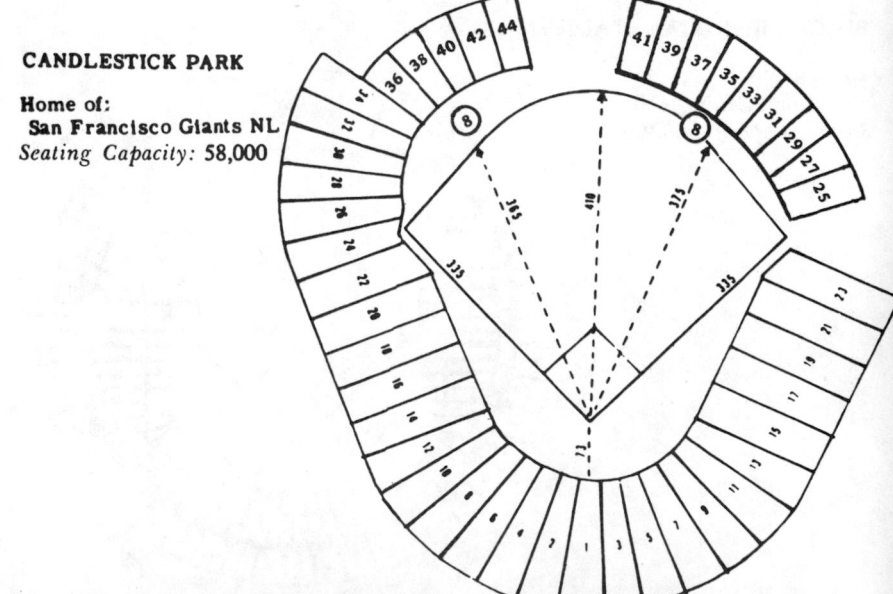

CANDLESTICK PARK